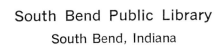

The Encyclopedia of Philosophy

Volumes 5 and 6
Complete and Unabridged

The
ENCYCLOPEDIA
of
PHILOSOPHY

PAUL EDWARDS, *Editor in Chief*

VOLUME FIVE

Macmillan Publishing Co., Inc. & The Free Press
NEW YORK
COLLIER MACMILLAN PUBLISHERS
LONDON

The Encyclopedia of Philosophy

L

[CONTINUED]

LOGIC, MANY-VALUED. It is common logical doctrine that every proposition is either true or false and that although there are intermediate possibilities between being certainly true and being certainly false, or between being known to be true and being known to be false, there are none between truth and falsehood themselves. This principle is one version of the law of excluded middle. Nowadays truth and falsehood are commonly described as the two possible truth-values of a proposition, the law of excluded middle, in the form just given, being referred to as the law of bivalence. At various times, however, logicians have entertained the view that there might be other possibilities—that there might be more than two truth-values. In the ancient and medieval periods this speculation was bound up with a specific philosophical problem. In the present century, although the starting point (at least with Jan Łukasiewicz) was the same philosophical problem, the emphasis has been on working out, in a rigorous mathematical way, the laws which a "multivalued" logic might contain, and the resulting systems and techniques have been seen to be susceptible of philosophical uses and interpretations quite different from the one that originally inspired this work.

PROBLEM OF FUTURE CONTINGENTS

Aristotle's treatise *De Interpretatione* concerns the division of statements into contradictory pairs, which are bound to have one member true and the other false. In the ninth chapter Aristotle asked, in effect, whether this can be done with future-tense statements about a "contingent" subject matter—that is, about a matter in which what will or will not occur is still in some way unsettled. His conclusion is obscure, but many commentators take him as having said that a statement like "There will be a sea battle tomorrow" when it has not yet been decided whether there will or will not be one is not yet actually true or actually false but is potentially either. Whether or not this is a correct interpretation of Aristotle, the Epicureans certainly held that the law of bivalence was false, this being one of their differences from Stoic logicians, such as Chrysippus. The problem was again taken up by medieval logicians, and some of them held that propositions about future contingencies are "neuter," neither true nor false. This gave rise to obvious problems about the extent of

God's foreknowledge. A particularly extensive debate on the subject, the records of which have been preserved (and, in this century, published), took place in Louvain in the middle of the fifteenth century, the main advocate of the three-valued system being Peter de Rivo.

Those who deny that Aristotle believed in neuter propositions take him as having held that truths about the past are now necessary (what has been cannot now not have been) but some truths about the future are contingent; in these cases neither "It will be that *p*" nor "It will not be that *p*" is in itself necessarily true, although one of them is in fact true, and the disjunction of the two propositions, "Either it will or it will not be that *p*," is necessarily true.

The main objection to this view is that it does not explain how Aristotle answered a certain line of reasoning which has repeatedly cropped up in the history of the subject and of which he was certainly not ignorant, as he adumbrates it himself in the course of his exposition. It proceeds as follows: If it be granted (and Aristotle certainly did grant) that all truths about the past are necessary (in the sense that whatever has come to pass cannot now not have come to pass), then if all propositions (even ones about the future) are already either true or false, all truths about the future must be necessary also (a conclusion which Aristotle certainly denied). Suppose it to have been true yesterday that there would be a sea battle in two days' time. Since it has already come to be true, it cannot now not have done so. But whatever necessarily follows from what is inevitable is itself inevitable, and it necessarily follows from its having been true yesterday that there would be a sea battle in two days' time that there will be a sea battle tomorrow; therefore, it is inevitable that there will be a sea battle tomorrow. And if it was already false yesterday that there would be a sea battle in two days' time, it will follow by analogous reasoning that it is inevitable that there will *not* be a sea battle tomorrow. This future sea battle cannot, therefore, be really a contingent matter, and the same type of argument will remove the contingency from all future events whatever. The only way of escaping this reasoning seems to be by denying that it was either already true yesterday or already false yesterday —or, indeed, that it is either already true today or already false today (for the precise interval involved is clearly immaterial)—that there will be a sea battle tomorrow.

We can, of course, escape the conclusion of this argument by denying one of its premises. Some of the ancients even denied the assumption that what necessarily follows from what is inevitable is itself inevitable. Others, and also some of the Scholastics (for example, Ockham and the theological opponents of Peter de Rivo), denied the premise that we have no power over the past. We have indeed no power over what might be called bona fide past events, but such oddly "past" states of affairs as the having been true of a statement about the future we *can* bring about or prevent by our present or future action. The argument can also be avoided by a distinction between two senses of "will not occur." "There will not be a sea battle tomorrow" may mean either "It is not now the case that there will be a sea battle tomorrow" or "It is already going to be the case tomorrow that there is no sea battle." In the former sense, if the eventuation of the sea battle is as yet undetermined, the negative statement is true; in the latter sense it is false; in neither sense is it neuter. And in the same circumstances the unambiguous affirmative "It is already going to be the case tomorrow that there is a sea battle" is simply false. This solution resembles the three-valued one in denying the principle that whatever is or will be true has always been going to be true, since it, too, admits that even though once the matter is settled "There will be a sea battle" is true, before it was settled this would not have been true. (On the present view it would have been false, on the three-valued view neuter.) It therefore raises similar problems about the possibility of foreknowing future contingencies (for one cannot be said to "know" what is not true).

ŁUKASIEWICZ'S MULTIVALUED CALCULI

Even those ancient and medieval writers who believed in a neuter truth-value did very little to work out what effect it would have on ordinary logical laws, although Ockham (not himself an advocate of three-valued logic) did make one or two suggestions about what the truth-value of "If p then q" would be if one of its components were neuter.

Modern logicians are able to be more precise about this, partly because they are accustomed to working with multivalued truth tables in order to establish the independence of axioms in a formal calculus. Consider, for example, a symbolism employing a capital C and an indefinite multiplicity of small letters, the small letters being well-formed formulas and the prefixing of C to any pair of well-formed formulas producing a new one. For example, $CCpqr$ is a well-formed formula (wff) because (*a*) p and q being wffs, Cpq is one, and (*b*) Cpq and r being wffs, $CCpqr$ is one. We may suppose our small letters to represent sentences and Cpq to represent the sentence "If p then q." Suppose we lay down as "axioms" the three wffs (1) $CCpqCCqrCpr$, (2) $CCCpqpp$, (3) $CpCqp$ and say that these axioms are "theses" and that whatever follows from given theses by substitution or detachment is also a thesis. Substitution is the replacement of a small letter in a thesis by a wff, the same replacement being made throughout the thesis. For example, $CCppCqCpp$ is the result of substituting Cpp for p in axiom (3). Detachment can be illustrated as follows: If

we have a formula α and also a formula $C\alpha\beta$ ("If α then β") as theses, then α may be detached and β on its own laid down as a new thesis. The rationale of these procedures is that the theses are supposed to be formulas which represent true propositions whether their contained small letters represent true ones or false ones. This property will clearly be preserved if a small letter is systematically replaced by any wff; if a wff α is in this sense always true and it is always true that α implies β, then β will be always true. If we regard wffs as taking the values 1 and 0 (which we can interpret as "true" and "false"), the value of any wff, given those of its small letters, can be worked out from the table: $C11 = C00 = C01 = 1$, $C10 = 0$. Graphically (with possible values for p written down the side and for q along the top):

C	1	0
1	1	0
0	1	1

It will be found that the axioms always have the value 1 when they are evaluated by this table, and it is obvious from the table that if α always equals 1, the only case in which $C\alpha\beta$ always equals 1 is that in which β always equals 1 (for if β ever equals 0, then $C\alpha\beta$ equals $C10 = 0$).

We now want to know whether any of the three axioms follows from the remaining two. We establish that the second does not by constructing for C the new table

C	1	$\frac{1}{2}$	0
1	1	$\frac{1}{2}$	0
$\frac{1}{2}$	1	1	$\frac{1}{2}$
0	1	1	1

With this table it is still true that if α always equals 1, then $C\alpha\beta$ always equals 1 only if β always equals 1, and any wff that we substitute for a small letter will still take a value within the range $(1,\frac{1}{2},0)$ that the small letter had. Hence, substitution and detachment cannot take us from a wff that always equals 1 to one that does not. However, if we evaluate axioms (1) and (3) by this table, they still always equal 1, but not so axiom (2), for $CCC\frac{1}{2}0\frac{1}{2}\frac{1}{2} = CC\frac{1}{2}\frac{1}{2}\frac{1}{2} = C1\frac{1}{2} = \frac{1}{2}$. Hence, (2) is not derivable from (1) and (3) by substitution and detachment.

This argument, clearly, holds regardless of what interpretation we put on the values 1, $\frac{1}{2}$, and 0 and, indeed, regardless of what interpretation we put on our formulas. In itself, therefore, it does nothing to show that propositions might be capable of a third value between truth and falsehood. If, however, we have independent reasons for entertaining such a supposition, we have an instrument at hand for working out what its consequence might be. In the early 1920s (the rudiments had been suggested even earlier) Jan Łukasiewicz, a Polish logician with uncommon skill in constructing independence proofs of this type, surmised that a logic with the above three-valued table for C might be used to express the ancient and medieval view that contingent future propositions are neither true nor false but neuter. To the table for C he added one for negation, represented by N—namely, $N1 = 0$, $N\frac{1}{2} = \frac{1}{2}$, $N0 = 1$

—and he defined "Either p or q," Apq, as $CCpqq$, and "p and q," Kpq, as $NANpNq$. These functions consequently have the tables

A	1	$\frac{1}{2}$	0		K	1	$\frac{1}{2}$	0
1	1	1	1		1	1	$\frac{1}{2}$	0
$\frac{1}{2}$	1	$\frac{1}{2}$	$\frac{1}{2}$		$\frac{1}{2}$	$\frac{1}{2}$	$\frac{1}{2}$	0
0	1	$\frac{1}{2}$	0		0	0	0	0

The tables for C and N together constituted what he called a "matrix," and his student Mordchaj Wajsberg established that the following axioms, with substitution and detachment, yielded precisely those theses which came out as always 1 when evaluated by the matrix: (1) $CpCqp$, (2) $CCpqCCqrCpr$, (3) $CCNpNqCqp$, (4) $CCCpNppp$.

With the future-contingency interpretation in mind, Łukasiewicz introduced the function Mp, "Possibly p," with the evaluation $M1 = M\frac{1}{2} = 1$, $M0 = 0$; that is, a proposition is definitely "possible" if it is either definitely true or neuter but definitely not possible if it is definitely false. Alfred Tarski observed that the complex $CNpp$ had these properties. The table for C, it may be noted, makes "If p then q" true as long as q is no further from truth than p is, which preserves the natural idea that a true implication will not lead us away from such truth as we already have. Tarski's definition makes p "possible" as long as p is no further from truth than its denial would be. The table for "Either . . . or . . ." fails to verify the law of excluded middle in the form "Either p or not-p" ($A\frac{1}{2}N\frac{1}{2} = A\frac{1}{2}\frac{1}{2} = \frac{1}{2}$). However, the table does not falsify it either, and it can be shown that no laws of two-valued logic are ever actually false in the Łukasiewicz system, although some of them come out as sometimes neuter.

The least satisfactory feature of this system is that it lacks not only the law of excluded middle but also the law of contradiction, "Not both p and not-p," since $NK\frac{1}{2}N\frac{1}{2} = NK\frac{1}{2}\frac{1}{2} = N\frac{1}{2} = \frac{1}{2}$. (In this it differs from the "intuitionistic" logic of L. E. J. Brouwer and Arend Heyting, which also lacks the law of excluded middle but has that of contradiction—see NEGATION.) Intuitively one is inclined to feel that in a system of this sort the conjunction of two propositions about the undetermined future should take different values in different cases. If they are independent possibilities, it will also be undetermined whether they will occur together ($K\frac{1}{2}\frac{1}{2} = \frac{1}{2}$), but if they are conflicting ones (like p and Np), one wants to say that their occurring together is already excluded ($K\frac{1}{2}\frac{1}{2} = 0$). But this would make "$p$ and q" no longer a truth-function; that is, its truth-value would not depend solely on the truth-values of its parts.

In 1954 the Chinese logician Moh Shaw-kwei suggested a more plausible interpretation of Łukasiewicz's three-valued system—namely, that the intermediate value should be read as "paradoxical" and should be assigned to propositions like "What I am now saying is false," which ordinarily would work out as false if it is true and true if it is false. It is reasonable to regard the negation of a paradoxical proposition, the conjunction of a paradoxical proposition with a paradoxical or a true one, the disjunction of a paradoxical proposition with a paradoxical or a false one, and the implication of a false one by a paradoxical one or of a paradoxical by a true, as all of them paradoxical; pre-

cisely these results are yielded by the Łukasiewicz matrix.

Łukasiewicz and others have also studied a system resembling the one above but admitting an infinity of truth-values instead of just three; they have considered the variety of additional truth-functions that become available when we have more than two truth-values to operate with; and they have examined the ways in which these propositional calculi may be combined with a suitable quantification theory.

OTHER INTERPRETATIONS AND USES

The particular evaluations assigned to C, K, etc., in the Łukasiewicz systems are clearly somewhat arbitrary, and innumerable variations are possible. Almost simultaneously with Łukasiewicz's early work, quite different many-valued systems were developed by E. L. Post. Intuitionistic logic has been shown to be interpretable as a system with an infinity of values, rather different from that of Łukasiewicz. The same is true of the various systems of modal logic—that is, the general theory of the necessary and the possible.

At this point it is worth observing that there is no necessity at all to regard the values assigned to functions of propositions by matrices as consisting of plain truth, plain falsehood, and various other things thought of as being between these two. We may very well insist that there is nothing at all between plain truth and plain falsehood but admit that there are other variable features of complex propositions which depend systematically on the same features in their components. For example, if we assume that there are precisely two possible states of affairs, we might divide all propositions into those true in both (value 1), those true in the actual state of affairs but not in its alternative (value 2), those true in the other state of affairs but not in the actual one (value 3), and those false in both (value 4) and evaluate Kpq ("p and q"), Np ("Not-p"), and Lp ("Necessarily p") by the following matrix:

K	1	2	3	4		N		L
1	1	2	3	4		4		1
2	2	2	4	4		3		4
3	3	4	3	4		2		4
4	4	4	4	4		1		4

For example, if p is true in both worlds but q only in the first, then "p and q" is true only in the first ($K12 = 2$), whereas if p is true only in the first and q only in the second, then "p and q" is true in neither ($K23 = 4$). "Necessarily p" is true in both worlds if p is true in both (that is, in all possible ones); otherwise it is true in neither. This matrix verifies (i.e., assigns the value 1 to the whole for all values of the components) all the laws of the modal system $S5$ (see LOGIC, MODAL), but it also verifies certain formulas which reflect the fiction that there are only two possible worlds and which are intuitively undesirable. It is thus not "characteristic" for $S5$ (it does not verify *all* and *only* the laws of $S5$). We would obtain a matrix characteristic for $S5$ if we employed an infinity of values, each value being an infinite sequence of 1's and 0's, each place in the sequence representing a possible world (p having a 1 in that place if it is true in that world and a 0 is false), the sequence for "Not-*p*" having a 0 wherever the sequence for *p* has a 1 and vice versa, the sequence for "*p* and *q*" having a 0 except at places where the sequences for *p* and for *q* both have 1's, the sequence for "Necessarily *p*" being all 1's when that for *p* is all 1's and all 0's otherwise, and a formula being a law if it comes out all 1's whatever the values of its components.

Again, purely geometrical propositions might be assigned an eight-valued matrix in which the value 1 means "true in Euclidean, Riemannian, and Lobachevskian geometry alike," 2 means "true in Euclidean and Riemannian but not in Lobachevskian," and so on through the other combinations. (This idea has been developed by Alan Rose.)

Another four-valued system would be obtained if we divided propositions according to whether they were purely abstract or mathematical in their subject matter or contained some reference to natural objects, assigning them the value 1 if they were both true and purely mathematical, 2 if true but "impure," 3 if false and "impure," and 4 if purely mathematical and false. Taking *Lp* to mean "It is a purely mathematical truth that *p*," we would have for *K, N,* and *L* the following matrix:

K	1	2	3	4	*N*	*L*
1	1	2	3	4	4	1
2	2	2	3	3	3	3
3	3	3	3	3	2	3
4	4	3	3	4	1	4

("Impurity" infects any proposition into which it enters. For example, the proposition "2 and 2 is 4, and grass is green" is "impure" because its second component is; *K*12 = 2.) With this matrix we need to "designate" the value 2 as well as 1; that is, we count as a law any formula that always has either the value 1 or the value 2. Otherwise "Not both *p* and not-*p*" would be no law, since "Not both (grass is green) and (grass is not green)" is impure; in fact, any formula at all will fail to take the value 1 when either 2 or 3 is assigned to a component.

Yet another four-valued system, the work of Łukasiewicz, is one in which the function *Mp* is *used ambiguously* for the plain *p* and for the tautological "If *p* then *p*." Here we have pairs of 1's and 0's as values, assigning to each function, at the first place, the value it would have if *Mp* were read the first way and, at the second place, the value it would have if it were read the second way. The matrix for *C, N,* and *M* will then be

C	11	10	01	00	*N*	*M*
11	11	10	01	00	00	11
10	11	11	01	01	01	11
01	11	10	11	10	10	01
00	11	11	11	11	11	01

(The column for *M* is the crucial one here; *Mp*'s first-place values are identical with the first-place values of *p*, whereas its second-place value is 1 regardless of the second-place value of *p*.) This is called the "product" of the two matrices

C	1	0	*N*	*M*		*C*	1	0	*N*	*M*
1	1	0	0	1		1	1	0	0	1
0	1	1	1	0		0	1	1	1	1

The laws are formulas which are always 1 on either interpretation of *M*—they are always 11—for example, *CpMp*.

Łukasiewicz in his later years thought that *M* here expressed the ordinary meaning of "possible," but this is doubtful. We would certainly agree that whatever *is* true *could* be true (*CpMp*), but the matrix also verifies, for example, *CMpCMNpMq*, "If *p* is possible, then if not-*p* is possible too, anything at all, say *q*, is possible," which seems odd. Ordinarily, in fact, we think of "Possibly *p*" as something less than the plain *p* (which means that *p* is not merely possible—it is a fact) but more than the mere "If *p* then *p*" (which is true even if *p* is *not* possible; for example, if 2 and 2 is 5, then 2 and 2 is 5). But this "possibly," which does not assert something between these limits but asserts the limits themselves ambiguously, is like the "possibly" of a politician answering a question and hoping that some of his audience will understand him to have said "yes" whereas others will understand him to have said nothing at all. The present four-valued system contains all those purely logical statements which such a man could get away with undetected (it being assumed that his use of "possibly" is consistent—for example, that when he says "If not possibly not-*p* then possibly *p*" he means either "If not not-*p* then *p*" or "If not (if not-*p* then not-*p*) then (if *p* then *p*)"). P. T. Geach has pointed out that it could be used to explore the logic of the propositions which Aristotle called "indefinite," such as "Men are cads," which has no sign of quantity to indicate whether it means that all men are cads or only that some are. If we define "Men are cads" as "Some men are cads, and possibly all are," in the above sense of "possibly," the present Łukasiewicz system, combined with the standard logic of "all" and "some," will enable us to work out just what laws involving "indefinites" we can be sure of. Human communication being what it is, tasks like this are worth performing.

Rose has found a use for multivalued calculi in designing signaling systems. It has sometimes been suggested that a multivalued logic would simplify and clarify quantum mechanics, although the suggestion has not yet been seriously taken up by physicists. What is surmised, with the historical origins of multivalued logic in mind, is that it would be helpful because of the notorious indeterminism of quantum mechanics, but it may very possibly be helpful, if it is so at all, rather because of its power (illustrated in the preceding paragraph) to formalize the reasoning that is possible where communication is imperfect. Or perhaps its use will consist, more philosophically, in its demonstration that the same technical devices can be used to cope with imperfect communication and with genuine indeterminism.

Bibliography

Aristotle's *De Interpretatione* is best read in J. L. Ackrill's edition of it with the *Categories* (Oxford, 1963), which contains a commentary on Ch. 9 with references to current discussions. On the medieval debates, see Philotheus Boehner's edition of Ockham's *Tractatus de Praedestinatione et de Praescientia Dei et de Futuris Contingentibus* (St. Bonaventure, N.Y., 1945) and especially L. Baudry's *La Querelle des futurs contingents* (Paris, 1950). There is a very acute survey of the possible positions and arguments in Francisco Suarez' *Opusculum de Scientia Quam Deus Habet in Futuris Contingentibus*, Book II. For a modern discussion, with attempted formalizations, see A. N. Prior's "The Formalities of Omniscience," in *Philosophy* (April 1962).

The details of Łukasiewicz's earlier systems are given in Alfred Tarski, *Logic, Semantics, Metamathematics* (Oxford, 1956), Paper IV; those of his later four-valued modal system are in "A System of Modal Logic," *Journal of Computing Systems*, Vol. 1, No. 3 (July 1953), reproduced in Polish in his *Z Zagadnien Logiki i Filozofii* (Warsaw, 1961). On the more detailed formal problems arising from many-valued systems, the standard text is J. B. Rosser and A. R. Turquette, *Many-valued Logics* (Amsterdam, 1952).

On particular applications of many-valued logics, see Alan Rose, "Eight-valued Geometry," in *Proceedings of the London Mathematical Society* (1952), and "Applications of Logical Computers to the Construction of Electrical Control Tables for Signalling Frames," in *Zeitschrift für mathematische Logik und Grundlagen der Mathematik*, Vol. 4 (1958); and A. N. Prior, "Curry's Paradox and Three-valued Logic," in *Australasian Journal of Philosophy*, Vol. 33 (December 1955), 177–182, and "Notes on a Group of New Modal Systems," in *Logique et analyse*, No. 6–7 (April 1959).

A. N. PRIOR

LOGIC, MATHEMATICAL. See LOGIC, HISTORY OF; LOGIC, MODERN.

LOGIC, MODAL.

Modal logic studies the logical features of necessity, possibility, impossibility, and related concepts. It was extensively treated by Aristotle and other ancient writers. After Christianity first conquered the ancient world modal logic appears to have been regarded as a theologically dangerous part of Greek philosophy, but it was again extensively studied by both the Arab and the Christian Scholastics. After the Renaissance it tended to be sketchily dealt with or ignored. Modal logic found little place in modern mathematical logic in the nineteenth and early twentieth centuries, but there has been a widespread revival of interest in it since the early 1930s, and it is now one of the most actively pursued branches of logic.

The basic concepts of modal logic are primarily expressed by certain adverbs and auxiliary verbs and verb phrases—possibility by forms like "Possibly p," "It is possible that p," "It could be that p"; necessity by "Necessarily p," "It is necessary (necessarily true) that p," "It is bound to be the case that p," "It must be that p." These words and phrases may be combined in various ways with others of the same type—for example, with those expressing negation—and the equivalences and implications that hold between these complexes were among the first laws of the subject to be recognized. In particular we have the following laws of modal "equipollence":

(1) It is necessary that p = it is impossible that not-p = it is not possible that not-p.

(2) It is necessary that not-p = it is impossible that p = it is not possible that p.

(3) It is not necessary that p = it is not impossible that not-p = it is possible that not-p.

(4) It is not necessary that not-p = it is not impossible that p = it is possible that p.

Of these, forms (2) imply forms (3), and forms (1) imply forms (4), but not vice versa. Also, forms (1) imply that p is true ("If necessarily p then p," or, as the Schoolmen put it, *ab oportere esse ad esse valet consequentia*, "from 'must be so' to 'is so' is a valid inference"); forms (2) imply that p is false ("If not possibly p then not-p"); forms (3) are implied by p's being false ("If not-p then not necessarily p"); and forms (4) are implied by p's being true ("If p then possibly p," *ab esse ad posse valet consequentia*).

When necessity is combined with implication a distinction must be made between the implication that something is necessary (*necessitas consequentis*, expressed by "If p then necessarily-q") and the necessity of the implication as a whole (*necessitas consequentiae*, expressed by "If p then-necessarily q" or, less ambiguously, by "Necessarily if-p-then-q"). For example, a proposition does not generally imply its own necessity (we do not generally have "If p then necessarily-p"), but every proposition necessarily implies itself (we do have "Necessarily if-p-then-p").

However, it has been recognized at least since Aristotle's time that what is necessarily implied by a necessary proposition is itself necessary: if necessarily (if p then q), then if necessarily p then necessarily q. Similarly, what is necessarily implied by something possible is itself possible: if necessarily if p then q, then if possibly p then possibly q. Conversely, whatever necessarily implies an impossible proposition is itself impossible.

When necessity is combined with disjunction (i.e., with "Either . . . or . . .") we must distinguish between the necessity of the disjunction ("Necessarily either p or q") and that of the disjuncts ("Either necessarily p or necessarily q"). For example, we necessarily have "Either p or not-p," but we may have neither "Necessarily p" nor "Necessarily not-p." Where neither a given proposition nor its denial is necessary—that is, where the proposition is neither necessary nor impossible—it is said to be contingent.

The conjunction (expressed by "and") of two separate assertions of possibility is to be similarly distinguished from the assertion that the whole conjunction is possible: "Possibly p and possibly q" does not entail "Possibly (p and q)." For example, both p and not-p may be separately possible (and will be so if p is contingent), but the combination "p and not-p" is not. Where propositions are not jointly possible, whether or not they are separately so, they are said to be inconsistent or incompatible; where they are jointly possible they are consistent or compatible.

Among contingent propositions, some are closer to being necessary than others; they are then said to be more likely or probable. The calculus of probabilities can be regarded as a metric extension of modal logic, just as modal assertions can be regarded as special cases arising in probability logic (Possibly p = There is some chance that p; Necessarily p = There is no chance that not-p). With this extension of modal logic we shall not, however, be further concerned.

MATERIAL IMPLICATION, STRICT IMPLICATION, AND ENTAILMENT

In the ancient, medieval, and modern periods modal concepts have been drawn upon to explain the "following" of one proposition from another which is expressed by the conditional form "If p then q."

In the fourth century B.C., Philo of Megara pointed out that truth and falsehood may be distributed in four ways between two propositions: either they will both be true, or the first true and the second false, or vice versa, or both false. Philo suggested that the form "If p then q" is true in all of these cases except the second; that is, it is true so long as we do not have p true and q false. There is no doubt that "If p then q" is false if p is true but q is not, nor that it could be true in each of the other cases (this much was observed by Aristotle), but that it automatically is true in all the other cases was widely questioned in Philo's time and was also questioned when the notion of material implication, with essentially the Philonian definition, was introduced by logicians of the nineteenth and twentieth centuries. Contemporary modal logic, in fact, began with C. I. Lewis' attempts to improve upon the Philonian definition of "if."

The trouble with the Philonian definition is that it makes any conditional automatically true if it has a false antecedent p or a true consequent q (for in neither of these cases will we have the combination of p with the falsehood of q). Lewis suggested that p genuinely or "strictly" implies q only if it not merely happens not to be the case that p is true and q false but could not be the case that p is true and q false. That is, "p strictly implies q" amounts not to merely "Not (p and not-q)" but to "Not possibly (p and not-q)"—symbolized $p \prec q := \sim \Diamond (p . \sim q)$. This definition of the relation of "consequence" was frequently given by medieval writers, who also arrived at the Philonian conception as a special case. If the combination of p with not-q is not realized at a particular moment, then it is not possible at that moment that it should be, so that at that moment, even if not always, the conditional "If p then q" in a sense holds; it is, as they said, a valid *consequentia ut nunc*.

Medieval logicians also noticed, as Lewis did, that "strict" implication has paradoxes of its own. The falsehood of p does not suffice to verify the strict conditional "If p then q," but its impossibility does, for if p cannot be true at all, we do not and cannot have the combination of p's truth with q's falsehood. Similarly, although the truth of q does not suffice to verify the strict "If p then q," its necessity does, for if q cannot be false at all, we do not and cannot have the combination of q's falsehood with p's truth. From these results it follows that all impossibilities strictly imply one another—i.e., are "strictly equivalent"—and similarly with all necessities.

Lewis simply regarded these results as discoveries (why should there not be surprises in logic as well as in other branches of mathematics?) but for many logicians they show that strict implication cannot give correctly the sense of "if" in which "If p then q" means that q logically follows from p. They have argued, for example, that if every necessary truth follows from all propositions whatsoever, the careful proofs of necessary truths that are presented in disciplines like geometry would be unnecessary, and the attempts of makers of logical systems to show that their axioms are "independent" (i.e., that no one of them follows from the rest) would all be doomed to failure. There is some confusion here, however. When an axiom set is shown to be "independent," what is shown is always that no axiom is derivable from the others by certain specified rules of inference; the independence is relative to the rules chosen. Strict implication has to do rather with what makes a rule of inference justified, valid, or "safe" in the sense that it cannot lead us from truth to falsehood, and no rule can lead us from truth to falsehood if it either starts from what is necessarily false or leads to what is necessarily true. Moreover, even if we use rules that will in fact enable us to prove all our theorems (necessary truths) from any arbitrarily chosen premises whatever (and there are now many logical systems constructed on just this principle), it still remains to show that a given proposition is such a necessary truth by so proving it. Those logicians who hold, for good reasons or bad, that p's strictly implying q is not the same as q's logically following from p describe the latter (following G. E. Moore) as p's entailing q. E. J. Nelson argued that entailment in this sense must express an inner connection between the propositions it relates, a relevance of the one to the other, and cannot hold merely on account of some property (falsehood or truth *or* impossibility or necessity) that one of the propositions may possess on its own. He suggested defining "p entails q" as "p is inconsistent with the denial of q," where "inconsistency" again means a relation involving both propositions and not merely the impossibility of their joint truth (for the latter would follow from the impossibility of either one of them and thus make Nelson's definition equivalent to Lewis').

Those who object to the identification of entailment with strict implication are not obliged to give an alternative definition of the concept they favor, for entailment may well be one of those undefinable notions in terms of which we define other things, rather than vice versa. They do, however, have an obligation to set out as systematically as possible the laws which they take entailment to obey, so that we can find out whether it, too, has its "paradoxical" features, and what they are. The only serious attempts to do this have been those of Wilhelm Ackermann, who in 1956 gave postulates for what he called "strong" or "rigorous" implication, and A. R. Anderson and N. D. Belnap, who have worked with a modification of Ackermann's conception. Their system satisfies Nelson's demand for "relevance," in the quite precise sense that it yields no laws of entailment except ones in which the entailing and entailed forms have at least one variable in common. For example, it is a law that for any p and q, p-and-q entails p (here p is common to antecedent and consequent), but not that for any p and q, p-and-not-p entails q (in which the one consequent-variable q does not appear in the antecedent). For specially chosen q's the second law does hold; for example, p-and-not-p does entail p, since even the first law yields this.

Anyone who sets himself the task of "formalizing" entailment has to face the following difficulty, which was noticed by the medieval logicians and, independently, by Lewis. If we use "If p then q" to express the entailment of q by p, the following laws would seem to be reasonable:

(1) If (if p then q) then if (if q then r) then (if p then r).

(2) If (p and r) then ((either p or q) and r).

(3) If (either p or q) and not-p, then q.

Here (1) expresses the "transitivity" of entailment, presupposed when we have a chain of proofs leading from one proposition to another. Principle (3) is one which the Stoic logicians said even dogs in the street recognized: when chasing their prey to a point where the road forks, they will sniff along one fork, and if they catch no scent there, they will chase along the other without further sniffing. But by (2) the impossible proposition "*p* and not-*p*" entails "(either *p* or *q*) and not-*p*," where *q* is any proposition you please; this, by (3), entails the plain *q*; hence, by (1), the impossible proposition "*p* and not-*p*" entails *q*, which can be any proposition at all. We can therefore avoid this last "paradox" only by denying (1), (2), or (3), and these denials seem just as "paradoxical" as what we are trying to avoid.

The Anderson–Belnap system, which has a certain formal elegance, turns out to lack the law (3). Intuitively more plausible, although the suggestion has not been developed very systematically, would be the denial of (1). Suppose we say that *p* entails *q* if and only if (*a*) *p* strictly implies *q* and (*b*) it does so in virtue of a "reasonable" general principle, one that *can* have instances in which the entailing proposition is not impossible and the entailed one not necessary. Then "*p* and not-*p*" will entail "Either *p* or *q*, and not-*p*" in virtue of the "reasonable" principle (2), and this will entail the plain *q* in virtue of the reasonable principle (3). However, if entailment were transitive we would then have "*p* and not-*p*" entailing *q*, and there is no "reasonable" principle that this exemplifies.

Some writers have suggested restricting the terms of the entailment relation to contingent propositions, so that where *p* or *q* is either necessary or impossible, "*p* entails *q*" is either false (according to one version of this view) or meaningless (according to another). It would be difficult to set out any laws at all for entailment thus restricted, and it would also exclude the kind of entailment used when we argue that some proposition is impossible because it entails something impossible.

SYSTEMS OF STRICT IMPLICATION

Various alternative sets of axioms and rules for possibility, necessity, and strict implication were given by Lewis and shown by him and others not to be equivalent—i.e., not to yield the same formulas as theorems. They were therefore given numbers—*S1*, *S2*, *S3*, *S4*, *S5*, *S6*, *S7*, and *S8*. Many alternative axioms and rules for these systems have been suggested by later logicians, and further systems, which are not equivalent to any of Lewis', have been developed. A particularly simple one, which Robert Feys called the system *T*, comes in essence from Kurt Gödel. It assumes the ordinary laws for material implication and negation, with the rule that if *X* is a law and "If *X* then *Y*" ("if" being the "if" of material implication) is also a law, then *Y* is a law; it adds an undefined symbol for "necessarily," defining "Possibly *p*" as "Not necessarily not-*p*" and "*p* strictly implies *q*" as "Necessarily (if *p* then *q*)" ("if" being the "if" of material implication, as it is in the axioms). The special axioms for necessity are simply

(1) If necessarily *p* then *p*;

(2) If necessarily (if *p* then *q*), then if necessarily *p*, then necessarily *q*.

There is a special rule, the "rule of necessitation," that if

a formula *X* is a law of the system, so is "Necessarily *X*." All the elementary modal principles set out in the first section of this article, and also the paradoxes of strict implication, can be derived as theorems in this system.

G. H. von Wright developed a system equivalent to *T*, calling it *M*. In *M* the undefined modal expression is "possibly," "Necessarily *p*" being defined as "Not possibly not-*p*." This is the procedure in Lewis' own systems, but still other procedures are possible. For example, strict implication itself may be taken as undefined and "Necessarily *p*" defined as "Not-*p* strictly implies *p*" (whatever is strictly implied by its own denial is necessarily true, and whatever is necessarily true is strictly implied by its own denial, since it is strictly implied by anything). In some of Lewis' stronger systems (*S4* and *S5*—their characteristic features will be sketched below), "Necessarily *p*" may be defined as "*p*'s strictly implying *p* strictly implies *p*" (whatever is strictly implied by a necessary truth, such as that it strictly implies itself, is itself necessary, and whatever is necessary is strictly implied by any necessary truth, since it is strictly implied by anything at all). It is then possible to distinguish those laws in which strict implication is the only logical notion that occurs. These are different for the different Lewis systems, and the full systems can be obtained from their pure strict-implication fragments by the addition of appropriate axioms (the same for all the systems) for "and" and "not" (E. J. Lemmon, or for "and," "or," and "not" (Ian Hacking), or for the material "if" and a standard impossible proposition (C. A. Meredith). (On the use of a standard false proposition instead of an undefined negation, see NEGATION.) Using the last procedure, we can give formal embodiment to the conception of material implication as a limiting case of strict implication, a favorite idea of C. S. Peirce's, which we have earlier noted as occurring also in medieval writings. Peirce said that in general the conditional form "If *p* then *q*" means that in no possible state of affairs is *p* true without *q*, but we may take into consideration a wider or a narrower range of possible states of affairs, and if we narrow the range down to the actual state of affairs our "if" becomes material.

Lewis' systems *S1* and *S2* are weaker than the system *T*; his *S3*, *S6*, *S7*, and *S8* possess laws that *T* does not have but lack some that it does have (they lack, for instance, the rule of necessitation), and his *S4* and *S5* contain *T*, adding to it certain principles about iterated and nested modalities—that is about the possibly possible, the necessarily necessary, the possibly necessary, and the necessarily possible. It might be maintained that although not everything is actually possible, anything at all could be possible; this view of the matter is embodied in *S6*, *S7*, and *S8*. Alternatively, it might be held that only what is actually possible could be possible—that is, that for any *p*, if possibly possibly *p* then possibly *p*. If this is so, it will follow by ordinary principles that whatever is actually necessary is necessarily necessary. These are the laws that distinguish the system *S4*. It may be held, further, that whatever is possible is necessarily possible, and whatever could be necessary is actually necessary. These principles are laid down in *S5*, and it has been found that the *S4* principles follow from the *S5* ones by ordinary modal laws, but not vice versa. In S5, although there is a place for contingent as well as necessary and impossible propositions, no assertions about the modality of propositions are contingent, since any statement that a proposition is necessary or impossible is necessarily true if it is true at all and necessarily false if it is false.

The pure strict-implication fragments of S4 and S5 are related to one another very much as are the implicational fragments of intuitionist logic and "classical" truth-functional logic, and there are similar analogies between the systems in their entirety. In recent years there has been some study of systems containing S4 and contained in S5 that parallel systems between intuitionist and classical propositional logic. One such system will be touched on in the next section. It is also possible, though a bit difficult, to give formal expression to the not uncommon view that nested modal expressions like "possibly possible" are meaningless.

INTERPRETATIONS OF MODAL SYSTEMS

The variety of alternative systems of modal laws which logicians now offer suggests that there is some obscurity in the meaning of the basic terms "possible" and "necessary" and that different laws among those proposed might hold good if these terms were given different precise meanings.

For example, we might take the possible to be that which either is or has been or will be true and the necessary as that which is and always has been and always will be true. This interpretation turns out, according to ordinary views concerning past and future truth, to verify S5. For example, "Whatever could be necessary is actually necessary" will amount to "If it is or has been or will be true that something is and always has been and always will be the case, then it is true right now that that thing is and always has been and always will be the case," and this is true.

The modal terms were given an interpretation of this general type by the Greek logician Diodorus Cronus; he, however, took account of the present and the future only—that is, he defined the possible as what is or will be true and the necessary as what is true and always will be. This does not verify all the S5 principles. For example, it is not always true that if it is or will be true that something is and always will be the case, then it is true right now that that thing is and always will be the case (it may not start its career of permanence until later); that is, in Diodorean modal logic it is not true that whatever is possibly necessary is actually necessary. However, Diodorean logic contains the S4 law that whatever is actually necessary is necessarily necessary, for if it is and always will be true that p, then this itself is and always will be true. Diodorean modal logic, however, is not quite identical with S4, as it contains certain laws which are not in that system (though they are in S5)—for instance, the law that whatever could be necessary must be possible (that is, if it is or will be that it is and always will be that p, then it is and always will be that it is or will be that p). The Diodorean system, in fact, lies between S4 and S5.

We do obtain precisely S4 if we suppose that the future is not quite fixed and that any state of affairs has a number of alternative futures which may issue from it (though it is too late, once it has become present, for a state of affairs to have alternative pasts) and then define "Possibly p" as "p either is true now or will be true in at least one of the alternative futures" and "Necessarily p" as "p is true now and throughout all the alternative futures."

Interpretations of this type have been brilliantly generalized by Stig Kanger (*Probability in Logic*, Stockholm, 1957), Jaakko Hintikka, and especially S. A. Kripke. Suppose we are furnished with a set of "worlds" (from an abstract mathematical point of view a "world" can be simply a set of propositions); we may define the possible as what is true either in the actual world or in some world accessible from it and the necessary as what is true in the actual world and in all worlds accessible from it (or, more abstractly, in all worlds to which this one stands in a certain relation R). We then obtain different modal systems by making different assumptions about the relation of accessibility (or R), and on different interpretations of this relation different such assumptions will be plausible. We may, for example, simply suppose that the relation is transitive—i.e., that what is accessible from any world that is accessible from a given one is itself accessible from the given one. Our last previous interpretation, in terms of alternative possible futures, is a special case of this (a possible future outcome of a possible future outcome of a given state of affairs will itself be a possible future outcome of this state of affairs); it gives us S4. Or we may assume that accessibility is symmetrical—i.e., that if any world A is accessible from a world B, then B is accessible from A. This yields a modal system between T and S5, containing the law (not in S4) that whatever is possibly possible is actually so. If we assume both symmetry and transitivity—conditions that would be realized if every world were accessible from every other and also if none were accessible from any other—we would have S5. If we assume that every world is "connected" by accessibility with every other—i.e., that for any worlds A and B either A is accessible from B or vice versa—we obtain another system between T and S5. Such connectedness would be one feature of the Diodorean system, for given any two momentary states of affairs A and B in the actual time series, either A is an actual future outcome of B or B is one of A. Where accessibility is defined in terms of alternative possible futures we do not have such connectedness, since A might be out on one limb and B on another and neither of them a possible outcome of the other.

SYNTACTICAL INTERPRETATIONS OF MODALITY

Attempts have also been made to give a "syntactical" interpretation to modal concepts, p's necessity being equated with its provability from specified axioms by specified rules. Such necessity would, of course, always be relative to the rules and axioms chosen, and the most straightforward way of developing this type of interpretation involves a certain subtle shift in the grammar of modal expressions. In systems such as Lewis', "necessarily" is an adverb like "not," which is attached to sentences to form other sentences, and the strict "if" is a "connective" that links two sentences to form a compound one. The compound sentences in each case are not about their components but about whatever the components are about.

"Blind men are necessarily men" is about men, not about sentences, not even about the sentence "Blind men are men," and "Caesar's conquering Gaul strictly implies Caesar's conquering something" is about Caesar, Gaul, etc., not about the sentences "Caesar conquered Gaul" and "Caesar conquered something." We have, indeed, in the course of this exposition, loosely used forms like " 'Grass is green' strictly implies 'Grass is colored,' " "*p* implies *q*," "*p* is necessary" (as if "*p*" and "*q*" stood not for sentences but for nouns), and we shall continue to do so. But in strict propriety one ought to write "*That p* is necessary" (i.e., "It is necessary that *p*") and "*That p* implies (or entails) that *q*." The necessity of sentences, and implication of sentences by sentences, is a secondary form that can easily be defined in terms of the primary one—for example, by saying that the sentence "Grass is green" is necessary if and only if "Grass is necessarily green" is true.

On the interpretation of modality now being considered, however, what is primary is the verb "is necessary," forming sentences not from sentences but from expressions that name sentences, the result being a sentence that is really about the named sentence; any other use of "necessary," if any other be admitted, is defined in terms of this one. Such a use of the modal words can be made precise only if we work with a language containing some systematic way of naming its own expressions, so that given any expression of the language, such as a sentence, we can discover which other expression of the language is the given one's name. If we write (*x*) for the name of the expression *x*, propositions of the form "If necessarily *p* then *p*" will have to be rewritten in this version of modal logic as "If (*p*) is necessary then *p*," and similarly with the exemplifications of other modal laws. "If (*p*) is necessary then *p*" is in its turn to be understood as "If (*p*) is provable then *p*," and "provable" is to mean "derivable by such-and-such transformations from the sentences (*q*), (*r*), (*s*)," whatever may be the sentences selected as axioms and the transformations selected as rules of derivation.

The possibility of presenting modal systems in this way was mentioned in the early 1930s by Gödel, who, however, also noticed one limitation to any such program. In view of his own proof that the consistency of Peano's arithmetic cannot be proved—at least not if Peano's arithmetic really is consistent—in Peano's arithmetic itself, it follows that we cannot prove in Peano's arithmetic that whatever is provable in Peano's arithmetic is true. Hence, if necessity means provability from axioms and by rules that are sufficient for Peano's arithmetic, one law that we cannot consistently have is "(If (*p*) is necessary, then *p*) is necessary," the counterpart of the modal law "Necessarily (if necessarily *p* then *p*)." If we are prepared to define necessity in terms of provability from a somewhat weaker basis than the postulates of Peano's arithmetic, we can consistently have a "modal" system (of the above sort) containing the above law, but not in combination with certain other laws whose counterparts are present in even the weakest Lewis system, S1. This has been recently shown by David Kaplan and Richard Montague, and Montague has added a number of allied results, such as that an inconsistency will result from the two postulates

(1) If (*p*) is necessary then *p*;

(2) If *α* is a law, "(*α*) is necessary" is also a law.

The proof depends on the possibility of finding, for any syntactical predicate *φ* in a language that contains its own syntax, a sentence *S* such that "*S* if and only if *φ*(*S*)" is provable. If for *φ* we take either "is not necessary" or "has a necessary negation," the proof from (1), (2), and the theorem about *S* is very easy. We can, for example, proceed thus:

(3) *S* if and only if (*S*) is not necessary.

(4) If not *S* then (*S*) is necessary (from 3).

(5) If not *S* then *S* (from 4 and 1).

(6) *S* (from 5).

(7) (*S*) is not necessary (from 6 and 3).

(8) (*S*) is necessary (from 6 and 2).

None of these consequences follow if we drop the attempt to make necessity a syntactical predicate attaching to names of sentences and use "necessarily" as an adverb attaching to sentences in the usual way. We shall revert to this more usual grammar in the sections that follow.

MODALITY AND QUANTIFICATION

Adverbial signs of modality may be placed not only before or after signs of negation, implication, conjunction, and disjunction but also before or after the signs of quantity, "all" and "some." Here again the order is often important. For example, "Everyone has a chance of winning" ("For all *x*, possibly *x* will win") does not say the same as "There is a chance that everyone will win" ("Possibly for all *x*, *x* will win"); the second implies the first, but not vice versa. In current discussions reference is often made at this point to the medieval distinction between *de dicto* and *de re* modalities. In "Everyone has a chance of winning" the possibility of winning is predicated of each individual object (*res*) being considered, but in the other form, "There is a chance that everyone will win," it is the entire *dictum*, or proposition, "Everyone will win" that is modified by a "possibly."

The combination of modal logic with the theory of the quantifiers "For all *x*" and "For some *x*" was pioneered in the early 1940s by Ruth C. Barcan, now Ruth Barcan Marcus ("Functional Calculus of First Order Based on Strict Implication," in *Journal of Symbolic Logic*, Vol. 11, 1946, 1–16). She added to the Lewis system S2 (*a*) one of the usual bases for quantification theory and (*b*) a special mixing axiom, to the effect that if it could be that something *φ*'s, then there is something of which it could be that it *φ*'s. From axioms of this sort she was able to prove a variety of laws, including the one-way implication mentioned in the preceding paragraph. Her special axiom (*b*) has since been shown to be superfluous, because it is provable from what is left, if we combine one of the ordinary bases for quantification theory with the stronger modal system S5.

The law (*b*), however, is, from some viewpoints, counterintuitive. What if the reason why "it could be that something *φ*'s" is not that "there is something which could *φ*" but rather that although nothing that actually exists could *φ*, the world might have contained different beings from the comparatively incapable ones that it does contain? Even in the later Middle Ages connected arguments were brought up against some of the derived laws in the Barcan system. For example, Jean Buridan argued that there are exceptions to the law "If possibly everything *φ*'s then everything possibly φ's," for from "It could be that everything is God" (true because God could annihilate all creatures) it does not follow that "Everything could be God" (for no creature could be).

Laws of this sort, in fact, can hold unrestrictedly only if we assume that whatever exists is bound to do so and whatever could exist does exist—that is, if we assume that however different may be the states of affairs which are possible alternatives to the actual one, they all contain the same individual objects. But a modal logic that dropped this postulate might well differ from the common systems even in its unquantified portion. For it might be argued that in a possible state of affairs not containing an object *A* there would be no positive or negative facts about *A,* so that "*A* is *A,*" for example, although not false in any possible circumstances, might in some be neither false nor true, and therefore its falsehood might be impossible without its truth being necessary. This would mean dropping the elementary "equipollences" listed earlier. A modal system called *Q,* with this and consequential modifications, was sketched by A. N. Prior and axiomatized by R. A. Bull. S. A. Kripke, in a further elaboration of his models for modal systems, sketched an alternative conception, in which, in a world not containing *A,* there are no simple positive facts about *A* but there are nevertheless negative and other complex ones. This also involves abandoning Barcan-type laws for quantified modal logic, but it modifies the unquantified basis much less drastically.

More radical objections, not just to the Barcan system but to the whole program of combining modal logic with quantification theory, have been made by W. V. Quine. Such a program, he argues, would involve us in reviving an outmoded piece of Aristotelianism. Aristotle distinguished between what he called "essential" and "accidental" predication, and at least since John Stuart Mill it has been widely held that a good sense can be given to this distinction when the statements involved are general but not when they are singular. We can say, for example, that man is essentially rational and accidentally earth-dwelling if all we mean by this is that being rational is part of what is meant by being a man but that being an earth-dweller is not. However, no such sense could be given to the statement that this object before me, say John Jones, is essentially rational but only accidentally earth-dwelling ("Individuals have no essences," as Mill put it). Translating this into the language of modal logic, we can say that it is a necessary truth that men are rational, since it is a necessary truth that whatever is a rational animal is rational, but we cannot say of any particular individual that it is necessary that *he* be either rational or anything else. Quantified modal logic, however, is a pointless complication unless we can give a meaning to such forms as "For some individual *x,* it is necessary that *x* should φ."

The only answer to this is that a view is not necessarily wrong because Aristotle held it, and the only "essential" attributes of individuals to which modal logic is committed are trivial ones like "φ'ing if one φ's." It is "essential" to an individual that he should φ-if-he-φ's; it is a truth of logic that he must do this—or if the considerations adduced earlier prevent us from saying quite this much, we can say of any individual *x* that it is not possible that he should not

φ-if-he-φ's (that he should φ-without-φ'ing). Also, with every individual object *x* it is necessarily true, or at least not possibly false, that it should be *that* object *x* (for if it were some other object instead it would be not *it* but that other object, which was that other object). But this introduces a new topic.

MODALITY AND IDENTITY: REFERENTIAL OPACITY

R. B. Marcus initiated studies of the effect of adding to modal logic not only quantification theory but also the ordinary postulates about identity, namely that everything is identical with itself and that if *x* and *y* are one and the same thing, then whatever is true of *x* is true of *y* (sometimes called "Leibniz' law" or the "indiscernibility of identicals"). The problems raised in the previous section crop up again here, together with some new ones. In particular, it is easy to prove, from ordinary assumptions, that if *x* and *y* are identical at all, their identity is a necessary truth. For if *x* is in fact identical with *y,* so that whatever is true of *x* is true of *y,* then since it is true that *x* is necessarily identical with *x* it must be true that *x* is necessarily identical with *y.*

Particularly strong objections have been made to this result by W. V. Quine. The morning star, he points out, is identical with the evening star, and the morning star is necessarily identical with the morning star, yet the evening star is not necessarily identical with the morning star but only contingently so. Contexts in which we can interchange identicals without loss of truth are called by Quine "referentially transparent," and ones in which we cannot are called "referentially opaque." Modal contexts, such as ". . . is necessarily identical with the morning star," are in general referentially opaque and in Quine's view have no place in a strictly scientific language.

Some writers—Hintikka, for example—have evolved forms of modal logic with identity in which it is a law not that if *x* is in fact identical with *y* then whatever is true of *x* is true of *y* but only that if *x* is necessarily identical with *y* then whatever is true of *x* is true of *y.* Alternatively, it may be argued (as it has been by Arthur Smullyan) that Leibniz' law holds only for *x*'s and *y*'s that directly *name* whatever they do name, not for *x*'s and *y*'s that pick out what they name merely as the thing, whatever it is, that answers to some definite description, such as "the morning star." If *x* and *y* simply tag the same object, so that "*x* is *y*" just comes to "This is this," then this (when it is true at all) is a necessary truth. But a definite description is a complex prefix like a quantifier, so that "The morning star is the evening star" is not really of the simple form "*x* is *y*"; it means either "Something is at once the one and only morning star and the one and only evening star" or "Whatever is the one and only morning star is the one and only evening star." From neither of these does it follow that because it is a necessary truth that whatever is the one and only morning star is the one and only morning star, it is a necessary truth that whatever is the one and only morning star is the one and only evening star. (See, on the difference between names and descriptions, PROPER NAMES AND DESCRIPTIONS.)

It seems clear, on any view of the matter, that when modal logic and identity theory are brought together Leibniz' law must be applied with caution, but we may be watchful at different points. We may look, with Quine, at the "contexts" we wrap around our identicals—the things that we say are true of *y* because they are true of *x*, which is identical with *y*—and insist that modal contexts, for example, are not covered by the law. In this case we need not be very meticulous about the expressions we take *x* and *y* to do duty for. We may, on the other hand, confine *x* and *y* rigorously to Russell's "logically proper names," and we can then afford to be free and easy with our "contexts."

Similar considerations apply when we attempt to combine modal logic with the theory of classes and numbers. Suppose that men are at once the only rational animals and the only featherless bipeds; it follows at once, on the ordinary view of class identity, that the class of rational animals is one and the same object—if it is an object at all—as the class of featherless bipeds. But it would seem that although the class of rational animals is necessarily the same as the class of rational animals, it is a merely contingent fact that it is the same as the class of featherless bipeds. If classes are genuine objects we are again compelled to restrict Leibniz' law to "referentially transparent" contexts, but if they are mere logical constructions and any talk of class identity is only a paraphrase of talk of functions' being satisfied by the same objects, the paradox disappears as soon as the paraphrase is made.

NONALETHIC MODALITIES

Syntactically, signs of modality are expressions that form sentences when attached to other sentences ("necessarily" forms the sentence "Necessarily 2 and 2 is 4" from "2 and 2 is 4"). In this they resemble signs of negation ("It is not the case that . . ."), but they differ from signs of negation in not being truth-functional, or, as it is sometimes put, in not being "extensional." The truth or falsehood of a modally qualified statement does not depend solely on the truth or falsehood of the original. Certainly if *p* is false so is "Necessarily *p*," and if *p* is true so is "Possibly *p*," but if *p* is false it may or may not be possible, and if true it may or may not be necessary. This feature (nonextensionality) is one that modal functions have in common with many others, and it is a natural extension of modal logic to take in some of these others as well.

G. H. von Wright describes the ordinary modal functions (necessity, possibility, etc.) as "alethic" modalities and compares them with the "deontic" modalities of obligatoriness, permittedness, etc. (see LOGIC, DEONTIC) and with the "epistemic" modalities of being known to be true, not being known to be false, etc. One can also treat tenses as modalities of a sort. In some of these further areas we can discern quite a firm logical structure, at once resembling and differing from that of ordinary modal systems. Just as nothing can be both necessary and impossible, for example, so nothing can be both obligatory and forbidden, nothing both known to be true and known to be false. On the other hand, although whatever is true is *ipso facto* possible, what is actually done need not be going to be done at any future time or have been done in the past.

Even quantifications could be regarded as modalities in this extended sense (von Wright calls them "existential" modalities). "*X*'s are universally *Y*'s" (or "*X*'s are always *Y*'s") has a similar ring to "*X*'s are necessarily *Y*'s" and similarly implies "This *X* is a *Y*," which in turn implies "*X*'s are sometimes *Y*'s." Again, the one-way implication "If something necessarily *ϕ*'s then necessarily something *ϕ*'s" is like the implication "If something *ϕ*'s everything then everything has something that *ϕ*'s it," with a second quantification in place of the modality. Some writers who are skeptical about ordinary modalities—for example, Russell—have suggested that they are quantifications in disguise. But Russell himself has pointed out that quantifications basically attach to properties (or "propositional functions") rather than to complete propositions: we say that *ϕ*'ing "universally" implies *ψ*'ing, but that a complete proposition *p* "necessarily" implies that *q*. We can, indeed, equate modalities with quantifications over "chances" or "possible worlds," but anyone who is skeptical about modalities is liable to be skeptical about these entities also, and even those who are skeptical about neither may prefer to explain the notion of a "possible world" in terms of particular things' being possible, rather than vice versa. C. A. Meredith, for example, has adopted Wittgenstein's definition of the actual world as "everything that is the case," conceiving this as a single comprehensive fact (i.e., a conjunction with all contingent facts as conjuncts) from which all more particular facts follow, so that any falsehood (i.e., the denial of any fact) is inconsistent with it. A "possible" world would then be any proposition which, though not implying so much as to be impossible (not implying, for instance, a proposition together with its negation), is so comprehensive that it either strictly implies or is strictly inconsistent with any given particular proposition. Being "true in" such a world would mean being strictly implied by it.

With regard to the general topic of functions that syntactically resemble modal ones, there are some, such as "It is believed that *p*," for which it is difficult to find any strict formal laws, but even these raise problems analogous to those that arise in modal logic proper, and it is sometimes easier to see in the case of these not strictly modal functions just what the issues are. For example, the difficulties that Kaplan and Montague found in the syntactical interpretation of modal systems were first unearthed when they were trying to use not "is necessary" but "is known" as a predicate attaching to sentences. Again, some of Quine's most instructive discussions of referential opacity are concerned with belief and allied topics rather than with possibility and necessity. He notes, for example, that if we admit expressions like "the morning star" as substitutable for the *x*'s and *y*'s in our formulas, there is a sharp difference with respect to referential opacity between the forms "*x* believes that *y* *ϕ*'s" and "*x* believes of *y* that it *ϕ*'s." If *x* believes that the evening star is not the morning star, it does not follow that he believes that the morning star is not the morning star, but if he believes of the evening star that it is not the morning star, it does follow that he believes of the morning star that it is not the morning star (this being, of course, a mistake on the part of *x*, but an empirical and not a logical one). The example brings out one of the disadvantages of this manner of handling such problems; it involves us in admitting two syntactically distinct kinds of believing, "believing that *p*" and "believing of *x* that it *ϕ*'s"—or, as Quine puts it, "believing *ϕ*'ing of *x*" ("ascribing *ϕ*'ing to *x*")—the connection between them being quite obscure. If, on the other hand, we restrict our *x*'s and *y*'s to direct identifications of individuals, we can equate "believing of *x* that it *ϕ*'s" with the simple "believing that *x* *ϕ*'s" and account for the difference between Quine's two cases by paraphrasing "*x* believes of the morning star that it is not the morning star" as "For some *y*, *y* is in fact the morning star but *x* believes that it is not."

In the quasi-modal areas the tightest logical structure is perhaps to be found among the tenses, although some logicians believe that a logically accurate language would dispense with tenses altogether (handling only dated sentences and sentences about the temporal order of events, which are timelessly true, rather than ones like "I have eaten my breakfast," which are false at one time and true at another). A certain amount of tense-logic is, of course, already involved in the Diodorean account of the ordinary modalities. If we write *Fp* for "It will be the case that *p*," "*Pp*" for "It has been the case that *p*," "*Gp*" for "It will always be the case that *p*," and "*Hp*" for "It has always been the case that *p*," we can construct complex tenses like the future perfect, "*FPp*," "It will be the case that it has been the case that *p*." There appear to be one-way implications between each of the following forms and its successor:

$$GHp, FHp, Hp, PHp, HPp, Pp, GPp, FPp.$$

Also, the plain *p* ("It is the case that *p*") is implied by *FHp* ("It will have always been the case that *p*") and implies *GPp* ("It will always have been the case that *p*"). Each of these laws also appears to have a "mirror image" in which *H* replaces *G* or vice versa and *P* replaces *F* or vice versa (for example, just as *PHp* implies *HPp*, so *FGp* implies *GFp*). Certain plausible reduction theses, such as that it will be that it will be that *p* if and only if it will be that *p* (*FF* = *F*), make it possible to condense all sequences of *F*, *P*, *H*, and *G*, however long, into one or another of the ones listed above or its mirror image.

These results, the findings of C. L. Hamblin, ignore certain problems concerning nonpermanent objects analogous to the problems (discussed earlier) concerning contingent objects in ordinary modal logic, and these may require complications of the system. It has been suggested by C. S. Peirce and Gilbert Ryle, for example, that there are definite singular facts, although perhaps no simple positive ones, about what no longer exists (Socrates is not now wise, but it is now a fact that he is not and that he once was) but only general facts about what does not exist as yet (before I existed it was neither a fact nor a falsehood that I was wise or that I was going to write this article, although it may have been a fact even then that there was going to be someone with such-and-such characteristics—ones that I in fact alone have—who would write it). This would mean that "If *p* then it will always have been the case that *p*" always holds but its mirror image "If *p* then it has always been that it will be that *p*" has exceptions, and

that future beings are to be treated like possible ones in Prior's modal system *Q* but past beings like possible ones in the alternative system of Kripke. Whether a consistent tense-logic (with quantification and identity) can be developed along these lines has yet to be established.

Bibliography

C. I. Lewis and C. H. Langford's *Symbolic Logic* (New York, 1932; new ed. with new appendix, 1951) is presupposed in most modern discussions of modal logic. Surveys of further problems are contained in G. H. von Wright's *An Essay in Modal Logic* (Amsterdam, 1951); and in A. N. Prior's *Formal Logic*, 2d ed., (Oxford, 1962), Part II, Ch. 1 and Appendix I, Sec. 11, and *Time and Modality* (Oxford, 1957). There is a particularly valuable collection of papers in *Acta Philosophica Fennica*, Fascicule 16 (1963), the proceedings of a colloquium on modal and many-valued logics held at Helsinki in 1962.

Aristotle's modal logic is presented mainly in *De Interpretatione*, Chs. 11 and 12, and *Prior Analytics*, Book I, Chs. 8–22; see also the *Metaphysics*, Book Γ, Chs. 4 and 8, and Book Δ, Ch. 4, and *De Caelo*, Book I, Ch. 12. On ancient and medieval treatments, see W. Kneale and M. Kneale, *The Development of Logic* (Oxford, 1962), Ch. 2, Sec. 7, Ch. 3, Secs. 2 and 3, and Ch. 4, Secs. 2, 3, and 5; and Nicholas Rescher, *Studies in the History of Arabic Logic* (Pittsburgh, 1964), Chs. 2, 8, and 10.

On entailment, the starting point is G. E. Moore's paper "External and Internal Relations," in his *Philosophical Studies* (London, 1922). On the distinction between entailment and strict implication, see E. J. Nelson, "Intensional Relations," in *Mind* (1930); Wilhelm Ackermann, "Begründung einer strengen Implikation," in *Journal of Symbolic Logic*, Vol. 21 (1956), 113–128; and A. R. Anderson and N. D. Belnap, "The Pure Calculus of Entailment," in *Journal of Symbolic Logic* (March 1962). On the difficulties of alternatives to strict implication, see J. F. Bennett, "Meaning and Implication," in *Mind* (1954), and T. J. Smiley, "Entailment and Deducibility," in *PAS* (1958–1959).

On calculi of pure strict implication, see Ian Hacking, "What Is Strict Implication?," in *Journal of Symbolic Logic* (March 1963), and C. A. Meredith and A. N. Prior, "Investigations Into Implicational S5," in *Zeitschrift für mathematische Logik und Grundlagen der Mathematik*, Vol. 10 (1964). On material implication as a special case of strict implication, see *The Collected Papers of C. S. Peirce*, Charles Hartshorne, Paul Weiss, and Arthur W. Burks, eds. (8 vols., Cambridge, Mass., 1931–1958), 2.348–354, 3.374–375, 3.440–445.

Interpretations of modal functions appear in Rudolf Carnap, *Meaning and Necessity* (Chicago, 1947), and in the following papers in *Acta Philosophica Fennica*, Fascicule 16 (1963): J. Hintikka, "The Modes of Modality," 65–82; S. A. Kripke, "Semantical Considerations on Modal Logic," 83–94; R. Montague, "Syntactical Treatments of Modality," 153–168; and T. J. Smiley, "The Logical Basis of Ethics," 237–246. See also D. Kaplan and R. Montague, "A Paradox Regained," in *Notre Dame Journal of Formal Logic*, Vol. 1, No. 3 (July 1960), and A. N. Prior, "Tense Logic and the Continuity of Time," in *Studia Logica*, Vol. 13 (1962).

On the modal system *Q*, see A. N. Prior, *Time and Modality* (Oxford, 1957) and "Axiomatisations of the Modal Calculus *Q*," in *Notre Dame Journal of Formal Logic*, Vol. 5, No. 3 (July 1964), 215–217; and R. A. Bull, "An Axiomatization of Prior's Modal Calculus *Q*," *ibid.*, 211–214.

On referential opacity, see W. V. Quine, *From a Logical Point of View* (Cambridge, Mass., 1953), Ch. 8, and *Word and Object* (New York, 1960), Chs. 4–6; P. T. Geach, "Quantification Theory and the Problem of Identifying Objects," in *Acta Philosophica Fennica*, Fascicule 16 (1963), 41–52; and A. N. Prior, "Is the Concept of Referential Opacity Really Necessary?," *ibid.*, 189–200.

A. N. PRIOR

LOGIC, MODERN. Modern logic, also known as symbolic or mathematical logic, is the latest stage in the development of a discipline that owes its founding to Aristotle.

What distinguishes modern from ancient and traditional logic is not only its reliance on symbolic techniques and mathematical methods but also its vastly greater formal power and range of application.

Form, validity, and arguments. Like its predecessors, modern logic is most widely studied as a means of testing the validity of arguments—specifically, *deductive* arguments (for "inductive" arguments, see INDUCTION). An argument is a sequence of statements one of which, the conclusion, is said to be logically deducible from, or a logical consequence of, the others, the premises. Examples of arguments are

(1) Sophocles was a philosopher or Socrates was a dramatist;
Sophocles was not a philosopher;
Therefore, Socrates was a dramatist.

(2) Some philosophers are Platonists;
Some mathematicians are philosophers;
Therefore, some mathematicians are Platonists.

Arguments thus make claims, namely that certain conclusions follow logically from, or are logical consequences of, certain premises. We count on logic to tell us just which arguments make valid claims and which do not.

Validity. What is a valid claim? Before this question can be answered a distinction must be made between the validity of an argument and the truth of its conclusion. These are not the same: Not all valid arguments yield true conclusions—see (1) above. Conversely, not all arguments that yield true conclusions are valid—see (2) above. Similarly, there are valid arguments with false premises, like (1), and invalid arguments with true premises, like (2). The question of the validity of an argument is therefore separate from that of the truth or falsity of its premises and conclusion. To say that an argument is valid is to say that its conclusion is a logical consequence of its premises, which is in turn to say simply that if the premises are all true, the conclusion must also be true. No claim is made with respect to the actual truth or falsity of any premise or conclusion; however, if the argument is valid, then it cannot be the case that the premises are all true and the conclusion false.

It is helpful to use another term, "sound," to refer to arguments that both are valid and contain true premises. Thus, sound arguments satisfy two conditions: (*a*) they are valid, and (*b*) they proceed from true premises. Since the logical consequences of true premises must be true, sound arguments necessarily have true conclusions. An example is the following:

(3) All human beings are mortal;
All Greeks are human beings;
Therefore, all Greeks are mortal.

Logic, whether modern, traditional, or ancient, limits its concern strictly to problems of validity; the task of obtaining true or well-confirmed premises it leaves to other disciplines. It is content to study the conditions under which certain conclusions may be validly drawn, or *inferred,* from certain premises. Indeed, the subject matter of logic may be described, not inaptly, as the theory of valid inference and of the consequence relation on which valid inference is based.

Form. In formulating its theory of inference, logic considers arguments solely with respect to their *form,* not with respect to their content. It regards the validity of arguments as being independent not only of the truth or falsity of their premises and conclusions but likewise of their infinitely varied subject matter. There is no attempt to supply a separate test of validity for each argument having a distinct content. On the contrary, validity is understood as *formal* validity and the conditions of valid inference as *formal* conditions of valid inference. Logic confines itself to those arguments whose validity rests exclusively on the *logical form* of the statements composing them and which may therefore be treated as instances of corresponding valid *argument forms.*

Although there is still no fully satisfactory account of logical form, present purposes may be served by comparing (1) and (3), respectively, with (1') and (3') below and noting that what each pair of arguments has in common is the form:

(1')   It is raining or the sun is shining;
It is not raining;
Therefore, the sun is shining.

(3')   All mathematicians are Platonists;
All algebraists are mathematicians;
Therefore, all algebraists are Platonists.

From this it is a small step to the representation of these forms by means of convenient symbols:

(1")   *P* or *Q*;
Not *P*;
Therefore, *Q*,

where "*P*" and "*Q*" denote statements;

(3")   All *M* are *P*;
All *S* are *M*;
Therefore, all *S* are *P*,

where "*S*," "*M*," and "*P*" denote classes.

Thus, modern logic, like its ancestors, is a *formal* logic: it considers the forms of statements, not their content, and some of its results are applied as *formal criteria* to identify certain classes of valid arguments. However, it far surpasses its forebears in the range of forms considered and even more in the rigor with which their study is prosecuted.

Modern logic since the publication of Gottlob Frege's *Begriffsschrift* in 1879 has been not only formal but also *formalized.* Its basic branches may be regarded as formal systems whose symbols, rules for combining symbols meaningfully, and rules for deriving certain combinations of symbols from other combinations are all fully specified. As a consequence, it is now often pursued not alone for its application to argument but in its own right as a (mathematical) theory of formal systems and their interpretations. Viewed thus abstractly, logic has found uses in areas as distant from argument and discourse as electrical switching circuits and computers.

Divisions of logic. The purpose of this article is to survey some of the main ideas and results of elementary modern logic. It therefore cannot—nor is it meant to—take the place of a full textbook treatment of the subject.

An account of modern logic is best begun not with elementary logic as a whole but with a certain fragment of it called *sentential*, or *propositional, logic*. This fragment, also known as the theory of truth-functions, deals only with unanalyzed simple sentences and certain forms, or ways, of compounding them. It formulates the theory of sentential inference, which serves to explicate the notion of "deducible from" or "consequence of" for a limited class of inferences. An informal survey of this fragment is given in the following section.

The section after that takes up elementary logic as a whole—that is, *first-order predicate logic*. In first-order predicate logic simple sentences are subjected to analysis; in particular, a logical account is given of the terms "some" and "all" (quantification theory), and the sentential fragment is absorbed into the much broader theory of inference of first-order logic. Again the discussion is informal.

The next two sections present formal treatments of sentential and first-order logic. Formal systems (axiomatic and natural deduction) and semantical characterizations are outlined for each. An attempt is made to summarize results obtained in investigating such properties of these systems as decidability, consistency, soundness, and completeness.

In addition to the elements, modern logic embraces a number of advanced fields. Only a few of these—predicate calculi of second and higher orders, for example—will be touched on, in a final section. (For the rest, the reader is referred to such articles as LOGICAL PARADOXES; RECURSIVE FUNCTION THEORY; SET THEORY; and SYSTEMS, FORMAL, AND MODELS OF FORMAL SYSTEMS.)

A more complete account of modern developments with respect to logic would include some discussion of the philosophy of logic. There is growing interest in this field, which lists among its concerns the nature of logical truths or principles, the relation of formal logic to natural language, extension and intension, and in general the relevance of formal logic and formal semantics to the solution of philosophical problems. (On these and related topics, the reader should consult MATHEMATICS, FOUNDATIONS OF; SEMANTICS; and related articles).

SENTENTIAL LOGIC: AN INFORMAL SURVEY

This informal account of the nature and uses of sentential logic is couched in ordinary language, supplemented by a few symbols, and is intended as a nontechnical introduction to the subject. Since ordinary language lacks precision, so will this account. In a later section a formal language will be specified, in terms of which sentential logic will then be expressed and studied with greater rigor.

Sentential logic limits itself to considering certain simple sentences, taken as unanalyzed wholes, together with certain of the connectives which operate on them or combine them to form compound sentences. It therefore finds application only to arguments whose validity or invalidity turns entirely on the forms, or ways, in which simple sentences are compounded (specifically, on the logical prop-

erties of some sentential connectives), not on the logical forms of the sentences themselves. Such arguments are called *sentential logic arguments*, and the corresponding argument forms are known as *sentential logic argument forms*. One such argument form, cited above, is

> *P* or *Q*;
> Not *P*;
> Therefore, *Q*,

where "*P*" and "*Q*" denote whole sentences. But

> All *M* are *P*;
> All *S* are *M*;
> Therefore, all *S* are *P*,

where "*S*," "*M*," and "*P*" denote classes rather than sentences, is not a sentential logic argument form. In view of its limited role sentential logic is properly described not as an independent branch of logic but as a fragment. As a fragment it is later absorbed into elementary logic, which considers *both* the logical form of simple sentences and some of the forms, or ways, of compounding them.

Sentences. Ordinary sentential logic restricts the term "sentence" to just those linguistic expressions (for example, "Socrates was a philosopher") which are capable of being true or false, in the usual sense. Accordingly, commands, questions, and the like are not dealt with. (For a discussion of these kinds of sentences, see LOGIC, DEONTIC; QUESTIONS.) The same restriction may be expressed by saying that a sentence is a combination of words which can serve as a complete utterance and that sentential logic treats just those sentences used to make true or false statements. A sentence is regarded as being true if the statement commonly made by it is true, false if the statement is false. Such a sentence is then said to have one or the other (but not both) of two *truth-values,* truth or falsity, and the standard sentential logic which studies sentences of this sort is called a *two-valued* logic. (For other logics, see LOGIC, MANY-VALUED and LOGIC, MODAL; for some of the problems raised by such notions as sentence and proposition, see PROPOSITIONS, JUDGMENTS, SENTENCES, AND STATEMENTS.)

A sentence is said to be *simple* if it contains no parts that are sentences; otherwise it is *compound*. Thus, "Life is short" is a simple sentence, whereas "Life is short, and art is long" is a compound sentence formed by means of the connective "and" from the two simple sentences "Life is short" and "Art is long."

Truth-functional connectives. Sentences in ordinary language are conjoined in many ways to form compounds. Of the various grammatical "conjunctions," connectives, or operators used in this process, only a handful—or, more exactly, their logical analogues—are considered in sentential logic. The most important are "and," "or," "not," "if–then," and "if and only if." Their common characteristic is that they are *truth-functional* sentential connectives. This means that they generate compound sentences that are *truth-functions* of their component sentences; that is, the truth-value of the compound is a function of (is determined solely by) the truth-values of the component sentences, not a function of the content of these components, the context in which the compound occurs, or anything else. For example, "Life is short, and art is long" is a truth-function of "Life is short" and "Art is long"—it is true if and only if its components are both true and is false otherwise. On the other hand, "Mr. Smith believes that poverty is ennobling" is not a truth-function of "Poverty is ennobling," since its truth-value is not determined by the truth-value of "Poverty is ennobling."

In sum, ordinary sentential logic studies only two-valued sentences and such of their connectives as form compounds that are truth-functions of their components. For this reason it is often called the *theory of truth-functions,* since its prime concern is the logical behavior of the words "and," "or," "not," etc.

In what follows it will be convenient to use nonverbal symbols for sentences, for their truth-values, and for truth-functional connectives. Let "*P*," "*Q*," "*R*," · · · stand for simple sentences that take the truth-values *T* for truth and *F* for falsity, and let "&" be the sign for "and," "∨" for "or," "¬" for "not," "→" for "if–then," and "↔" for "if and only if."

Then "*P* & *Q*" (read "*P* and *Q*") symbolizes the *conjunction* of the two sentences "*P*," "*Q*." Since "&" is a truth-functional connective, the truth-value of "*P* & *Q*" is determined solely by the truth-values of "*P*" and "*Q*." Specifically, "*P* & *Q*" is *T* if and only if both "*P*" and "*Q*" are *T*. For two sentences there are just four possible combinations of truth-values:

(1) *P* is *T*, and *Q* is *T*.
(2) *P* is *T*, and *Q* is *F*.
(3) *P* is *F*, and *Q* is *T*.
(4) *P* is *F*, and *Q* is *F*.

Thus, the rule or definition for conjunction states that "*P* & *Q*" is *T* in case 1 and *F* in all others.

Truth tables. Truth-functional connectives and compounds can be presented quite simply by the method of *truth tables.* This method, although it has a long history, was given special prominence by Ludwig Wittgenstein and E. L. Post in works published independently in 1921. A truth table for a given truth-functional compound consists of two parts: a tabular representation of all the alternative truth possibilities for the sentence or sentences that form the compound and a list in which opposite each such possibility appears the particular truth-value it determines for that compound. Truth table I is the truth table for a conjunction.

I

P	*Q*	*P* & *Q*
T	*T*	*T*
T	*F*	*F*
F	*T*	*F*
F	*F*	*F*

The sentence "¬*P*" (read "not *P*" or "It is not the case that *P*") is called the *negation* of "*P*." Since "¬" is a (singulary) truth-functional connective or operator, the truth-value of "¬*P*" is determined solely by the truth-value of its single sentential component, "*P*." The rule is that "¬*P*" is *F* if "*P*" is *T* and *T* if "*P*" is *F*. This is expressed by the two-line table II.

II

P	¬*P*
T	*F*
F	*T*

It should be noted that "&" and "¬" are quite close to their ordinary-language counterparts "and" and "not" (in fact, closer than the three other connectives). But they do not altogether coincide. For instance, "&" is commutative: "*P* & *Q*" and "*Q* & *P*" entail each other. However, "and" has non-truth-functional uses as well as truth-functional ones—in particular, it often expresses not merely a conjunction of sentences but a sequence of events—and in such contexts ("They were married, and they had a baby") it is obviously not commutative.

The connective "∨" is not very troublesome once a distinction is made between the two uses of "or," the inclusive ("and/or") and the exclusive ("alternation"). Logic defines "∨" as the *inclusive* "or": the *disjunction* "*P* ∨ *Q*" (read "*P* or *Q*") is *T* if "*P*" is *T* or if "*Q*" is *T* or if *both* are *T* and is *F* only if both are *F*. The exclusive "or" differs only in making "*P* or *Q*" false if "*P*" and "*Q*" are both true. Truth table III shows the contrast.

III

P	*Q*	*P* ∨ *Q*	*P* alternate *Q*
T	*T*	*T*	*F*
T	*F*	*T*	*T*
F	*T*	*T*	*T*
F	*F*	*F*	*F*

The paradoxes of (material) implication. The greatest difficulties, it seems, are offered by the connective "→," which generates the *conditional* "*P* → *Q*" (read "If *P*, then *Q*"), formerly called (material) implication. These difficulties, often referred to as "paradoxes," reflect the sharp divergence between the most common uses of "if–then," which are not truth-functional, and the logical definition of "→." Consider the *ordinary* conditional "If you take aspirin, your headache will disappear." It asserts a (causal) connection of content, a dependency of the *factual truth* of its second component, the consequent, on that of the first, the antecedent. By contrast, the *logical* conditional is a truth-functional compound; hence, there need be no relation at all between the subject matters of "*P*" and "*Q*." All that "*P* → *Q*" asserts is a dependency of its truth-value on those of "*P*" and "*Q*."

Now, if you take the aspirin and the headache disappears, you will pronounce the conditional true (*TT* yields *T*), and if you take the aspirin but the headache fails to disappear you will count the conditional false (*TF* yields *F*). In these cases the two conditionals—ordinary and logical—agree. It is in the remaining two cases that the divergence appears, and with it appear the difficulties. Suppose you do not take the aspirin (that is, suppose "*P*" is *F*). The tendency would be to regard the ordinary conditional as undetermined or perhaps pointless. In logic, on the other hand, when "*P*" is *F*, "*P* → *Q*" is *defined* as *T*. Let "*P* ∗ *Q*" represent, for the purpose of this discussion, the ordinary conditional. Table IV indicates how "*P* → *Q*" differs from "*P* ∗ *Q*."

IV

P	Q	P → Q	P ∗ Q
T	T	T	T
T	F	F	F
F	T	T	?
F	F	T	?

It follows from this definition that if "*Q*" is *T*, then "*P* → *Q*" is *T* no matter which truth-value "*P*" has, and if "*P*" is *F*, then "*P* → *Q*" is *T* no matter which truth-value "*Q*" has. These consequences may seem odd, but they are not paradoxes even in a loose sense. Any appearance of paradox that may exist is the result of a severalfold confusion. First, the expression "materially implies" is used in place of "→" or "if–then," thus yielding the familiar "paradoxes of material implication": a true sentence is *materially implied by* any sentence, and a false sentence *materially implies* any sentence. Second, the meaning of "materially implied by" is shifted from that of "if–then" to that of "follows logically from" (that is, from the truth-functional connective "→" to the relation of deducibility or logical consequence). Once this shift is made, the results are indeed "paradoxical": a true sentence *follows logically from* any sentence, and any sentence *follows logically from* a false sentence. However, such consequences flow not from the definition of "*P* → *Q*" but from a confusion between "*P* → *Q*" and "*P*; therefore, *Q*." The first set of symbols represents a truth-functional compound, the second an (obviously invalid) argument form—two quite different things, even though, as will appear later, they bear a centrally important relation to each other.

Biconditional. The last of the five connectives, "↔," may be disposed of briefly. It produces the *biconditional* "*P* ↔ *Q*" (read "*P* if and only if *Q*") and, as its reading suggests, can be expressed as the conjunction of "*P* → *Q*" and "*Q* → *P*" (table V).

V

P	Q	P ↔ Q	P → Q	Q → P	(P → Q) & (Q → P)
T	T	T	T	T	T
T	F	F	F	T	F
F	T	F	T	F	F
F	F	T	T	T	T

More about connectives. In table V parentheses have been introduced to indicate the scope of the connectives in "(*P* → *Q*) & (*Q* → *P*)." This or some other form of punctuation becomes necessary as soon as connectives are applied to compounds, unless the Polish parenthesis-free notation (see below) is adopted. For example, punctuation is required to differentiate between "¬*P* ∨ *Q*" and "¬(*P* ∨ *Q*)." Judicious use of parentheses, together with conventions concerning the relative strengths of the connectives (for instance, that "¬" be the weakest), generally suffices.

The same table also shows how to construct truth tables for the more complicated truth-functional compounds generated by the successive application of one or more connectives. Abbreviated tables for such compounds can be fashioned by listing the truth-values of a sentence letter ("*P*," "*Q*," and the like) under *each* occurrence of the letter and the truth-values of each compound under the principal connective employed in forming that compound, as in table VI.

VI

P ↔ Q	(P → Q)	&	(Q → P)
T T T	T T T	T	T T T
T F F	T F F	F	F T T
F F T	F T T	F	T F F
F T F	F T F	T	F T F

Since the literature of logic contains different symbols for the same connective, it may be useful to list those adopted here, alongside their most important alternatives:

	WHITEHEAD–RUSSELL	HILBERT	POLISH
Negation	¬P	~P	$\bar{P}$	Np
Conjunction	P & Q	P . Q	P & Q	Kpq
Disjunction	P ∨ Q	P ∨ Q	P ∨ Q	Apq
Conditional	P → Q	P ⊃ Q	P → Q	Cpq
Biconditional	P ↔ Q	P ≡ Q	P ~ Q	Epq

Of the five connectives that have been introduced, four are *binary*; that is, they connect two sentences. Now, given two sentences, there are 2^2, or 4, truth possibilities—*TT, TF, FT, FF*. (For *n* sentences there are 2^n possibilities.) By definition, a truth-functional compound involving just two distinct sentences is determined by specifying its truth-value for each of these four possibilities. This can occur in 4^2, or 16, different ways, as is indicated by table VII. Columns 1 to 5 contain the compounds formed by the four binary connectives, with "→" occurring twice, once in "*P* → *Q*" and once in "*Q* → *P*"; columns 6 to 10 contain their negations. Of the six remaining possibilities, 11 and 12

VII

P	Q	1 P & Q	2 P ∨ Q	3 P → Q	4 Q → P	5 P ↔ Q	6 ¬(P & Q)	7 ¬(P ∨ Q)	8 ¬(P → Q)	9 ¬(Q → P)	10 ¬(P ↔ Q)	11 P	12 Q	13 ¬P	14 ¬Q	15	16
T	T	T	T	T	T	T	F	F	F	F	F	T	T	F	F	F	T
T	F	F	T	F	T	F	T	F	T	F	T	T	F	F	T	F	T
F	T	F	T	T	F	F	T	F	F	T	T	F	T	T	F	F	T
F	F	F	F	T	T	T	T	T	F	F	F	F	F	T	T	F	T

are simply the tables for "*P*" and "*Q*" taken separately, and 13 and 14 are the negations of 11 and 12. This leaves two special cases, the columns containing either all *T*'s or all *F*'s. These will be discussed later.

What of ternary, quaternary, *n*-ary connectives? It turns out that all *n*-ary connectives ($n > 2$) can be represented by means of negation, conjunction, and disjunction. In other words, it has been shown that every truth-functional compound, no matter which connectives occur in it, is logically equivalent to (that is, has the same truth table as) some sentence in what is known as *normal form*. A sentence is said to be (*a*) in *disjunctive normal form* if it is a disjunction each of whose members is a conjunction of one or more simple sentences and negations of simple sentences and (*b*) in *conjunctive normal form* if it is a conjunction each of whose members is a disjunction of one or more simple sentences and negations of simple sentences.

It also turns out that the pairing of negation with conjunction, disjunction, or the conditional constitutes a *set* of connectives *adequate* to express all others. Table V indicated how to define "↔" in terms of "→" and "&," and it is easy to verify that "$P \to Q$" is logically equivalent to "$\neg P \vee Q$," and "$P \vee Q$" to "$\neg(\neg P \& \neg Q)$."

Finally, it was proved by H. M. Sheffer in 1913 that a *single* binary connective is adequate, provided it is either joint denial ("neither *P* nor *Q*") or alternate denial ("not both *P* and *Q*"). Negation is then obtained in the form of either "neither *P* nor *P*" or "not both *P* and *P*," and thereafter the other connectives are obtained.

Tautology. In table VII, above, there were two special cases: the columns that contained all *F*'s and all *T*'s. Compounds that have truth tables of the first sort are called *contradictions*, those of the second sort *tautologies*; all others are *contingent*.

Tautologies may thus be defined as truth-functional compounds that take the truth-value *T* for all possible assignments of truth-values to their components. They are "true" no matter what happens to be the case. So defined, tautologies play a decisive role in sentential logic, for they provide an explication of the notion of "logical truth" or "logical principle" in sentential logic and the basis for the theory of sentential inference. Examples of tautologies are "$P \vee \neg P$" (law of excluded middle) and "$\neg(P \& \neg P)$" (law of contradiction), illustrated in table VIII, and "$P \to (P \vee Q)$" (law of addition), in table IX.

	VIII				IX	
P	¬*P*	*P* ∨ ¬*P*	¬(*P* & ¬*P*)	*P*	*Q*	*P* → (*P* ∨ *Q*)
T	*F*	*T*	*T*	*T*	*T*	*T*
F	*T*	*T*	*T*	*T*	*F*	*T*
				F	*T*	*T*
				F	*F*	*T*

A few of the more important tautologies and the names they bear as logical principles are:

(1) $(P \& (P \to Q)) \to Q$ law of detachment.

(2) $(\neg Q \& (P \to Q)) \to \neg P$ *modus tollendo tollens*.

(3) $((P \to Q) \& (Q \to R)) \to (P \to R)$ law of hypothetical syllogism.

(4) $(P \to (Q \& \neg Q)) \to \neg P$ law of absurdity.

(5) $P \leftrightarrow \neg\neg P$ law of double negation.

(6) $(P \to Q) \leftrightarrow (\neg Q \to \neg P)$ law of contraposition.

(7) $\neg(P \& Q) \leftrightarrow (\neg P \vee \neg Q)$
     $\neg(P \vee Q) \leftrightarrow (\neg P \& \neg Q)$ De Morgan's laws.

These and all other truths or principles of sentential logic can easily be shown to be tautologies by the method of truth tables.

Tautology and valid inference. With the aid of the notion of tautology, the entire theory of sentential inference may be formulated in one rule: *a sentential logic argument form is valid if and only if its corresponding conditional*—consisting of the conjunction of its premises as antecedent and its conclusion as consequent—*is a tautology.* This is illustrated by the argument form given earlier:

$P \vee Q$;
$\neg P$;
Therefore, *Q*.

Its corresponding conditional is

$$((P \vee Q) \& \neg P) \to Q.$$

That this conditional is a tautology is apparent from the abbreviated truth table X. This argument form is therefore *valid*, as are all its instances.

X

((*P*	∨	*Q*)	&	¬*P*)	→	*Q*
T	*T*	*T*	*F*	*F*	*T*	*T*
T	*T*	*F*	*F*	*F*	*T*	*F*
F	*T*	*T*	*T*	*T*	*F*	*T*
F	*F*	*F*	*F*	*T*	*T*	*F*

In contrast, consider the following argument form, which expresses the elementary fallacy of "affirming the consequent":

$P \to Q$;
Q;
Therefore, *P*.

Its corresponding conditional is

$$((P \to Q) \& Q) \to P,$$

which, as truth table XI shows, is *not* a tautology. Hence, this argument form is *invalid*, as are all its instances.

XI

P	*Q*	*P* → *Q*	(*P* → *Q*) & *Q*	((*P* → *Q*) & *Q*) → *P*
T	*T*	*T*	*T*	*T*
T	*F*	*F*	*F*	*T*
F	*T*	*T*	*T*	*F*
F	*F*	*T*	*F*	*T*

Testing an argument for validity in sentential logic thus reduces to two steps: (*a*) ascertaining whether the argument is an *instance* of a sentential logic argument form and, if it is, (*b*) determining by truth tables whether the conditional that corresponds to that sentential logic argument form is a tautology. If the conditional turns out to be a tautology, the argument is valid; if not, it is invalid. The first step requires some ingenuity, since there is no algorithm, or precise set of instructions, by which to determine whether or not an arbitrary sequence of sentences in ordinary language is an argument in sentential logic. The second step, however, is purely mechanical. Sentential logic is *decidable* in the sense that the truth tables furnish an *effective procedure* (that is, a procedure that can be carried out in a finite number of steps) for deciding whether or not an arbitrary truth-functional compound is a tautology, and hence a truth in sentential logic. By the same token, the tables provide an effective means for deciding whether or not an arbitrary argument form in sentential logic is valid.

The relation between valid argument and tautology is sometimes formulated in a different way: an argument is said to be valid if and only if its premises tautologically imply its conclusion. Since a tautological implication is simply a conditional that is a tautology, this formulation is equivalent to the statement, above, that an argument is valid if and only if the corresponding conditional (which consists of the conjunction of the premises as antecedent and the conclusion as consequent) is a tautology.

Since sentential logic is decidable, there is no need, in principle, to arrange its truths (the tautologies) in the form of, say, a deductive system. Thus, in essence our account of sentential logic is now complete.

There are several reasons, however, why the discussion should not rest here. First, there is the practical problem that since arguments involving *n* distinct simple sentences require tables with 2^n lines, the truth-table method becomes much too cumbersome when *n* is greater than 4 or 5. Of course, truth-value analysis can be simplified by one or another technical device; it seems desirable, however, to explore a different, more natural way of testing the validity of sentential logic arguments. Second, it is necessary to consider the axiomatic approach to sentential logic, which largely dominated the early history of the subject. Apart from its great historical interest, this approach has the virtue of making possible the study of partial sentential logics based on partial sets of axioms. Finally, the ground covered in this informal survey should in any event be retraced in a more rigorous and formal manner in order to provide a clearer view of the sentential fragment and of elementary logic as a whole.

FIRST-ORDER PREDICATE LOGIC: AN INFORMAL SURVEY

Sentential logic considers only unanalyzed simple sentences and truth-functional compounds of these sentences. It provides a theory of inference only for a very narrow class of arguments, those whose validity or invalidity is determined exclusively by the logical properties of the connectives "not," "and," "or," and the like. Since the great majority of arguments fall outside this class, the as-

sessment of their validity is beyond the means of sentential logic. An example is the following:

> All human beings are mortal;
> All Greeks are human beings;
> Therefore, all Greeks are mortal.

From the standpoint of sentential logic this argument is made up of three quite *distinct* simple sentences; consequently, its form is

> *P*;
> *Q*;
> Therefore, *R*,

where "*P*," "*Q*," and "*R*" stand for simple sentences. Now, the conditional that corresponds to this argument form is "$(P \mathbin{\&} Q) \to R$." Obviously this is not a tautology, for a distribution of truth-values to its components that assigns *T* to "*P*," *T* to "*Q*," and *F* to "*R*" makes the conditional false. Yet the argument itself, of course, is perfectly valid.

The point is that in this case, as, indeed, in the case of most arguments, validity is not determined solely by the *way* in which simple sentences are combined. It also depends on the *internal structure* of these sentences—on the recurrence of the same terms in different sentences of the argument and, even more, on the role of the so-called *quantifiers*, "all" and "some" and their idiomatic variants.

A wider class of arguments requires a more comprehensive logical apparatus. This need is met by *predicate logic*, which, absorbing the sentential fragment, offers an account of (simple) sentence forms as well as sentence connectives. Predicate logic rests in general on an analysis of the logical forms of certain simple sentences and in particular on a theory of the logical properties of the quantifiers. Its elementary portion, *first-order* (predicate) logic, constitutes modern elementary logic. It is called first-order because in it "the notions of 'some' and 'all' are applied only to individuals and not also to classes or attributes of individuals" (Benson Mates, *Elementary Logic*, p. v).

Terms and predicates. Predicate logic begins its analysis with the very simplest type of sentence, the singular sentence. A singular sentence asserts either that a certain property is possessed by an individual object or that a certain relation holds between two or more individual objects. Examples are

> Aristotle is fallible.
> 3 is greater than 2.
> Baltimore is between Washington and Elkton.

Expressions that either name or describe individual objects ("Aristotle," "2," "the even prime") are called *terms*. Expressions that stand for particular properties or relations of objects ("is fallible," "is greater than") are called *predicates*. These may be one-place, two-place, or *n*-place predicates, depending on the number of terms needed to complete the given sentence. Thus, "is between" is a three-place predicate, whereas "is greater than" is a two-place predicate.

Capital letters from the middle of the alphabet—"*F*,"

"G," "H," etc.—are used as symbols for arbitrary predicates; they are called *predicate constants*. Lower-case letters from the beginning of the alphabet—"a," "b," "c," etc.—are used as symbols for arbitrary proper names; they are called *individual constants*. The three singular sentences above may then be symbolized with respect to their form as follows:

$$Fa;$$
$$Gab;$$
$$Habc,$$

where "F" is a one-place, "G" a two-place, and "H" a three-place predicate constant.

Thus, the internal structure of singular simple sentences is represented in predicate logic by expressions consisting of a single n-place predicate constant followed by n individual constants. Such expressions (and another variety to be dealt with shortly) are called *atomic formulas*. Being formulas, they are neither true nor false; only after they are interpreted do they take on truth-values. For example, if "F" is made to stand for "is fallible" and "a" for "Aristotle," then "Fa" results in the true singular sentence "Aristotle is fallible." (The same atomic formula "Fa" may, of course, result in a false singular sentence under another interpretation, as when "F" stands for "is fashionable" and "a" for "Atlantic City.") Since interpreted atomic formulas are sentences, they may, like all sentences, be combined to form truth-functional compounds. Accordingly, just as "$P \lor Q$" represents in sentential logic the disjunction of *any* two simple sentences, so "$Fa \lor Gb$" represents in predicate logic the disjunction of any two *singular* sentences (having different predicate constants and different individual constants).

Variables. The next step is to extend the analysis to certain classes of *nonsingular* simple sentences. Examples are the following:

(1)   Everything is material.
(2)   Something is material.

Since these sentences contain no sentence connectives, they are simple; since they contain no names or descriptions, they are also nonsingular.

The analysis of these nonsingular sentences requires the introduction of a second sort of term, *individual variables*, symbolized by the letters "x," "y," "z," with or without numerical subscripts. Individual variables do not name or refer to a particular object but, like pronouns, serve as placeholders for terms that do. Their presence makes it possible to redefine an atomic formula as an expression that consists of a single n-place predicate constant followed by n terms—constants *or* variables.

Expressions that are like true–false sentences except for the presence of at least one individual variable are sometimes called "open sentences." Instances are "Fx," "Gxy," "$Haxb$," or, interpreted, "x is material," "x is older than y," "5 is between x and 4."

Consider one such expression, say "Fx," and let "F" stand for "is fallible"; "Fx" then becomes

$$x \text{ is fallible.}$$

This expression, which could as well have been written "_____ is fallible," is obviously not a true–false sentence as it stands. But it becomes one if an appropriate name (or description), say "Aristotle," is put in the place of "x" or the blank.

Quantifiers. Replacing variables by names is not the only way to obtain true–false sentences from "open sentences." We may also use the *quantifiers* "For every x" and "There is an x such that." The first is called the *universal* quantifier and is frequently symbolized by enclosing the variable symbol in parentheses, "(x)"; the second is called the *existential* quantifier and is frequently symbolized by "$(\exists x)$." Prefixing these quantifiers to, say,

$$x \text{ is material}$$

will yield

(1')   For every x, x is material.
(2')   There is an x such that x is material.

Clearly (1') and (2') are true–false sentences. Indeed, they are essentially the very ones displayed above as examples of certain classes of nonsingular sentences:

(1)   Everything is material.
(2)   Something is material.

Hence, (1) and (2) may be represented symbolically as

(1") $(x)(Fx)$;
(2") $(\exists x)(Fx)$,

and this, in fact, constitutes the analysis of their internal structure.

It should be noted that (1) may also be written as

$$\text{All things are material,}$$

which exhibits more clearly the universal ("all") character of the first quantifier; similarly (2) may be written either as

$$\text{Some things are material}$$

or as

$$\text{Material things exist,}$$

thereby exhibiting the particular ("some") or existential character of the second quantifier.

Thus, the nonsingular sentences (1) and (2) are examples of *general* sentences obtainable from "open sentences" by prefixing one or more quantifiers. The symbolic representations (1") and (2") are referred to respectively as the *universal generalization* and the *existential generalization* of the *open* formula "Fx." The general theory of the quantifiers and related concepts, developed chiefly by Frege, is known as *quantification theory*.

There are several additional remarks to be made before presenting the theory of inference of first-order predicate logic.

First, variables occur in formulas in two different ways. An occurrence of "x" in a given formula is said to be *bound* if that occurrence is controlled by a quantifier using that variable; otherwise, the occurrence is *free*. For example, both occurrences of "x" in "$(x)(Fx)$" are bound; the occurrence of "x" in "Fx" is free. A variable may have both bound and free occurrences in different formulas and in the same formula. Thus, in "$Fxy \rightarrow (x)(Fx)$" the first occurrence of "x" and the lone occurrence of "y" are free; the second and third occurrences of "x" are bound.

Second, in the presence of negation the universal and existential quantifiers are interdefinable in standard first-order logic. If

(3) $\qquad\qquad (\exists x)(\neg Fx)$

is read as "There is an x such that x is not F" and

(4) $\qquad\qquad (x)(\neg Fx)$

as "For all x, x is not F," then clearly (3) is the negation of "$(x)(Fx)$," and (4) is the negation of "$(\exists x)(Fx)$." Accordingly, "$(x)(Fx)$" is the same as "$\neg(\exists x)(\neg Fx)$," and "$(\exists x)(Fx)$" is the same as "$\neg(x)(\neg Fx)$."

Third, quantifiers may be applied in formulas that contain more than one predicate constant. For example, the open sentence "If x is human, then x is fallible" when universally quantified becomes the sentence "For all x, if x is human, then x is fallible," or, in symbols, "$(x)(Hx \rightarrow Fx)$." Similarly, the open sentence "x is human, and x is fallible" when existentially quantified yields the sentence "There is an x such that x is human, and x is fallible," or, in symbols, "$(\exists x)(Hx \ \& \ Fx)$." Thus, in quantification theory the A-, E-, I-, and O-propositions of traditional logic,

All S are P;
No S are P;
Some S are P;
Some S are not P,

become, respectively,

$$(x)(Fx \rightarrow Gx);$$
$$(x)(Fx \rightarrow \neg Gx);$$
$$(\exists x)(Fx \ \& \ Gx);$$
$$(\exists x)(Fx \ \& \ \neg Gx).$$

Note, too, that

$$(\exists x)(Fx) \ \& \ (\exists x)(Gx)$$

is not the same as

$$(\exists x)(Fx \ \& \ Gx);$$

that is, "There are men, and there are mortals" is not the same sentence as "Some men are mortal."

Fourth, it has been indicated just above that the two quantifiers are interdefinable with the aid of the negation symbol. A similar duality holds for conjunction and disjunction in sentential logic, as De Morgan's laws express: "$P \ \& \ Q$" is logically equivalent to "$\neg(\neg P \lor \neg Q)$" and "$P \lor Q$" to "$\neg(\neg P \ \& \ \neg Q)$." This suggests an inquiry into the relation between the quantifiers and the connectives.

Suppose that the individual variable "x" ranges over a *finite* set of individuals, a set, for example, whose members are named by the individual constants "a," "b," "c," "d," and "e." Then to say that "$(x)(Fx)$" is simply to say that

$$Fa \ \& \ Fb \ \& \ Fc \ \& \ Fd \ \& \ Fe,$$

and to say that "$(\exists x)(Fx)$" is simply to say that

$$Fa \lor Fb \lor Fc \lor Fd \lor Fe.$$

In short, for finite domains of individuals, *universally* quantified formulas (general sentences) expand into equivalent finite *conjunctions* of atomic formulas (singular sentences), and *existentially* quantified formulas expand into equivalent finite *disjunctions* of atomic formulas. This, of course, applies in general only to finite domains; the subject of infinite domains will be touched on later.

It should be noted that the quantifier symbols are written in various ways. The following list gives the more important of these:

	WHITEHEAD–RUSSELL	HILBERT	OTHERS	POLISH
Universal	$(x)F(x)$	$(x)F(x)$	$\forall x F(x),$	$\Lambda x Fx$	$\Pi x \Phi x$
Existential	$(\exists x)F(x)$	$(Ex)F(x)$	$\exists x F(x),$	$\lor x Fx$	$\Sigma x \Phi x$

Inference and validity. The above analysis of simple sentences furnishes a broad range of sentence forms to which elementary logic may address its theory of inference. The theory is not completely general: first-order logic admits only *individual* variables and their quantifications; all other sorts (for example, predicate variables) are reserved for predicate logic of second and higher orders.

However, the class of first-order formulas or sentence forms is still a rather wide one. It includes the following:

(1) all formulas consisting of single n-place predicate constants and their n individual constants (these formulas, interpreted, are singular sentences);

(2) all universal and existential generalizations of open formulas—that is, those that contain one or more n-place predicate constants and at least one individual variable (these generalized formulas, when interpreted, become general sentences);

(3) all truth-functional compounds of (1) or (2) or both.

Such first-order formulas (sentences) serve as components for a correspondingly wide class of first-order argument forms (arguments) whose validity or invalidity it is the business of elementary logic to determine.

The key to inference in first-order logic is the notion of a *valid formula*. This, in turn, rests on the notion of *interpretation*. A sentence S is called an interpretation of a formula F relative to a domain of individuals D if S is obtained from F by (a) replacing the predicate constants of F with predicates defined for the individuals of D and (*b*) replacing the individual constants of *F* with proper names of individuals of *D*. Then a formula *F* in predicate logic is said to be *valid* (or universally valid) if it becomes a *true* sentence under *every* interpretation in *any* (nonempty domain of individuals.

Thus, the formula

$$Fa$$

is obviously not a valid formula. Let the domain of interpretation *D* (that is, the set of individuals over which the variable "*x*" ranges) be human beings, let "*F*" stand for "is French" and let "*a*" name Aristotle; under this interpretation "*Fa*" becomes the false sentence

Aristotle is French.

Consider, on the other hand, the formula

$$(x)Fx \rightarrow Fa.$$

Let the domain of interpretation *D* be human beings, let "*F*" stand for "is mortal," and let "*a*" name Aristotle. Under this interpretation the formula becomes the true sentence

If all men are mortal, then Aristotle is mortal.

Now retain the domain, but let "*F*" stand for "is French" and "*a*" again name Aristotle. The formula becomes the sentence

If all men are French, then Aristotle is French,

which is also true. Finally, take a different domain, say positive integers; let "*F*" stand for "is prime" and "*a*" name the number 4. The formula still yields a true sentence:

If all positive integers are prime, then 4 is prime.

In fact, the formula becomes a true sentence under every interpretation in any domain and is therefore a valid formula.

Just as an argument form in sentential logic is valid if its corresponding conditional is a tautology, so an argument form in predicate logic is valid if its corresponding conditional is a valid formula. The problem is to determine just which formulas are valid formulas—a problem not as easily solved as that of determining just which truth-functional compounds are tautologies.

In the first place, valid formulas cannot be identified with tautologies. Although all tautologies and instances of tautologies are valid formulas (and may therefore be adopted as "truths" of predicate logic), not all valid formulas are tautologies. For example, the formula

$$(x)Fx \rightarrow Fa$$

is a valid formula, yet it is not a tautology and, in fact, does not admit of a truth-table analysis—unless "*x*" is arbitrarily

restricted to finite domains including a member named "*a*," in which event "(*x*)*Fx*" dissolves into a finite conjunction one of whose members is "*Fa*," and the formula as a whole obviously becomes a tautology.

In the second place, predicate logic has no mechanical test for valid formulas analogous to the truth-table test for tautologies. Indeed, Alonzo Church proved in 1936 that there can be no general decision procedure for validity; predicate logic, unlike its sentential fragment, is **undecidable**. Consequently a deductive treatment of logical truths, dispensable in sentential logic, is essential in predicate logic.

A deductive system for first-order logic. It is convenient to treat first-order logic as a natural deduction system. There are no axioms; such a system draws all of its deductive strength from rules of inference. These rules are few, but they are so laden with conditions that a full description cannot be given in an informal survey. It suffices to sketch the general character of a system *S* and its use in testing the validity of arguments (citing, for purposes of illustration, the system offered in Patrick Suppes, *Introduction to Logic*, Ch. 5).

An argument form is valid in *S* if its conclusion is derivable in *S* from its premises. A formula *F* is *derivable in S from* certain premises if there is a sequence of formulas of *S* such that *F* is the last member and each member either is a premise or is obtained from preceding members of the sequence by means of the inference rules of *S*. These rules are as follows:

(1) Rule *P*: a premise may be cited at any point in a derivation.

(2) Rule *T*: a formula may be cited if it is *tautologically implied* by preceding formulas in the derivation.

(3) Rule *CP* (conditional proof): if a formula *G* can be derived in *S* from another formula, *F*, together with a set of premises, then the formula *F* → *G* can be derived from the premises alone.

In addition, there are four rules that permit, under stated conditions, the dropping and adding of quantifiers:

(4) Rule *US* (universal specification).

(5) Rule *UG* (universal generalization).

(6) Rule *ES* (existential specification).

(7) Rule *EG* (existential generalization).

As one instance: *US* says, in effect, that what is true for every individual is true for a specified individual; the rule thus permits inferring, for example, the formula "*Fa*" from the formula "(*x*)*Fx*" (the quantifier "(*x*)" being dropped in the process).

A useful strategy for constructing many derivations is as follows: ·

(*a*) Express the premises in symbols.

(*b*) Use *US* and *ES* (where applicable) to drop quantifiers.

(*c*) Use sentential inference (tautological implication) to obtain the desired conclusion, without quantifiers.

(*d*) Use *UG* and *EG* (where applicable) to restore quantifiers.

As an example of the procedure, consider the argument

All human beings are fallible;
Aristotle is a human being;
Therefore, Aristotle is fallible.

Expressed in symbols, the argument becomes the argument form

$$(x)(Hx \rightarrow Fx);$$
$$Ha;$$
$$\text{Therefore, } Fa.$$

The following derivation establishes the validity of this argument form (the numerals in the first column number the premises on which the particular line relies, and the numerals in the second column number the steps in the derivation):

{1}	(1)	$(x)(Hx \rightarrow Fx)$	P
{2}	(2)	Ha	P
{1}	(3)	$Ha \rightarrow Fa$	1, US
{1,2}	(4)	Fa	2, 3, T

This, of course, is the simplest sort of derivation, involving just one application of US and no restoration of quantifiers. Other derivations will call into play the other rules as well.

Theorems of first-order logic. Special interest attaches to those formulas derivable in S from the *empty* set of premises. Such formulas are called *theorems of S*. An instance is

$$(x)Fx \rightarrow Fa.$$

This is shown to be a theorem by the following derivation, where the premise "$(x)Fx$" is first assumed *conditionally* and then eliminated with the aid of Rule *CP*, and where "Λ" denotes the empty set of premises:

{1}	(1)	$(x)Fx$	P
{1}	(2)	Fa	1, US
Λ	(3)	$(x)Fx \rightarrow Fa$	1, 2, CP

The condition for the validity of argument forms in S can now be stated: an argument form is valid in S if the corresponding conditional is a theorem of S. Since, as was noted earlier, an argument form is valid in first-order logic if the corresponding conditional is a valid formula, the two criteria will coincide if S in fact captures as theorems all and only valid formulas.

If all theorems of S are valid formulas, S is said to be *sound*; conversely, if all valid formulas are theorems, S is said to be *complete*. The soundness of systems like S is readily established, and a completeness proof for systems of this sort was given by Kurt Gödel in 1930. Thus, elementary logic, though undecidable, is both sound and complete.

The significance of these results and of the contrast they reveal between first-order logic and its sentential fragment cannot be considered in this informal treatment. Further discussion must await the formal account, which follows.

FORMALIZED SENTENTIAL LOGIC: SENTENTIAL CALCULUS

In this section a formal language for sentential logic will be introduced; with its aid two kinds of deductive systems for sentential logic—the axiomatic and the "natural"—will be formulated and applied to arguments; finally, certain important properties of these systems or calculi will be examined.

As a preliminary, it is desirable to settle on some terminology.

The study *of* any language must be conducted *in* a (not necessarily different) language. The one that is studied is called the *object language* and the one in which the study is conducted its *metalanguage*. In the present case the metalanguage will be ordinary English, supplemented by a few (metalinguistic) symbols; the object language will be L_S, an uninterpreted formal language that is to be used in formalizing sentential logic.

A *formal language L* is given by specifying (*a*) a list of *symbols of L* and (*b*) a set of *formation rules* for combining these symbols into acceptable, or well-formed, expressions (terms, formulas, sentences) of L. The language L is said to be **uninterpreted** so long as no "meanings" are assigned to the symbols and well-formed expressions of L—that is, so long as these symbols and well-formed expressions are regarded merely as recognizably distinct shapes and as strings of these shapes. An **uninterpreted formal calculus** or *system S* is an uninterpreted formal language L for which a **deductive apparatus** has been specified consisting of (*c*) a distinguished subset (possibly empty) of well-formed formulas of L, called the *axioms of S*, and (*d*) a set of *rules of inference*, or "transformation" rules, for deducing or deriving certain well-formed formulas of L from other well-formed formulas of L. A good deal can be said about such uninterpreted calculi or systems without essential resort to their intended interpretations.

We must still define the terms "syntax" and "semantics" (see SEMANTICS). Syntax considers certain relations between symbols and other symbols without regard to their meanings; semantics, on the other hand, considers certain relations between symbols (linguistic signs) and nonlinguistic objects—in particular the relations of denoting, referring, meaning, and the like. To describe the syntax of a formal language L is to specify its symbols and formation rules; to describe syntactically a formal system S is to specify, in addition, its deductive apparatus. To provide L with a semantics is to give L an *interpretation*, which assigns meanings to its symbols (and expressions). Finally, if for a given interpretation I of the language L the axioms of a formal system S couched in terms of L turn out to be true, the interpretation I is said to constitute a *model* for S.

A formal language for sentential logic: L_S. The formal treatment of sentential logic begins with the construction of a formal language L_S. This construction, like that of any artificial language, is guided by the purpose that is to be served. Our purpose here is to furnish a precise means of talking about certain simple sentences and their truth-functional compounds. Since the intended interpretation covers such limited ground, L_S can be a very simple language, comprising a few symbols and only two or three formation rules.

(1) The symbols of L_S are of two sorts (corresponding to the sentence connectives and the sentences in the intended interpretation):

(*a*) *Logical constants*—that is, the *connective symbols*

$$\neg, \lor, \&, \rightarrow, \leftrightarrow,$$

which can, of course, be reduced to two *primitive* connective symbols, say ¬ and →, if we define the others in terms of these two.

(b) *Variables* — that is, the *sentence letters*

$$P_i$$

(with positive integers i as subscripts), to which are added the punctuation signs

$$(, \ ).$$

Then any string (of finite length) of symbols of L_S is an *expression of L_S*.

(2) The formation rules of L_S pick out those expressions of L_S that are to count as the well-formed formulas (wffs, for short) of L_S. In stating these rules it will be convenient to supplement the metalanguage, English, with the small Greek letters $\varphi, \psi, \chi, \cdots$, which serve as metalinguistic variables ranging over (but not belonging to) the set of expressions of L_S. The rules, then, are as follows:

(a) All sentence letters are wffs.
(b) If φ is a wff, so is $\neg\varphi$.
(c) If φ and ψ are wffs, so are $(\varphi \lor \psi)$, $(\varphi \ \& \ \psi)$, $(\varphi \to \psi)$, and $(\varphi \leftrightarrow \psi)$.

It is understood that nothing can be a wff of L_S except by virtue of the rules (a), (b), and (c).

At this stage, with only its syntax given, L_S is merely an uninterpreted formal language. Its symbols and expressions are nothing more than recognizably distinct shapes, without assigned meanings. These shapes acquire denotations only when L_S is supplied with a semantics. Roughly speaking, this involves two things. First, a domain of objects is specified over which the "P_i," the variables of L_S, are understood to range. Under the intended interpretation (which, of course, is not the only possible one) this domain is the set of simple sentences ordinarily used to make statements that are either true or false but not both. Second, meanings are assigned to the logical constants of L_S: "¬," "∨," "&," "→," "↔." In the present instance these symbols are understood to denote, respectively, the ordinary connectives "not," "or," "and," "if–then," and "if and only if," restricted, however, to their truth-functional uses—that is, to cases where they combine true–false sentences in such a way that the truth or falsity of the compound sentence depends only on the truth or falsity of its component sentences. The well-formed expressions of L_S now all have meanings; the wff

$$P_1 \lor P_2,$$

for example, stands for the disjunction of any two simple true–false sentences.

Deductive systems for sentential logic. The formal language L_S may now be used to formulate deductive systems for sentential logic. These systems serve to characterize logic syntactically, in particular by means of the concepts of *deducibility* (provability, derivability, "follow logically from") and *theorem*. This syntactical characterization must be clearly distinguished from a semantical one, in which the paramount concepts are (logical) *consequence* and *validity*. The relation between these two kinds of descriptions is at the base of the modern view of logic and will be considered in some detail later in this section.

The syntactical characterization of sentential logic (indeed, of elementary logic as a whole) can itself be given by either of two different procedures. One is *formal axiomatization*, in which the deductive apparatus laid down for the calculus consists of (logical) axioms and rules of inference. The other, known as *natural deduction*, dispenses with axioms and uses rules of inference alone. The axiomatic method, which became bound up with modern logic in the work of its principal creator, Frege, and whose intimate connection with modern logic was reinforced by A. N. Whitehead's and Bertrand Russell's *Principia Mathematica* (1910–1913), was long regarded as the only acceptable way of presenting the principles of logic. The alternative procedure, natural deduction, is a comparatively recent contribution, having been developed independently by Gerhard Gentzen and Stanisław Jaśkowski in 1934.

Axiom systems. The sentential calculus can be formally axiomatized in many different ways, depending on the particular choice of axioms, primitive symbols, rules of inference, and the like. A typical axiom system (adapted from Elliott Mendelson, *Introduction to Mathematical Logic,* pp. 29 ff.), here called S_A, will be given.

If φ, ψ, and χ are any wffs of L_S, then the following are axioms of S_A:

(A1) $(\varphi \to (\psi \to \varphi))$.
(A2) $((\varphi \to (\psi \to \chi)) \to ((\varphi \to \psi) \to (\varphi \to \chi)))$.
(A3) $((\neg\psi \to \neg\varphi) \to ((\neg\psi \to \varphi) \to \psi))$.

It will be observed that A1, A2, and A3 are axiom *schemas*; each has an infinite number of instances, and all of these are the axioms of S_A. Thus,

$$P_1 \to (P_2 \to P_1)$$

is an instance of A1 and hence an axiom of S_A.

The one rule of inference of S_A is *modus ponens* (MP), also called the *rule of detachment*:

From φ and $\varphi \to \psi$, where φ and ψ are wffs of L_S, to infer ψ.

Some additional terminology is needed. A proof in S_A is a sequence of wffs of L_S such that each either is an axiom of S_A or follows from some of the preceding wffs in the sequence by virtue of *modus ponens*. A *theorem of S_A* is a wff φ of L_S such that there is a proof in S_A whose last line is φ. Further, a wff φ of L_S is said to be *deducible (provable)* in S_A *from a set* Γ *of wffs of L_S* if and only if there is a sequence of wffs of L_S such that φ is the last member of the sequence, and each member of the sequence is an axiom of S_A or belongs to Γ or else follows from some of the preceding wffs in the sequence by virtue of *modus ponens*. Such a sequence is called a *deduction (or proof) of φ from* Γ, and the expression "φ is deducible or provable from Γ (in S_A)" is abbreviated as

$$\Gamma \vdash_{S_A} \varphi.$$

The sense of this is that in S_A there is a *conditional proof* of the wff φ from the wffs belonging to Γ, these latter being referred to as the *premises* or *hypotheses* of the proof. Finally, if φ is a *theorem*, then by definition it is deducible from the axioms alone. There being in that case no "premises," Γ is then the empty set, and

$$\vdash_{S_A} \varphi$$

says that φ is a theorem of S_A.

Once the axioms and the rule of inference are given, it is possible to proceed with the proofs of theorems in S_A. A simple example is the following:

For any wff φ, $\vdash_{S_A} \varphi \to \varphi$.

Proof

(1)	$(\varphi \to ((\varphi \to \varphi) \to \varphi)) \to$	
	$\quad ((\varphi \to (\varphi \to \varphi)) \to (\varphi \to \varphi))$	Instance of A2
(2)	$\varphi \to ((\varphi \to \varphi) \to \varphi))$	A1
(3)	$(\varphi \to (\varphi \to \varphi)) \to (\varphi \to \varphi)$	From 1, 2 by *MP*
(4)	$\varphi \to (\varphi \to \varphi)$	A1
(5)	$\varphi \to \varphi$	From 3, 4 by *MP*

An important procedural result for systems like S_A is the so-called *deduction theorem*, obtained independently by Jacques Herbrand (1929) and Alfred Tarski (1930). This theorem, which concerns conditional proofs, states that where Γ is a set of wffs and φ, ψ are wffs

$$\text{if } \Gamma, \varphi \vdash \psi, \text{ then } \Gamma \vdash \varphi \to \psi,$$

and, in particular,

$$\text{if } \varphi \vdash \psi, \text{ then } \vdash \varphi \to \psi.$$

In other words, if ψ is deducible in S_A from Γ and φ, then $\varphi \to \psi$ is deducible in S_A from Γ, and if ψ is deducible in S_A from φ, then $\varphi \to \psi$ is a theorem of S_A (that is, it is deducible in S_A from the axioms of S_A alone).

It should be noted that this result itself is *not* a theorem of S_A. Rather, it is a derived rule of inference, and the "proof" that it is valid for S_A is not a proof *in* S_A but a series of arguments *about* proofs in S_A, the details of which cannot be gone into here.

A word is needed on the use of axiomatic sentential calculus in testing the validity of sentential argument forms. Consider an example cited earlier, now expressed in the form of a sequence of wffs of L_S:

$$P_1 \vee P_2;$$
$$\neg P_1;$$
$$\text{Therefore, } P_2.$$

To say that this argument form is valid in S_A is to say that there is in S_A a proof of "P_2" from the premises "$P_1 \vee P_2$" and "$\neg P_1$," or

$$(P_1 \vee P_2), \neg P_1 \vdash_{S_A} P_2.$$

By the deduction theorem,

$$\text{if } (P_1 \vee P_2), \neg P_1 \vdash_{S_A} P_2, \text{ then } (P_1 \vee P_2) \vdash_{S_A} \neg P_1 \to P_2,$$

and again,

$$\text{if } (P_1 \vee P_2) \vdash_{S_A} \neg P_1 \to P_2, \text{ then } \vdash_{S_A} (P_1 \vee P_2) \to (\neg P_1 \to P_2).$$

This means that the wff

$$(P_1 \vee P_2) \to (\neg P_1 \to P_2)$$

is a theorem of S_A. But that wff is equivalent to

$$((P_1 \vee P_2) \,\&\, \neg P_1) \to P_2,$$

which is simply the conditional formed by taking the conjunction of the premises of the above argument form as the antecedent and its conclusion as the consequent.

Thus, to test the validity of any argument form composed of wffs of L_S is merely to determine whether or not the conditional that corresponds to that argument form is a theorem of S_A.

This requirement is easy enough to state, but the actual procedure of proving that a given wff of L_S is a theorem of S_A can be an extremely involved affair. Moreover, even the proofs of the simplest theorems—as the example of $\varphi \to \varphi$ shows—have a pronounced air of artificiality about them.

This inevitably raises a question: What is the point of axiomatizing (sentential) logic? Historically the point seems to have been to codify the principles of logic by obtaining them as the theorems of a deductive system. It was this aim that guided the selection of axioms and inference rules for Frege's original system and for all of its lineal descendants down to and including S_A. The problem of codifying "logical truths" had been posed afresh by the rebirth of logic and the enlargement of its domain in the second half of the nineteenth century. Frege and the other mathematicians responsible for this renaissance naturally assumed that they could best solve the problem by exploiting the axiomatic method which had been so successful in mathematics. Also, if, as Frege and, later, Russell supposed, arithmetic was to be deduced from logic, there must surely be "logical axioms" on which to base the deduction (on this, see William Kneale and Martha Kneale, *The Development of Logic*, p. 530).

Subsequent developments have called into question the whole enterprise of axiomatizing logic, on several grounds. First, for sentential logic axiomatization is unnecessary. Post and Wittgenstein in 1921 showed that to identify the "truths" of sentential logic with the set of tautologies and then to utilize truth tables as a decision procedure for determining just which wffs of L_S are tautologies is a far simpler way of certifying these truths.

Second, the axiomatization of logic tends to be misleading about the nature of logic. This became apparent in the 1930s, as a result of the pioneering work of Rudolf Carnap in formal syntax and Tarski in formal semantics. Their studies served, among other things, to clarify the distinctions between a theory and the logic in which it is formalized and between the syntactical and the semantical characterizations of logic. The danger is that the axiomatization of logic tends to create the presumption that logic is merely another theory to be axiomatized, like a geometry or an algebra. This, of course, is not so. The axiomatization of a geometry presupposes a logic that governs the deducing of theorems from geometrical axioms. This logic, when made explicit, is found to consist of *inference rules*; "logical axioms," unlike the "proper axioms" of the axiomatized (mathematical) theories, do not in fact enter as premises in any of the deductions in these systems.

Finally, the axiomatization of sentential logic results in cumbersome proof procedures. Hence, it is of uncertain value even for the limited purpose of characterizing the sentential fragment syntactically. For this reason most authors now prefer to use some form of natural deduction system.

Natural deduction systems. As an alternative syntactical characterization of sentential logic, a natural deduction system has marked advantages. For one thing, its deductive apparatus consists of inference rules alone, thus eliminating the awkward business of logical axioms. For another, its method of testing the validity of argument forms is much closer to ordinary patterns of reasoning.

The choice between logical axioms and rules of inference, as Carnap noted in 1934 (*Logische Syntax der Sprache*), is a practical one rather than one of principle, in that for any logical axiom an equivalent inference rule, or rules, can be stated. The same deductive strength can be built into both kinds of sentential logic systems. They are, so to speak, alternative ways of fixing syntactically the logical properties of the connective symbols. These properties can also be fixed semantically, by means of truth-table definitions. All three devices, when used properly, will impose the same behavior on the connective symbols.

Natural deduction systems themselves are of two sorts. The first employs a full set of rules of inference to obtain the desired behavior on the part of the connectives. An example is the system S_N (patterned after Donald Kalish and Richard Montague, *Logic: Techniques of Formal Reasoning*, Chs. 1 and 2). The inference rules of S_N are as follows:

For any wffs φ and ψ of L_S,

(1) *modus ponens*: from $\varphi \to \psi$ and φ to infer ψ.

(2) *modus tollens*: from $\varphi \to \psi$ and $\neg\psi$ to infer $\neg\varphi$.

(3) double negation (in two forms): from $\neg\neg\varphi$ to infer φ; from φ to infer $\neg\neg\varphi$.

(4) repetition: from φ to infer φ.

(5) simplification (in two forms): from $\varphi \& \psi$ to infer φ; from $\psi \& \varphi$ to infer φ.

(6) adjunction: from φ, ψ to infer $\varphi \& \psi$.

(7) addition (in two forms): from φ to infer $\varphi \vee \psi$; from φ to infer $\psi \vee \varphi$.

(8) *modus tollendo ponens* (in two forms): from $\varphi \vee \psi$, $\neg\varphi$ to infer ψ; from $\varphi \vee \psi$, $\neg\psi$ to infer φ.

(9) biconditional–conditional (in two forms): from $\varphi \leftrightarrow \psi$ to infer $\varphi \to \psi$; from $\varphi \leftrightarrow \psi$ to infer $\psi \to \varphi$.

(10) conditional–biconditional: from $\varphi \to \psi$, $\psi \to \varphi$ to infer $\varphi \leftrightarrow \psi$.

The system S_N provides a direct and natural means of testing the validity of argument forms of sentential logic. If Γ is a set (possibly empty) of wffs of L_S and φ is a wff of L_S, then the argument form

$$\Gamma;$$
$$\text{Therefore, } \varphi$$

is valid if there is a derivation in S_N of the conclusion φ from the premises Γ—that is, if

$$\Gamma \vdash_{S_N} \varphi.$$

Here by a derivation is meant a finite sequence of consecutively numbered lines, each consisting of a wff of L_S, such that φ appears on the last line and each line is vouched for by one of the following rules for the construction of S_N derivations:

(1) Any premise (that is, any member of Γ) may appear on a line.

(2) Any wff of L_S may occur as a line if it follows from previous wffs in the sequence (conditional assumptions excepted) by one of the inference rules of S_N.

(3) Any wff of L_S may occur as a line if it is obtained from previous wffs in the sequence by conditionalization. Conditionalization, or conditional derivation, rests on the deduction theorem for S_N, which states that if there is a derivation in S_N, say, of φ from Γ *together with* the additional assumption ψ, then there is a derivation in S_N of $\psi \to \varphi$ from Γ alone; $\psi \to \varphi$ is then said to have been obtained from Γ by conditionalization.

Finally, a wff φ of L_N is called a theorem of S_N if and only if φ is derivable in S_N from the empty set of wffs—that is, if and only if

$$\vdash_{S_N} \varphi.$$

The second sort of natural deduction system assumes the presence of truth-table definitions for the connectives and the notion of tautological implication. An illustration is the system $S_{N'}$ (adapted from Patrick Suppes, *Introduction to Logic*, Ch. 2), which requires only the following rules for the construction of derivations:

Rule *P*: a premise may be introduced at any point in a derivation.

Rule *T*: a wff φ may be introduced at any point in a derivation if there are preceding wffs in the derivation such that their conjunction *tautologically implies* φ.

Rule *CP* (conditional proof): if a wff φ can be derived from a wff ψ in the presence of a set of premises Γ, then $\psi \to \varphi$ may be derived from Γ alone.

The system $S_{N'}$ is well suited to testing argument forms that involve a large number of different sentence letters, for which the truth-table method becomes tedious. Consider the following argument form, which, since it involves four sentence letters, would require a truth table with sixteen rows:

$$P_1 \to (P_2 \to P_3);$$
$$\neg P_4 \vee P_1;$$
$$P_2;$$
$$\text{Therefore, } P_4 \to P_3.$$

That this argument form is valid is shown by the following derivation in $S_{N'}$ (the first column gives the numbers of the premises that tautologically imply the wff on the particular line, and the second column numbers the steps in the derivation):

{1}	(1)	$P_1 \to (P_2 \to P_3)$	Premise
{2}	(2)	$\neg P_4 \vee P_1$	Premise
{3}	(3)	P_2	Premise
{4}	(4)	P_4	Premise

{2,4}	(5)	P_1	2, 4, T
{1,2,4}	(6)	$P_2 \to P_3$	1, 5, T
{1,2,3,4}	(7)	P_3	3, 6, T
{1,2,3}	(8)	$P_4 \to P_3$	4, 7, CP

Note that "P_4" has been added as a conditional premise in the derivation and has been used in conjunction with the three original premises to derive "P_3"; the desired conclusion "$P_4 \to P_3$" is then derived by Rule *CP* from the three premises alone, and the argument form is thus valid.

In effect, the $S_{N'}$ derivation breaks down a complicated sentential argument form into a series of simple argument forms each of which can be tested in an obvious and simple manner.

Semantical aspect of sentential calculus. The system S_A (or S_N) is an uninterpreted formal language L_S for which a deductive apparatus has been specified. It is a formal calculus allowing the deduction or derivation of certain wffs of L_S from other wffs of L_S without regard to any "meanings" that may later be ascribed to the symbols of L_S. But just as the construction of L_S was guided by its intended interpretation, so the choice of axioms and inference rules for S_A (or S_N) has been motivated by its intended application (to sentences and arguments) and by the aim of obtaining as theorems just the "truths of logic." Whatever pertains to interpretation constitutes the semantical aspect of the sentential calculus, which must now be outlined.

The essential notions are interpretation, truth under an interpretation, (logical) consequence, validity, and model.

An *interpretation I* of L_S is an assignment of denotations to the symbols of L_S. In the present instance let the sentence letters "P_i" range over the set of true–false simple sentences, and let the connective symbols stand for the corresponding truth-functional connectives as defined by the standard truth tables. Then any wff φ of L_S will be a truth-function of its n different component sentence letters, and the truth tables will serve as semantical devices to generate all of the 2^n possible assignments of the truth-values T and F to the n components of φ, and hence to φ itself. If φ comes out T under at least one but not all value assignments to its components, it is a *contingent* wff; if under none, it is a *contradiction*; if under all, it is a tautology.

It is now possible to define "consequence of" and "valid wff," which are the semantical counterparts of the syntactical notions "deducible from" (or "derivable from") and "theorem." A wff φ of L_S is said to be a *consequence in sentential logic* of a set Γ of wffs of L_S if and only if all the value assignments that assign T's to all of the wffs of Γ also assign T to φ. This can be written as

$$\Gamma \models \varphi,$$

where the sign "$\models$" is an abbreviation of "has as its consequence." Note that if Γ is a set of premises and φ is its supposed conclusion, then if φ is a consequence of Γ, it will be impossible for all the wffs of Γ to be true and φ false.

Further, a wff φ of L_S is said to be *valid in sentential logic* if it comes out T under all possible value assignments to its component sentence letters. Such a wff (recall the definition of consequence) is then a consequence of any set of wffs, including the empty set, so that

$$\models \varphi$$

says that φ is valid in sentential logic. Clearly the set of wffs valid in sentential logic coincides with the set of tautologies, and the notion of "wff valid in sentential logic" or "tautology" explicates for sentential logic the notion of logical truth.

Finally, an interpretation of L_S is called a *model of S_A* (or S_N) if the (axioms and) theorems of the system are true under that interpretation. For the interpretation I, above, this means that I is a model of S_A (or S_N) provided that all theorems of the system are valid wffs; that is,

$$\text{if} \vdash_{S_A} \varphi, \text{then} \models \varphi.$$

If this condition is fulfilled, the system S_A (or S_N) is then said to be *sound*. Conversely, S_A (or S_N) is called *complete* if it captures as theorems *all* the truths of sentential logic. For the interpretation I this means that S_A (or S_N) is complete provided all valid wffs are theorems of the system; that is,

$$\text{if} \models \varphi, \text{then} \vdash_{S_A} \varphi.$$

That both of these conditions are satisfied will be shown shortly.

The use of the term "valid" in "valid wff" is different from but related to its use in "valid argument form." For example, consider the argument form

$$\Gamma, \psi;$$
$$\text{Therefore, } \varphi.$$

This will be valid if and only if

$$\Gamma, \psi \models \varphi.$$

The semantical form of the deduction theorem, which provides that

$$\Gamma, \psi \models \varphi \text{ if and only if } \Gamma \models \psi \to \varphi,$$

can then be applied as often as necessary to show that an argument form in sentential logic is valid if and only if the corresponding conditional is itself a valid wff in sentential logic (a tautology)—that is, if and only if

$$\models \Gamma \to (\psi \to \varphi).$$

The three characterizations of the sentential calculus may now be summarized as follows:

(1) To say that a wff φ of L_S is a logical truth in sentential logic is to say that it is

(a) a theorem deducible in S_A from the axioms alone:

$$\vdash_{S_A} \varphi,$$

that it is

(b) a theorem derivable in S_N from the empty set of premises:

$$\vdash_{S_N}\varphi,$$

or that it is
    (*c*) a wff valid in sentential logic—that is, a tautology:

$$\models\varphi.$$

(2) To say that a wff φ of L_S may be validly inferred from a set of premises Γ consisting of wffs of L_S is to say that it is
    (*a*) deducible from Γ in S_A :

$$\Gamma\vdash_{S_A}\varphi,$$

or that it is
    (*b*) derivable from Γ in S_N :

$$\Gamma\vdash_{S_N}\varphi,$$

or that it is
    (*c*) a consequence in sentential logic of Γ:

$$\Gamma\models\varphi.$$

Metatheory of the sentential calculus. The metatheory of a formal system is the study of certain properties of that system. Metatheoretic findings are metatheorems, or theorems *about* the system as contrasted with theorems *of* the system. The properties studied include decidability, consistency, and completeness, the last in two senses, a weaker and a stronger.

A formal system S expressed in a formal language L is called *decidable* if there exists an algorithm for deciding in a finite number of steps whether or not an arbitrary wff of L is a theorem of S. If such a *decision procedure* exists, the *decision problem* of S is said to have a *positive* solution. If it can be proved that no such procedure is possible, the decision problem of S is said to have a *negative* solution. If neither is the case, its decision problem is still open.

As it turns out, the sentential calculus is decidable, and this makes its metatheory quite simple. Consider S_A, or any similar axiom system for the sentential calculus. It can easily be shown that S_A is *sound*—i.e., that all of its theorems are tautologies, or, more specifically, that (*a*) any instance of the three axiom schemas is a tautology and (*b*) *modus ponens,* the one rule of inference, preserves tautologies (that is, if φ and $\varphi\rightarrow\psi$ are tautologies, so is ψ). Conversely, it can be shown that S_A is *complete* (in the weaker sense)—i.e., that all tautologies are deducible as theorems of S_A. Similar reasoning establishes that all theorems of S_N are tautologies and that all tautologies are derivable in S_N from the empty set of premises and hence are theorems. Consequently there will be a decision procedure for theorems if there is one for tautologies. And this is precisely what the truth tables furnish: a mechanical procedure for deciding in a finite number of steps whether or not an arbitrary wff φ of L_S is a tautology. Thus, the decision problem for the sentential calculus has a positive solution, and logical truths in sentential logic may be certified without having to be deduced or derived as theorems.

It should be noted that checking the correctness of a deduction or derivation is also a mechanical task. How-

ever, there is no decision procedure for determining whether or not an arbitrary wff φ of L_S is deducible in S_A or derivable in S_N. If φ is not a theorem, the search for a deduction or derivation of φ could in theory proceed endlessly without any assurance that the failure to find such a deduction or derivation arises because none exists rather than because the search has not been prosecuted far enough. Thus, despite their cumbersomeness, only the truth tables provide a mechanical test for validity in sentential logic.

The consistency and the (strong) completeness of the sentential calculus follow directly from its decidability. A formal system S expressed in a formal language L is said to be consistent if there is no wff φ of L such that both φ and $\neg\varphi$ are theorems of S. Since *all* theorems of the sentential calculus must be tautologies, and since the negation of a tautology is a contradiction, it is clear that φ will be a theorem if and only if $\neg\varphi$ is not a theorem. The consistency of the sentential calculus is thus assured. Further, S is said to be complete (in the stronger sense of the term, which originated with E. L. Post) if for any wff φ of L that is not a theorem of S, the addition of φ as an axiom would render S inconsistent. Since all tautologies are theorems, adding φ as an axiom would mean adding an axiom that is not a tautology; it can be shown that this would result in the loss of the consistency of S.

Finally, as noted above, there are proofs at hand that S_A (or S_N) is sound, i.e., that

$$\text{if } \vdash_{S_A}\varphi, \text{ then } \models\varphi,$$

and complete, i.e., that

$$\text{if } \models\varphi, \text{ then } \vdash_{S_A}\varphi.$$

When the two results are combined,

$$\models\varphi \text{ if and only if } \vdash_{S_A}\varphi.$$

This can also be expressed by saying that the syntactical and the semantical characterizations of the sentential calculus coincide. Since the set of logical truths of sentential logic is identical with the set of tautologies, the system S_A (or S_N) has thus been shown to codify *only* and *all* the logical truths of the sentential fragment of modern logic.

FORMALIZED ELEMENTARY LOGIC: FIRST-ORDER PREDICATE CALCULUS

The formal account of elementary logic opens with the presentation of a formal language. This language is then used to formulate axiomatic and natural deduction systems for the first-order predicate calculus, and certain varieties of first-order calculi are briefly noted. The account concludes with a summary of the metatheory of elementary logic, a metatheory which—first-order logic being in general undecidable—is considerably more complex than that of the sentential calculus.

The formal language L_P. A formal system for first-order logic requires a language which, absorbing that of the sentential fragment, goes well beyond it with respect both to its stock of symbols and to its formation rules. Such a language is L_p, of which L_s is essentially a sublanguage.

(1) The *symbols* of L_p are

(a) all the *logical constants* of L_s:

$$\neg, \vee, \&, \rightarrow, \leftrightarrow, (,),$$

to which is added

$$\exists,$$

(b) *nonlogical constants,* comprising

(i) *predicate constants*: capital letters with or without numerical subscripts and superscripts,

(ii) *individual constants*: the lower-case letters from "a" through "t," with or without numerical subscripts,

(c) *individual variables*: the small letters from "u" through "z," with or without numerical subscripts,

(d) *sentence letters*: capital letters standing alone (as distinguished from predicate symbols).

An *expression of L_p* is any sequence (of finite length) of symbols of L_p. A *term* is an individual variable or an individual constant. A predicate with superscript n is an *n-place* or *n-adic predicate*. An *atomic formula* is an expression of L_p consisting either of a sentence letter alone or of an n-place predicate followed by n terms.

(2) The *formation rules of L_p*, which define the phrase "well-formed formula (wff) of L_p," are

(a) every atomic formula is a wff;

(b) if φ is a wff, so is $\neg\varphi$;

(c) if φ, ψ are wffs, so are $(\varphi \vee \psi)$, $(\varphi \& \psi)$, $(\varphi \rightarrow \psi)$, $(\varphi \leftrightarrow \psi)$;

(d) if φ is a wff and α is a variable, then $(\alpha)\varphi$ and $(\exists\alpha)\varphi$ are wffs.

It is understood that nothing can be a wff of L_p except by virtue of rules a–d.

In addition, an occurrence of a variable α in a formula φ is called *bound* if it is within the scope of a quantifier—that is, if it is within an occurrence in φ of a formula of the form $(\alpha)\psi$ or the form $(\exists\alpha)\psi$; otherwise it is called *free*. The variable itself is called free (bound) if it has a free (bound) occurrence; hence, a variable may be both bound and free in the same wff. A term τ is said to be *free for a variable α in a wff φ* if and only if no free occurrences of α are within the scope of a quantifier (β), where β is a variable in τ. For example, "x_1" is free for "x_2" in the wff "Fx_2" but not in the wff "$(x_1)Fx_2$." Finally, by a *sentence of L_p* is meant a wff of L_p that contains no free variable.

That completes the syntax of L_p. At this point its expressions are simply recognizably distinct shapes to which no "meanings" have yet been assigned. The construction of L_p, like that of L_s, has, of course, been guided by an intended interpretation. But it is better to defer the semantics until after first-order logic (with the aid of L_p) has been characterized in terms of the purely syntactical concepts of deducibility (derivability) and theorem.

Deductive systems. In the absence of a decision procedure for first-order logic, the codification of its principles by means of deductive systems assumes special importance.

Axiom system, P_A. Illustrative of the axiomatic approach is the system P_A (adapted from Mendelson, *Introduction to Mathematical Logic,* Ch. 2).

The (logical) axioms of P_A are given by axiom schemas, as follows: if φ, ψ, χ are wffs of L_p, then the axioms of P_A are

(1) $\varphi \rightarrow (\psi \rightarrow \varphi)$.

(2) $(\varphi \rightarrow (\psi \rightarrow \chi)) \rightarrow ((\varphi \rightarrow \psi) \rightarrow (\varphi \rightarrow \chi))$.

(3) $(\neg\psi \rightarrow \neg\varphi) \rightarrow ((\neg\psi \rightarrow \varphi) \rightarrow \psi)$.

(4) $(\alpha)\varphi\alpha \rightarrow \varphi\tau$, if $\varphi\alpha$ is a wff of L_p and τ is a term of L_p free for α in $\varphi\alpha$; note that τ may be identical with α, in which case the axioms $(\alpha)\varphi\alpha \rightarrow \varphi\alpha$ result.

(5) $(\alpha)(\varphi \rightarrow \psi) \rightarrow (\varphi \rightarrow (\alpha)\psi)$, if φ is a wff of L_p containing no free occurrences of α.

The rules of P_A are

(1) *modus ponens (MP)*: from φ and $\varphi \rightarrow \psi$, to infer ψ.

(2) generalization *(GEN)*: from φ to infer $(\alpha)\varphi$.

It will be noted that the schemas and rules of P_A include all those of S_A. The sentential calculus is thus seen to be literally a fragment of first-order logic.

The definitions of *proof, deducibility,* and *theorem* parallel those for S_A. A theorem of P_A is any wff of L_p that is obtainable from the axioms by means of the rules. The expression "φ is deducible in P_A from a set of wffs Γ" is abbreviated as

$$\Gamma \vdash_{P_A} \varphi,$$

and "φ is a theorem of P_A"—that is, "φ is deducible in P_A from the axioms alone"—is abbreviated as

$$\vdash_{P_A} \varphi.$$

In general the proofs of theorems proceed as before, but the deduction theorem carries over only in a modified form.

Although a deductive treatment is essential for first-order logic, the choice between the two types, axiomatic and natural deduction, remains a purely practical one. The system P_A, which follows in the tradition of Frege and Russell, imposes the desired behavior on the quantifiers (and connectives) by means of axioms *and* rules. Today, however, many authors hold that a simpler and less artificial equivalent account is obtained by concentrating the deductive power of the system in the rules alone.

Natural deduction system, P_N. An example of a natural deduction system for first-order logic is the system P_N (modeled after that presented in Mates, *Elementary Logic,* Ch. 7). Its basic rules will be described and one or two sample derivations considered.

By a *derivation in P_N* is meant a finite sequence of lines; these are consecutively numbered, and each consists of a sentence (that is, a wff of L_p with no free variables) together with a set of numbers called the premise numbers of that line. The construction of the sequence is controlled by the following rules (φ and ψ being arbitrary wffs of L_p, α an individual variable, and δ an individual constant):

(1) Rule *P* (introduction of premises): any sentence may be entered on a line; the line number is taken as the only premise number.

(2) Rule *T* (tautological implication): any sentence may appear on a line if it is tautologically implied by a set of sentences that appear on previous lines; the premise numbers of the new line will be all the premise numbers of those previous lines.

(3) Rule *C* (conditionalization): the sentence $\varphi \rightarrow \psi$ may appear on a line if ψ appears on a previous line; the premise

numbers of the new line will be all those of that previous line, except (if desired) any that is the line number of a line on which φ appears.

(4) Rule *US* (universal specification): the sentence $\varphi\alpha/\delta$ (i.e., the sentence that results from substituting δ for all free occurrences of α in a wff φ) may appear on a line if $(\alpha)\varphi$ appears on a previous line; the premise numbers of the new line will be those of that previous line.

(5) Rule *UG* (universal generalization): the sentence $(\alpha)\varphi$ may appear on a line if $\varphi\alpha/\delta$ appears on a previous line and δ occurs neither in φ nor in any premise of that previous line; the premise numbers of the new line will be those of the previous line.

(6) Rule *E* (existential quantification): the sentence $(\exists\alpha)\varphi$ may appear on a line if $\neg(\alpha)\neg\varphi$ appears on a previous line, and vice versa; the premise numbers of the new line will be those of the old line.

It will be noted that this list includes all of the rules of the sentential calculus $S_{N'}$, to which are added the three rules *US*, *UG*, and *E*, regulating the behavior of the quantifiers.

A *derivation in P_N of a sentence φ from a set of sentences* Γ is a derivation in which φ appears on the last line and all the premises of that line belong to Γ, and φ is said to be *derivable* (in P_N) from Γ, abbreviated

$$\Gamma \vdash_{P_N} \varphi,$$

if and only if there is a derivation in P_N of φ from Γ.

The use of the rules is illustrated in the following derivation of "$(x)(Fx \to Hx)$" from the two premises "$(x)(Fx \to Gx)$" and "$(x)(Gx \to Hx)$":

{1}	(1)	$(x)(Fx \to Gx)$	P
{2}	(2)	$(x)(Gx \to Hx)$	P
{1}	(3)	$Fa \to Ga$	1, *US*
{2}	(4)	$Ga \to Ha$	2, *US*
{1,2}	(5)	$Fa \to Ha$	3, 4, *T*
{1,2}	(6)	$(x)(Fx \to Hx)$	5, *UG*

Finally, to say that a sentence φ of L_p is a theorem of P_N is to say that φ is derivable from the empty set of premises Λ, abbreviated

$$\Lambda \vdash_{P_N} \varphi.$$

For instance, the following derivation establishes that "$(x)(Fx \& Gx) \to ((x)Fx \& (x)Gx)$" is a theorem:

{1}	(1)	$(x)(Fx \& Gx)$	P
{1}	(2)	$Fa \& Ga$	1, *US*
{1}	(3)	Fa	2, *T*
{1}	(4)	Ga	2, *T*
{1}	(5)	$(x)Fx$	3, *UG*
{1}	(6)	$(x)Gx$	4, *UG*
{1}	(7)	$(x)Fx \& (x)Gx$	5, 6, *T*
Λ	(8)	$(x)(Fx \& Gx) \to$	
		$((x)Fx \& (x)Gx)$	1, 7, *C*

Semantical aspect of first-order logic. The (syntactical) systems for first-order logic, P_A and P_N, like those for sentential logic, have been set up with a view to obtaining as

theorems just the truths of logic. The next step is to characterize semantically the truths of first-order logic in terms of the basic notions of logical consequence and validity. It will then be possible to determine whether the two characterizations, syntactical and semantical, fully coincide.

One difficulty is that since L_p is a much richer formal language than L_S, its semantics is correspondingly much more involved. For this reason only a bare outline of its semantics can be given here.

The starting point once again is the notion of interpretation. Briefly, an interpretation I of L_p (*a*) specifies a nonempty domain of individuals or objects D as the domain of interpretation, (*b*) assigns to each individual constant of L_p as its denotation an individual member of D, and (*c*) assigns to each n-place predicate constant of L_p a class of (if $n = 1$), or an n-ary relation among, the members of D. Since any nonempty set may serve as D, the denotations of the expressions of L_p will vary from interpretation to interpretation, and many sentences true under one interpretation will be false under another.

The next problem is to indicate just what it means to say that a sentence φ of L_p is "true under an interpretation I." An atomic sentence φ will be "true under I" if the individual objects assigned by I to the individual constants of φ are in fact related by the relation I assigns to the predicate constant of φ. For example, let D be the positive integers; let "a_1," "a_2," $\cdots$, "a_n" name the first n of them; let "F" be "is less than" (that is, let "F" denote the set of ordered pairs of positive integers such that the first member is less than the second). Then under this interpretation "Fa_2a_3" will be true and "Fa_2a_1" false.

"True under I" is easily defined for sentences of L_p that are compounded from atomic sentences by means of the connectives. It is necessary to state only how the truth-values of the compounds depend on the truth-values of their components; this is done by assigning to the connective symbols of L_p—"$\neg$," "$\vee$," "$\&$," "$\to$," "$\leftrightarrow$"—their standard truth-table meanings.

The presence of quantifiers introduces into the truth definition certain technical complications that cannot be gone into here (for a full discussion, see Mates, *Elementary Logic*, Chs. 4 and 5). For our purposes it is enough to say that φ will be true under I if the individuals of the given domain D in fact belong to the classes or have the relations that φ, in virtue of I, says they have.

Once "true under I" is defined for an arbitrary sentence φ of L_p, the remaining semantical notions can be quickly set down. If φ is true under I, then I is said to be a *model* of φ, or to satisfy φ. The same applies to a set of sentences Γ.

The two concepts essential to the semantical characterization of first-order logic may then be defined. A sentence φ of L_p is a *consequence* of a set of sentences Γ, or

$$\Gamma \models \varphi,$$

if and only if there is no interpretation I in any nonempty domain D under which all the sentences of Γ are true and φ is false. A sentence φ of L_p is *valid*, or

$$\models \varphi,$$

if and only if φ is true under every interpretation in every nonempty domain D and hence is a consequence of the empty set of premises. The concluding steps, as in the case of sentential logic, are (*a*) to identify the intuitive concept of *logical truth* with the precise concept of *valid sentence* and (*b*) to certify those argument forms as valid whose conclusions are *consequences* of their premises. This completes the characterization.

The two critical questions can now be asked about any formal system for first-order logic: First, is it sound; that is, does it capture as theorems *only* valid sentences (logical truths)? Second, is it complete; that is, does it capture as theorems *all* valid sentences? If the answer to both questions is yes, then the syntactical relation of deducibility (in that system) has been shown to coincide with the semantical relation of consequence. Such an answer is immediately forthcoming for a decidable system. But elementary logic, being undecidable, presents a more complex problem; this will be dealt with shortly.

Some varieties of first-order calculi. Before the metatheory of first-order logic is discussed, mention must be made of certain kinds of first-order calculi that can be formulated in languages obtained from the language L_p by the addition or deletion of certain symbols or classes of symbols.

If a new logical constant "I" (identity) is added to L_p, the result is a language that permits the formulation of what is called the *first-order predicate calculus with identity*. This system contains, besides first-order logic, the theory of identity expressed in the form either of added axioms or of added rules. Accordingly it will have theorems beyond those of P_A or P_N. (Note that if identity is treated as part of the logic rather than simply as a possible denotation of a two-place predicate constant of L_p, the symbol "I" must *always* be taken as the relation of identity in the domain of interpretation under consideration.) First-order logic with identity is a standard means of formalizing mathematical and other types of theories, and those theories so formalized are called *elementary*.

Another method of supplementing L_p is to introduce operation symbols. These, however, are used not to formulate an enlarged system with new axioms or rules but merely to express first-order logic in a more convenient way.

Formal languages for other first-order calculi are obtained by dropping certain notations from L_p. Thus, if all individual constants are removed, the result is a language—call it L_p*—for the *pure* (as distinguished from the applied) *predicate calculus of first order*. If, in addition, all except one-place predicate symbols are eliminated, the result is a language for the (pure) *monadic* or *singulary predicate calculus of first order*. (A precise and full account of these systems appears in Church, *Introduction to Mathematical Logic*, Ch. 3.) Of special interest is the fact that although elementary logic as a whole is undecidable, certain portions of it—in particular the pure monadic calculus—turn out to be decidable.

Metatheory of pure first-order logic. The metatheory of pure first-order logic offers important results with respect to soundness, consistency, (weak) completeness, and decidability. Some of these will be briefly described.

The soundness of elementary logic, like that of its sentential fragment, is relatively easy to establish. All that is needed is to show that the axioms of P_A are themselves valid sentences of L_p and that the inference rules of P_A preserve validity (alternatively, that only valid sentences of L_p are derivable in P_N from the empty set of premises). It follows at once that all theorems of P_A (or P_N) are valid sentences of L_p, or

$$\text{if } \vdash_{P_A} \varphi, \text{ then } \vDash \varphi.$$

Consistency (in the sense that there is no sentence φ of L_p such that both φ and $\neg\varphi$ are theorems of the system) is an immediate consequence of soundness. If φ is a theorem, then φ is valid; by the definition of validity, $\neg\varphi$ cannot also be valid and hence cannot be a theorem. (There is a purely syntactical argument that establishes the consistency of P_A: Associate with any sentence φ of L_p a sentence ψ of L_S obtained by deleting from φ all individual symbols, quantifiers, and predicate superscripts. The axioms of P_A have the property that the sentences of L_S corresponding to them are tautologies, and the rules of P_A preserve this property; hence, if both φ and $\neg\varphi$ were theorems, then both ψ and $\neg\psi$ would be tautologies. But this is impossible; therefore, P_A is consistent.)

The problems of completeness and decidability, unlike those of soundness and consistency, are beset with complications that go far beyond the limits of an elementary account. (For a comprehensive treatment, see Church, *Introduction to Mathematical Logic*, Ch. 4; for a historical summary, see William Kneale and Martha Kneale, *The Development of Logic*, pp. 701 ff.) The most that will be attempted here is an indication of the general character of the more important results: the pioneering proof of the *decidability* of the monadic first-order calculus presented by Leopold Löwenheim (1915), the *completeness* proof for first-order logic presented by Kurt Gödel (1930), and the proof of the *undecidability* of general first-order logic presented by Alonzo Church (1936). For this purpose some further semantical refinements are required.

Let φ be any wff of L_p*, the language for pure first-order logic. Then φ is said to be *satisfiable in* a given nonempty set D if, when D is taken as the domain of interpretation, φ is satisfied by at least one system of values of its free variables—that is, if there is at least one interpretation I assigning individuals of D to the individual variables of φ and classes or relations of individuals of D to the predicate symbols of φ such that φ is true under that assignment. The wff "Fxy," for example, is satisfiable in the domain of positive integers: simply assign the relation "less than" to "F," the number 2 to the free variable "x," and the number 3 to the free variable "y"; this system of values satisfies "Fxy."

Similarly, φ is said to be *valid in* a given nonempty set D if, when D is taken as the domain of interpretation, φ is satisfied by *every* such assignment of individuals, classes, and relations of D to the symbols of φ. Thus, "Fxy" is obviously not valid in the set of positive integers: it is not satisfied, for example, by the assignment of the relation "less than" to "F," the number 3 to "x," and the number 2 to "y."

Finally, if φ is satisfiable in *some* nonempty set, it is called *satisfiable*; if it is valid in *every* nonempty set, it is called (universally) *valid*.

It is a consequence of these definitions that (for non-empty D) if φ is valid in D, then $\neg\varphi$ is not satisfiable in D, and if φ is satisfiable in D, then $\neg\varphi$ is not valid in D.

Further, the validity (or satisfiability) of a first-order wff in a nonempty domain D depends only on the *number* of individuals in D, not on their identity. This is best seen by considering the validity of wffs in *finite* domains. Let φ, for example, be the wff

$$(x)Fx \lor (x)\neg Fx.$$

Then φ is valid in any domain of just one individual, since in such a domain it asserts merely that the lone individual either does or does not belong to the class denoted by "F," and this assertion will be true of any one-member domain no matter how "F" is interpreted. However, φ is not valid in a domain of two (or more) individuals, since in such a domain it asserts that either both individuals belong to the class denoted by "F" or neither does, and this assertion will be false if it so happens that one individual belongs to the class and the other does not.

It can be shown that (*a*) if a wff is valid in a domain of $n + 1$ individuals, it must be valid in a domain of n individuals, and (*b*) if a wff is satisfiable in a domain of n individuals, it must be satisfiable in a domain of $n + 1$ individuals.

It was noted above that for finite domains universal (or existential) generalizations may be replaced by the conjunctions (or disjunctions) that are their truth-functional expansions; these conjunctions (or disjunctions) will have 2^n terms, where n is the number of individuals in the particular domain.

It is now possible to formulate the following rule for determining validity in finite domains: a wff φ of L_p^* is valid in a particular nonempty finite domain if and only if its truth-functional expansion for that domain is a tautology. For example, let φ again be the wff

$$(x)Fx \lor (x)\neg Fx.$$

For a domain of two individuals (designated by the letters "a" and "b"), the expansion is

(1) $(Fa \lor \neg Fa) \,\&\, (Fa \lor \neg Fb) \,\&\, (Fb \lor \neg Fa) \,\&\, (Fb \lor \neg Fb)$.

For a domain of just one individual (designated by the letter "a"), the expansion is

(2) $Fa \lor \neg Fa$.

Clearly, (2) is a tautology, whereas (1) is not. Thus, φ is shown to be valid in a domain of one individual but not valid in a domain of two (or more) individuals.

This leads directly to the problems of completeness and decidability. Here the earliest result seems to have been Löwenheim's positive solution of the decision problem for validity in the case of the pure monadic predicate calculus of first order. Improved solutions were given later by Heinrich Behmann (1922) and by Paul Bernays and Moses Schönfinkel (1928).

Bernays and Schönfinkel proved that if a monadic first-order wff φ is satisfiable at all, it is satisfiable in a domain

of 2^n individuals, where n is the number of distinct predicate symbols in φ. By the same token, they showed that if φ is valid in such a domain, it is (universally) valid. It follows that the validity of any monadic first-order wff φ can be decided merely by ascertaining whether φ is valid in a domain of a *finite* number of individuals. This can be done by applying the test for validity cited above: given a wff φ with n distinct predicate symbols, simply replace the quantifications occurring in φ with the appropriate conjunctions or disjunctions of 2^n members; then use the truth tables to determine whether or not the resulting sentential formula is a tautology. The decision problem for validity is thereby solved in the case of the monadic first-order calculus. (Other special cases have also been dealt with successfully by the above authors and by others; the results are reported in full in Wilhelm Ackermann, *Solvable Cases of the Decision Problem,* Amsterdam, 1955.)

This particular solution, of course, does not admit of extension to first-order logic as a whole, for there are (non-monadic) first-order wffs that are not satisfiable in finite domains but are satisfiable in infinite domains; their negations accordingly are valid in finite domains but are not valid in infinite domains. In other words, first-order logic is taken as quantifying over infinite as well as over finite domains.

The question then arises whether a logic that lacks a general decision procedure for validity can nonetheless be shown to be *complete*. The term "complete," it will be recalled, has at least two senses. A system is complete in the weaker sense if all valid wffs are provable as theorems in that system. In the stronger sense a system is complete if and only if for any wff φ, either φ is a theorem or the system becomes inconsistent if φ is added as an axiom without any other changes being made. (As was seen earlier, the sentential calculus is complete in both senses.)

It is easily shown that first-order logic is not complete in the strong sense. Noting this fact, David Hilbert and Wilhelm Ackermann, in the first edition (1928) of their celebrated text *Grundzüge der theoretischen Logik*, pointed to the question of *weak* completeness as an "as yet unsolved problem" (p. 66). Within two years, however, a solution was published by Gödel, then a young student in Vienna.

Gödel's completeness theorem, not to be confused with his theorems on the *in*completability of certain formal systems for the arithmetic of natural numbers (discussed in the article GÖDEL'S THEOREM), states that every valid first-order wff φ is a theorem of a system (such as P_A), or

$$\text{if} \models \varphi, \text{then} \vdash \varphi.$$

The proof uses a result obtained by Thoralf Skolem in 1920 to the effect that for every valid first-order wff φ there is a valid first-order wff ψ in "Skolem normal form" such that ψ is provable as a theorem if and only if φ is provable as a theorem (a wff is in Skolem normal form if it is so constituted that all of its quantifiers are at the beginning and all of its existential quantifiers, if any, precede its universal quantifiers). Hence, to prove completeness it suffices to show that all valid first-order wffs in Skolem normal form are provable as theorems. This Gödel did by relating validity in first-order logic to tautologicality in sentential logic; his method makes novel use of ideas developed by Löwenheim, Skolem, and Herbrand.

In the course of his proof Gödel obtained as a corollary an important theorem on domains first proved by Löwenheim in his 1915 paper. This theorem states that if a first-order wff is valid in a denumerably infinite domain (for example, the domain of natural numbers), then it is valid in every nonempty domain. Skolem later generalized this to read: if a set of wffs is simultaneously satisfiable in any nonempty domain, then it is so in a denumerably infinite domain. A consequence seems to be that a first-order theory is unable to characterize a mathematical structure involving a nondenumerable infinity of elements.

Another completeness proof for first-order logic was given by Leon Henkin in 1949 (a modified version appears in Mates, *Elementary Logic*, pp. 136–141). A set Γ of wffs is defined as *inconsistent* if there is a wff φ such that

$$\Gamma \vdash \varphi \text{ and } \Gamma \vdash \neg\varphi.$$

Otherwise Γ is consistent. It is then proved that any consistent set of wffs is simultaneously satisfiable in a denumerably infinite domain and that any simultaneously satisfiable set of wffs is consistent. Henkin exploits the close relation between the syntactical concept of consistency and the semantical concept of satisfiability suggested by the close relation between deducibility and consequence. Gödel's completeness theorem is here obtained as a corollary (as is Löwenheim's theorem). Specifically, if φ is a valid wff, then by the definitions of validity and satisfiability the set whose only member is $\neg\varphi$ is not "simultaneously" satisfiable; hence, it is not consistent, so that for some wff ψ,

$$\neg\varphi \vdash \psi \text{ and } \neg\varphi \vdash \neg\psi.$$

By the deduction theorem and sentential logic, it follows that

$$\vdash\varphi,$$

i.e., φ is a theorem, and first-order logic is complete. Since it is also sound,

$$\models\varphi \text{ if and only if } \vdash\varphi.$$

In 1936, six years after the publication of Gödel's completeness proof, Church obtained the important result already referred to—he proved the impossibility of a decision procedure for validity for elementary logic as a whole. Guided by his own and other explications of the notion of effective calculability, he was able first to show that no general decision procedure was possible for a certain portion of elementary number theory. He then established that if a decision procedure existed for first-order logic as a whole, there would necessarily be one for that very same portion of elementary number theory. Since the undecidability of the latter had already been proved, it followed that the solution to the general decision problem for elementary logic was negative.

ELEMENTARY AND NONELEMENTARY LOGIC

This final section has two purposes: to summarize what we have said about the general nature and uses of elementary logic and to indicate very briefly what is meant by nonelementary logic.

Elementary logic: a summary. Logic from Aristotle to Gödel has had three ends in view. The first is to explicate in precise terms various intuitive notions of "logical truth." The second is to codify, with the aid of formal systems and other devices, those statements or formulas that are to count as logical truths. The third is to apply these systems and devices as a means of testing the formal validity of certain arguments and inferences in the sciences and in everyday life.

Modern logic, since Frege, has sought to achieve these ends by exploiting a variety of mathematical methods and notions, in particular that of formal system. The creation of the formal disciplines of syntax and semantics by Carnap and Tarski added new tools and sharpened older ones. The syntactical notions—formal system, consistency, deducibility, and theorem—on which the original systematization of modern logic by Frege and Russell primarily relied have now been paired with their semantical counterparts: interpretation, (simultaneous) satisfiability, consequence, and validity. The combined use of syntactical and semantical characterizations has resulted in a clearer view of logic itself and of its role in formalizing mathematical and other types of theories.

The sentential fragment of modern logic considers only those true–false sentences that are truth-functional compounds of their simple component sentences. With respect to these compounds the intuitive notion of logical truth is explicated in terms of the precise concept of tautology, or wff valid in sentential logic.

Since the truth-table device supplies a decision procedure for tautology, sentential logic is decidable. This fact has important consequences. One is that the logical truths of sentential logic do not require the kind of codification furnished by a deductive system; the deductive treatment of logical principles, although historically significant, is theoretically superfluous. Another is that the metatheory of the sentential fragment is comparatively simple; consistency and (strong) completeness are corollaries of decidability, and it is easy to establish the soundness and (weak) completeness of the usual systems of sentential calculus.

The principles of sentential logic are readily applied to the testing of those arguments whose formal validity turns exclusively on the logical properties of the truth-functional connectives. The rule of application is simple: a sentential logic argument form is valid if the conditional that corresponds to that argument form is a tautology.

Elementary logic as a whole considers the wider class of true–false sentences made up of singular sentences and existential and universal generalizations involving only individual variables and of truth-functional compounds of all such sentences and generalizations. With regard to this class of sentences, elementary logic explicates the intuitive notion of logical truth in terms of the precise concept of wff (universally) valid in first-order logic.

It has been shown that elementary logic as a whole is undecidable: no general decision procedure is possible for validity in first-order logic. Two things follow: First, the codification of first-order logical truths seems best achieved with the aid of a deductive system, axiomatic or natural. Second, the metatheory of such a system is very complicated. Nevertheless, it has been proved not only that the usual deductive systems for first-order logic are sound but also that they are (weakly) complete. Thus for the first-order predicate calculus, as well as for the sentential calculus, a wff is valid if and only if it is a theorem. Despite its undecidability, first-order logic does admit of a codification in which the syntactical and the semantical characterizations of logical truth are seen to coincide.

The first-order predicate calculus accordingly provides a system of logical truths that may be used to test all arguments whose formal validity is determined entirely by the logical properties of the quantifiers and truth-functional connectives. Again the rule of application is simple: an argument form in elementary logic is valid if the corresponding conditional is a theorem of the first-order calculus—i.e., if it is a wff (universally) valid in first-order logic.

Nonelementary logic. Beyond elementary logic, and beyond the bounds of this article, lie the varied subject matters commonly referred to as advanced, or nonelementary, logic. This portion of modern logic embraces the predicate calculi of second and higher orders. In addition, it is usually understood to include (*a*) a number of specific fields, such as set theory, recursive function theory, and the theory of models, (*b*) various nonstandard logical systems—for instance, intuitionistic logic (which has been developed largely through the investigations of L. E. J. Brouwer and his followers into the foundations of mathematics)—and (*c*) the use of predicate calculi of various types to formalize arithmetical and other types of theories.

The higher-order calculi are necessary because of the restricted scope of elementary, or first-order, logic. In first-order logic, as has been pointed out, the only variables bound by quantifiers are those that range over individuals. Such a logic cannot deal, for example, with sentences that generalize with respect to classes or properties of individuals and consequently involve *predicate variables* as variables of quantification.

The need is met by a system which admits not only variables that range over individuals but also variables that range over classes (or relations) of individuals, variables that range over classes of classes of individuals, and so forth. The pure predicate calculus of order ω is such a system. It is constructed by adding to the formal language for pure first-order logic a notation for distinguishing (simple) *types* of variables and the *orders* of these types (see TYPES, THEORY OF) and by making appropriate changes in the formation rules of the language and in the deductive apparatus of the system. Calculi of orders less than ω are then regarded as fragments of the calculus of order ω. First-order logic gets its name from the fact that individual variables are assigned the order 1.

The second-order predicate calculus, which allows predicate variables (as well as individual variables) to be bound by quantifiers, has been studied in some detail (see Church, *Introduction to Mathematical Logic*, Ch. 5). There are consistency proofs for second-order predicate calculus and the higher-order calculi, and in 1947, Leon Henkin proved a (weak) completeness theorem for the second-order calculus by a method similar to that used in his proof of Gödel's completeness theorem for the first-order calculus. Henkin's proof can be extended to higher-order calculi.

Advanced modern logic has become a highly technical field, cultivated primarily by mathematicians and by philosophers of mathematics. Nevertheless, many of its results are regarded as having broader foundational significance, and some—most notably Gödel's incompletability theorems—have been the object of widespread philosophical discussion. For this and other reasons modern logic will continue to claim the attention of philosophers.

Bibliography

There is an extensive and rapidly growing body of literature devoted to elementary logic. The list of publications that follows is selective, not exhaustive. It includes (1) the more important histories and source books, (2) a variety of textbooks classified roughly as elementary, intermediate, and advanced, and (3) original papers, monographs, and treatises, many of which have been referred to in the text.

On symbolic logic as a whole, there is a complete bibliography for the period 1666–1935 prepared by Alonzo Church and published in the *Journal of Symbolic Logic*, Vol. 1 (1936), No. 4; additions and corrections appear in Vol. 3 (1938), No. 4, 178–212, and the bibliography is supplemented periodically.

HISTORIES AND SOURCE BOOKS

The best treatment of the history of modern logic is found in the second half of *The Development of Logic*, by William Kneale and Martha Kneale (Oxford, 1962). The main writings on modern logic from Gottlob Frege to Kurt Gödel, many translated into English for the first time, are collected in *A Source Book in Mathematical Logic, 1879–1931*, edited by John van Heijenoort (Cambridge, Mass., forthcoming). Useful more as a source book than as a history is I. M. Bocheński, *Formale Logik* (Freiburg and Munich, 1956), translated by Ivo Thomas as *A History of Formal Logic* (Notre Dame, Ind., 1961). Tadeusz Kotarbiński's *Wykłady z Dziejów Logiki* ("Lessons in the History of Logic," Warsaw, 1957) has been translated into French as *Leçons sur l'histoire de la logique* (Warsaw and Paris, 1964).

TEXTBOOKS

The simplest accounts of elementary modern logic are provided in Patrick Suppes and Shirley Hill, *A First Course in Mathematical Logic* (New York, 1964), which is limited to sentential logic and a portion of first-order logic and is intended for selected elementary school and high school students, as well as for college students; A. H. Basson and D. J. O'Connor, *Introduction to Symbolic Logic*, 3d ed. (London, 1959; New York, 1960); and W. V. Quine, *Elementary Logic*, rev. ed. (paperback, New York, 1965).

The long list of intermediate-level introductory texts is headed by two classics written by major contributors to the development of modern logic: *Principles of Mathematical Logic*, by David Hilbert and Wilhelm Ackermann (New York, 1950), translated from the second German edition of *Grundzüge der theoretischen Logik* (Berlin, 1938); and *Introduction to Logic and the Methodology of the Deductive Sciences*, 2d ed., by Alfred Tarski (New York, 1946), translated by Olaf Helmer, with extensions and modifications, from the Polish (1936) and German (1937) originals.

One widely used intermediate text is Patrick Suppes, *Introduction to Logic* (Princeton, N.J., 1957), which employs natural deduction techniques, as does the somewhat more difficult *Logic:*

Techniques of Formal Reasoning (New York, 1964), by Donald Kalish and Richard Montague. Others are W. V. Quine, *Methods of Logic,* rev. ed. (New York, 1959), notable, among other things, for its treatment of truth-table testing; and Irving M. Copi, *Symbolic Logic,* rev. ed. (New York, 1965). Two very recent texts that are likely to be much in demand are *Elementary Logic,* by Benson Mates (New York, 1965), and *Beginning Logic,* by E. J. Lemmon (London, 1965). The former is a compact, relatively advanced treatment emphasizing syntactical and semantical aspects; the latter, although quite rigorous, moves at a slower pace and makes fewer demands on the reader. Both of these use natural deduction techniques in the main, whereas a new text by Hugues Leblanc, *Techniques of Deductive Inference* (New York, 1966), undertakes to report on axiomatic and natural deduction procedures and on Gerhard Gentzen's techniques for proving *Sequenzen.*

There are numerous intermediate texts in languages other than English. *Introduction à la logique contemporaine,* by Robert Blanché (Paris, 1957), also contains material on nonclassical logics (intuitionistic, many-valued, modal), and *Formale Logik,* by Paul Lorenzen (Berlin, 1957), is a highly condensed account of standard elementary logic. Gunther Asser's *Einführung in die mathematische Logik,* Part I (Leipzig, 1959), covers sentential logic; there is now a second edition. Joseph Dopp has published *Notions de logique formelle* (Louvain and Paris, 1964), designed by the author to supersede his *Leçons de logique formelle* (3 vols., Louvain, 1950).

Finally, some of the better-known advanced texts and treatises should be mentioned. Alonzo Church's *Introduction to Mathematical Logic* (Princeton, N.J., 1956) is a comprehensive and authoritative axiomatic treatment of sentential, first-order, and second-order logic, with a 68-page introduction of special interest to philosophers. The extremely difficult treatise of S. C. Kleene, *Introduction to Metamathematics* (Princeton, N.J., 1952), examines in depth classical and intuitionistic elementary logic, formal number theory, recursive function theory, and Gödel's incompletability theorems. Kleene expresses his particular indebtedness to the basic work of David Hilbert and Paul Bernays, *Grundlagen der Mathematik* (2 vols., Berlin, 1934–1939; reprinted, Ann Arbor, Mich., 1944). For the mathematically oriented reader there is a swiftly paced recent textbook of advanced logic, *Introduction to Mathematical Logic,* by Elliott Mendelson (Princeton, N.J., 1964), which treats the topics of elementary logic, formal number theory, axiomatic set theory, and effective computability. A full system of logic, extending from elementary logic to classes, relations, and other advanced areas, is to be found in W. V. Quine, *Mathematical Logic,* rev. ed. (Cambridge, Mass., 1951; paperback ed., New York, 1961). A. N. Prior's *Formal Logic,* 2d ed. (Oxford, 1962), contains interesting material on the history of logic, as well as on various nonelementary phases of the subject. Of special interest is Rudolf Carnap's *Introduction to Symbolic Logic and Its Applications* (New York, 1958), translated, with some revisions, from his *Einführung in die symbolische Logik* (Vienna, 1954); this is an advanced work which contains in brief compass a wealth of syntactical and semantical considerations as well as numerous applications of symbolic logic to mathematics and natural science.

ORIGINAL PAPERS, MONOGRAPHS, AND TREATISES

Some of the landmarks in the development of logic are (in chronological order):

Frege, Gottlob, *Begriffsschrift.* Jena, 1879. The first English translation appears in van Heijenoort, above.

Whitehead, A. N., and Russell, Bertrand, *Principia Mathematica,* 3 vols. Cambridge, 1910–1913; 2d ed., 1925–1927; paperback ed. (to *56), 1962.

Sheffer, H. M., "A Set of Five Independent Postulates for Boolean Algebras." *Transactions of the American Mathematical Society,* Vol. 14 (1913), 481–488.

Löwenheim, Leopold, "Über Möglichkeiten im Relativkalkül." *Mathematische Annalen,* Vol. 76 (1915), 447–470.

Skolem, Thoralf, "Logisch-kombinatorische Untersuchungen über die Erfüllbarkeit oder Beweisbarkeit mathematischer Sätze." *Skrifter Utgit av Videnskapsselskapet i Kristiania,* I. Matematisk-naturvidenskapelig Klasse, No. 4. Christiana, 1920. Pp. 1–36.

Wittgenstein, Ludwig, *Tractatus Logico-philosophicus.* New York and London, 1922. Reprint and English translation, by C. K. Ogden, of "Logisch-philosophische Abhandlungen," in *Annalen der Naturphilosophie* (1921). New translation by D. F. Pears and B. F. McGuinness. London and New York, 1961.

Post, Emil L., "Introduction to a General Theory of Elementary Propositions." *American Journal of Mathematics,* Vol. 43 (1921), 163–185.

Behmann, Heinrich, "Beiträge zur Algebra der Logik insbesondere zum Entscheidungsproblem." *Mathematische Annalen,* Vol. 86 (1922), 163–229.

Bernays, Paul, and Schönfinkel, Moses, "Zum Entscheidungsproblem der mathematischen Logik." *Mathematische Annalen,* Vol. 99 (1928), 342–372.

Herbrand, Jacques, "Recherches sur la théorie de la démonstration." *Travaux de la Société des Sciences et des Lettres de Varsovie, Classe III,* No. 33 (1930) 33–160.

Gödel, Kurt, "Die Vollständigkeit der Axiome des logischen Funktionenkalküls." *Monatshefte für Mathematik und Physik,* Vol. 37 (1930), 349–360.

Gödel, Kurt, "Über formal unentscheidbare Sätze der Principia Mathematica und verwandter Systeme I." *Monatshefte für Mathematik und Physik,* Vol. 38 (1931), 173–198. Translations in Martin Davis, ed., *The Undecidable* (Hewlett, N.Y., 1965), and van Heijenoort, above.

Tarski, Alfred, "Über einige fundamentale Begriffe der Metamathematik." *Comptes rendus des séances de la Société des Sciences et des Lettres de Varsovie, Classe III,* No. 23 (1930), 22–29. Translation by J. H. Woodger in Alfred Tarski, *Logic, Semantics, Metamathematics.* Oxford, 1956.

Tarski, Alfred, "Der Wahrheitsbegriff in den formalisierten Sprachen." *Studia philosophica,* Vol. 1 (1936). German translation, with added *Nachwort,* of *Pojęcie Prawdy w Językach Dedukcyjnyck,* in *Travaux de la Société des Sciences et des Lettres de Varsovie, Classe III,* No. 34 (1933). Translated by J. H. Woodger as "The Concept of Truth in Formalized Languages," in Alfred Tarski, *Logic, Semantics, Metamathematics.* Oxford, 1956.

Carnap, Rudolf, *Logische Syntax der Sprache.* Vienna, 1934. Translated, with revisions, by Amethe Smeaton as *The Logical Syntax of Language.* New York and London, 1937.

Heyting, Arend, *Mathematische Grundlagenforschung. Intuitionismus. Beweistheorie.* Berlin, 1934. Rev. French ed., *Les Fondements des mathématiques. Intuitionnisme. Théorie de la démonstration.* Paris and Louvain, 1955.

Gentzen, Gerhard, "Untersuchungen über das logische Schliessen." *Mathematische Zeitschrift,* Vol. 39 (1934–1935), 176–210, 405–431.

Jaśkowski, Stanisław, "On the Rules of Suppositions in Formal Logic." *Studia Logica,* No. 1 (Warsaw, 1934), 5–32.

Church, Alonzo, "A Note on the Entscheidungsproblem." *Journal of Symbolic Logic,* Vol. 1 (1936), 40–41, 101–102.

Henkin, Leon, "The Completeness of the First-order Functional Calculus." *Journal of Symbolic Logic,* Vol. 14 (1949), 159–166.

Henkin, Leon, "Completeness in the Theory of Types." *Journal of Symbolic Logic,* Vol. 15 (1950), 81–91.

Ackermann, Wilhelm, *Solvable Cases of the Decision Problem.* Amsterdam, 1954.

ALBERT E. BLUMBERG

LOGIC, SYMBOLIC. See LOGIC, HISTORY OF; LOGIC, MODERN.

LOGIC, TRADITIONAL. In logic, as in other fields, whenever there have been spectacular changes and advances, the logic that was current in the preceding period has been described as "old" or "traditional," and that embodying the new material has been called "new" or "modern." The Stoics described themselves as "moderns" and the Aristotelians as devotees of the "old" logic, in the later Middle Ages the more adventurous writers were called *moderni,* and since the latter part of the nineteenth century the immensely expanded logic that has developed along more or less mathematical lines ("mathematical logic," "symbolic logic," "logistics") has been contrasted with the "traditional" logic inherited from the sixteenth and seventeenth centuries. In every case the logic termed "old" or "traditional" has been essentially Aristotelian, but with a certain concentration on the central portion of the Aristotelian *corpus*, the theory of categorical syllogism—the logic of Aristotle himself having been rather less circumscribed than that of the "tradition," especially of the sixteenth to the nineteenth century.

THE LOGIC OF TERMS

To begin with the categorical syllogism, an inference, argument, or syllogism (traditionally, all arguments are assumed to be syllogistic) is a sequence of propositions (premises followed by a conclusion), such as "All animals are mortal; all men are animals; therefore, all men are mortal." Propositions, in turn, are built up from terms—for example, "animals," "mortals," "men." The traditional order of treatment, therefore, begins with the study of terms (or, in writers with a psychological or epistemological bias, ideas) and goes on to the study of propositions (or judgments), concluding with that of syllogisms (or inferences).

The terms from which the propositions principally studied in the traditional logic are built up are common nouns (*termini communes*), such as "man" and "horse," although some attention is also paid to singular terms, such as "Socrates," "this man," and "the man next door." Much of the traditional theory is devoted to the arrangement of common nouns in an order of comprehensiveness, and here a distinction is made between two aspects of their functioning—their "extension" (as the logicians of Port-Royal called it) or "denotation" (John Stuart Mill) and their "intension" (Sir William Hamilton), "comprehension" (Port-Royalists), or "connotation" (Mill). The extension or denotation of a common noun is the set of individuals to which it applies, its intension or connotation the set of attributes which an individual must possess for the common noun to be applicable to it. Thus, the connotation of the term "man" consists of the attributes of being an animal, being rational, and perhaps possessing a certain bodily form; its denotation consists of all objects that possess these attributes. Broadly, the connotation of a term is its meaning, the denotation its application. The analysis of the meaning of a term is described as definition, and the breaking up of the set of objects to which it applies into subsets is described as division. The subsets of the set of individuals to which a given term applies are called the species of the genus denoted by the given term. The attribute that marks off a particular species from others of the same genus is called its differentia. The species is said by scholastic logicians to "fall under" its genus, and the standard way of defining a species is by giving its genus and its differentia.

The ordering of terms into species and genera is often thought of as having an upper and a lower limit. The upper limit, or *summum genus,* will be a broad category like "thing" (*substantia*)—horses are animals, animals are organisms, organisms are bodies, bodies are things. More

abstract terms will come to an end in more abstract categories, such as "quality" or "relation" (scarlet is a species or kind of red, red is a color, color is a quality). The *infima species,* or lower limit, is a more difficult concept. Man, for example, is commonly given as an *infima species,* but are not men divisible into, for instance, dark-haired and fair-haired men? This is answered, from the point of view of intension, by dividing the attributes of an individual into those that constitute its essence or nature and those that are merely accidental, and genuine species are said to be marked off by "essential" attributes only; further subdivisions differentiated by "accidental" attributes, such as the color of a man's hair, are not counted as genuine species. This distinction is not recognized by some writers. Leibniz counted all attributes of an individual as essential, so that someone would not be *that* individual if he were in the least respect different from what he is. At the other extreme, Mill said that "individuals have no essences," although he had a use for the term "essence" in connection with *general* terms: it is of the essence of being a man, for example, to be an animal, if being an animal is one of the attributes commonly employed in fixing the application of the word "man."

An allied doctrine of Mill's is that the proper names of individuals, by contrast with common nouns, have no connotation, only denotation. We may not be able to think of a named individual without thinking of him as having certain attributes, but the purpose of a proper name is not to convey the fact that he has those attributes but only to identify him as *that* individual. This view has been criticized by various writers, on the ground, among others, that we cannot identify an object at all without knowing at least its *infima species*. Mill has also been criticized for using the same term, "denotation," both for the application of a common noun and for what is named by a proper name.

Common terms can be simple or complex. Some kinds of complexity are of logical interest—for example, the conjunctive combination exemplified by "blind man" (i.e., what is both blind and human) and the disjunctive combination exemplified by "man-or-beast." This kind of complexity is of interest because, for one thing, it links up with the previous topic, a blind man being a species (in the broad though not the narrow sense) of man and a man being a species (again in the broad sense) of man-or-beast (i.e., of animal). Again, the term "son-of-Philip" is compounded of the relative expression "son of" and the proper name "Philip," and this, too, links with the preceding topic, a son of Philip being a species (in the broad sense) of son. But the logical behavior of complex terms of these types is a topic of modern rather than traditional logic. Even traditional logic, however, has something to say about negative terms, such as "non-man" (i.e., what is not human), as will be shown in what follows.

The distribution of terms is a subject that will be more intelligible after propositions and syllogisms have been considered.

THE LOGIC OF PROPOSITIONS

Opposition. The division of traditional logic called the logic of propositions is not to be confused with what is now called the propositional calculus. The propositional calculus studies the logical behavior of propositions formed from simpler propositions by means of various connectives (for example, "Either all men are liars or no men are"), as opposed to propositions formed not from other propositions but from terms (for example, "No men are liars"). The traditional logic of propositions or judgments, on the other hand, is chiefly concerned with the classification and simpler interrelations of precisely the second class of propositions, although it normally also touches on "compound" or "hypothetical" propositions, without going beyond their simplest types and the simplest inferences involving them.

Propositions not compounded of other propositions are called "categorical." This word has the force of "unconditional," the implied contrast being with forms like "*If* all that the Bible says is true, all men are mortal" or "*Either* not all that the Bible says is true, *or* all men are mortal." Categoricals have a *subject term* and a *predicate term* ("men" is the subject term and "mortal" the predicate term of "All men are mortal") and are subdivided in two main ways—according to *quantity*, into *universals* ("All men are mortal," "No men are mortal") and *particulars* ("Some men are mortal," "Some men are not mortal"), and according to *quality*, into *affirmatives* ("All men are mortal," "Some men are mortal") and *negatives* ("No men are mortal," "Some men are not mortal"). These are often displayed in a square, with universals at the top, particulars at the bottom, affirmatives on the left, negatives on the right:

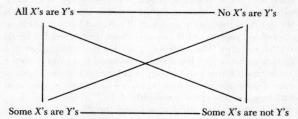

Universal affirmatives are called A-propositions, particular affirmatives I-propositions, universal negatives E-propositions, and particular negatives O-propositions (the vowels being taken from the words *affirmo* and *nego*). Two other "quantities" are commonly mentioned, namely *singular* and *indefinite*. Singular propositions, such as "Socrates is mortal," are a genuinely distinct type, which we shall touch upon at appropriate points; indefinites, such as "Men are mortal," seem merely to be universals or particulars in which the quantity is left unstated. The expressions other than terms which enter into these forms are called "syncategorematic"; they are divided into the signs of quantity "all" and "some" and the copulas "is" or "are" and "is not" or "are not." ("No" is both a sign of quantity and a sign of negation.)

These types of propositions—A, E, I, and O—are the traditional "four forms," and as a preliminary to logical manipulation it is customary to restate given sentences in some standard way that will make their quantity and quality immediately evident. The forms given above, with

"all," etc., and with plural common nouns for terms, are the most widely used, but it is in some ways less misleading to use "every," etc., and the terms in the singular— "Every *X* is a *Y*," "No *X* is a *Y*," "Some *X* is a *Y*," "Some *X* is not a *Y*." What is important is to understand that "some" means simply "at least one"; "Some men are mortals" or "Some man is a mortal" must be understood as neither affirming nor denying that more than one man is a mortal and as neither affirming nor denying that all men are (i.e., "some" does *not* mean "only some").

A square of the type shown earlier is called a *square of opposition,* and propositions with the same terms in the same order may be "opposed" in four ways. Universals of opposite quality ("Every *X* is a *Y*," "No *X* is a *Y*") are said to be *contraries;* these cannot be jointly true. Particulars of opposite quality ("Some *X* is a *Y*," "Some *X* is not a *Y*") are said to be *subcontraries;* these cannot be jointly false. Propositions opposed only in quantity are said to be *subalterns,* the *subalternant* universal implying (without being implied by) the *subalternate* particular ("Every *X* is a *Y*" implies "Some *X* is a *Y*," and "No *X* is a *Y*" implies "Some *X* is not a *Y*"). Propositions opposed in both quantity and quality ("Every *X* is a *Y*" and "Some *X* is not a *Y*," and "No *X* is a *Y*" and "Some *X* is a *Y*") are *contradictories;* they cannot be jointly true or jointly false—the truth of a given proposition implies the falsehood of its contradictory; its falsehood implies the contradictory's truth.

Equipollence. Closely connected with the theory of opposition is that of the *equipollence* of propositions with the same terms in the same order but with negative particles variously placed within them. Since contradictories are true and false under reversed conditions, any proposition may be equated with the simple denial of its contradictory. Thus, "Some *X* is not a *Y*" has the same logical force as "Not every *X* is a *Y*," and, conversely, "Every *X* is a *Y*" has the force of "Not (some *X* is not a *Y*)," or, to give it a more normal English expression, "Not any *X* is not a *Y*." Similarly, "Some *X* is a *Y*" has the force of "Not (no *X* is a *Y*)" and "No *X* is a *Y*" that of "Not (some *X* is a *Y*)"—i.e., "Not any *X* is a *Y*." Also, since "no" conveys universality and negativeness at once, "No *X* is a *Y*" has the force of "Every *X* is not-a-*Y*," and, conversely, "Every *X* is a *Y*" has the force of "No *X* is not-a-*Y*." Writers with an interest in simplification have seen in these equivalences a means of dispensing with all but one of the signs "every," "some," and "no." Thus the four forms may all be expressed in terms of "every," as follows: "Every *X* is a *Y*" (A), "Every *X* is not-a-*Y*" (E), "Not every *X* is not-a-*Y*" (I), "Not every *X* is a *Y*" (O).

Of singular propositions all that need be said at this point is that they divide into affirmatives ("Socrates is mortal," "This is a man," "This man is mortal") and negatives ("Socrates is not mortal," etc.) and that when their subject is formed by prefixing "this" to a common noun (as in "This man is mortal"), the singular form is implied by the corresponding universal ("Every man is mortal") and implies the corresponding particular ("Some man is mortal"). Some of the traditional logicians attempted to assimilate singular propositions to particulars, some to assimilate them to universals, but these attempts are not very impressive, and it is one of the few merits of the Renaissance logician Peter Ramus that he and his followers treated them consistently as a type of their own.

Conversion of propositions. With regard to pairs of propositions of the same form and with the same terms, but in reverse order—for example, "No *X* is a *Y*" and "No *Y* is an *X*"—these are sometimes equivalent and sometimes not. Where they are, as in the case just given, they are said to be *converses* of one another, and the forms are said to be convertible. E and I are convertible; A and O are not. That every man is an animal, for example, does not imply that every animal is a man, and that some animal is not a horse does not imply that some horse is not an animal. Conversion, the inference from a given proposition to its converse ("Some men are liars; therefore, some liars are men"), is a type of immediate inference—that is, inference involving only one premise (as opposed, for instance, to syllogisms, which have two). Other immediate inferences are those from a given proposition to an "equipollent" form in the sense of the preceding section (for example, "Every man is mortal; therefore, not any man is not") and from a subalternant universal to its subalternate particular ("Every man is mortal; therefore, some man is mortal").

The conversion just described is "simple" conversion; with universals (even A, though it is not "simply" convertible) there is also a conversion *per accidens*, or *subaltern* conversion—that is, a legitimate inference to the corresponding particular form with its terms transposed. Thus, although "Every man is an animal" does not imply that every animal is a man, it does imply that some animal is.

Other forms of immediate inference arise when negative terms are introduced. The simultaneous interchange and negation of subject and predicate is called *conversion by contraposition,* or simply contraposition. It is a valid process with A's and O's, not with E's and I's. ("Every man is an animal" implies "Every non-animal is a non-man"—whatever is not an animal is not a man—and "Not every animal is a man" implies "Not every non-man is a non-animal," but "No horse is a man" does not imply "No non-man is a non-horse"; "Some *X* is a *Y*" is true and "Some non-*Y* is a non-*X*" false if the *X*'s and the *Y*'s overlap and between them exhaust the universe.) All of the four forms may be "obverted" (Alexander Bain's term)—i.e., have their quality changed and the predicate negated ("Every *X* is a *Y*" implies "No *X* is a non-*Y*," "No *X* is a *Y*" implies "Every *X* is a non-*Y*," and similarly with the particulars). A variety of names are given to the results of repeated successive obversion and conversion.

THE LOGIC OF SYLLOGISMS

A categorical syllogism is the inference of one categorical proposition, the conclusion, from two others, the premises, each premise having one term in common with the conclusion and one term in common with the other premise—for example:

> Every animal is mortal;
> Every man is an animal;
> Therefore, every man is mortal.

The predicate of the conclusion (here "mortal") is called the *major* term, and the premise which contains it (here written first) the major premise. The subject of the conclusion ("man") is the *minor* term, and the premise which contains it (here written second) the minor premise. The term common to the two premises ("animal") is the *middle* term.

Figures and moods. Syllogisms are divided into four *figures,* according to the placing of the middle term in the two premises. In the first figure the middle term is subject in the major premise and predicate in the minor; in the second figure predicate in both; in the third figure subject in both; in the fourth predicate in the major and subject in the minor. The following schemata, with *P* for the major term, *S* for the minor, and *M* for the middle, sum up these distinctions:

Figure 1	Figure 2	Figure 3	Figure 4
$M - P$	$P - M$	$M - P$	$P - M$
$S - M$	$S - M$	$M - S$	$M - S$
$S - P$	$S - P$	$S - P$	$S - P$

Within each figure, syllogisms are futher divided into *moods,* according to the quantity and quality of the propositions they contain.

Not all of the theoretically possible combinations of propositions related as above constitute *valid* syllogisms, sequences in which the third proposition really follows from the other two. For example, "Every man is an animal; some horse is an animal; therefore, no man is a horse" (mood AIE in Figure 2) is completely inconsequent (even though all three propositions happen in this case to be true). During the Middle Ages those syllogistic moods that are valid acquired certain short names, with the mood indicated by the vowels, and all of them were put together in a piece of mnemonic doggerel, of which one of the later versions is the following:

> *Barbara, Celarent, Darii, Ferioque* prioris;
> *Cesare, Camestres, Festino, Baroco* secundae;
> Tertia *Darapti, Disamis, Datisi, Felapton,*
> *Bocardo, Ferison* habet. Quarta insuper addit
> *Bramantip, Camenes, Dimaris, Fesapo, Fresison.*

Here Bocardo, for example, means the mood OAO in Figure 3, of which an illustration (C. S. Peirce's example) would be

> Some patriarch (viz., Enoch) is not mortal;
> Every patriarch is a man;
> Therefore, some man is not mortal.

There is also a group of moods (Barbari and Celaront in Figure 1, Cesaro and Camestrop in Figure 2, Camenop in Figure 4) in which a merely particular conclusion is drawn although the premises would warrant our going further and making the conclusion universal (the "subaltern" moods). The Ramists added special moods involving singulars (if we write S and N for affirmative and negative singulars, we have ASS and ESN in Figure 1, ANN and ESN in Figure 2 and SSI and NSO in Figure 3). It may be noted that every syllogism must have at least one universal premise, except for SSI and NSO in Figure 3—the so-called "expository syllogisms," e.g., "Enoch is not mortal; Enoch is a patriarch; therefore, not every patriarch is mortal." Moreover, every syllogism must have at least one affirmative premise, and if either premise is negative or particular, the conclusion must be negative or particular, as the case may be ("the conclusion follows the weaker premise," as Theophrastus put it, negatives and particulars being considered weaker than affirmatives and universals).

Reduction. The mnemonic verses serve to indicate how the valid moods of the later figures may be "reduced" to those of Figure 1—that is, how we may derive their conclusions from their premises without using any syllogistic reasoning of other than the first-figure type. (This amounts, in modern terms, to proving their validity from that of the first-figure moods taken as axiomatic.) In the second-figure mood Cesare, for example, the letter *s* after the first *e* indicates that if we *simply convert* the major premise we will have a pair of premises from which we can deduce the required conclusion in Figure 1, and the initial letter *C* indicates that the first-figure mood employed will be Celarent. An example of a syllogism in Cesare (EAE in Figure 2) would be

> No horse is a man;
> Every psychopath is a man;
> Therefore, no psychopath is a horse.

This conclusion may equally be obtained from these premises by proceeding as follows:

No horse is a man —— *s* ——> No man is a horse;
Every psychopath is a man —> Every psychopath is a man;
    Therefore, no psychopath is
    a horse.

Here the right-hand syllogism, in which the first premise is obtained from the given major by simple conversion and the second is just the given minor unaltered, is in the mood Celarent in the first figure. Festino "reduces" similarly to Ferio, and Datisi and Ferison (in the third figure) reduce to Darii and Ferio, though in the third-figure cases it is the minor premise that must be simply converted. Darapti and Felapton reduce to Darii and Ferio by conversion of the minor premise, not simply, but *per accidens* (this is indicated by the *s* of the other moods being changed to *p*).

Camestres (Figure 2) and Disamis (Figure 3) are a little more complicated. Here we have not only an *s,* for the simple conversion of a premise, but also an *m,* indicating that the premises must be transposed, and a further *s* at the end because the transposed premises yield, in Figure 1, not the required conclusion but rather its converse, from which the required conclusion must be obtained by a further conversion at the end of the process. An example in Disamis would be the following:

> Some men are liars;
> All men are automata;
> Therefore, some automata are liars.

If we convert the major premise and transpose the two, we obtain the new pair

> All men are automata;
> Some liars are men,

and from these we may obtain in the first-figure mood Darii not immediately the conclusion "Some automata are liars" but rather "Some liars are automata," from which, however, "Some automata are liars" does follow by simple conversion.

Baroco and Bocardo are different again. In both of them neither premise is capable of simple conversion, and if we convert the A premises *per accidens* we obtain pairs IO and OI, and there are no valid first-figure moods with such premises—in fact, no valid moods at all with two particular premises. We therefore show that the conclusion follows from the premises by the device called *reductio ad absurdum.* That is, we assume for the sake of argument that the conclusion does *not* follow from the premises—i.e., that the premises can be true and the conclusion false—and from this assumption, using first-figure reasoning alone, we deduce impossible consequences. The assumption, therefore, cannot stand, so the conclusion does after all follow from its premises.

Take, for example, the following syllogism in Baroco (AOO in Figure 2):

> Every man is mortal;
> Some patriarch (viz., Enoch) is not mortal;
> Therefore, some patriarch is not a man.

Suppose the premises are true and the conclusion is not. Then we have

> (1) Every man is mortal;
> (2) Some patriarch is not mortal;
> (3) Every patriarch is a man.

(This is the contradictory of the conclusion.) But from (1) and (3), in the first-figure mood Barbara, we may infer

> (4) Every patriarch is mortal.

However, the combination of (2) and (4) is impossible. Hence, we can have both (1) and (2) only if we drop (3)—that is, if we accept the conclusion of the given second-figure syllogism.

It is possible to "reduce" all the second-figure and third-figure moods to Figure 1 by this last method, and although this procedure is a little complicated, it brings out better than the other reductions the essential character of second-figure and third-figure reasoning. Figure 1 is governed by what is called the *dictum de omni et nullo,* the principle that what applies to all or none of the objects in a given class will apply or not apply (as the case may be) to any given member or subclass of this class. As Kant preferred to put it, first-figure reasoning expresses the *subsumption* of *cases* under a *rule*—the major premise states some affirmative or negative rule ("Every man is mortal," "No man will live forever"), the minor asserts that something is a case, or some things are cases, to which this rule applies ("Enoch and Elijah are men"), and the conclusion states the result of applying the rule to the given case or cases ("Enoch and Elijah are mortal," "Enoch and Elijah will not live forever"). Hence, in Figure 1 the major premise is always universal (that being how rules are expressed) and the minor affirmative ("Something *is* a case"). Second-figure reasoning also begins with the statement of a rule ("Every man is mortal") but in the minor premise *denies* that we have with a given example the result which the rule prescribes ("Enoch and Elijah are *not* mortal," "Enoch and Elijah *will* live forever") and concludes that we do *not* have a case to which the rule applies ("Enoch and Elijah cannot be men"). It combines, in effect, the first-figure major with the contradictory of the first-figure conclusion to obtain the contradictory of the first-figure minor (compare the "reduction" of Baroco). A second-figure syllogism, in consequence, must have a universal major, premises opposed in quality, and a negative conclusion. Its practical uses are in refuting hypotheses, as in medicine or detection ("Whoever has measles has spots, and this child has no spots, so he does not have measles"; "Whoever killed *X* was a person of great strength, and *Y* is not such a person, so *Y* did not kill *X*"). In the third figure we begin by asserting that something or other does not exhibit the result which a proposed rule would give ("Enoch and Elijah are *not* mortal," "Enoch and Elijah *will* live forever"), go on to say that we nevertheless *do* have here a case or cases to which the rule would apply if true ("Enoch and Elijah *are* men"), and conclude that the rule is not true ("Not all men are mortal," "Some men do live forever"). A third-figure syllogism, consequently, has an affirmative minor (the thing *is* a case) and a particular conclusion (the contradictory of a universal being a particular); its use is to confute rashly assumed rules, such as proposed scientific laws.

This rather neat system of interrelations (first clearly brought out by C. S. Peirce) concerns only the first three figures; it was not until the later Middle Ages, in fact, that a distinct fourth figure was recognized. The common division of figures assumes that we are considering completed syllogisms, with the conclusion (and its subject and predicate) already before us; however, the question Aristotle originally put to himself was not "Which completed syllogisms are valid?" but "Which pairs of premises will yield a syllogistic conclusion?" Starting at this end, we cannot distinguish major and minor premises as those containing, respectively, the predicate and subject of the conclusion. Aristotle distinguished them, in the first figure, by their comparative comprehensiveness and mentioned what we now call the fourth-figure moods as odd cases in which first-figure premises will yield a conclusion wherein the "minor" term is predicated of the "major." Earlier versions of the mnemonic lines accordingly list the fourth-figure moods with the first-figure ones and (since the premises are thought of as being in the first-figure order) give them slightly different names (Baralipton, Celantes, Dabitis, Fapesmo, Frisesomorum).

Distribution of terms. Terms may occur in A-, E-, I-, and O-propositions as *distributed* or as *undistributed*. The rule is that universals distribute their subjects and particulars distribute their predicates, but what this means is seldom very satisfactorily explained. It is often said, for example, that a distributed term refers to all, and an undistributed term to only a part, of its extension. But in what way does "Some men are mortal," for example, refer to only a part of the class of men? Any man whatever will do to verify it; if any man whatever turns out to be mortal, "Some men are mortal" is true. What the traditional writers were trying to express seems to be something of the following sort: a term *t* is distributed in a proposition $f(t)$ if and only if it is replaceable in $f(t)$, without loss of truth, by any term "falling under it" in the way that a species falls under a genus. Thus, "man" is distributed in

> Every man is an animal;
> No man is a horse;
> No horse is a man;
> Some animal is not a man,

since these respectively imply, say,

> Every blind man is an animal;
> No blind man is a horse;
> No horse is a blind man;
> Some animal is not a blind man.

On the other hand, it is undistributed in

> Some man is keen-sighted;
> Some man is not disabled;
> Every Frenchman is a man;
> Some keen-sighted animal is a man,

since these do *not* respectively imply

> Some blind man is keen-sighted;
> Some blind man is not disabled;
> Every Frenchman is a blind man;
> Some keen-sighted animal is a blind man.

In this sense A- and E- propositions do distribute their subjects and E- and O-propositions their predicates. John Anderson pointed out that the four positive results above may be established syllogistically, given that all the members of a species (using the term widely) are members of its genus—in the given case, that all blind men are men. From "Every man is an animal" and "Every blind man is a man," "Every blind man is an animal" follows in Barbara; with the second example the syllogism is in Celarent, with the third in Camestres, with the fourth in Baroco. Note, however, that the mere prefixing of "every" to a term is not in itself sufficient to secure its "distribution" in the above sense; for example, "man" is not distributed in "Not every man is disabled," since this does not imply "Not every blind man is disabled."

For a syllogism to be valid the middle term must be distributed at least once, and any term distributed in the conclusion must be distributed in its premise (although there is no harm in a term's being distributed in its premise but not in the conclusion). Many syllogisms can quickly be shown to be fallacious by the application of these rules.

"Every man is an animal; every horse is an animal; therefore, every horse is a man," for example, fails to distribute the middle term "animal," and it is clear that any second-figure syllogism with two affirmative premises would have the same fault (since in the second figure the middle term is predicate twice, and affirmatives do not distribute their predicates). Other special rules for the different figures, such as that in Figures 1 and 3 the minor premise must be affirmative, can be similarly proved from the rules of distribution together with the rules of quality (that a valid syllogism does not have two negative premises, and that a conclusion is negative if and only if one premise is). Logicians have endeavored to prove some of these rules from others and to reduce the number of unproved rules to a minimum.

Euler's diagrams. One device for checking the validity of syllogistic inferences is the use of certain diagrams attributed to the seventeenth-century mathematician Leonhard Euler, although their accurate employment seems to date rather from J. D. Gergonne, in the early nineteenth century.

From the traditional laws of opposition and conversion it can be shown that the extensions of any pair of terms X, Y will be related in one or another of five ways: (α) every X is a Y and every Y is an X, i.e., their extensions coincide; or (β) every X is a Y, but not every Y is an X, i.e., the X's form a proper part of the Y's; or (γ) every Y is an X, but not every X is a Y, i.e., the Y's form a proper part of the X's; or (δ) some but not all X's are Y's and some but not all Y's are X's, i.e., the X's and Y's overlap; or (ϵ) no X's are Y's and so no Y's are X's, i.e., the X's and Y's are mutually exclusive. These five cases are represented by the following diagrams:

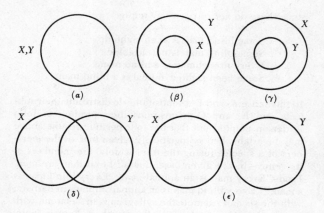

"Every X is a Y" (A) is true if and only if we have either (α) or (β); "Some X is not a Y" (O) if and only if we have either (γ) or (δ) or (ϵ); "No X is a Y" (E) if and only if we have (ϵ); and "Some X is a Y" (I) if and only if we have either (α) or (β) or (γ) or (δ). From these facts it follows that A and O are in no case true together and in no case false together, and similarly for E and I; that I is true in every case in which A is and also in two cases in which A is not, and similarly for O and E; that A and E are in no case true together but in two cases are both false; and that O and I are in no case both false but in two cases are both true. After working out

analogous truth conditions for the forms with reversed terms, we will see that they are the same for the two I's and the two E's (showing that these are simply convertible) but not for the two A's and the two O's (showing that these are not). Given which of the five relations holds between X and Y and which between Y and Z, we can work out by compounding diagrams what will be the possible relations between X and Z. For example, if we know that every X is a Y and every Y a Z, then we must have either (α)XY and (α)YZ or (α)XY and (β)YZ or (β)XY and (α)YZ or (β)XY and (β)YZ; that is, we must have

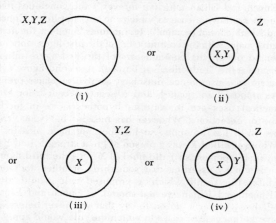

Inspection will show that for X and Z we have in every case either

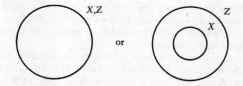

so in every case every X is a Z. Hence, Barbara is valid.

When employing this procedure it is essential to consider all the possible cases involved. Barbara is not validated, for example, by considering case (iv) alone, as popular expositions of this method sometimes suggest.

Polysyllogisms, enthymemes, and induction. In an extended argument the conclusion of one inference may be used as a premise of another, and the conclusion of that as premise of a third, and so on. In presenting such an argument we may simply omit the intermediate steps and list all the premises together. For example, the sequence of categorical syllogisms "Every X is a Y, and every Y is a Z, so every X is a Z; and every Z is a T, so every X is a T" may be condensed to "Every X is a Y, every Y is a Z, and every Z is a T; therefore, every X is a T." Such a condensed chain of syllogisms is called a polysyllogism or sorites. The theory of chains of two syllogisms was thoroughly studied by Galen, as reported in an ancient passage recently unearthed by Jan Łukasiewicz. Galen showed that the only combinations of the Aristotelian three figures that could be thus used were 1 and 1, 1 and 2, 1 and 3, and 2 and 3. His discovery of these four types of compound syllogism was misunderstood by later writers as an anticipation of the view that *single* syllogisms may be of four figures.

Even when it is not a conclusion from other premises already stated, one of the premises of an inference may often be informally omitted (for example, "Enoch and Elijah are men; therefore, Enoch and Elijah are mortals"). Such a truncated inference is often called an enthymeme. This is not Aristotle's own use of the term, though he did mention that a premise is often omitted in the statement of an enthymeme in his sense. An Aristotelian enthymeme is a merely probable argument—that is, one in which the conclusion does not strictly follow from the premises but is merely made more likely by them. When the claim made for an argument is thus reduced, the normal rules may be relaxed in certain directions; in particular, the second and third figures may be used to yield more than merely negative results. Thus, Figure 2 may be used not only to prove that something is not a case falling under a given rule but also to suggest that it is one—to use a modern example:

Any collection of particles whose movement is
  accelerated will occupy more space than it did;
A heated gas will occupy more space than it did;
Therefore, a heated gas may be a collection of particles whose movement is accelerated.

Figure 3 may be similarly used not only to prove that some rule does not hold universally but also to suggest that it does hold universally—for instance:

X, Y, Z are all of them white;
X, Y, Z are all of them swans;
Therefore, perhaps all swans are white.

If the second premise here is strengthened to "*X, Y, Z* are all the swans there are," the conclusion will follow without any "perhaps" (of course, the new premise is in this case a false one, and the conclusion is also false). The form of inference

X, Y, Z, etc., are all of them *P*'s;
X, Y, Z, etc., are all the *S*'s there are;
Therefore, all *S*'s are *P*'s

was called by Aristotle "induction"; more accurately, he used this term for a similar passage from all the subspecies to their genus ("The *X*'s, the *Y*'s, and the *Z*'s are all of them *P*'s and are all the *S*'s; therefore, . . ."). He observed that the "conversion" of the second premise to "All the *S*'s are the *X*'s, the *Y*'s, and the *Z*'s" will turn such an induction into a syllogism in Barbara.

The term "induction" being extended in the more recent tradition to cover the merely probable inference given just previously, we distinguish Aristotelian induction by calling it "formal" or "perfect" induction or (as W. E. Johnson called it) "summary" induction. The Figure 2 type of merely probable inference is one of the things meant by the term "argument from"—or "by"—"analogy" (or just "analogy"); C. S. Peirce called it "hypothesis."

Skeptical criticisms of syllogistic reasoning. In the latter part of the nineteenth century, under the influence of J. S. Mill, textbooks of the traditional type came to have two main divisions, "formal" or "deductive" logic (dealt with more or less as above) and "inductive" logic or "scientific method." With the details of inductive logic we are not concerned here, but we may glance at the view of some writers that merely probable induction and analogy are the only genuine types of reasoning, "formal" or syllogistic reasoning being useless or spurious because it is inevitably circular, assuming in the premises what it sets out to prove as the conclusion.

The second-century skeptic Sextus Empiricus suggested that in the syllogism "Every man is an animal; Socrates is a man; therefore, Socrates is an animal," the only way to establish the major premise is by induction; however, if the induction is incomplete the examination of a new instance—e.g., of Socrates—might prove it false, and if it is complete the conclusion ("Socrates is an animal") must already have been used in establishing it. This argument was repeated by such writers as George Campbell, in the eighteenth century, who supplemented it with another, to cover the case in which the major is established not by induction but simply by definition or linguistic convention: "Of course every man is an animal, for being an animal is part of what we mean by being a man." In this case it is the minor premise, "Socrates is a man," that cannot be established without first establishing the conclusion (that he is an animal). The same point was urged by another Scottish philosopher, Thomas Brown. It is allied to an argument used by Sextus to show not that syllogism is circular but that the major premise is superfluous. If, he said, every man is an animal because it *follows* from an object's being a man that it is an animal, then the allegedly enthymematic "Socrates is a man; therefore, Socrates is an animal" must be valid as it stands.

Richard Whately, answering Campbell's arguments in the early nineteenth century, complained that Campbell had confined himself to examples in which the syllogistic argument was indeed superfluous and countered them with some in which it was not—for example, the case of some laborers, ignorant of the fact that all horned animals are ruminant, digging up a skeleton which they, but not a distant naturalist, could see to be horned, the laborers and the naturalist thus separately providing premises which were both required to obtain the conclusion that the skeleton was of a ruminant animal. Whately admitted that the sense in which we may make a "discovery" by drawing a syllogistic conclusion is different from that in which we make a discovery by observation, but it can be a genuine discovery none the less; there are "logical" as well as "physical" discoveries.

After Whately, J. S. Mill took up the argument, but it is not entirely clear what side he was on. Sometimes he treated a universal major as already asserting, among other things, the conclusion:

Whoever pronounces the words, All men are mortal, has affirmed that Socrates is mortal, though he may never have heard of Socrates; for since Socrates, whether known to be so or not, really is a man, he is included in the words, All men, and in every assertion of which they are the subject. (*System of Logic*, Book II, Ch. 3, p. 8, note)

"Included in the *meaning* of the words," he must have meant (for it is obvious that neither Socrates the man nor "Socrates," his name, forms any part of the words "All men"), but this contradicts Mill's own insistence that the meaning of general terms like "men" lies wholly in their "connotation" and that "All men are mortal" means that wherever the *attributes* of humanity are present, mortality is present, too. He rightly chided Brown, who thought that the meaning of "Socrates is mortal" (like that of "Socrates is an animal") is already contained in the minor premise "Socrates is a man," for failing to distinguish the actual connotation of "man" (i.e., the attributes by which its application is determined) from other attributes (such as mortality) which we may empirically discover these to be attended with, but his own view in the passage cited is similarly negligent.

Mill's main point, however, is different and more defensible. When careful and extensive observation warrants the conclusion that, say, all men are mortal, and we then observe that the duke of Wellington is a man and conclude that he is therefore mortal, we have in effect an induction followed by a syllogism. Mill pointed out that if this procedure is justified at all, the introduction of the syllogistic major is superfluous. For if the original body of evidence really does warrant the inference that all men are mortal, it is certainly sufficient to warrant the inference that the duke of Wellington is mortal, given that he is a man. In other words, if we really are justified in the move from particular observations to the general proposition, and from there to new particulars, we would be equally justified in moving directly "from particulars to particulars." What the syllogistic major does, Mill argued, is simply to sum up in a single formula the entire class of inferences to new particulars which the evidence warrants. That is, "All men are mortal" means, in effect, that if we ever find anyone to be a man we are justified in inferring, from the observations we have previously amassed, that he is mortal. "The conclusion is not an inference drawn *from* the formula"—i.e., from "All men are mortal" thus understood—"but an inference drawn *according to* the formula" (*ibid.*, p. 4). Mill here anticipated Gilbert Ryle's treatment of "lawlike statements" as "inference licenses" and echoed Sextus' point that it is inconsistent to require that such licenses be added to the premises of the inferences they permit, since what they license is precisely the drawing of the conclusion from *those* premises.

Mill in fact here shifted the discussion from Sextus' first skeptical "topic" to his second—from the charge of circularity to the question of what distinguishes a rule of inference from a premise. On this point more was said later in the nineteenth century by C. S. Peirce. Peirce, like Mill, distinguished sharply between the premise or premises from which, and the "leading principle" according to which, a conclusion is drawn. He also noted, as did Mill, that what is traditionally counted as a premise may function in practice as a "leading principle." But it need not, and, indeed, what is traditionally counted as a "leading

principle" (say the *dictum de omni et nullo*) may sometimes be, conversely, treated in practice as a premise. Certainly, since *all men are mortal* (leading principle 1), we are justified in inferring the mortality of Socrates (or the duke of Wellington, or Elijah) from his humanity. But equally, since *all members of any class are also members of any class that contains the former as a subclass* (leading principle 2), we are justified in inferring the mortality of Socrates from his being a man *and* from men's being a subclass of mortals. For the very same reason (that all members of any class are also members of any class that contains the former as a subclass) we are justified in inferring the mortality of Socrates from his being a member of a subclass of the class of mortals *and* from the membership of any member of a class in all classes of which it is a subclass. In this last example we have one and the same proposition functioning as a premise and as a leading principle in the same inference (not merely, like "All men are mortal" in the preceding two examples, as a leading principle in one and a premise in another); to be capable of this, Peirce thought, is the mark of a "logical" leading principle.

It is not certain that Peirce's method of distinguishing "logical" from other sorts of "leading principles" will bear inspection. However, he seems to have established his basic point, that what it would be fatal to require in all cases—the treatment of a leading principle as a premise—we may safely permit in some. There may be useful and valid reasoning about subjects of all degrees of abstraction, including logic itself.

Hypothetical and disjunctive syllogisms. Traditional textbooks, aside from developing the theory of categorical propositions and syllogisms, have a brief appendix mentioning "hypothetical" (or "conditional") and "disjunctive" propositions and certain "syllogisms" to which they give rise.

"Hypothetical" syllogisms are divided into "pure," in which premises and conclusion are all of the form "If p then q" (notably the syllogism "If p then q, and if q then r; therefore, if p then r," analogous to Barbara), and "mixed," in which only one premise is hypothetical and the other premise and the conclusion are categorical. The mixed hypothetical syllogism has two valid "moods":

(1) *Modus ponendo ponens:* If p then q, and p; therefore, q.
(2) *Modus ponendo tollens:* If p then q, but not q; therefore, not p.

In both these moods the hypothetical premise is called the major, the categorical the minor. *Ponere,* in the mood names, means to affirm, *tollere* to deny. In (1), by affirming the antecedent of the hypothetical we are led to affirm its consequent; in (2), by denying its consequent we are led to deny its antecedent. The fallacies of "affirming the consequent" and "denying the antecedent" (i.e., of doing these things *to start with*, in the minor premise) consist in reversing these procedures—that is, in arguing "If p then q, and q; therefore, p" and "If p then q, but not p; therefore, not q."

"Disjunctive" syllogisms—i.e., ones involving "Either–or" propositions—have the following two "mixed" moods:

(3) *Modus tollendo ponens:* Either p or q, but not p; therefore, q (or, but not q; therefore, p).

(4) *Modus ponendo tollens:* Either *p* or *q*, and *p*;
therefore, not *q* (or, and *q*; therefore, not *p*).

Mood (4) is valid only if "Either *p* or *q*" is interpreted "exclusively"—i.e., as meaning "Either *p* or *q* but not both"—whereas (3) is valid even if it is interpreted as "Either *p* or *q* or both." There is also a *modus tollendo ponens* with the simple "Not both *p* and *q*" as major and the rest as in (4).

Dilemmas. Hypothetical and disjunctive premises may combine to yield a categorical conclusion in the *dilemma*, or "horned" syllogism (*syllogismus cornutus*), with its two forms:

(5) *Constructive:* If *p* then *r*, and if *q* then *r*, but either
p or *q*; therefore, *r*.

(6) *Destructive:* If *p* then *q*, and if *p* then *r*, but either
not *q* or not *r*; therefore, not *p*.

These basic forms have a number of variations; for instance, *q* in (5) may be simply "not *p*," making the disjunctive premise the logical truism "Either *p* or not *p*"; or *p* may imply *r* and *q* imply *s*, giving as conclusion "Either *r* or *s*" rather than the categorical *r*; or the disjunctive premise may be conditionalized to "If *s* then either *p* or *q*," making the conclusion "If *s* then *r*."

A typical dilemma is that put by Protagoras to Euathlus, whom he had trained as a lawyer on the understanding that he would be paid a fee as soon as his pupil won a case. When the pupil simply engaged in no litigation at all, Protagoras sued him for the fee. His argument was "If Euathlus wins this case, he must pay my fee by our agreement, and if he loses it he must pay it by the judge's decision (for that is what losing this case would mean), but he must either win or lose the case; therefore, in either case he must pay."

"Escaping between the horns" of a dilemma is denying the disjunctive premise; for example, Euathlus might have argued that he would neither win nor lose the case if the judge refused to make any decision. "Taking a dilemma by the horns" is admitting the disjunction but denying one of the implications, as Euathlus might have done by arguing that if he won he would still not be bound by the agreement to pay Protagoras, because this was not the sort of case intended in the agreement. "Rebutting" a dilemma is constructing another dilemma drawing upon the same body of facts but leading to an opposite conclusion. This is what Euathlus did, arguing that if he won the case he would be dispensed from paying by the judge's decision, and if he lost it the agreement would dispense him, so either way he was dispensed from paying. Rebuttal, however, is possible only if one of the other moves (though it may not be clear which) is also possible, for a single set of premises can lead by equally valid arguments to contradictory conclusions only if they contain some fault in themselves.

Dilemmatic reasoning obtains a categorical conclusion from hypothetical and disjunctive premises; the Port-Royalists pointed out that we may also obtain hypothetical conclusions from categorical premises. For in any categorical syllogism we may pass directly from one of the premises to the conclusion stated not categorically but conditionally on the truth of the other premise; for instance, from "Every man is mortal" we may infer that *if* Socrates is a man he is mortal, and from "Socrates is a man" that if every man is mortal Socrates is, and similarly with all other syllogisms. This "rule of conditionalization" is much used in certain modern logical systems.

TRADITIONAL AND MODERN LOGIC

Not only the "rule of conditionalization" but the whole subject of hypothetical and disjunctive reasoning fits more comfortably into modern than into traditional logic, being an inheritance from the Stoics, the first "modern" logicians, rather than from Aristotle. Traditionalists have often been worried at its finding any place at all in their general *corpus* and have sometimes attempted to justify it by "reducing" hypothetical and disjunctive propositions and syllogisms to "categorical" ones.

Disjunctives, to begin with, may be eliminated as a distinct form by equating "Either *p* or *q*" with the conditional "If not *p* then *q*," and the conditional form does sometimes look as if it might be a mere verbal variant of the categorical universal. This last is especially true where the conditional is introduced not by the plain "if" but by "if ever" or "if any"; "If ever a gas is heated it expands" and "If any gas is heated it expands" seem simply variants of "Every heated gas expands." But here the antecedent and consequent of the conditional are not, as J. N. Keynes put it, complete propositions with an "independent import"—"it expands" is not on its own a comprehensible sentence; the "it" refers back to the heated gas of the antecedent. Keynes suggested that the term "conditional" be used for precisely this type of "If–then" statement and the term "true hypothetical" confined to cases in which the antecedent and consequent do have "independent import," such as "If Socrates is damned, then there is no justice in heaven." And the representation of "true hypotheticals" as categorical universals is not easy.

In modern logic, from the Stoics through some of the medieval *moderni* to the "logisticians" of our own century, "the stone which the builders rejected has been made the head of the corner." "Pure hypotheticals," together with other forms in which entire propositions are linked by various "connectives," have been made the subject of the most elementary part of logic, the propositional calculus. Aristotelian universals and particulars are built out of these forms (by means of prefixes called "quantifiers") rather than vice versa. (Details are given in LOGIC, MODERN and RUSSELL, BERTRAND, section on logic and mathematics.) The essential procedure is to read "Every *A* is a *B*" as "For every individual *x*, if *x* is an *A* then *x* is a *B*" and "Some *A* is a *B*" as "For some individual *x*, *x* is an *A* and *x* is a *B*." Here, instead of a Keynesian "conditional" being explained as a categorical universal in disguise, the explanation is reversed, and the components which, as Keynes said, are "not propositions of independent import" are represented as "propositional functions" in which the place taken in a genuine proposition by an individual name is taken by a variable ("bound" by the initial quantifier "for all *x*"). But the "if" which links these components is the very same "if" which in the "pure hypotheticals" of the propositional calculus links genuine propositions. This "if" is not explained in terms of anything else (except perhaps other connectives) but is taken as fundamental.

In this way the traditional themes are not banished from modern logic but are incorporated into a much larger subject. When the Aristotelian forms are thus interpreted, however, their laws seem to require modification at some points. In particular, the A-form "For any *x*, if *x* is an *A* then *x* is a *B*" does not seem to imply the I-form "For some *x*, *x* is an *A* and *x* is a *B*," for the former does not imply that any *x* in fact is an *A* (it says only that *if* any *x* is an *A* it is a *B*), whereas the latter does imply this (if some *x* both is an *A* and is a *B*, then that *x* is at least an *A*). This eliminates inference by subalternation and whatever else in the traditional theory depends on it, such as subaltern conversion and syllogisms, like Darapti, which require this for reduction to Figure 1.

Modern logic, however, is not at all monolithic in character, and the sketch just given is a little stylized, depicting modern logic not as a living discipline but rather as a new "tradition" that has displaced the old and against which there are already dissentient voices that give the older tradition a measure of justification (rather like that accorded to pre-Copernican astronomy by the more radical forms of relativity theory). We cannot go back to the prison that would confine all logic to the Aristotelian syllogism, but it is possible to defend (*a*) something like the view that the form "Every *X* is a *Y*" is more fundamental than either "For all *x*, *f*(*x*)" or "If *p* then *q*" and (*b*) the traditional ignoring (in inference by subalternation, etc.) of terms that have no application.

As to (*a*), we now know how to define both "for all *x*" and "if" in terms of a single undefined logical operator which amounts to "for all *x*, if"; for we can take as our fundamental logical complex the form "Anything such that α is such that β" and read "If *p* then *q*" as the special case of this in which α and β are "propositions with independent import," and "For all *x*, β" as the special case in which α is logically true anyway (for instance, in which it has the form "Anything such that β is such that β") and so can be ignored as a "condition" of β's truth. C. S. Peirce—at almost every point the most imaginative and flexible of the "moderns," although he died in 1914—always regarded some such reduction as possible in principle and saw the difference between the "terms" out of which categorical propositions are constructed and the "propositions" out of which we construct hypotheticals as a point of little logical importance.

Peirce, moreover, gave a highly modern justification for the traditional view that within syllogistic logic only the first figure is strictly necessary. Traditional methods of "reducing" other figures to the first do indeed involve another form of inference, namely conversion, and although this can be represented as a kind of enthymematic syllogism, it comes out as syllogism that is already in the second and third figures. For we do it by letting the term *B* be the same as *A* in the two syllogisms

No *C* is a *B* (i.e., an *A*);
Every *A* is a *B* (i.e., an *A*);
Therefore, no *A* is a *C*

(Cesare, Figure 2) and

Every *B* (i.e., *A*) is an *A*;
Some *B* (i.e., *A*) is a *C*;
Therefore, some *C* is an *A*

(Datisi, Figure 3). The replacement of *B* by *A* turns the universal affirmative premise into the logical truism "Every *A* is an *A*," which can be dropped, and the conclusion into the converse of the remaining premise.

We can, however, derive second-figure syllogisms from first-figure ones by a variant of the *reductio ad absurdum* method, employing nothing but Barbara in its terminal and propositional forms, the forms

(*a*) Every *A* is a *B*, and every *B* is a *C*; therefore, every *A* is a *C*; and
(*b*) If *p* then *q*, and if *q* then *r*; therefore, if *p* then *r*,

together with freedom to rearrange our premises and to "conditionalize" and "deconditionalize" conclusions, i.e., to make such passages as that from (*a*) to, and to (*a*) from,

(*c*) Every *A* is a *B*; therefore, if every *B* is a *C* then every *A* is a *C*

and from (*b*) to, and to (*b*) from,

(*d*) If *p* then *q*; therefore, if (if *q* then *r*) then if *p* then *r*.

As a special case of (*d*) we have

(*e*) If every *B* is a *C* then every *A* is a *C*; therefore, if (if every *A* is a *C* I am much mistaken) then if every *B* is a *C* I am much mistaken.

Forms (*c*) and (*e*) will take us from the premise to the conclusion of

(*f*) Every *A* is a *B*; therefore, if (if every *A* is a *C* I am much mistaken) then if every *B* is a *C* I am much mistaken.

But "If *X* then I am very much mistaken" just amounts to "Not *X*," and (*f*) therefore amounts to

(*g*) Every *A* is a *B*; therefore, if not every *A* is a *C*, not every *B* is a *C*,

that is, a conditionalized form of Bocardo, Figure 3.

The equation of "Not *X*" with "If *X* then I am much mistaken" is Peirce's variant, at this point, of one account of denial (discussed more fully in NEGATION). It makes it possible to present the other traditional forms as complexes of "if" and "every" (and "if" and "every," as was shown, are basically the same form of linkage), as follows:

Not every *X* is a *Y* (O) = If every *X* is a *Y* I am much mistaken.
No *X* is a *Y* (E) = Every *X* is not-a-*Y* = Every *X* is such that if it is a *Y* I am much mistaken.
Some *X* is a *Y* (I) = Not (no *X* is a *Y*) = If every *X* is such that if it is a *Y* I am much mistaken, then I am much mistaken.

Syllogisms, in all figures, involving these forms are derivable from Barbara by methods similar to that used to obtain Bocardo above, although the derivations will often be more complicated than the one given. For some of them we require Barbara in yet another form besides (*a*) and (*b*) above, namely the mixed terminal and propositional

> Every *X* is a *Y*; therefore, anything such that if it is a *Y*, then *p*, is such that if it is an *X*, then *p*,

and a kind of terminal principle of *modus ponens,*

> Whatever is an *X* is a thing such that if its being an *X* implies that *p*, then *p*.

Modern logic will not admit that Barbara gives us all the logic there is, but its techniques do bring out anew the extreme fecundity of this ancient form.

Turning now to the failure of certain traditional forms of inference when terms without application are employed, there have been two recent lines of attack on the view that traditional logic is simply "wrong" in accepting such forms as "Every *X* is a *Y*; therefore, some *X* is a *Y*." One, used by Łukasiewicz, is formalistic in character; it is a mistake, Łukasiewicz says, to interpret the traditional propositional forms in terms of modern quantification theory in the ways above indicated, or in any other ways. If we just take them as they stand, without interpretation, we can find a rigorous symbolism for them and show that the traditional laws form a self-consistent system; worries about their interpretation are extralogical. T. J. Smiley, on the other hand, thinks the interpretation of the traditional forms in quantification theory worth attempting but points out that quantification theory, as now developed, offers us wider choices of interpretation than was once thought. For quantification theory now handles cases of the form "For all *x*, *f*(*x*)" in which the range of the variable *x* is restricted to objects of some particular sort, each sort of object having its own type of variable. We need not, therefore, interpret "Every man is mortal," say, in the standard modern way as "For any individual object *x*, if that object is human it is mortal" but may read it, rather, as "For any *human* individual *m*, that human individual is mortal" (with no "ifs" about it). This interpretation, when embedded in a suitable theory of "many-sorted" quantification, will yield all the traditional results.

Bibliography

Peter of Spain's *Summulae Logicales* (modern reprint, I. M. Bocheński, ed., Turin, 1947), Tractatus I–V and VII, is the best-known medieval compendium of the traditional material. In the post-Renaissance epoch the most influential work has been the so-called Port-Royal logic, Antoine Arnauld and Pierre Nicole's *Logique, ou L'Art de penser* (translated by T. S. Baynes as *The Port-Royal Logic,* London, 1851). Richard Whately's crisp, homely, and pugnacious *Elements of Logic,* which appeared in successive editions in the first half of the nineteenth century, is another classic. But the most comprehensive treatment of logic along traditional lines is J. N. Keynes's *Studies and Exercises in Formal Logic* (London and New York, 1884; last ed., 1906).

J. S. Mill's views on the denotation and connotation of terms are developed in his *System of Logic* (London, 1843), Book I, Chs. 2, 5, and 6; his views on the uses of the syllogism are in Book II, Ch. 3. The views of C. S. Peirce are in his *Collected Papers,* Charles Hartshorne, Paul Weiss, and Arthur W. Burks, eds. (8 vols., Cambridge, Mass., 1931–1958), 2.455–516 and 3.154–197, and in his article "Syllogism" in the *Century Dictionary* (6 vols., New York, 1889–1891).

For modern systematizations and interpretations, see Jan Łukasiewicz, *Aristotle's Syllogistic* (Oxford, 1951); J. C. Shepherdson, "On the Interpretation of Aristotle's Syllogistic," in *Journal of Symbolic Logic,* Vol. 21 (1956), 137–147; and T. J. Smiley, "Syllogism and Quantification," in *Journal of Symbolic Logic,* Vol. 27 (1962), 58–72.

A. N. Prior

LOGIC, TRANSCENDENTAL. See Kant, Immanuel.

LOGICAL ATOMISM. See Analysis, philosophical; Russell, Bertrand Arthur William; Wittgenstein, Ludwig Josef Johann.

LOGICAL EMPIRICISM. See Logical positivism.

LOGICAL NECESSITY. See Contingent and necessary statements.

LOGICAL PARADOXES. A paradox, in the original sense of the word, is a statement that goes against generally accepted opinion. In logic the word has taken on a more precise meaning. A logical paradox consists of two contrary, or even contradictory, propositions to which we are led by apparently sound arguments. The arguments are considered sound because when used in other contexts they do not seem to create any difficulty. It is only in the particular combination in which the paradox occurs that the arguments lead to a troublesome conclusion. In its most extreme form a paradox consists in the apparent equivalence of two propositions, one of which is the negation of the other. If for some proposition *A*,

$$A \supset \sim A,$$

this in itself simply leads to a proof of $\sim A$, by the valid law of the propositional calculus:

$$(A \supset \sim A) \supset \sim A.$$

If in turn we have

$$\sim A \supset A,$$

this establishes *A*. Hence, from

$$A \equiv \sim A$$

we obtain *A* and $\sim A$. This extreme form of a paradox is sometimes called an antinomy.

The major paradoxes. Greek philosophy knew the paradoxical arguments of Zeno of Elea, which were intended to show the unreality of motion. Today, with our knowledge of infinite series, the race between Achilles and the tortoise is much less apt to disconcert us. The Megarians cultivated an interest in paradoxes. Some of their aporias, like the Heap or the Bald Man, bear upon the problem of vagueness and are not today considered logical paradoxes. But one, the Liar, attributed to Eubulides, is still of great interest to us: "A man says that he is lying. Is what he says true or false?"

The medieval logicians showed great concern for *insolubilia,* but this interest died out after Paul of Venice (died 1429). Kant's antinomies deal with epistemological, rather than logical, problems.

Burali-Forti paradox. With the revival of logic in the second half of the nineteenth century the attention of logicians was again drawn to the paradoxes. The first published modern paradox was that of Cesare Burali-Forti ("Una questione sui numeri transfiniti" and "Sulle classi ben ordinate"). This is the paradox of the "greatest" ordinal. In Georg Cantor's set theory, to every well-ordered set an ordinal number is assigned. These ordinals can be compared: of any two, one is the smaller and the other the larger. Moreover, every set of ordinals, when it is ordered according to this order relation, is well-ordered, and its ordinal is greater than any element of the set. Let O be the set of all ordinals. It is well-ordered; hence, it has an ordinal number, w. Then, on the one hand, w is an element of O; on the other, w is greater than any element of O.

Burali-Forti's own presentation of the paradox was obscured by a misunderstanding of Cantor's notion of well-ordered set, but the misunderstanding can easily be remedied, and the paradox stands in its full force. Cantor himself had found the same paradox in 1895 and communicated it to David Hilbert in 1896 (see P. E. B. Jourdain, "On the Transfinite Cardinal Numbers of Well-ordered Aggregates," p. 70).

Cantor's paradox. Another paradox involving notions of set theory is that of the greatest cardinal. To every set there corresponds a cardinal number. For any two sets A and B, the cardinal number of A is less than the cardinal number of B if and only if A is equivalent to a subset of B and B is not equivalent to a subset of A. One of Cantor's fundamental results in set theory is that for any set A, the set of subsets of A, the power set $\mathscr{P}A$, is not equivalent to A, whereas A is equivalent to a subset of $\mathscr{P}A$. Therefore, the cardinal number of A is less than the cardinal number of $\mathscr{P}A$. Let S be the set of all sets. Its power set, $\mathscr{P}S$, has a greater cardinal number and contains more sets than S, whereas, on the other hand, all sets are in S. Cantor communicated this paradox to Richard Dedekind in a letter dated August 31, 1899 (*Gesammelte Abhandlungen,* p. 448), and it is now generally known as Cantor's paradox.

Russell's paradox. At the turn of the century the paradoxes of Burali-Forti and Cantor were the subjects of lively discussion among mathematicians interested in set theory. In June 1901, Bertrand Russell, reflecting on these two paradoxes and analyzing their structures, came upon a new paradox, that of the set of all sets that do not contain themselves as elements. A set r, the "Russell set," is defined by the following condition:

for every x, $x \in r$ if and only if $x \notin x$.

By substitution we obtain

$r \in r$ if and only if $r \notin r$.

Russell's paradox is remarkable for the fact that it employs only the notions "set" and "element of a set." The Burali-Forti and Cantor paradoxes could be ascribed to technical difficulties in Cantor's set theory; hence, they seemed to be the concern of the mathematician rather than of the logician or philosopher. Moreover, Cantor's theory was the object of many criticisms, independently of the paradoxes.

With Russell's paradox the situation is quite different. Rather than new and perhaps questionable results about sets, it involves just the bare notions of set and element. Russell communicated the paradox to Frege in a letter dated June 16, 1902 (John van Heijenoort, *A Source Book in Mathematical Logic*). Frege answered immediately (June 22, 1902; *ibid.*), stating that the discovery of the paradox had shaken the foundation of the system of logic on which he intended to build arithmetic.

The "contradiction," as Russell called his paradox, is dealt with in Chapter 10 of *The Principles of Mathematics.* The passage, apparently written in 1901, proposes a distinction in type between a class and the elements of the class and claims that "it is the distinction of logical types that is the key to the whole mystery" (Sec. 104). Before the book was published Russell felt that the problem deserved more attention, and he wrote Appendix B, almost six pages long, in which the doctrine of types is put forward "tentatively," since "it requires, in all probability, to be transformed into some subtler shape before it can answer all difficulties." In *The Principles of Mathematics,* Russell also dealt with the Burali-Forti paradox, which he proposed to solve by denying that the set of all ordinal numbers is well-ordered.

In December 1905 ("On Some Difficulties in the Theory of Transfinite Numbers and Order Types"), Russell abandoned the theory of types; to deal with the set-theoretic paradoxes in a somewhat unified manner he proposed three theories: (1) the zigzag theory, (2) the theory of limitation of size, and (3) the no-classes theory.

Russell's paradox would vanish if to the propositional function $x \in x$ there corresponded no class r such that

$$(x)(x \in r = x \notin x);$$

hence, not every propositional function would determine a class. In the zigzag theory the propositional function does not determine a class if the function is "complicated and recondite." Troublesome classes fail to exist, not because they would be too "big," but because they would exhibit a certain zigzag quality (x is in r if and only if x is *not* in x, and similarly for some of Cantor's arguments). A propositional function that determines a class was said to be predicative, and Russell proposed to set up axioms that would characterize predicative propositional functions. But he had to acknowledge that in attempting to do this he had found "no guiding principle except the avoidance of contradictions; and this, by itself, is a very insufficient principle since it leaves us always exposed to the risk that further deductions will elicit contradictions."

In the theory of limitation of size the test of predicativeness is no longer simplicity of form but a certain limitation of size. Classes fail to exist when they would be too "big."

The ordinals, for example, do not form a class, and thus the Burali-Forti paradox vanishes. However, Russell saw a difficulty in determining where to stop in the scale of ordinals.

In the no-classes theory propositional functions are not assumed to determine classes and relations. Propositions about classes and relations are rephrased in term of propositional functions. Although the reinterpretation is admittedly not possible for the whole theory of ordinal numbers, Russell considered it possible for ordinary mathematics. However, the reconstruction is difficult and cumbersome.

Russell presented the three theories without adopting any of them. But in a three-line note added at the very end of the paper and dated February 5, 1906, he declared that he now felt "hardly any doubt that the no-classes theory affords the complete solution of all the difficulties" caused by the paradoxes. This, however, is not the solution he finally adopted. He returned to the theory of types, only briefly sketched in 1903, and presented it in full-fledged form in 1908 ("Mathematical Logic as Based on the Theory of Types"). Two years later the theory was incorporated in *Principia Mathematica*. Before we explain what this theory is, we shall resume our historical presentation of the paradoxes.

Richard paradox. In 1905, Jules Richard, professor at the *lycée* in Dijon, published a new paradox ("Les Principes des mathématiques et le problème des ensembles"), dealing with definitions of real numbers: Consider all finite sequences, with possible repetitions, of the 26 letters of the alphabet (plus a number of typographical signs). Write these sequences in a table according to lexicographical order; that is, of two sequences of unequal length the shorter comes first, and for any two sequences of the same length the order is decided by the alphabetical order of their letters. Delete any sequence that is not the definition of a real number. We obtain denumerably many such definitions, and the set of finitely definable real numbers is denumerable. Now consider the following sentence: "Let d be the real number whose integral part is 0 and whose nth decimal place is 1 if the nth decimal place of the nth number in the table is 0, and is 0 otherwise." The sentence in quotation marks defines a real number, hence should occur in the table, and the number d should be finitely definable; on the other hand, d is distinct from any number appearing in the table.

Zermelo–König paradox. At the very time Richard's note was published Julius König made public a paradox bearing some analogy to that of Richard. Like Richard, König dealt with the set of finitely definable real numbers, but instead of using a diagonal construction, he considered the complement of that set. Since there are nondenumerably many real numbers and only denumerably many finitely definable real numbers, this complement is not empty. If the set of real numbers could be well-ordered, the set of real numbers not finitely definable could also be well-ordered and would have a first element, which would thus be finitely definable. This first element of the complement would be at the same time finitely definable and not finitely definable. From this König drew the conclusion that the set of real numbers cannot be well-ordered, contradicting a result obtained by Zermelo shortly before ("Beweis, dass

jede Menge wohlgeordnet werden kann"). After the discovery of the Richard paradox, in which the well-ordering problem plays no role, König's conclusion can hardly be accepted. Rather, taking for granted Zermelo's result that the set of real numbers can be well-ordered, we infer the existence of a first element in the complement of the set of finitely definable real numbers, and we thus have a paradox, sometimes called the Zermelo–König paradox, bearing on the notion of definability.

Berry's paradox. Berry's paradox was published by Bertrand Russell ("Mathematical Logic as Based on the Theory of Types," p. 223) and is related to both Richard's and König's. The name of any integer has a certain number of syllables, and only a finite number of such names can be made with a given finite number of syllables. Therefore, "the least integer not nameable in fewer than nineteen syllables" denotes a definite integer. But the phrase in quotation marks is a name consisting of 18 syllables, and the least integer not nameable in fewer than 19 syllables is thus named in 18 syllables. The paradox can be rephrased in terms of words rather than syllables: a definite lexicon is adopted, and we consider definitions of natural numbers containing, say, 50 words or fewer. In one form or another Berry's paradox has a simple formulation, not using involved set-theoretic notions.

Grelling's paradox. In 1908, Kurt Grelling presented a new paradox, that of "heterologicality" ("Bemerkungen zu den Paradoxien von Russell und Burali-Forti"). A word is said to be "autological" if and only if it applies to itself— that is, if it satisfies the schema "'w' is w." Examples of autological words are "English," "short," "polysyllabic." If a word is not autological, it is "heterological." Examples of heterological words are "French," "useless," "monosyllabic." Now, is the word "heterological" heterological? If we assume that "heterological" is heterological, then, by the schema above, "heterological" is autological; on the other hand, if we assume that "heterological" is autological, then, by the definition of "autological," "heterological" is heterological.

At about the same time, the Liar paradox, which dates back to the Megarians, was mentioned and discussed more and more and became the subject of a book, Alexander Rüstow's *Der Lügner: Theorie, Geschichte und Auflösung.*

Theory of types. The paradoxes mentioned so far are those that have exerted the greatest influence on the development of logic. They led to two major advances in logic—the theory of types and the axiomatization of set theory—and fostered, to some extent, the emergence of L. E. J. Brouwer's intuitionism.

Simple theory of types. The theory of types was presented by Russell in "Mathematical Logic as Based on the Theory of Types" and became an integral part of *Principia Mathematica.* Its basic idea is the distinction between a predicate and a predicate of predicates. A predicate holds of individuals; a predicate of predicates holds of predicates of individuals, but we cannot meaningfully assert that it holds or does not hold of an individual or individuals. If we follow this idea, we are led to distinguish predicates of various levels. We cannot, however, establish a hierarchy simply by using the numbers 0, 1, 2, · · ·, for predicate letters have different numbers of argument places, and the scheme has to be refined. We assign the type i to individual variables or constants, the type (i) to singular predicate variables or constants, the type (i,i) to binary predicate variables or constants. A predicate variable or constant of which the first argument place can be filled by a variable of type (i) and the second and third by variables of type i will be of type $((i),i,i)$. A type is thus assigned to every variable or constant. The formula $x_\beta(x_{\alpha_1}, x_{\alpha_2}, \cdots, x_{\alpha_n})$, where $x_\beta, x_{\alpha_1}, x_{\alpha_2}, \cdots, x_{\alpha_n}$ are variables or constants of types $\beta, \alpha_1, \alpha_2, \cdots, \alpha_n$, respectively, is well-formed if and only if β is precisely $(\alpha_1, \alpha_2, \cdots, \alpha_n)$. From these atomic well-formed formulas the other well-formed formulas of the system are obtained by truth-functions and quantification. Once types have been introduced in a system of logic, the analogue of Russell's paradox for predicates cannot be reproduced in the system because $x_\alpha(x_\alpha)$, for any type α, is not well-formed.

Ramified theory of types. To deal with the Liar and Richard paradoxes Russell found it necessary to introduce a further distinction, that of orders within each type, and he obtained what became known as the ramified theory of types. First, we define the *level* of a type. The type i is of level 0, the types (i), (i,i), (i,i,i), $\cdots$ are of level 1, the types $((i))$, $((i,i))$, $((i),i)$, $\cdots$ are of level 2, and so on. The level of a type is given by the number of nested pairs of parentheses. The levels somehow measure the complexity of the types, but for each level above 0 there are infinitely many types. Russell's presentation of the ramified theory of types suffers from several defects, the principal one being a confusion between notation and the objects that the notation is supposed to denote. A reconstruction of Russell's theory would involve giving an exact description of the formal system, which is beyond the scope of what we undertake here. We shall therefore simply take an example. Consider the open formula

$$(1) \qquad (x_{(i)})x_\beta(x_{(i)}, x_i),$$

where β is $((i),i)$, of level 2. The free variable x_i ranges over individuals; when some predicate is assigned to x_β the formula is true of some individuals and false of others and hence corresponds to a singular predicate of individuals. However, in that it contains a type of level 2 it differs from the formula

$$(2) \qquad y_{(i)}(x_i),$$

which corresponds also to such a predicate, because the highest level in (2) is 1. More specifically, formula (1), which purports to characterize a predicate of type (i), contains a quantifier, namely $(x_{(i)})$, ranging over all such predicates. In this Russell saw a breach of the vicious-circle principle (which he sometimes expressed as: no totality can contain members defined in terms of itself), and he introduced a distinction of orders between the predicate of type (i) characterized by (1) and the predicate of type (i) characterized by (2).

Let F be an open well-formed formula containing as argument exactly the free variable x_α, and let k be the level of α. If F contains no quantifier binding a variable of level greater than k, then F is said to be of order 1, or to be "predicative." This is the case for formula (2). If F contains a quantifier binding a variable of level $k + l$, with $l \geq 1$, and no quantifier binding a variable of greater level, F is said to be of order $l + 1$ and is "impredicative." Formula (1) contains a quantifier of level 1, while α is of level 0; hence, it is of order 2 and is impredicative. Analogous definitions can be given for formulas containing more than one free variable as argument, although the exact formulations become more complex.

Russell considered that the distinction of orders solves the Liar paradox, as well as the paradoxes of Richard and Berry. For the Liar, the liar's utterances will be distinguished according to their orders. Richard's "definitions" and Berry's "names" will also fall into different orders, and the paradoxes cannot be reproduced once the totality of definitions or of names has been split into orders. It turns out, however, that such a language would be extremely cumbersome; it would prohibit the very formulation, let alone the proof, of important theorems of mathematics, such as the theorem in calculus stating that if a nonempty set of real numbers has an upper bound, it has a least upper bound.

To remove these limitations Russell introduced the axiom of reducibility, which states that for every propositional function there is an equivalent predicative propositional function. For formula (1), above, the axiom would be

$$(\exists y_{(i)})(x_i)(y_{(i)})(x_i) \equiv (x_{(i)})x_\beta(x_{(i)}, x_i).$$

The axiom is anything but obvious. It restores some of the power that the system lost by the introduction of orders. In fact, it restores so much of that power that it becomes questionable whether anything is left of the distinction of orders (see W. V. Quine, "On the Axiom of Reducibility"). It is shown below how a suggestion by Ramsey allows us to dispense altogether with orders and the axiom of reducibility.

Axiomatization of set theory. It can be claimed with some justification that the distinction of types embodies some of our logical intuitions and would have to be introduced in logic independently of the paradoxes. In fact, Ernst Schröder anticipated the theory of types in 1890, although he was not at all concerned with the paradoxes. However, many mathematicians were reluctant to undertake a complete reconstruction of logic and were more inclined to deal with the paradoxes by giving a precise delimitation to the notion of set. The Cantor, Burali-Forti, Russell, and Zermelo–König paradoxes show that the intuitive point of view concerning the existence of sets cannot be maintained. All these paradoxes turn on the existence of some questionable set. Cantor had defined a set as "a collection, taken as a totality, of certain well-distinguished objects of our perception or our thought" (*Gesammelte Abhandlungen*, p. 282). This is not a mathematical definition; it cannot be used in a logical derivation. The words that it employs are as much in need of clarification as the word "set." Like Euclid's definition of a point as "that which has no parts," Cantor's definition of a set is merely a suggestion, and it cannot prevent the consideration of the set of all sets, of the set of all ordinals, or of the set of all sets that do not contain themselves as elements. Coming at almost the same time as Russell's theory of types, Zermelo's axiomatization of set theory ("Untersuchungen über die Grundlagen der Mengenlehre I") was an attempt to fix and delimit the notion of set. Russell's and Zermelo's approaches to a solution of the difficulties created by the paradoxes were quite different. The first was a far-reaching theory of great import for logic and even ontology, whereas the second was an immediate answer to the pressing needs of the working mathematician.

Zermelo's basic idea resembles, if anything, Russell's theory of limitation of size, set forth in 1905; both men refused to recognize as sets collections that are too "big." Zermelo fulfilled his goal by imposing axioms on sets. Sets are no longer "collections" that our intuition accepts; they are objects satisfying certain axioms. Zermelo used surprisingly few axioms. The null set, $\emptyset$, is introduced outright; given certain sets, the existence of the union, intersection, power sets are guaranteed for these sets by the proper axioms; "definite properties" cut subsets out of given sets; the set $(\emptyset,(\emptyset),((\emptyset)),\cdots)$ is introduced by the axiom of infinity; and so forth. No axiom allows the introduction of the set of all sets; that set just does not exist in the theory, and neither does the set of all ordinals or the Russell set. On the other hand, the axioms permit the derivation of the theorems that mathematicians want in a workable set theory. Admittedly, the consistency of the system remains unproved, and a new paradox may crop up in the theory. We can only check that the arguments leading to the known paradoxes cannot be reproduced in the system. In view of Gödel's theorem (1931), the very notion of consistency proof for set theory raises profound difficulties. After Zermelo, axiomatic set theory was developed by A. A. Fraenkel, Thoralf Skolem, and John von Neumann in the 1920s, by Paul Bernays and Kurt Gödel in the late 1930s, and by many others since then. It has become a lively and wide domain of investigation, and a return to a naive, intuitive view of sets seems impossible.

Syntactic and semantic paradoxes. Some light on the nature of the paradoxes is cast by a remark of Giuseppe Peano. Commenting on the Richard paradox, Peano wrote in 1906 ("Additione," p. 157): "Richard's example does not belong to mathematics, but to linguistics; a certain element, which is fundamental in the definition of *N*, cannot be defined in an exact manner (according to the rules of mathematics). From an element that is not well defined we can derive several conclusions contradicting each other." The element that cannot be precisely defined is ordinary language, and it enters into the definition of *N*, the set of numbers that are finitely definable in ordinary language. Peano's idea was developed by Ramsey in 1925 ("The Foundations of Mathematics"). In a discussion of the theory of types as presented in *Principia Mathematica*, Ramsey divided the paradoxes into two groups. The first group includes the paradoxes of Russell and Burali-Forti; the second includes the Liar paradox, as well as those of Berry and Richard. The principle behind Ramsey's division was that the paradoxes of the first group involve only syntactic and mathematical notions, whereas the formulation of those of the second group requires such notions as "truth," "definability," and "language." The paradoxes of the first group came to be called syntactic paradoxes, those

of the second group semantic paradoxes. The semantic paradoxes are due, it seems, not to any fault in logic but to the vagueness or ambiguity of some nonlogical notion; they raise problems concerning language, and they belong, as Peano said, to linguistics.

According to Ramsey, one effect of the distinction between syntactic and semantic paradoxes is a great simplification in the theory of types; the ramification of orders, which had been superimposed by Russell on the hierarchy of types, is necessary only in order to exclude the semantic paradoxes, and because one can deal with vagueness and ambiguity by simpler means, it can be dispensed with.

Ramsey's views were generally accepted, and the theory of types without the ramification of orders, which became known as the simple theory of types, has been widely used in logical investigations. Today one can question the distinction between the two kinds of paradoxes. Semantic notions have received precise definitions, generally in terms of set-theoretic notions, and it seems difficult to deny that these notions are "logical" without drawing arbitrary lines. The Liar paradox, Grelling's and Berry's paradoxes, and a few others are now generally solved not by the theory of types but by the distinction between language and metalanguage, a distinction emphasized and systematized by Alfred Tarski ("Der Wahrheitsbegriff in den formalisierten Sprachen"). If one compares Tarski's solution of the Liar paradox with Russell's solution of Russell's paradox, it seems difficult to draw a fundamental distinction between them. Both involve a refinement of our logical and set-theoretic intuitions. Ramsey's distinction had some content as long as the paradoxes were tied up with ordinary language, but with the development of a semantics in which the fundamental notions are defined in terms of sets the difference faded away.

Resolving the paradoxes. Since the last years of the nineteenth century the paradoxes have exerted a profound influence on the development of logic. For a while their effect on logic and the foundations of mathematics seemed devastating. After the advent of the theory of types and of axiomatic set theory they were, so to speak, domesticated, but they remained a constant source of concern to logicians. At first they were often considered to be due to the breach of some specific rule of logic, which explains Russell's invocation of the vicious-circle principle. Such injunctions to avoid breaches of logical rules undoubtedly guided Russell, Zermelo, and others in their construction of systems in which the known paradoxes could not be reproduced. However, no rule could be formulated that would by itself eliminate the paradoxes, and only the paradoxes. Even the notion of circularity could not be given a precise form that would be a necessary and sufficient condition for the existence of a paradox. It is impossible to characterize a circular argument in such a way that every circular argument leads to a paradox and every paradox is the result of a circular argument. The known paradoxes had to be eliminated by a radical and thorough reconstruction of logic and set theory that involved much more than merely plucking out the paradoxes.

There have been recurrent attempts to avoid such drastic solutions by looking in each specific case for the source of the difficulty in some definite mistake, some violation of the ordinary laws of logic. Such an attempt was made, for instance, by Paul Finsler. His analysis of the Liar paradox ("Gibt es unentscheidbare Sätze?") is as follows: When I assert the proposition A I assert by this very fact that A is true. Therefore, if by some device the proposition A states that it is itself false, the assertion of A actually is the assertion of the conjunction of two propositions, A is true and A is false. This conjunction is contradictory, hence false; the Liar is simply making a false statement, and there is no paradox at all. Heinrich Behmann ("Zu den Widersprüchen der Logik und der Mengenlehre") undertook to solve Russell's paradox by showing that the definition of the Russell set is non-Pascalian. That is, it does not satisfy the condition, stated by Pascal in *De l'Esprit géométrique* (1655), that a definition should allow us to replace the definiendum with the definiens: to say that r is in r is, according to the definition of r, to say that r is not in r; the definition of r does not enable us to eliminate r and hence is not Pascalian.

However interesting and judicious these observations are, they call for several remarks. First, what the ordinary logical laws are remains vague when these laws are not embodied in a formal system. One may feel, for example, that the distinction of types is an "ordinary" law of logic. Then Finsler's point, if we wanted to justify it thoroughly, would lead to a rather involved analysis of the notions of proposition and assertion. Behmann's remark immediately raises the question whether every non-Pascalian definition leads to a paradox whereas every Pascalian definition is perfectly safe. It is therefore doubtful that a mere appeal to "ordinary" logic will make the paradoxes vanish. Since, moreover, logic has been formalized for reasons other than the existence of paradoxes, these appeals to logical intuition have to be translated into formal terms if we want to dispose of the paradoxes that may crop up in formal systems.

The paradox, or pseudo paradox, of the Barber, published by Russell, will perhaps throw some light on what should constitute a solution of a paradox. A man of Seville is shaved by the Barber of Seville if and only if the man does not shave himself. Does the Barber of Seville shave himself? If we assume that the Barber of Seville is a man of Seville, the conclusion is that if he shaves himself he does not, and if he does not he does. Let $S(x)$ stand for "x is a man of Seville," $s(x,y)$ for "x shaves y," and b for "the Barber of Seville." The statement of the paradox becomes

$$(3) \qquad (x)(S(x) \supset (s(b,x) \equiv {\sim}s(x,x))).$$

By the rule of substitution, replacing x with b, we obtain

$$(4) \qquad S(b) \supset (s(b,b) \equiv {\sim}s(b,b)),$$

which, by the propositional calculus, yields

$$(5) \qquad {\sim}S(b).$$

With the additional assumption

$$(6) \qquad S(b)$$

we have a contradiction. But without this additional assumption we simply have the result that the Barber of Seville is not a man of Seville; he may be a woman or a boy of Seville or a man of some other town. Hence, the difficulty is merely apparent and is easily removed. The definition of the Barber of Seville as a man of Seville shaving all those and only those men of Seville who do not shave themselves is inconsistent, and there is no such barber. Presumably there are many inconsistent decrees, laws, and orders in the world. There is no paradox here, and that is why the puzzle is sometimes called a pseudo paradox.

However, the argument is worth reviewing. If we let the variable x range over the men of Seville, (3) becomes

$$(7) \qquad (x)(s(b,x) \equiv {\sim}s(x,x)),$$

which is quite similar to the definition of the Russell set:

$$(8) \qquad (x)((x \in r) \equiv {\sim}(x \in x)).$$

With this in mind we can attempt to skirt Russell's paradox by making a move similar to the one that takes us from (7) to (3)—that is, by writing, instead of (8),

$$(9) \qquad (x)(\Sigma(x) \supset ((x \in r) \equiv {\sim}(x \in x))),$$

where $\Sigma(x)$ stands for "x is a set." By instantiation we obtain

$$(10) \qquad \Sigma(r) \supset ((r \in r) \equiv {\sim}(r \in r)),$$

and by the propositional calculus,

$$(11) \qquad {\sim}\Sigma(r).$$

The conclusion is that the collection of sets that are not elements of themselves is not a set, just as the Barber of Seville is not a man of Seville. However, although this last fact can readily be accepted, it is not at all clear why the collection r is not a set. Confronted with a set-theoretic paradox, we could always, by denying the existence of some set, remove the paradox. But this would leave us with a chaotic notion of set, which would always be at the mercy of some new paradox and of which we would have no general understanding.

There is no one problem of the paradoxes. The problems are of different types. They are not due to some infraction of one specific law of logic ("vicious circle"), nor are they simply mistakes to be removed by some *ad hoc* corrective. The paradoxes actually reveal conflicts in our logical intuitions. Following a logical path, we reach a conclusion; following another path that seems equally natural to our logical insight, we reach a contrary conclusion. We then have to scrutinize these intuitions and undertake a systematic reconstruction of logic. But in this enterprise the avoidance of the paradoxes is not the only, perhaps not even the main, guide. Logic entered a process of systematization and formalization before the emergence of the modern paradoxes. Frege presented the notion of formal system independently of the problem of the paradoxes. In this process of systematization the paradoxes act as gadflies. They give us opportunities to sharpen our logical intuitions, but they do not constitute a problem in themselves.

Any given paradox rests on a number of definitions, assumptions, and arguments, and we can solve it by questioning any of these. That is why the literature on paradoxes is so rich and abounds with so many solutions. That is also why there is no one problem of the paradoxes. For the important paradoxes, the question is not of solving them by any means but of solving them by means that enlarge and strengthen our logical intuitions. It is to find, among the sometimes too numerous solutions, the one that fits our logic most smoothly and perhaps, to some extent, to adapt our logic to this solution.

Some further paradoxes. The paradoxes presented above are those that historically have had the greatest effect on the development of logic. But other paradoxes are known. Moreover, a puzzle or bewildering argument may or may not yield a paradox, depending on its exact formulation.

The paradox of denotation bears on the distinction between use and mention of an expression. It is presented here as stated by Evert W. Beth (*The Foundations of Mathematics*, p. 490). The inference

$$\frac{\log 343 > 2}{343 = 7^3}$$
$$\overline{\log 7^3 > 2}$$

would certainly not give rise to any doubt. But the similar inference

$$\frac{\text{``343'' contains three figures}}{343 = 7^3}$$
$$\overline{\text{``7}^3\text{'' contains three figures}}$$

is incorrect. The difficulty is solved by the introduction of proper rules for the use of quotation marks.

The prediction paradox has many forms—the Hangman, the Surprise Quiz, and so on. In the Hangman version a judge decrees on Sunday that a certain prisoner shall be hanged at noon on one of six following days and that he shall not know on which day he will be hanged until the morning of the hanging. It seems that the decree can be fulfilled and that it cannot. According to the exact formulation adopted, the paradox can be explained away (as by W. V. Quine, "On a So-called Paradox") or maintained (as by David Kaplan and Richard Montague, "A Paradox Regained").

What is sometimes called the Löwenheim–Skolem paradox is the result that although by Cantor's familiar diagonal argument there exist nondenumerable sets, any formalized set theory has a denumerable model. The Löwenheim–Skolem theorem raises deep questions about the very nature and the limitations of formalization, but it is misleading to speak of paradox in this context; the Löwenheim–Skolem theorem cannot be questioned.

The "paradoxes of implication" are not paradoxes either. The definition of the conditional is such that a false proposition implies any proposition, true or false, and that a true proposition is implied by any proposition, true or false. This result may be a departure from intuition, but it does not constitute a logical paradox.

Bibliography

Behmann, Heinrich, "Zu den Widersprüchen der Logik und der Mengenlehre." *Jahresbericht der Deutschen Mathematiker-Vereinigung,* Vol. 40 (1931), 37–48.

Beth, Evert W., *The Foundations of Mathematics.* Amsterdam, 1959.

Burali-Forti, Cesare, "Una questione sui numeri transfiniti." *Rendiconti del Circolo matematico di Palermo,* Vol. 11 (1897), 154–164.

Burali-Forti, Cesare, "Sulle classi ben ordinate." *Rendiconti del Circolo matematico di Palermo,* Vol. 11 (1897), 154–164.

Cantor, Georg, *Gesammelte Abhandlungen mathematischen und philosophischen Inhalts.* Berlin, 1932; Hildesheim, 1962.

Church, Alonzo, "Schröder's Anticipation of the Simple Theory of Types." Cambridge, Mass., 1939. Preprinted for the Fifth International Congress for Unity of Science as if from the *Journal of Unified Science,* Vol. 9, which never appeared.

Finsler, Paul, "Gibt es unentscheidbare Sätze?" *Commentarii Mathematici Helvetici,* Vol. 16 (1944), 310–320.

Grelling, Kurt, and Nelson, Leonard, "Bemerkungen zu den Paradoxien von Russell und Burali-Forti." *Abhandlungen der Fries'schen Schule,* N.S. Vol. 2 (1908), 301–334.

Jourdain, P. E. B., "On the Transfinite Cardinal Numbers of Well-ordered Aggregates." *Philosophical Magazine,* Series 6, Vol. 7, 61–75.

Kaplan, David, and Montague, Richard, "A Paradox Regained." *Notre Dame Journal of Formal Logic,* Vol. 1 (1960), 79–90.

Peano, Giuseppe, "Additione." *Revista de matematica,* Vol. 8 (1902–1906), 143–157.

Quine, W. V., "On the Axiom of Reducibility." *Mind,* Vol. 45 (1936), 498–500.

Quine, W. V., "On a So-called Paradox." *Mind,* Vol. 62 (1955), 65–67.

Ramsey, F. P., "The Foundations of Mathematics." *Proceedings of the London Mathematical Society,* 2d series, Vol. 25 (1926), 338–384. Reprinted in *The Foundations of Mathematics and Other Logical Essays.* New York and London, 1931.

Richard, Jules, "Les Principes des mathématiques et le problème des ensembles." *Revue générale des sciences pures et appliquées,* Vol. 16 (1905), 541. Reprinted in *Acta Mathematica,* Vol. 30 (1906), 295–296.

Russell, Bertrand, *The Principles of Mathematics.* Cambridge, 1903.

Russell, Bertrand, "On Some Difficulties in the Theory of Transfinite Numbers and Order Types." *Proceedings of the London Mathematical Society,* 2d series, Vol. 4 (1906), 29–53.

Russell, Bertrand, "Mathematical Logic as Based on the Theory of Types." *American Journal of Mathematics,* Vol. 30 (1908), 222–262.

Rüstow, Alexander, *Der Lügner: Theorie, Geschichte und Auflösung.* Leipzig, 1910. Originally a thesis at the University of Erlangen, 1908.

Tarski, Alfred, "Der Wahrheitsbegriff in den formalisierten Sprachen." *Studia Philosophica,* Vol. 1 (1936), 261–405.

Van Heijenoort, John, *A Source Book in Mathematical Logic.* Cambridge, Mass., forthcoming.

Whitehead, Alfred North, and Russell, Bertrand, *Principia Mathematica,* 3 vols. Cambridge, 1910–1913.

Zermelo, Ernst, "Beweis, dass jede Menge wohlgeordnet werden kann." *Mathematische Annalen,* Vol. 59 (1904), 514–516.

Zermelo, Ernst, "Untersuchungen über die Grundlagen der Mengenlehre I." *Mathematische Annalen,* Vol. 65 (1908), 261–281.

JOHN VAN HEIJENOORT

LOGICAL POSITIVISM is the name given in 1931 by A. E. Blumberg and Herbert Feigl to a set of philosophical ideas put forward by the Vienna circle. Synonymous expressions include "consistent empiricism," "logical empiricism," "scientific empiricism," and "logical neopositivism." The name logical positivism is often, but misleadingly, used more broadly to include the "analytical" or "ordinary language" philosophies developed at Cambridge and Oxford.

HISTORICAL BACKGROUND

The logical positivists thought of themselves as continuing a nineteenth-century Viennese empirical tradition, closely linked with British empiricism and culminating in the antimetaphysical, scientifically oriented teachings of Ernst Mach. In 1907 the mathematician Hans Hahn, the economist Otto Neurath, and the physicist Philipp Frank, all of whom were later to be prominent members of the Vienna circle, came together as an informal group to discuss the philosophy of science. They hoped to give an account of science which would do justice—as, they thought, Mach did not—to the central importance of mathematics, logic, and theoretical physics, without abandoning Mach's general doctrine that science is, fundamentally, the description of experience. As a solution to their problems, they looked to the "new positivism" of Poincaré; in attempting to reconcile Mach and Poincaré they anticipated the main themes of logical positivism.

In 1922, at the instigation of members of the "Vienna group," Moritz Schlick was invited to Vienna as professor, like Mach before him (1895–1901), in the philosophy of the inductive sciences. Schlick had been trained as a scientist under Max Planck and had won a name for himself as an interpreter of Einstein's theory of relativity. But he was deeply interested in the classical problems of philosophy, as Mach had not been.

Around Schlick, whose personal and intellectual gifts particularly fitted him to be the leader of a cooperative discussion group, the "Vienna circle" quickly established itself. Its membership included Otto Neurath, Friedrich Waismann, Edgar Zilsel, Béla von Juhos, Felix Kaufmann, Herbert Feigl, Victor Kraft, Philipp Frank—although he was by now teaching in Prague—Karl Menger, Kurt Gödel, and Hans Hahn. In 1926 Rudolf Carnap was invited to Vienna as instructor in philosophy, and he quickly became a central figure in the circle's discussions; he wrote more freely than the other members of the circle and came to be regarded as the leading exponent of their ideas. Carnap had been trained as a physicist and mathematician at Jena, where he had come under Frege's influence. Like other members of the circle, however, he derived his principal philosophical ideas from Mach and Russell.

Ludwig Wittgenstein and Karl Popper were not members of the circle but had regular discussions with its members. In particular, Wittgenstein was in close contact with Schlick and Waismann. Wittgenstein's *Tractatus Logico-philosophicus* had a profound influence on the deliberations of the circle, where it was interpreted as a development of British empiricism.

The circle ascribed to Wittgenstein the "verifiability principle"—that the meaning of a proposition is identical with the method of verifying it—that is, that a proposition means the set of experiences which are together equivalent to the proposition's being true. Wittgenstein, they also thought, had shown how an empiricist could give a satisfactory account of mathematics and logic. He had recognized that the propositions of logic and mathematics are tautologies. (The logical positivists paid no attention to Wittgenstein's distinction between tautologies and identities.) They are "independent of experience" only because they are empty of content, not because, as classical rationalists had argued, they are truths of a higher order than truths based on experience.

In the German-speaking countries, the Vienna circle was a small minority group. For the most part, German-speaking philosophers were still committed to some variety of "German idealism." Neurath, with his strong sociopolitical interests, was particularly insistent that the circle should act in the manner of a political party, setting out to destroy traditional metaphysics, which he saw as an instrument of social and political reaction.

In 1928 the significantly named Verein Ernst Mach (Ernst Mach Society) was set up by members of the circle with the avowed object of "propagating and furthering a scientific outlook" and "creating the intellectual instruments of modern empiricism." To welcome Schlick back to Vienna in 1929 from a visiting professorship at Stanford, California, Carnap, Hahn, and Neurath prepared a manifesto under the general title *Wissenschaftliche Weltauffassung, Der Wiener Kreis* ("The Scientific World View: The Vienna Circle"). This manifesto traced the teachings of the Vienna circle back to such positivists as Hume and Mach, such scientific methodologists as Helmholtz, Poincaré, Duhem, and Einstein, to logicians from Leibniz to Russell, utilitarian moralists from Epicurus to Mill, and to such sociologists as Feuerbach, Marx, Herbert Spencer, and Karl Menger. Significantly absent were any representatives of the "German tradition"—even, although somewhat unfairly, Kant.

In order to make its conclusions familiar to a wider world, the circle organized a series of congresses. The first of these was held in Prague in 1929 as a section of a mathematical and physical, not a philosophical, congress. It was jointly sponsored by the Ernst Mach Society and the Society for Empirical Philosophy, a Berlin group led by Hans Reichenbach and with such members as Walter Dubislav, Kurt Grelling and Carl Hempel, which stood close in its general approach to the Vienna circle.

Meanwhile, the international affiliations of the circle were increasing in importance. American philosophers like C. W. Morris emphasized the link between logical positivism and American pragmatism; Ernest Nagel and W. V. Quine visited Vienna and Prague. In Great Britain, logical positivism attracted the interest of such Cambridge-trained philosophers as L. Susan Stebbing and John Wisdom and the Oxford philosophers Gilbert Ryle and A. J. Ayer, the latter participating for a time in the deliberations of the circle. In France such philosophers of science as Louis Rougier were attracted by logical positivism, as were a group of Neo-Thomists led by General Vouillemin, who welcomed the positivist critique of idealism. In Scandinavia, where the way had been prepared by the antimetaphysical philosophy of Hägerström, a number of philosophers sympathized with the aims of the logical positivists; Eino Kaila, Arne Naess, Åke Petzäll, and Jørgen Jørgensen were prominent representatives of the international movement centering on logical positivism. The Polish logicians, especially Alfred Tarski, exerted a considerable influence on members of the circle, particularly on Carnap. German philosophers, except for Heinrich Scholz of Münster and the Berlin group, remained aloof. Undoubtedly, the organizational energies of the circle did much to bring into being in the 1930s an international community of empiricists; this was largely a consequence of the circle's isolation within the German countries themselves.

Meanwhile the circle was publishing. In 1930 it took over the journal *Annalen der Philosophie* and renamed it *Erkenntnis*. In the period from 1930 to 1940 it served as a "house organ" for members of the Vienna circle and their associates. In addition, the circle prepared a series of monographs under the general title *Veröffentlichungen des Vereines Ernst Mach* (from 1928 to 1934) and *Einheitswissenschaft* (edited by Neurath from 1934 until 1938).

During the 1930s, however, the Vienna circle disintegrated as a group. In 1931 Carnap left Vienna for Prague; in that year Feigl went to Iowa and later to Minnesota; Hahn died in 1934; in 1936 Carnap went to Chicago and Schlick was shot by a mentally deranged student. The meetings of the circle were discontinued. The Ernst Mach Society was formally dissolved in 1938; the publications of the circle could no longer be sold in German-speaking countries. Waismann and Neurath left for England; Zilsel and Kaufmann followed Feigl, Carnap, Menger, and Gödel to the United States. *Erkenntnis* moved in 1938 to The Hague, where it took the name *Journal of Unified Science;* it was discontinued in 1940. Logical positivism, too, disintegrated as a movement, absorbed into international logical empiricism.

CRITIQUE OF TRADITIONAL PHILOSOPHY

Mach denied that he was a philosopher. He was trying, he said, to unify science and, in the process, to rid it of all metaphysical elements; he was not constructing a philosophy. The general attitude of the Vienna circle was very similar. Schlick was the exception. With logical positivism, he argued, philosophy had taken a new turn, but logical positivism was nonetheless a philosophy. Carnap, in contrast, wrote that "we give no answer to philosophical questions and instead *reject all philosophical questions*, whether of Metaphysics, Ethics or Epistemology" (*The Unity of Science*, p. 21). Philosophy, on his view, had to be destroyed, not renovated.

Undoubtedly, this intransigent attitude to philosophy can in part be explained by the peculiar character of German idealism and its hostility to science. The logical positivists thought of themselves as extending the range of science over the whole area of systematic truth and as needing for that purpose to destroy the claim of idealist philosophers to have a special kind of suprascientific access to truth.

Metaphysics. Of the traditional branches of philosophy, the positivists rejected transcendental metaphysics on the ground that its assertions were meaningless, since there was no possible way of verifying them in experience. Nothing that we could possibly experience, they argued, would serve to verify such assertions as "The Absolute is beyond time." Therefore, the positivists held, it tells us nothing. The rejection of transcendental metaphysics was not a novelty; Hume had described transcendental metaphysics as "sophistry and illusion" and had alleged that it makes use of insignificant expressions; Kant and the Neo-Kantians had rejected its claim to be a form of theoretical knowledge; Mach had sought to remove all metaphysical elements from science. But whereas earlier critics of metaphysics had generally been content to describe it as empty or useless or unscientific, the logical positivists took over from Wittgenstein's *Tractatus* the rejection of metaphysics as meaningless. The propositions of metaphysics, they argued, are neither true nor false; they are wholly devoid of significance. It is as nonsensical to deny as to assert that the Absolute is beyond time.

Epistemology. Neo-Kantians had sometimes suggested that philosophy could be reduced to epistemology or "theory of knowledge," which discussed such topics as "the reality of the external world." But assertions about the external world, the positivists argued, are quite as meaningless as assertions about the Absolute or about things-in-themselves. For there is no possible way of verifying the assertion that there is, or the assertion that there is not, an external world independent of our experience. Realism and idealism, considered as epistemological theses, are equally meaningless. So far as epistemology has any content, it reduces to psychology, to assertions about the workings of the human mind, and these have nothing to do with philosophy.

Ethics. The logical positivists disagreed about ethics. Of course they all rejected any variety of transcendental ethics, any attempt to set up a "realm of values" over and above the world of experience. Assertions about values, thus conceived, fall within the general province of transcendental metaphysics and had therefore to be rejected as nonsensical. But whereas Schlick sought to free ethics from its metaphysical elements by converting it into a naturalistic theory along quasi-utilitarian lines, Carnap and Ayer argued that what are ordinarily taken to be ethical assertions are not assertions at all. To say that "stealing is wrong," for example, is neither, they suggested, to make an empirical statement about stealing nor to relate stealing to some transcendental realm. "Stealing is wrong" either expresses our feelings about stealing, our feelings of disapproval, or, alternatively (positivists' opinions differ about this), it is an attempt to dissuade others from stealing. In either case, "stealing is wrong" conveys no information (see EMOTIVE THEORY OF ETHICS).

Philosophical meaninglessness. In general, the positivists explained, when they said of philosophical assertions that they were meaningless, they meant only that they lacked "cognitive meaning." Ethical and metaphysical assertions have emotional associations; this distinguishes them from mere jumbles of words. Such statements as "God exists" or "Stealing is wrong" are, on the face of it, very different from a collocation of nonsense syllables. But the fact remains, the positivists argued, that such "assertions" do not convey, as they purport to do, information about the existence or character of a particular kind of entity. Only science can give us that sort of information.

Not all philosophers, however, have devoted their attention to describing pseudo entities like "the Absolute" or "values" or "the external world." Many of them have been mainly concerned with empirical-looking concepts like "fact," "thing," "property," and "relation." Russell's lectures on logical atomism and Wittgenstein's *Tractatus* are cases in point.

Wittgenstein suggested, however, that the sections in the *Tractatus* in which he talked about facts, or attempted to show how propositions can picture facts, must all in the end be rejected as senseless—as attempts to say what can only be *shown*. For it is impossible in principle to pass beyond our language in order to discuss what our language talks about. Philosophy is the activity of clarifying; it is not a theory.

Schlick carried to its extreme Wittgenstein's *Tractatus* doctrine that philosophy is an activity. Philosophy, he suggested, consists in the *deed* of showing in what the meaning of a statement consists; that is, philosophy is a silent act of pointing. The ultimate meaning of a proposition cannot consist in other propositions. To clarify, therefore, we are forced in the end to pass beyond propositions to the experience in which their meaning consists.

This view won few adherents. It was generally agreed that philosophers could not avoid making the sort of ontological assertions Wittgenstein made in the *Tractatus* and that it is altogether too paradoxical to suggest that all propositions about, for example, the relation between facts and language are nonsensical, even if "important" nonsense. Neurath, in particular, insisted that nonsense cannot be "important," cannot act as a ladder by which we arrive at understanding, as Wittgenstein had said.

Statements about language. Carnap suggested that Wittgenstein was mistaken in supposing that his ontological assertions were without any sense. They were, however, meaningful assertions about language, not about a world beyond language. No doubt, Carnap admits, ontological statements have the appearance of being about the world or, at least, about the relation between language and the world. But this is so only because they have been wrongly formulated in what Carnap calls "the material mode."

Carnap distinguishes three classes of sentences: object sentences, pseudo object sentences, and syntactical sentences. Any ordinary sentence of mathematics or science is an object sentence. Thus, for example, "Five is a prime number" and "Lions are fierce" are both object sentences. Syntactical sentences are sentences about words and the rules governing the use of words. For example, "Five is not a thing-word but a number-word" and "Lion is a thing-word" are syntactical sentences. Pseudo object sentences are peculiar to philosophy; they look like object

sentences but if rightly understood turn out to be syntactical sentences. To understand them rightly we have to convert them from the "material mode" into the "formal mode," that is, from sentences which look as if they are about objects into sentences which are obviously about words. Examples are "Five is not a thing but a number" and "Lions are things." Once these sentences are converted out of the "material mode" into the corresponding "formal" (or syntactical) mode, they can be discussed; in the material mode they are quite undiscussable.

But how are syntactical disputes to be settled? Suppose one philosopher asserts and another denies that "numerical expressions are class-expressions of the second level"—Carnap's "translation" of "numbers are classes of classes"—how is it to be determined which is correct? All such statements, Carnap argues, are relative to a language; they are either statements about the characteristics of some existing language or proposals for the formation of a new language. Fully expressed, that is, they have the form "In language *L*, such-and-such an expression is of such-and-such a type." It can be immediately determined whether such a syntactical statement is true by examining the language in question.

PROBLEMS OF POSITIVISM

Verifiability. The course taken by the subsequent history of logical positivism was determined by its attempts to solve a set of problems set for it, for the most part, by its reliance on the verifiability principle. The status of that principle was by no means clear, for "The meaning of a proposition is the method of its verification" is not a scientific proposition. Should it therefore be rejected as meaningless? Faced with this difficulty, the logical positivists argued that it ought to be read not as a statement but as a proposal, a recommendation that propositions should not be accepted as meaningful unless they are verifiable (see VERIFIABILITY PRINCIPLE). But this was an uneasy conclusion. For the positivists had set out to destroy metaphysics; now it appeared that the metaphysician could escape their criticisms simply by refusing to accept their recommendations.

Recognition of this difficulty led Carnap to suggest that the verifiability principle is an "explication," a contribution to the "rational reconstruction" of such concepts as metaphysics, science, and meaning, to be justified on the quasi-pragmatic grounds that if we ascribe meaning only to the verifiable we shall be able to distinguish forms of activity which are otherwise likely to be confused with one another. It is not, however, by any means clear in what way the verifiability principle can be invoked against a metaphysician who takes as his point of departure that his propositions clearly have a meaning. The most that can be said is that the onus is then on the metaphysician to distinguish his propositions from others which he would certainly have to admit to be meaningless.

A second set of problems hinged on the nature of the entities to which the verifiability principle applies. Since "proposition" had ordinarily been defined as "that which can be either true or false," it seemed odd to suggest that a *proposition* might be meaningless. Yet it was no less odd to suggest that a sentence—a set of words—could be verified, even if there was no doubt that it could be meaningless. Ayer suggested as an alternative the word "statement," and he wrote as if the problem were a purely terminological one. But it is a serious question whether "true," "false," and "meaningless" are alternative descriptions of the same kind of occurrence or whether to describe a sentence as "meaningless" is not tantamount to denying that any statement has been made, any proposition put forward. This would have the consequence that we can consider whether a statement is verifiable only *after* we have settled the question of the meaning of the sentence used to make the statement.

The logical positivists themselves were much more concerned about the fact that the verifiability principle threatened to destroy not only metaphysics but also science. Whereas Mach had been happy to purge the sciences, the logical positivists ordinarily took for granted the substantial truth of contemporary science. Thus, it was a matter of vital concern to them when it became apparent that the verifiability principle would rule out as meaningless all scientific laws.

For such laws are, by the nature of the case, not conclusively verifiable; there is no set of experiences such that having these experiences is equivalent to the truth of a scientific law. Following Ramsey, Schlick suggested that laws should be regarded not as statements but as rules permitting us to pass from one singular statement to another singular statement. In Ryle's phrase, they are "inference-licenses." Neurath and Carnap objected to this on the ground that scientific laws are used in science as statements, not as rules. For example, attempts are made to falsify them, and it is absurd to speak of "falsifying a rule." Furthermore, Carnap pointed out, ordinary singular statements are in exactly the same position as laws of nature; there is no set of experiences such that if I have these experiences there must be, for example, a table in the room.

For these and comparable reasons "verifiability" was gradually replaced by "confirmability" or by the rather stronger notion of "testability." Whereas at first the meaning of a proposition had been identified with the experiences which we would have to have in order to know that the proposition is true, now this was reduced to the much weaker thesis that a proposition has a meaning *only if it is possible to confirm it,* that is, to derive true propositions from it. Carnap, in accordance with his "principle of tolerance," was prepared to admit that a language might be constructed in which only verifiable propositions would count as meaningful. He was content to point out that such a language would be less useful for science than a language which admits general laws. But most positivists, interested as they were in the actual structure of science, simply replaced the verifiability principle by a confirmability principle.

If, however, the original principle proved to be too strong, the new principle threatened to be too weak. For, on the face of it, the new principle admitted as meaningful such metaphysical propositions as "Either it is raining or the Absolute is not perfect." Whether the confirmability principle can so be restated as to act as a method of distinguishing between metaphysical statements as meaningless and scientific statements as meaningful remains a question of controversy.

Unification of science. A further set of problems hinges on the question of what sort of things act as "verifiers" or "confirmers." One of Mach's main concerns, which the logical positivists shared, had been to unify science, especially by rejecting the view that psychology is about an "inner world" that is different from the "outer world" which physical science investigates. The doctrine that both physics and psychology describe "experiences" made such a unification possible. In his earlier writings Carnap tried to show in detail how "the world" could be constructed out of experience, linked together by relations of similarity. But then a new difficulty arose; one about how it is possible to show that one person's experiences are identical with another's. On the face of it, an experience-based science is fundamentally subjective; science is verified only at the cost of losing its objectivity.

To overcome this difficulty, Schlick drew a distinction between "content" and "structure." We can never be sure, he argued, that the content of our experience is identical with the content of any other person's experience, for example, that what he sees when he says that he sees something red is identical with what we see when we say we see something red. For scientific purposes, however, this does not matter in the slightest. Science is interested only in the structure of our experience, so that provided, for example, we all agree about the position of red on a color chart, it is of no importance whether our experience of red differs.

Yet Schlick still thought that such "experiences" are what gives content, meaning, to science, converting it from a conceptual frame into real knowledge. Thus, it appears that the ultimate content of science lies beyond all public observation. There is no way of verifying that another person is even experiencing a content, let alone a content which is like or unlike the content of my experience.

Physicalist theories. Profoundly dissatisfied with the conclusion that the ultimate content of scientific truths is private, Neurath was led to reject the view—which logical positivists had so far taken for granted—that it is "experiences" which verify propositions. Only a proposition, he argued, can verify a proposition. Carnap accepted this conclusion and developed the conception of a "protocol statement," the ultimate resting point of verifications, a statement of such a nature that to understand its meaning and to see that it is true are the same thing. Carnap still suggested, however, that a protocol statement records a private experience, even though every such statement—indeed every statement—can be translated into the public language of physics. Statements of the form "Here now an experience of red" can, he argued, be translated into statements about the physical state of the body of the person who has the experience of red. (Subsequently this "physicalist" thesis was expressed in the weaker form, that every statement is linked by means of correspondence rules with the statements of physics.)

Neurath was still dissatisfied. Protocol statements, he argued, must form part of science as distinct from merely being translatable into its language. Otherwise, science still rests on essentially private experience. In fact, protocol statements must take some such form as "Otto Neurath reports that at 3:15 p.m. there was a table in the room perceived by Otto." The effect of this suggestion, as Schlick remarked with horror, is to leave open the possibility that the basic protocol statements may not be true. They, rather than some natural law with which they are incompatible, can be rejected as false. Schlick persisted in arguing that the ultimate confirmations of scientific propositions must be experiences of the form "here, now, blue"—which he described as "the only synthetic statements which are not hypotheses." Carnap came to agree with Neurath, however, that all synthetic statements are hypotheses.

At first, indeed, Carnap replied to Neurath by invoking his principle of tolerance. One has a free choice, he argued, between a language which incorporates protocol statements and a language into which they can be translated. Subsequently he has moved more and more in Neurath's direction. Satements of the form "the body Carnap is in a state of green-seeing," he now suggests, are sufficient to act as confirmations, and it is not necessary at any point to use the "phenomenal language" which Mach had thought to be the basic language of science. But Carnap still writes as if the issue between physicalist and nonphysicalist hinges on the choice of a language. Logical positivism, we might say, split into three groups, one asserting physicalism, the second rejecting it, and the third expressing a preference for the physicalist language.

In his *Logical Syntax of Language* Carnap had argued that all statements about the "meaning" or "significance" of statements are of the "pseudo object" type and should be translated into a syntactical form. Thus, for example, "This letter is about the son of Mr. Miller" has to be read as asserting that in this letter a sentence occurs which has the expression "the son of Mr. Miller" as its subject. This was a highly implausible doctrine, since, clearly, a letter can be about the son of Mr. Miller without using the phrase "the son of Mr. Miller." Under Tarski's influence Carnap decided that his original thesis had been unduly restrictive; philosophy had to refer to the semantical as well as the syntactical characteristics of language in order to give a satisfactory explication of, for example, the conception of "truth." Now Carnap found himself in opposition to Neurath. To try to pass beyond language to what language signifies, Neurath argued, is at once to reintroduce the transcendental entities of metaphysics. The subsequent development of semantics at Carnap's hands would have done nothing to relieve Neurath's qualms. Languages can be constructed, Carnap argues, in a variety of ways, and the question whether, for example, one accepts a language which includes names for abstract entities is a matter of practical convenience, not admitting of argument at any other level. The influence of Mach on Carnap's thinking has now been almost entirely dissipated; he writes, rather, in the spirit of a Poincaré or a Duhem.

THE INFLUENCE OF POSITIVISM

Logical positivism, considered as the doctrine of a sect, has disintegrated. In various ways it has been absorbed into the international movement of contemporary empiricism, within which the disputes which divided it are still being fought out. Originally, it set up a series of sharp contrasts: between metaphysics and science, logical and factual truths, the verifiable and the nonverifiable, the corrigible and the incorrigible, what can be shown and what can be said, facts and theories. In recent philosophy, all these contrasts have come under attack, not from metaphysicians but from philosophers who would in a general sense be happy enough to describe themselves as "logical empiricists." Even among those philosophers who would still wish to make the contrasts on which the logical positivists insisted, few would believe that they can be made with the sharpness or the ease which the logical positivists at first suggested.

Logical positivism, then, is dead, or as dead as a philosophical movement ever becomes. But it has left a legacy behind. In the German-speaking countries, indeed, it wholly failed; German philosophy, as exhibited in the works of Heidegger and his disciples, represents everything to which the positivists were most bitterly opposed. In the United States, Great Britain, Australia, the Scandinavian countries, and in other countries where empiricism is widespread, it is often hard to distinguish the direct influence of the positivists from the influence of such allied philosophers as Russell, the Polish logicians, and the British "analysts." But insofar as it is widely agreed that transcendental metaphysics, if not meaningless, is at least otiose, that philosophers ought to set an example of precision and clarity, that philosophy should make use of technical devices, deriving from logic, in order to solve problems relating to the philosophy of science, that philosophy is not about "the world" but about the language through which men speak about the world, we can detect in contemporary philosophy, at least, the persistence of the spirit which inspired the Vienna circle.

(See also the following articles on some of the influential theorists of this movement: BASIC STATEMENTS; EMOTIVE THEORY OF ETHICS; LINGUISTIC THEORY OF THE A PRIORI; and VERIFIABILITY PRINCIPLE. See Logical Positivism in Index for articles on philosophers who are frequently classified as logical positivists or who strongly influenced the development of logical positivism.)

Bibliography

The essays by leading logical positivists included along with an introduction by Ayer and an extensive bibliography in Alfred J. Ayer, ed., *Logical Positivism* (Glencoe, Ill., 1959), are the best introduction to the movement as a whole. Other representative writings by members of the Vienna circle and its associates include the following: Alfred J. Ayer, *Language, Truth and Logic* (London, 1936; 2d ed., rev., 1946). Rudolf Carnap, *Der Logische Aufbau der Welt* (Berlin, 1928), translated by R. George as *The Logical Structure of the World* (London, 1965); "Die physikalische Sprache als Universalsprache der Wissenschaft," in *Erkenntnis*, Vol. 2, Nos. 5/6 (1932), 423–465, translated by Max Black as *The Unity of Science* (London, 1934); *Logische Syntax der Sprache* (Vienna, 1934), translated by Amethe Smeaton as *The Logical Syntax of Language* (London and New York, 1937); *Philosophy and Logical Syntax* (London, 1935); "Testability and Meaning," in *Philosophy and Science*, Vol. 3, No. 4 (1936), 419–471, and Vol. 4, No. 1 (1937), 1–40; *Meaning and Necessity* (Chicago, 1947); "Empiricism, Semantics and Ontology," in *Revue internationale de philosophie,* Vol. 4, No. 11 (1950), reprinted in Leonard Linsky, ed., *Semantics and the Philosophy of Language* (Urbana, Ill., 1952), pp. 208–228; and "Intellectual Autobiography" and "Reply to My Critics," in P. A. Schilpp, ed., *The Philosophy of Rudolf Carnap* (La Salle, Ill., 1963).

See Herbert Feigl and May Brodbeck, eds., *Readings in the Philosophy of Science* (New York, 1953), and Herbert Feigl and Wilfrid Sellars, eds., *Readings in Philosophical Analysis* (New York, 1949), for articles by Carnap, Feigl, Reichenbach, Hempel, Frank, and Zilsel. See also Philipp Frank, *Modern Science and Its Philosophy* (Cambridge, Mass., 1949); Victor Kraft, *Der Wiener Kreis, Der Ursprung des Neopositivismus* (Vienna, 1950), translated by Arthur Pap as *The Vienna Circle* (New York, 1953); Jørgen Jørgensen, *The Development of Logical Empiricism* (Chicago, 1951); Charles W. Morris, *Logical Positivism, Pragmatism and Scientific Empiricism* (Paris, 1937); Otto Neurath, *Einheitswissenschaft und Psychologie* (Vienna, 1933) and *Le Développement du Cercle de Vienne et l'avenir de l'empiricisme logique* (Paris, 1935); Hans Reichenbach, *The Rise of Scientific Philosophy* (Berkeley and Los Angeles, 1951); Karl Raimund Popper, *Logik der Forschung* (Vienna, 1935), translated with new appendices by the author, with the assistance of Julius Freed and Lan Freed, as *Logic of Scientific Discovery* (London, 1959); Moritz Schlick, *Allgemeine Erkenntnislehre* (Berlin, 1918), *Fragen der Ethik* (Vienna, 1930), translated by D. Rynin as *Problems of Ethics* (New York, 1939), and *Gesammelte Aufsätze* (Vienna, 1938), partially republished as *Gesetz Kausalität und Wahrscheinlichkeit* (Vienna, 1948); and Ludwig Wittgenstein, *Tractatus Logico-philosophicus,* German version as *Logisch-philosophische Abhandlung* in *Annalen der Naturphilosophie,* Vol. 14 (1921), 185–262, English translation by C. K. Ogden (London, 1922; rev. ed., 1961); *Philosophical Investigations* (Oxford, 1953).

See also Richard von Mises, *Kleines Lehrbuch der Positivismus* (The Hague, 1938), translated as *Positivism: A Study in Human Understanding* (Cambridge, Mass., 1951); G. Bergmann, *The Metaphysics of Logical Positivism* (London, 1954); Frederick C. Copleston, *Contemporary Philosophy* (London, 1956); Ernest Nagel, *Logic Without Metaphysics* (Glencoe, Ill., 1956); John Arthur Passmore, "Logical Positivism," in *Australasian Journal of Psychology and Philosophy,* Vol. 21 (1943), 65–92, Vol. 33 (1944), 129–153, Vol. 26 (1948), 1–19, and *A Hundred Years of Philosophy* (London, 1957); James O. Urmson, *Philosophical Analysis* (Oxford, 1956); and Julius R. Weinberg, *An Examination of Logical Positivism* (New York, 1936).

JOHN PASSMORE

LOGICAL TERMS, GLOSSARY OF. This glossary is confined, with few exceptions, to terms used in formal logic, set theory, and related areas. No attempt has been made to cover what is often called "inductive logic," although several terms in this field have been included for the convenience of the reader.

It should be noted that many topics dealt with very briefly here are treated in full in various other articles in the Encyclopedia. Cross references to these will be indicated by small capitals (e.g., "see article LOGIC, MODERN"); cross references to other glossary entries will be indicated by boldface italics (e.g., "see *relation*").

abduction. (1) A syllogism whose major premise is known to be true but whose minor premise is merely probable. (2) C. S. Peirce's name for the type of reasoning that yields from a given set of facts an explanatory hypothesis for them.

abstraction. (1) In traditional logic, the process of deriving a universal from particulars. (2) In set theory, the process of defining a set as the set of all objects that have a particular property.

abstraction, axiom of (axiom of comprehension). An axiom in set theory stating that for any predicate *P,* there exists a set of all and only those objects that satisfy *P.* It was the unrestricted use of this axiom that led to the paradoxes of set theory.

abstract term. In traditional logic, a term that is a name of the common nature of many individuals, considered apart from them or from what distinguishes them from one another. A common example of an abstract term is "humanity."

accident. See *predicables.*

actual infinite. The infinite regarded as a completed whole.

a fortiori. A nonsyllogistic mediate inference of the form "*B* is greater than *C; A* is greater than *B;* hence, *A* is greater than *C.*" It is clear that the validity of this argument follows from the transitivity of the relation "greater than," and therefore some authors extend the term to cover all relational syllogisms whose validity depends on the transitivity of the relation involved. See *relation.*

aggregate. A collection of objects satisfying a given condition.

alephs. The symbols, introduced by Georg Cantor, that designate the cardinality of infinite sets (see article SET THEORY). *Aleph-null* ($\aleph_0$) designates the cardinality of the smallest infinite set, aleph-one ($\aleph_1$) the cardinality of the next largest infinite set, etc. See *continuum hypothesis;* article CONTINUUM PROBLEM.

algebra of logic. A system in which algebraic formulas are used to express logical relations. In such a system many familiar algebraic laws that hold for numbers are not retained. The work of George Boole contains the first important example of an algebra of logic.

algorithm. A mechanical procedure for carrying out, in a finite number of steps, a computation that leads from certain types of data to certain types of results. See *decision problem; effectiveness.*

alternation. See *disjunction, exclusive.*

alternative denial. See *Sheffer stroke function.*

ambiguity. Capability of being understood in two or more ways. The term is strictly applied only in cases where the possibility of different interpretation is due not to the expression itself but to some feature of the particular use of the expression; when this possibility is due to the expression itself the expression is called *equivocal.* Many authors, however, do not make this distinction.

amphiboly. An equivocation that arises not out of an equivocation in a word or phrase but because the grammatical structure of the sentence or clause leaves the place of the phrase in the whole not entirely determinate. An example is "The shooting of the hunters was finished quickly."

ampliation. In medieval logic, the extension of a common term from a narrow supposition to a wider one.

analogy. A comparison between two or more objects that indicates one or more respects in which they are similar. An *argument from analogy* is an inference from some points of resemblance between two or more objects to other such points. The method of *refutation by logical analogy* is a method for showing that an argument is fallacious by giving an example of another argument of the same form whose invalidity is immediately apparent.

analysis, mathematical. The theory of real and complex numbers and their functions.

analytic. Used of a proposition whose denial is self-contradictory. Such a proposition is true either by virtue of its logical form alone (in which case it is called a *logical truth*, or *logically necessary*) or by virtue of both its logical form and the meaning of its constituent terms. An instance of a logical truth is "It is raining or it is not raining"; an example of an analytic truth that is not a logical truth is "All bachelors are unmarried." Analytic propositions cannot be false and are therefore said to be *necessary truths*. Whether there are necessary truths that are not also analytic truths is a matter of much dispute. See article ANALYTIC AND SYNTHETIC STATEMENTS.

ancestral relation. For a given relation R, the relation R^* that exists between two objects x and y if and only if y has every R-hereditary property that x has. A property is said to be *R-hereditary* when, if it is correctly predicated of b and if aRb, then it is also correctly predicated of a. For example, let R be the property "is the successor of." Then "is a natural number" (where this property also applies to 0) is R-hereditary, since if b is a natural number and a is the successor of b, then a is also a natural number. Given this fact, we can define the property "is a natural number" as the property of all objects that bear the ancestral relation to 0 for the relation "is the successor of"—that is, as the property of all objects that have every "is the successor of"-hereditary property that 0 has. One of these properties is "is a natural number," and therefore only the natural numbers can meet this definition.

It should be noted that the above definition is an example of an *impredicative definition*, since "is a natural number" is defined in terms of the class of "is the successor of"-hereditary properties, a class of which it is a member.

antecedent. The part of a hypothetical proposition that precedes the implication sign.

antilogism. A triad of propositions such that the joint truth of any two of the propositions implies the falsity of the third. Christine Ladd-Franklin's principle of the syllogism states that a valid syllogism is one whose premises taken with the contradictory of the conclusion constitute an antilogism. Thus, the syllogism whose premises are "All men are mortal" and "Socrates is a man" and whose conclusion is "Socrates is mortal" is a valid syllogism, for the joint assertion of any two of the three propositions that constitute the premises and the contradictory of the conclusion implies the falsity of the third proposition.

antinomy. See *paradox*.

apodictic (apodeictic) proposition. See *modality*.

appellation. In medieval logic a term is said to have appellation if it is applicable to some existing thing. Thus, "the present queen of England" has appellation, but "the present queen of the United States" does not.

A-proposition. In traditional logic, a universal affirmative categorical proposition. An example is "All men are mortal."

Archimedean property. The property of a system of numbers whereby for any two numbers a and b, if a is less than b, then there is a number c such that a multiplied by c is greater than b.

argument of a function. A member of the domain of a given function.

arithmetical predicate. A predicate that can be explicitly expressed in terms of the truth-functional connectives of propositional calculus, the universal and existential quantifiers, constant and variable natural numbers, and the addition and multiplication functions.

arithmetization of mathematics (arithmetization of analysis). The definition, which was developed by Karl Weierstrass, Richard Dedekind, and Georg Cantor, of the nonnatural numbers as certain objects construed out of the natural numbers and set-theoretic objects and the corresponding reduction of the properties of the former to the properties of the latter.

arithmetization of syntax. The process of correlating the objects of a formal system with some or all of the natural numbers and then studying the relations and properties of the correlated numbers so as to gain information about the syntax of the formal system. This was done systematically by Kurt Gödel in the researches that led to his incompleteness theorems. See article GÖDEL'S THEOREM.

ars combinatoria. A technique of deriving complex concepts by the combination of relatively few simple ones, which are taken as primitive. This technique was proposed by Leibniz as a valuable aid for the study of all subjects. He proposed the development of a universal language (*characteristica universalis*) containing a few primitive symbols in terms of which all other symbols would be defined. A universal mathematics (*mathesis universalis*)—that is, a universal system of reasoning—would then be added, and all subjects could be studied in this language. Leibniz' program is often viewed as an early forerunner of the formalization of various disciplines.

assertion sign. The sign ⊢, introduced by Gottlob Frege to indicate in the object language that a proposition is being judged as true and is not merely being named. Some authors now use this sign in the metalanguage to express that the formula to which it is prefixed is a theorem in the object language.

assertoric proposition. See *modality*.

associativity. The property of a relation R which consists in the identity of "$aR(bRc)$" and "$(aRb)Rc$," where a, b, and c are any elements of the field of R. Addition has this property, since "$a+(b+c)$" is the same as "$(a+b)+c$."

attribute. Although it is now often used synonymously with "property," this term was traditionally confined to the essential characteristics of a being.

Aussonderungsaxiom. An axiom in set theory, first introduced by Ernst Zermelo, which states that for any set a and any predicate P, there exists a set containing all and only those members of a that satisfy the predicate P.

axiom. A basic proposition in a formal system which is asserted without proof and from which, together with the other such propositions, all other theorems are derived according to the rules of inference of the system. See *postulate*.

axiomatic method. The method of studying a subject by beginning with a list of undefined terms and a list of axioms and then deriving the truths of the subject from these postulates by the methods of formal logic.

axiom schema. A representation of an infinite number of axioms by means of an expression containing syntactical variables and having well-formed formulas as values. Every value of the expression is to be taken as an axiom.

axiom schema of separation. See **Aussonderungsaxiom.**

Barbara. See **mnemonic terms.**

Baroco. See **mnemonic terms.**

biconditional. A binary propositional connective (↔, ≡), usually read "if and only if" (often abbreviated "iff"), whose truth table is such that "*A* if and only if *B*" is true when *A* and *B* are either both true or both false and is false when one is true and the other false. "*A* if and only if *B*" is equivalent to "if *A* then *B*, and if *B* then *A*."

binary connective. See **connective.**

Bocardo. See **mnemonic terms.**

Boolean algebra. The first algebra of logic. It was invented by George Boole and given its definitive form by Ernst Schröder.

Boolean functions. Functions that occur in Boolean algebra. The more important ones are the class-union function, the class-intersection function, and the class-complement function.

bound occurrence of a variable. An occurrence of a variable *a* in a well-formed part of a formula *A* either of the form "for all *a, B*" or of the form "there is an *a* such that *B.*"

bound of a set. For a given relation *R*, a *lower* bound (or first element) of a set *a* is any member of *a* that bears the relation *R* to all members of *a*; an upper bound of *a* is any member of *a* to which all members of *a* bear the relation *R*. A *greatest lower bound* of a set *a* (or *infimum* of *a*) is a lower bound of *a* to which all lower bounds of *a* bear the relation *R*; a *least upper bound* of *a* (or *supremum* of *a*) is an upper bound of *a* that bears the relation *R* to all upper bounds of *a*.

bound variable. A bound variable of a formula *A* is a variable that has a bound occurrence in *A*.

Bramantip. See **mnemonic terms.**

Burali-Forti's paradox. See **paradox.**

calculus. Any logistic system. The two most important types of logical calculi are *propositional* (or sentential) calculi and *functional* (or predicate) calculi. A propositional calculus is a system containing propositional variables and connectives (some also contain propositional constants) but not individual or functional variables or constants. In the *extended* propositional calculus, quantifiers whose operator variables are propositional variables are added. Among the *partial* propositional calculi, in which not all the theorems of the standard propositional calculus are obtainable, the most important are David Hilbert's *positive* propositional calculus (this contains all those parts of the standard propositional calculus that are independent of negation) and the *intuitionistic* propositional calculus (in this system axioms about negation acceptable from the intuitionistic point of view are added to the positive propositional calculus). A functional calculus is a system containing, in addition to the symbols of propositional calculus, individual and functional variables and/or constants, as well as quantifiers that take some of these variables and constants as their operator variables. In a *first-order* functional calculus (or *first-order logic*) the quantifiers have as their operator variables only individual variables, and the functions have as their arguments only individual variables and/or constants. In a *second-order* functional calculus (or second-order logic) the operator variables of the quantifiers can be functional variables. After that, each odd order adds functional variables and/or

constants some of whose arguments are of the type introduced two orders below, and each even order allows the use of the variables introduced one order below as operator variables for the quantifiers. When there are no individual or functional constants present the functional calculus is called *pure;* when either is present it is called applied. See articles LOGIC, MODERN; SYSTEMS, FORMAL, AND MODELS OF FORMAL SYSTEMS.

Camenes. See **mnemonic terms.**

Camestres. See **mnemonic terms.**

Cantor's paradox. See **paradox.**

Cantor's theorem. The theorem stating that for any given set *a*, the power set of *a* has a greater cardinality than *a* has.

cardinality (power). For a given set, the cardinal number associated with it.

cardinal number. An object *a* that is associated with all and only the members of a set of equipollent sets. Various authors disagree on what this object is. The *Frege–Russell definition* of cardinal number is simply the identification of *a* with the set of equipollent sets.

Cartesian product. For a given set *a*, the set whose members are all and only the sets that contain one member from each member of *a*.

categorematic. In traditional logic, used of a word that can be a term in a categorical proposition. In contemporary logic, used of any symbol that has independent meaning. An example of a categorematic word is "men." Cf. **syncategorematic.**

categorical proposition. See **proposition.**

category. A general or fundamental class of objects or concepts about whose members assertions can significantly be made which differ from those that can significantly be made about nonmembers of this class. The two most famous lists of categories are those of Aristotle and Kant. Aristotle's list comprises substance, quantity, quality, relation, activity, passivity, place, time, situation, and state. Kant's comprises unity, plurality, and universality (categories of quantity); reality, negation, and limitation (categories of quality); substantiality, causality, and reciprocity (categories of relation); and possibility, actuality, and necessity (categories of modality).

Celarent. See **mnemonic terms.**

Cesare. See **mnemonic terms.**

choice, axiom of (multiplicative axiom). An axiom in set theory stating that if *a* is a disjoint set which does not have the null set as one of its members, then the Cartesian product of *a* is different from the null set. It can be proved that this axiom is equivalent to the well-ordering theorem.

choice function. A function *R* whose domain includes (or, according to some authors, is identified with the set of) all the nonempty subsets of a given set *a* and whose value is a member of any such subset.

Church's theorem. The theorem, stated and proved by Alonzo Church, that there is no decision procedure for determining whether or not an arbitrary well-formed formula of the first-order functional calculus is a theorem of that system.

Church's thesis. The thesis that every effectively calculable function (effectively decidable predicate) is general recursive.

circular reasoning. See **fallacy.**

class. (1) An aggregate. (2) In Gödel–von Neumann–Bernays set theory, where a distinction is made between sets and classes, a class is an object that can contain members but cannot be a member of any object. See *set.*

classification. Two of the issues of concern to traditional logicians were the nature of the process of grouping individuals into classes of individuals (*species*), these classes into further classes, and so on (the process of classification), and the nature of the reverse process (the process of *division*)—breaking a class down into its subclasses, these into their subclasses, and so on, until the simplest classes are broken down into the individuals that are their members.

In the process of classification one begins with a group of individuals and arranges them into classes, called *infimae species,* none of which can be broken down into species but only into individuals. One then groups the *infimae species* into other classes, of which the *infimae species* are subclasses. (For any species the class of which it is a subclass is called the *proximum genus.*) The grouping continues until one reaches the class of which all the original individuals are members. This is the *summum genus,* and when one reaches it the process of classification is finished. (All the classes between the *infimae species* and the *summum genus* are called the *subaltern genera.*)

In the process of division one begins with the *summum genus* and breaks it down into its subclasses, continuing until one reaches the *infimae species.* Finally, these are broken down into the individuals that are their members.

Several rules were set up for classification and division: (1) at each step only one principle may be used for breaking down the classes or grouping them together; (2) no group may be omitted at any step; (3) no intermediate step may be omitted. When applied to division this last rule is known as the rule of *division non faciat saltum.*

A *dichotomy* is a form of division (or of classification) in which at each stage the genus is divided into species according to whether or not the objects possess a certain set of differentiae. The two species formed (*proxima genera*) are therefore mutually exclusive and jointly exhaustive.

closed sentence (closed schema). A sentence (or schema) that has no free variables.

closed with respect to (closed under) a relation. A set is closed under a relation R if and only if for all a, if aRb and if a is a member of the set, then b is a member of the set.

closure of a formula. A formula formed by placing before an original formula A quantifiers binding all variables that occur freely in A. A *universal* closure is the formula formed when only universal quantifiers are used, and an *existential* closure is the formula formed when only existential quantifiers are used.

collective term. In traditional logic, a term that denotes a collection of objects regarded as a unity. An example is "the Rockies."

combinatory logic. A branch of mathematical logic where variables are entirely eliminated, their place being taken by certain types of functions that are unique to this branch of logic.

commutativity. The property of a relation R that consists in the equivalence of aRb and bRa, where a and b are any elements of the field of R.

comparability, law of (law of trichotomy). The principle in set theory that the cardinality of two sets is always comparable; that is, for any two sets a and b, a is greater than b or equal to b or less than b.

complement of a set (negate of a set). The set of all and only those objects that are not members of a given set a.

completeness. The word "completeness" is used in varying senses. In the strongest sense (E. L. Post) a logistic system is said to be complete if and only if for any well-formed formula A, either A is a theorem of the system or the system would become inconsistent upon the addition of A as an axiom (without any other changes); in this sense propositional calculus, but not pure first-order functional calculus, is complete. In a second, weaker sense (Kurt Gödel) a logistic system is said to be complete if and only if all valid well-formed formulas are theorems of the system; in this sense both propositional calculus and pure first-order functional calculus are also complete. In a third, and still weaker, sense of completeness (Leon Henkin) a logistic system is said to be complete if and only if all secondarily valid well-formed formulas are theorems of the system; in this sense the pure second-order functional calculus and functional calculi of higher order are complete.

complete set. A set all of whose members are subsets of it.

composition, fallacy of. See *fallacy.*

comprehension, axiom of. See *abstraction, axiom of.*

computable function. See *Turing-computable.*

conclusion. That which is inferred from the premises of a given argument.

concrete term. In traditional logic, a term that is the name of an individual or individuals. An example of such a term is "Socrates."

condition. A *necessary condition* is a circumstance in whose absence a given event could not occur or a given thing could not exist. A *sufficient condition* is a circumstance such that whenever it exists a given event occurs or a given thing exists. A *necessary and sufficient condition* for the occurrence of a given event or the existence of a given thing is therefore a circumstance in whose absence the event could not occur or the thing could not exist and which is also such that whenever it exists the event occurs or the thing exists.

This terminology is sometimes extended to the formal relations that exist between propositions. Thus, the truth of a proposition A is said to be a necessary condition for the truth of another proposition B if B implies A, and the truth of A is said to be a sufficient condition for the truth of B if A implies B.

conditional. See *implication.*

conditional proof. A proof that begins by making certain assumptions, $A_1, A_2, \cdots, A_n$, deducing B from them, and then asserting on the basis of this the truth of the hypothetical proposition "if A_1, then if A_2, then if $\ldots$, then if A_n, then B." The *rule of conditionalization* is the rule that allows one to make this last step on the basis of the preceding ones.

conjunction. A binary propositional connective (&, .), usually read "and," whose truth table is such that "A and B" is false when A or B or both are false and is true when both are true.

connective. A symbol that is used with one or more

constants or forms to produce a new constant or form. When the constants or forms are propositional ones the connective is known as a *propositional connective* (or *sentential connective*). The most common propositional connectives are negation, conjunction, disjunction, implication, and biconditional. They are classified as *singulary*, *binary*, etc., according to the number of propositional constants or forms with which they combine. See article LOGIC, MODERN.

connotation. See *meaning, Frege's theory of.*

consequence. Any proposition that can be deduced from a given set of propositions. Thus, given the set of propositions {A, if A then B}, the proposition B is a consequence of the set, since it can be deduced from the members of the set by one application of *modus ponens.*

consequent. The part of a hypothetical proposition that follows the implication sign or the "then."

consequentia. The name given by medieval logicians to a true hypothetical proposition. *Formal* consequentiae (those which hold for all substitutions of the categorematic terms) were distinguished from *material* consequentiae (those holding only for particular categorematic terms).

consistency. A set of propositions has consistency (or is consistent) when no contradiction can be derived from the joint assertion of the propositions in the set. A logistic system has consistency when no contradiction can be derived in it. Two syntactical definitions of the consistency of a logistic system are Alfred Tarski's, that a system is consistent if not every well-formed formula is a theorem, and E. L. Post's, that a system is consistent if no well-formed formula consisting of only a propositional variable is a theorem. There is, in addition, a semantical definition of consistency, according to which a set of propositions (or a logistic system) is consistent if there is a model for that set of propositions (or for the set of all the theorems of the system). It must not be assumed that any of these definitions are equivalent; in any case where it is claimed that they are, a proof is required.

constant. A symbol which, under the principal interpretation, is a name for something definite, be it an individual, a property, a relation, etc.

constructive existence proof. A proof of the existence of a mathematical object having a property P which gives an example of such an object or at least a method by which one could find such an example.

contingent. Logically possible. See *logical possibility.*

continuity. An ordered dense class all of whose non-empty subsets which have an upper bound have a least upper bound has continuity (or is continuous). See article CONTINUITY.

continuum hypothesis. The hypothesis, proposed by Georg Cantor, that the cardinality of the power set of a set whose cardinality is aleph-null ($\aleph_0$) is aleph-one ($\aleph_1$)—that is, that there is no set whose cardinality is greater than aleph-null but less than the cardinality of the power set of a set whose cardinality is aleph-null. The *generalized continuum hypothesis* is the hypothesis that for the cardinality of any infinite set, the next highest cardinality is the cardinality of its power set.

contradiction. The joint assertion of a proposition and its denial.

contradiction, law of. See *laws of thought.*

contradictory. Two propositions are contradictory if and only if their joint assertion would be a contradiction. "All men are mortal" and "Some men are not mortal," for example, are contradictory propositions. Two terms are contradictory when they jointly exhaust a universe of discourse and are mutually exclusive. In the domain of natural numbers other than 0, for example, "odd" and "even" are contradictory terms. See *contrary.*

contraposition. In traditional logic, a type of immediate inference in which from a given proposition another proposition is inferred which has as its subject the contradictory of the original predicate. (It should be noted that a change of quality is involved in some cases.) *Partial* contraposition results in a new proposition that is the same as the subject of the original proposition; *full* contraposition results in a predicate of the new proposition that is the contradictory of the subject of the original proposition. The process of contraposition (whether partial or full) yields an equivalent proposition only when the original proposition is an A- or O-proposition; when it is an E-proposition traditional logicians allowed for contraposition *per accidens* (or by limitation)—that is, contraposition plus a change in the quantity of the proposition from universal to particular—claiming that the proposition formed is equivalent to the original proposition. The process of contraposition yields no equivalent proposition when the original proposition is an I-proposition. See article LOGIC, TRADITIONAL.

contrary. Applied to two propositions that cannot both be true but can both be false. "All men are mortal" and "No men are mortal," for example, are contrary propositions. Also applied to two terms that are mutually exclusive, but need not be jointly exhaustive, in a universe of discourse. In the domain of natural numbers, for instance, "less than 7" and "more than 19" are contrary terms. See *contradictory.*

contrary-to-fact (counterfactual) conditional. A conditional proposition whose antecedent is known to be false.

converse domain of a relation (range of a relation). For any relation R, the set of all objects a such that there exists an object b such that bRa.

converse of a relation (inverse of a relation). For any relation R, the relation R* such that aR*b if and only if bRa.

conversion. In traditional logic, a type of immediate inference in which from a given proposition another proposition is inferred which has as its subject the predicate of the original proposition and as its predicate the subject of the original proposition (the quality of the proposition being retained). The process of conversion yields an equivalent proposition only when the original proposition is an E- or I-proposition; when it is an A-proposition traditional logicians allowed for conversion *per accidens* (or by limitation)—that is, conversion plus a change in the quantity of the proposition from universal to particular. Thus, the E-proposition "No men are immortal" yields "No immortals are men," but the A-proposition "All men are mortal" can be converted only by limitation, yielding "Some mortals are men." The process of conversion yields no equivalent proposition if the original proposition is an O-proposition. See article LOGIC, TRADITIONAL.

copula. In traditional logic, the term that connects the subject and predicate in a categorical proposition. It is always a form of the verb "to be."

corollary. A proposition that follows so obviously from a theorem that it requires little or no demonstration.

counterfactual conditional. See **contrary-to-fact conditional.**

course-of-values induction. An argument from mathematical induction such that in the induction step one proves that "if the property P holds for all numbers before a, it holds for a as well," where a is any number.

Darapti. See **mnemonic terms.**

Darii. See **mnemonic terms.**

Datisi. See **mnemonic terms.**

decision problem. The problem of finding an algorithm (a *decision procedure*) which enables one to arrive, in a finite number of steps, at an answer to any question belonging to a given class of questions. For a logistic system in particular, this is the problem of finding a decision procedure for determining, for any arbitrary well-formed formula of the system, whether or not it is a theorem of the system.

A positive solution to a decision problem consists of a proof that a decision procedure exists. A negative solution to a decision problem consists of a proof that no such procedure is possible. An example of a positive solution is the proof that the truth tables provide a decision procedure for the propositional calculus; an example of a negative proof is Church's theorem. See articles LOGIC, MODERN; SYSTEMS, FORMAL, AND MODELS OF FORMAL SYSTEMS.

decision procedure. See **decision problem.**

Dedekind finite. See *finite set.*

Dedekind infinite. See *finite set.*

deducible. A set of propositions is said to be deducible from another set of propositions if and only if there is a valid deductive inference which has the latter set as its premises and the former set as its conclusion.

deduction. A form of inference such that in a valid deductive argument the joint assertion of the premises and the denial of the conclusion is a contradiction.

deduction theorem. For a given logistic system, the metatheorem that states that if there is a proof in the system of A_{n+1} from the assumptions $A_1, A_2, \cdots, A_n$, then there is also a proof in the system of the proposition "if A_n, then A_{n+1}" from the assumptions $A_1, \cdots, A_{n-1}$.

definiendum. That which is defined in a definition.

definiens. That which, in a definition, defines the definiendum.

definite descriptions, theory of. A definite description is a description which, by virtue of the meanings of the words in it, can apply to only one object. A standard example of a definite description is "the author of *Waverley.*" The theory of definite descriptions, introduced by Bertrand Russell, aims at eliminating definite descriptions. Unlike most other eliminative theories, Russell's does not attempt to offer a way of explicitly defining definite descriptions. Instead, it shows how in any given context the description together with the context can be eliminated in such a way that the resulting linguistic expression is equivalent to the original one. It is for this reason that Russell's theory is said to offer a way of contextually defining definite descriptions.

If we symbolize the definite description as "$(\imath x)P$" ("the unique x such that P," where P is any well-formed expression), Russell's theory can be stated as follows (unless otherwise indicated, it will be supposed that the scope of the occurrence of a definite description is the smallest well-formed part of the formula that contains that occurrence of the definite description): Let us symbolize the scope of the definite description as M and the whole formula as A. M is replaced by the expression "$(\exists y)(z)[(Pz \equiv z = y) . M']$," where y and z are the first two variables not occurring in A and M' is the result of substituting y for every occurrence of "$(\imath x)P$" in M. The resulting formula, A', is equivalent to A but lacks the definite description that we set out to eliminate.

The motivation for this theory is to be found in certain difficulties that arose for Russell's theory of meaning, the theory that the meaning of a term is its reference. It has been suggested, primarily by W. V. Quine, that since similar difficulties can arise for names in general, this theory should be extended to all names. Russell, however, thought that there was a class of names, *logically proper names,* for which these difficulties could not arise; he therefore favored retaining names of this class. See article PROPER NAMES AND DESCRIPTIONS.

definition. The description or explanation of the meaning of a word or phrase. Various types of definitions have been distinguished by logicians. To begin with, there is the distinction between a *lexical* definition (a report of a meaning the word already has) and a *stipulative* definition (a proposal to assign a meaning to a word). One must also distinguish, with traditional logicians, the following techniques for defining: (1) *dictionary* definition, giving a word or phrase that is synonymous with the definiendum; (2) *ostensive* definition, giving examples of objects to which the word or phrase is properly applied; and (3) definition *per genus et differentiam,* giving the genus of the objects to which a word or phrase is properly applied and the differentiae that distinguish these objects from the other members of the genus. See *predicables.*

Some new types of definition that have been discussed by contemporary logicians include (4) definition *by abstraction,* defining a class term by specifying the properties that an object must have in order to be a member of the class, and (5) *recursive (inductive)* definition, defining a number-theoretic function or predicate term by giving the value or values of the function or predicate when 0 is the argument and then giving the value or values when the successor of any number a is the argument in terms of a and the value when a is the argument (cf. *recursive function*). Finally, one must distinguish (6) *contextual* definitions, which give meaning to the definiendum only in particular contexts, not in isolation.

definition, Aristotelian theory of. See *predicables.*

demonstration (derivation). A deductive proof offered for a given set of propositions.

De Morgan's laws. The theorems of propositional calculus that assert the material equivalence of "not $(A$ or $B)$" with "not-A and not-B" and "not $(A$ and $B)$" with "not-A or not-B." De Morgan, in his book *Formal Logic,* did not actually state these laws; he gave, instead, the corresponding laws for the logic of classes. It should be noted that some of the medieval logicians stated these theorems for the logic of propositions.

denotation. See *meaning, Frege's theory of.*

dense. Used of an ordered set such that between any two elements of the set there is another element of the set.

denumerable set. A set whose cardinality is aleph-null ($\aleph_0$). Some authors extend "denumerable" so as to make it synonymous with "enumerable."

derivable. See *deducible.*

derivation. See *demonstration.*

derived rule of inference. A metalinguistic theorem asserting that under certain conditions there is a proof in the object language for a certain type of well-formed formula. The point of such theorems is that they enable us to state that certain well-formed formulas are theorems of the object language without having to find a proof in the object language for these formulas.

descending induction. An argument that shows that a certain property holds for no number by demonstrating that if it held for any number, it must hold for a lesser number.

diagonal proof. The proof, given by Georg Cantor, that there are infinite sets that cannot be enumerated.

dichotomy. See *classification.*

dictum de omni et nullo. The principle of syllogistic reasoning that asserts that whatever is distributively predicated (whether affirmatively or negatively) of any class must be predicated of anything belonging to that class.

difference of sets. For any two sets a and b, the set of all and only those objects that are members of a but not of b.

differentia. See *predicables.*

dilemma. An argument whose major premise is the conjunctive assertion of two hypothetical propositions and whose minor premise is a disjunctive proposition. If the minor premise alternatively affirms the antecedents of the major premise, the dilemma is said to be *constructive;* if the minor premise alternatively denies the consequents of the major premise, the dilemma is said to be *destructive.* Constructive dilemmas are divided into *simple constructive* dilemmas (the antecedents of the major premise are different and the consequents are the same) and *complex constructive* dilemmas (both the antecedents and the consequents of the major premise are different). Destructive dilemmas are divided into *simple destructive* dilemmas (the consequents of the major premise are different and the antecedents are the same) and *complex destructive* dilemmas (both the consequents and the antecedents of the major premise are different).

Dimaris. See *mnemonic terms.*

Disamis. See *mnemonic terms.*

discreteness. The property possessed by all ordered sets that lack the property of continuity.

disjoint sets. Sets that have no members in common.

disjunction, exclusive (alternation). A binary propositional connective, one possible interpretation of "or," whose truth table is such that "A or B" is true if and only if one of the two propositions is true and the other false.

disjunction, inclusive. A binary propositional connective (v), one possible interpretation of "or," whose truth table is such that "A or B" is true in all cases except where both A and B are false.

distributed term. In a categorical proposition the occurrence of a term is distributed if and only if the term as used in that occurrence covers all the members of the class that it denotes. In a universal categorical proposition the subject is distributed; in a negative categorical proposition the predicate is distributed.

distributivity. The relation that exists between two relations R and R^* when "$aR(bR^*c)$" is identical with "$(aRb)R^*(aRc)$."

division. See *classification.*

division non faciat saltum. See *classification.*

domain of a relation. For any relation R, the set of all objects a such that there exists an object b such that aRb.

domain of individuals. For a given interpretation of a given logistic system, the set of objects that is the range of the individual variables.

duality. The relation that exists between two formulas that are the same except for the interchanging of the universal with the existential quantifier, the symbol for the null class with that for the universal class, sum of sets with product of sets, and conjunction with disjunction (where conjunction, disjunction, and negation are taken as primitive, all other propositional connectives being defined in terms of them). The two formulas are said to be the duals of each other. "A and B" and "A or B," for example, are duals.

dyadic relation. A two-place relation.

effectiveness. A notion is said to be effective if there exists an algorithm for determining, in a finite number of steps, whether or not the notion applies to any given object. For example, in a logistic system the notion of a proof is effective, since there is a mechanical procedure for determining, in a finite number of steps, whether or not in that system a given sequence of well-formed formulas constitutes a proof of another given well-formed formula.

element. A member of a given set.

elementary number theory. The theory of numbers insofar as it does not involve analysis.

empty set. See *null set.*

entailment. The relation that exists between two propositions one of which is deducible from the other.

enthymeme. A syllogism in which one of the premises or the conclusion is not explicitly stated. An example of an enthymeme is the inference of "Socrates is mortal" from "All men are mortal," the missing premise being "Socrates is a man."

enumerable set. A set that either is finite or has a cardinality of aleph-null ($\aleph_0$). Cf. *denumerable set.*

epagoge. In traditional logic, the process of establishing a general proposition by induction.

epicheirema. A syllogism in which one or more of the premises is stated as the conclusion of an enthymematic prosyllogism. See *polysyllogism.*

episyllogism. See *polysyllogism.*

E-proposition. In traditional logic, a universal negative categorical proposition. An example is "No men are mortal."

epsilon. In set theory, the name of the symbol (ϵ) for set-membership.

equality. A relation that exists between two or more sets, equated by some authors with *identity* and by others with *equivalence relation.*

equipollent. Used of sets between which there exists a one-to-one correspondence.

equivalence relation. A relation that is reflexive, symmetric, and transitive (see *relation*). Identity is a standard example of an equivalence relation.

equivalent. Used of two propositions that are so related that one is true if and only if the other is true. Some authors also use this term, as applied to sets, synonymously with "equipollent."

equivocation. See *fallacy.*

eristic. The art of fallacious but persuasive reasoning.

essence. See *predicables.*

Euler's diagrams. The representations, generally attributed to Leonhard Euler, of relations among classes by relations among circles. See article LOGIC DIAGRAMS.

excluded middle, law of. See *laws of thought.*

existential generalization, rule of. The rule of inference that permits one to infer from a statement of the form "Property P holds for an object a" a statement of the form "There exists an object such that property P holds for it."

existential import. The commitment to the existence of certain objects that is entailed by a given proposition.

existential instantiation, rule of. The rule of inference that permits one to infer from a statement of the form "There exists an object such that property P holds for it" a statement of the form "Property P holds for an object a." Because this inference is not generally valid, restrictions have to be placed on its use.

existential quantifier. The symbol $(E\ )$ or $(\exists\ )$, read "there exists." It is used in combination with a variable and placed before a well-formed formula, as in "$(\exists a)$_____" ("There exists an object a such that _____").

extension. Although often used synonymously with "denotation," this term is sometimes used to refer to the set of species that are contained within the genus denoted by a given term. In the first sense the extension of "men" is the set of all men; in the second sense it is the set of sets into which mankind can be divided.

extensional. Used of an approach to a problem which in some respect confines attention to truth-values of sentences rather than to their meanings. Thus, a logic in which, for purposes of deductive relations, truth-values may be substituted for sentences is an extensional logic. Cf. *intensional.*

extensionality, axiom of. An axiom in set theory stating that for any two sets a and b, if for all c, c is a member of a if and only if c is a member of b, then a is identical with b.

fallacy. An argument which seems to be valid but really is not. There are many possible types of fallacy; traditional logicians have discussed the following ones: (1) *accentus,* a fallacy of ambiguity, where the ambiguity arises from the emphasis (accent) placed on a word or phrase; (2) *affirmation of the consequent,* an argument from the truth of a hypothetical statement and the truth of the consequent to the truth of the antecedent; (3) *ambiguity,* an argument in the course of which at least one term is used in different senses; (4) *amphiboly,* a fallacy of ambiguity where the ambiguity involved is of an amphibolous nature; (5) *argumentum ad baculum,* an argument that resorts to the threat of force to cause the acceptance of the conclusion; (6) *argumentum ad hominem,* an argument that attempts to disprove the truth of what is asserted by attacking the asserter or attempts to prove the truth of what is asserted by appealing to the opponent's special circumstances; (7) *argumentum ad ignorantiam,* an argument that a proposition is true because it has not been shown to be false, or vice versa; (8) *argumentum ad misericordiam,* an argument that appeals to pity for the sake of getting a conclusion accepted; (9) *argumentum ad populum,* an argument that appeals to the beliefs of the multitude; (10) *argumentum ad verecundiam,* an argument in which an authority is appealed to on matters outside his field of authority; (11) *begging the question* (*circular reasoning*), an argument that assumes as part of the premises the conclusion that is supposed to be proved; (12) *composition,* an argument in which one assumes that a whole has a property solely because its various parts have that property; (13) *denial of the antecedent,* an argument in which one infers the falsity of the consequent from the truth of a hypothetical proposition and the falsity of its antecedent; (14) *division,* an argument in which one assumes that various parts have a property solely because the whole has that property; (15) *equivocation,* an argument in which an equivocal expression is used in one sense in one premise and in a different sense in another premise or in the conclusion; (16) *ignoratio elenchi,* an argument that is supposed to prove one proposition but succeeds only in proving a different one; (17) *illicit process,* a syllogistic argument in which a term is distributed in the conclusion but not in the premises; (18) *many questions,* a demand for a simple answer to a complex question; (19) *non causa pro causa,* an argument to reject a proposition because of the falsity of some other proposition that seems to be a consequence of the first but really is not; (20) *non sequitur,* an argument in which the conclusion is not a necessary consequence of the premises; (21) *petitio principii,* see (11) *begging the question;* (22) *post hoc, ergo propter hoc,* argument from a premise of the form "A preceded B" to a conclusion of the form "A caused B"; (23) *quaternio terminorum,* an argument of the syllogistic form in which there occur four or more terms; (24) *secundum quid,* an argument in which a proposition is used as a premise without attention given to some obvious condition that would affect the proposition's application; (24) *undistributed middle,* a syllogistic argument in which the middle term is not distributed in at least one of the premises. See article FALLACIES.

Felapton. See *mnemonic terms.*

Ferio. See *mnemonic terms.*

Ferison. See *mnemonic terms.*

Fesapo. See *mnemonic terms.*

Festino. See *mnemonic terms.*

field of a relation. The union of the domain and the converse domain of a given relation.

figure. A way of classifying categorical propositions. According to most traditional logicians, since figure depends on the position of the middle term in the premises, there are four possible figures. In the first figure the middle term is the subject of the major premise and the predicate of the minor premise. In the second figure the middle term is the predicate of both premises and in the third figure the subject of both premises. In the fourth figure the middle term is the predicate of the major premise and the subject of the minor premise. Aristotle allowed only three figures and treated as being indirectly in the first figure those syllogisms that later logicians placed in the fourth. See article LOGIC, TRADITIONAL.

finitary method. The type of method to which David Hilbert and some of his followers restricted themselves in their metamathematical research. The clearest statement of the restrictions was made by Jacques Herbrand, who insisted that the following conditions be met: (1) One must deal only with a finite and determined number of objects and functions. (2) These are to be so defined that there is a univocal calculation of their values. (3) One should never affirm the existence of an object without indicating how to construct it. (4) One must never deal with the set of all the objects of an infinite totality. (5) That a theorem holds for all of a set of objects means that for every particular object it is possible to repeat the general argument in question, which should then be treated as only a prototype of the resulting particular arguments.

finite set (inductive set). A set that either is empty or is such that there exists a one-to-one correspondence between its members and the members of the set of all natural numbers less than a specified natural number. A set which is not finite is said to be *infinite.*

Richard Dedekind introduced a different characterization of finite and infinite sets. A *Dedekind finite* set is one that has no proper subset such that there exists a one-to-one correspondence between the elements of the set and the elements of that proper subset. A *Dedekind infinite* set (or *reflexive* set) is one that is not Dedekind finite. It can be shown that Dedekind's characterization is equivalent to the previous one; the proof, however, involves the axiom of choice.

first element of a set. See *bound of a set.*

first-order logic. First-order functional calculus. See *calculus.*

formalism. The doctrine, advanced as a program by David Hilbert and his followers, that the only foundations necessary for mathematics are its formalization and a proof by finitary methods that the system thus produced is consistent. See article MATHEMATICS, FOUNDATIONS OF.

formalization. The construction of a logistic system whose intended interpretation is such that under it the truths of a given body of knowledge are the interpreted theorems of the system.

formalized language. A logistic system with an interpretation.

formally imply. A proposition A is said to formally imply a proposition B in a given logistic system if there is, in that system, a valid proof of B from A taken as a hypothesis.

formal system. See *logistic system.*

formation rules. For a given logistic system, the rules that determine which combinations of symbols are well-formed formulas and which are not.

formula. For a given logistic system, any sequence of primitive symbols.

foundation, axiom of (Axiom der fundierung, axiom of regularity). An axiom in set theory stating that every nonempty set a contains a member b which has no member in common with a.

free occurrence of a variable. For a given variable a that occurs in a given well-formed formula A, an occurrence of a in no well-formed part of A which is of the form "For all a, B" or of the form "There exists an a, B."

free variable. A free variable of a formula A is a variable in A that has no bound occurrence in A.

Fresison. See *mnemonic terms.*

function. A many–one correspondence.

functional calculus. See *calculus.*

future contingents, problem of. The problem, first discussed by Aristotle, of whether any contingent statement about the future has a truth-value prior to the time it refers to.

Galenian figure. The fourth syllogistic figure, supposedly introduced by Galen.

generalization, rule of. The rule of inference that allows one to infer from every proposition another proposition that is the same as the original one except that it is preceded by a universal quantifier binding any variable.

general term. A term that is predicable, in the same sense, of more than one individual.

Gentzen's consistency proof. The proof, first given by Gerhard Gentzen in 1936, of the consistency of classical pure number theory with the unrestricted-induction postulate. The proof employs transfinite induction up to the ordinal ϵ_0.

Gentzen system. A system of logic characterized by the introduction into the object language of a new connective (symbolized by $\rightarrow$) that has properties analogous to the ordinary metalinguistic idea of "provable in the system." The rules of inference of such a system apply to *Sequenzen*—that is, to formulas of the form "$A_1, A_2, \cdots, A_n \rightarrow B_1, B_2, \cdots, B_m$," where m and n are equal to or greater than 0, and $A_1, A_2, \cdots, A_n, B_1, B_2, \cdots, B_m$ are formulas of ordinary logical systems.

genus. See *predicables.*

Gödel-numbering. The assignment of a natural number to each entity of a formal system. See *arithmetization of syntax.*

Gödel's completeness theorem. The theorem, first introduced by Kurt Gödel in 1930, that every valid well-formed formula of pure first-order functional calculus is a theorem of that system.

Gödel's incompleteness theorems. Two theorems which were first proved by Kurt Gödel in 1931. One states that any ω-consistent system adequate for elementary number theory is such that there is a valid well-formed formula of the system not provable in the system. J. B. Rosser, in 1936, extended this result to any consistent system. The second theorem states that any consistent system adequate for elementary number theory is such that there can be no proof of the consistency of the system within the system. See article GÖDEL'S THEOREM.

Gödel–von Neumann–Bernays set theory. The form of axiomatic set theory that avoids the paradoxes of set theory by distinguishing between sets (collections that can also be elements of other collections) and classes (collections that cannot be elements of other collections) and ensuring that all the objects leading to paradoxes (for example, the universal class) are classes and not sets.

Henkin's completeness theorem. The theorem, proved by Leon Henkin in 1947, that every secondarily valid well-formed formula of pure second-order functional calculus is a theorem of that system.

hereditary property. See **ancestral relation.**

Hilbert program. See **formalism.**

ideal mathematics. For David Hilbert, the nonfinitary part of mathematics, which, although necessary, was suspect and therefore required a consistency proof. See **real mathematics.**

idempotency. A binary operation is idempotent if and only if that operation, when performed on any element with itself, results in just that element.

identically false. Used of a well-formed formula of propositional calculus whose truth-value is falsehood for all possible values of its constituent well-formed formulas.

identically true. Used of a well-formed formula of propositional calculus whose truth-value is truth for all possible values of its constituent well-formed formulas.

identity. A relation that holds only between an object and itself.

identity, law of. See **laws of thought.**

identity of indiscernibles. Leibniz' principle that two objects are identical if for every class, one object belongs to the class if and only if the other does. This is not to be confused with what W. V. Quine has called the *indiscernibility of identicals,* the principle that if two objects are identical, they belong to the same classes.

iff. A common abbreviation for "if and only if." See **biconditional.**

ignoratio elenchi. See **fallacy.**

image. The members of the converse domain of a relation that are values of the relation when its argument is a member of a set that is part of its domain.

immediate inference. An inference of a conclusion from a single premise. Traditional logicians discussed two types: (1) *opposition of propositions,* the inference, from the truth or falsity of one proposition, of the truth or falsity of another proposition having the same subject and predicate (such inferences involve contradictory, contrary, subalternate, and subcontrary propositions), and (2) *eductions,* the inference, from one proposition, of another differing from it in subject or predicate or in both (these involve obversion, conversion, contraposition, and inversion).

imperfect figures. The second and third syllogistic figures, the valid arguments of which, according to Aristotle, are such that their validity can be known only by their reduction to valid syllogisms in the perfect first figure.

implication (conditional). A binary propositional connective ($\rightarrow$, $\supset$), usually read "if–then," of which there are two major interpretations: (1) *Material implication.* Under this interpretation, "If A then B" is true in all cases except when A is true and B false. (2) *Strict implication.* Under this interpretation, "If A then B" is true only when B is deducible from A. *Philonian* implication is the Stoic version of material implication, and *Diodorean* implication is the Stoic interpretation of "if–then" according to which "If A then B" is true if whenever (in the past, present, or future) A is true, B is also true.

implicit definition. A set of axioms implicitly define the undefined terms in them by, in effect, confining the references of these terms to the intended ones. The axioms do this by stating conditions satisfiable by only one set of objects.

The idea that a set of axioms can implicitly define the undefined terms in them is usually credited to J. D. Gergonne (1819). It was once thought that the basic terms of arithmetic could be implicitly defined by the axioms (namely, Peano's postulates) containing them; however, it is now known that this cannot be done, since Peano's postulates admit of more than one interpretation.

impredicative definition. Definition of an object in terms of a totality of which it is a member. For an example of impredicative definition, see **ancestral relation.**

inclusion. A relation that holds between two sets when all the members of one are members of the other. The relation of set-inclusion must be distinguished from that of set-membership.

inconsistent. Used of a set of propositions from which, or a logistic system in which, a contradiction can be derived.

indemonstrables. The Stoics' name for the axioms of their propositional logic.

independence. An axiom A of a given logistic system is independent (or has independence) if and only if in the system obtained by omitting A from the axioms of the given system, A is not a theorem. A rule of inference R of a given logistic system is independent if and only if in the system obtained by omitting R from the rules of inference of the given system, R is not a derived rule of inference.

indirect proof (reductio ad absurdum). An argument which proves a proposition A by showing that the denial of A, together with accepted propositions B_1, B_2, $\cdots$, B_n, leads to a contradiction. Strictly speaking, this fails to prove the truth of A, since one of the previously accepted premises may be false; the force of the argument therefore rests on using premises that are far better established than the denial of A, so that the denial of A will be rejected and A accepted.

individual (particular). (1) Anything considered as a unit. (2) In the theory of types, any member of the lowest type.

induction. Among acceptable inferences, logicians distinguish those in which the joint assertion of the premises and the denial of the conclusion is a contradiction from those in which that joint assertion is not a contradiction. The former are deductive inferences; inductive inferences are to be found among the latter.

Much has been written about the precise nature of inductive inferences, but few definite results have been obtained. It is likely that there is a wide variety of types of inductive inferences. Two quite different types are the inference from observational data to theoretical conclusions and the inference from the composition of a sample to the composition of a whole population.

induction, mathematical. An inference of the form "0 has the property P; if any natural number a has the property P, then its successor has the property P; therefore, every natural number has the property P." The first step is called the *basis,* or the *zero step,* of the induction, and the second is called the *induction step.*

inductive set. See **finite set.**

inference. Derivation of a proposition (the conclusion) from a set of other propositions (the premises). When the inference is acceptable the premises afford good reasons to assert, or render certain, the conclusion.

infima species. See **classification.**

infinite set. See **finite set.**

infinity, axiom of. An axiom in set theory that guarantees the existence of an infinite number of individuals. This axiom takes various forms, all having in common the property of being valid in at least one infinite domain of individuals while not being valid in any finite domain of individuals.

initial ordinal. An ordinal that is not equipollent with any smaller ordinal.

insolubilia. The medieval name for antinomies. The antinomies that are usually referred to by this name are variants of the Liar paradox.

intension. A term sometimes used by traditional authors as synonymous with "connotation." In contemporary logical works "intension" has come to be synonymous with "sense." See **meaning, Frege's theory of.**

intensional. (1) Used of an approach which in some respect considers the meaning as well as the truth-value of a formula. A characteristic of such systems is that some propositions in them are referentially opaque. Systems of modal logic are usually intensional systems.

(2) Used of a proposition that contains a referentially opaque part. Cf. **extensional.**

intention, first (primary). In medieval logic, signs that signify things and not other signs are said to have first intention. See article LOGIC, TRADITIONAL.

intention, second (secondary). In medieval logic, signs that signify other signs and not things are said to have second intention. See article LOGIC, TRADITIONAL.

interpretation. An interpretation of a set A of well-formed formulas consists of a nonempty set (the *domain of the interpretation*) and a function which assigns to each individual constant appearing in any of the members of A some fixed element in the domain, to each n-place predicate letter appearing in any of the members of A some n-place relation in the domain, and to each n-place function letter appearing in any member of A some function whose arguments are n-tuples of elements of the domain and whose values are also elements of the domain. The individual variables are thought of as ranging over the elements of the domain, and the connectives are given some meaning. Such an interpretation provides meaning for the members of A.

The *principal* interpretation is the intended interpretation. The *secondary* interpretations of a set of well-formed formulas are all the interpretations, other than the principal one, such that under them all the members of the set are true.

intersection of sets (product of sets). The set of all the objects that are elements of all the sets $a_1, a_2, \cdots, a_n$ (symbolized "$a_1 \cap a_2 \cap \cdots \cap a_n$").

intuitionism. The doctrine, advanced by L. E. J. Brouwer and his followers, whose key thesis is that a mathematical entity with a particular property exists only if a constructive existence proof can be given for it. As a result the actual infinite is ruled out of mathematics, and only denumerably infinite sets, viewed as potentially infinite, are allowed. Furthermore, the law of excluded middle is rejected in the sense that when infinite classes are being dealt with, a disproof of a universal statement is not automatically a proof of its denial—that is, an existential statement. See article MATHEMATICS, FOUNDATIONS OF.

intuitive set theory. The form of set theory that is based on an unrestricted use of the axiom of abstraction. The paradoxes of set theory were generated within a system of intuitive set theory.

inverse of a relation. See **converse of a relation.**

inversion. In traditional logic, a type of immediate inference in which from a given proposition another proposition is inferred whose subject is the contradictory of the subject of the original proposition. See article LOGIC, TRADITIONAL.

iota operator. The definite description operator, $\imath$. It is read: "The unique _____ such that _____."

I-proposition. In traditional logic, a particular affirmative categorical proposition. An example is "Some men are mortal."

joint denial. A binary propositional connective ($\downarrow$) whose truth table is such that "A joint-denial B" is true if and only if both A and B are false. Joint denial and the Sheffer stroke function are the only binary propositional connectives that are adequate for the construction of all truth-functional connectives.

judgment. (1) The affirming or denying of a proposition. (2) The proposition affirmed or denied.

Lambert's diagrams. The representation, introduced by J. H. Lambert, of relations among classes by relations among straight lines.

law of logic. Any general truth of logic.

laws of thought. Three laws of logic that were traditionally treated as basic and fundamental to all thought. They were (1) *the law of contradiction,* that nothing can be both P and not-P, (2) *the law of excluded middle,* that anything must be either P or not-P; and (3) *the law of identity,* that if anything is P, then it is P.

lekton. The Stoic name for the sense of a formula.

lemma. A theorem proved in the course of, and for the sake of, the proof of a different theorem.

level (order). In the ramified theory of types, a class of objects that is composed of all and only those objects such that the definition of one of them requires no reference to a totality containing other members of the class. A hierarchy of levels is built up by beginning with the class of those objects that can be defined without reference to any totality and continuing with succeeding levels, members of each of which are defined in terms of totalities of objects of the previous level.

Liar paradox. See **paradox, Epimenides' paradox.**

limit. For a given sequence of numbers, the number a such that for any arbitrarily small number b greater than 0 there exists a number c such that for any number d larger than c the absolute value of the difference between the dth member of the sequence and a is less than b.

limit number. An ordinal number that is not 0 and is such that if a is a member of it, then the successor of a is also a member of it.

limit ordinal. See **limit number.**

logic. The study of the validity of different kinds of inference. This term is often used synonymously with *deductive* logic, the branch of logic concerned with inferences whose premises cannot be true without the conclusion's also being true. The other major branch of logic, *inductive* logic, is concerned with inferences whose premises can be true even if the conclusion is false.

logical fiction. The apparent denotation of a symbol that really has no denotation. Formulas containing such symbols are translatable into formulas containing no symbol or symbols that even appear to have this denotation.

logical form. It is commonly said that logic is concerned with the form, not the matter, of a proposition or argument. The distinction between form and matter is, however, seldom made precise; it can therefore best be seen by consideration of an example:

> If it is raining, people will carry umbrellas.
> It is raining.
> _____
> People will carry umbrellas.

Analysis of this inference shows that it is valid because it is of the form "If A, then B; A; therefore, B." The values of the variables make no difference in the validity of the argument. Formal logic is concerned with inferences, like this one, whose validity depends on their form.

As the example shows, the form of a proposition is nothing more than the result of substituting, in the proposition, free variables for the constants, whereas the *matter of a proposition* is that for which the variables are substituted. The form of an argument is the result of substituting, in all the premises and in the conclusion of the argument, free variables for constants.

In some contemporary works any formula that contains one or more free variables is called a form.

logical implication. The relation that holds between two propositions when one is deducible from the other.

logically necessary. See *analytic.*

logical possibility (possible truth). A proposition that is not self-contradictory. Some authors restrict this term to propositions that are also not logically necessary.

logical truth. See *analytic.*

logic diagram. A diagram used to represent logical relations. See article LOGIC DIAGRAMS.

logicism. The doctrine, advanced by Gottlob Frege and Bertrand Russell, that all the concepts of mathematics can be derived from logical concepts through explicit definitions and all the theorems of mathematics can be derived from logical axioms through purely logical deduction. See article MATHEMATICS, FOUNDATIONS OF.

logistic method. The method of studying a subject by formalizing it.

logistic system (formal system). A system whose primitive basis is explicitly stated in the metalanguage. See article SYSTEMS, FORMAL, AND MODELS OF FORMAL SYSTEMS.

Löwenheim's theorem. See *Skolem–Löwenheim theorem.*

major premise. In a categorical syllogism, the premise that contains the major term.

major term. In a categorical syllogism, the term that is the predicate of the conclusion.

many–one correspondence. A relation R such that for every element a of its domain there is only one member b of its converse domain such that aRb. "Son of" is a many–one correspondence since for every member of its domain (for every son) there is only one member of the converse domain (his father) of which it is true that the member of the domain is the son of the member of the converse domain.

many-valued logic. A system of logic in which each formula has more than two possible truth-values.

map of one set into another. A one-to-one correspondence between two sets whose domain is the first set and whose converse domain is a proper subset of the second set.

map of one set onto another. A one-to-one correspondence between two sets whose domain is the first set and whose converse domain is the second set.

material implication. See *implication;* article LOGIC, MODERN.

mathematical induction. See *induction, mathematical.*

matter of a proposition. See *logical form.*

meaning, Frege's theory of. According to this theory, propounded by Gottlob Frege in 1892, the meaning of a proper name has two aspects, the *sense* and the *reference.* The reference of a proper name is that which it is a name of. Thus, the reference of "Sir Walter Scott" is Sir Walter Scott. Frege claimed that there must be, besides the reference, another aspect of the meaning of such a name. "Sir Walter Scott" and "the author of Waverley" have the same reference, but it would be most implausible to say that they have the same meaning. The aspect of meaning that distinguishes "Sir Walter Scott" from "the author of Waverley" is called the sense of the proper name.

It should be noted that this is a theory of the meaning of proper names, not common names. It is for common names that John Stuart Mill first introduced his distinction between *denotation* (the objects to which the common name is properly applied) and *connotation* (the characteristic or set of characteristics that determines to which objects the common name properly applies). Unlike Frege, Mill thought that the meaning of a proper name is simply that which it denotes.

mediate inference. An inference in which the conclusion follows from two or more premises.

membership. The relation that exists between a set and its elements. The relation of set-membership must be distinguished from the relation of set-inclusion.

mention of a term. An occurrence of a linguistic expression in quotation marks for the purpose of talking about that linguistic expression. For example, in " 'Cicero' has six letters" it is not the orator himself but the word referring to him that is being discussed.

This is to be contrasted with *use of a term,* the occurrence of a linguistic expression for the purpose of talking about something other than the expression.

metalanguage. A language used to talk about an object language; a *meta-metalanguage* is a language used to talk about a metalanguage, and so forth. Derivatively, a proposition is said to be in the metalanguage if and only if it is about an expression in the object language.

metamathematics (proof theory). The study of logistic systems. Some authors restrict this term to investigations employing finitary methods.

metatheorem. A theorem in a metalanguage.

metatheory. The metamathematical investigations relating to a given logistic system.

method of construction. Bertrand Russell's name for the method of introducing new types of numbers by defining them in terms of previously introduced numbers and the usual logical and set-theoretic notation. Opposed to the method of construction is the *method of postulation*, whereby one introduces new types of numbers as primitive terms with appropriate axioms.

middle term. In a categorical syllogism, the term that occurs in both premises but not in the conclusion.

minor premise. In a categorical syllogism, the premise that contains the minor term.

minor term. In a categorical syllogism, the term that is the subject of the conclusion.

mnemonic terms. The names that the medieval logicians introduced for the valid syllogisms. One such term is "Barbara." The key for these mnemonics is as follows: The three vowels respectively indicate the three constituent propositions of the syllogism as A, E, I, or O. For first-figure syllogisms the initial consonants are arbitrarily the first four consonants; for the other figures the initial consonants indicate to which of the first-figure syllogisms the syllogism in question may be reduced. Other consonants occurring in second-, third-, and fourth-figure mnemonics indicate the operation that must be performed on the proposition indicated by the preceding vowel in order to reduce the syllogism to a first-figure syllogism. The key for this is as follows: "*s*" indicates simple conversion, "*p*" indicates conversion *per accidens*, "*m*" indicates metathesis (interchanging of the premises), "*k*" indicates obversion, and "*c*" indicates *convertio syllogism* (that is, the syllogism is to be reduced indirectly). In mnemonic terms the only meaningless letters are "*r*," "*t*," "*l*," "*n*," and noninitial "*b*" and "*d*." More elaborate mnemonics have been devised for syllogisms in which two or more of the premises exhibit modality. See article LOGIC, TRADITIONAL.

MNEMONIC TERMS

Name	Figure	Major Premise	Minor Premise	Conclusion
Barbara	first	A	A	A
Baroco	second	A	O	O
Bocardo	third	O	A	O
Bramantip	fourth	A	A	I
Camenes	fourth	A	E	E
Camestres	second	A	E	E
Celarent	first	E	A	E
Cesare	second	E	A	E
Darapti	third	A	A	I
Darii	first	A	I	I
Datisi	third	A	I	I
Dimaris	fourth	I	A	I
Disamis	third	I	A	I
Felapton	third	E	A	O
Ferio	first	E	I	O
Ferison	third	E	I	O
Fesapo	fourth	E	A	O
Festino	second	E	I	O
Fresison	fourth	E	I	O

modality. (1) The characteristic of propositions according to which they can be described as "apodictic," "assertoric," or "problematic." An *assertoric* proposition asserts that something is the case; an *apodictic* proposition asserts that something must be the case; a *problematic* proposition asserts that something may be the case. This type of modality was called by the medieval logicians *modality sine dicto* (*de re*).

(2) The characteristic of propositions according to which they can be described as "necessary," "impossible," "possible," or "not-necessary." Medieval logicians called this type *modality cum dicto* (*de dicto*).

modal logic. The study of inferential relations among propositions which are due to their modality. Most logicians treat systems of modal logic as intensional, basing them upon strict implication. An alternative approach is to treat these systems as extensional, basing them upon a many-valued logic. See article LOGIC, MODAL.

model. An interpretation of a given set of well-formed formulas according to which all the members of the set are true. The *standard* model corresponds to the principal interpretation, and a *nonstandard* model corresponds to a secondary interpretation. See *interpretation*.

modus ponendo tollens. An inference of the form "Either A or B; A; therefore, not-B." This type of inference is valid only if "or" is interpreted as exclusive disjunction.

modus ponens. An argument of the form "If A then B; A; therefore, B." Some authors use the term to designate the rule of inference that allows arguments of this form.

modus tollendo ponens. An argument of the form "Either A or B; not-A; therefore, B."

modus tollens. An argument of the form "If A then B; not-B; therefore, not-A." Some authors use the term to designate the rule of inference that allows arguments of this form.

mood. A way of classifying categorical syllogisms according to the quantity and quality of their constituent propositions.

multiplicative axiom. See *choice, axiom of*.

name. In traditional logic, a word or group of words that can serve as a term in a proposition. A *general* name is one that can be significantly applied to each member of a set of objects, a *singular* name is one that can be significantly applied to only one object, and a *collective* name is one that can be significantly applied to a group of similar things regarded as constituting a single whole.

natural number. A member of a certain subset of the cardinal numbers. There are various ways of defining this subset so that it contains all and only the desired objects (namely 0, 1, 2, 3, · · ·); the most common way is to define it as the set of all objects that belong to all sets containing 0 and closed under the successor relation.

necessary condition. See *condition*.

necessary truth. See *analytic*.

negate of a set. See *complement of a set*.

negation. A singulary propositional connective (¬, ⁻, ~, —), usually read "not," whose truth table is such that "not-A" is true if and only if A is false.

negative name. In traditional logic, a name that implies the absence of one or more properties or that denotes everything with the exception of some particular thing or set of things. An example of such a name is "non-Briton."

non sequitur. See *fallacy*.

normal system of domains. A system of domains such that the axioms of second-order functional calculus are valid in them and the rules of inference of second-order functional calculus preserve validity in them.

null set (empty set). A set with no members.

number. See *cardinal number; natural number; rational number; real number;* article NUMBER.

object language. A language used to talk about things, rather than about other languages. Derivatively, a proposition is said to be in the object language if and only if it is not about any linguistic expression. "Socrates was a philosopher" is therefore in the object language, whereas " 'Socrates' has eight letters" is not.

obversion. In traditional logic, a type of immediate inference in which from a given proposition another proposition is inferred whose subject is the same as the original subject, whose predicate is the contradictory of the original predicate, and whose quality is affirmative if the original proposition's quality was negative and vice versa. Obversion of a proposition yields an equivalent proposition when applied to all four types (A, E, I, and O) of propositions that traditional logicians considered. See article LOGIC, TRADITIONAL.

omega. The smallest infinite ordinal (denoted by ω), the order type associated with the set of all natural numbers as ordered in their natural order.

omega-complete. Used of a system which, if it contains the theorems that property P holds of 0, of 1, of 2, and so on, contains the theorem that P holds of all numbers.

omega-consistent. Used of a system which, if it contains the theorems that property P holds of 0, of 1, of 2, and so on, does not contain the theorem that P holds of all numbers.

one–many correspondence. A relation R such that for every member a of its converse domain, there is more than one object b that is a member of its domain such that bRa. "Father of" is an example of a one–many correspondence, since for every member of its converse domain (everyone who has a father) there is only one member of its domain (that person's father) such that the member of the domain is the father of the member of the converse domain.

one-to-one correspondence. A relation R such that for every member a of its converse domain, there is only one object b that is a member of its domain such that bRa. A one-to-one correspondence is said to be *order-preserving* if both its domain and its converse domain are simply ordered and if, for all c and d that are members of its domain and are such that c precedes d in the ordering of the domain, it is the case that their respective images e and f in the converse domain are such that e precedes f in the ordering of the converse domain.

open schema. A formula containing free individual and functional variables.

open sentence. A formula containing free individual variables.

operator. A symbol or combination of symbols that is syncategorematic under the principal interpretation of the logistic system it occurs in and that may be used with one or more variables and one or more constants or forms or both to produce a new constant or form. Universal and existential quantifiers are the most common examples of operators.

O-proposition. In traditional logic, a particular negative categorical proposition. An example is "Some men are not mortal."

order. See *level.*

ordered, partially. A set a is partially ordered if and only if there is a relation R such that for all $b, c,$ and d that are members of a, (1) if bRc and cRd, then bRd, and (2) it is not the case that bRb.

ordered, simply. A set a is simply ordered if and only if there is a relation R such that a is partially ordered by R and for all b and c that are members of a and are not identical, either bRc or cRb.

ordered, well. A set a is well ordered if and only if there is a relation R such that a is simply ordered by R and for every nonempty subset of a, there is a first element of that nonempty subset.

ordered pair. For given objects a and b, the ordered pair $\langle a,b \rangle$ is the pair set of which one member is the unit set whose only member is a and the other member is the pair set whose members are a and b.

order-preserving. See *one-to-one correspondence.*

order type. The set of all sets that are ordinally similar to a given set.

ordinally similar. Two or more sets are ordinally similar if and only if there exists between them a one-to-one order-preserving correspondence.

ordinal number. An order type of a well-ordered set.

pairing axiom. An axiom in set theory stating that for any two objects a and b, there is a set c whose members are a and b only.

pair set. A set that contains exactly two members.

paradox (antinomy). A statement whose truth leads to a contradiction and the truth of whose denial leads to a contradiction. Since F. P. Ramsey it has been customary to distinguish between *logical paradoxes* (often called *paradoxes of set theory*), which can arise in the object language because they involve only the usual logical and set-theoretic symbols, and *semantic paradoxes*, which can arise only in the metalanguage because they involve semantic concepts.

The most prominent logical paradoxes are the following: (1) *Russell's paradox.* Consider the set of all objects that are not members of themselves. Is that set a member of itself? If it is, then it is not. If it is not, then it is. (2) *Cantor's paradox.* Consider the set of all sets. Is it equal to or greater than its power set? If it is equal, then there is a contradiction, since there is a proof that the power set of any set is greater than the set itself. If it is not, then there is a contradiction, since the power set of any set is a set of sets and must therefore be a subset of the set of all sets, and there is a proof that the subset of a set cannot be greater than the set itself. (3) *Burali-Forti's paradox.* Consider the set of all ordinals. Does it have an ordinal number? If it does not, there is a contradiction, since by the "less than" relation it is well ordered, and there is a proof that all well-ordered sets have ordinal numbers. If it does, there is a contradiction, since it can be proved that the set's ordinal number must be both equal to and less than its image in the mapping of the set of all ordinals onto the set of all ordinals less than its own ordinal.

The most prominent of the semantic paradoxes are the following: (1) *Berry's paradox.* Consider the expression "the least natural number not namable in fewer than 22 syllables." Is the number it denotes namable in fewer than 22 syllables? If it is, there is a contradiction, since by definition it cannot be. If it is not, there is a contradiction, since we can produce a way of naming it in 21 syllables— the way we named it in stating this paradox. (2) *Epimenides' paradox.* Consider the sentence "This sentence is not true." Is it true? If it is, then it is not; if it is not; then it is. (3) *Grelling–Nelson paradox of heterologicality.* A predicate is heterological if the sentence ascribing the predicate to itself is false. Is the predicate "heterological" itself heterological? If it is, then it is not; if it is not, then it is. (4) *Paradox of the Liar.* See *Epimenides' paradox* (although the name is often used to refer to the nearly identical paradox beginning with the sentence "This statement expresses a lie"). (5) *Richard's paradox.* Consider the set of all real numbers between 0 and 1 that can be characterized in a finite number of English words. This set has only denumerably many members. It can be shown, in a manner very similar to Cantor's diagonal proof, that we can specify in a finite number of English words a number that cannot belong to the set. Does it belong to the set? If it does, there is a contradiction, since it cannot. If it does not, there is a contradiction, since it can be characterized in a finite number of English words, and all such numbers belong to the set. See article LOGICAL PARADOXES.

paradoxes of material implication. These so-called paradoxes consist in the fact that if "if _____ then _____" is taken in the sense of material implication, then any proposition of that form is true if the antecedent is false no matter what the consequent is or if the consequent is true no matter what the antecedent is. Thus, "If Eisenhower were premier of France, then the moon would be made of cheese" and "If $2 + 2 = 17$, then Johnson is the president of the United States" are both true propositions if "if–then" is interpreted in the sense of material implication. See article LOGIC, MODERN.

paralogism. Any fallacious reasoning.

particular. See *individual.*

Peano's postulates. A system of five postulates from which one can derive the rest of arithmetic. The five postulates are (1) 0 is a number; (2) the successor of any number is a number; (3) there are no two numbers with the same successor; (4) 0 is not the successor of any number; (5) every property of 0 also belonging to the successor of any number that has that property belongs to all numbers.

per accidens. Used of a predication to the subject of one of its accidents.

perfect figure. The first figure of the syllogism. According to Aristotle, this is the only figure to which the *dictum de omni et nullo* is directly applicable.

per se. Used of a predication to the subject of one of its essential attributes.

petitio principii. See *fallacy,* (11) *begging the question.*

polysyllogism. A series of syllogisms so linked that the conclusion of one is a premise of another. In such a series

a syllogism is said to be a *prosyllogism* if its conclusion is a premise of the syllogism with which it is connected and an *episyllogism* if one of its premises is the conclusion of the syllogism with which it is connected. See *sorites.*

possible truth. See *logical possibility.*

post hoc, ergo propter hoc. See *fallacy.*

postulate. Although often used synonymously with "axiom," this term is sometimes confined to the basic propositions of a particular discipline, with the axioms being the basic propositions common to all disciplines (for example, the laws of logic). The distinction arises only when one is concerned not merely with a formal system but also with its interpretation.

postulation, method of. See *method of construction.*

potential infinite. The infinite regarded as a limiting concept, as something becoming rather than as something completed.

power. See *cardinality.*

power set. The set of all subsets of a given set.

power-set axiom. An axiom in set theory stating that for any given set, its power set exists.

pragmatics. See *semantics, formal.*

predicables. A classification of things and concepts as predicated of subjects, first made by Aristotle. His four predicables were definition, genus (in which he included differentia), proprium, and accident. Medieval logicians, following Porphyry, offered a list of five predicables—species, differentia, genus, proprium, and accident—which was adopted by most traditional logicians.

For Aristotle one defined a term by stating the *essence* of the object that it names (this statement is called the *definition*). The essence of a thing is that property which makes it the type of thing it is and not some other type of thing. The essence has two aspects: the *genus* is that which is predicable essentially of other kinds of things as well, and the *differentia* is that which is possessed essentially only by things of one type (members of one species) and not by things of any other type. Thus, in "Man is a rational animal" the genus is "animal," and the differentia is "rational."

Aristotle distinguished between the essence of a thing and other properties which belong only to that type of thing but are not part of its essence; such a property is called a *proprium.* The precise manner in which he hoped to make this distinction is not very clear. He also recognized that a thing might have a property that it need not have. He called such a property an *accident.*

predicate. Traditionally, the word or group of words in a categorical proposition which connote the property being attributed to the subject or denote the class which the subject is being included in or excluded from. The term is often extended, in contemporary works, to cover all words or groups of words that connote properties or relations in any type of proposition. Thus, in "All men are mortal" the predicate is "mortal."

predicate calculus. See *calculus.*

predication. The attributing of a property to a subject.

premise. A member of the set of propositions, assumed for the course of an argument, from which a conclusion is inferred.

primitive basis. The list of primitive symbols, formation rules, axioms, and rules of inference of a given logistic system.

primitive symbols. Those symbols of a given logistic system that are undefined and are not divided into parts in the course of operating within the system. One can, following John von Neumann, divide these symbols into constants, variables, connectives, operators, and bracketlike symbols.

privative name. A name that implies the absence of a property where it has been or where one might expect it to be.

problematic proposition. See *modality*.

product of sets. See *intersection of sets*.

proof. For a given well-formed formula *A* in a given logistic system, a proof of *A* is a finite sequence of well-formed formulas the last of which is *A* and each of which is either an axiom of the system or can be inferred from previous members of the sequence according to the rules of inference of the system.

proof from hypothesis. A proof from a given set of hypotheses $A_1, A_2, \cdots, A_n$ in a given logistic system is a sequence of well-formed formulas the last of which is the conclusion of the proof and each of which is either an axiom of the system or one of $A_1, A_2, \cdots, A_n$ or a formula that can be inferred from previous formulas in the sequence by the rules of inference of the system.

proof theory. See *metamathematics*.

proper class. An object which contains members but which cannot itself be a member of any object.

proper subset. A subset of a given set that is not identical with the given set.

proposition. There is no uniform use of the word "proposition" among logicians and philosophers. Many writers distinguish a proposition from a sentence; thus, "Socrates was a philosopher" and "Socrates war ein Philosoph" would be two different sentences that express the same proposition. Other writers use "sentence" and "proposition" interchangeably. To avoid some of the associations of the word "proposition" some contemporary philosophers abandon the term altogether in favor of "statement." For a discussion of some of the philosophical controversies arising in this connection, see article PROPOSITIONS, JUDGMENTS, SENTENCES, AND STATEMENTS. For present purposes it is assumed that the reader has a rough idea of what the term "proposition" means. This discussion will accordingly confine itself to an account of the different kinds of propositions distinguished by logicians.

Propositions may be classified in many ways. To begin with, one must distinguish *simple* (or *atomic* or *elementary*) propositions, propositions that do not have other propositions as constituent parts, from *compound* (or *molecular*) propositions, propositions that do have other propositions as constituent parts.

Among simple propositions the more important types are *categorical* (or *subject–predicate*) propositions, which affirm or deny that something has a property or is a member of a class, and *relational* propositions, which affirm or deny that a relation holds between two or more objects. A categorical proposition is *singular* when its subject is the name of an individual and *general* when its subject

is the name of a property or class, affirmative when its predicate is affirmed of the subject and *negative* when its predicate is denied of the subject. A general categorical proposition is *universal* when it is talking about all the members of the subject class or all the objects that have the subject property and *particular* when it is talking about only some of the members of the subject class or some of the objects that have the subject property.

Among compound propositions the most important types are *alternative* (or *disjunctive*) propositions, which are of the form "A or B," *conditional* (or *hypothetical*) propositions, of the form "If A then B," *conjunctive* propositions, of the form "A and B," and *negative* propositions, of the form "Not-A." Many propositions that seem to be simple turn out under proper analysis to be compound. Such propositions are known as *exponible* propositions.

Kant, and many logicians following him, distinguished a class of *infinite* (or *limitative*) propositions, affirmative propositions with a negative term as predicate. This distinction has been challenged by many authors. A more widely accepted addition to our classification is the *indefinite* proposition, a proposition that is equivocal because no indication is given of whether it is universal or particular. Finally, modality provides still another means of classifying propositions.

propositional calculus. See *calculus*.

propositional connective. See *connective*.

propositional function. A function whose range of values consists exclusively of truth-values. Thus, "*a* is the father of George Washington" is a propositional function, since for any argument for *a*, the value of the whole unit is truth or falsehood, depending on whether or not the argument is the name of George Washington's father. See article LOGIC, MODERN.

proprium. See *predicables*.

prosyllogism. See *polysyllogism*.

prototthetic. A form of the extended propositional calculus, first introduced by Stanisław Leśniewski, to which have been added variables whose values are truth-functions and a notation for the application of a function to its argument or arguments, and in which the quantifiers are allowed to have variables of any kind as operator variables. In the *higher* prototthetic, variables whose values are propositional functions of truth-functions are added.

proximum genus. See *classification*.

quality of a proposition. The characteristic that makes a proposition affirmative or negative. Kant, and logicians following him, added a third type, infinite propositions. See *proposition*.

quantification of the predicate. The prefixing of a sign of quantity, "some" or "all," to the predicate of a proposition in the same way as to the subject, a device introduced by Sir William Hamilton. The claim was that this would make explicit what was implicit in the proposition.

quantifier. An operator of which it is true that both the constant or form it is used with and the constant or form produced are propositions or propositional forms. Thus, an existential quantifier, when joined to a proposition or propositional form *A*, produces a new proposition or propositional form "$(\exists a)M$."

quantity of a proposition. The characteristic that makes a proposition universal or particular. Kant and others considered singular propositions as being a third, distinct type of quantity.

Quine's set theories. A group of set theories proposed by W. V. Quine, combining some of the features of type theory with some of the features of the Zermelo–Fraenkel and Gödel–von Neumann–Bernays set theories. As in the set theories, the axiom of abstraction is not retained in its full power, and the formation rules of intuitive set theory are not modified; as in type theory, the notion of stratification is used, since in certain key axioms only stratified formulas generate sets.

   range of a relation. See *converse domain of a relation.*

   range of values. The class of those things that are ambiguously named by a given variable.

   rational number. A number that can be put into the form a/b, where a is any integer and b any natural number.

   real mathematics. For David Hilbert, that part of mathematics that is finitary in character, has therefore a clear and intuitive meaning, and poses no problem about its foundation except for the fact that when ideal mathematics is adjoined to it the possibility of inconsistency arises. See *ideal mathematics.*

   real number. Any number which can be represented by an unending decimal.

   recursive function. There are various types of recursive functions. In order to explain them we must first introduce some terminology: a *constant function* is a function that has the same value for all of its arguments; a *successor function* has as its value for any given argument the successor of that argument; an *identity function* is a function of n arguments whose value is always the ith argument. All such functions are known as *fundamental functions.*

   A function of n arguments is defined by *composition* when, given any set of previously introduced functions of n arguments, the value of the new function is equal to the value of a previously introduced function whose arguments in any particular case are the values of each of the members of the set of functions when their arguments are the arguments of the newly introduced function in that particular case. In symbols, where P is the new function being defined by composition, $P(a_1,a_2,\cdots,a_n) = R(S_1(a_1,a_2,\cdots,a_n), S_2(a_1,a_2,\cdots,a_n),\cdots,S_m(a_1,a_2,\cdots,a_n))$, where R and S_1, $S_2,\cdots,S_m$ are previously introduced functions.

   A function is defined by *recursion* in the following circumstances: (1) A value is assigned to the function for the case where one of its arguments is 0 in terms of a previously introduced function whose arguments, except for 0, are in any particular case all and only the arguments of the new function in that particular case. In symbols, where P is the new function and R the previously introduced function, $P(a_1,a_2,\cdots,a_n,0) = R(a_1,a_2,\cdots,a_n)$. (2) A value is given to the new function when 0 is not one of its arguments and when one of its arguments is the successor of any number b, in terms of a previously introduced function S, whose arguments, except for the successor of b, are in any particular case all the arguments of the newly introduced function, b itself, and the value of the new function when its arguments are all and only the arguments already given for S. In symbols, $P(a_1,a_2,\cdots,a_n,b+1) = S(a_1,a_2,\cdots,a_n,b,P(a_1,a_2,\cdots,a_n,b))$.

Any numerical function which is a fundamental function or can be obtained, by composition or recursion or both, from the fundamental functions by a finite sequence of definitions is a *primitive recursive numerical function.* A function P is introduced by the *least-number operator* if its value for a given set of arguments is the least number b such that the value of a previously introduced function R, whose arguments in any particular case are the arguments of P in that case and b, is equal to 0 provided that there is such a b; if there is no such b, the function is undefined for those arguments. In symbols, $P(a_1,a_2,\cdots,a_n) =$ the least b such that $R(a_1,a_2,\cdots,a_n,b) = 0$, provided that there is a b such that $R(a_1,a_2,\cdots,a_n,b) = 0$. Any numerical function which either is a fundamental function or can be obtained from the fundamental functions by a finite sequence of definitions by composition, recursion, and the least-number operator (when this operator is used in defining a general recursive function, it must be the case that for all $a_1,a_2,\cdots$, a_n there is a b such that $R(a_1,a_2,\cdots,a_n,b) = 0$) is a *general recursive numerical function.*

   recursively enumerable. Used of a set or class that is enumerated (allowing for repetitions) by a general recursive function. That is, there is a general recursive function whose converse domain has the same members as the set when its domain is the set of natural numbers.

   recursive number theory. The development of number theory, instituted by Thoralf Skolem, in which no quantifiers are introduced as primitive symbols, in which universality is expressed by the use of free variables, and in which functions are introduced through definitions by recursion.

   recursive set. A set that is enumerated (allowing for repetitions) by a general recursive function and whose complement is also enumerated (allowing for repetitions) by a general recursive function.

   reducibility, axiom of. An axiom, introduced by Bertrand Russell and A. N. Whitehead in *Principia Mathematica*, which says that for any propositional function of arbitrary level there exists a formally equivalent propositional function of the first level.

   reductio ad absurdum. (1) See *indirect proof.* (2) The method of proving a proposition by showing that its denial leads to a contradiction. In this sense it is often known as a *reductio ad impossibile.*

   reduction of syllogisms. The process whereby syllogisms in imperfect figures are expressed in the first figure. Reduction is *direct* when the original conclusion follows from premises in the first figure derived by conversion, obversion, etc., from premises in an imperfect figure. Reduction is *indirect* when a new syllogism is formed which establishes the validity of the original conclusion by showing the illegitimacy of its contradictory. See article LOGIC, TRADITIONAL.

   reference. See *meaning, Frege's theory of.*

   referential opacity. An occurrence of a word or sequence of words such that one cannot in general supplant the word or sequence of words with another word or sequence of words that refers to the same thing while preserving the truth-value of the containing sentence. For example, although "9 is necessarily greater than 7" is true, the result of substituting for "9" a sequence of words that refers to the same thing, "the number of planets," is the false proposition "The number of planets is necessarily greater than 7." Therefore, in this occurrence "9" is referentially opaque.

reflexive relation. See *relation.*

reflexive set. See *finite set.*

regularity, axiom of. See *foundation, axiom of.*

relation. This term is not adequately defined in traditional logic. The failure to offer an adequate definition is symptomatic of the lack of serious consideration, on the part of traditional logicians, of the significant differences between categorical and relational propositions. Augustus De Morgan and C. S. Peirce were the first logicians in the contemporary period to study the logic of relational propositions. Since their time this subject has become an important part of logic. In contemporary works, particularly in works on set theory, a relation is defined as a set of ordered pairs.

A relation R is *reflexive* if "aRa" holds for all a that are members of the field of R, *irreflexive* if "aRa" holds for no members of the field of R, and *nonreflexive* if "aRa" holds for some but not all members of the field of R. For example, "is a member of the same family as" is a reflexive relation, "is not a member of the same family as" is an irreflexive relation, and "loves" is a nonreflexive relation.

A relation R is *symmetric* if for all a and b that are members of the field of R, aRb if and only if bRa, *asymmetric* if for all a and b that are members of the field of R, aRb if and only if not-bRa, and *nonsymmetric* when "aRb" and "bRa" hold for some but not all a and b that are members of the field of R. For example, "is a member of the same family as" is a symmetric relation, "is a child of" is an asymmetric relation, and "is a brother of" is a nonsymmetric relation.

A relation R is *transitive* when for all a, b, and c that are members of the field of R, if aRb and bRc, then aRc, *intransitive* when for all a, b, and c that are members of the field of R, if aRb and bRc, then not-aRc, and *nontransitive* when if aRb and bRc, then "aRc" holds for some but not all of the a, b, and c that are members of the field of R. For example, "is a descendant of" is a transitive relation, "is a child of" is an intransitive relation, and "is not a brother of" is a nontransitive relation.

The foregoing classifications are said to apply to a relation in a set if the corresponding properties hold for all members of the field of a relation that are members of the set. A relation is *connective* in a set if for all distinct a and b that are members of the set, either aRb or bRa.

The study of relational propositions has raised many philosophical issues—and has greatly influenced discussions of older issues—about the nature of relations. On these matters, see article RELATIONS, INTERNAL AND EXTERNAL.

replacement, axiom of (axiom of substitution). An axiom in set theory stating that for any set a and any single-valued function R with a free variable b, there exists a set that contains just the members $R(b)$, with b being a member of a.

representative of a cardinal number. A set that has a given cardinal number as its cardinality.

Richard's paradox. See *paradox.*

rule of inference (transformation rule). For a given logistic system, any rule in its metalanguage of the form

"From well-formed formulas of the form $A_1, A_2, \cdots, A_n$, it is permissible to infer a well-formed formula of the form B."

Russell's paradox. See *paradox.*

Russell's theory of definite descriptions. See *definite descriptions, theory of.*

Russell's vicious-circle principle. The principle according to which impredicative definitions are not allowed.

satisfiable. A well-formed formula that is satisfiable in some nonempty domain of individuals.

satisfiable in a domain. A well-formed formula is satisfiable in a given domain of individuals if and only if it has the value truth for at least one system of possible values of its free variables.

Schröder–Bernstein theorem. The theorem, first conjectured by Georg Cantor and proved by Felix Bernstein and Ernst Schröder, which states that if a and b are sets such that a is equipollent with a subset of b and b is equipollent with a subset of a, then a and b are equipollent.

scope of a quantifier. For a given occurrence of a quantifier as part of a well-formed part of a well-formed formula, the rest of that well-formed part.

secondarily satisfiable. Used of a well-formed formula that is satisfiable in some normal system of domains.

secondarily valid. Used of a well-formed formula that is valid in every normal system of domains.

second-order logic. Second-order functional calculus. See *calculus.*

section of a set. See *segment of a set.*

segment of a set (section of a set). The subset of a given set ordered by a given relation whose members are those members of the set that precede a given member in the given ordering.

selection set. A set that contains one member from each subset of a given set.

self-contradiction. A proposition that in effect both asserts and denies some other proposition.

semantical rule. Any rule in the metalanguage that concerns the meaning of expressions in the object language.

semantics, formal (semiotics). The study of linguistic symbols. Following C. W. Morris, it is customary to divide formal semantics into three areas: (1) *Syntax,* the study of the relations between symbols. The study of the ways in which the symbols of a given language can be combined to form well-formed formulas is one part of syntax. (2) *Semantics,* the study of the interpretation of symbols. Following W. V. Quine, it is customary to distinguish between the theory of reference, which studies the reference or denotation of symbols, and the theory of meaning, which studies the sense or connotation of symbols. (3) *Pragmatics,* the study of the relations between symbols, the users of symbols, and the environment of the users. Thus, the study of the conditions in which a speaker uses a given word is part of pragmatics. See article SEMANTICS.

sense. See *meaning, Frege's theory of.*

sentential calculus. See *calculus.*

sentential connective. See *connective.*

sequence. A function whose domain is a subset, not necessarily a proper one, of the set of natural numbers. Some authors extend the term to any function whose domain is ordered.

set. (1) An aggregate. (2) In Gödel–von Neumann–

Bernays set theory, where a distinction is made between sets and classes, sets are those objects that can both contain members and be members of some other object.

Sheffer stroke function (alternative denial). A binary propositional connective ($|$), whose truth table is such that "*A* stroke-function *B*" is false if and only if *A* and *B* are both true. The Sheffer stroke function and joint denial are the only binary propositional connectives adequate for the construction of all truth-functional connectives.

simultaneously satisfiable. A class of well-formed formulas is said to be simultaneously satisfiable if there is some nonempty domain of individuals such that for all the free variables in all the formulas that are members of the class, there exists at least one system of values in that domain for which every formula in the class has the value truth.

singular term. A term that, in the sense in which it is being used, is predicable of only one individual. For example, any definite description is a singular term.

singulary connective. See **connective.**

Skolem–Löwenheim theorem. In 1915, Leopold Löwenheim proved that if a well-formed formula is valid in an enumerably infinite domain, it is valid in every nonempty domain. A corollary is that if a well-formed formula is satisfiable in any nonempty domain, it is satisfiable in an enumerably infinite domain. In 1920, Thoralf .Skolem generalized this corollary—and thus completed the theorem—by proving that if a class of well-formed formulas is simultaneously satisfiable in any nonempty domain, then it is simultaneously satisfiable in an enumerably infinite domain.

Skolem's paradox. The seemingly paradoxical fact that systems in which Cantor's theorem is provable, and which therefore have nondenumerable sets, must, by virtue of the Skolem-Löwenheim theorem, be satisfiable in an enumerably infinite domain.

sorites. A chain of syllogisms in which the conclusion of each of the prosyllogisms is omitted. If each of the conclusions forms the minor premise of the following episyllogism, the sorites is an *Aristotelian* sorites; if each of the conclusions forms the major premise of the following episyllogism, it is a *Goclenian* sorites.

sound. Used of an interpretation of a logistic system such that under the interpretation all the axioms either denote truth or always have the value truth, and all the rules of inference are truth-preserving.

species. See **classification.**

square of opposition. A diagrammatic representation of that part of the traditional doctrine of immediate inferences between categorical propositions that went under the name of the opposition of propositions. See article LOGIC, TRADITIONAL.

stratification. The substitution of numerals for variables in a formula (the same numeral for each occurrence of a single variable) in such a way that the symbol for class-membership is flanked always by variables with consecutive ascending numerals.

subalternation. The relation between a universal and a particular proposition of the same quality. Traditionally this relation has been viewed in such a way that the universal proposition implies the particular proposition. The universal proposition is called the *subalternant;* the particular proposition is called the *subalternate.*

subaltern genera. See **classification.**

subcontrary propositions. Two propositions that cannot both be false but may both be true. Any I- and O-propositions with the same subject and the same predicate form a pair of subcontrary propositions.

subject. The word or words in a categorical proposition that denote the object to which a property is being attributed or the class which is either included in or excluded from some other class.

subset. Any set *b* such that all the members of *b* are members of a given set *a*.

substitution, axiom of. See **replacement, axiom of.**

substitution, rule of. A rule of inference that allows one to infer from a given formula *A* another formula *B* that is the same as *A* except for certain specified changes of symbols. The various rules of substitution differ in the types of changes they allow.

successor. For a given number, the number that follows it in the ordinary ordering of the numbers. In Peano's axiomatic treatment of arithmetic "successor" is treated as a primitive term. In the various set-theoretic treatments of arithmetic it is defined differently. For example, "the successor of *a*" is sometimes defined as the unit set whose only member is *a*.

sufficient condition. See **condition.**

summum genus. See **classification.**

sum of sets. See **union of sets.**

sum set. For a given set *a*, the set whose members are all and only those objects which are members of members of *a*.

sum-set axiom. An axiom in set theory stating that for any set *a*, its sum set exists.

supposition. Roughly, the property of a term whereby it stands for something; the doctrine of supposition was extensively developed by the medieval logicians. *Material* supposition is possessed by those terms that stand for an expression, and *formal* supposition is possessed by those terms that stand for what they signify. Among terms having formal supposition, those that are common terms have *common* supposition, and those that are properly applicable to only one individual have *discrete* supposition. When in a given occurrence a common term stands for the universal, it has *simple* supposition; opposed to this is *personal* supposition, a property possessed by a common term in those occurrences where it stands for particular instances.

syllogism. A valid deductive argument having two premises and a conclusion. The term is often restricted to the case where both premises and the conclusion are categorical propositions which have between them three, and only three, terms. More careful authors distinguish this case by referring to it as a *categorical* syllogism. A *hypothetical* syllogism is one whose premises and conclusions are hypothetical propositions, and a *disjunctive* syllogism is one whose premises and conclusion are disjunctive propositions. All of these cases, where the three propositions are of the same type, are *pure* syllogisms. A *mixed* syllogism is one in which there occur at least two types of propositions.

A *strengthened* syllogism is one in which the same conclusion could be obtained even if we substitute for one of the premises that is a universal proposition its subalternate. Thus, the syllogism whose premises are "All men are mortal" and "All baseball players are men" and whose conclusion is "Some baseball players are mortal" is a strengthened syllogism, since it would have been sufficient to have as a premise "Some baseball players are men." A *weakened* syllogism is one whose premises imply a universal proposition but whose conclusion is the subalternate of that universal proposition. The above example is also an example of a weakened syllogism, since the premises, as they stand, imply "All baseball players are mortal."

symbol, improper. A symbol that is syncategorematic under the principal interpretation of the logistic system it occurs in. An example of such a symbol is "and."

symbol, proper. A symbol that is categorematic under the principal interpretation of the logistic system it occurs in. Any individual constant is a proper symbol.

symmetrical relation. See *relation.*

syncategorematic. In traditional logic, used of a word which cannot be a term in a categorical proposition and which must be used along with a term in order to enter into a categorical proposition. An example of this is "all." In contemporary logic the term refers to any symbol that has no independent meaning and acquires its meaning only when joined to other symbols. Cf. *categorematic.*

syntactical variable. A variable ranging over the names of symbols and formulas.

syntax. See *semantics, formal.*

synthetic. Used of a proposition that is neither analytic nor self-contradictory.

systematic ambiguity (typical ambiguity). A convention, introduced by Bertrand Russell and A. N. Whitehead, whereby one does not specify the type or order to which the variables in a formula belong, thus allowing one formula to represent an infinite number of formulas, namely all those formulas that are exactly like it except for the fact that their variables are assigned orders and types in such a manner that the formula formed is well-formed according to the formation rules of the ramified theory of types.

tautology. A compound proposition that is true no matter what truth-values are assigned to its constituent propositions. Thus, "A or not-A" is a tautology, since if "A" is true, then the whole proposition is true, and if "A" is false, then "not-A" is true, and therefore the whole proposition is still true. See article LOGIC, MODERN.

term. Traditionally, the subject or predicate in a categorical proposition. Some authors extend the word "term" to cover all occurrences of categorematic words or expressions which, although not propositions by themselves, are parts of a proposition.

tertium non datur. The law of excluded middle. See *laws of thought.*

theorem. Any well-formed formula of a given logistic system for which there is a proof in the system.

theorem schema. A representation of an infinite number of theorems by means of an expression that contains syntactical variables and has well-formed formulas as values. Every value of the expression is to be taken as a theorem.

theory of types. The theory, introduced by Bertrand Russell and A. N. Whitehead in *Principia Mathematica,* which avoids the paradoxes of set theory by modifying the formation rules of intuitive set theory. In the *simple theory of types* the only modification is that every variable is

assigned a number that signifies its type, and formulas of the form "*a* is a member of *b*" are well-formed if and only if *a*'s type-number is one less than *b*'s. In *ramified type theory* each variable is also assigned to a particular level, and certain rules are introduced about the levels of variables; these rules are such as to exclude classes defined by impredicative definitions. See article TYPES, THEORY OF.

tilde. The name of the symbol for negation ($\sim$).

token. A specified utterance of a given linguistic expression or a written occurrence of it. An expression-*type,* on the other hand, is an entity abstracted from all actual and potential occurrences of a linguistic expression. In "John loves John," for example, there are three word-tokens but only two word-types.

transfinite cardinals. All cardinal numbers equal to or greater than aleph-null ($\aleph_0$).

transfinite induction. A proof by course-of-values induction where the numbers involved are the ordinal numbers. This type of proof is important because it can be used to show that a property holds not only for the finite ordinals but for the transfinite ordinals as well.

transfinite ordinal. The order-type of an infinite well-ordered set.

transfinite recursion. A definition of a function by recursion in such a way that a value is assigned not only when the argument is a finite ordinal but also when it is a transfinite ordinal.

transformation rule. See *rule of inference.*

transitive relation. See *relation.*

transposition. A rule of inference that permits one to infer from the truth of "A implies B" the truth of "Not-B implies not-A," and conversely.

trichotomy, law of. See *comparability, law of.*

truth-function. A function whose arguments and values are truth-values. A compound proposition is said to be a truth-functional proposition if the connective that is adjoined to the constituent propositions to form the compound proposition has a truth-function associated with it. In such a case, since the only arguments of the function are truth-values, the truth-value of the compound proposition depends only on the truth-values of its constituent propositions. See article LOGIC, MODERN.

truth table. A table that shows the truth-value of a compound proposition for every possible combination of the truth-values of its constituent propositions.

truth-value. One of two abstract entities, truth and falsehood, postulated in Fregean semantics to serve as the reference of true and false sentences. In many-valued logics other truth-values are introduced.

Turing-computable. Used of a function whose value for any given argument a Turing machine can compute. The notion of Turing computability, due to A. M. Turing, is often introduced as a way of making precise the notion of an effectively computable function.

Turing machine. A machine that is capable of being in any one of a finite number of internal *states* at any particular time. The machine is supplied with a linear tape divided into squares on which symbols (from a fixed finite alphabet) may or may not be printed. It scans one, and only one, square at any given time and can erase a symbol from the scanned square and print some other symbol on it. The machine's behavior (in terms of changing what is on the scanned square, changing its internal state, and moving the tape so as to scan a different square) is governed by a *table* of instructions that determines what the machine is to do, given any *configuration* (a combination of the state the machine is in and the symbol on the scanned square) of the machine.

type. (1) See *token.* (2) In the theory of types, a class of objects all of whose members are such that they can be members of the same object. The lowest type is composed of all individuals, the next type of all sets of individuals, and each succeeding type of sets whose members are objects of the immediately preceding type.

typical ambiguity. See *systematic ambiguity.*

union of sets (sum of sets). The set whose members are all and only those objects that are members of at least one of two or more sets.

unit set. A set with only one member.

universal generalization, rule of. The rule of inference that permits one to infer from a formula of the form "Property *P* holds for an object *a*" a formula of the form "Property *P* holds for all objects." Because this inference is not generally valid, restrictions have to be placed on its use.

universal instantiation, rule of. The rule of inference that permits one to infer from a statement of the form "Property *P* holds for all objects" a statement of the form "Property *P* holds for an object *a*."

universal quantifier. The symbol ( ) or ($\forall$), read "for all." It is used in combination with a variable and placed before a well-formed formula, as in "(*a*) _____" ("For all *a*, _____").

universal set. A set such that there is no object *a* that is not a member of the set.

universe of discourse. Those objects with which a discussion is concerned.

univocal. A linguistic expression is univocal if and only if it is neither ambiguous nor equivocal.

use of a term. See *mention of a term.*

valid formula. A well-formed formula that is valid in every nonempty domain. A well-formed formula is said to be valid for a given domain of individuals if it is true for all possible values of its free variables.

valid inference. An inference the joint assertion of whose premises and the denial of whose conclusion is a contradiction.

value. A member of the range of values of a given variable.

value of a function. That member of the converse domain of a function with which a given argument is paired under the function.

variable. A symbol that under the principal interpretation is not the name of any particular thing but is rather the ambiguous name of any one of a class of things.

Venn diagram. A modification, first introduced by John Venn, of Euler's diagrams. The key differences between Euler's diagrams and Venn's diagrams stem from the fact that Venn, and many other logicians, wanted to deny the traditional assumption that propositions of the form "All *P* are *Q*" or "No *P* are *Q*" imply the existence of any *P*'s. For details, see article LOGIC DIAGRAMS.

vicious-circle principle. See *Russell's vicious-circle principle.*

well-formed formulas. Those formulas of a given logistic system of which it can sensibly be asked whether or not they are theorems of the system. In any particular system, rules are given that define the class of well-formed formulas and enable one to determine mechanically whether or not a given string of symbols is a well-formed formula of the system.

well-ordering theorem. The theorem stating that for any set there is a relation that well-orders it. See *choice, axiom of.*

wff. A common abbreviation for "well-formed formula."

Zermelo–Fraenkel set theory. That form of axiomatic set theory that avoids the paradoxes of set theory by dropping the axiom of abstraction and substituting for it a set of axioms about set-existence.

BORUCH A. BRODY

LOGIC AND THE FOUNDATIONS OF MATHEMATICS.

The basic concepts of logic, as it is understood at the present time, are explained in LOGIC, MODERN; the main ideas of what is usually termed "traditional logic" are discussed in LOGIC, TRADITIONAL. A very detailed account of main developments of logic will be found in LOGIC, HISTORY OF. Brief explanations of many of the terms commonly used by logicians will be found in LOGICAL TERMS, GLOSSARY OF. The Encyclopedia also features the following articles dealing with questions in logic and the foundations of mathematics: ANY AND ALL; ARTIFICIAL AND NATURAL LANGUAGES; COMPUTING MACHINES; CONTINUITY; CONTINUUM PROBLEM; CRAIG'S THEOREM; DECISION THEORY; DEFINITION; EXISTENCE; FALLACIES; GEOMETRY; GÖDEL'S THEOREM; IDENTITY; IF; INFINITY IN MATHEMATICS AND LOGIC; LAWS OF THOUGHT; LOGIC, COMBINATORY; LOGIC, DEONTIC; LOGIC, MANY-VALUED; LOGIC, MODAL; LOGICAL PARADOXES; LOGIC DIAGRAMS; LOGIC MACHINES; MATHEMATICS, FOUNDATIONS OF; NEGATION; NUMBER; QUESTIONS; RECURSIVE FUNCTION THEORY; SEMANTICS; SET THEORY; SUBJECT AND PREDICATE; SYNONYMITY; SYNTACTICAL AND SEMANTICAL CATEGORIES; SYSTEMS, FORMAL, AND MODELS OF FORMAL SYSTEMS; TYPES, THEORY OF; and VAGUENESS. See Logic and see Mathematics, Foundations of, in Index for articles on thinkers who have made contributions in this area.

LOGIC DIAGRAMS

LOGIC DIAGRAMS are geometrical figures that are in some respect isomorphic with the structure of statements in a formal logic and therefore can be manipulated to solve problems in that logic. They are useful teaching devices for strengthening a student's intuitive grasp of logical structure, they can be used for checking results obtained by algebraic methods, and they provide elegant demonstrations of the close relation of logic to topology and set theory.

Leonhard Euler, the Swiss mathematician, was the first to make systematic use of a logic diagram. Circles had earlier been employed, by Leibniz and others, to diagram syllogisms, but it was Euler who, in 1761, first explained in detail how circles could be manipulated for such purposes. Euler's contemporary Johann Heinrich Lambert, the

German mathematician, in his *Neues Organon* (1764) used straight lines, in a manner similar to Euler's use of circles, for diagraming syllogisms.

Venn diagrams. The Euler and Lambert methods, as well as later variants using squares and other types of closed curves, are no longer in use because of the great improvement on their basic conception which was introduced by the English logician John Venn. The Venn diagram is best explained by showing how it is used to validate a syllogism. The syllogism's three terms, *S*, *M*, and *P*, are represented by simple closed curves—most conveniently drawn as circles—that mutually intersect, as in Figure 1. The set of points inside circle *S* represents all members of class *S*, and points outside are members of class not-*S*—and similarly for the other two circles. Shading a compartment indicates that it has no members. An X inside a compartment shows that it contains at least one member. An X on the border of two compartments means that at least one of the two compartments has members.

Consider the following syllogism:

Some *S* is *M*.
All *M* is *P*.
Therefore, some *S* is *P*.

The first premise states that the intersection of sets *S* and *M* is not empty. This is indicated by an X on the border dividing the two compartments within the overlap of circles *S* and *M* (Figure 2). The second premise states that the set indicated by that portion of circle *M* which lies outside of *P* is empty. When this area is shaded (Figure 3) the X must be shifted to the only remaining compartment into which it can go. Because the X is now inside both *S* and *P*, it is evident that some *S* is *P*; therefore, the syllogism is valid.

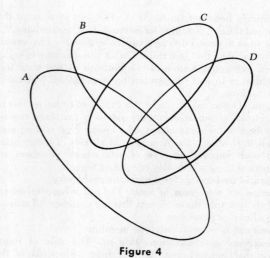

Figure 4

VENN DIAGRAM FOR FOUR TERMS

Rectangular charts. Statements involving a large number of terms are best diagramed on a rectangle divided into smaller rectangles that are labeled in such a way that the chart can be manipulated efficiently as a Venn diagram. Many different methods of constructing such charts were worked out in the late nineteenth and early twentieth centuries, each with merits and defects. The first to be published was that of Allan Marquand in 1881. Figure 5 shows a Marquand chart for four terms. Alexander Macfarlane preferred a narrow strip, which he called a "logical

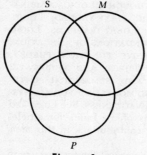

Figure 1

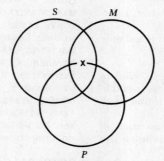

Figure 2

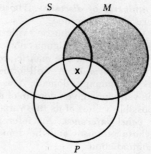

Figure 3

VENN DIAGRAM APPLIED TO A SYLLOGISM

Venn did not restrict this method to syllogisms. He generalized it to take care of any problem in the calculus of classes, then the most popular interpretation of what is now called Boolean algebra. For statements with four terms he used four intersecting ellipses, as shown in Figure 4. Since it is not possible for five ellipses to intersect in the desired manner, statements with five or more terms must be diagramed on more complicated patterns. Various methods of forming nonconvex closed curves for Venn diagrams of statements with more than four terms have been devised.

spectrum," subdivided and labeled as in Figure 6. Later, in "Adaptation of the Method of the Logical Spectrum to Boole's Problem" (in *Proceedings of the American Association for the Advancement of Science,* Vol. 39, 1890, 57 f.), Macfarlane used his chart for solving a complicated problem in George Boole's *Laws of Thought* (1854).

Other types of rectangular charts were devised by William J. Newlin, William E. Hocking, and Lewis Carroll. Carroll introduced his chart in a book for children, *The Game of Logic* (London and New York, 1886). Instead of shading compartments, he proposed marking them with

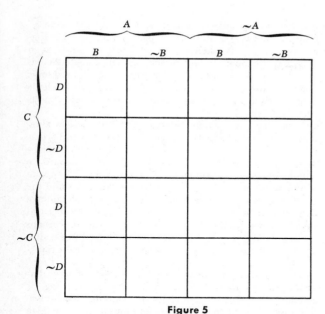

Figure 5

MARQUAND CHART FOR FOUR TERMS

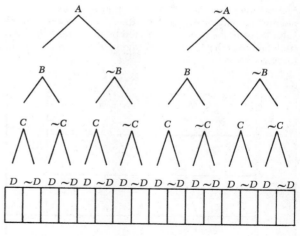

Figure 6

MACFARLANE CHART FOR FOUR TERMS

counters of two colors, one for classes known to have members, the other for null classes.

An elaborate diagrammatic method designed to cover all types of logic, including modal logics, was devised in 1897 by the American philosopher Charles Peirce and later discussed in several brief, obscurely written papers. Although Peirce considered these "existential graphs," as he called them, his greatest contribution to logic, they aroused little interest among later logicians and have yet to be fully explicated and evaluated.

Diagrams for the propositional calculus. In the early twentieth century the class interpretation of Boolean algebra was supplemented by a more useful interpretation in which classes are replaced by propositions that are either true or false and related to one another by logical connectives. The Venn diagrams, as well as their chart extensions, work just as efficiently for the propositional calculus as for the class calculus, but cultural lag has prevented this fact

from entering most logic textbooks. For example, the class statement "All apples are red" is equivalent to the propositional statement "If x is an apple, then x is red." The same Venn diagram is therefore used for both statements (Figure 7). Similarly, the class statement "No A is B" is equivalent to the propositional statement "Not both A and B," symbolized in modern logic by the Sheffer stroke. Both statements are diagramed as in Figure 8.

A major defect of the Venn system is that it is difficult to distinguish the shading of one statement from the shading of another, so that one loses track of individual premises. This is best remedied by diagraming each statement on a separate sheet of transparent paper and superposing all sheets on the same basic diagram. Such a method using cellophane sheets shaded with different colors and superposed on a rectangular diagram was recently devised by Karl Döhmann, of Berlin.

A network method for solving problems in the propositional calculus, designed to keep statements separate and to bring out visually the nature of the logical connectives, is given in Martin Gardner's *Logic Machines and Diagrams* (1958), Chapter 3. Each term is represented by two

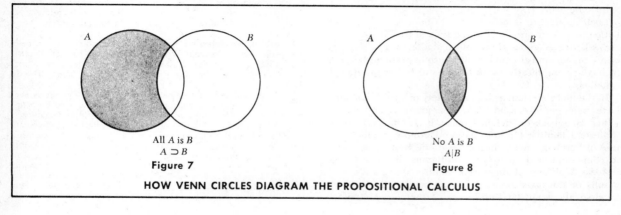

All A is B
$A \supset B$
Figure 7

No A is B
$A|B$
Figure 8

HOW VENN CIRCLES DIAGRAM THE PROPOSITIONAL CALCULUS

vertical lines, one for "true," the other for "false." A connective is symbolized by "shuttles" that connect truth-value lines in the manner indicated by the "true" lines of a truth table for that connective. Figure 9 shows the diagram for implication.

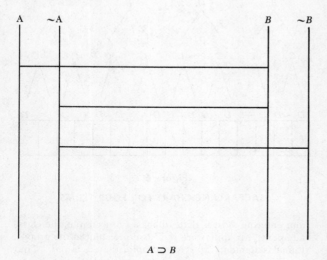

$$A \supset B$$

Figure 9

A NETWORK DIAGRAM OF IMPLICATION

A "Boole table," devised by Walter E. Stuerman, also keeps individual statements separate and can be used for graphing any type of Boolean algebra. It combines features of Macfarlane's chart with Lambert's linear method. John F. Randolph has developed a simple method of handling a Marquand diagram by sketching nested cross marks and using dots to indicate nonempty compartments.

Although the Venn circles and their various chart extensions can obviously be given three-dimensional forms, no three-dimensional techniques for diagraming Boolean algebra have been found useful because of the extreme difficulty of manipulating solid diagrams. In this connection, however, mention should be made of a curious cubical chart, devised by C. Howard Hinton in 1904, that is constructed with 64 smaller cubes and used for identifying valid syllogisms.

Boolean algebra is now known to be a special type of lattice, which in turn is a certain type of partially ordered set. A lattice diagram for a Boolean algebra of two terms is easily drawn, and although of little use in problem solving, it displays graphically many features of the propositional calculus.

In the logic of relations a large variety of useful diagrams have been widely used. The tree graph, for example, which goes back to ancient Greece, is an efficient way to indicate a familiar type of relation. Examples include the tree of Porphyry, found in medieval and Renaissance logics, the later tree diagrams of Peter Ramus, diagrams showing the evolution of organisms, family tree graphs, and graphs of stochastic processes in probability theory. The topological diagrams in Kurt Lewin's *Principles of Topolog-*

ical Psychology (1936), as well as modern "sociograms," transport networks, and so on, may be called logic diagrams if "logic" is taken in a broad sense. However, such diagrams are now studied in the branch of mathematics called graph theory and are not generally considered logic diagrams. In a wide sense *any* geometrical figure is a logic diagram since it expresses logical relations between its parts.

Areas for exploration. All diagrams for Boolean algebras work most efficiently when the statements to be diagramed are simple binary relations. Compound statements with parenthetical expressions are awkward to handle unless the statements are first translated into simpler expressions. Attempts have been made to extend the Venn diagrams and other types of Boolean graphs to take care of parenthetical statements directly, but in all cases the diagrams become too complex to be useful. Perhaps simpler methods will be found by which traditional diagrams can be made to accommodate parenthetical expressions.

Little progress has been made in developing good diagrammatic methods for minimizing a complex logical statement—that is, for reducing it to a simpler but equivalent form. Several chart methods for minimizing have been worked out. The closest to a diagrammatic technique is the Karnaugh map, first explained by Maurice Karnaugh in 1953. The map is based on an earlier diagram called the Veitch chart, in turn based on a Marquand chart.

Work on better methods of minimizing is still in progress. The work has important practical consequences because electrical networks can be translated into Boolean algebra and the expression minimized and then translated back into network design to effect a simplification of circuitry. It is possible that a by-product of new minimizing methods may be a diagrammatic method superior to any yet found.

Another field open to exploration is the devising of efficient ways to diagram logics not of the Boolean type, notably modal logics and the various many-valued logics.

Bibliography

Venn's *Symbolic Logic*, rev. 2d ed. (London, 1894), remains the best single source for the early history of logic diagrams. It also contains the fullest exposition of his own method, which he first presented in "On the Diagrammatic and Mechanical Representation of Propositions and Reasonings," *Philosophical Magazine*, Vol. 10 (July 1880), 1–18. For more recent history and references, consult Martin Gardner, *Logic Machines and Diagrams* (New York, 1958).

Euler's explanation of his circles can be found in his *Lettres à une princesse d'Allemagne*, Vol. II, letters 102–108 (St. Petersburg, 1768). Lambert's method, in an improved form, is explained in J. N. Keynes, *Studies and Exercises in Formal Logic*, 4th ed. (London, 1906), p. 243.

For Venn diagrams of statements with more than four terms, see W. E. Hocking, "Two Extensions of the Use of Graphs in Elementary Logic," in *University of California Publications in Philosophy*, Vol. 2, No. 2 (1909), 31–44; Edmund C. Berkeley, "Boolean Algebra and Applications to Insurance," in *The Record*, American Institute of Actuaries, Vol. 26 (1937), 373–414, and Vol. 27 (1938), 167–176 (reprinted, New York, 1952); Trenchard More, Jr., "On the Construction of Venn Diagrams," in *Journal of Symbolic Logic*, Vol. 24 (1959), 303–304; and Stephen Barr, *Experiments in Topology* (New York, 1964), p. 206. A method of drawing five irregular but congruent convex pentagons intersecting in the required manner is explained by David W. Henderson in "Venn Diagrams for More Than Four Classes," *American Mathematical Monthly*, Vol. 70 (1963), 424–426.

On rectangular Venn charts, see Allan Marquand, "A Logical Diagram for *n* Terms," in *Philosophical Magazine*, Vol. 12 (1881), 266–270; Alexander Macfarlane, "The Logical Spectrum," in *Philosophical Magazine*, Vol. 19 (1885), 286–289; William J. Newlin, "A New Logical Diagram," in *Journal of Philosophy, Psychology, and Scientific Methods*, Vol. 3 (1906), 539–545; and the Hocking paper mentioned above. Carroll's method is further developed in his *Symbolic Logic* (London and New York, 1896; paperback ed., New York, 1958). Peirce's papers are reprinted in the *Collected Papers of Charles Sanders Peirce*, Charles Hartshorne and Paul Weiss, eds., Vol. IV (Cambridge, Mass., 1933).

An explanation of how Venn circles can be used to handle problems in the propositional calculus appears in Gardner's *Logic Machines and Diagrams* (*op. cit.*), pp. 48–54. Döhmann explained his method in a privately printed booklet, *Eine logistische Farbenquadrat-Methode* (Berlin, 1962). Stuerman described his "Boole table" in "Plotting Boolean Functions," *American Mathematical Monthly*, Vol. 67 (1960), 170–172, and in "The Boole Table Generalized," *American Mathematical Monthly*, Vol. 68 (1961), 53–56. Randolph's method is given in "Cross-examining Propositional Calculus and Set Operations," *American Mathematical Monthly*, Vol. 72 (1965), 117–127. Hinton explained his cubical chart in his eccentric book *The Fourth Dimension* (London, 1904), pp. 100–106. John Evenden presented a two-term lattice diagram for Boolean algebra in "A Lattice-diagram for the Propositional Calculus," *Mathematical Gazette*, Vol. 46 (1962), 119–122.

Karnaugh first explained his map in "The Map Method for Synthesis of Combinational Logic Circuits," *Transactions of the American Institute of Electrical Engineers*, Part 1, Vol. 72 (1953), 593–599. E. W. Veitch explained his earlier diagram in "A Chart Method for Simplifying Truth Functions," *Proceedings of the Association for Computing Machinery* (May 2 and 3, 1952), 127–133.

Martin Gardner

LOGICISM. See Mathematics, foundations of.

LOGIC MACHINES. Because logic underlies all deductive reasoning, one might say that all computers are logic machines. In a wider sense, any mechanical device is a logic machine (for example, an egg beater spins clockwise "if and only if" its crank turns clockwise). Generally, however, the term is restricted to machines designed primarily or exclusively for solving problems in formal logic. Although a digital computer, or even a punch-card data-processing machine, can be programmed to handle many types of logic, it is not considered a logic machine in the strict sense.

The rotating circles of Ramón Lull, thirteenth-century Spanish mystic, cannot be called logic machines even though they were used as reasoning aids. The first true logic machine was a small device called a "demonstrator," invented by Charles Stanhope, third Earl Stanhope, an eighteenth-century English statesman. By sliding two panels (one of gray wood, the other of transparent red glass) behind a rectangular opening, he could test the validity of traditional syllogisms, as well as syllogisms with such quantified terms as "Most of *a*" and "8 of 10 of *a*." Stanhope also used his device for solving elementary problems in what he called the logic of probability.

Jevons' machine. The first logic machine capable of solving a complicated problem faster than a man could solve it without the aid of a machine was the "logical pi-

ano" invented by the nineteenth-century economist and logician William Stanley Jevons. The machine was built for him by a clockmaker at Salford in 1869 and first demonstrated by Jevons in 1870 at a meeting of the Royal Society of London. The device (now owned by the Oxford Museum of the History of Science) resembles a miniature upright piano, about three feet high, with a keyboard of 21 keys. On the face of the piano are openings through which one can see the 16 possible combinations of four terms and their negatives. A statement in logic is fed to the machine by pressing keys according to certain rules. Internal levers and pulleys eliminate from the machine's face all combinations of terms inconsistent with the statement. When all desired statements have thus been fed to the machine the face is inspected to determine what term combinations, if any, are consistent with the statements.

Jevons believed that this machine, designed to handle Boolean algebra, provided a convincing demonstration of the superiority of George Boole's logic over the traditional logic of Aristotle and the Schoolmen. John Venn's system of diagraming follows essentially the same procedure as Jevons' machine. In both cases the procedure gives what are today called the valid lines of a truth table for the combined statements under consideration. Neither the Venn diagrams nor Jevons' machine is capable of reducing these lines to a more compact form. This criticism of the machine was stressed by the English philosopher F. H. Bradley in his *Principles of Logic* (1883).

Other mechanical devices. Jevons' logical piano was greatly simplified by Allan Marquand, who built his first model in 1881, when he was teaching logic at Princeton University. Like Jevons', Marquand's machine is limited to four terms, but the 16 possible combinations are exhibited on its face by 16 pointers, each with a valid and an invalid position, arranged in a pattern that corresponds to Marquand's chart for four terms (see Logic diagrams, Figure 5). The number of keys is reduced to 10, and the device is about a third the height of Jevons' machine. Both Marquand and Jevons interpreted Boolean algebra primarily in class terms, but their machines operate just as efficiently with the propositional calculus.

A third machine of the Jevons type was invented in 1910 by Charles P. R. Macaulay, an Englishman living in Chicago. It is a compact, ingenious boxlike device with interior rods operated by tilting the box a certain way while pins on the side are pressed to put statements into the machine. Consistent combinations of four terms and their negatives appear in windows on top of the box.

A curious contrivance for evaluating the 256 combinations of syllogistic premises and conclusions was constructed in 1903 by Annibale Pastore, a philosopher at the University of Genoa. It consists of three wheels, representing a syllogism's three terms, joined to one another by an arrangement of endless belts appropriate to the syllogism being tested. If the syllogism is valid, all three wheels turn when one is cranked.

Grid cards. Logic grid cards are cards that can be superposed so that valid deductions from logical premises are seen through openings on the cards. A set of syllogism grid cards invented by the Englishman Henry Cunynghame, a contemporary of Jevons, was depicted by Jevons in Chapter 11 of *Studies in Deductive Logic* (London, 1884). A differently designed set is shown in Martin Gardner's "Logic Machines" (in *Scientific American*, Vol. 186, March 1952, 68–73). A more elaborate set, indicating the nature of the fallacy when a syllogism is invalid, can be found in Gardner's *Logic Machines and Diagrams* (New York, 1958) and Richard Lampkin's *Testing for Truth* (Buffalo, N.Y., 1962). Triangular-shaped grid cards, for binary relations in the propositional calculus, are described in Gardner's book and in H. M. Cundy and A. P. Rollett's *Mathematical Models* (2d ed., Oxford, 1961; see pp. 256–258). Gardner described a simple way to make punch cards that can be sorted in such a manner as to solve logic problems in "Mathematical Games" (in *Scientific American*, Vol. 203, December 1960, 160–168).

Electrical machines. Marquand sketched an electrical circuit by which his machine could be operated, but the electrical version was probably never built. Benjamin Burack, a psychologist at Roosevelt College, Chicago, was the first actually to construct an electrical logic machine, in 1936. His device tested all syllogisms, including hypothetical and disjunctive forms. Since then many different kinds of electrical syllogism machines have been constructed.

In 1910, in a review in a Russian journal, Paul Ehrenfest pointed out that because a wire either carries a current or does not, it would be possible to translate certain types of switching circuits into Boolean algebra. Work along such lines was done by the Russian physicist V. I. Šestakov in 1934–1935, but his results were not published until 1941. Similar views were set forth independently in 1936, in a Japanese journal, by Akira Nakasima and Masao Hanzawa. It was the mathematician Claude E. Shannon, however, who impressed the engineering world with the importance of this isomorphism by his independent work, first published in 1938.

Shannon's paper inspired William Burkhart and Theodore A. Kalin, then undergraduates at Harvard University, to design the world's first electrical machine for evaluating statements in the propositional calculus. The Kalin–Burkhart machine was built in 1947. Statements with as many as 12 terms are fed into it by setting switches. The machine scans a truth table for the combined statements, and a set of 12 small bulbs indicates the combination of true and false terms for each truth-table row as it is scanned. If the combination is consistent with the statements, this is indicated by another bulb. The machine is thus an electrical version of Jevons' device but handles more complex statements and presents valid truth-table rows in serial time sequence rather than simultaneously.

A three-term electrical machine was built in England in 1949 without knowledge of the Kalin–Burkhart machine. Advances in switching components made possible more sophisticated logic machines in the United States and elsewhere during the early 1950s. Of special interest is a ten-term machine built at the Burroughs Research Center in Paoli, Pennsylvania, using the parenthesis-free notation of Jan Łukasiewicz.

Digital computers. While the special machines were being developed it became apparent that statements in Boolean algebra could easily be translated into a binary notation and analyzed on any general-purpose digital computer. As digital computers became more available, as well as faster and more flexible, interest in the design of special-purpose logic machines waned. Since 1955 almost all machine-aided investigations in logic have been conducted with digital computers. In 1960, Hao Wang described how he used an IBM 704 computer to test the first 220 theorems of the propositional calculus in *Principia Mathematica*. The machine's total running time was under three minutes.

The similarity between switching circuits and the nets of nerve cells in the brain suggests that the brain may think by a process that could be duplicated by computers. Much work is being done in programming computers to search for proofs of logic theorems in a manner similar to the heuristic reasoning of a logician—that is, by an uncertain strategy compounded of trial and error, logical reasoning, analogies with remembered experience, and sheer luck. The work is closely related to all types of learning machines. Such work may prove useful in exploring logics for which there is no decision procedure—or no known decision procedure—but no special machines have yet been built for such a purpose. Work is also under way on the more difficult problem of designing a machine, or programming a digital computer, to find new, nontrivial, and interesting theorems in a given logic.

Attempts have been made to design machines capable of reducing a statement in Boolean algebra to simpler form. A primitive minimizing machine was constructed by Daniel Bobrow, a New York City high school student, in 1952. At about the same time, Shannon and Edward F. Moore built a relay circuit analyzer that makes a systematic attempt to simplify circuits, a problem closely related to the logic minimizing problem.

No special machines are known to have been constructed for handling many-valued logics, but many papers have been published explaining how such machines could be built, as well as how digital computers could be programmed to handle such logics. Kurt Gödel's undecidability proof has ruled out the possibility of an ultimate logic machine capable of following a systematic procedure for testing any theorem in any possible logic, but whether the human brain is capable of doing any kind of creative work that a machine cannot successfully imitate is still an open, much debated question.

Bibliography

For a history of logic machines, see Martin Gardner, *Logic Machines and Diagrams* (New York, 1958), and Rudolf Tarján, "Logische Maschinen," in Walter Hoffmann, ed., *Digital Information Processors* (New York, 1962), which includes a bibliography of 119 references. Stanhope's machine is discussed in Robert Harley, "The Stanhope Demonstrator," *Mind*, Vol. 4 (1879), 192–210.

Jevons described his logical piano in "On the Mechanical Performance of Logical Inference" (1870), reprinted in his *Pure Logic and Other Minor Works* (London, 1890); a briefer discussion appears in his *Principles of Science* (London, 1874; reprinted, New York, 1958). Marquand discussed his machine in "A New Logical Machine," *Proceedings of the American Academy of Arts and Sciences*, Vol. 21 (1885), 303–307. Marquand's machine was praised by C. S. Peirce in "Logical Machines," *American Journal of Psychology*, Vol. 1 (November 1887), 165–170. Pastore wrote an entire book about his device, *Logica formale, dedotta della considerazione di modelli meccanici* (Turin, 1906). The book was reviewed at length by André Lalande in *Revue philosophique de la France et de l'étranger*, Vol. 63 (1907), 268–275.

Wolfe Mays, "The First Circuit for an Electrical Logic-machine," in *Science*, Vol. 118 (1953), 281–282, and George W. Patterson, "The First Electric Computer, a Magnetological Analysis," in *Journal of the Franklin Institute*, Vol. 270 (1960), 130–137, describe Marquand's sketches. A description of Macaulay's device is in his U.S. patent, No. 1,079,504, issued in 1913.

Burack first described his 1936 machine in "An Electrical Logic Machine," *Science*, Vol. 109 (1949), 610–611. Shannon's historic paper on the isomorphism of Boolean algebra and certain types of switching circuits is "A Symbolic Analysis of Relay and Switching Circuits," in *Transactions of the American Institute of Electrical Engineers*, Vol. 57 (1938), 713–723. The Kalin–Burkhart machine is described in Edmund C. Berkeley, *Giant Brains* (New York, 1949). The English three-term machine is discussed in Wolfe Mays and D. G. Prinz, "A Relay Machine for the Demonstration of Symbolic Logic," *Nature*, Vol. 165 (1950), 197. The Burroughs machine is discussed in A. W. Burks, D. W. Warren, and J. B. Wright, "An Analysis of a Logical Machine Using Parenthesis-free Notation," *Mathematical Tables and Other Aids to Computation*, Vol. 8 (1954), 53–57, and in William Miehle, "Burroughs Truth Function Evaluator," *Journal of the Association for Computing Machinery*, Vol. 4 (1957), 189–192.

Hao Wang's description of his use of the IBM 704 is in "Toward Mechanical Mathematics," *IBM Journal of Research and Development*, Vol. 4 (1960), 2–22, reprinted in Kenneth Sayre and Frederick J. Crosson, eds., *The Modeling of Mind* (Notre Dame, Ind., 1963). On computer simulation, see Allen Newell and H. A. Simon, "Computer Simulation of Human Thinking," in *Science*, Vol. 134 (1961), 2011–2017, and references cited there. On the Shannon–Moore relay circuit analyzer, see Shannon and Moore's "Machine Aid for Switching Circuit Design," in *Proceedings of the Institute of Radio Engineers*, Vol. 41 (1953), 1348–1351.

MARTIN GARDNER

LOGISTIC SYSTEM. See LOGIC, MODERN; SYSTEMS, FORMAL, AND MODELS OF FORMAL SYSTEMS.

LOGOS.

The Greek noun *logos*, derived from the root found in the verb *lego*, "I say," in the classical period covered a wide range of meanings expressed by quite different words in most modern languages. Thus *word, speech, argument, explanation, doctrine, esteem, numerical computation, measure, proportion, plea, principle*, and *reason* (whether human or divine)—all represent standard meanings of the one Greek word. Earlier attempts to trace a logical progression of meanings in the history of the word are now generally acknowledged to lack any secure foundation, and even to try to trace out the history of a single "logos doctrine" in Greek philosophy is to run the risk of searching for a simple pattern when the truth was much more complex. But the extreme importance of the "logos doctrines" of different thinkers is clear, and there certainly were relationships between the ways in which successive thinkers used the term.

The logos doctrine of Heraclitus was as famous as it was obscure. Fairly certainly, he used the term both for his own distinctive doctrine and for that which his doctrine was attempting to describe, namely, the rational governing principle of the universe. The status of this governing principle for Heraclitus is in doubt, but he may have regarded it as a material force identical with or akin to fire, giving rational order to the universe, which it "steers" by its own divine power. If this is correct, then the term "logos" for Heraclitus combined at least three ideas which we tend to separate: our human thought about the universe, the rational structure of the universe itself, and the source of that rational structure. Heraclitus' logos as source of rationality in the universe was an immanent principle, and while it was itself a sort of intelligence, it does not seem to have been regarded as either conscious or intelligent, in the sense of itself indulging in the activity of thinking. A further step was taken by Anaxagoras through his doctrine of a principle of intelligence in the universe that was not mixed with all other things and so was not completely immanent, but he called this principle "nous" and not "logos."

The Sophists used the term "logos" both for arguments and for what arguments were about, so that "right reason" (*orthos logos*) tended to be used both of a correct argument or theory and of the rational structure or principle which the argument or theory was about, but it was used of particular cases rather than of any universal single principle.

In Plato the Forms, as completely rational elements, were the sources of such approaches to rationality as might be found in the phenomenal world and were also the objects of all true rational thinking, but they did not themselves think. The Platonic universe was itself organized on rational principles, but this organization was produced by an entity called Nous and not Logos, and Aristotle also used the term "nous" in connection with his own doctrine of the unmoved mover, an entity to which he did not hesitate to assign the activity of thinking. The identification of Logos and Nous was perhaps first made in the pseudo-Platonic *Epinomis* 986c4, although Plato had treated the two terms as meaning very nearly the same thing in his account of the human soul in the *Republic*.

It was in the system of Stoic thought that a doctrine of Logos achieved its greatest extension. For the Stoics, Logos was the principle of all rationality in the universe, and as such it was identified with God and with the source of all activity. It was material but could interpenetrate other matter, like a drop of wine diffused through the whole sea. It had various derivatives, which are better regarded as aspects of itself than separate entities. As active principle it was *logos spermatikos*, or seminal reason, which worked on passive matter to generate the world, and in plural form, as seminal reasons, it functioned as the universals which Plato and Aristotle had attempted to account for by their respective doctrines of transcendent and immanent Forms. In man it was the power of reason in his soul, "resident" in him, and also, when spoken, it became "uttered" reason. For the Stoics the principle of morality was "living in accordance with nature," and as the nature of man was to be rational and indeed nature as a whole was the rational product of Logos, living according to nature could be equated with living according to Logos. Logos was thus the source of law and morality, and in this connection the Sophistic doctrine of *orthos logos* acquired a new role in Stoic ethics.

In the New Testament the opening words of St. John's Gospel have given rise to a notable and far-ranging controversy. The doctrine of the Word, or Logos, at the beginning of all things seemed to many, including St. Augustine (*Confessions* VII.13), to have direct affinities with Heraclitus, with Plato, and with the doctrines of the Stoics. The identification of Christ with the Logos both of St. John and of the Stoics was greatly elaborated by early Christian apologists, and many details of Stoic thought were given a Christian setting in the process. All earlier manifestations of Logos, for example, in thinkers such as Socrates, were accepted as evidence that the persons concerned were Christians before Christ. Minucius Felix (*Octavius* V.10) identified God the Father with Nous, God the Son with Logos, and the Holy Ghost with Pneuma. Increasingly, as in Origen, the Second Person of the Trinity was subordinated to God the Father, and in Arianism the Logos ceased to be equated with God, since its function of cosmic creation was regarded as inconsistent with the necessary immutability of the deity.

But in the course of the present century there has been increasing discussion of non-Greek sources for the logos doctrine of St. John. A doctrine of the Word of God appears in the Old Testament in association with the Hebrew word *dābhār,* which is regularly translated by *logos* in the Septuagint, and the Word of God on occasion undergoes considerable personification. Moreover, in the Aramaic paraphrases, known as the Targums, the term *mēmrā,* meaning "Word of God," takes on many of the functions of God himself, although some suppose this is merely a device to avoid naming the deity. In the "Wisdom" literature (e.g., *Wisdom of Solomon* VII.25 ff.), Wisdom begins to take on the aspect of a being intermediate between God and man, and this also may have influenced the Johannine doctrine. If Greek influences were also at work, these would require some medium of transmission to the Gospel period, and this has often been found in Philo Judaeus (about 30 B.C. to A.D. 45). The term "logos" occurs repeatedly in his voluminous writings, and it covers a wide range of meanings. But sometimes, it is clear, he used it for a cosmological principle equated with the image or work of God but distinct from God himself and so intermediate between God and the world. While the direct influence of Philo upon St. John seems unlikely, he represents a kind of literature, now largely lost, some of which may well be connected with the opening words of the Gospel.

Plotinus' logos doctrine seems to have been as follows. Just as the ultimate One produced Nous and Nous produced Soul and finally the ordered material universe, so from the first Logos as creative power there flowed a series of subordinate logoi representing the powers of creation at subordinate levels, including the Stoic seminal logoi.

The problems concerning the sources of order and rationality in the universe discussed under the heading "logos" in antiquity are abiding problems, but their subsequent discussions have been conducted without the use of the term. Two exceptions are the discussions of certain Platonists and Neoplatonists during the Renaissance and the terminologies used in more recent times by Husserl and Gentile.

Bibliography

Aall, A., *Der Logos, Geschichte seiner Entwicklung in der griechischen Philosophie und der christlichen Literatur,* 2 vols. Leipzig, 1896–1899.

Boeder, H., "Der frühgriechische Wortgebrauch von Logos und Aletheia." *Archiv für Begriffsgeschichte,* Vol. 4 (1959), 82–112.

Heinze, M., *Die Lehre vom Logos in der griechischen Philosophie.* Oldenburg, Germany, 1872; reprinted, 1960.

Inge, W. R., "Logos," in James Hastings, ed., *Encyclopaedia of Religion and Ethics.* Edinburgh, 1915. Vol. VIII, 133–138.

Kelber, W., *Die Logoslehre von Heraklit bis Origines.* Stuttgart, 1958.

Kleinknecht, H., et al., "Lego," in Gerhard Kittel, ed., *Theologisches Wörterbuch zum neuen Testament.* Stuttgart, 1942. Vol. IV, pp. 69–140.

Leisegang, H., "Logos," in A. Pauly and G. Wissowa, eds., *Real-Encylopädie der classischen Altertumswissenschaft.* Stuttgart, 1927. Vol. XIII, pp. 1035–1081.

Toffanin, G., *La fine del Logos.* Bologna, 1948.

Walton, F. E., *Development of the Logos-doctrine in Greek and Hebrew Thought.* London, 1911.

G. B. KERFERD

LOISY, ALFRED (1857–1940), French Biblical exegetist, was the best-known and most controversial representative of the Modernist movement in France at the end of the nineteenth and beginning of the twentieth centuries. His scholarly investigation led him to the kind of destructive criticism of the Gospel narratives and Christian dogmas carried on earlier by such scholars as D. F. Strauss and Ernest Renan, whose lectures at the Institut Catholique Loisy attended from 1882 to 1885. Loisy's long career, from his entry into the priesthood in 1879 to shortly before his death, was one of much controversy and progressive estrangement from personal religion.

Loisy was born at Ambrière, Marne, and died at Ceffonds, Haute Marne. He became professor of Hebrew in 1881, and of Holy Scripture in 1889, at the Institut Catholique. Loisy's views on the date of the book of Proverbs soon aroused misgivings, and he was warned that continuation of such unorthodoxy would place him in danger of official censure.

Loisy's superior, Msgr. d'Hulst, was an enlightened man and not intolerant of the work of the modern critical school, but as head of the Institut Catholique he was in a responsible and difficult position. The head of the College of St. Sulpice had forbidden his students to attend the heterodox Loisy's lectures, and when in 1892 Loisy started his own periodical, *L'Enseignement biblique,* for the instruction of young priests, d'Hulst felt obliged to urge caution. In 1892, soon after Renan's death, d'Hulst himself wrote an article on Renan in *Le Correspondant.* Without condoning Renan's break with Catholicism, d'Hulst upheld his complaint, in *Souvenirs d'enfance et de jeunesse,* that the instruction given at such seminaries as St. Sulpice was out of touch with modern scholarship and the modern world. A further article by d'Hulst, aimed at promoting tolerance of the more searching kind of Biblical criticism, gave offense in orthodox quarters, and d'Hulst felt obliged to clear his institute of any suspicion of unorthodoxy. Therefore, when Loisy continued to declare his critical independence of dogma and revelation, and to present a historical Jesus apart from the Christ of faith, he was forced to resign his chair in 1893.

As a reply to modernist exegesis, the pope issued the encyclical *Providentissimus Deus* (November 18, 1893), denying that error is compatible with divine authorship. Loisy wrote to Leo XIII, professing submission to the encyclical's demand that the truth of the Bible should not be questioned. His insincerity can be inferred, however, for his activities remained unchanged. In fact, on receiving a reply in a mollified tone that invited him to devote himself to less contentious studies, Loisy openly expressed his impatience.

Loisy criticized the Protestant scholar Harnack's *Wesen des Christentums* (Leipzig, 1900) in his *L'Évangile et l'église* (Paris, 1902), which was condemned by the archbishop of Paris as undermining faith in the authority of Scripture and the divinity of Jesus Christ. Loisy wrote an apology, *Autour d'un petit livre* (Paris, 1903), which, with four other works of his, was condemned by the Holy Office and placed on the Index in 1903. The papal secretary of state required the archbishop of Paris to demand that Loisy withdraw the five offending volumes, but Loisy refused.

He wrote in conciliatory terms to Pope Pius X, but the development of his religious ideas—or, in Catholic eyes, the disintegration of his faith—could ultimately lead only to his exclusion from the Roman communion. He regarded such mysteries as the incarnation of God as mere metaphors and symbols, and described his own religious belief as pantheistic, positivistic, or humanitarian rather than Christian. He conceived the basic problem facing the man torn between belief and doubt to be whether the world contains or embodies any spiritual principle apart from man's own consciousness.

In 1907 the papal secretary of state called upon Loisy to repudiate certain propositions, attributed to him and condemned in the decree *Lamentabili* (July 2, 1907), and to disown Modernism, condemned in Pius X's encyclical *Pascendi Dominici Gregis* (September 6, 1907). Loisy replied that where his views were not misrepresented in the decree, he felt obliged to stand by them, since he regarded them as true. The demands were repeated, and Loisy was required to submit within ten days. He still refused and was thereupon excommunicated.

Loisy's break with the church in 1908 put an end to what had become a false and increasingly impossible position. In 1909 he was appointed professor of the history of religion at the Collège de France, a chair that he held until 1927 and that allowed him to continue publishing in freedom. He published memoirs of his most controversial years in *Choses passées* (Paris, 1913).

His *Naissance du christianisme* (Paris, 1933) drew together and presented more intransigently views that he had held and expressed earlier, but his disbelief in the truth of the Gospel narratives and the Acts of the Apostles was now more pronounced. The supernatural elements were discredited, and the view of the historical Jesus was not very different from those of Strauss and Renan. A prophet appeared in Galilee and was crucified while Pontius Pilate governed Judaea. The rest—the alleged events of Jesus' life and his subsequent deification by his followers—belonged, for Loisy as for Renan, to the realm of myth and Messianic aspiration in search of its symbolic figure.

Additional Works by Loisy

Histoire du canon de l'Ancien Testament. Paris, 1890.
Histoire du canon du Nouveau Testament. Paris, 1891.
Histoire critique du texte et des versions de l'Ancien Testament. Paris, 1892.

Le Quatrième Évangile. Paris, 1903.
Les Évangiles synoptiques. Paris, 1908.
Jésus et la tradition évangélique. Paris, 1910.
À propos d'histoire des religions. Paris, 1911.
Les Mystères païens et le mystère chrétien. Paris, 1914.
La Paix des nations et la religion de l'avenir. Paris, 1920.
La Morale humaine. Paris, 1923.

Works on Loisy

Petre, M. D., *Alfred Loisy: His Religious Significance.* London, 1944.
Vidler, A. R., *The Modernist Movement in the Roman Catholic Church.* London, 1934. Pp. 67–139.

COLIN SMITH

LOMBARD, PETER. See PETER LOMBARD.

LOPATIN, LEO MIKHAILOVICH (1855–1920), Russian philosopher and psychologist, was one of a number of Russian thinkers—such as A. A. Kozlov—to advance a pluralistic idealism or personalism inspired by the monadology of Leibniz. Lopatin was for many years professor of philosophy at Moscow University, president of the Moscow Psychological Society, and editor of the leading Russian journal, *Voprosy Filosofii i Psikhologii* ("Problems of Philosophy and Psychology"). He wrote extensively and is famous for the clarity and beauty of his style. His thought owed much not only to Leibniz (and to Lotze) but also to his longtime friend, the Russian philosopher Vladimir Solovyov.

Lopatin held that every activity or process presupposes an agent. In his metaphysics there is a plurality of agents, which are spiritual entities (monads), supratemporal, and thus indestructible (since destruction involves cessation of existence in time). He held that God is related to this plurality as its unifying ground, but he did not develop fully the character of this relationship. Lopatin's chief contributions to the general doctrine of monads are his view of the substantiality of the individual spirit and his doctrine of "creative causality." According to the former, the individual spirit is neither a substance which is separate from its phenomena nor a pure succession of absolute states; each of these conceptions is fundamentally self-contradictory. Rather, the spirit is a substance which is immanent in its phenomena; its phenomena are the direct realization of its nature. Each individual spirit, moreover, is a "creative" or productive cause; temporal, mechanical causality, and necessity, as well as all material properties—such as extension—are derivatives of the primary causality of supratemporal spirit.

Lopatin was the first of the Russian Leibnizians to give thorough attention to the moral sphere. The doctrine of creative causality gave him a basis for asserting the freedom of the will and for developing an ethical personalism in which moral phenomena represent the highest manifestation of the creative activity of individual spirit. Thus moral phenomena have metaphysical significance, and despite the evil and the inefficacy of good which we observe in the world, reality contains a moral order and is not "indifferent to the realization of the moral ideal."

Just as in ethics Lopatin maintained that unaided experience is not an adequate guide, so in epistemology generally, he discounted pure empiricism in favor of "speculative" principles, defining speculative philosophy as "the knowledge of real things in their principles and in their ultimate signification." Man's immediate inner experience is the source of his knowledge of real things, but philosophy works on this experience and goes beyond it through rational speculation.

Works by Lopatin

Polozhitel'nyye Zadachi Filosofii ("The Positive Tasks of Philosophy"), 2 vols. Moscow, 1886–1891.

Filosofskiye Kharakteristiki i Rechi ("Philosophical Characterizations and Addresses"). Moscow, 1911. The chapter entitled "Filosofskoe Mirosozertsaniye V. S. Solovyova" (pp. 120–156) was translated by A. Bakshy as "The Philosophy of Vladimir Soloviev." *Mind*, Vol. 25 (October 1916), 425–460.

Works on Lopatin

Ognev, A., *Lev Mikhailovich Lopatin.* Petrograd, 1922.

Zenkovsky, V. V., *Istoriya Russkoy Filosofii*, 2 vols. Paris, 1948–1950. Translated by George L. Kline as *A History of Russian Philosophy.* New York and London, 1953.

JAMES P. SCANLAN

LOSSKY, NICHOLAS ONUFRIYEVICH (1870–1965), Russian intuitionist philosopher, was born in the village of Kreslavka, Vitebsk Province, where he received his early education. He studied at the University of St. Petersburg and graduated from the faculty of arts and natural science there. He did postgraduate work in Germany under Wilhelm Windelband, Wilhelm Wundt, and G. E. Müller. In 1903 he obtained his master's degree and four years later was awarded his doctorate. Upon his return to Russia he was appointed lecturer and later associate professor at his alma mater in St. Petersburg, where he taught until 1921. In 1922 Lossky was exiled from Russia by the Soviet government because of his religious beliefs. He went to Prague upon the invitation of Tomáš Masaryk and was appointed professor at the Russian University in Prague. He also taught at the Charles University in Prague and at the University of Bratislava. In 1946 he emigrated to the United States and was professor for a number of years at the St. Vladimir Russian Orthodox Seminary in New York City. Lossky was a prolific writer and was regarded as the dean of contemporary Russian philosophers. His books have been translated into many foreign languages.

Lossky's philosophical system is a synthesis of a number of influences, the most pronounced being Leibnizian monadology and Bergsonian intuitionism. Lossky called his system intuitivism or ideal-realism. We shall examine his system from the three central themes inherent in his *Weltanschauung*—epistemology, metaphysics, and ethics.

Lossky's epistemological views were first outlined in his book *The Intuitive Basis of Knowledge* and were further expounded in "Sensory, Intellectual, and Mystical Intuition." His epistemology may be characterized as a synthesis of absolute immanentism and absolute intuitivism. It is based on his assertion that "everything is immanent in everything else."

According to Lossky, we know an object immediately, or intuitively. The object we intuit is not a copy or a representation but is the real original object. There is no causal relation between subject and object. The connection between subject and object is achieved by an "epistemological coordination" which is supertemporal and superspatial. It is this coordination which makes knowledge possible for all substantival agents in the world. According to Lossky, all human knowledge is experienced through sensory, intellectual, or mystical intuition. These three types of intuition correspond to three kinds of being. All events of a nonspatiotemporal nature, such as relations between a quality and its bearer, number, unity, or plurality, are ideal being. All events of a spatiotemporal character are real being. The third kind of being is metalogical being, or the Absolute, which transcends the laws of identity, contradiction, and the excluded middle. Intellectual intuition is to be understood in the Platonic sense of "beholding ideas." It is passive and purely contemplative. Lossky identified intellectual intuition with thought, which reveals transsubjective relations but does not create them. Although the Absolute is a supermundane being, it is also an object of intuition. It is cognized by the subject through mystical intuition. By substituting "epistemological coordination" for "causal relation," Lossky did not really succeed in explaining how this coordination operates in relating object and subject. In the final analysis, his epistemology is simply an ontology of cognition.

Lossky's metaphysics is essentially a variation of Leibnizian monadology. Leibniz' "windowless" monads became for Lossky substantival agents that can have mutual interaction through intuition.

Lossky developed an intricate system of beings, which he called hierarchical personalism. He began with the lowest and simplest form of being, such as an atom, and proceeded up the scale of being to higher forms, such as man. He then introduced a supermundane principle, or the Absolute, in order to avoid a radical plurality and to make the unity of the cosmos intelligible. The Absolute creates potential beings, called substantival agents. These agents are supertemporal and superspatial, and they possess freedom of choice. Through freedom of choice they strive to achieve a higher form of being. Thus, a human being may, through a period of billions of years, evolve from a proton. A potential agent becomes an actual person when he apprehends absolute values and recognizes the duty to apply them in his moral behavior.

The cosmos is the result of the constant mutual conflict between substantival agents. The cosmos in turn leads to the origin of space and time. Lossky regarded space and time as modes of activity of the agents. From this premise, which he considered to be self-evident, he concluded that the cosmos does not exist in space and time. Unity, or consubstantiality, is preserved by the Absolute, who is incommensurable with the cosmos. Lossky insisted on religious experience, or devotional communion, which enables a person to discover the Absolute as a living God. Man's ultimate destiny is to experience absolute fullness of being, which is achieved through mystical intuition with the triune God. Lossky's metaphysics is a synthesis of speculative philosophy and religious mysticism.

Lossky's ethical views flow directly from his metaphysics. They are based on the idea that existence and value are mutually related. The concept of freedom is central in his ethics. Since man as an ideal self possesses freedom of choice, he may choose God, who is a living reality, or he may choose the path away from God, which Lossky termed the "basic moral evil." Man's ultimate destiny is to become the ideal self, which is the normative principle of his moral behavior. Lossky left no room for a relative ethics. His is an absolutistic ethics applicable to the ideal self.

Works by Lossky

Die Grundlehre der Psychologie vom Standpunkte des Voluntarismus ("The Fundamental Doctrines of Psychology from the Point of View of Voluntarism"). Leipzig, 1904. Originally published in Russian in 1903. German translation by E. Kleuker.
Obosnovaniye Intuitivizma. St. Petersburg, 1906. Translated by N. A. Duddington as *The Intuitive Basis of Knowledge.* London, 1919.
Mir kak Organicheskoe Tseloe. Moscow, 1917. Translated by N. A. Duddington as *The World as an Organic Whole.* Oxford, 1928.
Svoboda Voli. Paris, 1927. Translated by N. A. Duddington as *Freedom of Will.* London, 1932.
Tipy Mirovozzreniy ("Types of World Views"). Paris, 1931.
Tsennost i Bytie. Paris, 1931. Translated by S. S. Vinokooroff as *Value and Existence.* London, 1935.
Chuvstvennaya, Intellektualnaya i Mysticheskaya Intuitsiya ("Sensory, Intellectual, and Mystical Intuition"). Paris, 1938.
Des Conditions de la morale absolue: Fondements de l'ethique. Translated by S. Jankélévitch. Neuchâtel, 1948. First published in Slovak in 1944.
Bog i Mirovoye Zlo ("God and Cosmic Evil"). Paris, 1941.

Works on Lossky

Askoldov, S. A., "Novaya Gnoseologicheskaya Teoriya N. O. Losskago." *Zhurnal Ministerstva Narodnago Prosveshcheniya,* N.S., Pt. V (1906), 413–441.
Askoldov, S. A., *Mysl i Deistvitelnost.* Moscow, 1914.
Berdyaev, Nikolai, "Ob Ontologicheskoi Gnoseologii." *Voprosy Filosofii i Psikhologii,* No. 93.
Boldyrev, D. V., *Znanie i Bytie.* Harbin, Manchuria, 1935.
Duddington, N. A., "Philosophy in Russia." *Journal of Philosophical Studies,* Vols. 1–3 (1926–1929), Vol. 6 (1931).
Duddington, N. A., "The Philosophy of N. O. Lossky." *Dublin Review,* Vol. 192 (1933), 233–244.
Harms, E., "Besprechung des Werkes Losskijs 'Handbuch der Logik.'" *Der russische Gedanke,* Vol. 1 (1929–1930).
Hessen, S., "Besprechung des Buches Losskijs 'Svoboda Voli.'" *Der russische Gedanke,* Vol. 1 (1929–1930).
Ivanovsky, I., "O Nekotorykh Nedoumeniakh Vyzvaemykh Intuitivizmom N. O. Losskago," in *Sbornik Statei v Chest D. A. Korssakova.* 1913.
Jakowenko, B., "Besprechung des Buches Losskijs 'The World as an Organic Whole.'" *Der russische Gedanke,* Vol. I (1929–1930), 109–110.
Karzes, I., "Nikolaj Onufriewitsch Losskij und seine Lehre," in F. Cohen, ed., *Festschrift N. O. Losskij zum 60. Geburtstage.* Bonn, 1932. This volume contains an extensive bibliography of Lossky's writings.
Kohanski, A. S., *Lossky's Theory of Knowledge.* Nashville, Tenn., 1936.
Lopatin, L. M., "Novaya Teoriya Poznaniya." *Voprosy Filosofii i Psikhologii,* No. 87.
Polanowski, Feiga, *Losskys erkenntnistheoretische Intuitivismus.* Berlin, 1931.
Povarin, S., *Ob Intuitivizme N. O. Losskago.* St. Petersburg, 1911.
Tomkieieff, S., "The Philosophy of N. O. Lossky." *Durham University Philosophical Society Proceedings,* Vol. 6 (1923), 375–393.
Vvedensky, A., *Logika, kak Chast Teorii Poznaniya.* St. Petersburg, 1912.
Wenley, R. M., "Mystical Realism." *Anglican Theological Review,* Vol. 24 (1929), 342–347.
Zenkovsky, V. V., "Besprechung der Schrift Losskijs 'Sein und Wert.'" *Put,* Vol. 30 (1931), 89–91.

Louis J. Shein

LOTZE, RUDOLF HERMANN (1817–1881), German idealist metaphysician, was born in Bautzen. He studied medicine and philosophy at the University of Leipzig, taking his doctorates in both fields. He studied mathematics and physics with E. H. Weber, W. Volckmann, and G. T. Fechner and philosophy with C. H. Weisse, who influenced him greatly. In 1841 he became instructor in medicine at Leipzig, where he subsequently taught philosophy. While at Leipzig he published two short works, the *Metaphysik* (Leipzig, 1841) and *Logik* (Leipzig, 1843), which adumbrated the essentials of his later philosophy. In 1844 Lotze succeeded Johann Friedrich Herbart as professor of philosophy at the University of Göttingen. He remained there until 1881, when he was called to the University of Berlin. Shortly after joining the faculty at Berlin, he contracted pneumonia and died.

Lotze pursued his interests in the medical sciences, psychology, philosophy, the arts, and literature throughout his life. As a result of his medical training, he developed a strong love for exact investigation and precise knowledge, but art and literature made him particularly sensitive to the central role of feeling and value in the total life of a culture. He wanted nothing to interfere with the growth of the exact sciences in all areas of human experience, yet he insisted that both intellect and scientific knowledge were essentially the means and tools of feeling, emotion, and intuition.

New conception of metaphysics. Like many thinkers born in the first two decades of the nineteenth century, Lotze faced three great schisms: the schism between science and Christianity, which was known at that time as the conflict between science and religion; the schism between reason and feeling; and the schism between knowledge and value. To Lotze, these schisms had to be rationally harmonized in some manner. It seemed impossible to him for any rational man to reject any one of the trinity that composes the total culture of man: science, art, and value. Each has its place in the life of man and the universe, and none can be eliminated without distorting and destroying that life. However, Lotze felt that their proper relationship cannot be established by the older metaphysical methods. There is no possibility of rationally deducing the basic categories and values of existence by any sort of logical dialectic, either Platonic or Hegelian. Knowledge of existence depends upon knowledge of fact acquired through observation and experimentation. Consequently, the empirical sciences are the proper investigators of existence. All that metaphysics can do is to analyze, clarify, and order those concepts and theories that the sciences create into as adequate a system as the facts permit. Metaphysics cannot go beyond this in any scientific sense. Nevertheless, Lotze admitted that metaphysics has another, broader purpose. The urge to be metaphysical is not to be found in metaphysics itself but in ethics, in the desire to know and attain some ultimate good. Thus, metaphysics involves speculating beyond what is scientifically warrantable in order to include that which drives men to write metaphysics: the experience of ultimate goodness.

Because metaphysics must be founded upon science, Lotze objected to any philosophical system that claimed completeness. All philosophical systems, like his own, must remain open and undogmatic. They must not even provide provisional answers to profound questions for which not even provisional answers exist. He thought it was far better for a philosopher to raise questions and to stimulate inquiry than to offer sterile answers lacking any reasonable foundation in fact.

Idealistic monadism, mechanism, and God. Lotze was essentially an idealist, but his idealism was tempered by his respect for science and his emphasis upon feeling as the dominant element guaranteeing meaning to the life of man.

From the beginning, Lotze considered thought as one aspect of the soul. Thought is aware only of ideas about reality; it does not know reality, for knowledge and reality can never be identical. Neither are experience and thought to be identified. Identity with reality or object can be achieved as experience, never as thought, for thought is purely representative. Truth is attained in ways different from thought. Thought must fuse with the total feeling experience, since it is in feeling that we have direct awareness of good and evil, beauty and ugliness, worth and unworth, contradiction and harmony; these rest in the soul's original capacity to experience pain and pleasure. Consequently, Lotze thought that feeling is the ultimate arbiter of consistency and intellectual harmony, the ultimate judge of the worth of anything, and the ultimate creator of imagination and its works. Moreover, feeling is the nisus that drives man to seek whatever total unity of comprehension and action is possible for him. His love of knowledge, goodness, and beauty arises from, and finds its fulfillment in, feeling. Thus, the essential nature of feeling is love, which constantly drives man toward a greater over-all comprehension of his life and the cosmos. "If . . . love did not lie at the foundation of the world . . . this world . . . would be left without truth and without law."

Feeling convinced Lotze that the world is psychical and thus consists of souls as well as a personal deity. A soul is not simply a stream of impressions united by memory; it is a substantival entity, causally related to the body and interacting with it. Nevertheless, the soul is the greater influence and governs the body in ways closed to it. Both soul and body act according to law, but the laws of bodies as such are purely physical. The laws of the soul are on a higher level; they are teleological and unite the physical and the mental. They do not contradict the laws of the physical world, but they do control and reorder them.

A personal deity, God, follows from the existence of souls and ends. How else can they be explained? The world and everything in it is the personal creation of God and the means by which he attains his ends and the ends of his creatures. However, Lotze tempered this conviction by insisting that God attains his ends through the mechanisms or causal nexuses that science discovers, and he further insisted that these mechanisms are characteristic of both the living and the nonliving.

Lotze rejected the notion that telic and nontelic explanations are incompatible with each other. He opposed the older forms of vitalism popular in his day. He argued that mechanisms are simply the instruments, or tools, by which God accomplishes his ends in the world. Although it is true that God might have used other means, he preferred mechanism as a way of establishing universal law in both the physical and psychic realms.

Lotze argued further that the thesis of mechanism should not be identified with materialism. Mechanism does not imply the nonexistence of ends or of psychic beings; it implies only the existence of uniform modes by which things come into being. The world can just as easily be psychic as material, but the psychic interpretation is rationally to be preferred because it does not make a mystery or a paradox of the presence of feeling and values in the world.

In the *Mikrokosmus*, Lotze continued to elaborate this position. Mechanism is simply a method of research; it is not a fundamental explanation of life and mind. Only the most exhaustive survey of the life of man can provide such an explanation and relate his life to the cosmos and God. Furthermore, mechanism does not repudiate free will; it is simply the necessary condition for the will to express its autonomy.

For Lotze, there are three realms of observations: the realm of fact, the realm of universal law, and the realm of values, which serve as standards of meaning for the world. These realms are only logically separable; they cannot be separated in reality. Fact and law are the means, the mechanisms, by which values are attained in this world; they are also the means by which men discover that certain values are foolish, contradictory, unrealizable, or in other words, false. Since fact and universal law are not existentially separable from value, God must also be the creator of everything and the quintessence of whatever deserves to exist for its own sake. Moreover, since feeling is fundamental, a sort of pluralistic idealism in which the only realities are living spirits and God in interaction is justified. All other realities are so only secondarily, as manifestations of these spiritual activities.

Lotze ultimately accepted a variant of Leibnizian monadism as a correct interpretation of experience. There is no single unity or oneness to existence. Direct experience reveals an irreducible multiplicity of things. Reality is always in flux, always involving constant doing and suffering. However, the flux, the doing, and the suffering occur within a fixed order, a pre-established harmony between God and the multitude of spirits.

Lotze recognized that this metaphysical theory is neither a logical deduction from experience nor completely intelligible, but he believed it to be a reasonable inference from the manner in which the valid experiential concepts of our thought, the flux of facts, and the order of values interconnect in our experience. To limit ourselves to what science understands is to exclude unjustifiably the realms of feeling and values, and to exclude the latter is to render our experience unintelligible.

Piety. To Lotze, nature and the social life are the two fundamental sources for religious ideas. From nature we derive the concept of God; from our social life, the concepts of ethical living. Paganism has tended to emphasize the cosmological; Christianity, the ethical. Christianity has sought to fuse both into one complete theological scheme. In this it is mistaken. To Lotze, the ethical element in religion is far more significant than the cosmological (which can properly be left to science), even though the emphasis upon cosmology leads to recognition of God. The true mark of the religious man is not his cosmology but his feeling for, and search after, what ought to be, his passion for, and loyalty to, the highest possible ideals. This passion and loyalty, however, are not so much activistic as contemplative.

Piety, for Lotze, is found in the inner life, in a feeling for the holy that attains so high a state of intuitive comprehension that logic, reason, becomes futile and inessential. Piety lies beyond any sectarian interest, Christian or not, for it drives men to seek a totality of feeling in which truth is completely fused with goodness and beauty. In consequence, the holy is not merely what men think it is; it is rather the unattained, the beyond in our lives that is without contradiction, defect, or dissonance. It is manifested in the endless striving for that immortal sea that is the infinite parent of all things. In this contemplative striving, in this endless search for total harmony and for the ought-to-be lies the possibility of progressively uniting science, religion, and art. However, the overwhelming realization of this unity occurs only at particular moments when one is moved by the experience of total beauty. In such moments, one knows absolutely that the fusion has, as far as possible, been accomplished.

Influence. Lotze's influence in Germany, France, and England was considerable during his lifetime. Philosophers became more empirical-minded, less dogmatic. More consideration was given to the feeling, experiential aspects of human life. Nevertheless, Lotze left few, if any, disciples, and no Lotzean school of philosophers arose.

In America, Lotze's influence during the 1870s and 1880s was felt both in church and philosophical circles. Reverend Joseph Cook of Boston made him widely popular, hailing him as the seer who had made the microscope the instrument of immortality and science the humble servant of the Bible. Leading American philosophers like B. P. Bowne, G. T. Ladd, and Josiah Royce were particularly influenced, for he offered them an experiential mode of reconciling their strong Christian commitments with the methods and conclusions of science.

Bibliography

The principal writings of Lotze include *Allgemeine Pathologie und Therapie als mechanische Naturwissenschaften* (Leipzig, 1842); *Medicinische Psychologie oder Physiologie der Seele* (Leipzig, 1852); *Mikrokosmus*, 3 vols. (Leipzig, 1856–1864), translated by E. Hamilton and E. E. C. Jones as *Microcosmus*, 2 vols. (Edinburgh, 1885–1886); and *Die Geschichte der Aesthetik in Deutschland* (Munich, 1868). Lotze planned a comprehensive account of his philosophy in three volumes entitled *System der Philosophie*. The first part was *Logik* (Leipzig, 1874), and the second, *Metaphysik* (Leipzig, 1879). These were translated into English and edited by Bernard Bosanquet as *Lotze's System of Philosophy* (Oxford, 1884). The third volume, which was to have covered religion, art, and practical philosophy, was incomplete at the time of his death. See also *Kleine Schriften*, D. Peipers, ed., 3 vols. (Leipzig, 1885–1891).

For literature on Lotze, see Karl Robert Eduard von Hartmann, *Lotzes Philosophie* (Leipzig, 1888); Henry Jones, *A Critical Account of the Philosophy of Lotze* (Glasgow, 1895); J. W. Schmidt-Japing, *Lotzes Religionsphilosophie in ihrer Entwicklung . . .* (Göttingen, 1925); E. E. Thomas, *Lotze's Theory of Reality* (London, 1921); and Max Wentscher, *H. Lotze. Lotzes Leben und Werke*, Vol. I (Heidelberg, 1913).

RUBIN GOTESKY

LOVE. Love as a concept enters philosophy at one point through religion, particularly when the origin of the world is expressed as an act of procreation or the Creator is conceived of as loving his creation either as a whole or in part (i.e., the human race). But the concept of love is also a subject for philosophic meditation in regard to ethical problems. Love, as one of the most powerful of human impulses, was early seen to be much in need of control, especially if man as rational animal was to be able to use his rational capacities. Much of the ethical writing on love is designed to suggest some means whereby the pleasures and other values of loving may be preserved without entailing the supposed evils of intemperate sexuality. This type of speculation ran from Plato through the Neoplatonists—those of both the early Christian period and the Italian Renaissance. In the Platonic tradition love had a unique metaphysical status, for it existed in both the material and the ideal worlds. Love can take on many forms, from gross sexual passion to a devotion to learning, but, it was argued, the ultimate object of love is the beautiful. The goodness that God sees in his creation is its beauty and to feel the beauty of the world is to love it and its Creator.

Classical mythology. The word "eros" as it is found in Homer is not the name of a god but simply a common noun meaning "love" or "desire." In Hesiod's *Theogony* Eros becomes one of the three primordial gods, the other two being Chaos and Earth. Although Eros has no offspring and seems to play no role in the genealogy of the gods, he has the greatest power over his fellow immortals. He unnerves the limbs and overcomes the reason of both gods and men. When Aphrodite is born from the sperm of Uranus (Heaven), Eros and Himeros (desire, longing, lust) accompany her into the council of the gods. Whether Hesiod was talking in terms of personalized abstractions or was actually thinking of anthropomorphic beings is not clear, for the *Theogony* is a curious mixture of both kinds of expression. For the history of philosophy, the importance of Hesiod's brief mention of Eros lies in the attribution to him of a power that is the enemy of reason. Something similar is to be found in Sophocles' *Antigone* in the chorus that is sung just after Creon has announced that Antigone must die for having buried her brother's body. Eros is addressed as the god who has brought about Antigone's tragedy. He is described as unconquerable, destructive, roaming over the sea and among the dwellers of the wilderness. Neither the gods nor ephemeral mankind can escape him; he drives his victims to madness and turns the just to evil. An even stronger denunciation of the god may be found in Euripides' *Hippolytus,* along with the additional warning that whether one surrenders to love or refuses to capitulate to it, one is doomed. And indeed, Phaedra, whose successors are obviously Vergil's Dido and

Racine's Phèdre, became the prototype of a woman ruined by Eros.

Such poetic passages reflect certain observations about human nature and human behavior. They point to a struggle within man's psyche between a rational, controllable, prudent, and wise agent and an irrational, uncontrollable, mad, and foolish agent. When the former is in control, man will behave in praiseworthy fashion, but when the latter gains the upper hand, he will act like a beast. He will abandon reason that, according to most of the ancients, alone distinguishes him from the beasts. Although man also has an animal nature, to yield to its demands is to betray his essential nature. The notion that Eros might reinforce the human element in man does not appear in the pre-Platonic writers.

Early philosophic reflections. The Greeks admitted several forms of love, including heterosexual and homosexual passion; parental, filial, and conjugal affection; fraternal feeling; friendship; love of country; and the love of wisdom. All were associated with either Eros or *Philia* (fondness or friendship). Love was believed to be a power capable of uniting people in a common bond. And since not only people but also animals and the elements were thus united, it was appropriate to conceive of this power as lodged in a single agent that governed the whole cosmos. According to Parmenides, Love was created by the goddess Necessity, and in the writing of Empedocles, love emerges as one of the two universal forces (the other being strife) that explain the course of cosmic history. These two agents—the one of union, the other of decomposition—are not simply names for the fact that composition and decomposition occur; on the contrary, love and strife are not resident in things but are external to them and act upon them. According to Empedocles, the cosmos, so to speak, is held in tension between the forces of harmony and disunion. Were the two forces to be synchronously present, the world would clearly be in a state of disorder. Hence, Empedocles introduced the idea of cycles into his philosophy, as well as the concept of world history as an alternation of the reigns of Love and Strife. When Love is in control, the elements form compounds out of which arise more complex units and, eventually, animate beings. In the primitive period of the cycle, men worship Aphrodite, are innocent of slaughter and, presumably, of war, and are, moreover, vegetarians. "The altar did not reek of the unmixed blood of bulls, but this was the greatest abomination among men, to snatch out the life and eat the goodly limbs" (Fragment 128). But when Strife is dominant, disorganization, the ultimate disaggregation of the elements, and war and all its attendant evils, take the place of the blessings of love. As far as we can tell from the surviving fragments, Empedocles believed that the cyclical process was everlasting.

The attribution of peace and harmony to the goddess Aphrodite (Empedocles' name for love) is clearly a renunciation of the early poets' idea of love. Empedocles' conception of her resembles the *alma* Venus of Lucretius. Yet she remains the goddess of sexual love, for sexual love has become one example of the universal power of union: it provides the philosopher with empirical evidence of a metaphysical principle.

Plato. For a complete expression of a philosophic concept of love, one must turn to Plato's *Symposium*. Probably no other document in European literature has had as much influence on the philosophy of love. The various speeches that are reported in this dialogue represent points of view with which Plato does not always agree but which he apparently thought important enough to be presented as typical. These speeches range from an encomium of love's effect on morality to a description of its effect on knowledge. Phaedrus likened the passionate attachment between Achilles and Patroclus to the conjugal affection between Alcestis and Admetus. In both cases it is the lover, not the beloved, who has gained virtue through his or her love. In the following speech, by Pausanias, two kinds of love are distinguished, that of the heavenly Aphrodite and that of the earthly Aphrodite, or the love of the soul and the love of the body. The former is more likely to be the love of a young man (not a boy) at the time when his reason begins to develop and his beard begins to grow. In this speech honorable love is clearly the attraction that a man has for a virtuous soul and is fused in the mind of the speaker with philosophy itself, which is the love of wisdom. It is this honorable love which Eryximachus then describes as the source of harmony and the preserver of the good. The conclusion drawn from these encomiums is that love is in essence the love of beauty and that beauty is nothing material; it is an ideal. But no man desires the ideal until he has been educated through philosophic training. In the final speech, which supposedly reports the philosophy of the seeress Diotima, we find that there is a scale of beauty, progressing from that of bodies through that of forms, thoughts, minds, institutions and laws, the sciences, to absolute or ideal beauty.

Beauty, for Plato, was the one bridge between the two realms of the material and the ideal, particulars and universals. (This appears clearly enough in the *Phaedrus;* what the *Symposium* adds is a discussion of the power that draws men to beauty in its many modes.) The two realms present not simply a duality of kind but also of value, for the ideal and the universal, which are perfect and eternal, are always to be preferred to the material and the particular. Sexual love itself, although lowest on the scale of love, is nevertheless the seed of ideal love, since what attracts a man to the beloved is beauty.

Aristotle. Plato's account of love, insofar as it concerns friendship, was amplified by Aristotle in the eighth and ninth books of the *Nicomachean Ethics*. But Aristotle treated chiefly the ethical and psychological aspects of the matter. He also utilized the metaphor of the attractive power of love in explaining the motion of the planetary spheres, the Unmoved Mover being the beloved and the planetary system the lover. With important differences that will be mentioned below, the Unmoved Mover became a part of the Christian concept of God.

Transition to Christianity. In the *Magna Moralia*, which was probably composed at least in part by Aristotle, it is written that "It would be strange if one were to say that he loved Zeus. . . . It is not love towards God of which we are in search . . . but love towards things with life, that is, where there can be a return of affection." God then is thought to be incapable of returning our love for him, assuming that we can have love for him. In fact, although there are myths in which gods and mortals have been in love with each other, the gods always first disguise themselves as mortals, as Aphrodite did when she fell in love with Anchises, or take on various other forms, which was the habit of Zeus. These myths all deal with sexual intercourse, not with friendship or paternal affection. Omitting the culture heroes, there was no god or goddess in ancient mythology who had any love for mankind. Prometheus is an exception, but he was punished for his help to mortals, and in all probability the historic Greeks thought of him as simply a personification of forethought.

There is no god in classical religion who could be called "our father in heaven." The attitude that Lucretius tried to foster in the minds of his fellow Romans was supposed to be an antidote to their fear of the gods. According to the legends, however, there was good reason to fear them. Ceres and Bacchus may have given men bread and wine, but most of the divinities did little more than take revenge on the human race for the injuries they had received from their fellow gods. In Judaism and Christianity, however, a new relationship to the divinity was established. As early as Deuteronomy 6.5 the commandment was laid down to love God "with all thine heart, and with all thy soul, and with all thy might," a commandment repeated by Jesus (Matthew 22.37) as the first and great commandment, followed by the second, "Thou shalt love thy neighbor as thyself." It will be observed that now love is not seen as a power that destroys man's reason, but rather, as an emotional attitude that can be voluntarily produced. It is praised in the Psalms (for example, 91.14) and also in the First Epistle to the Corinthians and the First Epistle of John (I John 4.16–20). Both epistles cite the power of love to heal discord and fear, and love is represented as a bond between God and man. According to the Gospel of John (3.16), it is because of God's love for the world that redemption is brought to man.

That man could love God, even if he could not love Zeus, had been seen by Philo Judaeus in his *Questions on Genesis* (XVIII, 16) in which he says that once a man has received a clear impression of God and God's powers, his soul is filled with longing for union with God. Thus, in the First Epistle of John, God is identified with love, "and he that dwelleth in love dwelleth in God, and God in him" (I John 4.16). This idea was also found in non-Christian theologians of Hellenistic times, for example, in the *Hermetica* (*Asclepius* II, Sec. 21), in which all things, including God, are said to be bisexual, a unity that is approximated by men and women in sexual love. This unity is admittedly incomprehensible and what "you might correctly call either Cupid or Venus." But in both Philo and the *Hermetica*, as in Plotinus and Cleanthes' "Hymn to Zeus," the original stimulus to the love of God is knowledge, not sexual love. In *Asclepius* (XIII, 9) the love of God is reduced to worship, sacrifice, prayer, and reverence, and these follow upon a knowledge of the divine nature. In Plotinus the union with God, although aided by ascetic practices, is nevertheless the climax of cognition. Since knowledge occurs only between similar beings, to know God is to be like him; since God is unique, one must become absorbed into his being in order to know him.

This may seem to be suggested in the verses from the First Epistle of John cited above, but actually in John the love of God, although it unites man and God, is an act of will similar to the love for one's fellow man. It would presumably be made manifest by one's acts and one's faith; it is not the conclusion or fulfillment of a metaphysical system.

Although the Church Fathers came closest to an identification of God with Aristotle's Unmoved Mover and later Christian philosophers gave God the attributes of that ontological principle, there were differences that have too often been obscured. The Unmoved Mover was neither a person nor a creator; he was uniquely able to produce change without being altered himself, and he could thus suffer no emotions whatsoever. The Biblical God was the very antithesis of this. But in order to give an analogy of the way in which the Unmoved Mover moves the world, Aristotle took recourse to the metaphor of the beloved who attracts the lover. This, of course, became in time Dante's "love which moves that sun and the other stars." For Aristotle, however, the Unmoved Mover could not return the love of the beings who are below him. In Christianity, as in Judaism, it was essential that God love his creatures as they love him, and, as previously mentioned, love seems to have been thought of as subject to volition. According to Plato (to limit the discussion to him), love arose involuntarily at the sight of a beautiful body. A man's erotic education consisted in a denial, after an analysis of the nature of beauty, of the acts that usually follow such a sight. Once that denial became a part of a man's character, he could rise to allegedly nobler beauties until the final goal—the contemplation of absolute beauty completely detached from anything corporeal—was reached.

The early Christians had more confidence in man's will than had their pagan contemporaries. Both love of God and religious faith were thought to be subject to volition. The concept of believing in order to understand, as St. Augustine put it, was based on the assumption that belief was not the effect but the source of understanding. To what extent the early Christian writers were aware of the psychological effect of practicing certain rites, as Pascal later was, is difficult to say. But since great emphasis was put upon ceremonious expressions of devotion and upon the refusal to carry out pagan rites, we can assume that the practices were believed to induce the appropriate emotions. The most famous of such ceremonies was the Christian agape, in which the devout met to share a supper and to rejoice in their common beliefs. The word "agape" means both love and the object of love, although the pagan satires treated it as if it meant a sexual orgy. The participants in the agape probably thought of it as a ceremony of brotherly love commemorating the Last Supper, although according to the testimony of the Epistle of Jude (12), it was abused at a fairly early date. Whatever its origin and its primitive significance, it is clear that it was supposed to be a ceremony of affection, and it reinforced the friendliness that members of the same religion might be expected to have toward one another. Two emotional factors that seem to have been absent from paganism thus came into prominence in early Christianity—fraternal love as an essential of piety and filial love to a divine father, both of which were reciprocated. These forms of love were strengthened by the persecutions to which the early Christians were subjected—persecutions that bound them together in a special community and led to self-sacrifice in the various forms of martyrdom.

Augustine. Of the Church Fathers, it is St. Augustine who gives us the most detailed analysis of love, ranging from his youthful sexual escapades to his final love of God. The famous opening of Book II of the *Confessions* described his condition as one of utter subservience to the flesh. Just as he was capable of enjoying sin (in his case, petty theft), not for the loot it brought him but for the joy of sinning, so he enjoyed love not for the sake of his beloved, but for the sake of his own self-centered pleasure. He described in vivid terms the loathing that invaded him while satisfying his passion. The death of a dear friend aroused in him a realization of the egocentricity of his passion, and in planning to organize a small group of fellow Christians who would live in charity and share their belongings (a plan that came to nothing), he first approached unselfish love. Through self-knowledge he learned to look upon the eternal light and ultimately came to the complete love of God, which he described in the tenth book of the *Confessions.* The fruit of this love was knowledge of the divine. Whereas for Plato and Philo cognition led to love, for Augustine it was love that led to cognition. This theme was developed in the twelfth century by such writers as William of Saint Thierry and St. Bernard of Clairvaux.

Middle Ages. The ecstatic loss of self that accompanies sexual love was also assumed to be one of the features of the beatific vision. It is apparent in mystical literature that erotic language is especially effective in communicating mystical experience, and the similarities between religious and sexual ecstasy are manifest in, for example, the Song of Solomon. One should not conclude, however, that the medieval mystics were actually aware of the similarity between the beatific vision and sexual union, for those who are supposed to have made "mystic marriages," like the two St. Catherines, had presumably never had a corporeal marriage. Nonetheless, in mysticism the climax of the love of God was self-annihilation, much as in the Indian *mithuna,* and although the church never encouraged mystic practices, it had to admit their importance when they led to the immediate knowledge of God.

Thus, love in itself became an object of study, and the casuistry of love was elaborated in textbooks and poems as early as the twelfth century. Most of these writings seem to have taken as their source the *De Amore* of André le Chapelain which, whether intended to be serious or not, was taken seriously by most of its readers. It would appear to be a manual on seduction and to have only the most remote relevance to love. The time of its publication, however, coincided with the appearance of many commentaries on the Song of Solomon, and its influence on the rituals of the courts of love has been admitted by most medievalists. As the etiquette of the courts of love developed, love became an end in itself and was not necessarily to be gratified by sexual experience. The lover was supposed to serve his lady with no recompense other than the consciousness of his having served her. One can only guess at how faithfully the precepts of courtly love were carried

out, but as a set of ideas they form an important part of European moral philosophy. By elevating women to a position of irrefragable sovereignty over men, the ideals of courtly love became interwoven with the religious ideal of unquestioned loyalty to church and to God. The sovereign woman became identified with the Blessed Virgin to whom were applied many of the epithets of the bride in the Song of Solomon—rose of Sharon, the closed garden, the tower of ivory—phrases whose symbolical meaning had already been elaborated by St. Bernard. In the thirteenth century the question of the relative primacy of God's reason and will was disputed. For those who believed in the primacy of God's will, it followed that obedience rather than understanding was to be given the higher value. This was also true of courtly love and of chivalry as a doctrine.

Dante. The culmination of the medieval writing on love is, for modern readers, Dante's *Vita nuova.* However else this book may be interpreted, it is the story of how love that begins with the sight of a girl's beauty ends with a vision which Dante intimated was to be that of the *Divine Comedy.* For Dante the Johannine phrase "God is love" was of essential importance in religion. In ending the *Divine Comedy* with the love that moves the sun and the other stars, he identified his own love and all love with the love that the cosmos has for its Creator. His "new life" was not to be fulfilled in a union with the woman whom he loved but in her guiding him through paradise. Few words occur more frequently in the poems of Dante than "amore." Sometimes he seems to be writing in the vein of courtly love, sometimes in the mystical vein of St. Bernard, but in both cases love is represented as a force that attracts man to a nobler life. Dante does not overlook the sufferings of a man in love; indeed, he emphasizes them. But to suffer because of love appears to be analogous to the sufferings of the martyrs—an abnegation of the self for a value that transcends egoism.

Renaissance Neoplatonism. In Plotinus a distinction was made between three forms of love—love as a god, as a daemon, and as a passion. The first of these was again divided into the celestial and terrestrial Aphrodite. The celestial Aphrodite inspires the love of ideas and is the soul of the intelligible world. The terrestrial Aphrodite presides over marriage and is the soul of the sensible world. Love as a daemon is identified with the souls of individual human beings. As a passion it is the love of beauty in temperate men and the love of sexual pleasure in those who dwell exclusively in the material world of ugliness. All love, however, is the love of some degree of beauty. Plotinus adopted the scale of beauties that had been outlined in the *Symposium* and read into it a hierarchy of being. At the apex stood the One; the "way up" to the One led from the beauty of material objects to that of ideas. In this instance one sees again the fusion of the erotic passion with the ecstasy of the mystic vision. Paradoxically, an experience that is intimately associated with our bodily life was thought of as the one escape from it.

This complex of confused ideas permeated Renaissance Neoplatonism. Philosophers such as Marsilio Ficino and Pico della Mirandola constantly emphasized the power of love to free the soul from its bodily prison. They took over the theme of the two Venuses, and they assigned separate human faculties to each. They gave different names to the kinds of love—namely, divine, human, and animal.

Leone Ebreo. The philosophy of love expounded by Ficino and Mirandola was most fully developed by Leone Ebreo (Judah Abrabanel) in his *Dialoghi d'amore* (1501–1502), a work that circulated extensively not only in Italy but (in translation) through all Europe. Leone tied together the religious, philosophic, and literary traditions into a single network of ideas.

In the *Dialogues* the two interlocutors are Philo and Sophia, obviously elements of the word "philosophia." Philo is the lover, and Sophia is the beloved. The first dialogue distinguishes between love and desire and describes the various forms of love; the second discusses the presence of love in all natural operations, from the synthesis of the four elements to the movements of the planetary spheres; and the third deals with the love of God as the force that holds the universe together. Thus, it is asserted that love is a single principle permeating all things, from the material through the spiritual, and that this principle is the dynamic factor in cosmic change. There is no difference in essence between the attraction the elements have for one another and the forms of love that exist in human beings. The appraisal of the kinds of love is based on the objects of love, and Leone, like most of his contemporaries, thought that wisdom was inherently more valuable than pleasure.

It should be noted that the concept of a single dynamic power, whether it was called love or force or attraction, became more and more widely used as time went on. Its most extreme form was the *Sehnsucht* ("longing") of some German romantic philosophers, the *Streben* ("striving") of Fichte, and Novalis' endless and unfulfilled search for the blue flower. One of the characteristics of love, at least in the mind of Leone, is its inability ever to be satisfied. Though Philo in the *Dialogues* pleads with Sophia to tell him that she responds to his love, she will not do so.

Modern period. During the seventeenth and eighteenth centuries the interest in love was largely psychological and was expressed mainly in novels, poems, and maxims. While love of neighbor and God was approved, sexual love was morally more problematic. The ideal of female chastity was still upheld; in English novels, such as those of Richardson, a man was allowed to love a woman as long as he did not infringe upon her virginity. Whereas André le Chapelain graded sexual relations according to the social ranks of the maiden and her seducer, Richardson put all men and women on the same level in this respect. Thus, love was democratized. Sexual love was not to be condoned unless sanctified by the sacrament of marriage.

In such French novels as *Le Grand Cyrus* by Magdeleine de Scudéry, *Les Liaisons dangereuses* by Laclos, and *La Nouvelle Héloïse* by Rousseau, one finds more subtle distinctions and analyses. These authors continue the Renaissance casuistry about the different kinds of love and their respective values, but it must be remembered that their psychology of love was developed against the background of Christian moral principles. There is a constant conflict between the fervent religious and moral desire not to satisfy one's longings (described in *La Nouvelle Héloïse*) and an awareness of the almost unlimited force of the individual's erotic desires (treated in *Les Liaisons dangereuses*).

Spinoza. The *Ethics* of Spinoza was published in Holland in 1677. In this posthumous work, as in earlier publications, Spinoza emphasized man's need of perfection—that is, the fulfillment of both his intellectual and his emotional powers, which indeed were not existentially separate. He maintained that the more adequate an idea, the more it is pleasing, liberating, and intrinsically human. The culmination of the ethical life—that is, the life devoted to freedom of the intellect—is found in the "intellectual love of God." This phrase may have come from Leone Ebreo, but the idea goes back to St. Augustine. Both the *Confessions* and the *Ethics* are built on premises that are discovered by the intuitive process. The God of Spinoza is far from being the God of St. Augustine, but the method of finding him in the inner life and becoming aware of his presence is curiously similar. Both philosophers present a similar paradox: One must lose oneself in order to find oneself, but in so doing, one finds that what one has really discovered is God.

Other writers. The analysis of love now passes into the hands of psychologists. Destutt de Tracy and the novelist Stendhal both wrote books on love in which they attempted to probe its motivation and its effects upon conduct, but neither attempted to do more than to discuss love as a sexual experience. Destutt de Tracy's *De l'Amour* was not published until 1926, although it may have been known in manuscript form; Stendhal's *On Love*, however, was published in 1822, and although it had no popular success at the time, it was later widely read. In Germany, on the other hand, such books as Goethe's *Sorrows of Young Werther, Elective Affinities,* and, of course, *Faust* gave a quasi-religious tone to the sexual experience. The impossibility of attaining complete satisfaction led men of this tendency to idealize Don Juan as a perfectionist who seeks a goal that he can never reach, for the ideal is precisely that which ought to be and never is. K. W. F. Schlegel's *Lucinde* is a perfect example of this interpretation of love as the ever-sought and unrealizable ideal.

Schopenhauer. Schopenhauer was unique in condemning all forms of love on the grounds that they tie one to the will-to-live. But he found this will even in the subanimate world of nature; thus, he was reverting to the ancient tradition of an omnipresent principle and was more interested in the metaphysical status of this principle than in the details of human psychology. Although Schopenhauer's condemnation of love follows from his general metaphysical position, he supplemented this condemnation with an essay, "Metaphysics of the Love of the Sexes," in which he tried to show that poets and novelists had recognized the evil of loving, although they had not formulated the abstract principles that would justify this point of view. Love drives men and women to suicide, madness, and extremes of sacrifice. Pointing out that he has no philosophic precedents to guide him, Schopenhauer flatly declares that all forms of love are rooted in sexuality and that, obviously, the existence of future generations depends upon its gratification. But the sexual instinct can disguise itself in various ways, especially as "objective admiration," although in reality the will-to-live is aiming at the production of a new individual. Because sexual union exists for the benefit of the species, not for the individuals involved in it, marriages should not be made for love but for convenience. Thus, he says, there is guilt in loving, for its culmination is simply the perpetuation of the will-to-live, with all its attendant miseries.

Freud. Historically, Schopenhauer's influence on Freud is more important than his theory of the will-to-live in itself. Freud renamed the will-to-live the libido and at one time even saw its goal as death. The concept of the death wish paralleled Schopenhauer's emphasis on art and pity as the two ways of escape from life, and it had no great success in psychological circles. The libido as a term for generalized desire, on the other hand, has become part and parcel of the terminology of psychodynamics. Like most philosophic concepts, it has been distorted by both its supporters and its adversaries, but by reintegrating humanity and its strivings into the natural world, it has revived in a new form the kernel of Diotima's speech in the *Symposium.* Freud, along with most Platonists, would deny this. However, since love in the *Symposium* is found not only in sexual attraction but also in scientific research and philosophic meditation, there is only a verbal difference between the two philosophies. Freud, to be sure, does not preach the denial of bodily love, but at the same time he never denied the need for self-restraint and self-discipline. Although he may have said that the scientist is dominated by an anal–erotic urge, he did not deprecate science in these terms; rather, he explained what he thought was its general etiology. He also opened the door to a franker discussion of human motivations, and his contribution to ethics can hardly be overestimated. He attempted to show men how to realize the ideal of self-knowledge that philosophers had advocated for centuries without indicating how one might attain it. By pointing out the universality of love in its various forms and suggesting how it becomes deformed and alienated from its natural goals, Freud laid the foundation for an ethics that would be freed from ecclesiastical dogmatism. Although his followers have modified some of his ideas, as was inevitable, they have not denied either the pre-eminence of the libido as a driving power in human affairs or its ability to mask itself. One cannot overlook Freud's contribution toward giving men the ability to understand both one another and themselves—a type of understanding that had been preached over the centuries but always on the assumption that human nature could be observed in conscious behavior.

As is always the case in intellectual history, ancient beliefs survive and take on new forms. This is as true of the history of the idea of love as it is of other ideas. It is obvious that although no one believes any longer in the myth of the two Aphrodites as anthropomorphic deities each of whom is accompanied by a special Eros, the distinction between the two still persists as the contrast between carnal and spiritual love. The First Epistle of John and the Gospel of John have been by no means discarded in the Occident, nor has the commandment to love God and one's neighbor been forgotten. *Caritas* as both brotherly love and charity is still preached, if not practiced, and the Neoplatonic notion that through love we shall have harmony and through harmony, peace, is as potent a force in social education as it has ever been. Philosophy sometimes takes as its goal the rationalization of common sense, or at least of widely held beliefs, and according to the available evidence, no one has ever maintained that the whole duty of man consists in hating, provoking disorder, and disobeying what are at various times called the laws of God or of nature. Philosophers writing on love have attempted in numerous ways, first, to describe the unique part it plays in human life; second, to seek its similarity to other impulses; third, to appraise the ends that it wishes to achieve; and finally, to work out a systematic account of all these distinctions and put them into a logical network of ideas.

Bibliography

PRIMARY SOURCES

Aristotle, *Nicomachean Ethics,* translated by W. D. Ross. Oxford, 1925. Books 7–8.

Augustine, *Confessions,* translated by E. B. Pusey. London, 1907. Book 1, Ch. 12; Book II, Chs. 1 and 6; Book III, Ch. 1; Book IV, Ch. 6; Book VI, Ch. 14; Book VII, Ch. 10; Book VIII, Ch. 2; Book X, Ch. 7.

Bernard, *De Diligendo Deo; Sermon, In Cantica Canticorum,* in J. P. Migne, ed., *Patrologia Latina.* Paris, 1844–1864. Vols. 182–183, respectively.

Chapelain, André le, *De Amore,* E. Trojel, ed. Havniae, 1892.

Cleanthes, *Hymn to Zeus.* Translated by George Boas in *Rationalism in Greek Philosophy.* Baltimore, Md., 1961. P. 251.

Dante, *Divine Comedy.* Translated by H. F. Carey, 2d ed. London, 1819.

Dante, *Vita nuova.* Translated by Dante Gabriel Rossetti as *The New Life of Dante Alighieri.* London, 1901.

Dante, *Il convivio.* Translated by P. H. Wicksteed as *The Convivio of Dante Alighieri.* London, 1903.

Empedocles, Fragments 115, 128, 130, in J. Burnet, *Early Greek Philosophy,* 3d ed. London, 1920; New York, 1957.

Euripides, *Hippolytus.*

Freud, Sigmund, *Three Contributions to the Theory of Sex* and *Totem and Taboo,* in *The Basic Writings of Sigmund Freud.* New York, 1938.

Freud, Sigmund, *A General Introduction to Psycho-Analysis,* translated by Joan Riviere. Garden City, N.Y., 1943.

Hermetica (Asclepius II, 21), A. D. Nock and A. J. Festugière, eds. Paris, 1960. Vol. II.

Laclos, Choderlos de, *Les Liaisons dangereuses.* Garden City, N.Y., 1961.

Leone Ebreo, *The Philosophy of Love,* translated by F. Friedberg-Seelye and Jean H. Barnes. London, 1937.

Lucretius, *De Rerum Natura,* Book I, 1–49, in W. J. Oates, *The Stoic and Epicurean Philosophers.* New York, 1957.

Plato, *Symposium,* in B. Jowett, ed., *Plato: Dialogues,* 4th rev. ed. Oxford, 1953.

Pseudo-Aristotle, *Magna Moralia,* translated by St. George Stock. Oxford, 1915. 1208 b, 31.

Schopenhauer, Arthur, *The World as Will and Idea,* translated by R. B. Haldane and J. Kemp. 6th ed., London, 1907. See especially Vol. III, Ch. 44, "Supplements to the Fourth Book." London, 1909.

Spinoza, Baruch, *Ethics,* Part 5, in *The Chief Works of Spinoza,* 2 vols., translated by R. H. M. Elwes. New York, 1955.

SECONDARY SOURCES

Bruyne, Edgar de, *Études d'esthétique médiévale.* Bruges, 1946. Vol. III, Book IV, Ch. 2.

Gilson, Étienne, *The Spirit of Mediaeval Philosophy,* translated by A. H. C. Downes. New York, 1940. Ch. 14.

Mackail, J. W., *Select Epigrams from the Greek Anthology.*

London, 1906. See especially the Introduction, Sections vi–vii, pp. 32–41.

Panofsky, Erwin, *Studies in Iconology*. New York, 1939. Chapters 5–6.

GEORGE BOAS

LOVEJOY, ARTHUR ONCKEN (1873–1962), American philosopher and historian of ideas, was born in Berlin, Germany, the son of the Reverend W. W. Lovejoy of Boston and Sara Oncken of Hamburg. Educated at the University of California (Berkeley) and at Harvard, where he received his M.A., Lovejoy began his teaching career at Stanford University (1899–1901) and then taught for seven years at Washington University in St. Louis. After short periods at Columbia University and the University of Missouri, he went to Johns Hopkins in 1910 as professor of philosophy, remaining there until his retirement in 1938. In 1927 he gave the Carus lectures, published as *The Revolt Against Dualism* in 1930, and the William James lectures, published as *The Great Chain of Being* in 1933. Lovejoy was widely known as an epistemologist, a philosophic critic, a historian of ideas, and a man of action. He helped to organize the Association of American University Professors, in which he served for many years as chairman of the group that investigated all charges of violation of academic freedom. In this connection he wrote the article "Academic Freedom" for the *Encyclopaedia of the Social Sciences*.

Lovejoy's works fall into two main groups—those on epistemology and those on intellectual history—although he also wrote essays on ethics, religion, and social problems.

Philosophical works. For many years Lovejoy confined his writings to articles, a great number of them critical. These were often directed against various forms of anti-intellectualism: "The Thirteen Pragmatisms" (1908), "Some Antecedents of the Philosophy of Bergson" (1913), and "The Paradox of the Thinking Behaviorist" (1922). However, these articles were frequently examinations of certain contemporary movements in philosophy, such as the New Realism: "Reflections of a Temporalist on the New Realism" (1911) and "On Some Novelties of the New Realism" (1913). Some were even on the supposed philosophical implication of the theory of relativity: "The Travels of Peter, Paul and Zebedee" (1932) and "The Paradox of the Time-Retarding Journey" (1931).

It was not until 1930 that Lovejoy published his major work, *The Revolt Against Dualism*, in which he attempted to defend epistemological dualism against the reigning modes of monism. He began by sketching what he called naive dualism, which assumes that (1) many possible objects of knowledge (*cognoscenda*) are at places external to the body of the percipient; (2) man must have real traffic with things that existed in the past and may exist in the future; (3) man can have knowledge of things as they would be if they were not directly known; (4) other minds and experiences exist; and (5) *cognoscenda* in other places and at other times are apprehensible by other knowers. The book analyzed this naive dualism and defended a corrected form of it. On the whole, although not in detail, Lovejoy was more interested in the duality of two exist-ents (of two 5-cent stamps, for instance) than qualitative duality such as of red and green. The duality of two things is demonstrated, he wrote, by the fact that one of the supposed pair has a spatial, a temporal, or a spatiotemporal position that is inconsistent with that empirically exhibited by the other. If, then, it can be shown that our ideas of objects have positions that can be shown not to be those of the objects, then the two cannot rightly be believed to be one. Qualitative duality would be demonstrated in analogous fashion, but the inconsistency would lie between two sets of qualities.

In his autobiographical essay, "A Temporalistic Realism," in Volume II of *Contemporary American Philosophy*, edited by G. P. Adams and W. P. Montague (London and New York, 1930), Lovejoy pointed out that one of his earliest philosophical theses was that experience itself is temporal. Any philosophical position that overlooks or denies this, or conflicts with it, would, in his opinion, be condemned as contradicting a manifest truth. (This does not, of course, assert that any philosophy—such as that of Bergson—that admits the empirical reality of time is thereby proved.) The various forms of monism fail to evade, and cannot evade, the consequences of this fact. For instance, the date at which a visual datum occurs is not the date of the object that one is seeing. There is a time lag between the emission of light rays from a star and their arrival at the retina of a human eye, to say nothing of the arrival of the nerve current stimulated by them at the cerebral cortex, where it apparently causes a visual image to appear. Indeed, some stars that we perceive now may have become extinct many light-years ago. Analogous statements can be made about sound, odor, and taste.

Although Lovejoy also used other criteria, this criterion of duality suffices to establish existential duality between object and sensum. To deny the duality, Lovejoy asserted, would be equivalent to asserting that two particulars can each be in two places at the same time, that one particular has or consists of many shapes and other inconsistent qualities at the same time, that it has two dates in the same temporal order, that it can be at the same time both the beginning and the end of a causal series, and, finally, that error is impossible. Lovejoy discussed each of these theses in connection with epistemological positions widely held at the time the book was written: the New Realism, objective relativism, Whitehead's denial of simple location, and Bertrand Russell's epistemology as given in *The Analysis of Mind* (London and New York, 1921) and *The Analysis of Matter* (London and New York, 1927).

Lovejoy's dualism differed from that of the naive dualist in that the latter is likely to believe that his objects are qualitatively, if not existentially, identical with the objects of others. Our ideas, Lovejoy held, do not necessarily have properties identical with the properties of anything in the physical world, but we are not therefore condemned to know nothing whatsoever of that world. We cannot prove beyond doubt that some of the properties of our ideas are also properties of the physical world, but such is "a natural assumption which no one can prove to be false" (*Revolt Against Dualism*, p. 273). Qualities that vary with percipients must be held to be subjective, but there are certain residual properties—extension, shape, relative position, temporal succession, and motion—that may reasonably be said to characterize both our ideas and their objects. The reasonableness of the hypothesis rests on its ability to give us grounds for framing a "coherent, simple, unifying, scientifically serviceable" set of hypotheses for explaining both the rise of our sensory data and their peculiar characteristics. It will, in short, account for a world that is causally efficacious, that exists between our perceptual moments, and that has a past and future independent of any percipients.

Intellectual history. To separate Lovejoy's philosophical views from his historical studies is artificial, for his philosophy is based on a wide knowledge of history, and his historiography is based on his belief in the existence and efficacy of ideas. However, such a distinction may be made for purposes of classification.

Lovejoy was the chief promoter in the United States of the historiography of ideas. His continuing interest in this area dated back at least to his monograph *The Dialectic of Bruno and Spinoza* (Berkeley, 1904). He was the originator and first editor of the *Journal of the History of Ideas*. He studied such general ideas as romanticism, evolutionism, naturalism, and primitivism, showing the ambiguities resident in them and their ingression into fields that have no ostensible logical connection with them.

In the preface to *Essays in the History of Ideas*, Lovejoy defined his conception of the historiography of ideas: (1) It studies the presence and influence of the same ideas in very diverse provinces of thought and in different periods; thus, an idea that may have originated in logic may turn up in biology, or vice versa. (2) There are certain catchwords, such as "nature," that have taken on new meanings over a period of time, although the people using them are seldom aware of their ambiguities. The historian of ideas will analyze these various meanings as they occur. An example from fairly recent history (not one of Lovejoy's own) would be the eulogistic usage of the word "organic." (3) It has also been noticed that a given author will prove susceptible to the emotional aura of certain terms and, probably because of this, will waver between a valid meaning of an idea and an incongruous meaning. It is usually assumed that the thought of a given writer must be consistent and unified; but by accepting this assumption, a historian may overlook precisely those thoughts expressed by a writer that were in fact influential. A fuller explanation of the program is given in Lovejoy's essay "The Historiography of Ideas," first published in 1938 and republished as the opening chapter in *Essays in the History of Ideas*.

"The Great Chain of Being." Lovejoy's most influential single contribution to the history of ideas is *The Great Chain of Being*. The idea whose fortunes he traced in this book was first expressed by Plato in the *Timaeus*. There Plato maintained that the Demiurge, being good, was not jealous and, not being jealous, wanted the world to lack nothing; therefore, if the world were to lack nothing, all possibilities must be realized. The realization of all possibilities is the great chain of being, and the principle it rests upon was called by Lovejoy the principle of plenitude.

This apparently simple idea, contained in a creation myth, was introduced into Christian theology through Neoplatonism and into cosmography by Hasdai Crescas with his supposition of many worlds, by Johannes Kepler, by Nicholas of Cusa with his theory of a boundless universe, and, above all, by Giordano Bruno with his open acceptance of the principle as it applies to stellar bodies. In Spinoza it appeared as the doctrine that all ideas of God must be realized, and in Leibniz as the principle of sufficient reason. Lovejoy showed how the principle entered into biological speculations in the eighteenth century and how it was "temporalized." In the idea of the great chain of being, which he presented with a richness of erudition, Lovejoy found one of the most fertile yet neglected ideas in Western philosophy and masterfully traced its ramifications and subsequent history.

Primitivism. A second dominant idea, the study of whose history Lovejoy initiated, is that cluster of notions known as primitivism. Primitivism has two forms—a chronological form, exemplified in the myth of the Golden Age, and a cultural form, best exemplified in cynicism and in all attempts to rediscover the so-called natural life. Each of these forms has two subspecies, "hard" primitivism and "soft" primitivism. Hard primitivism maintains that the state of nature (man's primordial condition) was rugged and unencumbered with superfluities, a state very close to that of the legendary noble savage. Soft primitivism, on the contrary, maintains that the state of nature was agreeably gentle, that earth gave man her fruits spontaneously without any labor on his part, and that there was no private property and hence no covetousness, no war, no foreign trade, none of the complications that the arts and sciences introduce.

Lovejoy urged as early as 1917 that there would be more progress in philosophical studies if there were more cooperation among philosophers ("On Some Conditions of Progress in Philosophical Inquiry"). A documentary history of primitivism provided, it seemed, an ideal opportunity for such cooperation. Lovejoy and three other scholars formed a team and agreed to publish a four-volume work, to be entitled *A Documentary History of Primitivism and Related Ideas*, covering the ground from early Greek times to the recent past. Of this projected work only one volume, *Primitivism and Related Ideas in Antiquity*, written by Lovejoy with George Boas, was completed, although a number of smaller works by various scholars came out as contributions to the subject. The published volume contained, along with documents and commentaries, two supplementary essays—"Primitivism in Ancient Western Asia," by W. F. Albright, and "Primitivism in Indian Literature," by P.-E. Dumont—and an appendix by Lovejoy—"Some Meanings of 'Nature.'" Although the original four-volume plan was never carried out, what did appear may have shown historians of philosophy that primitivism was a philosophic theme neglected by the historical tradition that had nevertheless permeated Occidental thought.

Works by Lovejoy

"The Thirteen Pragmatisms." *Journal of Philosophy*, Vol. 5 (1908), 1–12, 29–39.

"Reflections of a Temporalist on the New Realism." *Journal of Philosophy*, Vol. 8 (1911), 589–599.

"Some Antecedents of the Philosophy of Bergson." *Mind*, N.S. Vol. 22 (1913), 465–483.

"On Some Novelties of the New Realism." *Journal of Philosophy*, Vol. 10 (1913), 29–43.

Bergson and Romantic Evolutionism. Berkeley, 1914.

"On Some Conditions of Progress in Philosophical Inquiry." *Philosophical Review*, Vol. 26 (1917), 123–163.

"The Paradox of the Thinking Behaviorist." *Philosophical Review*, Vol. 31 (1922), 135–147.

The Revolt Against Dualism: An Inquiry Concerning the Existence of Ideas. La Salle, Ill., 1930.

"The Paradox of the Time-Retarding Journey." *Philosophical Review*, Vol. 40 (1931), 48–68, 152–167.

"The Travels of Peter, Paul and Zebedee." *Philosophical Review*, Vol. 41 (1932), 498–517.

Primitivism and Related Ideas in Antiquity, G. Boas, co-author. Baltimore, 1935.

The Great Chain of Being: A Study of the History of an Idea. Cambridge, Mass., 1936.

Essays in the History of Ideas. Baltimore, 1948. Contains a list of Lovejoy's articles up to and including 1947.

Reflections on Human Nature. Baltimore, 1961.

The Reason, the Understanding, and Time. Baltimore, 1961. Deals with the Romantic theory of knowledge.

Works on Lovejoy

Boas, George, "A. O. Lovejoy as Historian of Philosophy." *Journal of the History of Ideas*, Vol. 9, No. 4 (Oct. 1948), 404–411.

Mandelbaum, Maurice, "Arthur O. Lovejoy and the Theory of Historiography." *Ibid.*, 412–423.

Montague, W. P., "Professor Lovejoy's Carus Lectures." *Journal of Philosophy*, Vol. 25, No. 11 (May 24, 1928), 293–296.

Montague, W. P., "My Friend Lovejoy." *Journal of the History of Ideas*, Vol. 9, No. 4 (Oct. 1948), 424–427.

Murphy, Arthur E., "Mr. Lovejoy's Counter-revolution." *Journal of Philosophy*, Vol. 28 (1931), 29–42, 57–71.

Nicholson, Marjorie, "A. O. Lovejoy as Teacher." *Journal of the History of Ideas*, Vol. 9, No. 4 (Oct. 1948), 428–438.

Spencer, Theodore, "Lovejoy's *Essays in the History of Ideas.*" *Ibid.*, 439–446.

Taylor, H. A., "Further Reflections on the History of Ideas: An Examination of A. O. Lovejoy's Program." *Journal of Philosophy*, Vol. 40 (May 27, 1943), 281–299.

Wiener, Philip P., "Lovejoy's Rôle in American Philosophy," in *Studies in Intellectual History.* Baltimore, 1953. Pp. 161–173. A collection of essays by a group of Lovejoy's colleagues.

GEORGE BOAS

LÖWENHEIM-SKOLEM THEOREM. See SYSTEMS, FORMAL, AND MODELS OF FORMAL SYSTEMS.

LOYALTY. Loyalty, as a moral rather than a political concept, has received scant attention in philosophical literature. In fact, at the present time it seems banished from respectable ethical discussions, owing, no doubt, to its historical association with an obsolete metaphysics (idealism) and with such odious political movements as the extreme nationalism of Nazism. However, the supposed implications suggested by these disreputable associations are ill-founded. On the contrary, loyalty is an essential ingredient in any civilized and humane system of morals.

Philosophical issues regarding loyalty may be separated into the question of the object of loyalty, and the question of the moral value of loyalty.

The object of loyalty. Granted that loyalty is the wholehearted devotion to an object of some kind, what kind of thing is this object? Is it an abstract entity, such as an idea or a collective being? Or is it a person or group of persons? The idealist contends that loyalty is "the willing and

practical and thoroughgoing devotion of a person to a cause" (Josiah Royce, *The Philosophy of Loyalty*, p. 17). Its object is "a cause beyond your private self, greater than you are . . . impersonal and superpersonal" (*ibid.*, pp. 19–20). As a cause it is something that transcends the individual, "an eternal reality." Apart from familiar metaphysical and logical objections to this concept of a superpersonal reality, this view has the ethical defect of postulating duties over and above our duties to individual men and groups of men. The individual is submerged and lost in this superperson not only ontologically but also morally, for it tends to dissolve our specific duties and obligations to others into a "superhuman" good.

Opposing the idealistic position is the view, characteristic of social atomism (empiricism or utilitarianism, for example), that denies any distinctive status to loyalty on the grounds that metaphysically there can be no such superpersonal entity to serve as its object. Insofar as the concept of loyalty has any validity at all, it reduces to other kinds of relations and dispositions, such as obedience or honesty. Most empiricists are inclined to agree with Hume, however, that loyalty is a virtue that holds "less of reason, than of bigotry and superstition."

Thus, it is generally assumed that we must either accept the notion of a superperson or some other abstract entity as the object of loyalty or reject the notion of loyalty altogether as founded on an illusion. This assumption is open to question.

In answer to the idealists, it should be pointed out that in our common moral language, as well as historically, "loyalty" is taken to refer to a relationship between persons—for instance, between a lord and his vassal, between a parent and his children, or between friends. Thus, the object of loyalty is ordinarily taken to be a person or group of persons.

Loyalty is conceived as interpersonal, and it is also always specific; a man is loyal to *his* lord, *his* father, or *his* comrades. It is conceptually impossible to be loyal to people in general (to humanity) or to a general principle, such as justice or democracy.

The social atomist fails to recognize the special character and significance of the ties that bind individuals together and provide the basis for loyalties. Loyalty is not founded on just any casual relationship between persons, but on a specific kind of relationship or tie. The special ties involved arise from the twofold circumstance that the persons so bound are comembers of a specific group (community) distinguished by a specific common background and sharing specific interests, and are related in terms of some sort of role differentiation within that group. A friendship, a family, or such a highly organized group as a political, priestly, or military community illustrates the presence of these conditions. Special ties of this sort provide both the necessary and the sufficient conditions for a person to be a proper object of loyalty.

The impersonal or objective element mentioned by Royce and other idealists is explained by the fact that it is the ties, the mutually related roles, rather than any particular personal characteristics of the individuals involved that provide the grounds for loyalty. Why should I be loyal to X? Because he is *my R* (friend, father, leader, comrade).

More purely personal characteristics of *X,* such as his kindness, courage, amiability, honesty, or spirituality cannot serve as *grounds* for loyalty. That the conditions of loyalty abstract from the personal characteristics of the individuals concerned does not, of course, entail that loyalty must relate to a superpersonal entity (cause, whole) any more than the fact that an algebraic formula contains a variable within it (such as *Fx*) entails that there must be some kind of supernumber to satisfy the function.

The moral value of loyalty. Is loyalty something good in itself? Is it always good? Can there be bad loyalties?

On these questions the idealist takes an extreme position, for he holds that loyalty is the highest moral good. According to Royce, a man's wholehearted devotion to a cause is *eo ipso* good and becomes evil only when it conflicts with other loyalties. The supreme good is loyalty to loyalty: "so choose and so serve your individual cause as to secure thereby the greatest increase of loyalty amongst men" (*ibid.,* p. 121).

The view that loyalty has an inner value, "whatever be the cause to which this man is loyal," can be used to redeem the most evil acts of men. Such a belief outrages our moral feelings, for we want to say that a cause which demands injustice or cruelty as the price of devotion renders that devotion an evil in itself. It is impossible to separate logically the moral quality of devotion from the moral quality of its object, if that object is a cause. (Incidentally, a distinction must be made between devotion to a thoroughly evil purpose and devotion that is simply misdirected, in the sense that it is well-intentioned but wrong for some other reason.)

Even assuming that the problem of bad loyalties can be resolved by invoking "loyalty to loyalty," the idealist may still be accused of turning morality, which properly concerns man's relations to his fellows, into service of an abstract principle or a cause, thus treating man as a mere means rather than as an end-in-itself.

The social atomist, on the other hand, regards the moral value of loyalty, construed as devotion or obedience to persons or institutions, entirely as a function of its benign or mischievous consequences. This view, however, robs loyalty of any special moral significance. It fails to account, for example, for the admirable side of a mother's loyalty to her son even when, considering the total picture, it is not entirely justified morally.

We must ask what loyalty demands of a person. The etymology of the word "loyalty" gives a clue, for it comes from the French word *loi* and thus means something akin to "legality." Loyalty, strictly speaking, demands what is morally due the object of loyalty. A loyal subject is one who wholeheartedly devotes himself to his duties to his lord. What is due or owed is defined by the roles of the persons concerned. The fact that loyalty gives what is due also explains why we can demand the loyalty of others.

It follows that mere blind obedience to every wish of the person who is the object of loyalty is not loyalty; it is a perversion of loyalty. There is no moral value to it at all, since it is not something that is morally due. A loyal Nazi is a contradiction in terms, although a loyal German is not.

There are, to be sure, conflicts of loyalties, but this fact does not entail that any of the loyalties involved are improper or invalid. It is simply a logical consequence of the fact that there are conflicts of duties; my duty to my parents may conflict with my duty to my wife or to my fellow countrymen. Sometimes there are clear ways of resolving these conflicts and sometimes there are not, but we cannot eliminate the problem of conflicting loyalties either by a metaphysical trick or by the mechanical application of a value calculus.

One final observation must be made concerning the distinction between loyalty and fidelity. Loyalty includes fidelity in carrying out one's duties to the person or group of persons who are the object of loyalty; but it embraces more than that, for it implies an attitude, perhaps an affection or sentiment, toward such persons. Furthermore, at the very least, loyalty requires the complete subordination of one's own private interest in favor of giving what is due, and perhaps also the exclusion of other legitimate interests. In this sense, loyalty may often be one-sided, although it need not be. If we could not count on the loyalty of others or give them our loyalty, social life would be not only bleak but also impossible.

Bibliography

Aristotle, "On Friendship," in *Nicomachean Ethics.* Books VIII and IX.

Bryant, Sophie, "Loyalty," in James Hasting's *Encyclopaedia of Religion and Ethics.* New York, 1916. Vol. VIII, pp. 183–188.

Rashdall, Hastings, *Theory of Good and Evil.* Oxford, 1924. Vol. I, pp. 188 and 273. For the social atomist view of the moral value of loyalty.

Royce, Josiah, *The Philosophy of Loyalty.* New York, 1924.

Sidgwick, Henry, *Methods of Ethics,* 7th ed. London, 1922. P. 254. For the social atomist view of the moral value of loyalty.

JOHN LADD

LU CHIU-YÜAN. See LU HSIANG-SHAN.

LUCIAN OF SAMOSATA (c. 115–c. 200), philosophical satirist and satirist of philosophy, was born at Samosata (Samsat) on the Euphrates and was educated there. He then studied rhetoric in Asia Minor, after which he was a lawyer for a while, toured Greece and Italy as a lecturer, and held a chair of literature in France. In middle age he settled in Athens, where he wrote and gave public readings of his most successful dialogues, many of which were on philosophical themes. Late in life he joined the staff of the Roman governor of Egypt. Nothing is known of his death except that it occurred after 180.

Lucian's philosophical position is not easy to define because he expresses contradictory attitudes, and his persistent irony and his obvious wish to entertain make it hard to know how seriously to take his statements. The contradictions have been used as a basis for several different theories of his intellectual development, but the chronological order of his works is too uncertain for any such interpretation to be wholly convincing.

In *The Fisher,* Lucian claimed to be a champion of philosophy, which he described elsewhere as a civilizing and morally improving study; however, he constantly criticized pseudo philosophers for their greed, bad temper, sexual immorality, and the general inconsistency between their preaching and their practice. The historical occasion for such attacks was the encouragement of philosophy by Marcus Aurelius, which had made philosophers almost as numerous as monks and friars were in the Middle Ages.

Lucian's favorite target was the Stoic, but he also savagely attacked such Cynics as Peregrinus, and in *The Sale of Lives* he made fun of every school. However, he sometimes wrote approvingly of individual philosophies. The *Nigrinus* appears to be a eulogy of Platonism, although this may be ironical or simply an excuse for satirizing Roman society. The *Cynicus* is a less ambiguous defense of Cynicism, and in several dialogues Lucian speaks through a character called Cyniscus or through that of the Cynic Menippus. Diogenes is once mentioned favorably, and in the *Alexander* there is enthusiastic praise for Epicurus, "a really great man who perceived, as no one else has done, the beauty of truth."

The *Hermotimus* rejects all philosophical systems on the grounds that they are mutually contradictory and thus cannot all be right, and life is too short to discover which of them is nearest to the truth. The wisest course is to get on with the business of living, guided by common sense. Tiresias in the *Menippus* gives the same advice.

In general, Lucian disliked philosophies that encourage superstition, such as Platonism and Stoicism, and preferred materialists like Democritus and Epicurus. Although he made fun of the Skeptics, he was temperamentally inclined to skepticism, or to an eclecticism of the kind described in the *Life of Demonax.*

His own positive ideas included a conception of society free from racial, social, and economic distinctions. He valued such human qualities as sincerity, courage, cheerfulness, and kindness; and he continually stressed the importance of facing facts, especially the fact of death.

Lucian's influence on later thought was exerted largely, but not entirely, through the medium of literary technique. He facilitated the spread of humanism in the sixteenth century by suggesting one of the basic themes (the absurdity of plutocracy) and some of the incidental jokes in More's *Utopia,* but his main contributions were the lighthearted manner, the form (a fantastic journey described in a familiar dialogue), and the trick of using proper names that etymologically imply nonexistence or nonseriousness. He also aided in the Reformation by providing literary precedents and humorous devices for the satire on ecclesiastics, theologians, monks, and superstitions in Erasmus' *Encomium Moriae* and in the work of Rabelais. Voltaire's *Candide* is Lucianic in both manner and theme (the refutation of philosophical theory by reality), and its final moral is identical with that of the *Menippus.* The *Conversation between Lucian, Erasmus and Rabelais in the Elysian Fields* shows that Voltaire regarded Lucian as one of his masters in the strategy of intellectual revolution.

Bacon called Lucian a contemplative atheist, and as such Lucian evidently interested Hume, who described him as a very moral writer, quoted him with respect when discussing ethics and religion, and read him on his deathbed. Since then, professional philosophers have tended to ignore him, but perhaps his spirit is still alive in those who, like Bertrand Russell, are prepared to flavor philosophy with wit.

Bibliography

Lucian's complete works are collected in *Luciani Samosatiensis Opera,* C. Iacobitz, ed. (Leipzig, 1887–1888). An edition of Lucian's works with annotated English translation is *Lucian,* translated by A. M. Harmon, M. D. McLeod, and K. Kilburn, 7 vols. (London and New York, 1913–1961; series not complete). An English translation, complete except for passages considered spurious or indecent, with explanatory notes, is *The Works of Lucian of Samosata,* translated by H. W. Fowler and F. G. Fowler (Oxford, 1905). Selected works in English, with a glossary explaining philosophical allusions, is *Satirical Sketches,* translated with an introduction by Paul Turner (Harmondsworth and Baltimore, 1961).

Works on Lucian are J. Bernays, *Lukian und die Kyniker* (Berlin, 1879); W. H. Tackaberry, *Lucian's Relation to the Post-Aristotelian Philosophers* (Toronto, 1930); M. Caster, *Lucien et la pensée religieuse de son temps* (Paris, 1937); A. Peretti, *Luciano: Un intellettuale greco contro Roma* (Florence, 1946); and J. Bompaire, *Lucien écrivain: Imitation et création* (Paris, 1958).

PAUL TURNER

LUCRETIUS (c. 99–55 B.C.), whose full name was Titus Lucretius Carus, is known only as the author of a didactic poem, probably unfinished, *De Rerum Natura* ("On the Nature of Things"), consisting of some 7,400 hexameter lines divided into six books. According to an ancient biographer cited by St. Jerome, the poem was composed during the lucid intervals of a madness induced by a love philter, which culminated in the author's suicide. This uncorroborated testimony is virtually the sole external evidence for his life story. From internal evidence it may be inferred that he was a Roman of good family and education and a friend of the statesman Gaius Memmius; that he had traveled at least as far afield as Sicily; and that he held himself aloof from the murderous political strife of his day, probably living the life of a recluse. His poem was avowedly an attempt to expound and popularize, for the benefit of his fellow Romans, the "obscure discoveries" of Epicurus, for whom he expressed an unbounded and uncritical admiration throughout. Historically, *De Rerum Natura* is important as the fullest surviving exposition of the most coherent and influential system of materialistic philosophy produced in classical antiquity—an exposition, moreover, whose literary qualities have made Epicureanism familiar to multitudes of readers who might otherwise scarcely have heard of it.

But it is much more than this. There is reason to believe that Lucretius was a more original thinker than he professed to be or than he himself realized. Certainly there are aspects of his thought that cannot be traced to any earlier thinker and can therefore be most properly considered under his name. For at least three reasons, he was forced to rethink, rather than merely to restate, his master's teaching.

First, he wrote in Latin, and in this he explicitly claimed to be a pioneer, "blazing a trail through pathless tracts." Since he was not content merely to transliterate Greek terms, as Latin writers were often tempted to do, he devised his own technical vocabulary and thereby stamped Epicurean doctrine with something of the practical character of a language well adapted to the needs of law and administration but as yet lacking in metaphysical subtlety. This task was simplified, however, by Epicurus' own resolve (in contrast to Plato's, for instance) to eschew "empty words" and to hold onto the "underlying things" (Letter I, 37).

Second, while Epicurus modeled his bald prose style on that of Euclid's geometry and held that "a wise man would not write poetry," Lucretius' models were the Greek epic poets, and he employed the traditional epic devices of simile and metaphor to illustrate each step of his argument with a series of clearly visualized pictures. Here again he was true to the Epicurean emphasis on sense perception as the foundation of knowledge. But he evidently drew directly on his own observation—for example, of a Roman military exercise (II, 40–43) or of a theatrical display (IV, 75–83)—and for better or worse his ability to think in concrete images gives him a unique place among philosophers.

Third, he wrote not merely as a versifier but as a poet, with an imaginative grasp of his theme and an intense emotional involvement which, to more coldly logical minds, might seem to disqualify him as a philosopher entirely. It has been argued by N. W. de Witt in *Epicurus and His Philosophy* (Minneapolis, 1954, p. 98) that even in his most emotional outbursts Lucretius is a good Epicurean, "speaking by the book." This may well be true. It is also true that Epicurus himself taught that a man who had become truly wise could yield more fully to his emotions (*pathe*) without detriment to his wisdom and that in the Epicurean system there is no such central conflict between reason and passion as appears in Platonism and Stoicism. But Epicurus (at any rate in his maturer years, when he taught and wrote) was renowned for his tranquil disposition. In any case, throughout his entire poem Lucretius proclaims, even if he never states in explicit terms, that philosophy is something to be felt as well as thought.

Religion. His originality is perhaps most evident in his attitude toward religion. He may have meant to round off his poem with a full treatment of Epicurean theology, but his actual references to the subject scarcely suggest that he shared his master's devotion to the traditional Greek gods or fully grasped the reasoning which enabled Epicurus to combine his theology with a materialistic explanation of the universe. The Roman adoption of Greek mythology seldom constituted much more than a literary artifice. In Cicero's *Tusculan Disputations* the claim that Epicurus had freed man from the fear of Hell is simply laughed out of court. No educated Roman believed these old wives' tales, nor was the devout Roman expected to feel passionately about the gods any more than he was asked to subscribe to a creed. Acceptance of the state religion meant primarily service to the state (an obligation which Lucretius denounced as fostering insensate ambition and brutal militarism), coupled with a meticulous observance of omens and taboos, a practice which Lucretius condemned in a famous line, *Tantum religio potuit suadere malorum* ("So great the evils which religion could prompt" I, 101), as an incentive to the worst of crimes. Finding no outlet for his pent-up religious emotion through traditional Greek or Roman channels, Lucretius expressed it partly in idolization of Epicurus, which surpassed the normal enthusiasm of a disciple, and partly in a devotion to Nature as creatress and life-giver, which he clothed at times in lan-

guage more appropriate to the worship of a deity. Epicurus had spoken of gratitude to Nature, both as a giver of good things and as a teacher of true wisdom and justice. Lucretius not only personified nature, to the extent of telling us what she would say if she had a voice (III, 931–932); he entered personally into the joys and sorrows of the whole living creation. His Wordsworthian language may not amount to formal pantheism, but nature worship, psychologically if not logically, was an integral part of his philosophy. He is a witness to the fact that it is possible to investigate natural phenomena with no religious inhibitions and to explain them on purely materialistic lines, rejecting divine purpose, providence, and the immortal soul, without sacrificing the joys of reverence and adoration.

Materialism. Lucretius remains quite uncompromising in his materialism. He emphatically states that all knowledge is derived from sensations, which are caused by the impact of "images," or surface-films, emanating from external objects, on the mind-atoms in the human breast. "If a belief resting on this basis is not valid, there will be no standard to which we can refer any doubt on obscure questions for rational confirmation" (I, 422–423; cf. IV, 469–521). Nowhere does he attempt to explain the doctrine of "anticipation" (*prolepsis*) with which Epicurus himself qualifies this dogma. This omission may merely mean that in a popular exposition he felt the need to simplify. But it does suggest that, intellectually, if not emotionally, he was, if possible, more wholeheartedly mechanistic than his master and that he was bent on constructing a working model of the universe in which there was no place for anything that could not be seen and handled (except, of course, that much of the working was on too small a scale to be detectable by eye or hand).

As a sample of Lucretius' method, we may take his exposition (II, 216–293) of the doctrine of the "swerve" (Greek, *parenklisis;* Latin, *clinamen*), with which Epicurus sought to combat the determinism of the earlier atomists and thereby find a basis for the exercise of moral judgment. First, the dogma is clearly asserted as a fact: "When the atoms are traveling straight down through empty space by their own weight, at quite indeterminate times and places they swerve ever so little from their course, just so much that you can call it a change of direction." Then we are given the reason, in terms of Epicurean physics, for this being a necessary assumption: "If it were not for this swerve, everything would fall downwards like raindrops through the abyss of space. No collision would take place and no impact of atom on atom would be created. Thus nature would never have created anything." Next an alternative explanation (that heavy atoms overtake light ones) is considered and dismissed as inapplicable to the behavior of matter in a vacuum, where it encounters no obstacle. Following this, Lucretius disposes of the objection that the phenomenon of the swerve is never observed. This objection would be valid against a swerve big enough to be perceptible, but it does not hold against a minimal one. Then he turns to the psychological argument, based partly on our inner experience of free choice and partly on the observed behavior of conscious beings: "If all movement is always interconnected, the new arising from the old in a determinate order . . . what is the source of the free will possessed by living things . . . that will power snatched from the fates whereby we follow the path along which we are severally led by pleasure, swerving from our course at no set time or place but at the bidding of our own hearts?" By comparing with vivid precision the movement of a race horse at the start of the race with that of someone pushed by an external force, he seeks to demonstrate that voluntary action arises from within and ultimately from the unpredictable movement of a single atom. Thus, "besides weight and impact there must be a third cause of movement, the source of this inborn power of ours, since we see that nothing can come out of nothing."

Philosophy of history. Probably Lucretius' outstanding contribution to thought has been his sociology, or his philosophy of history. Greek philosophers agreed that the basis of human society, as of rational thought and moral judgment, was articulate speech. Accordingly, no question was more hotly disputed than that of whether the origin of language was "natural" or "conventional." Epicurus (Letter I, 75) argued that while speech must have originated in a physical reaction as natural as the instinctive cries of animals, the association of specific sounds with specific objects was the result of a long process, partly casual coincidence and partly agreement among the members of a community. And he took this as illustrating the more general principle "that [human] nature had all sorts of lessons driven into it by the pressure of events and that reasoning afterwards refined them and added new inventions, quickly or slowly." Lucretius' account of the origin of language (V, 1028–1090) elaborates Epicurus' argument, and he may have had equally good Epicurean authority for his whole description, based on the same general principle, of the growth of civilization. But it must have been his own genius that turned this description into a narrative so lifelike and convincing that it is hard to realize that it can have had little relation to any actual society known to either the Greeks or the Romans. An essential step in the development of this society was the growth of "natural justice," which Epicurus defined as "a bargain for mutual profit not to hurt or be hurt." In Lucretius the definition of natural justice is followed by the characteristic comment that not everybody kept this bargain, but that unless a substantial number had done so, the human race would have been wiped out (V, 1024–1027). Thus the fact that mankind has survived at all is adduced as a proof that there must have been such a compact. But it also serves to explain the occurrence of such a compact along Darwinian lines, as an example of survival of the fittest; communities that failed to achieve it must have perished like those ill-equipped forms of life, "trapped in the toils of their own destiny," which "nature had debarred from increase" (cf. V, 837–924). By this evolutionary approach to the problem, Lucretius escapes the absurdities of some later theories of "social contract." He finds the basis of social cooperation, not in calculated self-interest, but in a natural instinct that impelled the strong to take pity on the weak. The whole passage well illustrates the poet-philosopher's blend of close reasoning with controlled imagination and unsparing realism with sensitivity and compassion.

Influence. According to St. Jerome, Lucretius' poem was "emended" by Cicero, who certainly received a manuscript of it from his brother Quintus and was impressed by its unusual combination of artistry and illuminating genius. During the period of the Roman Empire, Lucretius was read and admired as a poet rather than as a philosopher, since his Epicurean philosophy conflicted with the prevailing Stoicism or Platonism of the ruling classes. The Christian apologists Arnobius and Lactantius (early fourth century) quoted with approval his denunciations of pagan *religio*. But later generations of Christians, who derived a guilty enjoyment from the pagan mythology and morals of Ovid, showed no interest in Lucretius. Perhaps they found too little point of contact with his beliefs even to be shocked by them. Four manuscripts of the *De Rerum Natura* are known to have existed in the ninth century, all based on a single defective codex, but there is little to suggest that these were copied or even read in the later Middle Ages. When the poem was rediscovered by the fifteenth-century humanists, its style was generally condemned as "harsh" and "obscure," while Catholics and Protestants alike could see little in the subject matter but the ravings of a madman.

It was not until the age of Galileo and Descartes that Epicureanism came into its own under the inspiration of Pierre Gassendi. Since then, although Lucretius has continued to be frowned upon by the orthodox down to the present century, his influence on the pioneers of Western thought has been pervasive and widespread.

Bibliography

TEXTS

The editions and translations of the *De Rerum Natura* are fully enumerated in Cosmo Gordon, *A Bibliography of Lucretius* (London, 1962). The *editio princeps* is that of Ferrandus (Brescia, c. 1473). Landmarks in the history and interpretation of the text are the editions of Denys Lambin (Paris, 1563–1564) and Karl Lachmann (Berlin, 1850). The editions that are of special value to English readers because of their detailed commentaries are those of H. A. J. Munro (Cambridge, 1864–1886) and Cyril Bailey (Oxford, 1947). The first complete English translation to appear in print was in rhymed couplets by Thomas Creech (Oxford, 1682). Among later translations the scholarly prose versions of Munro and Bailey are well known, and the extracts "in the metre of Omar Khayyam" by W. H. Mallock in *Lucretius on Life and Death* (London, 1900) represent perhaps the most successful attempt to convey the poetic force of the original. The latest versions are the prose translation of R. E. Latham (Harmondsworth, England, 1951) and the verse translation of A. D. Winspear (New York, 1955).

WORKS ON LUCRETIUS

For literature on Lucretius, G. D. Hadzsits, *Lucretius and His Influence* (New York, 1935) and P. H. DeLacy, "Lucretius and the History of Epicureanism," in *Transactions of the American Philological Association*, Vol. 79 (1948), 12–23. See also Wolfgang Bernard Fleischmann, *Lucretius and his Influence 1680–1740* (Paris, 1964) and Alban D. Winspear, *Lucretius and Scientific Thought* (Montreal, 1963).

RONALD E. LATHAM

LU HSIANG-SHAN (1139–1193), also called Lu Chiuyüan, started the idealistic trend in Chinese philosophy. He emphasized the supremacy and self-sufficiency of the mind, contrary to his contemporary Chu Hsi, who stressed the need to discover reason and to acquire knowledge of the external world. He lived in the province of Kiangsi. His father was a respected member of the gentry, and from his early youth Lu was able to devote himself to the study of Confucius and Mencius. He disagreed with the views of the scholar Ch'eng I of the Northern Sung Dynasty.

Lu Hsiang-shan is known for the following:

> When a sage arises in the East,
> The mind is the same,
> And so is reason.

The same is true of sages born in the West, the North, and the South and of those born thousands of generations earlier and later. What he meant is that mind is the same the world over and at all times. From this fundamental thesis he drew the conclusions that mind has priority over all things and that reason has a universal validity.

Yang Chien, a disciple of Lu and a submagistrate, asked him, "What is the Original Mind?" Lu quoted the words of Mencius concerning the four kinds of virtues—*jen* (benevolence), *i* (righteousness), *li* (decency), and *chi* (knowledge)—and said, "This is the Original Mind." But Yang failed to understand what Lu meant. Some time after, a lawsuit was brought by a salesman of fans for Yang's verdict, and Yang again came to Lu with the same question. Lu answered, "In trying the case of the fan salesman, you were able to judge right that which is right and wrong that which is wrong. This is the Original Mind." Yang was then convinced that the mind is self-conscious and self-evident.

Lu was firmly convinced that there is a universal mind and a universal rationality: "What fills the universe is rationality; what the scholars should search for is to render the idea of rationality clear to all. The scope of rationality is boundless." He also quoted Cheng Hao's words, "The universe is great; yet it has its limitation," and then inferred from them that what is more perfect than the universe is rationality.

Again he said: "Rationality in the universe is so evident that it is never concealed. The greatness of the universe lies in the existence of rationality which is an order publicly followed and without partiality. Man with Heaven and Earth constitutes the triad. Why should one be egocentric and not in conformity with rationality?" Lu's main idea is that since each one has a mind and reason is inherent in mind, mind is reason. Furthermore, he says: "What is the happening of the universe is the ought-to-do-duty of man; what is the ought-to-do-duty is the happening of the universe."

Bibliography

Works by Lu may be found in the typescript *The Philosophy of Lu Hsiang-shan, a Neo-Confucian Monistic Idealist*, translated by L. V. Cady in 2 volumes (Union Theological Seminary, New York, 1939), which also contains discussion.

CARSUN CHANG

LUKÁCS, GEORG (György), Hungarian Marxist philosopher and literary critic, was professor of aesthetics and the philosophy of culture at the University of Budapest from 1945 to 1956. Lukács was born in 1885 at Budapest into a rich and eminent family (before he became a communist he wrote under the family name "von Lukács"). He took a doctorate in philosophy in Budapest (1906) and then studied under Georg Simmel at Berlin and under Max Weber at Heidelberg. Since Lukács was recognized as one of Europe's leading literary critics when he joined the Communist party of Hungary in December 1918, he was offered the post of people's commissar for culture and education in the communist regime of Béla Kun (March–August 1919). After the fall of Kun, Lukács took refuge in Vienna, where he edited the review *Kommunismus* and carried on a struggle with Kun (exiled in Moscow) for control of the Hungarian underground movement. Publication in Berlin in 1923 of Lukács' collection of essays, *Geschichte und Klassenbewusstsein*, decided the issue in favor of Kun—for the book was denounced as "deviationist." Lukács was ousted from the central committee of the Communist party and from the editorship of *Kommunismus* after publishing his "self-criticism." He took refuge in Russia when Hitler came to power and, after a further and more thorough act of self-criticism, worked in the Institute of Philosophy of the Soviet Academy of Science from 1933 to 1944. Returning to Hungary, he became a member of parliament and professor of aesthetics. In 1956 Lukács was a leader of the Petofi circle, which played a role in the anti-Russian insurrection, and then minister for culture in the short-lived Imre Nagy government. After the defeat of the revolution, Lukács was deported to Rumania, but he was allowed to return to Budapest in April 1957 to live in retirement and to devote himself to a monumental work on aesthetics, of which one volume has appeared, in Hungarian.

Aesthetics and criticism. Lukács' fame as one of the few philosophers produced by the Marxist movement rests on a book that he repudiated soon after its publication, *Geschichte und Klassenbewusstsein* ("History and Class Consciousness"). His later work—some thirty books and hundreds of articles—constitutes an attempt to found a Marxist aesthetic which could be used to criticize modernist, formalist, and experimental art in the name of socialist realism. This critical work entailed some confusion of literary criticism with political polemic, of which the following judgment on Kafka is typical: ". . . no work of art based on *Angst* (anxiety) can avoid—objectively speaking—guilt by association with Hitlerism and the preparations for atomic war" (*The Meaning of Contemporary Realism*, p. 81). Lukács' influence as a critic has been intensely conservative, for he holds that "realism is not one style among others; it is the basis of literature" (*ibid.*, p. 48).

In his first aesthetic studies, *Die Seele und die Formen* ("The Soul and the Forms") and *Die Theorie des Romans* ("The Theory of the Novel"), Lukács was still a Neo-Kantian. He held that literature was the striving for expression of the irrational soul in and through an alien and hostile reality. He stressed the value of "inwardness" and the uselessness of society to the individual. These works have been claimed as among the sources of existentialism, but Lukács himself denounced them as "false and reactionary" upon his conversion to communism. Thereafter he contrasted Marxism, as a philosophy that integrated the individual in society, with all modern "philosophies of crisis and evasion," and in particular with existentialism, which isolated men outside social and economic relations.

Lukács' stress on social relationships became the basis of his aesthetics. Form, he argued, should be determined by content (therefore abstract art and formalism are degenerate), and "there is no content of which Man himself is not the focal point" (*ibid.*, p. 19). Since man exists only in a social and historical context, aesthetics inevitably is concerned with politics. If the subject of a work of art is man seen statically, then that work declines into subjectivism and allegory. Literature must be dynamic, setting characters in historical perspective in order that they might be shown as having direction, development, and motivation. For literature to be dynamic, the major historical movement of the day must be taken into account. In the twentieth century that movement is socialism. The only valid contemporary literary styles are socialist realism, which is practiced inside the socialist movement, and critical realism, which is practiced by authors sympathetic to socialism. Lukács' theories naturally entailed condemnation of most twentieth-century art, literature, and music, but they were fruitfully applied to the historical novel.

Social and historical analysis. *Geschichte und Klassenbewusstsein,* the censored masterpiece of communist thought, became the classic text of Western Marxism as contrasted with Soviet orthodoxy. It led to a revaluation of Marxism by setting it in a Hegelian context. Lukács was the first to see that Marx's theory of history and even his economics could be read as an application of the Hegelian dialectic. He did this a decade before the discovery and publication of Marx's *Economic and Philosophic Manuscripts of 1844,* which amply confirmed his theory, at least with regard to the young Marx. Having meanwhile disowned his book, Lukács could not claim credit for that brilliant piece of philosophical reconstruction, but he later could show the profound similarity between the philosophies of Hegel and Marx (*Der junge Hegel*). His idealist reading of Marx clashed with the accepted Leninist version, and, since Lukács worsened his case in 1923 by revealing the influence of Georges Sorel and Rosa Luxemburg on his thought, his book was condemned with a ferocity unusual even in communist polemics.

Lukács had rejected Engels' and Lenin's conception of the Marxist dialectic as a set of laws applying to nature, and he rejected too the notion that historical materialism deduces all social and moral life from the economic base. Historical materialism and the dialectic, he said, both mean the same thing, namely that in society subject and object are one. When men know (or enter into any other relation with) social entities—whether these are institutions or economic goods or another age's culture—the relation established is not the sort of relation they have with the natural objects studied by physical science. Social entities are reified personality or alienated spirit, while men themselves are the product of historical forces. The knower and the known, subject and object, are moments of one entity, society, and their relations are necessarily ambiguous, two-way, or dialectical.

Marx had said, "As personal interests become autonomous in the shape of class interests, the personal conduct of the individual becomes reified and alienated and thereby becomes a thing apart from him, an independent force." It is just such alienated forms of conduct that make up society. In the nineteenth century in particular, because of the development of industry, "material forces were saturated with spiritual life, while human existence was made animal, became a material force." Marx meant, said Lukács, that spirit had become thing and things were steeped in spirit, so that history was a fabric of meanings-become-forces. This dialectical relation of subject and object was most marked in the case of the proletariat because the proletariat had been reduced by capitalism to labor, a mere economic commodity, and yet it could still take cognizance of itself as a commodity by acquiring class consciousness. Thereupon, it saw through the supposed natural laws of economics and revolutionized capitalism. "For this class, self-knowledge means at the same time correct knowledge of the whole of society . . . so this class is at once subject and object of knowledge" (*Geschichte und Klassenbewusstsein*). Its self-knowledge is history knowing itself, and in that total clarity lies the promise of a return from alienation.

The difficulties raised by historical relativism—difficulties that had been seen by all who asked how Marxism alone among social opinions could escape being vitiated by its relation to a given class and age—can be resolved only by going right to the extreme of relativism. That is to say, historical materialism must be applied to itself until it is seen as relative and provisional. This means abandoning the notion of absolute truth and denying the complete opposition of true and false. History is a dialectical totality of knowers and things known, and every piece of culture, no matter how deformed by class position and historical situation, reflects that totality. Truth exists, but it exists only in the future tense; it is the presumptive totality to be attained by permanent self-criticism. "The criterion of truth is grasp of reality. But reality is not at all to be confounded with empirical being, what actually exists. Reality *is* not; it becomes—and not without the collaboration of thought" (*ibid.*). Rejecting the representative theory of knowledge made orthodox for Marxists by the examples of Engels and Lenin (the "concepts in our heads" are "true images of reality"), Lukács held that truth is not something to be reflected but something to be made by us by collaborating with what is new and progressive in historical forces. The vague notion of a moving totality of things, of the whole of history, is essential to this "relativization of relativism." Lukács did not clearly delineate this notion, but it evidently bears a resemblance to the Hegelian Absolute.

Lukács' three main doctrines—the dialectical unity of subject and object in society; the promise of a return from alienation when society, through the proletariat, attains self-knowledge; and the notion of truth as a totality yet to be achieved—were attractive to some Western existentialists. Lukács complained that their "treacherous" use of his work was a "falsification of a book forgotten for good reason." Another line of influence was through his former associate Karl Mannheim, who developed the relativization of all ideologies into the sociology of knowledge. Within the communist world, the only doctrine of Lukács' censored book to enjoy some surreptitious authority has been his "proof" of the communist intellectual's duty to accept the Communist party as the supreme expression of proletarian class consciousness and thus as endowed with the correct view of history. This doctrine Lukács himself practices rigorously, even to the extent of repudiating his own major contribution to modern thought.

Works by Lukács

PHILOSOPHY

Die Seele und die Formen. Berlin, 1911.
Die Theorie des Romans. Berlin, 1920.
Geschichte und Klassenbewusstsein. Berlin, 1923.
Der junge Hegel. Zurich, 1948; rev. ed., Berlin, 1954.
Existentialismus oder Marxismus? Berlin, 1951.
Beiträge zur Geschichte der Aesthetik. Berlin, 1954.
Die Zerstörung der Vernunft. Berlin, 1955.

LITERARY CRITICISM

Essays über Realismus. Berlin, 1948. Translated by E. Bone as *Studies in European Realism.* London, 1950.
Thomas Mann. Berlin, 1949. Translated by S. Mitchell as *Essays on Thomas Mann.* London, 1964.
The Historical Novel. Translated by H. Mitchell and S. Mitchell. London, 1962.
The Meaning of Contemporary Realism. Translated by J. Mander and N. Mander. London, 1963.

Works on Lukács

Carbonara, C., *L'estetica del particolare di G. Lukacs.* Naples, 1960.
Goldmann, Lucien, *Le Dieu caché.* Paris, 1955. Translated by P. Thody as *The Hidden God.* London and New York, 1964.
Goldmann, Lucien, "Introduction aux premiers écrits de Georges Lukacs," in Lukács' *La Théorie du roman.* Geneva, 1963.
Lukács, Georg, and others, *Georg Lukács: Zum Siebzigsten Geburtstag.* Berlin, 1955.
Merleau-Ponty, Maurice, *Les Aventures de la dialectique.* Paris, 1955.
Watnick, Morris, "Relativism and Class Consciousness: Georg Lukács," in Leopold Labedz, ed., *Revisionism.* London, 1962.
Zitta, Victor, *Georg Lukacs's Marxism.* The Hague, 1964.

NEIL McINNES

ŁUKASIEWICZ, JAN (1878–1956), Polish philosopher and logician, was born in Lvov. After studying mathematics and philosophy at the University of Lvov he graduated in 1902 with a Ph.D. in philosophy. Łukasiewicz taught philosophy and logic first at Lvov and from 1915 at the University of Warsaw. In 1918 he interrupted academic work to accept a senior appointment in the Polish ministry of education in Ignacy Paderewski's cabinet. At the end of that year, however, he returned to the university and continued as professor of philosophy until September 1939. During that period he served twice as rector of the university (1922/1923 and 1931/1932). Toward the end of World War II Łukasiewicz left Warsaw. After some time in Münster and then in Brussels, in 1946 he accepted an invitation from the Irish government to go to Dublin as professor of mathematical logic at the Royal Irish Academy, an appointment which he held until his death. Łukasiewicz held honorary degrees from the University of Münster and from Trinity College, Dublin. He was a member of the Polish Academy of Sciences in Cracow, the Society of Arts and Sciences in Lvov, and the Society of Arts and Sciences in Warsaw.

Early writings. Łukasiewicz studied under Kazimierz Twardowski, who was occupied with conceptual analysis. The rigorous, clear thinking Twardowski advocated is easily recognizable in the first major essays published by Łukasiewicz. Of these works, *O zasadzie sprzeczności u Arystotelesa* ("On the Principle of Contradiction in Aristotle," Cracow, 1910) was one of the most influential books in the early period of the twentieth-century logical and philosophical revival in Poland. It must have stood high in the author's own estimation, for in 1955 he began translating it into English. The main point of the book is that in Aristotle's work one can distinguish three forms of the principle of contradiction: ontological, logical, and psychological. The ontological principle of contradiction is that the same property cannot both belong and not belong to the same object in the same respect. The logical principle says that two contradictory propositions cannot both be true, and the psychological principle of contradiction holds that no one can, at the same time, entertain two beliefs to which there correspond two contradictory propositions. Łukasiewicz supported his findings with quotations from the writings of Aristotle and then examined the validity of Aristotle's argumentation. One chapter brought to the notice of Polish readers Russell's antinomy concerning the class of all classes that are not members of themselves. The appendix contains an elementary exposition of the algebra of logic, as well as an original and interesting methodological classification of the ways of reasoning, a problem with which at least two of Łukasiewicz's early papers were concerned.

Łukasiewicz's writings published before 1918 suggest that until that time he was in quest of topics to which he could devote all his intellectual resources. He found such topics in the logic of propositions and in the logic of the ancient Greeks. From 1918 onward, deviations from this double line of research are few and of little significance.

LOGIC OF PROPOSITIONS

Many-valued logics. The first and perhaps most important result obtained by Łukasiewicz in the logic of propositions was his discovery of three-valued logic in 1917. Our ordinary logic of propositions is two-valued, presupposing only two logical values, truth and falsity, and it tacitly adheres to the principle of bivalence, that a propositional function holds of any propositional argument if it holds of the constant true proposition (usually symbolized by 1) and if it holds of the constant false proposition (represented by 2). If we use δ as a functorial variable that, when followed by a propositional argument, forms a propositional expression, then we can express the principle of bivalence by saying "if $\delta 1$ then if $\delta 2$ then δp," where p is a propositional variable. The meaning of the logical constants forming such expressions as, for instance, Cpq ("if p then q"), Kpq ("p and q"), Apq ("p or q"), and Np ("it is not the case that p") are, in two-valued logic, conveniently and adequately determined by means of the familiar two-valued truth tables:

$$C11 = C21 = C22 = 1$$
$$C12 = 2$$
$$K11 = 1$$
$$K12 = K21 = K22 = 2$$
$$A11 = A12 = A21 = 1$$
$$A22 = 2$$
$$N1 = 2$$
$$N2 = 1$$

In three-valued logic the principle of bivalence does not hold. It is replaced by the principle of trivalence, which presupposes three logical values: the constant true proposition represented by 1, the constant false proposition by 3, and the constant "possible" proposition by 2. The principle then says "if $\delta 1$ then if $\delta 2$ then if $\delta 3$ then δp." As a consequence the meanings of implication, conjunction, alternation, and negation have to be readjusted, and the following three-valued truth tables suggest themselves for the purpose:

$$C11 = C21 = C22 = C31 = C32 = C33 = 1$$
$$C12 = C23 = 2$$
$$C13 = 3$$
$$K11 = 1$$
$$K12 = K21 = K22 = 2$$
$$K13 = K23 = K31 = K32 = K33 = 3$$
$$A11 = A12 = A13 = A21 = A31 = 1$$
$$A22 = A23 = A32 = 2$$
$$A33 = 3$$
$$N1 = 3$$
$$N2 = 2$$
$$N3 = 1$$

In this logic alternation and conjunction can be defined as follows: $Apq = CCpqq$, and $Kpq = NANpNq$. All expressions involving only C and N and verified by the new truth tables can be constructed into a deductive system based on the axioms $CpCqp$, $CCpqCCqrCpr$, $CCCpNppp$, and $CCNpNqCqp$. This was shown by Mordchaj Wajsberg, who had studied logic under Łukasiewicz in Warsaw. Wajsberg's system, however, does not enable us to define all the functors available in three-valued logic. In particular the functor T, whose truth table says that $T1 = T2 = T3 = 2$, cannot be defined in terms of C and N. Jerzy Słupecki, who had also been a pupil of Łukasiewicz, subsequently proved that by adding $CTpNTp$ and $CNTpTp$ to Wajsberg's axioms we get a functionally complete system of three-valued logic, in which any functor can be defined.

The conception of three-valued logic was suggested to Łukasiewicz by certain passages in Aristotle. Purely formal considerations, such as those that led E. L. Post to comparable results, played a subordinate role in Łukasiewicz's thinking. By setting up a system of three-valued logic Łukasiewicz hoped to accommodate the traditional laws of modal logic. He also hoped to overcome philosophical determinism, which he believed was entailed by the acceptance of the bivalence principle and which he had always found repulsive. Interestingly enough, he modified his views in the course of time and saw no incompatibility between indeterminism and two-valued logic.

Once a system of three-valued logic had been constructed, the possibility of four-valued, five-valued, . . ., *n*-valued, and, finally, infinitely many-valued logics was obvious. At one time Łukasiewicz believed that the three-valued and the infinitely many-valued logics were of greater philosophical interest than any other many-valued logic, for they appeared to be the least arbitrary. In the end, however, he interpreted Aristotelian modal logic within the framework of a four-valued system.

The philosophical significance of the discovery of many-valued logic can be viewed in the following way: The laws of logic had long enjoyed a privileged status in comparison with the laws propounded by natural sciences. They had been variously described as a priori or analytic, the purpose of such descriptions being to point out that the laws of logic were not related to reality in the same way as were the laws of natural sciences, which had often been corrected or discarded in the light of new observations and experiments. The laws of logic appeared unchallengeable. By discovering many-valued logics Łukasiewicz showed that even at the highest level of generality—within the field of propositional logic—alternatives were possible. By adhering to the principle of bivalence or any other *n*-valence principle we run the same risk of misrepresenting reality that the scientist does when he offers any of his generalizations.

The classical propositional logic. Although Łukasiewicz contemplated the possibility that a nonclassical logic of propositions applied to reality, he made the classical propositional logic the principal subject of his research. He showed that the axiom systems of the calculus of propositions proposed by Frege, Russell, and Hilbert each contained a different redundant axiom. He proved that all the theses of the *CN*-calculus could be derived from the three mutually independent axioms $CCNppp$, $CpCNpq$, and $CCpqCCqrCpr$. He solved the problem of the shortest single axiom for the *E*-calculus and the *C*-calculus by showing that the *E*-calculus, whose only functor means "if and only if," with $E11 = E22 = 1$ and $E12 = E21 = 2$ as its truth table, could be based on any of $EEpqEErqEpr$, $EEpqEEprErq$, and $EEpqEErpEqr$ and on no shorter thesis and by proving that $CCCpqrCCrpCsp$ is the shortest thesis strong enough to yield the *C*-calculus. The first single axiom for *CN*-calculus, consisting of 53 letters, was discovered by Alfred Tarski in 1925. It was soon followed by a series of successive simplifications devised by Łukasiewicz and by Bolesław Sobociński. The latest in this series is a 21-letter axiom, $CCCCCpqCNrNsrtCCtpCsp$, discovered by C. A. Meredith, Łukasiewicz's Irish colleague. It is likely to prove to be the shortest possible axiom for the *CN*-calculus.

Consistency, completeness, and independence. The metalogical study of deductive systems of the logic of propositions includes the study of consistency and completeness, and, in the case of systems based on several axioms, the mutual independence of the axioms has also to be considered. Independently of Post, Łukasiewicz developed both a method of proving consistency and one of proving the completeness of systems of the calculus of propositions. The completeness proof was based on the idea that if the system under consideration is not complete, there must be independent propositions, that is, propositions not derivable from the axioms of the system which on being adjoined to the axioms lead to no contradiction. If there are independent propositions, then there must be a shortest one among them. Following Łukasiewicz's method, one tries to show that any proposition that is meaningful within the system either is derivable from the axioms or is longer than another proposition inferentially equivalent to it. This method dispenses with the concept of "normal expressions" and is very useful for proving weak completeness of partial systems. Mutual independence of theses is usually established by an appropriate reinterpretation of the constant terms occurring in them. Many such reinterpretations have been provided by Łukasiewicz's many-valued logics. The wealth of metalogical concepts and theorems worked out in Łukasiewicz's logical seminar in Warsaw by Łukasiewicz himself, Tarski, Lindenbaum, Sobociński, and Wajsberg can best be seen in "Untersuchungen über den Aussagenkalkül," which summarizes the results obtained there between 1920 and 1930.

Functorial calculus. In Dublin, Łukasiewicz became interested in a two-valued calculus of propositions involving functorial variables. Since he used only functorial variables requiring one propositional argument to form a propositional expression, his new calculus was only a part of what Stanisław Leśniewski had called protothetic. A very strong rule of substitution invented by Łukasiewicz, together with the usual substitution rules for propositional variables, allows us, for instance, to use a thesis of the form $\delta\alpha$ to infer not only $N\alpha$ but also such theses as $Cp\alpha$, $C\alpha p$, $C\alpha CN\alpha p$, $C\alpha\alpha\cdot$ and α. By means of the new rule Łukasiewicz was able to base the calculus on the single axiom $C\delta C22C\delta 2\delta p$. This axiom is identical with the principle of bivalence, because $C22=1$. Meredith succeeded in showing that Łukasiewicz's axiom could be replaced by $C\delta\delta 2\delta p$ or by $C\delta pC\delta Np\delta q$. He was also able to prove completeness of the system.

ANCIENT LOGIC

Concurrently with his investigations of the logic of propositions Łukasiewicz was engaged in a thorough reappraisal of ancient logic. For centuries the logic of the Stoics had been regarded as a sort of appendage to the Aristotelian syllogistic. Łukasiewicz was the first to recognize in it a rudimentary logic of propositions. He found evidence that the main logical functions, such as implication, conjunction, exclusive disjunction, and negation, were known to the Stoics, who, following Philo of Megara, interpreted them as truth-functions, just as we do now. He pointed out that the Stoics, unlike Aristotle, had given their logic the form of schemata of valid inferences. Some of these schemata had been accepted axiomatically and others were rigorously derived from them. He subjected to severe but justified criticism the treatments of Stoic logic by such authorities as Carl Prantl, Eduard Zeller, and Victor Brochard. His preliminary investigations of medieval logic showed beyond doubt that in this field too there was room for fruitful research.

Equally successful was Łukasiewicz's inquiry into Aris-
totle's syllogistic. No sooner had he mastered the elements of symbolic logic for himself than he realized that the centuries-old traditional treatment of the Aristotelian syllogistic called for revision. A new presentation of the logic of Aristotle was before long included in his regular lectures at the university and then published in *Elementy logiki matematycznej* ("Elements of Mathematical Logic," Warsaw, 1929). Łukasiewicz completed a detailed monograph on the subject in Polish in the summer of 1939, but the manuscript and all printed copies were lost during the war. *Aristotle's Syllogistic* (1951) is a painstaking reconstruction undertaken by Łukasiewicz on his arrival in Dublin. The monograph can rightly be called revolutionary. In it Łukasiewicz argued that Aristotelian syllogisms are logical laws rather than schemata of valid inferences, as is taught in traditional textbooks. He put in historical perspective Aristotle's introduction of variables and, referring to a forgotten Greek scholium, gave a plausible explanation of the problem of the so-called Galenian figure. Among more formal results, we owe to Łukasiewicz the first modern axiomatization of syllogistic. The system he set up, based on the axioms Aaa ("every a is a"), Iaa ("some a is a"), $CKAbcAabAac$, and $CKAbcIbaIac$, seems to be in perfect harmony with Aristotle's own treatment of the subject in the *Analytica Priora*. The axioms are jointly consistent and mutually independent. Moreover, Słupecki has ingeniously solved the decision problem for the system.

MODAL LOGIC

During the last few years of his life Łukasiewicz devoted much attention to modal logic. The results are presented in "A System of Modal Logic," and in the second edition of *Aristotle's Syllogistic* (1957) they serve as the basis for a critical examination of Aristotle's theory of modalities. Łukasiewicz's principal idea is that of "basic modal logic," obtained by adding to the classical calculus of propositions the axioms $CpMp$ and $EMpMNNp$ and by axiomatically rejecting $CMpp$ and Mp. In these formulas Mp stands for "it is possible that p." According to Łukasiewicz any modal system must contain basic modal logic as a part. This condition is fulfilled by the four-valued modal system based on $C\delta pC\delta Np\delta q$ and $CpMp$ as the only axioms, with $CMpp$ and Mp axiomatically rejected.

The logical symbolism used in this article was worked out by Łukasiewicz in the early 1920s. It requires no punctuation signs, such as brackets or dots, which from the point of view of metalogical investigations is its greatest merit. At the same time Łukasiewicz worked out a simple and perspicuous method of setting out proofs in the logic of propositions and in syllogistic. Both his symbolism and his proof technique have been adopted by many logicians outside Poland.

Łukasiewicz was not only a resourceful and imaginative scholar but also a gifted and inspiring teacher. He was one of the founders, and the life and soul, of the Warsaw school of logic. Tarski, Lindenbaum, Stanisław Jaśkowski, Wajsberg, Father Jan Salamucha, Sobociński, Słupecki, and Meredith have been his most outstanding pupils or collaborators.

Principal Works by Łukasiewicz

"Analiza i konstrukcja projcia przyczyny" ("Analysis and Construction of the Concept of Cause"). *Przegląd Filozoficzny*, Vol. 9 (1906), 105–179.

O zasadzie sprzeczności u Arystotelesa. Cracow, 1910.

Die logischen Grundlagen der Wahrscheinlichkeitsrechnung. Cracow, 1913.

"Opojęciu wielkości" ("On the Concept of Magnitude"). *Przegląd Filozoficzny*, Vol. 19 (1916), 1–70.

"O logice trójwartościowej" ("On Three-valued Logic"). *Ruch Filozoficzny*, Vol. 5 (1920), 170–171.

"Logika dwuwartościowa" ("Two-valued Logic"). *Przegląd Filozoficzny*, Vol. 23 (1921), 189–205.

"Démonstration de la compatibilité des axiomes de la théorie de la déduction." *Annales de la Société Polonaise de Mathématique*, Vol. 3 (1925), 149.

Elementy logiki matematycznej. Warsaw, 1929; 2d ed., Warsaw, 1958. Translated by Olgierd Wojtasiewicz as *Elements of Mathematical Logic*. New York, 1963.

"Untersuchungen über den Aussagenkalkül." *Comptes rendus des séances de la Société des Sciences et des Lettres de Varsovie*, Classe III, Vol. 23 (1930), 30–50. In collaboration with Alfred Tarski. English translation by J. H. Woodger in Alfred Tarski, *Logic, Semantics, Metamathematics*. Oxford, 1956. Pp. 38–59.

"Philosophische Bemerkungen zu mehrwertigen Systemen des Aussagenkalküls." *Comptes rendus des séances de la Société des Sciences et des Lettres de Varsovie*, Classe III, Vol. 23 (1930), 51–77.

"Ein Vollständigkeitsbeweis des zweiwertigen Aussagenkalküls." *Comptes rendus des séances de la Société des Sciences et des Lettres de Varsovie*, Classe III, Vol. 24 (1931), 153–183.

"Zur Geschichte des Aussagenlogik." *Erkenntnis*, Vol. 5 (1935–1936), 111–131.

"Der Äquivalenzenkalkül." *Collectanea Logica*, Vol. 1 (1939), 145–169.

"Die Logik und das Grundlagenproblem," in *Les entretiens de Zurich sur les fondements et la méthode des sciences mathématiques 6–9 Décembre 1938*. Zurich, 1941. Pp. 82–100.

"The Shortest Axiom of the Implicational Calculus of Propositions." *Proceedings of the Royal Irish Academy*, Vol. 52, Section A (1948), 25–33.

"On Variable Functors of Propositional Arguments." *Proceedings of the Royal Irish Academy*, Vol. 54, Section A (1951), 25–35.

Aristotle's Syllogistic. Oxford, 1951; 2d ed., 1957.

"A System of Modal Logic." *The Journal of Computing Systems*, Vol. 1 (1953), 111–149.

Z zagadnień logiki i filozofii ("Problems of Logic and Philosophy"), Jerzy Słupecki, ed. Warsaw, 1961. Essays. Contains bibliography.

In addition to the above, Łukasiewicz published about twenty papers and over fifty notes and reviews.

Works on Łukasiewicz

Borkowski, Ludwik, and Słupecki, Jerzy, "The Logical Works of J. Łukasiewicz." *Studia Logica*, Vol. 8 (1958), 7–56.

Jordan, Z. A., *The Development of Mathematical Logic and of Logical Positivism in Poland Between the Two Wars*. Oxford, 1945.

Kotarbiński, Tadeusz, "Jan Łukasiewicz's Works on the History of Logic." *Studia Logica*, Vol. 8 (1958), 57–62.

Kotarbiński, Tadeusz, *La Logique en Pologne*. Rome, 1959.

Prior, A. N., "Łukasiewicz's Contributions to Logic," in *Philosophy in the Mid-century*, Raymond Klibansky, ed. Florence, 1958. Pp. 53–55.

Sobociński, Bolesław, "In Memoriam Jan Łukasiewicz." *Philosophical Studies* (Ireland), Vol. 6 (1956), 3–49. Contains bibliography.

Sobociński, Bolesław, "La génesis de la Escuela Polaca de Lógica." *Oriente Europeo*, Vol. 7 (1957), 83–95.

CZESŁAW LEJEWSKI

LULL, RAMÓN, or Llull, Ramón (c. 1232–1316), Franciscan philosopher, was born in Palma de Mallorca in the Balearic Islands. Lull received the education of a rich knight of the period, but was converted from dissipation to a devout life in about 1263. At that time Majorca was largely populated by Muslims, and Islam was still the great rival of Christianity. Lull resolved to dedicate himself to the conversion of Muslims and to seek martyrdom for their sake. After selling almost all his possessions and undertaking various pilgrimages, Lull spent nine years (c. 1265–1274) in Majorca, acquiring a profound knowledge of Arabic. In 1274 he had a vision which revealed to him the Principles on which his combinatory Art should be based. In 1275 James II of Majorca had Lull's early writings examined for orthodoxy, and in 1276 James founded at Miramar in Majorca a monastery where Franciscans could study Arabic and Lull's Art to prepare for missions to Islam.

Lull appears to have divided his time in the years 1276–1287 between Miramar and Montpellier. In 1287 he began a series of journeys to the courts of kings and popes with the hope of persuading them to support his missionary, his reforming, and (later) his crusading projects. Lull placed his hopes principally in the papacy and in the kings of France and Aragon. His only apparent success was when the Council of Vienne (1311–1312) ordained the creation of chairs for Hebrew, Arabic, and "Chaldean" in five centers. Lull also undertook missions to Tunis (1293), to Bougie, in Algeria (1307), and again to Tunis (1314–1315). The traditional account of his martyrdom at Bougie cannot be sustained. He seems to have died in Majorca before March 25, 1316. He has been beatified by the Roman Catholic church.

In the years 1288–1289, 1297–1299, 1309–1311, and probably 1306, Lull taught at the University of Paris; he also lectured publicly at Naples and Montpellier. Starting about 1272, he began to write incessantly. Some 240 of his approximately 290 works have survived. About 190 are only preserved in Latin (over 100 of these Latin works remaining unpublished until recently), although most of them were originally written in Catalan. Some of his works were originally written in Arabic; all these Arabic versions, however, are lost.

The desire to bring about the conversion of Muslims and Jews, as well as pagan Tartars, which inspired Lull's ceaseless activity, also inspired his writings. The desire for the reunification of the church (divided into hostile East and West), and for the complete reunification of mankind, through Christianity, dominated Lull's life. Lull's Art and his whole philosophy are apologetic and Franciscan, aimed at conversion by peaceful persuasion. Lull's advocacy of an armed crusade came late in his life; it was intended as subsidiary to missions. Lull's life was a continual battle with Islam, not only in Spain and North Africa, but also, from 1298, in Paris, with the "Averroists." In opposition to the "double-truth" theory imputed to such rationalist philosophers as Boethius of Dacia and Siger of Brabant, whose master was Aristotle as interpreted by Averroës, Lull sought to re-establish the unity of truth in philosophy and theology.

The "Ars Combinatoria." According to Lull, God, insofar as he can be known to men, consists of a series of divine attributes, or "Dignities," which are also the absolute Principles of Lull's Art. These Dignities (in the later works goodness, greatness, eternity, power, wisdom, will, virtue, truth, glory) are the instruments of God's creative activity, the causes and archetypes of all created perfection. The essence of the Art does not (as is often thought) consist in demonstration, but in the metaphysical reduction of all created things to the Dignities, which are Principles of knowing as well as of Being, and in the comparison of particular things between themselves in the light of the Dignities, by means of such relative predicates as difference, agreement, contrariety, beginning, middle, end, majority, equality, minority. The absolute and relative predicates together form the self-evident principles common to all the sciences. These principles are combined in circular figures, where letters are substituted for their names (B = goodness, and so on).

Lull's treatises on different sciences (cosmology, physics, law, medicine, astronomy, geometry, logic, psychology) are applications of his general Art. Lull made continual efforts to simplify and popularize his Art, from the primitive version in the *Ars Magna* of about 1274 to the final *Ars Generalis Ultima* of 1308. The latter work and also the *Arbre de ciència* (*Arbor Scientiae*) of 1296 are more philosophical and less polemical in purpose than the original Art. A vast encyclopedia which found favor in the Renaissance, the *Arbre* is an attempt to classify all knowledge under a unified plan. Lull's influence was acknowledged by Leibniz in the later philosopher's search for the *caracteristica universalis* and *ars combinatoria,* which he hoped would make possible the deduction of all truths from basic concepts. Despite the clear analogies between the two systems, Leibniz only took over part of Lull's ideas, omitting Lull's original purpose of the Art as a means of converting infidels.

Lull was the first Christian philosopher of the Middle Ages to use a language other than Latin for his major works. Although he did not receive a university training, he enjoyed advantages denied to the great Scholastics. Of the three Mediterranean cultures of his time he knew Latin Christianity and Islam well and was aware of Greek Christianity. The basis of Lull's philosophy was Neoplatonic realism as transmitted through the Augustinian tradition: his exact use of Scotus Erigena, Anselm, the Victorines, Bonaventure, and Roger Bacon is still debated. Lull was also familiar with the writings and beliefs of his Jewish and Muslim contemporaries.

All Lull's contemporaries shared a vision of the world based on Neoplatonism. The common belief in a hierarchy, or ladder, of creation, the theories of the four elements and of the spheres, the organization of reality by numerical–geometrical symbolism, the idea of man as a microcosm, were all incorporated by Lull into his system. That excellent scholars have seen the inspiration of Lull's theory of the Dignities in the Muslim *hadras* or in the Jewish cabalist *sephiroth* (both terms for the divine attributes) shows that Lull's doctrine (although of Christian derivation) provided a reasonable basis for a dialogue with the Muslim and Jewish elites. Much the same is true of the doctrine of correlative principles, developed in Lull's later works, by which each attribute unfolds into a triad of interconnected principles, agent, patient, and the action itself, expressing the relations between God, a creature, and God's action. Lull probably took this doctrine from the Arabic writer al-Ghazālī, whose *Logic* he translated. It is more probable that Lull derived the idea for the figures that illustrate his Arts from contemporary Spanish cabalists or from the circular figures of Isidore of Seville's well-known cosmological treatise *De Natura Rerum* than from Ibn al-'Arabi of Murcia, who has been suggested as his source.

Two of the most striking characteristics of Lull's philosophy and theology—his "rationalism" and his emphasis on the importance of action, shown in his constant appeals to Christian rules—owe their prominence in his system to its polemical inspiration. Lull's "necessary reasons," by which he proposed to "prove" the articles of faith, are reasons of congruence and analogy, not purely deductive principles. In opposition to Islamic scholastic theology (the *Kalām*), which tried to demonstrate the Faith, Lull sought to show that the Muslim, who began with a belief in monotheism and the divine attributes, must proceed to Christianity. Despite the nondeductive character of his works, Lull's thought is deeply rational. Only seldom in his mystical writings does love eclipse the intellect or obscure its powers. For him, contemplation issues in action. *Blanquerna* and *Felix* are the first philosophical–social novels of Europe. In *Blanquerna* Lull sketched his plan for a *Pax Christiana,* a society of nations presided over by the papacy.

Bibliography

Lull's works in Latin may be found in *Raymundi Lulli Opera Omnia,* edited by Ivo Salzinger, 8 vols. (Mainz, 1721–1742), which contains most of the works·concerned with the Art, but neither the *Arbor Scientiae* (Majorca, 1745) nor the *Ars Generalis Ultima* (Strasbourg, 1651). A new critical edition, *Raimundi Lulli Opera Latina,* is being edited by Fridericus (Friedrich) Stegmüller (Palma, 1959——); 35 vols. have been projected.

Lull's works in the Catalan language include: *Obres de Ramón Lull,* 21 vols. (Majorca, 1906–1950), in progress; and Ramón Llull, *Obres Essencials,* 2 vols. (Barcelona, 1957–1960). *Blanquerna* has been translated into English by E. Allison Peers (London, 1926).

A contemporary Latin account of Lull's life, edited by Baudouin de Gaiffier, may be found in *Analecta Bollandiana,* Vol. 48 (1930), 130–178. For other biographies, see E. Allison Peers, *Ramon Lull, A Biography* (London, 1929), and Armand Llinarès, *Raymond Lulle, philosophe de l'action* (Grenoble, 1963), both of which contain detailed bibliographies.

For studies of Lull's work, see Tomás y Joaquín Carreras y Artau, *Historia de la filosofía española,* Vol. I: *Filosofía cristiana de los siglos XIII al XV* (Madrid, 1939), pp. 231–640, which contains a detailed bibliography. Vol. II (Madrid, 1943) contains the best history of Lullism yet written. See also J. Tusquets, *Ramón Lull, pedagogo de la cristianidad* (Madrid, 1954); Frances A. Yates, "The Art of Ramon Lull," in the *Journal of the Warburg and Courtauld Institutes,* Vol. 17 (1954), 115–173; Robert Pring-Mill, *El microcosmos lul.lià* (Palma and Oxford, 1962); and Erhard W. Platzeck, *Raimund Lull,* 2 vols. (Düsseldorf, 1962–1964), contains detailed bibliography. Many valuable articles may also be found in the issues of the review *Estudios lulianos,* published in Palma since 1957.

JOCELYN NIGEL HILLGARTH

LUNACHARSKI, ANATOLI VASILYEVICH (1875–1933), Marxist philosopher and literary critic and Soviet administrator, joined the Russian Social Democratic party in Kiev in 1892. Because of his political activities as a secondary school student, he was denied admission to Russian universities. He attended lectures at Kiev University and at the University of Zurich, where in 1894/1895 he studied under Richard Avenarius, who converted him to empiriocriticism. Lunacharski returned to Moscow in 1897, was exiled to Vologda (1899–1902), and spent several years in western Europe between 1904 and 1917. He was the first Soviet people's commissar for education (1917–1929).

Lunacharski's contributions to philosophy are concentrated in value theory (which he rather misleadingly called biological aesthetics), ethics, and philosophy of religion. Like the positivists, he denied the adjudicability of value disputes. "In order to show," he wrote, "that a given type of valuation is in its very root worse than another type, the scientist must oppose one criterion to another, but the choice between criteria is a matter of *taste*, not *knowledge*" ("K Voprosu ob Otsenke" ["On the Question of Valuation"], 1904, reprinted in *Etyudy*, Moscow, 1922, p. 55).

In ethics and social philosophy Lunacharski was a "Nietzschean Marxist." He called himself an aesthetic amoralist and rejected the categories of duty and obligation, stressing instead free creative activity, the "artistic" shaping of ends and ideals. "Nietzsche," he declared, "and all the other critics of the morality of duty, have defended the autonomy of the individual person, the individual's right to be guided in his life solely by his own desires" ("'Problemy Idealizma'. . . ," in *Obrazovaniye*, Vol. 12, No. 2, 1903, p. 133).

Lunacharski called his individualism macropsychic, or "broad-souled," to distinguish it from "narrow-souled" (micropsychic) individualism. It approached collectivism in its stress on the historical community of the creators of culture.

Traditional religious attitudes and institutions, according to Lunacharski, could and should be given a new, socialist content. The old religions—supernatural, authoritarian, "antiscientific"—must be replaced by a new religion that will be humanistic, libertarian, and "scientific." The building of socialism and the shaping of the high human culture of the future will be a building of God (*bogostroitelstvo*). "Scientific socialism," Lunacharski declared, "is the most religious of all religions, and the true Social Democrat is the most deeply religious of men" ("Budushcheye Religii," p. 23). The religion of God-building will soften the sting of mortality by intensifying man's awareness of the "universal connectedness of life, of the *all-life* which triumphs even in death" ("Yeshchyo o Teatre i Sotsializme ["Once More on the Theater and Socialism"], in *Vershiny*, Vol. I, 1909, p. 213). The new religion, imparting a sense of "joyous union with the triumphant future of our species," will be full of drama and passion, having its own "saints and martyrs." It will be worthy to stand beside medieval Christianity in the "universal arsenal of art and inspiration" (*R. Avenarius: Kritika Chistovo Opyta v Populyarnom Izlozhenii A. Lunacharskovo*

["R. Avenarius: *Critique of Pure Experience*, Expounded for the Layman by A. Lunacharski"], Moscow, 1905, p. 154).

Bibliography

Other works by Lunacharski include "Osnovy Positivnoi Estetiki" ("Fundamental Principles of Positive Aesthetics," 1904), reprinted as a book (Moscow, 1923). See "Budushcheye Religii" ("The Future of Religion") in *Obrazovaniye*, Vol. 16 (1907), No. 10, 1–25, and No. 11, 30–67.

An eight-volume edition of Lunacharski's works is now being published. Vols. I–IV (Moscow, 1963, 1964) are devoted to literary criticism. See also the article on Lunacharski in *Filosofskaya Entsiklopediya*, Vol. III (Moscow, 1964), pp. 261–262.

GEORGE L. KLINE

LUTHER, MARTIN (1483–1546), German theologian and leader of the Protestant Reformation, was born at Eisleben, Saxony. His father came of peasant stock, but established himself during Luther's boyhood as a successful copper miner in Mansfeld. From 1501 to 1505 Luther attended the University of Erfurt, and then, at his father's wish, he began the study of law; but a spiritual crisis, occasioned by a violent thunderstorm, induced him to enter the Erfurt monastery of the Augustinian Friars. Despite conscientious and even overscrupulous attention to his monastic duties, Luther was obsessed by dread of God's anger, and his superior tried to direct the young man's energies and undoubted ability into a scholar's calling. From 1512 he was Biblical professor at the new University of Wittenberg, a position he held, despite interruptions, until his death.

THEOLOGICAL DEVELOPMENT

Three stages may be distinguished in Luther's theological development. Between 1512 and 1517, and probably (in the judgment of most scholars) not later than 1515, his Biblical studies led to a theological reorientation, at the center of which was an interpretation of the justice of God in Romans 1.17, not as a divine attribute expressed in punishment and reward, but as the activity by which God makes men just ("justifies" them). This justice of God is identical with His grace: it is not conditional upon human merit, but is received by faith alone (faith itself being a work of God in man). The working out of this basic insight made Luther increasingly critical of late scholastic theology and of ecclesiastical abuses. The appearance of the Ninety-five Theses on indulgences (1517), although they were not intended as "un-Catholic," was interpreted by Luther's opponents as ecclesiastically disloyal and subversive. Luther had, indeed, touched on the heart of medieval piety, the sacramental system, since indulgences belonged to the sacrament of penance.

The second period of Luther's development, from 1517 to 1521, was marked by his struggle with the Roman authorities, during which he abandoned the theory of papal, and even ecclesiastical, infallibility. In his *Babylonian Captivity* (1520), he made a systematic attack on the sacramental system, reinterpreting a sacrament as, like preaching, a form of the divine Word, by which God offers man His justice and creates the response of faith. The "church" is defined, not in terms of hierarchical authority, but as the communion of those whom Christ rules with His Word, all of whom are priests. Luther's basic insight into the character of Christian justice (or righteousness) was sharpened during this same period by greater precision in the distinction (already made before 1517) between Law and Gospel. The Law of God can only demand and condemn; it cannot be. used by man as a means of self-salvation through strict obedience. The security of man before God lies solely in the Gospel, with its word of free forgiveness.

During the third period, after 1521, Luther's attention was turned to rival reformers who departed from him on particular points, or who demanded a more radical transformation of the church than he was prepared to countenance. Many of the radicals sought to establish communities in which the ethic of the Sermon on the Mount should be the sole rule of social conduct. Against them, Luther again argued for the distinction between Law and Gospel. Just as it is wrong to place Law between God and the conscience, so it is wrong to regulate society by the Gospel. The conscience needs the gospel of forgiveness, but society can only be founded upon the law of retributive justice (though Law should always be the agency of love). The two "realms," or "kingdoms," of Heaven and Earth—that is, the two ways in which God rules over the world of men—are not to be confused.

In his controversy with the humanist leader Erasmus, which also belongs within the third stage of his development, Luther again believed himself to be fighting for the gospel of forgiveness. He acknowledged that Erasmus' selection of the theme to be debated—namely, the freedom of the will—came closer to the decisive issue than did the questions of the papacy, purgatory, and indulgences. Luther was not, of course, interested in the psychology of human action as such but in preserving his original insight into the agency of divine grace. He acknowledged a measure of human freedom in matters that do not concern salvation, but refused to make salvation depend at any point on the inherent possibilities of human nature. He therefore located the power of man's decision for God in the Gospel itself, and in the secret influence of the Holy Spirit. For Luther, this did not mean that God acts coercively, thereby doing violence to man's will, but that God is sovereign over the will and can direct it to His ends. Man acts voluntarily (that is, as he wills) even in those matters that concern his salvation. But the will itself is controlled by God. It cannot change itself from an evil to a good will: it must *be* changed under the influence of the Spirit.

Luther was not, of course, a philosopher. He was primarily a theologian, obliged by circumstances to become a rebel and a reformer. Indeed, it is often supposed that he was an implacable enemy of philosophy, and to this problem the remainder of this article will be devoted. It will appear how closely Luther's views on reason and philosophy are related to the central theological concerns (Christian justice and the two realms of Heaven and Earth) which have been sketched above. (For further details on Luther's theological views, see REFORMATION.)

ATTITUDE TOWARD PHILOSOPHY

It is not hard to document from Luther's own writings the common accusation that he was an anti-intellectualist. His description of reason as "the Devil's Whore" is well known, and he recommended that the faithful sacrifice reason, or slay it, as the enemy of God. Many have seen in this apparent antirationalism evidence of Luther's Ockhamist heritage, but this is an oversimplification of an intricate historical problem. Luther did not invariably decry reason. In his celebrated appearance before the Diet of Worms (1521) he seemed to appeal to a double norm—Scripture and reason. (He refused to recant unless convinced by "the testimonies of Scripture or by evident reason.") And sometimes he showered extravagant praise upon reason as the greatest of God's gifts, as the "inventress and mistress of all the arts, of medicine and law, of whatever wisdom, power, virtue and glory men possess in this life." Luther accepted the traditional view that reason set man apart from the brute beasts and gave him dominion over the world. Clearly, the problem is to explain, not an extreme one-sidedness, but a strange ambivalence. And the appeal to Luther's alleged Ockhamist heritage cannot help to explain his attitude until the Ockhamist understanding of reason is itself clarified and the extent of Luther's over-all dependence upon nominalism is carefully assessed. The persistent image of nominalist theology as antirational and un-Catholic requires reconsideration in the light of recent studies, and verbal echoes of nominalism in Luther's writing may prove of no great significance. In any case, the primary historical task is to examine Luther's actual utterances on reason and philosophy and to view them in relation to the inner structure of his thought.

The concept of reason. The apparent ambiguities in Luther's utterances on reason can be explained, in part, by his fundamental distinction between the two realms of human existence. At one and the same time, man lives toward God in the Heavenly Kingdom and toward his natural and social environments in the Earthly Kingdom. Luther judges human reason to be an adequate instrument for dealing with earthly affairs, that is, the maintaining of physical subsistence (*oeconomia*) and the regulation of life in society (*politia*). In this realm, reason is legitimately exercised and affords the only light man needs. But in spiritual affairs the situation is quite different. Reason has no understanding of what it is that commends a man to God. Therefore God has given His Word (in the Scriptures), and reliance upon reason could, in this realm, only be perverse and presumptuous. The way of salvation could never have been thought out by rational enquiry, for all God's works and words transcend reason. The Word of God is apprehended, not by reason, but by faith.

This does not mean that, for Luther, reason must be totally excluded from theology. He allowed for the possibility of taming reason's presumptuousness. It then becomes the handmaid of faith. Luther spoke of reason as illumined by faith, regenerated, or born anew. Sometimes the notion of regenerate reason tended to coalesce with the notion of faith itself. But generally, Luther seemed to think of regenerate reason as the human capacity for orderly thought being exercised upon material provided by the Word. Perhaps this is what he meant by the correlation of Scripture and reason in his answer before the Diet of Worms: he was willing to be persuaded either by direct Biblical citations or by plain inferences from them. He certainly did not mean to set reason beside Scripture as an independent and supplementary source of theological knowledge.

The doctrine of the two realms provides, then, the framework for a threefold distinction by means of which Luther's various utterances on reason may, for the most part, be harmonized. We have to distinguish between natural reason, ruling within its own domain (the Earthly Kingdom); presumptuous reason, encroaching on the domain of faith (the Heavenly Kingdom); and regenerate reason, serving faith in subjection to the Word of God. Luther does not represent an anti-intellectualist dismissal of disciplined thought; he tries to formulate a theological critique of reason, in which the boundary lines of reason's competence are sharply drawn. Only in the second of these three contexts does reason appear as "the Devil's Whore." In the first it is the greatest of God's gifts; in the third, an excellent instrument of godliness.

It is necessary, however, to carry the analysis further and to show that Luther's invective against reason is focused upon a quite specific blunder that reason makes when it trespasses, unregenerate, upon the domain of faith. It then appears that the *sacrificium intellectus* for which he calls cannot be understood simply as an epistemological doctrine, but rests upon a more strictly theological (or soteriological) concern. For in many passages from his writings, what Luther meant to express by his colorful invective against reason, was his constant astonishment at the heart of his own gospel: the unconditioned character of God's grace. Reason must be "put to death" because it cannot comprehend the miracle of divine forgiveness, and therefore stands in the way of man's receiving the justice of God. Reason became identified in Luther's mind with the religious attitude of the natural (that is, unregenerate) man, who can conceive only of a strictly legalistic relationship to God. *Ratio* became virtually synonymous with a definite *opinio*, and it is by no means accidental that the two words can be found side by side in several passages. Nor, of course, was this usage wholly eccentric, since Lewis and Short's Latin–English dictionary gives as one of the meanings of *ratio* a "view or opinion resting upon reasonable grounds." And Luther fully acknowledged a certain reasonableness about the assumption that a just God must require "good works" as the precondition of communion with Him. Consequently, the proclamation of an unconditioned grace—which demands nothing, save the acceptance of faith—can be greeted by reason only with incredulity. What needs to be "sacrificed," therefore, is not human rationality, without qualification, but rather the legalistic mentality of the natural man. As Luther put it, grace must "take us out of ourselves," and we must learn to "rise above reason." In short, Luther's concept of reason (at least, when his remarks about it are pejorative) is not formal, but material. *Ratio* is a concrete attitude rather than the faculty or structure of reasoning. When the natural man turns his thoughts to religion, he carries over into the Heavenly Kingdom presuppositions which, however appropriate in dealing with his social existence in the Earthly Kingdom, no longer apply. For the Kingdom of Christ is a realm, not of law, but of grace (*das Reich der Gnaden*).

The concept of philosophy. Because Luther's views on reason are set in a theological context, they are not always directly relevant to the problem of faith and reason as the philosopher normally understands it. But Luther's standpoint certainly had consequences for the philosophy of religion, and more particularly for the problem of a natural theology. For Luther there could be no question of treating the truths of reason as a kind of foundation for the truths of revelation. The continuity between nature and grace, as presented in the classical scholastic scheme, is broken. There is no rational preamble to faith, because reason is not a neutral instrument for the discovery of objective truths; it is misled by its own bias and even corrupted by sin—that is, by the egocentricity of the unredeemed man. For man in sin actually prefers a God of law, upon whom he can establish a claim. Revelation does not confirm or supplement reason: it stands in contradiction to reason, until the natural man is "born anew." The religion of reason is not merely insufficient or imperfect, but perverted and erroneous. Luther does not deny that a limited knowledge of God is available to reason; but the egocentricity of man in sin is a fatal defect, productive of idolatry and superstition. Reason makes God as it wills Him to be, and turns this natural knowledge into idolatry. The god of reason is a false God.

In general, Luther's direct statements about philosophy closely parallel his judgment on reason. As early as the Lectures on Romans (1515–1516) he had come to see his mission as a protest against philosophy, and his writings are interspersed with abusive descriptions of Aristotle ("the stinking philosopher," "the clown of the High Schools," "the blind pagan," etc.). Thomas Aquinas, who symbolized the attempt to synthesize Aristotle and the Christian faith, is treated with similar disrespect. Nevertheless, Luther could on occasion speak deferentially of philosophy and even of Aristotle. He approved of much that the Greek philosopher had written on social ethics and ranked Cicero's ethics even higher. He freely acknowledged that the Christian had much to learn from philosophy in this area. The key to Luther's ambivalence lies, as with his concept of reason, in the distinction between the two realms. The boundaries are carefully drawn. Philosophy is an excellent thing in its own place, but if philosophical categories are transferred into theology, the result can only be confusion. Luther saw philosophy as tied to the empirical world (the Earthly Kingdom), whereas theology is concerned with things unseen (the Heavenly Kingdom). He was not, strictly speaking, hostile to Aristotle, but to the theological application of Aristotelianism by the Schoolmen. Of course, some of the Greek philosopher's doctrines already had a theological bearing (for example, on the immortality of the soul and on divine Providence). These Luther dismissed. But he approved Aristotle's treatises on the sermonic arts (logic and rhetoric) and, with qualifications, those on moral philosophy.

Perhaps the most important illustration of Luther's attitude toward Aristotle is afforded by his discussions of moral "habit" (Latin, *habitus;* Greek, *hexis*). In the *Nicomachean Ethics,* Aristotle taught that "we become just by performing just acts." Luther's opponents apparently gave this doctrine a theological application: that is, it was used to support the claim that good works must precede justification. In assailing the concept of habit, Luther is not offering a philosophical critique of Aristotle, but rejecting the theological application of Aristotelian doctrines. A philosophical theory belongs within the Earthly Kingdom. The Schoolmen mix the kingdoms.

Comparison with nominalism. Luther's distinction between two spheres of knowledge (philosophy and theology) and between two organs of knowing (reason and faith) certainly invites comparison with late medieval Scholasticism. There is perhaps a prima facie probability that Luther's views on reason and philosophy were under the influence of the nominalists. His main instructors at Erfurt were nominalists, and it is noteworthy that Luther could speak of Ockham with apparent respect, even calling him "my dear master." He adopted the nominalist view of universals, and he explicitly owned a debt to the nominalist Pierre d'Ailly in the doctrine of the Real Presence. Other possible debts have been argued with more or less plausibility, although it can hardly be denied that Luther left nothing unchanged that he borrowed from others. At least the possibility is open that at the outset the sharp distinction between faith and reason may have been suggested to him by his familiarity with the Ockhamist school.

It may be that the separation of theology and philosophy in Luther is to be explained partly by his acceptance, along with the nominalists, of a strict Aristotelian concept of science. Against Thomas, Luther agreed with the nominalists that since theology rests upon assertions of faith, it cannot be classed as a science. Philosophy (which is the sum total of rational knowledge and embraces the various sciences) deals with the visible world, which is accessible to reason. Theology deals with an invisible world, accessible only to faith. Such points of agreement between Luther and the Ockhamists cannot, however, conceal the sharp differences between them. Quite apart from the fact that Luther developed a divergent concept of faith, his standpoint represents a different basic concern. The interest of the Ockhamists in the problem of faith and reason was primarily epistemological. Hence they devoted considerable thought to relating the cognition of reason to the cognition of faith, and sought in various ways to bridge the gap that they had apparently cut between the two. Nominalist theologians tried to comprehend both faith and reason within a single epistemological scheme. They regarded theological propositions (once established) as subject to rational scrutiny, believed that merely probable arguments could lead to faith when the will cooperates, and argued that revelation was given precisely to those who made maximum use of their rational capacities. Luther, on the other hand, was not interested in narrowing the epistemological gap. On the contrary, the problem for him was graver, because he allowed for the corruption of reason by human sinfulness. Hence his restrictions on reason, even if

they were built on a nominalist view of science, go beyond it in what is primarily a theological, rather than philosophical, concern.

The theory of "double truth." The nominalist distinction between the spheres of faith and of reason has commonly been interpreted as though there were a disharmony, or even a contradiction, between them. Indeed, the doctrine of a "double truth"—that is, that a proposition may be true in theology, but false in philosophy—has been attributed to the nominalist theologian Robert Holkot. Properly speaking, double truth seems never to have been a consciously adopted "doctrine" in the Middle Ages, but rather an accusation leveled against theological opponents. There does not seem to be adequate reason to attribute it to any of the nominalists. True, they admitted some apparent conflicts, for instance, that the Christian belief in the Trinity, when formulated according to the rules of Aristotelian logic, contained real contradictions. But this simply prompted the quest for a higher logic, which could embrace both the traditional Aristotelian rules and also the rules appropriate to the peculiarities of theological truth.

A doctrine of double truth could, however, be attributed to Luther with some plausibility, since he explicitly said that "the same thing is not true in different disciplines" (*Disputation on the Proposition, "The Word became flesh,"* 1539). But Luther himself did not use the expression "double truth," and a close inspection of his argument suggests that, despite appearances, he really had a rather different thesis in mind. What he was trying to defend might better be called a "theory of multiple meaning." Neither "twofold" nor "truth" quite pinpoints Luther's thesis, and perhaps even "manifold truth" (Bengt Hägglund's phrase) is still misleading. If we may paraphrase the drift of Luther's argument, he seems to be saying that *homo loquens* reflects and communicates, not by means of a single, universally valid language, but by means of several languages, which are relative to particular disciplines or areas of experience. Hence the meaning of a term or proposition is determined by the area of discourse: if transferred from one area of discourse to another, a term may acquire a different meaning, or have no meaning at all. To use Luther's own examples, it makes no sense to ask the weight of a line or the length of a pound. Whether correct or not, this argument bears a close resemblance to ideas which have played an important role in twentieth-century linguistic philosophy, and is therefore not likely to be dismissed as obscurantism or anti-intellectualism. Unfortunately, Luther's argument is not developed with adequate precision, either in this Disputation or elsewhere. But it is not an isolated argument. The basic thesis—that the same form of words may have different meanings in different disciplines—underlies many of his remarks about the relation of ethics and theology. For example, the proposition that fallen man can do no good is fundamental to Luther's teaching on justification. But Luther admits that this is true only in a theological, not in an ethical, context, for in each context the word "good" means something different. This is, perhaps, a statement of double truth, but only because it rests on a theory of multiple meaning. Thus interpreted, "double truth" does not imply contradiction, but excludes it, since real contradiction is possible only within a single realm of discourse. As Luther put it in the first thesis of the *Disputation:* "Although we must hold to the saying, 'One truth agrees with another,' nevertheless the same thing is not true in different disciplines."

Works by Luther

The definitive German edition of Luther's writings in Latin and German is *D. Martin Luthers Werke. Kritische Gesamtausgabe* (Weimar, 1883——). The most comprehensive English version is *Luther's Works: American Edition,* Jaroslav Pelikan and Helmut T. Lehmann, eds. (St. Louis and Philadelphia, 1955——, 55 vols. planned).

Works on Luther

RECENT STUDIES

Three recent books dealing with Luther's views on reason and philosophy are Bengt Hägglund, *Theologie und Philosophie bei Luther und in der occamistischen Tradition. Luthers Stellung zur Theorie von der doppelten Wahrheit* (Lund, 1955); Bernhard Lohse, *Ratio und Fides. Eine Untersuchung über die Ratio in der Theologie Luthers* (Göttingen, 1958); and B. A. Gerrish, *Grace and Reason: A Study in the Theology of Luther* (Oxford, 1962). One of the most adequate treatments of Luther's intellectual background is still Otto Scheel, *Martin Luther, Vom Katholizismus zur Reformation,* Vol. I, 1st ed. (Tübingen, 1916); Vol. II, 3d and 4th eds. (Tübingen, 1930).

LUTHER AND NOMINALISM

The literature dealing with the general question of Luther's relation to nominalism is sketched in Leif Grane, *Contra Gabrielem. Luthers Auseinandersetzung mit Gabriel Biel in der Disputatio contra scholasticam theologiam 1517* (Copenhagen, 1962). Grane's own discussion is focused on the theological rather than on the philosophical points, as is the work of Reinhard Schwarz, *Fides, Spes und Caritas beim jungen Luther unter besonderer Berücksichtigung der mittelalterlichen Tradition* (Berlin, 1962). The work of Heiko Augustus Oberman in *The Harvest of Medieval Theology: Gabriel Biel and Late Medieval Nominalism* (Cambridge, Massachusetts, 1963) is intended to lay the foundations for a study of nominalism in relation to the beginnings of Reformation theology.

ADDITIONAL BACKGROUND

For the wider aspects of Luther's thought, see the articles and bibliographies under "Luther" in *Die Religion in Geschichte und Gegenwart,* 3d ed. (Tübingen, 1960), Vol. IV, pp. 480–523, which may be brought up to date by the annual listings of the *Luther-Jahrbuch.*

B. A. GERRISH

M

MACH, ERNST (1838–1916), Austrian physicist and philosopher, was born at Turas, Moravia (now in Czechoslovakia). He studied in Vienna and became professor of mathematics at Graz in 1864. In 1867 he was appointed to a chair of physics at Prague and in 1895 to a chair of the history and theory of inductive science at Vienna. He held this chair until 1901, when he was appointed to membership in the upper house of the Austrian parliament. In 1879 and 1880 he was among those who opposed the replacement of German by Czech as the official language at the University of Prague. His interests were wide; in physics he made contributions to acoustics, electricity, hydrodynamics, mechanics, optics, and thermodynamics, and in psychology to perception and aesthetics. The influence he exerted with regard to the philosophy of science is still discernible in many discussions of the sciences. A modern view which owes a great deal to the work of Mach is the operationalism of Percy W. Bridgman, who showed how Mach and the new positivism influenced Einstein's work through the concept of operational definitions. On the other hand, because of the strong Berkeleian element in his work, Mach called down upon himself the fierce, often misguided criticisms of V. I. Lenin in, for example, the latter's *Materialism and Empirio-criticism*.

General aims. Philosophers usually think of Mach as having been closely connected with the Vienna circle. Philipp Frank, in his *Modern Science and Its Philosophy*, calls him "one of the spiritual ancestors of the Unity of Science Movement and, particularly, the real master of the Vienna Circle." Indeed, the public organization formed by several members of the Vienna circle was called the "Ernst Mach Verein." This fact is of the utmost importance, since besides suggesting that Mach was positivist, empiricist, and antimetaphysical in his attitude toward science, it also indicates the great diversity of his scientific interests. William James, who met Mach in 1882, reported that he appeared to have read and thought about everything. Moreover, Mach's writings cover a much wider field than was usual during this period. Apart from the work already mentioned, Mach wrote on the photographing of projectiles in flight, the chemistry of the ripening of grapes, and the place of classics in secondary education. This is not purely fortuitous, nor is it a sign of dilettantism. On the contrary, through all Mach's work there runs an interest in the logical and philosophical basis of science and the belief that the division of science into various branches, such as physics, psychology, and chemistry, is arbitrary and artificial, and very likely to be misleading if it is regarded as anything other than a matter of practical convenience. In the process of developing the empiricism of Berkeley and Hume and applying it to contemporary science, he reached the conception which underlies the *International Encyclopedia of Unified Science*, one of the major projects of the philosophers usually known as logical positivists. An appreciation of this conception is essential to an understanding of Mach's philosophy of science.

Much of Mach's work is historical, partly because he was interested in the history of science for its own sake, but also because he wished to keep his logical and philosophical account of the sciences as faithful as possible to the character of science as it is and has been. He believed, too, that his particular view could be supported by restating in the appropriate way the development of various concepts and theories. We are blinded, he thought, by certain traditional ways of stating things; we mistake conventions of speech for part of what is being asserted.

"The Science of Mechanics." The work for which Mach is perhaps best known is *The Science of Mechanics (Die Mechanik in Ihrer Entwicklung historisch-kritisch dargestellt, Leipzig, 1883)*. In the Preface to the first edition, he stated that the aim of the work was to elucidate the fundamental ideas and expose the real significance of mechanics, and to remove from the subject certain metaphysical obscurities. The book is very largely a historical treatise. But history does not just happen; it is made by historians. *The Science of Mechanics* is an attempt to rewrite the history of mechanics in such a way as to expose the logical principles and procedures upon which it depends.

The origins of science lie in our experiences in the manual arts and in our need to communicate these experiences. The need for communication involves the necessity of seeing connections and relations between the facts, and leads us to realize that nothing in the natural world can be understood in isolation from its context. Men also desire to simplify and abridge their descriptions, in order to reduce the labor of communication. They are thus led to the unitary conception of the world which underlies all scientific investigation.

Among other things, Mach attacked the physicists' respect for demonstration, or proof, which he referred to as "misplaced rigor." He attempted to show that the alleged proofs in mechanics rest on a foundation that is no surer than earlier, half-forgotten, and largely unappreciated experiences which he calls instinctive experiences and which are often, he said, mistaken for a priori knowledge.

This is the clue to his whole approach. There can be no a priori knowledge in mechanics; the basis and origin of all scientific knowledge is sense experience. Thus, an attempted mathematical demonstration can have no more rigor than a conclusion from observation. It can add nothing to observation and can tell us nothing about the world which sense experience cannot tell us. This being so, considerable stress is laid upon verification; it is verification rather than proof that is the appropriate method for establishing scientific conclusions or, indeed, any reasonable conclusions about the natural world.

We frequently remind one another, for example, that our conception of force is inclined to be animistic and subjective. Mach appeared to think that although this is a salutary warning, it should not lead us to reject our conception of force, for we cannot escape the animistic and subjective features of it. If a scientific conception is to be of any use in relation to the world, it must be derived from experience, and its anthropomorphic character is a sign that it is so derived. What we should do, however, in our effort to remove animistic and subjective elements from science, is to measure force by means of weight. Just as the thermometer provides a convenient "public" measure of our "private" perceptions of temperature, so weight can provide a "public" and communicable measure of our perceptions of force. In a similar way, Mach held, all the basic concepts of mechanics must ultimately be derived from, and related to, sense experience.

This view is antimetaphysical in aim and empiricist in origin. Mach's empiricism is of a special variety which may be called sensationalism, for he refers to his epistemological units as "sensations." In considering his sensationalism, it is well to bear in mind that one of the difficulties encountered in interpreting Mach is that he does not examine in sufficient detail, or state with sufficient clarity, the possible meanings of "sensation."

Sensationalism. Mach admitted a debt to Berkeley, Hume, Kant, and his contemporary Richard Avenarius among philosophers, and to Helmholtz, Kirchhoff, and Boltzmann among scientists. In regard to Mach's sensationalism, his most obvious debt is to Berkeley and Hume, since he based his whole philosophy of science upon the conception of "elements" or "sensations," which is a developed and refined form of the eighteenth-century empiricists' "ideas" and "impressions." The discussion of this basic concept is mainly to be found in his book *The Analysis of Sensations* (1886).

In his earliest papers Mach set out with a firm idea of the general character and purpose of science (see, for example, "The Economical Nature of Physics," 1882, in *Popular Scientific Lectures*). The aim of science is to reach concise, economical descriptions of phenomena, and its character is determined by the fact that in this context "phenomena"

has its Kantian sense and "description" necessarily refers to what is communicable. The only way of finding out about phenomena is through sense experience, and the only sound basis for communication about the external world is in the observation of it.

The world that we encounter in casual observation is a complex and unorganized flux. On closer inspection we find common qualities in radically different things: however else objects differ from one another, they may have the same color, or the same texture, or the same shape, or make the same sound when tapped, and so forth. There is a great variety of possible differences between objects which may lead us to give them different names or to wonder whether we *ought* to give them different names. If two different objects are of the same shade of red, however, we can, to this extent at least, describe them in the same way.

In fact, when we describe things, we do so by analyzing them into separately sensible qualities, such as particular colors, shapes, and textures. A uniform patch of color entirely within my visual field is, just because it is uniform and simple, what Mach called an element. Objects are made up of "elements" belonging to various classes and accessible to one or another of the five senses. The most accurate and economical description of the natural world is in terms of these elements.

Now these elements are known to us only through sense experience, and in this respect they depend entirely upon our senses. Considered from one point of view (indeed, the only point of view which is ultimately available to us), they are sensations. I cannot distinguish between the red color of a poppy and the sensation I have when I look at the poppy; or rather, if I do distinguish between these two phenomena, I am not making a distinction that is within my experience; indeed, I can make it only because I accept the fact that other people also have sensations when they look at this poppy and because I am prepared to draw an inference from this. For Mach, "the world consists only of our sensations" (*Analysis of Sensations*, p. 12).

One of the advantages of this view, it is alleged, is that it enables science to be built on a foundation of certainty. Throughout the history of philosophy, men have attempted to find certainty, the rationalist, like Descartes, searching for a priori truths upon which to base deductions, and the empiricist, like Hume, searching for unmistakable "atoms" of experience upon which to base inductions. Mach pursued the empiricist form of this search, in the belief that although I may be mistaken if I assert that there is a red book on the table before me, I cannot be mistaken if I confine myself to asserting that I am having various sensations—for example, one that I call red. No one is in a position to dispute this, and I myself cannot be mistaken about it. Moreover, everyone is in a similar position. There is perfect democracy in scientific contexts; all men's sensations are equal, and each sensation is to count for one and none for more than one.

Even if we accept the view that we can achieve some kind of certainty by reference to sensations (and it is by no means clear that Mach is correct about this), there are difficulties about the communicability of our certainties. By what right does Mach say that the world is *our* sensations rather than *my* sensations? Does his view not lead inevitably to solipsism? Mach saw this danger and attempted to avoid it by that familiar empiricist device, the argument from analogy. As I can observe, various features of my overt behavior go along with certain specific experiences of mine, so I can *infer* that similar features of other people's overt behavior go along with similar experiences of theirs. I can thus test for and discover a community of experience, and thereby the public basis of scientific agreement is assured. There are, of course, serious and familiar difficulties attached to this argument.

The fact remains that according to Mach, the world, for me, is constituted by my sensations. Sticks, stones, trees, stars, and animals are complexes analyzable into sensations and, ultimately, into my sensations. This, of course, also applies to other people, including my fellow scientists and their utterances; they, too, are collections of my sensations. Different branches of science, as we usually regard them, are distinguished by their subject matter: botanists study plants, while geologists study rocks. It is perfectly true that the physicist may study both plants and rocks, but this does not make his subject matter the same as that of the botanist or the geologist. The physicist studies plants and rocks only as examples of matter, and he does not, as the botanist does, study the growth of plants or, as the geologist does, the ways in which particular kinds of rocks are formed. From Mach's view it follows, however, that ultimately the subject matter of every branch of science is the same, since they must all study sensations and the relations between them. The only thing that distinguishes one branch of science from another is our attitude to our sensations, or what Mach called the direction of our investigation.

Suppose that I am studying a red flower. If I consider its red color in relation to light sources, the reflection of light rays, and other colors, then I am treating the color as a physical object, and I am in the realm of physics. If I consider it in relation to my retina, optic nerves, and so on, and in relation to the pleasure or pain the color gives me, then I am treating it specifically as a sensation, and I am in the realm of physiology and psychology.

We now see how Mach's premises led him to the conception of a unified science, and why he is linked with the Vienna circle and logical positivism. His successors in the twentieth century have tended to adopt the more neutral-sounding conception of sense data, rather than sensations, but in essentials the empiricism of the Vienna circle and its descendants is Machian. Mach's conception of unified science has connections with Russell's "neutral monism," the view that the material of which the world is constructed is neither mind nor matter, but a neutral "stuff" which can be treated, according to the context, as either mental or material. Mach's theory of the self as a bundle of "elements" reflects a similar approach, because the "elements" can be regarded, from one point of view, as physical, and from another point of view, as mental.

Scientific law. The premises of science are statements of the most elementary kind about sensations; they merely record the occurrence of specific kinds of sensations. The final aim of science is to give as complete a description of

phenomena as possible in terms of such sensations. Thus laws, which may figure among the conclusions of science, are, like its premises, concerned with sensations. They, in fact, state general relations between sensations.

Laws are descriptions of phenomena in terms of sensations, but because they are general they are abstract. In other words, a law covering a particular sort of phenomenon clearly cannot be a complete description of every detail of every instance of that kind of phenomenon; it is an abridged description. Its main function is to summarize past experience and to assist prediction; the detailed predictions, rather than the law, which is a mere aid to them, are of chief importance, since they will be an addition to our store of descriptions of actual facts.

The only hypotheses that are admissible are those that can be tested in sense experience; and until they have been tested, they must not be regarded as accepted scientific conclusions. Some hypotheses, which have been mistakenly regarded as scientific conclusions, are not testable in sense experience, according to Mach, and to regard these as conclusions is to misconstrue them. As examples of this he cited some of the statements which occur in the atomic theory of modern physics and chemistry. Since these statements refer to what is in principle unobservable, their role cannot be to describe, and that is why they cannot figure among the conclusions of the sciences. They are "explanatory" in a sense unacceptable to Mach.

He examined Newton's laws of motion in relation to his view of the nature of scientific laws, which are already firmly established and hence must be shown to be consistent with his view even if they do not appear to be so at first sight. There are two problems for Mach, which can be illustrated by Newton's first law, the law of inertia, namely, that "Every body perseveres in its state of rest or of uniform motion in a straight line except insofar as it is compelled to change that state by impressed forces."

The first problem is that this law appears to depend upon a conception of absolute space and absolute rest and motion that Mach regarded as unintelligible (*Science of Mechanics,* pp. 283 ff.). He attempted to remove this difficulty by regarding the law as having been arrived at directly from observation. In considering terrestrial motions, no error is introduced if we ignore the earth's rotation and so regard it as being relatively at rest; similarly, in considering the motions of the planets, no error is introduced by ignoring the motions of very distant stars and regarding them as being relatively at rest. All that is needed for seeing the truth of Newton's law in various contexts is the possibility of regarding some body as being relatively at rest for that particular context. We know no more of the behavior of bodies than what is observationally given; for all practical purposes, we need know no more than that.

The second problem is that no matter how the law of inertia is arrived at, it is in fact used in theoretical mechanics, and must be used, in its most general form when it cannot be regarded as merely summarizing observations. Used in this way, however, it appears to assert something about the behavior of bodies upon which no force acts. This is an unrealizable situation, and therefore an unobservable one; for Mach, it is consequently unacceptable in scientific contexts. He seeks to overcome this difficulty by regarding the law of inertia, used in the above way, as a definition of force, or rather, as a restatement of Newton's own definition of force. It is a definition which is grounded in the observed facts, in that it is part of the statement of the mathematical form of the observed behavior of moving bodies, although not a description of any observed motions. It is more abstract than any description; it gives not a picture of the phenomena but the pattern which must be contained in any picture of the phenomena. It is, in fact, part of a theory of motion.

Theories. We are inclined to think of theories as explanatory, and so as being the final achievements of scientific investigation. For Mach, however, a theory is entirely provisional, since it uses analogies as temporary substitutes for direct descriptions of phenomena in terms of sensations. When we meet an unfamiliar phenomenon which we do not understand, we first attempt to understand it in terms of phenomena with which we are already familiar, that is, by the use of analogy. For example, when scientists were unable to understand certain phenomena involving light, they made attempts to understand them by supposing that light moved the way waves move in water. The fact that the theory was successful in certain contexts does not mean that it had been discovered that light really is a wave motion. This conclusion we can neither assert nor deny, because we can never directly verify the assertion or denial; that is, we cannot give to either assertion or denial a meaning in terms of actual sensations. The theory functioned as a useful tool for predicting; we learned from it how to describe in terms of sensations further phenomena involving light. What is important in a theory is not the "picture" it gives us but the quantitative relations it represents. To say that the "picture" represents the reality underlying certain appearances is to speak metaphysically, in a context in which this type of discourse is absolutely out of place.

The theory's task is quantitative, not qualitative. In a qualitative sense, theory can tell us nothing about phenomena other than what we can learn by observation. If a feature of a theory cannot be found to correspond to a feature of the phenomena covered by it, then that feature of the theory cannot be part of the description of the phenomena. The particular feature may help us in the description of phenomena, however, for if the theory is predictively powerful, the feature will help us to find new phenomena or new details in familiar phenomena.

Mach illustrated his view of theories with the help of theories about the nature of heat (see "On Comparison in Physics" and "Conservation of Energy" in *Popular Scientific Lectures*, p. 243 and pp. 160 ff.). Scientists have disputed whether heat is a substance or a motion. Certain properties of heat do suggest a substantial view. For example, the fact that one body may become warmer at the expense of a neighboring body suggests that heat transfer involves the flow of a substance from one body to another. On the other hand, the fact that a piece of metal may be heated by hammering suggests that the "substantial" view is mistaken, and that it is more correct to regard heat as a form of motion.

In fact, Mach contended, neither "picture" can be finally supported by the observations, and it would be mere metaphysical speculation to regard either as the truth about what really goes on behind the observable phenomena of heat generation and transfer. Either picture may be heuristically valuable, but neither is essential to the theory; what is essential is the mathematical relations involved in heat phenomena. It does not matter what picture our theory uses, as long as it contains the correct quantitative relations between work done and heat generated, between the heat disappearing from one place and the heat appearing in another, and so on.

Theories are valuable only insofar as they lead us to observed descriptions of observed phenomena; if we take them to be descriptions of underlying realities, they can only mislead us. "Theoretical entities" are merely provisional, economical tools which help us to predict; theories are mathematical models for "facilitating the mental reproduction of facts."

It is clear that Mach attached considerable importance to the scientist's ability to predict; and it is only as devices for assisting predictions that Mach can admit many scientific theories. He steadfastly refused to believe in the existence of the physical atoms of modern atomic theory; if anyone found their postulation useful for predicting further phenomena, he was entitled to use them, but anyone would be equally entitled to use any other device which gave the same predictions. In fact, Mach was prepared to admit into science almost any device which would assist prediction. He showed, for example, how a teleological account of phenomena may sometimes be useful in this way. Perhaps because of the central position in science that Mach allotted to prediction, and because this evaluation led him to minimize the importance of explanation, his discussions of scientific explanation are most unsatisfactory.

Explanation. It is clear that Mach took an unusual view of explanation and, in particular, of what constitutes scientific explanation. As we have seen, he held that it is the aim of science to give concise, economical descriptions of phenomena. He was also prepared to say that these descriptions constitute scientific explanation. Whatever we do not understand (hence, whatever needs explaining) is what is unfamiliar to us. Thus, to make a phenomenon intelligible, we need only describe it in familiar terms. This concept is linked with Mach's sensationalism because, of course, the things that are most familiar to us are our elementary sensations. To describe phenomena in terms of our sensations is to remove their strangeness, to render them understandable, hence to explain them.

This is an unfamiliar meaning to give to "explanation," and it springs from Mach's hostility to the metaphysical. It has frequently been thought that explaining something is saying why it is as it is, and that this involves referring to some purpose it serves. In relation to natural phenomena, this is a metaphysical conception of explanation. Mach and his followers, intent as they were on avoiding metaphysics, regarded a concentration on description as being safer. If we say that our aim is to describe phenomena, we are unlikely to produce something which cannot be checked by observation; and if we admit only those explanations which are descriptions of phenomena, we shall avoid the likelihood of metaphysical entanglements.

There are, of course, difficulties involved in this view. In the first place, it is doubtful if we do in fact use the terms "explanation" and "description" in such a way that we can ever take an explanation to be merely a description—even a description of a very special sort. Of course, explanations often, and perhaps always, involve descriptions, but they also involve something more than descriptions, such as a particular relation between the description of what is to be explained and a description of something else. Followers of Mach who have perhaps noticed this fact have been inclined to say that it is the aim of science to describe rather than to explain, thereby avoiding the suspect identification of explanation with some kind of description. This development is sometimes referred to as the "descriptive view" of science. But whichever form of the view we consider, there is a further difficulty which Mach ought to have recognized. His account of scientific explanation does less than justice to the importance attached by working scientists to theories and theoretical concepts and their explanatory function. If scientists regard their aim as explanation in any sense in which it cannot be equated with description, then this is one good reason for supposing that Mach is mistaken on this point.

Works by Mach

"Über die Definition der Masse." *Repertorium für physikalische Technik,* Vol. 4 (1868), 355. Translated by P. E. B. Jourdain as "On the Definition of Mass," included in the English edition of Mach's *Die Geschichte und die Wurzel des Satzes von der Erhaltung der Arbeit.* Prague, 1872. Translated by P. E. B. Jourdain as *History and Root of the Principle of the Conservation of Energy.* Chicago, 1911.

Die Mechanik in ihrer Entwicklung historisch-kritisch dargestellt. Prague, 1883. Translated by T. J. McCormack as *The Science of Mechanics.* Chicago, 1893; latest (6th) English ed. from the 9th German ed., with a new introduction by Karl Menger, La Salle, Ill., 1960. From the philosophical point of view, this is usually regarded as Mach's most important work, but the preceding work, as well as *The Analysis of Sensations* and *Popular Scientific Lectures,* are perhaps equally important.

Die Prinzipien der Wärmelehre. Leipzig, 1886.

Beiträge zur Analyse der Empfindungen. Jena, 1886; 5th ed., greatly enlarged, *Die Analyse der Empfindungen,* Jena, 1906. Translated by C. M. Williams and Sydney Waterlow as *The Analysis of Sensations.* Chicago, 1914.

Populärwissenschaftliche Vorlesungen. Leipzig, 1894. Translated by T. J. McCormack as *Popular Scientific Lectures.* Chicago, 1894. The third and subsequent English editions contain additional lectures and essays dated between 1865 and 1897.

Erkenntnis und Irrtum. Leipzig, 1905. Translated by Marcel Dufour as *La Connaissance et l'erreur.* Paris, 1908. A collection of lectures and essays, some of which are of great interest.

Space and Geometry, translated and collected by T. J. McCormack. Chicago, 1906. Three essays originally published in *The Monist* (1901–1903).

Die Prinzipien der Physikalischen Optik. Leipzig, 1921. Translated by J. S. Anderson and A. F. A. Young as *The Principles of Physical Optics.* London, 1926. Mach wrote a preface to the first German edition just before he died in 1916, but its publication was considerably delayed.

Works on Mach

Adler, F., *Ernst Machs Überwindung des mechanischen Materialismus.* Vienna, 1918.

Ayer, A. J., ed., *Logical Positivism.* Glencoe, Ill., 1959. An ex-

cellent collection of original papers on the work of the Vienna circle, which contains, as an introduction, a useful historical sketch that links Mach with the logical positivists.

Bridgman, P. W., *The Logic of Modern Physics.* New York, 1927.

Carus, P., "Professor Mach's Philosophy." *The Monist,* Vol. 16 (1906), 331.

Carus, P., "Professor Mach and his Work." *The Monist,* Vol. 21 (1911), 19.

Dingler, H., *Die Grundgedanken der Machschen Philosophie.* Leipzig, 1924.

Frank, P., *Modern Science and its Philosophy.* Cambridge, Mass., 1949.

International Encyclopedia of Unified Science. Chicago, 1939–1952. Especially Vol. 1, Nos. 1, 5, 7, and 10, and Vol. 2, Nos. 7–9.

Kleinpeter, H., "On the Monism of Professor Mach." *The Monist,* Vol. 16 (1906), 161.

Kraft, V., *The Vienna Circle.* New York, 1953.

Lenin, V. I., *Materialism and Empirio-criticism,* translated by A. Fineberg. London, 1930.

Mises, R. von, *Ernst Mach und die empirische Wissenschaftsauffassung.* The Hague, 1938.

Mises, R. von, *Positivism.* Cambridge, Mass., 1951.

Popper, K. R., *The Logic of Scientific Discovery.* London, 1959.

Popper, K. R., *Conjectures and Refutations.* London, 1963.

Reinhold, F., *Machs Erkenntnistheorie.* Leipzig, 1908.

Russell, B., *An Outline of Philosophy.* London, 1927. American ed., *Philosophy.* New York, 1927.

Schlick, M., *Gesammelte Aufsätze.* Vienna, 1938.

PETER ALEXANDER

MACHIAVELLI, NICCOLÒ (1469–1527), Italian politician and political thinker, is famous for his treatise on princeship entitled *The Prince* (*Il principe*) and for a discussion of how to establish a good republican government, *The Discourses* (*Discorsi sopra la prima deca di Tito Livio*). Machiavelli also wrote poems and comedies (including the *Mandragola*), a *History of Florence,* and a book entitled *Art of War.* They contain many original ideas and were widely read, but today these writings arouse interest mainly because their author was the man who, with *The Prince* and *The Discourses,* inaugurated a new stage in the development of political thought.

When Machiavelli wrote *The Prince* and *The Discourses,* he was aware that he was saying things about politics which had not been expressed before; in the introduction to *The Discourses* he stated that he was resolved "to open a new route which has not yet been followed by anyone." Nevertheless, Machiavelli would not have claimed to be a systematic political philosopher. *The Prince* was written in 1512/1513; the date of *The Discourses* is less certain, but it was certainly completed by 1517. Machiavelli was then in his forties and, in the preceding years of his life, he had been a practical politician who had never shown interest in becoming a political writer or in embarking on a literary career.

In 1498, after the expulsion of the Medici from Florence and the fall of Savonarola, Machiavelli had entered the Florentine chancellery, where his special function was to serve as the secretary of The Ten, a group of magistrates charged with the conduct of diplomatic negotiations and the supervision of military operations in wartime. In this position Machiavelli carried out a number of diplomatic missions in Italy, France, and Germany. His ability attracted the attention of Gonfalonier Piero Soderini, the official head of the Florentine government, and Machiavelli became Soderini's confidant—his "lackey," according to Soderini's enemies. Machiavelli's close relationship with Soderini became a serious handicap when, in 1512, the republican regime was overthrown and the Medici returned to Florence. Other members of the chancellery were permitted to continue in office, but Machiavelli was dismissed and forced to withdraw to a small estate near Florence, where he lived in straitened economic circumstances.

It was at this time that Machiavelli turned to literary work in the hope that through his writings he would gain the favor of influential men who might help him to regain a position in the Florentine government. *The Prince* was dedicated to Lorenzo de' Medici, a nephew of Pope Leo X, who was the actual ruler of Florence. *The Discourses* was dedicated to members of the Florentine ruling group, and his *History of Florence* was written at the suggestion of Cardinal Giulio de' Medici, who in 1523 became Pope Clement VII. In the 1520s Machiavelli's efforts began to bear fruit. Clement VII entrusted him with a number of minor political commissions, and Machiavelli devoted himself to this kind of work, relegating the completion of his literary projects to the background. However, in 1527, before Machiavelli had been firmly re-established in a political position—actually, at a moment when his future had again become uncertain because the Medici had once more been driven from Florence—he died.

Thus, Machiavelli's attitude in composing *The Prince* and *The Discourses* was not that of a disinterested scholar; his aims were practical and personal. He wanted to give advice which would prove his political usefulness, and he wanted to impress those who read his treatises. Therefore, Machiavelli was inclined to make numerous startling statements and extreme formulations. A characteristic example is his saying that the prince "must abstain from taking the property of others, for men forget more easily the death of their father than the loss of their patrimony" (*The Prince*, Ch. 17).

Arts of war. Machiavelli's statements were startling not only because of their form of presentation but also because of their content. One aspect of political affairs with which Machiavelli had been particularly concerned and in which he was especially interested was the conduct of military affairs. He thought deeply about the reasons why the French had so easily triumphed over the Italians in 1494 and had marched from the north to the south of Italy without meeting serious resistance. Machiavelli's explanation was that the governments of the various Italian states, whether they were republican regimes or principalities, had used mercenary soldiers led by hired *condottieri*. He therefore recommended that in case of war the prince should lead his troops himself and that his army should be composed of his own men; that is, the Italian governments should introduce conscription. Moreover, Machiavelli polemicized against other favorite notions of his time on military affairs; for instance, he denied that artillery was decisive in battle or that fortresses could offer a strong defense against an invading army.

Morals and politics. Machiavelli's rejection of traditional political ideas emerged most clearly in his discussions of the relation between morals and politics. The most revolutionary statements on these issues are found in chapters 15–19 of *The Prince*, which deal with the qualities a prince ought to possess. In the Mirror of Princes literature of the ancient world and of the Middle Ages, a prince was supposed to be the embodiment of human virtues; he was expected to be just, magnanimous, merciful, and faithful to his obligations, and to do everything which might make him loved by his subjects. Machiavelli objected to such demands. According to him, a prince "must not mind incurring the scandal of those vices without which it would be difficult to save the state, and if one considers well, it will be found that some things which seem virtues would, if followed, lead to one's ruin and that some others which appear vices result in one's greater security and well-being." This sentence and chapters 15–19 have frequently been understood as meaning that instead of being mild a prince ought to be cruel; instead of being loyal, treacherous; instead of aiming to be loved, he should aim to be feared. But this is a misunderstanding. A closer reading shows that Machiavelli admonishes a prince to disregard the question of whether his actions would be called virtuous or vicious. A ruler ought to do whatever is appropriate to the situation in which he finds himself and may lead most quickly and efficiently to success. Sometimes cruelty, sometimes leniency, sometimes loyalty, sometimes villainy might be the right course. The choice depends on circumstances. To illustrate his point of view Machiavelli used as an example the career of Cesare Borgia, which he outlined in Chapter 7 of *The Prince*.

Machiavelli's views have frequently been interpreted as meaning that wickedness is more effective than goodness. This distortion of his views has been regarded as the essence of Machiavelli's teaching, as identical with what later centuries called Machiavellism. It should be stated that Machiavelli was not concerned with good or evil; he was concerned only with political efficiency. His rejection of the *communis opinio*—whether in the special area of military affairs or in the general field of ethics—was a reflection of a new and comprehensive vision of politics. Before Machiavelli, the prevailing view had been that the task of government was distribution and maintenance of justice. Machiavelli believed that the law of life under which every political organization existed was growth and expansion. Thus, force was an integral, and a most essential, element in politics.

Machiavelli's interest in military affairs had its basis in his conviction that possession of a powerful and disciplined military force was a requisite for the preservation of political independence. Moreover, because political life was a struggle, the conduct of life according to Christian virtues could endanger political effectiveness; Christianity, by preaching meekness and selflessness, might soften men and weaken a political society. Machiavelli directed some very strong passages against the effeminacy to which Christianity had led. Political man needed not virtues but *virtù*, "vitality." The possession of *virtù* was the quality most necessary for a political leader, but according to Machiavelli both individuals and entire social bodies could and should possess *virtù*. That is why, in *The Prince*, Machiavelli could write a "handbook for tyrants," while in *The Discourses* he could advocate a free republican regime. Every well organized, effective political organization must be permeated by one and the same spirit and must form an organic unit. There are few if any passages in Machiavelli in which he uses the word state (*stato*) in the modern sense of an organic unit embracing individuals and institutions. However, there can be no doubt that his concept of an organized society producing *virtù* among its members comes very close to the modern concept of state.

Method of argument. The new vision of the character of politics required a new method of political argumentation. Rules for the conduct of politics could not be formulated on the basis of theoretical or philosophical assumptions about the nature of a good society; successful political behavior could be learned only through experience. Machiavelli stated in his dedication of *The Prince* that he wanted to tell others what he had "acquired through a long experience of modern events and a constant study of the past." Thus, experience was not limited to those events in which a person participated but embraced the entire field of history. To Machiavelli the most instructive period of the past was that of republican Rome. Machiavelli thought that, because the Romans succeeded in extending their power over the entire world, no better guide for the conduct of policy could be imagined than that of Roman history. It is indeed true that previous writers on politics, particularly the humanists, had used historical examples, but to rely exclusively on historical experience in establishing political laws was an innovation; Machiavelli's writings implied that every true political science ought to be based on history.

It has been said that, in rejecting the validity of the doctrines of theology and moral philosophy for the conduct of politics, Machiavelli established politics as an autonomous field. He could do so because he regarded political bodies not as creations of human reason but as natural phenomena. In Machiavelli's opinion all political organizations, like animals, plants, and human beings, are subject to the laws of nature. They are born, they grow to maturity, they become old, and they die. Well organized political bodies might live longer than others, but even the best-constructed political society, even Rome, could not escape decline and death. This view of the instability and impermanence of all things gives Machiavelli's recommendations their particular tenor. Men or political bodies are entitled to use all possible means and weapons because the moments when they can flourish and triumph are brief and fleeting. Despite Machiavelli's claim that political success depended on acting according to the political laws he established in his writings, he was always conscious of the role of accident and fortune in human affairs.

Influence. It is of some importance to distinguish between the shocking novelty of Machiavelli's particular recommendations and his general concepts of politics from which his practical counsels arose. Such a distinction helps to explain the contradictory reception his ideas found in the following centuries. Machiavelli's writings soon became known in Italy and then in other European countries, particularly France and England, although in 1559 his works were placed on the Index. Generally he was considered an adviser of cruel tyrants, an advocate of evil; Cardinal Reginald Pole said that Machiavelli wrote "with the finger of the Devil." Although nobody in the sixteenth century dared publicly to express anything but abhorrence, a school of political writers arose in Italy who explained

that the criteria of a statesman's or ruler's actions were the interests of the state. These advocates of the doctrine of "reason of state"—even if they did not acknowledge their obligations to Machiavelli—followed the course Machiavelli had charted. The Enlightenment, with its belief in the harmony of morality and progress, could only condemn Machiavelli's view that political necessity permitted the neglect of ethical norms. An example is the *Anti-Machiavel* which Frederick II of Prussia composed as a young man. However, some eighteenth-century thinkers recognized truth in Machiavelli's approach to politics. For instance, Mably and Rousseau admired Machiavelli because he had realized that the strength of a political organization depends on the existence of a collective spirit which is more than a summation of individual wills.

In the nineteenth century, students of Machiavelli, following the interpretation which the German historian Leopold von Ranke had given, did not believe that Machiavelli had wanted to separate ethics and politics. Because the last chapter of *The Prince* contains an appeal for the liberation of Italy from the barbarians, they assumed that Machiavelli had permitted the violation of moral rules only for the purpose of a higher ethical goal; that his purpose had been to point the way toward the foundation of a unified Italy. Thus, in the nineteenth century Machiavelli became respectable as the prophet of the idea of the national state. In the later part of the century Machiavelli was also referred to by those who wanted to free man from the oppressive shackles of traditional morality and believed that man's faculties could be fully developed only if he placed himself "beyond good and evil." Nietzsche's superman was supposed to have "virtue in the style of the Renaissance, *virtù*, virtue free from morality."

Bibliography

The literature on Machiavelli is very extensive. The most recent critical edition of Machiavelli's works is that edited by Sergio Bertelli and Franco Gaeta and published by Feltrinelli in its Biblioteca di classici italiani. So far four volumes containing Machiavelli's literary works and three volumes containing his *Legazioni e commissarie* have appeared (1960–1964). This edition provides a critical discussion of the Machiavelli literature. The best recent translation is Allan Gilbert, *Machiavelli: the Chief Works and Others*, 3 vols. (Durham, N.C., 1965).

Older biographies have become obsolete since the appearance of Roberto Ridolfi's *Vita di Niccolò Machiavelli* (Rome, 1954), translated by Cecil Grayson as *The Life of Niccolò Machiavelli* (New York, 1963). Machiavelli's intellectual development is well analyzed by Gennaro Sasso in his *Niccolò Machiavelli: Storia del suo pensiero politico* (Naples, 1958). For the relation of Machiavelli's thought to that of his contemporaries, see Felix Gilbert, *Machiavelli and Guicciardini* (Princeton, 1965). The main lines of the influence of Machiavelli's ideas on the political thought of later centuries are traced in Friedrich Meinecke, *Die Idee der Staatsräson in der neueren Geschichte* (Berlin, 1924), translated by Douglas Scott as *Machiavellism* (New Haven, 1957). For Machiavelli's impact on English political thought, see Felix Raab, *The English Face of Machiavelli: A Changing Interpretation 1500–1700* (London and Toronto, 1964).

FELIX GILBERT

MACROCOSM AND MICROCOSM are philosophical terms referring, respectively, to the world as a whole and to some part, usually man, as a model or epitome of it. According to one version of this ancient analogy, man and the universe are constructed according to the same harmonic proportions, each sympathetically attuned to the other, each a cosmos ordered according to reason. By an imaginative leap, the universe itself was thought to be, like man, living and conscious, a divine creature whose nature is reflected in human existence. Animism and panpsychism also regard the world as alive throughout, but the microcosm idea is distinct in emphasizing the unity or kinship of all life and thought in the world. If man is the microcosm of the universe, then not only is everything animated by *some* soul or other, but there is *one* world soul by which everything is animated. Thus, the followers of Pythagoras and Empedocles held, according to Sextus Empiricus, that "there is a certain community uniting us not only with each other and with the gods but even with the brute creation. There is in fact one breath pervading the whole cosmos like soul, and uniting us with them" (W. K. C. Guthrie, *A History of Greek Philosophy*, Vol. I, p. 278).

Because the word *kosmos* can mean order as well as world or world order, "microcosm" can signify not only man in relation to the universe (or in relation to the state, as in Plato's *Republic*) but also any part of a thing, especially a living thing, that reflects or represents the whole it belongs to, whenever there is a mirroring relation between the whole and each of its parts. Nicholas of Cusa's doctrine of individuals as "contractions" of the form of the universe is a microcosm theory, as is Leibniz' theory of monads as "perpetual living mirrors of the universe"; similarly, to cite an example from nonphilosophical discourse, the composer Béla Bartók's collection of piano pieces *Mikrokosmos* is a little world of modern musical style and technique.

The idea of the microcosm appears in pre-Socratic philosophy in connection with the problem of relating the One and the many. Taking all of nature to derive ultimately from a single common substance, they supposed it to have inherent in it a principle of motion and change (which they identified with life, soul). Since some of the resulting entities possess consciousness, so too must their source. And if the universal soul is eternal and divine, then the human soul, which is a "fragment" of the One, as the Pythagoreans held, must also be eternal and divine. The return of the individual soul to its divine origin could be realized by philosophical understanding of the cosmos; since like is known by like, as the cosmos becomes known the knower is assimilated to it. Thus, man is, and discovers himself to be, the part that most perfectly reveals the nature of the whole.

Man the microcosm is a commonplace of Greek thought from Anaximenes, the Pythagoreans, Heraclitus, and Empedocles to the Stoics and Neoplatonists. It is a staple theme for variation in the Orphic, Gnostic, and Hermetic texts and in the literature of mysticism, pantheism, and the occult. That man is the microcosm was, in the Renaissance, widely taken to mean that cosmic knowledge and influence might be achieved through contemplation of the powers and tendencies men find in their own imaginations. Such knowledge would be based not on mere inference from resemblance but rather on the kinship or identity of human life and consciousness with the forces governing nature as a whole.

The notion that man is the microcosm has always played both rational and mystical roles in Western thought. Well into the period of the scientific revolution, the microcosm was an image of the order and harmony pervading the world. Saying that the universe is controlled by a single principle (in the way that rational thought is the controlling principle in man) expressed the unified and self-regulating character of the world as understandable in its own terms, fit for scientific investigation. Similarly, human thought itself was conceived to be self-regulating and self-correcting—thus entered the idea of the autonomy of reason that has played an important part in the history of rationalism and of Western philosophy generally. According to Plato's recollection doctrine, "All nature is akin, and the soul has learned everything, so that when a man has recalled a single piece of knowledge—*learned* it, in ordinary language—there is no reason why he should not find out all the rest" (*Meno* 81D, E). By recollection Plato meant the recovery of systematic knowledge of necessary truths from within oneself, but it is easy to see how it could also be thought of as an intuitive, nontheoretical process—a stream of consciousness leading to memory of past reincarnations or of the soul's celestial origin.

The thought that the universe is ordered not by chance but by one spiritual principle stimulated the wish for direct mystical union with this soul, and even for influence over things through it, as easily as it encouraged the pursuit of systematic understanding of the world. The first impulse produced such exalted sentiments as those lavished upon the universe in the Hermetic religious writings; the second pushed open the door to that underground world of magic, astrology, alchemy, and spiritualism which claimed to utilize the same unifying principles assumed in science and in the astral theology of the philosophers. Perhaps something may be said for a generous interpretation of this magical view of nature, which even in antiquity was distinguishable from its rationalistic and humanistic counterpart. For the practitioners of the occult and for their opponents, the view of the world as a "besouled" creature was neither an isolated hypothesis nor an idle conceit; the microcosm was an almost omnipresent presupposition, the basis of the very language in which the phenomena whose explanation was sought were represented. Yet there were always philosophical skeptics, and often the same writers who affirmed the world soul or the microcosm—for example, Plotinus, Pico della Mirandola, Kepler—also tried to restrict it in ways that precluded the possibility of undesirable magical application.

Ancient thought. In the *Timaeus* Plato presents a mythical account of the creation of the world according to which the world's soul and body are made by the Demiurge, who copies the Form of the ideal living creature (not itself any species of animate being but embracing the types of them all). The world soul is constructed according to a complex musical pattern, and, in order to be capable of thought, the elements of discourse—sameness, difference, and existence—are blended to form its mind. The body joined to the world soul is said to be unlike the human body or that of any animal in the world, being perfectly spherical, devoid of organs of sense, respiration, and ingestion; however, the processes of the universe are said to be reproduced even in the details of microcosmic processes, such as the moment of blood in humans. And because of the affinity between the divine part in humans and the thoughts and revolutions of the universe, the study of the rhythms of the macrocosm are recommended as a means of "correcting those circuits in the head that were deranged at birth."

A methodological discussion forms the context of a playful passage in the *Philebus* (27A–31B) in which the microcosm image also appears. All philosophers hold mind to be the king of heaven and earth, Socrates observes; "in reality they are magnifying themselves. And perhaps they are right." Socrates and Protarchus agree that the order of the world proves that the cosmos is governed by "Mind [*nous*] and a wondrous regulating Intelligence." Socrates argues further that the elements composing our bodies are but fragments produced and sustained by the elements in the universe. Because the unity of the elements in us makes up our bodies, the collective unity of elements in the universe must make up the world's body; because our bodies have souls, the body of the universe must have one, too; for where could our bodies have gotten their souls "if the body of the universe, which has elements the same as our own though still fairer in every respect, were not in fact possessed of a soul?" Strictly, this much of the argument concludes merely in the existence of a world soul which is the cause of the mixture of the body's elements—there is as yet barely a hint of the world soul's having a structure of its own apart from the body, of its being rationally ordered and the cause not just of all mixture but of all movement in the cosmos. Ultimately, the universal soul itself is said to be produced by Cause (later identified with Mind), yet this Mind cannot come into existence without soul (30C). To the extent that we can distinguish the Demiurge from the world soul (in the *Timaeus*), we can say that the Cause of the *Philebus* is probably more like the first of these.

Aristotle's physical system seems to have been designed to avoid the view of the cosmos as "besouled" or as alive in all its parts. Thus, in *De Caelo* the motion of the stars is explained not by any life in them but mainly in terms of the circular motion natural to the *aether* of which they are composed. In Book II (Ch. 2) Aristotle rejects the view that "it is by the constraint of a soul that it [the heaven] endures forever." The Demiurge as designer of the world is wholly excluded; no consciousness is needed of the rational (but unpremeditated) pattern to which nature adheres. Although there is a reference (to the views of others) in the *Physics* (Book VIII, Ch. 2), which may be the first occurrence of the Greek expression for "microcosm," Aristotle seems not to have organized his conception of nature around the view of it as an organism in any significant way. (For a contrasting account, see W. K. C. Guthrie, "Man as Microcosm.")

What is missing in Aristotle reappears (partly under Heraclitus' influence) in the thought of the Stoics—the sense of the world as an animate and conscious continuum each part of which affects all others by its *sympathy,* its "sharing of experience" with the others. The doctrine of sympathies and antipathies among the parts of the world animal guided the physical research of the Stoics and predisposed them to accept and to attempt to rationalize the particulars of astrology and divination. And man as

microcosm was the source of their efforts to locate the basis of human conduct in natural law; by playing one's assigned role in the cosmos, one's logos, his "inner self," would be linked to that of the whole (Hans Jonas, *The Gnostic Religion,* p. 248).

Plotinus, like the Stoics, treated the world as a single creature, "living differently in each of its parts." If the world soul of Plato's system is thought of as operating purposefully and consciously, and if the Nature of Aristotle's system is taken to work purposefully but unconsciously, we should say that for Plotinus the world as a whole is governed consciously yet produces individual things "as in a dream," spontaneously, without reasoning, choice, or calculation. According to Plotinus only a unity of soul among us could explain our sympathetic relations to one another, "suffering, overcome, at the sight of pain, naturally drawn to forming attachments" (*Ennead* IV, ix, 3). Plotinus denied that the unity he spoke of entailed the transference of a person's emotions to places outside his body; the souls of the sufferer and of the sympathizer do not feel as one. Rather, his model of unity is that of a science, where individual truths cannot be considered apart from the whole; ". . . the whole is in every part: . . . The one detail, when it is matter of science, potentially includes all" (IV, ix, 5). In geometry, for example, ". . . the single proposition includes all the items that go to constitute it and all the propositions which can be developed from it" (IV, ix, 5). Perhaps this very strict sense of unity, which asserts that each thing is internally connected with every other thing (or that there is one thing with which each is connected) has always been latent in the microcosm doctrine; if so, it is an aspect of the doctrine that seems to offer small encouragement to the search for the actual relations in nature. The question "Which things are causally connected, which are not?" has little point if all can affect all alike.

The general ancient view of the world as a perfect organism may have been responsible, as Samuel Sambursky suggests, for the insistence of ancient thinkers on the attempt to understand the world as a whole, in its entirety, and for their almost total avoidance of experimentation—the isolation of phenomena, or "dissection of nature," characteristic of modern science.

Medieval and modern thought. Man as microcosm of the universe is not integral to Jewish and Christian doctrine in the way that it is to the Gnostic religious system, for example; thus, Philo Judaeus and Moses Maimonides employed the idea of the world soul only dialectically. In *The Guide of the Perplexed* (Pt. I, Ch. 72) Maimonides at first argues that the world is like a human being, but he then presents so many points of difference between the two that in the end it is clear that he considers the possession of a rational order to be their only common factor. As a cosmological view, the microcosm has little or no place in Augustine or in Aquinas, who treats it as a mere figure of speech. By contrast, Joseph ibn-Zaddik states one of the microcosm's main attractions when he proposes to show how self-knowledge will lead to knowledge of the whole—a "short cut" through the study of man, bypassing the sciences. Bernard of Tours and other members of the school of Chartres assimilated the world soul of Plato's

Timaeus to the Third Person of the Trinity. Drawing upon Bernard, Hildegard of Bingen, in her visionary writings, represented detailed correspondences between heavenly motions, winds, elements, humors, and bodily and spiritual states in the individual.

Plato had typically employed the microcosm image to portray the transformation of consciousness through theoretical knowledge of whatever cosmic order science reveals; ibn-Zaddik reverses the process, seeking to discover in man what the cosmic order must be. Where Plato stressed the dissimilarity between the living cosmos and the structure and functioning of any particular animal, including man, Hildegard dwells on their supposed similarity in picturesque detail. The idea that inner experience of human nature supplies a direct route to reality is prone to magical extension in a way that Plato's view is not, but it was this conception that took hold in medieval and Renaissance microcosm literature.

Renaissance speculation on the microcosm centered on the idea that human nature partakes of bodily, intellectual, and divine existence, uniting in itself the whole of the sublunary, celestial, and supercelestial realms. Human consciousness, by which man can know all things, connects him with all things; consciousness is itself a link between thought and its objects. Through consciousness man can know and become all that he wills. A similar doctrine of connections drawn from the Cabala underlies the various magical theories of language which asserted that quasi-physical influences join names and things, beyond the conventions of the various natural languages. Partly controllable influences also form the structure of the elaborate identities and correspondences that Agrippa von Nettesheim and Paracelsus described between minerals, animals, heavenly bodies, psychic powers, and parts of the human body. Such influences are also involved in the interaction between thought and its objects that Giordano Bruno assumed in his search for direct awareness of the sympathies controlling nature through memory and the ideas of them in his imagination.

The occult "applications" of the microcosm idea did not survive the advance of the mechanistic world view. By the eighteenth century, occult qualities, or anything that seemed like them—for example, action at a distance—were in such wide disrepute that even Newton, to avoid the appearance of being committed to an occult doctrine, refrained from expressing fully his theory of the mode of action of atomic "Central Forces." But in the second edition of the *Principia* (1713), he described the ether as "a certain most subtle spirit which pervades and lies hid in all gross bodies . . . by the force and action of which spirit the particles of bodies attract one another at near distances and cohere . . . and all sensation is excited, and the members of animal bodies move at the command of the will, namely by vibrations of this spirit . . ."—a view not far from that of the Stoics, as Toulmin and Goodfield remark (*The Architecture of Matter*, p. 195).

Even later, belief in psychic planetary action had not lost all ground; thus, Franz Anton Mesmer's explanation of "animal magnetism," or hypnosis, assumed a "responsive influence . . . between the heavenly bodies, the earth, and animated bodies," which the hypnotist drew upon.

And the idea of a psychic force in the world beyond our immediate awareness, of which our conscious lives are parts or manifestations, endured, for example, in Goethe's Nature philosophy and in Schopenhauer's world will—ancestors of the concept of the unconscious. Perhaps some aspects of the microcosm idea can be found in Freud's attempts to explain the instincts in man as repetitions of the reactions of living matter to drastic changes in the prehistoric environment. (Thus, we might say that man's instincts are a microcosm of his evolution.) Among the known "enforced alterations in the course of life . . . stored for repetition," Freud, along with Sándor Ferenczi, noted the drying up of the oceans which left life to adapt on land and the cultural development necessitated by the glacial epoch. These are re-experienced at birth, in the diphasic onset of man's sexual life, and in the latency period. Freud invokes the contending forces, Love and Strife, of Empedocles' "Cosmic phantasy," pointing out their similarity to Eros and Destructiveness, the two primal instincts of his biopsychical theory. These instincts, which "present the delusive appearance of forces striving after change and progress" actually impel the organism toward the reinstatement of earlier, more stable states, ultimately to inorganic existence. The originally biological principle that ontogeny recapitulates phylogeny has received very wide psychological extension in psychoanalysis; most recently, Carl Jung has (somewhat cryptically) identified his doctrine of the collective unconscious with that of "the microcosm containing the archetypes of all ideas."

Perhaps the microcosm image is not entirely the scientific dead end it has understandably been taken for; as early attempts to construct models of the embodied soul's structure, development, and dynamics, some versions of the image may stand to scientific psychological research as alchemy stands to chemistry.

Bibliography

Three useful histories of the microcosm theme are G. P. Conger, *Theories of Macrocosms and Microcosms in the History of Philosophy* (New York, 1922), which includes a survey of critical discussions up to 1922; Rudolph Allers, "Microcosmus, From Anaximandros to Paracelsus," in *Traditio*, Vol. 2 (1944), 319–407; and W. K. C. Guthrie's "Man as Microcosm," in *Proceedings of the European Cultural Foundation* (Athens, 1966); all contain many references. W. K. C. Guthrie's discussion of the microcosm, to which this article is indebted, in *A History of Greek Philosophy* (Cambridge, 1962——), Vol. I, is the most important one for the period covered; this volume, *The Earlier Presocratics and the Pythagoreans,* also contains valuable remarks on Plato and Aristotle. The microcosm in Plato is discussed by F. M. Cornford throughout his commentary on the *Timaeus* in *Plato's Cosmology* (London, 1937); G. M. A. Grube discusses the microcosm as part of Plato's theory of the soul in *Plato's Thought* (London, 1935), Ch. 4; see also F. M. Cornford, "Psychology and Social Structure in the Republic of Plato," in *Classical Quarterly* (1912), 247–265; R. Hackforth's translation of the *Philebus*, with commentary, in *Plato's Examination of Pleasure* (Cambridge, 1945); and Gregory Vlastos, "Anamnesis in the *Meno*," in *Dialogue*, Vol. 4, No. 2 (September 1965), 143–167, which interprets the recollection theory with comments on its connection with the doctrine of reincarnation. Possible oriental influences on Plato are discussed in A. Olerud, *L'Idée de microcosmos et de macrocosmos dans la Timée de Platon* (Uppsala, 1951). Two valuable relevant studies of Aristotle are W. K. C. Guthrie's introduction to the text and translation of *Aristotle on* the Heavens (London, 1939) and Friedrich Solmsen's *Aristotle's System of the Physical World* (Ithaca, N.Y., 1961).

On the Stoics, see Samuel Sambursky, *The Physics of the Stoics* (New York, 1959).

On Plotinus, see the introductions and translations in E. R. Dodds, *Select Passages Illustrating Neoplatonism* (London, 1923), and A. H. Armstrong, *Plotinus* (London, 1953). Remarks bearing on the microcosm in ancient thought generally are contained throughout E. R. Dodds, *The Greeks and the Irrational* (Berkeley, California, 1960); Hans Jonas, *The Gnostic Religion* (Boston, 1963), especially Ch. 10, "The Cosmos in Greek and Gnostic Evaluation"; A.-J. Festugière, *Personal Religion Among the Greeks* (Berkeley, 1954); E. A. Lippman, *Musical Thought in Ancient Greece* (New York, 1964); and Samuel Sambursky, *The Physical World of the Greeks* (New York, 1956). See also E. W. Beth, *The Foundations of Mathematics; A Study in the Philosophy of Science*, rev. ed. (New York, 1964), Chs. 1 and 2, "The Prehistory of Research into Foundations" and "Aristotle's Theory of Science."

Hildegard of Bingen's life and writings are examined in Charles Singer, *From Magic to Science* (New York, 1958), Ch. 6, "The Visions of Hildegard of Bingen," a rewritten chapter from *Studies on the History and Method of Science*, Vol. I (Oxford, 1917). Ernst Cassirer, *Individuum und Kosmos in der Philosophie der Renaissance* (Leipzig and Berlin, 1927), translated by Mario Domandi as *The Individual and the Cosmos in Renaissance Philosophy* (New York, 1963), is the standard discussion of the microcosm in Renaissance thought. On the difficult subject of Renaissance occult literature, see D. P. Walker, *Spiritual and Demonic Magic From Ficino to Campanella* (London, 1958). Three chapters in Frederick Copleston's *A History of Philosophy*, Vol. III, *Late Medieval and Renaissance Philosophy*, Part 2 (Westminster, Md. 1953), are useful surveys; Ch. 15 discusses the microcosm in Nicholas of Cusa, Chs. 16 and 17 are on the philosophy of nature. An important interpretation of Bruno is Frances Yates, *Giordano Bruno and the Hermetic Tradition* (Chicago, 1964). There are also interesting discussions in Alexandre Koyré, *Mystiques, spirituels, alchimistes du XVIᵉ siècle allemand* (Paris, 1955), and in Werner Pauli, "The Influence of Archetypal Ideas on the Scientific Theories of Kepler," in *The Interpretation of Nature and the Psyche* (New York, 1955). Microcosm and macrocosm are discussed in the context of the idea of the chain of being in E. M. W. Tillyard, *The Elizabethan World Picture* (New York, 1941); see also W. C. Curry, *Shakespeare's Philosophical Patterns* (Baton Rouge, La., 1937). On the transition from animism to mechanism in science, see E. J. Dijksterhuis, *Mechanization of the World-picture*, translated by C. Dikshoorn (Oxford, 1961); M. B. Hesse, *Forces and Fields* (London, 1961); and Stephen Toulmin and June Goodfield, *The Architecture of Matter* (New York, 1962).

A brief account of Mesmer's ideas can be found in C. L. Hull, *Hypnosis and Suggestibility* (New York, 1933), pp. 6–11. Schopenhauer's doctrine of the microcosm and its influence on Wittgenstein are discussed in Patrick Gardiner, *Schopenhauer* (Baltimore, 1963). Wittgenstein's remark "I am my world. (The microcosm.)" appears in the *Tractatus*, but without the connection with the world-spirit doctrine it has in his *Notebooks* (pp. 84–85). Wittgenstein's idea of an internal connection between language, thought, and reality is discussed in Erik Stenius, *Wittgenstein's Tractatus* (Oxford, 1960), and Max Black, *A Companion to Wittgenstein's Tractatus* (Ithaca, N.Y., 1964).

A short discussion of the microcosm image as employed by Freud and other analysts is contained in Philip Rieff's Introduction to *General Psychological Theory* (New York, 1963), which is a volume in the paperback edition of Freud's *Collected Papers;* see pp. 9–17. Freud discusses Empedocles in "Analysis Terminable and Interminable," in the volume *Therapy and Technique*, Philip Rieff, ed. (New York, 1963), the paperback edition of Freud's *Collected Papers.* Jung's ideas are expressed in his *Naturerklärung und Psyche* (Zurich, 1952), translated by R. F. C. Hull as *The Interpretation of Nature and the Psyche* (New York, 1955). Ch. 3 of his essay "Synchronicity: An Acausal Connecting Principle" contains numerous quotations from earlier microcosm literature.

Problems that arise in trying to characterize the universe as a unified whole (or as a "whole" at all) on the basis of information concerning only a part and in trying to treat scientifically the nature of a necessarily unique object are presented in D. W. Sciama, *The Unity of the Universe* (New York, 1959), pp. 69–205. For further discussion and bibliography, see COSMOLOGY and RATIONALISM.

DONALD LEVY

MADHVA (1197–1276), Hindu metaphysician and theologian, was born in Udipi, near Mangalore on the west coast of India. The extant accounts of his life are largely legendary (some of the incidents resemble New Testament miracles, one reason why some have detected Christian influences upon him). He devoted his life to combating Śaṅkara's doctrines in favor of Vaiṣṇavite devotionalism (see HINDUISM). In this he resembled Rāmānuja, and his philosophical views were subservient to this main spiritual interest. His chief works include important commentaries on the *Brahma-Sūtra* and the *Bhagavad Gītā*, as well as other religious, metaphysical, and logical treatises.

The structure of his system depends on an ontological distinction of three kinds of entities—life monads or souls (*jīva*), nonintelligent substances (*acit*), and God (*Īśvara*). In addition, Madhva held that the cosmos (which is a complex conglomeration of nonintelligent substances) has nature (*prakṛti*) as its material cause—a concept whose chief function was to oppose the suggestion that God is the material cause of the world, a doctrine held by some schools. Madhva's view was borrowed from the Sāṃkhya school of Indian philosophy, and he also took over other elements from the evolutionary cosmology of that school. The distinction between God and the souls accounts for the fact that Madhva's system is known as Dualism (Dvaita), in opposition to the Advaita, or Nondualism, of Śaṅkara. However, Madhva was also concerned to stress the distinction between souls and nonintelligent substances and worked with a fivefold set of distinctions: God–soul; soul–soul; God–material substance; material substance–material substance; soul–material substance. While Rāmānuja considered souls as numerous but essentially alike (so that they become qualitatively indistinguishable in a state of release), Madhva held that each soul has its own peculiar properties.

This was one reason for his theory of relative particulars (*viśeṣa*). He objected to the doctrine of real universals and considered that qualities belonging to substances are aspects peculiar to them. Insofar as we use general terms, it is because the aspects of different substances are similar. (It was objected by Madhva's opponents that similarity itself must be a universal. His reply was that each case of similarity is unique—thus the similarity of A to B differs from the similarity of B to A.) On the other hand, one cannot identify the aspect with the substance, for then a change in quality would entail the disappearance of the substance. Thus, a substance can be regarded as a combination of particular aspects relative to the point of view from which we describe it. Every substance stands in relation to a host of others, so that a full description of its qualities must take account of these complex relationships. Nevertheless, it would be fallacious to think that because the qualities of a substance are determined by its causal and other relations, they do not properly belong to it. Since each entity has a different location in the whole structure of substances, it has its own peculiar character as determined by its relationships. This general thesis, it should be noted, applies to God and souls as much as to inanimate entities.

All this implies that there are ineluctable, if often very subtle, divergences between all entities in the universe. Hence, Madhva felt justified in adopting a radically pluralistic account of the substances in the cosmos as well as a doctrine of the sharp distinction between God and other entities. The most important characteristic distinguishing the Lord (*Īśvara*) from the world and souls is that he is self-dependent (*aparatantra*), while they are dependent on him. This distinction has two main applications. First, at a period when the cosmos is dissolved back into chaos (in accordance with the common Indian belief that the cosmos is "pulsating"—a period of organization being followed by one of chaos, and so on), nature (*prakṛti*) is catalyzed into a fine powdery substance, or virtual chaos, having only the property of generating instants of time. Thus, the material entities of the cosmos are subject to transformation through the creative, sustaining, and destructive power of God. On the other hand, God is changeless and not liable to evolutionary transformation. He affects the world but is not affected by it.

Second, the relation between God and souls is rather different. Regardless of the ignorance (*avidyā*) and materiality with which they are obscured and entangled during the process of transmigration, souls are internally changeless. Thus, the difference between the Lord and the cosmos does not hold in this case. However, the destinies of souls, and the ways in which they manifest themselves, are determined by God. It is God who determines whether a soul attains release (*mokṣa*) and what its status therein shall be; and it is God who operates the powers of ignorance and materiality which implicate them in the round of rebirth. Thus, the circumstances of the souls, in regard to what they suffer or enjoy, are affected by God; but the circumstances of the Lord in these respects are not affected by the souls or by other substances in the cosmos (indeed, the souls are strictly inactive, for their destiny is worked out through their karma, in accordance with their particular natures; and God is the controller of karma).

While for Rāmānuja the difference between selves is due to the operation of karma as an expression of God's will, the Dualists held that the differences in the destinies of different individuals can be explained through their individual idiosyncrasies. Each self has certain intrinsic properties which necessarily determine its course of existence. God, in governing and controlling the cosmos, arranges the destinies of souls in accordance with their patterns of existence.

For instance, in accordance with a common Indian conception, the cause of the soul's being bound to the round of rebirth is ignorance—lack of spiritual perception and detachment. In contrast to Śankara, who conceived of *avidyā* as a unitary cosmic phenomenon (the subjective correlate of *māyā*, illusion), Madhva conceived more naturalistically of each person's ignorance as being peculiar to him. Thus, God's imposition of ignorance on a life monad does not involve foisting upon it a spiritual darkness

foreign to it. Moreover, he held that there are various grades of release—and of nonrelease. Uniquely among Indian teachers, he held that some selves are destined for everlasting punishment in hell (Indian hells are normally more in the nature of purgatories, so that the soul is ultimately reborn in another state). Also, some souls will go on transmigrating forever, without arriving either at release or at everlasting punishment.

The doctrine of predestination to eternal punishment is one reason why some have suspected Christian influences on Madhva. Certainly, in the area where he was brought up there were Christian communities. Further, Madhva taught, at the mythological level, that the god Vāyu (literally, "Wind"—thus there is an analogy to the Holy Spirit) is a principal intermediary between the Lord and men. Also, a biography represents Madhva as walking on water. However, there are other ways of explaining these similarities to Christianity. Vāyu is a Vedic deity and has nothing historically to do with the Holy Spirit. Legendary miracles of all sorts abound in Indian literature. Madhva's predestinationism is more easily accounted for in terms of the internal dynamics of his system. Given that destinies differ, it is not surprising that some individuals should achieve the worst possible fate (with certain appropriate variations).

Like Rāmānuja, and in opposition to the illusionism of Śankara's Advaita Vedānta, Madhva was committed to the self-authentication of common-sense knowledge (for some of the arguments, see INDIAN PHILOSOPHY, section on Epistemological questions). He held that there is an inner faculty, the apperceiver or witness (*sākṣi*), which passes final judgment on what is presented in sense perception and induction (since methods of induction always leave room for marginal doubt and, theoretically, perception can be hallucinatory). The *sākṣi* is, further, the source of intuitive knowledge, such as of the self and of space and time. It is thus, in Western terminology, a faculty of a priori cognitions. The concept of the *sākṣi* was one of Madhva's means of resisting skeptical arguments and of validating his realistic pluralism.

It is worth noting that although, superficially, Madhva's doctrines are nearer to orthodox theism in the Christian tradition than are Rāmānuja's (the latter can be interpreted in a pantheistic sense), Rāmānuja's strong insistence on grace, and the Dualist doctrine that the Lord assigns destinies in accordance with the particular natures of souls, mean that there is a stronger sense of dependence in Qualified Nondualism than in Dualism. This is reflected religiously in the fact that Madhva stressed not merely the practice of devotion (*bhakti*) but also inner contemplation, a practice which elsewhere in the Indian tradition tends to ignore or modify doctrines of a supreme personal Lord and to be associated with a doctrine of the self-sufficiency of the aspirant. Naturally, however, Madhva interpreted such contemplation as bringing one close to God.

Of the successors of Madhva in the Dualistic school, the most important was Jayatīrtha (fourteenth century), whose chief work was in logic.

Works by Madhva

Vedānta-Sūtras With the Commentary of Sri Madhwacharya, translated by S. Subba Rao, 2d ed. Tirupati, 1936.

Madhva's Teachings in His Own Words, translated by B. N. K. Sharma. Bombay, 1961.

See also Sarvepalli Radhakrishnan, *The Brahma-Sūtra*. London, 1960.

Works on Madhva

Dasgupta, S. N., *A History of Indian Philosophy*. Cambridge, 1949. Vol. IV, Chs. 26 and 27.

Glasenapp, Helmuth von, *Madhva's Philosophie des Vishnu-Glaubens*. Bonn, 1923.

Raghavendrachar, Vidwan H. N., *The Dvaita Philosophy and Its Place in the Vedānta*. Mysore, 1941.

Sharma, B. N. K., *A History of the Dvaita School of Vedānta*, 2 vols. Bombay, 1960–1961.

NINIAN SMART

MAILLET, BENOÎT DE (c. 1656–1738), French diplomat, traveler, and natural scientist. Information concerning the place and date of his birth, details of his life, and the significance of his works is, at best, sketchy and contradictory. A member of the impoverished nobility, Maillet presumably received the customary classical education of the day. He seems to have led an apathetic existence until his appointment to the French consulate in Cairo at the age of 36. As consul, he handled the king's business well and, for services rendered, was named ambassador to Ethiopia in 1702. He declined the honor, ostensibly for reasons of health but actually because his duties would be less concerned with Franco-Ethiopian relations than with the formidable task of converting the natives to Christianity. In 1707, at his own request, he left his post in Cairo to assume charge of the French consulate in Livorno, Italy. He was so successful as consul and later as inspector of French settlements in other parts of the Mediterranean that, upon his retirement in 1724, he received a handsome pension and spent the remaining 14 years of his life in Marseille. There, besides attending to a large correspondence, most of which is now lost, he wrote several works, including *Description de l'Egypte* (1735) and the vastly more important *Telliamed, ou entretiens d'un philosophe indien avec un missionnaire françois* (1748), which appeared posthumously.

"Telliamed." The years of Maillet's consulships, his travels in the Mediterranean basin, and his wide readings and careful observations formed much of the background for *Telliamed* (the author's name spelled backward). First published in Amsterdam, it was closely followed by other editions in both French and English, the most important being that of the Abbé Le Mascrier (1755). The work consists of a series of conversations in which Maillet, speaking through his Indian philosopher, Telliamed, puts forth various geological and biological speculations about the earth's cosmogony and its evolution—together with the organic beings it supported—into its present state. According to Maillet's system, the earth, product of a whirlpool of cosmic dust, was for countless ages entirely covered with swirling waters. As the waters gradually receded, the primordial mountains formed by the currents of these waters slowly emerged from the depths. The crashing of the waves against these mountains formed new mountains, and with the appearance of life in the seas, fossil strata were formed.

Primitive forms of aquatic life, produced in ever-in-creasing abundance through the eons, underwent gradual modifications of structure and function in keeping with changing habits and new environments. Thus, creatures along the shallow coastal waters moved into the marshes and, after much trial and error, finally emerged with wings for flying or legs for walking. Beneath this speculation lay the work's basic theme that everything in the universe, through the processes of time, was undergoing constant change. Occasionally the author's boldly imaginative thought resulted in whimsey, which was interpreted by many of his critics as folly or childish fantasy.

Telliamed immediately became a center of controversy that extended well into the nineteenth century. Maillet's heretical views, which ran counter to the tenets of Genesis, aroused the theologians of the day, while many eighteenth-century rationalists and scientists, led by Voltaire, were violently opposed to his ideas on other grounds. Disparaging criticisms continued in the writings of such eminent men of science as Étienne Geoffroy Saint-Hilaire and Georges Cuvier, Nonetheless Buffon, Diderot, Lamarck, and Erasmus Darwin, among others, availed themselves of Maillet's theories as a starting point for even more daring concepts of their own.

Bibliography

Collier, Katherine, *Cosmogonies of Our Fathers*. New York, 1934.

Dufrenoy, Marie-Louise, *Benoît de Maillet, précurseur de l'évolution*. Paris, 1960.

Haber, Francis C., *The Age of the World. Moses to Darwin*. Baltimore, 1959.

Kohlbrugge, J. H. F., "B. de Maillet, Lamarck und Darwin." *Biologisches Zentralblatt*, Vol. 32 (1912), 508–518.

Wolf, A., *A History of Science, Technology and Philosophy in the XVIIIth Century*, 2d ed., Douglas McKie, ed. London, 1952.

OTIS FELLOWS

MAIMON, SALOMON (c. 1752–1800), the philosopher recognized by Kant as the most penetrating of his critics, was born in a village near Nieswiez in Lithuania (then part of Poland). Maimon received a Jewish religious education, and he was familiar at an early age with the vast field of rabbinic learning. He also read extensively in the Hebrew philosophical works of the Middle Ages, especially those of Maimonides and Ibn Ezra. At the age of 25 Maimon left for Germany, wandering from place to place until he reached Posen, where he was engaged as a tutor for two years. In the fall of 1779 Maimon went to Berlin and, with the exception of a short stay in Holland, remained in Germany until his death. He attended a Gymnasium in Hamburg for three years and there gained a fundamental knowledge of languages, mathematics, and science. From his Talmudic studies Maimon acquired a method of critical analysis which served him well in every field of study. He applied the same method to the study of Kant's *Critique of Pure Reason*. Throughout his life Maimon retained a high regard for the ethical and religious conceptions of prophetic and rabbinic Judaism.

Maimon's manuscript on the *Critique*, consisting of his comments and critical notes, was sent to Kant by the latter's student and friend Markus Herz. In his reply to Herz, Kant wrote, among other things: ". . . but a glance at the manuscript soon enabled me to recognize its merits, and to see not only that none of my opponents had understood me and the main problem so well, but that very few could claim so much penetration and subtlety of mind in profound inquiries of this sort as Herr Maimon . . . ." The manuscript was published in 1790 under the title *Versuch über die Transcendentalphilosophie*. In this work, which placed him in the philosophical arena of the time, Maimon reached a position that he was to maintain, except in regard to some minor points, throughout the entire course of his philosophical career. From the publication of his first work until his death (a span of only 11 years), he completed a series of works including essays and commentaries on other philosophers.

In his autobiography, which is of general interest apart from its philosophical significance (and the only work of Maimon's which was translated into many languages), Maimon defined his philosophy as a "coalition-system." Maimonides, Leibniz, Spinoza, Locke, Hume, and Kant contributed to the shaping of Maimon's thought. His position, however, was neither eclecticism nor syncretism; he did not attempt a reconciliation of irreconcilable principles. Rather, several motives of thought closely connected with one another constituted his main concern. He presented his views in the form of comments and criticisms of his contemporaries (Karl Leonhard Reinhold and Gottlob Ernst Schulze, for example), who, he held, misunderstood the essence of the critical philosophy. With the elimination of the thing-in-itself as dogmatic residuum from the critical philosophy of Kant, Maimon began a line of thought leading to Fichte and Neo-Kantianism.

The thing-in-itself. The thing-in-itself is not to be understood in the sense of realism, as Reinhold's and F. H. Jacobi's conceptions imply, nor according to the skepticism of Schulze, but in a sense compatible with the system of the critical philosophy. A thing-in-itself as a real object behind the phenomena, as some of Maimon's contemporaries presumed it to be, is not only unknowable but also unthinkable. An object is thinkable when its distinguishing features are defined. But the distinguishing mark of a thing-in-itself as the cause of the appearances is not thinkable without causality, a concept of the understanding; thus the distinguishing mark of the thing-in-itself really belongs to consciousness. In a strict sense, the thing-in-itself beyond consciousness, as the substratum of the appearances, would be an object without any distinguishing mark because any feature of an object that distinguishes it from other objects is defined by, and grounded in, a concept of understanding.

A thing-in-itself in the sense of realism would thus be a "no-thing"; it would be comparable to the imaginary magnitude in mathematics, such as the square root of -1. In a critical sense, the thing-in-itself is to be understood as that aspect of the object which is not mastered by our thought and which presents a problem for scientific thought. It is thus comparable to the irrational magnitude in mathematics, such as the square root of 2. The critical concept of the thing-in-itself is a limiting concept; it constitutes the limit of an endless series approaching its final value. The irrational magnitude is just as real as the rational; its solution in rational terms implies, however, an endless task. As a limiting concept, the thing-in-itself cannot

be the cause of the appearances, as could be presumed by a dogmatic realistic interpretation of Kant's *Critique*. The thing-in-itself is placed not in the external world beyond consciousness but in consciousness itself—namely, in the cognition of a problem, a task for further scientific penetration of the object. This idea of the thing-in-itself was derived by Maimon from the formulations of Kant's *Critique*, not in opposition to it, by grasping the essence of the critical philosophy and pursuing its tenets to their ultimate conclusions; his contemporaries Reinhold and Schulze understood the thing-in-itself as an entity underlying the phenomena. Such a conception of the thing-in-itself cannot be reconciled with the basic principle of the *Critique*.

The given. Locating the given in consciousness confronts us with a dilemma. On the one hand, a thing-in-itself as a given object is unthinkable; on the other hand, appearance implies something that appears, that is, something given from without. The solution of this dilemma is to be found in the realization that the given cannot be defined in terms of conscious elements of cognition; the given is grounded in "incomplete consciousness." The appearance (*Schein*) of a given object is due to the incompleteness of our cognition. The comparison of the thing-in-itself with the irrational number in mathematics (for instance, $\sqrt{2}$) implies that the thing-in-itself constitutes an endless task for scientific cognition striving toward final solution in the absolute identification of thought and being. The incompleteness of our knowledge is subject to gradation. The more the cognition of an object increases, the more the given decreases; and with the diminution of cognition, the given increases. Complete cognition of an object is a limiting concept of the highest degree of consciousness in which there is no given but all is thought; in the lowest degree of cognition of an object, all is given. Matter and form are not to be understood as belonging to two different realms, the object and the subject; rather, both are grounded in the subject. But while the generation of the form is grounded in a conscious act of cognition, the mode of the generation of the given material is not brought to our consciousness. Scientific experience, however, is never complete; there is thus an element of the given in every stage of cognition. The elimination of the given is an endless task. The thing-in-itself is a limiting concept; it is thinkable only as an idea of attaining complete cognition of an object.

Sensibility and understanding. Maimon was critical of Kant's distinction between the forms of sensibility (time and space) and the concepts of understanding (the categories). If sensibility and understanding are essentially different capacities, constituting two heterogeneous realms, the object given through sensibility could not be comprehended by the forms of understanding. If the object given through sensibility, which is entirely different from understanding, is a condition for the application of the categories of understanding, such application of pure forms of understanding to objects given through sensibility cannot be justified. Maimon maintained that sensibility and understanding are not two totally different sources of cognition. He consciously followed Leibniz and Wolff in the conception of sense knowledge as flowing from the same source as intellectual knowledge. They differ from each other only in clearness and completeness. While through understanding we attain clear and distinct concepts, sense knowledge is confused. Since sensibility and understanding differ from each other only with regard to the degree of clearness and distinctness, the application of a priori forms of understanding to objects given through sensibility is justified.

An infinite mind. Bound up with Maimon's treatment of sensibility and understanding was his idea of an infinite mind.

Let us assume, at least as an idea, an infinite reason in relation to which the forms of thought are simultaneously objects of understanding, or which produces out of itself all possible relations and associations of objects (i.e., their ideas). Our human reason will be of the same kind as the infinite reason, though in a limited degree. This sublime idea . . . will, I believe, solve the difficulty of the relation of the *a priori* forms to sensuous objects. (*Versuch über die Transcendental-philosophie*, pp. 64 f.)

The reality of synthetic propositions cannot be deduced from the principle of the "possibility of experience," as Kant proposed. Kant must assume the facts of scientific experience as real in order to grant certainty to the synthetic a priori propositions which make facts possible. But facts themselves are subject to doubt. According to Maimon, Kant did not answer the question concerning the reality of "facts," that is, facts of scientific experience. He therefore proposed that the reality of experiential knowledge can be maintained only on the assumption of an infinite reason, in relation to which our synthetic propositions are dissolvable into analytic propositions. There is no escape from this alternative: either we must doubt the reality of experiential knowledge in terms of synthetic propositions, or we must assume an infinite mind in relation to which our synthetic propositions are grounded in analytic thought. It is possible to understand the idea of an infinite reason, in a critical sense, as a limiting concept and an endless goal. But Maimon was inclined to understand it as an ontological entity. The alternative for Maimon is either skepticism or metaphysical idealism, and his philosophy presents a constant vacillation between these two positions.

Works by Maimon

Versuch über die Transcendentalphilosophie. Mit einem Anhang über die symbolische Erkenntnis. Berlin, 1790.

Philosophisches Wörterbuch, oder Beleuchtung der wichtigsten Gegenstände der Philosophie. Berlin, 1791.

Commentary to the *More Newuchim* of Maimonides. This work appeared anonymously in 1791 in Berlin, under the title of *Givat Hamoreh* (in Hebrew); 2d ed., Sulzbach, 1828.

Lebensgeschichte. Berlin, 1792. The second part of this work contains a presentation of the philosophy of Maimonides.

Anfangsgründe der Newtonischen Philosophie von Dr. Pemberton. Berlin, 1793. With comments and notes by Maimon.

Bacons von Verulam neues Organon translated by G. W. Bartholdy, with comments and notes by Maimon. Berlin, 1793.

Streifereien im Gebiete der Philosophie. Berlin, 1793.

Die Kategorien des Aristoteles. Mit Anmerkungen erläutert. Berlin, 1794.

Versuch einer neuen Logik oder Theorie des Denkens. Berlin, 1794. Republished, as edited by B. C. Engels. Berlin, 1912.

Kritische Untersuchungen über den menschlichen Geist. Leipzig, 1797.

Works on Maimon

Atlas, Samuel, "Solomon Maimon's Philosophy of Language." *Hebrew Union College Annual,* Vol. 28 (1957), 253–288.

Atlas, Samuel, "Solomon Maimon and Spinoza." *Hebrew Union College Annual,* Vol. 30 (1959), 233–285.

Atlas, Samuel, *From Critical to Speculative Idealism. The Philosophy of Salomon Maimon.* The Hague, 1964.

Baumgardt, D., "The Ethics of Salomon Maimon." *Journal of the History of Philosophy,* Vol. 1, No. 2 (December 1963).

Bergman, Hugo, *The Autobiography of Solomon Maimon With an Essay on Maimon's Philosophy.* London, 1954.

Cassirer, Ernst, *Die Geschichte des Erkenntnisproblems,* Vol. III. Berlin, 1920.

Gueroult, M., *La Philosophie transcendentale de Salomon Maimon.* Paris, 1929.

Kroner, Richard, *Von Kant bis Hegel,* 2 vols. Tübingen, 1921–1924.

Kuntze, Friedrich, *Die Philosophie Salomon Maimons.* Heidelberg, 1912.

Zubersky, A., *Salomon Maimon und der kritische Idealismus.* Leipzig, 1925.

SAMUEL ATLAS

MAIMONIDES (1135–1204), the most celebrated Jewish philosopher of the Middle Ages. "Maimonides" is the Latinized cognomen of Moses son of Maimon. Also called RaMBaM, the acronym for Rabbi Moses ben Maimon, he was born in Córdoba, which belonged at that time to Muslim Spain. His father, Maimon son of Joseph, was a distinguished scholar versed in traditional Jewish lore. At the age of 13, Maimonides left his native town after it was conquered by the army of the Almohads, an intolerant Muslim sect. After various journeys he and his family settled in northern Africa, under the oppressive rule of the Almohads. In 1165 they went to Egypt, where Maimonides became a court physician and leader of the Jewish community. He died in Cairo.

Maimonides was and is regarded as an outstanding authority on Jewish religious law, the Halachah. His writings in this field include a commentary in Arabic on the Mishnah that contains a treatise on ethics known as "Eight Chapters" and a list of the 13 fundamental dogmas of the Jewish faith as established by Maimonides; another of these works, known under the two titles *Mishnah Torah* and *Yad Hazakah,* is a voluminous codification of the Law written in Hebrew, whose first portion, the "Book of Knowledge," expounds a system of religious beliefs and is markedly influenced by philosophy.

The fact that a considerable portion of Maimonides' activity was devoted to legal doctrine is by no means irrelevant in a consideration of his philosophical attitude. In a sense this was a practical activity which can be assimilated to that of a statesman; it was accordingly consonant with Maimonides' Platonizing contention that certain superior individuals are able to combine a mode of existence given over to contemplation and intellection with a life of action.

Maimonides also wrote several medical treatises in Arabic. One of them, known as *Moses' Chapters* (*Fuṣūl Mūsā*), contains a critique of Galen, part of which deals with the Greek physician's animadversions on the Law of Moses. He also composed two popular tracts, "Treatise on Resurrection" and "Epistle to Yemen," the latter treatise rebutting the claims of a pseudo Messiah who had appeared in Yemen. Maimonides is also the author of one philosophical treatise on logic, composed in his early youth.

"Guide of the Perplexed." Maimonides' reputation as a philosopher rests squarely upon his *Guide of the Perplexed* (*Dalālat al-Ḥā'irīn* in Arabic), a work which its author did not regard as being of a philosophical nature. The "perplexed" to whom the *Guide* is supposed to have been addressed are men who are well grounded in the Jewish religious tradition and have some knowledge of certain philosophical sciences; the disciple to whom Maimonides addresses the "Introductory Epistle" at the beginning of the *Guide* is said to be conversant with logic and mathematics but not with physics or metaphysics. These semi-intellectuals are regarded by Maimonides as being in a state of mental confusion because they consider that the theses of the Greek sciences contradict religious faith. The word *ḥayra*, "perplexity," which is connected with the participle *ḥā'irīn* figuring in the title of the work under discussion, appears to have served as a technical term denoting the state of mind induced by a tug of war between two opposed beliefs. Both al-Fārābī and, in the generation before Maimonides, the Jewish philosopher Abraham ibn-Da'ud also used the term "perplexed" to describe people who hesitate between the conflicting claims of philosophy and religion. In one passage of the *Guide* Maimonides seems to indicate that his purpose in writing the work was to help such of the "perplexed" as were endowed with the requisite intellectual capacities to achieve a full knowledge of philosophical truths without giving up the observance of the religious commandments.

However, Maimonides, like his contemporary Averroës, was convinced that philosophy could constitute a terrible threat to the social fabric if a vulgarized version of its doctrines were to spread among ordinary people and destroy simple faith in authority. Systematic treatises, giving a step-by-step account of the Aristotelian doctrines, avoided this danger through recourse to technical terms and logical argumentation, which were incomprehensible to noninitiates. Maimonides employed another method, set forth in his introduction to the *Guide*. In the case of this work his very considerable gift for literary composition, which had enabled him to succeed in the extremely difficult task of producing a well-ordered code comprising the whole of Talmudic law, was called upon to disarrange and make a jumble of the systematic expositions of Aristotle and the Aristotelians. Maimonides makes it quite clear that in order to make understanding more difficult, he carefully tore apart conceptions which belong together. The reader is thus faced with the challenge of reconstructing the original whole out of pieces dispersed in various portions of the *Guide*. Maimonides even states that on certain points he deliberately makes two contradictory assertions. These and other precautions, which were intended to confuse readers of insufficient intellectual caliber or preparation, have turned the *Guide* into an enigma; any solution of the enigma can be impugned by an appeal to some statement of Maimonides' that may or may not have been meant to be taken at its face value.

Influences on Maimonides. There is a question whether the *Guide* was meant to be an apologetic attempt to render religion intellectually respectable by exposing the limitations of human reason, beyond which lies the domain of faith in things that may be true although they are unknown to philosophers; or, alternatively, whether it was meant to demonstrate that religion has a purely practical use. If the latter, then Maimonides meant to say that theoretical truth is essentially, although perhaps not completely, revealed by philosophy and to deny that religion has anything to offer except, in the most favorable cases, myths and parables to be interpreted with the help of scientific knowledge. A knowledge of the philosophical authors whose influence was avowed by Maimonides or may be discerned in his work may help to determine what actually was the main object of the *Guide*.

In a letter to Samuel ibn-Tibbon, who translated the *Guide* into Hebrew, Maimonides wrote that he considered Plato's writings to be superseded by those of Aristotle, which are the root and foundation of all philosophy. However, he thought that Aristotle should be studied only with the help of the commentators Alexander of Aphrodisias, Themistus, and Averroës (a contemporary of Maimonides, who was not acquainted with the Muslim philosopher's commentaries at the time the *Guide* was written). Maimonides esteemed al-Fārābī above all the other Islamic philosophers (a typical attitude of the philosophers of Spain), and also praised ibn Bājja, the Muslim Spanish Aristotelian. His reaction to Avicenna, who was the dominant philosophical influence in the Islamic East, was ambivalent.

Maimonides does adopt certain conceptions of Avicenna's. Thus, his view that existence is an accident derives from Avicenna's fundamental doctrine that essences per se are neutral with respect to existence, which supervenes on them as an accident. However, in points that have an obvious bearing on religious beliefs, Maimonides sometimes does not hesitate to prefer Aristotelian notions, although they appear to be incompatible with the Jewish tradition prevalent in his time, to views that are more easily reconcilable with this tradition and that, through Avicenna's adhesion, were given the hallmark of philosophical respectability. To cite an outstanding example, Maimonides holds no brief for Avicenna's opinion that the individual human soul survives the death of the body and is immortal. Like Alexander of Aphrodisias and other Aristotelians, he considers that in man only the actual intellect—which lacks all individual particularity—is capable of survival. In adopting this view, Maimonides clearly shows that, at least on this point, he prefers the philosophical truth as he sees it, however opposed it may seem to be to the current religious conceptions, to the sort of halfway house between theology and philosophy which, in the severe judgment of certain Spanish Aristotelians—notably Averroës—Avicenna had sought to set up.

To cite another instance, Maimonides does not give the slightest indication of recognizing, as Avicenna did, the mystical ecstatic way to God as being on the same level as the way of the intellect (the Muslim philosopher may have claimed even more for it than simple equality). According to the *Guide,* the religious commandment enjoining the love of God entails the duty of knowing whatever may be known of him, for love is proportionate to the knowledge which man has of the beloved.

Theory of divine attributes. What kind of cognition of God is possible to man? The *Guide* sets forth at considerable length and with stronger emphasis than in Avicenna the doctrine of negative theology. According to this doctrine, nothing positive can be known about God, who has nothing in common with any other being. No predicate or descriptive term can legitimately be applied to him unless it is given a meaning which is wholly different from the one the term has in common usage and is purely negative. All statements concerning God considered in himself should, if they are to be regarded as true, be interpreted as providing an indication of what God is *not*. This applies even to the statement that God exists. Maimonides maintains that progress in this kind of negative knowledge is of considerable value, for it does away with false ideas concerning God.

On the other hand, the positive knowledge which man is capable of is concerned with quite a different domain; it deals not with God in himself but with his governance of nature, or, in other words, with the order obtaining in the cosmos and determining the events which occur in it. According to Maimonides' interpretation of Exodus 33, only this knowledge is granted to Moses, and such are the limitations of human science. As far as this conception is concerned, the acts of God may be identified with the operations of nature (or with historical happenings brought about by natural causes). Maimonides' view of the world being by and large Aristotelian, these operations are subject to the rule that they do not destroy but, rather, safeguard the perpetuity of the immutable order of nature, including the preservation of mankind and of the various other species of living beings.

Some of the operations of God (or of nature) seem, from the human point of view, to be beneficent, for instance, the operation which instills into progenitors the impulse to care for their young; others, such as earthquakes or large floods, seem destructive. Because of the anthropomorphic tendency, men witnessing happenings of the first kind speak of God as being merciful and may impute havoc and death to God's being vengeful. These are two of the so-called divine attributes of action. Quite evidently they are not concerned with the essence of God but reflect a purely human evaluation of God's, or nature's, actions. In contrast with other medieval Aristotelian philosophers, Maimonides does not recognize the divine attributes of relation.

Divine intellection. As the Aristotelian system of physics requires, and as Maimonides demonstrates by means of a number of proofs taken over from earlier philosophers, this world is dependent upon God (who is the Prime Mover); but, contrary to Aristotle's conception (already modified by some of the late Greek Neoplatonists, whose views reached Maimonides through the Islamic philosophers), God is regarded as the efficient and formal as well as the final cause of the cosmos. This God is pure intellectual activity, to which (in Maimonides' view as well as in Aristotle's) man's intellection bears a certain resemblance.

Indeed, Maimonides seems to go out of his way to point out this similarity. In this connection a comparison between a statement of his and one of al-Fārābī's is instructive. In accordance with the doctrine of Book Λ of Aristotle's *Metaphysics,* the Muslim philosopher states quite unequivocally that it is because God intellects only himself that the subject, object, and act of divine intellection are identical. Maimonides, too, maintains this threefold identity with regard to God (*Guide,* Part I, Ch. 68); but he points out that it exists equally in the case of man's intellection of any object, for instance, a piece of wood, because according to an opinion of Aristotle, the actual intellect is identical with the object cognized by it. (This opinion was apparently quite unconnected with Aristotle's conception of God.) This comparison of man's cognition to God's, which argues similarity between the two, appears to be incompatible with Maimonides' negative theology. This point had already been made in the Middle Ages and must be taken into account in any interpretation of the *Guide.*

Furthermore, the fact that Maimonides uses as an example the intellection of a piece of wood seems to suggest that, unlike Aristotle and al-Fārābī but in accordance with many of the medieval Aristotelians, he tends to believe that God cognizes not only himself but all the intelligibles. Since cognition involves identity, this conception would appear to entail the identification of God with the intelligible structure of the universe, regarded both as the subject and as the object of cognition. The argument does not entail the identification of matter with God or with an attribute of the Deity. To call Maimonides' position or its logical corollaries "pantheism" would therefore be to go beyond the evidence.

Origin of the world. A main theme of the *Guide* concerns the contradiction between the idea of God upon which Judaism is founded and the philosophical view of God. The philosophical view for Maimonides is the conception of God as an intellect rather than as described by the speculations of negative theology. Maimonides is fully aware of the crucial character of the issue and of the impossibility of achieving a true reconciliation between the philosophical and the religious points of view. He remarks in the *Guide* (Part II, Ch. 20): "For to me the combination between [the world] existing in virtue of necessity and being produced in time in virtue of a purpose in the world . . . comes near to being a combination of two contraries." Maimonides points out the "very disgraceful conclusions" that follow from the first opinion:

Namely it would follow that the Deity, whom everyone who is intelligent recognises to be perfect in every kind of perfection, could as far as all beings are concerned, produce nothing new in any of them; if He wished to lengthen a fly's wing or shorten a worm's foot, He would not be able to do so. But Aristotle would say that He would not wish it and that it is impossible to will something different from what is; that it would not add to His perfection, but would perhaps from a certain point of view be a deficiency. (*Guide,* Part II, Ch. 22)

In Maimonides' interpretation of the Aristotelian position, God's will is assimilated to the divine Intellect, which is identical with God himself, and the world may be regarded as something like an intellection necessarily produced by this Intellect. A consequence of Aristotle's theory as understood by Maimonides is that every characteristic of things existing in the world must be supposed to have a cause grounded in the natural structure of the universe (as opposed to a supernatural cause not determined by this structure). It may be added that as far as bodies are concerned, Maimonides seems to believe that in cases in which a mechanistic explanation can be found, it might provide such a cause. If this were accepted, it would mean that no part of the natural order could be, or could ever have been, different from what it actually is, for its existence is guaranteed by the immutability of divine reason. In other words, the world could not have been created in time.

From this point of view Maimonides is quite consistent in describing temporal creation as the greatest of miracles and in stating that if this is admitted, the intellectual acceptance of other direct interventions of God in the natural course of events does not present any difficulties. Since it serves Maimonides' purpose to make out the best case possible for what he designates as the religious conception of God, he attempts to show that a structure of the universe which is necessary, because it is rationally determined in every respect, does not exist—or at least he seems to do so. In fact, he does not go beyond the demonstration, made at some length, that as far as the heavenly spheres are concerned, Aristotelian physics (although it gives satisfactory explanation of the phenomena of the sublunar world) is incapable of propounding a comprehensive scientific theory which can be regarded as certain and which provides cogent proof for the assumption that the cosmic order could not be different from what it actually is. In this critique of Aristotle's celestial physics he is helped by the much-debated discrepancy that exists between Aristotle's natural science and the Ptolemaic system.

Maimonides also puts forward an argument of somewhat different character. He points out that man's knowledge of the order of nature is based on the empirical data of which he is cognizant. It is, however, conceivable that the existence of the data that are known to man had a beginning in time. No man who studies this problem should ignore this possibility, for if he does so, his case would be analogous to that of a person who disbelieves on empirical grounds—because he has met only adults—that human beings are brought into the world through birth after having been embryos.

Maimonides' critique of the inconsistencies and the insufficiency of the Aristotelian physics is pertinent within its scheme of reference. However, the doctrine of the eternity of the world does not rest exclusively upon physical theory. It is also corollary to the conception of God as Intellect, and Maimonides is aware of this. It is certainly significant, and it may be a deliberate omission, that when Maimonides is dealing with the problem of the eternity of the world in the *Guide,* he does not mention this conception although other portions of the work prove he had adopted it. Thus he does not allude to God as Intellect when he proclaims in the *Guide* (Part II, Ch. 25) that he does not accept the doctrine of the eternity of the world for two reasons: (1) because it has not been demonstrated; (2) because its adoption would be tantamount to destroying the foundations of the Law, for it would mean denying the claims of the prophets and rejecting the belief in miracles.

Sources of knowledge. That Maimonides rejected the doctrine of the eternity of the world partly because (as his second reason) it would have destroyed the foundations of religious law may appear to affirm the claim of religious belief to have a decisive voice in theoretical questions that are of paramount concern to it. That is, it may appear to affirm this claim, provided that the intellect is unable to reach a fully demonstrable conclusion with regard to the moot points. Clearly such a claim can have far-reaching implications. It could be argued that this position leads to the recognition of suprarational theoretical truths or, alternatively, to the assertion of validity of conclusions in the sphere of theory adopted only on the basis of practical reason. However, Maimonides himself does not at all countenance such a demotion of theoretical reason. In the *Guide* (Part I, Ch. 2) he explains the superiority of theoretical reason, which is concerned with the difference between truth and falsehood, over practical reason, which deals with the distinction between good and evil. His allegorical interpretation of Adam's fall entails the conclusion that practical reason has the comparatively lowly function of curbing the appetite to which man is prone when he is not given over to theoretical contemplation.

As for prophecy and divine revelation, they cannot be regarded as sources of supraintellectual knowledge conceived as being independent of, and superior to, the system of sciences produced by theoretical reason. This comes out clearly in Maimonides' description of the characteristics peculiar to prophets. According to him, prophets must have both an outstanding intellectual capacity and an outstanding imaginative capacity. Given these two preconditions, and suitable conduct, prophecy is a natural phenomenon; the gift of prophecy can be withheld from a person having the required qualifications only by means of a miracle. The intellectual capacity of prophets is similar at least in kind to that of the philosophers; it enables them to receive what Maimonides terms a "divine overflow," an influx coming from the Active Intellect, which, according to the interpretation of the Aristotelian doctrine adopted by Maimonides, brings about the actualization of man's potential intellect. The Active Intellect is the last of the ten incorporeal Intellects; its special sphere of action is the sublunar world.

There is no suggestion that the conclusions reached by the prophets through the use of the intellect are in any way different from those of the philosophers, though the prophets may reach them more rapidly; all prophets are philosophers. This clearly applies also to Moses, in spite of a statement in the *Guide* that none of the author's assertions about the prophets pertain to Moses. In other writings Maimonides describes Moses as having attained union with the Active Intellect; according to the conception of certain Islamic Aristotelians, union with the Active Intellect represents the highest goal and is reached by the great philosophers.

Imagination is inferior to intellect for Maimonides, who

was on this point an orthodox Aristotelian. Imagination enables the prophet to see veridical dreams and visions, for the "divine overflow" spills over from the intellectual to the imaginative sphere. But it certainly does not give access to a supraintellectual truth. In fact the superiority of Moses over all other prophets is, according to Maimonides' interpretation, partly the result of the circumstance that in his prophecy he did not have recourse to imagination.

Political philosophy. Religious revelation thus does not procure any knowledge of the highest truth that cannot be achieved by the human intellect; it does, however, have an educative role—as well as a political one. In Maimonides' words, "The law as a whole aims at two things: the welfare of the soul and the welfare of the body" (*Guide,* Part III, Ch. 27).

Because of the great diversity of human character, a common framework for the individuals belonging to one society can be provided only by a special category of men endowed with the capacity for government and for legislation. Those who have only a strong imagination, unaccompanied by proportionate intellectual powers, are not interested in the intellectual education of the members of the state which they found or govern. On the other hand, the foremost example of an ideal lawgiver is Moses.

The law instituted by Moses had to take into account the historical circumstances—the influence of ancient Oriental paganism—and had to avoid too great a break with universal religious usage. To cite one example, sacrifices could not be abolished, because this would have been an excessively violent shock for the people. In spite of these difficulties, however, Moses succeeded in establishing a polity to which Maimonides, in the "Epistle to Yemen," applies the term *al-madina al-fādila* ("the virtuous city") used by the Muslim philosophers to designate the ideal state of Plato's *Republic*—a work which, perhaps mainly through the mediation of al-Fārābī, had a considerable impact on Maimonides' political thought.

Moral philosophy. The polity is not alone in regulating men's actions in the best possible way. The Scriptures by which the polity is ruled also contain hints that may guide such human individuals as are capable of understanding its hints to philosophical truths. Some of these truths are to be discovered in the beliefs taught to all those who profess Judaism; these dogmas are for evident reasons formulated in a language adapted to the understanding of ordinary unphilosophical people. There are, however, other religious beliefs that, although they are not true, are necessary for the majority of the people, to safeguard a tolerable public order and to further morality. Such are the belief that God is angry with those who act in an unjust manner and the belief that he responds instantaneously to the prayer of someone wronged or deceived (*Guide,* Part III, Ch. 28). The morality suited to men of the common run aims at their exercising a proper restraint over the passions of the appetite; it is an Aristotelian middle-of-the-road morality, not an ascetic one. The ascetic overtones which are occasionally encountered in the *Guide* concern the philosopher rather than the ordinary man.

There is a separate morality for the elite, which is or should be called upon to rule, to which Maimonides alludes in the *Guide* (Part I, Ch. 54; Part III, Chs. 51 and 54).

This ethical doctrine is connected with Maimonides' interpretation of what ought to be man's superior goal, which is to love God, and, as far as possible, to resemble him.

From the point of view of negative theology, love of God can be achieved only through knowledge of divine activity in the world, the only knowledge of God possible. This supreme goal can be reached through a study of natural science and of metaphysics, which appears to signify that the highest perfection can be attained only by a man who leads the theoretical life—the man whose superiority was proclaimed by Aristotle. However, Maimonides is at pains to show—and this seems to be a Platonic element in his doctrine—that the theoretical life can be combined with a life of action, as proved by the examples of the patriarchs and of Moses.

What is more, a life of action can constitute an imitation of God. For the prophetic legislators and statesmen endeavor to imitate the operations of nature, or God (the two are equivalent; the expression "divine or natural actions," which occurs in the *Guide,* may have been in Spinoza's mind when he first spoke of *Deus sive natura*). Maimonides emphasizes two characteristics that belong both to the actions of God–nature and to the actions of superior statesmen. First, however beneficent or destructive—or, in ordinary human parlance, however merciful or vengeful—the actions in question appear to be, neither God nor the prophetic statesman is actuated by passions. Second, the activity of nature (or God) tends to preserve the cosmic order, which includes the perpetuity of the species of living beings, but it has no consideration for the individual. In the same way the prophetic lawgivers and statesmen, who in founding or governing a polity should imitate this activity, must have in mind first and foremost the commonweal, the welfare of the majority, and must not be deterred from following a politically correct course of action by the fact that it hurts individuals.

The imitation of the works of God (or of nature) by the prophets means (*Guide,* Part III, Ch. 32) that the prophets imitate in leadership the indirect and complicated way through which nature obtains its desired results, as seen, for instance, in the extremely intricate mechanism of living organisms. Maimonides calls this indirect method a "gracious ruse" of God and his wisdom; he may have taken the expression over from Alexander of Aphrodisias' work "Principle of the All" (extant only in Arabic translation). It is reminiscent, not only on the verbal plane, of Hegel's "Cunning of Reason." According to the *Guide,* Moses used the indirect method in making the sons of Israel wander for forty years in the desert instead of leading them straight to the land of Canaan, for he wanted the people to shed slavish habits and acquire in the hard school of the desert the warlike virtues necessary for conquest. He also used it in adapting the commandments to the historical and geographical circumstances.

Influence of the "Guide." The *Guide* was first translated into Hebrew in Maimonides' lifetime, by Samuel ibn-Tibbon and a little later by al-Harizi. Its first translation into Latin was also produced in the thirteenth century. Maimonides' injunction to follow his example in writing the Arabic text of the work only in Hebrew characters (and thus to prevent its being read by non-Jews) was not always observed. The work is mentioned by some later Muslim writers but does not appear to have had more than a very slight impact on Muslim thought.

In the period after Maimonides the *Guide* was the fundamental text of medieval Jewish thought and was much debated. In the thirteenth and fourteenth centuries it was violently denounced for being antireligious and as vehemently defended against this charge; commentaries upon it were written by Shem-Tov Falaquera, Joseph ibn Kaspi, Moses of Narbonne, Isaac Abravanel, and others, and its theses are discussed at length in such capital philosophical works as Gersonides' "The Wars of the Lord" (*Milḥamot Adonai*) and Hasdai Crescas' "Light of the Lord" (*Or Adonai*). At first blush it is therefore rather surprising that among Jewish philosophers, relatively few of Maimonides' disciples have been content to adopt his apparently agnostic attitude toward fundamental metaphysical problems and thus to leave what he believed to be a necessary loophole for religious belief. In fact, no doubt partly because of the unsystematic mode of exposition of the *Guide,* some philosophically minded commentators (notably Moses of Narbonne) expounded Averroës' conceptions rather than Maimonides' in their commentaries on the *Guide.* Other commentators—for example, Abravanel—often criticized him from a traditionalistic religious point of view.

The *Guide* had a strong influence on later Jewish philosophers, many of whom owe their introduction to philosophy to the *Guide.* This can be seen in Spinoza (a considerable portion of the *Tractatus Theologico-politicus* is devoted to a critique of Maimonides, although the explicit references to him are few) and in Salomon Maimon, who wrote a commentary on the *Guide.*

The influence of Maimonides on the medieval Christian Schoolmen seems to have been considerable; the matter has not yet been sufficiently investigated, though several studies dealing with the subject do exist. It may be noted that by elaborating the doctrine of suprarational truths the systems of Thomas Aquinas and of other Scholastics found a way of legitimating from a theoretical point of view Maimonides' decision to opt for the belief in temporal creation, because the existence of religion hinged on this belief's being generally accepted.

Works by Maimonides

Le Guide des égarés, Salomon Munk, ed., 3 vols. Paris, 1856–1866. Arabic text and French translation, with many detailed notes. The French translation has been re-edited. Paris, 1960.
The Guide of the Perplexed, translated with an introduction and notes by Shlomo Pines. Chicago, 1963. Introductory essay by Leo Strauss.

Works on Maimonides

Altmann, Alexander, "Das Verhältnis Maimunis zur jüdischen Mystik." *Monatsschrift für Geschichte und Wissenschaft des Judentums,* Vol. 80 (1936), 305–330.
Baron, Salo, ed., *Essays on Maimonides: An Octocennial Volume.* New York, 1941.
Diesendruck, Z., "Maimonides' Lehre von der Prophetie," in G. A. Kohut, ed., *Jewish Studies in Memory of Israel Abrahams.* New York, 1927, Pp. 74–134.

Diesendruck, Z., "Die Teleologie bei Maimonides." *Hebrew Union College Annual,* Vol. 5 (1928), 415–534.
Epstein, I., ed., *Moses Maimonides: 1135–1204.* London, 1935.
Guttmann, Jakob, *Der Einfluss der Maimonideschen Philosophie auf das christliche Abendland.* Leipzig, 1908.
Rohner, A., *"Das Schöpfungsproblem bei Moses Maimonides, Albertus Magnus, und Thomas von Aquin.* Münster, 1913.
Roth, Leon, *The Guide for the Perplexed, Moses Maimonides.* London, 1948.
Strauss, Leo, *Philosophie und Gesetz.* Berlin, 1935.
Strauss, Leo, "Quelques Remarques sur la science politique de Maimonide et de Farabi." *Revue des études juives,* Vol. 100 (1936), 1–37.
Strauss, Leo, *Persecution and the Art of Writing.* Chicago, 1952. Includes "The Literary Character of *The Guide for the Perplexed,*" also published in Baron's *Essays on Maimonides* (see above).
Wolfson, H. A., "Maimonides and Halevi." *Jewish Quarterly Review,* N.S. Vol. 2 (1911–1912), 297–337.
Wolfson, H. A., "Maimonides on the Internal Senses." *Jewish Quarterly Review,* N.S. Vol. 25 (1934–1935), 441–467.
Wolfson, H. A., "Halevi and Maimonides on Design, Chance, and Necessity." *Proceedings of the American Academy for Jewish Research,* Vol. 11 (1941), 105–163.
Wolfson, H. A., "Halevi and Maimonides on Prophecy." *Jewish Quarterly Review,* N.S. Vol. 32 (1941–1942), 345–370, and N.S. Vol. 33 (1942–1943), 49–82.
Wolfson, H. A., "The Platonic, Aristotelian, and Stoic Theories of Creation in Hallevi and Maimonides," in I. Epstein, E. Levine, and C. Roth, eds., *Essays in Honor of the Very Rev. Dr. J. H. Hertz.* London, 1942. Pp. 427–442.
Wolfson, H. A., "Maimonides on Negative Attributes," in A. Marx and others, eds., *Louis Ginzberg Jubilee Volume.* New York, 1945. Pp. 419–446.

SHLOMO PINES

MAINE DE BIRAN (1766–1824), French statesman and philosopher. Maine de Biran was born Marie François Pierre Gonthier de Biran, receiving the name "Maine" from the name of his family's property (le Maine). He attended the *collège* at Périgueux, dominated by the secular, moderate constitutional Royalists called *Doctrinaires,* and excelled there in mathematics. In 1784 he joined the king's guard and in 1789 was wounded defending Louis XVI in a mob uprising. To escape the Reign of Terror, he retired to his estate in 1793 and began intensive psychological and philosophical investigations. In 1797 he was elected to the Council of Five Hundred, and this election of a moderate royalist was a symptom of the beginning of the end of the Reign of Terror. This post and other public duties did not keep him from reaping the fruits of his earlier meditations. He became acquainted with the *Idéologues* Cabanis and Destutt de Tracy by winning first prize in an essay contest sponsored by the Institute of France with the essay *L'Influence de l'habitude sur la faculté de penser* (*The Influence of Habit on the Faculty of Thinking*). He won membership in the institute in 1805 by gaining another first prize, for *Mémoire sur la décomposition de la penser* ("The Analysis of Thought"). While continuing to write outstanding philosophic and psychological essays, he intensified his political activities, became a member of the Chamber of Deputies, and was made commander in the Legion of Honor. Under the first restoration he returned to the National Assembly and was put in charge of liaison between the assembly and the king on financial matters. Despite these public activities, he was at the time of his death acknowledged by most of his distinguished contemporaries as their master *(maître à tous)* in philosophy.

His famous *Journal intime* reveals a melancholy, emotionally changeable person, of poor health, who was highly sensitive to climatic and personal surroundings. He spent much of his personal and philosophic life trying to understand and mitigate this sensitivity.

Philosophical development. Maine de Biran's philosophic development can be summarized briefly as a movement toward a more and more detailed conviction that man's inward experience is (1) different from his outwardly experienced "impressions," and (2) an important source and basis of knowledge. His most mature essays speak of an "inward sense" *(sens intime)* that reveals our experience of willed bodily movement *(effort voulu)*; in the course of his philosophic development he gave to this experience a more and more important role, progressively more subtly analyzed. The names of Locke, Condillac, and Charles Bonnet, all of whom emphasized outward impressions as the ultimate source of knowledge, occurred as frequently in his early notes as did the name of Rousseau, whose "Profession of Faith of a Savoyard Vicar" in *Émile* had aroused Maine de Biran's interest in the "inner light" *(lumière intérieure)*. But the outwardly oriented epistemologies of Condillac and Locke and their disciples, the *Idéologues*, soon grew less adequate for Maine de Biran, as did Bonnet's explanations of perception in terms of physiological mechanisms (explanations based upon outward "impressions"). After 1802 and his first great prize essay, *The Influence of Habit on the Faculty of Thinking*, which was similar in many ways to the writings of the *Idéologues*, Maine de Biran moved into his longest and most original period of philosophizing, during which he became quite critical of his former masters and developed and defended the key doctrine of his philosophy, that the *effort voulu* is a unique source of basic knowledge. In this stage he wrote "The Analysis of Thought" (which won him membership in the Institute of France) and his most mature completed philosophic work, *Essai sur les fondements de la psychologie* ("Essay on the Foundations of Psychology," 1812).

From 1814 to the end of his life he developed—but never with great precision—a doctrine derived from Kant (by way of Maine de Biran's friend André Marie Ampère), a doctrine that identified "belief" *(croyance)* as one of the inner sources of knowledge. At first Maine de Biran spoke of belief as revealing the transphenomenal substance of things, and from 1815 on he applied this notion of a "faculty of belief" to problems of theology. According to Maine de Biran, *croyance*, like the *effort voulu*, originates inwardly, but—unlike voluntary bodily movement—is always passive; its function is to receive God's grace. Still, he continued to speak of the importance of the *effort voulu*; the doctrine of the significance of the faculty of belief in relation to religious matters was not a repudiation of the significance of the activistic, individualistic capacity of the *effort voulu* in matters of natural knowledge. In fact, during this last period, from 1814 to 1824, he wrote some of his finest essays developing his doctrine that the *sens intime* is a unique and important source of knowledge. Two of his outstanding works on this subject were *Examen des leçons de philosophie de M. Laromiquière* ("An Examination of Laromiquière's Lessons in Philosophy," 1817) and his unfinished masterpiece, *Nouveaux Essais d'anthropologie* ("New Essays in Anthropology," 1824), both of which cast much light on the doctrine of *effort voulu*. In fact this doctrine was far more thoroughly developed than the doctrine of *croyance*. Nevertheless, the emphasis given to belief in the last stage of his thought confirms the generalization that the whole tendency of his philosophic development was toward a more profound conviction that inward experience—whether of willed effort or of belief itself—is the richest basis of knowledge.

Learning and experience. Condillac, the forerunner of the *Idéologues*, had insisted on clarifying terms and validating claims to knowledge by reference to simple, directly experienced outward "sensations" stripped of the increments of learning. The leader of the *Idéologues* in Maine de Biran's day, Destutt de Tracy, had continued Condillac's line of thought but had noticed that (1) some experiences get duller and vaguer by repetition, while others become more distinct; and that (2) there is a capacity to move our bodies voluntarily (Destutt de Tracy called it "*motilité*") that has a vital function in our learning to perceive objects. In addition, Destutt de Tracy's colleagues Cabanis and Bonnet had seen the importance of physiological conditions for an analysis of the human mind. In his first prize-winning essay Maine de Biran developed all of these suggestions. He not only distinguished between outer impressions and felt effort, but he distinguished what he called "sensations" (such as tastes and smells), wherein the impression is vivacious and our voluntary bodily movement is minimal, from what he called "perceptions" (such as talking aloud and hearing ourselves), wherein the outward impresssion is less important than the inward experience of moving our organs. But these distinctions might have no importance for an analysis of knowledge, he thought, if they do not help us to understand learning more fully. And so in his first essay he set about trying to discover whether habituation or repetition has a different effect on passive sensations than on active perceptions; if different effects were found to exist it could be assumed that the distinction between sensations and perceptions is important. He found that passively experienced sensations got vaguer with habituation, and perceptions which are involved with our willed bodily movement became more and more precise. Our sense of smell loses its refinement in a hothouse, but we walk, talk, play games better by practicing. Therefore, he concluded, in perceptions alone do we find the possibility of learning, of moving from the passive sensational confusion of the infant to the subtle distinctions of the adult mind. If Condillac's passively received outward impressions were all that was available to consciousness, the repetition of these impressions would have resulted in a vague blur. The development of mind is linked with willed bodily movement, with perceptions.

One of our most important perceptions is our experience of speaking and hearing our own words; this is the most active perception, and the least dependent upon adventitious external impressions. Sounds uttered by us are among the first signs we know; they are outwardly experienced signs of our own inward actions, and it is the inward action that constitutes the meaning of the sign. There are other signs too: We learn to associate two or more external impressions as natural, or physical, signs of each other. But for Maine de Biran the sign-relationship most directly involved in human reasoning is the relationship between spoken words or conventional signs and our inwardly experienced effort to move our organs of speech. In the course of acquiring by habituation a more subtle and distinct way of talking we acquire a more subtle and distinct mentality. Maine de Biran never lost sight of natural sign-relationships between impressions or between images of impressions as part of our learning process, but he insisted that oral, conventional sign-relationships were basic to human mentality. To describe human thinking only in terms of associated images of outward impressions is to ignore speech, the faculty that makes human thought peculiarly human.

In 1812, in his "Essay on the Foundations of Psychology," Maine de Biran set out to find a primary experience, a *fait primitif* antecedent to all learning or habituation (Condillac had sought such a fact and had claimed to find it in outward sensations). Maine de Biran held that such a basic experience must satisfy three criteria: First, it must be within the limits of awareness (although he sometimes talked of unconscious perceptions); second, it must, of course, not be learned or deduced, but must be directly experienced; finally, it must be persistent, for knowledge must have a firmer basis than the passing moment. He rejected outward impressions and inward emotions and affections because they were fleeting, and he rejected the physiological findings he had once been attracted to because they were the results of inferences or deductions, not immediately experienced. In the end he adopted as his primary experience the *effort voulu* he had found to be so crucial to the learning process: we are aware of it, although sometimes not vivaciously; it is not itself learned, although we learn how to move various members skillfully; and this experience persists in various degrees of tension (ranging from sensations up to perceptions) throughout our waking life. The most lucidly developed part of Maine de Biran's philosophy is his explanation and defense of this triple claim involved in calling the *effort voulu* a primary experience.

Selfhood, causality, and liberty. Philosophers such as Locke, Condillac, and the *Idéologues* had great difficulty accounting for our idea of a persistent, inwardly experienced self, because they assumed that experience was made up of nothing but fleeting, outward impressions. But the origin of this idea loses its mystery if we give our attention to our persistent, inward experience of our own willing against our varying bodily resistance to that willing. Throughout our lives we feel this relationship at the center of our experience in varying degrees of tension. The center is the self (*le moi*), the periphery, or the surrounding impressions, is the nonself. In fact, the unity of our own more or less resisting body as felt in the *sens intime* is the origin of our whole notion of unity or identity, whether it occurs in mathematics or elsewhere.

The felt relationship between the body and our more or less active willing to move that body is for Maine de Biran our basic experience of causation. In defending this claim he argued that the term "cause" cannot be explained by hazy references to "innate" ideas, or by question-begging, tautological assertions about effects presupposing causes; in this he agreed with Hume. He also agreed with Hume that our disparate impressions do not reveal any instance of necessary connection. But he flatly disagreed with Hume's double assumption that outward impressions are basically similar to and are the origin of any inward experience we may have. Maine de Biran insisted that in our *sens intime* we find a unique, primary experience of necessary connection.

Hume's main objections to this claim occur in his *Enquiries Concerning the Human Understanding and Concerning the Principles of Morals;* he points out that in cases such as palsy or amputation we cannot be sure our own bodily movement will follow our willing. Moreover, the means by which the will and our body are united is, in Hume's word, "mysterious." How then can we be said to experience an instance of necessary connection when neither connection nor necessity is experienced here? Maine de Biran responded to these objections by using his basic distinction between impressions and the *effort voulu*, or between images, or copies of outward impressions, and our idea of inward felt effort. To the first objection he replied that bodily movement is simultaneous with the willing that is its cause, and that if there is any failure or disappointment, it is the failure or disappointment of a plan involving memory and anticipatory images concerning a succession of experiences. Willed effort itself, involving the simultaneity of cause and effect, never fails; only plans involving successive outward impressions may fail. According to Maine de Biran, Hume mistakes our *pensées* for our *effort voulu*, confuses disparate outward impressions and their images with intimately related, inwardly simultaneous willing and movement.

Hume's second objection is that no connection or "means" connecting the will to the body is present in willed effort. By "means" Hume chiefly meant physiological means that can be demonstrated through outward impressions and derived hypotheses concerning the connection between the willed effort and bodily movement. Maine de Biran answered, however, that in the face of the plainly felt experience of inward causation, one need not ask for "connecting" entities deviously derived from a different sort of experience; Hume, in doing so, simply reasserted his old prejudice in favor of outward impressions and their images. No assertion concerning our physiological structures can diminish or put in question our inwardly experienced relationship between willing and our body. To say that it does is like claiming that remarks about a Caruso's anatomy diminish or put in question the greatness of his artistry. The greatness lies in the singing itself, just as our certainty in experiencing the *effort voulu* lies in this experience itself, not in any hypothetical structures based on quite different experiences. Finally, Maine de Biran pointed out that we apply the term "cause" or "necessary connection" to outward impressions by projecting our inward experience of simultaneity into the outward world of successive impressions; our original experience of causation or necessary connection is inward; all other uses of the term "causation" are derivative from it.

The certainty of the experienced relationship between will and bodily movement is the basis of man's liberty. Deterministic arguments that have been invoked to contest man's liberty depend on causal laws that are less certain than, and indeed irrelevant to, the experience of moving our bodies ourselves. Maine de Biran was willing to assert that in varying degrees strong motives or desires incline us to will certain movements. He was even willing to agree that our passions are sometimes overwhelming, for example, under the influence of hunger or fear, but he went on to say that there are times when the crucial causal factor in any action is our will, which is capable of rejecting any given desire or inclining motive. At those times we are free, and no dubious hypotheses concerning determining causes can hold up against the plain fact that we can and do withstand particular external or internal pressures. Our freedom does exist, although it is occasional and is tempered by the degree of inclination or pressure.

Works by Maine de Biran

The first published edition of Maine de Biran's works was *Oeuvres philosophiques de Maine de Biran*, Victor Cousin, ed., 4 vols. (Paris, 1841). This edition is incomplete and should be avoided, except by those who wish to account for the gross misunderstandings of Maine de Biran's thought that were current in the nineteenth century. The definitive edition of Maine de Biran's notes, essays, and letters is the one edited by Pierre Tisserand and Henri Gouhier: *Oeuvre de Maine de Biran*, 14 vols. (Paris, 1920–1942). Gouhier has also edited the definitive edition of Maine de Biran's philosophically revealing *Journal intime* (Neuchâtel, 1954–1957). Only one of Maine de Biran's works has been translated into English—his first prize-winning essay, translated by Margaret Boehm as *The Influence of Habit on the Faculty of Thinking* (Baltimore, 1929).

Works on Maine de Biran

No definitive biography has been written; the most detailed life now in print is that by Amable de La Vallett-Monbrun, *Maine de Biran: Essai de biographie historique et psychologique* (Paris, 1914). Sainte-Beuve's brief biography of him in *Causeries du Lundi*, Vol. VIII (Paris, undated), is famous for its eloquence. On the development of Maine de Biran's philosophy three excellent books have been written. Henri Gouhier's *Les Conversions de Maine de Biran* (Paris, 1947) is the best account we have of the influences upon him. *Maine de Biran et son oeuvre philosophique*, by Victor Delbos (Paris, 1931), is a lucid, impartial summary of the key works. *L'Expérience de l'effort et de la grâce chez Maine de Biran*, by George Le Roy (Paris, 1934), uses a Bergsonian approach but even so is faithful and perceptive; it is the best consecutive account of his development. A perceptive, memorable account of his thought occurs in *French Philosophies of the Romantic Period*, by George Boas (Baltimore, 1925).

A few useful works on specific topics include Henri Gouhier, "Maine de Biran et Bergson," in *Les Études bergsoniennes*, Vol. I (Paris, 1948); Philip Paul Hallie, *Maine de Biran, Reformer of Empiricism* (Cambridge, 1959); Jacques Paliard, *Le Raisonnement selon Maine de Biran* (Paris, 1925); Euthyme Robef, *Leibniz et Maine de Biran* (Paris, 1927).

PHILIP P. HALLIE

MAISTRE, COMTE JOSEPH DE (1754–1821), Savoyard philosopher and diplomat, was born in Chambéry. After the conquest of Savoy by the French revolutionary forces, he retired to Lausanne, where he lived for three years, devoting himself mainly to writing his *Considérations sur la France* (1796), an attack on the political philosophy of republicanism. He was then summoned to Turin by the king of Sardinia and later moved to Cagliari, the capital of the very diminished kingdom of Sardinia. In 1802 he was appointed Sardinian minister plenipoteniary to St. Petersburg and remained there for 14 years, composing his famous *Soirées de Saint-Pétersbourg*, which was not published until the year of his death.

Ultramontanism. De Maistre is best known for his ultramontanism and traditionalism, which are most forcibly stated in *Du Pape*, written in 1817, although anticipated in certain details in his *Considérations sur la France*. His presuppositions were those of any medieval Roman Catholic—the church is a divine institution; its foundation was given to St. Peter; St. Peter was the first pope; his successors have inherited the powers conferred on him by Jesus Christ himself. The book opens with a demonstration of papal infallibility. Identifying the sovereignty of the pope with that of any secular ruler, de Maistre argued that sovereignty implies infallibility, since no ruler is sovereign whose decisions can be set aside or be subject to appeal. He thus made no distinction between executive competence and validity. As parliaments exist simply to inform the sovereign of matters of which he might not be aware or to make requests and express occasional desires, so the church councils have no power to do more than this. They are convoked and presided over by the pope, who is not bound by their decisions, for they have no real power of decision. The notion that matters of faith and doctrine can be decided by a council is as absurd as the notion that a parliament can actually rule. De Maistre maintained that when the pontiff speaks ex cathedra and without restraint to the church, he has never erred nor can he ever err in questions of faith. He might be constrained to make a false pronouncement, or he might be speaking merely as a man and not as a pope, but in his function as a sovereign monarch, it is impossible that he should ever be in error.

The reason we require any kind of government is that we are born corrupt, yet with a sense of morality. Our souls are thus in a state of conflict. Sovereigns exist in order to prevent the disasters which arise from this conflict and to keep order within the state. No man is capable of governing himself, for no man can spontaneously quell the evil that is in him; therefore, the power to do so must reside in the hands of one ruler who will be above criticism and have absolute power. This ruler, whether he is a king or a pope, does not rule by the consent of his people but because of their needs. Kings, although infallible in regard to their own provinces, are nevertheless subject to the laws of God, and the pope is the only possible judge of whether they have been faithful to them. The pope is the deputy of God, and when a secular ruler has erred, he can be deposed and his subjects can be freed from their oaths of allegiance to him by papal decree. This power, de Maistre maintained, has been used only rarely where hereditary sovereigns were involved; it was used more freely against elected sovereigns, such as the Holy Roman emperors, for they were chosen by man, not by God. The pope, it should be noted, does not interfere in purely secular problems of administration; his intervention is invoked only in morals and religion.

Nevertheless, the pope is not a universal sovereign, for

his power is checked by the canons, the laws, the customs of nations, duty, fear, prudence, and opinion, "which governs the world." Is it not better, de Maistre asked, to settle disputes by the decision of a wise and prudent ruler, inspired by God himself, than by rebellions, civil wars, and all the evils which follow from them? Such an arbitrator will inevitably submit to the commands of duty and prudence, will be sensitive to custom and opinion, and will intuitively know which road to take when conflict arises.

Traditionalism. A reader of *Du Pape* will be impressed by de Maistre's use of tradition to justify his conclusions. The supremacy of the pope, he argued, has always been acknowledged, even by his critics. That is, they all admitted that he has done what de Maistre said he has the power to do, and, de Maistre added, no one except those who had suffered at his hands objected to his power. That something has always been done is to de Maistre proof that it has been done correctly. He even denied the right to liberty on the ground that slavery was the fate of most men until the rise of Christianity.

To de Maistre the human race is a single being, the soul of which is expressed in its language. Language develops, but so does tradition. The tradition of Catholicism is simply the fulfillment of the covenant God gave to Abraham; passed to Moses and then to Aaron, the high priest; and so on down to the promise made to Peter. But in every tradition, in spite of its development, there is a unity of idea, and the maintenance of that unity is entrusted to the pontiff.

Royalism. Concurrent with de Maistre's traditionalism was his royalism. He was so convinced of the need for absolute monarchs that he even maintained that since kings had a longer life expectancy than other men, royal families differ in nature from nonroyal families, as a tree differs from a shrub. A king is not a private individual and must not be judged as such. He is the nation in the same way that the pope is the church. Consequently, his power is also absolute, for when he speaks, it is the nation speaking through him. Kings alone preserve national unity. The word "unity" was a eulogistic term for de Maistre. To be unified is better than to be manifold; to remain the same is better than to change. And although de Maistre had to admit those changes that have obviously occurred and are not evil, he insisted on the unity which underlay them.

De Maistre usually carried his ideas to their logical conclusions. His famous apostrophe to the hangman in the *Soirées* is based on de Maistre's presupposition of the twofold nature of man. If the hangman is removed from society, order will give way to chaos, thrones will totter, and society will disappear. "God who is the author of sovereignty is also the author of punishment." He is the author of punishment so that corrupt man may still be redeemed. But if man is to be punished, there must be an absolute and unquestioned power to execute the punishment, and that power is the king's.

De Maistre was the first philosopher of the counterrevolution in France. With the vicomte de Bonald, he gave a set of arguments to legitimists and Catholics. But although de Maistre was admired by many for his consistency in both principle and inference, his variety of political philosophy was never popular, even during the restoration.

The anti-intellectualism of Chateaubriand and Mme. de Staël, as fully opposed to the extremes of revolution as was de Maistre's traditionalism, gained more adherents. Moreover, ultramontanism was disclaimed by the Vatican. This disclaimer, perhaps, was the main reason for the failure of de Maistre's thought to become popular in France.

Works by de Maistre

Oeuvres complètes, 14 vols. Lyons, 1884–1887.
Considérations sur la France. Neuchâtel, Switzerland, 1796.
Du Pape, 2 vols. Lyons, 1819.
Soirées de Saint-Pétersbourg, 2 vols. Paris, 1821.
The Works of Joseph de Maistre, translated by Jack Lively. New York, 1965. Selections.

Works on de Maistre

Boas, G., *French Philosophies of the Romantic Period.* Baltimore, 1925. See Ch. 3.
Ferraz, M., *Histoire de la philosophie en France au XIXe siècle,* Vol. II, *Traditionalisme et ultramontanisme.* Paris, 1880.
Gianturco, E., *Joseph de Maistre and Giambattista Vico.* Washington, D.C., 1937.
Laski, H. J., *Authority in the Modern State.* New Haven, 1919.
Lecigne, C., *Joseph de Maistre.* Paris, 1914.

GEORGE BOAS

MAJOR, JOHN, or Mair (1469–1550), was a Scottish theologian, active at the University of Paris for some years before and after he secured a license in theology in 1506. Major helped to revive, if only briefly, the spirit of fourteenth-century nominalism. He was entirely sympathetic with the approach of Ockham and Buridan, even though he adopted some doctrines of Scotus and other realists.

Major came to Paris in 1493 after studying at Cambridge. He taught at the University of Paris for most of his lengthy career, with the exception of seven years at the Scottish universities of Glasgow and St. Andrews. When he arrived at Paris, scholasticism, pietism, and humanism were rivals within the university itself. Late medieval pietism was reflected in the ascetic discipline instituted at the Collège de Montaigu, the school that so repelled Erasmus by its austerity and its logic-chopping. Major, with his frugal Scottish background, found the atmosphere of Montaigu less forbidding, and he responded with initial enthusiasm to its manner of disputing. He seems to have been little influenced by the sort of humanism being advocated at the time by Lefèvre d'Étaples, who stressed the value of knowing Aristotle and the Church Fathers in the original Greek. Major belonged to the scholastic tradition completely. His theological and philosophical works proceed entirely from a formal analysis of separate arguments. He made no use of Greek, although he clearly was conversant with Latin literature.

Major's earliest published work consisted of short treatises on terminist logic, published separately from 1500 to 1503, and then together at Lyons in 1505 as a commentary on Peter of Spain. Later he published commentaries on Aristotle's *Ethics* and *Physics*. In theology, he wrote commentaries on the *Sentences* of Peter Lombard and on the Gospels. All of these writings reflect his teaching duties, even in their style. Toward the close of his long life, Major complained mildly at having been forced to accommodate himself to the "manner of our ancestors" and admitted that students had not always found the disputatious style agreeable. In addition to the works already mentioned, Major wrote *A History of Greater Britain*, a landmark in the writing of Scottish history and a most unusual work for a nominalist theologian. Many passages in this work—such as those in defense of the "oaten bread" of Scotland or of ale as opposed to wine—suggest a personality by no means dry and pedantic. Nevertheless, Major's philosophical style has put off scholars, and his work still awaits total and mature evaluation. Almost all present-day accounts of Major are still colored by humanist criticisms of theology made in the spirit of Erasmus, with little sympathy for medieval logic.

Bibliography

A reliable, although sketchy, account of Major's philosophical opinions is given by Ricardo Garcia Villoslada in *La Universidad de Paris durante los estudios de Francisco de Vitoria* (Rome, 1938), pp. 127–164. Carl Prantl, in *Geschichte der Logik im Abendlande* (Leipzig, 1927), Vol. IV, pp. 247–250, gives a few excerpts from Major's logical writings. Major's views on church matters (he was a conciliarist and champion of Gallicanism) are sometimes dealt with briefly in histories of political theory. The details of his life are presented in Aeneas J. G. Mackay's biography, prefixed to an English translation of *A History of Greater Britain* (Edinburgh, 1892), which also contains a bibliography of Major's writings. This bibliography needs to be supplemented, however, by the additions given by Hubert Élie, *Le Traité "De l'Infini" de Jean Mair* (Paris, 1938).

NEAL W. GILBERT

MALCOLM, NORMAN, one of America's best-known philosophers, was born in Selden, Kansas, in 1911. After studying philosophy with O. K. Bouwsma at the University of Nebraska, he enrolled as a graduate student at Harvard in 1933. The decisive period for Malcolm's career, however, was probably the time he spent at Cambridge University in 1938/1939, when he met G. E. Moore and Ludwig Wittgenstein. Although Moore exerted a strong influence on him, it is perhaps not unfair to say that most of Malcolm's published work has been an attempt to understand Wittgenstein, to explain his thought to others, and to apply Wittgenstein's characteristic manner of approaching philosophical questions to areas the latter did not directly treat.

Malcolm's published work deals especially with the nature of necessary truth; empirical certainty; the connections between common sense, ordinary language, and philosophy; knowledge and perception; and such topics in the philosophy of mind as memory, dreaming, and the problem of other minds. He has also written on topics in the philosophy of religion (see ONTOLOGICAL ARGUMENT FOR THE EXISTENCE OF GOD). What follows will be confined to the first three topics. (For a discussion of Malcolm's views on the other topics, see, for example, CRITERION, MEMORY, DREAMS, and OTHER MINDS.)

Necessary truth. "Are Necessary Propositions Really Verbal?" and its companion piece, "The Nature of Entailment" (in *Knowledge and Certainty*), together form an interesting statement of the linguistic theory of the a priori. In the former, Malcolm points out that some philosophers (for example, C. D. Broad, Moore, and A. C. Ewing) hold that necessary propositions state very general truths about

reality—for instance, that nothing is both red and green all over. Others (for example, A. J. Ayer and the early Wittgenstein) apparently believe that if necessary propositions state anything at all, they state truths about language; they are "merely verbal." Malcolm tries to show that, although it is false, literally speaking, that necessary propositions are merely verbal, there is nonetheless considerable merit in saying that they are. He argues this point by claiming that we learn necessary truths by observing how people use certain expressions. Finding out that a pair of propositions are equivalent, for example, is the same thing as finding out that some pairs of expressions are used interchangeably. What makes a given statement necessary is some empirical fact about linguistic usage. (Although Malcom considers the objection that on this account any necessary statement turns out to be identical with or equivalent to some contingent statement about linguistic expressions, he does not, it seems, have a clear answer to it.) Accordingly, he says, it is false that necessary statements are merely verbal or are rules of grammar or are not really propositions; it is nonetheless worthwhile to say these things in that they prevent one from supposing, for example, that there are two kinds of facts or truths, necessary and contingent, a supposition which is, literally speaking, true but nonetheless misleading. Why? Perhaps Malcolm believes that in saying this one minimizes the vast and important difference between necessary and contingent truths, the difference being that the necessary truths depend upon or reflect facts of linguistic usage in a way that the contingent truths do not.

Empirical certainty. In "The Verification Argument" and "Certainty and Empirical Statements" (in *Knowledge and Certainty*), Malcolm objects to the view that no empirical statements are ever really certain. "The Verification Argument" is a careful, clear, and very impressive examination of the arguments philosophers (in particular, C. I. Lewis, who was a teacher of Malcolm's at Harvard) have offered for this skeptical view. Where *S* is any empirical statement, Malcolm points out that these arguments always invoke as a premise the claim that the consequences of *S* may not occur and deduce from this that it is not certain that the consequences of *S* will occur. What Malcolm shows is that there is no interpretation of the former statement according to which it both is true and entails the latter.

Ordinary language. In several essays, Malcolm deals with certain questions about the relationships between ordinary language, common sense, and philosophy. Essentially, what he says is that if a philosopher is investigating a concept of ordinary language (for example, *seeing*) and comes to conclusions at variance with ordinary language, then we may be sure that he has made a mistake. What is it to come to a conclusion that goes against ordinary language? One way of doing this is to hold that a sentence with an ordinary use expresses a logical impossibility: some philosophers, for example, appear to insist that it is logically impossible to see physical objects. We may recognize their error by noting that such sentences as "I see the table in the corner" have a perfectly good ordinary use and therefore cannot be self-contradictory. But it is impossible to convey the full power of Malcolm's arguments without a very detailed consideration of particular cases.

Works by Malcolm

"Defending Common Sense." *Philosophical Review* (1949).
"Philosophy and Ordinary Language." *Philosophical Review* (1951).
"Dreaming and Skepticism." *Philosophical Review* (1956).
Ludwig Wittgenstein: A Memoir. Oxford, 1958.
Dreaming. London, 1959.
Knowledge and Certainty. Englewood Cliffs, N.J., 1963.
"Behaviorism as a Philosophy of Psychology," in T. W. Wann, ed., *Behaviorism and Phenomenology.* Chicago, 1964.
"Is It a Religious Belief That God Exists?" in John Hick, ed., *Faith and the Philosophers.* London, New York, and Toronto, 1964.
"Scientific Materialism and the Identity Theory." *Dialogue* (1964).

ALVIN PLANTINGA

MALEBRANCHE, NICOLAS (1638–1715), one of the principal figures in the development of Cartesianism, was born in Paris and received his formal intellectual training in philosophy and theology at the Collège de La Marche and at the Sorbonne. Having a religious vocation, he entered the congregation of the Oratory and was ordained in 1664. In the same year, he came upon Descartes's posthumously published *Traité de l'homme* ("Treatise on Man"), an early, unfinished work describing the mechanics of human physiology and indicating Descartes's distinction between soul and body. Deeply impressed, Malebranche applied himself to the study of Cartesian philosophy, mathematics, and natural science, reading, besides the works of Descartes, the writings of some of his followers, notably the occasionalist Géraud de Cordemoy's *Discernement du corps et de l'âme*. Cartesianism and the philosophy of Augustine were the dominant influences in the formation of his philosophy. Four years after his encounter with Cartesianism, he decided to put his thoughts in order with a view to publication. In 1674 and 1675 there appeared, in two volumes, his first and indeed his most important work, *De la Recherche de la vérité* ("Search after Truth").

Cartesian in inspiration, the *Recherche* contained a number of the master's views skillfully developed and solidly supported. Among them were the definition of matter as extension; the exclusion from nature of the scholastic apparatus of substantial forms, real qualities, powers, virtues, faculties, and the like; the requirement in physics that the behavior of bodies be explained in terms of the configuration and movement of their parts; the denial that in bodies there is anything like our sensations of color, sound, heat, etc.; and the assertion that, clearly conceived, a body is an extended thing that is capable of assuming various shapes and movements and is of a certain kind by virtue of the configuration of its parts. Malebranche also agreed with certain of Descartes's views about the soul, or mind. Animals are machines; in man there is a soul, or mind, distinct and separable from the body; awareness of mental states is immediate and infallible, perception of bodies indirect and problematic; and knowledge of the nature of things comes, not from sensation or imagination, but from clear and distinct ideas perceived by the understanding. And he also thought that the existence of God follows from man's cognizance of infinity.

Yet, while Descartes's influence on him was considerable, Malebranche differed with Descartes on major matters, and the *Recherche* showed independence of mind and great originality both in the exceedingly ingenious arguments on particular points and, generally, in the underlying conception—expressed in the words of Paul and presented as literal philosophic truth—that in God we live and move and have our being. This basic conception involved two important views. The first was the doctrine of vision in God, strikingly expressed in the chapter heading *Que nous voyons toutes choses en Dieu* ("That we see all things in God"). According to this doctrine, we see in the intelligible world of the divine reason not only eternal and immutable essences but—in a certain sense and with certain qualifications—created and changing corporeal things as well.

The second view is occasionalism. Malebranche maintained that created things are in themselves causally inefficacious and that God is the sole true cause of change in the universe. Applied to human nature, this view was expressed in Malebranche's conception of man's dependence on God. It is God who creates us and conserves us from moment to moment and who alone acts on us and for us. Owing our existence and actions as well as our knowledge to God, we are truly united with him. The seemingly mystical notion of union with God is presented, both discursively and rigorously, as the deliverance of reason as well as of faith.

Controversy aroused by the *Recherche* and, five years later (1680), by his *Traité de la nature et de la grâce* ("Treatise of Nature and Grace") forced Malebranche to spend much of his life explaining and defending his views. The *Éclaircissements*, written to elucidate exceptionable points in the *Recherche*, showed his talent for philosophic argument. He examined and refuted objections and, in doing so, used the occasion to elaborate or revise some of his views; in particular, he developed his notion of intelligible extension, the archetype in God of the matter he created and the locus of man's ideas of extended things. After reworking his views in the light of critical reaction to them, he was able to present them in more concise and polished form, in 1683, in his *Méditations chrétiennes et métaphysiques* ("Meditations, Christian and Metaphysical"), and, in 1688, in his *Entretiens sur la métaphysique et sur la religion* (*Dialogues on Metaphysics and on Religion*). The *Dialogues on Metaphysics*, for which he has been called the French Plato, is the best introduction to his philosophy.

He was continually involved in polemics with, among others, Foucher, Le Valois (de la Ville), Fontenelle, Leibniz, Régis, and François Lamy. The most interesting and important polemic—and the most acrimonious and voluminous—was with that exceptionally keen critic, coauthor of the Port-Royal *Logic*, and philosophically talented Jansenist, Antoine Arnauld. Taking exception to Malebranche's theory of grace, Arnauld struck an opening blow, not directly at that theory, but at a fundamental thesis contained in the doctrine of vision in God—that knowledge of objects requires ideas that are independent of, and distinct from, the human mind and its perceptions. In his *Des Vrayes et des Fausses Idées* ("True and False Ideas," Cologne, 1683), Arnauld deemed chimerical the representative entities, or ideas distinct from perceptions, posited by Malebranche and offered an interesting explanation of how Malebranche and others, because of confusion in their notions of presence to the mind, came to think that knowledge of, so to speak, external objects requires representative entities to serve as surrogates. Later the controversy turned to its initiating cause, problems about grace, and to other matters of theological importance. The advantage of the last word went to Malebranche, who chose to reply to posthumously published letters of Arnauld's.

Malebranche was also involved in the controversy over the moon-illusion, arguing against Régis that the moon appears larger at the horizon than at the meridian because of the presence of intervening objects and the unreflective judgments (*jugements naturels*) we are led to make of its comparative distance and size. He was also attacked by Leibniz, who forced Malebranche to change his account of the laws of motion. Malebranche had at first adopted a modified version of Descartes's laws, but he came to acknowledge his mistakes. He did not, however, accept Leibniz' notion of an intrinsic force in created things; and Malebranche's occasionalism, as Leibniz realized, was incompatible with the doctrine of a pre-established harmony among substances that are inherently active.

In his later years Malebranche maintained his interest in the observation of natural phenomena, followed closely the development of the infinitesimal calculus, and worked out an explanation of color differences in terms of the frequency of vibrations. Theological controversies continued to occupy him. His views were not accepted by religious authorities: the *Traité de la nature et de la grâce* was on the Index in 1690 and the *Recherche* in 1709. Malebranche was even suspected of Spinozism, a suspicion generated in part by his view that we perceive intelligible extension in God. In the informative correspondence with Dourtous de Mairan, Malebranche spelled out his differences with Spinozism and, as in other places, dissociated himself from that abominated view. Although he was known as a *méditatif* and has been placed in the mystical tradition, he was very much a man of the intellectual world. His reputation was enormous, and his influence sufficient to give the term *malebranchiste* currency. His affect on posterity was, at least in one important instance, incongruous: Hume owed a great deal to Malebranche, as can be seen in his critique of the idea of power or necessary connection and in his celebrated failure to find a clear idea of the self.

Vision in God. The doctrine of vision in God was offered as the solution to a problem that arises about our knowledge of objects outside of us (*hors de nous, hors de l'âme*). Presenting the problem in the *Recherche*, Malebranche began by calling attention to, and expressing his agreement with, the accepted view that we do not perceive external objects (for instance, the sun) in themselves (*par eux-mêmes*). It is not likely, he added in a remark pounced upon by Arnauld, that the soul leaves the body and walks about in the heavens to look at the sun and the stars; on the contrary, there is of necessity something united with (*unie*) and present to the mind that exhibits these objects to it. The term "idea" (*idée*) was used for the immediate object of the mind; and in corroboration of the accepted view that objects themselves are invisible and that ideas

mediate our perception of them, he pointed out that we sometimes, as in fever, seem to see things that do not in fact exist. Though there is agreement that our perception of bodies is not immediate, there are differences of opinion about the origin and nature of the ideas we immediately perceive; and it is to this problem that Malebranche addressed himself. In the discussion that followed, he examined a number of theories and, by eliminating possible alternatives, supported his own view that the ideas we immediately perceive are the ideas, or archetypes, of objects in the mind of God.

Although the examples Malebranche used in stating the problem suggest that he was concerned about the nature of sense perception and, more particularly, the origination and status of sense data, to use a recent idiom, he in fact conceived the problem more generally. He was concerned not only about ideas of bodies present in sense perception but also about ideas needed, he believed, to imagine or think about bodies; and he was as much concerned about ideas of extended things in general (the idea of a triangle, for instance) as he was about ideas of particular bodies. In regard to sense perception, moreover, the problem was, in a certain respect, settled for him in advance. Having argued earlier in the *Recherche* that colors, sounds, heat, and the like are confused feelings and modifications of the soul, he took it for granted in the discussion of vision in God that these sensations cannot do the job of representing the bodies ostensibly causing them. In addition to sensation, there must be a representation. And he assumed that the representations of bodies are ideas of them as they really are, that is, ideas of them as extended things. Strictly speaking, in Malebranche's view, there cannot be ideas of colors; and in perception, the idea, though tinged, as it were, is intrinsically an idea of a geometrical solid, or portion of space.

In his survey of existing theories, he first took up the view, imputed to the Scholastics, that bodies emit species, or likenesses of themselves, which, transmitted through the intervening atmosphere and acted upon by various faculties of the soul, are the sources of ideas. As a true Cartesian, he found this theory unintelligible, noting—with evident relish—the problems involved in the emission and transmission of the hypothetical species. Would they not, for instance, collide and shatter? And would they not deplete the bodies supposed to be continuously emitting them? More serious attention was paid to the theory that the mind forms its own ideas. In one version of the theory, an impression in the brain activates a faculty of the mind, which produces an idea of the object perceived; and in imagination and abstract thought the mind presumably forms ideas at will. Against this theory, he used two arguments of signal importance to his proof of vision in God.

(1) Ideas of objects differ and have distinctive properties, an idea, say, of a circle having properties distinguishing it from an idea of a square. Since what has properties cannot be nothing, ideas are real beings (*êtres-réels*). Hence, to form an idea, the mind would have to bring into existence, or create, a real being. Although some ideas could perhaps be formed out of others, not all of them could; and at least some of them would have to be created *ex nihilo*. It is of no help, he added, to suppose that the mind forms these ideas

out of impressions in the brain; for an idea, admittedly not a corporeal but a spiritual thing (*chose spirituelle*), cannot be formed out of what is material. Since it is absurd to attribute to the mind God's power of creation *ex nihilo*, it is taken to follow by a *reductio* that the mind is not the originating cause of ideas.

(2) In order to represent or form an idea of an object, the mind must know what it is to represent. It cannot, so to speak, work in the dark, and there must be a model on which to base its representation. Objects themselves (including brain impressions) are invisible; so the model would have to be an idea of the object to be represented. But then, in order to form an idea of an object, the mind must already *have* an idea of the object. The putative formation of an idea of the object would be a pointless duplication of a pre-existing idea; and it follows by a regress argument that forming an idea of an object is impossible.

Having shown that ideas are, in the Cartesian vocabulary, neither adventitious nor factitious, Malebranche also dealt with the possibility that they are innate and created with the mind, as part of its equipment (*innées ou créés avec nous*). The following is an incomplete list of his reasons for rejecting a theory of innate ideas. (*a*) We are able to think of an indefinite number of triangles simply by varying the altitude on the base of any given triangle, and we can think of an infinite variety of geometrical figures, each admitting of infinite variations. To suppose that an infinity of infinite numbers of ideas (*infinité de nombres infinis*) are, as it were, stored in the mind is, at least, implausible. There is also a difficulty for the storehouse model in our apprehension of space as infinite. (*b*) How would the mind know which idea to select from the storehouse to represent an object? To select an idea requires having the idea, and again a regress threatens. (*c*) It is simpler and more in harmony with the divine economy to suppose that there is one set of ideas common to all minds, rather than many sets of ideas created with, and private to, individual minds. (*d*) The hypothesis of one set of ideas common to all minds accounts for the universality of knowledge, as seen in the fact, for instance, that the Chinese have the same arithmetic and geometry as Europeans. (*e*) On the assumption that the ideas we consult are in us, there are problems about the necessity of truths like "2+2=4"; for it seems that our ideas might have been other than they are and that there is at best a *de facto* relation to truth. Malebranche, in his account of necessary truths, rejected Descartes's view that they are created by God and, in line with this, denied that our perceptions of them need to be certified by God. From these critical considerations it is a relatively easy step to the conclusion that the ideas we immediately perceive—real beings, uncreated by bodies, minds, or God and exhibiting what is essential and also universal and necessary in our awareness of nature—are to be identified with the ideas, or archetypes, that God used in creating the world. Expressed in another way, the conclusion is that we see all things in God.

Several implications and qualifications of the conclusion warrant attention. (1) It clearly follows that we see the changing and corruptible as well as the eternal and immutable in God. And it also seems to follow, as an unwelcome consequence, that the intelligible world of the divine reason contains individual, intelligible duplicates of all the particular things, or at least the kinds of things, that God created. In the tenth *Eclaircissement* and in the polemic with Arnauld, Malebranche dealt with this problem. Introducing his notion of intelligible extension, he rejected the seeming implication that in the divine reason there are individual and separate ideas of particular bodies or kinds of bodies. Ideal, or intelligible, extension is said to be the archetype of all bodies. Undifferentiated in the divine reason, yet capable of representing any actual or possible extended thing, it is limited or determined by God to represent certain bodies; and applied to the human mind, determinations of it are seen as ideas, say, of the triangle in general and also of particular bodies.

(2) Strictly speaking, we do not see *all* things in God, notable exceptions being the self and God. According to Malebranche's account of the soul, or mind, neither its nature nor its modifications are known by way of ideas. Rejecting Descartes's view that we have a clear idea of the nature, or essence, of the mind, he maintained that although there is an archetype of the soul in the divine reason, we, in this life, cannot perceive it. Our awareness of the mind is limited to internal sensation (*sentiment intérieur*) or immediate consciousness (*conscience, sans idées*) of its particular states or modifications.

Nor are we aware of God by means of an idea in a strict sense of the term, that is, by way of a representation of him. An idea (in the strict sense) is an idea of a certain being, that is, of one being rather than another, and involves a limitation. Hence, there cannot be an idea (in this sense) of unlimited being, or of God. Yet a variant of Descartes's proofs of the existence of God is possible. Since we can think of God, or infinite, unlimited being, but cannot have an idea of him, we must be directly aware of him when we think of him, and so he must exist. As Malebranche stated the argument: if we think of the infinite, it must exist. According to his view, then, our vision of God, although very imperfect, is immediate and direct (*vûe immédiate & directe*); and while we see bodies in him by way of ideas, we see him, although imperfectly, in himself (*par lui-même*).

(3) Granted that we do not see bodies directly and that we live in an intelligible world of ideas, what need is there for, and what assures us of the existence of, an actually created, real corporeal world? Effectively demolishing Descartes's attempted proof in the sixth *Meditation*, Malebranche argued in general against the possibility of any strict demonstration on the grounds that in a strict demonstration of existence there must be a necessary connection between cause and supposed effect, whereas the world is not a necessary emanation from the Deity. Although the existence of a corporeal world is, from the viewpoint of reason, dubitable and indemonstrable, revelation through Scripture provides proof of its creation; and our sensations are natural revelations, giving us moral assurance of the existence of particular bodies. Berkeley was greatly indebted to Malebranche's negative teachings on this question.

Occasionalism. The occasionalist view of causation that Malebranche presented is not, as is sometimes supposed, a special theory dealing exclusively with, or devised *ad hoc* to explain, relations between mind and body, but a general view about relations between bodies as well as between minds and bodies. Neither was the view original with Malebranche, though he presented it with a fuller realization of its generality and consequences and in a distinctive setting, as part of his theocentric conception of God's relation to man and the universe. According to Malebranche, the notion that there are powers or faculties in bodies which produce the ostensible effects of bodies is the most dangerous error in the philosophy of antiquity. Believing that bodies have the power of affecting us, we come to love and fear them rather than the true cause of our well-being. And in philosophy we remain ignorant of the true principle of change in bodies: the movement of their parts in accordance with laws of motion established and administered by God.

But even in more enlightened views of nature, it is supposed that there is a power or force in bodies accounting for their motion. Against this supposition, Malebranche argued, in a manner to be followed by Hume, that we lack a clear idea of the supposed power or force in bodies. From an examination of an idea of a body, we cannot determine under what circumstances it will move or in what way it will move other bodies; and though we have experience of uniformities in the motion of bodies, we observe only a constant conjunction of events and not a necessary connection (*rapport, liaison nécessaire*) between them. Moreover, the lack of intrinsic power or force in bodies can be shown to follow from their dependence on God. If a body depends on God for its existence, it must not only be created by him but be conserved by him from moment to moment; that is, God must will not only that it come into existence but also that it continue to exist. When he wills that it continue to exist, he must will that it exist either in the same place at successive moments, that is, be at rest, or in different places at successive moments, that is, be in motion. Since nothing can move a body that God wills to be at rest or impede or alter the movement of a body that he wills to be in motion, bodies themselves are inefficacious; and since there is a necessary connection between the volition of an omnipotent being and the execution of that volition, God is the true cause of motion in bodies, and the action of his will is their moving force. Accordingly, when one ball strikes a second ball and the second ball moves, God is the real or true cause (*cause réelle, véritable*) of the second ball's moving. Since he acts, not at random, but in accordance with general laws of motion that he has enacted, the impact of the first ball may be called the occasional, or particular, cause (*cause occasionnelle, particulière*) of the second ball's moving.

Granted that bodies are inefficacious, it is true a fortiori that they cannot produce changes in the mind. And God being the true cause of movements in bodies, it follows that the mind cannot produce changes in the body. But since we are strongly inclined to suppose that the mind, especially in movements we call voluntary, does produce changes in the body, Malebranche offered additional considerations to show that the mind cannot be the true cause of these movements. (1) If a person were the true cause, say, of the movement of his arm, he would have to know how to produce this movement; and since movement of the animal spirits in his brain is necessary for the movement of his arm, he would have to know how to move the animal spirits in his brain. But jugglers, for example, move their arms with great agility, while in ignorance of physiology. And it is clear that we do not know how to bring about the movements prerequisite to the arm's moving. (2) Although we may think we have the power of acting on the body because our volitions are usually followed by the movements willed or because we have a feeling of effort in our volitions, there is no intrinsic relation between a volition or a feeling of effort and the movement accompanying it. We may, for instance, exert ourselves to do something without success, and it is possible that God might have conjoined to our volitions effects contrary to them. As it is, God acts according to laws connecting mental events and cerebral events in such a way that, if the body is suitably disposed, our volitions are executed.

Not only does the mind lack true power over the body and the material world, but also, being unable to form ideas of objects, it is not the true cause of its perceptions of ideas in the intelligible world. Since we are dependent on God in both action and thought, a question arises about the will and the possibility of freedom of the will. Malebranche conceived of the will as a movement caused by God toward the good-in-general (*le bien en général*) and determined in various ways toward particular objects. Movement toward the good-in-general is absolutely invincible, as is evident in the fact, Malebranche held, that we cannot will to be unhappy or desire something that does not appear to us to be a good. Determinations of the will, occasioned by sensations and thoughts, are not absolutely invincible. Although we do not initiate particular inclinations, we are immediately aware, by *sentiment intérieur*, of our power to refuse consent. And freedom in this sense is manifested even in our acceptance of grace.

Bibliography

An authoritative edition of Malebranche's complete works is in progress, under the direction of André Robinet, *Oeuvres complètes de Malebranche* (Paris, 1958——), scheduled for completion in 1965. (An asterisk indicates that the volume appeared prior to 1965.) Vols. 1*, 2*, and 3* contain *De la Recherche de la vérité* (1st ed., 1674–1675) and *Éclaircissements* (1678); Vol. 4*, *Conversations chrétiennes* (1677); Vol. 5*, *Traité de la nature et de la grâce* (1680); Vols. 6–9, replies to Arnauld (1684–1709); Vol. 10*, *Méditations chrétiennes et métaphysiques* (1683); Vol. 11, *Traité de morale* (1684); Vols. 12–13, *Entretiens sur la métaphysique et sur la religion* (1688) and *Entretiens sur la mort* (1696); Vol. 14*, *Traité de l'amour de Dieu* (1697) and letters to Lamy; Vol. 15*, *Entretien d'un philosophe chrétien et d'un philosophe chinois* (1708); Vol. 16*, *Réflexions sur la prémotion physique* (1715); Vols. 17-1*, 17-2, 18*, 19*, and 20, diverse writings, correspondence, and biographical and bibliographical material. A commonly used edition, *Oeuvres de Malebranche*, edited by Jules Simon (Paris, 1884), contains major works. *Entretiens sur la métaphysique et sur la religion* has been translated by Morris Ginsberg as *Dialogues on Metaphysics and on Religion* (London, 1923).

Y. M. André's biography, *La Vie du R. P. Malebranche*, written shortly after Malebranche's death, was first published in the *Bibliothèque Oratorienne* (Paris, 1886).

For material on Malebranche, see Pierre Blanchard, *L'Attention à Dieu selon Malebranche* (Paris, 1956), and L. Bridet, *La Théorie de la connaissance dans la philosophie de Malebranche* (Paris,

1929). Ralph Withington Church, *A Study in the Philosophy of Malebranche* (London, 1931), a critical study, contains an analysis of the controversy with Arnauld on the nature of ideas. See also Armand Cuvillier, *Essai sur la mystique de Malebranche* (Paris, 1954), and Victor Delbos, *Étude de la philosophie de Malebranche* (Paris, 1924). Ginette Dreyfus, *La Volonté selon Malebranche* (Paris, 1958), is an interesting interpretation based on Malebranche's conception of the will, divine and human. Henri Gouhier, *La Philosophie de Malebranche* (Paris, 1926 and 1948), is a masterful work on the theme of Malebranche's *philosophie chrétienne*. Gouhier's *La Vocation de Malebranche* (Paris, 1926) is extremely important, assessing Cartesian and Oratorian influences and examining Malebranche's view about the relation of faith and reason. Martial Gueroult's *Malebranche* (Paris, 1955–1959) is an exceedingly interesting, comprehensive, and detailed account in three volumes. Also by Gueroult is *Étendue et psychologie chez Malebranche* (Paris, 1939).

Other studies of Malebranche include: Henri Joly, *Malebranche* (Paris, 1901); Lucien Labbas, *La Grâce et la liberté dans Malebranche* (Paris, 1931); Lucien Labbas, *L'Idée de science dans Malebranche* (Paris, 1931); A. Le Moine, *Des Vérités éternelles selon Malebranche* (Paris, 1936); Léon Ollé-Laprune, *La Philosophie de Malebranche*, 2 vols. (Paris, 1870), the monumental work of the nineteenth century; Geneviève Rodis-Lewis, *Nicolas Malebranche* (Paris, 1963), the best introduction and general account; Beatrice K. Rome, *The Philosophy of Malebranche* (Chicago, 1963), a disputatious reinterpretation of Malebranche's occasionalism and theory of perception in view of his conception of method; and Joseph Viderain, *Le Christianisme dans la philosophie de Malebranche* (Paris, 1923).

For the relations of the views of Malebranche to those of Spinoza, Leibniz, Locke, Berkeley, and Hume, see *Correspondance avec J.-J. Dourtous de Mairan*, edited with an introduction, "Malebranche et le Spinozisme," by Joseph Moreau (Paris, 1947); P. Mouy, *Les Lois du choc des corps d'après Malebranche* (Paris, 1927); *Malebranche et Leibniz*, the relevant texts, edited and introduced by André Robinet (Paris, 1955); John Locke, "An examination of P. Malebranche's opinion of seeing all things in God," in his *Philosophical Works*, J. A. St. John, ed. (London, 1872), Vol. II; Arthur Aston Luce, *Berkeley and Malebranche* (London, 1934); and R. W. Church, "Malebranche and Hume," in *Revue internationale de philosophie*, Vol. 1, No. 1 (1938), 143–161.

WILLIS DONEY

MALRAUX, GEORGES-ANDRÉ, French author, critic, revolutionist, and statesman, was born in Paris in 1901 of a well-to-do family. He studied at the Lycée Condorcet and the Institut des Langues Orientales and early in life developed an enduring interest in archaeology, art, and Oriental languages and thought. His life and writing have been characterized by a restless, questioning, quasi-apocalyptic intensity that is fully understandable only in terms of the crisis with which Western thought was confronted in the first half of the twentieth century: at grips with a fast-accumulating mass of new knowledge, Western civilization was seeking to adjust to the violent changes that had disrupted its former social, intellectual, and spiritual framework of values.

In 1923 Malraux went on an archaeological expedition into the Cambodian jungle, and soon afterward he returned to the Orient to participate in the revolutionary struggle that was transforming the Asiatic world. He seems at the time to have been in sympathy with the Marxist ideology. *La Tentation de l'occident* (Paris, 1926), his first serious work, is a fictional dialogue between a Chinese and a European intellectual and shows how decisive was his first encounter with the Orient. It intensified Malraux's self-styled obsession with the notions of civilization and

culture. He has always been vitally concerned with the problems of the life and death of civilizations; the specificity, irreducibility, and relativity of all cultures; their determining action in shaping the mental structures of individuals; and the bearing on his own cultural world of the observations and conclusions of historians and anthropologists such as Oswald Spengler and Leo Frobenius. This initial obsession was nourished and substantiated by Malraux's legendary familiarity with all realms of art (painting and sculpture in particular); his avid and exceptionally broad grasp of literature; and his addiction to passionate debate with leading personalities in Europe and the Orient. Although his thought is always concentrated on a present unremittingly interrogated, it develops within vast perspectives both in time and space.

In the late 1920s Malraux, as art editor for the Gallimard publishing firm in Paris, traveled widely in search of art treasures, while actively participating in the unavailing struggle of the European intellectuals against fascism, Nazism, and anti-Semitism. He later commanded a group of aviators for the Republican forces in the Spanish Civil War, was active in the French resistance after 1940, and became, first, minister of information, then minister of cultural affairs, in the cabinet of General de Gaulle.

He was deliberately "committed" as a writer for intellectual reasons. Western science, he claimed, offers a set of relationships that define the cosmos but, by omitting the observer, it presents a cosmos in which man has no place. According to Malraux, psychoanalysis has revealed the blind, destructive forces at work within the self and has put into question the very notion of a fundamental human personality. To recover some concept of man, Malraux maintained that one must once again examine what man does, thereby redefining his powers. The image of the rational, detached observer—scientist or philosopher—placed outside the world he observes must therefore give way to the participant who is, as it were, a knot of relations with the world. Malraux has often reiterated that man "is what he does." Participation therefore was the first and necessary stage in his search for definition.

The elucidation of an action is the theme of his novels. All revolve around the question, "What can a man best do with his life?"; all are animated by the same answer that is given in *Man's Hope*: "Transform into consciousness an experience as broad as possible." Writing is the medium through which this transformation takes place; hence the intensity of the process, the inner questioning, and the many-faceted debate that it embodies. His six widely read novels all are wrenched from stages of his own experience: *Les Conquérants* (Paris, 1928); *La Voie royale* (Paris, 1930); *La Condition humaine* (Paris, 1933); *Le Temps du mépris* (Paris, 1935); *L'Espoir* (Paris, 1937); and *Les Noyers de l'Altenburg* (Lausanne, 1943), the first volume of a two-part novel whose second part was destroyed by the Nazis. These were followed by an impressive series of works on art: *Goya* (Geneva, 1947); *La Psychologie de l'art* (3 vols., Geneva, 1947, 1949, 1950); *Le Musée imaginaire de la sculpture mondiale* (3 vols., Paris, 1952, 1953, 1954); *Les Voix du silence* (Paris, 1953); and *La Métamorphose des dieux* (Paris, 1960). A number of reviews, prefaces, and speeches add to this abundant corpus of work.

Despite both the variety of his media and the obscurities

inherent in his manner of writing, there is a remarkable degree of consistency and lucidity in Malraux's thought, questionable though many of his assumptions and examples may be. He posits as premise the definitive disappearance from Western civilization of the structure of values established by the Christian *Weltanschauung*. Western man is thus left face to face with a cosmos to which he cannot relate. However, he is still in possession of the inner drive that, since the Greeks, has structured his world—the need to create a coherent, intelligible image of man's fate that gives significance to each individual life. Hence the double burden of lucidity and anguish characteristic of our time, hence its "temptations." The most prevalent is the nihilism whereby Western man, living in a state of "metaphysical distraction," renounces his drive toward lucidity and submits to blind necessity and to natural and social conditioning. This, according to Malraux, is an intolerable reversion to the "demons," that is, to the blind animal instinct within us. Malraux also examined and partially rejected the Oriental resorption of the individual into the cosmos (considered as divine). In preference to the Oriental view, he sought to define man's power in his capacity to "leave a scar on the planet," to transform his environment. For a while he understood the process in terms of the Marxist theory of history.

Malraux's final view emerged from his meditations on art. It is a complex outlook related to the study of art styles and their migrations and metamorphoses, an approach that is characteristic of such art historians as Élie Faure and Henri Focillon. In brief, for Malraux a new planetary civilization that has destroyed all significant cultures is now in the making. The structures of values whereby each individual within a human society relates to the cosmos, to the community, and to his own actions now exist only as "relativized absolutes." This is the first agnostic civilization, the first that does not relate to some form of the divine. It also presents a new phenomenon, the "imaginary museum," in which all works of art—whatever their origin—are available, to be perceived as significant in themselves and not for what they once signified. For Malraux this universal presence and significance testifies to a fundamental power of mankind: the power to dominate and transcend fate and to create a universe in some way accessible to all men, who are thereby freed from time, death, and blind necessity. The privileged potential image of mankind, therefore, that Malraux detects as indicative of our present orientation is that of man as creator and as forger of his own freedom. Malraux has thus formulated in new terms the age-old problem of freedom and destiny, to serve as the foundation for a new ethic. His work is fundamentally relevant in an age that is deeply preoccupied with the working of the mind, considered on one hand as a form of conditioned mechanism and on the other as a principle of free activity, order, and meaning.

Works by Malraux

The works listed below are English editions of Malraux's works in the order in which they appear in the text.
The Temptation of the West, translated with an introduction by Robert Hollander. New York, 1961.
The Conquerors, translated by W. S. Whale. New York, 1929.
The Royal Way, translated by Stuart Gilbert. New York, 1935.

Man's Fate, translated by Haakon Chevalier. New York, 1934.
Days of Wrath, translated by Haakon Chevalier. New York, 1934.
Man's Hope, translated by Stuart Gilbert and Alistair MacDonald. New York, 1938.
The Walnut Trees of Altenburg, translated by A. W. Fielding. London, 1952.
Saturn: An Essay on Goya, translated by C. W. Chilton. London, 1957.
The Psychology of Art, translated by Stuart Gilbert. Vol. I, *Museum Without Walls;* Vol. II, *The Creative Act.* New York, 1949–1951.
The Voices of Silence, translated by Stuart Gilbert. New York, 1953.
The Metamorphosis of the Gods, translated by Stuart Gilbert. New York, 1960.

Works on Malraux

Blend, Charles, *André Malraux: Tragic Humanist.* Columbus, Ohio, 1963. A biography and general critical study, with a bibliography of Malraux's work and a brief critical bibliography.
Frohock, Wilbur, *André Malraux and the Tragic Imagination.* Stanford, Calif., 1952. A basic work.
Lewis, R. W. B., ed., *Malraux.* Englewood Cliffs, N.J., 1964. A collection of critical essays.
Vandergars, André, *La Jeunesse littéraire d'André Malraux.* Pauvert, 1964. Contains a wealth of information on Malraux's Indochinese activities.

GERMAINE BRÉE

MALTHUS, THOMAS ROBERT (1776–1834), English economist and moral philosopher, is most famous for his contributions to population studies. In his *Principles of Political Economy* (1820) and in his controversies with David Ricardo, Malthus seems partly to have anticipated J. M. Keynes; and Keynes himself, in his *Essays in Biography,* generously remarked that "if only Malthus, instead of Ricardo, had been the parent stem from which nineteenth century economics proceeded, what a much wiser and richer place the world would be today!"

Malthus' work on population is contained in two books, misleadingly presented as if they were merely different editions of one. The first, best referred to as the *First Essay,* is actually titled *An Essay on the Principle of Population as It Affects the Future Improvement of Society, with Remarks on the Speculations of Mr. Godwin, M. Condorcet, and Other Writers.* The second, best thought of as the *Second Essay,* was, with some reserve, offered by Malthus as a much extended second edition. But it was retitled *An Essay on the Principle of Population, or a View of Its Past and Present Effects on Human Happiness with an Inquiry Into Our Prospects Respecting the Future Removal or Mitigation of the Evils Which It Occasions.* The *First Essay* is an occasional polemic against utopianism; the *Second,* a labored treatise full of detailed factual material. What they have in common is the same guiding and coordinating theoretical schema, although even this is in one respect importantly amended in the later book.

The fundamental principle is that unfreakish human populations possess a power of multiplying in a geometrical progression. The next step is to urge that this power always is and must be checked by countervailing forces; for, on the most optimistic supposition, means of subsistence could in the long run at best be increased only in an arithmetical progression. (The subsistence of checks could, of course, be inferred without recourse to this misleadingly arithmetized supposition, by referring directly to the fact that no human population ever does achieve its full multiplicative potential.) The questions then arise, What are these checks? what ought they to be?

Checks are classified in two different ways. First, they can be positive or preventive: the former by the time of the *Second Essay* being all causes of (premature) death; and the latter, correspondingly, all checks on the birth rate. The second classification is strongly normative: in the *First Essay* all checks must count as either misery or vice; but in the *Second Essay* a third option, moral restraint, is added. This is defined as "the restraint from marriage which is not followed by irregular gratifications." Malthus seems never to have entertained the possibility of restraint within marriage; and he categorically rejected any form of contraception, even within wedlock, as vice.

This scheme of ideas constituted an intellectual engine that was immensely powerful both for its primary purpose of confounding utopian optimism and for its secondary function of guiding social inquiry. We also have clear statements from both Charles Darwin and Alfred Russel Wallace that it was reading Malthus on population which independently led each to see the clue to the problem of the origin of species in natural selection through "a struggle for existence," a phrase used by Malthus himself. Against the utopians the argument was that our inordinate animal power of multiplication is bound—sooner or later, and usually sooner—to run up against the inexorably constricting walls of scarcity. All measures of intended amelioration which directly or indirectly encourage an increase of population that outstrips resources—and most do—will, in the not very distant end, merely multiply the number of bearers of misery and agents of vice. These harsh and gloomy conclusions were only modified, not upset, by the belated recognition of the option of moral restraint. For it was, and remains, hard to cherish high hopes from the preaching of such prudence; and in any society which did generally accept such preaching all but the richest would have to marry women nearing the evening of their reproductive powers.

It is, therefore, not surprising that generations of idealists hoping to reshape the present sorry scheme of things nearer to their heart's desire have released torrents of argument and abuse at "Parson Malthus" and his ideas. Yet, despite the apparent implication of his system—that God has placed mankind in a situation offering little promise of secure improvement—it would be wrong to assume that Malthus as a man or as a thinker was either insensitive or harsh. Compared with the optimistic utopians of his father's reading and acquaintance he could not but appear a jarring pessimist. But this was a matter of facing what he took to be the sober facts of the human condition, not of callous indifference to the relief of man's estate. To quote Keynes again, his work is really in "the tradition which is suggested by the names of Locke, Hume, Adam Smith, Paley, Bentham, Darwin and Mill, a tradition marked . . . by a prosaic sanity . . . and by an immense disinterestedness and public spirit." As against, say, Condorcet, who wrote of inevitable progress while under the shadow of the guillotine, Malthus was concerned first with finding what the facts are and then with discovering how,

in the light of those perhaps recalcitrant facts, we are to do the best we can. It is no accident that in the first chapter of the *First Essay* he acknowledges a debt to Hume and Adam Smith but not to the impossible and visionary Rousseau, whom his father had known and admired.

Theodicy. The same intellectual associations are seen in his theodicy. William Paley was one of the early converts to Malthus on population, and appropriately, Paley was one of Malthus' favorite theologians. So Malthus insists in the *First Essay* that "Evil exists in the world not to create despair but activity." (It was from this part of the work that Darwin and Wallace most directly derived the idea of a necessary struggle for existence.) What Malthus may have acquired from the dissenting Christians and Unitarians of his father's circle is a note of theological radicalism, a note not caught either by the hostile conventional left, represented then by Cobbett and Hazlitt, or by such sentimental conservative opponents as Coleridge and Southey. In the theodicy of the last chapter of the *First Essay* Malthus boldly steps away from Paley and from the whole tradition of Christian orthodoxy by insisting that "it is perfectly impossible to conceive that any . . . creatures of God's hand can be condemned to eternal suffering. Could we once admit such an idea, all our natural conceptions of goodness and justice would be completely overthrown, and we could no longer look on God as a merciful and righteous Being." (Malthus settles his own account with Christianity by accepting the Hobbist interpretation; that eternal death means eternal death and not eternal life in torment. The "doctrine of life and immortality which was brought to light by the gospel" is "the doctrine that the end of righteousness is everlasting life, but that the wages of sin are death." This plausible reading had been unanimously rejected by the orthodox Saints and Fathers, doubtless as being unacceptably merciful.)

Critique of population theory. As a heuristic and explanatory scheme, the population theory resembles bits of classical physics, although it might also be usefully compared with that of Darwinism. The fundamental principle is like the first law of motion in that both describe not what does go on but what would go on if there were no counteracting forces; and in both cases the main theoretical function of the basic law is to generate questions about such forces and checks. Again, Malthus in classifying checks always aims at complete, exhaustive lists; and his arguments often depend on his appreciation that the values of the various checks considered as variables will be, for a given population, inversely connected: the bigger the sum of the preventive checks, the smaller the sum of the positive checks; and so on. These are similarities of which Malthus himself—thanks to his mathematical training at Cambridge—seems to have been aware. (It is doubtless to the same training that we owe his introduction of the supposition of the arithmetical progression to which, and to the consequent comparison of the two progressions, is due much of the appearance of "mathematical certainty" in his demonstrations.)

Malthus never tied up all the various minor logical loose ends in his original conceptual scheme, although he added important appendices to the third and fifth editions of his work in 1806 and 1817 and wrote the article "Population" for the 1824 supplement to the *Encyclopaedia Britannica* (revised and published separately as his last word in 1830). But the main objections to Malthus that emerged from the enormous controversy are two, one moral and one logical. The moral objection repudiates Malthus' total rejection of contraception. It is this repudiation, combined with acceptance of Malthus' warnings on the dangers of overpopulation, which makes a Neo-Malthusian. The suggestion sometimes heard that the spread of contraception has made Malthusian ideas obsolete should be seen as manifestly absurd. Contraception is one kind of preventive check; none at all would be required if the multiplicative power was not still there to be checked.

The second objection insists on a distinction, which Malthus was forever inclined to overlook, between two senses of *tendency*. A tendency to produce something may be a cause which, operating unimpeded, would produce it. But to speak of a tendency to produce something may also be to say that the result is one which may reasonably be expected to occur in fact. This point seems to have been put against Malthus for the first time by Nassau Senior in his *Two Lectures on Population* (1831) and was grudgingly accepted. It was developed in the following year by Archbishop Whateley in *Lectures on Political Economy* (ninth lecture).

If both these objections are accepted, it becomes possible to recognize the Malthusian menace but to insist that the tendency to catastrophe does not have to be a tendency in the second sense—not if people can be persuaded to employ the means which science has and will put into our hands. Yet Malthus must have the last word. For it was he who most dramatically and powerfully drew attention to an absolutely vital fact, a fact which is still persistently and often disastrously ignored. It is, in the words of Senior, that "no plan for social improvement can be complete, unless it embraces the means both of increasing production, and of preventing population making a proportionate advance."

Works by Malthus

An Essay on the Principle of Population as It Affects the Future Improvement of Society, with Remarks on the Speculations of Mr. Godwin, M. Condorcet, and Other Writers. London, 1798. Facsimile edition (London, 1926); paperback edition with introduction by K. E. Boulding (Ann Arbor, Mich., 1959).

An Essay on the Principle of Population, or a View of Its Past and Present Effects on Human Happiness, with an Inquiry Into Our Prospects Respecting the Future Removal or Mitigation of the Evils Which It Occasions. London, 1803. There is an Everyman Library edition (London and New York); the version now in print has an introduction by M. P. Fogarty.

Glass, D. V., ed., *Introduction to Malthus.* London, 1953. Includes discussion by Glass and others and an appendix of two things by Malthus.

Works on Malthus

Bonar, J., *Malthus and His Work,* 2d ed. London, 1924.

Flew, Antony, "The Structure of Malthus' Population Theory," in B. Baumrin, ed., *Philosophy of Science: The Delaware Seminar,* Vol. I. New York, 1963.

Keynes, J. M., "Robert Malthus: The First of the Cambridge Economists," in *Essays and Sketches in Biography.* London, 1951.

Levin, S. M., "Malthus and the Idea of Progress." *Journal of the History of Ideas,* Vol. 27, No. 1 (1966), 92–108.

Senior, Nassau William, *Two Lectures on Population.* London, 1831.

Whateley, Richard, *Lectures on Political Economy.* London, 1832.

ANTONY FLEW

MANDEVILLE, BERNARD (c. 1670–1733), physician and moralist, was probably born in Rotterdam, Holland, where he was baptized on November 20, 1670. His family was a distinguished one, his father, grandfather, and great-grandfather having been noted physicians. The family name was originally de Mandeville, but Mandeville dropped the "de" in later life. He was educated at the Erasmian School in Rotterdam and then attended the University of Leiden, where he studied philosophy and medicine. He was granted the degree of doctor of medicine in 1691. His medical specialty was the treatment of nerve and stomach disorders, or, as he called them, the "hypochondriack and hysterick passions." Dr. Johnson is said to have had a high regard for a treatise Mandeville wrote on these diseases.

A short time after taking his degree Mandeville visited London to learn English, and liking the country and the people, he chose to settle in England. Little is known about his English life beyond the bare facts that he married, that he had a son and a daughter, that he practiced medicine, and that he apparently had plenty of time for writing. His success as a writer is all the more remarkable when one remembers that English was his adopted language. His best-known work is *The Fable of the Bees,* with its slogan "private vices, public benefits." It called forth a number of replies from the outraged defenders of virtue, including Berkeley in the *Alciphron* and Francis Hutcheson. The book was a regular source of public and private controversy in the eighteenth century. The notoriety that this work gained Mandeville doubtless explains why no very consistent account of his situation and character has come down to us from his contemporaries. But Benjamin Franklin, who once met Mandeville, reported that he was "a most facetious and entertaining companion." Mandeville died at Hackney in England.

The Fable of the Bees was 24 years in the making. It began as a poem of 433 lines called "The Grumbling Hive: Or, Knaves Turn'd Honest" (London, 1705). The many bitter attacks on the poem caused Mandeville to produce several expositions, elaborations, and defenses of it, all of which grew, over the years, into the book *The Fable of the Bees; Or Private Vices, Public Benefits.* In its final form, the sixth edition (1729), the *Fable* consists of two parts. Part I is the original poem followed by several essays: (1) "An Enquiry Into the Origin of Moral Virtue," consisting of 22 remarks on various lines or words in the poem, such as luxury, pride, and so on; (2) "An Essay on Charity and Charity Schools"; (3) "A Search into the Nature of Society"; and (4) "A Vindication of the Book" against a presentment of the grand jury of Middlesex and other abuse. Part II, which is as long as the first part, consists of six dialogues in which Cleomenes instructs Horatio in the true meaning of the *Fable.*

As might be expected in a book that was put together over a long period of time and whose later parts are a defense of the earlier, Mandeville's targets are several, and assessing the relative importance of his ideas is not easy. His economic doctrines are certainly more thoroughly worked out than his moral theories, and he wanted politicians to take his economic views seriously. Given that a politician desires the nation he governs to be great and wealthy and given that there is a large population to be kept in employment, then a certain kind of economic life must be permitted and even fostered. The production of necessities will neither employ very many people nor by itself make a nation great. Therefore, the production of luxuries must be permitted, and their consumption on the most lavish scale possible encouraged, thus simultaneously achieving splendor and full employment. Mandeville analyzes the making of hooped and quilted petticoats in order to show not only the opportunities for labor which the manufacture of this luxury provides in itself, but also the subsidiary employments (shipwright, sailor, dye-finder, and so on) which that fashion calls into being.

In "An Essay on Charity and Charity Schools" Mandeville gives some hint of the structure of the society that is required to produce a great and wealthy nation. In this essay, he opposes educating the poor on the grounds that knowledge enlarges and multiplies our desires and that the fewer things a person wishes for, the more easily may his necessities be supplied. As Mandeville understood the English economic system of the eighteenth century, it required a large number of laboring poor, and he feared that education would make them dissatisfied with their lot and would consequently disrupt the system.

But Mandeville goes on to show the mixed feelings that have always troubled the analytical observer of society who is also a decent human being. He tells us that he does not wish to be thought personally cruel, but he believes that proposing to educate the poor is ". . . to be Compassionate to excess, where Reason forbids it, and the general Interest of the Society requires steadiness of Thought and Resolution." It is, he argues, no harder on the poor to withhold education from them, even though they may have "natural parts and genius" equaling the rich, than it is to withhold money from them as long as they have the same inclinations to spend as the rich have.

Mandeville strongly favored free trade, seeing clearly that in order for one nation to buy another's goods, it must be able to sell its own. Any restriction in international trade must cause the loss of markets, with a consequent fall in the level of employment at home. In the eighteenth century Mandeville's writings became the chief source of arguments in favor of the manufacture of luxuries and against restrictions on trade, either within a given nation or between nations. Adam Smith owed much to his knowledge of *The Fable of the Bees*.

Mandeville did not choose, however, to publish these economic doctrines in a straightforward way. Instead, he offered them in his moralizing poem, "The Grumbling Hive." The bees in the poem have many vices, but their society thrives. Mandeville's notion of vice is a threefold one. First, he has in mind such character traits as envy, vanity, love of luxury, and fickleness in diet, furniture, and dress. These traits make buyers eager to spend lavishly and consume prodigiously, so that they will soon be ready

to spend again. Second, Mandeville calls vice that behavior which is necessary to profitable trade. The seller must conceal from the prospective buyer both the original cost of his goods and the lowest price at which he is willing to sell, while the buyer must conceal the highest price at which he will buy. Mandeville believes that success will certainly require deceit on the part of both buyer and seller, not to mention sharper practices that may descend to downright fraud. Third, Mandeville counts crime as a vice that provides public benefits. Thieves are valuable on two counts. The threat of them keeps locksmiths in business, and when they do succeed, they soon squander their gains, thus contributing to the circulation of wealth. Mandeville may therefore conclude, "The worst of all the Multitude/Did something for the Common Good." In this vein he regards even wars and natural disasters as valuable to the economic system, for by destroying goods, they provide an opportunity for labor to replace them.

Against his claims for the social utility of vice Mandeville sets the following picture of virtue:

It is certain that the fewer Desires a Man has and the less he covets, the more easy he is to himself . . . the more he loves Peace and Concord, the more Charity he has for his Neighbor, and the more he shines in real virtue, there is no doubt but that in proportion he is acceptable to God and Man. But let us be Just, what Benefit can these things be of, or what earthly good can they do, to promote the Wealth, the Glory and Worldly Greatness of Nations?

By a divine fiat the bees of the grumbling hive are all made honest, and their society declines into simplicity and insignificance.

Why did Mandeville present his economic doctrines in a poem praising vice, a poem which could only outrage his contemporaries? The most likely supposition is that in the first writing the motives of the moralist are uppermost. If English economic life is seen as it is and as it will be, then encouraging men to be honest and frugal is a disservice to both them and the continuation of the economic system. By praising those sorts of behavior which are ordinarily called vicious, Mandeville hoped to shock the moralist into seeing the world as it is. He gives the moralist the choice either of accepting the world as it is and changing his tune or of rejecting the world and admitting that the virtues the moralist praises require a context quite different from what is ordinarily supposed. What Mandeville takes to be economic truths thus become the basis for a program that is no less than the reform of moralizing.

As *The Fable of the Bees* grew, Mandeville came to offer bits of moral theory, largely because of his discovery of the writings of Shaftesbury. He attacked Shaftesbury bitterly. He calls the claim that men may be virtuous without self-denial "a vast Inlet to Hypocrisy." He says that Shaftesbury's search for "a real worth and excellence" in things "is not much better than a Wild-Goose-Chace that is but little to be depended on." Mandeville's own view is that "our Liking or Disliking of things chiefly depends on Mode and Custom, and the Precept and Example of our Betters and such whom one way or other we think to be Superior to us. In Morals there is no greater certainty."

The organization of men into a society arises from the multiplicity of each man's desires and the need to overcome the great man's desires and the need to overcome the great natural obstacles that stand in the way of satisfying these desires. In society each man achieves his own ends by laboring for others. Under a government each member of society is rendered subservient to the whole, and all men, by cunning management, are made to act as one. The key to social organization is man's pride and his consequent delight in flattery. Thus, governors may flatter men into putting public interest before private interest, and men are led to be pleased with themselves for being virtuous. Indeed, this satisfaction is the reward for virtuous actions, and it is ultimately this feeling that makes virtue possible.

These doctrines place Mandeville in the moral-sense school, but his presentation of them is desultory and unsystematic. A successor, such as Hume, would have been interested to find these views in the *Fable*. But there is something else in Mandeville's writings that is even more impressive—the large number of vignettes, anecdotes, and sketches that make the reader feel he is learning what people are really like and that must in the end make him a shrewder observer of human nature.

Bibliography

The premier modern edition of *The Fable of the Bees* is that prepared by F. B. Kaye, 2 vols. (London, 1924). Kaye's researches have provided us with a balanced account of Mandeville's life, and his introductory essay on Mandeville's thought and influence should be consulted.

Mandeville's other works include *The Virgin Unmask'd: Or, Female Dialogues Betwixt an Elderly Maiden Lady, and Her Niece* (1709); *Free Thoughts on Religion, the Church, and National Happiness* (1720); *A Modest Defence of Publick Stews* (1724); *An Enquiry Into the Causes of the Frequent Executions at Tyburn* (1725); *An Enquiry Into the Origin of Honour, and the Usefulness of Christianity in War* (1732); and *A Letter to Dion* [Berkeley], *Occasion'd by His Book Call'd Alciphron* (1732).

ELMER SPRAGUE

MANI AND MANICHAEISM.

Mani, "the apostle of God," founder of one of the most widely influential religions of the ancient world, was born in southern Babylonia about A.D. 216. Little is definitely known of his birthplace and parentage, since some statements should probably be discounted as malicious reports from his adversaries. He seems to have been of Persian descent and related, at least on his mother's side, to the royal house of Parthia, which was overthrown in 226 by the Sassanid Ardashir I. He is said to have received his first revelation at the age of 12, but he did not receive his formal call to apostleship until he was 24. His public activity began with a journey to India, where he founded his first community.

Upon the death of Ardashir in 241, Mani returned to Parthia, where he was welcomed by Ardashir's successor Shapur, for whom he wrote a book, the *Shapurakan*. When Shapur died thirty years later, Mani also enjoyed the favor of his successor, but when Bahram came to the throne in 272 the situation changed. Throughout Mani's career the Magian priests had been his most deadly enemies, and they now secured his impeachment and condemnation. He was executed about A.D. 276, and his death apparently was followed by persecution of his adherents.

At least seven works have been ascribed to him, including the *Shapurakan*, another work entitled "The Living Gospel," and the *Epistula Fundamenti*, which, on the evidence of Augustine, was used by north African Manichaeans as a handbook of doctrine. To these some Western authorities add the *Kephalaia*, which is extant in Coptic. Resources for the study of Manichaeism—once limited to the information supplied by such opponents as Augustine and Titus of Bostra and to excerpts in the works of Theodore bar Konai, in Hegemonius' *Acta Archelai*, and in such Arabic sources as the *Fihrist* of En-Nadim—have in the twentieth century been enriched by discoveries of original Manichaean documents in Turkestan and Egypt. The fragments discovered at Turfan include texts in several Iranian dialects, Turkish, and Chinese, while the Egyptian discovery includes Coptic versions of the *Kephalaia*, a psalmbook, and a collection of homilies.

The system of Mani. The chief characteristic of Mani's system is a consistent dualism which rejects any possibility of tracing the origins of good and evil to one and the same source. Evil stands as a completely independent principle against Good, and redemption from the power of Evil is to be achieved by recognizing this dualism and following the appropriate rules of life. The opposition of God and Matter is seen in the realm of nature as the conflict of Light and Darkness, Truth and Error. The present world, and man in particular, presents a mixture of Good and Evil, the result of a breach of the original limits by the powers of evil. The whole purpose of the founding of the universe was to separate the two principles and restore the original state of affairs, rendering Evil forever harmless and preventing any future repetition of the intermingling.

It is the special task of the Manichaean, the man who has been brought to the light, to collaborate in this separation. Through the God-sent mind that is in him and that sets him apart from the other creatures, he must become aware of the mixture present in all things. He must thus discover the true meaning and significance of the world and conduct himself accordingly, in such a way as to avoid any further contamination of the light and promote its release from its mixture with the darkness. The death of the body is thus redemption; and true life is the release of the soul, which is light, from its imprisonment in the body and its return to its true abode.

The Manichaean myth begins with the two primal principles of Light and Darkness, each dwelling in its own realm, coeternal but independent. Perception of the Light excites envy, greed, and hate in Darkness, and provokes it to attack the Light. In response the Father of Greatness calls forth the Primal Man, who arms himself with five powers and descends to battle with the Darkness. He is defeated, however, and the five powers of Darkness devour a part of his light and thus bring the mixture into being. In some versions this is explained as part of a deliberate plan to satisfy the powers of Darkness temporarily by the cession of a portion of the light and thus to prevent further attack. The captive portion of light, the armor of the Primal Man, is identified with the soul, which thus becomes subject to the affections of Matter.

The Primal Man appeals to the Father of Greatness, who sends the Living Spirit to deliver him. The archons, or powers of Darkness, are now overcome (although they do not lose their power of action), and heaven and earth are made from their carcasses. From the purest part of the Light in the archons the sun and moon are formed, but even so only a small part of the Light has been delivered. A fresh appeal from the powers of Light leads the Father of Greatness to send a Third Messenger, whose appearance inspires the Darkness to produce Adam and Eve in the image of his glorious form and to enclose in them the Light still at its disposal. The creation of Eve has a special purpose, in that she is more subservient to the demons and serves as their instrument for the seduction of Adam. Procreation serves the ends of Darkness, since each birth means a further dispersal of the Light, another subject for the realm of Darkness, and a prolonging of the captivity of the Light. The powers of Light accordingly send Jesus on a mission of revelation to Adam, who is still innocent but subsequently disobeys, is seduced by Eve, and so sets the chain of reproduction in motion. This protracts the drama of salvation, and with it the mission of Jesus, into the history of mankind. In one age the revelation comes to India through the Buddha, in another to Persia through Zoroaster, in a third to the West through the historical Jesus, and in the last age it comes through Mani himself, the apostle of the true God.

Manichaean ethics. The cosmogonic myth provides the basis and substructure for the Manichaean ethics and hope of redemption. The ethics are rigorously ascetic: since procreation only prolongs the reign of the powers of darkness, marriage must be rejected. The Manichaean must abstain from all "ensouled" things and eat only vegetables, so as to avoid, as far as possible, any injury to the Light. The full rigor of Manichaean ethics is reserved for the Elect, and the mass of adherents, the Hearers or Soldiers, are allowed to live under less rigorous rules. Correspondingly there is a difference in their destiny after death: the Elect pass at once to the Paradise of Light, but the Soldiers must return to the world and its terrors until their light is freed and they attain to the assembly of the Elect. The third class of men, the sinners who are outside the Manichaean religion, are doomed to remain in the power of Evil.

Manichaean Gnosticism. It is clear that Manichaeism may be regarded as a form of Gnosticism. Indeed, it has been called "the most monumental single embodiment of the gnostic religious principle, for whose doctrinal and mythological representation the elements of older religions were consciously employed" (Hans Jonas, *The Gnostic Religion*, pp. 207 f.). It differs, however, from such older forms of Gnosticism as Valentinianism in that here the dualism is from the beginning an integral part of the myth, and not the result of a development in the myth. In Jonas' words, "the tragedy of the deity is forced upon it from outside, with Darkness having the first initiative," whereas in the other type of Gnosticism, Darkness is the product of the divine passion, not its cause. Any attempt to identify the sources upon which Mani drew for the construction of his system is, however, fraught with difficulty, and it would be dangerous to try to establish any genetic

relationship. For example, attempts have been made, on the basis of the statement that his father belonged to a Baptist sect, the *Mugtasila*, to forge a link with Mandaeism; but although Mandaean elements have been found in the Manichaean psalmbook, the identity of the *Mugtasila* with the Mandaeans, or of either with some still older Jewish or Jewish–Christian Baptist movement, is still a matter of debate.

Another possible link is with the Zervanite heresy in Zoroastrianism, but here again caution is necessary. (On this whole subject, see Carsten Colpe, *Die Religion in Geschichte und Gegenwart*, Sec. 5). In a general way, it may be said that Mani incorporated Christian, Buddhist, and Zoroastrian elements into his religion, but Manichaeism seems to have adapted itself to the dominant religion of a particular area. Moreover, it has been held that he had little more than a hearsay knowledge of Christianity, although he had some acquaintance with the heresies of Bardesanes and of Marcion. It appears that he intended to found not merely a sect but a new religion which could embody the best of the older faiths, fusing elements from Buddhism, Christianity, and Zoroastrianism with his own teaching.

His success is evident from the fact that Manichaeism survived so long and for a time was a serious rival to Christianity. After Mani's death it spread through Syria into the West and spread eastward deep into central Asia. Centuries later Manichaean ideas were current among the Bogomiles in the Balkans (see Dmitri Obolensky, *The Bogomils*) and among the Albigenses and Cathari in Provence (see Steven Runciman, *The Mediaeval Manichee*). There may be debate as to the historical connection of these later movements with the original Manichaeism, but some influence appears beyond dispute. Nor should it be forgotten that Augustine himself was for a time an adherent of Manichaeism. A religion which could arouse the interest of such later thinkers as Bayle, Hume, and Voltaire must be regarded as one of profound significance for the history of thought.

Bibliography

Texts include A. Adam, *Texte zum Manichäismus*, Kleine Texte . . . 175 (Berlin, 1954); H. J. Polotsky and A. Böhlig, eds., *Kephalaia* (Stuttgart, 1940); H. J. Polotsky, *Manichäische Homilien* (Stuttgart, 1934); and *A Coptic Manichean Psalm-Book*, translated and edited by C. R. C. Allberry (Stuttgart, 1938). On the Manichaean Gospels, see H. C. Puech's section on Gnostic Gospels in E. Hennecke, *Neutestamentliche Apokryphen*, Wilhelm Schneemelcher, ed. This was translated as *New Testament Apocrypha* (London and Philadelphia, 1963); see Vol. I, esp. pp. 350 ff.

Secondary sources are H. J. Polotsky, "Manichäismus," in Pauly-Wissowa, *Real-Encyclopädie* . . . (Stuttgart, 1935), Supp. VI, pp. 240–271; Carsten Colpe, *Die Religion in Geschichte und Gegenwart*, 3d ed. (Tübingen, 1960), Vol. VI, pp. 714 ff., with full bibliography; H. C. Puech, *Le Manichéisme, son fondateur, sa doctrine* (Paris, 1949); Georg Widengren, *Mani und der Manichäismus* (Stuttgart, 1961); Torgny Säve-Söderbergh, *Studies in the Coptic Manichean Psalm Book* (Uppsala, 1949); D. Roché, *Études manichéennes et cathares* (Paris, 1952); Dmitri Obolensky, *The Bogomils* (Cambridge, 1948); Steven Runciman, *The Mediaeval Manichee* (Cambridge, 1947); and Hans Jonas, *The Gnostic Religion* (Boston, 1958), pp. 206 ff.

R. McL. Wilson

MANNHEIM, KARL (1893–1947), German sociologist, was born in Budapest and died in London. He studied at Berlin and Paris, and at Heidelberg under Max Weber, and later taught at Heidelberg, Frankfurt am Main, and, after 1933, in London.

Mannheim's thought resembles that of such philosophers as Comte and Hegel, who believed that in the past man had been dominated by the historical process whereas in the future he would gain ascendancy over it. Mannheim was deeply influenced by Karl Marx, but he deviated from Marxism in asserting that a better society might be achieved by nonrevolutionary means and also in de-emphasizing the interpretation of the development of society as being semiautomatic and stressing the importance of conscious political effort. He was, in addition, decisively influenced by German historicism and Anglo-Saxon pragmatism. From the former he took the belief that history is the *ens realissimum,* while from the latter he derived his criterion of truth. Both positions pointed toward a radical relativism, which, however, he strove to overcome.

In his first and most important book, *Ideologie und Utopie,* Mannheim asserted that the act of cognition must not be regarded as the effort of a purely theoretical consciousness, because the human consciousness is permeated by nontheoretical elements arising both from man's participation in social life and in the streams and tendencies of willing which work themselves out contemporaneously in that life. The influence of these active factors is all-important; even the categorial structure of the intellect does not escape it. Mannheim therefore maintained that epistemology (as practiced, for instance, by Kant) was outdated, and must be superseded by a new discipline, the sociology of knowledge. According to Mannheim, this new discipline revealed that all knowledge (at any rate, knowledge of things human) was situation-bound (*situationsgebunden*)—that is, tied to a given constellation of sociohistorical circumstances. Each age develops its own style of thought, and comparisons between these styles are impossible, since each posits a different basic (or, so to speak, relatively absolute) sphere. Even within each age there are conflicting tendencies toward conservation, on the one hand, and toward change on the other. Commitment to conservation tends to produce "ideologies"—to falsify thought by excessive idealization of the past and overemphasis on the factors making for stability. Intentness on change is apt to produce "utopias," which overvalue both the future and factors leading to change.

Between ideology and utopia there is at least the possibility of completely realistic (*situationsgerecht*) thought that functions without friction within the given framework of life, and is set neither on pushing forward nor on holding back the development of society. But Mannheim places little emphasis on this possibility. He sees a very strong tendency toward the polarization of society into hostile camps. Only the comparatively uncommitted intelligentsia is likely to approach nearer the truth. From its special and particularly favorable vantage point, it could, and should, elaborate a "total perspective" which would synthesize the conflicting contemporary world views and thereby neutralize, and to some extent overcome, their one-sidedness. Such a "dynamic synthesis" is the nearest possible approximation to a truly realistic attitude, within the limitations imposed upon a given epoch.

This estimate of human thought might seem to justify accusing Mannheim of skepticism, but Mannheim held himself innocent of the charge. To rebut it, he developed his doctrine of "relationism," which he opposed to skeptical relativism. Relationism, he argued, does not impugn the validity of an insight: it merely draws attention to the fact that the insight is dependent upon, and confined within, a specific sociohistorical situations. But this argument merely shifts the relativity, and does not remove it. Mannheim held that every sociohistorical situation is located at a specific point along a unilinear, ever-progressing and never-returning temporal continuum—history. Each situation is therefore unique, and the knowledge to which it gives birth, and which is true within it, is equally unique, bound to its time and place, and relative. But Mannheim was not primarily concerned with the truth of propositions. Rather, he operated with a radically different conception of "truth." To him, truth is an attribute, not so much of discourse, as of reality. The individual who is in contact with the living forces of his age has the truth, or better, is in the truth—a conception which shows at once Mannheim's Marxism, his historicism, and his pragmatism. He was moving close to the belief that the traditional *adaequatio rei et intellectus* (correspondence of thought and reality) should be replaced by a new test, the *adaequatio intellectus et situs* (correspondence of thought and situation). He was interested in the genuineness, rather than in the truth (properly so-called), of a given world view.

Mannheim was a confirmed progressivist, and he tended to prefer whatever was, at any time, emergent. After his immigration to England in 1933, he adopted a more practical and political orientation. He argued dialectically, especially in *Mensch und Gesellschaft im Zeitalter des Umbaus* (1935), that a completely unregulated society, such as he thought liberalism had created, was apt to produce its own opposite, totalitarian dictatorship. To secure the values of democracy, it was necessary to avoid the weaknesses of both liberalism and totalitarianism. As a viable synthesis, Mannheim advocated "planning for freedom," a social system which would insure economic stability by regulating the more objective aspects of life, such as production, but at the same time grant freedom to men's subjective strivings (for example, in matters of taste), thereby releasing cultural creativity. In this context, Mannheim became interested in education as the prime means of radical democratization. Toward the end of his career, he began to feel that a modernized Christianity held out some hope for a new integration of society's value system, which had become splintered and self-contradictory.

Bibliography

WORKS BY MANNHEIM

Ideologie und Utopie. Bonn, 1929. Translated by Louis Wirth and Edward Shils as *Ideology and Utopia.* London, 1936. The English edition also includes the article "Wissenssoziologie" from Alfred Vierkandt, ed., *Handwörterbuch der Soziologie.* Stuttgart, 1931.

Mensch und Gesellschaft im Zeitalter des Umbaus. Leiden,

1935. Translated by Edward Shils as *Man and Society in an Age of Reconstruction*. London, 1940.

Diagnosis of Our Time. London, 1943.

Freedom, Power and Democratic Planning, Hans Gerth and Ernest K. Bramstedt, eds. London, 1951.

Essays on the Sociology of Knowledge, Paul Kecskemeti, ed. London, 1952.

Essays on Sociology and Social Psychology, Paul Kecskemeti, ed. London, 1953.

Essays on the Sociology of Culture, Ernst Mannheim and Paul Kecskemeti, eds. London, 1956.

Systematic Sociology, J. S. Erös and W. A. C. Stewart, eds. London, 1957.

An Introduction to the Sociology of Education, W. A. C. Stewart, coauthor. London, 1962.

WORKS ON MANNHEIM

Lieber, Hans-Joachim, *Wissen und Gesellschaft*. Tübingen, 1952.

Maquet, Jacques Jerome, *Sociologie de la connaissance*. Louvain, 1949. Translated into English by John F. Locke as *The Sociology of Knowledge*. Boston, 1951.

Schoeck, Helmut, "Die Zeitlichkeit bei Karl Mannheim." *Archiv für Rechts- und Sozialphilosophie*, Vol. 38 (1949–1950), 371–382.

WERNER STARK

MANSEL, HENRY LONGUEVILLE (1820–1871), English philosopher and divine, was educated at Merchant Taylors' School, London, and St. John's College, Oxford. He became tutor in his college, the first Wayneflete professor of moral and metaphysical philosophy at Oxford University in 1859, Regius professor of ecclesiastical history there in 1866, and dean of St. Paul's in 1868.

Mansel was at Oxford during the period when, after more than a century of slumbers, it was again beginning to take philosophy seriously. But whereas his Oxford contemporaries, such as Benjamin Jowett and T. H. Green, looked to Germany for their philosophy, Mansel looked to France and Scotland.

Indebted to various thinkers, especially to William Hamilton and Victor Cousin, Mansel was remarkably successful in assimilating their influences. When—as on the question of the perception of an external world—he occupied common ground with Hamilton, Mansel's version was marked by a superior clarity and relevance. Likewise, he more than did justice to what was genuinely original and valuable in Cousin's critique of Locke's doctrine of judgment, making it the foundation of a subtle and thorough discussion of the relation of thinking to experience begun in the *Prolegomena Logica* and completed in the article "Metaphysics, or the Philosophy of Consciousness."

The point at issue was the relation of meaning to verification. Can we know a proposition to be true or false without first understanding the meaning of the terms involved, in the sense of being able to define each of them separately? Mansel dealt with this difficulty by making a sharp distinction between a *logical judgment*, in which the understanding of the terms precedes the judgment as to the truth or falsity of the proposition, and a *psychological judgment*, in regard to which this sharp distinction cannot be drawn, and in regard to which the understanding of the terms coincides with the judgment as to the truth of the proposition.

Mansel's main point was that the former sort of judgment must always, in the last analysis, rest upon the latter, of which the Cartesian *cogito* is the prime example. In this way the kind of clear-cut empirical knowledge with which science deals rests on the foundation of an essentially vague metaphysical knowledge embodied in the *cogito*. This doctrine, which descended through Cousin from Thomas Reid, was worked out by Mansel in the course of an excellent discussion of the problem of universals and particulars, contained in the article "Metaphysics." What nominalistic atomists had forgotten was that the individual thing is initially given in an essentially vague experience (for example, three objects seen in the far distance and just recognizably human) that withholds the details and reveals only general characteristics.

While this topic of the relation of thinking to experience was central in Mansel's work, he was equally stimulating on other questions. Somewhat in the French style, he held that the will, in the form of attention, forms an integral part of cognition. Following a suggestion of Dugald Stewart's, he tried to illuminate the difference between the presence and the absence of efforts of will by an interesting phenomenology of daydreaming and semiconsciousness. Again influenced by Reid, Mansel was aware—as few were in his time—of the complexities and difficulties of the problem of our knowledge of the existence of other minds, discussing it, appropriately enough, in connection with the moral judgment. Finally, Mansel dealt interestingly with the distinction between philosophy and science. Philosophy deals with what he called facts of consciousness, whose distinctive feature is that their *esse* is *percipi*, in the sense in which Descartes had said that, so far as philosophy is concerned, there is no difference between seeing something and thinking one sees it.

The result of this careful phenomenological analysis (the word "phenomenology" had been introduced by Mansel's masters, Hamilton and Cousin) was that Mansel saw human experience as inherently complex and mysterious. In the background of Mansel's philosophy there was always an explicit contrast with a rival kind of reductive analysis that regarded man as being as unmysterious in his inner workings as a pocket watch. This contrast was the key to the controversies aroused by Mansel's Bampton lectures, "The Limits of Religious Thought," delivered in 1858. Mansel held that reason tells us that if evil exists, then God cannot be both perfectly good and all-powerful. However, God's omnipotence and perfect goodness must be accepted as a matter of faith. Although God is perfectly good, we cannot know the nature of his goodness. Man's finite goodness cannot explain God's infinite goodness; they are the same by analogy, not identity.

Mansel's lectures were attacked by F. D. Maurice and Goldwin Smith, and by John Stuart Mill, who devoted Chapter 7 of his *Examination of Sir William Hamilton's Philosophy* to Mansel's views. Mill wrote, "I will call no being good, who is not what I mean when I apply that epithet to my fellow creatures, and if such a being can sentence me to hell for not so calling him, to hell I will go." Mansel replied in *The Philosophy of the Conditioned*, and Mill in turn replied in numerous footnotes in later editions of the *Examination*, listing Mansel first among his critics. For Mansel man's goodness was not clear and God's goodness was inscrutable; both were equally a mystery.

Mansel's *Letters, Lectures, and Reviews*, published posthumously, contains, among other things, interesting articles on the philosophy of language and on mathematical logic.

Works by Mansel

Prolegomena Logica. Oxford, 1851.

"Metaphysics, or the Philosophy of Consciousness," in *Encyclopaedia Britannica*, 8th ed. 1857. Published separately, Edinburgh, 1860.

The Limits of Religious Thought. Oxford and London, 1858.

The Philosophy of the Conditioned. London and Edinburgh, 1866.

Letters, Lectures, and Reviews, H. W. Chandler, ed. London, 1873.

Works on Mansel

Burgon, J. W., *Lives of Twelve Good Men.* London, 1888. Vol. II, pp. 149–237.

Mill, J. S., *An Examination of Sir William Hamilton's Philosophy.* London, 1865. Ch. 7.

Stephen, Leslie, "H. L. Mansel," in *Dictionary of National Biography.* London, 1893. Vol. 36, pp. 81–83.

GEORGE E. DAVIE

MANY-VALUED LOGIC. See LOGIC, MANY-VALUED.

MARBURG, SCHOOL OF. See NEO-KANTIANISM.

MARCEL, GABRIEL, French philosopher, dramatist, and critic, was born in Paris in 1889. His father, a highly cultured man, held important administrative posts in the Bibliothèque Nationale and the Musées Nationaux. Marcel's mother died when he was four. Raised in a home dominated by the cultured agnosticism of his father and the liberal, moralistic Protestantism of his aunt, and nurtured in a scholastic system concerned only with intellectual achievement, he later sought refuge in a modified type of idealism. The shaking experiences of World War I, during which he was an official of the Red Cross concerned with locating missing soldiers, brought home to him the failure of abstract philosophy to cope with the tragic character of human existence. His conversion to Catholicism in 1929 did not substantially alter the direction of his thought, although it intensified his conviction that the philosopher must take into consideration the logic interior to faith and hope.

Relationship to existentialism. Marcel's name has most often been linked with "theistic existentialism." Because of the ambiguities of this term and the association of existentialism in the popular mind with Sartre's philosophy, to which his is almost diametrically opposed, Marcel has preferred the designation "Neo-Socratic" for his thought. This should not obscure Marcel's contributions to existential philosophy or his similarity to other thinkers who are ordinarily associated with it.

Before publication of the major philosophical works of Jaspers and Heidegger, Marcel introduced into French philosophy, in his essay "Existence and Objectivity" (1925) and in his *Metaphysical Journal*, many of the themes which later became central to existentialism. Often

making use of an independently developed phenomenological method, he dealt with such themes as participation, incarnation, man as being in the world, and the priority of existence over abstraction (the *cogito*) as a starting point for philosophy.

Marcel's critique of idealism and his defense of faith resemble Kierkegaard's critique of Hegel; however, Marcel refuses to allow that faith is an irrational leap or that the individual stands alone in his faith. Heidegger and Marcel explore much of the same terrain in seeking to restore the "ontological weight to human experience" (*Being and Having*, p. 103). They share a common view of the nature of truth and language. However, Marcel, unlike Heidegger, includes within his ontology the assurance of fulfillment which is part of faith's apprehension of God as Absolute Presence. In many ways Buber has been Marcel's closest contemporary philosophical relative. Each has independently developed a philosophy of dialogue and communion in which the distinction between the relation of an I to a thou and an I to an it or a him plays a central part.

Philosophical method. A great injustice is necessarily done in any summary account of Marcel's thought, for the charm and the convincing power of his conclusions are inseparable from his itinerant, tentative, and exploratory philosophical method. One of the most characteristic features of his thinking is the vigor with which he has combated the spirit of abstraction and the conceptual sclerosis which he believes is an occupational hazard of systematic and academic philosophers. But despite his rejection of systematic philosophy, Marcel's work is based on an underlying principle of unity, or more accurately an underlying vision, which, seen dimly from the beginning, has been progressively more clearly apprehended. This vision, which is essentially both Platonic and Christian, expresses itself in the conviction that within the temporal and transient order *homo viator* is given a foretaste of eternal realities.

Marcel's philosophical explorations cannot be divorced from his dramatic writings or from his experimentation in music. His plays are not philosophical in the sense of being popular forums for the presentation of worked-out ideas. Rather, they present complicated situations in which persons find themselves trapped, challenged, and confused; and thus indirectly they explore the nature of the exile into which the soul enters as it becomes alienated from itself, from those it loves, and from God. Marcel believes that in music one finds a foretaste or presentiment of the perfect harmony and communion toward which all authentic human existence strives. Philosophy shares both in the tension that is the essence of drama and in the harmony which is the essence of music. Its starting point is a metaphysical "dis-ease" like that of a man in a fever who shifts around searching for a comfortable position. This search for a home in the wilderness, a harmony in disharmony, a transcendent source of assurance in a transient life takes place through a reflective process which Marcel calls secondary reflection.

The nature of thinking. Marcel distinguishes two degrees or types of thinking, primary and secondary reflection.

Primary reflection is characterized as abstract, analytical, objective, universal, and verifiable. The thinking subject in primary reflection is not the individual human person but the thinker qua mind (the *Bewusstsein überhaupt*). Primary reflection deals with the realm of the problematic. As the etymology of "problem" (*pro-ballo*) suggests, the distinguishing feature of the problematic approach to reality is the separation of the questioner from the data about which he questions. The data of primary reflection lie in the public domain and are equally available to any qualified observer. Once a problem is posed, primary reflection proceeds to abstract from the concrete data any elements that are not relevant to the solution of the particular problem under consideration. When a solution or an explanation has been found, the original curiosity and tension that motivated the thinker are alleviated.

Primary reflection, as exemplified in scientific and technical thought, has allowed us to possess and manipulate our world more completely and is therefore indispensable to human culture. However, intellectual and moral confusion results when primary reflection becomes imperialistic and claims the right to judge all knowledge and truth by criteria appropriate only to the realm of the objective and the problematic. When this happens, abstraction gives way to "the spirit of abstraction," the use of techniques gives way to technocracy, and the inexhaustible riches of a kaleidoscopic world are forced to conform to a black-and-white logic.

Secondary reflection is concrete, individual, heuristic, and open. Strictly speaking, it is concerned not with objects but with presences. Its contemplation begins not with curiosity or doubt but with wonder and astonishment. Hence, it is humble in its willingness to be conformed to categories created by that on which it is focused. It remains open to its object as a lover does to his beloved—not as a specimen of a class but as a unique being. This openness is not a methodological principle as in scientific thought but arises from the possibility of something new being created in the relationship. Secondary reflection is dialogical, not dialectical. Rather than searching for information about the other and dealing with it abstractly, secondary reflection seeks the revelation of total presence, whether the presence be that of my body, the world, the other person, or God. Thus, secondary reflection is brought to bear on data or questions from which the thinker as existing person cannot legitimately abstract himself: "Am I free?" "Is there meaning and value in life?" "Can I commit myself to this person?" In other words, secondary reflection is concerned not with problems but with mystery.

Mystery. According to Marcel, a mystery initially appears to be merely a problem that is difficult to solve. Reflection shows, however, that in dealing with a genuine mystery the distinction between subject and object, between what is in me and what is before me, breaks down. Faced with questions about freedom, the meaning of life, the existence of God, and so forth, no objective standpoint can be found from which a universally valid answer may be discovered. This does not mean that mystery is unknown or unknowable and lies in a realm of vague feelings over which thought has no grasp. Rather, knowledge of mystery presupposes an immediate participation, or what

Marcel also calls a "blinded intuition," but this participation is understood only with the aid of a conceptual process. Unaided intuition is not an adequate philosophical instrument. However, secondary reflection penetrates into the mystery of existence and being only when it works in conjunction with love, fidelity, faith, and the other "concrete approaches." It yields a kind of knowledge and truth which, if unverifiable, nevertheless is confirmed as it illuminates our lives. Two foci of mystery may be distinguished, although never separated, in Marcel's thinking. The mystery of existence is dealt with in "concrete" philosophy and the mystery of being in "concrete" ontology.

Concrete philosophy. Marcel denies that the detached, disincarnate, Cartesian *cogito* provides a possible starting point for a concrete philosophy. It is with the existing subject, the incarnate being who is already in the world, that philosophy must begin. The experience of the inexhaustible concreteness of the existing world can be neither deduced, doubted, nor demonstrated. Existence is not a thing, a quality, or a discrete content of thought which can be isolated and pointed out; rather it is that in which the subject participates and from which thought begins its quest for meaning. The assurance of existence which we have is not of the intellectual order but is an outcome of our direct participation in the world via sensation and feeling. Because sensation and feeling are inseparable from the body, our knowledge of existence is tied up with our being incarnate.

Incarnation is the "central given of metaphysic," the absolute starting point for an existential philosophy, because it is on the analogy of my experience of my body that the world is understood. I project into the world the sense of density and presence that I experience when I become aware of my own body. The world exists for me only in the measure that I am related to it in a way similar to the way in which I am related to my own body.

As I am not even ideally separable from my body, I am likewise inseparable from my situation. Those habitual surroundings and historical conditions which shape my life enter into the very fiber of what I am. Insofar as I recognize that my situation enters into the constitution of my being, and hence that I am not able to abstract myself from it completely and view it with the objective detachment of a spectator, I may speak of the family which nurtured me or of an illness that shaped me as having a mysterious character.

A concrete philosophy must also affirm the immediacy of our being with others. The principle of the intentionality of consciousness, Marcel holds, applies in our relations both to persons and to the world. Philosophy begins not with *I am* but with *we are*.

The significance of this intersubjectivity will be determined by the type of relations which characterize one's life. The self who treats other persons as objects to be manipulated and used is condemned because of its egocentricity to live in a world lacking in ontological depth, and hence it will be prey to despair when the thrill of possession wears thin. To endeavor to allow the other person to become present as a thou is to enter into a relationship within which the assurance of fulfillment is received.

Ontology. No word used by Marcel is more difficult to define or richer in meaning than "being." It refers neither to the sum total of all objects that exist nor to some universal substratum underlying all particulars. Being is eternal and inexhaustible. It is "that which does not allow itself to be dissolved by the dialectics of experience" (*Metaphysical Journal*, p. 181). Only by participation in being can isolation, despair, and tragedy be overcome. The quest for being is thus identical with the quest for salvation. To deny being is to say that "all is vanity," that nothing has intrinsic worth. To affirm being is to declare that corresponding to the deepest exigency of the human spirit is a fulfillment of which an earnest is given in experiences of creativity, joy, and love.

As defined by Marcel, the question of being cannot be approached objectively and problematically. Being can be affirmed only if I can discover within experience some presence which testifies to being. Two elements in human experience seem to offer such a testimony. First, at the heart of the human condition is an "ontological exigence," an impulse to transcendence which is present in all authentic human life, the exigence to penetrate to a level of experience saturated with meaning and value. The mere existence of such an exigence is no guarantee in itself that a corresponding satisfaction exists. It could be the case, as Sartre says, that man is a "useless passion." But Marcel has attempted to show, by way of a phenomenological analysis, that certain experiences of love, joy, hope, and faith, as understood from *within*, present a positive testimony to the existence of an inexhaustible presence. This assuring presence, which might be called the immanence of being in human experience, is never a possession but is constantly created anew as an I enters into relations with an empirical thou or the Absolute Thou (God). Although the assurance of being never becomes conceptually clear, it provides the illumination making creative, open existence possible.

In what might be called Marcel's ontological personalism, the concrete approaches to being are identical with the approaches to other persons and to God. To enter into a loving relationship requires that a person exorcise the spirit of egocentricity and possession and become spiritually available (*disponible*) to others. A vow of creative fidelity is likewise necessary if the unconditional demands of love are to be satisfied. In approaching God, fidelity becomes faith and *disponibilité* becomes hope. In love, fidelity, hope, and faith man approaches the mystery of being and is overtaken with the assurance that he is accompanied by the eternal fulfilling Presence that he seeks to know.

Works by Marcel

PHILOSOPHICAL WORKS

Journal métaphysique. Paris, 1927. Translated by Bernard Wall as *Metaphysical Journal.* Chicago, 1952.
Être et avoir. Paris, 1935. Translated by Katharine Farrer as *Being and Having.* London, 1949.
Du Refus à l'invocation. Paris, 1940. Translated by Robert Rosthal as *Creative Fidelity.* New York, 1964.
Homo Viator. Paris, 1945. Translated by Emma Craufurd. New York, 1962.
The Philosophy of Existence. Translated by Manya Harari, New York, 1949. Republished as *Philosophy of Existentialism.* New York, 1961. Previously uncollected essays written between 1933 and 1946. Perhaps the best short introduction to Marcel's thought.
Le Mystère de l'être, 2 vols. Paris, 1951. Translated by G. S. Fraser and René Hauge as *The Mystery of Being,* 2 vols. Chicago, 1950.
Les Hommes contre l'humain. Paris, 1951. Translated by G. S. Fraser as *Men Against Humanity.* London, 1952. Republished as *Man Against Mass Society.* Chicago, 1962.
L'Homme problématique. Paris, 1955.
Présence et immortalité. Paris, 1959.
The Existential Background of Human Dignity. Cambridge, Mass., 1963.

PLAYS

"The Lantern." *Cross Currents,* Vol. 8, No. 2 (1958), 129–143.
Three Plays, translated by Rosalind Heywood and Marjorie Gabain. New York, 1958; 2d ed., 1965. Contains "A Man of God," "Ariadne" (*Le Chemin de Crête*), and "The Funeral Pyre" (*La Chapelle ardente;* in the 2d ed., "The Votive Candle").

Works on Marcel

Cain, Seymour, *Gabriel Marcel.* London, 1963.
Prini, Pietro, *Gabriel Marcel et le méthodologie de l'invérifiable.* Paris, 1953.
Ricoeur, Paul, *Gabriel Marcel et Karl Jaspers.* Paris, 1947.
Troisfontaines, Roger, *De l'Existence à l'être,* 2 vols. Paris, 1953. Essentially a concordance of what Marcel has said on any subject. Contains a complete bibliography of Marcel's work until 1953.

SAMUEL McMURRAY KEEN

MARCION was one of the most significant and, in a way, perplexing figures of the second century A.D.—significant both for founding the Marcionite church and for providing the stimulus for the formation of the New Testament canon, and perplexing because of the difficulty of classifying him among contemporary thinkers. He is often called a Gnostic, and there are certainly distinct affinities with Gnosticism in his cosmology and soteriology; but his lack of a mythical anthropology and of any syncretistic tendency sets him apart.

A native of Sinope in Pontus, he was born c. 85 and must have died c. 159, since there is no suggestion in our sources that he survived until the reign of the emperor Marcus Aurelius (161–180). According to the ecclesiastical writer Hippolytus, Marcion was the son of a bishop, and indeed there are indications that he grew up within the Christian faith. Excommunicated by his own father because of his unorthodox views, he traveled first to Asia Minor, then to Rome (c.138–140), where he was at first closely associated with the church. In 144 he was again excommunicated, and he founded a church of his own which was for a time a serious menace to "orthodox" Christianity.

Marcion was a Bible critic and theologian rather than a philosopher; indeed, Harnack describes him as "fundamentally a Biblicist and an opponent of all philosophy." The root of his teaching lies in the Pauline antithesis of Law and Gospel, but he exaggerated this contrast to the extent of distinguishing the Creator (the God of the Old Testament) from the true God, in himself unknown and alien to this world but manifested in the person of Jesus. This conception of the "alienness" of the true God Marcion shared with the Gnostics, but for him this concept developed from the study of the Scriptures rather than from philosophical speculation. Rejecting allegorical interpretation, he was unable to reconcile the Old Testament description of God with the New Testament portrayal of God as the father of Christ. Unlike the Gnostics as well as some of his followers, Marcion himself held that the Creator is not evil but merely just. Only the true God is good, a God of love. From this initial contrast the whole of Marcion's system follows naturally. This world, which is the work of the Creator, is imperfect. The Jewish law, and indeed all positive morality, is a means by which the Creator exercises control over mankind and is therefore to be rejected. Marcion's conclusions, however, led not to licentious antinomianism but to asceticism: marriage and sexual intercourse, for example, were prohibited as devices for the continued procreation of subjects of the Creator. Salvation is deliverance from the world and its God and is effected at the price of Christ's blood, solely by God's grace and not because the redeemed were considered "akin" to the supreme good God, as the Gnostics believed.

The gospel brought by Jesus was misunderstood and falsified by the apostles: only Paul had the truth of the matter. Marcion therefore rejected not only the Old Testament but also those parts of the New Testament which, according to him, were contaminated by Judaism. His canon consisted of ten letters of Paul, beginning with Galatians, and an expurgated Gospel of Luke. He also set out his teaching in his *Antitheses,* which was largely composed of contrasts between the two Gods. Marcion's works have not survived, and we are dependent on information provided by his opponents (especially Tertullian). His followers (especially Apelles) later modified his teachings so that they were in closer conformity with ordinary Gnosticism. Some of the "Gnostic" elements in his own theology have been attributed to the influence of the second-century Gnostic Cerdo.

Marcionism was at its height in the latter half of the second century. Thereafter it tended to decline in the West, and the remnants of Marcionite churches were often absorbed into Manichaeanism. In the East it had a longer history, surviving down to the fifth century or later.

Bibliography

Blackman, E. C., *Marcion and His Influence.* London, 1948.
Harnack, A. von, *Marcion: Das Evangelium vom fremden Gott.* Leipzig, 1921. A classic.
Jonas, H., *The Gnostic Religion.* New York, 1958. Pp. 137 ff.
Knox, J., *Marcion and the New Testament.* Chicago, 1942.

R. McL. Wilson

MARCUS AURELIUS ANTONINUS (121–180), emperor of Rome, Stoic philosopher, and one of the noblest figures of antiquity, has been well described as "by nature a saint and a sage, by profession a warrior and a ruler." He was born of patrician stock in Rome as Marcus Annius Verus, and after the early death of his parents was brought up by his grandfather, of whom he wrote with admiration and gratitude. Among the tutors responsible for his education was the distinguished Marcus Cornelius Fronto, and the letters exchanged between them, still extant, throw much light on the young pupil's industrious and affectionate nature. His qualities so favorably impressed the emperor Hadrian that he advised Aurelius Antoninus (an uncle of Marcus usually known as Antoninus Pius), whom he had nominated as his successor, to adopt the boy and make him his heir.

At the age of 11, through the philosopher Diognetus, Marcus became acquainted with the doctrines of Stoicism. He assumed the dress of a Stoic and imitated the Stoics' austere way of life, eventually giving up his other studies to dedicate himself to the principles and practice of Stoicism. When Antoninus, now emperor, adopted him and betrothed him to his daughter Faustina. Marcus took the name of his new father and became Marcus Aurelius Antoninus. For the next 23 years, as the companion and colleague of Antoninus, he was occupied in learning the arts of government, until at the emperor's death in 161 the burden of sovereignty descended upon his shoulders. Against the wishes of the Senate he generously appointed the worthless Lucius Verus, the other adopted son of Antoninus, to share his throne as coemperor and gave him his daughter Lucilla in marriage.

The subsequent years of this gentle and peace-loving ruler were harassed by long and bloody wars, troubles of state, and domestic unhappiness. Floods, fires, and earthquakes devastated Rome. Verus and his troops, returning from a campaign in Syria, brought back the seeds of plague, which spread over the empire. Fierce hordes of Quadi and Marcomanni irrupted over the frontiers of Pannonia, compelling Marcus to quit Rome and take command of his hard-pressed legions on the Danube. In 169 Verus died, and Marcus was left sole emperor. In 175 the commander of the forces in Asia, Avidius Cassius, mutinied and proclaimed himself emperor. Marcus hastened to the east, but on finding that Cassius had been assassinated by his own officers, he magnanimously ordered all the traitor's papers to be burned unread and induced the Senate to pardon his family. During this expedition Faustina, who had accompanied her husband on his journey, died. She had borne him five sons, none of whom had survived except the ignoble Commodus, who lived to succeed his father as emperor. On Marcus' return from the east he resumed his exhausting struggle against the barbarians on the Danube, where, at last worn out by toil and anxiety, he died in the fifty-ninth year of his life and the nineteenth of his reign.

The "Meditations." The only extant work by Marcus Aurelius is the volume of *Meditations,* which has justly been called the highest ethical product of the ancient mind. Written in Greek during his lonely vigils in the Danubian marshes, its 12 books contain reflections on moral and religious topics, set down with little attempt at order or consecutive arrangement. It has been suggested that these may represent material collected by the author for a book which he contemplated writing, but the more general assumption is that they are private soliloquies intended for no eyes but his own. Though the philosophy of which the *Meditations* are the expression is that of the Stoic school, it is a Stoicism that would scarcely have commended itself to Zeno. It must be borne in mind that when the system had passed from the east into the west it had come to wear a different aspect. The practical Roman character valued it chiefly as ethical counseling and was impatient of its abstruse physical and metaphysical speculations.

Of this Neo-Stoicism the prime exponent had been Epictetus, whom Marcus held in the highest regard and whose sayings he quoted with especial fondness. To both men the great issue that overshadowed all other inquiries was the question of how life is to be lived well. But with the emperor, whose delicate and sensitive nature was essentially religious rather than scientific, this took the form of an intense preoccupation with the spiritual state of his own soul. Because it is difficult for such a temperament to escape its need for a sympathetic deity and for some assurance that there is a correspondence between the universe and its own moral strivings, the Stoicism of the *Meditations* inevitably betrays anomalies inconsistent with the cold doctrine of the Stoa. Marcus, however, was not an original thinker, and he made no real effort to reconcile these intellectual inconsistencies. Thus, under the superficial harmony of his philosophy we detect the constant struggle between science and personal faith. While Stoic orthodoxy committed him to a creed that is entirely materialistic and impersonal, all his religious instincts impelled him strongly toward the conception of a moral and benevolent power which can feel for humanity and concern itself with the troubles and aspirations of men. Thus, Marcus' language appears at one time to imply acceptance of a purely physical pantheism and at another to desert the dogmas of the schools for the impulses of his own heart.

The truth is that Marcus stands at a point of transition. Not only is the antique Stoic self-sufficiency replaced in him by a diffidence and a consciousness of his own imperfections which seem to anticipate the Christian virtue of humility, but also the whole tenor of his writings suggests forcibly that a very short step forward would have carried him across the gap that divides impersonal nature from a personal God. It was never given him, however, to take that step. In the words of Matthew Arnold, "the effusion of Christianity, its relieving tears, its happy self-sacrifice, were the very element, one feels, for which his soul longed; they were near him, they brushed him, he touched them, he passed them by."

Bibliography

The first printed text of the *Meditations*, with a Latin translation by William Xylander, was published in 1559 by Andreas Gesner at Zurich. In 1652, Thomas Gataker issued his great edition, with a translation and notes in Latin, which is still indispensable for the vast range and depth of its editor's learning. Among well-known English translations are those of Meric Casaubon (1634); Jeremy Collier (1701); George Long (London, 1862); G. H. Rendall (London, 1898), which has an excellent introductory essay on Stoicism; John Jackson (Oxford, 1906); and C. R. Haines (Loeb series; London, 1915). A. S. L. Farquharson's critical edition, 2 vols. (Oxford, 1944), with translation and commentary, is an admirable and comprehensive example of modern scholarship.

For a detailed analysis of the emperor's philosophy *Marcus Aurelius and the Later Stoics*, by F. W. Bussell (Edinburgh, 1910), should be consulted, and a useful historical study of his life and times, including an examination of his attitude toward Christianity, will be found in H. D. Sedgwick's *Marcus Aurelius* (Cambridge, Mass., 1920). Matthew Arnold wrote a sympathetic and perceptive character study of the emperor in the ninth essay of *Essays Literary and Critical*.

MAXWELL STANIFORTH

MARÉCHAL, JOSEPH (1878–1944), one of the most original and influential of Neo-Scholastic thinkers, was born at Charleroi, Belgium. He entered the Society of Jesus at the age of 17, and between 1895 and 1910, in spite of poor health, he not only successfully completed the long and exacting Jesuit course of studies in the humanities, philosophy, theology, and asceticism but also obtained his doctorate in the natural sciences from the University of Louvain (1905). After the completion of his Jesuit training, during the latter part of which he also taught biology to his younger confreres, he spent some time in Germany studying experimental psychology and psychotherapy. From the outset his main interest centered on the psychology of religious experience and its implications for metaphysics and the critical problem.

After the outbreak of war in 1914 he went to England with his Jesuit students. He did not begin teaching formally at the Jesuit scholasticate in Louvain until 1919. From then until 1935 he conducted courses in psychology, theodicy, and the history of modern philosophy. It was during these years that he published his most important works, the two-volume *Études sur la psychologie des mystiques* and the First, Second, Third, and Fifth Cahiers of the *Point de départ de la métaphysique* (the first three are somewhat abridged in his *Précis d'histoire de la philosophie moderne*). The Fourth Cahier, *Le Système idéaliste chez Kant et les postkantiens*, was published posthumously in 1947 from manuscripts left by the author.

After 1935 and until his death Maréchal ceased teaching and writing, mostly because of poor health but partly because he felt that his work was misunderstood and ineffectual. Concerning "my epistemology," he remarked, "I have never had the means of exposing, orally or by writing, my general conception of the problem of knowledge. The Fifth Cahier states once more this problem *in terms of Kant,* which retains something artificial demanded by immediate historical antecedents. My definitive position ought to appear only at the end of the Sixth Cahier, in which there remains a new stage to overcome" (*Mélanges Maréchal*, Vol. I, p. 13; all translations are the author's). Unfortunately, the Sixth Cahier was never published.

In an article, "À propos du Sentiment de présence chez les profanes et chez les mystiques," published in 1908, the year he was ordained a priest, and later reproduced in the first volume of his *Études sur la psychologie des mystiques* (2d ed., pp. 67–122), Maréchal for the first time indicated the distinctive trend of his philosophical thought. He pointed out that "the judgment of presence properly speaking affirms a spatial relation between a subject and an object," implying their reality, which is conditioned by "(1) a certain unity of mind, realized by (2) the coordination of representations, (3) with the concurrence of feeling" (*Études*, p. 110). Because the existential judgment cannot be founded solely on sensible experience, in view of sensible illusions, or on subjective feeling, the "psychologists" arbitrarily assume the anteriority of the subjective over objective knowledge, thus creating the pseudocritical problem of the "bridge" from thought to reality, the solution of which is thus prejudiced in favor of idealism. According to Maréchal the terms of the problem should be reversed. A more simple and more logical procedure would be "to posit as a primitive fact the *real, affirmation,* and the *objective* and to seek how this fact, in being broken up, gives birth to the secondary notions of the *unreal,* of *doubt,* and of the *subjective.* We shall thus rediscover, with a certain number of modern psychologists and under the impulse of experience, the point of view—very clear but insufficiently analyzed—of ancient Thomistic psychology" (*ibid.*).

Maréchal's principal work is his Fifth Cahier. The first four cahiers present a historical exposition and critical analysis of the problem of knowledge prior to Kant, in Kant, and in post-Kantian transcendental idealism and a "historical demonstration" of the Thomistic solution. A twofold antinomy emerges, of the sensibility and understanding and of the understanding and metaphysical reason. Kant resolved the first antinomy by refuting the exaggerated claims of both the empiricists and the rationalists and by effecting a synthesis of the sensibility and understanding. However, according to Maréchal, Kant failed to resolve the second antinomy because he did not take into consideration the role of finality and intellectual dynamism in objective knowledge, a failure revealed in his *Opus Postumum* and in Fichte's finalism. Maréchal held that Thomas' epistemology virtually contains the solution of the antinomy of the understanding and reason by their effective synthesis in terms of intellectual dynamism (though Thomas himself did not explicitly consider the modern critical problem). Hence, the Fifth Cahier, "Thomisme devant la philosophie critique," presents the Thomistic solution of the critical problem without pretending to present an anachronistic confrontation of Kant and Aquinas.

Maréchal agreed with Kant that we have no intellectual intuition of the noumenal, but he denied Kant's conclusion that the noumenal is therefore unknowable to human reason. Even though the human mind is not intuitive, but only abstractive and constructive, in its knowledge, yet in virtue of its innate active dynamism to Absolute Being it attains the noumenal or metaphysical in its synthetic elaboration of the object of knowledge by the "active intellect."

The Fifth Cahier has two main divisions. The first part is an examination, according to the demands of modern criticism, of "the theory of knowledge in the framework of Thomistic metaphysics," which Maréchal aptly termed "a *metaphysical* critique of the object"; it is preceded by a "critical preamble," in which the author explains Thomas' "universal doubt" and refutation of skepticism. The second part is "a Thomistic critique of knowledge transposed to the transcendental plane" and therefore "a *transcendental* critique of the object," an attempt to go beyond Kant on the basis of Kant's point of departure and transcendental method, which seeks the a priori conditions of the possibility of the objective contents of human consciousness, viewed precisely as objective.

How does Maréchal's metaphysical critique of the object differ from his transcendental one? Both have as their initial point of departure the object immanent in the mind, the mental content directly revealed in consciousness, what Descartes called the "objective reality" of the idea. However, according to the metaphysical critique, the presence of the object in the mind is intentional and therefore ontological or noumenal in its signification, whereas according to the transcendental critique there is present to the mind only a phenomenon. From either viewpoint, however, there can be no question but that this immanent object presents (1) a sensible aspect, (2) a conceptual aspect (involving the notes of universality and necessity), and (3) a transcendent aspect inexorably pointing toward Absolute Being. Unlike Kant, scholastic Thomism accepts the objective validity of the third aspect. As we shall presently see, the two critical approaches differ not as regards their philosophical methods but only as regards their formal object. The formal object of the metaphysical critique is being, viewed as being in all its fullness, universality, and necessity—namely, Absolute Being or God; the formal object of the transcendental critique is the phenomenon.

This is not to say that the transcendental method, as understood in too narrow a sense by Kant himself, does not differ from the metaphysical method of Thomism. The transcendental method seeks to determine the a priori conditions of the possibility of the "objective" contents of consciousness. But as Maréchal contended, the most important and salient of these a priori conditions (which Kant failed to recognize) is the intellectual dynamism of the subject, its activity in constructing the immanent object. This is revealed by "transcendental reflection," whereas "transcendental deduction" proves that the object immanent in consciousness cannot be truly "objective" except in terms of this a priori or objectivizing function of the dynamic intellect, whose formal object is Absolute Being. Needless to say, Kant himself never conceived the transcendental method in such a dynamic fashion. Thus, the most basic inconsistency of his methodology, according to Maréchal, is his stated purpose of disclosing by transcendental reflection the purely logical and static a priori conditions of knowledge, whereas, inadvertently or not, his procedure is often psychological and dynamic; he viewed the mind as constructive and synthetic, and therefore as active, but illogically concluded that the only a priori discoverable by transcendental reflection is purely logical, formal, and static. Hence, Maréchal refuted Kant in the first part of Cahier V by applying the transcendental method to the ontological object, thus legitimizing the Thomistic point of departure of metaphysics (namely, that the human mind directly attains the noumenal or intelligible in its necessary judgments), while in the second part he attempted to go beyond Kant's agnostic conclusions by proving the necessity of metaphysics, using this same transcendental method and basing the proof on Kant's own presupposition that the object immanent in consciousness is the phenomenal.

To constitute a noumenal "object in itself," that which is known must be something more than an abstract essence or form in the mind; it must go beyond the domain of *form* and be related to the sphere of *act.* An abstract essence can become a possible essence and therefore represent a real essence only when the immanent form becomes an act of the dynamism of the intellect, necessarily relating the abstract form to Absolute Being, as a partial fulfillment of this dynamism.

Maréchal was not maintaining "the ontological parologism" that the proposition "Truth is" is intuitive or analytical; rather, he held that what the discursive and abstractive intellect apprehends is that the connection between truth and being must be affirmed under pain of contradiction, when our intellectual dynamism to Absolute Truth is also apprehended. (The objective validity of our abstractive knowledge is thus assured.) Only the divine intellect is intuitive, but an abstractive intellect is capable of apprehending and reducing an abstracted form, inherent in the potentially intelligible data of sense, to act by virtue of its active dynamical tendency to Pure Act, thus approximating the perfection of the exemplary divine knowledge. Since our intellectual knowledge is not a purely passive reception of abstract forms, the self-consciousness of the synthesizing knowing subject as an intellectual dynamism is the key to Maréchal's doctrine on the objectivization of human knowledge.

Maréchal's distinction between the human intellect viewed as formally cognoscitive and the same intellect viewed as a natural being or entelechy (*ut res quaedam naturae*) is very important for an understanding of his epistemology of objectivization. The strictly intentional function of the abstractive intellect, whose formal object is being as such, must be basically identified with the entitative function of the same intellect viewed as a dynamic real tendency to Absolute Being or Truth. It is only in virtue of the intellect viewed as dynamic act that the formally cognoscitive and abstractive intellect can assimilate a representative form as objective being, that is, as a partial fulfillment of the intellect's natural dynamism to the acquisition of *all being*, the intuition of Being Itself.

Granted the sensible data, it is in the formation of the concept that the synthesizing function of the knowing subject reveals itself. Thus, metaphysical concepts present themselves in our consciousness as universal and necessary and therefore as connoting a relation to Absolute Being; though they may conceptually represent a multiplicity, they necessarily signify a universal, though analogical, unity of being that is intelligible only in terms of Absolute Being. How are we to explain these elements of universality and necessity?

In a Thomistic metaphysical critique of the object, the a priori is not simply a logical function, as in Kant. Rather, it designates, in terms of Maréchal's intellectual dynamism, an a priori that is at once both metaphysical and psychological; for Maréchal the formal object of the intellect as a natural entelechy, or *res quaedam naturae*, is Absolute Being. On the conscious, elicitive, and formally cognoscitive level, being is necessarily presented as an abstract being as such, but such a representation, Maréchal contended, is possible only because the intellect naturally tends to Absolute Being as its natural entelechy or end on the preconscious and pre-elicitive level. The substantial unity of the knowing subject makes possible the "conversion to the phantasm," without which it could not make a judgment concerning the concrete individual.

Maréchal's transcendental critique of knowledge can be more readily understood when it is viewed in the light of his posthumously published Fourth Cahier, especially his remarks on Kant's *Opus Postumum* (pp. 225–326) and on Fichte's "Intellectual Intuition of Act or Dynamic Intuition" (pp. 348 ff.) and his article "L'aspect dynamique de la méthode transcendentale chez Kant" (*Revue Néoscholastique*, Vol. 42, 1939, 341–384). In his analysis of Kant's *Opus Postumum* ("The Passage From the First Foundations of the Metaphysic of Nature to Physics")—which Kant once called his "masterpiece" but which was first published in 1920 by Erich Adickes under the title *Kants Opus Postumum, dargestellt und beurteilt*—Maréchal pointed out that Kant acknowledged that the "form" involved in human knowledge is not merely static or logical but dynamic and real in its implication. This same idea of intellectual dynamism is emphasized by Maréchal's analysis of Fichte's development of Kantianism, so much so that Maréchal has been accused of being too Fichtean and voluntaristic in his application of the Kantian transcendental method to the problem of knowledge. For Fichte, as for Maréchal, the self-reflecting self, the immediate intuition of the self as "a primary fact of consciousness . . . is the sole solid foundation of all philosophy" (Fourth Cahier, p. 349).

Bibliography

Works by Maréchal

Le Point de départ de la métaphysique. Leçons sur le développement historique et théorique du problème de la connaissance, 5 vols. Vols. I, II, III, Bruges and Paris, 1922–1923; Vol. IV, Brussels, 1947; Vol. V, Louvain and Paris, 1926.

Études sur la psychologie des mystiques, 2 vols. Vol. I, Bruges and Paris, 1924; Vol. II, Brussels, 1937. Translated in great part by Algar Thorold as *Studies in the Psychology of the Mystics.* London, 1927.

Précis d'histoire de la philosophie moderne, Vol. I, *De la Renaissance à Kant.* Louvain, 1933.

Mélanges Maréchal, Vol. I, *Oeuvres.* Brussels, 1950. Collected articles, with bibliography.

Works on Maréchal

Casula, M., *Maréchal e Kant.* Rome, 1955.

Gilson, Étienne, *Réalisme thomiste et critique de la connaissance.* Paris, 1939. Pp. 130–155.

Hayen, A., "Un Interpréte thomiste du kantisme: Joseph Maréchal." *Revue internationale de philosophie* (1954), 449–469.

Mélanges Maréchal, Vol. II (Paris, 1950), contains additional studies.

JAMES I. CONWAY, S.J.

MARIANA, JUAN DE (1535–1624), Neo-Scholastic political philosopher, was born at Talavera de la Reina, Spain, and died at Toledo. Entering the Society of Jesus at 18, he completed the Jesuit course of studies in philosophy and theology and taught theology in Rome from 1561 to 1569 and at Paris from 1569 to 1574. He then retired to Toledo to work on his "History" and other writings in practical philosophy. Mariana's *Historiae de Rebus Hispaniae* (Toledo, 1952; also published in elegant Spanish by the author, Toledo, 1601) was one of the first general histories of Spain. Also influential were his treatises *De Rege et Regis Institutione* (Toledo, 1599, translated by

G. A. Moore as *The King and the Education of the King*, Washington, 1948) and *De Mutatione Monetae* ("On Changing the Value of Money"), one of the *Tractatus Septem* (Cologne, 1609).

Accused of attacking the sovereign power of Spain in his criticism of its fiscal policies, Mariana was tried in 1609 by the Spanish Inquisition and acquitted. His philosophy is important for its handling of political, social, and economic problems. A strong advocate of the power of the people, Mariana argued that the citizens as a whole (*communitas civium*) are superior in power to the monarch. Men lived originally in an unorganized "state of nature," not needing political institutions to maintain justice; all possessions were held in common, and men naturally cooperated for their common welfare (*De Rege*, Chs. 8 and 13). With advances in arts and sciences, a division of goods developed into private possession; thus arose jealousy, pride, and strife among men. Tired of the struggle for domination, men then made a pact, delegating the ruling power to certain leaders. (Note that Mariana antedates both Hobbes and Rousseau.) The basic enactments of law can be changed only by the manifest will of the people. If the king fails to rule in accord with the law, he may be deposed by the people using prudent judgment; physical force may be employed for this purpose. Mariana was accused of trying to justify tyrannicide; his views did not endear him to the Spanish monarchists.

Bibliography

Laures, J., *The Political Economy of Juan de Mariana*. New York, 1928. Contains Latin text of *De Mutatione Monetae.*

Tallmadge, G. K., "Juan de Mariana," in Gerard Smith, ed., *Jesuit Thinkers of the Renaissance*. Milwaukee, 1939. Pp. 157–192.

Ullastres Calvo, A., "La teoria de la mutación monetaria del Mariana." *Anales de economia*, No. 15 (1944), 273–304; No. 20 (1945), 437–471.

VERNON J. BOURKE

MARÍAS, JULIÁN, is the best-known and most productive of the post-Civil War philosophers in Spain who have sought to reconcile the doctrines of their teacher, José Ortega y Gasset, with traditional theism. Born in Valladolid in 1914, Marías studied under Ortega in Madrid just before the Civil War. When Ortega returned from exile in 1948, they jointly founded the Institute of Humanities in Madrid. Marías has taught at the institute and, as visiting professor, at various American universities. The bulk of his published work concerns the history of philosophy, mainly Spanish and scholastic philosophy. His general *Historia de la filosofía* (1941), which he wrote at the age of 26, emphasizes the Aristotelian and scholastic traditions and gives a prominent position to Spanish thought. In *La escuela de Madrid* ("The Madrid School," Buenos Aires, 1959), Marías presented the most comprehensive study available of such contemporary Spanish thinkers as Ortega, Miguel de Unamuno, Xavier Zubiri, and Manuel García Morente.

As a Catholic disciple of Ortega, who was explicitly irreligious and anti-Catholic, Marías gave a theistic interpretation of Ortega's "ratiovitalism" (a reconciliation of rationalism and the vitalist doctrines of the 1920s). In his major work, *Introducción a la filosofía* (1947), Marías argued that certain intellectual and spiritual "ultimates" are true biological needs of mankind. To be lived at all humanly, life requires, in addition to food and other animal necessities, "the possession of a radical and decisive certitude." That certitude serves as the foundation for numerous "partial truths." It harmonizes all our beliefs into a single clear perspective, and it also provides society with a ruling view that is needed for social stability. Men turn to philosophy for this certitude, so there is nothing more "practical," vital, or socially relevant than metaphysics, which is called upon to give men a standard to live by.

Marías accepts all the pragmatist, relativist, and historicist implications of vitalism, which usually have been regarded as destructive of religious convictions, and he argues from them back to the traditional religious outlook. Truth is what answers a vital need by removing the feeling of insecurity and perplexity. It is always relative to particular life situations and historical periods. Truth fragments into a multitude of relative truths, which contain concrete concepts as distinct from general concepts, which are obtained only by an arbitrary and schematizing process of abstraction. Yet, if the quest for completely satisfying, radical certainty is pressed tenaciously enough, it will lead beyond this complete nominalism to God, who appears as the ground or basis of being. Although the ego that carries on that quest was, for Ortega, the incarnation of "vital reason," for Marías it is the person who owns both vitality and reason. At death, that person, or soul, loses vitality and psychic activity but does not necessarily cease to exist. The mortality of the soul is a theory that remains in need of proof.

Bibliography

Works by Marías are *Obras* ("Works"), 6 vols. (Madrid, 1958–1964), *Historia de la filosofía* (Madrid, 1941); and *Introducción a la filosofía* (Madrid, 1947), translated by Kenneth Reid and Edward Sarmiento as *Reason and Life* (New Haven, 1956).

On Marías, see Alain Guy, "Julián Marías," in *Philosophes espagnols d'hier et d'aujourd'hui* (Toulouse, 1956), pp. 330–339.

NEIL MCINNES

MARITAIN, JACQUES, French philosopher, has been a powerful force in twentieth-century philosophy and cultural life. The author of more than fifty philosophical works and of countless articles which have appeared in the leading philosophical journals of the world, he is widely regarded as a pre-eminent interpreter of the thought of Thomas Aquinas and as a highly creative thinker in his own right.

Maritain, born in Paris, in 1882, was reared in an atmosphere of liberal Protestantism. He attended the Sorbonne, where he fell briefly under the spell of teachers passionately convinced that science alone could provide all the answers to the questions that torment the human mind. It was at the Sorbonne that he met his wife-to-be, Raïssa Oumansoff, a young Russian Jewish student who was to share his quest for truth and to become an intellectual and poet of real stature in her own right. She was also to collaborate with Maritain on a number of books. Soon disillusioned with the scientism of their Sorbonne masters, the two attended the lectures of Henri Bergson at the Collège de France. Bergson liberated in them "the sense of the absolute," and, following their marriage in 1904, they were converted (1906) to the Roman Catholic faith through the influence of Léon Bloy.

The years 1907 and 1908 were spent in Heidelberg, where Maritain studied biology under Hans Driesch. He was particularly interested at the time in Driesch's embryogenetic theory of neovitalism, a theory then little known in France. Upon returning to Paris, Maritain undertook the task of directing the compilation of a *Dictionary of Practical Life.* During the three years that he worked on this project, he also undertook a serious study of the writings of Aquinas. In 1914, he was appointed to the chair of modern philosophy at the Institut catholique de Paris.

From 1945 to 1948 Maritain was French ambassador to the Vatican. Afterward he taught at Princeton University until his retirement in 1956. He has also taught at the Pontifical Institute of Mediaeval Studies in Toronto, Columbia University, the Committee on Social Thought at the University of Chicago, and the University of Notre Dame. The Jacques Maritain Center was established at Notre Dame in 1958 for the purpose of encouraging research along the lines of his philosophy.

Maritain's thought is based on the principles of Aristotle and Thomas Aquinas but incorporates many insights found in other philosophers, both classical and modern, and also profits greatly from data supplied by such sciences of man as anthropology, sociology, and psychology.

Theory of knowledge. The cardinal point in Maritain's theory of knowledge is his defense and critical elucidation of different ways of knowing reality. On the one hand, Maritain sees the richness and inexhaustibility of material reality as requiring that the mind let fall on it different noetic glances, each of which reveals to the mind a different universe of intelligibility to be explored. There is, first of all, the universe of *mobile being*—being imbued with mutability—which constitutes the sphere of the knowledge of nature and which itself calls for both an empiriological analysis, that is, a spatiotemporal analysis oriented toward the observable and measurable as such (science of nature), and an ontological analysis, that is, an analysis oriented toward intelligible being, toward the very being and intelligible structure of things (philosophy of nature). There is, second, the universe of *quantity* as such, which constitutes much of the sphere of mathematics. And there is, finally, the universe of *being as being,* which constitutes the sphere of metaphysics.

Much of Maritain's energy has been devoted to giving the philosophy of nature its epistemological charter, in contrast with many Thomists in a hurry who would have it almost totally eclipsed by metaphysics, and in contrast with the many scientists who think that the only object capable of giving rise to an exact and demonstrable science is that which is sense-perceivable and can be subjected to methods of experimental and mathematical analysis. Maritain's serious study of the work of modern physicists and biologists revealed to him that scientists are led by their science itself to discover within the mysterious universe of nature problems which go beyond the experimental and mathematical analysis of sensory phenomena. It also revealed to

him that the conceptual lexicon of the scientist is radically different from the conceptual lexicon of the philosopher. For these reasons, Maritain has emphasized the need for, and prerogatives of, both an ontological analysis and an empiriological analysis of the sensible real. He has also worked out a theory of physicomathematical knowledge that relates this knowledge to what the Scholastics called intermediary sciences (*scientiae mediae*), sciences which straddle the physical order and the mathematical order and which have more affinity with mathematics than with physics as to their rule of explanation and yet at the same time are more physical than mathematical as to the terminus in which their judgments are verified.

On the other hand, Maritain sees the human mind as having another life than that of its conscious logical tools and manifestations: "there is not only logical reason but also, and prior to it, intuitive reason." There is indeed not only the Freudian unconscious of instincts, tendencies, complexes, repressed images and desires, and traumatic memories; there is also a spiritual unconscious or preconscious, the preconscious of the spirit in its living springs. The acts and fruits of human consciousness and the clear perceptions of the mind—in other words, the universe of concepts, logical connections, rational discursus, and rational deliberation—emerge in the last analysis from the hidden workings of this preconscious life of the spirit; but there also emerge from them many genuine knowings, and many affective movements, which remain more or less *sur le rebord de l'inconscient,* as Bergson would have said—on the edge of the unconscious. Among such knowings we have the various kinds of knowledge by inclination (knowledge through connaturality)—notably, poetic knowledge, the "natural" or prephilosophical knowledge of moral values, and mystical experience. Maritain feels it to be most incumbent upon us to recognize not only the different kinds or degrees of conceptual and discursive knowledge but also these different nonconceptual and "immediate" forms of knowledge.

Metaphysics. Maritain holds the classical view that the object of metaphysics is *being as being,* and he stresses that it is in things themselves that metaphysics finds this object. It is the being of sensible and material things, the being of the world of experience, which is the immediately accessible field of investigation for metaphysics; it is this which, before seeking its cause, metaphysics discerns and scrutinizes—not as sensible and material but as being. Before rising to what may be a realm of spiritual existents, metaphysics must grasp empirical existence, the existence of material things—not as empirical and material but as existence.

For Maritain, at the starting point of metaphysics there lies an intuition, the "metaphysical intuition of being," which may be said to consist in the intellect's seeing—through an abstractive or eidetic (idea-producing) visualization—the intelligible value *being,* being in itself and in its essential properties. The word "intuition" here has caused much difficulty for some philosophers, but it seems to be demanded by the thought that Maritain is trying to express. What must somehow be preserved is, on the one hand, that it is as true to say that this "seeing" produces itself through the medium of the vital action of our intellect—of our intellect as vitally receptive and contemplative—as to say that we produce it; and, on the other hand, that it is being more than anything else which produces this "seeing."

In his scrutiny of the being of sensible and material things, Maritain has presented a highly original treatment of what Thomists and others have long considered to be the first principles of speculative reason—the principles of identity, sufficient reason, finality, and causality. He explains that the reality which is the object of the idea of being is richer than this idea, and it presses for multiplication in a manifold of notions, among them the notions of unity, of goodness, of truth: being is one, is good, is true. Each of these notions expresses to the mind nothing but being itself, to which it adds nothing but a conceptual difference. But precisely in virtue of this ideal element which differs from one to the other, these notions as such are different among themselves and are different from the notion of being; they are convertible notions but they are not identical with one another. There is thus a superabundance of being with regard to the notions in which it is objectified, and it is in terms of this superabundance that Maritain elucidates the intuitivity of the first principles.

When he turns his philosophical gaze to the problem of the "cause of being," Maritain is attentive both to specifically philosophical ways of establishing the existence of God and to nonphilosophical or prephilosophical ways of approaching God. Under the first heading he restates the five classical ways of Thomas Aquinas, divesting them of the examples borrowed from ancient physics and formulating them in a language more appropriate to modern times; then he proposes a "sixth way." In this "sixth way" we have first the complex primordial intuition, that the *I* who thinks, the *I* who is caught up in pure acts of intellect, cannot ever not have been, for both the intellect and the intelligible as such are above time: this *I* must always have existed, and in some personal existence, too, although not within the limits of its own personal being but rather in some transcendent and suprapersonal Being. Philosophical reflection can go on to establish how the *I* always existed in God, can establish that "the creature which is now I and which thinks, existed before itself eternally in God—not as exercising in Him the act of thinking, but as thought by Him."

But Maritain is quick to recognize prephilosophical approaches to God—the "natural," or instinctive and intuitive, approach proper to the first apperceptions of the human intellect, the approach through art and poetry, and the approach through moral experience. The inner dynamism of a man's first awakening to the intelligible value of existence causes him to see that the Being-with-nothingness that is both his own being and the being of the universal whole must be preceded by transcendent Being-without-nothingness. As concerns art and poetry, the poet or artist, in following the very line of his art, tends without knowing it to pass beyond his art; just as a plant, although lacking knowledge, directs its stem toward the sun, the artist, however sordid his life, is oriented toward the primary source of beauty. And finally, as concerns moral experience; when a man experiences, in a primary act of

freedom, the impact of the moral good, and is thus awakened to moral existence and directs his life toward the good for the sake of the good, then he directs his life, without knowing it, toward the absolute Good. In this way he knows God vitally, by virtue of the inner dynamism of his choice of the good, even if he does not know God in any conscious fashion or through any conceptual knowledge.

Moral philosophy. One of the most provocative sides to Maritain's thought is his theory of "moral philosophy adequately taken." His contention is that moral philosophy—however vast, necessary, and fundamental be the part that natural ethics plays in it—must, if it is to be adequate to its object (the direction or regulation of human acts), take into account the data of revelation and theology concerning the existential state of man. Human conduct is the conduct of an existent, not simply the conduct of a nature. Consequently, the moral philosopher must take into account all data which contribute to make the existential condition of man genuinely known to us. He must take into account the data of ethnology, sociology, and psychology. And he must also take into account theological data. For, in fact, as a result of the present state of human nature, man has more propensity to evil than the man of pure nature by reason of the original sin and of the concupiscence which remains even in the just; and, on the other hand, he has incomparably stronger weapons for good, by reason of divine grace. Maritain recognizes that the moral philosopher who does take this situation into account will not be a *pure* philosopher but maintains that he will still be able to use the method proper to philosophy and advance with steps, so to speak, of philosophy, not of theology.

Maritain's theory of natural law has been elaborated against the background of anthropological data. He holds that two basic elements must be recognized in natural law: the *ontological* and the *gnoseological;* and it is perhaps in considering the second of these two that Maritain makes his most fecund insights. The chief point he wishes to emphasize is that the genuine concept of natural law is the concept of a law which is natural not only in the sense that it is the normality of functioning of human nature or essence but also in the sense that it is naturally known, that is, known through inclination or through connaturality, not through conceptual knowledge and by way of reasoning. The inclinations in question, even if they deal with animal instincts, are essentially human and, therefore, reason-permeated inclinations; they are inclinations refracted through the crystal of reason in its unconscious or preconscious life. And since man is a historical animal, these essential inclinations of human nature either developed or were released in the course of time; as a result, man's knowledge of natural law developed progressively and continues to develop. Thus, the fact that there is considerable relativity and variability in the particular rules, customs, and standards of different peoples is in no way an argument against natural law.

It belongs, of course, to moral philosophy to provide a scientific justification of moral values by a demonstrative determination of what is consonant with reason and of the proper finalities of the human essence and of human society.

Social and political philosophy. Much of Maritain's effort has been directed to working out the character of authentically Christian politics. He lays primary emphasis on man as being both an *individual* and a *person*—an individual by reason of that in him which derives from matter, and a person by reason of that in him which derives from his subsisting spirit. Man must live in society both because of his indigence as an individual and because of his abundance or root generosity as a person. As an individual, man is only a part, and as such he bears the same relation to society as the part bears to the whole. His private good as an individual is in everything inferior to the common good of the whole, so that an individual may even be required to risk his life for the sake of the good of the community. But as a person, man is a whole; and the whole that the person is surpasses the whole that society is, because the person, by reason of the subsistence of his spiritual soul, is destined for eternal union with the transcendent Whole; whereas the particular society in which the person lives, by reason of its not having a spiritual soul, is not destined for union with the transcendent Whole, but will die in time. Man is above and superior to political society, and the political community must recognize the person's orientation to an end above time and facilitate his attainment of it.

Maritain's social and political philosophy also manifests a keen sense of history. For Maritain as for Pindar, man must become what he is—man must "win his being"; man must become, in the psychological and moral order, in the social and political order, the person he is in the ontological order. Among the many truths related to this fundamental exigency of man's being is one that Maritain sees as of absolutely essential importance—the fact that human history is made up of periods, each of which is possessed of a particular intelligible structure, and therefore of particular basic requirements.

It is Maritain's contention that the historical climate of the modern world is quite different from that of the medieval world. For him, medieval civilization was a sacral civilization, by which he means that the historical ideal of the Middle Ages was principally controlled by two dominants: on the one hand, the idea or myth of fortitude in the service of God—the lofty aim was to build up a fortress for God on earth—and on the other hand, the concrete fact that temporal civilization had a largely ministerial role as regards the spiritual—the body politic was to a large extent a function of the sacred and imperiously demanded unity of religion. In contrast, modern civilization is for Maritain a secular civilization, by which he means that the historical ideal of modern times is largely controlled by two other dominants: on the one hand, the idea or myth of the body politic as being by nature something of the natural order and something directly concerned, therefore, only with the temporal life of men and their temporal common good; and on the other hand, the concrete fact that in pursuing this temporal common good, modern man is most intent on the attainment of freedom and the realization of human dignity in social and political life itself.

Against the background of this view of medieval and modern civilizations, Maritain has reflected at length on the nature of the democratic ideal. He sees democracy as the only way of bringing about a moral rationalization of politics, and he insists that in order to accomplish this task

democracy needs the quickening ferment of Gospel inspiration. But he also insists, no less forcefully, that the "creed of freedom" which lies at the very basis of democracy is not a religious, but rather a civic or secular, one. Furthermore, this secular creed deals with practical tenets which depend basically on simple, "natural" apperceptions of which the human heart becomes capable with the progress of moral conscience and which can be similarly adhered to by minds that may differ greatly as to the speculative and theoretical justifications. In keeping with such a conception, Maritain repeatedly asserts that men belonging to very different philosophical or religious lineages can and should cooperate in the pursuit of the common good of political life. He also maintains that the supreme principles governing the relationship between church and state should today be applied less in terms of the social power than in terms of the vivifying inspiration of the church: "the superior dignity of the Church is to find its ways of realization in the full exercise of her *superior strength of all-pervading inspiration.*" This reflects a most basic premise in all of Maritain's thought: that immutable principles admit of, and even call for, analogical applications in different existential situations.

Philosophy of art. From his earliest years Maritain has been the friend and confidant of numerous artists, writers, poets, and musicians, and he is considered by many as having the finest aesthetic sensibility among the major figures of modern philosophy. His long reflection on almost every facet of the artistic process culminated in his monumental *Creative Intuition in Art and Poetry,* which grew out of six lectures given in 1952 at the National Gallery of Art, Washington, where he had been invited to deliver the initial series of the A. W. Mellon Lectures in the Fine Arts.

Maritain holds, like Dante, that human art continues in its own way the labor of divine creation. But he keeps reminding the modern artist that human art cannot create out of nothing; it must first nourish itself on things, which it transforms in order to make a form divined in them shine on a bit of matter. Maritain will admit that the widespread effort toward "pure art" in the latter part of the nineteenth century may have been a beneficent phase after the exasperation of sensibility provoked by impressionism, but he affirms that in the last analysis human art is doomed to sterility and failure if it cuts itself off from the existential world of nature and the universe of man.

The deepest concern of Maritain has been with the nature of poetic knowledge and poetic intuition, that is, with the nature of the knowledge immanent in and consubstantial with poetry, poetry as distinct from art and quickening all the arts. He holds that poetic knowledge is a typical instance of knowledge through connaturality. Poetic knowledge, as he sees it, is nonconceptual and nonrational knowledge; it is born in the preconscious life of the intellect, and it is essentially "an obscure revelation both of the subjectivity of the poet and of some flash of reality coming together out of sleep in one single awakening." This unconceptualizable knowledge comes about, Maritain maintains, through the instrumentality of emotion, which, received in the preconscious life of the intellect, becomes intentional and intuitive, and causes the intellect obscurely to grasp some existential reality as *one* with the self (of the knower) reality has moved; and at the same time the knower grasps all that which this reality calls forth in the manner of a sign. In this way the self is known in the experience of the world and the world is known in the experience of the self, through an intuition which essentially tends toward utterance and creation. Thus, in such a knowledge it is the object created—the poem, the painting, the symphony—in its own existence as a world of its own that plays the part played in ordinary knowledge by the concepts and judgments produced within the mind.

Poetic knowledge, then, is not directed toward essences, for essences are disengaged from concrete reality in a concept, a universal idea, and are an object for speculative knowledge. Poetic intuition is directed toward concrete existence as connatural to the soul pierced by a given emotion. In a passage of great beauty Maritain wrote:

> This transient motion of a beloved hand—it exists an instant, and will disappear forever, and only in the memory of angels will it be preserved, above time. Poetic intuition catches it in passing, in a faint attempt to immortalize it in time. But poetic intuition does not stop at this given existent; it goes beyond, and infinitely beyond. Precisely because it has no conceptualized object, it tends and extends to the infinite, it tends toward all the reality, the infinite reality which is engaged in any singular existing thing. . . . (*Creative Intuition in Art and Poetry*, p. 126)

Maritain is admired even by those who may be of very different philosophical convictions. He is admired not only for his lifelong zeal for truth and impassioned commitment to freedom but also for his exceptional qualities as a person—his humility, his charity, his fraternal attitude toward all that is. Increasingly he is being recognized as one of the great *spirituels* of his time.

Works by Maritain

THEORY OF KNOWLEDGE

La Philosophie bergsonienne. Paris, 1914; 3d ed., Paris, 1948. Translated by Mabelle L. Andison and J. Gordon Andison as *Bergsonian Philosophy and Thomism*. New York, 1955.
Réflexions sur l'intelligence et sur sa vie propre. Paris, 1924.
Le Docteur angélique. Paris, 1929. Translated by Joseph W. Evans and Peter O'Reilly as *St. Thomas Aquinas*. New York, 1958.
Distinguer pour unir, ou Les Degrés du savoir. Paris, 1932; 4th ed., Paris, 1946. Translated under the supervision of Gerald B. Phelan as *The Degrees of Knowledge*. New York, 1959.
Le Songe de Descartes. Paris, 1932. Translated by Mabelle L. Andison as *The Dream of Descartes*. New York, 1944.
La Philosophie de la nature; Essai critique sur ses frontières et son objet. Paris, 1935. Translated by Imelda C. Byrne as *Philosophy of Nature*. New York, 1951.
The Range of Reason. New York, 1952.

METAPHYSICS

Sept Leçons sur l'être et les premiers principes de la raison spéculative. Paris, 1934. Translated as *A Preface to Metaphysics: Seven Lectures on Being*. London and New York, 1939.
Court Traité de l'existence et de l'existant. Paris, 1947. Translated by Lewis Galantière and Gerald B. Phelan as *Existence and the Existent*. New York, 1948.

Approches de Dieu. Paris, 1953. Translated by Peter O'Reilly as *Approaches to God*. New York, 1954.

MORAL PHILOSOPHY

Science et sagesse. Paris, 1935. Translated by Bernard Wall as *Science and Wisdom*. London and New York, 1940.
Education at the Crossroads. New Haven, 1943.
Neuf Leçons sur les notions premières de la philosophie morale. Paris, 1951.
La Philosophie morale, Vol. I, *Examen historique et critique des grands systèmes*. Paris, 1960.

SOCIAL AND POLITICAL PHILOSOPHY

Humanisme intégral. Paris, 1936. Translated by M. R. Adamson as *True Humanism*. New York, 1938.
La Personne et le bien commun. Paris, 1947. Translated by John J. FitzGerald as *The Person and the Common Good*. New York, 1947.
Man and the State. Chicago, 1951.
The Social and Political Philosophy of Jacques Maritain, Joseph W. Evans and Leo R. Ward, eds. New York, 1955. Selected readings.
On the Philosophy of History. New York, 1957.
Reflections on America. New York, 1958.

PHILOSOPHY OF ART

Art et scolastique. Paris, 1920; 3d ed., Paris, 1935.
"Frontières de la poésie," in his *Frontières de la poésie et autres essais*. Paris, 1935. This and the above work were translated by Joseph W. Evans as *Art and Scholasticism and the Frontiers of Poetry*. New York, 1962.
Situation de la poésie. Paris, 1938. Written in collaboration with Raïssa Maritain. Translated by Marshall Suther as *The Situation of Poetry*. New York, 1955.
Creative Intuition in Art and Poetry. New York, 1953.
The Responsibility of the Artist. New York, 1960.

Works on Maritain

Bars, Henry, *Maritain en notre temps*. Paris, 1959.
Bars, Henry, *La Politique selon Jacques Maritain*. Paris, 1961.
Croteau, Jacques, *Les Fondements thomistes du personnalisme de Maritain*. Ottawa, 1955.
Evans, Joseph W., ed., *Jacques Maritain: The Man and His Achievement*. New York, 1965.
Gallagher, Donald, and Gallagher, Idella, *The Achievement of Jacques and Raïssa Maritain: A Bibliography, 1906–1961*. New York, 1962.
Maritain, Raïssa, *Les Grandes Amitiés*, 2 vols. New York, 1941. Vol. I translated by Julie Kernan as *We Have Been Friends Together*. New York, 1942. Vol. II translated by Julie Kernan as *Adventures in Grace*. New York, 1945.
The Maritain Volume of The Thomist. New York, 1943. Originally published as Vol. 5 (1943) of *The Thomist*, dedicated to Maritain on the occasion of his sixtieth birthday.
Phelan, Gerald B., *Jacques Maritain*. New York, 1937.
Tamosaitis, Anicetus, *Church and State in Maritain's Thought*. Chicago, 1959.

JOSEPH W. EVANS

MARKOVIĆ, SVETOZAR (1846–1875), Serbian socialist, philosopher, and publicist. After prolonged uprisings between 1804 and 1815 had liberated Serbia from Turkey, a cultural revolution took place, led by the reformer of the Serbian language and orthography Vuk Karadžich (1787–1864), and socialist ideas began to spread. The first Serbian socialist writers were the economist and philosopher Živojin Žujović (1838–1870) and Svetozar Marković. After technical studies in Belgrade, Marković continued his education in St. Petersburg, where he attended the lectures of Dmitri Pisarev and became acquainted with the ideas of the Russian revolutionary democrats. Marković went to France in 1869 and then to Zurich, where he became acquainted with the Western revolutionary workers' movement and with the works of Karl Marx. Marković became the correspondent for Serbia and the Balkans of the Marxist First International. In 1870 he returned to Serbia, where he gathered about himself a circle of young intellectuals and workers. He published *Radenik* ("The Worker," 1871–1872), the first socialist newspaper in the Balkans, and later the newspapers *Javnost* ("The Public") and *Glas Javnosti* ("The Public Voice"). After nine months' imprisonment for violating the press law, Marković, who had become seriously ill, was set free in 1875. He began publishing a new newspaper, *Oslobodjenje* ("Liberation"), but shortly afterward he died in Trieste.

The basic determinant of Marković's thought and activity was the Serbian social situation. The disoriented rural paupers and the small and unorganized urban proletariat had repudiated the patriarchal social order, but they disagreed on the means of improving their lot. In search of ways to solve the social problems of his countrymen, Marković developed a socialist ideology. This theory was greatly influenced by the Russian revolutionary democrats Nikolai Chernyshevski, Nikolai Dobrolyubov, and Dmitri Pisarev, and later by Marx, but its main sources were materialist philosophy and the natural sciences— French eighteenth-century materialism (particularly Holbach, Diderot, and d'Alembert); the vulgar materialism of Friedrich Büchner, Karl Vogt, and Jacob Moleschott; the positivism of Comte and John Stuart Mill; and the scientists Darwin, Ernst Haeckel, Wilhelm Wundt, and Ivan Mikhailovich Sechenov, the Russian physiologist. There are also traces in Marković's thought of the utopian socialists Saint-Simon, Fourier, and Étienne Cabet, as well as of other socialists such as Pierre Proudhon and Louis Blanc.

Atheism and materialism. Lacking a deep and systematic philosophical and sociopolitical education, Marković did not intend to become a philosopher or a literary figure but strove to be the ideologist and spiritual leader of a new trend in science and life—a publicist and propagator of new ideas. Nevertheless, his theoretical outlook was relatively original and presented an integral whole.

Marković's ideology embraced first of all the general principles of scientific atheism and natural—philosophical materialism expressed in the study "Realni Pravac u Nauci Iživotu" ("The Realistic Trend in Science and Life," in the journal *Letopis Matice Srpske*, 1871–1872) and other works. From Chernyshevski and Marx he borrowed the notion of the need for building up a philosophical theory as the basis of sociopolitical knowledge and practice. He called his view "scientific materialism and realism." All phenomena, as well as the processes of nature, society, and spiritual life, were interpreted in terms of matter and its laws. Nature and society were integrally connected. Only by means of science was the people's economic and political revival possible. Marković, like Marx, contrasted his view with Bakunin's. In spite of certain elements of mechanism and agnosticism in his outlook, Marković advocated the idea of dialectical development and an evolutionistic–

materialistic theory of knowledge as the basis of the social struggle of the socialist movement.

In his interpretation of man and society, Marković drew upon Darwin, Comte, the French materialists, Feuerbach, and Chernyshevski. Morals is founded on knowledge and science, and the development of morals is affected by the development of man's needs through the socialization of instincts. Moral feelings are not innate; man becomes individually moral and socially more morally minded as society develops. Only by constant labor can man raise himself to a height unreachable by any other organism. Marković condemned the morals of bourgeois society as being founded upon the exploitation of the lower classes. Because morality is the indispensable consequence of the social machine, only a socialist revolution can bring about a new socialist morality. Seeing the primary goal of the future socialist society as the morality of its members, Marković termed his ethical socialism "idealistic realism." He did not conceive of the idea as being determined by matter, but spoke of the idea as the primary motive force in the development of society.

Aesthetics. Believing that a spiritual revolution must precede the political and economic revolutions, Marković held that the social revival had to be supported by literature and art. In "Pevanje i Mišljenje" ("Songs and Thought," *Matica*, 1868), "Realnost u Poeziji" ("Reality in Poetry," *Matica*, 1870), and many other works, Marković expounded a materialist aesthetic modeled upon that of Chernyshevski. Literature should be realistic and rational, expressing the genuine life, needs, and interests of the people, and should have an effect upon the general social revival. Marković's views decisively affected the development of Serbian literature, turning it toward Russian and western European realism.

Sociopolitical views. In his voluminous book, *Načelo Narodne Ekonomije* ("The Principles of the National Economy," Belgrade, 1874), written in the vein of J. S. Mill and Chernyshevski, Marković praised Marx for his discovery of the law of social development, but he held that these laws could not be applied to Russia, Serbia, and other economically undeveloped countries, which, in Marković's opinion, could bypass capitalism and move from patriarchal cooperatives directly to socialism. Marković's teachings on society, state, and revolution, in spite of some elements of utopianism and historical idealism, showed a high degree of accuracy. Although he gave too much weight to the roles of social consciousness, science, and philosophy, and consequently to the revolutionary intelligentsia, in the development of socialist society, his program was revolutionary and democratic. In a series of works, especially in his most original work, *Srbija na Istoku* ("Serbia in the East," Novi Sad, 1872), Marković defended the Paris Commune and criticized the capitalistic social system of western Europe and the narrowness of the bourgeois democracies. Marković was convinced that the transition to socialism was possible only by means of a revolution of the whole people against foreign invaders and native capitalist exploiters. He developed a fragmentary theory of the smashing of the bourgeois state in the socialist revolution and the withering away of the socialist state in the process of building communism. Like Marx, he held that only in conjunction with revolutionary practice could revolutionary theory solve the social problem. He perceived the significance of the class struggle in the West, but in backward Serbia he thought that the revolutionary intelligentsia could play a more decisive role than the proletariat. He advocated federation and self-government for the southern Slav nations. He also advocated a system of cooperatives.

Although Marković was more a revolutionary democrat than a Marxist, his teachings nevertheless united general Marxian principles concerning revolution with theories concerning the specific national character of Serbia. Moreover, they stressed the need for joint action on the part of the revolutionary intelligentsia, the peasantry, and the workers. Thus, Marković was the founder and leader of the Serbian socialist movement, as well as its theoretician, philosopher, aesthetician, and literary critic.

Works by Marković

Many of Marković's scientific and periodical papers are collected in *Sabrani Spisi*, 4 vols. (Belgrade, 1960–1965).

Works on Marković

For literature on Marković, see Slobodan Jovanović, *Svetozar Marković* (Belgrade, 1904); Jovan Skerlić, *Svetozar Marković* (Belgrade, 1910); Veselin Masleša, *Svetozar Marković* (Belgrade, 1947); Dušan Nedeljković, "Lik Svetozara Markovića," in the journal *Glas SAN*, Vol. 3 (1951), 200–207; Dimitrije Prodanović, *Shvantanje Svetozara Markovića o državi* (Belgrade, 1961).

ANDRIJA STOJKOVIĆ

MARSILIUS OF INGHEN (?–1396), one of the two leading disciples of Jean Buridan in the second half of the fourteenth century. (Albert of Saxony was the other.) For over twenty years Marsilius was one of the outstanding figures at the University of Paris; he was rector in 1367 and again in 1371. As a result of the Great Schism, in 1383 he migrated to the new University of Heidelberg, and in 1386 he became its first rector. He thus helped to spread the new outlook associated with Ockhamism to Germany.

Marsilius, to an even greater degree than his confrères, combined philosophical speculation with scientific inquiry in the tradition of Ockham. In addition to his main theological work, a "Commentary on the Sentences," he wrote on Aristotle's *Prior Analytics* and composed a treatise on dialectic, a set of questions on *De Generatione*, and *Abbreviations* on the eight books of Aristotle's *Physics*. His outlook, like that of so many fourteenth-century thinkers, still awaits systematic study; but two aspects of it seem agreed upon. The first is that, without following the path to skepticism, he adhered to the distinction (given special currency by Ockham) between knowledge derived from natural experience and faith. The second is that he gave a more philosophical interpretation to the scientific concepts of his day.

Marsilius held that God's infinite power could not be proved by natural evidence alone; his omnipotence was a matter for faith. Similarly, belief in the fact that there will be a bodily resurrection was independent of our knowledge of how it will take place. Philosophically it was not possible to prove the creation of the world in time and *ex nihilo*, although it was certain as a matter of faith. At the same time, Marsilius also showed the influence of Duns Scotus in his acceptance of a metaphysical—as opposed to a mathematical—argument for God's existence, namely, that God is unique and the efficient and conserving cause of all things. This eclecticism was characteristic of fourteenth-century thought and Marsilius was not the first to combine Scotus with Ockham.

In his doctrine of *impetus* Marsilius followed Buridan, imparting to it his own more speculative emphasis. Like his master he rejected Aristotle's view that moving air was the cause of an object's movement in favor of a *virtus impressa* in the object, which he called *impetus*. It was in answering the question, What is *impetus?* that disagreement arose between the leading participators—Buridan, Nicholas of Oresme, Albert of Saxony. Marsilius was in fact the first among them to grapple fully with the nature of *impetus*. His conclusions were of subsequent importance. With Buridan, Marsilius began by asking whether *impetus* was identical with movement or whether it was different. He concluded, first, that it was different: a quality added to movement; second, that although it was of a permanent nature in itself it was as transitory as movement, ending when movement stopped; third, that it was not all of the same kind; there could be *impetus* upward, downward, or in other directions. Fourth, he concluded that *impetus* could be regarded as a habit, an action, or a sensible quality.

Marsilius' more speculative side is also to be seen in his view that quantity was an independent quality distinct from extension.

Works by Marsilius

Quaestiones Super Quatuor Libros Sententiarum. Argentoratum, 1501.
  Expositio Super Libros Priorum. Venice, 1516.
  De Generatione. Venice, 1518.
  Abbreviationes Libri Physicorum. Venice, 1521.

Works on Marsilius

Maier, A., *Die Vorläufer Galileis im 14. Jahrhunderts*. Rome, 1949.
Maier, A., *An der Grenze zwischen Scholastik und Naturwissenschaft im 14. Jahrhunderts*. Rome, 1951.
Maier, A., *Zwei Grundprobleme der scholastische Naturphilosophie*. Rome, 1951. Especially Ch. 9, for an extract of Marsilius' theory of *impetus* taken from his *Abbreviations on the Physics*.
Maier, A., *Metaphysische Hintergründe der spätscholastischen Philosophie*. Rome, 1958.
Maier, A., *Zwischen Philosophie und Mechanik*. Rome, 1958.
Ritter, G., *Studien zur Spätscholastik*, 2 vols. Heidelberg, 1921, 1922.

GORDON LEFF

MARSILIUS OF PADUA (Marsilio dei Mainardini), Italian political theorist, was born between 1275 and 1280 and died in 1342. He probably studied medicine at the University of Padua. In 1313 he was rector of the University of Paris, where he met such leading Averroists as Peter of Abano and John of Jandun. He is chiefly famous for his antipapalist treatise *Defensor Pacis* ("Defender of Peace," 1324), a landmark in the history of political philosophy. When his authorship of this work became known in 1326, he was forced to flee to the court of Louis of Bavaria in Nuremberg; Pope John XXII thereupon branded him a heretic. Marsilius subsequently assisted Louis in various imperial ventures in Italy.

"Defensor Pacis." The primary purpose of the *Defensor Pacis* was to refute the papalist claims to "plenitude of power" as these claims had been advanced by Pope Innocent IV, Egidius of Rome, and others in the thirteenth and fourteenth centuries. So crushing was the refutation produced by Marsilius that it completely reversed the papalist position. The papal position had held that secular rulers must be subject to the papacy even in "temporal" affairs, so that they must be established, judged, and, if necessary, deposed by the pope. Marsilius, in contrast, undertook to demonstrate that the papacy and the priesthood in general must be subject not only in temporal, but even in "spiritual," affairs to the whole people and to the secular ruler acting by the people's authority. The powers of the priesthood were to be reduced to the administration of the sacraments and the teaching of divine law, but even in these functions the priests were to be regulated and controlled by the people and its elected government. The upshot of Marsilius' doctrine was that the attempt to base human society on religious values under priestly control was decisively overthrown; instead, the way was opened for a purely secular society under the control of a popularly elected government. Hence, it is understandable that Marsilius has been hailed as a prophet of the modern world. His treatise exerted a marked influence during the period of the Reformation.

Theory of the state. Equally as important as these revolutionary conclusions are the premises from which Marsilius derived them. These premises are found in his general theory of the state, which is noteworthy for its fusing of three distinct themes. The first is the Aristotelian teleological view of the state as subserving the good life. The various parts of the state, including government, are defined by the contribution they make to the rational "fulfillment" of men's natural desire for a "sufficient life." This fulfillment proceeds through the "proper proportioning" of men's actions and passions, ranging from nutritive and sensitive acts to appetitive and cognitive ones. The function of government is to regulate men's transitive acts in accordance with the law as a standard of justice. The first theme, then, stresses an affirmative and maximal utilitarianism—what is required for the attainment of the highest ends of the "sufficient life," the common benefit, and justice.

The second theme of Marsilius' political theory, in contrast, is a negative and minimal utilitarianism. It emphasizes the inevitability of conflicts among men and the consequent need for the formal instrumentalities of coercive law and government in order to regulate these conflicts. Without such regulation, Marsilius repeatedly insists, human society itself must be destroyed. In developing this theme, Marsilius presents a positivistic concept of law, which stands in contrast with his nonpositivistic conception of justice (a distinction often overlooked in discussions of his ideas). He holds that there are objective criteria of justice, which he characterizes in terms of Aristotle's analysis of rectificatory justice—moderating the

excesses of men's transitive acts and "reducing them to equality or due proportion," thereby promoting the common benefit. But whereas Marsilius views law as a system of general rules concerned with the regulation of the same "excesses" and the resultant conflicts, as well as with other matters bearing on the common benefit, he emphasizes that these legal rules need not be based on "true cognitions of justice." On the contrary, laws may be based on "false cognitions of the just and the beneficial," so that Marsilius, unlike most medieval political philosophers, holds that justice is not a necessary condition of law. What is necessary is that the legal rules have coercive force, such that with regard to their observance "there is given a command coercive through punishment or reward to be distributed in the present world." These rules and the government which enforces them must be unitary in the sense that, if a society is to survive, it cannot have two or more rival coercive bodies of law and government.

The third theme of Marsilius' political theory is that the people is the only legitimate source of all political authority. It is the people, the whole body of citizens or its "weightiest part," which must make the laws either by itself or through elected representatives, and it is also the people which must elect, "correct," and, if necessary, depose the government. Marsilius presents many arguments for this republican position: (1) the whole people is intellectually and emotionally superior to any of its parts, so that only from its choice will emerge the best law and government, the ones most conducive to the common benefit, as against the ones that subserve the interests of some special group; (2) self-legislation is necessary for individual freedom; (3) only if the laws and government are chosen by the people will they be obeyed; (4) that which affects all ought to be subject to approval by all.

Although all three themes of Marsilius' general political theory were found in earlier medieval political philosophers, no other philosopher had given the second and third themes as central a position as did Marsilius. As a result of this, although Marsilius' first theme—about the ends of the "sufficient life," the common benefit, and justice—persists throughout his treatise, it is overshadowed by his emphases on coerciveness as the essence of political authority and on the republican bases of all such authority. The full consequence of these emphases emerges in the applications he makes of his general political theory to the problems of ecclesiastical politics.

Applications of the theory. In keeping with his first theme, Marsilius views the Christian priesthood as one of the parts of the state dedicated to achieving the "sufficient life" for all believers. Unlike the other parts of the state, however, the priesthood subserves the "sufficient life" to be attained primarily "in the future world" rather than the present one. Like the other Averroists, Marsilius manifests skepticism about the rational demonstrability of such a future life; nevertheless, he officially accepts the Christian doctrine that the future life is superior to the present life. He also holds, however, that secular and religious values are in basic opposition; here he seems to be applying in the realm of the practical the Averroist doctrine of the contrariety of reason and faith in theoretic philosophy.

Taken in conjunction with the maximal, affirmative

utilitarianism of his first theme, accepting that the priesthood subserves the highest end of man would have required Marsilius to accept also the papalist doctrine that the "secular" government, subserving the lesser end of this-worldly happiness, must be politically subordinate to the priesthood. At this point, however, Marsilius' second and third themes have their effect. Since the essence of political authority is the coerciveness required for the minimal end of preserving society, it follows that the higher end subserved by the priesthood does not entitle it to superior political authority. The question of the order of political superiority and inferiority is thus separated from the question of the order of moral and religious values. What determines the order of political authority is not the greater excellence of one end over another but, rather, the specifically political need for unified coercive authority in order to prevent unresolved conflicts from destroying society. Hence, the secular government, as bearer of this coercive authority, must be politically superior to the priesthood. If the priests refuse to obey the government and its laws, then they must be compelled to do so, because such disobedience threatens that unity of coercive authority without which society cannot survive. Indeed, it is because of this disobedience and because of its claim to a rival, superior "plenitude of power," that Marsilius convicts the papacy of being the gravest enemy of civil peace. In this context Marsilius presents his whole critique of the papacy as an application to fourteenth-century conditions of Aristotle's book on revolutions (*Politics* V), dealing with the ways in which threats to civil peace may be avoided.

In addition to this political argument against diverse centers of coercive power in any society, Marsilius also stresses, from within the religious tradition itself, that religious belief, in order to be meritorious, must be purely voluntary. Hence, in order to fulfill its mission, divine law and the priesthood which teaches and administers it cannot be coercive in this world.

Marsilius' third theme, republicanism, also plays an important role in the political subordination of the priesthood and papacy. The only rules and persons that are entitled to the status of being coercive laws and government officials are those ultimately chosen by the people; hence, there can be no crediting the claims of divine law and the priesthood to a separate derivation of coercive political authority from God. It is true that Marsilius subsequently holds that secular rulers govern by divine right, but he views this only as a divine confirmation of the people's ultimate electoral authority. This republicanism operates not only in the relation of the priesthood to the secular state but also in its relation to religious affairs. Because the whole people is superior in virtue to any of its parts and because freedom requires popular consent or election, the priesthood itself must be elected by the people of each community rather than being appointed by an oligarchically chosen pope, and the pope himself must be elected by the whole of Christendom. Similarly, the whole people must elect general councils to provide authoritative interpretations of the meaning of divine law. In these ways Marsilius' general political theory leads to a republican structure for the church as against its traditional monarchic structure. In effect, this also means that the secular government, acting by the people's authority, secures hegemony over the priesthood and papacy in all spheres.

Bibliography

The *Defensor Pacis* is available in two critical editions, one edited by C. W. Previté-Orton (Cambridge, 1928) and one edited by Richard Scholz, 2 vols. (Hanover, 1932–1933), in the series *Fontes Juris Germanici Antiqui* of the series *Monumenta Germaniae Historica.* There is an English translation by Alan Gewirth, *Defensor Pacis* (New York, 1956).

A comprehensive bibliography of studies published to about 1950 of Marsilius' doctrines is contained in Alan Gewirth, *Marsilius of Padua and Medieval Political Philosophy* (New York, 1951), pp. 323–326.

Bibliographical information on subsequent studies will be found in Georges de Lagarde's important study, *Marsile de Padoue*, 2d ed. (Paris, 1948), which is in the series *La Naissance de l'esprit laique au déclin du moyen âge*, 3d ed. (Paris, 1959——).

ALAN GEWIRTH

MARSTON, ROGER (c. 1250–1303), Augustinian Scholastic, was born in Marston near Oxford. He was educated at the Faculty of Arts and Theology at the University of Paris about 1270 and taught at Oxford and Cambridge between 1276 and 1285. He was the provincial of the English Franciscans between 1292 and 1298.

Roger Marston's career may be characterized as a conscious effort to restore St. Augustine to his position as the great leader of Christian philosophers and theologians. In carrying out the proposals of his teacher, John Peckham (also an Augustinian), Marston exhibited a phenomenal knowledge of the writings of Augustine, as well as a fine sense of historical and textual criticism. He must have been attacked as an archconservative, because he defended himself by remarking that he did not cling to tradition out of mere habit, but that after a reasonable scrutiny of the evidence, he had formed opinions that harmonized the writings of the "saints" with the wisdom of the philosophers. Marston knew the Greek and Muslim philosophers, and interpreted them with a great deal of subtle skill, sometimes calling attention to fundamental ambiguities in their thought.

Marston needed all the resources at his command to counter the attacks directed against the Augustinian theory of divine illumination, which he deemed necessary to explain certitude. Since the attacks were made under the guise of Aristotle's authority, Marston attempted to reconcile Augustine's theory of knowledge with that of Aristotle, as seen through the latter's Islamic commentators. Thus, Roger claimed that the Eternal Light of Augustine is the same as the separate agent intellect of Avicenna and Averroës. However, the English friar would not allow man to be "dispossessed" of his own individual agent intellect, and hence he posits a double agent intellect: divine and human. This was one of the medieval solutions to the idealist–empiricist dilemma.

In the realm of the philosophy of nature, there was one doctrine of Thomas Aquinas to which Marston took serious exception—namely, the Thomistic contention that each individual being had but one form. Prior to Aquinas, the far more common opinion had been that in material beings there was a plurality of forms. In man there were the forms of "vegetivity," "sensitivity," and "rationality," corresponding to the human functions of nutrition, sensation, and thought. Roger's solution to the question introduced a refinement which amounted to a synthesis of the Thomistic and traditional solutions, although it favored the latter. There is one substantial form for each being, but that single form admits of various subordinate and persisting degrees, or grades. Marston's theory of the grades of the form is the first organized version of this theory which has come down to us from the Middle Ages.

With respect to the majority of his philosophico-theological tenets, Marston followed the lead of Bonaventure. With Bonaventure (and against Aquinas), he considered an eternal creature an impossibility. Prime matter can exist apart from all forms by divine intervention, because God is the "Form of all things" who conserves his handiwork just as water conforms to the intricate convolutions of a mold, as long as it is contained by the mold. On the subject of God's foreknowledge of future human acts—a perennial problem in Christian philosophy—Marston remarks that since an individual's memory of a past event does not constrain his free will with regard to the past, neither does God's foreknowledge constrain his free will with regard to the future.

For a medieval, Marston has an unusually personal style, and his remarks are often a source of valuable information for the historian.

Works by Marston

Quaestiones Disputatae. Quaracchi, 1932.

Works on Marston

Etzkorn, F., "The Grades of the Form according to Roger Marston, OFM." *Franziskanische Studien*, Vol. 44 (1962), 318–354.

Gilson, Étienne, "Roger Marston, un cas d'Augustinisme avicennisant." *Archives d'histoire doctrinale et littéraire du moyen âge*, Vol. 8 (1952), 37–42.

Pelster, F., "Roger Marston. Ein englischer Vertreter des Augustinismus." *Scholastik*, Vol. 3 (1928), 526–556.

Prezioso, F., "L'attivita del soggetto pensante nella gnoseologia di Matteo d'Acquasparta e di Ruggerio Marston." *Antonianum*, Vol. 25 (1950), 259–326.

FERDINAND ETZKORN, O.F.M.

MARTINEAU, JAMES (1805–1900), English philosopher and religious leader, was born in Norwich. He was a brother of Harriet Martineau, the novelist and economist. Martineau attended school in Norwich and Bristol and went on to study for the ministry under the Unitarian auspices of Manchester New College at York. He accepted a call to a congregation in Dublin in 1828 and was married later the same year. In 1832 he became minister to a dissenting congregation in Liverpool. He occupied this post for 25 years, but for most of that period he was also teaching philosophy and other subjects at Manchester New College, and when the college was moved to London in 1857, he moved with it. From 1869 to 1885 he served as principal of the college. Despite the criticism aroused by his views on religious and theological matters, he was regarded as the foremost spokesman of Unitarianism in England and was revered by many in other religious groups as well for his impressive contributions to the literature of hymn, private prayer, and sermon.

In accordance with the then prevailing tendency of Unitarian thought, Martineau was brought up to accept the doctrines of associationism, egoism, and necessitarianism as taught by David Hartley and Joseph Priestley. In his early teaching he used works by James Mill and Thomas Brown as texts, but the difficulties he had in defending their views, together with his own growing sense of the inadequacy of their philosophy as a basis for a Christian outlook, led him rapidly toward a new general position. By 1839 he concluded that necessitarianism was incompatible with that sense of "the personal origin and personal identity of sin" which is central to Christianity. During the next half-dozen years he worked out the implications of this point. The results were first published in 1845 and 1846 in two long reviews (reprinted in *Essays, Reviews, and Addresses*) which outlined the positions he was to develop and defend for the rest of his life. Although he learned much from a year of study in Berlin in 1848 and 1849, German philosophy did not really change his thought. He remained far more a follower of Bishop Butler and Thomas Reid than of Kant or Hegel.

At the basis of all of Martineau's constructive thought is the view that we must accept as true certain deliverances of consciousness which appear to give us directly information about the external world, the self, and morality. Neither Kant nor William Hamilton nor J. S. Mill seemed to him to have given us reason to distrust the intuitions of the mind, and since these intuitions present themselves as reliable, we are entitled to have faith in them until reasons against them are produced. Martineau's intuitionism is the philosophical counterpart of the very great emphasis he placed, in interpreting religion, on personal religious experience. It is in such experience, he held, that one must look for revelation, not in messages delivered by others nor in traditions preserved by organized groups. Philosophically, both epistemology and ethics lead directly to justifications of religious belief.

From the very start of knowledge, Martineau argued, we are aware of a self and a not-self, and we are aware of these not as simply passively there but as being actively related. We thus intuit ourselves as willing and the world, in turn, as an expression of will. The former intuition is at the basis of our understanding of causality, which cannot be explained in terms of succession of phenomena, and the idea of causality finds its mature expression in the belief that God is the noumenal cause of the phenomenal order. Science, which deals only with phenomena, cannot upset our belief in God, but the increasing unity of the laws and theories which science discovers acts as a confirmation of our intuitive belief in the unity of the cause of nature.

If the "natural" attributes of God, such as omnipotence and intelligence, are revealed through our experience of the external world, the moral attributes are revealed to us primarily in our moral experience. Martineau argued very carefully that the central subject of moral judgment is motives or "springs of action," not acts or consequences. He held that whenever there is more than one motive competing to direct our action, we are intuitively aware that one of the motives is higher than the others.

"The moral faculty," he said, "is not any apprehension

of invisible qualities in external actions, not any partition of them into the absolutely good and absolutely evil, not any intellectual testing of them by rules of congruity or balances of utility, but a recognition, at their very source, of a scale of *relative* values lying within ourselves," relative because a given motive may be higher in relation to one alternative, lower in relation to another. To be good is to choose to act on the relatively higher motive. Once this choice is made, consideration of consequences comes in to aid in selecting the particular act which will best express the motive in the actual circumstances. It is the first choice only which is morally relevant, though the second is, of course, important. Since the moral value of both agent and act is wholly determined by his choice of motive, Martineau went to considerable pains to defend absolute freedom of the will. The arguments rely heavily on the concept of cause developed in his epistemology. In our own willing we learn something of the nature of God's activity; the realization that there is an authoritative demand on us to act on the relatively higher motive is the chief revelation of God within our moral experience. The authoritativeness of the demand can be explained only in theistic terms, and the content of the demand reveals to us God's moral nature.

Martineau's style is extremely florid and his exposition quite diffuse. In his epistemological and metaphysical writings he seems often to have missed the point of an opposing theory or to have been content with very weak arguments for his own. But his ethics, as an account of the ethics of motive, if not highly original, is in conception and in execution one of the finest that has ever been presented.

Bibliography

Works by Martineau include *A Study of Spinoza* (London, 1882); *Types of Ethical Theory*, 2 vols. (Oxford, 1885); *A Study of Religion*, 2 vols. (Oxford, 1888); *The Seat of Authority in Religion* (London, 1890); *Essays, Reviews, and Addresses,* selected and revised by Martineau himself (London, 1890–1891).

For an account of his life and philosophy, see James Drummond and C. B. Upton, *Life and Letters of James Martineau* (London, 1902); criticism of the ethics will be found in Henry Sidgwick, *Lectures on the Ethics of T. H. Green, Mr. Herbert Spencer, and James Martineau* (London, 1902).

J. B. SCHNEEWIND

MARTINETTI, PIERO (1872–1943), Italian metaphysician, was professor of theoretical philosophy at the University of Milan from 1906 until 1931, when he resigned in protest against the oath imposed on university professors by the fascist regime.

Martinetti sought to re-establish metaphysics as a valid science by a method whose validity would have to be recognized even by positivists. This project involved a refutation of positivism on its own grounds. The positivist attack on metaphysics, Martinetti claimed, is valid only against vulgar or dogmatic metaphysics. Scientific metaphysics meets all the requirements of scientific methodology. It adheres to data that all science must recognize; but it is no mere synthesis of the sciences, for it interprets scientific findings and determines their meaning rather than their mere truth. Consequently, a scientific metaphys-

ics would achieve, on a posteriori grounds, successive unifications of empirical data until the Absolute was achieved.

The first of the successive levels in this projected unification is that of the "I" or self as a unity of sensuous consciousness. This is the constant flux of sense perception, the central point around which all perception is synthesized. At this stage no distinction is made between subject and object. The self at this level possesses a rudimentary transcendental character in the invincible conviction that its sense perceptions are identical with those of all possible subjects, but this persuasion is itself a mere datum.

This intimation of the transcendental and a priori provides a means of passage to the next level of synthesis, the logical level. But the a priori forms of synthesis are not a priori in the Kantian sense; they are "con-natural" with their empirical content. Among these forms are substance and cause, which unify respectively the coexistent and the successive. The movement from the sensible forms of unity to the logical forms is not itself a logical process; rather, it is entirely natural. Logic is the "science of the natural conformations of human thought," and logical relations are therefore empirical relations.

The third stage of synthesis, that of absolute unity, cannot be achieved in thought; it is implied in the dynamic of thought. We can have no speculative concept, but only a symbolic intuition, of it. However, it cannot be concluded, therefore, that our knowledge is limited to phenomena. The absolute unity is always present, although in an imperfect way, because it enters structurally into all levels of synthesis. This omnipresence of the Absolute Martinetti called mystical: "Our knowledge is a mystic unity with the eternal Logos."

This process of synthesis applies also to the practical order, whose transcendental principle is liberty. Morality exhibits a primary synthesis in the form of necessity freely achieved—a synthesis that is continued and extended by art and religion.

Works by Martinetti

Introduzione alla metafisica, 2 vols. Milan, 1902–1904.
Emanuele Kant-Prolegomini. Turin, 1913. With a commentary by Martinetti.
La libertà. Milan, 1928.
Gesù Cristo ed il cristianesimo. Milan, 1934.
Ragione e fede. Turin, 1942.

Works on Martinetti

Alessio. F. P., *L'idealismo religioso di Piero Martinetti.* Brescia, 1950.
Gentile, Giovanni, "La teoria della conoscenza del Martinetti," in *Saggi critici,* 1st series. Naples, 1921.
Sciacca, M. F., *Piero Martinetti.* Brescia, 1943. Contains an excellent bibliography.

A. ROBERT CAPONIGRI

MARTY, ANTON (1847–1914), professor of philosophy at the German University of Prague and for forty years a close associate of Franz Brentano. Marty's most important work is the *Untersuchungen zur Grundlegung der allge-*

meinen Sprachtheorie (Halle, 1908), a treatise on the philosophy of language. His theory of meaning, or "semasiology," is based upon Brentano's descriptive psychology. From a contemporary point of view, the most interesting aspects of this theory are the distinction between categorematic and syncategorematic uses of words and the theory of emotive utterances.

Like Brentano, Marty appeals to the correctness of affirmation and rejection, and of love and hate (in a broad sense) to explicate the syncategorematic character of certain basic philosophical concepts. In the assertion "There is a horse," the words "a horse" *refer* to an object, but the words "there is" serve only to *express* the fact that the speaker is accepting or acknowledging the object. An object is said to have being if it may be correctly accepted; it has nonbeing if it may be correctly rejected; it is good if it may be correctly loved; it is bad if it may be correctly hated; the necessary is that which may be correctly accepted a priori; the impossible is that which may be correctly rejected a priori.

Marty rejected the view of Bernard Bolzano and Alexius Meinong, according to which there are objects that may be said to "subsist" and not to "exist." But he did contend that the objects that may be said to "exist" may be classified as being either "real" or "nonreal." Examples of nonreal objects that exist are gaps, deficiencies, holes, space, time, and what Marty called the content of a judgment. (If the judgment "There are horses" is correct, then there exists that nonreal object that is the being of horses; if it is incorrect, then there exists that nonreal object that is the nonbeing of horses.) According to Marty, nonreal objects have no causal efficacy, and their existence is always a function of the existence of certain concomitant real objects. Brentano objected to this view on the ground that sentences ostensibly referring to such nonreal objects may be translated into sentences referring only to the real objects that Marty conceded to be their concomitants ("There is an absence of food in the larder" serves only to express the rejection of food in the larder) and that hence all such "irrealia" are superfluous. But where Marty restricted "real" to a subclass of things that exist, Brentano said that judgments about unicorns are also judgments about "real objects"; these judgments are about things which, if they were to exist, would be real (in Marty's sense of "real").

The word "good," according to Marty, serves to express one's love of an object; "bad" serves to express one's hate of an object. Marty discussed the emotive function of ethical sentences in detail and noted the ways in which such sentences are related to commands, recommendations, questions, and optatives. However, unlike contemporary emotivists, Marty held with Brentano that the emotions expressed and incited by ethical sentences are emotions that are either correct or incorrect; his theory of ethical sentences could thus be said to be emotive and also objective. He discussed in detail the relations among emotive and nonemotive sentences and the respects in which sentences of the one type may presuppose sentences of the other (for example, a man who calls "Stop thief!" asserts implicitly that there is a thief and that he is trying to get away).

Bibliography

Marty's posthumously published *Raum und Zeit* (Halle, 1916) sets forth a comprehensive theory of space, time, and causality. His writings also include *Über den Ursprung der Sprache* (Würzburg, 1875); *Die geschichtliche Entwicklung des Farbensinnes* (Vienna, 1879); *Die logische, lokalistische und andere Kasustheorien* (Halle, 1910); *Gesammelte Schriften*, Josef Eisenmeir, Alfred Kastil, and Oskar Kraus, eds., 2 vols. (Halle, 1916–1920); *Nachgelassene Schriften*, Otto Funke, ed. (Bern, 1940–1950).

See also Oskar Kraus, *Anton Marty: sein Leben und seine Werke* (Halle, 1916); and *Die Werttheorien* (Brünn, 1937).

RODERICK M. CHISHOLM

MARULIĆ, MARKO (1450–1524), Croatian poet, historian, and philosopher, was born in Split, Dalmatia. Marulić's epic, *Istorija Svete Udovice Judit* ("The History of the Holy Widow Judith," Vinegia, 1521), is the oldest Croatian epic and the first printed Croatian literary work. Like all of Marulić's poetry, it is both epic and didactic. Marulić's philosophical works were written in Latin and translated into German, French, Italian, Portuguese, and other languages. His *De Institutione Bene Beateque Vivendi per Exempla Sanctorum*, first published in Venice in 1506, was reprinted, in the original or in translation, 15 times in the sixteenth and seventeenth centuries. His *Evangelistarium* (Venice, 1516) was printed 9 times.

Marulić was influenced by the Renaissance humanists and was also a student of the classical Greek philosophers, but he was at the same time an outstanding representative of then-modern Christian philosophical thought. He enriched Christian moral teaching with the abundant wealth of Stoic–Platonic moral thought and revived traditional philosophy in the spirit of humanism. Marulić regarded Epicurean and Stoic ethics as antithetically opposed and Stoic ethics as superior to Epicurean. In general, he rejected all forms of hedonism and utilitarianism, and with them ethical subjectivism and relativism.

Marulić's exposition of a Christian ethics combined with elements of Stoicism and Platonism was enlivened by examples from life. This original synthesis of ancient elements, rejuvenated by humanism, was greatly appreciated in its day, especially for its service in the Catholic fight against the Reformation.

Although ethical problems were Marulić's main concern, he also considered the fundamental problems of philosophy.

Bibliography

For additional philosophical works by Marulić, see *Quinquaginta Parabolae* (Venice, 1510); *De Humilitate et Gloria Christi* (Venice, 1519); and *Dialogus de Laudibus Herculis a Christianis Superacto* (Venice, 1524).

For works on Marulić, see *Zbornik Marka Marulića 1450–1950* (Zagreb, 1950), a commemorative volume honoring Marulić, published by the Yugoslav Academy of Arts and Sciences, with a complete bibliography of Marulić's works and of works about his life and writings.

VLADIMIR FILIPOVIĆ

MARX, KARL (1818–1883), German revolutionary socialist, social and economic theorist, and source of most of the important currents in modern socialism. Marx was born in Treves (Trier) in the Rhineland. His family was

Jewish but converted to Lutheranism when he was six. Marx studied law in Bonn and philosophy and history in Berlin, where the intellectual legacy of Hegel, dead five years earlier, "weighed heavily on the living," as Marx later said. He received a doctorate from the University of Jena in 1841 for a thesis on Epicurus and Democritus. As an undergraduate Marx had identified himself with the left wing of the young Hegelians and was known as a militant atheist whose creed was (and remained): "Criticism of religion is the foundation of all criticism." This reputation made an academic career impossible under the Prussian government. Instead he became editor of a liberal businessmen's newspaper in Cologne, the *Rheinische Zeitung.* This paper was suppressed in 1843, and Marx decided to continue the struggle against Prussian autocracy from Paris, thus beginning a lifelong exile. In Paris he became friendly with Friedrich Engels, and they began what was probably the most momentous literary partnership in history. In his *Economic and Philosophic Manuscripts of 1844,* written in Paris, Marx roughed out, in a more metaphysical form than his later work, a brilliantly original view of human society, whose three components were French socialism, English economics, and German philosophy (the Hegelianism of his student days corrected by Feuerbach's materialism).

Expelled from France in 1845, Marx went to Brussels, where he continued his economic studies and made his first contact with the workingmen's movement. Asked to draft a statement of principles for one of their leagues, he and Engels produced the immensely influential *Communist Manifesto* (1848). The *Manifesto* is an analysis of capitalism, a criticism of "false" socialism, an interpretation of history as the preparation for the coming of true socialism, and a call to revolutionary action. During the 1848 revolutions, Marx was expelled from Brussels; he went first to Paris and then to Cologne, where he edited the *Neue Rheinische Zeitung* during an abortive experiment in parliamentary democracy. Upon the defeat of the democracy, Marx was arrested, tried for sedition, acquit-ted, and expelled in 1849.

He lived the rest of his life in London, supported financially by Engels, who had returned to his prosperous textile business. Apart from some journalism for Horace Greeley's New York *Tribune,* Marx never had regular work. He lived a life of poverty that was complicated by his own notions of respectability, worsened by chronic illness, and saddened by the death of three children. His only notable political activity was domination of the International Working Men's Association (the "First International"), formed in 1864 and scuttled by Marx himself in 1872 after prolonged factional strife, notably between Marx and Michael Bakunin. Most of those years Marx spent in the British Museum, gathering material for his great historical analysis of capitalism, *Das Kapital,* of which he was able to publish only one volume (Hamburg, 1867); Engels had to construct the other two volumes from posthumous papers. Marx's other writings were mostly exercises in political pamphleteering, in which his keen but often overhasty analysis was backed by unusual gifts for rhetoric and invective. At his death Marx was, in his own words, "the best hated and most calumniated man of his time."

His life had been dedicated to political fanaticism and to a passionate quest for a vast synthetic view of all history and culture.

That synthesis was only partially achieved, yet it succeeded well enough to provide an ideology and a fairly coherent world view for attempts to produce a new civilization, supposedly better and more advanced than the one produced by democracy and industrialism in western Europe and North America. Philosophy played little part in the Marxian synthesis, which was intended to be positive, historical, and sociological—"scientific," as Engels called it. It has been argued that any such generalizing world view is by definition philosophical or even religious and that therefore Marx must be classed with such great metaphysical synthesizers as Aristotle, Aquinas, and Hegel. But that begs the very question Marx posed: whether the study of history and economics, free of all philosophical speculation, religious prejudice, and overt ethical promotion, cannot show us the course that humanity will follow on this earth.

Marx's system began with an economic theory. Goods were exchanged at rates decided by the amount of labor that went into them (the labor theory of value). The price of labor itself was no exception to this law; labor was paid subsistence wages, just what was needed to "make" workers, i.e., to keep them alive and reproducing themselves. Yet labor produced goods worth more than its wages, and the difference belonged to the capitalists. Thus the misery of the masses was not due to wickedness that might respond to preaching, but to the operation of economic laws. However, a critical study of political economy showed that these laws were peculiar to capitalism, which was merely one stage of historical development, one soon to be destroyed by its internal contradictions. As the masses became poorer and more numerous, the capitalists became fewer and controlled greater concentrations of productive equipment, whose full productiveness they throttled back for their own gain. The capitalists would soon be swept aside as a restraint on production, and the masses would take over the already socialized industrial economy, which had been carried to the edge of perfection by self-liquidating capitalism. There would succeed a progressive, rational society with no wages, no money, no social classes, and, eventually, no state—"a free association of producers under their [own] conscious and purposive control."

Marx was the author of the doctrine of historical materialism, the theory that the "material conditions of life" and specifically "the mode of production of the material means of existence" determine much else in human consciousness and society. Neither Marx nor any of his followers, in a century-long debate, ever succeeded in stating this theory both rigorously and plausibly at the same time. Yet, because it stressed economic and technological factors in human affairs that previously had been overlooked or veiled by hypocrisy, the theory has had an extensive and generally fruitful influence over much thinking and writing about society. Marx "flirted with" Hegel's triadic dialectic to express some parts of his economic and historical theories, but it was Engels who developed dialectical materialism as a metaphysics or a theory of reality. Marx remained, like many Germans in his day, marked by the influence of Hegel, which revealed itself in a taste for metaphysical bombast but also in certain specific doctrines, such as that history progresses by struggle and opposition and that change occurs in revolutionary leaps rather than in gradual, quantitative stages. Not surprisingly, the Hegelian imprint is clearest in the earliest work: Marx's Paris manuscripts are a fusion of political economy and Hegelianism, each interpreted in terms of the other. But as Marx extended his knowledge of history and economics, he abandoned the metaphysical-moral critique of capitalism for an approach that sought to be factual and scientific.

Works by Marx

The nearest approach to a complete edition of Marx's work is in Russian, Karl Marx and Friedrich Engels, *Sochineniya*, 32 vols. (Moscow, 1955——), of which the parallel German version is *Werke*, 30 vols. (Berlin, 1957——). Previously scholars used *Marx–Engels Gesamtausgabe*, 12 vols. (Berlin and Moscow, 1927–1935). Neither contains all of Marx's output, which is catalogued in Maximilien Rubel, *Bibliographie des oeuvres de Karl Marx* (Paris, 1956).

In English there are several selected editions: Marx and Engels, *Selected Works*, 2 vols. (London, 1942; and, slightly different, 1951); and Marx and Engels, *Selected Correspondence 1846–1895* (London, 1934). Selections dealing with philosophical subjects include Marx and Engels, *Selected Writings in Sociology and Social Philosophy*, Maximilien Rubel and T. B. Bottomore, eds. (London, 1956); and Marx and Engels, *Basic Writings on Politics and Philosophy*, L. S. Feuer, ed. (New York, 1959).

Separate works in English by Marx alone are: *Capital*, translated by S. Moore, E. Aveling, and E. Untermann, 3 vols. (Chicago, 1906–1909); *A Contribution to the Critique of Political Economy*, translated by N. I. Stone (Chicago, 1904); *Economic and Philosophic Manuscripts of 1844*, translated by M. Milligan (London, 1959); *Letters to Dr. Kugelmann* (New York 1934); *The Poverty of Philosophy*, translated by H. Quelch (Chicago, 1910); *Theories of Surplus Value* (London, 1951).

Separate works in English by both Marx and Engels are *The Holy Family* (Moscow, 1956) and *The German Ideology*, R. Pascal, ed. (New York, 1933); *The Communist Manifesto* has had numerous editions, whose history is told in Bert Andreas, *Le Manifeste communiste de Marx et Engels* (Milan, 1963); the most useful in English are those of Max Eastman (New York, 1932) and Harold Laski (London, 1948).

Works on Marx

Biographies include *Karl Marx: Chronik seines Lebens in Einzeldaten* (Moscow, 1934); Isaiah Berlin, *Karl Marx* (London, 1939); E. H. Carr, *Karl Marx, A Study in Fanaticism* (London, 1934); Franz Mehring, *Karl Marx*, 4th ed. (Leipzig, 1923), translated by E. Fitzgerald (London, 1936); Maximilien Rubel, *Karl Marx. Essai de biographie intellectuelle* (Paris, 1957); Otto Rühle, *Karl Marx*, translated by Eden Paul and Cedar Paul (New York, 1929); D. Ryazanov, *Marks i Engels* (Moscow, 1923), translated by J. Kunitz as *Karl Marx and Friedrich Engels* (London, 1927).

The literature on Marxism is enormous. See the section "Bibliographie marxologique" by Maximilien Rubel in the journal *Études de marxologie*, published in Paris since 1959. Notable theoretical studies include H. P. Adams, *Karl Marx in His Earlier Writings* (London, 1940); Jean-Yves Calvez, *La Pensée de Karl Marx* (Paris, 1956); Max Eastman, *Marxism: Is It Science?* (New York, 1940); Sidney Hook, *Toward the Understanding of Karl Marx* (New York, 1933); Sidney Hook, *From Hegel to Marx* (New York, 1936); Karl Korsch, *Karl Marx* (New York, 1938); Antonio Labriola, *Marx nell'economia e come teorico del socialismo* (Lugano, 1908); George Lichtheim, *Marxism* (London, 1961).

NEIL MCINNES

MARXISM. Marxist theories, insofar as they are of philosophical interest, are discussed in detail in the articles DIALECTICAL MATERIALISM; HISTORICAL MATERIALISM; and MARXIST PHILOSOPHY. Various Marxist ideas are also discussed in the articles ALIENATION; COMMUNISM; COMMUNISM, PHILOSOPHY UNDER; DIALECTIC; IDEOLOGY; and SOCIALISM. See Marxism in Index for thinkers who are usually regarded as Marxists.

MARXIST PHILOSOPHY is the aggregation of philosophical ideas developed from various aspects of Karl Marx's social theory by later thinkers. Marx did not intend to write a philosophy and would have regarded "Marxist philosophy" as a contradiction in terms. He considered his work to be scientific, historical, and sociological, as opposed to "philosophical" divagations on social affairs, which he rejected as class-biased ideology. Moreover, he held that his social theory showed that philosophy was about to end. Philosophy, he said, was a symptom of social malaise and would disappear when revolution put society on a healthier foundation. The young Marx thought that this would happen because revolution would "realize" philosophy, would give solid reality to the ideal phantoms of reason, justice, and liberty that philosophers in sick societies consoled themselves with. The older Marx thought that revolution would destroy philosophy, would simply make it unnecessary, by bringing men back to the study of "the real world." Study of that world is to philosophy "what sexual love is to onanism." In either case Marx never varied in the opinion that the reign of philosophy over men's minds was drawing to a close. Thus, he naturally would not have contributed to its survival by writing a "Marxist philosophy."

Marxism and traditional philosophies. Within a few years of Marx's death, however, there were attempts to turn Marxism into philosophy. These have continued ever since and, indeed, have gathered force since the discovery of Marx's earliest writings. There are two explanations for this posthumous transformation. First, there is the familiar paradox that efforts to get rid of philosophy by argument are themselves philosophical. Thus, Marx's antiphilosophy and the theory of historical materialism on which it is based blossomed into a veritable philosophical doctrine, to which Georg Lukács gave consummate form. Second, after the empirical social sciences had taken from Marx's work all that was useful to them (and it was a great deal), there remained much dross—disproven prophecy, hasty generalization, and plain error. Instead of being discarded, as the errors and absurdities of Newton and Pasteur were discarded in the physical and biological sciences, this nonempirical material was kept alive by a social movement committed to preserving intact the whole of Marx's legacy. It has been called Marxist philosophy.

Because Marxism is not explicitly a philosophy, those who have treated it philosophically have largely sought to find the philosophy to which it "corresponds," from which it "derives," or which it "implies." Solutions have been extremely varied and incompatible. Enrico Ferri put Marxism into the Spencerian system, and Karl Kautsky connected it with Darwinism. Eduard Bernstein and Max Adler found its philosophical complement in Kant, and

"Back to Kant!" became the slogan of the revisionists. Plekhanov noted Marx's Hegelian origins but preferred to ally Marxism with materialism, notably that of Feuerbach. This opinion was widely accepted by Marxian political activists but was ardently combated by intellectuals. Otto Bauer said that Marxism could not be annexed by materialism because it was compatible with any philosophical doctrine, "including Thomism." Henri de Man essayed a combination of Marx and Freud, whereas the Marburg school of Neo-Kantians made a synthesis of Kant's ethics and Marx's socialism. The Russians whom Lenin attacked in *Materialism and Empirio-criticism* had married Marxism to the positivism of Mach and Avenarius. Lenin himself followed Plekhanov in putting Marxism in the tradition of mechanist materialism, later adding a dialectical theory of development to distinguish it from classic materialism. Georges Sorel, René Berthelot, and various Italian writers found the extension of Marxism in pragmatism, and this view became influential in the United States through the writings of Sidney Hook. Antonio Gramsci and Giovanni Gentile, in their different ways, reacted against the "materialist debasement" of Marxism by coupling it with Italian neoidealism. The search for new philosophic settings for Marxism, such as existentialism, continues and is necessarily inconclusive.

The variety of opinions confirms that there is no Marxist philosophy. Nevertheless, some efforts to incorporate Marxism into philosophy are less successful than others, for Marxism is not philosophically neutral even if it does fail to define its position in respect to the major philosophical traditions. Least successful are alliances of Marxism with materialism, from Holbach to Büchner, or with positivism, whether Mach's or Spencer's. The tendency of decades of criticism has been to show that the idealist content of Marx's thought is too dominant to allow those confusions. Conversely, the alliance that has proven most fruitful and which has grown in authority over the years is that between Marxism and the Hegelian dialectic. Though Antonio Labriola had noted this, it was ignored for more than a generation until Lukács insisted that Marx belonged in the Hegelian tradition. In this Lukács has been followed by Karl Mannheim, Herbert Marcuse, Lucien Goldmann, Jean-Paul Sartre, and Maurice Merleau-Ponty. Everywhere, Marxism's principal philosophical consequence has been to stimulate the study of Hegel. Otherwise, it has had singularly little effect on philosophy, even on pragmatism, with which it has evident affinities.

Orthodox Marxism. The distinction between a materialist and an idealist reading of Marx does not exactly coincide with the division between the orthodoxy of the Communist parties and the independent criticism of the so-called Western Marxists but the history of the subject must be told in terms of the latter division. The orthodox tradition begins with Engels, not with Marx. It uses two principal texts, Engels' *Anti-Dühring* and Lenin's *Materialism and Empirio-criticism*. The name of Marx is very seldom mentioned in these discussions, for Marx never explicitly stated the doctrines set out by Engels, taken over and interpreted by Lenin, and then dogmatically systematized by Stalin. He sometimes appeared to hold opinions resembling those they expressed—for example, the rep-

resentationist theory of knowledge—yet his early manuscripts seem far removed in spirit from the materialism of these works. That is why the early works, which are the basis of most Marxist philosophy in the West, are dismissed by Soviet writers as juvenile hang-overs from Hegelianism which the mature Marx disowned.

Epistemology. Orthodox Marxist philosophy has developed very little over the years, being accepted as much by Rosa Luxemburg as by Lenin, as much by Trotsky as by Stalin, as much by Mao Tse-tung as by Khrushchev. Its epistemology is naive representationism: The "concepts in our heads" are images, reflections, or copies of "real things." Objections to that view have been familiar since Bishop Berkeley, but they are held by orthodox Marxists to be answered by a reference to practice. We can compare mental images and the things they copy by noting our success or failure in manipulating those things. This manipulation is primarily economic activity or is affected by it, so it must differ for each technological age and each class. There is therefore no nonpartisan science. There is a contradiction here, for it is contended that the mind has exact copies of reality and yet its knowledge is historically relative. This is admitted but is circumvented by asserting that absolute knowledge is the historical goal but relative knowledge is the present plight.

Metaphysics. In metaphysics the orthodox doctrine distinguishes itself from classic materialism by insisting on dialectic process, as opposed to mechanism, in the development of things. Matter is subject to laws that are causal and determinist but not mechanist. It evolves toward the better and more complex, and it does so in a series of revolutionary jumps, in which accumulations of quantitative difference produce sudden qualitative changes after a period of tension and conflict. Matter is the unique reality. Chance does not exist, and there is no breach in this absolute monism. Mind is an epiphenomenon producing, in consciousness, reflections of matter. Matter does not determine mind directly, as the medical materialists said, but indirectly, by way of society. Society, too, develops dialectically, in revolutionary jumps that resolve its recurrent self-contradictions or internal conflicts. Human liberty consists in awareness of the necessity of social process.

Religion, ethics, and aesthetics. Religion is doomed to disappear, being a symptom of unjust and self-negating social conditions. Ethics and aesthetics evolve as society changes, for there are no eternal, nonhistorical laws in either. Beauty is objective but appreciation is relative to class, so art is implicated in the class struggle.

In ethics the situation is more complex. At first the exclusion of eternal, suprahistorical laws was held to warrant amoralism, ethical indifference, or at least some experimentation in new ways of living. Soviet authorities found that attitude socially inconvenient, and eventually Stalin formally condemned all applications of historical relativism that suggested that the new polity could have a new ethics (or a special new logic). Since then the position has been that Marxist philosophy substantially accepts the ethical ideals preached in other contemporary societies but adds that only a communist nation can escape hypocrisy by living up to those ideals, by practicing what it preaches. Thus, not only is ethical innovation discouraged in communist countries, but ethical criticism in noncommunist countries—for instance, by existentialists—is strongly deplored as a diversion from the work of creating the social conditions for the application of the uncriticized ethical code common to all modern societies.

Western Marxism. The Western Marxists, whose first generation, in the 1920s, comprised Lukács, Karl Korsch, Bela Fogarasi, and Josef Revai, rejected the representationist theory of knowledge, but their quarrel with orthodoxy centered on the dialectic. On this issue the orthodox followed Engels, the Westerners the young Hegelian Marx.

Engels had posited the triadic dialectic of thesis, antithesis, and synthesis as an eternal law of cosmic development, applying as much to nature as to mind and society. Everywhere, one would find constant progress from lower to higher by way of objective tensions. The tensions are caused when something engenders its own opposite or negation and are resolved when the opposites merge in a synthesis (the negation of the negation). Engels' immediate successors, whether social democrats, revisionists, Austro-Marxists, or independent students like Benedetto Croce and Sorel, could make nothing of these ideas and simply ignored the dialectic. At first Lenin did the same, in 1894 dismissing it as a "vestige of Hegelianism." However, he later adopted Engels' dialectic as the badge that distinguished Marxist materialism from classic or vulgar materialism. This dialectic embellishment of materialism has remained a point of honor with subsequent Marxist philosophers even when the dialectic is seldom applied or evoked. The law of the negation of the negation has found little use, and the examples of it offered by Engels, August Thalheimer, and Paul Sandor have been generally rejected by philosophers and scientists. Stalin formally declared that the other law of dialectic, the law of the transformation of quantity into quality, did not have universal scope but applied only to class-divided societies. With the two laws in effect discarded, orthodox Marxist materialism no longer has a characteristic theory of development. There remains only the law of the union of opposites, which serves to reconcile contradictions (and to justify inconsistencies).

The role of the dialectic in Western Marxism is very different. It does not operate in physical nature and is not a law at all. It concerns the relation between mind and social history. That relation comes to the fore because of an evident difficulty encountered by the historical relativism of Marx. If all knowledge is partial, provisional, relative, class-biased, and historically limited, then is this not true of Marxism itself? The answer of Engels and Lenin was that everything was relative except a small number of absolutely true propositions which included logic and Marxist theory. Seeing the impossibility of maintaining this dualism of relative and absolute knowledge, Lukács abandoned absolute (or unconditionally true) knowledge and accepted the relative and partial character of all knowledge. The relation between our knowledge and all other world views that constitute cultural history is a dialectical one, meaning that none is completely true or completely false. More generally, all relations between subject and history are dialectical in the sense of being ambiguous, reciprocal relations which leave room for

"contrary and inseparable truths." This is true because, on the one hand, the subject is a social and historical product and, on the other hand, because historical forces are alienated spirit, reified personality. There is conflict and tension between the two terms of that relation, and they will be removed by revolution, which will effect the synthesis of the two and will represent the triumph of the human spirit over the alienation or reification of its products. In this view the crux of historical materialism is the relation between mind and history, the dialectic relation between the personal subject and the apparently impersonal, material forces of society. In showing that those forces are really alienated personality, the theory denounces the objectification of spirit in inhuman institutions. It foresees the victory of spirit over that dehumanization.

Marxist historical materialism, said Lukács, thus criticizes itself according to its own principles. It comes to hold itself as provisional, as, at most, a progress toward a truth that is yet to be attained. Because this relativization seemed to lower Marxism from the status of a dogma to that of one ideology among others, it was no doubt the main reason for the condemnation of Western Marxist philosophy by the orthodox. Yet even the relativism of Lukács (and also of Karl Mannheim) still claims to have dogmatic knowledge of the whole of history, which is the total process into which all partial ideologies fit dialectically and which they all reflect more or less faithfully. With this notion of totality the relativists have brought back the Absolute that they first threw out in favor of the historically relative.

Common features. Because of a dualism in Marx's own thinking, which he never cared to resolve, Marxist philosophy has thus divided into two broad streams. On the one side, there is emphasis on the determinist, evolutionist, materialist, and sociological themes. On the other side, there is the idealist strain that looks forward to the deliverance of humanity from economic determinism. This idealist strain, stressing the primacy of present human activity over the solidified, alienated products of past human activity, has aptly been called titanism by Nikolai Berdyaev. It is a powerful factor in all modern Marxist thought—not only in Western Marxism, where it is explicit, but also in orthodox Soviet Marxism. After a profession of materialist faith orthodox Marxism introduces the idealist element by attributing to matter a readiness to cooperate with progressive causes. (In other contexts such an attribution of spiritual purposes to matter is called magic.)

The two varieties of Marxist philosophy retain other common features. Both abandon the distinction between truth and falsity in favor of a relativist notion that sees truth as a historical goal and knowledge as never more than progress toward absolute truth. This relativist concept appears in all philosophical developments of Marxism, from Engels to Gramsci and Lukács. Moreover, both sorts of Marxist philosophy cling to the idea of an ultimate reality. Though this is called matter in one case and history in the other, the difference is not great wherever matter has tacitly been endowed with a purposefulness and spirituality (by evolving dialectically) that make it resemble history. Marxism started with the recognition of all things as events or processes that interact, and it emphasized, in the theory of historical materialism, some sorts of interaction that had been overlooked. In its philosophical extensions it has gone on from there to the concept of a moving totality of things to which single things are relative and within which single things have ambiguous, dialectical relations with one another. This view is as familiar to philosophers as the representationist theory of knowledge that Lenin revived and has been as thoroughly criticized. For this reason, among others, Marxist philosophy has seldom secured consideration or academic influence outside of countries where it is politically privileged.

Bibliography

WORKS BY MARX AND ENGELS

Engels, Friedrich, *Herr Eugen Dührings Umwälzung der Wissenschaft.* Leipzig, 1878. Translated by E. Burns as *Herr Eugen Dühring's Revolution in Science.* London, 1935. The *Anti-Dühring.*

Engels, Friedrich, *Ludwig Feuerbach und der Ausgang der klassischen deutschen Philosophie.* Stuttgart, 1888. Translated as *Ludwig Feuerbach and the Outcome of Classical German Philosophy.* New York, 1934.

Engels, Friedrich, *Dialektik der Natur.* Berlin, 1927. Translated by Clemens Dutt as *Dialectics of Nature.* New York, 1940. This work was first written in 1872–1873.

Marx, Karl, *Oekonomische-philosophische Ausgabe.* Frankfurt, 1932. Translated by Martin Milligan as *Economic and Philosophical Manuscripts of 1844.* Moscow and London, 1959.

Marx, Karl, and Engels, Friedrich, *Die deutsche Ideologie.* Berlin, 1932. Translated anonymously as *The German Ideology,* S. Ryazanskaya, ed. Moscow, 1964.

MARXIST WRITINGS

Gramsci, Antonio, *Il materialismo storico e la filosofia di Benedetto Croce.* Turin, 1948.

Lenin, N., *Materializm i Empirio-Krititsizm.* Moscow, 1908. Translated by David Kvitko and Sidney Hook as *Materialism and Empirio-criticism.* New York, 1927.

Lukács, Georg, *Geschichte und Klassenbewusstsein.* Berlin, 1923. Translated as *Histoire et conscience de classe.* Paris, 1960.

Mannheim, Karl, *Ideologie und Utopie.* Bonn, 1929. Translated by Louis Wirth and Edward A. Shils as *Ideology and Utopia.* London, 1936.

Mao Tse-tung, *On Contradiction.* New York, 1953.

Mao Tse-tung, *On Practice.* New York, 1953.

Mao Tse-tung, *Selected Works,* 4 vols. New York, 1954–1956.

Plekhanov, Georgi, *Osnovnie Voprosi Marksizma.* 1910. Translated by Eden and Cedar Paul as *Fundamental Problems of Marxism.* London, 1929.

Plekhanov, Georgi, *Izbranniye Filosofskie Proizvedenia v Piati Tomakh.* Moscow, n.d. Translated as *Selected Philosophical Works.* London, 1961.

Stalin, *Leninism, Selected Writings.* New York, 1938. Contains the essay "Dialectical and Historical Materialism."

Stalin, *Concerning Marxism and Linguistics.* Moscow, 1950.

WORKS ON MARXISM

Berdyaev, Nikolai, *The Origin of Russian Communism,* translated by R. French. London, 1937. This work has never been published in Russian.

Bocheński, I. M., *Der sowjetrussische dialektische Materialismus (Diamat).* Bern and Munich, 1950. Translated by Nicholas Solluhub as *Dialectical Materialism.* Dordrecht, Netherlands, 1963.

Carew Hunt, R. N., *Marxism Past and Present.* New York, 1954.

Fetscher, I., *Der Marxismus: Seine Geschichte in Dokumenten,* Vol. I, *Philosophie, Ideologie.* Munich, 1963.

Hook, Sidney, *Towards the Understanding of Karl Marx.* New York, 1933.

Hook, Sidney, *From Hegel to Marx.* London, 1936.

Korsch, Karl, *Marxismus und Philosophie.* Leipzig, 1923; 2d ed., 1930.

Leningrad Institute of Philosophy, *Textbook of Marxist Philosophy,* translated by A. Moseley. London, 1937.

Lichtheim, George, *Marxism: An Historical and Critical Study.* London, 1961.

Marcuse, Herbert, *Soviet Marxism: A Critical Analysis.* New York, 1958.

Merleau-Ponty, Maurice, *Les Aventures de la dialectique.* Paris, 1955.

Vranicki, P., *Historija marksizma.* Zagreb, 1961.

Wetter, Gustav, *Der dialektische Materialismus.* Vienna, 1952. Translated by Peter Heath as *Dialectical Materialism: A Historical and Systematic Survey of Philosophy in the Soviet Union.* New York, 1958.

NEIL MCINNES

MASARYK, TOMÁŠ GARRIGUE (1850–1937), Czech statesman and philosopher, and president of Czechoslovakia from 1918 to 1935. Masaryk was born in Hodonín, Moravia. His political career belongs to history; of interest to students of philosophy is the fact that he studied philosophy at the University of Vienna from 1872 to 1876 under Franz Brentano. He spent the year 1876/1877 at Leipzig, where Wilhelm Wundt was his teacher and Edmund Husserl and Richard Avenarius were fellow students. In 1879 Masaryk became *Privatdozent* at Vienna, submitting *Der Selbstmord als sociale Massenerscheinung* (Vienna, 1881) as his habilitation thesis. In 1882 Masaryk became professor of philosophy at the Czech University in Prague, where he soon made his mark as a politican and writer in Czech. *Základové konkretné logiky* ("The Foundations of Concrete Logic," Prague, 1885; German translation, *Versuch einer concreten Logik,* Vienna, 1887) and *Otázka sociální* ("The Social Question," Prague, 1898; German translation, *Die philosophischen und sociologischen Grundlagen des Marxismus,* Vienna, 1899) were followed by books on Czech history and politics and by an extensive Russian intellectual history, first published in German as *Russland und Europa* (2 vols., Jena, 1913; translated by Eden and Cedar Paul as *The Spirit of Russia,* 2 vols., London, 1919). World War I and the presidency of Czechoslovakia put an end to Masaryk's academic pursuits, but a book of memoirs, *Světová revoluce* ("The World Revolution," Prague, 1925; English translation, edited by H. W. Steed, *The Making of a State,* London, 1927) and *Hovory s T. G. Masarykem* ("Conversations with T. G. Masaryk," 3 vols., Prague, 1931–1935) by Karel Čapek (English translations by M. and R. Weatherall, *President Masaryk Tells His Story,* London, 1934, and *Masaryk on Thought and Life,* London, 1938) reformulate his convictions impressively.

Masaryk was a practical philosopher who believed that philosophy should not only contemplate the world but also try to change it. He thus had little interest in problems of epistemology or cosmology. In his early life he reacted against German idealism and accepted British empiricism (Hume) and French positivism (Comte). Later he argued for a type of realism that he called concretism. In every act of knowing, he believed, the whole man takes part. Concretism acknowledges not only reason but also the senses, the emotions, and the will—the whole experience of our consciousness. It is something like William James's radical empiricism without the exceptional experiences admitted by James. But Masaryk's main interest was in sociology and philosophy of history.

Masaryk's realism was combined with a deep religious belief—Masaryk was a theist who found the Unitarianism of his American wife congenial—and a strong conviction of the immutable difference between right and wrong. Masaryk's thinking centered on the crisis of civilization caused by the decay of religion. He diagnosed the diseases of modern man (indifference, suicidal mania, violence, war, etc.) and prescribed remedies for them. He believed that sociology is the foundation of any futher cultural advance but that its method must not be purely genetic and descriptive. Teleology, or explanation by purpose, is legitimate. The aim of history is the realization of the ideal of humanity. Masaryk's humanism was not, however, merely humanitarianism, although he often spoke of democracy as another term for his ideal. In spite of his sympathies for the concrete demands of socialism, Masaryk remained an individualist who disapproved of all forms of collectivism. He criticized Marx as a blind worshiper of determinist science. Nevertheless, Masaryk exalted the role of the right kind of science. In *Základové konkretné logiky*, his philosophically most ambitious book, he classified the sciences and showed how they are internally related and coordinated. The task of philosophy is to create a world view based on the results of the sciences. Masaryk desired a new "Advancement of Learning" that would save man from intellectual and moral anarchy.

Masaryk assigned an important role in the realization of his ideal to his own nation, the Czech, and interpreted its history, remembering the Hussites and the Bohemian Brethren as a preparation for this task. He thoroughly criticized Russia for being a breeding ground for all the European diseases, particularly romanticism and materialism. Dostoyevsky, whom he both admired and rejected as a thinker, was a lifelong concern. Masaryk always expressed the deepest sympathies for the English and American tradition of empiricism and moralism and, in politics, turned his nation resolutely toward the Anglo-Saxon West. In 1918 he liberated the Czechs not only politically but also intellectually.

Bibliography

For information on Masaryk as a thinker, see the bibliography and articles in B. Jakowenko, ed., *Festschrift Thomas G. Masaryk zum 80. Geburtstag*, 2 vols. (Bonn, 1930); W. P. Warren, *Masaryk's Democracy* (Chapel Hill, N. C., 1941); and René Wellek, "Masaryk's Philosophy," in *Essays on Czech Literature* (The Hague, 1963).

RENÉ WELLEK

MASS. The mass of a body is its inertia or resistance to change of motion. More precisely, it is a property of the body that determines the body's acceleration under the influence of a given force. Mass can therefore be measured either by the amount of force necessary to impart to the body a given motion in a given time or by the acceleration produced by a given force.

The absolute metric unit of mass is the gram, which is the mass of a body whose velocity increases by one centimeter per second each second if acted upon by a force of one dyne. Other common units are the kilogram (1,000 grams) and the pound (453.592 grams). For velocities that are small as compared with the speed of light, the mass of a body is a constant, characteristic of the body and independent of its location—in contrast to weight, which varies with the body's place on the earth or in the universe.

Although fundamental to science and, together with length and time, the basis of all measurements in physics, the concept of mass was unambiguously defined only at the end of the last century. However, its rudimentary sources, systematically employed long before by Newton and to some extent already by Johannes Kepler, can be traced back to early Neoplatonic ideas concerning the inactivity of matter as opposed to the spontaneity of mind. The ancient metaphysical antithesis of matter and spirit served as a prototype of the physical contrast of mass and force.

Concept of inertial mass. Antiquity, and Greek science, in particular, had no conception of inertial mass. Even the idea of quantity of matter (*quantitas materiae*), the antecedent of inertial or dynamic mass, was foreign to the conceptual scheme of Aristotelian natural philosophy. Paradoxically, it was Neoplatonism and its admixtures of Judeo-Christian doctrines, with their emphasis on the spiritual and immaterial nature of reality, that laid the foundations for the inertial conception of mass, which later became the basic notion of materialistic or substantial philosophy. To accentuate the immaterial, sublime source of all force and life in the intellect or God, Neoplatonism degraded matter to impotence and endowed it with inertia in the sense of an absolute absence of spontaneous activity. For Plotinus, Proclus, Philo, ibn-Gabirol, and the Platonic patristic authors, matter was something base, inert, shapeless and "plump," attributes that reappear in Kepler's characterization of matter as that which is too "plump and clumsy to move itself from one place to another."

The idea of a quantitative determination of matter different from, and ontologically prior to, spatial extension originated in scholastic philosophy in connection with the problem of the transubstantiation. The question of how accidents of condensation or rarefaction (volume changes) can persist in the consecrated *hostia* of the holy bread and wine of the Eucharist whereas the substances of the bread and the wine change into the Body and the Blood of Christ led Aegidius Romanus, a disciple of Thomas Aquinas, to the formulation of his theory of *duplex quantitas*. According to this theory matter is determined by two quantities; it is "so and so much" (*tanta et tanta*) and "occupies such and such a volume" (*et occupat tantum et tantum locum*), the former determination, the *quantitas materiae*, having ontological priority over bulk. Aegidius' early conception of mass as quantity of matter, expounded in his *Theoremata de Corpore Christi* (1276) was soon renounced and had little influence on the subsequent development of the concept of mass. It was primarily Kepler who ascribed to matter an inherent propensity for inertia in his search for a dynamical explanation of the newly discovered elliptical orbits of planetary motion; in need of a concept expressing the opposition intrinsic in matter to motory forces, Kepler formulated the inertial concept of mass. In his *Epitome Astronomiae Copernicanae* (1618) he declared that "inertia or opposition to motion is a characteristic of matter; it is stronger the greater the quantity of matter in a given volume.

A different approach to the same idea arose from the study of terrestrial gravitation. As soon as gravity was regarded no longer as a factor residing in the heavy body itself, as Aristotle taught, but as an interaction between an active principle, extraneous to the gravitating body, and a passive principle, inherent in matter, as Alphonso Borelli and Giovanni Baliani (author of *De Motu Gravium*, 1638) contended, the notion of inertial mass became a necessity for a dynamical explanation of free fall and other gravitational phenomena. Furthermore, Christian Huygens' investigations of centrifugal forces (*De Vi Centrifuga*, 1659; published in Leiden, 1703) made it clear that a quantitative determination of such forces is possible only if with each body is associated a certain characteristic property proportional to, but conceptually different from, the body's weight. Finally, the systematic study of impact phenomena, carried out by John Wallis, Sir Christopher Wren, and Huygens, enforced the introduction of inertial mass. With Newton's foundations of dynamics (*Principia*, 1687) these four categories of apparently disparate phenomena (planetary motion, free fall, centrifugal force, and impact phenomena) found their logical unification, through his consistent employment of the notion of inertial mass. Newton's explicit definition of this concept, however, as "the measure of quantity of matter, arising from its density and bulk conjointly" was still unsatisfactory from both the logical and the methodological points of view. It was probably the influence of Kepler or of Robert Boyle and his famous experiments on the compressibility of air that made Newton choose the notion of density as a primary concept in his peculiar formulation of the definition of mass, a formulation that was severely criticized in modern times, especially by Ernst Mach and Paul Volkmann.

Leibniz and Kant. Leibniz' original conception of mass (1669), in contrast to Newton's, defined it as that property which endows primary matter with spatial extension and antitypy, or impenetrability. In his later writings, especially in his doctrine of monads, Leibniz associated mass with secondary matter and saw in it a property of a collection of substances (monads) resulting from their being a collection. Finally, recognizing the insufficiency of purely geometric conceptions to account for the physical behavior of interacting bodies, Leibniz departed from the Cartesian approach and accepted the dynamic, or inertial, conception of mass. The trend of Leibniz' ideas was brought to its final consequences by Kant, with his rejection of the Newtonian *vis inertiae*, the dynamic opposition against impressed force. Refuting its legitimacy on the ground that "only motion, but not rest, can oppose motion," Kant postulated the law of inertia as corresponding to the category of causality ("every change of the state of motion has an external cause") and consequently defined mass as the amount of the mobile (*die Menge des Beweglichen*) in a given volume, measured by the quantity of motion (*Die metaphysischen Anfangsgründe der Naturwissenschaft*, 1786).

Definition of mass. Under the influence of the Kantian formulation, often incompletely understood, and primarily owing to the fact that in spite of the universal use of the concept in science as well as in philosophy no clear-cut definition of mass was available, most authors defined mass as quantity of matter without specifying how to measure it. Toward the middle of the nineteenth century, with the rise of modern foundational research and the critical study of the principles of mechanics, the logical deficiency of such definitions became obvious. It was primarily Ernst Mach, preceded by Barré de Saint-Venant and Jules Andrade, who insisted on the necessity of a clear operational definition of mass. In an essay, "Über die Definition der Masse" (1867; published in 1868 in *Carl's Repertorium der Experimentalphysik*, Vol. 4, pp. 355–359), and in the *Science of Mechanics* (*Die Mechanik in ihrer Entwicklung, historisch-kritisch dargestellt,* Leipzig, 1883; translated by T. J. McCormack, La Salle, Ill., 1942), Mach defined the ratio of the masses of two bodies that interact with each other but are otherwise unaffected by all other bodies in the universe as the inverse ratio of their respective accelerations ($m_1/m_2 = a_2/a_1$), thereby converting Newton's third law of action and reaction to a definition of mass. If a particular body is chosen as the standard unit of mass, the mass of any other body can be unambiguously determined by simple physical operations. The practical method of comparing masses by weighing is, of course, operationally still simpler but logically more complicated, since the notion of weight presupposes that of mass. Although Mach's definition is not quite unobjectionable, it has gained great popularity and is generally adopted in modern texts in science.

Inertial and gravitational mass. In addition to its inertial mass, every physical body possesses gravitational mass, which, in its active aspect, determines the strength of the gravitational field produced by the body and, in its passive aspect, the amount by which the body is affected by the gravitational field produced by other bodies. According to Newton's law of universal gravitation, the force of attraction is proportional to the inertial masses of both the attracting and the attracted bodies. The resulting proportionality of inertial and gravitational masses of one and the same body, experimentally confirmed by Newton, Friedrich Bessel, Roland von Eötvös, and others, remained in classical physics a purely empirical and accidental feature, whereas the strict proportionality between the active and the passive gravitational masses is a straightforward consequence of Newton's third law of action and reaction or, alternatively, of the very definition of inertial mass if the postulated interaction is of gravitational nature. In general relativity, however, the so-called principle of equivalence, which maintains the unrestricted equivalence between uniformly accelerated reference systems and homogeneous gravitational fields, implies the fundamental identity between inertial and passive gravitational masses. In addition, it can be shown that on the basis of general relativity the active gravitational mass of a body or dynamical system equals its inertial mass, so that in relativistic physics, in contrast to Newtonian physics, the identity of all three kinds of masses is a necessary consequence of its fundamental assumptions.

Mass and energy. Whereas general relativity led to an important unification of the concept of mass, special relativity, already with Einstein's paper *Does the Inertia of a Body Depend Upon Its Energy Content?* (1905; reprinted in *The Principle of Relativity,* New York, 1923), led to a vast generalization of the concept by showing the equivalence of mass and energy insofar as a body emitting radiative energy of an amount E loses mass to an amount of E/c^2, where c is the velocity of light. Subsequent research, especially in connection with energy transformations in nuclear physics, supported the general validity of the formula $E = mc^2$, according to which mass and energy are interconvertible and one gram of mass yields 9×10^{20} ergs of energy. It also became obvious that Antoine Lavoisier's law of the conservation of mass (1789) and Robert Mayer's (or Hermann Helmholtz') law of the conservation of energy were only approximately correct and that it was the sum total of mass and energy that was conserved in any physicochemical process.

Influence of the electromagnetic concept. The way to these far-reaching conclusions of relativity had been prepared to some extent already by the introduction of the electromagnetic concept of mass at the end of the nineteenth century (by J. J. Thomson, Oliver Heaviside, and Max Abraham). It seemed possible on the basis of Maxwell's electromagnetic theory to account for the inertial behavior of moving charged particles in terms of induction effects of purely electromagnetic nature. Walter Kaufmann's experiments (1902) on the deflection of electrons by simultaneous electric and magnetic fields and his determination of the slightly variable inertial mass of the electron seemed at the time to support the hypothesis that the mass of the electron, and ultimately the mass of every elementary particle, is of purely electromagnetic nature. Although such eminent theoreticians as H. A. Lorentz, Wilhelm Wien, and Henri Poincaré accepted these ideas, according to which the whole universe of physics is but an interplay of convection currents and their radiation, with physical reality stripped of all material substantiality, the electromagnetic conception of mass had to make way for the relativistic concept as outlined above. Certain aspects, of the electromagnetic conception of mass did survive, however, and reappeared in modern field theories—in particular the fundamental tenet that matter does not do what it does because it is what it is, but it is what it is because it does what it does.

Bibliography

Bainbridge, K. T., "The Equivalence of Mass and Energy." *Physical Review*, Vol. 44 (1933), 123.

Comstock, D. F., "The Relation of Mass to Energy." *Philosophical Magazine*, Vol. 15 (1908), 1–21.

Jammer, Max, *Concepts of Mass in Classical and Modern Physics.* Cambridge, Mass.; 1961; New York, 1964.

Lampa, A., "Eine Ableitung des Massenbegriffs." *Lotos*, Vol. 59 (1911), 303–312.

Mach, Ernst, *Die Geschichte und die Wurzel des Satzes von der Erhaltung der Arbeit.* Prague, 1872.

Pendse, C. G., "On Mass and Force in Newtonian Mechanics." *Philosophical Magazine*, Vol. 29 (1940), 477–484.

Whittaker, E. T., "On Gauss' Theorem and the Concept of Mass in General Relativity." *Proceedings of the Royal Society*, A, Vol. 149 (1935), 384–395.

M. JAMMER

MATERIALISM. Materialism is the name given to a family of doctrines concerning the nature of the world which give to matter a primary position and accord to mind (or spirit) a secondary, dependent reality or even none at all. Extreme materialism asserts that the real world consists of material things, varying in their states and relations, and nothing else. It is with such extreme materialist views that we are here concerned. In what follows "materialist" is to be understood as an abbreviation of "extreme materialist."

Philosophers have differed among themselves over what constitutes a body, over what states and relationships a body may enter, and over whether every material thing is a body. Thus, the cardinal tenet of materialism, "Everything that is, is material," covers several different claims.

To accommodate these differences, a material thing can be defined as being made up of parts possessing many physical properties and no other properties. The physical properties are position in space and time, size, shape, duration, mass, velocity, solidity, inertia, electric charge, spin, rigidity, temperature, hardness, and the like. This list is open-ended. It is composed of properties that are the object of the science of physics. The questions "What counts as a physical property?" and "What counts as possession of most of the physical properties?" have no determinate answers. In consequence, there are also no determinate answers for the questions "What is a material thing?" and "What does materialism claim?"

Consciousness, purposiveness, aspiration, desire, and the ability to perceive are not considered properties of matter. Materialism differs from panpsychism, the doctrine that every bit of matter is also at least partly spiritual, in that it denies these psychological properties to the world's basic entities. Materialists add that there is no second class of fundamental beings possessing such psychological properties and no others. Therefore, there are no incorporeal souls or spirits, no spiritual principalities or powers, no angels or devils, no demiurges and no gods (if these are conceived as immaterial entities). Hence, nothing that happens can be attributed to the action of such beings. The second major tenet of materialism is, accordingly, "Everything that can be explained can be explained on the basis of laws involving only the antecedent physical conditions." The differences among materialists over the type of effect material things can have on one another make the second tenet another slogan covering a variety of particular doctrines. Materialists have traditionally been determinists, adding the claim "There is a cause for every event." This claim, however, is not strictly entailed by materialism; recently, it has apparently been weakened by the development of quantum theory, and some contemporary materialists are opponents of determinism.

It should also be mentioned that metaphysical materialism does not entail the psychological disposition to pursue money and tangible goods despite the popular use of "materialistic" to describe this interest.

Nature and appeal of materialism. The enduring appeal of materialism arises from its alliance with those sciences which have contributed most to our understanding of the world we live in. Investigations in the physical sciences have a materialist methodology; that is, they attempt to explain a class of phenomena by appeal to physical conditions alone. The claim of materialists is that there is no subject matter which cannot be adequately treated with a materialist methodology. This claim cannot be established by any scientific investigation; it can be established, if at all, only by critical reflection on the whole range of human thought and experience.

Early philosophers proceeded dogmatically, aiming to prove the material nature of the world by mere reflection on what must be. Contemporary materialists are much more modest, offering the claim as a speculative but reasonable empirical generalization. Men have continued to embrace materialism in the face of the difficulties with which it is beset because it offers a comprehensive, unified account of the nature of reality which is economical, intelligible, and consistent with the most successful of the sciences.

HISTORY OF MATERIALISM

Classical period. Materialism has been a theme in Western speculative thought from the earliest recorded period to the present day.

Ionian philosophers in the tradition of Thales (sixth century B.C.) attempted to account for the origin and present state of the world by appeal to changes in the state of fundamental substances. Parmenides of Elea (fifth century B.C.) vigorously defended not only a monism of substances but also a monism of entities, maintaining that the world is One, uniform, eternal, homogeneous, indivisible, indestructible, and without any interior void.

These two threads of thought are combined in the true materialism of Leucippus and his pupil Democritus, who flourished at Abdera in the late fifth century B.C. Between them they worked out the first clear conception of matter, the first clear restrictions on the kind of natural interactions in which material particles could figure, and the first clear program of explanation by appeal to these material interactions alone. The "Great Diakosmos," a lost work written by one or the other (or both), expounded their position. Their basic idea was that the fundamental stuff was of just one kind (matter) and that the fundamental entities were material atoms having the characteristics (except uniqueness) of Parmenides' One and moving in an exterior void.

Insofar as it can be reconstructed, their doctrine embraced the following theses.

(1) Nothing exists but atoms and empty space.

(2) Nothing happens by chance (for no reason at all); everything occurs for a reason and of necessity. This necessity is natural and mechanical; it excludes teleological necessitation.

(3) Nothing can arise out of nothing; nothing that is can be destroyed. All changes are new combinations or separations of atoms.

(4) The atoms are infinite in number and endlessly varied in form. They are all of the same stuff. They act on one another only by pressure or collision.

(5) The variety of things is a consequence of the variety in number, size, shape, and arrangement of the atoms which compose them.

(6) The atoms have been in confused random motion from all eternity. This is their natural state and requires no explanation. (Some scholars dispute the attribution of random motion to the atoms and credit the "Great Diakosmos" with the Epicurean doctrine of an eternal fall through infinite space.)

(7) The basic mechanism whereby bodies are formed from atoms is the collision of two atoms, setting up a vortex. In the vortex motion is communicated from the periphery toward the center. In consequence, heavy atoms move to the center, light ones to the periphery. The vortex continually embraces new atoms which come near it in their random motion, and it thus begins a world.

According to this position, a mechanical account must be given of human sensation. The Leucippus–Democritus account seems to have been ingenious, speculative, and false. Objects perceptible by sight, hearing, or smell give off effluences, or images, composed of fine, smooth atoms. There are channels in the eyes, ears, and nose along which these effluent atoms pass to collide with the atoms of the soul. Thus, sensation occurs. Differences of color or of pitch are due to varying smoothness or roughness of the incoming image atoms. In touch and taste the size and shape of the atoms on the surface of the perceived object act on soul atoms in the relevant organs.

Sensory qualities (for example, sweetness, bitterness, temperature, color) are thus not qualities of the object perceived, which is a collection of atoms, but the effects of that collection of atoms on us. Here is an early appearance of the distinction between primary and secondary qualities, a distinction every subsequent materialist has also found it necessary to make.

Empedocles (fifth century B.C.) founded a medical school in Acragas (Agrigento) in Sicily. His aim was to account, in a naturalistic manner, for the special features of this world, particularly for the organized matter of living creatures. The first appearance of the famous four elements—earth, air, fire, and water—is in his theory. Empedocles seems to have believed that each of these elements consisted of a different type of atom. The creation and dissolution of the macroscopic objects of this world is brought about by the combination and separation of these atoms by two fundamental forces, love and hate, or harmony and discord.

Under the influence of love and hate the world goes through an endless cycle from complete random separation of elements (the triumph of hate), through gradually increasing order, to a complete, calm, spherical, harmonious union (the triumph of love). Hate then begins to exert itself once more. Disintegration sets in, and ultimately the world returns to the state of complete separation of elements. The present state of the world lies between these two extremes. The existence of planetary systems and the origin of animals are thus explained as the influence of love.

Empedocles can be considered a true materialist only if love and hate are either inherent forces in the elemental atoms or themselves material elements with a cementing or corrosive effect on combinations of the other elements; however, he probably thought of them as blind, powerful gods. The rest of his system is similarly ambiguous. On the one hand, he believed in the transmigration of souls and adhered to some kind of Orphic mystery religion; on the other, he gave a mechanical account of sensation, held that the soul was composed of fiery atoms, and said that the blood around the heart is the thought of men. Empedocles' thought thus perpetuated the materialist tradition but not in a rigorous or consistent form.

The misinterpretation of the ethics of Epicurus (342–270 B.C.) has made him the most famous of classical materialists. In his middle age Epicurus came to Athens and founded a school where materialism was taught as the sole foundation of a good life, a life calm, serene, and free from superstition.

He adopted the position of the "Great Diakosmos" but gave a modified account of the origin of worlds. There are an infinite number of atoms falling through an infinite space. In one construction of the Epicurean system the heavier, faster atoms occasionally strike the lighter, slower ones obliquely, giving them a slight lateral velocity. In another construction all atoms fall at uniform velocity, and the original deviations from parallel vertical motion are left quite unexplained.

However caused, the original lateral deviations result in more collisions and deviations and the establishment of vortexes. From these vortexes ordered arrangements of atoms arise. The number of atoms and the time available are both quite unlimited, so every possible arrangement of atoms must occur at some time or another. This world, with its marvelously organized living bodies, is thus just one of the infinite, inevitable arrangements into which the indestructible atoms must fall.

The only Roman author of note in the tradition of materialism is Lucretius (born c. 99 B.C.), whose long didactic poem *De Rerum Natura* gives imaginative sparkle to the metaphysics of Epicurus. Lucretius adopted the second account of the fall of atoms through the void and appealed to some form of voluntary action to explain the original deviations from vertical descent. He thus introduced a nonmechanical source of motion, inconsistent with the remainder of his system.

Like Epicurus, Lucretius was motivated by a wish to free men from the burdens of religious fear. He argued passionately and at length against the existence of any spiritual soul and for the mortality of man. These beliefs have been explicit features of materialism ever since.

Seventeenth century. From the close of the classical period until the Renaissance the church and Aristotle so dominated Western speculation that materialist theories virtually lapsed. The revival of materialism is attributable to the work of two seventeenth-century philosophers, Gassendi and Hobbes, who crystallized the naturalistic and skeptical movements of thought which accompanied the rediscovery of antiquity and the rise of natural science. Their most important forerunners were probably Telesio, Campanella, and Cyrano de Bergerac, all of whom attempted to combine materialistic views in physics with a sensationalist psychology.

Pierre Gassendi (1592–1655), who in the last part of his life taught astronomy at the Royal College in Paris, rejected the official Aristotelian philosophy of his time and set about the rehabilitation of Epicureanism. To bring the Epicurean system into closer conformity with Christian doctrine, he claimed that the atoms are not eternal but created. They are finite, not infinite, in number and are organized in our particular world by a providential determination of initial conditions.

Gassendi's materialism extended over physics and psychology, undertaking to account for all inanimate changes and for sensation on a materialist basis. He treated the coming into being of particular things as the accumulation of matter about a seed atom.

But his metaphysics was not, strictly speaking, materialistic, for outside the experienced world Gassendi admitted a creative and providential God and an immaterial and immortal intellect in man distinct from his corporeal soul. There are even some lapses in the physics, too, for Gassendi spoke of gravitation as some kind of movement for self-preservation and allowed that growth from seed atoms may be controlled by formative principles other than the natural motions of atoms.

Thomas Hobbes (1588–1679) was much more consistent and uncompromising. In 1629 he discovered Euclidean geometry and was captivated by its method. During the years that followed he strove to work out a rational philosophy of nature on the Euclidean model.

Hobbes's aim was to discover by cunning analysis of experience fundamental principles expressing the true nature of everything. The truth of these principles would be manifest to right reason and could thus serve as axioms from which a comprehensive theory of the nature of the world could be deductively derived.

The resulting system is almost pure materialism. Hobbes hoped to use the new physics as the basis of a final, complete account of reality. From definitions of space and motion he derived the laws of uniform motion. From these, together with a notion of the interaction of bodies, he hoped to proceed to an account of change, thence to an account of sensible change, thence to a theory of the senses and appetites of men, and finally to his notorious civil philosophy.

No part of the universe is not a body, said Hobbes, and no part of the universe contains no body. Hobbes was a plenist, holding all space to be filled by an intangible material ether if nothing else. This doctrine followed directly from his definition of a body as anything existing independently of our thought and having volume. Thus, Hobbes considered God to be a corporeal spirit difficult to distinguish from that incarnate space, the pervasive ether.

All change in the universe is motion of bodies, and nothing can cause a motion but contact with another moving body. The substance of anything is body, and "incorporeal substance" is therefore a contradiction in terms. Hobbes thereby disposed of angels, the soul, and the God of theology. Hobbes departed from strict materialism in his introduction of "conatus" and "impetus" (which are not physical properties) into his account of the initiation of motion and measurement of acceleration. Conatus is also appealed to in Hobbes's account of human sensation and action. Sensations are motions in a man's body, and changes of sensation are changes of that motion. Sensory qualities are really within the perceiver, but by conatus a "phantasm" is projected from the observer onto the observed.

Hobbes was the first to take seriously the problems which language, thought, and logic pose for materialism. He developed a nominalist theory of language and took the subject matter of thought and inference to be phantasms of sense or abstractions from these phantasms. He held, for example, that to remember is to perceive one has perceived. But Hobbes did not make clear just what contact mechanism is at work in mental operations nor whether the phantasms involved are genuinely corporeal. Thus, in spite of Hobbes's best efforts it is doubtful that he developed a fully consistent materialism.

The influence of Gassendi and Hobbes was diminished by the prestige of their brilliant contemporary, René Descartes (1596–1650), who accepted a materialist and mechanical account of the inanimate world and the brute creation but insisted that men had immaterial, immortal spirits whose essential nature lay in conscious thought undetermined by causal processes. According to Descartes, there are in the world two quite different sorts of things, extended (material) substances and thinking (spiritual) substances, which are mysteriously united in the case of mankind. He thus crystallized the tradition of dualism (the doctrine that there are just two fundamentally different kinds of things), which was until recently materialism's chief rival.

Eighteenth century. In Epicurus and Lucretius one motive for working out a materialist philosophy was opposition to religious terror. With Hobbes, and again in eighteenth-century France, it was opposition to religious oppression. Further, rapid growth of physiological knowledge gave rise to the hope that a complete doctrine of man in purely physiological terms was possible and so generated a medical materialism which made the path of the metaphysicians smoother.

Ever since the time of Democritus materialists had held that the soul consists of fine particles within a man. In the course of the eighteenth century this suggestion was taken up and amplified, and some attempt was made to give it an experiential basis.

An anonymous manuscript, the *Ame matérielle*, written between 1692 and 1704, contains many ingenious explanations of mental function on Democritean lines. Pleasure and pain consist, respectively, of the flow of finer or coarser particles through the channels of the brain. The passions are a matter of the temperature of the heart. Reason consists in the ordering of the soul's fine particles, and the effect of wine in its course through the body is to dislodge some of these fine particles from their proper places. The manuscript is panpsychic in its expression, crediting the atoms with a rudimentary consciousness and will, but it is materialist in substance, for these qualities are not credited with causative functions. Its doctrines were purely hypothetical and, as we now know, false. The *Ame matérielle* had successors in Dr. Maubec's *Principes physiques de la raison et les passions de l'homme* (Paris, 1709), which again gave a materialist vision of man a panpsychic dress and opposed Descartes's "thinking substance," and in Denis Diderot's many unsystematic writings, which took a progressively more materialistic turn. Diderot's *Le Rêve de d'Alembert* is a striking hypothetical account of heredity, growth, and the simpler forms of animal behavior in terms of interior motions of living bodies.

The most famous medical materialist is Julien de La Mettrie (1709–1751), a doctor with a philosophical bent whose radical views obliged him to leave a fashionable practice in Paris and live in Holland and Prussia. In *L'Homme machine* (Leiden, 1748) he presented a view of man as a self-moving machine.

After criticizing all views of the soul as spiritual, La Mettrie proceeded to review all the common-sense evidence for the physical nature of mental activity. He cited the effects of bodily needs, aging, and sleep; he pointed to the analogy of the human body to much lower forms. Anticipating Pavlov, he spoke of the mechanical basis of speech and of the possibilities of educating deaf-mutes and anthropoid apes. He explained learning how to perceive and how to make moral judgments by appeal to modifications of the brain. Human action is accounted for by the then new doctrine of the stimulus irritability of muscles. La Mettrie embarrassed those who held that the soul is a spiritual unity by observing the continuing function of organs removed from bodies, the muscular activity of dead or decapitated animals, and the ability of a bisected polyp to grow into two complete ones. He explained conscious sensation and the mental capacities of which we are introspectively aware by means of a magic-lantern analogy, but this was unsatisfactory, for the status of the images was not made clear.

The details of La Mettrie's physiology, depending as they do on supposed movements of nervous filaments, are false. However, his program of seeking in neural changes the explanation of mental activity has endured, and his claim that appeals to the soul can furnish only pseudo-explanations has gained wide support.

Jean Cabanis (1757–1808), a French doctor, continued this line of thought and in 1802 published *Rapports du physique et du moral de l'homme*, the most notable innovation of which was to treat the brain as analogous with the digestive system, making sensory impressions its aliments and thoughts its product.

The great metaphysical materialist of the period is Paul Heinrich Dietrich d'Holbach (1723–1789), a German nobleman who passed his life in Paris. His work the *Système de la nature* was published under a false name, "Mirabaud," at "London" (Amsterdam) in 1770. This "Bible of all materialism" is speculative philosophy in the grand style; in it the antireligious motive is again uppermost. Holbach maintained that nothing is outside nature. Nature is an uninterrupted and causally determined succession of arrangements of matter in motion. Matter has always existed and always been in motion, and different worlds are formed from different distributions of matter and motion. Matter is of four basic types (earth, air, fire, and water), and changes in their proportions are responsible for all changes other than spatiotemporal ones.

Mechanical causes of the impact type are the only intelligible ones, hence the only real ones. Since man is in nature and part of nature, all human actions spring from natural causes. Man's intellectual faculties, thoughts, passions, and will can all be identified with motions hidden within him. In action outward motions are acquired from these internal ones in ways we do not yet understand.

Holbach based the intellectual faculties on feeling and treated feeling as a consequence of certain arrangements of matter. Introspected changes are all changes in our internal material state. Thus, in remembering, we renew in ourselves a previous modification. He treated personal characteristics and temperament in terms of a man's internal structure and interpreted so-called free action not as motiveless action (an absurdity) but as action springing from an ultimately unchosen modification of the brain. Holbach's theory of mind is also interesting because in dealing with wit and genius, it suggests the first behavioral analyses of mental concepts. Not surprisingly, he held the soul to be mortal.

The purity of Holbach's materialism is marred only by his admission of relations of sympathy, antipathy, and affinity among material particles, in addition to the primary qualities, gravity and inert force.

The revolution in chemistry which was effected by Joseph Priestley in England and Antoine-Laurent Lavoisier in France in the 1770s and 1780s was of importance for the later development of materialism, for it established chemistry as a strictly physical science all of whose explanations appeal only to material substances and their natural interactions. Such a chemistry has since been extended to cover the processes of life, and the case for materialism has thereby been profoundly strengthened. Priestley is a curious figure in the history of materialism. A thoroughgoing determinist and materialist (he supported Roger Boscovich's concept of matter as points of force), Priestley nevertheless vigorously maintained his belief in Christianity. His religious views were far from orthodox, but he did insist that the existence of God and the resurrection of the body are not incompatible with a materialist and determinist position.

Nineteenth century. The philosophers of greatest influence in the nineteenth century—Kant, Fichte, Hegel, Schopenhauer, Lotze, and Mill, for example—were all of an idealist or phenomenalist bent. (The materialism of Engels and Marx, which is not an extreme materialism, is dealt with in DIALECTICAL MATERIALISM.)

Ludwig Büchner, a minor figure, deserves mention as the first to claim explicitly that materialism is a generalization from a posteriori discoveries. In *Kraft und Stoff* (1855) he claims that we have discovered (not proved a priori) that there is no force without matter and no matter without force.

There was during this period a continuation of inquiry and speculation on the physiological bases of mental function. Jacob Moleschott, Karl Vogt, and Emil Du Bois-Reymond proceeded with the investigation of physiological processes along physicochemical lines. The most important developments were scientific ones which all undermined the barrier between physical systems and living organisms and thus softened the natural resistances to materialistic theses.

In 1828 the synthesis of urea was achieved, and this refuted the idea that biochemistry was in some way special and distinct from chemistry. In 1847, Hermann Helmholtz established the conservation of energy in organic systems, making still less plausible any claims that living and non-living systems could not possibly be comprehended in one theory.

In 1859, Charles Darwin published his *Origin of Species*, in 1871 his *Descent of Man.* T. H. Huxley had produced *Man's Place in Nature* in 1863. These three works at last provided a plausible, empirically grounded case for two of the main planks of materialism, the claim that the organization of living things into forms admirably suited for survival and reproduction admits of explanation without appeal to immanent or transcendent purposes and the claim that man is a part and product of the natural world.

Since then biologists, physiologists, and pathologists have increasingly taken the truth of medical materialism for granted, couching their explanations in physicochemical terms without questioning the propriety or completeness of successful explanations in this form.

Contemporary materialism. The triumphant progress in the twentieth century of a materialistic biology and biochemistry has almost completely eliminated vitalist notions and supranatural views of life. The situation of earlier ages has been reversed; it now seems implausible to maintain that the vital functions of living organisms are different in kind from chemical (ultimately, physical) processes. In the attempt to demonstrate that something other than matter exists, it is on mind, rather than life, that immaterialists now rely.

But the rise of cybernetics (the abstract theory of machines) and its applications in computing machinery and objects which simulate some of the performances of living things are beginning to threaten the idea of a special status for mental activity. The gathering and interpretation of information, the employment of stored information, successful and spectacular problem solving, even analogues of fatigue, overload, and confusion, hitherto all monopolies of the animate, are now displayed by organizations of matter whose operations can be explained in terms of physical properties alone. And on the other hand, experimental study of the nervous systems of animals and men is showing, in ever increasing detail, how artificially induced changes in the electrochemical state of the nervous system issue in changes in the subject's "mental" activity. Displays of emotion, performance in perception and recall, and anxiety and tension are being tied down to brain function in this way.

Furthermore, many psychologists of this century have become disheartened by the difficulties of investigating hypothetical mental states and have turned to the study of behavior, relying on publicly observable and physical phenomena in their analyses and explanations of human activities. Indeed, there have been three distinct movements of a materialistic stamp in recent philosophizing about minds.

Some logical positivists, led by Rudolf Carnap and Otto Neurath, espoused an epistemic materialism. They held that statements about minds incontestably meant something. The meaning of any statement consisted in those directly testable statements deducible from it (protocol sentences). The protocol sentences must be intersubjectively testable, and the only intersubjectively testable sentences refer to physical properties of physical entities. Hence, those meaningful statements about minds which do not deal with hypothetical constructs must refer to such physical properties and entities, even though we cannot yet give their physical translations. The beginnings of translation into behaviorist terms was offered for some psychological expressions—for example, "is happy"—by directing attention to the way in which the use of such expressions is taught, by pointing to people behaving happily. In this the positivists anticipated a favorite strategy of Wittgenstein and moved away from complete dependence on their general doctrines of meaning and verification.

The analytic behaviorists, in particular Gilbert Ryle and his followers, offered to show that attributions of intention and intelligence, choice, desire, excitement, fear, and so on all are to be understood as attributions of a disposition to behave in a characteristic manner in suitable circumstances. Dispositions are held by most thinkers to issue from some standing or recurrent underlying state, and with these behaviorists the state was assumed to be a state of the body. Their manifest intention to exorcise the spiritual soul places them in the materialist tradition.

Ludwig Wittgenstein, although he disdained the title behaviorist, belongs to the same group. The conditions upon which he insisted in any acceptable analysis of a mental concept require that descriptions of a man's state of mind must make reference only to publicly detectable features of the organism and its behavior. His many subtle discussions of mental concepts are all attempts to identify that pattern of behavior whose display would constitute being in a given state of mind. To attribute that state of mind to a man is to describe him as disposed to display the relevant pattern of behavior. Talk of states and processes of a spiritual soul is, according to Wittgenstein, not merely false; it is unintelligible. On two key points the analytic behaviorists have not been entirely convincing. First, if mental states are names of particular patterns of behavior, they cannot cause the behavior in question; it cannot be said that a man's anger made him shout or that his pride made him stubborn. It is hard to believe expressions like these must be illegitimate. Second, the occurrences of some inner episodes—afterimages, pains, flashes of illumination—resist any plausible dispositional analysis. The mind does seem to be a collection of states, items, or events in addition to a syndrome of dispositions.

The third group of contemporary materialists embraces a theory of mind known as central state physicalism. They hold that the mental states, items, or events which cannot be understood dispositionally turn out, as a matter of fact, to be states of the central nervous system presented to itself in an opaque or covert fashion. Some, like Paul K. Feyerabend and Hilary Putnam, claim only that this is the most promising line investigation may now take. Others, like U. T. Place, J. J. C. Smart and Herbert Feigl, go further and maintain that any alternative view is already frankly incredible. David M. Armstrong has extended the range of mental concepts which are given a central state analysis to include some not strictly tied to introspection, such as intelligence, the emotions, and the will. He holds that the mind is the cause of the distinctive behavior of higher animals, and in his view this cause proves to be a neurological one.

The argumentation surrounding central state physicalism is not yet concluded. The fate of the doctrine seems to hang on its ability to deal adequately with the peculiarities of introspective knowledge and to clarify the identification of mental with neural states and on the continuing success of physiologists in their efforts to discover neural changes corresponding to every change in consciousness.

OBJECTIONS TO MATERIALISM

Materialist doctrines have never lacked critics and detractors, for they require that some of mankind's more cherished beliefs and hopes be abandoned. Of the many possible lines of attack, we will here review the more important.

Theology. Materialist theses contradict a large number of theological assertions. In a materialist theory there are no necessary beings and no supernatural interventions in the course of nature.

In order to defend materialism on these points, one must first show that there is no valid deductive argument for the existence of a necessary being. No mean task this, but one many philosophers now think can be completed. Next, one must deny to religious experience any supernatural significance. Adopting the critique made by skeptical empiricists, one can argue that religious experience presents no good and sufficient reasons for abandoning natural modes of explanation, in particular none for abandoning them in favor of hypotheses which face peculiar difficulties when it comes to putting them to the test. Furthermore, the materialist position is strengthened by the promise of continued success in finding concrete natural explanations of religious experience through developments in physiology and psychology.

If these positions can be established, claims to the existence of God and the occurrence of miracles are established neither by argument nor in experience and so must be considered as interpretative hypotheses laid upon the experienced world. The materialist must again urge that in framing hypotheses, as in seeking explanations, there is no sufficient reason for deserting the natural for the supernatural. In such circumstances as these considerations of parsimony exclude all supernatural entities from any reasonable ontology.

Materialists must show there is no reason to believe in survival of bodily death or in reincarnation. Plausible recent arguments have claimed that both doctrines are logically incoherent. These arguments do not impugn the possibility of resurrection, but that is compatible with materialism.

Physics. Materialism has in the past been assailed for leaving the origin, persistence, and motion of the fundamental particles unexplained, for failing to make intelligible that each fundamental interaction has had one result and not another, and for failing to admit the necessity in causal sequences. The reply, now very widely accepted, is that all chains of explanation must eventually come to a terminus and that to seek a terminus beyond contingent truths concerning the items and processes of the world is to go hunting a mare's-nest.

Psychology. Almost every distinctively human capacity has been pointed to as showing that a man is more than an assemblage of atoms. In understanding men, we cannot do without the concepts of perception, belief, and intelligence; action, decision, and choice; motive, drive, and need; feeling, emotion, and mood; temperament and character. We will also need to treat of consciousness and self-consciousness. The task of the materialist is to explain how merely material structures could qualify for description under all these categories. Two basic approaches, the behavioral and the topic neutral, have been adopted in attempting this. Contemporary materialists differ on which strategy is appropriate in particular cases, but they agree that one or the other is appropriate for every aspect of the mind.

Behavioral strategy. The attribution of some of the mental predicates (for example, intelligence, equanimity, or ambition) to an organism is claimed to be in reality the attribution of a disposition to behave in a characteristic way under suitable conditions. The form the behavior takes, the conditions under which it is manifest, and the organism which behaves are all specifiable in terms with no immaterialist implications. Also, the remarkable subtlety and complexity of human behavior no longer appear to have strong immaterialist implications, for now the development of machines with the ability to duplicate it seems possible. In particular, the self-monitoring features of conscious behavior can be displayed by material systems.

Topic-neutral strategy. For those mental descriptions which resist behavioral treatment (being in pain, seeing a color, feeling depressed) a different claim is made. It is held that to apply such descriptions is to assert that there is within the organism some state which typically arises from a given stimulus and/or typically issues in a characteristic kind of behavior. Mental predicates of this kind have been called topic-neutral because they do not specify as material or immaterial the nature of the inner state whose causes and/or effects we encounter. To say a man is in pain, the argument runs, does not of itself imply that he has or has not a soul. It implies that he is in a certain state, which arises from the state of his sensory system and issues in certain behavior patterns. When we explore this state, we find reason to believe that it is a state of the organism's central nervous system. If inner states admit of the topic-neutral treatment, they, too, have no immaterialist implications.

Inner states. The hardest part of the materialist program is to deal with introspective awareness. Consider sensations; a pain has a definite and distasteful felt quality, a color a definite presence to its observer. Neither colors nor pains present themselves in introspection as states of the person typically connected with stimuli and/or responses. The most promising materialist suggestion is that the intrinsic qualities of sensations are in reality purely schematic and enable us only to distinguish one sensation from another. The sameness or difference of inner states but not their nature is given introspectively. If this is so, sensations can very well be states of the central nervous system typically connected with stimulus and/or response, even though we are not aware of this.

The doctrine is strange but by no means clearly false. Inner states notoriously elude direct characterization. Our attempts to describe them proceed by comparison with other sensations directly or ultimately picked out by reference to their stimulus and/or response. For example, we describe smells as of cinnamon or of rotten eggs (stimulus) and as appetizing or nauseating (response); we speak of pains as jabbing, burning, like "pins and needles," as

crippling or distracting. Feelings of anger, shame, pride, and fear are all described in terms of body temperature. Many common descriptions of our inner states are in terms of the behavior they dispose us to display: "I could have jumped over the moon," "I could have bitten off my tongue," "You could have knocked me down with a feather," "I was ready to give up." All these ways of talking fit the suggested account of inner states.

A somewhat parallel claim is made concerning inner awareness of mental states which are not sensations. For example, nonsensory knowledge of my intention to go swimming is held to be direct knowledge of the causal properties of some inner state. It is true that an intention has no physical properties, but the causal character of anything whatsoever has no physical properties. Thus, the inner state known when I know of my intention to go swimming may be a state of the body.

If the behavioral and topic-neutral approaches to mental concepts are jointly adequate, it does not follow that men are exclusively material, only that they may be. To establish that men are material, it would have to be shown by empirical investigation that there were bodily states with the right physicochemical causal properties to account for all human capacities.

Parapsychology. Paranormal phenomena are a serious embarrassment to materialism; the evidence amassed in the investigations of S. G. Soal and L. L. Vasiliev, to name just two, cannot reasonably be ignored. At some times some people have access to information in ways not explicable within current scientific theory. A fortiori, these phenomena are not explicable within physics alone. It is not merely that the faculties dubbed "telepathy" or "clairvoyance" cannot yet be accommodated but that they seem to be positively excluded by our present understanding of the physical world. The same can be said of the very striking but less well controlled feats of trance mediums.

Although paranormal phenomena cannot be discounted, the spiritual constructions commonly put on them are altogether too hasty. Some revisions of scientific theory will be necessary, but it is not at all clear that we must credit the paranormally gifted with extraordinary souls capable of magic performances which "explain" this or that striking event.

There are two other avenues open. The first takes the paranormal phenomena to be indicative of some property of the fundamental physical particles undetected or even undetectable in studies of simpler systems than the human being. Unhappily, a postulated property of particles which shows itself only in the cognitive functions of immensely complex organisms is both implausible and apparently incapable of independent investigation. And to claim that such a property is a physical property, although it plays no part in any normal physical explanations, is to win a materialist victory by a hollow verbal maneuver.

The second line of approach, to consider paranormal phenomena to be consequences of the complexity of the physical structures involved, is more promising. To admit that paranormal capacities cannot be predicted to arise from concatenation of physical particles is not to admit that ghosts come into play at a certain level of complexity. For instance, even before we could explain the macroscopic phenomena of ferromagnetism as arising from juxtaposition of molecular magnets, it was not reasonable to suppose that "immaterial magnetism" was at work. The suggestion that "resonances" among complex systems could explain extrasensory perception has been made by Ninian Marshall. His speculations are most plausible in the cases of information passing from mind to mind without intermediary. However, clairvoyant successes (guessing what color light is on inside a box when nobody knows) and trance medium reports of the dead involve action at a distance without medium in both temporal directions. It is not going to be easy to develop the second line of approach in a convincing fashion.

There is no reason to think that these emergent capacities of complex systems will ever be predictable from knowledge of their physical elements. This does not mean that they are not physical emergences or that we could never learn that they were. To deviate into science fiction, we could reasonably claim to know that they were merely physical emergences if it were possible to assemble an electronic machine which demonstrated paranormal powers or to synthesize an organism which grew into something which could demonstrate them. Until then, materialism remains unproven.

Philosophy. Forms of materialism that offer knowledge immune from experiential refutation or knowledge of a reality beyond the reach of empirical investigation are vulnerable to empiricist and Kantian criticisms. But the physicalism which treats its doctrines as contingently true generalizations avoids the charge of purveying degenerate or transcendent hypotheses. There are several other objections of a logical kind which must be faced.

Argument from self-destruction. A popular argument for disposing with materialism is this:

All doctrines concerning the nature of the world are arrived at by inference.

Thus, a fortiori, materialism is so reached.

But if materialism is true, inference is a causally determined process in people's brains, and not a rational process.

Materialism is therefore a doctrine arrived at by nonrational causal processes.

Thus, if it is true, there can be no reason to think it so.

This argument is invalid. That a given process of inferring was determined by the structure of a man's brain does not entail that it was an unreasonable inference. Nor does it entail that the man could have no ground for thinking it reasonable. There is nothing in materialism to prevent our learning which inference patterns lead from true premises to largely true conclusions, applying this knowledge to the arguments for materialism, and reasonably (albeit determinedly) concluding that materialism is a worthy position.

Physical and mental properties. C. D. Broad in *The Mind and Its Place in Nature* formulates many people's reaction to the suggestion that mental events are physical events in a body:

About a molecular movement it is perfectly reasonable to raise the question "Is it swift or slow, straight or circular and so on?" About the awareness of a red patch it is nonsensical to ask whether it is a swift or slow awareness, a straight or circular awareness, and so on. Conversely, it is reasonable to ask about an awareness of a red patch whether it is a clear or a confused awareness; but it is nonsense to ask of a molecular movement whether it is a clear or a confused movement. Thus the attempt to argue that "being a sensation of so and so" and "being a bit of bodily behavior of such and such a kind" are just two names for the same characteristic is evidently hopeless.   (p. 623)

Indeed, this attempt is hopeless, but it is not one a materialist must make. The two "names" that materialists claim to name the same thing are "subject S having sensation P" and "subject S undergoing bodily changes Q." As for P, the sensation S has, this is dealt with by a topic-neutral strategy and held to be the covert presentation of bodily changes Q to the person S, who is having the sensation.

Knowledge of physical and mental states. Another common argument against materialism points to the fact that although the common man can recognize thoughts and feelings and knows what anger, fear, and his intention to go swimming are, he is completely ignorant of the processes in his central nervous system, and so the mental occurrences cannot be identified with any such physical events. Friedrich Paulsen, for example, argued to this effect in Chapter 1 of his *Introduction to Philosophy.*

This argument is also, as it stands, invalid. It is like arguing that because the police know some of the characteristics of a man who committed a crime but do not know anything about John Smith, John Smith could not possibly be the man who committed the crime. A reply along these lines is provided by Place and Smart in articles cited in the Bibliography.

As no physical processes are disclosed in introspective knowledge of mental events, the argument would be valid if another premise were added: In introspection the full nature of mental events is disclosed. But there seems to be no good reason for thinking this premise is true.

Generalized nature of reason. Keith Gunderson has recently revived an argument of Descartes's to the effect that men are not machines, even cybernetic machines, and therefore not merely material.

In all known machines the matching or surpassing of a human intellectual ability is a specific outcome of a specific structure. Each skill is a skill at some special task and no other.

But in human beings, intellectual skills are generalized and come in clusters; reason is a tool for all circumstances.

Thus, it is not proven that the man and the machine have a like given skill in consequence of a like inner structure.

On the contrary, the reasonable conclusion is that the machine's skill and the man's skill are to be explained in different ways—that is, man is not any kind of machine.

One reply available to materialists is that this argument is premature. The simulation of human performance by material assemblages is in its infancy. There seems no reason to suppose a machine with generalized skills impossible.

Another line of reply is also open. To show human abilities can be matched by a machine is sufficient to establish that men need not be credited with an immaterial side to their nature, but it is not necessary. There may be some irreducible biological laws which distinguish living things from artifacts. But, as was suggested for paranormal phenomena, these could be treated as emergent properties of special kinds of complex material structures and not as the operations of spiritual elements in those structures.

Intentionality. The argument from intentionality can be stated in this form:

A peculiarity of many mental states is their essential connection with an object. In intending, I must intend something, and in hoping, I must hope for something.

The thing intended or the thing hoped may or may not have any real existence.

Thus, intentions and hopes can be real mental states having as an essential part an object with no physical existence.

Thus, materialism cannot be true.

The materialist reply to this argument is that hopes or intentions are specified by reference to that which would fulfill them or that which would constitute their exercise. It is important to note that they are specified by way of that which *would* fulfill them; that is, they are specified by way of things conditionally claimed to exist. That which perhaps exists does not necessarily exist, but this does not at all mean that if it does, it is something other than a physical thing.

Logical connections. There is also the argument from logical connections between different items:

Where an intention is carried out, both the intention and the thing intended exist.

They are two different things.

Nevertheless, they are logically connected.

But any two different physical items are only contingently connected.

Hence, mental states cannot be physical items.

Materialists urge in rebuttal that this is a consequence of the peculiarly causal character of mental states. Often the only way of identifying a mental state is by reference to the behavior which it characteristically evokes. If a physical item *A* is specified as that which evokes *B*, then although *A* is in its own nature only contingently connected with *B*, the specification of *A* is logically connected with the specification of *B*.

Incorrigible knowledge of mental states. It is frequently claimed that:

Introspective knowledge of mental states is logically immune from error.

What I believe about my current mental state cannot be false.

But all knowledge of physical items is corrigible.

Thus, mental states cannot be physical states.

Materialists differ in their reply to this objection. Smart concedes this to be a feature of the logic of reports in which introspective knowledge is expressed but urges that it is inessential and will pass away when materialism is generally embraced. Armstrong takes the bull by the horns and argues that the doctrine of incorrigible introspective knowledge is a mistake.

Epistemic dualism. A much more wide-ranging argument has been advanced by some philosophers in the tradition of Kant. They argue that the categories of the physical and the mental are both necessary to a full understanding of human knowledge; that each presupposes the other; and that therefore neither can be eliminated in favor of the other. If they are right, the very statement of materialism presupposes its own falsehood. To defend themselves against this claim, materialists are therefore bound to develop a complete epistemology.

The most critical problem facing contemporary materialists is to provide an account of the mind which has some prospect of being at once adequate and compatible with materialism. Major advances have been made in this direction, but whether they will be fully successful remains to be seen.

(See also the following articles in which various materialistic theories are discussed: ANIMAL SOUL; ATOMISM; MECHANISM IN BIOLOGY; MIND–BODY PROBLEM; and NEWTONIAN MECHANICS AND MECHANICAL EXPLANATION. For a list of the articles that treat historical and dialectical materialism the reader should consult MARXISM. See Materialism in Index for thinkers who are commonly classified as materialists.)

Bibliography

GENERAL HISTORIES

Lange, Frederick Albert, *Geschichte des Materialismus* . . . . Marburg, Germany, 1865. Translated by E. C. Thomas as *The History of Materialism*. London, 1877–1892. Lucid, penetrating, and thorough, this classic is by far the most important secondary source in the history of materialist theories. All English editions since the London edition of 1925 include an introduction by Bertrand Russell entitled "Materialism."

Lewes, George Henry, *The Biographical History of Philosophy*. London, 1857. A lively, idiosyncratic one-volume history, with good comments on materialist philosophers.

CLASSICAL PERIOD

Aristotle, *Metaphysica*. Translated by W. D. Ross as *Metaphysics*, 2d ed. Oxford, 1928. Most easily accessible source for near-contemporary opinion on materialistic Greeks.

Burnet, John, *Greek Philosophy*. London, 1914. Standard account of ancient philosophy.

Burnet, John, *Early Greek Philosophy*, 4th ed. London, 1930.

Lucretius, *De Rerum Natura*, translated by R. C. Trevelyan. Cambridge, 1937. Great epic presentation of Epicurean doctrine.

SEVENTEENTH CENTURY

Brandt, Frithiof, *Den mekaniske Naturopfattelse hos Thomas Hobbes*. Copenhagen, 1921. Translated by Vaughan Maxwell and Annie Fairstøll as *Thomas Hobbes' Mechanical Conception of Nature*. London, 1928. Detailed and definitive.

Cyrano de Bergerac, Savinien de, *États et empires de la lune* and *États et empires du soleil*. Paris, 1657, 1662. Translated by Richard Aldington as *Voyages to the Moon and the Sun*. New York, 1962. Epitomize seventeenth-century movement toward materialism.

Gassendi, Pierre, *De Vita et Moribus Epicuri Libri Octo*. Lyons, 1647.

Gassendi, Pierre, *Animadversiones in Decimum Librum Diogenis Laerti*. Lyons, 1649.

Gassendi, Pierre, *Philosophiae Epicuri Syntagma*. Lyons, 1649.

Gassendi, Pierre, *Syntagma Philosophicum*. Lyons, 1658. Expounds and defends Epicurus except in cases of conflict with Catholic doctrine, where he is corrected.

Hobbes, Thomas, *English Works*, William Molesworth, ed. London, 1839.

Hobbes, Thomas, *Latin Works*, William Molesworth, ed. London, 1839.

Laird, John, *Hobbes*. London, 1934. Straightforward introductory account of Hobbes's thought.

Mintz, Samuel I., *The Hunting of Leviathan*. Cambridge, 1962. Narrates contemporary reaction to Hobbes.

Peters, Richard, *Hobbes*. Harmondsworth, England, 1956. Interesting and comprehensible introduction.

Rochot, Bernard, *Les Travaux de Gassendi sur Epicure et sur l'atomisme 1619–1658*. Paris, 1944. Most accessible modern treatment of Gassendi.

Spink, John S., *French Free-thought From Gassendi to Voltaire*. London, 1960.

Stephen, Leslie, *Hobbes*. Ann Arbor, Mich., 1961. Intellectual biography.

EIGHTEENTH CENTURY

Cabanis, Pierre-Jean-Georges, *Rapports du physique et du moral de l'homme*. Paris, 1802.

Diderot, Denis, *Oeuvres complètes*. Paris, 1875.

Holbach, Paul Heinrich Dietrich d', *Système de la nature . . . par Mirabaud*. "London" (Amsterdam), 1770. Translated by H. D. Robinson as *The System of Nature, Edited With Notes by Diderot, Translated by H. D. Robinson*. Boston, 1868. Classic text.

La Mettrie, Julien Offray de, *L'Homme machine*. Leiden, 1748. Translated with philosophical and historical notes by Gertrude C. Bussey as *Man a Machine*. La Salle, Ill., 1943. There is also a critical edition with notes by Aram Vartanian. Princeton, N.J., 1960.

Priestley, Joseph, *Disquisitions Relating to Matter and Spirit*. London, 1777.

NINETEENTH CENTURY

Büchner, Ludwig, *Kraft und Stoff*. Frankfurt, 1855. Translated by J. Frederick Collingwood as *Force and Matter*. London, 1884.

Darwin, Charles, *The Origin of Species*. London, 1859. Classic text.

Darwin, Charles, *Descent of Man*. London, 1871. Classic text.

Moleschott, Jakob, *Der Kreislauf des Lebens*. Mainz, Germany, 1852.

Passmore, John, *A Hundred Years of Philosophy*. London, 1957. Readable guide.

Vogt, Karl, *Physiologische Briefe*. Stuttgart, 1845–1846.

Vogt, Karl, *Köhlerglaube und Wissenschaft*. Giessen, Germany, 1854.

CONTEMPORARY MATERIALISM

Armstrong, David M., *A Materialist Theory of the Mind*. Forthcoming. A defense of central state physicalism.

Carnap, Rudolf, "Psychologie in physikalischer Sprache." *Erkenntnis* (1932–1933). Translated by Frederick Schick as "Psychology in Physical Language," in A. J. Ayer, ed., *Logical Positivism*. Glencoe, Ill., 1959. Epistemic materialism.

Eliot, Hugh, *Modern Science and Materialism*. London, 1919.

Feigl, Herbert, "The 'Mental' and the 'Physical,'" in Herbert Feigl et al, eds., *Minnesota Studies in Philosophy of Science*, Vol. II. Minneapolis, 1958. Identifies mental states and brain processes.

Feyerabend, Paul K., "Materialism and the Mind–Body Problem." *The Review of Metaphysics*, Vol. 17, No. 1 (1963), 49–66. Claims materialism is the only plausible view.

Hook, Sidney, ed., *Dimensions of Mind: A Symposium*. New York, 1960. Deals with the relations of mind, body, and machinery from many points of view.

Kotarbiński, T., "The Fundamental Ideas of Pansomatism." *Mind*, Vol. 64 (1955), 488–500.

Nagel, Ernest, "Are Naturalists Materialists?," in his *Logic Without Metaphysics*. Glencoe, Ill., 1957.

Place, U. T., "Is Consciousness a Brain Process?" *British Journal of Psychology*. Vol. 47 (1956), 44–50. Pioneering paper in central state physicalism.

Ray, N. N., *Materialism*, 2d ed. Calcutta, 1951. Vigorous popular statement of a materialist position.

Ryle, Gilbert, *The Concept of Mind*. London 1949. Readable and influential advocacy of analytic behaviorism.

Skinner, B. F., *Science and Human Behavior*. New York, 1953. Methodological behaviorism.

Smart, J. J. C., "Sensations and Brain Processes." *Philosophical Review*, Vol. 68 (1959), 141–156. Important paper for central state physicalism.

Smart, J. J. C., *Philosophy and Scientific Realism*. London, 1963. Amplification of Smart's materialism.

Wittgenstein, Ludwig, *Philosophical Investigations*. Oxford, 1953. Influential but difficult reappraisal of the logic of mental concepts.

PARAPSYCHOLOGY

Broad, Charlie Dunbar, *Lectures on Psychical Research*. London, 1962. Sagacious and well-informed commentary on parapsychology.

Marshall, Ninian, "ESP and Memory: A Physical Theory." *British Journal for the Philosophy of Science*, Vol. 10 (1959), 265–286.

Soal, S. G., and Bateman, F., *Modern Experiments in Telepathy*. London, 1954.

Vasiliev, L. L., *Experiments in Mental Suggestion*. London, 1963.

PHILOSOPHICAL OBJECTIONS

Armstrong, David M., "Is Introspective Knowledge Incorrigible?" *Philosophical Review*, Vol. 72 (1963), 417–432.

Broad, Charlie Dunbar, *The Mind and Its Place in Nature*. London, 1925. Readable review of various doctrines of the mind.

Ducasse, Curt John, *Nature, Mind and Death*. La Salle, Ill., 1951. Dualist attack on materialism.

Gunderson, Keith, "Descartes, La Mettrie, Language and Machines." *Philosophy*, Vol. 39 (1964), 193 ff. Revives argument from generalized nature of reason.

Lewis, C. S., *Miracles*. New York, 1947. Expounds argument from self-destruction.

Paulsen, Friedrich, *Einleitung in die Philosophie*. Berlin, 1892. Translated by Frank Thilly as *An Introduction to Philosophy*. New York, 1895. Idealist attack on materialism.

KEITH CAMPBELL

MATERIALISM, DIALECTICAL. See DIALECTICAL MATERIALISM.

MATERIALISM, HISTORICAL. See HISTORICAL MATERIALISM.

MATHEMATICS, FOUNDATIONS OF. The study of the foundations of mathematics comprises investigations, though probably not all possible investigations, that consist of general reflection on mathematics. The subject naturally proceeds by singling out certain concepts and principles as "fundamental" and concentrating attention on them, but of course the identification of fundamental concepts and principles is itself based on foundational research or may be revised in the light of it.

In this article considerable emphasis will be placed on philosophical questions about mathematics, which undoubtedly belong to foundations. However, many, perhaps most, foundational investigations are mainly mathematical. In the last hundred years an important role has been played by mathematical logic. We shall not give a detailed exposition of mathematical logic, but we hope that our discussion will give an idea of the relation between the logical problems and results and the philosophical problems and an idea of some of the results of recent work in logic (see also LOGIC, HISTORY OF; LOGIC, MODERN; RECURSIVE FUNCTION THEORY; and SYSTEMS, FORMAL, AND MODELS OF FORMAL SYSTEMS).

Two of the main qualities for which mathematics has always attracted the attention of philosophers are the great degree of systematization and the rigorous development of mathematical theories. The problem of systematization seems to be the initial problem in the foundations of mathematics, both because it has been a powerful force in the history of mathematics itself and because it sets the form of further investigations by picking out the fundamental concepts and principles. Also, the systematic integration of mathematics is an important basis of another philosophically prominent feature, its high degree of clarity and certainty. In mathematics systematization has taken a characteristic and highly developed form—the axiomatic method—which has from time to time been taken as a model for systematization in general. We shall therefore begin our main exposition with a discussion of the axiomatic method.

Foundational research has always been concerned with the problem of justifying mathematical statements and principles, with understanding why certain evident propositions are evident, with providing the justification of accepted principles which seem not quite evident, and with finding and casting off principles which are unjustified. A natural next step in our exposition, then, will be to consider mathematics from an epistemological point of view, which leads us to examine mathematics as a primary instance of what philosophers have called a priori knowledge. In this connection we shall give some logical analysis of two very basic mathematical ideas, class and natural number, and discuss the attempts of Gottlob Frege and Bertrand Russell to exploit the intimate relation between these two ideas in order to prove that mathematics is in some way a part of logic. We shall also discuss Kant's views on the evidence of mathematics and other conceptions of a priori knowledge. (The word "evidence" will often be used in this article in a way that is unusual outside philosophical writings influenced by the German tradition, to mean "the property of being evident"—German, *Evidenz*.)

The growth of modern mathematics, with its abstract character and its dependence on set theory, has caused the problem of evidence to be focused on the more particular problem of platonism. It is in this development and the accompanying growth of mathematical logic that modern foundational research has centered.

Throughout the nineteenth century, mathematicians worked to make arithmetic and analysis more rigorous, which required axiomatization and an attempt to use the concepts of the theory of natural numbers as a basis for defining the further concepts of arithmetic and analysis. The manner in which this axiomatization and definition

was undertaken was platonist, in the sense that both numbers and sets or sequences of numbers were treated as existing in themselves. The development of set theory by Georg Cantor provided a general framework for this work and also involved even greater abstraction and even stronger platonist assumptions.

The growth of mathematical logic introduced as further elements the axiomatization of logic (the basic step in which was completed by Frege in 1879), the effort to incorporate the axiomatization of logic into that of mathematics, and the accompanying tendency, on the part of Frege and Giuseppe Peano, to interpret rigorous axiomatization as formalization. Frege carried the development much further by undertaking to develop the whole of arithmetic and analysis in a formal system which is essentially a system of set theory.

At the turn of the century the entire development reached a crisis with the discovery of the paradoxes of set theory, which showed that the concept of class or set as it was then being used had not been sufficiently clarified. Much of the foundational research of the early twentieth century—and not only in the axiomatization of set theory—was directed at problems posed or believed to have been posed by the paradoxes.

In that period emerged three general viewpoints, each of which had its own program based on a distinctive attitude toward the question of platonism. The most radical was intuitionism, based on L. E. J. Brouwer's critique of the whole idea of platonism. In contrast to Brouwer, David Hilbert had a firm commitment to the platonizing tendency in mathematics, but he held epistemological views which were fundamentally in accord with Brouwer's critique of platonism. Making use of the fact that no matter how platonist the mathematics formalized, questions of provability in a formal system are meaningful from a narrow constructivist point of view, Hilbert's school sought to secure the foundations of platonist mathematics by metamathematical investigation of formalized mathematics—in particular, by a proof of consistency. This viewpoint was called formalism, although the designation is misleading, since Hilbert never maintained that even platonist mathematics could be simply defined as a "meaningless" formal system.

Proponents of the third viewpoint, logicism, whose leading figure was Russell, continued to believe in Frege's program of reducing mathematics to logic. Accepting this program involved taking some platonist assumptions as intuitively evident.

A great deal of work in mathematical logic was directed toward clarifying and justifying one or another of these points of view. We might mention Brouwer's (informal) results on the impossibility of constructively proving certain theorems in analysis, Arend Heyting's formalization of intuitionist logic, the development of finitist proof theory by Hilbert and his co-workers, and Russell and A. N. Whitehead's *Principia Mathematica* as a much further development of mathematics within a system of set theory.

Nonetheless, the trichotomy of logicism, formalism, and intuitionism has probably never been the best classification of points of view in foundations. It does not take account of one of the philosophically most important problems, that of predicativity, or of some mathematical developments—such as the development of the semantics of logic by Leopold Löwenheim, Thoralf Skolem, Kurt Gödel, and Alfred Tarski—which were crucially important for later work. At any rate the schools no longer really exist. All of them had programs which encountered serious difficulties; further experience with set theory and the axiomatizations of Ernst Zermelo and Russell deprived the paradoxes of their apparently apocalyptic character; and specialized work in mathematical logic led more and more to the consideration of problems whose significance cut across the division of the schools and to looking at the results of the schools in ways which would be independent of the basic controversies. A decisive step in this development came in the early 1930s, with the discovery of Gödel's incompleteness theorem and the coming of age of formal semantics.

Some areas of the foundations of mathematics will be passed over here—in particular, we shall not go far into the significance of the fact that mathematics has applications to the concrete world, although historically the relation between mathematics and its applications has been very close, and the present sharp distinction between pure and applied mathematics is a rather recent development. For instance, we shall omit a special consideration of geometry. If the pre-twentieth-century view that geometry is a purely mathematical theory which nonetheless deals with actual space is correct, then the omission is unjustified. However, even the question whether this view still has something to be said for it is more intimately related to the philosophy of physics than to the problems on which we shall concentrate. Geometry as understood today by the pure mathematician, as the general study of structures analogous to Euclidean space, raises no philosophical problems different from those raised by analysis and set theory (see GEOMETRY).

THE AXIOMATIC METHOD

As we said, we shall begin our discussion with the axiomatic method. Consideration of the notion of an informal axiomatic system leads to the notions of formalization and formal system. Through this process, especially through the last step, mathematical theories become themselves objects of mathematical study. The exploitation of this possibility is perhaps the specifically modern move in the study of the foundations of mathematics and has led to an enormous enrichment of the subject in the last hundred years.

Axiomatization. Ever since Euclid, axiomatizing a theory has meant presenting it by singling out certain propositions and deducing further ones from them; if the presentation is complete, it should be the case that *all* statements which could be asserted in the theory are thus deducible. Axiomatization has also come to mean a similar reduction of vocabulary, in that certain notions should be taken as primitive and all further notions which are introduced in the development of the theory should be defined in terms of the primitive ones. In essence this is the conception of an axiomatized theory which prevails today, although it has been developed in different directions.

There are important ambiguities concerning the means of deduction and definition to be admitted in the development of the theory. Here informal axiomatics always makes use of some general background which can be used in developing the theory but is not itself included in the axiomatization. In modern mathematics this background typically includes logic and arithmetic and usually also analysis and some set theory. For example, in an axiomatic theory concerning objects of a certain kind, one permits oneself very quickly to make statements about sequences and sets of those objects, to introduce concepts defined in terms of the primitives of the theory by means of these general mathematical devices, and to make inferences which turn on laws of arithmetic, analysis, or set theory. Such notions often enter into the statement of the axioms themselves. We shall presently say more about the significance of this procedure.

It might seem natural to require provisionally that the means of deduction and definition be restricted to those of pure logic, for logic is supposed to contain those rules of correct inference which have the highest degree of generality and which must be applied in all sciences. We would then regard an axiomatization as only partial if deductions from it required the use of methods of the special sciences—in particular, branches of mathematics (likewise if, in addition to the primitives, notions other than purely logical ones entered into the definitions). An axiomatic theory would then consist of just those statements which are deducible by purely logical means from a certain limited set of statements and of the statements which can be obtained from these by definitions expressible purely logically in terms of the primitives.

It seems possible that such an axiomatic system was the objective toward which Euclid was striving. He evidently did not intend to allow himself general mathematical notions, such as arithmetical ones, for he included propositions involving such notions among his axioms and undertook to develop some of number theory from the axioms in Books VII–IX. Even some of Euclid's well-known failures to achieve this degree of rigor—for example, his assuming in his very first proof that two circles with the center of each lying on the circumference of the other will have two points of intersection—might have arisen because he saw them as immediate deductions from the meaning of the concepts involved. Of course, a rigorous theory of definition would require definitions to be given or axioms to be explicitly stated in such a way that such deductions do proceed by mere logic.

A perfectly satisfactory axiomatization in this form certainly was not possible in Euclid's time; it probably had to wait for two developments that did not take place until the late nineteenth century, Frege's discovery and axiomatization of quantification theory and the Dedekind–Peano axiomatization of arithmetic. (Nonetheless, considerable progress was made prior to these developments.)

This remark points to a limitation of the conception we are considering, for it does not give a meaning to the idea of an axiomatization of logic itself, although such axiomatization has played a vital role in modern foundational studies. Appreciation of this point leads to the concept of a *formal system,* but before we consider this concept let us observe a consequence of the axiomatization of a theory.

The abstract viewpoint. Suppose a theory is so completely axiomatized that all concepts of the special theory which are used in statements and deductions are explicitly given as primitives and all special assumptions underlying the proofs are disengaged and either stated among or deduced from the axioms. This means that the validity of the deductions does not at all depend on the actual meaning of the primitive terms of the special theory. It follows that the formal structure determined by the primitive concepts and the axioms can have a more general application than they have in the given special theory, in the sense that we could by *any* choice of interpretation of the primitive terms obtain a deductive system of hypotheses concerning some subject matter, even though the hypotheses will in many cases be false.

This fact is of crucial importance in the study of axiom systems. We can then think of a *model* of an axiomatic theory as a system of objects and relations which provides references for the primitive terms so that the axioms come out *true*. We can think of axiomatization as having proceeded with a particular model in mind, but this need not have been the case; at any rate, interest attaches to the study of other possible models. (Although we may, in this discussion, allow means of deduction which go beyond pure logic, it ought to be the case that if a proposition is deducible from the axioms of the theory, then it must be true in *all* models of the theory. It might be reasonable to take this as a sufficient condition of deducibility, but if so it seems that the notion of model will have to have a relativity comparable to that of the notion of deducibility.) For example, suppose we consider absolute geometry—that is, Euclidean geometry without the parallel postulate. Then any model either of Euclidean geometry or of the standard non-Euclidean geometries will be a model of absolute geometry. If the parallel postulate is deducible from the other axioms of Euclidean geometry—that is, from the axioms of absolute geometry—then it must be true in every model of absolute geometry. The construction of models for non-Euclidean geometries showed that this is not the case. We call an axiom of a system independent if it is not deducible from the others. Thus, if the theory obtained by dropping an axiom $\mathscr{A}$ has a model in which $\mathscr{A}$ is false, then $\mathscr{A}$ is independent.

Another possibility, which has been much exploited in modern mathematics, is to replace a system of primitive terms and axioms by what amounts to an explicit definition of a model of the axioms. Thus, suppose Euclidean geometry is formulated with two primitive predicates (following Alfred Tarski in "What Is Elementary Geometry?," in Leon Henkin, Patrick Suppes, and Alfred Tarski, eds., *The Axiomatic Method,* Amsterdam, 1959):

$$\text{``}\beta(x,y,z)\text{''},$$

meaning "x, y, and z are collinear, and y lies between x and z or $y = x$ or $y = z$," and

$$\text{``}\delta(x,y,z,w)\text{''},$$

meaning "x is the same distance from y as z is from w." (The variables here range over points, which in the informal theory must be thought of as a primitive notion.) Then we can define a *Euclidean space* as a triple $\langle S,B,D \rangle$, where S is a set of entities called "points," B a ternary relation on S, and D a quaternary relation on S, such that the axioms of

Euclidean geometry hold. Then to any theorem proved from these axioms corresponds a statement of the form "Every Euclidean space is such that . . . ." A number of attempts to characterize mathematical structures axiomatically have led in a similar way to explicit definitions of abstract types of structure. This is regarded, for more than historical reasons, as a fruit of the axiomatic method. The search for an axiomatic basis for a mathematical theory is also the search for a formulation of the arguments in a fashion which will make them more generally applicable, giving them a generality which can be expressed in the definition of a general type of structure.

Formalization. Whereas one development of the axiomatic method tends to the replacement of axioms by definitions, another leads to the conception of a formal system. One result of the axiomatization of a theory was that the meaning of the primitive terms became irrelevant to the deductions. If we carry this abstraction from meaning to its limit, we can cover the case of axiomatizations of logic and resolve once and for all the question of what means of deduction are to be allowed. That is, we put into the construction of an axiom system a complete specification of all the means of inference to be allowed (for example, logic and basic mathematics) in the form both of further axioms and of rules of inference that allow us to infer from statements of certain given forms a statement of another given form. If this is done with utmost rigor, so that use can be made of only as much of the meaning of the terms as is specified in axioms and explicit definitions, then the system is specified simply in terms of the designs of the "linguistic" forms in which it is expressed. "Linguistic" is put in quotation marks because, invariably, much of the language has been replaced by an artificial syntax. We are left with a specification of certain strings of symbols as "axioms" and certain rules, each of which allows us to "infer" a new string from certain prior ones. The strings which we can obtain from axioms by successive application of the rules can be called *theorems*.

A proper explanation of the concept of a formal system requires somewhat more apparatus. The exactness of this procedure requires that the strings of symbols used be constructed out of preassigned material, which we can assume to be a finite list of symbols. Among the strings of these symbols we single out a subclass that we call *formulae* (or well-formed formulae, wffs), which are those strings to which, in an interpretation, we would give a meaning. (The non-wffs correspond to ungrammatical sentences.) Then a certain class of formulae is singled out as the *axioms*. The class of theorems can be defined as the closure of the axioms under certain operations; that is, rules of the following form are specified:

$$\mathscr{R}_i(\mathscr{A}_1,\cdot\cdot\cdot,\mathscr{A}_{r_i},\mathscr{B}) : (R_i). \text{ If } \mathscr{A}_1,\cdot\cdot\cdot,\mathscr{A}_{r_i} \text{ are theorems}$$
and $\mathscr{R}_i(\mathscr{A}_i,\cdot\cdot\cdot,\mathscr{A}_{r_i},\mathscr{B})$, then $\mathscr{B}$ is a theorem, where R_i is some relation on strings of the symbols of the system.

So the definition of "theorem" is an inductive definition with the clauses (R_i) and

every axiom is a theorem.

In this setting we can resolve another ambiguity of our original rough conception of axiomatization. The question arises concerning what conditions a class of statements must satisfy to be appropriate as the axioms of an axiomatic theory. Various epistemological desiderata, such as self-evident truth for the intended model, are put aside once we take the abstract point of view. Another requirement which has been found natural in the past is that both individual axioms and the class of axioms as a whole should have a certain simplicity. What there is in the way of general theory about the simplicity of individual axioms has not played much of a role in investigations of the foundations of mathematics, although much effort has been expended in replacing individual axioms with simpler ones or in finding systems of axioms which have particular advantages of "naturalness" for intended applications.

In order to characterize the important axiom systems which have been used in the past we shall have to place some limitation on the class of axioms. In the traditional cases the class has been finite. However, the formalization of such an axiomatic system can give rise to an infinite system—for example, if we take as axioms all instances of a certain schema.

The limitation which is used instead of a finite class of axioms is based on the fact that the notions of formula, axiom, and theorem are to be syntactically specified. Then the requirement is that there be a mechanical, or *effective,* procedure for deciding whether a given formula is an axiom and whether a given inference (of a formula from finitely many premises) is correct according to the rules of inference. This requirement is natural in the light of the idea that a proof of a statement in an axiomatic theory should contain all the mathematically significant information needed to show that the statement is indeed assertible in the theory. That would not be the case, it is argued, if something beyond mechanical checking were needed to determine the correctness of the proof. (It should be pointed out, however, that generalizations of the concept of formal system in which this condition is not satisfied are frequently used in mathematical logic.)

The notion of a formal system gives the highest degree of generality, in that there is *no* element of the symbolism whose interpretation is restricted. Indeed, it permits much of what we might want to say about an axiomatic theory to be formulated without reference to interpretation, since the formulae, axioms, and rules of inference are specified without reference to interpretation, and what is a theorem is then defined, again without such reference. An entire division of the theory of formal systems—what is usually called syntax—can thus be built up with no more than a heuristic use of interpretation. In particular, the intensional notions—concept, proposition, etc.—relied on so far in the informal exposition can be eliminated.

The concept of a formal system also brings to the formulation of the theory the highest degree of precision, at the cost of a still further idealization in relation to the concrete activities of mathematicians. Furthermore, the concept not only gives a refined formulation to axiomatizations and allows a mathematical study of axiom systems of a more general scope than was possible without it but also makes possible a precise formulation of differences about mathematical methods. Carrying the axiomatic method to this

limit makes possible a new approach to a wide variety of questions about the foundations of mathematics.

Inasmuch as axiomatization is a rendering of a theory in a more precise formulation (if not a singling out of some particular aspect of the theory), the axiomatized theory cannot be identified in every respect with what has gone before. However, it can *replace* what has gone before and actually has done so in many cases. The passage from axiomatization to formalization is in an important respect more radical than the various stages of informal axiomatization, and we can therefore regard a formalization of a theory as not so much a more precise formulation of the theory as an idealized representation of it. The process of replacing expressions of natural language by artificial symbols, which goes on in all mathematical development, is here carried to an extreme. For example, we lay down by a definition what are "formulae" and "proofs" in the system, whereas informally we rely for the notion of sentences on our more or less unanalyzed linguistic sense, and for proofs we rely on this sense, on mathematical tradition, and on intuitive logic. In particular, formulae and formal proofs are of unbounded length and complexity, without regard to the limits of what we can perceive and understand.

With this goes the fact that the basic general notions with which we operate in formulating and reflecting on theories —sentence, proposition, deduction, axiom, inference, proof, definition—are replaced in the formalized version by specifically defined, more or less simplified and idealized substitutes. In particular, although we "interpret" formalized theories, the relation between a sign or a formal system and its reference in some model is a "dead" correspondence, an aspect of a purely mathematical relation between two systems of objects. This enables one to avoid the intractable problems of how linguistic expressions come to have "meaning" and, with it, reference and is therefore an extremely valuable piece of abstraction. But it *is* an abstraction; moreover, it does not mean that the informal linguistic and intellectual apparatus disappears altogether, since it will still be used in the setting up and investigation of the formalized theory. In fact, one of the results of formalization is a sharper separation between what is within the theory and what belongs to discourse about it—that is, to the metatheory. If the metatheory is in turn axiomatized and then formalized, the same situation arises at the next-higher level.

The importance of this observation is difficult to assess, but it is relevant to a number of problems we shall discuss later—in particular, attempts to argue from results of mathematical logic to philosophical conclusions.

EPISTEMOLOGICAL DISCUSSION

A priori knowledge. We shall now put the matter of axiomatization and formalization aside and consider mathematics from the point of view of general epistemology. The guiding thread of our discussion will be the fact that a powerful tradition in philosophy has regarded mathematics, or at least a part of it, as a central case of a priori knowledge. This means that reflection on mathematics has been at the center of philosophical discussion of the concept of a priori knowledge.

The characteristics of mathematics which have led to the

conclusion that mathematics is a priori are its abstract character and accompanying enormous generality and its great exactitude and certainty, which, indeed, have traditionally been considered absolute. Thus, even before setting forth a developed logical analysis of the concept of number, we find that the effort to interpret "2 + 2 = 4" as a hypothesis which can be checked by observation runs into obvious obstacles. It is perhaps not so vital that the statement refers to abstract entities, numbers, which are not the sort of thing we observe. The concept of number certainly does apply to empirically given objects, in the sense that they can be counted and that the numbers thus attributed to them will obey such laws as "2 + 2 = 4." Therefore, the proposition could so far be taken as a law concerning such entities. Even then its range of application is so enormous, extending over the entire physical universe, that it seems evident that if it were taken as a hypothesis, it would be stated and used in a more qualified way, at least by critically minded scientists. In other words, the certainty which we attribute to elementary arithmetical propositions would be quite unwarranted if they were laws based on observation. Even in the case of mathematical principles to which we do not attribute this degree of certainty, such as the axiom of choice and the continuum hypothesis, the possible "contrary evidence" would arise from the deductive development of the theory involved (in the examples, set theory), not from observation.

Moreover, it seems that we ought to be able to conceive of a possible observation which would be a counterinstance. Although it is perhaps not evident that this is impossible, the ideas that come to mind lead either to descriptions of doubtful intelligibility or to the description of situations where it seems obviously more reasonable to assume some other anomaly (such as miscounting or the perhaps mysterious appearance or disappearance of an object) than to admit an exception to "2 + 2 = 4."

Another difficulty is that the concept of number must apply beyond the range of the concrete entities which are accessible to observation; such abstract entities as mathematical objects must be subject to counting, and this seems also to be the case for transcendent entities.

The foregoing considerations could be developed into decisive arguments only with the help of both a more developed formal analysis of number and a more detailed discussion of the relation between arithmetical laws and actual counting and perhaps also of the role of mathematics in empirical science. In any case, they do not tell against another form of the denial that arithmetic is a priori, the view that arithmetical laws are theoretical principles of a very fundamental sort, which we are therefore far more "reluctant to give up" in a particular situation than more everyday beliefs or impressions or even than fundamental theoretical principles in science. Such a view would nonetheless take it to be conceivable that in response to some difficulty in, say, particle physics a new theory might be formulated which modified some part of elementary arithmetic.

Mathematics and logic. The above considerations show why it is necessary to add technical analysis to the epistemological discussion. We shall take as our guiding thread the attempt to show that mathematics—in particular, arithmetic—is a part of logic. This attempt has led to some

of the most important results in the logical analysis of mathematical notions. The view that mathematics can be reduced to logic is one of the principal general views on the foundations of mathematics which we mentioned earlier; it goes generally by the name of logicism, and its classic expression is in the writings of Frege and Russell.

Even if successful, the reduction of mathematics to logic could not by itself give an account of how there can be a priori knowledge in mathematics, for it would only reduce the problem of giving such an account to the corresponding problem with regard to logic. Nonetheless, the a priori character of mathematics has traditionally been found perhaps slightly less certain than that of logic. The obvious fact that one of the primary tasks of mathematics is the deductive development of theories has been found to be one of the most powerful supports of the claim that mathematics is a priori. We can expect that a successful reduction of mathematics to logic will simplify the problem of a priori knowledge, and not only by replacing two problems by one. Logic is more unavoidable: we cannot get anywhere in thinking without using logical words and inferring according to logical rules. This would suggest that logic is in fact more basic than mathematics and more certainly a priori. (It would also suggest that philosophical treatments of logic are more liable to circularity.) Moreover, in the course of history philosophers have invoked sources of evidence for mathematics which are at least apparently special, such as Kant's pure intuition. Thus, a reduction of mathematics to logic might make superfluous certain difficult epistemological theories.

The claims of logicism are based in large part on mathematical work in axiomatics. A number of nineteenth-century investigations showed that the basic notions of analysis—for example, rational, real, and complex number—could be defined, and the basic theorems proved, in terms of the theory of natural numbers and such more general notions as class and function. At the same time, axiomatic work was done in the arithmetic of natural numbers, culminating in the axiomatization of Richard Dedekind (1888) and Peano (1889). The movement toward formalization began somewhat later, with the work of Frege and of the school of Peano.

Thus, the effort to reduce mathematics to logic arose in the context of an increasing systematization and rigor of all pure mathematics, from which emerged the goal of setting up a comprehensive formal system which would represent all of known mathematics with the exception of geometry, insofar as it is a theory of physical space. (But of the writers of that generation only Frege had a strict conception of a formal system.) The goal of logicism would then be a comprehensive formal system with a natural interpretation such that the primitives would be logical concepts and the axioms logical truths.

We shall be guided by Frege's presentation, although he did not go very far in developing mathematics within his system and of course the system turned out to be inconsistent. Nonetheless, it is already clear from Frege's work how to define the primitives and prove the axioms of a standard axiomatization of arithmetic.

We shall begin with some discussions of the notions of number and class, which are crucial for the reduction and for the foundations of mathematics generally.

Counting and number. In order to be clearer about the concept of number, we might start with the operation of counting. In a simple case of carefully counting a collection of objects, we perhaps look at and point to each one successively, and with each of these directions of the attention we think of or pronounce one of a standard series of symbols (numerals) in its place in a standard ordering of these symbols. We are careful to reach each of these objects once and only once in the process. We thus set up a *one-to-one correspondence* between the objects and a certain segment of the series of numerals. We say that the number of objects in the collection is _____, where the blank is filled by the last numeral of the series.

Before pursuing this matter further, let us examine the series of numerals itself. We have certain initial symbols and rules for constructing further symbols whose application can be iterated indefinitely. We could simplify the situation in actual language and suppose that there is one initial symbol, say "|", and a generating operation, concatenation of another "|", so that the numerals will be |, ||, |||, ||||, · ·. It is not clear, however, that it is merely a matter of "practical convenience" that ordinary numerals are, in the long run, considerably more condensed: if a string of several million "|'s" were offered as a result of counting, one would have to count *them* to learn what the number was.

However, it is worth asking whether the *pure* notion of natural number requires more than the possibility of generating such a string of symbols. By "symbols" do we mean here blobs of ink? Only with certain reservations. The particular blobs which we have produced are not at all essential; if we write others— |, ||, |||, ||||, · · ·—they will do just as well. In fact, we could have chosen symbols of quite different forms and still have produced something equivalent for our purposes, such as +, ++, +++, · · ·, or something not consisting of marks on paper at all, such as sounds, which are, of course, actually used. As long as it is capable of representing to us the process of successive generation by which these sequences of symbols are produced, anything will do—any collection of perceptible objects that can be placed in one-to-one order-preserving correspondence with our first sequence of symbols.

Thus, the blobs of ink serve as the representatives of a quite abstract structure. This abstraction allows us (even on a subordinate level) to disregard some limitations of the blobs besides their particularity and accompanying boundedness to a particular place and time. They are constructed according to a procedure for generating successive ones, and what matters is the structure embodied in the procedure, not any particular limitations that might be encountered in carrying it out. On a sufficiently abstract level we say that we *can* continue to generate symbols indefinitely, although life is too short, paper and ink run out, the earth perhaps disintegrates, etc.

Here we have already taken the step of introducing abstract entities. In a weak form this could be represented as taking certain abstract equivalence relations between entities (e.g., marks on paper) as criteria of *identity* for new kinds of entities (e.g., symbols as types or, further, numbers). But we have already reached a point where more is involved, since the abstract entities which are represented by all the marks of a given equivalence class belong to a series which can be continued far beyond any practical possibility of constructing representatives. We can create a "pseudo-concrete" model by appealing to space, time, and theoretical physics, but then we are already depending on abstract mathematical objects. Given that we do think of numerals as referring to numbers, it is natural to introduce the apparatus not only of identity but also of quantification. Certain uses of such quantification, however, will involve still stronger presuppositions than we have uncovered up to now, and we shall discuss these when we consider platonism and constructivism.

Axioms of arithmetic. We have so far taken for granted that the natural numbers are obtained by starting with some initial element 0 and iterating an operation of "successor" or "adding 1". This is the basis for an especially simple axiomatization of the theory of natural numbers, that of Dedekind and Peano, in which the primitives are "0", "number" ("NNx"), and "successor" (which we shall give as a relation: "Sxy" means "y is successor of x"). Then the axioms are

(1) $NN0$.
(2) $NNx \supset (\exists! y)(NNy \ \& \ Sxy)$.
(3) $\neg S0x$.
(4) $Sxz \ \& \ Syz \ . \supset x = y$.
(5) $(F)[F0 \ \& \ (x)(y)(Fx \ \& \ Sxy \ . \supset Fy) \ . \supset (x)(NNx \supset Fx)]$.

In (5), "(F)" may be read "for all properties F," but for the present we shall not discuss just what this means. We do not need to suppose that precisely what properties there are is determined in advance, but we have to acknowledge that if it is not determined what properties there are, then it may not be determined precisely what natural numbers there are.

We could think of the natural numbers as given by a kind of inductive definition:

(*a*) $NN0$.
(*b*) If NNx, then $NN(Sx)$.
(*c*) Nothing is a natural number except by virtue of (*a*) and (*b*).

However, in this case we have to suppose that the successor relation is given in such a way that axioms (2), (3), and (4) are evident. We might think of "0" as represented by "|" and the successor function as represented by the addition of another "|" to a string. Then there is apparently an appeal to spatial intuition in regarding these axioms as evident. (Cf. Paul Lorenzen, *Einführung in die operative Logik und Mathematik,* Berlin, Göttingen, and Heidelberg, 1955. The last remark is not necessarily an objection to Lorenzen's procedure, but it does seem doubtful that Lorenzen's procedure is superior to Brouwer's appeal to introspective construction or to Kant's appeal to pure intuition.) In that event the induction principle (5) will be in some way a consequence of (*c*). It could be regarded simply as an interpretation of (*c*), or one might argue, as Ludwig Wittgenstein apparently did at one time (see Friedrich Waismann, **Introduction to Mathematical Thinking,** Ch. 8), that the meaning of all natural numbers is not given to us by such specifications and our independent concept of "all" and that the induction principle functions as a *cri-*

terion for a proposition's being true of all natural numbers.

The concept of class. Before we discuss further the notion of number it is necessary to give some explanation of the notion of class or set. We shall consider two explanations, one suggested by Cantor and one suggested by Frege.

Frege's explanation. Instead of the term "class" or "set," Frege used the phrase "extension of a concept." Frege's usage is based on the tendency to regard the predicates of a language as standing in quantifiable places—

John is a Harvard man.

Henry is a Harvard man.

∴ John and Henry have something in common—

and the tendency to derive from general terms *abstract singular* terms, which are usually explained as referring to *properties* or *attributes.*

These two tendencies can be separated. Frege regarded predicates in context as in fact referring, but to concepts, not to objects. Concepts, like the predicates themselves, have argument places; Frege called both predicates and concepts "unsaturated" because only with the argument place filled by an object (in the case of a predicate, a proper name) could they "stand by themselves." A notation which expresses his conception is that of the second-order predicate calculus, in which the above conclusion might be symbolized (misleadingly) as $(\exists F)[F(\text{John}) \& F(\text{Henry})]$. An expression which is syntactically appropriate for denoting an object cannot denote a concept, and vice versa.

The extension of a concept, then, is simply an object associated with the concept in such a way that if two concepts apply to the same objects, they have the same extension—that is,

$$(6) \qquad \hat{x}Fx = \hat{x}Gx \,.\, \equiv (x)(Fx \equiv Gx),$$

where $\hat{x}Fx$ is the extension of the concept F. This is essentially Frege's famous axiom V (*Grundgesetze der Arithmetik*, Vol. I, p. 36; Frege's notion of concept can interpret the quantifiers in our axiom 5).

Cantor's explanation. Cantor characterized a set as "jedes Viele, welches sich als Eines denken lässt, d.h. jeden Inbegriff bestimmter Elemente, welcher durch ein Gesetz zu einem Ganzen verbunden werden kann" ("every many, which can be thought of as one, that is, every totality of definite elements which can be combined into a whole by a law"; *Gesammelte Abhandlungen,* p. 204). "Unter einer 'Menge' verstehen wir jede Zusammenfassung M von bestimmten wohlunterschiedenen Objekten m unserer Anschauung oder unseres Denkens (welche die 'Elemente' von M genannt werden) zu einem Ganzen" ("By a 'set' we understand any collection M of definite well-distinguished objects of our intuition or thought, which are called the 'elements' of M, into a whole"; *ibid.,* p. 282).

It is virtually impossible to explain Cantor's idea of set without using words of the same general type, only vaguer ("collection," "multitude," *Inbegriff*). We can perhaps approach it by mentioning a few ways in which multitudes are thought of as unities: by being thought of by means of a predicate—that is, by being brought under a concept in Frege's sense—so that Frege's extensions could perhaps

be regarded as sets, or by being in some way brought to the attention at once, even without the intervention of language; in particular, a finite number of objects of perception can constitute a set. That the objects must be "determinate and well-distinguished" means that it must be determinate what the elements are, that identity and difference be well-defined for the elements, and that a set must be determined by its elements.

One is inclined in this connection to think of a set as "composed" of its elements, but this is not essential and might lead to confusion of a set with a spatiotemporal sum, but a portion of space or time (for example, a geometric figure) can be partitioned in a number of ways, so the sets of the parts will be different but the sum will always be the same.

The picture of finite sets can be extended in such a way that one might imagine an "arbitrary" infinite set independent of any predicate. Suppose it is to be a set S of natural numbers. We go through the natural numbers one by one *deciding* for each n whether n is a member of S ($n \,\epsilon\, S$) or not. Although the determination takes infinitely long, it is determined for each n whether $n \,\epsilon\, S$. (Or we might imagine its being done all at once by God.)

Difficulties in these conceptions. Both Cantor's and Frege's conceptions of sets have difficulties which did not come clearly to the consciousness of logicians and set-theorists until the discovery of the set-theoretical paradoxes, discussed below. We shall merely mention here a source of difficulty. In both theories a set or extension is supposed to be an object, capable of being itself a member of sets. Cannot this give rise to circularities—that is, that a set is formed from or constituted by certain objects, among them itself? (Or, in Frege's terms, among the objects in the range of the quantifiers on the right side of formula 6 are $\hat{x}Fx$ and $\hat{x}Gx$ themselves, so that the identity condition for these objects, which from Frege's point of view was part of their essence, seems to depend on particular facts about them.)

We shall not say anything at the moment about the particular form the difficulties take or about how to resolve them. We shall continue to use second-order quantification somewhat vaguely; one can interpret the variables as ranging over Frege's concepts, in most cases over classes or even over intensional entities, as might have been suggested by our original word "property."

Frege's analysis of number. We can now proceed to the main steps of Frege's argument for the thesis that arithmetic is a part of logic. Frege observed that a necessary and sufficient condition for, say, the number of F's (which we shall write as "N_xFx") to be the same as the number of G's is that there should be a one-to-one correspondence of the F's and the G's. (In that case we say they are *numerically equivalent.*) This criterion, which is quite general—that is, not restricted to the case where there are only finitely many F's or G's—had already been exploited by Cantor to generalize the notion of cardinal number to infinite classes (see CANTOR, GEORG; SET THEORY). It can be justified by our discussion of counting and number, above.

On the basis of a one-to-one correspondence between the F's and $\{1,\cdot\cdot\cdot,n\}$ we are prepared to say that the number of F's is n. But no such correspondence can then exist with $\{1,\cdots,m\}$ for any $m \neq n$, and if by the same criterion there are n G's, then by composition we can set up a one-to-one correspondence between the F's and the G's. If there are m G's for $m \neq n$, we cannot. So we say that there are n F's if and only if a one-to-one correspondence *exists* between the F's and $\{1,\cdots,n\}$, and in that case there are n G's if and only if there is a one-to-one correspondence between the F's and the G's. Writing "there are n F's" as "$(\exists x)_n Fx$", we have that if $(\exists n)[(\exists x)_n Fx]$,

(7) $N_x Fx = N_x Gx$. $\equiv$ the F's and the G's are numerically equivalent.

Since we have no independent criterion for the case where there are infinitely many F's, we take (7) to be true by *definition* in that case. We then have Frege's criterion.

Frege then defined a relation H as a one-to-one correspondence of the F's and the G's if and only if for every F there is exactly one G to which it bears the relation H and vice versa—in symbols,

(8) $\qquad (x)[Fx \supset (\exists! y)(Gy \,\&\, Hxy)]$ &
$\qquad\qquad (y)[Gy \supset (\exists! x)(Fx \,\&\, Hxy)]$,

where "$(\exists! x)(\cdots x \cdots)$" can be defined in first-order logic:

(9) $\qquad$ "$(\exists! x)(\cdots x \cdots)$" for
$\qquad$ "$(\exists x)[\cdots x \cdots \,\&\, (y)(\cdots y \cdots \supset y = x)]$".

Thus, numerical equivalence can be defined by a formula "$(\exists H)\mathscr{S}(H,F,G)$", where "$\mathscr{S}(H,F,G)$" is an abbreviation for a first-order formula, namely, the expansion of (8) in terms of (9).

The relation of numerical equivalence is an equivalence relation; Frege's idea was, in effect, to define cardinal numbers as the equivalence classes of this relation. This definition, however, requires a powerful use of the notion of extension which is allowed by his axiom (6). In other words, $N_x Fx$ is to be the extension of the concept *concept numerically equivalent to the concept F*—that is, we define

(10) $\qquad$ "$N_x Fx$" for "$\hat{G}(\exists H)\mathscr{S}(H,G,F)$".

(In fact, in the *Grundgesetze*, Frege avoided applying the extension operator to a second-order variable by appeal to formula 6: G can be replaced by its extension. We define "$\hat{G}\mathscr{F}(G)$" as $\hat{y}(\exists G)[y = \hat{x}Gx . \mathscr{F}(G)]$".)

Formula (10) gives a definition of Cantor's general concept of cardinal number, so we can prove (7); no further use of axiom V is needed for the definition of the natural numbers and the proof of the axioms (1)–(5). We now define Peano's primitives—"0", "Sxy" ("y is the successor of x"), and "NNx" ("x is a natural number"):

(11) $\qquad$ "0" for "$N_x(x \neq x)$",

for then (7) yields $N_x Fx = 0 \equiv \neg(\exists x) Fx$.

Intuitively, $n+1 = N_x(x=0 \vee \cdots \vee x=n)$; this result will be reached if we define "Sxy" as follows:

(12) "Sxy" for
$\quad$ "$(\exists F)\{y = N_w Fw \,\&\, (\exists z)[Fz \,\&\, N_w(Fw \,\&\, w \neq z) = x]\}$".

Intuitively, the number of F's is one more than the number of G's if there is an F such that the number of the *rest* of the F's is precisely $N_x Gx$. Definition (12) implies that in this case $S(N_x Gx, N_x Fx)$.

The remaining primitive is defined by an ingenious device (already present in Frege's *Begriffsschrift*), which yields mathematical induction: we want to define "NNx" so that something true of 0 and of the successor of anything of which it is true is true of every natural number—that is,

(13) $\qquad F0 \,\&\, (x)(y)(Fx \,\&\, Sxy . \supset Fy) . \supset (x)(NNx \supset Fx)$.

But this will be immediate if we *define* "x is a natural number" as "x falls under *every* concept F which 0 falls under and which is such that any successor of whatever falls under it also falls under it"—that is,

(14) "NNx" for "$(F)\{F0 \,\&\, (x)(y)(Fx \,\&\, Sxy . \supset Fy) . \supset Fx\}$".

To prove the other axioms: (1) is immediate from (14); that S is one-to-one and that 0 is not the successor of anything follow from (12) together with (7).

Difficulties in logicism. The first difficulty with Frege's construction is certainly the use Frege made of the notion of extension. We have alluded to difficulties with the ideas of set theory; they affected Frege's system through Russell's deduction in 1901 of a contradiction from (6). (For Russell's exchange of letters with Frege, see John van Heijenoort, ed., *A Source Book in Mathematical Logic, 1879–1931*.) We shall discuss Russell's paradox and other paradoxes and the difficulties of the concept of class below.

Nonetheless, it turns out that a reasonably secure system of set theory can be developed in any one of a number of ways that are more than sufficient for the definition of Peano's primitives and proof of his axioms. In fact, no part of the axiomatic apparatus of a system of set theory which gives rise to any doubts as to consistency is really necessary for this reduction; we can say that if the development in set theory of a branch of mathematics necessarily involves the stronger and more problematic parts of set theory, this is due to the nature of the branch of mathematics itself, not the reduction to set theory.

This success is not without loss for the development of arithmetic: it seems that in the more natural set-theoretical systems (the theory of types, Zermelo's set theory) no definition of "$N_x Fx$" can be given with the same appearance of naturalness as in (10). The consequences of Russell's theory of types are more serious: the numbers must be duplicated at each type. What one usually ends up doing is identifying the numbers in a somewhat arbitrary way with a sequence of sets of the required order type.

Given that all this has been done, in what sense is the enterprise a reduction of arithmetic to set theory, and in what sense is it a reduction to logic? To take up the last question first, obviously the construction does not reduce arithmetic to logic unless the principles of the set theory involved can count as logical principles. The notion of class is not very far removed from concepts which played a role in traditional logic; from that point of view it is not at all evident why the first-order predicate calculus, which is already a considerable extension of the traditional formal apparatus, should count as logic and the theory of classes should not.

One difference is that whereas a valid formula of first-order logic will yield a truth if the quantifiers are interpreted to range over any domain of objects whatsoever, and without regard to its cardinal number in particular, set theory involves existence assumptions, so the domain over which the quantifiers range must be large enough to contain representatives for the sets whose existence is implied by the formula in question. In Frege's procedure these assumptions were embodied in the admission as a term of an abstract "$\hat{x}Fx$" for any predicate "F," and simple non-paradoxical instances of (6) already require that Frege's universe contain infinitely many objects.

Frege, of course, regarded (6) as a logical principle, a view which was fairly well refuted by its inconsistency. It would be much more reasonable to regard set theory as logic if its existence assumptions all followed from a single general principle, such as (6). But the analysis of the foundations of set theory stimulated by the paradoxes points to the opposite conclusion: any very definite system of existential postulates will prove incomplete in the sense that it is always possible to construct further existential postulates which are stronger (in the sense of first-order, or even second-order, logic). Moreover, these postulates assume a character not unlike principles of construction, so it is at least as natural to consider them hypothetical and analogical extensions of "constructions in pure intuition" as it is to consider them principles of logic. At any rate, if logic consists of the necessary principles of all coherent reasoning, then it seems evident that the stronger principles of set theory do not have this character; it is far from certain even that the weaker ones have it (perhaps even that all of first-order logic does). This being so, a reduction of arithmetic to set theory does little to increase the security and clarity of the foundations of arithmetic.

Kant's view. One of the purposes that Frege, Russell, and many later proponents had in mind in seeking to reduce arithmetic to logic was to show that no appeal to sensible intuition was necessary in arithmetic, as had been claimed by such empiricists as John Stuart Mill and by Kant in his theory of a priori intuition. Let us consider whether this purpose has been accomplished. Since Kant's view constitutes an independent effort to explain the a priori character of arithmetic, and since it is part of an extremely influential general philosophy, it deserves special mention. Kant began by insisting that mathematical judgments (at least the most characteristic ones) were synthetic, rather than analytic. We shall not enter into the question of just what he meant by that. Provided that one remembers that the scope of logic was much narrower for Kant than it is for us, it is plausible to suppose that his claim that mathematical judgments are synthetic implies that the propositions of a mathematical theory cannot be deduced from logical laws and definitions. The case of Kant's principal example, the geometry of space, seems clear, given, for instance, the fact that there are consistent geometrical theories which differ with respect to certain fundamental principles, such as the parallel postulate. (Even here, however, one might claim that the difference in principles corresponds to a difference in the meanings of the primitive terms. In application to real space this comes down to the question of "conventionalism" in geometry. W. V. Quine is probably right in holding that one cannot, in general, decide the question whether such a difference is *merely* a difference of meaning.)

The case of arithmetic presents a certain similarity if we deny that set theory is logic. The proofs in the set-theoretic development even of such elementary arithmetical laws as "$2+2=4$" depend on existential axioms of these theories. However, this does not mean that we can come as close to clearly conceiving the falsity of these principles as we can for the principles of geometry. Although we can easily enough set up a domain in which the existence postulates will fail, it is not clear that this counts as conceiving that the numbers $0, 1, 2, \cdots$ should not exist.

Kant went on to maintain that the evidence of both the principles of geometry and those of arithmetic rested on the "form of our sensible intuition." In particular, he said that mathematical demonstrations proceeded by "construction of concepts in pure intuition," and thus they appealed to the form of sensible intuition. Mathematical proof, according to Kant, required the presentation of instances of certain concepts. These instances would not function exactly as particulars, for one would not be entitled to assert anything concerning them which did not follow from the general concept. Nonetheless, conclusions could be drawn which were synthetic, because the construction of the instance would involve not merely the pure concept as of an abstract structure but also its "schematism" in terms of the general structure of our manner of representing objects to ourselves.

Thus, geometric figures would obey the axioms of geometry even though these axioms were not provable by analysis of the concepts. At the same time, the constructions would serve to verify any existence assumptions involved. (Indeed, instead of existential axioms Kant spoke of postulates asserting the possibility of certain constructions.)

In the case of arithmetic Kant argued that in order to verify "$7+5=12$" one must again consider an instance, this time in the form of a set of five objects, and add each one in succession to a given set of seven. It seems that although the five objects may be quite arbitrary, even abstract, they will, if not themselves present to perception, be represented by symbols which are present and which exhibit the same structure. In fact, we find this structure even in the symbolic operations involved in the formal proofs of "$7+5=12$" either within a set theory or directly from axioms for elementary number theory—or even in the proof of the formula of *first*-order logic

(15) $(\exists x)_7 Fx \,\&\, (\exists x)_5 Gx \,\&\, (x)\neg(Fx \,.\, Gx) \,.\, \supset (\exists x)_{12}(Fx \lor Gx),$

which is the key to the proof of "$7+5=12$" in Frege's construction. We think of "$(\exists x)_n(Fx)$" expanded as follows:

"$(\exists x)_0 Fx$" for "$\neg(\exists x)Fx$".
"$(\exists x)_{n+1}Fx$" for "$(\exists x)[Fx \,\&\, (\exists y)_n(Fy \,\&\, y \neq x)]$".

The arguments for the claim that intuition plays an essential role in mathematics are inevitably subjectivist to a degree, in that they pass from a direct semantical consideration of the statements and of what is required for their truth to a more pragmatic consideration of the operations involved in understanding and verifying them (and perhaps even "using" them, in a broad sense) and to a metalinguistic reflection on formulae and proofs as configurations of symbols. Leibniz had already emphasized the essential role of calculation with symbols in mathematics, and to Kant this role became an argument for the dependence of mathematics on sensible intuition.

We can see why the arguments must have this subjectivist character if we notice the complete abstractness of both set theory and arithmetic, which talk of objects in general in terms of logical operations (propositional combination, quantification) which are equally general. Even the specifically mathematical objects (sets and numbers) are subjected by the theory only to certain structural, relational conditions, so that they are not, as it were, individually identified by the theory. The content thus does not suggest any direct sensory verification; indeed, it seems that any proposition which is susceptible of such verification must contain some particular reference to space or time or to objects or properties which by nature occur only in space and time. Although it is Frege's construction and the development of set-theoretic mathematics which make this fact clear, Kant apparently was aware of it in the case of arithmetic, which he related closely to the pure categories and therefore to logic.

Nevertheless, it does not seem, at least in the light of philosophical and mathematical experience, that we can directly verify these propositions, or even understand them, independently of the senses. Determining the precise nature of the dependence of the operations of the mind in general on the senses is one of the central difficulties of all philosophies. But it is hard to maintain that we understand mathematical structures, or even the general notion of object which underlies them, without at least starting with a sensible representation, so that concrete explanations make use both of embodiments of the structures by perceptible objects and of reflection on symbolism. For instance, explanations of the notion of class can either make use of an appeal to language, as Frege's explanation does, or begin with the notion of a group of perceptible objects. (Indeed, it seems that even in the second case an appeal to language is sooner or later indispensable.)

Perhaps more decisive than these rather vague considerations is the fact that we cannot carry on any even fairly elaborate reasoning in mathematics without, as it were, placing ourselves at the mercy of a symbolic representation. Prior to the construction of a proof or calculation we do not know the answer to any substantial mathematical question. That the proof *can* be constructed, that the calculation turns out as it does, is, as it were, brute fact without which one cannot see any reason for the mathematical state of affairs' being what it is. In *Über die Deutlichkeit der Grundsätze der natürlichen Theologie und der Moral*, Kant gave this as his principal reason for asserting that mathematics proceeds by representing concepts in intuition, and in the *Critique of Pure Reason* the idea is again suggested in the discussion of "$7 + 5 = 12$" and the remarks about "symbolic construction" in algebra.

One might argue that the existence of a natural number n is verified by actually constructing a sequence of numerals up to that point. Such a construction provides a representation for the numbers up to n. It is noteworthy that either it or a mental equivalent is necessary for a full and explicit understanding of the *concept* of the number n. This gives some plausibility to the view that the possibility of such a representation rests on the "form of our sensible intuition," since everything belonging to the content of the particular realization is nonessential. It is perhaps permissible to speak, as Kant did, of "pure intuition," because we are able to take the symbols as representing or embodying an abstract order. This conception could be extended to the intuitive verification of elementary propositions of the arithmetic of small numbers. If these propositions really are evident in their full generality, and hence are necessary, then this conception gives some insight into the nature of this evidence.

However, the above description already ceases to apply when we pass to the construction, by a general rule, of the sequence of natural numbers and therefore when we consider large numbers, which we must describe in terms of general rules. Besides the "factor of abstraction" signalized in our being able to use sensory representations in thinking about the abstract structures they embody, there is also a factor of higher generality and the accompanying possibility of iteration, so that the sequence of natural numbers extends far beyond those represented by numerals it is possible actually to construct. Here the sense of the notion of "form of intuition" is less clear. Kant's idea, however, must surely be that the larger numbers are conceived only as an extension of the structures of our actual experience. The fact that the forms in question are, according to Kant, those of space and time means that the abstract extension of the mathematical forms embodied in our experience parallels an extension of the objective world beyond what we actually perceive.

Kant connected arithmetic with time as the form of our inner intuition, although he did not intend by this to deny that there is no direct reference to time in arithmetic. The claim apparently was that to a fully explicit awareness of number goes the *successive* apprehension of the stages in its construction, so that the structure involved is also represented by a sequence of moments of time. Time thus provides a realization for any number which can be realized in experience at all. Although this view is plausible enough, it does not seem strictly necessary to preserve the connection with time in the necessary extrapolation beyond actual experience. However, thinking of mathematical construction as a process in time is a useful picture for interpreting problems of constructivity (discussed below).

Kant's view enables us to obtain a more accurate picture of the role of intuition in mathematics, but, at least as developed above, it is not really satisfying, because it takes more or less as a fact our ability to place our perceptions in a mathematically defined structure and to see truths about this structure by using perceptible objects to symbolize it. The great attraction of Kantianism comes from the fact that other views seem unable to do any better: Frege, for example, carried the epistemological analysis less far than Kant in spite of his enormously more refined logical technique.

Conventionalism. Attempts to avoid dogmatism completely while still affirming the existence of a priori knowledge in mathematics have been made on the basis of conventionalism, the characteristic logical positivist view of a priori knowledge. This view in effect rejects the question of evidence in mathematics: mathematical statements do not need evidence because they are true by fiat, by virtue of the conventions according to which we specify the meanings of the words occurring in mathematics. Mathematics is therefore "without factual content" or even "empty."

Before we proceed to discuss this view we should distinguish it from two others which are associated with logical positivism, the view that mathematical statements are true by virtue of the meanings of the words in them and the view that they are analytic. The doctrine that mathematical statements are true by virtue of the meaning of the words they contain is somewhat vague and is likely to reduce to the doctrine that they are analytic, to conventionalism, or to something compatible with Kantianism or even with some form of direct realism. If there are objective relations of meaning which hold not merely by fiat, then there is as much need in this view for an account of the evidence of our knowledge of them as there is for the evidence of mathematics itself.

The view that mathematics is analytic has generally been associated on one side with logicism and on the other with conventionalism. The definitions of "analytic" which have been given have been such that logical truths were automatically analytic. If the thesis that mathematics is analytic was to say more than the thesis of logicism, the definitions had to be taken as explicating a concept which had a more direct epistemological significance, usually truth by virtue of meanings or truth by convention. (Once this has been done, the connection with logicism seems less important, in spite of the importance which the logical positivists attributed to it. Thus, one may explain the claim that the axioms of set theory are analytic by saying that they are "meaning postulates" in Carnap's sense, but one could argue equally well that the axioms of number theory are meaning postulates. Logicism was important to the logical positivists for other reasons: the reduction served as a methodological paradigm; it served the "unity of science.")

That the propositions of mathematics should be true by convention in a strong sense, that one should actually have set up conventions which determine that they should be true, seems possible only for "rational reconstructions" of mathematics by explicit construction of an axiom system and identification of the system with mathematics. If such a procedure could be carried out, there would still be room for discussion of the sense in which it showed that the mathematics practiced by those who are not interested in foundations is true by convention.

The usual conventionalist position appeals to *rules* specifying that certain propositions are to be true by convention or, more often, to rules of another sort (such as semantical rules of an interpreted formal system), from which it can be *deduced* that certain statements are true, the nature of the premises being such that they can be called conventions governing the use of expressions. (For example, the truth of any statement which is a substitution instance of a theorem of the classical propositional calculus can be deduced from the information contained in the truth tables for the propositional connectives. Then if the truth tables are regarded as semantical rules specifying the meanings of the connectives, then the theorems of classical propositional logic thus become true by virtue of these rules.)

In the simplest case—that of simply laying down, by rules or in individual instances, that certain sentences are to be taken as expressing true statements—something more seems to be required to justify this procedure as attributing "truth" to "statements." No serious philosopher, however, has been content to leave the matter at that.

Nonetheless, the procedure of specifying by rules runs into a difficulty essentially independent of the form of the rules and the manner in which they are interpreted. This difficulty, which was pointed out forcefully by Quine early in his career (in "Truth by Convention") and is perhaps implicit in remarks by Frege, is that the passage from the general statements which are the actual explicit conventions to the truth by convention of specific statements involves inference. So something essentially logical is not, on the face of it, reduced to convention by the analysis. The inferences will assume properties of generality (for example, the properties of the universal quantifiers) and of the conditional, since the rules will in all probability be of the form of conditionals—for instance, they may say that if a statement satisfies certain conditions, then it is true by convention. In the example that we gave, one needs in addition the laws of contradiction and of excluded middle: application of the truth tables already supposes that each statement has one, and only one, of the two truth-values.

Quine showed that the attempt to regard the rules by which this inference proceeds as themselves valid by convention leads to an infinite regress. For example, suppose a rule is *modus ponens:* from "p" and "$p \supset q$" infer q". This could be stated as the convention:

(16)   If A and C are true and C is the result of substituting A for "p" and B for "q" in "$p \supset q$", then B is to be true.

Now, suppose that for some A' and B' we have proved that A' and C' are true by convention, where

(17) C' is the result of substituting A' for "p" and B' for "q" in "$p \supset q$".

Then we have also

(18) A' is true;
(19) $A' \supset B'$ is true.

Therefore, by (16) and *modus ponens, B'* is true. However, in order to represent *this* inference as proceeding according to the convention, it is necessary to make *another* application of *modus ponens,* and so on.

The above argument would not prevent this form of conventionalism from being applied to further parts of mathematics, particularly to existential axioms. In view of the equivalences between derivability statements in logic and elementary propositions in number theory, as well as the above-mentioned element of brute fact in the existence of a derivation, it is not likely that such an approach will work for elementary number theory. But with the stronger axiom systems for set theory the view is on somewhat firmer ground, in that such axioms are often not justified by appeal to direct evidence and "pragmatic" criteria have played a role in the selection of axioms.

Nonetheless, the procedure also has much in common with the setting up of a hypothetical theory in science, and, indeed, as Whitehead and Russell already emphasized, the axioms are subject to a sort of checking by their consequences, since some propositions deducible from them are decidable by more elementary and evident mathematical means. It is not evident that if a system of axioms is replaced by another because its consequences come into conflict with intuitive mathematics, the meaning of "set" has changed and the original axioms can be interpreted according to a previous meaning so as to remain true. Moreover, set theory proceeds on the assumption that the truth-value of statements is determinate in many cases where it is not determined by the axioms—that is, by the conventions.

Quine, in fact, now argues, apparently even in the case of elementary logic, that there is no firm ground for distinguishing between making such principles true by convention and adopting them as hypotheses ("Carnap and Logical Truth"). This is as much an extension of conventionalism to the whole of science as a rejection of it in application to mathematics.

Wittgenstein's view. At this point we must consider the possibility that a priori truths, even the elementary ones, are thought of as true by convention, not in the sense that they may be made so by an explicit convention actually set up but in the sense that the conventions are, as it were, implicit in our practice with the logical and mathematical vocabulary. It might still be argued that the principles of mathematics are not in that way sufficiently distinguished from the principles of natural science or from other rather deep or fundamental principles which we firmly accept. But this objection could be met by a more detailed descriptive analysis of how logical and mathematical words are used.

However, this type of conventionalism must be careful not to slip into the situation of the more explicit conventionalism of requiring a necessary connection between general intentions and their application in particular statements which is not itself accounted for by the conventions. It appears that the only philosopher who has really faced these challenges has been Ludwig Wittgenstein, in his later period. In connection with Wittgenstein it would probably be better to speak of "agreement" than convention, since the reference to explicit conventions or to "decisions" seems metaphorical, as a picture which is contrasted with that against which he is arguing rather than as a fundamental theoretical concept. It is agreement in our *actions*—e.g., what we say follows from what—that is essential. We should also be cautious in attributing to Wittgenstein any explanatory theory of logical and mathematical knowledge, in view of his disclaimers of presenting a theory.

Even with these qualifications Wittgenstein's view seems highly paradoxical, for in order to avoid the above-mentioned pitfall the analysis in terms of agreement must extend even to the connection between general rules and their instances. This seems to be the point of the famous discussion of following a rule in Wittgenstein's *Philosophical Investigations*. What ultimately determines what is *intended* in the statement of a rule are facts of the type of what is *actually accepted* in the course of time as falling under it.

Wittgenstein (I, 185) gave the example of instructing someone in writing down the terms of the sequence of natural numbers 0, 2, 4, $\cdots$, $2n$, $\cdots$. At the start the instructor does not actively think that when the time comes the pupil is to write 1,000, 1,002, 1,004, $\cdots$, rather than 1,000, 1,004, 1,008, $\cdots$. Wittgenstein regarded it as conceivable that the pupil might do the second on the basis of a misunderstanding which we just could not clear up. Moreover, it is, as it were, just a fact of natural history that normally, in such a case, we accept the first and reject the second—indeed, continue in that way ourselves. It appears, further, that the same issue can arise for steps in the sequence which have been written before, since the recognition of symbols as tokens of an already understood type is itself an application of a rule (see I, 214).

Wittgenstein's criticism seems directed particularly against certain psychological ideas associated with Platonism and Kantianism. The manner in which the steps of writing numerals are determined by the rule cannot be explained by appealing to one's understanding of the relations of abstract entities expressed in the rule or even to the intentions of the instructor. According to Wittgenstein the criterion of how the pupil *does* understand the rule lies in the steps which he in fact takes. And what makes them right or wrong is their agreement or disagreement with what *we* do.

The steps are indeed determined by the rule, in the sense that at each stage there is only one number we accept as correct, and the force of social custom directs us to expand the series in the way we do. But this does not mean that Wittgenstein considered his appeals to custom and training as constituting a fully satisfactory explanation of either the agreement that exists or the fact that we feel "compelled" by the rule, for it is because we are made as we are that we react to custom and training as we do.

The paradoxical nature of Wittgenstein's position can perhaps be brought out by considering the case of a complex mathematical proof which contains steps which no one has thought of before. The proof may lead to a quite unexpected conclusion. Yet each step is recognized by every trained person as necessary, and their combination to form the proof is entirely convincing. (This is, of course, not inevitably the case: proofs as published can be obscure or doubtful and can rest on principles about which there are difficulties.) In spite of the fact that it is in principle possible for an irresolvable disagreement to arise at each point, this does not happen: irresolvable disputes among mathematicians are only about fundamental principles and about taste. Nonetheless, Wittgenstein, in *Remarks on the Foun-*

dations of Mathematics, used the metaphor of decision in speaking of our acceptance of the proof and spoke of the proof as providing a new criterion for certain concepts; his terminology suggests change of meaning.

The vast extent of the agreement on which mathematics rests seems to have astonished Wittgenstein; indeed, it is hard to understand, on his view, how such agreement is possible and why contradictions arise so seldom. We may be faced here with natural facts, but they are facts which show an extremely regular pattern.

Wittgenstein devoted a good deal of attention in the *Remarks* to discussions of calculation and proof, their relation to mathematical truth, and the ways in which they resemble and differ from experiment. In a number of examples he revealed an outlook which resembles Kant's in seeing a construction either of figures or of arrangements of formulae or propositions as essential to a proof. To the problem concerning how such a singular construction can serve to establish a universal and necessary proposition Wittgenstein suggested a quite different answer: in accepting the proof we accept the construction as a paradigm for the application of a new concept, so that, in particular, we have new criteria for certain types of judgments. (For example, if we have determined by calculation that $25 \times 25 = 625$, then a verification that there are 25×25 objects of a certain kind is also accepted as verifying that there are 625.) The same question arises in connection with the possibility of conflict in these criteria as arose in connection with agreement.

We shall close at this point our discussion of the a priori character of mathematics and the attempts to justify and explain it. In the sense that the concepts of mathematics are too general and abstract to refer to anything particular in experience, their a priori character is evident, at any rate after a certain amount of logical analysis of mathematical concepts. The a priori evidence of mathematics, on the other hand, is perhaps not raised, by our discussion, above the level of a somewhat vague conviction. In the case of the more powerful forms of set theory one is probably forced to admit that the evidence is less than certainty and therefore to admit that there is an analogy between the principles involved and the hypotheses of a scientific theory. In the case of arithmetic and elementary logic, however, this conviction can withstand the objections that might be posed, but in view of the difficulties we have discussed in relation to various accounts, it seems still not to have been analyzed adequately.

PLATONISM AND CONSTRUCTIVISM

The discussion in the preceding section suggests that the problem of evidence in mathematics will appear to differ according to the part of mathematics being emphasized. The form which discussion of these differences has tended to take is a distinction between two broad methodological attitudes in mathematics, which we shall call platonism and constructivism. This section will be devoted to a discussion of these attitudes.

Platonism. We begin with platonism because it is the dominant attitude in the practice of modern mathematicians, although upon reflection they often disguise this attitude by taking a formalist position. Platonism is the methodological position which goes with philosophical realism regarding the objects mathematics deals with. Mathematical objects are treated not only as if their existence is independent of cognitive operations, which is perhaps evident, but also as if the facts concerning them did not involve a relation to the mind or depend in any way on the possibilities of verification, concrete or "in principle."

This is taken to mean that certain *totalities* of mathematical objects are well defined, in the sense that propositions defined by quantification over them have definite truth-values. Thus, there is a direct connection between platonism and the law of excluded middle, which gives rise to some of platonism's differences with constructivism.

It is clear that there is a connection between platonism and set theory. Various degrees of platonism can be described according to what totalities they admit and whether they treat these totalities as themselves mathematical objects. These degrees can be expressed by the acceptance of set-theoretic existence axioms of differing degrees of strength.

The most elementary kind of platonism is that which accepts the totality of natural numbers—i.e., that which applies the law of excluded middle to propositions involving quantification over all natural numbers. Quite elementary propositions in analysis already depend on this law, such as that every sequence of rational numbers either tends to the limit 0 or does not, which is the basis for the assertion that any real number is either equal to 0 or not. We shall see that not even this assertion is immune to constructivist criticism.

What is nowadays called classical analysis advances a step further and accepts the totality of the points of the continuum or, equivalently, the totality of subsets of the natural numbers. The equivalence between these totalities and their importance in mathematics were brought out by the rigorous development and "arithmetization" of analysis in the nineteenth century. We recall that the theories of (positive and negative) integers and rational numbers can be developed from the theory of natural numbers by means of the notion of ordered pair alone and that this notion can in turn be represented in number theory. A general theory of real numbers requires general conceptions of a set or sequence of natural numbers to which those of a set or sequence of rational numbers can be reduced.

Following Paul Bernays ("Sur le Platonisme dans les mathématiques") we can regard the totality of sets of natural numbers on the analogy of the totality of subsets of a finite set. Given, say, the numbers $1, \cdots, n$, each set is fixed by n independent determinations of whether a given number belongs to it or not, and there are 2^n possible ways of determining this. An "arbitrary" subset of the natural numbers is fixed by an *infinity* of independent determinations fixing for each natural number whether it belongs to the subset or not. Needless to say, this procedure cannot be carried out by a finite intelligence. It envisages the possibility of sets which are not the extensions of any predicates expressed in a language.

Impredicative definitions. The strength of the assumption of the totality of arbitrary subsets of the natural numbers becomes clear if we observe that it justifies *impredicative definitions,* definitions of sets or functions in terms of totalities to which they themselves belong. A predicate of natural numbers involving quantification over all sets of natural numbers will have a well-defined extension, which will be one of the sets in the range of the quantifier.

Such definitions have been criticized as circular (for example, by Henri Poincaré), but they do not seem so if we understand the sets as existing independently of any procedure or linguistic configuration which defines them, for then the definition picks out an object from a pre-existing totality.

The resistance which impredicative definitions met with arose partly because their acceptance clashes with the expectation that every set should be the extension of a predicate, or at least of a concept of the human mind.

Given any definite (formalized) notation, we can by Cantor's diagonal method define a set of natural numbers which is not the extension of a predicate in the notation. Thus, no procedure of generating such predicates by continually expanding one's notation can possibly exhaust the totality. And the idea that every set is the extension of a predicate has little sense if it is assumed that in advance of the specification of notations there is a totality of possible predicates which can be arrived at by some generating procedure.

If the statements of classical analysis are interpreted naively, then quite elementary theorems, such as that every bounded set of real numbers has a least upper bound, require impredicative definitions. Nonetheless, in *Das Kontinuum*, Hermann Weyl proposed to construct analysis on the basis of mere platonism with respect to the natural numbers. He proposed an interpretation under which the least upper bound theorem is true. Later interpretations have preserved more of the statements of classical analysis than Weyl's, and it is an involved technical question how much of it can be given a natural predicative interpretation (see below).

Set theory and the paradoxes. Set theory as developed by Cantor and as embodied in the present standard systems involves a higher degree, or variety of degrees, of platonism. The axiom system of Zermelo and its enlargement by Fraenkel (which is called the Zermelo–Fraenkel system), for example, allows the iteration of the process of forming the set of all subsets of a given set and the collection into a set of what has been obtained by iterated application of this or some other generating procedure. This latter allows the iteration into the transfinite. If we assume we have transfinite ordinal numbers, then we can generate a transfinite succession of "universes" U as follows: Let $\mathscr{P}(A)$ be the set of all subsets of the set A.

$U_0 =$ a certain class, perhaps empty, of "individuals."
$U_{\alpha+1} = \mathscr{P}(U_\alpha) \cup U_\alpha$.
$U_\alpha =$ the union of all U_β, for $\beta < \alpha$, if α is a limit ordinal.

Then for certain ordinals α the U_α will form models for the different systems of set theory ($U_{\omega+\omega}$ for Zermelo's set theory, without Fraenkel's axiom of replacement).

The paradoxes of set theory imply that we must accept *some* limitations on forming totalities and on regarding them in turn as mathematical objects—that is, as sets. If,

for example, the totality of sets is a well-defined set, then it seems that it will be reasonable to ask of each set x whether it is a member of itself ($x \in x$) or not and to form $\hat{x}(x \notin x)$, the set of all sets which are not members of themselves. This will satisfy

$$(y)[y \in \hat{x}(x \notin x) . \equiv y \notin y],$$

which implies

$$\hat{x}(x \notin x) \in \hat{x}(x \notin x) . \equiv . \hat{x}(x \notin x) \notin \hat{x}(x \notin x),$$

a contradiction. This is Russell's paradox, the most shocking, because the most elementary, of the paradoxes of set theory.

On the same basis one can ask for the cardinal number of the set of all sets, which we shall call S. Then $\mathscr{P}(S)$, the set of all subsets of S, will have a cardinal number no greater than that of S, because $\mathscr{P}(S) \subseteq S$. But by Cantor's theorem the cardinal number of $\mathscr{P}(S)$ is properly greater than that of S (Cantor's paradox, 1895).

If the totality O of ordinals is a set, then, since it is well-ordered, there will be an ordinal number γ that represents its order type. But then O will be isomorphic to the set of ordinals less than γ—that is, to a proper initial segment of itself. This is impossible: γ must be the greatest ordinal, but there is no obstacle to forming $\gamma + 1$ (Burali-Forti's paradox, 1897).

These paradoxes do not imply that we have to stop or otherwise limit the process, described above, of generating larger and larger universes. On the contrary, we must never regard the process as having given us "all" sets. The totality of sets, and hence the totality of ordinal numbers, cannot be the terminus of a well-defined generating process, for if it were we could take all of what we had generated so far as a set and continue to generate still larger universes.

Thus, suppose we consider the arguments for the paradoxes applied to a particular U_α, as if it were the universe of all sets. The construction precludes $x \in x$, so $\hat{x}(x \notin x)$ is just U_α itself. But $U_\alpha \notin U_\alpha$ and hence is disqualified as a set. The same consideration applies to Cantor's paradox. Burali-Forti's paradox is avoided because the passage from U_α to $U_{\alpha+1}$ always introduces well-orderings of higher order types. Thus, for no α can U_α contain "all" ordinals, no matter how the ordinals are construed as sets. (A very natural way of construing them would be such that α occurs in $U_{\alpha+1}$ but not in U_β for any $\beta \leq \alpha$. But then only for certain ordinals will U_α contain an ordinal for each well-ordered set in U_α.)

For some time after they were first discovered, the paradoxes were viewed with great alarm by many who were concerned with the foundations of mathematics. In retrospect this seems to have been due to the fact that set theory was still quite unfamiliar; in particular, the distinction between the customary reasonings of set theory and those which led to the paradoxes was not very clear. The opposition which set theory had aroused had not yet died down. However, the marginal character of the paradoxes has seemed more and more evident with time; the systems which were soon devised to cope with the paradoxes (Russell's theory of types and Zermelo's set theory, both published in 1908) have proved satisfactory in that they are based on a reasonably clear intuitive idea, and no one today regards it as a serious possibility that they (or the stronger Zermelo–Fraenkel system) will turn out to be inconsistent. This does not mean that the security and clarity of set theory are absolute; in the sequel some of the difficulties will become apparent.

The above-described sequence of universes uses general conceptions of set and ordinal but applies the characteristic move of platonism only one step at a time. It renounces what Bernays calls "absolute platonism," the assumption of a totality of all mathematical objects which can be treated as itself a customary mathematical object—for example, a set. Such a conception seems definitely destroyed by the paradoxes. The totality of sets can be compared with Kant's "Ideas of Reason": it is an "unconditioned" or absolute totality which just for that reason cannot be adequately conceived by the human mind, since the object of a normal conception can always be incorporated in a more inclusive totality. From this point of view there is an analogy between the set-theoretic paradoxes and Kant's mathematical antinomies.

If we assume that every set will appear in one of the U_α, we have a conception which is adequate for all of modern mathematics except, perhaps, the recent theory of categories. The conception is by nature imprecise: there are limitations on our ability to circumscribe both what goes into the power set of a given set and what ordinals there are. It is perhaps unreasonable to apply classical logic to propositions involving quantification over all sets, since such an application seems to presuppose that it is objectively determined what sets (and a fortiori, on this conception, what ordinals) there are. Nonetheless, this additional idealization does not seem to have caused any actual difficulties.

This way of conceiving sets combines two of Russell's early ideas for resolving the paradoxes—the theory of types and the theory of "limitation of size." What are rejected as sets are the most inclusive totalities, such as the entire universe. (Our talking of "totalities" while rejecting them as sets is not incompatible with our conception; as John von Neumann observed, all that is necessary is to prohibit them from belonging to further classes. Von Neumann's observation was the basis for some new set theories, the principal one being that of Bernays and Gödel.) Moreover, the sets are arranged in a transfinite hierarchy: one can assign to each set an ordinal, its type or, as it is now called, *rank*, which will be the least ordinal greater than the ranks of its members. We have thus a transfinite extension of the cumulative theory of types. But we have dropped the more radical idea from which Russell proceeded: that each variable of a system of set theory should range over objects of a specified type, and that "$x \in y$" is meaningless unless the range of "y" is of a type one higher than that of "x," so that, in particular, "$x \in x$" is meaningless.

Predicativism. In the first 25 years or so after the discovery of the paradoxes a number of more radical proposals for their elimination were presented. These generally amounted to some further attenuation of platonism. We shall first consider the program of eliminating impredicative definitions, which amounts to a restriction of platonism to the natural numbers. This was the outcome of the general views of Poincaré and Russell. Russell's original theory, the ramified theory of types, which formed the basis of *Principia Mathematica,* was directed to the elimination of impredicative definitions, which he held to involve a "vicious circle" and to be responsible for the paradoxes. The effect was, however, nullified by his axiom of reducibility.

A greatly simplified version of the ramified theory is as follows: One has variables, each of which is assigned a natural number as its *level,* and the predicates of identity and membership. The logic is the usual quantification theory, except that in the rules for quantifiers allowance must be made for levels. Since the levels can be cumulative, we could have for the universal quantifiers the following:

(20) $(x^i)Fx^i \supset Fy^j$ if $j \leqslant i$;

(21) From "$p \supset Fy^i$" infer "$p \supset (x^i)Fx^i$", where for "p" only something not containing free "y^i" can be substituted.

The axioms are those of identity, extensionality, and the following schema of class existence:

(22) If "F" represents a predicate which does not contain free x^{i+1}, any free variables of level $>i+1$, or any bound variables of level $>i$,

$$(\exists x^{i+1})(y^i)(y^i \in x^{i+1} \equiv Fy^i).$$

One effect of this axiom is that a predicate involving quantification over objects of level n need not have an extension of level n. Therefore, the axiom does not assert the existence of any impredicative classes; in fact, it is compatible with the idea that classes are constructed by the construction of predicates of which they are the extensions.

Russell's actual theory combined that of a hierarchy of levels, applied in this case to "propositional functions," the objects over which the variables of a higher-order logic were to range, with the "no class" theory, the introduction of locutions involving classes by contextual definition in terms of propositional functions. In order to derive classical mathematics, however, he wanted to avoid dividing the classes into levels. This he did by postulating the axiom of reducibility, which asserts that for every propositional function there is a function of the lowest possible level (compatible with the nature of its arguments) extensionally equivalent to it. Russell admitted that this axiom was equivalent to the existence of classes, and he has never been satisfied with it. In effect, it yields even impredicatively defined classes and destroys the effect of the hierarchy of levels.

A formalization of mathematics on the basis of the ramified theory is the most natural formalization if a platonist theory of classes is repudiated but classical logic admitted. The construction of the natural numbers leads to the difficulty that the class quantifier needed to reduce induction to an explicit definition is no longer available. One must either assume the natural numbers or have a hierarchy of different concepts of natural number.

A ramified theory with the natural numbers as individuals and the Peano axioms would be a natural formalization of the mathematics allowed by platonism with respect to the natural numbers. But there is in principle no reason not to extend the hierarchy of levels into the transfinite. The question of the limits of predicative mathematics has become identical with the question of the transfinite ordinals that can be predicatively introduced.

We have said that quite elementary proofs in analysis already require impredicative definitions when naively interpreted. Nonetheless, from recent work it appears that a good deal of classical analysis is susceptible of a natural predicative interpretation, which, however, fails for some theorems. One can, on this basis, give a good approximation to classical analysis, but not to the whole of it. That part of mathematics which depends essentially on still more powerful set theory is completely lost. It seems that it would not be reasonable to insist on this limitation unless there were some quite powerful reason for rejecting platonism. We shall discuss some possibile reasons later.

Constructivism. We shall now consider the complete rejection of platonism, which we shall call constructivism. It is not a product of the situation created by the paradoxes but rather a spirit which has been present in practically the whole history of mathematics. The philosophical ideas on which it is based go back at least to Aristotle's analysis of the notion of infinity (*Physics*, Bk. III). Kant's philosophy of mathematics can be interpreted in a constructivist manner, and constructivist ideas were presented in the nineteenth century—notably by Leopold Kronecker, who was an important forerunner of intuitionism—in opposition to the tendency in mathematics toward set-theoretic ideas, long before the paradoxes of set theory were discovered.

Our presentation of constructivism relies heavily on the "intuitionism" of Brouwer, presented in many publications from 1907 on, but the ideas can also be found to some extent in other critics of platonism, including the French school of Émile Borel, Poincaré, and Henri Lebesgue, although in their work predicativity played a greater role than constructivity. These writers did not arrive at a very consistent position, but they contributed mathematically important ideas. Brouwer reached and developed a conclusion from which they shrank: that a thoroughgoing constructivism would require the modification of classical analysis and even of classical logic.

Intuitionism. Constructivist mathematics would proceed as if the last arbiter of mathematical existence and mathematical truth were the possibilities of construction. "Possibilities of construction" must refer to the idealized possibility of construction mentioned in the last section. Brouwer insisted that mathematical constructions are *mental.* The possibilities in question derive from our perception of external objects, which is both mental and physical. However, the passage from actuality to possibility and the view of possibility as of much wider scope perhaps have their basis in intentions of the mind—first, in the abstraction from concrete qualities and existence; second, in the abstraction from the limitations on generating sequences. In any case, in constructive mathematics the *rules* by which infinite sequences are generated are not merely a

tool in our knowledge but part of the reality that mathematics is about.

Why this is so can be seen from the problem of assertions about the infinite. We have suggested that the generation of a sequence of symbols is something of which the construction of the natural numbers is an idealization. But "construction" loses its sense if we abstract further from the fact that this is a process in time which is never completed. The infinite in constructivism must be "potential" rather than "actual." Each individual natural number can be constructed, but there is no construction which contains within itself the whole series of natural numbers. To view the series *sub specie aeternitatis* as nonetheless determined as a whole is just what we are not permitted to do.

Perhaps the idea that arithmetic rests on time as a form of intuition lies behind Brouwer's insistence on constructivity interpreted in this way. One aspect of sensibility from which we do not abstract in passing from concrete perception to its form is its finite character. Thus, whatever one may think of the notion of form of intuition, Brouwer's position is based on a limitation, in principle, on our knowledge: constructivism is implied by the postulate that no mathematical proposition is true unless we can in a nonmiraculous way *know* it to be true.

Because of its derivation from his own philosophical account of mathematical intuition (discussed in BROUWER, LUITZEN EGBERTUS JAN) Brouwer called his position, and the mathematics which he constructed on the basis of it, *intuitionism.* We shall use this name for a species of constructivism which answers closely to Brouwer's ideas.

In spite of the "potential" character of the infinite in mathematics, we shall not renounce assertions about all natural numbers or even, with some reservations, talk of infinite classes. A proposition about all natural numbers can be true only if it is determined to be true by the law according to which the sequence of natural numbers is generated. This Brouwer took to be equivalent to its possessing a *proof.* Thus, the intensional notions of "law" and "proof" become part of the subject matter of mathematics.

A consideration of existential propositions connects the broad philosophical notion of constructivity with the general mathematical notion. Roughly, a proof in mathematics is said to be constructive if wherever it involves the mention of the existence of something, it provides a method of "finding" or "constructing" that object. It is evident that the constructivist standpoint implies that a mathematical object exists only if it can be constructed; to say that there exists a natural number x such that Fx is to say that sooner or later in the generation of the sequence an x will *turn up* such that Fx. If x depends on a parameter y, this x must be determinable from y on the basis of the *laws* of the construction of the numbers and of the constructions involved in F. Proving $(\exists x)Fx$ means showing how to construct x, so one can say that the proof is not complete until x has been exhibited. (But then "proof" is used in an idealized sense.) To prove $(y)(\exists x)Fxy$ must involve giving a general method for finding x on the basis of y.

This point of view leads immediately to a criticism of the basic notions of logic, particularly negation and the law of excluded middle. That "$(x)Fx$" is true if and only if it can be proved does not mean that "$(x)Fx$" is a statement about certain entities called proofs in the way in which, on the usual interpretation, it is a statement about the totality of natural numbers. According to Brouwer we can *assert "p"* only if we have a proof; the hypothesis that $(x)Fx$ is the hypothesis that *we have* a proof, and it is a reasonable extrapolation to deny that we can say more about *what* "$(x)Fx$" asserts than is said in specifying what is a proof of it. The explanation of "$\neg(x)Fx$" as "$(x)Fx$ cannot be proved" does not satisfy this condition. Brouwer said instead that a proof of "$\neg p$" is a construction which obtains an absurdity from the supposition of a proof of "p".

An immediate consequence of this interpretation is that the law of excluded middle becomes doubtful. Given a proposition "p", there is no particular reason to suppose that we shall ever be in possession either of a proof of "p" or of a deduction of an absurdity from "p". Indeed, if the general statement of the law of excluded middle is taken as a mathematical assertion, a proof of *it* will have to yield a general method for the solution of *all* mathematical questions. Brouwer rejected this possibility out of hand.

It is evident that such a point of view will lead to changes in quite basic parts of mathematics. Many instances of the law of excluded middle, where the propositions involved can be shown constructively to be systematically decidable, will be retained. But Brouwer rejected even elementary instances in classical analysis. Let the sequence r_n of rational numbers be defined as follows: if there is no $m \leqslant n$ such that the mth, $(m+1)$st, $(m+2)$d terms of the decimal expansion of π are each 7, then $r_n = 1/2^n$; if there is such an m, then $r_n = 1/2^k$, where k is the least such m. Then r_n constructively defines a real number r. But a proof of either $r = 0$ or $r \neq 0$ would tell us whether or not there are three 7's in the decimal expansion of π. Thus, we cannot assert either $r = 0$ or $r \neq 0$.

For a satisfactory constructivist theory of analysis, an analysis is needed of the notion of an arbitrary set or sequence of natural numbers. Brouwer's analysis gives additional distinctiveness to intuitionism. Such a sequence is thought of as generated by a *succession* of independent determinations or "free choices," which may be restricted by some law. Obviously the succession of choices must be thought of as never being complete. In the absence of a law a statement about a sequence can be true only if it is determined to be true by some finite initial segment of the sequence. The consequence of this is that a function defined for all sequences of natural numbers whose values are integers must be continuous. It also leads to sharper counterexamples to the law of excluded middle: it is absurd that for all sequences α, either $(x)(\alpha(x) = 0)$ or $\neg(x)(\alpha(x) = 0)$. We can also sharpen the result of the preceding paragraph and state generally that not every real number is equal to or different from 0.

The intuitionist point of view thus leads to a distinctive logic and to a distinctive theory of the foundations of analysis. The latter contains another distinctive principle, the bar theorem, obtained by analyzing the requirement that if a function is defined for all sequences, there must be a constructive proof of this fact. It is roughly equivalent to the proposition that if an ordering is well-founded, transfinite induction holds with respect to it. Nonetheless, intuitionism is far from having shown itself capable of the

same rich development as classical mathematics, and it is often very cumbersome. Important as it is in itself, it does not provide a sufficient motive for renouncing platonism.

Finitism. So far our account of constructivism has been based entirely on Brouwer's intuitionism. However, intuitionism is not the only possible constructivist development of mathematics. Indeed, it makes some quite powerful assumptions of its own. As we have said, the intuitionists make the notions of construction and proof a part of the subject matter of mathematics, and the iteration of logical connectives, especially, renders it possible to make quite elaborate and abstract statements involving construction and proof. Thus, intuitionist mathematics seems to rest not merely upon intuition but upon rather elaborate reflection on the notion of intuitive construction. (It also does not obviously exclude impredicativity, since what counts as a proof of a given proposition can be explained in terms of the general notion of proof.) A constructivist might feel that intuitionism leads from the Scylla of platonist realism to the Charybdis of speculative idealism.

A weaker and more evident constructive mathematics can be constructed on the basis of a distinction between effective operation with forms of spatiotemporal objects and operation with general intensional notions, such as that of proof. Methods based on operation with forms of spatiotemporal objects would approximate to what the mathematician might call elementary combinatorial methods or to the "finitary method" which Hilbert envisaged for proofs of consistency. Formal systems of recursive number theory, in which generality is expressed by free variables and existence by the actual presentation of an instance or (if the object depends on parameters) a function, will accord with this conception if the functions admitted are sufficiently elementary—for example, primitive recursive functions. In such formalisms any formula will express a general statement each instance of which can be checked by computation. For this reason classical logic can be used. Moreover, the concept of free choice sequence can be admitted so that some analysis can be constructed.

The precise limits of this conception are perhaps not clear, although it is evident that some constructive arguments are excluded. The conception does not allow full use of quantifiers but probably does allow a limited use of them.

The Hilbert program. If one accepts the idea that from a philosophical point of view constructivist conceptions are more satisfactory than platonist conceptions—more evident or more intelligible—one is not necessarily constrained to abandon classical mathematics. The way is still open to investigating classical mathematics from a constructive point of view, and it may then prove to have an indirect constructive sense and justification.

Such an investigation was the objective of the famous program of Hilbert, which was the third main animating force—with logicism and intuitionism—in foundational research in the period before World War II. The possibility arises first from the fact that classical mathematics can be formalized (though not completely; we shall consider this fact and its implications later). Once it has been formalized, one can in principle drop consideration of the intended meaning of the classical statements and simply consider the combinations of the symbols and formulae themselves. Thus, if the proof of a certain theorem has been formalized in a system S (say Zermelo–Fraenkel set theory), it is represented as a configuration of symbols constructed according to certain rules. Whether a configuration is a proof can be checked in a very elementary way.

The concepts by which a formal system is described belong, in effect, to finitist mathematics. For example, the consistency of the system is the proposition that no configuration which is a proof will have a last line of a certain form—for example, $\mathcal{A}$ & $\neg\mathcal{A}$. Nonetheless, although in the mathematical study we abstract from the intended interpretation, this interpretation certainly guides the choice of the questions in which we are interested.

Hilbert sought to establish classical platonist mathematics on a firm foundation by formalizing it and proving the consistency of the resulting formalism by finitist means. The interest of the question of consistency depends on the fact that the formulae of the system represent a system of *statements;* that is, even if the meanings of the platonist conceptions are highly indeterminate, statements in terms of them are introduced according to an analogy with "real" (i.e., finitist) statements which is intended to preserve at least the notions of truth and falsity and the laws of logic.

In fact, Hilbert had a further motive for his interest in consistency: the fact that platonist mathematics is an extension of an extrapolation from finitist mathematics. Certain elementary combinatorial notions are also embodied in the formalism; formulae involving them express "real statements." Hilbert thought of the other formulae as expressing "ideal statements"—analogous to the ideal elements of projective geometry—introduced to give greater simplicity and integration to the theory. Within the system they have deductive relations to the real statements. It would be highly undesirable that a formula of the system should be seen by elementary computation to be false and yet be provable. One might hope to prove by metamathematical means that this would not happen. In the central cases a proof of consistency is sufficient to show that it would not. Thus, suppose we extend a quantifier-free recursive number theory by adding quantifiers and perhaps also second-order quantifiers. A proof of the consistency of the resulting system will show that no false numerical formula (stating a recursive relation of particular integers) will be provable. In fact, it will yield a *constructive* proof of any formula of the original system provable in the extension, in this sense showing the use of "ideal" elements to be eliminable. Since Hilbert it has been pointed out (chiefly by Georg Kreisel) that many further results relevant to the understanding of nonconstructive mathematics from a constructivist point of view can be obtained from consistency proofs.

Hilbert hoped to settle the question of foundations once and for all, which for him meant establishing the platonist methods of set theory on a firm basis. His hope was founded on two expectations: that all of mathematics (at least all of analysis) could be codified in a single formal system and that the consistency of this system could be proved by methods so elementary that no one could question them.

He was disappointed of both these expectations as a result of Gödel's incompleteness theorems (1931). Work on the program has nonetheless continued, with the limitations that one has to work with formalisms which embody only part of the mathematics in question and that the proofs must rely on more abstract, but still constructive, notions; and the work in finitist proof theory has achieved valuable results, some of which will be discussed later.

MATHEMATICAL LOGIC

Our remaining considerations on the subjects of the two preceding sections fit best into an independent discussion of mathematical logic as a factor in the study of the foundations of mathematics. Before World War II an important part of the work in logic was directed toward establishing, in the service of some general position such as logicism or intuitionism, a more or less final solution to the problems of foundations. Certain particular results, and probably also a more diffuse evolution of the climate of ideas, have discouraged this aim. Today nearly all work in mathematical logic, even when motivated by philosophical ideas, is nonideological, and everyone acknowledges that the results of this work are independent of the most general philosophical positions.

Starting from the axiomatic method in a more general sense, mathematical logic has become the general study of the logical structure of axiomatic theories. The topics selected from the great variety of technical developments for discussion here are Gödel's incompleteness theorems, recursive function theory, developments related to Hilbert's program, foundations of pure logic, and axiomatic set theory.

Gödel's incompleteness theorems. Research in mathematical logic took quite new directions as a result of the discovery by Kurt Gödel, in 1930, of his incompleteness theorems (see GÖDEL'S THEOREM). According to the first theorem (as strengthened by J. B. Rosser in 1936) any formalism S which is sufficiently powerful to express certain basic parts of elementary number theory is incomplete in the following sense: a formula $\mathcal{A}$ of S can be found such that if S is consistent, then neither $\mathcal{A}$ nor $\neg\mathcal{A}$ is provable in S. The conditions are satisfied by very weak systems, such as the first-order theory Q whose axioms are the Peano axioms for the successor function and the recursion equations for addition and multiplication. (This system is formalized in first-order logic with equality, having successor, addition, and multiplication as primitive function symbols. The axioms are versions of our axioms 1–4, recursion equations for addition and multiplication, and an axiom which says that every number not equal to 0 is the successor of something.) They are satisfied by extensions of systems which satisfy them and therefore by the full elementary number theory Z (the first-order version of the Dedekind–Peano axiomatization, obtained from Q by adding induction: in place of the second-order axiom 5 one adds all results of substituting a predicate of the formalism for "F" in 7), by analysis, and by axiomatic set theories in which number theory can be constructed. They are also satisfied by formalizations of intuitionist theories. Evidently adding further axioms offers no escape from this incompleteness, since the new theories will also satisfy the conditions of the theorem.

One of the conditions necessary for some general statements of the theorem is that which we mentioned earlier, that proofs can be checked mechanically. This must be interpreted more precisely in terms of one of the concepts of recursive function, discussed below.

The technique of Gödel's proof is of great interest and has since found wide application. It consists of a mapping of the syntax of the theory into the theory itself, through assigning numbers to the symbols and formulae of the system. Any syntactical relation will then be equivalent to some relation of natural numbers. For the crucial relation "$\mathscr{X}$ is a *proof* in S of the formula $\mathscr{A}$" the corresponding relation $P(x,a)$ can be *expressed* in the theory, and certain things about it can be proved in S. Then the undecidable formula $\mathscr{A}$ is a formula which has a number k such that what $\mathscr{A}$ says (about numbers) is equivalent to the unprovability of the formula number k, i.e., $\mathscr{A}$. (1) Then if only true formulae are provable, $\mathscr{A}$ is unprovable. But then $\mathscr{A}$ is true. Therefore, (2) by the same assumption $\neg\mathscr{A}$ is also unprovable. This appeal to the notion of truth was replaced in Gödel's detailed argument by the condition that S be consistent for (1) and ω-consistent for (2). By changing the formula Rosser showed that the assumption of ω-consistency could also be replaced by that of consistency.

The proof that if S is consistent, then $\mathscr{A}$ is unprovable is finitist. If S and the mapping of its syntax into S satisfy some further conditions, the argument can be formalized in S. This yields the second theorem of Gödel. If S is consistent, then the formula which, under the above mapping, corresponds to the consistency of S is unprovable in S.

The first theorem implies not only that mathematics as a whole cannot be codified in a single formal system but also that the part of mathematics which can be expressed in a specific formal notation cannot be so codified. This fact undermines most attempts at a final solution to the problem of foundations by means of mathematical logic. The second theorem was a blow to the Hilbert program in particular. The methods which the Hilbert school envisaged as finitary could apparently be codified in first-order number theory Z; indeed, that they can be so codified seems fairly certain, even though the notion of finitary methods is not completely precise. Therefore, not even the consistency of Z is provable by finitary means. Moreover, the consistency of stronger and stronger systems requires stronger and stronger methods of proof.

There has been much discussion of the broader philosophical implications of Gödel's theorem. We shall not enter into the discussion of such questions as whether the theorem shows the falsity of any mechanistic theory of mind. It should be remarked that there are a number of connections between the surpassing of any given formal system by possible means of proof and the inexhaustibility phenomena in the realm of mathematical existence. Gödel's argument can be viewed as a diagonal argument parallel to that by which Cantor proved that no countable set of sets of natural numbers can exhaust all such sets. Peano's axioms are categorical if the range of the quantifiers in the induction axiom (5) includes *all* classes of natural numbers, but in the context of a formal system one can use only the fact that induction holds for classes definable in the system, of which there are only countably many. In set theory the addition of axioms asserting the existence of very large classes can make decidable previously undecidable arithmetical formulae.

Recursive function theory. A number of problems in mathematical logic require a mathematically exact formulation of the notion of mechanical or effective procedure. For most purposes this need is met by a concept of which there are various equivalent formulations, arrived at by several writers. The concept of (general) recursive definition, introduced in 1931 by Jacques Herbrand and Kurt Gödel, was the first. A function of natural numbers which is computable according to this conception (the "computation" consists of the deduction of an evaluation from defining equations by simple rules) is called a general recursive, or simply a recursive, function. Other formulations are that of λ-definability (Alonzo Church), computability by Turing machine (A. M. Turing), algorithms (A. A. Markov), and different notions of combinatorial system (Emil Post and others).

The concept of recursive definition has proved essential in decision problems. Given a class of mathematical problems defined by some parameter, is there an effective algorithm for solving each problem in the class? As an example consider the tenth problem of Hilbert: given a polynomial with integral coefficients, is there a general method which tells us whether it has a zero among the integers? If such a question can be resolved in the affirmative, the resolution can generally be reached on the basis of the intuitive conception of an algorithm: if one can invent the procedure, then it is generally clear that the procedure is effective. But to give a negative answer to such a question one needs some idea of the *possible* effective procedures. The development of recursive function theory has made possible a large number of results asserting the nonexistence of decision procedures for certain classes of problems. This way of interpreting the results depends on a principle known as Church's thesis, which says that the mathematical conception of an effectively computable function in fact corresponds to the intuitive idea—i.e., that a number-theoretic function is (intuitively) effectively computable if and only if it is recursive.

An important type of decision problem is that concerning provability in formal systems. Given a formal system S, is there an algorithm for deciding whether a given formula $\mathscr{A}$ is a theorem of S? If there is, then S is said to be decidable. Although quite interesting examples of decidable systems exist, the systems to which Gödel's first incompleteness theorem applies are undecidable. In fact, Gödel's type of argument can also be used to prove that first-order logic is undecidable (as by Church in 1936).

Another important aspect of recursive function theory is the classification of sets and functions according to different principles related to recursiveness. One such principle, stated in terms of the complexity of possible definitions by recursive predicates and quantifiers (the Kleene–Mostowski hierarchy), not only is of wide application in logic but is closely related to older topological classifications. One can single out the arithmetical sets (those sets definable from recursive predicates by quantification over natural numbers alone), the hyperarithmetical sets (a certain transfinite extension of the arithmetical hierarchy—in effect, those sets definable in ramified analysis with levels running through the recursive ordinals), and the analytic sets (those sets definable from recursive predicates by quantification over numbers and functions, or sets, of natural numbers). The recursive ordinals, singled out by Church and Kleene, can most readily be characterized as the order types of recursive well-orderings of the natural numbers.

The theory of recursive functions is evidently valuable for explicating different notions of constructivity and for comparing classical and constructive mathematics. A constructive proof of a statement of the form "$(x)(\exists y)Fxy$" should yield an effective method of obtaining y from x. For example, Kleene and his collaborators have shown that any statement provable in formalized intuitionist number theory and analysis has a property called "realizability," which amounts roughly to interpreting "$(x)(\exists y)Fxy$" as asserting the existence of a recursive function giving y in terms of x. Although it is also intuitionistically meaningful, the construction gives a classical interpretation of the intuitionist formalisms. It also allows a sharpening and extension of Brouwer's counterexample technique. Certain classically provable formulas can be shown not to be realizable and therefore not to be provable in the intuitionist formalisms Kleene considers.

A problem arises with regard to the relation between the concept of recursive function and the fundamental concepts concerning constructivity—for instance, the concept of intuitionism. One cannot interpret Church's thesis as explicitly defining "effectively computable function" and therefore as giving the meaning of the intuitionist quantifiers. For by definition a function is general recursive if there is a set of equations from which for each possible argument one can compute the value of the function for that argument, a statement of the form "$(x)(\exists y)Fxy$". If this is interpreted constructively, the proposed definition is circular. The relation between "function constructively proved to be everywhere defined" and "general recursive function" is still not clear. One can ask whether every intuitionistically everywhere-defined number-theoretic function is general recursive or whether every (classically) general recursive function can be proved constructively to be such. Neither question has yet been resolved.

Development of the Hilbert program. For the study of constructivity it is also important to study more restricted types of recursive definition which can be seen by definite forms of argument to define functions. This is particularly important for the extended Hilbert program.

Gödel's second incompleteness theorem meant that the consistency even of elementary number theory Z could not be proved by the methods envisaged by Hilbert. A number of consistency results of the sort envisaged by Hilbert have since been obtained by stronger constructive methods. Gödel and Gentzen proved independently (and finitistically) that if intuitionistic first-order arithmetic is consistent, then so is classical first-order arithmetic. The proofs were based on a quite simple method of translating classical theories into intuitionist theories which is of wide application—for example, to pure logic. One renders an atomic formula P by $\neg\neg P$ (in elementary number theory, equivalent to P itself). If $\mathscr{A}$, $\mathscr{B}$ are translated into $\mathscr{A}°$, $\mathscr{B}°$, respectively, then $\mathscr{A} \vee \mathscr{B}$ is translated by $\neg\neg(\mathscr{A}° \vee \mathscr{B}°)$, $(\exists x)\mathscr{A}$ by $\neg\neg(\exists x)\mathscr{A}°$, $\mathscr{A} \supset \mathscr{B}$ by $\neg(\mathscr{A}° \& \neg\mathscr{B}°)$, $\mathscr{A} \& \mathscr{B}$ by $\mathscr{A}° \& \mathscr{B}°$, $\neg\mathscr{A}$ by $\neg\mathscr{A}°$, and $(x)\mathscr{A}$ by $(x)\mathscr{A}°$. Evidently the translation not only proves relative consistency but also gives each provable formula an intuitionist meaning according to which it is intuitionistically true. If $\mathscr{A}$ is a quantifier-free formula of number theory, or if it is composed with conjunction, negation, and universal quantification only, then if it is provable in Z, it is intuitionistically provable. This translation can easily be extended to ramified analysis. Since intuitionistically the consistency of the intuitionist systems follows from their soundness under the intended interpretation, the consistency of the classical systems has been intuitionistically proved.

A sharper result was obtained in 1936 by Gerhard Gentzen. New proofs, with various advantages and refinements, have since been found by several workers. Gentzen proved the consistency of Z by adding to finitist arithmetic the assumption that a certain recursive ordering of natural numbers, of order type ϵ_0 (the least ordinal greater than ω, ω^ω, ω^{ω^ω}, $\cdots$), is a well-ordering. This assumption could be proved in intuitionist ramified analysis using set variables only of level 1 but could not in elementary number theory.

Gentzen's result has made it possible to extract further information about the power of elementary number theory. Kreisel obtained information about the relation between elementary number theory and certain quantifier-free arithmetics and also obtained a characterization of the functions which can be proved in Z to be general recursive.

A corresponding result for ramified analysis for finite levels was obtained by Lorenzen in 1951 and sharpened by Kurt Schütte. It was extended by Schütte to transfinite levels.

On the basis of these results we can say that constructive consistency proofs are available for all of predicative mathematics. In well-defined senses they are the best possible results (for instance, the above-mentioned ordinal ϵ_0 cannot be replaced by a smaller one). Nonetheless, efforts to give such a proof for impredicative classical analysis, not to speak of axiomatic set theory, have proved fruitless.

Results of quite recent research have shed considerable light on this situation. Clifford Spector (1962) proved the consistency of classical analysis relative to a quantifier-free theory (Gödel, 1958) of primitive recursive functionals of arbitrary finite types, enriched by a new schema for defining functionals by "bar recursion." This amounted to generalizing Brouwer's bar theorem to arbitrary finite types. Such generalized bar recursion has not found a constructive justification, but the method has led to consistency proofs by the original bar theorem for subsystems of analysis which are, according to a reasonable criterion, impredicative.

Kreisel (1963) has shown that intuitionist analysis, with the bar theorem and a strong schema of "generalized inductive definitions" included, does not suffice to prove the consistency of classical analysis. Such a proof requires an essential extension of constructive methods beyond the established intuitionist ones.

Solomon Feferman and Schütte have given an analysis of

the notion of *predicativity* according to which established intuitionist methods go beyond predicative ones. According to their conception, inductive definitions such as that of the class O of numbers representing the recursive ordinals are impredicative.

What has been the fate of the Hilbert program? Put most broadly, its objective was to secure the foundations of platonist mathematics by a constructive analysis of classical formal systems. The incompleteness phenomena have made it impossible, in dealing with stronger and stronger systems, to avoid the introduction of more and more abstract conceptions into the metamathematics. However interesting the information obtained about the relation between these conceptions and the platonist ones, it is not evident that these conceptions are in all respects more secure. Moreover, in the present state of research it is not certain that strong enough constructive methods can be found even to prove the consistency of classical analysis.

This state of affairs is unfavorable to those methodological views seeking to restrict mathematics to the methods which have the greatest intuitive clarity. It is evident that such methods will not suffice to resolve certain mathematical questions whose content is extremely simple, namely those concerning the truth of certain statements of the form "(x)Fx", where "F" stands for a primitive recursive predicate of natural numbers. Proponents of the views in question seem forced to admit that even such questions can be objectively undetermined.

Foundations of logic. An important result concerning pure logic obtained in finitist metamathematics is a theorem, or cluster of related theorems—including Herbrand's theorem (1931) and Gentzen's theorem (1934)—to the effect that the proof of a formula of first-order logic can be put into a normal form. In such a normal-form proof the logical complexity of the formulae occurring in the proof is in certain ways limited in relation to the complexity of the conclusion; for instance, no formula can contain more nested quantifiers than the conclusion. The proof is, as it were, without detours, and *modus ponens* is eliminated. As a consequence, a quantifier-free formula deduced from quantifier-free axioms can be proved by propositional logic and substitution, which implies all the consistency results proved by the Hilbert school before the discovery of Gödel's theorem. Gentzen's theorem also applies to intuitionist logic and to other logics, such as modal logics.

These theorems, which are the fundamental theorems of the proof theory of quantification theory, are closely related to the fundamental theorem of its semantics, Gödel's completeness theorem. Every formula not formally refutable has a model—in fact, a model in which the quantifiers range over natural numbers; i.e., there are denumerably many individuals. This can be strengthened to the following: If S is any set (finite or infinite) of formulae of first-order logic, it has a denumerable model unless some finite subset of S is inconsistent—that is, unless the conjunction of the subset's members is formally refutable (Skolem–Löwenheim theorem).

This theorem has some quite startling consequences: in particular, it applies if S is the set of theorems of some system of set theory. Then if the system is consistent, S has a denumerable model even though S may contain a theorem which asserts·the existence of nondenumerable sets.

That is not a contradiction: if n represents a nondenumerable set in the model, there will indeed be only countably many m's such that m ε n is true in the model, but the assertion "n is nondenumerable" will be true in the model because the model will not contain an object representing the function which *enumerates* the objects m for which m ε n is true in the model. The model is denumerable only from "outside."

This is an example of a model which is nonstandard in that it differs in some essential way from the intended one. The Skolem–Löwenheim theorem also implies the existence of nonstandard models for systems of number theory. In fact, there is a nonstandard model even for the set S of all *true* formulae of elementary arithmetic. The number sequence cannot be characterized up to isomorphism by any countable set of first-order formulae.

The existence of denumerable models of set theory illustrates how essential the platonist conception of set, particularly of the set of subsets of a given set, is to set theory. If there is no more to the platonist conception than is specified in any particular formal system, then apparently the cardinal number of a set cannot be objectively determined. Indeed, the cardinal number of a set depends on what mappings there are and therefore on what sets there are.

The acceptance of this relativity has been urged by many, including Skolem. A fully formalist conception would give rise even to the relativity of the natural numbers themselves.

The completeness theorem and the construction of nonstandard models are fundamental tools in a now rapidly developing branch of logic called model theory. This subject can be viewed as a development of logical semantics, but what is perhaps distinctive about the point of view underlying recent work is that it regards a model of a formal theory as a type of algebraic structure and, in general, that it integrates the semantic study of formal systems with abstract algebra. Model theory takes mathematical logic a long way from the philosophical issues with which we have been mainly concerned, in particular by taking for granted a strong form of platonism. The leaders of this development have, in fact, emphasized the application of metamathematical methods to problems in ordinary mathematics.

There are other investigations concerning the foundations of pure logic. For example, we have mentioned that there can be no decision procedure for quantification theory. Nonetheless, there is interest in the question of what subclasses of formulae are decidable. As a striking result in this direction we might mention the proof of A. S. Kahr, E. F. Moore, and Hao Wang (1962) that the existence of models of formulae of the form "(x)(∃y)(z)M(x,y,z)" (or, equivalently, the provability of formulae of the form "(∃x)(y)(∃z)M(x,y,z)" where "M(x,y,z)" is an arbitrary quantifier-free formula, is undecidable. The development of appropriate concepts of model and completeness proofs for modal logics and intuitionist logic has come to fruition in recent years. In the case of the completeness of intuitionist logic, the situation is unclear. E. W. Beth (1956) has given a construction of models in terms of which he proves *classically* the completeness of intuitionist quantification theory. On the other hand, Kreisel has shown that the completeness of intuitionist logic cannot be proved by methods available in present intuitionist formal systems and, indeed, that it is incompatible with the supposition that all constructive functions of natural numbers are recursive.

Axiomatic set theory. We shall not undertake here to survey the different axiomatic systems of set theory. We shall, however, mention some developments in the metamathematics of set theory, developments concerning the axiom of choice and Cantor's continuum problem (see CONTINUUM PROBLEM).

The axiom of choice asserts (in one formulation) that for every set A of nonempty sets no two of which have a common element, there exists a set B which contains exactly one element from each of the sets in A. This axiom became prominent when Zermelo used it in 1904 to prove that every set can be well-ordered. Although it was much disputed, it came to be applied more and more, so that entire theories of modern abstract mathematics depend essentially on it. Naturally the question arose whether it was provable or refutable from the other axioms of various systems of set theory. A. A. Fraenkel (1922) showed that it could not be proved from Zermelo's axioms, provided that the axioms allowed individuals—that is, objects which are not sets—in the range of the quantifiers.

The continuum problem appears to be an elementary problem in the arithmetic of cardinal numbers: is there a cardinal between $\aleph_0$, the cardinal of the integers, and $2^{\aleph_0}$, that of the continuum; stated otherwise, does the continuum contain subsets of cardinal number different from that of the continuum and that of the integers? If the answer is negative, then $2^{\aleph_0} = \aleph_1$, the first cardinal larger than $\aleph_0$, and the cardinal of the first noncountable well-ordering. Cantor's conjecture that $2^{\aleph_0} = \aleph_1$ is called the continuum hypothesis.

Gödel, in 1938, proved that the axiom of choice and a generalization of the continuum hypothesis are consistent with the other axioms. The argument applies to a number of different systems, including the Zermelo–Fraenkel system (ZF). What is proved (finitistically) is that if, say, ZF is consistent, it is likewise consistent with a new axiom, the axiom of constructibility, which implies the axiom of choice and the generalized continuum hypothesis. For the constructible sets, which are the sets obtained by extending the ramified hierarchy of types through all the ordinals, can be proved in the system to satisfy all the axioms plus the axiom of constructibility, which says that every set is constructible. In terms of models, any model of ZF contains a subclass that is a model in which all sets are constructible. The constructible sets are of interest on their own account; Gödel has remarked that the idea behind them is to reduce all impredicativities to one special kind, the existence of large ordinals. However, he does not consider the axiom of constructibility plausible.

Thus, it has been known for some time that the axiom of choice and the continuum hypothesis are not refutable from the other axioms. Recently, Paul J. Cohen proved that they are not provable either. That is, if, say, ZF is consistent, it remains so by adding the negation of the axiom of choice or by adding the axiom of choice and the negation of the continuum hypothesis. Starting from Gödel's ideas, Cohen developed a quite new method for constructing models, which has led very quickly to a large number of further independence results.

The situation with respect to the axiom of choice and the continuum problem raises anew the question of how definite our idea of a set is, whether or not such a question as the continuum problem has an objectively determinate answer. Most mathematicians today find the axiom of choice sufficiently evident. But the continuum hypothesis—perhaps because of its more special character and because of the fact that the analogy of the infinite to the finite on which the conception of the set of all subsets of a given set is based does not suggest a justification of it—is left much more uncertain by considerations of intuitive evidence or plausibility. The role of the Skolem–Löwenheim theorem in Gödel's and Cohen's constructions might encourage the idea that the continuum hypothesis is in fact undetermined. Gödel himself believes that it is false and hopes that an axiom will be found which is as evident as the axiom of choice and which suffices to refute the continuum hypothesis. At present no one seems to have a good idea of what such an axiom would be like. It would have to be of a different character from the usual strong axioms of infinity, to which the method of Gödel's consistency proof applies.

The question of the continuum hypothesis is thus very close to the general epistemological question concerning platonism. If the general conceptions of set and function are given in some direct way to the mind, if, to echo Descartes, the idea of the infinite is in one's mind before that of the finite, there is no reason to expect a comparatively simple question like the continuum problem to be unanswerable. If, on the other hand, the platonist conceptions are developed by analogies from the area where we have intuitive evidence, if they are "ideas of reason" which, without having an intuition corresponding to them, are developed to give a "higher unity" which our knowledge cannot obtain otherwise, then it would not be particularly surprising if the nature of sets were left indeterminate in some important respect and, indeed, could be further determined in different, incompatible ways.

General Works

Beth, E. W., *The Foundations of Mathematics*. Amsterdam, 1959.

Fraenkel, A. A., and Bar-Hillel, Yehoshua, *Foundations of Set Theory*. Amsterdam, 1958.

Heyting, Arend, *Mathematische Grundlagenforschung. Intuitionismus. Beweistheorie*. Berlin, 1934. Expanded French version, *Les Fondements des mathématiques. Intuitionnisme. Théorie de la démonstration*. Paris, 1955.

Hilbert, David, and Bernays, Paul, *Grundlagen der Mathematik*, 2 vols. Berlin, 1934–1939.

Kleene, S. C., *Introduction to Metamathematics*. New York, Toronto, Amsterdam, and Groningen, 1952.

Körner, Stefan, *The Philosophy of Mathematics*. London, 1960.

Kreisel, Georg, "Mathematical Logic," in T. L. Saaty, ed., *Lectures on Modern Mathematics*, Vol. III. New York, 1965. Pp. 95–195.

Weyl, Hermann, *Philosophy of Mathematics and Natural Science*. Princeton, 1949.

TEXTBOOKS

Mendelson, Elliott, *Introduction to Mathematical Logic*. Princeton, 1964.

Wilder, R. L., *Introduction to the Foundations of Mathematics*. New York, 1952.

COLLECTIONS OF PAPERS

Benacerraf, Paul, and Putnam, Hilary, eds., *Philosophy of Mathematics: Selected Readings.* Englewood Cliffs, N.J., 1964.

Van Heijenoort, John, ed., *A Source Book in Mathematical Logic, 1879–1931.* Cambridge, Mass., forthcoming.

HISTORICAL STUDIES

Becker, Oskar, *Die Grundlagen der Mathematik in geschichtlicher Entwicklung.* Freiburg and Munich, 1954; 2d ed., 1964.

Kneale, William, and Kneale, Martha, *The Development of Logic.* Oxford, 1962.

AXIOMATICS

Beth, E. W., *The Foundations of Mathematics,* above. Parts II and III.

Blanché, Robert, *L'Axiomatique.* Paris, 1955.

Tarski, Alfred, *Introduction to Logic.* New York, 1941.

The Thirteen Books of Euclid's Elements, translated with commentary by T. L. Heath, 3 vols. Cambridge, 1908.

THE ABSTRACT VIEWPOINT.

Hilbert, David, *Grundlagen der Geomtrie,* 9th ed. Stuttgart, 1961. 2d ed. translated by E. J. Townsend as *Foundations of Geometry.* Chicago, 1902.

FORMALIZATION

Church, Alonzo, *Introduction to Mathematical Logic.* Princeton, 1956. Introduction.

Hilbert, David, and Bernays, Paul, *Grundlagen der Mathematik,* above.

Quine, W. V., *Mathematical Logic,* rev. ed. Cambridge, Mass., 1951.

Epistemological Discussion

A PRIORI KNOWLEDGE

Frege, Gottlob, *The Foundations of Arithmetic,* translated by J. L. Austin. Oxford, 1950; 2d ed., 1953. With German text.

MATHEMATICS AND LOGIC

Frege, Gottlob, *Grundgesetze der Arithmetik,* 2 vols. Jena, 1893–1903; reprinted, Hildesheim, 1962.

Hempel, C. G., "On the Nature of Mathematical Truth." *American Mathematical Monthly,* Vol. 52 (1945), 543–556. Reprinted, Benacerraf and Putnam, *op. cit.*

Russell, Bertrand, *The Principles of Mathematics.* Cambridge, 1903; 2d ed., London, 1937.

Russell, Bertrand, *Introduction to Mathematical Philosophy,* 2d ed. London, 1920.

Waismann, Friedrich, *Introduction to Mathematical Thinking.* New York, 1951.

COUNTING AND NUMBER

Frege, Gottlob, *The Foundations of Arithmetic,* above.

AXIOMS OF ARITHMETIC

Dedekind, Richard, *Was sind und was sollen die Zahlen?* Braunschweig, 1888.

Hilbert, David, and Bernays, Paul, *Grundlagen der Mathematik,* above.

Kleene, S. C., *Introduction to Metamathematics,* above.

Peano, Giuseppe, *Arithmetices principia nova methodo exposita.* Rome, 1889.

THE CONCEPT OF CLASS

Cantor, Georg, *Gesammelte Abhandlungen,* Ernst Zermelo, ed. Berlin, 1932; reprinted, Hildesheim, 1962.

Frege, Gottlob, *Funktion und Begriff.* Jena, 1891. Reprinted as *Funktion, Begriff, Bedeutung,* Günther Patzig, ed. Göttingen, 1962. Translated and edited by P. T. Geach and Max Black in *Translations From the Philosophical Writings of Gottlob Frege.* Oxford, 1952.

Frege, Gottlob, *The Foundations of Arithmetic,* above.

Frege, Gottlob, *Grundgesetze der Arithmetik,* above.

FREGE'S ANALYSIS OF NUMBER

Frege, Gottlob, *Begriffsschrift.* Halle, 1879; reprinted, Hildesheim, 1964. Translation, van Heijenoort, *op. cit.*

Frege, Gottlob, *The Foundations of Arithmetic,* above.

Frege, Gottlob, *Grundgesetze der Arithmetik,* above.

Quine, W. V., *Mathematical Logic,* above.

Quine, W. V., *Set Theory and Its Logic.* Cambridge, Mass., 1963.

Whitehead, A. N., and Russell, Bertrand, *Principia Mathematica,* 3 vols. Cambridge, 1910–1913; 2d ed., 1925–1927.

DIFFICULTIES IN LOGICISM

Carnap, Rudolf, "Die logizistische Grundlegung der Mathematik." *Erkenntnis,* Vol. 2 (1931), 91–105. Translation, Benacerraf and Putnam, *op. cit.*

Poincaré, Henri, *Science et méthode.* Paris, 1908.

Wittgenstein, Ludwig, *Remarks on the Foundations of Mathematics,* G. E. M. Anscombe, G. H. von Wright, and R. Rhees, eds. Oxford, 1956. German text with translation by G. E. M. Anscombe. Part II.

KANT'S VIEW

Kant, Immanuel, *Untersuchung über die Deutlichkeit der Grundsätze der natürlichen Theologie und der Moral.* Berlin, 1764. Printed in *Gesammelte Schriften,* Berlin Academy of Sciences, ed., 23 vols. Berlin, 1902–1955. Vol. II, pp. 273–301.

Kant, Immanuel, *Kritik der reinen Vernunft.* Riga, 1781; 2d ed., 1787. Translated by Norman Kemp Smith as *Critique of Pure Reason.* London, 1929. See especially Introduction, "Transcendental Aesthetic," "Axioms of Intuition," and "Discipline of Pure Reason in Its Dogmatic Employment."

CONVENTIONALISM

Carnap, Rudolf, *Logische Syntax der Sprache.* Vienna, 1934. Translated by Amethe Smeaton as *Logical Syntax of Language.* London, 1937.

Carnap, Rudolf, *Meaning and Necessity,* 2d ed. Chicago, 1956. Especially appendices.

Nagel, Ernest, "Logic Without Ontology," in Y. H. Krikorian, ed., *Naturalism and the Human Spirit.* New York, 1944. Partially reprinted, Benacerraf and Putnam, *op. cit.*

Quine, W. V., "Truth by Convention," in O. H. Lee, ed., *Philosophical Essays for A. N. Whitehead.* New York, 1936. Pp. 90–124. Reprinted, Benacerraf and Putnam, *op. cit.*

Quine, W. V., "Two Dogmas of Empiricism," in *From a Logical Point of View.* Cambridge, Mass., 1953; 2d ed., 1961. Reprinted, Benacerraf and Putnam, *op. cit.*

Quine, W. V., "Carnap and Logical Truth." *Synthese,* Vol. 12 (1960), 350–374.

WITTGENSTEIN'S VIEW

Wittgenstein, Ludwig, *Philosophical Investigations,* translated by G. E. M. Anscombe, R. Rhees and G. E. M. Anscombe, eds. Oxford, 1953. With German text.

Wittgenstein, Ludwig, *Remarks on the Foundations of Mathematics,* above.

Platonism

Bernays, Paul, "Sur le Platonisme dans les mathématiques." *L'Enseignement mathématique,* Vol. 34 (1935), 52–69. Translation, Benacerraf and Putnam, *op. cit.*

Gödel, Kurt, "Russell's Mathematical Logic," in P. A. Schilpp, ed., *The Philosophy of Bertrand Russell.* Evanston. Ill., 1944. Pp. 123–154. Reprinted, Benacerraf and Putnam, *op. cit.*

IMPREDICATIVE DEFINITIONS

Gödel, Kurt, "Russell's Mathematical Logic," above.
Poincaré, Henri, *Science et méthode,* above.
Weyl, Hermann, *Das Kontinuum.* Leipzig, 1918.
Weyl, Hermann, "Über die neue Grundlagenkrise der Mathematik." *Mathematische Zeitschrift,* Vol. 10 (1921), 39–79.

SET THEORY AND THE PARADOXES

Bernays, Paul, "Sur le Platonisme dans les mathématiques," above.
Fraenkel, A. A., and Bar-Hillel, Yehoshua, *Foundations of Set Theory,* above.
Gödel, Kurt, "Russell's Mathematical Logic," above.
Montague, Richard, and Vaught, R. L., "The Natural Models of Set Theories." *Fundamenta Mathematicae,* Vol. 47 (1959), 219–242.
Quine, W. V., *Set Theory and Its Logic,* above.
Whitehead, A. N., and Russell, Bertrand, *Principia Mathematica,* above. Introduction.

PREDICATIVISM

Wang, Hao, "The Formalization of Mathematics." *Journal of Symbolic Logic,* Vol. 19 (1954), 241–266.
Weyl, Hermann, *Das Kontinuum,* above.

Constructivism

INTUITIONISM

Heyting, Arend, *Mathematische Grundlagenforschung,* above.
Heyting, Arend, *Intuitionism: An Introduction.* Amsterdam, 1956. Both books by Heyting, especially the French version of the first, contain extensive bibliographies on intuitionism.
Kreisel, Georg, "Mathematical Logic," above.
Weyl, Hermann, *Philosophy of Mathematics and Natural Science,* above. Sec. 9.
For works by Brouwer, see the bibliography to BROUWER, LUITZEN EGBERTUS JAN.

FINITISM

Bernays, Paul, "Sur le Platonisme dans les mathématiques," above.
Gödel, Kurt, "Über eine bisher noch nicht benützte Erweiterung des finiten Standpunktes." *Dialectica,* Vol. 12 (1958), 280–287.

THE HILBERT PROGRAM

Hilbert, David, "Über das Unendliche." *Mathematische Annalen,* Vol. 95 (1926), 161–190. Translation, Benacerraf and Putnam, *op. cit.* (with an omission); van Heijenoort, *op. cit.*
Hilbert, David, "Die Grundlagen der Mathematik." *Abhandlungen aus dem mathematischen Seminar der Hamburgischen Universität,* Vol. 6 (1928), 65–85. Translation, van Heijenoort, *op. cit.*
Hilbert, David, and Bernays, Paul, *Grundlagen der Mathematik,* above.

Mathematical Logic

Hilbert, David, and Bernays, Paul, *Grundlagen der Mathematik,* above.
Kleene, S. C., *Introduction to Metamathematics,* above.
Mendelson, Elliott, *Introduction to Mathematical Logic,* above.

GÖDEL'S INCOMPLETENESS THEOREMS

Gödel, Kurt, "Über formal unentscheidbare Sätze der Principia Mathematica und verwandter Systeme I." *Monatshefte für Mathematik und Physik,* Vol. 38 (1931), 173–198. Translation, van

Heijenoort, *op. cit.* For detailed presentations of Gödel's proof, see Hilbert and Bernays, *op. cit.;* Kleene, *op. cit.;* and Mostowski, below.
Mostowski, Andrzej, *Sentences Undecidable in Formalized Arithmetic.* Amsterdam, 1952.
See also the bibliography to GÖDEL'S THEOREM.

RECURSIVE FUNCTION THEORY

Kleene, S. C., *Introduction to Metamathematics,* above.
Kleene, S. C., "Hierarchies of Number-theoretic Predicates." *Bulletin of the American Mathematical Society,* Vol. 61 (1955), 193–213.
Kleene, S. C., and Vesley, R. E., *The Foundations of Intuitionistic Mathematics.* Amsterdam, 1965.
See also the bibliography to RECURSIVE FUNCTION THEORY.

DEVELOPMENT OF THE HILBERT PROGRAM

Feferman, Solomon, "Systems of Predicative Analysis." *Journal of Symbolic Logic,* Vol. 29 (1964), 1–30.
Gentzen, Gerhard, "Die Widerspruchsfreiheit der reinen Zahlentheorie." *Mathematische Annalen,* Vol. 112 (1936), 493–565.
Gödel, Kurt, "Zur intuitionistischen Arithmetik und Zahlentheorie." *Ergebnisse eines mathematischen Kolloquiums,* Vol. 4 (1933), 34–38.
Gödel, Kurt, "Uber eine bisher noch nicht benützte Erweiterung des finiten Standpunktes," above.
Kleene, S. C., *Introduction to Metamathematics,* above.
Kreisel, Georg, "On the Interpretation of Non-finitist Proofs." *Journal of Symbolic Logic,* Vol. 16 (1951), 241–267, and Vol. 17 (1952), 43–58.
Kreisel, Georg, "Hilbert's Programme." *Dialectica,* Vol. 12 (1958), 346–372. Reprinted, with revisions, Benacerraf and Putnam, *op. cit.*
Kreisel, Georg, "Mathematical Logic," above.
Lorenzen, Paul, "Algebraische und logizistische Untersuchungen über freie Verbände." *Journal of Symbolic Logic,* Vol. 16 (1951), 81–106.
Schütte, Kurt, *Beweistheorie.* Berlin, Göttingen, and Heidelberg, 1960.
Spector, Clifford, "Provably Recursive Functionals of Analysis," in *Recursive Function Theory. Proceedings of Symposia in Pure Mathematics,* Vol. V. Providence, 1962. Pp. 1–27.

FOUNDATIONS OF LOGIC

Gentzen, Gerhard, "Untersuchungen über das logische Schliessen." *Mathematische Zeitschrift,* Vol. 9 (1934), 176–210, 405–431.
Gödel, Kurt, "Die Vollständigkeit der Axiome des logischen Funktionenkalküls." *Monatshefte für Mathematik und Physik,* Vol. 37 (1930), 349–360.
Herbrand, Jacques, "Recherches sur la théorie de la démonstration." *Travaux de la Société des Sciences et des Lettres de Varsovie, Classe III,* No. 33 (1930), 33–160. Excerpted, with important notes, van Heijenoort, *op. cit.* Material on Skolem in van Heijenoort is also highly relevant.
Hilbert, David, and Bernays, Paul, *Grundlagen der Mathematik,* above.
Kleene, S. C., *Introduction to Metamathematics,* above. See especially Part IV.
Robinson, Abraham, *An Introduction to Model Theory and the Metamathematics of Algebra.* Amsterdam, 1963.
Skolem, Thoralf, "Über die Nicht-charakterisierbarkeit der Zahlenreihe mittels endlich oder abzählbar unendlich vieler Aussagen mit ausschliesslich Zahlenvariablen." *Fundamenta Mathematicae,* Vol. 23 (1934), 150–161.
Tarski, Alfred, *Logic, Semantics, Metamathematics.* Oxford, 1956.

CONTINUUM PROBLEM

Cohen, Paul J., "The Independence of the Continuum Hypothesis," I and II. *Proceedings of the National Academy of Sciences,* Vol. 50 (1963), 1143–1148, and Vol. 51 (1964), 105–110.

Gödel, Kurt, *The Consistency of the Axiom of Choice and the Generalized Continuum-hypothesis With the Axioms of Set Theory.* Princeton, N.J., 1940; reprinted, with additional notes, 1951.

Gödel, Kurt, "What Is Cantor's Continuum Problem?" *American Mathematical Monthly,* Vol. 54 (1947), 515–525. Reprinted, with additions, Benacerraf and Putnam, *op. cit.*

Kahr, A. S.; Moore, E. F.; and Wang, Hao, "*Entscheidungsproblem* Reduced to the AEA Case." *Proceedings of the National Academy of Sciences,* Vol. 48 (1962), 365–377.

CHARLES PARSONS

MATHER, COTTON (1663–1728), scholar, clergyman, and author, was the oldest son of Increase Mather, one of the leading figures in the Puritan theocracy in Massachusetts. The younger Mather was so precocious that he entered Harvard College at the age of 12 and graduated at 15. Because he stammered, he felt unqualified to preach and therefore began to study medicine. After a few years, however, he overcame his speech handicap and became the assistant to his father at the Second Church, Boston. Ordained in 1685, he remained in the service of the Second Church for the rest of his life.

Mather was disappointed in many of the major quests of his life. Partly because he associated himself politically with the unpopular royal governor, Sir William Phips, partly because of the diminished prestige of the Puritan clergy, and partly because of his own often unpleasant personal qualities he lost the power to wield significant influence in public affairs. When he greatly desired to succeed his father, who retired in 1701 as president of Harvard College, he was not selected. Convinced that Harvard no longer represented the true Calvinist faith, he threw himself energetically into the foundation of Yale College, but its presidency was not offered to him until 1721, when he declined the position because of his age.

Mather's intellectual attitudes during his earlier years were extremely narrow, for he moved within the confines of a strict Puritan world view; later, however, he became more tolerant of the differing beliefs of others. Finally, especially in his *Christian Philosopher* (1721), he moved close to the natural religion characteristic of the Age of Reason. He interpreted the theological doctrine of divine Providence in philosophical terms by asserting that the order of the universe was planned for man's good by an all-wise, all-good God. Man's appreciation of natural beauty and his application of reason to observations drawn from nature are sufficient to prove the existence and beneficence of God. His scientific communications to the Royal Society of London led to his election as a fellow in 1713, one of the first Americans to be so honored. He was one of the earliest in the colonies to advocate inoculation against smallpox, and he ably defended his position in several pamphlets. The change in his mental attitude thus epitomizes the alteration in the intellectual life that pervaded his milieu.

Nowhere is this duality more apparent than in Mather's involvement in the witchcraft epidemic in Salem. He attempted to make a "scientific" study of the cases, but he came to the conclusion that they could be treated by prayer and fasting. He warned the judges in witchcraft trials to proceed very cautiously against the suspects and to be particularly careful in admitting "spectral evidence," yet in his *Wonders of the Invisible World* (1693) he argued that the verdicts in the Salem trials were justified. By 1700, however, he changed his mind about the fairness of the trials. In regard to the suspicion of witchcraft, as in other respects, Mather stood uneasily between traditional faith and the new scientific outlook.

Bibliography

Mather's most important works (of more than 450 published) are *Magnalia Christi Americana, or the Ecclesiastical History of New England* (London, 1702); *Essays to Do Good* (Boston, 1710; originally entitled *Bonifacius,* Boston, 1710); and *Christian Philosopher* (London, 1721). Kenneth B. Murdock has edited, with introduction and notes, *Selections from Cotton Mather* (New York, 1926; new ed., 1960).

Discussion of Mather may be found in Ralph P. and Louise Boas, *Cotton Mather, Keeper of the Puritan Conscience* (New York and London, 1928); Barrett Wendell, *Cotton Mather, the Puritan Priest* (New York, 1891; new ed., with introduction by Alan Heimert, 1963); and Otho T. Beall and Richard Shryock, *Cotton Mather, First Significant Figure in American Medicine* (Baltimore, 1954).

J. L. BLAU

MATTER. The term "matter" and its cognates ("material," "materialist," "materialistic," and the like) have played active parts in philosophical debate throughout intellectual history. Natural philosophers have studied material objects and contrasted them with such immaterial agencies as energy and fields of force; metaphysicians and mathematical philosophers have distinguished the material or tangible aspects of things from their formal or intangible aspects, their physical properties from their geometrical ones. Again, the terms "matter" and "material" have played a humble part not only in science but also in moral philosophy and even theology. Matter has thus been placed in opposition to life and mind, soul and spirit, and a preoccupation with worldly pleasures and bodily comforts, as opposed to the "higher" pleasures of the mind, has been condemned as "materialistic" and unworthy of spiritual beings. In thinking about matter, accordingly, the question of how far—if at all—these various distinctions can actually be justified and reconciled must always be borne in mind.

This question immediately poses a historical problem, for men's ideas about matter have not been static. On the contrary, they have been subject to continual development, and it is highly doubtful whether one can isolate a single concept of matter shared by, say, Anaximander and Aquinas, Democritus and Descartes, Epicurus and Einstein. Thus, for instance, a seventeenth-century philosophical thesis about the relations between mind and matter must be interpreted in relation to seventeenth-century ideas about physics and chemistry. Such a thesis can be transplanted into the intellectual environment of the twentieth century only by taking into account changes in the fundamental concepts of science during the intervening years. We must therefore consider how the concept of matter has been progressively refined and modified in the course of intellectual history.

GREEK PHILOSOPHY

As far as we can judge from the surviving texts and the testimony of Aristotle, the idea of a constituent or material ingredient (hyle) common to things of all kinds was a central concept of the Ionian school of philosophy. The Ionian philosophers, beginning with Thales of Miletus, disagreed about the nature of this common ingredient. Some likened it to water, others to air or breath, others to fire; some insisted that it could have no properties analogous to those of any familiar substance but must be entirely undifferentiated or unlimited. Yet they agreed, at any rate, in their statement of the basic philosophical problem: "What universal, permanent substance underlies the variety and change of the physical world?"

It would be a mistake, however, to think of the Ionians as materialists in the modern sense. As they conceived it, the universal material of things was far from being brute, inorganic, passive, mindless stuff intrinsically devoid of all higher properties or capabilities. Water, for instance, was, for them, not a sterile, inorganic chemical but a fertilizing fluid, and in their system it was quite open to consideration whether the basic stuff of the world might not be provided by either spirit (pneuma) or mind (nous). At this initial stage in philosophical speculation, indeed, the questions preoccupying philosophers cut across many of the distinctions which later generations were to treat as fundamental.

We first find these distinctions being drawn explicitly and insisted on by the Athenian philosophers, following the examples of Plato and Aristotle. For instance, Plato and his fellow mathematicians at the Academy explained the properties of homogeneous material substances in one way, those of organized, functional systems in another. Like the Sicilian philosopher Empedocles, they classified material substances into four contrasted states or kinds—solid (earth), aeriform (air), liquid (water), and fiery (fire)—but they added a novel mathematical theory to account for the contrasted properties of these four kinds of substance. Each kind, they supposed, had atoms of a distinct geometrical shape, and they hypothetically identified these shapes with four of the five regular convex solids—tetrahedron, cube, octahedron, and icosahedron—whose mathematical properties had been studied by Plato's associate Theaetetus. (The fifth solid, the dodecahedron, they associated with the twelve constellations of the outer heavens.) The characteristic properties of organisms, on the other hand, they explained in functional rather than material terms. The form of any bodily organ must be accounted for as reflecting its role in the life of the organism; this form should be thought of as created specifically to perform a particular function as effectively as the available materials permitted.

Aristotle went further. He distinguished sharply between the material substance of which an object was composed and the form imposed on it, and he questioned whether the characteristic properties of any substance or system could be usefully explained in either atomistic or geometrical terms. In order to understand the properties and behavior of any individual object, it was first necessary to recognize it as an object of a particular kind. Each kind of object existing in nature had properties determined by its own special form or essence, so that any universal primary stuff (hyle) must be devoid of any particular distinguishing characteristic. For Aristotle and his followers the problem of distinguishing substances became primarily a matter of taxonomy, of qualitative classification, rather than a quantitative, physicochemical problem. Weight, from this point of view, was just one possible quality among others. Aristotle's views went beyond those of Plato in one other respect which was to have profound implications for cosmology. He drew a clear distinction between the sublunary world, whose objects were composed of the four terrestrial elements—earth, air, fire, and water—and could be created and destroyed, and the superlunary or celestial world of the outer heavens, whose inhabitants were composed of the quintessence (fifth essence) and exempted from change and decay. Of all terrestrial things only the souls of rational beings in any way shared this immutability.

LATER CLASSICAL AND MEDIEVAL PERIODS

Subsequent philosophers—whether in Hellenistic Alexandria (200 B.C.–A.D. 550), the Islamic centers of learning (650–1150), or the newly founded universities of Western Europe (950–1500)—introduced a number of variations into the debate about matter without adding any fundamentally new themes. For both the Stoics and the Epicureans, ideas about matter were closely associated with religious beliefs. Epicurus and his followers—notably, the Roman poet Lucretius—developed the more fragmentary speculations of Democritus and Leucippus about the atomic structure of matter into a complete philosophical system. But the atoms of the Greek philosophers differed from those of nineteenth-century European science in three crucial respects. First, they had an indefinitely large range of sizes and shapes instead of a limited number of fixed forms, one for each chemical "element": next, they interacted only by direct contact or impact rather than by exerting forces of attraction or repulsion on one another; and, finally, they existed in special varieties—atoms of magnetism, of life, of mind, and of soul—to explain all sorts of activities—physical, biological, psychological, and even spiritual. The collisions and conjunctions of these atoms were regarded by Epicurus as an autonomous physical process, for his fundamental aim was to attack any belief in external interference by divine agencies in the affairs of the natural world.

The Stoics, such as Zeno of Citium and Chrysippus, rejected atoms in favor of three kinds of continuous physical medium or spirit (pneuma) for both scientific and religious purposes. The pneuma was an integrative agency, analogous to a field of force, capable of maintaining a stable pattern of properties and behavior in a physical system; in addition, it was capable of existing in separation from the solid and liquid frame of the "body" and could probably be identified with the soul. Instead of rejecting the traditional deities, like the Epicureans, the Stoics reinterpreted them as incorporeal agencies comparable to the pneuma. Yet though the Stoics and the Epicureans differed about many things, they agreed that every agency capable of producing physical effects—even the mind—must be regarded as a material body (soma). As a result for Lucretius pure mind was composed of very smooth and mobile atoms; for Chrysippus it consisted of undiluted fire.

The alchemical philosophers, for their part, introduced an experimental element into the study of matter. Beginning with the Democritean Bolos of Mendes (c. 200 B.C.), going on through Maria the Jewess and Zozimos of Alexandria (second and third centuries A.D.), the alchemists exploited the traditional craft techniques of the Middle Eastern metallurgists, dyers, and jewelers and attempted to find ways of separating and isolating the essences or spirits in things. In this way they were led to contrast volatile and chemically active substances, such as alcohol and ether (spirits), with solid and passive ones, such as earths and *calces* (bodies). The association of the soul and the body in living creatures was thus treated as analogous to the association of volatile and gaseous with solid and earthy substances in a chemical compound. When freed from this association, incorporeal spirits naturally tended to rise toward the heavens, corporeal bodies to sink to the earth, a fact which apparently harmonized with the traditional Aristotelian contrast between the celestial and terrestrial worlds.

Nevertheless, philosophers and theologians in the strictly orthodox Aristotelian tradition rejected Stoic, Epicurean, and alchemical ideas as being excessively materialistic. In their view the soul was not in any way a subject for chemical or quasi-chemical speculation. The forms or essences of things were not themselves composed of any material stuff, even of the highly tenuous kinds conceived by the Stoics and alchemists. Accordingly, for Aquinas and the other philosophers of the high Middle Ages, the relation between matter and form was a problem in metaphysics or theology rather than one in natural philosophy.

NEW THEORIES: 1550–1750

Thus, the revival of the physical sciences during the Renaissance started from a position in which no single doctrine about the nature of matter was clearly established and generally accepted. All supporters of the new mechanical philosophy were attracted to an atomistic or corpuscular view of matter, but most of them took care to dissociate themselves from the original atomistic doctrines of Democritus and Epicurus, which were still suspected of having atheistical implications. Thus, Kepler explained the crystalline structure of snowflakes by reference to a geometrical theory of atoms modeled on that of Plato, Galileo embraced atomism as a physical embodiment for the points of geometry, and Descartes treated all matter as corpuscular in structure at the same time denying the theoretical possibility of a void or vacuum. All of them regarded such mechanical interactions as collisions as the basic model for physical processes and sought to build up a theory of forces (dynamics) capable of explaining the established generalizations about the motions of physical objects.

However, attempts to work out an effective and comprehensive system of physical theory without going beyond the categories of atomism inherited from the Greeks encountered a number of difficulties. These sprang ultimately from the dual axiom that any agency capable of producing physical effects must be composed of a corresponding type of material object and that these objects could influence one another only by direct mechanical action, which required that the bodies be in contact. To deny the first half of this axiom implied accepting the notion of nonmaterial physical agencies; to deny the second implied accepting action at a distance. Both these notions were widely rejected as being incompatible with sound natural philosophy.

The immediate outcome of this dual axiom was to commit the advocates of the new mechanical corpuscular philosophy to a proliferation of new kinds of atom—for instance, magnetic, calorific, and frigorific corpuscles—introduced to account for the corresponding physical phenomena of magnetism, heat, cold, and so on. Although some philosophers, including Descartes, saw the possibility of cutting down the types of atoms—for example, by explaining heat as a consequence of the internal agitation of the material atoms composing hot bodies—even Descartes felt bound to accept that light, magnetism, and the like were carried by subtle fluids made up of corpuscles of insensible weight. Matter, he declared, came in three kinds, of which only "third matter" was subject to gravity and thus had any weight.

An indirect but even more profound outcome of the corpuscularian axiom was to support Descartes's fundamental division between mind and matter as absolutely distinct substances. The least plausible element in traditional atomism had been its psychology. Christian theology had added its own objections to any explanation of mental activity which regarded the mind as composed of atoms, no matter how light or mobile, for this, it was generally agreed, came perilously close to denying the immortality of the soul. The new physical science of the seventeenth and eighteenth centuries accordingly limited its aim. The realm of nature consisted of material bodies interacting mechanically by contact and impact and could be studied by science. The realm of spirit—including, at least, the intellectual activities of human beings—was a distinct and separate object of speculation to which the categories of physical science were not directly relevant. Much of the debate in subsequent epistemology can be traced to this point.

Accordingly, for two hundred years beginning around 1700, the concept of matter kept a central place in physical theory but was set aside as irrelevant to the study of mind. In physics the first major break with traditional ideas came through the work of Sir Isaac Newton. By his theories of dynamics and gravitation, Newton established a sharp distinction between material objects in a strict sense, whose mass conferred on them both inertia and weight, and forces, which were a measure of the way in which material objects interacted rather than a special kind of material thing. In the case of gravity, as he showed in his *Philosophiae Naturalis Principia Mathematica* (1687), these forces had to be supposed capable of acting over distances of many million miles, though Newton himself was inclined to believe that some invisible mechanical link existed by which the sun, for instance, exerted its gravitational action on the planets. In the later editions of his *Opticks* (especially those published after Leibniz' death in 1716) he extended this idea to explain other physical phenomena. Electrical, magnetic, and chemical action also, he argued, might prove to be manifestations of forces of attraction and repulsion acting across the spaces between the massive corpuscles of bodies. Thus, the traditional system of atoms and the void was amended to become a theory of material corpuscles interacting by centrally directed forces.

CLASSICAL PHYSICS

Newton's program for natural philosophy made its way only slowly to begin with, but it met with no grave check until the late nineteenth century. At first, his insistence on mass as the essential property of matter was not found universally convincing. Others continued to regard extension, impenetrability, weight, or the capacity to produce physical effects as the indispensable criterion. As a result, throughout the eighteenth century there was an element of cross purposes in debates about the corporeal nature of, for example, light and fire. Two developments particularly helped to clarify the intellectual situation and established the Newtonian categories as the basis of physical science. First, Antoine-Laurent Lavoisier and his followers—notably, John Dalton—demonstrated that the phenomena of chemistry as well as those of physics could be unraveled on the assumption that all genuine material substances possessed mass and were composed of corpuscles or atoms. Second, the mathematical work of Leonhard Euler and his successors transformed Newton's account of forces of attraction and repulsion into the modern theory of fields of force.

After 1800, then, physical scientists went ahead rapidly with the experimental and mathematical work which culminated in the so-called classical physics and chemistry of the late nineteenth century. In this system the agents responsible for physical action were divided into two sharply contrasted categories. On the one hand, there was matter; this consisted of massive atoms which combined to form molecules in accordance with the principles of chemical combination. The mechanical energy associated with the motion of the molecules within any body accounted for its temperature; the fields of force between them explained gravitational, electric, and magnetic attraction and repulsion. On the other hand, there were those agencies—such as light and radiant heat—which apparently lacked both mass and weight and which were transmitted in the form of waves across the empty space between the material atoms. Gravitation apart, these various agencies turned out, as was shown by James Clerk Maxwell's electromagnetic theory of light, to be all of one general kind. By combining the established theories of the electrical and magnetic fields of force into a single mathematical system having the same degree of generality as Newton's dynamics, Maxwell demonstrated that electromagnetic waves would share the known properties of light and radiant heat and would move across space with the same velocity that had actually been measured in the case of light. This interpretation gained greatly in strength when Heinrich Hertz used an intermittent electrical spark to produce artificial electromagnetic waves, the so-called radio waves.

Though devoid of mass, these various forms of radiation nevertheless carried energy. Numerically, the sum total of all forms of energy in any isolated system (like the sum total of the masses of all the material bodies involved) was apparently conserved unchanged throughout all physical and chemical changes. As a result it seemed for several decades that the whole of natural philosophy could successfully be built on the central distinction between matter and energy and on the two independent axioms of the conservation of mass and the conservation of energy. Thus, Newton's program for physical science came close to being finally fulfilled in classical physics and chemistry.

TWENTIETH-CENTURY RECONSIDERATIONS

This intellectual equilibrium was short-lived. As Sir John Squire put it:

> Nature and all her Laws lay hid in Night.
> God said "Let Newton be, and all was Light."

It could not last. The Devil, shouting "Ho! Let Einstein be," restored the *status quo*.

To do Albert Einstein justice, the difficulties in the classical system which he resolved had been considered residual embarrassments for some time, and many of the conceptual changes for which he argued have since established themselves as indispensable features of physical theory. Still, they did undoubtedly have the effect of blurring the sharp distinctions and tidy certitudes of nineteenth-century science.

The effect of these conceptual changes on our concept of matter has been profound. Physicists have been compelled to reconsider and modify all the fundamental planks in the program enunciated for natural science by the mechanical philosophers of the seventeenth century. To begin with, Einstein displaced the seventeenth-century model of mechanical action as the universal pattern for intelligible physical processes by a new model based on electromagnetic theory. The embarrassments facing physicists in the 1890s arose, he showed, from a mathematical conflict between Maxwell's theory of electromagnetism and the mechanics of Galileo and Newton. Einstein circumvented these difficulties in his theory of relativity by giving priority to the theory of electromagnetic fields and by amending the principles of Newtonian mechanics to conform to the Maxwellian pattern. As a result the attitudes of a representative late nineteenth-century physicist, such as William Thomson, Lord Kelvin (who declined to accept Maxwell's theories, declaring that he could embrace a physical explanation of a phenomenon wholeheartedly only if he could make a mechanical model to demonstrate it), have since come to seem excessively narrow.

As a result of this initial change, however, certain other fundamental elements in classical physics have had to be called in question. The absolute distinction between matter and energy, for instance, has gone by the board. It now appears that any quantity of energy (E) is in certain respects equivalent to a proportional quantity of mass ($m = E/c^2$, where c is Maxwell's constant, equal to the measured velocity of electromagnetic radiation); that for theoretical purposes the twin conservation principles of nineteenth-century physics and chemistry should be joined in a single axiom, according to which the sum total of energy and mass (combined according to the formula $E + mc^2$) was conserved in all physical processes; and that in appropriate circumstances a quantity of electromagnetic energy can be transformed into the corresponding quantity of matter or vice versa. This implication was confirmed in the 1930s from a detailed study of individual actions between atomic nuclei and other particles, and it was dramatically reinforced by the explosion of the first atomic bombs, whose energy was derived from the marginal loss of mass involved in the nuclear fission of such heavy elements as uranium.

Meanwhile, the earlier contrast between matter, which was assumed to exist in discrete atomic units, and radiation, which traveled in the form of continuous waves, was under criticism for quite different reasons. First, Max Planck showed that bodies exchanged light-energy in the form of bundles or wave-packets. Einstein, going further, argued that electromagnetic energy always existed in the form of these photons. Then, in the early 1920s, Louis de Broglie put forward the idea that the subatomic particles into which Niels Bohr and Ernest Rutherford had analyzed the fundamental material units of earlier chemistry might themselves manifest some of the properties of wave-packets. This was confirmed in 1927, when it was shown that a beam of electrons passed through a crystal lattice produced a diffraction pattern just as a beam of light of the corresponding wave length and velocity would have done. By the 1960s it began to appear that matter-particles might differ from the energy-packets of light or other kinds of radiation only in having part of their energy frozen in the form of inertial mass.

Finally, the theory of quantum mechanics, first formulated between 1926 and 1932 by Werner Heisenberg, Erwin Schrödinger, and P. A. M. Dirac, has radically undercut one last presupposition, which had underlain physical science since the time of Galileo. From 1600 on, the fundamental units of matter—whether called corpuscles, particles, or atoms—had been regarded as intrinsincally brute, inert, and passive. They might be constituted in such a way that they are capable of exerting forces on one another by virtue of their relative motions and positions, but one had to seek the ultimate source of this capacity—as of their motion—in God who created them. (This was one point on which Newton, Descartes, and Maxwell all agreed.) Since 1926 the final unit of analysis in physics has ceased to bear any serious resemblance to these inert corpuscles. Instead, the quantum physicists begin with certain wave functions or eigenfunctions, which characterize the activity of, say, an electron or an atom as much as they do its structure and position. Just as mass has ceased to be entirely distinct from energy, so the particles of Newton's physics have ceased to be absolutely distinct from the forces of attraction and repulsion acting between them. On the contrary, according to the principles of contemporary physical theory, every kind of fundamental particle—whether of matter or energy—should be associated with a corresponding mode of interaction and force field. Photons, electrons, mesons, nucleons—all these have a dual aspect, being characterized partly by their inertial mass or intrinsic energy and partly by their pattern of interaction

with the environment. One outstanding and at present unsettled question is whether the transmission of gravitational forces, from which the whole notion of a field began, also involves the propagation of particles ("gravitons") at a finite speed. If it proves that "gravitons" do in fact exist and travel at the same speed as photons, this will tie up one of the more notorious loose ends in mid-twentieth-century physics.

IMPLICATIONS OF NEW THEORIES

Today almost all the axioms of earlier natural philosophy have been qualified, if not abandoned. Mass has ceased to be the essential, unalterable characteristic of all physical objects and now appears to be one variant of the wider category of energy. No longer can any determinate amount of this energy be localized with absolute precision (Heisenberg's principle), and we are left with a picture of a natural world whose fundamental elements are not so much passive bricks as units of activity. This transformation—as S. Sambursky has argued—involves a reaction against the axioms of seventeenth-century physics as radical as the Stoics' rejection of the atomism of Epicurus. Indeed, Sambursky points out, there is a strong parallel between the two reactions. As in the Stoic theory, physicists today also consider matter essentially active rather than passive and explain its behavior as the outcome of patterns of energy and excitation associated with any given state or condition.

The full implications of this change for our other ideas are beginning to become apparent only now. In biology, at any rate, a considerable change has come about since 1950 by the extension of physical theories into the fields of genetics, embryology, and bacteriology. Here the intimate association of structure and function characteristic of modern subatomic theory is reproduced in the association of specific biological activities with particular configurations (and, thus, eigenfunctions) of the complex molecules involved. The extensions of the new ideas about matter into the theory of organic development and human behavior are still at a speculative stage.

This much can, however, be said. During the centuries which have elapsed since the revival of natural philosophy at the Renaissance, the concept of matter has changed its character quite fundamentally. In the present state of scientific thought, accordingly, all earlier questions about, for instance, the relation of matter, life, and mind need to be entirely reconsidered. When, for instance, Descartes classified matter and mind as distinct substances, he was putting the concept of mind and mental activities in opposition to a concept of matter as inert extension, a concept which is now discredited. To that extent the extreme dualism of Descartes's philosophy has been not so much refuted by later science as made irrelevant; its categories no longer fit our situation.

Similarly, other long-standing debates concerning, for example, the reality of the material world or the relation between material objects and our sensations will need to be reappraised in the light of changes in our concept of matter. But this is a task for the future.

Bibliography

In general, this article follows the argument of Stephen Toulmin and June Goodfield, *The Architecture of Matter* (London, 1962), in which the development of the concept of matter is fully analyzed but discussed without serious technicalities. For the various periods covered here the reader is referred to the following works.

GREEK PHILOSOPHY

S. Sambursky, *The Physical World of the Greeks* (London, 1956), is an outstanding survey for the general reader. W. K. C. Guthrie, *A History of Greek Philosophy*, Vol. I (Cambridge, 1962), and G. S. Kirk and J. E. Raven, *The Presocratic Philosophers* (Cambridge, 1958), are up-to-date scholarly discussions of the Ionian natural philosophers. F. M. Cornford, *Plato's Cosmology* (London, 1937), is the most convenient existing version of the *Timaeus*, in which Plato's views about matter are expounded. J. H. Randall, Jr., *Aristotle* (New York, 1960), provides an illuminating account of that philosophers's scientific ideas; it is useful for the nonspecialist.

LATER CLASSICAL AND MEDIEVAL PERIOD

S. Sambursky's *The Physics of the Stoics* (London, 1959) and *The Physical World of Late Antiquity* (London, 1962) complete the story begun in his *Physical World of the Greeks* (see above). Cyril Bailey, *The Greek Atomists and Epicurus* (Oxford, 1928), and A. J. Hopkins, *Alchemy, Child of Greek Philosophy* (New York, 1934), are scholarly but readable; both books remain stimulating and full of interest. E. J. Holmyard, *Alchemy* (London, 1957), and A. C. Crombie, *Medieval and Early Modern Science* (New York, 1959), are readable popular surveys.

NEW THEORIES: 1550–1750

H. T. Pledge, *Science Since 1500* (London, 1939; reprinted, New York, 1959), and A. R. Hall, *From Galileo to Newton* (London, 1963), are general histories, both of which include useful material on the new theories. Mary B. Hesse, *Forces and Fields* (Edinburgh, 1961); Marie Boas, *Robert Boyle and Seventeenth Century Chemistry* (Cambridge, 1958); Hélène Metzger, *Les Doctrines chimiques* (Paris, 1923) and *Newton, Stahl, Boerhaave* (Paris, 1930); I. Bernard Cohen, *Franklin and Newton* (Philadelphia, 1956); and E. J. Dijksterhuis, *The Mechanization of the World Picture*, translated by C. Dikshoorn (Oxford, 1961), are scholarly books dealing in a penetrating way with more detailed aspects of the subject.

CLASSICAL PHYSICS

Edmund Whittaker, *History of the Theories of Aether and Electricity*, 2 vols. (Edinburgh, 1951–1953), and Mary B. Hesse, *Forces and Fields* (see above), are the best specialist surveys. For the general reader Charles C. Gillispie, *The Edge of Objectivity* (Princeton, N.J., 1960), N. R. Campbell, *What Is Science?* (London, 1921; reprinted, New York, 1952), Albert Einstein and Leopold Infeld, *The Evolution of Physics* (Cambridge, 1938), and George Gamow, *Biography of Physics* (New York, 1963), may be selected from many others as being particularly useful.

TWENTIETH-CENTURY RECONSIDERATIONS

A great many books of general interest have been published about the twentieth-century transformation in physical theory. Apart from Einstein and Infeld, *op. cit.*, and Gamow, *op. cit.*, one of especial merit is Banesh Hoffmann, *The Strange Story of the Quantum* (New York, 1947). Many of the physicists directly involved have written interestingly about the changes—notably, Werner Heisenberg, *Philosophical Problems of Nuclear Science* (London, 1952). The analogy between Stoic matter theory and wave mechanics is pursued in Sambursky, *The Physics of the Stoics* (see above).

STEPHEN E. TOULMIN

MATTER AND PROBLEMS OF PERCEPTION. See APPEARANCE AND REALITY; ILLUSIONS; PERCEPTION; PHENOMENALISM; PRIMARY AND SECONDARY QUALITIES; REALISM; SENSA.

MATTHEW OF ACQUASPARTA (c. 1237–1302), Italian Franciscan scholastic philosopher and theologian, was born in Acquasparta, near Todi in Umbria, possibly of the illustrious Bentivenghi family. In 1254 he entered the Franciscan order, and about 1268 he began studies at the University of Paris, where he was profoundly influenced by Bonaventure's system. Matthew was lector in the Studium Generale at Bologna (at least for the year 1273/1274), and in 1276 he became master in theology at Paris. From 1279 to 1287, he was lector Sacri Palatii in Rome, succeeding John Peckham. He was general of the order from 1287 to 1289. In 1288 he was made cardinal, and in 1291 he was named bishop of Porto and Santa Rufina. Matthew died at Rome, where he is buried in the church of Ara Coeli.

Doctrine. Matthew taught and wrote during the time of conflict between the Augustinian–Franciscan doctrinal tradition and the rising Thomistic Aristotelianism. In this far-reaching controversy he proved himself to be exceptionally well-versed in Augustine's doctrines and in general a faithful follower of Bonaventure. Although he incorporated a few Aristotelian elements, Matthew's system in its entirety shows that he was among the purest adherents of Augustinianism in the last quarter of the thirteenth century. He had a calm, balanced mind, a sober style, and an exact manner of formulating his ideas. In discussion he was generally modest and perceptive. With these qualities he often achieved, at least in his *Quaestiones Disputatae de Fide et de Cognitione*, a level comparable to that of the greatest thinkers of his age.

In his theory of knowledge Matthew taught that our intellect knows the individual object not only by reflection, as St. Thomas held, but also by a direct perception, which precedes the formation of an abstract idea. By virtue of this perception, the intellect forms a *species singularis* of the concrete object with all the richness of detail it possesses in reality. In this way the mind prepares for knowledge of the essence of the object. Similarly, the soul knows its own existence and habits not only by reasoning and by reflection but also by a direct and intimate intuition. In *Quaestiones Disputatae de Cognitione*, Matthew presented a personal solution to the controversial question of the activity of the knowing subject. Rejecting the impressionism of Bonaventure and Thomas Aquinas, the innatism of Thomas of York and Roger Bacon, and the pure activism of William of Auvergne and John Peckham, Matthew defended a semiactivism, not an occasionalism. Whereas according to pure activism the *species intentionalis* is completely (matter and form) caused by the knowing subject, according to Matthew the matter comes from the object, the form from the subject. This opinion, however, was soon contested by Roger Marston as contradicting both Aristotle and Augustine. Matthew defended the theory of divine illumination almost in the same manner as did Bonaventure. The purely human faculties for knowing the extramental world do not give us either clear understanding or certainty. We need the aid of the divine *rationes aeternae* (divine ideas) to illuminate our mind during the process of knowledge. God is not simply the creator of human intelligence; he also conserves it and concurs in each of its actions. This collaboration of God by means of the divine illumination is possible because man in his mind bears a special likeness to his creator. Our intellect is illumed by the divine light that contains the eternal ideas and is the ground of all created beings. The divine light is not the object itself of our knowledge but the moving principle that leads us to the true knowledge of the created world. Following the Augustinian doctrine, Matthew believed that the object of knowledge never determines the election of the will.

Among Matthew's other philosophical theses, the following are worthy of mention. Matthew, like Bonaventure, rejected the possibility of a creation from eternity; the spiritual beings (souls and angels) are necessarily composed of matter and form, because if they were composed simply of essence and existence (as Aquinas taught), this would not account for their contingency. Also, the process of coming to existence must be explained by the Augustinian theory of the *rationes seminales*. The "being body" (*esse corporale*) constitutes a plurality of forms. The two elements of the beings, matter and form, are together the cause of individuality. Matthew upheld the Ontological Proof of the existence of God; he also argued that the knowledge of God that we attain through faith is compatible with scientific knowledge. Matthew was particularly interested in problems concerning the relations between the natural order and the supernatural order.

Importance. Matthew is undoubtedly to be ranked among the great scholastic thinkers. His importance, however, lies not so much in the originality of his thought as in the fact that he is, after Bonaventure, the ideal representative of Augustinianism. The only philosophers that are known to have been directly influenced by him are Roger Marston and Vitalis of Furno.

Bibliography

PRIMARY SOURCES

Matthew's most important philosophical works are *Introitus ad S. Scripturam* (1268–1269), in *Bibliotheca Franciscana Scholastica Medii Aevi*, Vol. I (Quaracchi, 1903; 2d ed., 1957), pp. 3–21; *Introitus ad S. Theologiam* (probably 1271–1272), *ibid.*, pp. 22–33; *Commentarius in I, II, et III Sententiarum* (1271–1272), unedited manuscript at Quaracchi; *Quaestiones Disputatae* (1267–1287), which is almost complete in *Bibliotheca Franciscana Scholastica Medii Aevi*, Vols. I–II, XI, XVII–XVIII (Quaracchi, 1903–1961); *Quaestiones de Anima VI*, in A.-J. Gondras, ed., *Archives d'histoire doctrinale et littéraire du moyen âge*, Vol. XXIV (Pariš, 1958), pp. 203–352; *Quaestiones Disputatae de Anima XIII*, A.-J. Gondras, ed., *Études de philosophie médiévale*, Vol. 50 (1961); VI Quodlibeta, about ninety questions (1276–1279), unedited manuscript at Quaracchi; *Concordantiae Super IV Libros Sententiarum*, unedited manuscript at Quaracchi.

SECONDARY SOURCES

Beha, H. M., "Matthew of Acquasparta's Theory of Cognition." *Franciscan Studies*, Vol. 20 (1960), 161–204; Vol. 21 (1961), 1–79, 383–465.

Bettoni, E., "Rapporti dottrinali fra M. d'Acquasparta e G. Duns Scoto." *Studi francescani*, Vol. 15 (1943), 113–130.

Bonafede, G., "Il problema del 'lumen' nel pensiero di Frate M. d'Acquasparta." *Rivista rosminiana*, Vol. 31 (1937), 186–200.

Doucet, V., *Matthaei ab Aquasparta, Quaestiones Disputatae de Gratia*. Quaracchi, 1935. See pp. 11*–163* for a general introduction.

Pacchierini, L., *La dottrina gnoselogica di M. d'Acquasparta*. Naples, 1949.

Pegis, A.-C., "Matthew of Aquasparta and the Cognition of Non-being," in *Scholastica Ratione Historico-critica Instauranda*. Rome, 1951. Pp. 463–480.

Simoncioli, F., "Il concetto di legge in M. d'Acquasparta." *Studi francescani*, Vol. 56 (1959), 37–50.

A. EMMEN, O.F.M.

MAUPERTUIS, PIERRE-LOUIS MOREAU DE

(1698–1759), French scientist and philosopher, was born in Saint-Malo, Brittany. Elected in 1723 to the Académie des Sciences (and to the Royal Society in 1728), he first became known for his work in geometry. The expedition which he led to Lapland in 1736 to measure a degree of meridian near the pole helped finally to prove that the earth was an oblate spheroid. With his early introduction of Newtonian theories into France, Maupertuis became a leading exponent among the *philosophes* of the ideal of experimentalism as opposed to the overly deductive method in science associated with the Cartesian tradition. In 1744 Frederick II of Prussia asked him to reorganize the Berlin Academy of Sciences and later appointed him as its president (1746–1759). The remainder of his career was intimately linked to the activities of this group, and the growth of the academy into an important center of research owed much to his efforts.

Principle of least action. Maupertuis's famous principle of least action, which contributed signally to the systematization of mechanics, was formulated in "Recherche des loix du mouvement" (1746) as follows: "Whenever any change occurs in nature, the quantity of action employed for this is always the smallest possible"—the "quantity of action" being proportional to the product of the mass of a body and its velocity and the distance traversed. Among the heated controversies provoked by this notion, Samuel Koenig's unfair (although understandable) attribution of it to Leibniz brought about a scandalous quarrel and lifelong enmity between Maupertuis and Voltaire. But all this proved irrelevant to the historic value of the principle of least action, which, clarified progressively by the applications it found in the works of Euler, Lagrange, Hamilton, Helmholtz, and others, emerged ultimately as a basic concept in the mathematical analysis of dynamic systems.

Cosmological Argument. In the *Essai de cosmologie* (1750), Maupertuis's extension of the principle of least action to the much debated problems of theodicy offered a compromise solution between the radical antifinalism of contemporary materialists and the naive finalism of those who saw God's wisdom in every manifestation of design in nature, however trivial or self-contradictory. By claiming that an actual mathematical equation showed God's regulation of nature through the parsimony of kinetic means employed in the production of all physical events, Maupertuis succeeded in giving an original and seemingly scientific version of the Cosmological Argument. But his assumption that there is logical necessity as such in the existence of mechanical laws, which was consistent with the example of Descartes and Leibniz, typified a rationalist attitude which, though prevalent at the time, was already undermined by those who, like Hume, alleged a merely empirical necessity for physical causation. Although Maupertuis's distrust of metaphysical reasoning led him to present his cosmological argument not as demonstrably certain, but only as the best that man's imperfect intellect was capable of, it remained perhaps less plausible than ingenious, particularly since it was affirmed without sufficient regard either to the epistemological difficulties it incurred or to the possible nontheological interpretations of its underlying minimal concept. Coming late in a current of thought that was to yield before long to new orientations in philosophy, the *Essai de cosmologie* had a limited historical impact. It was, in fact, in a form essentially free of teleological meanings that the principle of least action exercised its considerable influence on the development of physicomathematical science.

Biology: the structure of matter. A different science, biology, inspired Maupertuis's next major work (1751), the *Dissertatio Inauguralis Metaphysica de Universali Naturae Systemate* (known also as the *Système de la nature*). Study of the problem of heredity had led Maupertuis to reject, in the *Vénus physique* (1745), the then reigning doctrine of preformation and to favor instead a theory of epigenesis utilizing the law of attraction. But he had subsequently found this theory inadequate and had despaired altogether of accounting mechanistically for the origins and nature of life. In the *Dissertatio Inauguralis*, therefore, he sought to explain the formation of living things by supposing that all the elementary particles of matter are individually endowed in a proportionately elementary degree with "desire, aversion, and memory," by virtue of which they combine to form organic entities. Such a notion, no less than that of least action, betrays a marked Leibnizian background in Maupertuis's thinking, despite his outspoken criticism of the metaphysics of Leibniz. It is true, nevertheless, that Maupertuis did not assign the metaphysical status of the monads to his "percipient particles" but, rather, presented them as part of a general biological hypothesis; he accounted for the elemental coexistence of physical and psychic properties in nature by reference to a common unknowable substance. Thus, the philosophical basis of his biological theorizing may be described as either an "atomistic dualism" or a "corpuscular psychism," sustained by a phenomenological accord between matter and its presumed psychic qualities. These ideas were misinterpreted in materialistic terms by Diderot and contributed indirectly to the eventual success of naturalism in biology. Since Maupertuis's metabiological conception was also intended to explain the structural transformations of the various species by a process of genetic mutation, it merged, in that respect too, with an important current of evolutionist speculation that grew in France after about 1750.

Epistemology. The views of Maupertuis in epistemology can be judged from a number of his writings. While, like Condillac and most of the *philosophes*, he agreed with

Locke that sensation is the source of all our knowledge, his position was appreciably more sophisticated, probably because of his encounter with the Berkeleian critique. If this critique did not quite win him over to subjectivism, he at least became convinced that experience offers no more than the disjointed fragments of a merely phenomenal reality and that the substance presumed to excite in the mind the perceptions that in turn are projected cognitively toward the natural world remains itself beyond objective determination. Maupertuis ascribed even the evidence of mathematics not to any intrinsic veracity of such knowledge but to the fact that it is based on the repetition (*réplicabilité*) of certain simple ideas which consist of identical units and are abstracted from the heterogeneous totality of sensory impressions. In the same spirit, his *Réflexions philosophiques sur l'origine des langues et la signification des mots* (1748) raises the equally crucial question of the linguistic prefigurations of sense experience, from which scientific reasoning is unable completely to escape.

Ethics. Maupertuis's principal excursion into ethics, *Essai de philosophie morale* (1749), tried somewhat overambitiously to reconcile the Stoic, Epicurean, and Christian schools but succeeded only in reaching an eclectic view characterized by the author's own pessimism concerning the chances of human felicity. It offered, however, an early instance of the application of arithmetic to the problem of happiness by its attempt to express, in the analogy of statics, the equations of a "hedonistic calculus."

Importance. Generally, the thought of Maupertuis pursued the aim, shared by many of his contemporaries, of linking philosophy more concretely than in the past with the content of the particular sciences. Instead of presenting an over-all logical coherence, his work contributes various philosophical essays reflecting the different points of departure dictated by his primarily scientific interests. The cosmological thesis, speculative biology, and moral opinions of Maupertuis remained largely separate from each other; moreover, Maupertuis himself was often in the curious but historically symptomatic predicament of searching earnestly for metaphysical solutions while disbelieving in their possibility. Having elaborated the principle of least action and the notion of percipient particles of matter in a rather ambiguous zone between metaphysics proper and scientific theory, it is not surprising that he should have suffered much unmerited neglect from historians both of philosophy and of science. But it is now recognized that Maupertuis had a significant, even if secondary, role in the maturing of modern physics and biology alike, as well as in the transition of philosophical thinking from classical metaphysics to the critical position adopted by Kant.

Works by Maupertuis

Oeuvres, 4 vols. Lyons, 1756.
Lettres. 1752. Place of publication unknown.
Examen philosophique de la preuve de l'existence de Dieu, in *Memoirs of the Berlin Academy of Sciences*. 1756.

Works on Maupertuis

Abelé, Jean, "Introduction à la notion d'action et au principe de l'action stationnaire." *Revue des questions scientifiques*, Vol. 119 (1948), 25–42.

Bachelard, Suzanne, *Les polémiques concernant le principe de moindre action au XVIIIᵉ siècle*. Paris, 1961.

Brunet, Pierre, *Maupertuis, étude biographique* and *Maupertuis: l'oeuvre et sa place dans la pensée scientifique et philosophique de XVIIIᵉ siècle*, 2 vols. Paris, 1929. An authoritative study of Maupertuis's life and thought.

Brunet, Pierre, *Étude historique sur le principe de la moindre action*. Paris, 1938.

Crombie, A. C., "Maupertuis, précurseur du transformisme." *Revue de synthèse*, Vol. 78 (1957), 35–56.

Gossman, L., "Berkeley, Hume and Maupertuis." *French Studies*, Vol. 14 (1960), 304–324.

Guéroult, Martial, "Note sur le principe de la moindre action chez Maupertuis," in *Dynamique et métaphysique leibniziennes*. Strasbourg, 1934. Pp. 215–235.

Ostoya, Paul, "Maupertuis et la biologie." *Revue d'histoire des sciences*, Vol. 7 (1954), 60–78.

ARAM VARTANIAN

MAUTHNER, FRITZ (1849–1923), poet, novelist, literary critic, and philosopher, was born in Hořice, Bohemia, of German-speaking Jewish parents. He received his early education at the Kleinseitner Gymnasium in Prague. From 1869 to 1873 he attended the university there, where he studied law; however, he left the university without qualifying and never took any degree. Mauthner's earliest ambition was to become a poet, and his first published work was a book of poems, published at his own expense. He left Prague in 1876 for Berlin, where he lived until 1905, employed for most of this period by the newspaper *Berliner Tageblatt* as a theater critic. During this time he achieved a certain literary fame through his novels and especially through his parodies of German classical poems, of which the volume *Nach Berühmten Mustern* proved the most successful. However, Mauthner's main concern was his philosophical critique of language, an interest aroused earlier by Otto Ludwig's *Shakespeare-Studien*, Nietzsche's *Vom Nutzen und Nachteil der Historie für das Leben*, Ernst Mach's popular lectures, and by the example of Bismarck, who so successfully combined his contempt for words, theories, and ideologies with great success in the field of action. Mauthner completed his first major book, *Beiträge zu einer Kritik der Sprache* ("Contributions Toward a Critique of Language"), in 1902.

Mauthner lived in Freiburg from 1905 until 1907, when he settled for the remainder of his life in Meersburg, in the famed Glaserhäusle that was once the home of the early nineteenth-century poetess Annette von Droste-Hülshoff. During this period he devoted himself entirely to philosophy and wrote two major philosophical works. His *Wörterbuch der Philosophie* sought to clarify some central concepts in philosophy from the point of view of his critique of language and thus is to be regarded as a completion of the *Beiträge*. He also completed the four volumes of *Der Atheismus und seine Geschichte im Abendlande* ("Atheism and Its History in the West"). This work is essentially a history of the rejection of the God of Christianity, and its philosophical significance lies largely in its method. Mauthner's analysis of religious language in this work was one of the first attempts to use linguistic analysis as a tool of intellectual historiography. Mauthner always stood outside of academic life and therefore remained philosophically a rather lonely figure throughout his lifetime.

Although Ernst Mach and Hans Vaihinger appreciated his work, he had no following. His few friends came from among the radical intellectuals of his time, such as Gustav Landauer.

Mauthner's problem. Mauthner was probably the first philosopher to devote his full attention to ordinary language and to the philosophical problems raised by it. His work belongs to the mainstream of traditional nominalism, skepticism, and empiricism. He regarded himself as the thinker who consummated this tradition. He was scornful of the philosophy of the schools, which were the abodes of what he liked to call "word superstition." The delusion of "word-superstition" consists in believing that reality can be known through language, and it is equivalent to the belief that all words refer to some entity and that therefore from the existence of a word the existence of the corresponding entity can be inferred. Mauthner's problem was whether language is a suitable tool for gaining knowledge about the world. His negative answer involved a detailed examination of ordinary language, of its relation to the structure of artificial languages and the calculi used in various specialized disciplines, and of the psychological origins of language in general.

Ordinary language. Mauthner's point of departure was the view that our senses are accidental (*Zufallssinne*), and that therefore we notice only those qualities in the world that our senses can register. The words we possess in our language are designed to single out those qualities that are accessible to us. Moreover, as everyone is acquainted only with his own sense impressions, there is always a certain lack of correspondence between the impression and the public word that is used to describe it. It follows that we are able to describe correctly neither the outside world nor our own experiences. Artificial languages and calculi, if they are meaningful, originate in certain sense experiences and are consequently reducible to ordinary language. Ordinary language, the only language we have, is a tool designed to facilitate activity but not the communication of true information.

Language is essentially social; it is like a rule in a game (*Spielregel*) and gains increasing validity as more speakers submit to it. Language is identical with its use. The social character of language has certain tendencies inherent in it, of which the most important, and epistemologically most disastrous, is the speakers' desire to create a substantive world. Mauthner held that our original world is adjectival, but that because we notice only qualities, the social nature of language forces us to invent substances and to refer to these by substantives. The most important task of a critique of language is to show that what we regard as a substance, as a thing existing in itself, is nothing but a word invented for our convenience. Strictly speaking, there are no referring words at all. All referring is at most tentative, suggestive—possibly a hint, but never precise.

Speech is one of the natural functions of man. It has pragmatic but not epistemic value. Language is excellent as an instrument of poetry or as a medium for the expression of religious feeling, because in these pursuits the question of truth or falsity does not arise.

Epistemology. Mauthner's epistemological skepticism follows from his identification of knowledge with absolute certainty. Truth, in the sense of perfect correspondence, is an object of human desire that can never be satisfied. But why, within our language, do we habitually make a distinction between knowledge and ignorance on the one hand, and true and false statements on the other? Mauthner explained this by referring to the way in which language is actually used. The distinction between analytic and synthetic propositions lies not in some logical characteristic of the propositions themselves but in their role. A proposition is synthetic only if it expresses a new discovery or insight. If it expresses what is already known, it is analytic. Thus, all propositions that are known to be true are analytic; the predicate is already contained in the subject. Hence, all known true propositions are tautologies. The criterion of truth that enables us to recognize a proposition as true or false is not that of correspondence with reality, but that of agreement or disagreement with our prevailing mode of speaking.

Since Mauthner held that language is both social and individual—that is, it exists only *between* people in their communicating activities, although each man has his own version or variation of this common language—the test of truth is whether what the individual asserts is or is not the correct thing to assert within the culture whose language is being used. Thus, truth for Mauthner is nothing but the "common use of language" (*gemeine Sprachgebrauch*). This amounts to the adoption of a coherence theory of truth within the limits of ordinary language.

No empiricist before Mauthner had been so consistent in following the logic of his arguments from sensationalism to extreme linguistic conventionalism. He argued that traces of past sense experiences become conventionally associated with certain words that are used to refer to them. Thus, the very fact that just these and not other experiences have been singled out for naming by a culture determines, in a way, the kinds of things to which attention is paid in that culture. Moreover, those new discoveries that are generally accepted by speakers of the same language become part of their common fund of experience. Thus, a language always expresses a *Weltanschauung*, and what is true or false is necessarily decided by referring to the way language is used—that is, to the convention governing discourse on the topic in question.

Mauthner therefore held that whatever counted as true in the past was in fact true at some time; truth is historically relative. However, languages develop slowly, words shift their meanings, and the conventional association of a word with a certain kind of sense experience becomes dislocated. Languages develop through what Mauthner, in agreement with Vico, called "the growing pale of the metaphor." But the metaphorical character of language never disappears completely; it is continually reinforced through new sense impressions becoming associated with the old words. Ordinary language is, therefore, self-enclosing in two respects. It cannot give a true description of reality, because the criterion of truth within ordinary language is not correspondence but the actual use of language. Also, because every linguistic convention is an expression of a *Weltanschauung,* it cannot be used to assess the truth of another *Weltanschauung,* either of the past or of other cultures in the present. Accepting a linguistic convention

entails the rejection of any *Weltanschauung* that conflicts with it. For this reason, science, which is no more than a convention of discourse that is accepted at present, cannot correspond to reality, and thus it cannot be true.

Psychology. Mauthner's radical skepticism was also manifest in his view of psychology. He held that all inquiry into the nature of language is psychological in character because language is only a collective memory of innumerable sense experiences. All words originate in observation of the physical world. The inner world cannot be described, because all our words are designed for description of the outside world. Psychology proper is therefore impossible, and physiological psychology is "psychology without psyche." Mauthner held with Hume that the "self" cannot be found, that the term is only a man-made substantive that does not refer to anything real.

According to Mauthner's methodological principles, knowledge of the self is impossible. But only if psychology were to give us that knowledge could Mauthner recognize psychology as a science. His skeptical despair was the logical consequence of his putting his original demand in a traditional, and essentially unsatisfiable, way.

Logic. Mauthner rejected the idea that there is any connection between the structure of reality and the logic of discourse: the former is beyond the realm of possible knowledge, while the latter is no more than a series of linguistic conventions. Contradictions, as the word itself indicates, can occur only in discourse, not in reality. Formal logic is certain, but epistemically empty. Once formal logic is put to practical use it loses its certainty. If words are used with the intent of referring to things in the world, then the ambiguities and uncertainties that follow from the difference between the sense impressions of various individuals affect the meaning of the words used and, consequently, the "objective" truth of the conclusion. Even statements of identity, such as "cheese is cheese," if used in actual discourse, become more than mere substitution-instances of "$A = A$"; they acquire a point that can be contradicted with logical impunity. In all actual and purposeful discourse the point of view of the speaker is of decisive importance. Mathematical symbols are in no way connected with sense experience, and therefore mathematics is absolutely certain. It is also totally uninformative.

Mauthner's view of tautologies is not completely coherent. He classed as tautologies both the propositions of formal logic and mathematics and all other statements whose truth is known. Because he was not interested in the formal properties of propositions but rather in the question of whether they extend our knowledge or not, he labeled both kinds of propositions as tautologies on account of their noninformative character. The difference between tautologies in ordinary language and formal tautologies lies in the fact that the former can be pragmatically useful, while the latter cannot be. But once a formal tautology is used in actual discourse, it ceases to be different from a tautology in ordinary language.

Mauthner does not seem to have been acquainted with the work of Gottlob Frege and Bertrand Russell. He knew of Boole and Ernst Schröder, but he rejected their undertaking on the ground that improvement in the technicalities of logical symbolism would not affect the uninformative character of formal logic. He saw in the concomitant development of calculi of probability only a further retreat from the ideal of absolute certainty in matters of knowledge.

Religion and ethics. Religion, like science, is a *Weltanschauung*. The difference between them, from the point of view of knowledge and truth, is a matter of degree, not of kind. The religion of today is the science of yesterday. "Religion" is not the name of one thing, but rather encompasses cultural phenomena of a wide variety. What singles out some beliefs and attitudes in any given culture as religious is not their content but their pervasiveness and their great emotional appeal to the individual. Mauthner held that everyone is to some degree under the influence of some form of religion. His own *Der letzte Tod des Gautama Buddha* is a deeply religious book, even though its overt message is that religious truth cannot be articulated. While religion is, in a sense, inevitable, theology is not. Theology is a pseudo science that pretends to deal with entities that on analysis turn out to be substantives unsupported even by such kinds of sense experience as those that support the substantives of ordinary language. Theology, therefore, is the worst kind of word superstition, and it is the task of the critique of language to destroy it.

Mauthner held that morals is not a possible subject matter of knowledge. He rejected the Kantian position that what is morally right can be known through practical reason, and also the intuitionist claim that values can in some sense be known. He regarded values as the results of the substantivizing tendency of language. He distinguished between actual behavior, or custom (*Sitte*), and *Moral*, by which he meant ideals: "*Moral* is the custom we do not have." Mauthner was an ethical relativist, and his analysis of moral language was an attempt to show that moral terms function both as summaries of crystallized patterns of behavior in a given society and, through being used to recommend certain actions, as vehicles of change in standards of behavior. Terms of moral discourse do not refer to anything beyond themselves, but they possess great emotive appeal to the community of language users.

Critique of language. If by philosophy is meant an attempt to explore the nature and describe the structure of the world, philosophy is impossible. Our senses and our language defeat us at the outset. The only possible philosophical project is that of a critique of language. This "critical attention to language" is essentially a liberating and healing activity that reveals to us our delusions and their source in language. It does not increase our knowledge; it only helps us toward recognition of the fact that true knowledge is beyond our reach and that the quest for absolute certainty is merely an insatiable desire of the human spirit. The critique of language is not the solution of the "riddle of the Sphinx," but "it is at least the redeeming act which forces the Sphinx into silence." Mauthner conceived the critique of language as an activity, as a continual purging of language, not as a doctrine. He thought that the most he could accomplish in consistency with his linguistic conventionalism was to introduce a new convention of philosophical inquiry, to set up a new critical *Spielregel*. Mauthner envisaged a great cooperative enterprise in which scholars working in various fields would

attempt to purge their professional terminologies of traces of word superstition.

The highest degree of critical attitude is silence. The critique of language merely leads up to it, for the critique tries "to say the unsayable." Realizing that nothing really true can be said about the world as a whole does not mean that something really true cannot be felt. All that philosophers have endeavored and failed to say can become present in mystical silence. Mauthner declared himself an adherent of a "godless mysticism" (*gottlose Mystik*)—godless because, from the point of view of the critique of language, "God" is but another unwarranted substantive.

Mauthner's place in the history of philosophy. Mauthner belongs, like Alexander Bryan Johnson, to the lonely and forgotten precursors of later linguistic philosophers, but his lack of appreciation of the role of logic sets him apart from them as a radical, but not a logical, empiricist. Ludwig Wittgenstein, in the *Tractatus Logico-Philosophicus*, spoke, like Mauthner, of the proper task of philosophy as being a critique of language, but it is evident that for Wittgenstein, this was a very different task from what it was for Mauthner. Wittgenstein differed sharply from Mauthner in conceiving of the proposition as a picture of reality, and of the ordered system of propositions as corresponding to the structure of reality. Wittgenstein's later concern with ordinary language and his conception of it as a game played according to rules echoes Mauthner, but there remain many important differences in their outlooks. The true historical significance of Mauthner's work lies in the fact that his critique of language was probably the most completely worked out philosophy of language within the tradition of classical empiricism.

Works by Mauthner

Beiträge zu einer Kritik der Sprache, 3 vols. Stuttgart, 1901–1902; 2d ed., 1906–1912; 3d ed., Leipzig, 1923.
Die Sprache. Frankfurt, 1906.
Aristotle. Translated by D. Gordon. London, 1907.
Wörterbuch der Philosophie, 2 vols. Munich and Leipzig, 1910; 3 vols., 2d ed., Leipzig, 1923–1924.
Der letzte Tod des Gautama Buddha. Munich and Leipzig, 1913.
Erinnerungen. Munich, 1918.
Ausgewählte Schriften, 6 vols. Stuttgart, 1919.
Muttersprache und Vaterland. Leipzig, 1920.
Spinoza. Dresden, 1921.
Der Atheismus und seine Geschichte in Abendlande, 4 vols. Stuttgart and Berlin, 1921–1923.
"Fritz Mauthner," in Raymund Schmidt, ed., *Die Philosophie der Gegenwart in Selbstdarstellungen*, Leipzig, 1924. Vol. III. Pp. 123–146. Autobiography.
Die drei Bilder der Welt, M. Jacobs, ed. Erlangen, 1925.
Gottlose Mystik. Dresden, 1925.

Works on Mauthner

Eisen, Walter, *Fritz Mauthner: Kritik der Sprache*. Vienna, 1929.
Kappstein, Theodor, *Fritz Mauthner*. Berlin, 1926.
Krieg, Max, *Fritz Mauthners Kritik der Sprache*. Munich, 1914.
Kühtmann, Alfred, *Zur Geschichte des Terminismus*. Leipzig, 1911.
Landauer, Gustav, *Skepsis und Mystik*. Berlin, 1903.
Weiler, Gershon, "On Fritz Mauthner's Critique of Language." *Mind*, Vol. 67 (1958), 80–87.
Weiler, Gershon, "Fritz Mauthner—A Study in Jewish Self-

Rejection," in *Yearbook*, Leo Baeck Institute, Vol. 8 (1963), 136–148.

Weiler, Gershon, "Fritz Mauthner as an Historian," *History and Theory*, Vol. 4 (1964), 57–71.

Wein, Hermann, *Sprachphilosophie der Gegenwart*. The Hague, 1963. Ch. 4.

GERSHON WEILER

MAXWELL, JAMES CLERK (1831–1879), British physicist, came from a well-known Scottish family, the Clerks; his father adopted the name Maxwell on inheriting an estate originally belonging to that family. Maxwell was educated at Edinburgh University and the University of Cambridge, becoming a fellow of Trinity College in 1855. In 1856 he won the Adams prize at Cambridge for an essay in which he demonstrated that the rings of Saturn would be unstable if they were continuously solid or fluid and that they must be composed of discrete and separated parts. Maxwell was professor of natural philosophy at Marischal College in Aberdeen from 1856 to 1860 and professor of natural philosophy and astronomy at King's College in London from 1860 to 1865. His first paper on electromagnetism appeared in 1856; his electromagnetic field theory with the derivation of the velocity of light was first published in 1861–1862 and in more rigorous form in 1865; and he began work on the kinetic theory of gases in 1860. From 1865 to 1871 Maxwell remained at his country estate in Scotland where he worked on his *Treatise on Electricity and Magnetism,* which summarized the subject and his contributions thereto. In 1871 he became the first occupant of the Cavendish chair of experimental physics at Cambridge, supervised the construction of the Cavendish laboratory, and later guided the first research done there. During this period he edited the works of Henry Cavendish. During his lifetime Maxwell also did research on color vision, mechanics, and other topics, and although his fame rests on his theoretical achievements, his experimental work was noteworthy.

The electromagnetic field. Maxwell's greatest contribution to fundamental physics was his concept of the electromagnetic field, a concept that underwent much modification both in the course of his own researches and at the hands of his successors. In modern terms, a field—such as the electric field—is a condition in the space surrounding charged bodies that determines the force that a unit electric charge would experience if it were placed at any point. In field theory all actions are regarded as transmitted from point to point by the contiguous modification of the field between the points, and the field is regarded as the seat of energy. Contemporary physics is dominated by the field-theoretic viewpoint, whether or not it is reinterpreted in terms of quantum theory.

Maxwell aimed at embodying in mathematical notation the ideas of Michael Faraday and, in particular, Faraday's fruitful concept of lines of force. In this Maxwell was inspired by the work of William Thomson (later Lord Kelvin), who had demonstrated the mathematical analogy between the problems of heat flow and of the distribution of static electricity. Maxwell developed similar analogies in his first paper on the subject, "On Faraday's Lines of Force" (1855–1856), drawing separate analogies for different aspects of electromagnetism: between electrical and fluid currents, and between electric or magnetic lines of force and fluid currents. While suggestive, such an endeavor was of course not a unified theory. "I do not think," he wrote, "that we have any right at present to understand the action of electricity, and I hold that the chief merit of a temporary theory is, that it shall guide experiment, without impeding the progress of the true theory when it appears." The beginning of the paper is of interest as a statement of method; Maxwell points out the pitfalls of commitment to a mathematical formula, in which case "we entirely lose sight of the phenomena to be explained," or to a physical hypothesis, the irrelevant parts of which are liable to carry one beyond the truth. He advocates instead the use of physical analogy, "that partial similarity between the laws of one science and those of another which makes each of them illustrate the other."

In his "On Physical Lines of Force" (1861–1862), Maxwell's electromagnetic field theory appears for the first time, presented as a deduction from a detailed model of the ether. Magnetic lines of force are represented as molecular (microscopic) vortices in this ether, the matter of the ether whirling around in planes normal to the direction of the lines of force, so that the latter is the direction of the axes of the vortices. Maxwell found that in this fashion he could represent the properties of lines of force needed for magnetostatics, that is, that the lines should tend to contract along their length and repel each other laterally. But how can neighboring vortices spin in the same sense, since their neighboring boundaries move in opposite directions, and how are these motions initiated and communicated through the ether? Maxwell assumed a layer of tiny idle wheels between each pair of vortex cells in the ethereal substance. These wheels can rotate freely, so that a uniform magnetic field is represented by the vortex cells all spinning at the same rate and in the same sense, and the interspersed wheels rotating in place in the opposite sense. The idle wheels can also move from place to place in a conductor, but they are constrained to rolling contact without slipping with the neighboring vortices. The translatory motion of the wheels is identified with the electric current and used to explain the manner in which a magnetic field is created by an electric current (Hans Christian Oersted's discovery); it also is used to account for electromagnetic induction. Furthermore, in a dielectric, including the vacuum, the wheels are not free to move in translation, but can only be displaced slightly against the elastic forces of the material of the cells. This action of displacement is the displacement current that forms the new term Maxwell added to previous results, while transforming all of them into his theoretical language. Maxwell then proceeded to calculate the velocity of propagation of transverse waves in his elastic ether. The speed of these waves was proportional to the ratio between the electromagnetic and electrostatic units of charge.

The factor of proportionality between the speed of the waves and the ratio of the units depended in this calculation on the specific model chosen for the ether; the argument showing the two terms to be equal cannot be regarded as very satisfactory. In "A Dynamical Model of the Electromagnetic Field" (1865), the electromagnetic field equations are presented directly without recourse to the ether model, and the relation between velocity of waves and ratio of electrical units is derived directly from the equations. Since, according to Wilhelm Weber and Friedrich Kohlrausch (1857), the ratio between the units was 3.11×10^8 meters/sec., whereas, according to Armand Fizeau, the speed of light was 3.15×10^8 meters/sec., Maxwell drew the important conclusion that light consisted of waves in the electromagnetic ether. This finally gained general acceptance when Heinrich Hertz generated electromagnetic waves by electrical means and showed that they had all the properties of light except that they were of much lower frequency, a result of the conditions of generation.

In his later papers Maxwell no longer relied on specific models of the ether. In the *Treatise* he wrote:

The attempt which I then [in "On Physical Lines of Force"] made to imagine a working model of this mechanism must be taken for no more than it really is, a demonstration that mechanism may be imagined capable of producing a connexion mechanically equivalent to the actual connexion of the parts of the electromagnetic field. The problem of determining the mechanism required to establish a given species of connexion between the motions of the parts of a system always admits of an infinite number of solutions.

Nevertheless, he still regarded the underlying phenomena as motions and stresses in the mechanical ether, maintaining that the energy of magnetism "exists in the form of some kind of motion of the matter in every portion of space," apparently of a vortical character. Maxwell's views differ from those of the twentieth century in the following ways: the electromagnetic field was not regarded as a separate dynamic entity from matter, that is, a material ether; ordinary matter was treated macroscopically, phenomenologically, rather than from the atomic point of view; and the role of charge in the theory was ambiguous. Late in the nineteenth century H. A. Lorentz combined Maxwell's field theory with Continental conceptions of atomicity of charge to establish the classical theory of the dualism of matter and field.

Kinetic theory of gases. Also of fundamental importance was Maxwell's work on the kinetic theory of gases. In deriving the experimental gas laws, previous investigators had made the simplified assumption that all the gas molecules moved with the same speed. In "Illustrations of the Dynamical Theory of Gases" (1860), Maxwell first derived the equilibrium distribution of the velocities of the molecules: the components of the velocity along a given direction are distributed according to Gauss's error law. This paper also contained the startling result, later demonstrated experimentally, that the viscosity (internal friction) of a gas should be independent of its density. Maxwell wrote two other pathfinding papers on the kinetic theory; their main subject was the derivation of the transport coefficients of a gas (coefficients of diffusion, viscosity, and thermal conductivity) and, in the last of them, the discussion of radiometric phenomena.

Maxwell's work on the kinetic theory may be regarded as constituting the first important introduction of statistical reasoning into physics and the first steps in the development of statistical mechanics, later continued by Ludwig Boltzmann and Josiah Gibbs. In statistical mechanics the use of statistics is not a manifestation of any indeterminism in the purported fundamental laws of nature, as it is in quantum physics; rather it is the reflection of our ignorance of the exact motions of the enormous number of molecules in any macroscopic system. The very enormity of this number (there are about 6×10^{23} hydrogen atoms in one gram of hydrogen) and the minuteness of the individual molecules give assurance that in ordinary experiments the measurable properties will be statistical in character and thus will be exactly the properties singled out by a statistical theory.

Maxwell's demon, a hypothetical being that apparently could reverse the tendency of isolated systems toward increase of disorder or entropy and so would violate the second law of thermodynamics, appears in his *Theory of Heat* (London, 1872, pp. 308–309). The thermal equilibration of neighboring vessels containing gas, representing a state of maximum disorder, could be destroyed by a being capable of seeing the individual molecules of the gas who acts so as to let only the faster molecules in one container pass through a small hole into the other, and the slower ones in the latter to pass in the reverse sense. Since the temperature is determined by the mean energy of motion of the molecules, this process would result in the gas in one vessel becoming warmer than that in the other, without any interference from outside the system. The demon has been exorcised by L. Brillouin and others (see Brillouin's *Science and Information Theory*, New York, 1956, Ch. 13). To obtain the information about an approaching molecule that the demon needs in order to decide whether or not to open the hole, the demon must absorb at least one quantum of light, the energy of which is reasonably greater than the mean energy of the quanta of thermal radiation that are always present. The absorption of this quantum demonstrably leads to a greater increase in entropy in the total system (including the demon) than the decrease obtained by properly manipulating the hole.

Bibliography

The *Scientific Papers of James Clerk Maxwell*, including his semipopular lectures but not the *Treatise* and other books, appear in two volumes edited by W. D. Niven (Cambridge, 1890). See in particular his Bradford address, "Molecules," Vol. II, pp. 361–377, in which he expresses most lucidly his religious and metaphysical position. The *Treatise on Electricity and Magnetism*, 3d ed., edited by J. J. Thomas, was published in 1892 at Oxford. The standard biography is Lewis Campbell and William Garnett, *The Life of James Clerk Maxwell* (London, 1882).

ARTHUR E. WOODRUFF

MAYA. See INDIAN PHILOSOPHY.

McCOSH, JAMES (1811–1894), an influential representative of "common-sense realism," was born in southern Ayrshire, Scotland. He was educated at Glasgow and Edinburgh universities. McCosh was licensed for the ministry in 1834 and served as a pastor of the Established Church of Scotland until 1850, when he was appointed professor of logic and metaphysics at Queen's College of Belfast. In 1868 he came to America to serve as president of the College of New Jersey (now Princeton University), a position he held until 1888.

McCosh's philosophical outlook was in its largest features inherited from the "Scottish school" of Reid, Stewart, and others. On one side this meant the denial that our beliefs about the external world rest on any dubious inferences, causal or otherwise, from immediately presented ideas. Those beliefs are rather the natural, noninferential accompaniments of sensation, and their general reliability cannot sensibly be questioned. On another (and for McCosh, more important) side, common-sense philosophy meant apriorism. In *The Intuitions of the Mind, Inductively Investigated* (London and New York, 1860), McCosh undertook to enumerate certain fundamental principles (such as principles of causation and moral good) which belong to the constitution of the mind. Although persons are not necessarily or normally aware of these very general truths, their particular cognitions and judgments are regulated by them. In saying that these principles are to be discovered "inductively" McCosh did not mean that they are inductive generalizations. Certainly one is led to these principles by reflection on experience. But once before the mind, the principles are recognized as self-evidently and necessarily true. McCosh's realism, unlike that of H. L. Mansel and William Hamilton, was relatively free of the influence of Kant. Thus, in *An Examination of Mr. J. S. Mill's Philosophy* (London and New York, 1866), McCosh defended Hamilton's intuitional philosophy against Mill's criticism but took care to disassociate himself from the former's "agnostic" view that man's knowledge is limited to the finite.

The most original aspect of McCosh's philosophy was his effort to accommodate evolution and Christian theism. In one of his earliest works, *The Method of the Divine Government, Physical and Moral* (Edinburgh, 1850), he opposed the view that God's design exhibits itself entirely in the lawful development of nature. Such a view, he thought, amounted to a denial of divine providence. Divine government proceeds instead by a combination of law and particular, spontaneous interventions. When *The Origin of Species* appeared (1859), McCosh found it natural to identify his "special providences" with Darwin's "chance variations." In *Christianity and Positivism* (New York and London, 1871) he argued that evolution, properly understood, is not only compatible with a divine design but in fact magnifies the Designer. Unlike Darwin, McCosh found nothing abhorrent in the notion that God employs the struggle for survival as a technique of creation. He was confident that success in that struggle was a matter of moral rather than physical strength.

McCosh's writings enjoyed considerable popularity, particularly among the evangelical clergy who found in them a way of dealing with the difficulties raised by science and science-inspired philosophies.

Bibliography

Apart from those already mentioned, McCosh's chief works are *The Supernatural in Relation to the Natural* (Cambridge, 1862); *The Scottish Philosophy, Biographical, Expository, Critical, from Hutcheson to Hamilton* (London, 1874); and *First and Fundamental Truths, Being a Treatise on Metaphysics* (New York and London, 1889). An extensive bibliography by Joseph H. Dulles is appended to the autobiographical *The Life of James McCosh,* edited by William Milligan Sloane (New York, 1896).

DOUGLAS ARNER

McDOUGALL, WILLIAM (1871–1938), British-American proponent of hormic psychology, was born in Chadderton, England, the second son of a chemical manufacturer. He was educated at schools in England and Germany, and at Manchester and Cambridge universities, where he received first-class honors in biology. In 1897 he qualified in medicine at St. Thomas's Hospital, London. While working there with Charles Scott Sherrington, he read William James's *Principles of Psychology,* and returned to Cambridge to study psychology on a fellowship from St. John's College. He joined the Cambridge Anthropological Expedition (1899) to Torres Straits, collaborating with W. H. R. Rivers in sensory researches and with Charles Hose in anthropological studies, which resulted in *The Pagan Tribes of Borneo* (London, 1912). He worked at Göttingen with G. E. Müller and subsequently joined the psychology department of University College, London, under James Sully, where he published researches supporting Thomas Young's theory of color vision against those of H. L. F. von Helmholtz and Ewald Hering (*Mind,* Vol. 10, 1901, 52–97, 210–245, 347–382). In London, and in Oxford from 1904 as Wilde reader in mental philosophy, McDougall worked on reflexes, inhibition, and psychophysical relationships. In *Physiological Psychology* (London, 1905) he combined William James's view of instinctive action and emotion as objective and subjective aspects of the excitement of inherited perceptual dispositions, with Sherrington's theory of the nervous system as integrator of reflex and instinctive–impulsive actions. McDougall explained subjectivity and purposiveness through R. H. Lotze's "psychoneural parallelism," postulating psychic currents induced in etherlike soul-stuff by neural activity.

McDougall first outlined his hormic psychology in *An Introduction to Social Psychology* (London, 1908). He derived human behavior from instincts, which are innate psychophysical dispositions with specific cognitive, affective, and conative aspects (for example, perception of danger, fear, flight). In adult humans, instincts operate indirectly through socially acquired patterns, the sentiments, in which object(s) and instinct(s) have become enduringly associated. Sentiments increasingly remote from innate instincts are exemplified, for instance, by parental love, family feeling, patriotism. In the growth of character the developing sentiments become hierarchically ranged round a master sentiment (or ruling passion) whose nucleus in a stable character is the self-regarding sentiment.

In *Body and Mind* (London, 1911), subtitled *A History and Defense of Animism,* McDougall reviewed psychophysical theories. To explain heredity and evolution, memory and learning, the "body-memory" of growth and repair, and parapsychological evidences of personal survival, he now discarded Lotzean parallelism, and declared himself, unfashionably, a dualist, interactionist, vitalist, animist, and Lamarckian.

In World War I McDougall enlisted as a French army ambulance driver but was drafted into the Royal Army Medical Corps. His command of a British shell-shock unit provided the limited clinical material for his *Abnormal Psychology* (see below). In 1920 he became professor of psychology at Harvard, and in 1927 professor of psychology at Duke University. His American period was one of immense literary productivity. *The Group Mind* (New York, 1920) essayed to complete McDougall's social psychology by applying the hormic theory to "national mind and character." It was a work of subjective socio-political criticism rather than of objective scientific psychology, and resembled his many books of polemic and propaganda on national and international policy, from *Is America Safe for Democracy?* (New York, 1921) to *World Chaos* (London and New York, 1931). In these he advocated racial eugenics, a subsidized intellectual aristocracy, and a world air police, to defend the finest (explicitly North European–American) type of civilization.

In *An Outline of Psychology* (New York and London, 1923), *An Outline of Abnormal Psychology* (New York and London, 1926), and *Character and the Conduct of Life* (New York and London, 1927), McDougall elaborated his theory of personality built from sentiments that are powered by instincts, themselves channels of biological purposive energy (horme). The self-regarding sentiment governs conduct according to guidelines formed through identifications with admired persons or abstract ideals. Within the self-regarding sentiment, moral sentiments (conscience) control crude instinctive impulses, and thus, in McDougall's view, individual free will is truly exercised. The ordered hierarchy of sentiments completes the integration of personality. In *Abnormal Psychology*, McDougall reproached both Freud and Jung for neglecting the integration of personality—at that time Freud's "superego" and Jung's "self" were not yet formulated.

McDougall's theory still had to explain the occurrence of autonomous complexes apparently outside the hierarchy, and of dissociated activities and "multiple" personalities. Rejecting Freud's determinism, McDougall considered these unconscious mental functions purposive and goal-seeking. He then combined his personality theory with a revised view of body–mind relationships in an elaborate monadic theory based upon that of Leibniz. Every personality is integrated as a converging hierarchy of monads, each "potentially a thinking striving self, endowed with true memory." A supreme monad "which each of us calls 'myself'" exercises control by telepathic communication through the hierarchy. Failure of integration allows pathological conflicts, automatisms in sleep or hypnosis, or even revolt of a subordinate monad as a dissociated personality.

McDougall left open the question whether monads might be perceptible through the senses, and he considered the monadic theory to be consistent with either a monistic or a dualistic psychophysical theory. To reconcile a presumably purposive mind with an apparently causally determined body, he suggested that there might be two types of monad, one goal-seeking and the other cause-following, that were somehow interconnected, or one single series of monads with two aspects, causalistic and finalistic. Thus McDougall reconciled his theory both with

causal–mechanistic schemes of neurophysiological levels (Sherrington) and with more purposive views, neurological (Henry Head, *Studies in Neurology,* London, 1920) and psychological (hormism). However, he too hastily equated biological purpose (horme) with individual goal-seeking will, and acquired self-control with the capacity for choice and responsibility in conduct.

Once a noted experimental physiologist, McDougall later based hormic psychology increasingly upon his purposivist metaphysical beliefs, little upon verifiable observation or experiment. His great experimental work at Duke was designed to test Lamarck's hypothesis of evolution by inheritance of acquired characteristics. Eventually, after ten years and 23 animal generations, McDougall reported an apparently inherited facilitation of learning in laboratory rats. Subsequent workers have not confirmed his results.

A lucid and persuasive writer, McDougall wielded great if temporary influence, and guided many English-reading students toward dynamic, biological, and social psychology. His weaknesses were his fondness for intellectual and verbal solutions to empirical problems, and his temptation to premature systematization. Admiration tinges the epigram that, had the Creator but paused to consult William McDougall, there had been no need of redemption.

Additional Works by McDougall

Psychology, the Study of Behavior. London, 1912.
Ethics and Some Modern World Problems. New York and London, 1924.
The Battle of Behaviorism. New York and London, 1928. Written with J. B. Watson.
Modern Materialism and Emergent Evolution. New York and London, 1929.
Psycho-analysis and Social Psychology. London and Toronto, 1936.

Works on McDougall

Greenwood, Major, and Smith, May, "William McDougall," in *Obituary Notices of Fellows of the Royal Society,* Vol. III. London, 1939–1941. Pp. 39–62. Contains a complete bibliography.
Nicole, J. Ernest, *Psychopathology.* London, 1930; 3d ed., 1942. Chs. 15, 16, 21.
Woodworth, R. S., *Contemporary Schools of Psychology.* New York and London, 1931. Ch. 6.

J. D. UYTMAN

McGILVARY, EVANDER BRADLEY (1864–1953), American realist philosopher, was born in Bangkok, Siam. He received his B.A. from Davidson College in 1884, his M.A. from Princeton in 1888, and his Ph.D. from the University of California in 1897. He was appointed assistant professor of philosophy in California and then Sage professor of ethics at Cornell (1899–1905). From 1905 to 1924 he was professor of philosophy and head of the department at the University of Wisconsin, and in the year 1912/1913 he was the president of the American Philosophical Association. He was the Howison lecturer in 1927, the Mills lecturer in 1928, and the Carus lecturer in 1939.

Philosophical orientation. McGilvary's "first impulse" toward philosophy was a reaction against the theology in which he was schooled. He came under the Hegelian influence of George Howison at California, and his writings from 1897 to 1903 reflect this influence. But McGilvary, like other Hegelians of his time, eventually found Hegelianism unacceptable. From the start McGilvary held the view that every part of the world is what it is by virtue of its organic relation to every other part. And when he broke with Hegelianism, he took with him this theory of relations and the characteristically Hegelian view that two antagonistic ideas always suggest a third that synthesizes the truth of each.

Realist philosophers in America during the first two decades of the twentieth century were struggling to formulate an epistemology that would do justice both to those elements in experience that are clearly in the objective world and to those dependent upon the experiencing organism. Taking James's thesis that "the world is as it is experienced," the non-Hegelian new realists developed a monistic realism, but it always threatened to become pan-objectivism. In reaction the critical realists set forth a dualistic realism that always threatened to become pan-subjectivism. In his "perspective realism" McGilvary sought to combine the truth of new realism with the truth of critical realism. He, too, took James's thesis as his starting point and sought to combine epistemological monism with epistemological dualism and the theory of external relations with the theory of internal relations. McGilvary's synthesis of the objective and the relative—like Dewey's and Whitehead's—was dubbed "objective relativism" by A. E. Murphy.

To effect the synthesis of monism and dualism, McGilvary developed his theory of perspectives. It is summarized in the first three postulates of perspective realism: (1) "In our sense-experience there is presented to us in part the real world in which we all in common live"; (2) "Every particular in the world . . . is what it is only because of its context"; (3) "In the world of nature any 'thing' at any time is, and is nothing but, the totality of the relational characters, experienced or not experienced, that the 'thing' has at that time in whatever relations it has at that time to other 'things.' " McGilvary first hinted at such a theory in 1907, but he did not systematically state it until twenty years later, and in 1939 it became the core of his Carus lectures, *Toward a Perspective Realism*. This work is the key to understanding McGilvary's philosophy, and it grew out of his early thinking about the nature of consciousness.

The nature of consciousness. McGilvary believed that the question of the precise nature of consciousness was the fundamental question of philosophy. Like other realists, he agreed with James that consciousness is a relation. Since it was his view that things are what they are only in their relations to other things, he could not agree with realists who claimed that this relation was external. Consciousness, he held, is that relation by which anything becomes an experience. It is a unique kind of "togetherness" of, or between, things. It is neither a spatial nor temporal togetherness, nor is it any other distinguishable relation. The peculiar relation of feeling binds external objects together into an experiential unity we call "consciousness," "awareness," or "experiencing."

McGilvary thought this togetherness may have been what Kant meant by the synthetic unity of apperception. It has a unique center of reference in the body of the experiencing organism. This centering gives to the relation of togetherness a character and coloring all its own. Hence, consciousness exists in individualized instances, like other relations, yet each instance produces an individuality generically different from that of any other individualized relation. Each instance is its own kind of betweenness.

As he developed this theory, McGilvary increasingly described consciousness in terms of perspectives. In addition to the familiar perceptual perspectives of space and time, he said, consciousness is characterized by intellectual, moral, and aesthetic perspectives. All these perspectives have both a physical and an "epiphysical," a dynamic and an "epidynamic," causal and noncausal quality. The most distinctive characteristic of these perspectives is the absence of energy transaction between their station point (the organism) and objects in the perspective. The peculiar "epidynamic" relatedness of a perspective does not "go over" to the object or do anything to it. Yet it does "go over" in the way any other relation "goes over" from one term to another. It is a conditioning relatedness that is not itself a cause of the physical existence of its objects, nor is it itself an object in the relation complex. Thus, a perspective (seeing, for example) is not an act of the organism on its object. If it were, it would be difficult to understand how an organism can see now what antedates the seeing, such as a star which may have exploded eons ago. Like the verb "to relate," the verb "to see" does not name an act performed on the objects seen, any more than "having" a grandfather is an act performed on him. Physical objects become a field of vision when light from them stimulates an organism through its eyes, just as grandparents become grandparents only when a grandchild is born.

The organism, then, is a condition of vision, and as such it is not one of the members or terms in the relationship, just as common parents are a condition for the relationship of brotherhood but are not members in that relationship. Seeing the star that no longer exists is no more difficult for McGilvary to explain than how being an ancestor of a president of the United States is a quality that comes to belong to persons who die before the event that permits ascribing that characteristic to them. In the same way the perspective realist can hold that the physical object that initiated the series of physical conditions which ended in a perception of attributes occupying the position of that object still does not have those attributes. These attributes, however, can be considered part of the real world resulting from a real and natural relation between the organism and external objects. Not all physical qualities, then, are causally conditioned. Sense qualities, for example, can be considered part of their object but are not causally related to the organism that senses them.

It is the same for McGilvary with memory or knowledge of the past. The pastness of an event is not independent of all external standpoints. The pastness of consciousness is retro*spective*, a particular kind of perspectivity, but not retro*active*. Consciousness also is prospective, another kind of perspectivity, but not active on the future. This is the "epiphysical" or "epidynamic" quality of the consciousness relation that distinguishes it from other physical, dynamic, causal relations that act on their objects. Perspectives do not exist if that means being in space and time. Nor do they subsist. The being of a perspective is its being between—"inter-sistence," McGilvary called it—and each perspective is its own kind of "inter-sistence."

But it is not clear whether McGilvary thought that each perspective is an instance of consciousness and whether perspectives go to make up what we call consciousness. Nor does he show us how to distinguish between what the organism contributes to the perspective, as its station point, and what is there independent of the organism. At times he said nothing is there independent of the organism for the organism is the necessary condition of any perspective. But when Dewey said that the logical forms of our knowledge cannot be read back into nature (because they come into being only when inquiry is instituted and are only modes of operating upon subject matter), McGilvary disagreed. He argued that any logical form that serves to solve a problematic situation serves that purpose because it is actually the form of the subject matter under investigation, not of the subject matter as it was immediately experienced when inquiry started but as successful inquiry shows the subject matter to have been in the natural world. It is doubtful, then, that McGilvary, like the other objective relativists, was any more successful than other realists in doing justice to the objective and the relative found in experience.

McGilvary's few articles on ethics present familiar positions, but none of them is developed systematically, nor did McGilvary apply his perspective realism beyond epistemological and ontological problems.

Works by McGilvary

"Pure Experience and Reality: A Re-assertion." *Philosophical Review*, Vol. 16 (May 1907), 266–284.

"The Physiological Argument Against Realism." *Journal of Philosophy*, Vol. 4 (October 1907), 589–601.

"Realism and the Physical World." *Journal of Philosophy*, Vol. 4 (December 1907), 683–692.

"Experience and Its Inner Duplicity." *Journal of Philosophy*, Vol. 6 (April 1909), 225–232.

"Experience as Pure and Consciousness as Meaning." *Journal of Philosophy*, Vol. 8 (September 1911), 511–525.

"The Relation of Consciousness and Object in Sense Perception." *Philosophical Review*, Vol. 21 (March 1912), 152–173.

"A Tentative Realistic Metaphysics," in G. P. Adams and W. P. Montague, eds., *Contemporary American Philosophy*, 2 vols. New York, 1930. Vol. II, pp. 109–132.

"The Revolt Against Dualism." *Philosophical Review*, Vol. 40 (May 1931), 246–265.

"Perceptual and Memory Perspectives." *Journal of Philosophy*, Vol. 30 (June 1933), 109–132.

Toward a Perspective Realism. La Salle, Ill., 1956. His 1939 Carus lectures and his only book.

Between 1918 and 1926 McGilvary published only two book reviews. His publications after 1926 display a new interest in and command of mathematical physics. Two of these papers are reprinted in his book. In all he published 48 articles and 23 reviews in addition to 81 articles in *The New International Encyclopedia* (New York, 1902).

Works on McGilvary

Murphy, Arthur E., "McGilvary's Perspective Realism." *Journal of Philosophy*, Vol. 56 (February 1959), 149–165. Reprinted in W. H. Hay et al., eds., *Reason and the Common Good*. Englewood Cliffs, N.J., 1963.

Oliver, Donald W., "The Logic of Perspective Realism." *Journal of Philosophy*, Vol. 35 (April 1938), 197–208.

THOMAS ROBISCHON

McTAGGART, JOHN McTAGGART ELLIS (1866–1925), British metaphysician, was born in London, the son of Francis and Caroline Ellis. (His father later took the name McTaggart to fulfill a condition for inheriting a bequest.) He attended school at Clifton and went on to Trinity College, Cambridge, where he took first-class honors in the moral science tripos in 1888. He was made a fellow of Trinity in 1891. The next year he paid a visit to New Zealand, where his widowed mother lived, and there he met Margaret Elizabeth Bird, whom he married in 1899, during a second visit to New Zealand. Thereafter he resided at Cambridge. Active in the affairs of his college and the university, he was a busy and successful teacher from 1897 until he retired in 1923. He died suddenly in January 1925.

McTaggart's philosophy is a peculiar and quite personal variety of Hegelian idealism. Ultimate reality, he held, is spiritual: it consists entirely of individual minds and their contents. He understood this in a way that excludes space, time, and material objects from reality. What appear to us as being these things are really minds and parts of the contents of minds, but we "misperceive" these entities in a systematic way, and this misperception is the source of the whole apparent universe. Despite the unreality of time, McTaggart argued, there is an important sense in which it is true to say that individual persons are immortal, and that they are reincarnated in a succession of (apparent) bodies. He also held that in reality persons stand in relations either of direct perception, and consequently love, or of indirect perception, and consequently affection, to one another. Love is, indeed, the basically real emotional state. There is, however, no God in this heavenly city, for McTaggart did not think there is any reason to believe that there is or even can be an overarching mind that includes individual minds like ours but is still in some sense an individual mind itself. McTaggart was, in addition, a determinist, though he held that determinism is not incompatible with the existence of valid judgments of moral obligation.

On these basic points McTaggart never changed his mind. He argued in support of them both in his early writings on Hegel and in his great systematic work, *The Nature of Existence*. The main difference between his earlier and his later work is that in the former the arguments are dialectical in a Hegelian manner, whereas in the latter they are more straightforwardly deductive.

Writings on Hegel. McTaggart's commentaries on Hegel are all more or less critical of Hegel, and none is entirely reliable as pure exegesis. Two deal primarily with Hegelian methodology. The essays on the dialectic defend Hegel's method against what McTaggart took to be common misunderstandings and criticisms and offer an account of the way in which the Absolute Idea works to move thought from stage to stage. The *Commentary on Hegel's Logic* is a detailed and very careful examination of the validity of each step in the logical development of the categories. McTaggart frequently found Hegel to be mistaken or confused about his transitions and in some cases offered alternative modes of development.

The essays on cosmology are among McTaggart's most interesting work. He here discussed, more fully than anywhere else, a number of concrete topics—such as the moral criterion, sin, the organic nature of society, and the relations between Christianity and Hegelianism—in the light of his metaphysical position. He brought out his differences, not only with Hegel, but with many of the British Hegelians as well. And in the concluding chapter he presented with great clarity and power what is essentially his mature view of the relations between selves in ultimate reality.

"Some Dogmas of Religion." In *Some Dogmas of Religion* McTaggart examined, in a careful but nontechnical manner, a number of dogmas that are especially relevant to Christianity. (By "dogma" he meant "proposition having metaphysical significance.") He argued that dogmas of some sort are essential to any religion and that we must have reasoned proof of a dogma before we can be justified in believing in it. Then, without claiming to give conclusive arguments (for these would involve a whole metaphysical system) he argued in favor of immortality, pre-existence, and determinism, criticized the belief in a personal and omnipotent God, and attacked some of the arguments that have been alleged to support this belief. Finally, he tried to show that there is much less connection than is frequently held to be between the truth of theism and improved chances for personal happiness.

"The Nature of Existence." McTaggart's metaphysical system is presented in two parts. In the first, contained in Volume I of *The Nature of Existence*, he gave an extended argument to show that whatever exists must be of a certain nature and must, therefore, satisfy a certain requirement, to be explained below. In the second part, occupying Volume II, he examined various types of entities that our present experience shows us as existing to determine whether these entities can satisfy the requirement; he attempted to account for the apparent existence of those entities that do not really exist; and he evaluated the practical importance of the results he had thus reached.

The argument of Volume I is almost entirely a priori. McTaggart appealed to experience for only two propositions: that something exists, and that what exists has parts. His argument proceeds through the following stages: First, McTaggart offered a proof of the principle of the Identity of Indiscernibles. Second, he argued that every substance must have a "sufficient description," i.e., a description that uniquely identifies the substance and contains no reference to substances that are only identified (as by pointing or by the use of purely referring expressions), not described.

He next moved to the assertion that every substance, without exception, must be divisible into parts that are themselves substances, and hence into parts within parts to infinity. The crucial argument is then presented. The principle that every substance must have a sufficient description together with the principle that every substance is infinitely divisible into further substances would entail a contradiction unless the substances in question were such that from the nature of any existing substance there follow sufficient descriptions of all of its parts within parts to infinity. This can occur, McTaggart showed, if the substance stands in a certain extremely complex relation to its parts, which he called the relation of "Determining Correspondence"; it can occur, he held, in no other way. Hence,

whatever exists—and we know that something does exist—must satisfy the conditions necessary for it to stand in Determining Correspondence relations to its parts.

In Volume II McTaggart denied the existence of material objects, space, judgments, inferences, sense data, and certain other mental contents, on the ground that entities of these types cannot satisfy the conditions required for them to stand in Determining Correspondence relations. His denial of the existence of time, however, rests on a quite different argument. This argument is McTaggart's most widely discussed contribution to philosophy. Briefly, it is as follows: Temporal positions and events may be ordered either as earlier–later or as past–present–future. Ordered the first way, they form what McTaggart called a B-series; ordered the second way they form an A-series. In the first stage of the argument McTaggart tried to show that the A-series characteristics "past," "present," and "future" are essential to the existence of time. He assumed it to be admitted that change is essential to time, and he argued that unless the A-series characteristics can change, nothing can change. The B-series characteristics cannot change, for if an event is ever earlier than another, it is always earlier; and neither can the other characteristics of events change, for if it is ever true that an event is, for instance, the death of a queen, then it is always true that this event is the death of a queen. Hence, without the A-series there cannot be time, and in the second stage of the argument McTaggart tried to show that a vicious infinite regress is involved in affirming the existence of a series ordered by A-series characteristics. Each member of such a series must have all the A-series characteristics, he said, but those characteristics are incompatible. If we try to remove the contradiction by saying that each member possesses all the characteristics *at different times*, we are presupposing the existence of different moments of time at which the A-series characteristics are possessed. But each of these moments, to be temporal, must itself possess all of the A-series characteristics, which, again, is impossible; the attempt to relieve this contradiction by appeal to yet another set of moments only gives rise to another set of contradictions, and so on.

McTaggart's complicated and difficult account of the relations between appearance and reality centers on the concept of a C-series, analogous to the B-series in having its members related by an asymmetrical and transitive relation, but timeless. The model for the C-series relationship is the concept of "inclusion," and the terms that are included in and inclusive of each other are perceptions, i.e., parts of spirits. McTaggart argued that reality must be structured so as to form a set of related inclusion series which, however, are misperceived as temporal series. He drew the further conclusion that time had a first moment and will have a last moment. (See TIME.)

McTaggart went on to discuss the question of the value of the universe, both in its prefinal stages and at the stage when the appearance of time has ceased. Taking both "good" and "evil" to stand for simple, unanalyzable characteristics, and arguing that only what is spiritual can have value, he found that in the prefinal stages the relative proportions of good and evil will fluctuate considerably, though we can be confident that on the whole the proportion of good will steadily increase. In the final stage we will exist in a "timeless and endless state of love" far more profound and powerful than anything we now have any inkling of. We shall, McTaggart said, "know nothing but our beloved, those they love, and ourselves as loving them," and this will be our ultimate and unshakable satisfaction. If McTaggart's metaphysics thus concludes with a vision that he himself was not unwilling to call mystical, it is at least a vision that springs from one of the most brilliantly conceived and carefully executed attempts any philosopher has ever produced to grasp the nature of reality in purely rational terms.

Works by McTaggart

Studies in the Hegelian Dialectic. Cambridge, 1896; 2d ed., Cambridge, 1922.
Studies in Hegelian Cosmology. Cambridge, 1901; 2d ed., Cambridge, 1918.
Some Dogmas of Religion. London, 1906; 2d ed., London, 1930.
A Commentary on Hegel's Logic. Cambridge, 1910.
The Nature of Existence, 2 vols. Vol. I, Cambridge, 1921; Vol. II, C. D. Broad, ed., Cambridge, 1927.
Essays in S. V. Keeling, ed., *Philosophical Essays.* London, 1934.

Works on McTaggart

C. D. Broad delivered an obituary address to the British Academy which contains an admirable summary of McTaggart's work. It was published in the society's *Proceedings* for 1927 and reprinted in the second edition of *Some Dogmas of Religion,* as well as in Broad's *Ethics and the History of Philosophy* (London, 1952). *John McTaggart Ellis McTaggart,* by G. Lowes Dickinson (Cambridge, 1931), contains more information about McTaggart's life, in addition to interesting reminiscences and a chapter by S. V. Keeling on McTaggart's metaphysics. The standard commentary is C. D. Broad's exhaustive *Examination of McTaggart's Philosophy* (Vol. I, Cambridge, 1933; Vol. II, in two parts, Cambridge, 1938). This work is discussed at length by R. L. Patterson in *The Philosophy of C. D. Broad* (New York, 1959). (For discussion of McTaggart on time, see the bibliography for TIME.)

J. B. SCHNEEWIND

MEAD, GEORGE HERBERT (1863–1931), American pragmatist philosopher, was born in South Hadley, Massachusetts. He received his B.A. from Oberlin College in 1883 and did graduate work at Harvard in 1887/1888, where he studied under Josiah Royce and William James. From 1888 to 1891 he studied psychology and philosophy in Europe. He was married in 1891 and in the same year was appointed instructor at the University of Michigan. In 1892 he joined the staff of the University of Chicago and later became chairman of its philosophy department.

A major figure in American pragmatism, Mead has also had a large influence on psychologists and social scientists. Many thinkers, including Whitehead and Dewey, regarded Mead as a creative mind of the first magnitude. He published relatively few papers, however, and died before he was able to develop his many original ideas into an integrated philosophy. Large segments of his books were collated from his unfinished manuscripts and from his students' notes and hence are repetitious, unsystematic, and difficult.

Mead's main philosophic themes may be classified as follows: (1) the emergence of mind and self from the communication process between organisms (often termed his "social behaviorism"), discussed in *Mind, Self and Society;* (2) the psychological genesis of scientific categories in purposeful acts, discussed in *The Philosophy of the Act;* and (3) the social conception of nature and the location of reality in the present, discussed in *The Philosophy of the Present.*

Social behaviorism. Mead's thought stemmed from the impact of Darwinism on nineteenth-century ideas. Man was regarded as an organism functioning in accordance with natural laws. This approach opposed traditional philosophy and theology and sought to understand human nature by the methods of experimental science. The theory of evolution also gave impetus to the conception of the universe as a process rather than as a set of fixed, unalterable essences that remain invariant over time. In psychology the process concept was expressed in functionalism, which sought to comprehend all mental phenomena not as structures, traits, or attributes of the mind but as relations between the organism and its environment. These ideas were taken up by behavioristic psychology, which dismissed introspection as unscientific and confined itself to experimental data, particularly the responses of organisms to stimuli under varying conditions.

Mead challenged many of the crudities of behaviorism. In rejecting introspection, this school tended to regard it as a nonexistent phenomenon, since it could not be studied experimentally. Mead's social behaviorism sought to widen behaviorism to include the introspectively observed phenomena of consciousness. For Mead stimulus and response are meaningful only when viewed as aspects of communication; they cannot be studied in abstraction from the social process in which actions occur. Furthermore, organisms do not merely respond mechanically and passively to stimuli. Rather, the individual purposefully selects its stimuli. Mead here opposed associationism; the organism is a dynamic, forceful agent, not a mute receptacle for ideas which are later associated. For Mead organism and environment mutually determine each other. Mind emerges from this reciprocal determination.

Mead's naturalistic conception of introspection was based on the viewpoint that an idea is the early, inner stage in an ongoing act directed toward an environmental goal. The mistake of the behaviorists was to study merely one part of the complete act, the last, overt stage, thereby ignoring the initial phase of the act, which occurs privately, within the organism.

According to Mead actions occur within a communicative process. The initial phase of the overt stage of an act constitutes a gesture. A gesture is a preparatory movement which enables other individuals to become aware of the intentions of the given organism. The rudimentary situation is a conversation of gestures, in which a gesture on the part of the first individual evokes a preparatory movement on the part of the second, and the gesture of the second organism in turn calls out a response in the first person. On this level no communication occurs. Neither organism is aware of the effect of its own gestures upon the other; the gestures are nonsignificant. For communication to take place, each organism must have knowledge of how the other individual will respond to his own ongoing act. Here the gestures are significant symbols.

Communication is also based on the fact that actions are organized temporally. The consequences of behavior (final phases of the act) are present in imagery during the early phases of the action and control the nature of the developing movement. There are usually several alternative ways of completing a movement which has been started. Since the final phases of the act control the ongoing movement, the organism can select one of these alternative ways of conjoining means with the end. In this manner rational conduct is possible. Where organisms use significant symbols, the role of the other individual controls the ongoing act. In advance of our completion of a social action, we anticipate the response of the other individual. Since our behavior is temporally organized, the imported role of the other may cause us to select a course of action that is different from what we originally intended.

Mind is the ability of an organism to take the role of the other toward its own developing behavior. Reflexivity, the ability of a person to reflect upon himself, is the necessary condition for the emergence of mind within the social process. With reflexivity the social act is imported within the individual and serves to alter the person's ongoing acts. A complete social act can be carried out internally without external movements necessarily occurring. Mead denotes the internalized role of the other as the "me." Each organism has an "I," which is a capacity for spontaneity. The "I" is expressed when the individual alters his ongoing response or creates a new response to the "me." Individuality and originality arise from the inner conversation between the "I" and the imported role of the other. An inner forum comes to exist, consisting of a dialogue between the "I" and the "me." This inner rehearsal of projected actions constitutes introspection, or thinking.

In the organized group situation, such as is exemplified in games, the individual learns to take into himself the entire social organization which now exerts internal control over his ongoing acts. The "generalized other" is the group's attitudes imported into the individual. It is here that social institutions enter into an individual's thinking as a determinative factor and cause him to develop a complete self. Now the inner forum becomes an inner dialogue between the person and the group.

The religious experience occurs in situations where each person becomes closely identified with the other members of the group. In common efforts, such as in teamwork, where a sense of closeness develops among everyone involved, a feeling of exaltation arises. Here Mead refers to a "fusion" of the "I" and the "me."

Mead's social psychology is similar to the psychoanalytic theories of Freud and Harry Stack Sullivan in that it conceives personality as arising from the internalization of the roles of other persons and relates inner conflict to the tension between the spontaneous forces of the person and the introjected demands of society. The temporal organization of the act, stressed by Mead, is also a key concept in automatic control machinery and digital computers, where the later stages of a process feed back upon the earlier phases, modifying the ongoing process.

Philosophy of science. Mead sought to find the psychological origin of science in the efforts of individuals to attain power over their environment. The notion of a physical object arises out of manipulatory experience.

Perception is coordinated with the ongoing act: when we approach a thing we wish to manipulate, the imagery of handling that thing is present in the distance perception. Here again there is a temporal organization of the act, in that the later phase of the action, the contact experience, is present in the earlier stage when we are merely perceiving the distant object. Perception involves the readiness of the organism to manipulate the thing when the intervening distance has been traversed. The reality of a thing is in the consummatory phase of the act, the contact experience, and this reality is present in the experience of perceiving that thing at a distance.

There is a social relation to inanimate objects, for the organism takes the role of things that it manipulates directly or that it manipulates indirectly in perception. For example, in taking (introjecting or imitating) the resistant role of a solid object, an individual obtains cognition of what is "inside" nonliving things. Historically, the concept of the physical object arose from an animistic conception of the universe.

Contact experience includes experiences of position, balance, and support, and these are used by the organism when it creates its conceptions of the physical world. Our scientific concepts of space, time, and mass are abstracted from manipulatory experience. Such concepts as that of the electron are also derived from manipulation. In developing a science we construct hypothetical objects in order to assist ourselves in controlling nature. The conception of the present as a distinct unit of experience, rather than as a process of becoming and disappearing, is a scientific fiction devised to facilitate exact measurement. In the scientific world view immediate experience is replaced by theoretical constructs. The ultimate in experience, however, is the manipulation and contact at the completion of an act.

Cosmology. *The Philosophy of the Present* develops the conception that reality always exists in a present. However, as it is experienced, the present involves both the past and the future. A process in nature is not a succession of instantaneous presents or a sequence of spatial points. Instead there is both spatial and temporal duration, or continuity.

The developing action is the basis of existence. It is true that as we look back the present is determined by the past. But each new present, as it passes into the next present, is a unique emergent. A new future also arises as the result of the emerging present. Hence, we are always reconstructing our pasts and restructuring our future. Novelty stretches out in both directions from the present perspective.

Every object in the universe is seen from the perspective of a particular individual. What is seen from one person's perspective may be different from that which is seen by another individual. Mead was not solipsistic, however, for although a person sees nature only from his own perspective, he is able to import within himself the perspectives of others. Reality is the integration of different perspectives. Mead made use of the theory of relativity to project his theory of sociality and mind into nature. Sociality is the ability to be in more than one system at a time, to take more than one perspective simultaneously. This phenomenon occurs in emergence, for here an object in the process of becoming something new passes from one system to another, and in the passage is in two systems at the same time. During this transition, or transmutation, the emergent entity exists on two levels of nature concomitantly.

Mead's philosophy has been compared with that of Martin Buber. Although their approaches stem from different traditions, both thinkers have a social conception of nature and conceive of the self as arising from a social matrix. Certain affinities between Mead and Edmund Husserl have been suggested, in that the mind's reflexive examination of itself is an effort to describe the constitution and foundation of experience.

Works by Mead

The Philosophy of the Present, Arthur E. Murphy, ed. Chicago, 1932. Mead's Carus lectures. Prefatory remarks by John Dewey.
Mind, Self and Society From the Standpoint of a Social Behaviorist, Charles W. Morris, ed. Chicago, 1934. Based on Mead's lectures in social psychology. Introduction by Morris. Contains a listing of Mead's writings.
Movements of Thought in the Nineteenth Century, Merritt H. Moore, ed. Chicago, 1936. Notes from course lectures.
The Philosophy of the Act, Charles W. Morris, ed., in collaboration with John M. Brewster, Albert M. Dunham, and David L. Miller. Chicago, 1938. Unpublished papers and lecture notes. Introduction by Morris.
The Social Psychology of George Herbert Mead, Anselm Strauss, ed. Chicago, 1956. Introduction by Strauss.

Works on Mead

Lee, Grace Chin, *George Herbert Mead: Philosopher of the Social Individual.* New York, 1945. Includes bibliography of secondary literature.
Natanson, Maurice, *The Social Dynamics of George Herbert Mead.* Washington, 1956. Discusses affinities with Husserl's phenomenology. Includes bibliography. Introduction by Horace M. Kallen.
Pfuetze, Paul E., *The Social Self.* New York, 1954. Comparisons between Mead, Buber, and psychoanalysis.

WILLIAM H. DESMONDE

MEANING. The word "mean" and its derivatives have a great many different uses. For example:

(1) I mean to help him if I can.
(2) The passage of this bill will mean the end of second-class citizenship for vast areas of our population.
(3) Once again life has meaning for me.
(4) What is the meaning of this?
(5) Keep off the grass. This means you.
(6) That look on his face means trouble.
(7) "Procrastinate" means—to put things off.

Many of these uses are of interest to philosophers in one connection or another. In this article we shall concentrate on (7), on the use of "mean" that is involved when we say what a word, or other meaningful element of language, means. The basic philosophical task here is to make explicit what this use is—in other words, to bring out what it is for a word to have a certain meaning. As usual, the philosophical problem is basic to other problems concerning meaning. Social scientists and humanists deal with a variety of such problems. How do children learn the meanings of words? How are the meanings in a given language interrelated? What causes words to change their meanings over time? What are the best ways of setting out the meanings of various kinds of words? How many

different meanings should be listed, for example, for the word "run"? Do proper names have meaning? How many kinds of meaning are there? It is clear that none of these questions can be investigated unless one is working with some concept, perhaps implicit, of linguistic meaning. The philosopher sets himself the task of making explicit what it is for a word to have a certain meaning, thereby providing a firm foundation for these more special inquiries.

In addition to the interest in providing a conceptual foundation for more special investigations, there are motivations within philosophy itself. For one thing, the philosopher in the course of his own investigations comes to points at which he needs to make more explicit his own implicit ability to use the word "mean." In trying to get at the meaning of various crucial terms, he often encounters competing claims that cannot be resolved just by his intuitive sense of meaning. Does "I know that p" mean "I feel certain that p, I have sufficient grounds for this belief, and p is true"? Or is more involved? Does "feel sad" mean the same in "I feel sad" and "He feels sad"? In such cases there are real considerations pushing us in both directions, and in order to resolve the issue one is forced to become more explicit about the nature of meaning. Second, the word "meaning" shares with other words, such as "existence" and "causation," a certain lack of obviousness that has always been a challenge to philosophical reflection. With one of these terms, unlike "run" or "tree," there is no readily observable thing or aspect of things to which the word corresponds. What are we saying about an object when we say that it exists? What are we saying about Jones's harsh words when we say that they caused his daughter to cry? We cannot see, or otherwise sense, the existence of an object or the causal bond between the speech and the crying, so it becomes a challenge to specify just what we are attributing in these cases. Likewise, the meaning of a word is not a grossly observable feature like its length, phonetic content, or stress pattern, nor is it a more complicated, but still easily understandable, relational feature like its distribution in various sentence slots or its rhetorical effectiveness. The more we reflect on the matter, the more difficult it becomes to put our finger on the meaning. What is it that gives a certain pattern of sound the capacity to "point beyond itself" to its meaning?

It will be useful to discuss our problem in the form "What are we saying about a word when we say what it means?" Of course, clarifying specifications of meaning does not in itself suffice to analyze completely the concept of linguistic meaning, for specification of meaning is only one of the contexts in which that concept occurs. Of almost equal importance is talk about someone's knowing the meaning of a word and talk about something's having or not having meaning. Nevertheless, there is ground for supposing that if we could clarify *specifications* of meaning, this would enable us to clear up these other contexts as well.

THEORIES OF MEANING

Most of the attempts to deal with the problem can be grouped into three types of theories, referential, ideational, and stimulus–response. A critical presentation of each of these in turn follows.

Referential theory. The referential theory is, on the surface, the simplest, and it dominates most thinking about meaning. It usually stems from concentration on the proper name as the typical unit of meaning. With a proper name everything seems to be simple. Here is the name "John"; there is the man named. All the factors are out in the open; there is nothing mysterious about it (until we ask what makes the word "John" the name of this man). It is tempting to generalize this account and hold that for any word to have a meaning is for it to name, designate, or refer to something other than itself. Variations of the theory differ over whether the meaning of a word is to be identified with (1) what it refers to or (2) the relation between the word and its referent.

Difference between meaning and reference. The first form of the relational theory, though common in popular writings on semantics, can be shown to be untenable because two expressions can have the same referent but different meanings. This is by now a familiar point in the literature. Frege's classic example has to do with the expressions "the morning star" and "the evening star." They refer to the same extralinguistic entity, the planet Venus, but they do not have the same meaning. If they did, one could know that the morning star is the same entity as the evening star just by understanding the meanings of the terms (as with "The thermometer in my study is the same object as the instrument for measuring temperature in my study"). But this is not the case. It was an astronomical discovery that the morning star and the evening star are the same. More generally, anything to which we can refer can be referred to by a variety of nonsynonymous expressions. Thus, Winston Churchill can be referred to as "the prime minister of Great Britain during World War II" and as "the author of *The Gathering Storm*." Since meaning can vary without a corresponding variation in referent, having a certain meaning cannot consist in referring to a certain object.

Reference and other semantic relations. In view of the difficulties with the first form of the referential theory, the more careful versions identify the meaning of an expression with the relation between an expression and its referent. This account has the merit of focusing attention on the question of what that relation is, the question of what it is that gives a certain expression one referent rather than another. But like the first version it runs into difficulty over the assumption that every meaningful expression does refer to something. First, there are many classes of words, including prepositions and conjunctions, which do not seem to be individually connected with discriminable things or aspects of things in the extralinguistic world as a name is connected with the thing named. What does "and," "if," or "about" refer to? We would be hard pressed to say. Words like these may be set aside for special treatment. They were dubbed "syncategorematic" by the medieval logicians, on the ground that they make sense only when used with terms belonging to the "categories" (of Aristotle), which include, roughly, nouns, adjectives, verbs, and adverbs. In a similar vein more recent writers of a referential persuasion, like Bertrand Russell, have held that such words have no meaning "in isolation" but only modify the sense of whole sentences in which they occur. One

might well question the claim that conjunctions have meaning in a basically different sense of the term from that in which nouns and verbs do. At first blush, it seems that in saying "'If' means—provided that" we are saying just the same sort of thing as by uttering "'Procrastinate' means—to put things off." If so, we should not be so hasty in abandoning the attempt to give an account of meaning which applies equally to both.

But even if we exclude conjunctions from the scope of the theory, the referential theorist has trouble with the "categorical" terms themselves. At this point we should say explicitly what reference is. As soon as we try to do so we have to eliminate the fiction that words engage "on their own" in the activity of referring; speakers of a language *use* words to refer to something. (The same point is to be made about such terms as "designate," "name," and "denote.") To use an expression to refer to *x* is to utter the expression in order to make explicit what one is talking about. If this is what referring is, then it is proper nouns, pronouns like "he" and "this," common nouns in the plural ("trees") and nominal phrases of various sorts ("the typewriter," "your car") which are used to refer. Common nouns in the singular, adjectives, verbs, and adverbs do not have this function. One cannot use the verb "run" in any of its forms to make it explicit that one is talking about either the activity of running or a particular act of running. For the former one must use "running" and for the latter a phrase like "that run of his." One does not say "Run always tires me." These grammatical observations are pertinent because they show that referring is one linguistic function among others, a function performed by some kinds of linguistic expressions and not others. It is not something coextensive with meaning.

It may be that the referential theorist is using "reference" in a looser sense as a general type of word-world relation of which referring in the strict sense is only one special case, along with connoting, denoting, etc. Thus, although "run" cannot be used to refer to the activity of running, it could be said to *denote* that activity, which simply means that the word can be truly applied to *x* if and only if *x* engages in that activity. The difficulty here lies in specifying what all these relations have in common. What can be said other than that they are all relations between linguistic and nonlinguistic elements, which seem to have something to do with meaning? And that does not get us very far.

Attachment to the referential theory has led philosophers into many blind alleys. If to have a meaning is to refer to something, then it must be possible to find a referent for every meaningful expression, including whole sentences. We do not ordinarily think of a sentence as itself referring to something. One refers to something by a word or phrase in the course of uttering a sentence. But if one holds the referential theory one must find a referent. Some have held that a (declarative) sentence refers to the fact which makes it true or false; some have held that all true sentences have the same reference, which has been variously specified as the existing universe as a whole, and as Truth conceived as a single abstract entity. When answers to a question vary as wildly as these, we may well wonder whether the question makes sense.

Most discussions of meaning in referential terms suffer from superficiality because they do not take seriously enough the necessity of specifying what it is that connects an expression with its referent. Insofar as expressions do refer to something, this is clearly the heart of the problem, and it is clear that it is to be located somewhere in the activity of language users. It is obvious on reflection that no linguistic element has any meaning or reference or any other semantic status, except by virtue of what users of the language do with it. Apart from that, a word is just a sound pattern, devoid of special significance. The other two theories mentioned, the ideational and the stimulus–response, look within the activity of using language for the key to meaning. The ideational theory concentrates on the inner connection between conscious ideas and speech behavior, and the stimulus–response theory concentrates on outer, publicly observable connections between speech and the stimuli that evoke it, on the one hand, and responses to which speech gives rise, on the other. Either of these theories can be cast as a statement of the connections between words and their referents, in which case they are saddled with the assumption examined above, that all meaningful expressions refer to something. But they need not tie themselves to the referential theory by this assumption, and in examining particular theories of these types we shall abstract from this difficulty, insofar as this is possible.

Ideational theory. One of the classic statements of the ideational theory was given by the seventeenth-century British philosopher John Locke: "The use, then, of words is to be sensible marks of ideas; and the ideas they stand for are their proper and immediate signification" (*Essay Concerning Human Understanding*, Bk. III, Ch. 2, Sec. 1). The conception of language and speech that lies behind this statement is as follows: Language is essentially an instrument for the communication of thought. Thought consists of a succession of ideas in consciousness, these ideas being directly accessible only to their possessor. In order to make others cognizant of one's thoughts, one employs publicly observable sounds and marks as representations of these ideas. Communication is successful when my utterance arouses in you the same idea which led, in me, to its issuance. Thus the crucial fact about a word, semantically, is its regular association with a certain idea.

The conception of thought involved here has often been criticized, especially its assumption that thought exists independently of language, the latter coming in only because *interpersonal* communication is desirable. For present purposes, however, we shall concentrate on the more strictly semantic features of this view. The ideational theory of meaning can work only if for every meaningful linguistic expression—or, rather, for every distinguishable sense of every expression—there is an idea which is regularly associated with that expression. To say it is regularly associated is not to imply that the word is never uttered without being triggered by the idea; Locke is at pains to point out that most of the time we use language "unthinkingly." It implies only that there are occasions on which the occurrence of this idea gives rise to the utterance of the word and that these are the basic occasions by derivation from which the other occasions deserve the name of speech. One way of putting this is to say that the word is not being used with a specific meaning unless the speaker *could* call up the appropriate idea in connection with the word if he chose to do so. Unfortunately, this does not seem to be the case. Consider a sentence taken at random, "Increases in the standard of living have not been offset by corresponding increases in the income of clerical personnel." Ask yourself whether there was a distinguishable idea in your mind corresponding to each of the meaningful linguistic units of the sentence, "increases," "in," "the," "standard," etc. One can safely predict that most people not only would report no distinctive imagery actually occurring when they spoke or heard the sentence but would not be able to call up an idea distinctive of each of the constituent words. It may be that whenever I hear or speak a word whose meaning I know, such as "increases," I have a vague sense of familiarity with the word, and I might term this sense an "idea of 'increases.'" But this would not be the sort of "idea" required for Locke's theory. If we are to explain meaning in terms of word–idea association, we will have to bring in ideas which are identifiable apart from recognizing what the word means. Otherwise the explanation will be circular. That is why Locke and his followers have concentrated on sensory imagery; a given sensory image seems to be introspectively recognizable apart from language. Thus the ideational theorist is caught in a dilemma. If he insists on independently recognizable sensory ideas, he cannot find enough to make his theory work. If he uses "idea" as it is used in a phrase like "I get the idea," he can perhaps claim that every meaningful word is associated with a distinctive idea. But one can specify what an idea of "standard" is only by saying that it is what one gets when one is aware of the word "standard" and knows what it means; hence "ideas" of this sort cannot be brought into an account of the nature of meaning.

There are difficulties even for those words that are most closely linked to sensory imagery. Even here there is no one-to-one correspondence between associated image and meaning. The same image can be associated with words of different meaning, and the same word (in the same sense) can have widely different images associated with it. The image of a sleeping beagle might well accompany the utterance of "beagle," "sleep," "home," "quiet," "peace," "hound," "dog," "sports," or "animal," to mention only a few of the possibilities. The word "dog," in its usual sense, may at one time be accompanied by the image of a collie, at another time by the image of a terrier, on one occasion by the image of a dog sitting, on another by the image of a dog standing, and so on. Ideas are not distributed in the way required by the ideational theory.

Stimulus–response theory. A further deficiency in the ideational theory stems from the fact that we do not settle questions about meaning by looking for ideas in the minds of speakers and listeners. If I am in doubt about the exact sense in which you used the word "social" in something you said, I do not try to find out by asking you what imagery accompanied your utterance of the word. It is not clear what we do look for to settle such questions, but the fact that we have public consensus on what words mean strongly suggests that meaning is a function of publicly observable aspects of the language situation. This consideration has inspired a number of thinkers to develop a theory of meaning in terms of such aspects. Obvious candidates present themselves as soon as we recall that speech occurs in physical contexts and that it typically has some effect on the person(s) addressed. It is natural, then, to look for meaning in regularities of connection between utterances and publicly observable features of the communication situation. This tendency has been reinforced by the successes of psychologists in explaining certain aspects of behavior in terms of stimulus–response connections, thereby giving rise to a hope that the treatment can be extended to verbal behavior.

The crudest forms of the theory are to be found in the writings of linguists who have taken over concepts from behaviorally oriented psychology with little awareness of the difficulties involved. Thus, Leonard Bloomfield has said that the "meaning of a linguistic form" is "the situation in which the speaker utters it and the response which it calls forth in the hearer" (*Language*, p. 139). This formulation is absurdly oversimplified. A moment's reflection should suffice to bring out the great variety of situations in which almost any given word—"house," "impressive," "in," "whereas"—is uttered. It seems clear that there is nothing common to all these situations which is distinctive of the meaning of the word. Analogous comments apply to responses to utterances.

Sophisticated forms of the theory. Such psychologists as Charles Osgood and such behaviorally oriented philosophers as Charles Morris have developed more sophisticated accounts. Interestingly enough, they have focused exclusively on the responses to utterances and have ignored the situations in which the utterances occur. Perhaps this is because they have taken natural signs (for example, a certain noise as a sign of an improperly seated valve) as their model for the treatment of language. Natural signs are not intentionally *produced,* so the focus of a behavioral analysis would be on their interpretation construed in terms of responses. Working within these limitations, both Osgood and Morris try to take account of two difficulties facing a behavioral analysis: (1) On different occasions very different responses are made to the utterance of a given expression, even when used in the same sense. (2) Sometimes there is no overt response at all. Osgood tries to deal with these complexities by identifying meaning with an "implicit" response, Morris by concentrating on a "disposition" to respond.

Osgood's account intimately depends on the assumption (criticized earlier) that every meaningful linguistic expression refers to something (or, in his terms, is a "sign" of something). Furthermore, he assumes that there will be typical responses to the thing of which a given word is the "sign." In his view the word functions as it does through eliciting a fractional portion of the response normally called out by its object. Thus, the word "hammer" does its job by calling out in the listener implicit grasping and pounding responses. These "fractional" responses usually do not get as far as overt action. They are generally confined to purely internal muscular contractions, glandular secretions, and neural processes and hence are properly termed "implicit." Osgood then identifies the meaning of an expression with an appropriate set of such implicit fractional responses. Morris, on the other hand, finds the crucial semantic fact about language in the production of a disposition to respond rather than in the elicitation of an actual (even implicit) response. His idea can be explained as follows: Suppose I say to you, "There is beer in the refrigerator." As previously noted, we cannot find any overt response common to all, or even most, instances of this utterance. That is because the response, if there is any, is dependent on many factors other than the utterance, such as the desires and beliefs of the hearer and the social situation. If we think of the response of going to the refrigerator and getting beer, we can think of the utterance as supplying one of the conditions for that response, the knowledge that there is beer to be had there, though other conditions will still have to be satisfied—desire for beer, lack of scruples against drinking it, etc. This can be formulated thus: The utterance has produced a disposition to go to the refrigerator and get beer if one wants beer, has no scruples against drinking it, . . . To say that it has produced such a disposition is just to say that it has provided one of the conditions for such a response and hence has altered the situation in such a way that now the response will occur if the other conditions are satisfied.

The attempt to give behavioral analyses of meaning is still in an early stage, and it would be premature to deliver a final verdict. Nevertheless, one must recognize that at present they exhibit some glaring deficiencies. First of all, they are saddled with the assumption that every meaningful linguistic unit is a "sign" of some discriminable extralinguistic thing, aspect, or state of affairs. It may be that a behavioral account could be given which did not depend on the above assumption, but that this is possible is not clear, since the pertinent responses are singled out as those which are made to the "object." Second, we have the same difficulty as with the ideational theory, namely, identifying the proper sorts of entities with the right distribution. Osgood does not tell us how to get at the fractional implicit responses, and even if he could it is doubtful that they occur in such a way that for each meaning of each word there is a single such response which occurs (almost) invariably when that word is uttered in that sense.

Morris' account looks plausible as long as we stick to utterances which serve to provide information about practically relevant facts in the immediate environment. But what disposition would be produced by "The Peloponnesian War was a disaster for Greece"? Moreover, as Morris specifies dispositions, there may be an infinite number of dispositions produced by any utterance capable of producing a disposition. Consider all the actions that a person possessed of the information that the beer is in the refrigerator might perform if certain other conditions held. For example, if he could not resist pouring beer on his head, he would go to the refrigerator, get some beer, and pour it on his head. The number of such dispositions that could, by Morris' principles, be said to be produced by the utterance is limited only by the limits of our ingenuity.

Difficulties in traditional theories. Much can be learned from the unhappy fate that has befallen each of the traditional types of theory. Each is based on a real insight into the nature of language and meaning. (1) Language is used to talk about the extralinguistic world (referential), (2) it somehow expresses our thoughts and ideas (ideational), and (3) words have meaning by virtue of the ways in which they figure in human activity (stimulus–response). But all of these insights get perverted through oversimplification. Thus, (1) becomes the idea that each meaningful unit is connected with something discriminable in the extra-linguistic world in the same way as any other. On the basis of (2) it is supposed that each meaningful unit has a fixed association with a particular "idea," and (3) analogously leads to a search for regular stimulus–response associa-tions in which words figure. It is important to see that things do not work out in so piecemeal a fashion. More-over, the ideational and stimulus–response theories suffer from supposing that the meaning of a word is to be identified with something that *happens* every time it is used. In Roger Brown's happy phrase, they look for the "click of comprehension."

Accounts of meaning, as usually presented, suffer from another, more formal defect. They are generally formu-lated as answers to the question "What sort of an entity is a meaning, and how must an entity of that sort be related to a given word in order to be the meaning of that word?" Thus, the referential theory usually takes the form of say-ing that the meaning of a word *is* its referent or, alterna-tively, *is* the relation between a word and its referent; the ideational theory holds that the meaning of a word *is* the idea with which it is associated; the stimulus–response theory (in Osgood's form) holds that the meaning *is* the fractional implicit response which the word elicits. This way of viewing the problem stems from a misconception of the "logical grammar" of "means." When we say what a word means ("'Procrastinate' means—to put things off") the grammatical form of the sentence may lead us to sup-pose that we are specifying an entity which *is* the meaning of "procrastinate." But this construction of the statement is untenable, as can be seen from the fact that the activity of putting things off passes none of the tests for identity with the meaning of the word "procrastinate," or any other meaning. Thus, putting things off is an activity in which I often engage, but it makes no sense to say that I engage in the meaning of "procrastinate," or any other meaning. Phrases of the form "the meaning of *W*" simply do not operate that way. More generally, it is impossible to iden-tify the meaning of a word with any entity not already specified as a meaning. Whether we take ideas, responses, or referents (a class which obviously includes anything mentionable), many things will be true of them that it makes no sense to attribute to a meaning. Thus we might say of implicit hammering movements that they seldom occur, but what would it mean to say of the meaning of the word "hammer" that it seldom occurs? If meanings are entities, they are entities of such a *sui generis* character that they cannot be identified with any class of entities otherwise specified. Hence it is a misguided endeavor to try to clarify the concept of linguistic meaning by saying what kind of an entity a meaning is.

However, this is a purely formal criticism. It gives us no guidance in choosing between alternative theories. The substance of any theory can be preserved in other forms. Any theory put in the way we have just criticized can be restated as follows: the fact that a word has a certain mean-ing is a function of _____. Thus, according to the referen-tial theory, as so reformulated, a word has a certain mean-ing by virtue of the fact that it refers (perhaps in a certain way) to a certain object. And so for the others. Of course, these theories remain subject to all the difficulties brought out in the separate discussion of each.

MODERN ANALYSES OF MEANING

Meaning and use. In recent years a movement has de-veloped which bids fair to give birth to an analysis of meaning that avoids all these deficiencies. We may think of this movement as stemming largely from the work of Ludwig Wittgenstein at Cambridge University in the 1930s and 1940s. The prevailing attitude became crystal-lized into a slogan: "Don't look for the meaning, look for the use." In the background is a pragmatic view of the nature of language. As Wittgenstein put it, in the *Philo-sophical Investigations,* "Look at the sentence as an in-strument, and at its sense as its employment" (I, 421). In a sense this is the same emphasis we have in the ideational and stimulus–response theories, which also look for the clue to meaning in the way language figures in human behavior. But there are significant differences. For one thing, Wittgenstein and his followers, as the slogan indi-cates, are aware of the point made above, that it is a mis-take to try to locate "the meaning" of an expression in some realm of being or other. For another, they stress the diversity of uses of language and hence are protected against such oversimplifications as that language is always used to convey information or that every meaningful expression functions as a "sign" of something. Finally, they have focused on the behavior of the speaker as the place to look for the use of language. It is a striking fact that behaviorally oriented theorists have generally man-aged to ignore the fact that the speaker is doing something when he speaks. They have looked for the determinants of meaning either in the stimuli which elicit his utterance or in the responses to which it gives rise. This is undoubtedly because of the fact that they have been working with a severely limited concept of a verbal action. If we think of a speaker's behavior as made up solely of the production of sounds patterned in a certain way, we are obviously not going to find anything there that determines one meaning for his words rather than another. If our conception of what he is doing is so limited, we will be forced to look outside his action—in its causes, effects, or concomitants—for the determinants of meaning. But it is not necessary to be so impoverished. A great many of the things people are said to do when speaking—such as make a request, announce something, frighten someone, or convince someone of something—do not simply consist of uttering sentences. If we can enlarge our notion of linguistic behavior to include actions of these sorts and can provide an adequate account of what is involved in them, we may be able to exploit the common-sense notion that the sense in which a person employs words is a function of what he is doing with them in that employment, what he is using the words to do. John Austin's classification of linguistic behavior into "locutionary," "illocutionary," and "perlocutionary" acts has provided a strong impetus in this direction.

Meaning and linguistic acts. It should be remembered that the bearer of meaning, be it a word, phrase, or sentence, is a relatively abstract entity. A word is a pattern of temporally ordered sound types to which particular soundings may more or less approximate. Hence, meaning does not attach to particular activities, sounds, marks on paper, or anything else with a definite spatiotemporal locus. It is a fundamental mistake to say, as people often do, that one gives a word a meaning on a certain occasion by using it with a certain intention or purpose (of course, one can explicitly define a word in a certain way, but that happens rarely) or that the words one uses lose their meaning if one misuses them. A word is a common possession of the linguistic community, and it has the meaning(s) it has by virtue of some general facts about what goes on in that community. Hence, we must look for general trends in linguistic behavior if we are to exhibit the meanings of words as functions of what speakers do with them.

Approaching the matter this way, it is natural to begin with the sentence, for the sentence is the smallest linguistic unit with which a complete action can be performed. (One might define the notion of a sentence in this way.) Ordinarily one cannot *say* anything by just uttering a single word. This is possible only in special contexts. If you have said, "Do you want lemon or cream?" I can say something by just uttering the word "lemon." But in such cases the context functions so as to make the one word equivalent to the full sentence "I want lemon." There are various kinds of actions that people can perform by uttering sentences, and to exhibit meaning as a function of what people do with language, care must be taken to focus on the proper category. Using Austin's terms (but not in exactly the way he did), we can say that normally when a person says something he utters a certain sentence (locutionary act), he produces certain effects, such as informing, persuading, or frightening someone (perlocutionary act), and he does something else, the nature of which cannot be briefly explained except to say that it is not simply a locutionary act but also does not go beyond this by essentially involving a certain kind of effect the way a perlocutionary act does (illocutionary act). Examples of this last category are making a certain request, promise, or announcement, telling someone something, and congratulating someone on an accomplishment. Starting with the notion that a sentence's having a certain meaning is a function of its regularly being used to perform a certain action, it is obvious that the locutionary act is not what is crucial here, since that simply consists in uttering the sentence. The locutionary act essentially involves nothing further that could determine one meaning of the sentence rather than another. The perlocutionary act will not work either. The fact that "Mankind is on the verge of extinction" and "Boo" can both be used to frighten people does nothing to show that they have even partially the same meaning. On reflection we can see that it is the illocutionary act which provides what we are looking for. It is the fact that "Would

you open the door?" is regularly used to ask someone to open a certain door that gives the sentence the distinctive meaning it has and makes it roughly synonymous with "Please open the door." It is the fact that "What time is it?" and *Quelle heure est-il?* are both used to ask someone what time it is which makes one a translation of the other. As a first step we can say that for a sentence to have a certain meaning is for that sentence to be used to perform a certain illocutionary act.

Rules and regularities. At this point one of the major issues in contemporary semantic discussions looms before us: whether meaning is to be conceived in terms of rules or in terms of *de facto* regularities. If we try to think of the meaning of "You're not going out this evening" as a function of the fact that whenever someone utters the sentence he is ordering someone to stay in, we get into trouble. For there will be a significant number of occasions on which the sentence is uttered but no such illocutionary act is performed. Some of these we can handle by distinguishing different uses of the sentence. In one or another context it is used to make a prediction, give an example, be ironical. This is just the familiar point that most expressions in a language have more than one meaning. To accommodate the point in the present framework it will be necessary to develop some method of distinguishing contexts (something which has never been done); we can then regard each meaning of the sentence as determined by the fact that in a certain range of contexts it is regularly used to perform a certain illocutionary act. But there are other difficulties. Even if we are in the right context for ordering the addressee to stay in this evening, the sentence may be uttered without that illocutionary act's being performed. The speaker may be unfamiliar with the language and may be using the wrong words to say what he wanted to say, or there may be a slip of the tongue, and so on. Of course we could say that what gives the sentence a certain meaning on those occasions is the fact that usually when it is uttered in those contexts the speaker is ordering someone to stay in. But then we would have difficulty in distinguishing between by-and-large correlations which determine meaning and those which do not. (For a possible example of the latter, suppose that generally people scratch their heads when uttering "Maybe I will.") These problems naturally lead to the idea that a sentence is semantically connected to an illocutionary act by a rule rather than a *de facto* regularity. According to this view, what gives "You're not going out this evening" one of its meanings is the fact that in the English language community there is a rule in force which says that in certain contexts the sentence is to be used to order the addressee to stay in. Theorists who have worked with the construction and study of simple artificial languages (see ARTIFICIAL AND NATURAL LANGUAGES) have long treated meaning as a matter of rules, and there are actual features of speech behavior which would support the project of extending this practice to natural language. This interpretation easily handles deviations from the regularity, since the existence of a rule is compatible with a large number of violations. (The fact that tennis players often footfault does not alter the fact that this practice is forbidden by a rule.) When someone *misuses* a word or sentence, we do not just take this as an exception to a generally valid regularity the way we would the fact that on a particular occasion a certain young girl has not, as she usually does, blushed at the mention of love. On the contrary, we treat the deviation as something to be dealt with. If the person misusing the word is a small child or a foreigner learning the language we give him instruction in the correct use. If the deviation was a slip of the tongue we call the speaker's attention to it. And so on. That is, we treat such irregularities as deviations from a norm that it is in the interests of society to maintain in force. This would seem to justify our speaking of rules here. On the other hand, some philosophers have violently objected to this interpretation on the ground that one can properly use the term "rule" only where the supposed rules are explicitly formulated, or at least *could* be explicitly formulated, by the participants. At present the point is still a matter of controversy.

Uses of words. The analysis of sentence meaning is only a first step. The crux of the problem is word meaning. In fact, we rarely have occasion to say what a sentence means. One can explain this fact without supposing, with Gilbert Ryle, that the notion of the meaning of a sentence does not make sense. Specifications of meaning are provided in the course of helping another person to increase his mastery of the language, and it is obviously more economical to do this by telling him what words mean and then giving him rules (or depending on his prior knowledge of them) for putting these words together into sentences than by telling him the meaning of each sentence. Indeed, the latter is impossible, since no limit can be put on the number of sentences that can be formed in a language. However, it is not immediately obvious how we should proceed in explicating the notion of a meaning of a word in terms of what speakers do with the word. We do not have at hand a rich battery of terms for talking about what is done with words which is at all comparable to the almost indefinite variety of illocutionary act terms. One approach would involve building on the analysis of sentence meaning. If a sentence gets a meaning through being assigned by rule to the performance of a certain illocutionary act in a certain range of contexts, then, since the illocutionary act potential of the sentence is surely somehow a function of the words it contains plus the structure of their combination into the sentence, it is reasonable to suppose that a word gets a certain meaning through being assigned by a rule to make a certain distinctive contribution to the illocutionary act potential of sentences in which it occurs. Thus, according to this idea the fact that "shirt" is used in the same sense in "Bring me my shirt," "What a beautiful shirt," and "I need a new shirt," is a function of the fact that the word "shirt" makes the same contribution to the illocutionary act potential of each of these sentences. In order to make progress along this line we would need a more positive characterization of the nature of an illocutionary act than was provided above, when the notion was introduced in largely negative terms. That is, if we are to think of the different meaningful constituents of a sentence, each contributing a part of the capacity of the sentence to be used in performing a certain illocutionary act, we shall need an analysis of what it is to perform an illocutionary act that allows for an assignment of different parts of the act to

different parts of the sentence. Presumably what is involved in an illocutionary act in addition to the uttering of a sentence is a set of conditions in the context of which the sentence is to be uttered. If we could then construe the separate parts of the sentence as tied by rules to these several conditions (with the result that the whole sentence is tied by rule to the whole set of conditions), we would have the materials for a thoroughgoing analysis of meaning along these lines. Unfortunately, the most obvious ways of stating conditions that enter into an illocutionary act do not yield this kind of result. Thus, to say that in certain contexts "You're not going out this evening" is assigned by rule to ordering someone to stay in is to say that there is a rule specifying that it is not to be uttered in those contexts unless the following conditions hold:

(1) There is a possibility that the addressee will go out on the evening of the day of the utterance.

(2) It is the will of the speaker that the addressee not go out that evening.

(3) The speaker has authority over the addressee.

Clearly we have no one-to-one correspondence between conditions and meaningful units of the sentence. Intuitively we can see that the expressions "evening," "go out," and "this" all enter into the first and second conditions. This is a problem which still awaits solution.

Criteria of synonymy. Although at its present stage of development the foregoing kind of analysis cannot handle the notion of word meaning, it can provide an account of word synonymy. That is, we can say that two words are synonymous to the extent that they can be substituted for each other in sentences without altering the illocutionary act potential of the sentences. This criterion requires only that we make judgments of sameness and difference with respect to the illocutionary act potentials of sentences before and after substitution. It does not require us to analyze a particular illocutionary act potential in such a way as to make clear the contribution of each sentence constituent.

The criterion of synonymy most commonly put forward in the literature is that two expressions are synonymous to the extent that they can be substituted for each other in sentences without altering truth-values. The present criterion is in the same spirit, but it gets closer to fundamentals. This is partly because what basically has to remain the same through these substitutions is *what is said*. A change in truth-value is an indication of a change in what is said, for if one statement is true and another false they cannot be the same statement, but it is a relatively inadequate indication for the simple reason that statements with radically different content can have the same truth-value. The proponents of the criterion under discussion try to neutralize this factor by requiring (for complete synonymy) that the two expressions be substitutable in every sentence (where either can occur) without altering truth-value. The assumption is that even though two nonsynonymous expressions might be substituted for each other in many sentences without altering truth-value, they could not for the entire range of sentences in which either occurs. Whether this assumption is justified is a matter of controversy. Be that as it may, if it is true that what is said is directly a function of what illocutionary act is performed, we will be getting at this much more directly if we attend to the effect of substitution on illocutionary act potential. The second reason that this criterion is more fundamental is that it takes into account the whole range of sentential contexts in which an expression occurs. There are many sentences in which one expression can be substituted for another where questions of alteration of truth value do not arise because the sentence is not used to say something which is true or false (for example, "Bring me my shirt"). Yet alteration of what is said in these contexts should count against synonymy as much as alteration of what is said in statement-making contexts.

Synonymy and the concept of meaning. It is important to understand that the analysis of synonymy is sufficient for the analysis of specifications of meaning as they are ordinarily made. That is because what we do when we say what an expression means is to exhibit another expression which we are claiming to be (at least roughly) synonymous. Hence, if we have an effective criterion of synonymy, we are in a position to make explicit what we are saying about a word when we say what it means.

Of course, there is still much work to be done on this, and any other, account of synonymy. First, we have to decide what to do with substitution inside quotation marks. No matter how synonymous another word is (intuitively) with "shirt," we will not preserve illocutionary act potential if we substitute it for "shirt" in the sentence "'Shirt' contains the letters *s, h, i, r,* and *t,* in that order." Second, since even apart from very special contexts like this practically no two expressions are substitutable everywhere, pairs of expressions are going to differ in degree of synonymy. If a degree concept of synonymy is actually applied to particular cases, there must be some method of weighing the relevant factors, such as the proportion of types of sentential contexts in which substitution can be carried out without substantially altering illocutionary act potential and the extent to which alterations occur when they do occur. This calls for a number of developments, such as a classification of sentential contexts. And over and above all this, much more needs to be done with the notion of an illocutionary act before a general method for determining when illocutionary act potential has or has not altered can be developed. But at least a promising start has been made on the notion of synonymy along these lines.

Although an adequate notion of synonymy would suffice for an elucidation of specifications of meaning, it would not suffice for a complete analysis of the concept of linguistic meaning, for there are other important contexts in which the concept of linguistic meaning occurs which are not derivable in any obvious way from specifications of meaning. Thus, we often have occasion to talk about someone's knowing the meaning of a word, how the meaning of the word is learned, or what is required if one is to come to know what it means. And we talk about a sentence having a meaning or not having a meaning. None of these uses of the concept can be analyzed in terms of synonymy. One can know what a word means without knowing that it is synonymous with some other expression, and for a sentence to have a meaning it is not necessary that there be some other sentence with which it is synonymous. If these contexts are to be analyzed along the lines we have been exploring, it is not enough to specify the conditions under which one word is used to do the same thing as another. A way must be found to specify *what* it is used to do. If we could do that, we could make explicit what it is a person learns when he learns what a word means, and likewise for the other uses of the concept mentioned above. This brings us back to the unsolved task of developing a set of concepts that would illuminate the contribution a meaningful constituent of a sentence makes to the illocutionary act potential of the whole sentence.

Bibliography

Bertrand Russell has been one of the most influential writers on the topic of meaning in this century. His views, which have changed over the years and which incorporate elements from all the theories of meaning presented in this article, are to be found in the series of lectures entitled "The Philosophy of Logical Atomism" (reprinted in *Logic and Knowledge,* R. C. Marsh, ed., London, 1956), in *The Analysis of Mind* (London, 1921), Ch. 10, and in *An Inquiry Into Meaning and Truth* (New York, 1940).

The reference theory of meaning is found mostly in works on logic. From the nineteenth century there are J. S. Mill's *A System of Logic* (London, 1906), Bk. I, and Gottlob Frege's "On Sense and Reference," in *Philosophical Writings,* Peter Geach and Max Black, eds. (Oxford, 1952). More contemporary versions include Alonzo Church, "The Need for Abstract Entities in Semantic Analysis," in *Proceedings of the American Academy of Arts and Sciences,* Vol. 80 (1951), 100–112, and C. I. Lewis, *An Analysis of Knowledge and Valuation* (La Salle, Ill., 1946), Part I. Rudolf Carnap has used the referential concept of meaning to construct elaborate "semantic systems" in *Introduction to Semantics* (Cambridge, Mass., 1942) and *Meaning and Necessity* (Chicago, 1947).

The ideational theory received its classic formulation in John Locke's *Essay Concerning Human Understanding,* Bk. III. For a near-contemporary critique see George Berkeley, *Alciphron,* Book VII. Modern refinements include C. L. Stevenson's formulation in terms of dispositions of linguistic expressions to produce psychological effects in the hearer, in *Ethics and Language* (New Haven, Conn., 1944), Ch. 3, and a formulation in terms of intentions of speakers to produce such effects, in Henry Leonard's *An Introduction to the Principles of Right Reason* (New York, 1957), Unit 14, and in H. P. Grice's "Meaning," in *Philosophical Review,* Vol. 66 (July 1957), 377–388.

One of the earliest and most influential presentations of the stimulus–response theory (though contaminated by ideational elements) is to be found in C. K. Ogden and I. A. Richards, *The Meaning of Meaning* (New York, 1938), Chs. 3 and 9. Presentations of this kind of approach by linguists include Leonard Bloomfield, *Language* (London, 1935), and C. C. Fries, "Meaning and Linguistic Analysis," in *Language,* Vol. 30 (1951). Paul Ziff, *Semantic Analysis* (Ithaca, N.Y., 1960), and W. V. Quine, *Word and Object* (New York, 1960), contain different developments of the notion that the meaning of an expression is a function of the conditions under which the expression is uttered. Charles Morris, *Signs, Language, and Behavior* (Englewood Cliffs, N.J., 1946), Charles Osgood, *Method and Theory in Experimental Psychology* (New York, 1953), Ch. 16, and B. F. Skinner, *Verbal Behavior* (New York, 1957), are basic sources for a predominantly behavioral theory. Ch. 3 of Roger Brown's *Words and Things* (New York, 1958) is a valuable review of stimulus–response theories, and Ch. 7 of Max Black's *Language and Philosophy* (Ithaca, N.Y., 1949) is a penetrating criticism of Morris' views.

Among important discussions not readily classifiable in terms of our schema is J. J. Katz and J. A. Fodor, "The Structure of a Semantic Theory," reprinted in their anthology *The Structure of Language* (Englewood Cliffs, N.J., 1964). In this essay the authors attempt to elucidate semantic concepts by using devices developed in recent linguistic theory.

Ludwig Wittgenstein's *Philosophical Investigations,* translated by G. E. M. Anscombe (Oxford, 1953), is a source of seminal ideas concerning the relation between meaning and the use of language. The essays collected in *Ordinary Language,* V. C. Chappell, ed. (Englewood Cliffs, N.J., 1964), throw light on the way in which contemporary analytical philosophers are concerned with the *use* of expressions. The semantic view sketchily developed in this article is presented in more detail in W. P. Alston, "The Quest for Meanings," in *Mind,* Vol. 72 (January 1963), 79–87; "Meaning and Use," in *Philosophical Quarterly,* Vol. 13 (April 1963), 107–124; "Linguistic Acts," in *American Philosophical Quarterly,* Vol. 1 (April 1964), 1–9; and *Philosophy of Language* (Englewood Cliffs, N.J., 1964), Chs. 1 and 2. John Austin's stimulating discussion of linguistic action is contained in *How to Do Things With Words* (London, 1962).

Important discussions of the notion of synonymy include Nelson Goodman, "On Likeness of Meaning," and Benson Mates, "Synonymy," both reprinted in Leonard Linsky, ed., *Semantics and the Philosophy of Language* (Urbana, Ill., 1952). Michael Scriven, "Definitions, Explanations, and Theories," *Minnesota Studies in the Philosophy of Science,* Vol. II, Herbert Feigl and Michael Scriven, eds. (Minneapolis, 1958), contains a penetrating discussion of the relation of synonymy to specifications of meaning.

WILLIAM P. ALSTON

MEANING, EMOTIVE OR EXPRESSIVE. See EMOTIVE MEANING.

MEASUREMENT is the practice of applying arithmetic to the study of quantitative relationships. The logic of measurement is concerned with the principles that govern this practice and with the conditions for its possibility. This article will deal mainly with the logic of measurement.

History of the practice of measurement. The art of measurement is as old as recorded history. From earliest times men have been able to measure length, weight, time interval, and angle—the techniques used being essentially similar to those we use today—and to measure (or calculate) speed, area, volume, and density. Speeds and densities have always been calculated from the results of other measurements. Areas and volumes are either measured directly, by "stepping-off" procedures analogous to those used in length measurement, or calculated indirectly from the results of length measurements.

The development of geometry in early Greek science extended the range of shapes whose areas and volumes could be measured indirectly. By the time of Archimedes (c. 287–212 B.C.) the areas and volumes of quite complex geometric figures were rendered calculable from the results of length measurements. Archimedes showed, for example, how the volume of a paraboloid of revolution could be determined.

Although the techniques of calculation were well developed in Greek times, the art of making the required primary measurements was not enthusiastically pursued. Clocks capable of measuring short time intervals accurately were unknown to the Greeks. Universal weight and length standards were not employed. The result was, as A. C. Crombie put it, that the theory of quantitative relationships outstripped the practice of determining them experimentally. The result of this is nowhere more evident than in the field of dynamics.

In Aristotelian theory, for example, the speed of a body in violent motion was supposed to be directly proportional to the force acting on it and inversely proportional to the resistance of the medium. But the theory did not explain how to measure either the acting force or the resistance of the medium. Nor, for that matter, were the known techniques for measuring speed sufficiently refined to enable experimenters to make any decisive check on the Aristotelian law of motion—even supposing that ways of measuring force and resistance were well developed. The development of measuring techniques in this field—and, indeed, in most other fields—had simply not kept pace with the corresponding quantitative theory.

This gap did not begin to close again until the sixteenth century, when Tycho Brahe set up his remarkable observatory. From then on, an accelerating development and refinement of the techniques of measurement took place. In the seventeenth century the mechanical clock was invented, and the first real beginnings of temperature and pressure measurement were made. In the eighteenth century objective temperature scales were adopted, and considerable advances were made in the techniques for measuring almost every other physical quantity. In the nineteenth century the theory of error came under close scrutiny, the techniques of physical measurement were refined beyond anything imagined in the eighteenth century, and a start was made in psychophysical measurement. Particularly important in the nineteenth century was the work of Adolphe Quételet and later of Sir Francis Galton in applying elementary statistical methods to social, biological, and psychological data. This led to the vast expansion of the techniques of biometrics and sociometrics in the twentieth century and, through the work of Karl Pearson, J. M. Cattell, Alfred Binet, and others, to the development of objective mental tests.

Of similar importance was the work done in psychophysical measurement. The discovery of the so-called psychophysical laws of E. H. Weber and Gustav Fechner gave great impetus to psychometrics, for until the late nineteenth century there were (indeed, there are even today) many who believed that although the development of objective psychological scales might be possible, measurements on these scales could not possibly have any independent significance.

The progress in the twentieth century is already comparable only with that of the nineteenth century. Nineteenth-century measuring techniques in every field now seem crude as compared with those available to us today.

It is significant that the evolution of measuring techniques has accompanied the accelerated evolution of modern science. Although it certainly cannot be said that all scientific progress depends on the development of adequate ways of measuring, it is the development of measuring techniques, sufficiently refined to allow distinction between rival hypotheses and theories, which, above all else, distinguishes modern science from ancient.

History of the logic of measurement. The logic of measurement, as opposed to its practice, has a comparatively short history. Apart from the ancient Greek discovery of incommensurables, there were no major advances in this field until the nineteenth century. When philosophers spoke of measurement they did so within the framework of Platonic idealism, and this continued until the present century. Thus, a measuring technique was considered accurate or inaccurate depending on whether it yielded the true magnitude or degree of the quantity it was designed to measure. Even today we find that some philosophers think there is an absolute distinction between linear and nonlinear scales for the measurement of certain quantities. (What is a scale linear or nonlinear with respect to, if not another scale?)

Ernst Mach was the first to make a decisive break with this outlook. His analyses of quantitative physical concepts, particularly mass and temperature, were the first important advances in the logic of measurement since pre-Socratic times. They were important because they succeeded in changing men's views about the significance of the numerical assignments that are made in the course of measurement, a change of viewpoint that was necessary for the two great twentieth-century revolutions in physical theory—relativity and quantum theory. This article is written within an essentially Machian framework.

Quantities. We have said that measurement is concerned with quantitative relationships. Roughly speaking, a quantitative relationship is any that may be described as a "greater than," "equal to," or "less than" relationship. Thus, "heavier than," "as long as," "more than," "not so pretty as," and "more intelligent than" are all names of quantitative relationships, since we could as well use the terms "greater in weight than," "equal in length to," "greater in number than," "less pretty than," and "greater in intelligence than" to describe these same relationships. Some of these phrases are clumsy, but we should have no difficulty in understanding them to mean the same as their more colloquial equivalents. In place of the expressions "greater in p than," "equal in p to," and "less in p than," the terms "$>_p$," "$=_p$," and "$<_p$" will be used, and a set of three quantitative relationships for the same aspect will be called a set of quantitative relationships.

If one thing can be said to be greater than, equal to, or less than another in a certain respect, then this respect may be called a quantity. Thus, weight, length, density, intelligence, probability, and even prettiness are all quantities. This usage may not be universally acceptable. Some may wish to distinguish certain subclasses of aspects in which things may be connected by quantitative relationships and reserve the term "quantity" for aspects belonging to one of these subclasses. N. R. Campbell, for example, proposed to restrict the use of the word "quantity" in such a way when he distinguished between quantities and qualities. However, the existence of a set of quantitative relationships is at least a necessary condition for the existence of a quantity, and it will not be misleading to suppose that it is also a sufficient condition.

Under what conditions, then, is it appropriate to use expressions of the forms "$>_p$," "$=_p$," and "$<_p$" to designate a given set of relationships, which, for the moment, we shall designate by the logically neutral terms "R_1," "R_0," and "R_2"? Part of the answer is that it is appropriate to use the expressions "$>_p$," "$=_p$," and "$<_p$" to describe R_1, R_0, and R_2 only if R_1, R_0, and R_2 in fact possess the formal characteristics of the arithmetical relationships $>$, $=$, and $<$, respectively. Thus,

(1) R_0, R_1, and R_2 must be in fact a set of mutually exclusive binary relationships. That is, if A and B are any

two systems that may be connected by any one of these relationships, then

$$\sim(AR_iB.AR_jB), \qquad i \neq j.$$

(2) R_0, R_1, and R_2 must be in fact a set of alternative relationships. That is, if A and B are any two systems that could (logically) be connected by any one of these relationships, then

$$(AR_1B) \cdot \vee \cdot (AR_0B) \cdot \vee \cdot (AR_2B).$$

(3) R_0 must in fact be symmetrical and transitive.

(4) R_1 and R_2 must each in fact be asymmetrical and transitive.

(5) R_1 and R_2 must in fact be converse relationships.

These are certainly necessary conditions for describing R_1, R_0, and R_2 as a set of quantitative relationships, and hence they are also necessary conditions for the existence of quantity.

Can we also say that they are sufficient conditions? Suppose, for example, we construct an arbitrary set of questions that it is always appropriate to answer with "yes" or "no." Then it is obvious that any two subjects A and B who are required to answer these questions must be related by one or another of the following relationships:

(a) A gives as many "yes" answers as B.

(b) A gives more "yes" answers than B.

(c) A gives fewer "yes" answers than B.

These relationships clearly satisfy all of the conditions (1) to (5). But we should not ordinarily regard them as a set of quantitative relationships. Since the list of test questions is arbitrary, we should not be inclined to say that A was greater than, equal to, or less than B in any respect just because he gave more, as many, or fewer "yes" answers to these questions.

What additional requirements, then, would be needed to give us sufficient conditions for the existence of a quantity? Here we might fall back on the Maxwell–Bridgman criterion for physical reality. First, we should note that any relationships that satisfy the conditions (1) to (5) are order-generating relationships. Let R_0 be the symmetrical and transitive relationship satisfying the conditions (1) to (5) and R_1 and R_2 the asymmetrical relationships. Let A and B be any two things that are connected by R_0, R_1, or R_2. Then it is always, in principle, possible to arrange those things that are connected by these relationships into a linear order such that A occurs above, at the same level as, or below B, according as AR_1B, AR_0B, or AR_2B. Relationships that satisfy the conditions (1) to (5) may therefore be described as linear-ordering relationships.

According to the Maxwell–Bridgman criterion for physical reality, no quantity is "real" unless it is measurable by at least two logically independent procedures. Dropping the measurability requirement, which is clearly unnecessary, we might say that if two or more logically independent sets of linear-ordering relationships always generate the same order among the same things under the same conditions, then these relationships are sets of quantitative relationships—that is, they may be used to order things in respect of some quantity.

However, the Maxwell–Bridgman criterion is too restrictive, for there are many different reasons why a linear order may be an interesting one. And if it is interesting for any reason, we are likely to invent a quantity name to enable us to talk about it. That the same linear order may be generated by any of several logically independent sets of relationships would certainly make it worthy of further investigation. But the same would be true if, for example, it were highly correlated with some cruder order given in sense experience or, again, if the order were defined by the value of a system-dependent constant in a numerical law (for example, a refractive index or a dielectric constant). Consequently, the Maxwell–Bridgman criterion must be rejected. Instead, we shall say that the existence of a set of linear-ordering relationships entails and is entailed by the existence of a quantity. The problem of deciding which linear orders are sufficiently interesting to warrant the invention of special quantity names remains unsolved.

In general, it is true that things may be ordered in respect of some quantity by any of a number of logically independent sets of linear-ordering relationships. Things can be ordered in respect of temperature, for example, by any of a dozen or more logically independent procedures. The criteria for the identity of quantities, therefore, cannot be tied to the ordering relationships. It must be the order, not the ordering relationships, that is important for the identity of quantities. Accordingly, it will be said that two logically independent sets of ordering relationships are sets of quantitative relationships for the same quantity if and only if they always generate the same order among the same things under the same conditions.

SCALES

Measurement always involves the application of arithmetic. But every measurement is made on some scale. Consequently, we should expect a close connection between our concept of a scale and our concept of an application of arithmetic. We should expect, perhaps, to find that different kinds of scales represent different kinds of applications of arithmetic.

Scale of measurement. The classification of scales will be discussed later. But first, what is it to have a scale of measurement; second, what is it to have a scale for the measurement of any given quantity; and third, what are the criteria for the identity of scales?

According to S. S. Stevens (in "Measurement, Psychophysics and Utility," p. 19), to make a measurement is simply to make "an assignment of numerals to things according to a rule—any rule." Since every measurement must be made on some scale, if Stevens' criterion is accepted we have a scale of measurement if and only if we have a rule for making numerical assignments. But unless some restrictions are placed on the nature of the rule, it is possible that we will make different numerical assignments to the same things under the same conditions while yet following the same rule. For example, the instruction "Think of a number and write it down" is a rule for making numerical assignments. But no one could be said to be measuring anything, in any respect, on any scale at all, if this were his procedure. On what scale could he be said to be measuring?

Again, consider the rule that to any two substances A and B the numerals a and b are to be assigned in such a way that $a \gtreqless b$ according as A scratches B, A does not scratch and is not scratched by B, or A is scratched by B. If one simply makes numerical assignments according to this rule, one cannot yet be said to be making measurements. We may, indeed, make such assignments in setting up a scale of measurement, but these numerical assignments are not the results of measurements. No one has measured the hardness of diamond and found that on Mohs' scale it is 10. Nor has anyone measured the standard meter in Paris and found that it is exactly one meter long. We must distinguish between those numerical assignments which we must make in defining a scale and those which we make on a scale that is already established. Only the latter may be termed "measurements."

The reason we do not wish to say that the rules considered in the above examples define scales of measurement seems clear enough. It is simply that the rules are not determinative—i.e., such that anyone who follows them with sufficient care would be led to make the same numerical assignments to the same things under the same conditions. It will therefore be said that we have a scale of measurement if and only if we have a determinative rule for making numerical assignments.

Measurement of a quantity. What is it to have a scale for the measurement of a given quantity q? The answer that suggests itself is that we have a scale for the measurement of q if and only if we have a determinative rule for making numerical assignments to things possessing q, such that if those things are arranged in the order of the numerals that would be assigned to them according to this rule, then they are also arranged in the order of q.

It may be objected that this criterion is unduly restrictive, since it rules out the possibility of nominal scales (on the notion of nominal scales, see the two items by S. S. Stevens in the bibliography) for the measurement of a given quantity. But those nominal scales which have been described certainly cannot be said to be scales for the measurement of a quantity. Numbers assigned to football players, for example, cannot be said to be the results of measurements of anything (save, perhaps, sameness and difference).

It may also be objected that this criterion is not sufficiently restrictive, since it allows for the possibility of mass and length scales which are dissimilar—that is, not related by similarity transformations (explained below) to our ordinary scales for the measurement of these quantities. But no one has objected to E. A. Milne's mutually dissimilar time scales on the ground that no more than one of them can be a genuine time scale. Why, then, should anyone object to mutually dissimilar mass or length scales? The onus is surely on anyone who wishes to object in this way to say why he so wishes and to set up alternative criteria to those which have been given for the identity of quantities (for presumably he must say that at least one of Milne's "time" scales is a scale for the measurement of something other than time).

Identity of scales. What are the criteria for the identity of scales? What is it to say that two logically independent procedures are procedures for measuring on the same scale? Here it will be supposed that two procedures are procedures for measuring on the same scale if and only if they would always lead to the same numerical assignments (within limits of error) to the same things under the same conditions. This is at least a necessary condition, and it is not clearly inconsistent with ordinary usage to say that it is also a sufficient condition. It is true that the ideal-gas scale and Kelvin's thermodynamic scale of temperature are sometimes regarded as different scales. But as often as not they are treated as one and the same scale, and no distinction is made between different kinds of degree absolute. Accordingly, we shall simply adopt this criterion and leave it to others to prove that it is inappropriate.

Multidimensional scales. The concept of a scale that has been discussed above is that of a unidimensional scale. There are, however, multidimensional scales (see W. S. Torgerson, *Theory and Methods of Scaling*), arising from the fact that there are in nature more complex orders than the simple linear orders which give us our quantitative concepts. But the extensions to the criteria for the existence and identity of scales that should be made in the multidimensional cases are obvious enough, and they will merely be stated without discussion. We have an *n*-dimensional scale if and only if we have a determinative rule for assigning ordered sets of *n* numerals to things. Two procedures are procedures measuring on the same *n*-dimensional scale if and only if anyone who follows these procedures with sufficient care would be led to assign the same ordered sets of *n* numerals to the same things under the same conditions.

Classification of scales. In view of the close connection between the concept of a scale and that of an application of arithmetic, the most obvious approach to the classification of scales of measurement would be in terms of the kinds of application of arithmetic which they represent. This approach to the problem is the one chosen by C. H. Coombs (in *A Theory of Scaling*) and others. But other approaches have been taken, most notably by N. R. Campbell (*Physics: The Elements*) and S. S. Stevens ("On the Theory of Scales of Measurement"). Campbell's approach was operational. He proposed to classify scales according to the kinds of operations by which they may be set up. Stevens' approach was to classify scales according to the range of mathematical transformations which leave their "scale forms" invariant.

This section will not discuss these systems of classification in great detail or evaluate the various claims that have been made for them but will only follow out Coombs's approach and show its relation to Stevens'. A modified Campbellian classification will be presented later.

Arithmetical classification. Consider what is meant by an application of arithmetic. According to the formalist viewpoint, arithmetic is a purely formal system and must be applied before it can yield any information about the world. A formal system becomes applied, it is said, by its terms' being interpreted. Hence, it must be asked what it is to have an interpretation of the terms of arithmetic.

As a minimum we may demand that an interpretation of an arithmetical formula be a statement. But clearly this is not sufficient. The formula "$4+3=7$" might be read as "I like cheese very much" in a code, but we should not consider this to be an application of arithmetic. There must, therefore, be certain rules of interpretation to be satisfied before we can speak of an application of arithmetic.

No systematic attempt has been made to state these rules, but the following appear to be both necessary and sufficient conditions for saying that we have an application of arithmetic:

(1) The interpretation must be an interpretation of some formally defined class of arithmetical formulas, such as those of the form $a \gtreqless b$.

(2) The numeral terms must always be interpreted as referring to some objects or systems to which those numerals would be assigned on some specified scale of measurement.

(3) The relational terms—for example, ">," "=," "<"—must always be interpreted as referring to some relationships which connect these objects or systems, and which in fact possess the formal characteristics of the arithmetical ones.

(4) The operator terms, such as "+," "−," "×," "÷," must always be interpreted as referring to physical (or mental) operations performable on the systems connected by these relationships which in fact possess the formal properties of the arithmetical operations.

(5) The resulting statements must be true if and only if the arithmetical formulas of the interpreted class are theorems of the system of arithmetic.

The simplest kind of application of arithmetic involves only application of arithmetical formulas of the class

$$(1) \qquad a \overset{=}{\neq} b.$$

As an example of this, take the numbering of football players. In this case, "$a \overset{=}{\neq} b$" is interpreted as "a player *A* whose number is *a* (is)/(is not) the same person as a player *B* whose number is *b*." A determinative rule for assigning numbers to football players, which need satisfy only the condition that every such interpreted formula (which is a theorem of arithmetic) be a true proposition, may be said to define a nominal scale.

Ordinal scales are scales on which the only classes of arithmetical formulas that are applied are those of the form

$$(2) \qquad a \gtreqless b.$$

As an example of such a scale we may take Mohs' hardness scale. Here, "$a \gtreqless b$" is interpreted as "a substance *A* whose hardness is *a* (will scratch)/(will not scratch or be scratched by)/(will be scratched by) a substance *B* whose hardness is *b*." And the rule for assigning numerals to substances is such that (with a few exceptions) every such interpreted formula (which is an arithmetical theorem) is a true proposition.

Nominal-interval scales are scales on which only arithmetical formulas of the classes

(3a)
$$a \gtreqless b,$$
$$|a-b| \gtreqqless |c-d|$$

are applied. Ordinal-interval scales are those on which the following classes of formulas are applied:

(3b)
$$a \gtreqless b,$$
$$|a-b| \gtreqless |c-d|.$$

Clearly, many other subclasses of interval scales could be defined.

A common example of an interval scale is the date scale. Arithmetical formulas of the class $a \gtreqless b$ are interpreted in terms of our time-ordering relationships, "later than," "at the same time as," and "earlier than," and those of the class $|a-b| \gtreqless |c-d|$ are interpreted independently in terms of our time-interval-ordering relationships, "longer than," "as long as," and "shorter than."

On ratio scales we not only can apply arithmetical formulas of the classes (1), (2), and (3b), but we can also apply arithmetical formulas of the class

(4)
$$a/b \gtreqless c.$$

Examples of ratio scales are provided by our common scales of mass, length, time interval, electrical resistance, potential difference, and several other quantities.

Thus, a classification of scales on the basis of the kinds of applications of arithmetic which they represent can indeed be achieved. However, the system leads to a great proliferation of scale types, for there are clearly as many different classes of scales on this system as there are formal classes of arithmetical formulas. Also, it gives us no insight into the nature of the procedures by which our numerical assignments may be made.

Scale-form invariance. The system of Stevens to some extent overcomes the first of the above criticisms. It often happens that scales that are of different kinds according to Coombs's classification are of the same kind according to Stevens'. Stevens' method is to consider the effects of scale transformations and to classify a given scale according to the range of scale transformations that leaves invariant what he calls its scale form.

To explain this, let X and X' be any two scales for the measurement of the same quantity, and let x and x' be the results of any two measurements (assumed to have been perfectly executed) made on the same particular under the same conditions. Then, according to the above criteria for saying that we have a scale for the measurement of a given quantity,

$$x' = f(x),$$

where f is a strictly monotonic increasing function.

Hence, it appears that measurements on X can always be transformed into measurements on X' by some strictly monotonic increasing function f. The process of so transforming our measurements is called scale transformation, and the function f is called the transformation function connecting X and X'. If f is a constant, then the function is called a similarity transformation, and the scales X and X' are said to be similar.

Stevens remarked that the scale form remains invariant under a given scale transformation if and only if the new scale could "serve all of the purposes" of the old one ("On the Theory of Scales of Measurement," p. 680). He offered no further clarification. However, it is not difficult to supply more precise criteria for invariance of scale form. We may say that the scale form remains invariant under a given transformation if and only if the same classes of arithmetical formulas as those that are applied on the old scale may also be applied in the same way on the new scale.

Thus, to find the class of scale transformations that will leave the scale form of a nominal scale invariant, we must solve to find the range of functions f such that

$$f(a) \gtrless_{\neq} f(b), \qquad \text{according as } a \gtrless_{\neq} b.$$

This is simply the condition that the same classes or arithmetical formulas should be applicable in the same way on the new scale. The solution is simply that f must be a single-valued function with a single-valued inverse.

To find the class of scale transformations that will leave the scale form of an ordinal scale invariant, we must find the range of functions f such that

$$f(a) \gtreqless f(b), \qquad \text{according as } a \gtreqless b.$$

The solution is that f must be a strictly monotonic increasing function.

To find the class of permissible scale transformations for a nominal-interval scale, we must solve to find f such that

(5)
$$f(a) \gtreqless f(b), \qquad \text{according as } a \gtreqless b;$$

(6)
$$|f(a)-f(b)| \gtreqqless_{\neq} |f(c)-f(d)|,$$
$$\text{according as } |a-b| \gtreqqless_{\neq} |c-d|.$$

It is not difficult to prove that under these conditions f must be a linear increasing function (the proof is given in B. D. Ellis, *Basic Concepts of Measurement*, pp. 197–199). The same result, however, is obtained if we attempt to solve

(7)
$$f(a) \gtreqless f(b), \qquad \text{according as } a \gtreqless b;$$

(8)
$$|f(a)-f(b)| \gtreqless |f(c)-f(d)|,$$
$$\text{according as } |a-b| \gtreqless |c-d|.$$

The function f again turns out to be a linear increasing function (*ibid.*).

Consequently, there is no distinction to be drawn in Stevens' system of classification between these different kinds of interval scales. They are both scales whose scale forms remain invariant only under linear increasing transformations. Therefore, Stevens' system of classification of scales does provide more general scale classes than Coombs's. But neither is intended to give much insight into the nature of the processes of measurement or into the conditions for the possibility of carrying out these processes. It is no criticism of Stevens or Coombs to say that from this point of view the classical system of Campbell, or a modification of it, is much to be preferred.

PROCEDURES OF MEASUREMENT

In the following sections three procedures of measurement, which can be distinguished within Campbell's general framework, will be described.

Fundamental measurement. Fundamental measurement depends on the existence of fundamental measuring operations. A fundamental measuring operation, for any given quantity q, is any operation for combining any two systems that possess q to form a composite system that also possesses q, the operation having the formal characteristics of the arithmetical operation of addition in the field of real positive numbers.

Physical and arithmetical operations. What are the formal characteristics of the arithmetical operation of addition in the field of real positive numbers, and what is it for a physical operation to possess these characteristics? Let

$$f(x,y) = x + y, \qquad x > 0, y > 0.$$

Then clearly f satisfies the following conditions:

(a) $f(x,y) = f(y,x) =_{Df} f^{(1)}(x,y).$

(b) $f(x,y) \gtreqless f(x,z)$, according as $y \gtreqless z$.

(c) $f(x,y) > x$.

(d) $f(x,f(y,z)) = f(f(x,y),z) =_{Df} f^{(2)}(x,y,z).$

(e) If $a < b$, then there exists an integer N such that for all integers $n > N$

$$f^{(n)}(a,a,\cdots,a) > b.$$

(Compare Patrick Suppes, "A Set of Independent Axioms for Extensive Qualities.")

We may take these various conditions to exhaust the formal characteristics of the arithmetical operation of addition in the field of real positive numbers. Of course, they are not sufficient to restrict the function f to the solution

$$f(x,y) = x + y, \qquad x > 0, y > 0.$$

Other solutions are certainly possible—for example,

$$f(x,y) = (|\sqrt{x}| + |\sqrt{y}|)^2, \qquad x > 0, y > 0,$$

also satisfies the various conditions (a) to (e). But it seems that no purely formal characterization of the arithmetical operation of addition, in the field of real positive numbers, will yield the unique solution

$$f(x,y) = x + y, \qquad x > 0, y > 0.$$

Next, what is it for a physical operation to possess these various characteristics? Let O be any combination operation performable on any two systems S_1 and S_2 that possess q, and let $O(S_1,S_2)$ be the composite system that results from the performance of this operation on S_1 and S_2, taken in that order. As before, let ">$_q$," "=$_q$," and "<$_q$" signify any set

of linear ordering relationships for the quantity q. Then O will be described as a fundamental measuring operation for q if and only if

(a') $O(S_1,S_2) =_q O(S_2,S_1) =_{Df} O^{(1)}(S_1,S_2).$

(b') $O(S_1,S_2) \gtreqless_q O(S_1,S_3)$, according as $S_2 \gtreqless_q S_3$.

(c') $O(S_1,S_2) >_q S_1$.

(d') $O(S_1,O(S_2,S_3)) =_q O(O(S_1,S_2),S_3) =_{Df} O^{(2)}(S_1,S_2,S_3).$

(e') If A and B are any two systems possessing q such that $A <_q B$, then there exists an integer N such that for all integers $n > N$,

$$O^{(n)}(A,A,A,\cdots,A) >_q B.$$

It will be noted that these conditions are formally analogous to the conditions (a) to (e).

Suppose, then, that we have a fundamental measuring operation O for some given quantity q. A fundamental scale for the measurement of q is then set up in the following way:

(1) Some object, say S_0, possessing q, is chosen to act as an initial standard and is assigned a positive number a_0.

(2) The following rules for making numerical assignments are then adopted:

(a) If S_1 and S_2 are any two systems that possess q, and the system S_1 has already been assigned the number a_1, then the system S_2 is to be assigned a number a_2 such that

$$a_1 \gtreqless a_2, \qquad \text{according as } S_1 \gtreqless_q S_2.$$

(b) If S_1 and S_2 are any two systems that possess q to which the numbers a_1 and a_2 have already been assigned, then the composite system $O(S_1,S_2)$ is to be assigned the number $a_1 + a_2$.

It is not difficult to show that these rules will be determinative, at least to within the range $\pm <a_0$, if it is always possible to find or produce as many systems as we wish equal in q to S_0. If, further, it is possible to find two systems $S_{1/2}$ and $S'_{1/2}$ such that $O(S_{1/2},S'_{1/2}) =_q S_0$ and $S_{1/2} =_q S'_{1/2}$, then these rules will be determinative to within the range $<a_0/2$. The conditions under which these rules will be determinative to within any prescribed range should now be obvious, and no attempt will be made to state them here.

Problems of choice. It follows from the above analysis that there are three fundamental problems of choice in setting up a fundamental scale for the measurement of any given quantity q.

First, there is the problem of choice of fundamental measuring operation. There is nothing in our analysis of fundamental measuring operations which implies that there is not more than one fundamental measuring operation for any given quantity. As an illustration, consider the right-angled addition operation for length represented in the figure. The various conditions (a') to (e') are all satisfied by this operation. It is therefore as much entitled to be called a fundamental measuring operation for length as is the ordinary linear stepping-off procedure (see B. D. Ellis, "Some Fundamental Problems of Direct Measurement"). Our scale of length, or any other quantity, is therefore not completely determined by our choice of initial standard (as Campbell supposed).

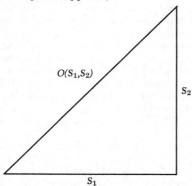

Second, there is the problem of choice of principle of correlation. This arises from the fact that there are many arithmetical operations which, in some prescribed range of the real number field, possess the formal characteristics of the arithmetical operation of addition in the field of real positive numbers. For example, the following functions satisfy the various conditions (a) to (e):

(9) $\qquad f(x,y) = x \cdot y, \qquad\qquad x > 1, y > 1.$
(10) $\qquad f(x,y) = x^2 + y^2, \qquad\quad x > \frac{1}{2}, y > \frac{1}{2}.$
(11) $\qquad f(x,y) = (|\sqrt{x}| + |\sqrt{y}|)^2, \quad x > 0, y > 0.$

Hence, any physical operation O satisfying the various conditions (a') to (e') may be interpreted arithmetically in a variety of ways. The choice of solution (9) would give us a multiplicative scale for the measurement of q. And the choice of solution (11) would give us a scale which is, as it were, the square of an ordinary additive scale for the measurement of this quantity.

Third, there is the problem of choice of initial standard. At first this may seem to be an utterly trivial choice, but such is not the case. Consider, for example, the problem of choice of an initial standard for the fundamental measurement of length. In order that we should be able to use any given object as an initial standard to set up a scale of length, it is required that this object be one member of an indefinitely large set of objects which always, in all circumstances (or at least in some specified circumstances), bear stable length relationships to each other (as determined by methods of direct length comparison). If this condition were not fulfilled we should not in fact be able to carry out the various procedures necessary to set up a fundamental scale. But there may be two or more sets of such objects—the various members of the one set changing in length with respect to those of the other. Hence, there arises the possibility of relatively dynamic fundamental scales for the measurement of the same quantity.

Associative measurement. A second kind of measurement to be distinguished within the Campbellian framework is associative measurement. The vast majority of scales used in psychology and sociology, and also a few, like temperature scales, used in the physical sciences, are set up by associative measurement.

Let p be any quantity, and let "$>_p$," "$=_p$," and "$<_p$" be any set of linear ordering relationships for that quantity. Let q be any other quantity that is always associated with p and is independently (e.g., fundamentally) measurable. Let q be such that under certain precisely specified conditions, if A and B are any two systems possessing p, then

$A \gtreqqless_q B$ according as $A \gtreqqless_p B$. Then in these circumstances

we may take the measure of q on some selected scale (in the given circumstances) as the measure of p and thus define a scale of p. A scale set up in this way will be called an associative scale.

Examples of associative scales are not hard to find. Our various scales of temperature, learning ability, retentiveness, interstellar and submolecular distances, morale, hunger, thirst, favorableness toward the church, and many other quantities are all of this kind (cf. L. L. Thurstone and E. J. Chave, *The Measurement of Attitude*). In each case some independently measurable quantity on some selected scale is taken under certain precisely specified conditions to be the measure of the quantity we are dealing with. The quantity p is, of course, distinguishable from the quantity q (by our criteria for the identity of quantities) by the fact that the order of q is not always the same as the order of p. For example, if gas samples are arranged in order of volume, then they are not thereby arranged in order of temperature. This will only be true under the special conditions that the various gas samples should all contain the same number of gram molecules and all be maintained at the same pressure. If this were not the case and the order of p were always the same as the order of q, then we should simply say that p is directly (e.g., fundamentally) measurable by the procedure for measuring q. In other words, we should make no distinction at all between p and q.

To make associative measurement possible we need only one associated and independently measurable quantity. (Associative measurement is thus to be distinguished from derived measurement.) If, for example, electrical resistance were the only known thermometric property, then a scale of temperature could still be set up. It is doubtful, of course, whether we should ever form a concept of temperature under these conditions, for we recognize the existence of thermal equilibrium by the fact that after sufficiently long isolation from heat sources and heat sinks the thermometric properties of objects cease to vary. And if electrical resistance were the only known thermometric property, we should probably prefer to say simply that the electrical resistance of objects ceases to vary under these conditions. Nevertheless, it would be logically possible to form a concept of temperature under these circumstances and to set up an associative scale for its measurement.

Derived measurement. The third principal kind of measurement is that which Campbell called derived measurement. Scales which are defined by this kind of measurement will here be called derivative scales.

According to Campbell, derived measurement is "measurement by means of constants in numerical laws" (*An Account of the Principles of Measurement and Calculation*, p. 94). To explain the nature of derived measurement we must, therefore, say something about numerical laws.

Numerical laws. The simplest kind of numerical law refers to some particular system and relates the measures of quantities possessed by that system under certain specified conditions. For example, let A_1 be a particular sample of gas maintained at constant volume. Let the conditions under which this sample of gas exists be so changed that its temperature is observed to change whereas its volume remains unchanged, and let measurements of the temperature and pressure of A_1 be made after each change on the scales T and P, respectively. Let t_1 and p_1 be the results of any simultaneous measurements of the temperature and pressure of the gas sample A_1 on the scales T and P. Then if T and P are scales similar to (that is, related by similarity transformations to) our absolute and dyne-per-square-centimeter scales of, respectively, temperature and pressure, it would be found that $p_1 = K_1 t_1$ (where K_1 is a constant) held approximately under all conditions. In this way a numerical law relating to the particular system A_1 (which is maintained at constant volume) would be discovered.

Now let us suppose that any scales T' and P' similar to T and P had been chosen instead. Let t be the result of any measurement on the scale T and t' be the result of the measurement of the same particular under the same conditions on the scale T'. Then since T and T' are similar scales, we have $t' = mt$, where m is the conversion factor from T to T'. Similarly, we have $p' = np$, where n is the conversion factor from P to P'. Hence, had the scales T' and P' been chosen initially, the empirically discovered numerical law would have been $p_1' = K_1' t_1'$, where $K_1' = (m/n)K_1$.

Thus, instead of expressing the law with respect to the particular scales T and P, we could, if we wished, express the law with respect to the classes (T) and (P) of scales similar to T and P, respectively. We need only write

$$(12) \qquad p_1 = k_1 t_1,$$

where now p_1 and t_1 are the results of any simultaneous measurements of the temperature and pressure of the system A_1 maintained at constant volume, the measurements being made on any scales of the classes (P) and (T), and where k_1 is what may be called a scale-dependent constant—that is, a constant whose value depends on the choice of scales within the classes (P) and (T).

Of course, there is no necessity for us to express the law in this way. We could, if we wished, express the law with respect to the classes $\{T\}$ and $\{P\}$ of scales related by linear transformations to T and P, respectively. In that case we should have to write

$$(13) \qquad p_1' = k_1' t_1' + k_2',$$

where p_1' and t_1' are the results of any simultaneous measurements of pressure and temperature made on the system A_1 on any scales of the classes $\{P\}$ and $\{T\}$, respectively, and where k_1' and k_2' are both scale-dependent constants.

In fact, it seems that we always prefer to express our laws either with respect to particular scales (as we do, usually, in the fields of electrostatics and electromagnetics) or with respect to classes of similar scales (as we do, almost invariably, in the field of mechanics). The reasons for this preference for classes of similar scales are not obvious (but see the account in B. D. Ellis, *Basic Concepts of Measurement*). For the remainder of this section let us simply adopt the convention that our laws will be expressed with respect to classes of similar scales.

So far we have considered only laws relating to a particular system A_1. Let (A) be the class of gas samples which are maintained always at constant volume, and let A_i be any arbitrary member of that class. Then by carrying out the same procedure as for the gas sample A_1, we should find that, in general,

$$p_i = k_i t_i,$$

where p_i and t_i are any simultaneous measurements of pressure and temperature made on the gas sample A_i on any scales of the classes (P) and (T) and k_i is, as before, a scale-dependent constant. But it should be noted that the value of k_i also depends on the choice of the system A_i. Hence, we should say that k_i is not only a scale-dependent but also a system-dependent constant.

Of course, it is not necessary that k_i be a system-dependent constant. It could turn out that for the same choices of scales within the classes (P) and (T) the value of k_i is the same for all systems of the class (A). In that case we should say that k_i is a universal constant. But for the purposes of this article it is the system-dependent constants that are important.

Nature of derivative measurement. Derivative measurement is measurement by means of constants in numerical laws. But we are in a position to say more precisely what this means. Forget for a minute the particular examples discussed and consider A_i to be any system that meets certain specifications, and suppose that

$$(14) \qquad f(p_i, q_i, r_i, \cdots) = k_i$$

is a numerical law which is found to be obeyed by all systems of the class (A), where $p_i, q_i, r_i, \cdots$ are the results of any simultaneous measurements made on the system A_i on any scales of the classes of similar scales $(P), (Q), (R), \cdots$. Let us suppose, further, that k_i is a system-dependent constant and that if the systems of the class (A) are arranged in the order of this constant (for any particular choice of scales from within the classes $(P), (Q), (R), \cdots$) they are also arranged in the order of some quantity d which we know to be possessed by these systems. Then clearly the conditions for saying that we have a scale for the measurement of d are satisfied. Hence, we may take k_i to be the measure of the quantity d which is possessed by the system A_i, on a derivative scale that depends on the choices of scales from within the classes $(P), (Q), (R), \cdots$. Under these conditions, and only under these, we may say that we have a derivative scale for the measurement of the quantity d.

Derivative measurement of a quantity d is possible, therefore, if and only if there exists some numerical law relating to systems that possess the quantity d in which there appears a system-dependent constant such that if these systems are arranged in the order of this system-dependent constant, they are also arranged in the order of d. A derivative scale for the measurement of d is, then, one that is defined by taking the value of the system-dependent constant (or some strictly monotonic increasing function of it) for some particular choice of independent scales as the measure of the quantity *d*.

Units and dimensions. Units are the names of scales. Simple unit names, such as "pound," "second," "ohm," "°C.," are used for fundamental and associative scales. Complex unit names, such as "gm. cm. sec.⁻²," are used for derivative scales. Occasionally, simple unit names are used for derivative scales ("erg," "dyne," "poundal"), but these names can always be replaced by complex equivalents and are introduced only for abbreviation.

Dimensions are the names of classes of similar scales. Simple dimension names, such as "(*M*)," "(*L*)," "(*T*)," "(*Q*)," are used for classes of similar fundamental and associative scales. Complex dimension names, or dimensional formulas, are used for classes of similar derivative scales.

As might be expected, the conventions which govern the naming of classes of similar scales are like those which govern the naming of scales. Accordingly, we find that dimensional formulas behave like generalized complex unit names. To explain the properties of dimensional formulas, however, we must first take account of several theorems.

Two derivative scales D_1 and D_2 will be said to be similarly defined if and only if they are defined on the basis of the same numerical law, expressed with respect to the same classes of similar scales. Thus, for example, the "gm. cm. sec.⁻²" and the "ft. lb. sec.⁻²" scales of force are similarly defined. We then have

Theorem 1. Similarly defined derivative scales are similar to each other.

This theorem (proved in B. D. Ellis, *Basic Concepts of Measurement,* p. 133) is important because it means that classes of similarly defined derivative scales are simply classes of similar scales and hence may serve as reference classes for the expression of numerical laws in the standard form of equation (14). Consequently, to each quantity there will correspond a unique dimension (class of similar scales) if enough numerical laws are known and we adopt the following conventions:

Convention 1: always to use similar fundamental or associative scales for the measurement of any given quantity; and

Convention 2: always to use similarly defined derivative scales for the measurement of any given quantity not measured on a fundamental or associative scale.

Moreover, in order to specify a scale system, we need only name the fundamental and associative scales on which it is based and state what laws are involved in the definition of the various derivative scales. Thus, the m.k.s. system is a system of scales based on the meter, kilogram, and second scales and in which, for example, force is defined on a derivative scale via Newton's second law of motion, rather than, say, the law of gravitation.

A second important theorem is this: let

(15) $$f(p,q,r,\cdots)=k$$

be a numerical law expressed with respect to the classes of similar scales (*P*), (*Q*), (*R*), · · ·, where *k* is the only system- and/or scale-dependent constant that appears. Let us say

that such a law is expressed in standard form. We then have

Theorem 2. Any law expressed in standard form must be of the form

(16) $$Cp^a q^b r^c \cdots = k,$$

where *C*, *a*, *b*, *c*, · · · are constants which are neither system-dependent nor scale-dependent.

(See P. W. Bridgman, *Dimensional Analysis,* and Ellis, *op. cit.,* pp. 204–206.)

The importance of this theorem is that it enables us to explain both the form and the significance of complex unit names and dimensional formulas. Thus, equation (16) defines a class of similar derivative scales (Theorem 1) for the measurement of some quantity *d*. To designate this class we could use a simple dimension name, say "(*D*)." But it is obviously more informative to use the dimensional formula "$(P)^a (Q)^b (R)^c \cdots$." By doing so we say something about the form of the law (16) on which our derivative scales of *d* are defined. Likewise, if $P_1, Q_1, R_1, \cdots$ are particular scales from within the dimensions (*P*), (*Q*), (*R*), · · ·, then this choice of scales would yield a particular derivative scale, say D_1, for the measurement of *d*. But obviously it is preferable to use the complex unit name "$P_1^a Q_1^b R_1^c \cdots$" instead of "D_1," and thus to indicate

(*a*) Which particular independent scales D_1 depends on; and

(*b*) The form of the law upon which the derivative scale D_1 is defined.

A third important theorem is

Theorem 3. Relative magnitude is invariant with scale transformations within any given dimension.

(See Ellis, *op. cit.,* pp. 140–141.)

This theorem forms the basis of the mathematical theory of dimensions. It serves instead of Bridgman's metaphysical postulate of the absolute significance of relative magnitude.

The theory of dimensional analysis cannot be developed here, but its power depends on the information that we pack into dimensional formulas. If we wish to increase this power we must include more information. This can be done only if we adopt the basic convention of expressing our laws with respect to classes of similar scales more widely than we do at present and adopt the Conventions 1 and 2 in fields other than mechanics. Thus, instead of expressing laws involving angular displacement with respect to the radian scale and saying (absurdly) that angular displacement is a dimensionless quantity, we should always express them with respect to the class of scales similar to our radian scale and introduce the dimension of angle into our dimensional formulas. As is demonstrated by Ellis (*op. cit.,* pp. 145–151), this would increase the power of dimensional analysis.

An attempt has been made here to discuss those concepts which are most basic in the logic of measurement—concepts which every writer on the logic of measurement must consider, whatever his primary field of interest. The concepts of scale and quantity, unit and dimension, are basic in this sense. Whether one is interested primarily in psychological, physical, psychophysical, or sociological measurement, one must discuss these concepts. The same applies to the concept of an application of arithmetic. For that is just what measurement is—the practice of applying arithmetic to quantitative relationships.

The problems of classifying scales of measurement is also basic, for the practices of measurement are so diverse that one cannot speak significantly about measurement without some prior classification system. One cannot, for example, give other than trivial conditions for the possibility of measurement in general. But given a suitable system of classification of scales, some more significant statements can be made concerning the conditions for the possibility of setting up a scale of a given kind for the measurement of any given quantity. Similarly, without a system of classification of scales of measurement, no important assertions can be made about the significance of the numbers which we assign to things by measuring operations. It is only when we have such a system of classification that we even begin to answer this important question.

Bibliography

Bergmann, Gustav, and Spence, K. W., "The Logic of Psychophysical Measurement." *Psychological Review,* Vol. 51 (1944), 1–24.

Boring, E. G., "The Beginning and Growth of Measurement in Psychology," in H. Woolf, ed., *Quantification* (see below).

Bridgman, P. W., *Dimensional Analysis.* New Haven, 1931. The classic presentation of the theory of dimensional analysis.

Campbell, N. R., *Physics: The Elements.* Cambridge, 1921. Reprinted as *Foundations of Science.* New York, 1957. Part II is still the most comprehensive discussion of the logic of measurement.

Campbell, N. R., *An Account of the Principles of Measurement and Calculation.* London, 1928. A development of Campbell's work in *Physics: The Elements.*

Coombs, C. H., "Psychological Scaling Without a Unit of Measurement." *Psychological Review,* Vol. 57 (1950), 145–158.

Coombs, C. H., *A Theory of Scaling.* Ann Arbor, Mich., 1952.

Crombie, A. C., "Quantification in Medieval Physics," in H. Woolf, ed., *Quantification* (see below).

Dingle, Herbert, "A Theory of Measurement." *British Journal for the Philosophy of Science,* Vol. 1 (1950), 5–26.

Ellis, B. D., "Some Fundamental Problems of Direct Measurement." *Australasian Journal of Philosophy,* Vol. 38 (1960), 37–47. Contains a fuller discussion of the concept of quantity and of the logical problems of choice in fundamental measurement.

Ellis, B. D., *Basic Concepts of Measurement.* Cambridge, 1965. A detailed analysis of all the issues discussed in this article.

Mach, Ernst, *Prinzipien der Wärmelehre,* 2d ed. Leipzig, 1900. Ch. 3, "Critique of the Concept of Temperature," is one of the most important contributions of the last century to the logic of measurement. A translation by M. J. Scott-Taggart and B. D. Ellis appears as an appendix to Ellis, *Basic Concepts of Measurement.*

Nagel, Ernest, "Measurement." *Erkenntnis,* Vol. 2 (1931–1932), 313–333. Reprinted in Arthur Danto and Sidney Morgenbesser, eds., *Philosophy of Science.* New York, 1960.

Stevens, S. S., "Measurement, Psychophysics and Utility," in C. W. Churchman and P. Ratoosh, eds., *Measurement: Definitions and Theories.* New York, 1959.

Stevens, S. S., "On the Theory of Scales of Measurement." *Science,* Vol. 103 (1946), 677–680. Reprinted in Danto and Morgenbesser, *op. cit.* Stevens' original presentation of his system of classification of scales.

Suppes, Patrick, "A Set of Independent Axioms for Extensive Quantities." *Portugaliae Mathematica,* Vol. 10, Fasc. 4 (1951), 163–172.

Thurstone, L. L., and Chave, E. J., *The Measurement of Attitude.* Chicago, 1929.

Torgerson, W. S., *Theory and Methods of Scaling.* New York, 1958. The most comprehensive work to date on the theory of scaling in psychological and sociological measurement. It contains an excellent discussion of the theory of multidimensional scaling.

Woolf, Harry, ed., *Quantification: A History of the Meaning of Measurement in the Natural and Social Sciences.* This volume, a collection of papers that originally appeared in *Isis,* Vol. 52, No. 168 (1961), contains many important articles on the history of measurement.

BRIAN ELLIS

MECHANICAL EXPLANATION. See MECHANISM IN BIOLOGY; NEWTONIAN MECHANICS AND MECHANICAL EXPLANATION.

MECHANISM IN BIOLOGY. The doctrine of mechanism in biology is a philosophical theory about the nature of biological systems. Not many biologists would characterize themselves as mechanists, although many—if not the great majority—would be mechanists in a certain sense. The term is often used by vitalists and organismic biologists to characterize the adherents of theories that they wish to reject, but this does not mean that other biologists, not members of either school, would thank them for the title. The term "mechanism" has no fixed meaning, although it is almost generally regarded as a term of abuse.

"Mechanism" and "machine." To retrieve "mechanism" as the name of a clear position in the philosophy of biology, it is necessary to reconstruct a doctrine that has a discernible connection with the concept of a machine. This doctrine would, in fact, be supported by many biologists but would be rejected by members of the vitalistic and organismic schools.

Mechanism is sometimes said to be the theory that living organisms and all of their living parts are machines. This is unfortunate for several reasons. There is a tendency, at least in everyday speech, to reserve the term "machine" for artificial devices of a certain sort, especially, as J. J. C. Smart has argued, for devices, such as sewing and milking machines, that perform tasks ordinarily performed by people. Organisms are obviously not machines in this sense. There is also a tendency in both the scientific and common vernacular to regard an object of a certain kind (for example, kind *K*) as a machine—whether or not it is an artificial device—only if there are certain activities that are regarded as characteristic of all objects answering to the definition of *K* and that can be described and explained solely by the principles of mechanics. Thus, for example, at the end of the seventeenth century, it was common to call the solar system a machine and to ascribe to Descartes the view that "brutes"—but not men—are machines; today, most people would be willing to call a pulley system or a bicycle a machine. A living organism, of course, is not a machine in this sense. No matter how we define the science of mechanics—and the usage of physicists is not decisive—mechanical action is to be distinguished from chemical action, which is certainly regarded as characteristic of living organisms.

Finally, there is a tendency among some physicists and engineers, especially those engaged in systems design and analysis, to use the terms "machine" and "system" interchangeably. This tendency can be traced to two linguistic facts. Many systems that they call machines are machines in one or both of the above senses; and those systems that are not machines in either of these senses may be "mechanisms." We ordinarily apply the term "mechanism" more broadly than "machine." Radios, watches, telephones, electric switches, and the like are, in the vernacular, regularly mechanisms and only sporadically machines. Since a scientist is unlikely to see any significant theoretical difference between systems that are paradigmatic machines (such as sewing machines) and systems that are paradigmatic mechanisms but not machines (such as telephones), he is willing to extend the term "machine" at least to cover mechanisms. Moreover, there seems to be no significant theoretical difference between the systems that are regularly called mechanisms and any assemblage of material parts that show causal interaction.

In everyday usage, a mechanism is a system whose parts are related in the following manner. (1) Changes in some of the parts cause changes in most of the others. (2) These causally connected changes are regarded as identical with some single activity. For example, when a switch that turns on a lamp is thrown, a bar changes position, a spring is stretched, a friction lock is activated, and a gap between two contacts is closed. These changes are all regarded as identical with the single activity of closing the switch. (3) This single activity is of some special interest. It is frequently the function that the mechanism was designed to serve; in this case we often use such expressions as "switching mechanism" or "starting mechanism." Sometimes, however, we are interested in an activity or process only for other, perhaps scientific, reasons. For example, a biologist interested in the segregation of genetic traits is willing to speak of the processes of meiosis as the mechanism of genetic segregation. It is always possible, however, to regard any repetitive pattern of changes as a single activity, whether or not that activity has any special theoretical or practical significance. The relaxation of the requirement of special interest leads to the extension of the term "mechanism" to any system that satisfies conditions (1) and (2).

To summarize these linguistic points: the common language, serving as it does a variety of purposes, draws a distinction between the terms "machine" and "mechanism," and restricts the application of "mechanism" on grounds that are irrelevant to the aims of scientific inquiry. There is no important principle, therefore, that would lead the scientist to apply the term "machine" to one system and to deny it to another that is like a machine in every relevant respect. Thus the tendency arises to use the terms "system" and "machine" interchangeably. The separation of the concept of a machine from the science of mechanics is aided by the concept of a mechanism, for "mechanism" is connected etymologically with "mechanics" but in ordinary application is not especially associated with mechanical systems.

"Mechanism" as a philosophical theory. If mechanism is interpreted to mean that living organisms are machines in the broadest sense (material systems), then the term marks no distinction in the philosophical beliefs of biologists. No biologist believes that organisms are machines in the colloquial sense, but even vitalistic and organismic biologists would agree that organisms are machines in the broader sense and that every organic process is accomplished by means of mechanisms. The important philosophical differences, which will be associated here with the term "mechanism," concern the nature of the principles needed in accounting for the behavior of living systems.

Two conceptions will be helpful in drawing the distinction between mechanisms and machines. The first is the notion of exemplification of a law in a system or process. One can say, for instance, that an object falling in an evacuated cylinder exemplifies Galileo's law of free fall $(s = \frac{1}{2}gt^2)$ and that the inheritance of a set of genetic traits may exemplify Mendel's laws of independent assortment and segregation. On the other hand, a football resting on a table top exemplifies neither law. If we think of a law as of the form "If conditions A are met, then so are conditions B," the law is then exemplified in every system that meets conditions A, but not necessarily by every system that satisfies the propositional function $Ax \supset Bx$. By this convention, then, Newton would have said that every body exemplifies the law of universal gravitation, but only some special systems, such as a falling body or the solar system, exemplify Galileo's and Kepler's laws. One can also say that the events themselves exemplify a law if they occur in a system that exemplifies the law.

The second conception may be explained as follows. It is, of course, a commonplace that numerically the same event may fall under conceptually distinct descriptions. A particular dive, executed by a contestant in a competition, might, for example, be described as a case of relatively free fall, a swan dive, a graceful performance, or the winning effort. The alternative descriptions here belong to different conceptual schemes, but they apply properly to numerically the same event. Evidently, slight differences in the event itself would make some of the descriptions inapplicable: for instance, one sort of difference could make the description "swan dive" inapplicable but leave the rest unchanged. Moreover—and this is philosophically of greater interest—there is a sense in which the event could be the same and yet some of the descriptions would be inapplicable, for some of the descriptions depend for their applicability on the circumstances of the event's occurrence. Thus, if the dive were not part of a competition, it could not be a winning effort. It will be assumed for the purposes of this article that sufficiently clear criteria are available for the term "same event." This will, in general, permit us to say whether E_1 and E_2 are numerically the same event, where E_1 and E_2 are distinct descriptions with their own criteria of application. In particular, one or both of the descriptions may be appropriate only under special circumstances of the event's occurrence.

Mechanism may now be defined as the view that every event E, which is describable as a biological event (by any reasonable criterion of "biological"), is numerically the same as the set of events $\{E_1, E_2, \cdots, E_n\}$, in which each E_i exemplifies no laws that are not also exemplified in nonbiological systems ("nonbiological" by the same criterion as "biological"). Stated less formally, mechanism is the view that every biological event is a pattern of nonbiological occurrences.

The above definition of mechanism specifies a sense in which biological phenomena might be reducible to the physicochemical. It differs, however, from some standard explications of reducibility. Without examining any of these explications in detail, we may, however, note some of the differences. It is usual to distinguish between conceptual and nomic reduction. Theory T_2 is conceptually reducible to T_1 if all the terms in the theoretical vocabulary of T_2 may be defined by the terms in T_1. Our definition leaves reducibility in this sense an open question. It is plausible to suppose that biology contains terms that could not be defined by reference to physics and chemistry, particularly if we count psychological phenomena as special cases of the biological, but perhaps even if we do not. Biological theory takes account of the circumstances of an event's occurrence in a way that the physical sciences do not. For example, it is a biological fact that lions hunt zebras. The biological mechanist ought to insist merely that everything that happens in a given case of zebra hunting is identical with a sequence of physicochemical events, not that the concept of hunting can be defined in physicochemical terms. Indeed, it may be the case that "hunting" can be defined only in intentional language.

A theory T_2 is nomically reducible to T_1 if all the laws of T_2 can be deduced from the laws of T_1 with the help of coordinating definitions and specifications of the structure of T_2 systems in the vocabulary of T_1. Again, a mechanist ought to say that biological phenomena are reducible to the nonbiological and still leave open the question of whether nomic reducibility is possible even in principle. It seems a priori that the nonbiological laws that alone are exemplified in the set of events $\{E_1, E_2, \cdot \cdot \cdot, E_n\}$ might have a degree of complexity that would render it impossible to specify their form under the initial and boundary conditions embodied in organic systems.

If one were to say that biological phenomena are, after all, not just physicochemical phenomena, he would be correct in any sense that could be important to him; and yet mechanism, even of the form that states that all biological phenomena are physicochemical, is also correct, in any sense that matters to the mechanist. "Is hunting a zebra a physicochemical process?" is too simple a question. The description "hunting a zebra" belongs to a conceptual scheme that is not physicochemical; however, an alternative description of the same event could belong to the physicochemical scheme.

Bibliography

Ashby, W. R., "The Nervous System as Physical Machine: With Special Reference to the Origin of Adaptive Behavior." *Mind*, Vol. 56 (January 1947).

Broad, C. D., *The Mind and Its Place in Nature*. London, 1951.

Haldane, J. S., *Mechanism, Life and Personality*, 2d ed. New York, 1923.

Nagel, Ernest, *The Structure of Science*. New York, 1961.

Woodger, J. H., *Biological Principles*. London, 1948.

Woodger, J. H., *Biology and Language*. Cambridge, 1952.

MORTON O. BECKNER

MEDIAVILLA, RICHARD OF. See RICHARD OF MEDIAVILLA.

MEDIEVAL AND EARLY CHRISTIAN PHILOSOPHY.

In addition to the general article MEDIEVAL PHILOSOPHY the Encyclopedia features the following articles having discussions of early Christian and medieval schools and movements: APOLOGISTS; AUGUSTINIANISM; AVERROISM; BYZANTINE PHILOSOPHY; CAROLINGIAN RENAISSANCE; CHARTRES, SCHOOL OF; GNOSTICISM; OCKHAMISM; PATRISTIC PHILOSOPHY; SAINT VICTOR, SCHOOL OF; SCOTISM; SUFI PHILOSOPHY; and THOMISM.

Particular aspects of early Christian and medieval thought are discussed in the Encyclopedia's general articles, including ETHICS, HISTORY OF; ISLAMIC PHILOSOPHY; JEWISH PHILOSOPHY; LOGIC, HISTORY OF; METAPHYSICS, HISTORY OF; MYSTICISM, HISTORY OF; SEMANTICS, HISTORY OF; and UNIVERSALS. See also CHRISTIANITY; ILLUMINATION; and LIBER DE CAUSIS.

See Medieval Philosophy and Christianity in Index for articles on important figures in this area.

MEDIEVAL PHILOSOPHY

began with the African Christian Augustine of Hippo (354–430), whose life and writings reflected the unsettled state of the declining Roman Empire long before the commencement of the Middle Ages proper. His rich and many-sided works display the Platonic otherworldliness of his theories of knowledge and world history. According to Augustine's vision, the true cosmic plan unfolds in the history of the City of God, and the local accidents of the Earthly City are of little account in comparison. Correspondingly, true wisdom and virtue are obtainable only in the light of the Christian faith and by the prevenience of divine grace; human nature, grossly corrupted since the Fall, is in need of a correspondingly complete divine remaking. Whereas for Plato and Aristotle the fulfillment of human capacities required the possession of a high degree of sophisticated intelligence, for Augustine such fulfillment depended on rightness of the will and the affections. These two features, a radical view of the transforming power of grace and a voluntaristic accent, may be regarded as the kernel of Augustinianism, at least insofar as it affected subsequent thought. The tremendous influence of Augustine on medieval thought is matched by that of Boethius, whose grandiose plan was to transmit to the Latin West the works of Plato and Aristotle—a plan rudely cut short by his execution in A.D. 524. However, he accomplished the translation of Aristotle's logical works into Latin; his commentaries on some of them, and on the Neoplatonist Porphyry's Introduction (*Isagoge*) to the *Categories* of Aristotle, were immensely influential in shaping the technical Latin vocabulary and turns of expression that prevailed in the Middle Ages, so much so that any appreciation of medieval thought must inevitably be inadequate without a thorough acquaintance with Boethius' logical output.

The intervention of the Dark Ages presented Western scholars with a gigantic task of rethinking and reconstruction. During these centuries of insecurity and uprootedness there was little intellectual endeavor, apart from the exceptional work of the Neoplatonist John Scotus Erigena in the ninth century. The logical, theological, and classical inheritance slumbered insecurely within the libraries of threatened Western monasteries. When Anselm of Canterbury (1033–1109) began to exploit Boethian logic in order to render his Christian faith intelligible, he had no immediate predecessor who in any way approached his stature as a thinker. Author of the Ontological Argument and fully alive to the power of linguistic analysis as a tool for clarifying conceptual problems, Anselm was the father of Scholasticism. Working within an Augustinian framework, Anselm and other logical theologians of the eleventh and twelfth centuries attempted to bring into order and coherence the body of doctrine to which they were committed by Holy Writ, dogmatic pronouncements, and the works of earlier authoritative church writers. The formidable dimensions of the enterprise were well known to them, as is shown in the lists of clashing antitheses made explicit in the *Sic et Non* ("For and Against") of the ill-fated logician Peter Abelard (1079–1142). A systematic collection of authoritative opinions, the *Sentences,* upon which all subsequent medieval thinkers exercised their logical and philosophical ingenuity in the form of commentary, was compiled by Peter Lombard (c. 1100–1160).

While the Latin West, employing a predominantly logical Aristotelianism, was engaged in the tasks described above, as well as in controversy on the topic of universals, the more advanced Islamic civilization spreading from the Middle East possessed the whole body of Aristotle's works. These received development, commentary, and a Neoplatonic flavor at the hands of a series of subtle thinkers, among whom were al-Fārābī (c. 870–950), Avicenna (980–1037), and Averroës (1126–1198). From about the middle of the twelfth century on, Latin translations of their works became available; and through these, as well as through translation directly from the Greek, Western thinkers eventually knew all of Aristotle's writings.

The Jewish philosophers ibn-Gabirol (1021–c. 1070) and Moses Maimonides (1135–1204) also contributed to the intellectual ferment of the thirteenth century, which was accompanied by the establishment of universities within which members of the recently founded orders of Dominican and Franciscan friars were soon competing with secular masters for professorships. Generally speaking, the Dominicans, following the lead of Thomas Aquinas (c. 1224–1274), attempted to assimilate Aristotle by adopting a framework within which divine grace was seen as completing and fulfilling human nature, rather than dramatically abrogating it in the Augustinian manner. Consequently, the Thomistic tradition represented a separation, at least in principle, of philosophy from theology and a more optimistic view of human nature, society, and the civil state, coupled with opposition to those Latin Averroists who were prepared to compartmentalize their thought to the extent of claiming that on certain points philosophy (Aristotle, as interpreted by Averroës) demonstrated conclusions incompatible with their personal Christianity. Those who preferred to remain within the Augustinian stream, especially St. Bonaventure (1221–1274), Duns Scotus (1266–1308), and William of Ockham (c. 1285–1349), nevertheless increasingly absorbed elements of the new Aristotelianism. Concerned as they were with the sense in which theology could be a science

(a form of knowing), Duns Scotus and William of Ockham evinced a tendency to bring epistemological considerations more to the forefront of their work.

NATURE OF SCHOLASTICISM

Aristotelian empiricism: matter, form, and substance. Medieval philosophy and logic are aspects of an effort to resolve conceptual puzzles (often, but not always, theologically inspired) and to underpin such resolutions with a satisfactory theory of how things are and why they are as they are. The dominant theory, although subjected to multiple variations and modifications during the medieval period, was basically Aristotelian and therefore involved an ultraempiricist effort (not always successful) to resist the abrogation of the pretheoretical common-sense aspect of the world by the theoretical. Before the consideration of any theory, whether scientific or metaphysical, human beings are inevitably confronted with a world populated by a multiplicity of diverse kinds and sorts of beings that are subject to generation, change, and death. These diverse beings are understood to the extent that "why?" questions about them or their kinds can be answered; they are the objects of evaluation insofar as they or their qualities, quantities, states, or relations are characterized as good, bad, and so on.

In accordance with the nonabrogatory policy, a technical vocabulary is required such that the pretheoretical picture does not forfeit its basic sense by relativization to a more fundamental theory that demands radical revision of that picture. For example, an ultraempiricist account of how things are must always leave place for the attribution of a literal (and not merely metaphorical) sense to questions regarding the "makings" of sense objects, states of affairs, or processes. The term "matter" represents an attempt to guarantee such a literal sense—it is the general reply to the always sensible question (in the context mentioned) "What is it made out of?" The detailed replies to such questions—"wood," "stone," "bones and flesh," "clay," "cloth," and so forth—all mention makings or materials out of which something is made, physical antecedents that are among the necessary conditions of a thing's being.

In the same context, however, explanations of why things are as they are can be given by reference to the kinds or sorts to which those things belong; for example, "Horses are self-moving because they are animals, and all animals are self-moving." Here a feature of a particular sort of being (horse) is explained by reference to its general kind (animal), and it is the notion of "form" (with its alternative medieval vocabulary, "nature," "essence," "quiddity") that represents a reminder of the fact that things fall into distinguishable sorts (species) that can in turn be subsumed under broader kinds (genera). Since truistic explanations can be given in terms of sorts and kinds, the form or essence is said to be the principle of the intelligibility, or explanation-worthiness, of things; and such general definitions as "Man is rational animal" are said to hold true in regard to the formal aspect of things. Whether or not the definitions are true of things in a scientific sense is of little import to the philosophical notion of form: its point is to insure the nonabrogation, by a general theory of how things are, of the pretheoretical picture of the diversity of things; realization of this point may lie behind Aquinas' agnosticism concerning the scientific value of such formal definitions.

It is plain that the replies to questions about the makings (matter) of things still involve a formal aspect, since not only are explanations in terms of the definitions of wood, stone, and the other sorts of material mentioned still possible, but it is also possible sensibly to ask what the wood or stone is made out of, or what "stuff" endures when wine becomes vinegar. In order to do justice to such possibilities—and to the pretheoretical conviction that in processes of change the successive sorts that occur are not totally new creations but rather a sequence of diverse activizations of a common substratum—the notion of "prime" matter is employed; this is matter as mere substratum, totally devoid of any formal aspect. Prime matter was viewed schematically, by a kind of extrapolation, as pure susceptibility upon which the various formal actualities supervene, and was said to be by some medievals the principle of individuation, whereby form, the principle of intelligibility and generality, is concretized to the particularity of the various individual "this-es" that belong to a given sort. Thus, one might say that a horse is an *equinizing* of prime matter, a stone is a *petrifying* of prime matter, and so on; this use of verblike nouns helps to bring out the fact that form is act, or actuality, as opposed to the mere susceptibility of prime matter. These verblike nouns are constant, since it never makes sense to say of a horse, for example, that is it more horse or less horse (using "more" and "less" in a nonquantitative sense). Some actualizations, however, are variable, such as whiteness; one can say of a white object that it is (or becomes) more white or less white.

The real correlates of certain of the constant actualizations are called substances, objects that are pretheoretically recognized as being constantly what they are over the whole span of their existence. A horse does not become a horse, and on ceasing to be a horse, it simply ceases to be, whereas a white object can be something that becomes white in varying degrees and may cease to be white, but it is not on that account said to cease to exist. When adjectival terms such as "white" are used to denote subjects in sentences, such as "A white thing is coming down the road," it always makes sense (although in many instances it may be superfluous) to ask a question like "What is the thing that is white and is coming down the road?" This is true because such terms leave open the possibility of asking a question regarding the nature of the "something else" (*aliquid aliud*, as Aquinas has it) that is qualified (in this instance by the whiteness). When the "something else" is a substance, such as "horse," the possibility of a further question having a similar sense, but with the substance name in place of the adjective, vanishes. For example, one would not ask, "What is the thing that is a horse and is coming down the road?" Thus, this notion of substance is unlike that with which Locke was concerned; for him it *did* make sense, even when a substantial sentence subject had been used, to carry on with requests for information about what he called a "something besides."

Technical language, meaning, and universals. Much of medieval philosophical and logical discourse involved the endowment of old words with new senses, as part of the artificialization of natural language that is characteristic of the Schoolmen, who, according to Locke, "covered their ignorance with a curious and inexplicable web of perplexed words." The Scholastics were in fact to some extent aware of the exigencies of discourse of this sort, which constitutes a kind of halfway house between the sort of philosophy that is careful to use only a completely jargon-free natural language, and the sort that is prepared to use the resources of some totally artificial language (such as those of modern symbolic logic) as a set of coordinates whereby sense and senselessness may be distinguished. When discussing the technical sense of "in" in sentences such as "Qualities inhere *in* substances," Boethius had distinguished no fewer than nine ways in which the word "in" could be used. It was clear to him that the "man" of the technical sentence "Man is a species" does not play the same role as does the name "man" in "Socrates is a man"; if it did, then one should be able to use these two sentences as premises whence "Socrates is a species" (which is false or nonsensical) could be inferred.

How, then, are such terms as "man," "animal," "genus," and "species," as they occur in sentences like "Man is a species" and "Animal is a genus," to be understood? These are sentences of a sort that must occur in the discussion of the principles of those definitions described as efforts to do justice to the formal aspect of things. Interpretation of such sentences as consisting of two names joined by "is" naturally leads to the question, transmitted by Boethius when commenting on Porphyry, of what the things are that these names name. Are the things named by such specific or generic names extramental entities additional to individual human beings and animals? An affirmative answer represents one medieval form of the option for a "realist" position in the problem of universals, and throughout the period thinkers were divided on this topic. Certain early medieval antirealists, such as Roscelin and Garland the Computist, developed a solution that had been suggested by Boethius: Words like "species" and "genus," said Boethius, may be interpreted as "names of names" (*nominum nomina*), so that "Man is a species" should be analyzed as " 'Man' is a species," with "species" naming the word "man" and indicating that it is predicable specifically of many individuals.

Herein lies one of the roots of the logical doctrine developed during the thirteenth and fourteenth centuries, the doctrine of *suppositio*.

Roscelin and Garland went further than Boethius and regarded "man" in "Man is a species" not as a mentioned name (a mentioned *significant* utterance) but as a *mere* utterance (*vox*) undergoing mention; thus St. Anselm accused Roscelin of having reduced universals to the "breath of an utterance" (*flatus vocis*). Other antirealists, observing that this extreme nominalism (as it is usually called) failed to account for the success of language as a representation of the formal aspect of things, adopted an intermediate position, according to which the universal is a natural (as opposed to a merely conventional) mental sign, or concept; such a position was designed to secure the objective reference of the universal while avoiding commitment to the plethora of extra entities demanded by realism. Abelard, Aquinas, and Ockham may be credited with having held, each in his own way, a doctrine of this type.

Extent of the artificialization of language. There are several facets of the general medieval concern with the study of meaning. In the writings of Anselm of Canterbury, for example, there is an immensely powerful and pervasive realization that the overt, apparent, or grammatical form of an utterance need not show its implicit, true, or logical form—a realization whose revival has been most prominently reinitiated in our own age by Bertrand Russell. Again and again Anselm's writings contain the contrast between forms of speech that are allowed by the loose texture of ordinary language (*usus loquendi*) and the forms to which a strict attention to the exact sense (*significatio per se*) commits one; the loose texture is methodically explored, and the results of this exploration are applied to the elucidation of difficulties raised by forms of speech found in Holy Writ and ordinary language. In their technical explanations Anselm and his successors felt compelled to make innovations that violated the grammar of the natural language (Latin) in which they wrote; for instance, in expressing the objective counterparts of assertions concerning the meaning of adjectival (as opposed to substantival) words, Anselm used the novel formula "Literate is literacy," which in its Latin version (*Grammaticus est grammatica*) is about as full of scandals, from the point of view of ordinary Latin grammar, as any three-word sentence could be.

Naturally the classicists of the time, like their counterparts of the sixteenth century, took alarm at these monstrous impurities of language; a classicist rear-guard action is shown in the *Metalogicon* of John of Salisbury (c. 1115 – 1180), who at one point explicitly argues against mixtures of abstract and concrete of the kind put forth by Anselm. A better-known example of this technical development, resulting in nonsense in respect to ordinary language, is found in Aquinas' assertion that a man *is* neither his humanity nor his existence, whereas God *is* both his essence (divinity) and his existence; these claims involve a like mixture of concrete and abstract nouns that in nontechnical speech just cannot be connected by the same "is" (or "is not").

Breakdown of communication. The semiartificial language of the Scholastics was excessively clumsy, and, in the absence of the precise definitional control that goes with a totally artificial language, required for its tolerably safe employment an intuitive power extending beyond the ordinary; even when this has been achieved, the history of the period demonstrates that there is no guarantee that communication will be maintained. For example, skill in the use of such language probably reached its peak in the writings of Duns Scotus, the Subtle Doctor. He rejected the theory that matter is the principle of individuation on the grounds that this attribution leaves the individual lacking in total intelligibility and even makes problematic the possibility of an omniscient being's (God's) radical understanding of the individual object. He therefore posited that individuation is performed not by a material, but by a formal, principle; for example, by "Socrateity" in

respect of the individual Socrates, and in general by the "thisness" (*haecceitas*) appropriate to each individual "this." We have already observed the connection between form and intelligibility presupposed in this operation, an operation that raises a further phase of the universals controversy and at the same time exemplifies the breakdown in communication.

Ockham criticized the Scotist thing-centered formal distinction (*distinctio formalis a parte rei*) alleged to hold between the universal nature in question (humanity in the case of a human being) and the individuating formal principle (Socrateity) that makes the individual into *this* individual. Ockham was at a loss to see how this distinction could be thing-centered (*a parte rei*) and yet not commit its proponent to the admission of extra entities (humanity, Socrateity) over and above, and distinct from, individuals, in spite of the fact that the existence of universals as extra entities of this sort was denied by Scotus.

It has already been suggested that form may be best expressed by means of verblike nouns ("equinizing," "petrifying"); hence, the abstract nouns often used to express formal principles could be viewed as being more verblike than namelike—a position taken by Aquinas from Boethius and apparently recognized by other Scholastics. If this view is accepted, then the statement that the Socrateity of Socrates is distinct from his humanity may be interpreted, using appropriate verblike forms, as asserting that *Socratizing* is not identical with *humanizing*, an analysis that yields a true thing-centered distinction and yet does not send one on a vain search for extra named entities over and above the man Socrates; this offers at least one way in which the Scotist contention may be consistently understood.

But Ockham assumed, in effect, that any distinction that holds in respect of things (a "real" distinction) can only be like that which holds between, for example, Socrates and Plato and which is expressed by a sentence such as "Socrates is not Plato," wherein "Socrates" and "Plato" are names (as opposed to the verblike "Socratizing" and "humanizing"). When, therefore, Ockham encountered the further Scotist tenet that although a thing-centered formal distinction holds between Socrateity and humanity (for example), it is nevertheless not the case that a *real* distinction holds between the two, he assumed that "Socrateity" and "humanity" could be treated in the same way as such names as Socrates, Plato, Cicero, and Tully, and that even as the negation of a real distinction between Tully and Cicero amounts to a statement of their real identity as the same individual object, so also the denial of a real distinction between Socrateity and humanity amounts to a statement of real identity of this sort. In point of fact, however, once the verblike nature of the form-expressing words "Socrateity" and "humanity" has been grasped, it becomes clear that a denial of a real distinction between Socrateity and humanity should be understood as the rejection of any attempt to treat those form expressions as though they were pure names. The whole weight of Ockham's subsequent attack, aimed as it was at the consequence that the Scotists were in such contexts stating the denial of a real identity (one framed in terms of names, as opposed to verbs) is therefore totally misplaced.

The same blindness, combined with the theological premise that God is omnipotent, and hence can effect anything that does not involve a contradiction, also played havoc with other distinctions patiently established by earlier thinkers. For example, the distinction between essence and existence, some of whose associated theses were described above as embodying novel uses of words, was attacked on the grounds that the essence of a thing (a man's humanity) and its existence are (if a *real* distinction holds between them) two things distinct in the way that Socrates and Plato are two distinct things. In consequence, the Ockhamists considered themselves licensed to assert that the admission of a *real* distinction between essence and existence has as a consequence the possibility of God's omnipotence producing something's essence without at the same time producing its existence, or vice versa; however, this is patently absurd, and therefore (they concluded) there is no real distinction between essence and existence.

In the presence of such misplaced criticism it is obvious that scholastic thought could have been better expressed in a fully artificial language, armed with precise definitions and a greater capacity for generating and identifying new parts of speech than that of the semiartificial language that was used.

Reaction against technical artificialization. Although the artificialization of natural language for the expression of technical truths beyond the capacity of natural language proceeded apace from the time of Anselm, the final major philosophical reaction, brought about by communication difficulties, was in the opposite direction. Ockham's attitude to the contrast between ordinary and technical discourse was the polar opposite of Anselm's attitude at the opening of the period. For Anselm, accounts of meaning could and did call for the use of, or have as consequences, technical assertions that were either nonsense from the point of view of ordinary usage, or at least involved radical departures therefrom—and his successors were similarly venturesome.

Ockham, although likewise constantly conscious of the contrast between ordinary speech and the technical forms of speech used by his predecessors, nevertheless placed propriety of expression on the side of ordinary speech, and *not* on the technical side, except in those instances where the novel locutions of his forerunners could be explained away or disarmed as mere stylistic ornament. His lists of sentences that are false if taken literally (*de virtute sermonis*) because words are not therein used properly (*secundum proprietatem sermonis*) are catalogues of the sort of technical assertions that for Anselm and following thinkers had been a necessary consequence of the special requirements of logical and philosophical discourse, and that for them enshrined propriety to a degree to which the looseness of ordinary speech could not aspire. This reversal of attitude, symptomatic of the breakdown of communication in terms of semiartificial language, did not, of course, immediately prevail; it was combated at great length, for instance, by John Wyclyf (c. 1324–1384). Nevertheless, Ockham's attitude, reinforced by Renaissance philology, ultimately triumphed and was represented in the strictures of Locke on "the frivolous use of uncouth, affected, and unintelligible terms" that made philosophy "unfit or uncapable to be brought into well-bred company and polite conversation."

Ethics and politics. Augustine's severe view of the effects of the Fall of man resulted in a largely negative view of the civil state. He held that save in the ideal case of a Christian commonwealth, earthly states are merely coercive institutions which would not exist had man not fallen, and serve simply to issue punishments and remedies for the corruption of human nature. Correspondingly, divine grace is seen by Augustine as playing a dramatically elevating part in the reformation and reordination of the will. However, the thirteenth-century revival of full Aristotelianism, coupled with the Thomist view of grace as a completion rather than an abrogation of nature, allowed that civil subordination was natural to man, would exist even if the Fall had not taken place, and hence could not be written off as an extraneous penal imposition; the state possesses a positive value in its own right. Aquinas' enormously detailed philosophical anthropology constituted the foundation of his version of Aristotelian humanist ethics and politics, to which he attempted to give a Christian completion; it cited the perfection and fulfillment of human nature in the intellect rather than in the will: accordingly, he viewed law as essentially a rule of right reason, rather than as a species of will-based command. This doctrine was in conflict with the teachings of the Augustinian voluntarists such as Ockham, whose view has endured through Hobbes and Austin down to modern times. Aquinas' system of rationally based natural law as a measure of the value of human actions in general, and of human law in particular, was in opposition to the absolutist tendencies evident in the coalescence of revived Roman law with Augustinianism, which were to come to final fruition in the sovereign nation-state of our own era. The distinction between the righteous prince (who remains within the bounds of the law) and the tyrant (who puts himself above the law) had been trenchantly enunciated by John of Salisbury, was supported by the non-Roman medieval legal tradition, and clearly presupposes limits to the powers of the chief legal authority. It is clear that Aquinas' natural-law theory supports this limiting attitude and justifies resistance to tyranny; he was therefore faced with the task of coming to terms with those features of Roman law (to be emphasized in the Renaissance) according to which the prince is above the laws. This he did by distinguishing between the coercive power (*vis coactiva*) and the directive, or rationally qualifying, power (*vis directiva*) of law: in respect of the first the prince is above the law, but in respect of the second he is voluntarily subject to it. In his theory of law Aquinas directly influenced Richard Hooker, to whom John Locke admitted his indebtedness.

It is in connection with Aquinas' defense of the right of resistance, as well as in his prima facie puzzling assertions on the relation of the papacy to civil power, that we may best see how he attempted to resolve the perennial problem of the relation between political principle and political fact through the use of exceptive (*nisi forte . . .*) clauses. Instead of rigidly carrying through principle to the bitter end and at all costs, without any regard for concrete or historical facts (in the manner, one might say, of Plato in the *Republic*), Aquinas suggested that the most rational course would be to make appropriate accommodations with local conditions, if necessary by recourse to empirically based anticipation of the results of political action. For example, it follows from natural law that tyranny may rightly be resisted by force; this justification of rebellion may be acted upon, said Aquinas, except perhaps (*nisi forte*) when the facts of the case make it plain that the revolution will generate worse evils than the tyranny which it is designed to displace. Again, in religious matters he declared that the ecclesiastical power is to be obeyed rather than the civil, and in civil matters the lay power is to be obeyed rather than the ecclesiastical, except perhaps (*nisi forte*) in the special case of the two powers' being amalgamated in one person, such as the Roman pontiff. Commentators discussing this last example, and not armed with a realization of the significance of its exceptive (*nisi forte*) structure, have inferred from it that Aquinas here committed himself to an extreme papalist position which would endow the pope with the fullness of spiritual and temporal power. However, once the significance of that structure has been gathered from the many other available textual examples, the conclusion may be drawn that Aquinas taught the separation of these powers as a matter of principle, yet he also observed the local fact that insofar as the pope is a temporal ruler of papal territory, he, exceptionally, holds both spiritual and temporal power. A like adaptability may be seen in Aquinas' concession that the secondary precepts of natural law are mutable in accordance with changing historical conditions and in his recommendation that laws should be tailored to fit the type of population for which they are intended; to attempt to legislate a people into full virtue is futile.

Augustinianism in general, and the Augustinian theory of law as essentially will-based command, received impetus and encouragement from the archbishop of Paris' condemnation in 1277 of certain Aristotelian theses of Arabic philosophical complexion, a condemnation which also bore upon some Thomist positions. The tendency of Averroism had been toward a pantheism which diminished the freedom of God in the act of creation. Aquinas' claim that moral evaluation consists of rational assessments based upon the intrinsic nature of the cases in question was also susceptible of being interpreted as constituting a restriction on divine omnipotence. Accordingly, Duns Scotus and Ockham, in varying degrees, claimed that the rules governing the attribution of rightness or wrongness to human actions were contingent in relation to the absolute power of God; the consequent contingency of connection between deed and merit has caused some historians to assume that in Augustinian thought one may find the basis of Luther's doctrine of justification by faith alone, as well as a source for the legal aspects of the Hobbesian theory of sovereignty.

Science and philosophy. Although the nonabrogatory policy of medieval philosophy outlined above served well enough to insure that philosophers took seriously the fully human realm of reasons, purposes, hopes, and so forth, thus avoiding the split between the thinker as a human being and the thinker as a philosopher, the extrapolation of that policy's attendant ultraempiricism to sciences such as physics and cosmology tended to a greater or lesser extent to inhibit their development as practical tools. A prime and early example of such ultraempiricist inhibition is to be found in the refusal of the second-century astronomer Ptolemy to consider a sun-centered planetary system because it so obviously is at variance with things as we find them to be, a refusal which was espoused by most but not all medieval philosophers. On this point Ptolemy was in agreement with the physics-based cosmology of Aristotle, but in general he represented a rival tradition, that of the mathematicians, who were usually regarded by the medievals as devisers of ingenious fictions that served merely to "save the observed appearances." Mathematical theories were accordingly believed to lack the necessity attributable to the vast and coherent background of Aristotelian physics and metaphysics, and this attitude prevailed until the time of Galileo. However, there was some support for the development of mathematical physics, insofar as it relies on thought experiments as opposed to exact experiment, in the very competent medieval enlargements on a point whose root lay ultimately in Aristotle's *Categories;* there, when attempting to differentiate between substances (such as man, tree, stone) and qualities (such as whiteness, roundness, hardness), Aristotle pointed out that the latter are susceptible of degree, while the former are not. To this remote starting point much of modern mechanics owes its origin, for through speculation on the various kinds, rates, and degrees of "intension" and "remission" of qualities, the ideas of constant motion and acceleration and deceleration (uniform or nonuniform), and their relations to time and distance were thoroughly explored by fourteenth-century philosophers, such as those of Merton College, Oxford. Nicholas of Oresme (1323–1382) related these aspects of motion to their graphical expressions and anticipated infinitesimal calculus and coordinate geometry. Herein lies the starting point of certain segments of Galileo's mechanics.

Bibliography

PRIMARY SOURCES

Abelard, Peter, *Opera*, Victor Cousin, ed. Paris, 1859.

Anselm of Canterbury, *Proslogion, De Grammatico,* and other works, in *S. Anselmi Opera Omnia,* F. S. Schmitt, ed. Secovii (Seckau), 1938. Vol. I.

Augustine, St., *City of God,* revised translation and edition by R. V. G. Tasker, 2 vols. New York, 1945.

Boethius, logical works in J. P. Migne, ed., *Patrologia Latina.* Paris, 1844–1864. Vol. 64.

Duns Scotus, John, *Opera Omnia,* 26 vols. Paris, 1891–1895. Extracts and translations in Allan B. Wolter, ed., *Duns Scotus, Philosophical Texts.* New York, 1962.

Erigena, John Scotus, *Works,* in J. P. Migne, ed., *Patrologia Latina.* Paris, 1844–1864. Vol. 122.

John of Salisbury, *Metalogicon,* C. C. J. Webb, ed. Oxford, 1929. Translated by D. D. McGarry. Berkeley, 1962.

Maimonides, Moses, *Guide of the Perplexed.* London, 1881.

Ockham, William of, *Summa Totius Logicae,* Philotheus Boehner, ed., 2 vols. St. Bonaventure, N.Y., 1957–1962. Extracts and translations in Philotheus Boehner, ed., *William of Ockham.* New York, 1957.

Thomas Aquinas, *Summa Theologica,* translated by the Fathers of the English Dominican Province, 24 vols. London, 1920–1924.

Thomas Aquinas, *Summa Contra Gentiles,* translated by the

Fathers of the English Dominican Province, 4 vols. London, 1924.
    Thomas Aquinas, *Selected Political Writings*, A. P. d'Entrèves, ed. Oxford, 1948.
    Wyclyf, John, *Wyclif's Latin Works*, issued in several volumes by the Wyclif Society. London, 1883——.

HISTORICAL BACKGROUND

    Southern, R. W., *The Making of the Middle Ages*. New Haven, 1953. Development of medieval thought.

MEDIEVAL THOUGHT IN GENERAL

    Copleston, Frederick, *A History of Philosophy*. New York, 1962. Vols. II and III.
    Knowles, David, *Evolution of Medieval Thought*. New York, 1964.

DETAILED COMMENTARY

    Clagett, Marshall, *The Science of Mechanics in the Middle Ages*. Madison, Wis., 1959. Medieval mechanics.
    Henry, D. P., *The "De Grammatico" of St. Anselm, the Theory of Paronymy*. Notre Dame, Ind., 1964. Application of artificial language for the elucidation of medieval philosophical and logical texts.
    McMullin, Ernan, ed., *The Concept of Matter*. Notre Dame, Ind., 1963. Full discussion of medieval view of matter.
    Morall, John B., *Political Thought in Medieval Times*. London, 1958.
    Santillana, Giorgio de, *The Crime of Galileo*. Chicago, 1955; London, 1958.

DESMOND PAUL HENRY

MEGARIANS, a philosophical school at Megara (one day's walk from Athens) from the late fifth to the early third century B.C., was founded under the influence partly of Eleaticism and partly of Socrates; it produced contemporary critics of Plato and Aristotle and influenced the beginnings of Stoicism. It was notorious for its logic-chopping and paradoxes and for question-and-answer forms of argument. It was the Megarian Alexius who tried, but failed, to extract a "yes-or-no" answer from Zeno the Stoic to the question "Have you stopped beating your father?"

Euclides (c. 430–c. 360 B.C.), the founder, was a friend of Socrates and was Plato's host at Megara for a time after Socrates' death. Euclides apparently fused Eleatic and Socratic views; he said the good was one and unchanging under many names—such as wisdom, God, and mind—and denied the existence of the opposites of the good. In debate he attacked the conclusion, not the premises, of an argument and rejected arguments from analogy. He appears in Plato's *Theaetetus*.

Eubulides, his successor, attacked Aristotle and propounded paradoxes about the number of grains required to make a heap (the "Sorites"), whether one "knows" a man in disguise, whether one has lost what one does not have, and (most famous) the "Liar"—if I say that I am lying, am I telling the truth?

Bryson denied that a plain word could be offensive if it meant the same as a circumlocution and squared the circle by methods regarded by Aristotle as sophistical. His friend Polyxenus introduced a variety of "third man" argument against Forms, the precise nature of which is perhaps now irrecoverable but which did not involve an infinite regress.

Stilpo (c. 380–c. 300 B.C.), a rival of Theophrastus and a teacher of the Stoic Zeno, "demolished Forms," saying that he who said "man," if he meant no one man more than any other, meant no man at all, and that if "lettuce" existed ten thousand years ago, then *this* lettuce is not "lettuce." (This point may be less subtle than another "third man" argument perhaps due to the Megarians: when I say "man walks," I mean neither the Form "Man" nor any particular man but some further "man.") Stilpo also denied predication: one cannot say "the man is good" because "man" does not mean the same as "good"; "the musical Socrates" and "the white Socrates" cannot be the same Socrates. (Others had used these last arguments.)

Diodorus Cronus was also a teacher of Zeno; a famous debate between Diodorus and Stilpo took place in 307 B.C. Aristotle referred to earlier Megarians who denied potentiality except when actualized; this, Aristotle said, prevented motion. Diodorus produced further arguments against motion and, perhaps attacking Aristotle's *De Interpretatione*, defined the possible as that which either is or will be true; the impossible as that which, being false, will not be true; the necessary as that which, being true, will not be false; and the nonnecessary as that which either is or will be false. He justified his definition of the possible by his "master argument," which asserted an incompatibility between the three propositions (1) everything which is past and true is necessary; (2) the impossible does not follow from the possible; (3) what neither is nor will be is possible. Diodorus accepted (1) and (2) and rejected (3). He apparently intended to provide a definition of possibility consistent with fatalism (which he maintained). Panthoides, another Megarian, chose to reject (1); Chrysippus the Stoic rejected (2). Diodorus' pupil Philo of Megara, a friend of Zeno, defined possibility quite differently, in terms of the "intrinsic nature of the assertion," as opposed to the external circumstances affecting its truth. The more complex Stoic view of possibility is partly derived from Philo's position.

The Stoics regarded an argument as valid when the conditional statement having the conjunction of the premises as antecedent and having the conclusion as consequent is true. Diodorus and Philo perhaps originated this view; certainly they debated the nature of conditionals. Philo said a "sound" or "true" conditional is one that does not "begin with a truth and end with a falsehood" (for example, when it is day and I am conversing, the statement "If it is day, I am conversing"). This anticipated the modern truth-functional definition of material implication and may mark a reaction to Diodorus' stricter requirement for a sound conditional as one in which it neither is nor ever was possible for the antecedent to be true and the consequent false; this requirement was even stricter in that it satisfied Diodorus' conditions for necessary truth. Requirements even more strict were suggested by others, probably Stoics.

Both Cleinomachus, who was the first to write about "propositions, predicates, and such topics" (Stoic terminology appears in our report on Cleinomachus, though he may have used earlier terminology of his own), and Panthoides, whose book on "ambiguities" was attacked by

Chrysippus, clearly shared the Stoics' interest in meaning. Diodorus had denied that any word in itself could be ambiguous.

No Megarian writings survive. The above facts and arguments are widely scattered in various ancient authorities, and many of them are reported in no more detail than is given here. Some arguments in Plato's *Euthydemus* or Aristotle's *Sophistical Refutations* resemble Megarian paradoxes, but not all seemingly "contentious" or "Eleatic" views mentioned by Plato or Aristotle should be ascribed to them. (They are *not*, as once was thought, the "Friends of the Forms" in Plato's *Sophist*.) Their skill as logicians is demonstrated by the work of Diodorus and Philo; earlier Megarian logic was perhaps more systematic than our evidence allows it to appear. The early paradoxes are proof that they were already interested in problems of refutative procedure, meaning and ambiguity, predication, and perhaps in many other topics.

Bibliography

Cherniss, Harold, *Aristotle's Criticism of Plato and the Academy*, Vol. I. Baltimore, 1944. Pp. 500–505.

Hintikka, Jaakko, "Aristotle and the 'Master Argument' of Diodorus." *American Philosophical Quarterly*, Vol. 1 (1964), 101–114.

Kneale, William, and Kneale, Martha, *The Development of Logic*. Oxford, 1962. Chs. 1–3.

Mates, Benson, *Stoic Logic*. Berkeley, 1953.

Pauly, A.; Wissowa, G.; and Kroll, W., eds., *Real-Encyclopädie der classischen Altertumswissenschaft*. Stuttgart, 1893——. See J. Stenzel and W. Theiler, "Megarikoi," Vol. 15, Part 1 (Halfband 29); K. von Fritz, "Megariker," Supp. 5; and under individual names.

Ryle, Gilbert, "Dialectic in the Academy," in Renford Bambrough, ed., *New Essays on Plato and Aristotle*. London, 1965. Pp. 39–68.

Zeller, Eduard, *Die Philosophie der Griechen*, 5th ed. Leipzig, 1922. Vol. II, Part 1, pp. 244–275.

DAVID B. ROBINSON

MEIER, GEORG FRIEDRICH (1718–1777), German philosopher and aesthetician. A pupil of A. G. Baumgarten, Meier succeeded Baumgarten as extraordinary professor at the University of Halle in 1740 and became a full professor in 1748, holding that position until his death.

Meier, a prolific writer, developed and commented on Baumgarten's doctrines as an extension and revision of Wolffianism and went far beyond Baumgarten in the reform of Wolffianism. His treatises, used as textbooks in many universities, were perspicuous, sophisticated, and modern renderings of Wolffian doctrine; by their thorough discussion of basic concepts and attention to details they give one of the best insights into the Wolffian system and its problems. Wolff's and Baumgarten's ideas were rendered more fluid by Meier's work, establishing connections between disparate problems and establishing new distinctions. Meier's style was closer to the style of the "popular philosophers" than to that of orthodox Wolffians, and he made little use of the Wolffian mathematical method in philosophy.

Meier's *Vernunftlehre* introduced into the traditional frame of Wolffian logic lengthy psychological and methodological discussions like those of the Pietist philosophers

A. F. Hoffmann and C. F. Crusius. He also presented a detailed typology of concepts. In a marked departure from Wolff, he stressed the limits of the human understanding, devoting an entire work to the subject (*Betrachtungen über die Schranken der menschlichen Erkenntniss*).

Meier's *Metaphysik*, although in general rather close to Baumgarten, shows the same individual features. For instance, in empirical psychology Meier advocated a subjectivism like that of Crusius. He held that the nature of our understanding determines what we can or cannot think. This determination, like the principle of *cogitabilis* in Crusius, is the foundation of the principle of identity.

Meier devoted several pamphlets to the immortality of the soul, which he held could not be theoretically demonstrated. Any a priori proof of God's existence must be completed by an a posteriori one. And in general Meier would not extend the power of reason much beyond basic truths and human experience.

Meier's most typical work was his *Anfangsgründe aller schönen Künste und Wissenschaften* ("Principles of All Beautiful Arts and Sciences"). He was opposed to the classical thesis that art imitates nature. He stressed the importance of sensitivity (the "lower faculty") and the indispensability of a knowledge of the beautiful within one's whole outlook on the world. Besides Baumgarten, whose views it is difficult to extricate from Meier's because of their close collaboration, Meier was influenced by the Swiss critics Bodmer and Breitinger and by English aestheticians. Like Baumgarten, he gave the term "aesthetics" a broad interpretation and, like Baumgarten's, his work contains an extensive discussion of scientific methodology.

Principal Works by Meier

Anfangsgründe aller schönen Künste und Wissenschaften, 3 vols. Halle, 1748–1750.

Gedanken über die Religion. Halle, 1749.

Vernunftlehre. Halle, 1752.

Philosophische Sittenlehre, 5 vols. Halle, 1753–1761. A much extended version of Baumgarten's *Ethica Philosophica*.

Metaphysik, 4 vols. Halle, 1755–1759.

Betrachtungen über die Schranken der menschlichen Erkenntniss. Halle, 1775.

Works on Meier

Bergmann, E., *Die Begründung der deutschen Aesthetik durch A. G. Baumgarten und G. F. Meier*. Leipzig, 1911.

Böhm, Hans, "Das Schönheitsproblem bei G. F. Meier." *Archiv für die gesamte Psychologie*, Vol. 56 (1926).

Langen, S. G., *G. F. Meier*. Halle, 1778.

GIORGIO TONELLI

MEINECKE, FRIEDRICH (1862–1954), German historian and political philosopher. Meinecke was small in stature and somewhat frail but remained mentally very vigorous and intellectually prolific until his death at the age of 92. His great charm and influence were due partly to his erudition, partly to his modesty, and partly to two conflicting tendencies in his thinking which he continually sought to reconcile.

One of these tendencies was his patriotism and loyalty to

Germany's best traditions of the past. As a boy he had been thrilled by the sight of the victorious German troops marching home through the Brandenburg Gate after the Franco-Prussian War. Later he admired the skill with which Bismarck established the long-desired unification of his country and saw with pride Germany's industrial and commercial expansion into a great power. After studying under the Prussian nationalist historian J. G. Droysen, Meinecke became an archivist and published in rapid succession several valuable historical works, including accounts of the German uprising against Napoleon and a two-volume biography of Feldmarschall von Boyen, one of the leading figures in the reorganization and liberalization of Prussia in the early nineteenth century. In 1893 he was appointed an editor of the leading German historical journal, *Historische Zeitschrift*, a post that he filled with distinction for forty years until ousted by the Nazis.

The second tendency in Meinecke's thinking asserted itself in 1901 when he became deeply occupied with the problems of European political philosophy. In that year he was promoted to a teaching position at the University of Strassburg, later moving to Freiburg. Here in these two cities in the beautiful Rhine valley Meinecke's eyes were opened to the charm of the countryside. His talks with the Roman Catholic population and scholars and his contact with French culture widened his outlook and quickened his philosophical interests. These were his happiest years. In 1914 he was appointed to a permanent professorship at Berlin.

Meinecke's dual preoccupation with liberal culture and with Prussia found expression in a perceptive account of German development. *Weltbürgertum und Nationalstaat* (1908) examines the views of many cosmopolitan liberals and political leaders and, at the same time, analyzes the characteristics and pretensions of the Prussian state, which had been exaggerated by Hegel. It was supplemented by some two dozen articles written by Meinecke in the following years and reprinted in *Preussen und Deutschland* (1918).

Can reason of state justify the employment of might against right? May a state properly do things that are ethically forbidden to the ordinary citizen? Does it enjoy a code of morals above and beyond that of the private individual? Meinecke's classic treatment of these old but perennial questions, *Die Idee der Staatsräson in der neueren Geschichte* (1924), examines meticulously the actions of various European rulers and statesmen and the writings of numerous political theorists from Machiavelli to Treitschke. Meinecke comes to the conclusion that, since power is the essence of its existence, the state is justified in using such means as are necessary to maintain and even extend its power, but that this power is limited by the state's obligation to protect the rights of its citizens and to promote their cultural and material welfare. It is, however, practically impossible to draw a precise line between state egoism and ideal morality.

Meinecke always preferred to till a small area where he could closely observe concrete facts and deal with them in a rigorously critical scientific manner. For Ranke and Burckhardt he had the highest regard. He rejected the grandiose theoretical constructions of Karl Lamprecht, Oswald Spengler, and Arnold Toynbee. If he could be said to have had any one primary underlying thought, it would be that of individuality—the unique individual character of every event, person, social group, nation-state, or idea. In addition he believed in evolution—the capacity of every individuality for development either by growth or decay. Hence his preoccupation with Machiavelli, Richelieu, Freiherr vom Stein, Schleiermacher, Wilhelm von Humboldt, Goethe, Joseph Maria von Radowitz, Bismarck, and Hitler. Meinecke's conceptions of individuality and evolution contributed to the new way of historical thinking, now known as "historicism," which developed in the age of Herder and Goethe and which Meinecke minutely unfolded in *Die Entstehung des Historismus* (1936). Historicism dealt a sharp blow to unquestioning belief in absolute values, optimistic positivism, religious creeds, and natural law. It opened wide the floodgates of relativism. Meinecke, however, was not unaware of the aberrations resulting from historicism and tried to counteract them by repeatedly insisting that the only sure and safe guide to morality and conduct is the individual's own conscience.

With the advent to power of the Nazis, Meinecke was forced to retire from active teaching, and under their tyranny he suffered spiritual agony and physical hardship. He might have escaped abroad as did so many others; but he remained in the country hoping to hasten Hitler's downfall and by his own advice and influence to help to lead Germany back to its older and better traditions. He was a close personal friend of General Beck and had some inkling of the plots to get rid of Hitler, but did not participate actively in them. His last contribution to an understanding of German history and his own interpretation of it was his little volume *Die deutsche Katastrophe* in 1946. Later, when the University of Berlin fell under communist control he took the lead in founding the new Free University in West Berlin of which he was appropriately chosen rector.

Bibliography

The principal works of Friedrich Meinecke are *Weltbürgertum und Nationalstaat* (Oldenburg, Munich, and Berlin, 1908; 7th ed., 1929); *Preussen und Deutschland* (Munich, Berlin, and Oldenburg, 1918); *Die Idee der Staatsräson in der neueren Geschichte* (Oldenburg, Munich, and Berlin, 1924), translated by D. Scott as *Machiavellianism: The Doctrine of Raison d'État and Its Place in Modern History* (London, 1957); and *Die Entstehung des Historismus*, 2 vols. (Munich and Berlin, 1936). *Die deutsche Katastrophe* (Wiesbaden, 1946), translated by Sidney B. Fay as *The German Catastrophe* (Cambridge, Mass., 1950, and Boston, 1962), written at the moment of Germany's utter defeat and deepest despair, contains Meinecke's penetrating reflections on the preceding hundred years, the causes of the Nazi disaster, and his faith in the future. Two short autobiographical volumes are *Erlebtes, 1862–1901* (Leipzig, 1941) and *Strassburg–Freiburg–Berlin, 1901–1914* (Stuttgart, 1949). A six-volume edition of part of his works was published for the Friedrich Meinecke Institute of the University of Berlin between 1957 and 1962; this edition contains a volume of his correspondence and a reprint, with valuable editorial introductions and notes, of his more important writings.

One of the best books on Meinecke and historicism is Walther Hofer, *Geschichtsschreibung und Weltanschauung: Betrachtungen zum Werk Friedrich Meineckes* (Munich, 1950). A bibliography of writings by and about Meinecke may be found in the *Historische Zeitschrift*, Vol. 174, 503–523.

SIDNEY B. FAY

MEINONG, ALEXIUS (1853–1920), studied under Franz Brentano at the University of Vienna from 1875 through 1878 and taught at the University of Graz from 1882 until his death. In 1894 he established at Graz the first laboratory for experimental psychology in Austria. Some of his psychological writings fall within this area, but most pertain to what Brentano called descriptive psychology. The philosophical works, referred to below, also pertain to descriptive psychology.

Meinong's most important contributions to philosophy concern the theory of objects, the theory of assumptions, the theory of evidence, and the theory of value. He also discussed, at considerable length, the nature of the emotions and their relation to intellectual phenomena, imagination, abstraction, wholes and other "complex objects," relations, causality, possibility, and probability.

Theory of objects. The two basic theses of Meinong's theory of objects (*Gegenstandstheorie*) are (1) there are objects that do not exist and (2) every object that does not exist is yet constituted in some way or other and thus may be made the subject of true predication. Traditional metaphysics treats of objects that exist as well as of those that merely subsist (*bestehen*) but, having "a prejudice in favor of the real," tends to neglect those objects that have no kind of being at all; hence, according to Meinong, there is need for a more general theory of objects.

Everything is an object, whether or not it is thinkable (if an object happens to be unthinkable then it is something having at least the property of being unthinkable) and whether or not it exists or has any other kind of being. Every object has the characteristics it has whether or not it has any kind of being; in short, the *Sosein* (character) of every object is independent of its *Sein* (being). A round square, for example, has a *Sosein*, since it is both round and square; but it is an *impossible object*, since it has a contradictory *Sosein* that precludes its *Sein*.

Of possible objects—objects not having a contradictory *Sosein*—some exist and others (for example, golden mountains) do not exist. If existence is thought of as implying a spatiotemporal locus, then there are certain subsistent objects that do not exist; among these are the *being* of various objects and the *nonbeing* of various other objects. Since there are horses, there is also the being of horses, the being of the being of horses, the nonbeing of the nonbeing of horses, and the being of the nonbeing of the nonbeing of horses. And since there is no Pegasus, there is the nonbeing of Pegasus, as well as the being of the nonbeing of Pegasus and the nonbeing of the being of Pegasus.

Meinong's theory must be distinguished from both Platonic realism, as this term is ordinarily interpreted, and the reism, or concretism, of Brentano and Tadeusz Kotarbiński. (Meinong noted that since his view is broader than realism, it might properly be called objectivism.) Thus, the Platonic realist could be said to argue: "(*P*) Certain objects that do not exist have certain properties; but (*Q*) an object has properties if and only if it is real; hence (*R*) there are real objects that do not exist." The reist, or concretist, on the other hand, reasons from not-*R* and *Q* to not-*P*; that is, he derives the contradictory of Plato's first premise by taking Plato's second premise along with the contradictory of Plato's conclusion. But Meinong, like Plato and unlike

the reist, accepted both *P* and *R*; unlike both Plato and the reist, he rejected *Q* by asserting the independence of *Sosein* from *Sein*; and therefore, again unlike both Plato and the reist, he said that the totality of objects extends far beyond the confines of what is merely real (*das Universum in der Gesamtheit des Wirklichen noch lange nicht erschöpft ist*).

This doctrine of *Aussersein*—of the independence of *Sosein* from *Sein*—is sometimes misinterpreted by saying that it involves recourse to a third type of being in addition to existence and subsistence. Meinong's point, however, is that such objects as the round square have no type of being at all; they are "homeless objects," to be found not even in Plato's heaven. Bertrand Russell objected that if we say round squares are objects, we violate the law of contradiction. Meinong replied that the law of contradiction holds only for what is real and can hardly be expected to hold for any object, such as a round square, that has a contradictory *Sosein*.

Russell's theory of descriptions is often thought to constitute a refutation of the doctrine of *Aussersein;* actually, however, his theory merely presupposes that Meinong's doctrine is false. According to Meinong, the two statements "The round square is round" and "The mountain I am thinking of is golden" are true statements about nonexistent objects; they are *Sosein* and not *Sein* statements. The distinction between the two types of statements is most clearly put by saying that a *Sein* statement (for example, "John is angry") is an affirmative statement that can be existentially generalized upon (we may infer "There exists an *x* such that *x* is angry") and a *Sosein* statement is an affirmative statement that cannot be existentially generalized upon; despite the truth of "The mountain I am thinking of is golden," we may not infer "There exists an *x* such that I am thinking about *x* and *x* is golden." Russell's theory of descriptions, however, presupposes that every statement is either a *Sein* statement or the negation of a *Sein* statement and hence that there are no *Sosein* statements. According to Russell, a statement of the form "The thing that is *F* is *G*" may be paraphrased as "There exists an *x* such that *x* is *F* and *x* is *G*, and it is false that there exists a *y* such that *y* is *F* and *y* is not identical with *x*." If Meinong's true *Sosein* statements, above, are rewritten in this form, the result will be two *false* statements; hence Meinong could say that Russell's theory does not provide an adequate paraphrase.

An *impossible object*, as indicated above, is an object having a *Sosein* that violates the law of contradiction. An *incomplete object*, analogously, is one having a *Sosein* that violates the law of the excluded middle. Of the golden mountains, which most readers will think of on reading the paragraph above, it will be neither true nor false to say that they are higher than Mount Monadnock. And some objects are even more poorly endowed. For example, if I wish that your wish will come true, then the *object* of my wish is whatever it is that you happen to wish; but if, unknown to me, what you wish is that *my* wish will come true, then this object would seem to have very little *Sosein* beyond that of being our mutual object. Meinong said that such an object is a *defective object* and suggested that the concept may throw light upon some of the logical paradoxes.

The theory of complexes—that is, the theory of wholes and other such "objects of higher order"—upon which Meinong wrote at length, also falls within the theory of objects.

None of the objects discussed above is created by us, nor does any of them depend in any way upon our thinking. Had no one ever thought of the round square, it would still be true *of* the round square that it does not exist; the round square need not be thought of in order not to exist. We draw these objects, so to speak, from the infinite depths of the *Ausserseienden,* beyond being and not-being.

Theory of assumptions. Meinong's theory of assumptions, or suppositions, is set forth in *Über Annahmen* ("On Assumptions"; first ed., Leipzig, 1902; 2d ed., Leipzig, 1910). The theory is best understood by contrasting it with two theses held by Franz Brentano, to which Meinong's theory may be said to be a reaction. The first of Brentano's theses is that of reism, or concretism, referred to above: every object is a concrete thing; there are no objects such as the being of horses or the nonbeing of unicorns; the object of a judgment, therefore, is not a proposition, fact, or state of affairs; it is, rather, a certain concrete thing that the judgment may be said either to accept or to reject. And according to the second of Brentano's theses, there are basically only two types of intellectual attitudes we can take with respect to any object: we can simply think about the object, in which case it is the object of a thought or idea, or we can take an intellectual stand with respect to the object, either accepting it or rejecting it, in which case it becomes the object of a judgment. Meinong rejected both these theses of Brentano.

The object of a judgment, according to Meinong, is not a concrete thing; it is an "objective" (*Objektiv*). "That there are horses," for example, designates an objective—an object of higher order, containing horses as a kind of constituent. (Thus, the nonexisting, nonsubsisting round square is a constituent of that subsisting objective which is the nonbeing of the round square.) Assumptions, like judgments, take objectives as their objects.

What Meinong intended by his term "assumption" (*Annahme*) is most clearly exemplified in deliberation: "Suppose I were to do A. What would happen then? And now suppose I were not to do A. What would happen then?" Assumptions belong to a category falling between ideas and judgments. Like mere ideas, they do not themselves involve commitment, belief, or conviction; therefore, as such, they do not involve any possibility of error. Like judgments, they are concerned with objectives (in the above example, with what is designated by "I shall do A"), which are either true or false (it is either true or false that I shall do A); and, like judgments, assumptions involve either affirmation ("Suppose I do A") or denial ("Suppose I do not do A"), but affirmation or denial without commitment.

Meinong argues that only by reference to assumptions can we understand such phenomena as the nature of inference, our apprehension of negative facts, communication in general, desire, art, and the nature of play and of games. *Über Annahmen,* which is probably Meinong's best book, contains important material on these and many other topics.

Theory of evidence. The concept of evidence involves three dichotomies: (1) direct and indirect; (2) a priori and a posteriori; and (3) "evidence for certainty" and "evidence for presumption." Meinong's conception of the first two dichotomies is similar to that of Brentano. Thus there are axioms of mathematics and logic and the theory of objects, which are directly evident and a priori; and there are facts of "inner perception"—for example, the fact that I am making such-and-such an assumption, or the fact that I take something to be a tree—which are directly evident and a posteriori. (Any psychological process that "presents" an object to us, as memory may be said to present certain objects of the past, is also a process that "presents itself"; "self-presentation" is thus the source of that evidence which is direct, certain, and a posteriori.) These directly evident judgments may confer evidence upon certain other judgments, which are then said to be indirectly evident.

For Meinong, paradigm cases of what is a priori evident would be expressed by "Round squares are both round and square" and "red is different from blue." Every a priori judgment has four characteristics: it is grounded in the nature of its object (*gegenständlich begründet*); it is certain; it is necessary; and it does not take into consideration the question whether its object exists. (Brentano had said that every a priori judgment is a judgment to the effect that a certain type of object does not exist.)

An evident presumption (*Vermutung*) may be directly evident but not certain. The concept is needed, according to Meinong, in order for us to understand memory, perception, and induction. In each of these three cases we have a source of knowledge that cannot be impugned as such but may on occasion mislead us. A particular memory judgment, for example, may not be certain, but it may be evident, especially if it is supported by other memory judgments, by perceptual judgments, or by inductive inferences from such judgments; analogously, this holds for any particular perceptual judgment or any particular inductive conclusion. Such items of a posteriori knowledge may be compared with the cards in a pack, "no one of which is capable of standing up by itself, but several of which placed together can serve to hold each other up. Or, for something more solid, consider a stack of weapons in the field. . . ." A consequence of this theory of evident presumptions is that a false judgment may yet be evident, a consequence that Brentano took to be absurd. Evidence does not guarantee truth; but, according to Meinong, evidence resembles truth in that if a judgment is evident, then its being evident—its *Evidentsein*—as well as the *Evidentsein* of this *Evidentsein,* and so on ad infinitum, is also evident.

An essential part of Meinong's epistemology is his theory of "emotional presentation." There is an analogy between the way in which we come to know, say, that the temperature is high and the way in which we come to know that the temperature is agreeable. Meinong proposed, as a "heuristic principle," that we try to carry the analogy as far as possible. If it is by means of a subjective feeling that we perceive the temperature to be agreeable, it is also by means of a subjective sensation that we perceive the temperature to be high. In neither case is the subjective experience the object of the presentation; in neither case is our apprehension a matter of inference or of reasoning from effect to cause. "The sense in which the sky is said to be 'beautiful,' for example, is precisely that in which it is said to be 'blue.' But the experience by means of which the first property is presented plays an important role in our psychical life in addition to that of enabling us to grasp something else. This fact is reflected in our language; we refer to the one experience directly, but in the other case we must go round about, by way of the object that is presented, and use some such expression as 'experience of blue.'" Meinong noted that the traditional arguments against a "subjectivistic" or "psychologistic" interpretation of ordinary sense perception apply equally to any such interpretation of emotional presentation.

Theory of value. In the final version of his theory of value, Meinong made use of the theory of emotional presentation considered above, as well as of Brentano's doctrine of correct and incorrect emotion—i.e., the doctrine according to which emotions, like judgments, may be said to be correct or incorrect, justified or unjustified, and according to which certain things may thus be said to merit or be worthy of certain emotions.

The basic concept of value theory is not that of desire, interest, or utility, but that of value feeling (*Wertgefühle*). Value feelings take objectives as their objects, more particularly, objectives consisting of the being or nonbeing of certain objects. One type of value feeling is *Seinsfreude*, pleasure or joy in the existence or being of a certain object; another type is *Seinsleid*, displeasure or sorrow with respect to the existence or being of a certain object. But the feelings of joy and sorrow may also be directed toward nonexistence and nonbeing; hence there are four fundamental types of value feeling, which may be illustrated by reference to the nature of good and evil. The good is that which merits *Seinsfreude* if it exists and *Nichtseinsleid* (sorrow with respect to its nonexistence) if it does not exist; evil, on the other hand, merits *Seinsleid* if it exists and *Nichtseinsfreude* (joy with respect to its nonexistence) if it does not exist. Meinong noted that human beings are not consistent in their emotional reactions. For example, as far as our health and ordinary comforts are concerned, we experience considerable *Nichtseinsleid* when they are absent, but not the appropriate amount of *Seinsfreude* when they are present.

Our actions have moral qualities other than those of being good, bad, or indifferent. Meinong introduced four moral categories, which he explicated by reference to good and bad. Actions that are good may be either meritorious or simply required; those that are bad may be either excusable or inexcusable. (Meinong's terms are, respectively, *verdienstlich, correct, zulässig,* and *verwerflich.*) One may say of any act that performance is meritorious if and only if nonperformance is bad but excusable; nonperformance is meritorious if and only if performance is bad but excusable; performance is required if and only if nonperformance is inexcusable; and nonperformance is required if and only if performance is inexcusable. Given this "law of omission" (*Unterlassungsgesetz*), Meinong's concepts of meritorious, required, excusable, and inexcusable, respectively, approximate what are sometimes called the supererogatory, the obligatory, misdeeds that are venial, and misdeeds

that are not venial. According to one of Meinong's followers (Ernst Schwarz), these four moral concepts are related to the concept of justified or correct emotion in the following way: the meritorious is that which it is incorrect to blame and incorrect not to praise; the required is that which it is incorrect to blame, correct to praise, but not incorrect not to praise; the merely excusable is that which it is incorrect to praise, correct to blame, and not incorrect not to blame; and the inexcusable is that which it is incorrect to praise and incorrect not to blame.

Works by Meinong

Meinong summarized his principal philosophical conclusions in Raymund Schmidt, ed., *Die deutsche Philosophie der Gegenwart in Selbstdarstellungen* (Leipzig, 1921), Vol. I, pp. 91–150. His purely psychological writings can be found in the first volume of *Gesammelte Abhandlungen* (2 vols.; Leipzig, 1913–1914).

THEORY OF OBJECTS

Meinong's theory of objects is discussed in "Über Gegenstandstheorie" (1904); this article was reprinted in Vol. II of his *Gesammelte Abhandlungen* and translated as "The Theory of Objects" in Roderick M. Chisholm, ed., *Realism and the Background of Phenomenology* (Glencoe, Ill., 1960). The theory is discussed also in *Über die Stellung der Gegenstandstheorie im System der Wissenschaften* (Leipzig, 1907) and, indeed, in almost all Meinong's writings after 1904.

EPISTEMOLOGY

His most important epistemological writings are *Zur erkenntnistheoretischen Würdigung des Gedächtnisses* (1886), reprinted in Vol. II of *Gesammelte Abhandlungen*; *Über die Erfahrungsgrundlagen unseres Wissens* (Berlin, 1906); *Über Möglichkeit und Wahrscheinlichkeit* (Leipzig, 1915); and *Über emotionale Präsentation* (Vienna, 1917).

VALUE THEORY

Meinong's principal writings in value theory are *Psychologisch-ethische Untersuchungen zur Werththeorie* (Graz, 1894) and the posthumously published *Zur Grundlegung der allgemeinen Werththeorie* (Graz, 1923).

Works on Meinong

Among the most useful writings on Meinong are Bertrand Russell, "Meinong's Theory of Complexes and Assumptions," three articles in *Mind*, Vol. 13 (1904), 204–219, 336–354, and 509–524; J. N. Findlay, *Meinong's Theory of Objects and Values* (2d ed., Oxford, 1963); G. Dawes Hicks, "The Philosophical Researches of Meinong," in *Critical Realism* (London, 1938); and Konstantin Radakovic et al., *Meinong-Gedenkschrift* (Graz, 1952).

Important material on all aspects of Meinong's philosophy can be found in Rudolf Kindinger, ed., *Philosophenbriefe: Aus der wissenschaftlichen Korrespondenz von Alexius Meinong mit Fachgenossen seiner Zeit* (Graz, 1965).

RODERICK M. CHISHOLM

MELANCHTHON, PHILIPP (1497–1560), German reformer, was born at Bretten, Baden, and died at Wittenberg. He was a grandnephew of the great humanist Reuchlin, who encouraged him in his studies and deeply influenced his outlook. After studying at Heidelberg and Tübingen, Melanchthon, on Reuchlin's recommendation, became professor of Greek at Wittenberg. Because of his persuasiveness in interpreting the humanist spirit, this appointment marked the beginning of a new era in German education. At Wittenberg, Melanchthon collaborated closely with Luther. He helped him both in translating the Bible and in giving systematic shape to the new theology which until that time had existed in a highly subjective form. Melanchthon's task was to reduce this theology to exact form and to set it forth as an integrated and persuasive system. In 1521 Melanchthon published his *Loci Communes Rerum Theologicarum,* a work that in its various editions was one of the most influential manuals of Protestant theology.

During the rest of his career, Melanchthon was much occupied with controversy and debate. In many of the famous conferences of the Reformation era, his influence was thrown on the side of moderation and peace. He was closely identified with some of the most important formularies of the period, such as the Augsburg Confession.

Such activities involved even a man of conciliatory spirit in vigorous debate, and Melanchthon's position in the history of thought is largely determined by the controversies in which he took part. Two of these demand consideration.

The Adiaphoristic controversy was concerned with "indifferent matters"—that is, religious practices or theological beliefs on which flexibility or compromise might be permissible. Melanchthon was unfairly charged with including among the "adiaphora" such major questions as justification by faith. Melanchthon did not minimize the importance of essentials, but he was inclined to veil them beneath a conscious indefiniteness of expression. This deliberate obscurity extended to many matters which were intensively canvassed in the sixteenth century. He was willing to concede that good works are necessary to salvation, but not in the way in which the connection had traditionally been taught. He was prepared to recognize seven sacraments, but only if most of them were regarded as rites which have no inherent efficacy in securing salvation. Later he retreated from the permissive position he had adopted on the "adiaphora" and maintained a strict interpretation of the doctrines set forth in the *Loci Communes.*

More acute and more important was the controversy about synergism. Here the central issue was the relation between God's grace and man's will in regeneration. In his early period, Melanchthon, strongly influenced by Luther and deeply impressed by the experience of dependence upon God, severely restricted the role of man's will. To defend free will was to rob God's grace of its unique supremacy. But Melanchthon naturally tended to adopt a mediating outlook, and ethical issues were of great importance to him. Erasmus, in his controversy with Luther concerning free will, had advanced views which served to modify Melanchthon's position. Melanchthon was now prepared to recognize the part played in conversion by man's will. The position which he reached (called synergism) precipitated a violent debate. Melanchthon's own statements were ambiguous and lacking in precision. His supporters (Pfeffinger and Stringel, for instance) and his opponents (Amsdorf and Flacius) were very explicit indeed. Synergism, however, can best be understood as an ethical protest against attitudes which paralyze the conscience and leave the church powerless in its struggle against moral chaos. Melanchthon's concern with God's moral purity led him to the belief that the problems of evil and of human responsibility have been aggravated by an extreme doctrine of predestination. He therefore abandoned the decree of eternal reprobation. The cause of sin lies in man himself; the hardening of his heart is due to his own perversity. Man has a real measure of responsibility for his spiritual condition. Man's will, therefore, can cooperate with God's grace, and does so. The human will, of course, is never the primary cause of man's regeneration—the Spirit of God and the preaching of the Word always maintain the initiative—but man's will is specifically granted a place, and unless there is consent on man's part there can be no effective regeneration. Melanchthon guarded himself against the charge of Pelagianism, but nevertheless he was accused of yielding to this heresy. The violence of the controversy was due to the seriousness of the issues involved. A wide range of theological views had to be re-examined, and every aspect of the Christian doctrine of man and of salvation was involved. The controversy was finally silenced by the Formula of Concord, which ruled against the Melanchthonist position.

Works by Melanchthon

"Works," in K. G. Bretschneider and E. Bindseil, eds., *Corpus Reformatorum,* Vol. I–XXVIII. Brunswick, Germany, 1834–1860.
Supplementa Melanchthoniana. Leipzig, 1910.
The Loci Communes of Philipp Melanchthon, translated by C. L. Hill. Boston, 1944.

Works on Melanchthon

Hartfelder, K., *Philipp Melanchthon als Preceptor Germaniae.* Berlin, 1889.
Hildebrandt, Franz, *Melanchthon, Alien or Ally?* Cambridge, 1946.
Richards, J. W., *Philipp Melanchthon, The Protestant Preceptor of Germany.* New York, 1898.

GERALD R. CRAGG

MELISSUS OF SAMOS (fifth century B.C.), Greek Eleatic philosopher, led the Samian fleet against the Athenians and defeated them (Plutarch, *Pericles* 26, quoting a lost work of Aristotle). The date of the battle was 441–440 B.C., and this is the only reliable date in the biography of Melissus. He was said to have been a pupil of Parmenides, but this may be an inference from his work, which gives ample evidence of dependence on Parmenides.

Portions of Melissus' book entitled "On Nature or What Exists," written in prose, were quoted and preserved by the Aristotelian commentator Simplicius. The total length of these fragments is a little under one thousand words—enough to provide evidence of the content and quality of Melissus' argument. No other fragments survive. The pseudo-Aristotelian treatise *On Melissus, Xenophanes and Gorgias* (c. A.D. first century) adds nothing useful.

Melissus' argument, as revealed by the fragments, was similar to Parmenides' in method and results, although it differed in some details. The starting point is the contradictoriness of descriptions of change. Any change ultimately implies the generation of something from nothing or its destruction into nothing, and Melissus, with Parmenides, held both of these to be impossible on the ground that "nothing" is absolutely nonexistent and unthinkable. Hence, what exists must have existed always and must continue to exist (Melissus seems to view eternity as a continual existence through time, whereas Parmenides thought of a timeless present).

From the eternity of what exists, Melissus deduced its spatial infinity. He argued that if what exists did not come into existence, it had no beginning or end, and being without beginning or end, it must be limitless or infinite. He seemed not to have noticed the ambiguity of "beginning" and "end" (or else his defense of the move from time to space has been lost); this is presumably the basis of Aristotle's criticism of the argument (*De Sophisticis Elenchis* 167b13 and 168b35), although he does not make it quite explicit.

From the spatial infinity of what exists, Melissus deduced its unity. If there are two things in existence, each must limit the extent of the other; there cannot be more than one limitless thing in existence. Thus, Melissus chose a different route to the monism of Parmenides—indeed, according to most interpreters of Parmenides, this route was closed to him since, unlike Melissus, he held that what exists is spatially limited. But this is a dubious interpretation of Parmenides.

Next, Melissus argued that if what exists is one, it cannot have parts and must therefore be incorporeal because any solid body has actual or imaginable parts. Moreover, what exists cannot vary in density since this, according to Melissus, could come about only if one area contained less of being—and hence more of nonbeing—than another, and nonbeing is absolutely nonexistent. For similar reasons there is no motion, since there is no "give" anywhere in the plenum (this is an argument against motion which may not have been used by Parmenides). Every form of change—whether of size, order, or quality—means the coming into existence of something which previously was nothing, or the annihilation of something that exists, and these are ruled out by the first stage of Melissus' argument.

In the eighth fragment Melissus applies his own criteria of existence to the plural beings of the sensible world. If these things, such as air and fire, exist, then they must *be* just what our senses tell us they are and nothing else. But our senses tell us that they do change into something else. Our senses must therefore be wrong about this; hence, we can conclude that they were wrong initially in telling us that things are many and not one. The sensible world is therefore illusion.

Melissus was the least important of the Eleatics. Zeno's arguments proved more influential than his, and Parmenides was the original genius who pioneered the way. If Melissus has any claim to special historical importance that is not shared by the other Eleatics, it is perhaps that by applying Eleatic criteria to the plural beings posited by his opponents, he produced a formula (in Fr. 8) which led Leucippus directly to the concept of atoms. In the absence of complete texts it is wiser to refrain from pronouncing on Melissus' originality. Aristotle criticized both Parmenides and Melissus for bad arguments (*Physics* 186a6) and was more severe on Melissus, but perhaps that was because Melissus' clear style made him an easier target.

Bibliography

Fragments of Melissus' writings in Greek with German translations have been published in Diels–Kranz, *Fragmente der Vorsokratiker,* 10th ed., Vol. I (Berlin, 1960); English translations, in J. Burnet, *Early Greek Philosophy,* 4th ed. (London, 1930).

Selected texts with English translation and commentary are in G. S. Kirk and J. E. Raven, *The Presocratic Philosophers* (Cambridge, 1957); the commentary should be treated with caution, especially on the subject of infinity and Melissus' relation with the Pythagoreans. The same is true of J. E. Raven, *Pythagoreans and Eleatics* (Cambridge, 1948).

See also Harold Cherniss, *Aristotle's Criticism of Presocratic Philosophy* (Baltimore, 1935); G. E. L. Owen, "Eleatic Questions," in *Classical Quarterly,* Vol. 10 (1960); and W. K. C. Guthrie, *A History of Greek Philosophy,* Vol. II (Cambridge, forthcoming).

DAVID J. FURLEY

MEMORY. The word "remember" appears in many different grammatical constructions and takes a wide variety of grammatical objects. One can say, "I remember that such and such happened," but also (and with a somewhat different meaning), "As I remember, such and such happened." One can remember an event, an action, a person, a place, a feeling, a procedure, a line of verse, a melody, or a person's name. One can remember doing such and such, seeing such and such, or thinking such and such. And one can remember where something is, when a certain event happened, why something happened, who did a certain thing, how to do something, and how something looks, sounds, or feels. Although memory is commonly said to be of the past, one can remember facts about the future ("I just remembered that there will be a meeting tomorrow"), facts about the present ("I just remembered that the debate is going on right now"), scientific laws and generalizations, and timeless truths of logic and mathematics.

Despite this variety of uses, philosophers writing on memory have tended, until recently, to concentrate on those uses of "remember" in which it takes as its object an expression referring to a particular past event or action. While they have paid some attention to memory of facts (memory *that* such and such), they have generally restricted this attention to memory of facts about remembered events. Thus they have tended to ignore, or rule out of consideration, cases in which the fact remembered is about the remote past (for example, the fact that Brutus stabbed Caesar), or about the future. For to say that a person remembers an event (and hence to say that he remembers a fact about an event he remembers) normally implies that he witnessed the event, or otherwise came to know of it, at the time of its occurrence, and this implication limits the possible objects of event-memory to past events and actions occurring within the lifetime of the rememberer. And of course it is only such events and actions that one can remember having witnessed or done. The notion of the past enters into the notion of memory in another way, for it is true in general that remembering involves having *previously* learned or acquired knowledge of what one remembers. But it should not be supposed that when a person is said to remember a fact about an event in the remote past or the future—that is, about an event to which he cannot have been a witness—what he "really" remembers is learning (for example, reading or being told) that fact; it commonly happens that one remembers a fact without having any recollection of the occasion on which one learned it. Memory of facts (what has been called "factual memory") cannot be reduced to memory of events experienced or witnessed by the rememberer (what has been called "personal memory"), and not all cases of factual memory are cases in which the remembered fact is a fact about a remembered event or action. (For the terms "factual memory" and "personal memory," and a more extended discussion of the points touched on here, see N. Malcolm, "Three Lectures on Memory," in *Knowledge and Certainty*.)

The preoccupation of philosophers with memory of events has led some of them to hold that what is expressed by many of the common uses of the word "remember" is, strictly speaking, not memory at all. Thus, in *Matter and Memory* Bergson held that much of what is called memory (for example, memory of how to do something) is simply the retention of a "motor mechanism," and that this "habit memory" is radically different from the spontaneous recollection of unique events that is "memory par excellence." Following Bergson, Bertrand Russell distinguished between "habit memory" and "true memory," the latter being "cognitive" while the former is not (*The Analysis of Mind*, p. 166). A. D. Woozley makes the same distinction, saying that it is the sense of "remember" in which "remembering is a cognitive act," that is, what Russell called true memory, that is of philosophical importance (*Theory of Knowledge*, p. 37). And it is commonly assumed that in "true" memory the remembering itself, as well as what is remembered, is always an event; remembering is said to be a "mental occurrence" or "mental act."

Philosophers have sometimes used the word "remember" in such a way that "I remember E (some event)" and "I remember that P (some proposition)" can be true even if E did not occur and P is false; they have also asked such questions as "When someone remembers that P, is there any reason to think that P is in fact the case?" and "When I remember an event of a certain kind, how am I to know that (or whether) such an event has actually occurred?" The ordinary use of the word "remember," however, is such that "I remember that P" entails "It is true that P" (in fact, it entails "I know that P"), and "I remember E occurring" entails "E occurred" (see Moore, "Four Forms of Scepticism," in *Philosophical Essays*, p. 214). Sometimes it is objected that if we insist on using "remember" in this "entailing sense" we beg important epistemological questions by making it true by definition that memory is infallible. But this is a mistake. To say that memory is fallible (which it certainly is) is not to say that one can remember what is not the case; it is to say that one can be mistaken in thinking that one remembers something, or, in other words, that one can seem (to oneself) to remember something and yet not actually remember it (because what one seems to remember happening did not actually occur). Using "remember" in the "entailing sense" does not prevent us from saying that there are false memories. A mistaken memory belief is still a *memory* belief. And while the statement "I remember that it was snowing" entails the statement "It was snowing," the statement "As I remember,

it was snowing" has no such entailment. When someone actually remembers something we may say that his memory is "veridical," and when we wish to speak of a memory without implying either that it is or that it is not veridical, we may speak of it as an "ostensible memory." The question that some have wanted to express by asking "How do I know that what I remember really happened?" may be expressed by asking "How do I know that what I ostensibly remember really happened?" or "How do I know that my ostensible memories are veridical rather than false?"

THE REPRESENTATIVE THEORY OF MEMORY

Until fairly recently, the dominant theory of memory has been what we shall call the representative theory. According to this theory, someone's remembering a past event consists at least partly in his apprehending (perceiving, viewing, being directly aware of, being acquainted with) something that is *not* past, that is, something existing or occurring at the time at which the person has the memory. What the person thus apprehends is something private to him, a content of his mind, and has been variously designated by different theorists as an "image" (St. Augustine, Bertrand Russell, and others), a "presentation" (Aristotle), an "impression" (Aristotle and others), an "idea" (Locke and Hume), and the "immediate" or "present" object in memory (A. D. Woozley and others). Usually it is thought to be or to include an image, in that sense of "image" in which one sees (or has) an image when visualizing something. Although this presentation is what one apprehends when one remembers and is sometimes spoken of as the object of (or in) memory, proponents of this theory have generally seen that it cannot be the object of memory in the sense of being what is remembered. Thus, Aristotle found it necessary in "On Memory and Reminiscence" to explain "how it is possible that, though perceiving only the impression, we remember the absent thing which we do not perceive." One remembers a past event or state of affairs, but one does this by apprehending, or "having before the mind," a present object. In C. D. Broad's terminology, the immediate object is the "objective constituent" of the memory situation, rather than the "epistemological object" (*Mind and Its Place in Nature*, p. 229). The present object serves as a "sign" (Russell) or "picture" (Aristotle) of the remembered event and is commonly held to provide the grounds or evidence on the basis of which the rememberer believes or knows that such an event has occurred.

Memory theorists sometimes speak of the memory presentation as a sense impression that has been "stored" in the memory. The image of memory as a storehouse goes back at least as far as Plato, who in the *Theaetetus* compares memory first to a wax tablet and then to an aviary. St. Augustine speaks of "the great cave of memory" within which images are laid away, to be "brought forth when there is need for them" (*Confessions* X, 13). In the first edition of the *Essay Concerning Human Understanding*, Locke said that memory is "as it were the storehouse of our ideas," in which ideas are "as it were laid out of sight." In the second edition, however, he added that "this laying up of our ideas in the repository of the memory signifies no more but this—that the mind has a power in many cases to revive perceptions which it has once had, with this additional perception annexed to them, that *it has had them before*." Even here, Locke's language suggests that one and the same thing is first presented in sense perception and later "revived" in memory, and this is likewise suggested by Hume's statement in the *Treatise of Human Nature* that "when any impression has been present with the mind, it again makes its appearance there as an idea." But it was clearly Hume's view, and seems to have been Locke's final view, that the memory-image of a past perception is not that perception itself, still existing in the mind, but a numerically different perception which resembles, or is in some way capable of representing, the no longer existing past perception. And this seems to be the most common view among advocates of the representative theory.

To remember an event occurring is certainly not the same as to imagine that event occurring, so remembering cannot consist simply in the occurrence of images. Hume proposed two differences between memory and imagination. First, the ideas of memory, according to Hume, are "much more lively and strong than those of the imagination" and have a "superior force and vivacity." Since Hume held that it is precisely the force and vivacity of ideas that constitutes belief, this difference may also be expressed by saying that whereas memory involves belief (namely, in the previous occurrence of a train of impressions having an "order and form" corresponding to that of the ideas), imagination does not. Second, whereas in imagination the ideas may occur in any order, and need not occur in the same order as did the original impressions of which they are "copies," the order of the ideas in memory cannot vary in this respect and must preserve the original "order and form" of the original impressions.

Hume eventually decided that it is the first of these differences that distinguishes memory from imagination. It cannot be the second that distinguishes them, "it being impossible to recall the past impressions, in order to compare them with our present ideas, and see whether their arrangement be exactly similar." It is clear from this that Hume was seeking a distinguishing difference that would enable a person to know whether he is remembering or imagining; he says of the first difference that it "is not sufficient to enable us to distinguish them [memory and imagination] in their operation, or make us know the one from the other." Hume apparently did not realize, however, that in stating the above-mentioned differences, he shifts between two different senses of "memory." Since he did not regard memory as infallible and did not suppose that the nature of one's present experiences (one's ideas) can inform one infallibly as to whether one's memories are veridical, the first difference mentioned must be offered as a difference between *ostensible* memory and imagination. In mentioning the second difference, however, Hume is clearly trying to state a distinguishing feature of *veridical* memory. For presumably the ideas in ostensible memory need not preserve the "order and form" of the impressions from which they are derived; they will not do so if (as can happen) the ostensible memory is false. The term "imagination" undergoes a corresponding shift in meaning. (See R. F. Holland, "The Empiricist Theory of Memory," in *Mind*, 1954, for a more extended criticism of the attempts of Hume and others to distinguish memory from imagination.)

The objection is often raised against Hume that the "force and vivacity" of the images that occur in "pure fancy" need not be inferior to, and sometimes exceed, that of memory images. But while few philosophers have been disposed to accept Hume's account of belief in terms of the force and vivacity of ideas, representative theorists have generally agreed with him in making the presence of belief one of the distinguishing features of memory, and in assuming that the distinguishing features of memory must be among, or have counterparts among, the introspectable features of the memory presentation. The latter assumption has led proponents of this theory to hold that the memory presentation, in addition to having some feature which marks what it represents as something believed rather than merely imagined or supposed, must have features which mark what it represents as something occurring in the *past* (thus distinguishing memory belief from expectation and belief about the present) and as something previously experienced *by the rememberer* (thus distinguishing memory belief from other belief about the past, that is, from belief based on records, testimony, scientific inference, and the like). James Mill held that remembering a past event involves "running over," very rapidly, a series of ideas corresponding to the series of sense impressions one has had since experiencing the event in question, this making it possible (according to Mill) for one to locate a remembered sense impression at some point in one's own past history by the position of its idea in this rapid succession of ideas (see *Analysis of the Phenomena of the Human Mind*, Vol. I, pp. 330–331). More recent writers have held that memory images are characterized, or accompanied, by an unanalyzable "feeling of pastness." William James said that memories are referred to the past history of the rememberer by feelings of "warmth and intimacy" and of "the past direction in time" (*Principles of Psychology*, Vol. I, p. 650). Bertrand Russell also makes a feeling of pastness an essential constituent of memory. Remembering is "a present occurrence in some way resembling, or related to, what is remembered" (*The Analysis of Mind*, p. 163). This consists partly in the occurrence of images, but it cannot consist solely in this, "for their mere occurrence, by itself, would not suggest any connection with anything that had gone before." We regard the images as "more or less accurate copies of past occurrences" because they are accompanied by two kinds of feelings, "feelings of familiarity," which lead us to "trust" the images, and "feelings of pastness," which lead us to refer the images to the past and to "assign places to them in the time order." According to the intensity of the feeling of pastness, we refer the image (or the event represented by it) to more or less remote times in the past. Russell also speaks (as does James) of a "feeling of belief" as a constituent of memory. But for Russell this feeling is apparently not something distinct from the feelings of pastness and familiarity; he says that the reference to the past in memory "lies in the nature of the belief-feeling, not in the content believed."

Sources of the representative theory. It is a common philosophical view that the ultimate grounds for any reasonable belief must consist of facts which the believer knows with complete certainty. It is also a common view that the only contingent facts that a person can know with complete certainty are facts about the present contents of his own mind. The sort of certainty demanded is that which is supposed to characterize the making of such statements as "I have a pain" and "I see a red patch"; in order for the truth of a statement to be known with this sort of certainty, the statement must be such that if it is sincerely asserted, there is not even a logical possibility of its being false, that is, of the belief expressed by it being mistaken. (Statements of which this is so are sometimes called "incorrigible statements.") It appears that statements about the past, including memory statements, never have this sort of certainty. We all know of cases in which our memories have "deceived us." And even if this were not so, even if our memories appeared always to be accurate, we would still be able to conceive of situations in which we would be prepared to say that a sincere and confident memory claim had turned out to be mistaken. But if reasonable beliefs must be based on facts known with complete certainty, and if no fact about the past can be known with complete certainty, it appears that memory beliefs can be reasonable only if they are grounded on certain knowledge of facts about the present. These facts, it seems, can be facts only about the present state of mind of the rememberer, facts of which the rememberer has "direct awareness," "direct apprehension," "direct acquaintance," or "direct perception" (these terms having been introduced by philosophers to designate the way in which we have our absolutely certain knowledge of the contents of our own minds, that is, of images, pains, and the like). Thus the representative theory can seem to give the only possible answer to the question, When a person remembers a past event, on the basis of what sort of grounds does he know, or at least believe, that such an event has occurred?

But it is not only to this question that the representative theory has been thought to provide an answer, and some representative theorists (Aristotle for one) hardly seem to have been concerned with it. If one asks what justifies a person in making a statement of the form "I remember that *P*," one may be asking about the justification, or grounds, of memory beliefs. But many philosophers who have asked this sort of question have used the word "remember" in the sense of "ostensibly remember," that is, in such a way that it can be true that a person remembers that *P* even if it is false that *P*. These philosophers appear to have been raising the question, How does one know (what justifies one in saying) that one ostensibly remembers that *P*, that is, that one at least seems to remember that *P*? We can most easily see the representative theory as an answer to this question by dividing the question into two parts: first, How does one know that one *remembers* (or at least seems to remember) that *P*, as opposed to imagining, supposing, expecting, or merely believing that *P*?, and, second, How

does one know that *what* one remembers (or at least seems to remember) is *that P*, and not something else? By positing an image, the representative theory attempts to provide something from which the rememberer can "read off" the content of his memory and thereby know what he (ostensibly) remembers. And by positing feelings of various kinds (of belief, pastness, familiarity, and so on) the theory attempts to provide something from which it can be "read off" that this content is a content of a memory (veridical or otherwise), rather than of an imagining, a supposition, or some other mental "act." The idea that there must be something from which memory claims are "read off" is connected with the more general idea which Locke expressed by saying that one cannot so much as "contemplate" (let alone have knowledge of) something that is not "present to the understanding," unless an idea, serving as a "sign or representation of the thing," is "present to the understanding" (*Essay Concerning Human Understanding*, Vol. II, p. 461).

Difficulties in the representative theory. Hume began his account of memory in the *Treatise of Human Nature* by saying that we "find by experience, that when any impression has been present with the mind, it again makes its appearance there as an idea." Thomas Reid charged that Hume makes an appeal here to a kind of memory (namely, "memory in the common acceptance of the word") which is not the kind of memory his theory "defines" and which his theory cannot account for (*Essays on the Intellectual Powers of Man*, p. 222). To say that we find "by experience" that there is such a relationship between impressions and subsequent ideas can only mean, according to Reid, that we remember that our impressions are frequently followed by ideas which resemble them. But this would involve having memory knowledge of the past that is not inferred from or grounded on present ideas; unless we could have such "immediate" and noninferential knowledge (which is what Reid believes is properly called memory), we could never discover the empirical generalizations we would need to know in order to be entitled to infer from present events to past ones. If we did discover a correlation between the occurrence of sense impressions and the subsequent occurrence of ideas (images) resembling them, we might be entitled to take the occurrence of an image as evidence of the previous occurrence of an impression resembling it. But in doing this, we would not be remembering the past impression, and if we do remember the past impression there is no need for us to infer its existence from anything.

Reid adds that Hume's account of memory, if accepted, "leads us to absolute scepticism with regard to those things which we most distinctly remember." If ideas are "the only immediate objects of thought," then, according to Reid, "there is the same need of arguments to prove that the ideas of memory are pictures of things that really did happen as that the ideas of sense are pictures of external objects which now exist. In both cases it will be impossible to find any argument that has real weight." Reid took it for granted, as did Hume, that there can be only a contingent (as opposed to logically necessary) relationship between the different "perceptions" (sense impressions, sensations, feelings, and so on) that a person has at various times during his life, and that this precludes the possibility of an a priori argument to show that ideas of a certain kind are "pictures" of past impressions. He also held that any empirical argument to show this will either beg the question, by assuming that some "ideas of memory" do correspond to past impressions and then taking the alleged information about the past given by these ideas as showing that there is such a correspondence, or else will make an implicit appeal to a kind of memory knowledge (not allowed for the representative theory) that does not involve the taking of present ideas as "pictures" of past events. Critics of the representative theory have generally followed Reid in charging that this theory, far from explaining how we can have knowledge of the past, has the consequence that such knowledge is impossible.

G. F. Stout differed from some representative theorists in holding that memory knowledge is "immediate in the sense that it is not inferential or representative in any ordinary or natural meaning of those terms," but held that this knowledge is nevertheless "logically rooted and grounded in actual present experience" (*Studies in Philosophy and Psychology,* p. 166). He says that if the latter is denied, "the only alternative seems to be clairvoyance or absolutely a priori knowledge of matters of fact," and he dismisses this alternative by adding "but we no longer believe in miracles." Stout thinks that the existence of memory knowledge would be a "miracle" if this knowledge were not grounded on present evidence. But why should he think this? He can hardly mean that the denial that memory knowledge is so grounded makes it impossible to give a scientific (for example, physiological) explanation of the phenomenon of memory. Even if we suppose that memory beliefs must have causes, and that the immediate cause of a memory belief must be something existing simultaneously with it (perhaps a state of the brain or nervous system which is the effect of previous sensory stimuli and the like), there seems to be no reason whatever to suppose that the cause of a memory belief must also be a ground of it, or that the cause must be something of which the rememberer is in any sense aware. And, supposing that beliefs can have causes, it does not seem impossible that a causal account could be given that would explain how it is that memory beliefs are (as we suppose) generally true. Stout's idea must be that unless our memory beliefs are grounded on present evidence, it cannot be explained how we are justified in having them, or how our having them, even if they are mostly true, can ever constitute knowledge. But if so, we must ask whether this is explained by the supposition that these beliefs are grounded on present experience. Reid's point was precisely that it is not, since there is no possible explanation (compatible with the view that memory beliefs are always so grounded) of how we could be entitled to take such and such present experiences as indicating the existence of such and such past events. A belief that is grounded on nothing at all cannot be less justified than one whose "grounds" are such that there is no warrant whatever for believing anything on the basis of them. (As we shall see, however, in denying that memory beliefs are based on the *present* experiences of the rememberer, one is not committed to holding that such beliefs always lack evidence or grounds.)

The representative theory undoubtedly gains some of its plausibility from the fact that remembering (especially remembering how something looked or sounded) is often accompanied by mental imagery. But many people report that they never have imagery of any sort, and even people who have exceptionally vivid mental imagery report that they often have no imagery at all on occasions on which they can truly be said to remember, or to be remembering, something. The belief that memory always involves imagery reflects an a priori requirement, rather than anything that can plausibly be regarded as an empirical discovery (and of course no conceivable deliverance of introspection could establish that the occurrence of imagery is a *logically* necessary condition of introspection). Yet this requirement is not one that we make in our ordinary employment of the terms "remember" and "memory." If we know that a man witnessed a certain event, that he has not subsequently been told about it or read about it and has not been in a position to infer its occurrence from its effects, and that he now claims to remember the event and is able to give a detailed and accurate description of it, we regard what we know as sufficient to show that he does remember it; we do not regard the question of what imagery (if any) he now has, or for that matter the question of what feelings (of "pastness," "familiarity," and so forth) he has, as even relevant to the question of whether he remembers.

If one rejects the view that remembering essentially involves having mental imagery, but attempts to hold on to the representative theory, one is bound to be hard put to say what the data are on which, according to that theory, memory beliefs are based. Stout says that the present "internal ground" of memory knowledge "is not capable of being known in such a way as to be asserted in a proposition distinct from the memory judgment itself as premiss is distinct from conclusion." But if this means that we can characterize the present ground of a memory judgment only by saying that it is something that is the ground of that judgment, and that no further description of it is possible, it is no longer clear what it means to say that such judgments have present grounds. (For a fuller discussion of this and related points, see G. E. M. Anscombe, "The Reality of the Past," pp. 43–45.)

As already noted, for some representative theorists the claim that there is a memory presentation is supposed to explain how one knows (or is enabled to say) that one ostensibly remembers something (as opposed to imagining it, expecting it, and so on), and how one knows what it is that one (ostensibly) remembers. Here the knowledge to be explained is not knowledge of the past; it is the rememberer's knowledge of his own present state of mind. This view involves the idea that when one has a memory belief one must, unless one is unaware of having the belief (if this is possible), be aware of a "presentation" from which one can "read off" that one has it. Let us suppose, following Russell, that this presentation consists, among other things, of a "feeling of belief" together with an image representing the content of the belief. Now unless we suppose that this presentation is the belief itself, rather than a mere sign of its existence, it would seem that positing its existence does not advance us toward an explanation of how a person knows that, and what, he believes; for otherwise we would need an explanation of how a person knows that a presentation of a certain sort indicates the existence of a belief of a certain sort. Yet it seems absurd to say that a memory belief *is* a feeling or a complex consisting of feelings and images. And this will be doubly absurd if it is held that memory presentations are the grounds of memory beliefs. For then the presentation will be both the belief and the ground on which the belief is based, and the belief, therefore, will be based on itself. And it seems absurd to speak of a belief as being based on itself. Perhaps it will be said that only part of the memory presentation—a part which excludes the feeling of belief—is the ground of the belief, and that this part is not identical with the belief that is grounded on it. But if so, why must there also be a feeling of belief? Apparently this is to be the ground, or part of the ground, for another belief, namely the rememberer's belief that he has the first belief. But it would seem to be a mistake to think that if one has grounds that entitle one to assert that *P*, and one asserts that *P* on the basis of those grounds, one needs additional grounds in order to be entitled to assert that one believes that *P*. It is absurd to say "*P*, but I don't believe that *P*," and it is no less absurd to say "*P*, but I don't know whether I believe that *P*"—yet the latter should make sense according to the view under consideration. Indeed, it is questionable whether it even makes sense to speak of a person as either having or lacking grounds for thinking that he believes something; we might say that someone is not entitled to say that he believes that *P*, but this would ordinarily mean either that he lacks grounds for *P* (not for "I believe that *P*") or that he is being dishonest in saying that he believes that *P*.

NAIVE REALISM

It is often assumed that the only alternative to the representative theory is a theory, commonly known as "naive realism," according to which what one is directly aware of in memory (what is "before the mind") is the remembered event itself and not a mere representation of it. Not many philosophers have explicitly endorsed this view, but in *Space, Time, and Deity*, Samuel Alexander held that when one remembers something, the object of memory (the past event remembered) is "before the mind, bearing on its face the mark of pastness" (Vol. I, p. 113), and H. H. Price once held that "some memory is knowledge in the strict sense, i.e. . . . is direct or immediate apprehension of past events or situations" ("Memory Knowledge," in *PAS*, Supp. Vol. 15, 1936, 24). (Whether Alexander and Price meant the same thing by these remarks is not at all clear.)

The advantage of naive realism over the representative theory is supposed to be that it avoids the difficulty raised by Reid, namely, that of explaining how we can be justified in inferring the occurrence of a past event from a present memory datum. If what we are directly aware of is the remembered past event itself, and not a present datum which serves as a representation of it, then no such inference is made and there is thus none to be justified. But naive realism is plainly mistaken if it holds that we are directly aware of past events in precisely the sense of

"directly aware" in which the representative theory holds that we are directly aware of present memory data. For this sense of "directly aware" is supposed to be the sense in which we are directly aware of such entities as pains and mental images; in this sense, it is logically impossible for a person to mistakenly think that he is directly aware of an object, and logically impossible for a person to be mistaken concerning the character of that of which he is directly aware. If we were directly aware of past events in this sense, there would be memory statements that are, like pain reports, "incorrigible," that is, such that it is logically impossible for a sincere assertion of them to be false. But it is evident that no memory statement is incorrigible in this sense, and that the mere fact that someone now has the memory belief that *X* happened can never *entail*, by itself, that *X* happened.

The sense of "directly aware" discussed above is a technical sense and only one of the senses that might be given to these words. And one could use the word "aware" in such a way that remembering itself would count as a mode of awareness (in ordinary speech "is aware" is often synonymous with "knows," and to remember something is clearly to have knowledge of it). If one used it in this way, one might want to distinguish between "direct" and "indirect" memory awareness—for example, by saying that one has direct memory awareness of a past event if one's knowledge of that event is not grounded on the memory of some other event. The assertion that in memory we are aware, and sometimes directly aware, of past events would then be a truism. But if it is only this truism that the naive realist is asserting, he is not contradicting anything asserted by the representative theorist. The representative theorist does not deny that we remember past events (for he is trying to explain *how* we remember them), and he therefore does not deny that we are "aware of" past events, or that we "apprehend" them, if this means simply that we remember them.

However, the claim of the naive realist can be interpreted in such a way that it is neither false nor a truism and is in disagreement with what the representative theory maintains. In saying that we have direct awareness of past events, the naive realist might be taken to be asserting that memory knowledge of the past is "immediate," in the sense of not being inferred from or grounded on private memory data of the sort posited by the representative theory. But if immediacy is all that naive realism asserts, then this "theory" is completely negative. It does not offer any explanation of how we have knowledge of the past in memory; it simply asserts that we do have such knowledge and rejects a certain kind of explanation (the sort offered by the representative theory) of how we have it. This point is worth stressing, for terms like "direct awareness" and "direct apprehension" are commonly used by philosophers as if they had explanatory force. Saying that we have direct awareness of *X*'s is thought to provide a sufficient explanation of how we have knowledge of *X*'s. But it is clear that the expression "directly aware" has no such explanatory force if it is used in such a way that "We have direct awareness of past events" means simply "We have knowledge of past events that is not grounded on present evidence." (For further discussion of naive realism, see C. D. Broad, A. D. Woozley, and A. J. Ayer, *The Problem of Knowledge*.)

REMEMBERING AS OCCURRENCE AND AS SOURCE OF KNOWLEDGE

The classical theories of memory can be seen as answers to the question, What happens when a person remembers, and how does what happens provide the person with knowledge of the past? This question presupposes that (1) remembering is a mental occurrence (taking place, as Russell said, "in the present") which (2) is a source of knowledge concerning the past. Both of these assumptions have been challenged in recent discussions of the topic.

When used in the present tense, the word "remember" normally does not report an occurrence. If one says, "John remembers being punished on his first day in kindergarten," one is not saying anything about what is presently occurring in John's mind; this statement could be true even if, at the time it was made, John were asleep or concentrating all of his thoughts on a mathematical problem. Memory theorists often suppose that this present tense use of "remember" is a secondary use of the word, and that to say that someone remembers in this sense is simply to say that *if* certain conditions were satisfied (for example, if he were asked certain questions, or gave thought to certain matters), he *would* remember in what is thought to be the primary sense of the word "remember," namely, a sense in which "He remembers" (or perhaps "He is remembering") reports a mental occurrence (a mental act or process). "Memory dispositions," or "memory powers," are contrasted with "memory acts" (see C. D. Broad, *Mind and Its Place in Nature*, p. 222), and it is with the "memory acts" that the classical theories of memory have been primarily concerned. But while it is true that to say that someone remembers something in the nonoccurrent sense of "remember" is to ascribe a disposition, it is not the case that this is, primarily or exclusively, a disposition to remember in an occurrent sense of the word "remember." If someone remembers something in the nonoccurrent sense, he will be disposed to give correct answers to certain questions and to behave in certain ways (for example, if what he remembers is putting the lawn mower in the garage, he will be disposed to look in the garage when he wants the lawn mower). But doing these various things is not remembering. There is no use of the word "remember" in which a person who has answered a question correctly and without effort, thereby showing that he remembers (still remembers) something in the nonoccurrent sense, can be said to have been remembering that thing while answering the question, and to have ceased remembering it as soon as he has finished answering the question and turned his mind to other matters.

Sometimes the word "remember" is used to report an occurrence. If I say that at noon yesterday John remembered the name of a childhood friend, I may mean simply that at noon he still knew (had not forgotten) the name, but this is not the same thing as reporting an occurrence. I may mean, however, what could be expressed by saying that at noon John suddenly recalled the name; and this, in fact, would be to report an occurrence. The occurrence would be one of coming to remember, or perhaps being reminded of, something previously forgotten (sometimes something only momentarily forgotten). Here remembering may involve an "act of mind"; remembering in this sense may be preceded by *trying to remember,* as when one "gropes for" the answer to a question, or "searches one's memory" for it. When this happens, and also in cases of sudden and spontaneous recollection, there often occur the "memory images" and "experiences of remembering" to which memory theorists have attached so much importance. But cases of trying to remember and coming to remember can hardly serve as paradigms of the operation of memory; on the contrary, these occur only when there has been a breakdown in the operation of memory, that is, only when something has been, to some degree, forgotten.

There are, no doubt, other occurrences that might be called occurrences of remembering: for example, sometimes "I was remembering" means roughly "I was reminiscing about," and reminiscing is a datable mental activity. But there seems to be no justification for the view that the occurrent uses of "remember" are primary and that the nonoccurrent ("dispositional") uses are to be analyzed in terms of them.

The idea that "true" remembering is a mental occurrence or act goes naturally with the idea that one's memory is a source of knowledge concerning one's past in much the same way that one's senses are a source of knowledge concerning one's present environment. The latter idea has been sharply challenged by various recent writers (G. Ryle, R. F. Holland, N. Malcolm, and C. Landesman). Coming to remember a fact after having forgotten it is indeed coming to know that fact, although we would not say of a man who came to remember a fact at time *t* that he *learned* that fact at time *t*. But consider a case in which a person now remembers a fact which he has never forgotten. If we say that he remembers it, we appear to be saying, not that he has just acquired his knowledge from a certain source (his memory), but that his knowledge is not a recent acquisition at all and is rather knowledge retained from some point in the past. If we think of remembering as the retention of knowledge rather than the acquisition of knowledge, we can deny that memory knowledge is grounded on private memory data, and also that it is acquired by some kind of inspection of the past (whatever that may mean), without having to deny that we ever have evidence or grounds for our memory beliefs. If yesterday I came to believe that *P* on the basis of evidence *E*, why should we not say (as indeed we do say) that my present belief that *P* is based on evidence, namely *E*? My belief that *P* can be described as a memory belief today, whereas it could not have been so described yesterday, but this seems to be no reason for denying that the belief I have today is based on the evidence from which it was acquired yesterday. (On this point, see N. Malcolm, *Knowledge and Certainty*, pp. 230 ff.)

If it be denied that knowledge and belief can be simply retained, and that a belief can be well grounded simply by virtue of having been acquired on the basis of good evidence or from a reliable source, the only alternative seems to be that we must be constantly *re*-acquiring, on the basis of a continuous supply of fresh evidence, every item of knowledge we possess and are said to remember. The latter seems a fantastic view, yet it appears to be implicit in the representative theory and other classical theories of memory.

SKEPTICISM AND THE JUSTIFICATION OF MEMORY

The problem of the "justification of memory" is often formulated in such a way as to make it appear that the problem exists only for those who accept a representative theory of memory. Thus we can avoid having to answer the question, "What entitles us to believe in the existence of past events on the basis of our present memories?" by denying, as it seems that we should deny, that memory beliefs are grounded on present data. But not all formulations of the problem can be dismissed in this way. Russell claimed in *The Analysis of Mind* that it is logically possible that "the world sprang into existence five minutes ago, exactly as it was then, with a population that 'remembered' a wholly unreal past." In support of this claim, Russell remarked that "there is no logically necessary connection between events at different times." This suggests that he would have assented, not simply to the claim that for any instant of time it is logically possible that all memory beliefs held at that time are false, but also to the stronger claim that it is logically possible that memory beliefs always have been and always will be false. To many it has seemed that these claims (especially the latter) lead to absolute skepticism about the possibility of memory knowledge, or any other sort of knowledge, about the past. The problem of the justification of memory can be regarded as the problem of showing that philosophical skepticism about memory is groundless and perhaps senseless. To show this, it seems, one must show either (1) that (contra Russell) it is not logically possible that memories should be always or generally false, or (2) that the admission that this is logically possible (as opposed to being possible in some stronger sense) does not imply that we do not or cannot have memory knowledge of the past.

A question frequently discussed is whether there can be an *inductive* justification of memory. Anyone who thinks that there can be such a justification presumably thinks it logically possible that memories should be generally false, but holds that we nevertheless have good empirical (inductive) grounds for thinking that in fact our memories are for the most part true. The following analogy lends this view some plausibility: It is logically possible that there should never have been fire where there is smoke (for it is only a contingent fact that smoke is generally produced by fire), but this does not prevent us from having excellent empirical grounds for thinking that smoke generally indicates the existence of fire.

It is often argued against the possibility of an inductive justification of memory that any such "justification" would be circular. In order to establish any correlation between memories and past events (that is, between the existence of memory beliefs and the truth of these beliefs), we would

need to have knowledge of the past, and this knowledge, it is said, would be based ultimately on memory. Thus, it has been argued by C. D. Broad, Bertrand Russell (in *An Inquiry Into Meaning and Truth*), and H. H. Price, that in trying to show that this is so, we would be assuming that memories (our own, or those of other persons on whose testimony we were relying) are generally true, and we would therefore be begging the question.

This argument, however, must be used with care. As noted earlier, philosophical discussions of memory have been concerned mainly (sometimes exclusively) with memory of particular past events. And if it is only the "reliability" of this sort of memory that someone purports to be able to establish empirically, the charge of circularity cannot be proved, at least not in any obvious way. Suppose that I try to show that event-memory is generally accurate by checking my event-memories, and those of others, against what I can infer about the past on the basis of present evidence (records, remains, and the like), and scientific laws and generalizations. It may be objected that my knowledge of scientific laws and generalizations rests ultimately on memory. But does it rest on the sort of memory in question, namely, on memories of particular past events? It is true that I would not have this knowledge if I had not had experiences of certain sorts in the past. But it is not the case that I must remember those experiences in order to have the knowledge (of laws and generalizations) that I have now. We would never say that a man does not know a general truth simply on the grounds that he is unable to remember learning it, or is unable to remember the observations or experiments that originally led him to accept it. (R. F. Holland makes a similar point; see "The Empiricist Theory of Memory," 475–477.)

But to the extent that a noncircular inductive justification of memory is possible, such a justification would be of no use in refuting a philosophical skeptic. Our knowledge of scientific laws and generalizations is not, and does not normally depend on, event-memory. But in a broad sense this knowledge is memory knowledge; if I know a general truth, and have not just learned it, I can, given an appropriate context, be said to remember it. (I would not be said to remember such a truth, or for that matter to know it, unless it were such, and the context were such, that there could be a real question as to whether I know it. Thus it would generally be inappropriate, though not generally false, to say of a normal adult that he remembers, or knows, that salt dissolves in water. This fact seems to be irrelevant to the question under discussion, but for a writer who takes a different view, see J. Nelson.) Any skeptical doubts that can be raised about event-memory can equally well be raised about memory in this broader sense. If one is led by the Russellian (and Humean) principle that "there is no logically necessary connection between events at different times" to believe that it is logically possible that we are mistaken whenever we think that we remember particular events, one will also be led to believe that it is logically possible that we are mistaken whenever we think that we remember (or know) such general facts as (to take an example from Price) that ink marks retain a more or less constant shape for long periods of time (this being the sort of fact one would be taking for granted in trying to check the accuracy of event-memory by making use of diaries and other written records). But if the words "remember" and "memory" are used in their broadest senses, so that a man can be said to remember anything he knows and has not just learned, then it seems quite absurd to suppose that we can give a noncircular inductive justification of memory. For the only facts that one could appeal to in giving such a justification would be a subset of those one had just come to know, namely, those one's knowledge of which was not in any way grounded on previously acquired knowledge. Possibly there are some facts of this sort—for example, observable facts about one's present environment. But it seems clear that such facts could never constitute, by themselves, evidence for the assertion that memory beliefs are generally true. (Unfortunately, space does not permit a discussion of R. F. Harrod's ingenious, though to this writer unconvincing, attempt to do what has been claimed here to be impossible.)

At least one writer, C. I. Lewis, has attempted to give what could be called an a priori justification of memory. He argues that the supposition that we are victims of a "systematic delusion of memory" is meaningless because unverifiable in principle; that "to doubt our sense of past experience as founded in actuality, would be to lose any criterion by which either the doubt itself or what is doubted could be corroborated and to erase altogether the distinction between empirical fact and fancy"; and that every ostensible memory must therefore be regarded as having, simply by virtue of being an ostensible memory, a "prima facie credibility." And if this is so, he holds, the "congruence" of different memories with one another, that is, the fact that two or more memories agree in testifying to the existence of a past state of affairs, can promote the prima facie credibility of a memory into a high degree of probability—rather as the agreement of someone's testimony with the independent testimony of other witnesses increases the likelihood that what he says is true. (For another attempt to give a noninductive justification of memory, see R. Brandt.)

Lewis appears to subscribe to a version of the representative theory of memory and to think that his argument establishes that we are justified in basing beliefs about the past on present memory data. But one can disagree with him about this and still agree that it does not make sense to suppose (and hence is not logically possible) that memory beliefs are universally or generally false. A strong case has recently been presented against the logical possibility of Russell's "hypothesis" that the world came into existence five minutes ago (see N. Malcolm, pp. 187 ff.). And the considerations which tell against this tell at least as strongly against the view that it is logically possible that memory beliefs in general—those that we will have in the future as well as those we have now—are universally or generally false. This view rests on the idea that it can only be contingently true, if it is true at all, that memory beliefs are for the most part true. If this were so, we ought to be able to imagine finding a people whose memories were seldom or never correct. But supposing that there could be such a people, how could we identify any of their utterances as memory claims (as we would have to be able to do in order to find that their memory claims are mostly false)? We

would not be satisfied that one of our own children had learned the correct use of the word "remember" and of the expressions that indicate past tense unless the sincere statements he made by the use of these expressions were normally true—just as we would not allow that someone knew the meaning of the word "blue" if he typically applied it to such things as grass and trees. In this case, as in many others, using an expression correctly necessarily goes together with using it to make statements that are (for the most part) true. It is only because this is true of many expressions that it is possible to decipher a strange language by seeing in what circumstances the expressions in that language are typically uttered. If the language of a people were translated in a certain way and it turned out that the utterances translated as memory claims nearly always had to be regarded as false, this would surely be conclusive grounds for saying that these utterances were not memory claims at all and that the language had been mistranslated.

Memory theorists often write as if there were a special skeptical problem about the existence of memory knowledge, over and above whatever skeptical problems there are about, say, the existence of perceptual knowledge of the "external world." But if we have any knowledge at all, we have memory knowledge, unless knowledge is never retained. Skepticism about memory, if it is distinct from skepticism about knowledge in general, is skepticism about the retention of knowledge. But what would it mean to say that while we sometimes acquire knowledge (for example, in sense perception) we never retain any of the knowledge we acquire? Someone might think that this is possible, because he accepts the principle that what occurs in a person's mind at any given time is logically independent of what occurs in that person's mind at any other time, and he takes this as implying that the set of a person's beliefs at a given time can be totally different from (that is, not overlap with) the set of his beliefs at any other time. For if beliefs were never retained, knowledge would never be retained. But the general principle is open to question, and in any case, believing (and therefore knowing) is not a mental occurrence in the sense in which, say, thinking about something is. The set of propositions I can be said to believe now does not consist only of propositions that I am presently thinking of; it includes a vast number of propositions that I have not thought of or acted on recently and will not think about or act on in the near future. It seems clear that neither I nor anyone else could have any basis for making the claim that five seconds ago, or even five minutes or five hours ago, I believed *none* of the propositions I believe now and believed instead an entirely different set of propositions. This claim would be quite unintelligible. What ought to seem puzzling is not the idea that beliefs can be simply retained once acquired, but the idea that they cannot be, that is, the idea that their retention, if possible at all, requires a special explanation (perhaps in terms of their constantly being reacquired on the basis of the memory data posited by the representative theory). No sense can be given to the notion of a belief lasting no time at all, and if someone is said to have believed something for only a few seconds or minutes, then what requires an explanation (if what is said is to be even intelligible) is not his retaining the belief for that length of time, but rather his losing it after so short a time. (The explanation might be that he acquired, or suddenly remembered, evidence against the truth of the belief—and obviously there is no comparable explanation that could make intelligible the claim that someone has lost *all* of the beliefs he had five seconds or five minutes ago.) But if beliefs can, indeed must, be retained for some period of time, the same must be true of knowledge. At any rate, this will be so if, as was suggested above, a person's belief can be well grounded (well enough grounded to qualify it for being knowledge if it is true) by virtue of its having been so grounded in the past—and certainly we do not require, in our ordinary use of the word "knowledge," that a person must constantly be acquiring new grounds for a belief, if his retention of it is to be the retention of knowledge. But if there is retained knowledge, then there is memory knowledge.

If it is not intelligible to say (and hence not logically possible) that memory beliefs are always or generally false, or that knowledge is seldom if ever retained long enough to become memory knowledge, perhaps showing this to be so could be called giving an "a priori justification of memory." But in any case, if this can be shown, by arguments of the sort sketched above, it is not clear what more can be demanded by way of a solution to the philosophical problem of skepticism about, and the justification of, memory.

Bibliography

Alexander, S., *Space, Time, and Deity*. London, 1920. Vol. I, Ch. 4.

Anscombe, G. E. M., "The Reality of the Past," in M. Black, ed., *Philosophical Analysis*. Ithaca, N.Y., 1950.

Aristotle, "On Memory and Reminiscence," in R. McKeon, ed., *The Basic Works of Aristotle*. New York, 1941.

Augustine, *Confessions*. Many translations and editions. Book X, 8–19.

Ayer, A. J., "Statements about the Past," in A. J. Ayer, *Philosophical Essays*. London, 1954.

Ayer, A. J., *The Problem of Knowledge*. Harmondsworth, England, 1956. Ch. 4.

Bartlett, F. C., *Remembering*. Cambridge, 1932.

Benjamin, B. S., "Remembering." *Mind*, Vol. 65 (1956), 312–331.

Bergson, H., *Matter and Memory*. London, 1912. Ch. 2, Pt. 1.

Brandt, R., "The Epistemological Status of Memory Beliefs." *Philosophical Review*, Vol. 64 (1955), 78–95.

Broad, C. D., *Mind and Its Place in Nature*. London, 1925. Ch. 5.

Earle, W., "Memory." *Review of Metaphysics*, Vol. 10 (1956–1957), 3–27.

Furlong, E. J., *A Study of Memory*. London, 1951.

Furlong, E. J., "Memory." *Mind*, Vol. 58 (1948), 16–44.

Furlong, E. J., "Memory and the Argument from Illusion." *PAS*, Vol. 54 (1953–1954), 131–144.

Harrod, R. F., *Foundations of Inductive Logic*. London, 1956. Ch. 8.

Harrod, R. F., "Memory." *Mind*, Vol. 51 (1942), 47–68.

Harvey, J. W., "Knowledge of the Past." *PAS*, Vol. 41 (1940–1941), 149–166.

Holland, R. F., "The Empiricist Theory of Memory." *Mind*, Vol. 63 (1954), 464–486.

Hume, D., *A Treatise of Human Nature*, L. A. Selby-Bigge, ed. Oxford, 1888. Book I, Pt. I, Sec. 3; Pt. III, Sec. 5.

James, W., *The Principles of Psychology*, 2 vols. New York, 1890. Chs. 15–16.

Landesman, C., "Philosophical Problems of Memory." *Journal of Philosophy*, Vol. 49 (1962), 57–65.

Lewis, C. I., *An Analysis of Knowledge and Valuation*. La Salle, Ill., 1946. Ch. 11.

Locke, J., *An Essay Concerning Human Understanding*, 2 vols., A. C. Fraser, ed. Oxford, 1894. Book II, Ch. 10.

Malcolm, N., "Three Lectures on Memory," in N. Malcolm, *Knowledge and Certainty*. Englewood Cliffs, N.J., 1963.

Mill, James, *The Analysis of the Phenomena of the Human Mind*, 2 vols. London, 1878. Chs. 2-3, 10-11.

Moore, G. E., "Four Forms of Scepticism," in G. E. Moore, *Philosophical Essays*. London, 1959.

Moore, G. E., *Some Main Problems of Philosophy*. London, 1953. Ch. 13.

Nelson, J., "The Validation of Memory and Our Conception of a Past." *Philosophical Review*, Vol. 72 (1963), 35–47.

Plato, *Theaetetus*. Many translations and editions.

Price, H. H., "Memory Knowledge." *PAS*, Supp. Vol. 15 (1936), 16–33.

Reid, T., *Essays on the Intellectual Powers of Man*, A. D. Woozley, ed. London, 1941. Essay 3.

Russell, B., *The Analysis of Mind*. London, 1921. Chs. 4, 9.

Russell, B., *An Outline of Philosophy*. London, 1927. Chs. 6, 18.

Russell, B., *An Inquiry Into Meaning and Truth*. London, 1940. Ch. 11.

Ryle, G., *The Concept of Mind*. London, 1949. Ch. 8.

Saunders, J. T., "Skepticism and Memory." *Philosophical Review*, Vol. 72 (1963), 477–486.

Stout, G. F., *Studies in Philosophy and Psychology*. London, 1930. Chs. 8, 16.

Taylor, R., "The 'Justification' of Memories and the Analogy of Vision," *Philosophical Review*, Vol. 65 (1956), 192–205.

Von Leyden, W., *Remembering*. London, 1961.

Wittgenstein, L., *Philosophical Investigations*. Oxford, 1953. Pt. I, Secs. 265, 305, 342–343, 648–649, 651; Part II, Sec. 13.

Woozley, A. D., *Theory of Knowledge*. London, 1949. Chs. 2–3.

Sydney Shoemaker

MENASSEH (MANASSEH) BEN ISRAEL

MENASSEH (MANASSEH) BEN ISRAEL (1604–1657), Jewish scholar, philosopher, and theologian. Menasseh was probably born in Madeira. His father, a victim of the Spanish Inquisition, escaped with his family to La Rochelle and then to Amsterdam, where Menasseh studied in the growing Jewish community. At 18 he became a teacher and preacher. Although very successful in his rabbinical career, Menasseh could not support his family with his salary and so became a printer, establishing Holland's first Hebrew press. He printed his own first published work, an index to the *Midrash Rabbah* (1628). Most of his subsequent works are in Spanish, Portuguese, or Latin.

Menasseh's vast erudition in Jewish and Christian theology and philosophy and classical and contemporary literature attracted notice in 1632, when the first part of his *El Conciliador* appeared in Frankfurt (the second, third, and fourth parts appeared in Amsterdam, 1641–1651; the book was translated into English by E. H. Lindo, London, 1842). This work attempted to reconcile the apparent conflicts and contradictions in the Bible and brought Menasseh into the company of Gerhard Johannes and Isaac Vossius, Hugo Grotius, and many other scholars, who came to regard him as the leading expositor of Jewish thought to the Christian world. He corresponded with Christian and Jewish scholars everywhere, and many came to Amsterdam to confer with him.

Menasseh ben Israel was greatly interested in the Jewish and Protestant cabalistic, mystical, and Messianic views of his time and was involved with some of the strangest seventeenth-century visionaries. This led to his most famous work and the best-known episode of his career. A Portuguese Jew from South America told him of finding some of the lost tribes of Israel in the jungles there. Using this material and other "data," Menasseh ben Israel published his *Hope of Israel* in Latin, Spanish, and English (1650), in which he argued that because the Israelites were spread almost everywhere on earth, the Messianic age was at hand. If the Jews were readmitted to England, then all might be ready for the Messiah. Several influential Puritans, including Oliver Cromwell, held similar views, and they invited Menasseh ben Israel to London to discuss the readmission of the Jews. Menasseh ben Israel stayed in England from 1655 to 1657, but after much controversy no official solution emerged, although the unofficial readmission of Jews to England did begin. Disappointed, Menasseh ben Israel died shortly after leaving England.

Although his works are not of the first rank, Menasseh ben Israel was extremely influential in developing and disseminating a modernized form of Jewish learning and in making Christian scholars aware of then-current streams of Jewish thought.

Bibliography

The Hope of Israel appeared in Spanish in 1650 (Amsterdam) and was translated by Menasseh ben Israel into Latin the same year. An English translation by M. Wall appeared in London in 1650. The latest English edition was published in London in 1901.

Cecil Roth, *A Life of Menasseh ben Israel* (Philadelphia, 1934), contains an excellent bibliography of works by and about Menasseh ben Israel. Also consult the articles "Manasseh ben Israel" in *Jewish Encyclopedia* (London and New York, 1904), Vol. VIII, pp. 282–284, and *Dictionary of National Biography* (Oxford, 1959–1960), Vol. XII, pp. 898–899.

RICHARD H. POPKIN

MENCIUS (372?–298? B.C.), known in China as Confucius' successor in transmitting the tradition of the Tao, was born in the kingdom of Chou and lived in the Period of the Warring States. After finishing his study under a disciple of Tzu Ssu, grandson of Confucius, he traveled to various feudal states—Liang, Chi, Chou, and Lu—and called on the respective kings. When he found that no ruler would take him into confidence, he devoted himself to writing.

His work *The Book of Mencius* consists of seven books with 261 chapters. It was first edited by Chao Ch'i, who lived from A.D. 108–201. In Chao's preface he says, "The seven books comprise the whole doctrine of Heaven and Earth, and make inquiries into thousands of topics which exist in the universe. Mencius' subjects of discussion are *jen* (benevolence, humanity), *i* (righteousness), Tao (reason, Way), *te* (virtue), the nature of man, the decree of Heaven, misery, and happiness." Whether this voluminous work was written by Mencius himself or by his pupils Wan Chang, Kung-sun Ch'ou, or others is still a question, but the style of the language does show the imprint of Mencius' strong character. It may be safely assumed that most of the dialogues in the book are derived from Mencius' own notes.

Mencius' philosophy was first recognized by Emperor Wen Ti of the Former Han Dynasty (reigned 179–157 B.C.), who also founded a professional chair for the study of *The Book of Mencius* before Chao Ch'i's commentary was written. His philosophical principles are summarized in the following paragraphs.

Goodness of human nature. Mencius believed that there is a beginning or a potentiality of goodness in human nature because of four kinds of virtue—*jen*, *i*, *li* (decency), *chih* (knowledge)—inherent in man. He said: "The feeling of commiseration is the beginning of *Jen*, that of shame and dislike is the beginning of *I*, that of modesty and complaisance is the beginning of *Li*, and that of approving and disapproving is the beginning of *Chih*" (Book II, Part 1, Ch. 6). This view of human nature presupposes that man as rational being has moral sense and knowledge.

Mind and thinking. Confucius gave the advice: "Learning without thinking is labor scattered; thinking without learning is dangerous." He meant to say that both learning and thinking are indispensable. Without learning there are no data for inquiry. Without thinking no principle or concept can be reached. Mencius penetrated more deeply and singled out the priority of the work of mind and thinking. He said: "The senses of hearing and seeing do not think and are obscured by external things. When one thing comes into contact with another, as a matter of course, one leads the other away." Mencius meant to say that senses never make man reflect upon himself. He added: "To the mind belongs the office of thinking. By thinking, it gives the right view of things; by neglecting to think, it fails to do this" (Book VI, Part 2, Ch. 15). By giving priority to the function of mind and thinking, Mencius built up an idealistic foundation for Chinese philosophy.

Moral rigorism. Mo Tzu's view of utilitarianism is based on his engineering works. Mo Tzu attacked the Confucian school by criticizing it for starting with the motive of doing what is right and neglecting the aspect of utility or advantages. Mencius, in defending moral rigorism, called Mo Tzu a heretic and condemned him as one who neglected his duty of serving the father. In Mencius' eyes Mo Tzu's principle of universal love neglected the priority of the duty of serving one's father. The Confucian school thinks that the duty of serving the members of one's family is the most important while Mo Tzu's school thinks that love for all is the first duty.

Intuitive knowledge. Mencius held the view that conscience is the wellspring from which rules of moral duty arise. He said:

The ability possessed by men without having been acquired by learning is their intuitive ability [*liang-nêng*], and the knowledge possessed by them without the exercise of thought is their intuitive knowledge [*liang-chih*]. Children carried in the arms all know to love their parents, and when they are grown, they all know to love their elder brothers. Filial affection for parents is [the working of] benevolence. Respect for elders is [the working of] righteousness. There is no other reason [for these feelings]; they belong to all under heaven. (Book VII, Part 1, Ch. 15)

The question of whether intuition alone is sufficient or whether knowledge and experience are necessary in order to distinguish right and wrong is controversial in Chinese philosophy. Philosophers such as Chu Hsi and others held that dictates of conscience alone are not sufficient and that experience and learning must supplement them. Wang Yang-ming, on the other hand, believed that intuitive knowledge provides a criterion of right and wrong.

Political philosophy. Mencius condemned contemporary strategists and diplomats and those who advocated the policy of fighting and of increasing food production. In opposing them, Mencius tried to convince the people that government by benevolence—that is, love of the people, fair distribution of land among the farmers, and better education—is the proper way.

Class concepts or universals. Mencius' method is to find a class concept or a universal for any universe of discourse. He said: "Thus all things which are the same in kind are like to one another. . . . In accordance with this the scholar Lung said, 'If a man makes hempen sandals without knowing the size of people's feet, yet I know that he will not make them like baskets. Sandals are all like one another because all men's feet are like one another.' " The term "class concept," repeatedly stressed by Mencius, indicates his fundamental method. Mencius' theoretical formulation exercised a more penetrating influence on the Sung and Ming thinkers, although Confucius, a founder of the same school, is much more respected than any other philosopher.

Works by Mencius

The Works of Mencius, translated by W. A. C. H. Dobson. Toronto, 1963.

Legge, James, *The Chinese Classics,* Vol. II, *Mencius,* 2d ed. Oxford, 1893–1895; 3d ed., 1960.

Works on Mencius

Chang, Carsun, "The Significance of Mencius." *Philosophy East and West,* Vol. 8 (1958), 37–48.

De Bary, W. T., Chan, W.-T., and Watson, B., *Sources of Chinese Tradition.* New York, 1960. See pp. 100–112. Contains selections.

Fung Yu-lan, *A Short History of Chinese Philosophy,* Derk Bodde, ed. New York, 1948; paperback ed., 1960. See Ch. 7.

CARSUN CHANG

MENDELSSOHN, MOSES (1729–1786), the greatest Jewish philosopher in the eighteenth century, was born in Dessau, the son of a poor Jewish copyist of sacred scrolls. His first studies were devoted to the Bible, the Talmud, and Maimonides' *Guide for the Perplexed.* He followed his teacher Rabbi David Fränkel to Berlin in 1745, where he learned to read German and Latin while living in great poverty. In 1750 he became a tutor in the household of the Jewish silk manufacturer Isaak Bernhard; he was later a bookkeeper and ultimately a partner in Bernhard's firm. In Berlin Mendelssohn became a close friend of G. E. Lessing, C. F. Nicolai, and Thomas Abbt. After 1755 his reputation as a philosopher and critic grew rapidly throughout Germany. By his contemporaries he was regarded as eminently kind and virtuous, and because of his wisdom and ugliness he was called "The Jewish Socrates." Lessing is said to have modeled the character of Nathan in his drama *Nathan der Weise* upon Mendelssohn. In 1763 Mendelssohn's *Abhandlung über die Evidenz in den metaphy-*

sischen Wissenschaften ("Essay on Evidence in Metaphysical Science," Berlin, 1764) won a prize from the Berlin Academy, and he was later elected to the academy, although his appointment was never confirmed.

In spite of his Jewish extraction, Mendelssohn's development as a philosopher was notably German in character; he was influenced mainly by Leibniz, Christian Wolff, Alexander Baumgarten, G. F. Meier, his Berlin friends, and among foreign philosophers, by John Locke, Shaftesbury, Edmund Burke, Jean Baptiste Dubos, and Maupertuis.

Mendelssohn was a typical "popular philosopher." He was empirically minded, refrained from final systematizations of his theories, wrote in an easy and attractive style, and was mainly interested in aesthetics, psychology, and religion (although he also discussed methodological and metaphysical questions). His contribution to the emancipation of the Jews was significant. Because of the continuous evolution of his ideas, a summary of his views can only cover the general trends of his thought. He exerted a great influence not only upon his closest friends but upon his whole generation in Germany, and upon Kant in particular.

Aesthetics and psychology were, in Mendelssohn's mind, closely interrelated. He continued the work of Baumgarten and Meier, but amalgamated their doctrines with the tenets of English and French aesthetics translated into the terminology of German psychology. Generally attributed to Mendelssohn is the first clear distinction between beauty and metaphysical perfection: he held that beauty was an inferior, subjective kind of perfection. Metaphysical perfection consists in unity in a multiplicity. Aesthetic perfection arises out of the limits of human understanding. Man is unable to conceive, as God can, the real, supreme unity in the enormous variety of things. He must therefore content himself with introducing an artificial unity (uniformity) into some objects in order to be able to perceive them as wholes; and this is beauty.

In this way, Mendelssohn began a trend away from Baumgarten's and Meier's aesthetic objectivism toward a subjective aesthetics that soon dominated German aesthetics: a beautiful object is not necessarily perfect in itself, but must be perfect in its capacity to be perceived. The perception of beauty strengthens the representative activity of the soul and makes it more perfect, thus causing a feeling of pleasure. The perception of beauty causes intuitive knowledge; in its highest stage it becomes the "aesthetic illusion" in which, for example, fable appears as reality. Mendelssohn's conception of beauty permitted him to explain the pleasurable effect of tragedy and of the sublime, whose distinction from beauty he was the first in Germany to explain clearly. In tragedy, murder is the representation of a morally and metaphysically imperfect event, but its representation may be subjectively perfect. Mendelssohn, clearly under the influence of Burke, held that in the sublime, the pleasure in awareness of immensity of distance, size, or number is mixed with some pain because of our inability to comprehend it completely. In both cases, aesthetic pleasure is the result of the "mixed feeling" (*vermischte Empfindung*) arising in our soul: even if some element of the perception is unpleasant, the perception as a subjective whole is pleasurable.

Mendelssohn's study of the perception of beauty led him to introduce a doctrine of mental faculties that was later adopted in modified form by Kant and others. Mendelssohn held that aesthetic feelings must be attributed to a faculty different from intellect and desire, a faculty that he called the faculty of approval (*Billigungsvermögen*). The beauty of an object escapes us if we subject it to a process of analysis and definition; therefore, experience of the beautiful cannot be an object of knowledge. A beautiful object gives us aesthetic pleasure even if we do not possess the object; thus, the approval of beauty must be distinct from desire. Metaphysical perfection, unlike beauty, is both known by intellect and an object of desire.

Beauty is produced by genius. Genius does not imitate nature, but "idealizes" it; that is, it exhibits natural objects as God would have created them if his aim had been aesthetic and not metaphysical perfection. Genius is independent of rules because it establishes its own rules. A genius' procedure is instinctive.

Mendelssohn believed that both the existence of God and the immortality of the soul could be demonstrated. Although his *Morgenstunden oder Vorlesungen über das Daseyn Gottes* ("Morning Hours, or Lectures on the Existence of God," Berlin, 1785) was written in awareness of Kant's previously published *Kritik des reinen Vernunft*, in it Mendelssohn accepted both the Ontological Argument and the Argument From Design.

Mendelssohn's *Phädon oder über die Unsterblichkeit der Seele* (" 'Phaedo,' or on the Immortality of the Soul," Berlin, 1767) was a dialogue on immortality in imitation of Plato's *Phaedo*. The soul is a simple substance and therefore indestructible. The soul might nevertheless lose its consciousness, but the divine wisdom and goodness of God would not allow this to happen.

Mendelssohn's plans to publish a work commemorating Lessing, who had died in 1781, prompted F. H. Jacobi to write to Mendelssohn asking whether he knew that Lessing was a Spinozist. The resulting quarrel, which soon involved Hamann, Herder, and Goethe as well as Mendelssohn and Jacobi, is discussed in the article PANTHEISMUSSTREIT.

Mendelssohn had been challenged in 1769 by the Swiss physiognomist and religious writer Johann Caspar Lavater either to demonstrate the falsity of Christian revelation or to become a convert to Christianity. Mendelssohn's answer was that the deism of the Enlightenment, which he had developed into a universal religion of reason, was in fact identical with Judaism. In his *Jerusalem oder über religiöse Macht und Judentum* ("Jerusalem, or on Religious Power and Judaism," 2 vols., Berlin, 1783), Mendelssohn supported religious and political toleration, and advocated separation of church and state and civil equality for the Jews. He always fought against both advocates of anti-Semitism and conservative Jews for a cultural and political union of Christians and Jews.

Works by Mendelssohn

Philosophische Gespräche. Berlin, 1755.
Briefe über die Empfindungen. Berlin, 1755.
Betrachtungen über die Quellen und die Verbindungen der schönen Künste und Wissenschaften. Berlin, 1757.
Moses Mendelssohn an die Freunde Lessings. Berlin, 1786.
Werke, E. G. B. Mendelssohn, ed., 7 vols. Leipzig, 1843–1844.
Gesammelte Schriften, D. Elbogen, J. Guttmann, and E. Mittwoch, eds. Berlin, 1929——.

Works on Mendelssohn

Bamberger, F., *Die geistige Gestalt M. Mendelssohns*. Frankfurt, 1929.
Cahn, N., *M. Mendelssohns Moralphilosophie*. Giessen, 1921.
Cassirer, Ernst, "Die Idee der Religion bei Lessing und Mendelssohn," in *Festgabe zum zehn jährigen Bestehen der Akademie für die Wissenschaft des Judentums*. Berlin, 1929. Pp. 22–41.
Cohen, B., *Über die Erkenntnislehre M. Mendelssohns*. Giessen, 1921.
Goldstein, L., *M. Mendelssohn und die deutsche Aesthetik*. Königsberg, 1904.
Hoelters, Hans, *Der Spinozistische Gottesbegriff bei M. Mendelssohn und F. H. Jacobi, und der Gottesbegriff Spinozas*. Bonn, 1938.
Kayserling, Moses, *Moses Mendelssohn, sein Leben und sein Wirken*. Leipzig, 1862; 2d ed., 1888.
Pinkus, F., *M. Mendelssohns Verhältniss zur englischen Philosophie*. Würzburg, 1929.
Richter, L., *Philosophie der Dichtkunst, M. Mendelssohns Aesthetik*. Berlin, 1948.
Ritter, J. H., *Mendelssohn und Lessing*, 2d ed. Berlin, 1886.
Sander, D., *Die Religionsphilosophie Moses Mendelssohns*. Erlangen, 1894.
Zarek, O., *M. Mendelssohn*. Amsterdam, 1936.

GIORGIO TONELLI

MERCIER, DÉSIRÉ JOSEPH (1851–1926), Thomist philosopher and Roman Catholic cardinal, was born in the Walloon section of Brabant, Belgium. At the end of his secondary education, Mercier decided to study for the priesthood; he studied philosophy and theology at the Malines Seminary for five years and subsequently at the University of Louvain. Ordained in 1874, he received the licentiate (equivalent to the current doctorate) in theology in 1877. The same year he was named professor of philosophy at the Malines Seminary, where he taught logic and psychology for the next five years.

The famous encyclical, *Aeterni Patris*, of Pope Leo XIII, urging the restoration of scholastic, particularly Thomistic, philosophy, was published in 1879. In 1882 a chair of Thomistic philosophy was established at Louvain, and Mercier was named to this post.

For the next several years, Mercier taught courses in the various branches of philosophy, always attempting to relate Thomism to contemporary issues; in the course of this effort, Mercier became convinced that the task of making Thomism a living philosophy would require the combined efforts of many specialists. Hence, he conceived the notion of establishing a special institute of philosophy, with the aim not only of offering courses in Thomistic thought but also of providing the staff and facilities for a genuine research center. After considerable difficulty the Institute of Philosophy was established in 1889 as an integral part of the University of Louvain, with Mercier as its first president. The Philosophic Society of Louvain (still active) was founded by Mercier in 1888; in 1894 this organization founded the philosophical quarterly *Revue néo-scolastique* (still published under the title of *Revue philosophique de Louvain*), with Mercier as its editor.

From 1893 to 1906, Mercier's life was intimately bound

up with that of the Institute. His teaching activity continued; he published widely; and in the face of many difficulties, he worked incessantly to build and maintain the quality of the Institute. His success in this area is measured by the fact that Louvain quickly became an internationally recognized center for philosophical work, attracting students from all over the world.

In 1906 Mercier's career in philosophy was interrupted by his being named archbishop of Malines; he was made cardinal the following year. From this time until his death, Cardinal Mercier's immense energies were directed toward the organizational and pastoral duties of his office. The seven volumes of his *Oeuvres pastorales* (Louvain, 1911–1928) give some indication of the extent of his writings on pastoral, religious, and theological matters. Chief among his interests were social, political, and scientific questions affecting religious life, the liturgy, and church unity. In 1921, at Malines, he initiated the "conversations" with members of the Anglican church, which continued at intervals until his death.

World War I broke out during Cardinal Mercier's episcopate, and he became a national and international leader in resisting German imperialism and in articulating the moral rights of peoples and nations during times of war. His death was the occasion of world-wide tributes to Mercier's immense moral stature and influence as an outstanding philosopher, ecclesiastic, and citizen of the world.

Mercier's philosophy. An examination of the life of Cardinal Mercier makes it evident that one dimension of his importance for the history of philosophy must be related to his key role in organizing and developing the Institute of Philosophy at Louvan. It becomes equally evident, however, that this dimension cannot be divorced from his originality and depth as a philosopher. Moreover, the significance of Mercier as a philosopher can be fully seen only in the context of the state of philosophy among Roman Catholic thinkers and teachers in Catholic institutions in the latter half of the nineteenth century, on the one hand, and in the light of Mercier's response to and understanding of the papal encyclical *Aeterni Patris*, on the other. Although there were scattered efforts at a renewal of Thomistic thought during this period, philosophy in Catholic circles was by and large eclectic and superficial. Little serious effort had been made to meet either the challenge of Kant or the Positivism of Comte and the skepticism of Hume and the British empiricists. Consequently, Catholic philosophy was generally in serious disrepute.

It is in this setting that the publication of *Aeterni Patris* must be viewed. This encyclical has been misinterpreted by Catholic and non-Catholic thinkers alike as calling for a return to the letter of thirteenth-century thought and as representing ecclesiastical approval, even sanction, of a particular philosophical doctrine. Recent scholarship has amply demonstrated the falsity of both these views and shows Leo XIII's intent to have been a renewal and articulation of a philosophy organically linked to a great philosophical tradition and compatible with Christian faith but rethought in relation to contemporary problems and issues (see J. Collins in Edward T. Gargan, ed., *Leo XIII and the Modern World*, New York, 1961, pp. 181–209).

No one seems to have caught the spirit of this intent or to have grasped the urgency and challenge of the intellectual crisis of the time more accurately than Cardinal Mercier. Perhaps this can best be seen by a brief exposition of Mercier's thought in three crucial areas: the nature of the philosophical endeavor in itself and in its relation to revealed truth and theology, the relation of Thomistic thought to modern philosophy, and the relation of philosophy to the discoveries of modern science.

For Mercier, philosophy is essentially an effort of reason reflecting on the data of experience. Included in this view is a strong affirmation that philosophy must take its point of departure and find its ultimate grounding in the evidence of the real, objective world, in contradistinction to all forms of idealism and theories of innate ideas. The role of reason is likewise strongly emphasized by Mercier, especially in his opposition to Positivism. For him, philosophy must be scientific in the classical Aristotelian sense; the mind is capable of going beyond the contingent order of the factually given and of finding real, general necessity and order underlying the sensibly grasped world. Hence, Mercier makes a strenuous effort to re-establish the viability of a realistic metaphysics in the face of the Kantian critique and the severe limitations placed on reason by Comtian Positivism. The doctrine of abstraction and the legitimate use of the analytic and synthetic activity of the mind constitute the operative principles in this effort. Nevertheless, philosophy for Mercier is a highly personal endeavor that must always remain open and be capable of organic growth in the light of new evidence. Thus, Thomistic philosophy is held by him as "neither an ideal which one is forbidden to surpass nor a barrier fixing the limits of the activity of the mind"; rather, it is a source of philosophical inspiration which provides a framework for entering into genuine dialogue with the contemporary situation.

Mercier is in fundamental agreement with St. Thomas in expressing confidence in the impossibility of real contradiction between revealed doctrine and philosophically established truth. Revealed truth functions for him as an extrinsic negative norm, but it provides neither the motivation for adherence to a philosophical truth nor a source of evidence or knowledge for the philosopher in his proper task. Thus, Mercier emphasizes the essential automony, the rigorously rational character, the intrinsic openness, and the need for internal growth of philosophy.

In his writings Mercier is manifestly impatient with the general tendency of his immediate predecessors among Roman Catholic philosophers to opt for one of two general positions—a superficial eclecticism or a dogmatic and naive realism based on common sense. In sharp contrast to these positions, Mercier felt it absolutely essential to examine the whole of modern philosophy with great sympathy and to integrate its sound insights into an integral and rethought Thomism. This principle did not, however, prevent Mercier from being highly critical of the various contemporary philosophical positions. His polemical writings are directed against fideism, traditionalism (the view that human reason without the aid of revelation necessarily falls into error), voluntarism, sentimentalism, pragmatism, Cartesianism, Positivism, and Kantian critical philosophy. He argued strenuously against the Cartesian principle of universal methodic doubt and against Cartesian dualism, undertaking to show that the Thomistic doctrine of the substantial unity of man could overcome the difficulties to which this dualism gives rise.

Positivism and Kantian philosophy, however, occupied most of Mercier's attention, and it was in relation to these views that Mercier developed his own epistemology (in *Critériologie générale*, 1899), which represents one of his most original contributions to the renewal of Thomistic thought. Against the positivist theories of H. A. Taine, John Stuart Mill, Herbert Spencer and Auguste Comte, which he undertook to refute in detail, Mercier insistently affirmed the primacy of the criterion of reason and the absolute value of "ideal judgments." Although the positivists of his day were his principal adversaries, Kant was probably the modern philosopher whom he most admired. His understanding of Kant was limited, however, to the interpretation of his times, and his criticism centers on what he considered to be the psychological subjectivism, hence relativism, of Kant. In the final analysis, then, he feels that both Kantian critical philosophy and Positivism lead to skepticism and agnosticism. His response was an attempt to establish a realistic metaphysics on the basis of a sophisticated epistemological critique and a development of a theory of certitude. In his own systematic thought, it is not clear that Mercier fully succeeded in formulating what he intended—that is, a middle term between empiricism and rationalism—for his effort begins with a vigorous defense of the absolute certitude of ideal judgments, and from this position he attempts to establish the degree of certitude proper to judgments of experience. In choosing this starting point, Mercier is forced to infer the reality of the external world on the basis of an ideal principle of causality. Nevertheless, it remains a fact that Mercier's epistemology in its attempt to establish a viable, realistic metaphysics represented a major advance in Thomistic thought.

Apart from his epistemology the most original and commanding dimension of Mercier's thought concerned the relation between philosophy and science. In this area he strongly advocates the necessity for philosophy to be intimately acquainted with the findings of modern science. His own efforts in this area were devoted to a synthesis of the new science of psychology and traditional philosophy; the detail with which he undertook to understand the work of such contemporary psychologists as Wilhelm Wundt and the developments in medical psychology were radically new for his time. Although he clearly held that science and philosophy represent two different modes of thought and although he attributed some real autonomy to science, Mercier probably did not fully appreciate the theoretical component of science (this is hardly surprising given the state of the psychological sciences and the philosophy of science in his day). Hence, his synthesis represents an attempt to understand the facts and laws established by science in the light of metaphysical principles. Once again, however partial Mercier's particular solution to this problem may be, it represents a major advance over the earlier tendency of scholastic philosophy to develop in complete isolation from contemporary thought.

Mercier's own philosophical work represents, then, a vigorous and sustained effort to rethink traditional Thomistic thought in the light of contemporary thought on all fronts; moreover, the spirit of this effort was embraced by colleagues whom Mercier chose to staff the Institute of Philosophy. The true philosophical importance of Mercier must be judged by the caliber of philosophical research and writing which has emanated from the Louvain Institute from his day to the present.

Works by Mercier

For a complete bibliography of Mercier's writings, see *Revue néo-scolastique*, Vol. 28 (1926), 250–258. Mercier wrote extensively for this and other philosophical journals, and much of his polemical writing appears in articles. His major books were written primarily as textbooks and frequently appeared in several mimeographed forms before publication; the published books were revised and frequently reprinted.

The following are his principal works: "La Psychologie expérimentale et la philosophie spiritualiste," in *Bulletin de la Classe des Lettres et des Sciences Morales et Politiques et de la Classe des Beaux-Arts* (Brussels, 1900), which was translated by E. J. Wirth as *The Relation of Experimental Psychology to Philosophy* (New York, 1902); *Psychologie*, 2 vols. (Louvain and Paris, 1892; 11th ed., 1923); *Logique* (Louvain and Paris, 1894; 7th ed., 1922); *Métaphysique générale ou ontologie* (Louvain and Paris, 1894; 7th ed., 1923); *Les Origines de la psychologie contemporaine* (Louvain and Paris, 1897; 5th ed., 1922), which was translated by W. H. Mitchell as *Origins of Contemporary Psychology* (New York, 1918); *Critériologie générale* (Louvain and Paris, 1899; 7th ed., 1918).

Mercier collaborated with M. de Wulf and D. Nys in writing *Traité Elémentaire de philosophie*, 2 vols. (Louvain and Paris, 1905; 5th ed., 1920), translated by T. L. Parker and S. A. Parker as *A Manual of Modern Scholastic Philosophy*, 3d ed., 2 vols. (London, 1926).

Studies on Mercier

The definitive personal and intellectual biography of Mercier is by L. de Raeymaeker, *Le Cardinal Mercier et l'Institut Supérieur de Philosophie de Louvain* (Louvain, 1952), which also contains a detailed account of the founding and history of the Institute. The best critical study of Mercier's thought is in G. Van Riet, *L'Epistémologie thomiste* (Louvain, 1946), pp. 135–178. Also to be noted is L. Noel, "Le Psychologue et le logicien," *Revue néo-scolastique*, Vol. 28 (1926), 125–152. Probably the best biography in English is by J. Gade, *The Life of Cardinal Mercier* (New York, 1934).

ALDEN L. FISHER

MERLEAU-PONTY, MAURICE (1908–1961), French philosopher, was born in Rochefort-sur-mer. He studied at the École Normale Supérieure in Paris, and after taking his *agrégation* in philosophy in 1931, he taught in a number of different *lycées* and at the École Normale itself. During World War II he served as an army officer. After 1945 he was appointed to professorships at the University of Lyon and then at the Sorbonne; and in 1952 he was named to fill the chair of philosophy at the Collège de France. During the postwar period he was also active as an editor of *Les Temps modernes,* a publication he founded with Jean-Paul Sartre and Simone de Beauvoir.

Philosophical orientation. Merleau-Ponty's career had two principal aspects. He was, first, a professional philosopher and teacher of philosophy whose main work was done in the field of philosophical psychology and phenomenology. In addition, he was a man of letters who wrote widely on political and aesthetic subjects and took an active part in the intellectual life of his time. Despite the fact that Merleau-Ponty is sometimes represented as a kind of junior collaborator of Sartre's, both his philosophical work and his more general writings reveal a mind and a mode of thought that developed in a fully independent manner and that are at once very different from Sartre's and, in point of intellectual rigor and elegance, often markedly superior.

Reaction to Cartesianism. To a considerable degree, Merleau-Ponty's philosophical development was dominated by a strong reaction against the Cartesian tradition and against the critical idealism of such contemporary thinkers as Léon Brunschvicg, which was, in his view, the ultimate issue of this tradition. His deepest objection to that philosophy (and one shared by many philosophers of his generation) was that by treating the objects of knowledge as completely susceptible to (a residueless) conceptualization, it reduced the world to the status of a term of thought and, in effect, assimilated it to the knowing mind. Idealism produced a harmonious logical systematization of our experience, but it failed to do justice to the fundamental discontinuities between consciousness and the world and between one consciousness and another. It was just these discontinuities that Merleau-Ponty and others came to regard as fundamental to an understanding of human subjectivity. Merleau-Ponty remained a lifelong student of Descartes, and his whole philosophy can be accurately characterized as a radical reinterpretation of the "Cogito"; but it was also an effort to work out a theory of mind that would do justice, as Descartes's had not, to the contingent and nonconceptual character of our encounters with the world and with other conscious beings.

Psychology. In constructing his theory of mind, Merleau-Ponty drew on two very different bodies of thought: scientific psychology and the phenomenology of Edmund Husserl. In both cases he freely readapted the ideas he borrowed for his own purposes. The psychological theory to which he owed the greatest debt was the Gestalt theory, but he gave its conception of perceptual wholes a much wider range of application than had the psychologists from whom he took it, and he regarded the attempt of W. Köhler to explain perceptual configurations by reference to supposedly isomorphic, transphenomenal brain states as a fundamental error. Similarly, the behaviorists' identification of mental activities with the functioning of the physical organism made a deep impression on him, but he denied that causal or quantitative analysis could do justice to these dimensions of bodily activity.

Phenomenology. Merleau-Ponty's relation to Husserlian phenomenology is still more complex. From Husserl he derived the idea of philosophy as a descriptive account of the structures of consciousness, but he never accepted Husserl's theory of phenomenological reduction, which required that the world as a phenomenon for consciousness be disconnected or "bracketed off" from any transcendent being it might have in its own right. In Husserl's own philosophy, this leaving open of existential questions eventually developed into a denial that the world could be anything more than the intentional object of consciousness. While Merleau-Ponty agreed with Husserl that there

can be no knowledge of things-in-themselves but only of things as they are accessible to human consciousness, he insisted that all perceptual experience carries with it an essential reference to a world that transcends consciousness. This transcendent reference can itself be made a theme for explicit reflection and, in that sense, be reduced to its being-for-consciousness; but this kind of reduction is radically different from Husserl's, for it involves no attempt to create an independent world of phenomenal immanence. Therefore, phenomenological description, as Merleau-Ponty conceived it, does not deal with sense data or essences alone; it also undertakes to render the self-transcending and referential character of our experience, by virtue of which it differs from conceptual thought. Because he believed that the nexus of conceptual thought and the world (or, as Sartre says, of essence and existence) is effected not by means of a deduction, as the classical tradition would have it, but through a perceptual encounter, Merleau-Ponty announced the "primacy of perception" as a mode of access to the real.

Strangely enough, it was in the writings of Husserl's last period, particularly in *Die Krisis der europäischen Wissenschaften und die transcendentale Phänomenologie* ("The Crisis of European Science and Transcendental Phenomenology," 1936), that Merleau-Ponty found some of the principal guidelines for his account of what he termed the "perceptual milieu." In that work, Husserl argued that the modern scientific world view that had developed since the seventeenth century had, in effect, resulted in a kind of systematic obliviousness to the familiar perceptual world from which, in Husserl's view, the mathematico-physical sciences of nature take their departure and on which they remain dependent for their final interpretation. This perceptual world he called the *Lebenswelt*. Merleau-Ponty, in his major works, elaborated, in very great detail and with a wealth of supporting psychological evidence, this conception of an original and unique perceptual relationship to the world that is presupposed by all further scientific construction but that cannot be retroactively explained or even described by means of the categories of the natural sciences. In particular, this distinctively human mode of "being-in-the-world" cannot, according to Merleau-Ponty, be understood in terms of the traditional dualistic model that represents perceptual experiences as effects produced in the mind by the action of extraphenomenal physical causes. In contrast with Husserl, Merleau-Ponty emphatically affirmed the reality of a world that transcends our consciousness of it; but he held that all our attempts (scientific and otherwise) to conceptualize that world remain dependent for their sense on that primordial perceptual milieu.

The two principal works in which Merleau-Ponty developed these views are *La Structure du comportement* (*The Structure of Behavior*, 1942) and *Phénoménologie de la perception* (*The Phenomenology of Perception*, 1945). The former is in large part a criticism of a variety of psychological theories which, according to Merleau-Ponty, give a distorted picture of perceptual consciousness because they use exclusively causal and behavioristic models. In attacking the attempts that have been made to analyze human behavior as a mosaic of reflexes, Merleau-Ponty made extensive use of the work of K. Goldstein, with its emphasis on the involvement of the organism as a whole in all its separate functions.

The physical and the mental. Perhaps the most important thesis of *La Structure du comportement* is Merleau-Ponty's reinterpretation of the distinctions between the physical, the biological (or vital), and the mental. These were treated by him as different levels of conceptualization at which human behavior can be studied, and they are distinguished by the degree to which the concepts used are meaningful (that is, purposive in character). While Merleau-Ponty was very insistent upon the irreducibility of these distinctions, he also held that they are logically cumulative, so that biological concepts presuppose physical concepts, and mental concepts presuppose both. But at the same time that he defended this thesis of the logical interdependence of the physical and the mental, Merleau-Ponty rejected in principle all attempts to interpret this relationship in causal terms.

Subjectivity. In *Phénoménologie de la perception,* his major work, Merleau-Ponty continued his critique of traditional psychology, but he also laid the basis of a general theory of human subjectivity that was closely comparable to the ontologies of Heidegger and Sartre. The book opens with a sustained assault upon the sense-datum theory of perception. This theory was objectionable to Merleau-Ponty because it represents as primary a level of experience composed of "pure" sensations, that is, sensations stripped of any transcendent reference to objects and the world. Like Bergson, Merleau-Ponty regarded sensations as the products of intellectual analysis, and he argued that it is impossible to reconstitute our experience of the world by means of artificial units that have been abstracted from the intentional structure of consciousness.

In subsequent chapters Merleau-Ponty developed his highly original theory of the role of the body in perception. The body, he argued, is not just an object among objects; nor is it just a contingent fact that our perceptual experience is specially conditioned by what occurs in one particular sector of the physical world. Instead, it is precisely because consciousness has a locus within the world that our knowledge of that world has the "perspectivistic" and uncompletable character which Merleau-Ponty so strongly insisted on. The functioning of the human body itself, at least at its higher levels, can be understood only if we attribute to it the intentional structures that Sartre (with whom Merleau-Ponty here differed sharply) would reserve for pure consciousness.

In the concluding chapters of the *Phénoménologie de la perception,* Merleau-Ponty presented, as a part of his general theory of human subjectivity, an account of human liberty and its deployment in historical action. This theory is further developed in his two books devoted to political philosophy, *Humanisme et terreur* (1947) and *Les Aventures de la dialectique* (1955). Like Sartre, Merleau-Ponty viewed liberty (in the sense of freedom from causal determination) as implicit in the capacity of human consciousness for objectifying its situation and setting it within a context of possible courses of action. But unlike Sartre, Merleau-Ponty denied that this liberty is ever total. By our choices we do indeed create our moral being; but we do so

progressively, and our point of departure is always the collectively accepted meanings by which our world is, so to speak, "pre-evaluated." Merleau-Ponty laid great emphasis on this stratum of funded meanings, which to him was the intermediate term between pure individual subjectivity and the blank opacity of things. He saw it not as an obstacle to individual moral autonomy but as an indispensable precondition for the exercise of freedom. His strong interest in philosophy of language reflected his recognition that our language is the chief repository of these established modes of conceptualizing our experience.

Marxism. Ethics, as Merleau-Ponty conceived it, is inescapably associated with political action; and in *Humanisme et terreur* and *Les Aventures de la dialectique,* he developed a theory of political action and of human history. This theory took the form of a revision of Marxism in the light of Merleau-Ponty's own conception of human subjectivity. What appealed to Merleau-Ponty in Marxism was its relentless realism with respect to the actual moral relations between human beings in modern industrial society and its profound sense of the dependence of consciousness on its material situation. What he could not accept was the Marxist's neglect, sometimes amounting to outright denial, of moral individuality and choice in favor of a self-propelling and preordained dialectic of economic development. In *Humanisme et terreur,* however, Merleau-Ponty went so far in the direction of Marxist historicism as to argue that historical undertakings are to be judged retroactively by their success or failure and that to act "historically" is inevitably to submit oneself to this "objective" judgment of events, in which personal intentions, good or bad, are irrelevant. At the same time, however, he rejected the orthodox Marxist view that a scientific theory of the logic of historical development is available as a basis for such action. According to Merleau-Ponty, political and social enterprises are always launched in ignorance or with uncertainty as to whether they will mesh with the course of history; but if he challenged the belief that we know what that course will be, he did not, at this stage in his thought, take issue with the notion of an "objective" logic of history.

In his more recent book, *Les Aventures de la dialectique,* Merleau-Ponty revealed again a very considerable sympathy for Marxism but also a strong contempt for the degeneracy of Marxist theory within the communist movement and a growing disposition to subject the stereotyped judgments of the intellectual left to critical analysis. The version of the dialectic that he espoused in this work has virtually no predictive function and seems to be simply an application of his general theory of consciousness to political action. Unlike Sartre, whose revision of Marxism Merleau-Ponty called "ultrabolschevism," he insisted that the action of a revolutionary party, instead of supervening upon a popular mass in which no revolutionary tendency may even be latent, actually presupposes tendencies or meanings in the movement of society—tendencies which it will act to develop and direct. In this book and elsewhere, Merleau-Ponty made it clear that he had come to regard history as irreducibly plural and contingent; he seemed disposed to believe that no single revolutionary movement against a particular class or economic structure can claim to be the unique agency of the historical process or immune to the stagnation and loss of initiative that the Marxists consider as the peculiar fate of the capitalistic bourgeoisie. In general, Merleau-Ponty saw in Marxism a powerful theoretical instrument, but one that had to be employed in a heuristic way and progressively revised in the light of the varying historical conditions to which it was applied.

Aesthetics and language. In his essays and articles Merleau-Ponty made contributions to two other fields of philosophical inquiry: aesthetics and the philosophy of language. In the visual arts, and above all in painting, he found the integral understanding of our perceptual rapport with the world that a science-oriented culture tends increasingly to suppress. His interest in the role of language in the constitution of our experiential world was one that, particularly in his last years, seemed almost to challenge the primacy he had previously claimed for perception. Unfortunately, he never completed the work in which this theme was to have been developed, but it is clear from the essay "On the Phenomenology of Language" (1952) that his studies were organized around the contribution that language makes to the intersubjectivity of our experience.

Principal Works by Merleau-Ponty

La Structure du comportement. Paris, 1942. Translated by Alden L. Fisher as *The Structure of Behavior.* Boston, 1963.

Phénoménologie de la perception. Paris, 1945. Translated by Colin Smith as *Phenomenology of Perception.* London and New York, 1962.

Humanisme et terreur. Paris, 1947.

Sens et non-sens. Paris, 1948. Translated by H. L. and P. A. Dreyfus as *Sense and Nonsense.* Evanston, Ill., 1964. Collected essays.

L'Éloge de la philosophie. Paris, 1953. Inaugural lecture at the Collège de France. Translated by John Wild and James M. Edie as *In Praise of Philosophy.* Evanston, Ill., 1963.

Les Aventures de la dialectique. Paris, 1955.

Signes. Paris, 1960. Translated by R. C. McCleary as *Signs.* Evanston, Ill., 1964.

The Primacy of Perception, James M. Edie, ed. Evanston, Ill., 1964. A collection of Merleau-Ponty's essays in English translation.

Le Visible et l'invisible, C. Lefort, ed. Paris, 1964. Notes by Lefort. This book consists of three chapters of the book Merleau-Ponty was working on at his death.

Works on Merleau-Ponty

Kaelin, Eugene, *An Existentialist Aesthetic: The Theories of Sartre and Merleau-Ponty.* Madison, Wis., 1962. A valuable study of one aspect of Merleau-Ponty's work.

Kwant, Rémy C., *The Phenomenological Philosophy of M. Merleau-Ponty.* Duquesne Studies, Philosophical Series. Pittsburgh, 1963. A general view of Merleau-Ponty's position.

Spiegelberg, Herbert, "The Phenomenological Philosophy of M. Merleau-Ponty," in *The Phenomenological Movement: A Historical Introduction.* The Hague, 1960. Vol. II, Ch. 11. A good short account with a bibliography.

Waehlens, Alphonse de, *Une Philosophie de l'ambiguité: L'Existentialisme de M. Merleau-Ponty.* Louvain, 1951. An excellent study of Merleau-Ponty's whole philosophy.

FREDERICK A. OLAFSON

MERSENNE, MARIN (1588–1648), French mathematician, philosopher, and scientist, was one of the most influential figures of the scientific and philosophical revolutions of the seventeenth century. Although he is remembered primarily for his relationship with Descartes, he was a significant figure in his own right and also, through his immense correspondence, publications, and personal acquaintances, a key figure in coordinating and advancing the work of the new philosophers and scientists.

He was born at Oizé, France, and studied at Le Mans and later at the Jesuit college of La Flèche, from 1604 to 1609. (Descartes, eight years his junior, was there from 1604 to 1612, but their friendship began later, around 1623.) He next studied in Paris and then entered the very pious and austere order of the Minimi. After further theological studies Mersenne taught philosophy at a convent in Nevers until 1619, when he was sent back to Paris by his order. He remained there until his death in 1648, except for some trips to the Netherlands, Italy, and the French provinces. His Parisian monastic cell was the center of the European scientific world. Scholars, scientists, philosophers, and theologians often made their way to Mersenne's quarters.

From 1623 to 1625 Mersenne published several enormous polemical works attacking all sorts of Renaissance outlooks and figures, ranging from atheists, deists, cabalists, astrologers, and numerologists to Pyrrhonists. These writings include the *Questiones Celeberrimae in Genesim* (Paris, 1623), *L'Impiété des déistes, athées et libertins de ce temps, combatuë, et renversée* (Paris, 1624), and *La Verité des sciences contre les septiques* [sic] *ou pyrrhoniens* (Paris, 1625). The last work, over one thousand pages long, was the culmination of this phase of Mersenne's career and the beginning of the scientific phase that was to continue until his death. Thereafter, his writings were on all sorts of scientific and mathematical subjects (including the famous *Harmonie universelle* [Paris, 1636–1637] on the theory of music, harmonics, and acoustics) and were compendiums of the knowledge in these areas. He became involved in the publication of fundamental works of his friends or correspondents, such as Galileo's *Mechanics* (translated by Mersenne), the objections to Descartes's *Meditations* (gathered by Mersenne), Herbert of Cherbury's *De Veritate* (in a translation by Mersenne), Hobbes's *De Cive* (the publication of which was arranged by Mersenne), and La Mothe Le Vayer's *Discours sceptique sur la musique* (published in Mersenne's *Questions harmoniques*). He also carried on a monumental correspondence, still in the process of being published, that provides a magnificent running record of the intellectual revolution of the time. Mersenne was actively interested in an enormous range of scientific and pseudoscientific questions, from the most complex ones in physics, mathematics, music theory, and Hebrew philology to such ones as "How high was Jacob's ladder?" and "Why do wise men earn less money than fools?"

His major philosophical contributions were his massive refutation of skepticism, *La Verité des sciences,* and his later discussions of the nature of scientific knowledge. *La Verité des sciences* is a dialogue between a skeptic, an alchemist, and a Christian philosopher (Mersenne). The skeptic uses his arguments to show that alchemy is not a true science. When he broadens his attack to encompass all claims to knowledge of the real nature of things, Mersenne's Christian philosopher offers his own resolution to the skeptical crisis, starting with a detailed examination of Sextus Empiricus' *Outlines of Pyrrhonism*. He repeatedly contends that although the Pyrrhonian arguments may show that we cannot know the real nature of things, we can gain knowledge of the apparent, phenomenal world in terms of how it seems to us and how the various appearances are related. Although our sense experiences vary and although we cannot tell what objects are really like, we can find laws that enable us to connect and, thus, to predict experiences. Although we cannot find any absolutely certain first principles, we can discover enough indubitable ones to enable us to construct systematic information about our experienced world. "This limited knowledge suffices to serve us as the guide for our actions." We are able to know something—namely, the sciences of phenomena—and this has adequate pragmatic value for us in this life. Francis Bacon was trying to find out too much and was raising too many insoluble skeptical problems with his Idols. Instead, the ultimate answer to skepticism was to show how much we could and did, in fact, know. The last eight hundred pages of the work is a listing of what is known in mathematics and mathematical physics—until the Pyrrhonist gives in. He has been conquered not by being refuted but by being shown what sort of knowledge we can have once we grant that knowledge about reality is unattainable.

Mersenne was willing to accept the skeptic's claims but was unwilling to see them establish that nothing can be known. Instead, he saw an epistemological skepticism as the prelude to a "constructive or mitigated skepticism," a scientific and systematic development of the truths of the sciences of the empirical world. The rest of Mersenne's life was devoted to his religious duty, exploring in phenomenalistic terms, what could be known about the world God had made. Mersenne's immense contribution to the scientific revolution was the result of his positive views. Although he had originally portrayed skepticism as one of the greatest menaces to mankind, he continued to insist in his scientific tracts that we can gain no certain knowledge about reality but can study only the surfaces of things as they appear to us and employ mathematics as a hypothetical system about things. Like his friend Pierre Gassendi (in whose arms he died), Mersenne saw scientific endeavors as a *via media* between complete skepticism and dogmatism. Mersenne tended to emphasize the antiskeptical aspect of this view, whereas Gassendi tended to emphasize the antidogmatic one.

In his formulations of the new science, Mersenne was probably the first to use a mechanical model to account for the world that we experience and to develop a thoroughgoing phenomenalism (although hardly as well worked out as Gassendi's) adequate to state the findings and assumptions of modern science. Mersenne's lifelong devotion to science and scientists can apparently be attributed to their common quest for more information and understanding of the phenomenal world. Hence, Mersenne could see in Descartes a major contributor to the scientific revolution but could see nothing important in his metaphysical revolution. Descartes, Hobbes, Herbert of Cherbury, Gassendi, Pascal, Galileo, and others were, for Mersenne, together in seeking the truth of the sciences,

although some of them still had illusions that more truth than that could be discovered. For Mersenne science had no metaphysical foundations and needed none. "Until it pleases God to deliver us from this misery," we can find no ultimate knowledge, but we can, if we are not destructively skeptical, proceed to gain and use scientific knowledge.

Bibliography

Seven volumes of the *Correspondance*, Mme. Paul Tannery, Cornelis de Waard, René Pintard, and Bernard Rochot, eds. (Paris, 1932——), have been published thus far.

For works on Mersenne see Robert Lenoble, *Mersenne ou la naissance du mécanisme* (Paris, 1943), and Richard H. Popkin, "Father Mersenne's War Against Pyrrhonism," in *Modern Schoolman*, Vol. 34 (1956–1957), 61–78, and *The History of Scepticism from Erasmus to Descartes* (Assen, Netherlands, 1960; New York, 1964).

RICHARD H. POPKIN

MESLIER, JEAN (1664–1729), perhaps the least restrained freethinker of the French Enlightenment, is also one of the most notorious examples of apostasy. As curé of the village of Etrépigny in Champagne from 1689 to his death, Meslier lived in complete obscurity, attending to his pastoral duties. But under the innocuous exterior of the humble Catholic priest, there seethed a violent hatred and passionate disavowal of the religion which it was his ironic profession to serve. Having resolved sometime in the 1720s to compose his only work, the *Testament*, with the aim of keeping it secret until his death, he felt free to vent fully the anti-Christian, atheistic, revolutionary—indeed, anarchistic—sentiments that he had been obliged to suppress beneath a lifelong mask of prudent duplicity. The available biographical facts are unfortunately too meager to clarify this extraordinary personality. It is known, however, that on one occasion Meslier's abhorrence of injustice and persecution brought him into bitter conflict with the local nobility and, indirectly, almost into rebellion against the archbishop of Rheims, who, siding (as might be expected) with feudal privilege in the dispute, had castigated the morally outraged but powerless curate.

Editions of the "Testament." The three autograph originals of the *Testament* addressed by its author to posterity were succeeded, in eighteenth-century France, by a profusion of manuscript copies that circulated briskly in the philosophical underworld of forbidden literature. The prolixity and other stylistic shortcomings of the work resulted, however, in its being edited in the form of various abridgments that proved more suitable for dissemination. The most important of these summaries was, without question, the *Extrait des sentiments de Jean Meslier*, prepared by Voltaire and published in 1762. This first printed version of the apostate priest's opinions was often reprinted, especially under the rubric of Holbach's *Le Bon Sens du curé Meslier*—a combination of one of his own atheistic tracts and of the *Extrait*—which saw many editions well into the nineteenth century. The integral text of the *Testament* was not published until 1864.

Thought. Meslier's entire critique follows from the assumption that religion is basically a political means whereby those in power consolidate their control over the vastly greater number of weak and poor members of society. All religious dogmas, beliefs, and rituals, supposedly devised by the ruling class as instruments of government, are considered to be nothing but errors and superstitions serving to dupe and paralyze the victims of tyranny, holding them in ignorant fear and keeping them from any effective action to alleviate their misery by overthrowing their oppressors.

Meslier thought primarily in terms of economic exploitation, asserting that the opulence and power of the few are, thanks to the protection of civil and religious laws, acquired and maintained at the expense of the near destitution of the people. There is little doubt that, in adopting this general view, he was motivated by deep feelings of sympathy for the sufferings of the poor, with whom he came into daily contact. His condemnation of Christianity therefore had at its root the eminently Christian virtue of pity for the downtrodden and helpless, joined, however, to a fiercely un-Christian zeal to right secular wrongs.

Although Meslier condemned all religions, he attacked Christianity in particular. The bulk of the *Testament* is devoted to fastidious refutations of the many different types of argument by which the "truth" of Christian revelation was presumed demonstrable. Meslier examines and rejects, in turn, the validity of faith, the historicity of miracles, the authenticity of Scripture, the authority of tradition, the accuracy of Biblical prophecies, the testimony of martyrdom, the morality of eternal rewards and punishments, and the meaningfulness of such dogmas as the Trinity, the Incarnation, and transubstantiation. The *Testament* is, indeed, a compendium of the historical, exegetical, textual, and logical objections concerning the essentials of the Christian creed discussed in the critical and apologetic literature from the time of Bayle through the early decades of the eighteenth century. Meslier was conversant with this literature, and although there is relatively little in his criticism that is entirely new with him, the forcefulness, breadth, and intransigence of his "case against Christianity," together with its politicoeconomic basis, give his work a unique character. Moreover, Meslier did not stop at exposing the fallacies of Christian belief and the social abuses of institutional religion but boldly pursued his train of thought to the affirmation of a materialistic system in which all phenomena can be traced to a physical basis and are subject to the laws of mechanics. He advocated atheism as the only outlook consistent with the interests of the majority of mankind in its struggle against the lust for domination of the unscrupulous few. Among the sources of the *Testament*, special importance should be given to Montaigne's skeptical treatment of time-honored social practices, to the philosophy of Spinoza, and to the Epicurean–Cartesian vision of a mechanistic, naturalistic universe in which the supernatural—particularly the doctrines of divine creation and spiritual immortality—no longer found any place.

Influence. The impact of Meslier's ideas still has to be studied carefully. During the eighteenth century it was merely his negation of Christianity that proved appealing, and his socioeconomic protest, with its overtones of popular revolution, went largely unheeded. Contrary to the philosophes' estimate of Meslier as compatible with middle-class *bon sens*, some Marxists have been able to see in

him an audacious spokesman for the economically repressed class of peasants and urban workers and the advocate of socialistic and egalitarian reform of society. But even if this was the true spirit of Meslier's thought, it did not play its intended role, for his influence was largely assimilated into the main stream of Enlightenment ideology, with its predominantly bourgeois, liberal, and deistic polemic directed at Christianity. Seen in retrospect, the principal weakness of Meslier's anti-Christian *summa* is his oversimplification of the extreme psychological and cultural complexity of the religious phenomenon and its social applications. Moreover, his ardent wish forever to abolish injustice and wretchedness from the world by the expedient (in his own words) of "hanging and strangling with the bowels of the priests all the nobles and rulers of the earth" was no less utopian than fanatical. Nevertheless, Meslier's indignant and savage denunciation of religion was meaningful at the historical moment that inspired and shaped it, when the Roman Catholic church of France, owing to its official status and immense riches, actually had a vested interest in the perpetuation of political and economic institutions related to the feudal oppression and exploitation of the people.

Bibliography

Le Testament de Jean Meslier, edited by Rudolf Charles, 3 vols. Amsterdam, 1864.

Marchal, Jean, *L'Étrange Figure du curé Meslier*. Charleville, France, 1957.

Morehouse, Andrew, *Voltaire and Jean Meslier*. New Haven, 1936.

Petitfils, E., *Un Socialiste-révolutionnaire au commencement du XVIIIe siècle, Jean Meslier*. Paris, 1908.

Porchnev, B. F., *Jean Meslier, et les sources populaires de ses idées*. Moscow, 1955.

Spink, J. S., *French Free-thought from Gassendi to Voltaire*. London, 1960.

Wade, I. O., *The Clandestine Organization and Diffusion of Philosophical Ideas in France From 1700 to 1750*. Princeton, N.J., 1938.

ARAM VARTANIAN

METAETHICS.   See ETHICS, PROBLEMS OF.

METAMATHEMATICS.   See MATHEMATICS, FOUNDATIONS OF.

METAPHOR   is a linguistic phenomenon of peculiar philosophical interest and importance because its use in various domains raises puzzling questions about the nature and limits of language and knowledge. The study of metaphor in its aesthetic aspects belongs to rhetoric and poetics. The present article is limited to what may be called, in a broad sense, the cognitive aspects of metaphor, that is, problems about its functions in the acquisition and communication of knowledge.

The term "metaphorical," as contrasted with "literal," is applied to words, uses of words, meanings, and sentences. For present purposes, the term "attribution" will be convenient and may be allowed to include both phrases and declarative sentences (statements). Thus, "Time is a child at play" (Heraclitus) will be called a metaphorical statement, or (equivalently) "child at play" will be said to have a metaphorical sense in this context. And "the river of time" will be called a metaphorical phrase, or (equivalently) "river" will be said to have a metaphorical sense. The noun "time" in both these attributions will be called the subject in the metaphor, and time itself will be called the subject-thing. The metaphorical predicate or term, whether noun or adjective, will be called the modifier. Grammar does not always decisively indicate which is the subject and which is the modifier; in "logical space" (Wittgenstein), "logic" is the (implied) subject and "space" is the metaphorical modifier. Every metaphor consists of, and can be analyzed into, these two parts. Compound metaphors may contain several pairs of parts: for example, when Plato, in the *Timaeus*, writes, "Intelligence, controlling necessity, persuaded her to lead towards the best the greater part of the things coming into being," we may say that intelligence metaphorically controls and persuades, necessity is metaphorically controlled and persuaded, and necessity metaphorically leads; so that there are five distinct metaphors in this passage. (The widely used terms "tenor" and "vehicle," introduced by I. A. Richards in *The Philosophy of Rhetoric*, Oxford, 1936, Ch. 5, are not adopted, because of their tendency to vary in sense.)

By common definition, and by etymology, a metaphor is a transfer of meaning, both in intension and extension. The metaphorical modifier acquires a special sense in its particular context (when conjoined with "logical," the word "space" means something different from what it means in its usual contexts); and it is applied to entities different from those it usually applies to, in any of its normal senses. Both of these features of metaphor have long been recognized, and some attempts have been made to explain them. The problem is to understand how that radical shift of intension comes about; how we know that the modifier is to be taken metaphorically; and how we construe or explicate its meaning correctly. The answers to these questions, and others, are in some dispute, and no fully satisfactory theory has been devised.

Theories of metaphor. An adequate theory of metaphor must explain the two properties of metaphor that are generally acknowledged to be most fundamental. First, a metaphorical attribution differs from a literal one by virtue of a certain tension between the subject and the modifier: we are alerted by something special, odd, and startling in the combination. Metaphor is a species of what Paul Ziff has termed "deviant discourse," in *Semantic Analysis* (Ithaca, N.Y., 1960, Ch. 1). This tension, difficult to describe and analyze, is present in the phrase "logical space" but not in "Minkowsky space." Where it is very weak, we are on or near the imprecise border between metaphorical and literal attributions. Second, a metaphorical attribution is not merely an odd conjunction, for it is intelligible. In nonsense combinations, the oddity is there, but the opening-up of meaning is not. It is very difficult to be certain that attributions involving "space" and "time" are utterly nonsensical, because both of these terms are so basic and abstract, but perhaps "ungrammatical space" and "Time is an uncle" will serve as examples of nonsense combinations.

One conceivable theory of metaphor, which has been broached, although never very thoroughly worked out, is the Emotive Theory. A number of philosophers, including some inclined toward logical positivism, have suspected that metaphorical statements are not capable of verification and hence, by their criterion, not genuinely meaningful. The nonsense examples above show that individually meaningful words can be combined into expressions that are not meaningful as a whole. The Emotivist suggests that the difference between acceptable and unacceptable deviant discourse ("the abating shadow of our conscript dust" versus Bosanquet's remark that "when the Absolute falls into the water, it becomes a fish") is that the former, but not the latter, somehow acquires a powerful emotive meaning in the process of relinquishing its cognitive, or descriptive, meaning. But since it is evident that metaphors do in fact differ cognitively from nonsense phrases, and since the Emotive Theorists do not explain how emotive meaning can rise out of the ruins of cognitive meaning, this theory does not seem very promising.

A second theory apparently fails for the opposite reason: it accounts for the intelligibility, but not for the tension, of metaphor. This proposal goes back to Aristotle, who suggested (*Rhetoric*, III, iv, 1–3; cf. x) that "the simile also is a metaphor; the difference is but slight." A metaphor, in this view, is an elliptical simile, that is, a collapsed comparison from which "like" or "as" has been omitted, for convenience or for heightened interest. Thus, Heraclitus meant that time is *like* a child at play; our problem in grasping his meaning is to see how these two things might be alike. This Comparison Theory evidently makes the metaphorical attribution intelligible, but it has difficulties in explaining what is so special about it. There are two related possibilities. One is to make a distinction between, say, "close" and "remote" comparisons, and explain the tension in terms of remoteness: the tension is present when time is compared to a river or to a child at play (or when Bergson says that "real duration is that duration which gnaws on things, and leaves on them the mark of its tooth"), but absent when time is compared with space. The criteria of remoteness have not proved easy to provide. A second possibility is to measure the degree of metaphoricalness (so to speak) as the inverse of relative frequency, as in Information Theory. But that, too, seems insufficient: even if one compared, for the first time, the color of a fruitcake to the color of a newly cleaned Rembrandt, a metaphor would not thereby be established.

The Iconic Signification Theory, proposed in recent years, grows out of the Comparison Theory, but goes beyond it in an interesting way. According to this third theory, a metaphor involves a double semantic relationship. The modifier, which is to be interpreted literally, directs us (sometimes obliquely) to an object, event, or situation; and the latter is proposed as an iconic sign of the subject-thing (an iconic sign, in Peirce's sense, being one that signifies in virtue of its similarity to what it signifies). The meaning of the metaphor is obtained by reading off the properties thus iconically attributed. For instance, when a river is offered as an iconic sign of time, certain notable features of rivers (for example, one-dimensional directionality) are ascribed to time. Criticisms that have been made of this theory, in which it has been considered a special case of the Comparison Theory, can perhaps largely be answered by further refinements of the theory itself.

A fourth theory aims to explain metaphor more simply in terms of an interplay between two levels of meaning. In many common words and phrases, we can roughly distinguish two sorts of meaning: (1) the central meaning, or meanings—what is called designation or (in Mill's sense) connotation, and may be recorded in a dictionary as standard; and (2) the marginal meaning, consisting of those properties that the word suggests or connotes (in the literary critic's sense of this term). Thus, "conscript" (adjective) designates the property of having been ordered into military service; it connotes such properties as being passive and subordinate, and being under control of a higher power. When "conscript" is applied to the body (also metaphorically described as "dust") we take the combination in a double way. First, we recognize that on the level of literal meaning it is impossible or absurd to speak of ordering dust into military service. (In some cases, the metaphor is self-contradictory on this primary level; in other cases, there is a conflict between properties presupposed by the subject and modifier, as, for example, that only something that is conscious can, in the full sense, be given an order.) Second, we select from the modifier's repertoire of marginal meaning (and from the nonconflicting part of the central meaning) those properties that can sensibly be attributed to the subject-thing, and so read the metaphor as making that attribution.

This theory, the Verbal-Opposition Theory, thus rests upon (1) a distinction between two levels of meaning, and (2) the principle that metaphor involves essentially a logical conflict of central meanings. The first point has been questioned on certain grounds: for example, whether it is proper to refer to "marginal meaning" as meaning at all, and whether the alleged "open texture" of language does not undermine the notion of "central meaning." A qualification of the second point has also been shown as being desirable: in some situations, as in pointing to a building and saying, "That's a dump," it is not the self-contradictoriness, but the obvious falsity, of the statement that requires it to be taken metaphorically. A more fundamental objection (best made by Paul Henle) is that metaphorical meanings cannot be limited to already known connotations of a modifier, because metaphor creates novel senses of words. The Verbal-Opposition Theory can be altered to allow, for example, that "conscript" takes on new meanings when first conjoined with "dust"; all the noteworthy properties of dust constitute a potentiality for metaphorical meaning. Then this theory comes close to the Iconic Signification Theory.

The uses of metaphor. The above discussion gives some indication, however sketchy, of the important roles that metaphor may play in the development of language and in poetry. Its cognitive roles are primarily two. First, metaphor is a convenient, extraordinarily flexible and capacious device for extending the resources of language, by creating novel senses of words for particular purposes and occasions. If there are no words or short phrases in English that convey with precision and conciseness a certain disparaging view of Descartes's dualism, then "the ghost in the machine" (Gilbert Ryle) may do so. Second, metaphor is a condensed shorthand, by which a great many properties can be attributed to an object at once. When Santayana says that "the mind is a lyric cry in the midst of business," a number of the features of his epiphenomenalistic materialism are stated together.

On the other hand, certain dangers appear as the price that may be paid for these virtues.

First, just because of the metaphor's complexity of meaning, it is especially susceptible to misunderstanding: the reader may overlook an important part of what is meant, or may read into the metaphor something that is not there. Thus, if a dispute were to arise as to whether the mind is indeed a lyric cry in the midst of business or whether time is really a child at play, it would be crucially important, but extremely difficult, to insure that both parties understood these statements in the same sense. Second, because the various properties involved in the marginal meaning of a word (or its potential marginal meaning, or in the iconic signification of an object) are of various degrees of noteworthiness, ranging from the obvious to the subtlest and most marginal, the meaning of a metaphor trails off at the edge, so to speak, with diminishing emphasis. This border indecisiveness is a species of vagueness, and therefore, so long as the dispute continued in these words, some of the questions that might arise in a discussion as to whether the Absolute becomes a fish when it falls into the water would be unanswerable. Third, because the actual meaning of a metaphor in a given context consists of those marginal meanings pushed into prominence, or at least not canceled out, a metaphor is highly sensitive to its context. Therefore, as metaphorical terms move through a changing context, they are highly susceptible to equivocation and cannot safely be used in inductive or deductive argument. Suppose all A are B, and suppose that B are metaphorically C; if we conclude that A are metaphorically C, there will probably be equivocation.

Metaphors used in the course of cognitive enterprises are frequently guarded, so as to take advantage of their values without courting their dangers. There are two main forms of control.

(1) If the metaphor is hedged about with protective rules and auxiliary explanations, it becomes less rich in meaning, but safer. When Leibniz chooses to describe his monads as being "windowless" but "mirroring" each other, he makes clear how we are to take these metaphors by using more technical terms of his system ("perception," "perspective," "clear and distinct," and so forth). And Santayana's metaphorical description of the mind is clarified and fixed by the whole course of his metaphysics.

(2) Although a term may be introduced metaphorically, for the sake of a new meaning, its metaphorical status can be negated by appropriate stipulations, and it can become simply a new technical term in a novel sense. Leibniz' term "perception," for example, has a metaphorical origin, since obviously not everything that happens in the world is perception. But when he explains that there are preconscious perceptions, and that perceptions differ in clarity and distinctness, and that they are all coordinated, the ordinary sense of "perception" is pushed into the background. The question remains open, of course, as to

whether the ordinary sense of the word is (or should be) excluded completely.

Epistemological problems. Metaphor, by the foregoing accounts, is at least a manner of speaking, and one of considerable scope and importance; with caution, it can also be said to be a manner of thinking. If we conceive of philosophy as a "disease of which it [philosophy] is the cure" (as Herbert Feigl once suggested), or as the task of "showing the fly the way out of the fly-bottle" (Wittgenstein), these figures may not only guide our subsequent thoughts in certain fruitful directions, but also lead us into mistaken ideas. But of course the metaphorical description, as its implications are pursued, can be checked at each step, and we need not feel committed to all of its implications merely because it has a general appropriateness. So the metaphorical description may least misleadingly, perhaps, be considered as an aid to thought rather than a special mode of thinking.

A good deal more than this, however, has been meant by those philosophers who have found in metaphor (and in related phenomena, to be considered shortly) a distinct logical and epistemological character. Ernst Cassirer in *Language and Myth* (translated by Susanne Langer, New York, 1946, Ch. 6) has argued for the existence of a primitive "metaphorical thinking," reflected in "radical metaphor," which is the source of myth and poetry. Philip Wheelwright's *The Burning Fountain* (Bloomington, Ind., 1954, especially Chs. 5 and 6) treats metaphor as a species of "plurisignative" discourse and defends "the ontological status of radical metaphor. That is to say, metaphor is a medium of fuller, riper knowing" than is possible in literal (that is, ordinary and scientific) language. The thesis is that there are two fundamentally different forms of language, the literal and the metaphorical, and that while the former is suited to the expression of empirical truths, the latter alone is capable of expressing transempirical, intuitive truths. In one form, this view may be traced back to those passages in Plato's dialogues in which Socrates, sometimes with a slight apology, abandons the mode of discursive argument and turns to speaking of the soul, or the Idea of Good, or the afterlife, "in a figure"—suggesting that figurative language can somehow outrun the nonfigurative.

This Double-Language thesis has one consequence that has evoked a great deal of discussion, namely, that if the two languages are so different, then they are not intertranslatable: that is, the meaning of metaphorical attributions must be, in large part, untranslatable into nonmetaphorical attributions. This is the problem of paraphrase. Wheelwright and others have argued for the autonomy and irreducibility of metaphorical language. Others (Urban and Herschberger) have argued that, in principle, everything that can be said metaphorically could also be said literally.

Disputed areas. A number of problems in four fields of philosophy have centered on metaphor, or have been connected with it.

Philosophy of mind. Peter Geach, in *Mental Acts* (London, 1957, pp. 75–79), argues that our descriptions of mental acts are metaphorical. He holds that this is true, not merely in the (philosophically less interesting) sense that many of the terms we use for mental acts are etymologically derived from physical terms (see W. K. Wimsatt, Jr., *Philosophic Words*, New Haven, 1948), but also in the sense that our concepts of mental acts are "analogical" extensions of concepts that apply natively to sensible objects, including utterances. Thus, for example, the concept of "judging that p" would involve the extension of the concept of "saying that p." (This view is closely connected with Geach's theory of concepts as mental activities and with his rejection of the abstractionist theory of concepts.) However, it seems that according to Geach's theory, metaphorical applications of terms are neither necessary nor sufficient for analogical extensions of concepts.

Philosophy of science. It has been remarked that metaphor plays a role in the historical development of empirical science. In the early stages of a science, terms may be taken over metaphorically from ordinary language ("field," "force"), and protolawlike generalizations may be stated in metaphorical terms ("Nature abhors a vacuum"). Such transfers are nearly always guarded, the metaphorical richness being severely cut down by special rules. Thus, for example, when Darwin, in the *Origin of Species* (Ch. 3), introduces the term "struggle for existence" in "a large and metaphorical sense," he immediately gives examples and an explanation of what he wishes it to cover (for example, "success in leaving progeny"). And although he notes (Ch. 4) that some of the readers of his first edition misunderstood him by taking "natural selection" too literally, he thinks that in context, such "metaphorical expressions" should be plain enough. In time, scientific metaphors are either reduced to literalness (dead metaphors), or replaced by technical neologisms. "Perhaps every science must start with metaphor and end with algebra; and perhaps without the metaphor there would never have been any algebra," as Max Black writes in *Models and Metaphors* (Ithaca, N.Y., 1962, p. 242). Sometimes, of course, the transition may take some time, and there is the danger of being misled—as Freud may have been misled by his personification of the parts of the self (see H. Nash, "Freud and Metaphor").

The issue of the function of metaphor in the development of science has been related to the question of the usefulness of models in science (see Black, *op. cit.*). Duhem argued in *The Aim and Structure of Physical Theory* (translated by Philip Wiener, Princeton, N.J., 1954) that models have no justification but "the pleasure of the imagination." A model can be thought of as a kind of controlled metaphor, but a statement like "Electricity is a fluid" is probably best understood either as a simile ("Electricity behaves, in some ways, *like* a fluid") or as a suggestive analogy ("Electricity can be treated *as though it were* a fluid").

Philosophy of religion. The epistemological problems of metaphor appear at the heart of the study of religious language. The attempt to express the otherworldly in terms drawn from this world is manifested in Biblical figures ("The Lord is my shepherd"), in parable, and in the imagery of the mystics. Recently, the tendency has been to bring together metaphor, symbol, and myth under the same general heading. And if they are all species, or aspects, of the same general striving for a transcendental or supernatural mode of expression, then the issues of whether metaphors are meaningful, whether they are transempirical, and whether they are paraphrasable are bound to reappear in the philosophy of religion.

One attempt to resolve these issues is to be found in the Thomistic doctrine of analogy. According to St. Thomas, a few abstract negative terms (such as "eternal," "simple," and "immaterial") can be univocally predicated of God. But since God is beyond genus and species, any positive concrete terms (such as "wise" and "good") must be predicated of him analogically. Analogical predication is grounded on the analogy of being—the principle that since God is the cause of the good in each genus, he can be called by the name of the perfection of these goods. Besides the "analogy of attribution," which is justified by the analogy of being, St. Thomas also recognizes an "analogy of proportion," which is to be understood as a comparison (God is to man as the shepherd is to his sheep).

The Thomistic analogy of being was split apart by Barthianism, with its attack on all natural theology, and post-Barthian theories of theological language reflect the Double-Language theory. For Barth, all theological statements are metaphorical, but they can be interpreted only after the word of God has spoken to the interpreter. Paul Tillich defended the view that religious language is "symbolic," and that in fact all statements about God are symbolic, except one—that God is "being itself" or "ground of being" (see his *Systematic Theology*, Vol. I, Chicago, 1951, Parts II and IIB). More recently, he said that even those are "metaphoric names," and he classified metaphorical descriptions of God ("The Lord is my shepherd") as a form of "secondary religious symbolism." F. W. Dillistone has distinguished the "metaphorical symbol" from the "analogical symbol" in *Christianity and Symbolism* (London, 1955, Ch. 1, pp. 160, 179, 273).

The important concept of myth, which has figured prominently in twentieth-century discussion, has also been connected with that of metaphor: a myth can be roughly described as an extended metaphor, and its accompanying ritual as a dramatized figure of speech. Even Rudolf Bultmann, who proposes to "demythologize" New Testament theology, has argued that myth is an expression of man's conception of the universe and of his place in it.

Ontology. The use of metaphor in metaphysical inquiry has long been the subject of dispute among philosophers. We can detect a certain uneasiness in Simplicius' report of Anaximander's theory that things "suffer punishment and make reparation to one another for their injustice according to the order of time, as he says in somewhat poetical language" (*Physics* 24, 13). The rise of science in the seventeenth century, with its demand for clear and vigorous expression, brought this suspiciousness toward poetical language to its highest pitch. One of the seven reasons given by Hobbes why "there can be nothing so absurd, but may be found in the books of philosophers" is "the use of metaphors, tropes and other rhetorical figures, instead of words proper" (*Leviathan*, Part I, Ch. 5). And Locke emphatically numbered among the abuses of language "figurative speeches, and allusion" (*Essay*, III, x, 34; cf. II, xi, 2). As Colin Turbayne points out in *The Myth of Metaphor* (New Haven, 1962, p. 12), metaphor seems easily subsumable under Ryle's definition of "category-mistake": "the presentation of the facts of one category in the idioms

appropriate to another" (*The Concept of Mind*, London, 1949, p. 8). Turbayne's book is itself an extended attack on the way philosophers let metaphors turn into myths.

On the other hand, a number of philosophers, from Plato through the German romantics to the present, may be counted among the defenders of metaphor. After his remark that "whenever anything lives, there is, open somewhere, a register in which time is being inscribed," Bergson adds, "This, it will be said, is only a metaphor.—It is of the very essence of mechanism, in fact, to consider as metaphorical every expression which attributes to time an effective action and a reality of its own" (*Creative Evolution*, translated by Arthur Mitchell, New York, 1911, p. 16). This is an interesting variation on the Double-Language view: it suggests that there is a language of mechanism and a wholly distinct language of the *élan vital*. Stephen Pepper, in *World Hypotheses* (Berkeley, 1942, p. 91; cf. p. 96), has presented what he terms a "root metaphor" theory of "world-hypotheses": that there are four basic ontological systems, each derived from a "basic analogy or root metaphor." Dorothy M. Emmett has argued, in *The Nature of Metaphysical Thinking* (London, 1949, pp. 5, 197–198), that "metaphysics is an analogical way of thinking" which generalizes from "some form of intellectual or spiritual relationship" judged to be significant. More recently, Douglas Berggren has argued that "metaphysics must be vitally metaphorical"; that is, it must preserve the "stereoscopic" vision necessary to creative thought, if it is to overcome such puzzling dualisms as mind–body, without losing the identity of the terms.

It seems clear that, in its first appearance at least, any universal ontological statement must involve a synecdoche, for any interesting word that is applied to everything must be one that has already acquired a usage in which the word is applied to less than everything. Such statements as "The real is the rational," "The world is Will," "All the states of the monads are perceptions," "Everything is material," and even "All events are actual occasions," extend the part metaphorically to the whole. From this point of view, such statements raise metaphilosophical questions as to whether they can claim meaning as essentially untranslatable "insights," or whether they can be recast by the metaphysician as literal technical statements, without losing their meaning.

Bibliography

BACKGROUND

Barfield, O., "Poetic Diction and Legal Fiction," in Max Black, ed., *The Importance of Language*. Englewood Cliffs, N.J., 1963.

Beardsley, M. C., *Aesthetics*. New York, 1958. Chs. 3, 5, 9.

Black, Max, "Metaphor," in *Models and Metaphors*. Ithaca, N.Y., 1962.

Edie, J. M., "Expression and Metaphor." *Philosophy and Phenomenological Research*, Vol. 23 (1962/1963), 538–561.

Henderson, G. P., "Metaphorical Thinking." *Philosophical Quarterly*, Vol. 3, No. 10 (1953), 1–13.

Horsburgh, H. J. N., "Philosophers Against Metaphor." *Philosophical Quarterly*, Vol. 8, No. 32 (1958), 231–245.

Lewis, C. S., "Bluspels and Flalansferes," in Max Black, ed., *The Importance of Language*. Englewood Cliffs, N.J., 1963.

Murdoch, I., Lloyd, A. C., Ryle, G., "Thinking and Language." *PAS*, Supp. Vol. 25 (1951), 25–82.

Stanford, W. B., *Greek Metaphor*. Oxford, 1936.

THEORIES OF METAPHOR

Alston, W., *Philosophy of Language.* New York, 1964. Ch. 7. Defense of the Iconic Signification Theory.

Beardsley, M. C., *Aesthetics.* New York, 1958. Ch. 3. Verbal-Opposition Theory. See also "The Metaphorical Twist," below.

Beardsley, M. C., "The Metaphorical Twist." *Philosophy and Phenomenological Research,* Vol. 22 (1962), 293–307.

Buchanan, S., *Poetry and Mathematics.* Philadelphia, 1929. Ch. 4. The Comparison Theory.

Henle, P., "Metaphor," in *Language, Thought, and Culture.* Ann Arbor, Mich., 1958. The Iconic Signification Theory.

Herschberger, R., "The Structure of Metaphor." *Kenyon Review,* Vol. 5 (1943), 433–443.

Rieser, M., "Brief Introduction to the Epistemology of Art." *Journal of Philosophy,* Vol. 47 (1950), 695–704. The Emotive Theory.

Urban, W. M., *Language and Reality.* New York, 1939. Chs. 9–10. Defense of Paraphrasability of Metaphor.

Wheelwright, P., *Metaphor and Reality.* Bloomington, Ind., 1962. Double-Language Thesis.

METAPHOR IN LANGUAGE AND POETRY

James, D. G., *Skepticism and Poetry.* London, 1937. Pp. 94–108.

Stern, G., *Meaning and Change of Meaning.* Göteborg, Sweden, 1937. Ch. 11.

Wellek, R., and Warren, A., *Theory of Literature.* New York, 1949. Ch. 15.

METAPHOR IN PHILOSOPHY OF SCIENCE

Braithwaite, R. B., *Scientific Explanation.* Cambridge, 1953. Ch. 4.

Freudenthal, Hans, ed., *The Concept and the Role of the Model in Mathematics and Natural and Social Sciences.* The Hague, 1961.

Harré, R. "Metaphor, Model and Mechanism." *PAS,* Vol. 60 1959–1960).

Hutten, E. H., "The Role of Models in Physics." *British Journal for the Philosophy of Science,* Vol. 4 (1953/1954), 284–301.

Nash, H., "Freud and Metaphor." *Archives of Psychiatry,* Vol. 7 (1962), 25–29.

METAPHOR IN PHILOSOPHY OF RELIGION

Barth, Karl, *Anselm: Fides Quaerens Intellectum; Anselm's Proof of the Existence of God,* translated by I. W. Robertson. New York, 1960.

Bultmann, Rudolf, *Kerygma and Myth,* H. W. Bartsch, ed. New York, 1953.

Emmett, D. M., *The Nature of Metaphysical Thinking.* London, 1949. Chs. 5–8. On Thomistic analogy.

Hepburn, R. W., "Demythologizing and the Problem of Validity," in Antony Flew and Alasdair MacIntyre, eds., *New Essays in Philosophical Theology.* New York, 1955.

McInerny, R. M., *The Logic of Analogy.* The Hague, 1961. On Thomistic analogy.

Tillich, Paul, "The Meaning and Justification of Religious Symbols," in Sidney Hook, ed., *Religious Experience and Truth.* New York, 1961. P. 7.

METAPHOR IN ONTOLOGY

Berggren, D., "The Use and Abuse of Metaphor." *Review of Metaphysics,* Vol. 16 (1962/1963), 237–258, 450–472, esp. 470–472.

Nemetz, A., "Metaphysics and Metaphor," in R. Houde and J. P. Mullally, eds., *Philosophy of Knowledge.* Philadelphia, 1960.

MONROE C. BEARDSLEY

METAPHYSICS. The Encyclopedia contains two general articles on this subject: METAPHYSICS, HISTORY OF and METAPHYSICS, NATURE OF. It also features the following articles: ABSOLUTE, THE; APEIRON/PERAS; APPEARANCE AND REALITY; ARCHE; BEING; CATEGORIES; CAUSATION; CHANCE; CHANGE; CHAOS AND COSMOS; CONTINUITY; DETERMINISM; DIALECTIC; EMANATIONISM; ESSENCE AND EXISTENCE; ETERNAL RETURN; ETERNITY; HEN/POLLA; IDEALISM; IDENTITY; INEFFABLE, THE; INFINITY IN THEOLOGY AND METAPHYSICS; LOGOS; MACROCOSM AND MICROCOSM; MATERIALISM; MONAD AND MONADOLOGY; MONISM AND PLURALISM; NATURALISM; NATURE, PHILOSOPHICAL IDEAS OF; NOTHING; NOUS; ONTOLOGY; PANPSYCHISM; PANTHEISM; PERSONAL IDENTITY; PERSONALISM; PERSONS; PESSIMISM AND OPTIMISM; PHYSIS AND NOMOS; POSSIBILITY; RELATIONS, INTERNAL AND EXTERNAL; SOLIPSISM; SUBSTANCE AND ATTRIBUTE; TIME; UNCONSCIOUS; UNIVERSALS; VITALISM; VOLUNTARISM; WHY.

Differing schools of metaphysical thought are represented in the articles ARISTOTELIANISM; AUGUSTINIANISM; CARTESIANISM; HEGELIANISM; NEOPLATONISM; OCKHAMISM; PLATONISM AND THE PLATONIC TRADITION; SCOTISM; SPINOZISM; STOICISM; THOMISM.

METAPHYSICS, HISTORY OF. The word "metaphysics" derives from the Greek *meta ta physika* (literally, "after the things of nature"), an expression used by Hellenistic and later commentators to refer to Aristotle's untitled group of texts that we still call the *Metaphysics.* Aristotle himself called the subject of these texts first philosophy, theology, or sometimes wisdom; the phrase *ta meta ta physika biblia* ("the books after the books on nature") is not used by Aristotle himself and was apparently introduced by the editors (traditionally by Andronicus of Rhodes in the first century B.C.) who classified and catalogued his works. Later, classical and medieval philosophers took this title to mean that the subjects discussed in the *Metaphysics* came "after the things of nature" because they were further removed from sense perception and, therefore, more difficult to understand; they used Aristotle's frequent contrast of things "prior and better known to us" with things "prior and better known in themselves" to explain why the treatises on first philosophy should come "after the books on physics." In medieval and modern philosophy "metaphysics" has also been taken to mean the study of things transcending nature—that is, existing separately from nature and having more intrinsic reality and value than the things of nature—giving *meta* a philosophical meaning it did not have in classical Greek. Especially since Kant "metaphysics" has often meant a priori speculation on questions that cannot be answered by scientific observation and experiment. Popularly, "metaphysics" has meant anything abstruse and highly theoretical—a common eighteenth-century usage illustrated by Hume's occasional use of "metaphysical" to mean "excessively subtle." The term has also been popularly associated with the spiritual, the religious, and even the occult. In modern philosophical usage "metaphysics" refers generally to the field of philosophy dealing with questions about the kinds of things there are and their modes of being. Its subject matter includes the concepts of existence, thing, property, event; the distinctions between particulars and universals, individuals and classes; the nature of relations, change, causation; and the nature of mind, matter, space, and time. In the eighteenth and nineteenth centuries "metaphysics" was used broadly to include questions about the reality of the external world, the existence of other minds, the possibility of a priori knowledge, and the nature of sensation, memory, abstraction, and so on. In present usage these questions are included in the study of epistemology.

THE CLASSICAL PERIOD

The history of metaphysics in Western philosophy (taking "metaphysics" in the contemporary sense) began with speculations by the Ionian cosmologists in the sixth century B.C. about the origin of the physical universe, the matter or stuff from which it is made, and the laws or uniformities everywhere present in nature. Our knowledge of these early cosmologists comes mostly from Aristotle and other classical authors; the main figures were the Milesians (Thales, Anaximander, and Anaximenes), Pythagoras, and Heraclitus.

Parmenides. The beginning of metaphysics, however, is most conveniently dated from Parmenides (fl. c. 475 B.C.), since some of the typical characteristics of metaphysics as a distinct philosophical inquiry are present in, or at least suggested by, his surviving writings. These characteristics are, first, the conception of philosophy as an attempt to understand the universe by means of a logical investigation that is a priori, appealing to meanings of terms rather than to the evidence of the senses. This method is in contrast to the method of natural science, which relies on sense perception. Second is a more or less explicit use of very general principles viewed as sufficient to arrive at a true account of reality. Such principles were, for example, noncontradiction and something like a principle of sufficient reason, which is expressed in Parmenides' poem: "Also, what necessity impelled it, if it did spring from Nothing, to be produced later or earlier? Thus it must Be absolutely, or not at all." Philosophy was therefore conceived as a deductive science like mathematics. Third is the paradoxical contrast between apparent reality and true reality and the association of the truly real with singleness and unchangingness. Of these features of Parmenides' writings, the first is fundamental; it can be taken as a defining characteristic of metaphysics. Like the natural scientist, the metaphysician gives an account of the universe; unlike the scientist, he does not base his account on observations and experiments, at least not on any special observations and experiments made for the purpose. His account is based primarily on analysis of concepts; if he does appeal to the evidence of the senses, he appeals to something generally familiar, not to new evidence he is adding to knowledge. Parmenides himself apparently believed he had done all that could be done by way of a philosophical account of the universe. His account consists in pointing to what he believed were the logical consequences of saying "It is." He dismissed everything else either as poetic imagery with no claim to truth or as empirical science; he indiscriminately referred to both as opinion. His position was not naive; it is not easy to see

how a metaphysician can give an account of reality based on logic alone unless reality in some sense has the features of necessity and vacuous generality belonging to logical truths. And doctrines similar to Parmenides' logical monism have frequently reappeared in the history of metaphysics—for example, in Neoplatonism, in Spinoza, and in nineteenth-century Hegelianism. There is more than a superficial resemblance between Parmenides' Being, the Neoplatonists' One, Spinoza's God or nature, and Hegel's Absolute as understood by a metaphysician like F. H. Bradley. Perhaps the underlying reasoning is that recognizing that metaphysics gives an account of the world based on analysis of concepts rather than on empirical evidence, these philosophers have felt that logic alone should be sufficient basis for making assertions about the world; since whatever is logically true is thought to be necessarily and always true, they have concluded that the world itself must be unchanging and in some sense necessarily what it is.

Later pre-Socratics. Parmenides apparently believed he had said all that a metaphysician could say about the world. Accordingly, his followers Melissus and especially Zeno are more critical than constructive—a trait shown by many later metaphysicians who are more often concerned to demonstrate what they take to be logical failures in the ordinary or scientific understanding of reality than to give a positive account of reality. We learn from Plato's *Parmenides* that Zeno's paradoxes of motion were meant to support Parmenides' system by showing contradictions in the ordinary concept of change. (When does the arrow move? Not now, because at any given instant it is in one place and hence not moving; not at some other time, because if it is moving, it must be moving now.)

Parmenides' general effect, however, was to interest philosophers in following what seemed to be the logical implications of their assumptions. An example is Anaxagoras, who apparently argued from the assumption that reality is many and changing to the conclusion that the things we ordinarily call real are composed of unendingly smaller parts similar to the whole things, that "all things are together," that "everything contains a part of every other thing," and that although there are rearrangements of things, nothing is ever really created or destroyed. Like his contemporaries Empedocles and the atomists Leucippus and Democritus, Anaxagoras did rely on observation and experiments to give an account of nature, but the surviving fragments suggest that his cosmology was arrived at largely by a priori reasoning in the way Parmenides' was, although the resulting account of reality is the opposite of Parmenides' account. And in the same way that something like Parmenides' logical monism is repeated in Neoplatonism, in Spinoza, and in nineteenth-century Hegelianism, something like Anaxagoras' logical pluralism is repeated in Leibniz' theory of monads and Russell's logical atomism. The common feature of this kind of system is that on logical grounds reality is described as composed of elements viewed as the limit of an unending process of division; the least parts of things are, so to speak, real infinitesimals —things smaller or simpler than any given thing one can mention. The atomism of Leucippus, Democritus, and, later, Lucretius is, by contrast, primarily a physical theory.

These thinkers believed that the existence of atoms can be shown empirically; their atoms have finite sizes and such recognizable physical properties as shape and motion and, perhaps, weight, and the theory anticipates Galileo and Newton rather than Leibniz and Russell.

Plato. In Plato's *Phaedo* Socrates is made to say he once studied Anaxagoras but gave up this study and all empirical investigations of nature, deciding instead to "have recourse to conceptions and examine in them the truth of realities." Anaxagoras, Parmenides, and others had also had recourse to conceptions in contrast to the evidence of the senses; what is new in the *Phaedo* is the theory of Ideas or Forms, which historians of philosophy sometimes ascribe to Plato (c. 427–347 B.C.) and sometimes to Socrates himself. For Plato, at least, ideas exist independently of the things we see and touch; moreover, they are considered the source of existence of things we see and touch, somewhat as a man is the cause of his shadow or of his reflection in a mirror or a pool of water. Popularly, Plato's metaphysics means the theory of Ideas in this sense, and in this way the theory has had a great influence in the history of thought. Plato's own evaluation, however, was considerably more critical than that of many of his followers. The theory of Ideas in this form is presented in the *Phaedo* as a hypothesis that cannot be known to be true; in the *Parmenides* its logical weaknesses are pointed out; in the *Timaeus* it is used as part of a "probable" or "likely" cosmology. Nevertheless, Plato does consistently argue for the existence of mind or soul as a kind of entity distinct from, and in some sense prior to, physical objects. This thesis is developed, notably in the *Phaedo,* where the theory of Ideas is used as a step in proving the immortality of soul, in the *Phaedrus,* and in Book X of the *Laws.* In these contexts Plato argues that since bodies cannot move themselves (apparent self-motion is reduced to one part's moving another) whereas soul can, the ultimate source of observed motions must be soul or mind. In the *Laws* this argument is used to prove the existence of the gods, who are understood as sources of observed motions and changes in the visible universe.

Plato's technical contributions to metaphysics are contained in the difficult later dialogues, especially the *Parmenides* and *Sophist.* Both dialogues purport to be a criticism of Eleatic philosophy, by Parmenides himself in the *Parmenides* and by an "Eleatic stranger" in the *Sophist.* In the *Parmenides* Parmenides is represented as illustrating the method of dialectic by scrutinizing his own hypothesis that "the One exists" and deducing the logical consequences both of asserting and of denying this hypothesis. The point is that what follows depends on how the hypothesis is understood—in particular, on how one understands unity and existence. If, for example, unity is thought to be in no way compatible with plurality, a thing which has unity can hardly have anything else. Thus, it cannot have spatial extension, for it would then have a right and a left, an up and a down. The more straightforward *Sophist* classifies philosophers into materialists and idealists according to their criteria of reality. A general criterion of reality as power is suggested, and a number of concepts of equal generality with that of being are introduced and discussed—sameness, difference, rest, and motion. The

apparent paradox in negation is explained by distinguishing absolute nonbeing (*A* does not exist) from relative nonbeing (*A* is non-*B*) or otherness and by distinguishing the existential is (*A* exists) from the is of predication (*A* is characterized by *B*). In the *Timaeus* the generic concepts are used in the mythical account of the construction of the physical universe by a godlike artisan using an ideal pattern as a blueprint.

Aristotle. Aristotle (384–322 B.C.) is indirectly the source of the term "metaphysics"; he is also the source of a systematic list of metaphysical issues, a technical language in which these issues are stated, and a metaphysical system that has had followers down to the present and has proved immensely fruitful. In part, the importance of this system has been in serving as an object of criticism, although this function has been served by Plato as much as by Aristotle and Aristotle himself illustrates Plato's importance as an object of criticism in the history of metaphysics.

The problems of "first philosophy," or metaphysics, listed by Aristotle in books Beta and Kappa of the *Metaphysics* are partly about metaphysics itself: Does its subject matter include all the basic concepts and assumptions of all the special sciences? Does it include the principles of logic? Is there metaphysical knowledge in contrast to opinion? These questions ask, in effect, whether metaphysics is a superscience proving the assumptions made by the special sciences and also the assumptions it itself uses—whether, in short, it is a logically self-contained body of knowledge contrasting with the logically incomplete special sciences. This concept of metaphysics was held, for example, by Descartes, but on the whole Aristotle rejected this view. Metaphysics is less the capstone of a hierarchy of sciences than a discussion of problems left over by the special sciences. Physics, for example, assumes there is motion, but it is not part of the metaphysician's job as Aristotle saw it to prove this assumption; at most, he should explain it or defend it from criticism. Aristotle thought of metaphysics as explaining things we already know to be true rather than as giving reasons for the assumptions we make in the sciences and everyday life, thereby providing the underpinnings of science and common sense.

Some of the problems of metaphysics listed by Aristotle are questions about the kinds of things there are. In addition to physical objects perceived by the senses, do such abstractions as Plato's Ideas or the mathematician's numbers, points, lines, and so on also exist? Are all existing things particulars, or do universals like man or whiteness exist, too? Do particulars of the same kind have anything in common, and if so, what and how? Are physical objects something more than the material parts that compose them, and if so, what?

For Aristotle, however, the most fundamental questions of metaphysics concerned the concepts of being and unity. Are being and unity properties of things (since everything both is and is one thing), or are they entities or substances of some kind (as Parmenides seemed to have thought)? If being and unity are things in their own right, what kind of things are they? These questions are suggested by Plato's *Parmenides* and *Sophist.* Aristotle's answers are his most important contribution to metaphysics. In the *Sophist*

Plato suggested a general definition of being as power but gave little by way of an explicit analysis of this sense of being, which does not correspond to the use of the word in ordinary language. Such an explicit analysis is the center of Aristotle's metaphysics; his contribution can be summarized as the view that although there are many ways in which things are and are one (and there are therefore many senses of being and unity) and although these ways are irreducibly distinct, they nevertheless depend on one basic kind of being. Being is neither an attribute nor a thing and cannot therefore be defined in the ways "triangular" or "horse" can be defined. But we can pick out a basic sense of being, illustrated in such statements as, "This is a horse" or "This is a man," and show how the other senses of being depend on it. "Being a horse," "being a man," and, in general, "being an *X*" in the basic sense of being means to have attributes and therefore to be a subject of thought and discourse without in turn being an attribute of something else; "being a horse" is not, for Aristotle, an attribute of some more basic subject of thought and discourse. Primarily, what there is, is this horse, this man, and so on when we are speaking of an individual; secondarily, what there is, is horse, man, and so on understood as species or kinds of things. Qualities, dates, locations, motions, relations, and the like are attributed to the things that exist in the basic sense; they themselves do not have independent existence and "are" only in a derivative and borrowed sense of being.

Aristotle's analysis of being is the heart of his metaphysics; it is not the whole of it or the part most stressed by his later followers. What is often referred to as Aristotle's metaphysics is his account of the universe. Roughly, it states that there are a large but finite number of things that for the most part (with exceptions such as the sun, the only thing of its kind, and biological "mistakes" resulting from mutation and crossbreeding) belong to definite kinds—for example, plant and animal species. In most cases the individual members of these kinds or classes are born and die, but the classes themselves do not change. Some things— for example, the stars—exist forever and apart from uniform motions do not change at all. There is an ultimate prime mover which is the source of all observed motion and change but is itself completely immaterial and therefore completely motionless and changeless. This set of ideas is in the *Metaphysics,* and the pluralism and some theory of natural kinds do follow from Aristotle's analysis of being. But the theory of prime movers and the Unmoved Mover is also in the *Physics* as a scientific—that is, demonstrable—account of the physical universe; it is not therefore a true part of his metaphysics, which is dialectical (arguing from common opinion and logic) rather than scientific.

The central chapters of the *Metaphysics* elucidate and defend the claim that such common-sense things as this horse, this man, and so on are the fundamental subjects of discourse. Aristotle upheld this claim against (1) the view that the ultimate material parts of things are the ultimate subjects of discourse (so that "This is a horse" would be understood as "These material elements have horselike attributes"); (2) the view that Platonic Ideas are the ultimate subject of discourse (where "This is a horse" is un-

derstood as "The horse is exemplified by these sensible qualities"); and (3) the view that the basic sense of being is illustrated in, for instance, "There is a horse in the barn"—the view according to which "there is" means "it is true that" or "it is a fact that." For Aristotle to be is to be an individual, and the being of a thing is primarily its nature or identifying features rather than the fact that it is. Aristotle hardly even recognized the sense of being involved in such sentences as "There are good men, and there are wicked men," which can be read as "Among all the things that are, some are—that is, have the identifying features of—good men; others are wicked men." Such sentences suggest that what exists primarily are featureless particulars, which can be referred to collectively as "the things that exist," not common-sense things.

In general, the question "What is being?" became for Aristotle "What is an individual?," a horse, a man, a house, and so on being understood as paradigms of an individual. And, positively, the central argument of the *Metaphysics* is that an individual is primarily the distinguishing features by which we identify and classify it. Aristotle himself believed that these classifications are learned through experience; he was a realist in the sense that he thought the groups and classes of things are there to be learned by observation and are not simply mental constructions. Therefore, there is a sense in which we learn empirically what being is. But metaphysics is not itself an empirical study of being; Aristotle did not, for instance, think of metaphysics as a science of high-level generality describing the properties that all beings (individuals) have.

Aristotle's *Metaphysics* in its present form—and there is no reason to think it ever had a very different form—is barely readable in large stretches. Other parts read like outmoded astronomy; still other parts read like rather tedious lexicography. The devastating criticism of Plato is largely borrowed from Plato himself. However, the *Metaphysics* gives a surprisingly coherent set of answers to the questions it raises, and the questions themselves are those that metaphysicians still ask.

Neoplatonism. The Neoplatonists in the late classical period were metaphysicians of great power and originality. They were also of great importance in the development of metaphysics since they formed a link between ancient and medieval philosophy. The main figure of this movement, Plotinus (c. 204–270), associated metaphysics with mysticism and personal asceticism. The mystical and religious side of his philosophy was stressed by his disciple and editor Porphyry (c. 232–304), and such later Neoplatonists as Iamblichus and Proclus gave a further religious and even occult and superstitious emphasis to the movement. But the intellectual power of the movement is shown in as late a philosopher as Boethius (c. 480–524), and through Boethius Neoplatonism had a very strong influence on medieval philosophy and, therefore, indirectly on modern philosophy.

Plotinus. Plotinus' philosophy is a paradigm case of a metaphysical system according to one common conception of metaphysics. It asserts the unreality or half reality of the things of everyday experience; the illusory character of change, motion, and even space and time; the superior reality of soul or mind over matter. It conceives of goodness and intelligence as substantial things and stresses personal mysticism and an ascetic way of life. The line of thought by which Plotinus arrived at this position is not easy to follow, but, briefly, it seems to have been somewhat as follows. Whatever is, is one thing (even a collection of things is said to "be" only when counted as one thing—a collection); the answer to the question "What is being?," understood as a request for a description of being, is therefore unity or singleness. But unity or singleness cannot be described any further, although a direct, intuitive experience of it is in some sense possible. Since being is equivalent to unity and since things can have unity to a greater or lesser degree, we can speak of degrees of being. Although unity is itself ineffable, it does duplicate itself in a kind of descending series of things—in goodness and intelligence—in a lesser way in disembodied spirits, in a still lesser way in human souls, least of all in physical objects and their properties and relations. The emanation of successively less real things from unity is to be understood in a logical rather than a physical sense. Speaking accurately, unity or singleness (the One) is not a cause at all, although it can be described metaphorically, for example, as an inexhaustible fountain of being bringing existence to all the things that are by its continuous overflow. Plotinus' writings are full of these metaphors, but he recognized them as metaphors, and the underlying position is rigorously argued, granting the not implausible identification of being with unity or singleness.

Plotinus' line of thought begins with the assumption that being and unity are properties that things have—properties of utmost generality, to be sure, but still properties in the same way that black or being four-legged are properties of a horse. Combined with this seems to be the Platonic assumption that properties are not simply modifications of particulars or ways that particulars exist; properties are entities in their own right that particular things instance or exemplify. The first of these two assumptions is clearly made in the *Isagoge*, Porphyry's short introductory treatise on Aristotle's *Categories*. In Porphyry's account—and in this account he is presumably expressing a typically Neoplatonic point of view—the theory of categories or types of predication is a theory of kinds of predicates: genus, species, difference, property (that is, essential property), and accident. These kinds of predicates (the predicables) are distinguished from individuals. But even expressions designating individuals are predicates of a sort according to Porphyry; such expressions as "Socrates," "this man here," and "this thing here" are attributes, differing from the predicables because they are "only said of a single thing" whereas the predicables "are said of several things." The distinction is between attributes belonging to several things and attributes belonging to only one thing. But of individuals themselves, in contrast to attributes, nothing is said; they can apparently be characterized only indirectly, as the ultimate subjects of predication.

This account of predication makes the distinction between thing and property peripheral to metaphysics. The important distinction is between relatively less general and relatively more general attributes, culminating in the most general attributes, being and unity. Porphyry spoke of substance as "the most general genus" and in a sense

the only real genus, since unlike animal, for example, which is a genus relative to man but only a special case relative to "living thing," substance is not itself a special case of some higher genus. Neoplatonic metaphysics is largely an analysis, similar to Plato's *Parmenides*, of these ultimate genera; the main force of Plotinus' writings is the argument that the ultimate genera cannot be described in any ordinary way but are in some sense manifest in lower orders of being. Neoplatonism thus easily lends itself to religious interpretation; in the late classical world it actually was a theological system associated with a religious way of life competing with Christianity.

THE MIDDLE AGES

Porphyry's *Isagoge*, translated into Latin by Boethius in the sixth century, gave philosophers some basic tools and stimulated speculation on two questions in particular: (1) What is a thing considered just by itself, as a bare existent, apart from all its attributes? (2) Do attributes exist (or subsist) separately from human thought and discourse and from the things that are said to have attributes? The first question, implicit in Porphyry's account of predication, is roughly the problem of distinguishing essence from existence, what a thing is from the fact that it is. The second question (really, group of questions) was explicitly raised but not answered by Porphyry; it is the problem of universals much discussed throughout medieval philosophy.

For Aristotle the contrast between what a thing is and the fact that it is, is at best peripheral to metaphysics. Aristotle recognized that the question "Does X exist?" is distinct from "What is X?," but he attached no metaphysical importance to the distinction. Particular questions of the form "Does X exist?" are decided by sense perception or by proof; there is no general metaphysical question about the nature of existence ("thatness") in contrast to essence ("whatness"). The metaphysician is concerned with what things are rather than with their existence or nonexistence. Aristotle's position was that what things are—that is, their being—is primarily what is contained in their definitions; the definition of a thing describes its essence, which is equivalent to its species (the traits that identify it as the kind of thing it is) which is in turn identified with its genus, differentia, and essential properties. But when, as in Porphyry, genus (mammal), difference (solid-hoofed), species (horse), property (neighs), and accident (gray) are indiscriminately called attributes of the thing itself, it is natural to ask what it is that has these attributes or what it is that gives this collection of attributes an actual rather than a merely possible existence.

The problem of universals dominated metaphysics in the early Middle Ages; it was discussed by metaphysicians from Boethius in the sixth century to Roscelin and Abelard in the twelfth century. The main philosophical tradition during this period was the Augustinian tradition, represented by Boethius himself, John Scotus Erigena (died c. 877), St. Anselm (1033–1109), William of Champeaux (died c. 1120), St. Bonaventure (1221–1274), and many others. This tradition favored realism; species and genera like horse and animal were thought to exist not only apart from human thought and discourse (epistemological realism) but also apart from particular horses and animals. Species and genera were regarded as paradigms, archetypes, or exemplars of particular things; as such, they exist in the mind of God and are used by him as models in creating nature. As in St. Augustine and Plato, the fundamental contention is that particulars cannot be recognized and identified as one of a general type unless we first have independent knowledge of the type; the inference is that these general types must exist apart from, and in some sense prior to, the particulars exemplifying them.

St. Anselm's proof of God's existence (anticipated by St. Augustine), has had an important history in its own right; it is also an illuminating example of Christian Platonism in the early Middle Ages. The argument cannot be appreciated apart from its context of religious meditation, but it can be picked out and studied (as it has been by philosophers to this day) as a kind of supreme test case of Platonic (or Neoplatonic) metaphysical assumptions. Briefly, the argument is that (1) we have a concept of a supreme being (a being "than which nothing greater can be conceived") so that (2) the Supreme Being "exists in the understanding." Since (3) it is greater to exist in reality than merely in the understanding, it is contradictory to say the Supreme Being exists only in the understanding; hence, we can infer that (4) the Supreme Being does exist in reality. Kant's objection seems decisive. The existence (as contrasted with the concept of existing) of the Supreme Being cannot be a part of our concept of the Supreme Being. If it were, our concept would be the Supreme Being, not its concept. But the argument seems inevitable if one assumes, as the Neoplatonists did, that existence is an attribute that things have and, in consequence of having it, are, as things are red in consequence of having the attribute redness. Combined with the assumption that attributes have an independent existence, this line of thought leads to the conclusion that existence or being is itself an existing thing; the existence of things in nature is thought of as being due to their receiving a part of the inexhaustible thing, being, somewhat as an illuminated object receives its light from a source of illumination. Furthermore, it seems to follow that existence must itself necessarily exist as an analytic consequence of what it is (just as "Redness is red" seems to state an analytic necessity). Given these assumptions, the Ontological Argument for God's existence, as Kant later called it, is at least a strong temptation; the argument has had a history identical with the history of logical monism in metaphysics, from Parmenides to Hegel and beyond, as well as a close association with Christian theology.

REVIVAL OF CLASSICAL PHILOSOPHY

Although the realism–nominalism controversy occupied philosophers in the eleventh and twelfth centuries, new ways of thinking in metaphysics were being prepared by translations of Greek and Arabic texts into Latin, especially translations of Aristotle and his Arabian commentators. In the early Middle Ages there was very little firsthand knowledge of the Greek philosophers. Plato's *Timaeus, Phaedo,* and *Meno* were known, but the important later dialogues, including *Parmenides* and *Sophist,* were not.

The Greek texts had been preserved, however, and, especially after the capture of Constantinople by crusaders in 1204, were slowly recovered in the West. In the thirteenth century William of Moerbeke made a literal Latin translation of Proclus' *Commentary on the Parmenides;* the commentary contained the text of the *Parmenides* through the first hypothesis, thereby giving philosophers some firsthand knowledge of that important dialogue.

Aristotle was even less known and understood in the early Middle Ages. Only his logic, the text of *De Interpretatione,* and the other logical treatises in Neoplatonized versions through Boethius were known. As late as the thirteenth century, two Neoplatonic texts—the "Theology of Aristotle" (actually a compilation from Plotinus' *Enneads,* IV–VI) and the *Liber de Causis* (a work based on Proclus' *Elements of Theology)*—were wrongly attributed to Aristotle. However, Aristotle's writings had been translated into Syriac by Nestorian Christians in the fifth century and from Syriac into Arabic in the ninth century; Latin translations of Arabic texts were made in the twelfth century and directly from Greek texts by Robert Grosseteste and William of Moerbeke in the thirteenth century. By the end of the thirteenth century most of Aristotle was translated into Latin and was generally available to philosophers. In effect, Aristotle was a new philosopher who appeared on the scene and dominated it as if he were a contemporary; the *Metaphysics* was the stimulus for such metaphysicians as Albert the Great, St. Thomas Aquinas, Duns Scotus, William of Ockham, and others in the thirteenth and fourteenth centuries.

Aquinas. Aquinas' metaphysics is an attempt to explain the distinctions between essence and existence, necessary and contingent existence, and particulars and universals, using the language and much of the metaphysical outlook of Aristotle. For Aquinas common-sense things like horses and houses do exist in a literal and straightforward sense apart from human observers and also apart from God and paradigms of things in the mind of God. The existence of these common-sense things is not an attribute that they receive from outside; it is not like the light the earth receives from the sun. The existence of finite things in nature is an intrinsic act of existing that these things exercise. But Aquinas also held that the ordinary things we experience exist contingently in the sense that their existing is not an analytic consequence of what they are; it is not something they do by nature. There must therefore be a cause (in a metaphysical, not a physical, sense of "cause") of their existence; this must be a necessary being, identified with God, who exists by his own nature. Contingent beings, like horses and houses, are obviously contingent because being composed of matter, their existence is finite—they begin to exist and cease to exist. Matter also accounts for the individuality of things; things that are identical insofar as what they are, or, in other words, things that have the same nature, are still different things because the matter of which they are composed is different. God, on the contrary, is immaterial and, hence, one and unchanging. Aquinas, like the Neoplatonists, associated finitude, contingency, plurality, and change with matter. He differed from the Neoplatonists chiefly in his view that finite things—in particular, human persons—exist in their own right (by virtue of a delegated power, as it were) and do not merely participate in the existence of a higher order of being. In this view Aquinas agreed with Christian theology and was close to Aristotle.

Duns Scotus. Duns Scotus (1266–1308) seems to have agreed with Aquinas that being is not an attribute or a thing in some sense shared by all the things said to be. On the other hand, he criticized Aquinas' contrast of essence with existence, arguing that whatever we are aware of must be an essence in some sense, including even individuality or "thisness," which he treats as an attribute of individuals ("this horse here"), distinguishing them from indeterminate beings ("a horse" or "the horse" in general).

William of Ockham. William of Ockham (c. 1300–1349) held that general or indeterminate expressions like "a horse" or "the horse" do not correspond to general beings either in the mind or in reality but refer indifferently to individual horses. He was therefore conventionally called a nominalist in contrast to Scotus, a realist. But Ockham's main point seems to be that logical distinctions between universal, particular, and singular are not distinctions between kinds of things—not an enumeration of what there is—but are, rather, ways of referring to the one and only one kind of thing that does exist—namely, the common-sense things we encounter in everday experience. For this reason Ockham was probably closer to Aristotle's own view than either Aquinas or Scotus; unlike them his explicit aim was to state Aristotle's original position as accurately as he could. But Ockham's successors—notably, John of Mirecourt and Nicholas of Autrecourt—pushed Ockham's views in a direction that anticipated Hume and even twentieth-century logical positivism. We can talk meaningfully only about what we are acquainted with through the senses, and we are acquainted only with particulars, so that all discourse about things refers ultimately only to particulars. The existence of a particular is never an analytic necessity or an analytic consequence of the existence of some other; hence, all meaningful statements about things are only probable.

DESCARTES TO KANT

Descartes. The revival of metaphysics in the seventeenth century begins with René Descartes (1596–1650), who has been traditionally considered the originator of modern philosophy. The ideas most commonly associated with Descartes are not original with him. In St. Augustine's writings can be found the *cogito ergo sum* argument and the view that our own existence is the ultimate certainty since we can be certain of it while the existence of all other things is in doubt. The argument that nothing less than God could have produced the idea of God in the human mind can also be found in St. Augustine. The Ontological Argument had a famous history in the Middle Ages, and the view that physical objects have only geometrical attributes of shape and motion was held by early Greek atomists. The concept of mind as a substantial thing more or less externally attached to the body is hardly original with Descartes. But to say this is to say only that Descartes used a good deal of material from old ruins in his work of "building from the foundation" in metaphysics in

order "to establish a firm and abiding superstructure in the sciences."

Descartes was most original in his conception of philosophical method and philosophical truth. No metaphysical assertion is to be believed unless (1) it is understood with the kind of clarity and distinctness that mathematical propositions have and (2) its truth is either so intrinsically obvious that, like the postulates of geometry, it cannot be doubted or it is proved with the same rigor with which theorems are proved in geometry. Descartes's philosophy can be viewed in large part as an effort to reduce the second criterion to the first—that is, to show that at least in the case of metaphysical propositions, if we understand them clearly and distinctly, we are thereby certain of their truth. These claims made for his or any other metaphysical assertion were revolutionary and most influential. As Descartes and his followers understood them, they amounted to a demand that metaphysics be scientific, understanding by the word "scientific" being subject to a kind of rigorous intellectual discipline best illustrated in mathematics and the exact physical sciences.

Spinoza. Baruch Spinoza (1632–1677), following one interpretation of Descartes's demand for clarity and distinctness in metaphysics, thought of metaphysics as a deductive account of the universe to be developed from a few definitions—notably, the definition of substance as a being that requires nothing outside itself to be or to be conceived—and self-evident assumptions. His inferences are that there must logically be one and only one substance, uncreated and everlasting; there are an infinite number of attributes of the one substance, only two of which, thought and extension, are known to us; attributes are faces of the one substance—self-contained ways of describing it—rather than properties inhering in it the way we commonly think of colors as inhering in physical objects; the universe, described in terms of the attribute extension, is a mechanical system in which all happenings are links in a chain of physical causation; an equally complete causal determinism holds when the universe is conceived in terms of the attribute thought.

Leibniz. Gottfried Wilhelm von Leibniz (1646–1716) was also a follower of Descartes in the sense that he agreed with the demand for a rigorously scientific metaphysics and for clear and distinct ideas in contrast to scholastic verbiage. But while Leibniz agreed that metaphysical assertions are true if clearly and distinctly understood, he interpreted this to mean that metaphysical truths (and truths of reason generally, in contrast to contingent truths of fact) are logically necessary; their denial involves a self-contradiction. Leibniz understood clarity and distinctness in a logical rather than a psychological sense; for him "the true mark of a clear and distinct notion of an object is the means we have of knowing therein many truths by *a priori* proofs." And we know a truth by an a priori proof when "by the help of definitions or by the resolution of concepts" we "reduce" it to an explicit tautology of the form "*A is A*" or "*A is not non-A*."

Leibniz' metaphysical system is, in effect, an effort to get a clear and distinct idea of the universe in his own rather special sense of clarity and distinctness. And his technical writings in metaphysics consist largely of a series of somewhat different a priori proofs of a number of metaphysical assertions, including the following: there are an infinite number of substances, each of which is logically complete in that it contains in some sense all the properties it ever has exhibited or will exhibit; no two substances exhibit exactly the same properties ("identity of indiscernibles"); a complete description of any one substance would be a description of the entire universe "from a point of view"; space and time are relations among things, not things in their own right; the appearance of causal relations between things is illusory, reflecting God's deliberate prearrangement rather than any real influence exerted by one thing on another. In proving these assertions, Leibniz relied on a principle of sufficient reason stating, in effect, that there is always a rational explanation for a fact. But the principle of sufficient reason is not really a description of the universe for Leibniz. What it really expresses is the idea that in principle any truth can be given an a priori proof; the underlying thought is that when any statement is understood with perfect clarity and distinctness, it will be seen to be an explicit tautology.

Locke. Spinoza and Leibniz are usually grouped with Descartes as rationalists, as contrasted with British empiricists, represented in the seventeenth century by John Locke (1632–1704). But in an important way Locke, too, was a follower of Descartes; he was also mainly interested in replacing scholastic jargon with clear and distinct ideas and opening the way for the sciences. Locke's main contribution to metaphysics lies in his critical discussion of substance and essence. Descartes had laid it down as an indubitable common notion that "nothing is possessed of no attributes, properties, or qualities," so that "when we perceive any attribute, we therefore conclude that some existing thing or substance to which it may be attributed, is necessarily present." Locke did not deny that this is a valid inference; he does not question the distinction between thing and property. But he asked what we know (or, as he phrased it, "What is our idea") of a thing beyond its attributes, powers, and so forth. His answer was that we have no clear and distinct idea at all; we know only what the common notion itself says—namely, that if there are attributes, there must be something underneath that has them. We have no clear idea what is underneath or what underneath means in this context. We know only the attributes, powers, and so on (indiscriminately called qualities by Locke) of things, not the things in themselves. Here, however, Locke was criticizing only the notion of substance as substratum underlying properties. And this is a concept of substance minimized by Aristotle and never stressed by metaphysicians. Hobbes, for example, argued that the accidents of body, such as shape or hardness, are the very "manner of our conception of body." To ask for a description of body apart from its accidents would be, for Hobbes, a senseless request. Locke's more important and original criticism concerns the notion of essence—the notion of what a thing is in contrast to what it is made of, how big it is, its location, its age, and the like. Locke argued at length that the distinction is a useless one; the question "What is X?" can be answered only by enumerating X's observed properties, and (most important) we cannot see any logical necessity for the coexistence of just these and not some other combination of properties. We do not therefore have any knowledge of real essences except in cases where we ourselves construct the thing in question, as in mathematics. Locke reasoned, roughly, that we know the attributes and powers of things only through the simple sense impressions we have of them. Since, for the most part at least, there are no noticeable necessary connections between simple sense impressions, we cannot explain why things appear as they do but can only describe how they do appear. Locke never denied there is a reason for things' having just the attributes and powers they have and not some others, but he denied our ability ever to have clear and distinct ideas of these reasons. The effect of Locke's view is to deny the possibility of metaphysical knowledge when metaphysics is conceived of in the way Francis Bacon, for example, conceived of it, as a very general but still empirical and even experimental study of the formal causes of things, as distinguished from natural science, which studies material and efficient causes.

Berkeley and Hume. Locke never questioned the distinction between ideas of things and the qualities in things that cause ideas, and he thought we have at least a "relative and obscure" idea of a thing in contrast to its qualities. But George Berkeley (1685–1753) questioned both distinctions, partly on grounds of fact but more especially on grounds of a general theory of meaning. For Berkeley the grammatical distinction between subject and predicate has no counterpart in a distinction between things and properties; we can talk meaningfully only about what we are acquainted with, and we are acquainted only with individual colors, sounds, tastes, and the like. Since these individual colors, sounds, and tastes have characteristics that are admittedly mental, such as pleasantness and painfulness, and are relative to the human observer in various ways, Berkeley concluded we can talk meaningfully only about mental entities or, as he called them, following the usage of Descartes and Locke, ideas in the mind. In this way Berkeley arrived at phenomenalism (things exist exactly as they appear to the senses) and idealism (things exist only as objects of conscious perception; their being consists in being perceived). Berkeley was not thoroughgoing in these positions; he thought it meaningful to talk about other minds and about God even though we cannot directly perceive such phenomena.

These qualifications, however, were swept aside in the thoroughgoing phenomenalism of David Hume (1711–1776). Hume criticized the notion of a mind as distinguished from the ideas said to be in the mind for the same reasons that Berkeley criticized the notion of matter. According to Hume, the notion of existence itself signifies nothing beyond a greater or less degree of force and vivacity attaching to sense impressions and mental images. Our beliefs in the continuous existence of physical objects and the presence of causal connections between them are explained as effects of habitual associations of ideas for which there is, strictly speaking, no evidence. Although Hume is usually and correctly called an empiricist in contrast to speculative metaphysicians like Leibniz or Spinoza, there is a sense in which he was as much a rationalist as his contemporary Christian Wolff. Hume assumed that the ultimate subject of thought and discourse must be something we are directly conscious of, that we are directly conscious only of individual sensations (or their more or less faint copies), and that whenever we can discriminate one sensation or feeling from another, these exist separately and hence count as different things. These assumptions amount to a theory of empiricism, but they are not themselves empirical assertions. Nor, on the other hand, are they necessary truths in Leibniz' sense—propositions whose denial involves a self-contradiction. In effect, they demonstrate how Hume understood Descartes's demand for clarity and distinctness in metaphysics and are analogous to Leibniz' principle of sufficient reason, which expressed his understanding of the same demand. For Leibniz clarity and distinctness meant, in the end, reduction to an explicit tautology; for Hume clarity and distinctness meant, in the end, reduction to directly verifiable assertions about sensations and feelings.

Kant. By the time of Hume's death, in 1776, the difficulties and ambiguities in Descartes's program for metaphysics were apparent. Cartesianism inspired both the speculative constructions of Spinoza, Malebranche, Leibniz, and others and the critical and—at least, on the surface—increasingly skeptical philosophies of Locke, Berkeley, and Hume. This, at least, was the view taken by Immanuel Kant (1724–1804). It led Kant to ask whether metaphysics could be scientific—whether metaphysical knowledge is even possible and if not, how the questions that gave rise to metaphysics in the past could be answered. In discussing these problems, Kant made a very penetrating analysis of metaphysics as a discipline and a set of assertions and as a "human propensity"; Kant's contribution, apart from his own system, was to raise questions about what metaphysical assertions, as distinguished from scientific assertions, are, about the sense in which they claim truth, and about the grounds on which they are to be believed or disbelieved.

From Kant's point of view the history of metaphysics (insofar as metaphysics had claimed to be a science) had been a story of dogmatism versus skepticism. Dogmatists like Leibniz have held that metaphysics can, on the basis of purely logical or conceptual considerations, answer with absolute certainty questions about the origin of the universe, the existence of God, and the immortality of the soul. "Dogmatists," as Kant used the word, can be materialists, panpsychists, or dualists, monists or pluralists. What they share is a confidence that a metaphysician can give an account of the nature of reality using a priori reasoning. Skeptics, on the other hand, are empiricists; for them there are no universal and necessary truths of fact and reasoning alone, in contrast to observing and experimenting, is of no use whatsoever in answering questions about the existence or natures of things. For Kant this alternating dogmatism and skepticism was the effect of alternating overconfidence and lack of confidence in the abilities of the human mind. Accordingly, his critical philosophy is an effort to show what human knowledge is like and what its limits must necessarily be.

Dogmatic metaphysics in Kant's sense is not mere *ad hoc* speculation; it is an understandable and correctable misuse of basic concepts. The dogmatic metaphysician rightly sees that we actually use concepts like substance (in contrast to accidents) or causation (in contrast to mere succession). He also correctly saw that we are a priori certain of such things as the irreversibility of time or the impossibility of two physical objects' occupying the same space. But he uncritically concluded that we have a power other than sense perception of knowing what things are like, whereas the true conclusion is that we ourselves determine in advance what any object of knowledge must be like. The questions we ask about things and the answers we look for are determined by our own a priori forms of perceiving (space and time) and of judging (every attribute must belong to some substance, every event must have some cause and so on). Mistaking these a priori forms of perceiving and judging for descriptions of things-in-themselves, the dogmatic metaphysician is led to speak of ultimate subjects and first causes. In Kant's view these speculations are misguided and even meaningless. But metaphysical ideas, such as an ultimate subject or a first cause, do have a regulative use in encouraging us never to be satisfied with what we actually know at any given time. And Kant did not infer that the beliefs that metaphysicians have tried to prove—beliefs in personal immortality or in the existence of God—are illusory. These beliefs are not like belief in perpetual motion machines; they can be justified and can even be supported by arguments—but by moral arguments, not speculative arguments. Dogmatic metaphysics can thus be explained and even in a sense vindicated. It cannot be taken seriously as a source of knowledge, however.

METAPHYSICS SINCE KANT

Kant's own metaphysical position was idealistic. Aristotle's categories reappear somewhat altered in Kant's philosophy as forms of judgment. The most immediate and obvious effect of Kant's thought can be seen in the idealistic systems of his younger German contemporaries and successors, Johann Fichte (1762–1814), Friedrich Schelling (1775–1854), Arthur Schopenhauer (1788–1860), and, above all, Georg Friedrich Hegel (1770–1831).

Hegel. Among the idealists, however, it was Hegel whose metaphysical outlook has probably had more general intellectual influence than that of any other single recent philosopher. Kant's critical idealism assumes a clear-cut contrast between what is given in experience (sense impressions) and the forms we use to arrange and interpret what is given. In general, Kant assumed a clear distinction between what is directly perceived and what is inferred or constructed by the mind. Hegel's absolute idealism consists largely in denying this contrast; for him the underlying notion of a plurality of separately existing particulars, uniquely located in space and time (conceived as containers in which things are unambiguously placed), was a false, even a logically incoherent notion. He appears to have arrived at this conclusion from the assumptions that things-in-themselves cannot be distinguished meaningfully from things as we know them and that things as we know them gradually take shape in our consciousness and become defined only in contrast to other things. On this basis he concluded that all things shade off into their opposites and that the connections between things we establish in thought are as much a part of the things as their so-called inherent properties. Hegel was thus led to the monistic position that there is only one kind of substance and only one truly substantial entity. His idealism is an evolutionary pantheism in which the only self-subsistent reality is spirit; it contrasts not only with materialism in the traditional sense but with any metaphysical position associating reality with some kind of hard definiteness.

Outside of philosophy proper Hegel's influence was apparent mainly in inspiring a view of things as phases of a living and growing history; institutions, languages, ideas, even philosophies themselves, were seen as quasi-living and even quasi-personal phenomena whose histories were to be sympathetically grasped and appreciated rather than appraised by themselves on the basis of a priori standards. This widely held view has been encouraged by Hegel's absolute idealism, in which reality is associated with self-expression and all-inclusiveness, not with given things or facts. Within philosophy Hegel's influence can be seen in the many evolutionary idealisms of the nineteenth and early twentieth centuries. It can also be seen in the more rigorous and critical thought of Hegelians like F. H. Bradley (1846–1924) and J. M. E. McTaggart (1866–1925). Bradley in particular stressed the negative side of Hegelianism, finding logical antinomies in the ordinary concepts of things, properties, relations, causation, and space and time. McTaggart, on the other hand, attempted to rephrase Hegelianism as a clear and straightforward speculative system; this tradition is continued by such contemporary metaphysicians as Brand Blanshard.

Metaphysics and pragmatism. Largely through the influence of German idealism and especially of Hegel, metaphysics in the nineteenth century generally meant a priori cosmology and, in particular, an idealist cosmology contrasted and even opposed to the alleged mechanistic and materialist assumptions of science. Auguste Comte's positive—that is, nonmetaphysical—philosophy did not attack metaphysics as such; it attacked speculative philosophy as a way of providing substitutes for religious beliefs. Popularly, metaphysics was associated with religion, idealism, and spiritualism and opposed to science, which was associated with empiricism and materialism. But this concept of metaphysics, although still popular, was only a temporary alignment in the history of metaphysics and was strongly challenged even in the nineteenth century.

A notable example is the American philosopher C. S. Peirce (1839–1914). Peirce was a Hegelian to the extent that he believed there are no self-identical particulars that can be unambiguously located or identified. Reality is indeterminate both in the sense that it is characterized by novelty and unpredictability and in the sense that things are not just what they are but shade off continuously into other things; reality is an evolutionary process that is in some sense rational. But for Peirce this outlook is required by reflection on experience and the sciences, metaphysics itself being an observational science whose job is "to study the most general features of reality and real objects" and whose backward condition is due chiefly to the fact that "its leading professors have been theologians." Science and experience force us to give up the concept of definite,

unambiguous facts and fixed a priori assumptions; science is a community of inquirers sharing methods and a kind of moral and intellectual discipline rather than a body of knowledge or a set of assumptions (as Kant, for example, had thought). Metaphysics for Peirce was an attempt to describe how reality must seem to men imbued with science; reality is what will eventually be agreed on by the community of inquirers; general laws and relations among things are real since these, rather than particular facts, are the objects of scientific research. Peirce's concept of metaphysics influenced John Dewey (1859–1952), and largely through Dewey it has had considerable importance in recent American philosophy. Like Peirce, Dewey hoped metaphysics could be a descriptive account of generic traits exhibited in all experience.

Logical positivism. The main stream of metaphysics in the nineteenth and early twentieth centuries was idealistic; metaphysicians responded to Kant by constructing systems meant to extend or deepen Kant's critical idealism. But another response was to question dogmatic metaphysics more profoundly than Kant himself. This more radical questioning was begun by such nineteenth-century philosophers of science as Ernst Mach (1839–1916), who criticized the notion that general concepts of science (for example, force) described unobserved entities or that scientific laws are more than convenient formulas for summarizing observations. This line of criticism has been most forcefully and systematically carried out by twentieth-century logical positivism. For the logical positivists metaphysics has a special meaning; an assertion is metaphysical if it purports to make a statement of fact but fails to do so —and therefore fails to have a meaning—since no observations count as evidence for or against it. This special use of metaphysics should be understood in the context of the belief of logical positivists that traditional questions of metaphysics do have a point but a point that traditional formulations of the questions obscures. They are not questions about things at all but about language—in particular, about the types of words and sentences and the logical vocabulary needed to express the findings of the sciences. The hope of some logical positivists was that if traditional metaphysical questions were translated into questions about the language of science, the answers would be immediately and clearly seen. If, for example, "Does nonbeing exist?" is phrased as "Are sentences of the form '*X* is not an *F*' ever true?," the answer is obviously "Yes." But it became increasingly clear that in the construction of languages expressing the findings of the sciences problems analogous to traditional metaphysical problems occur. For example, some positivists suggested that sentences such as "Two plus two equals four" owe their truth to linguistic usage rather than to a necessary connection between things, perceived by reason, as past metaphysicians often assumed. Critics pointed out, however, that since it is an empirical fact that we use language as we do, the substitution of "true by virtue of linguistic convention" for "necessary truth" threatens to make "Two plus two equals four" a merely empirical statement. Thus, a distinction is needed between what we merely do not say and what our language will not allow us to say. This does not, of course, mean that nothing was gained over traditional metaphysics, but it does mean that the achievement of logical positivism has been to elucidate or reconstruct traditional metaphysical issues rather than give a method for easily solving them. Accordingly, logical positivists now tend to accept metaphysics in its conventional sense, as the name of a legitimate part of philosophy, along with the special use of metaphysical to refer to pseudoinformative assertions that in reality are meaningless.

Ordinary-language philosophy. The logical positivists were strongly influenced by Bertrand Russell's view that much of traditional metaphysics resulted from a superficial and hasty analysis of ordinary language as well as by the view of Russell and Peirce that past failures of metaphysicians were due to a narrowly restricted logic that prevented them from analyzing ordinary language correctly. The notion that traditional metaphysics resulted from a superficial understanding of ordinary language has been developed independently of logical positivism (although sometimes popularly confused with it) by Ludwig Wittgenstein, Gilbert Ryle, and a large number of contemporary British and American philosophers. Like the logical positivists the ordinary-language philosophers agree that traditional metaphysical questions are in some sense intelligible but need to be radically reformulated; unlike the positivists they are not concerned with rephrasing them as questions about the language of science. They want to show, rather, how metaphysical questions can be solved (or dissolved) by exhibiting the less obvious but essential presuppositions that give linguistic expressions the meanings they actually have in ordinary discourse. Positively, ordinary-language philosophers use linguistic analysis (for example, naming, referring, describing, and so on) to deal with traditional metaphysical issues, and like logical positivists they accept metaphysics in this positive sense as a legitimate area of philosophy.

Phenomenology and existentialism. Both logical positivism and ordinary-language philosophy could be viewed as extensions of Kant's criticism of dogmatic metaphysics; they both sharply contrast with Hegelianism and, in general, with the more or less speculative metaphysical systems inspired by Kant's idealism. A third major development in nineteenth-century and twentieth-century metaphysics, represented by phenomenologists and existentialists, agrees with Hegelians that metaphysics is not an observational science in any ordinary sense and also agrees with analytically minded philosophers that a priori reasoning cannot establish anything about the nature of reality. Accordingly, these philosophers have sought new and unconventional ways of experiencing or encountering reality. This response is shown by more conventional metaphysicians like Henri Bergson (1859–1941), who stressed the inability of spatializing and static conceptual thinking to represent correctly the reality of immediate experience, especially its temporal flow, or by Alfred North Whitehead (1861–1947), who stressed imaginative feeling and emotion as a way of gaining access to the inner natures of things. Phenomenologists hold that common sense and science presuppose a more primitive experience that can be grasped by a deliberately naive description of how things actually appear to us; existentialists argue that the subject of metaphysics is a reality that cannot be described in an emotionally neutral way but is in some sense possessed or encountered in personal commitment to a cause or in facing the certainty of one's own death. Phenomenology and existentialism have been combined by systematic philosophers like Martin Heidegger and Jean-Paul Sartre, whose systems attempt to express an intuitive understanding of time, contingency, and particularity as these are experienced in human life.

Philosophical analysis. In the English-speaking world at least, the most original and important contributions to metaphysics at the present time come from analytic philosophers largely influenced by logical positivism or ordinary-language philosophy. These philosophers see the present situation in metaphysics somewhat as Aristotle did when he reviewed the history of metaphysics up to his own time. In a sense, Aristotle thought, everything had been said, but in a sense nothing had been said because the early philosophers were vague and inarticulate. Contemporary metaphysicians, however, are in a better position to review and analyze the history of their subject than was Aristotle, partly because the history itself is so much richer and partly because contemporary insights make the work of past metaphysicians more intelligible.

Bibliography

GENERAL WORKS

Copleston, F. C., *A History of Philosophy*, 7 vols. London, 1946——. A careful, detailed work requiring close study; probably the most comprehensive and scholarly general history available. Includes excellent bibliographies and sections on metaphysics in chapters on individual philosophers.

De George, Richard T., ed., *Classical and Contemporary Metaphysics: A Source Book*. New York, 1962. A book of readings emphasizing contemporary authors but also including selections from classical texts.

Gilson, Étienne, *Being and Some Philosophers*, 2d ed. Toronto, 1952. A challenging essay on the history of metaphysics argued with great subtlety by an outstanding Roman Catholic philosopher.

Kaufmann, Walter, ed., *Philosophical Classics*, 2 vols. Englewood Cliffs, N.J., 1961. A comprehensive source book for the history of philosophy, with some excellent introductory essays.

Lovejoy, Arthur O., *The Great Chain of Being*. New York, 1936. Traces some main themes of metaphysics from the Greeks to the nineteenth century; a wide-ranging essay in the history of ideas rather than the conventional history of philosophy.

Smith, T. V., ed., *Philosophers Speak for Themselves*, 4 vols. Chicago, 1957. A collection of readings from Thales to Kant.

Whitehead, A. N., *Adventures of Ideas*. New York, 1933. Suggestive and sometimes profound nontechnical essays on movements in science and philosophy by a great twentieth-century metaphysician.

PRE-SOCRATICS

Burnet, John, *Early Greek Philosophy*, 4th ed. New York, 1930. Lucid and authoritative; contains translations of some important fragments.

Freeman, Kathleen, *Ancilla to the Pre-Socratic Philosophers*. Cambridge, Mass., 1952. English translations of the surviving pre-Socratic writings collected in Hermann Diel's monumental *Fragmente der Vorsokratiker.*

PLATO

Cornford, F. M., *Plato and Parmenides*. New York, 1957. Translations with running commentaries of Parmenides' *Way of Truth* and Plato's *Parmenides;* for advanced students.

Cornford, F. M., *Plato's Theory of Knowledge.* New York, 1959. Translations with running commentaries of Plato's *Theaetetus* and *Sophist.*

Lynch, William F., *An Approach to the Metaphysics of Plato Through the Parmenides.* New York, 1959. An attempt to see the *Parmenides* as a straightforward assertion of "basic positions in Platonic metaphysics."

Ryle, Gilbert, "Plato's *Parmenides.*" *Mind,* Vol. 48 (1939), 129–151, 302–325. Article by a leading contemporary British ordinary-language philosopher; suggests a modern reading.

Vlastos, Gregory, "The Third Man Argument in the *Parmenides.*" *The Philosophical Review,* Vol. 63, No. 3 (1954), 319–349. Technical but clear and acute analysis of the third-man argument against the theory of ideas in the first half of the *Parmenides.*

ARISTOTLE

Aristotle, *Metaphysics,* translated by Richard Hope. Ann Arbor, Mich., 1960. With an analytical index of technical terms; a useful edition for advanced students. Index contains Greek terms with Latin equivalents.

Brumbaugh, Robert S., "Aristotle's Outline of the Problems of First Philosophy." *The Review of Metaphysics,* Vol. 7, No. 3 (1953). A brief but very helpful analysis of the organization of the *Metaphysics.*

Owens, Joseph, *The Doctrine of Being in the Aristotelian Metaphysics.* Toronto, 1951. Highly technical but original and forcefully argued interpretation of the *Metaphysics.*

NEOPLATONISM

Bréhier, Émile, *The Philosophy of Plotinus,* translated by Joseph Thomas. Chicago, 1958. Readable sympathetic account of Plotinus and his school by a modern French historian of philosophy.

Porphyry, *Isagoge,* translated by J. Tricot. Paris, 1947. A translation into French of the complete text, with introduction and notes.

EARLY MIDDLE AGES

Anselm, *Proslogion and Monologium,* translated by S. N. Deane. La Salle, Ill., 1948.

Malcolm, Norman, "Anselm's Ontological Arguments." *The Philosophical Review,* Vol. 69, No. 1 (1960), 41–62. A closely reasoned analysis of Anselm's argument and medieval and modern criticisms.

LATE MIDDLE AGES

Aquinas, Thomas, *Concerning Being and Essence,* translated by George C. Leckie. New York, 1937. Difficult but important treatise on a basic distinction in Thomistic metaphysics.

Copleston, F. C., *Aquinas.* Harmondsworth, England. Clearly written, relatively simple introduction to Aquinas; contains a useful bibliography.

Moody, Ernest A., *The Logic of William of Ockham.* New York, 1935. A scholarly study of Ockham and medieval logic and metaphysics; difficult but searching and persuasive.

SEVENTEENTH CENTURY

Aaron, R. I., *John Locke.* London, 1955.

Balz, A. G. A., *Descartes and the Modern Mind.* New Haven, 1952.

Beck, Leslie J., *The Method of Descartes.* Oxford, 1952.

Descartes, René, *Selections,* edited by R. M. Eaton. New York, 1927.

Hampshire, Stuart, *Spinoza.* Harmondsworth, England, 1953. An excellent exposition and criticism with a general concluding chapter on the nature of metaphysics.

Jackson, Reginald, "Locke's Distinction Between Primary and Secondary Qualities." *Mind,* Vol. 37 (1929), 56–76. Explains and criticizes Locke's contrast between ideas in the mind and qualities in things and between primary and secondary qualities.

Leibniz, Gottfried Wilhelm von, *The Monadology and Other Philosophical Writings,* Robert Latta, ed. London, 1948.

Leibniz, Gottfried Wilhelm von, *New Essays Concerning Human Understanding,* translated, with notes, by Alfred G. Langley, 3d ed. La Salle, Ill., 1949. A standard edition containing some very interesting but little-known essays by Leibniz in an appendix.

Locke, John, *An Essay Concerning Human Understanding.* New York, 1958.

Whitehead, A. N., *Science and the Modern World.* New York, 1926. Early chapters contain a brilliant critique of seventeenth-century and eighteenth-century science and philosophy.

EIGHTEENTH CENTURY

Kant, Immanuel, *Prolegomena to Any Future Metaphysics,* Lewis White Beck, ed. New York, 1951. A good introductory text by a leading authority on Kant; contains a useful bibliography.

Smith, N. K., *Immanuel Kant's Critique of Pure Reason,* 2d ed. New York, 1933. A classic translation of Kant's major work.

Warnock, G. J., *Berkeley.* Harmondsworth, England, 1953. An exceptionally good introductory work; highly critical of some of Berkeley's leading arguments.

METAPHYSICS SINCE KANT

Ayer, A. J., ed., *Logical Positivism.* Glencoe, Ill., 1959. A collection of the most important and influential papers in the logical positivist movement; includes an unusually complete bibliography covering the entire range of twentieth-century analytic philosophy.

Findlay, J. N., *Hegel.* London, 1958. A very clearheaded sympathetic exposition of Hegel's system.

Passmore, John, *A Hundred Years of Philosophy.* London, 1957. A useful and very well written survey of philosophy since 1860; emphasizes metaphysics and theory of knowledge in English-speaking countries.

Royce, Josiah, *The Spirit of Modern Philosophy.* Boston and New York, 1926. Lectures on post-Kantian philosophy, especially nineteenth-century German idealism.

White, Morton, *Toward Reunion in Philosophy.* Cambridge, Mass., 1956. A forceful and lively essay on main issues in recent British and American philosophy; Part I is devoted to recent metaphysics.

Wolheim, Richard, *F. H. Bradley.* Harmondsworth, England, 1959. An introduction to Bradley; quite critical but closely and skillfully argued.

ROGER HANCOCK

METAPHYSICS, NATURE OF. Almost everything in metaphysics is controversial, and it is therefore not surprising that there is little agreement among those who call themselves metaphysicians about what precisely it is that they are attempting. In beginning a discussion of the nature and validation of metaphysical arguments and theories, the best course we can follow is to list some of the standing preoccupations and ambitions of metaphysicians. For this purpose we need to make the assumption that there is a distinct class of metaphysical philosophers, a class into which such thinkers as Plato, Aquinas, Descartes, Spinoza, and Hegel would fall and. from which purely critical or analytic philosophers like the later G. E. Moore would be excluded. It has to be admitted, however, that the line between metaphysical and nonmetaphysical philosophy is exceedingly hard to draw, for many metaphysicians from Plato on have been expert in the supposedly nonmetaphysical pursuit of analyzing or clarifying ideas, while few self-styled analysts have contrived to stick to pure analysis without the open or covert advocacy of a metaphysical point of view.

Setting these difficulties aside, we may note three main features of metaphysics as traditionally practiced. First, metaphysicians have constantly aspired to say what there is in the world or to determine the real nature of things; they have been preoccupied, that is, with the concepts of existence and reality. Their interest in these concepts springs from a double source: from the reflection that the surface show of things often misrepresents them, with the result that we are set the task of determining their real as opposed to their apparent constitution, and from the need to specify what ultimately different kinds of things there are in the world, a need which presses itself on our attention when we wonder whether, for example, minds or numbers are independent existents. The first of these tasks might seem to belong to the scientist rather than the philosopher, for science, too, makes constant use of the distinction between the apparent and the real; we shall indicate in the next paragraph why metaphysicians have not been ready to accept this proposal for lightening their labors.

Second, metaphysics has been commonly presented as the most fundamental and also the most comprehensive of inquiries. It claims to be fundamental because questions about what there is or about the ultimate nature of things underlie all particular inquiries. If you are to assess the results of mathematical investigations, for instance, you need to determine the ontological status of mathematical objects, and according to the theory, this is a task for the metaphysician. The claim of metaphysics to be comprehensive is more difficult to justify. One possible line of support for it, followed by Aristotle, is found in the reflection that questions about existence and reality, along with those about potential and actual being and about causation which are also raised by metaphysicians, cut across the boundaries of particular sciences and arise in connection with every sort of subject matter. Thus, metaphysics is comprehensive just because of its extreme generality. But there is another way in which the claim to comprehensiveness has been advanced. It has been customary to say that whereas sciences like physics and mathematics are departmental studies each of which deals only with a part or particular aspect of reality, metaphysics, by contrast, is concerned with the world as a whole. This explains why philosophers have been unwilling to accept the suggestion that scientists might be left to determine the true nature of things. A scientific theory purports to explain, for example, the real constitution of matter or the fundamental mechanisms of the human body but not to draw the distinction between appearance and reality in an entirely general way, not to tell us, to give an instance, whether matter is the ultimate reality, as materialists suppose, or whether it is itself a manifestation of spirit, as Hegel tried to argue.

This contrast between metaphysics and the particular sciences is sometimes developed in yet another way, again, as will be apparent, to the great advantage of metaphysics. It is said that inquiries in the individual sciences are carried out under assumptions which it is the business of metaphysics to make explicit and either to justify or to correct. Metaphysics, by contrast, proceeds without assumptions and is thus fully self-critical where the particular sciences are in part credulous. This line of argument goes back to Plato, who tells us that mathematicians postulate the existence of "odd and even numbers" and "three kinds of angles," and implies that these "hypotheses," taken as "starting points" or "bases" in mathematics, could find their justification and thus lose their hypothetical character in the comprehensive "synoptic" study which Plato called dialectic. The dialectician is a man who leaves nothing unquestioned, and just because of this the results of all other inquiries must be seen as no more than provisional; they await ratification or correction from the dialectician. The apparently arbitrary and obviously vague character of this suggestion has not prevented its having a continued appeal to philosophers. Even today, we sometimes hear it said that we need not be unduly disturbed by, for example, the findings of physiologists and psychologists, since the proponents of these sciences work under assumptions which it is the business of philosophers to uncover and correct in the light of their knowledge of the whole man (for an argument on these lines see J. S. Haldane, *The Philosophy of a Biologist,* Oxford, 1935).

If metaphysics is to make good its claim to be uniquely self-critical, its propositions must be shown to be exempt from intellectual challenge as those of no other study are. Descartes, in fact, tried to offer such a demonstration. He argued first that common-sense assertions like "There is a table under the window" were in every case open to theoretical doubt: However much I seemed to perceive a table, it might be that I was under perceptual illusion or was dreaming. Next, he maintained that even propositions whose truth appeared to be evident, such as those of mathematics, could not be accepted as necessarily in order. An evil demon could be deceiving me into thinking them clear and distinct when they did not really deserve this description. But matters were different when we came to the fundamental metaphysical truth "I think, therefore I am." This truth was such that in the very act of doubting it, one reaffirms it. To doubt is to think, and in thinking that I might not exist, I make clear that I do. Hence, there is at least one truth about whose correctness I could not be in error, and this is a truth of metaphysics. But Descartes was not content to stop at this point. He went on to argue that if I, a being with obvious limitations, certainly exist, then just as certainly there exists a perfect being whose nature is such that he would never deceive me into thinking that true which is not in fact so, once I have satisfied myself that it is by the test of clear and distinct perception. The effect of this move was to provide a guarantee for the findings of the sciences, which were otherwise open to "hyperbolical" doubt. We could henceforth be assured on metaphysical grounds that whatever was clearly and distinctly perceived was true. As for the propositions of metaphysics itself, their truth was guaranteed by their connection with the *cogito,* which, as we have seen, could not be intelligibly questioned.

The interest of these arguments for our present purpose lies not in their details but in the basic claims they involve. The propositions of metaphysics, according to Descartes, are intellectually impregnable, and in this respect they contrast not only with the beliefs of common sense but also with the pronouncements of the sciences, at least when these are considered apart from their metaphysical guarantee. But from where can they derive their unique certainty? The only possible answer is from their being the products of reason when that faculty is put to work in the fullest and freest way. The result will be that metaphysics is not only the most fundamental of studies; it is also one which relies for its results on the efforts of reason alone.

Metaphysics and the supersensible. Thus far, we have observed three main features in the projected science of metaphysics. It claims to tell us what really exists or what the real nature of things is, it claims to be fundamental and comprehensive in a way in which no individual science is, and it claims to reach conclusions which are intellectually impregnable and thus possess a unique kind of certainty. Now, many critics of metaphysics have suggested that these claims could be justified only if metaphysics were a factual science providing us, on the strength of rational insight, with knowledge of things or aspects of reality which lie beyond the range of the senses. Nor is this view without support from practicing metaphysicians. Plato drew a contrast between "things seen" and "things unseen" and argued that only things unseen were proper objects of knowledge. From his time on there was a standing tendency to identify the province of the metaphysician with what was vaguely called the supersensible, or the realm of the intellect. Aristotle, for example, distinguished between sensible and insensible substance and assigned the investigation of insensible substance to "first philosophy," or metaphysics. Medieval and early modern philosophers thought of God, the "being of beings," as an entity without bodily extension or shape and for that reason considered him outside the province of the empirical sciences. More generally, it was widely believed that behind the phenomena which present themselves in everyday experience, there lie realities whose existence and properties can be established only by use of the intellect and which can hence be described as noumena, or intelligible objects. In this view, the proper concern of metaphysics was to give us news about noumena.

From the eighteenth century on much ingenuity has been displayed in showing the untenability of this position. The idea that there might be a science which was at once factual and purely intellectual drew its firmest support from the example of mathematics. Hume suggested, however, that the concern of the mathematician was not with matters of fact and existence but solely with "relations of ideas": His aim was only to make explicit what was already implicit in the premises from which he started. The propositions of mathematics were indeed necessary truths, but by the same token they gave no information about the world. If an inquiry was to pronounce on matters of fact, its method must be empirical, not conceptual, and this meant that its results could not possibly claim to be intellectually impregnable, for anything established on the strength of experience might need to be amended or even withdrawn in the light of further experience. There were no final empirical truths.

A natural reply to this is to argue that even if every factual inquiry must begin from experience, it need not necessarily terminate there. Why should not the metaphysician argue from the characteristics of things sensible to the existence and the nature of things supersensible, as, for instance, Aquinas and Locke thought they could? Kant was much concerned about the proper answer to this question. He allowed—and here he showed more sympathy with metaphysicians than empiricists then or now—that such concepts as cause and substance, which figure prominently in supposed inferences from the phenomenal to the noumenal, have a necessary character; in Kant's terminology they are a priori, as opposed to empirical, concepts. But he denied as stoutly as Hume that they can therefore be used to carry us beyond the range of possible experience. The question "What brought that about?" is a necessary question, one which we cannot rationally refuse to ask, but the answer to such questions must always be sought within experience. If we try, as, for example, Descartes did, to maintain that there must be a First Cause, a necessary being entirely different from the contingent things with which we are familiar, we cease to attach any clear meaning to the concept of cause, for, as Hume saw, it is an essential part of the idea of cause that a cause precede its effect. We can talk about causes as long as we remain within the sphere of the temporal; once we step outside it, the concept loses its determinate character. And what is true of cause here is also true of substance and other metaphysical notions. We can give sense to the concept of substance if we understand it as the permanent which persists through change, but if we eliminate the reference to time, we are left with no more than the logical notion of that which is always a subject and never a predicate, an idea which in its pure form is too indeterminate to be put to metaphysical or, indeed, any other use.

Another attack on metaphysics as the supposed science of intelligible reality was made by the logical positivists. It is a mark of those propositions which belong to accredited sciences like mechanics or genetics, they argued, that we know in principle how to test them; we can see what difference it makes that they are true rather than false. But if a metaphysician comes along and tells us that what really exists is not trees or tables but, say, monads, what tests can we apply to determine the truth of his statement, and what difference does it make if it is true? By definition monads are entities which could never be encountered within experience, nor is their presence supposed to have particular empirical consequences like that of electrons and similar unobservables postulated by natural scientists. Thus, a metaphysical thesis will be compatible with any state of affairs whatsoever, just as the propositions of logic and mathematics are. But if this is so, how can it possibly be maintained that metaphysics gives us information about the world, even the unseen world? The news which it purports to bring can only be news from nowhere.

These highly general refutations of a particular conception of metaphysics have seldom been found convincing by metaphysicians. One reason for this is that they fail to come to grips with individual metaphysical arguments, for example, with the *cogito*. Another is that they appear to prejudge the case against this sort of metaphysics. Why, for example, should it be supposed that a metaphysical thesis must make an empirical difference? Another cause of their failure to carry conviction, however, may be found in the fact that many metaphysicians have worked with a different concept of their subject, one which does not involve it in the claim that it provides information or rivals the empirical sciences. This conception will be considered below.

Metaphysics without ontology. We have already seen that metaphysicians have wanted to say both that their propositions possess a peculiar certainty and that they are significant as a purely analytic proposition is not. In Kantian terminology they pretend to the status of synthetic a priori truths. Now, many critics of metaphysics have made the assumption that a proposition could be synthetic a priori only if it at once stated a truth of fact and was established by conceptual means alone, a combination which they regard as impossible. Facts must be established empirically; pure thinking can lead to the knowledge only of analytic truths. But if we look at Kant's alleged synthetic a priori judgments, particularly those which he called principles of the understanding, we see that they make no claim to state facts, even very general facts. A principle like the principle of causality is not a very wide empirical truth, mysteriously known in a nonempirical way; it is, on the contrary, the expression of a rule of procedure which serves to tell us not what properties things have but how to interpret them. Kant supposed that principles of this sort had a special sort of necessity, though they did not logically compel; they owed this, he thought, to the fact that they are prescribed by the human mind as principles specifying what is to count as objective in our experience. Thus, we take it to be a feature of what is objectively there that no quality is present except in a determinate degree, that nothing ever goes entirely out of existence (all change is transformation), that nothing happens except for a reason, and so on.

Kant himself intended this doctrine to have limited application. He thought of the principles of the understanding as prescribing the form of the phenomenal world which we know by means of the senses and investigate in the natural sciences. In his view there were other aspects of experience, in particular the activities of the moral agent, in regard to which they had no legislative force. But it is possible to think of an extension of Kant's doctrine and imagine a set of principles which would prescribe the form not just of one department of experience, but of experience as a whole. A set of principles of this kind would tell us how to organize the data of our experience in such a way that we could give a unitary account of them; it would thus help us make sense of the scheme of things entire. Possessed of concepts of this sort, we could hope to resolve the apparent inconsistencies of science and common sense, together with the more serious conflicts between science and religion and science and morality. We should then be masters of an over-all point of view enabling us to see things synoptically or have a set of ideas which would allow us to differentiate the real nature of the universe from its merely superficial aspects. We should, in short, be in possession of a metaphysics.

There can be no doubt that many of the classical metaphysical systems can be thought of as conforming to this schema. In the system of Aristotle, for instance, the key concepts are teleological, and their articulation is to be found in the doctrine of the four causes. It is axiomatic in Aristotle's thought that everything serves a purpose; Aristotle's ambition is to find the point of each phenomenon and thus specify its place in the articulation of the whole. He attempted to carry through his program not only at the biological level, the most obvious source of the concepts involved, but also above and below it—in moral, political, and social life, on the one hand, and in physical science, on the other. His success in these spheres is unequal, but that does not affect the general character of the enterprise.

The popular philosophy of materialism, again, can be seen as an attempt to make sense of the world as a whole on the basis of a distinctive set of first principles. The primary thought of the materialist might be expressed in the axiom that there is nothing which cannot be satisfactorily explained in natural terms; belief not merely in the competence, but also in the omnicompetence, of natural science is a prominent item in his credo. The materialist sees the world as a vast mechanism; whatever happens is the result of natural causes, and all other phenomena must be assessed and understood on this basis. Thus, the phenomena that characterize religious and moral life can be taken in psychological and social terms as things whose causes are ultimately natural, though scarcely in the terms favored by those who engage in them. Religion, as Freud said, is an illusion but not an unintelligible illusion; science can account for it, as it can account for everything else.

Finally, Hegelianism made a conscious attempt to produce a metaphysics which constitutes an over-all reading of experience. The central concept here is the concept of spirit; it is alleged that everything can be understood in terms of this concept once we take account of the fact that spirit cannot fulfill its potentialities except by working on and against something not itself—in Hegel's peculiar language, "its own other." Thus, we can make sense of the existence of a world of nature in this system; it is there to subserve the purposes of spirit. We can make sense of the social world, too, for many of the characteristics of mind are intelligible only when people are aware of one another and know that others are aware of them. Self-respect and self-contempt would be cases in point.

Each of the systems mentioned could be said to rest on a basic idea or intuition, an idea articulated in a series of concepts taken as definitions of reality and applied, with greater or less success, to the whole range of experience. To appreciate the force of such a system, we need to grasp the basic idea as well as understand the articulated concepts; we have to see the world as the metaphysician in question saw it. The deviser of a metaphysical theory thus becomes a man with a vision of the scheme of things entire. It is important to add, however, that he is not merely a man with a vision, in which case he would be indistinguishable from a philosophical poet. He needs to work his vision out in a theory; he needs to argue his case both by adducing those facts which immediately support it and by explaining those which on the face of things do not.

It seems clear that most of the standard claims for metaphysics can be understood with this account of the matter. Since the first principles of a metaphysical system have prescriptive force, exactly as Kant's principles of the understanding had in regard to the world of nature, they can be properly thought to compel every rational thinker.

Their certainty is not the certainty of logic, and yet it exceeds that of any individual statement of fact, for facts are descried only within a framework which these principles provide. Again, even if a system of this kind does not tell us precisely what there is, it nevertheless pronounces on the real character of the world as opposed to the surface show. According to the materialist, for instance, there seem to be features of experience which transcend the natural realm, but in the end it turns out that this is not so. Everything, including men's thoughts and actions, can be accounted for satisfactorily in natural terms. That a scheme of this kind is comprehensive, wider than that of any particular science, goes without saying; that it is fundamental because it is concerned with the coordination of ways of thinking in widely differing spheres is also obvious. True, there is no straightforward counterpart in this type of theory for the criticism by metaphysics of the assumptions of the particular sciences: Metaphysics not being a source of knowledge in itself, it cannot be claimed that other studies are dependent on it as, say, chemistry is dependent on physics. But this circumstance will not prevent this type of metaphysician from putting his own construction on the results of the sciences, as the example of Hegelianism shows. He may have no warrant to question such results, but all the same he may insist on interpreting them in his own way when he offers his reading of experience as a whole. Hegel was doubtless too brusque in his treatment of Newton and Dalton, but it does not follow that the whole project for a philosophical treatment of natural phenomena is a mistake.

Argument and truth in metaphysics. If metaphysics answers the description given above, a description which would fit many if not quite all of the best-known metaphysical systems, two questions immediately arise. First, we may be asked what sort of a study metaphysics is in this account. Is it a priori or empirical, and to what sorts of argument does it appeal? Second, there is the question of what criteria to use in choosing among metaphysical systems. Seeing that many systems are possible, are there any objective ways of deciding that one system embodies the true or the proper way to look at the world?

Argument. The answer to the first query is that metaphysics, according to this account, is neither a priori nor empirical, though it makes constant use of both deductive and probable reasoning. A metaphysician is concerned to advocate, articulate, and apply a set of basic interpretative principles, categorical principles we might call them, and principles of this kind cannot be grounded in either conceptual considerations or an appeal to empirical fact. They cannot be supported conceptually since no contradiction is involved in disputing them; they cannot be deduced from facts since they claim to apply with unrestricted validity, no matter what data turn up in experience. They may indeed be suggested by experience and commonly are, but that is not to say that they can be shown to be acceptable or unacceptable by simple empirical methods. Apart from anything else there are no absolutely neutral data to which we can appeal when supporting or attacking a metaphysical theory. For though it is the case that every metaphysician has the duty of explaining all the facts as he sees them, he also has the privilege of being able to decide

what really is to count as fact. To see the importance of this we have only to reflect on the different views of religious phenomena taken by materialists and their opponents.

However, though it is true that a metaphysical theory on this account can be established neither deductively nor inductively, deductive and inductive argument both bulk large in metaphysical discussion. Like any other thinker the metaphysician is much concerned with consequences and consistency. He often wants to make the point that since p is true and p implies q; which in turn implies r, we are logically committed to r or to contending that since q is false and p implies q, p must also be false. The very fact that a metaphysician has a theory to put forward means that he must be preoccupied with the logical connections between the concepts which constitute his system. To say this, however, is not to deny his preoccupation with fact or with probable arguments. Unlike an empirical scientist he establishes no new facts, but all the same he has a double interest in fact. First, he is concerned, more than any specialized inquirer, to see similarities in widely different areas of fact, a process which is relevant to both the formulation and the application of his theory and which involves him in much reasoning by analogy. Second, he needs to pay constant attention to the state of factual knowledge in working out and pressing home his central insight. He promises, after all, to make sense of all the data of experience, and he must consequently take continuous account of these data. The legend that metaphysicians are indifferent to fact has no foundation; on the contrary, they have a primary interest in facts of all sorts even though they do not originate any factual propositions. The extent to which advances in cybernetics have been discussed in recent years by philosophers interested in the truth of materialism affords an apt and striking illustration of this point.

Truth. We saw that one charge made against metaphysics as a doctrine of what there is was that no decisive considerations can be adduced either for or against such a theory; the monads of Leibniz and the Forms of Plato make no empirical difference. In this respect are things any better in our revised form of metaphysics? It must be confessed that the initial appearance is not favorable. We have emphasized that the first principles of such a system are neither analytic nor empirical; the temptation to conclude that they must accordingly be no more than arbitrary prescriptions, representing a point of view taken up for no good reasons, is strong. And though we have also urged that metaphysicians of this sort have a special interest in fact, the force of that contention is considerably weakened by the admission that they claim the right to decide for themselves what really is fact. If we arm them with this veto—and it is hard to see how they could be refused it—the question of metaphysical truth seems wholly intractable.

It could be, however, that we are setting an impossible standard for metaphysics in requiring it to possess a decision procedure as clear-cut as those of mathematics and the natural sciences. One reason that we can get a straight answer about the acceptability of a theory in physics is that physics works on principles which it does not question (such as that every natural happening will have a sufficient natural explanation). In metaphysics, by contrast, we are concerned with the comparison and assessment of precisely this type of principle. As the widest and most general of all forms of thinking, metaphysics can appeal to no fixed criteria beyond itself except to the requirements of internal consistency which any theory must satisfy. Nor is it true that every reputable branch of knowledge possesses obvious and easily applicable decision procedures. If, for example, we compare metaphysics with history instead of physics, we may begin to see that there are areas of study where dispute and disagreement play a prominent part and which still can claim to proffer understanding and enlightenment. Once we pass beyond the mere ascertaining of fact, there are many histories written from many points of view and resting on many judgments about what is historically important; it is not really possible to hope for a final decision about which, if any, is correct or even about the relative merits of any two equally sophisticated interpretations. However, we do not conclude from this that history is a pointless pursuit which rational men would do well to avoid. We realize that a study like history can enlarge the mind and educate the understanding even when it does not add to the sum of public knowledge.

A comparison with metaphysics which is in some respects even closer is provided if we consider the interpretation of a literary text. The data which the literary critic confronts—I am thinking of someone who offers a reading of a controversial literary work like *Hamlet* or *Faust*—are "harder" than in the case of metaphysics, but this does not prevent the appearance of a wide variety of conflicting theories. And it happens that there are no accepted criteria for deciding among the various theories; all that each critic can do, in the last resort, is explain his way of looking at the text, marshal the points in its favor, and invite the reader to test the matter for himself. But we need not conclude from this that it will be a matter of luck or, perhaps, of psychology which theory will win the reader's approval. At the end of the day, he can be entirely convinced of the authenticity of one particular reading, and he can be persuaded that it offers more enlightenment, covers the central points more impressively, and does better justice to the evidence than its rivals. He may not be able to produce knock-down grounds in favor of his choice, but that is not to say that he has made it for no reason at all.

Metaphysical argument is like literary argument in that it reaches no apparent end; it is like it again in terminating, insofar as it ever does terminate, in an insight which is more personal than public. The old dream of a demonstrated metaphysics whose propositions were even more certain than those of mathematics could scarcely be further from realization. But it would be wrong on that account to think that the concepts of truth and falsity have no application in metaphysics. At the lowest estimate we can describe one system of metaphysics as more illuminating than another. We must, however, decide for ourselves what is really illuminating and what is not. As in the case of the humanities in general, we cannot just learn the truth from another.

Contemporary antimetaphysics. Theories which profess to deal with "the world as a whole," however they are meant to be taken, are today more often objects of suspicion than of interest, thanks to the influence of G. E.

Moore and the later work of Wittgenstein. Moore himself never attacked metaphysics explicitly, and indeed his early work, both in logic and in moral philosophy, showed pronounced metaphysical leanings of a generally Platonic kind. But the "Defence of Common Sense" with which he came to be most prominently associated was evolved as a counterblast to views put forward by contemporary metaphysical philosophers, views which, as Moore saw them, could be maintained only by someone prepared to disregard what he evidently knew to be true. When F. H. Bradley, for instance, argued that time is not real, Moore thought this an absurd paradox since the reality of time is taken for granted in any statement containing a temporal expression. If time is not real, it cannot be true that yesterday was Friday or that I had my breakfast before leaving for work. Moore's procedure here, which is to call the metaphysician's bluff by reminding him of what in an off-duty moment he will himself acknowledge that he knows, was generalized by some of his followers into an all-round exposé of metaphysics, which they represented as necessarily consisting of paradoxes and evident falsehoods. For this purpose the thesis that everything is material did not differ from its rival that everything is spirit; both were, when taken seriously, obviously false. There might be a point in maintaining such a thesis (it could be a revealing paradox, according to John Wisdom, or serve a deep-seated psychological purpose, according to Morris Lazerowitz), but in no sense could it express what was really the case.

Moore and his followers assume here that there can be only one correct description of a situation and that in matters like dating or temporal precedence it is known to all of us. It is not obvious that this view is correct, for it could be, as Bradley thought, that a description which was valid and serviceable at the common-sense level would need to be superseded when wider considerations were taken into account. One way of putting Bradley's view is to say that metaphysics claims to offer a conceptual scheme in terms of which we can give a description of the world which is ultimate and comprehensive but that it also recognizes the existence of many subordinate and more limited schemes, each of which has its point in the characterization of appearances. The Bradleian doctrine of degrees of truth and reality is obviously relevant here, and it cannot be said that Moore gives it very serious consideration. But even if this point had to be granted, the respectability of metaphysics might still be in doubt, for the whole notion of an ultimate description of the world is itself suspect thanks to the work of Wittgenstein.

According to Wittgenstein, a principal source of philosophical error has been the idea that the primary function of language is to describe. The truth is, rather, that we engage in many different "language games," each of which serves its own purpose and each of which is authentic at its own level. There can be no question of ruling any such game out of court; the fact that it is played is sufficient evidence that it is appropriate. Nor are different sets of language users rivals; it could not be said, for instance, that physics gives a truer picture of the world than common sense or that the naivetés of everyday moral language are corrected by the psychologist. If we keep these diverse languages apart, we see that each has its own point and utility. The idea of a finally correct language which would embrace and replace them all is clearly the height of absurdity, and, hence, metaphysics in its revised form is no more acceptable than was metaphysics in the shape of news from nowhere.

But this analysis, too, is built on questionable assumptions. First, is it really clear that language games or areas of linguistic activity are as distinct as Wittgenstein says they are? The point is by no means clear as far as the language games of science and common sense are concerned, for most scientists and many plain men think that the scientific account of the physical world gives a truer picture of it than that embodied in the ordinary man's everyday beliefs. Nor can we agree without further argument with the thesis that sufficient authentication is found for a language game when we note that it is played. There are, after all, games and games. In a form of game much played in the ancient world, elaborate formulas to appease the god of the sea were devised by those about to embark. As a result, a certain way of talking commanded a wide use and approval. But could that fact alone be invoked to show that it was legitimate? Surely, we should want to object that however much such language was used, its use could not be legitimate if in fact there was no god of the sea or if he exercised no influence on whether seafarers reached their destinations safely. To do this, however, is to make the propriety of a language game subject to the tenability of the factual assumptions on which it rests. Although this is not to maintain that the only use of language is to describe (which would be absurd), it is to claim a certain priority for the language game in which we say how things are.

Metaphysics as we have expounded it is concerned with resolving conceptual conflicts by finding a way of speaking which will enable us to express the true nature of the world. If we possess such a way of speaking, we have a yardstick by which to measure the ultimate tenability, as opposed to the immediate use, of particular language games—the languages of religion, science, law, and so on. It is not self-evident that each of these is in order as it is, and though the fact that they are constantly used and understood is enough to show that they serve some purpose, it does not in itself show that they are suited for the purposes which those who use them have in mind. These games are indeed played, but they could, for all that, be played on false pretenses. To decide whether they are, we must have recourse to metaphysics.

Metaphysics as analysis. Even if the foregoing account of the nature of metaphysics were accepted as generally unobjectionable, there are many philosophers who would deny that it covers everything that metaphysicians have attempted or are attempting to do. In particular, it fails to accommodate an activity pursued by many contemporary analytic and linguistic philosophers which has a clear affinity with the work of some of the classical metaphysicians. The classical metaphysicians were led to ask what there is partly because of puzzles about the status of numbers and qualities. Plato had produced arguments to show that these must be independently real, and Aristotle elaborated the doctrine of categories as an answer to them. Now, there are plainly parallels to this controversy in contemporary philosophy, both in the discussions among logicians about names and descriptions (which revive the ancient dispute about the relative priority of universals and particulars) and in the arguments about the relation of the mind and body which have recently been so prominent in British and American philosophy. What is notable about these issues, as opposed to those mentioned above, is that matters of fact appear to have no relevance to their solution. If we can solve them at all, we can solve them only by thinking.

This contrast is both genuine and important; there certainly are philosophical activities which are traditionally connected with metaphysics and which cannot be subsumed either under the schema given above or under that which it was meant to replace. These activities are in essence logical or analytic, and insofar as it is confined to them, metaphysics is indistinguishable from analysis. But there is no reason to confine metaphysics to such inquiries. That metaphysicians have been speculative theorists as well as ontologists in the restricted modern sense is almost too obvious to need mention; to decide, as some commentators do, that the speculation can be set aside as regrettable and the ontology played up is at best arbitrary. Nor is it true that we can make an entirely clear-cut distinction between the two. If we look at recent work on the mind–body problem, for instance, we see that much of it is indeed logical in a wide sense of that word but that considerations of substance also come in, for example, when we discuss the nature of consciousness or of thought bearing in mind the properties and possibilities of thinking machines. An all-important motive which impels men to persist with these questions is the need to take account once more of the claims of materialism against a background in which new scientific and technical discoveries seem to lend increased support to those claims. However fascinating logical problems may be, interest in them cannot be long sustained without some external stimulus. It is such a stimulus that metaphysics of the broad kind argued for above may be expected to provide.

Bibliography

CLASSICAL WORKS

Plato, *Republic,* A. D. Lindsay, ed. New York, 1958. See especially VI–VII.

Plato, *Sophist,* in F. M. Cornford, ed., *Plato's Theory of Knowledge.* London, 1935. See especially 253 ff.

Aristotle, *Works,* Vol. VIII, *Metaphysics,* J. A. Smith and W. D. Ross, eds. Oxford, 1928. See especially Γ 1–2; E 1; Λ 1–2, 6. Compare also W. D. Ross, *Aristotle's Metaphysics,* Vol. I. Oxford, 1924. See pp. lxxvii ff.

Descartes, René, *Meditations on First Philosophy* (1641), in *The Philosophical Works of Descartes,* translated by E. S. Haldane and G. R. T. Ross, 2 vols. New York, 1931. See especially "Reply to Second Objections."

Wolff, Christian, *Philosophia Prima Sive Ontologia.* Frankfurt, 1729; J. Ecole, ed., Hildesheim, 1962.

Baumgarten, A. G., *Metaphysica.* Halle, 1739.

Hume, David, *A Treatise of Human Nature* (1739–1740), L. A. Selby-Bigge, ed. Oxford, 1888; 1941.

Hume, David, *Enquiry Concerning Human Understanding.* London, 1748. There are many modern editions.

Kant, Immanuel, *An Inquiry Into the Distinctness of the Principles of Natural Theology and Morals* (1764), in L. W. Beck, ed., *Kant's Critique of Practical Reason.* Chicago, 1949.

Kant, Immanuel, "Inaugural Dissertation" (1770), in *Kant's Inaugural Dissertation and Early Writings on Space,* translated by J. Handyside. Chicago, 1929.

Kant, Immanuel, *Critique of Pure Reason* (1781), translated by N. Kemp Smith. London, 1929.

Kant, Immanuel, *Prolegomena to Every Future Metaphysics* (1783), translated by P. G. Lucas. Manchester, 1953.

Hegel, Georg Friedrich, *Phenomenology of Mind* (1807), translated by J. B. Baillie, 2d ed. New York, 1931.

Bradley, F. H., *Appearance and Reality,* Oxford, 1893. See especially the Preface and Introduction.

MODERN WORKS

Ayer, A. J., *Language, Truth and Logic.* London, 1936. Lively brief account of the logical positivist criticism of metaphysics. See also the Introduction to the second edition (1945) for replies to objections.

Broad, C. D., "Critical and Speculative Philosophy," in J. H. Muirhead, ed., *Contemporary British Philosophy,* Vol. I. London, 1924. An influential article.

Carnap, Rudolf, *Philosophy and Logical Syntax.* London, 1935.

Carnap, Rudolf, "The Elimination of Metaphysics Through Logical Analysis of Language," in A. J. Ayer, ed., *Logical Positivism.* Glencoe, Ill., 1959. An important and influential article; originally published in 1932.

Collingwood, R. G., *An Essay on Metaphysics.* Oxford, 1940. Written in reaction to Ayer but also of independent interest.

Emmet, D. M., *The Nature of Metaphysical Thinking.* London, 1945.

Lazerowitz, Morris, *The Structure of Metaphysics.* London, 1955. Mainly influenced by Moore.

Moore, G. E., "The Conception of Reality," in his *Philosophical Studies.* London, 1922. Sharp criticism of Bradley.

Moore, G. E., *Some Main Problems of Philosophy.* London, 1953. Expounds at length the doctrine of "A Defence of Common Sense"; written in 1911.

Moore, G. E., "A Defence of Common Sense," in his *Philosophical Papers.* London, 1959.

Pears, D. F., ed., *The Nature of Metaphysics.* London, 1957. A series of modern discussions of metaphysics.

Walsh, W. H., *Metaphysics.* London, 1963.

Wittgenstein, Ludwig, *Tractatus Logico-philosophicus.* London, 1922.

Wittgenstein, Ludwig, *Philosophical Investigations.* Oxford, 1953.

Wittgenstein, Ludwig, *The Blue and Brown Books: Preliminary Studies for the Philosophical Investigations.* Oxford, 1958.

W. H. WALSH

METEMPSYCHOSIS. See REINCARNATION.

METHOD IN PHILOSOPHY. See PHILOSOPHY.

METHODOLOGY. See SCIENTIFIC METHOD.

MEYERSON, ÉMILE (1859–1933), French epistemologist and philosopher of science, was born in Lublin, Poland (at that time Russia). He was educated in Germany where, after completing his classical studies, he studied chemistry under Robert Wilhelm Bunsen. In 1882 he settled in Paris; following a disappointing experience with industrial chemistry, he served as foreign editor of the Havas news agency and later as director of the Jewish Colonization Association for Europe and Asia Minor. After World War I he became a naturalized French citizen.

Meyerson never held an official teaching position. But a group of philosophers and other scholars, attracted by his celebrated erudition, formed an eager and attentive audience. He was especially well-versed in the history of the sciences (chiefly, but not exclusively, the physicochemical sciences) from their origins to their most recent developments. His command of language, his clarity of thought, and his extraordinary capacity for work served him well. Both his writings and his person gave an impression of great robustness—"solid as a Roman wall," as André Lalande once remarked.

Meyerson's philosophy was offered not as a philosophy of nature but as a "philosophy of the intellect." He set himself the tasks of disentangling the principles that govern the advance of thought and of extracting from reason the kernel that constitutes the *intellectus ipse.* This search for a priori, he held, this new critique of pure reason, should not itself be conducted in an a priori manner. It had to proceed empirically—not directly, through a psychological analysis of the activity of thought, but indirectly, through reflection on the products of thought. These products may be true or false, so long as they bear witness to a serious effort of the intellect. From this point of view, the history of the sciences provides unique documentation. Thus it is that, of Meyerson's three major works, the first (*Identité et réalité,* Paris, 1908) is almost exclusively epistemological; but in the second, *De l'Explication dans les sciences* ("Explanation in the Sciences," 2 vols., Paris, 1921), and especially in the third, *Du Cheminement de la pensée* ("The Ways of Thought," 3 vols., Paris, 1931), the scope is widened to encompass the whole of knowledge. In the last two works it is shown that the mind works always and everywhere in the same fashion, and this catholicity of reason proves that it does indeed include a portion that is a priori.

Each of Meyerson's works begins with an attempt to dispel the positivist bias that weighed so heavily on his years of apprenticeship. Science requires the concept of thing; science searches for explanation. It is not content simply to bind together by laws the phenomena given us in sense experience in order only to predict and control them. Science tends to dissolve the qualitative datum—but only to reach behind it for a more lasting and more objective, substantial *real.* Science not only seeks to know the how, but also to understand the why. Its aim is speculative. Its theories are not merely edifices built of laws; they claim to reveal to us the innermost causes of things. Realism and causalism are two fundamental tendencies that, taken together, govern the entire activity of the scientist. For the scientist, "phenomenism" and "legalism," when he submits to them, are only provisional stages. His ambition is to get to the bottom of things, his ultimate purpose is an ontological one.

In what does explanation consist? It is at this point that the Meyersonian theory proper begins. In every domain, whether it be philosophy, science, or everyday life, to explain is to identify. Causality is nothing but a form of logical identity. We understand a change only when it becomes evident to us that, at bottom, nothing has happened, that the entire effect was already present in the cause—or at least that the change has been reduced to the minimum, to a simple displacement. The old adage *causa aequat effectum,* mechanistic theories, and chemical equations all manifest this identifying tendency. As the

Eleatic paradoxes attest, we are troubled even by change of place and by the mere passage of time. Reason is satisfied only to the degree that it succeeds in eliminating time. The principle of inertia, the reversibility of mechanical phenomena, the conservation of matter and energy, the permanence and immutability of the ultimate elements, show in what direction we insistently turn as we strive for intelligibility.

Yet in a world thus rigidly set, there still remains a qualitative diversity which is the source of new attempts at identification: the elimination of "secondary qualities," the explanation of apparent differences in terms of combinations of quite similar elements from which all but geometrical properties have been removed. Thus the world is fully intelligible to us only if we succeed in assimilating it, in the final analysis, to homogeneous space. Being, like becoming, tends to turn into its opposite when our reason seeks to explain it.

But reality resists this persistent will to identify. Carnot's principle defeats any hope of eliminating time. It proves that the irreversibility of the course of time is not a subjective illusion, that the future is not interchangeable with the past, in brief, that something really does happen. Furthermore, in denying sense qualities any place in the physical world, mechanism has not thereby made them disappear. The heterogeneity of the data of sense exists unexplained and indeed inexplicable from a mechanistic point of view. In addition, atomic discontinuity puts an obstacle in the way of geometrization. Reality rejects the identity to which reason would reduce it. The real is only partly intelligible; it contains elements that are irreducible, and hence irrational. It is in fact the presence of these irrational elements, contradicting the rationalist idealism of the philosophers, which can serve to define the real in opposition to the structures erected by our thought. Thus while reason may well move from success to success in the quest for identity that essentially motivates its activities, it can never win a definitive victory. In the end, it is condemned to defeat.

Indeed, how could matters be otherwise? There is something odd and almost absurd about this endeavor of reason, for its complete success would betoken its ultimate failure. To explain reality fully would amount precisely to denying it as real, to dissolving it into a motionless and undifferentiated space, that is, into nothingness. A perfect explanation of the world would end up in acosmism. And the conflict would be met with again even if the object studied were only an ideal one, as in the case of mathematical speculation. Reasoning, even that which is apparently formal, is never tautological. Thought, at work, advances; it does not just repeat interminably that A is A. Meyerson came to emphasize more and more reason's need for something diverse to assimilate, and he tended to define reason not so much by its end, identity, as by its activity, identifying. Reason is thus essentially divided against itself. This is the epistemological paradox.

Meyerson later extended these views to other domains, from scientific reason to philosophical reason, from the modern physicist to primitive man and the medieval thinker; but they were first suggested to him by reflection upon classical science. Have the revolutions in physics served to confirm or contradict them? In *La Déduction relativiste* (Paris, 1925), Meyerson easily showed that relativity theory was inspired throughout by the same ideal of objectivization and geometrization. Like Parmenides' sphere or Descartes's world, Einstein's universe is resorbed into space. However, quantum physics, because it sets bounds to continuity and objectivity, contains something "unassimilable." Meyerson believed, nonetheless, that quantum theory, in the interpretation given it by the Copenhagen school, was a passing "aberration," and that as soon as the physicists recognized the possibility of doing so, they would hasten to return to traditional views—a conjecture which was in part subsequently verified.

If the detail is rich, the broad outlines of Meyerson's philosophy are simple and clear. It enjoyed great prestige about 1930. Since then, it has been somewhat overshadowed by the philosophy of the scientific theorists of the Copenhagen school, although Louis de Broglie retains the high estimate of it stated in his preface to Meyerson's *Essais*. Meyerson's philosophy has also been neglected because of the general shift of interest among contemporary philosophers from epistemological to existential problems.

Bibliography

Meyerson's writings include the small work *Réel et déterminisme dans la physique quantique* (Paris, 1933) and a posthumously published collection, *Essais* (Paris, 1936). An English translation of *Identité et réalité* by Kate Loewenberg appeared under the title *Identity and Reality* in London and New York in 1930.

See also André Lalande, "L'Épistémologie de M. Meyerson," in *Revue philosophique de la France et de l'étranger*, Vol. 96 (1922), 259–280; Léon Brunschvicg, "La Philosophie d'Émile Meyerson," in *Revue de métaphysique et de morale*, Vol. 33 (1926), 39–63; George Boas, *A Critical Analysis of the Philosophy of Émile Meyerson* (Baltimore, 1930); Jacob Loewenberg, "Meyerson's Critique of Pure Reason," in *Philosophical Review*, Vol. 41 (1932); Albert E. Blumberg, "Émile Meyerson's Critique of Positivism," in *Monist*, Vol. 42 (1932), 60–79; André Metz, *Meyerson, une nouvelle philosophie de la connaissance*, 2d ed. (Paris, 1934); Thomas R. Kelly, *Explanation and Reality in the Philosophy of Émile Meyerson* (Princeton, N.J., 1937), with bibliography; *Bulletin de la Société française de philosophie* (April, 1961), an issue devoted to Meyerson in celebration of the centenary of his birth.

ROBERT BLANCHÉ
Translated by *Albert E. Blumberg*

MICHAEL SCOT. See SCOT, MICHAEL.

MICHELS, ROBERT (1876–1936), German–Italian political sociologist, was born in Cologne but spent most of his life as a university teacher and writer in Italy. Michels was neither an acute nor a rigorous social theorist. He indiscriminately coupled different forms of social groupings and collectivities; he attempted no close examination of the different types of authority; and his method is too descriptive and anecdotal to be theoretically interesting. Subsequent work on political parties and on the forms and functions of power, influence, leadership, bureaucracy, and ruling elites in modern societies are far more adequate and sophisticated than those of Michels, but his many detailed accounts of working-class and socialist organizations in the late nineteenth and early twentieth centuries and his studies of socialist thought in his own day are still worth reading. Michels also wrote voluminously on problems of political sociology, on the theoretical aspects of Marxism, and on such diverse topics as political economy, social ethics, imperialism and colonialism, and Italian fascism. After the advent of Mussolini to power, Michels—unlike Gaetano Mosca—did not manifest overt opposition to the methods or the policies of the Fascist regime. He continued to travel widely abroad, lecturing on a variety of subjects. He appears to have attracted neither the friendly nor the hostile attention of the government, but references in some of his later writings suggest that he was not ill-disposed toward the regime.

Michels' most famous and important book was *Zur Soziologie des Parteiwesens in der modernen Demokratie* (*Political Parties*). Like Vilfredo Pareto and Mosca, Michels was concerned to demolish "some of the facile and superficial illusions which trouble science and lead the masses astray" (*Political Parties*, p. 404). He subscribed fully to Mosca's doctrine of the political class, and in *Political Parties* he tried to demonstrate, by painstaking accumulation of examples from the history and practice of European working-class and socialist parties and organizations, that a small minority always rules and the large majority is ruled. He propounded the famous "iron law of oligarchy" that "society cannot exist without a dominant class"; that "oligarchy is, as it were, the preordained form of the common life of great social aggregates"; and that "class struggles consist merely of struggles between successively dominant minorities" (*ibid.*, pp. 389–390). Michels sought to explode the "democratic illusion" that democracy consists in a high degree of equality between all members of an association or collectivity and in the full and constant participation of the rank and file in the direction or policy-making of the collectivity. (Michels regarded representation and therefore parliamentarianism as being not truly democratic but oligarchic.)

Michels, unlike Mosca, was strongly influenced by Marx. He largely accepted the Marxist conception of social class and the class struggle, and spoke of the struggle between the proletariat and bourgeoisie much as Marx did. He differed from Marx in holding that the proletariat produces its own oligarchy, or ruling elite, in its trade unions, parties, and other organizations, and he argued that class struggle always puts another ruling minority in place of the older ruling class. Or, more exactly, there is produced a proletarian oligarchy or aristocracy which comes to resemble and to be absorbed by the older ruling minority. Thus, Michels rejected Pareto's doctrine of the circulation of elites on the ground that one ruling class is rarely superseded by another; rather, he held, new ruling elites tend to coalesce with the existing ruling group, often with important effects on the character and attitudes of the ruling group they enter. This view is not incompatible with the main elements of Marx's theory of political and social change, but it is incompatible with the belief that any social struggle can culminate in the achievement of democracy.

Michels was also influenced by the strain of nineteenth-century social thinking stemming from Saint-Simon that emphasized the essential role of organization and bureaucracy, and the functions of leadership, administration, and management as constituting a base for authority or power. He insisted that "the principal cause of oligarchy in the democratic parties is to be found in the technical indispensability of leadership" (*ibid.*, p. 400) and that "social wealth cannot be satisfactorily administered in any other manner than by the creation of extensive bureaucracy. . . . In this way, we are led by an inexorable logic to the flat denial of a state without classes. The administration of an immeasurably large capital, above all when this capital is collective property, confers upon the administrator influence at least equal to that possessed by the private owner of capital" (*ibid.*, p. 380).

In *Political Parties* Michels was not antidemocratic in the sense that he employed the iron law of oligarchy as a support for authoritarian or dictatorial forms of government. His view is that although the ideals of democracy can never be realized, they should forever be pursued. Democracy counts most not as a goal to be attained but as an ideal to inspire and suffuse political struggle. All societies and social movements are strongly oligarchical, bureaucratic, and authoritarian, but they are more or less so: Persistence in the search for democracy helps to ensure that they will be less oligarchical rather than more.

Works by Michels

Zur Soziologie des Parteiwesens in der modernen Demokratie. Leipzig, 1911. Translated by Eden and Cedar Paul as *Political Parties: A Sociological Study of the Oligarchical Tendencies of Modern Democracy.* New York, 1915; reprinted, New York, 1959.
   Probleme der Sozialphilosophie. Leipzig and Berlin, 1914.
   La teoria di Carlo Marx sulla miseria crescente e le sue origine. Turin, 1922.
   Sozialismus und Fascismus in Italien. Munich, 1925.
   Storia critica del movimento socialista italiano dagli inizi fino al 1911. Florence, 1926.
   Corso di sociologia politica. Milan, 1927.
   Introduzione alla storia delle dottrine economiche e politiche. Bologna, 1932.
   First Lectures in Political Sociology, translated with an introduction by Alfred de Grazia. Ann Arbor, Mich., 1949.

Works on Michels

There are discussions of Michels' theories of oligarchy in H. Stuart Hughes, *Consciousness and Society* (New York, 1958); James Burnham, *The Machiavellians* (London, 1943); and Thomas B. Bottomore, *Elites and Society* (London, 1964).

P. H. PARTRIDGE

MICROCOSM. See MACROCOSM AND MICROCOSM.

MIDDLETON, CONYERS (1683–1750), English historian and clergyman. Middleton entered Trinity College, Cambridge, in 1700. He took orders in the Church of England and became a fellow of his college, but he had to resign his fellowship at the time of his first marriage in 1710. He held various livings but never obtained any considerable preferment in the church. The course of Middleton's life unfortunately provides several grounds for questioning his integrity and ingenuousness.

Middleton's first major publication was *A Letter from*

Rome, showing an exact conformity between Popery and Paganism (London, 1729). His theme was certainly not entirely original. It can, for instance, be traced to Part IV of Hobbes's *Leviathan* (1651), and there is even some suspicion of plagiarism at the expense of a little known French treatise, *Conformité des cérémonies modernes avec les anciennes* (Leiden, 1667). What was remarkable was the force and skill with which Middleton traced the relics of the worship of Vesta in the cult of the Virgin and deployed passages from the Christian Fathers that excoriated as heathen such practices as the erecting of votive tablets or the use of holy water.

Daniel Waterland, in his *Scripture Vindicated* (London, 1731–1732), had attacked the deist Matthew Tindal's *Christianity as Old as the Creation* (London, 1730). In 1731 Middleton published an anonymous *Letter to Waterland*, in which he urged that it was unwise to insist on the literal truth of every sentence in the Bible, and in particular ridiculed bits of the book of Genesis. His authorship was discovered, and during the ensuing uproar the public orator of Cambridge was heard to cry for a book-burning. Middleton next wrote a very profitable *Life of Cicero;* in this instance the charge of plagiarism seems to have been borne out.

After writing an *Introductory Discourse* (1747), Middleton published *A Free Enquiry into the Miraculous Powers, which are supposed to have subsisted in the Christian Church from the Earliest Ages, through several successive Centuries* (London, 1748). Coincidentally, David Hume's first *Enquiry*, containing the section "Of Miracles," which later became notorious, was published in the same year. Many years later, in *My Own Life* (London, 1777), Hume confessed his chagrin: "On my return from Italy, I had the mortification to find all England in a ferment, on account of Dr. Middleton's *Free Enquiry*, while my performance was entirely overlooked and neglected."

There was every reason to compare the two books, for the tendency of both was to undermine belief in the miraculous. But whereas Hume was raising methodological difficulties about the possibility of providing adequate historical proof of such occurrences, especially in a religious context, Middleton was concerned primarily with the historical evidence actually available. His argument was addressed in the first instance to those, including the great majority of educated Protestants, who believed both that the occurrence of miracles was a guarantee of religious truth and that the age of miracles was now past. This position was obviously precarious, for where precisely was the crucial dividing line to be drawn? Middleton directed his onslaught at this weak point. It was, as Leslie Stephen said, "incomparably the most effective of the whole deist controversy." Although Middleton himself never ventured to question the miracle stories of the New Testament, he attacked the credibility of similar accounts in the early Christian church. In a series of damaging quotations, he displayed the credulity of the Fathers, including some of the most respected, such as St. Augustine, and even cited passages in which others seem to have been deliberately approving pious frauds. The impact of Middleton's attack would have been smaller on a position that was less inherently precarious. Arguments of this kind would not have been effective, for instance, with Protestant "enthusiasts" such as the Wesleys or with the Roman Catholics, who insisted that the age of miracles was not past. As a historian, Middleton displayed the faults characteristic of his period, particularly the naive view that stories must be either wholly and straightforwardly true or else just lies. His importance lies in the contributions he made toward undermining the arbitrary barriers between secular and sacred history.

Bibliography

Apart from the works of Middleton mentioned in the text, see Sir Leslie Stephen's article on Middleton in the *Dictionary of National Biography* (London and New York, 1909), Vol. XIII, pp. 343–348, as well as his *English Thought in the Eighteenth Century* (3d ed., London, 1902), Ch. 4.

ANTONY FLEW

MIDDLETON, RICHARD OF. See RICHARD OF MEDIAVILLA.

MIKHAILOVSKY, NICHOLAS KONSTANTINO-VICH (1842–1904), Russian philosopher, social thinker, and literary critic, was a theorist of Russian Populism and an exponent of a form of positivism first advanced by his contemporary, Peter Lavrov.

Mikhailovsky was born near Meshchovsk, Russia, the son of a landowner of moderate means. After his parents' death, he was enrolled in the St. Petersburg Mining Institute in 1856. Expelled in 1861 for leading student protests against the government, he became a writer on social and literary topics for progressive St. Petersburg reviews. From 1869 to 1884 he edited *Otechestvennye Zapiski* ("Annals of the Fatherland"), at that time the chief organ of Russian radicalism. Mikhailovsky was periodically banished from the capital by the tsarist authorities, but he sufficiently tempered the expression of his views to avoid imprisonment and permanent exile. He remained an influential radical spokesman until his death in St. Petersburg.

Mikhailovsky's humanistic, democratic outlook took shape early in his career, under the influence of John Stuart Mill, Pierre Proudhon, and the Russian thinkers Alexander Herzen and Vissarion Belinsky. The most direct and extensive philosophical influence on Mikhailovsky was that of Lavrov, whose combination of an antimetaphysical positivism with an emphasis on the "subjective," moral demands of the human consciousness provided Mikhailovsky with his basic philosophical orientation. In his numerous philosophical essays, chief of which is *Chto Takoye Progress?* ("What Is Progress?," 1869–1870), Mikhailovsky strongly developed the ethical foundation and the individualism of this orientation and defended it against the views of Spencer, Comte, Darwin, and later against those of Marx and Engels.

In opposition to Spencer, Mikhailovsky argued that human progress cannot be understood "objectively," or nonteleologically, and that in general the phenomena of man's historical and social life can only be approached through a "subjective method" which takes into account the feelings and aims of the individual and makes moral evaluations. Mikhailovsky protested the stunting of the individual by the division of labor in modern industrial society, maintaining that the goal of progress should be a more homogeneous social order in which each individual would be able to develop his diverse abilities comprehensively and harmoniously. Against the social Darwinists he maintained that in human society a struggle for survival is neither inevitable nor desirable, and he asserted that as the division of labor was eliminated, economic competition would yield to cooperation. During the last quarter of the nineteenth century, Mikhailovsky was a leading exponent of Russian Populism—a form of agrarian socialism that emphasized the *obshchina,* or peasant village commune.

Like Comte, Mikhailovsky viewed historical progress as occurring in three stages. Adhering to the "subjective method," however, he distinguished these stages by reference to their teleology. In the objectively anthropocentric stage man sees himself as the end or purpose of nature. In the eccentric stage he still finds ends in nature but no longer regards himself as their unique focus. In the subjectively anthropocentric stage man finally realizes that ends or purposes do not inhere in nature but are produced by him; the individual dispenses with supernaturalism and metaphysics of every sort and relies on his own active energies for the promotion of his moral ideals.

Mikhailovsky's doctrines, and in particular his emphasis on the autonomous moral individual, brought him into sharp conflict with nascent Russian Marxism. In the 1890s his critiques of Marxism were extensively attacked by both Plekhanov and Lenin.

Works by Mikhailovsky

Polnoye Sobraniye Sochineni ("Complete Works"), E. Kolosov, ed., 4th ed., 10 vols. St. Petersburg, 1906–1914.
Selections from "What Is Progress?" and from other essays in *Russian Philosophy,* James M. Edie, James P. Scanlan, Mary-Barbara Zeldin, and George L. Kline, eds., 3 vols. Chicago, 1965.

Works on Mikhailovsky

Billington, James H., *Mikhailovsky and Russian Populism.* Oxford, 1958.
Zenkovsky, V. V., *Istoriya Russkoy Filosofii,* 2 vols. Paris, 1948–1950. Translated by George L. Kline as *A History of Russian Philosophy,* 2 vols. New York and London, 1953.

JAMES P. SCANLAN

MIKI KIYOSHI (1897–1945), Japanese philosopher of history and leading intellectual in the stormy years before World War II. Miki was born in Isseimura, Hyogo Prefecture. He was a student of Nishida Kitarō and of Hatano Seiichi at Kyoto University. He developed an early interest in the philosophy of history and studied in Germany (1922–1924) under Heinrich Rickert and Martin Heidegger, absorbing also some socialist ideas. In 1927 he accepted a chair of philosophy at Hōsei University, Tokyo, but he had been rejected as a teacher by his alma mater for dubious reasons—he had a love affair with a widow, in his day a more than sufficient reason to be excluded from a state university. Feeling resentment, and moved by the social climate of the time, he became Japan's first spokesman for philosophical Marxism. His essays on historical materialism (1927–1930) created a stir in academic circles

and in the general public. His Marxism, however, was strongly colored by Heidegger's *Anthropologie* and by Pascal's conception of man, two views he had studied as a youth. His later works are not at all Marxist. In 1930 he was briefly imprisoned for contributing money to leftist causes; as a result he had to give up his teaching career and make a living as a social critic. During the crucial years before World War II, as ultranationalism became pervasive, Miki at first held to liberal principles without compromise. In 1936, he joined the Shōwa Research Society, which was led by Prince Konoe Fumimaru and which strove to moderate though not to oppose the mounting militarist trend. As the Shōwa became more and more nationalistic, Miki, though liberal at heart, had to compromise. For opposing Japan's entry into World War II and for aiding prosecuted leftists, he was returned to prison toward the war's end, and there he died.

Miki's best works are *Rekishi tetsugaku* ("Philosophy of History," Tokyo, 1932) and *Kōsōryoku no ronri* ("The Logic of the Power of Imagination," Tokyo, 1939). In the first work Miki's starting-point is the subjective existential and sensible experience of life. From this he proceeds to formulate the structure of "history-in-the-making." Fundamental experience of life, he says, creates selfhood, the historical subject which is the only maker of history, since in selfhood there are not subjective and objective factors, but only lived experience. "The Logic of the Power of Imagination" reflects Miki's use of Kant's *Einbildungskraft* ("imaginative power") as it was revived by Heidegger and also reveals the evolution of Miki's thought away from the logos as social rationality that dominated the "Philosophy of History" and toward a major role for pathos, the subjective inspiration that in Japan led to ultranationalist feelings. Miki was perhaps hinting that rationality was losing ground to ultranationalist passion. At any rate, for Orientals, the logic of the imagination, with its creation of myths and of what Miki calls "forms" of technocultural systems, is said to have some advantages, such as artistic inventiveness and creativity, over conceptual knowledge and usual logic. Miki uses terms borrowed from his master Nishida, the originator of the Oriental "logic of field."

Bibliography

For works in Japanese, see *Miki Kiyoshi Choshaku-shū* ("Miki Kiyoshi's Collected Works"), 16 vols. (Tokyo, 1945–1951), and Miyagawa Tōru, *Miki Kiyoshi* (Tokyo, 1958). For works in English see Gino K. Piovesana, "Miki Kiyoshi: Representative Thinker of an Anguished Generation," in *Studies in Japanese Culture,* J. Roggendorf, ed. (Tokyo, 1963), pp. 141–161.

GINO K. PIOVESANA, S.J.

MILETUS, SCHOOL OF. See PRE-SOCRATIC PHILOSOPHY.

MILHAUD, GASTON (1858–1918), French philosopher, came to philosophy by way of mathematics, which he taught for nearly ten years in the *lycées* before becoming a professor of philosophy at the University of Montpellier. In 1909 he went to the University of Paris, where the chair of history of philosophy in its relationship to the sciences was created especially for him.

His courses on Cournot and Renouvier were published (*Études sur Cournot*, Paris, 1927; *La Philosophie de Charles Renouvier*, Paris, 1927). Under the influence of Paul Tannery, his works on the history of science were at first devoted to Greek science: *Leçons sur les origines de la science grecque* (Paris, 1893) and *Les Philosophes géomètres de la Grèce* (Paris, 1900). Later they were extended to include modern science. Examples are *Études sur la pensée scientifique chez les Grecs et chez les modernes* (Paris, 1906); *Nouvelles Études sur l'histoire de la pensée scientifique* (Paris, 1911); and *Descartes savant* (published posthumously, Paris, 1923).

Milhaud was both a historian and an epistemologist. With Henri Poincaré, Pierre Duhem, and Édouard Le Roy he belongs to that group of French scholars who around 1900, following the path opened for them by Émile Boutroux, denounced scientific dogmatism, using as a basis the precise analysis of past and contemporary examples in history of science. They emphasized the role of spiritual initiative, and thus the element of contingency, in the construction of scientific theories. Milhaud himself generally avoided the dangerous words *convention* and *commodité* used by Le Roy and Poincaré. He spoke, rather, of free creations, of the activity of the mind, and of the spontaneity of reason (*Le Rationnel*, Paris, 1898). In his thesis, *Essai sur les conditions et les limites de la certitude logique* (Paris, 1894), he maintained that certitude, which is founded on the principle of noncontradiction, is limited to the domain of pure mathematics. He believed that it was thus possible to establish a radical break between the realm of mathematical knowledge and the realm of knowledge of the real world.

However, almost immediately thereafter (2d ed., 1897), he regretted having shown himself to be too much the logician: "I see today that even in the extreme example of absolute rigor dreamed of by the mathematician, the living and dynamic identity of thinking always takes precedence over the static immobility of the principle of identity." The fundamental concepts and principles of all sciences result from rational decisions that simultaneously transcend both experience and logic, in the sense that they are not determined by either external or internal necessities. Positivism is, therefore, outmoded. A "fourth stage" consists of the liberation of thought from the obstacles imposed on it by the dogmatism of Comte (*Le Positivisme et le progrès de l'esprit*, Paris, 1902). Nonetheless, scientific contributions are not arbitrary, and they have a universal value, in that they have matured on a basis of fact and have gradually imposed themselves upon the mind as a network of relations in which logical exigencies are composed and harmonized with the demands of a practical and aesthetic order.

Bibliography

For selections from Milhaud, see R. Poirier, *Philosophes et savants français*, Vol. II, *La Philosophie de la science* (Paris, 1926), pp. 55–80. A. Nadal, "Gaston Milhaud," in *Revue d'histoire des sciences*, Vol. 12 (1959), 1–14, has a bibliography.

ROBERT BLANCHÉ

MILL, JAMES (1773–1836), Scottish philosopher, historian, and economist, was born in a village near Forfar, Scotland, the son of a shoemaker. He attended Montrose Academy and in 1790, with the help of his patron, Sir John Stuart, entered Edinburgh University, where he studied philosophy under Dugald Stewart. In 1794 he began a course of study in divinity and obtained a license to preach in 1798, but he never exercised the right. Indeed, before long he lost his belief in God, on grounds that were, according to his son, John Stuart Mill, "moral, still more than intellectual": to James Mill the world seemed too full of evil to have been created by an infinitely good being. In 1802 he set out for London to earn his living as a free-lance journalist. He contributed to the *Anti-Jacobin Review*, which is surprising in view of his later political opinions, and to other journals. He also edited two periodicals (the *Literary Journal* and the *St. James' Chronicle*) published by a bookseller called Baldwin, translated books, and did other literary hack work. In 1805 Mill married Harriet Burrow; they had nine children, John Stuart Mill being the eldest. In 1806 Mill began his *History of India*, with the avowed object of concentrating on social conditions and underlying social forces rather than on details of battles and the lives of rulers. This book, which was published in London in 1817 in three volumes, became the standard work on the subject and earned Mill a post with the East India Company.

In the meantime Mill had become a friend and disciple of Jeremy Bentham and soon emerged as one of the leaders of the growing utilitarian movement. Mill was more practical than Bentham, and although debarred by his office from active political agitation, he did much to define the policy of the group which became known as the "philosophical radicals," and which included David Ricardo, who was a member of Parliament as well as an economist; Joseph Hume, another M.P.; John Black, editor of the *Morning Chronicle*; J. R. McCulloch, editor of the *Scotsman*; George Grote, the historian; John Austin, the jurist; and others who were influential in various ways. The philosophical radicals exerted the kind of influence that the Fabian Society exerted on a later generation. Primarily intellectuals and theorists, they nevertheless proved to be a force that could not be ignored by practical politicians.

Writings. Mill's writings included contributions to William Allen's journal *The Philanthropist* and to the *Westminster Review*, the utilitarian journal launched by Bentham in 1824. He also wrote an influential series of articles for the supplement to the *Encyclopaedia Britannica*, which appeared between 1816 and 1823; these articles applied Benthamite principles to such subjects as government, education, liberty of the press, and colonies and expounded Bentham's views on his favorite topics, jurisprudence and prisons. In 1821 Mill published *Elements of Political Economy*, which owes more to Ricardo than to Bentham, in spite of Bentham's claim, "I was the spiritual father of Mill, and Mill the spiritual father of Ricardo." The *Fragment on Mackintosh*, in which Mill defended utilitarian ethical theory against Mackintosh's *Encyclopaedia Britannica* article on ethics, was privately printed in 1830 and issued publicly in 1835. Mill's most ambitious work, apart from the *History of India*, was his *Analysis of the Phenomena of the Human Mind*, which appeared in 1829.

Importance. Mill is important chiefly for his role as Bentham's lieutenant and for his influence on the philosophical radicals in general and his son John Stuart in particular. He was not an original thinker: there is little in his writings that cannot be found either in Bentham or in the forerunners of utilitarianism, such as David Hartley. His chief contributions to utilitarian theory are to be found in his *Britannica* articles on government and education and in his elaboration of Hartley's associationist psychology.

Political thought. Mill held that the greatest happiness of the greatest number is not necessarily attained by majority rule: it is conceivable that an enlightened and benevolent despot might secure it more efficiently than the ignorant masses. On Benthamite principles, however, the despot will not remain benevolent unless he has reason to associate his own happiness with that of others, and some constitutional machinery is necessary to ensure this. Consequently Mill advocated the extension of the franchise. Everyone need not vote, however, since husbands can be trusted to consider the interests of their wives and men over forty to be concerned about their sons. On the other hand, the interests of the owner of property may very well conflict with those of the propertyless. In general, Mill maintained that individuals rather than social classes should be represented. He did not doubt, however, that the poor would choose members of the middle classes to represent them.

Although the philosophical radicals identified themselves with the cause of the people, they were never revolutionaries. Mill would not have agreed with G. E. Moore that utilitarianism favors the preservation of the *status quo*, since the disadvantages of departing from custom are certain and the advantages are only problematical. Nevertheless, the hedonic calculus was bound to lead, at most, to a moderate, cautious, and constitutional radicalism. The true revolutionary needs to feel that his cause is wholly good and his opponents' cause wholly evil. If he is tough-minded, he will believe that the suffering of oppressors is itself a good; if he is tender-minded, he will believe that the oppressors themselves are the victims of the system and will benefit from the new regime no less than the oppressed. But it is central to utilitarian theory that interests clash and that the best that can be hoped for is a compromise in which the pluses in the hedonic calculus outnumber the minuses. Men are unlikely to die on the barricades for a few extra items on the credit side of the balance sheet.

Psychology. In the *Analysis of the Phenomena of the Human Mind*, Mill elaborated the associationist epistemology of Hartley and Hume. Sensations, he said, occur either "synchronously" (simultaneously) or successively. Sensations experienced synchronously give rise to synchronous ideas, and sensations experienced successively give rise to successive ideas. For example, the smell of a rose and the sight and touch of a rose are frequently synchronical; hence any one of these simple ideas is likely to call up the other. As a result we are aware, not of the sim-

ple ideas as such, but of a composite "cluster of ideas," that is, the idea of a rose. These clusters of ideas, Mill said, are called objects. Mill's nominalism thus seems to be different from that of Bentham, who regarded ideas of qualities as "fictions," obtained from the reality by abstraction. For Mill, simple ideas (or at least "sensations" or impressions) were the building blocks from which all else is constructed. However, he did agree with Bentham about the unreality of classes and universals in general.

Mill attempted to explain all mental phenomena in terms of association. Belief, for example, is either memory or expectation, both of which result from association. All belief in propositions (hence in testimony) arises from the association of words with their referents. To assent to a proposition is to associate both the subject and the predicate term with the same referent. All reasoning can be explained in the same way, as Hobbes had shown.

Associationism had enabled Hartley to bridge the awkward gap between ethical egoism and utilitarianism. What a man takes pleasure in depends largely on the associations he happens to have formed. It is therefore possible for him to associate his own pleasure with that of his fellows. In Mill's opinion, it is the task of the educator and the legislator to see that he does. For Hartley, however, the associations between our own pleasures and those of others are not entirely factitious. Pleasure is not entirely subjective: although you take pleasure in a thing as the result of your past conditioning, it is an objective fact that if you had been conditioned to like a different kind of thing, your total pleasure would have been either greater or less. Certain sources of pleasure cut us off from other kinds of pleasure: the pleasure of wife-beating, for example, is incompatible with many other domestic pleasures. Hartley went on to erect an elaborate "ladder of pleasures," with the pleasures of benevolence very near the top because of their ramified associations with many other kinds of pleasure. Mill did not follow him the whole way: he was content to say that there are many associations between our own pleasure and that of our fellows, partly because of the facts of social life to which Hobbes had called attention and partly because of the pleasure we all take in being praised by others.

Education. Since the main task of the educator was, in Mill's view, to ensure that the pupil formed the right associations (the ones most conducive to his own happiness and to that of others), he advocated what has since been called the education of the whole man. The mind and character, he said, began to be formed at birth, or perhaps even at conception. When this fact was taken into account, Mill thought, Helvétius' claims that there were no bounds to what could be achieved by education and that "the whole of this great mass of mankind" was "equally susceptible of mental excellence" might not have been too extravagant. It followed that education included such matters as diet and, indeed, the manipulation of the whole environment. The great obstacle, Mill said, was that most men had too little to eat and too much work to do. Moreover, one important educational influence was the political system under which men lived.

Views of this kind have led modern progressive educators to play down the training of the intellect by means of the traditional mental disciplines. Mill's *Encyclopaedia Britannica* article on education suggests that he might have agreed with them. In this instance he seemed to have regarded education as being primarily moral training, and its main object as the inculcation of the virtues of temperance, fortitude, justice, and benevolence. On the other hand, he also said that intelligence is one of the virtues capable of cultivation; and, despite his associationism and his belief in the great importance of the largely unconscious effects of environment, he valued reasoning and skill in argumentation. It is odd, therefore, that he should have devoted a lengthy footnote to praise of a missionary scheme for a kind of synopsis of learning (including "a view of the solar system, a synopsis of geography, a collection of facts relative to natural objects, an abstract of general history and a compendium of ethics and morality") in the form of pithy aphorisms that were to be dictated to pupils who would, presumably, commit them to memory.

The education that Mill personally gave his eldest son was rigorously intellectual. According to John Stuart Mill's *Autobiography*, he was made to learn Greek at the age of three, and by the time he was eight he had read, among other authors, "the whole of Herodotus" and six dialogues of Plato, including the *Theaetetus*, which, he remarked with admirable restraint, "I venture to think would have been better omitted, as it was totally impossible I should understand it." He added, however,

Mine was not an education of cram. My father never permitted anything which I learnt to degenerate into a mere exercise of memory. He strove to make the understanding not only go along with every step of the teaching, but, if possible, precede it. Anything which could be found out by thinking I never was told, until I had exhausted my efforts to find it out for myself.

Bibliography

Bain, A., *James Mill*. London, 1882.
Halévy, Élie, *La Formation du radicalisme philosophique*. Paris, 1904. Translated by Mary Morris as *The Growth of Philosophic Radicalism*. London, 1928.
Mill, J. S., *Autobiography*. London, 1873.
Stephen, L., *The English Utilitarians*, 3 vols. London, 1900. Vol. II.

D. H. MONRO

MILL, JOHN STUART (1806–1873), English philosopher, economist, and administrator, was the most influential philosopher in the English-speaking world during the nineteenth century and is generally held to be one of the most profound and effective spokesmen for the liberal view of man and society. In the belief that men's opinions are the dominant influence on social and historical change, Mill tried to construct and to propagate a philosophical position which would be of positive assistance to the progress of scientific knowledge, individual freedom, and human happiness. Despite numerous flaws in his theories, he succeeded in providing an alternative to existing views on morals and politics and their foundations which was both specific and cohesive enough to give a markedly liberal tendency to social and political opinion,

and also sufficiently tolerant and inclusive to gain it access to an extraordinarily large and diverse public. Mill cannot be ranked among the greatest of pure philosophers, either for his originality or for his synthesizing power. His work in logic, however, broke new ground and gave a badly needed impetus to the study of the subject, while his reformulations of classical British empiricism and Benthamite utilitarianism gave these positions a relevance and continuing vitality which they would not otherwise have had.

Although Mill's views on economics will not be discussed in the present article, an excellent summary of them is contained in the article on Mill by F. Y. Edgeworth in Palgrave's *Dictionary of Political Economy*.

Life. John Stuart Mill was born in London, the son of James and Harriet Burrow Mill. Outwardly his life was not eventful. He was educated by his father and never attended school, although for a short time he read law with John Austin. In 1823 he became a clerk in the East India Company, where his father was a high official, and worked there until 1858. Eventually he became chief of his department, a post involving considerable administrative responsibility. In 1831 he was introduced to Harriet Taylor, the wife of a successful merchant and mother of several children. Friendship between Mill and Mrs. Taylor rapidly developed into deep though Platonic love, and for the next twenty years they saw each other constantly, despite the increasing social isolation this involved. Mill was convinced that Mrs. Taylor was a great genius: he discussed all of his work with her and attributed to her an enormous influence on his thought. Her husband died in 1849, and three years later she married Mill. In 1858, while the Mills were on a tour of France, Harriet died in Avignon. Mill bought a house nearby so that he could always be near her grave.

In 1857 Mill had written a brilliant defense of the East India Company for the parliamentary debate on renewal of the company's charter. When renewal was not granted, Mill retired, refusing an offer of a position in the government as an official for Indian affairs. In 1865 he was invited to stand for election to Parliament as an independent member for Westminster. He accepted, and although he refused to campaign, contribute to expenses, or defend his views, he won, and served until the next election, in 1868, when he was defeated. Thereafter he spent his time alternately in London and in Avignon, admired and sought after by many, accessible to few. He died after a very brief illness, attended by his wife's daughter Helen, who had looked after him since her mother's death.

Education and philosophical radicalism. Until 1826 Mill's thought was completely controlled by his father. James Mill gave him one of the most formidable educations on record, starting him on Greek at the age of three and Latin at eight. By the age of fourteen he had read most of the major Greek and Latin classics, had made a wide survey of history, and had done intensive work in logic and mathematics. He had also been prepared for acceptance of the central tenets of philosophical radicalism, a set of economic, political, and philosophical views shared by the group of reformers who regarded Jeremy Bentham and James Mill as their intellectual leaders. When at the age of fifteen Mill read Bentham's *Traité de législation,* it had the effect on him of a religious revelation. It crystallized his thoughts and fixed his aim in life—to be a reformer of the world. Guided by his father, he threw himself into the work of the radicals; he edited Bentham's manuscripts, conducted a discussion group, wrote letters to the press and articles critical of laws, judicial decisions, and parliamentary debates and actions.

Depression and change of views. Late in 1826, Mill suffered a sudden attack of intense depression, which lasted for many months. The attack led him to reconsider the doctrines in which he had been raised and to seek other than Benthamite sources of thought. He believed that his capacity for emotion had been unduly weakened by strenuous training in analytic thought, with the result that he could no longer care for anything at all. In the poetry of Wordsworth he found something of a cure—an education of the feelings that helped to balance the education of intellect given to him by his father. In 1828 he met Gustave d'Eichthal, a French follower of Saint-Simon, who sent him an early essay by Auguste Comte and a great deal of Saint-Simonian literature. He also met John Sterling, a disciple of Coleridge. Mill came to admire both the Saint-Simonians and the Coleridgeans, and he attempted to incorporate into his own thinking what he took to be sound in their doctrines. In 1829 he published nothing at all, but by the following year he had reached a philosophical position that seemed to him far more adequate than the older Benthamism. He never again changed his philosophical views so radically.

Comte and Saint-Simon. The historical standpoint of the Saint-Simonians, as well as the appreciation of the value of old institutions emphasized by Coleridge, impressed Mill as important additions to Benthamism, which, he thought, simply neglected such factors. He accepted the outlines of the Saint-Simonian–Comtian philosophy of history, and particularly its theory that in social change there is an alternation between "critical" periods, in which society destroys outmoded forms of life and tends toward disintegration, and "organic" periods, in which new forms of common life are evolved and social cohesion is re-established. He agreed also with the French view that in his own times society had come to the end of a critical period. From Coleridge he learned to think of the cultured class as the leader of opinion in a nation. He also came to believe that the problem he had in common with other intellectuals was that of assisting the world, and especially England, to emerge from the critical period and progress toward a new organic period. Unless this was done, he thought, the tendency toward disintegration might possibly grow too strong to be controlled.

Three important consequences followed from this. First, merely negative remarks upon institutions, laws, and political arrangements were no longer sufficient. Although much remained that needed to be changed, it was necessary now to replace what had been destroyed with something better. Second, the views of those who defended the old and outmoded could no longer be dismissed, in Benthamite fashion, as mere lies used in defense of vested interests. What is now outmoded must, at one stage of historical development, have served a valuable purpose;

otherwise it could not have survived. Those who defend it are those who see the good still in it; hence we must seek for the truth in their views, and not merely reject the falsity. The particular vice plaguing social thought is not the tendency to make mistakes of fact or faulty inferences from facts, but the great ease with which data can be overlooked: in a word, one-sidedness. Hence, if we are to obtain sound social views, our greatest need is for a complete survey of data, and this is possible to achieve only if we can appreciate the truth that our opponents have learned. For each man is naturally one-sided and can overcome this only by education and effort. Third, the tactics of a reformer must be adapted to the period in which he lives. In particular, during a critical period there is no point in promulgating an entire system: no one will listen, and the ideas will not serve to improve social cohesion. One must proceed cautiously, piecemeal, educating one's public as one goes. One must—especially in England, Mill held, where any appearance of system is abhorrent—confine oneself to particular issues, only slowly insinuating more general principles; or else work only from points on which there is general agreement, so as to avoid any shocking appearance of novelty.

This set of views dictated the program that Mill followed for the next twenty or more years. He did not abandon his early epistemology or ethical beliefs, but in developing them he always tried to emphasize their inclusiveness and their constructive power, rather than their critical and destructive powers. He refrained (with one major exception) from publishing a systematic account of his ideas, but wrote instead occasional essays dealing with fairly specific issues, in which he always tried to bring out the value of the books he was criticizing. (These tactics are largely responsible for the common view of Mill as a wavering, halfhearted, muddled thinker, appreciative of what others had to say but holding no clear opinions of his own.) He defended what he held to be sound views on philosophy, but he did not explicitly link these views together, except in his *System of Logic,* which was an entirely different case. Methods of investigation, Mill held, could be relatively neutral as regards political and moral opinion. Since these methods could be discovered from analysis of subjects like physical science, in which there was widespread agreement on results, there was a good chance of obtaining general agreement on the methods. The methods could thus serve as a cohesive, rather than a disruptive, social force.

The "System of Logic." Mill's *Logic* is in fact by no means neutral with regard to substantive issues. It is the first major installment of his comprehensive restatement of an empiricist and utilitarian position. It presents (sometimes, to be sure, only as "illustration") a fairly complete outline of what would now be called an "empiricist" epistemology, although Mill himself used "empiricist" in a deprecatory sense to mean "miscellaneous information," as contrasted with "scientific knowledge." It begins the attack on "intuitionism" which Mill carried on throughout his life, and it makes plain his belief that social planning and political action should rely primarily on scientific knowledge, not on authority, custom, revelation, or prescription. The *Logic* had a rapid and wide success. Adopted as a text first at Oxford and eventually at Cambridge, it was also read by many outside the universities, including workmen. Its success can be explained in part by its enormous superiority to any book then existing in the field, but credit must also be given to its clear and unmistakable relevance to social problems (and to religious questions: it was attacked as atheistic by some of its earliest reviewers).

With the publication of the *Logic*, Mill took a major step toward showing that the philosophy of experience, which had hitherto been identified primarily as a skeptical position, could offer at least as much in the way of constructive thinking as any other kind of view. His treatment of deductive inference was far more sympathetic to formal logic than that of previous empiricists; and by arguing that, with care, certainty could be attained even in inductive reasoning, he made it plain that empiricism was not committed to a Humean standpoint. Mill held that the philosophy of experience was more likely than any other to encourage the development of society along liberal lines. He therefore held that it was a matter of considerable importance to show that empiricism was a viable alternative to the less progressive views—notably, Scottish common-sense philosophy and German idealism—which were then dominant. The *Logic* succeeded in doing this.

The *Logic* is primarily a discussion of inferential knowledge and of the rules of inference. (The discussion of noninferential, or as Mill also called it, immediate or intuitive, knowledge belongs, in Mill's view, to metaphysics.) It contains six books. In the first two, Mill presented an empiricist theory of deductive inference, and, since mathematics is the chief deductive science, a discussion of the nature of the truth of mathematics, especially of its axioms. In Book III, Mill discussed induction, its grounds, its methods (the well-known four methods described in the article MILL'S METHODS OF INDUCTION in this encyclopedia), and its results. Book IV, entitled "Of Operations Subsidiary to Induction," contains chapters on observation and description, abstraction, naming, and classification. Book V is a discussion of fallacies. Book VI contains Mill's attempt to extend the methods of the physical sciences, as derived in Book III, to what were then called "moral sciences," that is, psychology and sociology. He argued for the possibility of a science of human nature and action, and assessed the value of the various methods for attaining it. He concluded with a chapter on the logic of morality, discussing primarily the relation between rules for actions and the factual statements which serve as their foundations.

No adequate summary of the contents of the *Logic* can be given here, but some of Mill's leading views may be indicated.

Deductive reasoning. Mill's argument in Book I of the *Logic* is intended to show the mistake of those who say that deductive inference (as found, for example, in the syllogism) is entirely useless because it involves a *petitio principii*, but at the same time to make it clear that deduction in general is never the source of new knowledge. Mill agreed that the conclusion of a syllogism may not contain more than is contained in the premises and that "no reasoning from generals to particulars can, as such, prove anything, since from a general principle we cannot infer any particulars, but those which the principle itself assumes as known."

It is useless to defend deduction by saying that it shows us what was "implicit" in our premises, unless we can go on to explain how something can be implicitly contained in what we already know. Mill's solution to this problem and his explanation of the value of rules of deduction rest on his view that "all inference is from particulars to particulars." When we reason "All men are mortal; Jones (not yet dead) is a man; so Jones is mortal," our real evidence for the assertion that Jones will die is our knowledge that Smith, Peters, Wilkins, and many other individuals who resemble Jones in many respects did die. We infer from their deaths to his. The general premise that all men are mortal is not itself our evidence. It is rather a note, or register, of the particular evidence on which the conclusion really depends, together with the prediction that what we have found in cases which we have already observed will also hold in similar cases not yet observed. The real inference, Mill thought, comes in constructing the general proposition on the basis of observation of particular cases. Deduction is to be understood as a way of interpreting the note that has been made of our previous inference. It is valuable because misinterpretation is very easy; but it no more gives us new information than do propositions that are true by definition. Such propositions, which Mill called "verbal," only pull out of a word what was previously put into it; and in the same way, a syllogism simply retrieves from a general proposition a particular one that was previously assumed to be in it. Since there is no real progress of thought in deduction, deductive inference is merely *apparent* inference. Induction is the only procedure that gives us nonverbal general propositions that go beyond what has actually been observed. Hence, only in induction do we make *real* inferences.

Mathematical knowledge is no exception to this. Taking geometry first, as the deductive science par excellence, Mill argued that its conclusions are necessary only in the sense that they necessarily follow from the premises from which they are deduced. But the premises themselves—ultimately, the axioms—are grounded on observation and are generalizations from what we have always experienced. (The definitions are in a somewhat different position, although an experiential element is involved in the belief that the entities they define, such as a geometric point or line, really exist.) That two straight lines do not enclose a surface is evident to us every time we look at two straight lines which intersect. The laws of psychology, operating on such experiential data, are sufficient to explain the production in us of the belief that such lines cannot possibly enclose a surface: hence we need not appeal to intuition or to some other nonexperiential source to explain the belief. Even the inconceivability of the denial of the axioms of geometry does not show, Mill argued, that they are not based on experience. For inconceivability is psychological, and the fact that we cannot think of something does not show that that thing cannot exist. Mill went on to offer an account of the way in which arithmetic and algebra are founded on experience. Here the essential point is that groups of four items, for example, may be rearranged into, or formed from, two groups of two items each, or a group of three items together with a group of one item. Seeing that this is always so, we come, through the operation of psychological laws, to believe that 2 + 2, or 3 + 1, *must* be the same as 4. Algebra is simply a more abstract extension of this sort of belief.

With these explanations Mill hoped to show how mathematics can yield propositions which are not merely verbal and which are certainly true of the world of experience, but which do not depend on any nonexperiential sources of knowledge. His account has never been accepted by philosophers as it stands, but there have been some attempts, among thinkers influenced by pragmatism, to work out a philosophy of mathematics along lines analogous to Mill's.

Inductive reasoning and scientific explanation. In Mill's view, induction is clearly of central importance, since it is the only possible source of substantive general propositions. While the details of his theory are complicated, its main lines may be concisely indicated. All methodical and critical induction rests on the fundamental principle of the uniformity of nature; namely, that what has happened once will happen again, if circumstances are sufficiently similar. Mill thought that this is a factual proposition which is itself derived by a primitive and natural process of induction: we first note a few limited regularities and predict that they will hold in the future. After our predictions come true, we spontaneously generalize, saying that since some events have been found to occur in repeating patterns, all events will be found to occur in repeating patterns. Belief in the uniformity of nature is thus derived from, and resolvable into, belief in the existence of less sweeping patterns of occurrences, or into particular causal laws. Mill defined "cause of a phenomenon" as "the antecedent, or concurrence of antecedents, on which it is invariably and unconditionally consequent." Like the "axiom" of the uniformity of nature, the principle that every occurrence has a cause is confirmed by all our experience. It is, in fact, simply a more precise way of stating the principle of the uniformity of nature. The hope of science is to formulate propositions about specific sequences of phenomena that can be relied on to the same degree as the law of causation. And the problem of methodical induction—which is the core of the problem of scientific reasoning—arises when it is discovered that the simplest method of induction (that of assembling positive instances of a sequence of phenomena and generalizing directly from them) often leads to general propositions which turn out to be false. We then seek ways of obtaining better results. The fundamental technique is to obtain evidence which will allow us to argue as follows: either A is the cause of a, or else there are some events which have no cause; and since we are certain that every event has a cause, we may be certain that A causes a.

According to Mill, there are four inductive methods: the method of agreement, the method of difference, the method of residues, and the method of concomitant variations. He also discussed a combination of the first two, calling it the joint method of agreement and difference. We use the first two methods in this way. If we find that A under circumstances BC is followed by abc, while under circumstances DE it is followed by ade, then A cannot be the cause either of bc or of de, since they sometimes do not occur when A occurs (and hence by the definition of "cause," cannot be caused by it). But a occurs under both sets of conditions; hence it could be the effect of A: this illustrates the method of agreement. To ascertain if something other than A might be the cause of a we use the method of difference. Will BC without A be followed by a? If not, we have so far confirmed our view that A causes a, for, in the cases we have examined, A is always followed by a and a never occurs without being preceded by A. Hence, by the definition of "cause," A is, so far as our evidence goes, the cause, or part of the cause, of a—or else there are events without any regular cause.

Science does not rely upon induction and experiment alone. It is only infrequently, Mill thought, that we will find genuine causal laws, that is, absolutely invariable sequences. More frequently we will find regularities which hold as far as a limited experience shows but which, we have reason to believe, might well not hold under quite different circumstances. These "empirical laws" are not to be considered basic laws of nature. Much of the practical application of science depends on them, but we cannot claim to have truly scientific knowledge until we can deduce empirical laws from basic laws of nature, showing why the combination of circumstances and laws renders inevitable the limitations within which the empirical laws hold. This makes clear the aim of science: to discover laws of nature and empirical laws, and to connect them, in a deductive system, in such a way as to show how the unrestricted laws would give rise to the regularities reported by the empirical laws. The various sciences are differentiated by the ways in which these two types of laws must be discovered and connected. In some sciences it is possible to discover laws of nature directly, deduce what the empirical laws must be, and then proceed to verify the deductions by checking against experimental data. In others, empirical laws are discovered first, and laws of nature are presented as hypotheses to explain them. These alleged laws of nature are then tested by deducing further empirical laws from them and testing these deductions. In any science, however, explanation comes to an end when laws of nature are reached: these are simply ultimate facts which are to be accepted.

The moral sciences. In the last book of the *Logic*, Mill argued that the phenomena of individual or social human life are no exception to the law of causation, and that consequently it must be possible to determine what are the natural laws of human behavior. He investigated the various modes of inquiry used in the different physical sciences to determine which are most suited to this sort of investigation, and he sketched an outline of what a completed science of man will be. Here as elsewhere, Mill thought that "however complex the phenomena, all their sequences and co-existences result from the laws of the separate elements." Since the separate elements in this instance are men, it is the basic laws of psychology from which, when the science is completed, all the laws and regularities concerning social phenomena must be deduced. Because of the enormous number of interacting elements, however, the complexity of social action is so great that no direct deduction of its regularities from basic psychological laws will be possible. In order to make this deduction it will be necessary first to construct a science of human character that will cover both the development of human character and the tendencies to action of different types of persons. From the laws of this science, which Mill called "ethology," we may hope eventually to get sociological laws. Even then, however, we will at best obtain statements of tendencies toward action, for the enormous number of factors involved in determining social action will not allow any more accurate predictions. Still, Mill held, "knowledge insufficient for prediction may be most valuable for guidance" in practical affairs. His chief interest lay in the possibility of obtaining scientific guidance for the direction of political decisions.

How far, then, had social science actually progressed? Mill thought that the basic laws of psychology were by then well established: they were the laws put forward by psychologists of the associationist school, among whom James Mill was pre-eminent. But the science of ethology, which John Stuart Mill had hoped to found himself, eluded him, and he gave up work on it shortly after he published the *System of Logic*. Although the absence of the intermediate laws that this science was designed to contribute made impossible the completion of sociology, Mill thought that at least one basic law of social change had been discovered and substantially proven: Auguste Comte's Law of Three Stages. One element, Mill argued, is more important than any other single factor in causing change in society: "This is the state of the speculative faculties of mankind, including the nature of the beliefs which . . . they have arrived at concerning themselves and the world by which they are surrounded. . . . the order of human progression in all respects will mainly depend on the order of progression in the intellectual convictions of mankind." Comte had shown that opinion always passes through the same three phases. Men first try to understand their universe in theological terms, then in metaphysical terms, and finally in scientific or, as he called them, positive terms. He had also shown that correlated with these three stages of opinion are types of social organization, which change as opinions change. This generalization, for Mill, was enormously important to our understanding of history and to our practical decisions, and up to that time it was the sole example of a well-founded sociological law. But Mill had high hopes that, with work, much progress could be made in constructing a social science; and he looked forward to a time when "no important branch of human affairs will be any longer abandoned to empiricism and unscientific surmise."

Epistemology and metaphysics. With respect to metaphysics in the contemporary sense of systematic knowledge transcending experience, Mill claimed to have none; and his epistemology consists largely of an account of experiential knowledge in which he intended to show why nothing beyond such knowledge is either possible or necessary. Mill presented an empiricist theory of our knowledge of the external world and of persons which is equally free of the skepticism of Hume and the theology of Berkeley. He consequently covered quite thoroughly a good deal of the ground that was gone over again in the discussions among empiricists and logical positivists in the second and third decades of the twentieth century.

Aim and method. Mill held that we must know some things intuitively, without inference, if we know anything at all, and he rejected skepticism as failing to make a relevant distinction between knowledge and doubt ("In denying all knowledge it denies none"). For if all knowledge were inferential, there would be no firm starting point for inference, and we should be led into a vicious infinite regress of premises. But because whatever can be known only by intuition is beyond the realm of rational discussion and experimental test, such intuitive knowledge is not easily distinguished from dogmatic opinion. Hence, it was Mill's aim to reduce to an absolute minimum the number of points at which intuitions are required. In the *Logic* he argued that no intuitions are necessary for mathematics, logic, or the procedures of natural science. In the *Examination of Sir William Hamilton's Philosophy* (1865), he pursued these questions further and explicitly took up the questions he had claimed to avoid in the earlier work—especially those concerning the foundations and nature of our knowledge of bodies and of minds.

Mill argued that we cannot tell by intuition or by introspection what we know intuitively. In order to distinguish what is directly given to consciousness from what is there as a result of inference, we must try to investigate the *origins* of the present contents of our minds. And again, this cannot be done directly, because the minds of infants are not accessible to us. Hence, Mill concluded, "the original elements can only come to light as a residual phenomena, by a previous study of the modes of generation of the mental facts which are confessedly not original." This is the psychological method that was originated by Locke. In using it, Mill attempted always to show how experience, acting in accordance with known laws of psychology, can explain all of our knowledge. If successful, such accounts make unnecessary (and therefore unwarranted, according to sound scientific methodology) any appeal to extraordinary faculties or to nonexperiential sources of knowledge.

Matter and mind. Mill attempted to explain our belief in the existence of matter and in the existence of our own and other minds by using a psychological method. The "Psychological Theory of the Belief in an External World," as he called it, postulates first, a mind capable of expectation (that is, of forming the conception of possible sensations which would be felt if certain conditions were realized), and second, the psychological laws of association. The claim is that these two factors, operating on experienced sensations and reminiscences of them, would generate not only a belief in an external world but, in addition, a belief that this belief was immediate or intuitive. Mill argued first that by an external object we mean only something that exists whether it is thought of or not, that stays the same even if the sensations we get from it change, and that is common to many observers in a way that sensations are not. One's concept of the external world, Mill said, is made up only to a slight degree, at any moment, of actual sensations, but to a large degree of possible sensations—not of what I am sensing, but of what I would sense *if* I moved, or turned my head, and so forth. These possible sensations, moreover, are thought of as being in groups: numbers of them would be present if I did this, numbers of others if I did that. Contrasted with any particular actual sensation, these groups of possible sensations seem stable and permanent. Moreover, there is not very much regularity in the sequences of our actual sensations, but there is considerable regularity associated in our minds with the groups of possible sensations: we will regularly get this sensation following that one if we do this following that. Hence ideas of cause and power, which (as had been argued in the *Logic*) depend on regularity and succession, are associated with the groups of possible sensations, and not with the actual sensations. At this stage we begin to refer any actual sensation to some group of possible sensations, and even to think of the possibilities as the cause or root of the actual sensation. The groups of possibilities, having permanence and causal power, are so different from fleeting actual sensations that they come to be thought of as being altogether different from them. When it finally becomes clear that the permanent possibilities are publicly observable, we have a concept answering in all respects to our definition of externality. Hence, Mill said, matter "may be defined, a Permanent Possibility of Sensation"; this is all, he held, that the plain man believes matter to be, and indeed, Mill shared this belief. Mill's aim, however, was not so much to defend the belief, as to account for it. And his account, which appeals only to psychological laws known to operate in many other kinds of cases, is simpler than accounts that would make the belief in matter an original part of our mind or an intuitive belief: consequently, he held, it is a better account.

Mill went on to ask how far a similar theory is adequate to account for mind. The theory will work, he thought, to a large extent, since we know nothing of our mind but its conscious manifestations, and since we know other minds only through inference from the similarities of other bodies and their actions to ours. But memory and expectation pose a fatal difficulty. They involve a belief in something beyond their own existence, and also the idea that I myself have had, or will have, the experience remembered or expected. Hence, if the mind is really a series of feelings, it is an extraordinary series, for it is one that is "aware of itself as a past and future." And if it is not this paradoxical series, it is something more than a series—but what that can be we have no idea. Mill concluded that at this point we are "face to face with that final inexplicability at which . . . we inevitably arrive when we reach ultimate facts," and all we can do is accept the facts as inexplicable. Hence, mind is not simply a permanent possibility of sensation.

Sensations and feelings—the data of experience—are, then, intuitively known; the fact of memory (a consequence of which Mill thought to be expectation) is also known directly; and the kind of link between past and present involved in memory (which Mill took to be the central inexplicable reality about the self) is known directly. Aside from these, there is only one additional inexplicable fact, and that is belief—the fact that there is a difference between contemplating, or imagining, or supposing, and actually believing. Mill rejected his father's analysis of belief, but could develop no adequate account of his own.

Ethics. According to Mill, agreement on moral beliefs is the most important single factor making for cohesion in society, and where it is lacking society cannot be unified. In his own times he saw and recognized the significance of the first serious widespread breakdown of belief in the Christian moral scheme. He thought it a task of first importance to provide an alternative view of morality which would be both acceptable to those who still clung, in part, to their older views, and capable of redirecting these older moral attitudes into newer paths. He was a utilitarian in ethics: that is, he held that an action is right if, and only if, it brings about a greater balance of good over bad consequences than any other act open to the agent, and he also believed that only pleasure is intrinsically good and only pain intrinsically bad. Bentham and James Mill had held a similar position, but John Stuart Mill modified their view in a number of ways, attempting always to show that utilitarianism need not be a narrow or selfish view and that it did not force one to rely, for social progress, purely on impersonal institutional arrangements and thereby compel one to leave human personality out of account. By arguing that the utilitarian could appreciate the wisdom embodied in traditional morality as well as offer rational criticism of it, and that he could also accept and account for the high value of self-sacrifice and could make the development and perfection of individual character the key obligation of morality, Mill sought to rebut the most frequent criticisms of the Benthamite morality and thereby make it more generally acceptable. Although his ethical writings (especially *Utilitarianism*) have been much criticized, they contain the most influential philosophical articulation of a liberal humanistic morality that was produced in the nineteenth century.

In his ethical writings, Mill pursued the attack on intuitionism which was so constant a feature of his other work. This issue is especially important with regard to moral problems. Intuitionism, he said in the *Autobiography*, is "the great intellectual support of false doctrines and bad institutions" because it enables "every inveterate belief and every intense feeling . . . to dispense with the obligation of justifying itself by reason. . . . There never was such an instrument devised for consecrating all deep-seated prejudices." The intuitionists supposed, Mill believed, that only their view could account for (1) the uniqueness of moral judgments, (2) the rapidity with which the plain man passes moral judgments, and (3) the authority to be given to common-sense moral judgments. To the first point, Mill answered with the theory that moral feelings may have unique properties, just as water has, and yet may still be derived, by a chemical compounding process, from simpler elements which do not have those properties. Hence, so far there is no need to say that these feelings are caused by unique intuitions. To the second point he replied that rapidity of judgment may be due to habit and training as well as to a faculty of intuition. And with regard to the third point, which is the crucial one, he argued that the utilitarian can give at least as good an account as the intuitionist of the authority of common sense in moral matters. Rules such as those that enjoin the telling of truth, the paying of debts, the keeping of promises, and so forth (Mill called these "secondary rules") were taken by him to indicate, not widespread intuitions, but the results of hundreds of years of experience of the consequences of actions. These rules, based on so much factual knowledge, are of considerable value in helping men to make correct decisions when time or data for a full calculation of the results in a particular case are lacking. The wisdom of the ages, thus embodied in the rules and precepts of common-sense morality, is an indispensable supplement to the limited knowledge and almost inevitable one-sidedness of any single person. It is for these reasons, utilitarians claim, that these rules and precepts have a certain cognitive authority. There is no need to appeal to a faculty of intuition to explain the authority, and therefore such an explanation is, from a scientific point of view, unwarranted.

Mill thus gave a prominent place to moral directives other than the utilitarian principle. But he was basically an act-utilitarian, believing that each particular obligation depends on the balance of pleasure and pain that would be produced by the act in question. The utilitarian principle is so abstract, Mill thought, that it is unlikely to be actually used, except in cases where two secondary rules come into conflict with each other. But it serves the invaluable function of providing a rational basis for the criticism of secondary rules (this is brought out especially well in the essay on justice, Ch. 5 of *Utilitarianism*), and there was no doubt in Mill's mind that there can never be a right act which contravenes the principle. This is true even with regard to the rule (to which Mill gave so much emphasis) dictating the development and perfection of individual character. It often seems that Mill placed more stress on individuality, or self-realization, than on general welfare, and critics frequently claim that he contradicted himself by saying that both of these constitute the sole highest good. But there is no contradiction in his views, for he held that self-development is the best way for an individual to work for the common good.

Mill's concern with the problem of free will sprang from his view of the importance of self-development. (He presented this view both in the *Logic* and in the *Examination of Hamilton*.) The doctrine of necessity, which he had been taught to believe, seemed to him to make a man a creature of his environment, and this doctrine depressed and disturbed him for many years. When he realized that the desire to improve oneself could be a powerful motive and that actions dictated by this desire, although not contravening the law of causation, are properly said to be due to oneself rather than to one's environment, he felt "as if an incubus had been raised off him." He thought that this view enabled him to make determinism compatible with his emphasis on the individual's responsibility for his own character.

Two aspects of Mill's *Utilitarianism* have been attacked more frequently than any others. The first is his attempt to broaden utilitarianism by making a distinction between *kinds* of pleasure, so that an act producing a smaller amount of a more valuable kind of pleasure might be obligatory, rather than an act producing a larger amount of a less valuable kind of pleasure. This line of reasoning has been said to involve him in flagrant contradictions, or else to be sheer nonsense.

The second aspect is his attempt to give some sort of reasoned support to the utilitarian principle itself, which led G. E. Moore to accuse him of committing the "natural-istic fallacy." Moore thought Mill was trying to give a conclusive proof of a first moral principle, but he was mistaken. Throughout his life, Mill consistently held that no such proof of the principle was possible, either deductively or inductively. There is, however, no agreement as to the manner in which Mill attempted, in the fourth chapter of *Utilitarianism*, to support his first principle so that he would not be open to the same reproach of dogmatism that he had made against the intuitionists. Mill's remarks here are extremely unclear. His problem arises because, while he insisted that there must be a factual basis for moral judgments, he held that moral judgments are different in kind from factual propositions and therefore cannot be strictly derived from them. Although he failed to solve this problem, he at least propounded it in precisely the form in which it has perplexed (not to say obsessed) recent moral philosophers.

Social and political philosophy. Mill was more aware than were the older Benthamites of the importance of nonrational and noninstitutional factors to an understanding of society and was consequently less disposed to rely on legal and governmental reforms for the improvement of it. He believed in democratic government, but he was convinced that it could not work well unless the citizens who lived under it were reasonably well educated, tolerant of opposing views, and willing to sacrifice some of their immediate interests for the good of society. He was profoundly worried about the tendency of democracies to suppress individuality and override minorities: indeed, this, and not the problem of forcing those who control government to work for the interests of the people, seemed to him the crucial problem of his times. Hence, in his writings on social and political philosophy, his central concern was to show the importance of personal freedom and the development of strong individual character and to devise ways of encouraging their growth.

Economic theory. With regard to economic theory Mill at first supported a general policy of laissez-faire, but increasing awareness of the uselessness to the individual of political freedom without economic security and opportunity led him to re-examine his objections to socialism. By the end of his life he had come to think that as far as economic theory was concerned, socialism was acceptable. His reservations about it sprang from his fear that it would give overwhelming strength to the tendencies of the age toward suppression of individuality.

"On Liberty." Mill thought that his essay *On Liberty* was the most likely of all his works to be of enduring value. In it he maintained the view, which he had expressed as early as 1834, that "the sole end for which mankind are warranted, individually or collectively, in interfering with the liberty of action of any of their number, is self-protection." Mill argued for this view especially in regard to freedom of thought and discussion. "We can never be sure," he wrote, "that the opinion we are endeavoring to stifle is a false opinion; and if we were sure, stifling it would be an evil still": these are the lines of his defense, which rests ultimately on his assessment of the importance of sociological knowledge to the direction of social action and on his view of the peculiar difficulties in obtaining it. In the third chapter, Mill argued at length

for the importance of "individuality," which, he held, comes from, or indeed is identical with, continued effort at self-development. Even eccentricity is better, he held, than massive uniformity of personality and the stagnation of society that would result from it. Mill's strong emphasis on this point stems from his conviction, here strongly influenced by de Tocqueville, that the chief danger of democracy is that of suppressing individual differences and of allowing no genuine development of minority opinion. Democratic tyranny would be far worse, he held, than aristocratic or despotic tyranny, since it would be far more effective in utilizing the most efficient of means of social control, the pressure of public opinion. Against this the only reliable safeguard would be the development of personalities strong enough to resist such pressures.

Representative government. In more specifically political matters the same concerns are evident. Mill defended representative democracy, but not solely on the grounds used by the older Benthamites. Representative government, he held, is ideally the best form of government because it does more to encourage the growth and development of individuality than any other form of government. By leading people to participate in the processes of governing, representative government makes them more active, intelligent, and well rounded than even the best-intentioned of despotisms could. It thereby gives them vitally important moral training, by cultivating their public sympathies, strengthening their habit of looking at social questions from an impersonal point of view, and aiding their identification of personal interests with the interests of society. Care must be taken, however, to get a true democracy, one in which minorities as well as majorities are represented. For this reason Mill enthusiastically endorsed Thomas Hare's scheme of proportional representation. He also favored plural voting, which would allow educated and responsible persons to have more influence than the uneducated, by giving the former several votes. Mill's view of the function of the representative also shows his concern to get as much intelligence as possible into government. A properly educated constituency, he held, would be able and willing to select the best men available; and since those elected would be better informed and wiser on particular issues than the electorate, it would be absurd to bind the representatives to anything but a very general agreement with the beliefs and aims of the electors.

Individuals and society. Mill is frequently criticized for overlooking the organic elements in society and for thinking of society as a mere aggregate of units in which each unit is what it is regardless of its membership in the whole. Mill certainly held this view as far as the most fundamental laws of psychology are concerned. But his view of individual character involves new considerations. Individuals, he held, are radically affected by their membership in society and inevitably formed by the customs, habits, morality, and beliefs of those who raise them. There is, however, no impersonal assurance, metaphysical or otherwise, that the individual will feel himself an organic member of any group. He will do so, Mill thought, only if he is educated to do so. Mill cannot be accused of underestimating the importance of ensuring that men are

so educated, and it is not clear that an organic theory has anything better to offer on a practical level.

Religious views. Mill maintained for the most part a determined silence on religious questions. Although he had written "On Nature" and "The Utility of Religion" by 1858, and although he lived during a period of increasingly free discussion of all possible religious subjects, he thought that the British public would not listen patiently to what he had to say on these questions and that he could not publish his views without alienating readers and losing public influence. And this, as he made quite clear in his correspondence with Auguste Comte, he was determined not to do. Despite his precautions, however, he was generally taken to be atheistic, and he was sometimes criticized for not openly stating the views which, so it seemed, he insinuated but did not defend. The consternation of his followers and the delight of his opponents was therefore considerable when it became apparent from the posthumously published *Three Essays on Religion* (1874) that Mill did not entirely condemn religious aspirations and hopes and even thought that there might be some faint possibility of the existence of rational support for a religious view of the world. Admirers felt betrayed, and religious critics proclaimed that Mill's secular education and materialistic position here issued in collapse and evident moral and intellectual bankruptcy.

Goodness of God. Mill's most famous pronouncement on religion occurs not, however, in the *Three Essays*, but in the *Examination of Hamilton*. Discussing the use made by one of Hamilton's philosophical followers, Mansel, of Hamilton's view that we cannot know the Absolute, Mill particularly criticized Mansel's theory that even the moral terms we apply to God do not mean what they mean when we apply them to men. Mill objected to this theory in the name of logic: if terms are not to be used in their usual sense, they ought not to be used at all. But, more strongly, he went on to say that a being, no matter how powerful, whose acts are not sanctioned by the highest human morality conceivable, is not deserving of worship. If Mill were convinced of the existence of such a being he would not worship him. "I will call no being good," Mill proclaimed, "who is not what I mean when I apply that epithet to my fellow creatures, and if such a being can sentence me to hell for not so calling him, to hell I will go."

Nature. Of the *Three Essays*, the first two, at least, show no reversal or collapse of Mill's views. In "On Nature" Mill argued that the maxim "Follow Nature" is of no use as a guide to action. For "Nature" either means "everything that happens, good as well as bad," in which case it offers no guidance whatsoever; or it means "what happens without any human interference," and in that case the maxim is self-contradictory. Nature in the second sense, Mill went on to argue, offers at least as much evil to our observation as good; it is rather a challenge to amendment than an ideal for imitation. From this, two conclusions follow. First, it is our job to improve nature, especially human nature; for it is only insofar as men have intervened to change things that the world has become civilized, safe, and happy, even to the limited extent that it has. Human virtues are not natural: they are pre-eminently the results of cultivation. Even justice is an artificial virtue, Mill said, and the idea of natural justice does not precede, but follows, it. Second, in view of the suffering and ugliness presented by much of the natural world, the only religious view that is at all tenable is one which holds that the deity is not omnipotent, that "the Principle of Good *cannot* at once and altogether subdue the powers of evil," and that, consequently, men should think of themselves as the far from useless helpers of a limited but benevolent God.

Utility of religion. In "The Utility of Religion," Mill argued that much of the social usefulness attributed to religion is actually due to the influence of a widely accepted and instilled moral code, and to the force of public opinion guided by that code. The belief in the supernatural origin of morality may once have helped it to gain acceptance, but is no longer needed, or indeed, even effectual, in maintaining this acceptance. The effect of religion on individuals springs largely from our need to have ideal conceptions that move us to action. "The essence of religion is the strong and earnest direction of the emotions and desires towards an ideal object, recognized as of the highest excellence, and as rightfully paramount over all selfish objects of desire." But a religion of humanity, Mill argued, can have this effect to an even greater extent than a supernatural religion. The religion of humanity would cultivate our unselfish feelings and would free us from any need for intellectual juggling or willful blindness with regard to its tenets, since it would rather point out than deny the evil in the world and urge us to work to remove it.

God. Thus, the first two essays of the *Three Essays* together suggest that the alternative to a supernatural religion is not simple acceptance of Nature, but the construction of an alternative way of living based on education and convention; and these themes are to be found throughout Mill's thought. The third essay, "Theism," drafted from 1868 to 1870, which assesses arguments in support of a supernatural religious view, seems to make more concessions to traditional religiosity than the other essays; but even these are slight. In this essay, Mill discussed the possibilities of rational support for supernatural beliefs. Dismissing all a priori reasoning, he found only the Argument from Design at all convincing, and this argument gives us at best "no more than a probability" that some intelligent creator of the world exists. For the same evidences that thus support the existence of a creator also go to show that he was not omnipotent and do not prove that he was omniscient. Mill suggested that we think of a limited deity faced with the independent existence of matter and force. To this picture of a Platonic demiurge, Mill thought we are entitled to add that benevolence may have been one (although surely not the only) moral attribute of the creator. But Mill emphasized strongly the importance of the work of man in improving the world. "If man had not the power," he said, "by the exercise of his own energies for the improvement both of himself and of his outward circumstances, to do for himself and other creatures vastly more than God had in the first instance done, the Being who called him into existence would deserve something very different from thanks at his hands."

Immortality and miracles. Mill argued that there is no evidence for the immortality of the soul and none against

it. After a lengthy discussion of Hume's arguments on this point he found that roughly the same is true of miracles. But in each case he pointed out that there is room for *hope:* one may, if it is comforting and encouraging, hope that the soul is immortal and that the revelations attested by miracles are true. And it is this point more than any other in the essay that upset Mill's admirers. For while he concluded that the proper rational attitude to supernatural religion is skepticism rather than belief or positive disbelief and that "the whole domain of the supernatural is thus removed from the region of Belief into that of simple Hope," he also held that it may be valuable and justifiable to encourage religious hopes. This, he said, can be done without impairing the power of reason; and indulgence in such hopes may help some men to feel that life is more important and may strengthen their feelings for others. Furthermore, to construct a picture of a person of high moral excellence, such as Christ, and form the habit of seeking the approval of this person for one's acts, may aid that "real, though purely human, religion, which sometimes calls itself the Religion of Humanity, and sometimes that of Duty." Critics may wish to call these views objectionable, but in Mill at least they are not inconsistent. They hark back to his early discovery of the importance of cultivating the feelings and develop the further implications of his idea of the moral importance of educating the emotions. His assessment of the degree to which scientific support can be given to a supernaturalist theory by evidences of design, low though it is, may seem far too high; but his interest in the theory of a limited deity with whom we must cooperate to bring about improvement in the world is hardly great enough or personal enough to lend credence to the accusations that he had undergone an emotional collapse.

Works by Mill

Mill's works have not yet been collected. Even the projected University of Toronto Press edition of his *Works* will probably not contain all of them. Mill's own *Bibliography*, edited by M. MacMinn, J. R. Hainds, and J. M. McCrimmon (Evanston, Ill., 1945), is not quite complete.

Mill's books (all of which were published in London, unless otherwise noted) are as follows: *System of Logic*, 2 vols. (1843; 8th ed., 1872); *Essays on Some Unsettled Questions of Political Economy* (1844; written 1830–1831); *Principles of Political Economy*, 2 vols. (1848; 7th ed., 1871; variorum ed., W. J. Ashley, ed., 1909); *On Liberty* (1859); *Dissertations and Discussions*, periodical essays, 2 vols. (1859), 4 vols. (1875); *Considerations on Representative Government* (1861); *Utilitarianism*, reprinted from *Frasers Magazine*, 1861 (1863); *An Examination of Sir William Hamilton's Philosophy* (1865; 6th ed., 1889); *Auguste Comte and Positivism* (1865); *Subjection of Women* (1869; written in 1861); *Autobiography* (1873; more complete edition, J. J. Coss, ed., New York, 1924).

Among Mill's shorter writings of philosophical interest (most reprinted in *Dissertations and Discussions*) are the following: "Whately's Elements of Logic," *Westminster Review* (1828); "The Spirit of the Age," in the *Examiner* (1831), included in F. Hayek, ed., *The Spirit of the Age* (Chicago, 1942); "Prof. Sedgwick's Discourse" (1835); "Civilization" (1836); "Bentham" (1838); "Coleridge" (1840); "M. de Tocqueville on Democracy in America" (1840); "Bailey on Berkeley's Theory of Vision" (1842); "Michelet's History of France" (1844); "Dr. Whewell on Moral Philosophy" (1851); "Bain's Psychology" (1859); "Austin on Jurisprudence" (1863); "Plato" (1866); "Inaugural Address to the University of St. Andrews" (1867); "Berkeley's Life and Writings," *Fortnightly Review* (1871); "Grote's Aristotle" (1873);

"Chapters on Socialism," *Fortnightly Review* (1879), reprinted as *Socialism*, W. O. P. Bliss, ed. (Linden, Mass., 1891).

Of Mill's literary essays, the best known are "What Is Poetry?" and "The Two Kinds of Poetry," in *Monthly Repository* (1833), reprinted in part in *Dissertations and Discourses* as "Thoughts on Poetry and Its Varieties."

Works on Mill

LIFE

For Mill's life, see his *Autobiography;* F. E. Mineka, ed., *Earlier Letters,* 2 vols. (Toronto, 1963); H. S. R. Elliott, ed., *Letters,* 2 vols. (1910); J. Stillinger, ed., *Early Draft of Mill's Autobiography* (Urbana, Ill., 1961). See F. Hayek, ed., *John Stuart Mill and Harriet Taylor* (1951), for their correspondence. See also the standard M. St. John Packe, *The Life of John Stuart Mill* (1954); A. Bain, *John Stuart Mill* (1882); and W. L. Courtney, *Life of John Stuart Mill* (1886); H. O. Pappe, *John Stuart Mill and the Harriet Taylor Myth* (Melbourne, 1960); A. W. Levi, "The Writing of Mill's Autobiography," in *Ethics,* Vol. 61 (1951),

Among many estimates of Mill's life and character are those by R. H. Hutton, reprinted in *Criticism on Contemporary Thought and Thinkers,* Vol. 1 (1894); J. Martineau, in *Essays,* Vol. 3 (1891); J. Morley, in *Critical Miscellanies,* Vol. 2 (1877); B. Russell, in *Proceedings of the British Academy* (1955); W. Ward, in *Men and Matters* (1914).

GENERAL WORKS

For general commentary on the thought of Mill see Sir Leslie Stephen, *English Utilitarians,* Vol. 3 (1900); R. P. Anschutz, *Philosophy of John Stuart Mill* (Oxford, 1953); Karl Britton, *John Stuart Mill* (1953).

LOGIC

See O. A. Kubitz, *Development of John Stuart Mill's System of Logic,* Illinois Studies in the Social Sciences, VIII (Urbana, Ill., 1932); R. Jackson, *Deductive Logic of John Stuart Mill* (Oxford, 1941); W. Whewell, *Of Induction, with especial reference to Mr. J. Stuart Mill's System of Logic* (1849), and see E. A. Strong, "W. Whewell and John Stuart Mill," *Journal of the History of Ideas* (1955). Classic criticisms include: T. H. Green, "The Logic of John Stuart Mill," *Works,* Vol. II (1886); F. H. Bradley, *Principles of Logic* (Oxford, 1883), Bk. II, Part II, Chs. 1–3; W. S. Jevons, "John Stuart Mill's Philosophy Tested," reprinted in *Pure Logic* (1890).

METAPHYSICS

Among older studies of interest are: W. L. Courtney, *The Metaphysics of John Stuart Mill* (1879); C. M. Douglas, *John Stuart Mill, A Study of His Philosophy* (Edinburgh and London, 1895); J. McCosh, *An Examination of Mr. John Stuart Mill's Philosophy* (London and New York, 1866); and John Grote, *Exploratio Philosophica* (Cambridge, 1865; 2 vols., 1900). Few recent discussions center explicitly on Mill.

ETHICS AND UTILITARIANISM

E. Halévy, *La Formation du radicalisme philosophique,* 3 vols. (Paris, 1901–1904), translated into English by Mary Morris as *Growth of Philosophic Radicalism* (London, 1928), is the basic study of the development of Benthamite doctrine; see also E. Albee, *History of English Utilitarianism* (1900) and J. Plamenatz, *The English Utilitarians* (Oxford, 1949). Especially valuable older critical works are John Grote, *Examination of the Utilitarian Philosophy* (Cambridge, 1870) and F. H. Bradley, *Ethical Studies* (Oxford, 1876), Ch. 3. Recent discussions start from the criticisms of G. E. Moore, *Principia Ethica* (Cambridge, 1903), Chs. 1 and 3. Compare J. Seth, "Alleged Fallacies in Mill's Utilitarianism," in *Philosophical Review,* Vol. 17 (1908); E. W. Hall, "The 'Proof' of Utility in Bentham and Mill," in *Ethics,* Vol. 9 (1949); J. O. Urmson, "Interpretation of the Moral Philosophy of John Stuart Mill," in *Philosophical Quarterly,* Vol. 3 (1953). I. Berlin's lecture, "John Stuart Mill and the Ends of Life" (London, 1962), is more general.

POLITICAL PHILOSOPHY

See G. H. Sabine, *History of Political Theory,* 3d ed. (New York, 1961); M. Cowling, *Mill and Liberalism* (Cambridge, 1963). J. F. Stephen, *Liberty, Equality, Fraternity* (1873) is an interesting early attack; others are summarized in J. C. Rees, *Mill and His Early Critics* (Leicester, 1956). B. Bosanquet, *Philosophical Theory of the State* (1899) and D. G. Ritchie, *Principles of State Interference* (1891) present representative criticism. J. H. Burns, "John Stuart Mill and Democracy," in *Political Studies,* Vol. 5 (1957), traces the development of Mill's views. For criticisms of Mill's views on sociological method, see K. Popper, *Open Society and Its Enemies,* 2 vols. (1945), Ch. 14, and P. Winch, *Idea of a Social Science* (1958), especially Ch. 3.

J. B. SCHNEEWIND

MILLER, DICKINSON S. (1868–1963), was an American ethical philosopher and epistemologist who published both under his own name and under the pseudonym R. E. Hobart. He was born in Philadelphia and studied at the University of Pennsylvania, Clark University, the universities of Berlin and Halle, Hobart College, and Harvard University. He held a doctorate in philosophy from Halle and a D.Sc. from Hobart.

At Harvard, Miller was a student of William James, who became his long-time friend and with whom he often discussed and argued points of philosophy. James was instrumental in getting Dickinson an appointment as associate professor of philosophy at Bryn Mawr College in 1893, the year after Miller's graduation from Harvard.

Miller left Bryn Mawr in 1898 to become first an instructor and then a professor of philosophy at Harvard. He subsequently joined the Columbia faculty, where he remained until the 1920s. He had also received a D.D. at Berkeley (California) Divinity School and in 1911 started to teach apologetics at the General Theological Seminary in New York City.

In his later days he lived for several years (1927–1932) close to his friend the critical realist Charles Augustus Strong, in Fiesole, near Florence, Italy. Strong appreciated Miller's company, especially because of Miller's neorealistic tendencies as opposed to Strong's different epistemological outlook. Their discussions were lively and interminable. George Santayana occasionally joined them, coming to Florence from Rome. Miller was a visitor during 1926 at the Vienna circle of logical positivists; although mostly a silent listener at the circle's sessions, he was an intensely interesting and challenging discussant in individual conversations. During his last 25 years he lived in Boston.

Miller's was an extremely penetrating and constructively critical mind. In a number of remarkable articles he addressed himself mainly to such topics as direct realism, the philosophy of mind, and also the controversy between William James and E. A. Singer on behaviorism. Especially interesting is "Is Consciousness 'A Type of Behavior'?" (1911), mainly about the "automatic sweetheart" puzzle. In 1951, Miller wrote "'Descartes' Myth' and Professor Ryle's Fallacy," a sharp critique of Gilbert Ryle's logical behaviorism. He also wrote on Hume's views on causality and induction, on various topics in moral philosophy, and most notably, on the free-will–determinism issue. Miller's article provocatively entitled "Free Will as Involving Determination and Inconceivable Without It" (1934), published, for obscure reasons, under the name R. E. Hobart, has become a *locus classicus* of the free-will controversies. With remarkable lucidity and perspicacity Miller brought up to date the essentials of the point of view of Hume and J. S. Mill. He argued that once we realize the clear distinctions between causality and compulsion and between indeterminism and free will, the traditionally vexing problem disappears, and a fully adequate account of human freedom, responsibility, reward, and punishment can be given. Miller's views on religion and theology were extremely liberal and modern, close to the outlook of Unitarianism (in fact, he occasionally served as a Unitarian minister in the Boston area).

Miller's contributions to the epistemological controversies of his time may now seem a bit old-fashioned, but they are worthy of renewed attention because the same issues are still being debated, albeit in a different style and terminology.

Works by Miller

"Is Consciousness 'A Type of Behavior'?" *Journal of Philosophy,* Vol. 8 (1911), 322–327.

"The Pleasure-quality and the Pain-quality Analysable, Not Ultimate." *Mind,* Vol. 38 (1929), 215–218.

"Is There Not a Clear Solution of the Knowledge-problem?" *Journal of Philosophy,* Vol. 34 (1937), 701–712; Vol. 35 (1938), 561–572.

"An Event in Modern Philosophy." *Philosophical Review,* Vol. 54 (1945), 592–606.

"Hume's Deathblow to Deductivism." *Journal of Philosophy,* Vol. 46 (1949), 745–762.

"'Descartes' Myth' and Professor Ryle's Fallacy." *Journal of Philosophy,* Vol. 48 (1951), 270–280.

UNDER THE NAME R. E. HOBART

"Hume Without Scepticism." *Mind,* Vol. 39 (1930).

"Free Will as Involving Determinism and Inconceivable Without It." *Mind,* Vol. 43 (1934), 1–27.

HERBERT FEIGL

MILL'S METHODS OF INDUCTION. John Stuart Mill, in his *System of Logic* (Book III, Chapters 8–10), set forth and discussed five methods of experimental inquiry, calling them the method of agreement, the method of difference, the joint method of agreement and difference, the method of residues, and the method of concomitant variation. Mill maintained that these are the methods by which we both discover and demonstrate causal relationships, and that they are of fundamental importance in scientific investigation. Mill called these methods "eliminative methods of induction." In so doing, he was drawing an analogy with the elimination of terms in an algebraic equation—an analogy which is rather forced, except with respect to the various methods that are classed under the heading of method of difference. As will be demonstrated, it is perhaps best to use the term "eliminative methods" with reference to the elimination of rival candidates for the role of cause, which characterizes all these methods.

ILLUSTRATIONS OF THE METHODS

The general character of Mill's methods of experimental inquiry may be illustrated by examples of the two simplest ones, the methods of agreement and of difference. Mill's canon for the method of agreement is this: "If two or more instances of the phenomenon under investigation have only one circumstance in common, the circumstance in which alone all the instances agree is the cause (or effect) of the given phenomenon."

For example, if a number of people who are suffering from a certain disease have all gone for a considerable time without fresh fruit or vegetables, but have in other respects had quite different diets, have lived in different conditions, belong to different races, and so on, so that the lack of fresh fruit and vegetables is the only feature common to all of them, then we can conclude that the lack of fresh fruit and vegetables is the cause of this particular disease.

Mill's canon for the method of difference is this: "If an instance in which the phenomenon under investigation occurs, and an instance in which it does not occur, have every circumstance in common save one, that one occurring in the former; the circumstance in which alone the two instances differ, is the effect, or the cause, or an indispensable part of the cause, of the phenomenon."

For example, if two exactly similar pieces of iron are heated in a charcoal-burning furnace and hammered into shape in exactly similar ways, except that the first is dipped into water after the final heating while the second is not, and the first is found to be harder than the second, then the dipping of iron into water while it is hot is the cause of such extra hardness—or at least an essential part of the cause, for the hammering, the charcoal fire, and so on may also be needed. For all this experiment shows, the dipping alone might not produce such extra hardness.

The method of agreement, then, picks out as the cause the one common feature in a number of otherwise different cases where the effect occurs; the method of difference picks out as the cause the one respect in which a case where the effect occurs differs from an otherwise exactly similar case where the effect does not occur. Both are intended to be methods of ampliative induction, that is, methods by which we can reason from a limited number of observed instances to a general causal relationship: the intended conclusion is that a certain disease is always produced by a lack of fresh fruit and vegetables, or that dipping iron into water while it is hot always hardens it, if it has been heated and hammered in a particular way. And the other three methods are intended to work in a similar manner.

These methods have been criticized on two main counts: first, it is alleged that they do not establish the conclusions intended, so that they are not methods of proof or conclusive demonstration; and second, that they are not useful as methods of discovery. Such criticisms have been used to support the general observation that these methods play no part, or only a very minor part, in the investigation of nature, and that scientific method requires a radically different description.

In order to estimate the force of such criticisms, and to determine the real value of the eliminative methods, Mill's formulation need not be discussed in detail. Instead, one need only determine what would be valid demonstrative methods corresponding to Mill's classes, and then consider whether such methods, or any approximations of them, have a place in either scientific or common-sense inquiry.

METHODS OF AGREEMENT AND OF DIFFERENCE

To avoid unnecessary complications, let us assume that the *conclusion* reached by any application of the method of agreement or of difference is to have the form "Such-and-such is a cause of such-and-such kind of event or phenomenon." For a formal study of these methods and the joint method we could regard a cause as a necessary and sufficient condition of the effect—or, in some cases, as a necessary condition only, or as a sufficient condition only—where to say that X is a necessary condition for Y is just to say that wherever Y is present, X is present, or briefly that all Y are X; and to say that X is a sufficient condition for Y is just to say that wherever X is present Y is present, or briefly that all X are Y.

In general we shall be looking for a condition that is both necessary and sufficient for the phenomenon, but there are variants of the methods in which we look for a condition that is merely necessary or merely sufficient. In practice, however, we are concerned with conditions that are not absolutely necessary or sufficient, but that are rather necessary and/or sufficient in relation to some *field,* that is, some set of background conditions, which may be specified more or less exactly. We are concerned, for example, not with the cause of a certain disease in general, but with what causes it in human beings living on the earth, breathing air, and so forth. Again, we are concerned not with the cause of hardness in general, but with that of a greater-than-normal hardness in iron in ordinary circumstances and at ordinary temperatures. The field in relation to which we look for a cause of a phenomenon must be such that the phenomenon sometimes occurs in that field and sometimes does not. We may assume that this field is constituted by the presence of certain qualities or at least of some general descriptive features, not by a specific location.

The *observation* that supports the conclusion is an observation of one or more instances in each of which various features are present or absent. An instance may be one in which the phenomenon in question occurs, which we may call a *positive instance,* or one in which the phenomenon does not occur, which we may call a *negative instance.*

To reason validly, however, from any such observation to a general causal conclusion, we require an additional general premise, an *assumption.* We must assume that there is some condition which, in relation to the field, is necessary and sufficient (or which is necessary, or which is sufficient) for the phenomenon, and also that this condition is to be found within a range of conditions that is restricted in some way. For these methods fall within the general class of eliminative forms of reasoning, that is, arguments in which one possibility is confirmed or established by the elimination of some or all of its rivals. The assumption will state that there is a cause to be found and will limit the range of candidates for the role of cause; the task of the observation will be to rule out enough of the candidates initially admitted to allow some positive conclusion.

Possible causes. It follows from the above that the assumption must indicate some limited (though not necessarily finite) set of what we may call *possible causes.* These are the factors (Mill calls them *circumstances* or *antecedents*) which, it is initially assumed, may be causally relevant to the phenomenon. Any possible cause, any factor that may be causally relevant in relation to the field in question, must, like the phenomenon itself, be something that sometimes occurs and sometimes does not occur within that field.

But are we to assume that a possible cause acts singly, if it acts at all? If the possible causes are A, B, C, etc., the phenomenon is $P,$ and the field is $F,$ are we to assume that the cause of P in F will be either A by itself or B by itself, and so on? Or are we to allow that it might be a conjunction, say $AC,$ so that P occurs in F when and only when A and C are both present? Are we to allow that the necessary and sufficient condition might be a disjunction, say (B or D), so that P occurs in F whenever B occurs, and whenever D occurs, but only when one or other (or both) of these occurs? Again, are we to allow that what we have taken as possible causes may include counteracting causes, so that the actual cause of P in F may be, say, the absence of C (that is, the negation not-C, or $\overline{C}$) or perhaps $B\overline{C}$, so that P occurs in F when and only when B is present and C is absent at the same time?

There are in fact valid methods with assumptions of different sorts, from the most rigorous kind, which requires that the actual cause should be just one of the possible causes by itself, through those which progressively admit negations, conjunctions, and disjunctions of possible causes and combinations of these, to the least rigorous kind of assumption, which says merely that the actual cause is built up out of these possible causes in some way.

Classification of these methods. There will be, then, not one method of agreement, one method of difference, and one joint method, but a series of variants of each. A complete survey could be made of all possible methods of these types, numbered as follows: A number from 1 to 8 before a decimal point will indicate the kind of assumption. Thus, it is assumed that there is an actual cause which is

(1) one of the possible causes;

(2) one of the possible causes or the negation of a possible cause;

(3) a possible cause or a conjunction of possible causes;

(4) a possible cause or a disjunction of possible causes;

(5) a possible cause or the negation of a possible cause, or a conjunction each of whose members is a possible cause or the negation of a possible cause;

(6) a possible cause, or the negation of a possible cause, or a disjunction each of whose members is a possible cause or the negation of a possible cause;

(7) a possible cause, or a conjunction of possible causes, or a disjunction each of whose members is a possible cause or a conjunction of possible causes;

(8) a possible cause, or the negation of a possible cause, or a conjunction each of whose members is a possible cause or the negation of one; or a disjunction each of whose members is a possible cause or the negation of one, or a conjunction each of whose members is a possible cause or a negation of one.

The first figure after the decimal point will indicate the sort of observation, as follows:

(1) a variant of the method of agreement;

(2) a variant of the method of difference;

(3) a variant of the joint method;

(4) a new but related method.

The second figure after the decimal point will mark further differences where necessary, but this figure will have no constant significance.

The complete survey cannot be given here, but a few selected variants will be considered, numbered in the manner set forth above.

Positive method of agreement. Let us begin with an assumption of the first kind, that there is a necessary and sufficient condition X for P in F, that is, that for some X all FP are X and all FX are P, and X is identical with one of the possible causes A, B, C, D, E. (It may be noted that a condition thus specified may sometimes not be what we would ordinarily regard as the cause of the phenomenon: we might rather say that it *contains* the real cause. However, in our present account we shall call such a condition the cause; it is explained below how the cause of a phenomenon may be progressively located with greater precision.)

We obtain a variant of the method of agreement (1.12) by combining with this assumption the following observation: a set of one or more positive instances such that one possible cause, say A, is present in each instance, but for every other possible cause there is an instance from which that cause is absent. This yields the conclusion that A is necessary and sufficient for P in F.

For example, the observation might be this:

	A	B	C	D	E
I_1	p	a	p	·	a
I_2	p	p	a	a	·

where p indicates that the possible cause is present, a that it is absent, and a dot that it may be either present or absent without affecting the result. I_1 and I_2 are positive instances: I_1 shows that neither B nor E is necessary for P in F, I_2 that neither C nor D is necessary, and hence, given the assumption, it follows that A is necessary and sufficient.

Since this reasoning eliminates candidates solely on the ground that they are not necessary, there is another variant (1.11) which assumes only that there is some necessary condition for P in F identical with one of the possible causes, and (with the same observation) concludes that A is a necessary condition for P in F.

Negative method of agreement. Besides the positive method of agreement, in which candidates are eliminated as not being necessary because they are absent from positive instances, there are corresponding variants of a negative method of agreement in which candidates are eliminated as not being sufficient because they are present in negative instances. This requires the following observation: a set of one or more negative instances such that one possible cause, say A, is absent from each instance, but for every other possible cause there is an instance in which it is present. For example:

	A	B	C	D	E
N_1	a	p	·	·	·
N_2	a	·	p	p	·
N_3	a	·	·	·	p

If the assumption was that one of the possible causes is sufficient for P in F, this observation would show (1.13) that A is sufficient, while if the assumption was that one of the possible causes is both necessary and sufficient, this observation would show (1.14) that A is necessary and sufficient.

Method of difference. For the simplest variant of the method of difference (1.2) we need this observation: a positive instance I_1 and a negative instance N_1 such that of the possible causes present in I_1, one, say A, is absent from N_1, but the rest are present in N_1. For example:

	A	B	C	D	E
I_1	p	p	p	a	·
N_1	a	p	p	·	p

Here D is eliminated because it is absent from I_1, and hence not necessary, and B, C, and E are eliminated because they are present in N_1 and hence not sufficient. Hence, given the assumption that one of the possible causes is both necessary and sufficient for P in F, it follows that A is so. (Note that since it would not matter if, say, E were absent from I_1, the presence of the actual cause in I_1 need not be the only difference between the instances.) We may remark here that the method of difference, unlike some variants of the method of agreement, requires the assumption that there is some condition which is both necessary and sufficient for P. It is true, as we shall see later with variants 4.2 and 8.2, that the "cause" detected by this method is often not itself a necessary condition, or even a sufficient one; but the assumption needed is that *something* is both necessary and sufficient.

Joint method. The joint method may be interpreted as an indirect method of difference, that is, the job done by I_1 above may be shared among several positive instances, and the job done by N_1 among several negative instances. That is, we need (for 1.3) the following observation: a set S_i of one or more positive instances and a set S_n of one or more negative instances such that one of the possible causes, say A, is present throughout S_i and absent throughout S_n, but each of the other possible causes is either absent from at least one positive instance or present in at least one negative instance. Given that one of the possible causes is both necessary and sufficient, this yields the conclusion that A is so.

Simple variants of these methods. With an assumption of the second kind (that the requisite condition is either a possible cause or a negation of a possible cause) we need stronger observations. Thus, for variants of the positive method of agreement (2.11 and 2.12) we need this: two or more positive instances such that one possible cause (or negation), say A, is present in each instance, but for every other possible cause there is an instance in which it is present and an instance from which it is absent. This is needed to rule out, as candidates for the role of necessary (or both necessary and sufficient) condition, the negations of possible causes as well as the possible causes other than A themselves.

For the corresponding variant of the method of difference (2.2) we need this: a positive instance I_1 and a negative instance N_1 such that one possible cause (or negation), say A, is present in I_1 and absent from N_1, but each of the other possible causes is either present in both I_1 and N_1 or absent from both. For example:

	A	B	C	D	E
I_1	p	p	a	a	p
N_1	a	p	a	a	p

Since B is present in N_1, B is not sufficient for P in F; but since B is present in I_1, not-B is not necessary for P in F; thus neither B nor not-B can be both necessary and sufficient. Similarly, C, D, E, and their negations, and also not-A, are ruled out, and thus the necessary and sufficient condition must be A itself. This is the classic difference observation described by Mill, in which the only (possibly relevant) difference between the instances is the presence in I_1 of the factor identified as the actual cause; but we need this observation (as opposed to the weaker one of 1.2) only when we allow that the negation of a possible cause may be the actual cause.

The joint method needs, along with this weaker assumption, a similarly strengthened observation: that is, each of the possible causes other than A must be either present in both a positive and a negative instance or absent from both a positive and a negative instance, and then this variant (2.3) still yields the conclusion that A is both necessary and sufficient.

(What Mill and his followers describe as the joint method may be not this indirect method of difference, but rather a double method of agreement, in which a set of positive instances identifies a necessary condition and a set of negative instances identifies a sufficient condition. Such a combination is redundant with an assumption of either of the first two kinds, but not when the assumption is further relaxed.)

More complex variants. We consider next an assumption of the third kind, that the requisite condition is either a possible cause or a conjunction of possible causes. (This latter possibility seems to be at least part of what Mill meant by "an intermixture of effects.") This possibility does not affect the positive method of agreement, since if a conjunction is necessary, each of its conjuncts is necessary, and candidates can therefore be eliminated as before. But since the conjuncts in a necessary and sufficient condition may not severally be sufficient, the negative method of agreement as set forth above will not work. The observation of (1.13 or) 1.14 would now leave it open that, say, BC was the required (sufficient or) necessary and sufficient condition, for if C were absent from N_1 and B from N_2, then BC as a whole might still be sufficient: it would not be eliminated by either of these instances. This method now (in 3.14) needs a stronger observation, namely, a *single* negative instance N_1 in which one possible cause, say A, is absent, but *every* other possible cause is present. This will show that no possible cause or conjunction of possible causes that does not contain A is sufficient for P in F. But even this does not show that the requisite condition is A itself, but merely that it is either A itself or a conjunction in which A is a conjunct. We may express this by saying that the cause is $(A\underline{...})$, where the dots indicate that other conjuncts may form part of the condition, and the dots are underlined, while A is not, to indicate that A *must* appear in the formula for the actual cause, but that other conjuncts may or may not appear.

The corresponding variant (3.2) of the method of difference needs only the observation of 1.2; but it, too, establishes only the less complete conclusion that $(A\underline{...})$ is a necessary and sufficient condition of P in F. For while (in the example given for 1.2 above) B, C, D, and E singly are still eliminated as they were in 1.2, and any conjunctions

such as BC which, being present in I_1, *might* be necessary, are eliminated because they are also present in N_1 and hence not sufficient, a conjunction such as AB, which contains A, is both present in I_1 and absent from N_1, and might therefore be both necessary and sufficient. Thus this assumption and this observation show only that A is, as Mill put it, "the cause, or an indispensable part of the cause." The full cause is represented by the formula $(A\underline{...})$, provided that only possible causes that are present in I_1 can replace the dots.

In the corresponding variant of the joint method (3.3), we need a *single* negative instance instead of the set S_n, for the same reason as in 3.14, and the cause is specified only as $(A\underline{...})$.

With an assumption of the fourth kind (that the requisite condition is either a possible cause or a disjunction of possible causes), the negative method of agreement (4.13 and 4.14) works as in 1.13 and 1.14, but the positive method of agreement is now seriously affected. For with the observation given for 1.12 above, the necessary and sufficient condition might be, say, $(B$ or $C)$, for this disjunction is present in both I_1 and I_2, though neither of its disjuncts is present in both. Thus the observation of 1.12 would leave the result quite undecided. We need (for 4.12) a much stronger observation, that is, a single positive instance in which A is present but all the other possible causes are absent together; but even this now shows only that the cause is $(A$ or...$)$. This assumption (that the cause may be a disjunction of possible causes) allows what Mill called a "plurality of causes," for each of the disjuncts is by itself a "cause" in the sense that it is a sufficient condition; and what we have just noted is the way in which this possibility undermines the use of the method of agreement.

The method of difference, on the other hand (4.2), still needs only the observation of 1.2; this eliminates all possible causes other than A, and all disjunctions that do not contain A, either as being not sufficient because they are present in N_1 or as not necessary because they are absent from I_1. The only disjunctions not eliminated are those that occur in I_1 but not in N_1, and these must contain A. Thus this observation, with this assumption, shows that a necessary and sufficient condition is $(A$ or...$)$, that is, either A itself or a disjunction containing A, where the other disjuncts are possible causes absent from N_1. This, of course, means that A itself, the factor thus picked out, may be only a sufficient condition for P.

The joint method with this assumption (4.3) needs a *single* positive instance, but can still use a set of negative instances and it specifies the cause as $(A$ or...$)$.

As the assumptions are relaxed further, the method of agreement requires stronger and stronger observations. For example, in 6.12, which is a variant of the positive method with an assumption allowing that the necessary and sufficient condition may be a disjunction of possible causes or negations, the observation needed is a set S_i of positive instances such that one possible cause, say A, is present in each, but that for every possible combination of the other possible causes and their negations there is an instance in which this combination is present (that is, if there are n other possible causes, we need 2^n different instances). This observation will eliminate every disjunction that does not contain A, and will show that the requisite necessary and sufficient condition is (*A* or...), and hence that *A* itself is a sufficient condition for *P* in *F*. A corresponding variant of the negative method of agreement (5.14) shows that (*A*...) is a necessary and sufficient condition, and hence that *A* itself is necessary—a curious reversal of roles, because in the simplest variants, the positive method of agreement was used to detect a necessary condition and the negative one a sufficient condition.

In the method of difference, however, the observation of 1.2 (or, where negations are admitted, that of 2.2) continues to yield results, though the conclusions become less complete, that is, the cause is less and less completely specified. For example, in 8.2, where we assume that there is a necessary and sufficient condition for *P* in *F* which may be one of the possible causes, or a negation of one, or a conjunction of possible causes or negations, or a disjunction of possible causes or negations or of conjunctions of possible causes or negations—which in effect allows the actual condition to be built up out of the possible causes in any way—the observation of 2.2 establishes the conclusion that the requisite condition is (*A*... or...). that is to say, it is either *A* itself, or a conjunction containing *A*, or a disjunction in which one of the disjuncts is *A* itself or a conjunction containing *A*. Since any such disjunct in a necessary and sufficient condition is a sufficient condition, this observation, in which the presence of *A* in I_1 is the only possibly relevant difference between I_1 and N_1, shows even with the least rigorous kind of assumption that *A* is at least a necessary part of a sufficient condition for *P* in *F*—the sufficient condition being (*A*...).

The joint method, as an indirect method of difference, ceases to work once we allow both conjunctions and disjunctions; but a double method of agreement comes into its own with this eighth kind of assumption. In 8.12, as in 6.12, if there are *n* possible causes other than *A*, the set of 2^n positive instances with *A* present in each but with the other possible causes present and absent in all possible combinations will show that (*A* or...) is necessary and sufficient, and hence that *A* is sufficient. Similarly in 8.14, as in 5.14, the corresponding set of 2^n negative instances will show that (*A*...) is necessary and sufficient and hence that *A* is necessary. Putting the two observations together, we could conclude that *A* is both necessary and sufficient.

A new method, similar in principle, can be stated as follows (8.4): if there are *n* possible causes in all, and we observe 2^n instances (positive or negative) which cover all possible combinations of possible causes and their negations, then the disjunction of all the conjunctions found in the positive instances is both necessary and sufficient for *P* in *F*. For example, if there are only three possible causes, *A*, *B*, *C*,

A	*B*	*C*	*P*
p	*p*	*p*	*a*
p	*p*	*a*	*p*
p	*a*	*p*	*p*
p	*a*	*a*	*a*
a	*p*	*p*	*a*
a	*p*	*a*	*p*
a	*a*	*p*	*a*
a	*a*	*a*	*a*

and we have the observations listed in the accompanying table, then ($AB\overline{C}$ or $A\overline{B}C$ or $\overline{A}B\overline{C}$) is a necessary and sufficient condition for *P* in *F*. For if these are the only possibly relevant conditions, each combination of possible causes and negations for which *P* is present is sufficient for *P*, and these are the only sufficient conditions for *P*, since in all the relevantly different circumstances *P* is absent; but the disjunction of all the sufficient conditions must be both necessary and sufficient, on the assumption that there is some condition that is both necessary and sufficient.

Many valid methods. We thus find that while we must recognize very different variants of these methods according to the different kinds of assumptions that are used, and while the reasoning that validates the simplest variants fails when it is allowed that various negations and combinations of factors may constitute the actual cause, nevertheless there are valid demonstrative methods which use even the least rigorous form of assumption, that is, which assume only that there is some necessary and sufficient condition for *P* in *F*, made up in some way from a certain restricted set of possible causes. But with an assumption of this kind we must be content either to extract (by 8.2) a very incomplete conclusion from the classical difference observation or (by 8.12, 8.14, the combination of these two, or 8.4) to get more complete conclusions only from a large number of instances in which the possible causes are present or absent in systematically varied ways.

An extension of the methods. An important extension of all these methods is the following: since in every case the argument proceeds by eliminating certain candidates, it makes no difference if what is *not* eliminated is not a single possible cause but a cluster of possible causes which in our instances are always present together or absent together, the conclusion being just as we now have it, but with a symbol for the cluster replacing *A*. For example, if in 2.2 we have, say, both *A* and *B* present in I_1 and both absent from N_1, but each possible cause either present in both or absent from both, it follows that the cluster (*A*,*B*) is the cause in the sense that the actual cause lies somewhere within this cluster. A similar observation in 8.2 would show that either *A*, or *B*, or *AB*, or (*A* or *B*) is an indispensable part of a sufficient condition for *P* in *F*.

METHOD OF RESIDUES

The method of residues can be interpreted as a variant of the method of difference in which the negative instance is not observed but constructed on the basis of already known causal laws.

Suppose, for example, that a positive instance I_1 has been observed as follows:

	A	*B*	*C*	*D*	*E*
I_1	*p*	*p*	*a*	*p*	*a*

Now if we had, to combine with this, a negative instance N_1 in which *B* and *D* were present and *A*, *C*, and *E* absent, we could infer, according to the kind of assumption made, by 2.2 that *A* was the cause, or by 8.2 that (*A*... or...) was the cause, and so on. But if previous inductive inquiries have already established laws from which it follows that given $\overline{ABCDE}$ in the field F, P would not result, there is no need to observe N_1; we already know all that N_1 could tell us, and so one of the above-mentioned conclusions follows from I_1 alone along with the appropriate assumption.

Again, if the effect or phenomenon in which we are interested can be quantitatively measured, we could reason as follows. Suppose that we observe a positive instance, say with the factors as in I_1 above, in which there is a quantity x_1 of the effect in question, while our previously established laws enable us to calculate that with the factors as in N_1 there would be a quantity x_2 of this effect; then we can regard the difference $(x_1 - x_2)$ as the phenomenon P which is present in I_1 but absent from N_1. With an assumption of kind (1) or (2) or (4) or (6)—that is, any assumption that does not allow conjunctive terms in the cause—we could conclude that the cause of P in this instance I_1 was A alone, and hence that A is a sufficient condition for P in F. With an assumption of kind (1) or (2) we could indeed infer that A is both necessary and sufficient, but with one of kind (4) or (6) we could conclude only that a necessary and sufficient condition is (A or...).

To make an assumption of any of these four kinds is to assume that the effects of whatever factors are actually relevant are merely additive, and this lets us conclude that the extra factor in I_1, namely A, by itself produces in relation to F the extra effect $(x_1 - x_2)$. But with an assumption of kind (3) or (5) or (7) or (8), which allows conjunctive terms, and hence what Mill calls an "intermixture of effects," we could only infer that the cause of $(x_1 - x_2)$ in this instance was (A...). With the other factors that were present in both I_1 and N_1, A was sufficient to produce this differential effect, but it does not follow that A is sufficient for this in relation to F as a whole.

(Though Mill does not mention this, such a use of constructed instances along with some observed ones is in principle applicable to all the methods, not only to the method of difference in the way here outlined.)

METHOD OF CONCOMITANT VARIATION

The method of concomitant variation, like those already surveyed, is intended to be a form of ampliative induction; we want to argue from a covariation observed in some cases to a general rule of covariation covering unobserved cases also. To interpret this method we need a wider concept of cause than that which we have so far been using. A cause of P in the field F must now be taken, not as a necessary and sufficient condition, but as something on whose magnitude the magnitude of P, in F, functionally depends. For our present purpose this means only that there is some true lawlike proposition which, within F, relates the magnitude of the one item to that of the other. The *full cause*, in this sense, will be something on which, in F, the magnitude of P wholly depends, that is, the magnitude of P is uniquely determined by the magnitudes of the factors that constitute the full cause.

A full investigation of such a functional dependence would comprise two tasks: first, the identification of all the factors on which, in F, the magnitude of P depends, and second, the discovery of the way in which this magnitude depends on these factors. The completion of the first task

would yield a mere list of terms, that of the second a mathematical formula. Only the first of these tasks can be performed by an eliminative method analogous to those already surveyed.

We should expect to find concomitant variation analogues of both the method of agreement and the method of difference, that is, ways of arguing to a causal relationship between P and, say, A, both from the observation of cases where P remains constant while A remains constant but all the other possibly relevant factors vary, and also from the observation of cases where P varies while A varies but all the other possibly relevant factors remain constant. And indeed there are methods of both kinds, but those of the second kind, the analogues of the method of difference, are more important.

As before, we need an assumption as well as an observation, but we have a choice between two different kinds of assumption. An assumption of the more rigorous kind would be that in F the magnitude of P wholly depends in some way on the magnitude of X, where X is identical with just one of the possible causes A, B, C, D, E. Given this, if we observe that over some period, or over some range of instances, P varies in magnitude while one of the possible causes, say A, also varies but all the other possible causes remain constant, we can argue that none of the possible causes other than A can be that on which the magnitude of P wholly depends, and thus conclude that X must be identical with A, that in F the magnitude of P depends wholly on that of A. (But *how* it depends, that is, what the functional law is, must be discovered by an investigation of some other sort.)

An assumption of the less rigorous kind would be that in F the magnitude of P wholly depends in some way on the magnitudes of one or more factors X, X', X'', etc., where each of the actually relevant factors is identical with one of the possible causes A, B, C, D, E. Given this, if we again observe that P varies while, say, A varies but B, C, D, E remain constant, this does not now show that B, for example, cannot be identical with X, etc.; that is, it does not show that variations in B are causally irrelevant to P. All it shows is that the magnitude of P is not *wholly* dependent upon any set of factors that does not include A, for every such set has remained constant while P has varied. This leaves it open that the full cause of P in F might be A itself, or might be some set of factors, such as (A,B,D) which includes A and some of the others as well. All we know is that the list must include A. This observation and this assumption, then, show that a full cause of P in F is (A, ...); that is, that A is an actually relevant factor and there may or may not be others. Repeated applications of this method could fill in other factors, but would not *close* the list. (And, as before, it is a further task, to be carried out by a different sort of investigation, to find *how* the magnitude of P depends on those of the factors thus shown to be actually relevant.)

To close the list, that is, to show that certain factors are actually irrelevant, we need to use an analogue of the method of agreement. If we assume, as before, that the full cause of P in F is some set of factors (X,X',X'', etc.), but also that P is *responsive* to all these factors in the sense that for any variation, in, say, X while X', X'', etc. remain constant P will vary, and that X, X', X'', etc. are identical with some of the possible causes A, B, C, D, E, then if we observe that P remains constant while, say, A, C, D, and E remain constant but B varies, we can conclude that B is causally irrelevant, that none of the X's is identical with B.

USES AND APPLICATIONS OF THE ELIMINATIVE METHODS

We have so far been considering only whether there are demonstratively valid methods of this sort; but by stating more precisely what such methods involve, we may incidentally have removed some of the more obvious objections to the view that such methods can be applied in practice. Thus, by introducing the idea of a *field*, we have given these methods the more modest task of finding the cause of a phenomenon in relation to a field, not the ambitious one of finding conditions that are absolutely necessary and sufficient. By explicitly introducing the possible causes as well as the field, we have freed the user of the method of agreement from having to make the implausible claim that his instances have only one circumstance in common. Instead, he has merely to claim that they have in common only one of the possible causes, while admitting that all the features that belong to the field, or that are constant throughout the field, will belong to all the instances, and that there may be other common features too, though not among those that he has initially judged to be possibly relevant.

Similarly, the user of the method of difference has only to claim that no *possibly relevant* feature other than the one he has picked as the cause is present in I_1 but not in N_1. Also, we have taken explicit account of the ways in which the possibilities of counteracting causes, a plurality of causes, an intermixture of effects, and so on, affect the working of the methods, and we have shown that even when these possibilities are admitted we can still validly draw conclusions, provided that we note explicitly the incompleteness of the conclusions that we are now able to draw (for example, by the method of difference) or the much greater complexity of the observations we need (for example, in variants of the method of agreement or method 8.4).

Eliminative methods and induction. By making explicit the assumptions needed and by presenting the eliminative methods as deductively valid forms of argument, we have abandoned any pretense that methods such as these in themselves solve or remove the "problem of induction." Provided that the requisite observations can be made, the ultimate justification of any application of one of these methods of ampliative induction will depend on the justification of the assumption used; and, since this proposition is general in form, it will presumably have to be supported by some other kind of inductive, or at least nondeductive, reasoning. But we must here leave aside this question of ultimate justification.

Eliminative methods and determinism. Some light, however, can be thrown on the suggestion frequently made that causal determinism is a presupposition of science. If these eliminative methods play some important part in scientific investigation, then it is noteworthy that they all require deterministic assumptions: they all work towards the identification of a cause of a given phenomenon by first assuming that there is some cause to be found for it. However, it has emerged that what we require is not a single universally applicable principle of causality, namely, that every event has a cause, but something at once weaker in some ways and stronger in other ways than such a principle. The principle assumed is that the particular phenomenon P in the chosen field F has a cause, but that a cause of P in F is to be found within a range of factors that is restricted in some way. We have also found that different concepts of a cause are required for concomitant variation and for the other methods. The complaint that the phrase "uniformity of nature" cannot be given a precise or useful meaning, incidentally, has been rebutted by finding in exactly what sense our methods have to assume that nature is uniform.

Employment of the methods. Such assumptions are in fact regularly made, both in investigations within our already developed body of knowledge and in our primitive or common-sense ways of finding out about the world. In both these sorts of inquiry we act on the supposition that any changes that occur are caused; they do not "just happen." In a developed science, the causal knowledge that we already have can limit narrowly the range of possibly relevant causal factors. It can tell us, for this particular phenomenon, what kinds of cause to be on the lookout for, and how to exclude or hold constant some possibly relevant factors while we study the effects of others.

In more elementary discoveries, we restrict the range of possibly relevant factors mainly by the expectation that the cause of any effect will be somewhere in the near spatiotemporal neighborhood of the effect. The possible causes, then, will be features that occur variably within the field in question in the neighborhood of cases where the effect either occurs, or might have occurred, but does not.

Use of method of differences. As an example of the above, singular causal sequences are detected primarily by the use of variants of the method of difference. Becquerel discovered that the radium he carried in a bottle in his pocket was the cause of a burn by noticing that the presence of the radium was the only possible relevant difference between the time when the inflammation developed and the earlier time when it did not, or between the part of his body where the inflammation appeared and the other parts.

Similar considerations tell us that a certain liquid turned this litmus paper red: the paper became red just after it was dipped in the liquid, and nothing else likely to be relevant happened just then. The situations before and after a change constitute our negative and positive instances respectively, and we may well be fairly confident that this is the only possibly relevant factor that has changed. We do not and need not draw up a list of possible causes, but by merely being on the lookout for other changes we can ensure that what would constitute a large number of possible causes (identified as such by their being in the spatiotemporal neighborhood) are the same in I_1 as in N_1.

Repeating the sequence—for example, dipping another similar piece of litmus paper into the liquid—confirms the view that the liquid caused the change of color. But it is not that in this case we are using the method of agreement; the repetition merely makes it less likely that any other change occurred to cause the change of color simultaneously with each of the two dippings, and this confirms our belief that the instances are what the use of the method of difference would require.

Since, in general, it will not be plausible to make an assumption more rigorous then one of kind (8), the conclusion thus established will only be that this individual sequence is an exemplification of a *gappy* causal law, of the form that (A... or...) is necessary and sufficient for *P* in *F*. But this is exactly what our ordinary singular causal statements mean: to say that this caused that says only that this was needed, perhaps in conjunction with other factors that were present, to produce the effect, and it leaves it open that other antecedents altogether (not present in this case) might produce the same effect.

General causal statements, such as "The eating of sweets causes dental decay," are to be interpreted similarly as asserting gappy causal laws. Anyone who says this would admit that the eating of sweets has this effect only in the presence of certain other conditions or in the absence of certain counteracting causes, and he would admit that things other than the eating of sweets might produce tooth decay. And such a gappy causal law can be established by the use of method 8.2, or the method of concomitant variation, or by statistical methods which can be understood as elaborations of these. Such general causal statements are, however, to be understood as asserting gappy causal laws, not mere statistical correlations: anyone who uses such a statement is claiming that in principle the gaps could be filled in.

Use in discovering effects. The use of the above methods is not confined to cases where we begin with a question of the form "What is the cause of so-and-so?" We may just as well begin by asking "What is the effect of so-and-so?"—for example, "What is the effect of applying a high voltage to electrodes in a vacuum tube?" But we are justified in claiming that what is observed to happen is an effect of this only if the requirements for the appropriate variant of the method of difference are fulfilled.

Use of method of agreement. The simpler variants of the method of agreement can be used to establish a causal conclusion only in a case in which our previous knowledge narrowly restricts the possible causes and justifies the belief that they will operate singly. For example, if the character of a disease is such as to indicate that it is of bacterial origin, then the microorganism responsible may be identified through the discovery that only one species of microorganism not already known to be innocent is present in a number of cases of the disease. Otherwise, the observation of what seems to be the only common factor in a number of cases of a phenomenon can be used only very tentatively, to suggest a hypothesis which will need to be tested in some other way.

Where, however, we have a very large number of extremely diverse instances of some effect, and only one factor seems to be present in all of them, we may reason by what is in effect an approximation to method 8.12. The diverse instances cover at least a large selection of all the possible combinations of possibly relevant factors and

their negations. Therefore it is probable that no condition not covered by the formula (A or...) is necessary, and hence, if there is a necessary and sufficient condition, (A or ...) is such, and hence A itself is a sufficient condition of the phenomenon.

Similarly, by an approximation to 8.14, we may reason that the one possibly relevant factor that is found to be absent in a large number of very diverse negative instances is probably a necessary condition of the phenomenon (that is, that its negation is a counteracting cause).

Use of method of concomitant variation. The method of concomitant variation, with statistical procedures that can be considered as elaborations of it, is used in a great many experimental investigations in which one possibly relevant factor is varied (everything else that might be relevant being held constant) to see whether there *is* a causal connection between that one factor and the effect in question. (Of course, what we regard as a single experiment may involve the variation of several factors, but still in such a way that the results will show the effects of varying each factor by itself: such an experiment is merely a combination of several applications of concomitant variation.)

Further uses. The "controlled experiment," in which a control case or control group is compared with an experimental case or experimental group, is again an application of the method of difference (or perhaps the method of residues, if we use the control case, along with already known laws, to tell us what would have happened in the experimental case if the supposed cause had not been introduced.)

An important use of these methods is in the progressive location of a cause. If we take "the drinking of wine" as a single possible cause, then an application of 8.2 may show that the drinking of wine causes intoxication: that is, this factor is *a* necessary element in *a* sufficient condition for this result. But we may then analyze this possible cause further and discover that several factors are included in this one item that we have named "the drinking of wine," and further experiments may show that only one of these factors was really necessary: the necessary element will then be more precisely specified. But the fact that this is always possible leaves it true that in relation to the earlier degree of analysis of factors, the drinking of wine was a necessary element in a sufficient condition, and the discovery of this (admittedly crude) causal law is correct as far as it goes and is an essential step on the way to the more accurate law that is based on a finer analysis of factors.

CRITICISM OF THE METHODS

The sort of example presented above helps to rebut one stock criticism of these methods, which is that they take for granted what is really the most important part of the procedure, namely, the discovery and analysis of factors. Any given application of one of these methods does presuppose some identification of possible causes, but it will not be completely vitiated by the fact that a finer analysis of factors is possible. Besides, the use of the methods themselves (particularly to discover singular causal sequences and hence the dispositional properties of particular things) is part of the procedure by which factors are further distinguished and classified. Also, the assumptions used, especially with regard to the range of possible causes allowed, are corrigible, and in conjunction with the methods they are self-correcting. A mistaken assumption is likely to lead, along with the observations, to contradictory conclusions, and when this happens we are forced to modify the assumption, in particular, to look further afield than we did at first for possibly relevant factors.

A fundamental and widely accepted objection to the claim that these methods form an important part of scientific method is that science is not concerned, or not much concerned, with causal relations in the sense in which these methods can discover them. It may be conceded that the formulation and confirmation of hypotheses and theories of the kind that constitute the greater part of a science such as physics is a scientific procedure quite different from the actual use of these methods. Even the discovery of a law of functional dependence is, as was noted, a task beyond what is achieved by our method of concomitant variation. It may also be conceded that many sciences are concerned largely with the simple discovery of new items and the tracing of processes rather than with causal relationships. Further, it was noted that these methods logically *cannot* be the whole of scientific procedure, since they require assumptions which they themselves cannot support.

In reply to this objection, however, it can be stressed, first, that a great deal of common-sense everyday knowledge, and also a great deal of knowledge in the more empirical sciences, is of causal relations of this sort, partly of singular causal sequences and partly of laws, especially of the incomplete or gappy form at which these methods characteristically arrive.

Second, it is largely such empirical causal relations that are explained by, and that support, the deeper theories and hypotheses of a developed science. But if they are to be used thus, they must be established independently.

Third, although descriptions of the eliminative methods of induction have often been associated with a kind of ground-floor empiricism which takes knowledge to be wholly concerned with empirical relations between directly observable things, qualities, and processes, the methods themselves are not tied to this doctrine but can establish causal relations between entities that are indirectly observed. For example, as long as there is any way, direct or indirect, of determining when a magnetic field is present and when there is an electric current in a wire, the methods can establish the fact that such a current will produce a magnetic field.

Finally, even where such causal relations are not the main object of inquiry, in investigation we constantly make use of causal relations, especially of singular causal sequences. In measuring, say, a voltage, we are assuming that it was the connecting of the meter across those terminals that caused this deflection of its needle, and the precautions that ensure that this is really so are to be explained in terms of our methods.

In fact, these methods are constantly used, explicitly or implicitly, both to suggest causal hypotheses and to confirm them. One should not, of course, expect any methods of empirical inquiry to establish conclusions beyond all possibility of doubt or all need of refinement, but in using these methods we can frequently say at least this: we have reason to suppose that for an event of this kind in this field there is some cause, and if the cause is not such-and-such, we cannot see what else the cause might be.

Bibliography

WORKS ON INDUCTION

The classical study of eliminative induction remains that of J. S. Mill, *A System of Logic* (London, 1843), Book III, Chs. 8–10. Mill acknowledges that his study owes much to John Herschell, *A Preliminary Discourse on the Study of Natural Philosophy* (London, 1831), Part II, Ch. 6, and both are fundamentally indebted to Francis Bacon, *Novum Organum* (London, 1620), Book II. Since Mill, the literature has become extensive, but mostly in textbooks rather than in original works on logic or philosophy. There have been many worthwhile treatments of eliminative induction that are far above the textbook level—notably those of John Venn, *Empirical Logic* (London, 1889), Ch. 17; Christoff von Sigwart, *Logic*, 2d ed. (Freiburg, 1893), translated by Helen Dendy as *Logic* (London, 1895), Vol. II, Part II, Ch. 5; and H. W. B. Joseph, *An Introduction to Logic* (Oxford, 1906), Ch. 20. But there are only a small number of writers who, either by criticizing Mill or developing his account, have added something new and substantial to either the logic or the philosophy of eliminative induction.

CRITICISMS OF MILL'S METHODS

Mill's most important critics are William Whewell, *The Philosophy of Discovery* (London, 1860), Ch. 22; W. S. Jevons, *The Principles of Science* (London, 1874), Chs. 11, 19, and 23; F. H. Bradley, *The Principles of Logic* (London, 1883), Book II, Part II, Ch. 3; and M. R. Cohen and Ernest Nagel, *An Introduction to Logic and Scientific Method* (New York, 1934), Ch. 13.

ELABORATIONS ON MILL'S METHODS

The main writers who have tried to develop Mill's ideas on the logical side are W. E. Johnson, *Logic* (Cambridge, 1924), Part II, Ch. 10; C. D. Broad, "The Principles of Demonstrative Induction" in *Mind,* Vol. 39 (1930) 302–317 and 426–439; and G. H. von Wright, *A Treatise on Induction and Probability* (London, 1951). Broad, following Johnson, undertakes a demonstrative reconstruction of Mill's methods and tries to extend eliminative methods to reasonings that terminate in quantitative laws. Von Wright's is the most thorough treatment so far published and studies the conditions under which "complete elimination" can be achieved even with what are here called the "less rigorous" kinds of assumptions. His account, however, seems somewhat unclear.

FURTHER STUDIES

The only major addition to the pure philosophy of induction is that of J. M. Keynes, *A Treatise on Probability* (London, 1921), Part III. Three recent books which contain some discussion of it are J. O. Wisdom, *Foundations of Inference in Natural Science* (London, 1952), Ch. 11; S. F. Barker, *Induction and Hypothesis* (Oxford and Ithaca, 1957), Ch. 3; and J. P. Day, *Inductive Probability* (London, 1961), Sec. 5.

J. L. MACKIE

MILTON, JOHN (1608–1674), English poet, author, and political writer. Milton was born in London, the son of a prosperous scrivener. He was educated at St. Paul's School in London and Christ's College, Cambridge. After receiving an M.A. in 1632, he spent six years in study at his father's estate in Horton. In 1638 and 1639 he traveled to Italy, where he met Galileo, and on his return to London he found employment as a tutor. He wrote five pamphlets (1641–1642) attacking episcopacy, and his unhappy marriage in 1642 lent intensity to his subsequent tracts on divorce. In 1644 he published the tract *Of Education,* as well as *Areopagitica,* his famous attack on censorship of the press. His pamphlet justifying regicide, *Tenure of Kings and Magistrates* (1649), probably brought him the post of secretary for foreign tongues to the Council of State. He wrote several defenses of the revolutionary government, but after 1652 total blindness forced him to withdraw gradually from public life. He turned to the completion of his theological treatise, *De Doctrina Christiana,* and his *History of Britain* and to the fulfillment of his poetic ambitions. Despite a brief return to public controversy in 1659 and 1660, Milton was treated leniently by the Restoration government. His epic, *Paradise Lost,* was published in 1667; *Samson Agonistes* and *Paradise Regained* appeared together, in one volume, in 1671. He died in 1674, survived by his third wife.

Approach and method. Milton was essentially a religious and ethical thinker, and his views are a striking blend of Christian humanism and Puritanism. The fullest statement of his position is *De Doctrina Christiana,* which was complete in all but certain details by 1660.

Milton believed that the Bible is divine revelation, plain and perspicuous in all things necessary to salvation. In matters of religion Scripture is the only outward rule or authority, and conscience, illuminated by the spirit of God, the only guide within. This scrupulous Biblicism, however, is linked (as in Socinianism) with a strong emphasis on reason. Conscience, even when illuminated by the spirit, operates in rational terms rather than through mystical insight, so that "right reason" becomes the guide to Scripture. At the heart of this view, authorizing yet limiting the role of reason, is the doctrine that Scripture is an accommodation of God's will to the limited understanding of man. God has made in the Bible as full a revelation of himself as man is capable of receiving, and the safest approach is thus to form in the mind "such a conception of God, as shall correspond with his own delineation and representation of himself." This view eliminates speculations of a transcendental kind, reserving an area of mystery into which reason may not trespass; at the same time it encourages reason to assimilate Biblical revelation to the categories of ethics. Thus, the theological treatise, like *Paradise Lost,* is a theodicy; its aim is to discover a view of God which is both worthy of him and consistent with revelation.

Theology. Milton's aim led him to some unorthodox conclusions, the most striking of which is his rejection of the doctrine of the Trinity. Embracing a loosely Arian position, he insisted on the unity of God and the consequent subordination of the Son and the Holy Spirit to the Father. The Son is the first of the creatures, and although he is the perfect image of the Father and even made of the same substance, he is not of one essence with the Father. The Spirit, a rather supernumerary figure, was created at a later date than the Son. Milton maintained that the doctrine of the Trinity is a purely man-made mystery, with no scriptural foundation; it defies logic and degrades our conception of deity.

There was a second deviation from orthodoxy in the direction of monism. Milton rejected the Augustinian doctrine of the creation of the world *ex nihilo* and presented a theory of creation *de Deo.* Drawing support from both Scripture and reason, he argued that the universe was made out of the substance of God. This view, he claimed, is not only more logical than the alternative position, but in its assertion of the goodness of matter it underlines more emphatically the benevolence of the creator. The same antiascetic impulse is present in Milton's theory of body and soul; he argued that the higher comprehends the lower, that spirit contains matter, and that the body should thus be seen not as the prison house of the soul but as integral to it: "The whole man is soul, and the soul man." From this conclusion two corollaries proceed: first, the human soul is not created immediately by God but is propagated from father to son in a natural order; second, the whole man dies, body and soul, and does not live again until the end of time. Milton's view of spirit and matter probably encouraged both his rejection of traditional Eucharistic theory and his radical endorsement of divorce and polygamy.

Free will. The doctrines we have examined, which are departures from the main traditions of Christianity, were designed to avoid dualism and to make theology conform to the canons of logical thought. A second group of doctrines emerged as a defense of free will against Calvinism. Milton rejected the orthodox Calvinist view of predestination and reduced the decree of predestination to a general offer of salvation to all men who are willing to believe. Other Arminian views reinforced his conviction that man is free to pursue or refuse salvation. Milton wished to show that regeneration is a matter neither of faith nor of works but of works of faith. Faith, it is true, is a gift of God, but every man is given sufficient grace to put a saving faith within his reach. Finally, the object of a saving faith is God the Father rather than Christ, so that such a faith is possible beyond the bounds of the Christian religion.

Ethics. The relation of the individual to the community absorbed Milton's attention during two decades of public controversy (1640–1660). His tracts, written in response to the disturbing events of the period, received force and direction from his lasting concern with liberty. Reason is "but choosing"; it is the power of ethical action, and man must therefore be free to choose between good and evil. Only by knowing evil and rejecting it can one become virtuous, for, as Milton remarked in *Areopagitica,* "That which purifies us is trial, and trial is by what is contrary." Prescriptive morality, enforced by church or state, prevents both the real understanding of truths already known and the discovery of new truths.

Milton defended the autonomy of reason by appealing from man-made authorities—positive law, canon law, custom, or tradition—to the law of nature. The work of John Selden probably encouraged him to develop a distinction between the primary law of nature, given to Adam at the creation, and the secondary law, the imperfect remnants of the primary law in fallen man. Secondary law allows for the "hardness of heart" which was introduced by the Fall and thus prescribes for such aspects of man's fallen state as war, servitude, divorce, and private property. In *De Doctrina Christiana,* however, Milton stressed the importance of the primary or unwritten law of nature which was "given originally to Adam, and of which a certain remnant, or imperfect illumination, still dwells in the hearts of all mankind; which, in the regenerate, under the influence of the Holy Spirit, is daily tending towards a renewal of its primitive brightness." This law teaches whatever is intrinsically good and agreeable to right reason, and in making it the final authority, Milton gave his ethic a religious orientation.

Thus, Milton's ethical position was that of the Christian humanist. Grace, he believed, comes to perfect nature, not to destroy it; by means of grace reason is illuminated and natural virtue sanctified. In this emphasis he resembled the Cambridge Platonists, writers like Benjamin Whichcote, John Smith, and Nathanael Culverwel, who sought to unify man's natural and religious experience by insisting that reason is, "the candle of the Lord." Milton also resembled these philosophers in his habit of drawing upon Platonic writings, particularly on Plato's myths, in order to enrich his treatment of reason and the passions. Although his stress on the Bible prevented classical philosophy from making a direct contribution to his theology, Platonism nonetheless played a major and continuous part in shaping his ethical idealism.

The influence of Puritanism, as well as of humanism, led Milton to stress the importance of liberty. Believers are a "royal priesthood," and those who force the conscience of the individual are guilty of forcing the spirit of God. Central to Milton's conception of Christian liberty is the distinction between the Mosaic law, a law of bondage which extorts servile obedience through fear, and the gospel, which offers a free, elective, and spiritual service based on man's filial relation to God. Spiritual regeneration, moreover, brings about a renewal of man's natural powers; the understanding is restored in large measure to its primitive clearness, the will to its primitive liberty. This strong emphasis on inner law led Milton to the antinomian view that Christ, by his life and death, abrogated the whole Mosaic law, the moral parts as well as the judicial and ceremonial parts. The sum of the law—love God and love your neighbor—remains and must be fulfilled by following the spirit, or the "internal scripture" (*De Doctrina Christiana*, I, xxvii). At this point, in spite of a continuing emphasis on reason, Milton had moved toward a position similar to the Quaker doctrine of inner light.

Church and state. Despite his early support of Presbyterianism, Milton soon came to believe that "*New Presbyter* is but *Old Priest* writ large." He defended the growth of religious sects on the ground that God requires unity of spirit rather than unity of doctrine, and he denied both the claim of the church to exercise secular power and that of the state to wield ecclesiastical power. His final view was that a particular church is a purely voluntary association of believers. Ministers should be elected by their congregations and supported by free offerings, and no ceremonial observances, such as the Sabbath, should be made obligatory. Despite his separation of the powers of church and state, however, Milton could not follow his more radical contemporaries in divorcing civil good from the good of religion. Although he denied the magistrate "compulsive" powers in matters of religion, he left him the

"defensive" function of protecting Protestant Christianity from the threat of open "popery and idolatry."

Milton's view of the state varied in accordance with the changing conditions in which he was called upon to defend the revolutionary party. A basic line of his argument founds the state upon a social contract. Men are born free, but the effects of the Fall cause them to agree to a common league to bind one another from mutual injury. The people are thus the sovereign power in the state and have the right to revoke the power that they have delegated. When it became apparent that the Puritan party represented a small part of the nation, Milton resorted to a further argument which was not entirely consistent with the social contract theory. The revolutionary party, he maintained, was guided by providence and consisted of those most worthy to rule and to interpret the good of the people. The minority must force the majority to be free.

Poetry. The themes and preoccupations of Milton's prose gain in power when expressed in the "more simple, sensuous, and passionate" language of poetry. All the major poems center on the theme of temptation and move toward a clarification of true heroism. Temptation works through passion, in its simplest form through sensuality and anger but more subtly through specious reasoning and the lure of evil means to good ends. The definition of true heroism involves the exposure of such false forms as the romantic sensuality of Comus in the early "Masque" (1634) or Satan's courage of despair in the late epics. *Paradise Lost*, which was written to justify God's ways to man by dramatizing man's freedom and responsibility, ends with Adam setting out to imitate the spiritual heroism of the Son of God—revealed to him in a vision—and thus to achieve a "paradise within" which will be "happier far" than the outward paradise he has lost. Samson, in *Samson Agonistes*, also achieves a victory over himself through suffering and discovers that freedom is enjoyed only in the service of God. *Paradise Regained*, which has as its subject the temptation of Jesus in the wilderness, presents Milton's final and most complete study of heroism. Avoiding the temptations to distrust and presumption, the Son rejects Satan's offers of worldly power and authority and realizes the spiritual sense in which he is Messiah.

Arts and sciences. In his literary theory Milton emphasized the importance of genres and of decorum and urged the power of literature to create moral order in the individual and the society. (See his Preface to Book II of *The Reason of Church Government*, the Preface to *Samson Agonistes*, and the invocations to Books I, III, and IX of *Paradise Lost*.) His view of education (*Of Education*) was humanistic in its stress on languages and classical texts, its dislike of scholasticism, and its ethical aim. He showed no deep interest in the new science, and he used the traditional science in his poetry because it was for him a better source of metaphor. As a historian he had a critical sense of the value of evidence, but his view of history moved from millenarian optimism to the pessimism which informs the survey of history in the last two books of *Paradise Lost*.

Works by Milton

The definitive edition of the text is *The Works of John Milton*, Frank Allen Patterson et al., eds., 18 vols. (New York, 1931–1938), with an index, 2 vols. (New York, 1940). A variorum commentary on the poems is in preparation, with Merritt Y. Hughes as the general editor, and it will be published as a supplement to the Patterson edition.

There are editions of the poetry and selected prose by Frank Allen Patterson, *The Student's Milton* (New York, 1930; rev. ed., 1933); Merritt Y. Hughes, *Complete Poems and Major Prose* (New York, 1957); and others. Editions of the poetry include those by James Holly Hanford, *Poems* (New York, 1937; 2d ed., 1953); Harris Francis Fletcher, *Complete Poetical Works* (Boston, 1941); and Helen Darbishire, *Poetical Works*, 2 vols. (Oxford, 1952–1955).

Scholarly introductions provide continuous commentary on the prose in the closely annotated *Complete Prose Works,* Donald M. Wolfe et al., eds. (New Haven, 1953——), of which there are eight projected volumes.

Works on Milton

GENERAL CRITICISM

Douglas Bush provides a penetrating review of Milton's life and works in *English Literature in the Earlier Seventeenth Century* (Oxford, 1945; rev. ed., 1962); a survey of the scholarship is found in James Holly Hanford, *A Milton Handbook*, 4th ed. (New York, 1946). The standard biography is still David Masson's *The Life of John Milton*, 6 vols. (London, 1859–1880; rev. ed., with index, 1881–1896).

MILTON'S THOUGHT

Pioneer work is found in Denis Saurat's stimulating if erratic *Milton: Man and Thinker* (London, 1925; rev. ed., 1944) and in the more literary *Milton* (London, 1930) by E. M. W. Tillyard. G. N. Conklin considers theological method in *Biblical Criticism and Heresy in Milton* (New York, 1949), and the growth and significance of Milton's theology are examined authoritatively by Maurice W. Kelley in *This Great Argument* (Princeton, N.J., 1941). On Milton's political and ethical views, see A. S. P. Woodhouse, "Milton, Puritanism and Liberty," in *University of Toronto Quarterly*, Vol. 4 (1934–1935), 483–513; William Haller, *The Rise of Puritanism* (New York, 1938) and *Liberty and Reformation in the Puritan Revolution* (New York, 1955); Arthur Barker, *Milton and the Puritan Dilemma, 1641–1660* (Toronto, 1942; reprinted, 1955); Michael Fixler, *Milton and the Kingdoms of God* (London, 1964); Ernest Sirluck, "Milton's Political Thought: The First Cycle," in *Modern Philology*, Vol. 61 (1964), 209–224.

Other aspects of Milton's thought are covered in Kester Svendsen, *Milton and Science* (Cambridge, Mass., 1956); Howard Schultz, *Milton and Forbidden Knowledge* (New York, 1955); Walter C. Curry, *Milton's Ontology, Cosmogony and Physics* (Lexington, Ky., 1957); and Irene Samuel, *Plato and Milton* (Ithaca, N.Y., 1947). Further criticism is listed in a selective bibliography by Douglas Bush, *op. cit.;* in the bibliographies by David H. Stevens, *A Reference Guide to Milton, From 1800 to the Present Day* (Chicago, 1930); Harris Francis Fletcher, *Contributions to a Milton Bibliography, 1800–1930* (Urbana, Ill., 1931); and Calvin Huckabay, *John Milton: A Bibliographical Supplement, 1929–1957* (Pittsburgh, 1960); and the annual bibliographies of *Studies in Philology* and *PMLA*.

H. R. MacCallum

MIMESIS.

The Greek *mimēsis* covers two meanings, that of imitation and that of artistic representation. A mimesis theory of music, according to which music imitates numbers, and thus things, has been attributed to certain Pythagoreans of the fifth century B.C., but it is in Plato that the term became important. Holding, at least at one stage of his thought, that particulars resemble or imitate the Forms which give rise to them, he claimed that this was one reason for the inferiority of the phenomenal world: it consisted of imitations instead of originals.

In the *Republic* he developed the view that art corrupts the consumer because it stands in relation to the phenomenal world as the latter stands to the Forms. Because art is thus an imitation of an imitation, it is even further removed from the truth than the world it imitates. It is a matter of controversy whether Plato admitted the exception that some art may be nonrepresentational and thus nonimitative, or that a true artist may imitate the Forms directly.

Aristotle in his *Poetics* took from Plato the concept of mimesis and the importance of the universal in art, but, perhaps because his universals were immanent ones, he did not regard art as inferior because it was imitative. His views influenced Hellenistic, Roman, and modern writers until the rise of romanticism in the eighteenth century.

Bibliography

Butcher, S. H., *Aristotle's Theory of Poetry*, 4th ed. London, 1923. Ch. 2.

Koller, H., *Die Mimesis in der Antike*. Bern, 1954.

Tate, J., "Plato and Imitation." *Classical Quarterly*, Vol. 26 (1932), 161–169.

G. B. Kerferd

MINAGAWA KIEN (1734–1807), Japanese Confucianist, painter, and writer. Minagawa was born in Kyoto. At the age of 28, having established himself as a Confucianist, he became the official scholar for Lord Matsudaira Nobumine. His literary skill made him an outstanding figure in Kyoto circles; he had a following of 3,000. For a Confucianist his life was unusually dissipated. His era was a time of moral decline, but this was eventually checked by several edicts. The 1790 edict against "heterodox doctrines" affected Minagawa and he reformed his habits, though his ideas did not change.

Minagawa's philosophical reputation has recently grown among Japanese philosophers because of his positivist approach to Confucian studies. He is considered an eclectic because he upheld neither the official Chu Hsi school of Neo-Confucianism nor the rival Wang Yang-ming school. Minagawa was analytic and positivist, which made him a kind of forerunner of Western philosophy in Japan. This assessment stems largely from two of Minagawa's works, *Ekigaku kaibutsu* ("The Learning of the Book of Changes on the Discovery of Things") and *Meichū rokkan* ("Six Chapters on Categories").

Ekigaku kaibutsu starts from the Chinese classic *I Ching*, the "Book of Changes" or "Book of Divination," which despite its esoteric nature stimulated Minagawa and other Confucianists to make a study of celestial phenomena. *Ekigaku kaibutsu* clearly manifests his lifetime search for the nature of things. However, for him "things" are mainly human affairs seen from the ethicopolitical point of view, and their "discovery" or investigation is in relation to the ruling of the realm.

The "Six Chapters on Categories" analyzes the origins of basic concepts or categories. Starting with words, Minagawa shows that they are abstract expressions of reality itself. He believes that we grasp reality objectively through its manifestation in words. This rather naive realist epistemology is an attempt to penetrate the nature of things without employing *ri*, Chu Hsi's abstract "principle," or the "innate knowledge" of Wang Yang-ming. Among Minagawa's categories, significant ones are learning or science (*gaku*) and wisdom (*tetsu*). Although he did not wholly grasp modern science or philosophy, he came very close.

Another topic of interest to Minagawa is the samurai class, which he criticizes in many of his writings. He hoped the samurai would survive as the intellectual and moral leaders of the ordinary people.

Bibliography

For Minagawa's works see *Nihon Tetsugaku Shisō Zensho* ("Library of Japanese Philosophical Thought"), Saigusa Hiroto, ed. (Tokyo, 1957), Vol. I, pp. 109–119, and Saigusa Hiroto, *Nihon Yuibutsuronsha* ("Japanese Materialists"; Tokyo, 1956), pp. 95–107.

GINO K. PIOVESANA, S.J.

MIND. See IDEALISM; MIND–BODY PROBLEM; OTHER MINDS; PERSONAL IDENTITY; PSYCHOLOGY; REASON; THINKING.

MIND–BODY PROBLEM. The mind–body problem, in the first instance, concerns the question whether a valid distinction can be made between the mind and the body. If such a distinction can be made, then we can ask whether in fact any things exist to which we can apply either term, or both terms. Finally, if there are things to which both terms can be applied, we can, for those cases, ask what the relation is between the mind and the body.

DISTINCTION BETWEEN MIND AND BODY

Is the distinction between mind and body valid? To begin, it is generally agreed that we can distinguish two sorts of statements made about people. There are those statements which describe a person's body, his bodily states and dispositions, and events that occur in and to his body. It is characteristic of such statements that they can be made of any physical object whatsoever. There are, however, statements that are made exclusively about people (and, in some cases, animals). These statements describe thoughts and feelings, hopes and fears, memories and expectations, moods and humors, features of personality and character, acts of deliberating, judging, and choosing, motives and intentions, and so on. It is to such things as these that the words "mind" and "mental" usually refer.

It is further very widely agreed that these two sorts of statements, which we shall call physicalistic statements and mentalistic statements, differ in meaning, so that neither can be translated into the other. There have been philosophers who have denied this and attempted to provide translations. Thus, Berkeley argued that physicalistic statements should be construed as mentalistic statements. More recently the physicalists and logical behaviorists have argued the reverse, maintaining that mentalistic statements should be construed as physicalistic statements. No one, however, has provided a translation schema that has stood up under criticism. Even so formida-

ble a foe of any mental–physical dualism as Gilbert Ryle, who analyzes many sorts of mentalistic statements in terms of physicalistic ones, has maintained that reports of sensations and feelings cannot be so analyzed.

Some philosophers, admitting the difference in meaning, deny that what we have called mentalistic statements are really statements at all. Utterances such as "I feel bored" and "I am depressed," according to this view, are not used to describe or report (any more than "Ho hum" and "Alas, alack" are so used). They are bits of behavior that are symptoms, expressions, or effects of inner (physical) conditions, rather than ways of making assertions. Although this view does correctly indicate one aspect of such utterances, it cannot account for the obvious fact that such utterances are often also used to make true or false statements. One can say "I feel bored" and be lying (whereas one cannot say "Ho hum" and be lying).

If it is agreed that there are genuine mentalistic statements as well as physicalistic statements, then it should be noted that there are many statements of the one sort that in no way logically entail any statements of the other sort. Therefore, it is at least a logical possibility that some mentalistic statements but no physicalistic statements are true, or vice versa. In his *Meditations* (1641), Descartes brought this out clearly in two ways: by saying that one could be sure of the existence of mental events while being in complete doubt about the existence of bodies, and by saying that God could make the mind exist in separation from the body. Thus, survival in a disembodied state after the death of the body is at least a logical possibility. Furthermore, it is logically possible for complex physical behavior to occur without any mental events at all. As we shall see below, Descartes held that this was precisely the case for animals, which he believed to be automata devoid of thought (although capable of feelings); he also raised the possibility that it might be the case for his fellow men. We have here the problem of other minds, namely, What reasons might there be for thinking that anything other than oneself has mental events? The possibility of solipsism as well as that of disembodied existence is derived from the fact that mentalistic statements and physicalistic statements are not logically connected.

Even if there are no direct logical connections, there still may be empirical facts that indicate a relation between mentalistic and physicalistic statements. Perhaps such statements, despite their difference in meaning, refer to one and the same set of facts, substances, events, or properties. Or perhaps they refer to different sets of properties, but the properties belong to one and the same set of substances. Or perhaps they refer to quite different substances. All these possibilities, and more, remain to be chosen from when we attempt to solve the mind–body problem. The fact that mentalistic statements and physicalistic statements differ in meaning in no way favors one solution or another. Rather, it establishes that there is a problem here.

What is a mind? It was Plato who was the first to make a sharp distinction between the mind and the body, holding that the mind could exist both before and after its residence in the body and could rule the body during that residence. St. Augustine further developed this distinction and theorized in more detail about the relation between the two. But it was Descartes who first developed a systematic theory of the natures and interrelationship of mind and body.

For Descartes both body and mind were substances, but with utterly different basic natures. Body is extended and unthinking; mind is thinking and unextended. Of the two concepts, that of body was the more original and enduring. Descartes rejected the currently popular Aristotelian concept of body, which was, with its form – matter and actuality – potentiality dimensions, an essentially biological concept of matter. By isolating extension and ignoring all else, Descartes succeeded in purging the concept of body of its spiritualistic, teleological, and animistic features. In this way he arrived at a concept much more consistent with the new science of physics.

Mental-substance theory. In comparison with this clear concept of body, Descartes's concept of mind, often called the mental-substance, or pure-ego, concept, is somewhat obscure. It is the view that the mind is an enduring, immaterial, nonextended stuff that undergoes changes consisting in the performance of various acts. These acts are all acts of thinking, understood very broadly, for a thing which thinks "is a thing which doubts, understands, conceives, affirms, denies, wills, refuses, which also imagines and feels" (*Meditations,* II). Since it is the essence of mental substance to think, this substance is always engaged in the performance of one or another of the above activities.

The basic difficulty here is to give some content to the notion of "substance." Locke charged that it was a most confused idea, little better than the idea of a something-I-know-not-what, which acts in some-way-I-know-not-how. Hume argued that it could be given no meaning at all. And Kant, in his discussions of the paralogisms (*Critique of Pure Reason*), showed how the concept is based on confusing logical requirements for the subject of judgments with a metaphysical determination of some sort of absolute subject.

Bundle theory. Because it seems unlikely that the concept of mental substance can be made clear, many philosophers have turned to the most promising alternative, championed by Hume. It is called the "bundle" concept, since it is the view that the mind is "nothing but a bundle or collection of different perceptions, which succeed each other with an inconceivable rapidity, and are in a perpetual flux and movement" (*Treatise of Human Nature*, I, iv, 6). The problem is to say how events are related so as to belong to one bundle rather than another. Hume suggested that they are related by resemblance, contiguity, and causation, but in the Appendix to his *Treatise* (1739) he admitted that he had failed to account for the "real simplicity and identity" of the mind. Another proposal is that it is memory that is the key condition; events are said to be in the same mind if they are capable of being remembered at a later date. This is at best a sufficient condition rather than a necessary one, since, as Hume pointed out, there are many past thoughts that we cannot remember.

No bundle theory has yet withstood criticism. Accounts in terms of resemblance, contiguity, or causation are too weak because it is merely an empirical fact that only

events in the same mind tend to be so related; it is not impossible for mental events to be so related and still be undeniably in different minds. Hume diagnosed the basic difficulty here when he said, again in the Appendix, that if we take mental events to be separate existences, then any principles of connection will be extrinsic and accidental, yielding only an artificial unity rather than that natural unity which minds possess. On the other hand, the proposal that mental events are linked by memory does provide a more natural unity, but only at the cost of circularity. Something can be a genuine memory of an earlier mental event only if the earlier event was experienced by the same person. Thus, memory already presupposes the concept of the mind and cannot be used to explain that concept.

Stream-of-consciousness theory. In an attempt to find an intermediary between the mental-substance and the bundle theories, William James proposed that the mind is a "stream of consciousness." We can see that this view fails to solve our difficulties, however, when we note the occurrence of states of unconsciousness. If we assert that the stream continues during states of unconsciousness, then we face the problems involved in the substance theory; if we assert that there are genuine gaps in consciousness, then we have the problems of the bundle theory in trying to relate the separate segments.

Finally, we may try to find the unity of the mind not in internal connections between mental events but in their relation to something else—for example, the body. The precise account we gave would depend upon how we conceived the relation between mind and body. We might define a mind, for example, as that set of mental events which is produced by any one particular body. Any such view defining the mind in terms of the body faces the difficulty of ruling out even the logical possibility that the mind continues to exist, in disembodied form, after the death of the body. It should be noted, however, for the slight consolation it might bring, that disembodied mental events would, by this account, remain a logical possibility if we allowed that mental events could occur without being a part of any mind.

Essence of the mental. The fact of the matter is that there does not as yet exist a very satisfactory account of our concept of the mind. We know that for each person a series of mental changes occurs, but if we try to say exactly what it is that changes we fall into utter obscurity; if we take the mind to be simply the collection of those changes, we seem to be leaving out precisely what ties them together into the mind. Because of this inability to say what a mind is, many philosophers prefer to speak not of minds as such but simply of mental facts, mental states, mental properties, mental acts, mental processes, mental events, etc. We can indicate roughly what we mean by each of these terms by indicating the expressions we use to report such things. Thus, to take the last mentioned, mental events—the most important of all for the mind – body problem—we may say that it refers to the class of events we report when we say such things as "A name just came to me," "I just had the thought that . . . ," "I have just decided that . . . ," "I just had the wish that . . . ," "Just now I had the fear that . . . ," "I feel feverish," "My foot hurts," "I just felt a glow of pride when I thought of my son's accomplishment," etc. These are all reports of mental events.

Since reports like these are only a small part of those we make about ourselves, what is it about them that leads us to call the events they report mental? One popular suggestion is that they are made immediately, without any sort of inference. But this does not distinguish them from many simple judgments about physical events, where the judgments are made easily and without inference; for example, we often judge without inference that one event followed another. Another suggestion is that they are incorrigible—that is, not open to correction in the light of other experience. But it is a familiar fact that such reports are often corrected either by the reporter himself or by others. For example, one may say, "I thought the pain was in my shoulder, but now I realize it is my neck that hurts." The most that can be said about reports of mental events is that the person reporting need not do so on the basis of perceptions via his five senses or on the basis of inferences from such perceptions; the mere occurrence of the event *eo ipso* puts the person to whom it occurred in a position to report it. This is sometimes expressed by saying that the person has "privileged access" to these events. A person is in this privileged position only with respect to his own mental events, and only while they are occurring or immediately afterward. It is this feature of privileged position that may be said to define at least one important sense of "mental": it can be applied not only to events, as we have done, but to states, properties, acts, etc., as well. This definition, however, covers a somewhat narrow set of characteristics; in this sense being good at arithmetic and being ambitious would not qualify as essentially mental, since they are not cases in which the person himself is in the privileged position of deciding whether he has those properties.

We should take note of another proposal for characterizing the mental, that of Franz Brentano. He claimed that mental phenomena are "intentional"; that is, they have content or contain an object in themselves, whether or not such content or object actually exists. Wanting something would be an example of an intentional phenomenon, since the content or object of that want may not exist, as in the case of wanting a flying horse. Other examples are hoping, seeking, believing, doubting, and imagining. It was Brentano's claim that intentional phenomena cannot be analyzed into purely physical terms. At present this claim is still a matter of controversy.

MONISTIC THEORIES

Having come to some notion of what the mind is, or at least of what mental events are, we may now raise the following question: When a person experiences a mental event, what is the relation, if any, between that mental event and the person's body? There are, in general, two sorts of theories: monistic theories, which deny that there are two things to be related, and dualistic theories, which admit that there are two things to be related and offer various accounts of this relation. These will be taken in order.

Extreme materialism. The oldest mind – body theory is an extreme form of materialism. Materialism has many variants, but it always holds that matter is fundamental and that whatever else exists is dependent on matter; in its most extreme form materialism is the view that whatever exists is physical. From this radical view is derived the thesis, already discussed, that utterances reporting mental events are either meaningless or else synonymous with utterances reporting physical events. In psychology this position has been called behaviorism (although it might be called logical behaviorism, to distinguish it from a methodological behaviorism that recommends merely that psychologists confine their investigations to physical phenomena). Philosophically this position is known as physicalism. It was supported by some of the members of the Vienna circle, notably Otto Neurath and Rudolf Carnap, although not by the founder, Moritz Schlick. This position no longer has many supporters, primarily because it has proved impossible to provide a plausible translation into physical terms of even so simple a mentalistic report as "I have a pain."

A more moderate but no less shocking version of materialism is the claim that mentalistic reports have their own special meaning, to be sure, but are always and everywhere false. According to this view, there have never existed thoughts, feelings, sensations, images, etc., and the vast majority of us who have believed these things to exist were simply mistaken, just as those who believed witches to exist were mistaken. Some have attempted to dismiss this view as self-refuting, as follows: anyone who holds such a view thinks it to be true, so that there will be at least one thought, namely that there are no thoughts; therefore, the view cannot be true. This argument fails because a serious proponent, determined to be consistent, would deny that he or anyone else had thoughts about this theory or anything at all. The argument does have the value, however, that it reminds us of how drastically we must revise our beliefs (assuming we are allowed to keep the concept of "beliefs") if we accept this view. And for what? Is it not as obvious as anything can be that our reports of the occurrence of feelings, thoughts, etc., are at least some of the time true—that is, that feelings and thoughts do occur? Surely it is undeniable.

Descartes did believe that animals are totally devoid of mental events. He called them automata, comparing them to clocks and other machines whose movements are solely determined by physical forces. He concluded this from the fact that their capacities and range of behavior are severely limited, and he was particularly struck by the fact that animals never develop languages. He was strengthened in the conviction that animals lack mental events by the thought that if some animals have mental events, then all do, which implied for him that all animals have immortal souls, including oysters and sponges, creatures "too imperfect to make it possible to believe it of them."

Difficult as it is to accept the view that animals are all automata, it is much more difficult to believe that all humans (including oneself) are automata, devoid of all mental events. Even the aggressive materialists of the French Enlightenment shrank from drawing this conclusion. La Mettrie did entitle one book *Man a Machine* (1748), but he also wrote "Animals More than Machines" (1750); his view seems to have been epiphenomenalistic, that both animals and men have mental events, but these are completely causally dependent on bodily activity. Holbach seemed to hold an identity theory, that thoughts and feelings occur, to be sure, but are physical in nature. Even the most extreme, Pierre Cabanis, who characterized man in the saying *Les nerfs – voilà tout l'homme,* admitted that thoughts exist when he said that the brain secretes thought just as the liver secretes bile. We may express these views by saying that if man is an automaton, he is a *"conscious* automaton," to use the phrase of T. H. Huxley. The occurrence of thoughts and feelings is not denied. What is denied is the Cartesian doctrine that in the case of humans, thoughts and feelings constitute a separate, nonphysical substance that can affect the body. We find this view even in the self-styled "materialism" of Marx. In *The German Ideology* he wrote: "Men's conceptions, thoughts, spiritual intercourse, here still appear as the direct emanation of their material conduct." Such a view will be discussed below under the heading of epiphenomenalism.

Identity theory. A version of materialism that is much discussed today is the identity theory, recently presented and defended by J. J. C. Smart and H. Feigl, among others. The identity theorist uses the familiar philosophical distinction between significance and reference, or connotation and denotation, to make the claim that mentalistic and physicalistic expressions differ in significance or connotation but will turn out as a matter of empirical fact to refer to or denote one and the same thing, namely *physical* phenomena. Other examples of this kind of *de facto* identity would be the morning star and the evening star, water and H_2O, and lightning and a particular sort of electrical discharge. In all these cases the discovery of identity was not merely a philosophical discovery but, at least in part, an empirical discovery. Thus, the statement by Hobbes—who can be said to have held an identity theory, although not explicitly—that the feeling of pleasure is "nothing really but motion about the heart, as conception is nothing but motion in the head" can be understood not as an analytic claim about the synonymy of meaning of "a feeling of pleasure" and "motion about the heart" but as the synthetic hypothesis that the referent of "a feeling of pleasure" will turn out to be a motion about the heart.

Formulated in terms of *de facto* identity rather than logical identity, this theory survives many of the standard refutations of the older materialisms. For example, it has often been argued that a thought cannot be identical with a brain event because a man can know very well what his thought is without knowing anything about his brain. But this shows only that there is no logical identity; the identity must be an empirical discovery.

The identity theory is in part, then, an empirical theory, hypothesizing that each particular mental event occurs if and only if some particular brain event occurs. It is still too early to say whether this hypothesis is probable, but it is a hypothesis that many scientists take seriously and use to guide their research. However, even if this hypothesis turns out to be true, it would not establish the identity theory, which holds not just that mental and neural events are correlated in some regular, lawful way but that they are one and the same event, and, moreover, that these events are, basically, physical. These latter speculations are sup-

ported by conceptual considerations, appeals to Ockham's razor, simplicity, analogies with the rest of our scientific procedures, and the goal of a unified science. One must appreciate these laudable and honest considerations, but the real question is whether the identification is plausible.

One objection to the identity theory comes from the fact that it makes sense to ask of a neural event where it occurred in the body (even if the answer is that it occurred in no local place but throughout the nervous system), whereas it makes no sense to ask where in the body the thought occurred. Since two putatively different things can turn out to be one and the same only if they have the same location, it cannot be the case that thoughts and neural events are identical. It is true that some bodily sensations have anatomical designation, but we rarely, if ever, feel sensations in our brain.

Another objection to the identity theory is that it cannot account for that feature indicated above as an essential feature of the mental, namely the privileged position of the subject with respect to his own mental events. If they were ordinary physical events, why should the subject be in a position to report their occurrence without having to make the observations or inferences the rest of us would have to make? That they can be known, but not in the way physical events can be known, suggests that they are not physical events.

Idealism. Descartes found that the one thing he could not doubt was the existence of his own mind. Bishop Berkeley went on to maintain that minds and the perceptions of those minds are the only things that do exist: to be is either to be perceived or to be a perceiver. So-called physical objects exist only in the mind, as classes of perceptions. This view is labeled idealism. It is sometimes called subjective idealism, to distinguish it from various post-Kantian idealisms that take reality to be a single, all-embracing superconsciousness.

Although it is often not clear exactly what Berkeley was trying to prove in his classic, *Principles of Human Knowledge* (1710), his main contention seems to be a claim about meaning, namely that statements about physical objects are meaningful if and only if they are taken as statements about the perceptions of perceivers. To account both for those objects that exist unperceived and for veridical perception (as contrasted with illusory perceptions), Berkeley appealed to a supreme perceiver.

Berkeley's idealism has never had many followers. Despite the skill and elegance of the argument, it has always seemed most unlikely to think that a simple statement about the desk in the next room is really equivalent in meaning to a complicated theological statement about the sense perceptions of God. In the popular mind, Berkeley is interpreted as having claimed that what we take to be the physical world is a kind of pervasive hallucination or dream; even Kant suggested this when he accused Berkeley of "degrading bodies to mere illusion." Although it is intriguing and instructive to attempt to see the world in Berkeley's way, this yields in the end an incoherent picture. One must say that all objects exist only in the mind, but at the same time the standard distinction between what exists only in the mind and what does not is obliterated.

Double-aspect theories. Some philosophers have held the view that the mental and the physical are simply different aspects of something that is itself neither mental nor physical. Spinoza is the most famous example. He held that man could be considered an extended, bodily thing and, equally well, a thinking thing, although neither characterization, nor even both taken together, exhausted the underlying substance of man. These different aspects are intended not as different properties of man but rather as full descriptions of man under different categories. Gustav Fechner proposed the analogy of an undulating line that at a given moment would be concave from one point of view and convex from the other; the line would be the underlying reality, but it could be given different (although isomorphic) descriptions. Similarly, a man can be considered and described from a physical viewpoint and also from a psychological viewpoint; some prefer to say that these are "different levels" rather than different viewpoints.

Although it is possible to hold that the double-aspect theory is true only of man (and perhaps the higher animals), many supporters of this view are also panpsychists, holding that every physical entity has a corresponding mental aspect. Spinoza certainly held this view, although he believed that in many cases the mental aspect was so crude as not to deserve the name of "mind." And W. K. Clifford held that "a moving molecule of inorganic matter does not possess mind or consciousness; but it possesses a small piece of mind-stuff" (*Lectures and Essays*, 3d ed., London, 1901, Vol. II, pp. 69–70).

There are two crucial obscurities in the double-aspect theory. First, what is the underlying unity that admits of the various aspects? Spinoza called it "God or Nature," but the unending controversy over whether Spinoza was an atheist or a "God-intoxicated man" shows that it is not clear how he used either of these terms. Herbert Spencer, calling a spade a spade, referred to it simply as the Unknowable. Contemporary philosophers suggest that the underlying unity is the "person." But when it is asked what a person is, the best that can be said is that it is, in the words of P. F. Strawson, "a type of entity such that *both* predicates ascribing states of consciousness *and* predicates ascribing corporeal characteristics, a physical situation etc. are equally applicable to a single individual of that single type" (*Individuals*, 1959, p. 102). This brings us back to our starting point.

The second obscurity in the double-aspect theory is that it is not clear what an "aspect" is. The point of talking about different aspects (literally, "looking at") or viewpoints is to suggest that the differences are not intrinsic to the thing but only exist in relation to human purposes, outlook, conceptual scheme, frame of reference, etc. This point is even reflected in Spinoza's definition of "attribute" (for example, extension or thought) as "that which the intellect perceives as constituting the essence of a substance" (*Ethics* I, Def. 4). But if someone wishes to claim that the difference between the mental and physical is a matter of viewpoint, then it is essential that he explain what he means by "viewpoint." Sometimes it is suggested that we are looking at the same thing "from the inside" (the mental) and "from the outside" (the physical), but this

is incoherent, since it already presupposes extended bodies with insides and outsides. If these expressions are only metaphors, then we are still left with the question of how to interpret them. Another account of the different "aspects" is that they are two different languages or conceptual schemes. Two-language accounts are misleading, based as they are on a comparison with, say, French and German, for these are translatable, each into the other, whereas mentalistic and physicalistic expressions are not. But worse still, these accounts are unilluminating, since it is precisely the existence of two sets of expressions for describing people that must be explained. In general, double-aspect theories fail to improve our understanding of the mind – body relationship.

Neutral monism. There is a variety of monistic theory in which minds and bodies are each conceived as complex collections composed of things of the same sort. The difference between mind and body is seen to lie not in the nature of the atomic constituents but in the way these constituents are arranged. Minds and bodies are different sorts of bundles of the same sort of things.

Many philosophers have tried to defend such a theory. One attempt may be found in Hume's *Treatise*. Minds and bodies are both bundles of what Hume called "perceptions." We have already mentioned his bundle theory of the mind. Hume suggested that bodies also are simply bundles of perceptions, where the perceptions have a consistency and coherence that lead us to call them the appearances of a single, unified thing. William James expressed a similar view, calling the neutral stuff pure experience, and Ernst Mach called his neutral entities sensations. Russell introduced the term "sensibilia" and argued that mind and matter were "logical constructions" out of sensibilia. More recently, A. J. Ayer, in his textbook on logical positivism, *Language, Truth and Logic* (London, 1936; 2d ed., 1946), defended a neutral monism in claiming that statements about the mental and statements about the physical could both be translated into statements about sense contents.

We have already indicated the basic difficulties in the bundle theory of the mind. Bundle theories of matter, of which phenomenalism is today the most favored, also have grave difficulties. First there is the problem of the neutral entities themselves. Discussions of them are very obscure. These neutral entities must be capable of being both elements of my mind and elements of objects outside my mind at the same time. How could anything be that neutral? But even if it were possible to give a clear account of these neutral things, there would still be the problem of establishing the conditions for their being elements of one and the same physical object. Much ingenuity has gone into this endeavor, especially on the part of recent phenomenalists, but no account has as yet succeeded. The reason seems to be that no entailment relations exist between statements about physical objects and statements about neutral entities, such as the sense data of the phenomenalists, of a sort that given the one, the other must be true. Therefore, it seems that statements about physical objects cannot be analyzed into statements about such neutral entities, as the neutral monists claim.

DUALISTIC THEORIES

Dualistic theories may be generally characterized as holding that mentalistic and physicalistic expressions differ not only in meaning but in reference as well. But there are diverse theories of referential nonidentity. Some have held that the mental and physical are different substances or stuffs, others that they are different sorts of events, others that they are different properties or relations, others that they are different states.

Interactionism. Interactionism is the thesis that mental events can sometimes cause bodily events and also that bodily events can sometimes cause mental events. As examples of the former the interactionist would claim pains that cause winces, thoughts that cause the heart to pound or a man to take to his heels, and feelings that cause a person to tremble; as examples of the latter the interactionist would claim blows that cause dull aches, flashes of light that cause a person to have a certain afterimage, pieces of music that cause a person to have certain feelings or memories, and electrical brain stimulations that cause a person to have a certain thought.

Descartes gave interactionism its classic formulation. He claimed there are two sorts of substances in the world, mental substances and corporeal substances. The essence of a mental substance is that it is a thing that thinks; the essence of a corporeal substance is that it is extended in space. Man is composed of both substances so intimately combined that events in the one can affect events in the other. Thus, in man (and in man alone) these two substances form a single system of mutually interacting components.

Although Descartes formulated his interactionist views in terms of a duality of substances, the interactionist does not necessarily have to accept the notion of a mental substance. He may talk simply of "mental events," leaving open the question whether there are mental substances. Mental events do not presuppose a substratum any more than meteorological events do. If we are asked what changes when meteorological events occur—for example, when it begins to rain or snow—we may say (trivially) that the weather changes, although no one should take this to mean that the weather is some sort of substance. Similarly, we may say that it is the mind (or its contents) that changes as mental events occur, but this does not commit us to a mental-substance theory in any serious sense. Just mental "events" will do for the interactionist's purposes, for it is perfectly clear that an event is the sort of thing that may be a cause or an effect.

Objections to interactionism. The two major objections that have been repeatedly raised against interactionism arise precisely as a consequence of the sharp distinction Descartes drew between the mental and the physical. The first is an empirical objection, namely that interactionism would have the unacceptable result of forcing us to abandon the physical principle of conservation of matter and energy, since physical energy would be lost when physical events produced mental effects and would be gained when mental events produced physical changes. Once we begin thinking of interactionism in this detailed way the second objection, an a priori one, arises, namely that mental events and physical events are so utterly dissimilar that there could never be a causal connection between them. If they are essentially different, one could never give rise to the other; it is simply impossible that a change in brain cells could produce a thought or vice versa.

Neither of these objections is decisive. So far as the first is concerned, the interactionist has many alternatives. He can deny the sacredness of the conservation principle, holding that it does not apply to the area of complex brain phenomena. Or he can claim that the loss or gain of energy is so slight in relation to our means of detection that it is negligible and can be ignored. Or he can hold to the conservation principle and deny that physical energy is gained or lost in interactions. He could point out that it does not necessarily take physical energy to do work on the nonphysical; for example, there is no strictly physical inertia to overcome in getting the mind to start going in the morning. Similarly, there could be changes in the physical system (produced by the mental) that would not involve increases in the total energy of the system; for example, a particle might move in one direction or another after a collision without changing the total mass-energy of the system. Therefore, the mind could produce from a particle collision in the brain one outcome rather than another, resulting in major differences in behavior without changing the total mass-energy of the brain. So mind–body interaction can be consistent with the conservation principle.

The second objection, that the mental and physical are too dissimilar to be causally connected, figured importantly in producing as immediate reactions to Descartes's interactionism two new theories, which will be discussed below, the occasionalism of Geulincx and Malebranche and the parallelism of Leibniz. Descartes himself held the traditional view that there could be nothing in the effect that was not already contained in the cause ("The stone . . . cannot now commence to be unless it has been produced by something which possesses within itself . . . all that enters into the composition of the stone," *Meditations*, III), thinking of causality as a kind of drawing forth or educing. This is very close to Spinoza's view that causality is a precise analogue of deduction. Since the mental and physical have quite different essences, by such views of causality it is hard to see how either can come from the other.

The doctrine on which these objections rest, that the cause must contain whatever properties the effect has, is no longer taken seriously in very many quarters. Electrical activity may produce a magnetic field, which may produce a change in location of a piece of iron. What similarities are there here between cause and effect? Yet would we be prepared to deny that causal connection is possible here? Causal connections are where we find them, and we are not entitled to have a priori convictions about what events can and cannot enter into causal relations. Nor are we required to explain how the cause produces the effect before we are entitled to assert a causal relation.

There is a more troublesome objection, however, which gives rise to the theory of epiphenomenalism. It is that the postulation of mental events as causes may be superfluous.

Mental events may be not causes of physical events but only symptoms of underlying physical events that are the real causes. If the science of physiology continues to develop in its present direction, it may be possible some day to give a full account of human behavior in terms of bodily states, with special attention to brain states. In such circumstances the purported efficacy of mental events may prove to be an illusion. But it must be admitted that our present scientific knowledge is too limited to appraise this possibility.

Occasionalism. Many philosophers accepted Descartes's bifurcation of the natural world into the mental and the physical but, also accepting the concept of cause and effect as having a necessary connection, rejected the possiblity that there could be causal interaction between the mental and the physical. Yet experience did seem to show the existence of recurrent sequences, which called for explanation. A number of philosophers, of whom Arnold Geulincx and Nicolas de Malebranche are the best known, proposed the theory that God is the intermediary link that connects them; when, for example, I will to move my arm, that is the occasion for God to make my arm move, and when an object is in my field of vision, that is the occasion for God to produce a visual appearance in my mind. The occasionalists, as they were called, used the analogy of two clocks that keep in phase not because they have direct causal connection but because they have the same maker. Thus, mental and physical events do not ever affect each other but are each of them effects of God's causal activity. It is an implication of the two-clock analogy (which was exploited by Leibniz) that the clocks keep in time because of the inner works of each. But this implication was denied by the occasionalists, who claimed that there could be no real causal connection between any natural events whatsoever. God's causal intervention is required even for one billiard ball to move another. God is the one true cause, and it is solely due to his providence that the regularities in experience occur. A more appropriate analogy than the two clocks would be two clock faces with hands that are synchronized by God's constant actions.

Occasionalism is an inherently unstable theory that seemed plausible only for a moment in the history of philosophy, as a desperate attempt to maintain Descartes's system despite the internal conflict between his two-substance doctrine and his concept of causality. Thus, occasionalism has historical importance as a transitional view. We can look upon Spinoza's more enduring system as an alternative attempt to maintain the concept of cause (as containing the effect) and the doctrine that God is the one true cause by abandoning the two-substance doctrine. Berkeley simply dropped corporeal substance out of the occasionalist scheme. Hume omitted God as the intermediary and simply identified causality with the regularities in experience. Each of these represents a desirable simplification of the cumbersome machinery of occasionalism.

Parallelism. The theory that mental and physical events are correlated in a regular way but without any causal connection, either direct or indirect, is known as psychophysical parallelism. The main motive for this theory is to avoid the perplexities, already noted, of postulating causal interaction. How could events so utterly dissimilar affect each other, or if they were only indirectly connected, how could some third thing (whatever that would be) produce such utterly different effects? Deciding that causal connection is impossible, the parallelist holds that every mental event is merely correlated with some physical event(s) in such a way that whenever the former occurs, then in fact the latter does also.

How is it possible that there should be these noncausal correlations? Leibniz offered a model by taking over the two clocks of the occasionalists but making them perfect mechanisms synchronized by God at their origin so that by this pre-established harmony they remain forever in phase without any further intervention. Leibniz actually used this analogy to arrive at a deeper level of analysis in which the mind – body dualism itself disappears to be replaced by an infinity of spirits each going inexorably through its own development and all coordinated by the pre-established harmony. But it is not necessary that we follow him into the peculiarities of his own system; the analogy is intelligible as it stands.

For this analogy to be of use in explaining the noncausal correlations of the mental and physical, we need to point to synchronous mechanisms. In the case of the physical we do have something that is like a mechanism in which later states and events are explainable in terms of earlier ones. But can we say the same of the mind? First, on this analogy there must be a one-to-one correspondence such that for every physical event there corresponds some mental event. Descartes believed that the mind always thinks, and if it does there might be such a correspondence. Or we might ensure the correspondence by accepting panpsychism. For the two-clock model to apply we need not only the assumption that the mind always thinks but also the assumption that it works as an isolated mechanism whose later states and events are explainable in terms of earlier states and events. Both these assumptions are implausible as a matter of empirical fact. The mind does not always think; there are comas and deep sleeps in which apparently no mental events occur, at least as we have conceived of mental events in this discussion. Nor is the mind an isolated system; the first noises one hears in the morning are not always a function of the earlier contents of one's mind alone. So the two-clock analogy is not one that the parallelist can use to explain the constant correlation.

This brings us to the major objection to parallelism. It is at variance with the rest of our empirical procedures. Parallelists are forced to conceive of the postulated constant correlations of mental and corresponding physical events as sheerly accidental, whereas the whole of modern scientific method and statistical technique would say that it is quite impossible for such a degree of correlation to occur accidentally. If we admit that such uniform correlations could really occur by chance, then we must admit that the most solid results of science could really occur by chance. This would undermine the whole of science. We understand the parallelist's scruples about drawing from the degree of correlation the natural inference that the relation is causal, but if we are not entitled to draw that inference here we are not entitled to draw it anywhere.

Epiphenomenalism. If we reject parallelism because the evidence for causal connection between physical and mental events is overwhelming, we must still ask what kind of causal relation it is. An old but still attractive theory is epiphenomenalism, the theory that the causal connection goes in only one direction, from body to mind, so that mental events are effects only, never causes, of brain events. This view is sometimes mistakenly thought to be a kind of extreme materialism, and the standard analogies encourage this. Thus, when Cabanis said that the brain secretes thought, just as the liver secretes bile, or when the mind is compared with the smoke of a steam engine, a movie on a screen, or the shadows of a shadow show, we are encouraged to think of the mind as quasi-physical. However, epiphenomenalism, strictly speaking, is a dualistic theory that asserts the occurrence of peculiarly mental events but makes their occurrence completely dependent on physical events. Thus, physical events are the primary phenomena; mental events are by-products.

Epiphenomenalism is identical with interactionism for those cases where the physical allegedly causes the mental, and it shares the strengths and weaknesses of the other theory in those respects. It differs in denying any causal efficacy to mental events. Why should it do so?

Epiphenomenalists believe the evidence indicates that the physical world is an autonomous system. Impressed by the advances that have been made in the physical and biological sciences, especially in such fields as neurophysiology, they foresee the day when, in principle at least, it should be possible to give a full account of the events in the physical world, including the behavior of human bodies, simply by appealing to other physical events and physical laws. This is at present only a hope, but the epiphenomenalist does not want to hold a mind–body theory incompatible with such a hope; he does not wish to postulate nonphysical events that intrude themselves into the physical world with the result that it would not be possible to give a full explanation of every physical event in merely physical terms.

How does the epiphenomenalist account for the apparent causal efficacy of mental events? He argues that it is an illusion arising from the fact that the brain events that cause a wince, for example, also cause the mental event that is the sensation of pain. Since the pain occurs (very slightly) before the wince and since we know nothing of events going on in our brain, we make the mistake of thinking it was the mental event, the sensation of pain, that caused the wince. It is a simple case of the fallacy of *post hoc, ergo propter hoc*. In general, mental events are symptoms of brain processes and may be taken as signs of later events but not as causes of them.

This explanation depends on a distinction between invariable sequences that are causal and invariable sequences that are noncausal. There is much controversy to this very day about the concept of causality, but it would appear that the distinction is a sound one and, in many instances, can clearly be applied. The question is whether it can be applied in this case, since it is very difficult to see how we could devise a test to tell us whether the mental event is a cause or merely an inevitable precursor.

The question whether to prefer interactionism or epiphenomenalism is therefore still an open one. When we have invariable accompaniment, it is most reasonable to assume a direct causal connection unless there are special reasons for accepting a more complicated model. The development of the science of neurophysiology to the point where a full explanation could be given without resort to mental events might give us such a reason. But we are still a long way from that. Until we are closer, perhaps the most reasonable thing to do is to continue to believe what we ordinarily mean when we say that it is the pain that causes us to wince.

RELATED EMPIRICAL ISSUES

Neuropsychology. There has recently been a tremendous increase in our knowledge of how the brain works, how it is functionally related to the rest of the body and behavior, and what the mental correlates of brain events are. There are a number of approaches that have superseded the original technique of noting abnormalities and trying to correlate them with the findings of subsequent autopsy. One new technique, used extensively by K. S. Lashley, among others, is to remove parts of the brain (of experimental animals) systematically and to note the effect of this on behavior. Another, developed and used by the brain surgeon W. G. Penfield, is to stimulate directly parts of a conscious patient's brain and ask him to report any mental events that occur. Finally, there are the large-scale, statistically sophisticated studies made by H.-L. Teuber over a number of years on men who suffered wartime brain damage; these studies involve such new techniques as electroencephalography and pneumoencephalography. Drugs, too, are now beginning to be used in the study of the brain.

Despite this progress, we are at present far from understanding the brain. Results indicate that earlier theories of exact isomorphisms of mind and brain and of precise locations in the brain of the correlates of memory, speech abilities, emotions, etc., are unlikely to be true. Whatever correlations are found will probably be very complicated and involve very large portions of the brain. Nevertheless, it seems probable that mental functioning is correlated with identifiable mechanisms in the brain. This is presupposed by all of the mind–body theories here discussed, and to that extent they all gain some confirmation from the emerging facts. But the facts do not seem to support one theory rather than another. For example, there is no way of deciding at present whether the experience known as searching one's memory is merely a by-product of brain mechanisms (as epiphenomenalists believe) or whether the experience somehow influences those brain mechanisms (as interactionists might hold). Nor can it be expected that results in the near future will be decisive.

Parapsychology. Some of the mind–body theories we have discussed assert that mental events can have effects either on other mental events or on physical events. But they have confined these effects, at least for the interaction of mental events, within the person (although these mental effects might incidentally result in further effects outside the person). Cases where a mental event of one person directly affects the thought of another person or directly affects some body other than his own would be cases of parapsychological phenomena—telepathy and psychokinesis, respectively. There is grave doubt that such phenomena ever occur, but their implications must be discussed.

Are they logically possible? If interactionism is possible, then it seems that these, too, are possible. Supposing they occurred as genuine phenomena, this would be strong confirmation for the interactionist theory of mind and body.

However, there is a peculiar twist to this matter, which becomes apparent if we ask how we would establish the existence of such phenomena. Suppose certain people are able to tell what thoughts another is having, and we cannot explain this in any usual way or attribute it to chance. Now if parallelism or epiphenomenalism, for example, is true, then corresponding to the nonchance correlations of the mental events of "sender" and "receiver" there will be nonchance correlations of the brains of the two. Even if we rule out the usual forms of energy transmission, we may postulate a new sort of energy transmission or even a new kind of action at a distance. If mind and brain are in one-to-one correspondence, then corresponding to the curious psychic phenomena there will be curious physical phenomena. In such a case there would be no reason to take the psychic phenomena as autonomous, or "basic," as the parapsychologist might wish us to do.

In short, before we can decide that something is a parapsychological phenomenon we must rule out such theories as epiphenomenalism and parallelism. Even the physicalist could allow that two physical systems could so affect each other that certain sorts of noises produced by one (that is, reports of one's own thoughts) would be surprisingly similar to the noises produced by the other (that is, reports of the other person's thoughts). So we cannot use the results of parapsychological investigation to help us choose a mind–body theory.

Disembodied existence. If it were the case that when what we call death occurred a person continued to have feelings, thoughts, images, etc., this would have important bearing on the mind–body problem. Materialism, the identity theory, the double-aspect theory, parallelism, and epiphenomenalism would all have to be rejected; idealism, neutral monism, and interactionism would still stand. On the other hand, that no such thing occurs is compatible with any of these theories.

Some philosophers have argued that mental events after death are logically impossible. They contend that a mind or mental events presuppose a person who has them, and what is meant by "a person" entails a body. A typical line of reasoning would be the following: the concept of a person presupposes criteria for identifying the person, and in the end the criteria will have to be physical if we are to identify people.

It does, however, seem perfectly possible and quite graphically describable, too, that I should survive my own death and witness my own funeral. So the disembodied existence of a person seems to be logically possible. Yet, on the other hand, there does appear to be a difficulty in conceiving of disembodied existence as the general rule, since it is hard to see how we would even have a concept of persons in such a situation. It is only through their bodies that we come to know of the existence, identity, and nature of other persons. Perhaps the concept of a person

logically requires that there be at least some cases of people with bodies, but it does not require that all persons have bodies.

Since we are here dealing with a question of great personal importance to many people, it is not surprising that there have been an enormous number of arguments. We shall in this article ignore the metaphysical and moral arguments and discuss only some of the empirical considerations.

In favor of the hypothesis of survival, there is the large number of reports, investigated with varying degrees of neutrality, of messages from and apparitions of people who have died. In many of these cases it is reported that information was transmitted that only the dead person could have had. It is argued that such occurrences are best explained by postulating that the persons involved survived their physical deaths and are able to communicate with us. Even if such cases did stand up under scrutiny, we would be faced with the difficult problem of distinguishing them from retrospective clairvoyance and telepathy, which in turn, as we saw in our discussion of parapsychology, cannot easily be distinguished from unusual forms of physical causation.

Evidence against the hypothesis of disembodied existence is the fact that certain neural mechanisms are necessary for consciousness. When these mechanisms are interfered with, there is temporary loss of consciousness. Since all neural mechanisms cease functioning entirely in death, it is reasonable to think that consciousness ceases entirely. It is true that there is still the possibility that only as long as a person has a body is his consciousness dependent on it and when the body dies the person is freed from this dependency. But this simply points out an inductive argument from known cases to as yet unknown cases, and such induction runs some risk of going wrong. General inductive procedures justify not giving much weight to this possibility.

Cybernetics. We have recently seen the emergence of a new science, cybernetics, devoted to the theory and construction of self-governing machines. Especially important are the development of feedback mechanisms, which allow the device to achieve and maintain some predetermined state, and the development of programming, which enables devices to solve large ranges of problems by following a detailed set of instructions. Here we have machine analogues of two features—namely, purposeful behavior and reasoning—traditionally taken to be of the essence of what is mental. Therefore, many believe that we can gain insight into the mind–body problem by considering the analogous issues involved in these machines.

The achievements in machine technology are truly remarkable. Machines are able to store enormous amounts of information and perform calculations at incredible speeds. Machines have been developed that prove theorems (sometimes more ingeniously than their designers), play games (sometimes more skillfully than their inventors), translate spoken words into different languages, compose music, and write poems. Machines have been constructed that learn from past experience, adapt their programs to new circumstances, and develop new ways of solving problems.

One question here is whether there is any human achievement that could not, in principle, be matched by the output of a suitably designed machine so closely that the two would be indistinguishable. Many experts in this field, including A. M. Turing, who first raised this question (in "Computing Machinery and Intelligence," *Mind*, Vol. 59, 1950, 433–460), believe there is no human achievement that could not be matched by a machine output.

Some philosophers have argued that Kurt Gödel's results concerning the existence of undecidable propositions show a fundamental limitation of the machine, since a machine is a model of a formal system, and formal systems complex enough to be interesting are incomplete. Others have replied that since the proposition that if the system is consistent it is incomplete can be proved within the system, the machine could prove its own incompleteness as well as we can. Thus, we are not superior to the machine in this respect.

So far we have confined the discussion to the behavior of humans and machines. What relevance does this have to mental events and the mind? The suggestion might be made that if we can explain machine output solely in physical terms, and if there is no difference in principle between machine output and human behavior, then it follows that we can explain human behavior in physical terms. This would count against interactionism but not against epiphenomenalism, parallelism, and the rest.

This argument assumes that if we had machines whose output could in fact match human behavior, we would still be able to understand their output solely in terms of the physical mechanisms. Might it not be that when we got machines that complex, we would have just as much reason for believing in the intervention of mental events in the case of machines as we have in the case of humans? This remains to be seen. Meanwhile it is reasonable to think that such complex machines would operate in the same ways as the simpler ones we have now.

The mind–body problem remains a source of acute discomfort to philosophers. There have been many attempts to prove that it is a "pseudo problem," but none has stood up under scrutiny. There have been many attempts to solve it, but at present no solution stands out as markedly superior to the others. Nor does it seem that new empirical information will furnish a decisive test for one theory or another. It may well be that the relation between mind and body is an ultimate, unique, and unanalyzable one. If so, philosophical wisdom would consist in giving up the attempt to understand the relation in terms of other, more familiar ones and accepting it as the anomaly it is.

Bibliography

GENERAL DISCUSSIONS

A most detailed and exhaustive treatment of many of the issues involved in the mind–body problem is to be found in C. D. Broad, *The Mind and Its Place in Nature* (London, 1925). Other general discussions of the problem are C. A. Strong's *Why the Mind Has a Body* (New York, 1903); John Laird's *Our Minds and Matter* (Cambridge, 1934); J. B. Pratt's *Matter and Spirit* (New York, 1926); Durant Drake's *Mind and Its Place in Nature* (New York, 1925); G. F. Stout's *Mind and Matter* (Cambridge, 1931); and C. J. Du-

casse's *Nature, Mind and Death* (La Salle, Ill., 1951). For a treatment that is much briefer, yet comprehensive and penetrating, see John Hospers' *An Introduction to Philosophical Analysis* (New York, 1953), Ch. 5, Part 2. A. C. Ewing has a lively and provocative discussion in *The Fundamental Questions of Philosophy* (London, 1951), Chs. 5 and 6. Gilbert Ryle, in *The Concept of Mind* (London, 1949), has attempted to show that the whole mind–body problem is spurious, arising from a series of mistakes; the book is of great importance in its details, even if it fails in its grand purpose. A very interesting collection of essays by contemporary philosophers of different persuasions is Sidney Hook, ed., *Dimensions of Mind* (New York, 1961). For Franz Brentano's doctrine of intentionality, see Oskar Kraus, ed., *Psychologie vom empirischen Standpunkt*, Vol. II (Leipzig, 1925). This edition contains useful notes that trace the development of Brentano's philosophy.

NATURE OF THE MIND

The nature of the mind was discussed by Plato in various dialogues, especially the *Phaedo*, translated by R. Hackworth (Cambridge, 1955), the *Phaedrus*, translated, with an Introduction and commentary, by R. Hackworth (Cambridge, 1952), the *Republic*, translated by F. M. Cornford (Oxford, 1941; New York, 1945), and the *Timaeus*, in B. Jowett, ed., *Plato: Dialogues*, 4th rev. ed. (Oxford, 1953). In these dialogues Plato suggested a mental-substance view of the mind. Such a view was defended more explicitly by René Descartes in his *Meditations*, in *Philosophical Works*, translated by E. S. Haldane and G. R. T. Ross (New York, 1955), especially the Second and Sixth. David Hume's *A Treatise of Human Nature*, D. G. C. Macnabb, ed. (Cleveland, 1962), contains his bundle theory and his attack on the substance theory of the mind; see especially Book I, Part IV, Secs. 5–6, and the Appendix. William James presented the concept of the "stream of consciousness" in *The Principles of Psychology* (New York, 1890), Ch. 9.

MATERIALISM

Materialism may be found in the writings of many of the early Greek philosophers, especially Democritus and, later, Lucretius in *De Rerum Natura*, translated by H. A. J. Munro as *On the Nature of Things* (Cambridge, 1864–1868). Hobbes expounded such a view in the *Leviathan*, edited, with an Introduction, by R. Peters (New York, 1962). Variations on this theme are found in the French Enlightenment figures La Mettrie (*L'Homme machine*, A. Vartanian, ed., Princeton, N.J., 1960); Diderot ("D'Alembert's Dream," in Jonathan Kemp, ed., *Diderot, Interpreter of Nature*, selected writings translated by Jean Stewart and Jonathan Kemp, London, 1937; New York, 1938); and Holbach (*Système de la nature*, 2 vols., London, 1771). They are also found in the nineteenth-century German materialists J. Moleschott (*Der Kreislauf des Lebens*, Mainz, 1852); L. Büchner (*Kraft und Stoff*, Frankfurt, 1855); and K. Vogt (*Vorlesungen über den Menschen*, Giessen, 1863). Marxist "materialism" is best represented by V. Lenin's *Materialism and Empirio-criticism* (1908; Vol. XIII of *Collected Works*, New York, 1916–1917). Most of the above express views more akin to epiphenomenalism than to materialism. The whole development of materialism from the early Greeks through the nineteenth century was carefully detailed by F. A. Lange in his monumental *The History of Materialism* (1865); the third edition (London, 1925) has an Introduction by Bertrand Russell. Not without interest is the latter part of this book, in which Lange presents his own view, a modified Kantian position.

In recent years materialism has had different labels. As behaviorism it was defended by the psychologists J. B. Watson, in *Psychology From the Standpoint of a Behaviorist* (Philadelphia, 1919) and *Behaviorism* (New York, 1924); and K. S. Lashley, in "The Behavioristic Interpretation of Consciousness," in *Psychological Review*, Vol. 30 (1923), 237–272, 329–353. For an excellent critique of behaviorism by another psychologist, see Wolfgang Köhler, *Gestalt Psychology* (New York, 1947). As physicalism the theory was defended by Rudolf Carnap, in *The Unity of Science* (London, 1938). A very lucid presentation of physicalism is Carl G. Hempel's "The Logical Analysis of Psychology," in *Revue de synthèse*, Vol. 10 (1935), reprinted in Herbert Feigl and

Wilfrid Sellars, eds., *Readings in Philosophical Analysis* (New York, 1949), pp. 373–384. This last volume also contains an excellent attack on physicalism by C. I. Lewis, "Some Logical Considerations Concerning the Mental," an article originally published in *The Journal of Philosophy,* Vol. 38 (1941), 385–392.

IDENTITY THEORY

The identity theory had an early formulation in Feigl's "The Mind–Body Problem in the Development of Logical Empiricism," in *Revue internationale de philosophie,* Vol. 4 (1950), 612–626, reprinted in Herbert Feigl and May Brodbeck, eds., *Readings in the Philosophy of Science* (New York, 1953). The same author surveys the whole mind–body problem, amplifying his own theory and making a number of interesting comments on other theories, in "The 'Mental' and the 'Physical,'" in Herbert Feigl et al., eds., *Minnesota Studies in the Philosophy of Science,* Vol. II (Minneapolis, 1958); this article contains a very extensive bibliography. The clearest presentations of the identity theory are found in J. J. C. Smart's "Sensations and Brain Processes," in *The Philosophical Review,* Vol. 68 (1959), 141–156, and "Materialism," in *The Journal of Philosophy,* Vol. 60 (1963), 651–662. This theory is criticized by Jerome A. Shaffer in "Could Mental States Be Brain Processes?," in *The Journal of Philosophy,* Vol. 58 (1961), 813–822, and "Mental Events and the Brain," in *The Journal of Philosophy,* Vol. 60 (1963), 160–166.

OTHER MONISTIC THEORIES

Turning to other monistic theories, we find subjective idealism best stated and defended in Berkeley's *Treatise Concerning the Principles of Human Knowledge* (New York, 1957). The double-aspect theory can be found in Spinoza's *Ethics,* translated by W. H. White and A. H. Stirling, 2d ed. (London, 1894). These two great thinkers are exceedingly well discussed in G. J. Warnock's *Berkeley* (London, 1953) and S. Hampshire's *Spinoza* (London, 1951). W. K. Clifford defended a double-aspect theory in his *Lectures and Essays* (London, 1879), and more recently P. F. Strawson has suggested in *Individuals* (London, 1959) a modern version of a double-aspect theory in which the person is the underlying unity. Neutral monism can be found in Hume's *A Treatise of Human Nature* (Oxford, 1888; reprinted 1958), Book I; William James's *Essays in Radical Empiricism,* in Vol. I of *Works* (New York, 1943); and Ernst Mach's *The Analysis of Sensations* (New York, 1959). More recently it has been defended by Bertrand Russell in a number of works, especially *Our Knowledge of the External World* (London, 1914), Chs. 3 and 4; *Mysticism and Logic* (London, 1917), Chs. 7 and 8; and *The Analysis of Mind* (London, 1921), Ch. 1. The same doctrine, but put as a thesis about language and meaning, is presented in A. J. Ayer's *Language, Truth and Logic,* 2d ed. (London, 1946), Ch. 7.

DUALISTIC THEORIES

Of the dualistic theories, Descartes's interactionism has its classical exposition in his *Meditations* and *The Passions of the Soul.* More recent defenses of it are in J. B. Pratt's *Matter and Spirit* (New York, 1922) and Michael Maher's *Psychology* (London, 1940). Occasionalism is presented in Malebranche's *Dialogue on Metaphysics and Religion.* A parallelist position is taken by Leibniz in his *New System of Nature and of the Interaction of Substances.* Harald Höffding advocated this position in *The Problems of Philosophy* (New York, 1905), as did Friedrich Paulsen in *Introduction to Philosophy* (New York, 1906). Epiphenomenalism was defended by T. H. Huxley in his 1874 essay "On the Hypothesis That Animals Are Automata and Its History," to be found in his *Collected Essays* (London, 1893–1894). For other accounts, see Shadworth Hodgson, *The Metaphysics of Experience* (London, 1898), Vol. II; and George Santayana, *The Realm of Essence* (New York 1927) and *Reason and Common Sense* (New York, 1922). C. D. Broad defended a more sophisticated version of this theory in *The Mind and Its Place in Nature,* mentioned earlier.

JEROME SHAFFER

MIRACLES. The term "miracle," like the word "nice," is often used to refer primarily to the responses of the user.

In this usage, a miracle is merely some event which astounds the speaker, with perhaps some presumption that others will or should react to it in the same way; just as in the parallel case "nice" means simply "agreeable to me," with perhaps again some suggestion that all right-minded people will feel the same. But the senses of "miracle" that are of philosophical and methodological interest are stronger and less subjectively oriented. Although they include the idea that wonder is called for as at least part of the appropriate response, the crux as well as the ground for the wonder is that a miracle should consist in an overriding of the order of nature. A miracle is something which would never have happened had nature, as it were, been left to its own devices.

This idea of overriding is essential; however, it is certainly subject to various variations and additions. Some writers, for instance, insist that the word "miracle" should be used in such a way that it becomes necessarily true that a miracle can be worked only by God or by his specially deputed agents. Others even build into their very definition of "miracle" some reference to the purposes for which Authority is supposed to be prepared to consider making such an exception. Certainly, most theist theologians are also at great pains to maintain that a miraculous event could not properly be considered a violation, since it would not really represent any infringement, of the fundamental hierarchical order. "It is not against the principle of craftsmanship (*contra rationem artificii*) if a craftsman effects a change in his product, even after he has given it its first form" (Aquinas, *Summa Contra Gentiles,* III, 100). But these very labors to show that and how such "violations" need involve no ultimate irregularity still admit and presuppose the essentially overriding character of the miraculous. There would be no point in trying to show in this way that a miracle must ultimately be no violation of regularity unless it were taken for granted that it apparently is such a violation.

This point is fundamental, and it needs to be stressed more heavily today than in the past. For in addition to the traditional theist reluctance to ascribe to the Deity anything savoring of unseemly irregularity, it is nowadays usual to encounter a certain shyness about any apparent repudiation of scientifically accepted modes of explanation. Aquinas, earlier in the chapter referred to above, gave a perfectly clear and unequivocal definition of "miracle" that makes no bones at all about the crux of the matter, namely, that "those things are properly called miracles which are done by divine agency beyond the order commonly observed in nature (*praeter ordinem communiter observatum in rebus*)." Again, in the twentieth century, Dr. Eric Mascall, remaining in the same forthright tradition, insisted in his article in *Chambers' Encyclopaedia* that the word "miracle" "signifies in Christian theology a striking interposition of divine power by which the operations of the ordinary course of nature are overruled, suspended, or modified."

MIRACLES AND NATURAL ORDER

To seize the fundamental point that a miracle is an event which violates the "ordinary course of nature" is to appreciate that the notion of a miracle is logically parasitical on the idea of an order to which such an event must constitute some sort of exception. This being so, a strong notion of the truly miraculous—a notion involving something more than the notions of the merely marvelous, the significant, or the surprising—can only be generated if there is first an equally strong conception of a natural order. The inevitable tension between the ideas of rule and of exception thus gives concepts of the miraculous an inherent instability. It is perhaps relevant to notice how this tension has been felt in the history of ideas. Where there is as yet no strong conception of a natural order, there is little room for the idea of a genuinely miraculous event as distinct from the phenomenon of a prodigy, of a wonder, or of a divine sign. But once such a conception of a natural order has taken really firm root, there is a great reluctance to allow that miracles have in fact occurred or even to admit as legitimate a concept of the miraculous.

An interesting early case of this is provided by Spinoza in his *Tractatus Theologico-Politicus,* in which he tried to reconcile his vision of a natural order (*Deus sive natura*) with an acceptance of the Bible as in some sense a privileged document. He did this partly by admitting the limitations of observatory powers of the men of Biblical days, but mainly by urging that conventional interpreters of the Bible read far more miracles into it than it contains, because they constantly read poetic Hebrew idioms literally. Today, more and more theologians seem to be noticing the exact words used by the New Testament writers in describing the sorts of alleged events which, in more scientific ages, have been characterized (and perhaps dismissed) as miraculous. These words are τερατὰ ("wonders," or "prodigies"), δυναμεῖς ("powers"), σημεῖα ("signs"); and, particularly in St. Paul, χαρισματὰ ἰαμάτων ("graces of healing") and ἐνεργήματα δυνάμεων ("effects of powers"). None of these words seems to carry any entailments about the overriding of a natural order. On the other hand, once a really strong conception of natural order has arisen, its adherents tend to dismiss out of hand all stories of putative occurrences in the belief that if they allowed that these occurrences had taken place at all, they would have to admit them to have been miraculous. One may refer here to R. M. Grant's recent *Miracle and Natural Law in Graeco-Roman and Early Christian Thought* (Amsterdam, 1952) and to William E. H. Lecky's classic study *History of the Rise and Influence of Rationalism in Europe* (London, 1890). The former summarizes its own thesis as follows: "Credulity in antiquity varied inversely with the health of science and directly with the vigor of religion" (p. 41). This, however, was later qualified by the important observation that "at least in some respects Christians were far less credulous than their contemporaries, at least in the period before Augustine" (p. 120). Lecky traced a development in which stories of the ostensibly miraculous, from being accepted as a chief guarantee of the authenticity of the Christian revelation, become instead "a scandal, a stumbling block, and a difficulty" (Vol. I, p. 143). In the nineteenth century the radical Biblical critic David Strauss announced in the introduction to his *Das Leben Jesu* (2 vols., Tübingen, 1835; translated by Mary Ann Evans as *Life of Jesus Critically Examined,* London, 1848), "We may summarily reject all miracles, prophecies, narratives of angels and demons, and the like, as simply impossible and irreconcilable with the known and universal laws which govern the course of events." And in the twentieth century there has even been a bishop of the Church of England capable of saying of the author of Mark, "He was credulous inasmuch as the miracles, as they are narrated, cannot, in the light of our modern knowledge of the uniformity of nature, be accepted as historical facts" (F. W. Barnes, *The Rise of Christianity,* London and New York, 1947, p. 108).

Dilemma of holding strong rules while admitting exceptions. The spokesman for the occurrence of the miraculous faces a dilemma that arises from the very essence of the concept he espouses. It is tempting, but wrong, for the believer in the miraculous to think that he can afford to gloat over any little local difficulties and embarrassments which may from time to time beset the forward march of science. But insofar as a miracle involves an alleged overriding of a law of nature, he too is committed to showing the subsistence of a natural order. Exceptions are logically dependent upon rules. Only insofar as it can be shown that there is an order does it begin to be possible to show that the order is occasionally overridden. The difficulty (perhaps an insoluble one) is to maintain simultaneously both the strong rules and the genuine exceptions to them. The oscillations in the history of thought are to be understood by reference to this tension (amounting perhaps to a contradiction) that is inherent in the concept of the miraculous, and it is on this same tension that the various logical and methodological problems also center.

LOGICAL AND METHODOLOGICAL PROBLEMS

It is with logical and methodological problems that we are primarily concerned. The classical, and by far the best, approach is by way of the notorious section X, "Of Miracles," in Hume's *Enquiry Concerning Human Understanding* (1748). This and Section XI of this *Enquiry*, both of which were parts of a single coordinated case, constitute Hume's answer to what was, in his day, the stock program of Christian apologetic. This program had two stages: the first was an attempt to establish the existence and certain minimal characteristics of God by appealing only to natural reason and experience, the second was an attempt to supplement this rather sketchy religion of nature with a more abundant revelation. This program, in its characteristically eighteenth-century form, received its archetypal fulfillment in Archdeacon William Paley's *Natural Theology* (London, 1802) and also in his *Evidences of Christianity* (London, 1794). In the eighteenth-century form, the weight of the first part of the case was borne primarily by the Argument to Design. If from a watch we may infer a watchmaker, then the orderliness of the universe entitles us to infer, by parity of reasoning, a Maker of the universe. The second part of the case rested on the claim that there is ample historical evidence to show that the Biblical miracles, including the crucial physical resurrection of Jesus bar Joseph, did in fact occur, and that this in turn proved the authenticity of the Christian revelation.

Paley's style of systematic rational apologetic has no doubt gone out of fashion, at least among Protestants. But Hume's challenges to the whole idea of a substantial natural theology and to the project of establishing the authenticity of any alleged revelation by proving that its claims have been supported by miracles are not, and are not likely to become, dead issues. For in 1870 the third session of the First Vatican Council defined as constitutive dogmas of the Roman Catholic religion both of the positions which Hume had challenged. The relevant passage of the canon dealing with the second reads, "If anyone shall say . . . that miracles can never be known for certain, or that the divine origin of the Christian religion cannot properly be proved by them: let him be cast out" (*si quis dixerit . . . aut miracula certo cognosci numquam posse nec iis divinam religionis christianae originem rite probari: anathema sit*; H. Denzinger, ed., *Enchiridion Symbolorum*, 29th ed., Sec. 1813, Freiburg im Breisgau, 1953).

Problem of supernatural revelation. Hume's main contention was thus, in his own words, that "a miracle can never be proved so as to be the foundation of a system of religion." For him, all other questions about the miraculous were, officially at least, merely incidental to this basic tenet. He defined a "miracle" as "a transgression of a law of nature by a particular volition of the Deity, or by the interposition of some invisible agent." This definition has been attacked on various counts, but the criticism is misconceived, for two reasons. First, this was in fact the way in which the opponents whom Hume had in mind defined the term "miracle." Thus, Dr. Samuel Clarke, in his famous Boyle lectures (*The Works of Samuel Clarke*, Vol. II, London, 1738, p. 701), had defined "miracle" as "a work effected in a manner . . . different from the common and regular method of providence, by the interposition either of God himself, or of some intelligent agent superior to men." Second, if, as Clarke and the orthodox tradition would have it, the occurrence of a miracle is to serve "for the proof or evidence of some particular doctrine, or in attestation of the authority of some particular person," then surely a miracle must be conceived in this way. It is only and precisely insofar as it is something really transcendent—something, so to speak, which nature by herself could not contrive—that such an occurrence could force us to conclude that some supernatural power is being revealed.

In this context it would be worse than useless to appeal to revelation for criteria by which genuinely miraculous events may be identified, and thus distinguished from the unusual, the untoward, or the merely ordinary. For if the occurrence of a miracle is to serve as the endorsement of a revelation, then we have to find some means entirely independent of that revelation by which the endorsement itself may be recognized. Exactly the same point applies, of course, if, with what is now a rather fashionable school of apologetic, it is urged that miracles are not essentially overridings, but signs. If a sign is to signify to the unbeliever, then there must be some means independent of the doctrinal system itself by which the signs may be identified and read. As has been suggested already, there is much to be said for trying to interpret the records of τερατὰ and σημεία in the New Testament in terms of some notion of sign, rather than as miracle stories proper. But it is necessary to insist on two facts that seem to be often overlooked—namely, that part of the price which must be paid for this method of interpretation is the sacrifice of the use of these stories as independent evidence of the genuinely revelatory character of the doctrines; and that such a sacrifice presumably entails the rejection of at least one defined dogma of the Roman Catholic church, and hence of the truth of Roman Catholicism as a theological system.

A similar, but different, point applies if a relativistic definition of "miracle" is adopted, as was done, for instance, by John Locke. In his *Discourse of Miracles* (written 1702, published posthumously), he defined the word "miracle" as "a sensible operation, which, being above the comprehension of the spectator, and in his opinion contrary to the established course of nature, is taken by him to be divine." It was also done, in a slightly different way, by St. Augustine, who insisted that "nature is the will of God" (*Dei voluntas rerum natura est*), and hence that "a portent is not contrary to nature, but contrary to our knowledge of nature" (*Portentum ergo fit non contra naturam, sed contra quam est nota natura*; *De Civitate Dei*, XXI, 8). To operate with a relativistic notion of this sort is necessarily to be deprived of the possibility of arguing that a miracle is a miracle regardless of whatever anyone may happen to know or to believe about it, and hence to rob the attempt to base an apologetic on the occurrence of miracles of whatever initial plausibility it might otherwise possess. For the occurrence of events which are merely inexplicable *to us*, and *at present*, provides no good ground at all for believing that doctrines associated with these occurrences embody an authentic revelation of the transcendent. There is, of course, no particular reason why Locke himself should have been disturbed about this. The case of Augustine, however, is more interesting, for he is a recognized saint and one of the four great doctors of the church. And yet insofar as he held to a relativistic notion of a miracle, he was safeguarding the vital doctrine of the total dependence of the whole creation—but at the price of subverting a sort of apologetic which it has since become essential for Roman Catholics to believe in as a possibility.

Problem of identifying an event as miraculous. Up to this point it has been insisted that if the occurrence of a miracle is to serve—as Clarke and the orthodox tradition would have it—"for the proof or evidence of some particular doctrine, or in attestation of the authority of some particular person," then in a traditional sense, miracles must be conceived of as involving the overriding of some natural order that is at least partly autonomous. The importance of this crucial point is often overlooked. Another immediately consequential point, however, is overlooked perhaps even more often, namely, that if an occurrence that is miraculous in the traditional sense is to serve as evidence for anything, it must be possible to identify it as being miraculous. Furthermore, as was urged above, if its occurrence is to serve as an endorsement of some doctrinal system, the method of identification must be logically independent of that system. The difficulty of meeting this last requirement is often concealed by the acceptance of what seems, for many people, to be an almost unquestionable assumption. Protagonists of the supernatural, and opponents too, take it for granted that we all possess some natural (as opposed to revealed) way of knowing that and where the unassisted potentialities of nature (as opposed to a postulated supernature) are more restricted than the potentialities which, in fact, we find to be realized or realizable in the universe around us.

This is a very old and apparently very easy and tempting assumption. It can be found, for instance, in Cicero's *De Natura Deorum,* and hence presumably much earlier, in Cicero's Greek sources. Nevertheless, the assumption is entirely unwarranted. We simply do not have, and could not have, any natural (as opposed to revealed) criterion which enables us to say, when faced with something which is found to have actually happened, that here we have an achievement which nature, left to her own unaided devices, could never encompass. The natural scientist, confronted with some occurrence inconsistent with a proposition previously believed to express a law of nature, can find in this disturbing inconsistency no ground whatever for proclaiming that the particular law of nature has been supernaturally overridden. On the contrary, the new discovery is simply a reason for his conceding that he had previously been wrong in thinking that the proposition, thus confuted, did indeed express a true law; it is also a reason for his resolving to search again for the law which really does obtain. We certainly cannot say, on any natural (as opposed to revealed) grounds, that anything that actually happens is beyond the powers of unaided nature, any more than we can say that anything which any man has ever succeeded in doing transcends all merely human powers. For our evidence about the powers of nature in general, and of men in particular, is precisely and only everything that things and people do. For a scientist to insist that some recalcitrant fact constitutes an overriding of a still inviolably true law of nature is—to borrow Carnap's mischievous analogy—as if a geographer were to maintain that the discrepancies between his maps and their objects show that there is something wrong with the territories concerned.

The insistence of the scientist, insofar as he is simply a scientist, on always seeking strictly universal laws is itself rooted in the fundamental object of the whole scientific quest: if scientists are to find comprehensive explanations, they must discover universal laws. A scientist's refusal to accept the idea that in any single case nature has been overridden by supernatural intervention is grounded partly on precisely the above-mentioned lack of any natural (as opposed to revealed) criterion for distinguishing natural from supernatural events, and partly on his commitment—which is chiefly what makes him a scientist—to continue always in the search for completely universal laws, and for more and more comprehensive theories. In view of this, it need be neither arbitrary nor irrational to insist on a definition of a "law of nature" such that the idea of a miracle as an exception to a law of nature is ruled out as self-contradictory.

The seductive but erroneous idea that we do possess some natural means for the identification of the supernatural is one that, in some respects, parallels the notion that it is logically possible to derive prescriptive norms from knowledge of what is, in some purely descriptive sense, natural. In each case there are adherents for whom the division between natural and supernatural, or between natural and unnatural, is nothing but an incoherent muddle. Likewise, in each case there are others who, in support of their choice, are prepared to deploy some more or less elaborate structure of theoretical justification.

Problem of evidence. All of this argumentation, although both relevant and (in spirit at least) thoroughly Humean, has little in common with the line of argument which Hume chose to develop in the section "Of Miracles." Although this line of argument is equally methodological, it treats the question of miracles as it arises in the field of history rather than as it might impinge upon natural science. Hume was primarily concerned, not with the question of fact, but with that of evidence. The problem was how the occurrence of a miracle could be proved, rather than whether any such events ever had occurred. Consequently, even if Hume was successful, the way would still remain clear for people to believe in miracles simply on faith. In his own mordant way, Hume himself was happy to allow for this, but he always insisted that "a wise man proportions his belief to the evidence."

This concentration on the evidential issue means that Hume's thesis, however offensively expressed, is nevertheless at bottom defensive. Hume hoped that he had discovered "a decisive argument . . . which must at least silence the most arrogant bigotry and superstition, and free us from their impertinent solicitations . . . an argument which . . . will . . . with the wise and learned, be an everlasting check to all kinds of superstitious delusion. . . ." These words were very carefully chosen. The whole argument was directed to the wise—to those, that is, who insist on proportioning their belief to the evidence. It did not show that the substantive claims of the bigoted and superstitious are in fact false. It was intended to serve as a decisive check on any attempt to solicit the assent of rational men by producing proof of the occurrence of the miraculous. In particular, the object was to interdict the second movement of the standard apologetic attack as outlined above.

If for present purposes a certain amount of misguided psychologizing is ignored, the following would appear to be the gist of Hume's "everlasting check." There is, he remarked, "no species of reasoning more common, more useful, and even necessary to human life than that derived from the testimony of men and the reports of eye-witnesses and spectators." Yet all testimony must ultimately be subject to assessment by the supreme court of experience. Certainly there are, as Hume observed, "a number of circumstances to be taken into consideration in all judgments of this kind." Yet "the ultimate standard by which we determine all disputes . . . is always derived from experience and observation." (Of all people, Hume, as the author of that most famous paragraph in the *Treatise of Human Nature,* should have said not *"is,"* but *"ought"* always to be so derived.)

The weight of the testimony required must depend on the apparent credibility of the events reported. If the events are in some way marvelous and rare, then the testimony for them has to be treated with more circumspection than the witness to everyday occurrences. But supposing that the testimony is for events which, had they occurred, would have been genuinely miraculous: we are then confronted with a paradoxical dilemma, proof balanced against proof. However overwhelming the testimony might have appeared were it not being considered as evidence for a miracle, in this peculiar case the testimony must always be offset against a counterproof. In Hume's own words, "A miracle is a violation of the laws of nature; and as a firm and unalterable experience has established these laws, the proof against a miracle, from the very nature of the fact, is as entire as any argument from experience can possibly be imagined."

In the first part of section X, Hume argued generally from the concept of the miraculous—from, as he put it, "the very nature of the fact." In the second he deployed several more particular assertions about the corruptions to which testimony is liable, urging that such corruptions are exceptionally virulent where any religious issue is involved. He also added a further consideration relevant to any attempt "to prove a miracle and make it a just foundation for any . . . system of religion."

This consideration was expressed badly and was entangled in one or two inessential errors and confusions. But a letter makes clear Hume's intent. The point is that if the occurrence of some sort of miracle is to serve as a guarantee of the truth of a system of religion, then there must not have been any similar miracle under the auspices of a rival system, the truth of which would be incompatible with the truth of the first. Consequently, insofar as we are considering a miracle not as a putative bald fact but as a possible endorsement of the authenticity of a revelation, we have to throw into the balance against the testimony for the miracles of any one candidate revelation all the available testimony for all the miracle stories presented by all the rival systems that are inconsistent with the first. In its appeal to a necessary conflict of evidence, this argument resembles the paradoxical dilemma expounded above.

MIRACLES AND THE PHILOSOPHY OF HISTORY

Enough already has been said to suggest that there is more to Hume's check than a trite insistence that since the occurrence of a miracle must be very improbable, it would have to be exceptionally well evidenced in order to be believed. C. S. Peirce was in possession of the vital clue (which he seems never to have exploited fully) when he remarked, "The whole of modern 'higher criticism' of ancient history in general, and of Biblical history in particular, is based upon the same logic that is used by Hume" (*Values in a Universe of Chance*, P. P. Wiener, ed., New York, 1958, pp. 292–293). When we follow this clue, it becomes obvious that Hume himself saw "the accounts of miracles and prodigies to be found in all history, sacred and profane" as presenting a methodological problem. This section on miracles constitutes the outer ring of Hume's defenses against the orthodox religious apologetic. But at the same time it is also part of his contribution to an understanding of the presuppositions and the limitations of critical history.

This fact seems not to have been appreciated as it should have been. There is, for instance, no reference to Hume's section "Of Miracles" in R. G. Collingwood's *The Idea of History* (Oxford, 1946); and neither Collingwood nor F. H. Bradley seems to have had any idea of the extent to which Bradley's own essay, "The Presuppositions of Critical

History" (*Collected Papers*, Vol. I., Oxford, 1935), echoed arguments first developed by Hume. It is worthwhile to consider possible causes of this neglect. In part it is to be attributed to the insistence (at one time universal) on treating section X, "Of Miracles," as though it were a separate and disingenuous essay, irrelevantly inserted into the first *Enquiry* simply to cause scandal and thereby push up sales. This perverse and gratuitously offensive notion has misled interpreters to overlook some extremely relevant remarks in Part I of section VIII which concern the inescapably uniformitarian presuppositions of both the natural and the social sciences. Even those who have succeeded in appreciating section X as a very considerable piece of argumentation have been inclined to pigeonhole it as being a contribution to the philosophy of religion only. Certainly Hume's argument does, in the first instance, belong to the philosophy of religion; and this, of course, is how Hume presented it. Yet, as we have already seen, it also has a place in the philosophy of science. The fact that Hume appreciated this is perhaps suggested by his proposal that if, against all reasonable expectation, there were to be sufficient historical evidence to establish that the "miracle" of a universal eight-day eclipse had occurred in January 1600, "then our present philosophers [scientists], instead of doubting the fact, ought to receive it as certain; and ought to search for the causes whence it might be derived." It is surely significant that in this one context, and inconsistently with his own official definition of "miracle," he spoke not of "a violation of the laws of nature," but rather, and more weakly, of "violations of the usual course of nature."

The same nodal argument which thus has a place in both the philosophy of religion and the philosophy of science belongs equally in the philosophy of history. For what Hume was contending (with certain lapses and hesitations) is that the criteria by which we must assess historical testimony, and the general presumptions which alone make it possible for us to interpret the detritus of the past as historical evidence, must inevitably rule out any possibility of establishing, upon purely historical grounds, that some genuinely miraculous event has indeed occurred. Hume concentrated on testimonial evidence because his conception of the historian, later illustrated in his own famous *History of England*, was of a judge assessing with judicious impartiality the testimony set before him. But the same Humean principles can be applied more widely to all forms of historical evidence.

The fundamental propositions are first, that the present detritus of the past cannot be interpreted as historical evidence at all, unless we presume that the same basic regularities obtained then as today; and second, that in trying his best to determine what actually happened, the historian must employ as criteria all his present knowledge, or presumed knowledge, of what is probable or improbable, possible or impossible. In his first work, the *Treatise of Human Nature* (II, iii, i), Hume had argued that it is only on such presumptions that we can justify the conclusion that ink marks on old pieces of paper constitute testimonial evidence. Early in the first *Enquiry*, in the first part of section VIII, he urged the inescapable importance of having such criteria. In a footnote to section X, he quoted with approval the reasoning of the famous physician De Sylva in the case of a Mlle. Thibaut: "It was impossible she could have been so ill as was proved by witnesses, because it was impossible she could, in so short a time, have recovered so perfectly as he found her."

Flaws in Hume's account. Two very serious faults in Hume's presentation of his argument may obscure the force and soundness of De Sylva's reasoning, as well as the fact that this sort of application of canons to evidence is absolutely essential to the very possibility of critical history.

The first fault is a rather wooden dogmatism of disbelief. For against all his own high, skeptical principles, Hume tended to take it for granted that what in his own day he and all his fellow men of sense firmly believed about the order of nature constituted not just humanly fallible opinion, but the incorrigible last word. He was thus betrayed into categorically dismissing as downright impossible certain reported phenomena which the later progress in the study of abnormal psychology and of psychosomatic medicine has since shown to have been perfectly possible. But the moral to be drawn from these lapses into dogmatism is not that Hume was mistaken in insisting that the critical historian must apply canons of possibility and probability to his evidence, but that he failed to appreciate that all such canons are themselves subject to criticism and correction.

The second major fault in Hume's treatment is both more serious and more excusable. He was unable to provide an adequate account of the logical character of a law of nature. Hence, he could not offer any sufficiently persuasive rationale for employing, as canons of exclusion in historical inquiry, propositions which express, or which are believed to express, such natural laws. The way may thus seem to be open for a historian who holds different presuppositions, yet still remains truly a historian, to endorse as veridical stories of events which, had they occurred, would have been truly miraculous. (For a recent sustained study of such attempts to have it both ways, see T. A. Roberts, *History and Christian Apologetic,* London, 1960.)

This problem of the logical nature of natural laws has, of course, many more aspects than those which immediately concern us here. But it is important first to emphasize that it is at least as much a problem for Hume's immediate opponents as for Hume. For it is his opponents who need a strong sense of "miracle," in which the miraculous can be distinguished from the merely marvelous. It is tempting, but entirely wrong, for the spokesman for the miraculous to think that he can afford to triumph over Hume's difficulties without being himself committed in any way to producing his own account of the character of laws of nature—an account which shall be more satisfactory as an analysis and yet, at the same time, consistent with the things the spokesman himself wants to say about the miraculous. His dilemma, to repeat, is that he needs to be able to accommodate simultaneously both the strong laws and the spectacular transgressions.

Nomological propositions. Casting back to the reasoning of De Sylva, it can now be seen that (and how) it constitutes a paradigm of critical history. For it is only and precisely by presuming that the laws that hold today held in the past and by employing as canons all our knowledge—or presumed knowledge—of what is probable or improbable, possible or impossible, that we can rationally interpret the detritus of the past as evidence and from it construct our account of what actually happened. But in this context, what is impossible is what is physically, as opposed to logically, impossible. And "physical impossibility" is, and surely has to be, defined in terms of inconsistency with a true law of nature. Or rather, since this sense of "impossible" is prior to the development of science proper, it might be said that what is physically impossible is whatever is inconsistent with a true nomological proposition.

Both causal propositions and those expressing laws of nature fall under the genus nomological. Although Hume himself concentrated on the causal species, what he said can easily be extended. In his view, when we say that A is the cause of B, the main thing we are saying is that B's are constantly conjoined with A's—never as a matter of fact A and not B, or, in modern terminology, A materially implies B. Of course, he went on, people think they are asserting not a mere constant conjunction, but some real connection, and in a way this is right. The fact is, according to Hume, that there *is* a connection, but that it is a psychological one: we have formed a habit of associating the idea of an A with the idea of a B.

Yet this account of causal propositions cannot be adequate. All causal propositions entail subjunctive conditionals. (A subjunctive conditional, appropriately enough, is a proposition of the form, "If it were . . . it would.") Thus, "A's are the only things which cause B's" entails "If A were not to occur (or to have occurred) B would not occur (or have occurred)." But no variation on the material implication theme, with or without benefit of associationist psychological speculation, can be made to entail any such subjunctive conditional. Furthermore, the same essential inadequacy afflicts any extension of a Humean analysis to cover nomologicals in general. For a nomological is, by the above definition, a contingent proposition which entails some contingent subjunctive conditional.

The essential difference between the contingent "All X are ϕ" and the equally contingent "Any X must be ϕ" is that the former can be expressed as a material implication, "Not both X and not ϕ," whereas the latter cannot be so expressed, because it is a nomological, entailing such subjunctive conditionals as "If there were to have been an X (which in fact there was not) it would have been a ϕ." The nomological goes far beyond the statement of a mere conjunction of X and ϕ as a matter of fact. It asserts also a (contingent) connection between X and ϕ. For although the nomological is no more logically necessary than the corresponding material implication, it says not merely that, as it happens, a constant conjunction has been, is being, and will be maintained, but also that it would be and would have been maintained regardless of what anyone did or might have done. To assert the nomological is to assert that the conjunction is one which can be relied upon. It is for this reason that experimental evidence is so essential to our knowledge of nomologicals: the obvious and ultimately the only satisfactory test of the reliability of a law is to subject it to strains. It is for the same reason that a knowledge of nomologicals provides, at least in principle, a guarantee of repeatability. To say that the conjunction of *B*'s with *A*'s is reliable is to say that any time anyone likes to produce an *A* he will thereby bring about a *B*.

The historian's approach. In the light of the above discussion, we can again consider the question of historical evidence for the miraculous. The critical historian, confronted with some story of a miracle, will usually dismiss it out of hand, asking first only whether it can be used as evidence, not for the occurrence reported, but for something else. To justify his procedure he will have to appeal to precisely the principle which Hume advanced: the "absolute impossibility or miraculous nature" of the events attested must, "in the eyes of all reasonable people . . . alone be regarded as a sufficient refutation." Our sole ground for characterizing the reported occurrence as miraculous is at the same time a sufficient reason for calling it physically impossible. Contrariwise, if ever we became able to say that some account of the ostensibly miraculous was indeed veridical, we can say it only because we now know that the occurrences reported were not miraculous at all.

Objections to the historian's approach. To this representation of the procedure of the critical historian there are two main objections. First, it will be argued that such an approach to what purports to be historical evidence for the miraculous is irrationally dogmatic, for in this instance the historian seems to be represented as dismissing all evidence that conflicts with his own fundamental prejudices and as defending a closed system in which his professional predilections are guaranteed against falsification by a "Heads-I-win: tails-you-lose" argument. This is a very understandable objection. It is made more plausible by the regrettable fact that there have been, and still are, many historical writers whose actual procedures correspond rather too closely to this suggested representation. Also it is, of course, true that the dilemmas generated by the tension implicit in the concept of the miraculous must necessarily seem to their victims to have a "Heads-you-win: tails-I-lose" aspect. Nevertheless, the critical historian is not committed to the sort of bigoted dogmatism which the present objection attributes to him.

Nomological laws and reports of miracles. As Hume was insisting from first to last, the possibility of miracles is a matter of evidence and not of dogmatism. For, to proceed beyond Hume, the nomological proposition that provides the historian's canon of exclusion will be open and general and of the form "Any *X* must be ϕ." The proposition reporting the (alleged) occurrence of the miracle will be singular, particular, and in the past tense; it will have the form "This *X* on that particular occasion was not ϕ." Propositions of the first sort can in principle be tested at any time and in any place. Propositions of the second sort cannot any longer be tested directly. It is this that gives propositions of the first sort the vastly greater logical strength that justifies their use as criteria of rejection against the latter. It will indeed be only and precisely insofar as we have evidence sufficient to warrant our assertion of the general nomological that excludes the particular historical proposition that we shall have sufficient reason to claim that the event which it reports would have been genuinely miraculous.

The logic of evidence. Suppose that in some particular case the evidence for a miracle appears extremely strong. Then perhaps the historian may ask himself whether the nomological proposition that precludes this event is after all true. It could, in principle at any rate, be further tested. If, as is possible, it were shown to be false after all, then perhaps the event so strongly evidenced did indeed occur. But by the same token, that event could now no longer be described as truly miraculous. This, surely, is what has happened in the case of so many of the reports of astonishing psychosomatic cures, which Hume himself, in his capacity as a historiographer, too rashly dismissed. (Consider, for example, his contemptuous rejection of the stories of faith healings by the Emperor Vespasian and of the many cures associated with the tomb of the Jansenist Abbé Paris, all in section X of his first *Enquiry*.) Alternatively, the nomological proposition might survive even our further tests. Hume should be the last one to deny that it must remain always conceivable—logically, that is, as opposed to physically possible—that the event in question did in fact occur. Yet in this case, no matter how impressive the testimony might appear, the most favorable verdict that history could ever return must be the agnostic, and appropriately Scottish, "not proven."

Need for canons of evidence. The second objection to the above representation of the procedure of the critical historian suggests that there is something arbitrary or at least optional about the appeal to canons provided by some of our knowledge, or presumed knowledge, of what is probable or improbable, possible or impossible. Once again there is some ground for this objection. Certainly we can choose whether or not we will try to act as critical historians. But once that fundamental choice is made, there is nothing arbitrary and nothing optional about insisting on the employment of these canons. For the essential aim of the historian is to get as near as he can to a full knowledge of what actually happened, and why. To do this he must find and interpret evidence, for belief unsupported by evidence may be true, but it cannot constitute knowledge. Yet to interpret the detritus of the past as evidence, and to assess its value and bearing as such, we must have canons. And for a rational man, these canons can only be derived from the sum of his available knowledge, or presumed knowledge. It is not the insistence on the systematic employment of these always corrigible canons which is arbitrary; what is arbitrary is to pick and choose in the interests of your ideological predilections among the available mass of miracle stories, or to urge that it is (psychologically) impossible that these particular witnesses were lying or misinformed and hence that we must accept the fact that on this occasion the (biologically) impossible occurred. If one once departs in such arbitrary ways from these canons of critical history, then anything and everything goes. (For examples of precisely this sort of arbitrariness, see M. C. Perry, *The Easter Enigma,* London and New York, 1959.)

Possible justifications for belief in miracles. Nothing that has been said in this article decisively closes the door on faith. We have been concerned only with questions about the possibilities of having good reasons for belief in the miraculous. Again, nothing has been said to preclude the production of nonhistorical and nonscientific considerations which might, either by themselves or with the aid of historical or scientific evidence, justify our belief that certain miracles did indeed occur. Perhaps one might develop some defensible system of rational theology which would provide criteria both for identifying particular occurrences as miraculous and for separating the true miracle stories from the false. Hume tried to rule this out also, of course, in section XI of his *Enquiry,* and elsewhere. But it has been no part of our present task to examine arguments against natural theology. Finally, it is perfectly possible to develop a new concept and to apply to it the word "miracle." There is never anything to keep anyone from simply changing the subject.

Bibliography

HISTORICAL STUDIES

Grant, R. M., *Miracle and Natural Law in Graeco-Roman and Early Christian Thought.* Amsterdam, 1952.

Lecky, W. E. H., *History of the Rise and Influence of Rationalism in Europe.* London, 1865. Chs. 1–3. These chapters carry on approximately from where Grant leaves off.

Stephen, Leslie, *English Thought in the Eighteenth Century,* 3d ed. London, 1902. Vol. I. Contains the classic account of the entire controversy of which Hume's "Of Miracles" formed a part.

LOGICAL AND METHODOLOGICAL STUDIES

Augustine, *The City of God,* XXI, 8.

Aquinas, Thomas, *Summa Contra Gentiles,* III, 98–107.

Spinoza, B., *Tractatus Theologico-Politicus,* VI.

Hume, D., *An Enquiry Concerning Human Understanding,* VIII–XI.

Mill, J. S., *A System of Logic,* III, 4 and 25.

Mozley, J. B., *On Miracles.* London, 1865.

Tennant, F. R., *Miracle and Its Philosophical Presuppositions.* Cambridge, 1925.

Lewis, C. S., *Miracles.* London and New York, 1947. Mozley, Tennant, and Lewis all give Anglican views, of which Tennant's is perhaps the most liberal and Lewis' the most conservative. The latter employs a theoretical structure of the type referred to in the discussion of the problem of identifying the supernatural in order to uphold the possibility of miracles. For a discussion and development of the ideas touched on in that section, see the exchanges between H. H. Dubs, A. Lunn, and P. Nowell-Smith in *The Hibbert Journal* (1950–1952).

Smith, G. D., ed., *The Teaching of the Catholic Church,* 2d ed. London, 1952.

Roberts, T. A., *History and Christian Apologetic.* London, 1960.

King-Farlow, J., "Miracles: Nowell-Smith's Analysis and Tillich's Phenomenology." *International Philosophical Quarterly,* Vol. II (1962). Although this article appeared in a Jesuit journal, it seems to accept most of the sort of methodological criticism presented in the present article. The bibliography of recent Roman Catholic literature on the subject is especially valuable.

ILLUSTRATIONS OF MAIN METHODOLOGICAL POINTS

Middleton, Conyers, *A Free Inquiry into the Miraculous Powers which are supposed to have subsisted in the Christian Church from the earliest ages through several successive centuries.* London, 1748. A pivotal work in the great eighteenth-century controversy described by Stephen.

Newman, J. H., "Essay on the Miracles Recorded in Ecclesiastical History," in *The Ecclesiastical History of M. L'Abbé Fleury.* Oxford, 1842. This essay by the future cardinal deserves to be read alongside Middleton's *Free Inquiry.*

Huxley, T. H., "Agnosticism and Christianity," in *Lectures and Essays.* London, 1902. An attack on Newman.

Schweitzer, Albert, *The Quest for the Historical Jesus, from Reimarus to Wrede.* London, 1911. A classic history of a historiographical subject. It is interesting to note that the work contains no reference to Hume.

Thomson, J. M., *Miracles in the New Testament.* London, 1911. An important but neglected work by a historian who later achieved distinction in the field of secular history.

Morrison, F., *Who Moved the Stone?* New York, 1930. A gripping, if very unsophisticated, study of New Testament evidence.

West, D. J., *Eleven Lourdes Miracles.* London, 1957. A study of the best evidence by a psychiatrist and sometime research officer of the Society for Psychical Research.

Perry, M. C., *The Easter Enigma.* London, 1959. An attempt to apply the findings of psychical research to the interpretation of the New Testament documents. It illustrates both an admirably undogmatic flexibility about what in fact is and is not possible and a certain inconsistency in applying the canons of critical history.

ANTONY FLEW

MIRANDOLA, COUNT GIOVANNI PICO DELLA.
See PICO DELLA MIRANDOLA, COUNT GIOVANNI.

MIURA BAIEN (1723–1789), Japanese Confucianist who in the era of Tokugawa rule most closely approached Western philosophy. Miura was born in Ōita Prefecture on the island of Kyūshū. After the usual training in Chinese classics, Miura went to Nagasaki and learned astronomy, physics, medicine, and economics and developed a great admiration for Western experimental methods. This explains in part his rationalism in opposition to the general reliance on the authority of the classics. He devoted his life to scholarship, refusing several offers to serve feudal lords. To help the poor he organized a relief society based on communal principles. Miura's encyclopedic knowledge also included economics. In *Kagen* ("The Origin of Price") he discussed currency like his contemporary Adam Smith. Miura wrote "if bad money finds wide circulation, good money will go into hiding," a statement similar, in words at least, to Gresham's Law.

Miura's main philosophical works are three: *Gengo* ("Abstruse Words"), an exposition of logic; *Zeigo* ("Superfluous Words"), an exposition of the philosophy of nature; and *Kango* ("Presumptuous Words"), an exposition of ethics. *Gengo* is highly esteemed as original because in it he expounds his ideas of *jori*, or the logic of "things" (an abstract concept covering everything). This logic is based not on ancient authority but on rational or experimental grounds. Miura built his logic according to the laws of nature and things. In these he saw a unity and order of antithetic natural elements. He called his dialectic *hankan gōitchi*, or "synthesis of the contraries." This dialectic is both a logical device and the inner reality of things. Things, which are always in the process of becoming, pass from unity to multiplicity and back again, through antithesis and synthesis. His merits as the forerunner of modern trends in science and philosophy notwithstanding, Miura had rather staid political and theological ideas. His criticism of Christianity, in *Samidare-shō*, focuses on the idea that a foreign religion that puts God before devotion to one's lord and one's father cannot be tolerated.

Bibliography

Miura's works are available in Japanese in *Baien zenshū* ("The Collected Works of Miura Baien"), 2 vols. (Tokyo, 1912). See also G. K. Piovesana, "Miura Baien, and his Dialectical and Political Ideas," in *Monumenta Nipponica*, Vol. 20 (1965), 389–443, which contains a translation of Miura's letter "Answer to Taga Bokkyō." See also W. T. de Bary, Ryusaku Tsunoda, and Donald Keene, eds., *Sources of Japanese Tradition* (New York, 1958), pp. 489–497; N. S. Smith, "An Introduction to Some Japanese Economic Writings of the 18th Century," in *Transactions of the Asiatic Society of Japan*, 2d series, Vol. 11 (1934), 80–88; L. Hurvitz, "The *Samidare-shō*," in *Monumenta Nipponica*, Vol. 8 (1953), 289–326; Vol. 9 (1953), 330–356.

GINO K. PIOVESANA, S.J.

MODAL LOGIC. See LOGIC, MODAL.

MODELS AND ANALOGY IN SCIENCE. The term "model" has become fashionable in the literature and philosophy of science, with the result that the many different senses of the term need to be distinguished before the philosophical problems connected with models in the sciences can be understood. This article will begin with a classification of some of the more important senses of "model" before discussing the relevant philosophical issues.

Logical models. Formal logic is concerned with sets of axioms and their deductive consequences and also with the interpretations of these axioms and theorems in "models"—that is, sets of entities that satisfy the axioms. These relationships are most easily exemplified in terms of elementary geometry. Suppose a formalized geometry contains as an axiom the sentence "Any two points lie on one and only one straight line." In a fully formalized system there will be no definition of the terms "point" and "straight line" apart from this axiom and others in which these terms appear. As far as the formal system is concerned, the use of these terms is wholly defined by their relationships as given in the axioms and their deductive consequences. If we ask what the axioms are about, the only answer that can be given is that they are about just those sets of entities that satisfy the axioms.

One such set of entities clearly consists of the points and straight lines drawn in geometrical diagrams, or, rather, idealizations of these, which accurately reproduce the relationships specified in the axioms. However, it does not follow that this obvious interpretation of the axioms is the only possible one. In the geometric example the axiom may otherwise be interpreted in terms of certain sets and their members, so that the axiom would read "Any two individuals are comembers of one and only one set." Similarly, a formalized Boolean algebra can be interpreted as a calculus of classes, as a calculus of propositions, or in terms of spatial areas as in the Venn diagrams. Any set of entities that constitutes an interpretation of all the axioms and theorems of a system and in which those axioms and theorems hold true is called a model (in the logician's sense) of that system.

Such an informal characterization of this sense of "model" is, of course, entirely inadequate for the logician's purposes. But it is sufficient to indicate, first, how the term "model" has become attached to certain semiformal and nonformal systems in the empirical sciences and, second, what crucial differences exist between these logical models and those that are of interest in science. Some uses of "model" in science, such as nineteenth-century mechanical "models" of the ether, antedate the logician's use; others are consequences of it. It can be said as a preliminary that most uses of "model" in science do carry over from logic the idea of interpretation of a deductive system. Most writers on models in the sciences agree, however, that there is little else in common between the scientist's and the logician's use of the term, either in the nature of the entities referred to or in the purposes for which they are used.

Replicas and analogue machines. There is a sense of "model" in science that is both nearest to its sense in ordinary language and furthest from the logician's sense. Replicas, scale models, and analogues are familiar in various contexts and may be said to provide, after logical models, the second main source of ideas associated with the term "model" in the sciences. They may be used in science for expository purposes or even as calculating devices in cases where the building of a replica or analogue of a system as a working model is the simplest method of investigating the consequences of those natural laws that the system is believed to satisfy. Various examples include wind-tunnel experiments, crystallographic models, electronic models of nerve nets, and hydraulic models of economic supply and demand. Not all these are examples of straightforward replicas, however; some of them do not resemble in substance the thing modeled but are merely similar in certain of the relations between its parts. It is perhaps better, therefore, to call them analogue machines. Thus, economic supply and demand does not consist of pipes carrying colored fluids, but the relations exhibited by such a model may enable conclusions to be drawn in an economic system when the appropriate interpretations are made. In such cases the similarity of relations between model and system modeled may be called isomorphism. This relation of isomorphism may be linked with the concept of logical model by remarking that if the laws of the system were explicitly set out in a formal system, then model and thing modeled would both be models of that system in something like the logical sense. The relation of isomorphism between the model and the thing modeled would therefore be the relation between two interpretations of the same formal system. But this way of looking at analogue machines may be highly artificial in many practical cases, because such machines are often constructed precisely for cases where there is no known mathematical specification of a system or where this specification is so complex that the explicit drawing of deductive consequences is impossible or impracticable. Where this is the case, it is dangerous to attempt to apply to scientific models those arguments that are valid in connection with logical models of formal systems.

Before describing the senses of "model" that are more central to the structure of theoretical science and that contain some of the features of both logical and replica models, it is useful to give some account of the associated notion of analogy in terms of which different kinds of models can best be categorized.

Analogy in science. The relation between model and thing modeled can be said generally to be a relation of analogy. Two kinds of analogy relation can be distinguished in connection with models in the sciences. First, in the case of a logical model of a formal system, there is analogy of structure or isomorphism between model and system, deriving from the fact that the same formal axiomatic and deductive relations connect individuals and predicates of both the system and its model. This isomorphism consists of the correspondence between individuals and predicates of the system and the terms that are their interpretations in the model. Derivatively, we may say that there is an analogy of the same kind between two different models of the same formal system. A swinging pendulum and an oscillating electric circuit, for example, are analogous by virtue of the formal relations described in a wave equation satisfied by both. Let us call this type of analogy between systems formal analogy.

Second, however, we must consider the analogy exhibited by a replica with its parent system, which consists in something more than formal analogy. In a formal analogy there may be no similarity between the individuals and predicates of two models of the same formal system other than their relation of isomorphism. But in a replica model there are also what might be called material similarities between the parent system and its replica. The wings of an aircraft and its replica, for example, may have similar shape and hardness and may be made of the same material although they differ in at least one respect, size. Where two systems exhibit such similarities, which are not—or not simply—similarities by virtue of being logical models of the same formal system, we shall say that they have material analogy.

Two systems may have formal but not material analogy; two examples are the hydraulic model of economic systems and the various mechanical and electrical models of the wave equation. The systems may have both kinds of analogy, as do such replicas and near replicas as crystallographic models. It does not seem possible to conceive of a material analogy without some formal analogy; if there is material analogy, there is presumably some consequent structural similarity that could—at least in principle—be formalized. The distinction between formal and material analogy is difficult to make precise, but its significance will become clearer in considering the functions of theoretical models.

The relation of analogy, whether formal or material, generally implies differences as well as similarities. In analogous systems let us denote the set of similarities by the term "positive analogy" and the set of differences by "negative analogy."

The types of models to be described with the aid of these concepts of analogy are classified mainly in accordance with their function in relation to theories rather than with their intrinsic character. Thus, a model having various functions on the same or different occasions may very often come under different categories, and models of very different intrinsic kinds may come under the same cate-

gory. Many other types of classification of models can be and have been produced (depending on whether they are mechanical or electrical, micromodels or macromodels, and so on). The categorization to be given now, however, seems to raise the most interesting philosophical questions in regard to the functions of models in science.

Semiformal or mathematical models. The logical sense of "model" has led to widespread use of the word in connection with a variety of mathematical theories developed in the sciences. No element of a replica is involved in these theories, and their interpretation is in terms of mathematical concepts such as probability or the elements of a geometry. It has become common to speak of "probabilistic models" of, for example, psychological learning theory or population dynamics. In this context "model" refers to a mathematical theory containing the axioms of probability together with an interpretation of all or some of the nonlogical constants and variables of the theory into empirical observables. In these cases use of the word "model" seems to borrow most of its appropriateness from the logical sense, and the analogy involved is almost wholly formal. Insofar as it is merely formal, some writers, such as Max Black, have denied that it has any causal or explanatory force, since the theories involved are no more than convenient mathematical expressions of the empirical data. In some cases, however, these theories do seem to have some element of material as well as formal analogy. For example, the "probability" that is a limiting-frequency interpretation of the axioms of probability exhibits some material analogy with the logical or range model of probability, for the similarity or correlation of the two notions in, for instance, games of chance exists not only by virtue of formal analogy with the same axiom system but also might well be apprehended independently of knowledge of that system. Where such material analogy does exist in connection with theoretical models, we may well say that a mathematical model does have causal, predictive, and explanatory force as an interpretation of a formal system.

Simplifying models. The term "model" is sometimes used to denote systems that deliberately simplify and even falsify the empirical situation under investigation for purposes of convenience in research or application. Such idealizations as ideal gases come into this category, as do such simplifying statistical approximations as "smoothed-out universes" in cosmology. It is also convenient to include in this category archaic models, which have been developed in now falsified theories but which still have some use as convenient approximations in applied rather than pure science. Examples are the model of heat as a fluid or of faculty psychology, in which man is seen as a nexus of interacting faculties of reason, will, and emotion. Archaic models are those that have a large and deliberate element of negative analogy with the relevant empirical system, in respects sufficiently important to have led to abandonment of these models in connection with current theories. But insofar as they are still at all useful, they must retain sufficient positive analogy in other respects to enable some correct conclusions to be drawn from the comparison of system and model.

Theoretical models. There are kinds of models, which we shall conveniently group as theoretical models, that are much more intimately associated with the structure of theories than simplifying models. Roughly speaking, these are models that appear—at least at first sight—to be identical with the relevant theory, as may be indicated by means of some examples. The explanation of light phenomena in terms of light corpuscles may be spoken of indifferently as a corpuscular model or a corpuscular theory of light. Similarly, the model of the DNA molecule, in at least one sense of "model," is identical with the theory of the molecular structure of DNA. We speak of Bohr's model of the atom, referring to the theory that was proposed to account for certain quantum phenomena. In cosmology we refer to "world models," which are theories of the structure of the universe. If there is any difference in such cases between the uses of the terms "model" and "theory," it is probably connected with the degree of acceptability of the theory. Thus, Bohr's theory, which is a rather radical departure from previous physics, or a theory of light that is not fully established and to which there are viable alternatives, may be called a model. It would, however, be odd to speak today of a wave model of sound, since a theory of sound in terms of wave motion is fully established and is even regarded as factual rather than theoretical.

The question of the degree to which a theory is accepted does not, however, seem to be the most important consideration in leading some philosophers to maintain a distinction between theoretical models and the theories of which they are models. To understand their motives, let us try to abstract from the previous examples the salient features of theoretical models. First, these frequently are models in something like the logical sense of being interpretations of a formal or semiformal theoretical system from which the phenomena are deducible. Thus, a system of mechanical corpuscles is an interpretation of Newton's laws of motion, and in this interpretation the linear propagation and reflection properties of light can be deduced from Newton's laws. If the Bohr model of the atom had turned out to be acceptable in a more developed quantum theory, it also would have been an interpretation of the formal structure of quantum theory. In the case of the DNA molecule, it is not so clear that there is any formal theory of which it is a model; the presumption is that a wave mechanics adequate to describe such complex structures as organic molecules would be such a theory. This example indicates that in science, unlike logic, the notion of model is not dependent on prior development of a formal theory.

The second notable feature of theoretical models is that they are dependent on some system or, if it is known, on the theory of the system, which is epistemologically prior to and independent of the particular phenomena that the model is invoked to explain. In other words, models of this kind provide explanation in terms of something already familiar and intelligible. This is true of all attempts to reduce relatively obscure phenomena to more familiar mechanisms or to picturable nonmechanical systems (such as Bohr's atom), and it is true of geometrical models of the expanding universe and in topological models of brain structure, to give only a few examples. Basically, the theoretical model exploits some other system (such as a mechanism or a familiar mathematical or empirical theory

from another domain) that is already well known and understood in order to explain the less well-established system under investigation. This latter may be called the explanandum. What chiefly distinguishes theoretical models from other kinds is a feature that follows from their associating another system with the explanandum. This is, that the theoretical model carries with it what has been called "open texture," or "surplus meaning," derived from the familiar system. The theoretical model conveys associations and implications that are not completely specifiable and that may be transferred by analogy to the explanandum; further developments and modifications of the explanatory theory may therefore be suggested by the theoretical model. Because the theoretical model is richer than the explanandum, it imports concepts and conceptual relations not present in the empirical data alone.

The last point can be used to characterize the difference between theoretical models and models in other categories. Almost any model or interpretation carries some surplus meaning. If, however, a model is used in a way that exploits this surplus meaning in prediction and explanation, we shall call it a theoretical model. Here another distinction must be made. Any model derived in an unsophisticated way from a familiar system (such as a mechanism) inevitably has negative as well as positive analogies with the explanandum. When a billiard ball model of gases is proposed, it is not intended that every feature of billiard balls—for example, their size or color—should be ascribed to gases. There is always a negative analogy that is implicitly recognized and tacitly ignored. We can therefore make a distinction between the model as exhibited by the familiar system and the model as it is used in connection with the theory. The latter is a conceptual entity arrived at by stripping away the negative analogy, and it is only this that can plausibly be identified with the theory. It is only this that we shall in future speak of as the theoretical model proper.

The sense in which the theoretical model and the theory can be identified can now be brought out in the following way. The model is first proposed because there is some obvious positive analogy (usually material as well as formal) between it and the explanandum. But the theoretical model that results from ignoring the negative analogy has more than simply a remaining positive analogy with the explanandum. If this were not so, the theoretical model would be identical with the explanandum and not richer, as we have required. In addition to the known positive analogy, there is a set of properties of the model whose positive or negative analogy is not yet known. Let us call this set the neutral analogy. Exploitation of the model consists in investigating this neutral analogy and in allowing the neutral analogy to suggest modifications and developments of the theory that can be confirmed or refuted by subsequent empirical tests.

Function. Few philosophers would deny that theoretical models may have the heuristic function in relation to theories that has just been described. The main philosophical debate about models concerns the question of whether there is any essential and objective dependence between an explanatory theory and its model that goes beyond a dispensable and possibly subjective method of discovery.

The debate is an aspect of an old controversy between the positivist and realist interpretations of scientific theory. Many episodes in the history of science may be regarded as chapters in this controversy, including application of Ockham's razor to scientific theories, the Newtonian–Cartesian controversy over the mechanical character of gravitation, nineteenth-century debates about the mechanical ether and the existence of atoms, and Machian positivism. In its modern form the argument for the essential dependence of theories on models was first developed in 1920 by N. R. Campbell in *Physics, the Elements,* and it is convenient to state the argument mainly in his terms.

Campbell's interpretation. Campbell attacked the contemporary positivist view, expressed by Heinrich Hertz, Ernst Mach, Pierre Duhem, and others, that models are merely dispensable aids to theory construction and can be detached and discarded when the theory is fully developed. In *Physics* Campbell first sets out explicitly the structure of a particular theory (the elementary kinetic theory of gases) in what later came to be called the hypothetico-deductive form. This form exhibits theories as made up of three elements—a formal deductive system (hypothesis) of axioms and theorems; a "dictionary" for translating some of the terms of the formal system into experimental terms; and experimental laws such as, in this example, the Boyle and Charles gas laws, which are confirmed by empirical tests and also can be deduced from the system of hypothesis plus dictionary. This structure is roughly what positivists and formalists regard as the essence of an explanatory theory. As distinct from various views demanding explicit definability in empirical terms of every nonlogical concept in a theory, Campbell points out that the hypothetico-deductive structure does allow for "hypothetical ideas," the interpretations of which were later called theoretical concepts. These concepts appear in the formal theory as part of the machinery of deduction; they do not appear in the theory's dictionary and are therefore given no explicit empirical interpretation. Further, Campbell argues that the hypothetico-deductive form is insufficient to account for an explanatory theory as understood in science. There is, he maintains, an essential fourth element in theories—namely, the analogy, which is exemplified in gas theory by the model of point particles moving at random in the vessel containing the gas. In this model all the theoretical concepts such as molecule, as well as the position, velocity, and mass of molecules receive an interpretation in particle mechanics, although they are not directly observable.

Campbell has two main arguments for his view that the particle model is essential to the structure of the theory of gases. First, it is intellectually satisfying as an explanation of the empirical data. Here Campbell implicitly contradicts the later analysts of explanation who regard the hypothetico-deductive structure itself as sufficiently explanatory and reject further criteria, such as familiarity or intellectual satisfaction, for explanation. Second, and more cogently, Campbell draws attention to the dynamic character of theories and their use in prediction. Using the particle model, he shows that it allows modifications and extensions of the theory that issue in empirical predictions over a wider domain of phenomena than those initially ex-

plained. Furthermore, his arguments implicitly demand a model that, in the above terminology, has not only formal but also material analogy with the explanandum; such would be a vessel containing a gas (for example, a balloon) as model for an elastic Newtonian particle. Predictivity is one of the characteristics demanded of satisfactory scientific theories, and Campbell argues that without material analogy there are no rational, nonarbitrary grounds for prediction. His argument has been extended and developed (by E. H. Hutten, M. B. Hesse, R. Harré, and others); it has also been subject to various objections, and formalist alternatives have been proposed by R. B. Braithwaite and others. Three distinct problems can be distinguished in these subsequent discussions—the predictivity of theories, the meaning of theoretical concepts, and the question of the realistic interpretation of models.

Predictivity. Most disputants are agreed that predictivity in some sense is a requirement for satisfactory explanatory theories, but some deny that theoretical models are essential or even helpful for the satisfaction of this requirement. First, it is argued that even if there is such a model for a given theory, no argument by analogy with the model guarantees the truth of the predictions thereby derived. This must be conceded, for no empirical predictions can be guaranteed, however derived. But the objection presupposes that there are no grounds for holding that arguments by analogy have at least some inductive force and that these grounds may be stronger than for other methods of making predictions from theories. The truth of this presupposition is by no means obvious (see P. Achinstein, "Variety and Analogy in Confirmation Theory," and M. B. Hesse, "Analogy and Confirmation Theory").

Second, it is argued that theories without theoretical models may use criteria other than analogy for the purposes of extension and prediction. Such formal characteristics as simplicity, symmetry, or mathematical elegance may be exploited to modify or extend the theory and thus to derive from it new consequences that can be empirically tested. Introduction, in the interests of symmetry, of the displacement-current term in Maxwell's equations is cited as an example of this process. Furthermore, although it is pointed out that in modern physics it has been shown conclusively that no models of the classical type are possible, the quantum theory does seem to have all the required characteristics, including predictivity, even though no other type of model has been introduced. Further discussion of this point demands a closer analysis of what is meant by predictivity and also of the assumption that quantum theory, where it is predictive, does not still make essential use of models in some sense.

The meaning of theoretical concepts. In the hypothetico-deductive scheme theoretical concepts are not given explicit meaning in terms of observables. Thus, there is the question of how theoretical concepts are meaningful or, expressed more precisely, if the rules of the formal hypothesis give the syntax of the system, what gives its semantics. In the Campbellian tradition the answer has been that the semantics is given by the model, which is intelligible independently of the explanandum; hence, the model contributes to the meaning of the theoretical concepts an element not derived from any direct connection with the observable explanandum. Those who wish to relegate models to mere heuristic devices argue, on the other hand, that no such nonempirical element in the meaning of theoretical concepts is required. An extreme version of this formalist view would hold that no interpretation at all of the theoretical terms is required, that the theory can, in fact, be viewed as a black box into which data are fed and out of which predictions emerge without any question arising as to the meaning of the intervening deductive machinery or its axioms. Thus, such theoretical terms as "electron" and "electromagnetic field" are nothing more than arbitrary names for certain parts of the deductive machinery and must be entirely divested of any associations with a model. A somewhat less extreme view, which Braithwaite labeled contextualism, holds that theoretical concepts have meaning that is wholly derived from the empirical consequences which can be drawn from the theory; meaning in this sense must be regarded as implicit or contextual, in contrast to the explicit empirical meaning of observables. Thus, in this view "electron" means just that entity that has the relations to the other entities of atomic physics that are specified in the formal system of physics; this formal system is such that empirically confirmed relations between observables can be deduced from it, although "electron" does not appear explicitly among these observables. In this view the interpretation of theoretical terms clearly has some of the features of an interpretation into a logical model but has no reference to the further, familiar system required for theoretical models. Whether such an analysis of "meaning" sufficiently accounts for the use of theoretical concepts remains controversial. It must also be said that the notion of "contextual meaning" has by no means been fully worked out.

A different kind of denial of the relevance of the Campbell account comes from those who hold that there is no problem of the meaning of theoretical concepts because these are learned like any other linguistic terms by their use in the development of theoretical science. Theoretical terms in this view are in some way extensions of the language about observables used to refer to nonobservables. The potentiality for such extensions is said to be always present in language—for instance, even in as childish an example as "people too little to see." Again, however, no adequate account of these linguistic extensions has been given, and in particular it has not been shown that they are independent of exactly the kind of analogical meaning that Campbell began to analyze.

Realism. It might be agreed that models are essential for prediction and for giving semantic interpretation to theories, although one can still deny that they are intrinsically part of the theory in the sense of being its real reference. Campbell himself was in fact nearer to the formalists than the realists on this point, for in answer to the question "Are there molecules?" he denied that the particle model implied the existence of molecules as real constituents of gases. According to him, if we answer the question affirmatively, all we intend is a shorthand assertion of all that has been said about the essential function of the analogy between the gas theory and particle systems. Contextualists, on the other hand, in answering the question

affirmatively, intend only to assert the existence of entities that, by means of their relations to other entities specified by the theory, issue in empirically confirmed laws as deductive consequences.

It would seem more natural to hold, as was naively held by almost all theorists before the nineteenth century, that when a theory is developed in terms of a model, the model is the description of the way the world is conceived by that theory. That is, gases are really made up of molecules, light is really transmitted by wave motion in the ether, and so on. In other words, the model containing the positive and neutral analogy with the explanandum (and not the negative analogy) is identifiable with the theory of the explanandum, and this theory has a real reference to the domain of the explanandum. There are several reasons why some writers wish to deny such an identification. First, it is considered dangerous to identify or confuse model with theory, because the model may have implications that turn out to be untrue of the explanandum. This is a weak objection, because it can be made against any theory having implications beyond what has been directly confirmed—that is, against any theory with predictive potentialities. It also overlooks the possibility of conceiving a model from which the negative analogy has been excluded. If there are implications that are known not to be true and if these are not central to the model, they can be deliberately ignored and are therefore not dangerous.

Second, it is held that models are used in situations where deliberate simplification and distortion are intended and that therefore they cannot be identified with the theory of which they are imperfect interpretations. Some models are undeniably used in this way, as has been described, but it does not follow that all are. In some cases it is even possible to show how initially distorting models have been modified and refined so as to become consistent with theory and explanandum, to become, in the phrase of R. Harré, "candidates for reality."

A third argument is that even if models are accepted as essential ingredients of theories, there is no evidence (other than their functions in relation to prediction and meaning) for endowing them with "reality." This objection may be associated with the stronger presupposition that only that which is in some way directly observed can be real. But in both versions there is still the question of what is involved in ascribing physical reality to entities and what is the relation between the theoretical and observational in science. These problems are dealt with in LAWS AND THEORIES.

Bibliography

Achinstein, P., "Variety and Analogy in Confirmation Theory." *Philosophy of Science,* Vol. 30 (1963), 207–221.

Beament, J. W. L., ed., "Models and Analogues in Biology." *Symposium of the Society for Experimental Biology.* Cambridge, 1960. Discussions of various kinds of model in biology.

Black, M., *Models and Metaphors.* Ithaca, N.Y., 1962. See Chs. 3 and 13 for an important analysis of linguistic metaphor and application to theoretical models.

Braithwaite, R. B., *Scientific Explanation.* Cambridge, 1953. Chs. 1–4.

Braithwaite, R. B., "Models in the Empirical Sciences," in E. Nagel et al., eds., *Proceedings of the Congress of the Interna-*

tional Union for the Logic, Methodology and Philosophy of Science. Stanford, Calif., 1960. P. 224.

Bunge, M., "Phenomenological Theories," in M. Bunge, ed., *The Critical Approach to Science and Philosophy*. London, 1964. See p. 234 for an analysis and rejection of the sufficiency of black-box theories.

Campbell, N. R., *Physics, the Elements*. Cambridge, 1920. Ch. 6. Reprinted as *Foundations of Experimental Science*. New York, 1957.

Cohen, M. R., and Nagel, E., *An Introduction to Logic and Scientific Method*. New York, 1934. Ch. 7 is an introduction to logical models.

Duhem, P., *The Aim and Structure of Physical Theory*, translated by P. P. Wiener. Princeton, N.J., 1954. Part I, Ch. 4. First published as *La Théorie physique*. Paris, 1905. A classic source of the view that models are dangerous and dispensable adjuncts to theories.

Feyerabend, P. K., "Problems of Microphysics," in R. G. Colodny, ed., *Frontiers of Science and Philosophy*. Pittsburgh, 1962. Pp. 191–283.

Freudenthal, H., ed., *The Concept and Role of the Model in Mathematics and Natural and Social Sciences*. Dordrecht, Netherlands, 1961. Most of the articles interpret models in the sciences only in the logical or mathematical sense.

Harré, R., *Theories and Things*. London, 1961.

Hertz, H., *The Principles of Mechanics*, translated by D. E. Jones and T. E. Walley. London, 1899. Introduction. First published in 1894, this work is a classic statement of the formalist position.

Hesse, M. B., "Models in Physics." *British Journal for the Philosophy of Science*, Vol. 4 (1953), 198–214.

Hesse, M. B., *Models and Analogies in Science*. London, 1963. Includes a discussion of meaning and predictivity.

Hesse, M. B., "Analogy and Confirmation Theory." *Philosophy of Science*, Vol. 31 (1964), 319–327.

Hutten, E. H., "On Semantics and Physics." *PAS*, Vol. 49 (1948–1949), 115–132.

Hutten, E. H., "The Role of Models in Physics." *British Journal for the Philosophy of Science*, Vol. 4 (1953), 284–301.

Nagel, E., *The Structure of Science*. New York, 1961. Chs. 5–6 attempt to reconcile the realist and instrumentalist views of theories.

Putnam, H., "What Theories Are Not," in E. Nagel et al., *op. cit.* Pp. 240–251.

Suppes, P., "A Comparison of the Meaning and Uses of Models in Mathematics and the Empirical Sciences," in H. Freudenthal, *op. cit.* Claims that these uses are essentially the same in mathematics and the sciences.

MARY HESSE

MODEL THEORY. See SYSTEMS, FORMAL, AND MODELS OF FORMAL SYSTEMS.

MODERNISM was a movement in Catholic religious thought, and particularly in Biblical criticism, that developed in the late nineteenth century and spent itself, as a distinctive movement, before World War I. It aimed at bringing Catholic traditions into closer accord with modern views in philosophy and in historical and other scholarship and with recent social and political views. Modernism ran parallel to liberal Protestantism; both tended to reject authority and rigid forms and, in their more extreme versions at least, to aspire to a kind of Christianized rationalism.

The kind of Christology and Biblical exegesis undertaken in Germany by D. F. Strauss and in France by Ernest Renan, aided and encouraged by such philosophical currents as positivism and evolutionism, culminated in the late nineteenth century attempt to reconcile science with religion and historical criticism with belief. Renan's rejection of the supernatural, combined with his vague evolutionary religiosity, anticipated much that was to be written during the 15 years following his death in 1892.

Modernism was represented in England by George Tyrrell, Friedrich von Hügel (a friend of Alfred Loisy), and Maude Petre; in Italy by Antonio Fogazzaro, Romolo Murri, and Salvatore Minocchi; and in Germany by Franz Xavier Kraus and Hermann Schnell. However, most of the controversy centered in France, on account of the writings and influence of Loisy, Édouard Le Roy, and Lucien Laberthonnière, who brought to their approach to religion the spirit of contemporary science and philosophy. Loisy, like Renan, rejected the supernatural and explained religion in terms of an immanent rather than a transcendent principle. Le Roy circumvented the difficulties inherent in Catholic dogmas by treating them as pragmatically true. Laberthonnière edited the *Annales de philosophie chrétienne*, a journal that was committed, according to its program, to a rationalistic interpretation of religion, recognizing "the duty to submit to reflection what we believe no less than what we do and think." The review's general policy favored the view that religion is progressively revealed, primitive revelation being only potentially complete. The maneuverings necessitated by the desire to reconcile faith and reason led to some inconsistency and self-contradiction.

From its inception, modernism was in constant trouble with the ecclesiastical authorities, but orthodoxy did not become militant until the accession of Pope Pius X in 1903. In 1907 the papal decree *Lamentabili Sane Exitu*, a collection of 65 condemned propositions aimed chiefly at Loisy, and the more general and philosophically grounded encyclical *Pascendi Dominici Gregis*, condemned the modernists' views. The requirement in 1910 that all clerics take the antimodernist oath, known as *Sacrorum Antistitum*, marked the end of the movement as such, although its spirit persisted and prospered in less rebellious forms.

Bibliography

Riviere, J., *Le Modernisme dans l'église*. Paris, 1929.

Vidler, A. R., *The Modernist Movement in the Roman Church*. London, 1934.

COLIN SMITH

MOIRA/TYCHE/ANANKE. The term *moira* (fate) in Greek probably meant originally the share or lot granted to an individual. In Homer it is usually an impersonal power stronger than the gods; in subsequent literature it is sometimes an unpredictable, essentially nonmoral force and at other times the embodiment of universal justice. In either case it inescapably determines some course of events, but it was originally only one among several controlling or overriding forces in the universe. It is in the Stoics that *moira* is first identified with a fully generalized principle of fate.

Tyche (chance), which is not found in Homer, was originally a principle not very different from *moira*; it was the force responsible for "what happens." But Thucydides, for whom *tyche* covers events that are fully caused, although unpredictable, anticipates Plato's approach in *Laws* (X) where all events spring from three causes—nature (*physis*), chance, and art or design. For Aristotle, *tyche* is what happens exceptionally and yet fulfills a possible purpose (*Physics* II, 4–6, *Metaphysics* Z, 9; K, 8), as distinct from a spontaneous accident (*automaton*).

Ananke (necessity), like *moira*, is inescapable in its operations but originally controlled only specified events and not the whole range of necessitated occurrences. Plato (*Timaeus* 47E ff.) opposes necessity to reason; necessity as "errant cause" is the irrational element in the universe—it can be rationalized by persuasion, but not wholly eliminated. In itself it is a blind and aimless force, and for both Plato and Aristotle it is akin to *tyche*.

Bibliography

On *moira*, see F. M. Cornford's *From Religion to Philosophy*, Ch. 2 (London, 1912); S. Eitrem's article "Moira" in *Real-Encyclopädie der classischen Altertumswissenschaft*, A. Pauly and G. Wissowa, eds., Vol. XV (Stuttgart, 1932), pp. 2449–2497; and W. C. Greene's *Moira, Fate, Good and Evil in Greek Thought* (Cambridge, Mass., 1944).

On *tyche*, see G. Herzog-Hauser's article "Tyche" in *Real-Encyclopädie der classischen Altertumswissenschaft*, A. Pauly and G. Wissowa, eds. Vol. VII A (Stuttgart, 1948), pp. 1643–1689.

On *ananke*, see F. M. Cornford's *Plato's Cosmology* (London, 1937), pp. 159–177; H. Schreckenberg's *Ananke, Untersuchungen zur Geschichte des Wortgebrauchs* (Munich, 1964).

G. B. KERFERD

MOLESCHOTT, JACOB (1822–1893), physiologist and philosopher, often regarded as the founder of nineteenth-century materialism. He was born in Holland. After studying at Heidelberg, Moleschott practiced medicine in Utrecht. He later became lecturer in physiology at Heidelberg. The controversial doctrines expressed in his book, *Der Kreislauf des Lebens* ("The Circuit of Life," Mainz, 1852), and the materialistic tendencies of his teaching forced him to move to Zurich. He later became professor of physiology at Rome, where his lectures were popular and his important research on diet earned him respect and many honors.

Materialism at that period was a philosophical trend with political, social, and scientific implications. The state-controlled German universities had produced an official philosophy (a watered-down Hegelianism) that was used as a defense against social reform and as a shield for religion or the spiritual life. Certain important scientists held conservative views about the role of science. The biologist Rudolf Virchow, for example, believed that all speculation about consciousness should be left to the church or even to the state. The German materialists, attempting to free scientific inquiry from such control, saw these conventional philosophical tendencies as obstructing intellectual and social progress.

Philosophic monism. Moleschott's *Der Kreislauf des Lebens* went through many editions and helped to spur the materialist movement. The book was directed against Justus von Liebig's theologizing views as he had expressed them in his *Chemischen Briefen*. Liebig had especially objected to Moleschott's famous statement epitomizing materialist monism: "No thought without phosphorus." The German materialists of this period criticized dualists as being engaged in a system of philosophic double-entry bookkeeping.

Moleschott maintained, as did Ludwig Büchner, that force and matter were inseparable. Force cannot be viewed in an Aristotelian way, nor teleologically, nor as a vital force. It is not an entity separate from a material substratum, but is rather "one of its eternal indwelling properties." Matter cannot occur or be conceived without force, and vice versa: "A force unconnected with matter, hovering loose over matter, is an utterly empty conception."

Thus, any materialism attributing existence to matter independently of force was rejected. Moleschott maintained that to call his theory materialistic in this sense would be as wrong as to call it spiritualistic: "I myself was well aware that the whole conception might be converted, for since all matter is a bearer of force, endowed with force or penetrated with spirit, it would be just as correct to call it a spiritualistic conception." On the other hand, once the restriction of the term "material" to "dead matter" is given up, Moleschott appears materialistic indeed. He regarded the brain as the source of consciousness and emphasized physical conditions as the major determinants of human life. He was fascinated by circular processes, such as the miner digging lime phosphate from the earth, and the peasant later fertilizing his field with the same chemical. Life circulates through all parts of the world, and with life goes thought.

As was also typical of the materialists of the time, Moleschott emphasized the doctrine of the conservation of matter. This notion, he held, was discovered by the eighteenth-century encyclopedists. Recent science had confirmed it, and future science had to be built upon it. Chemistry is the basic science, and the solution to social questions depends on our discovering the proper way to distribute the matter with which thought and will are bound up. A rigid determinism was emphasized: "Natural law is the most stringent expression of necessity."

Theory of knowledge. Moleschott inveighed against the Kantian thing-in-itself and emphasized the importance of what things could be known as rather than what they are alleged to be. All knowledge, he maintained, presupposes someone who knows and, thus, a relation between the object and the observer. The observer could be an insect or other creature; there is no restriction to man. All existence is by means of qualities; there is no quality that exists other than through a relation. In the case of a man's perceiving a tree, "it is just as necessary for the tree as for the man that it stands to him in a relation that manifests itself by the impression upon his eye."

Moleschott maintained a certain relativism, but also a certain objectivism: "Steel is hard as opposed to soft butter, ice is only cold to the warm hand, trees only green to a healthy eye." He argued that a vorticella with an eye having only a cornea must receive different representations of objects than a spider, which has a more complex eye with lenses. Yet, "Because an object is [exists] only through its relation to other objects, for instance, through its relation to the observer, because the knowledge of the object resolves itself into the knowledge of their relations, all my knowledge is an objective knowledge." Although there are difficulties in understanding Moleschott's doctrine here, it appears to have a strong family resemblance to recent objective relativism.

Ethics. The German materialists were frequently criticized for promulgating doctrines subversive of received morality, especially theologically sanctioned morality. In general, they did protest against duty-centered, puritanical views of morality and adopted a kind of utilitarian hedonism. However, they did not advocate a continuing round of sensual pleasures. Moleschott argued that even a misguided hedonism was socially less dangerous than some other views of morality: "The erroneous theory of seeking after pleasure will scarcely find half as many disciples, as the rule of priests of all shades had claimed unfortunate victims."

As was true of other contemporary materialistic theories, many of Moleschott's doctrines that once aroused immense wrath seem relatively mild today. His insistence that scientific inquiry is relevant to the solutions of many problems is now a commonplace, but it caused shudders a century ago. The materialists' struggle against giving theological answers to scientific questions seems to have been largely successful.

Additional Works by Moleschott

Die Physiologie der Nahrungsmittel. Darmstadt, 1850.
Physiologie des Stoffwechsels in Pflanzen und Thieren. Erlangen, 1851.
Lehre der Nahrungsmittel. Erlangen, 1853. Translated by Edward Bronner as *The Chemistry of Food and Diet.* London, 1856.
Eine physiologische Sendung. Giessen, 1864.
Für meine Freunde. Lebenserinnerungen von Jacob Moleschott. Giessen, 1894.

Works on Moleschott

Lange, Frederick A., *Geschichte des Materialismus*, 2 vols. Iserlohn, 1866. Translated by E. C. Thomas as *The History of Materialism*, 3 vols. London, 1877–1892. Gives an account of Moleschott.
Merz, John T., *A History of European Thought in the Nineteenth Century.* Edinburgh, 1903. Discusses Moleschott briefly and contemporary issues in considerable detail.

ROLLO HANDY

MOLINA, LUIS DE, AND MOLINISM. See SCI-ENTIA MEDIA AND MOLINISM.

MOLINA GARMENDIA, ENRIQUE (1871–1962), Chilean spiritualist philosopher, was born at La Serena, Chile. After several years of practicing law and teaching on the faculty of the Liceo de Chillán, he became the first rector of the University of Concepción in 1919. He was one of the leading members of the generation of Latin American intellectuals who, under the influence of William James, Bergson, and the French spiritualists, reacted against the positivism that had dominated the political and cultural life of Latin America for half a century.

Throughout the 11 books which he published between 1912 and 1952, Molina was basically concerned with philosophical anthropology and with offering "an interpretation of [the human spirit], acceptable even to the skeptics, formulating a consideration of the spiritual in human life

where it is constructive and creative, and where it is involved with ethical exigencies" (*De lo espiritual en la vida humana*). This concern raised the problem of the nature of consciousness and its relation to being, as well as the problem of the origin and status of values in the natural order.

Rejecting both idealistic and materialistic ontologies, Molina maintained the priority of being over consciousness, although he noted that the emergence of the latter within natural processes indicates the potentiality for consciousness within being. Following the German philosopher Edmund Husserl, Molina declared that being and consciousness are integrally united within experience. The priority of being "is affirmed, because it is first *lived* by consciousness as a totality of which consciousness forms a part" (*ibid.*). Molina restated Descartes's basic premise as "I think, therefore I exist *and Being exists*." An adequate conception of being must incorporate both the subjective and the objective poles of experience.

It is in man that spirit has become most fully actualized. Closely associated with consciousness, spirit is the locus of values and is characterized by the freedom that makes activity leading toward the realization of value possible. The realm of the spirit embraces all the realms that are the result of human creativity—morality, religion, the sciences, the arts, "all the work of enlightened intelligence." Spirit is that element within each of these realms which aspires to be, which strives to perfect itself and to go beyond itself. Reason is the highest structure of spirit. Through reason, the presence of being is recognized, mere automatic functioning of the organism is overcome, and the horizons of consciousness are opened to the possibilities for creative advance.

Works by Molina

De lo espiritual en la vida humana ("Concerning the Spirit in Human Life"). Concepción, 1936.
Confesión filosófica ("Philosophical Confession"). Santiago, 1942.
Tragedia y realización del espíritu. Del sentido de la muerte y del sentido de la vida ("Tragedy and Realization of the Spirit. The Meaning of Death and Life"). Santiago, 1952.

Works on Molina

Millas, Jorge, *Panorama de la filosofía chilena.* Washington, D.C., to be published.
Vidal Muñoz, Santiago, "Apuntes sobre la filosofía en Chile." *Cursos y conferencias*, Vol. 48, No. 272 (1956), 39–60.

FRED GILLETTE STURM

MOLYNEUX PROBLEM. See VISION.

MONAD AND MONADOLOGY. The Greek term μονάς, from which the word "monad" is derived, means a "unit" or a "one." In Pythagorean writings it is the unity from which the entire number system, and therefore—as a consequence of the doctrine that "everything is number"—all things, are derived. Through Plato, who applied the Pythagorean term to the Ideas or Forms (*Philebus* V, 15B), it entered the tradition of Neoplatonism and Christian Platonism to mean a simple, irreducible, self-determining entity whose activity is the source of all composite beings.

In this sense it was sometimes used to designate God as the simple source of all being and sometimes to signify the simplest irreducible entities in the created order out of whose harmonious action all existence is compounded.

A monadology is a metaphysical system that interprets the world as a harmonious unity encompassing a plurality of such self-determining simple entities. The term was first used in the early eighteenth century of the metaphysics of Gottfried Wilhelm von Leibniz.

In its modern meaning since Leibniz, a monad is held to be (1) a simple, irreducible, and sometimes indestructible entity; and (2) the minimal unity into which the cosmos and all composite things in it can be resolved; yet (3) containing within itself, in contrast to material atoms, powers and relations of which it is itself the source. It is therefore conceived after the analogy of a mind or a *res cogitans* rather than a material substance. It is held to constitute, along with other monads, an all-inclusive unity or harmony of the cosmos as a whole.

A monadology may thus entail a theory of cosmic harmony, based upon a mathematical or scientific functionalism or upon a psychology of intersubjective relations, as well as a theory of relations, in which the relations constituting this cosmic harmony are brought into being through monadic action, although they do not affect the monads or organizations of monads that are the objects of the acts (Leibniz' perceptions and Whitehead's prehensions are examples of such relations).

This intermonadic harmony may itself be regarded as a unity, or cosmic Monad, and this view may involve pantheism or a theistic theory of creation. The relation of the minimal monads to the supreme Monad is one of mirroring rather than being a part of; since the supreme Monad must itself be simple, each monad may be held to be a finite (unclear and indistinct) reflection of the attributes of the supreme Monad. (The metaphors of mirroring, of echoing, and of the infinite circle whose center is everywhere have commonly been used in monadologies.)

Monadologies may disagree in their fundamental categories. Monads are active substances and, therefore, also processes; Leibniz attempted, but with incomplete success, to unite a logical and a psychological analysis of the monad by applying the notions of intensionality and extensionality. The finite monads may be of a temporal nature; the cosmic order may be either eternal or temporal, or—as Whitehead and Hartshorne held—both eternal and temporal. The finite monads themselves may be eternal changeless souls (McTaggart). The cosmic harmony may be thought of as a divine Person or merely as the unitary society of monads.

In the history of modern monadologies, three conceptions have been operative: the Christian Platonist tradition of the soul as a simple substance possessing self-certainty in immediate unity (Augustine, *De Trinitate*, IX, 3; X, 9, 10); the Neoplatonic–Stoic conception of the One that is essentially represented in each of its parts; and a spiritualized form of atomism ultimately derived from this Neoplatonic–Stoic conception. The first tradition, mediated by Boethius, the Franciscans, and other medieval Platonists, became prominent in the seventeenth century in Suárez,

Descartes, and others. The second tradition emerged in the Renaissance in the concepts of the microcosm and macrocosm after a long history during which the Stoic doctrine of the Logos had been combined with the Neoplatonic theory of the One and the subordinate intelligences. This tradition involved the principle of plenitude, according to which the universe can achieve its maximal being only when God multiplies or reduplicates his nature in every created being. This principle was suggested by Meister Eckhart and explicated by Nicholas of Cusa in his doctrine of the coincidence of maximum and minimum in God. Giordano Bruno developed the principle of plenitude into a theory of material monads as spherical atoms that are spiritual reflections of the Divine Nature (*De triplice minimo et mensura . . . Libri quinque,* 1591; *De monade, numero, et figura Liber,* 1591).

Leibniz' concept of monad is variously ascribed to Giordano Bruno, Henry More, or Franciscus Mercurius van Helmont, all of whom had made use of the term. But the terms "Monas" and "monadica" appear in the early papers of Leibniz, written long before he had come to know any of these thinkers or had developed his mature metaphysics.

Leibniz' monadology involves a harmonious universe composed of an infinite number of monads, each of which was an infinite series of perceptive acts defined by a unique point of view or a unique law of series; each such law, in turn, was a particular finite combination of the perfections of God expressed in his creation. Leibniz presented a succinct but incomplete account of this system in his *Principles of Nature and of Grace* and the so-called *Monadology,* both written in 1714; he then devoted the last twenty years of his philosophical activity to a defense and amplification of his monadology through various papers and a vast correspondence. His system and that of Alfred North Whitehead, who ascribed greater spontaneity and creativity to the monads and interpreted them as mindlike entities of limited duration, are the most detailed modern monadologies.

Trained in the Leibniz–Wolff tradition, Immanuel Kant wrote *Physical Monadology* in his precritical period (1756), in which the monads were treated as sources of motion in a Newtonian space. In the *Critique of Pure Reason* (1781), Kant called his second antinomy "the dialectic principle of monadology" (1st ed., p. 442). This antinomy is directed at the metaphysical claims for a monadology made by the Wolffian school. In their development of a realistic, spiritualistic metaphysics, Johann Friedrich Herbart, Hermann Lotze, and Gustav Theodor Fechner developed monadologies on a Kantian basis. In his third *Essai de critique générale* (Paris, 1859), and in *La Nouvelle Monadologie* (Paris, 1899), Charles Renouvier built a monadology upon his relativized interpretation of Kant, making the highest attainable harmony in "the best of all possible worlds" depend upon the freedom of human monads or persons. In contrast to this relativized monadism, Edmund Husserl, in his *Cartesian Meditations* (1929–1931), suggested a monadic completion of his transcendental phenomenology, describing a type of "indirect experience which possesses its own modes of verification" within one's own monadic experience and which also provides "the transcendental base" for an objective natural order; implied in this is a "sphere of monadological inter-subjectivity." Other recent monadologies include Dietrich Mahnke's attempt to reconcile Leibniz' monadology with recent science and philosophy; H. Wildon Carr's *Theory of Monads* (London, 1922), influenced by the British person-alistic tradition; and William Stern's hierarchical system of persons and things, inspired by Spinoza, Fechner, and Lotze.

Bibliography

Discussions of monadologies are to be found in Heinz Heim-soeth, *Atom, Seele, Monade. Historische Ursprünge und Hin-tergründe von Kant's Antinomie der Teilung* (Wiesbaden, 1960). W. Cramer, in *Die Monade* (Stuttgart, 1954), begins with Kant's antinomy and treats him in terms of intermonadic relations. P. F. Strawson subjects a Leibnizian monadology to critical analysis in *Individuals: An Essay in Descriptive Metaphysics* (New York, 1963), pp. 114–133.

See also Dietrich Mahnke, *Eine Neue Monadologie* (*Kantstu-dien,* Erganzungsheft 39; Berlin, 1917) and *Unendliche Sphäre und Allmittelpunkt* (Halle, 1937) by the same author; Edmund Husserl, *Cartesianische Meditationen und Pariser Vorträge,* S. Strasser, ed. (The Hague, 1950), especially Sections 55–56; Wil-liam Stern, *Person und Sache,* 3 vols. (Leipzig, 1906–1924), Vol. I (Leipzig, 1906); and A. N. Whitehead, *Process and Reality* (New York, 1929).

L. E. LOEMKER

MONISM AND PLURALISM.

How many things are there? Or how many kinds of thing? Monism is the doc-trine that the answer to one or other of these questions is "Only one." Opposed to monism is the doctrine of plural-ism, which is that there are many kinds of thing, or that there are many things. It will be apparent, on reflection, that this weaker form of pluralism, that there are many things, is quite consistent with the weaker form of mon-ism, that there is only one *kind* of thing to which the many particular things belong. For instance, materialism, in the sense that everything existent is material, is a form of monism because it insists that all existent things are of a single *kind,* the material kind. Thus monism and plural-ism, though opposed, do not always exclude each other.

A doctrine which might be regarded as a form of plural-ism, possibly the most important form of it, is dualism, the belief that there are two things or two types of thing. In view of its importance, it will be treated below in a sepa-rate section.

Monism. "Monism" is a name for a group of views in metaphysics that stress the oneness or unity of reality in some sense. It has been characteristic of monism, from the earliest times, to insist on the unity of things in time (their freedom from change) or in space (their indivisibility) or in quality (their undifferentiatedness). Such a view of the world is already found in a developed form in the pre-Socratic philosopher Parmenides and was nicknamed the "block universe" (by Thomas Davidson, a friend of William James), that is, the universe thought of as a single closed system of interlocking parts in which there is no genuine plurality and no room for alternative possibilities. Al-though this world view and similar ones are now classified as forms of monism, they may not have been seen as fall-ing into a single category at all until the term "monism" had itself been invented. The term was coined by Chris-tian Wolff (1679–1754), and he used it only in a narrow sense, applying it to the two opposite theories that ev-erything is mental (idealism or mentalism) and that every-thing is material (materialism). The term was subsequently applied to a particular doctrine of the relation between mind and matter, namely, the theory of their absolute identity (the *Identitätsphilosophie* so often mentioned by William James). The main proponents of this doctrine were Schelling and Hegel, although it actually originated with Spinoza and is sometimes known as the double-aspect theory. It holds that mind and body are only modes of the same substance, and it is this substance to which they are both reducible, not one to the other. A more recent version of this theory is the "neutral monism" of William James, which Russell at one time also adopted. On the other hand, it should be noted that the *Identi-tätsphilosophie* and neutral monism differ from the "iden-tity theory," which is a form of materialism recently set forth by J. J. C. Smart, Herbert Feigl, and others. The identity theory holds that the mind is not some third thing, some "neutral stuff" like sensation, but is literally identical with the brain. (See MIND–BODY PROBLEM.)

In the nineteenth century the word "monism" came to be given wider application and so to have a systematic ambiguity, that is, a consistent variation of meaning ac-cording to context. Since then any theory that tries to re-duce all phenomena to a single principle, or to explain them by one principle, or to make statements about reality as a whole, has been labeled "monism." The ambiguity is not harmful, provided that theories about how many sub-stances there are (substantival monism) are distinguished from theories about what *kinds* of substance exist (attribu-tive monism). This distinction also needs to be observed in the case of pluralism (see below).

Substantival and attributive monism are logically inde-pendent views, and the various possible combinations of attitude to these questions are actually found in the doc-trines of major philosophers. Thus if by "substantival mon-ism" we mean the theory that the apparent multiplicity of substances is really a manifestation of only a single sub-stance in different states or from different points of view, then Spinoza, with his God-or-Nature, and Bradley, with his Absolute, are typical substantival monists. Indeed, Part I of Spinoza's *Ethics* is the classic exposition of substan-tival monism, offering a proof that there can be only one self-subsistent and independent thing. But Spinoza rejected attributive monism, which maintains that all the substances that there are, whether one or many, are ultimately of a single kind. He believed in an infinity of real attributes. An opposite case is that of Leibniz, who rejected substanti-val monism but accepted a monism of attributes, for in his philosophy all the monads are of one kind, being souls.

A further possible doctrine, that might be called partial monism, is the belief that even if there is more than one realm of being, there is only one substance within some particular realm. For example, Descartes, who is the clas-sic dualist insofar as he divides the world into the two realms of mind and matter, accepted partial monism about matter, which he treated as a unitary substance, while he rejected partial monism about minds.

If monism in one or other of these various senses keeps

on turning up in quite diverse philosophical systems, that is not really surprising. A striving for unity in a world description, perhaps for the sake of easier comprehensibility and greater economy of explanation, perhaps resulting from the direct appeal of simplicity, is a perennial urge in human thought. Even a substantival pluralist, Leibniz for instance, usually maintains that the plurality of substances in his world do form a systematic unity "ideally" or when looked at from the viewpoint of an omniscient being. To many minds, a monistic theory is always the most attractive option if the obstacles to holding it can be removed.

Dualism. Dualism is the position of those thinkers who find some radical and irreducible difference in the world, an insuperable gulf between two realms of being. Any philosophical system that divides the world into two categories or types of thing, or uses two ultimate principles of explanation, or insists that there are two substances or kinds of substance is a form of dualism. (The same ambiguity is found here as with the other labels.) Even the presence of a cardinal though not all-embracing contrast in a philosophical system may justify calling it a dualism in a looser sense, as when we speak of the dualism of Plato, in whose works the world of flux presented to the senses is sharply contrasted with the world of Forms known by the intellect, or when we consider the corresponding dualism of phenomena and noumena in Kant.

Although superficially dualism can be seen as a special case of pluralism, it should be clear from the foregoing that it has often been, so to speak, the expression of failed monism. Nor is it merely that monism has to many minds the attractiveness described earlier; the dualistic position is inherently unstable and puzzle-generating. Once we have divided the world into two—for example, into natural and supernatural, temporal and eternal, material and mental, particular and universal—we have on our hands the problem of the relation between the two resulting worlds. These bridging problems have bulked large in both ancient and modern philosophy. Even though dualism of mind and body, for instance, may be said to reflect the time-honored view of common sense and was adopted by philosophers at least as early as Anaxagoras, Descartes's version of it, with thinking substances operating mysteriously on bits of extended substance, set the problem for all subsequent philosophers until Gilbert Ryle, in *The Concept of Mind* (1949), dismissed it as a "category-mistake" (see CATEGORIES).

There may be thinkers for whom oppositions themselves have an attraction, just as triads certainly do for some others. If so, the series of opposites set up by the Pythagoreans may have had this motivation. Since, however, they reduced the two sets to two fundamental principles, the Limit and the Unlimited, they may have been forced by their mathematical discoveries to acknowledge a difference that blocked the way to monism. Whatever the correct interpretation in their case, it is plain that no philosopher would in advance adopt dualism as an ideal at which to *aim,* in creating his world picture.

What in fact drew attention to dualism as a type of theory was theology, where doctrines like Manichaeism, with its two ultimate principles of good and evil, or darkness and light, are found. Those who put forward such doctrines were labeled "dualists" by Thomas Hyde, writing in Latin about 1700. Later the term found its way into philosophy in various languages.

Pluralism. If there is more than one kind of existent, why not any number instead of just two? The unsuccessful would-be monist may, through thinking in this way, lapse into pluralism. Others, like William James, may find they have a temperamental objection to monism, with its emphasis on the totality and its exclusion of individuality and quirkiness. Yet others may from the start see the world as having some kind of disconnectedness as an essential feature, without which motion, change, and free will, for example, would be impossible. The rejection of any form of monism of course entails adopting the corresponding pluralist viewpoint. There may, however, be different types of rejection. Pluralism may arise from the rejection of the metaphysical conception of the "block universe" or of the logical doctrine that all true statements are, in the last analysis, logically necessary. For if there are some truths of a merely contingent nature, the doctrine of internal relations, that all relations are grounded in the natures of the related terms, must be false, and this doctrine is fundamental to the idealist versions of monism. The case of Leibniz, who is often taken as a standard pluralist, does not illustrate this point, but an instance of this sort of conversion to pluralism is afforded by Bertrand Russell, who writes of his early position, "I came to disbelieve Bradley's arguments against relations, and to distrust the logical bases of monism" (*The Philosophy of Bertrand Russell*, P. A. Schilpp, ed., Evanston, Ill., 1944, pp. 11–12). Russell later adopted a full-blown pluralism associated with logic: for instance, "When I say that my logic is atomistic, I mean that I share the common-sense belief that there are many separate things" ("The Philosophy of Logical Atomism," 1918; reprinted in his *Logic and Knowledge,* New York, 1956, p. 178). Though this phase of Russell's philosophy is usually known as logical atomism, he also described it himself as "absolute pluralism." Even after abandoning logical atomism, Russell remained an enthusiastic pluralist; in 1931 he wrote of the proposition that the world is a unity, "the most fundamental of my intellectual beliefs is that this is rubbish. I think the universe is all spots and jumps, without unity, without continuity, without coherence or orderliness or any of the other properties that governesses love" (*The Scientific Outlook,* New York, 1931, p. 98).

Bibliography

Helpful general discussions of monism, dualism, and pluralism are rather few in number. The only good general account of all three is A. M. Quinton, "Pluralism and Monism," in the *Encyclopaedia Britannica*. The best sources, though more difficult to use, are the actual works of the philosophers mentioned as proponents of the various doctrines.

MONISM

On monism see the works of philosophers named in the text, such as Parmenides, Spinoza, and Bradley. A useful discussion is C. E. M. Joad, "Monism in the Light of Recent Developments in Philosophy," in *PAS*, Vol. 17 (1916/1917), 95–116. Now somewhat antiquated is A. Worsley, *Concepts of Monism* (London, 1907). A typical short account from the heyday of monism in British philosophy is A. E. Taylor, *Elements of Metaphysics* (London, 1902), Chs. 2–3. Compare J. A. Smith, "The Issue Between Monism and Pluralism," in *PAS*, Vol. 26 (1925/1926), 1–24. See also Marvin Farber, "Types of Unity and the Problem of Monism," in *Philosophy and Phenomenological Research*, Vol. 4 (1943/1944), 37–58, and postscript, *ibid.*, Vol. 6 (1945/1946), 547–583; Raphael Demos, "Types of Unity According to Plato and Aristotle," *ibid.*, 534–545; Abraham Edel, "Monism and Pluralism," in *Journal of Philosophy*, Vol. 31, No. 21 (Oct. 1934), 561–571; Jonathan Bennett, "A Note on Descartes and Spinoza," in *The Philosophical Review*, Vol. 74, No. 3 (July 1965), 379–380. Such nineteenth-century works as Ernst Haeckel, *Der Monismus als Band zwischen Religion und Wissenschaft* (Bonn, 1893; translated by J. Gilchrist as *Monism as Connecting Religion and Science*, London, 1894), are not now of much philosophical interest, for they are not about monism in general but are presentations of an outdated type of materialism.

DUALISM

On dualism see the main works of Descartes. The difficulties of the dualist position in general are well brought out by John Passmore in his *Philosophical Reasoning* (London, 1961), Ch. 3. See also Simone Pétrement, *Le Dualisme chez Platon, les gnostiques, et les manichéens* (Paris, 1947).

PLURALISM

The most readable book on pluralism and other theories is William James's *A Pluralistic Universe* (London, 1909). For further reading, there is James Ward, *The Realm of Ends, or Pluralism and Theism* (Cambridge, 1911). A dry but clear account is to be found in C. D. Broad, *The Mind and Its Place in Nature* (London, 1925), Introduction. More difficult and technical but classic is G. E. Moore, "External and Internal Relations," in *PAS*, Vol. 20 (1919/1920), 40–62, reprinted in his *Philosophical Studies* (New York, 1922). Compare Bertrand Russell, "The Nature of Truth," in *Mind*, Vol. 15 (1906), 528–533, reprinted as "The Monistic Theory of Truth," in Russell's *Philosophical Essays* (London, 1910). See also J. H. Muirhead, F. C. S. Schiller, and A. E. Taylor, "Why Pluralism?," in *PAS*, Vol. 9 (1908/1909), 183–225; and P. Laner, *Pluralismus oder Monismus* (1905).

ROLAND HALL

MONTAGUE, WILLIAM PEPPERELL (1873–1953), American realist philosopher. Montague received his B.A. from Harvard in 1896, his M.A. the following year, and his Ph.D. in 1898. He taught briefly at Radcliffe, Harvard, and the University of California. In 1903 he began teaching at Barnard and from 1907 to 1910 was an adjunct professor and a member of the Columbia University graduate faculty of philosophy. He became associate professor in 1910, professor in 1920, and was the Johnsonian professor of philosophy from 1920 to 1941. In 1928 he was Carnegie visiting professor in Japan, Czechoslovakia, and Italy. He served as chairman of several delegations to the International Congress of Philosophy (1920, 1934, 1937) and as president of the eastern division of the American Philosophical Association in 1923.

Realism. Montague advocated a frankly Platonic "subsistential realism." He called it a right-wing realism, in contrast with left-wing realism, whose adherents included the behaviorists, objective relativists, and—to some extent—pragmatists. At the turn of the twentieth century, the idealist claim that the object of knowledge was dependent on the knower and thus was "ideal" had come increasingly under attack in England and America. Montague, in "Professor Royce's Refutation of Realism" (1902), was one of the first to attack idealism by means of the realist theory of independence. This theory—that the object of knowledge is not dependent for its reality on the knowing relation—became one of the cardinal tenets of the New Realist movement, of which Montague was a charter member. However, by itself it was not enough to establish that the known is independent of the knower. It also had to be shown how a conscious, knowing organism could be in such a unique kind of rapport with events whose loci and dates were different from its own. Thus the central issue in epistemology for Montague was to establish the independence and the immanence of the object of knowledge.

Montague proposed his "subsistential realism" as a resolution of this issue. Subsistence included everything that could be made an object of discourse. The objects of knowledge then are subsistently real, that is, propositions and terms rather than common-sense objects, and as such they are directly present to mind (immanent), though independent of it. Montague thus brought the things of the earth into the realm of ideas by interpreting existence as a subclass of subsistence, hence also as a set of propositions.

With his idea of subsistent and existential propositions, Montague could distinguish nonveridical and unreal objects from the veridical and real. Existential propositions are the objects of true or real knowledge, and the "merely subsistent" propositions are the objects of false or unreal knowledge. Thus there is a tendency in Montague's thinking to identify the true, real, and existent on the one hand, and the false, unreal, and nonexistent on the other.

What, then, is the cause of error? Truth and falsity attach to our judgments, Montague said, because of their content, not because they are stated or believed. Error is the result of the selective action of sense perception and conception. He attributed error to these factors of the "personal equation" (as realists called the subjective aspect of knowledge) because he had said existential subsistent propositions cause themselves to be known in a way the "merely subsistent" cannot. But how can a proposition cause itself to be known?

The answer apparently was in the difference between the "merely subsistent" propositions and the existential subsistent propositions. Montague identified existential propositions with facts, and he described a fact as "something done," a *fait accompli*. But this was as far as he went.

Animistic materialism. Epistemology was secondary, however, to Montague's preoccupation with the psychophysical problem of the nature of mind and its relation to the body. Naturalistic monism, strongly supported by science, could not, Montague claimed, adequately account for such characteristics of mind as purpose, privacy, duration, and integration. Traditional dualism could account for them, but it was scientifically sterile in its reliance on concepts of spirit. Montague's answer, which he called "animistic materialism," was the hypothesis of a physical soul possessing all of the traits of mind although still physically describable.

Throughout his career, Montague considered the soul to be the only answer to the psychophysical problem. After proposing the idea of a substantial soul in his first published writing, Montague soon rejected it in favor of considering the soul as a new kind of energy, purely private, and internally observable as sensation. This "potential" energy comes into existence when and where the kinetic energy of a stimulus ceases to be externally observable as motion. Sensations (or consciousness) and their externally observable causes are thus qualitatively identical. The potentiality of the physical is the actuality of the psychical, and vice versa. Just as when successive twists are imposed upon a coiled spring there is left unobservable potential energy, so too the potential energies of sensations leave traces superposed on one another. These traces constitute the memory system and modify the organism's responses to later stimuli.

Thus, within the organism there arises a field of potential energy that is externally unobservable yet is causally effective upon the visible cerebral matrix; this inner organism possesses all the characteristics of mind. In Montague's relational dualism, therefore, mind and body are in radical contrast as relations but not as substances. The truths of psychophysical dualism were thus saved without departing from material categories. Montague in general maintained this materialistic dualism, yet at one point (in "A Realistic Theory of Truth and Error," 1912) he admitted to what he called a qualified panpsychism: matter had something psychical about it.

Religious views. Montague's "Promethean challenge to religion" (as he called it in *Belief Unbound*) was a challenge to authoritarianism, supernaturalism, and asceticism in religion. Montague denied what he termed the "pseudo creativeness" that idealism and pragmatism attribute to man. Man has no transcendent power to legislate for nature, or to support infinite space and time by his consciousness. Realism instead gives to man an even greater responsibility of membership in the independent order of nature. Realism also adds to existent things the "quiet and infinitely great immensities of the realm of subsistence" where mind gains access to new and imperishable sources of joy and peace. Philosophy's one certainty is that ideals are eternal things, and the life that incarnates them attains an absolute value that time alone could not create and that death is powerless to destroy.

Ideals are not dependent on God's will. God is neither finite nor infinite in all things. He is infinite and eternal like the universe which is his body, all-perfect in himself and in his will but limited in power by that totality of actual and possible things which is within him yet not himself. God is to be loved because he is good, not because he is powerful.

Montague had a genuinely speculative and daring mind that explored not only the fields of philosophy but also such areas as time perception, mathematics, relativity theory, and quantum mechanics. At the beginning of Montague's career, philosophy suffered from what he called "internalism," a subjectivism sometimes carried to the point of solipsism, which, if it perhaps contained a grain of truth, was sterile. By the end of his life Montague feared that philosophy had gone to the other extreme. In "The Modern Distemper of Philosophy" (1951), he expressed his concern that it now suffered from an "externalism," a "distemper" that was eliminating important philosophical problems from discussion because they were insufficiently empirical.

Bibliography

Works by Montague include the following: "A Plea for Soul-Substance," in *Psychological Review*, Vol. 6, No. 5 (September 1899), 457–476; "Professor Royce's Refutation of Realism," in *Philosophical Review*, Vol. 11 (January 1902), 43–55; "A Realistic Theory of Truth and Error," in E. B. Holt and others, *The New Realism* (New York, 1912), pp. 251–300; *The Ways of Knowing; or The Methods of Philosophy* (New York, 1925), a good example of Montague's desire to save the truths in all philosophies; *Belief Unbound; a Promethean Religion for the Modern World* (New Haven, 1930); "Confessions of an Animistic Materialist," in W. P. Montague and G. P. Adams, eds., *Contemporary American Philosophy*, Vol. II (New York, 1930), pp. 135–158; *The Ways of Things; A Philosophy of Knowledge, Nature and Value* (New York, 1940), the best single source for an over-all view of Montague's philosophy; "The Human Soul and the Cosmic Mind," in *Mind*, Vol. 54, No. 213 (January 1945), 50–64; *Great Visions of Philosophy; Varieties of Speculative Thought in the West From the Greeks to Bergson* (La Salle, Ill., 1950), Montague's Carus lectures; and "The Modern Distemper of Philosophy," in *Journal of Philosophy*, Vol. 48, No. 14 (1951), 429–435.

See also Helen Huss Parkhurst and others, "The Philosophic Creed of William Pepperell Montague," in *Journal of Philosophy*, Vol. 52, No. 21 (1954), 593–637, which consists of articles on Montague and tributes to him by former colleagues and students.

THOMAS ROBISCHON

MONTAIGNE, MICHEL EYQUEM DE (1533–1592), French essayist and skeptical philosopher, was born near Bordeaux. His father was an important merchant, and his mother belonged to a wealthy Spanish–Portuguese Jewish family that had fled to Toulouse. Montaigne was raised a Catholic and was given special training by his father, who would not allow him to hear any language other than Latin until he was six. At this time he was sent to the Collège de Guyenne at Bordeaux, where he studied with some of the leading humanistic teachers of the time. Montaigne also apparently studied at the University of Toulouse, a leading center of humanism and unorthodox religious ideas. For 13 years he was a member of the *parlement* of Bordeaux and made several trips to Paris and the court seeking a more important position. His closest friend at this time was the stoic humanist and poet, Étienne de La Boétie. Montaigne's first significant writing was a letter describing La Boétie's death (1563), published at the end of the latter's *Oeuvres* in 1570.

In 1568 Montaigne published his French translation of *Theologia Naturalis sive Liber Creaturarum* ("Natural Theology or the Book of Creatures") by Raimond Sebond (Raymond of Sabunde), a fifteenth-century Spanish theologian who had taught at Toulouse. In his translation he somewhat modified Sebond's rationalistic claims that unaided human reason could comprehend the universe and establish the existence and nature of God. Montaigne also published La Boétie's works before retiring from public life in 1571. The following year he began writing his most important work, the *Essays*, a series of rambling, erudite, witty discussions on a variety of topics, serving as a self-portrait. The longest of the essays, the "Apology for Raimond Sebond," was written about 1576 while Montaigne was studying the recently rediscovered treasury of Greek skepticism—the works of Sextus Empiricus—and undergoing a personal skeptical crisis. He had mottoes from Sextus carved into the rafter beams of his study and adopted as his own motto, "Que sais-je?" ("What do I know?"). In 1580 the first two books of the *Essays* were published. Besides writing, Montaigne tried in vain during the 1570s to mediate between the Catholics and the Protestant leader, Henri of Navarre (later Henri IV).

In 1580 Montaigne went to Paris to present a copy of his *Essays* to the king; he then set out on a trip to Germany, Switzerland, and Italy, which he describes in his *Travel Journal*. The following year he was called back from Italy to become mayor of Bordeaux, a post he held for four years. He then added material to his earlier *Essays* and wrote a third volume of them; the complete edition was first published in 1588 in Paris. Montaigne went there and probably negotiated on behalf of Henri of Navarre concerning his succession to the throne, his conversion to Catholicism, and the temporary settlement of the religious wars, which was later incorporated into the Edict of Nantes. Illness apparently prevented Montaigne from joining Henri IV's court, but he continued to revise his *Essays*. The final version was published posthumously in 1595.

"Apology for Raimond Sebond." Montaigne's most important philosophical work, the "Apology for Raimond Sebond," had an enormous influence on the subsequent history of thought. A superbly written presentation of skepticism, it formulated a challenge that affected Descartes, Pierre Gassendi, Bacon, and many others and inspired monumental efforts to meet it. The "Apology" gradually reveals a series of waves of doubt, continuously coupled with a new type of Christian fideism.

The essay begins with an account—probably not very accurate—of Montaigne's reasons for translating Sebond's *Theologia Naturalis*. Pierre Bunel, a Renaissance scholar, gave Montaigne's father a copy of the book, saying that it had saved him from Lutheranism. Long afterward, Montaigne's father asked his son to render it into French (from what Montaigne claimed was Spanish with Latin endings). After the translation appeared, Montaigne reported that some readers—mainly female—needed help in comprehending Sebond's contention that all the articles of the Christian faith could be established by reason. Two major objections to this thesis had been raised: the first held that Christianity should rest on faith rather than reason, and the second maintained that Sebond's reasons were not good ones. Montaigne purported to defend Sebond by showing that since all reasoning is unsound, Sebond's is no worse than anyone else's and, therefore, religion should rest on faith alone.

Montaigne held that men are vain, stupid, and immoral, and he pointed out that they and their achievements do not appear very impressive when compared with animals and their abilities. The "noble savage" of the New World seemed to possess an admirable simplicity and ignorance that did not involve him in the intellectual, legal, political, and religious problems of the civilized European.

Montaigne suggested that our sole contact with the truth was due not to our intellect or reason, but rather to the grace of God; he agreed with St. Paul that ignorance is more useful than learning in acquiring truth. To show this, Montaigne examined the teachings of the ancient schools of philosophy and argued that those of the Pyrrhonists were the best and the most compatible with the Christian religion. All of the other philosophies were in conflict with one another, contained contradictions and absurdities, and relied on fallible human faculties and questionable premises to reach their conclusions. Only Pyrrhonists showed man as naked and empty, portrayed his natural weakness, and by ridding him of his false or dubious opinions, left his mind a blank tablet, ready to receive whatever God might wish to write upon it. The modern Pyrrhonist would not be led into heresy, since he would accept no reasons or arguments that are open to question. In contrast to the Pyrrhonists, who suspended judgment on all matters, other philosophers offered their own opinions as genuine truths. They thought that they had discovered the real nature of things and had measured the universe in terms of their own systems; they were only deceiving themselves.

In the later portions of the "Apology," Montaigne presented the Pyrrhonistic evidence that everything is dubious and that genuine knowledge must be gained either by experience or by reasoning. We do not, however, know the essence of what we experience (for example, the real nature of heat), and we do not even know the nature of our own faculties. We are constantly changing as our physical and emotional conditions alter, and the judgments we make and accept at one time, we find doubtful at another. Not only does this seem to happen to each of us, but it also appears to be the fate of man in general. Each alleged scientific discovery is superseded by another, and what is thought true at one time is regarded as false or silly at another.

The new sciences of Copernicus and Paracelsus claimed that the ancient sciences of Aristotle, Ptolemy, and others were false. How could we know, Montaigne asked, that some future scientist would not make similar claims, on equally firm grounds, about these new discoveries? These same variations and disagreements occur in every area of human concern.

Montaigne then presented the more theoretical objections that Sextus Empiricus had raised about the possibility of gaining knowledge. All of our alleged knowledge, he argued, appears to come from sense experience, but perhaps we do not possess the requisite number of senses for gaining knowledge. Even if we do possess all of them, the information we gain through them is deceptive and uncertain. Illusions lead us to wonder when our senses are accurate. Dreams are often so similar to sense experiences that we cannot tell if sense experience itself is not really a dream. Each of our experiences differs from that of animals, from that of other human beings, and even from our other experiences; we cannot, therefore, know when to accept an experience as accurate. Such conditions as illness or drunkenness distort what we perceive. Perhaps normal experience itself is a kind of distortion.

In order to determine the accuracy of our experiences, we require a criterion. But we need some way of testing that criterion, and this requires a second criterion to establish how to test it, and so on. If reason is to be the judge of our experiences, then we need reasons to justify our reason, and so on, to infinity. Thus, if our ideas come from our sense experiences, we are hardly in a position to use our ideas to judge the nature of objects. Our experiences and our ideas tell us only how things seem to be, but not necessarily how they are in themselves. Trying to know reality, Montaigne concluded, is like trying to clutch water. We can deal with the world only in terms of appearances, unless and until God decides to enlighten us. In our present state, we can only try to follow nature, living as best we can.

Intentions and influence. Montaigne questioned and cast doubt upon almost all of man's beliefs in philosophy, theology, science, religion, and morality, and criticized almost every supersision and accepted view. He insisted that he was merely showing man's inability to find truth by means of his natural capacities and his need to rely on faith as his sole access to truth. Montaigne's own portrayal of the human predicament succeeded in intensifying the doubts already produced by the religious crisis of the Reformation, the humanistic crisis of the Renaissance, and the philosophical-scientific crisis of revived Pyrrhonism. The three currents were fused into a massive and forceful onslaught in his "Apology." Montaigne's formulation of skepticism and the more didactic one of his disciple, Pierre Charron, provided the issues for seventeenth-century thought. Some, like La Mothe Le Vayer, were to follow out the more destructive and anti-intellectual tendencies of Montaigne's doubt. Others, like Mersenne and Gassendi, were to formulate a mitigated skepticism that could accept its doubts while seeking information about the world of appearances. Still others, like Bacon, Herbert of Cherbury, and Descartes, were to seek new philosophical systems to provide for human knowledge a basis impervious to Montaigne's doubts.

Some have seen Montaigne as a skeptic, questioning religion with everything else, and as the founder of the critical spirit of the Enlightenment. They have taken his fideism as a mask for his actual views and have portrayed him as a genuine freethinker and free spirit. Others have interpreted his fideism as an expression of his own resolution of his doubts. Although Montaigne lacked the religious fervor of Pascal, who regarded him as a skeptical nonbeliever, many of his contemporaries and later admirers took his skepticism as part of the Counter Reformation, since it opposed the reasons and arguments of the Reformers by undermining the validity of all reasoning.

Montaigne played a vital role in the development of both Christian skeptical fideism and of the so-called libertinage, a later movement of critical freethinking that preceded the Age of Reason. His views are compatible with both roles, in that his doubts neither imply nor contradict either a religious or an irreligious conclusion. He was probably mildly religious, accepting Catholicism in the light of the religious wars of his time. He apparently opposed fanaticism and wished for toleration of all sides, recognizing man as a fallible, limited creature struggling to live and comprehend with weak and uncertain capacities. Without God's assistance, man could only try to understand himself, guided by the past and the present. To understand himself and his situation would at least make him doubtful of radical proposals for solving everything, make him more tolerant, and—most important—make him capable of accepting himself and his fate. To philosophize, Montaigne said, was to learn to die.

Works by Montaigne

FRENCH EDITIONS

Journal de Voyage, Louis Lautrey, ed. Paris, 1906.
Essais, Pierre Villey, ed., 3 vols. Paris, 1922–1923.

ENGLISH EDITIONS

The Essayes, translated by John Florio. London, 1603. Still reprinted. The first English edition, probably known to Shakespeare and Francis Bacon.
The Essays, translated by Jacob Zeitlin, 3 vols. New York, 1934–1936. Very good introduction and notes.
The Complete Works of Montaigne, translated by Donald M. Frame. Stanford, Calif., 1958. The best modern translation, containing the *Essays, Journal,* and *Letters,* plus an excellent introduction and annotated bibliography.

Works on Montaigne

Boase, Alan M., *The Fortunes of Montaigne: A History of the Essays in France, 1580–1669.* London, 1935. A study of Montaigne's impact.
Brunschvicg, Léon, *Descartes et Pascal, lecteurs de Montaigne.* New York and Paris, 1944. Shows the influence of Montaigne on both.
Busson, Henri, *Le Rationalisme dans la littérature française de la renaissance (1533–1601).* Paris, 1957. Interprets Montaigne as a freethinker and as part of an irreligious, rationalistic milieu.
Dréano, Maturin, *La Pensée religieuse de Montaigne.* Paris, 1936. An interpretation of Montaigne as sincerely religious.
Frame, Donald M., *Montaigne's Discovery of Man. The Humanization of a Humanist.* New York, 1955. A study of the development of Montaigne's thought.
Frame, Donald M., "What Next in Montaigne Studies?" *French Review,* Vol. 36 (1963), 577–587. A survey of the state of scholarship on Montaigne and an evaluation of various interpretations.
Frame, Donald M., *Montaigne: A Biography.* New York, 1965.
Malvezin, Théophile, *Michel de Montaigne, son origine, sa famille.* Bordeaux, 1875. Contains much data about Montaigne's background and environment.
Popkin, Richard H., "Skepticism and the Counter-Reformation in France." *Archiv für Reformationsgeschichte,* Vol. 51 (1960), 58–87. The role of Montaigne's skepticism in French Catholic theology of the time.
Popkin, Richard H., *The History of Scepticism from Erasmus to Descartes.* New York and Assen, 1964. Ch. 3 discusses Montaigne in the context of sixteenth-century skepticism.
Strowski, Fortunat, *Montaigne,* 2d ed. Paris, 1931. The best-known scholarly modern French interpretation of Montaigne.
Villey, Pierre, *Les Sources et l'évolution des essais de Montaigne.* Paris, 1908. Basic study of Montaigne's sources and the development of the *Essays.*
Villey, Pierre, *Montaigne devant la posterité.* Paris, 1935. A study of how Montaigne has been interpreted.

RICHARD H. POPKIN

MONTESQUIEU, BARON DE (1689–1755), philosopher and political theorist. Charles-Louis de Secondat, afterward baron de la Brède et de Montesquieu, was born at Labrède, near Bordeaux, in the year of the English revolutionary settlement that established the pre-eminence of Parliament. He was a follower of Locke and the outstanding champion in France of the supposedly "English" notions of freedom, toleration, moderation, and constitutional government. He was also a pioneer in the philosophy of history and in the sociological approach to problems of politics and law. Honored in his own country, Montesquieu was even more revered in the English-speaking world. He described the constitution of England as "the mirror of liberty," and although his analysis of the English principles of government was generally considered defective by later historians, it was hailed as marvelously penetrating by English readers of his own time. Charles Yorke, the future lord chancellor, told Montesquieu, "You have understood us better than we understand ourselves." Moreover, the founders of several new political societies, notably of the United States, were profoundly affected by Montesquieu's teaching. Especially influential was his theory that the freedom of the individual could best be guaranteed by the division of the powers of the state between three distinct organs which could balance and check one another—a separation of powers which Montesquieu, rightly or wrongly, believed to be characteristic of the English system.

Montesquieu belonged to the *noblesse de robe*. Part of his design in recommending the separation of powers in France was to elevate the French aristocracy to a position comparable to that of the English, for whereas Rousseau believed that political liberty could be achieved only in a democracy and Voltaire believed it could best be achieved by a philosopher-king, Montesquieu held that liberty was most secure where there was a potent aristocracy to limit the despotic tendency of both the monarch and the common people. He believed that the way to preserve freedom was to set "power against power."

No one wrote with greater eloquence against despotism than did Montesquieu, yet he was far from sharing the conventional liberal outlook of the eighteenth-century *philosophes*. He had all the conservatism which is characteristic of the landowner and the lawyer. In many respects he was positively reactionary; for instance, he wished to strengthen rather than diminish hereditary privileges. But like Edmund Burke, whom he influenced considerably, Montesquieu was able to reconcile his reforming and reactionary sentiments by insisting that he sought to restore old freedoms, not promote new ones. He argued that the centralizing monarchistic policy of Louis XIV had robbed Frenchmen of their ancient liberties and privileges. The only kind of revolution Montesquieu advocated was one which would give back to the French Estates —and to the nobility and the *parlements* in particular—the rights they had enjoyed before the seventeenth century. The actual French Revolution, which sought to enfranchise the bourgeoisie and the common people and to bring about a variety of other innovations, was far from the sort of change that Montesquieu had favored, although he inadvertently did help to inspire the events of 1789 and after.

Montesquieu's parents were not well off. He inherited his title and much of his wealth from an uncle who at the same time bequeathed him the office of *président à mortier* of the *parlement* at Bordeaux. About the same time his worldly position was further secured by a prudent marriage to a Protestant named Jeanne de Lartigue, who, although exceedingly plain in appearance, was heiress to a considerable fortune. Even so, Montesquieu remained an ambitious man, and, after 12 years as *président* in Bordeaux, he forsook his chateau and vineyards, to which he was deeply attached, and his wife, whom he loved perhaps rather less, to seek fame in Paris and to travel to other countries collecting material for his books. He was a success in the Paris salons, and although there seem to be no recorded examples of his wit in talking, he was celebrated as a conversationalist. He made friends with influential people and became the lover of the marquise de Grave, among others. She inspired one of his early anonymous works, *Le Temple de Gnide*, a mildly indecent erotic fantasy which was also a satire on the court of the infant Louis XV. After some difficulties Montesquieu was admitted to the French Academy in 1728.

He was on the whole a popular, but certainly not a generous, man. As a landowner he was most rigorous in the collection of even the smallest debts; at the same time he was slow to pay money he owed to others. In Paris he had a reputation for parsimony; more than one contemporary remarked that he "never ate at his own table." At his chateau, La Brède, English guests were struck by what they politely called the "plainness" of the fare, and Montesquieu even economized on the arrangements for the wedding of his daughter Denise. He once warned his grandson, "La fortune est un état et non pas un bien."

"Les Lettres persanes." Montesquieu made his name as a writer at the age of 32 with the publication of *Les Lettres persanes* (1721). Presented in the guise of a series of letters sent from France by two Persian visitors, Usbek and Rica, and translated into French by Montesquieu, this book is a satirical attack on French values and institutions. It is written with great wit and skill. The Persian visitors begin by remarking on the strange customs of the French in such matters as cutting their hair and wearing wigs and reversing the Persian rule of giving trousers to women and skirts to men. They then proceed by degrees to express delicate amazement at the things the French choose to respect or hold sacred. They comment on the mixture of grossness and extravagance in the manners of Parisian society. Their sly digs at French politics are even more telling. They describe Louis XIV as a "magician" who "makes people kill one another even when they have no quarrel." The Persians also speak of "another conjuror who is called the Pope . . . who makes people believe that three are only one, and that the bread one eats is not bread or that the wine one drinks is not wine, and a thousand other things of the same sort." The Spanish Inquisitors are described as a "cheerful species of dervishes who burnt to death people who disagreed with them on points of the utmost triviality." The revocation of the Edict of Nantes is likewise mocked, Louis XIV being said to have contrived "to increase the numbers of the faithful by diminishing the numbers of his subjects."

In the same book Montesquieu sought to establish two important principles of political theory—first, that all societies rest on the solidarity of interests and, second, that a free society can exist only on the basis of the general diffusion of civic virtue, as in the republics of antiquity.

Although Montesquieu attacked the manners of polite society in France, he did not fail to give *Les Lettres per-*

sanes a fashionable appeal. The two Persian travelers offer piquant descriptions of the pleasures of the harem and the sufferings of the women they have left behind them. Satire is nicely spiced with wit and the wit with impropriety, although this book is not quite so risqué as *Le Temple de Gnide*. Montesquieu was said by Rutledge, one of his many admirers, to have "conquered his public like a lover; amusing it, flattering its taste, and proceeding thus step by step to the innermost sanctuary of its intelligence."

"De l'Esprit des lois." Montesquieu's *Considérations sur les causes de la grandeur des Romains et de leur decadence* (1734), is a brilliantly written attempt to apply a scientific method to "historical understanding," to set forth—admittedly in a distinctly literary style—a sociological explanation of one phase of historical experience as a model for a new kind of positivistic history. This book is perhaps best read as a prolegomenon to Montesquieu's masterpiece, *De l'Esprit des lois*, on which he worked for 17 years.

De l'Esprit des lois was first published in Geneva in 1748 against the advice of all the friends to whom Montesquieu had shown the manuscript. It was promptly placed on the Index, but it sold 22 editions in less than two years. It was a resounding success. Even so, it is a long, rambling, ill-arranged book which reflects the developments and changes in the author's point of view in the 17 years he took to write it. But like *Les Lettres persanes* and the *Considérations*, it is the work of an unmistakable master of French prose and of a man who knows how to entertain his readers as well as to instruct them.

By the *esprit des lois*, Montesquieu meant the *raison d'être* for laws, or the rational basis for their existence. Like Locke, he believed in natural law, but he was a much more thoroughgoing empiricist in his method than was Locke. Montesquieu believed that the way to learn about law was to look at the actual legal systems in operation in various states. Formal recognition of natural rights did not mean that men had positive rights. Mere a priori principles have little real value; it is important, he argued, to have the actual verifiable facts of the situations in which men find themselves.

Similarly, in his approach to the question of freedom, Montesquieu was less interested in abstract assertions of a general concept than in the concrete circumstances in which freedom had been or was being enjoyed. "Liberty," he wrote, "has its roots in the soil." He noted that freedom is more easily maintained in mountainous countries, like Switzerland, than in fertile plains, and on islands, like England, than on continents. Island and mountainous states find it easier to defend themselves from foreign invasion; in mountainous countries the very poverty of the soil encourages industry, frugality, and independence and so promotes individualism among the people. Another condition of freedom, he suggested, is that tranquillity which comes from security. This can be enjoyed only where the constitution sets inviolable limits to the action of the state and where the law itself guarantees the rights of the individual. Montesquieu always insisted that political liberty could never be absolute. "Freedom," he wrote, "is the right of doing whatever the laws permit." For example, he maintained that free trade did not mean that traders should do what they liked, for that would be to enslave the nation. Restrictions on traders were not necessarily restrictions on trade but might well be measures conducive to the liberty of all. Good laws were those which protected the common interest, and it was the mark of a free society that all the people be allowed to follow their own inclinations as long as they did not disobey the laws.

The concept of law. Montesquieu gives a rather bewildering definition of laws as "necessary relations," or "the relations which necessarily follow from the nature of things." Like most philosophers before Hume, he failed to distinguish clearly between the normative laws of morals and the descriptive laws of science, but he was nevertheless conscious of having two tasks in seeking the *raison d'être* of laws. On the one hand, he was embarking on a sociological study of existing legal and political institutions, including the institutions of positive law. Here Montesquieu the empiricist came to the front. On the other hand, Montesquieu the rationalist and the votary of natural law was seeking beyond his inductive generalizations for some general principles of justice and conduct, which he believed to be founded on reason.

I first of all examined men, and I came to the conclusion that in the infinite diversity of their laws and customs they were not guided solely by their whims. I formulated principles, and I saw particular cases naturally fitting these principles; and thus I saw the histories of all nations as the consequence of these principles, with every particular law bound to another law and dependent on a further more general law.

At the highest level of abstraction, Montesquieu saw a uniform law—"Men have always been subject to the same passions"—but in various societies this higher natural law is expressed in differing systems of positive law. The systems differ because the external conditions differ. Montesquieu made much of the differences of climate and attempted to describe how different climates promote different customs, habits, economic arrangements, and religions. Much of political wisdom consists in adapting general principles to local circumstances. Solon was right to give people "the best laws they could bear."

The measure of relativism in Montesquieu affronted his friends among the *philosophes*, who believed in a kind of abstract universal individualism, but Montesquieu's method proved the more acceptable to social theorists of later generations. Émile Durkheim said it was Montesquieu who gave modern sociology both its method and its field of study. Montesquieu was ahead of his time in regarding social facts as valid objects of science, subject to laws like the rest of nature; he was also ahead of his time in seeing social facts as related parts of a whole, always to be judged in their specific contexts.

Views on religion. Montesquieu resisted the notion that a "scientific" approach to problems of human conduct entailed determinism. He believed that God existed and that God had given men free will. "Could anything be more absurd," he asked, "than to pretend that a blind fatality could ever produce intelligent beings?" Assuredly, God had laid down the laws which govern the physical world, and "man, as a physical being, is, like all other bodies, governed by immutable laws." On the other hand, precisely because he is a rational, intelligent being, man is capable of transgressing certain laws to which he is subject. Some of the laws he transgresses are his own laws, namely positive laws, but governing the conduct of men are other laws which are antecedent to positive laws, and these are the general "relations of justice" or, in a more conventional term, natural law.

Montesquieu's attitude toward religion was very like that of Locke. He did not believe in more than a few simple dogmas about the existence of God and God's benevolence, but to that minimal creed he clung with the utmost assurance. On the other hand, Montesquieu grew to be much more cautious than Locke in his criticisms of religious institutions. In *Les Lettres persanes*, Montesquieu did not hesitate to mock the Roman Catholic church and clergy, but in later years he took care to avoid provocative utterances on the subject. In his biography of Montesquieu, Robert Shackleton gives an example of the philosopher's increasing wariness as revealed in successive drafts of the *Esprit des lois*. In the first draft of the chapter on religion, Montesquieu wrote, "Under moderate governments, men are more attached to morals and less to religion; in despotic countries, they are more attached to religion and less to morals." In the second draft Montesquieu introduced at the beginning of that sentence, "One might perhaps say that . . . ." In the published version he cut out the remark altogether.

Much has been made of the fact that Montesquieu was reconciled to the Church of Rome on his deathbed. An Irish Jesuit named Bernard Routh got into the chateau at La Brède during Montesquieu's last illness, and in spite of the efforts of the duchess d'Aiguillon to prevent him from "tormenting a dying man," the priest succeeded (or, at any rate, claimed to have succeeded) in leading the philosopher back to the path of devotion and repentance. The pope himself read Father Routh's account of Montesquieu's death "with the deepest reverence and ordered it to be circulated." Madame d'Aiguillon was able to rescue from the clutches of the Jesuits only one manuscript, that of the *Lettres persanes*. "I will sacrifice everything for the sake of reason and religion," Montesquieu had told the duchess, "but nothing to the Society of Jesus."

These dramatic scenes are perhaps less important to an understanding of Montesquieu's religious sentiments than is his behavior in less emotional times. He never asked his wife to give up her Protestantism, and he was always a fervent champion of religious toleration. At the same time, he remained on the best of terms with his several relations who were in holy orders in the Catholic church. Besides, according to his "sociological" principle that every country had the religion which its geographical and climatic conditions demanded, Montesquieu held that Catholicism was the "right" religion for France, just as Anglicanism was the "right" religion for England. This is not to say that Montesquieu inwardly believed in more than a fraction of the teachings of the Catholic church or that—until his deathbed repentance—the church regarded him as a true son. But he always detested atheism. To him the idea of a universe without God was *effroyable*. The concept of a loving creator played as prominent a part in his political theory as it did in that of Locke; indeed, whereas Locke had been content to see the church apart from the state, Montesquieu favored an alliance of organized religion with the government. In *Esprit des lois* he suggested that Christian principles, well engraved in the minds of the people, would be far more conducive to a good political order than either the monarchist notion of honor or the republican notion of civic virtue. Montesquieu was thus a deist in his heart and an Erastian in his politics.

Works by Montesquieu

Oeuvres complètes, A. Masson, ed., 3 vols. Paris, 1950–1955.
Oeuvres de Montesquieu, E. Laboulaye, ed., 7 vols. Paris, 1875–1879.
De l'Esprit des lois, G. Truc, ed., 2 vols. Paris, 1945.
Spirit of the Laws, translated by Thomas Nugent. New York, 1949.

Works on Montesquieu

Actes du Congrès Montesquieu. Paris, 1956. Introduction by L. Desgraves.
André, Desiré, *Les Écrits scientifiques de Montesquieu*. Paris, 1880.
Barrière, P., *Un Grand Provincial*. Bordeaux, 1946.
Cabeen, D. C., *Montesquieu: A Bibliography*. New York, 1947.
Cotta, S., *Montesquieu e la scienza della societa*. Turin, 1953.
Dedieu, J., *Montesquieu, l'homme et l'oeuvre*. Paris, 1913.
Dodds, Muriel, *Les Récits de voyages: Sources de l'Esprit des lois de Montesquieu*. Paris, 1929.
Durkheim, Émile, *Montesquieu et Rousseau*. Paris, 1953. Translated by Ralph Manheim as *Montesquieu and Rousseau*. Ann Arbor, Mich., 1960.
Fletcher, F. T. H., *Montesquieu and English Politics*. London, 1939.
Shackleton, Robert, *Montesquieu: A Critical Biography*. Oxford, 1961. The outstanding work on Montesquieu.
Sorel, A., *Montesquieu*. Paris, 1887.

MAURICE CRANSTON

MONTGOMERY, EDMUND DUNCAN (1835–1911), Scottish-American philosopher, anticipated in his "philosophy of vital organization" ideas of emergent evolution, the energetic nature of matter, and the pragmatic functioning of knowledge. Born in Edinburgh, he studied medicine in Germany in the 1850s, did research on cell pathology in London in the 1860s, and immigrated to America in 1870 with his sculptress wife, Elisabet Ney.

After a short-lived communitarian experiment at Thomasville, Georgia, the Montgomerys settled on Liendo Plantation, near Hempstead, Texas. There Montgomery wrote most of his philosophical articles and, in his later years, took an active role in community affairs. As chairman of the Waller County Democratic party in the Bryan–McKinley campaign, he argued the dependence of political liberty upon economic reforms.

By 1867 Montgomery saw life as a power of certain compounds to reintegrate their chemical unity after damage, a power evolved by the inherent creativity of matter interacting in new combinations. He tested views of matter, mentality, selfhood, knowledge, and morality by this touchstone in over sixty articles in such journals as *Mind*, *The Monist*, *The Index*, *The Open Court*, and *The International Journal of Ethics* and in five books. His major book was *Philosophical Problems in the Light of Vital Organization.*

Even inorganic compounds, Montgomery said, are inherently reactive, evolving in unpredictable ways by virtue of their peculiar composition and organization. Conservation of energy is thus wrongly viewed as requiring inertness of matter. Mentality is not dependent on a separate substance but is a capacity of certain complex organisms (chemical unities of a high order), heirs of evolution through foregone ages. Human knowledge and action are products of man's interplay with environment; they are instruments in preserving and enhancing well-being.

Some data of consciousness, such as kinesthetic and emotive states, seem to derive in each of us only from his own body, even though the body's activity thus perceived is in turn activated by outside stimuli. Others of our conscious states (such as visual data) are occasioned by features of either our own bodies or of external objects. Montgomery denied that this difference warrants the inference that there are two distinct kinds of substance, mental and material. All inferences from sensory data are conjectural. Data do not copy things but give "hieroglyphic signs" that permit discovery, prediction, and testing of natural relations among things.

Montgomery argued for a "naturalistic humanitarianism," a "religion of life," stressing ethical self-determination in a struggle against indifferent and hostile forces, to convey to the next generation a heritage nobler than the one received. Making common cause with those who wanted a religion and an ethic consistent with scientifically established knowledge, he added to classic criticisms of prevailing theologies and moral systems his own emphasis upon their failure to heed the full potentialities of men, the pre-eminent heirs of an evolution far from completed.

Works by Montgomery

On the Formation of So-called Cells in Animal Bodies. London, 1867.

Die Kant'sche Erkenntnislehre widerlegt vom Standpunkt der Empirie. Munich, 1871.

The Vitality and Organization of Protoplasm. Austin, Tex., 1904.

Philosophical Problems in the Light of Vital Organization. New York and London, 1907.

The Revelation of Present Experience. Boston, 1910.

Works on Montgomery

A complete bibliography of writings by and about Montgomery before 1950 and an index of writings by and about him appear in Morris Keeton, *The Philosophy of Edmund Montgomery* (Dallas, Tex., 1950). The definitive biography is I. K. Stephens, *The Hermit Philosopher of Liendo* (Dallas, Tex., 1951).

MORRIS KEETON

MOORE, GEORGE EDWARD (1873–1958), was born into moderately affluent circumstances in Upper Norwood (a suburb of London), the third son of D. Moore, M.D., and Henrietta Sturge Moore. The Sturges were prominent Quaker merchants and philanthropists. On his father's side there had been some tendency toward, and some prominence in, the practice of medicine.

Upon reaching eight, Moore commenced attendance at Dulwich College, a boarding and day school of excellent reputation located within walking distance of his home. In the ten years of his attendance there he acquired a thorough mastery of the classics. It was also at this time that he underwent a very painful experience. Having been converted around the age of 12 to "ultra-evangelism," he felt it his duty to preach the word of Jesus and to distribute religious tracts. He found these activities extremely repugnant and suffered much inward torment in carrying them out. This experience, which lasted two years or more, may account in some measure for his subsequent coolness to religious enthusiasms of any sort. Before leaving Dulwich College he was persuaded, through discussions with his eldest brother, the poet Thomas Sturge Moore, to adopt the view that was then known as "complete agnosticism." This seems to have been the view that there is no evidence in support of a belief in God's existence and almost as little in support of a belief in his nonexistence. So far as can be determined from his writings, Moore never departed from this view.

In 1892 Moore entered Trinity College, Cambridge, as a student in classics. At the beginning of his third year he changed his major concentration to philosophy and completed the moral science tripos in 1896. On the basis of a dissertation treating Kant's ethics he was elected in 1898 a fellow for a term of six years. During the period 1898–1904 he carried on frequent and consequential discussions with Bertrand Russell, wrote *Principia Ethica*, presented several papers to the Aristotelian Society (to which he had been elected), and published a number of reviews and articles.

With the termination of his fellowship in 1904, Moore left Cambridge. Because of an inheritance he was still able to pursue his philosophical activities. He wrote articles, papers, and reviews, as well as the small volume *Ethics,* and gave a series of private lectures at Richmond. In 1911 he was invited to return to Cambridge as university lecturer. He lectured regularly at Cambridge from 1911 to 1925, first on philosophical psychology and later on metaphysics. In 1925 he succeeded James Ward as professor of mental philosophy and logic. His courses appear to have enjoyed a good deal of popularity among the more serious students of philosophy and had an immense influence upon the philosophizing going on in England at the time, as did his publications (notwithstanding that they consisted entirely of articles and papers).

In 1939, having reached the mandatory age of retirement, Moore gave up his professorship at Cambridge, though not his philosophical activities. These, with a few interruptions due to illness, he carried on to almost the very last years of his life, writing articles, editing his previous writings, working on problems, and holding discussions with friends and students. He died at Cambridge at 85, survived by his wife, Dorothy Ely, whom he had married in 1916, and two sons, Nicholas, a poet, and Timothy.

Although Moore's life was extremely active in academic and philosophic spheres, it was almost without incident otherwise. Except for a brief sojourn in Germany in the summer of 1895, a somewhat longer stay in Scotland from around 1904 to 1908, and a couple of years spent during World War II lecturing in the United States, he resided entirely in England, mainly in or near Cambridge. His most noticeable personal trait appears to have been his intense and passionate absorption in philosophy. It is said, for example, that when discussing a question, whether with his professional peers or with a student, he gave himself wholly to the inquiry and viewed its progress with the constant fresh surprise of one considering a matter for the first time. Another trait that has been commented on was his lack of any intellectual pretensions (in spite of a formidable erudition) and an almost childlike naïvete concerning ordinary affairs.

Moore served as editor of the philosophical journal *Mind* from 1921 to 1947. The major honors that he received during his lifetime were the Litt.D. from Cambridge (1913), the honorary degree of LL.D. from the University of St. Andrews and election as a fellow of the British Academy (1918), and appointment to the Order of Merit (1951).

FORMATIVE PERIOD OF MOORE'S PHILOSOPHY

Moore's published philosophy falls into two distinct parts, divided by the year 1903. Although the writings published prior to 1903 are few and cover no more than five years, at least three different philosophical positions can be detected in them. In his first publication, a paper titled "In What Sense, if Any, Do Past and Future Time Exist?" (1897), Moore agreed wholly with F. H. Bradley. He argued that time does not exist, and he did so using Bradley's methods and premises, in particular the dogmas of internal relations and concrete universals and the principle that identifies reality with the absence of contradiction. When his conclusions, like the one that time does not exist, proved to outrage common sense, Moore was prepared to say that common sense is simply wrong, and he did so more than once.

One year later, in the essay "Freedom," Moore replaced Bradley with Kant as the philosopher with whom he was "in most agreement." What he agreed with most in Kant was the method of the transcendental exposition and the doctrine of synthetic necessary truths. He did not agree with the critical restrictions of Kant's philosophy or with what he took to be its psychological bias. He contended, for instance, that Kant was wrong in trying to conceive freedom in terms of the will (a psychological concept); freedom is rather to be understood and explained in terms of the idea of Transcendental Freedom, into which temporal relations do not enter. Thus, while accepting much of Kant's system and terminology, Moore continued to speculate in the critically unrestricted manner of the absolute idealists, maintaining that a reality transcending time and the senses is something that can be theoretically known and that must be theoretically known before the major problems of philosophy can be solved.

The next year, 1899, in the article "The Nature of Judgment," Moore adopted a third position. As part of his continuing attack upon psychologism in philosophy (an attack he shared at the time with Russell), he proposed the doctrine, adumbrated in Thomas Reid, that mental acts and their objects are entirely separate existences. Applying this doctrine to Bradley's analysis of judgment, Moore concluded that the entire world—everything we can either think of or perceive with our senses—consists in qualitative universals, or what he called "adjectival concepts."

These universals compose propositions, material objects, minds, and all other "complex objects." Not only do some universals (for example, red) exist through time, but some propositions also exist through time and are even objects of perception (for instance, the proposition that this book is red). Such universals and propositions are designated "empirical universals and propositions," as opposed to those that do not exist through time, such as the concepts *two* and *attribute,* which are called "a priori." This bizarre metaphysics, which might be termed "absolute realism" because according to it universals not only exist but, in fact, comprise everything that does exist, obviously repudiates all the major philosophical tenets to which Moore subscribed in his first essay: the dogmas of the nonreality of time, internal relations, concrete universals, and the transcendent monism that springs from them. Just as obviously it cannot be harmonized with the two-story world of phenomena and noumena that is attributed to Kant or with Kant's critical conclusions. Moore did, however, attempt to show that his realistic principles were compatible with, and even substantiated, Kant's method of transcendental exposition and distinction between a priori and empirical propositions and the doctrine of synthetic necessity. This Moore did by attempting to show that the possibility of a priori and empirical propositions, along with synthetic necessary truths, can be accounted for in terms of the realistic distinction between temporally existing (empirical) universals and nontemporal (a priori) universals and by shaping some of the arguments supporting this demonstration along the lines of a transcendental exposition. On the whole, though, the argumentation of "The Nature of Judgment," as well as of the articles and reviews that immediately followed (1899–1902), proceeds in the legislative, dogmatic manner of Bradley.

With this unstable amalgam of Bradley, Kant, and absolute realism, the first period of Moore's philosophizing came to a close. Marked by abrupt changes of doctrine, by either derivativeness (as in the first two positions adopted) or bizarreness (as in the third), it is recognizably an effort to find, rather than to express, a philosophy. It is therefore with some justice that these writings have been generally ignored by succeeding generations of philosophers, as they were ignored by Moore himself in his subsequent summations and compilations of his work. On the other hand, a complete understanding of Moore's later philosophy is difficult to arrive at without some familiarity with these earlier works. It will then be understood, for instance, that the charge sometimes leveled against Moore that he criticized the metaphysical theses of philosophers like Bradley piecemeal, without attempting to comprehend them fairly and in their entirety, is groundless. It will be understood, for instance, that in attacking items of Bradley's metaphysics Moore was attacking not only a system of thought with which he was thoroughly conversant but one to which he had himself once been most strongly attracted.

MOORE'S PHILOSOPHY PROPER

The system of philosophical thought and method that has come to be associated with Moore's name and that he was alone concerned to defend issued fully formed in the volume *Principia Ethica* and the essay "The Refutation of

Idealism," in 1903. This is not to say that no alterations thenceforth took place in the body of Moore's philosophical doctrines and aims. They did. For example, with the passage of time Moore became increasingly concerned with eliminating from the world various entities, such as propositions, that his principles generate. The theory proposed in "The Refutation of Idealism," that we directly perceive material things, was replaced by a disjunction of theories respecting the relation between sense data and material things. And the note of philosophical optimism that expressed itself in *Principia Ethica* and "The Refutation of Idealism" in the view that solutions to the problems under discussion have either been completed in their pages or are on the brink of completion finally gave way to a note of philosophical pessimism and puzzlement. But in its main outlines what might be called Moore's philosophy proper was now permanently formed.

As will be seen in subsequent discussion, the tenets of this philosophy are largely based on the principle that sentences like "I think of *X*" describe (*a*) mental acts and (*b*) objects related to but distinct from those acts. From 1903 until the late 1930s Moore almost invariably interpreted this principle realistically, and even after the late 1930s, when he was prepared to admit that the *esse* of sense data is *percipi*, this realist tendency continued to make itself felt in his philosophizing, especially with respect to universals. Moore's philosophy proper resembles, therefore, the absolute realism of "The Nature of Judgment." There exists, however, a fundamental metaphysical difference between the two positions. This difference lies in the fact that Moore's absolute realism of 1899 is reductionistic, being the view that everything can be resolved into qualitative universals, whereas the realism he enunciated in 1903 and afterward is, in intention at least, nonreductionistic. Thus, within the compass of things that are, Moore now included both particulars—for example, material things—and universals, and though he was not perfectly clear about just what a universal or a particular is, he wanted to maintain neither that universals can be resolved into particulars nor that particulars can be resolved into universals. His new view was that each sort of thing is what it is and nothing else (or, in the words of Bishop Butler, quoted on the frontispiece of *Principia Ethica*, "Everything is what it is, and not another thing").

The most striking and significant difference between Moore's philosophizing prior to 1903 and his philosophy proper lies not, however, in doctrine or even in the mechanics of method (though differences here are pronounced) but in the attitude and style of his philosophizing. These now project the familiar picture of Moore: the picture of a cautious and probing observer, attempting by the patient dissection and scrutiny of minute and hardly distinguishable objects to set straight the confused descriptions by philosophers of what is the case. This posture of Moore's lends to his philosophizing the appearance of a completely empirical inquiry whose conclusions represent only what is found or not found to be the case, as opposed to what is merely thought to be or not to be the case. It is in the solvent of this empiricist posture that Moore's initial philosophical optimism, as one might predict, evaporated into pessimism and puzzlement. For the principle from

which it originated, that sentences like "I perceive *X*" describe acts of mind and distinct objects, is itself something no amount of observation would seem to confirm or lend substance to.

In the first of the lectures that he delivered in 1910–1911, some forty years later published under the title *Some Main Problems of Philosophy*, Moore listed the main topics of philosophy as three. The first and primary aim of philosophy, he said, is to provide a metaphysical inventory of the universe, that is, "a general description of the *whole* of this universe, mentioning all the most important kinds of things which we *know* to be in it, considering how far it is likely that there are in it important kinds of things which we do not absolutely *know* to be in it." The second aim is epistemological: to classify the ways in which we can know things. The third topic of philosophy is ethics.

In "A Reply to My Critics," published in 1942, Moore again divided his philosophical discussion into three parts: ethics, theory of perception, and method. Although this alteration in the classification of topics indicates certain real alterations in Moore's interests and views, it will be convenient to treat his philosophy proper under the five heads mentioned: method, metaphysics, general epistemology, theory of perception, and ethics.

Method. By Moore's "method" will be understood the topics encompassed by the following: (1) The question What did Moore believe he was doing in philosophizing, i.e., what project did he think he was engaged in? (2) The question How did he attempt to carry out this project? (3) Certain questions that are often raised in specific connection with Moore's method, such as: What is the role of common sense in his method? What is the role of analysis?

Moore's intentions. It has been suggested by some of his commentators that what Moore was trying to do was to analyze ordinary language, to defend common sense, or to recommend ways of speaking. As an answer to the question What was Moore *actually* doing? it is possible that one or all of these suggestions may be true. But it is clear that none of them describes what Moore believed he was doing.

Moore's conception of what he was doing originated in the following two principles, to which he consistently subscribed: the principle that sentences like "I think that *P*" and "I perceive *X*" designate acts of consciousness, on the one hand, and objects related to but distinct from those acts, on the other; and the principle that every object of consciousness is either a simple, in which case it is unanalyzable, or a complex, in which case it always possesses a definable essence in terms of which it is the sort of thing it is and not some other sort of thing. The first principle makes it appear as if there should be discoverable as the objects of consciousness a great many more kinds of entities and properties than persons ordinarily envisage, and these entities and properties should comprise, at least in part, what is objectively in the universe. When applied to these entities, the second principle makes it appear as if every complex object should be unequivocally reducible to simples. But this picture of things raises a question: If the constitution of the universe is both so determinate and so open to consciousness, why is it that there has been so much disagreement and confusion in the attempts of philosophers to describe it? And to this question the most obvious answer seems to be that past errors and confusion in philosophy have arisen either from inattention on the part of philosophers to the objects of their consciousness or from a lack of clarity and preciseness in their statements and questions.

In fact, the two major concerns of Moore through the period 1903–1911 directly correspond to the above outline of subject matter. Primarily, Moore wished to determine what sorts of entities or properties fall within the province of his particular inquiry, for example, ethics, theory of perception; to classify these entities (where deemed necessary) as simples or complexes; and to analyze the essences of the complexes. Second, and always as a project subordinate to the first, he wished either to direct the reader's attention to the objects of consciousness that pertain to the inquiry at hand or to lay bare the ambiguities and unclarities of the terms customarily used by philosophers in conjunction with the inquiry at hand, and to supply "precising" definitions of the terms that he intended to use.

After the lectures of 1910–1911 an increasing concern with terminological questions was detectable in Moore's writing. This concern is traceable to an apparently growing conviction on his part (as well as on the part of his contemporaries) that the terminological sources of philosophical error and confusion are much more subtle, deeply rooted, and pervasive than he had originally thought and much more intimately connected with the logical grammar of ordinary language. In the last connection it is worth recalling that certain of Moore's contemporaries eventually decided that the root and cure of all philosophical problems lay in terminological confusion and clarification.

Moore never went so far as to assent to the last conclusion. He did, however, relinquish his earlier view that the primary concern of philosophy is to observe and delineate the entities objectively making up the universe. By 1940, when he composed his "Reply to My Critics," he described himself as engaged, not in the analysis of facts, but in the analysis of concepts. Although he was unclear about what the relation is between concepts, the entities objectively making up the universe, and verbal expressions, he appears to have thought that concepts are not only distinct from and (at least from their side) independent of their verbal expressions but also distinct from the entities objectively making up the universe (for otherwise, in analyzing concepts, he would be resolving philosophical doubts and questions in a way that he agreed that one cannot do and that he was not doing). But just what, then, are concepts according to Moore? In "A Reply to My Critics" he did not say. It is not improbable, however, that Moore had come full circle, back to something like Bradley's psychologically grounded view of concepts, which, ironically, served in "The Nature of Judgment" as the launching platform for Moore's philosophy of realism.

Moore's procedure. In much the same way that Moore's doctrine of mental acts and objects dictated his conception of what he was trying to do, it also dictated his conception of how to accomplish what he was trying to do. It is evident, for instance, that once sentences like "I think that P" and "I perceive X" are interpreted according to that doctrine, it must seem unjustified to argue in the legislative manner of Bradley, which Moore employed in "The Nature of Judgment" and the essays previous to it. If the objects of acts of judging, perceiving, and thinking are entities distinct from, and indeed independent of, those acts, then whatever we can learn about those objects must be by means of synthetic observations, not a priori thought. Moore throughout his philosophy proper adhered to this viewpoint. Where he conceived himself as primarily engaged in reporting, classifying, and analyzing the entities objectively constituting the universe, he assumed that he was basing his reports and analyses on observation. Where, as in "A Reply to My Critics," he conceived himself as engaged rather in analyzing concepts, it is evident that he thought of concepts as comprising some sort of object he was engaged in observing.

As was noted previously, this picture of philosophical inquiry suggests that philosophical questions have determinate and easy solutions that it might be expected all philosophers will agree on. Moore's explanation of this discrepancy between expectation and fact—that the disagreements and failures of philosophers stem either from a lack of attention to what is present to their consciousness or from terminological unclarities—suggests, in turn, that in order to be certain we are observing what we think we are we must make sure both that our attention is directed to the right objects and that we know the precise meanings of the terms we are employing in our thoughts.

It turns out, however, that even with this supplement observation fails to bring about the results that Moore anticipated or that his assumptions might have led him to anticipate. The answers to philosophical questions remain stubbornly shrouded in obscurity and disagreement. Moore was therefore compelled to add to his methods and procedures. In cases where he felt there was no conclusive answer to a question, he resorted to what might be termed the principle of weighted certainties. If, for instance, he felt that proposition A possessed more certainty than proposition B, or if he felt that he knew the truth of A with more certainty than that of B, he would refuse to deny the truth of A on account of some argument based on B. In short, a lesser certainty (according to this principle) cannot rationally overturn a greater certainty per se (though a number of lesser certainties, cohering together, may). Moore also employed, in the same connection, the scholastic method of citing all the plausible arguments that can be advanced for or against a thesis in order to indicate its degree of credibility. And finally, in order to discredit a thesis (usually a thesis of skepticism), he employed either a *reductio ad absurdum* argument or what might be called a paradigm argument. He pointed out, for example, that the skeptic who maintains that we cannot know there are other persons is already contradicting himself by supposition in referring to the plural, *we.* Or he argued that if such-and-such is not an instance of knowing, then no one has ever known anything and there cannot be such a thing as knowing.

When these norms for evaluating philosophical conclusions are arranged in order of their indefeasibility, it would seem that where observation unequivocally reveals just what a thesis represents to be the case, according to Moore the thesis is indefeasible. Thus, Moore maintained that when we look at an inkwell we directly perceive a sense datum and that this claim is indefeasible in that observation unequivocally presents us with a sense datum. Where a thesis can be shown to contain an evident contradiction, according to Moore it is conclusively disproved. Thus, one can affirm with certainty that the skeptic who maintains that *we* cannot know other persons exist is wrong. Where the principle of weighted certainties or the method of citing plausible arguments has to be invoked, Moore would generally grant that answers are not conclusive or indefeasible, although there may be more to be said in favor of one answer than another. In certain cases, however, it would appear that the certainties or feelings of certainty (Moore rarely distinguished between the two) attaching themselves to a thesis are so absolute or overpowering that no denial of the thesis is either psychologically or rationally (in view of the principle of weighted certainties) possible.

Common sense. It is tempting, but wrong, to suppose that because Moore defended common sense, common sense constitutes a court of last appeal in his philosophy. Indeed, the very fact that he described himself as defending common sense indicates that it cannot.

In his works Moore used the term "common sense" to refer to two different, but related, things. He sometimes meant by it, he said, simply those beliefs that men universally or almost universally subscribe to at some particular epoch. At other times he meant either those beliefs that we are naturally inclined to hold or the propensity that issues in such beliefs.

Although there may exist a very intimate causal connection between these two forms of common sense, they are not one and the same thing. As the "universal" belief of men at a particular epoch, common sense can change, and Moore in fact argued that it can. As a natural tendency to believe something, common sense would not seem susceptible of change. It must be remarked, however, that Moore never explicitly drew the above distinction or attempted to "analyze" the notion of common sense beyond saying that it consists in the universal belief of men at a particular time. In practice, however, he would seem to have maintained that although both forms of common sense possess a certain amount of presumptive credibility, it is essentially as a natural tendency that common sense provides a foundation for philosophical conclusions. It does this in two ways. When we try to deny the latter form of common sense we find it virtually impossible to do so because what we naturally tend to believe keeps slipping into our assertions. We thus find ourselves contradicting ourselves by supposition, like the skeptic who says that *we* cannot know persons exist. On the other hand, what we naturally tend to believe will have attached to it some degree of certainty. This degree varies, it seems, from an absolute quantity, which makes dissent really impossible, to a quantity that only inhibits dissent. For example, Moore said he was naturally disposed to think that what he always saw directly when viewing a material thing was the surface, or part of the surface, of the material thing, but he

finally decided it would be nonsense to maintain that he did.

Moore, then, defended common sense by showing that certain beliefs that we are naturally inclined to hold, and consequently that most men do hold, are supported by the principle of weighted certainties or by showing that the traditional counterclaims of skeptics are self-contradictory. He did not argue conversely that because a certain belief is a belief of common sense it is *ipso facto* indisputably true or need not be subjected to assessment.

Analysis. When Moore described himself as "analyzing," he conceived of himself as picking out and naming the essential constituents of complex objects. In his earlier works he viewed himself, when analyzing, as picking out and naming the essential constituents of various objective entities and facts; in his later works, as picking out and naming essential constituents of various complex concepts. In his reply to Langford in "A Reply to My Critics," he explicitly denied that he ever engaged in the analysis of verbal expressions.

This last denial may not be disingenuous, but it is misleading. Moore maintained that the only proper meaning of the term "analyzing verbal expressions" is merely counting the letters in a sentence, noting the order of the letters, etc. If this is true, then obviously Moore never engaged in analyzing verbal expressions, and just as obviously his denial that he did is trivial.

It may therefore be more significant to ask whether Moore engaged in linguistic analysis, where "linguistic analysis" is used as a technical term designating the following practices or inquiries: the determination of the meaning of a word or expression (not excepting the determination of its dictionary meaning); the determination of the various senses of a word or expression; the determination of the ordinary use of a word or expression; and the determination of discrepancies between the philosophical and ordinary uses of a word or expression. In all these senses of the technical term "linguistic analysis" Moore, it is clear, engaged frequently in linguistic analysis. However, as was pointed out previously, he engaged in linguistic analysis never as an end in itself but always as an inquiry subordinate to the ascertainment of facts or the determination of the essential constituents of things or concepts.

Metaphysics. By the term "metaphysical" Moore sometimes meant to refer to nonnatural objects or qualities, that is, objects or qualities that are constituents of the universe but not of temporal events (or nature); sometimes he meant to refer to the sort of philosophical inquiry that concerns itself with the over-all constitution of the universe. It is in the latter sense that the term "metaphysics" is being used here.

Although not without expressing some doubts on the matter, Moore inclined to the view that the things to be *found* in the universe are broadly of two sorts: those things that exist and those that simply *are* but do not exist. A third class of things consists of those that neither exist nor are; they simply are not. As Moore conceived of these categories, the main ontological division is between the things that are and those that are not. For the former, whether they exist or simply are, comprise the objective constituents of the universe and have equal claim to philosophical investigation. The latter are merely "chimeras" or "imaginary objects."

Moore suggested at least three ways of distinguishing between things that are and things that are not. First, the former possess the property of being; the latter do not. Second, borrowing from Russell's theory of descriptions, Moore claimed that whereas an object that *is* or possesses *being* can be the bearer of a name, imaginary objects can be described only by incomplete symbols. Thus, for example, "centaur" is not the name of anything (for there is nothing to bear the name), whereas "chair" is a name. Third, if a thing's *esse* is *percipi,* then it is an imaginary object and actually *is not.* There are only thoughts of centaurs, for example; there are not centaurs independent of our thoughts. Hence, centaurs are imaginary objects. Moore, however, discovered difficulties with the last description in that he thought it likely that the *esse* of acts of consciousness and sense data is *percipi,* and at the same time he did not want to say that acts of consciousness and sense data *are not.*

Where he did distinguish between mere being and existence (and in places he did not), Moore generally cited two grounds as the basis for the distinction. Sometimes he argued that whatever endures through parts of time exists; what does not endure through parts of time does not exist. He also sometimes argued that whatever can be an object of sensory perception exists. Although he never discussed the connection between these two criteria for existence, it seems from what he said on other matters that the temporal criterion states both a necessary and a sufficient condition for existence, whereas the sensory criterion states but a sufficient condition. For in Moore's system it is possible that material things are never the contents of sensory perception, but they are, par excellence, things that exist.

In addition to existence, being, and nonbeing, Moore treated at length and in detail the category of *reality.* Although painstakingly carried out, his thoughts on this subject possessed little over-all coherence. In *Principia Ethica* he equated reality with existence; in the lectures of 1910–1911 he equated it simply with *being.* In the same lectures he referred to reality as a property; on the other hand, in *Philosophical Studies,* in the essay "The Conception of Reality" (1917), he denied that reality is a property. What he consistently maintained is expressed in his rejection of Bradley's view that reality possesses degrees and that the highest degree of reality is at an extreme remove from material things. Moore denied that reality possesses degrees. But if it does, he said, then he wanted to maintain, in opposition to Bradley, that material things possess the highest degree of it.

Within the category of *being* Moore distinguished between three kinds of objects: particulars, truths or facts, and universals. He generally, though not always, argued as if particulars may be divided into five sorts: material things, sense data (for instance, *patches* of yellow), acts of consciousness, volumes of space, and intervals of time. He did not appear to think that the term "mind" refers to a particular substance in which acts of consciousness inhere.

The theory he seemed to favor is that acts of consciousness are located in material bodies and are properties of material bodies and that the word "mind" stands for something like a logical construction from acts of consciousness. Truths or facts are the objects of true beliefs and comprise such things as mathematical equations—for example, 2 plus 2 equals 4—and the references of indicative sentences, such as "Tom stood to the left of Henry." Universals are again divisible into three sorts: relations, relational properties, and a third sort of universal that is neither a relation nor a relational property. Moore never provided an essential description of this third sort of universal, but he cited as clear-cut examples of it numbers and nonnatural qualities or objects, such as *good,* and as possible examples of it shades of color.

Of the three sorts of *being*—i.e., particulars, facts, and universals—particulars alone exist; facts and universals merely *are:* this, at least, was Moore's view when he was prepared to grant that a significant distinction holds between existence and mere being. It was also his view that the only *substantial* things we are acquainted with are material bodies and acts of consciousness.

It should be remarked that the above inventory of the universe was not considered by Moore to be exhaustive. There may be things in the universe that we are in fact ignorant of or must even necessarily remain ignorant of. For example, Moore thought it is not impossible that God exists but found no evidence for maintaining that he does. Moore described himself as being certain, though, that all the things that have been mentioned as *being* or *existing* do constitute at least some of the constituents of the universe.

General epistemology. Although a number of the topics that have been treated under the heading of Moore's methodology might as reasonably be considered under the heading of his general epistemology, and vice versa, under his methodology it was asked what Moore in his philosophizing was attempting to do and how he was attempting to achieve his aims, whereas under his epistemology these quite different questions are being asked: (1) What, according to Moore's philosophic account, does knowledge consist in? (2) Does knowledge, as so conceived, exist, and if it does, what is it knowledge of?

(1) What does knowledge consist in? Moore's basic metaphysical and methodological principles dictate that in order to discover what knowledge is, it is necessary to distinguish between the different senses (if there are different senses) of the verb "to know" and then to pick out and analyze the particular objects denoted by these senses of "to know" and the relations (if any) that hold between them.

Throughout his earlier writings and the lectures of 1910–1911, Moore was convinced that careful observation of facts and careful differentiation of terms provide us with the following results. First, every instance of cognition ultimately consists in an act of consciousness and, distinct from the latter, in an object. Second, an act of consciousness can exist only as long as the corresponding instance of cognition exists. Thus, when I cease to see a sense datum, my *seeing* of it ceases to exist. The object of cognition, however, may or may not exist after the act of consciousness to which it is related ceases. This is a matter to be decided by empirical considerations. Third, it is conceivable that an act of consciousness and its related object—for example, a sense datum—exist in two different locations. "It seems to me conceivable," wrote Moore in *Some Main Problems of Philosophy*, "that this whitish colour is really on the surface of the material envelope. . . . My seeing of it is in another place—somewhere within my body."

Reflecting this analysis of cognition and its objects, Moore thought that he could pick out four different ways of knowing and, corresponding to them, four different senses of the verb "to know." First and basic to an understanding of any other sense of "to know" is the sense in which "to know" stands for cases in which the relation between the object cognized and its correspondent act of consciousness is similar to or identical with the relation that a patch of color has to the consciousness of a person seeing that patch of color. This is knowledge by direct apprehension or knowledge by acquaintance. A second sense of "to know" represents cases in which the relation between the object cognized and the correspondent act of consciousness is similar to or identical with the relation that, for example, a hat on a table has to the act of consciousness of a person who is remembering that his hat was on the table. Thus, he knows that his hat was on the table, but neither the hat and table nor any sense data that were connected with the hat and table are directly present to his consciousness. This is knowledge by indirect apprehension. At least until 1911, Moore described himself as uncertain whether knowledge by indirect apprehension always necessitates direct apprehension of a proposition, by means of which, following Russell's theory of knowledge by description, one is made aware of the object indirectly apprehended, but he was inclined to think it does. Third, there is a sense of "to know" that represents cases in which the following complex relation between acts of consciousness and objects holds: there is an act of consciousness; there is a proposition directly apprehended; this proposition is in fact true; we believe that it is true; and we believe that it is true because of some further relation or condition that it satisfies. What this further condition is Moore left undecided, though one might plausibly suppose that it had to do with conclusive evidence. In any event, Moore termed this way of knowing "knowledge proper." Last, and involving the previous senses of "to know," is that sense of "to know" in which we describe a person as knowing something, such as the multiplication table, even though he may not at the time be conscious of anything. We imply, in such cases, that the person in question has at some time known, in one of the other three senses of "to know," the multiplication table.

Moore also distinguished between what he termed "immediate knowledge" and "knowledge by direct apprehension." Immediate knowledge is a species of "knowledge proper." Thus, immediate knowledge is distinguished from knowledge by direct apprehension in that the latter does not require the presence of a proposition (for instance, I can directly apprehend sense data), whereas the former does. It is specifically the "kind of way in which you know a proposition to be true—really know

it, not directly apprehend it—when you *do not* know any other proposition from which it follows" (*Some Main Problems of Philosophy*).

(2) Does knowledge exist? and of what things? Since Moore, purportedly on the basis of observation, resolved knowledge into a certain complex of objects, it is evident that knowledge, or "acts of knowing," exists in his view. The question of its existence becomes, indeed, a psychological or introspective question (it would seem) rather than an epistemological one.

In dealing with the question of what sorts of things are known, Moore generally, however, treated it as a *de jure* or epistemological, rather than a *de facto* or psychological, question. Thus, in defense of asserting that such-and-such a sort of thing can be known, he would sometimes appeal to the principle of weighted certainties (for example, he would ask, "Which is more certain—that I know that I am holding a pencil in my hand or that the principles of the skeptic are true?") and sometimes to paradigm arguments of the sort "If I do not know that *P*, then I can know nothing." In this connection, it is worth noting that Moore sometimes argued *de jure* that we know such-and-such a sort of thing exists although he was unable to discover by introspection the way in which we know it. For instance, he insisted that we know the existence of material things, such as the earth and our own body and other bodies like it, but he was unable to determine with any certainty in just what way we know their existence.

Moore claimed that in addition to the existence of material things, we know the existence of our own acts of consciousness and our own sense data, past events in our lives, the being of universals and nonnatural qualities or entities (such as good), the existence of other minds, synthetic necessary truths, and practically all matters of fact that are commonly thought to be known—for instance, that Caesar crossed the Rubicon, that the earth goes around the sun, and so on. Thus, in contrast to the skeptic, who traditionally maintains that the circumference of knowledge is much smaller than people ordinarily think, Moore appears to have maintained that it is much larger than people ordinarily think. For it is doubtful that people ordinarily think they know the existence of some things called sense data and acts of consciousness or the being of some things called nonnatural qualities or universals.

Theory of perception. It is apparent that Moore's general epistemological principles and the premises that he operated with in his methodology enforce an empiricist approach to knowledge. They imply that all knowledge must finally be based on the observation of objects presented in experience. In three respects, however, Moore consistently parted company with traditional empiricists. He refused to limit the term "experience" to mean simply sensory experience. That is, he wanted to maintain that many sorts of objects other than those discovered by the senses are the objects of acts of consciousness—for example, timeless facts, relational universals, and nonnatural qualities. He also wanted to maintain (following Kant) that there are necessary synthetic truths and that we can apprehend these truths. And finally, he was never willing to reject what seemed to him a certain truth—for instance, that he was holding a pencil—because some less certainly true analyses or philosophical principles were incompatible with it. Thus, he consistently refused to acquiesce in the skeptical conclusions that traditional empiricism and indeed, it seems, his own empiricist principles tend to establish.

At the same time, these principles seem to have had two distinct effects on Moore's over-all philosophizing. First, as time passed his interests converged on theory of perception and questions concerning our knowledge of an external, material world. Second, the skeptical conclusions that empiricism appears to foster produced a constantly widening cleavage in his philosophy between what he wanted to assert preanalytically to be certainly true and what his analyses permitted him to assert to be certainly true. This ever-growing cleavage is nowhere more apparent than in his theory of perception.

In his essay of 1903, "The Refutation of Idealism," Moore maintained that material things can be directly apprehended and therefore can be known to exist with as much certainty as one's own acts of consciousness. Soon afterward, however, Moore was led to change his mind on this crucial point, apparently by what has sometimes been referred to as the argument from synthetic incompatibility. This argument assumes that the looks of things are the objects a person directly perceives, and then, because the looks of things change when the thing itself is not presumed to be changing, the argument concludes that what a person directly perceives is not the material thing or a part of its surface but some other kind of object that possibly exists only when he is perceiving it. This "other kind of object" is called by Moore a sense datum.

Moore had trouble in deciding just what a sense datum is: whether it is a particular or a universal, whether it is something like a color (in the case of visual sense data) or some other sort of thing. His final position on this question would seem to be that a visual sense datum is a *patch* of some color: the patch, which is a particular, is related to the color, which is a universal of the third sort (that is, it is neither a relation nor a relational property) in the way something is related to that which, in part, is spread over it.

The main problem concerning Moore in his theory of perception was not this, however, but the question of the relation between sense data and the material things to which they "belong." Although Moore concerned himself with this question in a series of remarkably closely reasoned essays, commencing with "The Status of Sense-data" (1914) and concluding with his last published article, "Visual Sense-data" (1958), he was never able to arrive at a definite or even a very plausible answer. Throughout most of these essays he presented three alternative theories as possibly true: phenomenalism, or what he termed the Mill–Russell theory—that is, the view that a material thing is simply a "logical construction" of sense data; some form of representational theory (varying from the theory that the relation between sense data and material things is an unanalyzable relation of "appearing" to causal theories resembling Locke's); and the theory that visual sense data are identical with parts of the surfaces of material things. With all these alternatives he found grave difficulties and, indeed, was led in the end to dismiss the last as constituting, at least in most cases of perception, nonsense. But if we do not directly perceive material things or their surfaces (and Moore was willing to grant that perhaps we never do), and if by "material things" is meant nothing so Pickwickian as a logical construction of sense data (and Moore would have tended to agree that nothing so Pickwickian is meant), how can we possibly know that material things exist? Moore, in one of his last lectures, "Four Forms of Scepticism," suggested none too plausibly that we know their existence by analogical or inductive arguments.

Ethics. As in the other branches of his philosophy, Moore was confident in his earlier works on ethics of the correctness and finality of the results he set forth; this confidence diminished constantly in the solvent of his empiricist methods of inquiry and was replaced in his later works by no more than tentative agreement with his earlier views. Also, as in the other branches of his philosophy proper, Moore's viewpoint toward both the proper method of ethical inquiry and the nature of the findings to be anticipated stemmed directly from his originally realist presuppositions.

Ethics, as Moore conceived of the discipline, takes the form of a partly definitional, partly descriptive science, resting on observation and induction. His theory is not, however, naturalistic. The fundamental object of observation for ethics, goodness, is a nonnatural quality or entity, according to Moore, and thus is one that neither exists through parts of time nor presents itself through sensory experience. On the other hand, his theory is not "metaphysical": it does not purport to *define* this fundamental entity or quality of ethics in terms of some *other* nonnatural entity or quality. Indeed, a main point of Moore's theory is that the fundamental entity of ethics cannot be defined at all and that any attempt to define it must commit what he termed "the naturalistic fallacy." This is essentially the fallacy that results from construing the "is" of attribution as an "is" of identity, and thus supposing, for example, that because pleasure is (attributive "is") good, good is identical with pleasure.

The fundamental object of ethics is the simple quality or entity good; being simple, good is unanalyzable and indefinable. One can only say that good = good. This is the outcome of the first and most basic inquiry any science of ethics must engage in, the answer to the question What is good?, where this ambiguous question is understood to ask for a definition.

A second important inquiry that the science of ethics undertakes is to determine what are the pre-eminent goods obtainable by men. Since the term "good" is here being used substantively (and not adjectively) to refer to complex wholes to which the quality or entity *good* attaches, definitions or analyses of such goods are possible, in the sense that the parts making up the wholes in question can be set forth. On the other hand, because the quality "good" is indefinable, it is not possible to determine which things are and which are not good analytically. This can be determined only by perceiving which wholes possess good, and to what degree or amount. Since they do not rest on any external evidence, such perceptions were termed by Moore "intuitions," and it is for this reason that his theory of ethics is sometimes called "intuitionistic." A further character of these perceptions is that when we perceive that a certain whole possesses in itself a certain amount of good, we perceive at the same time that any similar whole must possess in itself an equal amount of good. Thus propositions of the sort "Such-and-such possesses in itself such-and-such amount of good" or "Such-and-such is intrinsically good" express truths that are both synthetic and necessary.

The determination of what things are pre-eminently good is complicated by two factors. First, substantive goods are organic unities or wholes; that is, the good of a whole is not simply equal to the sum of the goods of its parts. This makes it impossible to determine what things are good and in what amount merely by determining previously the amount of good attaching itself to basic units of experience and adding up these units. Second, it is in fact difficult to separate, in our perceptions or intuitions, organic wholes from their consequences; hence, in assessing goods-in-themselves we are likely to include the good accruing to causal consequences of those wholes. In order to avoid the last sort of error, Moore proposed that we isolate the organic unity we are concerned with by imagining it as alone existing in the universe and then asking whether it is better that it exists or does not.

Applying this method to the question What are the pre-eminent goods obtainable by men? Moore maintained that "it is obvious that personal affection and aesthetic enjoyments include by far the greatest goods with which we are acquainted."

The third major inquiry of ethical science encompasses the questions of traditional casuistry: What are our duties? What is their order of precedence? What actions as a rule are right, etc.? The answers to all these questions are predicated, in Moore's system, on the assumption that unlike the term "good," the terms "right," "duty," "virtue," and so on are definable. They are all, in fact, definable in terms of good. When we say that a certain sort of action is right or our duty *we mean* that it is productive of the greatest amount of good in comparison with any possible alternative action. Thus, in determining duties and right actions we must not only determine what things are good in themselves but what causal effects actions will have, and this is an almost impossible task, except when conceived in rather short-term measures. As so conceived, Moore generally argued that the rights and duties enjoined and sanctioned in conventional morality are indeed just what the science of ethics shows to be our rights and duties.

CRITICISM OF MOORE'S PHILOSOPHY PROPER

Moore, in his last writings, confessed that he had not been a good answerer of questions, and if by a "good answerer to a philosophical question" is meant one who leaves the question settled or seemingly close to being settled, it is hard not to agree. In his ethics Moore provided simple, clear-cut answers to the problems and questions of traditional ethics, but their very simplicity (like saying the world is made of water) produces its own disbelief, and this disbelief is borne out by subsequent reflection. For example, if good is a simple objective quality of some sort, why should persons be concerned with maximizing it? In

the other branch of inquiry with which he was primarily concerned, theory of perception, Moore failed even to provide clear-cut answers or decisions.

Again, if by "good philosophical answers" are meant answers that can be formed into a consistent system, it must be agreed that Moore is not a good answerer. In his philosophy there are a great many loose ends that he never tied together or attempted to tie together. For instance, he made no attempt to tie together his discussions of the two questions What is the relation of sense data (i.e., patches) to universals? and What is their relation to material things? In the same connection, Moore sometimes admitted that he was inclined to hold at one and the same time two incompatible views (as on the question whether the surfaces of material things are directly seen) and was unable to choose between them.

On the other hand, if a good philosophical answer is conceived as one that is closely reasoned and demands and instills close reasoning on the part of its auditor or reader, then Moore was a good answerer. Studying Moore, it can be fairly said, is like holding one's mind to a whetstone: a mind composed of good stuff is bound to be sharpened (and one of poor stuff to be dulled).

Further, if philosophy is conceived as an inquiry rather than a closed system, Moore was a good answerer. It is the essence of inquiry that every problem considered be freshly considered, that pat answers be abjured, that truth be placed ahead of remaining consistent or reaching conclusions, and that alternatives be given a hearing and their merits weighed. These are precisely the virtues of Moore's philosophizing.

A more serious objection that can be urged against Moore is that there is a certain number of philosophical prejudices that he adopted without question, but that he ought to have questioned. It is arguable, for instance, that he adopted without question the principle that there is something called an act of consciousness and something called an object of that act. Applied to the various topics of philosophy, this principle produces all sorts of obvious nonsense: a ridiculous proliferation of entities, etc. Why, it may be asked, did not Moore seriously question this presupposition and remove it? And if he had, might he not have arrived at sound conclusions instead of the perplexity that he does in fact arrive at?

There is unquestionably a good deal of justice in this last objection. Yet, with some justice too, one may retort on Moore's behalf: "What other principle *seems* as certainly true as the above principle? Has some alternative assumption permitted philosophers to arrive at indisputably true conclusions? And if not, why should not Moore explore the resources of this principle, which seems true to him, just as other philosophers explore the resources of the principles they have accepted, which seem equally true to them?"

Works by Moore

Except in ethics, Moore's major published philosophical writings consist almost entirely of articles, papers (to be delivered), reviews, and compilations of articles and lectures. Exceptions would be his autobiography (a minor masterpiece in its genre) and "A Reply to My Critics," included in the collection of critical essays concerning Moore's philosophy entitled *The Philosophy of G. E. Moore.* In this bibliography, the more important or influential articles of Moore's are noted in the compilations in which they occur.

Principia Ethica. Cambridge, 1903.

Ethics. London and New York, 1912.

Philosophical Studies. London and New York, 1922. Collection of papers, including "The Refutation of Idealism" (1903), "The Status of Sense-data" (1914), "The Conception of Reality" (1917), "Some Judgements of Perception" (1918), and "External and Internal Relations" (1919). It is in the last paper that the term "entailment" is first used and defined philosophically.

The Philosophy of G. E. Moore, P. A. Schilpp, ed. Chicago and Evanston, Ill., 1942; 2d ed., New York, 1952. Contains "An Autobiography" and "A Reply to My Critics." In the second edition is the "Addendum to My 'Reply.'"

Some Main Problems of Philosophy. London and New York, 1953. Contains Moore's lectures of 1910 and 1911.

Philosophical Papers. London and New York, 1959. With an obituary notice by C. D. Broad. Includes "A Defense of Common Sense" (1923), "Is Existence a Predicate?" (1936), and "Proof of an External World" (1939).

The Common Place Books, 1919–1953, Casimir Lewy, ed. Edinburgh, 1962.

Works on Moore

Bridge, Ursula, ed., *W. B. Yeats and T. Sturge Moore, Their Correspondence, 1901–1937.* London, 1953. In this correspondence the two well-known poets (one of them Moore's brother) refer at some length to Moore's philosophy and some of Moore's comments on their interpretations of his philosophy. Although of little philosophical interest, their references provide an amusing picture of nonphilosophers trying desperately to understand Moore. Typical is Yeats's remark "I find your brother extraordinarily obscure."

Keynes, John Maynard, *Two Memoirs.* London, 1949. In the second memoir, "My Early Beliefs" (pp. 78–103), Keynes describes the members and discussions of the "Bloomsbury Club," c. 1903–1914. This is a fascinating, witty, and informative account of the tremendous influence Moore's *Principia Ethica* had on some of the finer and younger intellects of the early twentieth century in England; of their attempts, largely verbal, to put Moore's ethical theories into some sort of practice; and of Moore's role in the group, his method of verbal argument, and the "pure and passionate intensity" of his realistic "vision."

Malcolm, Norman, *Knowledge and Certainty.* Englewood Cliffs, N.J., 1963. "George Edward Moore," pp. 163 ff. In the first part of this important essay Malcolm presents a penetrating and intimate description of Moore's character as a man and as a philosopher, based in large part on personal recollections and impressions. In the remaining parts he discusses the relationship of certain of Moore's "common-sense propositions" to the concept of common sense, traditional philosophy, and to Wittgenstein's views on the proper role of philosophy with respect to ordinary language. Included is a philosophic evaluation of Moore's purported defense of common sense. This essay is notable not only for the light it sheds on some central aspects of Moore's philosophizing but for the original philosophizing that it contains on the topics of ordinary language, the concept of common sense, and traditional skepticism concerning perception.

Passmore, John, "Moore and Russell," in *A Hundred Years of Philosophy.* London, 1957. Passmore presents a very searching account of Moore's earlier philosophy (especially as set forth·in the 1899 essay "The Nature of Judgment") and his later views on the "analysis of meaning." Passmore also discusses, in an interesting and illuminating way, Moore's theory of sense data and his essays "The Refutation of Idealism" and "Proof of an External World."

Schilpp, P. A., ed., *The Philosophy of G. E. Moore* (see above). Contains critical essays on Moore's ethics by C. D. Broad, Charles L. Stevenson, William K. Frankena, H. J. Paton, Abraham Edel, and A. Campbell Garnett; on his theory of perception by O. K. Bouwsma, C. J. Ducasse, Paul Marhenke, and C. A. Mace; on what might broadly be called his method by Arthur E. Murphy, C. H. Langford, Norman Malcolm, Morris Lazerowitz, Alice Ambrose,

John Wisdom, Richard McKeon, and V. J. McGill; and on his influence by L. Susan Stebbing. A number of the essays referrred to, such as Bouwsma's "Moore's Theory of Sense-data," are in their own right important contributions to the topics under discussion. But even when not intrinsically important, these essays constitute a particularly valuable commentary on Moore's philosophy in that Moore, in his "Reply," entered into several detailed discussions of their contents in an attempt to clarify his views. See especially his replies to the essays by Broad, Stevenson, Frankena, Bouwsma, Ducasse, and Langford.

Urmson, J. O., *Philosophical Analysis, Its Development Between the Two World Wars.* Oxford, 1956. A penetrating work on the "analytic movement" that helps one place Moore in his later philosophical setting. Although only fragmentary references are made to Moore's philosophy, many of the points of view and many of the topics that Moore was concerned with and that influenced his own philosophizing (from 1910 on) are brought into the open and clarified.

Warnock, G. J., "G. E. Moore," in *English Philosophy Since 1900.* London, 1958. This thin commentary propagates the thesis that Moore's philosophy can best be understood and appreciated through an understanding and appreciation of his temperament and character. The claim is made that Moore was a "man with no metaphysical quirks of temperament."

White, A. R., *G. E. Moore, A Critical Exposition.* Oxford, 1958. This work—the only English work of book length devoted exclusively to commentary on the philosophy of Moore—collects and collates most of the things Moore had to say on method, theory of ethics, and theory of perception.

JOHN O. NELSON

MORAL ARGUMENTS FOR THE EXISTENCE OF GOD. From the time of Kant to the present day, a great many attempts have been made to base arguments for God's existence not upon the mere fact that there is a world, nor on the general orderliness it manifests, but on a very special feature of that world—human moral experience. The popularity of moral arguments is not hard to understand. Hume and Kant had produced powerful and apparently disabling criticisms of the traditional arguments of natural theology, criticisms that seemed decisive against any conceivable type of argument to God as the explanation of the world. Hume had no alternative theistic argument to offer and, insofar as theoretical reasoning is concerned, Kant had none either. The structure of Kant's ethical philosophy, however, accorded to "practical reason" privileges not shared by theoretical reason. If God was to retain any place in the Kantian system, the weight of apologetic had to be shifted from the theoretical to the practical, to exploring the implications of our moral situation. Between Kant's day and the middle of the twentieth century, skepticism about the theoretical arguments has tended to deepen rather than to lighten; hence, there has been no lack of religious apologists following Kant's new "moral route" to God.

Another reason for the popularity of moral argument is religious rather than philosophical. Even if the argument to God as First Cause or "necessary being" were valid, these notions of deity can be more of an embarrassment than a help to the religious imagination. They present us with a divine object or superobject, whereas religion demands that God be primarily known as *person.* A moral argument offers hope of overcoming that external and thinglike character: it insures that concepts of God will be, from the outset, personal concepts.

Typical moral arguments. Among the many varieties of moral argument, the following are both historically important and recurrent patterns. Several of them may be found in a single author.

First, if one understands moral rules as "commands," one may argue to the existence of a "commander." The commander cannot be the individual human moral agent, for what today I command myself to do, I can tomorrow command myself not to do. I can have absolute moral obligations only if a God exists to command them. Because I do have absolute moral obligations, it follows that God exists.

Second, a minor variant of this moral argument claims that if we recognize moral authority, we must *ipso facto* recognize the existence of God as alone able to confer that authority. We judge that the moral law retains its authoritativeness whether particular human wills are at any time actually accepting its rules and principles or not; therefore, the source of its authority must lie altogether outside those human wills.

Third, the notion of "moral law" itself is said to be incomplete without reference to God, for law implies "lawgiver," a divine legislator. Our very acknowledgment of a moral law, therefore, presupposes theism.

Fourth, it has been claimed that there is a remarkable degree of agreement among the moral judgments made by men in widely different cultures and historical periods. Many apparent disagreements can be attributed to differences in belief and thus held to be not fundamental. This impressive measure of agreement, it is argued, can be accounted for only on the supposition that God has written his law in the hearts of men.

Certain of the most interesting and influential moral arguments take as their premise some part of the content of the moral law itself. We are under moral obligation to perfect ourselves and to attain a "highest good" (*summum bonum*) that is manifestly unattainable in a life lived under the conditions we know here and now. We can, at best, make a start to a moral development that requires very different conditions for its completion. But since that complete development is demanded of us as duty, it must be attainable. God and immortality are thus presupposed in our actual moral experience.

Analysis of moral arguments. Let us briefly consider each of the varieties of moral arguments again and attempt to estimate their strengths and weaknesses.

Of the moral commander argument we can pertinently ask: Is the notion of command basic to ethics? Certainly not in the sense of parade-ground commands, commands passively received and acted upon unreflectively. Such obedience is a long way from moral deliberation and judgment. An immature moral agent may see his duties as commands (parental, for example); but the mark of mature moral judgment is self-commitment to a policy on which one has deliberated. This policy may or may not be in harmony with someone's command; in any case, it does not owe its authenticity to its being commanded. "Here I stand," one may say; and this can express a settled resolution, one not to be made one day and rescinded the next.

Even if it were established that a celestial being unvaryingly commanded a certain policy as obligatory in an absolute sense, the unvaryingness of his command could not itself furnish the ground for the absoluteness of the obliga-

tion. For it is at least logically possible that this celestial being ought not to command unvaryingly what he does so command. If he commands what is right and obligatory, that is cause for thankfulness; but one could scarcely be thankful over a truth of logic. "Unvaryingly" must not equal "stubbornly" or "with chronic moral blindness"; these are unthinkable possibilities for Christian theism. But this does not affect the point being made: that absoluteness is not analyzable in terms of unvaryingness of command. Moreover, the Christian wishes to make one all-important moral judgment that could not possibly have its absoluteness reduced to commandedness by God—the judgment, namely, that God is morally perfect. But if a human being can make this moral judgment uncommanded, why can he not make others also?

Analogous criticisms can be made of the argument from the authority or authoritativeness of the moral law to the need for a divine source of authority. To put the main objection boldly: It is of the very nature of a fundamental moral judgment that it should be made on no authority but that of the agent who makes it. Certainly there are occasions when I may believe that another person has a superior measure of insight into the situation in which I have to act; I may then properly accept his judgment in lieu of my own. Yet if this is not to be a culpable moral abdication, I must have good grounds for trusting my temporary "authority": I must judge him to be morally reliable. But this is itself a moral judgment—one that I can make on nobody's authority but my own; or if on someone's authority, then this new person must be judged reliable on my own authority, and so on. A legitimate appeal to authority presupposes that autonomous moral judgments have already been made. Our argument held that we must postulate God as the authorizer of all our moral judgments—otherwise they would carry no authority; but we find, contrariwise, that God can play the role of authority only if we are able to make certain moral judgments without appealing to any external authority whatsoever.

The third version alleged that the notion of "moral law" is incomplete unless God is postulated as lawgiver. "Law," however, is a word with many strands to its meaning; and it is only by failing to distinguish certain of the strands that this can appear to be a plausible line of argument. It is perfectly intelligible to say that some person or group of persons has laid down positive laws, rules for a community, backed by penal sanctions. The existence of a developed body of such laws normally implies the existence of lawmakers or codifiers. It is quite another thing (and not really intelligible) to speak of anyone, human or divine, "laying down" the moral law itself. Laws, rules, and regulations are of the right logical type to be laid down in accordance with, or in conflict with, the moral law. But the moral law itself is not the sort of thing that needs to be, or that logically can be, laid down or promulgated by anyone. No conceivable story about men or gods could be taken, without absurdity, to describe the inauguration (or the annulling) of the moral law. Commands might be uttered, inscriptions miraculously appear; but it would never become a trivial or tautological question to ask of their content, "Is this in fact morally binding?" The distinctively moral authority of a rule or law does not lie in the prestige or power of its initiator, nor in the circumstances of its first recognition.

The argument from the convergence of moral codes is most often set forth in an objectivist ethical context. The existence of objective moral qualities "seen" to be there, or "intuited," by different moral agents in widely different places and times remains inexplicable unless we posit a God who creates and morally guides. It is less often noticed that the argument is perhaps stronger—certainly no weaker—if it is set forth in a subjectivist context instead. This was apparently noted by F. R. Tennant, who (in a conversation reported by R. B. Braithwaite) argued on the following lines. Failing the existence of any objective moral properties or moral relations, it is all the more remarkable that there should be such a measure of congruity among moral judgments or decisions: sufficiently remarkable to point the way, again, to divine activity. Yet this argument is not at all conclusive. The supernatural hypothesis that it puts forward is not the only hypothesis available to account for the data; and it has the disadvantage that it is not empirically confirmable or refutable. Powerful competitors would be arguments from the relative stability of basic human needs, desires, and aversions or from the pervasiveness of aggressive and social drives in the personality. These alone might well account for the actual agreements among moral judgments and would account for them without invoking the immensely problematic notion of divine causality.

Presupposition of the highest good. Our last group of arguments began its history in modern philosophy with a statement of Kant: "The idea of the highest good . . . cannot be realized by man himself . . . ; yet he discovers within himself the duty to work for this end. Hence he finds himself impelled to believe in the cooperation or management of a moral Ruler of the world, by means of which alone this goal can be reached (*Religion Within the Limits of Reason Alone*).

Kant was not betraying the austerity or rigor of his moral philosophy; he was not offering religious inducements to moral behavior. He would have denied distinctively moral worth to someone whose "dutiful" actions were aimed at securing his own post-mortem happiness. The emphasis in his argument is wholly on the intelligibility and rationality of the moral demand; it was inconceivable to him that the categorical imperative should be a mocking voice, laying obligations upon us and at the same time denying the environment in which alone the obligations could be fulfilled. (It has been claimed that Kant had abandoned these moral arguments by the time he wrote the *Opus Postumum*, but the contrary view has been argued more forcibly; see G. A. Schrader, "Kant's Presumed Repudiation . . . .")

The strength of Kant's moral argument is clearly dependent on the strength of his ethical theory as a whole. It is only because he saw moral judgment as the work of practical reason (not as a matter of emotive reactions or responses) that he was able to make plausible use of those judgments as a basis for theological demands. Any fundamental criticism of the Kantian ethic would *ipso facto* imperil the theology.

The argument is equally imperiled if we deny that we are under obligation to attain the highest good and our individual moral perfection, saying that we are obliged only to strive toward these unrealizable ends. We might indeed reverse Kant's argument as follows. From our observation of the world we conclude that the highest good and our moral perfection are unattainable; therefore, we can have no obligation to attain these but, at best, only an obligation to strive toward them. We can interpret them in Kant's own term, "regulatively," as Kant himself sometimes did. (See John R. Silber, "Kant's Conception of the Highest Good . . . .")

The postulating of God and immortality is aimed at solving an antinomy—of making intelligible what, without the postulate, is inexplicable. But does the postulation of God in fact produce intelligibility, a lifting of mystery? Or is there not so much mystery in the postulate itself that the final effect is a deepening, not a lightening, of perplexity? If independence, autonomy, and freedom are essential to a moral agent, that autonomy will presumably remain essential in a hereafter as well as in the here and now. But, if so, the postulation of God and immortality can by no means insure that the ultimate moral goals will, in fact, be reached, even though it was precisely to insure their attainment that the postulates were made.

Kant's theory of time as a "form of sensibility" makes it very dubious whether he could have spoken meaningfully of a continuing moral development and the attainment of the highest good in a hereafter. Granted that he disclaimed all theoretical insight into what such an existence would be like (this measure of agnosticism is part of the force of "postulate" as distinct from "demonstrate"), the notion of time still remains essential to Kant's moral argument. If we are unable to give meaning to it in that context, the argument cannot but suffer.

It is possible to reject some portions of Kant's detailed argumentation and yet to advance a moral argument of a definitely Kantian type. This was notably done in W. R. Sorley's *Moral Values and the Idea of God* and in A. E. Taylor's *The Faith of a Moralist*. Neither of these writers held the moral argument to be the sole and all-sufficient theistic proof, but they did believe that without it the case for theism is weak and dubious.

Sorley attempted first to show that "the moral order is an objectively valid order, that moral values belong to the nature of reality," and that "the history of the world-process is fitted to realise this order." If we were to assume that the goal of the world-process is the realizing of happiness, there would be the weightiest empirical evidence against us. With moral worth and goodness it is different. Conditions that work against happiness may work for, not against, the developing, trying, and testing of moral fiber. "The very imperfection of the world [is] an argument pointing to the theistic conclusion." There remains yet a gap between the claim that the universe works toward a moral purpose and the full claim that God exists. Sorley seeks to fill this gap by arguing that belief in God is presupposed by belief in an objective and "eternally valid" morality. If the moral law is eternally valid, and valid whether we recognize it or not, "how could this eternal validity stand alone, not embodied in matter and neither seen nor realized by finite minds, unless there were an eternal mind whose thought and will were therein expressed?"

One can readily agree that the world as we experience it is better adapted to be a vale of soul-making than a hedonistic holiday camp. Yet there are difficulties about even the soul-making view. Some human suffering (the unmerited suffering of young children, for instance) cannot always be treated plausibly as developing moral fiber, or as realizing any other moral value. The natural environment can figure as the destroyer of moral personality as well as its preserver and nourisher. Sorley's further argument, from the validity of the law to an eternal mind, surely contains a confusion of the logical and the psychological. Questions about validity and about truth are logically independent of questions about the propositions that are actually entertained in someone's mind. Whether or not there exists a person who says (or thinks) *p*, has no bearing on the truth of *p* or, if *p* is a moral principle, upon its bindingness or validity in the relevant sense.

A. E. Taylor saw the moral life not as a mere conforming to given static principles and rules but as directing the moral agent along certain paths of self-development. There is development within the moral ideal: "We discover tomorrow that today's ideal 'had more in it' than we had supposed." The goal transforms itself as we approach it. The further we pursue it, the less able we become to conceive the human good in purely this-world, secular terms. There is development also within our awareness of time. Purposeful, valuable activity produces an extension of our "conscious present"; it delivers us from the dullness of "one thing after another." The limiting case in this development would be well expressed by Boethius' account of eternity—"the complete and simultaneous fruition of a life without bounds."

'We may argue," Taylor then claimed, " . . . from the existence of a function to the reality of an environment in which the function can find adequate exercise." But no view of the world, short of theism, can guarantee the completion of these directions of development that Taylor has described.

Whatever is decided about the validity of the argument as an argument, Taylor's *The Faith of a Moralist* is a lastingly impressive and eloquent account of a religiously oriented morality. On validity, however, some searching criticisms were made by C. D. Broad in his review of Taylor's work published in *Mind* (1931). Taylor had taken as his premises certain moral judgments and certain trends of development in our experience of value. He then had asked what these entailed; whatever they entailed was to be added to our true beliefs about the universe. Broad argued that, in order to avoid a vicious circle, we must be sure that our premises do not already covertly assume the theistic conclusion. We must know that we have these duties and aspirations without already presupposing God and immortality. Only in this way could the existence of God and immortality be the conclusion of our argument. It is hard to be sure that these value judgments and aspirations are not the *consequence* of a prior theism. And a further point must be added: Only such a previously held theism, or cryptotheism, could entitle us to argue, with Taylor, "from the existence of a function to the reality of an

environment in which [it has] adequate exercise." (Or, if this is true by definition of "function," only such a theism can justify calling those value pursuits "functions.") Once again it might be added that the directions of moral development, although unrealizable *in toto*, could still be taken as targets for ever-nearer approximation. That they can be taken in this way, however, tells against Taylor's argument, for he wished to deny that we can be morally serious about these unless complete realization is possible.

Moral theories dominant in the mid-twentieth century do not tend to lead naturally into moral arguments for God. In Britain and the United States, at any rate, they have been characteristically this-worldly. But exceptions do occur. Austin Farrer offered, if not a moral argument, then certainly a moral "persuasion" toward theism in the first chapter of *Faith and Logic*, "A Starting-point for the Philosophical Examination of Theological Belief." His argument is that we are incontestably under an obligation to love our neighbor—that is, to hold him in highest regard; and that this is not impossible if our neighbor is a lovable person. If our neighbor occasionally lapses from lovability and from goodness, we may still manage to love his "normal" self, although it is temporarily obscured. If, however, he lapses chronically and grossly, how are we to love him? To love what he might be is now to love a fiction only; but it is persons, not fictions, that we ought to love. Farrar claimed Christianity provides a uniquely helpful way in which we can see the unlovable neighbor, admit his deficiencies, and yet succeed in loving him. In praying for and about our neighbor, we bring our view of him into relation with God's action—his action in creating our neighbor and his constant and costly redemptive action on our neighbor's behalf. Farrer insisted that, if these reflections help to give plausibility and impressiveness to the Christian view itself, they are not to be taken as a refurbishing of strong Kantian claims to establish God's existence.

Farrer appears to have assessed the capacity of this type of argument far more realistically than those who used it before him. If we judge that certain attitudes or evaluations are supremely worth realizing—for example, that "people ought to be held in the utmost regard"—then it is reasonable, even mandatory, to take up whatever stance will best further our task of realizing them. In our present example, we are required to meditate upon those reflections that uniquely put our neighbor in a regard-furthering light. Of course, provisos must be added. There must, for instance, be no logical incoherence in the description of the stance or of the context that furthers our neighborly love; otherwise, what we called the light or the stance might be in fact only a fugitive, quasi-aesthetic movement of feeling. To provide a point of entry to traditional Christianity, the stance must be capable of being expressed in a set of meaningful affirmations about reality. Another obvious proviso is that our premises must be sound. We must in fact be under obligation to hold our neighbor in highest regard, and all non-Christian ways of seeing our neighbor must be less helpful than the Christian way. It is particularly upon the second of these premises that, in a fuller discussion, argument necessarily would concentrate.

Bibliography

The chief sources for moral arguments to God are the following works of Kant: *Kritik der praktischen Vernunft* (Riga, 1788), translated by T. K. Abbott (London and Dublin, 1879) and by L. W. Beck (Chicago, 1949), and *Die Religion innerhalb der Grenzen der blossen Vernunft* (Königsberg, 1793), translated by T. M. Greene and H. H. Hudson as *Religion Within the Limits of Reason Alone*, 2d ed. (New York, 1960).

Post-Kantian works in which moral arguments to God play an important part are Austin Farrer, "A Starting-point for the Philosophical Examination of Theological Belief," in B. G. Mitchell, ed., *Faith and Logic* (New York, 1957); John Henry Newman, *A Grammar of Assent* (London, 1901), especially pp. 109–110; Hastings Rashdall, *The Theory of Good and Evil*, 2 vols. (Oxford, 1907), and *God and Man* (Oxford, 1930); W. R. Sorley, *Moral Values and the Idea of God* (Cambridge, 1918); and A. E. Taylor, *The Faith of a Moralist* (London, 1930), reviewed by C. D. Broad in *Mind*, Vol. 40 (1931), 364–375.

Among contemporary studies of the Kantian argument are the following: H. P. Owen, *The Moral Argument for Christian Theism* (London, 1965); G. A. Schrader, "Kant's Presumed Repudiation of the 'Moral Argument' in the Opus Postumum," in *Philosophy*, Vol. 26 (1951), 228–241; John R. Silber, "Kant's Conception of the Highest Good as Immanent and Transcendent," in *The Philosophical Review*, Vol. 68 (1959), 469 ff.; and W. H. Walsh, "Kant's Moral Theology," in *Proceedings of the British Academy*, Vol. 49 (1963), 263–289.

RONALD W. HEPBURN

MORALITY. See RELIGION AND MORALITY.

MORAL LAW, THE. See KANT, IMMANUEL.

MORAL PHILOSOPHY. See ETHICS, HISTORY OF; ETHICS, PROBLEMS OF.

MORAL RESPONSIBILITY. See RESPONSIBILITY, MORAL AND LEGAL.

MORAL SENSE. In the first half of the eighteenth century certain British philosophers argued that the moral sense is the faculty by which we distinguish between moral right and wrong. The deliverances of this faculty are feelings or sentiments; hence, it is counted as a sense. Our observation of an instance of virtuous action is the occasion for a feeling of pleasure or satisfaction, which enables us to distinguish that action as virtuous. Similarly, our observation of an instance of vicious action is the occasion for a feeling of pain or uneasiness, which enables us to distinguish that action as vicious. The moral sense is also an influencing motive in our pursuit of virtue and our avoidance of vicious behavior, and it plays a part in our bestowal of praise and blame.

Historical background. Arguments for and against the moral sense take their character from the larger social and intellectual context in which they were advanced. The late seventeenth century and early eighteenth century in Europe saw the culmination of certain lines of thought which had their origin in earlier times. The Protestant insistence on individual conviction in purely religious matters had an effect on other areas of thought as well. The rejection of external authority as the guarantor of religious truth and the consequent reliance of each believer on his own inner light led to a full-blown theory of knowledge in which the different ways a person can know different kinds of subject matter were definitively catalogued. The way of knowing a given subject was appealed to as the foundation or guarantee of truth. The first account of this theory of knowledge was John Locke's *Essay Concerning Human Understanding* in the late seventeenth century. The most comprehensive statement of it was the *Treatise of Human Nature* by David Hume in the eighteenth century. These developments in theory of knowledge were closely related to a growing interest in feelings and their expression. The new theory of knowledge was also closely connected with changes in beliefs about God's relation to the world. Speculations about the will of God were no longer a necessary preliminary to doing physics. When the notion of a physics without God met in men's minds with a resistance to religious authority in all matters, including morals, the problem was posed of the possibility of accounting for morality without an appeal to a divine source. But if morality is not founded on God's will, where is the foundation laid? In line with the new theory of knowledge, the most promising direction for a search appeared to be in human nature itself.

The first Englishman to search for the foundation of morals in human nature, Thomas Hobbes, returned with a brilliantly stated but outrageous report. He found that "good" and "evil" are relative to the person who uses these words; and when people are joined together in a commonwealth, then good and evil are subject to the determinations of the commonwealth. As for our motives for pursuing good and avoiding evil, they may be summed up as self-interest. Were it to our own interest to pursue what others, or the commonwealth, have designated as evil, we certainly would; but, for the most part, our appreciation of the convenience which follows from everyone's following the same rules and, at the worst, our fear of punishment on being caught deter us from the practice of evil.

Hobbes's unflattering picture of human nature and his relativistic account of morals, which he presented in *Leviathan,* are the ominous and ever-present background of all discussions of moral philosophy for the next hundred years. They called forth their contradictory counterpart in the writings of the third earl of Shaftesbury. Shaftesbury argued that Hobbes had made a shortsighted survey of human nature. There is benevolence in human nature, as well as selfishness; and indeed, if men were not originally endowed with a disposition to be sociable, the formation of a commonwealth would be impossible. Shaftesbury was the first to attribute to a moral sense our ability to distinguish between good and evil, virtue and vice. This sense, along with our natural affection for virtue, accounts for the possibility of morality. Shaftesbury, however, did not make clear how the possession of a moral sense enables us to avoid relativism in moral judgments; and indeed the specter of relativism must inevitably haunt the proponents of the moral sense.

Development of the doctrine. The systematic development of the doctrine of a moral sense was left to Shaftesbury's successors: first Francis Hutcheson and later David Hume. Their first move was to fit the moral sense into the mainstream of eighteenth-century philosophy by finding a place for it in Locke's theory of knowledge. Looking into the human mind, Locke found that all knowledge consists of perceptions, which must arrive in the mind by one of two routes, either sensation or reflection. Whatever can be known must be accounted for as a perception; and whatever cannot be accounted for in this way is not knowledge. The proponents of the moral sense accounted for our knowledge of moral right and wrong as Lockean reflexive perceptions. When someone observes a given action or considers a certain character trait, these first perceptions are immediately followed by a secondary set of feelings of either pleasure or uneasiness, according to whether the action or character is virtuous or vicious. By consulting these secondary perceptions, we can make our moral judgments. The proponents of the moral sense were careful to point out that actions are not virtuous *because* they please. Rather we know them to be virtuous because we are pleased in a *certain manner*. Thus, moral pleasures and pains are distinctive feelings. Hume argued for the possibility of distinguishing different kinds of pleasure by pointing out, for example, that someone may be pleased both by a good musical composition and by a good bottle of wine, and their goodness is determined merely by the pleasure they give; but we do not say on that account that the wine is harmonious or the music of good flavor.

Besides accounting for our knowledge of right and wrong, the moral sense closes the gap between moral knowledge and moral behavior by providing a motive for moral behavior. Since moral knowledge consists of feelings of pleasure and uneasiness, the prospect of enjoying or avoiding these feelings is a sufficient motive for pursuing virtue and avoiding vice. If moral knowledge were not ultimately a matter of feelings, it would be possible for someone to know that a certain kind of action is virtuous but still have no motive for doing it. The moral sense also enables us to account for our approval and condemnation of actions and characters as following from our being pleased or pained by them.

Criticism. The moral sense was subjected to two sorts of criticism. The first sort was directed against supposed defects in the doctrine of the moral sense itself. The second sort of criticism advanced the claims of rival candidates for the title of moral faculty.

Defects in the doctrine. The bluntest form of the first sort of criticism was to interpret the proponents of the moral sense as talking about an extra organ of sense, "a moral nose" or "a moral ear." How acute they were to have discovered a new human organ which no one had noticed until they came along! Merely to mention the possibility was enough to show the nonexistence of such an organ and to render the doctrine of a moral sense laughable. Hutcheson was especially plagued with this kind of criticism. But he spoke of the moral sense as a determination of the mind; which left the way open for viewing the moral sense not as an organ but as a faculty which can be looked for only in the way memory or will can be looked for. Hume's defenses against this criticism were somewhat better. He boldly asserted the principle that our acquaintance with our senses or faculties can never be anything but an acquaintance with their characteristic perceptions. Hence, he was justified in confining himself to talk of moral feelings and sentiments; and indeed, he never actually used the phrase "moral sense" in any argument but relegated it to a section title.

The next most severe criticism was to point out that although all men are said to be endowed with a moral sense, there is no universal agreement about moral right and wrong. Hutcheson turned aside this criticism by arguing that the moral sense may be inoperative or defective, just as human eyes may be. Hume added that differences in moral judgments may be attributed to differences in experience and education and to a failure to pass judgment from a disinterested point of view; and he hoped that by additional experience or by a greater effort to achieve disinterestedness moral disputants might be able to reach agreement.

But the critics of the moral sense thought that by far the most serious fault in the doctrine was its apparent foundation of the distinction between moral right and wrong on human nature itself. This opened the door to Hobbesian relativism: Whatever action pleases is virtuous, and whatever displeases, vicious. Actually, Hutcheson based the distinction between virtue and vice on the will of God, one step removed from human nature. It just so happens, he held, that God determined us to be pleased by benevolent actions; and when nothing interferes with the moral sense, we count benevolence a virtue and malevolence a vice. But, his opponents argued, to base the distinction between moral good and evil on God's will is no less arbitrary than to base it on human nature itself. If, by divine fiat, we count benevolence a virtue, we might very well have done the opposite, had God so pleased. What is more, the distinction between good and evil cannot possibly rest on God's will, for if good and evil have not some real character in themselves, what is there to determine his will in the first place?

Hume based the distinction between moral right and wrong directly on human nature—that is, our power to be pleased and displeased by different ways of acting—without an appeal to any divine determination of this power. But if there is to be a stability in the distinction between moral right and wrong, then there must be a consistency in human nature. This is no easy thing to show, for the slightest inspection of human affairs appears to tell against it. Yet Hume argued that, on balance, man is more of a social being than not. Indeed, this contention had always been strongly supported by proponents of the moral sense; but Hume added the refinement that man's very inclination to be social leads him to be pleased by those actions and character traits which tend to make society possible and to be displeased by those which tend to disrupt society. Thus, while the distinction between virtue and vice does indeed rest on human nature, it is not an arbitrary distinction. We do have a good reason for preferring one sort of action to another, namely the action's tendency to maintain society. Should someone ask, "And why should I prefer the maintenance of society to its destruction?" Hume had no answer in the form of a logical argument. He certainly recognized the possibility of someone's preferring the destruction of society over its maintenance; but on such a fundamental issue, he held, there can be no arguments pro or con, but only an appeal to feelings. Society exists because, as a matter of fact, by far the greater number of people have the kind of feelings that make it possible.

Rival moral faculties. Another set of objections to the moral sense was advanced by those who argued that the faculty by which we discern moral right and wrong must be reason, or the understanding. The most notable members of this school were Samuel Clarke, John Balguy, and Richard Price. Their most characteristic doctrine was that moral right and wrong are unchanging and unchangeable and, thus, independent of any human, or even divine, determination. This school accepted Locke's theory of knowledge with the modification that the understanding is capable of originating new simple ideas for itself by considering those it gets by way of the two great avenues of sensation and reflection. Thus, according to Clarke, the understanding can discern a certain eternal fitness which things and actions bear to one another in their natures. He likened these moral discoveries to mathematical reasoning in which one discovers the consistency of certain concepts. The implication is that the absolute and immutable character of moral distinctions is such that they can be known only by reason. Therefore, the moral faculty could not possibly be a sense.

Hume endeavored to answer these arguments by pointing out that, strictly considered, reason is capable only of comparing ideas. Since moral knowledge is a sentiment or feeling which arises on the observation of an action or character trait, it is not the result of comparing ideas, and thus it cannot be a conclusion of reason. What is more, since our moral sentiments about certain actions may excite us to perform or to avoid these actions, it is even more doubtful that our moral knowledge comes from reason, for, according to Hume, the conclusions of reason alone can never be an exciting motive to action. A person may know that a certain way of acting may have a certain result, but in order for him to act to achieve that result, he must first find it pleasing.

The moral sense and reason were not the only candidates for a moral faculty proposed at that time. Joseph Butler argued for conscience; and Adam Smith chose to argue for sympathy—which had also figured in Hume's moral philosophy—as the source of moral distinctions. Considering the arguments advanced on behalf of the different candidates for the moral faculty, one can see that the issue was never one that could be settled by empirical investigation. The search for a moral faculty had its origin in the general acceptance of a faculty psychology, supplemented with the Lockean assumption that the acts attributed to our mental faculties are to be accounted for as the occurrence of various sorts of perceptions. When one recognizes the *ad hoc* character of the conceptual framework in which the disputes over the nature of the moral faculty took place, one can see why there was no resolving them. When one no longer finds a need for a faculty psychology, the need to search for a moral faculty goes too.

The present-day moral philosopher no longer casts his study as an investigation of the deliverances of a moral faculty, but rather as a study of the logic of moral discourse. Despite their central preoccupation, the proponents of the moral sense have made a contribution to the development of modern moral philosophy. In particular, they contributed the points that morality assumes the value of society and is incomprehensible apart from this presupposition; that conduct must be judged by general rules; and that a general rule of definitive importance to morality is the injunction to act for the greatest good of the greatest number. But perhaps the most important contribution to moral philosophy by the proponents of the moral sense was their insistence that feeling has a place in morals and that to miss this fact is to omit a distinctive element in moral discourse.

(For a further discussion of theories of moral sense, see ETHICAL OBJECTIVISM and ETHICS, HISTORY OF.)

Bibliography

For original statements of the moral sense doctrine, see Shaftesbury (Anthony Ashley Cooper), *An Inquiry Concerning Virtue or Merit* (1699), to be found in *Characteristics of men, morals, opinions, times*, 3 vols. (London, 1711), Vol. II; Francis Hutcheson, *An Inquiry into the Original of our Ideas of Beauty and Virtue* (London, 1725) and *An Essay on the Nature and Conduct of the Passions and Affections with Illustrations upon the Moral Sense* (London, 1728); and David Hume, *A Treatise of Human Nature* (London, 1740), Book III.

For rival moral faculties, see, for reason, Samuel Clarke, *A Discourse Concerning the Unchangeable Obligations of Natural Religion and the Truth and Certainty of the Christian Revelation* (London, 1706); John Balguy, *The Foundation of Moral Goodness* (London, 1728); and Richard Price, *A Review of the Principal Questions and Difficulties in Morals* (London, 1758). For conscience, see Joseph Butler, *Fifteen Sermons upon Human Nature, or Man Considered as a Moral Agent* (London, 1726). For the rival moral faculty of sympathy, see Adam Smith, *Theory of Moral Sentiments* (London, 1759).

For modern studies, see James Bonar, *Moral Sense* (London and New York, 1930) and D. Daiches Raphael, *The Moral Sense* (London and New York, 1947).

ELMER SPRAGUE

MORE, HENRY (1614–1687), philosopher, poet, and Cambridge Platonist, was born at Grantham, Lincolnshire. His father, "a gentleman of fair estate and fortune," was a strict Calvinist but supported church and king against the Puritans. He introduced his son to Spenser's *Faerie Queene*, and Spenser's Platonism, allegorizing, and moral attitudes persist in More's own writings. At Eton, where More was educated, the religious atmosphere was latitudinarian; More abandoned the Calvinist doctrine of predestination without losing what he called "an inward sense of the divine presence." In December 1631 he entered Christ's College, Cambridge, where he was elected to a fellowship in 1639. He remained at Cambridge until his death, refusing preferments, except those he could pass on to such fellow Platonists as Edward Fowler and John Worthington. Unlike most of the Platonists he took no part in public affairs or in university administration. In *An Explanation of the Grand Mystery of Godliness* (1660) he defended what he called a "neutrality and cold indifference in public affairs."

When More entered Christ's College, it was split into three factions—the high church party, the Calvinistic Puritans, and the Medians, so called because they stood for a moderate church and had as their leader Joseph Mede, or Mead (1586–1638), author of *Clavis Apocalyptica* (1627), an allegorical interpretation of the Scriptures. More's tutor Robert Gell, whose *Remaines* were published in 1676, was a member of Mede's party; he emphasized even more strongly than Mede that salvation depended upon "good works," not on blind faith, and he shared Mede's fascination with demonology and Scriptural interpretation. More himself described Mede as an "incomparable interpreter of Prophecies," and in *The Grand Mystery of Godliness* defends his Biblical interpretations against the criticisms of Hugo Grotius.

Neoplatonism. Developing a passion for philosophy, More read widely in Aristotle and the Scholastics. However, he became impatient with their failure, as he thought, to provide a satisfactory account of the relation between God and the individual self. He therefore turned to the Neoplatonists and to mystical writings, especially the *Theologia Germanica,* an anonymous fourteenth-century mystical handbook which Luther republished in 1516. From the mystics and Neoplatonists More derived his belief that to acquire knowledge, one must first seek moral perfection and his definition of perfection as the process of becoming godlike by subduing egoism. More did not refer to Benjamin Whichcote, none of whose writings was published until just before More's death, but he told his biographer that 1637 was the date of his conversion to his "new way of thinking"; this was the year of Whichcote's appointment as Sunday lecturer at Trinity Church. More shared certain fundamental epistemological and metaphysical ideas with Ralph Cudworth. These were ultimately derived from Platonism, and how far Cudworth's formulation of them influenced More or vice versa is impossible to determine.

More's first philosophical writings were allegories in Spenser's manner, collected in 1647 as *Philosophical Poems.* They present a complicated world view in which the basic concepts of Neoplatonism are interpreted in Trinitarian terms. Christ is presented as a living demonstration that a human being can be wholly possessed by God, rather than as a Calvinistic redeemer. More's poems preach the lesson common to Cambridge Platonism that the life we live, not the creed we preach, is our path to salvation, but their obscure allegorical manner is quite remote from Whichcote's direct, epigrammatic style.

Metaphysics. In atmosphere the *Philosophical Poems* carry us back to the Renaissance. More saw Plato through the eyes of Plotinus and Plotinus through the eyes of Renaissance humanists like Marsilio Ficino, who set out with the help of allegory to Christianize Neoplatonic metaphysics. Yet on December 11, 1648, More wrote the first of four Latin letters to Descartes, in which he not only expressed the highest admiration for Descartes's work but added that Descartes's views "appear indeed to be my own—so entirely have my own thoughts run along the channels in which your fertile mind has anticipated me." Nor was this a merely transient enthusiasm. In the general preface to his *A Collection of Several Philosophical Writings* (1662), he still spoke with admiration of Descartes. Yet in the *Divine Dialogues* (1668) and even more severely in *Enchiridion Metaphysicum* (1671) More criticized "the superstitious admiration" for Descartes and alleged that his views led to atheism, a charge against which he had previously defended Descartes.

Not surprisingly, More's French critics accuse him of irresponsible fickleness. But if *Enchiridion Metaphysicum* is the first of More's writings to be officially an anti-Cartesian tract, the fact remains, as Descartes realized from the beginning but More only slowly, that More's leading ideas had always been in complete opposition to Cartesianism. The central point in More's metaphysics as it is developed in *The Immortality of the Soul* (1659) and the metaphysical sections of *Divine Dialogues* and *Enchiridion Metaphysicum* is that extension is a characteristic of all substances and not, as Descartes had argued, a peculiarity of matter. Substances fall into two classes—spirits and material objects. Spirits are physically indivisible, can penetrate both other spirits and material objects, and can initiate motion; material objects are physically divisible, impenetrable, and capable of motion only when it has been communicated to them. But both spirits and material objects are extended. There are familiar objections to such an ontology; these concern, particularly, the compatibility of the two properties of being extended and being spiritual. In meeting these objections, More began by making two logical points. The first is that since we are never acquainted with essences but only with attributes, it is no objection to the extendedness of thinking beings that we "cannot see why" a being which thinks should also be extended. The second is that the intellectual separability of the properties of being extended and being spiritual is no proof of their incompatibility.

More's opponents have to show, he argued, that it is logically impossible for anything to be extended and yet to think. Most of the arguments which are supposed to establish this impossibility depend, according to More, upon the tacit identification of extension and materiality; the rest can be met by distinguishing between two forms of extension—metaphysical and physical. Metaphysical extension—pure space—is eternal, infinite, physically indivisible; physical extensions are finite, physically divisible, mutable. We can break up a particular cylinder, and we can easily imagine it not to exist, but we cannot take a piece out of space or imagine it not to exist. These properties it shares with God; indeed, space is an "obscure representation of the essence or essential presence of the divine being."

More came to see in Descartes the leader of what he calls the nullibists, who deny extension to spirits. And although Descartes had set out to defend God and immortality—this was one main reason why More approved of him—More finally concluded that nullibism is atheistic in tendency. For More the essential feature of the soul is that it initiates movement. To do this, however, it must be where body is. This is possible because unlike material objects spirits can penetrate both other spirits and material objects, contracting or expanding like Newton's "aether," as the occasion makes necessary. Thus, God, an individual mind, and a material object can all be present in the one place without losing their independence as substances. Spirit can be regarded, More argued, as a sort of fourth dimension; a body which contains a spirit has a certain "spissitude," or density of substances.

More's criticism of mechanical explanation is along the same general lines. At first, he had welcomed Descartes's mechanical explanations; by carrying ingenuity, so More thought, as far as it could be carried, they made it clear just what the limits of mechanical explanation were. But his conclusion is that mechanical explanation is never possible and that to suppose otherwise leads to atheism. (The emergence of Spinoza from the Cartesian school encouraged More in this belief.)

A material object, he said, is nothing but a "congeries of physical monads"—that is, a collection of atomic particles. To explain how these particles are held together in solid objects, we have to introduce a nonmaterial, although spatial, spiritual agent. Equally, he argued, gravity is inexplicable in mechanical terms; mechanics—he meant, of course, Cartesian mechanics—cannot explain why a bullet once fired from a gun should ever return to the earth's surface. Even more obviously, the behavior of living organisms cannot be derived from a collection of particles.

Indeed, in order to explain any natural process, we have to refer to spirit as something additional to material particles; spirits are the true cause of all activity. This does not mean that all activity is the work of conscious rational beings. Spirit exists at various levels; "seminal forms," which are neither sensitive nor rational but are still capable of initiating motion, are responsible for actions at a level lower than animal feeling.

Religion and ethics. More's metaphysical theories are not worked out in detail. His main interests, indeed, were religious rather than metaphysical: to defend Christianity against its three main enemies—namely, atheists, Roman Catholics, and "enthusiasts." *An Antidote Against Atheism* (1653) reformulates the Ontological Argument but mainly relies upon anecdotes about animals to establish an Argument from Design and upon anecdotes about witches and apparitions to establish that spiritual forces are at work in the world. *Conjectura Cabbalistica* (1653), with the aid of the Jewish cabala, discerns Platonism and Cartesianism in Genesis; indeed, More expressed his regret that he had ever wasted his time on philosophy seeing that all fundamental truths are contained in the Bible. *A Brief Discourse of the Nature, Causes, Kinds and Cure of Enthusiasm* (1656) is directed against "enthusiasm," defined as "a full but false persuasion in a man that he is inspired." More found the origin of enthusiasm in "melancholy"—that is, in a manic–depressive constitution. *The Grand Mystery of Godliness* defends the Cambridge Platonist concept of religion against Calvinists, atheists, and Roman Catholics alike; *An Antidote Against Idolatry* (1674) attacks Roman Catholics. More had a special animosity against Quakers which increased in intensity when his disciple and admirer Anne Finch, Lady Conway, at whose home in Ragley, Warwickshire, he had been a frequent guest, became a convert to Quakerism.

More's *Enchiridion Ethicum* (1667), translated into English by Edward Southwell in 1690 with the appropriate title *An Account of Virtue*, was the most popular of More's writings in his own time but has since been neglected. It can be most succinctly described as a Christian version of Aristotle's *Nicomachean Ethics*, although the detail is influenced by Descartes's account of the passions and by mathematical ideals. (More set out a number of "moral axioms," which incorporate an ethical calculus.) Virtue, More argued, consists in pursuing what seems to be in accordance with right reason, but both our capacity to discover what actions accord with reason and our inclination toward those actions flow from a special "boniform" faculty. Reason itself cannot incite action; virtuous action

can be instigated only by the passional side of our nature. The ultimate ground of all virtue is intellectual love. Thus, More hoped to weld the Christian doctrine of love and the Aristotelian doctrine of intellectual activity into a single ethical system.

Influence. More devoted the last seven years of his life to translating his English works into Latin in the hope of attracting wider interest on the Continent. They caught the attention of Leibniz, but although he took an occasional phrase from More, he was interested in him mainly as a representative of the sort of view he particularly wished to avoid. In fact, More, the only one of the Cambridge Platonists to publish at all extensively, quite failed in what he conceived as his main task—to halt the advance of the mechanical world view. More's metaphysics, however, had a considerable influence on Newton even if mathematicians, not metaphysicians, were Newton's principal masters. Newton did not refer explicitly to More—the Cambridge group almost never referred to one another—but the resemblances are conspicuous. Newton was taught mathematics at Grantham, More's birthplace, by a former pupil of More's; Newton's correspondence reveals that he and More stood close to one another.

Works by More

More's *Philosophical Poems* are reprinted in Alexander Balloch Grosart, *The Complete Poems of Henry More* (Blackburn, 1878). Geoffrey Bullough, *Philosophical Poems of Henry More* (Manchester, 1931), is a selection with a valuable introduction and notes. More's main philosophical writings are included in *A Collection of Several Philosophical Writings* (London, 1662) and his theological writings in *Theological Works* (London, 1708); the Latin version, *Opera Omnia* (London, 1675–1679), contains in addition a number of controversial pamphlets. Sections of the *Enchiridion Metaphysicum* were translated by Joseph Glanvill in his *Saducismus Triumphatus* (London, 1681) and are included in Flora Isabel MacKinnon, *Philosophical Writings of Henry More* (New York, 1925), with a useful bibliography and expository essays. Edward Southwell's translation of *Enchiridion Ethicum* has been reprinted by the Facsimile Text Society (New York, 1930). The correspondence with Descartes is partly translated by Leonora D. Cohen in *Annals of Science,* Vol. 1, No. 1 (1936), 48–61, and is included in Geneviève (Rodis-) Lewis, *Correspondance avec Arnaud et Morus* (Paris, 1953).

Works on More

For works on More see Bibliography under CAMBRIDGE PLATONISTS. See also Richard Ward, *The Life of Dr. H. More* (London, 1710); M. F. Howard has edited this life, but his introduction is not reliable (London, 1911). See also Marjorie Nicolson, ed., *The Conway Letters* (London, 1930), and Paul Russell Anderson, *Science in Defense of Liberal Religion* (New York and London, 1933). For More's relation to Newton see Edwin Arthur Burtt, *The Metaphysical Foundations of Modern Physical Science* (London, 1925; rev. ed., 1950), and Alexandre Koyré, *From the Closed World to the Infinite Universe* (Baltimore, Md., 1957). On the opposite side see Edward William Strong, *Procedures and Metaphysics* (Berkeley, Calif., 1936), and Stephen Edelston Toulmin, "Criticism in the History of Science: Newton on Absolute Space, Time and Motion," in *Philosophical Review,* Vol. 68, No. 1 (1959), 1–30, and No. 2 (1959), 203–228.

JOHN PASSMORE

MORE, THOMAS (1478–1535). Sir Thomas More, later canonized St. Thomas More, was a lawyer and statesman rather than a philosopher. More was born the son of a London lawyer who later became a judge. He was educated at

St. Anthony's School and was appointed a page in the household of Archbishop (later Cardinal) Morton, who sent him to Canterbury Hall, Oxford, in the early 1490s. More left without a degree to study at New Inn and Lincoln's Inn in London. His lectures dealt not only with law but also with St. Augustine's *City of God*. He early composed various English poems and Latin epigrams that were not printed for years. However, a Latin translation of four Greek dialogues of Lucian appeared in 1506, and an English translation of the Latin life of his model, Giovanni Pico della Mirandola, in 1510. Increasingly involved in public affairs, More became a member of Parliament in 1504, beginning the career that led to the well-known events of his chancellorship and his martyrdom. By the time of the *Utopia* (1516), he had long since mastered Greek and enjoyed the friendship of such humanists as Erasmus, Thomas Linacre, William Grocyn, John Colet, Cuthbert Tunstall, and St. John Fisher.

Philosophical orientation. With respect to his philosophy, Thomas More belonged very much to the early or Erasmian period of the English Renaissance in his emotional and intellectual attitudes—toleration of eclecticism, search for simplicity, stress on ethics, return to Greek sources, and desire for reform: social, political, educational, religious, and philosophical. These traits appear not only in his highly imaginative and durably significant creation, *Utopia*, but also in his most pertinent pronouncements in real life. The latter may be divided into two philosophical periods, roughly separated by the year 1521, the year of publication of Henry VIII's *Defense of the Seven Sacraments* (*Assertio Septem Sacramentorum*), which More undertook to defend by his pseudonymous diatribe (1523) against Luther's strictures.

During his first period, in his justly famous letters to Martin Dorp (1515), to the University of Oxford (1518), and to a monk (1519–1520), More opted for a simplified logic, the study of all Aristotle's works in Greek with their classical Greek commentaries, and the mastery of the Greek New Testament and Greek Fathers as well as the pagan classics in the original language. He praised the Aristotelian paraphrases of Jacques Lefèvre d'Étaples and, in a letter to Erasmus (May 26, 1520), expressed complete agreement with Juan Luis Vives' *False Dialecticians* (*Pseudodialectici*). His attack on contemporary Schoolmen centered on their preoccupation with logic, the universals, and a mere fragment of the Aristotelian corpus.

In his second, controversial period, More rose to the defense of Thomas Aquinas and the scholastic theologians, whose doctrine he showed to agree with that of the earlier church. However, since the interest of these works, even of *A Dialogue of Comfort against Tribulation* (1534), is almost entirely theological, there is no need to dwell on them, except to point out that he held the common scholastic views on the mutual relationship, harmony, and assistance between reason and revelation, with philosophy as the propaedeutic to theology and as the handmaid of theology. This synthesis appears in a fundamental form even on the island of Utopia, where ethical norms are bolstered by religious truths and where the true religion can prevail in an atmosphere of free and calm reasoning.

"Utopia." Since *Utopia* is More's major, or at least most influential, writing, its philosophical elements will be discussed in detail.

Background. Renaissance thinkers usually held that there were four great philosophical schools: Platonism, Aristotelianism, Stoicism, and Epicureanism, which differed mainly according to their opinions of the *summum bonum*. The Christianization of Aristotle was accomplished in the thirteenth and fourteenth centuries by the Schoolmen, and that of Plato in the fifteenth century by Marsilio Ficino and other humanists. Stoicism had found expression in almost boundless humanistic admiration for the writings of Seneca and especially Cicero before reaching definite formulation later in the Christian Stoicism of Justus Lipsius. It was therefore inevitable that humanistic attempts, if only rhetorical ones, should be made to Christianize Epicurus, too. The latter's rehabilitation had been much accelerated in the early fifteenth century by Ambrogio Traversari's Latin translation of his life by Diogenes Laërtius. Lorenzo Valla had set forth Epicurus' doctrine favorably in *De Voluptate ac de Vero Bono* (*Pleasure and the True Good*). Finally Erasmus undertook his thorough baptism in *De Contemptu Mundi* (*The Contempt of the World*, written c. 1490) and the colloquy *The Epicurean* (published 1533). In both these works, Erasmus manipulated the concept of pleasure and the principles of selection to establish a Christian Epicureanism.

Epicureanism in "Utopia." More's main sources for classical Epicureanism were undoubtedly the *Lives* of Diogenes Laërtius and the *De Finibus* of Cicero, with minor borrowings from Seneca, Quintilian, Lucian, and Aulus Gellius. The "Christian" modifications already introduced by such humanists as Lorenzo Valla and Erasmus should not be minimized. The preoccupation of Renaissance men with the problem of pleasure is evident from the many humanistic treatments of the subject, including that by Ficino. Consequently Epicurus and Epicureanism are here viewed not according to their historical reality but according to the light in which they appeared to Thomas More through his reading and conversation.

In spite of the great to-do in the *Utopia* about the philosophy of pleasure and in spite of the deliberate but superficial rejection of Stoicism, the emphasis on virtue and virtuous living is disproportionate, even extraordinary, and therefore suspicious. This respect for Stoicism also becomes explicit in the stress on the guidance of nature, the assumed existence of natural law, and the natural community of mankind.

There are several contacts between Utopian and Epicurean hedonism. The most evident, naturally, is the exaltation of pleasure as the *summum bonum*, to which all human activities, including the operations of the virtues, are directed and subordinated. But the term "pleasure" (*voluptas*) is so manipulated in the *Utopia* that it embraces everything from scratching an itch to enjoying eternal bliss with God. Like Epicurus, the Utopians hold to both kinds of pleasure: pleasure as a state and pleasure as motion. Hence health for them is a true pleasure. Like Epicurus, they belittle neither the joy arising from conferral of a benefit, nor the testimony of a good conscience as the reward for just deeds, nor the importance of mental pleasures. There is a common emphasis with Epicúrus on the simple life, which in Utopia leads to the ridicule of false, unnatural delight in fine clothing, noble ancestry, glittering jewelry, gold and silver, gambling, and hunting. Perhaps the most important connection is the enunciation of the principles of selection; the single positive criterion is that a pleasure be natural—a criterion recognized as so obscure that it is delimited by three negative norms: that no pain follow the pleasure chosen, that no greater pleasure be lost, and that no social harm result.

Divergences from classical Epicureanism. The departures from the postulates of classical Epicureanism are so radical that the Utopian philosophy in action can be labeled Epicurean, or even hedonistic, only in the broadest sense. For example, good Utopians must believe in the providence of God, the immortality of man's soul, and divine retribution in a future life. These Utopian principles are taken not from Epicurus but from More's great favorite, Plato, especially his *Laws.* Utopian ascetics, with their hope of reward in a future life, would be ridiculous to Epicurus. The Platonic origin of Utopian communism also is evident, for Epicurus thought that the holding of property in common by friends implied mutual mistrust. Minor points of divergence are the emphasis upon marriage (in contrast with its disapproval by Epicurus in spite of his traditional devotion to his parents), upon euthanasia (in comparison with Epicurus' denial of suicide even to the blind), and upon learning (Epicurus urged his disciples to fly from learning in the swiftest ship available). Utopians love their gardens, but for practical rather than philosophical purposes, so that, surprisingly, no reference is made in *Utopia* to the connection between Epicurus and gardens.

Raphael Hythlodaeus. The unconscious pull of Platonism and Stoicism, not to mention Christianity, is too great to allow a full-fledged Epicureanism in Utopia. This is perfectly consistent, however, with the engrossing character of the main narrator, Raphael Hythlodaeus, who is a philosopher by nature and profession and interjects mild expressions of disapproval of Utopian hedonism. He is unattached: his only commitment is to freedom, truth, and justice. Negligent in dress, he has divested himself of the cares of riches by giving his patrimony to his relatives. He now lives as he pleases (according to Cicero's definition of freedom), and he must speak his mind openly. In spite of being accused of too great speculativeness and idealism by Thomas More, he travels and searches for something quite practical: the good state and the good citizen. In this emphasis on the useful, and in his return to the sources (especially the Greek), Hythlodaeus is at one with the early English, as well as the northern, Renaissance. In his chosen field of philosophy, he finds nothing of value in Latin except Seneca and Cicero. But he is far from being narrow. The great books in Greek that he carries with him include Plato and Plutarch, as well as Aristotle and Theophrastus, dramatists, poets, historians—and Lucian. Devotion to Lucian undoubtedly helped to mark More's philosophical character as his friends saw him—as "another laughing Democritus." More's emphasis upon the Greek

sources in medicine (Galen and Hippocrates) and science (Aristotle's *Meteorology*) makes him, in a sense, an unwitting scientific reactionary.

Plato's influence. Of all the Greek authors, Plato is cited most frequently in the *Utopia* proper and in its preliminary materials. This is hardly surprising, since its true title may be translated as *The Best Order of Society (De Optimo Reipublicae Statu).* More is indebted, however, as much to Plato's *Laws* as to his *Republic.* His obvious but modified borrowings from Plato are dialogic form, but with a monologue in Book II; communism, which he broadens to embrace a whole nation, not merely an élite class; pre-eminence of learning, with transformation of the philosopher-king into the scholar-governor; the almost complete equality of men and women; and the connections between goodness and religion. The differences are radical: Utopia is a casteless democracy, not an aristocracy; and the family, not a ruling class with common wives and children, is the basic social and political unit. It is significant that More also briefly introduces the Aristotelian objections to communism of property.

Pleasure and the best society. It is a tribute to More's rhetoric (not philosophy) that the unwary reader is left under the impression that the Utopians espouse thoroughgoing hedonism. But this does not involve merely a humanistic *jeu d'esprit* or even a literary *tour de force,* for pleasure is related intimately to the main subject of the *Utopia,* the best society. The best society is one whose aim is the temporal well-being or happiness—or pleasure, as defined and described in Utopian terms—of all the citizens, not only of the rich or of the well-born. All are to share equally and equitably in all the good things—or pleasures—of this life and this world: food, clothes, houses, work, play, sleep, and education. More bridges the gap between Utopian philosophy and Utopian communism by the use of the basically Aristotelian phrase "the matter of pleasure" (*materia voluptatis*). Vital commodities (food, clothing, housing) constitute the pleasurable *matter,* which must be determined by a *form* (either private ownership or common possession). The Utopians have chosen communism, not private property, to bring the greatest pleasure to the whole nation. Only in this way will justice be introduced into an unjust society. In this at least theoretical espousal of communism, More agreed with Erasmus and many fellow humanists.

Weaknesses. On the debit side of the *Utopia* might be listed the deliberately static nature of this ideal society and the failure to recognize the individual person and his basic instincts, liberties, and even imperfections. The removal of all struggle and all insecurity would logically and psychologically lead· to the prayer: "Give me something to desire."

Influence. The major influence of the *Utopia* lies not in its philosophic hedonism, with its concomitant communism, but in its establishment of a pattern for ideal commonwealths. Historically the type proliferated into a thousand different forms that can be found discussed in bibliographies and commentaries. In particular, the *Utopia* itself set an example for what might be termed the philosophical utopia that continued well into the eighteenth century. The most notable productions are Bacon's *New Atlantis*, Campanella's *City of the Sun*, and Johnson's *Rasselas*.

Bibliography

The best modern edition of More's Latin and English writings will be the Yale edition: *The Complete Works of St. Thomas More*, R. S. Sylvester, executive ed. (New Haven, 1963——), projected in 14 volumes. Vol. IV, *Utopia* (New Haven, 1965), is edited by Edward Surtz and J. H. Hexter. Also see the Selected Works edition (New Haven, 1961——), planned in seven volumes, of which two have appeared: *Selected Letters*, E. F. Rogers, ed. (1961), and *Utopia*, Edward Surtz, ed. (1964). E. F. Rogers had previously edited More's *Correspondence* (Princeton, N.J., 1947). Only the first two volumes of a contemplated seven-volume modern version of More's *English Works* (1557), W. E. Campbell, ed., were issued (London, 1927–1931).

More's best biographers are the earliest: William Roper, *The Lyfe of Sir Thomas Moore*, E. V. Hitchcock, ed. (London, 1935); and Nicholas Harpsfield, *The life and death of Sʳ Thomas Moore*, E. V. Hitchcock and R. W. Chambers, eds. (London, 1932). The best modern life is still R. W. Chambers, *Thomas More* (London, 1935), to be supplemented by E. E. Reynolds, *Saint Thomas More* (London, 1953).

Bibliographical data can be found in *St. Thomas More: A Preliminary Bibliography . . . to the Year 1750*, compiled by R. W. Gibson, with a bibliography of Utopiana compiled by R. W. Gibson and J. M. Patrick (New Haven, 1961). Also see F. and M. P. Sullivan, *Moreana, 1478–1945* (Kansas City, Mo., 1945). In 1963, the international Amici Thomae Mori began publication of *Moreana: Bulletin Thomas More* (Angers).

Illuminating studies of the background can be found in W. E. Campbell, *Erasmus, Tyndale, and More* (London, 1949); Fritz Caspari, *Humanism and the Social Order in Tudor England* (Chicago, 1954); Pearl Hogrefe, *The Sir Thomas More Circle* (Urbana, Ill., 1959); R. P. Adams, *The Better Part of Valor: More, Erasmus, Colet, and Vives on Humanism, War, and Peace* (Seattle, 1962); and especially G. Marc'hadour, *L'Univers de Thomas More* (Paris, 1963), corrected and supplemented currently in *Moreana*.

The principal interpretations of *Utopia* are those by Karl Kautsky, *Thomas More and His Utopia* (1888), translated by H. J. Stenning (reprinted New York, 1959); H. W. Donner, *Introduction to Utopia* (London, 1945); Russell Ames, *Citizen Thomas More and His Utopia* (Princeton, N.J., 1949); J. H. Hexter, *More's "Utopia": The Biography of an Idea* (Princeton, N.J., 1952); Edward Surtz, *The Praise of Pleasure: Philosophy, Education, and Communism in More's "Utopia"* (Cambridge, Mass., 1957); and Edward Surtz, *The Praise of Wisdom: A Commentary on the Religious and Moral Problems and Backgrounds of St. Thomas More's "Utopia"* (Chicago, 1957).

The fate of the utopia as a literary form can be followed in Richard Gerber, *Utopian Fantasy* (London, 1955); J. O. Hertzler, *The History of Utopian Thought* (New York, 1923); and G. R. Negley and J. M. Patrick, eds., *The Quest for Utopia* (New York, 1952).

EDWARD SURTZ, S.J.

MORGAN, AUGUSTUS DE. See DE MORGAN, AUGUSTUS.

MORGAN, C. LLOYD (1852–1936), English biologist and philosopher, was born in London. His early education "was almost exclusively literary," but he later became attracted to scientific studies, attended the Royal School of Mines, and received a diploma in metallurgy. His deepest interest, however, was in the bearing of science on philosophical issues. This interest was given encouragement and direction by T. H. Huxley, under whom he studied biology. Henceforth, Morgan's vocation was to be that of

an investigator of "borderland problems of life and mind" and the expositor of a philosophy of "emergent evolution." After teaching for five years at a small college near Cape Town, South Africa, he was appointed in 1884 to the chair of geology and zoology at University College, Bristol. When the college received a university charter in 1909, Morgan agreed to serve temporarily as its first vice-chancellor. At his own request, however, he resigned the next year and resumed his chair, now designated the chair of psychology and ethics. He retired in 1919. During his career at Bristol Morgan devoted himself to the study of animal psychology and published such books as *Animal Life and Intelligence; Habit and Instinct; Animal Behavior;* and *Instinct and Experience*.

When he was elected a fellow of the Royal Society in 1899, he became the first person to be thus honored for scientific work in psychology. After his retirement he was invited to deliver the Gifford lectures and used the occasion to expound his philosophical ideas, which subsequently appeared in *Emergent Evolution* and *Life, Mind, and Spirit*. Two other works, *Mind at the Crossways* and *The Emergence of Novelty*, contain elaborations of his position.

Morgan's psychological studies had a Darwinian background. Accepting the view that evolution is a continuous process, he sought to trace the development of mental characteristics in the world of living things. The focal point of his investigations was the behavior of those organisms which showed some capacity to learn from experience. He contended that the rudiments of intelligence are to be found wherever learning results from "the method of trial and error"—a phrase which he coined in the 1894. Much of his experimental work was designed to show how this method is employed, even by relatively simple forms of life. Unlike his predecessors in animal psychology, Morgan was alert to the dangers of using casual reports of animal behavior, especially reports from untrained observers. He urged the importance of a methodological "law of parsimony," according to which we should never interpret what an animal does as the outcome of a higher psychical power if the action "can be interpreted as the outcome of the exercise of a power which stands lower in the psychological scale." Morgan's experiments usually were not strictly laboratory ones but involved artificially produced situations in the natural habitat of animals. His accurate and detailed observations of their behavior in these situations, however, gave comparative psychology a new scientific status.

The conceptual background of Morgan's work was neither mechanistic nor finalistic. He rejected the view that biological processes are to be understood in physicochemical terms and that physiology can give an adequate account of animal behavior. Radical behaviorism was likewise unacceptable to him. On the other hand, he rejected the view that teleology is operative throughout the living world and that even reflex action and instinctive responses must be explained teleologically.

In *Instinct and Experience* Morgan criticized Bergson's teleological speculations. Morgan's own position, which he described as "naturalism," was that in all behavior there occurs an "unrestricted concomitance" of physical and psychical events. Hence, each behavior episode is susceptible of interpretation in both physiological and psychological terms. There are two stories to be told, each throwing light on the other, "but neither story as such *makes* the other what it is."

Philosophically, Morgan adopted the hypothesis that the twofold story was really about *one* natural order of events. Moreover, that one order of events has a progressive natural history designated by the word "evolution." An adequate description of this process requires us to recognize that evolution has not been uniformly continuous, as Darwin believed, but has involved from time to time major discontinuities or "critical turning points." These turning points are marked by the abrupt appearance of certain phenomena which Morgan called "emergents," a term used by G. H. Lewes in 1874. An emergent (1) supervenes upon what already exists, (2) arises out of what already exists, (3) is something genuinely new in the history of the universe, (4) occurs in a manner that is unpredictable in principle since it conforms to no general laws, and (5) cannot be naturalistically explained but must be accepted "with natural piety." The successive emergents in the panorama of evolution mark stages of progress from lower to higher. Hence, Morgan followed Alexander in picturing the totality of nature as "a pyramidal scheme."

The full significance of emergent evolution cannot be grasped, however, as long as one remains at the level of "a philosophy based on the procedure sanctioned by the progress of scientific thought." It was essential, Morgan thought, to construct a metaphysical system within which the naturalistic version of evolution could be set. This system would formulate certain fundamental concepts and presuppositions by whose aid an "ultimate explanation" of the evolutionary process could be given. Nothing affirmed in this constructive scheme was to be at variance with science, but it would "complete the otherwise incomplete delivery of strictly scientific thought."

A necessary basic presupposition of the system Morgan proposed was the existence of a physical world that "is nowise dependent on being perceived or thought of by any human or sub-human mind." Since no conclusive proof of this contention had ever been given, it was simply "accepted under acknowledgment." Morgan then elaborated a psychophysiologically oriented theory of how organisms perceive the external world. Physical events exert an "advenient influence" on the sense receptors of organisms. By virtue of their psychical power, the organisms respond by referring the signs arising within the psychophysical system to regions of physical space in a process which Morgan called "projicient reference." The result is an emergent object correlated with the external event in such a way as to be biologically useful to the organism.

Morgan's second presupposition was that the pyramid of emergent evolution is a hierarchy of kinds of relatedness. Four basic concepts are needed to unfold its consequences—stuff, substance, quality, and property. The ultimate stuff consists of psychophysical events, and the mode of their relatedness in a given system is that system's substance. Each system has intrinsic qualities grounded in its substance and extrinsic properties grounded in its relation to other systems. Besides the emergents there are

"resultants," or phenomena that are repetitive, predictable, and the source of quantitative continuity. Emergence generates progress in continuity, but through resultants there is continuity in progress.

The third presupposition that Morgan acknowledged was the universal correlation of physical and psychical events. He recognized a similarity between his system and that of Spinoza in this respect, yet Morgan's view that "mind" is "a quality emergent at a high level of evolutionary advance" would have been quite unacceptable, or possibly unintelligible, to Spinoza. Even that from which mind in this sense emerges—the pervasive psychical correlate—is scarcely to be compared with a Spinozistic attribute.

The last presupposition introduced by Morgan affirmed that a directing activity, otherwise called "spirit" or "God," is manifested everywhere. Thus, "the whole course of events subsumed under evolution is the expression of God's purpose," which embraces all that has been and all that will be brought about in the course of evolutionary advance. This postulate can be neither proved nor disproved but only adopted to satisfy the need for an ultimate explanation of things.

Morgan's philosophy of evolution gave wide currency to the idea of emergence. Yet when compared with later discussions, his treatment of the idea lacks precision. He was not a close reasoner, and his speculative scheme was much less carefully worked out than that of Alexander, to whom he was indebted. A hostile critic might well question Morgan's policy of "acknowledging," rather than arguing for, important principles in his system. And, although he opposed Darwinism by insisting that evolution is "jumpy" and not continuous, each jump is, in Morgan's view of evolution, a mystery, unexplained and inexplicable except, perhaps, to God.

Works by Morgan

Animal Life and Intelligence. London, 1890.
An Introduction to Comparative Psychology. London, 1894.
Habit and Instinct. London and New York, 1896.
Animal Behaviour. London, 1900.
Instinct and Experience. London and New York, 1912.
Emergent Evolution. London, 1923.
Life, Mind, and Spirit. London, 1926.
Mind at the Crossways. London, 1929.
The Animal Mind. London and New York, 1930.
The Emergence of Novelty. London, 1933.

Works on Morgan

McDougall, William, *Modern Materialism and Emergent Evolution.* London, 1929.
MacKinnon, Flora I., "The Meaning of 'Emergent' in Lloyd Morgan's 'Emergent Evolution.'" *Mind*, Vol. 33 (1924), 311–315.

T. A. GOUDGE

MORGAN, LEWIS HENRY (1818–1881), American anthropologist and social philosopher. After graduating from Union College in 1840, Morgan practiced law in Rochester, N.Y., from 1844 to 1864, but he devoted much of his time to anthropological research, which eventually became his exclusive interest. One of the most celebrated American scholars of his time, Morgan was elected a member of the National Academy of Sciences in 1875 and president of the American Association for the Advancement of Science in 1879. The results of his investigations into the life of various Indian tribes appeared in his *League of the Ho-dé-no-sau-nee or Iroquois* (Rochester, N.Y., 1851) and his later work, *Systems of Consanguinity and Affinity* (Washington, D.C., 1871); these two books were hailed as pioneering achievements of the first order in the study of kinship systems by even the most outspoken of his critics.

Morgan's aim was not merely to describe how different civilizations had evolved; he wished to elicit from their history a general pattern of institutional progress. In his most ambitious work, *Ancient Society* (New York, 1877), Morgan sought to establish that human history falls into three main stages—savagery, barbarism, and civilization—and that each stage reflects a close correlation between economic and cultural achievements. Savagery was the period before pottery; barbarism was the ceramic era; civilization began with writing and the phonetic alphabet. The first two periods are further subdivided, and each subperiod is defined in terms of its characteristic technological innovations. The discovery of fire and the beginning of fishing, for example, are characteristic of the second subperiod of savagery, the invention of the bow and arrow of its third subperiod.

Although Morgan shared the view of his Swiss contemporary and fellow anthropologist Johann Jakob Bachofen that society had emerged from a state of primitive communism and also accepted the Bachofen hypothesis of matrilineal descent, he had little interest in ancient myths and religions. His principal attention was focused on technological factors, kinship systems, and property systems, and their relations to social and political institutions. In spite of gaps and distortions, Morgan's account of the growth of civilization has been considered by so severe a critic of his ethnological theories as Robert H. Lowie to be a comprehensive scheme of cultural wholes far beyond anything attempted up to that time. Lowie has written, "Morgan's *Ancient Society* was a synthesis of sociological material that for the first time brought together material on Australian and American natives, on ancient Greece and Rome; and all this in an orderly arrangement prescribed by an evolutionary doctrine" (*The History of Ethnological Theory*, London, 1937, p. 56).

Moreover, *Ancient Society* speaks for a distinct social philosophy and philosophy of history. The collation and comparison of human institutions, inventions, and discoveries convinced Morgan of mankind's unity of origin, of the similarity of human wants in different societies at comparable stages of advancement, and of the uniformity in the operations of the human mind in similar conditions of society. He formed the view that the human race was "one in source, one in experience and one in progress" (*Ancient Society*, p. vi). The problem that preoccupied Morgan in his historical researches was the existence of social and economic inequality. He could not conceive that "a mere property career" was the final destiny of mankind. Man's obsession with private property, he felt, was only a transient stage of human civilization. For if it was not, it was bound to lead to society's self-destruction. If progress was to be the law of the future as it had been of the past, prop-

erty would have to be diffused and if necessary controlled, so that "democracy in government, brotherhood in society, equality in rights and privileges, and universal education" would foreshadow the next higher plane of society, "to which experience, intelligence and knowledge are steadily tending" (*Ancient Society*, p. 552).

Morgan recognized that civilization could be aggressive as well as progressive. But his theory of social evolution has nothing in common with such imperialist notions as Kipling's concept of the white man's burden. Progress, Morgan insisted, echoing Herder, is inherent in all cultures, civilized or not, and each has to advance along its own lines. Culture is a process, not an administrative imposition.

Although Morgan's theories were invoked by Marx and by Engels (notably in his *Origin of the Family, Private Property and the State*) in support of their interpretation of history, Morgan's social message only bears superficial similarities with Marxist doctrines. Nonetheless, the optimistic flavor of his evolutionism had a powerful appeal to social reformers. At the same time this very quality made it suspect to the uncommitted social scientist.

Additional Works by Morgan

Diffusion Against Centralization. Rochester, N.Y., 1852.
The American Beaver and His Works. Philadelphia, 1868.
Houses and House Life of the American Aborigines. Washington, D.C., 1881.
Pioneers in American Anthropology: The Bandelier–Morgan Letters, Leslie A. White, ed. Albuquerque, N.M., 1940.

Works on Morgan

Childe, V. Gordon, *Social Evolution.* New York, 1951.
Lowie, Robert H., "Evolution in Cultural Anthropology." *American Anthropologist,* Vol. 48 (1946), 223–233.
Lowie, Robert H., *The History of Ethnological Theory.* London, 1937.
Resek, Carl, *Lewis Henry Morgan, American Scholar,* Chicago, 1960. Contains a full bibliography.
Stern, Bernhard J., *Lewis Henry Morgan, Social Evolutionist.* Chicago, 1931.
White, Leslie A., "Evolutionism in Cultural Anthropology." *American Anthropologist,* Vol. 53 (1951), 11–18.
White, Leslie A., "Morgan's Attitude toward Religion and Science." *American Anthropologist,* Vol. 46 (1944), 218–230.

FREDERICK M. BARNARD

MORGAN, THOMAS (d. 1743), Welsh deist, dissenting minister, doctor of medicine, freethinker, and religious controversialist, was born of a poor family but received a free education from the Reverend John Moore, a dissenter. Morgan was ordained in 1714 and became minister of Burton two years later and subsequently of Marlborough; in 1720 he was dismissed from this last post for his growing unorthodoxy. He then took up the study of medicine and produced several books on that subject—*Philosophical Principles of Medicine* (1725), *The Mechanical Practice of Physic* (1735), *Letter to Dr. Cheyne in defence of the "Mechanical Practice"* (1738).

Morgan is chiefly remembered, however, for his deistical tracts, or "Christian deistical," as he preferred to call them, in which he described himself as "M.D. and Moral Philosopher." *The Moral Philosopher, in a Dialogue be-*

tween Philalethes, a Christian Deist, and Theophanes, a Christian Jew (1737) is his major work. Controversy produced two further works under the same title, the second of 1739, subtitled "Being a farther Vindication of Moral Truth and Reason," and the third of 1740, subtitled "Superstition inconsistent with Theocracy." In 1741 he published *A Vindication of the Moral Philosopher; Against the False Accusations, Insults, and Personal Abuses, of Samuel Chandler, Late Bookseller and Minister of the Gospel.*

In general, Morgan was a rationalist espousing the five Common Notions of Lord Herbert of Cherbury. He was also one of the pioneers of historical criticism of the Bible, particularly of the Pentateuch, and was considerably influenced by John Toland and to some extent by Thomas Chubb. The latter's advocacy of free will, however, he strongly attacked in 1727 in *A Letter to Mr. Thomas Chubb, occasioned by his "Vindication of Human Nature"* and in 1728 in *A Defence of Natural and Revealed Religion.*

Morgan believed in the corruption of human nature and defended suicide for the "weary or satiated with living." His criticism of the Scriptures centered on the fact that so many different interpretations are possible and are accepted by so many different and sincere believers. Traditional religion, therefore, is not infallible but only probable, as is all history. Priestcraft, which instituted superstition, enthusiasm, and finally persecution, is the culprit for the erroneous notion of the infallibility of a catholic church. Reason and tolerance are the only cures.

Bibliography

Additional works by Morgan include *A Collection of Tracts . . . occasioned by the late Trinitarian Controversy* (1725); *A Philosophical Dissertation upon Death. Composed For the Consolation of the Unhappy* (1732); *The History of Joseph Considered . . . by Philalethes* (1744). See also Sir Leslie Stephen's *History of English Thought in the Eighteenth Century* (London, 1876; the paperback edition, 2 vols., New York, 1963, follows the revised edition of 1902), and the general bibliography under DEISM.

ERNEST CAMPBELL MOSSNER

MOSCA, GAETANO (1858–1941), Italian legal and political theorist and statesman. Mosca was born in Palermo. He was one of several social theorists, including Vilfredo Pareto and Robert Michels, who gave currency to the conception of ruling elites and their circulation as being the basic characteristic of politically organized societies. Mosca outlined his conception in *Sulla teorica dei governi e sul governo parlamentare* and elaborated it in his major work, *Elementi di scienza politica*, first published in 1895 and considerably expanded in the third edition, which appeared in 1923 (translated as *The Ruling Class*).

The *Elementi* ranges over a large number of problems in the philosophy of history and in the analysis of political organization and development. Mosca speculated about the stages of political and social development, the types of political and social systems, the role of moral forces and religions in political organization and change, the function of international and civil wars, the causes and types of revolutions, race and nationality, and the causal significance of economic factors. However, the notion of the "political class," or "ruling class," is central to the *Elementi.*

Mosca asserted that every politically organized society of any degree of complexity is characterized by the existence of an organized minority that rules and a majority that is ruled. He rejected the Marxist position that the ruling class always derives from the organization of the economy. He held that in different types of societies, different qualities and functions characterize the members of the ruling class. In certain societies, warriors occupy a central role within the ruling class; in others, economic functions are important in determining membership; and still other societies have been characterized by a hereditary ruling class. In modern societies an important section of the ruling class is always the bureaucracy, the body of salaried officials professionally entrusted with the administration of the machinery of political, economic, and social life. (Mosca was particularly interested in the emergence of modern bureaucratic states and treated bureaucratic societies as one of the chief social types.)

It appears that Mosca loosely identified the ruling class with those who occupy the controlling or governing positions within the political organization of society. At times, however, he spoke as if the ruling class were a multiplicity of political, social, and economic elites, as when he wrote, for example, that "below the highest stratum of the ruling class there is, even in autocratic systems, another that is much more numerous and comprises all the capacities for leadership in the country." Without a ruling class, Mosca claimed, all forms of social organization would be impossible. He added that the democratic tendency—the tendency to replenish ruling classes from below—"is constantly at work with greater or less intensity in all human societies." Mosca, unlike Marx, did not think of classes as necessarily conflicting social forces; nor did he think of the ruling class as always imposing its will on, and maintaining its distinctive class interests against, the rest of society.

He said that every organized political society has its "political formula," a doctrine or body of belief which legitimizes the political structure and the authority of the ruling class; there are, for example, the doctrines of divine right, and of democracy. It may often be the case that the power of the ruling class requires the use of force or violence; but Mosca thought that in stable, progressive, and flourishing societies the position of the ruling class may be founded on its intellectual and moral pre-eminence as well as on its care for the collective interests of the nation; the political formula which legitimizes the authority of the ruling class may be accepted by all members of the society.

In fact, in arguing that all developed societies are governed by a ruling class (and that the idea of democracy in the literal sense of government by the majority is an illusion) Mosca did not wish to imply that all societies are authoritarian or autocratic. Throughout the *Elementi* he argued strongly in support of a society marked by a high measure of what he called "juridical defence"—a society in which members of the ruling class are limited in their exercise of authority and power by moral codes which protect individual rights and liberties; a society which is pluralistic, or "open," in the sense that power is widely diffused throughout the community, and hence many different interests or social forces are able to express themselves within the political framework. Mosca was critical of parliamentary government in his early work, but later, especially in the material added to the 1923 edition of the *Elementi*, he spoke strongly of its merits; he saw it as the one form of organization able "to utilise almost all human values in the political and administrative departments of government, . . . [in which] the door has been left open to all elements in the governed classes to make their way into the ruling classes" (*The Ruling Class*, p. 389). Thus, although Mosca thought that recognition of the inevitable existence of the ruling class in any society was sufficient to destroy the illusions of democratic ideologies, his conclusions are not easy to distinguish from the standard doctrines of liberal-democratic political philosophy.

Works by Mosca

Sulla teorica dei governi e sul governo parlamentare. Turin, 1884; 2d ed., Rome, 1925.

Le costituzioni moderne. Palermo, 1887.

Elementi di scienza politica. Rome, 1895; 2d ed., Rome, 1896; 3d ed., Turin, 1923; 4th ed., with preface by Benedetto Croce, Bari, 1947. There is a translation by Hannah D. Kahn of the third edition, edited and revised and with introduction by Arthur Livingstone, titled *The Ruling Class.* New York and London, 1939.

Lezioni di storia delle istituzioni e delle dottrine politiche. Rome, 1932. A revised, corrected, and retitled edition appeared in 1937 as *Storia delle dottrine politiche* (Bari, Italy).

Works on Mosca

Bobbio, Norberto, "Liberalism Old and New," *Confluence,* Vol. 5 (1956), 239–251.

Bottomore, T. B., *Elites and Society.* London, 1964.

Meisel, James H., *The Myth of the Ruling Class: Gaetano Mosca and the Elite.* Ann Arbor, Mich., 1958.

Piane, Mario delle, *Gaetano Mosca: Classe politica e liberalismo.* Naples, 1952.

Piras, Quintino, *Battaglie liberali: Profili e discorsi di Benedetto Croce, Gaetano Mosca, Francesco Ruffini.* Novara, Italy, 1926.

P. H. PARTRIDGE

MOTION, or movement, in its modern meaning, is change—or more precisely, change of the relative positions of bodies. The concept of motion thus involves the ideas of space and time. Kinematics, in the nineteenth century usually called "kinetics" or "phoronomics," is the science that deals exclusively with the geometrical and chronometrical aspects of motion, in contrast to dynamics, which considers force and mass in relation to motion. In medieval terminology, following Aristotelian tradition, "motion" (*motus* or *kinesis*) had a much wider significance, denoting any continuous change in quality, quantity, or place.

Early concepts of motion. Ever since the beginning of philosophical speculation and scientific analysis, the concept of motion has played a predominant role in Western thought. Anaximander of Miletus (sixth century B.C.) saw in motion an eternal agent of the cosmos. For Heraclitus motion was a cosmological principle underlying all physical reality (*panta rhei,* "everything is in perpetual flow"). Yet in spite of their insistence on the universality of motion, neither Anaximander nor Heraclitus seems to have inquired into the nature of motion itself. The Eleatics were probably the first to do so, when they discovered the contradiction inherent in the idea of motion and consequently denied the reality of motion, relegating its appearance to the realm of illusions and deceptions. A body, they argued, can move neither where it is nor where it is not; hence, reality is motionless and unchanging. Zeno's famous antinomies (Aristotle, *Physics* 239), such as the "Arrow" and "Achilles," seem to have been aimed, at least in part, at a refutation of the possibility of motion. On the other hand, for the atomists, such as Democritus and Leucippus, motion was a fundamental property of the atoms. All changes in nature were reduced to the movements of atoms in the void, and with the eternity and uncreatedness of the atoms their motion was eternal and uncreated; this motion itself, in the atomists' view, was not further analyzable. It remained a primary concept until Epicurus searched for a causal explanation. This (according to Lucretius) he thought to have found in weight, the cause of the downward movements of atoms, and in their little "swerves," by which he explained the otherwise incomprehensible collisions and redistributions of atoms without which physical processes could not be accounted for.

Aristotle. In Aristotle's natural philosophy the concept of motion played a decisive role, since for him nature was the principle of movement or change: "We must understand what motion is; for, if we do not know this, neither do we understand what nature is" (*Physics* 200b12), a statement recurrent in Peripatetic philosophy under the motto *Ignato motu, ignatur natura* ("To be ignorant of motion is to be ignorant of nature"). For Aristotle, in contrast to his predecessors, motion raised a profound problem—not merely from the logical point of view. Expressing the deeply rooted metaphysical conviction of Western thought that motion is neither logically nor ontologically self-sufficient but requires an explanation, Aristotle contended that motion is neither in the causal, or genetic, nor in the ontological sense a primary concept. Causally, every motion originates in another motion; only animate organisms possess an inherent power to move. Hence his famous dictum *Omne quod movetur ab aliquo movetur* ("All things that move are moved by something else"). To avoid infinite regression and to find a satisfactory explanation of the existence of motion, Aristotle reduced the ultimate origin of all movements to an eternal mover who is himself unmoved. (*Physics* 258b). Ontologically, Aristotle derived motion from the basic notions of his metaphysics of substance and form by defining it as "the progress of the realizing of a potentiality *qua* potentiality" (*Physics* 201a10). Motion as the actualization of that which exists in potentiality may produce a substantial form (*generatio*), may change qualities (*alteratio*) and quantities (*augmentatio* or *diminutio*), or, finally, may be a change of place (*motus localis*). Although Aristotle did not reduce qualitative differences to quantitative relations of size and position, as did the atomists, his physics is essentially a physics of qualities. He did regard local motion as of a more fundamental character than the other kinds of motion (*Physics* 208a31); it is "the primary and most general case of passage and prior to all other categories of change" (*Physics*

260b22). Yet in spite of this preferential status, local motion for Aristotle is only a necessary concomitant of change, not, as the mechanistic physicists of the post-Newtonian era maintained, the essential and exclusive constituent of change.

In kinematics Aristotle distinguished between circular and rectilinear motion (*De Caelo* 268b17), the former, the more perfect, being the motion of the celestial bodies (*De Generatione et Corruptione* 338a18). Dynamically, motion is either natural or violate. Natural motion is circular for celestial and rectilinear for terrestrial objects; violate motion is the removal of a body from its natural place (*locus naturalis*) through the action of an external force.

Ancient and medieval concepts. Aristotle's kinematics, like his physics in general, was a qualitative science, incapable of providing a precise definition of such notions as velocity and acceleration. In fact, Greek mathematics, with its insistence on the illegitimacy of proportions or ratios between heterogeneous quantities, did not provide even the formal means of defining velocity as the ratio between distance and time; only topological, not metrical, determinations of motion could be formulated. Thus, Aristotle said that a body is quicker than another if it traverses equal spaces in less time or greater spaces in equal time (*Physics* 215a26). As related by Simplicius, Strato of Lampsacus, in a lost treatise "On Motion" (*De Motu*), was apparently the first to analyze in great detail these kinematic notions, in particular the concept of acceleration, although without trespassing the boundaries imposed by the Aristotelian conceptual scheme. The kinematics of uniform motion could be fully developed and rigorously formulated at least *in abstracto,* as exemplified by the treatise "The Motion of the Sphere" (300 B.C.), written by the astronomer Autolycus of Pitane. Nevertheless, as far as is known, the earliest kinematicist to associate concrete numerical designations with velocities was Gerard of Brussels, in the thirteenth century (*Liber de Motu*).

The formulations of the basic concepts in the science of motion did not, however, evolve out of practical necessities, the study of simple machines, or other scientific or technical considerations; they were, rather, the outcome of a curious development that originated in connection with a purely philosophical, ontological, and even theological problem. The point of departure was the much discussed problem of the increase and decrease of qualities (*intensio et remissio formarum*), the question of how such qualities as warmness or blackness could vary in their intensities. Aristotle explicitly admitted (*Categories* 10b26) such alterations, but he also described such qualities as numbers (*Metaphysics* 1044a9) as immutable and unchangeable. One of the solutions, as listed by Simplicius, is that of Archytas, who suggested that every quality possesses a certain range of indeterminacy, or margin of variability (*platos*).

In Peter Lombard's "Books on the Sentences" (*Libri Quatuor Sententiarum,* c. A.D. 1150) the same problem reappears in the realm of theology when it is asked, with reference to Scripture, how an intensification or diminution of the Holy Spirit or of the *caritas* is possible in man. Until well into the thirteenth century the Christian concept of *caritas* was par excellence the subject of discussions on the intension and remission of qualities and served as the standard example for intricate analyses of the notions of change and motion. One solution, advanced by Henry of Ghent in one of his *Quodlibeta,* referred in this connection explicitly to Archytas' previously mentioned conception of margin of variability, now termed the "latitude" (*latitudo*) of quality or change, a notion that was destined to play an important role in the foundation of classical kinematics.

Growth of the science of kinematics. In order to understand the subsequent development of the concept of motion another problem that engaged the thirteenth century to a great extent must be mentioned, the question of what category change, or motion, belongs to. Aristotle was usually interpreted as having advocated an identification of *motus* with *terminus motus*—i.e., viewing motion as an evolving process in the same category as the terminal, or the perfection, of this process. According to this view motion is a *forma fluens,* to use the terminology of Albert the Great, whereas the opposing view, which relates motion and its terminus to different categories, is the *fluxus formae* conception of motion. In the special case of local motion the *forma fluens* interpretation regards the process of motion as merely the continuous and gradual acquisition of the final *terminus motus,* just as the qualitative change of *nigrescere* (to become black) is merely the gradual acquisition of the *nigredo* (blackness). The concept of motion obtained its final and most radical formulation along these lines in the nominalistic statement of William of Ockham that motion is merely a name for the set of successive positions occupied by the mobile.

The nominalistic interpretation, often epitomized as *motus est mobile quod movetur,* met with considerable opposition, curiously enough among the Parisian terministic philosophers, such as Jean Buridan. One of the arguments for its rejection was undoubtedly its logical inapplicability to the motion of the outermost sphere, which, not further surrounded by any object, possessed neither place nor space, according to the Aristotelian–scholastic theory of space; thus its motion clearly could not be interpreted as a set of successive positions. No wonder, then, that the *fluxus formae* interpretation of motion, which distinguished between the process, on the one hand, and the terminus or position (*locus*), on the other, and regarded motion as a specific quality inherent in the mobile, became predominant. Buridan, for example, defined motion, or *moveri,* as an inherent property in the mobile—*intrinsice aliter et aliter se habere*—and Blasius of Parma characterized local motion as a quality that is capable of gradual intensification or remission and is inherent in the moving object (*motus localis est qualitas gradualis intensibilis et remissibilis, mobili inhaerens subjective*).

Meanwhile the notorious *calculatores* of Merton College at Oxford, including Thomas Bradwardine, Richard Swineshead, and William Heytesbury, established their famous formalism of subjecting qualities of all kinds, but primarily the quality of *caritas,* to mathematical analysis and quantification. It was there, at Merton College, that the different trends converged. For motion, itself a quality according to the *fluxus formae* conception, soon became the favorite subject of mathematical description and took the place of *caritas* in these discussions. Employing the notion of latitude, the calculators analyzed the various possibilities of changes of motion and illustrated their theorems by graphical representations. Thus, through the conflux of various conceptual trends the foundations of modern kinematics were laid at Oxford: the concept of velocity was clarified by the introduction of the notion of instantaneous velocity, uniformly accelerated motion was unambiguously defined, the distance traversed by a body in uniformly accelerated motion was calculated, and, finally, a clear distinction between kinematics and dynamics was drawn. The results thus obtained seem, however, never to have been applied to any motions encountered in nature; they were, rather, a theory for the classification of possible motions.

The new knowledge soon spread to France, Germany, and Italy. Only Galileo, and possibly Dominic de Soto, applied these results to the study of specific natural phenomena, such as free fall. Since kinematic investigations formed the point of departure for the subsequent development of mechanics and physics in general, the analysis and clarification of the concept of motion may rightfully be regarded as of primary importance for the rise of modern science as a whole. With the establishment of a scientific kinematics the notion of motion also became purified from certain connotations that it carried from ancient times. Thus, according to the Aristotelian theory of motion the movement of any object presupposes the existence of an immobile body. Themistius, Averroës, and other commentators interpreted this statement as a proof of the immobility of the earth. In fact, for Averroës the immobility of the center was a necessary prerequisite not only for the motion of the spheres but also for the very spatiality of the outermost sphere (*caelum est in loco per centrum*). Not only was the earth unique as being the abode of man; its distinction was due also to the fact that it served as the basis for the localizability of the celestial spheres.

However, as soon as the *fluxus formae* conception characterized motion as a property inherent solely in the mobile, the Aristotelian presupposition of an immobile correlate lost its logical legitimacy. Celestial motions no longer needed to be conceived of as dependent on the immobility of the earth, and a severe obstacle to the Copernican doctrine could easily be removed.

Relativity of motion. It is a curious fact that the modern conception of motion, though historically and conceptually connected most intimately with the Copernican revolution, led to a partial reinstatement of the Aristotelian presupposition. Not the immobility but the existence of a correlate is the indispensable requirement for any physical significance of the concept of motion. For the relativization of the notion demands a body of reference. The question whether absolute motion, motion without reference to a physical object extraneous to the mobile, is a scientifically or philosophically meaningful conception or whether motion is only relative—that is, whether the statement "*A* moves" makes sense only if it means "*A* moves relative to *B*"—is the problem of the relativity of motion and has a long history of its own.

Aristotle's distinction between ordinary motion and

motion *per accidens* may be regarded as the first implicit differentiation between absolute and relative rest, an idea further developed by Sextus Empiricus (*Adversus Mathematicos* 2, 55). The dynamical equivalence, under certain conditions, between relative rest and absolute rest was essential to the acceptance of the Copernican theory and, in fact, was explicitly stated by Copernicus himself: *Inter motu ad eadem, non percipitur motus* (*De Revolutionibus Orbium Coelestium,* Nuremberg, 1583, Bk. 1, Ch. 3). It was further elaborated by Galileo (*Dialogo sopra i due massimi sistemi del monde,* second day) into what is now called the Galilean principle of relativity. Descartes, fully aware of the implications of the relativity of motion for the Copernican controversy, adopted a compromise position by distinguishing between "the common and vulgar conception of motion" as the passing of a body from one place to another and the "true or scientific conception" of motion as the transfer of matter from the vicinity of those bodies with which it was in immediate contact into the vicinity of other bodies (*Principia Philosophiae,* Part 2, Section 24). He thereby associated the relativity of true, or scientific, motion with the Aristotelian contiguity as the determinant of localization. Descartes is often credited with having been the first to enunciate explicitly the relativity of motion, and Leibniz is cited as one of its most enthusiastic proponents.

For Newton and his doctrine of absolute space the notion of absolute motion was, of course, of physical significance, being "the translation of a body from one absolute place into another" (*Principles*). He defined relative motion, corresponding to the concept of relative space, as "the translation from one relative place into another." In spite of his professed adherence to Galileo's principle of relativity, Newton maintained the possibility of distinguishing absolute from relative motion by their "properties, causes and effects." His belief in the reality of absolute motion was based on his thesis that real forces create real motion. The reality of absolute motion, he argued, is manifested by the effects that such motions produce, for example, the appearance of centrifugal forces or effects. For Newton forces are metaphysical entities, and the motions they produce are therefore more than merely geometrico-temporal or kinematic phenomena. Thus, rotation is an absolute motion, as he thought to have proved by an analysis of his famous pail experiment.

Apart from Christian Huygens, who since 1688 maintained the relativity of circular motion on physical grounds, and Leibniz, who rejected the Newtonian conception on philosophical grounds, it was primarily Berkeley who treated the epistemological aspects of the problem (*Treatise Concerning the Principles of Human Knowledge; De Motu*). He concluded:

> It does not appear to me, that there can be any motion other than *relative:* so that to conceive motion, there must be at least conceived two bodies, whereof the distance or position in regard to each other is varied. Hence if there was one only body in being, it could not possibly be moved. This seems evident, in that the idea I have of motion doth necessarily include relation.

However, in the eighteenth and early nineteenth centuries, primarily as a result of Leonhard Euler's justification of absolute motion on the basis of the principle of inertia (*Mechanica; Theoria Motus,* Secs. 84, 99) and Kant's argumentations in his "Metaphysical Foundations of Natural Science" (*Metaphysische Anfangsgründe der Naturwissenschaft,* 1786), absolute motion was regarded by the majority of philosophers as a meaningful concept, not only in physics but also in philosophy. Toward the middle of the nineteenth century the situation changed. At first it was admitted that rotational motion is absolute but translational motion is relative (James Clerk Maxwell, P. G. Tait, H. Streinitz, L. Lange), and later all motion was regarded as relative. One of the most ardent proponents of the universal relativity of motion was Ernst Mach (*Die Mechanik in ihrer Entwicklung,* Leipzig, 1883); he refuted Newton's argument concerning the rise of centrifugal forces as evidence of the absolute nature of motion and explained it as an induction effect produced by the motion relative to the fixed stars. Whether Mach's conjecture can be corroborated rigorously is still a problem that engages modern research, especially in the theory of general relativity.

The question of the relativity of motion, initiated, as we have seen, by Descartes, gained increased importance, owing to the fact that the concept of motion became the basic element of physical explanation. In fact, it was Descartes's insistence on the exclusive admissibility of local motion that was decisive in this development. As is suggested in the *Principles of Philosophy* (Pt. 2, Sec. 23) and expounded in a letter to Marin Mersenne (1643), Descartes refused to attribute any reality to the so-called qualities of substances. The conception of such qualities, he contended, complicates and confuses rather than simplifies the explanation of physical phenomena in natural philosophy. In concluding such deliberations, Descartes declared local motion to be the only admissible element for physical explication. Descartes's rejection of the Aristotelian physics of qualities had a great appeal to philosophers (see, for example, Hobbes, *Elementorum Philosophiae Sectio Prima,* 1655; *De Corpore,* Sec. 8, Ch. 9) and was instrumental in the development of the mechanistic orientation of modern classical physics, which tried to reduce all natural phenomena to motions of masses in space.

Characteristic of this conception of classical physics is a statement by Maxwell: "When a physical phenomenon can be completely described as a change in the configuration and motion of a material system, the dynamical explanation of that phenomenon is said to be complete" (*Scientific Papers,* Cambridge, 1890, Vol. 2, p. 418). The predominant role of the concept of motion in physical science poses a problem of great importance to philosophy. Why is it that all processes, laws, and formulas of physics—and modern physics is no exception—ultimately refer to motion, and why is it that even problems in statics, the science of equilibrium and absence of motion, are solved in terms of fictitious motions and virtual velocities? Is the answer to be found only in the historical circumstances, namely that kinematic investigations were the earliest successful approach to the establishment of a physical theory and that consequently forces were regarded as manifesting themselves only through motions? The answer probably lies in a vestige of ancient Eleatic philosophy that seems still to motivate our mode of thinking: a physical explanation of a natural phenomenon becomes more satisfactory the nearer it approaches the statement that nothing has happened. Motion, as Wilhelm Wundt pointed out, is the only conceivable process in which an object, so to speak, both changes and remains the same: it changes by assuming a different position relative to other objects; it remains the same by preserving its complete identity.

Bibliography

PRIMARY SOURCES

Aristotle, *Works,* J. A. Smith and W. D. Ross, eds. Oxford, 1908–1952. See especially the *Physics.*

Berkeley, George, *The Works of George Berkeley, Bishop of Cloyne,* A. A. Luce and T. E. Jessop, eds., 9 vols. London, 1948–1957. See especially the *Treatise . . . of Human Knowledge* (1710), *De Motu* (1721), and *Siris* (1744).

Copernicus, Nicolas, *De Revolutionibus,* in *Opera Complete.* Warsaw, 1873. Translated by C. G. Wallis in *Great Books of the Western World,* Vol. XVI. Chicago, 1952.

Descartes, René, *Philosophical Works,* translated by E. S. Haldane and G. T. R. Ross, 2 vols. Cambridge, 1911–1912; 2d ed., 1934. See especially the *Principia Philosophiae.*

Euler, Leonhard, *Opera Omnia,* 3 series. Leipzig, 1911–1942; Lausanne, 1942––. See especially *Opera Mechanica et Astronomica.*

Galileo Galilei, *Dialogue Concerning the Two Chief World Systems,* translated by S. Drake. Berkeley, 1953.

Kant, Immanuel, *Sämtliche Werke,* edited by the Preussiche Akademie der Wissenschaften, 22 vols. Berlin, 1902–1955.

Mach, Ernst, *Science of Mechanics,* translated by T. C. McCormack. Chicago, 1902.

Newton, Isaac, *Sir Isaac Newton's Mathematical Principles of Natural Philosophy and His System of the World,* Florian Cajori, ed. Berkeley, 1947.

Sextus Empiricus, *Philosophical Works,* 4 vols. Loeb Classical Library. Cambridge, Mass., 1939–1957. See nos. 273, 291, 311, 382.

SECONDARY SOURCES

Lange, L., *Die geschichtliche Entwicklung des Bewegungsbegriffs.* Leipzig, 1886.

Wundt, Wilhelm, *Die physikalischen Axiome und ihre Beziehung zum Causalprinzip.* Erlangen, 1886.

M. JAMMER

MOTIVES AND MOTIVATION. The topic of motivation is connected with many perennial philosophical interests, particularly in ethics and the philosophy of mind. Moral philosophy has long been concerned with the question of what sorts of things can motivate people to do what they do, and more especially with the question of whether such things as a sense of duty or a desire for the well-being of others can be motivating. Psychological hedonism, the view that all actions are motivated by a desire for pleasure and the absence of pain, has figured heavily in arguments for various forms of ethical hedonism. In discussions concerning free will and determinism, arguments have been given for and against the thesis that when action is motivated, it is thereby causally determined. More recently, questions about the nature of motivation have been central in philosophical discussions of the character, significance, and feasibility of attempts by psychologists to explore systematically the causes of human behavior. This article will survey a variety of views on the nature of motivation and explore some of the problems involved.

Formulation of the problem. At the outset we can formulate our question as follows: "What is it for a person (P) to be motivated to perform an action (A)?" But it would be unwise to tie the problem too closely to the word "motivation." That which philosophers seek to understand under the heading of "motivation" could also be indicated by such locutions as "doing something for a purpose," "acting to realize an end or achieve a goal," or "doing something in order to so-and-so." This last formulation provides the most exact delimitation of the topic, for whereas every case of acting for a purpose or of goal-seeking can be formulated in terms of "in order to," there are other cases of motivation which can be expressed in this last way but not in the other two. These include doing something out of a sense of duty, doing something to keep a promise, doing something in order to get revenge, and doing something because it is the polite thing to do. In explaining an action in any of these ways, we are specifying what it is that motivated the person to do what he did as much as if we said that he did it in order to get something, such as a job; but in none of the cases are we specifying any goal he was seeking to achieve or any (further) purpose in the interest of which he did what he did. The "end" of the action (that is, what replaces "y" in "P did A in order to y") is something which exists, if at all, at the same time as A and is simply another aspect of the "piece of behavior" of which doing A is one aspect. If I go to a meeting because I am obligated to do so ("in order to fulfill certain obligations"), then going to the meeting *is* fulfilling those obligations; fulfilling the obligations is not something further in time to which going to the meeting might or might not lead. Again, if I refrain from responding to a plea for help from A in order to get revenge on A, then refraining from responding *is* getting revenge.

Motivational explanations and wants. The problem, then, is "What is it to do A in order to y?" One way to make a start on this problem is to notice that in saying something like this we are giving a certain kind of *explanation* of the action A. That is, the concept of motivation is an abstraction from the concept of a motivational explanation, and the task of specifying the nature of motivation *is* the task of bringing out the salient features of this kind of explanation.

To explain a fact is to show that it is related in an appropriate way (appropriate for the kind of explanation involved) to certain other facts. To what sorts of facts are we relating the action, A, when we give a motivational explanation of it? We may get a clue to this by noting that the following pairs are equivalent:

A. (1) He got up early in order to get some yard work done.
   (2) He got up early because he wanted to get some yard work done.

B. (1) He invited Jones to the party in order to repay an obligation.
   (2) He invited Jones to the party because he wanted to repay an obligation.

This suggests that to give a motivational explanation of an action is to explain it as in some way due to a "want" or a "desire." There may be subtle differences between the terms "want" and "desire," but we will have to ignore them in this article. This suggestion is further reinforced by the fact that the members of the first pair are also equivalent to

A. (3) He got up early out of a desire to get some yard work done.
   (4) What motivated him to get up early was his desire to get some yard work done.

Likewise, B (1) and (2) are each equivalent to each of the following:

B. (3) He invited Jones to the party out of a desire to repay an obligation.
   (4) What motivated him to invite Jones to the party was his desire to repay an obligation.

The same conclusion can be reached by comparing "in-order-to" explanations with others. The following answers might conceivably be given to the question "Why did Jones get up early this morning?"

(5) He has always been an early riser.
(6) He was very nervous and couldn't stay still.
(7) He had a violent argument with his wife and got up in a fit of anger.

None of these answers represent the action as having been motivated by anything (though none of them rule out the possibility that a motivational explanation could also be given). (5) could be termed a "habit explanation." It explains the action by showing it to be an instance of a fairly specific situation-response regularity. (6) and (7) are different types of "agitation explanations." They explain the action by relating it to a condition of general upset, of which the action can be viewed as one manifestation. In none of these cases do we set out to show the action to result from any want or desire.

Thus we can take the problem of the nature of motivation to be the problem of how a want can give rise to an action. However, this equivalence holds only with certain qualifications.

Explanations that imply desire. It is possible to provide a motivational explanation without explicitly mentioning a want or desire (and without using the "in-order-to" form), provided that what is said implies that the action was due to a certain desire (or at least a certain kind of desire). Thus all the following would count as motivational explanations.

(8) P did A out of a sense of duty.
(9) P did A out of gratitude to Q.
(10) P did A because he had promised Q he would.
(11) P did A because Q had asked him to.
(12) P did A because he was afraid of the consequences of not doing it.
(13) P did A because he couldn't stand to stay in that place another minute.

In each case the statement made implies that a certain desire (or a certain kind of desire) gave rise to A. The relevant desires are

(8) A desire to do one's duty.
(9) A desire to repay Q for past favors.
(10) A desire to keep one's promise to Q.

(11) A desire to comply with Q's request.

(12) A desire to avoid the consequences of not doing A.

(13) A desire to get away from the place in question.

The treatment of (12) and (13) shows that "avoidance" or "negative" motivation falls within the area as here defined. For whenever I do A in order to avoid so-and-so, I can be said to have done A out of a desire to avoid so-and-so.

The widest sense of "want." The words "want" and "desire" are used in wider and narrower senses, and here they must be interpreted in the widest sense. Thus, in one sense of "want," "He didn't *want* to do that yard work" is compatible with "He got up early in order to get the yard work done." But in a wider sense of the term, the latter is equivalent to "He got up early because he wanted to do the yard work." Again, in one sense of "want," going to the library because one wants to read a certain book can be contrasted with going to the library because one has to read a certain book. But in another sense of "want," the latter state implies the former.

Restrictions on the use of "motive." It will be noted that in our formulations there has been no mention of "motives." It is often supposed that when something, x, motivates P to do A, it is *ipso facto* correct to speak of x as P's motive for doing A. In that case, we might have formulated the problem of motivation as the problem of how motives give rise to actions. It is true that desires—in the broad sense of the term, in which one is always motivated by some desire—are of the right order of entity to function as motives. It seems that one can always answer the question "What was his motive for doing A?" by specifying some desire, though one can also answer by using some desire-implying phrase like "To get even with Q." Of course motives do not exist apart from (actual or envisaged) actions of which they are motives. It makes no sense, apart from reference to some particular action(s), to ask "What motives do you have?" or "What are your strongest motives at the moment?," while it makes perfectly good sense to ask "What do you want most now?" or "What desires do you feel most keenly?" But this last point is perfectly compatible with the view that a desire acquires the status of a motive for a particular action, A, by virtue of the fact that it motivates the person to do A.

The reasons for avoiding the term "motive" in a general account of motivation lie in the restrictions there are on its employment. The case in which asking for a motive seems most clearly appropriate is one in which (a) the action is a relatively important one, and (b) we suppose that an explanation of the "in-order-to" sort is available, but (c) it seems to us that the action was not done for any of the reasons which are standard and/or socially acceptable for such actions in such circumstances. Thus, we might ask what P's motive was for buying a large number of shares of a certain stock, if we have reason to think that he did not make the purchase for the standard reason of receiving regular dividends or realizing capital gains and hence suspect some "devious motive" or "ulterior motive," for example, to gain control of the company and neutralize it as a competitor in a certain field. Where one of these conditions does not hold, talk of "motives" becomes puzzling. It sounds odd to ask what P's motive was for getting up and going into the kitchen (a relatively unimportant action),

unless we are seriously envisaging the possibility that this is a part of some "deep dark plot." Again, it would be odd to ask what P's motive was for going to Europe if we are *not* presupposing that his reason does not fall within the "standard" range of sightseeing, doing research, transacting business, and so forth. The clearest application of all is "What was the motive for the crime?"; and it is noteworthy that here we are dealing with a sort of action for which there are no socially acceptable reasons. Because of these limitations we would do well to steer clear of the term in a general discussion of motivation.

The use of "motivation" in psychology. A word is in order concerning uses of the terms "motive" and "motivation" by psychologists. It is not uncommon for psychologists to think of motivation as "the process (a) of arousing or initiating behavior, (b) of sustaining an activity in progress, and (c) of channeling activity into a given course." The study of motivation then becomes the study of "all factors which arouse, sustain, and direct behavior" (P. T. Young, in *Encyclopedia of Psychology*). On this very wide conception, the psychology of motivation is concerned with any laws and theories which take behavior as a dependent variable. Any explanation of an action is then, by definition, a motivational explanation; and any factors brought into such explanation could be called motives, although that term is often restricted to a subclass of such factors, such as drives (C. L. Hull), affective associations (D. C. McClelland), or higher-level dispositions to strive for a certain goal state (J. W. Atkinson).

From this point of view, our distinction between motivational, habit, and agitation explanations washes out, and a stimulus-response psychology, like that of Hull, which has no place for ultimate factors like wants, can still be said to put forward a theory of motivation. In Hull's system, the "motivating" factors which determine whether any behavior takes place in response to a certain stimulus, and if so, what kind of behavior, consist of a "drive state," which is, roughly, a state of physiological tension and which can vary in intensity, and a set of habits (of varying strengths) of responding to various kinds of stimuli in various ways. To oversimplify the account, the amount of drive currently in the organism determines whether there will be any activity at all, and if so, what its strength and persistence will be, while what the activity will be is determined by the relative strengths of different habits, each of which consists in a certain response to stimulation like the current stimulation. In the sense of "motivation" we have specified, such a psychology tries to bypass motivation altogether and provide a habit explanation for all behavior. On the other hand, many psychologists tie the term "motivation" to something like the "in-order-to" model. This is true of, for instance, Freud and Kurt Lewin and the many developments that have been inspired by their theories.

Questions in the analysis of motivation. The main problems involved in working out an analysis of motivation are the following:

What is a want?

How does a want give rise to an action? (What sort of explanation is a motivational explanation?)

What kinds of wants are there?

We shall discuss the questions in this order, although they are so closely interrelated that we cannot prevent aspects of one from spilling over into the consideration of another. We will also find it useful to distinguish between accounts of motivation in terms of their differing answers to these questions.

The nature of wants. First we must make explicit a crucial distinction, that between latent and aroused wants. Consider the difference between the following:

(14) "All his life he has wanted very much to be liked by people."

(15) "He went to the party because he wanted to make an impression on Dr. Z."

In the latter case, in referring to a want we are citing a factor which plays a role in his psychological economy at that time, which has to be taken into account, in one way or another, if we are to understand what he was doing at that time. In the first case, in specifying the want we are attributing to him a personality characteristic; we are claiming that something is true of him throughout a relatively long period of time. But we are not saying that at any particular time (much less at every time) within this period he will have a tendency to do something in order to satisfy this want. The fact asserted by the first statement is quite compatible with there being many times at which this want is not "active" or "aroused," at which he doesn't care, for the moment, whether people like him or not. It may be that in asserting the first statement we imply that there were many times in his life at which he actively wanted people to like him, at which he had a strong tendency to do something in order to get people to like him. Thus, we might think of a want in the "latent" sense as a disposition frequently to have the corresponding aroused want. But the two senses must be distinguished. In trying to understand motivation we shall be concentrating on "aroused" wants.

Phenomenological view. Most recent writers on motive and motivation have been reacting against a firmly entrenched tradition, according to which a desire is a kind of conscious state or content of consciousness, something which has the same ontological status as a feeling, sensation, or thought. This tradition stems from the epistemological primacy given to introspection in the seventeenth century by Descartes and Locke. Prior to that time, thinkers, particularly those in the Aristotelian tradition, such as Thomas Aquinas, thought of desire as a "movement of the appetite," an inclination of the person toward something apprehended as good. This inclination was typically manifested in consciousness, but it was not supposed that it revealed its full nature to introspection. A contemporary reconstruction of this approach would, presumably, come close to the conception of desire as a "hypothetical construct," to be expounded later in this article.

With the development of the Cartesian notion that one's own states of consciousness are better known to one than anything else, combined with the eagerness of British empiricists to get rid of traditional metaphysical concepts, eighteenth-century and nineteenth-century thinkers tried to find desire, along with other psychological states, among the immediate contents of consciousness. In this tradition a desire has been conceived as

(16) A felt urge or impulse to get *x* (Hume).

(17) An uneasiness occasioned by the absence of *x* (Locke).

(18) An idea of *x* as pleasant, or with pleasant associations; or an expectation that *x* will be pleasant (Mill).

(19) An idea of *x* as an end (T. H. Green).

Objections to phenomenological accounts. If we are thinking of latent wants, it is clear that none of the views just listed will do, for a latent want can exist over a period of time during which nothing related to the object of the want appears in consciousness. With respect to aroused wants, these views are not prima facie absurd. Nevertheless, none of them are adequate, a fact increasingly recognized in recent philosophical discussions of the topic. There are special problems with individual items on the list. (17) and (18) assume some form of a hedonistic answer to our third major question, "What kinds of wants are there?" It is difficult to apply (16) where, as with wanting to get a job, the object of the want might conceivably be attained by a number of different courses of action. How can that want consist in an impulse to do one particular thing rather than another? In other words, one–one correlations between wants and actions designed to satisfy them are the exception rather than the rule. Of course we could speak of an impulse to work toward getting a job. But this term "work toward" reintroduces just the kind of concept we are trying to analyze. As for (19), it does not seem to advance the inquiry. How are we to explain what it is to have an idea of something *as an end,* except to say that it is to have an idea of something one wants?

There is a more general difficulty with these views. With respect to a want for *x,* it is simply not the case that any particular conscious state—be it a felt urge to get *x,* an idea of *x* as pleasant, or whatever—is present during all the time the want is in existence and/or operative, even restricting ourselves to its "aroused form." To make this clear, let us consider a particular desire, my desire to plant some shrubs as a screen for a wire fence in my back yard. Antecedent to working out an adequate account of the nature of wants and the nature of motivation, we will be unable to determine exactly when this desire could be said to be in existence and operative. But at least this much can be taken as antecedently clear: the desire is in existence during any continuous stretch of activity which is designed to satisfy it. If, in order to satisfy this desire, I drive out to a nursery one morning, select some shrubs, bring them home, and plant them in front of the fence, it must surely be admitted that the desire in question is in existence throughout all this period. For at any time while this is going on, one could truthfully reply to the question "Why is he doing A (such as driving to the nursery)?" by saying "Because he wants (present tense) to put up some shrubs as a screen." But in the normal case it would not be true that this object was constantly before my mind in any form—be it impulse or idea. Much of the time my mind will be taken up with other matters.

The basic mistake of the "phenomenological" account is to construe a want as a much more concrete and directly accessible entity than it is. Felt impulses, and ideas of something as pleasant or attractive, are ways in which wants manifest themselves in consciousness from time to time. And different wants, under different circumstances, will be manifested consciously in different ways. No doubt some wants give rise to more or less insistent felt urges or impulses; this is typical of sexual desires and other desires based on identifiable states of physiological tension, as well as of desires for things that are very important to us, such as a desire to finish a paper which is very important to one professionally. But such manifestations are not the rule for more routine wants. My desire to keep my promise to take Jones to the airport is unlikely to give rise to any felt impulse or craving. Its appearance in consciousness will most likely be restricted to a passing, nonemotionally toned recollection that I had made that promise.

We have rejected the phenomenological account of the nature of wants without appealing to unconscious wants of the sort investigated by psychoanalysis, that is, wants which, by reason of repression, a person does not know he has. We shall return to this topic. What we have shown is that even if we restrict ourselves to garden-variety wants which are perfectly accessible to their possessor, we cannot identify such a want with any particular conscious state.

Wants as dispositions. If to want *x*, during a certain period, is not to be actually conscious of any particular item throughout that period, then it may be that it is to be liable or likely to be in certain conscious states (and also to respond in certain ways to certain circumstances) during that period. That is, it may be that to have a want is to have certain dispositions. Recent philosophy of mind, partly because of the influence exerted by Gilbert Ryle's *The Concept of Mind,* has been making extensive use of the notion of a dispositional pattern of analysis. Applying this pattern to the desire under discussion, we would say that to have the desire is to be disposed to find the prospect of shrubs in front of the fence attractive if it is brought to mind, to try to get to a place if I have learned that suitable shrubs are to be found there, and so on.

As at many points in philosophy, it is easier to demonstrate some plausibility for the general program than it is to spell out the analysis in detail for a particular case. The dispositional view has been embraced largely, though not exclusively, by thinkers of a behavioristic bent, who have been strongly motivated to show that so-called mental states can be construed as sets of dispositions to engage in overt behavior when certain publicly observable conditions are satisfied. (Gilbert Ryle does, or did, give half-hearted allegiance to this program. More enthusiastic advocates are to be found in the ranks of such psychologists as B. F. Skinner and E. C. Tolman.) It is important to realize that at best a dispositional analysis will be enormously, perhaps infinitely, complicated. No limit can be set on the number of actions which might conceivably be performed in order to satisfy some particular desire. In the course of trying to get some appropriate shrubs in front of my fence, I might consult any one of a number of books, ask various questions of various friends, drive to a nursery, walk to a nursery, buy some shrubs, steal some shrubs, dig some holes, and so on. The only way to give a concise definition of this class of actions is to say that they are actions which might be performed in order to get some appropriate shrubs in front of a given fence. But this makes

the account circular; for, as we have seen, in order to explain what it is to do *A* in order to get *x*, we have to bring in the notion of wanting *x*.

Objections to behavioral disposition theory. The main difficulty with a behavioral disposition theory is not its indefinite complexity. It lies in the fact that with respect to any one action *A*, the desire for *x* will necessarily give rise to *A* (in appropriate circumstances) only on the assumption of further conditions which are either not formulable in terms of publicly observable facts, or are indefinitely complex, or both. Once again, consider my horticultural desire and envisage a situation which, so far as publicly observable features go, is maximally conducive to that desire's giving rise to the action of going to Frank's Nursery and buying some shrubs. That is, I have some free time, means of transportation are at my disposal, and I am not incapacitated. (It might be doubted that these conditions could be stated in terms which would satisfy strict behaviorist standards for direct check by public observation, especially the first, which brings in notions of obligation and commitment; but let us waive these difficulties). It is clear that there are a number of factors which, if present, would prevent the performance of this action, however keen the desire:

(20) I do not know about Frank's Nursery.

(21) I do not believe that there are appropriate shrubs at Frank's Nursery.

(22) I am ill-disposed toward Frank's Nursery (because I feel that their merchandise is overpriced, or because I believe that the proprietor is dishonest, or because I object to his discriminatory hiring practices).

(23) I have a stronger desire which I am using the time to satisfy, for instance, a desire to finish a book or a desire to lie in a hammock and do nothing.

(24) I believe that I can get the shrubs much more cheaply by waiting two weeks until they are on sale.

(25) I have a strong aversion to this particular action for reasons unconnected with this particular desire. For example, I very much dislike getting into the crowds at nurseries on Saturday mornings in the late spring.

To say that desire can be analyzed dispositionally is to say that any statement attributing a desire to someone is synonymous with a conjunction of hypothetical statements; if it is a behavioral disposition analysis, there is the further requirement that the consequent of each of the hypotheticals asserts that the person in question performs some action or other. Now the desire attribution can be synonymous with a given conjunction of hypotheticals only if it logically implies each of them. For if it did not imply one of them, it would be possible for it to be true and the hypothetical to be false, in which case it could not have the same assertive force as a conjunction containing the hypothetical in question.

Applying these considerations to the case under discussion, if we are to make any hypothetical of the form "If ———, then *P* will go to Frank's Nursery" follow logically from the proposition "*P* wants to have some shrubs in front of his fence," we shall have to make the antecedent such that it will rule out possibilities of this sort. Otherwise, it can happen that the original want-proposition is true, the conditions specified in the antecedent of the hypothetical hold, and yet the action is not performed. But that would mean that the want-proposition could be true and the hypothetical false, which is to say that the latter does not follow from the former. Now apart from the question of the possibility of getting a complete list of such conditions, it is noteworthy that the ones we have listed contain psychological concepts of the same order as the concept of desire, namely, knowledge, belief, disapproval, aversion, and dislike. Presumably these are as far away from concepts of observable features of actions and situations as the concept of desire itself. Of course, the behaviorist could try to frame in observational terms a condition which would rule out these possibilities, but to do so he would have to give behavioral analyses of belief, dislike, and so on. And the chances are that in trying to do so, he would land in difficulties quite analogous to those facing us at present.

If we do not accept behaviorist restrictions on the content of the hypothetical propositions involved, the dispositional theory is not subject to these objections. But the attempt to identify a want with one or more dispositions is still open to the following objections.

Features of any dispositional analysis. Let us first restrict our attention to behavioral disposition of the sort we have been considering thus far, and consider a hypothetical proposition which formulates such a disposition: "If $C_1, C_2, \ldots$, then P will do A." As the preceding discussion makes clear, if such a proposition is to be true of a given P when and only when he has a certain want, W, there will have to be a large number of conditions in the antecedent. The most important item in such a list is a belief that doing A will (probably) satisfy or lead to the satisfaction of W; also there must be conditions which rule out the existence of factors which would prevent someone with such a want and such a belief from doing A. (It is not clear that it is possible to make sure that any list of such conditions is exhaustive.) Moreover, to specify these conditions in such a way that together with the want they will guarantee the performance of just this action, A, but at the same time not be too strong for this purpose, we shall have to have some reasonably exact way of specifying the strength of the desires and aversions involved. For example, we need a condition, or set of conditions, which will rule out the existence of any aversion to doing A which is *stronger* than the tendency to do A brought about by the want W, together with the associated relevant beliefs. But at present we do not have methods of measuring wants and aversions which are subtle enough to do this job. Such considerations may well make us doubt our ability to construct a hypothetical of this sort which is true when and only when P has the want W.

Moreover, included in the list of relevant conditions will be specifications of the relative strength of other wants. (Indeed, as pointed out earlier, an aversion is a special kind of want, in the broad sense in which we are using the term "want.") No matter how much I want to get a paper finished, I will not actually get to work on it if I have a stronger desire to play tennis and it is open to me to do so

at the moment. What this means is that we cannot use hypotheticals of this sort to specify the nature of a particular want without using the term "want" in the hypothetical. Thus, an action-disposition analysis of wants is infected with a vicious circularity. It is systems of wants, rather than any one want in isolation, which give rise to action. Indeed, the system which is involved in the motivation of any particular action includes a system of beliefs as well as a system of wants. From the fact that I want to finish a paper more than I want to do anything else at the moment, and the fact that I believe that I can do so by going to the office, it does not follow (even granting the absence of disturbing factors) that I will go to the office. For I may also believe that I can do it by working in my study at home, a course of action requiring less effort.

All these difficulties could be avoided by taking as the consequent of our hypothetical an action tendency or an action probability. A good case could be made for saying that a hypothetical of the following form is true of a person, P, when and only when he has a desire for a state of affairs, S.

(26) "If P believes that doing A either will be an attainment of S or has some considerable likelihood of leading to S, then if A is within his power, this belief will add to the probability of his trying to do A."

With this move, we have deviated even further from the behaviorist program. Now the consequent as well as the antecedent of the hypothetical contains reference to nonpublicly observable factors. An increment to a probability of an action is at least as abstract a notion as that of a want itself; and at present we do not have the resources to give it precise application to particular cases. However, this formulation does embody the important insight that whatever else a want may be, it makes action tendencies susceptible to increase by beliefs; in other words, it brings it about that our beliefs have an effect on what we do.

Analytic and synthetic hypotheticals. Further complexities are introduced into the dispositional analysis by the existence of other sorts of dispositions which seem to be more or less intimately connected with wants. Consider the following hypothetical propositions, in relation to a desire for a state of affairs, S.

(27) If S comes to mind, the thought of it will be pleasant.

(28) If P is aware of something associated with S, the thought of S is likely to be called up.

(29) If S-related objects are present in the environment, they are more likely to be noticed than other objects.

(30) If S occurs, P will be pleased.

Each of these hypotheticals calls for at least as much supplementation as an action hypothetical before it could plausibly be claimed that it is true when and only when one has a desire for A. Thus, with respect to (27) and (30), whether P is in a pleasant state of mind at a given moment will depend on what he is doing at the moment, as well as on what is specified in the antecedents of these propositions. But with such qualifications, these hypotheticals, as well as action hypotheticals, reflect typical ways in which the presence of a want will affect the behavior and experience of a person. Thus, the dispositional view must deal with the following question: Which of these connections are to be taken as making up the nature of a want and which are to be taken as connections in which wants stand as a matter of fact? To formulate the problem in linguistic terms, let us take a set of hypotheticals formed by prefacing to those we have been considering the antecedent "If P has a desire for S . . . ." Thus (30), as so amended, will read: "If P has a desire for S, then if S occurs, P will be pleased." The question then becomes: Which of these statements is analytic (true by virtue of the meanings of the words involved), and which are synthetic (true as a matter of fact, and subject to empirical test)? Any answer to this question is fraught with difficulties.

One possibility is that one of the hypotheticals is analytic and the others synthetic. (26) would seem to have the strongest claim to this position. The difficulty here is that the verification of some of the other hypotheticals would seem to give us as direct and conclusive a confirmation of the fact that P wants S as does the verification of (26). Thus, if it can be shown that whenever I see that Mr. X is humiliated, I am pleased, this would seem to be as strong evidence for the proposition that I want Mr. X to be humiliated as the fact that whenever I believe that my doing A is likely to lead to Mr. X's being humiliated, this increases the likelihood of my trying to do A. Hence, it is difficult to maintain that (26) tells us what a want *is*, while the other hypotheticals only tell us what is true of wants as a matter of fact. In this connection it is worthy of note that one of the standard methods in psychology for measuring the strength of a desire for something, such as achievement, is based on (28). Pictures which may well produce achievement-related associations are presented to subjects, and they are asked to write stories suggested by the pictures. Strength of the desire is measured by counting the achievement-related items in the stories.

Another possibility is that several of the statements are analytic. If this is the case, "P wants S" is equivalent to the conjunction of those statements. But then the falsity of any one of them will entail that P does not want S. However, we do not seem to use the term "want" in such a way that this is true. If I discovered that humiliating Mr. X was not on your mind very much, or at all, I would not conclude that you did not want Mr. X to be humiliated, provided that there were very strong indications drawn from the other hypotheticals. It seems that as we conceive wants, the lack of any one typical manifestation might be explained without having to give up the hypothesis that the want is present.

Wants as "hypothetical constructs." Despite the difficulties in establishing one or more of the hypotheticals as analytic, it seems that if we take all the hypotheticals to be straightforwardly synthetic, we will be left without any way of saying what a want is. What we need is a way of conceiving the matter which will allow us to make reference to such hypotheticals in explaining what a want is, without having to regard any of them as analytic in a strict sense. To adequately represent the logical state of affairs here, we need to replace the analytic–synthetic dichotomy with a notion of the degree to which a statement has the truth status it has because of the meanings of the terms

involved. There are some statements involving "want" or "desire" which, if they are true, do not enjoy that status through embodying some feature of the meanings of the words involved. Consider

(31) "When a person is frustrated in his attempts to satisfy a desire, he has a tendency to act aggressively."

If this is generally true, it is a fact which will have to be established by empirical research. It is surely no part of what we *mean* when we say that Jones wants to play golf today, that he will tend to act aggressively if he is prevented from doing so. This purely synthetic statement is at one end of the continuum. At the other end there are purely analytic statements like

(32) "If a person wants a state of affairs, S, he is not indifferent to the question of whether S comes about."

This statement is such that we could not deny it without radically changing the meanings of some of the terms involved. In between we have the statements, like those on our previous list of hypotheticals, which do the most to bring out what it is to want something. Each of these statements makes explicit some aspect of the meaning of "want," yet none of them is straightforwardly analytic on the model of "All squares have four sides."

There are several reasons for denying (complete) analyticity to any of them. First, as we have seen, it is difficult, if not impossible, to formulate any of them so as to exclude all factors that would prevent it from being generally true. Second, even if this could be done, any one of them could be rejected, with the possible exception of (26), without any basic change in our concept of a want. One might say that in using "want" as we do, we commit ourselves to most of these statements being true (if properly hedged in), but we do not unequivocally commit ourselves to any one—again, with the possible exception of (26). Third, it seems that some of these statements are more intimately involved in the concept than others. To give up (26) would seem to involve more of a modification of the concept than to give up (29). In other words, if one were to deny that what we want has an influence on what we do in the manner specified in (26), we would take his concept of desire to deviate more strikingly from the normal one than if he denied that our desires affect our perceptions via a principle like (29). Fourth, we want to leave open the possibility of new truths acquiring this same intermediate status. Thus, if the frustration-aggression hypothesis (31) became a securely established part of our knowledge, it might come to be involved in the concept of a want in the same way as the fact that objects of desire tend to be on our minds.

Thus, what a want is can be made clear only by bringing out how a want tends to manifest itself in behavior, thought, and experience; nevertheless, a want cannot be identified with any specifiable set of such tendencies. Because of its similarity to a view worked out by recent philosophers of science (such as C. G. Hempel and Hilary Putnam) concerning the way theoretical concepts in science are related to empirical evidence, we might dub this the "hypothetical construct" theory of the nature of wants, without thereby implying that the set of hypotheticals involved constitutes an explicitly worked-out theory in any strict sense of that term. To make this view more precise, we would need a more subtle and complex logic than any in existence—one which would replace the analytic–synthetic dichotomy with the notion of the degree to which a statement makes explicit some aspect of the meanings of one or more of the terms involved.

Knowledge of one's own wants. The main objection to the hypothetical construct view comes from a consideration that lends weight to phenomenological theories—the apparent fact that a person has immediate knowledge of his own desires. We ordinarily regard the individual himself as the final authority on the question of what he wants. Of course, he may not be sincere in what he says, but we do not ordinarily think that one can be *mistaken* in supposing that he wants to play golf this afternoon. Moreover, it does not seem that one has to engage in any research or make any observations in order to find out what he wants. He seems to know this "straight off," not on the basis of anything else. But if a want is anything like a hypothetical construct, something which lies behind manifestations and specifiable only through them, how could there be such knowledge?

At this point we must come to grips with the phenomenon of repression. According to psychoanalytic theory, behavior can be motivated by desires of which the agent has no knowledge, immediate or otherwise; in these cases, psychic mechanisms have come into operation to prevent this knowledge, which would be painful and/or dangerous. For example, a mother who overprotects her daughter may actually be doing so in order to prevent the daughter from developing into a rival, although she is quite unaware that she has this aim. Those who claim that it is of the essence of a desire that the possessor know that he has it, try to counter this move by claiming that a repressed desire is not a desire in the usual sense of the term. But this claim can be defended only by relying on the very thesis at issue, namely, that a desire, in the ordinary sense of the term, is by its very nature known as such to its possessor. In any event this much is clear: If we regard desires as *ipso facto* known to their possessors, then in speaking of repressed desires we are using the term in a different, though perhaps closely related, sense. If, on the other hand, a repressed desire is a desire in the ordinary sense of the term, then it is not part of that ordinary sense that a desire be known to its possessor. If there were no other grounds for deciding the matter, we could rule in favor of the latter position by invoking the principle that senses should not be multiplied beyond necessity. But in addition there is the fact that the hypothetical construct analysis, which has much else to recommend it, applies to repressed desires as much as to conscious ones, provided we recognize that such psychological factors as beliefs and perceptions can be repressed also.

We are still faced with the question of how a person can have immediate knowledge of a desire in cases where he does. On the hypothetical construct view, my knowledge that I want to play golf this afternoon is based on my knowledge of certain of the "manifestations" of this desire. But how can this be, since I am not aware of inferring the desire from the manifestations? We may find this problem less perplexing if we set it in the context of other cases in which my knowledge that something is the case is based on something, without my being able to specify this something and without my making any conscious inference from the one to the other. I know that what I see out the window is a tree because I make use of certain subtle variations in color patterns in my visual field; but I am unable to specify in detail what these are, and I certainly make no conscious inference from the one to the other. The same thing can be said of my seeing that you don't like something by observing the expression on your face. Similarly, it is not implausible to suppose that when I know "straight off" that I want to play golf, I am actually going on subtle features of the state of feeling and the incipient action tendencies that are aroused when the subject comes up. No doubt there is a variety of problems about such kinds of knowledge; but reference to the less problematic cases from visual perception should suffice to establish the possibility of construing first-person knowledge of wants in such a way that it is consistent with the hypothetical construct view.

How wants give rise to actions. Different conceptions of the nature of wants naturally carry with them differing conceptions of motivational explanation. If we think of wants phenomenologically as felt urges, impulses, uneasinesses, or attractions, it is natural to describe motivation in mechanistic metaphors. This was quite common in the British associationist tradition, in which an act of will (which then gave rise to action) was thought of as a resultant of the interplay of conscious forces, much as the motion of a body is a "compromise" resultant of a variety of forces operating upon it. However, this was, and remains, nothing but a metaphor. It undoubtedly provides an imaginatively stimulating way of representing motivation. Any further value it has lies in the suggestion that it is possible to devise methods of measuring wants in such a way that principles can be established which are like those of mechanics, in that they represent quantitative features of actions as a certain kind of mathematical function of the strengths and interconnections of the wants currently operative. However, this possibility remains unrealized, despite the fact that such recent psychological theorists as Hull and Lewin display attachment to a Newtonian model in their programmatic pronouncements.

The hypothetical construct view has a built-in answer to the question. Principles like (26), which partially make explicit what a want is, also bring out what it is for a want to give rise to an action, and conversely, what it is for an action to be explainable by reference to a want. Wants give rise to actions by virtue of the fact that it is a lawful generalization that given a desire for S and a belief that doing A is (or will lead to) bringing about S, there will be a tendency to do A, whether or not the agent actually does A being further dependent on what other action tendencies simultaneously exist, as well as on whether factors which prevent any action at all are present. When we have laws of this sort stated as adequately as possible, we will have completed the most fundamental part of the job of understanding what motivation is. However, some problems will still remain.

Is motivation essentially a process? In order to be able to say correctly that P did A in order to get S, must we be able to specify something that happened "in" P which could be identified as his *being* motivated by a desire for *S*? Of course, even on a pure disposition view, according to which *P* does *A* in order to get *S* if and only if *P*'s doing *A* is the activation of a certain disposition, we at least have the process of activation. Something must have happened, in the environment if not in the person, which resulted in the antecedent conditions being realized at that moment; otherwise there would be no explanation, along these lines, of the fact that the action was performed at this moment rather than just before or just after. Nevertheless, the question would still remain as to whether there is necessarily any psychological process which leads up to the action and which could appropriately be called *P*'s *being motivated* to do *A*.

There is no doubt that such processes do often occur. I feel the need to discuss an epistemological problem with someone. Various possibilities occur to me; finally I settle on one and call the person on the telephone. But it may still be doubted that a process is involved in every case of motivation. In view of the fact noted earlier—that we cannot identify a felt desire in every case of motivation—it is clear that we do not invariably get a process of just this form. But though there may be no occurrence of a conscious desire in a given case of motivation, what about the other major aspect—belief? Is it possible for *P* to be motivated to do *A* without the performance of *A* having been closely preceded by the occurrence of a conscious belief that *A* would be, or would lead to, the satisfaction of some desire? I can go into Frank's Nursery in order to get some shrubs, without its being the case that this entrance was immediately preceded by a felt desire for shrubs, or even by my saying to myself that I want some shrubs. But it might still be claimed that the action could not have been so motivated without having been led up to by the *occurrence* of a conscious belief that shrubs are (probably) to be obtained at Frank's Nursery. (This occurrence could take various forms—seeing that shrubs are there, remembering that shrubs are for sale there, the possibility that shrubs are for sale there occurring to me, hearing someone tell me that shrubs are for sale there, . . .)

There are two sorts of cases which provide possible counterexamples for this claim. First, there is habitual goal-directed activity. Suppose that I am in the habit of turning down Y Street on my way home whenever I want to stop by a drugstore. Consider a case where I am taking you home on the way and am planning to stop by a drugstore. En route I turn down Y Street, in a direction away from your house. You ask me why I did that, and I answer (truthfully) that I did so in order to go by a drugstore. Yet my action was not closely preceded by any conscious realization that turning down Y Street would be likely to result in my going by a drugstore. We might deal with this case in various ways. Although it seems clear that an "in-order-to" explanation can be correctly given here, it might still be denied that anything *motivated* me to turn down Y Street because this action was one which clicked off automatically in accordance with a fixed habit. Making this move would save the claim that motivation is always a conscious process at the expense of loosening the tie between motivation and "in-order-to" explanations. Alternatively, we might modify the requirement that the relevant cognition has to occur immediately before the action.

It seems plausible to suppose that during the formation of the habit, it had consciously occurred to me many times that turning down Y Street is a good way of getting to a drugstore on the way home.

A more serious difficulty concerns "unconscious motivation" of the sort studied by psychoanalysts. Let us consider the woman motivated to overprotect her daughter by her (repressed) desire to prevent the daughter from developing into a rival. Not only are her actions *not* preceded by a conscious realization that doing the sorts of things she is doing is likely to impede her daughter's development, but the repression makes it impossible that any such realizations should occur. However, if we look closely at the way psychoanalysts describe such cases, we will see that in order to retain motivational conceptions, they have construed the situation on the model of conscious motivation. That is, the woman is said to do what she does because she (unconsciously) sees that doing so will tend to prevent her daughter's development. Thus, by enlarging the thesis to allow for unconscious analogues of conscious occurrence of beliefs, it can accommodate psychoanalytic material. Further discussion of this problem would require an extensive investigation of alternative conceptual frameworks for psychoanalytic explanation. (See PSYCHOANALYTIC THEORIES, LOGICAL STATUS OF.)

In the foregoing we have restricted ourselves to the question of whether motivation always involves a distinctive kind of *conscious* process. No doubt other sorts of processes will be involved in one way or another. Physiological processes presumably always play a role in the initiation of action, and there might well be distinctive features of the physiology of the antecedent stages of *motivated* behavior. Moreover, various theoretical models of motivation in psychology specify distinctive processes involving theoretical entities. Thus, according to Lewin's model, motivation always involves the acquisition of "valences" by objects in the "psychological field" of the individual. Such accounts, although possibly useful for scientific theory construction, have little relevance to the elucidation of motivation as viewed in common-sense terms, the traditional concern of the philosopher.

Are motivational explanations causal? Concern with the question of whether motivational explanations are causal has stemmed from the long-term preoccupation of philosophers with problems of free will and determinism. Actions which we are inclined to regard as free seem to fall within the class of motivated actions. Hence, if for *P* to be motivated to do *A* is for the occurrence of *A* to be caused by the motivating factors, and if causal determination of an action is incompatible with its being done freely, we are in trouble.

Discussion of the question has been hampered by obscurities in the notion of cause and causal explanation. Moreover, crudities and inadequacies in the traditional "interplay of consciously felt urges" conception of motivation have made the causal interpretation seem weaker than it actually is. Thus, it has been argued that we cannot regard motivation of behavior as causation of behavior, because desires are not in general conscious occurrences, and even if they were, we cannot suppose that a momentary feeling can give an adequate explanation of an intentional action. On the more adequate hypothetical construct view, these difficulties disappear, once we rid ourselves of the lurking superstition that only momentary occurrences can function in causal explanations. The difficulties which remain are twofold.

First, there are legitimate doubts as to the applicability to motivation of "cause" in any ordinary sense of that term. We most naturally speak of causes where some agent does something which results in an interference with the natural operations or condition of some other agent or substance. These conditions are satisfied when a piece of spoiled meat causes a stomach ache or an overload causes a bridge to collapse. As we depart from such paradigms, the identification of causes becomes increasingly problematic. The situation in which someone does something because of what he wants and believes is very far indeed from primary cases of causality, most strikingly in that here we cannot identify two different substances. The causal relation, if any, holds between states and operations of one and the same agent. This may account for the strain involved in the use of "cause" here. However, it is worth noting that physical laws do not generally specify causes in this sense. To know that the strength of electric current through a wire is a determinate function of certain other quantities is not to know that something causes something or other to happen, in the basic sense of "cause" specified above. However, if human actions were determined by wants and beliefs in basically the same way as that in which the strength of electric current is determined by certain physical factors, this would undoubtedly satisfy the proponents of determinism and dismay its opponents, whether "causes" be involved or not. Hence the crucial question would seem to be "Are the principles in accordance with which motivated actions result from wants and beliefs 'natural laws' in the sense of that term in which physics establishes natural laws?" A negative answer has been given to this question on the grounds that such principles simply make explicit part of the meaning of words like "want" and therefore cannot be understood to specify relations in which things in the world stand as a matter of empirical fact. However, earlier we saw grounds for denying that such principles are analytic in any straightforward way. Moreover, the most anyone could possibly claim to establish just by reflecting on the meaning of such words as "want" is some relatively unspecific principle like (26). But to get a principle that makes fully explicit the actual relations involved, we will have to go beyond this and find some way of measuring the factors involved and then specify the exact functions by which the probability of action varies with variations in these factors. And all this is surely a job for empirical investigation.

Motivation and reasons. A number of contemporary philosophers influenced by Ludwig Wittgenstein, such as A. I. Melden and G. E. M. Anscombe, have been working toward a conception of motivational explanation which is radically different from any so far considered. According to this view, it is a mistake to think of a motivational explanation as specifying the process which led up to an action, or indeed as specifying anything which actually existed in the spatiotemporal environment of the action. Instead, the explanation throws light on the action by bringing out how the agent does conceive, or would conceive, the action—by bringing out the reason(s) he had for acting as he did. It is not denied by these thinkers that such an explanation can take the verbal form "*P* did *A* because he wanted *S*." But it is denied that in saying this we are claiming that the action, *A*, is related to a psychological entity existing just before the action.

There is no doubt that being motivated to do *A* is very closely connected with doing *A* for a reason. It is only in "unconscious motivation" that a motivational explanation would not specify the agent's reason for doing what he did, and those who take the above position will naturally deny that "motivation" is used in the same sense in "unconscious motivation." But if we try to elucidate motivation in terms of the notion of a reason, we are left with the question as to what it is to do something for a reason. One way to answer that question is to say that *R* was *P*'s reason for doing *A* if and only if a belief that *R* is the case figured in the determination of the action in accordance with a principle like (26). But obviously this move is not open to those who want to interpret motivational explanations in terms of reasons; with this move we would be taking the reverse route.

Traditionally, doing something for a reason has been thought of in terms of a "judicial decision" model. The will surveys a variety of considerations and then chooses in accordance with whatever consideration "weighs" most heavily with it. But, apart from the fact that this model seems to be just a metaphor, Wittgensteinians are anxious to avoid construing motivation in terms of antecedent processes of any kind, and especially anxious to avoid bringing in such entities as "the will." No fully worked-out version of this position exists at present, but the dominant tendency is to relate doing something for a reason, and hence motivation, very closely to justification. Thus, one might try to explicate "*P* did *A* for reason *R*" by equating it with "If *P* were asked to justify his doing *A*, he would cite *R*." This will not work in so unqualified a form. One can have a reason for doing something without supposing that the reason justifies what he is doing. It could be the case that my reason for stealing some money is that I need it in order to buy a boat, without its being the case that I am prepared to offer this in justification of what I did. This position must be developed further before it can be regarded as a serious contender.

The kinds of wants. Another respect in which accounts of motivation differ from one another concerns "content" rather than "form," what sorts of wants there are rather than what it is to be a want or how wants affect action. Of course, as wants are usually specified there is an indefinite plurality of them; the variety of things wanted is almost as great as the range of human powers of conception. Nevertheless, the possibility remains that this diversity can be shown to stem from one or a few basic principles. Historically, the most important view of this sort is psychological hedonism, according to one of the forms of which the only thing which men desire for its own sake is pleasure (and the absence of pain); anything else is desired only because it is thought either to involve pleasure or to lead to pleasure. Some hedonists go so far as to *define* desire in terms of pleasure. Thus, J. S. Mill in *Utilitarianism* holds that to desire something and to find it pleasant are, strictly speaking, the same thing. When this happens, hedonism becomes a view concerning the "form" of motivation as well as its "content." More usually, however, hedonism is not put forward simply as a consequence of the meaning of "desire."

The most popular monistic view of motivation in contemporary psychology is the drive-reduction view. The term "drive" is variously explained in different systems, but it is generally used to denote some state of organic tension, which is often felt as unpleasant. Drive reduction figures prominently in systems, such as that of Hull, which try to explain behavior without using what we are thinking of as motivational concepts; but the notion has acquired wide currency in psychology. In any event, it is not difficult to translate the emphasis on drive reduction into motivational terms. When this is done, it becomes parallel with psychological hedonism, with drive reduction replacing pleasure. Alternative forms are

(33) Only drive reduction is desired for its own sake.

(34) One desires something only to the extent that it has in the past involved or led to drive reduction.

(35) One desires something only if he expects it to involve or to lead to drive reduction.

Most drive-reduction psychologists would prefer the second formulation. It is possible to combine this view with hedonism by the simple device of defining pleasure as the reduction of drive.

This view has become popular largely because it seems to fit relatively easily manipulable desires, like hunger and thirst, which, since they are easily manipulable, appeal to experimentalists. Here the desire arises when a state of organic need sets up readily identifiable states of tension. It is a speculative leap of considerable magnitude to maintain that the same pattern is to be found in desires for wealth, power, approval, and recreation, where the tension-reduction pattern is not introspectively identifiable, much less experimentally manipulable. The most promising suggestion along this line is that the tension involved in these "social" desires is something like anxiety, which has become conditioned to the felt absence of the object in question. When one becomes aware of a lack of approval, this gives rise to anxiety, which is then reduced when approval is forthcoming. It remains to be shown, however, that this is in fact what lies behind desires of these sorts.

Bibliography

Aristotle's discussions of motivation are to be found in *On The Soul*, Book III, Chs. 9–11, and *Nicomachean Ethics*, Book III, Chs. 3 and 4. Both are in *The Basic Works of Aristotle*, Richard McKeon, ed. (New York, 1941).

Philosophical accounts of motivation from the medieval period through the nineteenth century typically take the form of analyses of the operations of the will. For important accounts, see Thomas Aquinas, *Summa Theologica*, translated by the Fathers of the English Dominican Province, 3 vols. (New York, 1947), Part I, Ques. 80–83; Thomas Hobbes, *Leviathan*, Michael Oakeshott, ed. (Oxford, 1947; New York, 1962), Part I, Ch. 6; John Locke, *Essay Concerning Human Understanding*, J. W. Yolton, ed., 2 vols. (London, 1961), Book II, Chs. 20–21; and David Hume, *Treatise of Human Nature*, L. A. Selby-Bigge, ed. (Oxford, 1888 and 1955), Book II, Part 3.

For typical treatments of motivation in introspectively oriented psychology, see William James, *The Principles of Psychology*, 2 vols. (New York, 1890), Ch. 26; G. F. Stout, *Manual of Psychology*, 5th ed. (London, 1938), Book IV, Ch. 9; and Karl Duncker, "Pleasure, Emotion, and Striving," in *Philosophy and Phenomenological Research*, Vol. 1 (1940), 391–430.

Sigmund Freud's powerfully influential ideas on motivation, especially unconscious motivation, can best be approached through his *General Introduction to Psychoanalysis*, translated by Joan Riviere (New York, 1943), *Beyond the Pleasure Principle*, translated by James Strachey (London, 1922), and the essay "Instincts and Their Vicissitudes," translated by Cecil M. Barnes, reprinted in Freud's *Collected Papers*, Vol. IV (London, 1925).

For a variety of experimental approaches to motivation, see C. L. Hull, *Principles of Behavior* (New York, 1943); E. C. Tolman, *Purposive Behavior in Animals and Men* (New York, 1932); Kurt Lewin, *A Dynamic Theory of Personality*, translated by D. K. Adams and K. E. Zener (New York, 1935), and *Field Theory in Social Science*, Dorwin Cartwright, ed. (New York, 1951); and J. W. Atkinson, ed., *Motives in Fantasy, Action, and Society* (Princeton, N.J., 1958). A very useful recent survey and integration of the psychology of motivation is provided by J. W. Atkinson, *An Introduction to Motivation* (Princeton, N.J., 1964). K. B. Madsen, *Theories of Motivation* (Cleveland, 1961), is a more methodologically oriented survey of psychological theories. Philosophical accounts heavily influenced by developments in psychology are to be found in R. B. Perry, *General Theory of Value* (New York, 1926), and S. C. Pepper, *The Sources of Value* (Berkeley and Los Angeles, 1958).

Important discussions of psychological hedonism include J. S. Mill, *Utilitarianism* (London, 1861), Ch. 4; Henry Sidgwick, *The Methods of Ethics* (London, 1874), Book II; and Richard Brandt, *Ethical Theory* (Englewood Cliffs, N.J., 1959), Ch. 12.

Important recent treatments of motivation by analytical philosophers include Gilbert Ryle, *The Concept of Mind* (London, 1949), Chs. 4 and 5; R. S. Peters, *The Concept of Motivation* (London, 1958); A. I. Melden, *Free Action* (London, 1961); Anthony Kenny, *Action, Emotion, and Will* (London, 1963); D. S. Schwayder, *The Stratification of Behavior* (London, 1965); G. E. M. Anscombe, *Intention* (Oxford, 1959); the symposium "Motives and Causes," in *PAS*, Supp. Vol. 26 (1952), 139–194; Donald Davidson, "Actions, Reasons, and Causes," in *Journal of Philosophy*, Vol. 60 (1963), 685–700; and C. G. Hempel, "Rational Action," in *Proceedings of the American Philosophical Association* (1961–1962), 5–23. More specifically on the nature of desire are Brian McGuinness, "I Know What I Want," in *PAS* (1956–1957), 305–320, and Richard Brandt and Jaegwon Kim, "Wants as Explanations of Actions," in *Journal of Philosophy*, Vol. 60 (1963), 425–435.

Wᴵᴸᴸᴵᴬᴹ P. Aʟsᴛᴏɴ

MO TZU (c. 470–c. 391 B.C.), also called Mo Ti, was the founder of one of the classical systems of Chinese philosophy, Moism, as well as of a religious community. After serving for a brief period as a civil servant, Mo Tzu spent a number of years as a traveling counselor to feudal lords and princes, and, having never been given the opportunity to put his teachings into practice or the world in order, he had eventually to be contented with conducting a school and preparing his disciples for public office. He left a work consisting of 71 chapters, known as *The Mo Tzu*. It is said that Mo Tzu was at first a follower of Confucianism but later renounced it to found a system of thought of his own. He was critical of Confucianism for its emphasis on the codes of rituals and social elegance, which were to him burdensome and wasteful.

The rigoristic temperament of Mo Tzu made him also a man who practiced what he preached. A chief concern for Mo Tzu, for instance, was to reduce the recurrent military conflicts among the feudal states. There are records of his taking distant journeys to prevent the outbreak of impending wars. On one of his journeys, according to the record, he had to walk ten days and ten nights and tear off pieces of cloth from his garments to wrap up his sore feet.

A distinctive characteristic of Mo Tzu's thought was his stress on methodology. He declared: "Some standard of judgment must be established. To make a proposition without regard for standard is similar to determining the directions of sunrise and sunset on a revolving potter's wheel." He attached great importance to the threefold test and the fourfold standard. The threefold test refers to the basis, the verifiability, and the applicability of a proposition. Explained in present-day language, this test is employed to examine a proposition for its compatibility with the best of the established conceptions, its consistency with experience, and its conduciveness to desirable ends when put into operation. The benefits resulting from the application of a proposition, the last part of the threefold test, are conceived in terms of the fourfold standard, namely, enrichment of the poor, increase of the population, removal of danger, and regulation of disorder. Mo Tzu evidently would employ these tests and standards on all propositions without exception, and contemporary scholars have sometimes called him a pragmatist, and sometimes a utilitarian. There is a section of six chapters in *The Mo Tzu* that has come to be spoken of as the section on Moist logic. Most of the material contained therein has little utilitarian application, but it must have been written in Mo Tzu's tradition, if not by his hand. This logical development is an outgrowth of Mo Tzu's insistence on "standard of judgment" but is generally regarded as constituting a Neo-Moist movement.

A common problem that confronted all the thinkers of the classical age was how to bring order out of chaos. The system of feudalistic hierarchy instituted at the beginning of the Chou dynasty had crumbled, the Period of Warring States (403–222 B.C.) was setting in, and the people were living in suffering and bewilderment. By Mo Tzu's diagnosis, the chaotic condition was brought about by selfishness and partiality. And the cure? "Partiality should be replaced by universality." Universal love is the keystone of Mo Tzu's teaching. Mo Tzu was dissatisfied with Confucianism for its gradation in benevolence, and he exhorted everyone to regard the welfare of others as he regarded his own. He was convinced that the practice of universal love would bring peace to the world and happiness to man, and he took pains to demonstrate that the principle of universal love was grounded simultaneously in its practicability on earth and its divine sanction from Heaven. Universal love for Mo Tzu was at once the way of man and the way of God.

In contrast to most Chinese philosophers, Mo Tzu spoke of Heaven with feeling and conviction; his conception of it was similar to the Western conception of God. The will of Heaven was to be obeyed by man and was to be the standard of human thought and action. Heaven loved all men, and it was the will of Heaven that men should love one another. Soon after Mo Tzu's death the teacher's system became embodied in an organized church with a succession of elder masters and a considerable following.

As a religious congregation Moism did not last long, but as a system of thought and teaching Moism ranked with Confucianism for some two centuries as one of "the eminent schools of the day." Moism was pushed into the background if not into complete oblivion by the ascendancy of Confucianism for the next two thousand years and was rediscovered only in recent decades.

Bibliography

Mo Tzu's works were translated by Y. P. Mei as *The Ethical and Political Works of Motse* (London, 1929) and also by Burton Watson in *Mo Tzu, Basic Writings* (New York, 1963).

For literature on Mo Tzu, see Y. P. Mei, *Motse, the Neglected Rival of Confucius* (London, 1934).

Y. P. MEI

MOUNIER, EMMANUEL (1905–1950), French personalist philosopher, was born in Grenoble. He studied philosophy from 1924 to 1927 in Grenoble and in Paris, where he was successful in the *agrégation* examination of 1928. After teaching philosophy in schools during 1931 and 1932, he collaborated with others in bringing out a work on the thought of Charles Péguy, whom Mounier as a Roman Catholic greatly admired. This collaboration was extended to plans for a review to carry on Péguy's work, and *Esprit* was launched in October 1932. Mounier continued to edit the review in the face of difficulties, not least of which was the feeling of some Catholics that his position was virtually Marxist. He taught at the French *lycée* in Brussels from 1933 to 1939. He was called up for military service on the outbreak of war and was demobilized shortly after the fall of France in 1940. Mounier contrived to continue the production of *Esprit* until August 1941, when the Vichy government banned it.

Suspected of subversive connections, he spent some months in prison in 1942, but was eventually acquitted and settled with his family, incognito, near Montélimar. Mounier returned to Paris in 1945, and until his death he continued to produce books and a resuscitated *Esprit*, inspired by the times and his personalist response to them.

Mounier is the chief representative of the movement known as personalism. It is closely related, in the ideas it propounds, to existentialism. Personalism, however, is distinctively Christian and sees the personal "vocation" as seeking communication between unique persons, whereas existentialism is often divorced from religious belief, rejects the possibility of shared values, and is often strongly pessimistic concerning human relationships.

Mounier held that the person is entirely distinct from the political individual, who is "an abstract, legal, self-seeking entity, asserting his rights and presenting a mere caricature of the person." The person is "a spiritual being . . . subsisting by his adherence to a hierarchy of values freely adopted, assimilated, and lived through, thanks to a responsible commitment and a constant process of conversion."

The "unique vocation" of the person has little more specifiable content than Sartre's "original project." Mounier, however, insisted on the distinctive character of legitimate commitment, which is both personalist and *communautaire*, or directed toward a fellowship of other persons. Man's chief task, Mounier wrote in *Qu'est-ce que le personnalisme?*, is not to master nature but increasingly to bring about communication leading to universal understanding.

Personalism is a natural product of the kind of French philosophy that has, since Maine de Biran, stressed the notion of a self that in some measure owes its being to an external reality which it apprehends or upon which it acts. Such thinking led Mounier to say that "as the philosopher who first shuts himself up within thought will never find a door leading to being, so he who first shuts himself up in the self will never find a path to others." Mounier criticized Descartes, despite his modernity, for first adumbrating the solipsism which has since hung over modern man. In the economic field, bourgeois values "exalt the isolated individual and strengthen that economic and spiritual individualism" that still bedevils us. Mounier pointed the way from spiritually sterile self-absorption to the apprehension of reality in the form of not-self, particularly in the form of the other person with whom we communicate. The primitive experience of the person is the experience of the second person. The thou, including the we, precedes the I, or at least accompanies it. Mounier's objection to egoism was not only to economic individualism but also to its subtler forms, such as a fastidious withdrawal from modern vulgarity into the purity of the self. All true living is a transaction with the reality of the world and others in a process of mutual enrichment. There is no true inwardness that is not nourished by its interaction with an outer reality. "We must find our way out of our inwardness in order to sustain that inwardness."

Works by Mounier

La Pensée de Charles Péguy. Paris, 1931.
Révolution personnaliste et communautaire. Paris, 1935.
De la Propriété capitaliste à la propriété humaine. Paris, 1936.
Manifeste au service du personnalisme. Paris, 1936.
L'Affrontement chrétien. Neuchâtel, 1944.
Introduction aux existentialismes. Paris, 1946.
Liberté sous condition. Paris, 1946.
Traité du caractère. Paris, 1946.
Qu'est-ce que le personnalisme? Paris, 1947.
L'Eveil de l'Afrique noire. Paris, 1948.
Le Personnalisme. Paris, 1949.
Carnets de route, 3 vols. Paris, 1950–1953.

Works on Mounier

Copleston, Frederick, *Contemporary Philosophy.* London, 1956. Pp. 109–115.
Guissard, Lucien. *Mounier.* Paris, 1962.
Moix, Candide, *La Pensée d'Emmanuel Mounier.* Paris, 1960.

COLIN SMITH

MUKAMMAS, DAVID BEN MERWAN AL-, was one of the first medieval Jews to respond to the philosophical challenge of Muslim rationalism. Nothing about his life is known with any certainty, but he probably flourished in the early years of the tenth century. According to the account given by the tenth-century Karaite historian Kirkisani, David al-Mukammas was a native of Raqqa, in Mesopotamia. Born into the Jewish faith, Kirkisani stated, al-Mukammas became a Christian and then studied philosophy and theology at the well-known school of Nisibis, in Syria. Later, as reported by Kirkisani, he returned to

Judaism but is supposed to have made good use of his Christian learning in his commentaries on Genesis and Ecclesiastes, which have been lost. In the latter part of the nineteenth century some quoted fragments of al-Mukammas' philosophical work were discovered in Judah ben Barzilai's Hebrew "Commentary on the *Sefer Yezirah*" (early twelfth century). In addition, a substantial section of al-Mukammas' major work, *Ishrun Makalat* ("Twenty Chapters"), in the original Arabic, was found by Abraham Harkavy in 1898 in the Russian Imperial Library at St. Petersburg, but it was never published.

This fragmentary and incomplete knowledge enables us to assert that al-Mukammas' thought was deeply rationalistic, influenced in this direction by the Mu'tazilites (Arab theologians). His philosophy was, like theirs, generally cast in an Aristotelian mold, modified by some Neoplatonic elements. He shared with all Muslim philosophers a rigorous view of the divine unity; possibly it was the crystallization of this conviction that led to his rejection of Christianity and his return to Judaism. His discussion of the nature of the concept of unity as applied to God led him to distinguish between several ways of speaking about unity in ordinary language and to realize that none of these ways suggests what we mean in speaking of the unity of God, which is unique. More generally, al-Mukammas argued, whenever we use the language of description we imply comparison and classification; however, God is incomparable and unclassifiable. Strictly, then, whether we speak of God in the language of the Bible or in that of philosophy, our language cannot be understood in any ordinary sense. If God is One, then each expression we use in speaking of him must be synonymous with every other expression. To use a variety of different expressions adds nothing, therefore, to our description of God. Al-Mukammas suggested, however—anticipating Moses Maimonides in this suggestion—that although the different attributions add nothing positive, they do have the value of denying their antonyms.

In al-Mukammas, then, we have the first suggestion in medieval Jewish philosophy of the theory of negative attributes. On other matters, such as the doctrine of rewards and punishments, al-Mukammas seems to have had no difficulty in blending the traditional thought of the rabbis into his rational system.

Bibliography

Blau, Joseph L., *The Story of Jewish Philosophy.* New York, 1962.
Husik, Isaac, *History of Medieval Jewish Philosophy.* New York, 1916.
Vajda, Georges, *Introduction à la pensée juive du moyen âge.* Paris, 1947.

J. L. BLAU

MULLĀ SADRĀ is the name usually given to Muhammad ibn-Ibrāhīm Sadr al-Dīn Shīrāzī (1571/1572–1640), the most outstanding of the later Muslim philosophers. (*Mulla* means teacher.) He is also known by the honorific title Sadr al-muta'allihin, "the foremost among the theosophers." Born in Shiraz into an aristocratic family, he received his early education in that city and his advanced training in Ispahan, the Safavid capital, where he studied with Mīr Dāmād and Bahā' al-Dīn 'Amilī. After completing his formal education he retired to a village near Qum, where he spent ten years in asceticism and self-purification. Then, upon the demand of the Persian king, he returned to Shiraz as a professor in the school of Allāhwirdī Khān, where he taught and wrote for the rest of his life. He died in Basra on the return journey from his seventh pilgrimage to Mecca.

Mullā Ṣadrā wrote over fifty books, most of them after leaving his spiritual retreat. All his books are in Arabic except his "spiritual defense," the *Sih aṣl* ("Three Principles") and a few poems and letters, which are in Persian. His works can be classified into those dealing primarily with religion, such as his commentaries on the Qu'rān and the *Uṣūl al-Kāfī* ("Principles of Kāfī") of Kulainī, and those which deal mostly with philosophy and theosophy. In the latter category the most important is *Al-Ḥikmat al-muta-'āliyah fi'l-asfār al-arba'ah* ("The Exalted Wisdom Concerning the Four Journeys of the Spirit"), or simply *Asfār* ("The Journeys"), a work of monumental proportions and the most advanced work on Islamic philosophy. Mullā Ṣadrā also wrote a large number of shorter treatises, such as *Al-Mashā'ir* ("The Book of Metaphysical Penetrations"), *Al-Shawāhid al-rubūbiyah* ("Divine Witnesses"), and *Al-Ḥikmat al-'arshiyah* ("The Book of Theophany Inspired by the Throne"), which treat specific metaphysical and philosophical questions.

In Mullā Ṣadrā's work Muslim Peripatetic philosophy, especially that of Avicenna, the illuminationist theosophy of Shihāb al-Dīn Suhrawardi, the gnostic doctrines of Muhyī al-Dīn ibn-'Arabi and certain themes of Muslim theology (*Kalām*) became unified in the background of Shī'ism and the teachings of the Shī'ite imams. The philosophy of Mullā Ṣadrā, however, is synthetic rather than eclectic, because out of these various threads he created a new intellectual perspective in which reason, revelation, and mystic vision are harmonized into a total, unified view of things.

Mullā Ṣadrā brought to fruition the attempt of Muslim thinkers from the beginning of the Middle Ages to harmonize religion and philosophy. In his thought the tenets of revelation, the dicta of reason, and the verities of gnosis discovered through illumination are all considered possible sources of knowledge and are blended together. His writings in fact bridge discursive and intuitive knowledge by making the discoveries of reason the necessary background of spiritual knowledge, which is above reason without being irrational. Mullā Ṣadrā also revised many of the tenets of Peripatetic and illuminationist philosophy and established philosophy upon a set of principles, many of which were derived from Sufism, that had not been demonstrated as such and had not existed in philosophy before.

These principles include the unity, gradation, and principality of being, by which is meant that it is being rather than the quiddity or essence of things that is ultimately real. Moreover, being is inwardly unified as a single reality which possesses states and gradations. It is upon this principle that Mullā Ṣadrā built his "metaphysics of being." Another principle of his philosophy is the unity of the intellect, or intelligence, and the intelligible, of the knower and the known. At the moment of intellection the intellect becomes identified with the intelligible form of the object perceived. Thus, knowledge is intimately connected with being and affects the ontological state of the knower.

Mullā Ṣadrā also posited the principle of substantial motion. According to the previous Muslim philosophers and going back to Aristotle, motion is possibly only in the accidents of things, not in their substance. Mullā Ṣadrā thought that, on the contrary, motion implies an inner becoming within the substance of things and therefore a continuous development toward higher states of being (without in any way implying the modern theory of evolution).

Another important principle asserted by Mullā Ṣadrā is the catharsis and independence of the imaginative faculty from the body. There is an intermediate "imaginal world" (*mundus imaginalis*) not to be confused with the "imagination" of current usage. The human imagination is a microcosmic aspect of this cosmic imagination and it is precisely in this domain possessing a reality of its own that eschatological problems whose solution escaped earlier philosophers take place and can be understood. These and many other principles, some of whose roots are to be found in the writings of the earlier Sufis and philosophers, Mullā Ṣadrā systematized and developed to their full conclusion.

Mullā Ṣadrā had many students, of whom the most famous are Mullā Muhsin Faiḍ Kāshānī and 'Abd al-Razzāq Lāhījī, who were among the leading Shī'ite thinkers. His disciples propagated his works and teachings in both Persia and India, and in fact he founded a school which has dominated the intellectual life of Persia for the past three-and-a-half centuries. It is, however, against his world view that the founder of the Shaikhī movement, Shaikh Ahmad Ahsā'ī, wrote his criticisms. The Bāb, the founder of Babism, also belongs to the current against Mullā Ṣadrā and should by no means be considered as a product of his school. The school of Mullā Ṣadrā is still alive in Iran today and is the most important traditional school of philosophy and theosophy there.

Works by Mullā Ṣadrā

Kitāb al-Ḥikmat al-'arshiyah ("The Book of Theosophy Inspired by the Throne"). Teheran, 1278 H./A.D. 1861.

Al-Ḥikmat al-muta'āliyah fi'l-asfār al-arba'ah ("The Exalted Wisdom Concerning the Four Journeys of the Spirit"). Teheran, 1282 H./A.D. 1865; new ed., M. H. Ṭabāṭabā'ī, ed., Teheran, 1378 H.——/A.D. 1958——.

Al-Shawāhid al-rubūbiyah ("The Divine Witnesses"). Teheran, 1286 H./A.D. 1869.

Rasā'il ("Treatises"). Teheran, 1302 H./A.D. 1884.

Ta'līqāt 'alā ilāhīyāt Kitāb al-Shifā' ("Glosses Upon the Metaphysics of the Book of the Remedy of ibn-Sīnā). Teheran, 1303 H./A.D. 1885.

Sharh al-hidāyat al-athīrīyah ("Commentary Upon the Guide of Athīr al-Dīn Abharī"). Teheran, 1313 H./A.D. 1895.

Kitāb al-mabda' wa'l-ma'ād ("The Book of Origin and Return"). Teheran, 1314 H./A.D. 1896.

Ta'līqāt 'alā Kitāb Hikmat al-ishrāq ("Glosses Upon the Theosophy of the Orient of Light [of Suhrawardi]). Teheran, 1315 H./A.D. 1897.

Asrār al-āyāt ("Secret of Quranic Verses"). Teheran, 1319 H/A.D. 1901.

Sih aṣl ("The Three Principles"), S. H. Nasr, ed. Teheran, 1380 H./A.D. 1960.

Kitāb al-mashā'ir, edited and translated by Henry Corbin as *Le*

Livre des pénétrations métaphysiques. Teheran and Paris, 1964. Contains Arabic text, Persian version, and French translation.

Mafātīḥ al-ghaib ("Keys to the Hidden World"). Teheran, n.d.

Sharḥ al-uṣūl min al-Kāfī ("Commentary Upon the Principles of Kāfī"). Teheran, n.d.

Works on Mullā Ṣadrā

Āshtiyānī, S. J., *Sharh-i ḥāl wa ārāy-i falsafi-i Mullā Ṣadrā* ("The Biography and Philosophical Views of Mullā Ṣadrā"). Meshed, 1382 H./A.D. 1962. In Persian.

Corbin, Henry, *Terre céleste et corps de resurrection: De l'Iran mazdéen à l'Iran shī'ite.* Paris, 1961.

Corbin, Henry, "La Place de Mollā Ṣadrā Shīrāzī dans la philosophie iranienne." *Studia Islamica,* Vol. 18 (1963).

Horten, Max, *Das philosophische System von Schirazi (1640) übersetz und erläutert.* Strassburg, 1913.

Langarūdī, Muḥammad Ja'far, *Sharḥ al-mashā'ir* ("Commentary Upon the Book of Metaphysical Penetrations"), S. J. Āshtiyānī, ed. Meshed, 1384 H./A.D. 1964.

Nasr, S. H., ed., *Mulla Ṣadra Commemoration Volume.* Teheran, 1380 H./A.D. 1960.

Nasr, S. H., *Islamic Studies.* Beirut, 1966.

Nasr, S. H., "Ṣadr al-Dīn Shīrāzī," in M. M. Sharif, ed., *A History of Islamic Philosophy,* Vol. II. Wiesbaden, 1966.

Sajjādī, S. J., *Muṣṭalaḥat-i falsafi-yi Ṣadr al-Dīn Shīrāzī mashhūr bi Mullā Ṣadrā* ("The Philosophical Vocabulary of Ṣadr al-Dīn Shīrāzī"). Teheran, 1380 H./A.D. 1960. In Persian.

SEYYED HOSSEIN NASR

MURO KYŪSŌ (1658–1734), Japanese Confucianist who was instrumental in defending the Chu Hsi school of Neo-Confucianism as the official learning of the Tokugawa government. Muro was born in Edo (Tokyo) and was a pupil of Kinoshita Junan (1621–1698) in Kyoto. In 1711 he became, through the recommendation of the scholar-statesman Arai Hakuseki (1657–1725), the official scholar of the Tokugawa government. He was commissioned to compile the *Rikuyu engi-tai* ("Outline of Principles of Confucianism") that in 1724 became the standard textbook on Chu Hsi's doctrine for all official schools. Muro in his early years was not a follower of the Chu Hsi school; as he tells us in his *Shundai zatsuwa* ("Conversations at Surugadai"), it was only at the age of 40, after a long period of doubt, that he embraced Chu Hsi's thought. The doctrine was then under heavy attack by such of the "ancient learning" scholars as Yamaga Sokō, Itō Jinsai, and Ogyū Sorai. Muro believed he had been chosen to defend the teaching of Chu Hsi, and to this task he dedicated the rest of his life with unsparing zeal.

Muro's ideas are not strikingly original, but they have the power of sincerity and conviction. Typical are his denunciations of hypocrisy, a trait not so uncommon among formalist Confucians, and his insistence upon virtue as springing from the inner self; two of his favorite maxims were "Be true to the self" and "The root of evil lies in the innermost recesses of the mind." His ideas on the Godhead bear a similarity to the Christian conception of the attributes of God. The deity (or deities) is omnipresent and omniscient. He stressed self-vigilance and the realization of heavenly reason in human life. The heavenly order was to be reflected in the social one, thus consolidating the immutability of Tokugawa society. His sense of the indebtedness (*gi*) and the gratitude (*on*) man owes to Heaven, the earthly lord, the parent, and the teacher was bound to foster obedience

rather than self-assertiveness. Muro opposed the scholars of the "ancient learning" school, who, with others, supported the emperor; Muro stood solidly for the Tokugawa government. He was also critical of Buddhism and Shinto. But the tide was against him; especially in vain was his effort to preserve the ancient spirit of the samurai who more and more assimilated into the merchant class.

Bibliography

Muro's *Rikuyu engi-tai* ("Outline of Principles of Confucianism") was published in Kyoto in 1722. His *Shundai zatsuwa* ("Conversations at Surugadai") is available in Inoue Tetsujirō, ed., *Nihon rinri ihen* ("Library on Japanese Ethics"; Tokyo, 1903), Vol. VII, pp. 81–122; it has been translated by G. W. Knox as "A Japanese Philosopher," in *Transactions of the Asiatic Society of Japan,* Vol. 20. Part I (1893), pp. 28–133. See also W. T. de Bary, Ryusaku Tsunoda, and Donald Keene, eds., *Sources of Japanese Tradition* (New York, 1958), pp. 433–442.

GINO K. PIOVESANA, S.J.

MURPHY, ARTHUR EDWARD (1901–1962), American philosopher, creator of the phrase "objective relativism." Murphy was born in Ithaca, N.Y., and received his training in philosophy at the University of California (A.B. in 1923, Ph.D. in 1926). He taught successively at California, Chicago, Brown, Illinois, Cornell, Washington, and Texas; at the last four he was department chairman.

Murphy attracted attention at an early age with his article "Objective Relativism in Dewey and Whitehead" (1927). He argued that the writings of these two influential philosophers exhibited a convergence on a common doctrine, which reversed a tradition of treating "objects as primary, as substantives, and events as characters of objects." In contrast, for Dewey and Whitehead "the event is substantive and objects are characters of events. Thus relatedness, in all its complexity and interconnections, is made basic for the objective world." Murphy, himself, supported this doctrine, which had a vogue for a time.

In 1930, however, Murphy attacked Whitehead's *Process and Reality* in his article "The Development of Whitehead's Philosophy." In later writings he repeatedly charged both Dewey and Whitehead, among other metaphysicians, with attempting to prove by speculative metaphysics what would better be offered as sheer speculation, to be tested in appropriate contexts. Commenting on Dewey, he wrote: "What Mr. Dewey says about cognition is true of it as he defines it and false of it as more ordinarily understood" ("Dewey's Epistemology and Metaphysics," in *The Philosophy of John Dewey,* edited by P. A. Schilpp, p. 210, Evanston and Chicago, 1939).

Throughout his career Murphy maintained an acquaintance with philosophers of varied opinions. As a graduate student on a traveling fellowship, he explored the philosophical currents of Europe in 1924/1925, when realism was at its height. During the 1930s his work as book editor of the *Journal of Philosophy* gave him occasion to examine and to pass judgment on the purpose and achievements of his generation and the previous one.

Murphy spent the year 1937/1938 in England, and from his remarks it is apparent that he was directly influenced by Ludwig Wittgenstein through reading the *Blue Book,* as well as indirectly through Wittgenstein's colleagues in

England. He grew increasingly dissatisfied with speculative metaphysics, as may be seen in his contributions to the Dewey, Moore, and Whitehead volumes of the Library of Living Philosophers. His disillusionment with his own creation, objective relativism, is reported in "What Happened to Objective Relativism." Yet, to the end, it was his opinion that the speculative philosophers had opened roads to "a better understanding of the values that are basic to human life" than had most of the so-called analytic philosophers.

Murphy's strong convictions on the importance of philosophy in a liberal education led him to expend a great deal of time on the work of the Commission on Philosophy in American Education of the American Philosophical Association. His opinions on this subject are to be found in the chapters that he contributed to *Philosophy in American Education* (1945) and in his own essays.

Much of his work illustrates his expressed intent "to write philosophy . . . with explicit reference to contemporary issues" (*The Uses of Reason,* p. 5). His early concern with epistemology and metaphysics changed to a dominating preoccupation with the uses of reason in ethical and social enterprises. His last twenty years were directed toward the working out of a systematic account of ethics. Sketches of this attempt appear in the chapter, "The Context of Moral Judgment," in *The Uses of Reason,* and in his essays. Murphy made good use of his powers of assimilation and criticism in examining the great moralists with a view to extracting and identifying points that must be taken account of in any subsequently defensible ethical theory. At his death, he left a long manuscript, *The Theory of Practical Reason,* which elaborates his Carus lectures of 1955, originally known as "An Enquiry Concerning Moral Understanding."

Bibliography

Murphy's *The Uses of Reason* was published in New York in 1943. He contributed Chs. 2, 3, and 10 to *Philosophy in American Education* (New York, 1945). *Reason and the Common Good. Selected Essays of Arthur E. Murphy,* edited by W. H. Hay and M. G. Singer (Englewood Cliffs, N.J., 1963), includes a bibliography and the papers on objective relativism and Whitehead mentioned in this article. See also *The Theory of Practical Reason,* edited by A. I. Melden (La Salle, Ill., 1965).

WILLIAM H. HAY

MUSLIM PHILOSOPHY. See ISLAMIC PHILOSOPHY.

MUST. What must be true or must be done is as various as the possible meanings of "must." The variety of these meanings is discouragingly large, but if it is kept in mind that "must" is basically a modal term, closely related to "can," its philosophically interesting meanings may be classified and then clarified without excessive difficulty.

There are, broadly speaking, two fundamentally different sorts of "cans," one relating to permissions and the other to possibilities. (The "cans" of permission are, of course, used interchangeably with "may," the latter being preferred by most grammarians.) Corresponding to these "cans" are two basic sorts of "musts," one relating to obligations and the other to necessities. Formal logicians,

concerned with alethic and deontic modalities, have mapped out the structure of this correspondence in a very neat, if highly abstract, way. According to the usual account, the "must" of absolute necessity, a priori or nomological, is interdefinable with the "can" of absolute possibility, a priori or nomological. Thus, "A must happen, or *p* must be true" may be taken to mean "Non-A cannot happen, or not-*p* cannot be true." The "must" of obligation is analogously related to the "can" of permission: "A must be done or is obligatory" means the same as "Non-A cannot (may not) be done or is not permitted." Given these relations, it may thus be said that anyone who is clear about the basic uses of "can" should have no difficulty understanding the corresponding uses of "must" (see CAN).

The "musts" of necessity. There are five basic senses of the term "possibility" (see POSSIBILITY). Since the word "can" is used in all five of these senses, one would expect, in view of the above-mentioned correspondence, that there are five related senses of "must." This is indeed the case. For convenience these five senses of the word may be listed as (1) the "must" of absolute necessity, both a priori and nomological; (2) the "must" of relative necessity, both a priori and nomological; (3) the "must" of epistemic necessity; (4) the "must" of overwhelming probability; and (5) the "must" of inveterate tendency or propensity.

"Musts" of absolute and relative necessity. In ordinary life we may express the fact that whatever is colored is necessarily extended by the words "Whatever is colored must also be extended." Here the "must" is used to indicate a priori necessity. When, however, we express the fact that unsupported bodies necessarily fall to the ground by saying, "An unsupported body must fall to the ground," we are using the word in the sense of nomological necessity. One may also use "must" to indicate relative necessity, as in saying, "If Jones is not here, he must be somewhere else." But familiar as this locution is in everyday life, it is unlikely that the "must" it contains is normally used in such a sophisticated sense. The logic of the relative modalities is, in fact, highly intricate, and careful writers, aware of the extreme ease with which modal fallacies are committed, generally employ "must" in the consequent of their conditional statements as a sign that the consequent follows from the antecedent either by logical necessity or by some other firmly established principle of inference.

"Must" of epistemic necessity. A state of affairs is deemed epistemically necessary when it follows from our knowledge at a given time that the state of affairs did, does, or will certainly obtain. Examples of this use would be "He must have committed the crime; our evidence rules out any other possibility" and "Having examined the room, I can assure you that he must have entered by the window."

"Must" of overwhelming probability. It is obvious that the last use of "must" is very close to what may be called the "must" of overwhelming probability, an example of which is "He must fail this time; no one's luck can last forever." The point in distinguishing these last two "musts" may, in fact, appear wholly academic, but it has considerable significance for the task of distinguishing different orders of certainty (as in epistemology, probabil-

ity theory, and so on), and it is actually forced upon us by the fact that the corresponding uses of "can" with which these "musts" are interdefinable are very different indeed.

"Must" of inveterate tendency. The "must" of inveterate tendency corresponds to the "can" of ability. We sometimes use the word "can" to indicate what a person has the ability to do without implying that he has the opportunity to exercise that ability; thus, "He can swim, read French, play chess." The corresponding sense of "must" is used to indicate that a particular ability is exercised whenever possible or that an agent is prone to, even compulsive about, exercising it. Some familiar examples of this use are "Our dog must bark at every stranger that comes to the door"; "Why must he always tell the same old story?"; "Tom must fish every spring and hunt every fall."

"Must" of circumstantial compulsion. Closely related to this last sense are various uses of "must" having roughly the force of "being compelled by the circumstances." These are not technical uses, reflecting, for instance, a sophisticated concept of physical necessity, absolute or relative. They correspond, rather, to the "can" of opportunity, which reflects a fairly rough and ready idea of what one might reasonably expect to happen or be done under certain circumstances. In this use of "must" we deem certain events or actions to be out of the question with respect to given circumstances. Thus, it may be said that a man must do what he is forced to do by threats or punishment. In such cases there need be no implication that it is strictly impossible, physically, for the man to have done other than what he did do or that had he tried harder to resist, he would necessarily have failed. On the contrary, if a man does all that we can reasonably expect of him by way of resisting coercion, then even if it is strictly possible for him to resist until he falls unconscious, we can still truly say that he had to do what he did, that he had no real alternative.

Normative uses of "must." The last use of "must" mentioned above shades into the normative or "regulative" uses, for the circumstances that may compel an action are sometimes defined in normative terms. Thus, it may be said that a man must enter the army if he is drafted, that he has no alternative but to report for induction. This claim, however, need not be equivalent to the claim that he was under a legal obligation to enter the army. If it can be shown that he had no satisfactory alternative to entering the army, going to jail not being a satisfactory alternative, then the man might truly say, "I must go into the army; I have no real choice in the matter."

Hortatory "must." Before turning to the purely normative uses, it is worth observing that "must" is very commonly used in a mainly hortatory sense, as in "You must stop that noise; it's driving me crazy" or "You must read this novel; the author is really first rate." These uses have philosophical interest because the "must" of moral obligation also has a hortatory force, so much so that philosophers holding an emotivist theory of ethics have argued that this is the only force that the word actually possesses. This theory seems plainly untenable, but there is no denying that the hortatory force of "must" in such deontic uses as "One must pay one's debts" is extremely significant, both for the speaker and the hearer. With reference to the

significance of such statements for the speaker, it has been forcefully argued in recent years that a man who recognizes that he must (in the distinctive moral sense) perform a certain action is *ipso facto* moved to perform it. We commonly explain a man's behavior by reference to the practical reasoning, moral and otherwise, that evidently prompted it, and if a man's sense of his own obligations did not move him to act in roughly the manner that his active intentions move him to act, explanations of this sort would be impossible. (Compare INTENTION.) In other words, if Aristotle were right that the intellect cannot itself move one to act, then reference to a man's moral or other reasons for acting as he does would not, as we normally assume it does, strictly answer the question of why he acts this way.

"Must" of obligation. Coming now to what might be called the purely normative uses of the word, it can be said that a man must do what is required of him by law, morality, custom, or convention or even what he is commanded or requested to do by some appropriate authority. Moral philosophers would, of course, argue that all these cases are to be classified in some special way, and different logics of obligation have been advanced to deal with special features of a particular case. Thus, it is sometimes held that very few things are unconditionally obligatory, as doing one's duty presumably is; other actions are said to be obligatory only relative to special conditions. This distinction between absolute and relative obligations parallels the distinction between absolute and relative necessity, and moral philosophers sometimes tend to use the formal apparatus designed for the logical modalities to formalize the logic of moral and other obligation as well. In general, it can be said that the logic of obligation is extremely complicated and problematic, as are the problems of moral philosophy generally, and no attempt to analyze these notions will be made here.

Is one sense fundamental? Although this article began with the claim that there are two basic sorts of "musts"—those of necessity and of obligation—the question arises whether these two sorts are really on the same level or whether one is actually more basic than the other. This question is an enormously complicated one, going to the heart of some of the oldest issues in philosophy. In view of the extreme complexity of the issue, only a few brief remarks can be made here.

Considering the analogous points made about the "cans" of possibility, it can be said that the fundamental uses of "must" in the sense of necessity concern a priori and nomological necessities. Now, empiricist philosophers have traditionally taken a very dim view of nomological necessities (see IF); for them such necessities (or "real connections") simply do not exist in nature. If, accordingly, we can legitimately speak of nomological necessities, our remarks must be interpreted as somehow elliptical for talk about laws of nature, where these laws are conceived as statements or principles concerning the regularities that actually obtain in the natural order. Many such interpretations of nomological necessities have been defended in the literature (on this see IF and LAWS OF SCIENCE AND LAW-LIKE STATEMENTS), but their general import can perhaps be indicated more concretely by the following claim: To say that it is nomologically necessary that all *A*'s are *B*'s is to say, very roughly, that our inductive evidence concerning *A*'s and *B*'s is such that the statement "All *A*'s are *B*'s" may be affirmed without reservation and that the negation of this statement—namely, "Some *A*'s are not *B*'s," must (in the sense of ought to) be disregarded as false. In other words, according to some empiricists, to speak of certain states of affairs as physically or nomologically necessary (to say that they must occur or obtain) is to express one's reasoned confidence that the facts of the world are such that statements describing these states of affairs may be safely affirmed in all contexts of discussion and that denials of these statements must (ought to) be rejected as false. If views of this general sort are at all tenable, it would therefore follow that the "must" of nomological necessity is ultimately reducible to the "cans" and "musts" of permission and obligation—that is, to the purely normative uses of these words.

In connection with the "must" of a priori necessity, nominalists are typically anxious to make a similar move. According to these thinkers, there is no Platonic domain of necessary truths. Statements to the effect that such and such is a priori necessary must rather be interpreted as in some way conveying essentially linguistic information. A. J. Ayer once expressed this view by saying that necessary statements simply record our determination to use symbols in a certain way, and more recently it has been argued that such statements are best understood as "object language surrogates for linguistic rules." However exactly this nominalist position is best stated, it is clear that if the general position is sound, the "must" of a priori necessity is also reducible to the "cans" and "musts" of permissions and obligations. For linguistic rules prescribe what may or must not (ought not) be inferred from certain premises or what may or may not be affirmed, given the formal structure of a particular language.

Bibliography

Austin, J. L., "Ifs and Cans," in his *Philosophical Papers*, J. O. Urmson and G. J. Warnock, eds. Oxford, 1961.

Edwards, Paul, and Pap, Arthur, eds., *A Modern Introduction to Philosophy*, 2d ed. New York, 1965. Should be consulted for more detailed information; see especially Ch. 1 and pp. 99–108.

Hook, Sidney, ed., *Determinism and Freedom in the Age of Modern Science.* New York, 1958.

Morgenbesser, Sidney, and Walsh, James, eds., *Free Will: A Book of Readings.* Englewood Cliffs, N.J., 1962.

Pears, D. F., ed., *Freedom and the Will.* London, 1963.

Taylor, Richard, *Metaphysics.* Englewood Cliffs, N.J., 1963. See Chs. 4–5.

Von Wright, G. H., *An Essay in Modal Logic.* Amsterdam, 1951.

BRUCE AUNE

"MY DEATH." Philosophers, psychologists, and novelists have written a great deal on the topic of "one's own death." It is hardly debatable that most human beings view their own deaths with more concern than they do the deaths of others—at least of those to whom they are not bound by any strong affection. A number of writers have, however, claimed a great deal more than this. According to some, a person cannot even imagine or conceive his own death, although he has apparently no difficulty in imag-

ining or conceiving of someone else's death. According to another account, in statements about one's own death the meaning of the word "death" is not the same as in statements about the deaths of others. The aim of the present article is to examine both these views.

"Our own death is unimaginable." "Our own death," writes Freud, "is unimaginable." "It may be considered axiomatic," in the words of Karl Menninger, "that the human mind cannot conceive of [its] non-existence." It is impossible for an individual, write N. L. Farberow and E. S. Shneidman, two leading students of the psychology of suicide, "to imagine his own death . . . a state where there is no more *I*, after death." All these writers are psychologists or psychoanalysts, but the same view is advanced by thinkers with very different affiliations. Thus, according to Chancellor von Müller, Goethe made the following "quite definite pronouncement": "It is entirely impossible for a thinking being to think of its own nonexistence, of the termination of its thinking and life." Goethe apparently took this to be evidence for personal immortality, for he went on to remark that "to this extent everybody carries within himself, and quite involuntarily at that, the proof of his own immortality." Similarly, the American pragmatist Sidney Hook observes that "we cannot imagine ourselves dead," apparently regarding this as a statement not in need of defense or proof. Unlike Goethe, however, Hook denies that the unimaginability of one's own death is any evidence for immortality. As far as is known, none of the writers just quoted maintains that our nonexistence before we were born is either unimaginable or inconceivable.

At first sight at least, there seems to be something exceedingly odd about all these statements. It seems quite plain that human beings not infrequently imagine and conceive of their own deaths without the least difficulty, as, for example, when they take out life insurance or when they admonish themselves to drive more carefully. Nor is it at all difficult to explain what a person imagines when he thinks of his own death. "When I die," wrote Bertrand Russell in a famous passage (in "What I Believe"), "I shall rot and nothing of my ego will survive"; and it is surely this that people wish to avoid or put off. A person thinking of his own death is thinking of the destruction or disintegration of his body and of the cessation of his experiences.

Yes, it will be remarked, to conceive of one's own death, it would be quite sufficient to conceive of the cessation of one's experiences; but that is precisely the trouble: a person cannot, no matter how hard he tries, conceive of or imagine such a cessation. "Whenever we make the attempt to imagine our death," in the words of Freud, we can, on reflection, "perceive that we really survive as spectators." We are not, then, really imagining our own death, since *as spectators* or witnesses we are still around; and the attempt to eliminate ourselves as spectators is bound to fail. It is bound to fail because as long as we do the imagining, we are still present.

This argument surely confuses the content of a thought with the fact of its occurrence at a certain time in the life of a human thinker. It is analytically (and trivially) true that a person must be alive in order to think of anything at all, just as it is analytically true that his thinking must take place at some moment or moments and must be conducted by means of symbols of some kind. But nothing whatsoever follows from this about the content of his thoughts: it does not follow that he is thinking *about* the moment at which the thinking takes place or about the symbols he uses. To take a simple illustration: it is now 3:23 P.M., August 12, 1965, and I am wondering how and when the war in Vietnam will come to an end. My thought here is clearly not about the moment at which I am thinking it or about the fact that I am employing certain English words. Similarly, the fact that I must be alive in order to think about my death does not mean that my continued existence is part of the content of my thoughts. Occasionally, I do indeed think about my (still) being alive or my going to be alive at some later time, but my own present or future existence is certainly not the subject matter of all my thoughts, although all my thoughts must occur while I am alive.

It should be pointed out that in Freud's argument the word "spectator" is used in a very special sense which must be carefully distinguished from another, more familiar sense. In this more familiar sense, thinking of oneself as a spectator does imply that one is thinking of oneself as not dead. Thus, let us suppose that I make plans to visit London next summer and to go to look at Goldie, the famous freedom-loving eagle in the London Zoo. In thinking about this visit I deliberately include myself among the spectators. Subsequently, it turns out that I cannot visit London, and I think again about Goldie and the people who will watch her, but this time I deliberately *exclude* myself from the spectators. Let us call these two thoughts T_1 and T_2, respectively. It surely makes perfectly good sense to say that in T_1 I did, but in T_2 I did not, include myself as spectator, and to include oneself as spectator in this sense implies that one imagines or conceives of oneself as being alive. Here, it should be noted, my being or not being a spectator *is* part of the content of my thoughts. However, this is clearly not the sense in which Freud uses the word; for in his sense the mere fact that I am thinking T_1 and T_2 makes me a spectator in *both* of them, quite regardless of their content: in T_2 I am present as spectator in Freud's sense although I deliberately excluded myself as a spectator in the other, more familiar sense. If the argument of the preceding paragraph is sound, we may characterize Freud's procedure in the following way: he invalidly concludes that because a person must be present as spectator in all his thoughts in the special sense in which this logically follows from the mere fact that he is thinking them, the person must also be present as spectator in the more familiar sense in which this tells us something about the content of his thoughts.

The confusion of writers like Freud and Goethe can perhaps also be brought out in the following way: It is maintained that I cannot imagine or conceive of my own death, but it is granted that another person, say, *B*, can imagine and conceive of my death. But what is *B* thinking of when he is thinking of my death? Anything more than the dissolution of my body and the cessation of my experiences? Surely not. Furthermore, *B*'s being alive while he is thinking of my death is not regarded as a dis-

qualification: it is not taken to affect the content of his thought. He is not, just because he is alive, thinking about my death *as well as* about his own being alive. He may, of course, think about both, but thinking about the former does not require him to think at the same time about the latter. But if the fact that *B* is alive while he thinks about my death does not affect the content of his thought, why should the fact that I am alive when I think of the dissolution of my body and the cessation of my experiences affect the content of my thought and require one to say that I, unlike *B*, am not then thinking of my death?

Again, it is granted that we can imagine or conceive of our nonexistence before we were born. However, just as we have to be alive when we think of our death, so we have to be alive when we think of our nonexistence before birth; and yet the writers who maintain that our death is unimaginable or inconceivable do not regard this as a reason for concluding that our nonexistence before birth is unimaginable or inconceivable.

To achieve a complete diagnosis of the confusion we have been discussing it would be necessary to supply an account of the various ways in which the words "imagine" and "conceive" are used in different kinds of situations. However, no such account is required to see *that* the writers in question are confused. For in whatever sense or senses the deaths of others and the nonexistence of oneself before birth can be imagined and conceived, in precisely this sense or senses can the death of oneself also be both imagined and conceived.

Annihilation of the spectator. Let us now turn to the other of the two views mentioned at the beginning of this article—that "death" does not mean the same in statements about one's own death as in statements about the death of other people. From reading Heidegger one gets the impression that this is one of the conclusions he reaches in Division Two, Section I, of *Being and Time*. Unfortunately, his terminology is so obscure that it is impossible to be sure. However, Peter Koestenbaum, one of his American disciples, has recently presented a lucid defense of this view, which moreover seems to express very well what many existentialists have been trying to say on this subject.

Unlike Freud, Koestenbaum maintains that a person *can* eliminate himself as spectator and hence that his own death is not unimaginable or inconceivable. However, if and insofar as somebody succeeds in eliminating himself as spectator, the word "death" takes on a different meaning. "Our death," writes Koestenbaum, "is generically different from the death of others"; we encounter here "a very serious and altogether fundamental ambiguity in the word 'death.'" A "phenomenological" analysis discloses that when we think of the death of another we eliminate "an object within the world" without at the same time eliminating "the observing ego or subject." If a man examines closely what he means by the death of another person, "he recognizes that *he himself is still in the picture*: he is the observer contemplating the scene, even if the scene may be only in his imagination. Death is an event within the world, while the life-world, the world of human experience, perdures" ("The Vitality of Death," p. 141). Our meaning is altogether different, however, when we think of our own death. A careful phenomenological analysis must examine more than the physical disintegration of the individual's body. It will then be seen that "my own death means the total disintegration and dissolution of my *world.* The death of myself is well described phenomenologically by the terms 'void' or 'encounter with Nothingness'" (*ibid.,* p. 142). In my thoughts about the deaths of others the "central fact" is "the continuous presence of my own self or ego as the inescapable observer"; in my thoughts about my own death "the central fact is that the *observer himself dies or vanishes*" (*ibid.*). It is for this reason that a candid "confrontation with my own death submerges me into the deepest state of anxiety." When I fully realize what my own death means I seem to myself "like a falling body in a dark and infinite abyss" ("Outlines of an Existential Theory of Neuroses," p. 13).

The disappearance of the observer in the thought of one's own death "entails, in a sense, the disappearance of the world itself." If anxiety is not allowed to interfere with "honest analysis," and if I "think of my death as the end of everything, then, in a manner of speaking, I must think as well of the termination of the universe itself." It is a "phenomenological error" to regard the thought of my death as simply being a thought of the cessation of my heartbeats, my burial, and similar events accompanied by the continuation of the world. "That is *not* how the threat of my own death presents itself to me" ("The Vitality of Death," pp. 142–143). If I leave the continuation of the world in my picture, then I have surreptitiously and erroneously slipped myself back into the situation as "some sort of eternal observer." To avoid this phenomenological error I must remember that my death is the death of the observer himself and that "with the extinction of the observer, the entire scene vanishes as well." Hence, "my image of the death of myself is tantamount to asserting the end of the world" (*ibid.*).

It can hardly be denied that there is some truth in this account. When people think about their deaths they do get pictures of voids, of falling through dark abysses, and the like. To bring home to themselves the utter finality of death, people say things like "With my death, my world comes to an end." Sometimes, perhaps, they even say "With my death, the world comes to an end." It is also true that while it is at least logically and at times also physically possible for me to witness the death of others, it is not even logically possible for me to witness my own death. Nevertheless, Koestenbaum's presentation involves the same confusion as Freud's argument considered earlier, and nothing he says has the slightest tendency to show that as applied to me and to others the word "death" is used in different senses. However many pictures of voids and abysses may accompany my thoughts, it is not these pictures which make them thoughts of my death. My thoughts are thoughts of my death insofar as they are thoughts of the disintegration of my body and the cessation of my experiences. In thinking these thoughts I am, of course, present as the thinker, but this does not mean that I have surreptitiously introduced my living self into the *content* of my thought. Nor does the fact that it is logically possible for me to witness the death of others but impossible for me to witness my own death show that "death" means something different in the two cases. It is also logi-

cally impossible for me to experience somebody else's anger or pleasure, but this does not show that "anger" and "pleasure" have different meanings when attributed to somebody else and to me. In fact, as we saw in the last section and as we again saw a moment ago, it is quite clear that what a person means by "death" (not in the sense of associated images or feelings, but in the only relevant sense of referential or descriptive meaning) is exactly the same in both cases: the disintegration of the individual's body and the cessation of his experiences. The word "death" is not one whit more ambiguous in such a case than, say, the word "father." If *A* says about himself that he is a father, this may be associated with feelings of pride or anxiety which he does not experience when he says about his colleague *B* that he too is a father, but this does not make the word "father" ambiguous. Koestenbaum notwithstanding, we do not have in the case of death, any more than in the case of fatherhood, "generically different phenomena."

It is true that in order to think of my death, it is not enough to think of the cessation of my heartbeats or of other bodily functions—I must also think of the cessation of my experiences. However, I do *not* also have to think of the annihilation of the world. In this connection Koestenbaum is guilty of an illicit transition from "*my* world" to "*the* world." It must indeed be granted that with my death my world comes to an end; for in this context "my world" is just a rhetorical way of referring to me or my life. It may also be granted that the end of my life or my world is, *in a manner of speaking,* the end of everything or the end of the world. It is the end of everything if the "manner of speaking" amounts to the qualification that it is the end of everything *for me* or *in my experience.* If the "manner of speaking" is deleted, as happens in the later stages of Koestenbaum's account, then the transition from "my world" to "the world" becomes illegitimate. If I die, if my world comes to an end, it does not follow that *the* world comes to an end—at least not unless solipsism is true, and solipsism here means *my* solipsism, not anybody else's. In fact, to judge by what happened after the death of others, each of us has extremely good grounds for supposing that after his world comes to an end, *the* world will go on. Koestenbaum's phenomenological analysis appears to be in error here. In thinking of our own death we do not suppose that the world is going to come to an end also. To give just two examples: people who envy the young because they have many years ahead of them certainly do not suppose that the world will be annihilated when they die, and the same is unquestionably true of anybody who makes his will. Even existentialist philosophers, it may be noted in passing, appoint literary executors. If, however, phenomenological analysis really disclosed that human beings believe *the* world to come to an end upon their death, then phenomenological analysis would disclose that when human beings "candidly" think of their death, they habitually believe a false proposition.

Bibliography

Freud's discussion of death is found in "Reflections Upon War and Death" (1915), reprinted in *Collected Papers,* 5 vols. (New York, 1959) and in *Character and Culture* (paperback ed., New

York, 1963). The Menninger quotation is from his *Man Against Himself* (New York, 1938). The passage by Shneidman and Farberow is from their essay "Suicide and Death," in Herman Feifel, ed., *The Meaning of Death* (New York, 1960). Goethe's remarks are quoted from T. Vogel, ed., *Goethes Selbstzeugnisse über seine Stellung zur Religion* (Leipzig, 1888). The line quoted from Sidney Hook occurs in his review of Heidegger's *Being and Time* in the *New York Times Book Review* (November 11, 1962), pp. 6 and 42. Morris Lazerowitz, in *The Structure of Metaphysics* (London, 1955), offers criticisms of Freud similar to those advanced in the present article.

Heidegger's discussion is found in *Being and Time,* translated by John Macquarrie and Edward Robinson (New York, 1962), Div. 2, Sec. I. Peter Koestenbaum's views are presented in "The Vitality of Death," in *The Journal of Existentialism,* Vol. 5 (1964), 139–166, and in "Outlines of an Existential Theory of Neuroses," in *Journal of the American Medical Women's Association,* Vol. 19 (1964), 472–488. Another treatment of the subject of one's own death which was strongly influenced by Heidegger can be found in P. L. Landsberg, *The Experience of Death* (London, 1953). We have not, in this article, concerned ourselves with the interesting psychological observations by Heidegger and various of his followers about the stratagems which human beings employ in order to evade the need for thinking about their death. Landsberg, who died very young in a Nazi concentration camp, offers some singularly acute observations about various human attitudes toward death and dying. Unfortunately, his work is almost completely unknown outside Germany.

PAUL EDWARDS

MYERS, FREDERIC W. H. (1843–1901), English essayist, minor poet, and psychical researcher. After a brilliant career at Trinity College, Cambridge, and after teaching there for a few years, he worked as a government school inspector. He married in 1881 and lived most of his life in Cambridge. Myers was one of the founders of the Society for Psychical Research (1882).

Myers is perhaps best known today for a passage in his essay on George Eliot which relates how, when speaking to him of God, immortality, and duty, she "pronounced, with terrible earnestness, how inconceivable was the *first,* how unbelievable the *second,* and yet how peremptory and absolute the *third.*" It is typical of Myers that he should have thought she withdrew from him "the two scrolls of promise, and left [him] with the third scroll only, awful with inevitable fates," for he possessed to a high degree the Victorian wish to retain a belief in God and exemplified one of the more extreme forms of the Victorian obsession with immortality. The chief aim of his life was to find evidence to support the belief in immortality or, as he preferred to call it, survival of bodily death. In particular he wished to find "scientific" evidence for immortality, holding that the time had passed when any other sort of support for beliefs could be at all convincing. Underlying this aim was the conviction that the restlessness, the spiritual dryness, and the increasing *Weltschmerz* of the nineteenth century could be removed only by discovering some way of giving an acceptable proof of the ancient truth that there is a profound kinship between the human soul and the nature of the universe. He devoted his energies chiefly to the investigation of psychic phenomena and to the elaboration of a theory in terms of which their significance could be estimated, and he finally reached the comforting conclusions that there are disembodied spirits, that we ourselves are spirits who can survive bodily death, and that some of us are even now sometimes in touch with

the spirit world. "The worst fear is over; the true security is won," he wrote at the end of his major work, *Human Personality and Its Survival of Bodily Death.* "The worst fear was the fear of spiritual extinction or spiritual solitude; the true security is in the telepathic law."

The bulk of *Human Personality* consists of reports of various types of supernormal experiences, some taken from the literature of mental disease, some from reports of earlier ages or from autobiographical writings, but most taken from cases investigated by the Society for Psychical Research and reported in its *Proceedings.* The facts are organized by the hypotheses that (1) if there is a spiritual world, we can expect it to manifest itself; (2) if there is a spiritual realm, it is governed by discoverable scientific laws; and (3) the self or personality of which each of us is consciously aware is only a fragment of a much larger self, manifestations of which are hindered but not rendered impossible by our present connection with a physical organism. The considerable vagueness of Myers' statement of the crucial third hypothesis makes it difficult to estimate the soundness of much of his reasoning.

He held that his hypotheses were borne out by the facts, and therefore he felt himself able to suggest further, very tentative, conclusions. "The religious upshot of observation and experiment," as he called it, is not corroborative of any exclusive theology, although in some respects the Buddhist view is more nearly correct than the Christian. Evolutionary development, he said, is the law of the spirit world as it is of our world, and the development is continuous from this world to that: as men here grow in holiness, so spirits there grow in love and wisdom. Myers thought that although there may be something like an "inconceivable union with the Divine," the growth in the spiritual realm is endless. He believed that the spirits see more of the laws of the spiritual realm than we do; they see enough to know that despite the existence of evil the universe is basically good. And because love and joy and wisdom are rooted in the nature of things, the egoist, Myers believed, can be refuted and a sound morality can be established.

Bibliography

For Myers' poetry, see *St. Paul* (London, 1867) and *The Renewal of Youth* (London, 1882). For Myers' prose, see *Wordsworth* (London, 1881); *Essays Classical; Essays Modern* (London, 1883); *Science and a Future Life* (London, 1893); *Human Personality and Its Survival of Bodily Death,* 2 vols. (London, 1903), with an abridged one-volume edition (London, 1906); and *Fragments of Prose and Poetry* (London, 1904). Myers also collaborated with Edmund Gurney and Frank Podmore on *Phantasms of the Living,* 2 vols. (London, 1886).

There is a study of Myers by William James in *Memories and Studies* (New York, 1911).

J. B. SCHNEEWIND

MYSTICISM, HISTORY OF. Mystical experience is a major form of religious experience, but it is hard to delineate by a simple definition for two main reasons. First, mystics often describe their experiences partly in terms of doctrines presupposed to be true, and there is no one set of doctrines invariably associated with mysticism. Some of the definitions of mysticism advanced by Western writers are quoted by W. R. Inge in his *Mysticism in Religion* (p. 25): "Mysticism is the immediate feeling of the unity of the self with God" (Otto Pfleiderer); "Mysticism is that attitude of mind in which all relations are swallowed up in the relation of the soul to God" (Edward Caird); "True mysticism is the consciousness that everything that we experience is an element and only an element in fact, i.e. that in being what it is, it is symbolic of something else" (Richard Nettleship). Quite clearly, such definitions import a religious and philosophical interpretation to the phenomenon of mysticism that would not be shared by all contemplatives. For instance, the Buddhist mystic, not believing in a personal God, would reject the first two of these definitions; and he might well be skeptical about the third—in what sense is the experience of nirvana symbolic of something else?

Second, there is quite a difference between mystical experience and prophetic and, more generally, numinous experience, but it is not easy to bring out this phenomenological fact in a short definition. (A numinous experience is an experience of a dynamic external presence—described classically in Rudolf Otto's *The Idea of the Holy* as that of a *mysterium tremendum et fascinans,* an awe-inspiring and fascinating mystery.) Sidney Spencer says, for instance, "What is characteristic of the mystics is the claim which they make to an immediate contact with the Transcendent" (*Mysticism in World Religion,* p. 9). Such a definition includes under mysticism the experiences of the Old Testament prophets, those of Muhammad, and the theophany described in the *Bhagavad-Gītā.* However, these differ so markedly from the interior illumination of such figures as Eckhart, Teresa of Ávila, Śankara, and the Buddha that it is misleading to bracket the two kinds of experience. This article will explicitly exclude the prophetic and numinous experience, save where it becomes relevant to the experiences and doctrines of those properly called mystics. It is thus best to indicate what is meant by "mysticism" by referring to examples, such as Eckhart and the others cited above, and by sketching some of the important features of the type of experience in question without interpreting it doctrinally.

Generally, mystics as typified by Eckhart, Teresa of Ávila, Śankara and the Buddha feel that their experience is somehow timeless, that it involves an apprehension of the transcendent (of some thing, state, or person lying beyond the realm of things), that it gives them bliss or serenity, and that it normally accrues upon a course of self-mastery and contemplation. These are certainly features of what has been called introvertive mysticism by W. T. Stace (*Mysticism and Philosophy,* p. 60). There are other experiences, however; those of extrovertive mysticism, where, according to R. C. Zaehner, one gains a kind of rapport with the world, or "panenhenic" feeling (*Mysticism Sacred and Profane,* Ch. 1). These neither coincide with prophetic experiences nor strictly with those of introvertive mysticism, but since they sometimes occur in conjunction with the latter, it is convenient to treat them as mystical. Various abnormal mental states, such as those induced by mescalin, lysergic acid, and alcohol are sometimes considered mystical, but they are far enough removed from mainstream mysticism for it to be reasonable to neglect them here.

In the light of all this, we can distinguish various aspects of mysticism: the experiences themselves, the paths or systems of contemplative techniques often associated with them, and the doctrines that arise from mysticism or are affected by it. Also, such paranormal phenomena as levitation are sometimes ascribed to mystics, although they usually regard these as of secondary significance.

There is no single history of mysticism because some of the major religious traditions have been largely independent of one another. Further, there is no way of knowing the real origins of mysticism, since for such an intimate type of experience we must rely chiefly on written records and thus have no access to prehistoric mysticism. Studies of contemporary nonliterate cultures—in Africa, for instance—do not reveal the presence of much or any mysticism proper; for example, the religious experiences of the Nuer in the Sudan are more akin to those of Old Testament prophecy. It is thus convenient to confine attention to the main literate religious traditions: Indian religions (Hinduism, Buddhism, Jainism, Sikhism); Chinese and Japanese religions; and the Semitic faiths (Judaism, Christianity, and Islam). It may be noted that early Christian mysticism was influenced by Greek, notably Platonist, ideas.

THE INDIAN TRADITION

The mainstream of Indian mysticism centers on the practice of yoga, which in its general sense involves techniques of pacifying the mind and of attaining interior insight. Evidence from the pre-Aryan Indus Valley civilization indicates that it may have been practiced in the second millennium B.C. or earlier. By contrast, the religion of the Aryans who settled in north India centered on sacrifice set in a polytheistic framework. As this ritual religion became more complex, questions arose concerning the inner meaning of the sacrificial rites. The *Upaniṣads* (the chief of which date from about 800 B.C. to about 500 B.C.) were in part concerned with extending and deepening sacrificial ideas in the quest for *vidyā,* or knowledge of sacred reality. Quasi-magical ideas surrounded this notion—for instance, that knowledge gives power over the thing known and that one can become identified with the thing known. At the same time, mystical ideas began to permeate religious thinking, notably the idea that through austerity and self-control one could attain a realization of one's eternal self. A confluence of these streams of religious thought resulted in the famous central identification expressed in the *Upaniṣads,* "That art thou"; the sacred reality embracing and sustaining the cosmos ("That") and the eternal self ("thou") are one. In brief, inner mystical knowledge brings a union with the Divine.

This union is described in various ways: "Just as a man embraced by his dear wife knows nothing at all, outside or inside, so does the eternal life-monad [*puruṣa*], embraced by the supreme spiritual Self, know nothing at all, outside or inside" (*Bṛhadāraṇyaka Upaniṣad,* IV. 3.21); "As rivers flow to their rest in the ocean and there leave behind them name and form, so the knower, liberated from name and form, reaches that divine Person beyond the beyond" (*Chāndogya Upaniṣad,* 6). Sometimes the lack of duality between the divine Being and the soul is stressed: "Where there is a duality, as it were, one sees another, tastes another, speaks to another. . . . But when everything has become one's own self then whom and how would one see? . . . The Self is not this, not that" (*Bṛhadāraṇyaka Upaniṣad,* IV. 5.15). Mystical consciousness is also said to be like a state beyond dreamless sleep. These passages hint at what is virtually universal throughout Indian yoga, the fact that the contemplative state in its highest form involves going beyond ordinary perceptions, mental images, and thoughts. It is thus not describable by the ordinary expressions for mental states. It is no doubt partly for this reason that the distinction between perceiver and perceived is not regarded as applicable, and so the contemplative who conceives himself as "seeing" *Brahman* (the divine Being) thinks of this as a kind of union with *Brahman.* By contrast, in atheistic systems of Indian religion, where there is nothing for the self to be identified *with,* the contemplative state is conceived in a rather different way.

Although identification between the self and *Brahman* is a central theme in Upaniṣadic religion, some of the writings, notably the *Kaṭha* and the *Śvetāśvatara Upaniṣads,* are more theistic in spirit and less inclined to speak in terms of identification. These differences of emphasis are partly the reason for the divergences in interpretation found in different types of Vedānta in the medieval period.

Jainism and yoga. Jainism, Buddhism, and the tradition later formulated as classical yoga involved an atheistic or agnostic interpretation of mystical experience. Jainism and classical yoga (the long-extinct Ājīvika school) were monadistic: they believed in an infinity of eternal life monads or souls, and the aim of the ascetic was to bring about the isolation of the soul from its material environment. Such an isolation would involve the cessation of reincarnation and thus final deliverance from suffering. Jainism, because it held that karma, the force determining people's situations as a result of their previous deeds, is a subtle form of matter, considered extreme *tapas* (austerity), which had the effect of annihilating this material force, the central means of liberation. Nevertheless, it seems that the Jain teacher Vardhamāna (known also as Mahāvīra), a contemporary of the Buddha, and his disciples claimed to attain a certain kind of experience analogous to the experience of nirvana in Buddhism. Thus, in Jain doctrine the life monad in its emancipated state gains omniscience, a concept reflecting the intense sense of insight accruing upon the contemplative experience.

Buddhism. The accounts of the Buddha's enlightenment—a crucial event in the history of Indian religion and likewise centrally important in the history of Indian mysticism—are elaborate and circumstantial. During the first night, the Buddha, seated under the bo tree, remembered the series of his former births; during the second, he acquired the "heavenly eye," which enabled him to view the entire world and the whole cyclical process of rebirth; during the third, he saw how the latter depended upon grasping and ignorance—if living beings were liberated from these, they would escape rebirth; and in the fourth, he attained supreme insight after going through the various stages of meditation (Sanskrit, *dhyāna;* Pāli, *jhāna*). In all this he gained supreme peace. No doubt the scriptural records are a formalized account, hardly based on the Buddha's autobiographical report, but they certainly point to the type of inner experience early Buddhism prized. Something can be learned from the *Theragāthā* and *Therīgāthā,* verses composed by monks and nuns and expressing the flavor of early Buddhist contemplative experience. These poems often show the sensitivity of the recluse to the beauty of nature:

The peacocks shriek. Ah, the lovely crests and tails
And the sweet sound of the blue-throated peacocks.
The great grassy plain with water now
Beneath the thunder-clouded sky. Your body is fresh;
  you are vigorous now and fit
To test the teaching. Reach now for that saintly rapture,
So bright, so pure, so hard to fathom,
The highest, the eternal place.
                              (*Theragāthā* clxvi)

The eternal place is, of course, nirvana.

The achievement of inner peace and insight, as opposed to the use of complex psychological categories in explaining human nature, was given comparatively little doctrinal elaboration in early Buddhism because the Buddha apparently felt that the concepts of the transcendent state (nirvana) and the cessation of rebirth through the perception or attainment of nirvana were sufficient means of interpreting mystical experience. Certainly, he did not give the more elaborate type of interpretation found in the *Upaniṣads* and in theistic mysticism. It is clear, however, that the experience or experiences involved both the attainment of a marvelous serenity and a kind of knowledge or insight (something regarded as knowledge, given the presuppositions of the Buddhist mystical quest). Grasping and ignorance are dispelled by this peace and knowledge.

Buddhism rejected the doctrine of a plurality of eternal souls, but in a sense it can be seen as a transcendence of monadism, with the concept of the eternal soul replaced by that of the capacity to attain release. Thus early Indian mysticism is typically monadistic, except in the *Upaniṣads,* where the interior experience is related to the *Brahman* and where, therefore, the *Brahman–ātman* (self) equation is formulated. Only because the eternal self of the mystic is identified with the presupposedly single divine Being is the plurality of souls denied. The numinous religion of Brahmanism overlays that of the contemplative mysticism of yoga, and the mystical experience is interpreted in terms of union with the unitary divine Principle.

Mahāyāna Buddhism, from the first century B.C. on, moved toward a more elaborate interpretation of the contemplative path. Nirvana was identified with the Absolute, variously named Suchness (*tathatā*) and the void (*śūnya*). These terms served to bring out the ineffability and undifferentiated nature of ultimate reality, which in turn corresponded to the undifferentiated and "void" nature of the contemplative experience itself. The Absolute was also identified, from the standpoint of the ordinary worshipers, with the Truth Body of the Buddhas—the transcendent and essential aspect of Buddhahood—and thus the mystical path involved being a Bodhisattva (Buddha-to-be). The distinctionless, nondual experience of ultimate reality, the goal of the path, was the achievement of identity with the Absolute, which was equated with Buddhahood. This is why the Mahāyāna path of contemplation was thought of as the path of Bodhisattvahood, so that on his enlightenment the mystic would himself become a Buddha.

As a preliminary, the aspirant practices individual worship (*pūjā*) of the celestial Buddhas and Bodhisattvas and can gain assurance from a living Buddha that his aspiration to Buddhahood will be fulfilled. He practices the perfections of the path, culminating in supreme wisdom or insight (*prajñā*).

There are three chief differences between Mahāyāna and Hīnayāna, now represented by the Theravāda (in Burma, Ceylon, and parts of Southeast Asia). First, the Mahāyāna stresses self-giving more strongly, so that the aspirant continually looks to the welfare of others; second, it is a path accessible to laymen as well as to monks; third, contemplation is supplemented by the use of sacramental and ritual practices, at least in certain phases of the Mahāyāna. Some of these practices, known as tantra, became well developed in the middle of the first millennium A.D. in both Hinduism and Buddhism and deeply affected the Buddhism of Tibet. It sometimes involved the ritual breaking of tabus (against meat-eating and against sexual intercourse outside marriage): such a breaking of tabus was regarded as a means of testing and developing detachment. Coordinate with this type of Buddhism was a highly ritualistic use of sacred texts and recitations. The most outstanding figure of Tibetan mysticism was the poet and yogi Milarepa (1040–1123).

Hinduism. The theistic religion implicit in some of the *Upaniṣads*, reinforced by popular cults and by an emphasis on *bhakti,* or loving adoration of God, led to a different valuation of mysticism in the *Bhagavad-Gītā.* The poem speaks of three paths to salvation: the way of knowledge (primarily contemplative knowledge), the way of works, and the way of devotion (*bhakti*). The three paths are stressed in different parts of the *Gītā*, but two significant lessons emerge. First, the pursuit of works (religious and moral duties) need not bind one to the world if they are performed in a spirit of self-surrender to God; the way of works should be seen in the light of the way of devotion. Second, the yogi who pursues knowledge (*jnana*) can become *Brahman* (VI.27). Elsewhere, however, *Brahman* is spoken of as part of God; the personal aspect of God is more important than his impersonal aspect. Thus the yogi, in pursuing a strictly contemplative path, can only unite himself with the lower, rather than the more important, aspect of the Lord's nature. This doctrine represented a higher evaluation of *bhakti* than of contemplative yoga. (It must be pointed out that traditional Indian commentators are divided on the question of what is the correct interpretation of the *Gītā*. However, there is little doubt that extraneous theological and philosophical presuppositions have played a large part in determining interpretations.)

The continued growth of devotional or *bhakti* religion led to a similar interpretation of mysticism during the medieval period. Thus, in the twelfth century Rāmānuja reversed the doctrinal priorities of Śankara (ninth century). Śankara's monism represented the most radical interpretation of the Upaniṣadic identity texts, asserting a numerical identity between the soul and the divine Being. While for Śankara the personal Lord was a lower manifestation of the Absolute, so that worship and devotion could be transcended when one had attained the apprehension of identity with Brahman, Rāmānuja, although recognizing identity as one religious goal, conceived it as an inferior form of release. The higher form was the vision of the personal God, in which the soul was in a state of loving dependence on the Lord. Both Madhva (thirteenth century) and the theistic Śaivite schools of Indian philosophy interpreted mystical experience in terms of union with God, but not a union involving the numerical identity of the soul and God. Thus, mystical experience was interpreted by reference to the duality of the soul and God implicit in the religion of *bhakti:* the worshiper has a strong sense of the majesty and glory of God, and thus of the difference between himself and the object of worship. Various analogies were used, including that of the marriage of the soul and God, since sexual love symbolizes the intimate union between the lover and the beloved while presupposing the difference between the two. This analogy tied in with the cult of Krishna: the legend of Krishna's amorous dalliance with the milkmaids was seen as an allegory of the relation between God and men's souls.

The interiorization of religion involved in both devotionalism and contemplation influenced Nānak (1469–1538), founder of the Sikh religion, who preached doctrines combining the anti-idolatrous monotheism of Islam and such characteristic Hindu ideas as reincarnation and karma.

There have been a number of outstanding contemplatives in modern Hinduism. Chief among them was Ramakrishna Paramahamsa (1834–1886), whose disciple Vivekananda (1862–1902) did much to popularize his teachings in both the East and the West; Vivekananda's organizing ability was chiefly responsible for the flourishing state of the Ramakrishna movement, in which the contemplative life is geared to social service and also provides a pattern of living that can, according to the teachings of the movement, transcend the differences between the great living faiths. A twentieth-century mystic who tried to adapt traditional teachings to modern thought was Aurobindo. Contemplation and yoga, through the activities of numerous recluses, holy men, and gurus, continue to play a prominent role in Indian religion.

CHINA AND JAPAN

Chinese mysticism has two main sources, Taoism and Buddhism. A product of their interaction was Ch'án, better known under its Japanese name, Zen. The teachings of Confucius were not much concerned with the contemplative quest for inner illumination, although certain mystical ideas were expressed in the *Book of Mencius* of the Confucian tradition. On the whole, however, early Confucianism was indifferent to the contemplative ideal.

Taoism. The chief early mystical writing in China was the *Tao-te-ching,* traditionally ascribed to Lao-tzu, who is thought to have been an older contemporary of Confucius. It is likely, however, not only that the book was later but also that it was the work of several men. The anthology expresses a roughly consistent viewpoint, one which, on the most natural account of it, has its roots in contemplation (although some commentators give it a nonmystical interpretation).

The Way, or Tao, referred to in the *Tao-te-ching* is both a principle underlying natural processes and a mode of life whereby the sage can gain identity or harmony with nature. Since nature acts spontaneously and effortlessly, the book claims that the sage likewise can be effective through inaction (*wu-wei*) and effortlessness. Thus, the pattern of life suggested is one of withdrawal and passivity. In these themes the *Tao-te-ching* reflects some of those found elsewhere in mystical literature: the sense of identification with the Principle (li) underlying the world and the need for an unworldly mode of existence. Because the attainment of harmony with Tao was seen as living in accord with nature, the Taoists reacted against what they considered the artificialities of social life and etiquette as practiced by the Confucians, and from the doctrine of *wu-wei* they derived political views not far from anarchism.

In practice the effortlessness of the Taoist contemplative was modified by the use of techniques of meditation, such as controlled breathing, analogous to those employed in Indian yoga. The Taoist aim of an immediate, intuitive, inner illumination was sufficiently close to the aim of Buddhist meditation for it to be natural that the two streams of religion should influence each other in the period after Buddhism's arrival in China, in the first century A.D. In particular, it was during the sixth and following centuries that this interplay was most marked.

Neo-Confucianism. The success of Buddhism, which in part resulted, at least among intellectuals, from the subtlety of its metaphysical doctrines, was a factor in stimulating the so-called Neo-Confucian revival, in which a metaphysics was elaborated to underpin the Confucian ethic.

One main phase of this revival was the growth of philosophical idealism, which owed something to mystical ideas. Thus, Lu Hsiang-shan (1139–1193) argued that there is a single underlying principle, li, that explains all things and is spiritual. Thus, he claimed, his mind and the universe were one. It followed that one can discover the truth by introspection.

Such an idealism was further developed by Wang Yang-ming (1472–1529), about whom a significant story is told. He and a friend were concerned about the method by which one should purify the mind, for Chu Hsi (1130–1200) had said that one should investigate the nature of things. Wang and his friend decided to contemplate a bamboo in the front courtyard but gave up after several days. It is notable that this attempt corresponds to one of the preliminary methods of Buddhist contemplation. Although unconvinced by such "external" contemplation, Wang nevertheless considered the interior quest—the purification of consciousness—important. He believed that through looking inward at one's own nature one could gain an intuitive knowledge of the whole of reality. It is said that while in banishment and living under poor and menial conditions, Wang had a mystical experience in which he realized this doctrine existentially. However, Wang was far from abandoning the traditional Confucian emphasis on ethical behavior; he did not advocate quietism and passiv-

ity but saw in mysticism a way of enhancing moral goodness. Inner illumination would shine through in active concern for others. However, in such Neo-Confucianism the influence of Ch'ān Buddhism can be detected.

Buddhism. Ch'ān, or Zen, Buddhism embodies the most distinctive feature of both Chinese and Japanese mysticism, since it incorporated Taoist ideas into Buddhist mysticism. Other schools of Far Eastern Buddhism in varying ways carried on and developed the Buddhist tradition and therefore incorporated Buddhist contemplative ideals. A powerful aspect of Far Eastern Buddhism was the success of the Pure Land school, which centered its teachings on the faith and devotion whereby the ordinary person could receive supernatural aid from the Buddha Amitābha and gain rebirth in the paradise of the Pure Land. With its stress on devotion and the efficacy of the Buddha's grace, this school tended to bypass contemplative mysticism and to focus religion upon worship.

JUDAISM

Although the Hebrew Bible contains virtually no expression of contemplative religion, mysticism developed within Judaism by the first century B.C. It centered mainly on the imagery of the *merkabah* (chariot), described in Ezekiel as a complex vision of the manifestation of divine power in the shape of supernatural beings riding on a mysterious four-wheeled chariot (Ezekiel 1). The Talmud indicates that some of the early rabbis practiced asceticism and self-purification as a preparation for a mystical "ascent into heaven." Philo Judaeus (c. 20 B.C.–c. A.D. 50) mentioned a community of Therapeutae near Alexandria who practiced a form of contemplative monasticism, and likewise mysticism may have been part of the Essene way of life. Philo himself was the greatest figure in these early phases of contemplative Judaism, although he was so deeply affected by Greek ideas that he is outside the mainstream of Jewish thought and piety. According to Philo, man, through his intellect, has an affinity with God; and through the contemplative life he can in principle attain a state where he can see God's essence. In accordance with Platonist and mystical ideas, Philo expounded a negative theology: God eludes the affirmations we try to make about him. Consequently, Philo's interpretation of Scripture was not at all literalistic, and he made lavish use of the allegorical method. He attempted, moreover, to show that the experiences of the prophets were mystical.

The most important period of Jewish mysticism was the Middle Ages. Beginning in the twelfth century there developed Hasidism, which made a lasting imprint on central European Judaism, and Cabalism, mainly in Spain and southern France. The former takes its name from the term *Hasidim* ("devout ones"), a name originally applied to a movement of the second century B.C. that was a forerunner of Pharisaism. Medieval Hasidism concentrated on the cultivation of the sense of divine presence. Modern Hasidism, dating from the eighteenth century, is more directly contemplative and is indebted to Cabalism.

Cabalism. Cabalism centered on the esoteric teachings known as the Cabala, which found their chief expression in the *Zohar* ("splendor"), a work traditionally ascribed to the second century but actually dating from the thirteenth century or a little earlier, that conceives of God as the En-Sof, the "Endless" or "Infinite." In itself the En-Sof is qualityless, but there are ten ideal qualities, known as the *Sefiroth*, that emanate from the Infinite—wisdom and power, for instance. These are used to explain the creation of the world. The cosmos that man inhabits, however, is the lowest sphere in which the *Sefiroth* operate—a doctrine that expresses the way in which the perfect Infinite is far removed from the imperfect world we inhabit. The hierarchy of stages between God and the material world is reminiscent of Gnosticism. Nevertheless, the En-Sof, being infinite, does in some sense embrace lower forms of existence; and every entity in the universe reflects and interpenetrates everything else.

How is all this related to traditional Jewish teachings? According to the Cabala, the doctrine of interpenetration implies that lower events will stimulate corresponding activity from on high. The fall of Adam brought about a rupture in the cosmos; the Shekinah, or Divine Presence, became exiled from the En-Sof. No longer does the Presence pervade the whole world; it appears intermittently here and there—for instance, in ancient Israel—and has continued to be especially associated with the Jewish people. The aim of the pious should be to bring about a reunion of the En-Sof with the Shekinah. Since the human soul contains some of the *Sefiroth*, the individual experience of such a reunion will have its cosmic effects and help to restore universal harmony. Consequently, the mystical life was given a dramatic and central place in the operations of the universe.

It will be apparent that some of these ideas, such as the ineffability of the En-Sof and the rather impersonal description of God, echo similar notions in Neoplatonism and other forms of mystical theology. Despite the unorthodoxy of much of their speculation, the Cabalists continued the detailed observance of Jewish law, ascribing to it a mystical significance.

Isaac Luria. An important figure in the development of Cabalism was Isaac Luria (1534–1572), of a Spanish Jewish family living in Palestine. He believed in reincarnation, which would give men ever fresh chances of living the pure life and would provide a framework for the punishment of those who had transgressed. Luria conceived of Adam as a universal being who before the Fall embraced the universe, then in an ideal state. With his fall, the material world was created, and the light of his divine nature was fragmented into the sparks that illuminate the myriads of living souls. In the final consummation, all will be reunited. Asceticism and the practice of *kavannah*—concentrated devotion in all one's acts—were the means of purifying the soul. Social conditions may have helped the growth of such doctrines, for the emphasis on meekness, love, and a quiet interior life were well adapted to the unhappy outer circumstances of the Jewish people, and the Cabalistic reinterpretation of the Messianic hope gave the contemplative a cosmic role.

Modern Hasidism. The founder of modern Hasidism was Israel Baal Shem-Tov (c. 1700–1760), who lived in Carpathia in eastern Europe. He gathered round him disciples who were devoted to the mystical life. His succes-

sor, Baer of Meseritz (1710–1772), was an energetic organizer and missionary who spread the movement among Jews throughout east Europe and the Ukraine. Stress was laid on the concept of the zaddik, or perfectly righteous man, through whom the favor of God is channeled. Only he can attain union with the divine Being; less perfect folk must find their spiritual development through his guidance. This doctrine is reminiscent of Hindu ideas about the guru as conveyor of illumination. In any event, Hasidism implied that the zaddik, rather than the rabbi or learned person, was the immediate source of authority. This gave Hasidic mysticism a popular following and organization, and the essential simplicity of its message—that salvation can be attained through prayer and pious acts—made it adaptable to the experience of people of no great sophistication or learning.

As elsewhere in the history of mysticism, antinomian tendencies made their appearance. Thus Sabbatianism, named after Sabbatai Zevi (1626–1676), a self-styled Messiah who preached apostasy from Judaism, made use of Cabalistic ideas in order to justify the concept of the God–man who is "beyond good and evil," as in the teachings of Jacob Frank (c. 1726–1791).

Although the Hasidim often attacked official rabbinical teaching, the revival of Jewish learning in the nineteenth century paved the way for a reconciliation between orthodoxy and Hasidic piety, so that the latter still remains a force within the fabric of Jewish religion.

CHRISTIANITY

Origins. As has been mentioned, there was little mysticism in the traditions of Judaism until the time of Christ, and there also seems to have been little in the experience of the earliest church. It is true that Paul underwent a powerful experience of being "caught up to the third heaven," which could have had a mystical character, although it is also reminiscent of certain prophetic experiences, such as those of Muhammad. The origins of Christian mysticism can more plausibly be sought elsewhere, in the rise of monasticism and the influence of Neoplatonism. Some stimulus to such a development may also have been given by the existence of Gnostic sects both within and outside Christianity, from the end of the first century A.D.

Gnosticism. Gnosticism—a term derived from the word *gnosis,* meaning knowledge, particularly the immediate inner knowledge of the divine Being—tended to be ascetic and esoteric. Its asceticism was expressed by the doctrine that matter is evil, so that liberation of the soul is achieved through withdrawal from the world. Because of the evil nature of the world, Gnostics frequently postulated a hierarchy of beings below God and concerned with the creation of the world. Thus God himself was not contaminated, so to speak, by direct contract with matter. Such a doctrine was heretical, for it did not square with the Christian doctrine of creation or with Christian attitudes to the world, but it was one factor in stimulating an orthodox asceticism and mysticism within Christianity.

Monasticism. Monasticism grew out of eremitic practices, mainly in Egypt. Famous among early hermits was Anthony the Great, whose asceticism became almost legendary. Early in the fourth century monasticism proper was established in Egypt, the key figure being Pachomius. Thereafter the movement spread rapidly in Egypt and the Eastern church. It was further organized by Basil the Great (c. 330–379), whose rule formed the basis of Orthodox monasticism. John Cassian (c. 360–c. 434) brought Egyptian-style monasticism to the West, founding two monasteries in the south of France. His rule underlay that of St. Benedict, who lived in the following century. The connection of monasticism with mysticism was a straightforward one, for a main rationale of monasticism was the cultivation of the spiritual life, whereby a foretaste of the beatitude of the blessed in heaven could be gained. Thus the ultimate destiny of man was seen in contemplative terms, and it was thought possible to anticipate this destiny by a regulated life withdrawn from the world.

Neoplatonism. Neoplatonism, which expressed a view of the world in part stemming from, and in part providing a rationale for, mystical experience, made a lasting imprint upon Christian contemplation. A sign of this was the composition of the Pseudo-Dionysian writings, which were ascribed to Dionysius the Areopagite, a convert of St. Paul, but really date from approximately the beginning of the sixth century. These writings had a wide impact upon medieval mysticism. The negative theology expounded in them was not merely the result of logical difficulties involved in the ascription of ordinary predicates to God but, more importantly, was geared to the expression of the contemplative's inner experience of a "darkness clearer than light." Thus the mystical experience, being different from, and not expressible in terms of, perceptual and related forms of experience, seemed to imply that its object was likewise indescribable and therefore better conveyed by negations than by positive affirmations.

Neoplatonism also, of course, deeply influenced St. Augustine, and he has been a principal source of the notion, enshrined in monastic practice, that introvertive contemplation can give a foretaste of the heavenly life. Thus the highest state of Christian blessedness was increasingly identified with contemplation, and mysticism became the pattern after which eternal life was conceived.

Eastern Orthodox mysticism. The Pseudo-Dionysian writings also formed an important part of the fabric of Eastern Orthodox mysticism, for there were also features of the general theology of Orthodoxy that favored the contemplative ideal. John of Damascus, who in the eighth century summed up the work of the Cappadocian Fathers (fourth century), expressed in his writings a doctrine of deification that was both typical and formative of Eastern Orthodox theology. Man was considered the connecting link between the visible and invisible worlds. He was created perfect but through the Fall lost his immortal, incorruptible, and passionless nature. A certain scope for free will remained, however. The image of God, although defaced, was not entirely lost. The restoration of man to the true end for which he was made—the contemplation of God—was effected through Christ's incarnation. Christ, by uniting the Godhead to human nature, restored that nature to its perfection; and by sharing in his perfect humanity, men also can be raised up and deified. In terms of Dionysian mysticism, this deification takes place through the

illumination of the soul; its divinization, through the divine Light. Virtually throughout Eastern mysticism this imagery of light was to play a central part, and thus St. Simeon (949–1022), perhaps the most important of Eastern Orthodox mystics, identified the inner light with the glory emanating from God.

Hesychasm. Simeon was also a forerunner of the significant contemplative movement known as Hesychasm (from the Greek word *hesychos,* "quiet"), whose methods of training had some analogy to those found in Indian yoga.

The Hesychasts (eleventh–fourteenth centuries) held that their methods were conducive to the inner vision of the uncreated Light, identified with that which suffused Christ at the Transfiguration on Mount Tabor. This Light was conceived as emanating from God and was not to be identified with his essence, which is unknowable (this was a means of retaining orthodox teaching, by safeguarding mysticism from a full doctrine of union with, or knowledge of, God). Among the training methods used were breathing exercises and the continued repetition of the Jesus Prayer— "O Lord Jesus, Son of God, have mercy on me, a sinner." In a mysterious manner, the very repetition of the sacred name of Jesus was supposed to contain the divine power.

Gregorius Palamas (c. 1296–1359), the most noted and controversial exponent of Hesychasm, considered the Jesus Prayer as the central act of piety; and although the use of breathing techniques, which persisted until the eighteenth century, has been discontinued, the Jesus Prayer has survived as a characteristic part of Orthodox religion. Palamas and the Hesychasts were not, however, unopposed. Some opponents thought that the doctrine of the uncreated Light made a division within the Godhead—Palamas had even spoken of "divinities." Thus the attempt to soften the idea of mystical union by regarding it as identification not with the divine essence but with the divine illuminative energy, was criticized on the ground that it transferred the difficulty to another locus by introducing something like polytheism. Nevertheless, Hesychastic teaching came to be recognized officially, and the movement was the mainspring of medieval Orthodox contemplation.

Roman Catholicism. The mystical life served to counterbalance the worldly tendencies that had permeated the early medieval church in the West. Pope Gregory the Great (c. 540–604) discovered in his own experience something that could be expressed in terms of the irradiation of the divine Light; and Gregory VII, elected pope in 1073, undertook extensive ecclesiastical and monastic reforms that were partly inspired by the intense cultivation of the personal and contemplative life he had discovered in the Cluniac movement—a monasticism whose rules and ideals emanated from the monastic center at Cluny in Burgundy.

The most important figure in monastic reform was Bernard of Clairvaux (1091–1153). Although he was influenced by Augustine, his concerns were not primarily expressed in metaphysical language. He believed that in the mystical experience the soul is emptied and wholly lost in God, but he did not conceive this as an actual union with the Godhead. The soul and God remain distinct in substance, although they are joined by the "glue of love." Through man's love flowing up to God and through the downward movement of God's grace, the two become united. Bernard combined this intense mysticism with great powers of leadership and played a large part in the forward movement of the Cistercian order.

Other important mystics were Hugh and Richard of St. Victor, an Augustinian abbey in Paris in the twelfth century, and St. Bonaventure (1221–1274) in the following century. St. Bonaventure evolved a theory of mysticism that set forth the three ways of the spiritual life: purgative, illuminative, and unitive. In the first stage, the individual purifies himself through meditation; in the second, he is illuminated by the divine mercy; in the third, he gains a continuing union with God through love. This love is nourished by concentrating upon God, to the exclusion of mutable things. Thus, Bonaventure's path typically followed that of introversion, while his theological doctrines leaned upon Augustine and Pseudo-Dionysius.

There were ways, however, in which mystical teachings, especially where they strongly emphasized the negative theology of Pseudo-Dionysius, could seem unorthodox. The work of Thomas Aquinas (1224/1225–1274), in excogitating a novel synthesis between Christian theology and Aristotelianism, accentuated differences of emphasis between some of the mystics and orthodox doctrine. Thus Meister Eckhart (c. 1260–c. 1327), a Dominican and therefore versed in Thomism, fell under condemnation.

The greatest of the German contemplatives, Eckhart spoke in ways which suggested not merely that there is an ontological distinction between the Godhead, which is beyond description, and the Trinity of describable Persons but also that it is possible for the contemplative to go "beyond God" in achieving identity with the Godhead. Despite his unorthodox language, Eckhart inspired a strong following, and the mysticism of Johannes Tauler (c. 1300–1361), Heinrich Suso (c. 1300–1366), Jan van Ruysbroeck (1293–1381), and the partly lay group known as the Friends of God in Germany, the Low Countries, and Switzerland owed much to him.

It was out of the Friends of God that the anonymous but famous mystical treatise, the *Theologia Germanica,* originated, stressing the abandonment of the soul to God. The corruption of the church and the disillusioning events of the Great Western Schism were motives for the Friends of God to attempt to revitalize faith through the inner life, and this sometimes involved a highly critical attitude toward ecclesiastical authority. It is worth noting, however, that the rather sudden flowering of mysticism in Germany during the fourteenth century owed much to the fact that in 1267 the Dominican friars had been charged by Pope Clement IV with the spiritual direction of the nuns in the numerous convents in the Rhineland. Hitherto they had frequently been without proper religious supervision.

Mysticism could lead in directions that seemed to be the reverse of Christian piety. The sect known as the Brethren of the Free Spirit, which dated from the early thirteenth century, believed that men are of the same substance as God: every man is capable of becoming divine. It followed that when this divinization was achieved, a person could no longer sin, for God is sinless. Thus, whatever one did, it would not be a sin. Commandments and conventional tests of morality could no longer apply, and mysticism was therefore interpreted as justifying antinomianism. (Thus, it was not surprising that some of Eckhart's language, although not intended in this sense, could be regarded as dangerous—as when he said that God is beyond good.) Despite the efforts of the Inquisition, the Brethren of the Free Spirit spread, partly because they were able to organize themselves into a secret society.

The asceticism often associated with mystical religion may also be seen in another heretical movement of the twelfth and thirteenth centuries—the Albigensians or Cathari, found in southern France, northern Italy, and parts of Spain, who held doctrines close to those of Manichaeism.

The fourteenth century also saw a marked development of mysticism in England, as exemplified by the writings of Richard Rolle de Hampole (c. 1290–1349), who led the life of a hermit; the anonymous author of the famous *Cloud of Unknowing,* which was influenced by Pseudo-Dionysius; Julian of Norwich (c. 1340–1415); Walter Hilton (d. 1396), and others. On the whole, the temper of their mysticism was nonspeculative, and they emphasized the practical means of developing the inner life.

A movement closely related to the Friends of God was that of the Brethren of the Common Life, which was deeply influenced by Ruysbroeck. Its best-known fruit was the widely read *Imitation of Christ,* attributed to Thomas à Kempis. With its stress on practical love, it was well adapted to the needs of those who did not necessarily feel the call to the cloister and was a means of giving mysticism a wider social impact. Similarly, Catherine of Siena (1347–1380) exhibited a dynamic concern for social and ecclesiastical service. She ministered to victims of the Black Death and played a part in the attempt to strengthen the ailing papacy, persuading Gregory XI to return from Avignon to Rome.

Catherine of Siena spoke vividly of mystical experience in terms of spiritual marriage, paralleling the symbolism whereby the church was looked on as the bride of Christ. Another woman mystic, Teresa of Ávila (1515–1582), gave further expression to this imagery. Her accounts of her own experiences in pursuing the contemplative life, in such works as *The Interior Castle* and in her autobiography, are valuable and sensitive sources for understanding the inner phenomena of mysticism.

Another important mystic who used the imagery of marriage was a younger contemporary of St. Teresa, John of the Cross (1542–1591). He gave detailed expression to the experience of the "dark night of the soul," an experience also recorded by Ruysbroeck and others. The mystic has, according to St. John, periods of despair in which he feels deserted by God. This he interprets as a means of purgation sent by God. The experience probably reflects the contrast between the bliss of union and the condition of striving for that bliss. It is not much written about in nontheistic mysticism, although Buddhist meditation involves the attempt to repress the feeling of bliss accruing on the attainment of higher states of consciousness, in order to obviate the depression liable to occur upon their cessation.

Protestantism. In one way, Protestantism provided a favorable milieu for mysticism, but in another and ultimately more important way, it provided an unfavorable one. The Protestant emphasis on personal experience of God could easily link up with the ideals of the contemplative life. Thus, the writings of the most famous Protestant mystic, Jakob Boehme (1575–1624), were widely diffused. Groups of followers known as the Behmenists flourished in England and were later absorbed in the Quaker movement, whose doctrine of the "inner light" was characteristically mystical. However, the type of experience that figured so centrally in early Protestantism and that has continued to be stressed in evangelical Christianity was that which gives the individual certitude of salvation. Such a "conversion" experience differs from the imageless rapture that is at the center of mystical religion. Moreover, Protestantism was organizationally unfavorable to the contemplative life, since this had flourished principally in monasteries and indeed had provided a main rationale for their existence. Protestantism could be puritanical, but it did not favor withdrawal from the world.

The antinomian tendencies exhibited by the Brethren of the Free Spirit in the thirteenth and fourteenth centuries were reproduced in various offshoots of Protestant mysticism, as in the movement known as the Ranters, who were strong in seventeenth-century England. Their doctrines were held by opponents to be pantheistic, but more correctly they believed in the essential divinity of all human beings. Since God cannot sin, neither can divinized men, however wrong their actions may look from the standpoint of conventional morality. This was another instance in the history of religion where mystical teachings, normally nurtured in the context of asceticism and unworldliness, were interpreted to justify the opposite. Other important mystics in the Protestant tradition were George Fox (1624–1691), the founder of Quakerism; William Law (1686–1761); and the eccentric poet William Blake (1757–1827).

Although contemplative writings have been less prominent in more recent times, there have been a number of striking mystics since 1850, among them the pseudonymous Lucie-Christine (1844–1908), whose experiences are recorded in her *Spiritual Journal;* the converted French army officer Charles de Foucauld (1858–1916), and the Indian Christian Sadhu Sundar Singh (1889–1929).

Moreover, there has been a renewed scholarly interest in mysticism, as seen in the writings of William James, Evelyn Underhill (1875–1941), and William Inge (1860–1954). Further stimulus to the study of mysticism has been provided by the increased interaction between Eastern religions and Christianity.

ISLAM

Early Islam was not especially conducive to mysticism, since its main spirit was that of the prophetic dynamism of Muhammad's numinous experiences. Nevertheless, by the eighth century mysticism was developing within Islam. Greek philosophy had already made its impact on the Arabs and thus had opened the way to speculation about God that was partly contemplative. More important, the ex-Christians who had been absorbed into the faith in many Middle Eastern areas carried with them a respect for the ascetic life. Further, the culture of the Arabian desert had encountered the rich and sophisticated standard of living of the conquered, and this confrontation had induced tensions within Islam. Those who held to the older tradition were moved to accentuate the puritanism of early Islam, and such asceticism accorded with the practice of contemplation. Moreover, it was possible for Muslims to interpret Muhammad's prophetic experience in a mystical sense.

Muslim mysticism is generally known as Sufism. The word "*Ṣūfī*" is probably derived from the term "*ṣūf*," "undyed wool," which was the material of a garment worn as a sign of simplicity and austerity. Although complete world denial was scarcely in accord with Muhammad's teachings, the world acceptance expressed in the struggle for power among his successors brought conformity with mere orthodoxy into disrepute among the pious. This represented an opportunity for the growth of an ascetic otherworldliness. Those who adopted the contemplative life could withdraw from politics and could harness self-mortification to the task of concentrating solely upon Allah.

The general structure of Islamic faith was adapted to the service of the inner life. The repetition of prayers enjoined by Islam could be extended from that normally required of the faithful until every moment could be spent in remembrance of God and adoration of him. Almsgiving, one of the seven "pillars of Islam," could be interpreted in terms of thoroughgoing self-denial. The whole of life could be seen as a pilgrimage to a spiritual Mecca. Although the earliest teachings of Islam had laid duties on the individual as a member of the community—conceived as a brotherhood—tendencies later developed that made religion essentially a matter for the individual alone.

The new asceticism was regarded primarily as a means toward inner illumination. Fear and obedience of God melted into a burning interior love of him that carried with it the hope that union with him might be gained through negation of the self. This interior knowledge was described in terms of light, and an important passage in the Qu'rān (Koran), the so-called Light Verse, was quoted as a backing for mysticism: "God is the light of the heavens and of the earth; His light is like a niche wherein there is a lamp, a lamp encased in glass, the glass as it were a glistening star." Also, the Sufis came to use the imagery of love as some Christian mystics did. An early example of this is to be found in the life and teachings of Dhū'l-Nūn (d. 861), an Egyptian influenced by Greek speculation.

Heretical aspects. The knowledge prized by the Sufis was not the rational knowledge developed by the scholastic theologians (in Islam this meant mainly those who had come into contact with Greek philosophy); rather, it was the direct knowledge of Allah, or *ma'rifa*. This *ma'rifa* or gnosis was the crown of the Sufi path. However, the idea of direct acquaintance with God could have consequences that were scandalous to the orthodox.

Thus, Abū Yazīd of Bistam (d. 875) was so convinced of his identity with God in the experience of *ma'rifa* that he could say "Glory to me—how great is my majesty." This seemed like claiming divinity, which was blasphemous and strictly contrary to the orthodox opposition to any doctrine of incarnation. Abū Yazīd also put forth an idea destined to play a large part in subsequent Islamic mysticism—that of *fanā'*, the passing away and extinction of the empirical self, which follows self-control through asceticism and contemplative techniques. The "passing away" involved the loss of the consciousness of one's own individuality and helps to explain why the Sufis sometimes spoke in terms which suggested that they became merged or identified with God. As has been seen, similar ideas were expressed on occasion by Christian mystics such as Eckhart and are found in Hindu and Buddhist mysticism.

The most notable example of this trend was the experience of al-Hallāj (854–922) of Baghdad, who spoke as though he were an incarnation of the divine Being through mystical experience and consciously and overtly modeled himself upon Jesus. Such ideas were intolerable to the orthodox and he was (appropriately) crucified.

Although at first the Sufis operated individually, they later associated in loose groups. The elaboration of contemplative techniques and the trend toward celibacy (scarcely in accord with the spirit of the revealed law contained in the Qu'rān) brought about the creation of orders of Sufis who could work, and often live, together. It was common for such a group to be under the spiritual direction of a *shaykh* or *pīr,* and very often his residence would turn into a monastic community. The prestige of such holy men became great, and miraculous powers were ascribed to them. This prestige, combined with concepts clustering around *ma'rifa,* brought the ideal of the divine human and the cult of saints into Islam.

Persecution, as in the case of al-Hallāj, was no lasting answer to threats to orthodoxy; what was required was a synthesis between the new ideas and traditional theology that could harness Sufi piety to Qu'rānic ends. Al-Ghazālī (1058–1111) provided the most acceptable and influential solution to the problem. In his *The Revival of the Religious Sciences* he dealt with the question of how *fanā'* could most properly be interpreted. He held that the mystic, in experiencing the vision of God, is so overwhelmed that he imagines he is united with him. However, this is a sort of illusion, analogous to the belief of a person who sees wine in a transparent glass and thinks that wine and glass are a single object. When the contemplative returns from the state of ecstasy ("drunkenness," as Ghazālī called it—metaphors of drinking were common in Sufi writings), he recognizes that there is a distinction between the soul and God. In such ways, Ghazālī tried to do justice both to the actual experience of the contemplative and to a religion's requirements of worship, which presupposes a dualism between the worshiper and the object of worship. Ghazālī stressed the way in which self-purification, as part of the Sufi path, follows penitence, which in turn depends on the recognition of the awe-inspiring majesty and holiness of Allah. Thus he tried to show that contemplation and orthodox religion go hand in hand. Hence, he also did not believe in a mysticism that involved withdrawal from the world. The mystic returns to ordinary life, revitalized by the dazzling vision of the divine Reality. Ghazālī's synthesis meant that henceforth Sufism had an accepted place within orthodox Islam, but contemplative and philosophical thought were not restricted.

Pantheist tendencies. Notable among those who expressed a poetical and metaphysical Sufism was ibn-'Arabī (1165–1240) of Spain. He influenced Dante, who adopted the outline of 'Arabī's description of the ascent into heaven (combining astronomical theory and the story of Muhammad's journey to heaven). His doctrines were pantheistic, and he considered human beings as offshoots of the divine essence that exist because of God's desire to be known; and in the realization of the divine Being, the contemplative reflects in his own person the structure of the universe. He also made use of the logos idea: the logos as the creative principle in the universe was identified with the spirit of Muhammad. However, there are hints in 'Arabī's work that he considered himself superior to Muhammad, having realized identity not with the logos but with the Godhead.

His voluminous writings, although regarded with distaste by the orthodox, were influential, especially in Persia, among such mystical poets as Jalal ad-Din Rūmī (1207–1273) and Mawlana Nur ad-Din Jāmī (1414–1492). Rūmī, who founded one of the *darwīsh* orders (*darwīsh* literally means "mendicant," and is commonly transliterated "dervish"), also wrote poetry expressing the longing of the soul for its return to God. However, he was also keenly appreciative of the beauties of nature, and he saw in the ritual of the Mevlevi order, which he founded, with its solemn swirling dance to the sound of drum and pipe, a reflection of the movements of the planets and of nature in general.

It may be noted that some of the orders experimented with various external means of inducing ecstatic experiences, and the dance was one. (The term "dervish" should properly apply to all mendicant orders, and not just to the Mevlevi "dancing dervishes.")

Certain features of Sufi teaching are reminiscent of Indian mysticism, and it has been argued, although not conclusively, that there were borrowings from India. (See R. C. Zaehner, *Hindu and Muslim Mysticism,* on this question.) For instance, Abū Yazīd's language is similar to that of the *Upaniṣads;* and ibn-'Arabī argued, with a logic like that of Śankara, that it is inappropriate to speak of *becoming* God through mystical experience, since one is already essentially identical with God—mystical realization involves no change of ontological status. Again, like nearly all Hindu theologians, 'Arabī treated hell as a purgatory, rather than as a place of everlasting punishment. Various similarities of this kind can probably best be explained not so much as borrowings but rather as reflections of similar patterns of experience and speculation.

Modern Sufism. In the modern period, Sufism has undergone a considerable decline, and the revitalization of Islam has come about through other forces—the puritanism of the Wahhābī, Pan-Arabism, and political advance. Sir Muhammad Iqbal (1877–1938), however, an important figure in Muslim modernism, was influenced by Sufi thought. Since he wished to distinguish sharply between religion and science—the former having to do with personal life—he found the interior quest of Sufism attractive.

Bibliography

A good introduction to mysticism is Sidney Spencer, *Mysticism in World Religion* (Baltimore, 1963). Evelyn Underhill's *Mysticism,* 6th ed. (London, 1916), is a classic, although dated in some respects and confined largely to theistic mysticism. The same is true of William James, *Varieties of Religious Experience* (New

York, 1902). See also W. R. Inge, *Mysticism in Religion* (London, 1907); R. C. Zaehner, *Mysticism Sacred and Profane* (Oxford, 1957); and W. T. Stace, *Mysticism and Philosophy* (Philadelphia, 1960).

On Indian mysticism, see Edward Conze, *Buddhist Meditation* (London, 1961); S. N. Dasgupta, *Hindu Mysticism* (London, 1927); D. T. Suzuki, *Mysticism Christian and Buddhist* (London, 1957); Rudolf Otto's classical *Mysticism East and West,* translated by B. L. Bracey and R. C. Payne (New York and London, 1957, in paperback); and Ninian Smart, *Doctrine and Argument in Indian Philosophy* (London, 1964), Ch. 10. See also bibliography to YOGA.

On Chinese and Japanese mysticism, see K. L. Reichelt, *Meditation and Piety in the Far East* (London, 1953) and *Religion in Chinese Garment* (London, 1952); Henri Maspero, *Le Taoisme* (Paris, 1950); and Fung Yu-lan, *A History of Chinese Philosophy,* 2 vols. (Princeton, N.J., 1952–1953). The *Tao-te-ching* has numerous English translations, ranging from that of Lionel Giles (London, 1911) to that of D. C. Lau (London, 1964). See also bibliography to ZEN.

For mysticism in Judaism, see G. G. Scholem, *Major Trends in Jewish Mysticism* (London, 1955); E. Müller, *History of Jewish Mysticism* (London, 1956); and Martin Buber, *The Legend of the Baal-Shem,* translated by Maurice Freedman (London, 1956).

On Christian mysticism, see R. M. Grant, *Gnosticism and Early Christianity* (London, 1959); W. R. Inge, *The Philosophy of Plotinus,* 2 vols. (London, 1918); A. J. Festugière, *Personal Religion Among the Greeks* (Berkeley, 1945); Cuthbert Butler, *Western Mysticism,* 2d ed. (London, 1922); Evelyn Underhill, *The Mystics of the Church* (London, 1925); Vladimir Lossky, *The Theology of The Eastern Church,* translated by the members of the Fellowship of St. Alban and St. Sergius (London, 1957); Jon Gregerson, *The Transfigured Cosmos* (New York, 1960); Margaret Smith, *Studies in Early Mysticism in the Near and Middle East* (London, 1931); R. M. Jones, *Studies in Mystical Religion,* 3d ed. (London, 1909); and E. A. Peers, *Studies of the Spanish Mystics,* 3 vols. (London, 1927–1960).

On mysticism in Islam, see A. J. Arberry, *Sufism—An Account of the Mystics of Islam,* 2d impression (London, 1956); R. A. Nicholson, *Studies in Islamic Mysticism* (Cambridge, 1921); A. J. Wensinck, *La Pensée de Ghazzali* (Paris, 1940); and R. C. Zaehner, *Hindu and Muslim Mysticism* (London, 1960).

NINIAN SMART

MYSTICISM, NATURE AND ASSESSMENT OF.

Attempts to define mystical experience have been as diversified and as conflicting as attempts to interpret and assess its significance. This is not surprising, for the language used to express and describe mystical experience is richly paradoxical, figurative, and poetical. Even if at times a mystic chooses what look like austere and precise metaphysical terms, this may be only an apparent concession to logic, for he will employ these terms in senses far from normal. Mystics have called the Godhead a sheer "Nothing" and yet the ground of all. They have affirmed simultaneously that the world is identical with God and that the world is not identical with God.

Some discriminations are possible, even if exact definition is not. Mystical experience is religious experience, in a broad but meaningful sense of "religious." It is sensed as revealing something about the totality of things, something of immense human importance at all times and places, and something upon which one's ultimate well-being or salvation wholly depends. More specifically, a mystical experience is not the act of acquiring religious or theological information but is often taken to be a confrontation or encounter with the divine source of the world's being and man's salvation. An experience is not held to be mystical if the divine power is apprehended as simply "over-against" one—wholly distinct and "other." There

must be a unifying vision, a sense that somehow all things are one and share a holy, divine, and single life, or that one's individual being merges into a "Universal Self," to be identified with God or the mystical One. Mystical experience then typically involves the intense and joyous realization of oneness with, or in, the divine, the sense that this divine One is comprehensive, all-embracing, in its being. Yet a mystical experience may be given much less theological interpretation than this description suggests. A mystic may have no belief whatever in a divine being and still experience a sense of overwhelming beatitude, of salvation, or of lost or transcended individuality.

Some mystical experiences occur only at the end of a lengthy, arduous religious discipline, an ascetic path; others occur spontaneously (like much nature-mystical experience); others are induced by drugs such as mescalin or take place during the course of mental illness.

An important distinction can be made between the extrovertive (outward-looking) and introvertive (inward-looking) types of mystical experience. In the first of these, the subject looks out upon the multiplicity of objects in the world and sees them transfigured into a living, numinous unity, their distinctness somehow obliterated. In nature mysticism, a form of extrovertive experience, the items of nature are not lost to consciousness; rather they are seen with unusual vividness and all as "workings of one mind, the features/Of the same face, blossoms upon one tree . . ." (Wordsworth, *The Prelude,* Book 6). In the introvertive type, the mystic becomes progressively less aware of his environment and of himself as a separate individual. He speaks of being merged in, identified with, dissolved into, the One. The subject–object distinction vanishes altogether. Some of the best-known mystics testify to experiences of both types, but the introvertive, being at the furthest remove from ordinary experience, is usually held to be the more developed of the two.

Although we can call mystical experience a kind of religious experience, we do not discover agreement among mystics about the nature and status of the mystical goal. Christian and Islamic mysticism, for example, interpret the experience theistically, although not with complete consistency; the Upaniṣads and Theravāda Buddhism are not theistic. Pantheist, monist, and agnostic interpretations have been offered, all with some prima facie plausibility.

Alternative religious interpretations. The pantheist argues that mystical experience compels us to strip away anthropomorphic conceptions of deity and that although theism begins this work of refining, it stops long before it should. The theistic notion of God remains that of an infinite, supernatural individual. But apart from being intellectually unsatisfactory (infinity and individuality go awkwardly together), this picture contradicts the mystic's own experience, which is one not of an external face-to-face meeting with a deity but rather one of merging with, and realizing one's own basic identity with, the mystical One. The theist has to set a great gulf between himself and his God; the mystic's experience testifies both to the existence of this gulf and, paradoxically, to its elimination. Brahman is both far and near.

Why have so many of the greatest Christian mystics used theistic language to describe their obviously intense mystical experiences? The pantheist will say that either they have simple-mindedly used the only religious terms they had been taught—despite their unsuitability—or else that the desire to conform to orthodox Christian dogma about God's transcendence has led them to muffle those parts of their individual experience that were opposed to it.

A pantheist interpretation claims that it alone does full justice to God's infinity and that its theology eliminates the last primitive remnants of deism. Since a mystical experience is a discovery, a realization, of what is eternally true, there need be no perplexing doctrines about special divine self-revelations and self-communications nor any interference with natural law. Accordingly, a mystical experience induced by drug or disease does not have to be judged illusory or demonic. In the determination of whether it is authentic or not, its causal circumstances are simply beside the point.

The theist, however, is not without a reply. He will reject the pantheist's conception of religious development. There has not been any general historical trend toward pantheism or monism in religion; and although early theisms were crudely anthropomorphic, this does not by itself entail that all personal language about God is equally false and crude. The doctrine of the Incarnation should teach the contrary—at least within Christendom.

Pantheism and monism, argues the theist, map only the lower slopes of the mystic's ascent. They are concerned with the preliminary purging of the senses and intellect; their raptures do not testify to an achieved union with God but only to what is perhaps an unusually fresh, innocent, and aesthetically intense awareness of the created world and its beauty. The mescalin-user and the temporarily psychotic, who make extravagant claims for their own identity with the mystical One, ought to—often do—think more humbly of their experiences once normality returns. To the theist, the *unio mystica* is an objective that cannot be taken by assault; in the end, it is only the initiative, the grace, of God that bestows it. Causation does matter in this interpretation, and the inner, felt nature of the mystical experience cannot alone determine its authenticity.

Paradoxes of religious interpretations. Short decisive arguments can hardly be invoked to settle the dispute between these interpretations of mystical experience. The experiences themselves seem able to bear either interpretation; the choice between pantheism and theism is a choice between two massive conceptual systems. Neither account can claim the merit of being free from internal difficulties both conceptual and religious. Theism has somehow to combine the notions that God is immeasurably "other" to man and, yet, that mystical union is possible. Pantheism identifies world and God while maintaining their distinctness; it denies that "God" is simply another way of saying "world."

Still more perplexingly, some mystics of great eminence speak the languages of both pantheism and theism. Eckhart's writings give full-blooded examples of each, as do those of the Indian mystic Śankara. Even in the Upanishads, although Brahman is said to be beyond relation, featureless, unthinkable, it (or he) is acknowledged to have personal aspects.

No precise or determinate idea, no particularized image, is allowed to be adequate to the mystical One. Although the ontological status of God seems at times to be that of a numinous individual being, at other times all hints of such a status are repudiated. "Simple people," said Eckhart, "imagine that they should see God, as if He stood there and they here. That is not so." The Divine is a "desert," a "void," an "abyss," a "wheel rolling out of itself," a "stream flowing into itself."

Mystics will not always allow one even to say unequivocally that God exists. The pseudo-Dionysius, for example, denied that either the category of existence or of non-existence applied to the Divine. These tensions and this indeterminateness—God is, or is not, a particular being, he is, or is not, an existent—can also be found in nonmystical theologies, but mysticism can enormously magnify them. Even Theravāda Buddhism contains deep-running paradox, despite its comparative reluctance to speculate at all. Attaining nirvana, for instance, is like the extinguishing of a flame, yet nirvana is not sheer simple extinction.

What attitude is it reasonable to adopt toward this display of tensions and antinomies? Four possibilities are worthy of serious discussion. (1) The paradoxes cannot be eliminated; they are to be taken literally and at their face value. Without paradox, we cannot speak of the mystic's experiences or of his God, but this is no argument against the truth of the mystic's claims. (2) The paradoxes are necessary in the same way that distortions of grammar and syntax are necessary to a poet attempting to say something that cannot be encompassed by ordinary language. They are not to be taken literally but are to be construed as analogies, hyperboles, metaphors, or oxymorons. (3) Since no logically coherent account of mystical vision seems attainable, it is more sensible to admit this fact and to believe the mystic's claim that his experience is ineffable and that all language falsifies it. We would now have a mysticism without a theology. A very high value could still be set upon mystical experience, but we should be reverently agnostic on all questions of interpretation. (4) The appearance of paradox in a piece of discourse is very often taken by philosophers as a *reductio ad absurdum* of its claims. (Compare the logician's story of the barber who shaves only those who do not shave themselves. When paradox arises over the question "Does the barber shave himself?" it is reasonable to infer that there logically cannot be a barber, so described.) Because the mystic says so many contradictory things about God, this demonstrates the logical impossibility of God's existence, so described. Criticisms charging illogicality can be supported by attempts to explain in naturalistic terms the mystical experiences themselves.

Evaluation of responses to paradoxes. Whether or not the paradoxes are finally to be judged literal and irreducible, we must clearly reject some of the speculations that are aimed at reducing their offense. For example, how God can be, but not by being an individual entity, is profoundly obscure. The mystery is not removed if we say that God is Being Itself or Being as such. Even if our ontology allowed such universals as "courage itself" or "blueness itself," we still could not meaningfully include Being Itself among their number; there is no characteristic named "being" that is common to all actual entities and that should figure in their complete description. "Being Itself" cannot logically refer to anything either particular or universal, divine or nondivine.

Similarly, if we are offended by the claim that God neither exists nor does not exist, we might try a familiar palliative and say that he is above being. Our concepts fail to grasp him precisely for that reason. "Above being" carries echoes of "above the turmoil," "above suspicion," "above praise," with "above" indicating distance from and superiority to something. But in order to be "above," one must first of all be—and continue to be. "God is above being" really fails to satisfy the conditions under which any "above" sentence of this kind can have meaning. It can, of course, be given a sense if "being" here means finite and dependent being. But if God is superior to this sort of being, if he is infinite and independent, then that is a superiority of his nature, and to learn this about him gives us no help with the original paradox.

Literal versus figurative language. The paradoxes and enigmas may have to stand, but why not take them as poetical, metaphorical, or symbolic language? Against that suggestion, it may be argued that if the paradoxes are metaphors, it should be possible to translate them—at least roughly—into direct, nonmetaphorical language. The only language available to the mystic, however, seems to be a language of irreducible paradox.

This argument is not very powerful. There are nonmystical topics about which it is impossible to speak without metaphor, such as important topics within the philosophy of mind. The history of conceptions of the mind is, in many of its facets, the history of changing metaphors, myths, and analogies. To defend a parallel account of mystical discourse would be less of a scandal to reason and logic than to insist on the literal view.

The literalist will reply that there is, in fact, no scandal to reason. The laws of logic work admirably for every situation where multiplicity is present. In the mystic's unique case, all multiplicity has vanished and with it, therefore, the applicability of those laws. The mystic's discourse is about the One that has no other; it lies beyond the province of logic.

This leaves us with a discomforting worry. If logic is inapplicable to the mystic's discourse, does that not come very close to saying that discriminations cannot be made in this field between sense and nonsense, the sound and the unsound?

The literal approach must be, for a philosopher, a desperate measure, a last resort only. To treat it as anything else would be methodologically perverse. Apart from the difficulties of discrimination, where logic is inoperative, the approach demands an unshakable prior conviction that the mystic's paradoxes are to be taken at their face value as reports of veridical insights. Here there is much that can be challenged.

We refused to dismiss the figurative account for not being able to translate its metaphors, or to give literal equivalents for its symbols and analogies. Yet that inability is nonetheless an embarrassment to it. When the mystic says, "God is a desert"; "God is a blinding light"; "God is, and is not, identical with the world"; or "The mystical enlightenment is an absolute emptiness which is absolute fullness"; we are compelled to accept these metaphors and paradoxes on the faith—if we accept them at all—that they can be true in some inscrutable way of one and the same deity. This cannot be shown, although the mystic *feels*

intensely that it is so. The skeptic complains that he cannot begin to see how such wildly incompatible predicates can refer to any one being, whereas he can understand with relative ease how they might, in fact, be the expression of some ecstatic inner experience of a quite noncognitive kind. He does not deny that some apparently incompatible predicates may be revealed as ultimately compatible. A psychoanalytic story can reveal how love and hate, desire and fear, can be harbored simultaneously by a person for a single object; the same can be true with conflicting analogies and metaphors. The last word of the mystic, however, is "ineffable"; he does not profess to have a reconciling story.

An objector might now suggest that it is easy enough to see how we could choose senses for the words "abyss," "desert," "light," that would give us at least a glimmer of insight into their metaphorical reference to the same divine being. The words are rich enough in their connotations and implications, both near and remote. This is true, but it cannot be a key to all the paradoxes. Certain ones (like that of identity and difference between God and world) offer no scope at all for such imaginative siftings and surmisings—unless we paraphrase the mystic's claim so freely that he will disown our translation. "The world is, and is not, identical with God" does not mean to the pantheistic mystic that the world is godlike in some respects and not in others.

If a city were referred to as a desert, a trap, or a furnace, the selection of appropriate meanings for these words in their metaphorical use would be possible because of the knowledge of the given fixed point of reference: a city. However, the concept of city is ontologically stable and intelligible in a way that the concept of God is not. The mystic's paradoxical discourse is related ultimately to his basic assertions about God's metaphysical status; this makes his semantic situation enormously more complex and precarious. (See also RELIGIOUS EXPERIENCE, ARGUMENT FOR THE EXISTENCE OF GOD. This and the present article are mutually relevant at many points.)

Once again, these reflections do not attempt to disprove the mystic's statements or even to show that they cannot be figurative as well as semantically sound. If the mystic had independent grounds for believing in God, then one could readily accept the claim that he could speak about this God only in oblique language. Some mystics would say that they do have such independent grounds, but for others the mystical experiences themselves, reported in the language of paradox, furnish the grounds of belief. Here the risk of delusion is higher.

Mystical experience and agnosticism. "According to our scale of values," Rudolf Otto wrote, we shall consider the mystic's intuition "either a strange fantasy or a glimpse into the eternal relationships of things" (*Mysticism East and West*, p. 42). Need these be the only options? Might it not be possible to reject all the traditional interpretations of mystical experience but yet accord it very high intrinsic value? If the mystic cannot interpret his experience theologically without talking nonsense, it is then better for him not to attempt theology or metaphysics at all, lest he bring his experience itself into needless disrepute.

An approach of this kind would have strong sympathy with the agnostic elements of early Buddhism. Buddha taught the path to nirvana but turned away any question about deities or the nature of a life hereafter. His emphasis was upon the moral quality of a life and upon attitudes toward life, death, suffering, and release from suffering. Mystical experience was attained in the course of a personal, practical discipline. It was understood as the culmination of such a discipline and given only the minimal theoretical interpretation. The lack of speculation did not, however, make the mystical experience unavailable to one who followed the Buddha's prescription for attaining it.

To insist that mysticism is possible without interpretation has the merit of avoiding unnecessary intellectual offense; it also allows us to admit as mystical the experiences of people outside both the theistic and monistic traditions but whose testimony, at the phenomenological level, shows great affinities with the mysticism of both traditions. Nevertheless, the mystical experiences of an agnostic are surely bound to differ in important respects from those of a Christian, a Buddhist, or a Muslim. The concepts used in interpretation help to determine the mystic's expectations of future experiences and to determine his map of the mystical path and the plotting of his position upon it. They shape the actual quality of his experience itself in a most intimate way. This does not imply that, but for the interpretative concepts, no experience could occur.

It may be feared that the theologically uninterpreted experience would tend to become a mere psychological curiosity, a luxury or consolation, isolated from all other parts of the subject's life. This can happen, but need not. Mystical experience basically involves a powerful urge toward the reconciliation, unification, and harmony of all with all, a feature that can readily be integrated with a moral outlook in which primacy is given to love. "Integrated," in fact, is really too weak a term; that moral ideal may receive its fullest and most splendid development in the mystical vision, and the moral agent gains a source of energy for the pursuit of the moral life.

These reflections may show, at least, that we cannot fairly assess the importance of mystical experience solely in terms of the interpretations that may be offered of it, whether speculatively pretentious or modest. An equally relevant question is what the mystic does with his experience, that is, what place he gives it in his total personal and moral existence. Evaluations based on this issue may often be at variance with those based upon a comparison of theories. A mystic may interpret elaborately and use his mystical experience as a mere refuge from responsibility, or he may be quite at a loss for interpretation, while recognizing in his experience the center and spring of a morally dedicated life.

Other philosophical criticisms. Our fourth type of response to the phenomena of mysticism was that offered by the radical philosophical critic, determined to call nonsense by its name, who takes the mystic's antinomies as a *reductio ad absurdum* of his claims. To those logical objections philosophers have added various epistemological and psychological difficulties.

The problem of objectivity. The mystic (and we are no longer thinking of the agnostic mystic) normally claims that his experience is not only a way of being inwardly, subjectively moved, but also that it discloses the nature of reality, that it is a cognitive, objective experience. To support this he may appeal to the impressive convergences of testimony on fundamentals among mystics of different periods and parts of the world. The critic may contest this. In reports upon perceptual illusions, for instance, even unanimity does not remove their illusoriness.

That the experiences are disclosures about the entire universe in its ultimate nature may be an almost irresistible conclusion for the mystic. Nonetheless, it must involve interpretation of a demonstrably fallible kind. To feel that the experience is revelatory is one thing; to judge confidently that it is so is quite another. A dream under nitrous oxide may strike the dreamer with the force of a satanic revelation, but on awakening and correlating the nightmare with the shock of tooth extraction, he may have little temptation to judge the experience as a genuine disclosure. The feeling of revealedness can attach itself with equal intensity to incompatible contents.

W. T. Stace has argued that mystical experience is neither objective nor subjective but that it transcends this distinction and is best classified as transsubjective. To be objective, an experience must be orderly and law governed; the criteria of subjective experience are disorderliness and incoherence. Mystical experience fits neither category. It is an experience of unity, untouched by plurality; and without plurality there can be neither order nor disorder.

This is an ingenious treatment, but it seems open to criticism at least on two points. First, the criterion of objectivity may be questioned. We may be quite properly convinced that certain phenomena are objective before we have assured ourselves of their orderliness, and they may indeed remain anomalous. The subjective events of dreams and fantasies are not disorderly, although the laws governing dreams are very different from those governing events in the public world. Second, we may wish to deny that mystical experience is, in fact, experience of a totally undifferentiated unity. There is, no doubt, a stage in which the mystic not only apprehends the world of plurality as issuing from a single divine source but sees that source and the world as a unity. Mystical experiences, however, cannot usefully be restricted to this one type. Perception of multiplicity does play a role, even if it is a subordinate one, in many other types. This is obviously so with extrovertive mystical experience in general, which is an experience not simply of oneness but of oneness in multiplicity. It is also apparent in the statement from Śri Aurobindo that "those who have . . . possessed the calm within can perceive always welling out from its silence the perennial supply of the energies which work in the universe" (*The Life Divine,* 1949, p. 28). The most favorable verdict we can pass upon claims to objectivity is "not proven."

Epistemological problems. When we ask more particularly what sort of apprehension, what modes of knowing are involved in mysticism, the answers swell our fund of paradoxes. If one mystic claims to perceive the cosmic energies welling forth from the One, another denies that anything like perception takes place. St. John of the Cross speaks of a "supernatural knowledge and light" that is so completely "detached and removed from all intelligible forms, which are objects of the understanding, that it is neither perceived nor observed" (*The Ascent of Mount Carmel*, Vol. I, p. 123). Nor is mystical insight a purely intellectual act, for "the higher and more sublime the Divine light, the darker is it to our understanding." Union with God "transcends all knowledge." The difficulty is increased by the doctrine that in mystical experience the subject–object distinction breaks down, and with it, naturally enough, go all our thought models for cognitive activities. Faced with the risk of a complete failure in communication, the mystic usually resorts to a characteristic complex use of language. This works in part by negations ("not ordinary perception," "not simply emotion") and in part by descriptions of his religious situation as he interprets it in metaphysical and theological terms, enhanced with poetical imagery; God now dwells in him, or has "absorbed" him "in the embrace and abyss of His sweetness." It is easy to see why the mystic resorts to these forms of discourse and also why they offer little comfort to the epistemologist. For the interpretations assume precisely what is at issue: that mystical experiences are objective and reliably cognitive in nature.

Some critics maintain that the mystic's claim to "know" must at least be suspected of being spurious. When such expressions as "objectivity," "discovery," and "vision" are used in senses so radically far from normal and applied with obscure and idiosyncratic criteria, it is legitimate to ask whether some quite different (and noncognitive) thought model might give a more intelligible clue to what is being described.

For example, it is sometimes suggested that the mystic's language might be best understood not as a description of reality but as the expression of a state of mind. Certainly, some of the mystic's language is clearly emotive, and even when it seems to describe his "situation," as we have been using the word, this may still be an indirect expression of his state of mind. Instead of saying, "I have an oppressive, worried feeling," one may say, "I feel as if there were something terribly wrong." Instead of "I feel uneasy, insecure," he may say, "There is no sure footing; everything and everybody is working against me." Instead of "I have a feeling of unreality," he may say, "I am not real anymore." The use of such examples does not imply that the mystic is psychotic. Some psychotic experiences are mystical experiences, but it hardly follows that all mysticism is psychosis. The critic could confine himself to pointing out this disturbing parallel in the use of language: both mystics and psychotics use situation-descriptive language for what, in the latter case at any rate, is a serious misperception of one's situation, a projection of inner disturbances upon the outer world. Furthermore, the projection occurs, partly at least, because the disturbances are not understood for what they are, and there is a failure of insight.

In the mystic's defense, it must be pointed out that to analyze his experience as a state of mind is not necessarily to discredit it. States of mind can be—and normally are—elicited by objective states of affairs, properly interpreted. People do, on occasion, fall victim to real persecution; their fears and anxieties can be very well founded.

But decisiveness, either in criticism or defense, is once more not to be had. Of course one's fears can be well-founded, but a person who says he does not really exist any more *must* be deluded. Significantly, as soon as such remarks verge on the paradoxical, we cease to take them at their face value and treat them as certain signs of disorder.

Content and quality of mystical experience. We have been considering some epistemological and linguistic problems set by mysticism and some ways in which a philosophical critic can assault, although probably not overthrow, the mystic's claims. Of the central mystical experience, characterized by loss of individuality and dissolution in a limitless divine totality, little or nothing has been said from a philosophical or psychological viewpoint. How far could a naturalistic account of mystical experience cope with these central features? Or could justice be done to them only in a thoroughgoing mystical philosophy, reared upon the paradoxes themselves? Here a suggestion or two must suffice.

In the first place, the mystical experience is a vision of the world that is free, to a very unusual extent, from the interposition of concepts. Normal perception is closely linked to practical projects; we see the world in terms of our needs and desires and our intentions to manipulate it in various ways. Aesthetic experience provides a sharp contrast. One may succeed briefly in contemplating a pastoral landscape not in terms of land utilization or of the practical problems of traveling across it, but simply as colors, shapes, or volumes. Seen in this way, the landscape can be excitingly and startlingly different from its everyday utilitarian appearance. Mystical experience is even more disturbingly strange because it suspends the application of still more basic concepts and categories. "As long as a man has time and place and number and quantity and multiplicity, he is on the wrong track and God is far from him" (Meister Eckhart, *Sermons,* p. 202).

When concepts are withdrawn and fundamental distinctions obliterated, it is understandable that our ordinary sense of the limits and boundaries between thing and thing, person and person, should also temporarily disappear. In this we may have an important clue to the mystic's claims about the overcoming of finite individuality, the cessation of the subject–object relation, and mergings and meltings into the infinite. Because our normal sense of our powers and their limits is fostered by the utilitarian and practical view of the world, when that view is suppressed, there can come the sense of exhilarating expansion or liberation that is often described in the mystical literature.

Similarly, if the practical orientation is suspended and, with it, the related conceptual framework of normal experience, we may lose awareness of the passage of time. We are not demarcating event from event in the normal time-articulating manner. In introvertive mystical experience the awareness of space is also obliterated, for there is a still more thoroughgoing withdrawal from perception and even from sensation. The intensity and strangeness of mystical experience reinforce the effect of timelessness; the experience is dramatically discontinuous with the flow of events before and after and hence is felt as not belonging to it.

The mystic himself can afford to be sympathetic to many

such naturalistic explanations. He can refuse to admit that they discredit his experience. They are simply (he will say "necessarily") incomplete, for they cannot account for the qualitatively unique tone of mystical feeling, and they do not disprove his claim that the Object of mystical vision itself must elude the categories of naturalistic philosophy.

Mysticism can be upgraded or downgraded with bewildering ease through the choice of a metaphor or a simile; its paradoxes are unutterable truths or blatant contradictions; its clearest affinities are with trustworthy modes of knowing or with psychotic, delusory states of mind; of all human experience it is the most valuable or it is a psychological curiosity, fashioned by the unconscious from infantile materials. The excesses of these opposite poles are avoided in our remarks about an "agnostic" or "noninterpreting" mysticism, although this is perhaps more of a practical compromise than the germ of a full-fledged theory. It tries at least to stress the potential human importance of mystical experience—when yoked to moral vision—and it expresses the wishful thought that the paradoxes of mystical interpretation should not be altogether allowed to mask that importance.

Bibliography

PRIMARY SOURCES

Boehme, Jakob, *Works,* 4 vols. London, 1764–1781. An English translation.
Eckhart, Meister, *Selected Treatises and Sermons,* translated by J. M. Clark and J. V. Skinner. London, 1958.
St. John of the Cross, *The Ascent of Mount Carmel.* London, 1943.
Progoff, Ira, ed., *The Cloud of Unknowing.* New York, 1957. An anonymous fourteenth-century treatise on contemplative prayer.
Ruysbroeck, Jan van, *The Chastising of God's Children . . . ,* J. Bazire and E. Colledge, eds. Oxford, 1957.
Underhill, Evelyn, ed., *The Cloud of Unknowing.* London, 1912. Contains introduction.

GENERAL STUDIES

Butler, C., *Western Mysticism.* London, 1922.
Hügel, F. von, *The Mystical Element in Religion.* London and New York, 1908.
Hügel, F. von, *Eternal Life.* Edinburgh, 1912.
Inge, W. R., *Christian Mysticism.* London, 1899.
Inge, W. R., *The Philosophy of Plotinus,* 2 vols. London, 1918.
Otto, R., *Das Heilige.* Breslau, 1917. Translated by J. W. Harvey as *The Idea of the Holy.* London, 1923.
Otto, R., *Mysticism East and West,* translated by B. L. Bracey and R. C. Payne. New York, 1932.
Underhill, Evelyn, *Mysticism.* London, 1911. Contains a substantial bibliography.

PSYCHOLOGY OF MYSTICISM

James, William, *The Varieties of Religious Experience.* London, 1902. Lectures XVI–XVII.
Leuba, J. H., *The Psychology of Religious Mysticism.* London, 1925.

ACCOUNTS OF MYSTICISM

Smart, Ninian, *Reasons and Faiths.* London, 1958. Particularly valuable for its discussions of various non-Christian as well as Christian forms of mystical and numinous religion.
Stace, W. T., *Mysticism and Philosophy.* Philadelphia, 1960.
Zaehner, R. C., *Mysticism Sacred and Profane.* Oxford, 1957.

PHILOSOPHICAL DISCUSSIONS

Glasgow, W. D., "Knowledge of God." *Philosophy,* Vol. 32 (1957), 229 ff.
Horsburgh, H. J. N., "The Claims of Religious Experience." *Australasian Journal of Philosophy,* Vol. 35 (1957), 186 ff.
Kennick, W. E., review of Stace's *Mysticism and Philosophy. Philosophical Review,* Vol. 71 (1962), 387–390.
Martin, C. B., *Religious Belief.* Ithaca, N.Y., and London, 1959.

RONALD W. HEPBURN

MYTH. The relation between philosophy and mythology can be usefully set out under three main headings. There is first the period in Greek philosophy, when philosophers wanted to discard and to criticize mythological modes of thought but when they were still so close to those modes of thought that mythology recurred in philosophical contexts. Then in modern thought there is the period from Vico to Comte, when mythology was taken seriously as a clue to the primitive history of thought, and from the nineteenth century on, when there was a variety of systematic attempts at a science of mythology. Finally, there is the role of myth in modern irrationalisms.

To this scheme three objections may be made. The first is that in discussing the Greeks what is said will inevitably be conditioned by the writer's beliefs about what modern scientific approaches to mythology have yielded. Thus, the second section should precede the first. To this objection everything can be conceded except the conclusion, for it would be equally difficult to discuss the growth of the science of mythology before anything had been said about mythology itself.

A second objection might be that no initial definition of mythology has been offered. But here the danger is that by delineating the field of mythology too sharply, one biases one's account in favor of one sort of theory. And any definition broad enough to escape this charge would be either vague or a mere catalogue.

The third objection would be that the Christian Era until the time of Vico appears to be neglected by this schematism. For this there is good reason, however. In that era mythologies were predominantly treated as false theological accounts, rivals to the one true theological account, the Christian.

Greek philosophy. Greek myths, like those of other Mediterranean and Near Eastern cultures, include cosmogonies and accounts of great discoveries and inventions, such as that of fire; of the founding of cities; and of the ancestry of kings, in which relationships between gods and men are codified. In different stages of the mythology, such as in the distinction between the Olympian gods and the dark, chthonic deities, one can distinguish different social origins. From the time of Durkheim and Jane Harrison anthropologists have stressed the function of myths as explanations of rituals which express the social consciousness of a group. In Greek society the public ritual continued to express the life of the community long after belief in gods had become questionable.

Greek philosophy only gradually separated itself from mythology. Personification, for example, was common in pre-Socratic philosophy, but at the same time rationalist criticism of mythology originated with writers like Xenophanes, who attacked anthropomorphic representation of the gods, and Euhemerus, who argued that myths were to be explained as stories about men who had been deified. Heraclitus attacked Homer and Hesiod for their dependence on myth.

Plato. Plato used myths and allegories for a variety of purposes. Frutiger draws a distinction between myths properly so called and allegories, which, for example, lack the element of story; among allegories he would include the account of the Cave in the *Republic* or the noble lie about precious and base metals in the souls of different types of men. He divides myths in the full sense into those which function as allegories, those which function as genetic explanations, and those which function as other types of parascientific explanations. An example of allegorical myth is Diotima's account of the birth of Eros in the *Symposium;* among genetic explanations is the account of the creation in the *Timaeus;* and typical examples of what Frutiger calls parascientific are the accounts of a future life and of rewards and punishments for virtue and vice given in the *Republic, Gorgias, Phaedo* and *Phaedrus.* Frutiger sees three features of Platonic myth as outstanding: the use of symbols, the freedom exhibited in the handling of the narrative, and what he pleasantly calls a prudent imprecision. The last is important. Plato uses myth where he wishes the precise extent of his own intellectual commitment to remain unclear. Thus, Plato's use of myth helps us to understand how the break with mythological thought forms involves the raising of sharp questions about truth and falsity which the mythological forms themselves are able to evade. This throws light on certain characteristics of mythology.

The subject matter of mythological narratives is no different from that of later philosophy and science; what differentiates myth from these is not merely its narrative form or its use of personification. It is, rather, that a myth is living or dead, not true or false. You cannot refute a myth because as soon as you treat it as refutable, you do not treat it as a myth but as a hypothesis or history. Myths which could not easily coexist if they were hypotheses or histories, as, for example, rival accounts of creation, can comfortably belong to the same body of mythology. There are often gradual processes of reconciliation and of integration into a single narrative, but the discrepancies which give so much pleasure to the anthropologist are not discrepancies at all from the standpoint of the narrator.

Thus, Plato, by falling back into myth, may be deliberately avoiding too direct an encounter not only with certain philosophical difficulties but also with rival religious traditions. For myth is not theology any more than it is hypothesis or history. Indeed, the dominance of theology in later religious thought and the insistence in the mystery religions and in Christianity on treating myth as theology are as responsible for the death of mythology as is any philosophical rationalism bred by the pre-Socratics and Plato. Of course, it was not only Greek mythology that was treated by Christianity in this way. Both Norse and Celtic mythology met the same fate, although they both survived in medieval literature as beliefs and not just as a source for tale telling.

Modern thought. The first serious modern treatment of mythology occurs in Giambattista Vico's *Scienza nuova.* In Vico's theory of history each period has its own unity and character, and periods succeed one another in a determinate order. The beginnings of civilization occur in "the age of the gods," when men live in families and center their lives around religion, marriage, and the burial of the dead; this period is followed by the "age of heroes," in which aristocratic states arise. Only then comes the "age of men," the age of democratic republics. By the third stage rational inquiry is established, but in the early stages poetry and myth express the vulgar wisdom of a people. Only from mythology can we discover the religion, morals, law, and social life of early society. Myths are not false narratives, nor are they allegories. They express the collective mentality of a given age.

Vico's treatment of myth is far closer to that of modern anthropology than is that of his immediate successors. The Enlightenment's belief in progress and attack on superstition produced an unsympathetic climate for such interests. Even Herder, whose sympathy was awakened by seeing in primitive poetry and song the spirit of the folk, was inclined to treat myths as pardonably false beliefs. In the nineteenth century this assumption underlay the first systematic attempts at a science of mythology, but there was also a new consciousness of the widespread prevalence of mythology and a wish to apply comparative methods.

In 1856, Max Müller published his *Comparative Mythology,* in which he tried to interpret mythologies by means of principles derived from philology. All Aryan languages are derived from Sanskrit, in which originally there were certain words named sun, sky, clouds, rain, and dawn. But language became diseased, the original meanings were lost, the words became treated as the names of divine beings, and what had been accounts of the sun ushering in the dawn and ending the reign of night were transformed into myths about battles between gods, heroic quests for gold, and the like. To understand a myth, asserted Müller, discover the etymology of the names.

Andrew Lang pointed out that rival philologists would give different etymological explanations of the same myth with apparently equal plausibility. Lang himself regarded myths as survivals of earlier social norms. The classical Greeks recount myths in which cannibalism and human sacrifice occur, although they practiced neither; however, among Polynesian and African peoples, of whom Lang's contemporaries were newly aware, just such customs and accompanying myths are found. In classical Greece the custom had vanished, but the myth remained. Or a nature myth may be found with its meaning plain in its Maori form today, whereas in its Greek version the story has been so changed that the original meaning has been lost. The anthropology which Lang and his school used was that of E. B. Tylor, who himself criticized Müller's theorizing by showing how convincingly the nursery rhyme "Sing a Song of Sixpence" could be explained as a solar myth in Müller's terms.

Recurrent themes and comparative methods. Lang took it for granted that the "same" myth could turn up both in Greece and in New Zealand. The modern collection of mythologies has emphasized nothing so much as the strikingly similar themes and stories which recur in widely different places and times. Myths of the creation of the world are widespread; myths of the creation of mankind occur everywhere. But even in detail myths resemble one another. Clyde Kluckhohn has written that he knows of no culture lacking myths of witchcraft in which were-animals move about at night; poisons can be magically introduced into the victim, causing illness and death; and there is some connection between incest and witchcraft. Rank has discussed the common myth pattern of a hero, born of noble parents, against whose birth an oracle warns his father, so that the child is left to die of exposure; the child is saved by shepherds or animals, grows up to return, perform great deeds, avenge himself, and finally be recognized. In the Far East, among the Navaho, and in Greece, as well as in many other places, we find this pattern. What is the explanation of its recurrence? We can distinguish three main types of explanation.

The first is psychoanalytic. Otto Rank, a Freudian, explains the hero as the ego of the child who rebels against his parents. His father, on whom the child's hate is projected, is pictured as exposing the child in a box on water. The box symbolizes the womb; the water, birth. The order of the story follows a sequence analogous to that of dreams in which natural events and symbols are combined in a single fantasy. The myth is the expression of all paranoid characters who hate the father who ousted them from the maternal love and care. Because such a character is widespread, the myth which expresses it is widespread, too; in general, it is the common biological, and, consequently, psychological, inheritance of mankind which underlies the common stock of mythology.

By contrast, the Jungian approach to mythology rests upon belief in a common human access to the collective unconscious. The individual continually finds himself giving expression to an archetypal symbolism which dominates not only the mythology but also much of the sophisticated literature of the world. The same myths recur in different times and places because all mythology has a common source. Modern man, who has overdeveloped the rational side of his nature, encounters in his dreams the same figures that appear in ancient and primitive mythology.

The difficulties in the Jungian account of mythology are difficulties which confront all Jungian theory. If the existence of the collective unconscious is a hypothesis designed to explain the recurrence of certain themes and symbols in myths and dreams, then it must be formulable in a way that is testable. But if such a hypothesis is to be testable, we must be able to deduce from it predictable consequences over and above the data which it was originally formulated to explain. Yet no such consequences seem to follow from the hypothesis of the collective unconscious. It seems to be untestable; it certainly remains untested. As an explanation of the recurrence of mythological themes and symbols, it is also unnecessary, for there are simpler and less incoherent explanations.

Joseph Campbell has used the Jungian theory of archetypes to interpret the story *The Frog King*, one of the myths collected by the brothers Grimm. He sees the frog as a small-scale dragon whose outward ugliness conceals the depths of the unconscious, in which unrecognized and unknown treasure is to be found. The frog king summons the child to attain maturity and self-knowledge by exploration of the unconscious. Fortunately, we also have a Freudian interpretation of *The Frog King* by Ernest Jones according to which the frog is a symbol for the penis and the myth represents the child's overcoming disgust in approaching the sexual act. Max Müller had, of course, long before interpreted *The Frog King* as one more solar myth.

In the face of these rival interpretations the need for a criterion of correct interpretation is clearly urgent, and with this need goes the need for a criterion for deciding when two myths are and are not versions of the "same" myth. The first step toward providing such criteria is the collection and tentative classification of as many bodies of mythology as possible. The most interesting work here has been done by Kluckhohn, who has systematically established not only the recurrence of plots and characters but also the existence of constant tendencies within this recurrence. For example, we can discover cases where a myth is reinterpreted to fit a new cultural or social situation. Clearly, where we can distinguish the original from the reinterpreted version, we are in a stronger position to compare a myth with similar myths for other cultures. We can study and compare not merely one version of a myth with another but the development of one myth through a series of versions with the development of another; from this it is clear that even if we wish to stress certain psychological functions of myth (Kluckhohn has thrown light on Navaho myth making by showing how it exemplifies mechanisms of ego defense), it is only when we put myth into a social context that we are likely to understand what the nature of myth making and recounting is.

Anthropology. The work of Claude Lévi-Strauss is important not only because its treatment of myth does not abstract myths from the social and economic relationships of those who tell and hear them but also because by invoking a wider context he has been able to pick out hitherto unnoticed features of mythology. In *Totemism*, for example, Lévi-Strauss shows how a myth of the North American Ojibwa and a myth from Polynesian Tikopia both express relationships between nature and culture, between the species which provide food and the kinship system. In each case the myth helps to express both continuity and discontinuity in these relationships; both myths also stress that no direct and simple connection between the one type of relationship and the other is possible. The myths, as it were, warn anthropologists not to oversimplify.

If one did not notice the connection of these myths with foodstuffs and with kinship but simply abstracted the "story," one would certainly not necessarily conclude that the Ojibwa myth and the Tikopia myth were the same myth. The resemblances between them appear fully only because Lévi-Strauss poses certain questions about the myths. These questions are formulated in the light of his general theory of kinship systems and invoke the notion of relationships which are specified in purely formal terms. Lévi-Strauss elsewhere has analyzed other myths with a view to showing that in their structure formal properties are both exhibited and implicitly commented upon. Perhaps not surprisingly, these formal properties parallel the formal properties exhibited by kinship systems and also parallel to some extent, much more surprisingly, the formal properties of certain linguistic structures.

What emerges from these studies is the thesis that myths incorporate and exhibit binary oppositions which are present in the structure of the society in which the myth was born. In the myth these oppositions are reconciled and overcome. The function of the myth is to render intellectually and socially tolerable what would otherwise be experienced as incoherence. The myth is a form in which society both understands and misunderstands its own structure. Thus, Lévi-Strauss gives a precise meaning to Vico's contention that "The fables of the gods are true histories of customs."

This judgment is perhaps inverted in the work of Lévi-Strauss's most important rival, Mircea Eliade. The customs of men, in Eliade's view, often turn out to be the expression of their beliefs about the gods. Thus, the behavior of shamans, who in a state of trance imitate animal sounds (birds' song, for example, among many peoples) is a re-enactment and an attempt to restore man's primitive, paradisal, unfallen state in which he not only did not die or have to work but also communicated with the animals and lived in peace with them. Hence, Eliade concludes both that shamanism is part of the central religious tradition of mankind, stretching from primitive African myths to Christian theology, and that it is therefore not, as it first appears to be, an irrational phenomenon. Eliade distinguishes sharply between the particular cultural and social trappings which may surround a myth and what he calls the ideology behind the trappings which is exhibited in the myth itself. Thus, where Lévi-Strauss analyzes the content of a myth in terms of what is local and particular to a given society, Eliade wishes to relate the content to general human religious interests and as far as possible divorce it from the local and particular.

Irrationalism. "Myths must be judged as a means of acting upon the present," said Georges Sorel in 1908. Sorel distinguishes those beliefs which it is appropriate to characterize in terms of truth and falsity and those which is appropriate to characterize in terms of effectiveness and ineffectiveness. A myth is essentially a belief about the future which embodies the deepest inclinations of some particular social group. The myth which Sorel himself wanted to propagate was the syndicalist project of a general strike. Other socialists treated their beliefs about the future as predictions; Sorel regards this as for the most part irrelevant. The only predicates in which he is interested are self-fulfilling ones.

Yet to regard beliefs about the future in this way is paradoxical. For example, when I try to propagate a myth, I am inviting people to believe. But insofar as I do this, I invite them to treat it as true rather than false and as susceptible to truth or falsity. It is difficult to resist the conclusion that anyone who holds a view like Sorel's will fall into a form of doublethink, treating the myth as true or false in certain situations but retreating into the assertion that questions of its truth or falsity are inappropriate in other situations. Certainly, just this kind of doublethink characterizes modern irrationalist myth makers after Sorel. They wish to avoid hard questions that philosophers or social scientists might raise about their myths, but they also wish to claim some kind of truth for their utterances. Thus, we also get a concomitant doctrine of special kinds of truth or special criteria for truth—for example, in works as different as Alfred Rosenberg's *Myth of the Twentieth Century* and D. H. Lawrence's *The Plumed Serpent*. Rosenberg's version of Houston Stewart Chamberlain's amalgam of anti-Semitism, racism, and authoritarian German nationalism is, of course, utterly different in content and implications from Lawrence's appeal to "the dark gods" and his attempt to restore an imagination violated by the wrong kind of arid rationalism. However, the difficulty with all irrationalism is that the abandonment of the criteria of rationality leaves us defenseless before the most morally outrageous appeals to emotion. In such appeals the revival of myth has a key place.

Bibliography

Eliade, Mircea, *Aspects du mythe*. Paris, 1963.

Frutiger, P., *Les mythes de Platon: Étude philosophique et littéraire*. Paris, 1930.

Hooke, S. H., ed., *Myth, Ritual, and Kingship*. Oxford, 1958.

Jones, Ernest, *Essays in Applied Psychoanalysis*, Vol. II, *Essays in Folklore, Anthropology and Religion*. London, 1951.

Jung, C. G., and Kerényi, Carl, *Essays on a Science of Mythology*, translated by R. F. C. Hull. New York, 1944.

Lang, Andrew, *Custom and Myth*. London, 1901.

Lévi-Strauss, Claude, *Structural Anthropology*, translated by Claire Jacobson and Brooke Grundfest. New York, 1963.

Lévi-Strauss, Claude, *Totemism*, translated by R. Needham. Boston, 1963; London, 1964.

Müller, Max, *Chips From a German Workshop*. New York, 1872.

Murray, Henry A., ed., *Myth and Mythmaking*. New York, 1960.

Rank, Otto, *The Myth of the Birth of the Hero*, translated by F. Robbins and S. E. Jellife. New York, 1952.

Sebeok, Thomas A., ed., *Myth: A Symposium*. Bloomington, Ind., 1955.

Stewart, J. A. *The Myths of Plato*. London, 1905.

Vico, Giambattista, *The New Science*, translated by T. B. Bergin and M. H. Fisch. New York, 1948; paperback ed., 1961.

ALASDAIR MacINTYRE

N

NĀGĀRJUNA, Buddhist metaphysician who lived sometime in the early second century, was probably born a Brahman in south India. His main work was done at Nālandā, the Buddhist university in north India. He was the founder of the Mādhyamika school of Mahāyāna (Greater Vehicle) Buddhism and can be reckoned the subtlest and most original philosopher that this wing of Buddhism has produced. Although in part he developed earlier ideas, his systematic application of the dialectical method was novel in Buddhism and had a lasting influence. He harnessed what appeared to be a total philosophical skepticism to a positive interpretation of Buddhism.

The Mādhyamika, or "Middle," school that Nāgārjuna founded claimed to give a correct interpretation of the Buddha's intentions in refusing to answer certain questions—for instance, the question of whether the saint who has attained nirvana persists after his decease—on the ground that they were wrongly put. The Buddha rejected the views that the saint does, that he does not, that he both does and does not, and that he neither does nor does not. Nāgārjuna generalized and reinterpreted this procedure, trying to show that all points of view about reality are contradictory. Thus his position is at the "middle" between the possible alternative theories about the world. Therefore, nothing can properly be said about reality, although the term "Void" (śūnya) could be used to signify its ineffability. Thus, the doctrine of the school is also referred to as Voidism (śūnyavāda). "Void" also served to express the emptiness of contemplative experience, so that it had a religious meaning as well as a philosophical one. Indeed, the term "the Void" came to function in the Mādhyamika system as the name of an admittedly insubstantial Absolute, embracing phenomena and constituting their inner nature.

The view that all views are self-contradictory should in effect invalidate ordinary language. For instance, Nāgārjuna criticized all theories of causation, which are themselves presupposed by ordinary concepts. Although at a higher philosophical level common-sense discourse is misleading, we can legitimately use it at a conventional level for the ordinary purposes of living. Thus Nāgārjuna held a two-level theory of truth, which was incorporated some eight centuries later into the epistemology of Śankara, who, ironically, used Mādhyamika concepts in the formulation of a renascent and rival Hinduism. Nāgārjuna's position here certainly corresponded to a theme running through Buddhism from very early times, namely, that ordinary language is misleading (for instance, it suggests that there is a permanent self underlying physical and mental processes). On the other hand, it was paradoxical for Voidism to hold, as a consequence of its skepticism, that the central teachings of the Buddha himself, such as that about the causes of rebirth, were false at the higher level.

Some Indian philosophers held the view that the effect is identical with the cause (that is, it is merely a transformation of the cause). But this view, according to Nāgārjuna, is absurd. First it implies that a thing produces itself. But if it already exists, it is wrong to speak of something's being *produced*. Second, a cause is either eternal or temporary. If eternal, there is no reason, other than some separate temporary condition, why it should produce its effect at one time rather than another. Since the eternal cause is unchanging, it is rational to explain the change through a temporary condition. But if the cause is temporary, it can be distinguished from, and is not identical with, the effect.

The nonidentity theory, which asserts that the cause and effect are distinct, is equally open to criticism. If the cause is totally extraneous to the effect, then anything can come out of anything, and this negates causal connection. But if there is something intrinsic to the effect, then the identity theory must hold. Further, a combination of these theories can be countered by a combination of these arguments. A similar type of critique is directed at other pairs and combinations of philosophical theories.

The gist of all these arguments is that the concept of relation involves a contradiction. If two things are externally related, the relation cannot be made sense of; and if they are internally related, they cannot be two. Because the empirical world, both as described in Buddhist doctrines and as experienced in ordinary life, seemingly comprises states and events in relation to one another, any statement about it will be incoherent. But how can even this be said? Does this not involve a view about the world that ought to come under Nāgārjuna's ban? Here his standpoint claimed to be negative: it was a series of *reductiones ad absurdum* of other viewpoints. In theory, therefore, the dialectic was not open to the criticisms it leveled at common sense and other philosophical positions.

Nevertheless, as his position was developed, especially by his successors, it became clear that some sort of thesis was implied. In religious terms, this could be expressed as follows. Ultimate reality is the Void: of this nothing can be predicated. But fortunately this empty Absolute phenomenalizes itself at the lower or empirical level as the Buddha. Thus a revelation fills the gap left by philosophical skepticism. And, as has been seen, the ineffability of the Void reflected the highest stage of mystical experience, so that one could have a kind of direct knowledge of the Absolute.

Nāgārjuna's work was carried on in the late second century by his pupil Āryadeva; and in the fifth century the school split over the issue of whether the *śūnyavāda* should be established simply by a negative dialectic or by positive arguments in favor of the religious interpretation. Partly as a result of the work of Candrakīrti (sixth century), the school coalesced with Buddhist idealism (*vijñānavāda*). This mixed form of the Mādhyamika became the dominant metaphysics in Tibetan Buddhism.

Bibliography

A work attributed to Nāgārjuna and relevant to Tibetan and Chinese Buddhism is *Mahāyānaviṃśaka*, edited and translated by Vidhushekhara Bhattacharya (Calcutta, 1931).

Works in which Nāgārjuna is discussed are Edward Conze, *Buddhist Thought in India* (London, 1964); T. R. V. Murti, *The Central Philosophy of Buddhism* (London, 1955); and Fedor I. Stcherbatsky, *The Central Conception of Buddhism and Meaning of the Word "Dharma"* (London, 1924). Stcherbatsky's *The Conception of Buddhist Nirvana* (Leningrad, 1917) includes a translation of Nāgārjuna's key text "Treatise on Relativity" and ancient commentary.

NINIAN SMART

NAGEL, ERNEST, John Dewey professor of philosophy at Columbia University, was born in 1901 at Nove Mesto, Czechoslovakia. Nagel came to the United States at the age of ten and was naturalized in 1919. He graduated from City College in 1923 and received an M.A. in mathematics from Columbia in 1925 and a Ph.D. in philosophy in 1930. He has expressed indebtedness to the teachings of Morris R. Cohen, John Dewey, and Frederick J. E. Woodbridge and to the writings of Charles S. Peirce, Bertrand Russell, and George Santayana.

Philosophy of science. Nagel belongs to the naturalist and logical empiricist movements, and he is primarily noted for his contributions to the philosophy of science. In 1934 he published, with Morris R. Cohen, *An Introduction to Logic and Scientific Method.* This noted text has been praised for its high level of rigor and for its enrichment of the traditional dry fare of logic with illustrations of the functions of logical principles in scientific method, in the natural and social sciences, and in law and history.

Nagel's book *The Structure of Science* is a unified and comprehensive distillation of many years of teaching and of his many publications on special aspects of scientific thought. It is the most complete exposition of Nagel's analysis of the nature of explanation, the logic of scientific inquiry, and the logical structure of the organization of scientific knowledge, and it illuminates the cardinal issues concerning the formation and the assessment of explanation in physics and in the biological and social sciences.

Two other contributions by Nagel to logic and the philosophy of science are *Principles of the Theory of Probability* (1939) and *Gödel's Proof* (1958), written in collaboration with James R. Newman. These studies range over many issues, from the logic of probable inference to the basic conditions of the structure of formal systems.

General philosophy. Two philosophical essays of a general scope by Nagel have been widely acclaimed. In "Logic Without Ontology" Nagel defended a naturalistic interpretation of logic. He argued that logico-mathematical principles must be understood according to their functions in specific contexts, namely, in inquiries, and he criticized attempts to adduce an ontological ground or transcendent authority for the meaning, warrant, and necessary character of logical laws. Nagel had already repudiated his early view that logical principles "are inherently applicable because they are concerned with ontological traits of utmost generality" (*An Introduction to Logic and Scientific Method*, p. v). In "Logic Without Ontology" he showed that the view that logic is ontologically determined or entails ontological commitments arises primarily from a failure to heed certain contextual and operational qualifications of the sense in which logical principles are supposed to possess "necessary truth."

In "Sovereign Reason" Nagel presented a penetrating critique, focused on the doctrine of internal relations, of Brand Blanshard's rational idealism. This critique exemplifies one of Nagel's strongest philosophical convictions and a main theme of "Logic Without Ontology": logical principles (and even pure Reason), just because they are analytic, are necessary but not sufficient instruments for acquiring knowledge or discovering truths about reality. The task of logic, according to Nagel, is to disclose the assumptions and clarify the methods on which responsible claims to knowledge are based and by which they are critically assessed. All claims to knowledge, even those most impressively supported by evidence and experiment, are subject to revision or rejection in the light of new advances in knowledge. This empiricist tenet led Nagel to accept contingency as a real trait of nature and fallibility as an inescapable feature of human inquiry.

Science and society. Nagel's technical interest in the logic and history of scientific knowledge has not prevented him from appreciating the social consequences and problems of science and technology in a democratic society. Much of his critical activity as a speaker, reviewer, and essayist has been devoted to imparting a clearer understanding of the nature of science and to dispelling philosophical vagaries and bizarre notions concerning such matters as causality and indeterminism in physics; the alleged paradoxical character of abstract science or its utter disparity with common sense; the frequent claims that science is value-free, or metaphysically inspired, or mere codified sense data; and the revulsion or despair and the impassioned remedies that science has occasioned in some literary and theological circles.

Materialism, determinism, and atheism. Nagel's philosophical naturalism has led him to take a decisive stand on certain broad philosophical issues, notably materialism, determinism, and atheism. It has been charged that naturalists, being materialists, are unable to account for mental phenomena. Nagel has replied, fully aware of the many senses of the word "materialism," that naturalists are not materialists if materialism is taken to mean that such psychological predicates as "fear" or "feeling of beauty" logically entail or are reducible to physical terms such as "weight," "length," or "molecule." Although he repudiates reductive materialism, Nagel holds that mental events are aspects of and contingent on the organization of human bodies. Events, qualities, and processes are dependent on the organization of spatially and temporally located bodies. In this sense, naturalism is committed to materialism: organized matter has a causal primacy in the order of nature. It follows that there can be no occult forces or disembodied spirits directing natural events and no personal immortality when bodily organizations disintegrate.

To assess the role of determinism in history and in ethical theory, Nagel formulated the meaning of "determinism" in natural science. A scientific theory is deterministic with respect to a set of properties when, given a specification of the set at any initial time, a unique set of the properties for any other time can be deduced by means of the theory. The theory might be a mechanical theory, and the sets of properties mechanical states. This theory might conceivably be of use in calculating the mechanical states of a human organism, but only its *mechanical* states. Whether *other* properties of the organism and its history were deterministic would remain an open empirical question. Nor would determinism in human history, if it were established, automatically empty moral endeavor and responsibility of significance. Which modes of human experience and behavior, if any, are subject to deterministic theory remains an empirical question; and the sense in which these conditions might be characterized as "deterministic" remains an issue of analysis.

In several places, including his influential paper "The Causal Character of Modern Physical Theory," Nagel has concerned himself with the philosophical implications of quantum theory. Like Einstein and Planck, but unlike the majority of writers on the subject, Nagel denies that quantum theory has indeterministic consequences. He also shows in some detail how intellectual confusion thrives when distinctions of context and the relevance of theoretical language to specific contexts are ignored; for example, when "particle" in the context of Newtonian theory is transported into discussions of the uncertainty principle in modern physics. In another well-known essay, "Russell's Philosophy of Science," Nagel argues that the physical and physiological facts of perception do not require the abandonment of common sense in favor of the strange conclusions held by Russell and Eddington.

Nagel is one of the few naturalists to present a forthright statement of the naturalist critique of theism. His formulation of atheism is not couched as a sheer negation of theism but proceeds from a positive moral position according to which, while it is granted that there are inevitable tragic aspects of life, knowledge of life and nature is to be preferred to illusions. On matters of such supreme moment, the truth rather than fiction is the more fitting ideal of rational men.

Nagel has not, however, denied the value and authenticity of other than purely cognitive pursuits. He has never argued that aesthetic qualities, ideals, suffering, and enjoyments are not genuine aspects of experience. On the contrary, he has urged that naturalism, although obliged to render a competent account of scientific knowledge, also include in its scope a place for imagination, liberal values, and human wisdom.

Bibliography

The Logic of Measurement. New York, 1930.
An Introduction to Logic and Scientific Method. New York, 1934. Written with Morris R. Cohen.
Principles of the Theory of Probability. Chicago, 1939. Vol. I, No. 6, of *The International Encyclopedia of Unified Science.*
"Russell's Philosophy of Science," in P. A. Schilpp, ed., *The Philosophy of Bertrand Russell.* Evanston, Ill., 1944. Reprinted in *Sovereign Reason.*
"Logic Without Ontology," in Y. H. Krikorian, ed., *Naturalism and the Human Spirit.* New York, 1944. Reprinted in *Logic Without Metaphysics* (see below).
"Are Naturalists Materialists?" *Journal of Philosophy,* Vol. 42 (1945), 515–530. Reprinted in *Logic Without Metaphysics.*
"Sovereign Reason," in Sidney Hook and Milton R. Konvitz, eds., *Freedom and Experience. Essays Presented to Horace M. Kallen.* Ithaca, N.Y., 1947. Reprinted in *Sovereign Reason.*
"The Causal Character of Modern Physical Theory," in S. W. Baron, Ernest Nagel, and K. S. Pinson, eds., *Freedom and Reason.* Glencoe, Ill., 1951. Reprinted with revisions as part of Ch. 10 in *The Structure of Science.*
Sovereign Reason. Glencoe, Ill., 1954.
Logic Without Metaphysics. Glencoe, Ill., 1956.
Gödel's Proof. New York, 1958. Written with James R. Newman.
"A Defense of Atheism," in J. E. Fairchild, ed., *Basic Beliefs.* New York, 1959.
The Structure of Science. New York, 1961.

H. S. THAYER

NAIGEON, JACQUES-ANDRÉ (1738–1810), French writer and associate of Diderot. Naigeon was not an original thinker; he became an editor, compiler, and commentator after having tried painting and sculpture, but he considered himself a philosopher and was proud of his classical erudition. A bibliophile, too, he accumulated one of the great collections of Greek and Latin classics of his time. Having been accepted into the group of Encyclopedists surrounding Baron d'Holbach, he became an aggressive atheist. He attached himself to Diderot as a disciple and tried to imitate his tone, his manner, and his ideas. Diderot in turn enjoyed Naigeon's wit and tolerated his bad temper, stiffness, and pedantry; Naigeon helped Diderot with the *salons* and the *Encyclopédie.* Naigeon later persuaded Diderot to make him his literary executor. He preserved and edited many of Diderot's manuscripts but did not publish others. He put out an incomplete edition of Diderot's works in 1798 and wrote a valuable but unfinished commentary on his life and writings, *Mémoires historiques et philosophiques sur la vie et les ouvrages de Diderot* (Paris, 1821). He also arranged the clandestine printing of several of Holbach's works in the Netherlands, and in 1770 published *Mélange de pièces sur la religion et la morale,* which contained some minor pieces by Holbach and other writers.

Naigeon edited the works of Seneca, completing the translation begun by N. La Grange and adding notes; he published it with Diderot's defense of Seneca, *Essai sur les règnes de Claude et de Néron* (Paris, 1778). A one-act musical comedy, *Les Chinois* (1756), is sometimes attributed to him, perhaps in collaboration with Charles-Nicolas Favart. His only "original" work was *Le Militaire philosophe, ou Difficultés sur la religion, proposées au P. Mallebranche* (London and Amsterdam, 1768), which is based on an earlier anonymous manuscript and has a final chapter by Holbach. This dull work is of minor value as an example of dogmatic atheism and materialism, but it merely repeats the same ideas and arguments that had run throughout the radical writings of the entire century. Naigeon supports hatred of priests and the church with the doctrine of materialism and a naturalistic utilitarian morality. He denounces Christian ethics (asceticism, humility, etc.), demanding fulfillment of legitimate natural demands and a moral code based on social well-being. He points out contradictions in Christian ethics and doctrine, stressing its cruelty and its failure. He argues that Christian ethics leads to an inversion of the natural order of values, hence to intolerance, inhumanity, and crimes. The earth would be peaceful and happy if the idea of God were eliminated.

Naigeon continued this attack in his contributions to C. J. Panckoucke's *Encyclopédie méthodique*. This work consisted of separate dictionaries, and Naigeon edited the *Dictionnaire de la philosophie ancienne et moderne* (3 vols., Paris, 1791–1793), which was largely a compilation. In *Adresse à l'Assemblée nationale sur la liberté des opinions* (1790) he demanded absolute freedom of the press and again gave vent to his hatred of priests.

There are no studies on Naigeon, except in relation to his publication of Diderot's manuscripts, nor is any needed.

L. G. CROCKER

NAIVE REALISM. See REALISM.

NAKAE TŌJU (1608–1648), "the sage of Ōmi" (his native town in Shiga Prefecture), the most respected Confucianist in the Tokugawa era, was an advocate of the Wang Yang-ming school. The ideas of Wang Yang-ming (in Japanese, Ōyōmei) were made known in Japan by the Chu Hsi scholar Fujiwara Seika (1561–1619), but only with Nakae did the Wang Yang-ming doctrine become a school of thought. The importance of this school lies in its impact on Japanese thinking and the nonconformists it produced. Its stress on *ryōchi* (literally, "good conscience"; more exactly, the innate knowledge which every man has from Heaven) favored the formation of strong individualists guided by the inner light of conscience without the formalistic restraints of Chu Hsi Confucianism. The cultivation of the mind combined with a stress on deeds rather than formal learning was another aspect of Nakae's teaching. His upright character showed in practice what it meant to be a Confucian sage, that is, almost a saint.

Nakae's intuitive and practical morality centering on filial piety had a great attraction for his pupils as well as for many later followers who for different reasons claimed him as their master. His outstanding followers were Ku-

mazawa Banzan (1619–1691) and such men prominent in the nineteenth-century movement to restore the emperor as Ōshio Heihachirō, Yoshida Shōin, and Saigō Takamori. Kumazawa tried to persuade his master to leave the obscure village of Ogawa and enter the service of the lord of Okayama, but the humble Nakae shunned the proposal. In addition, Nakae's inclinations were ethico-religious rather than politico-economic, the characteristic of many of his followers. Nor was he a radical, although some of his admirers were.

Nakae strove for a middle way, mildly criticizing other points of view. He spoke of *ri*, the "principle," and *ki*, Chu Hsi's material force (which Nakae interpreted as matter-life), as two aspects of the "supreme ultimate." Nakae's terminology recalls the ancient Chinese sages and suggests Christian influence; *Jōtei*, the "Supreme Lord Above," he called "the absolute truth and the absolute spirit," and he ascribed almost personal attributes to this Being. However, Nakae also had pantheistic leanings, and he used anthropomorphic expressions to ally his *Jōtei* with Shinto deities. His moral ideas, though, are much more important than his cosmological views. Filial piety (*kō*) is the pivotal virtue, for him both the universe's moral power and its reason for being. Everyone, from the emperor to the most despised woman—Nakae being quite an equalitarian—was affected by filial piety, the creative force descending by degrees from Heaven. This virtue became in his late followers patriotism toward the emperor. Still, for Nakae, it was a cosmic and religious force not limited to one family or nation.

Bibliography

See *Tōju sensei zenshū* ("The Complete Works of Nakae Tōju"), 5 vols. (Tokyo, 1940). A secondary source in Japanese is Bitō Masahide, *Nihon hōken shisōshi kenkyū* ("Studies on the History of Feudal Thought in Japan"; Tokyo, 1961), pp. 136–216. See also G. M. Fisher, "The Life and Teaching of Nakae Toju," in *Transactions of the Asiatic Society of Japan*, Vol. 36, Part 1 (1908), 24–94; W. T. de Bary, Ryusaku Tsunoda, and Donald Keene, eds., *Sources of Japanese Tradition* (New York, 1958), pp. 378–384, which offers selections, with an introduction.

GINO K. PIOVESANA, S.J.

NAMES, PROPER. See PROPER NAMES AND DESCRIPTIONS.

NATIONALISM. In defining the word "nationalism," at least five senses can be identified: (1) a sentiment of loyalty to a nation (a variety of patriotism); (2) a propensity, as applied to policies, to consider exclusively the interests of one's own nation, especially in cases where these compete with the interests of other nations; (3) an attitude which attaches high importance to the distinctive characteristics of a nation and, therefore, (4) a doctrine which maintains that national culture should be preserved; and (5) a political and an anthropological theory which asserts that mankind is naturally divided into nations, that there are determinate criteria for identifying a nation and for recognizing its members, that each nation is entitled to an independent government of its own, that states are legitimate only if constituted in accordance with this principle, and that the world would be rightly organized, politically speaking, only if every nation formed a single state and every state consisted exclusively of the whole of one nation.

Nature and criteria of nationality. Nationalist doctrines and theories of the kinds referred to in (4) and (5) date from the end of the eighteenth century. Attachment to one's nation and the belief that, for instance, all Englishmen constitute an English nation are, no doubt, much older. Men have always had this kind of attachment to an in-group—whether tribe, city, or nation—and a corresponding awareness of (and perhaps hostility toward) nonmembers as foreigners. But what characterizes nations, distinguishing them from groups of other kinds?

The nation defined by the state. A nation, wrote the French revolutionary ideologist the Abbé Sieyès in 1789, is "a union of individuals governed by *one* law, and represented by the same law-giving assembly." Thus conceived, a nation's unity and identity derive from political organization, and the state would thus be logically prior to the nation. This view was consistent with the individualist or atomistic interpretation of group phenomena of which Locke was a typical exponent and which was characteristic of much of the social theorizing of the eighteenth-century Enlightenment. Writers like Diderot and Condorcet considered that individuals must be taken to concur in the setting up of a political order because (or insofar as) it is in their interests, several and collective. A public interest, thus created, is the ground of a duty to preserve and defend the order, and the state, as the subject of this interest, becomes a proper object of loyalty. Those sharing in such a common interest would constitute one people, or nation. This view of nationality is supported by the way in which, in ordinary speech, citizenship and nationality are interchangeable in many contexts. (This was once true of legal usage, too; however, many states now distinguish the rights and duties of a citizen from those of a national.) If, however, we do distinguish nationality from citizenship in ordinary speech, it is principally by narrowing citizenship to matters of political and legal status, whereas to determine nationality, we take into account criteria like place of birth, parentage, language, and cultural tradition.

The nation defined by language and culture. The conception of nationality as language and culture became articulate, as an element in nationalist ideology, at the end of the eighteenth century, mainly through the work of German writers such as Herder, Novalis, Schleiermacher, and Fichte. Whereas for the French revolutionaries a nation was a group of individuals subject to a single political order, for the Germans nations were distinguished from one another by God and nature. Each had its peculiar character closely related to its common language. Since language is the vehicle of a tradition, preserving and transmitting sentiments, symbols, emotional associations, and myths, to share a native language is to share a common culture. "Every language," wrote Schleiermacher, "is a particular mode of thought, and what is cogitated in one language can never be repeated in the same way in another." This concept of nationality tended to be associated with a metaphysical doctrine that saw every nation as the expression of a spirit or idea, which in turn expressed a particular aspect of the divine image. The diversity of nations was a reflection of the diversity of reality, and each nation made its necessary contribution to the progress of mankind. Its members therefore had a moral duty to preserve and foster it. Thus, in reacting against the Francophile cosmopolitanism of the *Aufklärung* (German Enlightenment), the German cultural nationalist nevertheless continued to see the nations against the backcloth of humanity, each with a role to play in what, in the end, was a drama of mankind.

As these writers saw it, a nation's existence did not depend on its members' choice or recognition; or, rather, because it formed their consciousness, they could hardly choose not to be members. If the German nation was a natural fact, it was because men reared in a German tradition would be essentially different from Englishmen or Frenchmen. Thus, a German who tried to ape the French inhibited the expression of his own nature and made do with what for him were artificial second bests.

The nation defined by common heritage. The conception of nationality as language and culture was challenged by Ernest Renan in the famous lecture *Qu'est-ce qu'une nation?* of 1882. It is a mistake, says Renan, to confuse nations with ethnographic and linguistic groups. Common racial origin, language, or religion, common economic interests, or the facts of geography are not sufficient to constitute a nation. There are nations like the Swiss, who do not share such characteristics, and there are linguistic groups like the English-speaking peoples, who do but who do not form a single nation. According to Renan, what constitutes a nation is the possession, first, of a common history, particularly of sufferings—of a store, that is, of common memories which are a source of common sympathy and pride. But it is important that some things be forgotten, too, for until old wounds have healed, the sense of sharing a common heroic tradition will be lacking. Thus, the second condition of nationality is a will to live together and to keep the common heritage alive. "To have done great things together, and the will to do more, these are the essential conditions for a people. . . . The existence of a nation is . . . a daily plebiscite."

Granted the importance of personal identification with a common tradition in the life of a nation, the metaphor of common memories does little, perhaps, to elucidate what gives a national tradition its unity and continuity. In the sense in which memory is important for individual self-knowledge and identity, individuals cannot remember what happened before they were born. Nor need their heroic ancestors stand in any generative relation to them. It is only in a figurative sense that a Frenchman could claim Joan of Arc for an ancestor. It is only because he is already a participant in a national tradition that he knows whom to call ancestor. Different situations call out different loyalties, and the ancestors a man acknowledges may differ accordingly. An American Jew of German descent might identify himself now with Jefferson, now with Judas Maccabaeus, now with Frederick the Great. Again, although men may share memories simply by having been present at the same event, to share a common history is not just to know the same historical facts; it is to identify with the same historic symbols, feel vicarious pride in the same achievements, and feel indignation at the same affronts. A Frenchman may *know* as much about Frederick as about Joan; it is because Joan is *his* and Frederick *theirs* that he is a Frenchman. A nation exists, then, where there is a group of individuals, attached in this way to a common body of symbols, who recognize one another as fellow members sharing similar attitudes to these symbols and who, because of this, feel a loyalty and concern for one another that they would not extend to outsiders. Linguistic, religious, or physiognomic features may have a part in determining who is so recognized, and the importance of any one of them may be different in different situations.

The nation defined by territory. A characteristic of nationality distinguishing it from most other kinds of group attachment is its relation to territory. For a group to have no special territorial affinity would not prevent one from calling it a sect, a family, or a social class. The idea of a homeland, however, seems essential to the idea of a nation. The true cosmopolitan has no place where he belongs. This illumines the close conceptual relation between nation and state, for a state is also territorially based and will admit nonmembers only on its own terms.

Where an area has a history of conflict among religious, linguistic, or racial groups each concentrated in a particular territory, the members of each will be conscious of themselves as a separate group with a history of supremacy or suffering associated with that territory; the characteristics which significantly differentiate the group from those around it will come to be thought of as those of people who belong to that territory, even when they are also found outside it. Any such group excluded from political power may be expected to aspire to independence and to want to settle in its own territory the terms on which power and prestige are enjoyed. There is, then, a wide range of features by which a national group might identify itself and its members. Which of them becomes the focus of nationality in any given case will depend on how the group has come to self-consciousness; that feature will very often correspond to the criterion by which it has been singled out as an object of oppression. Its homeland will be the territory in which the group so defined now predominates or predominated in some earlier period to which its common recollections go back.

The nation defined by common aim. However, because nationalism is so often a form of protest, the concept of the nation to which it is tied may depend as much on the definition of the out-group against which it is aimed as on the positive delineation of the in-group. In the twentieth century African and Asian nationalisms, for instance, rely heavily on the repudiation of white colonialism and on an aspiration to count as the white man's equal. However, on its own this cannot be enough to constitute a nation, for though the same sentiments are found throughout Black Africa, only a few Africans see themselves as a single nation aspiring to unity in a single state. Nationalism, in fact, can exist before the nation, as the aspiration of a European-trained elite aiming at native independence in a territory defined by an imperial power for administrative convenience, not by any native tradition or symbolic attachment. Having transformed a colony into a state, nationalists in

countries like Ghana must then create a nation. That states can be as important in making nations as nations can be in making states is borne out by the success of the United States and the Soviet Union. The failure of the Austro-Hungarian Empire to create a nation was the cause of its distintegration.

National self-determination. The twin sources of modern nationalist doctrine are the French conception of popular sovereignty and German romantic anthropological nationalism. In eighteenth-century political theory the attribution of sovereignty to the people instead of the monarch gave the people the right to determine its own mode of government. This implied no threat to the existing order of states and gave rise to no Irredentisms in France and England, where the territorial boundaries of the self-conscious nation corresponded more or less with the established frontiers of the state and where the state itself was already a national symbol. In Germany and Italy, however, nationality spilled across frontiers. If the people, being sovereign, might choose the political order it wished and if "the people" was defined by nationality irrespective of existing states, then a national will to unity and independence was self-justifying even though it dismembered existing states, upset dynastic legitimacy, and sanctioned the invasion of one sovereign state by another in the interest of national liberation. The Italian nationalist Giuseppe Mazzini put the case in extreme terms, professing the belief that the political unity and independence of every nation within its natural boundaries was ordained by God. A characteristically more moderate view was stated by J. S. Mill in *Representative Government* (1861):

> Where the sentiment of nationality exists in any force, there is a *prima facie* case for uniting all the members of the nationality under the same government, and a government to themselves apart. This is merely saying that the question of government ought to be decided by the governed. One hardly knows what any division of the human race would be free to do if not to determine with which of the various collective bodies of human beings they would choose to associate themselves.

There are very great difficulties, however, in the notion of a right to self-determination, whether individual or collective. The idea of a state as an organization exercising authority over everyone within its boundaries is not compatible with the idea of conceding to each man a right to choose whether to give it his allegiance. Of course, everyone may have a right to some influence on how and by whom he will be governed. But this amounts to a right to participate in certain constitutional decision procedures that take the political framework for granted, not to a right to take or leave it as one likes. Nor is a collective right any easier. On the practical level no amount of fragmentation or partition could put every individual in an area like the Balkans into the right state.

A more fundamental problem, however, is to decide what constitutes a national group for the purpose of self-determination. In the name of national unity Ghanaian nationalists deny self-determination to the Ashanti as the Congolese denied it to Katanga. If Germans claim that all

German-speaking people, as members of the German nation, ought to be included in Germany, would the principle of national self-determination leave so-called Germans abroad any choice in the matter? And if they demurred, would it be as Germans or as non-Germans? If as Germans, would this be compatible with the self-determination of the whole German people? Clearly, if nationality is to be judged by objective criteria like language, the principle of national self-determination would support Irredentist expansion policies irrespective of the wishes of the subgroup concerned since the nation's will would presumably be more authoritatively expressed by the greater part than by the lesser. But if nationality is judged by subjective criteria, like a will to live under one government, repudiation by the subgroup would appear to be ground enough for saying that it was not part of the same nation after all. But a dissentient minority within that subgroup could then equally well claim a separate national identity and so on. If one accepts subjective criteria for group self-determination, there is no reason for stopping short of individual self-determination.

The objective criteria, though often difficult to apply in actual cases, do provide clear principles for the proper constitution of states. However, they can claim no support from the individualist doctrine that political obligation must rest on consent. This principle has played its part in the history of nationalist doctrine. Kant maintained that the principle of moral freedom and autonomy implied that men, as self-legislating members of the kingdom of ends, must impose political obligation upon themselves and that authority must derive from and be subject to the general will as expressed in law. Nationalists like the German political economist Adam Müller transformed the argument, however, by identifying the individual with the nation, insisting that the individual's permanent will was more truly expressed in the *Volksgeist*, or national spirit, than in any particular individual preference. Thus, the general will, which for Rousseau and Kant reconciled individual moral autonomy with political authority and obligation, became a way of denying the relevance of personal choice when it ran counter to the national spirit.

Early nineteenth-century nationalism was nevertheless liberal and humane in intention. Fichte and Mazzini would have argued that unless a nation was united in an independent sovereign state, its members, unable to command the respect of others as equals, would be lacking in dignity and self-respect. Much of the persuasive charm of nationalism in Africa and Asia has a similar source. Colored men repudiating white superiority feel that for their own self-respect they must be ruled by men of their own color and kind with whom they can identify and who will be received on equal footing by the leaders of other sovereign states.

However, the moral uncertainty out of which nationalism is born and which is perhaps its main justification, readily turns, once unity and independence has been won, into an aggressive assertiveness and national egoism, akin to what in France Charles Maurras called "integral nationalism," "the exclusive pursuit of national policies, the absolute maintenance of national integrity, and the steady increase of national power." The nation-state is no longer set in the context of a larger humanity; it is its own sufficient justification. Nationalism in this key is frankly irrationalist, delighting in the symbolic rhetoric of "blood and soil." Enormously important as it is for the historian and sociologist, it would be absurd to treat it as if it invited serious rational criticism.

Bibliography

HISTORICAL STUDIES

Hayes, Carlton J. H., *Historical Evolution of Modern Nationalism.* Chicago, 1948.
Kohn, Hans, *The Idea of Nationalism.* New York, 1945. History of nationality and nationalism before 1789.
Kohn, Hans, *Nationalism: Its Meaning and History.* Princeton, N.J., 1955. Introductory study with readings and selected bibliography.

GENERAL STUDIES

Hertz, Frederick, *Nationality in History and Politics.* London, 1944. Sociological and historical study of nationalist ideology.
Shafer, Boyd C., *Nationalism—Myth and Reality.* London, 1955. Has twenty-page bibliography.
Snyder, Louis L., *The Meaning of Nationalism.* New Brunswick, N.J., 1954.

CLASSIC EXPOSITIONS

Fichte, J. G., *Reden an die deutsche Nation.* Berlin, 1808. Translated by R. F. Jones and G. H. Turnbull as *Addresses to the German Nation.* Chicago, 1922.
Maurras, Charles, *Enquête sur la monarchie.* Paris, 1924. Originally published in 1900.
Mazzini, Giuseppe, *Doveri dell'uomo.* London, 1860. Translated by Ella Noyes as "The Duties of Man," in Ernest Rhys, ed., *The Duties of Man and Other Essays, by Joseph Mazzini.* London and New York, 1907.
Reiss, H. S., ed., *The Political Thought of the German Romantics, 1793–1815.* Oxford, 1955. Contains readings from Fichte, Novalis, Adam Müller, Schleiermacher, and Savigny; also has selected bibliographies.
Renan, Ernest, *Qu'est-ce qu'une Nation?*, in Henriette Psichari, ed., *Oeuvres complètes de Ernest Renan,* Vol. I. Paris, 1947. Originally published in 1882.

CRITICAL STUDIES

Acton, John Emerich Edward, "Nationality," in Gertrude Himmelfarb, ed., *Essays on Freedom and Power by Lord Acton.* Glencoe, Ill., 1948. For criticism of Mazzini.
Cobban, Alfred, *National Self-determination.* Chicago, 1948.
Kedourie, Elie, *Nationalism.* London and Toronto, 1960; 2d rev. ed., London and New York, 1961. Has notes for further reading; examines metaphysical foundations of nationalism and its influence on Europe and the Middle East.
Kohn, Hans, *Prophets and Peoples.* New York, 1957. Studies of J. S. Mill, Michelet, Mazzini, Treitschke, Dostoyevsky.

STANLEY I. BENN

NATIONAL SOCIALISM. See GERMAN PHILOSOPHY AND NATIONAL SOCIALISM.

NATORP, PAUL (1854–1924), German Neo-Kantian philosopher, was born in Düsseldorf and studied at the universities of Berlin, Bonn, and Strassburg. He became a *Privatdozent* at Marburg in 1881 and an extraordinary professor in 1885, and he was a full professor there from 1892 until his death. In 1888 he became editor of the *Philosophische Monatsheften,* in 1895 of the *Archiv für systematische Philosophie* (New Series), and in 1906 coeditor with Hermann Cohen of a series of philosophical works, *Philosophische Arbeiten.* He visited America briefly in 1921.

Natorp's thought, when judged by his more than one hundred complex and not always easy to read publications—books, essays, journal articles, encyclopedia entries, and speeches—may appear constant, but it underwent a genuine revolution, revealed especially in his posthumously published writings.

While still a student, Natorp felt the philosophical superficiality of materialism, "which transformed the world into a single great calculation which, as a result of an immense intertwining of factors, finally produced the calculator as well as the calculation" ("Selbstdarstellung," p. 2). Dissatisfied with the other academic philosophies, he was contemplating work in different fields—perhaps even music—when he discovered the Neo-Kantianism of Friedrich Albert Lange and Hermann Cohen. After comparing the critical and anti-Platonic positivism of Ernst Laas with the thought of Kant, he decided on a philosophical vocation and adherence to critical-methodological idealism. He dedicated his life to "the critical method applied to scientific, ethical, aesthetic, and religious idealism," a program influenced both by Kant and by Plato.

Natorp, who remained at Marburg even after Cohen's departure for Berlin in 1912, defined both the position of the Marburg school of Neo-Kantianism with respect to Kant and his own position with respect to Cohen and the entire Neo-Kantian movement. For Natorp, what was important in Kant was the discovery of the transcendental method as a critical foundation and justification of the great "facts" of science, morality, art, and religion and of the generative laws of logic immanent in the various forms of objectivication in an unending progressive undertaking. Natorp nevertheless saw much to be corrected in Kant, beginning with the dualisms of intuition and thought and of form and matter. He realized that some doctrines of the Marburg school resembled the idealism of Fichte and Hegel, but he pointed out profound differences, especially with respect to Hegelian panlogism and its absolutism of the conclusiveness of the dialectical process. The process is, he claimed, infinite, and it branches out into various methodical forms, each of which is a type of logic.

In 1918, upon the death of Cohen, Natorp drew up a kind of balance sheet of Kantian exegesis and of Cohen's contribution "from the point of view of the system": *Hermann Cohens philosophische Leistung unter dem Gesichtspunkt des Systems* (Berlin, 1918). He asked when Cohen first felt the need of system. It began to appear, Natorp claimed, in Cohen's study of Kant's *Critique of Practical Reason* (*Kants Begründung der Ethik,* Berlin, 1877), when he had to broaden the concept of experience to include moral experience and to place beside the legislation of the understanding that of the ideas of reason and of their regulative value. Other types of knowledge and of worlds of objects (*Gegenstandswelten*) or cultural experiences, such as that of art, were soon recognized. Cohen's *Das Prinzip der Infinitesimal-Methode* (Berlin, 1883), with its introduction and utilization in the explication of mathematical physics of the notion of the generative unity of the base, was another step forward. Natorp pointed out that in the

second edition of *Kants Theorie der Erfahrung* (Berlin, 1885) Cohen spoke of the system of critical idealism, but that Cohen's system contained gaps (it lacked the sciences of morals, culture, and history) and uncertainties about whether the sciences should be unified at the root or at the top. Natorp regarded not so much *Logik der reinen Erkenntnis* (Berlin, 1902) as *Ethik des reinen Willens* (Berlin, 1904) as Cohen's principal contribution to systematization. In the first work the systematic division of scientific, moral, and aesthetic consciousness was entrusted to psychology rather than logic, and the "logic of origins" concerned only mathematical natural science. On the contrary, in the second work there is a systematic foundation on "pure will"—a search for truth and tendency which gives both direction and anticipation, both method and content. It motivates self-consciousness and separates and reconciles being and duty (what ought to be) from the unitary origin to the last individualization. Natorp substantially accepted Cohen's foundation but would have liked to see the concepts of psychology and logic clarified and examined more deeply.

Natorp's basic work on Plato, *Platons Ideenlehre, Eine Einführung in den Idealismus* (1902), was preceded by 15 years of exhaustive philological and theoretical research and 10 years of correction and integration. A thorough exploration of the history of the problem of knowledge and of general philosophical problems among the Greeks was accompanied by methodical research on the founders of modern science and philosophy.

Both in the preliminary works and in *Platons Ideenlehre* the influence of Cohen is obvious. Plato had to be freed from the psychological and metaphysical trappings on which the traditional interpretation had been based from the time of Aristotle. Ideas are not things, not even things of another world, but laws and methods; they are the logical foundation of science. This is Plato's true discovery, whose progressive development can be seen in his works. Natorp's interpretation, which made of Plato "a Kantian before Kant, indeed a Marburg neo-Kantian before Marburg" (*Platons Ideenlehre,* 2d ed., 1921, p. 462), provoked much controversy, but in 1913 Natorp defended it brilliantly in a speech at the university of Berlin that took into account the then most recent and important Platonic studies.

By that time there were forming in Natorp's mind the seeds of a development accelerated by his experience in World War I, which led him to a systematization new in form and content, reached by means of the delineation of "practical philosophy and its culmination, social pedagogy, the new transcendental foundation of psychology and religion." In an appendix to the second edition of *Platons Ideenlehre* (1921) Natorp emphasized Plato's theme of the *epēkeina,* of the *agathōn–kalōn–sophōn,* which was regained in the pre-Kantian notion of the *transcendentalia.* Natorp traced back the plurality of Ideas to the unity of the *Logos* that both differentiates and unifies, and he recognized in this the ancient metaphysical problem of being and becoming. He restored the living psychological dimension to the Ideas and illuminated the relationship in Plato's thought between *logos, psyche,* and *eros.* He reaffirmed the mystical background of Platonic philosophy and placed it in a development running from Heraclitus to

Plotinus, through Pseudo-Dionysius, Erigena, Meister Eckhart, and Nicholas of Cusa to Leibniz' monads and the mystical philosophy of the post-Kantians.

The Kantian and Platonic components of Natorp's thought developed thus. They form less an amalgam than a restless dialectical response to different needs. Yet in a painful effort to examine thoroughly the varied thought of his era (positivism, impressionism, *Lebensphilosophie, Wertphilosophie,* phenomenology, Neo-Fichteanism, and Hegelianism), he was always ready to receive ideas and accept criticism and to go beyond his previous views.

Natorp's methodological transcendentalism was at first concerned only with mathematics and physics. In his major work, *Die logischen Grundlagen der exacten Wissenschaften* (Leipzig, 1910), he sought their logic and examined the resolution of the "fact of the sciences" into their *fieri,* a resolution that was brought about by the revolution in the physical sciences. But he also felt the need to deal with the biological and the historical and sociological sciences. Still another facet of Natorp's thought was his interest in pedagogical, social, and political studies, first discussed in *Sozialpädagogik* (1899) and touched upon in his studies of Plato and Pestalozzi. The foundations for these disciplines were to be laid by Kant's practical reason and even more by surpassing Kant's ethical formalism through indicating the logic of individual and collective concrete life. The problem of the "individual human personality" was indeed perhaps the impetus for his subsequent systematic development.

Natorp's *Allgemeine Psychologie nach kritische Methode* (1912) and his project for an *Allgemeine Logik* indicate his progress away from Cohen, who was somewhat distrustful of psychology and left the study of it to such natural sciences as physiology. Natorp saw that the subjective act could not be neglected and that it could be treated philosophically and transcendentally, so to say, by turning the transcendentalism of objectivication upside down. The importance of this idea, which at first Natorp himself did not recognize, soon became clear. The unity of consciousness gave unification and support to the triple objectivication of the worlds of science, morality, and art, and one could study the correlation between subjective and objective dimensions and methods. Natorp's proposed *Allgemeine Logik* would unify and define objectivication as a Fichtean positioning of the object (*Gegenstandssetzung*) and trace out every logically traceable position, "even if it be extra-, sub-, or super-objective," in all realms and dimensions, abstract and concrete, of spirit.

World War I and the German revolution directed Natorp's attention to the real contrasts of practice and to history, and led him to impassioned "synthetic" speeches and writings, not products of lengthy and tranquil meditation, on the philosophy of history (*Die Weltalter des Geistes,* Jena, 1918); social and political philosophy (*Sozialidealismus,* 1920, which advocated an idealist socialism); and a philosophy of education (*Genossenschaftliche Erziehung,* Berlin, 1920; *Individuum und Gemeinschaft,* 1921).

Natorp's analytical and systematic zeal are further revealed in the meticulous courses of lectures, given in his last years, on practical philosophy and on philosophical systematics; they were published posthumously by his son

Hans in 1925 and 1958. Ernst Cassirer, visiting Natorp on his seventieth birthday in 1924, was amazed by the inexhaustibility of his thinking: for example, he had plans for a course on the philosophy of *poiesis.* In 1925 Cassirer examined Natorp's posthumous work on practical philosophy by putting it in its historical perspective and showing its importance, and by stressing its agreement with the speculative principle and dialectical method of Hegel.

The two posthumous volumes, *Vorlesungen über praktische Philosophie* (1925) and *Philosophische Systematik* (1958), have much in common in their logical and metaphysical composition of a dialectic of fundamental categories and of phases of active realization which seek not only the content but also the concreteness of existence. Both works have a Hegelian rhythm which goes beyond Hegelian panlogism. *Philosophische Systematik* fills some of the lacunae in *Praktische Philosophie* in its conception of a "third dimension of logic," the dimension of subject-objectivity (*Subjekt-Objektivität*) and in its discussion of the limits of transcendental philosophy. This last problem is the problem of religion, which Natorp no longer saw as "within the limits of" human reason (as in his *Religion innerhalb der Grenzen der Humanität,* 1894) but "at the limit" of human reason.

Works by Natorp

Descartes' Erkenntnistheorie. Marburg, 1882.
Forschungen zur Geschichte des Erkenntnisproblems im Altertum. Berlin, 1884.
Einleitung in die Psychologie nach kritischer Methode. Freiburg, 1888.
Die Ethika des Demokritos. Marburg, 1893.
Religion innerhalb der Grenzen der Humanität. Freiburg, 1894.
"Berichte über deutsche Schriften zur Erkenntnistheorie." *Archiv für systematische Philosophie,* N.S. Vols. 3, 6, 7 (1896–1900).
Sozialpädagogik. Stuttgart, 1899.
Platons Ideenlehre. Leipzig, 1902; 2d ed., 1921.
Philosophische Propädeutik. Marburg, 1903.
Jemand und Ich. Ein Gespräch über Monismus, Ethik und Christentum. Stuttgart, 1906.
Gesammelte Abhandlungen zur Sozialpädagogik. Stuttgart, 1907; 2d ed., 1922.
Pestalozzi. Sein Leben und seine Ideen. Leipzig, 1909.
Philosophie und Pädagogik. Marburg, 1909.
Die logischen Grundlagen der exakten Wissenschaften. Leipzig and Berlin, 1910.
Philosophie, ihr Problem und ihre Probleme. Göttingen, 1911.
"Religion? Ein Zwiegesprach." *Weltanschauung,* 1911, 305–325.
Allgemeine Psychologie nach kritischer Methode, Vol. I. Tübingen, 1912.
"Kant und die Marburg Schule." *Kant-Studien,* Vol. 17 (1912), 193–221.
Sozialidealismus. Berlin, 1920.
Individuum und Gemeinschaft. Jena, 1921.
"Selbstdarstellung," in Raymund Schmidt, ed., *Die Philosophie der Gegenwart in Selbstdarstellung,* Vol. I. Leipzig, 1921. With bibliography of his works.
Vorlesungen über praktische Philosophie. Erlangen, 1925.
Philosophische Systematik. Hamburg, 1958.

Works on Natorp

Bellersen, Heinrich, *Die Sozialpädagogik Paul Natorps.* Paderborn, 1928.
Buchenau, A., *Natorps Monismus der Erfahrung und das Problem der Psychologie.* Langensalza, 1913.

Cassirer, Ernst, "Paul Natorp." *Kant-Studien*, Vol. 30 (1925), 273–298.

Festschrift für Paul Natorp zum 70. Geburtstage von Schülern und Freunden gewidmet. Berlin, 1924.

Gadamer, H. G., "Die philosophische Bedeutung Paul Natorps," Preface to Natorp's *Philosophische Systematik.* Hamburg, 1958.

Gschwind, Hermann, *Die philosophische Grundlagen von Natorps Sozialpädagogik.* Leipzig, 1920.

Kinkel, Walter, "Paul Natorp und der kritische Idealismus." *Kant-Studien*, Vol. 28 (1923), 398–418.

Klein, J., *Die Grundlegung der Ethik in der Philosophie Paul Natorps.* Dissertation. Bonn, 1942.

Knittermeyer, Heinrich, "Zur Entstehungsgeschichte der *Philosophische Systematik,*" Preface to Natorp's *Philosophische Systematik.* Hamburg, 1958.

Krüger, P., "Zur Erinnerung an Paul Natorp." *Kant-Studien*, Vol. 45 (1953/1954), 314–317.

Levy, Heinrich, "Paul Natorps praktische Philosophie." *Kant-Studien*, Vol. 31 (1926), 311–329.

Lugarini, L., "Coscienza e autocoscienza nella filosofia di Paul Natorp." *Rivista critica di storia della filosofia,* 1950, 40–49.

Prager, H., "Paul Natorp und das Problem der Religionsphilosophie." *Logos*, Vol. 13 (1924), 186–190.

Mariano Campo

Translated by *Robert M. Connolly*

NATURALISM, in recent usage, is a species of philosophical monism according to which whatever exists or happens is *natural* in the sense of being susceptible to explanation through methods which, although paradigmatically exemplified in the natural sciences, are continuous from domain to domain of objects and events. Hence, naturalism is polemically defined as repudiating the view that there exists or could exist any entities or events which lie, in principle, beyond the scope of scientific explanation. In all other respects naturalism is ontologically neutral in that it does not prescribe what specific kinds of entities there must be in the universe or how many distinct kinds of events we must suppose to take place. Accordingly, naturalism is merely compatible with the various forms of materialism it has been confused with; materialism is logically distinct from naturalism and requires independent support unless (as is not the case) materialism is the sole ontology compatible with the ubiquitous employment of scientific method. There is thus room within the naturalistic movement for any variety of otherwise rival ontologies, which explains the philosophical heterogeneity of the group of philosophers who identify themselves as naturalists: it is a methodological rather than an ontological monism to which they indifferently subscribe, a monism leaving them free to be dualists, idealists, materialists, atheists, or nonatheists, as the case may be.

The tenets of naturalism. Despite the official toleration of ontological diversity, the typical naturalist is likely to endorse, with whatever individual refinements he might require, most and perhaps all of the following tenets:

(1) The entire knowable universe is composed of natural objects—that is, objects which come into and pass out of existence in consequence of the operation of "natural causes." A rock, a cloud, a frog, a human being, are all instances of natural objects, however they may otherwise differ and however important these differences may be. Every natural object exists within the spatiotemporal and the causal orders. The universe *may* in addition contain one or another sort of *nonnatural* object, but we have no reason for allowing the existence of nonnatural objects unless they have impact on the observable behavior of natural objects, for natural objects are the only objects about which we know directly, and it would be only with reference to their perturbations that we might secure indirect knowledge of nonnatural objects, should there be any.

(2) A natural cause is a natural object or an episode in the history of a natural object which brings about a change in some other natural object. Each natural object owes its existence, continuance, and end to the constant operation on it of natural causes, and it is solely with reference to natural causes that we explain changes in the behavior of natural objects. This may require reference to objects we cannot directly experience, but these will nevertheless still be *natural* objects, and we need never go outside the system of natural objects for explanations of what takes place within it. Reference to nonnatural objects is never explanatory.

(3) A natural process is any change in a natural object or system of natural objects which is due to a natural cause or system of natural causes. There are no nonnatural processes.

(4) The natural order—or nature—is not simply a collection of all the natural objects but a system of all natural processes. Nature is in principle intelligible in all its parts, but it cannot be explained as a whole. For this would presumably require reference to a natural cause, and outside nature as a whole there are no natural causes to be found. Or else it would require reference to a nonnatural object, but such reference is never explanatory. Nature is self-contained as a system with reference to the furnishing of natural explanations, which means not that there will ever necessarily be natural explanations of everything but only that there are no intrinsic limits placed on which natural processes can be naturally explained. Thus, they are *all* in principle naturally explainable.

(5) Natural method is simply (*a*) explaining natural processes through identification of the natural causes responsible for them and (*b*) testing any given explanation with regard to consequences that must hold if it is true. Truth is merely a matter of consequences, and nature is in each of its parts susceptible to the natural method. The natural method is the way in which one set of natural objects—men—operate upon the rest of nature.

(6) Nature could not be both intelligible everywhere and random everywhere: no natural process could be intelligible if in each instance it were produced by dissimilar natural causes or if each natural process were dissimilar to every other. The thesis that nature is intelligible is equivalent to the claim that natural processes are *regular*. The natural method seeks, accordingly, to establish natural laws. Human beings, as natural objects, are no less subject to natural laws than are other parts of nature, and the natural processes that make up the mental and social life of human beings are equally with the rest of nature subject to the application of the natural method, within the scope of the natural laws it seeks to establish.

(7) Whatever may be their official persuasions, all philosophers must function in the natural order as other humans do and, in order to do this successfully, must sponta-

neously apply the natural method. Farmers and mechanics do not suppose that events have no explanation. Neither do policemen or politicians. Whether in human or in nonhuman contexts, men everywhere naturally seek natural explanations. Recourse is taken to nonnatural explanation only in moments of despair. But a nonnatural explanation merely underscores the fact that something cannot be explained or made intelligible at the moment —it does not provide an alternative kind of explanation or intelligibility. All nonnatural explanations, the result of using nonnatural methods, are in principle replaceable with natural explanations. Nonnaturalists contradict in their practice what they profess in their theories. Naturalists alone hold theories consonant with their practice.

(8) Reason is the consistent application of natural method, and natural science is the purest exemplar of reason. Science reflects while it refines upon the very methods primitively exemplified in common life and practice. Science is thus a way of acting rather than a set of doctrines, and science is, as such, not committed to any specific scheme of intelligibility. Its theories are held to the degree that they serve to explain natural processes, but it is consonant with the commitment to natural method that any theory is perpetually subject to revision or rejection in view of further test. Any scheme of intelligibility may be abandoned without thereby abandoning the principle that nature is intelligible throughout. Science is naturally self-corrective if we think of it as it is, as a method to which its own doctrines are unremittingly subjected.

(9) Knowledge of the world at a given time is what science tells us at that time about the world. For the doctrines of science have presumably been achieved through the most rigorous and consecutive application of the natural method. Should there be a conflict between common sense and science, it must be decided in favor of science, inasmuch as it employs, but more rigorously, the same method that common sense does and cannot, therefore, be repudiated without repudiating common sense itself. Conflicts within science are settled through deriving testable consequences from rival theories until a basis for rational differentiation appears. But because any theory remains infinitely testable, no ultimate certitude attaches to what science holds at any given time. Hence, there is nothing ultimate or eternal about knowledge, and, by naturalistic criteria, "*p* may be false" is compatible with "We know that *p*," since knowledge is what science says, and what science says may always be rejected in the light of further applications of natural method.

(10) Whatever further or other distinctions there may be between the (so-called) formal and the empirical sciences, they are alike in that the truths of the former no more entail a Platonistic ontology than the latter, nor are we, in using algorithms, committed to the existence of numerical entities as nonnatural objects. If the formal sciences are *about* anything, it will at least not be a realm of timeless numerical essences, and at any rate logic and mathematics are properly appreciated in terms not of subject matter but of function, as instruments for coping with this world rather than as descriptions of another one. A theory of logic is a theory of inquiry, which is reason in action.

(11) To say that outside science there is no knowledge to be had is *not* to say that it is only through science that men should relate to nature, for there are many ways of experiencing the world. Nevertheless, the only mode of experience which is *cognitive* is scientific, and no cognitive claims are to be accepted if they are based on other experiential modes. It is not the aim of naturalism to impoverish experience.

(12) Nor is it the aim of naturalism to insist that all natural objects are really reducible to one favored *sort* of natural object or that only the objects or the descriptions of objects recognized by the natural sciences are *real*. All natural objects are equally real, and the descriptive vocabulary of the sciences does not exhaust the reality of nature.

(13) The universe at large has no moral character save to the extent that it contains human beings among its objects and thus contains entities that have and pursue values. Men are integral though distinctive components of nature and, though part of the natural order, are not reducible in any way to other parts, save in the sense that along with the rest of nature, human beings are explainable through the methods of the natural sciences. Human institutions and practices, the modes of experience of men, the goals and values of individuals and groups, are all natural, and no less so than the wheeling of galaxies and the evolution of species. The natural method alone, not some special moral intuition, provides the key to dissolving moral disputes, and moral theories may be treated no differently from scientific theories with respect to determination of their strength through testable consequences. Naturalism, although otherwise morally neutral, *is* committed to institutions that permit the operation of natural method in moral and political decision in which, qua naturalist, the naturalist otherwise takes no sides.

(14) Naturalistic philosophy, unlike other philosophies, claims no special subject matter and uses no special tools. Its method is the natural method, and its problems are the problems of men. Positively, then, naturalists will be engaged in helpful clarifications of problems which arise in the course of human life rather than with anything otherwise identifiable as a philosophical problem. Negatively, the naturalist is a polemicist, defending naturalism and the natural method against antinaturalism of all varieties and types.

Criticism. These tenets, however crudely stated, constitute perhaps the main components of the naturalistic program. Each is obviously subject to question and contest. Naturalists have typically used one or another of the theses to support one under attack, and in the polemical literature truly philosophical arguments in support of the program are rare. Naturalists have tended to be philosophers *of* this or that discipline—*of* science, *of* history, *of* law, etc.—in consonance with their view of what philosophy ought to be, and in these spheres of specialized competence they have made their major contributions, which have been considerable. There nevertheless exists a vacuum between their special inquiries, on the one hand, and their polemics, on the other, where philosophy as such, as an independent inquiry, is in large degree neglected. Thus, Arthur Murphy, an otherwise sympathetic critic, has written that while there is little question of what is the naturalistic *position*, it remains the case that "the Naturalists, who have so much that is good to offer, still lack and need a philosophy." This implies that it is philosophical justification which naturalists have failed to furnish for their views. But of course, and consonantly with these views, naturalists have characteristically understressed matters of presupposition and the like. For they have argued that no philosophy can get on without presuppositions of one sort or another, that its own presuppositions are minimal, and that if any of its presuppositions *should* prove dubious, naturalism is at all events committed to an unrelenting self-criticism and is on the alert for unlikely consequences. But this is precisely to insist that naturalistic criteria be used in the adjudication of philosophical issues and in the determination of philosophical doctrine—and hence to insist that naturalism settle in its own way the issues between naturalism and its rivals. This has led to charges of circularity or disingenuousness. But such criticisms leave the naturalist undismayed, since he insists that he uses no method in philosophy that his critics do not employ in life. But critics have proposed that issues in philosophy are different from issues in life or even in science, for that matter, and the continuity of method is exactly what is at issue. And here matters more or less stand, the chief divisions being not so much between naturalists and antinaturalists—the latter being chiefly those who have proposed limits to science on ontological grounds and in combat with whom the naturalist has always been most comfortable—but between competing views of what *philosophy* is. And here the critics of naturalism are not necessarily antinaturalistic in the comfortable sense of being unhappy with science, in proposing that there are nonnatural entities, etc., but rather in the sense of supposing philosophy has its own problems and techniques, to the neglect of which naturalism owes its own neglect at the hands of contemporary nonnaturalist philosophers.

Naturalism flourished in American universities and in the pages of American philosophical journals in the late 1930s and through the 1940s. In the following decade, chiefly in consequence of movements originating in England and on the Continent, the vacuum which the polarization of naturalist philosophizing created was increasingly filled with the sorts of philosophical inquiries that the naturalist typically viewed with distaste and suspicion as being remote from the issues of the specialized disciplines and the problems of men. Despite some notable efforts to bring naturalism forward in recent times as a respectable metaphysics and an adequate system of philosophy, the typical professional philosopher appears no longer to find the form in which these issues are presented especially challenging. The dominant contests in contemporary philosophy have been cast in other terms and are fought on seemingly different fields. On the other hand, to a great extent many of the fashionable problems are merely disguises for questions which could as easily, and perhaps even more directly, be represented as arising in connection with the claim of the continuity of scientific method. (See ETHICAL NATURALISM.)

Bibliography

Some historians of naturalism trace the ancestry of the movement back to Aristotle and Spinoza. Still others regard it as but the coming to self-consciousness of the presuppositions inherent in the American temper. In any case, George Santayana's *The Life of Reason* appears to have exercised the dominating influence on the first generation of American naturalists, especially F. J. E. Woodbridge and Morris R. Cohen. Their writings, together with those of John Dewey, must constitute the primary obvious sources of the doctrine. For contributions by naturalists on various topics, see Yervant Krikorian, ed., *Naturalism and the Human Spirit* (New York, 1944). Interesting issues are raised in the following papers: John Dewey, Ernest Nagel, and Sidney Hook, "Are Naturalists Materialists?," in *Journal of Philosophy*, Vol. 42 (1945), 515–530; A. Edel, "Is Naturalism Arbitrary?," *ibid.*, Vol. 43 (1946), 141–152; R. W. Sellars, "Does Naturalism Need an Ontology?," *ibid.*, Vol. 41 (1944), 686–694; W. D. Oliver, "Can Naturalism Be Materialistic?," *ibid.*, Vol. 46 (1949), 608–615.

The best statements of naturalistic philosophy are in Ernest Nagel's presidential address to the American Philosophical Association, Eastern Division, "Naturalism Reconsidered" (1954), frequently reprinted, and his "Towards a Naturalistic Conception of Logic," in Horace Kallen and Sidney Hook, eds., *American Philosophy Today and Tomorrow* (New York, 1935), pp. 377–391; and Sidney Hook, "Naturalism and First Principles" and "Nature and the Human Spirit," in his *The Quest for Being* (New York, 1961), pp. 172–208.

For some important philosophical criticisms of naturalism, see Arthur Murphy's review of *Naturalism and the Human Spirit*, in *Journal of Philosophy*, Vol. 42 (1945), 400–417; Henry Aiken, "Notes on the Categories of Naturalism," *ibid.*, Vol. 43 (1946), 517–526; and O. K. Bouwsma, "Naturalism," *ibid.*, Vol. 45 (1948), 12–22.

ARTHUR C. DANTO

NATURALISM IN ETHICS. See ETHICAL NATURALISM; ETHICAL OBJECTIVISM; ETHICS, PROBLEMS OF.

NATURALISTIC RECONSTRUCTIONS OF RELIGION. See RELIGION, NATURALISTIC RECONSTRUCTIONS OF.

NATURAL LAW. Phrases like *ius naturale, diritto naturale, droit naturel, Naturrecht*, and "natural law" have been used over the centuries to designate a remarkably persistent doctrine concerning the moral basis of law. However, it would be wrong to assume either that whenever these phrases are used, they designate this doctrine or that the doctrine itself has endured without variants or modifications. Accordingly, a minimal characterization of the doctrine of natural law would seem called for.

CHARACTERISTICS OF NATURAL-LAW DOCTRINE

There is a view, attributed with differing degrees of reliability to certain Sophists and to Hobbes, that in any society the criterion of justice is provided by what the laws decree and that to ask of these laws whether they are just or unjust is an absurdity. "No Law can be Unjust," Hobbes asserted (*Leviathan*, Ch. 30). It is obviously a necessary condition of any natural-law doctrine that this view should be rejected. But does this suffice, or are there certain further propositions that must be entertained, over and above the claim that enacted or "positive" law is a suitable object of moral evaluation, before we have a doctrine that can reasonably be called one of natural law? Historically, at any rate, it would seem that there are.

Natural law as a legal code. First, it seems an intrinsic part of the doctrine (as the word "law" in its title is there to suggest) that the criterion by reference to which positive laws are to be judged should itself possess some of the characteristics of a legal code. In particular, it should exhibit some complexity or be capable of formulation as a comparatively extended set of rules or precepts, against which existing codes can then be matched item by item. Thus, a doctrine that the content of justice could not be expressed in anything more specific than one or two general adages would scarcely be one of natural law. Again, the criterion of justice must, like a system of law, be internally coherent; the rules that constitute it must exhibit consistency. To a natural-law theorist it would be unacceptable, for instance, that the content of justice should be expressed in a series of maxims each of which had some a priori obligatoriness but which might issue in conflicting judgments as to the moral validity of a given law.

The interpretation of "nature." Second, the ideal or ethical law, which is contrasted with positive law and provides the norm in terms of which it is evaluated, is regarded by natural-law theorists (and this is what the word "natural" is there to indicate) as grounded in something wider or more general or more enduring than the mere practical needs of men, whether these be expressed in custom or in convention and agreement. It is grounded in "nature," and the various interpretations that have been placed on this word have generated the principal transformations through which natural-law theory has passed. And here it is pertinent to observe that the two aspects of the theory—the logical aspect, "What is justice?," and the epistemological aspect, "How do we discover what justice demands?"—move close together.

Physical laws and laws of conduct. The simplest and oldest account of the "naturalness" of justice is to be found in a conception of the universe which originated with the Stoics Zeno and Chrysippus but is also to be found in thinkers as late as Montesquieu and Blackstone. The whole universe, on this view, is governed by laws which exhibit rationality. Inanimate things and brutes invariably obey these laws, the first out of necessity, the second out of instinct. Man, however, has the capacity of choice and is therefore able at will either to obey or to disobey the laws of nature. Nevertheless, owing to the character of these laws, it is only insofar as he obeys them that he acts in accord with his reason. "Follow nature" is therefore, on this view, the principle both of nonhuman behavior and of human morality; and in this last category justice is included. The laws which apply to man and which he can and should obey are not identical in content with those which apply to, for example, planets or bees and which they cannot but obey. Nevertheless, since the universe is a rational whole, governed by a unitary principle of reason, the analogies between the laws of nonhuman behavior and those of human morality are very strong and readily penetrated by the rational faculty with which man has been endowed.

Critics of this simple variant of natural-law doctrine (for example, John Stuart Mill, T. H. Huxley, and Vilfredo Pareto) have usually relied on pointing out an alleged confusion, which they claim is inherent in it, between two senses of "law"—law as the formulation of regularities in nature and law as the norms or rules to which voluntary behavior ought to conform. To infer the laws that men ideally ought to obey from the laws that animals visibly do

obey or to think that the former can be based on the latter is (the argument runs) to fall victim to a simple ambiguity.

Although natural-law doctrine in the form under consideration has undoubtedly gained adherents from a confusion between prescriptive and descriptive laws, it can avoid that confusion if certain other propositions are accepted. For instance, it might be held that the universe is the work of a supreme ruler, whose will we ought always to obey insofar as we can discern it. His will, however, is not transparent, but since the universe is his creation, it would be only reasonable (some would say mandatory) to assume that the phenomena he has placed in it evince his will in their behavior. Accordingly, if we want guidance about what we should do, we cannot do better than to look to what they do. Here the distinction between the two kinds of law is fully respected, and the inference from the one to the other is warranted only by the metaphysical premise that both kinds are, and are known to be, expressions of a divine or supernatural will. Thus, coherence is restored to the doctrine, although only at the price of further assumptions and greater complexity.

There is, however, another difficulty in the doctrine as stated, and the various other formulations the doctrine has received might be regarded as so many attempts to circumvent this difficulty. The difficulty concerns how we are to select those aspects of natural behavior or those laws of nature (in the descriptive sense) which can legitimately serve as guides to moral behavior. For it is idle to pretend that we can extract a uniform message from nature. Are we, for instance, to model ourselves upon the peaceful habits of sheep or upon the internecine conflicts of ants? Is the egalitarianism of the beaver or the hierarchical life of the bee the proper exemplar for human society? Should we imitate the widespread polygamy of the animal kingdom, or is there some higher regularity of which this is no more than a misleading instance? In the light of these and similar questions, it becomes impossible to regard the maxim "Follow nature" as a substantive guide to conduct. Moreover, although these discrepancies in nature considerably reduce the value of natural-law doctrine from an epistemological point of view, the damage they do to it as a logical theory would seem fatal, for the nature in terms of which the norms of justice are defined turns out to be internally inconsistent.

One's nature and one's end. Accordingly, for natural-law doctrine to be viable, we need a criterion for distinguishing within nature (where this is equated with the whole range of natural phenomena) those aspects to which we can, and those aspects to which we cannot, attach normative significance. Even in Stoic thought we find some reference to an ideal nature, but the most sustained effort in the history of Western thought to make a discrimination of this kind derives ultimately from the teaching of Aristotle. It involves a further appeal to or invocation of nature, in a more limited and specific sense—the sense, that is, in which every kind of thing or species has its own nature or end and its characteristic excellence is realized in performing whatever conduces to this end. It was the achievement of St. Thomas Aquinas that he managed, within a certain framework of thought, to solve what might be called the "selectivity" problem of natural-law theory by grafting on to the Stoic principle of "Follow nature" the Aristotelian concept of nature as a teleological system. The general principles of the law of nature are, St. Thomas argued, known equally to all through their use of reason, though with the derivative principles, which are exercises in practical not speculative reason, the same consensus cannot be expected.

If the Stoic version of natural-law doctrine is open to criticism on grounds of its implicit metaphysical assumptions, this would seem to be even truer of the Thomist version. That phenomena are divided into natural kinds, that each natural kind is distinguished by the possession of an essence, that the essence stipulates an end, that virtue and goodness are necessarily linked with the fulfillment of these ends—these are some of the assumptions behind St. Thomas' *lex naturae*. And none of them are, in an evident way, part of common-sense belief. Nevertheless, the remarkable persistence of a teleological mode of thinking can be accounted for only by the fact that it does in many respects accord with the ways in which we think and speak about the world. We talk of the natural functions or the proper development of man, of the needs that it is right to satisfy, or of how certain privations stunt or damage the personality.

Nature and reason. It was characteristic of much post-Reformation thought to abandon a teleological metaphysic, and in the juristic writings of Hugo Grotius, Samuel von Pufendorf, and Jean-Jacques Burlamaqui natural-law theory was correspondingly reformulated. The nature or essence of man was now identified *tout court* with the possession of reason, and natural law was held to be whatever is found acceptable by *recta ratio* or *sana ratio*. At this stage the logical and epistemological aspects of the theory come totally together—natural law was what reason discovers, and natural law was discovered by reason. But difficulties remained (as they did in the general philosophy of the age) over how to interpret "reason," which was sometimes equated with intuition, sometimes with the cool observation of nature, sometimes with the decisions of the law of noncontradiction. In this respect it is instructive to compare the different arguments employed by Grotius and Pufendorf in their treatment of, for example, the obligations that attend speech or the rights of testamentary capacity.

The state of nature. With the attenuation of the metaphysic that accompanied natural-law theory, the theory at the same time annexed to itself another sense of "nature." For natural law became increasingly associated with the state of nature, which was talked of, possibly even thought of, as a prehistoric or presocietal phase of human development. Theorists may differ on whether natural law was observed in the state of nature or merely recognized and respected in the heart, but we find an association between the two firmly asserted by Hobbes and Locke.

Law common to many legal codes. There remains, however, one further sense in which the norms of justice have been held to be grounded in nature, distinguished from the preceding by its comparative freedom from metaphysical overtones: This sense is that in which nature is identified with the common element in a large variety of codes and conventions. Such would seem to have been the view of the earlier generation of Roman jurists whose pronouncements on the nature of law were collected in the *Digest* at the order of Emperor Justinian (A.D. 533).

The Roman legal system contained a remarkable body of law, the *ius gentium,* which was employed in those cases in which either one of the litigants was not a Roman citizen or both were resident aliens of different nationalities. Although Roman in character, the *ius gentium* lacked the formality and technicality of the Roman *ius civile* and shared some features with the systems of rules and laws belonging to the peoples whom the Roman Empire had absorbed. It was apparently the *ius gentium* that Gaius (c. A.D. 160) took for his model when he contrasted the laws that each people had given itself (*ius civile*) with a law of nations—a law practiced by all mankind and dictated to all men by natural reason. As one would expect, such a highly empirical account of natural law did not remain like this for long, and it drew to itself a philosophical theory. In Ulpian, a century later, the *ius naturale* is presented separately from the *ius gentium* so as to form, with the *ius civile,* a tripartite division of law, and was clothed in the grandiose terminology of Stoicism.

The status of positive laws. A third characteristic of natural-law theory is the status that it imputes to particular laws that fail to comply with the norms of justice. Such laws, although they satisfy all the acknowledged criteria of legal validity, are held not to be, properly speaking, laws at all. True, certain natural-law theorists have qualified this judgment. For instance, the later Scholastics Francisco Suárez and Cardinal Bellarmine maintained that whereas positive laws that run counter to prohibitive natural law are null and void, those which fall short of affirmative natural law are still obligatory although not binding in conscience. However, by and large it would seem to be intrinsic to the theory to hold that conformity to natural law is the criterion not merely of a just law but of law itself. In this respect there is a clear and perennial conflict between natural-law theory and (in, at any rate, one sense of that phrase) legal positivism where this is defined in terms of Austin's dictum "The existence of law is one thing; its merit or demerit another" (*The Province of Jurisprudence Determined,* 1832, Lecture V).

However, on one aspect of this conflict obscurity has been cast by those who write on "the relation between law and morals" (see, for example, the works of Roscoe Pound). For it may well be the case that in certain legal systems, such as that of the United States, such conformity to natural law is one of the criteria of legal validity acknowledged by the system. It is no part of legal positivism to deny that in such cases a putative law that runs counter to natural law is, in point of fact, no law at all; all that is denied is that its invalidity is directly due to its divergence from natural law. Or to put the matter the other way around, the claim of natural-law theory is not that a putative law that is discrepant with natural law but satisfies all the *other* legal criteria of validity is invalid, for that is universally accepted. The claim is that a putative law that is discrepant with natural law but satisfied *all* the legal criteria of validity is still invalid. And this is a more radical claim.

It has been asserted by some critics, notably Hans Kelsen, that natural-law theory at this point becomes inconsistent. For a certain set of norms is first introduced as valid legal rules and then declared to be invalid. Now, certainly this criticism points to a genuine difficulty that does confront natural law here—namely, how the so-called laws whose invalidity it asserts are initially identified. Obviously, they cannot be identified as laws, nor, it seems, can they be identified as putative laws, for the criteria in terms of which they are putatively valid are themselves called in question. However, it seems possible that natural-law theory can accommodate itself to this criticism by an adjustment of terms.

On the other hand, it would be wrong to think of the conflict between natural-law theory and legal positivism as merely verbal, a dispute between a narrower definition of law that excludes unjust laws and a broader one that includes them. There are, as H. L. A. Hart (*The Concept of Law,* Ch. 9) has effectively demonstrated, substantive reasons for preferring one definition to the other. The narrower definition is likely to appeal to a society that has just emerged from an iniquitous regime and wishes neither to accept the laws of that regime nor to indulge in retrospective legislation. It avoids the dilemma by declaring the laws void—hence, the popularity of natural-law theory in post-Hitler Germany. But the narrower definition also has its dangers. It suggests that issues of justice are as readily decidable as those of legality. It totally denies the painful choices that sometimes have to be made, by magistrates as well as ordinary citizens, between an evil law and no law at all. And it has one important consequence which is the opposite of that intended—it makes any law once accepted as valid free of all further assessment.

CRITICISMS OF THE THEORY

Besides the internal difficulties that beset natural-law theory, there are two important criticisms to which it has been subjected.

Relativity of laws. It has been argued that natural-law theory cannot admit that the demands of justice may be relative to time and place so that what ought to be positive law in one society ought not to be in another. Kelsen thus contrasted the static character of natural-law theory with the dynamic character of positivism. Supporters of natural-law theory, however, often reject the supposition on which this imputation is based. In this century there has been a specific attempt by Rudolf Stammler to evolve a theory of "natural law with variable content." Even St. Thomas, in a passage (*Summa Theologica* II, 2, 57) which Pius XII commended to the attention of Catholic jurists in 1955, allowed that the secondary precepts of natural law might vary with the mutations of human nature, although it is arguable that the only sense in which he conceded human nature was mutable was that it could become depraved.

However, here, as with most disputes about relativism, the issue is unclear. Presumably, no absolutist would deny that circumstances may be relevant to judgments about justice, but, equally, no relativist would deny that what is just in one set of circumstances would be so if these circumstances were faithfully reproduced. So the only issue—and this is not a theoretical issue—is precisely what effect a particular change of circumstances would have on

the morality of a specific action. Perhaps, however, it could be held that a natural-law theorist who admitted very freely that circumstances change the ethical character of actions had departed considerably from the original inspiration of the theory. The theory of "natural law with variable content" certainly seems to transgress the first requirement laid down above for a natural-law theory.

Law and morality. Second, it might be argued that a natural-law theory has a tendency to blur the distinction between the two questions "What ought men to do in society?" and "What actions ought to be enforced at law?" In other words, it blurs the issue traditionally (though confusingly) referred to as that of sin and crime. And it has this tendency because, presumably, it is never quite clear whether natural law is a criterion of just action or of just law.

Many natural-law theorists have given at least some recognition to this problem. For instance, St. Thomas argued that the law can pass judgment only on "external action," for only God is able "to judge the inner movements of the will" (*Summa Theologica* I, 2, 100). And in the writings of Christian Thomasius, and again in Kant's, the distinction between the inner character of morals and the external character of law or between imperfect and perfect duties was made a fundamental principle.

Even so, it might be argued that natural-law theory is misleading in that it takes as the starting point for a discussion of what the law ought to enforce a consideration of what men ought to do, even if it goes on to exempt from the sphere of legislation certain areas of morality as incongruent with the actual means of enforcement the law has at its disposal. To many it might seem apparent that the law has no right, let alone obligation, even of a prima-facie or attenuated kind, to enforce morality as such.

Bibliography

TEXTS

The basic texts of natural-law theory are presented here in the order in which they were written.

Cicero, *De Re Publica,* translated by C. W. Keyes, ed. Loeb Classical Library. London, 1928. Book III.

Cicero, *De Legibus,* translated by C. W. Keyes, ed. Loeb Classical Library. London, 1928. Book III.

Aquinas, *Summa Theologica,* in A. P. d'Entrèves, ed., *Selected Political Writings.* Oxford, 1948. I, 1, 90–97.

Suárez, Francisco, *De Legibus, ac Deo Legislatore,* translated by G. L. Williams et al., eds. Classics of International Law. Oxford, 1944. Book II.

Pufendorf, Samuel von, *De Jure Naturae et Gentium, Libri Octo,* translated by F. G. Moore, ed. Classics of International Law. Oxford, 1927. Book II, Chs. 1–3; Book VIII, Ch. 1.

Locke, John, *Essays on the Law of Nature,* W. von Leyden, ed. Oxford, 1954.

Stammler, Rudolf, *Die Lehre vom richtigen Recht.* Berlin, 1902. Translated by Isaac Husik as *The Theory of Justice.* New York, 1925.

Hall, Jerome, ed., *Readings in Jurisprudence.* Indianapolis, Ind., 1938. Part I, Ch. 1.

HISTORICAL WORKS

Cairns, Huntington, *Legal Philosophy From Plato to Hegel.* Baltimore and London, 1949.

Entrèves, A. P. d', *Natural Law.* London, 1951.

Gierke, Otto von, *Das deutsche Genossenschaftsrecht,* Vol. IV.

Berlin, 1913. Translated by Sir Ernest Barker as *Natural Law and the Theory of Society: 1500–1800.* Cambridge, 1934.

Haines, C. G., *The Revival of Natural Law Concepts.* Cambridge, Mass., 1930.

Pollock, Sir Frederick, "A History of the Law of Nature," in his *Essays in the Law.* London, 1922.

Salmond, J. W., "Law of Nature." *Law Quarterly Review,* Vol. II (1895), 121–143.

CRITICAL WORKS

Bryce, James, "The Law of Nature," in his *Studies in History and Jurisprudence.* Oxford, 1901. Vol. II.

Hart, H. L. A., *The Concept of Law.* Oxford, 1961. Ch. 9.

Kelsen, Hans, *Naturrechtslehre und das Rechtspositivismus.* Berlin, 1928.

Kelsen, Hans; Perelman, C.; Bobbio, N.; et al., *Le Droit naturel.* Paris, 1959.

Mill, John Stuart, "Nature," in his *Three Essays on Religion.* London, 1874.

RICHARD WOLLHEIM

NATURE, PHILOSOPHICAL IDEAS OF. In its widest sense "nature" can mean "the totality of things," all that would have to appear in an inventory of the universe. It can also refer to the laws and principles of structure by which the behavior of things may be explained. These two senses cannot be kept independent of each other at any sophisticated level of inquiry, for to state in any of the sciences what an entity is involves describing what it does, its patterns of activity or behavior, and the activity of its constituent elements, as far as they can be known and subsumed under laws.

In a particular philosophical context the sense in which nature is being used can be brought out most clearly by insisting upon the question "What is nature (or the natural) being contrasted with in this context?" In one group of cases the natural is contrasted with the artificial or conventional. This contrast requires some conception of how the object or organism would behave by reason of its immanent causality alone, the causal factors that are peculiar to that type of thing and make it whatever it is—a stone, a fish, or a man. The artificial and conventional are seen as interferences, modifying by an alien causality the characteristic patterns of behavior. In the sphere of human nature this distinction is at the center of an ancient and continuing controversy, for it is by no means easy—if, indeed, possible—to delineate a human nature free of interferences, left to itself. Organism and environment, individual and cultural climate, are in ceaseless interplay. An activity (like moral evaluation or social organization) that seems to some theorists on the "convention side" of the boundary may be represented by others, with no less reason, as a development of natural potentialities. The controversy is further complicated by the intrusion of evaluative nuances in the distinction itself, so that the natural, for instance, may come to be more highly esteemed than the artificial and conventional, as the spontaneous or the basic is contrasted with the labored and derivative. The preference may be reversed, however; the natural can be taken as the mere raw material, the unfinished and preparatory, requiring artifice to complete and crown it.

In some contexts man is contrasted with nature; in others he is taken as part of nature. The difference is not trivially linguistic. To set man against nature is to emphasize his distinctiveness—his rationality, creativity, and freedom. But it may also support an unwarranted and distorting anthropocentricity. To count man as part and parcel of nature emphasizes the continuity of the human, animal, organic, and inorganic worlds and suggests that human behavior may be amenable to the same kinds of investigation that are effective in studying other domains of nature. Similarities as well as differences can be exaggerated, however, and overfacile generalizations can be made from the behavior, say, of rats to human behavior. Human distinctiveness and complexity may be overlooked in a tempting reductive analysis like that of behaviorism.

In still other contexts the natural world, man included, is contrasted with the supernatural. In part at least, the idea of the supernatural has tended to be constructed from allegedly miraculous events, events which, it is claimed, the power and laws of nature could not bring about. (There can be also an a priori element in the grounding of belief in the supernatural. Belief in a transcendent creator-God, who may be himself the subject of a priori proofs, implies the belief that nature's laws and processes can be overruled.)

It is anything but easy, however, to elaborate coherently the nature–supernature distinction. Crucial to it is the claim that we can distinguish what lies within the capacities of nature from what lies beyond them. Our knowledge of nature's powers and laws is itself derived from our experience and observation of events. What we judge to be possible depends upon what we have reason to believe actually occurs or has occurred. When we assemble the experiences out of which we are to construct these judgments about the possible, what shall we do with the happenings that, eventually, we wish to label miraculous? To exclude them would be to imply that we *already* know what nature's powers are, that there are criteria prior to experience by which we interpret our observations. But to include them makes it impossible for us to treat them later as miraculous exceptions to natural laws.

Certainly, it is not legitimate to move from saying, "This event is inexplicable in terms of our scientific knowledge of nature," to saying, "This event must be a supernatural intervention." The scientist is by no means committed to claiming that he has at any particular moment the concepts and theories adequate for every explanatory task. He is constantly revising and adding to these. We are not, therefore, forced to conclude that an event has a supernatural source on the grounds that it is inexplicable or anomalous in terms of present-day science. Indeed, it is only with the help of an independently established set of beliefs about God that one could plausibly interpret an event as supernatural. (See P. H. Nowell-Smith, "Miracles," in A. G. N. Flew and A. MacIntyre, eds., *New Essays in Philosophical Theology,* New York, 1955; and A. G. N. Flew, *Hume's Philosophy of Belief,* London, 1961.)

Although it has been implied above that God must be conceived in contradistinction to nature, this is true only if God is transcendent, not immanent (or, if immanent, then transcendent as well). In a pantheistic view if nature may be distinguished from God, it is only as different views or aspects of one and the same reality.

Historical transformations. The history of philosophical ideas of nature almost coincides with the history of philosophy itself. Where a philosophy is at all systematic, even if it is avowedly antimetaphysical, it cannot avoid stating or implying some interpretation of nature. This makes it impossible to compress the history of these interpretations into one article. The comments which follow are thus no more than indications that the philosophers named made significant contributions to the development of the idea.

When the Ionian pre-Socratic philosophers asked, "What is nature?" they assumed that the question demanded an answer in terms of a primitive substance or substances out of which the world is constructed. One of the more reasonable answers was that of Anaximander, who claimed that the ultimate world stuff must be indeterminate and indefinite (apeiron) and could not be identified with familiar stuffs like water, air, and so on. But although plausible, Anaximander's answer was also unhelpful precisely because the apeiron lacked all determinateness and explanatory power. Far more fruitful was the Pythagorean concern not primarily with the question "What is nature made from?" but with "What is its structure?" where "structure" means geometrical form. We need to know only that the constituents of the world are able to receive mathematically describable form, and the way is opened for investigating how natural objects are related, in detail, to their underlying geometrical structure.

To Plato the possibility of knowledge of nature (or of the natures of things) rests on the intelligibility of the Forms that things imitate (or in which they participate). The creation story in the *Timaeus* (which came to have enormous influence) represents God and the Forms as distinct from each other, the spatiotemporal world—mutable nature—being created after the model of the eternally unchanging Forms. It is a world necessarily deficient in important respects; the very existence of time makes it unstable and incomplete. On the other hand, it is the product of a *divine* creativity. God in his goodness does not withhold being from anything that might exist, and thus nature displays his fecundity. Here is the initial statement of the vision of nature as a great chain, or ladder, of being.

Aristotle's Unmoved Mover stands to nature as its final or teleological cause, inspiring nature to imitate the divine activity as far as its various constituents are able. Particular things, therefore, are seen as striving to realize their appropriate forms, and in so doing, they realize their own natures. Underlying this view of nature is a clear analogy with biological growth.

To Christian thinkers the primary distinction has, of course, been between the underivative creativity of God and the derivativeness and dependence of nature. Augustine, for instance, contrasts the divine "first cause that causes all and is not caused itself" with "the other causes" (the world of nature) that "both cause and are caused" (created spirits) or are primarily passive effects, corporeal causes (*City of God* V, 9). This does not preclude a wider use in which mutable spatiotemporal nature is contrasted with divine nature, "the Nature which is immutable is called Creator" (*Epistolae*, 18, Sec. 2). In Thomas Aquinas, too, God can be called *natura naturans* and the contrast made with *natura naturata*, the creating contrasted with the created nature (*Summa Theologica* IIa-IIae, 85, 6).

It was the Pythagorean–Platonic strand in philosophy of nature that furthered and came to dominate the rise of modern science. In Kepler, for example, nature appears as

the realm of the quantitative, a realm amenable to mathematical study and, indeed, to more precise study than ancient philosophy ever demonstrated. Such a view of nature could coexist with a religious interpretation of things, for the mathematical structure could be taken as supplied and sustained by the mind of God.

Although in one way the growth of a mathematical science promised most impressively to unify nature by bringing widely diversified phenomena under laws, in another way it produced new problems about the relation of man to his world, problems that led to various dualisms—bifurcations of nature—such as Descartes's. Those aspects of our experience that were not amenable to exact measurement were no longer to be identified with objectively real, accurately cognized features of the world. The measurable qualities were primary, the rest secondary, qualities—colors, sounds, tastes, and the like. Although materialist metaphysics boldly attempted (and still attempts) to reunite nature and man by describing the full range of his perceptual, moral, and imaginative life in terms of matter and motion, in a writer like Hobbes, for example, such explanations were only promissory notes. A great deal of development in physiology had to occur before the details of the mechanisms involved could be conjectured with any real plausibility.

Descartes gave the world of mind distinct ontological status alongside corporeal nature. Although this dualism saved mind from loss of reality or reduction to the nonmental, it introduced the problem, unsolvable in Cartesian terms, of how this bifurcated nature can yet be one, how the processes of mind and of matter can impinge on each other. The philosophies of nature in Spinoza and Leibniz both try strenuously to deal with this problem. Spinoza affirms a monistic and pantheistic position (*Deus sive natura*), but the dualism breaks out again in the inexplicable relation between extension and thought—a dualism not of substances but of attributes. In Leibniz' pluralist world the relation between material and mental aspects of monads is no more intelligible.

Berkeley's account of nature involves a radical criticism and rejection of the notion of material substance. Our experience could, he argued, be explained simply in terms of minds and their ideas, including, crucially, the divine mind, in which the totality of sensible things exists.

In the philosophy of Kant the burden of creativity further shifts to the human percipient. If we ask Kant why nature presents to us the persistent basic structure that it does present (such as the ubiquity of cause-effect relations and the spatiotemporal nature of all experience), his answer is that we are here dealing with the inescapable conditions for any experience of nature at all because "the understanding is itself the source of the laws of nature" (*Critique of Pure Reason*, A 127). The natural world, in the sense of the totality of things, is not in Kant's view a given whole, not an object of knowledge; for instance, whether we try to show that the world is finite or infinite, our thought runs into an impasse.

In Hegel the dominant language is of development, nisus, toward the realization of Absolute Spirit, the end for which nature exists. Necessary transitions, logical rather than temporal, are made from level to level, from nature as inert matter with its externality to life, consciousness, the inwardness of spirit. Subsequent philosophies of nature, however, like those of Bergson, Alexander, and Whitehead, were avowedly evolutionary, understandably so in an age that saw rapid development of the biological sciences, particularly biological evolutionary theory, and that had a new historical consciousness of human existence. Samuel Alexander saw the evolutionary process as the continuing "emergence" of the qualitatively new: God was to be conceived not as the initial creator or sustainer of nature but as the extrapolation of the evolutionary process to an ideal limit.

Theories involving a life force or other speculative, teleological accounts of nature have been strenuously opposed by various forms of materialism and antimetaphysical positivism.

Use of analogies. Successive conceptions of nature (like conceptions of the state) can be seen as a procession of images or controlling analogies. Dominant in Greek cosmology, for instance, was the image of nature as suffused with life and intelligence, like a living and growing organism. At the opposite pole, as in some seventeenth- and eighteenth-century cosmologies, nature is pure machine, directed from without by the divine intelligence. Or, again, nature is neither permeated by mind nor is it a mechanism in the hand of its Mechanic; it is a self-transforming system, essentially temporal, whose development is best understood through the analogies of biological evolution or human history. To make explicit the guiding analogy is an important step in appraising an account of nature. For example, it is a standing temptation for a philosopher who is working out such an account to overextend an explanatory principle that is proving dramatically fruitful in some limited area of investigation to make it seem to cover nature as the totality of things and processes.

Nature as norm. Corresponding to different philosophies of nature are markedly different answers to questions about the relation of nature to value: Can values be in any way derived from descriptions of nature? does nature set any norms for man? can appeals to nature and the natural properly settle moral or aesthetic perplexities? Various answers to these questions have been suggested in naturalistic ethical theories and in discussion of the naturalistic fallacy.

If, on the one hand, nature is seen as irreducibly complex, the theater not of a simple cosmic process but of countless and diverse processes, and if these processes have produced mind but are not themselves guided by intelligence, then there will be little plausibility in arguing directly from "natural" to "good" or "obligatory."

On the other hand, where nature is taken as created by a wholly good, wise, and omnipotent deity, to be natural is prima facie, to be *worthy* of being created by such a deity. But the existence of evil, however accounted for, makes the inference, even in this context, unreliable. The natural man may now be contrasted with the regenerate man, and "natural" thus come to have a depreciatory sense. Alternatively, the sinful can be held as unnatural—that is, as perverting the divinely appointed course of nature. The question "What *is* natural?" cannot now, however, be answered from a simple inspection of what actually happens in the world.

Historical examples. The demand that we should follow nature occurs in a wide variety of ethical theories, not only in Christianity. It was against an ethic of following nature that J. S. Mill eloquently argued in his "Essay on Nature" (in *Three Essays*). To Mill nature means either (1) "the sum of all phenomena, together with the causes which produce them" or (2) those phenomena that take place "without the agency . . . of man." Which of these senses can be intended when someone is enjoined to follow nature or when some act is condemned as unnatural? In the first sense *every* action is natural; no ground is given for discrimination between alternative courses. But is the second sense more helpful? "For while human action cannot help conforming to Nature in the one meaning of the term, the very aim and object of action is to alter and improve Nature in the other meaning." Behind the injunction to follow nature lies a dim belief that "the general scheme of nature is a model for us to imitate." Look at nature in some detail, however. Its processes are quite indifferent to value and desert. "Nearly all the things which men are hanged or imprisoned for doing to one another, are nature's every day performances." Even if it were true that some good ends were ultimately and obscurely served and realized by nature's processes, that would give no license to men to follow nature as a moral exemplar (to "torture because nature tortures," for example).

In any case, Mill argues, the presence of evil and indifference to value in nature cannot be reconciled with theistic claims about the omnipotence and perfect goodness of God. It is nonsense to argue that such a God has to bend to stubborn necessities since he "himself makes the necessity which he bends to."

With regard to *human* nature, as with nature at large, Mill's imperative is "not to follow but to amend it." Morality cannot be founded on instinct but on a strenuously achieved victory *over* instinct, as courage is a victory over fear. Similar views are found in T. H. Huxley and even, with important qualifications, in the later Freud.

Philosophical views of nature can be relevant to problems of evaluation in much more complex ways than we have thus far noted. One's conception of how man is related to the rest of the natural world may help to determine —in conjunction with many other factors—one's sense of the importance or unimportance of human life, the roles judged reasonable and unreasonable for men to adopt. Here are some historical examples.

Did a geocentric astronomy give a uniquely privileged place to the earth and to humanity? The symbolism was ambiguous; to be in the center was certainly to be the focus of the cosmic drama of fall and redemption. "Man is but earth," said John Donne. " 'Tis true; but earth is the centre" ("Sermon Preached at St. Paul's, Christmas Day, 1627"). Yet the center, the sublunary region, was nevertheless the humblest position, the realm of mutability, in contrast to the unchanging heavens. The shift to a heliocentric view was not, therefore, a catastrophic and disorienting demotion. It could be seen as an equally effective symbolic expression of creatureliness, earth being placed in a proper subordination to the sun (for example, see Copernicus and Kepler). "The sun, seated on his royal throne, [does] guide his family of planets . . ." (Kepler, *De Revolutionibus*, Book I, Ch. 10).

A far more radical shift in sixteenth- and seventeenth-century cosmology was the move toward acceptance of the universe as infinite and with that the obliterating of a locatable center or circumference. But this view, which, in fact, had no effective *scientific* backing, was largely a late development of the metaphysical Platonic idea of God's infinite fecundity, a view that also guaranteed humanity a position of dignity in the ladder of being (see A. O. Lovejoy, *The Great Chain of Being*, Ch. 4). This well shows how (at least in a period of metaphysical confidence) the importance or unimportance of man has not been a matter of attempted inference from observations of nature alone.

The same point can also be illustrated from sixteenth- and seventeenth-century arguments about the alleged "cosmic fall." If nature is inclement and hostile, this is because nature participated in the effects of man's fall into sin. It follows that the proper, God-intended destiny of man cannot be found in this fallen nature; it must be discovered in the revealed word of God.

More generally, reference to man's place in nature, for instance to his physical minuteness, could be used to depreciate the quest for "worldly" glory as a preparation for spiritual discipline. "Who can be great," asked Drummond of Hawthornden, "on so small a Round as is this Earth?" And Pascal asked: "Qu'est ce qu'un homme dans l'infini?" ("What is a man in face of the infinite?"). The vastness of nature could equally well be taken as evidence of man's importance in God's eyes; for on independent theological grounds the whole of nature could be seen as primarily a dwelling place for man. As Pierre de la Primaudaye expressed it, ". . . I cannot marvell enough at the excellencie of Man, for whom all these things were created and are maintained . . . ." Most of these arguments, with their ingredients capable of endless variation, assume that "in order to form a correct estimate of ourselves we must consider the results of the investigations . . . into the dimensions and distances of the spheres and stars" (Maimonides)—*mutatis mutandis* for later cosmologies.

In sharp contrast, at a time when there is little or no metaphysical and theological confidence and when deriving value judgments from statements of fact is deemed logically impossible, it is tempting to deny that accounts of nature can have any bearing on problems of value. F. P. Ramsey wrote: "My picture of the world is drawn in perspective, and not like a model to scale. The foreground is occupied by human beings, and the stars are all as small as threepenny bits" (*Foundations of Mathematics*). It is possible to make one's judgments about the value of human life independently of cosmic reflections and then to adopt an imaginative picture of the natural world that harmonizes rather than conflicts with that evaluation. There can be no logical or philosophical objections to that as long as one realizes exactly what is being done. Such an imaginative exercise, however, must be distinguished from a thoroughgoing anthropocentric philosophy of nature, and Ramsey himself has been criticized for falling into exactly that (see J. J. C. Smart, *Philosophy and Scientific Realism*, New York, 1963, p. 25). For Ramsey went on to say: "I

don't really believe in astronomy, except as a complicated description of human . . . and possibly animal sensation."

It is worth noting, finally, that arguments about aesthetic judgments have also relied on the vocabulary of "nature" and "natural" and relied on it in many differing and conflicting ways. Presenting or being true to nature has sometimes meant the faithful mirroring of the empirical world *or* the pursuit of the ideal type *or* the pursuit of the average type *or* a concern with whatever has not been modified by man (see A. O. Lovejoy, *Essays in the History of Ideas*, "Nature as Aesthetic Norm"). Works of art have been commended as sharing the characteristics of nature through being regularly patterned (compare to nature's mathematical intelligibility), through being rich in content, or through being austerely simple. To be natural can be to show spontaneity, to be unfettered by artificial rules, to reach toward the unspoiled and primitive. Where there is such extraordinary conflict of senses, only a scrutiny of the context can determine what criteria are being applied in any particular case, and a writer who is aware of this web of ambiguities in "natural" and "nature" may well decide to choose—wherever possible—words of greater precision and stability of meaning.

Bibliography

Because of the almost unlimited scope of the topic, references are for the most part confined to works mentioned in the text of the article or to which the article is in some general way indebted.

BACKGROUND TO GREEK PHILOSOPHIES OF NATURE

Aristotle, *Metaphysics*, W. D. Ross, ed., rev. ed., 2 vols. Oxford, 1924. Δ (V), 4.

Burnet, John, *Greek Philosophy: Thales to Plato*. London, 1914; paperback ed., 1962.

Crombie, I. M., *An Examination of Plato's Doctrines*, 2 vols. London, 1962–1963. Vol. II, Ch. 2.

Guthrie, W. K. C., *A History of Greek Philosophy*, Vol. I. Cambridge, 1962.

Heinemann, F., *Nomos und Physis*. Basel, 1945.

Kirk, G. S., and Raven, J. E., *The Presocratic Philosophers*. Cambridge, 1957.

Pohlenz, M., "Nomos und Physis." *Hermes*, Vol. 81 (1953), 418–438.

Popper, Karl, *The Open Society and Its Enemies*, 2 vols. London, 1945. Vol. I, especially Ch. 5, on nature and convention.

Ross, W. D., *Aristotle*. London, 1923; 2d ed., 1930. Ch. 3.

WIDE-RANGING HISTORICAL INTERPRETATIONS

Burtt, E. A., *The Metaphysical Foundations of Modern Physical Science*. London, 1925.

Collingwood, R. G., *The Idea of Nature*. Oxford, 1945.

Lovejoy, A. O., *The Great Chain of Being*. Cambridge, Mass., 1936.

Lovejoy, A. O., *Essays in the History of Ideas*. Baltimore, 1948. See "Nature as Aesthetic Norm."

Lovejoy, A. O., and Boas, George, *Primitivism and Related Ideas in Antiquity*. Baltimore, 1935. See "Some Meanings of 'Nature.'"

OTHER STUDIES

Dewey, John, *Experience and Nature*. La Salle, Ill., 1925; paperback ed., New York, 1958.

Maritain, Jacques, *La Philosophie de la nature*. Paris, 1935.

Mill, John Stuart, *Three Essays on Religion*. London, 1874; reprinted, 1904.

Ramsey, F. P., *The Foundations of Mathematics.* London, 1931; paperback ed., Paterson, N.J., 1960. See Epilogue.

Russell, Bertrand, *Mysticism and Logic.* London, 1918. See especially Ch. 3, "A Free Man's Worship."

Russell, Bertrand, *Why I Am Not a Christian, and Other Essays,* Paul Edwards, ed. New York, 1957.

Sherrington, Charles, *Man on His Nature.* Cambridge, 1940.

Weizsäcker, C. F. von, *Die Geschichte der Natur.* Göttingen, 1948. Translated by F. D. Wieck as *The History of Nature.* London, 1951.

Whitehead, Alfred North, *The Concept of Nature.* Cambridge, 1920.

Whitehead, Alfred North, *Nature and Life.* Cambridge, 1934.

RONALD W. HEPBURN

NECESSITY. See CONTINGENT AND NECESSARY STATEMENTS.

NEGATION. Negation, or denial, is the opposite of affirmation. It may be something that somebody does ("I deny what you have said") or the answer "No" to a question, but its full expression is generally a sentence. One sentence or statement may be the negation or denial of another, or we may call a statement simply a negation, or a negative statement, as opposed to an affirmative one, or affirmation. A negation in the last sense will contain some sign of negation, such as the "not" in "Grass is not pink" or "Not all leaves are green," the "no" in "No Christians are communists," or the phrase "it is not the case that" in "It is not the case that grass is pink." The negation of a sentence may simply be the same sentence with "it is not the case that" prefixed to it, or it may be some simpler form equivalent to this. For example, it might be said that "It is not the case that grass is pink" is negated or denied not only by "It is not the case that it is not the case that grass is pink" but also by the plain "Grass is pink" and that "If he has shut the door, it must have been open" is negated or denied by "He could have shut it even though it was already shut." Contradictory negation, or contradiction, is the relation between statements that are exact opposites, in the sense that they can be neither true together nor false together—for example, "Some grass is brown" and "No grass is brown." Contrary negation, or contrariety, is the relation between extreme opposites (which may very well both be false)—for example, "No grass is brown" and "All grass is brown." Incompatibility is the relation between statements which cannot both be true, whether or not they stand at opposite ends of a scale ("This is black all over" is incompatible with "This is green all over" as well as with "This is white all over"). Incompatibles imply one another's denials (what is black all over is not green all over or white all over).

Some of these technical expressions apply to terms as well as to statements. The terms "black," "green," and "white," for example, are incompatible; nothing can be more than one of these at once, at least not at the same time, at the same point, from the same angle, and so on. There are also "negative terms," usually formed by prefixing "non" or "not" to the corresponding positive term—for instance, "non-red," "not-red."

The concept of negation is closely related to that of falsehood, but they are not the same. Sometimes it is the negation that is true and the corresponding affirmation that is false. But in denying a statement, we implicitly or explicitly assert that the statement in question is false, though, of course, the assertion that something is false may itself be true.

There is also a connection between the concept of negation, especially as applied to terms, and that of otherness or diversity. What is not red is other than anything that is red, and what is other than anything that is red is not red. The class of things that are other than all the things included in a given class—that is, whatever exists besides the members of that class—constitutes the remainder or complement of the given class.

Internal and external negation. When a proposition is complex, it is often important to distinguish the negation of the proposition as a whole ("external" negation) from propositions resulting from the negation of some component or components of it ("internal" negation). The Stoics noted, for example, that the contradictory denial of an implication "If p, then q" should not be formulated as "If p, then not-q" but as "Not (if p, then q)"—"That p does not imply that q." "If p, then q" and "If p, then not-q" are not even incompatible, although when they are both true, it follows that the component p (since it has contradictory consequences) must be false. Again "Not (p and q)," which is true as long as p and q are not true together, is not to be confused with "Not-p and not-q," which is true only if p and q are both false and is equivalent to "Neither p nor q"—that is, "Not (p or q)." "Either not-p or not-q" is similarly equivalent to "Not (p and q)." These relations between the internal and external negations of "and" and "or" statements are called De Morgan's laws, although they were well known to the medieval Scholastics long before the birth of the nineteenth-century logician Augustus De Morgan.

Some of the distinctions made in the preceding section are now commonly treated as special cases of external and internal negation. For instance, propositions with negative terms are thought of as involving the negation, not perhaps of internal propositions strictly so called, but of internal "propositional functions" ("open sentences")—for example, "Every non-A is a non-B" may be paraphrased as "For any x, if it is not the case that x is an A, then it is not the case that x is a B"; the difference between "No A is a B," the contrary opposite of "Every A is a B," and the contradictory opposite of the latter, "Some A is a B" or "Not every A is a B," is perhaps simply that between the internally negated form "For every x, if x is an A, then not (x is a B)" and the external negation "Not (for every x, if x is an A, then x is a B)." It is obviously possible to place a sign of negation either inside or outside a variety of other qualifying phrases; for example, we may distinguish "It will be the case that (it is not the case that p)" from "It is not the case that (it will be the case that p)" and "It is thought that (it is not the case that p)" from "It is not the case that (it is thought that p)."

By the use of open sentences all the varieties of negation are reduced to the placing of "not" or "it is not the case that" before some proposition or propositionlike expression, the whole being either contained or not contained within some wider propositional context. This reduction assumes that with the basic singular form "*x* is an *A*" or "*x* φ's" there is no real distinction between the internal negation "*x* is not an *A*" (or "*x* is a non-*A*") or "*x* does not φ" and the external negation "Not (*x* is an *A*)" or "Not (*x* φ's)." When the subject "*x*" is a bare "this," such an assumption is plausible, but when it is a singular description like "The present king of France," we must distinguish the internal negation "The present king of France is not bald" (which suggests that there is such a person) from the external negation "It is not the case that the present king of France is bald" (which would be true if there were no such person). The thesis that all forms of negation are reducible to a suitably placed "it is not the case that" can be maintained only if the last two cases have an implicit complexity and may be respectively paraphrased as "For some *x*, *x* is the sole present king of France, and it is not the case that *x* is bald" and "It is not the case that (for some *x*, *x* is the sole present king of France and is bald)."

Positive presuppositions. It is sometimes held that no negation can be bare or mere negation and that whenever anything is denied, some positive ground of denial is assumed, and something positive is even an intended part of what is asserted. It is trivially true that even in denials, such as that grass is pink, something is made out to be the case—namely, that it is not the case that grass is pink. But something more than this is usually intended by the contention.

One thing that could be meant is that every denial must concern something which, whatever else it is not, is itself and, indeed, simply is (exists). We have seen that some types of denial—"This is not a man" and "The man next door does not smoke" (also "Some men do not lie")—do assert or presuppose the existence of a subject of the denial. But this does not seem to be the case with all forms; for example, no existing subject seems to be involved when we say that there are no fairies. Or if this is taken to mean that among existing things no fairies are to be found (thus presupposing a body of "existing things"—of values for the bound variable *x* in "For no *x* it is the case that *x* is a fairy"), even this positive presupposition seems absent from "There could not be round squares."

It is also sometimes said that in denying that something is red, we at least assume that it is some other color (counting white, black, and gray as colors); in denying that something is square, we assume that it is some other shape. In general (to use the terminology of W. E. Johnson), in denying that something has a "determinate" form of some "determinable" quality, we assume that it has some other determinate form of it. Sometimes a distinction is made at this point between the predication of a negative term and the simple denial of a predication; for example, it is argued that in saying that a thing is non-blue, we do assume that it is some other color but we do not assume this in simply saying that it is not blue. Others contend that we assume that a thing is some other color even in simply denying that it is blue. All denial, it is said, is implicitly restricted to some universe of discourse; if we deny that something is blue or classify it as non-blue, it is assumed that we are considering only colored things.

Against the weaker form of the theory that the predication of a negative term has positive implications which the denial of a predication does not have, it may be objected that there is no more than a verbal difference between "*x* is a non-*B*" and "Not (*x* is a *B*)." Against the stronger form the objection is that it is perfectly proper to say that virtue is not blue simply on the ground that it is not the kind of thing that could have any color at all. We must always distinguish between what we say and our reasons for saying it (otherwise, there could be no inference at all, as premises and conclusion would coalesce), and there may be diverse reasons for saying exactly the same thing of different subjects—Jones's favorite flower is not blue because it is pink, and virtue is not blue because being an abstraction, it is not colored at all. But it is perfectly true of each of these subjects, and true in the same sense, that it is not blue.

It may be answered that "This flower is blue" and "Virtue is blue" fail to be true in profoundly different ways—the former because it is false, and the latter because it is meaningless, as meaningless as, for example, "Virtue is but" would be—and, further, whereas the denial of a false statement is true, the denial of a meaningless form of words (that is, the result of attaching a negation sign to it) is itself a meaningless form of words. To this, one possible reply (made by J. M. Shorter in "Meaning and Grammar") would be to deny that the negation of a meaningless form of words is meaningless; even "Virtue is not but" might be defended as true precisely because it is not only false, but also meaningless, to say that virtue is but. Less desperately, it could be argued that "Virtue is (is not) blue" is not on a par with "Virtue is (is not) but" since the former is at least a grammatically correct sentence while the latter does not even construe. Perhaps, however, the conception of grammar which suggests this distinction is a rather superficial one. Grammar concerns what words go with what; it is not a set of commands directly fallen from heaven but reflects at least partly the feeling we already have for what does and what does not make sense. Perhaps we need only let this feeling lead us to slightly finer distinctions than the crude one between an adjective and a conjunction to see that "is (is not) blue" no more goes with "virtue" than "is (is not) but" goes with anything.

What is important is the line between falsehood (the negation of which is true) and nonsense (the negation of which is generally agreed to be only further nonsense), wherever this line be drawn. It is also important that what looks like true or false sense may on closer inspection turn out to be nonsense.

Negative facts. Many philosophers who have found negation a metaphysically embarrassing concept have expressed this embarrassment by denying that there are any negative facts. There are obviously negative as well as affirmative statements, but according to these philosophers, it is incredible that the nonlinguistic facts that make our statements true or false should include negative ones. (The linguistic fact that there are negative statements is, of course, not itself a negative, but a positive, fact.)

This question should not be confused with the question of whether there are objective falsehoods—that is, whether the universe contains such objects as the falsehood that Charles I died in his bed even if no one has ever believed or asserted this falsehood (whether there are falsehoods which are, as it were, waiting around to be asserted or believed, or even denied or disbelieved, just as there are facts waiting to be discovered and stated). For such objective falsehoods, if there were any, would not be facts—a fact is what is the case, not what is not the case. The present question is, rather, whether there are special facts that verify true negative statements, whether, for example, there is any such fact as the fact that Charles I did not die in his bed. There is nevertheless some connection between the two questions. For if there is any such language-independent and thought-independent fact as the fact that it is not the case that Charles I died in his bed, then, that Charles I died in his bed, which in itself is not a fact but a falsehood, would nevertheless seem to have some kind of existence "out there" as a constituent of this more complex object that is a fact.

In both cases, moreover, what deters the philosophers is partly the multiplicity of the objects involved. They cannot believe that there should be not only the fact that Charles I died on the scaffold but also, over and above that fact, the additional facts that he did not die in his bed, that he was not immortal, that he did not die by drowning, and, furthermore, the facts that he did not die in his bed of appendicitis, that he did not die in his bed of consumption, that he did not die by drowning in six minutes, that he did not die by drowning in six and a half minutes, and so on. This causes an embarrassment of the same sort as the idea that, over and above the fact that he died on the scaffold, there are "out there" the falsehoods that he died in his bed, that he was immortal, that he was drowned in six and a half minutes, and so on.

The most obvious way to reduce this excessive metaphysical population, and the one taken by Raphael Demos (one of the main opponents of negative facts), is to hold that what makes it false to say that Charles I died in his bed and true to say that he did not, false to say that he died by drowning and true to say that he did not, and similarly with all the other alternatives is simply the one positive fact that he died on the scaffold. Against this, however, it may be said that what is asserted by any true statement would seem to be some fact, and the true statement that Charles I did not die in his bed does not assert that he died on the scaffold (even if this is also true). It may be suggested that what the true statement asserts is that Charles died in some positive way that was incompatible with his dying in his bed. This suggestion has the disadvantage (a) that it only exchanges negative facts for facts that are vague and general in the way that assertions about something or other (but nothing in particular) are always vague and general and that philosophers who are uneasy about the former (because whatever is real must be particular and positive) are likely to be equally uneasy about the latter. The suggestion also presupposes (b) that there are facts of incompatibility—for example, the fact that Charles I's dying on the scaffold is incompatible with his dying in his bed and that these would seem, like straightforwardly negative facts, to contain objective falsehoods as constituents and would have the same dismaying multiplicity as negative facts or objective falsehoods do.

One way of answering objection (b) is to argue that the facts of incompatibility which explain the truth of negative statements never concern incompatibilities between propositions but always concern incompatibilities between qualities, like the incompatibility between red and blue or between one way of dying and another. This is to make a certain sort of internal negation the fundamental form in terms of which all other types of negation are to be defined. This eliminates the horde of positive falsehoods that are incompatible with the actual positive facts in favor of a possibly smaller and anyway more acceptable horde of incompatible qualities, each capable in itself of qualifying a real object but unable to do so at the same time as the others. But although there is some plausibility in accounting for simple singular negations in this way (that is, in taking the simple "x is not A" to be true, when it is true, because x is something incompatible with being A), it is hard to deal similarly with the negations of more complex forms—for example, "Not everything is A" or "It is not the case that if x is A, then y is B."

Difficulties in dealing with more complex negations also arise with the suggestion that the facts that verify negative statements are facts not so much about incompatibility as about otherness. It is important to note that the otherness account cannot take quite the same form as the incompatibility one; although the fact that x is something incompatible with being red will suffice to verify "x is not red," "x is something other than red" will not, for x may be something other than red (for instance, round) and be red as well. The otherness account would have to claim that what verifies "x is not A" is the fact that x is other than everything that is A. This account, like the preceding one, seems to be applicable only to simple singular negation. However, if the complexities that can arise are capable of being listed, it might be possible to give a separate account of the negation of each kind of complexity. Thus, having said what the simple "x is not A" means, we may say that in forms like "Not (not-p)," "Not (p and q)," "Not (p or q)," "Not (everything ϕ's)," and "Not (something ϕ's)" (that is, "Not anything ϕ's"), the apparently external "not" is to be defined in terms of a comparatively internal "not" as follows:

Not (not-p) = p,
Not (p or q) = (Not-p) and (not-q),
Not (p and q) = (Not-p) or (not-q),
Not (for every x, x ϕ's) = For some x, not (x ϕ's),
Not (for some x, x ϕ's) = For every x, not (x ϕ's).

In any given complex formed in these ways the innermost negations—the only ones that remain when all the reductions have been performed—will be simple singular negations explainable as above in terms of otherness or incompatibility.

Negation, facts, and falsehood. Another way of eliminating negative facts might be by defining negation in terms of disbelief or falsehood. Affirmative statements, we might say, express beliefs whereas negative ones express disbeliefs. Disbelief, however, is not just the absence of belief, and like belief it must have an object—it must be disbelief in something or disbelief of something—and it must be justified or unjustified; if justified, whatever justifies it must be either a negative fact or whatever we replace negative facts with when using some other and more objective method of dissolving them.

In terms of falsehood we might say that the contradictory

negation of a statement is the statement that is true if the given one is false and false if the given one is true. This amounts to defining negation by means of its truth table, a course advocated by Wittgenstein in the *Tractatus*. To this it may be objected that talk of the statement which is true when a given statement is false and false when it is true is legitimate only if we know that there is one and only one statement which meets these conditions, and this seems unlikely; for example, since "Oxford is the capital of Scotland" is false in any case, "Either Oxford is the capital of Scotland or grass is not green" is true if "Grass is green" is false and false if it is true, but what is stated by this complex does not seem to be simply the negation of "Grass is green." It may also be objected that statements are not simply true and false in themselves, as if truth and falsehood were simple properties requiring no further explanation. By the usual definition "Grass is green" is true if grass is green and false if it is not, but to say this is to define falsehood in terms of negation rather than vice versa.

Perhaps the whole problem about negative facts—and the problem about the objective falsehoods that would be parts of such facts if there were any—arise from thinking of facts (and falsehoods) too literally as objects or entities. It is not merely that there are no negative facts but, rather, that there are no facts. That is, expressions of the form "The fact that *p*" do not name objects, whether or not our "*p*" is negative in form. The word "fact" has meaning only as part of the phrase "it is a fact that" (that is, "it is the case that"), and "It is a fact that grass is (or is not) green" is just another way of saying the simple "Grass is (or is not) green." "There are negative facts" is true and, indeed, makes sense only if it means "For some *p*, it is not the case that *p*." But in this sense it is true and metaphysically harmless; it does not mean that there are objects called "That *p*" which go through a performance called "not being the case," and still less does it mean that there are objects called "The not-being-the-case of that *p*."

Even with this caution, however, one can sensibly inquire whether signs of negation are really indispensable—whether what we say when we use them cannot also be said, and more directly, without them—and whether signs of negation are not just convenient abbreviations for complex forms into which no such signs enter. Putting the question in this way, modern logic has evolved other devices for eliminating negation besides the ones thus far mentioned, devices which are worth examining, even though they are a little technical, and which require some preliminary account of negation as the logician sees it.

Laws of negation. Negation figures in formal logic primarily as the subject of certain laws, of which the best known are those of contradiction and excluded middle. The law of contradiction asserts that a statement and its direct denial cannot be true together ("Not both *p* and not-*p*") or, as applied to terms, that nothing can both be and not be the same thing at the same time ("Nothing is at once *A* and not-*A*"). The law of excluded middle asserts that a statement and its negation exhaust the possibilities—it is either the case that *p* or not the case that *p*—or, as applied to terms, that everything either is or is not some given thing—say, *A*. Each of these laws may be put in the form of an implication, or "if" statement; the law of contradiction

then appears as "If *p*, then not not-*p*," and the law of excluded middle as "If not not-*p*, then *p*." Sometimes the combination of these two, "*p* if and only if not not-*p*," is called the law of double negation.

Each of these laws involves a number of derived or related laws. From the law of contradiction it follows that what has contradictory consequences is false; if *p* implies *q* and also implies not-*q* (and so implies "*q* and not-*q*"), then not-*p*. From the law of excluded middle it follows that what is implied by both members of a contradictory pair is true; if *p* implies *q* and not-*p* equally implies *q*, then *q*. Again, because of the law of contradiction whatever implies its own denial is false, for if *p* implies not-*p*, it implies both *p* and not-*p* (since it certainly implies *p*) and thus cannot be true. This is the principle of *reductio ad absurdum*. To take an ancient example, if everything is true, then it is true (among other things) that not everything is true; hence, it cannot be the case that everything is true. Perhaps we can also argue that if it is a fact that there are no negative facts, then that is itself a negative fact; thus, it cannot be that there are no negative facts. Correspondingly, from the law of excluded middle it follows that whatever is implied by its own denial (that is, what we are compelled to affirm even when we try to deny it) is true. (The later Schoolmen called this the *consequentia mirabilis*.)

Another important law involving negation is the law of contraposition, or transposition, that if *p* implies *q*, then the denial of *q* implies the denial of *p* or, for terms, if every *A* is a *B*, then every non-*B* is a non-*A*. If this is combined with the first law of double negation ("If *p*, then not not-*p*"), we obtain "If *p* implies not-*q*, then *q* implies not-*p*"; if it is combined with the second law of double negation ("If not not-*p*, then *p*"), we obtain "If not-*p* implies *q*, then not-*q* implies *p*," and with both we obtain "If not-*p* implies not-*q*, then *q* implies *p*."

Many logicians have questioned the law of excluded middle and the laws associated with it. In particular, the intuitionist logic of L. E. J. Brouwer and Arend Heyting contains none of the laws "Either *p* or not-*p*," "If not not-*p*, then *p*," "If *p* implies *q* and not-*p* also implies *q*, then *q*," "If not-*p* implies *p*, then *p*," "If not-*p* implies *q* (not-*q*), then not-*q* (*q*) implies *p*."

Formal definitions of negation. The laws just discussed and many others figure in modern symbolic calculi as theorems derived by stated rules of inference from given axioms. Some of them, indeed, may themselves appear as axioms, different formulas being taken as axiomatic in different symbolic presentations. The symbols used, moreover, will be divisible into "primitive" symbols that are introduced without explanation and other symbols that are introduced by definition as abridgments of complexes involving other symbols. Which symbols are taken as primitive and which are defined will vary with the particular systematic presentation adopted.

Frege, for example, took symbols corresponding to "if" and "not" as undefined and introduced the form "*p* or *q*" as a way of writing "If not-*p*, then *q*" ("Either I planted peas, or I planted beans" = "If I did not plant peas, I planted beans"). Russell at one stage did the same, but he later took "not" and "or" as his primitives, defining "If *p*, then *q*" as "Either not-*p* or *q*" ("If you smoke, you'll get a cough" = "Either you won't smoke, or you'll get a cough") and "*p* and *q*" as "Not either not-*p* or not-*q*." Other writers have defined all the other symbols in terms of "not" and "and." For example, they have defined "If *p*, then *q*" as "Not (*p* without *q*)"—that is, "Not (*p* and not-*q*)" and "*p* or *q*" as "Not both not-*p* and not-*q*."

In all these examples the negation sign appears as one of the primitive or undefined symbols, but there are also systems in which this is not the case and in which "not" is defined in terms of something else. For example, Jean Nicod uses a single undefined stroke in such a way that "*p*|*q*" amounts to "Not both *p* and *q*" and "Not-*p*" is defined as "*p*|*p*" (Not both *p* and *p*). Russell sometimes attempts to avoid even the appearance of complexity in his verbal rendering of Nicod's stroke by reading "*p*|*q*" as "*p* is incompatible with *q*," but this would ordinarily be understood as a little stronger than what is intended. We would not normally say that "London is the capital of England" was incompatible with "Berlin is the capital of France," but it is correct to say "London is the capital of England|Berlin is the capital of France," since the two components are not both true.

An earlier and more interesting device was that of C. S. Peirce, who defined negation as the implication of something false. This is not quite a definition of negation in terms of falsehood. Formally, what is meant is that we arbitrarily choose some false proposition—say, "The ancient Romans spoke Polish"—and introduce "Not-*p*" as an abbreviation for "If *p*, then the ancient Romans spoke Polish." It is also possible to take as our standard false proposition for this purpose a formula which itself has some logical significance. In his later years Peirce himself liked to use the proposition "For all *p*, *p*," which is, roughly, "Everything is true" (which was shown to be false in the previous section of this article). In common speech we come close to defining "Not-*q*" as "If *q*, then for all *p*, *p*" when we say of something we wish to deny, "If you believe that, you would believe anything." A similar definition of "Not-*p*," used by Russell in his early writings, is "For all *q*, if *p*, then *q*." Starting in this way, it is possible to define all the symbols of logic in terms of "if" and the quantifier "for all *x*." Certain further technical devices make it possible to define both "if" and "for all *x*" in terms of a single operator that can be read as "For all *x*, if . . . , then . . ." or "If ever . . . , then . . ." (Russell's "formal implication," perhaps better called "universalized implication").

Given definitions of this type, the characteristic laws of negation fall into place as special cases of the characteristic laws of implication or of universality (or both). For instance, the law of transposition, "If (if *p*, then *q*), then (if not-*q*, then not-*p*)," expands to "If (if *p*, then *q*) then if (if *q*, then anything-at-all), then (if *p*, then anything-at-all)," which is just a special case of the law of syllogism, "If (if *p*, then *q*), then if (if *q*, then *r*), then (if *p*, then *r*)." Moreover, the peculiarities of the intuitionistic negation of Brouwer and Heyting turn out simply to reflect those of intuitionistic implication.

Intuitionistic logic, for example, contains the law "If *p* implies *q*, then if *p* also implies that *q* implies *r*, *p* implies *r*"; therefore, it contains the special case "If *p* implies *q*,

then if *p* also implies that *q* implies the falsehood, then *p* implies the falsehood"—that is, "If *p* implies *q*, then if *p* also implies not-*q*, then not-*p*." But it does not contain the law "If *p* implies *r*, then if *p*'s implying *q* also implies *r*, then *r*" (this law, being verified by the usual truth-tables for "if" and "not," does appear in nonintuitionistic or classical implicational logic) and therefore does not contain the law "If *p* implies *r*, then if *p*'s implying the falsehood also implies *r*, then *r*" ("If *p* implies *r*, then if not-*p* also implies *r*, then *r*").

It is also possible in both intuitionistic and classical logic to separate those laws of negation which are (or may be represented as) merely special cases of laws of implication (as in the above examples) and those which reflect the special features of what a proposition is being said to imply when we negate it. For example, both versions of logic contain the law (1) "If *p*, then if also not-*p*, then anything-at-all." But neither logic contains as a law the implicational formula of which this would be (if they had it) a special case, "If *p*, then if *p* implies *r*, then anything-at-all." However, they do both have, quite naturally, (2) "If *p*, then if *p* implies that everything is true, then anything-at-all." To get (1), in other words, it is important not only that we should see "Not-*p*" as something of the form "If *p*, then *r*" but also as this particular thing, "If *p*, then everything is true." If we drop from intuitionistic logic those laws of negation which require attention to this more special point, we obtain the "minimal" calculus of I. Johannson ("Der Minimalkalkül," *Compositio Mathematica*, Vol. 4, 119–136).

Technical eliminations of negation. Do the developments just sketched mean that we can dispense with negative facts by saying that the facts stated by true negative statements are ones which do not involve any special concept of negation but only (in one version) Nicod's stroke or (in the other) implication and universality? The suggestion, especially in its Peircean form, has its attractions. Peirce's definition would at least explain why negation is a proper subject of study for pure logicians. Logic studies universal rules of implication; even the purest logic must study whatever is involved in the very notions of implication and universality; and what Peirce means by negation is thus involved. Facts as to what is not the case are in this view only an instance of a more general type of complex fact without which logic would be impossible—namely, facts as to what leads to what.

Against this suggestion one might adduce the extreme artificiality and arbitrariness of these symbolic devices. Consider the fact that it is equally possible in a symbolic system to define "and" in terms of "or" and "not" and "or" in terms of "and" and "not." Whatever this fact signifies, it cannot signify that "Not (not-*p* or not-*q*)" is the real meaning of "*p* and *q*" and that the very form "*p* or *q*" that is used in this explanation has for its real meaning "Not (not-*p* and not-*q*)." This procedure would obviously be circular, and for this reason we cannot, even symbolically, have both definitions in the same system. It is obvious that the form "or" cannot be both simple and unanalyzable and a complex built up out of "and" and "not"; at least, it can only be this by being used ambiguously and, similarly, *mutatis mutandis*, with "and." The systems with the different definitions are equivalent in the sense that, given suitably chosen axioms, the same formulas will appear in them as theorems, and the undefined "and" (or "or") and the defined one are equivalent in the sense of having the same truth tables. But if there is an intuitively simple meaning of the form "p and q," "and" in this sense simply does not appear (is not symbolized) in a system which has only "or" and "not" as its undefined symbols and introduces "p and q" as short for "Not (not-p or not-q)." Primitiveness in a convenient calculus is one thing; intuitive or conceptual simplicity, another. No one symbolic system, we may surmise, can express everything, and in any given system we can take whatever we please as undefined, even if its intuitive meaning is complex.

Turning now to the calculi in which "not" is defined, it is notoriously difficult to explain the meaning of Nicod's stroke except by saying that "$p \mid q$" means "Not both p and q" or that it means "Either not-p or not-q"; furthermore, the "not" that is introduced by defining "Not-p" as "$p \mid p$" cannot be the "not" which is used in this explanation, though for purposes of logical calculation it may serve just as well. It could similarly be said that the "if" which Peirce uses in his definition of "not" cannot be understood without a more primeval "not" being presupposed. For Peirce did not use "If p, then q" in the familiar sense in which it means that q would be a logical consequence of p; it is not true that whenever p happens not to be the case, it would logically follow from it that everything whatever is true. Even the colloquial "If you believe that, you would believe anything" is not said of anything we wish to deny but only of particularly outrageous items (things which not only are not, but also could not, be the case). What Peirce meant by "If p, then q," it might be said, can be explained only by saying that it means "Not at once p and not-q," and this explanation uses a "not" that cannot be derived from his definition because the definition presupposes that "not."

On the other hand, it might be argued that our intuitions as to what is a construction from simpler conceptions and what is itself simple are not very reliable and that if a definition introduces new economies into a calculus and, still more, if it brings a new unity to a whole subject, this may well be a symptom that it also reveals what is conceptually fundamental. The treatment of "not being the case" as an extreme case of implication—as "implying too much," so to speak—does at least reflect something important about the relation between the two concepts. A proposition's implying something, having consequences, is like its taking a risk, and its not being the case is its having too strong consequences.

Bibliography

For clear summaries of the stock problems see J. N. Keynes, *Formal Logic,* 4th ed. (London, 1906), Part I, Ch. 4; Part II, Ch. 3; and Appendix B. See also W. E. Johnson, *Logic* (Cambridge, 1921), Part I, Chs. 5 and 14.

For the special insights of certain major writers see C. S. Peirce, *Collected Papers,* Charles Hartshorne, Paul Weiss, and Arthur W. Burks, eds., 8 vols. (Cambridge, Mass., 1931–1958), II.356, 378–380, 550, 593–600; III.381–384, 407–414. See also Peirce's article "Syllogism," in *Century Dictionary* (New York, 1889–1901); Gottlob Frege, "Negation," in P. T. Geach and Max Black, eds., *Trans-lations From the Philosophical Writings of Gottlob Frege* (Oxford, 1952); and Bertrand Russell, *Introduction to Mathematical Philosophy* (London, 1919), Ch. 14; "The Philosophy of Logical Atomism," Lectures I–II, in *Logic and Knowledge* (London, 1956); *An Inquiry into Meaning and Truth* (London and New York, 1940), Ch. 4; and *Human Knowledge, Its Scope and Limits* (London and New York, 1948), Ch. 9.

See also Ludwig Wittgenstein, *Tractatus Logico-philosophicus,* translated by D. F. Pears and B. F. McGuinness (London, 1961), 1.12, 2.06, 4.06–4.1, 4.25–4.463, 5.254, 5.43–5.44, 5.451, 5.512, 5.5151, 6.1201–6.1203.

On Wittgenstein (and Russell and Frege) see also G. E. M. Anscombe, *An Introduction to Wittgenstein's Tractatus* (London, 1959), Chs. 1–4.

On falsehood and meaninglessness see J. M. Shorter's classic piece, "Meaning and Grammar," in *Australasian Journal of Philosophy,* Vol. 34 (1956), 73–91.

Various philosophical problems concerning the nature of negation are discussed in the following works: F. H. Bradley, *Principles of Logic* (London, 1883; 2d ed., 1922), Vol. I, Book 1, Ch. 3, and Terminal Essay 6; Bernard Bosanquet, *Logic or the Morphology of Knowledge,* 2 vols. (London, 1888), Vol. I, Ch. 7, Secs. 1–3, 5; Raphael Demos, "A Discussion of a Certain Type of Negative Proposition," *Mind,* Vol. 24 (1917), 188 ff; Ralph M. Eaton, *Symbolism and Truth* (Cambridge, 1925); J. Cook Wilson, *Statement and Inference,* 2 vols. (Oxford, 1926), Vol. I, Ch. 12; J. D. Mabbott, Gilbert Ryle, and H. H. Price, symposium, "Negation," *PAS,* Supp. Vol. 9 (1929); F. P. Ramsey, "Facts and Propositions" (1927), in his *Foundations of Mathematics* (London, 1931), pp. 138–155; A. J. Ayer, "Negation," *Journal of Philosophy,* Vol. 49 (1952), 797–815, reprinted in his *Philosophical Essays* (London, 1954); Morris Lazerowitz, "Negative Terms," *Analysis,* Vol. 12 (1951/1952), 51–66, reprinted in Margaret MacDonald, ed., *Philosophy and Analysis* (Oxford, 1954); R. L. Cartwright, "Negative Existentials," *Journal of Philosophy,* Vol. 57 (1960), 629–639, reprinted in Charles E. Caton, ed., *Philosophy and Ordinary Language* (Urbana, Ill., 1963); and Gerd Buchdahl, "The Problem of Negation," *Philosophy and Phenomenological Research,* Vol. 22 (1961), 163–178.

A. N. PRIOR

NELSON, LEONARD (1882–1927), German critical philosopher and the founder of the Neo-Friesian school. Nelson was born in Berlin. After studying mathematics and philosophy he qualified for teaching as a *Privatdozent* in the natural science division of the philosophical faculty at Göttingen in 1909. In 1919 he was appointed extraordinary professor.

The critical school. Nelson's philosophical work was concerned mainly with two problems: the establishment of a scientific foundation for philosophy by means of a critical method and the systematic development of philosophical ethics and philosophy of right and their consequences for education and politics.

Nelson's search for a strictly scientific foundation and development of philosophy soon led him to critical philosophy. Nelson took the *Critique of Pure Reason* to be a treatise on method and regarded the critical examination of the capacities of reason as its decisive achievement. Through this critique alone could philosophical concepts be clarified and philosophical judgments traced back to their sources in cognition. Therefore, Nelson undertook a close examination of the thought of Jakob Friedrich Fries (1773–1843), the one post-Kantian philosopher who had concentrated on Kant's critical method, carried it further, and tried to clarify its vaguenesses and contradictions.

While Nelson was still a student, he began to collect Fries's writings. These were not easily available, for Fries was hardly known at that time; when he was mentioned at all in philosophical treatises, it was as the representative of an outmoded psychologism. In his own first works Nelson attempted to defend Fries against this reproach. Together with a few friends whom he had interested in Fries's philosophy, he began to publish a *neue Folge* (new series) of *Abhandlungen der Fries'schen Schule* in 1904—the same year in which he wrote his doctoral dissertation on Fries. A few years later he founded, together with these same friends, the Jakob-Friedrich-Fries-Gesellschaft to promote the methodical development of critical philosophy.

CRITICAL METHOD AND CRITIQUE OF REASON

In his own writings devoted to the critical method, Nelson distinguished between the critique of reason and two misinterpretations of it, transcendentalism and psychologism. The critique of reason was to prepare the grounds for a philosophical system and to give this system an assured scientific basis by means of a critical investigation of the faculty of cognition. Posing the problem in this way seems to require the critique of reason and the system of philosophy to be adapted to each other in such a way that either the critique of reason must be developed a priori as a philosophical discipline, because of the rational character of philosophy, or philosophy must be conceived as a branch of psychology, since the investigation of knowledge by means of the critique of reason belongs to psychology. Transcendentalism sacrifices the main methodical thesis of the critique of reason, that the highest abstractions of philosophy cannot be dogmatically postulated but must be derived from concrete investigation of the steps leading to knowledge. Psychologism fails to recognize the character of philosophical questions and answers, which is independent of psychological concepts.

Kant did not unequivocally answer the question whether the critique of reason should be developed as a science from inner experience of one's own knowledge or as a philosophical theory from a priori principles. His subjective approach, according to which philosophical abstractions should be introduced by a critique of the faculty of cognition, indicates the first interpretation, but in carrying out his investigations—and in the asserted parallelism between general and transcendental logic as well as in the demand for a transcendental proof of metaphysical principles—Kant tacitly assumed the second interpretation and interpreted the theorems of the critique as a priori judgments. Fries, who was mainly concerned with countering the contemporary tendency to develop Kant's teaching in the direction of transcendentalism, took the subjective approach and developed it consistently from inner experience, without, however, transforming philosophical questions and answers into psychological ones. The boundary between Fries's work and psychologism is not so clear, and for this reason most of his critics misunderstood his philosophy as a psychologistic system, albeit not a consistent one.

Nelson solved the problem that philosophy based on the critique of reason seemed necessarily to lead either to transcendentalism or to psychologism by proving that both tacitly assume that a basis of knowledge must consist of proving philosophical principles from theorems of the critique of reason. If the theorems of the critique and the foundations of the philosophical system were in fact related to each other in the same way that the premises and conclusions of logical problems are related, then indeed the critique of reason and philosophy would have to be identical—that is, they would both have to be either empirical and psychological or rational and a priori. By investigating the problem of the critique of reason Nelson showed that and why this premise is mistaken: the critique serves to clarify one's understanding of the origin of philosophical notions and of their function in the human cognition of facts. Cognition is an activity of the self, motivated by sensual stimulation; data acquired by sensual stimulation are related to one another by cognition of the surrounding world. The function of the critique of reason is to demonstrate the connecting ideas in this process and the assumed criteria by which these ideas are applied by analyzing the concrete steps in cognition and to follow these connecting ideas back to their origin in the cognitive faculty by means of psychological theory; it is not its function to prove the objective validity of the principles in which these criteria are expressed. These principles themselves are of a philosophical rather than a psychological nature. They cannot be derived from the statements of the critique; indeed, since they are the basic assumptions of all perception, they cannot be derived from any judgments more valid than they are.

Critique of reason and philosophy. The connection between the critique of reason and the system of philosophy, according to this theory, is not one of logical proof; it is derived, rather, from "reason's faith in itself," as Fries put it, from the fact that all striving for knowledge assumes faith in the possibility of cognition. This faith is faith in reason, inasmuch as reason is the faculty of cognition instructed by the stimulation of the senses. This faith is maintained by the agreement of cognitions, but it cannot be further checked or justified by a comparison of cognitions with the object cognized. This sets an unsurpassable limit to the provability of cognitions. Nelson expressed this in his paper on the impossibility of the theory of knowledge, in which he understood the theory to be an attempt to investigate scientifically the objective validity of cognition. In contrast, the critique of reason should limit itself to investigating the direction in which faith in cognition is in fact turned.

In carrying out this investigation Fries and Nelson distinguished between indirect cognition, supported by some other claim to truth, and direct cognition, which simply claims the faith of reason and which therefore neither needs nor has any justification, even when it is obscure and enters consciousness only in its application as a criterion for the unity of sensually perceivable isolated cognition. Fries and Nelson, in agreement with Kant, considered the criteria which belong solely to reason to include the pure intuition of space and time and their metaphysical combinations according to the categories of substance, causality, and reciprocal action.

Natural philosophy. Nelson's interpretation of cognition led him to the problem of a mathematical natural philosophy that had been sketched by Kant and further developed by Fries; this philosophy established a priori an "armament of hypotheses" for the empirical-inductive investigation of natural laws. It coincided in fact with the basic principles of classical mechanics and thereby came into conflict with modern physics. Nelson neither minimized this conflict nor confused it with problems of the principles of critical natural philosophy. He saw physics as being in the process of a radical changeover to modern theories, which had by no means yet been ordered into a conflict-free system comparable to that of classical physics. He was sure that every physical theory must go beyond the data provided by observation and experiment in developing concepts and making assertions. And he was convinced that the positivistic, antimetaphysical tendencies of contemporary physicists promoted a tacit and therefore uncritical metaphysics. Without himself being able to solve the conflict that had arisen within critical philosophy, he was convinced the progressive clarification of modern theories would lead back to a physics based on classical mechanics.

CRITICAL ETHICS

Basic principles. Nelson systematically applied the critical method in his studies in practical philosophy—ethics in the broadest sense of the word, including philosophy of right and philosophically based educational and political theory. He added his own critique of practical reason to those of his predecessors. He developed his own processes, both for what he called abstraction (analysis of the assumptions underlying practical ethical value judgments) and for determining, by an empirical study of value judgments, "the interests of pure practical reason," that is, ethical demands put to the human will by reason itself. It is these interests which make value judgments possible. Nelson derived two basic ethical principles from these interests: the law of the balanced consideration of all interests affected by one's own deeds and the ideal of forming one's own life independently, according to the ideas of the true, the beautiful, and the good. These two principles were linked by the fact that, on the one hand, the law of balanced consideration, as a categorical imperative, determines the necessary limiting condition for the ideal value of human behavior; on the other hand, the ideal of rational self-determination leads to the doctrine of the true interests of man and finds in these interests the standard for a balanced consideration of conflicting interests.

Nelson's system. From these two principles alone Nelson developed his system of philosophical ethics; he limited himself to such consequences as could be derived from these principles purely philosophically—without the addition of experience—but he attempted to grasp them completely and systematically. In this he was influenced, first, by his interest in systematically and strictly justifying the assumptions used in every single step and the logical connections of the concepts appearing in the principles and, second, by his interest in applying this practical science. The principles demonstrated are formal and permit determination of concrete ethical demands only through their application to given circumstances as justified by experience. But it is precisely this application of the principles to the world of experience which requires

preparatory philosophical investigation if the application is to be guarded against hasty generalization of single results, in which changing circumstances are not taken into account, and against opportunistic adaptation to circumstances without regard for the practical consequences of ethical principles. In the system as a whole, ethics and philosophy of right appear side by side. Nelson distinguished between them according to different ways of applying the law of balanced consideration. As a categorical imperative, this law demands of the human will the balanced consideration of other persons' interests affected by its actions. By its content it determines the duties of the individual by the rights others have with regard to him; in this respect it is related to communal life and thereby provides a criterion for the value of a social order. Nelson defined this criterion as the concept of the state of right, by which he meant the condition of a society in which the interests of all members are protected against wrongful violation. Ethics, by this definition, is concerned with the duties of the individual; philosophy of right is concerned with the state of right. To each of these disciplines Nelson added another concerned with the conditions of realizing the values studied by them: philosophical pedagogics, as the theory of the education of man to the ethical good, and philosophical politics, as the theory of the realization of the state of right.

Validity of ethical principles. The logically transparent construction of the entire system reveals clearly that the principles behind all further developments are strictly valid in all cases but can be applied only through full consideration of the concrete circumstances in each individual case; since they are objectively valid, they are not subject to arbitrary decisions and are valid even in cases where human insight and will fail to understand them; but they are justified only by reference to reason, which makes possible for each individual the autonomic recognition of these standards and the critical examination of their applications. Thus, the demands of equality for all before the law and of equality of rights are compatible with the demand to differentiate according to given circumstances; and the demands of force against injustice remain linked to those of freedom of criticism and of public justification for the legal necessity of certain coercive measures. Such coercive measures are particularly necessary when the freedom of man to form himself rationally within the framework of his own life is threatened; this freedom can be threatened because man's true need for it is at first obscure and can therefore be mistaken and suppressed.

Nature and chance. One conclusion appears again and again, determining the structure of the whole system. In each case it is a question of fighting with chance, to which the realization of the good is subject in nature. What happens in nature is, according to the laws of nature, dependent on the given circumstances and on the forces working through them, which are indifferent to ethical values: Under the laws of nature it is a matter of chance whether what should happen is in fact what happens or whether ethical demands are ignored. But what ethics demands should not be subject to chance but assured by the human will. Following this line of thought, Nelson derived the law of character in ethics, which demands from man the establishment of a basic willingness to fulfill his duty, by which he makes himself independent of given concrete circumstances; his inclinations and the influences on his will may or may not be in agreement with the commands of duty.

In the philosophy of right Nelson correspondingly finds certain postulates. These determine the forms of reciprocal action in society which alone assure just relations between individuals; among them are public justice, prosecutability, the law of contract, and the law of property. The transitions from ethics to pedagogy and from philosophy of right to politics are made in the same spirit. Education, among the many influences on man, should strengthen or create those elements which develop his capacity for good and oppose those that could weaken this capacity. Politics is concerned with the realization and securing of the state of right determined by the postulates of philosophy of right. This problem leads to the postulation of a state seeking the rule of law and having the power to maintain itself against forces in society opposing the rule of law. A sufficiently powerful federation of states is necessary to regulate the legal relationships between states.

The same conclusion is reached in the last section of Nelson's *System der philosophischen Rechtslehre und Politik*. Here again, in a state of nature it is a matter of chance to what degree states realize the rule of law or violate its demands, unless men having insight into justice and moral will work to transform the existing state into a just state. These men must interfere in the struggle between social groups and parties and must themselves band together into a party. In this case, therefore, the ideal of a just state leads to that of a party working to achieve it.

Freedom and necessity. The conflict between natural necessity and man's freedom and responsibility impelled Nelson's thinking. Ethical standards are valid for human action in nature and are therefore directly relevant to two apparently mutually exclusive forms of legality: the theoretical form, according to which everything that happens in nature (including human behavior) is determined by natural laws working through the existing powers, and the practical one, which presents the human will with duties that can either be violated and ignored or become man's purpose.

Thus on the one hand Nelson insisted that demonstrated ethical standards be maintained without compromise and rejected the skeptical assumption that man, as a limited creature of nature, was incapable of maintaining them; this assumption he considered a sacrifice of known ethical truth, a mere excuse for those who were able but not willing. On the other hand, he expected the human will to act according to the strongest motivation of the moment, without any guarantee from nature that this motivation would direct man toward what is ethically required. For this reason he rejected any speculation that in a state of nature the good would pave its own way.

Within the framework of the critique, Nelson thoroughly examined the question of how man's freedom could be reconciled with this natural law. He sought the answer in the doctrine of transcendental idealism that human knowledge is limited to the understanding of relationships in the sphere of experience but cannot achieve absolute perception of reality itself. In the consciousness of his freedom, which is indissolubly bound to the knowledge of his responsibility, man relates himself by faith to the world of that which is real in itself and superior to the limitations of nature. Nelson unified the two points of view by connecting two results of his investigations of the critique of reason: the principle of the existence of pure practical reason, which as a direct moral interest makes moral insight and moral motivation possible, and the principle of the original obscurity of this interest, according to which it does not determine judgment and will by its very existence but rather requires enlightenment and is dependent on stimulation.

Education and politics. Concern with the realization of ethical requirements led Nelson beyond his philosophical work to practical undertakings, in which he gave primary emphasis to politics, particularly to political education.

Toward the end of World War I Nelson collected a circle of pupils and co-workers who were willing to undergo intensive education and discipline in preparation for the political duties imposed by ethics and philosophy of right. Together with these pupils he founded the Internationaler Jugendbund and in January 1926 developed his own political organization, the Internationaler Sozialistischer Kampf-Bund. In 1924 he opened a "country educational institution," Landerziehungsheim Walkemühle, directed by his co-worker Minna Specht. Here youths and children were trained in a closely knit educational and working community for activity in the workers' movement, until the school was closed and appropriated by the National Socialists in 1933.

As a teacher and educator Nelson had a strong effect on his pupils. He led them by masterly Socratic discussions to a clarification and critical examination of their own convictions, and he required them to carry out what they had recognized as just and good in their actions with the same consistency which he demanded of himself. "Ethics is there in order to be applied."

Works by Nelson

"Die kritische Methode und das Verhältnis der Psychologie zur Philosophie." *Abhandlungen der Fries'schen Schule*, N.F. Vol. 1, No. 1 (1904), 1–88.

"Jakob Friedrich Fries und seine jungsten Kritiker." *Abhandlungen der Fries'schen Schule*, N.F. Vol. 1, No. 2 (1905), 233–319.

"Bermerkungen über die nicht-Euklidische Geometrie und den Ursprung der mathematischen Gewissheit." *Abhandlungen der Fries'schen Schule*, N.F. Vol. 1, No. 2 (1905), 373–392, Vol. 1, No. 3 (1906), 393–430.

"Inhalt und Gegenstand, Grund und Begründung. Zur Kontroverse über die kritische Methode." *Abhandlungen der Fries'schen Schule*, N.F. Vol. 2, No. 1 (1907), 33–73.

"Ist metaphysikfreie Naturwissenschaft möglich?" *Abhandlungen der Fries'schen Schule*, N.F. Vol. 2, No. 3 (1908), 241–299.

"Über das sogenannte Erkenntnisproblem." *Abhandlungen der Fries'schen Schule*, N.F. Vol. 2, No 4 (1908), 413–850.

"Bemerkungen zu den Paradoxien von Russell und Burali-Forti." *Abhandlungen der Fries'schen Schule*, N.F. Vol. 2, No. 3 (1908), 301–334. Written with Kurt Grelling.

"Untersuchungen über die Entwicklungsgeschichte der Kantischen Erkenntnistheorie." *Abhandlungen der Fries'schen Schule*, N.F. Vol. 3, No. 1 (1909), 33–96.

"Die Unmöglichkeit der Erkenntnistheorie." *Abhandlungen der Fries'schen Schule,* N.F. Vol. 3, No. 4 (1912), 583–617.

"Die Theorie des wahren Interesses und ihre rechtliche und politische Bedeutung." *Abhandlungen der Fries'schen Schule,* N.F. Vol. 4, No. 2 (1913), 395–423.

"Die kritische Ethik bei Kant, Schiller und Fries." *Abhandlungen der Fries'schen Schule,* N.F. Vol. 4, No. 3 (1914), 483–691.

Die Rechtswissenschaft ohne Recht. Kritische Betrachtungen über die Grundlagen des Staats- und Völkerrechts, insbesondere über die Lehre von der Souveränität. Leipzig, 1917.

Die Reformation der Gesinnung durch Erziehung zum Selbstvertrauen. Gesammelte Aufsätze. Leipzig, 1917; 2d enlarged ed., Leipzig, 1922.

Vorlesungen über die Grundlagen der Ethik, 3 vols. Leipzig, 1917–1932. Vol. II translated by Norbert Guterman as *System of Ethics.* New Haven, 1956.

Die Reformation der Philosophie durch die Kritik der Vernunft. Gesammelte Aufsätze. Leipzig, 1918.

Demokratie und Führerschaft. Leipzig, 1920.

Spuk, Einweihung in das Geheimnis der Wahrsagerkunst Oswald Spenglers. Leipzig, 1921.

"Kritische Philosophie und mathematische Axiomatik." *Unterrichtsblätter für Mathematik und Naturwissenschaft,* 34th year, Nos. 4 and 5 (1927), 108–115 and 136–142.

"Sittliche und religiöse Weltansicht." *XXVI Aasaner Studentenkonferenz.* Leipzig, 1922. Pp. 7–25.

"Die Sokratische Methode." *Abhandlungen der Fries'schen Schule,* N.F. Vol. 5, No. 1 (1929), 21–78. Translated by Thomas K. Brown in *Socratic Method and Critical Philosophy.* New Haven, 1949. Selected essays.

Fortschritte und Rückschritte der Philosophie; von Hume und Kant bis Hegel und Fries. Frankfurt, 1962.

Works on Nelson

Specht, Minna, and Eichler, Willi, eds., *Leonard Nelson zum Gedächtnis,* Frankfurt, 1953. Contains essays.

GRETE HENRY-HERMANN
Translated by *Tessa Byck*

NEMESIS, a goddess in ancient Greece associated with forests, fertility, and the soil, whose character and role were very much like those of Artemis of the woods. Her innocence was dramatized in a story according to which she transformed herself into a goose to avoid the amorous pursuits of Zeus. In sharp contrast to this picture, Nemesis was also taken to signify, in popular morals, a less benign power. She was thought to be the embodiment of divine revenge, the personification of retribution and the expression of righteous indignation by the gods at human arrogance and presumption. It seems that as the heroic conception of man's nature gave way to a morally more self-conscious view of his destiny, Nemesis became intimately associated with the sentiment of resentment toward all moral offense. Thus, the key ideas that accounted for the causes of moral transgression soon came to imply a special conception of Nemesis: the disapproval of excess, of temerity, of insolence, and of any violation of duty. Nemesis thereby joined such practical notions as *aidos* (shame), *thymos* (self-assertiveness), *koros* (gratification of desire), and *hybris* (overweening pride) in providing a rational background for the assessment of men's actions and character. From heroic poetry to classical philosophy shifts in the meaning of Nemesis parallel gropings toward the idea of an agent bent on punishing moral infringement—an agent committed to righting all wrong.

Even though Nemesis as a benign goddess in archaic times was not related to revenge—being primarily the dispenser of good to men—her sanctuary, a clearing in the woods (*nemos*), was regarded by everyone as an *adyton,* a place no ordinary mortal could enter. It was believed that trespassers met with Nemesis' anger; that she was always ready to avenge profanations. Once this implicit feature of Nemesis was emphasized it was apparently a short step for the popular mind to see Nemesis more and more as the avenger of all violations. When (for example, in Homer's *Iliad*) Nemesis is associated with *aidos* (the inborn sense of shame), her more anthropomorphic mythical associations begin to fade away and her new role as moral overseer comes into prominence. It is possible that as the ancient sanctuaries of the goddess fell into disuse and the new controversies about *nomos* (law)—what must be done within proper limits—became pressing, Nemesis was unconsciously converted by the popular mind into the protectress of all *nomos,* into the power that punishes whatever is not done lawfully, into the avenger of evil in general. The primitive idea of divine envy of man's superciliousness at last gave way to the abstract idea of righteous censure. Nemesis came to mean the cosmic gratification at man's getting his just deserts. As the Greeks realized that man could lose his sense of shame and that through the gratification of desire his self-assertiveness could lead him to *hybris,* man needed Nemesis (just punishment) to balance his moral violations, to cancel out evil if what was ultimately good in the world were to be preserved. In this framework Nemesis came to represent an impersonal corrective force, the expression of the universal concern with the problem of retribution. Greek lyric, tragic, and philosophical literature clearly reflect the consequences of this historical transformation.

Bibliography

Cornford, F. M., *From Religion to Philosophy; A Study in the Origins of Western Speculation.* London, 1912.

Farnell, L. R., *Cults of the Greek States,* 5 vols. Oxford, 1896–1909.

Greene, W. C., *Moira: Fate, Good and Evil, in Greek Thought.* Cambridge, Mass., 1944.

Jaeger, Werner, *Paideia.* Translated by Gilbert Highet from the 2d German ed. as *Paideia; The Ideals of Greek Culture,* Vol. I, *Archaic Greece, and the Mind of Athens.* Oxford, 1939.

"Nemesis," in *The Oxford Classical Dictionary.* Oxford, 1949. P. 601.

Nilsson, M. P., *Greek Popular Religion.* New York, 1940.

Rohde, Erwin, *Psyche,* 8th ed. Tübingen, 1921. Translated from the 8th German ed. by W. B. Hillis as *Psyche; The Cult of Souls and Belief in Immortality Among the Greeks.* London and New York, 1925.

P. DIAMANDOPOULOS

NEMESIUS OF EMESA (fl. c. 390), the author of a treatise, "On the Nature of Man" (*De Natura Hominis*), which is the earliest extant handbook of theological or philosophical "anthropology." All that is known of his life is that he was probably bishop of Emesa in Syria.

As a Christian, Nemesius viewed the Bible as his primary authority, but he derived the content of his work chiefly from Galen's *On the Use of the Parts of the Body,* which is superior to Nemesius' treatise both in thoroughness and originality; from Origen's *Commentary on Genesis;* and from some commentators on Aristotle, a few works by the Neoplatonist Porphyry, and doxographical materials. His subjects and sources can be outlined as follows: Ch. 1, man in the creation (Galen, Origen); Chs. 2–3, the soul and the body (doxographical, Porphyry, Galen); Chs. 4–5, the body and the elements (Galen); Chs. 6–14, the faculties of the soul, including human development, the senses, thought and memory, reason and speech (Galen, Porphyry); Chs. 15–28, the parts of the soul, the passions, and such matters as the nutritive and generative faculties and respiration (mostly Galen); Chs. 29–41, freedom, possibility, and fate (commentaries on Aristotle, Neoplatonists); Chs. 42–44, providence (in part ultimately from Posidonius, in part from Christian theologians).

In the last part of his book (Chs. 35 ff.), Nemesius turns from minimizing the function of free will in human affairs (deliberation concerns only indifferent possibilities) to an elaborate attack upon the Stoic doctrine of fate and teaching about destiny. Utilizing Aristotle's distinction between voluntary and involuntary acts, he insists that men actually have free will, that its extent can be discovered (interrelated with the action of providence), and that it was given to mutable men so that they might become immutable. The work ends abruptly and seems to lack a conclusion.

Nemesius argued that the soul is an incorporeal being and is therefore immortal (in his opinion the latter point is also proved by the Bible). The problem of how it is united with the body is solved (Chs. 20–21) by following the Neoplatonist Ammonius. "Intelligibles" are capable of union with things adapted to receive them, but in such a union they remain confused and imperishable. The soul is "in a body" not locally but "in habitual relation of presence." From this analysis Nemesius turns in Ch. 22 to discuss the union of the divine Word with his manhood—as William Telfer points out, thus reversing the usual patristic argument. Nemesius claims that the union in Christ is therefore not by "divine favor" but is "grounded in nature."

Bibliography

The Greek text, with Latin translation, of *De Natura Hominis* is in J. P. Migne, ed., *Patrologia Graeca* (Paris, 1857–1866), Vol. XL, Cols. 508–818. There is an English translation by William Telfer in *Cyril of Jerusalem and Nemesius of Emesa,* Vol. IV of the Library of Christian Classics (Philadelphia, 1955).

For works on Nemesius, see Werner Jaeger, *Nemesios von Emesa* (Berlin, 1914); H. A. Koch, *Quellenuntersuchungen zu Nemesius von Emesa* (Berlin, 1921); Johannes Quasten, *Patrology* (Westminster, Md., 1960), Vol. III, pp. 351–355, which includes a full bibliography. See also the articles by E. Skard, "Nemesiosstudien," in *Symbolae Osloenses,* Vols. 15–16 (1936), 23–43; Vol. 17 (1937), 9–25; Vol. 18 (1938), 31–41; Vol. 19 (1939), 46–56; Vol. 22 (1942), 40–48; and Skard's article "Nemesios," in *Realencyclopädie der classischen Altertumswissenschaft,* Supp. Vol. VII (Stuttgart, 1940), Cols. 562–566.

ROBERT M. GRANT

NEO-KANTIANISM is a term used to designate a group of somewhat similar movements that prevailed in Germany between 1870 and 1920 but had little in common beyond a strong reaction against irrationalism and speculative naturalism and a conviction that philosophy could

be a "science" only if it returned to the method and spirit of Kant. These movements were the fulfillment of Kant's prophecy that in a hundred years his philosophy would come into its own.

Because of the complexity and internal tensions in Kant's philosophy, not all the Neo-Kantians brought the same message from the Sage of Königsberg, and the diversity of their teachings was as great as their quarrels were notorious. At the end of the nineteenth century the Neo-Kantians were as widely separated as the first-generation Kantians had been at its beginning, and the various Neo-Kantian movements developed in directions further characterized by such terms as Neo-Hegelian and Neo-Fichtean. But whereas Hegel, Schelling, Fichte, and others had used the words of Kant while being alien to their spirit, the Neo-Kantians were, on the whole, faithful to the spirit while being revisionists with respect to the letter. Attempting to legitimize their revisions by the *ipsissima verba* of Kant, they established the craft of "Kant-philology" and began an analysis of Kant's texts that had not been equaled in microscopic punctiliousness except in the exegesis of the Bible and of a few classical authors. Hans Vaihinger's immense commentary on the first seventy pages of the *Critique of Pure Reason* (*Commentar zu Kants "Kritik der reinen Vernunft,"* 2 vols., Berlin and Leipzig, 1881–1893) is an exemplar of this craft and industry.

Neo-Kantianism grew out of the peculiar social–cultural situation of German science and philosophy, and in turn it constituted a new academic situation with many characteristics of a long intellectual fad. Most of the groups of Neo-Kantians had their own journals—the *Philosophische Arbeiten* at Marburg, *Logos* at Heidelberg, the *Annalen der Philosophie und philosophischer Kritik* of Vaihinger, and the *Philosophische Abhandlungen* at Göttingen. (*Kant-Studien,* like the Kant *Gesellschaft,* was open to all.) Doctrines were known by the names of the universities where they originated; men entered and left the movement as if it were a church or political party; members of one school blocked the appointments and promotions of members of the others; eminent Kant scholars and philosophers who did not found their own schools or accommodate themselves to one of the established schools tended to be neglected as outsiders and contemned as amateurs. As many as seven distinct schools have been described by historians, but they do not agree on the programs, heresies, and bona fide membership of each school.

THE BEGINNINGS

So far as an intellectual movement can be said to have a beginning at a specific moment of time, Neo-Kantianism began with the publication at Stuttgart in 1865 of Otto Liebmann's *Kant und die Epigonen,* whose motto—"Back to Kant!"—has become famous. German philosophy was generally weak toward the middle of the nineteenth century; there was less interest in it, and less ability among its practitioners, than at perhaps any other time in modern German history. Earlier in the century, when Kant's philosophy had been submerged first in the great idealistic systems and then in those of nature-philosophy, there had been modest calls for a return to Kant (for instance, by I. H. Fichte, the son of J. G. Fichte, and by Ernst Reinhold, the son of K. L. Reinhold) as a means of escape from the kinds of philosophy that Kant would have held to be impossible and that seemed more and more to offer nothing of value to German cultural life as a counterbalance to the materialism attendant upon the flourishing of natural science, technology, and national economy. However, in the decade preceding Liebmann's book there had been signs of change.

Zeller and Fischer. Eduard Zeller (1814–1908), in his Heidelberg lecture, *Ueber Bedeutung und Aufgabe der Erkenntnistheorie* (published Heidelberg, 1862), called for a return to epistemology; and this, he spelled out explicitly, meant a return to Kant. Kuno Fischer (1824–1907), the greatest historian of philosophy at that time and the teacher of Liebmann, Johannes Volkelt, and Wilhelm Windelband, in 1860 published a monumental book on Kant (*Kants Leben und die Grundlagen seiner Lehre*, Mannheim and Heidelberg) that presented, in a form still useful although outmoded in details, a picture of Kant that could not but excite interest in and study of Kant. In 1865 Fischer initiated a great controversy with Adolf Trendelenburg on the proper interpretation of Kant's theory of space; this controversy mobilized most of the philosophical public in Germany on one side or the other, including Trendelenburg's pupil Hermann Cohen, who had hitherto concentrated mostly on Plato.

Helmholtz and Lange. Two other men, Hermann von Helmholtz and F. A. Lange, almost simultaneously with Liebmann made their spiritual pilgrimage to Königsberg.

Helmholtz. Hermann von Helmholtz (1821–1894), then Germany's greatest scientist, had been arguing for years for a view whose origin he found in Kant. The doctrine of specific energies of sensory nerves had led him to a theory of the subjectivity of sensory qualities, which he regarded as signs of unknown objects interacting with our sense organs; he then extended this commonly held view to the conclusion that space itself is dependent upon our bodily constitution. This theory made it possible for Helmholtz to argue that there could be alternative spaces and geometries, each appropriate to a particular kind of nervous apparatus and necessary to the being so constituted, but none of them picturing the real structure of the world. Thus, while Helmholtz gave up Kant's theory of the unique status of Euclidean geometry, he held that his own theory of space was in keeping both with Kant's theory and with the most modern work in mathematics, physics, and physiology. Moreover, in his theory of unconscious inferences he accepted the Kantian theory that perception involves judgment. The guiding principle in such unconscious inference is the a priori principle of causation, which extends our knowledge no farther than possible experience, but gives us the right to posit unknown causes of our sensations. Helmholtz vigorously rejected metaphysics but extolled philosophy as an ancilla to science. Both the strengths and the obvious weaknesses of Helmholtz' Kantianism were effective in making a return to Kant seem fruitful to science, for it meant that the greatest of German thinkers could be used on the side of science, against metaphysics.

Lange. The year 1866 saw the publication of Friedrich Albert Lange's *Geschichte des Materialismus* (Iserlohn and Leipzig; translated by E. C. Thomas as *History of Materialism*, 3 vols., London, 1877–1879). Lange, who was born in 1828 and died, while professor of philosophy at Marburg, in 1875, wrote his massive but readable book to point out the metaphysical mysteries and pretensions of materialism, which traditionally claimed to be only a courageous but unspeculative extension of the results of science into regions previously occupied only by theology and superstition. Like Helmholtz, Lange held that the sensible world is a product of the interaction between the human organism and an unknown reality. The world of experience is determined by this interaction, but the organism itself is only an object of experience, and it is to be understood by psychology and physiology. Causality, needed in all such sciences, is a mode of thought necessary to a mind constituted like ours; processes and principles of thought have physiological bases. Thus, materialism (although a phenomenal materialism, since matter itself is only a phenomenon) is the most likely truth about reality so far as it can be known. But what of Kant's intelligible world? Lange completely rejected Kant's teaching of the rational necessity of the structure of an intelligible but unknowable world; he held that our views of it are only products of poetic fancy (*Dichtung*). While Lange defended materialism as a doctrine of reality (phenomena) that serves as a bulwark against theology and metaphysics, he held that because knowledge is not man's whole goal, *Dichtung* is also important. "Man needs to supplement reality [about which materialism is the best truth we know] with an ideal world of his own creation," and this is a world of value "against which neither logic nor touch of hand nor sight of eye can prevail" (*History of Materialism*, Vol. III, pp. 342 and 347).

Two things stand out in the works of these precursors—if not direct progenitors—of Neo-Kantianism. Their Kantianism was exclusively theoretical, oriented entirely around the *Critique of Pure Reason* and neglectful or disdainful of Kant's practical philosophy. This puts them in the line of development of German positivism, a line that goes from them through Alois Riehl and the fictionalist Hans Vaihinger to Ernst Mach and Moritz Schlick. Their Kantianism was also psychological and even physiological—the a priori elements they acknowledged were dependent upon the human constitution; the transcendental and logical aspects of Kant's work were neglected or rejected. In this respect they were followed by Hans Cornelius (1863–1947) and by Richard Hönigswald (1875–1947), a pupil of Riehl.

METAPHYSICAL NEO-KANTIANISM

Theoretical and physiological Kantianism was in the air when the 25-year-old Liebmann published his manifesto. *Kant und die Epigonen* argued that Kant made one great mistake: believing in the existence of the thing-in-itself. This belief, however, was not an essential part of Kant's doctrine, but only a dogmatic residue that could be removed without damage to the rest of the system. However, Fichte, Schelling, Hegel, Fries, Herbart, and Schopenhauer either did not recognize the belief that there is a thing-in-itself as an error (for instance, Schopenhauer) or, while recognizing it as an error, made analogous errors in their efforts to correct it (Fichte's transcendental ego is as unknowable and unthinkable as the thing-in-itself). The weaknesses thus introduced into their systems were fatal, since they depended upon a concept that Kant had only inadvertently admitted. Hence, none of them could be followed; one had to return to their common source, remove its error, and apply this improved Kantianism to present problems.

While Liebmann's first book showed remnants of a psychological interpretation of Kant, his next book, *Zur Analysis der Wirklichkeit* (Strasbourg, 1876) argued for a strictly transcendental "logic of facts" whose inspiration was as much Spinozistic as Kantian. In this book Liebmann stood close to the Marburg school, at least in his conclusions. However, in his later *Gedanken und Tatsachen* (2 vols., Strasbourg, 1882–1901) he admitted the need and argued for the possibility of a "critical metaphysics" as a "rigorous consideration of human views and hypotheses about the essence of things," growing out of "deep-rooted, ineradicable spiritual needs and intellectual duty" (*ibid.*, 2d ed., Vol. II, p. 113). His critical metaphysics makes hypotheses about the transcendent and the unknowable, but leaves open a field for value decisions that do not depend on claims to valid knowledge, but only on our wills as they are nurtured by culture. In this line of thought Liebmann seemed to draw closer to the Heidelberg school, but even in his earlier work there were anticipations of Windelband's famous analysis of the differences between historical and scientific knowledge.

Riehl. Less openly metaphysical than Liebmann's was the realistic Neo-Kantianism of Alois Riehl (1844–1924). In contrast to Liebmann, Riehl insisted that Kant held to the real existence of things-in-themselves and that this concept is essential to Kant's—and to any sound—theory of knowledge. He asserted that Kant proved only that things-in-themselves cannot be known by pure reason, not that they are not known mediately in sense perception. Phenomena are simply their modes of appearance; they are not in a different ontological realm, but are merely actualizations of their Aristotelian potentialities in the context of a mind. The laws of the organization of phenomena are transcendentally (not psychologically) based on the activity of self-consciousness; their specific characteristics depend on the reality of that of which they are appearances. All knowledge is or can become scientific; philosophy is nothing but a theory of science; metaphysics is "an opiate of the mind."

Nevertheless, Riehl believed it both unavoidable and legitimate to reason hypothetically from phenomena to reality, for metaphysical hypotheses cannot be entirely excluded from science itself. He argued, for instance, for a double-aspect psychophysical theory of the relationship between mind and the world, for a partial duplication of phenomenal laws in the real world, and for complete determinism. The tone of his philosophy, however, was somewhat positivistic; he said he acknowledged "the metaphysical" but not "metaphysics." With *wissenschaftliche* (scientific) philosophy he contrasted *unwissenschaftliche* philosophy, or classical speculative metaphysics, which he

rejected; and with both he contrasted *nichtwissenschaftliche* philosophy as a practical discipline for the realization of humanly created values (*Wertbegung* and *Geistesführung*). In his later life he was most concerned with the latter.

Other metaphysical interpretations. Another realistic metaphysical interpretation of Kant was given by the Kant philologist Erich Adickes (1866–1928) in his *Kants Lehre von der doppelten Affektion unseres Ich* (Tübingen, 1929).

Other attempts at "critical metaphysics" on a Kantian basis were made by Johannes Volkelt (1848–1930) and by Friedrich Paulsen (1846–1908). The former's *Kants Erkenntnistheorie* (Leipzig, 1879) and the latter's *Entwicklungsgeschichte der Kantischen Erkenntnistheorie* (Leipzig, 1875) tried to show that Kant himself was an idealistic metaphysician *malgré lui*. Later works designed to bring out the metaphysics in Kant were by Max Wundt (*Kant als Metaphysiker*, Stuttgart, 1924), Heinz Heimsoeth (articles collected in *Studien zur Philosophie Immanuel Kants*, Cologne, 1956), and Gottfried Martin (*Kant, Ontologie und Wissenschaftslehre*, Cologne, 1951; translated by P. G. Lucas as *Kant's Metaphysics and Theory of Science*, Manchester and New York, 1955). Martin Heidegger's *Kant und das Problem der Metaphysik* (Bonn, 1929; translated by J. S. Churchill as *Kant and the Problem of Metaphysics*, Bloomington, Indiana, 1962) presented an extreme form of this view but falls outside the scope of Neo-Kantian intentions.

MARBURG NEO-KANTIANISM

By the standards of recent philosophy Marburg Neo-Kantianism, or panlogistic transcendental philosophy, was no less metaphysical, but by the standards of the time its orientation around the "fact of science" seemed to make it at least antispeculative. In launching the journal of the Marburg school, Hermann Cohen and Paul Natorp wrote: "Whoever is bound to us stands with us on the foundation of the transcendental method. . . . Philosophy, to us, is bound to the fact of science, as this elaborates itself. Philosophy, therefore, to us is the theory of the principles of science and therewith of all culture" (*Philosophische Arbeiten*, Vol. I, No. 1, 1906).

Hermann Cohen. Hermann Cohen (1842–1918), a younger colleague of Lange's at Marburg, rejected the naturalism he believed to be inherent in the Kantianism of Helmholtz, Lange, and Liebmann. They were wrong in thinking philosophy should begin with an analysis of consciousness and should show how conscious human beings apply concepts to the data of sensation in order to produce phenomenalistic world pictures that are distinguished from things as they are. The fact to be understood is not this highly dubious psychological process; the fact is science itself and, in ethics, it is not human motives and aspirations and feelings of duty but the fact of civil society under law as constructed in the science of jurisprudence. Kant himself had tried to understand "the fact of science and culture," but he failed to separate this fact from dubious psychological and phenomenological facts he seemed to be dealing with.

Logic for Cohen is not at all psychologistic; it is not even formal. The very notion of formal logic presupposes something not formal: data drawn from some other source, be it pure intuition or perception. Logic, as Cohen saw it, is the logic of knowledge, not the logic of empty thought; it is the logic of truth, in which any assertion gains its status as true solely by virtue of its systematic position in a body of universal laws that, in turn, require each other on methodological grounds. Thought, Cohen taught, accepts nothing as given and is not true of anything independent of it—certainly not of intuitional data, as Kant believed. Thought generates content as well as form, and the content of self-contained thought is reality itself as object and goal of knowledge. This extravagant panlogism was based on Cohen's ingenious interpretation of the history of the differential calculus, which he saw as the logic of mathematical physics. Not number and not observed motion, as Kant believed, are given as raw data to science; rather, the mathematical differential, which is not given at all but is created by thought, is the necessary device for the creation of nature as object of possible experience: "This mathematical generation of motion [by integration of the derivative] and thereby nature itself is the triumph of pure thinking" (*Logik der reinen Erkenntnis*, Berlin, 1902, p. 20). Through an interpretation of Kant's teachings concerning intensive magnitudes of sensations, Cohen saw in the method of the calculus a paradigm of the category of origin (*Ursprung*) and the logical process of production (*Erzeugung*) to which every fact owes its reality; that is, its position in a logically necessary scheme.

Through the work of thought on its own materials, Cohen believed he could dispense with all independent givens in knowledge. Nothing is given (*gegeben*); all is problematic (*aufgegeben*). Fact is that which is completely determined by thought. The thing-in-itself is not a thing at all. It does not exist, but is only a thought of a limit (*Grenzbegriff*) to our approach to a complete determination of things as they are; that is, as they would fully satisfy systematic thought.

Cohen's pupil Cassirer spoke of him as "one of the most resolute Platonists that has ever appeared in the history of philosophy." When Cohen said, for example, "Thinking itself produces what is to be held to be" (*ibid.*, p. 67; cf. p. 402), he was not speaking of thought as a process in an individual. "Thought" is not the name of a process, but refers only to the corpus of the unending history of science. To be, then, is to be thought, but not to be thought in somebody's consciousness; to be thought means to be asserted under valid and immanent a priori principles that inescapably determine the unique structure of mathematical physics. Cohen was as much of a dogmatist as Kant himself with regard to the structure of science.

The original stages of Cohen's teachings are found in his three commentaries on Kant (*Kants Theorie der Erfahrung*, Berlin, 1871; *Kants Begrundung der Ethik*, Berlin, 1877; *Kants Begrundung der Aesthetik*, Berlin, 1889), one on each *Critique*. They are continuous criticisms of all of Kant's "givens"; for example, experience, intuition, categories, duty, things-in-themselves. The final stages are contained in his three systematic works (*Logik der reinen Erkenntnis*, Berlin, 1902; *Ethik des reinen Willens*, Berlin, 1904; *Aesthetik des reinen Gefühls*, 2 vols., Berlin, 1912), which parallel the three *Critiques*. At its midpoint Cohen's thought was close to the contemporary rejections of psychologism by Meinong and Husserl; at its end it would have taken only the "bathos of experience," to use Kant's words, to change it, in principle, into a kind of positivism or even historicism.

Natorp. The principal thinker among the second generation of Marburg Neo-Kantians was Paul Natorp (1854–1924). It fell to him to deal with the new developments in science (especially the theory of relativity, in his *Die logischen Grundlagen der exakten Wissenschaften*, Leipzig, 1910) by penetrating to a deeper level of methodology than Cohen could reach in his own work, which was largely restricted to classical mathematics and physics.

More important, it was Natorp's task to introduce the whole field of psychology into the body of knowledge considered and understood in Cohen's way, and thereby to fill the lacuna Cohen left between *Bewusstsein überhaupt* (consciousness in general, the "fact" of science) and the limited individual human consciousness. Natorp's *Einleitung in die Psychologie* (Freiburg, 1888) and his *Allgemeine Psychologie nach kritischer Methode* (Tübingen, 1912) attempted, first, to apply Cohen's transcendental method to psychology instead of leaving it exposed to the naturalistic methods of Cohen's and Natorp's rivals, such as Riehl. In this attempt Natorp came close to results like those of Dilthey without, he thought, having to draw his relativistic, skeptical, and historicistic conclusions. And, second, these books attempted to bridge the gap between the objective world of phenomena and the nonphenomenal, nonnatural self that possessed the knowledge of the phenomenal world. Cohen had moved so far from Kant toward Hegel that it was for him an almost insignificant accident that individual men and women know anything; *Bewusstheit* (known-ness), not *Bewusstsein* (consciousness), was important for him. Natorp had to undertake another almost Copernican revolution against objective panlogism without at the same time naturalizing the knowing subject, which would have led to relativism and skepticism.

He performed the first part of his task by the classical Kantian move of seeing empirical ego and empirical object as standing in a necessary correlation with each other, not as independent phenomena; the latter part he accomplished by insisting that the pure ego cannot be an object—it is as much a *Grenzbegriff* as the thing-in-itself. For Natorp the objective and the subjective were not two realms, either opposed to each other or one including the other. Rather, they were two directions of knowledge, objectification and subjectification, each starting from the same phenomenon and each employing the transcendental method of categorial constitution, resolution into *Ursprung* and *Erzeugung*. Just as Cohen's antipsychologistic panlogism had brought him close to Husserl's *Logische Untersuchungen*, Natorp's linking of psychology and panlogism brought him close to Husserl's *Ideen*; and it is easy to see how Nicolai Hartmann, Natorp's pupil, could move over into the phenomenological camp (J. Klein, "Hartmann und die Marburger Schule," in Heinz Heimsoeth and Robert Heiss, *Nicolai Hartmann, der Denker und sein Werk*, Göttingen, 1952).

Cassirer. The last great representative of Marburg Neo-Kantianism was Ernst Cassirer (1874–1945), whose works on the philosophy of science continued the line of argument initiated by Natorp and show some close resemblances to positivism. Cassirer's most important contribution, however, was to extend the Marburg conception of *Erzeugung* to the whole range of human culture (language, myth, art, religion, statecraft), ending not in panlogism but in "pansymbolism."

Other important Marburg Neo-Kantians were Rudolf Stammler (1856–1938) in the philosophy of law; Karl Vorländer (1860–1928), the historian of philosophy and the leading Kantian socialist (*Kant und der Sozialismus*, Berlin, 1900; *Kant und Marx*, Tübingen, 1911); Artur Buchenau (1879–1946), Albert Görland (1869–1952), and Arthur Liebert (1878–1946). A moderate form of Marburg Neo-Kantianism is represented in America by W. H. Werkmeister (*The Basis and Structure of Knowledge*, New York, 1948).

GÖTTINGEN NEO-KANTIANISM

In strong reaction against Marburg there arose, at the beginning of the twentieth century, the Neo-Friesian school in Göttingen, under the leadership of Leonard Nelson (1882–1927). Jakob Friedrich Fries (1773–1843) had interpreted Kant psychologically, not transcendentally; in this he was followed by Jürgen Bona Meyer (1829–1897) in his *Kants Psychologie* (Berlin, 1870). Lange and Helmholtz were psychologistic in their Kantianism, taking the results of experimental psychology as having a bearing on the a priori. Nelson, on the contrary, professed to avoid psychologism and its attendant skepticism by using psychological introspection to discover the principles of experience in the spontaneity of reason; these principles could then be deduced (in the Kantian sense) from the analysis of experience into its necessary conditions. In this, Nelson developed the views of Fries, whom he defended against the accusation of psychologism, and opposed the psychological or physiological interpretations of the experimental and empirical psychologists.

Kant's transcendental deduction was regarded by Nelson as circular if it was meant as a proof; it began with the experience (science, mathematics, morality) it was meant to justify. The circle might have been broken by Kant's subjective deduction, but this was jettisoned in the second edition of the *Critique*. Nelson proposed to re-establish it, or rather to put his own deduction into its place. Upon introspection, we find principles we know immediately to be true and that we hold by a Cartesian-like "principle of the self-confidence of reason." The discovery of these self-evident principles is a psychological process; the principles, however, are not psychological but metaphysical in Kant's sense; that is, as a priori synthetic truths based on concepts, not on intuition. They are shown to be the same as those uncovered by a transcendental analysis of science and ordinary experience. (In ethics Nelson followed an analogous procedure.) In this way Nelson thought he could use psychology without falling prey to either naturalism or skepticism. A good example of his method is to be found in the well-known *Das Heilige* (Gotha, 1917; translated by J. W. Harvey as *The Idea of the Holy*, New York, 1958) by Nelson's colleague Rudolf Otto. Nelson never had the influence in Germany that was enjoyed by many other Neo-Kantians, although he was revered by many disciples in fields related to philosophy. There has recently been an increased interest in his work, and several English translations have appeared.

HEIDELBERG NEO-KANTIANISM

The Heidelberg school of Neo-Kantianism, led by Windelband and Rickert, was not restricted to the University of Heidelberg, and is sometimes known as the Baden school or the Southwest German school of Neo-Kantianism. Wilhelm Windelband (1848–1915) was the most eminent historian of philosophy of his time, with the possible exception of Dilthey. Like Dilthey, he did not succeed in working out a complete system of philosophy, but certain of his ideas were decisive for the more systematic work of his followers in Heidelberg. His most characteristic doctrine was that the epistemological problem is really a problem in axiology; a judgment is known to be true not by comparison with an object (thing-in-itself) but by its conformity to an immediately experienced obligation to believe it. The teaching for which Windelband is chiefly remembered, however, was his distinction between natural and historical sciences as nomothetic and ideographic (law-giving and picturing the unique individual), respectively. The elaboration of these two points led to the systematic priority of axiological criteria to epistemological criteria, to the theory of the parallelism of norms and cultural consciousness, and to efforts to develop a Kantian categorization of historical and cultural experience.

Rickert. The great system builder of the Heidelberg school was Heinrich Rickert (1863–1936), professor in Freiburg and then Windelband's successor in Heidelberg. Rickert, like Windelband, regarded judging as a form of valuing, truth being the value intended by this act. There are two realms of objects that may be judged; that is, that are objects of knowledge—the sensible world of science (about which Rickert accepted most of Kant's views) and an intelligible world of nonsensuous objects of experience that we know not by perception but by understanding (*Verstehen*). These latter are cultural objects (history, art, morality, institutions). Although not reducible to sense and thus not under the categories of nature, they are not metaphysical but are within experience and correspond, roughly, to Hegel's objective spirit. Both cultural objects and nature, as objects, require (in the Kantian manner) a correlative subject that cannot be objectified. This is "the third realm of being," which Rickert calls "pro-physical"; it is Kant's transcendental ego and Hegel's subjective spirit. There is a fourth realm of being, the metaphysical proper, which is only an object of faith (in the Kantian sense) and which we refer to in religion and in the transition from scientific philosophy to *Weltanschauung*.

By keeping the ethical "this side" of the division between the experiential and the metaphysical, Rickert was able to bring about a closer liaison between the theoretical and the practical than Kant had established. The primacy of practical reason does not, for Rickert, mark the supremacy of valuing over knowing, but signifies the valuational dimension of knowing itself. Autonomy is thus the basis not only of ethics but also of thought even in science.

Rickert criticized the Kantian conception of experience as too thin; not only nature, but also history, must be categorized out of the heterogeneous continuum of data, and from these categorizations arise the nomothetic and ideographic disciplines. In all these points Rickert was under the influence of both Fichte and Hegel, but his conceptual framework remained Kantian: a transcendental nonobjectifiable basis (realm 3) for experience (realms 1 and 2) and an unknown realm of objects of faith (realm 4).

Others. Other important Heidelberg Neo-Kantians were Hugo Münsterberg (1863–1916), Jonas Cohn (1869–1947), Bruno Bauch (1877–1942; *Wahrheit, Wert und Wirklichkeit*, Leipzig, 1923), and Richard Kroner (*Von Kant bis Hegel*, 2 vols., Tübingen, 1921–1924). Kroner's *Kant's Weltanschauung* (Tübingen, 1914; translated by J. E. Smith, Chicago and Cambridge, 1956) is the only presentation in English of the characteristic Heidelberg interpretation of the historical Kant.

SOCIOLOGICAL NEO-KANTIANISM

Several philosophers close to *Lebensphilosophie* and concerned with the methodology of the *Geisteswissenschaften* were influenced by Kant's doctrine that we categorially construct the world of experience and that speculative metaphysics is impossible as science, but instead of having theories concerning the transcendental origin of the structural factors, they found the origin of the world of experience in the social situation. The most important of these philosophers were Wilhelm Dilthey (1833–1912), who is not usually characterized as a Neo-Kantian although Kantian elements are present in his thought, and Georg Simmel (1858–1918).

At various times Simmel took different attitudes toward, or at least emphasized different aspects of, Kantianism —the psychologistic and pragmatic, the transcendental, and the sociohistorical. He held that categories develop in the course of history, and that the structures of Hegel's objective spirit are historical products that cannot be taken ready-made for analysis in the Marburg manner. "[Even] the kind of science humanity has at any given moment depends upon the kind of humanity it is at that moment" (*Hauptprobleme der Philosophie*, Leipzig, 1910, Ch. 1). Because forms cannot be discerned except in the specific contents in which they appear, no categorial system is capable of structuring all experience. Different types of individuals have different styles for this structuring, and cultures are identified by their production of specifie a priori forms for knowledge, the experience of values, and images of the world as a whole (systems of metaphysics).

Between the Heidelberg tradition and the Dilthey–Simmel position there were Max Weber (1864–1921) and Eduard Spranger. Neo-Kantian elements in the sociology of knowledge are especially clear in the works of Max Adler (*Das Soziologische in Kants Erkenntniskritik*, Vienna, 1924) and Karl Mannheim (1893–1947).

Windelband said, "To understand Kant means to go beyond Kant." Most of the philosophers dealt with here did go beyond Kant, and their later works contained little that was specifically Kantian. Even the movements as a whole were more explicitly Kantian in their early periods than in their later ones. All this was to be expected of active and creative minds and groups. By the end of World War I, Neo-Kantianism as an institution ceased to be a dominant force in German intellectual life, partly through the death of most of its leaders and partly through defection. Rapid changes in logic and natural science favored the more pragmatic systems of positivism in Berlin, Prague, and Vienna; the greater experiential resources of phenomenology favored the rival school in Freiburg, Munich, and Cologne; the German cultural crisis called for *Lebensphilosophie* and speculative metaphysics. None of these movements, however, was free of Kantian elements, which might not have been passed on to them but for the Neo-Kantians' rediscovery of Kant. Their Neo-Kantian heritage has given repeated confirmation of an aphorism attributed to Liebmann: "You can philosophize with Kant, or you can philosophize against Kant, but you cannot philosophize without Kant."

Bibliography

Studies of and works by individual Neo-Kantians are listed in the respective articles. There is very little material in English on Neo-Kantianism, but see Ernst Cassirer, "Neo-Kantianism," in *Encyclopaedia Britannica*, 14th ed. (1930), Vol. XVI, pp. 215–216 and R. B. Perry, *Philosophy of the Recent Past* (New York, 1926), pp. 145–160. A complete history is being written by Mariano Campo; Vol. I of his *Schizzo storico della esegesi e critica kantiana* (Varese, 1959) covers the period up to about 1900. The most complete study, with excellent bibliographies, is K. Oesterreich in *Friedrich Überwegs Grundriss der Geschichte der Philosophie*, 12th ed. (Berlin, 1923), Vol. IV, pp. 410–483.

G. Lehmann reports the beginnings of the movement in "Kant im Spätidealismus und die Anfänge der neukantischen Bewegung," in *Zeitschrift für philosophische Forschung*, Vol. 17 (1963), 438–457; see also his "Voraussetzungen und Grenzen der systematischen Kantinterpretation," in *Kant-Studien*, Vol. 49 (1957), 364–388. Almost all books on recent German philosophy in the bibliography to GERMAN PHILOSOPHY have chapters on Neo-Kantianism.

Good comparative studies of Neo-Kantianism are included in Wolfgang Ritzel, *Studien zum Wandeln der Kantauffassung* (Meisenheim, 1952) and H. Levy, *Die Hegel-Renaissance in der deutschen Philosophie* (Berlin, 1927). Johannes Hessen, *Die Religionsphilosophie des Neukantianismus* (Freiburg, 1924) gives a Catholic criticism.

Authoritative presentations of two school programs are Paul Natorp, *Kant und die Marburger Schule* (Berlin, 1912; also in *Kant-Studien*, Vol. 17, 1912, 193–221) and Heinrich Rickert, *Die Heidelberger Tradition und Kants Kritizismus* (Berlin, 1934). The posthumously published (and incomplete) work by H. Dussort, *L'École de Marburg* (Paris, 1963) is excellent on the movement up through Cohen.

LEWIS WHITE BECK

NEO-MANICHAEISM. See MANI AND MANICHAEISM.

NEOPLATONISM is the philosophy of Plotinus and Platonists influenced by him without necessarily accepting all his doctrines. Neoplatonism absorbed virtually all nonmaterialist and religious doctrines of earlier systems (especially the Pythagorean, Peripatetic, and Stoic) and is the only significant school of antiquity since the beginning of the fourth century, a school that undertook to satisfy all intellectual and religious aspirations of man. Its end in the East was marked by the Arab conquest of Alexandria, in

642, rather than by the closing of the school of Athens, in 529. But it survived in some form in the Islamic world and also in Byzantium. There, only a few decades before the conquest, Stephanus, a member of the Alexandrian school, was appointed to the University of Constantinople (where Platonism had been taught before his appointment anyway). Furthermore, Latin Neoplatonism continued without a break in the Western Roman Empire and its medieval successor states. The resurgence of Neoplatonism in the Renaissance (Pletho in the East, Ficino in the West) and in seventeenth-century England (the Cambridge Platonists) is remarkable. It should be stressed that these Neoplatonists considered themselves, and were considered to be, orthodox Platonists. Only in the seventeenth century did a reaction set in. It reached its apogee in the nineteenth century, when Platonism became sharply distinguished from Neoplatonism. At present some counterreaction can be observed.

This article will present only the post-Plotinian Platonism of the Greco-Roman world. Following Karl Praechter, it will distinguish as the main currents of Neoplatonism (1) the metaphysical-speculative version, (2) the "theurgic" school of Pergamum, (3) the "scholarly" school in Alexandria, and (4) Latin Neoplatonism. It will stress doctrines different from those of Plotinus.

Metaphysical-speculative Neoplatonism. The metaphysical-speculative version of Neoplatonism included within it the school of Plotinus, represented mainly by Porphyry; the Syrian school of Iamblichus; and the school of Athens.

School of Plotinus. Whereas Plotinus rejected Aristotle's categories as inapplicable to the realm of the Intelligible and modified them as they pertained to the realm of the Sensible, Porphyry accepted them and wrote several commentaries on Aristotle's work on the subject, *Categories.* He thus started the wholesale reception of Aristotle by Neoplatonism that made commentaries on Aristotle's works as common as those on Plato. An opposite tendency of pre-Plotinian Platonism, represented by Atticus, who had declared that the philosophies of Plato and Aristotle were utterly incompatible (and that of Aristotle worthless), was rejected. Eventually the opinion prevailed in Neoplatonism that Aristotle should be studied as an introduction to the higher wisdom of Plato, though with exceptions Neoplatonists remained conscious of some fundamental differences between the two. Porphyry's "Introduction" to the study of categories (introducing genus, species, specific difference, *proprium,* and accident as five basic concepts) became one of the fundamental philosophical books of the Middle Ages.

A bitter enemy of Christianity, Porphyry wrote "Against Christians"; his anti-Christian attitude continued in the schools of Syria, Pergamum, and Athens. Porphyry was more interested in soteriology than Plotinus had been (he stressed more than his master the element of will and guilt implied in the "fall" of the soul resulting in its incarnation) and recognized in oracles a source of philosophic wisdom (he particularly admired the so-called *Chaldaean Oracles*) and in theurgy a means to achieve salvation (that is, the return of the soul to god). It is assumed that under the influence of Plotinus he adopted a more spiritual interpretation of religion, which led him to criticize the theurgy and other aspects of the Egyptian religion (for which he, in turn, was criticized by his pupil Iamblichus). But his plea for asceticism, including vegetarianism, written after his acquaintance with Plotinus, still contained some magical reasons for abstinence. However, he limited theurgical practices to the lower degrees of salvation while demanding strictly spiritual means for the highest degree. Porphyry also wrote a number of strictly scholarly works on philology, history, astronomy, and acoustics.

Syrian school of Iamblichus. Iamblichus' favorable attitude toward theurgy has already been mentioned. His religious interest also led him to identifications of abstract principles with divinities of Greek and non-Greek polytheism and to theologizing numbers in the footsteps of the Pythagorean Nicomachus of Gerasa (Iamblichus considered Plato, Aristotle, and himself to be Pythagoreans). Developing some tendencies of Plotinus, he subdivided his three hypostases (One, Intelligence, Psyche) by assuming a higher and a lower One. Perhaps following Porphyry, he interpreted every step of the emanative process as a triad of moments: the inferior emanating from its superior remains in it (*moné*), in that it is still similar to it; leaves it (*proodos*), in that it differs from it; and returns to it (*epistrophé*), in that it "desires" it. Iamblichus developed an entirely unphilological system of Plato exegesis: he accepted the division of reality (and therefore of all knowledge), ascribed to Plato by Aristotle, into physics, mathematics (equated with "psychology" by many Platonists since Posidonius), and metaphysics (theology) and then felt entitled to interpret every part of a dialogue from all or any of the corresponding points of view. In all respects he profoundly influenced the school of Athens.

School of Athens. The school of Athens was Plato's Academy turned Plotinian, with Plutarch of Athens (c. 350–433) being its first scholarch known to us to have been of this persuasion. He interpreted Aristotle's noetics, which Platonists, at least since Albinus, had adopted in most of its psychological and theological aspects. Syrianus, who succeeded Plutarch about 431 or 432, defended Plato and the Pythagoreans from Aristotle and made full use of their dualism, as Aristotle presented it.

The school culminated in Proclus (c. 409–c. 487). Two of his works, *Elements of Theology* and *Plato's Theology,* are systematic expositions of Neoplatonism. He greatly enriched the emanative schema of Neoplatonism, particularly by adding to the "vertical" emanation a "horizontal" one: in every hypostasis (and its subdivisions) the first vertically derived member acts as a monad engendering a horizontal series of monads belonging to the same hypostasis—for example, Intelligence as a monad engenders a series of monadic intelligences. This is true even of the Ineffable One: it engenders Ones, called henads (probably corresponding to Plato's Ideal Numbers). In each of these horizontal series, in addition to its peculiar monad, which corresponds to the Platonic–Pythagorean concept of limit, another principle, indeterminateness, plays a role. The result is a system that, paradoxically, is "vertically" monistic but "horizontally" dualistic. The great number of entities resulting from this double emanation, all in some way concatenated, Proclus identified with divinities of polytheism, beginning with the identification of henads with highest gods. Proclus and his predecessors probably started from a belief in the existence of all gods of polytheism and tried to construct a philosophic system that could accommodate and "hierarchicize" all of them. After all, the titles of his books mentioned above clearly indicate that their ultimate concern is theology. That Proclus fervently admired the *Chaldaean Oracles* and wrote a number of prayers in hymn form agrees with this.

As Proclus developed the triad "remaining–proceeding–returning," the whole emanative process acquired a static aspect: procession and return proceed *pari passu*. Only as far as man's soul is concerned does process have a temporal and kinetic quality: the soul may or may not return to the One in a condition of ecstasy. It can do so because in addition to Soul and Intelligence man possesses a faculty superior to Intelligence. There is no trace of gnostic pessimism in Proclus: matter is not evil, nor has evil any subsistence, and there is nothing wrong with the soul's complete descent into a body. Like Porphyry, Proclus also wrote on many strictly scholarly problems in the fields of mathematics, astronomy, physics, and literary criticism.

Proclus, the enemy of Christianity, was the fountainhead of much of medieval Christian philosophy, both scholastic and mystical. One of the reasons was that a man who pretended to be, and was for centuries believed to have been, Dionysius the Areopagite (Acts 17.19–34) filled the schema of Proclus, sometimes simply replacing pagan deities with Old and New Testament concepts of cherubim, seraphim, thrones, powers, Christ, the Holy Ghost, etc. If, as some scholars have it, the *Sefer Yezira* ("Book of Creation") was inspired by Proclus, then he must be considered one of the originators of Jewish mysticism, too. In this context it deserves mention that Domninus, who probably preceded Proclus as scholarch, and Marinus, who succeeded Proclus, originally professed Judaism, thus forming a link between Neoplatonism and Judaism. The last Athenian scholarch, Damascius, carried to its extremes the principle that the One is ineffable and can therefore be spoken of only in similes and asserted that the same was true of all steps and products of the emanative process. Thus, neither similarity nor difference, neither priority nor posteriority can be properly attributed to them, so that they all are actually unknowable. Rationalism abdicated to agnosticism.

Damascius' contemporary, Simplicius, deserves particular mention. He tried to harmonize Plato and Aristotle to such an extent that according to him Aristotle never criticized Plato but attacked only misinterpretations of Plato's philosophy.

"Theurgic" school of Pergamum. The school of Pergamum, an offshoot of the school of Iamblichus, seems to have been particularly interested in theurgy. To it belonged Sallust, whose presentation of Neoplatonism related to myths, gods, and the universe was probably intended to help another member of the school, Julian the Apostate (emperor 361–363), in his struggle with Christians. (Julian wrote a book refuting Christianity and promoted paganism by severely restricting the right of Christians to teach.)

Alexandrian school. The Alexandrian school began with Hierocles, Plutarch's pupil. But Hierocles' Platonism had only faint traces of Plotinus and often remained close to pre-Plotinian Platonism. He agreed, for instance, with Origen the Pagan in refusing to recognize a divinity superior to the demiurge. Some of Hierocles' doctrines indicate that he might have been influenced by Christianity, as when he spoke of creation out of nothing or of providence in terms of personal intervention in human affairs by god and his messengers.

Hermias imported the ideas of his master Syrianus into the school. His son Ammonius exhibited a conciliatory attitude toward Christianity, to which he eventually became a convert, though probably in name only. Much of Ammonius' teaching was devoted to interpreting Aristotle's logical writings, where it was easier to remain noncommittal with regard to problems sharply controversial between Christians and Platonists, such as transmigration of souls and the eternity of the world. His exegetical method differed entirely from that of Iamblichus in being sober and "philological," and the same was true of his many students. Of these, some were Christian (Elias, David, Stephanus); some, such as Asclepius and Olympiodorus, were pagan. Olympiodorus, however, tried to present his views with a minimum of offense to Christians.

Most remarkable among the Christians was the Monophysite Johannes Philoponus (a member of a sect of Christian lay brothers calling themselves *philoponos,* "lovers of work"). Philoponus' literary activity was divided between philosophy and theology; in the latter he originated a doctrine known as tritheism (which asserts that the *three* persons of *one* God are on the verge of becoming three gods). He criticized Iamblichus and Proclus and wrote a book against Proclus in which he tried to prove that the world originated temporally and that this was the doctrine of Plato (whom he tried to reconcile with Christianity in other ways, too). Proclus was defended by Simplicius (he spoke of Philoponus with utter disdain), and this polemic between the two excellently illustrates the difference between Athens and Alexandria: at Athens hostility to Christianity to the bitter end, at Alexandria a gradual blending. The students of Ammonius were the last generation of Alexandrian Platonists before the Islamic conquest.

Latin Neoplatonism. In the West, too, some Neoplatonists (fourth–sixth century) were convinced pagans (Praetextatus, Macrobius); others, like Marius Victorinus, the first to explain the Trinity in Neoplatonic categories, were Christians. Most famous among the Christians was Boethius (c. 480–525), who was strongly influenced by Ammonius. In his theological writings on the Trinity, Boethius coined a number of terms that profoundly influenced medieval theology; his translations from and commentaries on Aristotle similarly influenced medieval philosophy. The most famous of his writings, *De Consolatione Philosophiae* (*The Consolation of Philosophy*), is puzzling in its lack of references to Christianity and its inclusion of some doctrines incompatible with Christianity. Yet the book was written while Boethius was imprisoned under suspicion of plotting with Justinian to overthrow Theodoric, a situation in which we might expect a Christian seeking consolation to turn to his religion rather than to Stoic, Peripatetic, or Neoplatonic philosophy. None of the attempted solutions of the puzzle has as yet been universally accepted.

Bibliography

Courcelle, P., *Les Lettres grecques en occident.* Paris, 1948. See especially for Boethius and Ammonius.

Klibansky, Raymond, *The Continuity of the Platonic Tradition During the Middle Ages,* 2d ed. London, 1951.

Ueberweg, Friedrich, and Praechter, Karl, *Die Philosophie des Altertums,* 12th ed. Berlin, 1926. The best introduction to the topic.

Vogel, J. C. de, *Greek Philosophy,* Vol. III. Leiden, 1959. Selection of texts from Porphyry, Iamblichus, Proclus, Damascius.

Westerink, L. G., *Anonymous Prolegomena to Platonic Philosophy.* Amsterdam, 1962. Contains an important introduction on the school of Alexandria. Also on Ammonius' attitude toward Christianity.

Whittaker, T., *The Neoplatonists,* 2d ed. Cambridge, 1918. Includes summaries of some works by Proclus.

Zeller, Eduard, *Die Philosophie der Griechen,* 5th ed., Part III, Vol. II. Leipzig, 1923. Part edited in Italian by Eduard Zeller, Rodolfo Mondolfo, and Giuseppe Martano under the title *La filosofia dei Greci,* translated by Ervino Pocar, Part III, Vol. VI. Florence, 1961. Zeller does not distinguish the Alexandrian school from the Athenian. The Italian edition brings the text up to date; it covers Iamblichus and the post-Iamblichean period.

PHILIP MERLAN

NEO-PYTHAGOREANISM. See PYTHAGORAS AND PYTHAGOREANISM.

NEO-SCHOLASTICISM. See SCOTISM; THOMISM.

NEO-THOMISM. See THOMISM.

NEUMANN, JOHN VON (1903–1957), American mathematician, physicist, and economist. Von Neumann was born in Budapest, Hungary. He showed an early precocity in mathematics and was privately tutored in the subject; his first paper was written before he was 18. He studied at the universities of Berlin, Zurich, and Budapest and received his doctorate in mathematics from Budapest in 1926, almost simultaneously with an undergraduate degree in chemistry from Zurich. After serving as *Privatdozent* at Berlin, he accepted a visiting professorship at Princeton in 1930. Following three years there, he became a professor of mathematics at the Institute for Advanced Study, a position which he held for the rest of his life. In 1955 he was appointed one of the commissioners of the U.S. Atomic Energy Commission, on which he served brilliantly until his death.

Von Neumann made fundamental contributions to mathematics, physics, and economics. Furthermore, these contributions were not disjointed and separate but arise from a common point of view regarding these fields.

Mathematics was always closest to his heart, and it is the field to which he contributed the most. His earliest significant work was in mathematical logic and set theory, topics which occupied him from 1925 to 1929. His accomplishments were of two sorts; they concerned the axiomatics of set theory and David Hilbert's proof theory. In both of these subjects he obtained results of extraordinary importance. He became the first to set up an axiomatic system of set theory that satisfied the two conditions of allowing the development of the theory of the whole series of cardinal numbers and employing axioms that are finite in number and are expressible in the lower calculus of functions. This work contained a full classification of the significance of the axioms with regard to the elimination of the paradoxes. With regard to Hilbert's proof theory, von Neumann clarified the concept of a formal system considerably.

His work on the theory of Hilbert space and operators on that space was probably stimulated by what he had done on rigorous foundations for quantum theory. Essentially, von Neumann demonstrated that the ideas originally introduced by Hilbert are capable of constituting an adequate basis for the physical consideration of quantum theory and that there is no need for the introduction of new mathematical schemes for these physical theories. Von Neumann's papers on these subjects constitute about one-third of his printed work and have stimulated extensive research by other mathematicians.

Von Neumann was one of the founders of the theory of games; since the publication of von Neumann's first paper in 1928 it has become an important combinational theory, applied and developed with continuing vigor. Von Neumann's first paper contains rigorous definitions of the concepts of pure strategy (a complete plan, formulated prior to the contest, that makes all necessary decisions in advance) and of mixed strategy (the use of a chance device to pick the strategy for each contest). The central theorem in this theory, the minimax theorem, was not only enunciated and proved by von Neumann but in his hands became a powerful tool for obtaining new methods for combinatorial problems.

A decade after this fundamental paper was written, von Neumann began a collaboration with Oskar Morgenstern that led to *The Theory of Games and Economic Behavior,* a book that has decisively affected the entire subject of operations research.

Von Neumann's principal interest in his later years was in the possibilities and theory of the computing machine. He not only conceived the concept of the so-called stored program computer in 1944 but he made three other signal contributions. First, he recognized the importance of computing machines for mathematics, physics, economics, and industrial and military problems; second, he translated this insight into active sponsorship of a machine (it was called JOHNIAC by his collaborators) that served as a model for several important computers; third, he was one of the authors of a series of papers that provided a theoretical basis for the logical organization and functioning of computers. These papers set out the complete notion of the flow diagram and contained the genesis of many programming techniques.

Bibliography

Much of von Neumann's work, with the exception of certain still classified reports or papers that are essentially duplicates of other works, is published in *John von Neumann, Collected Works,* 6 vols. (New York, 1961–1963). Other important books by von Neumann are *Continuous Geometry* (Princeton, N.J., 1960); *Mathematical Foundations of Quantum Mechanics* (Princeton, N.J., 1955); *The Computer and the Brain* (New Haven, Conn., 1958).

For a survey of von Neumann's life and work, see the memorial volume *John von Neumann, 1903–1957, Bulletin of the American Mathematical Society*, Vol. 64, No. 3, Part 2 (May 1958).

HERMAN H. GOLDSTINE

NEURATH, OTTO (1882–1945), Austrian sociologist and philosopher, one of the originators of logical empiricism and an independent Marxist socialist. A man of great vitality, intelligence, and good humor, Neurath was a polymath and an energetic organizer of academic, educational, and economic affairs. His major work was in sociology, economic and social planning, scientific method, and visual education, this last especially by means of an international language of simplified pictures ("isotypes"), but he was also interested in the history of science, political and moral theory, economic history, and statistical theory and was engaged in recurrent efforts to create a new encyclopedism.

Economic and comparative history. Neurath's first article, published in 1904, was "Geldzins im Altertum" ("Commercial Interest in Antiquity"), and in 1909 he published a popular history of the economic systems of classical Greece and Rome, *Antike Wirtschaftsgeschichte* (Leipzig, 1909), which he supplemented by shorter studies of ancient economic thought. His historical interests then turned to physical science. A little-known paper of 1915, "Prinzipielles zur Geschichte der Optik," compared the ideas on optics of Newton, Descartes, Malebranche, Grimaldi, Huygens, Young, Fresnel, Biot, and Malus with respect to their conceptual images of periodicity, polarization interference, and Huygens' principle of continuity of centers of force. Neurath generalized the logic of this analysis to compare systems of hypotheses by a procedure which selects basic notions to be calculated and then enumerates all theories that may be constructed from permutations of these notions. The simple view that theories of light may be divided into wave theories and corpuscular theories is replaced by a more accurate, complex, and systematically clear historical development. To Neurath this use of basic explanatory notions, which are sometimes images and sometimes abstractions, illustrated the value of philosophical understanding for the historian of natural and social science. Neurath's own philosophical understanding anticipated later reliance on alternative sets of epistemologically basic sentences in the structural elucidation of scientific theories.

In 1916, Neurath wrote a general paper on classification, "Zur Klassifikation von Hypothesensystemen," and elaborated on this topic in his monographs *Empirische Soziologie* (1931) and *Foundations of the Social Sciences* (1944). Classification by hypotheses seemed to Neurath to be a principal method for comparative studies of theories and explanations and a crucial tool for rational understanding of cross-cultural phenomena.

Economic planning, war, and socialism. During 1919, Neurath served in the Central Planning Office of the Social Democratic government of Bavaria and of its successor, the short-lived Bavarian Soviet Republic. Although he was a civil servant and not a party man, he was imprisoned when the Communist regime was overthrown; upon his release in 1920 he went to Vienna. He there took up again an earlier career as a publicist for socialist economics by efforts on behalf of a socialist conception of civic education, moral and religious reform, and individual responsibility. With Josef Popper-Lynkeus, Neurath was one of the first socialists to call for a centrally planned, rational economy based on Marxist concepts but deriving its policy recommendations from welfare goals and a statistical analysis of the production and distribution of goods and of standards of living.

Less clear to Neurath than equitable distribution of wealth was how a community spirit could be developed while the workers themselves were still overwhelmed by the established culture and the habits of the competitive capitalist order. Nevertheless, he fused his hypotheses about social–economic planning with a moral optimism about the acceptance by the workers of enlightened and rational attitudes toward all life's problems. Neurath's *Lebensgestaltung und Klassenkampf* poignantly tried to teach the reader about a transformed way of life in which he could realistically experience something of the peaceful and cooperative future at least in his private life, and at the same time come to sober realization of the obstacles placed by exploitative society in the way of a rich inner life and good personal relations as well as in the way of the transformation of society by rational socioeconomic planning.

Empirical sociology. In the 1930s and early 1940s, between the publication of the two monographs on sociology (the *Empirische Soziologie* and the *Foundations*), Neurath published several smaller papers on sociological topics. The most important were "Soziologie im Physikalismus," a physicalist restatement of sociological theories and problems, "Soziologische Prognosen," on social–historical predictions, and "Inventory of the Standard of Living," on the problem of making a rational calculation of the standard of living.

To make sociology scientific, Neurath urged the use of a physicalist language in which all the possible empirical statements would be descriptive of space-time things and properties; this was, roughly, a demand for behaviorism in social theory. He believed that this social behaviorism carried out Marx's claim that historical materialism was empirical, starting from the factual situation of real men in objective circumstances and basing theories upon hypotheses which are free of wishful or evaluative assumptions. Human beings, streets, religious books, prisons, gestures can be so described, and they may be grouped in accord with physicalist theoretical systems. Happiness and suffering, too, may be described empirically, even in a manner similar to a mechanical description of space-time entities. But man, in some situations, dominates the lawlike mechanism of the natural environment. In Neurath's typical formulation: formerly when there was a swamp and man, man disappeared; nowadays the swamp disappears.

But the language of mechanism is laden with myth and metaphysical presuppositions, and Neurath tried to eliminate all impure or careless terminology. Just as he would ban metaphysics as a misuse of unverifiable but grammatically correct word-signs, so he wished to forbid social theorists to use words which carry multiple meanings and assumptions; he himself never used the word "capital." Sociological descriptions demand arguments over the entire range of environmental and causal science; biological, geological, ethnological, and chemical statements must join social, psychological, economic, legal, and other statements of purely human reference. Hence it would be useful to invent an empirical language suited to all the sciences, one which avoids descriptive distinctions that are the result of mere linguistic convention. Neurath hoped that empirical sociology might be formulated with clear and univocal physicalist predicates. However, we start with inexact "clots," with indistinct and unanalyzed evidence, and we must tolerate and even carefully devise a correspondingly rich vocabulary which is also amenable to analysis of regularities and at times to the creation of a calculus.

Neurath often wrote of an essential uncertainty in all scientific description and predication, of the probabilistic nature of learning from experience. Historians should explain the present from knowledge of portions of the past, but to predict the future with precision is beyond us. There are too many variables; at least some of these are unknown, and the greater the anticipated change, the less our scientific assurance about its realization. We may, in Neurath's view, strive to construct a future state of affairs, but whether we feel hesitant or confident, we have in sociological lawlike historical statements no rational ground for predictions that are certain. Moreover, some predictive statements, notably self-fulfilling or hortatory prophecies, are codeterminant; they carry causal weight which disturbs their subject matter. Other predictions seem impossible on their face. How should a nation that could not invent the wheel predict the invention of the wheel? Others are too complex. Will painters in misty regions paint misty pictures or, just because of the mistiness, sunny ones? Neurath carried out this analysis of pseudorational certainty throughout his work, using it with a moral force. Decisions cannot be replaced by calculation or by reasoning—not in practical life, and not in scientific work.

Scientific method. Physicalism was developed mainly by Neurath and Rudolf Carnap. It may be seen as Neurath's attempt to express, in epistemological terms, the materialist (objective) foundation of knowledge, since the persistent recognition he gave to the natural fact of socially intersubjective agreement was a principal source of his antiphenomenalist role within the Vienna circle. Despite Neurath's insistence on a sharp distinction between scientific and metaphysical expressions by means of criteria for empirical meaning, it was his view that intersubjective agreement provides approximate unanimity about the grounds for judgments, not for meanings. By use of a physicalist language, skeptical inquirers display and share a common standard for confirmation. Physicalism had the further merit for Neurath that it was a linguistic doctrine which overcame any systematic mutual incomprehension of special disciplines not by reduction to the special discipline of physics but by a doctrine of reference to the generalized physics of public space-time states (in the human macroscale).

Neurath freely admitted that this doctrine was a hypothesis; the world was assumed to be unified, a causal network whose multiplicity of descriptions should tend toward a unified language that includes the social, biological, and physical sciences. Moreover, as an analysis of the process of scientific knowledge, physicalism programmatically explicated (for any special science) the relations among the physiology and social psychology of sensuous perception, the physics of experimental and measurement technology, and the known scientific or common-sense entities. Neurath saw physicalism as the further hypothesis that the world is knowable in principle everywhere and throughout. Finally, in "Protokollsätze" (1932) Neurath represented physicalism as providing a sophisticated revision of the doctrine of atomic bits of knowledge, conveyed by individual reports, or "basic sentences," also known at the time as "protocol sentences," by demanding that they, too, be intersubjective and, however psychologically certain, logically tentative and empirically testable. Indeed, the truth of protocol sentences was attributable to their cohering role in a theory (or system of theories) to which empirical evidence gave confirmatory evidence, and consequently the possibility existed that a conflict between a particular protocol statement and a theoretical statement of more complex form and function might, by choice and for convenience, be resolved by discarding the protocol. Neurath found his early analysis of alternative hypothesis systems and their fact-fitting auxiliary statements borne out within this empirical conventionalist interpretation of the physicalist basis.

Visual education. Both the union of scholars and ordinary workers and the overcoming of national and linguistic divisions were in Neurath's mind when he began to develop his "Vienna method" of visual education. In rudiment, he used an invariant and self-explanatory pictorial sign for a given thing, so as to give quick information, unencumbered by irrelevancies and easily remembered. Neurath's maxims were simple: he who knows what best to omit is the best teacher; to remember simplified pictures is better than to forget accurate figures.

Unity of science and encyclopedism. Neurath was the principal organizer of several related philosophical enterprises. By 1929 the regular but informal Thursday meetings of philosophers and scientists who met for discussion with Moritz Schlick in Vienna had gathered sufficient force to produce a noted manifesto of a scientific world conception, signed by Neurath, Hans Hahn, and Carnap although it was largely Neurath's work. This led in the same year to the first of a series of international congresses for scientific philosophy. Neurath's stress upon the unification of the sciences by means of a unifying language, unity of method, and interdisciplinary dialogue led him to plan the *International Encyclopedia of Unified Science,* edited by himself, Carnap, and Charles Morris as the principal effort of the new Institute for the Unity of Science (founded in The Hague in 1936 and later removed to Boston, Massachusetts), directed chiefly by Philipp Frank. The first two introductory volumes appeared in parts, but even these were still incomplete nearly two decades after Neurath's death. Only the Institute for Visual Education (Isotype) continued with vigor after 1945, directed by Neurath's colleague and third wife, Marie Reidemeister Neurath.

Works by Neurath

"Geldzins im Altertum." *Plutus,* Vol. 29 (1904), 569–573.
"Prinzipielles zur Geschichte der Optik." *Archiv für die Ge-*

schichte der Naturwissenschaft und die Technik, Vol. 5 (1915), 371–389.

"Zur Klassifikation von Hypothesensystemen." *Jahrbuch des Philosophischen Gesellschafts an der Universität Wien.* Liepzig, 1916. Pp. 27 ff.

Durch die Kriegswirtschaft zur Naturalwirtschaft. Munich, 1919.

Lebensgestaltung und Klassenkampf. Berlin, 1928.

Wissenschaftliche Weltauffassung: Der Wiener Kreis. Vienna, 1929. Written jointly by Neurath, Rudolf Carnap, and Hans Hahn.

"Wege der wissenschaftlichen Weltauffassung." *Erkenntnis,* Vol. 1 (1930), 106–125.

Empirische Soziologie: Der wissenschaftliche Gehalt der Geschichte und Nationalökonomie. Vienna, 1931.

"Soziologie im Physikalismus." *Erkenntnis,* Vol. 2 (1931), 393–431.

"Protokollsätze." *Erkenntnis,* Vol. 3 (1932), 204–214. Tr. into English in A. J. Ayer, ed., *Logical Positivism,* by Frederick Schick (who is there listed as "George").

"Soziologische Prognosen." *Erkenntnis,* Vol. 6, No. 5/6 (1936), 398–405.

"Inventory of the Standard of Living." *Zeitschrift für Sozialforschung,* Vol. 6 (1937), 140–151.

Foundations of the Social Sciences. Chicago, 1944. This is Vol. 2, No. 1, of the *International Encyclopedia of Unified Science.*

Selected Papers of Otto Neurath. Marie Neurath and R. S. Cohen, eds. New York and London, forthcoming. With a biographical memoir and a complete bibliography.   ROBERT S. COHEN

NEW ENGLAND TRANSCENDENTALISM.

The New England transcendentalists were an influential but decidedly heterogeneous group of young writers, critics, philosophers, theologians, and social reformers whose activities centered in and around Concord, Massachusetts, from about 1836 to 1860. Insofar as they can be considered to have subscribed to a common body of doctrine, their leader and spokesman was Ralph Waldo Emerson (1803–1882). Apart from Platonism and Unitarian Christianity, the chief formative intellectual influence on the group was German idealism. It was not, however, the dense and difficult epistemological works of Kant, Fichte, Schelling, and Hegel that primarily attracted the transcendentalists; although nearly all had made some attempt to read the German philosophers, very few had persevered to the point of mastering them. Rather, it was the more personalized and poetic expressions of Goethe, Novalis, Wordsworth, Coleridge, and Carlyle, together with the belletristic expositions of Mme. de Staël's *De l'Allemagne* (New York, 1814) and Victor Cousin's *Introduction à l'histoire de la philosophie* (English translation, Boston, 1832) that provided Emerson and his disciples with whatever philosophical nourishment they possessed. Thus, far from being in any strict sense a primarily philosophical movement, New England transcendentalism was first and foremost a literary phenomenon. It was a passionate outcry on the part of a number of brilliant and highly articulate young Americans who had become so intoxicated with the spirit of European romanticism that they could no longer tolerate the narrow rationalism, pietism, and conservatism of their fathers.

After Emerson and Henry David Thoreau (1817–1862), the more important early transcendentalists were William Ellery Channing (1780–1842)—"Dr. Channing," as Emerson called him—distinguished clergyman and social reformer, leader of the Unitarian revolt against Calvinism; Amos Bronson Alcott (1799–1888), mystic, educationalist, and reformer; George Ripley (1802–1880), Ger-

manist, disciple of Fourier, and one of the founders of the Brook Farm community and of *The Dial* (the chief transcendentalist periodical); Orestes Augustus Brownson (1803–1876), journalist and clergyman whose lifelong attempt to reconcile religious conviction with radical views about social reform led him to embrace, in turn, nearly every available variety of Christianity from Presbyterianism to Catholicism; Frederic Henry Hedge (1805–1890), scholar, authority on German philosophy, founder in 1836 of the informal Transcendental Club for "exchange of thought among those interested in the new views in philosophy, theology and literature"; Margaret Fuller (1810–1850), literary critic, political radical, feminist, author of *Woman in the Nineteenth Century* (1845), and first editor of *The Dial* (1840–1844); Theodore Parker (1810–1860), dissenting Unitarian preacher and abolitionist whose ordination discourse, "The Transient and Permanent in Christianity" (delivered in Boston in 1841), denied the necessity of believing in Biblical inspiration and in miracles and led Emerson to nickname him the Savonarola of transcendentalism; Jones Very (1813–1880), poet and eccentric; James Freeman Clarke (1810–1888), Unitarian minister and religious pamphleteer; and Christopher Pearse Cranch (1813–1892), minister, painter, critic, and poet. Among the later transcendentalists were John Weis (1818–1879), Samuel Longfellow (1819–1892), J. E. Cabot (1821–1903), O. B. Frothingham (1822–1895), and Moncure D. Conway (1832–1907). It is debatable whether Nathaniel Hawthorne should be counted as a transcendentalist, but it is certain that, with other major imaginative writers like James Russell Lowell, John Greenleaf Whittier, Henry Wadsworth Longfellow, and Walt Whitman, Hawthorne owed much to his contact with transcendentalist modes of thought and feeling.

The nature of transcendentalism. "What is popularly called Transcendentalism among us," Emerson explained to a Boston audience in 1842, "is Idealism; Idealism as it appears in 1842" ("The Transcendentalist"). Yet we must add that it was a form of idealism that included and frequently confused the technical or epistemological idealism of the post-Kantian philosophers and the more vaguely understood "idealism"—in the sense of romantic aspirationism—of Wordsworth's "Intimations" ode and Novalis' *Fragmente.* The term "transcendental" was derived, Emerson claimed, from the use made of it by Kant, who had demonstrated that there was "a very important class of ideas, or imperative forms, which did not come by experience, but through which experience was acquired; that these were intuitions [*sic*] of the mind itself"; and that Kant had called them "Transcendental forms." This somewhat subjective exposition (contrast, for example, *Critique of Pure Reason,* B 25, A 11–12) led Emerson to conclude that consequently "whatever belongs to the class of intuitive thought, is popularly called at the present day *Transcendental.*" Here, of course, the word "intuitive" is being employed in its most general sense, quite dissociated from any philosophical use, so that Emerson could immediately go on lamely to characterize the "Transcendentalist" as one who displays a predominant "tendency to respect [his] intuitions."

The failure on the part of the movement's leader to give any really informative definition of transcendentalism is nevertheless instructive. Because of their intellectual eclecticism and avowed individualism, their subjective fads and eccentricities, and, above all, their wide range of activities, which embraced almost every aspect of American cultural life in the mid-nineteenth century, any attempt to express the outlook of the New England transcendentalists in a single formula is bound to fail. O. B. Frothingham was certainly right when he admitted that transcendentalism was not a systematic theory of life but something more like a state of mind, "an enthusiasm, a wave of sentiment, a breath of mind that caught up such as were prepared to receive it, elated them, transported them, and passed on—no man knowing whither it went." In a clear sense, however, the transcendentalists were the inheritors of certain forms of sensibility already well developed within the European romantic movement: a vague yet exalting conception of the godlike nature of the human spirit and an insistence on the authority of individual conscience; a related respect for the significance and autonomy of every facet of human experience within the organic totality of life; a consequent eschewal of all forms of metaphysical dualism, reductivism, and positivism; nature conceived not as a vast machine demanding impersonal manipulation but as an organism, a symbol and analogue of mind, and a moral educator for the poet who can read her hieroglyphics; a sophisticated understanding of the uses of history in self-culture; in general, the placing of imagination over reason, creativity above theory, action higher than contemplation, and a marked tendency to see the spontaneous activity of the creative artist as the ultimate achievement of civilization—these were the more pervasive principles shared by all thinkers of the New England school. Yet if "idealism," or, better still, "romanticism," serves roughly to denote the genus of transcendentalism, it is important to determine the specific characteristics of the American version.

American characteristics. American transcendentalism differed from its European counterparts in at least two important ways. First, unlike most forms of European idealism in the nineteenth century, transcendentalism was not simply closely allied with contemporary theological speculation and debate but arose directly out of it. The majority of its original adherents, including Channing, Emerson, Parker, Ripley, and Cranch, were, or had been, Unitarian clergymen, and from the point of view of cultural history the advent of transcendentalism must be seen as the final liberation of the American religious consciousness from the narrow Calvinism that Unitarianism had already done much to ameliorate. This is not, however, to imply that transcendentalism was primarily a movement within the Christian church. For its outcome, as the works of Emerson and Thoreau, for example, amply testify, was essentially secular and humanist in the widest sense.

Second, the later inception of romantic idealism in the United States led its exponents to less fluctuating and at the same time less radical programs of social reform. If the typical German or English romantic began with an enthusiasm for the ideals of the French Revolution, became disillusioned by the Terror, and ended his career a conservative, Emerson's disciples felt the outcome of the Revolution as something more distant and, in any case, European. Their social philosophy was the natural outcome of their reactions to the very different American scene. The majority of transcendentalists never wavered in their active opposition to slavery, imperialism, bureaucratization, and cultural philistinism; yet, partly because the United States had already achieved a democracy and partly because Western expansion kept economic conditions relatively good, the transcendentalists were not incited to the more extreme forms of political protest characteristic of such European inheritors of idealism as Marx and Proudhon.

Bibliography

Perry Miller's two collections, *The Transcendentalist: An Anthology* (Cambridge, Mass., 1950) and *The American Transcendentalists: Their Prose and Poetry* (New York, 1957), provide excellent selections of transcendentalist writings; they also contain bibliographies. O. B. Frothingham, *Transcendentalism in New England: A History* (New York, 1876), is still the best intellectual history of the movement.

MICHAEL MORAN

NEWMAN, JOHN HENRY (1801–1890), English philosopher of religion and cardinal of the Roman Catholic church. He was born in London, the son of a banker (later a brewer) who gave his children a love of music and literature. The young Newman was thoroughly familiar with the writings of both the romantic poets and the English deists. Raised as an Anglican, he underwent a deep religious experience when he was 15, and thenceforth he was strongly convinced of God's interior presence and providence. The mottoes chosen by Newman at this time foreshadowed his religious quest and interest in development: "Holiness rather than peace," and "Growth the only evidence of life."

He matriculated in 1816 at Trinity College, Oxford, where he read strenuously in the classics and mathematics. A fellowship at Oriel College at Oxford won him entrance to its common room, which proverbially "stank of logic." In 1824 Newman took holy orders.

The Oriel noetics, led by Richard Whately, gave Newman a taste for cool logical analysis of religious problems. His greatest influence at Oxford was exerted in company with Richard Froude, John Keble, and Edward B. Pusey. The Oxford movement sought to revive a living, full sense of the church and tradition through a series of incisive *Tracts for the Times* (1833–1841), culminating in Newman's *Tract 90*, which earned him an official censure. Newman's historical research in the Church Fathers and his theory of development in Christian doctrine eventually convinced him that the ideal of an Anglican *via media* was illusory. In 1845 he was received into the Roman Catholic church, in 1847 he was ordained, and in 1848 he established the Birmingham Oratory as a center for those who shared his aspirations.

Newman struggled futilely during the years 1851–1858 to succeed as rector of the new Catholic University of Ireland, but political forces were too strong for him. Out of this defeat, however, came his main educational work, *The Idea of a University* (1852, 1859), which looked forward to a new synthesis of scientific, humanistic, and theological studies. Newman's strongly felt defense of his religious integrity and conversion expressed in his *Apologia Pro*

Vita Sua (1864) restored his rapport with educated readers in England. It also cleared the path for the presentation of his basic philosophical views on knowledge and his defense of the reasonable character of the act of religious faith. Newman regarded his *Essay in Aid of a Grammar of Assent* (1870) as his way of discharging an intellectual debt to his generation and to religious seekers of every age. In recognition of his distinguished service to the church, Pope Leo XIII created him a cardinal in 1879. Even in his last years, Newman kept up an active interest in questions of science, Biblical criticism, and religious beliefs.

Newman belongs in the tradition of British churchmen who have contributed to philosophical thought. This he did in the course of dealing with certain problems of a religious and theological nature. He was well read in such Enlightenment sources as Hume, Voltaire, and Paine and had an early awareness of the modern philosophical difficulties propounded against Christianity. Under pressure from such critics, Newman felt obliged to sift the grounds for his own adherence to theism and the Christian faith. He made a close study of the rationalistic apologetic used by William Paley and by Whately in defense of the existence of God and the basic articles of the Christian creed. Although Newman appreciated their search for rigor, he remained unconvinced by their particular way of achieving it. Their formalism remained completely impersonal and abstract, leaving out of account the process whereby the individual mind comes to see the import of an argument and gives its assent to the statements under discussion. Newman found a much more realistic account of mental operations in the analyses of inquiry made by three sources: Aristotle (especially in the *Nicomachean Ethics*), the Greek Fathers, and Joseph Butler. These sources all stressed the importance of probable reasoning and analogy, especially in cases involving contingent realities and moral questions. Somewhat to his surprise, Newman also discovered a similar stress in Bacon, Newton, and the Newtonians as soon as they faced the problem of relating their formal structures to concrete nature.

Formal and informal reasoning. Groping during his Oxford years for a way of stating the difference between the sequence of logical steps and the path of the mind in discovery, Newman came to the distinction between formal and informal reasoning. In mathematics and formal logic, the regulative principle is furnished by the formal relations among the elements of the argument and the internal consequence of steps. The relations can be stated in a general way without taking into account the difficulties that individual minds may have in following the formal entailments. From the logicomathematical standpoint, questions about our way of grasping the proof are either deemed irrelevant or assigned to the psychological order. Newman accepted this position insofar as it was meant to preserve the integrity of the standpoint of formal reasoning and the rigor of its deductive method. But he was unable to accept Whately's rationalistic conclusion that nothing more is ever required for establishing a doctrine than to exhibit its conformity with a pattern of formal reasoning. If a statement asserts something about existent things and if we are invited to accept this assertion, then something more is involved than the application of a general pattern of formal argument. The particular ways of backing the argument must be considered, and they must be considered by individual minds called upon to weigh their agreement with the world we experience.

When Newman himself tried to set down in the *Apologia Pro Vita Sua* the stages in his religious journey toward Catholicism, he found further evidence of his contention that the grounds and stages of argument in concrete matters cannot be fully formalized. He did not regard religious inquiry as being peculiar in this respect, but rather as agreeing with the common human condition of informal reasoning. The religious inquirer uses his mind in much the same way as does the jurist, the historian, and the biologist: all share in a common pattern of inquiry that demands a distinctive and responsible use of intelligence moving in a region somewhere between formalism and psychologism. A prominent task of Newman's main philosophical book, *An Essay in Aid of a Grammar of Assent*, was to explore the middle ground of inference that eludes complete formalization and yet achieves results capable of surviving the formal tests. In a general way, he described this region as a concrete personal mode of reasoning, which he customarily divided into natural and informal inference.

"Concrete" reasoning. The reasoning is called "concrete" as an indication of its ultimate terms of reference and control. Newman was strongly convinced that ours is a world of individual unit things, each of which has its unique nature and history. There is sufficient likeness among individuals to permit comparison and general statements, but there is no real identity and hence no completely general way of following the logical rules to establish our statements about them. In the study of individual entities, a gap eventually opens between general rules and concrete matters of fact. It cannot be closed by carrying on some further manipulation of the formal procedures in logic, and one is forced to bring into play the personal discernment of the living mind working upon what it experiences. Man's reasoning becomes concrete in response to this situation.

When he inquires about concrete existents, each man assumes personal responsibility for the conduct of his own understanding. Although he cannot violate the logical system or the pattern of the language, he must determine issues that cannot be settled solely in their formal terms. In the ordinary course of life, a man does not stop to reflect upon the methodological issues involved but plunges directly into the particular matters at hand. Newman refers to this unreflective and implicit sort of concrete thinking as a natural mode of inference, one that is not burdened by any second-level questioning about the kind of use being made of the mind. Every person is faced with practical decisions and moral choices that require a personal assessment of the circumstances and particular means and end in view. There is a point at which even a great military leader cannot rely solely upon the rules of strategy and his formal conception of warfare; he must place all these aids at the service of his personal estimate of a particular military situation in order to make a responsible decision. He is directly engaged in concrete reasoning in the natural mode of inference.

Yet Newman did not restrict concrete reasoning to conditions of great practical stress, where reflection on one's method is a luxury that cannot be indulged. He recognized the pattern of concrete intelligence in the judgments made by the historian, the art critic, the jurist, and the scientist. Here there is often an opportunity for attending to the problem of method. In the degree that men who make these judgments reflect upon their procedures and make an explicit theme of them, they are involved in what Newman calls concrete reasoning in the informal mode of inference. The concrete uses of intelligence are now thematized and critically controlled. The reasoning is informal insofar as it deals with questions that cannot be settled by appealing simply to the formal logical rules, but still it is a quite deliberate and reflective way of reasoning. Informal reasoning is required by our world of particulars, but this world does not prevent us from reflecting upon the way in which we explore and interpret it.

The illative sense. Newman proposed the theory of the illative sense to account for the certitude that may be attached to informal judgments. Here he was not trying to burden the mind with a new and esoteric faculty but sought instead to account for a definite feature of our intellectual activity. Hence he remarked that illative sense is only a grand name for designating a very ordinary way of using the mind.

A distinction is needed between certainty and certitude. Newman regarded certainty as a formally determinable quality of propositions and assigned its study to the logician. Newman's own interest centers upon certitude as a quality of the mind when it is engaged in concrete reasoning of both the natural and the informal sort. Concrete reasoning yields certitude when it enables us to recognize and affirm the truth of some proposition. Certitude is not achieved, as the rationalists maintain, through an impersonal coercion of the mind by the force of the formal elements contained in it. In all reasoning, but especially in concrete inference, certitude consists in an active response of the mind to the weight and tenor of the argument, a living recognition of the meaning and the truth of the proposition that states some findings. Furthermore, this certitudinal apprehension of the truth of the proposition is an inalienably individual act. I come to grasp the import of an argument; I see the bearing of the evidence; I give my assent to the proposition as true.

For my warrant in accepting the proposition, I cannot fall back exclusively upon the general canons of logic and the common structure of the language. Although Newman recognized their indispensable contribution by way of opposition to sentimentalism in thought, he believed that in the final analysis these elements cannot settle issues about the concretely existent. The illative sense refers to the type of operation of the human mind as it engages in concrete reasoning, reaches a conclusion of inference, and determines whether to give its certitudinal assent to the inferred proposition about a concrete reality:

The sole and final judgment on the validity of an inference in concrete matter is committed to the personal action of the ratiocinative faculty, the perfection or virtue of which I have called the Illative Sense. . . . It is the mind that reasons, and that controls its own reasonings, not any technical apparatus of words and propositions. This power of judging and concluding, when in its perfection, I call the Illative Sense. (*Grammar*, Ch. 9)

Thus when Newman claimed to be developing a theory of the mind more empirical than Locke's, he instanced this functional analysis of the illative sense.

The illative use of the mind is observable not only in the concluding act of an inference in concrete issues but also at the outset and along the way of the reasoning. Newman pointed out the need for a personal use of intelligence—especially in creative work as done, for example, by Newton or Gibbon—in order to suggest the governing hypothesis, to gauge the strength of some particular stage in the inquiry, and to discern the bearing of many outlying investigations upon the main problem. We seek to conduct ourselves responsibly in all these operations, and the term "illative sense" refers to the intellectual mastery or perfection that an individual develops for inquiries in some concrete field. It comes close to the Aristotelian habit of prudence or practical wisdom, except that it can reach into the speculative order and attain certitude there. Newman added that despite a similar pattern of concrete logic for different fields, the personal mastery cannot simply be transferred from one area to another. A man may give us good grounds for trusting his judgment in military affairs or biological questions, whereas he may be utterly lacking in sagacity in respect to political legislation.

Newman did not isolate religious inquiry from other concrete uses of intelligence but required it to conform to the common requirements of concrete inquiry. The religious man is not concerned solely with abstract and general issues but seeks the truth about the reality of God, the person of Christ, the complex life of the church, and the individual soul's response to them all. These matters belong in the region of concrete existence and thus impose their own requirements upon the searcher's mind. The interested individual cannot do justice to the issues if he confines himself to what can be ascertained exclusively from the use of formal reasoning. Such a restriction is bound to lead to a noncommittal attitude, not because of the religious issues as such but because of the failure to make use of the concrete reasoning required by the situation.

Probability and assent. At this juncture, however, Newman was confronted with a strong objection propounded by William Froude (brother of Richard Froude) and other members of the Victorian scientific community. They noted Newman's statement in the *Apologia* about his agreement with Joseph Butler that probability is the guide of our life. In addition they noted the function assigned by Newman to the illative sense of discerning the convergence of probabilities among several strands of argument. To Froude, it seemed that the unavoidable result is that Newman's way of concrete reasoning can yield nothing higher than a probable conclusion, which is essentially open to constant revision. This falls considerably short of the certitude claimed by Newman for the act of religious faith.

Newman's treatment of this difficulty constitutes another

major topic in the *Grammar of Assent*. Indeed, the book's title derives from his wrestling with this issue, as recorded in the following entry in his journal. "At last, when I was up at Glion over the Lake of Geneva, it struck me 'You are wrong in beginning with certitude—certitude is only a kind of assent—you should begin with contrasting assent and inference.' On that hint I spoke, finding it a key to my own ideas" (*Journal*, August 11, 1865). In fixing upon assent as something different from inference, Newman was able to clarify his position with respect to Froude's objection. His terminology was geared to the earlier, Lockean era in British empiricism, but the thrust of his argument concerns the relationship between religious faith and what Charles Peirce was already calling the ideal of scientific fallibilism.

Newman felt that at least one difficulty rested upon a linguistic confusion. His critics treated probability as a trait belonging to propositions and arguments, in which respect they contrasted it with the certainty of propositions. But just as he considered certitude a quality of the mind, so Newman viewed probability as a relationship involving the mind in an existential situation, rather than as a relationship among propositions in an argument. In Newman's conception, reasoning is probable to the extent that it is nonformal. Whenever inference is carried on in a context other than that of formal logic and mathematics, it is probable in the sense of not being governed by the intention of yielding a logicomathematical sort of proof. So understood, the probable is not contrasted with the demonstrative and the certain as such, but rather with the formal kind of demonstration and the abstract kind of certitude. Whenever the mind is inquiring about a concrete matter of fact, it is engaged in probable reasoning. This means that we are adapting our investigation to the conditions of particular existents, not that we are seeking only a weaker form of evidence and consequence in our reasoning. Thus probability, as understood by Newman, does not exclude certitude of assent but permits it to be achieved in matters pertaining to the concrete world and its connections in being.

Historically, Newman had to face Locke's restriction of probability to those inevident relations among ideas that permit neither intuitive nor demonstrative knowledge. Locke also held that belief is an act of assent that cannot rise above the probability of the inference leading to it and hence cannot enjoy the certainty of intuition or demonstration. Newman had two grounds of disagreement with this teaching. First, there is no general rule necessarily subsuming religious assent under Lockean probability. Whether there is certitude in an act of religious faith cannot be settled by general stipulation about the meaning of probability and the judgment of belief. There must be a direct examination of the particular case and its grounds for claiming something about the order of concrete fact. Second, the act of assent is no mere shadow or reduplication of the conclusion of the inferential process. Using J. S. Mill's canons of induction, Newman sought to show the distinctive nature of assent as an act of the mind that remains irreducible to either the formal conclusion of an inference or to its psychological correlate in the act of concluding. We always conclude in a referential and con-

ditional way, in view of what the premises state. But assent is made directly to the proposition as true; hence assent intends the certitudinal acceptance of the proposition in itself as being a true one. Newman made an extensive analysis of such expressions as "half assent," "conditional assent," and "hesitating assent." These describe circumstances surrounding the assent or features of the content to which assent is given rather than the act of assent itself.

The drift of Newman's reply to Locke and Froude is fairly clear. The sort of probability that he accepts as a guide and about which the illative sense must make an appraisal consists in a relation of the human mind to concrete modes of being. We follow the way of probability when we adapt our analysis to the concrete particulars and make a personal appraisal of the particular evidence. Our concrete personal thinking does not always attain certitude, but there is no a priori reason drawn from the definition of assent and probability that prevents us in principle from attaining it. Furthermore, there remains a difference in structure and intention between the inferential process and the act of assent. The revisability attaching to the former, especially in scientific inquiries, does not prevent the achievement of assent with certitude in some concrete instances. Newman's defense of the certitude in the act of religious faith depends upon keeping inference and assent distinct, as well as upon interpreting probability in terms of his theory of concrete reasoning.

Notional and real assent. Within the order of assent itself, Newman distinguished between notional and real assent. His view cannot be understood if it is taken as implying an opposition in principle between these modes of assent, or as assigning all the intellectual worth to real assent. The distinction is a functional one, arising from Newman's study of the interpretative operations of the mind. In assenting to a proposition, we can intend to accept the statement itself as true or to accept the real thing intended by the statement. A notional assent is one made to the truth of the proposition itself, whereas a real assent is one made to the reality itself intended by the proposition. Thus one may give a notional assent to God in terms of some abstract divine attributes and also give a real assent to God considered as a personal being who cares for one as an individual person. This is a matter of interpretation on the part of the mind that is considering the statement. In the case of purely ideal inquiries, a notional assent is sufficient. But we live in a translinguistic world, and our questions reach out to the community of real existents, especially to other persons. Here, the mind's notional assent must be integrated with, and further perfected by, a real assent to the very realities under investigation.

For Newman, the fully appropriate intellectual response to our human situation is unavoidably a complex one, involving both notional and real assents. Taken by itself, the way of real assent is intense but unclarified. We need to engage in both formal and informal inference, weighing the evidence carefully and arriving at a careful act of notional assent. Inference and notional assent are indispensable elements in human cognition; otherwise we could not weigh the pertinent evidence on an issue, do justice to the difficulties, or formulate the theoretical findings with cool precision of statement. Thus Newman assigned a large role to the modes of formal and informal inference and to notional assent in the total composition of human knowledge.

But he also insisted upon the need for directly relating the mind to individual existents. The act of real assent achieves our intellectual orientation toward the domain of concrete existents and their values. It does so by furnishing a concrete image of the individual being under consideration and by establishing the relevance of that imaged reality to the inquirer's own personal life. Real assent does not necessarily ensure action, but it does furnish a necessary condition for our practical responses by directing our mind toward the real existent, grasped in an image that can appeal to our passions and will.

There is a strongly theistic motive behind Newman's insistence upon blending inference, notional assent, and real assent. Man's relationship to God is not yet one of direct vision; hence we must engage in inference. Since theistic inquiry concerns a real existent, it is not enough to employ formal inference, even though its resources must be used to analyze and test our arguments. A concrete personal mode of reasoning is also required in order to proportion our inquiry as fully as possible to the situation of man's search after the truth about God. Our aim must be the complex one of attaining some definite and well-grounded propositions to which we can legitimately give our notional assent, and also of forming a concrete image of the personal, morally good, and providential God to whose reality we can then give our real assent and practical attachment.

Conscience and the moral life. Newman's final philosophical problem in the *Grammar* was to describe the area where he personally could realize this synthesis of intellectual acts bearing on the being of God. He readily admitted that there are many ways to God and that many natural informants lead us to him: the way of causality and purpose, the meaning of human existence and history, and the import of our moral life. As a reader of Hume and a contemporary of Darwin, however, Newman refused to grant independent value to the design argument, which he regarded as a supplementary way of looking at nature on the part of those who already accept God on other grounds. To reach the transcendent, personal God, Newman examined the witness of our moral life, for this is a personal region where relations with other persons are best established. It is here that we have the experience of conscience, of being under command to do and not to do, of being responsible to a just and caring person who transcends our human reality but does so in a way that keeps him personally concerned about our conduct. Conscience as a commanding act discloses the full human situation of our responsibility toward the good God.

Three features of the living command of conscience recommend it to Newman as the best way of achieving real as well as notional assent to God: its intentional character, its personal significance, and its practical ordination. The dictate of conscience by its very structure refers the conscientious man beyond himself, pointing him toward the reality of the supreme lawgiver and judge of his moral actions. This is not a purely abstract orienting of our mind but involves a concrete image of God as our concerned father. Another advantage of the way of conscience is that the moral relationship in which it consists is personal in both poles of reference. Conscience engages me precisely as a personal self; hence it enables me to give a real assent to God as a morally concerned person. Finally, the acts of conscience relate us to the personal God in a concrete way that leads to moral and religious actions. Hence the approach to God from conscience encourages us to assent to the truth about God not only notionally but really, not only in respect to our propositions but also in respect to the personal, provident reality of God himself as the practical goal of our knowledge and love.

As a reader of Hume and Mill, Newman was very sensitive to the naturalistic criticism based upon physical and moral evil in our world. He suggested that the moral problem of theism be treated within a moral context. One cannot pose an objection to theism on moral grounds and then rule out the conditions that would permit theism to present its moral type of interpretation. Real assent to God as the lord of conscience furnishes a frame of reference for wrestling with evil and discerning his providential presence. A mind that is carefully formed upon the theistic implications of conscience "interprets what it sees around it by this previous inward teaching, as the true key of that maze of vast complicated disorder; and thus it gains a more and more consistent and luminous vision of God from the most unpromising materials. Thus conscience is a connecting principle between the creature and his Creator" (*Grammar*, Ch. 5). Whereas the naturalistic critic appeals to the vast disorder as an antecedent reason for withholding our assent from God, Newman asks us to secure first of all the inward principle of interpretation provided by the personal and moral relation of men to the lord of conscience. The work of this principle is not to soften or gloss over the power of evil, but to bring in the other considerations concerning God and moral man that will enable us to understand and work with hope against physical and moral evil in our world.

Historical development and social principles. Like other nineteenth-century thinkers, Newman was dissatisfied with the older empiricism's emphasis on the solitary and static individual perceiver. Hence he widened his horizon to include the social, developmental, and historical aspects of human experience. His *Essay on the Development of Christian Doctrine* (1845) opens with a chapter on the general nature and kinds of development among ideas. Here Newman explores the logic of those social ideals that grip the minds of men and account for developments in their beliefs and institutions.

For Newman, two questions are of prime importance in understanding the social growth of ideas and institutions: Why do certain ideas display themselves only through historical development? What pattern is common to diverse sorts of developing social principles? As an answer to the first question, Newman points to the interpretative activity of many minds as they are engaged in judging, relating, evaluating, and dealing practically with our complex world. There are some meanings that can be worked out only in this gradual social way. Historically important ideas are those that contain many facets and require the interpretative activity of many minds, testing and developing them over many years. "Ordinarily an idea is not brought home to the intellect as objective except through this variety; like bodily substances, which are not apprehended except under the clothing of their properties and results, and which admit of being walked around, and surveyed on opposite sides, and in different perspectives, and in contrary lights, in evidence of their reality" (*Development*, Ch. 1). We can grasp the intentional structure of basic human meanings only through studying their various perspectives, forcing them to enter the battlefield of critical discussion, and sometimes embodying them in visible, powerful social institutions.

Newman also suggested that there is a common pattern of development that has certain traits distinguishing a healthy growth from a sickly one. His seven criteria for genuine development are preservation of the type of principle that is socially influential, continuity of these principles, their capacity for assimilation of new data, their logical sequence in organizing a complex social process, their anticipation of their own future, conservation of their past achievements, and their chronic vigor. He deliberately illustrated these criteria by showing their development in kingdoms, economic policies, religious convictions, scientific hypotheses, and philosophical theories. Although the entire analysis is applied ultimately to the theological question of development among Christian doctrines, Newman's comparative use of empirical materials indicates the wider significance of his study of the dynamics of human thought and institutional forms. He himself, in fact, makes an explicit application of this theory of development to the ideas of civilization, the political constitution, and the university.

The university. Newman's effort at interpreting the Western ideal of the university in the context of his theory of development is revealed in *The Idea of a University*. He was more keenly aware than most of his contemporaries that the crucial decisions affecting the course of cultural development were being made within the university. It was replacing the episcopal palace, the banking house, and the parliamentary floor as the real center for determining the long-range direction of human history. Newman looked for a fresh synthesis of tradition and originality in the university community. The task of such a community is to educate men for the world by gradually introducing them to the full complexity of our humanistic, scientific, and religious interpretations. This it should try to do by cultivating an understanding of the various methods and ways of knowing, along with an awareness of their differences, limitations, and possibilities for unification.

As a Catholic churchman, Newman devoted the bulk of his writings to problems raised by the Christian faith and its practical institutions, especially as they are brought into close relation with modern humanistic and scientific ideas. His contributions to these issues might be considered as a sustained effort at education that draws its strength from both Christianity and the other components in the university ideal.

Works by Newman

The following are modern editions of Newman's works: *Two Essays on Biblical and on Ecclesiastical Miracles* (New York, 1924); *An Essay in Aid of a Grammar of Assent*, C. F. Harrold, ed. (New York, 1947); *The Idea of a University*, C. F. Harrold, ed. (New York, 1947); *Essays and Sketches*, 3 vols., C. F. Harrold, ed. (New York, 1947); *Apologia Pro Vita Sua*, C. F. Harrold, ed. (New York, 1949); *An Essay on the Development of Christian Doctrine*, C. F. Harrold, ed. (New York, 1949); *Sermons and Discourses*, 2 vols., C. F. Harrold, ed. (New York, 1949); and *The Letters and Diaries of John Henry Newman*, C. S. Dessain, ed. (New York, 1961——; to be published in 30 vols.).

Works on Newman

Benard, E. D., *A Preface to Newman's Theology*. St. Louis, 1945.

Boekraad, A. J., *The Personal Conquest of Truth According to J. H. Newman*. Louvain, 1955.

Boekraad, A. J., *The Argument from Conscience to the Existence of God according to J. H. Newman*. Louvain, 1961.

Bouyer, Louis, *Newman: His Life and Spirituality*. New York, 1958.

Collins, James, *Philosophical Readings in Cardinal Newman*. Chicago, 1961. A presentation of Newman's philosophical views in terms of his theory of personal knowledge, his concrete inference to God, his notion of social development, and his account of the relationship between faith and reason.

Culler, A. D., *The Imperial Intellect: A Study of Newman's Educational Ideal*. New Haven, 1955. An interpretation of the liberal and traditional strains in Newman's mind and educational outlook.

Walgrave, J.-H., *Newman the Theologian*. New York, 1960. An advanced analysis of the theory of development and the psychological aspect of Newman's approach.

Ward, Wilfrid, *The Life of John Henry Cardinal Newman*, 2 vols. New York, 1912. A reliable, standard life, with many letters and documents.

JAMES COLLINS

NEW REALISM arose at the turn of the twentieth century in opposition to the Idealist doctrines that the known or perceived object is dependent for its existence on the act of knowing and that the immediately perceived object is a state of the perceiving mind. The Austrian philosophers Franz Brentano and Alexius Meinong first enunciated the cardinal tenet of this new realism: that what the mind knows or perceives exists independently of the acts of knowing and perceiving. Developing mainly as a polemic against Idealism, this new realism was represented prior to 1900 in England in the works of such men as John Cook Wilson, Thomas Case, H. W. B. Joseph, and H. A. Prichard. Similar realist polemics were taking place in Sweden and Italy.

In America the movement known as New Realism dates from the critical writings of William P. Montague and Ralph Barton Perry in 1901–1902. Their immediate aim was to refute Josiah Royce's "refutation" of realism, which he had based on the claim that the knower and the known could not be independent of each other and still be related. The movement took definite form when Montague and Perry were joined by four others in a statement of a New Realist program ("The Program and First Platform of Six Realists") in 1910.

In England, New Realism took explicit form in the works of T. P. Nunn, Bertrand Russell, and G. E. Moore.

In both America and England, New Realists asserted the independence of consciousness and its object, but serious differences soon appeared between the two groups and between individuals within each group. The differences were particularly noticeable in their statements about the nature of consciousness and of its object, and of the relation between them. Moore claimed that the act of consciousness included both a nonmental, independent object and a transparent, or "diaphanous," mental act of consciousness. He agreed with Brentano and Meinong that consciousness involved awareness in the form of an act of intending something other than itself. To have an idea, to perceive or be aware at all, is already to be beyond consciousness and to be confronted by an independent object. American New Realists, on the other hand, took their view of consciousness from William James. While he, too, described consciousness as a relation, James denied that there was anything uniquely mental or psychic about it at all, and associated consciousness rather with the behavioral responses or functions of the organism.

But there were also differences between Moore, Nunn, and Russell. Nunn argued that both primary and secondary qualities not only exist as they are perceived, but also are really *in* their objects, whether perceived or not. He even argued that pain is something independent of mind, with which mind may come into various relations. In this he was closer to the American New Realism of Perry and E. B. Holt. Russell was influenced by Nunn's view, but his New Realism took a frankly Platonic turn that brought it closer to the New Realism of Montague. Russell's Realism, however, was soon significantly altered. Another variant of English New Realism, perhaps more a development from it than a version of it, was Samuel Alexander's. It, too, resembled American New Realism.

AMERICAN NEW REALISM

Although American, English, and, to a lesser extent, European New Realists influenced one another, it was among the Americans that New Realism flourished, particularly as a movement. Their aim was to produce an account of how a real object could be present in consciousness and knowledge and still be independent of that relation, and they sought to do this without a dualistic separation of knower and known. "The independence of the immanent" was their manifesto. Their first platform statement consisted of six lists of doctrines that had been discussed at length, revised, and agreed to by all, and that all thought were consistent. The lists were signed by Holt and Perry at Harvard, Walter T. Marvin at Rutgers, Montague and Walter B. Pitkin at Columbia, and Edward G. Spaulding at Princeton.

At a Philosophical Association meeting in 1909, five of these six had found themselves in agreement against a common foe that still spoke with authority and was listened to with deference: Idealism. Pitkin and Montague are credited with the idea of translating their agreement into an articulate statement, and papers soon began circulating. F. J. E. Woodbridge at Columbia gave encouragement, although he declined an invitation to join. Montague, in "Confessions of an Animistic Materialist,"

described E. B. McGilvary, Morris R. Cohen, J. E. Boodin, J. Lowenberg, and Douglas C. Macintosh as "unofficial" New Realists. Believing that philosophic disagreements were the result chiefly of a lack of precision and uniformity in the use of words, plus a lack of planned cooperation in research, the original six banded together in the hope of revealing the genuine philosophic disagreements that were more than mere differences of personal opinion. They hoped thereby to open the way to the solution of genuine philosophic disputes. They called for a new alliance between philosophy and science and formulated a statement of principles and doctrines, a program of constructive work with a method based on these, and an agreed-upon system of axioms, methods, hypotheses, and facts.

In 1912 they published their cooperative volume, *The New Realism; Cooperative Studies in Philosophy.* Although they were still preoccupied with polemics, the six authors hoped to go beyond criticism to produce a complete philosophy that would play a major part in human thought. They saw themselves as proponents of a doctrine concerning the relation between the knowing process and the thing known. They described their most urgent problem (one that had not been resolved by naive realism, dualism, or subjectivism) as how to give an adequate account of "the facts of relativity" in the knowing process from a Realist point of view; how, in other words, to reconcile the apparently hopeless disagreement of the world presented in immediate experience with the true or corrected system of objects in whose independent reality they believed. While New Realism succeeded in showing the fatal weaknesses in dualistic answers to this problem, it nonetheless failed to provide an adequate answer of its own.

The "facts of relativity." New Realism faced the above problem not just because Idealism had failed to resolve it but also because Idealism had made it impossible to ignore these "facts of relativity." Thus, any attempt by New Realists to return to the naïveté of earlier doctrines of realism, to a primitive notion that nothing intervenes between subject and object (particularly nothing attributable to the subject), was out of the question. Equally closed to them was any recourse to a Lockean or Cartesian dualism which, they thought, never escaped the subject's own mental states. The third traditional answer to the problem, subjectivism, was also impossible. Of the three approaches, subjectivism was most often the object of criticism by New Realists, and they identified it as the fatal doctrine of Idealism. They saw it as an illicit argument from the "ego-centric predicament," an argument based on the difficulty of conceiving known things to exist independently of their being known. New Realists refuted Idealism by refuting this argument; but then it became their turn to reconcile the facts of relativity, of which the predicament was one, with their theory of the independent existence, or reality, of objects of consciousness and knowledge.

New Realist writings thus were largely devoted to such facts of relativity as illusion, error, secondary qualities, and—later—choosing, valuing, meaning or intending, and purposing. The New Realists also thought that Idealism had gone too far in its view of the subject's role. However, if Idealism went too far in that direction, New Realism went too far in the opposite direction; its polemical theory of independence could not be reconciled with the facts of relativity. This in turn provoked such reactions as Critical Realism, Perspective Realism, and Objective Relativism.

Chief among the positive aspects of the doctrines of the New Realists was what they called the "emancipation of metaphysics from epistemology," the result of their theory of independence. Contrary to the Idealist claim that knowing was the universal condition of being and hence constitutive of it, the New Realists argued that knowing and being were independent. This, Perry showed, did not mean they were therefore unrelated, as Royce had argued, but simply that there was not the particular relation of dependence between them. Dependence is a special type of relation in which the dependent element contains, implies, or is exclusively caused or implied by that on which it is dependent. Between knowing and being, therefore, it was possible for there to be relations both of independence (external relations) and of dependence (internal relations). In holding out this possibility against the Idealist claim that all relations are internal, New Realism became identified with a theory of external relations.

In "immediate and intimate connection" with this theory was the doctrine that the content of knowledge is numerically identical with the thing known; things, when consciousness is had of them, become contents of consciousness, thus figuring both in the external world and in "the manifold which introspection reveals." This view was very close to James's Neutral Monism, but only Holt worked out its fullest implications. The theory of numerical identity soon became the target of critics of New Realism, and it was difficult to determine whether, and to what extent, any New Realist other than Holt maintained it. Yet for a time, at least, it was said to be fundamental to New Realism. If there was a numerical identity between consciousness and its contents, then the "things" of thought would have to be given full ontological status along with the "things" of sense. This the New Realists claimed to do in their volume. They said they were Platonic Realists in granting this status to subsistents as well as existents. Here, again, a belief held by all in the beginning became in the end the belief of but a few, notably Montague and Spaulding.

The egocentric predicament. The facts of relativity haunted New Realism throughout the life of the movement. That the New Realists ultimately failed in their professed aim of doing justice to these facts was in part the result of their constant polemical concern with asserting their doctrine of independence against Idealism and in part the result of their failure to recognize some possibly constitutive elements within the knowing relation. One such fact was the egocentric predicament, described by Perry as the fact that the "extent to which knowledge conditions any situation in which it is present cannot be discovered by the simple and conclusive method of direct elimination" ("The Ego-centric Predicament"). Perry thought this was merely a methodological difficulty, one faced by all philosophers. Idealism had used it to argue that since it was impossible to discover anything that is, when discovered, undiscovered by someone, therefore it is impossible to discover anything that is not thought. The argument, Perry contended, rested on a confusion between "everything which is known, is *known*," and "everything which *is*, is known."

Perry concluded that the predicament could not be used to support either Idealism or Realism. Idealists could not use it as an argument for dependence, or internal relations, and New Realists could not use it as an argument for independence, or external relations. But while exposing its illicit use, New Realists did not offer a convincing way out of the predicament. As a test for the dependence or independence of any element in consciousness, Perry proposed that insofar as the element was deducible from anything other than consciousness, it was independent. To be dependent, or subjective, the element would have to be exclusively determined by consciousness. However, it was pointed out, the predicament would prevent us, by the very test Perry proposed, from reaching an object that we could be sure was independent of consciousness, for we would be using consciousness (deduction) in order to get to it.

Spaulding maintained that New Realism had provided a solution to the predicament and that this solution was its most important doctrine. He argued that any sort of analysis purporting to discover—and not merely create—what is *there* would be impossible if it did not presuppose a Realist position; that is, presuppose relatedness with independence. Even a theory that argued against the Realist position would have to take that position toward the very state of affairs it described, assuming that it was a genuine state of affairs, not one created, altered, or modified by virtue of the knowing relation. Every philosopher, knowingly or not, solves the predicament by the Realist attitude he assumes toward his subject. But the question remained: What warrant do we have for such an assumption?

Pitkin attempted to support the doctrine of external relations by refuting the assertion that biology provided evidence for the internalist view. On the contrary, he argued, biology supports the externalist view through the discovery that organic parts do not depend upon the whole in which they naturally occur; and an organic whole does not depend upon its individual parts for its total specific organic character.

Beyond this, and apart from showing that independence did not rule out relatedness, the New Realists did not demonstrate how the knowing relation was external and independent, nor did they show how the facts of relativity were to be reconciled with externality and independence. In their cooperative volume they had refused to recognize ultimate immediacies, or any nonrelational or indefinable entities other than the simples in which they claimed analysis terminates. Their view that the knowing relation was external required such simples, or "neutral entities," that would maintain their identity no matter what relations they entered into. But it was never clear why analysis had to stop where the New Realists said it did—usually with the simples of mathematics and logic. Nor was it clear whether these simples were the product of their analysis or a genuine discovery by it.

Epistemology and ontology. In its constructive phase, New Realism proposed an epistemological monism and an ontological pluralism. James had argued that consciousness was not a substantive entity, and Moore similarly argued that it was diaphanous and transparent. In both cases, consciousness of something was viewed as a direct, unmediated, immanent affair. All content of consciousness, with the exception of Moore's psychical, diaphanous element, was thus objective in the sense that it consisted of objects in the real, external world. This was New Realism's epistemological monism: thought and its object are numerically the same.

Its ontology was pluralistic, however: some elements of the object would not be found in the consciousness of that object. Any elements in consciousness not found in the object would give consciousness a constitutive role beyond mere selection or grouping. The problem was to account for all of the "facts of relativity" through the selective and grouping function of consciousness without jeopardizing the New Realist theory of immanence which asserted that it was the "real" objects of the external world that were present in consciousness.

There were two principal positions taken on this matter among New Realists. Montague called them the left and right wings of New Realism. One was Neutral Monism, developed by Holt and, to a lesser extent, by Perry, but eventually abandoned by both. The other was a Platonic Realism developed by Montague into what he called Subsistential Realism.

Holt and Perry. Neutral Monism derived from James's idea of "pure experience." Pure experience was pure because it was uncontaminated by such distinctions as "object," "content," "subject," or "knower and known." It was "neutral" in terms of these distinctions; such distinctions could only be made later in terms of the relations between portions of pure experience. A "thing" could be said to be one portion of pure experience that was represented by another portion. A "thought" could be said to be one portion of pure experience that represented another portion. The dualisms of "inner" and "outer," mind and body, thus were undercut. All such distinctions were a matter of relations between bits of pure experience, but these relations had to be external. Hence, "mental," "nonmental," "real," "external," and "physical," are accidental features. New Realists thus were driven back to a realm of indefinable simples that come into and go out of various relations but never change their original identities. Where could such a realm be found? And what could these simples be?

Where James thought they were bits of pure experience (and may have been working toward an identification of experience with nature), Holt and Perry, influenced by developments in mathematics and symbolic logic, found these entities in a mathematical–logical realm of "being." It was a realm of entities having no definition or identity: neutral entities. These entities were similar to the simples that the New Realists had said analysis ultimately discloses. What we call consciousness is a grouping of these entities resulting from the selective (although not constitutive) response of the nervous system. This explanation enabled Holt and Perry to maintain the New Realist claim that consciousness and its objects were identical: error and illusory experiences were no less objective or real than

veridical experience. However, it failed to give an account of the difference between objects grouped and objects not grouped by consciousness. And it was still no easier to give an account of the organism's response to objects that were spatially or temporally distant.

Although he espoused Neutral Monism in his early years, Perry never went as far as Holt. He admitted that error and other nonveridical experiences were cases of "mis-taking" entities for something other than what they are. In a later development he identified this mis-taking as an anticipation or expectation of an event that does not, when acted on or verified, occur as expected. By this time, however, Perry had departed from the New Realist theories of independence and immanence.

Spaulding and Montague. Spaulding also identified error as a mis-taking, but he described it as a case of taking something to be existential that was only "subsistential." This mis-taking was the only subjective feature in consciousness. Therefore, he concluded, illusory objects and errors are objective and real because both the existential and subsistential are objective and real. It is the taking of a thing to be what it is not that is the psychic or subjective element in consciousness, and the problem of error—why error occurs—is one for psychologists and not for philosophers. Along with Pitkin, Spaulding also took a behaviorist view of consciousness, describing its objects as nonspatial projections or dimensions of spatial objects resulting from the interaction of organism and environment.

The second major attempt to formulate a New Realist epistemology and ontology consistent with the doctrines of independence and immanence was developed furthest by W. P. Montague, the only one of the New Realists who argued for uniquely mental, subjective elements in knowledge and experience. While admitting this was dualism, he insisted it was not the psychophysical dualism rejected by New Realism. He invoked a realm of subsistents, identifying them as propositions of which existential propositions, and hence existence, were a part. Error was a case of mis-taking the "merely" subsistential to be an existent as well.

Critiques of New Realism. All of these attempted solutions raised the question of whether New Realism's epistemology, based on an independently real object immanent in experience, could coexist with its view that the real object was part of the common-sense world. When the independence of the object of knowledge was emphasized, the facts of relativity were slighted, but the object could more easily be identified with common-sense objects. On the other hand, when immanence of the object was emphasized, it tended to lose its common-sense quality, becoming instead a neutral entity, or subsistent, or simple, supposedly disclosed by a rather sophisticated analysis. At the same time, however, the facts of relativity could more easily be taken into account. The former emphasis moved in the direction of dualism; the latter in the direction of monism.

Criticisms of New Realism in the second decade of the twentieth century were concerned mainly with showing that the organism intervenes in a considerably less naive way than the New Realists had thought and that their theories of external relations, independence, and immanence did not adequately account for what was given in knowledge and experience. Describing New Realism as the first phase of the "revolt against dualism," A. O. Lovejoy said its constructive program argued that since nothing "mental" could be admitted without leading to subjectivism and skepticism, therefore no content could be held to be psychically generated or dependent upon percipient functions. New Realism was left with things in a purely external relation to consciousness, or at best a bare and sterile awareness of them. In rejecting all mediated knowledge, he argued, New Realism could only hold the position that all content of experience must be identical with reality; everything before or "to" mind or consciousness was "objective." When this claim collided with the manifestly disparate content of nonveridical experience, an objective but "subsistent" content was said to be directly present or immanent; or, alternatively, this content was said to be no less objective than veridical content because it was at bottom ("neutrally") the same as it. But, Lovejoy concluded, this was little more than what the earlier naive, or commonsense, realism had said.

Although the New Realists hoped to produce other collections of studies, and although their discussions continued through 1914, according to Perry disagreements that had been subordinated and only imperfectly concealed, divergence of interests, and the ambition of each to write his own book soon divided them. As a movement, New Realism was soon displaced by the second major realist movement of the twentieth century, Critical Realism, which also developed and published a platform and joint program.

Works by New Realists

Holt, Edwin B., et al., "The Program and First Platform of Six Realists." *Journal of Philosophy*, Vol. 7 (July 21, 1910), 393–401. Reprinted in their cooperative volume *The New Realism: Cooperative Studies in Philosophy.* New York, 1912.

Montague, William P., "Professor Royce's Refutation of Realism." *Philosophical Review*, Vol. 11 (January 1902), 43–55.

Montague, William P., "Confessions of an Animistic Materialist," in W. P. Montague and G. P. Adams, eds., *Contemporary American Philosophy.* New York, 1930. Vol. II, 135–158. Pieces by other New Realists, "official" and otherwise, will be found in both volumes of this work.

Moore, G. E., "The Refutation of Idealism." *Mind*, N.S. Vol. 12 (1903), 442–453. Reprinted in Moore's *Philosophical Studies.* London, 1922.

Perry, Ralph B., "Professor Royce's Refutation of Realism and Pluralism." *Monist*, Vol. 12 (1901–1902), 446–458.

Perry, Ralph B., "The Ego-centric Predicament." *Journal of Philosophy*, Vol. 7, No. 1 (1910), 5–14. Reprinted in W. G. Muelder and L. Sears, eds., *The Development of American Philosophy.* Boston, 1940; 2d ed., Boston, 1960.

Perry, Ralph B., "William Pepperell Montague and the New Realists," in "William Pepperell Montague." *Journal of Philosophy*, Vol. 51, No. 21 (October 14, 1954), 593–637.

Spaulding, Edward G., *The New Rationalism.* New York, 1918.

Works on New Realism

Bowman, Lars, *Criticism and Construction in the Philosophy of the American New Realism.* Stockholm, 1955. One of the two extant studies devoted entirely to American New Realism, this work is mainly expository, utilizing the tools of modern philosophical analysis in order to determine the central doctrines of New Realism. It includes one of the better short bibliographies.

Chisholm, Roderick M., *Realism and the Background of Phenomenology.* Glencoe, Ill., 1960. A collection of readings, with probably the best bibliography of the works of all major Realists and their critics.

Harlow, Victor, *A Bibliography and Genetic Study of American Realism.* Oklahoma City, 1931. One of the best separate bibliographies of American Realism.

Hasan, Syed Zafarul, *Realism: An Attempt to Trace Its Origins and Development in Its Chief Representations.* Cambridge, 1928. An extensive treatment of New Realism (particularly of E. B. Holt) that includes a useful bibliography.

Hill, Thomas E., *Contemporary Theories of Knowledge.* New York, 1961. Although limited to theories of knowledge, this work includes an extensive critical treatment of American New Realists, centering on Perry ("polemical"), Holt ("radical"), and Montague ("conservative").

James, William, "Does Consciousness Exist?" *Journal of Philosophy*, Vol. 1, No. 18 (September 1, 1904). Reprinted in James's *Essays in Radical Empiricism.* New York, 1938.

Kremer, René, *Le Néo-réalisme américain.* Louvain and Paris, 1920. Devoted exclusively to New Realism.

Lapan, Arthur, *The Significance of James' "Essay."* Ph.D. dissertation, Columbia University. New York, 1936.

Lovejoy, Arthur O., *The Revolt Against Dualism; An Inquiry Concerning the Existence of Ideas.* Chicago, 1930. Lovejoy is probably the most persistent and incisive critic of New Realism.

Morris, Charles W., *Six Theories of Mind.* Chicago, 1932. A discussion of the relationships of the various realisms, Pragmatism, and Objective Relativism.

Passmore, John, *A Hundred Years of Philosophy.* London, 1957. The chapter on New Realism is mainly concerned with English New Realism, most particularly Alexander's. Selected bibliography.

Royce, Josiah, *The World and the Individual.* New York, 1912.

Schneider, Herbert W., *Sources of Contemporary Philosophical Realism in America.* Indianapolis, Ind., 1964.

Werkmeister, W. H., *A History of Philosophical Ideas in America.* New York, 1949. A good survey of the development of New Realism, including a detailed account of the polemical exchanges beginning with early New Realist statements in 1907.

THOMAS ROBISCHON

NEWTON, ISAAC (1642–1727), was the English mathematician and physicist whose fundamental work revolutionized the study of the physical world. Newton was born at Woolsthorpe, near Grentham. He attended Trinity College, Cambridge, graduating, apparently without special distinction, in 1665. In the autumn of that year, the university was closed because of the plague, and Newton retired to Woolsthorpe, where he remained for about 18 months. During this period he formulated the basic features of his great work in mathematics, mechanics and astronomy, and optics: his theories of "fluxions" (calculus), motion and gravitation, and the composition of light. In 1667 he returned to Cambridge, where, on the retirement of his former teacher, Isaac Barrow, and with the latter's backing, he was appointed Barrow's successor as Lucasian professor of mathematics. Not until 1669 did he communicate any of the results of his Woolsthorpe period; in that year, however, some of his mathematical work was circulated, and his genius was soon recognized.

In 1684, Edmund Halley asked Newton what the orbit of a planet would be, assuming it was attracted to the sun in accordance with an inverse-square law of force. Newton's immediate reply was "an ellipse," implying that he could connect the inverse-square supposition with Kepler's empirical first law of planetary motion. Unable to find his calculations, Newton promised to redo them. These he sent to Halley, together with the treatise *De Motu Corporum*, which Halley persuaded him to expand and publish. The result, completed in about 18 months, appeared in 1687 as *Philosophiae Naturalis Principia Mathematica*, or more briefly, *Principia*. The work was immediately and universally acclaimed. (For a description of this work, see NEWTONIAN MECHANICS AND MECHANICAL EXPLANATION.)

In 1689 Newton was elected member of Parliament to represent the university, and he served for about a year. In 1696 he was appointed warden of the mint, a post in which he revealed marked administrative abilities in supervising coinage reform. He became master of the mint in 1699 and was elected president of the Royal Society in 1703, holding both positions until his death. His later years were marred by quarrels with the astronomer John Flamsteed and by controversy over whether Newton or Leibniz had priority in the invention of the calculus.

In personality Newton was quiet and only rarely given to laughter. He did not communicate his ideas readily and was far from being a quick or facile speaker. Morbidly sensitive to criticism, he was so possessive about his own work that not only was he reluctant to publish it, but when he did, he only rarely acknowledged the specific contributions of others. This was the case despite his statement—made as much in an attempt to pacify Robert Hooke as in modesty—that what he accomplished was done because he had stood "on the shoulders of giants." When his priority was questioned or when he was crossed in other ways, he grew resentful and even vindictive, threatening to withdraw entirely from science. On more than one occasion, he used the power of his reputation or office to crush others. Even some of his closest friends, John Locke and Charles Montague (earl of Halifax), suffered from his suspicions. In the dispute over the discovery of the calculus, he masterminded the words and actions of his younger followers, who questioned not only Leibniz' priority but also his honesty, as he was accused of stealing Newton's ideas. (It is now granted that Newton and Leibniz arrived at the calculus independently.)

Work in optics: scientific method. In experiments with prisms, Newton separated white light into a spectrum and demonstrated the different refractive indexes of different colors. He was thus led to believe that an achromatic refracting telescope was impossible, since all the colors could not be focused at one point through a glass lens; as an answer to the difficulty he built the first reflecting telescope. His first published paper (1672) was an account of the "philosophical discovery" that had led him to construct the telescope: his exhaustive prism experiments and his doctrine of the heterogeneous composition of white light. Newton became embittered and his natural reluctance to publish was exaggerated by the strong criticism that this paper provoked from Robert Hooke, Christian Huygens, and other advocates of a Cartesian wave theory of light. Their criticisms were made largely on the ground that Newton had declared light to be a body and that he had failed to prove that no alternative hypothesis could account as well for the experimental facts. In reply, Newton declared that he had advanced his hypothesis "without any

absolute positiveness," and that, inasmuch as he was aware that the facts could be accounted for by many hypotheses, he "chose to decline them all," relying only on what was proved by the facts. He often expressed this attitude toward hypotheses in later works, most notably in the General Scholium to *Principia*, in the statement "*Hypotheses non fingo*" ("I feign no hypotheses"). The dictum provided an answer to critics (like Leibniz) who maintained that since *Principia* offered no explanation (cause) of gravitation (unless in terms of an occult quality), it was inadequate as a physical theory. Newton was perfectly clear on this point: "To us it is enough," he wrote, "that gravity does really exist, and act according to the laws which we have explained, and abundantly serves to account for all the motions of the celestial bodies, and of our sea."

It is not clear, however, how far Newton meant to carry his principle. It is taken by some merely as an injunction to avoid metaphysical or occult-quality speculations, although Newton says explicitly in the General Scholium that it applies to physical or mechanical as well as to metaphysical or occult-quality hypotheses. Newton's words have been taken by some as advocating a Baconian philosophy, according to which facts are collected and then the only possible explanation deduced (or induced). Others interpret it as a statement of the view that scientific explanations must be mere descriptions in terms of mathematical correlations of facts. However, apart from the question of whether these views of scientific method are defensible, it must be kept in mind in evaluating them as interpretations of Newton's view of scientific method that he himself—tentatively, it is true—advanced "hypotheses" and used this word in full self-consciousness to refer to them, as in his corpuscular view of light (and later in his "fits of easy reflection and easy transmission" view, which attributed wave as well as corpuscular properties to light) and in his views about an "aetherial medium." Indeed, he himself admitted the need to provide an "explanation" of gravity in mechanical (contact action) terms. In particular, the "Queries" appended to the *Opticks* (1704) are filled with hypotheses.

History, alchemy, and theology. Newton devoted a considerable effort throughout his life to such activities as trying to reconstruct the chronology of ancient times by combining astronomical methods with clues from the Bible, and attempting to interpret the prophecies of Daniel. He did not maintain that the future could be predicted on the basis of Biblical prophecies but only that, once the events had occurred, they could support the Bible by revealing themselves as the events that had been foretold. Newton also engaged in extensive alchemic experiments, but his purposes in these investigations are unknown.

His own religious beliefs, although strong, were heterodox; his anti-Trinitarianism was suppressed until well into the nineteenth century. He was influenced by Henry More's view that space is an attribute of God and is his sensorium. He maintained that after the creation, God retained at least two functions: to keep the stars from collapsing into one mass under the influence of gravitation, and to maintain the stability of the solar system in the face of perturbations of planetary motions by other planets.

Image and influence. Descartes's physical theory continued to vie with Newton's for primacy on the Continent throughout the first quarter of the eighteenth century. Newton's views finally triumphed, however, due not only to the defects of Cartesianism but also to the efforts of popularizers like Voltaire. Newton's views began to have an impact on areas outside science itself. Mechanics came to be regarded as the ultimate explanatory science: phenomena of any kind, it was believed, could and should be explained in terms of mechanical conceptions, and the scientific method of *Principia* could and should be extended to all fields of human endeavor.

Newton's mechanical theory was used to support both the deistic view that God had created the world as a perfect machine that then required no further interference from him, and the theistic view that he had to interfere continually in order to preserve the stability of the universe. Newton himself favored the latter view, but God's function of maintaining the stability of the solar system was dispensed with by Pierre Simon de Laplace, who showed that on the basis of the Newtonian theory the system was stable despite perturbations. Thus the Newtonian theory came increasingly to favor deism and, eventually, a view of the universe as determined by inexorable laws. Mechanism thus became equated with determinism, and the Newtonian world picture came to be thought of as a picture of a Newtonian world machine. These ideas are typified in Laplace's view that a Supreme Intelligence, armed with a knowledge of the Newtonian laws of nature and a knowledge of the positions and velocities of all particles in the universe at any moment, could deduce the state of the universe at any other time.

To the eighteenth and much of the nineteenth centuries, Newton himself became idealized as the perfect scientist: cool, objective, and never going beyond what the facts warrant to speculative hypotheses. The *Principia* became the model of scientific knowledge, a synthesis expressing the Enlightenment conception of the universe as a rationally ordered machine governed by simple mathematical laws. To some, even the fundamental principles from which this system was deduced seemed to be a priori truths, attainable by reason alone.

There was, however, another image of Newton in the eighteenth century: the Newton of the *Opticks*, the patient, cautious experimenter. This image led to an experimentalist trend, which manifested itself, for example, in the gathering of data in other areas of science—electricity, magnetism, heat, and chemistry. In many respects, this image was incompatible with that associated with *Principia*, for it led to sensitivity to the complexities of facts, a distrust of overarching, simple theories, the development of empiricist philosophies, and ultimately, to the development of sciences that would challenge the central place of mechanics in human knowledge.

Bibliography

An incomplete edition of Newton's *Opera,* edited by S. Horsley, was published in five volumes (London, 1779–1785). The only available English edition of *Principia* (*Mathematical Principles of Natural Philosophy*) was translated by A. Motte, F. Cajori, ed. (Berkeley, 1946); it is sparsely annotated. A critical edition, with the texts of the three editions prepared during Newton's lifetime, has been in preparation for several years by I. B. Cohen and the late Alexandre Koyré; it is approaching completion and is to be published jointly by Harvard and Cambridge University Presses. Other available works of Newton include *Opticks* (New York, 1952); *Papers and Letters on Natural Philosophy,* I. B. Cohen, ed. (Cambridge, Mass., 1958); *Unpublished Scientific Papers of Isaac Newton,* A. R. Hall and M. B. Hall, eds. (Cambridge, 1962), which contains excellent essays and commentaries by the editors; *Correspondence of Isaac Newton,* Vols. I – III, H. W. Turnbull, ed. (Cambridge, 1959–1961); subsequent volumes to be edited by J. F. Scott.

Early biographies, such as David Brewster's *The Life of Sir Isaac Newton* (London, 1831), tended to paint Newton as a paragon of morality and Christianity. This is avoided by L. T. More's *Isaac Newton* (New York, 1962), which, although valuable, suffers from several deficiencies of its own, among them its age (it was first published in 1934). A new biography by R. S. Westfall, incorporating the results of the enormous research of recent years, is in preparation. E. N. da Costa Andrade's *Sir Isaac Newton* (London, 1961) is brief but very good.

I. B. Cohen's *Franklin and Newton* (Philadelphia, 1956) is a study of the experimentalist tradition of Newtonianism. G. Buchdahl's *The Image of Newton and Locke in the Age of Reason* (London, 1961) is good although short; it contains a large number of illustrative passages from eighteenth-century writers.

Two excellent essays reviewing the vast recent literature and problems concerning research on Newton are I. B. Cohen, "Newton in the Light of Recent Scholarship," in *Isis,* Vol. 51 (1960), 489–514; and D. T. Whiteside, "The Expanding World of Newtonian Research," in *History of Science,* Vol. 1 (1962), 16–29.

DUDLEY SHAPERE

NEWTONIAN MECHANICS AND MECHANICAL EXPLANATION.

Expressions such as "mechanical explanation," "mechanical conception of nature," and "mechanical model" are often used so broadly and ambiguously as to include practically any kind of explanation, conception, or model. More careful philosophical discussions, however, restrict the usage considerably. Indeed, when philosophers refer to "mechanical explanation," they generally mean explanations within the context of one type of physical theory described as mechanical, namely, Newtonian or classical mechanics.

The first reasonably complete development of this subject in mathematical form was given by Isaac Newton in his *Philosophiae Naturalis Principia Mathematica* (1687). Presented on the model of Euclid's *Elements* (which, however, it does not approach in rigor), this work begins with a statement of eight definitions and three "axioms or laws" of motion from which theorems and corollaries are subsequently deduced. Following are the "axioms or laws," in Newton's words (as translated by A. Motte):

I. Every body continues in its state of rest, or of uniform motion in a right [i.e., straight] line, unless it is compelled to change that state by forces impressed upon it.

II. The change of motion is proportional to the motive force impressed; and is made in the direction of the right line in which that force is impressed.

III. To every action there is always opposed an equal reaction; or, the mutual actions of two bodies upon each other are always equal, and directed to contrary parts.

In accordance with Newton's Definition II, the word "motion" may be replaced by the later term "momentum," which is mass multiplied by velocity. The second law is usually expressed in the following form: force equals mass multiplied by acceleration, or, in the language of differential calculus, force equals mass multiplied by rate of change of velocity with respect to time $(F = m \; dv/dt)$, "rate of change of velocity with respect to time" being the definition of "acceleration"; "velocity" itself is defined as "rate of change of position with respect to time."

Insofar as the term "mechanical" is restricted to contexts concerning Newtonian mechanics, a mechanical explanation may be said to be one given in terms of the concepts and theorems of the Newtonian system or in terms of their equivalents. More specifically, physical systems in Newtonian mechanics are treated as "masses" in motion (changing position in time), affecting each other by "forces," which in turn are specified in terms of the spatiotemporal relations of masses and certain constants associated with those masses. The three axioms and their consequences specify the behavior of such masses, motions, and forces. However, the specific natures of the forces involved are not laid down by the laws, and further restrictions have often been imposed on what can truly qualify as a "mechanical" explanation or as a "complete" mechanical theory by restricting the admissible characteristics of those forces. Thus the seventeenth-century "mechanism" of Descartes and others insisted that the forces involved in any ultimately valid mechanical explanation must be contact forces, as action at a distance was considered impossible. This requirement provided the basis for much early criticism of Newton, who himself tended to agree that his theory was incomplete in this respect: gravitation, being a force acting at a distance, required a deeper "mechanical" explanation. Newton, in those moments when he did not mind feigning "hypotheses," favored the view that gravitational forces are propagated by contact through an "Aetherial Medium." Contact-action explanations of gravity continued to be sought long after Newton; the most popular was proposed by Georges Lesage in 1747 and was revived in the nineteenth century by Lord Kelvin and others. However, explanations in terms of action at a distance became respectable and even preferred in the eighteenth century. Thus Roger Boscovich developed a version of Newtonian mechanics in which all forces—even those by which one body repels another on contact (impenetrability)—were reduced to attractive and repulsive forces acting at a distance. So natural did action at a distance become that Kant in *Metaphysical Foundations of Natural Science* (1786) incorporated the notion into the a priori conception of matter, explaining contact action, as did Boscovich, in terms of forces centered in mass points.

Other types of restrictions on the forces admissible in mechanical explanations have also been imposed. One usual demand is that all forces be specifiable ultimately in terms of masses (sometimes ascribed certain characteristics besides mass) located in space and time. In order to account for all the phenomena usually dealt with in mechanics, it becomes necessary under this requirement to postulate microphysical entities and processes. Thus, a connection is established between mechanics and microphysics. Another commonly imposed requirement is that only central forces are admissible.

Historical remarks. Although the second law of motion is usually expressed in the form $F = m \; dv/dt$, there is considerable textual evidence that Newton himself had no such formulation in mind but rather was thinking of an impulsive force resulting in an instantaneous change of motion—a kick or push rather than a continuously operating force such as gravity. The explicit formulation in terms of differential calculus or $F = ma$, applicable to mechanical problems of all kinds, was first presented by Leonhard Euler in 1749. In this as in other respects, the inadequacy of Newton's development of "Newtonian" mechanics belies the assertion of Ernst Mach in the *Science of Mechanics* that Newton "completed the formal enunciation of the mechanical principles now generally accepted. Since his time no essentially new principle has been stated."

The first half of Book I of the *Principia* presents a mathematical unification of the achievements of the preceding century, but the remainder of that book as well as Book II—Newton's own original contribution beyond his mathematical unification of previous work—was largely inadequate. Book III constitutes an application of Book I to astronomical questions. Only rarely does the *Principia* resort to calculus, preferring to rely on geometrical argument. It is certainly not true that the work formulates the principles of mechanics that we learn today, for the mechanics one learns today (and in Mach's day) is the mechanics of Joseph Louis Lagrange, W. R. Hamilton, and a host of other successors of Newton, rather than of Newton himself. Those developments were unquestionably new as compared with Newton's formulations; the question of whether and in what sense they were essentially new (that is, whether or not they are "equivalent" to Newton's formulations) will be discussed below.

Inertia. The key principle of "Newtonian" mechanics is the principle of inertia, as embodied in the first law of motion. The basic principle of motion according to the Aristotelian tradition had been that an external force is required to maintain a body in violent motion (for simplicity we shall ignore the case of "natural" motion): *omne quod movetur ab alio movetur* (everything that moves is moved by something else). This view, however, faced numerous difficulties, particularly as to why projectiles continued to move "violently" after being released by the propelling agent. To meet this difficulty, the fourteenth-century supporters of the impetus theory (Jean Buridan, and Nicholas Oresme), anticipated by the sixth-century Byzantine John Philoponus, held that the force that maintains a body in violent motion need not be external but may be internal, being an "impetus" transferred from the propelling agent to the body. This view had a profound influence on the development of the concept of inertia and thereby on the development of Newtonian mechanics.

The next major step in the development of the concept of inertia came with Galileo's view that a body on a smooth (frictionless) level surface would, once in motion, continue to move "with a motion which is uniform and perpetual provided that the plane has no limits." Galileo, however, did not have a true principle of inertia, as he apparently held that the moving body, if not acted on by external forces, would continue to move at a uniform rate along a great circle on the surface of the earth. There is some question as to how much influence the work of Galileo actually had on Newton, and it has been claimed that the laws of motion were derived rather from Cartesian physics via the principle of the conservation of momentum.

The principle of inertia was given its first modern formulation by Descartes, who declared that "Any given piece of matter considered in itself tends to go on moving, not in any oblique path, but only in straight lines" (*Principles of Philosophy*, Part II, Par. 39). However, according to Descartes, since matter fills all parts of space (and indeed is identified with space) and is incompressible, this tendency is always impeded, and the only motions that ever actually take place are circular. Hence neither Galileo nor Descartes fully succeeded in escaping the Greek ascription of a fundamental role to circular motion in nature. Only with an atomistic view of matter as distinct from space and not filling it was it possible to maintain that inertial motion can be realized in nature, and even then, only if bodies can be free of all external forces (for example, by being at sufficiently great distances from other bodies).

Descartes's view embodies the heart of the modern conception of inertia, usually referred to as the "Newtonian" conception: that uniform rectilinear motion (or rest) in general does not require a cause or force, either external or internal, for its maintenance; what requires such causal explanation is, in general, accelerated motion. In brief, for the Aristotelian tradition and its critics, it is change of *position* (in a "violent" direction, at least) that requires a causal explanation (although the force may, according to the Impetus Theory, be internal rather than external); for the Newtonian conception, on the contrary, it is change of *motion* that requires a force. The extent to which Newton himself was clear about this shift, however, is questionable. In Definition III he speaks of a "*vis insita*, or innate force of matter," which is "a power of resisting by which every body, as much as in it lies, continues in its present state, whether it be of rest, or of moving uniformly in a right line." This *vis insita* is identified with the *vis inertiae* (not to be confused with the modern conception of "inertial force") and, insofar as it is conceived of as an internal force maintaining the body in its stage of uniform motion, it is still in the tradition of the *impetus* of the fourteenth century and Galileo's *vis impressa*.

Status of the laws of motion. Controversy has raged from Newton's day to the present regarding the kind and degree of justification, if any, for accepting the Newtonian laws of motion; the relations between them; the role they play in mechancs; the interpretation of the fundamental terms occurring in them; the presuppositions, if any, of these laws; and whether these laws and the terms occurring in them are fundamental in mechanics or, indeed, in all science.

According to Kant, the three laws of motion (or, rather, his own analogues thereof, since he omits Newton's second law and adds the principle of conservation of matter) are deducible, respectively, from the synthetic a priori principles of the permanence of substance, of causality, and of

reciprocity. Arguments purporting to show that the laws are a priori were also advanced by Jean Le Rond d'Alembert and James Clerk Maxwell. Against these views, arguments have been advanced that there is no a priori reason why change of velocity should require explanation in terms of the application of an external force or cause. Why should it not be change of position or change of acceleration—or even some higher derivative of distance with respect to time— that requires explanation in these terms? Similarly, what a priori reasons are there for supposing that the motion does not depend on the mass or even on the color of the body? Indeed, the Aristotelian view was that all (violent) motion (change of position rather than change of motion) requires a cause. As for natural motions, those Aristotelians who held that bodies speed up as they approach their natural places maintained in effect that acceleration is, at least in some cases, natural. Such arguments are also valid against the view that all alternatives to the Newtonian laws are psychologically inconceivable or self-contradictory.

The view that the laws are empirical has been a common one. Some have claimed, for example, that the laws are merely summaries of past observations, or that they are generalizations based on past observations. Critics, however, have argued that the laws cannot be empirical in either of these senses. The first law, for example, is said to make reference to abstractions or idealizations (such as mass points and force) that cannot be observed. Furthermore, it is argued, the necessary conditions for inertial motion cannot be realized even in principle. Thus one author maintains that in Galileo's inclined plane experiments, elimination of the friction of the plane is impossible, even for the idealized horizontal case, "since only a weightless body could move without friction, and according to the law of gravitation there are no weightless bodies (Arthur Pap, *The A Priori in Physical Theory*). The empirical basis of the laws has also been questioned on the ground that since gravitation does not vanish except at infinite distances, no body can be removed entirely from the action of external forces, and thus inertial motion cannot occur. This objection cannot easily be countered by holding that one can extrapolate via thought experiment to the case of a single body infinitely far from other bodies, that is, effectively alone in space. For, first, the notion of a single body in motion appears to be meaningless if motion can be determined only with respect to a material reference frame. Second, if one adopts Mach's definition of mass, according to which a particle possesses mass only insofar as it interacts with other particles, such a body would have no mass whatever and hence no inertia. In the face of such difficulties, many have concluded that "extrapolation from actual cases to an empirically impossible one is not inductive generalization in the ordinary sense, where one simply generalizes from the observed to the observ*able*" (Pap, *op. cit.*; see also G. J. Whitrow, "On the Foundations of Dynamics," *British Journal for the Philosophy of Science*, Vol. 1, 1951).

In view of such objections, as well as in the light of recent developments in empiricist philosophies, it has been maintained that the laws are empirical in a broader sense. This argument holds that although the laws are, in some sense, based on or suggested by past observations, they are not merely generalizations: they contain theoretical terms whose meanings go beyond what can be specified in purely observational terms. However, the exact relationships between such principles and the observations which suggest them or on which they are based have not yet been sufficiently clarified. This fact, together with the appeal of other interpretations of the laws, has resulted in only limited acceptance of even the broader empiricist interpretation.

Among these alternative interpretations, perhaps the most prominent today is the view that the laws are conventional, definitional, or regulative (these terms are often used interchangeably). In addition to interpretations that make the second law a disguised definition of force (Gustav Kirchhoff) or of equal time interval (William Thomson and P. G. Tait, *Treatise on Natural Philosophy*), the first law has been called an "ideal of natural order" and a "standard of rationality and intelligibility" (Stephen Toulmin, *Foresight and Understanding*) determining what needs to be explained and what does not. In advancing such views, many writers have alleged that the introduction of the law of inertia, far from having been brought about because of the acquisition of new factual evidence, "required a different kind of thinking-cap . . . a different attitude, so to speak, in the observer" (Herbert Butterfield, *The Origins of Modern Science*). According to the most extreme versions of this view, the concepts, problems, and criteria of success of one theory are relative to the fundamental ideals, paradigms, or principles of that theory; those fundamental principles themselves are nonempirical and even, for some writers, arbitrary. Such fundamental ideals, including the principle of inertia, are held to determine what counts as a phenomenon or a fact for the scientists who accept that principle. Such interpretations go hand in hand with interpretations (such as A. Koyré's) of the seventeenth-century scientific revolution as essentially a Platonic or rationalistic reaction against Aristotelianism.

Views intermediate between those described, as well as views combining them, have also been proposed. According to William Whewell, each of the three laws is a composite of two distinct but mutually supporting elements: one is necessary, and depends on "the way in which we can and do reason concerning causes"; this element is "of absolute and universal truth, and is independent of any particular experiment or observation whatever"; the other element is empirical. For Poincaré, the laws were originally empirical generalizations, but later were constructed as "conventional" principles. Émile Meyerson claimed that they are "intermediate between the *a priori* and the *a posteriori*." Arthur Pap called them "functionally *a priori*," in the sense that they are "regulative laws that tell us how to arrive at descriptive laws." Needless to say, many writers have not given the same interpretation of all three laws.

Logical relations. Views of the epistemological status of the laws affect the interpretation of the logical relations between them. According to some writers, the first law is merely a special case of the second, for the case $a = 0$ (in which case $F = 0$). This is certainly true if the second law is taken as giving a definition of force as mass times acceleration. However, if the second law is interpreted as stating that the exertion of a force is a sufficient condition for change of momentum, and the first law as stating that it is also a necessary condition, the two laws become logically independent. On this interpretation, the second law alone does not exclude the possibility that the momentum can, for example, decrease spontaneously, as was supposed by the Aristotelian tradition.

Again, if it is supposed that there are means of determining the presence of forces independently of the accelerations they produce, then, as Newton argued, the third law follows from the first for forces acting between parts of the same body or for bodies separated only by a rigid body. If the action and reaction between the parts (or the two bodies) were unequal, an acceleration not due to an external force would be produced, and the body (or system of bodies) would "in free space . . . go forwards *in infinitum* with a motion continually accelerated; which is absurd and contrary to the first Law." For forces acting between spatially separated bodies, however, the laws would be independent, although Newton may have thought, erroneously, that his argument could be extended to bodies separated from one another. In any case, if the first (or second) law is taken as the definition of force or as the operational test of the presence of forces, then the third law becomes empirical, asserting as it does that bodies and systems of bodies obey the law of conservation of momentum.

Function. Questions have also been raised concerning the role or function of the laws of motion; such questions are not always separated from questions about the epistemological status of the laws. Among the functions attributed to one or more of the laws are that they define scales of measurement of quantities (such as force or mass); that they demarcate the notation we accept; that they provide methods of defining, selecting, organizing, and/or summarizing facts; and that they serve as patterns of explanation, as rules of inference, as principles of instrument construction, or as empirical correlations between facts. One widely held view is that these diverse roles are not incompatible, but that the laws are used in all these and other ways—sometimes in one way, sometimes in another.

Force and mass. Newton (like Max Planck later) regarded forces as causes of accelerations, so that the presence of accelerations is merely the criterion of, or evidence for, the presence of forces. Thus he viewed the second law as a correlation between two physically real magnitudes, force and acceleration. However, positivistic criticisms of the notion of forces as real entities observable solely through their accelerative effects, have led to the claim that such a conception of force is meaningless. To such thinkers, the view of Gustav Kirchhoff and others that the second (and/or first) law is a definition of force as mass times acceleration has proved appealing. It is not true, however, that all forces are measurable only through their accelerative effects. For example, the forces involved in a situation may already have been measured by statical methods, so that the expression "This (statically determined) force is twice as great as that one" has a meaning independent of whether the forces will cause a body to move. Kirchhoff's interpretation also presupposes that it is possible to define mass and uniform rectilinear motion independently of force.

Newton defined quantity of matter, in Definition I, as a measure of matter "arising from its density and bulk conjointly," and then equated "mass" with quantity of matter. Mach criticized this notion of mass as being circular, since he held that density is definable only as the quotient of the total quantity of matter (mass) divided by its volume. However, in an atomistic conception, density can be defined as the ratio of the volume that material particles occupy in a body to the total volume of the body. Such a definition, however, appears to be generally unusable, and hence Mach's criticism continues to carry weight.

Many alternative definitions of mass have been proposed, the most famous and most often cited being that of Mach himself, who defined it in terms of the negative inverse ratio of the accelerations produced by two bodies. (He carefully tried to separate the empirical from the conventional elements involved in this definition.) Thus, if a standard body is taken as having unit mass, the mass of any other body can be determined by the mutual accelerations produced when that body interacts with the standard mass. In a simple and elegant mathematical argument, however, C. G. Pendse has shown that the Mach definition of mass cannot be applied to determine the ratios of the masses of the bodies in a system—even if it is isolated—if the system contains more than seven bodies.

Absolute space, time, and motion. Newton believed that the laws of motion presupposed the existence of an absolute space and time in which bodies could truly, rather than merely relatively, be said to be in motion. A body that appears to be in accelerated motion relative to some material reference frame would only appear to be in the presence of forces relative to that frame and would appear to be free of forces relative to some other reference frame. Although Newton admitted that, in general, measurements of velocity must be made relative to a material reference frame, he claimed that the presence of absolute motion could be distinguished from relative motion in certain cases by its "properties, causes, and effects." However, after a brief discussion, he seems to have abandoned the attempt to detect absolute motions through their properties and causes, and he based his main argument on a consideration of their effects. This was a new principle since it now turns out that forces appear not only as causes of accelerations, but also as their effects.

In his most famous argument along these lines, a water-filled bucket hanging from a rope is subjected to the following sequence of events. (1) The rope is twisted and then released so that the bucket begins to rotate; in the initial stages of this rotation, the bucket is in motion relative to the water, and the water surface is flat. (2) Shortly thereafter, the water begins to rotate also, until it finally reaches a state in which it is at rest relative to the bucket; now its surface is curved. (3) The bucket is stopped abruptly; again the water is rotating relative to the bucket, as in (1), but this time its surface is curved. (4) Finally, the water again comes to rest relative to the bucket, but unlike the situation in (2), its surface is now flat. Newton argued that since the surface of the water can be either flat or curved regardless of the state of the bucket to which its motions are referred, the water's rotation cannot be made a function of the reference frame and so must be real, not only

relative, and that this absolute motion implies the existence of an absolute space and time in which this motion takes place. In this argument, the accelerated (absolute) motion has as its effect a force which is revealed in the deformed surface. Similarly, Newton argued that absolute rotation may be revealed in the tension of cords attaching two spheres rotating about a common point on the cord, or in the flattened poles of a rotating body like Jupiter. Mach presented a detailed critique of the bucket experiment, arguing that it shows only that there is no correlation between the depression of the water surface and the motion of the water relative to the bucket, not that there may not be a correlation relative to some other body or set of bodies, such as the fixed stars, thus obviating the need for postulating an absolute space and time. In any case, Newton's argument is peculiar in that it applies only to accelerated motions, whereas absolute uniform velocity remains undetectable. Other arguments purporting to show that the laws of motion presuppose the existence of absolute space and time have been advanced, for example, by Euler and Bertrand Russell (*Principles of Mathematics*).

Post-Newtonian developments. The eighteenth century saw the extension of Newton's work and the development of alternative fundamental mechanical principles, among them the Principle of the Conservation of Force (that is, energy, in the modern sense), the Principle of Virtual Velocities, d'Alembert's Principle, the Principle of Least Action, and the dynamical equations of Euler and Lagrange. The work of Hamilton in the nineteenth century also belongs to this tradition. The nineteenth century also witnessed growing dissatisfaction with the foundations of mechanics. Not only were general critiques, like those of Mach, Karl Pearson, John Stallo, and Poincaré, prevalent but formulations of mechanics were developed that claimed to be epistemologically more satisfying than other versions. Heinrich Hertz's work is an example. In the case of some formulations, such as those utilizing "minimum principles," the question arises as to whether they imply a teleological view of nature, and Hertz was concerned with developing a formulation that would avoid such implications. He also rejected the Newtonian concept of force as a fundamental notion.

The alternate versions of mechanics which have been constructed are equivalent mathematically to Newton's, but the question remains of whether they are also equivalent in all other important respects. Certainly Hertz wished to develop a mechanical theory that would be superior (in other than a purely mathematical sense) to previous versions. C. Truesdell has argued that the mechanics of Newton and Euler is basically different from that of d'Alembert and his successors. He claims that the development of mechanics after Newton involved "abstraction, precision, and generalization of Newtonian concepts," and even the creation of "new principles and methods" and "new concepts." This suggests the possibility that classical mechanics consisted of a body of theories (of which Newtonian mechanics was only one) rather than a single one with variations and raises obvious questions concerning the relations between those theories.

Classical mechanics is sometimes said to be a special case of relativistic mechanics, applicable to bodies moving at velocities which are low as compared with the velocity of light. On the other hand, some writers claim that the theory of relativity has changed or altered the classical mechanical concepts of space, time, and mass, thus raising questions as to how classical mechanics can be a special case of relativistic mechanics. To complicate the issue still further, advocates of the Copenhagen Interpretation of quantum mechanics, such as Werner Heisenberg, have argued that "the concepts of classical physics [i.e., mechanics] are just a refinement of the concepts of daily life and are an essential part of the language which forms the basis of all natural science" (*Physics and Philosophy*). Those concepts, they argue, while inadequate for a complete description of microphysical phenomena, nevertheless are inescapable and incapable of being modified by any scientific theory. Thus we find that there remain controversies not only regarding the fundamental concepts and propositions of Newtonian mechanics, but also concerning the relations between that and other versions of classical mechanics and between classical mechanics and other types of mechanical theories.

Bibliography

(For a list of available works of Newton, see the bibliography to NEWTON, ISAAC.)

Two excellent general works on the historical background of Newtonian mechanics are E. J. Dijksterhuis, *The Mechanization of the World Picture* (Oxford, 1961), and A. R. Hall, *From Galileo to Newton* (New York, 1963). Other fine works in this area are E. A. Burtt, *The Metaphysical Foundations of Modern Science* (Garden City, N.Y., 1955); H. Butterfield, *The Origins of Modern Science* (New York, 1958); A. Koyré, *From the Closed World to the Infinite Universe* (New York, 1958); and T. S. Kuhn, *The Copernican Revolution* (Cambridge, Mass., 1957). M. B. Hesse's *Forces and Fields* (London, 1961) is an excellent historical and philosophical study of the question of action at a distance. The following works contain much valuable factual information but are less satisfactory in their treatment of the conceptual issues involved: R. Dugas' two works, *A History of Mechanics* (Neuchâtel, 1955) and *Mechanics in the Seventeenth Century* (Neuchâtel, 1958); and M. Jammer's three books, *Concepts of Force* (Cambridge, Mass., 1957); *Concepts of Space* (Cambridge, Mass., 1957); and *Concepts of Mass* (Cambridge, Mass., 1961).

Post-Newtonian mechanics has not yet been so extensively examined by historians. The chapters on mechanics in R. J. Forbes and E. J. Dijksterhuis, *A History of Science and Technology* (Baltimore, 1963), and A. Wolf, *A History of Science, Technology, and Philosophy in the 18th Century* (New York, 1961), are very good but sketchy. A penetrating survey of the period from Newton to Lagrange is found in C. Truesdell, "A Program Toward Rediscovering the Rational Mechanics of the Age of Reason," in *Archive for the History of Exact Sciences*, Vol. 1 (1960), 3–36. The great pre-Relativity critiques of classical mechanics are E. Mach, *The Science of Mechanics* (La Salle, Ill., 1960); K. Pearson, *The Grammar of Science* (New York, 1957); H. Poincaré, *The Foundations of Science* (Lancaster, Pa., 1946); and J. B. Stallo, *The Concepts and Theories of Modern Physics* (Cambridge, Mass., 1960).

The most comprehensive contemporary treatment of the philosophical issues concerning classical mechanics is E. Nagel, *The Structure of Science* (New York, 1961), Chs. 7–12. Specific issues are well treated in C. D. Broad, "Mechanical Explanation and Its Alternatives," in *PAS*, Vol. 19 (1919), 86–124; papers by N. Hanson and B. Ellis in R. Colodny, ed., *Beyond the Edge of Certainty* (Englewood Cliffs, N.J., 1965); P. Frank, *Philosophy of Science* (Englewood Cliffs, N.J., 1957), Ch. 4; N. R. Hanson, *Patterns of Discovery* Cambridge, 1958), Ch. 5; and A. Pap, *The A Priori in Physical Theory* (New York, 1946), Part II, Section I. W. Whewell, *The Philosophy of the Inductive Sciences* (London, 1847), is still well worth reading.

See also the following textbooks on classical mechanics. Nonmathematical: A. d'Abro, *The Rise of the New Physics* (New York, 1951), Vol. I; G. Holton and D. H. D. Roller, *Foundations of Modern Physical Science* (Reading, Mass., 1958). Intermediate: R. B. Lindsay and H. Margenau, *Foundations of Physics* (New York, 1957), Chs. 1–3. Advanced: H. Goldstein, *Classical Mechanics* (Reading, Mass., 1950).

C. G. Pendse's critique of Mach's definition of mass appears in *Philosophical Magazine*, Series 7, Vol. 24 (1937), 1012–1022; Vol. 27 (1939), 51–61; and Vol. 29 (1940), 477–484.

Two contemporary axiomatizations of classical mechanics, utilizing the techniques of modern mathematical logic, are J. C. C. McKinsey, A. C. Sugar, and P. Suppes, "Axiomatic Foundations of Classical Mechanics," in *Journal of Rational Mechanics and Analysis*, Vol. 2 (1953), 253–272, and H. A. Simon, "The Axioms of Newtonian Mechanics," in *Philosophical Magazine*, Series 7, Vol. 33 (1947), 888–905; see also Simon, "The Axiomatization of Mechanics," in *Philosophy of Science*, Vol. 21 (1954), 340–343. Further discussions of axiomatization are found in L. Henkin, P. Suppes, and A. Tarski, eds., *The Axiomatic Method* (Amsterdam, 1959).

Further bibliographical references may be found in M. B. Hesse, "Resource Letter PhM-1 on Philosophical Foundations of Classical Mechanics," in *American Journal of Physics*, Vol. 32 (December 1964).

DUDLEY SHAPERE

NICHOLAS OF CUSA, also known as Nicholas Kryfts or Krebs (1401–1464), theologian, philosopher, and mathematician, was born at Kues on the Moselle River between Trier and Koblenz. After attending the school of the Brothers of the Common Life in Deventer, Holland, he studied philosophy at Heidelberg (1416), canon law at Padua (1417–1423), and theology at Cologne (1425). Nicholas received a doctorate in canon law in 1423. About 1426 he gave legal assistance to Cardinal Orsini, papal legate to Germany. At about the same time began his lifelong interest in collecting classical and medieval manuscripts. Among his notable discoveries were 12 lost comedies of Plautus. He took an active part in the Council of Basel, first as a lawyer of Count von Manderscheid and later as a member of the deputation *De Fide*. Nicholas' *De Concordantia Catholica*, a vast program for reform of the church and the empire, supported the conciliar theory of the supremacy of the council over the pope. Later, disillusioned by the council's failure to reform the church, he abandoned the conciliar theory and supported the papal cause.

Nicholas carried out several missions for the pope in an effort to unify and reform the church. He was a member of the commission sent to Constantinople to negotiate with the Eastern church for reunion with Rome, which was temporarily effected at the Council of Florence (1439). In 1450 Nicholas was sent to Germany as a legate to carry out church reforms. He was created a cardinal in 1448 and appointed bishop of Brixen (Bressanone) in 1450. He died in Todi, Umbria.

Knowledge. According to Nicholas, a man is wise only if he is aware of the limits of the mind in knowing the truth. Knowledge is learned ignorance (*docta ignorantia*). Endowed with a natural desire for truth, man seeks it through rational inquiry, which is a movement of the reason from something presupposed as certain to a conclusion that is still in doubt. Reasoning involves a relating or comparing of conclusion with premises. The greater the distance between them, the more difficult and uncertain is the conclusion. If the distance is infinite, the mind never reaches its goal, for there is no relation or proportion between the finite and infinite. Hence, the mind cannot know the infinite. The infinite is an absolute, and the absolute cannot be known by means of relations or comparisons.

Accordingly, the mind cannot comprehend the infinite God. By rational investigation we can draw ever nearer to him but cannot reach him. The case is the same with any truth, for every truth is an absolute, not admitting of degrees. Since reason proceeds by steps, relating conclusion to premises, it is relational and hence never arrives at absolute truth. According to Cusa, "our intellect, which is not the truth, never grasps the truth with such precision that it could not be comprehended with infinitely greater precision" (*De Docta Ignorantia* I, 3). As a polygon inscribed in a circle increases in number of sides but never becomes a circle, so the mind approximates to truth but never coincides with it.

Thus, knowledge at best is conjecture (*coniectura*). This is no mere guess or supposition that may or may not be true; it is an assertion that is true as far as it goes, although it does not completely measure up to its object. Reason is like an eye that looks at a face from different and even from opposite positions. Each view of the face is true, but it is partial and relative. No one view, nor all taken together, coincides with the face. Similarly, human reason knows a simple and indivisible truth piecemeal and through opposing views, with the result that it never adequately measures up to it.

The weakness of human reason was evident to Cusa because its primary rule is the principle of noncontradiction, which states that contradictories cannot be simultaneously true of the same object. He insisted that there is a "coincidence of opposites" (*coincidentia oppositorum*) in reality, especially in the infinite God. He criticized the Aristotelians for insisting on the principle of noncontradiction and stubbornly refusing to admit the compatibility of contradictories in reality. It takes almost a miracle, he complained, to get them to admit this; and yet without this admission the ascent of mystical theology is impossible.

Cusa preferred the Neoplatonists to the Aristotelian philosophers because they recognized in man a power of knowing superior to reason which they called intellect (*intellectus*). This was a faculty of intuition or intelligence by which we rise above the principle of noncontradiction and see the unity and coincidence of opposites in reality. He found this faculty best described and most fruitfully cultivated by the Christian Neoplatonists, especially St. Augustine, Boethius, Pseudo-Dionysius, St. Anselm, the School of Chartres, St. Bonaventure, and Meister Eckhart. Following their tradition, he constantly strove to see unity and simplicity where the Aristotelians could see only plurality and contradiction. He frequently expressed his views in symbols and analogies, often mathematical in character, because the rational language of demonstration is appropriate to the processes of reason but not to the simple views of the intellect.

God. Cusa was most concerned with showing the coincidence of opposites in God. God is the absolute maximum or infinite being, in the sense that he has the fullness of perfection. There is nothing outside him to oppose him or to limit him. He is the all. He is also the maximum, but not in the sense of the supreme degree in a series. As infinite being he does not enter into relation or proportion with finite beings. As the absolute, he excludes all degrees. If we say he is the maximum, we can also say he is the minimum. He is at once all extremes, the absolute maximum as well as the absolute minimum. In short, in God, the infinite being, all opposition is reconciled in perfect unity.

The coincidence of the maximum and minimum in infinity is illustrated by mathematical figures. For example, imagine a circle with a finite diameter. As the size of the circle is increased, the curvature of the circumference decreases. When the diameter is infinite, the circumference is an absolutely straight line. Thus, in infinity the maximum of straightness is identical with the minimum of curvature. Or, to put it another way, an infinite circle is identical with a straight line.

Cusa offered several a priori proofs for the existence of the absolute maximum, or God. The first argued that the finite is inconceivable without the infinite. What is finite and limited has a beginning and an end, so that there must be a being to which it owes its existence and in which it will have its end. This being is either finite or infinite. If it is finite, then it has its beginning and end in another being. This leads either to an infinite series of actually existing finite beings, which is impossible, or to an infinite being which is the beginning and end of all finite beings. Consequently, it is absolutely necessary that there be an infinite being, or absolute maximum.

The second proof argued that the absolute truth about the absolute maximum can be stated in three propositions: It either is or is not. It is and it is not. It neither is nor is not. These exhaust all the possibilities, so that one of them must be the absolute truth. Hence there is an absolute truth, and this is what is meant by the absolute maximum.

As the absolute maximum, God contains all things; he is their "enfolding" (*complicatio*). He is also their "unfolding" (*explicatio*) because they come forth from him. Creatures add nothing to the divine reality; they are simply limited and partial appearances of it. As a face reproduces itself more or less perfectly in a number of mirrors, so God reflects himself in various ways in his creatures. In this case, however, there are no mirrors.

God transcends the universe but is also immanent in it, as a face is present in its mirrored images. Each creature is also present in every other, as each image exists in every other. Thus, as Anaxagoras said, everything is in everything else. Leibniz recalled this doctrine of Cusa's in his *Monadology* when showing that each monad mirrors every other.

Like all medieval Platonists, Cusa upheld the reality of universal forms. According to him, the most universal of all created forms is the form of the universe, called the Soul of the World. This form embraces in its unity all lower forms, such as those of genera and species. These lower forms are "contractions" of the form of the universe; they are the universe existing in a limited way. They exist in the universe, and it in turn exists in a limited way in them. Individuals are further contractions of universal forms—for example, Socrates is a contraction of the form of humanity. The universe as a whole is a contraction of the infinite God. Thus, all things exist in a unified manner in the universe, and the universe in turn exists in the unity of God. Oppositions and contradictions that appear on the level of individuals and lower universal forms are reconciled in the unity of the universe and ultimately in the unity of God.

Cosmology. Since the universe mirrors God, it too must be a maximum—not the absolute maximum, to be sure, but the relative maximum, for it contains everything that exists except God. Cusa denied that the universe is positively infinite; only God, in his view, could be described in these terms. But he asserted that the universe has no circumference and consequently that it is boundless or undetermined—a revolutionary notion in cosmology. (See Alexandre Koyré, *From the Closed World to the Infinite Universe*, Baltimore, 1957.) Just as the universe has no circumference, said Cusa, so it has no fixed center. The earth is not at the center of the universe, nor is it absolutely at rest. Like everything else it moves in space with a motion that is not absolute but is relative to the observer.

Nicholas of Cusa's cosmology in some respects broke with the Ptolemaic and Aristotelian cosmological views of the Middle Ages and anticipated those of modern times. He was above all concerned with denying the absolute oppositions in the world of Ptolemy and Aristotle. In Cusa's world there was no center opposed to its circumference, no maximum movement of the spheres opposed to the fixity of the earth, no movement of bodies in absolutely opposed directions, such as up and down. Cusa also denied that the heavenly bodies are composed of a substance different from that of sublunar bodies.

Cusa extended his principle of the coincidence of opposites to religion. In his irenical work *On the Peace of Faith*, while maintaining the superiority of Christianity over other religions, he tried to reconcile their differences. Beneath their oppositions and contradictions he believed there is a fundamental unity and harmony, which, when it is recognized by all men, will be the basis of universal peace.

In a century of social, political, and religious unrest, Nicholas of Cusa revitalized Neoplatonism as the most effective answer to the needs of his time. His thought was firmly rooted in the philosophy of Proclus and Christian medieval Neoplatonism and was opposed to the Aristotelianism that had prevailed in western Europe since the thirteenth century. It was also highly original and expressed in a language abounding in symbolism and paradox. Nicholas of Cusa had many of the traits of the Renaissance man: love of classical antiquity, all-encompassing curiosity, optimism, cultivation of literary style, critical spirit, preoccupation with the individual, and love of mathematics and science. His works were widely read for several centuries, and they influenced the philosophy of the Renaissance and of early modern times.

Bibliography

Nicholas' religious–political works are *De Concordantia Catholica* (1433–1434); *De Pace Fidei* (1453); and *Cribratio Alchorani* (1461).

His theological–philosophical works are *De Docta Ignorantia* and *De Coniecturis* (1440); *De Deo Abscondito* (1444); *De Quaerendo Deum* (1445); *De Genesi* (1447); *Apologia Doctae Ignorantiae* (1449); *Idiotae Libri* (containing *De Sapientia, De Mente,* and *De Staticis Experimentis;* 1450); *De Visione Dei* (1453); *De Beryllo* (1458); *De Possest* (1460); *Tetralogus de Non Aliud* (1462); *De Venatione Sapientiae* (1463); *De Ludo Globi* (1463); and *De Apice Theoriae* (1463).

His mathematical–scientific works are *De Staticis Experimentis* (1450); *De Transmutationibus Geometricis* (1450); *De Mathematicis Complementis* (1453); and *De Mathematica Perfectione* (1458).

Editions of Nicholas' works are *Opera* (Basel, 1565); *Opera,* 3 vols. (Paris, 1514; reprinted Frankfurt am Main, 1962); *Nicolaus von Cues, Texte seiner philosophischen Schriften,* A. Petzelt, ed., Vol. I (Stuttgart, 1949); *Opera Omnia,* 14 vols. (Leipzig and Hamburg, 1932–1959); and *De Pace Fidei,* R. Klibansky and H. Bascour, eds. (London, 1956).

Translations include *The Vision of God,* translated by E. G. Salter (New York, 1928); *The Idiot,* translated by W. R. Dennes (San Francisco, 1940); *Of Learned Ignorance,* translated by G. Heron (London, 1954); and *Unity and Reform; Selected Writings of Nicholas de Cusa,* J. P. Dolan, ed. (Notre Dame, Ind., 1962).

Literature on Nicholas includes P. Duhem, "Nicholas de Cues et Léonard de Vinci," in *Études sur Léonard de Vinci,* Vol. II (Paris, 1909); E. Vansteenberghe, *Le Cardinal Nicolas de Cues* (Paris, 1920); P. Rotta, *Il cardinale Nicolò di Cusa, la vita ed il pensiero* (Milan, 1928); and *Nicolò Cusano* (Milan, 1942); A. Posch, *Die "Concordantia Catholica" des Nikolaus von Cusa* (Paderborn, 1930); H. Bett, *Nicholas of Cusa* (London, 1932); M. de Gandillac, *La Philosophie de Nicolas de Cues* (Paris, 1941); J. Koch, *Nikolaus von Cues und seine Umwelt* (Heidelberg, 1948); P. Mennicken, *Nikolaus von Kues* (Trier, 1950); Étienne Gilson, *Les Métamorphoses de la cité de Dieu* (Paris, 1952); K. H. Volkmann-Schluck, *Nicolaus Cusanus* (Frankfurt am Main, 1957); E. Meuthen, *Die letzten Jahre des Nikolaus von Kues* (Cologne and Opladen, 1958); G. Santinello, *Il pensiero di Nicolò Cusano nella sua prospettiva estetica* (Padua, 1958); G. Heinz-Mohr, *Unitas Christiana* (Trier, 1958); E. Zellinger, *Cusanus-Konkordanz* (Munich, 1960); P. E. Sigmund, *Nicholas of Cusa and Medieval Political Thought* (Cambridge, Mass., 1963); and Ernst Cassirer, *Individuum und Kosmos in der Philosophie der Renaissance* (Leipzig and Berlin, 1927), translated by Mario Domandi as *The Individual and the Cosmos in Renaissance Philosophy* (Oxford, 1963).

ARMAND A. MAURER

NICHOLAS OF ORESME. See ORESME, NICHOLAS.

NICOLAI, CHRISTIAN FRIEDRICH (1733–1811), German publisher, editor, and author. He was born in Berlin and studied there and at a Pietist institution in Halle, but he never attended a university. Nicolai spent three years as a business apprentice in Frankfurt an der Oder. Upon his father's death in 1752, he took over the family bookstore, managing it—except for a short period—until his death and expanding it into a very successful and lucrative publishing house. He became a close friend of G. E. Lessing and of Moses Mendelssohn, and was active in Berlin intellectual life. He edited the *Bibliothek der schönen Wissenschaften und freien Künste* ("Library of Aesthetics and Fine Arts") from 1757 to 1758, The *Literaturbriefe* ("Letters on Literature") from 1759 to 1765, and the *Allgemeine deutsche Bibliothek* ("Universal German Library") from 1765 on. The last-mentioned journal became the most famous German literary review of its time and was widely influential in theology as well.

Nicolai's own works, like those of many Enlightenment figures, were largely higher journalism consisting mainly in forceful and lively attacks on contemporary intellectual and literary personalities and trends. His *Briefe, den jetzigen Zustand der Schönen Wissenschaften betreffend* ("Letters on the State of the Arts," Berlin, 1755) were directed against the influential literary critic J. C. Gottsched. His philosophical novel *Sebaldus Nothanker* (3 vols., Berlin, 1773–1776) was an attack on certain reactionary circles in Halle. In various articles in his journals he attacked J. G. Hamann, Johann Caspar Lavater, Christian Garve, and others. He quarreled with J. G. Herder and F. H. Jacobi. The novels *Daniel Säuberlich* (Berlin, 1777–1778) and *Die Freunden des jungen Werthers* (Berlin, 1775) were parodies of Goethe, Herder, G. A. Bürger (author of the ballad *Lenore*), and the *Sturm und Drang*. He attacked Catholicism as a source of superstition and Jesuitism; and, although he was himself a member of the Order of the Enlightened (*Illuminaten*) and of the Freemasons, he accused both of being secret instruments of the Jesuits (which resulted in his forced resignation). In the philosophical novels *Geschichte eines dicken Mannes* ("The Story of a Fat Man," 2 vols., Berlin, 1794) and *Sempronius Gundibert* (Berlin, 1798) and in other works, he accused Kant and his school and Fichte of being crypto-Catholics. His *Vertraute Briefe von Adelheid B. an ihre Freundin Julie S.* ("Confidential Letters from Adelaide B. to Her Friend Julie S.," Berlin, 1799) was directed against Schleiermacher.

Nicolai wrote many other works, notably a large work devoted to the economic, cultural, social, and religious life in Germany and Switzerland, *Beschreibung einer Reise durch Deutschland und die Schweiz im Jahre 1781* ("Description of a Journey Through Germany and Switzerland in 1781," 12 vols., Berlin, 1783–1796). Although Nicolai was awarded an honorary doctorate by the Helmstedt Theological Seminary in 1799 and was made a corresponding member of the Academy of St. Petersburg in 1804, his hostility toward the most influential persons of his time and his lack of understanding of the new critical philosophy and of romanticism led to a negative evaluation of his work by his leading contemporaries and by the following generation.

Nevertheless, Nicolai was one of the most typical representatives of "popular philosophy." Basing his theories on common sense, he avoided abstract thought and complex speculation and favored useful and easy knowledge. He opposed orthodoxy, intolerance, enthusiasm, mysticism, and secret machinations. He attacked the scholastic Wolffian philosophy; the newer critical and idealistic philosophies; Protestantism, both orthodox and mystical, and Catholicism; secret societies; Gottsched's classicism in literature as well as the glorification of the peasant by J. H. Voss and Bürger; *Sturm und Drang*; and early romanticism. He considered them all to be reactionary and pernicious, and his writings were full of misunderstandings, misrepresentations, and exaggerations.

His religious views incorporated his rejection of intellectualism, dogmatism, and mysticism. He held that religion and science should not be confused. Orthodox religion corrupted morality and tended toward an obnoxious hierarchical system. He denied original sin and eternal damnation and accepted the doctrines of free will and of the immortality of the soul. Religion should be based on the individual conscience and not on revelation—on common sense and not on enthusiasm.

According to Nicolai, religion and morality are not the same. Morality is based on social sense and experience; religion is a feeling for God's goodness and providence as mirrored in the goodness and beauty of the Creation. Although Nicolai was a deist himself, he did not believe that a purely natural religion would suffice for the common people, and therefore he refused to reject publicly the Christian tradition.

Nicolai was influenced in aesthetics by the classicists Nicolas Boileau and Jean Baptiste Dubos and by the Swiss critics J. J. Bodmer, J. J. Breitinger, and J. G. Sulzer. He tried to find a middle ground between the classical doctrine of the imitation of nature and the newer stress on the imagination. He opposed the classical ideal of literature as deduced from a set of rules, the sentimental school of literature, and the *Sturm und Drang* emphasis on intuitive genius. He held that poetry should be simple and reasonable and designed chiefly for moral improvement.

Additional Works by Nicolai

Ueber meine gelehrte Bildung. Berlin, 1799.
Philosophische Abhandlungen. Berlin, 1808.

Works on Nicolai

Aner, K., *Der Aufklärer Friedrich Nicolai.* Giessen, 1912.
Fichte, J. G., *Fr. Nicolais Leben und sonderbare Meinungen.* Tübingen, 1801.
Meyer, Friedrich, *Friedrich Nicolai.* Leipzig, 1938.
Ost, G., *Fr. Nicolais Allgemeine Deutsche Bibliothek.* Berlin, 1928.
Philips, F. C. A., *Nicolais literarische Bestrebungen.* The Hague, 1926.
Sommerfeld, M., *Nicolai und der Sturm und Drang.* Halle, 1921.
Strauss, Walter, *Nicolai und die kritische Philosophie.* Stuttgart, 1927.

GIORGIO TONELLI

NICOLAS OF AUTRECOURT (c. 1300–after 1350), also called Nicolaus de Ultracuria, was a leading anti-Aristotelian philosopher of the fourteenth century. The condemnation of extreme Aristotelianism at Paris in 1277 was probably responsible for the critical tendencies in many fourteenth-century philosophers and theologians. An extreme form of this critical tendency is to be found in the writings and lectures of Nicolas of Autrecourt. He was at the Sorbonne as early as 1328, lectured on the *Sentences* at Paris, and in 1340 was summoned by the Roman Curia to answer charges of heresy and error. His trial was interrupted when Pope Benedict XII died, and was resumed under Pope Clement VI by Cardinal Curty. In 1346 the trial was concluded, Nicolas was forced to recant many of his published statements, his works were publicly burned, and he was declared unworthy of advancement and unworthy to continue teaching. We last hear of him as a deacon at the cathedral of Metz in 1350.

His literary remains consist of (1) two complete letters to

the Franciscan Bernard of Arezzo, a reply to a certain Giles (whose letter to Nicolas is also extant), and the fragments of seven other letters to Bernard of Arezzo; (2) a theological discussion concerning the increase of cognitive powers; and (3) the "universal tractate of Master Nicolas of Autrecourt for seeing whether the statements of the Peripatetics are demonstrative" (usually called *Exigit Ordo Executionis* from its *incipit*), which survives in a single manuscript that breaks off toward the end.

The continuing research on fourteenth-century thought will probably show that many other Schoolmen of the period expressed doctrines similar to those of Nicolas. In fact, similar doctrines have already been found in Robert Holkot and John of Mirecourt on epistemological issues, and in Henry of Harclay, Gerard Odo, and some others on atomism and the constitution of the continuum. Nevertheless, there is some reason to attribute to Nicolas a considerable measure of originality and of persistent thought. For one thing, his contemporary John of Mirecourt attributes to Nicolas the proof that causal connections cannot be demonstrated. This may mean merely that Mirecourt was making an acknowledgement to a colleague and was unaware that similar doctrines were taught at Oxford. But there must be some significance in the fact that Nicolas was singled out for attack by the decrees of the Paris faculty in 1339 and 1340 and was one of those summoned to the Curia in 1340.

The main historical origin of Nicolas' skeptical and critical views about the extent of natural knowledge was undoubtedly the prominence given to the article of the Creed "I believe in one God, Father Omnipotent, Maker of heaven and earth, . . ." after the condemnation of 1277. As the theologians of the fourteenth century interpreted this article, it meant that God can accomplish anything the doing of which involves no logical contradiction. Now, the miracles of the Old Testament and New Testament are incompatible with the doctrines of Aristotle and his strict interpreters, especially Averroës, in ways which touch directly on the point. Whereas Aristotle denies the possibility of accidents without substrata, the Eucharist involves the supernatural existence of the accidents of bread and wine after the substance no longer exists (that is, after the substance of bread and wine has been converted into the body and blood of Christ when the priest consecrates the Host). Again, whereas Aristotle had held that effects inevitably arise from their causes unless there is some natural impediment, the episode of the three Israelites who were not consumed in the fiery furnace involves the miraculous interruption of the natural effects of causes where there is no impediment. Consideration of these and like cases led theologians to the following result: the common course of nature can, without logical absurdity, be interrupted by divine power. Hence, the relation of causes and effects or of substances and their accidents is not logically necessitated.

Certitude, substance, and cause. Nicolas of Autrecourt must have begun his reflections from the consideration of the theological doctrine just mentioned. He maintained that, excepting the certitude of faith, there is but one kind of certitude and this certitude depends on the principle of contradiction: Contradictories cannot be simultaneously true. Nothing is prior to this principle and it is the ultimate basis of all certitude. This certitude is absolute and no power can alter it. It has no degrees and all certitude is reducible to it. Thus, all reasoning by syllogism depends on the principle of contradiction. In every implication (*consequentia*) which is reducible to the principle of contradiction either immediately or by a number of intermediate steps, the consequent of the implication and the antecedent (or a part of the antecedent) are really identical. Otherwise it would not be evident that the antecedent is inconsistent with the denial of the consequent. From all this Nicolas derives the following result: From the fact that one thing is known to exist it cannot be inferred with an evidence reducible to that of the principle of contradiction that another thing exists. Neither the existence nor the nonexistence of one thing can be evidently inferred from the existence or nonexistence of any other thing. The consequences of this discovery, Nicolas thought, were enough to destroy the whole intellectual enterprise of the Schools. Not only is it impossible that the existence of effects entails the existence of causes, but there is no way to have any evident knowledge of any substance other than one's own soul starting from the objects of sensation or of inner experience. Things apparent to the senses are not substances, and therefore substance cannot be evidently inferred from sensibly appearing objects. Hence the existence of material substances or of other spiritual creatures cannot be inferred with certitude from the evidence of the senses. But this is not all. In *one* sense of "probable," there is not even a probability that there are any substances. For, in the sense in which the probable is what happens frequently, we can say, for example: When I in the past put my hand toward a fire, it was warmed; it is now probable that if I put my hand toward a fire, it will be warmed. But since there has never been (and could never be) a conjunction in my experience between any appearance and a substance, there is no appearance which renders the existence of a substance so much as *probable* in *this* sense of the word.

Some of Nicolas' critics urged that substance is deducible from appearances and that causes are deducible from their effects. But he replied that all such deductions depend upon descriptions of appearances and effects which, implicitly or explicitly, contain reference to substances or causes. The deductions from such descriptions are perfectly valid, but nothing in experience or in our stock of self-evident propositions provides the slightest evidence that anything corresponds to such descriptions. In a word, every attempt to prove the existence of substances or causes from appearances or effects begs the question. This point was made in other philosophical writings both before and after Nicolas. The Muslim theologian al-Ghazālī, in his *Tahāfut al-Falāsifah* ("Incoherence of the Philosophers"; see *Averroes' Tahafut al-Tahafut*, edited and translated by Simon van den Bergh, London, 1954, pp. 329–333), pointed out that logically guaranteed inferences concerning causes depend on the description and definitions of terms and so, in a sense, are mainly verbal arguments. Nicolas could not have had access to this work because the relevant sections were not translated until sometime later. Hume's negative critique of belief in causation and belief in substance parallels that of Nicolas very closely, but Hume had no possible access to the writings of Nicolas because these were not discovered until the nineteenth and twentieth centuries in the Bibliothèque Nationale and the Bodleian Library.

Critique of Aristotle. The purpose of Nicolas' critique of Aristotle and his followers is set forth in the prologue to his *Exigit Ordo Executionis.* He tells us that he read the works of Aristotle and his commentator Averroës and discovered that the demonstrations of their doctrines were defective, that arguments for the opposite of these doctrines can be found which are more plausible than arguments for them. (The word "plausible" here is intended to translate the Latin word *probabilis* because, in this usage, it does not mean "frequent" but "plausible.") Moreover, men have spent their entire lives studying Aristotle to no avail while neglecting the good of the community. Men would live better lives and contribute to the common good, in matters religious and moral, if only they knew that very little certitude about things can be learned from natural appearances and that what little can be learned can be obtained in a short while, provided men attend to things rather than the treatises of Aristotle and Averroës. In a word, the intellectual culture of Nicolas' age is condemned as largely vain; and the purpose of his criticism is simply to show this in detail. This is not to say that Nicolas is opposed to empirical investigation, but it would be a mistake to see in his attack on Aristotle an interest in empirical investigation such as we find in the promoters of natural science in the sixteenth and seventeenth centuries.

The criticism of Aristotle as set forth in the *Exigit* has an aspect not indicated in his controversy with Bernard of Arezzo. In the letters to Bernard he declared that nothing which is said about infrasensible reality is even probable. In another sense of probability, introduced in the *Exigit* (but one of the accepted senses of the term in the Middle Ages and derived, in fact, from Aristotle), a proposition or opinion is probable if there are arguments in its favor which, although inconclusive, would be approved by an impartial judge. In this sense, a proposition or opinion has a probability which varies as our information increases. Accordingly, Nicolas begins with a conception that is accepted by his adversaries: the principle that the Good exists in our minds as a kind of measure for evaluating things. According to this, we may assume that the things in the universe are so arranged that whatever is good exists and whatever is bad does not exist. Since there is no way of demonstrating that things exist in a certain arrangement, we are obliged to depend on the principle of the Good in order to determine what is probably the case. Following this principle we can suppose that (1) all things in the universe are mutually connected so that one thing exists for the sake of another (like Aristotle's view that all things are ordered to one ultimate end, that is, God; cf. Aristotle, *Metaphysics* 1075a15 ff.); (2) there is systematic subordination of all things to a single end so that nothing exists which does not somehow contribute to the good of the entire universe; (3) the universe, so conceived, must be at all times equally perfect.

Atomism. From the above, Nicolas concludes that any particular thing which now exists has always existed and will always exist. For whatever now exists, exists for the good of the whole, and because this whole is always and everywhere equally perfect, all its parts must always exist. Hence, on the principle of the Good, every ultimate entity in the universe is eternal.

The eternity of things is obviously incompatible with Aristotle's thought, in which the generation and corruption of substances and their accidents is an essential feature. Here Nicolas is content to show that all the Aristotelian arguments to prove the occurrence of generation, corruption, or other kinds of change are inconclusive. For example, we cannot prove conclusively that sensible qualities cease to exist. The only method of proving this is to argue that a quality ceases to exist because it no longer appears to us, and this is obviously inconclusive. Hence, Nicolas argues, the atomic theory in its most radical form is more plausible than Aristotle's nonatomistic theory of change. The *appearance* of change can be accounted for in terms of the aggregation and separation of atomic particles.

There is much of interest in the finer details of Nicolas' atomism, particularly in his defense of indivisible minima as the ultimate constituents of the continuum, his defense of the vacuum, and his theory of motion. But here he is by no means original. His theory of the nature of motion, for example, is taken over from William of Ockham, and his views about indivisibles owe much to other fourteenth-century Scholastics. Moreover, there are radical deficiencies in his views on these subjects. Nicolas also adopted the radical Ockhamist thesis that relations are reducible to their terms, so that there are no extracognitive referents to our relational concepts. The denial of extracognitive relations is mistaken, and this part of Nicolas' speculations suffers from this error.

The *Exigit* also develops a theory of knowledge in terms of which whatever appears to be the case is the case, that is, that the objects of cognition are all in some way real. Nicolas also develops a positive theory of causation, and there is a related theory of eternal recurrence. Whether he derived this from Stoic sources is not clear.

Influence and importance. The skeptical and critical views, as well as Nicolas' probabilistic defense of atomism, produced some responses among his contemporaries and successors. Albert of Saxony, Jean Buridan, and others replied to his critical views on causation and substance, and Thomas of Strasbourg discussed his atomism. Many references to his views on the nature of propositions occur in later fourteenth-century theologians. Moreover, although Nicolas' views were formally condemned by the Curia in 1346, at the end of the century Cardinal Pierre d'Ailly not only adopted many of these views but also wrote that "many things were condemned against [Nicolas] because of envy which were later publicly stated in the schools."

The importance of Nicolas of Autrecourt in the history of thought can best be summarized as follows: He was a radical representative of an increasing tendency in fourteenth-century thought to reject the idea that any of the principles of natural theology admit of demonstration, and he thus contributed to the decline of the authority of Aristotle. Although some of his reflections are both important and valid, they seem not to have had any direct effect on the development of philosophy in early modern times.

From one point of view, he and some of his contemporaries achieved a clarity about the nature of beliefs in causation and substance which was neither equaled nor surpassed until the eighteenth century in the writings of Hume.

Bibliography

Editions of Nicolas of Autrecourt's writings are found in J. Lappe's "Nicolaus von Autrecourt," in *Beiträge zur Geschichte der Philosophie des Mittelalters*, Vol. 6, No. 2 (Münster, 1908), and J. Reginald O'Donnell's "Nicholas of Autrecourt," in *Medieval Studies*, Vol. 1 (1939), 179–280, which contains an edition of the *Exigit*.

A study of Nicolas' work is found in Lappe's article. Other studies have been made by P. Vignaux, "Nicolas d'Autrecourt," in *Dictionnaire de théologie catholique,* Vol. XI (Paris, 1931); J. Reginald O'Donnell, "The Philosophy of Nicholas of Autrecourt and His Appraisal of Aristotle," in *Medieval Studies*, Vol. 4 (1942), 97–125; J. R. Weinberg, *Nicolaus of Autrecourt* (Princeton, N.J., 1948); Mario del Pra, *Nicola di Autrecourt* (Milan, 1951); and V. Zoubov, "Nicolas iz Otrekura i Drevnegrecheskie Atomisti," in *Trudi Instituta Istorii Estestvoznaniia i Tekhniki* (SSSR Akademiia Nauk), Vol. 10 (1956), 338–383.

JULIUS R. WEINBERG

NICOLE, PIERRE (1625–1695), French theologian and philosopher, was born in Chartres. Although unsuited by nature and temperament for leadership of a zealous religious faction, he nevertheless served the Jansenists of Port-Royal brilliantly with his pen. A keen polemicist, an able scholar, and a distinguished theologian and moralist, Nicole was so intimately associated in authorship with Antoine Arnauld that portions of works appearing under the latter's name were in fact written by Nicole. Unlike Arnauld, Nicole had the credentials neither of priest nor of doctor; although a bachelor of theology, he remained all his life in minor orders.

With Arnauld he prepared *La Logique ou l'art de penser*, the famous *Port-Royal Logic*. Under the pseudonym William Wendrock, he produced a much-praised Latin translation of Pascal's *Lettres provinciales*. His *Essais de morale* earned him a considerable reputation as a moralist. Several of these essays were translated by John Locke for Lord Shaftesbury but apparently were not published until the nineteenth century.

In the final phase of the Jansenists' controversy with the Roman Catholic church, Nicole—always physically weak and constantly tormented by fear—successfully sought an accommodation with the ecclesiastical authorities. This subjected him to vicious attack from several Jansenists but not, however, from the exiled Arnauld. During these years, Nicole put his pen at the service of Jacques Bossuet in the latter's controversy with quietism.

As an antagonist of the Calvinists, Nicole stands as one of the last great warriors. The arguments had been rehearsed for over a century, ever since the intellectual consequences of the Reformation were seen to include skeptical difficulties. In challenging the credentials of the Church of Rome as the true church, the Reformers had created a situation appropriate for questioning the criteria of religious truth and one in which the skeptical methodology of the Greek Pyrrhonists was applicable. Two of Nicole's controversial writings, *Préjugés légitimes contre les Cal-*

vinistes and *Prétendus réformés convaincus de schisme* (against opponents including Jean Claude and Pierre Jurieu), Pierre Bayle claimed, "may unhappily confirm in their evil dispositions, all who have any tendency towards Pyrrhonism."

Nicole tried to show that the way of examination, the technique of scrupulously examining a religion's claim to truth, ought to be practiced both by the Protestants, who usually only preached it, as well as by those Roman Catholics who contemplated abandoning their faith. In his three queries: Is the religion's claim drawn from a canonical Biblical book? Does the text under examination conform to the original? Are there not other ways of reading the original that weaken the argument to the religion's claim? Nicole raised innumerable difficulties for the Protestants, although not making it immediately apparent that the Catholic "way of authority" had triumphed. As Bayle commented, "A man who would be justly assured that he ought to submit to the authority of the Church, is obliged to know that the Scriptures enjoin this. Thus he is obliged to go through all the examinations laid down by Nicole. . . ."

Accordingly, Nicole, who some years before had sought to meet Pyrrhonism's challenge in his *Art de penser*, later tried to show that reason alone could give no conclusive answers to his own three questions. But since his own "way" was subject to the same difficulties of deriving Scriptural support for itself and since he even sought to show its reasonablenesss, the applicability of his argument to itself seemed evident to many. The realization, more appreciated by Bayle than by most, that nothing but mutual destruction and then perhaps religious skepticism and indifference followed from these sorts of disputes, led to their going out of style. In due course, there evolved more sophisticated ways of meeting or ignoring the skepticism that had been unleashed a century before.

Bibliography

In addition to his principal works, already referred to, Nicole produced a multitude of other writings that are of no great philosophical interest. For detailed bibliographical information, see *A Critical Bibliography of French Literature*, D. C. Cabeen and J. Brody, general eds., Vol. III, N. Edelman, ed. (Syracuse, N.Y., 1961), on Port-Royal, although little is primarily of philosophical interest. See also Gregor Sebba, *Bibliographia Cartesiana: A Critical Guide to the Descartes Literature 1800–1960* (The Hague, 1964) and *Nicolas Malebranche: A Preliminary Bibliography* (Athens, Ga., 1959) by the same author. *The Art of Thinking: Port Royal Logic* is a translation by James Dickoff and Patricia James of *La Logique ou l'art de penser* (Indianapolis and New York, 1964).

HARRY M. BRACKEN

NIEBUHR, REINHOLD, is eminent in two fields. One is social action and analysis of current social problems; the other is the interpretation of the Christian faith. This article will concentrate on his religious and ethical thinking.

Niebuhr was born in 1892 in Wright City, Missouri. His father was Gustave Niebuhr, a minister in the Evangelical Synod of the Lutheran church, who came to the United States when he was 17 years old. His mother was the daughter of the Reverend Edward Jacob Hosto, a second-generation German American of the same religious sect. Niebuhr studied at Elmhurst College, Eden Theological Seminary, and Yale University. He was ordained in 1915 and was pastor at the Bethel Evangelical church of Detroit until 1928. He was then appointed professor at the Union Theological Seminary in New York. He now lives in retirement.

Religious views. The central theme of Niebuhr's religious teaching can be stated as follows: a divine, forgiving, and timeless love "beyond history" gives meaning to human life. Nothing actually operating in human history can ever be sufficiently dominant over sinful pride and sensuality to deliver men from despair, although men attempt to conceal reality with optimistic illusions. But if we look beyond the temporal process to transcendent being, we find, through faith, a forgiving and perfect love which gives to human life a grandeur beyond the reach of despair and a zeal beyond the reach of apathy. This love from beyond history has been revealed to us in Jesus Christ. We know it is from beyond history because in history this kind of love, called agape, is ineffective before the powers that rule this world. It is futile and meaningless except when, as in the Christian faith, it reveals the ultimate purpose of our existence by an evaluation which transcends history.

Sin and anxiety. Sin arises from anxiety, although anxiety is not sinful in itself. Man is rendered anxious by criticizing himself and his world, by recognizing his own limitations and the contingencies of his existence, and by imagining a life infinitely better than what actually is.

Anxiety would not lead to sin if we brought it under control by trusting ourselves to God's forgiving love and ultimate power. But instead of this, we seek to bring anxiety under control by pretending to have power or knowledge or virtue or special favors from God, which we do not have. This pretense leads to pride, cruelty, and injustice. Or we seek to escape anxiety by dulling the awareness of it with sensuality. All this is sin because it is a turning away from God to a self-centered existence. Sin thus induced is not inevitable, but it is universal. Also Niebuhr has obscurely suggested that sin was in the world before men became sinners, this prehuman sin being symbolized by Satan.

In this predicament we have two alternatives. We may trust ourselves along with the whole of human history to God's forgiving love. The other alternative is twofold: to sink into annihilating despair or to conceal our predicament with illusions that render our condition even more desperate in the end. If we take the first alternative, we live not only for whatever love can be attained in history but also and primarily for the divine love beyond history. In this way the whole of history takes on meaning. Otherwise we have only glimpses of meaning in developments occurring here and there but no meaning for the whole of history.

Transcendence. Themes continuously recurrent throughout Niebuhr's writing are transcendence, freedom, reason, and love. Niebuhr's language often suggests that by "transcendence" he means the timeless ideal of perfect love. But for Niebuhr this love is not merely an ideal. It is a God who loves, yet is beyond time, cause, and world.

Self-transcendence is a central theme in Niebuhr's thought. If this merely meant that the self can change into a better self, the meaning would be obvious. But Niebuhr seems to mean that the self, while never escaping finitude in one dimension, does somehow, in another dimension, transcend time and causation and self. It does this by surveying past and future and by self-criticism. But to survey past and future is to be aware of one's involvement in time; and in self-criticism the self in retrospect is criticized by the present self; and this criticizing self may in turn be criticized by the self at a later time. Niebuhr would seem to be wrong, therefore, in claiming that in self-criticism the self can transcend time and causation.

Freedom and reason. Niebuhr affirms man's freedom by paradox: man is both bound and free, both limited and limitless; he is, and yet is not, involved in the flux of nature and time. As spirit he "stands outside" time, nature, world, and self, yet is involved in them. Freed of paradox, these affirmations assert that man is free in the dimension of spirit but not in the dimension of natural existence. The human spirit transcends the self, time, and nature because the individual can know himself as an object, can judge himself to be a sinner, can survey past and future. "The ultimate proof that the human spirit is free is its recognition that its will is not free" (*Nature and Destiny of Man*, Vol. I, p. 258).

Niebuhr would seem to be making contradictory statements. The self is not free if only the "spirit" transcending the self is free. The critical comment made above on his concept of transcendence would apply here also.

Reason is an instrument, says Niebuhr, which can be used for either good or evil. One evil use of reason is to impose rational coherence upon reality and to reject as unreal what cannot be fitted into that coherence. But Niebuhr is mistaken in thinking that one who insists on subjecting every affirmed belief to the tests of reason is thereby claiming that reason comprehends all reality. To the contrary, such a person fully admits that unknown reality extends beyond his knowledge; but he refuses to conceal his ignorance by superimposing religious beliefs where knowledge cannot reach. Niebuhr defends such beliefs because they relieve anxiety by providing courage and hope.

Another sinful use of reason, says Niebuhr, is to make it the basis of a false security, thus turning away from the one sure ground of security, which is a belief beyond the tests of reason, namely, that God in forgiving love will overrule all evil "at the end of history." Here again the question arises: Is true security to be found in beliefs exempt from the tests of reason or is it to be found by rejecting such beliefs and recognizing the unknown without concealing it beneath beliefs that cannot be rationally defended?

On the other hand, Niebuhr uses to the full his own magnificent powers of rational intelligence in dealing with problems arising in the temporal process of human existence. He completely accepts the powers of reason in dealing with such problems. For him reason has the further use of demonstrating its own incapacity for dealing with those religious beliefs which Niebuhr affirms while admitting that they cannot be rationally defended.

In June Bingham's book *Courage to Change* (p. 224) she

reports that Niebuhr wrote to a friend that he (Niebuhr) adheres to the religious pragmatism of William James. He validates Christian belief, when it cannot be rationally defended, by the courage, hope, peace, zeal, love, sense of being forgiven, and other psychological effects resulting when these beliefs are affirmed. Niebuhr has identified these psychological effects as the grace bestowed upon us by God when we affirm these beliefs with the total self. Thus are we assured that we are loved and forgiven by God while we are yet sinners. Niebuhr also affirms that beyond all the incoherence of our existence and beyond all our rational powers to know there is an all-comprehending and perfect coherence which somehow overcomes and absorbs all the manifest incoherences that we experience.

Love. Niebuhr has distinguished three kinds of love: heedless love (agape), which seeks nothing in return; mutual love; and calculating love. Heedless love is God's way of loving; and human beings by God's grace may have it to some degree. Since it seeks nothing in return, it cannot have the intention of awakening responsive love, although this may be its unintended result. Suffering endured with intention to awaken responsive love would be calculating love. Hence God's suffering love in Christ is not to awaken responsive love, although this may be its unintended result; but the intention is to protect God's righteousness in forgiving sin because forgiveness without atonement would be condoning sin.

Political views. In making political judgments, the individual is inevitably biased by the social position and historical process in which he finds his security and personal identity. No one can be entirely free of this bias, but its distortions are reduced by a faith which finds its ultimate security not in any social position or historical process but in the God of love and mercy who rules supreme over the whole course of history, determining its final outcome as no plan or purpose of man can ever do. Such a faith in God's power and forgiveness enables one to practice "Christian realism," whereby one is able to see the evil in the self and in the historical process with which the self is identified, as well as the depth of evil in all of human life. Political judgment can then be more free of the illusions generated by false pride, on the one hand, and by despair, on the other.

Justice requires the coercions of government to support moral demands; and the power of opposing parties must be equalized if one is not to be subordinated unjustly to the interests of the other. Also, to have justice, freedom to criticize is required. Justice serves love by providing the social conditions required for the practice of love. Love is the final norm but cannot by itself guide political action, because every project set forth in the name of love amid the contests for political power is infected with self-interest whereby the needs of others are falsely identified with those of self.

With his highly developed rational powers and critical intelligence, Niebuhr has sharply distinguished between problems subject to rational treatment and religious beliefs that cannot be rationally defended. This gives us what at times seems to be two Niebuhrs: one, the naturalist struggling with the problems of our existence with all the tools of human reason; the other, the mystic upholding a superstructure of religious belief beyond the tests of reason. Whether one of these, or both, will prevail in the course of history, only time can tell. However, the impact of Niebuhr's thought and action on our civilization will continue in one form or another for a long time.

Works by Niebuhr

Does Civilization Need Religion? A Study of the Social Resources and Limitations of Modern Life. New York, 1928.

Leaves from the Notebook of a Tamed Cynic. Chicago, 1929; new edition, Hamden, Conn., 1955. A diary of experiences when pastor in Detroit.

Moral Man and Immoral Society, A Study in Ethics and Politics. New York and London, 1932.

Reflections on the End of an Era. New York, 1934.

An Interpretation of Christian Ethics. New York, 1935.

Do the State and Nation Belong to God or the Devil? London, 1937.

Beyond Tragedy, Essays on the Christian Interpretation of History. New York, 1937. Sermons.

Europe's Catastrophe and the Christian Faith. London, 1940.

Christianity and Power Politics. New York, 1940.

The Nature and Destiny of Man, A Christian Interpretation, 2 vols. New York, 1941–1943. The most complete statement of his thought.

The Children of Light and the Children of Darkness, A Vindication of Democracy and a Critique of Its Traditional Defence. New York, 1944.

Discerning the Signs of the Times, Sermons for Today and Tomorrow. New York, 1946. Sermons.

Faith and History, A Comparison of Christian and Modern Views of History. New York, 1949.

The Illusion of World Government. New York, 1949.

Christian Realism and Political Problems, Essays on Political, Social, Ethical, and Theological Themes. New York, 1953.

The Self and the Dramas of History. New York, 1955.

Pious and Secular America. New York, 1958.

The Structure of Nations & Empires. New York, 1959.

Works on Niebuhr

Bingham, June, *Courage to Change.* New York, 1961.

Kegley, Charles, and Bretall, Robert, eds., *Reinhold Niebuhr: His Religious, Social and Political Thought.* New York, 1956.

HENRY NELSON WIEMAN

NIETZSCHE, FRIEDRICH (1844–1900), German philosopher and poet, is one of the most original and influential figures in modern philosophy. His life has attracted more attention from interpreters of his thought, major novelists, psychiatrists, and others than the life of other major philosophers. Misrepresentations of almost every facet of his life have been crucial, for they bear on an understanding of his significance. It is also difficult to obtain reliable information on the authenticity and relative importance of his works and his posthumously published notes, on his madness, and on his relation to Wagner. These problems will therefore be stressed in the following discussion.

LIFE AND PATHOLOGY

Nietzsche was born in Röcken, Prussia. His father, Ludwig Nietzsche, a Lutheran minister and the son of a minister, was 31, and his mother, the daughter of a Lutheran minister, was 18. His paternal grandfather had written several books, including *Gamaliel, or the Everlasting Duration of Christianity: For Instruction and Sedation . . .* (1796). Many of Nietzsche's ancestors were butchers; none of them seem to have been, as he believed, Polish noblemen. His father christened him Friedrich Wilhelm after King Friedrich Wilhelm IV of Prussia, on whose birthday he was born. The king became mad a few years later; so did Nietzsche's father. Nietzsche later shed his middle name, along with his family's patriotism and religion, but in January 1889 he, too, became insane.

In an early autobiographical sketch Nietzsche wrote, "In September 1848 my beloved father suddenly became mentally ill." When Elisabeth Förster-Nietzsche (born 1846) published this sketch in her biography of her brother (1895), she changed the wording to read, ". . . suddenly became seriously ill in consequence of a fall." (She also published, as addressed to her, letters actually addressed to her mother and drafts of letters to others, but there is no evidence of any forgery that affects Nietzsche's philosophy.) In fact, the diagnosis of Ludwig Nietzsche's doctor was softening of the brain (*Gehirnerweichung*), and after the elder Nietzsche's death in 1849, his skull was opened, and the diagnosis was confirmed. Nevertheless, most experts agree that the philosopher's later insanity was not inherited.

In January 1850, Nietzsche's widowed mother lost her youngest son (who was born in 1848) and moved her family to Naumburg. The household there consisted of Friedrich, his mother (who died in 1897) and sister, his father's mother, and two maiden aunts. This, as well as his sister's character, helps to account for some of Nietzsche's snide remarks about women.

In 1858 Nietzsche accepted free admission to Pforta, a famous boarding school a few miles from Naumburg. He was often at the head of his class and acquired an excellent classical education. In 1861 he wrote an enthusiastic essay on his "favorite poet," Hölderlin, "of whom the majority of his people scarcely even know the name." Hölderlin had spent the last decades of his life in hopeless insanity, but sixty years after Nietzsche wrote his essay, Hölderlin was widely recognized as Germany's greatest poet after Goethe. The teacher wrote on the paper, "I must offer the author the kind advice to stick to a healthier, clearer, *more German* poet."

The medical records of the school contain an entry, recorded in 1862: ". . . shortsighted and often plagued by migraine headaches. His father died early of softening of the brain and was begotten in old age [actually, when his father was 57, his mother 35]; the son at a time when the father was already sick [most experts deny this]. As yet no grave signs are visible, but the antecedents require consideration."

In 1864 Nietzsche graduated with a thesis on Theognis. He studied theology and classical philology at the University of Bonn, but in 1865 he gave up theology and went to Leipzig. There is no evidence that he contracted syphilis in Cologne while he was a student at Bonn, although this story has gained currency; there is, however, inconclusive evidence that two physicians in Leipzig treated Nietzsche for syphilis without telling him their diagnosis. Wilhelm Lange-Eichbaum, a psychiatrist, writes that a Berlin psychiatrist told him this and added that the names of the two doctors were known. Another psychiatrist, P. J. Möbius, is said to have possessed letters which were written by these two men but which no longer exist. Be that as it may, Nietzsche evidently never thought he had syphilis, and most of his life he was sexually a complete ascetic. The most that has been claimed is that as a student he may have visited a brothel once or twice. The matter has been much debated because his madness was probably tertiary syphilis, and Thomas Mann's novel *Doktor Faustus*, which draws on Nietzsche's life, has given these questions additional prominence.

Throughout his life Nietzsche's health was poor. His doctors kept warning him to preserve his very bad eyesight by reading and writing less. He disregarded this advice, fought severe migraine and gastric pains with long walks and much writing, and took pills and potions to purchase a little sleep. His books became his life. As they found no response, his style became shrill, and losing his inhibitions, he said in his later books what he had said earlier only in some of his letters. Out of context some phrases sound mad. Many of Nietzsche's dicta are redeemed by his wit, which has escaped many translators and interpreters.

In January 1889, Nietzsche collapsed in a street in Turin while embracing a horse that had been flogged by a coachman. His last letters, mailed on the first days of 1889, are mad but meaningful and moving. After the first week of 1889 nothing of even this pathetic brilliance relieved the utter darkness of his mind. He vegetated until his death. But none of his books can be discounted as a product of madness; all repay close study.

The various accounts of Nietzsche's pathology disagree on many points, but none of them illuminates Nietzsche's philosophy. When the novelist Arnold Zweig wanted to write a book on Nietzsche, Freud wrote him that Nietzsche's psychological development could not be reconstructed, and according to Ernest Jones, Freud's biographer, Freud "several times said of Nietzsche that he had a more penetrating knowledge of himself than any other man who ever lived or was ever likely to live." Lesser psychologists and would-be psychologists have been more condescending.

As a student at Leipzig, Nietzsche discovered Schopenhauer and Richard Wagner, the two greatest influences on his early thought, as well as F. A. Lange's *History of Materialism*. In a letter dated November 1866, Nietzsche wrote, "Kant, Schopenhauer, and this book of Lange's—more I don't need." But he also worked on Aeschylus and published papers on Theognis (1867) and a prize-winning essay on Diogenes Laërtius (1868–1869). Although the appearance of these articles in Professor Friedrich Ritschl's journals was a triumph, Nietzsche wrote his friend Erwin Rohde (later a famous classical philologist) that he found his prize paper "repulsive" and utterly inadequate. "What is Diogenes Laërtius? Nobody would lose a word over the philistine physiognomy of this scribbler if he were not by accident the clumsy watchman guarding treasures whose value he does not know. He is the night watchman of the history of Greek philosophy: one cannot enter it without obtaining the key from him."

In October 1867, Nietzsche commenced his military

service. In March 1868, while jumping on his horse, he hit the pommel of the saddle with his chest and was badly hurt, but he rode on as if nothing had happened. In August 1868, after prolonged suffering from the injury, he returned home and was formally discharged from the army in October.

Back in Leipzig, he complained, in a letter to Rohde of November 20, "I must again see the swarming philologists' breed of our day from nearby, and daily have to observe the whole molish business, the full cheek pouches and blind eyes, the delight at having caught a worm, and indifference toward the true and urgent problems of life." He published scholarly book reviews but at one point considered writing a doctoral thesis on Kant. Early in 1869 he even thought of taking up chemistry, "throwing philology where it belongs, with the household rubble of our ancient ancestors."

During the following winter the chair of classical philology at the University of Basel fell vacant, and Ritschl recommended him for the post: he had never published contributions from another student nor seen a student like Nietzsche in 39 years of teaching. Nietzsche had not yet written a doctoral thesis, let alone the dissertation generally required before a doctor of philosophy becomes a *Privatdozent*, or the additional book required for an associate professorship, yet he was appointed an associate professor at Basel at the age of 24. Ritschl wrote that "in *Germany* that sort of thing happens absolutely never" but reassured the authorities at Basel that although Nietzsche had concentrated on Greek literature and philosophy, "with his great gifts he will work in other fields with the best of success. He will simply be able to do anything he wants to do." Leipzig conferred the doctorate without thesis or examination, and in April 1869, Nietzsche went to Basel and became a Swiss subject. In 1870 he became a full professor.

In August 1870 he received leave to volunteer as a medical orderly in the Franco-Prussian War. Early in September he returned to Germany with dysentery and diphtheria; he may also have infected himself with syphilis while ministering to sick soldiers. Without waiting to regain his strength, he returned to Basel in October to teach at both the Gymnasium and the university. During the following months he also audited the lectures of Jakob Burckhardt, the art historian, visited Richard Wagner in Tribschen near Lucerne whenever possible, and finished his first book.

In summing up this account of Nietzsche's first 28 years, three points merit emphasis. First, although the historical-critical edition of Nietzsche's *Werke* (discontinued after five volumes) only includes material published before 1869 and the literature on the young Nietzsche keeps growing, this period commands attention only as the background of his later work. However, legions of errors about Nietzsche's early period have been used in support of false claims about his philosophy. Second, Nietzsche's eventual insanity seems overdetermined; no explanation of it has been proved, but so many explanations are available that what requires explanation is not so much why he became mad but how he could ever have written over ten books that stamp him as one of Germany's greatest masters of prose as well as the most influential and inexhaustible

German philosopher since Kant and Hegel. Third, he might never have subjected himself to all the requirements for a professorship had it not been offered to him practically gratis.

WRITINGS

"The Birth of Tragedy." Nietzsche's first book, *Die Geburt der Tragödie aus dem Geiste der Musik* (1872), advances theories about the birth and death of Greek tragedy that are unsupported by footnotes or Greek quotations; in 1874 a version with slight textual changes appeared. In 1886 both versions were reissued with a new introduction and a title page that read *The Birth of Tragedy, or Hellenism and Pessimism: A New Edition with an Attempt at a Self-Criticism.* This self-criticism is the best critique ever written of the book, which for all its faults has the touch of genius. Only the later introduction shows human greatness.

In 1872, immediately after *The Birth of Tragedy* was published, Ulrich von Wilamowitz-Moellendorff, who had just received his doctorate and much later was to achieve great fame as a Greek philologist, published a pamphlet, *Philology of the future! A reply to Friedrich Nietzsche's birth of tragedy* (*Zukunftsphilologie!*). Rohde replied with a polemic called *Afterphilologie*, which means "pseudophilology"; but *After*, a word Luther liked to use abusively in various combinations, also means posterior, and the title suggests a perversion of philology. Nietzsche wrote Rohde that his friend Franz Overbeck, church historian at Basel, had suggested this title. He did not mention that Schopenhauer, in his diatribe against *Die Universitätsphilosophie*, had spoken of Hegel's *Afterphilosophie*. In 1873 Wilamowitz published another reply. All three pamphlets were unworthy of their authors; they were never reprinted and have since become rarities.

Wilamowitz was utterly blind to the merits of *The Birth of Tragedy*, of which F. M. Cornford was to write in *From Religion to Philosophy* (1912) that it was "a work of profound imaginative insight, which left the scholarship of a generation toiling in the rear." Wilamowitz tried to establish his own erudition by cataloguing faults, and Rohde then tried to show that they were not faults. But Rohde, who had just received the title of professor, constantly called Wilamowitz "our Dr. phil." or "the pasquinader" and quite failed to see that Wilamowitz had a point in being worried about the future of philology if purple prose were to become a fashionable substitute for exact scholarship. (By now the Nietzsche literature offers many horrible examples.)

More than any other single work, *The Birth* changed the prevalent conception of the spirit of Greece, which owed much to Winckelmann and Goethe, and replaced "sweetness and light" (to use Matthew Arnold's phrase) with a more complex analysis, since further developed by Cornford, Jane Harrison, and E. R. Dodds (see Dodds's *The Greeks and the Irrational*, Berkeley, Calif., 1951, for recent literature).

Nietzsche distinguishes two tendencies: the "Apollinian," stressed hitherto—the genius of restraint, harmony, and measure that found expression in Greek sculpture and architecture—and the "Dionysian," a cruel longing to exceed all norms that found an outlet in the drunken frenzy of the Dionysian festivals and the music associated with them. Nietzsche argues that the Apollinian achievements cannot be fully appreciated until one realizes what powers had to be harnessed to make them possible. This point was missed by many interpreters because, in his later works, Nietzsche identified himself with Dionysus. In the late works, however, Dionysus is no longer opposed to Apollo; he stands for a synthesis of both gods and is played off against the crucified Christ. In Nietzsche's *Twilight of the Idols,* written in 1888, the old Goethe, who was certainly not anti-Apollinian, could therefore be celebrated as superbly Dionysian.

In *The Birth* the contrast between the Dionysian and Apollinian is indebted to Schopenhauer's contrast between will and representation. Even so, the book is a declaration of independence from Schopenhauer. Nietzsche explains the birth of Greek tragedy out of the music and dances of the Dionysian cult as a triumph of Apollinian form. He envisages "the sublime as the artistic conquest of the horrible," and he celebrates the Greeks who, facing up to the terrors of nature and history, did not seek refuge in "a Buddhistic negation of the will," as Schopenhauer did, but instead created tragedies in which life is affirmed as beautiful in spite of everything.

Ideally, the book should end, as a draft did, with Section 15; the remaining sections are a rhapsody on the rebirth of tragedy in Wagner's operas and obscure the conclusions of the original analysis. In *Ecce Homo,* written in 1888, Nietzsche said of *The Birth,* "It smells offensively Hegelian, and it is only in a few formulas affected by the cadaverous perfume of Schopenhauer." As Nietzsche pointed out, Dionysus and Apollo are "*aufgehoben* into a unity" in tragedy (*aufgehoben* is a characteristic Hegelian term meaning "canceled," "preserved," "lifted up"); this synthesis is then confronted by another idea, rationalism, symbolized by Socrates. Euripides was "a mask only: the deity who spoke out of him was . . . Socrates."

Rationalism antedated Socrates but "gained in him an indescribably magnificent expression." Even as the Greeks had needed tragedy to survive, they needed Socratism a little later. "If one were to think of this whole incalculable sum of energy . . . as *not* employed in the service of knowledge," Greek culture might have perished in "wars of annihilation," in "suicide," and in "pessimism." Rationalism brought about the demise of Greek tragedy, yet "the influence of Socrates necessitates ever again the regeneration of art." The two sections (14–15) that contain these conclusions suggest the need for a further synthesis—an "artistic Socrates."

Here one might think of Plato, but the *Republic* and *Laws* illustrate Nietzsche's claim that Socrates' rationalist-moralist heritage was opposed to the spirit of Aeschylus and Sophocles. The "artistic Socrates" is Nietzsche himself. Far from denouncing the development he described, he found his own task suggested by its projected culmination. What is wanted is a philosophy that faces what the Greek tragedians knew without sacrificing sharp rational analysis; a philosophy that does not share Socrates' optimistic assurance that knowledge, virtue, and happiness are inseparable; a philosophy that avails itself of the visions and resources of art.

The four meditations. From 1873 to 1876, Nietzsche published his four meditations.

First meditation. In 1873 Nietzsche published the first of his four "untimely meditations" (*Unzeitgemässe Betrachtungen,* translation published as *Thoughts out of Season*), a polemic entitled *David Strauss, The Confessor and Writer.* Strauss is best remembered for his influential *Life of Jesus* (1835). What enraged Nietzsche, however, was the immense success of Strauss's *The Old Faith and the New* (1872; 6th ed., 1873). It was the *Zeitgeist* that Nietzsche meant to attack, not Strauss, whom he was soon sorry to have hurt.

In his attack on the *Kulturphilister* ("cultural philistine"), Nietzsche abandoned the patriotism of his childhood, foresaw "the extirpation of the German spirit in favor of the 'German *Reich,*'" and denounced all "deification of success." Strauss "proclaims with admirable frankness that he is no longer a Christian, but he does not want to disturb any comfortableness of any kind." He praises Darwin, but his "ethics is quite untouched," as we see when Strauss exhorts us never to forget "that you are a human being and not merely something natural." Strauss fails to recognize that "preaching morals is as easy as giving reasons for morals is difficult."

Second meditation. In *Of the Use and Disadvantage of History for Life* (1874), Nietzsche distinguished three types of historiography. "Antiquarian history," cultivated at the universities, aims reverently to consolidate our knowledge of the past; "critical history" passes sentence; and "monumentalistic history" concentrates on past heroes in order to confront contemporary mediocrity with the possibility of greatness. While each type has its uses and disadvantages, Nietzsche dwelled particularly on the life-inhibiting consequences of the hypertrophy of the historical sense and on the usefulness of monumentalistic history, which was later cultivated under his influence by the Stefan George Circle in Germany. Their best studies include Friedrich Gundolf's monographs; their worst, Ernst Bertram's influential *Nietzsche: versuch einer Mythologie* ("Nietzsche: Attempt at a Mythology").

Nietzsche then introduced the suprahistorical (*überhistorisch*) man "who does not envisage salvation in the process but for whom the world is finished in every single moment. . . . What could ten new years teach that the past could not teach?" Nietzsche denounced "admiration for success" and "idolatry of the factual" as leading to a "yes" to "every power, be it a government, public opinion, or a majority of numbers." He rejected the optimism of nineteenth-century Hegelians and Darwinists. "The *goal of humanity* cannot lie in the end [*Ende*] but only *in its highest specimens.*"

Like the Greeks, confronted with a chaotic flood of older cultures, some of us might yet "*organize the chaos*" and appropriate the Greek "conception of culture as another and improved *physis* . . . culture as a harmony of living, thinking, appearing, and willing." In a later note Nietzsche complained that "the Germans alternate between complete devotion to the foreign and a vengeful craving for originality," as if originality consisted "in the complete and over-obvious *difference;* but the Greeks did not think that way about the Orient . . . and they *became* original (for one *is* not original to begin with, but one is raw!)" (*Werke,* Musarion edition, Vol. XI, p. 110).

Third meditation. *Schopenhauer as Educator* (1874) picks up the motif of self-perfection. "The man who would not belong in the mass needs only to cease being comfortable with himself; he should follow his conscience which shouts at him: 'Be yourself! You are not really all you do, think, and desire now.' " As Nietzsche put it later, one must become what one is. To find what one is in this sense, it helps to ask oneself what one has loved until now. The answer reveals your "true self," which is not within "but immeasurably high above you, or at least above what you usually take for your ego." Nietzsche then introduces Schopenhauer as the educator whom he has loved, in order to reveal his own true self.

State and church intimidate us into conformity; a new conception of humanity is needed. In the second meditation Nietzsche had already said of the Darwinian doctrine "of the fluidity of all . . . species, of the lack of any cardinal distinction between man and animal," that it was "true but deadly" and that in another generation, when the full implications would become apparent, a widespread practical nihilism would probably result (he did not use the word "nihilism" until later). Nietzsche was roused from his dogmatic slumber by Darwin, as Kant had been roused by Hume a century earlier, and he sought to serve humanity and humaneness by resurrecting "*the image of man.*"

He criticized Rousseau's image of man as representative of a Dionysian return to nature and the unleashing of savage and destructive forces. Schopenhauer's man—the kind Nietzsche decided then and there to become—"destroys his earthly happiness through his courage; he must be hostile even to the human beings he loves and the institutions from whose womb he issued; he may spare neither human beings nor things, though he himself suffers with them in hurting them; he will be mistaken for what he is not and long be considered an ally of powers he abominates."

Later, Nietzsche asked to be read with consideration for context in order to avoid misunderstanding—*rück- und vorsichtig* (Preface to *The Dawn*). He warned that his meaning was "plain enough, assuming—as I do assume—that one has first read my earlier writings and not spared some trouble in doing this" (Preface to *Genealogy of Morals*). He pleaded, "*Above all, do not mistake me for someone else!*" (Preface to *Ecce Homo*). This is the reason for giving so much space to Nietzsche's earlier writings, which are less familiar and accessible in English. A brief essay cannot adequately summarize Nietzsche's thought; it can serve only as an introduction.

Philosophically, the third meditation is not sophisticated. Its ethic is based on the intuition of conscience, which commands us to realize our true self, and a complementary intuition of the purpose of nature, which "wants to make the life of man significant and meaningful by generating the philosopher and the artist." We are asked to help nature, which will not succeed without our assistance. This is similar to the challenge of Zarathustra, the founder of Zoroastrianism, according to which we should help Ormuzd, the god of light, whose eventual triumph over Ahriman, the force of darkness, depends on us. In his earlier works Nietzsche does not mention the Persian prophet, but nine years later he used him as his mouthpiece in his best-known book.

Fourth meditation and break with Wagner. Nietzsche had now come up against philosophic problems he could not solve. During the next three years he published only one short book, his meditation on *Richard Wagner in Bayreuth* (1876). From 1878 to 1889 he published one book a year. But in 1875 he approached a crisis that was not only philosophical but also personal.

The first three meditations had appeared about six months apart; the fourth, on Wagner, was postponed several times and finally was published after a two-year interval. Meanwhile, Nietzsche anticipated in his notes some of the basic points of his later attack on Wagner, *The Case of Wagner* (1888). In 1878 their friendship came to an end.

Three reasons suffice to account for the break, although others may have contributed. First, according to Nietzsche, "one cannot serve two masters, when one is called Wagner" (*The Case of Wagner*). Wagner appreciated Nietzsche as an apostle of Wagnerism, as a professor who brought prestige to the cause, and as a young friend who could be asked to do one's Christmas shopping and other chores. Wagner had asked for changes in the endings of *The Birth* and the third meditation and had frowned on the second meditation, which made no special reference to him. In order to come into his own, Nietzsche had to break with Wagner.

Second, Nietzsche had had growing misgivings about many of Wagner's pet ideas, such as his nationalism and his hatred of the French and the Jews. As long as the composer lived at Tribschen, Switzerland, such idiosyncrasies could be discounted. After all, it meant a great deal to have a close relationship with the greatest German artist of the time. But when Wagner moved to Bayreuth, made his peace with the new German Empire, and became a cultural influence of the first order, Nietzsche had to take a stand.

His objection to Wagner's *Parsifal,* which is widely held to have precipitated the break between them, was that coming from Wagner, it was a betrayal of integrity. How could the self-styled modern Aeschylus celebrate the anti-Greek ideal of "pure foolishness"? How could Schopenhauer's foremost disciple, hitherto an avowed atheist, use Christianity for theatrical effects? Yet the break was not sealed in January 1878, when Wagner sent Nietzsche his *Parsifal;* it was sealed in May when Nietzsche sent Wagner *Human, All-too-human,* with a motto from Descartes and a dedication to Voltaire. In August, Wagner attacked Nietzsche in the *Bayreuther Blätter.* The third reason for the break, then, is that Nietzsche's development from Schopenhauer to Voltaire and from essays with romantic overtones to aphorisms after French models, as well as his abandonment of nationalism for the ideal of the "good European," were at least as unforgivable from Wagner's point of view as *Parsifal* was from Nietzsche's.

Nietzsche "never forgave Wagner . . . that he became *reichsdeutsch*" (*Ecce Homo*). In fact, Wagner's anti-Semitic essays profoundly influenced his son-in-law H. S. Chamberlain, author of *The Bases of the Nineteenth Century* (*Die Grundlagen des neunzehnten Jahrhunderts*); the Nazis' official philosopher, Alfred Rosenberg, author of *Der Mythus des 20. Jahrhunderts* ("The Myth of the Twentieth Century"); and, above all, Hitler. Nietzsche's cleanliness vis-à-vis Wagner's influence and vis-à-vis Bernhard Förster, the Wagnerian anti-Semitic leader whom the philosopher's sister married in 1885, merits emphasis.

The five aphoristic books. *Human, All-too-human* (*Menschliches, Allzumenschliches*, 1878) was subtitled "A Book for Free Spirits." During the winter of 1877/1878, Nietzsche's ill health had forced him to obtain leave from the Pädagogium. His eyes, head, and stomach continued to make him so miserable that in May 1879 he resigned from the university. In June he was granted a modest pension. Henceforth, he was entirely free and alone and devoted all his remaining strength to his writing.

Two sequels appeared in 1879 and 1880—"Mixed Opinions and Aphorisms" (*Vermischte Meinungen und Sprüche*) and "The Wanderer and His Shadow" (*Der Wanderer und sein Schatten*). In later editions all three books were subsumed under the general title, *Human, All-too-human*. All three consist of aphorisms, mostly a page or less in length, with little continuity between them. Also aphoristic are *The Dawn: Reflections on Moral Prejudices* (*Morgenröthe: Gedanken über die moralischen Vorurteile*, 1881, translated as *The Dawn of Day*) and *The Gay Science* (*Die fröhliche Wissenschaft*, 1882, translated as *The Joyful Wisdom*), surely Nietzsche's best books up to that time. Readers who are put off by the shrillness of his later style may find them more likable; the prose is superb, and they abound in penetrating observations.

Having reached a philosophical impasse in his meditations, Nietzsche tried a new tack, which some have called positivistic. In an exceptionally open-minded and experimental spirit, he assembled observations on which his later suggestions were built—for example, the psychology of the will to power and the contrast of master and slave moralities.

In *The Dawn*, Nietzsche tried to determine, among other things, to what extent behavior might be explained in terms of power and fear. In one long aphorism (number 113) he argued in some detail that "the striving for excellence is the striving to overwhelm one's neighbor, even if only very indirectly or only in one's own feelings," and also that "there is a long line of degrees of this secretly desired overwhelming, and a complete list of these would almost amount to a history of culture." At the top of the ladder stands "the ascetic and martyr." In other aphorisms Nietzsche stresses his contempt for the German Empire and those who worship strength; "Only the degree of reason in strength" can establish "worthiness of being honored." Corresponding to the early dualism of Dionysus and Apollo, of empirical and true self, we now have strength and reason, but there are many suggestions that self-integration evinces greater power than either asceticism or undisciplined strength.

In *The Gay Science* (290) "giving style to one's charac-

ter" is shown to be a sign of power, while "it is the weak characters without power over themselves who hate the constraint of style," who "become slaves as soon as they serve," and who "hate to serve." The one thing needed is "that a human being attain his satisfaction with himself"; those who do not will make others pay for it. In the same book we find the dictum "The secret of the greatest fruitfulness and the greatest enjoyment of existence is: *to live dangerously*" (250). Rilke's later poetry rings beautiful variations on this theme.

"Thus Spoke Zarathustra." *Thus Spoke Zarathustra* (*Also sprach Zarathustra*) contains the first comprehensive statement of Nietzsche's mature philosophy. Nietzsche called it "the most profound book" of world literature, and an apologist has asked which books, excepting the Bible, are more profound. It is widely considered Nietzsche's magnum opus. The Victorian style of the early English translations misrepresents the original, which in itself does not sustain the stylistic perfection of *The Gay Science* or *Nietzsche Contra Wagner*. Magnificence alternates with parodies, epigrams with dithyrambs, wit with bathos. Part IV derides the holy mass, as well as various types of men who were attracted to Nietzsche's philosophy. Unlike the first three parts, it relates a continuous story. It is full of laughter, some at Zarathustra's expense. Philosophically, there is an utter lack of sustained argument, but Nietzsche's later works support and develop the same ideas with attention to detail and ramifications.

The last seven books. Most British and American philosophers find *Beyond Good and Evil* (*Jenseits von Gut und Böse*, 1886) and *Toward a Genealogy of Morals* (*Zur Genealogie der Moral*, 1887) Nietzsche's most philosophic works. *Beyond Good and Evil* offers about 200 pages of 296 consecutively numbered aphorisms, framed by a preface and a poem. This book covers the whole range of Nietzsche's interests in nine chapters, each of which deals consecutively with one group of topics, such as religion and "the natural history of morals."

The *Genealogy* comprises three essays. The first contrasts good and evil as characteristic of slave morality with good and bad as characteristic of master morality. Nietzsche argues that slave morality is born of resentment and that evil is its primary concept, with good as an afterthought. In master morality, which is basically affirmative, "good" is primary and "bad" is an afterthought, a term of contempt for what is undistinguished and not noble. Nietzsche plainly prefers master morality to slave morality, without accepting or preaching either; these are merely two types of morality. Contemporary Western morality, according to Nietzsche, is an inconsistent mixture. The second essay deals with guilt, bad conscience, and related matters, and the third with the meaning of "ascetic ideals."

In 1888 Nietzsche published *The Case of Wagner* (*Der Fall Wagner*) and completed four other short books. *The Twilight of the Idols* (*Die Götzen-Dämmerung*, 1889), a 100-page summary of Nietzsche's philosophy, originally was to be entitled "A Psychologist's Leisure." Peter Gast, a disciple, pleaded for a more flamboyant title, and the master obliged with a dig at Wagner's *Götterdämmerung*, adding the subtitle "How One Philosophizes With a Hammer." This alludes to an image in the Preface, which was written before the title was changed: idols "are here touched with a hammer as with a tuning fork" to determine whether they are hollow.

The Antichrist (*Der Antichrist,* 1895) was subtitled *Attempt at a Critique of Christianity,* but shortly before his collapse Nietzsche struck out this subtitle, substituting "Curse on Christianity." It seems reasonable to retain the earlier subtitle.

Ecce Homo, Nietzsche's incomparably sarcastic review of his work, was withheld by his sister until 1908. Its four chapter headings are "Why I Am So Wise," "Why I Am So Clever," "Why I Write Such Excellent Books" (which comprises reviews of all his books through *The Twilight of the Idols*), and "Why I Am a Destiny." The similarity to George Bernard Shaw is striking, but many critics have discounted the book and failed to profit from its exceedingly interesting self-interpretation. Indeed, most interpreters have lacked an appreciation of Nietzsche's sense of humor and irony, and without that, *Ecce Homo*—and Nietzsche in general—cannot be understood.

The Preface to *Nietzsche Contra Wagner,* which is the last book Nietzsche completed, is dated Christmas 1888. Nietzsche's intent in the 25-page work was to show that *The Case of Wagner* involved no betrayal of his previous thought and that he had not waited for Wagner's death to publish his criticisms of him. So, according to the Preface, he assembled relevant passages from his earlier books, "perhaps clarified here and there, above all shortened. Read one after another, they will leave no doubt either about Richard Wagner or about myself: we are antipodes." If it had been better known, the book, whose prose is superb, might have obviated many misunderstandings.

In sum, the books of 1888, which are very short, are among Nietzsche's best, and they afford a good approach to his thought.

Poetry and forgery. Nietzsche was also a highly influential poet. *The Gay Science* begins with a section of verse, and in the second edition another chapter, as well as another section of poetry, was appended. *Zarathustra* contains several long poems, and Nietzsche's *Dionysus-Dithyramben* were appended with separate pagination to Part IV of *Zarathustra* (1891). These dithyrambs have been often reissued, with slight textual changes. The poems are all by Nietzsche, but he did not prepare any final version for the printer, and he considered using some of them to conclude his books of 1888. Although the poems are very uneven, they influenced Rilke's *Duino Elegies.*

My Sister and I (New York, 1951) was published over Nietzsche's name. Allegedly, the original was lost, and only a vermin-eaten carbon copy of a translation survived. The book is a clumsy forgery with no literary or philosophic value whatsoever.

"The Will to Power." The book published under the title *Der Wille zur Macht* (*The Will to Power*) consists of some of the notes Nietzsche accumulated from 1884 to 1888, systematically arranged by his sister. Her first version (Vol. XV of the "collected works," 1901) contained some 400 "aphorisms." In 1904, 200 pages of further notes were included in the last volume of her biography of her brother. Finally, a second edition in two volumes (1906) offered 1,067 notes, the new material being mixed with the

old. In the best edition, *Gesammelte Werke* (Musarion edition), the approximate date of every note is given in an appendix. The systematic arrangement makes it easy to see what Nietzsche had to say about religion, morality, epistemology, art, and so forth, although many notes might equally well be placed in another section. But those who regard *The Will to Power* as Nietzsche's magnum opus overlook that he utilized many of these notes in his later books, often giving them an unexpected twist, and that many of the notes not used by him presumably did not satisfy him.

For a time Nietzsche planned to write a book to be called "The Will to Power," but he never finished a single chapter. He later decided to call his main work "Revaluation of All Values" (*Umwertung aller Werte*), and he referred to *The Antichrist,* which draws heavily on notes included in *The Will to Power,* as Book I of the "Revaluation."

Friedrich Würzbach's rearrangement of the notes according to a scheme of his own has met with no acclaim. Karl Schlechta's arrangement, offered as part of a three-volume edition of the *Werke,* has been widely accepted and also widely criticized. By printing the material as found in the notebooks, in which Nietzsche sometimes wrote on right-hand pages first, then on left-hand pages, and sometimes started from the back, Schlechta eliminates all order, along with any pretense that this is a major work, and makes these notes almost unreadable. His claim that they contain "nothing new" and merely duplicate the books is exaggerated; for example, much of the material on nihilism, with which Nietzsche's sister's arrangement begins, is not found elsewhere. In sum, *The Will to Power* is of very great interest, but it must be used cautiously and compared with Nietzsche's later books and with the notes the sister did not include—notes that are to be found, for instance, in the Musarion edition of the *Werke* but not in Schlechta's edition.

PHILOSOPHY

The will to power. The conception of the will to power is central in Nietzsche's philosophy. In his aphoristic books he had found the will to power at work in all sorts of human behavior and valuations; in *Zarathustra* he proclaimed it man's basic motive and suggested that it is to be found in all living things (in his later works, he even ascribed it to inorganic nature). This is frankly presented as a "hypothesis," one which Nietzsche does not claim to have proved even in the realm of psychology—the only field in which he assembled a great deal of evidence. As a metaphysical theory about the universe or ultimate reality, the doctrine need not be taken seriously, not even in an effort to understand Nietzsche. Heidegger's interpretation of Nietzsche, which makes this metaphysic the center of his thought and significance, depends on a complete disregard for the context of the passages he cites and the *Gestalt* of Nietzsche's thought generally. He assigns to Nietzsche a totally uncongenial role in the history of Western thought, disregards the bulk of his writings, and stresses a few formulations in which Nietzsche opposes the will to power to Schopenhauer's blind will. Like all serious interpreters, however, Heidegger rejects the notion that the will to power is protofascist.

Nietzsche's psychological theory depends on his concept of sublimation (a word Nietzsche himself used), and he found more power in self-control, art, and philosophy than in the subjugation of others. Nietzsche's notion of resentment (*Ressentiment*) is another facet of the psychology of the will to power; so is the discussion of slave morality, created by "the resentment of those who are denied the real reaction, that of the deed, and who compensate with an imaginary revenge" (*Genealogy*). The noble man, being powerful, "shakes off with one shrug much vermin that would have buried itself deep in others"; free of resentment, he can respect and even love his enemies.

Nietzsche's doctrine developed out of his early reflections on the contest (agon) among the Greeks. The tragic poets sought triumphs over one another and also power over their audience, the language, and themselves. Socrates before his judges, Socrates in prison, Socrates meeting death is a paragon of power. But the weak also seek power; Nero, unsuccessful as an artist, became a tyrant, burned Rome, and fiddled on the roof.

Nietzsche's belief that Socrates is more powerful than Nero—the example is that of the present writer—is far clearer than his right to translate cultural power into *more* power. It seems that he reasoned more or less as follows. The only thing that all men want is power, and whatever is wanted is wanted for the sake of power. If something is wanted more than something else, it must represent more power. Men would rather be Socrates in prison than Nero on the roof; hence, Socrates must be more powerful. No argument of this form is found in Nietzsche's writings, and he may have found it evident, at least at times, that the acme of power is embodied in the perfectly self-possessed man who has no fear of other men, of himself, or of death and whose simple personality, unaided by any props, changes the lives of those who meet him and even imposes itself on the minds of those who encounter him only at second hand, in literature. Some of Nietzsche's objections to Socrates fit this account perfectly. We must surpass even Socrates insofar as he "suffered life"; "to *have* to fight the instincts—that is the formula for decadence." In Nietzsche's view Goethe was superior even to Socrates.

Nietzsche's admiration for Julius Caesar bears out our account: it is Caesar's personality and his rarely equalled self-mastery that he found exemplary. Nietzsche had reservations about Napoleon, calling him "this synthesis of the inhuman and superhuman." Cesare Borgia was not one of Nietzsche's heroes; he merely suggested that there was more hope "even" for the Borgia than for Parsifal because a man of passion might come to master his passions, while a pure fool, destitute of passion, is hopeless. When Nietzsche expressed the wish that Cesare Borgia might have become pope (*Antichrist*), his point was that this might have finished the church. Among his heroes there was not one he admired for conquests; all were men of surpassing intelligence, passionate men who mastered their passions and employed them creatively.

What is open to criticism is Nietzsche's assumption that the only thing wanted for its own sake is power. To be sure, it is not true that by finding the will to power at work everywhere, he necessarily empties "power" of all meaning. On the contrary, it is surprising how much of human behavior Nietzsche illuminates by calling attention to the will to power and its hidden workings; in this respect he invites comparison with Freud. What he overlooks is the point Freud made in *The Interpretation of Dreams* (1900), in the footnote about *Hamlet*. Neurotic symptoms, dreams, works of literature, and, one might add, human behavior generally "are capable of overinterpretation, and indeed demand nothing less than this before they can be fully understood." Even if almost all behavior can be illuminated by finding the will to power at work in it, it does not follow that this is the only ultimate motive and the only way of illuminating such behavior. Moreover, in some cases an appeal to the will to power is farfetched and not very illuminating. Nietzsche never gave systematic attention either to apparently negative instances or to possible alternative hypotheses.

Another objection could be met, at least partially, by Nietzsche. Would all men really rather be Socrates in prison than Nero on the roof or be Goethe rather than Hitler? Nietzsche's psychology would stress that Hitler, like Nero, was an artist *manqué* and that his behavior was, again and again, typical of frustration. No poll could settle the question of what all men would prefer. What matters is not what they might say they prefer but what they really prefer, and we could say that something is really wanted if, and only if, failure to get it results in frustration that disappears with attainment.

The overman. The overman (*Übermensch*) is the type approximated by Goethe—the human being (*Mensch* includes women as well as men) who has organized the chaos of his passions, given style to his character, and become creative. Aware of life's terrors, he affirms life without resentment. Except for an ironic, self-critical passage in the chapter "On Poets" in *Zarathustra,* the word "overman" is used in the singular; it is always intended as a this-worldly antithesis to God. Instead of conceiving perfection as a given, man should conceive it as a task (not as *gegeben,* Kant might have said, but as *aufgegeben*). The term is never applied to an individual, and Nietzsche plainly considered neither himself nor Zarathustra, whom he often ridiculed, an overman.

The concept of the overman involves no bifurcation of humanity; neither does the contrast between master and slave moralities, which is a sociological distinction and refers to the origin of moral valuations either in a ruling group or among the oppressed. Indeed, no sooner has Nietzsche introduced these terms (in *Beyond Good and Evil,* 260) than he feels compelled to "add immediately" that mixed types are common and occur "even in the same human being, within a single soul."

In *Ecce Homo* Nietzsche says that only "scholarly oxen" could have construed the overman Darwinistically. But some of the metaphors in the Prologue to *Zarathustra* invite this misunderstanding if one has not read Nietzsche's other books.

Still, Darwin did influence Nietzsche's conception of the overman, and at times Nietzsche did approximate a bifurcation of humanity, albeit not in the manner usually supposed. Unlike David Strauss and legions of other moralists,

Nietzsche concluded that if we renounce supernatural religions and accept a scientific approach to man, we lose the right to attribute to man as such a unique supranatural dignity. Such dignity is not *gegeben* but *aufgegeben,* not a fact but a goal that few approach. There is no meaning in life except the meaning man gives his life, and the aims of most men have no surpassing dignity. To raise ourselves above the senseless flux, we must cease being merely human, all-too-human. We must be hard against ourselves and overcome ourselves; we must become creators instead of remaining mere creatures. Therefore, Nietzsche wishes to those whom he wishes well "suffering, being forsaken, . . . profound self-contempt, the torture of mistrust of oneself, and the misery of him who is overcome" (*Will to Power,* 910). He has no pity for his "disciples" when they endure all this, for there is no other way in which one can attain or prove one's worth.

The bifurcation implicit in this position was formulated by Ortega y Gasset:

> The select man is not the petulant person who thinks himself superior to the rest, but the man who demands more of himself than the rest. . . . The most radical division that it is possible to make of humanity is that which splits it into two classes of creatures: those who make great demands of themselves, piling up difficulties and duties; and those who demand nothing special of themselves, but for whom to live is to be every moment what they already are, without imposing on themselves any effort towards perfection; mere buoys that float on the waves. (*The Revolt of the Masses,* Madrid, 1930; English translation, New York, 1932, Ch. 1)

Nietzsche acknowledged that a man's contemporaries may be poor judges of his nobility.

Eternal recurrence. The Nietzschean doctrine of the eternal recurrence of the same events may be summarized as follows. After our planet has been destroyed, it will eventually be reconstituted as the power quanta that make up the universe once again reach a previous configuration and thenceforward repeat all the following patterns, to the point where Nietzsche is born again in 1844 and so forth. What is, has been and will be innumerable times at immense intervals. As a young scholar Nietzsche had encountered essentially the same doctrine among the Greeks. In 1882, while taking a walk, it suddenly struck him with the force of a revelation that this was the most scientific of all hypotheses and that the prospect of eternal recurrence is gruesome unless one has succeeded in giving style to one's character and meaning to one's life to such an extent that one can joyously affirm one's existence and say, unlike Goethe's Faust: Abide, moment—but if you cannot abide, at least return eternally!

The Will to Power contains attempts to show why eternal recurrence is the most scientific hypothesis. If we assume a finite number of power quanta in a finite space and an infinite time, only a finite number of configurations are possible. But no end state has been reached yet; hence, unless we follow Christianity in positing a beginning of time, the same configurations must recur eternally. Georg Simmel has pointed out in his *Schopenhauer und Nietzsche* (Leipzig, 1907, pp. 250 f.) that even if there were only a very few things in a finite space in an infinite time, they need never repeat the same configuration. Imagine three wheels of equal size, rotating on a single axis, one point marked on the circumference of each and the three points lined up in one straight line. If the second wheel rotated twice as fast as the first and if the speed of the third was $1/\pi$ of the speed of the first, the initial line-up could never recur. In his books Nietzsche attempted no scientific proof of this doctrine but stressed its potential ethical impact and, even more, the experience of believing it—the horror that will be felt as long as one's life is all-too-human and the joy that can be felt by the exceptional person. The claim that this doctrine is incompatible with Nietzsche's conception of the overman arises from a misunderstanding of both doctrines, according to which the doctrine of eternal return held that history is punctuated by constant repetitions and the doctrine of the overman proclaimed that there is progress in history (see ETERNAL RETURN for other criticisms of Nietzsche's doctrine).

Religion. *The Antichrist* is Nietzsche's most sustained attempt at a critique of Christianity, but most of his books contain related material. Nietzsche thought that Jesus was like Prince Myshkin in Dostoyevsky's *The Idiot* (he alludes to the novel without citing it)—wonderfully pure and free of resentment but profoundly pathological. Jesus' disciples misunderstood him, and Christianity was, from the start, opposed to Jesus' spirit; it stressed faith and was deeply resentful toward unbelievers and, indeed, toward "the world." Nietzsche criticizes the Christian faith both as an illicit alternative to Jesus' way of life and as opposed to reason. These two criticisms are also important for an understanding of Nietzsche's attitude toward reason, which he esteemed highly. His most original criticism of Christianity is his attempt to show how from the very start resentment has been central in the so-called religion of love. (This point is made most succinctly in *The Antichrist,* Sec. 45, where Nietzsche quotes, *inter alia,* Mark 6.11, 9.42, and 9.47, and I Corinthians 1.20 ff.)

As for Judaism, he sometimes speaks of the Old Testament with the utmost enthusiasm as being infinitely superior to the New Testament, and even to the literature of the ancient Greeks, but elsewhere he tries to show how Christianity is the culmination of all that was worst in Judaism and traces back resentment and dishonesty to what he considers the priestly editing of the Old Testament. He rarely speaks of Jews and Judaism without using them, one way or another, to attack Christians and Christianity. Anti-Semitism, however, he derided consistently.

Nietzsche occasionally refers to Buddhism and Hinduism, usually to suggest that for all their faults they were also preferable to Christianity in some ways. Personally, he rejected all religions. He considered supernaturalism opposed to reason, sought the roots of otherworldiness in a resentment against this world, found Buddhism a religion of weariness, and objected to the Hindus' treatment of the untouchables as an outrage against humanity.

Metaphysics and epistemology. Nietzsche did not see himself as a metaphysician and opposed all two-world doctrines (for example, in the chapter "On the Afterworldly"—"afterworldly" was probably intended as a translation of "metaphysicians"—in *Zarathustra;* and in the chapters "'Reason' in Philosophy" and "How the 'True World' Finally became a Fable" in *The Twilight of the Idols*). His own concept of the will to power is primarily a psychological notion, but in a few passages, directed at Schopenhauer, it becomes a theory about ultimate reality. The doctrine of eternal recurrence is also a metaphysical theory, although this is not the aspect that most concerned Nietzsche. Nietzsche might therefore be called a metaphysician in spite of himself. But he insisted that we must turn to the sciences for knowledge of reality, and he had high hopes for the future development of psychology and physiology and their relevance to issues previously considered philosophical.

If metaphysics is understood as reflection about categories rather than about ultimate reality, then the chapter "The Four Great Errors" in *The Twilight of the Idols* is metaphysics because it deals with the error of confusing cause and effect, the error of a false causality, the error of imaginary causes, and the error of free will. But even here Nietzsche's concern is primarily with morality and religion, and his intent is antimetaphysical. Morality and religion teach, for example, that if you are good, you will be happy. Nietzsche argues that virtue is the effect of happiness or that vice is bred by unhappiness—a commonplace in the twentieth century but not in the nineteenth. Against the "error of a false causality" Nietzsche argues that "there are no mental causes at all," no spirits as entities or agents. "Imaginary causes" include events in dreams that "explain" ex post facto such events as noises outside, but they also include "sin" as a supposed cause of suffering. Here Nietzsche includes Schopenhauer in his critique. There is more material about metaphysical questions in *Beyond Good and Evil* and in the notes, especially in *The Will to Power.*

There is also more about epistemology in the notes than in the books, for Nietzsche was never sufficiently satisfied with his thoughts on these topics to put them into print. Two of his more interesting suggestions might be summed up as a not very thoroughly worked out perspectivism and a theory of fictions comparable to that of Hans Vaihinger, who conceived his independently and published it nine years after his book on Nietzsche.

On classifying Nietzsche. Nietzsche's philosophy is not readily separable into metaphysics, epistemology, ethics, aesthetics, and other fields (frequently, the same passage is relevant to many such areas), and most attempts to classify his philosophy are untenable. His ethics, for example, is definitely not evolutionist; neither was he an irrationalist. Positivistic elements appear side by side with existentialist concerns.

The poet Gottfried Benn (1886–1956) wrote in an essay on Nietzsche, "Really everything my generation discussed, thought through—one could say, spun out [*breittrat*]—all that had already been expressed and exhausted by Nietzsche; he had given the definitive formulations, all the rest was exegesis."

Nietzsche's 1886 Preface to the second edition of *Human, All-too-human* begins, "One should speak only where one may not remain silent, and speak only of that which one has overcome—everything else is chatter."

Wittgenstein had probably read this years before he concluded his *Tractatus* with the statement "Of what one cannot speak, one must remain silent" (his ladder metaphor is also reminiscent of Nietzsche's "has overcome"). Still, Nietzsche was perhaps replying to an ancient author quoted by Wittgenstein. In any case, Nietzsche was not content to remain silent about subjects that cannot be discussed with scientific precision. His myriad suggestions have an existential unity, but this unity includes the determination to bring to bear science, especially psychology, on traditional philosophic concerns and not to let religion and morality escape unscathed.

Nietzsche was also an influential poet and offered many interesting remarks about language—for example, "epistemologists who have got stuck in the snares of grammar (the metaphysics of the people)" (*Gay Science,* 354); "language . . . talks of opposites where there are only degrees and many refinements of gradation" (*Beyond Good and Evil,* 24); "the misleading errors of language (and the fundamental fallacies of reason which have become petrified in it), which understands, and misunderstands, all activity as due to an agent, a 'subject'" (*Genealogy,* I, 13; the parentheses show where Nietzsche differs from many analytic philosophers). Other remarks may be found in *The Will to Power,* 484; *Beyond Good and Evil,* 16 f.; and the chapter "'Reason' in Philosophy" in *The Twilight of the Idols,* especially Section 5, which ends, "We are not rid of God because we still have faith in grammar."

Influence. Under the Nazis an expurgated edition of *The Antichrist,* a few anthologies of Nietzsche's works, and some unconscionable books about him gained currency, but Plato and quotations about "the Jews" from the Gospel of John were used far more. Hitler, who was steeped in Wagner, probably never read one of Nietzsche's books, nor could any of them have been used by the Nazis in an unexpurgated form. Some of Nietzsche's coinages and even whole sentences torn out of context could have been made serviceable, but his ideas and spirit were clearly opposed to those of the National Socialist German Labor Party. In fact, few writers have been so hard on nationalism, socialism, the Germans, labor movements, and "party men" (see, for example, *The Twilight of the Idols* and, on the last point, *Antichrist,* 55: "Of necessity, the party man becomes a liar").

Nietzsche's influence on literature has been incalculable. It is especially marked in the poetry of Rainer Maria Rilke, Stefan George, Christian Morgenstern, and Gottfried Benn; in the novels of Thomas Mann, Hermann Hesse, André Gide, and André Malraux; in Shaw and Yeats; and in psychoanalysis and existentialism. Besides the many philosophers who have written books on him, Albert Camus, Jean-Paul Sartre, Max Scheler, Oswald Spengler, and Paul Tillich, are especially indebted to him.

At the age of 83, Martin Buber published *Begegnung; Autobiographische Fragmente* (Stuttgart, 1961) and included "encounters" with two philosophers, Kant and Nietzsche. In a footnote he revealed that at 17 he was so impressed by *Zarathustra* that he began to render it into Polish "and actually did translate the First Part." It is to be expected that in years to come it will be shown how many major writers were much more deeply influenced by Nietzsche than had been suspected.

After Freud's death Ernest Jones published a letter in which his master, at 78, said of Nietzsche, "In my youth he signified a nobility which I could not attain."

Nietzsche's appeal was confined neither to men of only one type nor to those who have published essays on him. To use the weighty word he applied to himself in *Ecce Homo*, he really became a "destiny" for many, including some of the leading spirits of the twentieth century.

Works by Nietzsche

COLLECTED WORKS

Gesammelte Werke, Musarionausgabe, 23 vols. (Munich, 1920–1929), features a chronological arrangement of Nietzsche's works and notes with indexes. Only the 20-volume *Grossoktavausgabe*, 2d ed. (Leipzig, 1901–1913), is nearly as good. Karl Schlechta's edition, *Werke in drei Bänden* (Munich, 1954–1956), contains all of the books, but far fewer of Nietzsche's notes than several previous editions. It also contains 278 letters, a 50-page philological postscript in which Elisabeth Förster-Nietzsche's petty forgeries (none of which affect his philosophy) are detailed, and a 24-page chronological table covering Nietzsche's life. Schlechta finds small faults in previous editions, but his own editing has been sharply criticized by E. F. Podach in his edition, *Nietzsches Werke des Zusammenbruchs* (Heidelberg, 1961). None of the disputed points, however, affects our understanding of Nietzsche's philosophy.

LETTERS

Gesammelte Briefe, Elisabeth Förster-Nietzsche, Peter Gast, et al., eds., 5 vols. in 6 (Leipzig, 1900–1909), was later supplemented by separate editions of *Nietzsches Briefwechsel mit Franz Overbeck*, C. A. Bernoulli and Richard Oehler, eds. (Leipzig, 1916); E. Förster-Nietzsche, *Wagner und Nietzsche zur Zeit ihrer Freundschaft* (Munich, 1915), translated by C. V. Kerr as *The Nietzsche–Wagner Correspondence* (London, 1922); and Karl Strecker, *Nietzsche und Strindberg, mit ihren Briefwechsel* (Munich, 1921). There are additional letters in various places. *Historisch-Kritische Gesamtausgabe der Werke und Briefe*, Wilhelm Hoppe, Karl Schlechta, Hans Joachim Mette, and Carl Koch, eds. (Munich, 1933–1942), includes five volumes of works up to 1869 and four volumes of letters to 1877. This edition was discontinued during World War II.

TRANSLATIONS

The Complete Works, Oscar Levy, ed., 18 vols. (Edinburgh and London, 1909–1913, reissued 1964), is marred by poor and unreliable translations. *The Portable Nietzsche* (New York, 1954), translated and edited by Walter Kaufmann, contains *Thus Spoke Zarathustra, Twilight of the Idols, The Antichrist*, and *Nietzsche Contra Wagner* (all complete) and selections from the other books, the notes, and the letters, with 60 pages of editorial material. *Basic Writings of Nietzsche* (New York, 1966), edited and in part newly translated, with notes, by Walter Kaufmann, contains *The Birth of Tragedy, Beyond Good and Evil, The Genealogy of Morals, The Case of Wagner, Ecce Homo* (all complete) and additional selections. *The Will to Power* (New York, 1966), translated by Walter Kaufmann and R. G. Hollingdale, and edited, with notes, by Walter Kaufmann, furnishes the approximate date of every note and cross references to parallel passages in the books Nietzsche finished.

Works on Nietzsche

BIOGRAPHY

C. A. Bernoulli, *Franz Overbeck und Friedrich Nietzsche*, 2 vols. (Jena, 1908), important for its biographical material, takes issue with the version of Nietzsche's life presented by his sister.

Elisabeth Förster-Nietzsche, *Das Leben Friedrich Nietzsches*, 3 vols. (Leipzig, 1895–1904), contains much important material, but, like all her publications, is quite unreliable. By far the best biography in English is R. G. Hollingdale, *Nietzsche: The Man and His Philosophy* (Baton Rouge, La., 1965), in which Nietzsche's ideas are discussed in the context of his life. E. F. Podach, *Nietzsches Zusammenbruch* (Heidelberg, 1930), translated by F. A. Voigt as *Nietzsche's Madness* (London and New York, 1931); *Gestalten um Nietzsche* (Weimar, 1931); and *Friedrich Nietzsche und Lou Salomé* (Zurich, 1938), are three books containing important biographical documents and information.

COMMENTARIES

Martin Heidegger, *Nietzsche*, 2 vols. (Pfullingen, 1961), and "Nietzsches Wort 'Gott ist tot,'" in *Holzwege* (Frankfurt, 1952), are interesting for students of Heidegger who know Nietzsche well enough to appreciate Heidegger's approach. Karl Jaspers, *Nietzsche* (Berlin and Leipzig, 1936), translated by C. F. Walraff and F. J. Schmitz as *Nietzsche* (Tucson, Ariz., 1965), exposes oversimplifications about Nietzsche in a stunning array of quotations, but Jaspers discounts all of Nietzsche's conclusions. Without regard for chronology or context, apparently contradictory statements from books and notes are methodically contrasted to persuade us of the inadequacy of all positions and of the need for Jaspers' existentialism. In the English version all page references are omitted, so the Nietzsche quotations cannot be located. Karl Jaspers, *Nietzsche und das Christentum* (Hameln, 1938), translated by E. B. Ashton (Chicago, 1961), is similar in approach to the preceding, but is less than one tenth its length. Walter Kaufmann, *Nietzsche* (Princeton, N.J., 1950; rev. ed., New York, 1956), is the book on which the present article is based; the original edition contains a long bibliography. Walter Kaufmann, *From Shakespeare to Existentialism* (Boston, 1959; rev. ed., New York, 1960), British edition entitled *The Owl and the Nightingale* (London, 1960), contains five chapters on Nietzsche, including three chapters on his relation to Rilke and to Jaspers. Walter Kaufmann, *Twenty German Poets: A Bilingual Collection* (New York, 1962), contains 11 of Nietzsche's poems and assigns him a place in the development of German poetry from Goethe to Benn. Walter Kaufmann, "Nietzsche Between Homer and Sartre: Five Treatments on the Orestes Story," in *Revue internationale de philosophie*, No. 67 (1964), 50–73, demonstrates Nietzsche's immense influence on Sartre's play *The Flies*. Walter Kaufmann, "Nietzsche in the Light of His Suppressed Manuscripts," in *Journal of the History of Philosophy*, Vol. 2 (1964), 205–225, includes discussions of *The Antichrist* and *Ecce Homo* and of the way Nietzsche's works have been edited. Ludwig Klages, *Die psychologischen Errungenschaften Nietzsches* (Leipzig, 1926), is an extremely interesting work in which Nietzsche is criticized for his Socratism and rationalism. George Allen Morgan, *What Nietzsche Means* (Cambridge, Mass., 1941), is a systematic epitome that deliberately ignores how Nietzsche came to think as he did; informed, avoids criticism of Nietzsche, useful for reference. A valuable commentary is Hans Vaihinger, *Nietzsche als Philosoph* (Berlin, 1902). Vaihinger's "Nietzsche und seine Lehre vom bewusst gewollten Schein," in *Die Philosophie des Als-Ob* (Berlin, 1911), translated by C. Ogden as *The Philosophy of As-If* (New York, 1924), is a chapter containing interesting material on Nietzsche's epistemology.

BIBLIOGRAPHY

H. W. Reichert and Karl Schlechta, *International Nietzsche Bibliography* (Chapel Hill, N.C., 1960), lists 3,973 items about Nietzsche in over 24 languages, arranged in alphabetical order by author within each language. It is selective, with some unfortunate oversights, and includes some very brief summaries and evaluations.

WALTER KAUFMANN

NIHILISM. The term "nihilism" appears to have been coined in Russia sometime in the second quarter of the nineteenth century. It was not, however, widely used until after the appearance of Ivan Turgenev's highly successful novel *Fathers and Sons* in the early 1860s. The central character, Bazarov, a young man under the influence of the "most advanced ideas" of his time, bore proudly what most other people of the same period called the bitter name of nihilist. Unlike such real-life counterparts as Dmitri Pisarev, Nikolai Dobrolyubov, and Nikolai Chernyshevski, who also bore the label, Bazarov's interests were largely apolitical; however, he shared with these historical personalities disdain for tradition and authority, great faith in reason, commitment to a materialist philosophy like that of Ludwig Büchner, and an ardent desire to see radical changes in contemporary society.

An extreme statement by Pisarev of the nihilist position as it developed in the late 1850s and 1860s in Russia is frequently quoted: "Here is the ultimatum of our camp: what can be smashed should be smashed; what will stand the blow is good; what will fly into smithereens is rubbish; at any rate, hit out right and left—there will and can be no harm from it" (quoted in Avrahm Yarmolinsky, *Road to Revolution*, p. 120). Bazarov echoes this idea, though a bit feebly, when he accepts a description of nihilism as a matter of "just cursing."

Use of the term spread rapidly throughout Europe and the Americas. As it did, the term lost most of its anarchistic and revolutionary flavor, ceasing to evoke the image of a political program or even an intellectual movement. It did not, however, gain in precision or clarity. On the one hand, the term is widely used to denote the doctrine that moral norms or standards cannot be justified by rational argument. On the other hand, it is widely used to denote a mood of despair over the emptiness or triviality of human existence. This double meaning appears to derive from the fact that the term was often employed in the nineteenth century by the religiously oriented as a club against atheists, atheists being regarded as *ipso facto* nihilists in both senses. The atheist, it was held, would not feel bound by moral norms; consequently, he would tend to be callous or selfish, even criminal. At the same time he would lose the sense that life has meaning and therefore tend toward despair and suicide.

Atheism. There are many literary prototypes of the atheist-nihilist. The most famous are Ivan in Dostoyevsky's *Brothers Karamazov* and Kirilov in Dostoyevsky's *The Possessed.* It was into Ivan's mouth that Dostoyevsky put the words, "If God does not exist, everything is permitted." And Dostoyevsky made it clear that it was Ivan's atheism which led him to acquiesce to his father's murder. Kirilov was made to argue that if God does not exist, the most meaningful reality in life is individual freedom and that the supreme expression of individual freedom is suicide.

Nietzsche was the first great philosopher—and still the only one—to make extensive use of the term "nihilism." He was also one of the first atheists to dispute the existence of a necessary link between atheism and nihilism. He recognized, however, that as a matter of historical fact, atheism was ushering in an age of nihilism. "One interpretation of existence has been overthrown," Nietzsche said, "but since it was held to be *the* interpretation, it seems as though there were no meaning in existence at all, as though everything were in vain" (*Complete Works,* Edinburgh and London, 1901–1911, Vol. XIV, p. 480). Albert Camus later dealt with this historical fact at some length in *The Rebel* (1951).

The tendency to associate nihilism with atheism continues to the present. It is to be found, for instance, in a work by Helmut Thielicke entitled *Nihilism,* which first appeared in 1950. During the course of the twentieth century, however, the image of the nihilist has changed, with a corresponding change in the analysis of nihilism's causes and consequences. Professor Hermann Wein of the University of Göttingen writes, for instance, that the members of the younger generation today tend to think of the nihilist not as a cynical or despairing atheist but as a robotlike conformist. For them nihilism is caused not so much by atheism as by industrialization and social pressures, and its typical consequences are not selfishness or suicide but indifference, ironical detachment, or sheer bafflement. The literary prototypes are not the romantic heroes of Dostoyevsky but the more prosaic and impersonal heroes of Robert Musil's *Man Without Qualities* (first volumes published 1931–1933) or Kafka's *The Trial* (1925).

Moral skepticism. If by nihilism one means a disbelief in the possibility of justifying moral judgments in some rational way and if philosophers reflect the intellectual climate of the times in which they live, then our age is truly nihilistic. At no period in Western history, with the possible exception of the Hellenistic age, have so many philosophers regarded moral statements as somehow arbitrary. For many Continental philosophers, especially the atheistic existentialists, moral values are products of free choice—that is, of uncaused, unmotivated, and nonrational decisions. The most notable statement of this view is in *Being and Nothingness* (1943) by Jean-Paul Sartre. In England and America, on the other hand, most philosophers tend to the view known as emotivism, according to which moral statements are ultimately and essentially products of pure social conditioning or brute feeling. The most noted, though not the most extreme, representatives of this position are A. J. Ayer and Charles Stevenson.

It is impossible to state here with reasonable detail and accuracy the positions so summarily described in the last paragraph, much less to discuss their logical merits. For an understanding of nihilism, however, it is important to note how these positions relate to the ideas of those to whom nihilism of this kind is anathema. As already indicated, the most vociferous antinihilists were originally theologians, like Dostoyevsky, who feared that disbelief in God would lead to selfishness and crime. If, they argued, there is no divine lawgiver, each man will tend to become a law unto himself. If God does not exist to choose for the individual, the individual will assume the former prerogative of God and choose for himself. For these antinihilists the principal enemy today would be Sartre. The later antinihilists, however, tend to save their fire for the emotivists, whom they accuse of sanctioning moral indifference and mindless conformity. If all moral codes are essentially matters of feeling and social pressure, then no one would be better or worse than another. The wise man, like the Sophists of Plato's day, would simply adjust as best he could to the code of the society in which he happened to be living.

John Dewey's fervid insistence upon critical individual intelligence as the prime agent of social and moral reconstruction places him squarely in the second group of antinihilists.

Whether belief in atheistic existentialism or emotivism does in fact have the kinds of consequences suggested above is not at issue here. The point is simply that antinihilists of the older variety do not regard conventional morality, especially in its other-regarding aspects, as adequately justified unless it has a cosmic or divine sanction, whereas more contemporary antinihilists do not regard any moral code as adequately justified unless there is some standard or touchstone more universal than pure feeling or social pressure to which it may be shown to conform. The pertinent question here is whether the antinihilists have a good case for these views.

It would appear that the demand for justification of conventional moral rules by appeal to a divine or cosmic power cannot be logically admitted without abandoning widespread and deeply felt notions about the nature of moral justification. If the higher power which presumably legitimizes our moral code is by definition good and just, an appeal to that power would involve us in a vicious circle. How would we know that that power was good and just unless there were some purely human ideas about the good and the just to which we felt entitled independently of that power's sanction? If, on the other hand, the presumed higher power is not by definition good or just, if, for instance, it were defined merely as a creator and sustainer of life, by what right could we appeal to it to legitimize our moral views? Might or power, even the power to create and sustain life, is not to be confused with right or legitimacy.

The demand that moral codes be justified by more universal standards than pure feeling or social dictate is, on the contrary, much more consonant with widespread, intuitive notions about the nature of moral justification. If social pressure is taken as the touchstone of morality, we once again court a confusion between might and right; if feeling is taken as the touchstone, we must apparently abandon not only the notion of a universal morality, feelings being notoriously fluctuating and individual, but also the notion that one of the functions of morality is to refine, direct, and control individual feelings. It may, of course, be the case that there is no universal morality and that whatever power morality possesses must derive from individual feeling and social conditioning alone. It would be surprising, however, if even the emotivists did not experience a certain chagrin that the truth in ethical theory should be so contrary to human hopes.

Meaninglessness of life. Passing to the second meaning of the term "nihilism," we find that the pertinent questions are less logical or technically philosophical than psychological or sociological. There are two questions here, corresponding to the two forms of antinihilism. Is it true that a loss of faith in God or cosmic purposes produces a sense of despair over the emptiness and triviality of life, consequently stimulating selfishness and callousness? Is it true that industrialization and conformist social pressures have trivialized life in a similar way, causing us to adopt an attitude of ironic detachment? A negative answer to these questions would appear to fly in the face of most contemporary social criticism and analysis as well as the testimony of most contemporary literature.

It is doubtful, however, whether a simple yes would be a proper response to the first question. When it is assumed that man needs a sense of divine or cosmic purpose in order to lead a rich and morally wholesome life, one is generalizing far beyond the evidence. The most that the evidence can be made to support is that relatively large numbers of men in certain societies at certain times have felt this need. No one who has read, for instance, Tolstoy's account of his religious crisis in middle age could doubt the depth of his despair or the reality of his need for a vital relationship to an eternal being. One can reasonably doubt, however, whether that need and despair spring from universal and firmly rooted human aspirations. Some psychologists regard Tolstoy's conversion crisis as a symptom of involutional melancholia, and there are many who believe it to be a consequence of Tolstoy's social position as a member of Russia's decaying aristocracy.

Bertrand Russell went through a similar crisis earlier in life. He not only survived that crisis without reverting to faith in God or cosmic purpose; he also survived it, as his essay "A Free Man's Worship" (1902) attests, by deliberately espousing a world outlook which emphasizes the finitude and cosmic isolation of mankind. And no one who is familiar with the facts of his life would dare to suggest that the later Russell was less morally earnest than the young believer or less wholeheartedly and happily engaged in the process of living.

Those who attribute the nihilistic malaise of our time to industrialization and conformity are less vulnerable to the charge of overgeneralization. This is not because they limit their analysis to a given historical epoch, for they, too, are making an implicit generalization about universal human needs. Their point is that all men need, if they are to be whole and healthy, the sense that they can by a unique and personal effort contribute to the social process and that society will appreciate and reward this individual effort. This generalization is less vulnerable than the first simply because there is more evidence for it. Novels and biographies, ethnographic reports and individual clinical histories, not to mention common-sense attitudes of most men in all societies at all historical periods, tend to support it. And the issue raised by nihilism in this sense of the term is one of the great unresolved political and social problems of the twentieth century. Whether philosophers in their professional capacity are competent to contribute to its solution is a question we shall not attempt to answer here.

Bibliography

On Russian nihilism of the 1850s and 1860s see Avrahm Yarmolinsky, *Road to Revolution* (New York, 1959), and Ivan Turgenev, *Fathers and Sons* (New York, 1958).

For interpretations of nihilism reflecting a theological or religious point of view, see Helmut Thielicke, *Nihilism* (London, 1962); Ernst Benz, *Westlicher und östlicher Nihilismus* (Stuttgart, 1948); Nikolai Berdyaev, *Sinn und Shicksal des russischen Kommunismus* (1937); and Lester G. Crocker, *An Age of Crisis* (Baltimore, Md., 1959).

For emotivism see A. J. Ayer, *Language, Truth and Logic*, 2d rev. ed. (New York, 1952); Charles Stevenson, *Ethics and Lan-*

guage (New Haven, 1944); and Ingemar Hedenius, "On Law and Morals," in *Journal of Philosophy,* Vol. 56 (1959), 117–125.

For existentialist nihilism see Jean-Paul Sartre, *Being and Nothingness* (New York, 1956).

See also Friedrich Nietzsche, *Will to Power,* in Oscar Levy, ed., *Complete Works* (New York, 1964); Albert Camus, *The Rebel* (New York, 1956); Hermann Wein, "Discussion on Nihilism," in *Universitas,* Vol. 6, No. 2, 173–182; C. F. von Weinzaecker, *The History of Nature* (Chicago, 1949), pp. 71 ff.; Bertrand Russell, "A Free Man's Worship," in his *Mysticism and Logic* (London, 1918), and "What I Believe," in his *Why I Am Not a Christian* (New York, 1957), Ch. 3; Leo Tolstoy, "My Confession" and "What Is To Be Done," in *Complete Works* (New York, 1898), Vol. VII; and Hermann Rauschning, *The Revolution of Nihilism* (London, 1939).

ROBERT G. OLSON

NIRVANA is a term used primarily to refer to the state of release or salvation in Buddhism. It is also one among a number of words used in the Hindu tradition (the most common of which is *mokṣa*) for the corresponding states in the various systems of Hindu soteriology. In modern usage "nirvana" almost always refers to Buddhist nirvana. The word is Sanskrit (*nirvāṇa*); its Pāli version, as found in the Theravādin canon (the scriptures of the Buddhism of Ceylon, Burma, and parts of southeast Asia) is *nibbāna*.

Literally *nirvāṇa* means the "going out" or "extinguishing" of a flame. The imagery here is related to the Buddhist doctrine of rebirth and karma. An individual's series of lives is compared to the lighting of successive lamps, one lamp from another. The state of nirvana is achieved when the saint (*arhat*), by uprooting craving, eliminates the fuel on which the flames feed, thereby achieving a state in which he will be reborn no more. The destruction of craving is typically attained by treading the Noble Eightfold Path, which includes not merely ethical self-training but also, and importantly, techniques of yoga or contemplative mysticism. Through the attainment of higher states of consciousness, the saint gains serenity and insight into the nature of reality.

The above doctrines give rise to a distinction between two phases of nirvana: nirvana "with substrate" and nirvana "without substrate." That is, one can distinguish between the saint's state while he is still alive and the state following his death. While he is alive, there remains the "substrate," the physical and mental states which constitute him as an individual. The "without substrate" phase of nirvana aroused doctrinal problems, mainly because the Buddha refused to answer the question of whether the saint survives after his death. This was one of the so-called undetermined questions—undetermined because the question was defective in some way, and therefore unanswerable. The Buddha compared it to the question "Where does a flame go when it goes out?" It is not correct to affirm that a flame goes north or that it does not, that it both does and does not, that it neither does nor does not. Likewise, it is not correct to assert that the saint survives or that he does not, and so on.

Both earlier and more recent commentators have given a pragmatic interpretation of the Buddha's silence on this issue. On this view the question is defective simply because speculation on these matters is not conducive to salvation. This interpretation is not without support in the texts, but it neglects two important points. First, the

Buddha's comparison of the question of the saint's survival to the question about the flame strongly suggests that he (or at least the early Buddhist tradition) considered the question defective independently of its not being conducive to salvation. Second, the texts also treat the Buddha as omniscient in spiritual matters and report him as having declared that he was not close-fisted like many teachers, who hold back knowledge from their pupils. Given that it was natural for serious questions to be asked about the nature of salvation, it is unlikely that the Buddha merely wished to put a pragmatic bar upon them.

It is probable that the question was considered defective because of an important feature of early Buddhist metaphysics, the doctrines of impermanence and nonself. The individual was analyzed as being constituted by a complex series of impermanent physical and mental states. In place of then current views, which asserted the existence of an eternal soul underlying such events, and such that it could in principle exist in a pure state (the state of release), the Buddha substituted the doctrine of an impermanent individual capable in principle of achieving a permanent state (nirvana). In nirvana the series of temporal states is replaced by a permanent state. But with the vanishing of the psychophysical states there is no longer an individual to be named or referred to. Thus, the question about survival is like "Is the king of France bald?" except that it is only a contingent fact that there is no king of France, whereas it is a metaphysical necessity that the saint does not survive after his death. Nevertheless, the Buddha strongly insisted that there is a transcendent state of nirvana.

The development of Mahāyāna (Greater Vehicle) Buddhism provided some striking interpretations of nirvana. Since Mahāyāna thought tended toward belief in an Absolute (albeit a tenuous one, referred to by such expressions as *tathatā*, or "Suchness," and *śūnya*, or "the Void"), as constituting the inner essence of phenomena, it became natural to identify nirvana with it. Moreover, the Absolute came to be interpreted religiously as the *dharmakāya*, or "Truth Body," of the Buddha. That is, the essence of Buddhahood is Suchness or the Void. Consequently, in attaining nirvana one becomes identified with this Buddha essence. This view related to the Mahāyāna evaluation of the Buddhist path; centrally the path involves being a Bodhisattva, or Buddha-to-be. The path of the Bodhisattva, who sacrifices himself on behalf of the welfare of other living beings, replaces the Hīnayāna (Lesser Vehicle) ideal of the saint who serenely, but not necessarily through suffering and self-sacrifice, attains nirvana. The Mahāyāna identification of nirvana with the essential Buddha nature meant that anyone seeking nirvana was a potential Buddha and thus was a Buddha-to-be in intention.

Further, there was the identification of nirvana not only with the Absolute but also with *saṃsāra*, the flow of empirical events and the round of rebirth. The Theravāda (like the other Hīnayāna schools) was dualistic, in the sense that a firm distinction was drawn between empirical events, which are conditioned and impermanent, and nirvana, which is uniquely unconditioned and permanent (although questions arose whether, for instance, space ought to be included in the same category). But the logic of Mahāyāna metaphysics impelled a kind of monism. Since the Absolute constitutes the underlying nature of phenomena, nirvana also constitutes that inner nature. Consequently it became possible to assert the paradox that nirvana equals *samsāra*—although, needless to say, the ordinary view of *samsāra*, which treats people and objects as substance and does not recognize their "voidness," is full of error, for it implies the need to escape *samsāra*. By removal of that error one can intuitively see that nirvana does equal *samsāra*.

Although these trends retained nirvana as a central concept in the Buddhist doctrine of salvation, there were other forces at work in the opposite direction. The Mahāyāna cult of the Buddha Amitābha (Japanese, Amida—the cult is sometimes known as Amida Buddhism) involved the belief that the Buddha can, out of his infinite store, confer merit freely upon the otherwise unworthy faithful, if they but call upon him in loving trust. They will then be reborn in the Pure Land, a splendid paradise created by Amitābha, where conditions for the attainment of nirvana are especially propitious. Gradually paradise, rather than nirvana, came to be the key hope in the religious imagination of Pure Land Buddhists.

In the traditional conceptions, however, nirvana transcends even the most refined forms of heavenly existence. Therefore, according to the Buddhist conception of divine beings as inhabiting the cosmos, rather than as being transcendent to it, the gods are ultimately irrelevant to salvation, that is, to the attainment of nirvana.

Bibliography

Jayatilleke, K. N., *Early Buddhist Theory of Knowledge.* London, 1964.

Poussin, Louis de la Vallée, *The Way to Nirvana.* Cambridge, 1917.

Slater, Robert L., *Paradox and Nirvana.* Chicago, 1951.

Stcherbatsky, Fedor I., *The Conception of Buddhist Nirvana.* Leningrad, 1917.

NINIAN SMART

NISHI AMANE (1829–1897), the pioneer in bringing Western philosophy to Japan. Nishi was born in Tsuwano, Shimane Prefecture. After the usual Confucian training he went to Edo (Tokyo) for further studies and was attached to Bansho Torishirabe-sho (Center for the Investigation of Western Books). In 1862 he was sent with other promising Japanese to Holland to study Western law and military science. In Holland his interest in philosophy was reawakened, and with his friend Tsuda Masamichi he became acquainted with the positivism of Comte, the utilitarianism of J. S. Mill, and Kant's *On Eternal Peace.* He returned to Japan in 1865 and was appointed to the Kaisei School in Edo, where the government of the shogun requested him to translate books on law. After the Meiji restoration, Nishi was put in charge of educational matters for the Ministry of Military Affairs. At this time he also wrote most of his philosophical books. He became a member of the *Meirokusha*, the group of leading intellectuals of the time, who advocated Western culture and mores. Nishi was several times president of the Tokyo Academy. He was made a baron and was appointed to the upper chamber of the legislature, the House of Peers, in 1890.

Nishi's importance as the "father" of Western philosophy in Japan lies in the new terminology he created—from his Japanese term for philosophy, *tetsugaku*, to his various translations—and in the original works that established a new tradition of speculative thinking. His positivist bent is revealed in *Reikon ichigenron* ("Monism of the Soul"), one of his earlier works. More famous are his panoramic treatments of Western learning and philosophy in *Hyakugaku renkan* ("Encyclopedia," written in 1874), a kind of philosophical or cultural dictionary, and *Haykuichi shinron* ("A New Theory on the Many Doctrines," written in 1874). In these Nishi prefers Mill's inductive method to Comte's positivism. In 1874 Nishi also wrote *Chichi keimō* ("Logic, An Introduction"), the first of its genre in Japan. His utilitarian ethics is clearly manifested in "Jinsei sampō-setsu" ("The Three Treasures Theory of Man's Life"), which appeared in the *Meiroku Journal* in 1875. He replaced Confucian ethics with a quest for the three treasures: health, wealth, and knowledge.

As a translator Nishi has to his credit Mill's *Utilitarianism* and a work titled *Mental Philosophy* by Joseph Haven, an American philosopher influenced by Scottish realism.

In later life Nishi became more conservative in his view of Western ideas, an attitude consonant with the country's post-1886 reaction against ultra-Westernization. As a director of a teacher's college, Shihan Gakkō, he proposed a combination of East and West in ethics; but in the last analysis he remains an expositor of Western philosophy who never really tried to combine East and West in his thought and writing.

Bibliography

Nishi's collected works are available in two editions. One is Okube Toshiaki, ed., *Nishi Amane zenshū* ("The Complete Works of Nishi Amane"; Tokyo, 1960——). Vol. I contains Nishi's philosophical works; two more volumes are planned. The other edition is Asō Yoshiteru, ed., *Nishi tetsugaku chosakushū* ("Collected Philosophical Works of Nishi Amane"; Tokyo, 1933).

Studies of Nishi can be found in M. Kōsaka, ed., *Japanese Thought in the Meiji Era,* translated into English by D. Abosch (Tokyo, 1958), pp. 99–113; Gino K. Piovesana, *Recent Japanese Philosophical Thought, 1862–1962* (Tokyo, 1963), pp. 5–18; and R. F. Hackett, "Nishi Amane, A Tokugawa–Meiji Bureaucrat," in *The Journal of Asian Studies,* Vol. 18, No. 2 (1959), 213–225.

GINO K. PIOVESANA, S.J.

NISHIDA KITARŌ (1870–1945), generally considered to be the foremost modern Japanese philosopher. Nishida was born in a small village on the Sea of Japan near the city of Kanazawa, Ishikawa Prefecture. He received his early education in local schools but completed his studies as a special student at Tokyo University. Upon graduation he became a country middle-school (high school) teacher but was later appointed to a post at Kanazawa Junior College, where for ten years he was engrossed in reading, philosophical speculation, and Zen meditation. It was then that he developed his basic philosophical views, and for the remainder of his life he merely broadened and deepened them.

His major concern throughout his life was to provide a framework, consistent with traditional Western philosophical methodology, for his essentially Zen intuition into the nature of reality. His first work, *Zen no kenkyū* (Tokyo, 1911; translated as *A Study of Good,* 1960), which he developed from his school lectures, attempted such a harmonious philosophical system, including a theory of reality, a study of ethics, and an outline of a philosophy of religion. It was hailed by the academic world as the first truly original philosophical work by a Japanese thinker in the modern period, which began in 1868 with the Meiji restoration. Almost all the works prior to it had hardly risen above crude eclecticism or the introduction of various aspects of Western philosophy in Confucian or Buddhist contexts.

In 1910 Nishida was appointed to Kyoto University, where he taught until his retirement in 1928. He gathered many brilliant students around him, and together with Tanabe Hajime he established what has come to be known as the Kyoto, or Nishida–Tanabe, school of philosophy. He continued his philosophical career even after his retirement and remained active throughout World War II, until his death, despite attacks from nationalists on his liberal views.

In *A Study of Good* Nishida developed his basic concept of "pure experience," which is not in opposition to thought and intellect but lies at the base of all oppositions. For example, a poet's viewing a flower is "pure experience," which is prior to the subjectivity of the poet and the objectivity of the flower; Nishida reverses the usual mode of thought and contends that subjectivity and objectivity are two ways of looking at the identical experience. Such experience is not established in the self but rather the self is established by it. Nishida proceeded beyond the usual Western distinctions between subject and object and mind and body to what is prior to these distinctions, thereby attempting to understand them. But since *A Study of Good* presented largely a psychology of pure experience, in his subsequent works Nishida tried to develop a logic of pure experience. In *Jikaku ni okeru chokkan to hansei* ("Intuition and Reflection in Self-Consciousness"; Tokyo, 1917), under the influence of the Neo-Kantian school and showing sympathy with Fichte and Bergson, he expanded "pure experience" into "self-consciousness," seeing "self-consciousness" as a truly concrete and universal thing and all things as various aspects and developments of it. In this complex and profound work he used "I am I," the form of "self-consciousness," which he considers to be the root of the logical "A is A," to trace the continuity of pure logic, mathematics, and experience generally, especially aesthetic and religious experience. He broadened his scope to treat epistemological and metaphysical problems, concluding his work by defining the ultimate character of self-consciousness as "absolute free will." This absolute free will, when genuine, cannot be reflected upon, for it transcends reflection and is that which causes reflection. The center of this will, the self, is always "the eternal now"; paradoxically it is also unlimited development. From this standpoint Nishida wrote his next two important works, *Ishiki no mondai* ("The Problem of Consciousness"; Tokyo, 1920), and *Geijutsu to dōtoku* ("Art and Morality"; Tokyo, 1923).

And yet, since even in the doctrine of absolute free will he had not wholly avoided a subjective bias, Nishida sought that which would transcend subjectivity completely. In his epoch-making work *Hataraku mono kara miru mono e* ("From the Acting to the Seeing"; Tokyo, 1927) he formulated the concept of *basho no ronri* ("logic of place" or "logic of field") as a solution. Although this concept is suggested by Plato's *topos* and Aristotle's *hypokeimenon,* it is still essentially a product of the thoroughness of Nishida's own thinking. Place is the substratum within which all forms become actualized. He had seen absolute free will as "emerging from creative nothingness and returning to creative nothingness," and therefore as possessing the character of "nothingness." Further, it must be basically "a certain *place wherein*" everything else exists. He made this transcend subjectivity completely and termed it "the place of nothingness." Nishida's nothingness, however, is not merely nothingness in opposition to phenomenal existence, that is, *relative* nothingness; since it is that wherein all phenomenal existences appear as determinations of it, it is *absolute* nothingness. With the idea of "place" Nishida provided the conceptual and logical framework for a position that is usually considered mysticism in the West.

In the last stage of his work Nishida developed the idea of "the self-identity of absolute contradiction," or, more simply, "the unity of opposites," through his investigation of the relationship between the self and the world. Moreover, he used this concept to probe the problems of a philosophy of religion: the contradictions of man's existence, where the satisfaction of desire means the extinction of desire and the will makes its own extinction its object. In these problems is religion established, for in the awareness of the absolute contradictoriness and nothingness of the self's existence we first touch the absolute and God. It may be noted that there are many striking parallels between Nishida and Hegel; however, the starting point for Nishida is always Zen intuition.

Nishida's thought has exerted great influence on contemporary Japanese intellectual life, although it has been vigorously attacked by Marxist thinkers. Several of his works have been translated into major Western languages, and he has begun to be recognized as among the first philosophers to make a genuine contribution to the establishment of a world philosophy transcending the usual East–West distinctions.

Works by Nishida

Nishida Kitarō zenshū ("The Complete Works of Nishida Kitarō"), 12 vols. plus 6 supplementary vols. Tokyo, 1947–1953. Hitherto unpublished material, letters, and Nishida's diary are included in the supplementary volumes.

Intelligibility and the Philosophy of Nothingness: Three Philosophical Essays, translated and with an introduction by R. Schinzinger. Tokyo, 1958.

A Study of Good, translated by V. H. Viglielmo, with an introduction by D. T. Suzuki and Shimomura Toratarō. Tokyo, 1960.

Works on Nishida

Kōsaka Masaaki, *Nishida Kitarō Sensei no shōgai to shisō* ("The Life and Thought of Professor Nishida Kitarō"). Tokyo, 1947.

Noda Matao, "East–West Synthesis in Nishida." *Philosophy East and West,* Vol. 4 (1955), 345–359.

V. H. VIGLIELMO

NJEGOŠ. See PETROVIĆ-NJEGOŠ, PETAR.

NOMINALISM. See GOODMAN, NELSON; HOBBES, THOMAS; QUINE, WILLARD VAN ORMAN; ROSCELIN; UNIVERSALS; WILLIAM OF OCKHAM.

NOMOS. See PHYSIS AND NOMOS.

NONCOGNITIVISM. See EMOTIVE THEORY OF ETHICS; ETHICS, HISTORY OF; ETHICS, PROBLEMS OF.

NONNATURALISM. See ETHICS, HISTORY OF; ETHICS, PROBLEMS OF; MOORE, GEORGE EDWARD.

NONSENSE. Thomas Hobbes, after equating the absurd with nonsense, remarked that one of man's distinctive abilities was "the privilege of absurdity to which no living creature is subject, but man only. And of men, those are of all most subject to it that profess philosophy" (*Leviathan*, Ch. 5). On both these counts philosophers have reason for an interest in nonsense—in nonsense as a peculiarly human product and in nonsense as the philosopher's occupational danger.

During this century both interests have been intensified. The concern with nonsense as a human phenomenon whose nature illuminates the nature of language has been deepened and furthered by recent advances in linguistic theory and by analyses provided by literary critics of those poetic uses of language which successfully risk the appearance of nonsense to achieve their special effect. The concern with nonsense as a philosophical phenomenon was stimulated by the logical positivist verifiability theory of meaning and the consequent rejection of all metaphysical claims as meaningless. As difficulties in this position accumulated, the demand for verifiability gradually gave way to the much less stringent requirement that if any expression is to count as meaningful, there must be some rules governing its use, some recognized conventions adhered to. The extent of the change from verificationist theories to more recent theories is most strikingly seen in the contrast between Ludwig Wittgenstein's early views, in the *Tractatus Logico-philosophicus* (New York, 1922), and his later views, in *Philosophical Investigations* (London, 1953).

This increased permissiveness does not, however, solve the problem of how to state the criteria for distinguishing the unverifiable sense of the metaphysician from the unverifiable nonsense into which he may lapse. The slogan "meaning as use," or even meaning as rule-governed or convention-guided use, does not, without further specification and elaboration, provide us with such a criterion, since a piece of undisguised nonsense may have its own conventions and its own use. Nonsense need be neither useless nor lacking in order and discipline. On the contrary, some of the clearest cases of nonsense, such as children's skipping rhymes, are cases where the use of the words spoken is exceptionally evident and where the rules decreeing which words may be spoken at each point are exceptionally rigid. It becomes essential, then, to attempt some sort of classification of the different sorts of rules or conventions to which language is subject in order to isolate those rules whose absence, alteration, or violation gives rise to nonsense.

That a variety of types of rules is involved is evidenced also by the variety of types of utterances (including the written as well as the spoken word) labeled as nonsense by different people in different contexts. To the man in the street, and to Dr. Johnson, nonsense includes everything plainly at variance with obvious fact. The philosopher is usually more discriminating and tries to distinguish fairly sharply between the false and the nonsensical, although there is no general agreement concerning just where the line is to be drawn. What one philosopher will class as senseless—for example, "Virtue is green"—another will class as false, and the literary critic may well find the same words, in a suitably enriching context, illuminating and apt. In listing the variety of things that can count as nonsense, and the related variety of linguistic requirement, the simplest strategy is to take a perfectly acceptable utterance as the point of departure and to note the directions and degrees in which deviant utterances may depart from it. In so doing we will be drawing up a rough hierarchy ranging from sense, through some contested cases, down to uncontroversial cases of nonsense.

Types of nonsense. Taking as the paradigm of sense the utterance "The water is now boiling" spoken when the water is in fact boiling, to an audience ignorant of and intererested in that fact, we may list the following main departures from the standard:

(1) The same words spoken when contrary to fact: In such circumstances a natural rejoinder would be "Nonsense, I can see that it is scarcely simmering yet." We may call this, which is nonsense in the colloquial sense, "nonsense as obvious falsehood."

(2) The same words spoken when no one knows which water is spoken of or cares if it boils—for instance, when spoken in the middle of a marriage ceremony or occurring without quotation marks in the middle of an entry in this encyclopedia: In such a context the words make no sense. The rules or conventions violated are those tying this well-formed sentence to certain nonlinguistic contexts, so we may call this "semantic nonsense."

(3) The words "The water is now toiling" spoken in almost any circumstances (at this point in the history of the English language): This would constitute nonsense of the sort which fascinates the philosopher, since although it is in most respects a well-formed sentence, it attaches to its subject, "water," a predicate in some way unsuitable. In just what way it is unsuitable is a contested point. What is involved is what has been called a category mistake. The principles disregarded in such utterances are difficult to state or to characterize. They may be regarded simply as very specific rules of syntax or as ontological truths. The difficulty in citing or establishing them is increased by the fact that the very same rules can be broken without producing nonsense, in all figurative language. "The kettle is boiling" makes perfect sense in any suitable semantic context, despite the metonymy and consequent category mistake embedded in it (the kettle, as distinct from its contents, cannot boil). Even "The water is toiling" can make sense when said of the water turning a mill wheel. The problem here is to find the decisive factor which

makes some category mixing successful in communication and the rest nonsense. Many nonsense verses rely on such category mistakes for their effect, such as

> He thought he saw a Garden-Door
> That opened with a key:
> He looked again, and found it was
> A Double Rule of Three.
>
> (Lewis Carroll, *Sylvie and Bruno*)

We may, following usage in current linguistics, call these deviant utterances "semisentences."

(4) Strings of familiar words which lack, to a greater or lesser extent, the syntactic structure of the paradigms of sense or any syntax translatable into the familiar—for example, "Jumps digestible indicators the under": Phrases in which, as in the example, no vestige of familiar syntax remains we may call "nonsense strings." Such nonsense strings may be seen as differing only in degree from the semisentences of level 3.

(5) Utterances which have enough familiar elements to enable us to discern a familiar syntax, but whose vocabulary, or a crucial part of it, is unfamiliar, and untranslatable into the familiar vocabulary: Nonsense verse is often of this sort. "All mimsy were the borogoves" (Lewis Carroll) contains enough familiar elements to enable us to parse the sentence. Sometimes the occurrence of only one unfamiliar word, if it is crucial enough, will suffice to make a poem a nonsense poem (for example, Edward Lear's "The Pobble Who Has No Toes"). We may call this "vocabulary nonsense."

(6) Last, those cases where we can find neither familiar syntax nor familiar vocabulary, still less familiar category divisions or semantic appropriateness: Nonsense of this extreme type, such as the utterance "grillangborpfemstaw" may be termed "nonsense as gibberish."

Even at this level nonsense shares with sense a familiar alphabet or phonetic system. Nonsense is parasitic upon sense and never departs so far from sense that it ceases to be part of some language, to the minimal extent of sharing its alphabet with that language.

Several general points can now be made with reference to this tentative hierarchy.

Nonsense, type, and token. At levels 1 and 2 what can be classified as nonsense is not a form of words, or utterance type, but those words on a particular occasion, an utterance token. At levels 4–6 we can classify as nonsense a form of words on whatever occasion it is used. Some of the difficulty in specifying the nonsensical character of the semisentences of level 3 may arise from the attempt to find rules or generalizations for sentence types, when all that may be possible at this level is a characterization of utterance tokens. The stubborn fact is that in propitious circumstances (verbal context or nonverbal context) tokens of these semisentence types may be not nonsense but figures of speech, and figures of fully successful speech.

Nonsense, falsity, and logical relatedness. It can be argued that ordinary empirical falsity (level 1) is simply one case of semantic nonsense (level 2), that speaking falsely is one of the ways in which we may utter a form of words at the wrong time, on the wrong occasion. To distin-

guish the semantic inappropriateness of the false claim from the semantic inappropriateness of the contextually irrelevant remark ("Please pass the salt" spoken at a board meeting), we can characterize the latter as presupposing an empirically false claim (that there is salt somewhere present), although it itself is not true or false—even when it is an indicative sentence such as "The present king of France is bald." (See P. F. Strawson, "On Referring," in *Mind*, Vol. 59, No. 235, July 1950, 320–344.) In a similar way, the senselessness of utterances at level 3 can be seen to lie in the fact that they presuppose something which is not empirically but necessarily false. "Vigorous green ideas sleep furiously" presupposes that ideas can sleep, and this, by the meaning rules of "sleep" and "idea," is necessarily false. "Virtue is green" presupposes that virtue has color, and this is of necessity false.

Such a characterization of nonsense utterances of levels 1, 2, and 3 marks them off in a fairly important way from the remaining levels: they have definite logical links with the paradigms of sense. At level 5 there may of course be logical links between different pieces of nonsense at that level but no links with paradigm utterances. "All mimsy were the borogoves" contradicts "The borogoves were not all mimsy" but has no logical relation to any paradigm sentence. This means we have a dichotomy between the sort of nonsense which has logical relations with sense and that which does not.

There are, however, difficulties in the suggestion that the semisentence "Virtue is green," which is, according to some, neither true nor false, presupposes the false sentence "Virtue is the sort of thing which has color." The difficulty is this, that logical relations are usually defined in terms of truth relations but truth relations hold only between statements which can be true or false. What, then, can be this logical relation of presupposition which can hold between the meaningless and the false? It seems that we cannot consistently hold all the following five theses, each of which some philosophers have wanted to hold:

(1) Everything which has logical relations with the meaningful is itself meaningful.

(2) Logical relations can be defined in terms of truth relations.

(3) "Virtue is green" is a piece of nonsense.

(4) "Virtue is not the sort of thing which can have color" is true.

(5) There is a logical relation between "Virtue is green" and "Virtue is not the sort of thing which can have color."

At least one of these theses must be abandoned, and different philosophers abandon different ones. The issues involved here essentially concern the demarcation of the field within which logical relations hold, within which sense can be spoken, in such a way as to allow us still to talk sense about those relations themselves (see Wittgenstein, *Tractatus Logico-philosophicus*, 5.61).

Nonsense and the uncomprehended. A final point needs to be made about the nature of our original hierarchy, and of any improved version of it. What this hierarchy attempts, and what the linguist in his more technical and detailed way attempts, is to set up a formal or quasi-formal hierarchy that will correspond with the actual scale ranging from the clearly understood acceptable utterance, through the difficult deviant but comprehensible utterance, down to the completely unintelligible. This scale is obtained by observing what the speakers of a language in fact understand and what they reject. This will be determined in part by how well-read they are, the sorts of situations they are familiar with, the lives they lead, and the words they have spoken and heard in the past. The set of utterances accepted by a language society is constantly changing: some combinations of words lose currency as others attain it (either by deliberate innovation, as in new technical terminologies, or, very differently, as in successful metaphors that "catch on"). What hope has any formal analysis of capturing the essential features of sense and nonsense when what determines whether a given utterance counts as sense or as nonsense seems to be so much a matter of history and of brute psychological fact? For Descartes the suggestion that machines could think was absurd. For us it is at least a discussible issue. What formal features does the sentence "Machines can think" now possess that it did not possess in the seventeenth century and that explain its contemporary status as controversial but not nonsensical?

The difficulties of finding any formula that can encapsulate the sense-nonsense factor leads many contemporary philosophers to turn from the attempt to give any calculus-like interpretation of language and instead to treat language as a psychological and historical phenomenon. Paul Ziff, in his article "About Ungrammaticalness," has introduced the useful but highly informal concept of "balking." An utterance is nonsensical in a given language at a given time if an average member of that language society "balks" at it. But who can predict what people will or will not balk at? Such an approach is a far cry from formal analyses of meaning, such as Rudolf Carnap's *Logical Syntax of Language* (London, 1937). It is, however, an approach that does not altogether rule out the usefulness of the linguist's attempt to find some schema into which can be fitted all the rich and changing varieties of sense and of nonsense and which could give us insight into their relations. Such a schema would not enable us to predict or legislate which actual words can count as sense; it could merely help us to vivisect the sense that language users confer upon certain combinations of words and to perform post-mortems on those discarded as total nonsense.

What, according to such a view, is the status of the metaphysical claims which earlier positivist theories excluded as senseless? Do we, or should we, balk at the Heidegger sentence "The Nothing itself nothings," rejected by Rudolf Carnap? (See "The Elimination of Metaphysics Through Logical Analyses of Language," in A. J. Ayer, ed., *Logical Positivism*, Glencoe, Ill., 1959.) The answer is that some of us balk, some do not. This sentence, by the previous classification, must count as at best a semisentence that may achieve meaning in a kindly setting. Presumably its original context (*Was ist Metaphysik?*, 1929) provided this, as a good poem may illuminate its own difficult metaphors. But most good philosophy, unlike most good verse, does not have to be recited *in toto* to succeed as intelligible speech. As philosophers and as metaphysicians we hope to use words in ways whose intelligibility is not completely context dependent; we try to speak in sentences which can be paraphrased, taken from their original context, and used to illuminate a range of related issues. This is not always possible. To make a new point it may be necessary for the philosopher, as much as for the poet or the scientist, to speak in a new form of words not simply translatable into any of the old forms. But the philosopher who speaks too often in semisentences runs the risk of semiunderstanding from only a semiaudience.

Bibliography

For recent linguistic theories, see Jerry A. Fodor and Jerrold J. Katz, eds., *The Structure of Language* (Englewood Cliffs, N.J., 1964), especially Noam Chomsky's "Degrees of Ungrammaticalness." See also Paul Ziff, *Semantic Analysis* (Ithaca, N.Y., 1960) and "About Ungrammaticalness," in *Mind,* Vol. 73, No. 290 (April 1964), 204–215; Gustav Stern, *Meaning and Change of Meaning,* Göteborgs Högskolas Arsskrift, XXXVIII (Goteborg, Sweden, 1932); and B. F. Skinner, *Verbal Behavior* (New York, 1957).

For recent discussions from a logician's point of view, see A. N. Prior, "Entities," in *Australasian Journal of Philosophy,* Vol. 32 (December 1954), 159–168; V. Presley, "Arguments About Meaninglessness," in *British Journal for the Philosophy of Science,* Vol. 12, No. 47 (1961), 225–234; and L. Goddard, "Sense and Nonsense," in *Mind,* Vol. 73, No. 291 (July 1964), 309–331.

For a more general philosophical treatment, see L. Jonathan Cohen, *The Diversity of Meaning* (New York, 1963).

For a literary approach, see Elizabeth Sewell, *The Field of Nonsense* (London, 1952); and Allen Tate, ed., *The Language of Poetry* (New York, 1960).

A. C. BAIER

NORMATIVE ETHICS. See ETHICS, PROBLEMS OF.

NORRIS, JOHN (1657–1711), English philosopher and disciple of Malebranche, was associated with the Cambridge Platonists. Norris was born in Collingbourne-Kingston, Wiltshire. His father was a clergyman and at that time a Puritan. Educated at Winchester and at Exeter College, Oxford, which he entered in 1676, Norris was appointed a fellow of All Souls in 1680. During his nine years at All Souls, he was ordained (1684) and began to write, mostly in a Platonic vein and often in verse. In 1683 he published *Tractatus adversus Reprobationis absolutae Decretum,* in which he attacked the Calvinist doctrine of predestination. His Platonism and anti-Calvinism naturally attracted Norris to the Cambridge Platonists; in 1684 he began to correspond with Henry More and Damaris Cudworth, the daughter of Ralph Cudworth.

The philosophical essays included in *Poems and Discourses* (1684)—renamed *A Collection of Miscellanies* in the 1687 and subsequent editions—could, indeed, have been written by a Cambridge Platonist. Their main argument is that since truth is by its nature eternal and immutable, it must relate ideas which are also eternal and immutable; this condition, according to Norris, can be fulfilled only by ideas which are "in the mind of God"—that is, manifestations of God's essence. Thus, the existence of God is deducible from the very nature of truth; the atheist is involved in a self-contradictory skepticism.

In Norris' *The Theory and Regulation of Love* (1688)—for all that Norris dedicated it to the former Damaris Cudworth, now Lady Masham, and included as an appendix his correspondence with More—the influence of Malebranche began to predominate. At first, it reinforced rather than weakened Norris' sympathy with Cambridge Platonism. Norris followed Malebranche in distinguishing two kinds of love—desire, which seeks to unify itself with the good it pursues, and benevolence, which seeks good for others. But, as also in *Reason and Religion* (1689), Norris explicitly rejected Malebranche's view that the only proper object of desire is God. The objects of desire, Norris said, form a hierarchy—God, the good of the community, intellectual pleasures, and sensual pleasures are all in some measure good. God is the highest but not the only good.

In 1689, Norris married and resigned his fellowship to become rector of Newton St. Loe in Somerset. In his *Reflections on the Conduct of Human Life* (1690), addressed to Lady Masham and intended as an admonition to her, he condemned the life he had lived at Oxford on the ground that he had interested himself in public affairs and in intellectual pursuits; in the future he proposed to dedicate himself in retirement to the "moral improvement of my mind and the regulation of my life." This is Malebranche's, not the Cambridge Platonists', ideal of conduct; even the pursuit of knowledge is conceived of as a worldly enticement.

In 1691, as a result of Locke's influence, Norris became rector of Bemerton, near Salisbury, where he died on February 5, 1711. He did not win the approval of his Cambridge Platonist bishop, Gilbert Burnet, who would certainly not have appreciated Norris' attack on toleration in *The Charge of Schism continued* (1691). Norris' *Discourse concerning the Measures of Divine Love* (*Practical Discourses*, Vol. III, 1693) and *Letters concerning the Love of God* (1695) reveal the complete disciple of Malebranche; we ought, Norris now said, to love nobody but God. Substantially reversing Kant's dictum, he argued that we should treat other human beings as means—occasions of happiness to us—and never as ends. Lady Masham was naturally indignant; in her anonymous *Discourse concerning the Love of God* (1696), a reply to Norris, she argued that men are "made for a sociable life" and should love their fellow men in the same way they love God.

Thought. Norris' metaphysical views, sketched in *Reason and Religion,* are set out in detail in his *Essay towards the Theory of the Ideal and the Sensible World* (Vol. I, 1701; Vol. II, 1704), which fully justifies his nickname "the English Malebranche." Yet the argument of the first volume of the *Essay* would still entitle Norris to be described as a Platonist—or as a Thomist or an Augustinian. Plato, the "Platonic father" Augustine, Suárez, and Aquinas all taught, he tried to show, the same lesson as Malebranche—that knowledge is of the eternal and, therefore, of God.

In the second volume, however, when Norris came to consider in more detail how our knowledge of "the world of sense" is related to our knowledge of "the intelligible world," his break with the Platonist tradition, arising out of his allegiance to Malebranche, is at once apparent. It is true that when he did (mildly) criticize Malebranche, it is on the Platonic ground that his theory of the imagination allows too much to sensation; Malebranche's phrase "We see all things in God," he also thought, might suggest to

the careless reader that sensation is our analogue for knowledge. "Divine ideas," Norris preferred to say, "are the immediate objects of our thought in the perception of things." But these are minor reformulations. Of much greater significance is the fact that he agreed with the Cartesians that "the world is a great mechanism and goes like a clock" and even accepted, although with some little hesitation, the Cartesian doctrine of animal mechanism. He did not even bother to refer to the Platonist theory of "plastic powers" or to More's criticism of Descartes's extension–thought dualism. He is a Platonist only where Malebranche is a Platonist—for example, in his rejection of the Aquinas–Locke account of abstraction.

Norris' philosophy might properly be described, in the phrase commonly applied to Spinoza, as "God-intoxicated." God, for him as for Malebranche, is the efficient cause of all happenings, the only good, the only object of knowledge. We know God directly; everything else is known by way of our apprehension of God's nature as revealed in the ideas which emanate from him. Norris could not explain, he confessed, how spiritual ideas can represent a material world; the material world is, indeed, an embarrassment to him, fading into the empty concept of "that which occasions our apprehensions" that Berkeley criticized. He was so concerned to leave nothing lovable in the world, nothing which could be a source of happiness to us, that he reduced it to a nonentity; it exists only as something to be shunned. The relation between our mind and God's is left in equal obscurity.

In 1692 Locke and Norris quarreled on a matter involving Lady Masham; Locke came to be very impatient with Norris' views, which probably provoked his *Examination of Malebranche* (first published in *Posthumous Works,* Peter King, ed., London, 1706); he directly criticized Norris in an essay first published in *A Collection of Several Pieces of Mr. John Locke* (1720). In general, Locke thought of Norris as a completely reactionary thinker.

Other of Norris' works deserving mention are *An Account of Reason and faith in relation to the Mysteries of Christianity* (1697), in which he argued—in reply to John Toland's deistic *Christianity not Mysterious* (1696)—that it is not unreasonable to believe the incomprehensible, and *A Philosophical Discourse concerning the Natural Immortality of the Soul* (1708), which makes use of Platonic–scholastic arguments against Henry Dodwell's *Epistolary Discourse proving . . . that the Soul is naturally Mortal* (1706). Many of his works, although not *The Ideal World,* were extremely popular, but it is usually impossible to distinguish his influence from Malebranche's. One of the least original of philosophers, he still displays considerable powers of criticism and exposition. He had a direct influence on Arthur Collier.

Bibliography

There is no modern edition of Norris. Norris brought together several of his minor works, including *Reason and Religion,* as *Treatises Upon Several Subjects* (London, 1697). For his *Poems* see the edition by Alexander Balloch Grosart in the *Fuller Worthies' Library,* Vol. III (Blackburn, 1871), pp. 147–348; John Wesley included an abbreviated version of *Treatise on Christian Prudence* and *Reflections upon the Conduct of Human Life* in his *Christian Library,* Vol. XXX (London, 1827).

See also Frederick James Powicke, *A Dissertation on John Norris* (London, 1894); Ernest Trafford Campagnac, *The Cambridge Platonists* (London, 1901); Flora Isabel MacKinnon, *The Philosophy of John Norris of Bemerton, Philosophical Monographs*, No. 2 of the *Psychological Review* (October 1910); John Henry Muirhead, *The Platonic Tradition in Anglo-Saxon Philosophy* (London, 1931); John K. Ryan, "John Norris, a Seventeenth Century Thomist," in *New Scholasticism*, Vol. 14, No. 2 (1940), 109–145; and Charlotte Johnston, "Locke's *Examination of Malebranche* and John Norris," in *Journal of the History of Ideas*, Vol. 19, No. 4 (1958), 551–558.

JOHN PASSMORE

NORWEGIAN PHILOSOPHY. See SCANDINAVIAN PHILOSOPHY.

NOTHING is an awe-inspiring yet essentially undigested concept, highly esteemed by writers of a mystical or existentialist tendency, but by most others regarded with anxiety, nausea, or panic. Nobody seems to know how to deal with it (he would, of course), and plain persons generally are reported to have little difficulty in saying, seeing, hearing, and doing nothing. Philosophers, however, have never felt easy on the matter. Ever since Parmenides laid it down that it is impossible to speak of what is not, broke his own rule in the act of stating it, and deduced himself into a world where all that ever happened was nothing, the impression has persisted that the narrow path between sense and nonsense on this subject is a difficult one to tread and that altogether the less said of it the better.

This escape, however, is not so easy as it looks. Plato, in pursuing it, reversed the Parmenidean dictum by insisting, in effect, that anything a philosopher *can* find to talk about must somehow be there to be discussed, and so let loose upon the world that unseemly rabble of centaurs and unicorns, carnivorous cows, republican monarchs and wife-burdened bachelors, which has plagued ontology from that day to this. Nothing (of which they are all aliases) can apparently get rid of these absurdities, but for fairly obvious reasons has not been invited to do so. Logic has attempted the task, but with sadly limited success. Of some, though not all, nonentities, even a logician knows that they do not exist, since their properties defy the law of contradiction; the remainder, however, are not so readily dismissed. Whatever Lord Russell may have said of it, the harmless if unnecessary unicorn cannot be driven out of logic as it can out of zoology, unless by desperate measures which exclude all manner of reputable entities as well. Such remedies have been attempted, and their effects are worse than the disease. Russell himself, in eliminating the present King of France, inadvertently deposed the present Queen of England. Quine, the sorcerer's apprentice, has contrived to liquidate both Pegasus and President Truman in the same fell swoop. The old logicians, who allowed all entities subsistence while conceding existence, as wanted, to an accredited selection of them, at least brought a certain tolerant inefficiency to their task. Of the new it can only be said that *solitudinem faciunt et pacem appellant*—they make a desert and call it peace. Whole realms of being have been abolished without warning, at the mere nonquantifying of a variable. The poetry of Earth has been parsed out of existence—and what has become of its prose?

There is little need for an answer. Writers to whom nothing is sacred, and who accordingly stop thereat, have no occasion for surprise on finding, at the end of their operations, that nothing is all they have left.

The logicians, of course, will have nothing of all this. Nothing, they say, is not a thing, nor is it the name of anything, being merely a short way of saying of anything that it is not something else. "Nothing" means "not-anything"; appearances to the contrary are due merely to the error of supposing that a grammatical subject must necessarily be a name. Asked, however, to prove that nothing is *not* the name of anything, they fall back on the claim that nothing *is* the name of anything (since according to them there are no names anyway). Those who can make nothing of such an argument are welcome to the attempt. When logic falls out with itself, honest men come into their own, and it will take more than this to persuade them that there are not better cures for this particular headache than the old and now discredited method of cutting off the patient's head.

The friends of nothing may be divided into two distinct though not exclusive classes: the know-nothings, who claim a phenomenological acquaintance with nothing in particular, and the fear-nothings, who, believing, with Macbeth, that "nothing is but what is not," are thereby launched into dialectical encounter with nullity in general. For the first, nothing, so far from being a mere grammatical illusion, is a genuine, even positive, feature of experience. We are all familiar with, and have a vocabulary for, holes and gaps, lacks and losses, absences, silences, impalpabilities, insipidities, and the like. Voids and vacancies of one sort or another are sought after, dealt in and advertised in the newspapers. And what are these, it is asked, but perceived fragments of nothingness, experiential blanks, which command, nonetheless, their share of attention and therefore deserve recognition? Sartre, for one, has given currency to such arguments, and so, in effect, have the upholders of "negative facts"—an improvident sect, whose refrigerators are full of nonexistent butter and cheese, absentee elephants and so on, which they claim to detect therein. If existence indeed precedes essence, there is certainly reason of a sort for maintaining that nonexistence is also anterior to, and not a mere product of, the essentially parasitic activity of negation; that the nothing precedes the not. But, verbal refutations apart, the short answer to this view, as given, for instance, by Bergson, is that these are but petty and partial nothings, themselves parasitic on what already exists. Absence is a mere privation, and a privation of something at that. A hole is always a hole *in* something: take away the thing, and the hole goes too; more precisely, it is replaced by a bigger if not better hole, itself relative to its surroundings, and so tributary to something else. Nothing, in short, is given only in relation to what is, and even the idea of nothing requires a thinker to sustain it. If we want to encounter it *an sich*, we have to try harder than that.

Better things, or rather nothings, are promised on the alternative theory, whereby it is argued, so to speak, not that holes are in things but that things are in holes or, more generally, that *everything* (and everybody) is in a hole. To be anything (or anybody) is to be bounded, hemmed in, defined, and separated by a circumambient frame of vacuity, and what is true of the individual is equally true of the collective. The universe at large is fringed with nothingness, from which indeed (how else?) it must have been created, if created it was; and its beginning and end, like that of all change within it, must similarly be viewed as a passage from one nothing to another, with an interlude of being in between. Such thoughts, or others like them, have haunted the speculations of nullophile metaphysicians from Pythagoras to Pascal and from Hegel and his followers to Heidegger, Tillich and Sartre. Being and nonbeing, as they see it, are complementary notions, dialectically entwined, and of equal status and importance; although Heidegger alone has extended their symmetry to the point of equipping *Das Nichts* with a correlative (if nugatory) activity of noth-ing, or nihilating, whereby it produces *Angst* in its votaries and untimely hilarity in those, such as Carnap and Ayer, who have difficulty in parsing "nothing" as a present participle of the verb "to noth."

Nothing, whether it noths or not, and whether or not the being of anything entails it, clearly does not entail that anything should be. Like Spinoza's substance, it is *causa sui;* nothing (except more of the same) can come of it; *ex nihilo, nihil fit.* That conceded, it remains a question to some why anything, rather than nothing, should exist. This is either the deepest conundrum in metaphysics or the most childish, and though many must have felt the force of it at one time or another, it is equally common to conclude, on reflection, that it is no question at all. The hypothesis of theism may be said to take it seriously and to offer a provisional answer. The alternative is to argue that the dilemma is self-resolved in the mere possibility of stating it. If nothing whatsoever existed, there would be no problem and no answer, and the anxieties even of existential philosophers would be permanently laid to rest. Since they are not, there is evidently *nothing to worry about.* But that itself should be enough to keep an existentialist happy. Unless the solution be, as some have suspected, that it is not nothing that has been worrying them, but they who have been worrying it.

Bibliography

Modern writers who have had something to say about nothing include:

Barrett, William, *Irrational Man.* New York, 1958.

Bergson, Henri, *L'Évolution créatrice.* Paris, 1907. Translated by Arthur Mitchell as *Creative Evolution.* London, 1911.

Carnap, Rudolf, "The Elimination of Metaphysics," in A. J. Ayer, ed., *Logical Positivism.* Glencoe, Ill., 1959. Pp. 69–73.

Edwards, Paul, "Professor Tillich's Confusions." *Mind,* N.S. Vol. 74 (1965), 192–214.

Findlay, J. N., *Meinong's Theory of Objects and Values,* 2d ed. Oxford, 1963.

Heidegger, Martin, *Sein und Zeit.* Halle, 1927. Translated by John Macquarrie and Edward Robinson as *Being and Time.* New York, 1962.

Heidegger, Martin, *Was ist Metaphysik?* Bonn, 1929; 4th ed., Frankfurt, 1943. Translated by R. F. C. Hull and Alan Crick as "What Is Metaphysics?," in W. Brock, ed., *Existence and Being.* London, 1949.

Heidegger, Martin, *Einführung in die Metaphysik.* Tübingen, 1953. Translated by Ralph Manheim as *An Introduction to Metaphysics.* New Haven, 1959.

Lazerowitz, Morris, *Structure of Metaphysics.* London, 1955.

Munitz, M. K., *Mystery of Existence.* New York, 1965.

Prior, A. N., "Non-entities," in R. J. Butler, ed., *Analytical Philosophy I.* Oxford and New York, 1962.

Quine, W. V., *From a Logical Point of View.* Cambridge, Mass., 1953.

Russell, Bertrand, "On Denoting." *Mind,* N.S. Vol. 14 (1905), 479–493.

Sartre, Jean-Paul, *L'Être et le néant.* Paris, 1943. Translated by Hazel E. Barnes as *Being and Nothingness.* London, 1957.

Taylor, Richard, "Negative Things." *Journal of Philosophy,* Vol. 49, No. 13 (1952), 433–448.

Tillich, Paul, *The Courage to Be.* New Haven, 1952.

Toms, Eric, *Being, Negation and Logic.* Oxford, 1962.

P. L. HEATH

NOUS. Homer used the term *nous* to refer to the mind and its functions generally, but in the pre-Socratics it became increasingly identified with knowledge, and with reason as opposed to sense perception. The term subsequently developed in two ways. For Plato it was equated generally with the rational part of the individual soul (*to logistikon*), although in the *Republic* it has a special function within this rational part. Plato always tended to treat *nous* as the only immortal part of the soul. Aristotle also considered *nous* as intellect distinguished from sense perception. In *De Anima* (III.3–5) he divides *nous* into a passive intellect which is affected by knowledge, and an active intellect, which alone is immortal and eternal.

The idea of a cosmic or divine mind represents the other way in which the concept of *nous* developed. Anaxagoras used *nous* to initiate the process of cosmic development. In the *Timaeus,* Plato identifies *nous* as the principle within the world soul that is responsible for the rational order in our universe. Aristotle (*Metaphysics,* Λ. 7) identifies the Prime Mover with a Nous that thinks itself. The Stoics equated *nous* with the Logos, so that for them it was both cosmic reason and the rational element in man; the two streams of development were thus united. Later Platonists distinguished a hierarchy of three separate manifestations of Nous, and in Plotinus *nous* is a second god, the direct image of the Good, containing within itself the world of intelligible being.

Bibliography

Armstrong, A. H., *The Architecture of the Intelligible Universe in the Philosophy of Plotinus.* Cambridge, 1940.

Fritz, K. von, "νόος and νοεῖν in the Homeric Poems." *Classical Philology,* Vol. 38 (1943), 79–93.

Fritz, K. von, "νοῦς and νοεῖν and Their Derivatives in Pre-Socratic Philosophy." *Classical Philology,* Vol. 40 (1945), 223–242; Vol. 41 (1946), 12–34.

Hamelin, O., *La Théorie de l'intellect d'après Aristote.* Paris, 1953.

G. B. KERFERD

NOVALIS (1772–1801), pseudonym of Friedrich Leopold Freiherr von Hardenberg, lyric poet and leader of the early German romanticists. Novalis was born of Pietistic parents on the family estate, Oberwiederstedt, in Saxony. In preparation for a civil service career, he studied jurisprudence, philosophy, chemistry, and mathematics at Jena, Leipzig, and finally at Wittenberg, where he completed his studies in 1794. In Jena, Novalis came under the influence of Goethe, Schiller, and especially Fichte. Soon afterward he became friendly with Friedrich and August Wilhelm von Schlegel, Ludwig Tieck, Friedrich von Schelling, and Johann Wilhelm Ritter. While apprenticed to a local official in Tennstedt, Novalis became engaged to 13-year-old Sophie von Kühn in 1795. Her death in 1797 reinforced his romantic mysticism and culminated in a poetic transfiguration of his loss, in which his love and his desire to follow her into death are mingled (*Hymnen an die Nacht,* first published in 1800). From 1796 on, Novalis worked in the administration of the Saxon salt works at Weissenfels. From 1797 to 1799 he studied mining at Freiburg, where he became engaged to Julie von Charpentier. He died at Weissenfels.

With Friedrich Schlegel, Novalis is the most characteristic spokesman of early romanticism. In opposition to the ideals of the Enlightenment and early classicism he presented his vision of the romantic life. In his novelistic fragment *Heinrich von Ofterdingen*, which was written in opposition to Goethe's *Wilhelm Meister,* he furnished the age with a poetic description of the poet. The self-consciousness implicit in such an undertaking is characteristic of Novalis. Thinking about his own situation, the poet tries to answer the more general question of the destiny of mankind; the poet is a seer who leads man home. The homelessness presupposed in this theme is also manifest in Novalis' characterization of the modern age as fragmented. By contrast, according to Novalis' idealized picture, the Middle Ages was a time of unity. These ideas are further developed in *Die Christenheit oder Europa* (1799), an essay on the history of Western civilization, in which Novalis attacks the Protestant Reformation and the Enlightenment for having destroyed medieval unity. Also, he proposes that the most important reason for the homelessness of man is simply that he is a finite being. To be finite is to be in search of the infinite, which can be recovered in the depths of the human soul, a concept which develops ideas derived from Fichte's *Wissenschaftslehre*. Meaning, being, and truth are identified with the absolute ego. When the adept in *Die Lehrlinge zu Sais* (1798) lifts the veil of Isis which hides the meaning of human existence, he discovers only his true self. At the same time, this discovery is an escape from all that separates man from nature and from others. The poet, through knowledge of his true self, is intuitively able to grasp the meaning of the world, which is veiled by mechanistic explanations, and to reveal this meaning to others. Poetry is an attempt to draw away the veil of the finite, which hides the mysterious meaning of everything. It thus has an apparently negative effect. The claims of the finite must be destroyed for the sake of the infinite. Romantic irony negates the ordinary significance of things and paves the way for a magic transformation of reality. Novalis' magic idealism may be described as an esoteric game in which relationships are suggested that may seem fantastic but are designed to reveal a higher meaning. The best example of this is *Heinrich von Ofterdingen,* in which past and present, fairy tale and everyday reality, mingle in such a way that the reader loses his bearings. This loss liberates his imagination. The world reveals its meaning when it is transformed into something man has freely chosen, and the opposition between man and nature is thereby overcome. Salvation lies in the godlike freedom of the artist.

Meaning escapes adequate conceptualization; it can only be hinted at. Fragment and aphorism (*Blütenstaub,* published in 1798) lend themselves particularly well to this purpose, as they point to meanings beyond themselves which must remain unstated. The romantic's refusal to mediate between the finite and the infinite, his assertion that there is no relationship between mere facts and transcendent meanings, makes it impossible to give any definite content to that reality which is said to be the goal of man's search. The movement toward salvation becomes indistinguishable from a flight into nothingness. Thus, in his *Hymnen an die Nacht* Novalis celebrates the night, in which all polarities are reconciled, and opposes it to more shallow day—a theme taken up by Schopenhauer, Nietzsche, and their more recent followers.

Works by Novalis

GERMAN EDITIONS

Editions of Novalis' collected works are Ludwig Tieck and Friedrich Schlegel, eds., 2 vols. (Berlin, 1802); Paul Kluckhohn and Richard Samuel, eds., 4 vols. (Leipzig, 1929; 2d ed., Stuttgart, 1960——); C. Seeling, ed., 5 vols. (Zurich, 1945); and E. Wasmuth, ed., 4 vols. (Heidelberg, 1953–1957).

For Novalis' philosophical works, see *Das philosophische Werke,* Richard Samuel, ed., Vol. I (Stuttgart, 1965), the first volume of a projected four-volume critical edition.

ENGLISH TRANSLATIONS

The Devotional Songs of Novalis, Bernard Pick, ed. Chicago, 1910. Also contains German text.

Henry of Ofterdingen: A Romance. Cambridge, 1842.

Hymns to the Night and Other Selected Writings, translated by C. E. Passage. New York, 1960.

The Novices of Sais, translated by R. Manheim. New York, 1949.

Works on Novalis

Biser, E., *Abstieg und Auferstehung, Die geistige Welt in Novalis Hymnen an die Nacht.* Heidelberg, 1954.

Carlyle, Thomas, "Novalis," in *Critical and Miscellaneous Essays,* in *Works,* H. D. Trail, ed. London, 1896–1899; New York, 1896–1901.

Dilthey, W., *Das Erlebnis und die Dichtung: Lessing, Goethe, Novalis, Hölderlin,* 3d ed. Leipzig, 1910.

Friedell, E., *Novalis als Philosoph.* Munich, 1904.

Kuhn, H., "Poetische Synthesis oder ein kritischer Versuch über romantische Philosophie und Poesie aus Novalis Fragmenten." *Zeitschrift für Philosophische Forschung* (1950–1951), 161–178; 358–384.

Küpper, P., *Die Zeit als Erlebnis des Novalis.* Cologne, 1959.

Rehm, W., *Orpheus, Der Dichter und die Toten.* Düsseldorf, 1950.

KARSTEN HARRIES

NUMBER. All human societies possess at least some partial conception of number as used in counting, for every language has some terminology for the first few numbers (even if only words for "one," "two," and "many"). Whether carried out by means of number words, fingers and toes, knots, notches, or numerals, the procedure of counting consists in correlating items to be counted with the elements of some readily surveyable standard sequence. For this counting to be correct the correlation effected must be one to one; if in trying to count the sheep in a field I called out the same number word while pointing in turn to two different sheep, or I call out two different number words pointing twice to the same sheep, I shall have miscounted the sheep in the field, and the final number word I utter will not then enable me to make reliable comparisons between the size of this flock and other sets of things. For the procedure to be considered counting in the full sense the standard sequence employed must be a progression; that is. it must have a first element but no last, each element must have a unique position in the sequence, and each element must have only finitely many precursors. Also, although this is so obvious as commonly to escape notice, the progression employed must be recursive in the sense that for any pair of its elements, which of the pair belongs earlier in the sequence must be decidable either by inspection or by some effective routine of steps.

MATHEMATICS OF NUMBER

The mathematical study of numbers has long been recognized as a keystone in the edifice of mathematics. The mathematics of number originated with the Babylonians and Hindus. To them we owe our powerful positional notation for numbers, in which the value of a symbol varies according to its place, so that "12" can mean the result of adding 1 times 10 to 2, and in which a symbol for zero plays an indispensable role, so that "102" can mean the result of adding 1 times 100 to 2. Important contributions to number theory were made by the Greeks, especially Euclid, Archimedes, and Diophantus, and after them by the Arabs. In the modern period Pierre de Fermat raised number theory to a new level. The work of Leonhard Euler and Adrien Legendre is noteworthy, and Karl Gauss's *Disquisitiones Arithmeticae* (1801) is the systematic treatise which, more than any other, established number theory as a modern mathematical discipline in its own right.

The numbers involved in counting—1, 2, 3, etc.—are of course the simplest and most fundamental kind. At least since late classical times these have been called the natural numbers, thereby being contrasted with the "artificial" kinds of numbers, such as rational numbers (all numbers expressible as fractions), real numbers (all numbers that measure lengths and areas—for example, the ratio of hypotenuse to side in an isosceles right triangle, $\sqrt{2}$, although real, is not rational, as the Pythagoreans proved to their horror), complex numbers (those having "imaginary" components based on $\sqrt{-1}$), and transfinite numbers (numbers uncountably large). A trifling ambiguity in the term "natural number" arises because some writers choose to call zero a natural number, whereas others do not. The theory of the natural and rational numbers is usually called number theory or arithmetic, whereas the theory of the real numbers is known as analysis.

Philosophical puzzlement about the various kinds of numbers, especially about the status of the more "artificial" ones, was much reduced by the work of Richard Dedekind and other nineteenth-century mathematicians who developed a unified theory of numbers. They showed how the mathematical theories concerning the artificial numbers can be reduced to (or constructed from) a theory concerning the natural numbers. That is, they showed how each of the artificial kinds of numbers, together with the operations (such as addition and multiplication) performable on numbers of that kind, can be defined in terms of the natural numbers and the operations performable on them, and they showed that this can be done in such a way that the laws which govern the artificial numbers can then be deduced from the laws of the natural numbers.

There are alternative schemes of definition that make all this possible; one approach is as follows: The rational numbers may be defined as a certain kind of sets of ordered pairs of natural numbers, the real numbers as a certain kind of sets of rational numbers, the signed (positive and negative) real numbers as a certain kind of sets of real numbers, and the complex numbers as ordered pairs of signed real numbers. By using Georg Cantor's theory of infinite sets this scheme of numbers can be extended to yield a hierarchy of larger and larger infinite numbers (with infinite numbers the distinction becomes important between cardinal numbers, which measure the sizes of sets, and ordinal numbers, which are types of order in series). The resulting unified theory of numbers enables us to regard the various kinds of numbers as belonging to a single family, all springing from one parent kind and all governed by laws that are strict deductive consequences of those governing that simple parent kind. If we accept this unified theory, we no longer need feel any special philosophical concern about the artificial numbers; our philosophical problems will be concentrated in the natural numbers.

Before turning to those philosophical problems, however, let us note that this unified theory of numbers makes heavy use of the notion of set (see SET THEORY). It is also important to investigate the narrower theory, called elementary number theory, that is obtained if we exclude all mention of sets and ordered pairs and concentrate solely on the natural numbers and such operations as addition, multiplication, and exponentiation that are performable on them; only the logic of truth-functions, of quantification, and of identity is used. The sorts of truths expressible in this notation include "For all x and for all y, x plus y is identical to y plus x," "There is an x such that for all y, x plus y is identical to y," and "For all x, if there is a y such that x plus y is identical to y, then for all z, x times z is identical to x."

Within the area of elementary number theory the prime numbers are of especial interest (a prime number is a natural number greater than 1 that is evenly divisible by no natural number other than 1 and itself). Euclid established that there are infinitely many prime numbers. It is known that every natural number can be decomposed in only one way into its set of prime factors (this proposition is called the "fundamental theorem of arithmetic"). Much attention has been devoted to the difficult problem of how primes are distributed within the sequence of natural numbers. Two notorious propositions of elementary number theory are C. Goldbach's conjecture that every even number greater than 2 can be expressed as the sum of two primes, and Fermat's last theorem, which states that there are no natural numbers x, y, and z satisfying the equation x^n plus y^n equals z^n when n is a natural number greater than 2. These two propositions are of philosophical interest because they seem true, no counterexamples ever having been found, yet they remain unproved despite strong efforts by many mathematicians.

Elementary number theory has been the focus of some especially important twentieth-century work in mathematical logic, by which long-standing preconceptions have been shattered. People used to picture the mathematics of number as a field in which, in principle, sheer calculation ought to be able to solve all problems. We now know that this picture does not fit even elementary number theory, which cannot have a decision procedure; that is, no mechanical routine of steps can suffice as a general test of the truth of statements expressible in the notation of elementary number theory. This fact is a corollary to another, far more surprising result, Kurt Gödel's famous proof (1931) that elementary number theory is not even completable, that is, that there can be no consistent set of axioms for elementary number theory from which every truth expressible in the notation of the theory would be deducible (see GÖDEL'S THEOREM). Another fundamental result is the Löwenheim–Skolem theorem (1920), which states that if a set of quantificational schemata are consistent, they all come out true together under some interpretation in the universe of natural numbers. This theorem does not mean that the Pythagoreans were right after all and that everything somehow really consists of natural numbers; it does mean that the logical structure of any theory (its truth-functions and quantification) is insufficient to distinguish the objects of the theory from the natural numbers.

LITERALISTIC PHILOSOPHIES OF NUMBER

The main philosophical issues with regard to number theory concern the kinds of meaning, truth, and knowledge that are involved in it. Through the ages philosophers have been inclined to regard number theory, along with geometry, as yielding knowledge of exemplary clarity and certainty. But what is the nature of the entities known, and by what means is this knowledge attained? In discussing these issues it is necessary to consider the question of mathematical existence, for some of the laws of number theory assert the existence of specific numbers (in this respect number theory differs from geometry—the other branch of mathematics that has most concerned philosophers—all of whose laws can be regarded as hypothetical and as not necessarily asserting the existence of anything).

One broad category of philosophical views of number comprises views according to which the laws of number theory are somehow literally true. To the question "Do numbers exist?" these viewpoints do not offer figurative answers, such as "Yes, in the sense that the term 'number' occurs in the talk of mathematicians" or "Yes, in the sense that number talk proves useful for science." Instead, they try to hold that things deserving the name of numbers, things of which the laws of number theory literally hold true, do exist and are in no sense imaginary or fictional,

that these things should be said to exist in the same logical tone of voice in which we speak of the existence of whatever we regard as belonging among the "ultimate furniture of the universe." Literalistic views about the metaphysical status of number may be divided into nominalistic, conceptualistic, and platonistic views.

Nominalism. Nominalism is the view that there are no abstract entities, and as a literalistic view of number it holds that numbers are literally concrete items in the world, occurring at particular times. Two unsophisticated forms of this view have enjoyed popularity: a crude version of formalism holds that numbers are literally particular marks occurring on paper and on blackboards, and a crude sort of psychologism identifies numbers with particular ideas occurring in people's minds. Gottlob Frege criticized these positions with brilliant savagery, pointing out that according to number theory each natural number exists and is unique, whereas these nominalistic views do not provide for the uniqueness of the smaller numbers (there would be as many distinct numbers 1 as there are occurrences of numerals for 1 or as there are ideas of 1) or for the existence of the larger numbers (numbers so great that no numerals for them are ever written down, so great that no particular ideas of them have occurred in the minds of men). Much more sophisticated than these crude forms of nominalism are the ingenious efforts of W. V. Quine and Nelson Goodman ("Steps Toward a Constructive Nominalism," *Journal of Symbolic Logic*, Vol. 12, 1947, 105–122), who successfully carry nominalism much further in many respects than might have been supposed possible. However, no series of actual concrete items in the world seems capable of being known to constitute a progression in the full sense required by number theory, and for this reason nominalism fails to provide a complete literalistic interpretation of number.

Conceptualism. Conceptualism may roughly be characterized as the view that abstract entities exist, but only insofar as they are created by the activity of human thought. As a literalistic view of number conceptualism may be regarded as holding that numbers literally exist as timeless abstract things yet are mental constructions and have no being independent of the mind. Kant is historically the outstanding representative of this difficult viewpoint. He connected number with time (a "pure intuition," the "form of inner sense") and seems to have believed that knowledge of number rests on the mind's awareness of its own capacity to repeat the act of counting, time after time. In knowing the laws of number the mind is gaining insight only into its own workings, which in principle must be perfectly knowable; therefore, the propositions of number theory, although synthetic (that is, not derivable from mere logic alone), can be known with a priori certainty. Kant actually said that facts about specific numbers, such as that 5 plus 7 equals 12, are known through synthetic a priori insight, but as Frege observed, this is not plausible, for these facts surely can, and especially for the larger numbers must, be proved. Kant might better have deployed his theory as an attempt to explain the status of the basic general laws of number theory.

In recent times a group of mathematicians, of whom L. E. J. Brouwer has been the central figure, have defended a philosophy of number closely akin to Kant's. Brouwer, like Kant, has maintained that a pure intuition of temporal counting serves as the point of departure for the mathematics of number; for this reason the name "intuitionism" has been given to the philosophy of the group. Believing that numbers are creatures of the mind, the intuitionists follow Kant in supposing that whatever the mind creates it must be able to know through and through. This leads to the belief that nothing is true about numbers except what is verifiable by counting or kindred constructive procedures and that nothing is false about numbers except what is constructively refutable. Fermat's last theorem and Goldbach's conjecture must then be regarded as propositions which, so far as we know, are neither true nor false. Thus, intuitionism rejects the traditional law of excluded middle, according to which no proposition is neither true nor false, and with it all use of indirect proof (reasoning by *reductio ad absurdum*) in mathematics. As a result much of classical mathematics goes by the board.

Is the philosophical position convincing enough to justify this sacrifice? Few philosophers or mathematicians would now think so. The central philosophical notion about the mind's activity in pure intuition is lamentably hazy. Moreover, a serious ambiguity infects the view of numbers as abstract creations of the mind. In order for a number to exist, is it necessary that someone actually have counted up to it, or is it sufficient that it be reachable by counting? No one ever counts infinitely high, so the first interpretation is of course incompatible with the principle of number theory which states that the series of natural numbers has no last member. The second interpretation, however, does not harmonize with the picture of numbers as creatures of the mind, for it allows the existence of numbers never thought of by anyone. To equate constructive verifiability with creation by the mind, as conceptualism does, seems a serious confusion. A further difficulty is that if numbers were viewed as mental constructions, it would then seem doubtful that numbers could be known to apply to what exists outside the mind—yet to suppose that they do not do so is incoherent.

Platonism. By platonism is understood the realistic view, akin to that of Plato himself, that abstract entities exist in their own right, independently of human thinking. According to this view number theory is to be regarded as the description of a realm of objective, self-subsistent mathematical objects that are timeless, nonspatial, and nonmental. Platonism conceives it to be the task of the mathematician to explore this and other eternal realms of being. Among modern philosophers of mathematics Frege is the pre-eminent representative of platonism, distinguished by his penetrating lucidity and his intransigence; Bertrand Russell's advocacy of platonism has often been equally forceful, although his dedication to the view has been less steady.

In recent thought platonism as a view of number has been associated with the logistic thesis, the claim that the theory of numbers is reducible to logic; however, the two positions are not linked by any strict necessity. Frege was the original proponent of the logistic thesis, which Russell and Alfred North Whitehead subsequently expounded in their monumental three-volume *Principia Mathematica*

(1910–1913). The reduction of the natural numbers to logic is a procedure of exactly the same sort as the reduction of the artificial to the natural numbers, but in this case the natural numbers themselves, and the operations on them, are defined in terms of concepts of logic, and their laws are deduced from laws of logic. Set theory is here regarded by Frege and the authors of *Principia* as a part of logic rather than of mathematics; the reduction is in effect a reduction to set theory.

Frege insisted on an elemental point that earlier philosophers had not recognized: Having a number (for example, being two) is not a feature of individual things or heaps of things (as being red is) but pertains rather to concepts or sets. To a pile of boots as such no number can be attributed. But to the set of boots in the pile, or to the concept "boot in this pile," a number does belong—although it will be different from the number belonging to the set of pairs of boots in the pile or to the concept "pair of boots in the pile." In line with this, Frege identified the natural number 2 with the set containing all and only those concepts under each of which fall something, another thing distinct from the first, and nothing else. Russell and Whitehead identified the number 2 not with a set of concepts but with a set of sets—the set of all couples.

Frege and Russell, like Kant, regarded our knowledge of the laws of number as a priori. But for them the philosophical significance of the logistic thesis that number theory is reducible to logic was that the mathematics of number need not be regarded as involving any special type of rational insight, as Kant claimed when he declared arithmetic to be synthetic, rather than analytic, a priori knowledge. According to their logistic thesis the type of rational apprehension by which we attain our knowledge in logic must be the same as that by which we come to know the laws of logic. Platonism enters in because they took a platonistic view of logic.

Platonism requires us to suppose that the numbers have their own definite nature, and when platonism is combined with the logistic thesis it requires us to suppose that the natural numbers are sets of some specific kind. From a platonistic viewpoint the definitions involved must be regarded not as stipulative but as descriptive of pre-existing reality. Here difficulties arise. For one thing, various ways of reducing the theory of natural numbers to set theory are available; a slight divergence between Frege's definitions and those of *Principia* has already been noted, and quite different schemes of definition have since been proposed by other mathematical logicians. All these schemes of definition succeed equally in characterizing set-theoretic entities having the required structural properties; we have no reason at all for regarding one of these as the correct scheme of definitions and the others as false. Another, far more serious difficulty for platonism is posed by modern developments in set theory. In response to paradoxes several distinctly different forms of set theory have been evolved, each having some advantages and some disadvantages but none being free of arbitrary limitations. This tends to undermine the view that in set theory we discover and describe the structure of a realm of abstract reality. These considerations make implausible the position which combines platonism with the logistic thesis. If platonism is to be maintained as a philosophy of number, it would seem that the logistic thesis had better be rejected and number theory not reduced to set theory. Even then platonism will possess but little plausibility, for it affords a misleading picture of the nature of mathematical knowledge by suggesting that without extrasensory insight into Plato's heaven we could not understand the laws of number—whereas in fact a mastery of the technique of counting surely does suffice for such understanding.

NONLITERALISTIC PHILOSOPHIES OF NUMBER

None of the main literalistic philosophies of number is convincing. This forces us to consider nonliteralistic philosophies of number, according to which the significance of number theory does not consist in its literal truth. At least two nonliteralistic views deserve attention.

Formalism in its thoroughgoing form is a philosophy of number which holds that number theory is only a scheme of marks, with rules for their manipulation; no attempt should be made to regard combinations of these marks as expressing meaningful statements. According to this view no meaning, truth, or knowledge is embodied in number theory; it is an abstract game, the study of whose rules is intellectually stimulating (rather like chess, but more intricate). This game (unlike chess) can be turned to practical use, for certain ways of applying combinations of its marks have been evolved that are very helpful to people who carry out practical activities of counting and measurement.

Such thoroughgoing formalism is an extreme view in its complete denial that the formulas of number theory ought to be assigned any meaning. Another nonliteralistic viewpoint holds that although the laws of number theory should not be regarded as literally describing mathematical objects, they should be regarded as indirectly expressing generalizations concerning the nature of correct counting. These would presumably be necessary truths explicative of the concept of correct counting rather than inductive generalizations about actual counting. In this spirit, "5 plus 7 equals 12" could be regarded as indirectly asserting that whenever the words "one" through "five" are called out in one-to-one correlation with the items of a group and then the words "one" through "seven" are called out in correlation with the items of another, quite separate group, the words "one" through "twelve" would be required if the two groups were to be pooled and all the items counted together. The law "For all x and y, x plus y equals y plus x" can be regarded as indirectly asserting that the result of counting two groups of items is the same no matter which group is counted first. In this fashion the laws of elementary number theory can be construed as expressing our knowledge of the counting process, and by extension many, but not all, of the laws of the artificial numbers can be regarded as doing the same. By giving to number theory some real, although nonliteralistic, content this viewpoint succeeds in being less abstractly arid than formalism and can give a more direct account of why mathematical theory can assist our practical activities of counting and measuring.

Bibliography

In addition to works listed here, see the bibliography to MATHE-MATICS, FOUNDATIONS OF.

Introductory accounts of number theory are given in A. A. Fraenkel, *Integers and Theory of Numbers* (New York, 1955), and Ore Oystein, *Number Theory and Its History* (New York, 1948). More advanced standard works in the field include I. M. Vinogradov, *Elements of Number Theory*, translated from the 5th Russian ed. (1952) by Saul Kravetz (New York, 1954); and G. H. Hardy and E. M. Wright, *An Introduction to the Theory of Numbers*, 4th ed. (Oxford, 1960). A classic is Richard Dedekind, *Was sind und was sollen die Zahlen?* (Brunswick, Germany, 1888), included in *Essays on the Theory of Numbers*, translated by Wooster Woodruff Beman (Chicago, 1901; New York, 1963).

On the philosophical side, two readable classics are Gottlob Frege, *Die Grundlagen der Arithmetik* (Breslau, 1884), translated by J. L. Austin as *The Foundations of Arithmetic* (Oxford, 1950); and Bertrand Russell, *Introduction to Mathematical Philosophy* (London, 1919). See also E. W. Beth, *The Foundations of Mathematics* (Amsterdam, 1959); Paul Benacerraf, "What Numbers Could Not Be," in *Philosophical Review*, Vol. 74 (1965) 47–73; and C. G. Hempel, "On the Nature of Mathematical Truth," in *American Mathematical Monthly*, Vol. 52 (1945), 543–556. An elementary philosophical survey appears in S. F. Barker, *Philosophy of Mathematics* (Englewood Cliffs, N.J., 1964), and a broad selection of writings is contained in Paul Benacerraf and Hilary Putnam, eds., *Philosophy of Mathematics: Selected Readings* (Englewood Cliffs, N.J., 1964).

STEPHEN F. BARKER

NUMENIUS OF APAMEA, second-century Greek philosopher perhaps best known for his description of Plato as an Atticizing Moses, was a precursor of Plotinus and Neoplatonism and also had affinities with Gnosticism and the Hermetic tradition. Of his life practically nothing is known, and even the approximate dates of his birth and death are uncertain. Since his description of Plato is quoted by Clement of Alexandria (*Stromateis* i, 22.93), he cannot have survived much later than A.D. 200, while the latest writers cited in the fragments of his works belong to the time of Nero (A.D. 37–68). He may have been of non-Greek origin, and his name, like that of Porphyry, may have been a Greek translation of a Semitic original. Our sources commonly describe him as a Pythagorean, but Iamblichus and Proclus call him a Platonist, which comes to much the same thing in an age when Plato was considered a disciple of Pythagoras. Certainly Numenius is best grouped with such Middle Platonists as Albinus. His work was based primarily upon exegesis of Plato and presents a systematization of Plato's thought with a dualist emphasis. It is possible that he had some knowledge of Christianity, but what is truly remarkable is his knowledge of Judaism. It has been suggested that he himself was a Jew, but this is far from certain. What is clear is that he sought to go back before Plato and Pythagoras to the teachings of the ancient East, the Brahmins, the Jews, the Magi, and the Egyptians. In this respect there are links with the Hermetic books and with the *prisca theologia* of such Renaissance writers as Marsilio Ficino and Pico della Mirandola, although scholars differ as to the extent to which Numenius' philosophy was actually influenced by Oriental ideas and the extent to which it was purely Greek.

A notable feature of his thought is his doctrine of the Demiurge. He postulates two opposed principles, God and matter, the monad and the dyad, but whereas the Pythagoreans adhered to monism by making the dyad emanate from the monad, Numenius developed a dualistic theory. Matter is evil, and the supreme God can therefore have no contact with it; hence the need for a second god, the Demiurge, who is of dual nature, an *anima mundi* related both to God and to matter (cf. the Philonic Logos). There are also two souls in the world, one good and one evil, and two souls in man, a rational and an irrational; and the only escape from this dualism is by deliverance from the prison of the body. Astrological elements in Numenius' anthropology suggest an attempt to give astrology a rational basis.

Numenius is important for his influence on later Neoplatonists, although some of his views were to be rejected by them. The allegation that Plotinus merely plagiarized Numenius prompted Plotinus' disciple Amelius to write a book pointing out the differences between them (Porphyry, *Vita Plotini* 17). The hierarchy of three gods, for example, appears to be similar to Plotinus' hierarchy of being, but the three entities in each case do not correspond exactly in detail. Moreover, Plotinus rejected Numenius' dualistic and Gnosticizing tendencies.

Bibliography

Armstrong, A. H., *The Architecture of the Intelligible Universe in the Philosophy of Plotinus.* Cambridge and New York, 1940.

Beutler, R., "Numenios," in Pauly-Wissowa, *Real-Encyclopaedie.* Supp. VII (1940), pp. 664 ff.

Dodds, E. R., "Numenius and Ammonius," in *Les Sources de Plotin.* Entretiens Hardt, Vol. V. Geneva, 1957.

Festugière, A. J., *La Révélation d'Hermes Trismégiste.* Vol. III, *Les Doctrines de l'âme.* Paris, 1953. Vol. IV, *Le Dieu inconnu.* Paris, 1954.

Leemans, E. A., *Studie over den Wijsgeer Numenius van Apamea.* Mémoires de l'Académie Royale de Belgique, Vol. 37. Brussels, 1937. Includes fragments and testimonia.

Puech, H. C., *Mélanges Bidez.* Brussels, 1934. Vol. II.

Vogel, C. J. de, *Greek Philosophy.* Leiden, 1959, Vol. III, pp. 421 ff.

R. McL. Wilson

O

OBJECTIVISM. See ETHICAL OBJECTIVISM.

OCCASIONALISM. See CARTESIANISM; GEULINCX, ARNOLD; MALEBRANCHE, NICOLAS; MIND—BODY PROBLEM.

OCKHAM, WILLIAM OF. See WILLIAM OF OCKHAM.

OCKHAMISM is a term used by some historians of medieval philosophy to characterize the critical and skeptical attitude toward natural theology and traditional metaphysics that became prevalent in the fourteenth century and is ascribed to the influence of William of Ockham (c. 1285–1349). There is little historical basis for speaking of an Ockhamist school, since Ockham had scarcely any avowed disciples; nor was the critical attitude toward natural theology initiated by him, although his logical criteria of demonstration and evidence undoubtedly gave it a powerful implementation. With these reservations one may, in a general sense, attach Ockham's name to the movement of thought that, in the fourteenth century, closed out the medieval enterprise of synthesizing Aristotelian philosophy with Christian theology and initiated new lines of development that led toward the scientific empiricism of the seventeenth century. The Ockhamist or nominalist movement was known in the fourteenth and fifteenth centuries as the "modern way" (*via moderna*), and was contrasted with the "old way" (*via antiqua*) associated with thirteenth-century Scholasticism.

One may distinguish two main phases of this movement of fourteenth-century thought. The first phase, occurring between 1330 and 1350, was marked by the rapid spread of Ockham's doctrines and method among the theologians and philosophers teaching at the universities of Oxford and Paris, where Ockham's logical techniques were used in criticism of the older scholastic tradition. The second phase, less directly associated with Ockham's own teachings, commenced around 1350 and involved what may be described as a reconstruction of philosophy, and of theology as well, on foundations compatible with Ockham's empiricism and nominalism.

Critique of Scholasticism. The influence of Ockham's logic and of his nominalistic critique of the thirteenth-century metaphysical syntheses of philosophy and theology was exhibited at Oxford in the work of Adam Wodham (d. 1349), a Franciscan who had studied with Ockham, and of Robert Holkot (d. 1349), a Dominican theologian who lectured at Oxford around 1330 and later taught at Cambridge. Holkot was an outspoken nominalist who minced no words in stating that theology is not a science and that its doctrines can in no way be demonstrated or even comprehended by human reason. Christian dogma, for Holkot, was accepted by an act of will, on the authority of the church.

Thomas Bradwardine (c. 1290–1349) reacted against what he regarded as a new Pelagianism embodied in the Ockhamist interpretation of revealed theology, but he utilized Ockham's logical techniques to draw deterministic consequences from the doctrine of divine omnipotence, invoking the authority of Augustine for his views. Other Oxford teachers influenced by Ockham, and particularly by his logical methods, included Richard Swineshead ("the Calculator"), John Dumbleton, William Heytesbury, and Richard Billingham.

The "modern way." It was at Paris, more than at Oxford, that Ockham's influence led, after an initial resistance, to establishment of a relatively stable, and in some respects scientifically fruitful, philosophical school that endured and spread through central Europe in the late fourteenth and early fifteenth centuries.

One of the first Parisian theologians to embrace Ockham's doctrines was John of Mirecourt, a Cistercian monk who lectured on Peter Lombard's *Sentences* in 1344–1345. His skeptical treatment of the arguments of traditional theology led to a condemnation by the theological faculty at Paris of articles taken from his lectures. In many respects Mirecourt's positions resembled those of Holkot, by whom he may have been influenced.

Another victim of disciplinary action by the authorities of the University of Paris was Nicolas of Autrecourt, who was condemned to burn publicly, in November 1347, his letters to Bernard of Arezzo and his treatise *Exigit ordo executionis*. Nicolas, reacting to the Ockhamist thesis that God, by his absolute power, could cause an intuitive cognition of a nonexistent object, or could cause sensible qualities to exist without any substance being qualified by them, held that the only things of which man can have certain knowledge are the qualities perceived by his five senses, the acts or affections of his own mind, and those propositions logically evident by the principle of contradiction. From this he argued that we have no ground for belief in substances or for making inferences on the basis of causal relations, and he asserted that the whole philosophy of Aristotle is a fictitious construction devoid of any evidence or even of probability, since it rests on the assumption of substances and of causal necessities that are neither logically nor empirically evident. Preferring certainty to the Ockhamist "hypothesis of nature," Nicolas turned Ockham's critique of metaphysical necessity against Ockham's own empiricism and was rebuked by Jean Buridan for demanding absolute evidence, or logical necessity, in a domain of inquiry in which only conditional evidence based on the assumption of a common course of nature is appropriate.

In the hands of Jean Buridan, a teacher on the faculty of arts at Paris, Ockham's logic, theory of knowledge, and nominalistic ontology were made the basis of a natural philosophy or physics of empirical type, within which Buridan developed the impetus theory of projectile motion and gravitational acceleration and subjected the assumptions of Aristotelian physics and cosmology to critical analysis in terms of empirical criteria of evidence. Buridan's reconstruction of natural philosophy as a positive and empirically based science of observable phenomena undermined the Aristotelian tradition and provided some of the main starting points for the development of modern mechanics in the seventeenth century.

At the same time a theologian of Paris, Gregory of Rimini (d. 1358), who became general of the order of Augustinian Hermits, made a constructive use of Ockhamist methods and doctrines in a theological synthesis of nominalism and Augustinianism; although he took issue with both Ockham and Buridan on some issues of metaphysics, the later Scholastics regarded him as a modern theologian of the nominalist group.

Natural philosophy, as distinguished from theology, was dominated by the moderately Ockhamist tradition established at Paris by Buridan, developed by Albert of Saxony and Nicholas of Oresme, and carried to the new universities of central Europe by Albert, Marsilius of Inghen, Henry of Hainbuch, and Henry of Oyta. A document drawn up by the faculty of the University of Cologne in 1425 speaks of the period of pre-eminence of the *via moderna* as the century of Buridan (*saeculum Buridani*), indicating that the Ockhamism of the later fourteenth century had become associated with Buridan and his followers more than with Ockham.

Religious influence. The Ockhamist divorce of Christian theology from Aristotelian metaphysics, with the corresponding emphasis on religious faith and the tradition of the Church Fathers as foundation of Christian doctrine, was reflected in the popular religious movement associated with the school of Deventer and the *devotio moderna* and in the criticisms of the scholastic methods of theological disputation and argument made by Jean Gerson at the end of the fourteenth century. Gabriel Biel (c. 1425–1495) was the last influential theologian of the Ockhamist school, and in his work the influence of Gerson, Gregory of Rimini, Holkot, and of Ockham himself brought together the diverse strands of this nominalist tradition in a doctrine with strong religious emphasis.

Ockhamism, as a well-developed philosophical and religious tradition, was submerged by the Reformation and the Counter Reformation, as well as by the humanist revolt against the medieval cultural tradition. However, its leading ideas, in the liberation of both the Christian faith and the scientific investigation of nature from dogmatic Aristotelianism, remained operative outside the schools and bore fruit in the seventeenth and eighteenth centuries.

Bibliography

Copleston, F. C., *History of Philosophy*, Vol. III, *Ockham to Suárez*. Westminster, Md., 1953. Chs. 9–10.

Duhem, Pierre, *Études sur Léonard de Vinci*, Vol. III. Paris, 1913.

Élie, Hubert, *Le Complexe significabile*. Paris, 1936.

Ehrle, Franz, *Die Sentenzkommentar Peters von Candia*. Münster-in-Westfalen, 1925. Treats of the whole Ockhamist movement.

Lagarde, Georges de, *La Naissance de l'esprit laïque au déclin du moyen âge*. Paris, 1946.

Leff, Gordon, *Gregory of Rimini*. Manchester, 1961.

Maier, Anneliese, *Die Vorläufer Galileis im 14. Jahrhundert*. Rome, 1949.

Michalski, Konstanty, *Les Courants philosophiques à Oxford et à Paris pendant le XIVᵉ siècle*. Cracow, 1921.

Michalski, Konstanty, *Le Criticisme et le scepticisme dans la philosophie du XIVᵉ siècle*. Cracow, 1926.

Michalski, Konstanty, *La Physique nouvelle et les différents courants philosophiques au XIVᵉ siècle*. Cracow, 1928.

Moody, E. A., "Ockham, Buridan and Nicholas of Autrecourt." *Franciscan Studies*, Vol. 7 (June 1947), 113–146.

Oberman, H. A., *The Harvest of Medieval Theology: Gabriel Biel and Late Medieval Nominalism*. Cambridge, Mass., 1963.

Ritter, Gerhart, *Studien zur Spätscholastik*, Vol. I, *Marsilius von Inghen und die Okkamistische Schule in Deutschland*. Heidelberg, 1921.

Weinberg, Julius, *Nicolaus of Autrecourt*. Princeton, N.J., 1948.

ERNEST A. MOODY

OGYŪ SORAI (1666–1728), or Butsu, Japanese Confucianist of the *kogakuha* ("school of ancient learning") famous as a political thinker. Ogyū was born in Edo (Tokyo). He was a gifted pupil and soon mastered classical Chinese; the classical style is characteristic of his writings. Proud by nature, Ogyū distinguished himself in the defense of official Chu Hsi Neo-Confucianism in polemics against Itō Jinsai. However, in 1716 his views changed, and in *Bendō* ("Defining the Way") and *Bemmei* ("Definitions of Terms") he supports most of Itō's ideas. All of Ogyū's other works were inspired by the ancient sages in accord with the maxim "back to antiquity," a maxim applicable to many of his innovations. These innovations were expressed in *Taiheisaku* ("A Policy for Great Peace") and *Seidan* ("Discourses on Government"). Ogyū's cosmological views differ little from Itō's; Ogyū, too, rejects the dichotomy of *ri*, the principle, and *ki*, the material energy.

Ogyū holds a positivist and historicist conception of the Way (*dō*); it became for him the factual order of society, with its positive laws and institutions. He rightly points out how Confucius stressed the societal implications of the Way. Ogyū goes much further, excluding personal ethics until only "rites," that is, propriety and social behavior, combined with obedience to the government, remain. In this sense he comes very close to the Chinese Legalists in utilitarian ethics. Although he was apparently inspired by Hsün Tzu (c. 298–c. 212 B.C.), he does not mention the name. For Ogyū, human nature cannot be much corrected; in this only social institutions are of any use. The sole meaning of "humaneness" is the giving of peace and prosperity to the people, and "virtue" is the virtue of the ruler in discerning able men. His political and economic ideas have little in common with Confucian moralizing. Government is a practical technique (*jutsu*), and the economy is not based on thrift but on sound social policies. He was against the idea of fanatic loyalty to the lord and advocated some social mobility, believing that the lower samurai but not the common people should be allowed to improve their status.

Ogyū's views of history are distinguished by the same practical approach. The founder of a dynasty plays a great role because of the public institutions he has to establish, yet rulers often fall because of the difficulty of preventing economic decline. Living under the Tokugawa shogunate, Ogyū rejected even the nominal sovereignty of the emperor (an opinion his best pupil, Dazai Shundai (1680–1747), concurred in). Shintoism for Ogyū was an invention of Yoshida Kanetomo (1435–1511). Ogyū's stand in favor of the Tokugawa government and his rejection of Shintoism explain why he was not repressed for his daring ideas and anti-Chu Hsi doctrine.

Bibliography

The principal works of Ogyū Sorai can be found in several collections. See *Nihon rinri ihen* ("Library on Japanese Ethics"), Inoue Tetsujirō, ed. (Tokyo, 1902), Vol. VI, pp. 11–203; *Nihon keizai taiten* ("Classics on Japanese Economics"), Takimoto Seiichi, ed. (Tokyo, 1928), Vol. IX, pp. 3–375; *Ogyū Sorai-shū* ("Collected Works of Ogyū Sorai"; Tokyo, 1937).

Two secondary sources in English are J. R. McEvan, *The Political Writings of Ogyū Sorai* (Cambridge, 1962) and W. T. de Bary, Ryusaku Tsunoda, and Donald Keene, eds., *Sources of Japanese Tradition* (New York, 1958), pp. 342–343, 422–433.

GINO K. PIOVESANA, S.J.

OKEN, LORENZ (1779–1855), German biologist and philosopher, was born at Bohlsbach, Baden. He graduated from the faculty of medicine at Freiburg in 1804 and obtained his first professorship in medicine at Jena in 1807. Oken left Jena in 1819 because as editor of the liberal periodical *Isis* he had incurred the disfavor of the authorities. He traveled in Germany and France, lectured at the University of Basel in 1821 and 1822, and after a brief appointment at the University of Munich he became professor of physiology in Zurich, where he remained until his death.

After a few years in Jena, Oken was asked to transfer from medicine to philosophy. Yet ten years later, in his second term at Basel, he was listed as professor of medicine only, with no reference to philosophy. These changes reflect Oken's development and the superseding of romantic nature philosophy by a more objective study of natural phenomena. Under the influence of Schelling and the thinkers of the romantic school, Oken's imagination—rather than a genuine philosophical bent—swept him on to his own version of philosophy of identity. If in his time Oken was thought to be a greater philosopher than even Schelling, it was because he had a much wider knowledge of the natural sciences to illustrate and support his metaphysics. His most significant book in this connection is the *Lehrbuch der Naturphilosophie* (*Elements of Physiophilosophy*). This work aroused great interest, especially among the New England transcendentalists. Oken tried to establish a correspondence between mathematical structures and nature, and between metaphysical essences and nature. Fond of Pythagorean mysticism, he argued that all life is cast in the mold of mathematical symbols. Zero is nothingness and the infinite at the same time. The evolution of positive and negative numbers out of zero is the counterpart of a descending and ascending order of things—the descent being from matter (heavenly bodies, rocks, minerals, etc.) to some primeval mucus, while the ascent is from this mucus, seminated by infusoria and helped along by galvanism, through the whole scale of plant and animal life to man.

Metaphysically, zero is God. The disintegration of matter to mucus and the evolution of living beings illustrate God's desire to manifest himself in nature—when he comes to man, he meets himself; man is a god created by God. Theogony turns into hylogeny, the creation of matter. By the same token, all that exists is embedded in and permeated by an everlasting stream of vitality—pantheism and vitalism combine in Oken's view of the universe and its parts.

A poet in science, Emerson called Oken admiringly. The appropriateness of this remark is underlined by Oken the physiologist, who regarded man as an assembly of all the sense organs and other bodily parts developed along the ascending path; and by Oken the psychologist, who saw all animals as contributing to the psychology of the crowning organism, man. Mollusks gave man prudence and caution; from the snails man received seriousness and dignity; courage and nobility came from the insects; and the fish brought him the dowry of memory. Oken as a scientist with imagination may have had his merits, but as a philosopher he was unable to raise thought from the level of matter, chemistry, physiology, and cosmogony to a level of creative independence. Mind for Oken was merely a mirror in which God and nature could behold themselves.

In his less poetic moods, Oken came close to being a modern scientist. He held, with Goethe but independently of him, that the cephalic bones are a repetition of the vertebrae, and he was not far from establishing the cellular structure of living organisms. His publications after *Physiophilosophy*—*Lehrbuch der Naturgeschichte* and *Allgemeine Naturgeschichte für alle Stände*—reverted to the method of his earlier works: close observation and faithful description. If in Oken's days the natural sciences had to extricate themselves from preconceived mystical notions wrongly called philosophy, they beg today to be understood again in some wider context. The wheel has come full circle, as it must according to Oken's belief in the alternating processes of dynamic expansion and nostalgic reduction to a state of absolute quietness, a belief reminiscent of Nietzsche's eternal recurrence of the same. The difference is that for Oken the fascination of this unending spectacle ended where Nietzsche's interest in it began, with the arrival of man and the search for values.

Principal Works by Oken

Lehrbuch der Naturphilosophie, 3 vols. Jena, 1809–1811; improved and final ed., 1843. Translated by Alfred Tulk as *Elements of Physiophilosophy.* London, 1847.

Lehrbuch der Naturgeschichte, 5 vols. Leipzig and Jena, 1813–1826.

Allgemeine Naturgeschichte für alle Stände, 13 vols. Stuttgart, 1833–1841.

Works on Oken

Ecker, Alexander, *Lorenz Oken. Eine biographische Skizze.* Stuttgart, 1880.

Hübner, Georg Wilhelm, *Okens Naturphilosophie prinzipiell und kritisch bearbeitet.* Borna-Leipzig, 1909.

Schuster, Julius, *Oken. Der Mann und sein Werk.* Berlin, 1922.

HERMANN BOESCHENSTEIN

OLIVI, PETER JOHN (1248 or 1249–1298), French Franciscan philosopher and theologian, was born at Sérignan in Languedoc. He entered the order at Béziers about 1261. From about 1267 to 1273 he studied at Paris, where he was acquainted with William de La Mare, John Peckham, and Matthew of Acquasparta. He received the *Baccalarius biblicus* about 1270 but did not go on for a doctorate. He became a lector at Montpellier in 1273 and later was lector at Narbonne. After 1275 he gradually became the intellectual leader of the Spirituals, a group of rigorists in the order who interpreted the vow of poverty with great strictness. Hence the order's moderate Community party tried to undermine Olivi's authority, accusing him (with the aid of evidence drawn from his writings) of rash and heretical doctrines. Olivi thus became involved in a long struggle with several generals of the order, which lasted from 1277 to 1285. In 1283 about 50 of his theses were censured, and his writings were forbidden. In 1287 he regained his good standing and became lector at Florence (1287–1289) and at Montpellier (1289–1292). From 1292 on he lived at Narbonne. Even after his death the Community party tried to break his influence by presenting 33 suspect theses to the Council of Vienne (1311–1312), but only three of his opinions were rejected. In 1319 the general chapter of the order again prohibited his writings, and in 1326 Pope John XXII censured his *Postilla in Apocalypsim.*

Doctrine. Olivi was an original and dynamic thinker who was deeply religious, with mystical tendencies, but also passionate and somewhat intemperate. His style is overcharged but inspired, and his thoughts are often captivating, in that they anticipate something of modern intellectual development. Although he participated in the Augustinian tradition, Olivi had a tendency toward nonconformist opinions (for example, he advocated the *impetus* theory of John Philoponus). He was not so much a systematic metaphysician as an intuitionist and a psychologist. He excelled in introspection, often appealed to experience, and was one of the first writers to use elements of the phenomenological method. His thought was centered on the idea of spiritual contemplation, which is essentially an act of the will leading to a charitable union with God. In the light of this union the philosopher considers the created universe. Although Olivi was neither a skeptic nor a fideist, he sharply rejected Aristotelianism in the sense of a purely natural standard for science and culture. His theological insight produced three master ideas from which almost all his particular philosophical opinions devolved.

Transcendence of God. Olivi's theodicy is dominated by the concept of God's transcendence. God is "the entirely other": a metaphysical abyss divides him from all other beings. He alone is the eternal; all the rest is temporary and mutable. God's power, liberty, and independence are unlimited. His omnipotence is not qualified by the existence of demigods. Hence Olivi rejected certain theses that were much discussed in his time, namely, creation from eternity; actual infinity outside of God; the impossibility of succession in eternity; and the opinion that every angel possesses infused universal ideas and forms a species apart. However, Olivi accepted St. Anselm's ontological argument for the existence of God.

Ontological and conceptual orders. Olivi's metaphysics and epistemology were based on the idea that there is a sharp distinction, or even a separation, between the ontological order and the conceptual order; each is ruled by its own laws and exigencies. In ontology, Olivi emphasized the principle "Entities are not unnecessarily multiplied" and he sharply attacked the idea that from the multiplicity of concepts we can deduce a corresponding multiplicity in the realm of beings.

Olivi interpreted the conceptual order according to his theory of the *ratio realis,* which postulates logical distinctions that are grounded in reality. (A similar theory was held by Henry of Ghent.) This sort of mediate distinction exists between essence and the individual existence; between a being and its transcendental attributes; and, in abstract knowledge, between general and specific concepts. (This last point in particular influenced Peter Aureol and William of Ockham.) Following this principle of real distinction (which is admitted only between things existing in real separation or at least able to so exist), Olivi came to the conclusion that created spirits are composed of matter and form; that man is composed of matter and spirit; and that there is a plurality of forms in corporal beings.

Nature of man. Olivi proposed a unique doctrine concerning the composition of man. The human body is actualized by corporal matter and the *formae corporeitatis* before its union with the soul. The soul, although a unity, has three partial forms—the vegetative principle, the sensitive principle, and the rational principle. He held that the body is informed directly by the vegetative and sensitive principles, but not by the rational principle, which moves the other parts only through the mediation of spiritual matter. He reasoned that if the rational part of the soul informed the body directly, the soul would no longer be purely active. The view that the rational principle does not inform the body directly was condemned by the Council of Vienne as heretical in denying the unity of man; by implication Olivi's doctrine was seen to contradict the doctrine of the full humanity of Christ.

Principle of intrinsic development. Another basic postulate was that every substance is a wholly active and dynamic principle which continually unfolds its intrinsic forces, thus reaching its perfection. Olivi chiefly applied this concept in his psychology and his doctrine of knowledge. He rejected the theories of divine illumination, of the active and passive intellect, and of sensible and intelligible species. Instead, he accentuated the intentional direction of the knowing subject to the object, so that it actively seizes the object. But since Olivi excluded the possibility of any causal influence of the object on the active potencies, some interpreters claim that he considered the object only as a *causa terminativa* (final cause) of knowledge; other scholars maintain that he intended the object to be a kind of *causa cooperans* (cooperative cause).

Olivi explained the development of higher knowledge from lower by the connection of the potencies of the soul (*colligantia potentiarum*). By virtue of the unity of the spiritual matter of the soul, the act of knowledge that originated in the vegetative and sensitive parts continues in the rational part of the soul, causing a spiritual image to form there. Olivi also insisted that it is primarily the free will which elevates man above all other creatures and energetically stressed the will's self-determination. His introspective arguments in this field are important.

Significance. In the Franciscan school, Olivi is the principal link between Bonaventure and Duns Scotus, who repeatedly cited Olivi's opinions. Although Scotus in general appeared to combat rather than to follow Olivi, an important point in which he may have followed him is that in Olivi's system there is considerably less necessity for the Augustinian concept of divine concursus in the natural operations of man. Olivi's principal contribution to philosophy was probably his description of the relations between the knowing subject and the object. In the field of human psychology, in which he presented a personal Augustinianism, many of his views show an outstanding originality. He helped to initiate the dissolution of the scholastic synthesis, and because of his influence on Ockham, he may be considered a remote precursor of Hegelian idealism and of phenomenology.

Works by Olivi

Olivi was one of the most prolific authors of his age. A complete list of his works (some 64 pieces) may be found in D. Pacetti, *P. I. Olivi, QQ. Quatuor de Domina* (Quaracchi, 1954).

Olivi's more important philosophical writings include *Commentarius in IV Libros Sententiarum*, c. 1287–1290, preserved only in an account of 193 questions at Padua, University Library, Mss. 637, 1540, 2094. *Summa Quaestionum Super Sententiarum*, probably put in definitive form only in 1295 (incomplete); Book II (118 questions) and some questions from Book I, in B. Jansen, ed., Bibliotheca Franciscana Scholastica Medii Aevi, Vols. IV–VI (Quaracchi, 1922–1926); Books III and IV are in preparation at Quaracchi. F. Delorme, ed., *De Perlegendis Philosophorum Libris*, in *Antonianum*, Vol. 16 (1941), 31–44; its thesis is that the pagan philosophers in certain questions are to be criticized rather than followed. F. Delorme, ed., *De Signis Voluntariis*, in *Antonianum*, Vol. 20 (1945), 309–330; exposes the real meaning of human signs. *V Quodlibeta*, 96 questions (Venice, 1509); 15 other questions in Ms. 2094 at Padua. *Contra Dicta Doctoris* in *Quodlibeta*, folio 42a–53a. *Epistola ad Raymundum Gaufredi*, in *Quodlibeta*, folio 51c–53a. D. Laberge, ed., *Tria Scripta Apologetica*, 1283–1285, in *Archivum Franciscanum Historicum*, Vol. 28 (1935), 115 ff.; Vol. 29 (1936), 98 ff.

Works on Olivi

For literature on Olivi, see F. Simoncioli, *Il problema della libertà umana in Pietro di Giovanni Olivi e Pietro di Trabibus* (Milan, 1956); E. Bettoni, *Le dottrine filosofiche di Pietro Gio-* *vanni Olivi* (Milan, 1956; pp. 521–527 give a bibliography through 1958); E. Stadter, "Das Glaubensproblem in seiner Bedeutung für die Ethik bei P. J. Olivi," in *Franziskanische Studien*, Vol. 42 (1960), 225–296, with a complete bibliography to 1959; C. Partee, "Peter John Olivi: Historical and Doctrinal Study," in *Franciscan Studies*, Vol. 20 (1960), 215–296; W. Hoeres, "Der Begriff der Intentionalität bei Olivi," in *Scholastik*, Vol. 36 (1961), 23–48; V. Heynck, in *Lexikon für Theologie und Kirche*, 2d ed., Joseph Höfer and Karl Rahner, eds., Vol. VII (Freiburg, 1962), Col. 1149; A. Emmen and F. Simoncioli, "La Dottrina dell'Olivi sulla contemplazione," in *Studi Francescani*, Vol. 60 (1963), 382–445; Vol. 61 (1964), 108–167.

A. EMMEN, O.F.M.

OMAN, JOHN WOOD (1860–1939), philosopher of religion and theologian, was a Scotsman from the Orkney Islands. After being educated at Edinburgh and Heidelberg universities and serving for 17 years in a rural pastorate in Northumberland, he taught for 28 years at Westminster College, Cambridge, the seminary of the English Presbyterian church. The chief influence on his developing thought was that of Friedrich Schleiermacher, whose *Reden* Oman translated into English.

In the massive *The Natural and the Supernatural* (1931) Oman portrays the root of religion as man's immediate sense of the Supernatural. The primary religious awareness is not inferential but is, in words which Oman used to describe the similar conception of Schleiermacher, "intuition of reality, an intercourse between a universe, present always in all its meaning, and a spirit, responding with all its understanding" (p. 36). By the Supernatural, Oman does not mean the mysterious, the uncanny, or the miraculous but a larger environment than physical nature, "a special kind of environment, which has its own particular sanctions" (p. 23), through commerce with which man receives his characteristically human degree of independence within his natural environment.

The Supernatural is variously conceived in different types of religion, as is the character of the redemption that the supernatural makes possible. In primitive religion redemption is found by seeking the Supernatural in nature as an animistic force indefinitely many and yet vaguely one. In polytheism the Supernatural consists of individual spirits that rule different parts of nature, and redemption means the managing of nature through its many divine masters. Cosmic pantheism accepts nature in its wholenesss as the Supernatural, while the acosmic mysticism of India wholly excludes nature from the Supernatural, as illusion. Religions of the ceremonial–legal type, such as priestly Judaism and Islam, divide the Natural into a sacred realm and a secular realm, cultivating the sacred or religious while leaving the secular outside the sphere of redemption. Finally, for the prophetic monotheism of the Hebrew prophets and of Christianity redemption is reconciliation to the Natural by finding within it the purpose of the one personal Supernatural. To be reconciled to God is to accept all the experiences of one's life as of God's appointing, and one's duties as divine commands. Thus, prophetic religion is intensely practical and this-worldly. Speaking of its Old Testament representatives, Oman says, "What determines their faith is not a theory of the Supernatural, but an attitude towards the Natural, as a sphere in which a victory of deeper meaning than the visible and of more abiding purpose than the fleeting can be won" (p. 448).

Oman emphasizes that knowledge of our environment, whether the natural or the Supernatural, does not consist in the mere registering of "impacts" but always consists in a perception of "meaning." In order to become aware of our environment, we must rightly interpret its impingements upon us. "Thus knowledge is not knowledge as an effect of an unknown external cause, but is knowledge as we so interpret that our meaning is the actual meaning of our environment" (p. 175). In this interpretative process, the mind exercises a degree of freedom. That degree is established by the individual frontiers of each mind, which are largely controlled from within and across which the meaning of the environment can pass only as a meaning recognized by the individual.

The Supernatural presents itself to the human mind with the quality of the sacred or of absolute worth. To be aware of the Supernatural is to recognize some sacred value that lays an absolute claim upon us, even if in the early stages of man's dealings with the Supernatural this is only an irrational taboo. Religion is "essentially a dealing with an unseen environment of absolute worth, which demands worship" (p. 23). This recognition of and allegiance to the sacred frees man from the dominance of his physical surroundings: "He obtained firm footing to deal with his environment the moment he regarded anything as sacred, because he could say 'No' and was no longer its mere creature" (p. 85).

While man's sense of the Supernatural gives him a fixed point amid the evanescent and a degree of freedom in relation to the natural, he can gain this only by exercise of his own freedom. For "The peculiarity of the supernatural environment is that we cannot enter it except as we see and choose it as our own" (p. 309).

Oman makes no use of the attempted logical coercion of the traditional theistic proofs. He does not try to establish the truth of religion independently of religious experience. Rather he starts from the fact of the religious man's awareness of a larger supernatural environment, in terms of which he lives, and argues that this awareness has no greater need or possibility of philosophical justification than has our awareness of the natural environment. "Among Western thinkers from Descartes onwards, attempts have been made to prove the existence of a material world by other evidence than the way it environs us, but the result was no more reassuring for the reality of the natural world than for the reality of the supernatural" (p. 51).

The same basic standpoint is evident in Oman's contributions to doctrinal theology, especially his *Grace and Personality* (1919). Oman was the first of a series of twentieth-century Christian thinkers—such as Karl Heim, Emil Brunner, H. H. Farmer, and John Macmurray—to treat as a normative principle of his theology the insight that God is the supremely personal reality, that his dealings with men take place in the personal realm, and that the great central Christian terms—revelation, faith, grace, sin, reconciliation—are to be understood as part of the language of personal relationship and are perverted when construed in nonpersonal ways. Oman taught that religious truths are not infallibilities declared authoritatively from heaven but claim acceptance only because they irresistibly impress our minds as true, and that God seeks our trust only by showing himself to be trustworthy.

There are in Oman's works the elements of a religious philosophy that might well appeal to many today because it is consistently empiricist, being based upon what is given in human experience. However, it is often expressed in Oman's pages on a higher level of generality, and with less detailed precision, than has become customary since he wrote, and there is therefore scope for the development of these same themes in more contemporary terms.

Works by Oman

Vision and Authority. London, 1902; 2d ed., 1928.
The Problem of Faith and Freedom in the Last Two Centuries. London, 1906.
The Church and the Divine Order. London, 1911.
The War and Its Issues. Cambridge, 1915.
Grace and Personality. Cambridge, 1919; 4th ed., 1931.
The Paradox of the World: Sermons. Cambridge, 1921.
The Book of Revelation. Cambridge, 1923.
The Office of the Ministry. London, 1928.
The Text of Revelation. Cambridge, 1928.
The Natural and the Supernatural. Cambridge, 1931.
Concerning the Ministry. London, 1936.
Honest Religion. Cambridge, 1941.
A Dialogue With God. London, 1950. Sermons.

Works on Oman

Healey, F. G., *Religion and Reality: The Theology of John Oman.* Edinburgh, 1965.
Tennant, F. R., "John Wood Oman, 1860–1939." *Proceedings of the British Academy,* Vol. 25 (1939), 333–338.

JOHN HICK

ONTOLOGICAL ARGUMENT FOR THE EXISTENCE OF GOD. The Ontological Argument for the existence of God was first propounded by Anselm (c. 1033–1109), abbot of Bec and later archbishop of Canterbury, in his *Proslogion* (Chs. 2–4) and in his *Reply* to a contemporary critic.

He begins (*Proslogion* 2) with the concept of God as "something than which nothing greater can be conceived" (*aliquid quo nihil maius cogitari possit,* and other equivalent formulations). It is clear that by "greater" Anselm means "more perfect." (Sometimes he uses *melius,* "better," instead of *maius,* "greater": for instance, *Proslogion* 14 and 18.) Since we have this idea, it follows that "Something than which nothing greater can be conceived" at least exists in our minds (*in intellectu*) as an object of thought. The question is whether it also exists in extramental reality (*in re*). Anselm argues that it must so exist, since otherwise we should be able to conceive of something greater than that than which nothing greater can be conceived—which is absurd. Therefore "Something than which nothing greater can be conceived" must exist in reality.

In *Proslogion* 3 Anselm adds that "Something than which nothing greater can be conceived" exists in the truest and greatest way (*verissime et maxime esse*); for whereas anything else can be conceived not to exist (and thus exists only contingently), "Something than which nothing greater can be conceived" cannot be conceived not to exist (and thus exists necessarily). For that which cannot be conceived not to exist is greater than that which *can* be conceived not to exist, and therefore only that which cannot be conceived not to exist is adequate to the notion of "Something a greater than which cannot be conceived."

Anselm explains (in his *Responsio*) that by a being which cannot be conceived not to exist he means one that is eternal in the sense of having no beginning or end and always existing as a whole, that is, not in successive phases. He argues that if such a being can be conceived, it must also exist. For the idea of an eternal being which has either ceased to exist or has not yet come into existence is self-contradictory; the notion of eternal existence excludes both of these possibilities. This latter argument has been revived and developed in our own day (see below).

Many of the earliest manuscripts of the *Proslogion* contain a contemporary criticism (attributed in two of the manuscripts to one Gaunilo of Marmoutier) together with Anselm's reply. The criticism, summed up in the analogy of the island, is directed against Anselm's argument as presented in *Proslogion* 2. Gaunilo sets up what he supposes to be a parallel ontological argument for the existence of an island more perfect than any known island: such an island must exist, since otherwise it would be less perfect than any known island, and this would be a contradiction. In reply Anselm develops the reasoning of *Proslogion* 3. His argument cannot be applied to islands or to anything else whose nonexistence is conceivable, for whatever can be conceived not to exist is *eo ipso* less than "Something than which nothing greater can be conceived." Only from this latter notion can we (according to Anselm) deduce that there must be something corresponding to it in reality.

Perhaps the most valuable feature of Anselm's argument is its formulation of the Christian concept of God. Augustine (*De Libero Arbitrio* II, 6, 14) had used the definition of God as one "than whom there is nothing superior." The Ontological Argument could not be based upon this notion, for although it is true by definition that the most perfect being that there is, exists, there is no guarantee that this being is God, in the sense of the proper object of man's worship. Anselm, however, does not define God as the most perfect being that there is but as a being than whom no more perfect is even conceivable. This represents the final development of the monotheistic conception. God is the most adequate conceivable object of worship; there is no possiblity of another reality beyond him to which he is inferior or subordinate and which would thus be an even more worthy recipient of man's devotion. Thus metaphysical ultimacy and moral ultimacy coincide; one cannot ask of the most perfect conceivable being, as one can of a first cause, necessary being, unmoved mover, or designer of the world (supposing such to exist) whether men ought to worship him. Here the religious exigencies that move from polytheism through henotheism to ethical monotheism reach their logical terminus. And the credit belongs to Anselm for having first formulated this central core of the ultimate concept of deity.

Descartes's argument. Anselm's argument was rejected by Aquinas in favor of the Cosmological Argument and as a consequence was largely neglected during the remainder of the medieval period. It was, however, again brought into prominence by Descartes in the seventeenth century, and most subsequent discussions have been based upon Descartes's formulation. Descartes made explicit the presupposition of the argument that existence is an attribute or predicate which, like other predicates, a given x can meaningfully be said to have or to lack. He claims that just as the idea of a triangle necessarily includes among the defining attributes of a triangle that of having its three internal angles equal to two right angles, so the idea of a supremely perfect being (a different formula from Anselm's) necessarily includes the attribute of existence. Consequently we can no more think, without contradiction, of a supremely perfect being which lacks existence than of a triangle which lacks three sides.

Descartes considers the following objection: from the fact that in order to be a triangle a figure must have three sides it does not follow that there actually are any triangles; and likewise in the case of the concept of a supremely perfect being. His reply is that whereas the notion, or essence, of a triangle does not include the attribute of existence that of a supremely perfect being does, and that therefore in this special case we are entitled to infer existence from a concept.

Kant's criticism. Descartes's version of the Ontological Argument had some important contemporary critics—for example, Gassendi and Caterus—but the classic criticism is that of Immanuel Kant. This moves on two levels. First, leaving the argument's presuppositions for the moment unchallenged, he grants the analytic connection which Descartes had affirmed between the concept of God and that of existence. In the proposition "A perfect being exists" we cannot without contradiction affirm the subject and reject the predicate. But, he points out, we can without contradiction elect not to affirm the subject together with its predicate. We can reject as a whole the complex concept of an existing all-perfect being.

Second, however, Kant rejects the assumption that existence is a real predicate. If it were a real, and not merely a grammatical, predicate, it would be able to form part of the definition of God, and it could then be an analytic truth that God exists. But existential propositions (propositions asserting existence) are always synthetic, always true or false as a matter of fact rather than as a matter of definition. Whether any specified kind of thing exists can be determined only by the tests of experience. The function of "is" or "exists" is not to add to the content of a concept but to posit an object answering to a concept. Thus, the real contains no more than the possible (a hundred real dollars are the same in number as a hundred imagined ones); the difference is that in the one case the concept does and in the other case it does not correspond to something in reality.

Russell's analysis. Essentially the same point—so far as it affects the Ontological Argument—has been made in the twentieth century by Bertrand Russell in his theory of descriptions. This involves an analysis of positive and negative existential propositions, according to which to affirm that x's exist is to affirm that there are objects answering to the description "x," and to deny that x's exist is to deny that there are any such objects. The function of "exists" is thus to assert the instantiation of a given concept. "Cows exist" is not a statement about cows, to the effect that they have the attribute of existing, but about the concept or description "cow," to the effect that it has instances. If this is so, then the proper theological question is not whether a perfect being, in order to be perfect, must together with its other attributes have the attribute of existence but whether the concept of an (existing) perfect being has an instance. This question cannot be determined a priori, as the Ontological Argument professes to do, by inspection of the concept of God. The nature of thought on the one hand and of the extramental world on the other, and of the difference between them, is such that there can be no valid inference from the thought of a given kind of being to the conclusion that there is in fact a being of that kind. This is the fundamental logical objection to the Ontological Argument.

Hegelian use of the argument. Prior to Kant, the Ontological Argument had been used by Spinoza and Leibniz. Since Kant, the form of it which he discussed has remained under the heavy cloud of his criticism. However, Hegel and his school put the argument to a somewhat different use. As Hegel himself expressed it, "In the case of the finite, existence does not correspond to the Notion (*Begriffe*). On the other hand, in the case of the Infinite, which is determined within itself, the reality must correspond to the Notion (*Begriffe*); this is the Idea (*Idee*), the unity of subject and object" (*Vorlesungen über die Philosophie der Religion,* Vol. II, p. 479). Otherwise stated, Being itself, or the Absolute, is the presupposition of all existence and all thought. If finite beings exist, Being exists; when beings think, Being comes to self-consciousness; and in the reasoning of the Ontological Argument, finite thinking is conscious of its own ultimate ground, the reality of which it cannot rationally deny.

The defect of this argument is that its conclusion is either trivial or excessively unclear. It is trivial if the reality of Being is synonymous with the existence of the sum of finite beings; but on the other hand, it is so unclear as to be scarcely interesting if Being is regarded as a metaphysical quantity whose distinction from the sum of finite beings cannot be explicated.

The use of the argument in early twentieth-century French "reflexive" philosophy (see bibliography) has affinities with the Hegelian use.

Contemporary discussions. Discussion of the Ontological Argument has continued throughout the modern period and is perhaps as active today as at any time in the past. For there is perennial fascination in a piece of reasoning which employs such fundamental concepts, operates so subtly with them, and professes to demonstrate so momentous a conclusion.

Among theologians, attempts have been made to maintain the value of the argument, not as a proof of God's existence but as an exploration of the Christian understanding of God. Thus, Karl Barth regards the proof as an unfolding of the significance of God's revelation of himself as One whom the believer is prohibited from thinking as less than the highest conceivable reality. On this view Anselm's argument does not seek to convert the atheist but rather to lead an already formed Christian faith into a deeper understanding of its object. Again, Paul Tillich treated the theistic proofs as expressions of the question of

God that is implied in our human finitude. They analyze different aspects of the human situation, showing how it points to God. Thus, the Ontological Argument "shows that an awareness of the infinite is included in man's awareness of finitude." This is in effect a Hegelian use of the argument.

Hartshorne and Malcolm. At the same time, some contemporary philosophers—especially Charles Hartshorne and Norman Malcolm—have revived the second argument, or second form of the argument, found in Anselm's *Proslogion* (3) and in his *Responsio* to Gaunilo. As they have reconstructed it, this argument starts from the premise that the concept of God as eternal, self-existent being is such that the question whether God exists cannot be a contingent question but must be one of logical necessity or impossibility. A being who exists, but of whom it is conceivable that he might not have existed, would be less than God; for only a being whose existence is necessary rather than contingent can be that than which nothing greater is conceivable. But if such a necessary being does not exist, it must be a necessary rather than a contingent fact that he does not exist. Thus God's existence is either logically necessary or logically impossible. However, it has not been shown to be impossible—that is, the concept of such a being has not been shown to be self-contradictory—and therefore we must conclude that God necessarily exists.

Hartshorne formalizes the argument as follows:

(1)	$q \rightarrow Nq$	"Anselm's principle": perfection could not exist contingently
(2)	$Nq \lor {\sim}Nq$	Excluded middle
(3)	${\sim}Nq \rightarrow N{\sim}Nq$	Form of Becker's postulate: modal status is always necessary.
(4)	$Nq \lor N{\sim}Nq$	Inference from (2, 3)
(5)	$N{\sim}Nq \rightarrow N{\sim}q$	Inference from (1): the necessary falsity of the consequent implies that of the antecedent (modal form of *modus tollens*)
(6)	$Nq \lor N{\sim}q$	Inference from (4, 5)
(7)	${\sim}N{\sim}q$	Intuitive postulate (or conclusion from other theistic arguments): perfection is not impossible
(8)	Nq	Inference from (6, 7)
(9)	$Nq \rightarrow q$	Modal axiom
(10)	q	Inference from (8, 9)

In this formalization q stands for $(\exists x)Px$ ("There is a perfect being" or "Perfection exists"); N means "analytic or L-true, true by necessity of the meanings of the terms employed"; and $\rightarrow$ signifies strict implication.

Criticism. The above argument seems to depend upon a confusion of two different concepts of necessary being. The distinction involved is important for the elucidation of the idea of God and represents one of the points at which study of the Ontological Argument can be fruitful even though the argument itself fails. The two concepts are those of logical necessity and ontological or factual necessity. In modern philosophy, logical necessity is a concept which applies only to propositions; a proposition is logically necessary if it is true in virtue of the meanings of the terms composing it. And it is a basic empiricist principle that existential propositions cannot be logically necessary. In other words, whether or not a given kind of entity exists is a question of experiential fact and not of the rules of language. On this view, the notion of a logically necessary being is inadmissible, for it would mean that the existential proposition "God exists" is logically true or true by definition. However, Anselm's principle, which is used as the first premise of Hartshorne's argument, was not that God is a logically necessary being (in this modern sense) but that God is an ontologically or factually necessary being, For, as noted above, Anselm was explicit that by a being whose nonexistence is inconceivable he meant a being who exists without beginning or end and always as a whole. (This is virtually the scholastic notion of *aseity*, from *a se esse*, "self-existence," that is, eternal and independent existence.) Interpreting "For God to exist is for him to exist necessarily" (prop. 1) in this way, we can validly infer from it that God's existence is ontologically either necessary or impossible (prop. 6). For if an eternal being exists, he cannot, compatibly with the concept of him as eternal, cease to exist: thus his existence is necessary. And if such a being does not exist, he cannot, compatibly with the concept of him as eternal, come to exist: thus his existence is impossible.

However, it does not follow from this that an eternal being in fact exists but only that if such a being exists, his existence is ontologically necessary, and that if no such being exists, it is impossible for one to exist. Hartshorne's argument can advance from proposition 6 to its conclusion only by assuming at this point that it has been established that the existence of God is (not, or not only, ontologically but) *logically* necessary or impossible. He can then rule out the latter alternative (prop. 7), and conclude that God necessarily exists (prop. 8) and hence that he exists (prop. 10). Thus, in propositions 1–6 "necessary" means "ontologically necessary"; in propositions 6–10 it means "logically necessary"; and proposition 6 itself is the point at which the confusion occurs. (The same illicit shift between the notions of ontological and logical necessity can be observed in Malcolm's version of the argument.)

The conclusion to be drawn is that the Ontological Argument, considered as an attempted logical demonstration of the existence of God, fails. In both of the forms which are found in Anselm, and which are still matters of discussion today, the flaw in the argument is that while it establishes that the concept of God involves the idea of God's existence, and indeed of God's necessary (in the sense of eternal) existence, it cannot take the further step of establishing that this concept of an eternally existent being is exemplified in reality.

Bibliography

For the general history of the Ontological Argument, see M. Esser, *Der ontologische Gottesbeweis und seine Geschichte* (Bonn, 1905); J. Kopper, *Reflexion und Raisonnement im ontologischen Gottesbeweis* (Cologne, 1962); and C. C. J. Webb, "Anselm's Ontological Argument for the Existence of God," in *PAS*, Vol. 3, No. 2 (1896), 25–43. On its alleged origin in Plato, see J. Moreau, "L' 'Argument ontologique' dans le *Phédon*," in *Revue philosophique de la France et de l'Étranger*, Vol. 137 (1947), 320–343, and J. Prescott Johnson, "The Ontological Argument in Plato," in *The Personalist* (1963), 24–34. The main passage in Augustine which

may have influenced Anselm (in relation to the Ontological Argument) is *De Libero Arbitrio*, Book II, translated by J. H. S. Burleigh as "On Free Will," in J. H. S. Burleigh, ed., *Augustine: Earlier Writings* (London and Philadelphia, 1953).

Anselm's version of the argument occurs in *Proslogion*, Chs. 2–4, and in his exchange with Gaunilo. The Latin text is in Dom F. S. Schmitt's critical edition of the *Opera Omnia*, Vol. I (Edinburgh, 1945), pp. 101–104 and 125–139. The best English translations of the *Proslogion* as a whole are those of Eugene R. Fairweather in *A Scholastic Miscellany: Anselm to Ockham* (London and Philadelphia, 1956); A. C. Pegis in *The Wisdom of Catholicism* (New York, 1949); M. J. Charlesworth, *St. Anselm's "Proslogion" With "A Reply on Behalf of the Fool" by Gaunilo and "The Author's Reply to Gaunilo,"* with an introduction and philosophical commentary by Charlesworth (Oxford, 1965); and A. C. McGill in John Hick and A. C. McGill, eds., *The Many Faced Argument* (New York, 1966), where McGill, as well as translating *Proslogion* 2–4, has translated Anselm's exchange with Gaunilo, arranging the texts so as to present Anselm's replies in relation to the specific criticisms to which they refer. The translations by S. N. Deane in *St. Anselm: Basic Writings*, 2d ed. (La Salle, Ill., 1962) include, in addition to the *Proslogion*, Gaunilo's *On Behalf of the Fool* and Anselm's *Reply*. Anselm's dialogue *De Veritate* is also relevant; there is an excellent English translation by Richard McKeon in *Selections From Medieval Philosophers*, Vol. I (New York, 1929).

On the interpretation of Anselm, the most important older writings are Charles Filliatre, *La Philosophie de saint Anselme* (Paris, 1920); Alexandre Koyré, *L'Idée de Dieu dans la philosophie de S. Anselme* (Paris, 1923); Karl Barth, *Fides Quaerens Intellectum: Anselms Beweis der Existenz Gottes in Zusammenhang seines theologischen Programms* (Zurich, 1930; 2d ed., 1958), translated by Ian Robertson as *Anselm: Fides Quaerens Intellectum* (London and Richmond, Va., 1960); A. Stolz, "Zur Theologie Anselms im Proslogion," in *Catholica* (1933), 1–21, translated by A. C. McGill in Hick and McGill, eds., *op. cit.*; Étienne Gilson, "Sens et nature de l'argument de saint Anselme," in *Archives d'histoire doctrinale et littéraire du moyen âge*, Vol. 9 (1934), 5–51; and Adolf Kolping, *Anselms Proslogion—Beweis der Existenz Gottes im Zusammenhang seines Spekulativen Programms: Fides Quaerens Intellectum* (Bonn, 1939).

For more recent historical studies, see *Spicilegium Beccense*, Proceedings of the Congrès International du IXe Centenaire de l'arrivée d'Anselme au Bec (Paris, 1959).

For the view that there are two different arguments in *Proslogion*, see Charles Hartshorne, Introduction to *St. Anselm: Basic Writings* (see above); "What Did Anselm Discover?," in *Union Theological Seminary Quarterly Review* (1962), 213–222; and *The Logic of Perfection* (La Salle, Ill.), Ch. 2. See also Norman Malcolm, "Anselm's Ontological Arguments," in *Philosophical Review*, Vol. 69, No. 1 (1960), 41–62, reprinted in Malcolm's *Knowledge and Certainty* (Englewood Cliffs, N.J., 1963). St. Thomas' criticism of the argument occurs in his *Summa Contra Gentiles* I, 10 and 11, and *Summa Theologica* I, 2, 1.

For the argument after Anselm, see O. Paschen, *Der ontologische Gottesbeweis in der Scholastik* (Aachen, 1903); Duns Scotus, *De Primo Principio*, translated by E. Roche (New York, 1949); I. Hislop, "St. Thomas and the Ontological Argument," in *Contemplations Presented to the Dominican Tertiaries of Glasgow* (London, 1949), pp. 32–38; P. L. M. Puech, "Duns Scotus et l'argument de saint Anselme," in *Nos Cahiers* (1937), 183–199; A. Runze, *Der ontologische Gottesbeweis, kritische Darstellung seiner Geschichte seit Anselm bis auf die Gegenwart* (Halle, 1882); O. Herrlin, *The Ontological Proof in Thomistic and Kantian Interpretation* (Uppsala, 1950); Robert Miller, "The Ontological Argument in St. Anselm and Descartes," in *The Modern Schoolman* (1954–1955), 341–349, and (1955–1956), 31–38; and Alexandre Koyré, *Essai sur l'idée de Dieu et les preuves de son existence chez Descartes* (Paris, 1922).

Descartes's own version of the argument occurs in his *Meditations* (V, but see also III). Spinoza uses the argument in his *Ethics*, Part I, Props. 7–11. Leibniz' version is found in his *New Essays Concerning Human Understanding*, Book IV, Ch. 10 and Appendix X, and in his *Monadology*, Secs. 44–45. Kant's criticism of the argument (in its Cartesian form) occurs in his *Critique of Pure Reason,* Transcendental Dialectic, Book II, Ch. iii, Sec. 4.

The Hegelian use of the argument is to be found in Hegel's *Vorlesungen über die Philosophie der Religion,* P. Marheineke, ed. (Berlin, 1832), Appendix: "Beweise für das Dasein Gottes," Vol. II, pp. 466–483, translated by E. B. Speirs and J. B. Sanderson as *Lectures on the Philosophy of Religion* (London, 1895), Vol. III, pp. 347–367; and in *Vorlesungen über die Geschichte der Philosophie,* K. L. Michelet, ed. (Berlin, 1836), Vol. III, pp. 164–169, translated by E. S. Haldane and F. H. Simson as *Lectures on the History of Philosophy* (London, 1896), Vol. III, pp. 62–67; Edward Caird, "Anselm's Argument for the Being of God," in *Journal of Theological Studies,* Vol. 1 (1899), 23–39; E. E. Harris, *Revelation Through Reason* (New Haven, 1958); Paul Tillich, "The Two Types of Philosophy of Religion," in his *Theology of Culture* (New York, 1959); and R. G. Collingwood, *An Essay on Philosophical Method* (Oxford, 1933). Collingwood's use of the argument was criticized by Gilbert Ryle in "Mr. Collingwood and the Ontological Argument," in *Mind,* N.S. Vol. 44, No. 174 (1935), 137–151. There is a reply to Ryle by E. E. Harris in *Mind,* N.S. Vol. 45, No. 180 (1936), 474–480, and a rejoinder by Ryle in *Mind,* N.S. Vol. 46, No. 181 (1937), 53–57. This discussion is reprinted in Hick and McGill, eds., *op. cit.*

For the argument in recent French "reflexive" philosophy, see M. Blondel, *L'Action* (Paris, 1893 and 1950), *L'Être et les êtres* (Paris, 1935), and *La Pensée* (Paris, 1934 and 1948); J. Paliard, *Intuition et réflexion* (Paris, 1925); and A. Forest, "L'Argument de saint Anselme dans la philosophie réflexive," in *Spicilegium Beccense,* pp. 273–294, translated by A. C. McGill in Hick and McGill, eds., *op. cit.*

Some important contemporary philosophical discussions are C. D. Broad, "Arguments for the Existence of God," in *Journal of Theological Studies,* Vol. 40, No. 157 (January 1939); J. N. Findlay, "Can God's Existence Be Disproved?," in *Mind,* N.S. Vol. 57, No. 226 (1948), 176–183, reprinted in A. G. N. Flew and Alasdair MacIntyre, eds., *New Essays in Philosophical Theology* (London, 1958); Nicholas Rescher, "The Ontological Proof Revisited," in *Australasian Journal of Philosophy,* Vol. 37, No. 2 (1959), 138–148; William P. Alston, "The Ontological Argument Revisited," in *Philosophical Review,* Vol. 69, No. 4 (1960), 452–474; Norman Malcolm, "Anselm's Ontological Argument" (see above); Charles Hartshorne, *The Logic of Perfection* (see above); Jerome Shaffer, "Existence, Predication and the Ontological Argument," in *Mind,* N.S. Vol. 71, No. 283 (1962), 307–325, reprinted in Hick and McGill, eds., *op. cit.;* and a discussion by R. E. Allen, Raziel Abelson, Terence Penelhum, Alvin Plantinga, and Paul Henle in *Philosophical Review,* Vol. 70, No. 1 (1961), 56–109.

On the notions of "existence" and "necessary existence," see Bertrand Russell, "The Philosophy of Logical Atomism" (1918), in his *Logic and Knowledge,* R. C. Marsh, ed. (London, 1956); G. E. Moore, "Is Existence a Predicate?," in *PAS,* Supp. Vol. 15 (1936), reprinted in A. G. N. Flew, ed., *Logic and Language,* 2d series (Oxford, 1959); William Kneale, "Is Existence a Predicate?," in *PAS,* Supp. Vol. 15 (1936), reprinted in Herbert Feigl and Wilfrid Sellars, eds., *Readings in Philosophical Analysis* (New York, 1949); George Nakhnikian and W. C. Salmon, "'Exists' as a Predicate," in *Philosophical Review,* Vol. 66, No. 4 (1957), 535–542; John Hick, "God as Necessary Being," in *Journal of Philosophy,* Vol. 57, Nos. 22–23 (1960), 725–734; and Terence Penelhum, "Divine Necessity," in *Mind,* N.S. Vol. 69, No. 274 (1960), 175–186.

JOHN HICK

ONTOLOGY. The term *ontologia* was coined by scholastic writers in the seventeenth century. Rudolf Goclenius, who mentioned the word in 1636, may have been the first user, but the term was such a natural Latin coinage and began to appear so regularly that disputes about priority are pointless. Some writers, such as Abraham Calovius, used it interchangeably with *metaphysica;* others used it as the name of a subdivision of metaphysics. Johannes Clauberg (1622–1665), a Cartesian, coined instead the term *ontosophia.* By the time of Jean-Baptiste Duhamel (1624–1706), ontology was clearly distinguished from natural theology. The other subdivisions of metaphysics are cosmology and psychology, from which ontology is also distinguished. Thus, *ontologia* as a philosophical term of art was already in existence when it was finally canonized by Christian Wolff (1679–1754) and Alexander Gottlieb Baumgarten (1714–1762).

Wolff. For the authors mentioned above, the subject matter of ontology was being as such. "Being" was understood univocally, as having one single sense. Ontology can therefore claim as ancestors Duns Scotus and William of Ockham, rather than Aquinas. In the case of Wolff himself, Leibniz was a stronger influence than scholasticism, but in his *Philosophia Prima Sive Ontologia,* Wolff refers explicitly to Francisco Suárez. According to Wolff, the method of ontology is deductive. The fundamental principle applying to all that is, is the principle of noncontradiction, which holds that it is a property of being itself that no being can both have and not have a given characteristic at one and the same time. From this, Wolff believed, follows the principle of sufficient reason, namely, that in all cases there must be some sufficient reason to explain why any being exists rather than does not exist. The universe is a collection of beings each of which has an essence that the intellect is capable of grasping as a clear and distinct idea. The principle of sufficient reason is invoked to explain why some essences have had existence conferred on them and others have not. The truths about beings that are deduced from indubitable first principles are all necessary truths. Thus, ontology has nothing to do with the contingent order of the world.

The influence of late scholasticism (or of what Étienne Gilson calls "essentialism") on rationalist metaphysics was repaid in kind, for the division of metaphysics into ontology, cosmology, and psychology found its way back into scholastic manuals, where it has persisted until very recently. Along with this division, there persisted the view that being constitutes an independent subject matter over and above the subject matter of the special sciences. The persistence of this view is perhaps to be explained by cultural rather than by intellectual factors. In the eighteenth and nineteenth centuries scholasticism was isolated in seminaries until Pope Leo XIII guided Thomism back into intellectual debate. Only in this way was scholasticism able to avoid the nemesis (in the form of Kant) that awaited rationalist metaphysics.

Kant. In the written announcement of lectures given from 1765 to 1766, Kant treated ontology as a subdivision of metaphysics that included rational psychology but was distinguished, in his case, from empirical psychology, cosmology, and what he called the "science of God and the world": "Then in *ontology* I discuss the more general properties of things, the difference between spiritual and material beings." But when Kant came to write the *Critique of Pure Reason,* he settled matters with ontology once and for all. The two key passages are the discussion of the second antinomy of pure reason and the refutation of the ontological argument. Wolff had argued a priori that the world is composed of simple substances, themselves neither perceived nor possessing extension or shape, and each of them different, and that physical objects are composite, collections of such substances. In the second antinomy the thesis is that "every composite substance in the world consists of simple parts, and nothing exists anywhere that is not either simple or composed of simple parts"; and the proof that Kant presented is effectively Wolffian. But he presented an equally powerful proof for the antithesis, namely, that "no composite thing in the world consists of simple parts, and there exists nothing simple anywhere." In exposing the shared fallacy of both proofs, Kant made it impossible ever again to accept ontology as a deductive body of necessary truths that is akin to geometry in form but has being as its subject matter. His analysis of existence in his refutation of the Ontological Proof is a counterpart to this.

Since Kant, the most influential use of the term "ontology" outside scholastic manuals has been in the writings of Heidegger and Quine. Both have been greeted by scholastic writers as engaged in essentially the same enterprise as they themselves, Father D. A. Drennen taking this view of Heidegger, and Father I. M. Bocheński of Quine.

Heidegger. In regard to Heidegger's ontology, Father Drennen is perhaps partly correct. Heidegger wished to explain what character being must have if human consciousness is to be what it is. He began by quarreling with the principle of sufficient reason in its Leibniz–Wolff form. This, he said, is an inadequate starting point for ontology because the question "Why is there something rather than nothing?" presupposes that we already know what being and nothing are. Heidegger treated "Being" and "Nothing" as the names of contrasted and opposed powers whose existence is presupposed in all our judgments. In negative judgments, for example, to speak of what is not the case is implicitly to refer to Nothing. Heidegger's ontology, however, was not deductive or even systematic in form. It proceeds at times by the exegesis of poetry or of the more aphoristic fragments of the pre-Socratic philosophers and is thus very different from scholastic ontology.

Quine. In the case of Quine, the name "ontology" has been in fact given to a quite different set of preoccupations. Quine has been concerned with two closely allied questions: To the existence of what kind of thing does belief in a given theory commit us? And what are the relations between intensional and extensional logic? His answer to the first question is that to be is to be the value of a variable: we have to admit the existence of that range of possible entities for which names could occur as values for those variables without which we could not state our beliefs. His answer to the second question is that intensional logics and extensional logics involve the admission not merely of different but of incompatible types of entity. "Both sorts of entity can be accommodated in the same logic only with the help of restrictions such as Church's, which serve to keep them from mixing, and this is very nearly a matter of two separate logics with a universe for each" (*From A Logical Point of View*, p. 157).

It is clear that Quine's logical preoccupations are in fact relevant to Wolff and the scholastics only in that an understanding of Quine's inquiries would preclude one from trying to construct a deductive ontology in the mode of Suárez or Wolff.

Bibliography

PRIMARY SOURCES

Baumgarten, Alexander Gottlieb, *Metaphysica*. Halle, 1740.

Clauberg, Johannes, *Opera Omnia*, J. T. Schalbruch, ed., 2 vols. Amsterdam, 1691. P. 281.

Duhamel, Jean-Baptiste, *De Consensu Veteris et Novae Philosophiae*. Paris, 1663.

Duns Scotus, *Opera Omnia*, 12 vols. Paris, 1891–1895. Vol. III, *Quaestiones Subtillissimae Super Libros Metaphysicorum Aristotelis*.

Heidegger, Martin, *Existence and Being*, translated by D. Scott, R. Hall, and A. Crick. Chicago, 1949.

Heidegger, Martin, *Being and Time*, translated by John Macquarrie and Edward Robinson. New York, 1962.

Kant, Immanuel, *Critique of Pure Reason*, translated by Norman Kemp Smith. London, 1929.

Quine, Willard Van Orman, *From a Logical Point of View*. Cambridge, Mass., 1953.

Wolff, Christian, *Philosophia Rationalis, Sive Logica Methodo Scientifica Pertractata et ad Usum Scientiarum Atque Vitae Aptata*. Frankfurt and Leipzig, 1728.

Wolff, Christian, *Philosophia Prima Sive Ontologia*. Frankfurt and Leipzig, 1729.

SECONDARY SOURCES

Bocheński, I. M., *Philosophy—An Introduction*. Dordrecht, Netherlands, 1962.

Drennen, D. A., ed., *Modern Introduction to Metaphysics*. New York, 1962.

Ferrater Mora, José, "On the Early History of Ontology." *Philosophy and Phenomenological Research*, Vol. 24 (1963), 36–47.

Geach, P. T.; Ayer, A. J.; and Quine, W. V., "Symposium: On What There Is." *PAS*, Supp. Vol. 25 (1951), 125–160.

Gilson, Étienne, *Being and Some Philosophers*. Toronto, 1949.

Martin, Gottfried, *Immanuel Kant: Ontologie und Wissenschaftstheorie*. Cologne, 1951. Translated by P. G. Lucas as *Kant's Metaphysics and Theory of Science*. Manchester, 1955.

Marx, Werner, *Heidegger und die Tradition*. Stuttgart, 1961.

Owens, Joseph, *The Doctrine of Being in the Aristotelian Metaphysics*. Toronto, 1951.

ALASDAIR MacINTYRE

OPERATIONALISM is a program which aims at linking all scientific concepts to experimental procedures and at cleansing science of operationally undefinable terms, which it regards as being devoid of empirical meaning. Scientists adopted the operational approach to their subject before the principles of operationalism were made articulate. Operationalist theory was erected not on the basis of independent philosophical considerations but upon what was already implicit in the working practice of scientists. P. W. Bridgman, the Nobel prize-winning physicist who is commonly regarded as the founder of operationalism, emphasized this point when he said, "it must be remembered that the operational point of view suggested itself from the observation of physicists in action" ("The Present State of Operationalism," in Philipp Frank, ed., *The Validation of Scientific Theories*, Boston, 1956, p. 79).

A fairly nontechnical illustration of the kinds of development in science in which one can discern an implicit operational point of view is the manner in which physicists treated the concept of physical length. In the nineteenth century it was discovered that Euclid's geometry was not logically unique and that other geometries based on different axioms were not necessarily internally inconsistent. The question was raised about the nature of physical space. Do lines and figures in physical space obey the theorems of Euclid?

At first sight this seems a perfectly sensible question to which there must be a definite answer. Even today some amount of sophistication is required to ask whether we have a clear notion of what could be done to find out whether space has a certain set of properties. Unless we can give an affirmative answer to this question, we should not take it for granted either that space has or that it lacks certain geometrical properties. By the end of the nineteenth century, however, scientists had accepted the view that if we cannot devise operations which would disclose whether or not space was Euclidean, then no definite geometrical properties can be assigned to space at all.

It is clear that in order to determine the geometrical properties of physical figures we must be able to compare distances. If we are unable to say whether distance AB is greater, smaller, or equal to distance CD, where AB and CD do not lie alongside one another, then we cannot even begin to investigate the geometrical nature of space. We take it for granted, however, that in order to compare distances we need a rigid measuring rod, that is, a rod which can be relied upon not to change in length while being transported from place to place. But the question whether the lengths of transported rods are preserved cannot be settled unless we presuppose the possession of some other standard of measurement to which these rods could be compared, but it is agreed that the sole standard of length is a rigid rod. Thus, there are no rigid rods except by fiat, and distances consequently cannot be spoken of as being objectively equal or unequal to one another, and the nature of space cannot uniquely be determined. From an operational point of view, therefore, space has no intrinsic metric, and it is a matter of convention whether we say space obeys this or that set of geometrical axioms.

The operationalist thesis. Although the idea that physical entities, processes, and properties do not have an independent existence transcending the operations through which we may ascertain their presence or absence played an influential role in the thoughts of scientists before the 1920s, it was not until 1927 that Bridgman, in his celebrated *Logic of Modern Physics,* stated operationalism as an explicit program, made an articulate case for it, and undertook extensive operational analyses of the foundations of numerous physical concepts.

Bridgman soon had to retreat from his first extreme statement of operationalism. He had maintained that every scientifically meaningful concept must be capable of full definition in terms of performable physical operations and that a scientific concept is nothing more than the set of operations entering into its definition. The untenability of this view was quickly noticed—for example, by L. J. Russell, who in 1928 pointed out that in science one often speaks of certain operations as being better than others and that one cannot do so except in relation to something existing over and above them. Moreover, useful physical concepts do not as a rule lend themselves to an exhaustive definition. Any connection they have with instrumental

operations may be loose and indirect: statements in which the concepts appear may, in the context of a set of other statements (but not on their own), entail statements describing physical operations. Consequently, in his later writings Bridgman freely permitted "paper and pencil operations," by which he meant mathematical and logical maneuverings with the aid of which no more is required of a concept than that it should be "indirectly making connection with instrumental operations."

It is not hard to see how by taking as one's model a physical concept like the length of a body one arrives at Bridgman's original position. But suppose someone objected that the stepping-off procedure carried out by measuring rods is not the only way to compute the length of a body. We may, for example, define it equally well in terms of the result obtained by timing the body's oscillation when it is allowed to swing as a pendulum and by using the well-known equation connecting the length with the period of oscillation. Length, after all, may enter into all sorts of relationships with other physical parameters, some of which we perhaps have not yet discovered.

To this objection it would have been replied that there is a fundamental difference between the ways in which the two sets of operations are related to the concept of length. The length of a body is "synonymous" with the number of times one can lay a rigid standard of length alongside it; when we speak of the length of a body we mean no more nor less than the number obtained through the stepping-off procedure performed by a measuring stick. When, however, we time a pendulum and then make the appropriate calculations, we merely measure length indirectly, via the relationship of length to other physical parameters. The second approach does not define length but rather inserts the already defined concept of length into an equation accepted as representing a genuine physical relationship.

It is much more difficult to maintain this distinction in the case of such concepts as temperature. One way to give an operational definition of temperature is in terms of measurements made by a mercury thermometer; another way is in terms of measurements made by a platinum-wire thermometer. The first way relies on the theory that the length of bodies varies with temperature; the second, on the theory that electrical resistance varies with temperature. It is easy to see that the concept of temperature is no more than partially interpreted through each of these, and doubtless other, sets of operations to which it is linked by relevant theories. This same position is today generally adopted toward all physical concepts.

We may thus distinguish three stages in scientific theorizing. In the first, preoperational stage, the universe was thought to contain many things and processes that transcend our theories about them and the operations and manipulations through which we may catch a glimpse of them in the mirror of experience. In the second, "naive" operational stage, the other extreme was taken, and all the terms of science were regarded as no more than abbreviations for our experimental results. In the third stage, scientific terms are still not regarded as standing for things and processes having an independent existence of their own, but the meaning of scientific terms is given by a more or less elaborate system of empirical theories in which the terms appear, together with the observations on which the theories embodying the terms are grounded. It is recognized that the concepts of science can never be fully grasped as long as the theories which contain them are open to further development.

The three stages in scientific theorizing are perhaps more dramatically accentuated in psychology than in the physical sciences. Until the early twentieth century the prevailing view was that psychology is a unique discipline dealing with a very special class of events, processes, and entities: the constituents of the realm of consciousness, to which no one but the experiencing individual has access. Although this realm is out of the reach of objective public operations and experimentations, many theorists regarded it as real—indeed, as more real than anything else—and believed that it should be studied by a unique method, introspection.

The radical behaviorism which replaced this mentalistic psychology is a form of naive operationalism and is based on the tenet that psychology is the study not of mental events, processes, or entities but of behavior. Psychologists were not to be concerned with publicly unobservable phenomena, and introspection—at best a private method of inquiry—was completely outlawed.

Today, in the third stage, sensations, images, and thought processes are no longer regarded as beyond the reach of scientists. They are studied through overt behavior, just as in physics nonobservables are studied indirectly through what is observed. The situation in psychology is very much like that in physics. That which is conceptualized need not be completely defined in terms of operations, although it must make contact with the world of public experience.

Operationalism and verificationism. Operationalism is a movement within the philosophy of science. It is instructive to study its development in conjunction with a parallel movement in general philosophy: logical positivism, or logical empiricism (see LOGICAL POSITIVISM). Central to logical positivism is the principle of verifiability, according to which any statement that is not a tautology must be verifiable or else is meaningless. It was thought that through the extensive employment of this principle it would be possible to show that many of the traditional unsolved problems of philosophy could be dealt with by demonstrating that they are simply meaningless. It was soon found, however, that the principle as originally conceived would get rid not only of troublesome problems but also of much useful discourse. The principle consequently underwent a number of revisions in rapid succession.

Rudolf Carnap's paper "The Methodological Character of Theoretical Concepts" embodies all the significant revisions. Carnap clearly exhibits a desire not to prescribe what should be regarded as meaningful from some metascientific or philosophical point of view but rather to describe what is commonly and usefully regarded as empirically meaningful. As mentioned earlier, operationalism from the beginning sought to explicate an approach already implied in the work of practicing scientists. Whereas verificationists previously tried to embrace all human discourse, they now, like the operationalists, confine their attempts to designing a criterion that will faithfully reflect what is meaningful discourse within empirical science. It has been realized that meanings are contextual and that one is therefore not to inquire whether a given sentence or word has or lacks meaning by itself but rather whether it has or lacks meaning relative to a specified system of theoretical, observational, and mixed statements.

A third important change, also clearly enunciated for the first time in Carnap's paper, is the departure from the original policy of inquiring directly into the meaningfulness of whole sentences. Instead, like the operationalists, Carnap deals with individual terms. He distinguishes between logical and empirical terms and also between observational-empirical and theoretical-empirical terms. Theoretical-empirical terms are not admitted into empirical discourse unless they can be shown to be anchored in observation. They need not be completely defined observationally, but a sentence must be constructible that, in conjunction with other sentences, logically implies that certain observations take place. A theoretical-empirical term is then regarded as having passed the test of empirical meaningfulness. The empirical significance of a sentence is now made dependent on the possession of significance by the terms it contains: any syntactically well-formed sentence in which every term is significant (that is, is either a logical, an observational-empirical, or a theoretical-empirical term which has passed the test of empirical meaningfulness) is itself significant in the context of the group of sentences forming our system of science.

The only issue which divides operationalism from logical positivism is that operationalism seems to associate meaningfulness with linkability to experimental activities, whereas the principle of verifiability is satisfied if an expression is anchored to mere passive observation. However, this particular requirement of operationalism can safely be discarded, leading to a complete merger of these two contemporary offshoots of empiricism.

Criticism. Even in its present form, operationalism has not gone uncriticized. The chief complaint is that in the course of weakening its demands in order to accommodate highly theoretical but useful terms which would otherwise have been excluded from science, it has become so watered down as to lose all significance. Operationalism, according to its critics, says nothing we did not know all along. Even in a discipline less precise than physics—for example, in the social sciences—and in a period when standards of rigor had not reached their present stringency, if anyone had advanced a theory employing concepts which had no bearing whatsoever on observables, his theory would have been rejected. It is admitted that operationalism as originally conceived did have practical impact; there are concrete results, especially in psychology, whose production was motivated by the naive operationalistic distrust of anything remote from experience—for example, results obtained in the investigation of subaudible speech. Psychologists came to this area of inquiry chiefly through their search for objective, nonmentalistic alternatives to thought processes. But now, with the liberalization of the criterion for empirical significance—so the complaint goes—when all that is stipulated is that no term qualifies for membership in the vocabulary of science unless it is in some way connected to the universe of operations, observables, and experience, the principle of operationalism is merely platitudinous.

In attempting to reply to this, we must not forget that the scope of operationalism is not confined to the weeding out from scientific vocabulary of terms devoid of empirical significance. Once we have adopted the operational point of view, we have formed in our own minds a particular image of the nature of scientific concepts, which colors our expectations and influences in all sorts of ways our practical approach and methodology.

The world of experience and observation was at one time looked upon as containing mere dim reflections of the world that is conceptualized in physics and whose real existence was on a transcendental plane ultimately beyond our reach. Admittedly, that which is without any observable manifestations whatsoever, which, so to speak, casts no shadow onto the plane of experience, would never have been considered as being of any use to science. Nevertheless, it is not unimportant whether we regard our operations as capturing at most the shadows of the furniture of the universe or as dealing with the furniture itself. Objects totally dissimilar in substance and even in size and shape may under particular circumstances cast identical shadows. Therefore, from the similarity of shadows one cannot infer a similarity in the corresponding objects or even that these objects always cast similar shadows. Similarly, so long as we regard as mere reflections the observations to which physical concepts are linked, the finding of resemblances between some of them will not give rise to the expectation that they resemble in all particulars. On adopting the operational point of view, on the other hand, we think we are looking not at reflected shadows but at the very entities and processes that are conceptualized in science, and our attitude changes accordingly.

To give an illustrative example, the properties of gravitational force and the laws governing it had been exhaustively investigated in the seventeenth and eighteenth centuries. Electromagnetic forces were comparative newcomers in science. Were they to be expected to behave like mechanical forces? There are excellent grounds for saying no: the sources from which electromagnetic forces arise, the systems with which they are associated, and the means by which they are generated are totally different from those involving mechanical forces. However, operationalists tend to see in the product of mass and acceleration (that is, in the measure of force) the very substance of force, although others might see in it no more than force's most immediately apparent reflection. Indeed, as soon as it was observed that electromagnetic phenomena are accompanied by the forcelike effect of accelerating masses, it was taken for granted that they are fully governed by all the laws of Newtonian mechanics, even though the latter was developed to deal with an effect of totally different origin.

An important aim of operationalism besides the practical one is philosophical. For philosophical purposes, it is far from sufficient to state generally that every empirically significant term must somehow be linked to observables—one must precisely articulate the nature of this link and construct in full detail a criterion of meaningfulness. Therefore, many concepts in the various sciences were analyzed in detail in order to clarify the exact role instrumental operations and observations play in the definition or explication of them. Believers in the ultimate formalizability of empirical significance hoped that the results would be generalized and expressible in a philosophically satisfactory way. It is, however, by no means clear that such work has been entirely successful. In fact, some philosophers are of the opinion that such efforts are altogether in vain and that although when faced with any individual term we are able quite easily to judge whether it is empirically significant, we shall never succeed in explicating the general criterion distinguishing meaningful from meaningless utterances.

There is thus unquestionably much scope for operationally clarifying basic concepts. The skeptic might try to show that just as there are no formal criteria by which to distinguish a fertile from a sterile theory, so there is no criterion by which to distinguish the empirically significant from the meaningless. One who believes that the contact empirical concepts must make with operations or experience in general can be precisely formalized might try to show that if our demands are modest enough and we do not expect the criterion of empirical significance to provide guidance for future scientific research, there are in principle no obstacles in the way of such formalization. Their next step would be to execute this formalization in a manner that would stand up to all criticism.

Bibliography

Bridgman, P. W., *The Logic of Modern Physics.* New York, 1927.

Bridgman, P. W., *The Nature of Physical Theory.* Princeton, 1936.

Bridgman, P. W., *The Nature of Thermodynamics.* Cambridge, Mass., 1941. Carefully analyzes many individual concepts.

Bridgman, P. W., *Reflections of a Physicist.* New York, 1950. A collection of papers.

Bridgman, P. W., *The Nature of Some of Our Physical Concepts.* New York, 1952. Many individual concepts carefully analyzed.

Bures, C. E., "Operationism, Construction, and Inference." *Journal of Philosophy,* Vol. 37 (1940), 393–401.

Carnap, Rudolf, "Testability and Meaning." *Philosophy of Science,* Vol. 3 (1936), 419–471 and Vol. 4 (1937), 1–40.

Carnap, Rudolf, "The Methodological Character of Theoretical Concepts," in Vol. I, pp. 38–76, of *Minnesota Studies in the Philosophy of Science,* Herbert Feigl and Michael Scriven, eds., Minneapolis, 1956.

Crissman, P., "The Operational Definition of Concepts." *Psychological Review,* Vol. 46 (1939).

Dingle, Herbert, "A Theory of Measurement." *British Journal for the Philosophy of Science,* Vol. 1 (1950). An extreme operationalist viewpoint.

Feigl, Herbert, "Operationism and Scientific Method." *Psychological Review,* Vol. 52 (1945). A lucid and fair assessment of operationalism. Written as a contribution to "Symposium on Operationism," presented in the same issue.

Frank, Philipp, *Modern Science and Its Philosophy.* Cambridge, 1950. On p. 44 the work of Bridgman is likened to that of Carnap.

Frank, Philipp, ed., *The Validation of Scientific Theories.* Boston, 1956. Various writers assess the significance of operationalism in the 1950s.

Hearnshaw, L. J., "Psychology and Operationalism." *Australasian Journal of Psychology and Philosophy,* Vol. 18 (1941).

Hempel, C. G., "A Logical Appraisal of Operationalism." *Scientific Monthly,* Vol. 79 (1954), 215–220. Reprinted with modifications in his *Aspects of Scientific Explanation.* New York, 1965. Pp. 123–133.

Lindsay, L. B., "A Critique of Operationalism in Science."

Philosophy of Science, Vol. 4 (1937). Important and fair criticism of operationalism.

Margenau, Hans, *The Nature of Physical Theory*. New York, 1952. On p. 232, expresses impatience with operationalism.

Pap, Arthur, "Are Physical Magnitudes Operationally Definable?" in C. West Churchman, ed., *Measurements, Definitions, and Theories*. New York, 1959. Argues for the abolition of the demand for active operations.

Peters, Richard, "Observationalism in Psychology." *Mind*, Vol. 68 (1959).

Reichenbach, Hans, *Experience and Prediction*. Chicago, 1938.

Russell, L. J., review of Bridgman's *The Logic of Modern Physics*. *Mind*, Vol. 47 (1938).

Schlesinger, Georg, *Method in the Physical Sciences*. London, 1963. Chapter 4 is devoted to a discussion of the practical scope of operationalism.

Skinner, B. F., "The Operational Analysis of Psychological Terms." *Psychological Review*, Vol. 52 (1945), 270–277.

Skinner, B. F., "Behaviorism at Fifty." *Science* (1963).

Spence, K. W., "The Postulates and Methods of 'Behaviorism.'" *Psychological Review*, Vol. 55 (1948), 67–78.

Stevens, S. S., "The Operational Basis of Psychology." *American Journal of Psychology*, Vol. 46 (1935).

Stevens, S. S., "The Operational Definition of Psychological Concepts." *Psychological Review*, Vol. 42 (1935). A major spokesman for operationalism in psychology.

G. SCHLESINGER

OPTIMISM AND PESSIMISM. See PESSIMISM AND OPTIMISM.

ORDER. See CHAOS AND COSMOS; MEASUREMENT; TELEOLOGICAL ARGUMENT FOR THE EXISTENCE OF GOD.

ORESME, NICHOLAS (c. 1325–1382), French scientist and bishop. Only meager details are available on the life of Nicholas (or Nicole) Oresme. He was probably born between 1320 and 1330 in Normandy, perhaps in the village of Allemagne, near the city of Caen. The first known mention of his name is on a list of students of the Norman nation at the University of Paris, dated November 29, 1348, the year of his entry into the College of Navarre. In 1356 he became grand master of his college and perhaps received his doctorate in theology, a prerequisite for the mastership.

Sometime before 1359 Oresme was brought into contact with the royal family of France as teacher to the dauphin, the future Charles V (1364–1380). Perhaps as reward for various services to the crown, Oresme became archdeacon of Bayeux in 1361, a position he was compelled to resign in the same year because it conflicted with the grand mastership. He was appointed canon of the cathedral of Rouen in 1362, canon of the Sainte-Chapelle in Paris in 1363, dean of Rouen Cathedral in 1364, and, finally, bishop of Lisieux in 1377. His appointment as bishop, which he held until his death, was a grateful king's reward for a series of translations into French that Oresme had made by royal request during the years 1369–1377. In succession he translated and commented upon Aristotle's *Ethics* (*Le Livre de ethiques d'Aristote*), *Politics* (*Les Politiques*), *Economics* (*Le Livre de yconomique d'Aristote*), and *De Caelo et Mundo* (*Le Livre du ciel et du monde*).

The numerous commentaries and treatises written by Oresme bear witness to his wide range of interests, embracing theology, physical science, economics, and politics;

but there is little doubt that physical and mathematical problems were of central importance to him. Philosophical issues were discussed largely in connection with scientific questions.

Science and tradition. Partly from theological temperament and partly because of the condemnations of extreme Aristotelianism in 1277, Oresme diligently combated claims that strict demonstrative proofs were possible in physical science and repeatedly attacked the extravagant presumptions of astrologers whose persuasive arguments influenced affairs of state. In order to reveal the inadequacy of demonstrative proofs in physical science, Oresme employed the tactic of rendering equally plausible alternative solutions to physical questions. Adopting, for the sake of argument, positions deemed absurd within the context of the scholastic tradition, Oresme strove to "demonstrate" that the repudiated view was as tenable as the traditional opinion. Two notable examples may be cited. In *Le Livre du ciel et du monde* (Book II, Ch. 25), Oresme argues that neither by experience nor by reason could it be decided whether the earth was stationary at the center of the universe with the celestial spheres undergoing a daily rotation, or whether the earth performed a diurnal rotation on its axis while the heavens remained stationary. Oresme was the only Scholastic thus far known who insisted that both astronomical and physical phenomena could be accounted for on either hypothesis, although he concluded his discussion by opting for the traditional position. In similar fashion Oresme argued (*Le Livre du ciel et du monde*, Book I, Ch. 24) that, Aristotle notwithstanding, there is nothing illogical or absurd about the concept of a plurality of worlds, for had God so desired, he could have created several coexistent worlds. Having shown that "proofs" for the existence of one world are in no way compelling, Oresme then adopted the usual view that there is, and can be, only one physical world.

Geometry of qualities. Oresme made notable contributions in treating the problem of "intension and remission of qualities," that is, the way qualities vary in intensity. The general solution reached earlier in the fourteenth century at Oxford was to treat qualitative variation quantitatively by addition or subtraction of qualitative degrees. At Merton College this approach was numerical; but Oresme's technique was geometrical, involving the application of two-dimensional figures in which the horizontal line, or base, represented the extension of a quality in a subject, and perpendiculars erected on that base represented the intensity of the quality at that point. The total area of the figure was taken as the quantity of the quality in the particular subject. While this method of graphing variation of qualities may not have been original with Oresme, it was given its fullest development in his *De Configurationibus Qualitatum*.

In this treatise is also found a significant geometric proof in which a uniform acceleration commencing from rest, or some initial velocity, is equated with a uniform motion equal to the mean speed of the accelerated motion. The two motions traverse equal distances in equal times. The proof is equivalent to $S = [V_0 + (V_f - V_0)/2]t$, where S is distance, V_0 initial velocity, V_f final velocity, and t time. When acceleration begins from rest, $V_0 = 0$ and $V_f = at$

(where a is acceleration), so that $S = at^2/2$. Should there be an initial velocity, then $V_f - V_0 = at$ and $S = V_0 t + at^2/2$. This is the famous mean-speed theorem enunciated in the first half of the fourteenth century at Oxford, although the geometric proof seems to have been original with Oresme. Galileo later employed a very similar geometric demonstration for the same theorem, which, in contrast to Oresme, he applied to freely falling bodies. Oresme's proof was actually applied to uniformly increasing qualities, but he says that it also applies to velocities. Indeed, Oresme also anticipated Galileo's distance theorem, wherein a body uniformly accelerating from rest will, in equal time intervals, traverse distances that are related to each other as the sequence of odd numbers beginning with unity.

Mathematics. Aristotle's law of motion, usually represented as $V \propto F/R$, where V is velocity, F force, and R resistance, was rejected by Oresme in favor of the function $F_2/R_2 = (F_1/R_1)^n$ enunciated by Thomas Bradwardine and accepted by most Parisian Scholastics. In this function, where F and R represent the same quantities as above, the exponent n, which Oresme called a "ratio of ratios" (*proportio proportionum*), relating the two ratios of force and resistance, represents a ratio of velocities because $n = V_2/V_1$. In his *De Proportionibus Proportionum* Oresme not only provided a mathematical foundation for this function but also elaborated many new propositions that he applied to dynamics and kinematics. More significantly, and perhaps for the first time in the history of mathematics, Oresme arrived at the concept of an irrational exponent. Indeed, he argued that in any sequence of ratios of integers not constituting a geometric series, there will be more irrational than rational exponents if the ratios are related exponentially two at a time. By way of example he took one hundred ratios in the sequence $r/1$ where $r = 2, 3, 4, 5, \cdots, 101$. Taking them two at a time, there will be $100 \cdot 99/2 = 4,950$ possible exponential relationships. Of these, only ratios in the same geometric series are relatable by rational exponents. Oresme calculated the ratio of irrational to rational exponents as 197 to 1 and held that the disparity would increase as more terms are taken in the sequence $r/1$.

Oresme unhesitatingly applied this mathematical conclusion directly to physical phenomena, to ratios of velocities, distances, and times. This was, perhaps, the earliest attempt to deal formally with mathematical probability and to apply it to physical phenomena. Its application to celestial motion provided Oresme with an unusual weapon against astrology. He assumed that any two planetary velocities are probably incommensurable, from which it would follow that precise planetary positions are unpredictable. Numerous propositions in his *Ad Pauca Respicientes* and *De Commensurabilitate* demonstrate that, according to the assumption of incommensurable celestial motions, every celestial configuration is unique and the regularity essential for astrological prediction is nonexistent. Although Oresme was not the first to consider the incommensurability of the celestial motions, he may have been the first to discuss it formally and at length. The detailed arguments and propositions had relatively little impact on subsequent writers, but the central theme did influence Henry of Hesse, Jean de Gerson, and perhaps Nicholas of Cusa.

Bibliography

No definitive, authoritative corpus of works has yet been established for Oresme, but those of probable authenticity are impressive in range and scope. There are French commentaries mentioned above: *Le Livre de ethiques d'Aristote*, A. D. Menut, ed. (New York, 1940); *Les Politiques* (Paris, 1489), with a new edition in preparation by A. D. Menut; *Le Livre de yconomique d'Aristote*, translated and edited by A. D. Menut, in *Transactions of the American Philosophical Society*, N.S. Vol. 47, Part 2 (Philadelphia, 1957); and *Le Livre du ciel et du monde*, A. D. Menut and A. J. Denomy, eds., in *Mediaeval Studies*, Vols. III–V (Toronto, 1941–1943), a revised edition of which with English translation by Menut will soon be published by the University of Wisconsin Press. In addition, there are extant Latin questions on the following Aristotelian treatises: *Physics*, *De Caelo*, *Meteorologica*, *De Generatione et Corruptione*, *De Anima*, and *Parva Naturalia*. Almost exclusively mathematical but containing some physical discussion are the *De Proportionibus Proportionum*, translated and edited by Edward Grant in *Nicole Oresme: De Proportionibus Proportionum and Ad Pauca Respicientes* (Madison, Wis., 1965); *Algorismus Proportionum*, M. Curtze, ed., translated as *Der Algorismus Proportionum des Nicolaus Oresme* (Berlin, 1868); and *Quaestiones Super Geometriam Euclidis*, H. L. L. Busard, ed., 2 fascicles (Leiden, 1961).

Two treatises, *Ad Pauca Respicientes*, translated and edited by Edward Grant in *Nicole Oresme: De Proportionibus Proportionum and Ad Pauca Respicientes* (Madison, Wis., 1965), and *De Commensurabilitate vel Incommensurabilitate Motuum Celi*, being translated and edited by Edward Grant, although to some extent mounting attacks against astrology, are largely concerned with the kinematics of circular motion, that is, with bodies and planets assumed to move with commensurable or incommensurable velocities. The lengthy and important *De Configurationibus Qualitatum*, being translated and edited by Marshall Clagett, treats of the intension and remission of qualities. Other physical works are the *Questiones de Sphera*, translated and edited by G. Droppers as a Ph.D. dissertation, University of Wisconsin (Madison, Wis., 1965); the *Inter Omnes Impressiones*, R. Mathieu, ed., which appeared as "L'Inter Omnes Impressiones de Nicole Oresme" in *Archives d'histoire doctrinale et littéraire du moyen âge*, Vol. 34 (1959), and is devoted to the nature and character of comets; and the *Traitié de l'éspere*, edited by L. McCarthy as a thesis at the University of Toronto (1942), which Oresme described as an introduction to his *Le Livre du ciel et du monde*.

Sometime between 1356 and 1360, Oresme may have translated into French the *Quadripartitum*, a Latin translation of Ptolemy's astrological work *Tetrabiblos*. Arguments against the prophesying arts, especially astrology, were formulated in the *Livre de divinacions* and the Latin *Tractatus Contra Judiciarios Astronomos*. These two basically similar treatises have been edited, and the *Divinacions* translated into English, by G. W. Coopland in *Nicole Oresme and the Astrologers* (Cambridge, Mass., 1952); the *Tractatus* has also been edited by H. Pruckner in *Studien zu den astrologischen Schriften des Heinrich von Langenstein* (Leipzig, 1933). Oresme's lengthiest attack against astrology is the *Questio Contra Divinatores Horoscopios*, written in 1370. Perhaps linked with this treatise is the *Quotlibeta Annexa Questioni Premisse*, in which Oresme discusses not only astrology but also natural marvels and causation.

In theology, Oresme wrote a lost *Commentary on the Sentences* and the *De Communicatione Idiomatum*, edited by E. Borchert in *Beiträge zur Geschichte der Philosophie*, Vol. 35, Nos. 4–5 (Münster in Westfalen, 1940).

The *Tractatus de Origine, Natura, Jure, et Mutationibus Monetarum*, an influential and oft-reprinted treatise on coinage, was written around 1356 and later translated into French by Oresme. It was edited, with an English translation, by C. Johnson as *The De Moneta of Nicholas Oresme and English Mint Documents* (London, 1956).

The reader may also consult Vols. IV, VII, VIII, and IX of Pierre Duhem's *Le Système du monde*, 10 vols. (Paris, 1913–1959), in which Duhem devotes lengthy and important sections to Oresme's physical ideas. Significant excerpts from Oresme's *De Configurationibus Qualitatum* and *Le Livre du ciel et du monde* are translated and fully discussed in Marshall Clagett's *The Science of Mechanics in the Middle Ages* (Madison, Wis., 1959). A work devoted solely to Oresme's natural philosophy is O. Pedersen's *Nicole Oresme og hans naturfilosofiske System* (Copenhagen, 1956); a French résumé is appended. A five-volume study by A. Maier, *Studien zur Naturphilosophie der Spätscholastik* (Rome, 1949–1958), contains much on Oresme's physics and mathematics.

EDWARD GRANT

ORGANISMIC BIOLOGY. The term "organismalism" was coined by the zoologist W. E. Ritter in 1919 to describe the theory that, in his words, "the organism in its totality is as essential to an explanation of its elements as its elements are to an explanation of the organism." Subsequent writers have largely replaced "organismal" with the more euphonious "organismic" as a title for this theory, for the many variations on its main theme, and for some subordinate but supporting doctrines concerning the teleological and historical character of organisms.

Ritter regards Aristotle as the founder and most distinguished exponent of the organismic theory. But Aristotle is also claimed as the father of vitalism, a view that organismic biologists in general reject. In fact, there is considerable affinity between the two schools. They both agree that the methods of the physical sciences are applicable to the study of organisms but insist that these methods cannot tell the whole story; they agree that the "form" of the single whole organism is in some sense a factor in embryological development, animal behavior, reproduction, and physiology; and they both insist on the propriety of a teleological point of view. On all of these points, Aristotle not only agrees but presents, in his own terminology, careful and persuasive arguments in their favor. But organismic biology and vitalism differ in one fundamental respect: the latter holds (and the former denies) that the characteristic features of organic activity—all of which fall under the heading of "regulation"—are caused by the presence in the organism of a nonphysical but substantial entity. There are different interpretations of Aristotle, (which we cannot examine here) on the question whether he believes there are such vital entities. In this writer's view, Aristotle is clearly a vitalist.

The affinity between vitalism and organismic biology is more than an accident. In the history of biology it is difficult to disentangle vitalistic and organismic strands, since both schools are concerned with the same sorts of problems and speak the same sort of language. The distinction between them was drawn clearly only in the twentieth century. Organismic biology may be described as an attempt to achieve the aims of the murky organismic–vitalistic tradition, without appeal to vital entities.

The writings of contemporary organismic biologists present a number of difficulties for a philosophical commentator. The position of organismic biology is usually stated in a vocabulary that plays little or no theoretical role in the working language of biology. For example, "whole," "unity," "integrity," "part," "form," "principle," "understanding," and "significance" all occur frequently in their works. Now any biologist will use these terms occasionally in the course of his professional writing, just because they are perfectly good words in the English language. But they are not technical expressions; they are not, in ordinary usage, laden with biological theory; and they are trouble-free only when employed in contexts that make clear their function as items in the common language. The organismic biologist, however, makes them bear a heavy burden in the description of the nature of living organisms. And many, but by no means all, organismic biologists also assign a great deal of weight to some rather mysterious formulas. Here are a few: "The whole acts as a causal unit . . . on its own parts" (W. E. Agar); "The living body and its physiological environment form an organic whole, the parts of which cannot be understood in separation from one another" (J. S. Haldane); "No part of any organism can be rightly interpreted except as part of an individual organism" (W. E. Ritter). And here are a few more that are characteristic but not direct quotations: "The organic whole is greater than the sum of its parts"; "Knowledge of the goal of an animal's behavior is necessary for understanding its significance"; "Biological theory should be autonomous, with concepts and laws of its own." These formulas may be termed "mysterious" because, according to their most natural interpretations (as will be argued), they are all the barest of truisms.

Two additional points should be mentioned. Organismic biologists have employed some of the more obscure technical conceptions of speculative philosophy, such as "formal cause," "emergence," "hormic," "telic," and so on. And since their writings are a minority report on biological phenomena, organismic biologists are often polemical, engaging in denunciations of other biologists—"mechanists," "elementalists," and "reductionists"—whose positions they leave just as obscure as their own. For all of these reasons, an account of the organismic position which aims at answering the questions likely to be raised by philosophers of science involves elements of reconstruction and interpretation. Thus, a fuller description of the position and an interpretation designed to do justice both to the letter and spirit of the organismic tradition follows.

The position of organismic biology. All organismic biologists hold that there is a gulf between organic and inorganic phenomena in one or more of the following respects.

Organic unity. Organic systems are so organized that the activities of the whole cannot be understood as the sum of the activities of the parts. All members of the school agree on this point. As the term "organismic" implies, the most important example of such wholes is the single organism, but there are others, such as cells, organs, colonies, and some populations.

J. H. Woodger, whose *Biological Principles* is the most careful and extensive exposition of organismic biology, explains the conception of organic unity in the following way. Consider a system *W* that is *totally* composed of physicochemical parts—elementary particles, for example. The activities of these parts are described by the laws of physics. These particles may be the sole constituents of other systems (for example, molecules) which also totally compose W and which exhibit, in addition to activities described by the laws of physics, other activities described by the laws of chemistry. Molecules may similarly be the sole constituents of other systems, which are in turn the constituents . . . , up to the whole system W. In Woodger's terminology, W exhibits a series of "levels of organization." The parts of W belong to a particular level, its physical parts to the physical level, its chemical parts to the chemical level, and so on. System W constitutes a perfect "hierarchy" of parts from levels 0 (zero) to n (a finite number), if 0-level parts are the sole constituents of all 1-level parts, and if every part at each level i (any given level) except the 0-level is totally composed of parts at level $i-1$. Woodger points out that organisms are not perfect hierarchies, since some parts of the organism at an i-level may have parts at the $i-2$ level, while the $i-2$ parts are *not* organized into $i-1$ parts (for instance, blood has cellular *and* chemical but noncellular parts). Nevertheless, he contends, organisms approximate to a hierarchical organization. If we ignore deviations from the perfect hierarchy, we may let W represent a whole organism, and we may say that its 0-level parts are physical parts. Now this analysis permits us to say that the organism is composed totally of physical parts. Perhaps some philosophical materialists would be content with this thesis; at any rate, if it is true, it rules out vitalism. But it is false that the organism is composed *only* of physical parts, for there are parts at higher levels of organization. It is Woodger's contention, and a general thesis of organismic biology, that the laws which determine the behavior of the parts at a given level of organization are silent about some aspects of the behavior of the parts at the higher levels. To use an extreme example, the laws of quantum physics have nothing to say on the question of why honey bees kill their drones. According to Woodger, it is necessary to study the relations between the relata at *each* level of organization. In order to understand the behavior of cells during morphogenesis, for example, we must develop a theory of cell relations and not be content, for example, with only a theory of the relations between molecules.

Determining features of the whole. The parts of organic wholes not only exhibit patterns of behavior in virtue of their relations to other parts at the same level of organization, but in addition, *some* of the features of the parts at a given level are determined by the pattern of organization at *higher* (and, of course, at lower) levels of organization. This is the general form of the special thesis that the properties of the whole determine the properties of the part; and it seems to have the methodological consequence that a theory of the elements at a given level could not be complete without a theory of the elements at the higher levels. Woodger puts the point this way: the parts of organisms must be studied *in situ*, for we cannot learn how they would behave *in situ* by studying them in isolation.

Teleological behavior of organisms. One kind of activity, which is a consequence of organization at a level higher than that of the organism's physical parts, is directive or teleological behavior. Directiveness is an aspect of organisms that is shown in their physiology, in the behavior of

individual animals, and in the social systems of some animals; and an account of directiveness is not only legitimate but necessary. E. S. Russell argues that since directiveness (processes aimed at the production and maintenance of organic unities) is a fact, then a physiological process, or piece of animal behavior, cannot be understood until we understand its function or its goal.

Interpretation of organismic biology. It was remarked above that if we give the slogans of organismic biology their most direct interpretations, they are nothing more than truisms. Consider, for example, the statement that the whole (if it is an organic unity) is more than the sum of its parts. This looks like a simple warning against the fallacy of composition: we are being warned, for example, that from the premise "No part of a bird can fly" we cannot infer "No whole bird can fly." No weighty volume is required to convince us that a whole may have numberless properties that its parts lack. Of course, there are other possible interpretations of the slogan. It might be taken to mean, especially in the form "The behavior of the whole is more than the sum of the behavior of its parts," that no description of the behavior of the parts could be a description of the behavior of the whole. So far from being a truism, this is obviously false. Finally, it might be taken to mean something like the following. Employing an analysis of Ernest Nagel, we might say that the behavior B of a system S is more than the sum of the behavior b_1, $b_2, \cdots, b_n$ of its parts $s_1, s_2, \cdots, s_n$, with respect to an antecedently specified theory T, if (1) B is an instance of a law L; (2) L is not part of T; (3) the laws in T describe s_1, $s_2, \cdots, s_n$ in such a way that they explain $b_1, b_2, \cdots$, b_n; and (4) L is not deducible from a description of s_1, $s_2, \cdots, s_n$ together with laws in T. An important point to notice here is that B can be identical with events b_1, $b_2, \cdots, b_n$, and yet the law of which B is an instance is not derivable from the laws of which $b_1, b_2, \cdots, b_n$ are instances. This account makes the "more than" relation relative to a body of theory. Relative to existing physical and chemical theories, it is true (but perhaps not a truism) that much organic activity is more than the sum of the physical and chemical activities of its parts. The thesis that there are cases of higher-level behavior that will remain greater than the sum of the behavior of its physical parts, for all possible physical theories, is the doctrine of emergence, which many organismic biologists believe to be true. But it is essential to note two points—first, that the thesis is dubious and unproved, and second, that one can be an organismic biologist without believing it (L. von Bertalanffy is an example).

Let us now look at two more formulas of the organismic biologists. Woodger holds that an organic part, such as a cell, has properties in the organism that it does not have in isolation from the organism. This, too, is a truism: an excised eye lacks the property of contributing to the sight of its former owner. Now if we add, as Woodger does, that the properties of the part in the whole could not be uncovered by studying the part outside the whole, the thesis reduces to the thesis of emergence. And certainly, one of the commonest scientific procedures consists in predicting the behavior of a part in a system that has not yet been studied, although this prediction is assuredly made on the basis of knowledge gained by studying the part—not in "isolation," but as a part of other systems. For instance, the behavior of an electron in a cathode ray tube allows us to predict the electron's behavior in a cyclotron.

Finally, we may consider E. S. Russell's remark that understanding the significance of an animal's behavior requires understanding its goal. This, at least on Russell's interpretation, is a truism, for he connects the notion of a goal with the notion of adaptive value for the animal and identifies "significance" with adaptive value.

Omitting specific discussion of the other formulas cited, the general point is clear: organismic biology seems to collapse either into doctrines that are not controversial or into unclarified, unproved, and dubious assertions about emergence, unpredictability, and irreducibility. Nevertheless, organismic biology is an important and valuable movement, for the following reasons.

First, organismic biology is perfectly correct in pointing out that there are levels of organization above the chemical level which exhibit laws of behavior that are not exhibited at lower levels (for example, molecules do not sting other molecules to death). Higher-level behavior can be treated without reference to behavior at lower levels, which means that the biologist can (and indeed does) construct concepts that are tailored to the description of higher-level behavior. The principles at the higher levels must be formulated before the question of their reducibility to lower level principles can even be considered. A biochemical geneticist is not only a biochemist; he is also a geneticist, because he is involved in elucidating the processes involved in the sort of gross biological phenomena studied by Mendel.

Second, the insistence of organismic biologists on the importance of functional analysis is well founded. Focusing on the biological ends of physiological and behavioral processes provides the only means for developing the conceptual schemes that are needed in morphology, ethology, evolution theory, and other branches of biology. This point is developed in detail in Morton Beckner's *Biological Way of Thought*.

Third, although organismic biology is a set of truisms, it is none the worse for being so. The trouble with truisms is their great number: there are so many that we easily overlook, sometimes systematically, some of the most important ones. Even though in fact many biologists agree with the organismic position, they will say that they disagree. This leads to the position (generally deleterious in the sciences) of the scientist's doing one thing and describing it as if he were doing something else.

To sum up, organismic biology is to be interpreted as a series of methodological proposals, based on certain very general features of the organism—namely, the existence in the organism of levels of organization with the biological ends of maintenance and reproduction. These features are sufficient to justify "a free, autonomous biology, with concepts and laws of its own," whether or not the higher levels are ultimately reducible to the lower ones.

Bibliography

Agar, W. E., *A Contribution to the Theory of Living Organisms*, 2d ed. Melbourne, 1951.

Beckner, Morton, *The Biological Way of Thought*. New York, 1959.

Bertalanffy, Ludwig von, *Modern Theories of Development*. London, 1933.

Haldane, J. S., *Mechanism, Life, and Personality*, 2d ed. New York, 1923.

Lillie, R. S., *General Biology and Philosophy of Organism*. Chicago, 1945.

Nagel, Ernest, "Mechanistic Explanation and Organismic Biology," in *Philosophy and Phenomenological Research*, Vol. 11 (1951), 327–338.

Ritter, W. E., *The Unity of the Organism*, 2 vols. Boston, 1919.

Russell, E. S., *The Behaviour of Animals*, 2d ed. London, 1938.

Woodger, J. H., *Biological Principles*. London, 1948.

MORTON O. BECKNER

ORIGEN (c. 185–253), Christian theologian and exegete of the Bible, was the foremost member of the catechetical school at Alexandria. Born of Christian parents in Alexandria, he was made head of a Christian school there in 204. He taught until 231, when conflict with the bishop forced him to leave for Caesarea in Palestine, where he taught until his death. He apparently heard lectures by Ammonius Saccas, founder of Neoplatonism, although he regarded philosophy as essentially preparatory to theology in the same way that other studies were prerequisite to philosophy itself. However, the influence of philosophy (primarily Platonic but also Stoic) on his thought was highly significant; it can be observed much more clearly in his presuppositions and arguments than in explicit quotations, which are relatively unusual except in the apologetic treatise *Contra Celsum*. The most important of his voluminous writings are *De Principiis*, a treatise on first principles and the earliest extant Christian systematic theology; the treatise *On Prayer*; and *Contra Celsum*.

"De Principiis." A relatively early work, *De Principiis* begins with the statement that apostolic doctrine, as found in the New Testament, is incomplete because the apostles intentionally left some matters untouched for the sake of their spiritual successors. Origen devotes the first book to a consideration of the spiritual hierarchy consisting of the Father, who acts on all beings; the Logos (Word or Reason), who acts upon rational beings; the Spirit, who acts upon those rational beings who are sanctified, and the angels. The second book deals with the material world. Man, created because the angels fell, is a pre-existent fallen spirit in a material body. After Adam's transgression came redemption by the incarnate Logos; later there will be resurrection, the last judgment, and the life of all men restored to spiritual bodies (a succession of other worlds may follow as it has gone before). The third book discusses freedom, characteristic of creatures but not of the Creator. When a soul is in a body, it can struggle for victory, helped by angels and hindered by demons. Since it possesses free will, it is capable of choosing the good. After a brief summary, Origen turns in the fourth book to an explanation of how the Scriptures can be shown to have various levels of meaning. Like man himself, they have flesh (literal meaning), soul (moral meaning), and spirit (allegorical–spiritual meaning). The exegetical difficulties in Scripture were placed there by their ultimate author, God, in the way that similar obstacles to faith were placed in the cosmos so that man could use his mind.

Origen's work, written in Greek, is extant only in fragments (Book IV is almost entire). The Latin version by Tyrannius Rufinus was severely criticized by St. Jerome on the ground that it lacks unorthodox passages that were in the original, but it has come to be regarded more favorably by modern scholars. The title *De Principiis* has parallels in second-century philosophy, as do many of the subjects Origen discusses; his approach, however, seems to be essentially Christian.

"On Prayer." In *On Prayer*, written later in his life, Origen discusses prayer in general (Chs. 3–17) and the Lord's Prayer in particular (Chs. 18–30). The principal problem is that presented by prayer to an omniscient God who has foreordained everything. Once again, Origen insists upon God's gift of free will; the primary purpose of prayer is not petition as such but sharing in the life of God. Origen classifies prayer as petition, adoration (only of the Father), supplication, and thanksgiving. In each case he emphasizes—as do contemporary middle Platonists—the spiritual attitude of the one who prays.

"Contra Celsum." The late apologetic treatise against Celsus, written in 248, reveals the extent to which Origen was able to argue on grounds shared by his philosophical opponents; there is actually a wide measure of agreement between him and Celsus. Both are opposed to anthropomorphism, to idolatry, and to any crudely literal theology. Origen, however, consistently defends Christianity as he sees it and does not hesitate to attack philosophies and philosophers.

Origen and philosophy. The precise extent of Origen's debt to philosophy was discussed in antiquity; the Neoplatonist Porphyry claimed (according to Eusebius, *Historia Ecclesiastica* VI, 19, 8) that Origen drew upon Plato, Numenius, Cronius, Apollophanes, Longinus, Moderatus, Nicomachus, Chaeremon the Stoic, and Cornutus. Since Origen does refer to many of these writers, whose names occur in Porphyry's description of the Neoplatonic curriculum, Porphyry may be attempting to demonstrate both the extent and the correctness of Origen's Neoplatonism. The systems and works of various philosophers—except for the "atheists"—were studied thoroughly in Origen's school. Origen himself often made use of philosophical dictionaries for the definitions of various terms, but he also studied the writings of the philosophers themselves, not only those of Plato and the Platonists but also those of the Stoics and, occasionally, the Peripatetics.

It is sometimes claimed that there were two Origens, one a pupil of Ammonius Saccas and the other the Christian theologian. It is more likely that both aspects were combined within one person, the first Christian to be a genuinely philosophical theologian.

Works by Origen

Die griechischen christlichen Schriftsteller der drei ersten Jahrhunderte, Origenes, Vols. I–II (*Contra Celsum, De Oratione*) and Vol. V (*De Principiis*), translated by P. Koetschau. Leipzig, 1899–1930.

Origen on First Principles, translated by G. W. Butterworth. London, 1936.

Origen: Contra Celsum, translated by H. Chadwick. Cambridge, 1953.

Origen's Treatise on Prayer, translated by E. G. Jay. Naperville, Ill., 1954.

Works on Origen

Bigg, C., *The Christian Platonists of Alexandria.* Oxford, 1913.

Cadiou, R., *La Jeunesse d'Origène.* Paris, 1935.

Crouzel, H., *Origène et la "connaissance mystique."* Paris, 1961.

Crouzel, H., *Origène et la philosophie.* Paris, 1962.

Daniélou, J., *Origène.* Paris, 1948.

Kettler, F. H., "Origenes," in *Die Religion in Geschichte und Gegenwart,* 3d ed. Vol. IV, pp. 1692–1701.

Koch, H., *Pronoia und Paideusis.* Leipzig, 1932.

Tollinton, R. B., *Alexandrine Teaching on the Universe.* London, 1932.

ROBERT M. GRANT

OROBIO DE CASTRO, ISAAC (1620–1687), was born Balthazar Orobio de Castro in Braganza, Portugal. He became an important Spanish doctor and a professor of metaphysics. The Inquisition arrested him for secretly practicing Judaism. After three years in prison he escaped to France and became professor of pharmacy at Toulouse. Finally, deciding to abandon living as a Christian, he moved to Holland, where in 1662 he changed his name from Balthazar to Isaac and became one of the leading intellectual figures in the Spanish-Portuguese Jewish community. He wrote poetry and philosophical defenses of Judaism. The latter include his letters against Juan de Prado—apparently one of those who led Spinoza away from orthodoxy. (Prado, ten years Spinoza's senior, was excommunicated with him.) Prado had argued that the law of nature should take precedence over the law of Moses. Orobio de Castro's three letters, two against Prado and one against Prado's son, offer a rationalistic defense of Judaism. He also wrote a metaphysical defense of his religion, based mainly on Spanish-Catholic scholastic works and in answer to Alonso de Cepeda. His most famous works are an extremely rationalistic and scholastic answer to Spinoza in geometrical form, *Certamen Philosophicum Propugnatum Veritatis Divinae ac Naturalis* (1684), which was published with Fénelon's *Demonstration de l'existence de Dieu* and his own defense of Judaism in a debate with Philip van Limborch. Limborch met Orobio in Amsterdam in the 1680s and was much affected by his report of the Inquisition, which, through Limborch's *Historia Inquisitionis,* became for the next two centuries the best-known study of Inquisitorial investigation and torture methods. Limborch was troubled by Orobio's anti-Christian views and debated with him (apparently in the presence of Limborch's friend John Locke). The debate was published by Limborch under the title *Amica Collatio cum Erudito Judaeo* (1687) just after his opponent died. One of Locke's first publications is a long review of this debate. Portions of Orobio's strongest anti-Christian work, *Prevenciones divinas contra la vana idolatria de las gentes,* were published in French under the title *Israel vengé* (1770). This work was used as important ammunition by French atheists against Christianity.

Throughout his works, Orobio de Castro showed an extremely acute understanding of metaphysics, using his knowledge of Spanish Scholasticism to buttress his religion against freethinkers and liberal and orthodox Christians. Some of his arguments against the doctrine of the Trinity are close to Spinoza's arguments against the plurality of substance.

Bibliography

Additional works by Orobio de Castro include *La observancia de la divina ley de Mosseh* (Coimbra, 1925), which has a preface by Moses Bensabat Amzalak.

For works on Orobio de Castro see Joaquim de Carvalho, *Orobio de Castro e o espinosismo*, in *Memórias da Academia das Ciências de Lisboa, Classe de letras*, Vol. II (Lisbon, 1937), a study on Orobio de Castro that includes the 1721 Spanish translation of *Certamen Philosophicum*. See also I. S. Révah, *Spinoza et Juan de Prado* (The Hague, 1959), and Enrico De Angelis, "Crisi di coscienza fra i seicentisti per il metodo geometrico," in *Annali della Scuola Normale Superiore di Pisa, lettere, storia e filosofia*, Series II, Vol. 31 (1962), 253–271.

Richard H. Popkin

The Encyclopedia of Philosophy

The

ENCYCLOPEDIA
of
PHILOSOPHY

PAUL EDWARDS, *Editor in Chief*

VOLUME SIX

Macmillan Publishing Co., Inc. & The Free Press
NEW YORK
COLLIER MACMILLAN PUBLISHERS
LONDON

The Encyclopedia of Philosophy

O

[CONTINUED]

ORPHISM is a modern term attached to two connected phenomena of Greek religion. The first is a body of traditional poetry, possibly from as early as the seventh century B.C., ascribed to a mythical singer called Orpheus and containing an account of the creation of the world and of the afterlife of the soul, its judgment and punishment for sins on earth, and its final reincarnation in another living body. The second is the way of life adopted by those who accepted the truth of these writings, such truths being regarded with as much respect as the revelations in the traditional Greek "mysteries" at Eleusis and elsewhere.

Contents of Orphic writings. A number of fragments of the Orphic poems have survived, some of which belong to the poems as they were known in Athens in the fifth and fourth centuries B.C. However, these writings, in the manner of popular poetry, were constantly growing by accretion, and they seem to have become a general compendium of poetical accounts of theogony, cosmogony, and the soul's nature and fate. The contents of the poems as they existed in the fifth and fourth centuries B.C. must be derived mainly from evidence in contemporary literature and, to a certain extent, in painting and sculpture.

Orpheus. It was in Greek art and literature of the sixth century B.C. that Orpheus first appeared as a famous singer. The tradition that Orpheus sang while Musaeus wrote down his master's songs may reflect the moment of transition from oral to written literature—which probably occurred in the second half of the seventh century B.C—and this may be the time when these songs were composed.

To the poets of classical Greece, Orpheus was the singer possessed of supernatural powers. As such, he was enrolled among the Argonauts. According to an Alexandrian poet, Orpheus soothed his quarreling companions by singing to them of the creation of the world and of the dynasties of the gods. Euripides wrote of Orpheus' special connection with the underworld. A Naples bas-relief, executed at the end of the fifth century B.C., depicts his attempt to bring back his wife Eurydice from the dead. A little earlier in the same century, Polygnotus executed his famous picture of the underworld in which Orpheus was shown, lyre in hand, amidst a group of legendary musicians.

It seems likely that this figure of Orpheus reflected the existing body of Orphic poetry, that his traits in fact represent its contents—a theogony which is an account of creation and a description of the underworld and of the soul's fate there.

Theogony. Plato's quotation of passages from an Orphic poem (in the *Cratylus* and *Philebus*) and Isocrates' description (in the *Busiris*) of what Orpheus wrote about suggest an Orphic theogony very like the one which is preserved as the work of Hesiod, the eighth-century B.C. oral poet. From much later writers (Athenagoras, of the second century A.D., and Damascius, of the fifth century A.D.) we learn of Orphic theogonies which contain non-Hesiodic elements—the cosmic egg and the creator Phanes. Since Phanes seems to be identifiable with the figure Eros which appears, together with the cosmic egg, in a cosmogony related in Aristophanes' fifth-century play *Birds,* both elements may accordingly be regarded as ancient. Three Orphic fragments joined by Otto Kern, which present a picture of the universe, may also be early, since this picture bears a marked resemblance to Plato's image of the universe in the myth of Er at the end of the *Republic.* According to these fragments, the heaven, the earth, the sea, and the "signs with which the heaven is ringed" are bound round with a bond of Aether.

Afterlife of the soul. Whereas Hesiod's *Theogony* contained a description of the underworld, inserted nominally in connection with the story of Zeus's overthrow of the Titans, this possibly traditional element was developed in the Orphic poems into a detailed account of the soul's fate after death, its judgment and its reincarnation. Plato, throughout his writings, plainly drew on an account of the soul's fate which he had read about in Orphic literature. In the *Gorgias* (493B) he refers to "one of the wise, who holds that the body is a tomb," and he also reports the story that the soul of an uninitiated man is like a sieve: In Hades the uninitiated is most miserable, being doomed to an eternity of filling sieves with water, by means of other sieves. Quoting the same story in the *Republic* (363D), he speaks of Musaeus and Eumolpus enlarging on the rewards of the righteous in the other world, and he also speaks of others who "when they have sung the praises of justice in that strain . . . proceed to plunge the sinners and unrighteous men into a pool of mud in the world below, and set them to fetch water in a sieve." In the *Phaedo* (69E) he says that "the man who reaches Hades without experiencing initia-

1

tion will lie in mud, whereas the initiated when he gets there will dwell with the gods." In the *Cratylus* (402B) Plato attributes specifically to the Orphic poets the theory that the body is the tomb of the soul. Two surviving Orphic fragments (Kern Fr. 222) speak of the differing fates of the just and the unjust in the afterlife, and several (Kern Fr. 223 ff.) deal with the rebirth of the soul in various forms. Plato must certainly have been referring to Orphic poems when he said in the *Meno* (81A) that among others "Pindar and many another poet who is divinely inspired . . . say that the soul of man is immortal, and at one time comes to an end, which is called dying, and at another is reborn, but never perishes. Consequently a man ought to live his life in the utmost holiness."

The Orphic life. For those who believed the eschatological dogma contained in the Orphic poems, there followed certain consequences for the conduct of life.

Prohibitions. Adikia, injustice against any living creature, had to be strictly avoided. In Euripides' *Hippolytus* the diet "of food without soul," which was required of followers of Orpheus, is mentioned. Herodotus referred to the Orphic practice, which was also Pythagorean, of avoiding the use of wool (robbed from sheep) in burial. Men who observed these scruples might be described as living an "Orphic life," in the words of Plato in the *Laws.*

Initiations. Proclus spoke of those who were initiated under Orpheus' patronage with Dionysus or Kore (in the case of the latter, at Eleusis). In Euripides' play *Rhesus,* Orpheus' amanuensis Musaeus is an Athenian, and Orpheus himself is closely connected with the Eleusinian initiations. It is certainly to these initiations that Aristophanes referred in his play *Frogs* when a character says, "Orpheus taught *teletai* [initiations] and abstinence from killing."

Evidently, the Orphic initiation had an essentially written character. Euripides referred to the person who observes Orphic scruples as "honoring the smoke of many writings." Plato mentioned "a mass of books" of Orpheus and Musaeus. Later writers contrasted this written initiation with the visual revelation at Eleusis, as when Pausanias wrote, "Whoever has seen an initiation at Eleusis or read the writings called Orphic knows what I mean." The Orphic literature seems to have borne the same relation to visual and oral instruction as a correspondence course bears to "live" teaching, and it appears to have been freely available.

Initiation into the mysteries was supposed to give a revelation of truth which would enable men to reach the next world in a state of guiltlessness. Plato reported that mendicant seers, who "frequented the doors of the rich," capitalized on this belief by offering cities and individuals the means of purification from sins committed. Among these are no doubt to be reckoned the *Orpheotelestai,* of whom Theophrastus spoke.

Significance of Orphism. Was Orphism, then, either a philosophy or a religion? It certainly was not a philosophical system, since it had no developed doctrine—merely a mythical account, derived from the popular oral poetry of the past, of the nature of the universe and of the afterlife of the soul. The philosophical importance of the Orphic

literature lies in its influence, first on Pythagoras and Empedocles and then on Plato.

Pythagoras seems to have taken over the Orphic stories so completely that they could be referred to by Aristotle as Pythagorean stories, and, earlier, Ion of Chios could say that Pythagoras had fathered his writings on Orpheus. The immortality and transmigration of the soul is the one doctrine which can certainly be attributed to the earliest Pythagorean society; Plato spoke of a Pythagorean way of life, based, as we know from other sources, on ritual prescriptions designed to ensure the purity and blamelessness of the soul.

Empedocles, who lived in Sicily in the fifth century B.C., exhibited a similar belief in the soul's immortality and transmigration.

In the *Symposium* Plato does not appear to believe in the soul's immortality, but in the *Meno* he accepts the pre-existence and survival of the soul on the authority of "divinely inspired poets," among whom Orpheus is certainly to be reckoned. This doctrine became a cornerstone of Plato's entire metaphysical system.

Orphism was not in itself a religion, although it was closely related to the initiations at Eleusis and elsewhere, which were perhaps the most striking religious manifestations of classical Greece. The Orphic element was, however, merely a traditional poetical account which provided the eschatological dogma that was the basis for certain observances to be described as a way of life. The religious depth of this way of life should not be exaggerated. There were no organized rituals, religious communities, or priesthood. In the sense in which we ordinarily use the word "religion" in the study of the ancient world, Orphism was not a religion.

Bibliography

Guthrie, W. K. C., *Orpheus and Greek Religion.* London and New York, 1935.

Kern, Otto, *Orphicorum Fragmenta.* Berlin, 1922; reprinted 1963.

Linforth, Ivan M., *Arts of Orpheus.* Berkeley, 1941.

Nilsson, M. P., "Early Orphism and Kindred Religious Movements." *Harvard Theological Review,* Vol. 28 (1935), 181–230.

JOHN MORRISON

ORTEGA Y GASSET, JOSÉ (1883–1955), Spanish essayist and philosopher, was born in Madrid of a patrician family. He was educated at a Jesuit college near Málaga and at the University of Madrid, where he received a doctorate in philosophy in 1904. Ortega spent the next five years at German universities in Berlin and Leipzig and at the University of Marburg, where he became a disciple of the Neo-Kantian philosopher Hermann Cohen. Appointed professor of metaphysics at the University of Madrid in 1910, he taught there until the outbreak of the Spanish Civil War in 1936. During those years he was also active as a journalist and as a politician. In 1923 he founded the *Revista de occidente,* a review and series of books that was instrumental in bringing Spain into touch with Western, and particularly German, thought. Ortega's work as editor and publisher, as a contribution toward "leveling the Pyrenees" that isolated Spain from contemporary culture, ranks high among his achievements.

Ortega led the republican intellectual opposition under the dictatorship of Primo de Rivera (1923–1930), and he played a part in the overthrow of King Alfonso XIII in 1931. Elected deputy for the province of León in the constituent assembly of the second Spanish republic, he was the leader of a parliamentary group of intellectuals known as *La Agrupación al servicio de la república* ("In the service of the republic") and was named civil governor of Madrid. This political commitment obliged him to leave Spain at the outbreak of the Civil War, and he spent years of exile in Argentina and western Europe. He settled in Portugal in 1945 and began to make visits to Spain. In 1948 he returned to Madrid, where, with Julián Marías, he founded the Institute of Humanities, at which he lectured. By the time of his death, Ortega was the acknowledged head of the most productive school of thinkers Spain had known for three centuries, and he had placed philosophy in Spain beyond the reach, not of opposition and criticism, but of the centuries-old reproach that it was un-Spanish or antinational and therefore either a foreign affectation or a subversive danger.

Writings and style. Ortega was a prolific writer. His numerous volumes consist mostly of essays and newspaper or magazine articles of general cultural interest. He wrote fewer strictly philosophical works; his vast influence on Spanish philosophy was exercised chiefly through his teaching.

All of Ortega's works are written in magnificent prose. He wrote in a clear, masculine style, and his mastery of Castilian has seldom been surpassed. On the other hand, he had a tendency to be wordy and to be content with literary brilliance and striking metaphor when argument and explanation were crucial.

Ortega's literary gifts had other, more important consequences. He used them to create a philosophical style and technical vocabulary in a tongue that until then had lacked models for philosophical writing and words for many modern concepts. But his literary virtuosity disarmed criticism in much of the Spanish-speaking world, so that his followers have often confounded philosophy with fine writing and emotional declamation.

Ratio-vitalism. Ortega called his philosophy the "metaphysics of vital reason," or "ratio-vitalism." By metaphysics he meant the quest for an ultimate or radical reality in which all else was rooted and from which every particular being derived its measure of reality. He found this ultimate reality in Life, a word that he first used in a biological sense, like the vitalists, but which soon came to mean "my life" and "your life"—the career and destiny of an individual in a given society and at a certain point in history. In his first philosophical book, *Meditaciones del Quijote* (1914), Ortega sought to go beyond the opposition of idealism (which, he claimed, asserted the ontological priority of the self) and realism (which asserted the priority of the things the self knows). He asserted that in truth self and things were constitutive of each other, each needing the other in order to exist. The sole reality was the self-with-things: *Yo soy yo y mi circunstancia* ("I am I

and my circumstances"). The things around me, he said in the *Meditaciones,* "are the other half of my personality." The experience-matrix comprising self and things is not simply one of coexistence, because the self acts on things and realizes itself in so doing. This activity is life, the dynamic interaction of mutually dependent self and things in the course of which the self carries out a mission of self-fulfillment.

Perspectivism. Ortega called his theory of knowledge "perspectivism." The world can be known only from a specific point of view. There is no possibility of transcending one's relative perspectives through absolute or impartial knowledge. "The definitive being of the world is neither mind nor matter nor any determinate thing but a perspective." Each perspective is unique, irreplaceable, and necessary, and all are equally true: "The only false perspective is the one that claims to be the one and only perspective." Ortega joined perspectivism to his notion of life as comprising the matrix self-with-things in the declaration, "Each life is a point of view on to the universe."

Reason and life. Although the *Meditaciones* seemed to place Ortega in the vitalist tradition, he dissociated himself from its antirationalism. Rather, just as he reconciled idealism and realism, he proposed to reconcile rationalism and vitalism. He agreed with the vitalists to "dethrone Reason," to dismiss abstract reason and bring it back to its rightful role as "only a form and function of Life." Yet Ortega stressed so strongly the rationality of the *élan vital* at the human level and underscored so firmly man's dependence on reason as an instrument for coping with life that he appeared to enthrone reason again beneath a vitalist disguise. He used the terms "Life" and "Vitality" to describe man's restless search for knowledge, understanding, and spiritual satisfaction, which others would have called "intelligence" or "practical reason." In fact, Ortega seemed to identify vitality and reason: thus, in *En torno a Galileo* (1933), he wrote, "Living means being forced to reason out our inexorable circumstances." Therefore, ratio-vitalism was more rationalism than vitalism, and Ortega's thought was far removed from the irrationalist, romantic vitalism that flourished after World War I.

Existentialism. Later, when Ortega appeared to have joined the existentialists (or, as he would have said, was joined by them), his insistence on the role of reason in the existential predicament gave his theories a distinctive color and allowed him to pour scorn on the sentimentalism of French existentialism. Ortega's dissociation from vitalism became complete when he took account of "the historical horizons of human life"—that is, of the social and cultural conditions of vitality in mankind. He gradually came to prefer the term "historical reason" to "vital reason." Life for Ortega now meant not biological vitality but "one man's life," and the vocation of the self was now conceived as what it must do with things—a mission of self-realization. This is the language of existentialism, and Ortega spoke it with a rare eloquence.

Man does not have a nature, but a history. . . . Man is no thing, but a drama. . . . His life is something that has to be chosen, made up as he goes along, and a man consists in that choice and invention. Each man is the novelist of himself, and though he may choose between being an original writer and a plagiarist, he cannot escape choosing. . . . He is condemned to be free. . . . Freedom is not an activity exercised by an entity that already possessed a fixed being before and apart from that activity. Being free means . . . being able to be something else than what one is and not being able to settle down once and for all in any determined nature. . . . Unlike all the other things in the universe which have a pre-fixed being given to them, man is the only and almost inconceivable reality that exists without having an irrevocably pre-fixed being. . . . It is not only in economics but also in metaphysics that man must earn his living [*ganarse la vida*, win his life]. (*Historia como sistema*)

Each man has one best choice, and this is his imperative vocation or mission. " 'Mission' means the awareness that each man has of his most authentic self which he is called upon to realize. The idea of mission is a constitutive ingredient of the human condition. . . . The being of man is at one and the same time natural and extranatural, a sort of ontological centaur" (*Obras completas*, Vol. V, pp. 209, 334). Ortega's moral theory thus derives directly from his anthropology; and indeed it is difficult, as with other existentialists, to separate his metaphysics from his anthropology and ethics. The moral life is the authentic one, the one that stays faithful to a life project or vocation; the immoral life is to abandon oneself to transient, outside influences, to drift instead of realizing a personal destiny. The choice of one personality out of the various possible personalities engages the whole of a man's reasoning powers and requires perpetual lucidity and concentration. This helps to explain Ortega's emphasis on the rationality of the *élan vital* at the human level. It is by intelligent reckoning with his circumstances that a man gains his being and becomes himself. Reasoned choice is constitutive of human personality.

Social theory. Life is always a problem, an insecurity, a "shipwreck," not only for the individual but for societies too. The desperate measures society takes to struggle against perpetual foundering constitute human culture. It was Ortega's social theory, set forth in *La rebelión de las masas* in 1930 (*The Revolt of the Masses*, New York, 1931), that first brought him international recognition. Ortega started from the belief that culture is radically insecure and that a constant effort is required to prevent it from lapsing into barbarism and torpor. That effort is beyond most men, who can merely contribute to it by accepting the leadership of a liberal aristocracy, which does most of humanity's works. The fact that men have no essence or fixed nature but each must choose himself implies their inequality. "Because the being of man is not given to him but is a pure imaginary possibility, the human species is of an instability and variability that make it incomparable with animal species. Men are enormously unequal, in spite of what the egalitarians of the last two centuries affirmed and of what old-fashioned folk of this century go on affirming" (*Meditación de la técnica*, p. 42).

Ortega distinguished interindividual from social relations. In the former, which include love and friendship, individuals behave as rational and responsible persons, whereas in social relationships, which include customs, laws, and the state, we encounter the irrational and impersonal, the imposed and anonymous. The resulting contrast of man and people (*El hombre y la gente*), of the individual and the collectivity, betrayed Ortega's aristocratic distrust of democracy and contemporary mass society. There is no collective soul, he said, because "society, the collectivity, is the great soulless one, because it is humanity naturalized, mechanized and as if mineralized." Everything that is social or collective is subhuman, intermediate between genuine humanity and nature; it is a "quasi-nature." Nevertheless, social relationships have their uses; they make other people's behavior predictable, they carry on inherited traditions, and by automatizing part of our lives, they set us free for creation in the important interindividual sphere. These gains of socialization need constant defense, for men's antisocial drives are never vanquished. Society is neither spontaneous nor self-perpetuating. It has to be invented and reinvented by a minority which, however, must be able to procure the cooperation of the masses. The elite is essential to any society; by proposing a project for collective living, it founds the community and then governs and directs it.

The masses are incapable of framing a project, for they live without plan or effort. When they revolt and claim to govern themselves, society is threatened with dissolution. Ortega thought this was happening in twentieth-century democracies, whether totalitarian, communist, or parliamentary. Nationalism was exhausted as a collective project, and the next plan had to be supranational. Ortega favored the "Europeanization of Spain" in a supranational entity governed by an irreligious intellectual elite. Catholicism was to be extirpated, but gradually and cautiously, with a first stage of "liberal religion" leading toward the secular state.

The sensitive intellectual would have as little as possible to do with governing, for it was inevitably degrading. "There is no political health when the government functions without the active cooperation of majorities. Perhaps this is why politics seems to me a second-class occupation" (*Invertebrate Spain*, p. 201).

Aristocratic logic. The notion of an aristocracy of talents is the key to Ortega's logic. In *Ideas y creencias* ("Ideas and Beliefs," in *Obras completas*, Vol. V, pp. 377–489), he claimed that ideas are the personal creation of the thinking minority, while the mass lazily accepts plain commonsense beliefs that in reality are vulgar ruling opinions imposed by "a diffuse authoritarianism." The archetype of mob belief is empiricism, or as Ortega called it, "sensualism." Sensualism is a reliance on the evidence of the senses, on self-evident truisms, on experiments in science or on documents in history. Philosophy since Parmenides has been a reaction against the vulgar prejudice in favor of the senses. "Against the *doxa* of belief in the senses, philosophy is, constitutionally and not accidentally, *paradox*" (*La idea de principio*, p. 285).

These views were developed with remarkable vigor in his unfinished, posthumously published magnum opus, *La idea de principio en Leibniz y la evolución de la teoría deductiva* ("The Idea of Principle in Leibniz and the Evolution of Deductive Theory," Buenos Aires, 1958). He assailed every form of the belief that principles or axioms can be founded on sensible intuition, taking Aristotle as the first representative of this belief and following its transmission through the Stoics and Scholastics. Such a belief, Ortega declared, is "idiot," "plebeian"; it results from a mental derangement akin to catalepsy, in that it entails sitting bemused before brute reality instead of thinking creatively. The only principles available to us, he held, are posed arbitrarily by the mind. They are assumptions that cannot be proved to the satisfaction of the senses, but "prove themselves" by allowing the deduction of a coherent corpus of propositions. This is the advance of post-Cartesian thought over traditional realism. "Modern philosophy no longer begins with Being but with Thought" (*La idea de principio*, p. 263). The only proof modern philosophy knows is theoretical use: if axioms or methods give good results, there is no more to be said.

> Principles can only come from the understanding itself as it is before and apart from any acquaintance with sensible things. From these purely intellectual principles may be deduced consequences that form a whole world of intellectual determinations, that is, of ideal objects. . . . The activity of knowing used to seem to consist in an effort to reflect, mirror, or copy in our mind the world of real things, but it turns out to be just the opposite, namely, the invention, construction, or fabrication of an unreal world. (*Ibid.*, p. 394)

Since he considered this idealist logic a characteristically aristocratic attitude, Ortega thought it significant that Plato and Descartes, the two men who did most to construct it, were of noble blood. In contrast, the empiricism of Aristotle was popular, vulgar, "demagogic." "It is the criteriology of Sancho Panza. Faith in the senses is a traditional dogma, a public institution established by the irresponsible and anonymous opinion of the People, the collectivity" (*ibid.*, p. 286). Even the principle of contradiction, "that dogma of ontological sensualism," was a mere commonplace of the collective mind, unsupported by reasons and anything but self-evident. Aristotle had failed to prove the principle of contradiction, that *A* could not both be and not be *X*, and Kant's transcendental deduction of it had no force. Ortega was not seeking to dispense with that principle but to argue that it could not be proven. Logic is a calculus tested by coherence, not an abstraction from sensible experience. Principles are assumptions that are useful for particular purposes.

Philosophy, science, and mathematics are "pure exact fantasy" based on principles that are arbitrary conventions. They are phantasmagoria, not far removed from poetry. They are the creation of an aristocracy of intellect that reveals the characteristics of all aristocracies: playfulness, lack of seriousness, and love of sport and games. Ortega meant quite literally that logic and science were games played according to strict but perfectly gratuitous rules by a minority that seeks to escape the tedium, vulgarity, and deadly seriousness of the world of beliefs. We never really believe in science or philosophy; they remain "mere ideas" to play with, and they are always somewhat spectral and unserious compared with the visceral faith we put into beliefs. Theory, like any fantasy, is by definition always revocable. Therefore, we ought to play at philosophy, jovially and without pathos, with the mock seriousness required to "obey the rules of the game."

Works by Ortega

Obras completas, 3d ed., 6 vols. Madrid, 1953. Contains Ortega's work up to 1943, except for certain political writings, such as *Rectificación de la República* (Madrid, 1931) and *La redención de las provincias y la decencia nacional* (Madrid, 1931).

Obras inéditas, 7 vols. Madrid and Buenos Aires, 1957–1961. Contains the later and posthumously published works.

Meditaciones del Quijote. Madrid, 1914. Translated by E. Rugg and D. Marín as *Meditations on Quixote*. New York, 1961.

España invertebrada. Madrid, 1922. Translated by M. Adams as *Invertebrate Spain*. New York, 1937.

El tema de nuestro tiempo. Madrid, 1923. Translated by James Cleugh as *The Modern Theme*. London, 1931.

La deshumanización del arte. Madrid, 1925. Translated by W. Trask as *The Dehumanization of Art*. New York, 1956.

En torno a Galileo. Madrid, 1933. Translated by M. Adams as *Man and Crisis*. New York, 1958.

Meditación de la técnica. Madrid, 1933.

Estudios sobre el amor. Madrid, 1939. Translated by T. Talbot as *On Love*. New York, 1957.

Del imperio romano. Madrid, 1940–1941. Translated by H. Weyl as *Concord and Liberty*. New York, 1946.

Historia como sistema. Madrid, 1941. Translated by H. Weyl, E. Clark, and W. Atkinson as *Toward a Philosophy of History*. New York, 1941; 2d ed., *History as a System*. New York, 1961.

El hombre y la gente. Madrid, 1957. Translated by W. Trask as *Man and People*. New York, 1959.

Qué es filosofía? Madrid, 1957. Translated by M. Adams as *What Is Philosophy?* New York, 1960.

Works on Ortega

Borel, J., *Raison et vie chez Ortega y Gasset*. Neuchâtel, 1959.

Cascalès, Charles, *L'Humanisme d'Ortega y Gasset*. Paris, 1956.

Ceplecha, C., *The Historical Thought of José Ortega y Gasset*. New Haven, Conn., 1957.

Guy, Alain, *Ortega y Gasset, critique d'Aristote*. Paris, 1963.

Marías, Julián, *Historia de la filosofía*. Madrid, 1941.

Marías, Julián, *Ortega y tres antípodas*. Buenos Aires, 1950.

Marías, Julián, *La escuela de Madrid*. Buenos Aires, 1959.

Marías, Julián, *Ortega, circunstancia y vocación*. Madrid, 1960.

Ramírez, Santiago, *La filosofía de Ortega y Gasset*. Barcelona, 1958.

Ramírez, Santiago, *Un orteguismo católico*. Salamanca, 1958.

Ramírez, Santiago, *La zona de seguridad*. Madrid, 1959.

NEIL McINNES

OSTWALD, WILHELM (1853–1932), German chemist, philosopher, and historian of science. Ostwald's main scientific achievement was his pioneer work in physical chemistry, particularly in electrochemistry. With J. H. van't Hoff he founded the *Zeitschrift für physikalische Chemie* in 1887. He was awarded the Nobel prize in chemistry in 1909.

Energetism. Ostwald's philosophical outlook, known as energetism or energetic monism, was strongly influenced by his scientific background and by the state of physical science at the end of the nineteenth century. In particular, the first and second laws of thermodynamics—the law of conservation of energy and the law of entropy—decisively influenced his thought. Ostwald claimed that energy is the substrate of all phenomena and that all observable changes can be interpreted as transformations of one kind of energy into another. This claim was based on both epistemological and physical considerations. Ostwald pointed out that we never perceive anything but energy, or more accurately, differences in energy. One never perceives a material substance itself, but only its energetic interaction with his own organism. In an argument similar to a classical argument of Descartes's, Ostwald showed that even impenetrability, which, according to mechanists, is the constitutive feature of matter, is a mere sensory quality that is perceived only when there is a difference in kinetic energy between a piece of matter and one's own organism. No sensation of hardness would arise if a piece of matter which one tried to touch retreated at the same velocity with which his finger moved toward it. Ostwald interpreted all aspects of matter in terms of energy: mass is the capacity of kinetic energy; occupancy of space is "volume-energy"; gravity is energy of distance. Thus, matter is nothing but a "spatially ordered group of various energies" which do not require any material substrate. Material substance belongs with caloric, phlogiston, and electric and magnetic fluids in the category of discarded and useless fictions. Ostwald prophesied that ether too would soon disappear from science, as the increasing difficulties in constructing a satisfactory model of it indicated.

This difficulty was for Ostwald only one symptom of mechanism's general failure to provide a satisfactory explanation of physical phenomena. He even doubted the usefulness of kinetic explanations of thermal phenomena, although the mechanical theory of heat had been extremely successful. The atom itself was for Ostwald only a convenient methodological fiction, which he refused to reify. (Only around 1908, under the growing pressure of new experimental confirmations of the discontinuous structure of matter, did he modify his view.)

The ubiquity and constancy of energy make it "the most general substance," and the conservation of energy underlies the validity of the law of causation. The succession of cause and effect is nothing but the transformation of one form of energy into another, the total amount of energy remaining constant. The law of conservation of energy guarantees the quantitative equality of cause and effect; and the direction of transformations is determined by the law of entropy, according to which all forms of energy are being gradually transformed into heat. Ostwald rejected all attempts to limit the application of the law of entropy; opposition to applying it to the whole of cosmic history was, in his view, nothing but emotional reluctance to accept the eventual death of civilization and even of mankind. The mechanistic view, which regards all processes as in principle reversible, fails to account for the irreversibility of time embodied in the law of entropy.

Ostwald belonged to a generation of philosophers of science that included Ernst Mach, Pierre Duhem, and J. B. Stallo, who were acutely aware of the limitations of mechanistic explanations. They overlooked the power and fruitfulness of mechanical and particularly of corpuscular models even on the molecular level, and atomic physics was not yet advanced enough to show the inadequacy of corpuscular models of subatomic phenomena. When this inadequacy became apparent, the crisis of the traditional scheme proved to be far more profound than Ostwald expected. While claiming to reduce all manifestations of matter to energy, he still retained mass, the basic concept of mechanism, under the disguised form of "capacity of energy." He anticipated the later relativistic fusion of mass and energy only in a hazy and qualitative way.

In this respect Ostwald can be compared with Herbert Spencer, with whom he shared other ideas: the substantialization of energy, the deduction of the causal law from the law of conservation of energy, an energetist approach to social science and ethics, and a determinist monistic metaphysics disguised by positivistic and agnostic formulas. Ostwald, however, lacked Spencer's philosophical sophistication; this is especially visible in his approach to the mind–body problem. Ostwald believed that he had refuted materialism by identifying consciousness with neural energy; he did not realize that his view was only a variant of physicalism. Like Ernst Haeckel, whom he greatly respected, Ostwald believed that his view was identical with Spinoza's double-aspect theory, but this is not true. The haziness of Ostwald's monism invited criticism from antagonistic camps; Hans Driesch called it disguised materialism, and Lenin denounced it as "sheer idealism."

Ostwald devoted much time to propagating his views on monism. He founded the pantheistically oriented League of German Monists in 1906, and in 1911 he began to publish the series Monist Sunday Sermons (*Monistische Sonntagspredigten*).

Ethics and social thought. Ostwald regarded the law of entropy as the basis for the theory of values. What we term "mind" or "consciousness" is nothing but a form of neural energy and is subject to the same laws as other forms of energy. In a temporally reversible world the concept of value would be meaningless, whereas it acquires a precise scientific meaning in the framework of energetism. Evolutionary advance consists in the fact that increased coordination between increasingly specialized organs results in increased efficiency of the organism and a minimum waste of energy. The same law—increased coordination resulting in maximum efficiency—determines the progress of civilization. Kant's categorical imperative should be replaced by the "energetic imperative": "Do not waste your energy." Ostwald's applications of his energetic imperative to social thought were even more ambiguous than his views on the mind–body problem. Prior to 1914 Ostwald regarded war and conflict as a wasting of energy, and he favored internationalism and pacifism. But during World War I he justified his militant nationalism by claiming that the organization, efficiency, and minimum waste of energy of the German state represented the highest existing evolutionary form of human society.

History of science. In history of science Ostwald deserves credit for editing *Ostwalds Klassiker der exacten Wissenschaften,* a series of reprints of important scientific writings. His own classification of creative scientific minds into "classics" and "romantics," however, is probably oversimplified although interesting. Ostwald also founded and edited the journal *Annalen der Philosophie* (1901–1921).

Works by Ostwald

Die Überwindung des wissenschaftlichen Materialismus. Leipzig, 1895.

Vorlesungen über die Naturphilosophie. Leipzig, 1895; 2d ed., Leipzig, 1902.

Individuality and Immortality. Boston and New York, 1906. The Ingersoll lecture.

Grundrisse der Naturphilosophie. Leipzig, 1908.

Die energetische Grundlagen der Kulturwissenschaften. Leipzig, 1909.

Der energetische Imperativ. Leipzig, 1912.

Monism as the Goal of Civilization. Hamburg, 1913.

Die Philosophie der Werte. Leipzig, 1913.

Lebenslinien, 3 vols. Leipzig, 1926–1927. Autobiography.

Wissenschaft und Gottesglaube, F. Herneck, ed. Leipzig, 1960.

Works on Ostwald

Adler, F. W., *Die Metaphysik in der Ostwaldschen Energetik.* 1905.

Delbos, Victor, *Une Théorie allemande de culture: W. Ostwald et sa philosophie.* Paris, 1916.

Driesch, Hans, *Naturbegriffe und Natururteile.* Leipzig, 1904.

Duhem, Pierre, *L'Évolution de la mécanique.* Paris, 1903. Esp. p. 179.

Lasswitz, K., "Die moderne Energetik in ihrer Bedeutung für die Erkenntniskritik." *Philosophische Monatshefte,* Vol. 39, 1–30, 177–197.

Lenin, V. I., *Materializm i Empirio-krititsizm.* Moscow, 1908. Translated by David Kirtko and Sidney Hook as *Materialism and Empirio-criticism.* New York, 1927. Esp. Ch. 5.

Meyerson, Émile, *L'Identité et réalité,* 5th ed. Paris, 1951. Esp. Ch. 10. Translated from the 1908 edition by Kate Loewenberg as *Identity and Reality.* London, 1930.

Rey, Abel, *La Théorie de la physique chez les physiciens contemporains,* 2d ed. Paris, 1923.

Rolla, A., *La filosofia energetica.* Turin, 1908.

Schnehen, Wilhelm von, *Energetische Weltanschauung.* Leipzig, 1908.

MILIČ ČAPEK

OTHER MINDS. The question of how each of us knows that there are other beings besides himself who have thoughts, feelings, and other mental attributes has been widely discussed, especially among analytic philosophers in the English-speaking world. At least three of the most influential German philosophers—namely, Husserl, Scheler, and Heidegger—have also dealt with this problem. The problem of other minds becomes a serious and difficult one because the traditional and most obvious solution to it, the argument from analogy, is open to grave objections. At the present time it would seem that a majority of the philosophers who have concerned themselves with the question consider the traditional solution—that our belief in other minds can be adequately justified by an analogical argument—at least inadequate, if not radically and unremediably defective.

ARGUMENT FROM ANALOGY

In general terms to argue by analogy is to argue on the principle that if a given phenomenon A has been found to be associated with another phenomenon B, then any phenomenon similar to A is very likely to be associated with a phenomenon similar to B. In the particular case of other minds, it is said, I observe that there is an association between my mental states, on the one hand, and my behavior and the physical state of my body, on the other. I then notice that there are other bodies similar to mine and that they exhibit behavior similar to my own. I am

justified, therefore, in concluding by analogy that mental states like the ones I experience are associated with those other bodies in the same way that my mental states are associated with my body. I notice, for example, that when I have a pain in my tooth, it is likely to be decayed and that I am likely to groan, complain, and hold my jaw. Observing another body like my own that has a decayed tooth and behaves as my body behaves when I have a toothache, I conclude that this body, like mine, is the body of a being that has a toothache.

Objections to the analogy argument. The first and least radical objection to the argument from analogy is that it does not establish its conclusion with an adequate degree of certainty. The argument, it is said, would be relatively strong if the correlation of the mental and the physical was observed to hold in a large and varied collection of instances before it was concluded that it also held in other similar cases. But this is not so. If I use the argument from analogy, I have only one case, my own, as a basis for my inference. Moreover, the characteristics and behavior of the other bodies vary markedly from my own. How can I be sure that the differences between myself and others are not associated with the presence of mental attributes in my own case and with the absence of them in other cases?

The other difficulties in the argument from analogy concern two features of that argument—first, that it is logically impossible to check up on the correctness of the conclusion of the argument and, second, that the argument's validity implies that one must learn from one's own case alone what it is to have a mental attribute. Let us elaborate a little on each of these points.

In the case of a normal analogical argument, it makes good sense to suppose that one might check up directly on the conclusion of the argument; in principle one could always dispense with reasoning by analogy, even though this may not be practicable in some cases. Of course, one who says that we know of the existence of other minds by analogy must deny that we can check up on our conclusion in some more direct way, for if we could, the argument by analogy with ourselves could be dispensed with. It also seems that he cannot say that our inability to check up is merely a practical matter. Such checking up cannot consist in making further observations of a person's behavior and body; this we can often do sufficiently well in practice. It would have to consist in some other operation which we cannot in fact perform but which we can conceive of ourselves performing; perhaps it would be something like telepathy. But aside from any difficulty in making clear sense of the notion of telepathy, why should telepathy be regarded as a more direct way of checking up than ordinary observation of behavior? Indeed, it seems that one's grounds for thinking that one has telepathic knowledge of another person's state of mind must include the knowledge that what one seemed to know telepathically generally correlates well with what one knows as a result of ordinary observation. The same would also seem to apply to any other extraordinary but conceivable way of knowing about another's mental state. Granted, then, that the supporter of the argument from analogy must hold that the impossibility of checking the conclusion more directly is not any variety of empirical impossibility, why is this held to destroy the argument? Perhaps there is a difference here between this argument and other valid analogical arguments, but why does this difference make this argument unacceptable? The answer given is that this difference renders the conclusion of the argument senseless. What can the phrase "He is in pain" mean to me if no conceivable observation I could make would show that it was true or false, if I have no criterion for its truth, and if I have no idea of what would count for or against it? It will not do to say that the sentence means that he has the same as I have when I am in pain, for, again, what counts as being the same here?

The other main difficulty in the analogical argument centers, as we have said, on the necessity, implied by that argument, for each of us to learn from his own case alone what it is to have a mental attribute. Two arguments have been advanced to show that this is impossible.

According to the first, which derives from Wittgenstein, the analogical argument requires that one be able to pick out something (for example, a pain or a state of anger) and thereafter to identify it, when it recurs, as a pain or a state of anger. The trouble is, however, that this account leaves no room for a distinction between a correct and an incorrect identification. Behavioral and other checks are ruled out, leaving no conceivable means of deciding whether a mistake has been made. But a distinction between a correct and a mistaken identification is surely essential to the very notion of identification itself. In this way the analogical argument, which requires that we be able to make correct identifications of our inner states, also deprives the notion of identification of any meaning.

The second argument, which has been advanced by P. F. Strawson, is more complex. According to him, the idea of a predicate involves the idea of a range of individuals to which that predicate can be significantly applied. In the case of mental attributes, this range includes both oneself and others; one cannot have the notion of a mental attribute unless one has a notion of oneself and a notion of another. Since the notion of oneself is the notion of a subject of mental and other attributes, one cannot have the notion of oneself without the notion of some mental attributes. Therefore, one cannot have a notion of oneself without also having the notion of another subject of mental attributes. This notion, however, can be possessed only if one knows how to ascribe mental attributes to such subjects. Hence, until one knows how to do this, one has no notion either of oneself or of another. But the argument from analogy requires that one should first have a notion of oneself, of one's own case, and then discover how to ascribe mental attributes to others by arguing analogically from correlations that are found to hold in one's own case. A person without a notion of his own case could indeed argue analogically. He could find that pain was to be expected when a certain body (his own, as *we* say) was branded with a hot iron. He could infer that there would also be a pain when another similar body was similarly affected. But he would soon find out that he was mistaken in this conclusion, for he would detect no pain when the hot iron was applied to any body other than his own.

Defenses of analogy argument. Some persistent attempts (especially by A. J. Ayer) have been made to defend the argument from analogy against the charges laid against it. To counter the charge of weakness, the following suggestions have been made. Emphasis has been laid upon the special feature of the argument from analogy—that people can speak and that their descriptions of their mental states are very like those I would give of some of my own. This, it is claimed, is something more telling than a mere similarity of behavior. Against this it is pointed out that speech can be regarded as something understood by the speaker only if it is accompanied by the appropriate nonverbal behavior.

Another defense is that conclusions drawn analogically from behavioristic similarities are powerfully reinforced by like conclusions drawn by arguments based on similarities in the state of the nervous system. This consideration hardly meets the main complaint—namely, that I base my inference on one case only, my own.

According to a rather more convincing attempt to meet this complaint, no more can be asked of any method of inference than that I be able to test its conclusion more directly in some cases and that when I do so, the conclusion usually turns out to be correct. The argument from analogy satisfies this test. I can suppose that there are, as there seem to be, other people besides myself and that these people argue analogically that I have certain thoughts and feelings. I can check on these imagined inferences and find that their conclusions are generally true. Whether these inferences are in fact made is neither here nor there; I can see that the method would work if it were used. Nor need I be worried because I can check only those cases in which the conclusion is about myself. In all or most inferences there will be a restricted class of cases that I can check up on. It is, for instance, logically impossible that I should make a direct check on a change of color that occurred where I could not observe it. But it would be a mistake to argue that any analogical argument that a color change had occurred was weak because it was based upon one sort of case only—the sort that I was able to observe. Why should it make a difference to the strength of the other minds argument that the relevant class of case is my own mental states as opposed to what I myself observe?

An argument similar to this one can also be used to rebut the charge that there is no conceivable means of checking up on the conclusion of the argument from analogy. There are in fact some cases in which I can make a check—namely, those cases that concern myself. Moreover, although it is logically impossible for me to be some other person and hence to make a direct check on that other person's mental states, this is unimportant, for it is never logically impossible that I should check on the truth of a psychological statement when the subject is referred to by a descriptive phrase, even though that description fits someone other than myself. It is logically impossible, perhaps, that I should be Robinson, but it is not logically impossible that I should now be the man flying a certain aircraft, even though Robinson is in fact that man. Moreover, it is claimed, when I make a statement about Robinson, what is stated is, in effect, that someone who answers to such and such a description has had such and such an experience. To this it has been objected that the only interpretation of this claim that yields the desired conclusion is untrue, namely, the interpretation that "Robinson has a pain" means the same thing as some sentence of the form "The so and so has a pain." However, this objection clearly fails to settle the matter, as can be seen by considering the following statements:

(1) The man sitting in this chair is angry.
(2) Robinson is the man sitting in this chair.
(3) Robinson is angry.

Statement (1) cannot be said to be unintelligible to me on the ground that I, not being the man in question, cannot check up directly, for it is conceivable that I might have been sitting in the chair; statement (2) can also be checked on by me; statement (3) follows from (1) and (2). It is surely quite implausible to hold that statement (3) is unintelligible to me, whereas statements (1) and (2) are not.

There is, however, another possible difficulty in the argument from analogy which is usually not at all clearly distinguished from the one just considered—namely, that it is in principle impossible for more than one person to check directly on the conclusion. It is often said that publicity is the essential requirement. But does this mean that it must be logically possible for each person to make the check, or is it the more stringent requirement that it be possible for everyone, or at least more than one, to do so? If the latter, then the difficulty has not been overcome. Equally it has not been shown clearly why publicity should be required in the more, rather than in the less, stringent form.

This brings us to the reasons given for holding that one cannot understand psychological predicates from one's own case alone, which is a requirement of the argument from analogy. One of these reasons, as we have seen, is that there is no sense in the idea of an identification that is subject to no check, where there is no criterion of correctness. This view has been questioned on two grounds. P. F. Strawson has argued that a criterion of correctness is not needed in all cases of identification, and according to A. J. Ayer, an identification of a sensation can be satisfactorily checked, without recourse to anything publicly observable, by means of other private sensations.

OTHER SOLUTIONS TO THE PROBLEM

Behaviorism. Assuming that the argument from analogy is unacceptable, the most obvious alternative is to adopt some form of that variety of behaviorism according to which all psychological expressions can be fully understood in terms of behavior. If behaviorism is correct, there is clearly no room or need for the argument from analogy. In ascribing a pain to someone, for example, one is asserting something that is in principle subject to a public check—something about the way the individual is behaving, about how he would behave in certain circumstances, about what the circumstances in fact are, or the like. There is no need to make any inference from the publicly observable to something radically different.

This is not the place for a general discussion of behaviorism. Any objection to a given form of behaviorism will, of course, be an objection to that form of behaviorism as a solution to the problem of other minds. There is, however, one difficulty that has given rise to a number of closely related attempts to deal with the problem—namely, that it is implausible to give a behavioristic account of some first-person psychological statements. When, for example, I say that I have a terrible pain, I do not say this on the basis of observation of my own behavior and the circumstances in which I am placed. Nor am I speculating about how I would behave in other, hypothetical circumstances. This difficulty has become of central importance for many philosophers who are impressed by some or all of the arguments that purport to refute the argument from analogy. They regard such arguments as showing, not only that this argument fails, but, more positively, that the connection between mental states, on the one hand, and behavior and circumstances, on the other, is logical or conceptual, not contingent. What is needed to remove the difficulty about our knowledge of other minds, it is thought, is to clear away the obstacles that prevent us from seeing clearly that this connection *is* a conceptual one. The primary obstacle in this instance is the peculiar nature of first-person psychological statements. It is this obstacle that prevents us from wholeheartedly accepting the true view and that makes us always hark back to the picture of mental states as objects to which the owner has privileged access.

There are at least two points involved here. First, if my own statements about my mental states are not about private happenings to which only I have access and if they are not about my behavior either, then what account *is* to be given of them? Second, the statement "I am in pain," made by me, contradicts the statement "He is not in pain," made about me by someone else. If one admits that the former is not about my behavior, how can one avoid the conclusion that the latter also is not about my behavior? But if the latter is not about my behavior, how can it be maintained that the connection between my pain and my behavior is a logical one?

Wittgenstein. In dealing with the question "How do words refer to sensations?" Wittgenstein suggested, "Here is one possibility: words are connected with the primitive, the natural, expressions of sensation and used in their place" (*Philosophical Investigations,* Sec. 244). This suggestion, which is not elaborated much by Wittgenstein, has sometimes been treated as an attempt to deal with the first point stated above and has had certain merits ascribed to it—for example, by Norman Malcolm. It explains how the utterance of a first-person psychological statement can have importance for us; such an utterance has the importance that natural expressions of sensation and emotion have. It is also said to explain certain features of the logic of psychological statements, the absurdity of someone's concluding that he has a pain from the observation of his own behavior, and the impossibility of someone's being mistaken about whether he has a pain or of wondering whether he has a pain. However, whatever its merits, this stress on the likeness of first-person sensation statements to natural expressions of emotion and sensation merely sharpens the second of the difficulties noted above—namely, that "I am in pain" can contradict "He is not in pain." It even makes it hard to see how the former can be a statement at all; a cry of pain is not a statement.

This difficulty is obviously insuperable for one who, unlike Wittgenstein, adopts the extreme position that apart from being verbal and learned responses, first-person sensation statements are *exactly* like natural expressions of sensation. Wittgenstein, however, appears to hold that a statement like "My leg hurts" is never in all respects like a cry of pain but is sometimes more like it and sometimes less, depending on the context of utterance. There seem to be three main likenesses that he wanted to stress in all first-person present-tense expressions of sensation and in many such expressions of emotion—namely, (1) the impossibility of these expressions being mistakenly uttered; (2) the possibility of their being insincere or pretended; and (3) the fact that such statements can justifiably be made without a basis of self-observation. The problem that arises in formulating a successful defense of his views is showing how a statement that bears the above likenesses to a cry of pain can yet be different enough to contradict another statement for which the criteria of truth lie in the realm of the publicly observable—that is, in the behavior of the speaker. It cannot be said that Wittgenstein himself made a serious attempt to cope with this difficulty. Others have made the attempt, but no attempt has been very convincing. The second and third points of likeness present no great difficulty (see Douglas Gasking, "Avowals"). Any statement can be made insincerely, and there are many nonautobiographical statements that a person can justifiably make without observing that the criteria for their truth are satisfied. For example, some people can tell you that a certain note is middle C without first carrying out the tests that determine whether it has the appropriate frequency. For such statements to be justified, it is necessary only that those who make them are usually right in such cases.

Alleged incorrigibility. The first difficulty, which arises from the alleged incorrigibility (as it is termed) of first-person present-tense statements, is not so easily disposed of. The most hopeful approach—indeed, the only approach—is to exploit the fact that the natural expressions of sensation and emotion can be feigned. An insincere groan is akin to a lie, and a lie is a false statement. Perhaps a verbal expression can reasonably be called false if it is insincere and true if it is sincere, the distinction between sincerity and insincerity being a matter of the behavior of the speaker. In this way a plausible account could be given of how something very like a groan could also in some ways be like a statement and be regarded as such. The incorrigibility of such statements would then be accounted for. But this is not enough; it does not explain how such a "statement" can be the contradictory of another statement that is logically connected with statements about the behavior of the maker of the "statement." For (1) "I have pain," said by me about myself, is the contradictory of (2) "I have not a pain," said by me about myself. Therefore, since (3) "He has a pain," said about me by someone else, is also the contradictory of (2), (1) and (3) must both be the same statement. Consequently, if (3) is logically connected with certain behavioral statements, (1) must also have these connections. This makes it difficult to see how (1) can be incorrigible. If I can be mistaken about my own behavior, as is the case, and if there is a logical connection between my pain and my behavior, then, it would seem, I can be mistaken about my pain. This difficulty is not overcome by assimilating the truth of a first-person pain statement to the sincerity of a groan. For (4) "I am sincere in saying I have a pain," said by me about myself, is the same statement as (5) "He is sincere in saying he has a pain," said about me by someone else. Therefore, if (5) is logically connected with statements about my behavior, so is (4), and, if (4) is so connected, it must, it seems, be corrigible. For to claim sincerely that *p* is to think that *p* when one makes the claim, and to claim insincerely that *p* is to think that not-*p* when one makes the claim. If (4) is corrigible, then someone might think he is sincere in claiming he has a pain when in fact he is insincere—that is to say, he might think that he thinks that he has a pain, although in fact he thinks that he has not a pain. If, however, one cannot be mistaken about one's own pain, then to think that one thinks one has a pain is to think one has a pain, and to think one has not a pain is not to have a pain. It follows that if (4) is corrigible, someone might think that he has a pain although, in fact, he has not a pain. In short, if (4) is corrigible and (1) is not, then (1) is corrigible.

There are apparently only two ways out of these difficulties that do not involve abandoning the thesis of the incorrigibility of first-person psychological statements and thus ceasing to attach much value to the assimilation of such statements to natural expressions of emotion and sensation. One might deny that (1) and (3) are the same statement, or one might maintain that although (1) is logically connected with behavioral statements about which I can be mistaken, yet I cannot be mistaken about (1). The first of these alternatives would involve finding a satisfactory explanation of why I cannot assert the same thing that someone else does when he asserts (3). The second would require an account of the notion of a logical connection that would allow for the existence of statements which, when made by myself, are incorrigible, but which are logically connected with other statements that, when made by myself, are not incorrigible. In fact it has been argued by some that there are no psychological statements that are incorrigible and that the problem we have just been discussing is therefore an unnecessary one. It seems to be quite true that there are some ways in which one can be mistaken when one says one has, say, a pain. But the matter has not yet been clarified sufficiently for anyone to be justified in saying with confidence that this renders the problem unnecessary. Even if first-person present-tense pain statements are corrigible, this does not show that they are corrigible in all the ways that other statements are corrigible. Nor has it been shown convincingly that they are corrigible in such a way as to obviate any difficulty which may arise from the fact that "I have a pain," said by me, contradicts "He has a pain," said about me.

In addition to the above objections to Wittgenstein's views on the subject of psychological statements, there is another one which is of a less definite character and to which Wittgenstein himself alludes when he puts into the mouth of an imaginary objector such words as " . . . and yet you again and again reach the conclusion that the sensation itself is a *nothing*" (*Philosophical Investigations*, Sec. 304). He protests, of course, that this is not the sort of impression he wishes to create and that it arises from his "setting his face against the picture of the inner process."

Nevertheless, it cannot be said that he altogether succeeds in dispelling this impression. His problem might indeed be described in just these terms—to set his face against the inner process picture without creating the impression that he wishes to deny the existence of sensations. It does not seem that he succeeds in this.

P. F. Strawson. It is perhaps Wittgenstein's failure that in part gives rise to another attack on the problem—namely, that of P. F. Strawson. Strawson, like Wittgenstein, is convinced that the argument from analogy is mistaken and that skepticism about other minds is senseless or at least empty and pointless. Like Wittgenstein, he holds that the relation of the behavior of other people to their mental states is not contingent: " . . . the behavior-criteria one goes on [in assigning P-predicates—that is, psychological predicates] are not just signs of the presence of what is meant by the P-predicate, but are criteria of a logically adequate kind for the ascription of the P-predicate" (*Individuals*, p. 106).

In spite of this he is out of sympathy with Wittgenstein in many ways. He considers that the assimilation of first-person present-tense psychological statements to the natural expressions of sensation and emotion "obscures the facts and is needless" (*Individuals*, p. 107). He is unconvinced by Wittgenstein's reasoning against the idea of a private language that might serve as a basis for the argument from analogy (see PRIVATE LANGUAGE PROBLEM). He sees little difficulty in the notion of a person's inventing for himself a private language in which he has names for his sensations even when such sensations have no outward expressions: "He might simply be struck by the recurrence of a certain sensation and get into the habit of making a certain mark in a different place every time it occurred" (*Individuals*, p. 85). Nor does he consider the notion of a person's continuing to exist in a disembodied state as logically absurd (*Individuals*, pp. 115–116). He accuses Wittgenstein of hostility to the idea of what is not observed and of a "a prejudice against the inner" ("Critical Notice," p. 91).

All these criticisms of Wittgenstein suggest that Strawson holds the view that the connection between behavior and mental states is, after all, a contingent one. But this, as we have seen, is not so. How, then, does Strawson reconcile these apparently conflicting aspects of his thought? His line of thought appears to be approximately that general agreement in judgment is necessary before it is possible to have a common language. Such general agreement exists about, for example, "what it looks like here," and this agreement makes possible our common impersonal language of, for example, color. There is no such general agreement about "whether or not 'it's painful here,'" and there is thus no possibility of a common impersonal pain language. However, there is something available (namely, pain behavior) on which general agreement *is* possible, and if we are therefore to have a common pain language, we must each ascribe pain to others on the basis of their behavior. In this way a common personal language becomes possible.

In discussing Strawson's thought, it is crucial to emphasize that until a person decides to ascribe pains to others on the basis of their behavior, he has not got and cannot have *our* concept of pain, for part of that concept is that a pain is something that someone possesses. Nevertheless, he can have a concept (or perhaps something more rudimentary than a full-fledged concept) that is akin to our concept of pain but does not involve the idea of something that is had or possessed by either himself or others. Perhaps this can be made more intelligible by considering a conceivable though unlikely case, that of a young child who has not yet got our concept of pain but is on the way to getting it. When he falls and knocks his head or scrapes his knee, he says, "It hurts." He has learned this sentence, perhaps as a replacement for natural cries of pain, and he uses it to get picked up and otherwise comforted. However, when his twin brother or a brick falls off the table, and the child is asked, "Does it hurt?" he replies, "No." Nevertheless, he cannot be said to mean by "It hurts" what is meant by "It hurts me," even though he says the former only when the latter is true, for he attaches no sense to "Does it hurt John?," as opposed to "Does it hurt me?" Nor, with regard to what he calls hurting, does he see any difference between John and a brick. If John says, "It hurts," when he himself is feeling all right, he regards what John says as simply untrue. In order for this child to make the transition to the concept of pain as something that either he or someone else has, he must learn to say, "It hurts John," when John bumps his head and cries and to say, "It hurts me," when formerly he said only, "It hurts." Until this linguistic convention is acquired, the child cannot be said to have the concept of pain as a property of persons at all, not even as a property of himself. Thus, the argument from analogy breaks down because it assumes not only that a person can have a private language but that this language contains our concept of pain (ascribed pain). But such a language could contain at best only a concept of what we may call unascribed pain. The connection between unascribed pain and my behavior is a contingent one, but the connection between behavior and ascribed pain is not. We can see now why Strawson says, "I have argued that such a . . . 'justification' [of our beliefs about others] is impossible, that the demand for it cannot be coherently stated" (*Individuals*, p. 112). To talk about other people's pains at all is to accept and use the concept of ascribed pain, and it is an integral part of this concept that behavior shows any person whether that concept applies to other people.

Criticisms of Strawson. Strawson's views are open to some of the criticisms that have been directed against opinions that are the same as his own. In addition, A. J. Ayer has directed a number of criticisms specifically against Strawson's positions, asserting that his notion of logical adequacy is obscure and arguing that this obscurity is irremediable. It is certainly true that Strawson does not make the notion of logical adequacy as clear as he might, but Ayer's reasons for thinking that this obscurity could not be remedied are themselves inconclusive. Ayer's other main criticism is directed against Strawson's reason for holding that neither the argument from analogy nor the philosophical skepticism that arises from this argument can be stated coherently. This criticism is based on a failure properly to understand Strawson's position, which in turn leads to the mistaken idea that Strawson cannot allow for the existence of someone with the concept of a person "who was invariably mistaken in ascribing states of consciousness to others" (*The Concept of a Person and Other Essays,* p. 106).

There is nothing in Strawson's position to prevent him from holding that analogy is used in the ascription of states of consciousness to others; the only thing that he rules out is analogical *argument* of the traditional pattern. To understand this, let us use the words "upain" and "utickle" for the concepts of unascribed pains and tickles. According to Strawson, in order to pass from these concepts to those of (ascribed) pains and tickles, I must adopt verbal rules according to which I say "I have a pain" when there is a "upain" and "He has a pain" when another body exhibits certain behavior, etc. But what sort of behavior, etc.? There is no reason that Strawson's answer should not be along some such lines as "behavior, etc., that is like the behavior, etc., that this body (i.e., mine) exhibits when there is a upain." In accepting such a rule, I am not *arguing* by analogy. Now, I can adopt such a rule and thus have the concept of a person, but I can still fail to realize that all the objects I regard as persons are in fact unlike myself in ways that I have not noticed. Ayer describes an imaginary child who is brought up and taught to speak by lifelike robots and who never meets real people. He argues, quite correctly, that this child would have the concept of a person and yet always be mistaken when he ascribes mental attributes to anything. But no consequences fatal to Strawson's views follow from this. The child has adopted the verbal rule whose acceptance, according to Strawson, is necessary for the possession of the concept of a person. The child mistakenly thinks that the robots are persons because he believes that they are much more like himself than in fact they are. This gives no ground for the skeptical conclusion that I may here and now be mistaken in my belief that there are other people besides myself. If one accepts Strawson's position, such skepticism need be justified only if what I think to be other people are a great deal less like me in behavior, etc., than I take them to be. If there is a doubt left here, according to Strawson it can have nothing very specifically to do with other minds. The basis of Ayer's misunderstanding is his mistaken belief that Strawson "infers that any attempt to justify the belief that there are other persons by relying on the premiss that one knows oneself to be a person would be circular; the premiss would already assume what the argument is supposed to prove" (*ibid.,* p. 104). But Strawson's objection to the argument from analogy is not that it is a circular argument. According to him, the trouble is that the argument both uses the concept of a person and rejects the verbal rule that is a necessary part of that concept, namely, the rule that mental attributes are to be ascribed to things on the basis of their behavior, etc.

John Wisdom's views. Finally, something should be said of John Wisdom's very important work on this problem. It is quite impossible to summarize Wisdom's contribution as another solution to the problem of other minds. This impossibility is inherent in his views about philosophy and in the method he uses in conformity with these views. All that can be done here is to give some idea of what is to be found in his writings on the problem of other minds by sketching his method of dealing with it. Wisdom has been much influenced by Wittgenstein, especially in regard to the idea that the treatment of a philosophical problem is in some ways like the treatment of an illness. Such a problem or puzzle is a symptom of deep-seated intellectual disorder that consists in a persistent tendency to think about a certain area of thought and language in accordance with a misleading and partially inappropriate model. The puzzle is dissipated when one is "cured" of this tendency. Inattention, however, is not the only remedy, nor is the taking of drugs. The only "cure" available to a philosopher qua philosopher is a certain form of insight. The misleading model that distorts one's thinking is largely an unconscious one. Insight and freedom from its grip are obtained by bringing it into the open, by making quite clear in detail how our thought is governed by it, and by giving us a proper view of the nature of, for example, our knowledge of other minds.

Thus, Wisdom's first aim is to induce and sharpen philosophical perplexity by showing how it arises precisely out of the sort of position that is at first sight the most attractive to us. For example, the most natural answer to the question about other minds is the traditional one. But it is from this answer and the way of thinking that goes with it that philosophical skepticism most easily arises. Skepticism is satisfactorily removed only when we are brought to see that knowing about other minds is not altogether like other ways of knowing that are by analogy and that it need not be. It might be thought that the aim of a philosopher should be to find a correct model that does not mislead. But according to Wisdom, this is not so. Although every statement has its own logic, the logic of every statement is in some degree like that of every other. We cannot usefully create a limited set of pigeonholes into one of which goes our knowledge of other minds along with, say, our knowledge of the past, while our knowledge of any theoretical entity goes into another. The matter cannot come to this sort of a conclusion. There will be important differences that will make inappropriate any such pigeonhole, as well as the likenesses that make it possible. To get a true grasp of the nature of our knowledge of other minds, it is necessary to make a very large number of detailed comparisons between the various ways in which we know or might know things and between the logic of various types of statements. Only then will we see psychological statements and the ways in which we know of the existence of other people's thoughts and feelings in all their idiosyncrasies and in all their similarities to other statements and to other ways of knowing things. Until this is done, we cannot be entirely freed from our tendency to see things as they are not.

As may be deduced, Wisdom's writings about other minds are almost as much about induction, the past, perception, philosophy of science, and so on as they are about other minds. He uses his method with subtlety, inventiveness, and imagination. Many points made by later writers on the problem of other minds are little more than elaborations or oversimplifications of points already made by Wisdom.

Bibliography

ENGLISH-SPEAKING PHILOSOPHERS

Ayer, A. J., *The Concept of a Person and Other Essays*. London, 1963. Ch. 4. Criticizes Strawson's views.

Ayer, A. J., *The Problem of Knowledge*. London, 1956. Ch. 5. Defends the argument from analogy.

Gasking, Douglas, "Avowals," in R. J. Butler, ed., *Analytical Philosophy*. Oxford, 1962. Pp. 154–169.

Malcolm, Norman, "Wittgenstein's Philosophical Investigations." *Philosophical Review*, Vol. 63, No. 4 (1954), 530–559. Defends Wittgenstein's views on private languages.

Malcolm, Norman, "Knowledge of Other Minds." *Journal of Philosophy*, Vol. 55 (1958), 969–978. A radical criticism of the argument from analogy and the traditional viewpoint.

Mill, J. S., *An Examination of Sir William Hamilton's Philosophy*. London, 1865. Ch. 12. Contains a straightforward version of the argument from analogy.

Strawson, P. F., "Critical Notice of Wittgenstein's Philosophical Investigations." *Mind*, Vol. 63, No. 249 (1954), 70–99. A criticism of Wittgenstein's views on private languages.

Strawson, P. F., *Individuals*. London, 1959. Ch. 3.

Wisdom, John, "Other Minds." *Mind*, Vol. 49, No. 196, 369–402; Vol. 50, No. 197, 1–22; Vol. 50, No. 198, 97–122; Vol. 50, No. 199, 209–242; Vol. 50, No. 200, 313–329; Vol. 51, No. 201, 1–18 (1940–1942).

Wisdom, John, "Other Minds." *Logic and Reality, PAS*, Supp. Vol. 20 (1946), 122–147.

Wisdom, John, *Other Minds*. Oxford, 1956. Reprints all the above.

Wittgenstein, Ludwig, *Philosophical Investigations*. Oxford and New York, 1953.

GERMAN PHILOSOPHERS

Husserl, Edmund, *Cartesianische Meditationen. Husserliana*, Vol. I. The Hague, 1950. Meditation V. Translated by Dorion Cairns as *Cartesian Meditations; An Introduction to Phenomenology*. The Hague, 1960.

Scheler, Max Ferdinand, *Zur Phänomenologie und Theorie der Sympathiegefühle und von Liebe und Hass*. Halle, 1913. Appendix.

J. M. SHORTER

OTTO, RUDOLF (1869–1937), German theologian, was born at Peine in Hanover. He studied at Erlangen and Göttingen, where he became a *Privatdozent* in systematic theology in 1897. In 1904 Otto was appointed professor of systematic theology at Göttingen. He accepted similar posts at Breslau in 1914 and at Marburg in 1917, where he remained until his death. In addition to his philosophical work, Otto published works on Christ, on Indian religious thought and its relation to Christianity, and on various theological topics.

Religious feeling and religious knowledge. Otto's most significant philosophic contribution is to be found in his discussion of religious feeling and religious knowledge —a discussion which begins with his earliest work and culminates in *The Idea of the Holy*.

In *Naturalism and Religion* (1904) Otto discusses the relation of religion to a naturalism which demands that everything be explained on the basis of mathematical–mechanical laws, thus excluding the beyond, purpose, and mystery, which are essential to religion.

Cognitive claims of religion. Religion makes certain claims—that the world is conditioned and dependent, that there is a providence, that there is a side other than that which appears to us. These claims are not put forward as poetry but as truths. They cannot, however, be justified by, nor derived from, a consideration of nature in any straightforward sense. Reason may show that science does not conflict with these claims and even that science is unable to consider their truth value. Reason may also point out hints in nature which suggest that these claims are true; reason cannot, however, justify them. These truths differ in kind from those of science and common sense and have their own grounds—the heart and conscience, feeling and intuition. Correlations can be made between various feelings, on the one hand, and religious claims, on the other. Corresponding to the claim that the world is conditioned and dependent is the feeling of the dependence and conditionality of all things. The claim that there is a providence, or teleological order, in things implies that certain value judgments are true and these value judgments rest on feeling and intuition. Corresponding to the claim that there is a beyond is piety—a feeling and intuition, which is bound up with our experience of the beautiful and the mysterious, that there is a reality behind appearances.

Religious feelings and intuitions. In *Naturalism and Religion* it is not entirely clear just what these feelings and intuitions are. Otto sometimes talks of them as if they were feelings in a straightforward sense. At other times he talks of them as if they were half-formulated judgments which carry with them an inescapable sense of conviction, and at still other times he talks of them as if they were cognitive experiences in somewhat the same way that visual experiences are cognitive.

Categories and ideas. The notion of religious feelings and intuitions receives a more complete treatment in *The Philosophy of Religion Based on Kant and Fries* (1909), in which Otto follows the position of J. F. Fries. We have an immediate knowledge of reality, the noumenal world, which shows itself in "feelings of truth." These feelings can be brought to full consciousness as ideas. An idea is a concept which can be applied to reality. When temporally schematized, the categories of theoretical reason can be applied to appearances and can also, when schematized by the principle of completeness (a principle based on reason's "perception and knowledge" that real existence is necessary, one, and complete), be applied to reality itself. A category thus schematized is an idea. These ideas are essentially negative. In effect, they exclude certain characteristics—temporality, contingency, and so on—from reality.

In the case of the practical reason the "feeling of truth" cannot be completely conceptualized. Practical reason does, however, derive the idea of reality as "the reign of purpose" from the principle of the dignity of the person which underlies the concept of duty. The idea is again presumably negative.

The negative judgments obtained through applying the ideas of theoretical and practical reason to reality must be supplemented by positive knowledge, which is gained through feelings or perceptions that cannot be adequately expressed although they can be communicated. These feelings, or perceptions, again seem to be, simultaneously, feelings in an ordinary sense, the ability to make judgments according to criteria which cannot themselves be formulated, and a direct perception of an objective existence—in this case, reality. Otto distinguishes between the feeling of beauty and of the sublime, on the one hand, and religious feelings, on the other. Although the discussion is somewhat obscure, it would seem that all three of these feelings either directly or indirectly disclose reality.

Numinous feelings. In *The Idea of the Holy,* Otto attempts to make a clear distinction between numinous, or religious, feelings and feelings which might be confused with them, such as the feeling of the sublime. Numinous feelings have two primary aspects—a feeling of religious dread and a feeling of religious fascination. The closest analogue to religious dread, or awe, is the feeling of uncanniness—the feeling one has when the hair on the back of one's neck rises, the shudder or terror on hearing a ghost story, the dread of haunted places. The feeling of fascination by, attraction to, and prizing of the object which arouses the feeling in question creates both the desire to approach the object and the feeling that one possesses no value when considered in relation to the fascinating and prized object.

Otto's attempt to describe the various feelings must be distinguished from his theory about numinous feelings. Numinous feelings are unique; they cannot be analyzed as a complex of such nonnuminous feelings as love, fear, horror, a feeling of sublimity, and so on. Second, the capacity for numinous feelings is unexplainable; although the capacity may appear in the world only when certain conditions are fulfilled, the conditions do not constitute an adequate explanation of the capacity in question.

Numinous feelings are also cognitive. Two claims are made at this point. First, the feelings are the source of the concept of the numinous—the concept of something which is both a value and an objective reality. The numinous feelings are also cognitive in the sense that they are like visual experiences. They have "immediate and primary reference to an object outside the self"—the numinous quality or object, which is an object of numinous feelings in somewhat the same way that visible objects and qualities might be said to be the object of visual experiences.

Interpretations. The relation between these two claims is not clear. At least two interpretations are possible. The first interpretation makes central the claim that numinous feelings disclose the numinous object. The encounter with the numinous object through numinous experiences gives rise to the concept of the numinous in much the same way that encounters with objects and qualities through visual experiences are thought to give rise to the concepts of those objects and qualities. The concept of the numinous is, then, a posteriori in the sense that it is derived from the experience of an object or quality. It is, however, a priori in the sense that it is not derived from any sense experience. In this interpretation the feeling is the source of the concept only in the sense that it discloses the object of the concept, the encounter with the object producing the concept of the object.

In the second interpretation the feeling gives rise to both the concept and the disclosure of the numinous object, yet it is not the encounter with the numinous which gives rise to the concept of the numinous. Rather, the feeling furnishes the concept in much the same way that Kant's theoretical reason furnishes the various a priori categories. The concept of the numinous is, then, a priori in a standard sense. The feeling does more than this, however. The feeling which furnishes the concept also discloses the object to which the concept applies. How are these two functions of numinous feelings related? Neither the concept nor the object is, it would seem, given in isolation. Rather, the object is given through the concept or as structured by the concept. The two are given together although one is not derived from the other. In either interpretation Otto makes the claim that feeling puts us in contact with, discloses, is an awareness of, intuits something outside ourselves. In this respect feeling is like visual and auditory experiences. It has an objective referent whether this is structured by an a priori concept or whether it simply gives rise to a concept. Unfortunately, the difficulties involved in this claim are not discussed. Obvious disanalogies with ordinary perception (the absence of tests for "mis-seeing," the fact that no sense organ is tied to numinous experiences, the fact that nonpsychological predictions cannot be based on numinous experiences in the way in which they can be based on visual experiences, and so on) are ignored.

The numen. Otto calls the object of numinous feelings the numen, something which is both value and object but which can be only indirectly characterized by means of "ideograms"—that is, by designating properties which would appropriately call forth a feeling response analogous to that evoked in the encounter with the numen. For example, the encounter with the numen evokes religious dread. This is analogous to fear. Accordingly, we indicate the property of the numen which arouses religious dread by "wrath," a term which refers to a property which often produces fear. In addition to this, however, we can and should "schematize" the numen by means of such rational concepts as goodness, completeness, necessity, and substantiality. That is, concepts of this sort may be predicated of the numen. The resulting judgment is synthetic a priori. It may be suggested that the cash value of the last claim is that we just "see" the connection to be appropriate if we possess numinous feelings.

The holy. When the concept of the numinous and the schematizing concepts are brought together in this way, we have the "complex category of the 'holy' itself." The category is a priori in the sense that (1) the connection between the notion of the numinous and the schematizing concepts is a priori, (2) the concept of the numinous is a priori in that although it arises "amid the sensory data . . . of the natural world, . . . it does not arise out of them," and (3) the schematizing concepts are a priori.

The last claim is difficult to maintain, however, for Otto's examples of the schematizing concepts seem to make this impossible. It could perhaps be argued that schematizing concepts like completeness, necessity, substantiality, and goodness are a priori. Otto also wishes to say, however, that the concepts of love, mercy, and moral will can function as concepts which schematize various aspects of the numinous. It is difficult to maintain that a concpt like love is a priori. What Otto maintains is that although "love" as applied to the numen and "love" as applied in ordinary situations have the same content, their form differs. When referred to the numen, the term is taken absolutely; when it is applied in ordinary situations, it is not. Otto seems to mean that love in the ordinary sense admits of degrees that can be arranged on a scale. The love of the numen is the limit of this scale. Since the limit (whatever this might be) is not given to us in sense experience, we may call it a priori.

Religious feelings and the numen. We can now explicate more fully the role which religious or numinous feelings play in religious knowledge. They disclose the numen to us. They are the source of the concept of the numinous. Finally, they appear to warrant the synthetic a priori judgments which link the schematizing concepts to the concept of the numinous.

The relation between the account presented in *The Philosophy of Religion* and *The Idea of the Holy* is, I think, clear. The ideas have become the "Idea of the Holy" (which breaks down into the concept of the numinous and the schematizing concepts), reality has become the numen, and feelings and intuitions have become numinous feelings.

Autonomy of the spirit. Another theme, although less philosophically interesting, is of central concern to Otto himself—the autonomy of the spirit and of the spirit's religious capacities. In asserting that the spirit is autonomous, Otto is claiming that the laws of the spirit are fundamentally different from those of the natural world. In effect, they are the prescriptive laws of logic and ethics (and of religion?) rather than the descriptive laws of physics and psychology. Insofar as a spirit determines itself by prescriptive laws, it is free. Otto is further claiming that spirit is the source of concepts, principles, intuitions, and valuations which cannot be derived from sense experience. And, finally, he is claiming that although spirit develops under the influence of external stimuli, it is something unique in its own right. Spirit cannot be explained by, nor can its occurrence be predicted on, the basis of a consideration of sense experience alone. Spirit and its operations "emerge" under certain conditions but are not explained by these conditions.

Books by Otto

Naturalistische und religiöse Weltansicht. Tübingen, 1904. Translated by J. A. Thomson and M. R. Thomson as *Naturalism and Religion.* New York, 1907.

Goethe und Darwin. Darwinismus und Religion. Göttingen, 1909. *Darwinismus und Religion* translated by S. G. Cole and E. M. Austin as "Darwinism and Religion" in *The Crozer Quarterly,* Vol. 8 (1931), 147–161.

Kantisch-Fries'sche Religionsphilosophie und ihre Anwendung auf die Theologie. Tübingen, 1909. Translated by E. B. Dicker as *The Philosophy of Religion Based on Kant and Fries.* London, 1931.

Das Heilige; über das Irrationale in der Idee des Gottlichen und sein Verhältnis zum Rationalen. Breslau, 1917; 25th ed. Munich, 1936. The later editions contain additional material. Translated by J. W. Harvey as *The Idea of the Holy: An Inquiry into the Nonrational Factor in the Idea of the Divine and Its Relation to the Rational.* New York, 1958.

Aufsätze das Numinose betreffend. Stuttgart and Gotha, 1923.

West-Östliche Mystik. Vergleich und Unterscheidung zur Wesensdeutung. Gotha, 1926. Translated by B. L. Bracey and R. C. Payne as *Mysticism, East and West. A Comparative Analysis of the Nature of Mysticism.* New York, 1932.

Das Gefühl des Überweltlichen (Sensus Numinis). Munich, 1932. The first part of the fifth and sixth editions of the *Aufsätze* with some added material.

Sunde und Urshuld und andere Aufsätze zur Theologie. Munich, 1932. The second part of the fifth and sixth editions of the *Aufsätze* with some added material.

Religious Essays. A Supplement to the "Idea of the Holy," by Rudolf Otto, translated by B. Lunn. London, 1931. This consists primarily of translations of essays found in the *Aufsätze* and the two preceding works.

Freiheit und Notwendigkeit. Ein Gespräch mit Nicolai Hartmann über Autonomie und Theonomie der Werte. Tübingen, 1940.

Books on Otto

Davison, R. F., *Rudolf Otto's Interpretation of Religion.* Princeton, N.J., 1947.

Feigel, F. C., *"Das Heilige." Eine kritische Abhandlung über Rudolf Otto's gleichnamiges Buch.* Haarlem, Netherlands, 1929.

Haubold, W., *Die Bedeutung der Religionsgeschichte für die Theologie Rudolf Ottos.* Leipzig, 1940.

Moore, J. M., *Theories of Religious Experience with Special Reference to James, Otto and Bergson.* New York, 1938.

Siegfried, T., *Grundfragen der Theologie bei Rudolf Otto.* Gotha, 1931.

Sommer, J. W. E., *Der heilige Gott und der Gott der Gnade bei Rudolf Otto.* Frankfurt, 1950.

WILLIAM J. WAINWRIGHT

P

PAINE, THOMAS (1737–1809), author, deist, and American revolutionary leader. He was born at Thetford, Norfolk, in England. After an inconspicuous start in life as corset maker and customs officer, Paine emigrated at the age of 37 from England to Philadelphia, carrying a letter of recommendation from Benjamin Franklin. Caught up almost immediately in the turmoil of the developing revolution, Paine published *Common Sense* (January 1776), the first public appeal for American independence as well as the pioneer enunciation of the diplomatic doctrine of avoiding European entanglements. In addition to attacking hereditary aristocracy, Paine expounded the theory that government and society are distinct entities and are not to be confounded, a theory also developed by Jean-Jacques Rousseau and later by William Godwin.

During subsequent stages of the American Revolution, Paine wrote a number of influential newspaper essays, including a famous series, the *Crisis,* concerned with particular political, economic, and military issues. In order to extend his reputation to Europe, Paine wrote the *Letter to the abbé Raynal, on the Affairs of North America* (1783), refuting among other concepts of the French *philosophes,* the assertion that the Revolution concerned only economic issues and had no moral foundation. A confident affirmation of the idea of progress was incorporated in Paine's notions that the circle of civilization was soon to be completed and that commerce and science had already combined to improve the world to the point where there no longer existed a need to make war for profit.

After the American victory, Paine proceeded to France to seek financial support for an iron bridge of his own invention, once again carrying letters of recommendation from Franklin. In January 1790 he began a work defending Lafayette and the principles of the revolution that had broken out in France, a work that he later converted to an attack on Edmund Burke's highly critical *Reflections on the French Revolution.* The resulting treatise, *The Rights of Man* (Part I, 1791; Part II, 1792), gave a solid theoretical basis to the contingent appeals of Paine's American journalism. Affirming that government should be founded on reason rather than on tradition or precedent, Paine argued that democracy—a society in which all men have equal rights and in which leadership depends upon talent and wisdom—is superior to aristocracy. Although his political

principles resemble those of John Locke, Paine later maintained that they were based entirely on his own reasoning and that he had never read the works of the English philosopher.

As a result of his republican writings, Paine was made an honorary citizen of France and in September 1792 he was elected to the French National Convention, taking his seat later that month.

Disturbed by the dogmatic atheism of the French revolutionary leaders, Paine began a treatise on religion, *The Age of Reason,* ostensibly a defense of deism but primarily an attack on Christianity. In Part I (1794), he rejected all forms of supernatural revelation in favor of the religion of nature, elevating, as he put it, reason and scientific observation over the three modes of superstition in Christianity: mystery, miracle, and prophecy. In Part II (1795), Paine continued to praise "the Perfection of the Deity," even though he exposed the abuses of Christianity with such vehemence that he brought upon himself the inaccurate accusation of opposing religion itself.

Although Paine dismissed the miracles of Christianity, he was later ready to believe that providence intervened in his own life. The story is incredible, but it reflects Paine's egoism. Because of his moderate policies in the Convention, particularly in an appeal to save Louis XVI from the guillotine, he was dismissed from the Convention and incarcerated in Luxembourg Prison. On his return to America, Paine explained that the cell doors of prisoners destined for execution were customarily marked with a number, and he argued that divine providence had protected him by causing his jailor to place the fatal number by mistake on the inside of his door so that it could not be seen the next morning.

One must turn to Paine's minor works to discover the positive side of his deism. His proof of the existence of God (in "A Discourse at the Society of Theophilanthropists") adopts essentially the same reasoning that Isaac Newton had used in a series of letters to an Anglican clergyman, Richard Bentley. Since the laws of mechanics, the argument runs, cannot explain the origin of motion, there must have been an external first cause to give the planets their original rotation. Paine stressed the concept of the plurality of worlds and assumed absolute moral laws. In "Private Thoughts on a Future State," he expressed a faith in an immortality strikingly different from that of most deists. The good people, he believed, would be happy in another world; the wicked would be punished; and those in between—the indifferent ones—would be "dropped entirely." Although contending that religion should be a private affair between each man and his creator, he insisted that no rational mind could logically reconcile new science and old Christianity.

Unable to adjust to French political life under Napoleon, Paine returned to America in 1802, where he was welcomed by liberal Jeffersonians but excoriated by most Federalists. Although he contributed extensively to newspapers under his revolutionary pseudonym of "Common Sense," he failed to regain his earlier influence and died in obscurity.

Paine, as much as any thinker of his age, was obsessed with the notion of the order and uniformity of nature, and he delighted in establishing parallels between one branch of learning and another. He believed that the fundamental laws of nature operative in religion, natural science, and politics were clear, simple, and within the reach of the average man. He developed no epistemology as such but combined a type of Quaker inner light with deistic reason. The fundamental weakness of his system—a weakness shared by most deists—is that he nowhere took up the problem of evil. Although he lavishly praised God for the regularity of the universe, the only suffering he noticed is that caused by social injustice.

Yet even though Paine was more influential as an agitator than as a theorist, he certainly understood and upheld the ideals of the Enlightenment and deserves to be ranked as one of America's outstanding *philosophes.*

Works by Paine

Writings of Thomas Paine, Moncure D. Conway, ed., 4 vols. New York, 1894–1896.
Complete Writings of Thomas Paine, Philip S. Foner, ed., 2 vols. New York, 1947.

Works on Paine

Aldridge, Alfred Owen, *Man of Reason: The Life of Thomas Paine.* New York, 1959.
Conway, Moncure D., *Life of Thomas Paine,* 2 vols. New York, 1892.
Russell, Bertrand, "The Fate of Thomas Paine," in *Why I Am Not a Christian.* London and New York, 1957.

ALFRED OWEN ALDRIDGE

PALÁGYI, MENYHERT or Melchior (1859–1924), scientist, literary critic, and philosopher, was born in Paks in west central Hungary. He studied science at Budapest, but his main activity there was as a literary critic. After 1900 he spent much time in Germany, studying informally with philosophers in many places. For a time he held a readership in physics and mathematics in Kolozvár, Hungary (now Cluj, Rumania). He had little contact with Hungarian philosophers, however, and eventually returned to Germany, where he died in Darmstadt.

Throughout Palágyi's philosophical works, psychological doctrines and speculations on theoretical physics are mingled with his main interest in epistemology. He interpreted and criticized the then new theory of relativity from the point of view of epistemology, and epistemology from the point of view of his psychological theory. As he expressed his views in response to the new developments in these fields, he became somewhat lost in their transitional stages, and the fact that he criticized them from his own particular standpoint hindered his understanding of them. The central dominating idea throughout his works is a broadly Hegelian principle of polarity. It asserts an interdependence of opposites, a sort of cooperative unity, and it was applied by Palágyi with no apparent consistency and even more liberally than Hegelian dialectics would be. Palágyi was a monist who held a curious version of the denial of the distinction between the a priori and a posteriori.

His most purely philosophical work is *Der Streit der Psychologisten und Formalisten in der modernen Logik* (Leipzig, 1902). In it, among other things, he criticized Husserl for "tearing" logic away from psychology and "submerging" it in mathematics, and for his "ideal meaning" and his distinction between real and ideal laws. (Husserl himself reviewed this book in *Zeitschrift für Psychologie und Physik des Sinnesorgane,* Vol. 31, 1903.) In the same year Palágyi wrote his *Die Logik auf dem Scheidewege* ("Logic at the Crossroads," Berlin and Leipzig, 1903). In these works Palágyi's main concern was not, despite his criticisms of Husserl, a return to psychologism but his principle of polarity. In his psychology, in fact, he tried to rescue from psychologism that which he termed "mental" (even though he only obscurely described the term). The source of all error is to mistake what is mental for what is merely vital (and, in the spirit of "polarity," what is vital for what is merely mental). He distinguished between mechanical and vital processes and consciousness. The mechanical is publicly observable, and the vital indirectly observable, but consciousness escapes observation by the methods applicable to the other processes: consciousness "punctuates" the vital process and is discontinuous. (He nevertheless explicitly affirmed the unity of the self, although it is doubtful how he could maintain this.) Our knowledge depends on the speed of these punctuations. God is the limiting case who grasps the whole time process instantaneously; for him all punctuations are one. This led Palágyi to such metaphysical claims as that our knowledge catches eternity in the fleeting moment, which is both temporal and eternal.

At the base of this theory of perception was his notion of imagined movement. Touch being the basic sense, all perception depends on our ability to trace the object in the imagination. He mistakenly supported this view by reference to the Kantian role of imagination in perception. His theoretical physics, in which his main interest was our perception of space time (space time being a unity in polarity), can best be understood if approached through this theory of perception.

Bibliography

Ausgewahlte Werke, 3 vols. (Leipzig, 1924–1925), contains Palágyi's most important works.
Works on Palágyi are Werner Deubel, "Die Philosophie und Weltmechanik von Melchior Palágyi," in *Preussische Jahrbuch,*

Vol. 203 (1926), 329–356, with complete bibliography; W. R. Boyce Gibson, "The Philosophy of Melchior Palágyi," in *Journal of Philosophical Studies*, Vol. 3 (1928), 15–28, 158–172; L. W. Schneider, *Der erste Periode in philosophischen Schaffen M. Palágyis* (Würzburg, 1942); and A. Wurmb, *Darstellung und Kritik der logische Grundbegriffe der Naturphilosophie Melchior Palágyis* (Leipzig, 1931).

JULIUS KOVESI

PALEY, WILLIAM (1743–1805), English theologian and moral philosopher. His father, William, was vicar of Helpston, Northamptonshire, and a minor canon of Peterborough; he later became headmaster of Giggleswick grammar school, where the younger Paley was educated. Paley entered Christ's College, Cambridge, in 1759, where he studied mathematics and became a senior wrangler. After an interlude of schoolteaching, he was elected a fellow of his college in 1766 and was ordained a priest in the established church in 1767. He taught at Cambridge for nine years, leaving the university only on his marriage. He held successively a number of different offices in the church, rising to be the archdeacon of Carlisle. Paley was the author of three books, one on morals and two defending Christian belief, all of which were widely read and accepted as textbooks. As late as 1831, Charles Darwin, studying for his B.A. examination at Cambridge, had to "get up" Paley's *A View of the Evidences of Christianity, The Principles of Moral and Political Philosophy,* and *Natural Theology.* The *Moral and Political Philosophy* contains Paley's famous satire on property, in which he describes the plight of a flock of pigeons in which private property is permitted. Although he immediately proceeds to list the advantages of a system of private property, his satire is savage ("the weakest perhaps, and worst pigeon of the flock" controls and wastes all the grain as he pleases), and Paley's friends are said to have assured him (correctly) that the publication of the passage would cost him a bishopric. It did earn him the nickname "Pigeon Paley."

Paley's *The Principles of Moral and Political Philosophy* (London, 1785) is a handbook on the duties and obligations of civil life rather than a philosophical treatise. The subtlety of the work may be gauged by its opening sentence: "Moral philosophy, Morality, Ethics, Casuistry, Natural Law, mean all the same thing; namely, that science which teaches men their duty and the reasons of it." Paley's definition of duty follows from his theological utilitarianism. The nature of the human frame implies that it is God's will for us to be happy in this life as well as in the next. Virtue is doing good to mankind, in obedience to the will of God and for the sake of everlasting happiness. Allegiance to God's will and a desire for everlasting happiness are sufficient grounds for moral obligation. Paley offers this account of moral obligation after finding that such obligation follows from the command of a superior, which is made persuasive by the prospect of a reward.

We may discover the will of God by consulting either Scripture or "the light of nature," both of which lead to the same conclusion. The will of God with regard to any action may be found by inquiring into its "tendency to promote or diminish the general happiness." We should carry out those actions which promote the general happiness and avoid those which diminish it. Promoting the general happiness requires paying attention to the general consequences of our actions. Paley offers a rule for assessing general consequences that resembles Kant's categorical imperative: "The general consequence of any action may be estimated by asking what would be the consequence if the same sort of actions were generally permitted."

Paley believed that no special faculty is required to enable us to have moral knowledge. Thus he dismissed the views of those who have argued that morality requires either a moral sense, or an intuitive perception of right and wrong, or any other innate or instinctive capacity. All that is required for the foundation of morality is that each man have the wit to see that certain actions are beneficial to himself. Then the sentiment of approbation that naturally arises when these actions benefit him will continue to accompany his perception of these actions when they benefit someone else. Thus the custom of approving certain actions is begun, and children, who learn everything by imitating their elders, carry it on.

The bulk of the *Principles* is a detailed discussion of our duties to others, to ourselves, and to God. The final part is an outline of the elements of political knowledge. The wide acclaim accorded Paley's work is said to have stirred Bentham to bring out his own version of the utilitarian doctrine in *Introduction to the Principles of Morals and Legislation* (1789).

Paley is the author of two theological works with the word "evidence" in their titles. The first, *A View of the Evidences of Christianity* (2 vols., London, 1794), is an essay in apologetics. The second, *Natural Theology; or, Evidences of the Existence and Attributes of the Deity, Collected from the Appearances of Nature* (London, 1802), is, as its title implies, an essay on natural theology. The books, which are similar in tone (they are both presented as judicious, lawyerlike statements of a case) doubtless owe much to Paley's lifelong interest in trials and the art of advocacy.

A View of the Evidences of Christianity demonstrates what can be said on behalf of Christian belief by an appeal to the behavior of the earliest Christians. Paley asks his readers to grant the possibility that God should have destined his human creation for a future state and that he should acquaint human beings with their destiny. If these possibilities are granted, then the need for miracles is clear, for they are the certification of revelation. The credibility of the Christian revelation hangs, therefore, on the issue of whether its miracles are genuine.

It is Paley's claim that the miracles on which Christianity is based (including those of the Old Testament) are genuine; and that indeed the only genuine miracles are those of Christianity (including its Jewish origins). Paley accepts Hume's contention that the believability of Christianity rests ultimately on the reliability of the testimony of the earliest Christians, but he rejects Hume's thesis that no testimony for a miracle can ever be relied on because such testimony goes against universal experience. He argues that universal experience is too strong a test. By definition, miracles must be exceptions to universal experience or they would not be miracles. The real issue is whether there is a test for the reliability of witnesses who report an event that necessarily only they could have experienced.

Paley finds such a test in our observation of whether the person who reports a miracle will cling to his report at the risk of his comfort, his happiness, and even his life. According to Paley, the original witnesses of the Christian miracles pass this test, since they labored and suffered "in attestation of the accounts which they delivered, and solely in consequence of their belief of these accounts."

Paley's hospitality for miracles is not quite so broad as we might at first think. The miraculous event must be in support of a revelation that is important to human happiness. Mere wonders are thus ruled out; and Paley also holds out against any event that may be resolved into a false perception and against any report that is guilty of exaggeration. But even after setting these limits, Paley maintains that a significant core of miracles stands as the guaranty of the Christian revelation. But the acceptance of these miracles must finally rest on the steadfastness of the original Christians; and the weakness of Paley's argument can be seen when we consider its close resemblance to a lawyer's defending his client by calling for the testimony of none but character witnesses. *A View of the Evidences of Christianity* had a huge success, and the bishops made Paley a prebendary of St. Pancras in the Cathedral of St. Paul's and the subdean of Lincoln.

In his *Natural Theology,* Paley appeals to a number of natural phenomena to establish the existence of a god. He states his argument at the very outset, and the remainder of the work is a train of examples illustrating that argument. The line of the argument runs as follows. If I found a stone while crossing a heath, and if I "were asked how the stone came to be there, I might possibly answer, that, for any thing I knew to the contrary, it had lain there forever; nor would it perhaps be very easy to show the absurdity of this answer. But suppose I had found a watch upon the ground, and it should be enquired how the watch happened to be in that place, I should hardly think of the answer which I had before given, that, for anything I knew, the watch might have always been there. Yet why should not this answer serve for the watch, as well as for the stone?" Paley answers, "For this reason, and for no other, viz. that when we come to inspect the watch, we perceive (what we could not discover in the stone) that its several parts are framed and put together for a purpose"—that is, to tell the time. The care with which the parts have been made and the fineness of their adjustment can have only one implication, namely, that the watch must have had a maker who understood its construction and who designed it for the use for which it is fitted. The conclusion would not be weakened if we had never seen a watch being made or could not conceive of how to make one. Nor would it be weakened if there were parts of the watch whose purpose we could not understand, or even if we could not ascertain whether these parts had some effect in the general purpose of the watch. Nor should we be satisfied if we were told either that the existence of the watch is to be explained by a principle of order which exists in things and disposes the parts of the watch into their present form and situation, or that the watch is the result of the laws of "metallic nature." Finally, we should be surprised to hear that the mechanism of the watch is no proof of contrivance, but "only a motive to induce the mind to think so." In short, where

there is mechanism, instrumentality, or contrivance, there must have been an intelligence who designed and made the machine, the instrument, the contrivance.

Paley then turns to nature with this argument in hand and, in his own words, applies it to adduce evidences of the existence of God. The bones and muscles of human beings, animals, and their insect equivalents, are of special interest to Paley, for the fitting together of joints and the adaptation of muscles are mechanisms which imply most forcefully a designing intelligence. The chemical side of physiology does not interest him much, for chemical action does not suggest the work of a divine mechanic. But Kiell's *Anatomy* is ransacked for appropriate examples, and the hare's backbone is picked apart at the end of the meat course to show the finesse of divine contrivance. The example that most interests Paley, and to which he often returns, is the eye, in its various parts and in the combination of these parts and their adaptation to function as an instrument of sight. As he remarks, he offers many examples of natural mechanism, but a single instance, the eye alone, should suffice to convince us of the existence of the divine intelligence that designed it.

The evidence drawn from nature, in addition to establishing the existence of God, permits us to infer certain of his characteristics. Because God has a mind, he must be a person. That there is a single intelligence at work is shown by the uniformity of the divine plan, as it is applied to all parts of the world. Finally, God's goodness is shown both by the fact that most contrivances are beneficial and by the fact that pleasure has been made an animal sensation.

At bottom, Paley's argument rests on his original decision to regard certain parts of nature as mechanisms or contrivances. If this decision is unquestioned, then his argument takes a long stride toward plausibility. Everything depends, however, on whether the human eye, for example, is analogous to a machine, and if so, how far this analogy takes us in the inference of other characteristics that the analogy might imply. These questions are raised and examined with devastating effect by Hume in the *Dialogues Concerning Natural Religion,* a work published a quarter of a century before Paley's *Natural Theology.* It is to be regretted that Paley does not meet Hume's arguments head-on in the *Natural Theology,* in the same way that he meets Hume squarely on the issue of the believability of miracles in *A View of the Evidences of Christianity.*

Bibliography

William Paley's collected writings are in *Works,* 8 vols. (London, 1805–1808). See also his *Natural Theology,* Frederick Ferré, ed. (Indianapolis, 1964).

ELMER SPRAGUE

PALMER, ELIHU (1764–1806), was a radical spokesman for the Age of Reason and Revolution in America, who along with Thomas Paine and Ethan Allen gave expression to the ideals of deism and republicanism. Born in Canterbury, Connecticut, Palmer graduated from Dartmouth in 1787. Originally a minister, he was persecuted for his extreme religious views and forced to flee the pulpit. In 1793 he was admitted to the bar. Blinded by disease, he spent the last years of his life defending deism. He edited the deistic weekly journal *Prospect, or View of the Moral World* and helped to organize The Deistical Society in New York.

Palmer's religious radicalism stemmed from his reaction to Calvinism. He rejected the doctrine of original sin as well as the idea of a punitive and arbitrary divine being. This reaction developed into a militant anti-Christianity and anticlericalism. Palmer rejected the claims of divine revelation, miracles, and prophesies, and he accused the Bible of inconsistency, contradiction, and vagueness. Not only did he deny the divinity of Christ, but he considered Jesus, Moses, and Muhammad indecent and immoral and Christian salvation absurd and irrational. He attacked organized and institutionalized religion for its hypocrisy and self-interest.

Like other deists, Palmer defended a religion of nature, in which the order and harmony of the universe is believed to proclaim the existence of one supreme being, the divine creator. Palmer maintained that evil is not inherent in man or in nature but is due to corrupt social institutions and to defective human knowledge, which can both be corrected. He had boundless faith and optimism in reason, science, and education, believing that man possesses the capacities for intellectual and moral progress. In place of the traditional religious depreciation of human ability and dignity, he proposed a humanistic ethics. With others of this period, he held an empiricist epistemology, locating the source of all knowledge in sensation, and he was sympathetic to scientific and materialistic philosophy. Palmer was an ardent supporter of liberty and republicanism and saw in the American Revolution the inception of a new era for humanity.

Bibliography

Palmer's works include *Political Miscellany* (New York, 1793); *The Examiners Examined: Being a Defence of the Age of Reason* (New York, 1794); *An Enquiry Relative to the Moral and Political Improvement of the Human Species* (New York, 1797); *The Political Happiness of Nations: An Oration* (New York, 1800); *Principles of Nature: Or, a Development of the Moral Causes of Happiness and Misery Among the Human Species* (New York, 1801); *Prospect, or View of the Moral World for the Year 1804* (New York, 1803–1805), which he edited; and *Posthumous Pieces* (London, 1826).

For literature on Palmer, see G. Adolf Koch, *Republican Religion. The American Revolution and the Cult of Reason* (New York, 1933).

PAUL KURTZ

PALMER, GEORGE HERBERT (1842–1933), American philosopher and moralist. Palmer was born in Boston, attended Harvard College, and received a B.D. degree from Andover Theological Seminary in 1867. He spent most of the next two years in Europe, acquainting himself with recent German philosophy, but the poor health which had plagued him since infancy caused lengthy interruptions in his studies. While visiting in Scotland, he formed a friendship with Edward Caird, with whom he later studied Kant and Hegel. In 1870 Palmer became an instructor of Greek at Harvard, an appointment which resulted in his translation of Homer's *Odyssey*, published in Boston and New York in 1884. Palmer was married first to

Ellen M. Wellman, who died in 1879 after eight years of marriage, and then to Alice Freeman, president of Wellesley College.

From 1872 until 1913, Palmer taught philosophy at Harvard. Although he was eclipsed in the field of philosophy by the work of his more brilliant colleagues, William James, Josiah Royce, and George Santayana, his own contributions were pedagogically important and were expressed through his teaching, in his books on the art of teaching, and in his continued interest in Harvard's administrative affairs.

Palmer acknowledged that he was strongly influenced by and grateful to New England Puritanism. He was a philosophical idealist and a religious man, but not a philosophic innovator or system builder. Palmer's main interest was ethics. His best philosophical work is *The Nature of Goodness* (Boston and New York, 1903), in which he begins by distinguishing between extrinsic goodness (an object's usefulness for something other than itself) and intrinsic goodness (that organic character of a whole in which every part is extrinsically good for every other part). The distinguishing mark of a human being, Palmer maintained, is self-consciousness, and the moral aim of life is self-realization, which is expressed in perpetual self-development. The driving force behind this development is the individual's sense of limitation. An important mode of moral action is self-sacrifice, conceived by Palmer as a genuine diminishing of one's possessions or powers.

These views obliged Palmer to undertake the reconciliation of, on the one hand, self-realization with the social function of ethics, and on the other hand, rationality and self-interest with the moral reality of self-sacrifice. He achieved this dual reconciliation by means of his conceptions of the "separate self" and the "conjunct self." "Rationality is the comprehending of anything in its relations," and the conjunct self is a person rationally conceived as constituted by his relations with other selves and with the whole universe. The separate self, distinct from everyone and everything else, is basically unintelligible. Therefore, self-sacrifice is wholly rational, since it is action which furthers the interest of one's rational, conjunct self. Likewise, self-realization is not egoistic, since it is also concerned with the development of one's social, conjunct self.

The Nature of Goodness concludes with an explanation of three stages of goodness. The first is that of unconsciousness, in which reflection has no command over impulse. The second stage is that of spirit, and is manifested in the conscious direction of one's impulses. The third and highest stage of goodness, which represents moral maturity, is that of "negative consciousness," in which nature and spirit are reconciled, in the sense that our consciousness has successfully turned impulses into moral habits, thus freeing itself for higher moral tasks.

In *The Problem of Freedom* (Boston and New York, 1911) Palmer cautiously defends a libertarian position with a theory of final causation which he calls "antesequential" causation, as distinct from ordinary, or "sequential," causation. Antesequential causes of a person's actions are conscious ideals, and therefore lie in the future rather than the past. Palmer strove to reconcile the universality of natural causes, which he acknowledged, with the efficacy of human freedom, or final causation. To this purpose he argued that while separate chains of causation—such as the flight of a bird and that of a thrown stone—unrolled inevitably, their convergence was not inevitable and hence constituted a genuinely ambiguous future, available for exploitation by free human action.

Bibliography

Palmer published 15 books. Works of interest, in addition to those cited above, are *The Field of Ethics* (Boston and New York, 1901); *The English Works of George Herbert* (Boston and New York, 1905), which Palmer edited and annotated; *The Life of Alice Freeman Palmer* (Boston and New York, 1908); *Altruism, Its Nature and Varieties* (New York, 1920); and *The Autobiography of a Philosopher* (Boston and New York, 1930). He was a contributor to *Contemporary Idealism in America* (New York, 1932).

For literature on Palmer, see *George Herbert Palmer, 1842–1933: Memorial Addresses* (Cambridge, Mass., 1935), compiled by the Harvard University department of philosophy.

ANDREW OLDENQUIST

PANAETIUS OF RHODES, founder of the Roman or Middle Stoa, was born between 190 and 180 B.C. and died about 109 B.C. A wealthy gentleman, he studied at the great library at Pergamum (with Crates the Stoic, who was head of the library) and from there went to Athens and studied with Diogenes of Seleucia, who had represented Greek Stoicism to the Romans in the famous embassy of philosophers of 155 B.C. Panaetius then visited Rome and became a close friend of Scipio the Younger (the friendship began sometime before 140 B.C.); around the two men the most gifted Roman thinkers gathered, including Polybius the Greek historian, then a hostage in Rome. After Scipio died in 129 B.C., Panaetius became the head of the Stoic school in Athens and remained its leader until his death about twenty years later.

He was profoundly influenced by Carneades the Skeptic, to the extent of accepting Carneades' basic attack on Stoic physics concerning the Conflagration (the fire that ends each cycle of world history); Carneades had said that if everything turned into fire, the fire would go out for lack of fuel. Panaetius did not share the view of the Early Stoa that the world was a vast animal of which the deity was the soul, and he suspended judgment on divination, a notion quite crucial to most Stoics, since it summarized their belief in providential determinism (God providentially helps us to see the predetermined future). But he did believe with the Peripatetics and other Stoics that the universe is immortal. In short, he radically altered Stoic physics, incorporating many Skeptical arguments.

We know his ethics through Cicero's work on duties, *De Officiis,* which is apparently a very free translation (more of an adaptation) of Panaetius' *Peri Kathekontos.* The heart of Panaetius' ethics is orthodox Stoicism: virtue is basically knowledge, the power to give assent only to true beliefs, and virtue is the only good a man needs. But past this point Panaetius softens the old ascetic ethic, makes health, riches, and fame worth pursuing both as aids in attaining virtue and for their own sake. In his thought, the wise man is less important than *ho prokopton,* the probationer who regularly performs his duties. Instead of

emphasizing knowledge of the universe and self-control as the key to virtue, he emphasized knowledge of the self and *prepon*, decorum, the harmony of all parts of a man's life. But he was still a Stoic, not a Skeptic or an Epicurean; he held firmly to the belief that man's reason alone shows the way to inner tranquillity and public concord. His innovation lay in his skeptically chastened notion of reason as a harmonizer of phenomena into aesthetical and ethical wholes; the old Stoics saw reason as an instrument for elucidating the depths of reality. His pupil Posidonius brought the spirit of the old scientific Stoicism to Rome, but the practical and aesthetic approach of Panaetius eventually set the tone of Roman Stoicism.

Bibliography

Arnold, E. V., *Roman Stoicism.* London, 1958. Pp. 100–104, 144, 227, 267, 280, 303. The most thorough discussion of Panaetius in English.

Cicero, *De Officiis,* translated by W. Miller. London, 1913. It is difficult to tell how much of this is Panaetius and how much is Cicero's version of other philosophers' doctrines, but in the first book, which treats of the cardinal virtues, a powerful ethic is stated, which seems to be very close to that of Panaetius.

Schmekel, A., *Die Philosophie der mittleren Stoa in ihrem geschichtlichen Zusammenhange dargestellt.* Berlin, 1892. The most thorough treatment of the subject now available.

PHILIP P. HALLIE

PANENTHEISM. See EMANATIONISM; KRAUSE, KARL CHRISTIAN FRIEDRICH.

PANPSYCHISM is the theory according to which all objects in the universe, not only human beings and animals but also plants and even objects we usually classify as "inanimate," have an "inner" or "psychological" being. The German philosopher and psychologist G. T. Fechner wrote:

> I stood once on a hot summer's day beside a pool and contemplated a water-lily which had spread its leaves evenly over the water and with an open blossom was basking in the sunlight. How exceptionally fortunate, thought I, must this lily be which above basks in the sunlight and below is plunged in the water—if only it might be capable of feeling the sun and the bath. And why not? I asked myself. It seemed to me that nature surely would not have built a creature so beautiful, and so carefully designed for such conditions, merely to be an object of idle observation. . . . I was inclined to think that nature had built it thus in order that all the pleasure which can be derived from bathing at once in sunlight and in water might be enjoyed by one creature in the fullest measure. (*Religion of a Scientist,* pp. 176–177)

To many readers this may seem to be merely charming poetry, but Fechner was writing in defense of a philosophical theory for which he argued with great passion and resourcefulness. "Where we see inorganic Nature seemingly dead," wrote the American panpsychist Josiah Royce, "there is, in fact, conscious life, just as surely as there is any Being present in Nature at all" (*The World and the Individual,* Second Series, p. 240). "All motion of matter in space," in the words of Hermann Lotze, "may be explained as a natural expression of the inner states of beings that seek or avoid one another with a feeling of their need. . . . The whole of the world of sense . . . is but the veil of an infinite realm of mental life" (*Microcosmus,* Vol. I, p. 363).

PANPSYCHISM AND RELATED DOCTRINES

Although panpsychism seems incredible to most people at the present time, it has been endorsed in one way or another by many eminent thinkers in antiquity as well as in recent times. Among those who were either outright panpsychists or who inclined to a position of this kind, in addition to Fechner, Royce, and Lotze one may count Thales, Anaximenes, Empedocles, several of the Stoics, Plotinus and Simplicius; numerous Italian and German Renaissance philosophers (including Paracelsus, Girolamo Cardano, Bernardino Telesio, Giordano Bruno and Tommaso Campanella); G. W. Leibniz, F. W. J. von Schelling, Arthur Schopenhauer, Antonio Rosmini, W. K. Clifford, Harald Høffding, C. B. Renouvier, Eduard von Hartmann, and Wilhelm Wundt; the German freethinkers Ernst Haeckel, Wilhelm Bölsche, and Bruno Wille; C. A. Strong, Erich Adickes, Erich Becher, Alfred Fouillée, C. S. Peirce, and F. C. S. Schiller; and, in our own day, A. N. Whitehead, Samuel Alexander, Bernardino Varisco, Paul Haeberlin, Aloys Wenzel, Charles Hartshorne, and the biologists Pierre Teilhard de Chardin, C. H. Waddington, Sewall Wright, and W. E. Agar.

Few panpsychists, writing in recent years, would make the claim that their position can be proven, but they do assert that the available evidence favors their theory or at the very least enables it to be a serious contender. According to Fechner, it is the best, clearest, most natural, and most beautiful account of the facts of the universe. According to Schiller, who was both a pragmatist and a panpsychist, the doctrine "renders the operation of things more comprehensible" and also enables us to "act upon them more successfully" (*Studies in Humanism,* p. 443). Similarly, Whitehead, after quoting a passage in which Francis Bacon declared his belief that "all bodies whatsoever, though they have no sense . . . yet have perception," claims that this line of thought "expresses a more fundamental truth than do the materialistic concepts which were then being shaped as adequate for physics" (*Science and the Modern World,* p. 56). Agar, who was a follower of Whitehead's, conceded that there can be "no coercive demonstration" of the truth or falsehood of panpsychism, but it "leads to a more consistent and satisfying world picture than any of the alternatives"; and, unlike these alternatives, panpsychism is not committed to the paradoxical view that "the mental factor . . . made its appearance out of the blue at some date in the world's history" (*The Theory of the Living Organism,* pp. 109–110).

Modern panpsychists have been quite aware that their theory ran counter to what Fechner's distinguished follower Friedrich Paulsen called "the obstinate dogmatism of popular opinion and of the physical conception of the universe" (*Introduction to Philosophy,* p. 93). This obstinacy they attributed to the prevalence of the "night-view"

of the universe—an outlook natural in a mechanized civilization in which people are incapable of noticing and appreciating anything that cannot become the subject of measurement and calculation. In arguing for panpsychism, Fechner and Paulsen (among others) believed that they were counteracting a pernicious tendency in modern life, not merely defending a philosophical viewpoint. Fechner conceived of himself as "awakening a sleeping world" (*Religion of a Scientist,* p. 130) and frequently appealed to his readers to "meet nature with new eyes" (p. 211). Whether plants have souls or not, in the opinion of these writers, an idle or trivial question but on the contrary has a "broader bearing," and its answer decides many other questions and indeed determines one's "whole outlook upon nature" (Fechner, *op. cit.,* p. 163). It is only by accepting panpsychism that a modern man (who finds it impossible to believe in the claims of traditional religion) can escape the distressing implications of materialism.

Unlike Fechner and Paulsen, Lotze supported the traditional religious doctrines of a personal, immaterial deity and a substantival, immortal soul; and hence he did not claim that we had to embrace panpsychism in order to avoid materialism. Lotze also repeatedly insisted, quite unlike Royce and Schiller, that we must not introduce panpsychism into science. Nevertheless he, too, greatly emphasized the emotional benefits accruing from the acceptance of panpsychism. Although science may and should set aside all reference to the "pervading animation of the universe," the "aesthetic view of Nature may lawfully fill out the sum of what exists." If we are panpsychists we no longer "look on one part of the cosmos as but a blind and lifeless instrument for the ends of another," but, on the contrary, find "beneath the unruffled surface of matter, behind the rigid and regular repetitions of its working, . . . the warmth of a hidden mental activity." Lotze was particularly concerned to vindicate "the fullness of animated life" in such lowly things as "the dust trodden by our feet [and] the prosaic texture of the cloth that forms our clothing." Dust, Lotze declares, is "dust only to him whom it inconveniences," and he asks us to remember that human beings who are "confined" in a low social position, in which the outflow of intellectual energy is greatly impeded, are not by any means deprived of their "high destiny." If in the case of such "oppressed fragments of humanity," of "this dust of the spiritual world," we may yet affirm a divine origin and a celestial goal, then we have far less reason to deny an inner life to physical dust particles; uncomely as these "may appear to us in their accumulations, they at least everywhere and without shortcoming perform the actions permitted to them by the universal order" (*Microcosmus,* Vol. I, pp. 361–363).

Hylozoism. Panpsychism is related to but not identical with hylozoism. "Hylozoism" is sometimes defined as the view that matter is "intrinsically" active and in this sense is primarily opposed to the view of philosophers, like Plato and Berkeley, who asserted that matter is "essentially" inert or passive. More frequently, it refers to the theory that all objects in the universe are in some literal sense alive. Any panpsychist who endorses the usual view that mind implies life would automatically be a hylozoist in the latter sense, but the converse does not hold. In fact most panpsychists have been quite ready to have themselves labeled hylozoists, but there are some exceptions, of whom Schopenhauer is perhaps the most famous. According to Schopenhauer, all objects have an inner nature which he calls "will," but although this will may be described as psychic or mental, it is not necessarily a form of life. "I am the first," Schopenhauer wrote, "who has asserted that a *will* must be attributed to all that is lifeless and inorganic. For, with me, the will is not, as has hitherto been assumed, an accident of cognition and therefore of life; but life itself is manifestation of will" (*On the Will in Nature,* p. 309).

William James is responsible for some terminological confusion that should be cleared up before we go any further. In several of his later writings James strongly supported a theory which he stated in the following words: ". . . there is a continuum of cosmic consciousness, against which our several minds plunge as into a mother-sea or reservoir. . . . we with our lives are like islands in the sea, or like trees in the forest" (*Memories and Studies,* p. 204). Not only psychical research, he held, but also metaphysical philosophy and speculative biology are led in their own ways to look with favor on some such "panpsychist view of the universe as this." Elsewhere he remarks that the evidence from normal and abnormal psychology, from religious experience and from psychical research combine to establish a "formidable probability in favor of a general view of the world almost identical with Fechner's" (*Varieties of Religious Experience,* p. 311). It is true that Fechner held to a theory of a cosmic reservoir of consciousness, regarding God as the universal consciousness in which all lesser souls are contained, but it was not the acceptance of this theory that made him a panpsychist, and James himself was *not* a panpsychist. He nowhere maintained that plants and inanimate objects have an inner psychic life, and it is not easy to see how the reservoir theory by itself logically implies panpsychism.

World soul. It should also be pointed out that the theory of the "world soul" is not identical with and does not necessarily follow from panpsychism. A number of panpsychists have in fact maintained the existence of a world soul, and they regarded it as a natural extension of panpsychism. Thus, Fechner in his *Zend-Avesta* (Vol. I, p. 179) concluded that "the earth is a creature . . . , a unitary whole in form and substance, in purpose and effect . . . and self-sufficient in its individuality." It is related to our human body as "the whole tree is to a single twig, a permanent body to a perishable, small organ." "Nothing," in the words of Zeno the Stoic (as approvingly quoted by Cicero), that "is destitute itself of life and reason, can generate a being possessed of life and reason; but the world does generate beings possessed of life and reason; the world therefore is not itself destitute of life and reason" (*On the Nature of the Gods,* Bk. II, Sec. VIII). In a very similar vein Paulsen argues that the earth, since it "produces all living and animated beings and harbors them as parts of its life," may itself be plausibly regarded as "alive and animated." Only the person who is "not open to the inner life of things" will find it difficult to regard the earth as a unitary organism with an inner life as well as a body (*Introduction to Philosophy,* p. 108). To demand to be shown the eyes and ears, the mouth and digestive system, the skin and hair, the arms and legs, the nervous system and the brain of the earth is quite improper. Unlike an animal, the earth does not need a mouth and a stomach because it does not have to take in substances from outside. An animal pursues its prey and in turn attempts to escape its pursuers, and hence it needs eyes and ears, but the earth is not a pursuer and is also not pursued. An animal needs a brain and nerves in order to regulate its movements in response to its environment, but the earth moves around without any such aid. Much like Fechner, Paulsen concludes that "it has regulated its relations to the external world in the most beautiful and becoming manner." "Please do not," he adds, slightly hurt by the irreverent objections of some critics, "please do not ask it to do what is contrary to its nature and cosmical position" (*ibid.*). This elevated idea of the earth soul has not won general acceptance among panpsychists. Charles Hartshorne, a contemporary panpsychist who, like Fechner, is a friend of religion, pays tribute to the "eloquence" of Fechner's account but questions whether "the advances of science since his time have served to confirm" his view. While it may be plausible to regard an electron as "a rudimentary organism," the larger systems that Fechner and Paulsen dealt with so enthusiastically "seem to contemporary knowledge rather too loosely integrated to be accepted as sentient subjects." A tree, it seems plausible to argue, has less unity than one of its own cells, and, similarly, the earth has less unity than the animals which inhabit it ("Panpsychism," p. 447). Hartshorne, as just observed, is a religious thinker, but there have also been atheistic and agnostic panpsychists, and there is no doubt that they would dismiss the theory of the world soul as quite absurd and as an illegitimate extension of panpsychism.

Degrees of consciousness. There is one other terminological confusion against which we should be on guard. Eisler, in the article on panpsychism in his *Wörterbuch der Philosophischen Begriffe,* first supplies the definition that we have adopted here and which is the one generally accepted. Later, however, he remarks that many panpsychists merely assert that all matter has a "disposition towards the psychological"—that is, that they ascribe to inorganic things no more than a "hypothetical" *or* low-grade mentality. Now, panpsychists have indeed generally emphasized that there are degrees of "mentality" or "soul life" and that the mentality or psychic nature of inanimate objects is of an exceedingly simple order, but a low degree or level of mentality must be distinguished from "hypothetical mentality" or the capacity to become the subject of mental activities. To qualify as a panpsychist a person must claim that all bodies *actually* have an inner or psychological nature or aspect. That all matter is potentially the subject of mental activities or characteristics is something that many other philosophers, including not a few materialists, would concede. To say that a stone is made of elements which, when suitably combined, form an entity that thinks and feels is not the same thing as to say that the stone itself has an inner, psychological being.

Royce is a notable exception to the statement that panpsychists regard the psychic character of inorganic bodies as much lower than that of human beings or animals. He thought that the difference was mainly one of speed and that the "fluent" nature of the inner life of inorganic systems tends to go unnoticed because of its "very vast slowness." To this he added, however, that slowness does *not* mean "a lower type of consciousness" (*The World and the Individual*, Second Series, pp. 226–227).

Naive. and critical panpsychism. Eisler distinguishes between "naive" and "critical" panpsychism—by the former he means the animism of primitive peoples and of children, by the latter he means panpsychist theories which are supported by arguments. In this article we are, of course, concerned exclusively with the "critical" or philosophical variety of panpsychism. Most critical panpsychists would probably endorse Agar's judgment that although primitive animism was "in its analogical way of thinking basically sound," it was also "full of errors" and "ludicrously mistaken in detail" (*The Theory of the Living Organism*, p. 109).

It should be observed that some philosophical panpsychists are not consistently "critical" in the sense just indicated. Thus, while offering elaborate arguments and conceding quite explicitly on numerous occasions that the inner psychic processes of plants and inanimate objects are not given to us in immediate experience but have to be inferred, both Schopenhauer and Fechner occasionally take the opposite position. In a remarkable passage, Schopenhauer tells us that if we consider various inanimate objects "attentively," we shall *observe* (among many other things) the "strong and unceasing impulse with which the waters hurry to the ocean, [the] persistency with which the magnet turns ever to the North Pole, [the] readiness with which iron flies to the magnet, [the] eagerness with which the electric poles seek to be reunited, and which, just like human desire, is increased by obstacles [as well as] the choice with which bodies repel and attract each other, combine and separate, when they are set free in a fluid state, and emancipated from the bonds of rigidity." Furthermore, if we attend to the way in which a load "hampers our body by its gravitation towards the earth," we shall "feel directly [that it] unceasingly presses and strains [our body] in pursuit of its one tendency." This passage is taken from the early first volume of *Die Welt als Wille und Vorstellung* (Bk. II, Sec. 23). His later work *Über den Willen in der Natur* consists largely of lists of scientific facts "proving" Schopenhauer's assorted philosophical theories, including his panpsychism. Here we are told to "*look* attentively at a torrent dashing headlong over rocks," whose "boisterous vehemence" can arise only from an "exertion of strength" (p. 308). As for the celestial bodies, if we observe them carefully we shall see that they "play with each other, betray mutual inclination, exchange as it were amorous glances, yet never allow themselves to come into rude contact" (p. 305). Fechner, a milder man than Schopenhauer and more interested in plants than in boisterous torrents or burdensome loads, records experiences in which "the very soul of the plant stood visibly before me," in which he "saw" not only a special "outward clarity" of the flowers but also "the inward light" which in all likelihood caused the outer appearance (*op. cit.*, pp. 211–212).

To see what is at issue between panpsychists and their opponents, it is important to point out that passages such as these are aberrations. It may indeed be held that in addition to the more familiar properties, to which philosophers refer as the primary and secondary qualities, physical objects possess a further set of qualities that are not noticed by observers who lack certain gifts or a suitable training. Such a view need not be mystical and has been plausibly defended in the case of the so-called "tertiary" qualities, especially those of artistic productions and performances. However, the initial definitions of "soul," "psychic," and "inner," or of any of the other terms used by panpsychists in statements of their position, preclude them from adopting a position of this kind. The "soul," the "inner" nature of an object, its "mental side" is *by definition*—a definition to which the panpsychists subscribe—something private which only the object itself can experience or observe. Hence, even if one grants that panpsychists possess gifts of which other mortals are deprived, these cannot possibly be the means of directly perceiving the inner qualities or states of any object external to the observer. Moreover, the great majority of panpsychists, including Schopenhauer and Fechner, do not, in their more considered presentations, claim any special faculty for themselves which the opponents of panpsychism supposedly lack. On the contrary, it is implied that, starting from certain generally accessible facts, sound *reasoning* will lead a person to a panpsychist conclusion.

ARGUMENTS FOR PANPSYCHISM

The arguments for panpsychism may be conveniently grouped according to whether they presuppose the acceptance of a particular metaphysical system or some controversial epistemological theory or whether they are or purport to be of an empirical or inductive character. Some of the arguments of Leibniz and Royce are based on their respective versions of metaphysical idealism, and some of the arguments of Schopenhauer and Paulsen presuppose a Kantian theory of knowledge. It is impossible to evaluate any such arguments without getting involved in an appraisal of their particular metaphysical or epistemological framework, and we shall therefore confine our discussion to arguments of the other kind. It is perhaps worth noting in this connection that especially during the last hundred years, many panpsychists have regarded themselves as opponents of metaphysics, or, if they did not object to being labeled metaphysicians, they took care to add that theirs was an "inductive," not a speculative, variety of metaphysics. Fechner in particular prided himself on dispensing altogether with "a priori constructions," and he was a leading figure, along with von Hartmann and Wundt, in a movement to renounce any claim to a special philosophical method distinct from the method employed in the natural sciences. The only method which, on his view, could lead to a tenable theory about the universe as a whole was "generalization by induction and analogy, and the rational combination of the common elements gathered from different areas," as he observes in *Zend-Avesta*. Furthermore, even some of the panpsychists who were also speculative metaphysicians appealed to empirical considerations. They thought that panpsychism could be supported in different ways that were logically independent of one another. Royce was one of the philosophers who adopted this approach. Insisting that his "Idealistic Theory of Being . . . furnishes a deep warrant" for panpsychism, he nevertheless regarded panpsychism as also resting on "a merely empirical basis" (*op. cit.*, p. 213). "Wholly apart from any more metaphysical consideration of the deeper nature of Reality," certain empirical facts suggest panpsychism as the conclusion of "a rough induction." In this connection, the theory should be treated as a "hypothesis for further testing" (*ibid.*, pp. 223–224).

Genetic arguments. The arguments which have been most widely urged in defense of panpsychism and which go back at least as far as Telesio and Campanella rely, in one way or another, on the assumption that mental facts can be causally explained only in terms of other mental facts. Philosophers who have arrived at a parallelistic answer to the body–mind problem have been specially prone to endorse such arguments, but these can be stated independently of any commitment to parallelism. It is perhaps interesting to note in passing that many early champions of Darwinism (for example, Clifford in England and Haeckel and Büchner in Germany) were attracted by reasoning of this kind, although they were frequently repelled by the analogical arguments considered later in the present article. We shall here examine two such genetic arguments—one advanced by Paulsen, the other by a contemporary British scientist.

How, asks Paulsen, did soul life originate? Modern biology assumes, quite rightly in Paulsen's opinion, that organic life had a beginning on earth and that the "first creations" arose from inorganic matter. The question then arises how "psychic life" came into being. "Is the first feeling in the first protoplasmic particle something absolutely new, something that did not exist before in any form, of which not the slightest trace was to be found previously?" (*Introduction to Philosophy*, pp. 99–100). To suppose that the first feeling in the first protoplasmic particle was something "absolutely new" would, however, imply a "creation out of nothing," which would be totally at variance with the basic (and well-founded) principles of science. You might as well, Paulsen remarks, ask the natural scientist "to believe that the protoplasmic particle itself was created out of nothing." The natural scientist rightly assumes that natural bodies arise from pre-existing elements. These enter into new and more complicated combinations, and as a result the bodies are capable of performing "new and astonishing functions." Why does the natural scientist "not make the same natural assumption" in the case of the inner psychic processes as well? Why does he not say that "an inner life was already present in germ (*keimhaft*) in the elements, and that it developed into higher forms?"

It is not easy to appraise this line of reasoning because of the vagueness of the expression "absolutely new." As Ernest Nagel and others have pointed out, it is frequently not at all clear whether two processes or occurrences are to be counted as different instances of the same property or as different properties—whether they are or not usually depends on the purpose of the particular investigation. Furthermore, what may be "absolutely new," in the sense of not being predictable from certain initial conditions in conjunction with a certain set of laws, may at the same time not be absolutely new in the sense of being predictable from these initial conditions together with a different set of laws. However, let us assume that in a given case all parties agree that if at a moment T_1 the features of a system were of a certain kind and if at a subsequent moment T_2 they were of a certain different kind, something "absolutely new" came into being at T_2. More specifically, let us assume that the conditions at T_1 do not include any mental fact but that at T_2 they include "the first feeling" in the first protoplasmic particle. Now, according to Paulsen's argument, anybody who supposes that this is the kind of thing which actually happened—and a person who accepts certain scientific facts while rejecting panpsychism has to suppose that this is what happened—is committed to the view that something came from nothing. But to suppose that something came from nothing is unscientific and absurd.

There is a simple answer to this. By saying that something must always come from something and cannot come from nothing, we may mean either (1) that every phenomenon or event has a cause or (2) the scholastic principle that any property residing in an effect must also have been present in its cause. If we suppose that at time T_1 there was no mental fact in the universe while at a later time T_2 the first feeling occurred in a protoplasmic particle, we would indeed be violating proposition (2), but we would not at all be violating proposition (1). Yet if anything can here be regarded as "unscientific" or "absurd" it would be exceptions to (1). For reasons explained earlier, it is not easy to state (2) or its denial with any precision, but, in the most familiar sense of "new," experience seems to show that there are any number of effects possessing new properties—properties not present in the cause. The very course of evolution, to which Paulsen and other proponents of the genetic argument appeal, provides a multitude of illustrations of this. At any rate, an opponent of panpsychism would deny proposition (2) and would insist that such a denial is in no way unempirical or unscientific. To assume the opposite without further ado would surely be to beg one of the basic questions at issue.

Let us now consider a more recent version of a genetic argument: "Something must go on in the simplest inanimate things," writes the distinguished British geneticist C. H. Waddington, "which can be described in the same language as would be used to describe our self-awareness" (*The Nature of Life*, p. 121). It is true, he continues, that we know nothing of its nature, but the conclusion is forced on us by the "demands of logic and the application of evolutionary theory" (p. 122). Waddington's argument opens with the declaration that the phenomenon of self-awareness is a "basic mystery." This is so because awareness "can never be constructed theoretically out of our present fundamental scientific concepts, since these contain no element which has any similarity in kind with self-consciousness." But self-awareness undoubtedly exists, and hence we must infer that the mode we experience "evolved from simple forms which are experienced by non-human things." It is not difficult to accept this conclusion as far as animals like dogs and cats are concerned. But, Waddington proceeds, we cannot stop there if we take the theory of evolution seriously. According to the initial premise it is inconceivable that self-awareness "originated from anything which did not share something in common with it and possessed only those qualities which can be objectively observed from outside." Hence, we are forced to conclude that "even in the simplest inanimate things there is something which belongs to the same realm of being as self-awareness." Waddington's argument is not overtly based, as Paulsen's was, on the contention that somebody who accepts evolution but rejects panpsychism is committed to the absurd proposition that something comes from nothing. According to Waddington such a person would be committed to the view that self-awareness is not a mystery—that is, that it is explicable in physical terms—and this Waddington takes to be plainly false.

In reply it should be pointed out that Waddington appears to use the word "explanation" in two very different senses in the course of his argument. Sometimes when we ask for the explanation of a phenomenon we are looking for an account of its make-up, of how its parts are related and how they work. We use the word "explanation" in this sense when we want to have the nature of a car or a clock or perhaps a human eye explained to us. At other times, and more frequently, in asking for the explanation of a phenomenon we are looking for its cause. It is not easy to see why awareness should be said to be a "mystery" just because it cannot, in the first sense of "explanation," be explained in physical terms (this betrays a strange materialistic bias which regards a phenomenon as properly explicable, in the first sense, only if it is something material—one wonders why physical objects are not equally mysterious, since they cannot be explained in terms of predicates that are applicable only to mental states). But waiving this point—allowing, that is, that awareness cannot be adequately characterized by the kinds of predicates usually applied to material objects and that this makes awareness incapable of explanation in the first of the two senses distinguished, none of this implies that awareness cannot be explained, in the second sense of the word, in terms of purely physical factors. Avoiding the word "explanation," the point can be expressed very simply: granting that awareness *is not* a physical phenomenon, it does not follow that it *cannot be produced* by conditions that are purely physical. When the matter is put in this way, it becomes clear that we are back to the difficulty besetting Paulsen's form of the argument. Waddington's argument does not, aside from the acceptance of the evolutionary theory, depend merely on the admission that awareness is not a physical phenomenon, that it "cannot be constructed" out of physical concepts: it also depends on the maxim that any property of the effect must also be present in the cause. We have already mentioned reasons for rejecting this principle, but perhaps it is worth adding that in the context of the body–mind relationship it seems particularly implausible. Brain tumors and other damage to the body, to give some very obvious examples, lead to all kinds of psychological states, but we do not for this reason refuse to regard them as explanations of the latter.

Analogical arguments. The second set of arguments commonly employed by panpsychists, independently of any metaphysical system, purport to be of an analogical kind. Here the more systematic panpsychists usually proceed in two steps: the first consists in arguing that plants are in "essential" respects so much like animals that one cannot consistently attribute a psychic or soul life to animals but refuse it to plants; it is then maintained that the borderline between animate and inanimate objects is not sharp and that a careful examination of inanimate objects reveals them to have many impressive likenesses to animals and plants, indicating the existence of inner psychic being there also.

Plants manifest many of the same vital processes that are found in animals: nutrition, growth, reproduction, and many more. Like animals, plants are born and also die. Moreover, it is simply not true that plants lack the power of spontaneous movement which we observe in animals. "Does not the plant," asks Paulsen, "turn its buds and leaves to the light, does it not send its roots where it finds nourishment, and its tendrils where it finds support? Does it not close up its petals at night or when it rains, and does it not open them in sunshine?" If there is so great a "correspondence" between the visible processes, why should there not be a similar correspondence in "the invisible processes"? (*op. cit.*, pp. 96–97). If it is argued that these analogies are too vague and trifling, because plants have neither a brain nor a nervous system, the answer is surely that there are animals which also lack brains and nervous systems. Fechner was particularly concerned to exhibit the weakness of this counterargument. He observes that if we remove the strings of a piano or a violin it becomes impossible to obtain any harmonic sounds from these instruments. If somebody concluded from this that the presence of strings is essential to the production of musical tones, he would be completely mistaken, because there are many instruments, like flutes and trombones, with which we can produce musical sounds although they have no strings; but this argument would be not one whit worse than that of the critic of panpsychism.

There are, to be sure, differences between plants and animals, and these a panpsychist has no wish to deny, but, according to Paulsen, they "may be conceived as indicating a difference in inner life also" rather than the absence of any inner processes. The differences indicate "that plants possess a peculiar inclination to receptivity and a decentralized extensity, whereas the psychical life of the animal shows more spontaneity and centralized intensity" (*ibid.*, p. 98). Fechner is even more specific and compares the difference in psychical life between animals and plants to the difference in the psychology of men and women. Elsewhere he compares the former difference to that between the emotions of travelers and those who are "home-bodies," between the pleasures associated with "running hither and thither" and those accompanying a "quiet and sedentary sphere of endeavor" (*Religion of a Scientist*, pp. 178–179). However, Paulsen adds, it does not really matter what we think about the details of the inner processes, since all such attempts at conceiving the nature of the psychic life of plants are "at best feeble." It should be remembered that we do not really fare any better if we try to "interpret" the psychical life of animals, especially that of the lower species. We know very little, Paulsen remarks, "about the inner experiences of a jelly-fish or the feelings of a caterpillar or a butterfly."

When we come to inanimate objects, Paulsen continues, the first thing to note is that organic and inorganic bodies must not be regarded as belonging to two separate worlds. There is constant interaction between them. They are composed of the same ingredients and acted on .by the same forces. If this were all, however, the analogy would not be strong enough. It would be objected that unlike animals and plants, objects like stones are lifeless and rigid, that they lack all spontaneous activity. This opinion, Paulsen argues, is totally mistaken and is based on the Aristotelian–scholastic theory, taken over by materialistic scientists of the eighteenth and nineteenth centuries, that matter is inherently and absolutely passive. This theory, whether in its original or in its modern atomistic form, is quite untenable. In fact a stone is not an "absolutely dead and rigid body" and devoid of "inner impulses." Modern physics has discarded such a view. Its molecules and atoms are "forms of the greatest inner complexity and mobility." Not only are the constituents of an apparently rigid object like a stone in continuous motion, but the entire system is "in constant interaction with its immediate surroundings as well as with the remotest system of fixed stars" (pp. 101–102). In the light of this it is not only not absurd but quite plausible to conclude that "corresponding to this wonderful play of physical forces and movements" there is a system of inner psychic processes "analogous to that which accompanies the working of the parts in an organic body." We thus arrive, on the basis of scientific evidence, at a view substantially like that of Empedocles that "love and hate form the motive forces in all things"—not, to be sure, quite as we know them in ourselves, but nevertheless in a form that is "at bottom similar" to these human emotions.

It is natural to object to such arguments that the analogies are altogether inconclusive. It is true that there are certain similarities between, say, a stone and a human body, but there are also all kinds of differences. Paulsen assures us that the similarities are "essential," but if "essential" here means that, as far as the inference to an inner psychic process is concerned, the similarities count and the differences do not, that they are relevant whereas the differences are irrelevant, one may well ask how Paulsen knows this. Surely no proposition has been or could have been established to the effect that inner physical movement is always and necessarily connected with psychic activity. Any such general proposition is precisely what the opponent of panpsychism would deny or question. Furthermore, leaving aside any discussion of whether those who regard matter as "active" and those who maintain it to be "passive" are engaging in a factual dispute (so that one party could be said to be right and the other wrong), it must be emphasized that in rejecting panpsychism one is in no way committed to the view that matter is devoid of "inner activity." The view that matter has no inner *psychic* aspect in no way precludes the admission of inner *physical* processes such as those postulated by modern physical theory.

These criticisms, however, do not go far enough. They assume, what seems very doubtful, that the arguments under discussion are of a genuinely empirical character. In this connection it is pertinent to raise the question of what

the universe would have to be like so that there would be no evidence for panpsychism, or, more strongly, so that the evidence would clearly favor the opposite position. We saw that Paulsen considered the fact that human bodies and inanimate objects are composed of the same elements to be evidence for his position. He also regarded the internal movements of the particles of apparently stationary objects as evidence of their inner life. But suppose that stones and human bodies were not composed of the same elements; would this constitute evidence against panpsychism or would it at least deprive panpsychism of evidence which is at present supporting it? Suppose that electrons were not buzzing inside the stone; would this show or would it be any kind of evidence for the view that the stone does *not* have a psychic life? From the writings of panpsychists it seems probable that the answer to these questions would be in the negative: If the elements of stones were quite different from those of human bodies, it might be an indication that the psychic processes in stones are even more different in detail from those of human beings, and if the internal constituents of the stones were not in constant motion it might indicate a more restful psychic life, but it would not indicate that no psychic life at all is going on. If this is an accurate presentation of the panpsychist position, it shows that the analogical arguments we have been considering are not genuinely empirical, that the facts pointed to are not, in any accepted sense, evidence for the conclusion. This is a far stronger criticism than the claim that the analogies are weak or the arguments inconclusive.

IS PANPSYCHISM AN INTELLIGIBLE DOCTRINE?

Some contemporary philosophers who have given more thought to the conditions of meaningful discourse than was customary in previous times are inclined to dismiss panpsychism not as false or unproven but as unintelligible. Thus, in his *Philosophical Investigations* Wittgenstein raises the question "Could one imagine a stone's having consciousness?" and comments that if anyone can imagine this, it would merely amount to "image-mongery" (Sec. 390, p. 119 e). Such image-mongery, Wittgenstein seems to imply, would not show at all that in attributing consciousness to a stone one is making an intelligible statement. It would probably be pointless to try to "prove" that panpsychism is a meaningless doctrine. Any such attempt is liable to involve one in an elaborate and inconclusive defense of some controversial meaning criterion. However, it may be of some interest to explain more fully, without intending to settle anything, why not a few contemporary philosophers would maintain that the panpsychists do not succeed in asserting any new facts and in the end merely urge certain pictures on us.

To this end let us first consider the following imaginary disputes about the "inner" nature of a tennis ball. A holds the common view that the ball is made of rubber and not of living tissue, while B holds the unusual opinion that if we were to examine the inside of the tennis ball under a powerful microscope we would find a brain, a nervous system, and other physiological structures usually associated with consciousness. Furthermore, B maintains that if we listened very attentively to what goes on while tennis balls are in their can we would hear one ball whispering to the other, "My brother, be careful—don't let them hit you too hard; if you roll into a bush on the other side of the fence you may spend the rest of your days in blissful peace." There is genuine empirical disagreement betweeen *A* and *B* and, as far as we know, *A* would be right if the ball or balls in question are of the familiar kind. Let us next suppose that *C*, after reading Paulsen and Waddington, becomes converted to panpsychism and starts saying such things as "the tennis ball is not a mere body—it has an inner psychic life, it is moved by love and hate, although not love and hate quite as we know them in human beings." To an uncritical outsider it may at first appear, chiefly because of the images one associates with the word "inner," that *C*, like *B*, is asserting the existence of strange goings-on inside the ball, never suspected by the ordinary man or the physicist. In fact, however, if *C* is a philosophical panpsychist, he will not expect to find a brain or a nervous system or any kind of living tissue inside the ball, and he will disclaim any such assertion. Nor will he expect that tennis balls whisper gentle warnings to one another when they are alone. If he should start serving less forcefully in order to avoid hurting the ball, a professional panpsychist would undoubtedly advise him not to be silly, explaining that although their lives are governed by love and hate, balls do not get hurt in any sense that need concern a sympathetic human being. In other words, *C* does not disagree with *A* about what would be found inside the ball or about the ball's behavior while it is in the can, and he is also not treating the ball any differently from the way *A* does—or at any rate no different treatment is logically implied by his opinion that the ball has an inner psychic life. *B* really contradicts *A* and, at least in the case of the balls we all know, he is quite certainly mistaken. *C* is not mistaken, but one begins to wonder whether he is asserting any facts not allowed for in the ordinary, non-panpsychist view of the ball. A semantically sensitive observer might comment that ordinary people (and uncritical philosophers) are apt to suppose that they understand well enough what panpsychism asserts and that they proceed to dismiss it as silly or incredible (that is, as plainly false) because they regard panpsychism as a theory like *B*'s unusual opinion about the tennis ball. In fact, panpsychism is not like *B*'s opinion but like *C*'s, and the appropriate criticism seems to be not that it is a false theory but that one does not really know what, if anything, has been asserted.

Schiller. Let us now turn to the procedure of an actual panpsychist to see the full relevance of the preceding reflections. F. C. S. Schiller argued that inanimate objects, contrary to the usual opinion, take notice of other inanimate objects, as well as of human beings. "Inanimate objects," he wrote, "are responsive to each other and modify their behavior accordingly. A stone is not indifferent to other stones" (*Logic for Use*, p. 447). Nor are stones indifferent to human beings: "In a very real sense," he wrote elsewhere, "a stone must be said to know us and to respond to our manipulation" (*Studies in Humanism*, p. 443). It is "as true of stones as of men" that if you treat them differently they behave differently (*Logic for Use*, p. 447). It must be emphasized, however, that the respon-

siveness, the nonindifference, of stones is not quite what we mean when we talk about the responsiveness and nonindifference of human beings. How does a stone exhibit its nonindifference to other stones? Very simply: in being gravitationally attracted to them (*ibid.*). Nor are we "recognized" by the stone "in our whole nature." It does not "apprehend us as spiritual beings," but this does not mean that the stone takes no note whatever of our existence. "It is aware of us and affected by us on the plane on which its own existence is passed." In the physical world which we and stones share, " 'awareness' can apparently be shown by being hard and heavy and colored and space-filling, and so forth. And all these things the stone is and recognizes in other bodies" (*Studies in Humanism*, p. 442). The stone "faithfully exercises" all its physical functions: "it gravitates and resists pressure, and obstructs ether vibrations, etc., and makes itself respected as such a body. And it treats us as if of a like nature with itself, on the level of its understanding, i.e., as bodies to which it is attracted inversely as the square of the distance, moderately hard and capable of being hit." The stone does not indeed "know or care" whether a human being gets hurt by it; but in those operations which are of "interest" to the stone, as, for example, in housebuilding, "it plays its part and responds according to the measure of its capacity." What is true of stones, Schiller continues, is also true of atoms and electrons, if they really exist. Just as the stone responds only "after its fashion," so atoms and electrons also know us "after their fashion." They know us not as human beings but "as whirling mazes of atoms and electrons like themselves." We treat stones and atoms as "inanimate" because of "their immense spiritual remoteness from us" and "perhaps" also because of "our inability to understand them" (*ibid.*, pp. 442, 444).

Some of his readers, Schiller realizes, will "cry" that the views just reported amount to "sheer hylozoism," but he does not regard this as any reason for concern. "What," he answers, "if it is hylozoism or, still better, panpsychism, so long as it really brings out a genuine analogy," and this, he is convinced, it does. "The analogy is helpful so long as it really renders the operations of things more comprehensible to us, and interprets facts which had seemed mysterious" (*ibid.*, p. 443). Schiller illustrates his claim by considering the chemical phenomenon of catalytic action. It had "seemed mysterious" and "hard to understand" (presumably prior to the publication of Schiller's "humanistic" panpsychism), that two bodies *A* and *B* may have a strong affinity for each other and yet refuse to combine until the merest trace of a third substance *C* is introduced, which sets up an interaction between *A* and *B* without producing an alteration in *C* itself. But, asks Schiller, "is not this strangely suggestive of the idea that *A* and *B* did not know each other until they were introduced by *C*, and then liked each other so well that *C* was left out in the cold?" To this he adds—and here surely not even the most hostile critic would disagree—that "more such analogies and possibilities will probably be found if they are looked for." However, panpsychism does not merely render the operation of things more comprehensible. It has a further virtue, to which Schiller alludes later in the same discussion: "The alien world which seemed so remote and so rigid to an inert contemplation, the reality which seemed so intractable to an aimless and fruitless speculation, grows plastic in this way to our intelligent manipulations" (*ibid.*, p. 444).

Perhaps the most striking features of Schiller's presentation are the constant modifications or retractions of what at first appear truly remarkable assertions. Inanimate objects are "responsive to each other," but not the way in which human beings or animals are—they are responsive in being gravitationally attracted by other inanimate objects. The stone is "aware of us," but not, of course, in the sense in which human beings are aware—it is aware on "*its* plane"; the stone "recognizes" other bodies and is "interested" in operations like housebuilding, but "on the level of *its* understanding"; it "plays its part," but "according to the measure of *its* capacity"; atoms and electrons know us no less than we know them, but "after *their* fashion." It is not, perhaps, unfair to say that Schiller takes away with one hand what he gives with the other, and it may be questioned whether anything remains. When one is told that the stone is aware of us one reacts with astonishment and is apt to suppose that a statement has been made which contradicts what an ordinary nonpanpsychist believes; but this turns out to be more than doubtful since the stone's awareness, on its plane, seems to consist simply in being hard, heavy, space-filling, and colored. The stone makes itself respected and is interested in operations like housebuilding, but in its own fashion, and this consists in gravitating, resisting pressure, and all the usual characteristics of stones, which are not questioned by those who do not subscribe to panpsychism. Schiller plainly believed that the panpsychist asserts (if he has not in fact discovered) facts about stones and atoms which are denied by, or whose existence is unknown to, the ordinary person and the materialist. He evidently did not believe that it was just a question of using words in different senses. But, if so, what are the facts which he asserts and which his opponents deny? Schiller's qualifications remind one of a song in the musical *Kiss Me, Kate* in which a light-hearted lady sings of her numerous and constantly changing amorous involvements, adding at the end of each verse, "But I'm always true to you, darling, in my fashion; yes, I'm always true to you, darling, in my way." How does the stone's awareness in its own way differ from what other people would refer to as absence of awareness?

Empirical pretensions of panpsychists. Even if one is disinclined to go so far as to dismiss panpsychism as meaningless, there is surely good reason to dispute the empirical and pragmatic pretensions of certain panpsychists. We saw that Royce regarded panpsychism (among other things) as a hypothesis "to be tested," but unfortunately he did not tell us anything about the way or ways in which this was to be done. Royce did indeed guard himself by maintaining that the mental processes in physical systems occur over "extremely august" temporal spans (*The World and the Individual*, Second Series, p. 226), so that a human being would be unable to detect a process of this kind. However, making the fullest allowance for this qualification and granting ourselves or some imaginary observer the "august" time span required by Royce's "hypothesis," this would still not do, since Royce omitted to inform us what such an observer should look for.

Schiller, it will be remembered, assured us that as a result of accepting panpsychism the previously "remote" and "rigid" reality "grows plastic . . . to our manipulations." But he did not explain how and where these happy transformations would take place. Is a bricklayer who has been converted to panpsychism going to lay bricks more efficiently? Does a tennis player's game improve if he becomes a disciple of Schiller? No, but perhaps the chemist will find catalytic action more comprehensible, and "more such analogies and possibilities" will make other "intractable" processes less "mysterious." Regrettably, the opinion that panpsychism makes any of these phenomena easier to understand is the result of a confusion which hinges on an ambiguity in "comprehensible" and related expressions. Sometimes we attempt to make *phenomena* or correlations of events more comprehensible. In this sense, a phenomenon (for example, a certain disease or a plane crash) is comprehended or understood if its cause is discovered, and a correlation or a law becomes comprehensible if it is subsumed under a wider law (if, for example, the administration of a certain drug has in many cases been followed by the cure of a given condition, the correlation becomes comprehensible if we determine what it is about the drug that has this effect; and this is another way of saying that we subsume the correlation under a law). But at other times when we talk about making something comprehensible, we are concerned with explaining the meaning of *theories* or *statements,* not with the explanation of phenomena or of correlations. Unlike the first, this kind of problem may be regarded as pedagogical, and here all kinds of analogies may be helpful which do not or need not shed any light on the causes of the phenomena dealt with in the statements we are trying to make more comprehensible. It cannot, of course, be denied that an analogy such as the one Schiller offers may well make catalysts more comprehensible in this pedagogical sense—it may, for example, help school children to understand what a chemist is talking about. It is equally clear that such an analogy does absolutely nothing to make catalytic action more comprehensible in the earlier sense we mentioned, and it was surely in this sense that Schiller claimed panpsychism to make things less mysterious and easier to understand. It is difficult to believe that either Schiller or any other champion of panpsychism would be satisfied to have the theory regarded as no more than a pedagogical device in the teaching of natural science.

Bibliography

The fullest systematic defenses of panpsychism during the last hundred years are found in the writings of Paulsen, Fechner, Lotze, and Royce. Paulsen's arguments are presented in his very influential *Einleitung in die Philosophie* (21st ed., Stuttgart and Berlin, 1909), translated by F. Thilly as *Introduction to Philosophy* (2d American ed., New York, 1906, with a preface by William James). Fechner's main writings on the subject are *Nanna: oder über das Seelenleben der Pflanzen* (3d ed., Leipzig, 1903) and *Zend-Avesta: oder über die Dinge des Jenseits* (2d ed., Hamburg, 1906). There is an English translation of selections from Fechner's works by W. Lowrie entitled *Religion of a Scientist* (New York, 1946). Fechner's ideas are discussed in some detail in G. Stanley Hall, *Founders of Modern Psychology* (New York, 1912); G. F. Stout, *God and Nature*, A. K. Stout, ed. (Cambridge, 1952); Otto Külpe, *Die Philosophie der Gegenwart in Deutschland* (Leipzig,

1902), translated by M. L. Patrick and G. T. W. Patrick as *Philosophy of the Present in Germany* (London, 1913); and G. Murphy, "A Brief Interpretation of Fechner," in *Psyche*, Vol. 7 (1926), 75–80. Although Wilhelm Wundt condemned Fechner's speculations about the souls of the stars and the earth as "a fantastic dream," he himself concluded that mental life can arise only out of conditions which are themselves mental (*System der Philosophie*, Leipzig, 1889). Lotze's defense of panpsychism is contained in Vol. I of *Mikrokosmus* (Leipzig, 1856–1864), translated by E. Hamilton and E. E. C. Jones as *Microcosmus* (New York, 1890). Royce's panpsychism is presented in Lecture V of *The World and the Individual*, Second Series (London and New York, 1901). The American neorealist W. P. Montague, a student of Royce, relates how he "jumped with almost tearful gratitude" at Royce's "hypothesis about the varying time-spans in nature." He regarded this "hypothesis" as "a new and challenging contribution to the great panpsychist tradition," as "a clear and great thought" which "might even be true" (*The Ways of Things*, London, 1940, p. 669). Montague referred to his own position as "animistic materialism," and he is sometimes classified as a panpsychist, but in fact it is very doubtful whether his animism implies panpsychism as we have here defined it.

Little was said in this article about A. N. Whitehead, probably the most distinguished champion of panpsychism in the twentieth century, chiefly because his views on the subject could not have been discussed without consideration of other features of his difficult system. Whitehead would have disagreed with many other panpsychists about the "units" that are to be regarded as the bearers of psychic life. These, he held, are not stars or stones but the events out of which stars and stones are constituted and which Whitehead calls "occasions." His views are presented in *Science and the Modern World* (London and New York, 1925), *Process and Reality* (London and New York, 1929), and, most fully, in "Nature Alive," Lecture 8 of *Modes of Thought* (London and New York, 1938). Panpsychistic views strongly influenced by Whitehead are put forward in Charles Hartshorne, *Beyond Humanism* (Chicago, 1937) and *Man's Vision of God* (Chicago, 1941), and in W. E. Agar, *The Theory of the Living Organism* (Melbourne, 1943). Samuel Alexander, whose metaphysical position has many similarities to Whitehead's, also expresses views akin to panpsychism in his British Academy lecture "The Basis of Realism," reprinted in R. M. Chisholm, ed., *Realism and the Background of Phenomenology* (Glencoe, Ill., 1960).

Of works by earlier panpsychists, special mention should be made of G. W. Leibniz, *Monadology* (various editions), and Arthur Schopenhauer, *Die Welt als Wille und Vorstellung*, 3 vols. (Leipzig, 1818), translated by R. B. Haldane and J. Kemp as *The World as Will and Idea* (London, 1883), as well as his *Über den Willen in der Natur* (Frankfurt, 1836), translated by K. Hillebrand as *On the Will in Nature* (London, 1889).

Giordano Bruno's panpsychist views are presented in the second dialogue of *De la causa, Principio e uno*; for translations see Sidney Greenberg's *The Infinite in Giordano Bruno* (New York, 1950) and Jack Lindsay's version in *Cause, Principle and Unity* (New York, 1964). The works by Telesio and Campanella in which their panpsychism is expounded are not available in English. There is a very clear summary of their arguments in Harald Høffding, *A History of Modern Philosophy*, Vol. I (London, 1908). The texts of the pre-Socratics, some of whom were hylozoists rather than panpsychists, are available in English translation in G. S. Kirk and J. E. Raven, *The Presocratic Philosophers* (Cambridge, 1957). Because of his remarks about the "plastic nature in the universe" in *The True Intellectual System of the Universe*, Ralph Cudworth is described as a panpsychist in various reference works, but it is doubtful that this classification is accurate. Cudworth appears to have postulated the "plastic nature" for living things only and he should be labeled a "vitalist" in a sense in which this theory does not automatically imply panpsychism. C. B. Renouvier's panpsychism, which is in many ways similar to that of Leibniz, is expounded in several of his works, most fully in *La Nouvelle Monadologie* (Paris, 1898). Eduard von Hartmann advocates the view that even atoms possess an unconscious will in *Grundriss der Naturphilosophie*, Vol. II of *System der Philosophie im Grundriss* (Bad Sachsa im Harz, 1907). Spinoza and Bergson

were not listed as panpsychists in the text because there is some doubt as to how some of their remarks are to be interpreted. In Spinoza's case there is at least one passage (*Ethics*, Pt. II, Note 2, Prop. XIII) supporting such a classification. Similarly, some of the remarks in "Summary and Conclusions," in Bergson's *Matter and Memory* (London, 1911), may be construed as an endorsement of panpsychism.

C. H. Waddington's genetic argument is presented in *The Nature of Life* (London, 1961). W. K. Clifford advocates very similar arguments in his essays "Body and Mind" and "On the Nature of Things-in-themselves," in *Lectures and Essays*, Vol. II (London, 1903). The American critical realist C. A. Strong also employs genetic arguments in support of panpsychism in *The Origin of Consciousness* (London, 1918). Sewall Wright, a distinguished contemporary biologist, defends panpsychism on scientific grounds in "Gene and Organism," in *The American Naturalist*, Vol. 87 (1953). Haeckel's views are found in *Natürliche Schöpfungsgeschichte* (4th ed., Berlin, 1892), translated by E. Ray Lankester as *The History of Creation* (London, 1892), and in *Zellseelen und Seelenzellen* (Leipzig, 1909). Panpsychism is also defended on the basis of an appeal to continuity in nature in Harald Høffding, *Outlines of Psychology* (London, 1919). Høffding, however, is rather more diffident than the other writers mentioned in this paragraph. Schiller's defenses of panpsychism are contained in his *Studies in Humanism* (London, 1907) and *Logic for Use* (London, 1929). There is a full discussion of William James' views on panpsychism and various related theories in W. T. Bush, "William James and Panpsychism," in *Columbia University Studies in the History of Ideas*, Vol. II (New York, 1925).

A defense of the scholastic doctrine that an effect cannot possess any perfection which is not found in its cause is contained in G. H. Joyce, *Principles of Natural Theology* (London, 1923), Ch. 3. The question of what may be meant by the claim that an effect contains a "new" property is discussed in Arthur O. Lovejoy, "The Meanings of 'Emergence' and Its Modes," in *Proceedings of the Sixth International Congress of Philosophy* (New York, 1927); Ernest Nagel, *The Structure of Science* (New York, 1961); and Arthur Pap, *An Introduction to the Philosophy of Science* (New York, 1962). Certain contemporary arguments about the alleged causal inexplicability of human actions, similar to the genetic arguments, are examined in Bernard Berofsky, "Determinism and the Concept of a Person," in *Journal of Philosophy*, Vol. 61 (1964), 461–475.

General surveys of panpsychism are found in A. Rau, *Der moderne Panpsychismus* (Berlin, 1901), and Charles Hartshorne, "Panpsychism," in V. T. A. Ferm, ed., *A History of Philosophical Systems* (New York, 1950). Almost all extended discussions of panpsychism occur in the works of writers who accept the theory or who are at least sympathetic to it. One of the few highly critical discussions is contained in Alois Riehl, *Zur Einführung in die Philosophie der Gegenwart* (Leipzig, 1903). Eisler's article on panpsychism in his *Wörterbuch der Philosophische Begriffe* (4th ed., Berlin, 1929) contains a very elaborate list of panpsychists and their writings.

PAUL EDWARDS

PANTHEISM is a doctrine that usually occurs in a religious and philosophical context in which there are already tolerably clear conceptions of God and of the universe and the question has arisen of how these two conceptions are related. It is, of course, easy to read pantheistic doctrines back into unsophisticated texts in which the concept of the divine remains unclarified, but it is wise to be skeptical about the value of such a reading. Some commentators have confidently ascribed pantheistic views to the Eleatics simply because they assert that what is, is one. But even if one considers Xenophanes, the most plausible candidate for such an ascription, it is clear that considerable care must be exercised. Thales and Anaximenes had some idea of objects in the world being infused with a divine power or substance which conferred life and movement. Xenophanes took over this idea and added to it a critique of Homeric and Hesiodic polytheism, attacking both their anthropomorphism and the immorality in which they involved the gods; his own consequent view of deity remains mysterious, however. Aristotle said that Xenophanes "with his eye on the whole world said that the One was god," but he also complained that Xenophanes "made nothing clear." It seems likely that Xenophanes, like other early Greek thinkers, did not distinguish clearly between asserting that an object was divine and asserting that a divine power informed the object's movement.

A failure by commentators themselves to observe this distinction makes it misleadingly easy to present both earlier pre-Socratic and later Stoic philosophers as recruits to the ranks of pantheism. But even Marcus Aurelius, the only notable thinker among them who can plausibly be represented as a pantheist, when he addressed the Universe itself as a deity did not clearly address it in the sense of all that is rather than in the sense of some principle of order that informs all that is.

Vedic pantheism. As in Greek thought, the approach to pantheism in Indian thought is a systematic critique of polytheism. Although there are also conceptions of a god who reigns as the highest deity—Indra at one time held this position—what emerged with the growth of theological reflection was the notion of Brahman. Brahman is the single, infinite reality, indefinable and unchanging, behind the illusory changing world of perceived material objects. The equation of plurality and change with imperfection is an assumption of the Vedānta teachings. From it there is drawn a proof of the illusory character of the material world, as well as of its imperfection. Were the material world real, it must, being neither self-existent nor eternal, have originated from Brahman. But if Brahman were such that from within it what is multifarious, changing, and therefore imperfect could arise, then Brahman would be imperfect. And what is imperfect cannot be Brahman.

We take the illusory for the real because our knowledge is itself tainted with imperfections. Our ordinary knowledge is such that knower and known, subject and object, are distinct. But to know Brahman would be for subject and object to become identical; it would be to attain a knowledge in which all distinctions were abolished and in which what is known would therefore be inexpressible. Two features of the pantheism of the Vedānta scholars deserve comment. The first is the affinity between their logical doctrines and those of F. H. Bradley, whose treatment of the realm of appearance is precisely parallel to the Vedānta treatment of the realm of illusion (*māyā*); Bradley's Absolute resembles Brahman chiefly in that both must be characterized negatively. As with Bradley's doctrine, the natural objection to Vedānta pantheism is to ask how, if Brahman is perfect and unchangeable, even the illusions of finitude, multiplicity, and change can have arisen. The Vedānta doctrine's answer is circular: ignorance (lack of enlightenment) creates illusion. But it is, of course, illusion that fosters the many forms of ignorance.

Yet if the explanation of illusion is unsatisfactory, at least the cure for it is clear; the Vedānta doctrine is above all practical in its intentions. It will be noteworthy in the discussion of other and later pantheisms how often pantheism is linked to doctrines of mystical and contemplative practice. The separateness of the divine and the human, upon which monotheists insist, raises sharply the problem of how man can ever attain true unity with the divine. Those contemplative and mystical experiences, common to many religions, for whose description the language of a union between human and divine seems peculiarly appropriate—at least to those who have enjoyed these experiences—for that very reason create problems for a monotheistic theology, problems which have often been partly resolved by an approach to pantheistic formulations. It is at least plausible to argue that the essence of the Vedānta doctrine lies in its elucidation of mystical experience rather than in any use of metaphysical argument for purely intellectual ends.

Western pantheism to Spinoza. The pantheism of the Vedānta argues that because God is All and One, what is many is therefore illusory and unreal. The characteristic pantheism and near pantheism of the European Middle Ages proceeded, by contrast, from the view that because God alone truly is, all that is must in some sense be God, or at least a manifestation of God. Insofar as this view implies a notion of true being at the top of a scale of degrees of being, its ancestry is Platonic or Neoplatonic. It would be difficult to call Neoplatonism itself pantheistic because although it views the material world as an emanation from the divine, the fallen and radically imperfect and undivine character of that world is always emphasized.

Erigena and Averroës. However, the translation of Neoplatonic themes of emanation into Christian terms by John Scotus Erigena (c. 810–c. 877) resulted in *De Divisione Naturae,* which was condemned as heretical precisely because of its break with monotheism. It might be argued that Erigena does not seem to be wholly pantheistic in that he did not treat every aspect of nature as part of the divine in the same way and to the same degree. This would be misleading, however, for on this criterion no thinker could ever be judged a pantheist.

According to Erigena the whole, *natura,* is composed of four species of being: that which creates and is not created, that which is created and creates, that which is created and does not create, and that which is not created and does not create. The first is God as creator; the last, God as that into which all created beings have returned. The second and third are the created universe which is in process of passing from God in his first form to God in his last form. Erigena wrote as if each class of beings belongs to a different period in a historical unfolding, but he also treated this as a misleading but necessary form of expression. *Natura* is eternal; the whole process is eternally present; and everything is a *theophania,* a manifestation of God.

Pope Honorius III condemned *De Divisione Naturae* in 1225 as "pullulating with worms of heretical perversity," and much earlier Erigena's other work had been described by the Council of Valence (855) as "Irish porridge" and "the devil's invention." Clearly, part of what perturbed them was Erigena's ability to interpret in a pantheistic sense both the Biblical doctrine of creation and the Biblical notion of a time when God shall be all in all.

A similar problem arose for the Islamic interpreter of

Aristotle, ibn-Rushd (Averroës), whose discussions of the relation of human to divine intelligence aroused suspicion of pantheism and whose assertions of fidelity to the Koran did not save him from condemnation. A Christian Aristotelian such as Meister Eckhart, the Dominican mystic, was also condemned. Both Eckhart and Johannes Tauler spoke of God and man in terms of a mutual dependence which implies a fundamental unity including both. However, in every medieval case after Erigena the imputation of pantheism is at best inconclusive. Only since the sixteenth century has genuine pantheism become a recurrent European phenomenon.

Bruno. Giordano Bruno (1548–1600) was an explicitly anti-Christian pantheist. He conceived of God as the immanent cause or goal of nature, distinct from each finite particular only because he includes them all within his own being. The divine life which informs everything also informs the human mind and soul, and the soul is immortal because it is part of the divine. Since God is not distinct from the world, he can have no particular providential intentions. Since all events are equally ruled by divine law, miracles cannot occur. Whatever happens, happens in accordance with law, and our freedom consists in identifying ourselves with the course of things. The Bible, according to Bruno, insofar as it errs on these points, is simply false.

Boehme. Jakob Boehme (1575–1624) was a shoemaker, a mystic, and a Lutheran whose wish to remain within the church was shown by the fact that to the end he received the sacraments. The pantheism of Erigena or Bruno was founded upon a view that the universe must necessarily be a single all-inclusive system if it is to be intelligible. Their pantheism derived from their ideal of explanation. Boehme, by contrast, claimed that he was merely recording what he has learned from an inward mystical illumination. He saw the foundation of all things in the divine *Ungrund,* in which the triad of Everything, Nothing, and the Divine Agony which results from their encounter produces out of itself a procession of less ultimate triads which constitute the natural and human world. Boehme made no distinction between nature and spirit, for he saw nature as entirely the manifestation of spirit. It is not at all clear in what sense the propositions that Boehme advanced can have been the record of vision; it is clear that both in claiming authority for his vision and in the content of his doctrine he was bound to encounter, as he did, the condemnation of the Lutheran clergy.

Spinoza. Spinoza's pantheism had at least three sources: his ideal of human felicity, his concept of explanation, and his notion of the degrees of human knowledge. His explicit aim was to discover a good that would be independent of all the ordinary contingencies of chance and misfortune. Only that which is capable of completely filling and occupying the mind can be the supreme good in Spinoza's sense. The only knowledge which could satisfy these requirements would be the knowledge that the mind is part of the total system of nature and is at one with it when recognizing that everything is as it must be. Felicity is the knowledge of necessity, for if the mind can accept the necessity of its own place in the whole ordering of things, there will be room neither for rebellion nor for complaint.

Thus, from the outset Spinoza's characterization of the supreme good required that his philosophy exhibit the whole universe as a single connected system.

So it is with his concept of explanation. To explain anything is to demonstrate that it cannot be other than it is. To demonstrate this entails laying bare the place of what is to be explained within a total system. Spinoza made no distinction between contingent causal connections and necessary logical connections. A deductive system in which every proposition follows from a set of initial axioms, postulates, and definitions mirrors the structure of the universe, in which every finite mode of existence exemplifies the pattern of order which derives from the single substance, *Deus, sive natura* (God, or nature). There can be only one substance, not a multiplicity of substances, for Spinoza so defined the notion of substance that the relation of a property to the substance of which it is a property is necessary, and therefore intelligible and explicable; however, the relation of one substance to another must be external and contingent, and therefore unintelligible and inexplicable. But for Spinoza it is unintelligible that what is unintelligible should be thought to exist. Hence, there can be only one substance; "God" and "Nature" could not be the names of two distinct and independent substances.

It follows that God cannot be said to be the creator of nature, except in a sense quite other than that of Christian or Jewish orthodoxy. Spinoza did distinguish between nature as active (*natura naturans*) and nature as passive product (*natura naturata*), and insofar as he identified God with nature as creative and self-sustaining rather than with nature as passive, he could speak of God as the immanent cause of the world. But this is quite different from the orthodox conception of divine efficient causality. Also, in Spinoza's view, there can be no divine providential intentions for particular agents and there can be no miracles. What, then, of the Bible?

Spinoza regarded the Bible as an expression of truth in the only mode in which the ordinary, unreflective, irrational man is able to believe it or be guided by it. Such men need images, for their knowledge is of the confused kind which does not rise to the rational and scientific explanation of phenomena, let alone to that *scientia intuitiva* (intuitive knowledge) by which the mind grasps the whole necessity of things and becomes identical with the *infinita idea Dei* (infinite idea of God). Freed from all those passions which dominated his actions so long as he did not grasp them intellectually, man is moved only by a fully conscious awareness of his place in the whole system. It is this awareness which Spinoza also identified as the intellectual love of God.

In using theological language to characterize both nature and the good of human life, Spinoza was not concealing an ultimately materialistic and atheistic standpoint. He believed that all the key predicates by which divinity is ascribed apply to the entire system of things, for it is infinite, at once the uncaused *causa sui* and *causa omnium* (cause of itself and cause of everything) and eternal. Even if Spinoza's attitude to the Bible was that it veils the truth, he believed that it *is* the truth that it veils. He considered his doctrine basically identical with both that of the ancient Hebrew writers and that of St. Paul. This did not save him from condemnation by the synagogue in his lifetime, let alone from condemnation by the church afterward.

German pantheism. Erigena, Bruno, Boehme, Spinoza—each of these, no matter how much he may have made use of material drawn from earlier philosophical or religious writing, was a thinker who was independent of his specifically pantheist predecessors and who revived pantheism by his own critical reflections upon monotheism. It was only in the eighteenth century that something like a specifically pantheist tradition emerged. The word "pantheist" was first used in 1705 by John Toland in his *Socinianism truly stated.* Toland's hostile critic, Fay, used the word "pantheism" in 1709 and it speedily became common. With the increased questioning of Christianity, accompanied by an unwillingness to adopt atheistic positions, pantheism became an important doctrine, first for Goethe and Lessing, both of whom were influenced by Spinoza, then for Schleiermacher, and finally for Fichte, Schelling, and Hegel.

Goethe and Lessing. Goethe's aim was to discover a mode of theological thinking, rather than a theology, with which he could embrace both what he took to be the pagan attitude to nature and the redemptive values of Christianity. Suspicious as he was of Christian asceticism, he also recognized a distinctive Christian understanding of human possibility, and his various utterances about Christianity cannot be rendered consistent even by the greatest scholarly ingenuity. In the formulas of pantheism, which he was able to interpret in the sense that he wished precisely because he failed to understand Spinoza correctly, Goethe found a theology which enabled him both to identify the divine with the natural and to separate them. The infinite creativity which Goethe ascribed to nature is what he took to be divine; but while the seeds of a consistent doctrine can be discerned in this aspect of Goethe's writings, it would be wrong to deny that part of pantheism's attraction for him was that it seemed to license his will to be inconsistent.

Lessing, by contrast, was consistent. He found the kernel of truth in all religions in a neutral version of Spinozism, which allowed him to see Judaism, Christianity, and Islam as distorted versions of the same truth, distorted because they confuse the historical trappings with the metaphysical essence.

Schleiermacher. Schleiermacher's quite different preoccupation was to make religion acceptable to the cultured unbelievers of his own time. The core of religion, on his view, is the sense of absolute dependence; to that on which we are absolutely dependent he gave a variety of names and titles, speaking of God in both monotheistic and pantheistic terms. However, he committed himself to pantheism by asserting that it is the Totality that is divine.

Fichte. It is clear from Goethe, Lessing, and Schleiermacher that Spinoza's writing had become a major text for philosophical theology, but for these writers he was an inspiration rather than a precise source. With the advent of German idealism, the attempt to criticize the deductive form of Spinoza's reasoning while preserving the pantheistic content became a major theme of German philosophy. Nowhere is this more evident than in Fichte's writ-

ing, in which God and the universe are identified because the world is nothing but the material through which the Ego realizes its infinite moral vocation, and the divine is nothing but the moral order that includes both world and Ego. The divine cannot be personal and cannot have been the external creator of the world. Fichte poured scorn on the unintelligibility of the orthodox doctrine of creation *ex nihilo* (out of nothing). He distinguished sharply between the genuinely metaphysical and the merely historical elements in Christianity. It is the theology of the Johannine Gospel which he treated as the expression of the metaphysical, and to this he gave a pantheistic sense.

Schelling and Hegel. Schelling's pantheism was cruder than Fichte's—according to him, all distinctions disappear in the ultimate nature of things. The divine is identified with this ultimate distinctionless merging of nature and spirit, a unity more fundamental than any of the differences of the merely empirical world.

Hegel was subtler and more philosophically interesting than either Fichte or Schelling. Like Boehme and Schleiermacher, he remained within orthodox Protestant Christianity, claiming to be engaged in the interpretation rather than the revision of its dogmatic formulas. The Hegelian Absolute Idea pre-exists its finite manifestations logically but not temporally, and it receives its full embodiment only at the end of history, when it is incorporated in a social and moral order fully conscious of its own nature and of its place in history. This phase of self-consciousness is already reached at the level of thought in Hegel's *Logic.* But the Absolute Idea has no existence apart from or over and above its actual and possible manifestations in nature and history. Hence, the divine is the Totality.

After Hegel pantheism was less in vogue. The critique of Christianity became more radical, atheism became a more acceptable alternative, and Spinoza dominated the intellectual scene far less. In England a poetic pantheism appeared in Shelley and Wordsworth, but in Shelley it coexisted with something much closer to atheism and in Wordsworth with a Christianity that displaced it. In any case, the intellectual resources of such a pantheism were so meager that it is not surprising that it did not survive in the nineteenth century.

Criticisms of pantheism. Pantheism essentially involves two assertions: that everything that exists constitutes a unity and that this all-inclusive unity is divine. What could be meant by the assertion that everything that exists constitutes a unity? It is first and most clearly not a unity derived from membership of the same class, the view that seems to have been taken by Boehme. "There is no class of all that is," wrote Aristotle. Why not? Because existence is not a genus. To say that something exists is not to classify it at all. When Boehme asserted that the universe includes both existence and nonexistence, he both anticipated a long tradition that culminated in Heidegger and remained unintelligible. The notion of *a* unity that includes all that exists—or even all that exists and all that does not exist—is a notion devoid of content. What could be unitary in such an ostensible collection?

The unity might be of another kind, however. In Spinoza the unity of the universe is a logical unity, with every particular item deducible from the general nature of things. There is a single deductive web of explanation—there are not sciences; there is science. About such an alleged unity two points must be made. First, the contingent aspect of nature is entirely omitted. Even a total description of the universe in which every part of the description was logically related to some other part or parts (assuming for the moment such a description to be conceivable) would still leave us with the question whether the universe was as it was described; and if it was as it was described, this truth would be a contingent truth which could not be included in the description itself and which could stand in no internal conceptual relationship to the description. The fact of existence would remain irreducibly contingent. Second, the actual development of the sciences does not accord with Spinoza's ideal. The forms of explanation are not all the same; the logical structure of Darwinian evolutionary theory must be distinguished from the logical structure of quantum mechanics. Thus, the kind of unity ascribed by Spinoza to the universe seems to be lacking.

In Fichte and Hegel the unity ascribed to the universe is one of an over-all purpose manifest in the pattern of events, as that pattern is discovered by the agent in his social and moral life. In order for this assertion to be meaningful it must be construed, at least in part, in empirical terms; in Fichte's case as a hypothesis about moral development, in Hegel's case as a hypothesis about historical development. Neither hypothesis appears to be vindicated by the facts.

Suppose, however, that a unity of some kind, inclusive of all that is, could be discovered. In virtue of what might the pantheist claim that it was divine? The infinity and the eternity of the universe have often been the predicates which seemed to entail its divinity, but the sense in which the universe is infinite and eternal is surely not that in which the traditional religions have ascribed these predicates to a god. What is clear is that pantheism as a theology has a source, independent of its metaphysics, in a widespread capacity for awe and wonder in the face both of natural phenomena and of the apparent totality of things. It is at least in part because pantheist metaphysics provides a vocabulary which appears more adequate than any other for the expression of these emotions that pantheism has shown such historical capacity for survival. But this does not, of course, give any warrant for believing pantheism to be true.

Bibliography

Boehme, Jakob, *Works*, C. J. Barber, ed. London, 1909——.

Bruno, Giordano, "Concerning the Cause, Principle, and One," translated by Sidney Greenberg in *The Infinite in Giordano Bruno*. New York, 1950.

Bruno, Giordano, "On the Infinite Universe and Worlds," translated by D. W. Singer in *Giordano Bruno: His Life and Thought*. New York, 1950.

Eckhart, *Meister Eckhart*, edited, with introduction, by O. Karrer. Munich, 1926.

Erigena, John Scotus, *Opera*, in J. P. Migne, ed., *Patrologia Latina*. Paris, 1844–1864. Vol. 122.

Fichte, J. G., *The Science of Knowledge*, translated by A. E. Kroeger. Philadelphia, 1868.

Fichte, J. G., *Die Schrifte zu J. G. Fichte's Atheismusstreit*, H. Lindau, ed. Munich, 1912.

Flint, Robert, *Antitheistic Theories*. London, 1878. Baird lectures.

Hegel, G. W. F., *Lectures on the Philosophy of Religion*, translated by E. B. Speirs and J. B. Sanderson, 3 vols. London, 1895 and 1962.

Schelling, Friedrich, *Werke*, M. Schröter, ed., 8 vols. Munich, 1927–1956.

Schleiermacher, Friedrich, *On Religion: Speeches to Its Cultured Despisers*, translated by J. W. Oman. London, 1893.

Spinoza, Benedict, *The Chief Works*, translated by R. H. M. Elwes, 2 vols. New York, 1951.

ALASDAIR MACINTYRE

PANTHEISMUSSTREIT, or the pantheism controversy, came to the attention of the public in 1785 when Friedrich Heinrich Jacobi published *Ueber die Lehre des Spinoza*, his correspondence with Moses Mendelssohn concerning Lessing's late Spinozist phase. Other prominent writers, including Kant, Herder, Goethe, Johann Kaspar Lavater, and Johann Georg Hamann, became involved in this dispute, which led to an objective reappraisal of Spinozism. The first important reaction to Spinoza's influence in Germany had been Leibniz' *Theodicy* (1710). At the time of the pantheism controversy, the distorted image of Spinoza, the "satanic atheist," was definitely destroyed. This image had been created by Pierre Bayle and cultivated in Germany by Theophil Gottlieb Spitzel (1639–1691), Johann Christophorus Sturm (1635–1703), Johann Konrad Dippel (c. 1672–1734), and Christian K. Kortholt (1633–1694), whose *De Tribus Impostoribus Liber* (1680) had attacked Herbert of Cherbury, Hobbes, and Spinoza as "impostors."

Inception of the controversy. Jacobi's book constituted one stage in the struggle waged by the supporters of Johann Georg Hamann (whose sentimentalist faith Jacobi attempted to combine with Kant's criticial philosophy) against the religious rationalism of the Berlin Enlightenment, whose proponents were grouped around Friedrich Christian Nicolai and the *Berlinische Monatsschrift*. In his *Golgotha und Scheblimini* (1784), Hamann had attacked the theistic rationalism of Mendelssohn's *Jerusalem* (1783). A work prized by Kant, Herder, Mirabeau, and Christian Garve, *Jerusalem* was directed against state-imposed creeds and religions of revelation.

Jacobi's hasty publication of his correspondence with Mendelssohn, too, was indirectly inspired by Hamann. The latter informed Jacobi on June 29, 1785, that the first part of Mendelssohn's *Morgenstunden* was already being printed. Wrongly suspecting that Mendelssohn had mentioned their controversy over Lessing in this work, Jacobi committed a dual breach of trust. To his *Ueber die Lehre des Spinoza* he appended anonymously a fragment from Goethe's unpublished "Prometheus" (1774) that Jacobi had shown Lessing during a conversation at Wolfenbüttel on July 7, 1780.

It was this conversation that served as the starting point and focus of the pantheism controversy. To the report of this conversation Jacobi added a digest of an argument with Mendelssohn that had ensued from a report by Elise Reimarus (February 1783) to the effect that Mendelssohn was busy with a work on Lessing. Through her, Jacobi led Mendelssohn to believe that "Lessing had been a Spinozist" but had never admitted it to his friend Mendelssohn because the latter had never taken seriously a relevant hint concerning the Spinozist purport of Paragraph 73 of Lessing's *Erziehung des Menschengeschlechts*. Mendelssohn, through Elise Reimarus, then addressed precise questions to Jacobi regarding the character of Lessing's alleged Spinozism. He considered it unlikely that, one, Lessing had been a Spinozist and that, two, he would have remained silent about it to a friend of many years' standing (Mendelssohn) while confiding it to the first stranger that had come along (Jacobi). Mendelssohn suggested courteously that perhaps Lessing, as was his nature, had made in jest certain paradoxical statements to Jacobi. However, if Jacobi could conclusively demonstrate Lessing's Spinozism, then, Mendelssohn allowed, he would have to give precedence to the truth in the work he planned to write about his friend.

In his reply of November 4, 1783, Jacobi again gave details of his conversations with Lessing. But in so doing, he misjudged his own situation. It was obvious that Lessing, tired of hearing Spinoza treated "like a dead dog," had been attempting to provoke Jacobi into a refutation of Spinozism. Jacobi, however, had declared himself helpless against the geometrical reasoning of Spinoza, which seemed unanswerable to him. Although he rejected Spinoza's "fatalism" and the concept of a God who created without insight and without will, he could find no counterarguments. To this Lessing had replied, "I note that you would like to have your will free; I do not crave free will." Lessing characterized the tendency to give thought the precedence over other life forces as a human prejudice. He asked Jacobi whether he thought he could derive the concept of an extramundane rationally creative deity from Leibniz. "I fear," Lessing added, "that Leibniz himself was fundamentally a Spinozist." He recalled "a passage in Leibniz where it is said of God that he himself is in a state of everlasting expansion and contraction, and that this constitutes the creation and existence of the world." Hard pressed by the logic of Lessing as well as that of Spinoza, which "admits of no cause of things separate from the world," Jacobi saved himself by a leap into a sentimentalist faith in the God of Christianity who orders the world teleologically. With unconcealed irony, Lessing remarked that such a leap of faith ending up in a somersault was something he could no longer exact of his "old legs and heavy head." Derisively, he professed to find agreements with his own system even in Charles Bonnet's *Palingénésie,* which Lavater—without the author's permission—had translated and had dedicated to Mendelssohn in an illfated attempt at proselytizing. Lessing also claimed to discern "obvious Spinozism" in Hemsterhuis' *Aristée.* Jacobi himself believed he recognized in the disputed Paragraph 73 of Lessing's *Erziehung des Menschengeschlechts* his Spinozist interpretation of Christ as reality (*natura naturata*) and of God as the infinite substance (*natura naturans*).

Seven months after his reply to Mendelssohn (June 1784), Jacobi learned from Elise Reimarus that Mendelssohn had put aside his *Lessing* "in order first to venture a round with the Spinozists or 'all-in-one'rs.'" In August of that year, Mendelssohn wrote his *Erinnerungen* and sent them to Jacobi without, however, publishing them at that time. (They first appeared in 1786 in *Moses Mendelssohn an die Freunde Lessings,* pp. 36–56). In the *Erinnerungen* Mendelssohn marshaled rationalistic arguments against Spinoza and again expressed his disbelief in Lessing's Spinozism. He dealt sarcastically with Jacobi's "honorable retreat under the flag of faith" as a device necessary for Christian philosophers; Mendelssohn's own religion, on the other hand, allowed him to "raise doubts on grounds of reason" and did not dictate to him "any belief in eternal verities." Mendelssohn left unanswered Jacobi's *Lettre à M. Hemsterhuis,* a copy of which the author had sent him on September 5, 1784. But he notified his correspondent once again that pantheism would indeed come under discussion in the first part of the *Morgenstunden,* although their mutual correspondence would be disregarded. Mendelssohn requested that Jacobi delay publishing his "counterrecollections" until after the publication of the *Morgenstunden.*

Jacobi again sent Mendelssohn an exposition of Spinozism, in 44 paragraphs, which ended in an enthusiastic identification of Christian faith, love, and—surprisingly—knowledge (in the sense of knowledge of nature). Mendelssohn, astonished at Jacobi's proselytizing zeal, called on Reimarus to act as arbiter in the matter of the controversy over Lessing. Reimarus counseled silence about the whole affair so as not to dishonor the memory of Lessing. Still another exegesis of Spinozism by Jacobi in six paragraphs began with the traditional thesis: "Spinozism is atheism."

Despite Mendelssohn's renewed assurances to Elise Reimarus on May 24, 1785, that he would not make use of his correspondence with Jacobi, the latter with an utter lack of consideration published the letters on August 28, 1785. Jacobi's account reads like an exorcism of the magnetic powers of Spinozism, whereas Mendelssohn's concern in the controversy was only to clear Lessing of the charge of Spinozism and to contrast his own religion of reason with Jacobi's visionary religion of sentiment, as well as to polemicize against Spinoza with Wolffian arguments. Mendelssohn's main proof for the existence of a rational God (in Part I of the *Morgenstunden*) was that all that is real must first be thought as real by some being, hence there exists an infinite intellect.

Results of the controversy. The pantheism controversy spread to wider circles of German intellectual life with the anonymous publication in 1786 of *Die Resultate der Jacobi'schen und Mendelssohn'schen Philosophie* by Thomas W. Wizenman, a young follower of Hamann and a Pietist, who had been induced by Jacobi to read Spinoza. Wizenman, under the guise of a disinterested spectator, openly took Jacobi's side. As Kant later revealed it, Wizenman launched into an *argumentum ad hominem* against Mendelssohn, attempting to destroy deism with atheism, and atheism with deism. For the fideist Wizenman, it was impossible to demonstrate the existence or the nonexistence of God and his relationships to the world. He tried to define the concept of reason in such a fashion that the rationality of a belief in revealed religion would proceed from this definition, once historical evidence of the revelation was at hand.

Compelled by Wizenman's publication to express an opinion, Kant in "Was heisst: sich im Denken orientieren?" (*Berlinische Monatsschrift,* October 1786) rejected both Jacobi's sentimentalist faith and Mendelssohn's rationalist faith as subjective views that conceal in themselves the danger of fanaticism. As in the later *Critique of Judgment* (Paragraph 80), Kant declared that pantheism did not provide a teleological explanation of things, so in the *Monatsschrift* article he defended himself against the reproach that his *Critique of Pure Reason* had promoted Spinozism: "Spinozism speaks of thoughts that themselves think and thus of an accidental thing that still at the same time exists for itself as subject—a concept that is not to be found at all in the human understanding and cannot be brought into it." Kant disapproved of Mendelssohn's attempt to reduce the quarrel of freedom of will versus determinism to a matter of pure logomachy (*Einige Bermerkungen zu Jakobis Prüfung der Mendelssohnschen Morgenstunden,* Leipzig, 1786).

More important than the polemics of the pantheism controversy were its effects on Herder and Goethe and later on Schleiermacher, Schelling, and Hegel. Herder, in his five conversations entitled *Gott* (1787), deplored Spinoza's terminological dependence on Descartes, but he accepted Spinoza's concept of God, whom he regarded as the primal power from which all other powers derive. Thus in his own way he came close to the concept of the primal phenomenon that Goethe, as a metaphysical philosopher of nature, was seeking to investigate.

Goethe himself had reread Spinoza in January 1785 and had found in him the foundations for his own holistic or antimechanistic, anti-Newtonian concept of the universe. He had already, on June 4, 1785, objected to Jacobi: "You acknowledge the highest reality, which is the basis of Spinozism, on which all else rests, from which all else flows. He does not prove the Being of God, Being *is* God. And if for this reason others scold Spinoza for being an atheist, I should like to name him and praise him as *theissimum,* indeed, *christianissimum.*" On October 21 of the same year, Goethe sharply attacked Jacobi's play on the word "believe" as the behavior of a "faith-sophist," admonished him to apply himself to "clarity and distinctness of expression," and admitted "that while by nature I do not share Spinoza's mode of conception, if I had to cite a book that, more than any I know, agrees most fully with my own conception, I should have to name the *Ethics.*" On May 5, 1786, he expressed his disagreement with Jacobi:

I cling more and more firmly to the reverence for God of the atheist [Spinoza] . . . and I cede to you [Christians] all that your religion enjoins and must enjoin . . . When you say that one can only *believe* in God . . . then I say to you that I lay great weight on *looking and seeing* and when Spinoza, speaking of *scientia intuitiva,* says *Hoc cognoscendi genus procedit ab adaequata idea essentiae formalis quorundam Dei attributorum ad adaequatam cognitionem essentiae rerum* [This manner of knowing moves from the adequate idea of the formal essence of some attributes of God to the adequate knowledge of the essence of things], these words give me courage to devote my entire life to the contemplation of the things that I can reach and of whose *essentia formali* I can hope to fashion an adequate idea.

Just as Goethe, who, inspired by the pantheism controversy to make a study of Spinoza, became conscious of his own holism while reading the *Ethics,* so pantheism, thanks to its contact with Spinozism, progressed from its traditional manifestation as Neoplatonic emanation to a concept of evolution, which in Hegel's philosophy (and in the twentieth century, that of Bergson) entails the development of the Absolute in and with the world.

Bibliography

Jacobi, Friedrich Heinrich, *Ueber die Lehre des Spinoza in Briefen an den Herrn Moses Mendelssohn.* Breslau, 1785. 2d ed., revised and enlarged, Breslau, 1789.
Mendelssohn, Moses, *Morgenstunden, oder über das Daseyn Gottes.* Berlin, 1785.
Mendelssohn, Moses, *An die Freunde Lessings.* Berlin, 1786.
Scholz, H., *Die Hauptschriften zum Pantheismusstreit zwischen Jacobi und Mendelssohn.* Berlin, 1916.

KURT WEINBERG
Translated by *Albert E. Blumberg*

PAPINI, GIOVANNI (1881–1956), Italian pragmatist philosopher and literary figure, was born in Florence into a family of modest means and had no formal education. Papini described himself in his *Un uomo finito* (Florence, 1913; translated by Virginia Page as *Failure; Un Uomo Finito,* New York, 1924), a book which was frankly and painfully biographical, as self-taught, urged on by an insatiable curiosity and a burning desire to investigate the various forms of knowledge. He quickly made a name for himself in Italian culture at the beginning of the twentieth century with his attack on the then prevailing positivist philosophy of Roberto Ardigò and his support of nationalistic tendencies and opposition to the ideals of democracy. He became a close friend of Giuseppe Prezzolini and other young writers who advocated doing away with the old oligarchies and giving a new impetus to the spiritual life of the country. The fruit of this collaboration was the birth in 1903 of *Leonardo,* a nonconformist review that published the most important contemporary thinkers. They chose Nietzsche, Bergson, James, and F. C. S. Schiller as their exemplars and leaders, but the interests of the *Leonardo* group embraced the avant-garde currents in art and literature as well.

In his writings, later gathered together in a book entitled *Pragmatismo* (Milan, 1913), Papini defined the essential aspects of his thought. His is a kind of magic pragmatism, markedly different from the logical and scientific pragmatism of C. S. Peirce. This pragmatism rejects the positivists' agnosticism concerning issues that go beyond experience; that metaphysical problems lack meaning does not indicate a lack in our intellectual capabilities but rather how very human the nature of knowing is. Instead of striving for definitive explanations in the manner of the traditional philosophies, the pragmatist is concerned with the methods and instruments which aid in defining the various forms of knowledge and activity. He does not believe in absolute principles or immutable truths; neither does he stop at mere description and generalization of the facts of experience. His aim is to develop laws and predictions, with the sole purpose of increasing the power of man over nature. No metaphysical hypothesis, observed Papini, is more valuable than another, and none can be recognized as true. On the contrary, the pragmatist viewpoint is one of maximum freedom and advocates a plurality of attitudes. Papini's celebrated definition of pragmatism was praised and quoted by William James:

> Pragmatism is a *corridor theory*, a corridor of a great hotel where there are 100 doors that open onto 100 rooms. In one there is a faldstool and a kneeling man who wants to regain his faith, in another a writing-desk and a man who wants to kill every metaphysic, in a third a laboratory and a man who wants to find new vantage points on the future. (*Pragmatismo*, p. 82)

Papini's *Leonardo* period, with Neo-Hegelians such as Benedetto Croce and Giovanni Gentile aiding the attack on positivism, terminated in 1906. But this was only the beginning of a painful intellectual journey in which Papini sought, without success, to give form and coherence to his thought. He participated in the battle of ideas of *La voce*, directed by his friend Prezzolini; then he broke away and in 1911, in collaboration with Giovanni Amendola, directed a review with a strong moral bent, *L'anima;* and finally he founded *Lacerba,* an avant-garde journal violently opposed to the prevailing order of things. In the meantime, his literary output was enriched by numerous works, including *Il crepuscolo dei filosofi* ("The Twilight of the Philosophers," Milan, 1906), *La cultura italiana* (Florence, 1906), written in collaboration with Prezzolini, and *L'altra metà* ("The Other Half," Ancona, 1912). In addition to these books, a great number of articles testify to his zeal and his cultural interests. In this period Papini drew further away from the idealism gaining popularity in Italy, intensified his dissent with the school of Croce, and supported the futurist movement in accordance with his rebellion against traditional aesthetic rules.

Papini strongly favored Italian intervention in World War I because he saw the war as a decisive conflict between the old and the new. However, the war led him to a reassessment of Christian values and to embrace the works of the fathers of the church, and in particular those of St. Augustine. He regarded Augustine, to whom he devoted a book (*S. Agustino,* Florence, 1929), as a defender of the faith, an uncompromising polemicist, and an unsurpassable model of humanity reaching out toward the divine. Papini's activity did not diminish after his religious "conversion," but gradually became less and less concerned with philosophical matters, and concentrated instead on literary and scholarly subjects. Stricken by a disease which deprived him almost completely of the use of his senses but left his mind as active as ever, Papini bore up bravely until his death.

Bibliography

See Michele Federico Sciacca, *Il secolo XX,* 2d ed. (Milan, 1947), Vol. I, pp. 22–25; Eugenio Garin, *Cronache di filosofia* (Bari, 1955); Antonio Santucci, *Il Pragmatismo in Italia* (Bologna, 1963).

ANTONIO SANTUCCI
Translated by *Robert M. Connolly*

PARACELSUS, the pseudonym of Philippus Aureolus Theophrastus Bombastus (Baumastus) von Hohenheim (1493–1541), reformer of medicine and pharmacology, chemist, philosopher, iconoclast, and writer. If he himself assumed this name, it could signify "higher than high," or "higher than Hohenheim," a jibe at his illegitimate paternal grandfather. Born in Einsiedeln, Switzerland, where his father practiced medicine, Paracelsus later lived at Villach in Carinthia (Austria), a center of mining, smelting, and alchemy—metal lores that were to occupy him for the rest of his life. From the age of 15 his life was migratory. After medical studies at various German and Austrian universities, he seems to have completed his doctorate in 1515 at Ferrara under a faculty that was Scotist, Platonist, and humanist.

For the next 11 years, Paracelsus traveled throughout Europe, jeopardizing his authority as a physician by practicing surgery (then a craft, not a learned profession) in the army of Charles V and by experimental prescriptions. He visited spas, analyzed the waters, treated by hypnosis, and sometimes alleviated pain with laudanum. At Salzburg he narrowly escaped execution for participating in a peasants' revolt. When, in 1526, he settled at Strasbourg to establish himself in medical practice, he was famous as an object of superstitious distrust. But his spectacular cure of the printer Frobinius quickly led to friendships with such men as Erasmus and Oecolampadius and an appointment—against the will of the faculty—as medical lecturer at the University of Basel.

His eminence was short-lived. Lectures in German (rather than Latin), rejection of the canonical theory of Avicenna and Galen, denunciation of the apothecaries, and a public burning of the works of Avicenna were topped by the death of Frobinius. Those whose vested interests had been threatened tricked Paracelsus into behavior that could justify dismissal and arrest.

From 1528 until his death, his life was once again nomadic. Unkept promises and unstable patronage led him to Colmar, Nuremburg, Saint Gall, Villach, Vienna, and finally to Salzburg, where he died, probably of cancer, perhaps of metal poisoning.

Among his medical innovations were chemical urinalysis; a biochemical theory of digestion; chemical therapy; antisepsis of wounds; the use of laudanum, ether (without awareness of its anesthetic properties), and mercury for syphilis; and the combining of the apothecary's and surgeon's arts in the profession of medicine.

Paracelsus' numerous books are mostly variants on the theme of man (the microcosm) in relation to nature (the macrocosm). The most important are *Archidoxis* (c. 1524); the treatises on syphilis (c. 1529); *Opus Paragranum* (c. 1529); *Opus Paramirum* (c. 1530); *Philosophia Sagax* (c. 1536); and *Labyrinthus Medicorum* (1538).

Paracelsian philosophy was both traditional and new. Its medieval elements are traceable to alchemy and Cabalism, which are branches of a trunk rooted in Hellenistic Neoplatonism, the Corpus Hermeticum, and Gnosticism. These occult lores shared the concept of creation through corruption; the axiom "That which is above is one with that which is below"; belief in a bisexual, homogeneous, hylozoic universe; a cyclic theory of time; and an animism approximating pantheism.

A mystery religion of life rather than merely of gold, medieval alchemy employed Semitic and Greco-Roman mythology as a screen against the unenlightened and as a vehicle of private communication for adepts. Although Paracelsus counted himself an adept, he abandoned the tradition of reserve and discarded most of the mythological symbolism. Unlike his predecessors, he wrote to clarify. He explained that alchemy's real desideratum was the secret of life.

Like Cabalists and alchemists, Paracelsus believed in the theory that decay is the beginning of all birth. Nature emerges through separations: first, prime matter separates out of ultimate matter (also called *Yliaster* or *Mysterium Magnum*), which is eternal and paradoxically immaterial. "The first was with God . . . that is *ultima materia;* this *ultima materia* He made into *prime matter* . . . that is a seed and the seed is the element of water [fluid]." God spins ultimate matter out of himself. This yields, by separation, the prime matter of individual objects, a watery matrix, perpetually spawning nature, perpetually resolvable back into ultimate matter. Human creativeness in art, alchemy, or pharmacology repeats the primal act. The human demiurge, like God, separates rather than combines.

The Paracelsian theory of time resembles that of Plotinus. Time is qualitative change: growth, transition—even fate. Given the basic concept of cyclic generation and decay, Paracelsian time would be for the material cosmos a cycle of becoming. But there are two orders of time: force time (within) and growing time (without). Like the Paracelsian concept of "prime matter" in relation to "ultimate matter," this theory of time is essentially dualist. "Above" and "below" are substantially the same: "Heaven is man and man is heaven, and all men together are the one heaven," but microcosm and macrocosm are contained by membranes or partitions.

Paracelsus rejected the concept of humors as governed by planets and substituted a chemical theory of humors as properties: salt, sweet, bitter, and sour. He retained the medieval alchemistic variant of the four elements and a quintessence, the fifth element, that is life. He tended to treat fire as less elementary than the combustible principle, sulphur. Medieval alchemy had stressed the sexual polarity of two elements, fire (identified with the male principle) and water (identified with the female principle), and contrasted flame with flow and sulphur with mercury. Paracelsus reinterpreted these as principles rather than as elements and added a third principle, salt. These are properties or states—combustible, fluid or vaporous, and solid; each confers on matter its structure, corporality, and function. As constituents of ultimate matter, these are absolutes; as components of nature, they are infinitely variable in all sensuously discernible properties. Every natural object has its own sulphur, salt, and mercury, as well as its own quintessence.

Absolute life comes from *Ens Seminis,* the cosmic protoplasm. *Ens Astrale* is to the microcosm (man) as the firmament is to the macrocosm (nature). It can sustain or poison from within, as a toxic atmosphere can poison sea water and fish. *Ens Veneni* is the poison from without. Nature lives by dying; life eats life. Man may eat the flesh of an animal whose food would poison him, but within every living body there is an alchemist that selects what is food for that body. *Ens Naturale* is the bodily harmony of the chemical humors. *Ens Spirituale* has its equivalent in what psychiatry calls the psyche. Against the common belief of his day, Paracelsus argued that madness was not demonic possession and that evil dreams were not intercourse with incubi or succubi. Mind produces diseases both in itself and its own body or in another mind or body through hypnosis, fetishism, or demonstrable ill will. Most diseases are positive evils, but there is *Ens Dei,* God's will, which no doctor can circumvent.

Although accused by Erastus of dualist heresy because of the importance he gave primal matter and because he described illness as intrinsically evil, Paracelsus died in the Church of Rome, and his burial place became a shrine.

Works by Paracelsus

Opera Omnia, John Huser, ed., 12 vols. Basel, 1589–1591. The original German text.

Opera Omnia, F. Bitiskius, ed., 3 vols. Geneva, 1658. In Latin.

Sämtliche Werke, Karl Sudhoff and E. Matthiessen, eds., 15 vols. Munich, 1922–1933. In German; the standard critical edition.

Four Treatises of Theophrastus of Hohenheim, Henry Sigerist, C. Lilian Temkin, George Rosen, and Gregory Zilboorg, eds. Baltimore, 1941.

Selected Writings, Jolande Jacobi, ed., translated by Norbert Guterman. New York, 1951 and 1958. Contains an introduction by the editor. Excellent.

Works on Paracelsus

Browning, Robert, *Paracelsus.* London, 1835.

Debus, Allen G., "The Paracelsian Compromise in Elizabethan England." *Ambix,* Vol. 8 (June 1960), 71–97.

Donne, John, *Ignatius His Conclave.* London, 1613.

Pachter, Henry M., *Magic Into Science.* New York, 1951. Represents Paracelsus as a proto-Faust; readable.

Pagel, Walter, *Paracelsus. An Introduction to Philosophical Medicine in the Era of the Renaissance.* New York, 1958. Excellent.

Pagel, Walter, "Paracelsus and the Neoplatonic and Gnostic Tradition." *Ambix,* Vol. 8 (October 1960), 125–166.

Pagel, Walter, "The Prime Matter of Paracelsus." *Ambix,* Vol. 9 (October 1961), 117–135.

Stillman, John Maxson, *Paracelsus.* London, 1920. Emphasis on science.

Stoddart, Anna M., *The Life of Paracelsus.* London, 1911. Browning's interpretation.

LINDA VAN NORDEN

PARADIGM-CASE ARGUMENT is a form of argument against philosophical skepticism found in contemporary analytic philosophy. It counters doubt about whether any of some class of things exists by attempting to point out paradigm cases, clear and indisputable instances. A distinguishing feature of the argument is the contention that certain facts about language entail the existence of paradigm cases. This claim, however, has been disputed in recent years, and the future status of the argument depends upon whether it can be upheld.

The paradigm-case argument has been used against a

wide range of skeptical positions. A typical example is doubt about our ability to perceive directly material objects. Such doubt can be raised by reflection upon the physiological and physical facts about perception. For example, since seeing involves the transmission of light waves to our eyes and these waves are what immediately affects our eyes, it may appear that we are mistaken in thinking that we see objects. If anything, we should say that we see light waves. The fact that it takes a certain amount of time for light to travel from an object to our eyes lends support to this. How can we see something unless we see it as it is at the present moment? While considerations such as these show how skepticism can arise, one striking fact about the paradigm-case argument is that if it is valid, the skeptic can be refuted directly without the necessity of examining in detail the reasons behind his position.

The first step in the argument is to make the skepticism bear on particular cases. If we cannot perceive material objects, then, presumably, we cannot see the table we are working on or the pen with which we write. Next, a situation is sketched in which, ordinarily, no one would hesitate to affirm just the opposite. If the light is excellent, our eyes open, our sight unimpaired, the table directly before us, and so on, then we should ordinarily have no qualms about stating that we see a table.

The argument would be weak if it relied merely on the fact that people would ordinarily have no doubts in such situations, for it does not follow from this that they state the truth. But the argument claims something more for the kind of situations it describes. It holds that they are indisputably examples of seeing a table because of their relationship to the meaning of the expression "seeing a table." Typically, this relationship is brought out by saying that such a situation is just what we call "seeing a table" or that it is just the sort of circumstances in which one might teach someone the meaning of the expression "seeing a table." Generalizing and taking the strongest interpretation of the force of these remarks, one might ask: "If this *is* just what we call *X*, then in saying that it is *X*, how can we fail to state the truth? If this *is* a situation in which we might teach the meaning of *X*, then how can it fail to be a case of *X*? In denying that anyone ever sees a table, the skeptic seems to be placed in the position of refusing to apply the expression "seeing a table" to the very situation to which that expression refers.

If the skeptic concedes that the situation presented is an instance of that which he doubted to exist, then he admits defeat. But if, despite what has been said, he will not concede this, the final stage of the argument poses a dilemma. When the skeptic wonders whether we ever really see such things as tables, we naturally understand the words he uses in their usual sense. By "usual sense" is meant no more than what we should have understood by his words "see" and "table" if, instead, he were describing some scene he had witnessed. But how can his words be construed in this way when he refuses to use them of a typical situation in which their usual meaning might be taught and which is just what we ordinarily call "seeing a table"? On the other hand, if the skeptic claims some different or novel meaning for his words, the original shock of his

skeptical conclusion is blunted. For in some special sense of the words, it may be true that we never see tables. In fact, what often happens is that the skeptical position maintains its plausibility only through an unnoticed fluctuation between the usual sense of the key expressions and some special sense. The paradigm-case argument may serve to bring out into the open the fact that an unusual meaning must be looked for.

Further applications. Other examples of philosophical doubt to which the paradigm-case argument has been applied include skepticism about the validity of inductive reasoning, about man's free will, about the possibility of knowledge concerning empirical facts generally, and about the reality of the past. In many cases these skeptical positions are founded entirely on a priori considerations, and their stand is not merely that, as a matter of fact, there are no instances of some class of things, but that, as a matter of logical necessity, there could not be any. Philosophers who have argued that we can never genuinely know anything about the empirical world, for example, have almost invariably thought such knowledge a logical impossibility. Their reason is often the supposed impossibility of complete verification of any empirical assertion about the world. But this they take to be a necessary truth following from the fact that there are an infinite number of possible observations and investigations relevant to any such assertion. Similarly, the impossibility of justifying inductive reasoning (that which goes from examined cases to a general conclusion or from past instances to a prediction) has been held on the grounds that there is a logical obstacle in the way of all attempts at justification.

Against such a priori skepticism the argument need not produce an actual paradigm case. The mere fact that a hypothetical case can be described is sufficient. This in part accounts for the fact that philosophers who have employed the argument in practice do not bother to describe an actual occurrence. So, for example, one writer, in using the argument to refute skepticism about induction, asks us to imagine that "the observed confirmatory instances for the theory of gravitation were a million or ten million times as extensive as they now are" (Paul Edwards, "Bertrand Russell's Doubts About Induction," p. 65). By its very statement this is only a hypothetical case. But the skeptic about induction cannot admit that if this were to happen, we should *then* be justified in accepting the law of gravitation, because if justification were a logical impossibility, no paradigm case of justified inductive inference would even be conceivable.

But not all philosophical skepticism is completely a priori. Doubts about man's ability to choose among genuine alternatives is often supported, for example, by citing the success of the behavioral sciences and arguing that they will eventually be able to describe and predict human actions through causal laws. Here the philosopher appears to argue from empirical premises. But here, also, the descriptions of paradigm cases offered to the skeptic have usually been hypothetical. A writer, for example, who pointed to a marriage where there has been no pressure and the like placed on the two people as a paradigm case of choosing freely would not feel compelled to prove the existence of some actual marriage fitting this description.

The reason why a purely hypothetical instance can be given even where the skepticism is based on empirical premises is that there is a sense in which the skeptic does not deny the existence of paradigm cases. In this example he would not, for instance, dispute the frequent occurrence of the sort of marriage described. And he would be prepared to admit that in such cases the appearances are in favor of a free choice having been exercised. But, he thinks, the other considerations provided by his skeptical argument show that, in fact, it is doubtful or impossible that such an occurrence should be an instance of genuinely free choice. This is why the appeal to the connection between such situations and the meaning of, in this example, the expression "free choice" is the vital step in the paradigm-case argument. It is that which, if anything, shows that whatever the skeptical argument, these circumstances *must* be counted as instances of free choice.

Background. The idea that philosophy cannot cast doubt on the applications ordinarily made of everyday expressions is not a new one. It can be seen, for example, in Berkeley's refusal to draw skeptical consequences from his radical thesis that nothing exists apart from the mind. He did not conclude that we are mistaken in talking of material objects such as trees and tables; instead, he attempted to show how his thesis could be used to analyze the meaning of statements about these things. Everyday language succeeds in saying something true about the world; the only question for him was, *What* does it say?

But what is perhaps novel is the erection of this idea into an explicit philosophical argument. And this is largely the product of what has been called the "revolution in philosophy," which began in England shortly before World War II and which has subsequently dominated much of Anglo-American philosophy. The possibility of defeating skepticism by reference to particular cases, however, was already present some time before this in the many essays on the subject, dating from the first decade of this century, by G. E. Moore.

G. E. Moore. Moore thought of his opposition to skepticism in any form as a defense of common sense. The statements of common sense which he wished to defend were of two kinds: such context-free statements as "The Earth has existed for many years" and such context-bound statements as "Here is a human hand" and "This is a pencil." Moore held that he knew with certainty the truth of statements of both kinds. Any skeptical argument, therefore, which entailed that he did not or could not know them must be mistaken. To his critics this has seemed a strange sort of defense of common sense, for how can one defend a position merely by reaffirming it? In answering this, some writers have suggested that Moore was implicitly using the paradigm-case argument. While it is difficult to interpret Moore's affirmation of context-free statements in this way, the suggestion is quite plausible, for example, when we find him attacking skepticism about the existence of material objects by holding up his hand and saying that it is quite certain that this is a human hand and that at least one material object therefore exists ("Proof of an External World," pp. 145–146).

Moore himself, however, apparently saw his procedure in a different light. He thought of it as a challenge to the skeptic: Which is more certain, the (usually esoteric) premises of your argument or the common-sense statements which you are compelled to deny? Moore also pointed out that whereas the skeptic has an argument that leads to the denial of some common-sense statement, a counterargument can be constructed using the common-sense statement as a premise and the denial of the skeptical reasons as a conclusion. The question then seems to resolve into who has the more certain premises. And in this conflict common sense surely seems to be on firmer ground. In an examination of four assumptions from which Bertrand Russell had drawn skeptical conclusions, for example, Moore ends by saying: "I cannot help answering: 'It seems to me more certain that I *do* know that this is a pencil and that you are conscious, than that any single one of these four assumptions is true, let alone all four'" ("Four Forms of Scepticism," p. 226). And at a much earlier time he wrote: "I think the fact that, if Hume's principles were true, I could not know of the existence of this pencil is a *reductio ad absurdum* of those principles" (*Some Main Problems of Philosophy,* p. 120).

In this interpretation of his procedure, Moore defends common sense as the more certainly true view of the world. The paradigm-case argument, in contrast, appeals to language to show that skepticism conflicts with the facts about the use of expressions needed to state it. Although Moore pointed to the importance of particular cases, it is necessary to look at the ideas which have subsequently come to the forefront of Anglo-American philosophy to see why a connection with language should be thought relevant.

Wittgenstein. Of central importance are the views of Ludwig Wittgenstein, whose work has heavily influenced many of those who have used the paradigm-case argument. (It is, however, debatable whether Wittgenstein himself employed the argument.) One of his central contentions, in opposition to his own earlier work, the *Tractatus Logico-philosophicus,* was that while rules can be formulated for language, it is a mistake to view the particular uses of language as deriving their correctness from being in accord with rules. Rather, the fact that those who speak the language agree that *this* is the correct thing to say here and *that* incorrect there shows what the rules are. If anything, this agreement in judgment about particular cases is primitive. So, in the notes he dictated to some of his students in 1933–1934 (subsequently known as the *Blue Book*), Wittgenstein said, "It is part of the grammar of the word 'chair' that *this* is what we call 'to sit on a chair.'" It would be a mistake to take it as a consequence of such remarks that if the users of a language agree in calling *this* an example of X, then, in the sense which the expression has in their language, this *must* be a case of X. Such a principle would indeed immediately yield the validity of the paradigm-case argument. But there is an obvious objection which an example will illustrate. There was a time, perhaps, when all agreed in calling the earth flat, although it was not. They were in agreement, but they were all mistaken. This, however, is a situation in which people were relying upon certain evidence which proved misleading. And in holding that there is a connection between the situations in which we should use a description and the meaning, or "grammar," of the description, Wittgenstein was probably thinking of circumstances in which we are not relying on evidence. It was one of his important ideas that where it makes sense to speak of having evidence that something is so, it must be (logically) possible to get beyond mere evidence. Thus, while we may sometimes have evidence that someone is sitting in a chair (from, for example, a report that he is), Wittgenstein would argue that when we are standing in a well-lit room looking at the person so seated, it would be a mistake to suppose we then have mere evidence. This idea runs directly counter to long traditions in philosophy. For philosophers, even those who are not skeptics, have most often held that one gets beyond evidence only in a very small class of statements—in general, only first-person, singular, present-tense assertions about one's own mental life. It appears reasonably certain, however, that some such general claim as Wittgenstein's must be substantiated before the paradigm-case argument can be declared valid, because a paradigm case of, for example, a free choice must be one in which there is *more* than just good evidence that a free choice has been made. Otherwise, the skeptical reasons may be sufficient to show that the evidence is misleading.

Whether Wittgenstein's view, if correct, is sufficient to show the validity of the paradigm-case argument is another question. It will depend, for example, upon whether a situation in which we have got beyond mere evidence is also one in which we cannot be mistaken.

It is important to note that the idea that we must be able to get beyond evidence presupposes that we are dealing with a concept free from logical inconsistency. We cannot, for example, ever be confronted with a round square or a genuine trisection of an angle. But a priori skepticism is based on a "proof" that a certain concept could have no instantiation because there would be some inconsistency in supposing it did. The paradigm-case argument, if it is to be generally employed, may need a proof of its own that no expression in everyday use can turn out to designate a self-inconsistent idea. While this has sometimes been held, more needs to be said about it. It seems impossible that anyone should prove, for example, that the idea of a table is self-inconsistent, but it is not so implausible to suppose that someone might show that the idea of a time machine or of transmigration of souls, which are ordinary expressions in the sense intended, contain contradictions. And is it beyond doubt that the concept of a free choice, for example, is logically irreproachable? Moreover, if it were to be demonstrated independently that no expression in ordinary language can designate a self-inconsistent idea, this would be sufficient by itself to discredit any a priori skepticism concerned with such expressions and would render the subsequent use of a paradigm-case argument superfluous.

There is a further difficulty in supposing Wittgenstein's view—that what we say in particular circumstances is determinant of what we mean—to entail the validity of the paradigm-case argument. This arises from the fact that particular cases can be related to the meaning of an expression without necessarily being paradigm cases.

This may be brought out by an illustration. Suppose someone doubts the existence of elephants. Very likely the surest way to convince him of his mistake would be to show him the elephants at a zoo or circus. That we call *these* elephants shows something about the meaning of the word "elephant." If the skeptic about elephants sees no connection between what he has been shown and the existence of elephants, we have grounds for suspecting that he does not know what the word "elephant" means. But the connection need not be that having seen these things, he must admit that elephants exist. All he must admit is that these things have the *appearance* of elephants (see Wittgenstein, *Philosophical Investigations*, Paragraph 354). If he maintains, for example, "These certainly look like elephants, but I am sure that they are in reality camels with false noses and padding," he has acknowledged a connection between what he has been shown and the meaning of the word "elephant." His skepticism, however, remains.

At this time it is an open question whether the important general ideas about the connection of language to particular cases which have fostered the use of the paradigm-case argument also entail its validity.

Criticisms and variations. Critics of the paradigm-case argument have questioned the legitimacy of the move from "This is just what we call *X*" to "Thus, it is a genuine case of *X*." Some reasons for doubt about this transition have already been mentioned. It should be pointed out, however, that there are times when the transition is legitimate, although the paradigm-case argument can draw no comfort from this fact.

Suppose, for example, that someone doubted that there are any bachelors but admitted that there are unmarried males of marriageable age. We might naturally say to him, "But this is just what we call 'being a bachelor.' " Here, however, the doubter has no reply (other than to question whether this *is* how the word is used) because "this" refers to a description which logically entails "being a bachelor." In the paradigm-case argument, however, especially where the case is actually pointed out instead of described, no such entailment is normally claimed.

If there is not an entailment, however, then there seems room for the skeptic to maneuver. How can one hold that no matter what the skeptic's reasons may be, he must admit *this* as an instance of what he doubted to exist? Faced with such difficulties, some proponents of the paradigm-case argument have placed restrictions on its use. They have said that it is valid only for expressions designating concepts which must be taught ostensively—that is, taught through examples. Philosophers have often held, for example, that color words can be taught only in this fashion. The usual reason given is that the concept of a particular color is simple and that its meaning cannot be captured by a verbal definition. Hence, it must be taught by pointing out things which are of that color. When the paradigm-case argument is confined to such concepts, a special reason is supplied for why there must be indisputable instances. If there were not (or had never been) any red objects, how could the concept get into the language?

The appeal to what must be taught ostensively is frequently presented as if it were merely an elucidation of the force of the paradigm-case argument. But it seems, instead, to be a separate and distinct form of argument.

There is, for example, no need to describe or point out particular circumstances. The conclusion that there are instances of, for example, red objects is drawn directly from the premise that the concept can be taught only ostensively. There would, perhaps, be point in calling this form of argument by a different name.

Argument from ostensive teaching. Whether such an argument is valid against a skeptic will depend upon several questions which have yet to be conclusively answered. First, are there any concepts which can be taught only ostensively? Is it logically impossible for someone to have the concept of, for example, redness without having obtained it through ostensive teaching? Second, even if a concept must be taught through such methods, must there be exemplifications of the concept? It seems possible, for example, to teach someone the meaning of "is red" by using objects which merely appear to be red as long as this fact is concealed from the student. Third, even if the answer in the above cases is affirmative, are the important concepts which give rise to skepticism of the required kind? Is the concept of choosing freely, for example, one which can be taught only by such methods?

Sometimes it is said that the paradigm-case argument need be confined only to those concepts which can be taught ostensively. When this is done, no conclusion can be immediately drawn about the existence of cases falling under the concept. The concept of a unicorn could be taught ostensively if only there were such a creature, but as things stand, it never has been. What, then, is the value of such a restriction? The idea seems to be that if a concept can be taught ostensively, then there must be conceivable circumstances, at any rate, in which something falls under the concept—those circumstances in which it could be taught in this fashion. Such an argument, in general, has force only against an a priori skeptic. But it is possible that the circumstances in which, it is claimed, the concept could be taught ostensively actually occur and that the skeptic may not wish to dispute their existence. It might be urged, for example, that the concept of acting freely can be taught ostensively in circumstances which the skeptic about freedom would have to admit do occur. Some of the same problems about ostensive teaching arise for this kind of argument as for the previous one.

Evaluative concepts. Still another restriction on the use of the paradigm-case argument has been proposed by some writers. J. O. Urmson questions the legitimacy of applying it to evaluative expressions such as "good (inductive) reasons" ("Some Questions Concerning Validity"). His point is that the use of evaluative expressions has a dimension that the use of purely classificatory expressions lacks. Evaluative expressions not only sort out things and situations but also signify approval or condemnation. The skeptic, therefore, may be willing to grant that there are differences between what we call, for example, "good inductive reasons" and "bad inductive reasons" and that he has said nothing to show that these differences are not exemplified. But he may question whether these differences support our approval of the one and our rejection of the other. Thus, to take Urmson's analogy, he may grant a difference between what we call "good apples" and what we call "bad apples" but urge that our standards are faulty. How can pointing out that *this* is just what we call a "good apple," he may ask, show that we would not do better to approve of some other kind?

Two sorts of skepticism. Urmson's point, if valid, appears to have many consequences. The dispute concerning whether we can exercise genuine freedom of choice about our own actions does not seem on the surface to be a dispute involving evaluative concepts. Philosophers, however, have been particularly uneasy about the use of the paradigm-case argument in this area, in contrast, for example, to its employment against skepticism about the existence or perception of material objects. The explanation may be that there are two sorts of skepticism involved. It may be that the skeptic about man's freedom is not, in fact, denying that many of the ordinary relevant expressions mark genuine distinctions but, rather, querying the purpose to which we put these distinctions. In contrast, the skeptic about the existence of material objects does appear to deny that there is, for example, a distinction between a material object and the mere appearance of one.

We contrast seeing material objects with seeing hallucinatory or imaginary objects. By describing circumstances in which we ordinarily are in no doubt about which member of these distinctions is present, the paradigm-case argument may be construed as pointing out that the everyday expressions do, after all, serve a function. The fact that we do make these contrasts in practice and, more importantly, that we generally agree in our judgments shows that some genuine distinction is being made. Moreover, the skeptic does not usually dispute the fact that we can independently reach agreement about particular cases. Thus, it might be said to him, "Whatever your arguments to show that we never see material objects, for example, after we have looked at them and debated them, there will still be that difference between what we have called 'a real object' and what we have called 'hallucinations,' 'illusions,' or 'imaginary objects.' We shall still need to mark that distinction and so return to our usual way of describing things."

While this seems quite powerful against, for example, skepticism about the perception of material objects, the same sort of explanation of the paradigm-case argument is not so convincing when tried out on disputes about evaluative terms or the existence of genuinely free choices. The trouble may be that although the skeptic's arguments cannot destroy the correctness of contrasting what we should call cases of freely choosing from those we should not, his argument may still destroy what we thought to be the point of making the distinction. To say that a choice was free often involves the ascription of responsibility and the possibility of praise and blame. We behave differently toward persons who have made a free choice than we do toward those who have been coerced. If we knew all our "choices" to be the product of prior conditioning or hereditary traits—a possibility that appears often to generate skepticism about our freedom—would we still be on solid ground in behaving differently toward those who have made a "free choice"? Although we could continue to make the same distinctions we do now as far as classification goes, we might think that to call certain choices "free" would have a hollow ring.

Whatever the ultimate verdict on the paradigm-case argument as a refutation of skepticism, there can be no doubt that its use in recent philosophy has generated very important questions about the relationship of language to the world.

Bibliography

BACKGROUND

Austin, J. L., "Other Minds," in Antony Flew, ed., *Essays on Logic and Language,* 2d series. Oxford, 1953.

Chappell, V. C., "Malcolm on Moore." *Mind,* Vol. 70 (1961), 417–425.

Malcolm, Norman, "Moore and Ordinary Language," in Paul A. Schilpp, ed., *The Philosophy of G. E. Moore,* 2d ed. New York, 1952.

Malcolm, Norman, "George Edward Moore," in his *Knowledge and Certainty.* Englewood Cliffs, N.J., 1963.

Moore, George Edward, *Some Main Problems of Philosophy.* London, 1953. See especially Chs. 1, 5–6.

Moore, G. E., *Philosophical Papers.* New York, 1959. See especially "A Defence of Common Sense," "Proof of an External World," "Four Forms of Scepticism."

White, A. R., *G. E. Moore.* Oxford, 1958.

Wisdom, John, "Philosophical Perplexity," in his *Philosophy and Psycho-analysis.* Oxford, 1953.

Wittgenstein, Ludwig, *Philosophical Investigations,* translated by G. E. M. Anscombe. New York, 1953.

Wittgenstein, Ludwig, *The Blue and Brown Books.* Oxford, 1958.

APPLICATIONS AND CRITICAL DISCUSSIONS

Black, Max, "Making Something Happen," in Sidney Hook, ed., *Determinism and Freedom.* New York, 1958. Application to freedom of the will and causation.

Bouwsma, O. K., "Descartes' Evil Genius." *The Philosophical Review,* Vol. 58 (1949), 141–151. Application to skepticism about the external world.

Danto, Arthur C., "The Paradigm Case Argument and the Free-Will Problem." *Ethics,* Vol. 69 (1959), 120–124. Critical.

Edwards, Paul, "Bertrand Russell's Doubts About Induction," in Antony Flew, ed., *Essays on Logic and Language,* 1st series. Oxford, 1951. Application to skepticism about induction and a sympathetic analysis.

Findlay, J. N., "Time: A Treatment of Some Puzzles," *ibid.* Application to skepticism about the passage of time.

Flew, Antony, "Philosophy and Language," in Antony Flew, ed., *Essays in Conceptual Analysis.* London, 1956. Sympathetic.

Flew, Antony, "'Farewell to the Paradigm-Case Argument': A Comment." *Analysis,* Vol. 18 (1957), 34–40. Defense against criticism by Watkins.

MacIntyre, A. C., "Determinism." *Mind,* Vol. 66 (1957), 28–41. Contains criticism of application made to freedom of the will.

Mackie, J. L., *Contemporary Linguistic Philosophy—Its Strength and Weakness.* Otago, New Zealand, 1956.

Malcolm, Norman, "Moore and Ordinary Language," in Schilpp, *op. cit.* Sympathetic analysis and several applications.

Nagel, Ernest, "Russell's Philosophy of Science," in Paul A. Schilpp, ed., *The Philosophy of Bertrand Russell.* Evanston, Ill., 1944. Application to several of Russell's views.

Passmore, John, *Philosophical Reasoning.* New York, 1961. See Ch. 6 for a critical analysis.

Richman, Robert J., "On the Argument of the Paradigm Case." *Australasian Journal of Philosophy,* Vol. 39 (1961), 75–81. Critical.

Richman, Robert J., "Still More on the Argument of the Paradigm Case." *Australasian Journal of Philosophy,* Vol. 40 (1962), 204–207.

Stebbing, L. Susan, *Philosophy and the Physicists.* London, 1937. See Ch. 3 for application to skepticism about the properties of material objects.

Urmson, J. O., "Some Questions Concerning Validity," in Antony Flew, ed., *Essays in Conceptual Analysis.* London, 1956. Critical of application to evaluative concepts.

Watkins, J. W. N., "Farewell to the Paradigm-Case Argument." *Analysis,* Vol. 18 (1957), 25–33. Critical.

Watkins, J. W. N., "A Reply to Professor Flew's Comment." *Analysis,* Vol. 18 (1957), 41–42.

Will, F. L., "Will the Future Be Like the Past?," in Antony Flew, ed., *Essays in Logic and Language,* 2d series. Oxford, 1953. Application to skepticism about induction.

Williams, C. J. F., "More on the Paradigm Case Argument." *Australasian Journal of Philosophy,* Vol. 39 (1961), 276–278. Defense of the argument against criticisms of Richman.

KEITH S. DONNELLAN

PARADOXES. See LOGICAL PARADOXES; ZENO OF ELEA.

PARANORMAL PHENOMENA. See ESP PHENOMENA, PHILOSOPHICAL IMPLICATIONS OF; PRECOGNITION.

PARETO, VILFREDO (1848–1923), Italian economist, sociologist, and philosopher, was born in Paris, where his father, the marchese di Pareto, a supporter of Mazzini, was living as a refugee. In 1858 the family returned to Italy, where Pareto received a mixed mathematical and classical secondary education. In 1870 he graduated with a degree in engineering from the Turin Istituto Politecnico. He embarked on a career with the Italian railways and soon became a director. He was deeply, though ambivalently, influenced by his father's involvement in radical politics. Throughout his life Pareto believed in the superiority of liberal free trade, but his disillusionment with the economic protectionism of the Italian government developed into a fierce hatred of the political and social side of liberal ideology, which he thought had resulted in indefensible economic policies. This hatred led Pareto into intemperate attacks on the government, which retaliated by banning his lectures, and Pareto was eventually forced to abandon his career in government service. At about this time he became acquainted with the mathematical economist Léon Walras, professor at Lausanne. In 1893 Pareto was appointed lecturer at Lausanne and succeeded to Walras' chair the following year. He lived in Switzerland for the rest of his life, eschewing political activity until Mussolini's advent to power in 1922. The fascists acknowledged a large debt to Pareto's writings and conferred numerous honors on him, but since he died after only one year of the fascist regime, his considered attitude to it must be a matter of conjecture.

Logical and nonlogical conduct. Pareto's social thought was largely conditioned by his reactions to contemporary political developments in Italy. He claimed to provide an impartial presentation and explanation of the facts of social existence without commitment to any particular sectional interest. In fact, however, his writings constitute a violently polemical defense of economic liberalism and political and social authoritarianism. This gulf between his professions and his practice is ironically in tune with his skepticism about the extent of men's understanding of their own behavior. In his economic writings, *Cours d'économie politique* (2 vols., Lausanne, 1896–1897) and *Manuel d'économie politique* (Paris, 1909), he tried to prove mathematically that the system of free trade provides maximum social benefit. In *Les Systèmes socialistes*, (2 vols., Paris, 1902), he attempted to refute the claims of socialism that it provided a superior solution to economic problems. But if the logical case for economic liberalism was as overwhelming as it seemed to Pareto, he had to show why it was not generally practiced. This led him from economics to sociology and to the distinction between logical and nonlogical conduct, which constitutes one of his most distinctive contributions to sociological theory.

Pareto introduced this distinction in the course of a discussion of the nature of a scientific sociology. His conception of "logico-experimental" science was largely Baconian, and his methodological desiderata for a scientific sociology were that all its concepts should have strictly controlled empirical reference; that all its theories should be subject to rigorous experimental or observational control; and that all its inferences should follow with strict logic from the data. He set himself to show how these norms should be applied in the sociological investigation of the ideas and systems of thought current in a given society, which, because they bear "the image of social activity," are an important part of the sociologist's data. Pareto thought it important not to accept such ideas and theories at their holders' valuations but to ask two questions about them: (1) Are their explanatory claims justified by logico-experimental standards? (2) Why are they accepted, and what are the social consequences of this acceptance? The question of acceptance became particularly pressing for Pareto in the case of widely held theories that did not seem to measure up to logico-experimental criteria. He thus regarded the logical critique of sophistries as only a prolegomenon, although a necessary one, to the real problems of sociology.

Many of Pareto's own criticisms of sophistries, especially of those committed by his political opponents, are extremely cogent and witty. However, his general account of the distinction between sound explanation and sophistry is less satisfactory. He held that an action was logical if it was performed by the agent with the intention of achieving an empirically identifiable end, if it actually tended to result in the achievement of that end, and if the agent had sound logico-experimental grounds for expecting this end to result. He designated as nonlogical any action that failed to measure up to any of these diverse criteria, and proceeded to classify what seemed the most characteristic ways in which this failure could occur.

Pareto regarded economic activity directed at maximizing profit, clearheaded Machiavellian political activity, and scientific work as the three most important types of logical conduct. But he left largely unasked most of the fundamental philosophical questions to which such an account gives rise. In particular, unlike his contemporary Émile Durkheim, he did not investigate the possibility that established forms of social behavior are themselves presupposed by the concepts most fundamental to his account—concepts such as "empirical reference," "respect for logic," and "setting oneself an end." However, Pareto's important insight, contained in his idea of "nonlogical conduct," that there are many forms of activity concerning

which it makes no sense to ask what reasons people have for performing them, could naturally have led to such an investigation, had Pareto been more of a philosopher and less of a brilliant political pamphleteer. His failure to press this line of inquiry impeded him from maintaining a clear distinction between nonlogical and illogical actions, and what he claimed to be a dispassionate account of the nature of social life became a massive polemical indictment of alleged human folly. It is also one of the roots of his uncritical acceptance of science as the mother and guardian of logic, notwithstanding his repeated attacks on worshipers of "the Goddess Science."

Residues and derivations. If the reasons offered by men for many of their own actions are not logically compelling, a different kind of explanation seems to be needed. To find this explanation Pareto undertook a wide-ranging, but unsystematic and biased, historical and comparative survey of human social behavior. In the course of it, he claimed to detect a contrast between kinds of conduct that constantly recur with very little variation and those that are highly diverse and changeable. The former he labeled "residues," the latter "derivations." The variable elements, or derivations, prove to be the theories with which people attempt to justify their residues. The alleged persistence of the same residue, even after the agent's abandonment of the derivation that had been supposed to justify it, gave Pareto an additional reason for claiming that the derivation was not the real explanation of the existence of the residue.

This theory has obvious affinities with Marx's concept of "ideology," with Freud's "rationalization" (although Pareto seems to have been ignorant of Freud's work), and with Durkheim's "collective sentiments." Unlike these writers, however, Pareto offered no systematic account of why men have recourse to derivations, contenting himself with the observation that among the residues is to be found a tendency of men "to paint a varnish of logic over their conduct."

The theory of residues is similarly incomplete. His most consistently held view seems to have been that the residues are constants and must be accepted as brute facts. At times he said that they were determined by certain congenital psychological "sentiments," although he failed clearly to distinguish these from the residues themselves. Nor did he explain how sentiments differ from the "interests" that he supposed to underlie logical economic activities. At other times he suggested that residues change as a result of social conditions. "A number of traits observable in the Jews of our time, and which are ordinarily ascribed to race," he wrote, "are mere manifestations of residues produced by long centuries of oppression." Moreover, in his Machiavellian advice to statesmen to reinforce in their subjects those residues that are politically advantageous to themselves, by means of propaganda in favor of suitable derivations, Pareto even implied that derivations could influence residues. Such difficulties stemmed largely from Pareto's failure to face the philosophical questions about the nature of logic that his theories should have led him to ask.

Elites and the cycle of history. The two classes of residues most important for Pareto's sociological theory were combinations and persistence of aggregates. Men dominated by combinations are the innovating, risk-taking experimenters, the "foxes," linked by Pareto with the economic class of speculators. At the other extreme are the "lions," dominated by persistence of aggregates, wedded to the status quo and willing to use force in its defense. These are to be found among the *rentier* class. Pareto thought that all societies are ruled by elites, composed of those naturally most able in the various forms of social activity. The balance between combinations and persistence of aggregates in the elites and the lower social strata respectively determines the general character of a society. Inconsistently with his insistence on the nonlogical character of value judgments, Pareto thought there was an objective distinction between healthy and decadent social states, a distinction strongly influenced by his own attachment to free trade and political authoritarianism. Elites must be enterprising and innovative but also ready to use force in defense of their authority. However, the latter propensity tends to hinder the "circulation of the elites," leading to an accumulation of ability among the masses. Alternatively, the former tendency may degenerate into a flabby humanitarianism that weakens authority. In either case, a revolution results, leading to government by new elites. Pareto's belief in the constant repetition of this process led him to a cyclical view of history.

Works by Pareto

Trattato di sociologia generale, 2 vols. Florence, 1916. 2d ed., 3 vols. Florence, 1923. Translated by A. Bongiorno and A. Livingston as *The Mind and Society,* 4 vols. London, 1935.

Works on Pareto

Borkenau, Franz, *Pareto.* London, 1936.
Burnham, James, *The Machiavellians.* New York, 1943.
Curtis, C. P., and Homans, G. C., *An Introduction to Pareto: His Sociology.* New York, 1934.
Parsons, Talcott, *The Structure of Social Action.* New York and London, 1937.

PETER WINCH

PARKER, THEODORE (1810–1860), American theologian and social reformer, was the grandson of Captain John Parker, who led the Lexington minutemen. Parker was born in Lexington, Massachusetts, and, except for scattered months of formal schooling during the winter, was almost entirely self-taught. Although unable to afford tuition, he was allowed to take the Harvard examinations, and in 1834 he was admitted to the Harvard Divinity School. He was ordained minister of a small parish in West Roxbury, Massachusetts, in 1837. In 1845, after he had become a controversial figure and commanded a large audience, his supporters created the 28th Congregational Society in Boston and later rented the Boston Music Hall, where Parker preached to one of the largest congregations in the country. He became equally famous as a scholar, preacher, theologian, and reformer. Parker died in Florence, Italy.

In his religious thought Parker's radicalism was partly instinctive and partly the result of environmental influences. In an autobiographical essay completed just

before his death, Parker remembered how he had been taught as a boy to respect the voice of conscience as the "voice of God in the soul of man" and encouraged to develop a spirit of free inquiry "in all directions." His religious upbringing was extremely liberal, and when he entered upon his formal theological studies, he had not only rejected the doctrine of the Trinity but was already suspicious of the validity of miracles and the "infallible, verbal inspiration of the whole Bible." Profiting by the encouragement of the liberal Unitarian professors at Harvard, he began an intensive study of the Bible which ultimately led him to a knowledge of twenty languages and did much to confirm his earlier suspicions regarding Biblical authority.

As a young minister Parker was a great admirer of William Ellery Channing and Ralph Waldo Emerson. He responded to Emerson's Divinity School Address with enthusiasm and was an anonymous contributor to the polemical pamphlet war which followed.

Parker's own religious philosophy was strongly influenced by Immanuel Kant and by the critical studies of Biblical scholars like Wilhelm Martin DeWette and theologians like David Friedrich Strauss and Ferdinand Christian Baur. Academic study and his own religious experience convinced him that the foundation of religion was based on "great primal intuitions of nature which depend on no logical process of demonstration." The three most important were the intuition of God, the intuition of morality, and the intuition of immortality. Basing his theology on these facts of consciousness, Parker emphasized the infinite perfection of God and the perfectibility of man.

His ideas first received wide publicity in 1841, when he delivered an ordination sermon entitled "The Transient and the Permanent in Christianity." In this sermon Parker contrasted the transiency of theology and Scripture with the permanence of the great moral truths of Christianity, truths which depended for their validity not on the authority of Christ but on the voice of God in the human heart. Parker spoke as a Unitarian minister, but the reception he received from organized Unitarianism was as wrathful as Channing's reception had been at the hands of the Calvinists twenty years earlier. As his more conservative followers faded away, Parker developed his radical ideas at greater length in a series of lectures which he published in 1842 as *A Discourse of Matters Pertaining to Religion.* The following year he published his own edition and translation of DeWette's critical study of the Old Testament, *Beiträge zur Einleitung in das Alte Testament.*

Emerson referred to Parker as "our Savonarola," and Parker's essay on transcendentalism is one of the clearest expressions that we have of the American rejection of the empirical philosophy of the Enlightenment. Modern scholarship has established, however, that Parker's transcendentalism was not identical with Emerson's, for Parker relied less completely on intuition and more on the critical study of history and theology.

Parker's extraordinary capacity for sustained scholarly endeavor was almost matched by his capacity for action. The "Absolute Religion" which he advocated required the application of religious truth to social problems, and Parker often preached on subjects like crime, poverty, temperance, and prostitution. Long before the proponents of the social gospel, Parker recognized the power of organized evil in the world and sought to marshal religious sentiment against it. He was inevitably drawn into abolitionism. A friend of Wendell Phillips and William Lloyd Garrison, he helped to lead the resistance to the Fugitive Slave Law in Boston and was a supporter of John Brown before Harper's Ferry.

Parker traveled widely on lecture tours, making about one hundred appearances a year during the last decade of his life. His influence on the public mind was at its peak just before his death.

Bibliography

Parker's work is collected in Frances P. Cobbe, ed., *Theodore Parker's Works*, 14 vols. (London, 1863–1870). A centenary edition was published by the American Unitarian Association, 15 vols. (Boston, 1907–1911). Henry Steele Commager has edited *Theodore Parker: An Anthology* (Boston, 1960).

Biographical studies include Henry Steele Commager, *Theodore Parker, Yankee Crusader* (Boston, 1936), John Dirk, *The Critical Theology of Theodore Parker* (New York, 1948), and John Weiss, *Life and Correspondence of Theodore Parker*, 2 vols. (New York, 1864).

IRVING H. BARTLETT

PARMENIDES OF ELEA, the most original and important philosopher before Socrates, was born c. 515 B.C. He changed the course of Greek cosmology and had an even more important effect upon metaphysics and epistemology. He was the first to focus attention on the central problem of Greek metaphysics—What is the nature of real being?—and he established a frame of reference within which the discussion was to be conducted. The closely related problem of knowledge, which to a great extent dominated philosophy in the fifth and fourth centuries, was raised at once by his contrast between the Way of Truth and the Way of Seeming. His influence can be found in Empedocles, Anaxagoras, and the atomists; it is strong in most of Plato's work, particularly in the vitally important dialogues *Parmenides, Theaetetus,* and *Sophist.*

Plato in his dialogue *Parmenides* describes a meeting in Athens of Parmenides, Zeno, and Socrates. Parmenides was then about 65, Zeno about 40, and Socrates "very young." Though the meeting is probably fictitious, there is no reason why the ages should be unrealistic. Since Socrates died in 399, when he was about 70, and since he was old enough in Plato's dialogue to talk philosophy with Parmenides, the meeting would have to be dated about 450, making Parmenides' birth about 515. An alternative dating (Diogenes Laërtius, *Lives* IX, 23, probably from Apollodorus' *Chronica*) puts his birth about 25 years earlier, but this can be explained away.

Plato's remark (*Sophist* 242D) that the Eleatic school stems from Xenophanes is not to be taken seriously. Parmenides founded the school in the Phocaean colony of Elea in southern Italy, and its only other noteworthy members were his pupils Zeno and Melissus (the tradition that the atomist Leucippus was from Elea is probably false).

Writings. The work of Parmenides is not extant as a whole. Plato and Aristotle quote a line or two; from later writers, particularly Sextus Empiricus and Simplicius, about 150 lines can be recovered. Parmenides wrote in hexameter verse. All the fragments seem to come from a single work, which may have been called *On Nature;* it is unlikely to have been very long, and the fragments may amount to as much as a third of the whole. The survival of a long consecutive passage of more than sixty lines (Fr. 8) is of the greatest importance; it is the earliest example of an extended philosophical argument.

The poem begins with a description of the poet's journey to the home of a goddess, who welcomes him kindly and tells him that he is to learn "both the unshakeable heart of well-rounded Truth, and the beliefs of mortals, in which there is no true reliability" (Fr. 1). The rest of the poem consists of the speech of the goddess in which she fulfills these two promises.

The interpretation of Parmenides is thoroughly controversial, and a short article cannot do more than offer one possible account, with a brief mention of the more important and plausible variants. In the interests of brevity many expressions of doubt have been omitted.

The proem. Sextus Empiricus (*Adversus Mathematicos,* VII, 111 ff.) quotes 32 lines which he asserts to be the beginning of Parmenides' *On Nature* (Fr. 1). The poet describes his journey in a chariot, drawn by mares that know the way and escorted by the Daughters of the Sun. The Sun Maidens come from the Halls of Night and unveil themselves when they come into daylight. There is a gateway on the paths of Night and Day, with great doors of which the goddess Justice holds the key. The Sun Maidens persuade Justice to open the gates for themselves and Parmenides, and they pass through. "The goddess" welcomes him kindly as a mortal man in divine company, shakes his hand, and sets his mind at rest by telling him that it is right and just that he should have taken this road. He must now learn both the truth and the unreliable beliefs of mortals.

Although few examples of contemporary poetry have survived for comparison, it is safe to say that this proem is a mixture of tradition and innovation. The "journey" of the poet is a literary figure closely paralleled in an ode by Pindar (*Olympian* 6). There, as for Parmenides, the journey is an image of the course of the song; the poet rides in a chariot, a gate has to be opened, the team knows the way, and the road is notably direct. The route followed by Parmenides' chariot, although straight and swift, is impossible to chart. The details are vague. What is clear is that the whole journey is nowhere on earth, but in the heavens, and that it begins in the realm of darkness and ends in the realm of light. This imagery is confirmed by other indications— the escort of Sun Maidens and their unveiling.

It can hardly be doubted that the journey symbolizes progress from ignorance to knowledge on a heroic or even cosmic scale. The epic verse form signifies a deliberately heroic context, for earlier philosophers probably wrote in prose (though Parmenides may also have chosen verse as being more memorable). Parmenides' journey in search of knowledge must recall Odysseus' journey to Hades (*Odyssey* XI) to get directions from Teiresias to guide him on his way home. The location of Parmenides' journey recalls the magic regions of this part of the *Odyssey,* where in one place dawn follows immediately upon nightfall because "the ways of night and day are close together" (X, 86) and where in another place there is no daylight at all, since Night envelops everything (XI, 19). There may also be reminiscences of the journey of Phaethon in the chariot of the Sun.

Sextus, after quoting Fragment 1, gives a detailed allegorical interpretation of it, and in this he has been followed by some modern scholars. But this is wrong; it is impossible to trace a consistent allegory, and in any case detailed allegory was a later invention.

The identity of the goddess is puzzling. The wording of the proem itself suggests that she is the same as the goddess Justice who holds the keys of the gates; in a later fragment, however, she speaks of Justice in the third person (possibly even in Fr. 1.28; certainly in Fr. 8.14). It may be that Parmenides left the identification intentionally vague. Simplicius does not mention the goddess at all but introduces his quotations as if the first person referred to Parmenides himself. The Neoplatonists appear to have called her "the nymph Hypsipyle" (that is, High Gate; Proclus, "Commentary on the *Parmenides*" Book IV, Ch. 34).

It is probably wrong to say that in his proem Parmenides is setting himself up as a mystic or that he is claiming to have received a divine revelation. If mysticism entails some privileged access to truth through nonrational means, then Parmenides was no mystic. The fragments show that he argued for his conclusions; his goddess tells him to use his reason to assess her words (Fr. 7.5). A single visionary experience is ruled out by the opening of the proem, in which the tenses show that the journey is a repeated one—perhaps repeated every time the poem is recited. Unless the claim of every poet to be inspired by the Muses is itself a claim to a divine revelation, this seems to be an inappropriate description of Parmenides' experience.

At the time of its composition, the proem was probably understood as a claim that the poet had something of great importance to say. The course of his divinely inspired song was a path that led to the light of knowledge. By making Justice responsible for opening the gate for him, he claimed that this was a right and proper path for him to follow and, therefore, a path that led to truth. By putting the whole of his doctrine into the mouth of a goddess, he claimed objectivity for it; it was not beyond criticism, since the goddess instructed him to judge it by reason, but it was not to be regarded as a merely personal statement by Parmenides.

The three ways. The goddess begins by telling Parmenides what are the only possible ways of inquiry. She describes three ways, produces reasons for ruling out two of them, and insists on the remaining one as the only correct one.

First two ways are stated, each being defined by a conjunctive proposition. The first is "that it *is*, and cannot not be; this is the way of Persuasion, for she is the attendant of Truth." The second is "that it *is not*, and must necessarily not be, this I tell you is a way of total ignorance" (Fr. 2).

The literal meaning of Parmenides' Greek in these propositions is hard to see. The verb "to be" is used in the existential sense. He uses it in the third person present indicative without any subject expressed. Some interpreters say that there is no subject to be understood; however, without any subject the sentence is incomplete, and no doubt the impersonal subject "it" is to be regarded as contained in the verb, as it often is. What this "it" refers to has to be derived from the rest of the argument and will be discussed shortly.

Immediately after the statement of the first two ways, the second way is ruled out on the ground that it is impossible to know or to utter what does not exist: "Whatever is for thinking and saying *must* exist; for it can exist [literally, 'is for being'], whereas nothing cannot" (Fr. 6). The line of thought seems to be that the object of thought *can* exist, and since "nothing" cannot exist, the object of thought cannot be nothing. But it must either exist or be nothing; hence, it *must* exist. The basic premises then are that "nothing" is nonexistent (presumably regarded as tautological) and that the object of thought *can* exist (that is, it is possible to think of something).

Parmenides makes it quite plain, by the use of inferential particles, that there *is* an argument in this passage (though this has been denied) along the lines described. It is therefore legitimate to fill in the basic proposition of the Way of Truth ("it is") from the grounds on which it is based. The unexpressed subject of this proposition must be "the object of thought or knowledge" (this is convincingly shown by G. E. L. Owen, "Eleatic Questions"). The Way of Truth will therefore show what can be said of a thing if it is to be a proper object of thought; the first step is to assert that it must *be,* that it should not *be* is unthinkable. Subsequently, the subject is referred to as τὸ ἐόν ("that which is," "what is real," "what exists").

After ruling out the second way, the goddess continues with a warning against a third way, the way followed by mortal men, who wander about senselessly, knowing nothing and getting nowhere. Their characteristic error is that they have made up their minds that "to be and not to be is the same and not the same" (Fr. 6). The third way can be identified with "the beliefs of mortals" mentioned at the end of the proem and discussed in detail in the main body of Parmenides' work, after the Way of Truth (this identification is often denied). Mortals treat existence and nonexistence as the same in that they attach them both to the same objects by supposing that things sometimes exist and sometimes do not (that is, that there is change) and by supposing that some things exist which contain less of being than others and therefore contain some nonexistence (that is, that there is difference). They treat them as not the same in that they suppose they have different meanings. The language in which the censured doctrine is expressed is reminiscent of Heraclitus, but Heraclitus is certainly not the only mortal who suffers from Parmenides' lash here.

The third way is ruled out by pointing to an alleged contradiction in it. It asserts that "things that are not, are" (Fr. 7). From the arguments of the recommended way, described later, it would appear that what is objectionable in the third way is its assumption of intermediate degrees of existence, of things that exist at one time but not another, at one place but not another, or in one way but not another. Ordinary habits of speech and the data of sense perception would lead a man along this path; the goddess gives a warning to "judge by *reason* the hard-hitting refutation that I have uttered."

The Way of Truth. The Way of Truth has now been shown by elimination to be the right way. The long Fragment 8 proceeds to make deductions from the basic proposition that "it" (the object of thought and knowledge if the analysis given above is correct) "exists and must exist."

Its first property is that it is ungenerated and indestructible. It cannot have come into being out of what does not exist since what does not exist is absolutely unthinkable and since there would, moreover, be no explanation of why it grew out of nothing at one time rather than another. There is no growth of what exists (and no decay either, but Parmenides offers no separate argument for that); hence, "either it is or it is not" (Fr. 8.16)—and that decision has already been made. It *is*, as a whole, entirely.

Since there is no growth or decay of what exists Parmenides argues that no distinctions can be made within it. There are no degrees of being—differences of density, for instance; the whole is full of continuous being. What exists is single, indivisible, and homogeneous. Here Parmenides apparently moves from the temporal continuity of being to its spatial uniformity; in the same way Melissus, his pupil, argues for the absence of a beginning or end in time and then assumes the absence of a beginning or end in space (Melissus, Frs. 3–4).

Next follows an assertion that since there is no generation or destruction, there is no motion or change in what exists. This argument is expanded by Melissus (Fr. 7). Any form of change or rearrangement implies the destruction of a state of affairs that exists and the generation of one that does not exist. Thus, Parmenides concludes that what exists "remains the same, in the same . . . held fast in the bonds of limit by the power of Necessity" (Fr. 8.29). It already is whatever it can be. Motion, as a species of change, is apparently denied by the same argument.

The last section of the Way of Truth is particularly difficult. Parmenides repeats his assertion that there is no not-being and there are no different degrees of being; what exists is equal to itself everywhere and reaches its limits everywhere. From this he concludes that it is "perfect from every angle, equally matched from the middle in every way, like the mass of a well-rounded ball" (Fr. 8.42–44). There is no agreement among modern scholars as to whether this is a literal assertion that what exists is a sphere (a view held by Burnet and Cornford) or only a simile indicating that it is like a ball in some respect other than shape (a view held by Fränkel and Owen). The latter view seems more probable. Parmenides' stress lies on the qualitative completeness, or perfection, of what exists, not on its spatial extension. The point of the simile might be put like this: As a ball is equally poised about its center so that it would make no difference which direction you took if you examined it from the center outward, so what exists is all the same from any center.

The Way of Seeming. Having completed her account "about truth," Parmenides' goddess fulfills her promise to describe mortal beliefs. Only about forty lines survive from this part of the poem. The fundamental difference from the Way of Truth is made clear at the outset: Mortals give names to two forms, and that is where they are wrong, for what exists is single. They assume the existence of two opposites, Fire and Night, probably characterized in terms of sensible opposites such as hot–cold, light–dark, light–heavy, soft–hard. Using these two forms as elements, the Way of Seeming apparently offered a detailed account of the origin of the stars, sun, moon, earth and all the things on the earth "as far as the parts of animals" (Simplicius, *In de Caelo* 559.25), some embryology, sense perception, and doubtless other things. The details are unimportant (though Parmenides is credited with the first assertion that the morning star is identical with the evening star, according to Diogenes Laërtius, *Lives* IX, 23); the interesting and puzzling thing is that he should have added a cosmogony to the Way of Truth at all. Modern scholars differ about his intention.

Zeller took the cosmogony to be an account of the beliefs of Parmenides' contemporaries; Burnet called it "a sketch of contemporary Pythagorean cosmology." However, there is no evidence for this. Such a review would seem to be pointless, and in antiquity the cosmogony was recognized as Parmenides' own. One can ignore the suggestion that it represents those of his early beliefs which were later superseded. The discussion now turns on this point: Is the Way of Seeming granted relative validity as a sort of second best, or is it wholly rejected? If it is wholly rejected, why did Parmenides write it?

Recently, the first view has been defended as follows by, for example, Verdenius, Vlastos, Schwabl, and Chalmers. The goddess in the prologue promised that Parmenides would learn about mortal beliefs as well as truth and would hardly have done so if they had no validity at all. Unless the phenomenal world is granted some degree of reality, the philosopher himself, the learner of truth, appears to be condemned to nonexistence; however, the mind, described in physical terms in the Way of Seeming (Fr. 16), is the faculty which grasps what is real in the Way of Truth. Moreover, some of the language of the way of Seeming deliberately echoes that of the Way of Truth. The two opposites, Fire and Night, transgress the canons of truth by being distinguished from each other, but they are each described as self-identical and as containing no non-existence, like the real being of the Way of Truth (Frs. 8.57–59, 9.4). Later writers in antiquity, notably Aristotle (*Metaphysics* A5, 986b27–34), took Parmenides to be yielding to the necessity of providing his own account of the phenomenal world. For reason, Aristotle said, there was just one being, but for sense perception more than one. Others have argued that the Way of Truth is the way an immortal looks at the world *sub specie aeternitatis*, whereas the Way of Seeming is the way mortals see the same world in time. Many variations on these themes have been suggested.

The contrary view, defended recently in differing forms by Owen, Long, and Taran, has more justification in the text of Parmenides. The goddess makes it clear enough that the Way of Seeming is wholly unreliable (Frs. 1.30, 8.52) and that the Way of Truth leaves no room whatsoever for intermediate degrees of reality. The text itself contains a statement of the intention: "Thus no judgment of mortals can ever overtake you" (Fr. 8.61; the metaphor is from chariot racing). Although this is ambiguous, the likeliest sense is that Parmenides is equipped by the Way of Seeming to defeat any mortal opinion about the phenomenal world. All descriptions of the phenomenal world presuppose that difference is real, but the Way of Truth has shown that what exists is single and undifferentiated. The transition to the Way of Seeming is made by pointing to the fundamental mistake in assuming even the minimum of differentiation in reality—that is, in assuming that two forms of what exists can be distinguished (Fr. 8.53–54). Once this assumption is made, a plausible description of the phenomenal world can be offered, but anyone who has followed Parmenides thus far will recognize the fundamental fallacy in even the most plausible description. This explanation is more consistent with the later history of Eleaticism, for Zeno and Melissus showed no interest in positive cosmology.

Parmenides and Greek philosophy. There is general agreement that Parmenides followed the Milesians, Heraclitus, and Pythagoras and preceded Empedocles, Anaxagoras, and the atomists (the thesis of Reinhardt that Heraclitus answered Parmenides has been generally rejected). Ancient tradition credits him with a Pythagorean teacher, Ameinias (Diogenes Laërtius, *Lives* IX, 21). It is often said that the rigorous deductive method of the Way of Truth was learned from the mathematicians, who at that time in Italy were likely to be Pythagoreans, but the truth is that too little is known of the mathematics of the time to allow this to be more than a guess.

In general, the relevance of Parmenides to earlier philosophy is fairly clear, though there is room for doubt about his attitude toward individual men. (Various scholars have found in the text attacks on Anaximander, Anaximenes, Heraclitus, and the Pythagorean school.) All previous systems had assumed the reality of change in the physical world and attempted to explain it. Thales, Anaximander, and Anaximenes held that the world evolved from a simpler state into a more complex one. Anaximander's view was that different substances ("the opposites") grew out of a primitive undifferentiated "indefinite"; Anaximenes gave a more precise description of the manner of differentiation and said that the original substance, air, turned into other substances by rarefaction and condensation. Heraclitus apparently abandoned the idea of an original simple state, asserting that everything in the world is always changing—"an ever-living fire." In somewhat less materialistic language the Pythagoreans produced a cosmogony based on the imposition of limit upon the unlimited. Parmenides' critique was equally damaging to all of these theories, since his argument, if accepted, condemned all difference as illusory.

It is often said that Parmenides' attack on the reality of the physical world depends on his confusion of two senses of the verb "to be"—the existential and copulative. It cannot logically be true that a subject *is* and at the same time *is not* (existentially); from this Parmenides is supposed to have concluded that it cannot be true that a subject *is* black and at the same time *is not* white and hence that all differentiation is impossible. The surviving text does not bear this out. Parmenides' premise (and his fundamental fallacy) was, rather, that "what is not" is absolutely unthinkable and unknowable. Every change would involve the passage of what is into what is not, and hence every attempt to describe a change would involve the use of an unintelligible expression, "what is not."

The argument of the Way of Truth is metaphysical and would apply to any subject matter whatsoever; it is false to suppose that it applied only to Pythagorean cosmogony or only to the materialist cosmogonies of the Ionians. But that Parmenides' primary intention was to criticize the earlier cosmogonists seems clear from the addition of the Way of Seeming to the Way of Truth. His own Real Being was certainly not a ball of matter, as Burnet and others thought. On the other hand, it was not something to which spatial terms were wholly inapplicable. It filled the whole of space and thus was in some sense a competitor of other accounts of the cosmos. The main effects of his work, too, were on cosmology.

The error of Parmenides' ways was not seen immediately, perhaps not until Plato's *Sophist.* Their immediate effect was to produce theories which attempted to save the natural world from unreality without transgressing Parmenides' logical canons. In brief, they produced theories of elements. Empedocles envisaged a cosmos made of the four elements which were later made standard by Aristotle—earth, water, air, and fire. He satisfied some of Parmenides' criteria by making his elements unchangeable and homogeneous. What he refused to accept from Parmenides was that difference was impossible without diminution of reality; his four elements were asserted to be different from one another yet equally real. He explained apparent change as the rearrangement in space of the unchanging elements. Anaxagoras went further to meet Parmenides by asserting that all natural substances, not just a privileged four, were elementary and unchangeable. The atomists responded in a different way; they accepted that no qualitative difference is possible but rescued the phenomenal world by asserting that "what is not" exists in the form of void—that is, as empty space separating pieces of real being from each other. (The equation of void with "what is not" is sometimes attributed to Parmenides himself, but it was probably first made by his follower Melissus, who explicitly denied its existence in his Fragment 7.)

Plato inherited from Parmenides the belief that the object of knowledge must exist and must be found by the mind and not by the senses. He agreed that the object of knowledge is not something abstracted from the data of sense perception but a being of a different and superior order. He differed, however, in that he allowed the sensible world to have an intermediate status, as the object of "belief," rather than no status at all (*Republic* 477B and elsewhere). He differed more significantly, too, in that he reimported plurality into the real and knowable by distinguishing different senses of "not-being" (*Sophist* 237B ff. and 257B ff.).

Bibliography

Fragments and ancient testimonia are in H. Diels and W. Kranz, eds., *Fragmente der Vorsokratiker*, 10th ed. (Berlin, 1961), the standard collection. Fragments with English translation and commentary are in G. S. Kirk and J. E. Raven, *The Presocratic Philosophers* (Cambridge, 1957), but the commentary is rather inadequate. They are also found in Leonardo Taran, *Parmenides* (Princeton, N.J., 1965), and in Italian, with a long bibliography, in Mario Untersteiner, *Parmenide* (Florence, 1958).

The most important recent studies are H. Fränkel, "Parmenidesstudien," in his *Wege und Formen frühgriechischen Denkens* (Munich, 1955), and G. E. L. Owen, "Eleatic Questions," in *Classical Quarterly*, N.S. Vol. 10 (1960), 84–102.

Other studies are H. Diels, *Parmenides Lehrgedicht* (Berlin, 1897); John Burnet, *Early Greek Philosophy* (London, 1892); K. Reinhardt, *Parmenides und die Geschichte der griechischen Philosophie* (Bonn, 1916); W. Kranz, "Über Aufbau und Bedeutung des Parmenideischen Gedichtes," in *Sitzungsberichte der Deutschen Akademie der Wissenschaften zu Berlin*, Vol. 47 (1916), 1158–1176; Eduard Zeller, *Die Philosophie der Griechen*, 6th ed., Vol. I (Leipzig, 1919), Ch. 1; F. M. Cornford, "Parmenides' Two Ways," in *Classical Quarterly*, Vol. 27 (1933), 97–111, and *Plato and Parmenides* (London, 1939); G. Calogero, *Studi sul eleatismo* (Rome, 1932); and Harold Cherniss, *Aristotle's Criticism of Presocratic Philosophy* (Baltimore, 1935).

Some more recent studies are W. J. Verdenius, *Parmenides: Some Comments* (Groningen, the Netherlands, 1942); Olof Gigon, *Der Ursprung der griechischen Philosophie von Hesiod bis Parmenides* (Basel, 1945); Gregory Vlastos, "Parmenides' Theory of Knowledge," in *Transactions of the American Philological Association*, Vol. 77 (1946), 66–77; Hans Schwabl, "Sein und Doxa bei Parmenides," in *Wiener Studien*, Vol. 66 (1953), 50–75; C. M. Bowra, *Problems in Greek Poetry* (Oxford, 1953); Eric A. Havelock, "Parmenides and Odysseus," and Leonard Woodbury, "Parmenides on Names," in *Harvard Studies in Classical Philology*, Vol. 63 (Cambridge, Mass., 1958); W. R. Chalmers, "Parmenides and the Beliefs of Mortals," in *Phronesis*, Vol. 5 (1960), 5–22; A. A. Long, "The Principles of Parmenides' Cosmogony," in *Phronesis*, Vol. 8 (1963), 90–107; J. Mansfeld, *Die Offenbarung des Parmenides und die menschliche Welt* (Assen, 1964); and W. K. C. Guthrie, *A History of Greek Philosophy*, Vol. II (Cambridge, 1965).

DAVID J. FURLEY

PASCAL, BLAISE (1623–1662), French mathematician, physicist, inventor, philosopher, and theologian. Pascal was born in Clermont in Auvergne, the son of a minor noble who was a government official. Pascal's mother died in 1626. In 1631 the family moved to Paris but fled in 1638 because of the father's opposition to the fiscal regulations of Richelieu. The next year Pascal's younger sister, Jacqueline, successfully acted in a children's play performed for Richelieu and thus gained a pardon for her father, who then became the royal tax commissioner at Rouen.

Mathematics and physics. Pascal was a prodigy, educated solely by his father, an excellent mathematician, who did not want to teach his son mathematics until the boy had mastered Latin and Greek for fear it would distract him. At 12, however, Pascal began working out the principles of geometry as far as the 32d proposition of Book I of Euclid. When his father discovered this, he gave him a copy of Euclid; soon son and father became regular participants at weekly mathematical lectures organized by Father Marin Mersenne. At 16, Pascal wrote his first major work, *Essai pour les coniques* (published in 1640), which his sister reported was "considered so great an intellectual achievement that people said that they had seen nothing as mighty since the time of Archimedes." In 1642, Pascal invented the calculating machine, originally designed to help his father in his tax work. This machine was one of the first applied achievements of the "new science." Pascal's writings on the calculating machine from 1645 to 1652 indicate the inordinate difficulties of putting theory into practice, the wide divergence between the levels of metallurgical and mathematical skill, and the monumental importance of this early contribution to the industrial revolution.

For the rest of his life Pascal continued to make major mathematical contributions in probability theory, number theory, and geometry. Although he gave up serious concern with mathematical problems after his religious conversion in 1654, a notable analysis of the nature of the cycloid grew out of a night's insomnia in 1658. Pascal's important work in the philosophy of mathematics, *L'Esprit géométrique*, was probably written in 1657/1658 as a preface to a textbook in geometry for the Jansenist school at Port-Royal.

The vacuum. In 1646, Pascal learned of Torricelli's experiment with a barometer, which involved placing a tube of mercury upside down in a bowl of mercury. Having successfully repeated the experiment, Pascal inquired what kept some of the mercury suspended in the tube and what was in the space above the column of mercury in the tube. Many scientists believed that the pressure of the outside atmosphere was responsible for holding up the column of mercury, but they had no proof. All agreed that the space at the top of the tube contained some kind of rarefied and invisible matter; hence, no vacuum. In 1647, Pascal published *Experiences nouvelles touchant le vide*, a summary of a series of experiments with variously shaped and sized tubes and different liquids, in which he set forth the basic laws about how much water and how much mercury could be supported by air pressure and about how large a siphon had to be to function. He also sketched out the reasons why a genuine vacuum could and did exist above the column of mercury or other liquid supported in the barometer. Father Estienne Noel, rector of the Collège de Clermont in Paris, challenged Pascal, insisting that nature abhors a vacuum and therefore would not allow one to exist; thus, the alleged empty space created in Pascal's experiments actually contained a special kind of matter. Pascal's reply, in which he gave the conditions for judging a hypothesis, is one of the clearest statements on scientific method made during the seventeenth century. Pascal asserted that a hypothesis could be disproved if one could elicit either a contradiction or a conclusion counter to fact from the affirmation of the hypothesis. However, if all the facts fit the hypothesis or follow from it, this merely shows the hypothesis is probable or possible. "In order to show that a hypothesis is evident, it does not suffice that all the phenomena follow from it; instead, if it leads to something contrary to a single one of the phenomena, that suffices to establish its falsity." Pascal showed that Noel's and Aristotle's hypothesis that there is no vacuum is false because conclusions contrary to experimentally established facts follow from it, whereas his own theory of a genuine vacuum is a possible or probable explanation of the facts in question.

In 1648, Pascal's brother-in-law performed the experiment of carrying a barometer up a mountain. This established the change in the level of the column of mercury. Pascal checked the results at various heights on a church tower in Paris. He then declared these results established "that Nature has no abhorrence of a vacuum, that she makes no effort to avoid it; that all the effects that are ascribed to this horror are due to the weight and pressure of air; . . . and that, due to not knowing this, people have deliberately invented that imaginary horror of a vacuum, in order to account for them." Combining his ingeniously derived experimental data with a clear analysis of the possible explanatory hypotheses, Pascal arrived at one of the major achievements of seventeenth-century science. His theory of the vacuum and air pressure played an important role in the development of the mechanical theory of nature and the elimination of some of nature's alleged occult qualities and personal characteristics. The Preface to the *Traité du vide* (which is all that has survived of the *Traité*) contains a defense of the new science and a discussion of the nature of scientific progress. In the study of nature Pascal insisted that respect for authority should not take precedence over reasoning or experience (in theology, however, he maintained that it should). The secrets of nature, he said, are hidden from us, and although it is always active, we do not always discover its effects. In the course of time, through experience and understanding, we come to learn more about the natural world. Hence, as more data are accumulated, we should expect to find previously accepted hypotheses replaced by newer ones. Our conclusions about nature are always limited by the amount of experience gathered up to now. In time we seek for truths in terms of our experience and comprehension. What is sought for may be unchanging, but the results of the quest are the variable developments that constitute the history of science. Thus, there is no reason for preferring the ancient scientific views of Aristotle or anyone else to the latest achievements of scientific reasoning, based on the most recent data.

Pascal and Jansenism. Pascal's mathematical and scientific accomplishments are among the most important of his time, but his religious and philosophical views have overshadowed them. His writings in religion and philosophy grew out of his involvement with the Jansenist movement. This involvement began in 1646, after Pascal's father had an accident and was cared for by two followers of Cornelis Jansen (1585–1638), the bishop of Ypres, and his French ally, the abbé de Saint-Cyran, spiritual director of the Port-Royal movement. Pascal's deep interest in the teachings of the Jansenists led to his family's interest. After his father's death in 1651, Pascal's sister became a nun at Port-Royal in spite of her brother's strong opposition. From 1652 to 1654, Pascal turned away from religious interests, spending his time mainly with libertine friends who were gamblers, womanizers, and probably freethinkers. Toward the end of this period, Pascal often visited his sister at Port-Royal, indicating to her that he had a great contempt for the world and people but that he did not feel drawn to God. However, on the night of November 23, 1654, Pascal had a profound religious experience which led him to devote the rest of his life principally to religious activities. The experience so overwhelmed Pascal that he wrote a *Mémorial* of it, which he thereafter carried, sewn into his clothes, to remind him of the event. It said: "From about 10:30 at night until about 12:30. FIRE. God of Abraham, God of Isaac, God of Jacob, not of the philosophers and of the learned. Certitude, certitude, feeling, joy, peace. God of Jesus Christ . . . Jesus Christ. . . . Let me never be separated from Him."

In January 1655, Pascal went to Port-Royal-des-Champs, the older of the two Port-Royal convents, for a two-week retreat. There a famous discussion with the Jansenist theologian Isaac Le Maistre de Saci took place, published in the *Entretien avec M. de Saci*. This text indicates that

Pascal had already formulated many of the views later developed in the *Pensées*. During the next several months Pascal often visited the two Port-Royal convents. On one of these visits Pascal met Antoine Arnauld, the leading Jansenist philosopher and theologian, who was about to be condemned by the Sorbonne for his views. In *Lettres provinciales*, a series of 18 letters published in 1656–1657, Pascal defended Arnauld and satirized his Jesuit opponents and their theological and moral views. These letters, published under the pseudonym Louis de Montalte, were probably the cooperative work of Pascal, Arnauld, and Pierre Nicole, though they were principally by Pascal. One of the great French literary masterpieces, the *Lettres provinciales* mercilessly ridicules the casuistry of various Jesuit moralists for what Pascal considered their lax, inconsistent, and unchristian views and defends Jansenism against charges of heresy. The arguments of various sixteenth-century and seventeenth-century scholastics are torn apart, and the charges against the Jansenists rebutted in a dazzling display of wit, irony, abuse, argument, and literary brilliance. Nevertheless, the *Lettres provinciales* was placed on the Index in 1657, and shortly thereafter the Jansenist movement was condemned by the pope. In 1661 the schools at Port-Royal were closed, and the nuns and *solitaires* had to sign a submission to the church.

Until 1659, Pascal worked on a wide variety of subjects, defending Jansenism, composing his *Écrits sur la grâce*, *De l'Esprit géométrique*, *De l'Art de persuader*, and the works on the cycloid and preparing his *Apologie de la religion chrétienne*, the unfinished work posthumously published as the *Pensées*. In 1659, seriously ill, Pascal practically stopped writing. In 1660, he was somewhat better and wrote his *Trois Discours sur la condition des grands*. The next year, after the suppression of Jansenism and the death of Jacqueline, Pascal wrote his final work on Jansenism, *Écrit sur la signature du formulaire*, urging the Port-Royalists not to give in. He then withdrew from all further controversy. His last achievement, illustrating another side of his genius, was the invention of a large carriage with many seats and the inauguration of what was in effect the first bus line, carrying passengers from one part of Paris to another for a fixed fare. One of his motives was to gain money to give to the poor, since he had already disposed of almost all his worldly possessions. Much of his will is devoted to bequeathing portions of the bus revenues to various hospitals.

Philosophy of mathematics and science. Pascal left unpublished his two most important philosophical works, the *Pensées* and *De l'Esprit géométrique*. *De l'Esprit géométrique* was first published in the eighteenth century. In it Pascal dealt with the problem of the method for discovering truths. The ideal method, he declared, would be one which defined all of the terms employed and demonstrated all propositions from already established truths, but this is impossible, since the basic terms to be defined presuppose others to explain their meaning, and the fundamental propositions to be proved presuppose still others. Thus, it is impossible to reach first terms and principles. Instead, we find primitive terms that admit of no further definitions that clarify them and principles that are so clear that nothing clearer can be found to aid in proving them. "From which it seems that men are naturally and unalterably powerless to deal with any science whatsoever in an absolutely perfected manner."

Given this state of affairs, geometrical procedure is the most perfect known to mankind—a balanced one in which those things that are clear and known to everyone are not defined and everything else is defined and in which those propositions known by all are assumed and other propositions are derived from them. Pascal insisted that this did not mean either that human beings could know by natural means that the premises of geometry were really true or that the fundamental concepts were thoroughly understood. Rather, the geometrical method provided the greatest certitude attainable by use of our limited capacities. Essentially, it developed an axiomatic system in which, from primitive terms and axioms, a set of propositions could be logically derived. Such a set would be true if the axioms were true.

In the companion piece to *L'Esprit géométrique, De l'Art de persuader,* Pascal explained how we come to be convinced of first principles and of conclusions from them. Conclusions are explained via the geometrical method. The problem of first principles raises a basic point for Pascal's theory of knowledge that is developed in the *Pensées.* Our reason and understanding can only work out axiom systems. Since we cannot prove the first principles, we can always cast skeptical doubts upon their truth, no matter how certain they may appear to us at various times. We can overcome this constant tendency toward skepticism (which also occurs in scientific research, since we can never know the secrets of nature but only plausible and as yet unrefuted hypotheses about the world) only by recognizing that principles are gained through instinct and revelation. This recognition requires admitting the importance of feelings and of submission to God in the quest for truth.

Religion. Pascal left the *Pensées* unfinished, with many notes of varying sizes pinned together. The first editors copied all the materials exactly as Pascal left them but published only those portions that they felt were completed, organizing them as they saw fit. Later editors assumed that the *Pensées* was a collection of fragments, left in a disordered state by their author, and that each editor could arrange the fragments as he wished. Victor Cousin in 1842 pointed out that only selections of the *Pensées,* often somewhat embellished by the various editors, existed in print, and he urged a definitive edition based on the manuscripts in the Bibliothèque Nationale. One of these, the *Recueil original* consists of the fragments in Pascal's own handwriting, pasted on large sheets of paper. For the next century editors used this manuscript for varying presentations of the text. In the 1930s and 1940s Zacharie Tourneur and Louis Lafuma established that the *Recueil* was pasted together after Pascal's death and that another manuscript, a copy by one of Pascal's relatives, represented the actual state of the work as organized and partially completed by the author. This led to Lafuma's definitive edition in 1952, which radically changed the order of the fragments, finally presenting the development of the themes in the *Pensées* as Pascal had intended them to be read.

The human condition. In the Lafuma edition the initial sections, "Order," "Vanity," "Misery," "Boredom," and "Causes of Effects," all portray the human condition by showing man's ways of dealing with and reacting to his ordinary world. The sixth and seventh sections turn to the core of man's philosophical problem—how to find truth and happiness. If man is a miserable, vain creature, unable by his own resources to find first truths from which to derive others, he has to realize that "we know truth not only by reason but more so by the heart. It is in this latter way that we know first principles, and it is in vain that reason, which plays no part in this, tries to combat them" (110 and 292, Lafuma and Brunschvicg numberings, respectively). The principles of geometry are known instinctively by the heart, and reason employs these principles to establish theorems. Both heart and reason yield results that are certain, but by different routes, and it would be ridiculous to require proofs of the heart's instincts and intuitions or intuitive knowledge of what is proved. The inability of reason to establish first principles serves to humiliate reason but not to undermine our certainty. The realization of the limitations of reason helps us, Pascal declared, to recognize our wretchedness, and the greatness of man is that he alone is capable of such a recognition.

The climax of this attempt to show the ultimate nonrational foundation of our knowledge of first principles comes in the next section, "Contradictions." In a famous passage on skepticism (131 and 434) Pascal began by pointing out that the strongest contention of the Pyrrhonists was that we have no assurance of the truth of any first principles apart from faith and revelation except that we feel them within us. This natural feeling is no convincing proof of their truth, since apart from faith we cannot tell whether man was created by a good God, an evil demon, or by chance. The truth-value of the principles depends upon their source. Pascal then explored the depths of complete skepticism and showed that if one had no assurance or any principles, one could be certain of nothing but at the same time one could not even become a complete skeptic.

What then will man do in this state? Will he doubt everything? Will he doubt whether he is awake? Whether he is being pinched, whether he is being burned, will he doubt that he doubts, will he doubt that he exists?

We cannot go so far as that; and I set it forth as a fact that there has never been a complete perfect Pyrrhonist. Nature sustains our feeble reason and prevents it from raving to that extent. . . .

What kind of a chimera then is man? What novelty, what monster, what chaos, what subject of contradictions, what prodigy? Judge of all things, imbecile worm of the earth, depository of truth, sink of uncertainty and error, glory and scum of the world.

Who will unravel this tangle? Certainly it surpasses dogmatism and Pyrrhonism; and all human philosophy. . . .

Nature confounds the Pyrrhonists and reason confounds the dogmatists. . . .

Know then, proud man, what a paradox you are to yourself. Humble yourself, weak reason. Silence yourself, foolish nature, learn that man infinitely surpasses man, and hear from your master your real state which you do not know.

Hear God.

The problem of knowledge thus becomes, for Pascal, a religious one. Only through submission to God and through acceptance of his revelation can we gain completely certain knowledge. The greatest achievements in science and mathematics rest on a fundamental uncertainty, since the basic principles employed, known through instinct and intuition, are open to question. Skeptical probings can only reveal the human predicament in its fullest and prepare us to submit and accept a religious foundation of knowledge.

The *Pensées* then proceeds to show how men try to avoid recognizing their situation through diversion and philosophy. Philosophy can only lead us continually to skepticism, from which we are saved by our own intuitive knowledge of truth. We seek for happiness but cannot find it apart from religion. Pascal then tried to show in the famous wager argument (418 and 233) that it is not unreasonable to believe in God and to seek for religious guidance. If there is a God, he argued, he is infinitely incomprehensible to us. But either God exists or he does not exist, and we are unable to tell which alternative is true. However, both our present lives and our possible future lives may well be greatly affected by the alternative we accept. Hence, Pascal contended, since eternal life and happiness is a possible result of one choice (if God does exist) and since nothing is lost if we are wrong about the other choice (if God does not exist and we choose to believe that he does), then the reasonable gamble, given what may be at stake, is to choose the theistic alternative. He who remains an unbeliever is taking an infinitely unreasonable risk just because he does not know which alternative is true.

Next, Pascal tried to show how belief can be achieved by curbing the passions, submitting to God, and using reason as a means of realizing that true religion is beyond reason and is known only through Jesus. We are suspended between two infinities, the infinitely small (the void) and the infinitely great (the Divine). Reason exposes our plight to us. Our desire for truth and happiness makes us see the futility of science, mathematics, and human philosophy as ways of finding the answers man seeks.

The Christian religion. The later sections of the *Pensées* are devoted to apologetics, arguing that the Christian religion is the true religion. From historical data, moral precepts, miracles, and the fulfillment of prophecies Pascal argued that the Bible is the source of true religious knowledge. He contended that the Old Testament foretold Christ's coming and the Jewish rejection of him. Using the recently rediscovered Spanish anti-Semitic classic by Raymundus Martinus, *Pugio Fidei*, Pascal took material from many Jewish sources to claim that "God used the blindness of the Jewish people for the benefit of the elect" (469 and 577) and that "if the Jews had been completely converted by Jesus Christ, we would not have had any but

suspect witnesses. And if they had been exterminated, we would not have had any at all" (592 and 750). The apologetic argument, Pascal admitted, was not logically decisive but only persuasive. The real problem was to *be* a Christian, and here reason could not help. Man could submit, but he still desperately required God's Grace.

The prophecies, the miracles themselves, and the proofs of our religion are not of such a nature that it could be said they are absolutely convincing, but they are also of such a kind that it cannot be said that it would be unreasonable to believe them. Thus there is evidence and obscurity to enlighten some and confuse others, but the evidence is such that it surpasses or at least equals the evidence to the contrary, so that it is not reason that can determine men not to follow it, and thus this can only be as a result of lust or malice of heart. . . . [So] that it appears that in those who follow it [religion], it is grace and not reason which makes them follow it, and that in those who shun it, it is lust and not reason that makes them shun it. (835 and 564)

Pascal's views hardly constitute an organized system. Most of his works are fragmentary, and he apparently made no effort to put the fragments together. His career first as a mathematical prodigy, then as a student of physics, and finally as a religious thinker made continuous intellectual development difficult. From the vantage point of his fideistic religious views his mathematical and scientific efforts appeared to him as of small significance. Throughout the *Pensées* Pascal tried to characterize the role and limits of mathematical and scientific achievements, in keeping with what he himself had accomplished. But his religious views were essentially antiphilosophical. Among philosophical views he found skepticism the most congenial insofar as it revealed most clearly "the misery of man without God" and prepared men for faith and grace.

Pascal's religious concerns have overshadowed his other contributions and as a result his impact has been mainly on thinkers concerned with religious subjects. In recent years Pascal has been studied seriously by existentialists because of his brilliant portrayal of the human condition, and he has often been compared with Kierkegaard, especially in terms of his antiphilosophical and fideistic statement of Christianity. Pascal's works on scientific method and the philosophy of mathematics have tended to be neglected, but in these areas he was one of the clearest and most advanced thinkers of his age. His many-sided genius and his unequaled command of the French language make him one of the most inspiring and thought-provoking of writers. Pascal fills a major place in the history of ideas both for his work in mathematics, physics, and philosophy of science and for his insights into human nature and his analysis of Christianity.

Works by Pascal

FRENCH TEXTS

Oeuvres complètes, publiées suivant l'ordre chronologique, avec documents, complémentaires, introductions et notes, Léon Brunschvicg, P. Boutroux, and F. Gazier, eds., 14 vols. Paris, 1904–1914. The most complete edition.

Oeuvres complètes, Louis Lafuma, ed. New York and Paris,

1963. Preface by Henri Gouhier; best one-volume edition, with Lafuma's text of the *Pensées*.

Pensées sur la religion et sur quelques autres sujets, 3d ed. Paris, 1960. Lafuma's annotated edition of the original form of the *Pensées*.

Le Manuscrit des Pensées de Pascal 1662, Louis Lafuma, ed. Paris, 1962. A photoreproduction of the manuscript text with a preface by Jean Guitton.

ENGLISH TRANSLATIONS

Great Shorter Works, translated with an introduction by Émile Cailliet and John C. Blankenagel. Philadelphia, 1948. Includes all important works except *Pensées* and *Provinciales*.

Pensées. The Provincial Letters, translated by W. F. Trotter and Thomas McCrie. New York, 1941.

Pensées, translated by W. F. Trotter. New York, 1958. With an introduction by T. S. Eliot.

Pensées, translated with an introduction by Martin Turnell. London, 1962. Translation of Lafuma text.

The Physical Treatises of Pascal: The Equilibrium of Liquids and the Weight of the Mass of Air, translated by I. H. B. Spiers and A. G. H. Spiers, Frederick Barry, ed. New York, 1937.

Works on Pascal

Abercrombie, Nigel, *Pascal and St. Augustine*. Oxford, 1938.

Bishop, Morris, *Pascal: The Life of Genius*. New York, 1936. Excellent intellectual biography.

Bishop, Morris, and Hubert, Sister Marie Louis, "Pascal Bibliography," in David C. Cabeen and Jules Brody, *A Critical Bibliography of French Literature*, Vol. III, Nathan Edelman, ed. Syracuse, 1961. Pp. 417–456.

Boutroux, Émile, *Pascal*. Paris, 1900. A brief biography in French.

Bremond, Henri, *Histoire littéraire du sentiment religieux en France*, 12 vols. Paris, 1916–1933. See Vol. IV (1921) for Pascal's religious views.

Brunschvicg, Léon, *Le Genie de Pascal*. Paris, 1924. A collection of essays on Pascal.

Brunschvicg, Léon, *Descartes et Pascal, lecteurs de Montaigne*. New York and Paris, 1944.

Busson, Henri, *La Pensée religieuse française de Charron à Pascal*. Paris, 1933. A study of skepticism, fideism, and apologetics up to Pascal.

Busson, Henri, *La Religion des classiques (1660–1685)*. Paris, 1948.

Cahiers de Royaumont, *Blaise Pascal, l'homme et l'oeuvre*, Paris, 1956. A series of papers by specialists.

Cailliet, Émile, *Pascal: The Emergence of Genius*, 2d ed. New York, 1961. A full-length intellectual biography.

Chestov, Léon (Leo Isakovich Shestov), *La Nuit de Gethsémani; Essai sur la philosophie de Pascal*. Paris, 1923. An interpretation by a twentieth-century fideistic Christian.

Drox, Édouard, *Étude sur le scepticisme de Pascal*. Paris, 1886.

Goldmann, Lucien, *Le Dieu caché*. Paris, 1955. Translated by Philip Thody as *The Hidden God*. New York, 1964. A stimulating Marxist interpretation of Pascal and Jansenism.

Humbert, Pierre, *L'Oeuvre scientifique de Blaise Pascal*. Paris, 1947.

Jovy, Ernest, *Études pascaliennes*, 9 vols. Paris, 1927–1936. A series of special studies on aspects of Pascal.

Julien-Eymard d'Angers (Charles Cheshenau), *Pascal et ses précurseurs*. Paris, 1954. On Pascal's place in the apologetic tradition.

Lafuma, Louis, *Histoire des Pensées de Pascal (1656–1952)*. Paris, 1954. A good survey of the various editions.

Laporte, Jean, *Le Coeur et la raison selon Pascal*. Paris, 1950. An examination of Pascal's theory of intuition and reason.

Mesnard, Jean, *Pascal, l'homme et l'oeuvre*. Paris, 1951. Translation by G. S. Fraser as *Pascal, His Life and Works*. London, 1952. Excellent biography and introduction.

Mortimer, Ernest, *Blaise Pascal: The Life and Work of a Realist*. New York, 1959.

Strowski, Fortunat, *Pascal et son temps*, 3 vols. Paris, 1907. Major study of the background and development of Pascal's views.

Works on Jansenism

Abercrombie, Nigel, *The Origins of Jansenism*. Oxford, 1936.

Orcibal, Jean, *Les Origines du Jansénisme*, 5 vols. Louvain and Paris, 1947–1962.

Sainte-Beuve, Charles A., *Port-Royal*, 7 vols. Paris, 1840–1859; 3 vols., Paris, 1954.

RICHARD H. POPKIN

PASTORE, VALENTINO ANNIBALE (1868–1956), Italian philosopher and logician, was born at Orbassano (Teramo), Italy. He educated himself in literary studies, and then obtained a degree in letters from the University of Turin, under Arturo Graf, with a thesis on *La vita delle forme letterarie* ("The Life of Literary Forms"), which was published at Turin in 1892. Pastore then turned to philosophy and was influenced by Hegelianism through the teachings of Pasquale d'Ercole. At the same time he was influenced by such scientists as Friedrich Kiesow, A. Garbasso, and Giuseppe Peano. In 1903 he published in Turin his thesis in philosophy, *Sopra le teorie della scienza: logica, matematica, fisica* ("On the Theories of Science: Logic, Mathematics, Physics"). In 1911 he began teaching theoretical philosophy at Turin, where he was full professor from 1921 until 1939 and where he instituted a laboratory of experimental logic.

Pastore's thesis was published in the same year in which Benedetto Croce's *La critica* appeared and in which irrationalism burst out in Italy in diverse forms—as a revolt against positivism, as a rebirth of idealism, as an expression of the "bankruptcy of science." Having been educated in an environment in which Hegelianism was not ignored but was linked with the point of view of classical positivism, Pastore became aware of the impossibility of separating the sciences (mathematical and natural) from philosophy, or of substituting the sciences for philosophy. In the first case, if philosophy were severed from the conditions which render it possible and nourish it, it would become empty and would wither; in the second case, the sciences themselves would eventually lose consciousness of their relationships, their fundamental rationale, and their methods and goals. Pastore therefore sought to assess the meaning of scientific knowledge and of its logical procedures.

Turning his attention to logical problems in particular, Pastore was at first drawn toward Russell's thesis of the identity of logic and mathematics, as is shown in *Logica formale e dedotta dalla considerazione dei modelli meccanici* ("Formal Logic Deduced by the Consideration of Mechanical Models," Turin, 1906) and *Sillogismo e proporzione* ("Syllogism and Proportion," Turin, 1910). His principal work of this period, *Il problema della causalità, con particolare riguardo alla teoria del metodo sperimentale* ("The Problem of Causality, With Particular Attention to the Theory of Experimental Method," 2 vols., Turin, 1921), which deals with causality, shows his systematic effort to single out the mutual relationship between scientific investigation and philosophical research. Pastore examined three aspects of causality—experience, science, and philosophy—and distinguished and analyzed the idea of cause, the concept of the causal relation, and the principle of causality.

After 1922, Pastore's interests were still focused on

scientific knowledge, but he clarified his conception of philosophy as the study of "pure thought," as "not of that which is common to all particular systems, by being inherent in each one, but of that which results from all the particular systems, even though not being inherent in each one." From this conception he evolved his idea of a "general logic" whose basis lies "outside of particular logical systems." Around 1936, assisted by Ludovico Geymonat, he investigated the "logic of strengthening" as a "theory of primal systems," that is, as a search for "the process of construction of the most elementary forms of thinking and of their relationships," by means of a distinction between logic as logicality (general presystematic logic) and logic as a particular system, joining, as he himself said, "the deduction of the discourse (*D*) with the logical intuition of the universe (*U*)." Pastore did not seek to reach a demonstration of intuitive principles, nor to propose an ontological intuition, but rather to establish the laws of the relationship between *D* and *U*, between the analysis of the discourse and a synthetic vision of the universe.

In the final phase of his work Pastore's concern with the sense of mystery became marked ("logic has always two allies at its side: sadness and mystery"). In the light of this concern he examined and discussed both the existentialist movements and the historical materialism of Marx and Lenin.

Bibliography

Additional works by Pastore are *Il solipismo* (Turin, 1923); *La logica del potenziamento* (Naples, 1936); *Logica sperimentale* (Naples, 1939); *L'acrisia di Kant* (Padua, 1940); "Il mio pensiero filosofico," in M. F. Sciacca, ed., *Filosofi italiani contemporanei* (Como, 1944), pp. 333–349; *La filosofia di Lenin* (Milan, 1946); and *La volontà dell'assurdo. Storia e crisi dell'esistenzialismo* (Milan, 1948).

Works on Pastore are Carmelo Ottaviano, "La 'logica del potenziamento' della scuola di Torino," in *Logos*, Vol. 17 (1934), 277–289; Francesco Crestano, "Intorno alla logica del potenziamento e alla logica dei comportamenti," in *Archivio di filosofia*, Vol. 5 (1935), 322–331 (and in *Idee e concetti*, Milan, 1939); and Filippo Selvaggi, *Dalla filosofia alla tecnica: La logica del potenziamento* (Rome, 1947), with bibliography.

EUGENIO GARIN
Translated by *Robert M. Connolly*

PATER, WALTER HORATIO (1839–1894), English essayist and critic, lived mainly in Oxford, where he read classics at Queens College and later became a fellow of Brasenose. He was a central figure of and inspiration for English *fin de siècle* art and art criticism and a profound influence on Oscar Wilde. He is of importance in philosophical aesthetics for his association with and championing of the *l'art pour l'art* doctrine of his age and for his insistence on "aesthetic criticism" of literature and the fine arts, stressing the subjective sensitivity of the critic and his power to paint evocative pictures of moments of intense experience in finely wrought, decorative prose. He is important in general philosophical history for his aphoristic but consistent statements that a relativist position was the only appropriate position for the modern temperament.

In the course of his career he proposed a highly personal conception of Platonism (*Plato and Platonism*, New York and London, 1893), playing down the immutable aspect of the theory of forms and emphasizing the imaginative sweep of Plato's more informal thinking. Pater maintained that moral values and moral standards were relative to the achievements and conditions of an age. Although he was formerly a Christian, he did not believe that Christian revelation had a privileged status, and he stressed the anthropological interpretation and psychological significance of all religious ritual. His tendency to ethical relativism, his inclination to praise goodness for its beauty, and his attitude toward religion as an aesthetically satisfying experience without final commitment made him many enemies in Oxford. The Paterian temperament was identified with aestheticism, or the hedonistic enjoyment of the intensely lived moment of beauty, the "exquisite passion," regardless of formal and moral standpoints. He was blamed for much of the moral eccentricity and artistic preciousness and pretentiousness of his followers, who deliberately courted decadence. However, he himself led a rather carefully balanced, withdrawn life, to which the famous sentence from the Conclusion to *The Renaissance*, "To live always with this hard, gemlike flame, to maintain this ecstasy, is success in life," can be applied only with some difficulty.

In his *Imaginary Portraits* (London, 1887), Pater developed the genre of imaginative presentation of personalities embodying certain philosophies of life. His novel, *Marius the Epicurean*(London, 1885), regarded by many as his major work, is one such imaginary portrait on a large scale, picturing the religious development of a highly civilized, aesthetically sensitive agnostic at the time of Marcus Aurelius and probably indicating Pater's own attitude toward religion.

Pater's importance for English letters might be said to lie largely in his having cultivated the essay form to a high level of competence combined with elegance, making a fine art out of deliberate abstention from judgment, out of tentativeness and the impressionistic recording of subjective states of mind. His best criticism occurs in the collection *The Renaissance*, in his essay on Coleridge in *Appreciations* (London, 1889), and in the essay on style (appended to *Appreciations*).

Pater understood the "historical method" to be the attempt to understand artistic phenomena in relation to the conditions which produced them and to commend them to the sympathetic imagination of the reader. Unlike Matthew Arnold, who had contrasted personal and historical assessment with the "real" assessment of art, Pater did not believe in any fully objective standards but only in the completely honest account of personal impressions against the background of historical relativity. While ostensibly agreeing with Arnold that one must see the object "as it really is," he insisted that this can be done only on the basis of knowing one's own impressions "as they really are." The critic needs a certain kind of temperament, the power of being deeply moved by the presence of beautiful objects. Pater acknowledged no distinction here between beautiful things in and apart from art. Yet he offered some fine insights into the autonomy and interdependence of the various arts, especially in the implications of his much-quoted passage from the essay "The School of Giorgione" in *The Renaissance:* "All art aspires constantly towards the condition of music." In the preceding paragraph of the essay, Pater wrote that each art has "its own specific order of impressions, and an untranslatable charm." Yet each art form, as art, needs the complete fusion of matter and form which music exemplifies in its purity.

Principal Works by Pater

Works, 8 vols. London, 1900–1901.
Essays from the "Guardian." London, 1897. Published uniformly, may be regarded as Vol. IX of the works.

Works on Pater

Benson, A. C., *Walter Pater.* London, 1906.
Cecil, Lord David, *Walter Pater.* Cambridge, 1955.
Eliot, T. S., "The Place of Pater," in Walter de la Mare, ed., *The Eighteen-eighties.* Cambridge, 1930.
Gaunt, William, *The Aesthetic Adventure.* London, 1945.
Greenslet, Ferris, *Walter Pater.* London, 1905.
Hough, Graham, *The Last Romantics.* London, 1949.
Iser, Wolfgang, *Walter Pater.* Tübingen, 1960.

EVA SCHAPER

PATRISTIC PHILOSOPHY is the term used to refer to the philosophical presuppositions, motifs, and structures in the writings of the early Christian apologists and Church Fathers. These writers were essentially theologians rather than philosophers, for their starting point lay in God and his self-revelation. Their use of philosophy can be divided into three periods: (1) the beginnings (roughly the first and second centuries A.D.), in which ideas derived from Platonism, Stoicism, and (to a lesser extent) Skepticism were employed chiefly for apologetic purposes, largely under the influence of Hellenistic Judaism; (2) the early Alexandrian period, during which Middle Platonism and Stoicism were dominant, especially in the thought of Clement and Origen; and (3) the development of Christian Neoplatonism, first under the influence of Porphyry and later under that of Proclus. The influence of Philo of Alexandria may have been felt during the first period and certainly was an important factor in the second.

BEGINNINGS

The New Testament. In the New Testament, as in the Apocrypha (for example, in the Wisdom of Solomon), there are ideas that are at least latently philosophical. As early as Paul's first letter to the Corinthians (8.6), the Christian faith was being formulated with the use of prepositions that in Greek philosophy indicated causal relations. For Christians there was "one God the Father, from whom is everything and for whom are we, and one Lord Jesus Christ, through whom is everything and through whom are we." The Father was thus represented as the first and final causes (see Romans 11.36, a doxology), the Lord as the instrumental cause. Such an analysis was presumably derived from Hellenistic Judaism; Philo spoke thus concerning God and the Logos. In Romans 1.19–21 Paul discussed the primal knowledge of God's eternal power and deity, which he revealed by means of what he created. Men capable of receiving revelation knew God but turned away to worship the creation instead of the Creator (Romans 1.25; cf. Philo, *De Opificio Mundi,* Bk. 7). The theme of a revelation implicit in the structure of the created world is further developed in sermons ascribed to Paul in Acts 14.15–17 and 17.22–31 (the setting of the latter ser-

mon contains reminiscences of the charges brought against Socrates and other philosophers at Athens), and in Colossians 1.15–20 the causal functions of Christ are further elaborated. The idea of the Logos, or creative Word of God, in John 1.1–14 is not necessarily philosophical either in its origin, which is probably not Philo, or in its expression. Later Christian theologians, however, interpreted it as philosophical, thus creating a bridge between Christianity and philosophy. These later theologians may perhaps have relied on Philo.

Second-century Christianity. In the apocryphal *Preaching of Peter,* God is described by means of adjectives clearly philosophical in origin. God is uncontained, without needs, incomprehensible, eternal, imperishable, and invisible. These negative adjectives reflect ideas current not only in the Platonism of the time but also in Hellenistic Judaism. They are close to later Gnostic developments, and it has been suggested that both are derived from a rather fully developed doctrine of God current in early second-century Christianity. This view is confirmed by what Ignatius of Antioch (early second century) says of Christ as God and man: "the timeless, the invisible who for us was visible, the intangible, the impassible who for us was passible" (*Polycarpi* 3.2). Ignatius is obviously employing current language about God to describe Christ. About 140 the doctrine was more fully expressed in the *Apology* of Aristides (Ch. 1). God is the unmoved mover and ruler of the universe, for "everything that sets in motion is more powerful than what is moved, and what rules is more powerful than what is ruled." God is eternal, without beginning (what begins also ends) or end (what ends is destructible); he is therefore ungenerated, uncreated, immutable, and immortal. He has no defects or needs; he is not contained or measurable but contains all; he is immobile (he could not move from one place to another); and he is positively Wisdom and wholly Mind. According to Philo and others, God has no name, form, or parts.

A problem arose when such negative attributes were combined with traditional Jewish and Christian ideas about God as the Creator active in history. Basilides, a Christian Gnostic, tried to avoid any kind of analogical statement by arguing that the doctrine of emanation would make God spiderlike, whereas the doctrine of creation would make him anthropomorphic. Basilides claimed instead that originally there was absolutely nothing, and then the nonexistent God made, so to speak, a nonexistent universe out of the nonexistent. Like certain Middle Platonists, Basilides held that God was completely transcendent, since "the universe cannot speak of him or contain him in thought"; he cannot even be called ineffable.

Christian thinkers, however, were generally less audaciously speculative. The apologist Justin Martyr (c. 160) wrote an account of conversion from Platonic religious philosophy to Christian truth. Justin had experienced the teaching offered by Stoics, Peripatetics, Pythagoreans, and Platonists but had little insight into any but the last. While a novice in Platonism he encountered a Christian who—apparently with Peripatetic arguments—demolished his defenses of the innate immortality of the soul and its reminiscence of the eternal world. After his conversion Justin continued to quote from Plato's dialogues (which in his view were partly based on the Old Testament), although his position was now fully eclectic: "Whatever has been said well by anyone belongs to us" (*Apologies*, Bk. 2, Ch. 13). He criticized the Stoic doctrines about fate and the *ekpyrosis* (destruction of the cosmos by fire) but expressed his admiration not only for Heraclitus and Socrates but also for the first-century Stoic moralist Musonius Rufus. Justin's disciple Tatian was much less friendly to philosophers, although he tried to create a theology largely Platonic in inspiration. His incidental reference to "the God who suffered" suggests that at a crucial point he had to rely on paradox.

The writings of the later apologists show that philosophy continued to influence theology. In the *Legatio* of Athenagoras (c. 178), there is an important attempt to demonstrate the oneness of God and consequently an approach toward a doctrine of the Trinity. In another treatise the logical necessity of corporeal resurrection is upheld on grounds that are largely Peripatetic. About the same time, Theophilus of Antioch set forth the doctrine that God is known only through his activities, to which his attributes and appellations refer; God is without beginning because uncreated, immutable because immortal. The word *theos* is derived from verbs referring to his creative acts. His invisibility is explained by analogies to the soul, a pilot, the sun, and a king. God is not "contained" but is the locus of the universe. He is known only through his Logos, originally existing within him as reason (*endiathetos*), then expressed as word (*prophorikos*) at creation.

Philosophical ideas influenced not only the apologists but other Christians as well. Irenaeus of Lyons (c. 185) was no philosopher, but in five passages he accepted a description of God originally derived from Xenophanes, "seeing entirely, knowing entirely, hearing entirely" (Fr. 24 in H. Diels and W. Kranz, eds., *Fragmente der Vorsokratiker*, 10th. ed., Berlin, 1961) and amplified it, ascribing it both to "religious men" and to "the Scriptures." In three instances he added the Platonic phrase "the source of all good things."

During the crucial second century, then, Christian theologians generally shared their doctrine of God with Platonists. Their doctrine of the Logos resembled that of the Stoics, although Christian theologians believed in one Logos (as in Philo) rather than many. They used Skeptical arguments against the pagan gods. Their ethical teaching was often close to that of the Roman Stoa as represented by Musonius (and Epictetus). Like non-Christians of various schools, they tended to believe that there had once been a unified religious philosophy, Oriental in origin, from which later philosophers had deviated. This first philosophy, it was thought, had been based on the inspiration of the divine Logos or on borrowing from Moses, or on both. The views of the Christian theologians were thus close to the kind of Hellenistic Judaism represented by Philo. Few writers took up the philosophical problems presented by the Incarnation; several of them do not even mention Jesus.

THE CHRISTIAN PLATONISTS OF ALEXANDRIA

In the cultural center of Alexandria, Christian philosophical theology came into its own, first in the writings of Clement of Alexandria (late second century) and later in the fuller treatment of Origen. The rather disdainful attitude of both writers toward "simpler believers" illustrates the tension between traditional and philosophical theology in their time. Philosophy was often viewed elsewhere as a seedbed of heresy; such was the case at Rome with Hippolytus and at Carthage with Tertullian, even though both these writers used philosophical definitions and arguments. Clement and Origen made use of the writings of Philo and other Hellenistic Jews, although both were directly acquainted with most of the works of Plato, some Middle Platonic writings, a few Aristotelian treatises, and a great deal of Stoic literature. Clement's learning was both broader and more superficial than Origen's. His philosophical ideas apparently developed away from the boldness of his semi-Gnostic *Hypotyposes* (now lost) toward the greater caution reflected in the *Stromata,* in which philosophy became the handmaid of a theology traditional in essence if not always in expression. The principal points at which the influence of philosophy is obvious are the doctrine of transcendence of God and the ideal world, analysis of the divine nature of Christ, divine impassibility as a model for human conduct, and Platonic and Stoic ethical conceptions. Following Philo, Clement made use of the allegorical method in order to relate his theology to the Bible. He was the head of a private philosophical school, training pupils to become Christian Gnostics. In later times he was far less influential than Origen, head of an authorized church school first at Alexandria and later at Caesarea. The ideas of both teachers, however, continued to create theological ferment as late as the sixth century.

LATER PATRISTIC PHILOSOPHY

We can hardly view Eusebius of Caesarea as a philosopher, but in the writings of the Cappadocian Fathers (especially Gregory of Nazianzus and Gregory of Nyssa) technical philosophical arguments are frequently adapted for theological use, as they are throughout the patristic period. During the fourth century the attack upon Christianity by Porphyry was largely forgotten (a new attack was produced by the emperor Julian), and the logical rigor of his eclectic Neoplatonism was viewed as supporting theology. Extensive quotations from Porphyry and his master Plotinus appear in Eusebius' writings as well as in the later treatise *Against Julian* by Cyril of Alexandria. Toward the end of the fourth century, a faintly Christianized Neoplatonism appeared in the West in the commentary on Plato's *Timaeus* by a certain Calcidius, who relied primarily on Porphyry. Before being baptized, Marius Victorinus had translated one of Porphyry's works into Latin; he made frequent use of Porphyry's teaching in his later treatises *On the Trinity*. Both Ambrose and Augustine were deeply influenced by Porphyry, whose writings paved the way for Augustine's conversion. In the late fifth century the ideal world of the Neoplatonist Proclus was Christianized in the influential writings ascribed to Dionysius the Areopagite.

(See also APOLOGISTS and ORIGEN.)

Bibliography

For works by the Church Fathers, see the individual articles devoted to them.

For the beginnings of patristic philosophy and for general discussions, see G. Ebeling, in *Die Religion in Geschichte und Gegenwart*, Vol. VI (3d ed., 1962), pp. 789–819; W. Pannenberg, in *Zeitschrift für Theologie und Kirche*, Vol. 70 (1959), 1–45; Robert M. Grant, in *Journal of Biblical Literature*, Vol. 83 (1964), 34–40; W. C. van Unnik, in *Theologische Zeitschrift*, Vol. 17 (1961), 166–174; G. L. Prestige, *God in Patristic Thought* (London, 1936; 2d ed., 1952); Harry A. Wolfson, *Philo*, 2 vols. (Cambridge, Mass., 1947), and *The Philosophy of the Church Fathers*, Vol. I, *Faith, Trinity, Incarnation* (Cambridge, Mass., 1956; 2d rev. ed., 1964); and Werner Jaeger, *Early Christianity and Greek Paideia* (Cambridge, Mass., 1961).

For second-century Christianity, see E. R. Goodenough, *The Theology of Justin Martyr* (Jena, 1923); C. Andresen, *Logos und Nomos* (1955); R. Holte, in *Studia Theologica*, Vol. 12 (1958), 109–168; M. Spanneut, *Le Stoïcisme des pères de l'église* (1957).

On the Christian Platonists of Alexandria, see bibliography to ORIGEN.

For later patristic philosophy, see Endre von Ivánka, *Hellenisches und christliches im frühbyzantinischen Geistesleben* (Vienna, 1948); P. Courcelle, *Les Lettres grecques en occident* (Paris, 1948), *Recherches sur les confessions de saint Augustin* (Paris, 1950), and *Les Confessions de saint Augustin dans la tradition littéraire* (Paris, 1963); and J. H. Waszink, *Timaeus a Calcidio Translatus* (1962).

ROBERT M. GRANT

PATRIZI, FRANCESCO (1529–1597), also known as Patritius, was a vigorous defender of Platonism and an unremitting foe of Aristotelianism. He was versatile even for his time, being at once philosopher, mathematician, historian, soldier, and literary critic. Born in Dalmatia, he studied at Padua (Francesco Robertelli was a teacher-friend) and Venice. Having been an early and avid reader of Ficino's *Theologia Platonica*, he turned from careers in business and in medicine to develop further his interest in Platonism.

After some years in France, Spain, and Cyprus in the service of various noblemen, in 1578 Patrizi was appointed by Duke Alfonso II as professor of Platonic philosophy at the University of Ferrara—which, with Florence and Pisa, was an important center of Platonism in Italy. In 1592 he was called to the University of Rome by Pope Clement VIII. He considered the privilege of expounding Platonism at Rome his crowning achievement, and he held that position until his death.

Although intellectual activity was his chief concern, Patrizi also showed interest in practical matters: he offered means for diverting a river threatening Ferrara, and presented plans for improving military strategy against the Turks and naval plans against the British.

In 1553 Patrizi's *Discorso* on types of poetic inspiration appeared, followed by his dialogues on history (1560). After visiting France, Spain, and Cyprus, he published *Discussiones Peripateticae* (1581), which violently attacked Aristotelianism. His achievement dates largely from his appointment at Ferrara, although correspondence with Telesio (1572) indicates an earlier interest in the study of nature. In *Della Poetica* (1586), he produced the first modern study of literary history, which also was an attack on Aristotle's *Poetics*. In 1587 there appeared several polemics defending his friend Orazio Ariosto against Torquato Tasso and Jacopo Mazzoni and upholding Patrizi's Platonic view of art as transcendental against their Aristotelian theory of poetry as imitation.

Patrizi's chief philosophical work, *Nova de Universis Philosophia* (1591), contained four parts: *Panaugia*, on

light; *Panarchia*, on first principles; *Pampsychia*, on souls; and *Pancosmia*, on mathematics and natural science. Dedicated to Gregory XIV, who had been a fellow student at Padua, its aims were the linking of Christianity with the teachings of Zoroaster, Hermes, and Orpheus; the derivation of the world from God through emanation; and the insistence on a quantitative study of nature. His last work was *Paralleli Militari* (1594).

Patrizi's metaphysics of light is suggestive of ibn-Gabirol and Grosseteste, and places him in the company of Cardano and Telesio. Defending the cognitive value of mathematics (as did Cusanus), Patrizi helped to establish the subsequent priority of space over matter in the study of nature. His doctrines, fanciful yet impressive, failed (as did those of Bruno and Telesio), for want of an adequate method, to overthrow the well-entrenched Aristotelians. The decisive attack came only in the seventeenth century, when Galileo and others postulated a new physics of quantities that was related to astronomy and was based on experiments and calculations.

Works by Patrizi

Discorso. 1553.
Della Historia. Venice, 1560.
Discussiones Peripateticae. Basel, 1581.
Della Poetica. Ferrara, 1586.
Nova de Universis Philosophia. Ferrara, 1591.
Paralleli Militari. 1594.

Works on Patrizi

Brickman, B., *An Introduction to Francesco Patrizi's Nova de Universis Philosophia*. New York, 1941.
Kristeller, P. O., *Renaissance Thought: The Classic, Scholastic, and Humanistic Strains*. New York, 1961.
Robb, N., *Neoplatonism of the Italian Renaissance*. London, 1935.
Salata, F., "Nel terzo centenario della morte di F. Patrizi." *Atti e memorie della Società Istriana di Archeologia e Storia Patria*, Vol. 12 (1897), 455–484.

JASON L. SAUNDERS

PAULER, AKOS (1876–1933), Hungarian philosopher, the son of an archivist and historian and the grandson of a professor of law, grew up in an intellectual and bookish environment. Even before he matriculated, he published his first article in the scholarly journal *Bölcseleti Folyoirat* in 1893. It was a defense of metaphysics against positivism—metaphysics starts from what is given and goes back to that without which the given cannot be thought. This is, in germ, Pauler's "reductive method" (as against induction and deduction), which became his main preoccupation in later life. However, influenced by his university professor Imre Pauer, he was first a positivist for about a decade. After obtaining his doctorate at Budapest in 1898, he spent a year at Leipzig and another at the Sorbonne. In 1902 Pauler became *Privatdozent* at Budapest and, in 1906, lecturer in ethics on the faculty of law at Pozsony (Bratislava). His departure from positivism seems to have started during this period, since his work on ethics published in 1907 at Budapest, *Az Etikai Megismerés*, is close to the Kantianism of Rickert. In 1912 Pauler became professor of philosophy at Kolozsvár, and from 1915 he occupied the chair of philosophy at Budapest.

Most expositions of Pauler mention his division of philosophy into five parts—logic, ethics, metaphysics, aesthetics, and ideology—presented in the first seven paragraphs of his *Bevezetés a Filozofiaba* ("Introduction to Philosophy," Budapest, 1920; revised 3d ed., Budapest, 1933). However, it will be sufficient to discuss only his logic and metaphysics.

For Pauler, logic is the most important part of philosophy, which is not surprising in view of his broad notions of logic, the scope and nature of which can be seen from his four "laws of logic"—the law of identity: "Everything is identical only with itself," from which follow the laws of contradiction and excluded middle; the law of connection: "Everything is connected with other things," which includes the law of sufficient reason; the law of classification: "Everything can be classified," which includes the *dictum de omni et nullo*; and the law of correlativity: "There is nothing relative without an absolute." Only the first three laws, in a slightly different version, are found in earlier works. The fourth law was added in the "Introduction to Philosophy."

Pauler's metaphysics is a combination of Aristotelian and Leibnizian elements, but by the end of his life it had moved toward Platonism and Neoplatonism. A substance is a center of self-activity based on intention or wish (*vágy*); the body is a manifestation of this activity. The interaction of substances not only proves their plurality but also provides the unity of the world. Since all change is from potentiality to actuality, the whole world process is a self-realization and self-liberation. All substances strive toward the first principle of their development, the principle of self-liberation, which is the Absolute. Moreover, substances exist insofar as they strive toward the Absolute. At first, God was described as something other than the Absolute, but Pauler later developed this Absolute into a theistic concept. He also introduced the Platonic *anamnesis* and the Augustinian *illuminatio* into his theory of knowledge.

Toward the end of his life he seems to have identified his reductive method with the Platonic dialectic, and his reductive method ultimately leads us to the notion of Good. He also criticized Aristotle for having misunderstood Plato. According to Pauler, Aristotle was mistaken in assuming that the Ideas are in the field of reality. They are, in fact, in the field of validity; that is, we do not come to them in the search for new entities, but in the search for those presuppositions without which we cannot think validly. We do this not by induction or deduction but by reduction.

Bibliography

There is a full bibliography of Pauler's published and unpublished works in *Pauler Akos Emlékkönyv* (Budapest, 1933), a special number (No. 6) of the publications of the Hungarian Philosophical Association that is devoted to Pauler.

See also J. Somogyi, "Die Philosophie Akos Paulers," in *Kantstudien*, Vol. 30 (1925), 180–188, and C. Carbonara, "Akos von Pauler e la logica della filosofia dei valori," in *Logos*, Vol. 3 (1931).

German translations of Pauler's works are *Grundlagen der Philosophie* (Berlin and Leipzig, 1925) and *Logik* (Berlin and Leipzig, 1929).

JULIUS KOVESI

PAULSEN, FRIEDRICH (1846–1908), German philosopher and educational theorist. He was born in the village of Langenhorn, Schleswig-Holstein, to a farming family descended from generations of seamen of the North Frisian Islands. In his autobiography Paulsen described his early life in detail, attributing to it the firm moral character and concern for people that marked his later work in philosophy and education. After attending the Altona Gymnasium, he entered the university at Erlangen in 1867. The following year he went to the University of Berlin, where a reading of F. A. Lange's *History of Materialism* and participation in Adolf Trendelenburg's seminar on Aristotle induced him to abandon theology for philosophy. After studies in Berlin, Bonn, and Kiel, Paulsen taught at Berlin. The professorship of philosophy to which he later succeeded there was, due to his own interests and the needs of the university, expanded to include pedagogy.

Philosophy could not, for Paulsen, be detached from the moral and cultural issues of private and public life, and the needs of the general public determined both the language and the content of his teaching and writing. Although far from negligent of the critical problems of theoretical and practical philosophy, he always tested the validity of their solutions by common sense and the public well-being. His collection of essays and addresses *Zur Ethik und Politik* (1905) shows the range of his interests and his public concern. Although he was temperate and reasonable, his efforts to distinguish good from evil in contemporary political and social life subjected him to political attack and involved him in public controversy.

Although Paulsen influenced all levels of German education, his published works deal chiefly with German universities and preparatory schools. His *Geschichte des gelehrten Unterrichts auf den deutschen Schulen und Universitäten* (1885) pioneered in the history of higher education and aroused wide controversy, helping to effect a liberalization of preuniversity education.

Paulsen usually described his philosophical position as idealistic monism but sometimes described it as pantheism. Participating in the revival of Kant and Aristotle in the second half of the nineteenth century, Paulsen found in both an epistemological realism, an emphasis upon practical reason over theoretical reason, and a teleological metaphysics. His own position was formulated in opposition to the two extremes of a rigid Christian orthodoxy and scientific materialism. Irrational supernaturalism and mechanistic naturalism are the enemies in his two textbooks, *System der Ethik* (1889) and *Einleitung in die Philosophie* (1892), and in his *Philosophia Militans* (Berlin, 1901). He rejected Christian supernaturalism because of its dualism in theoretical philosophy and its legalism and rigorism in practical philosophy. Materialism was discarded because its denial both of human freedom and of the reality of purposes is offensive to man's ethical demands.

Paulsen's two textbooks were addressed not merely to students but to the thoughtful layman. Simply written with many concrete applications and references to contemporary ethical and social problems, they appeared in many editions in German and in translation and set a pattern for introductory textbooks and courses in philosophy for at least four decades. In them Paulsen formulated his method as (1) analysis of problems and the construction of possible solutions, (2) a survey of the historical development of philosophical thought on each problem, and (3) a choice of the solution most coherent with an inclusive world view.

This method brought Paulsen close to a pragmatic and personalistic viewpoint. In his ethics he supported a modern utilitarianism or eudaemonism that repudiated the hedonism of the British school, replacing it with the goal of human welfare and an objective perfection of the ends of life. The good life is thus grounded in the will, not in feeling. In determining the valid ends of conduct, the individual must be guided by the historical tradition, which may be trusted ultimately to destroy evil and to bring about the survival of the good. Book I of the *System*, devoted to such historical evaluation, is still a most useful introduction to the history of ethics. Paulsen stressed the distinctions between the ascetic ethical ideals of early Christianity and the humanism of classical Greece, but he regarded as necessary the modern effort to reconcile them.

Ethical thought involves the problems of evil, of freedom, and of God. Evil is justified in a monistic world, because by overcoming evil we find the way and the will to the good. Although human freedom is real, it is never a motiveless freedom of action. The psychological theory of freedom is correct in finding the ground of free action in the human will or in man's determining his conduct through deliberation and resolution. The metaphysical theory of freedom, which denies that there are causes of the will, must itself be denied. Morality, in its historical development of responsibility and a sense of duty, comes to require a higher will with a right to command and thus provides an argument for the existence of a deity who is also implicit in the evolutionary account of nature.

In such later ethical writings as the article "Ethik" in Paul Hinneberg's *Systematische Philosophie* (Berlin and Leipzig, 1907), Paulsen moved closer to Hegel by introducing an "objective will" as the manifestation in the social forms of life of a universal reason to which individual conscience is a cognitive response. Paulsen held that the principles of ethics are rational in the sense that they arise from the conditions of life. They need not determine one's metaphysics, but teleological ethics demands an evolutionary teleology in which the purpose of nature is fulfilled in human reason.

Paulsen's *Introduction to Philosophy* was devoted to metaphysical and epistemological questions. In it he is led to monism by the Lotzean argument from finite interaction, Hartmann's vitalism and energism, and by a creative vitalistic interpretation of evolution. His solution to the mind–body problem is a theory of panpsychistic parallelism, showing the influence of Spinoza and Fechner. Mind and body are distinct aspects of a unified "All-One," a mental process of which history and nature are the two series of "modifications." This identity is affirmed of God in relationship to nature and to history. Science is limited to the phenomenalistic aspect of nature. Although God enters into interaction with lesser spirits, the concept of personality must be purged of its human limitations before it can be ascribed to God, who is to be thought of rather as a superpersonal source of energy and reason in nature and man. (See also PANPSYCHISM.)

Works by Paulsen

Geschichte des gelehrten Unterrichts auf den deutschen Schulen und Universitäten vom Ausgang des Mittelalters bis zur Gegenwart. Leipzig, 1885. 3d ed., 2 vols., Berlin, 1919–1920, translated by E. D. Perry as *The German Universities: Their Character and Historical Development.* New York, 1895.

System der Ethik mit einem Umriss des Staats und Gesellschaftslehre. Berlin, 1889. Translated from the 4th German edition by Frank Thilly as *A System of Ethics.* New York, 1899.

Einleitung in die Philosophie. Berlin, 1892. Translated from the 3d German edition by Frank Thilly as *Introduction to Philosophy.* New York, 1895.

Immanuel Kant: Sein Leben und seine Lehre. Stuttgart, 1898. Translated from the 3d German edition by J. E. Creighton and A. Lefevre as *Immanuel Kant: His Life and Doctrine.* New York, 1902. Paulsen's most important and influential historical study. Interprets Kant as a realist.

Philosophia Militans. Gegen Klerikalismus und Naturalismus. Berlin, 1901.

Zur Ethik und Politik: Gesammelte Vorträge und Aufsätze, 2 vols. Berlin, 1905.

Aus meinem Leben. Jugenderinnerungen. Jena, 1909. Translated by Theodor Lorenz as *Friedrich Paulsen: An Autobiography.* New York, 1938. Gives details of Paulsen's academic career and political influence as well as bibliographical data. Part II of this work, never published in German, was translated from Paulsen's manuscript.

Works on Paulsen

Schulte-Hibbert, B., *Die Philosophie Friedrich Paulsens.* Berlin, 1914.

Speck, Johannes, *Friedrich Paulsen. Sein Leben und sein Werk.* Langensalza, 1926.

Spranger, Eduard, ed., *Gesammelte pädagogische Abhandlungen.* Stuttgart, 1912. Contains a complete bibliography.

L. E. LOEMKER

PAVLOV, IVAN PETROVICH (1849–1936), Russian physiologist and originator of conditioned-reflex method and theory, was born the eldest son of a priest in Ryazan. After home tutoring, church school, and theological seminary (where he read G. H. Lewes' *Physiology*), he entered the University of St. Petersburg, where I. F. Tsyon confirmed his physiological interests. At the Military Medical Academy, as assistant to Tsyon and later to S. P. Botkin, the experimental pharmacologist, he excelled in surgery and in experimental physiological research, which he continued in Botkin's laboratory after qualifying as an approved physician in 1879. In 1881 he married a fellow student, and despite desperate financial struggles, he received his M.D. in 1883 with a dissertation on the heart's innervation. With a traveling fellowship, he worked in Leipzig with Karl Ludwig and in Breslau with Rudolf Heidenhain; he returned to Botkin's laboratory in 1886 to continue research on nervous control of circulation and digestion. In 1888 he discovered the secretory nerves of the pancreas, and the following year he wrote on "sham feeding" and gastric "psychic secretion" (at sight of food).

In 1890 he became professor of pharmacology at the Military Medical Academy and director of the physiological department of the new Institute of Experimental Medicine donated by the prince of Oldenburg. In 1895 he was named professor of physiology at the Military Medical Academy, although the rector, Pashootin, delayed confirmation of the appointment till 1897. *The Work of the Digestive Glands* (1897), which reported the research that won Pavlov the Nobel prize in physiology in 1904, was widely translated. Next he investigated salivary "psychic" secretion, devising a neat surgical technique to enable collection and measurement of the saliva of dogs. Reflex salivation was measured upon ingestion (natural stimulus) and sight ("psychic" stimulus) of food, and also upon application, to hungry dogs before feeding, of artificial ("conditioned") stimuli—visual, auditory, olfactory, and tactile. The "conditioned reflex"—a term coined by I. E. Tolochinov—was thus a simple unit of acquired behavior, as involuntary as salivation itself; its formation, persistence, and disappearance followed rules which Pavlov elucidated in meticulous experiment for over thirty years, gradually constructing a neurophysiological theory of behavior and learning. Pavlov's work attracted pupils and collaborators, produced a plentiful literature, and continued without significant interruption through World War I and the Russian Revolution.

A reflex theory of behavior accorded well with Marxist dialectical materialism, and Pavlov's researches received governmental encouragement and financial support. Pavlov was never a Marxist or a communist; he resigned his professorship in 1924 in protest against anticlerical discrimination at the academy, but he continued to enjoy state support, including new laboratories, and official foreign-language publication; his research village, Koltushy, was even renamed Pavlovo. When conditioned-reflex theory was extended to human behavior, Pavlovian doctrine became the Soviet Union's official "psychology," basic to psychiatry, pedagogy, industrial research, and other fields ranging from criminal re-education to space exploration.

Pavlov's collected lectures appeared in English, French, and German translations in the 1920s, with a further volume, *Conditioned Reflexes and Psychiatry,* in 1941. He observed that a conditioned reflex might comprise excitation (secretory or motor) or inhibition, both processes located in the cerebral cortex. Concentration and irradiation of excitation, enabling discrimination and generalization of response, followed laws of induction, conceived as resembling ionic polarization, with excitation and inhibition spreading wavelike over a largely unspecialized cortex. Specialization occurred in the analyzers, or cortical receptor areas (visual, auditory, etc.), which sorted stimulus signals and regulated responses.

Pavlov found that for permanence a conditioned reflex required reinforcement with the unconditioned stimulus. Disturbance of an already established temporal or spatial pattern of stimuli, including excessive requirement of discrimination, produced disordered responses in the three successive phases of (*a*) equalization of response to all stimuli, (*b*) paradoxical responses, and (*c*) ultraparadoxical responses, involving reversal of positive and inhibitory responses. Ultimate derangement ("neurosis") was behavioral breakdown in uncontrolled excitement or complete inhibition, depending upon the type of the nervous system. An increasing preponderance of inhibition was evident in the progression from (*a*) controlled activity, to (*b*) delayed activity, corresponding to deliberation or thought, to (*c*) hypnotic states with concentrated activity bounded by general inhibition, to (*d*) sleep considered as generalized inhibition. Nervous systems were classified as strong excitable, weak inhibitable, and two central "balanced" types, lively and stolid, analogous to the "Hippocratic temperaments," choleric, melancholic, sanguine, and phlegmatic, respectively. Conditioned reflexes were most stable in the two more inhibited types of dog (and probably of humans).

From 1928 until his death Pavlov surveyed human psychology and psychiatry, drawing bold analogies between psychiatric syndromes and the reactions of dogs to experimental laboratory situations. Manic-depressive psychosis was viewed as an excitation–inhibition disorder and paranoia as a pathologically persistent excitatory process in a circumscribed cortical area. Later work by others has shown the value of conditioning theory for a "how" explanation and for an empirical treatment for certain phobias and compulsions, but Pavlov's formulations, without direct experimental or adequate clinical basis, are subjective intuitions clothed in pseudophysiological vocabulary. His experimental observations were objective and sound, and his apparently prosaic method allowed repeatable exact measurement, although what else was being measured by measuring saliva remains unclear. When he wrote of "reflexes" of freedom and slavery in dogs and humans, or of an animal's "strong" or "weak" cortex, or of ripples of excitation or inhibition, he failed to recognize the subjective nature of his interpretations. Insight was hindered by his premature oversimplification and an increasingly militant materialist monism.

Pavlov's was the principal and most developed of the several physiopsychologies of his time. His priority was disputed by V. M. Bekhterev, a neurologist whose "reflexology" of "associated reflexes" was developed simultaneously although independently in the same academy; Pavlov undoubtedly published first, however. Pavlov yielded experimental priority to the American E. L. Thorndike and admitted the theoretical influence of V. M. Sechenov, a former professor of physiology in St. Petersburg, whom Pavlov styled "father of Russian physiology." Sechenov's *Reflexes of the Brain* (1863, in *Selected Physiological and Psychological Works,* Moscow, 1952–1956) followed his studies in Berlin, where Wilhelm Griesinger taught a psychology of temperamental types and psychic reflexes which was philosophically based upon Schopenhauer and Descartes (*Mental Pathology and Therapeutics,* Berlin, 1845 and 1861; translated by C. L. Robertson and J. Rutherford, London, 1867).

Pavlov's influence continues paramount in Russia. Elsewhere it is an important component in behavior theory and therapy, but with a strong admixture of Bekhterev and John B. Watson in practical techniques and a preponderance of C. L. Hull's learning theory in vocabulary.

Works by Pavlov

The Work of the Digestive Glands, translated by W. H. Thompson. London, 1902.

Conditioned Reflexes; an Investigation of the Physiological Activity of the Cerebral Cortex, translated and edited by G. V. Anrep. London, 1927; New York, 1960. The best English translation of the early papers.

Lectures on Conditioned Reflexes, Vol. I, *Twenty-five Years of Objective Study of the Higher Nervous Activity (Behavior) of Animals,* translated and edited by W. Horsley Gantt, with

G. Volborth, New York and London, 1928, Vol. II, *Conditioned Reflexes and Psychiatry,* translated and edited by W. Horsley Gantt, New York and London, 1941.

Selected Works, translated by S. Belsky, edited by J. Gibbons under the supervision of K. S. Koshtoyants. Moscow, 1955.

Experimental Psychology and Other Essays. New York, 1957; London, 1958. A reprint of *Lectures on Conditioned Reflexes,* omitting Pavlov's patriotic and political speeches.

Essays in Psychology and Psychiatry. New York, 1962. A selection from *Experimental Psychology and Other Essays* in paperback.

Psychopathology and Psychiatry; Selected Works, compiled by Y. Popov and L. Rokhin, translated by D. Myshne and S. Belsky. Moscow, 1962.

Conditioned Reflexes, Lectures on Conditioned Reflexes, and *Selected Works* contain some of the same papers in different translations. *Lectures on Conditioned Reflexes* and *Selected Works* have some later "psychiatric" papers, and *Selected Works* has some early papers on circulation and digestion preceding Pavlov's work on conditioned reflexes. *Psychopathology and Psychiatry* is selected entirely from his "psychiatric" work.

Works on Pavlov

Asratyan, E. A., *I. P. Pavlov, His Life and Work.* English ed., Moscow, 1953. An early and approved biography.

Babkin, B. P., *Pavlov: A Biography.* Chicago, 1949 and 1960; London, 1951.

Cuny, H., *Ivan Pavlov: The Man and His Theories.* London and Toronto, 1964. Brief, semipopular outline of Pavlov's life and work.

Frolov, Y. P., *Pavlov and His School—The Theory of Conditioned Reflexes,* translated by C. P. Dutt. New York and London, 1937.

Gray, J. A., editor and translator, *Pavlov's Typology.* Oxford and New York, 1964. Includes a detailed authoritative survey of this field by B. M. Teplov.

Platonov, K. I., *The Word as a Physiological and Therapeutic Factor—The Theory and Practice of Psychotherapy According to I. P. Pavlov,* translated by D. A. Myshne. Moscow, 1959. This work applying Pavlov's teachings openly acknowledges a debt to Bekhterev's.

Scientific Session on the Physiological Teachings of I. P. Pavlov. Moscow, 1951.

Simon, B., ed., *Psychology in the Soviet Union.* Stanford, Calif., 1957.

Wells, H. K., *Pavlov and Freud,* 2 vols. New York and London, 1956–1960; reprinted 1962.

J. D. Uytman

PEACE, WAR, AND PHILOSOPHY. Speculation about war and peace as conditions of interstate relations has tended to divide thinkers into two groups—those who regard war as inevitable, perhaps even desirable, and those who consider it an evil capable of being replaced by lasting peace through good will or improved social arrangements. The first group is sometimes described as "realist" and the second as "idealist," but these terms have the drawback that such idealist philosophers (in the ontological sense) as Plato and Hegel often accept war as a permanent condition of human existence. It is therefore proposed here simply to call the first group "conservatives" and the second "abolitionists," though a wide spectrum of opinion clearly exists within each subdivision.

THE CONSERVATIVE TRADITION

The Greeks. Ancient Greek thought commonly accepted war between the city-states themselves and between Greeks and "barbarians" as part of the order of nature. The Greek gods were a warlike breed who had come to power after a brutal struggle with the Titans. Ares was one of their leading figures, but the goddess of peace, Irene, was merely a subordinate deity attendant on the great gods. A view of war widely prevalent in Greece was that of Heraclitus of Ephesus. War, Heraclitus taught, was the "father of all and king of all," and it was through war that the present condition of mankind, some men free and some enslaved, had evolved. If strife between the warring elements in nature were abolished, nothing could exist; "all things," according to Heraclitus, "come into being and pass away through strife."

It was not until the later phases of the war between Athens and Sparta (431–404 B.C.) that a pacifist note unusual in the Greek world was struck in such works as Euripides' *The Trojan Women* (performed in 415 B.C.) and Aristophanes' *Lysistrata* (411 B.C.). Even so, the conclusion drawn by Plato from the Peloponnesian War was that the state must be organized for violent survival in an unruly world. Plato's *Republic* is, in effect, a design for a military community on the Spartan model. Plato does, however, distinguish between war among Greeks and war between Greeks and outsiders; the former, according to the *Republic,* is to be legally regulated whereas any excess is permissible in the latter.

Christianity and natural law. The conservative acceptance of war as a fact of life was also basic to the intellectual attitudes of the Roman Republic and Empire and was sustained during the Middle Ages, when Catholic writers wrestled with the problem of the conditions on which ecclesiastical approval could be given to the wars of secular monarchs. St. Thomas Aquinas in *Summa Theologica* (Question 40), while claiming that peace was the greatest aim toward which man should strive in fulfillment of his natural ends, nevertheless placed on monarchs the duty to defend the state. Similarly, Dante contended in *De Monarchia* that "peace was the target at which all shafts were sped" but that it was to be attained by the imposition of a world law, if necessary by force, issuing from a revived Roman Empire. The legacy of Christian teaching which had the most lasting influence, however, concerned the application of natural law, strongly tinged by Christian ethics, to the conduct of war.

The Spanish Jesuit theologian Francisco Suárez held that war is not intrinsically evil and that just wars may be waged. Suárez defined three conditions of legitimate war. It must be waged by lawful authority—that is, by the supreme sovereign; the cause of making war must be just, and other means of achieving justice must be lacking; and war must be conducted and peace imposed with moderation. A similar view was taken by Hugo Grotius, who held that far from war's being a breakdown of the law of nations, it is, in fact, a condition of life to which law is as applicable as it is to the conditions of peace. War, Grotius argued in his *De Iure Belli ac Pacis Libri Tres* (1625), should not be fought except for the enforcement of rights and, when fought, should be waged only within the bounds of law and good faith. This conception survives in the assumption behind such twentieth-century international organizations as the League of Nations and the United Nations that only wars fought on behalf of international interests, such as the maintenance of world peace, are just.

The advent of nationalism. In the era of European secular nationalism following the Renaissance the idea of war as a necessary or desirable institution strengthened. The Italian city-states of the Renaissance, whose diplomatic practice formed the model for the early European national states, were continually at war with one another; these were, however, limited conflicts which aroused no great indignation among philosophers. A typically acquiescent view of war was that of Sir Thomas More in his *Utopia* (1518). The Utopians have a pragmatic, not particularly heroic idea of war, which they regard as a normal event; war is to be fought as economically and safely as possible when one's lands are invaded or one's allies are oppressed.

A more profound view was that of the Florentine statesman and writer Niccolò Machiavelli. Like all conservatives, Machiavelli assumed that armed conflict was part of the human lot not because man was evil—Machiavelli was inclined to regard man as weak and stupid rather than evil—but because of the activity of malign fate (*fortuna*), which is always forcing man to arm himself against adversity. Machiavelli, unlike Heraclitus, held out no hope that war raised man to a higher plane; the prince is condemned to seek victory in war merely in order to survive in the hostile world. In peace a ruler should not sit with hands folded but should always be improving his state's military power against the day of adversity.

At the same time the formation of great national states in England and France was forcing men to speculate on the justification of government, especially since the acceptance of the papacy as the ultimate and sacred authority had been considerably weakened. The concept of a "state of nature" in which men exist without a common superior and in a state of internecine war was introduced to help explain the growth and functions of government. Thomas Hobbes explained in his *Leviathan* (1651) that war is not the act of fighting but the disposition to fight which exists where there is no common superior to ensure that violence shall not be permitted. Only through the establishment of a commonwealth—that is, a superior law-enforcing agency to which all men are subject—can peace and civilization be ensured. Hobbes did not regard the state of nature as a historical condition which had occurred in the past; he inferred that such would be man's state if the commonwealth did not exist.

John Locke differed from Hobbes in holding that there were natural rights in the state of nature which it was government's function, after its establishment, to protect; hence, war was not a universal condition in the state of nature but occurred only when force was exercised without right. For Locke there was an intrinsic difference between war waged for natural rights and war waged without this sanction. For Hobbes war in the state of nature, as well as war between sovereign states, could be neither right nor wrong since these categories exist only within the commonwealth. Baruch Spinoza shared Hobbes's view of the inevitability of war where men are without a common government, but, like Locke, he could not reconcile himself to the total absence of morality or law in the state of

nature. The Hobbesian argument has nevertheless been of immense importance in shaping modern Western man's attitude toward war and peace. It is that peace is the result of man's determination, deriving from fear of death and the wish for what Hobbes called "commodious living," to create an overriding government. Hobbes did not make clear whether he thought that man could sustain peace in his international relations, but it is clear that, unlike Locke, he considered that nothing short of a world state with a monopoly of power over the nations would suffice to ensure such peace.

Before the Napoleonic Wars, however, war, owing to its limited scale, could not be regarded as the decisive factor in the health or illness of nations. But with the Messianic fervor unleashed by the French Revolution, all Europe appeared to be caught up in revolt against the existing order, internal and external, and the expansion of national wealth showed for the first time the potentialities of nationalistic wars for good or evil. It was in the aftermath of the revolution that the more extreme conservative attitude toward war came into its own in certain countries and war began to be thought of as a positive principle of national regeneration. Germany in particular fostered these views, possibly because that country entered the struggle for national ascendancy somewhat late so that its militarism was proportionately more intense.

Georg Wilhelm Friedrich Hegel is well known for his conception of history as a struggle of opposites from which a synthesis emerges that transcends the two original conflicting forces. For Hegel the national state was the means by which the Idea realized itself in history. Since the Idea can materialize itself only if the state is allowed to live out its predetermined functions, it follows that the individual's life has no meaning except insofar as it serves the state's ends and that no principle is left by which the relations between states can be subject to moral criteria. Hegel had no patience with the notion of a league of nations for the establishment of permanent peace because he believed war was the catalyst through which history unfolded its purpose. Man must accept war or stagnate.

Arthur Schopenhauer rejected Hegel's idea of the state as the divine expression of justice. For him the state exists because there is injustice; the state is needed to protect man against the effects of his own egotism. In turn, man's egotism and his generally evil nature are a reflection of the dissonances of the Will which for Schopenhauer lies behind the world's realities. Under these conditions war is inevitable, but Schopenhauer, unlike Hegel, did not see war as a progressive factor in history but as a result of the immaturity and weakness of the masses and the love of luxury and power of their strong-willed leaders. Schopenhauer saw no hope of lasting peace.

The militarists. Friedrich Nietzsche may be judged as an extreme representative of the romantic cult of war and as marking the transition to modern totalitarian militarism. Nietzsche was capable of deploring the wastefulness of war; however, in his fully mature writings, *Thus Spake Zarathustra* (1892) and *The Will to Power* (first published in 1901), he glorified war and the dangerous life. The phrase "a good war hallows every cause" (*Thus Spake Zarathustra*), may be taken as typical of this attitude. For

Nietzsche's supermen war is a natural activity, the supreme witness to their superior quality; they should never succumb to the "slave morality" of Christianity, with its accent on humility, submissiveness, and turning the other cheek.

In the teaching of Heinrich von Treitschke the functions of the state were unlimited, as was the individual's duty to submit to its commands. The state's first duty was to maintain its power in its relations with other states and to maintain law within its own borders; its second duty was the conduct of war, the crucible in which the elements in a state's greatness are fused. The hope of a world state or permanent peace is vain; the Aryan race can only keep by the sword what it has won by the sword. Treitschke admitted that the cost of war had risen steeply and, hence, that wars should be shorter and less frequent. But this did not affect the basic axiom that war is the "one remedy for an ailing nation."

Treitschke's ideas were absorbed by the German military writer Friedrich von Bernhardi, who used them to foster the militantly nationalist mood in which Germany entered World War I. In *Germany and the Next War*, Bernhardi repeated the basic notions of Treitschke: War is the process by which the truly civilized nations express their strength and vitality, life is an unending struggle for survival, war is an instrument in biological evolution. And Bernhardi drew on other conservative writers: Heraclitus; Frederick the Great, whose writings represented war as bringing out man's finest qualities; and Karl von Clausewitz, who described the nation's place in the world as a function of the interplay between its national character and its military tradition.

The conservative-militarist tradition, with its racist overtones, was inherited by the German Nazi and Italian fascist writers of the interwar period, though these added little to the work of their forebears. More recently, the advent of nuclear weapons has made nonsense of the glorification of war, though belief in its inevitability is still not uncommon. Almost the only considerable section of contemporary opinion which believes that national survival after nuclear war is conceivable is that of the Chinese communists. Even these, however, are careful to insist that they would never initiate a nuclear war, and it is, moreover, a feature of all communist thought that the final global victory of communism will remove all cause of war. Communists therefore differ from the conservatives we have considered in that although they regard war as contingent (or perhaps inevitable) in a capitalist system, they have no doubt that permanent peace is attainable under communism.

THE ABOLITIONISTS

The premodern age. As we have seen, the ancient Greeks (and the same may be said of the writers of the Roman world) were not distinguished for protests against war, though the Stoics of the Roman Empire preached a cosmopolitanism which assumed the oneness of all mankind, making war between its members an affront. When Stoicism was embraced by the Roman emperors, however, it lost its pacifist element, and the same may be said for the early Christian doctrine of nonviolence. Also, during the Middle Ages the fact that the papacy was both the supreme fount of church doctrine and a temporal power of considerable military strength ruled out complete pacifism as a church doctrine.

The outstanding opponent of war during the Renaissance was the great humanist Desiderius Erasmus, though it is incorrect to speak of him as an absolute pacifist. In his *Anti-polemus, or the Plea of Reason, Religion and Humanity Against War* (1510), Erasmus argued that every man's duty was to spare no pains to put an end to war. War was directly opposed to every purpose for which Erasmus conceived man to have been created; man is born not for destruction but for love, friendship, and service to his fellow men.

Projects for European peace. During the seventeenth century speculation in Europe about the possibility of permanent peace began to develop, stimulated by growing international commerce and the desire to bind Europe together in a final effort to expel the Turks. This anti-Muslim aim had already figured prominently in the plan for the unification of Europe designed by Pierre Dubois in *De Recuperatione Terre Sancte* (1305–1307) and in the celebrated proposal for a federation of Christian princes which George of Poděbrad, king of Bohemia, had presented to his fellow monarchs in 1461. The seventeenth-century proposals were immensely varied, ranging from utterly Utopian ideas to some which might have achieved realization as limited international alliances. Some were limited to western Europe, others included all Europe, and some embraced the whole Christian world. "The Grand Design" (1620–1635), probably compiled by the duke of Sully, the chief minister of Henry IV of France, and *Some Reasons for an European State* (1710) by John Bellers both proposed to divide Europe into provinces of roughly equal size under a common government. A few schemes, such as Emeric Cruce's *The New Cyneas, or Discourse of the Occasion and Means to Establish a General Peace and the Liberty of Commerce Throughout the World* (1623), aimed at the formation of a single world state with all the races and religions under its jurisdiction. In these plans provision was generally made for some form of representative government. William Penn in *An Essay Towards the Present and Future Peace of Europe* (1693) contemplated annual European parliaments; the abbé de Saint-Pierre in *A Project for Settling an Everlasting Peace in Europe* (1713) preferred a perpetual congress in order to reflect the viewpoints of the states in his European federation; Cruce called for world assemblies. These confederations were chiefly advocated as defenses of peace, though other aims were also mentioned; Henry IV and the duke of Sully, for instance, had in mind, besides European peace, wars against the Muscovites and Turks and the weakening of the Hapsburgs as the preliminary steps to uniting Europe under French hegemony.

In the eighteenth century these peace plans were given a new lease of life with the French and German Enlightenment. Jean-Jacques Rousseau took the peace project of the abbé de Saint-Pierre and applied it to the Europe of his own day in *A Project of Perpetual Peace* (1761), with the insistence that unless the proposed central authority was powerful enough to overawe all the constituent states, the proposal would fail. Rousseau recommended the plan to governments on the ground that a single European authority strong enough to enforce peace would also ensure internal stability in the constituent states. He admitted, however, that governments were probably too shortsighted to appreciate the merits of the plan. A similar project of European confederation was that of Immanuel Kant, entitled *Eternal Peace* (1795). Kant's recipe is notable for its claim that the maintenance of peace requires the achievement of constitutional government by the states.

Nineteenth-century peace movements. The nineteenth century was even more prolific in its plans for organizing the nations to ensure peace. In Europe and the United States there arose strong unofficial peace movements which urged the creation of agencies for the arbitration of interstate differences and the equitable settlement of political issues, together with the strengthening and codification of international law. In the atmosphere of harmony that followed the Congress of Vienna the Great Powers of Europe met regularly to deal with threats to peace, while such functional organizations as the European river commissions and the Universal Postal Union (1875) dealt quietly with matters of practical concern to the nations. The hope of a permanent international assembly which might develop into a world legislature was held out at the Hague conferences of 1899 and 1907, and it seemed likely that the growing stake of nations in peaceful intercourse would soon render war obsolete.

The English utilitarians, such as Jeremy Bentham, James Mill, and John Stuart Mill, provided much of the theoretical background of the peace movements. They contended that war was an anachronistic encumbrance on a free society, benefiting no one but aristocrats and professional soldiers. Richard Cobden voiced the commerical classes' distaste for war in his pamphlet *Russia* (1836). Herbert Spencer, an extreme exponent of laissez-faire society, denounced war in his *Social Statics* (1851) as an outcome of excessive government authority; with the functions of government reduced and individual liberty restored, all reason for war would disappear. This liberal, economic case for peace culminated in the striking claim by Norman Angell in *The Great Illusion* (1908) that war had become so destructive of all economic values that nations would never again engage in it.

Pacificism and internationalism. World War I disastrously falsified Angell's prophecy; nevertheless, it reinforced the conviction of liberal-minded people that war was an absolute evil and that the creation of expedients to keep the peace, such as the League of Nations and collective security, was the most urgent task of the twentieth century. A strong cleavage now became apparent between absolute pacifists—for example, H. M. Swanwick, Gerald Heard, Aldous Huxley—and those who supported "just" wars fought under the league's aegis—for example, Gilbert Murray, Lord Cecil of Chelwood, P. J. Noel-Baker. Few of the abolitionists, however, considered a world federation necessary to ensure permanent peace. John Dewey, for instance, argued in the 1920s that it would be sufficient for

states to agree to declare war illegal and to prosecute countries which resorted to it as criminals.

The advent of World War II and the invention of nuclear weapons, followed by the failure of the great powers to act unanimously in the United Nations Security Council, raised the question of whether the abolitionists' aim can be attained short of the total surrender of national sovereignty. One curious effect of the nuclear stalemate has been to drive many abolitionists into the somewhat conservative belief that peace must be kept by the maintenance of a military balance between the two world camps. Others, like John Strachey in *On the Prevention of War* (London, 1962), contend that the two superpowers must go beyond this and exercise a kind of condominium over the rest of the world.

The outstanding British philosopher Bertrand Russell continues to believe that the rational conviction of the utter futility of nuclear war can in itself maintain peace provided that the realities of thermonuclear war are widely enough publicized (*Common Sense and Nuclear Warfare*, London, 1959). As a long-term measure, however, Russell sees no alternative to a world state, which must in the first instance be imposed by one nation or group of nations; only after the world authority has been in power for a century or so will it feel confident enough to base its power on consent rather than force (*New Hopes for a Changing World*, London, 1951, p. 77). It is not clear, however, whether Russell really wishes to pay the price of global despotism in return for peace; elsewhere, he writes that a new war would be preferable to a universal communist empire (Robert E. Egner and Lester E. Denonn, eds., *The Basic Writings of Bertrand Russell*, London, 1961, p. 691). Here, in essence, is the issue facing the abolitionist in the nuclear age: whether war is a greater or lesser evil than the imposition on himself and his nation of hostile values which the present anarchic world, with its attendant threat of war, allows him to keep at a distance.

Bibliography

The following are sources for some of the views discussed above.

CONSERVATIVES

Aquinas, Thomas, *Aquinas: Selected Political Writings*, A. P. d'Entrèves, ed. Oxford, 1959. Especially pp. 159–161.

Bernhardi, Friedrich von, *Germany and the Next War*, translated by Allen H. Powles. London, 1914.

Clausewitz, Karl von, *On War*, translated by J. J. Graham. London, 1940.

Guthrie, W. K. C., *A History of Greek Philosophy*, Vol. I. Cambridge, 1962. Ch. 7 contains quotations from Heraclitus.

Hegel, Georg Wilhelm Friedrich, *Hegel's Philosophy of Right*, translated by T. M. Knox. Oxford, 1942. Especially pp. 209–223.

Hobbes, Thomas, *Leviathan*, Michael Oakeshott, ed. Oxford, 1960. Especially Ch. 13.

Schopenhauer, Arthur, *The World as Will and Idea*, translated by R. B. Haldane and J. Kemp, 3 vols. London, 1909. Especially Vol. III, Ch. 46.

Spinoza, Baruch, *Spinoza: The Political Works*, A. G. Wernham, ed. London, 1958. Especially p. 23.

Treitschke, Heinrich von, *Politics*, translated by Blanche Dugdale and Torbende Bille, 2 vols. London, 1916. Especially Vol. I, pp. 61–70.

ABOLITIONISTS

Dewey, John, *Characters and Events*, 2 vols. London and New York, 1929. Vol. II, p. 670.

Kant, Immanuel, *Eternal Peace*, translated by W. Hastie. Boston, 1944.

Rousseau, Jean-Jacques, *A Project of Perpetual Peace*, translated by Edith M. Nuttall. London, 1927.

SECONDARY SOURCES

Adams, Robert P., *The Better Part of Valor: More, Erasmus, Colet and Vives, on Humanism, War, and Peace*. Seattle, 1962.

Aron, Raymond, *Paix et guerre entre les nations*. Paris, 1962. A sociological and historical inquiry into the conditions in international relations which make for war and peace, together with an assessment of proposals for maintaining international equilibrium.

Beales, A. C. F., *The History of Peace*. London, 1931. A survey of movements, predominantly unofficial, for the promotion of world peace since the creation of the first "peace societies" in 1815. The book includes some useful chapters on nineteenth-and early twentieth-century ideas on the maintenance of peace.

Hemleben, S. J., *Plans for World Peace Through Six Centuries*. Chicago, 1943. A handy abstract of famous plans for the maintenance of peace since the late Middle Ages.

McDonald, L. C., *Western Political Theory in the Modern World*. New York, 1962. A useful survey of modern Western political ideas, including thinking on war and peace; the book deals with both secular trends and individual thinkers.

Meinecke, Friedrich, *Machiavellism: The Doctrine of Raison d'État and Its Place in Modern History*, translated by Douglas Scott. London, 1957. A translation of *Die Idee der Staatsräson in der neueren Geschichte* (1924), a treatise on the perennial conflict between the power impulse in human nature and the search for a higher ethical rule in political relations.

Stawell, F. M., *The Growth of International Thought*. London, 1929. A concise history of pacifism and internationalism.

Vagts, Alfred, *A History of Militarism*. New York, 1937. Mainly a study of the ideas and practices of the eighteenth- and nineteenth-century European social movements that sought to make military men the dominant power in the state.

F. S. NORTHEDGE

PEANO, GIUSEPPE (1858–1932), Italian mathematician and logician, was a professor of mathematics at the University of Turin from 1890 to 1932 and also taught at the military academy in Turin from 1886 to 1901. In 1891 he founded the *Rivista di matematica*, which was later also published in French (*Revue de mathématique*) and in Interlingua (an international language developed from Latino sine flexione, an auxiliary language based on Latin), which Peano propounded in 1903. In 1898 Peano acquired a small printing establishment in Turin, and he soon became an accomplished printer; his skill seems to have been of help to him in the process of simplifying logico-mathematical symbolism.

Peano's contributions to mathematics include the first statement of vector calculus (*Elementi di calcolo geometrico*, Turin, 1891) and the first example of integration by successive approximations within the theory of ordinary differential equations; with the single hypothesis that the data were continuous he proved the existence of the integrals of such equations. He submitted to rigorous criticism the foundations of arithmetic, of projective geometry, and of the general theory of sets. Peano's postulates (1899) were a set of five postulates for the arithmetic of natural numbers that allowed arithmetic to be constructed as a hypothetical–deductive system. In 1882 Peano first arrived at the principle that rigorous language can be separated from ordinary language both within and without mathematics. As Bertrand Russell wrote, Peano's method "extended the region of mathematical precision backwards towards regions which had been given over to philosophical disagreement" ("My Mental Development," in *The Philosophy of Bertrand Russell*, Paul A. Schilpp, ed., Evanston, Ill., 1951, p. 11).

In 1890 Peano introduced the symbols ι and $\bar{\iota}$ to distinguish a one-member class from its member, which permitted him to overcome previous confusion between ϵ ("being a member of"), $\supset$ ("contained in"), and = ("equal to"). In general, Peano showed the importance of distinguishing the properties of a class from those of the individuals of that class, a need shown, for example, by his "sophism" (actually, a paralogism): "Peter and Paul are apostles; the apostles are twelve; therefore Peter and Paul are twelve."

Peano's work in mathematical logic is to be found in his "Formulario completo," which includes, among other items, the well-known *Formulaire de mathématiques*, a compendium of mathematics derived from a set of postulates by means of a new notation. The "Formulario," in its encyclopedic, high-level approach, anticipated the thorough expositions of Bourbakism. In using a notation at least as rigorous as those of C. S. Peirce and Gottlob Frege, and more comprehensive and expedient than theirs, Peano's work marked a transition from the old algebra of logic to contemporary methods. His notation is still partially in use, mainly through its adoption by Russell and A. N. Whitehead in *Principia Mathematica*.

After 1913 Peano ceased to follow developments in symbolic logic. He regarded as artificial Russell's interpretation of numbers as classes of classes. Peano made several hints concerning the need for analyzing the relation of formal language to ordinary language, but he was not himself interested in undertaking such analysis. A philosophical interpretation of some of Peano's techniques is to be found in the work of his pupil Giovanni Vailati, who pointed out the general importance of Peano's discoveries concerning recursiveness, implicit definitions, and the theory of postulates. The "Formulario completo," however, still offers suggestions for research.

Works by Peano

Opere scelte, 3 vols., Ugo Cassina, ed. Rome, 1957–1959. Includes much of what is referred to as the "Formulario completo": the 5 vols. below plus minor publications of 1888–1913.

Formulaire de mathématiques, Vol. I, Turin, 1895; Vol. II, in 3 parts, Turin, 1897–1899; Vol. III, Paris, 1901.

Formulaire mathématique, Vol. IV. Turin, 1903.

Formulario mathematico, Vol. V. Turin, 1905–1908. In Latino sine flexione.

Works on Peano

Cassina, Ugo, "Vita et opera de Giuseppe Peano." *Schola et Vita*, Vol. 7, No. 3 (1932), 117–148. In Interlingua.

Cassina, Ugo, "L'Oeuvre philosophique de Giuseppe Peano." *Revue de métaphysique et de morale*, Vol. 40, No. 4 (1933), 481–491.

Couturat, Louis, "La Logique mathématique de M. Peano."

Revue de métaphysique et de morale, Vol. 7, No. 4 (1899), 616–646.

Jourdain, P. E. B., "Giuseppe Peano." *The Quarterly Journal of Pure and Applied Mathematics*, Vol. 43 (1912), 270–314.

Russell, Bertrand, *The Principles of Mathematics*. London, 1903.

Stamm, E., "Józef Peano." *Wiadomości Matematyczne*, Vol. 36 (1933), 1–56.

Terracini, Alessandro, ed., *In memoria di Giuseppe Peano*. Cuneo, 1955. Essays by various authors.

FERRUCCIO ROSSI-LANDI

PEARSON, KARL (1857–1936), British scientist and philosopher of science, was born in London. He studied mathematics at King's College, Cambridge, where he became acquainted with James Clerk Maxwell, Sir George Stokes, and Isaac Todhunter and developed an interest in history, religion, and philosophy. He became a fellow of his college in 1880 and also studied law at Heidelberg and Berlin. Although he was called to the bar in 1881, he never practiced law. In 1884, at the age of 27, he was appointed to the chair of applied mathematics and mechanics at University College, London, a post which he held until 1911. For part of this time he also held a lectureship in geometry at Gresham College, London, where he developed his ideas in the philosophy of science for a popular audience. Through his friend Francis Galton he became interested in statistical problems in the biological sciences, helped to lay the foundations of modern statistical theory and biometry, and, in 1901, with Galton and Weldon, founded the journal *Biometrika*. In 1896 he was elected a fellow of the Royal Society and in 1911 was appointed to the new chair of eugenics at University College. Pearson was an enthusiastic socialist and humanist. He retired in 1933 and died three years later.

Pearson published many scientific papers, as well as essays on most of the subjects in which he was interested. His philosophical work is contained mainly in *The Grammar of Science* (1892) and *The Ethic of Freethought* (1888), a collection of essays and lectures. He is usually regarded as an important early figure in modern positivism, but his contribution in this field has perhaps been overrated. Much of his work derives from that of Ernst Mach.

He accepted and developed Mach's sensationalist, antimetaphysical standpoint, but he was not afraid to talk with approval of "a sound idealism" replacing "the crude materialism" of earlier physics. His concern was to emphasize the social background of science and to urge that good citizenship demanded the application of the scientific habit of mind to everyday living. He appears to have regarded this as a large part of the justification of scientific activity, but he also held that science "justifies itself in its methods." Like Mach he dwelt on "the unity of science," which depends upon its method rather than upon its material. This method, based as it is upon verification, rules out metaphysics. The metaphysician is a poet, who does no harm so long as he is recognized as such, but he is often taken to be something more. According to Pearson, an acceptable moral theory is more likely to develop from the experiments of the biologist than from the speculations of the philosopher.

He saw scientific laws as brief formulas representing complex relationships between many phenomena. Their "discovery" is the work of a creative but disciplined imagination; they are products of the human mind. Following Lloyd Morgan, he said that an external object is a construct; that is, "a combination of immediate with past or stored sense-impressions." He asserted, mysteriously and unsatisfactorily, that the distinction between real objects and imaginary ones is that only the real objects depend upon immediate sense impressions.

A fundamental distinction in his work is that between perception, the "physical association" of stored sense impressions, and conception, their "mental association." This appears to mean that perception is merely the copresentation of impressions, while conception is the "recognition" of relations. But the physical and the psychical differ only in degree, not in kind, because both physics and psychology deal with relations between sense impressions, although from different standpoints. On the whole, human brains work in the same way, and thus one receives the same sense impressions and forms the same constructs as another. This ensures the universal validity of science. The field of study of the various sciences is, in fact, immediate sense impressions; these are the phenomena which scientific laws relate, so that "the field of science is much more consciousness than an external world." The consciousness of others is established by an argument from analogy.

We tend to project our sense impressions and to regard them as existing externally to and independently of ourselves, but this is a mistake. The distinction between external and internal is arbitrary and no more than a practical convenience. It is based on distinguishing between classes of sense impressions, not between sense impressions and something else. We cannot assert the existence of causes of sense impressions, but Pearson wanted to leave open the possibility of such existents. He therefore used the term "sensation" in an unusual way: Sensation is "that of which the only knowable side is sense-impression." This is intended to express agnosticism about the causation of sense impressions while allowing him to say, "The outer world is for science a world of sensations, and sensation is known to us only as sense-impression."

Some scientific concepts are not of immediate sense impressions; for instance, atom and molecule. There are just two possibilities: Scientists may regard the atom as real and thus capable of being a direct sense impression, or as ideal and thus merely a "mental conception assisting them in formulating laws." In contrast, a metaphysical conception is of what is both real and independent of sense perception.

Pearson concluded that science is not explanatory but merely descriptive. For instance, Newton's law of gravitation is a description in the simplest possible terms of a wide range of phenomena; that is, of the "routine" of our perceptions. To talk of it as ruling nature is to confuse other senses of "law" with the scientific sense. Causal statements are records of regular sequences in past experience and cannot assert any necessity in them. Using Humean arguments, Pearson held that forces, because they are not discoverable in sense experience, cannot be regarded as causes. "Force" is but a name hiding our ignorance of the explanation of motion. The idea of necessity is appropriate only to relations between conceptions, not to relations between perceptions. Prediction and knowledge are possible only because we find repetition in our sense impressions. Even so, our knowledge is only probable and should, strictly speaking, be called "belief."

The whole of science involves the distinction between the perceptual and the conceptual. Scientific concepts generally are ideal limits of concepts originating in perception. This is especially obvious in the mathematical treatment of the world. Empirical space and time are "modes of perception." Space is "a mental expression for the fact that the perceptive faculty has separated coexisting sense impressions into groups of associated impressions"; time indicates "the progression of perceptions at a position in space." Neither space nor time is infinite or infinitely divisible, since each must be limited by our powers of perception and discrimination. Conceptual space and time, and the space and time of mathematics, are idealizations of their empirical counterparts and do not suffer from their limitations.

The aim of science is to construct conceptual models of the universe, devices to assist us in describing the correlation and sequence of phenomena. The failure to recognize this has led scientists to accept definitions of force, mass, atom, and—in the biological sciences—life which are riddled with metaphysical obscurities. Much of Pearson's philosophical writing consists in the empiricist elucidation of these fundamental concepts, in an attempt to remove these obscurities.

Bibliography

Pearson's main philosophical work is *The Grammar of Science* (London, 1892). The second edition (1900) contained two new chapters. The third (1911) contained only the first eight chapters (physical sciences) of the first two editions but had a new chapter on causation and a new final chapter on modern physical ideas, written largely by E. Cunningham. The Everyman edition (London, 1937) contains a more detailed account of the various editions.

Other works by Pearson are *The Ethic of Freethought, a Selection of Essays and Lectures* (London, 1888 and 1901); *The Chances of Death and Other Studies in Evolution* (London, 1897), a volume of essays and lectures; *National Life From the Standpoint of Science* (London, 1901); and *The Life, Letters and Labours of Francis Galton*, 3 vols. (Cambridge, 1914–1930).

Pearson edited and completed Isaac Todhunter, *A History of the Theory of Elasticity and of the Strength of Materials from Galilei to the Present Time*, 2 vols. (London, 1886–1893), and W. K. Clifford, *Common Sense of the Exact Sciences* (London, 1885), for which he wrote the chapter "Position" and much of "Quantity" and "Motion."

Works on Pearson include V. I. Lenin, *Materialism and Empirio-Criticism*, translated by A. Finchberg (Moscow, 1937); G. M. Morant, *A Bibliography of the Statistical and Other Writings of Karl Pearson* (London, 1939); E. S. Pearson, "Karl Pearson, an Appreciation of Some Aspects of His Life and Work," in *Biometrika*, Vol. 27 (1936), 193–257, and Vol. 29 (1937), 161–248; C. S. Peirce, *Collected Papers* (Cambridge, Mass., 1931——), *passim*, but especially Vol. VIII, which contains a long review of *The Grammar of Science*; and G. U. Yule and L. N. G. Filon, "Karl Pearson," in *Obituary Notices of Fellows of the Royal Society*, Vol. II (London, 1936–1938), pp. 73–110.

For reviews of *The Grammar of Science*, see those by C. G. K. (probably C. G. Knott) in *Nature*, Vol. 46 (1892), 97–99, with replies by Pearson on pp. 199 and 247; by F. A. D. (of 2d ed.) in *Nature*, Vol. 62 (1900), 49–50; by E. A. Singer, Jr. (of 2d ed.) in *Philosophical Review*, Vol. 9 (1900), 448–450; and an unsigned review in *Mind*, N.S. Vol. 1 (1892), 429–430.

There are numerous casual references to Pearson's views in books on the philosophy of science but few detailed discussions.

PETER ALEXANDER

PECKHAM, JOHN (c. 1225–1292), or Pecham, English philosopher and theologian, defender of Augustinian doctrines, was born in Patcham, near Brighton, Sussex. Educated at the monastery at Lewes, he continued his studies at Oxford and Paris, and sometime during the 1250s he joined the Franciscan friars at Oxford. Subsequently he became a master of theology in Paris in 1269 and returned to Oxford in 1272. Peckham was provincial of the English Franciscans from 1275 to 1277 and then lectured at the papal court for two years. In 1279 he was appointed archbishop of Canterbury and held this office until his death.

Peckham's philosophical career represents a concentrated effort to counteract the growing allegiance to Aristotle through a return to the thought of Augustine. There seems little doubt that he was motivated to take this stand by the Lenten sermons of St. Bonaventure, who in the late 1260s had alerted his friars to the growth of heterodox Aristotelianism—which was apparent, for example, in the work of Siger of Brabant. Peckham did not reject all philosophy that stemmed from Greek and Arabic sources—as a matter of fact, he systematically used Aristotelian terminology—but his approach was a highly selective use of non-Christian philosophers to the extent that their works could be made to harmonize with the thought of Augustine. Among the disciples of Peckham who perpetuated this attitude were Matthew of Acquasparta, Roger Marston, and, later, Vital du Four.

Peckham's theory of knowledge shows the persistence of a special type of apriorism in the Franciscan school of this period. Clues to this apriorism are to be found in the *Summa* of Alexander of Hales, which taught that the human intellect is incapable of a satisfactory a posteriori analysis of the first principles or of the most basic "perceptibles," such as time and space. Similarly, Augustine said: "If we both see that which you say to be true, and both see that which I say to be true, where, I ask you, do we see it? Neither I in you, nor you in me, but both in the unchangeable Truth itself, which is above our minds" (*Confessions* XII.24). Peckham concludes that more is required for the operation of the intellect than mere sensation that "contacts" accidents but does not reach the essence of things. Even granting the intellect's power of abstracting essences, Peckham says that the mind does this either knowingly or unknowingly. If knowingly, then the mind knows before abstracting, and hence it is useless to abstract. If unknowingly, then the mind is at the mercy of chance and can hardly be called an intellect at all. Consequently, the intellect is not a passive Aristotelian *tabula rasa*, but a beam moving outward and casting its light on things. However, this explanation is not sufficient because in matters of intellectual knowledge, certitude, and evidence, man must be assisted by a divine illumination—a divine active intellect—in addition to his own human active intellect. This assistance by divine illumination is not a direct vision of God or an infusion of ideas. Rather, it is an assistance over and above that given by God as the conserving cause of all that exists. Its purpose is to guarantee necessity and certitude (considered irrevocably unobtainable through sensation) for our knowledge.

In the realm of natural theology, there was one key axiom that pervaded Franciscan philosophical circles in Peckham's time—that creatures are entirely dependent upon the First Cause with regard both to the fact of existing and to their ability to act. From this it follows that whatever causal powers a creature may possess are ontologically delegated to it by the First Cause. The important corollary of this principle is that the First Cause can bypass the agency of the creature and intervene to produce the effect immediately. Peckham invokes this principle to some extent in the illumination theory of knowledge. He also uses it to defend the autonomous existibility of prime matter without any form against the contrary opinion of Aquinas.

Peckham also took rather strong exception to Aquinas' opinion that no single thing ever has more than one form. All medieval philosophers were agreed that the First Cause was pure form and that prime matter was completely formless. Against Aquinas, Peckham and his confreres held that in each thing there are many forms, or at least many grades of one form. The dispute soon fossilized into two schools—the Dominicans and the Franciscans—and as often as not their arguments generated more heat than light. In any case, Peckham held that in man there are several forms—vegetative, sensitive, and rational—in a gradated order that cooperates toward the good and unity of the being as a whole.

John Peckham's career represents a sincere effort to perpetuate and to update the doctrines of Augustine. He suffered much distress as archbishop of Canterbury when, as a stubborn defender of Augustine, he incurred the wrath of the equally stubborn Dominican defenders of Aquinas.

Many of the points that were merely hinted at in Peckham's philosophy were taken up by his disciples and elaborated in full-length treatises. A final judgment of this English Franciscan must await the publication of many of his works that are still in manuscript.

Works by Peckham

Quaestiones Tractantes de Anima, Hieronymus Spettmann, ed., in Vol. XIX of *Beiträge zur Geschichte der Philosophie des Mittelalters*. Münster, 1918.

Summa de Esse et Essentia, Ferdinand Delorme, ed. *Studi francescani*, Vol. 14 (1928), 1–18.

Quodlibet Romanum, Ferdinand Delorme, ed. Rome, 1938.

Tractatus de Anima, Gaudentius Melani, ed. Biblioteca di studi francescani. Florence, 1949.

Works on Peckham

Callebaut, André, "Jean Peckham O.F.M. et l'augustinisme." *Archivum Franciscanum Historicum*, Vol. 18 (1925), 441–472.

Crowley, Theodore, "John Peckham O.F.M., Archbishop of Canterbury, Versus the New Aristotelianism." *Bulletin of the John Rylands Library*, Vol. 33 (1951), 242–255.

Douie, Decima L., *Archbishop Pecham*. Oxford, 1952. Includes a good bibliography.

Ehrle, Franz, "J. Peckham über den Kampf des Augustinismus und Aristotelismus in der zweiten Hälfte des 13 Jahrhunderts." *Zeitschrift für katholosche Theologie*, Vol. 13 (1889), 172–193.

Spettmann, Hieronymus, "Die Psychologie des Johannes Pecham," in Vol. XX of *Beiträge zur Geschichte der Philosophie des Mittelalters*. Münster, 1919. Pp. 1–102.

FERDINAND ETZKORN, O.F.M.

PEIRCE, CHARLES SANDERS (1839–1914), American philosopher, physicist, and mathematician and the founder of pragmatism, was born in Cambridge, Massachusetts. His father, Benjamin Peirce, was the leading American mathematician of the time and Perkins professor of mathematics and astronomy at Harvard. Young Charles was born and bred a scientist, and from his earliest years he showed great promise in mathematics and the physical sciences. He attended Harvard, graduated in 1859, and subsequently studied at the Lawrence Scientific School, from which he received his degree in chemistry *summa cum laude* in 1863. During the next 15 years, Peirce simultaneously pursued several distinct careers. He worked as an astronomer at the Harvard Observatory, where he did pioneer work in photometric research. He also worked as a physicist for the United States Coast and Geodetic Survey, of which his father was superintendent, and achieved some distinction for his discovery of hitherto undetected errors in pendulum experiments used to determine the force of gravity. And he worked, more or less privately, at philosophy and logic, steadily publishing works on these subjects from 1866 on. By 1879 he had achieved sufficient stature in these last two fields to be appointed lecturer in logic at the newly organized Johns Hopkins University in Baltimore, Maryland. He remained at Johns Hopkins from 1879 until 1884, meanwhile continuing to work for the Coast and Geodetic Survey—a connection which he sustained until 1891. In 1887, after having inherited some money, he retired to Milford, Pennsylvania, where he lived in relative isolation until his death. Peirce was twice married—in 1862 to Harriet Melusina Fay, whom he divorced in 1883, and in 1883 to Juliette Froissy, who survived him. He had no children.

Philosophical orientation. Peirce was a systematic philosopher of great breadth, and his writings cover almost all fields of philosophy. His greatest contributions were in the field of logic, but he wrote extensively on epistemology, scientific method, semiotics, metaphysics, cosmology, ontology, and mathematics, and less extensively on ethics, aesthetics, history, phenomenology, and religion. Since Peirce's views underwent considerable change as he grew older, it is not possible to speak of his philosophy as a single system: rather, he formulated several systems, each of which represents a different phase in his development. These different systems, however, deal with the same problems and embody the same fundamental concept of philosophy.

Peirce came to philosophy as a student of Kant, from whom he had acquired the architectonic theory of philosophy. In brief, this theory holds that the domain of knowledge can be so characterized that general assertions can be proven true of all possible knowledge; the theory also holds that it is the dependence of all knowledge upon logic that makes such a characterization possible. Accordingly, the doctrine holds that it is possible to derive from logic the fundamental categories and principles which form the basis of all that can ever be known. In formulating this theory, Kant assumed that logic was a completed, unchanging science. But Peirce was one of that group of men, including George Boole, Augustus De Morgan, Gottlob Frege, and others, who revolutionized logic and prepared the way for Whitehead and Russell's *Principia Mathematica*. Hence, for Peirce, logic was a growing, changing subject, and as it changed, so, according to the architectonic theory, Peirce's philosophy had to change with it. Thus the major shifts in Peirce's system are correlated with his major discoveries in logic and reflect the modifications that he thought those discoveries entailed. In the following exposition, Peirce's work will therefore be dealt with chronologically, and each system will be treated in order.

THE FIRST SYSTEM, 1859–1861

Pierce's first system is a form of extreme post-Kantian idealism. The sources of this idealism are not known: whether he evolved it himself or derived it from some other source, such as Emersonian transcendentalism, cannot now be determined. What is clear is that by 1857 he was seeking to combine the Transcendental Analytic with Platonic idealism.

Categories. From Kant's doctrine of the Transcendental Sciences, Peirce derived a threefold ontological classification of all there is into matter (the object of cosmology), mind (the object of psychology), and God (the object of theology). Peirce referred to these three categories as the It (the sense world), the Thou (the mental world), and the I (the abstract world), respectively; and it was from these pronouns that he subsequently derived the names Firstness, Secondness, and Thirdness, by which he usually called his categories.

Having divided all there is into these three categories, Peirce's problem was then to define the relations among them. Specifically, the problem of knowledge as it appears in the first system is how the ideas in the mind of God can be known by human minds. Peirce thought he had found the solution to this problem in the Kantian principle that all phenomena and all concepts—all that can be before the mind—are representations, for he understood this to imply that the ideas in the mind of God, which Peirce conceived as Platonic archetypes, are first given a material embodiment in the form of the objects of our experience and are then derived by us from those objects by abstraction. So Peirce took the Transcendental Analytic to be a description of this process: the synthesis in intuition is the synthesis of the divine idea (already present in an unconscious form within the soul) with "the matter of sensation" to form the empirical object which is also, by virtue of the divine idea, the transcendental object; and the concept is derived by abstraction from the object given in intuition. But when it came to explaining just how the Kantian categories served to effect so un-Kantian a synthesis as that demanded by his own semiotic idealism, Peirce found himself in grave difficulties, and after struggling with the problem for some time he was forced to conclude that the Kantian table of categories was simply inadequate.

TRANSITIONAL PERIOD: STUDY OF LOGIC

According to the architectonic principle, the inadequacy of the table of categories implies the inadequacy of Kant's logical classification of propositions. In 1862, therefore, Peirce began the serious study of logic, and he naturally turned to the Scholastics for instruction. Although he began his study in the belief that the fundamental problem was the classification of propositions, he soon learned from Duns Scotus that the classification of arguments, or forms of inference, was more fundamental, since the significance of propositions depends upon the role they play in inference. He was therefore led to investigate the irreducible forms of inference, and so to study Kant's famous paper "The Mistaken Subtlety of the Four Syllogistic Figures," in which Kant argued that all inference is reducible to Barbara or to a combination of Barbara and immediate inference. In the "Memoranda Concerning the Aristotelian Syllogism," which he published in 1866, Peirce showed that Kant's argument is invalid, for the syllogism by which the reduction of the second and third figures is made is itself in the figure from which the reduction is being made. Peirce therefore concluded that the first three figures are irreducible. Moreover, Peirce noted that if the first figure is defined as the deduction of a conclusion from a major and a minor premise, then the second figure can be described as the inference of the major from the minor and conclusion and the third figure as the inference of the minor from the major and conclusion. Accordingly, Peirce held that the first figure is purely deductive, the second figure inductive, and the third figure hypothetical.

For Peirce this discovery had great importance. His previous belief in the existence of synthetic a priori propositions had rested on the two doctrines, derived from Kant, that all thought involves inference and that all inference is in Barbara. Granting these doctrines, it is clear that the major premises must be innate in the mind. But with the discovery of the role of hypothesis and induction, all synthetic propositions can be regarded as inferred, and so the problem shifts to the process of synthetic inference and to scientific inquiry.

At about the same time that he discovered the irreducibility of the three figures, Peirce made another important discovery in logic—namely, that the copula can be interpreted as the sign relation. This view, which was probably derived from the scholastic theory of supposition, enabled him to regard all propositions as instances of a single fundamental relation, and the analysis was quickly extended to inferences also by treating the conclusion as a sign that is determined by the premises to represent the same state of affairs which they themselves represented. Such a result was thoroughly in line with Peirce's early semiotic idealism, and it meant that the fundamental logical relation from which the categories must be derived is signhood.

THE SECOND SYSTEM, 1866–1870

In 1867 Peirce published a paper entitled "On a New List of Categories," in which he attempted to solve the problem of relating his three ontological categories of mind, matter, and God.

The sign relation. Starting from Kant's position that knowledge occurs only when the manifold is reduced to the unity of a proposition, Peirce asked what that unity consisted in. Since he conceived the proposition in subject–predicate form, this is equivalent to asking how the predicate is applied to the subject. On the basis of the reduction of the copula to signhood, Peirce argued that the predicate is applied to the subject by being made to stand for the same object for which the subject stands. Thus a proposition would be impossible without reference to some object. But how does the predicate come to stand for this object? Only, Peirce held, by being interpreted as standing for it by some interpreting representation, or mind, so that no proposition is possible unless such an interpretant also exists. And how does the mind make this interpretation? Only, Peirce held, by the sign's representing its object in some respect, that is, by referring to some attribute of the object. Hence, propositions would be impossible if there were no pure abstract attributes embodied in the object to form the basis of comparison among them. So his argument, in essence, was that all synthesis involves the sign relation, that the sign relation consists in a sign standing for something to someone in some respect, and therefore that unless there are things, minds, and abstractions, there is no knowledge. But since the pure abstract attribute is the Platonic Form in the mind of God, what Peirce was really arguing is that without his three ontological categories signhood would be impossible.

Aspects of reference. In the "New List," Peirce did not present his categories directly as ontological classes; rather, he began with the problem of unifying the manifold by joining the predicate to the subject through the sign relation and then analyzed signhood into the three aspects of reference: reference to abstraction, reference to an object, and reference to an interpretant. These three aspects are then made the basis for a systematic classification of signs according to the prominence given to each reference, and this mode of classification is applied to terms, propositions, and arguments. In the case of arguments, Peirce rederived the division into hypothesis, induction, and deduction, thus presenting the three forms of syllogistic as consequences of his analysis of signs.

Logic, however, is not the only science of signs; indeed, it is but one of three, each of which studies a particular aspect of the subject. The first is speculative grammar, which studies the relation of signs to the abstraction; the second is logic, which investigates the relation of signs to their objects; and the third is speculative rhetoric, which investigates the reference of signs to their interpretants. Peirce could therefore derive his three ontological categories by abstraction from the three references of signs, but he had to show further how we can know the objects referred to and whether or not they are real. For these purposes he needed a theory of cognition and a theory of reality.

Cognition. Peirce stated his new theories of cognition and reality in three articles published in 1868 in the *Journal of Speculative Philosophy*. These papers simply develop the implications of the "New List." Since the reference of a sign to its object is established by its being predicated of another sign which already refers to that object, and since the predication exists only because there is an interpreting sign which so interprets it, it is clear that the series of signs is doubly infinite. Peirce accepted this conclusion and asserted that there is neither a first nor a last cognition. While this doctrine appears bizarre, it has a clear purpose. What Peirce was trying to avoid was the classic dilemma of the empiricist who, having tracked cognition back to an original impression of sense, finds himself completely unable to prove the accuracy of that first impression.

Peirce held that if we examine what actually occurs in cognition, we find the process to be something like the following. In the flood of sensory stimuli that pours in upon us, we detect certain relations which lead us to segregate some stimuli and to interpret these as having a common referent. We do not know what the first such stimulus having that referent may have been, and the question is meaningless, since it is only after many stimuli have occurred that we note their relations. As experience progresses and we acquire more relevant stimuli, we further conceptualize this referent, and in time we acquire a progressively more and more complete and precise idea of it. But our knowledge is never fully complete, so that this process of learning and inquiry is endless. It is true that once we have a relatively detailed concept of the referent, we assume that the object antedated our experience of it and in fact caused that experience; epistemologically, however, it is the experience which comes first and the notion of the object which comes later. The object, then, is a hypothesis designed to give coherence to our experience, and this hypothesis is derived by hypothetical and inductive reasoning; hence, the process of cognition can be fully described by the three forms of inference. Moreover, it follows that the object must be as we conceive it, since it is only as we conceive it that it is postulated at all, and therefore there can be no such thing as an incognizable cause of cognition, for the postulate that an object exists is warranted only by the coherence it gives to experience. Accordingly, whatever is, is cognizable.

Reality. The above theory of cognition leads at once to a theory of reality. The object is real, Peirce held, only if as the number of cognitions goes to infinity, the concept of the object tends to a limiting form. It follows, therefore, that although the object is not independent of being thought (since it is only as it is thought that it exists at all), it is nevertheless independent of the thought of any particular man and represents what would be agreed upon by an ideal community of investigators if inquiry were to go on forever.

Many empiricists would agree with Peirce that if the object is real, then if inquiry does go on forever, our hypotheses will converge to a final true description. But few would follow him in holding that the object is real because inquiry converges. What Peirce was attempting to do in this instance was to propound a doctrine which was at once phenomenalistic and realistic. To do this, he had to give a phenomenal definition of reality which would compromise neither the inexhaustibility of the real nor the particularity of the phenomenal, and the infinite series of cognitions seemed to do just that. But could Peirce prove that the infinite series is convergent? In 1868 he thought he could do this by means of an argument which purported to show that the concept of a universe in which induction and hypothesis would not lead to agreement was self-contradictory. When he subsequently discovered that this argument was fallacious, his theory of reality had to be substantially revised.

Universals. Peirce's theory that reality consists in the convergence of inquiry led to a further consequence. For it follows that the real object must be as we conceive it to be, and since, as the "New List" showed, the predicate of a judgment is always general, it further follows that universals are real. On this basis Peirce declared himself a scholastic realist of the moderate, or Scotist, school. The claim is misleading, for whereas the scholastic doctrine rests on the assertion that the universal in the mind and the individual out of the mind have a common nature, Peirce's argument rests on the fact that no cognition is wholly determinate—that is, that there is no true individual, and that therefore everything is to some degree general. Peirce's "realism" was thoroughly idealistic throughout.

THE THIRD SYSTEM, 1870–1884

By 1870 Peirce had propounded, in outline at least, an architectonic philosophy based upon the principles that all cognition involves the sign relation; that the sign relation involves three classes of referents; and that these referents are real and can be adequately known by scientific inquiry. But this theory depended upon logical doctrines that Peirce was forced to abandon when he discovered the logic of relations.

The logic of relations. The first work on the new logic had been done by Augustus De Morgan, but little progress was made with the subject until Peirce entered the field in 1870. It was in this area that Peirce made his greatest contributions to logic, and it is no exaggeration to say that it was he who created the modern logic of relations. Philosophically these new discoveries in logic had important consequences, for the logic of relations forced Peirce to abandon the subject–predicate theory of the proposition which underlies the "New List," and so required that he overhaul his basic position. Probably the most notable revisions directly attributable to the new logic are the doctrines of pragmatism and the doubt–belief theory of inquiry.

The doubt–belief theory of inquiry. Peirce formulated the doubt–belief theory in 1873, but it was first published in a series of six papers in *Popular Science Monthly* in 1877 and 1878. These papers do not constitute a rejection of the earlier theory of cognition; rather, they elaborate the earlier theory and set it in the context of biological evolution.

Any organism that is to survive, Peirce held, must develop habits of behavior that are adequate to satisfy its needs. Such habits are rules of behavior that prescribe how we should act under given conditions in order to achieve a particular experiential result. Now such habits, when thoroughly adopted, Peirce called beliefs. Since to possess beliefs is to know how to satisfy one's wants, belief is a

pleasant state: doubt, or the absence of belief, is an unpleasant state, since one is then uncertain how to act and is unable to attain the desired goals. The organism will therefore seek to escape from doubt and to find belief. The process by which the organism goes from doubt to belief Peirce defined as inquiry. Clearly, there are various methods of inquiry, and the most satisfactory method will be that which leads most surely to the establishment of stable belief—that is, to beliefs that will stand in the long run.

Pragmatism. From the standpoint of the inquiring organism, a belief concerning a particular object is significant because it permits the organism to predict what experiences it will have if it acts toward the object in a given way. Recalling Kant's use of the term "pragmatic," namely, ". . . contingent belief, which yet forms the ground for the actual employment of means to certain actions, I entitle *pragmatic belief*" (*Critique of Pure Reason*, A 824, B 852), Peirce propounded what he called the pragmatic theory of meaning, which asserts that what the concept of an object means is simply the set of all habits involving that object. This doctrine involves a major change in Peirce's thinking, and one which is directly due to the logic of relations.

Prior to 1870, Peirce conceived the meaning of a term as the embodied abstraction that it connotes. The meaning of the concept of an object is therefore the same abstraction that is the essence of the object. But once relations were admitted as propositional constituents coordinate with quality, it became possible to conceive the object not only in terms of indwelling qualities but also in terms of relations among its states and with other objects—that is, in terms of its behavior. Accordingly, instead of regarding the behavior of the object as determined by its qualitative essence, the behavior itself may now be regarded as the essence. The meaning of the concept of an object may therefore be given by the set of laws completely specifying the behavior of the object under all conditions. These laws are conditional statements relating test conditions to phenomenal results, and such laws, considered as governing behavior, are habits relating action to experiential effects. Hence, the principle of pragmatism asserts that the concept of the object is synonymous with the set of all such conditionals. Since actual synonymy is asserted, it follows that the concept of a real object can be completely translated into phenomenal terms, but only, it should be noted, into dispositionally phenomenal terms—a point which was to cause Peirce considerable trouble.

Pragmatism: a theory of meaning. Pragmatism is Peirce's most famous philosophical doctrine, although it was made famous by William James rather than by Peirce. As Peirce defined it, pragmatism is purely a theory of meaning—not of truth. Moreover, it is a theory of meaning which combines two rather distinct emphases. First, Peirce intended pragmatism to be a principle of scientific definition. By permitting the translation of a concept into phenomenal results that are observable under stated test conditions, the principle legitimizes the use of theoretical constructs in science and thus does much to clarify the nature and status of scientific theory and proof. But when Peirce chose to call the doctrine pragmatism and insisted that the concept must be translatable into "practical effects," the choice of Kantian terminology was not accidental. Peirce was also stressing the utilitarian aspect of science and of all knowledge—that is, the fact that significance lies in the relation to ends desired. Peirce drew no distinction between these two aspects of pragmatism: for him they formed a single doctrine.

Scientific method. Taken together, pragmatism and the doubt–belief theory imply that the stable beliefs sought by inquiry are in fact the laws of science. The problem of finding the best method of inquiry therefore becomes that of the justification of scientific method, which in Peirce's terms means the justification of induction and hypothesis. Although Peirce formally presented this justification in terms of the operating characteristics of the procedures, he admitted that the relative frequency with which inductive and hypothetical inferences lead to the truth cannot be calculated; hence, our assurance that synthetic inference does ultimately lead to truth comes from the fact that inquiry will converge to a limiting result which is true by definition. Thus, in this instance Peirce admitted that the convergence of inquiry to a final opinion cannot be proven but must be assumed, and since his definition of reality rests upon the convergence of inquiry, this is equivalent to saying that the existence of the real is unprovable and must be assumed. But even as an assumption the doctrine presents problems, for it amounts to saying that if inquiry were to go on forever it would converge, and thus involves fundamental questions concerning counterfactuals.

Counterfactuals. The problem of counterfactuals is central to Peirce's philosophy, and his failure to solve it was one of the chief reasons that his system of the 1870s had to be rejected. Pragmatism requires that the concept of a real object be wholly translatable into a set of conditionals relating test conditions to observations. But then it would seem that the concept of the real object is devoid of content: that is, if the concept of the real object is synonymous with the set of conditionals, each of which is purely phenomenal, then the assertion of reality adds nothing to which a nominalist might object. Peirce, however, did not regard the concept of reality as vacuous; he argued that the conditionals are asserted to be true always, whether actually under test or not. The real, therefore, is a permanent possibility of sensation—not merely a series of sensations. But this leads directly to the counterfactual problem, or the equivalent problem of real possibility. Peirce's theory requires that there be real possible sensations—an assertion that is not only unprovable but pragmatically meaningless, since possible sensations are pragmatically equivalent to actual sensations. Thus, far from proving phenomenalism realistic, Peirce found his position reduced to a subjectivism which was the exact antithesis of the scholastic realism he had hoped to establish.

THE FOURTH SYSTEM, 1885–1914

During the years he spent at Johns Hopkins, Peirce was extremely productive in the field of logic. He further developed and extended the calculus of relations and applied it to problems in mathematics. He also clarified and revised his theory of synthetic inference, began the study of the Cantor set theory, and in 1885, with the help of his student, O. H. Mitchell, discovered quantification—a discovery in which Frege had anticipated him by six years. These new developments in logic, together with the rather serious difficulties in his own philosophical position which had become apparent by the end of the 1870s, led Peirce to attempt a radical reformulation of his position in 1885. This reformulation involved a complete revision of the categories, the theory of cognition, and the theory of reality.

The categories. In the 1885 version of the categories, Peirce distinguished sharply between their formal and material aspects. Formally considered, the categories (Firstness, Secondness, and Thirdness) are simply three classes of relations—monadic, dyadic, and triadic. Moreover, Peirce held that these classes are irreducible and that all higher relations (quartic, quintic, etc.) are reducible to some combination of these three. The irreducibility of monadic and dyadic relations is generally admitted. The irreducibility of triadic relations is argued on the ground that all combinatorial relations are triadic, since they involve a relation between two elements and a resulting whole. Granting this, it follows that triadic relations are irreducible, because analysis could only resolve them into components and a combinatorial relation, and that combinatorial relation would itself be triadic. But once the notions of element and combination are given, relations of more than three correlates are easily generated, and so all higher relations may be regarded as being constructed from the three basic types.

Among triadic relations Peirce distinguished pure and degenerate species. A pure triadic relation is one in which no two of the correlates would be related without the third. His example of such a relation is signhood, for the sign relates object and interpretant, the interpretant relates sign and object, and the object, by establishing the identity of the extensional domain, relates sign and interpretant. Since Peirce held that all thought is in the form of signs, it follows that all thought is irreducibly triadic, which is another way of stating the Kantian doctrine that all thought is synthetic.

Since a monadic relation is a one-place predicate, the material aspect of Firstness must be qualitative, and Peirce therefore called it quality; what he meant by this term in 1885, however, was not the embodied abstraction that he had described in 1867. Quality now refers not to a concept but to a phenomenal suchness which is the immediate, nonconceptual given of sensation. In the 1885 version, not the concept red, but that suchness of an object which leads us to classify it as red, is a quality.

Peirce called the material aspect of Secondness haecceity, a term derived from Scotus' *haecceitas,* meaning "thisness." As experienced, haecceity is known as shock or brute resistance: Peirce described it as an immediately given, nonconceptual experience of dyadic opposition or "upagainstness." The fact that the experience implies the dynamic interaction of two things, and is therefore dyadic in structure, permits it to qualify as the material aspect of Secondness. For Scotus, haecceity was the principle of individuation, and Peirce accepted this meaning: only individual things have haecceity. It was apparently the discovery of quantification theory which led Peirce to this formulation, for in the variable of quantification theory he found a sign capable of referring directly to an object without describing it, and "thisness" was intended as that property of the object by virtue of which such a reference can be made.

The material aspect of Thirdness is less clearly defined than that of the other two categories. Peirce described it as combination, or mediation, where the latter term signifies either connection or means–ends relations among things. Signhood may also be regarded as part of the material aspect of Thirdness, and so too may generality, since the general constitutes a connection among particulars. Clearly, what Peirce was describing in this instance has much less the character of the immediately given than is the case for the other two categories. The reason is that Peirce not only regarded all thought as triadic—he also regarded all pure triads as conceptual. The material aspect of Thirdness is therefore the experience of thought or rationality. One of Peirce's problems was to explain just how so immaterial a thing can be perceived.

Cognition. The revision of the categories raised some important problems in regard to cognition. Not only did Peirce have the problem of demonstrating how Thirdness can be perceived, but he also had the problem of explaining how quality and haecceity could be perceived. For in his earlier writings on cognition, Peirce had explicitly denied the existence of first impressions of sense of precisely the sort that he now introduced as the material aspects of his first two categories. Moreover, a further set of problems relating to cognition arose from the doubt–belief theory itself. For in that theory, logic, both deductive and synthetic, is treated as a method whereby an inquiring organism seeks belief. The status of logic, therefore, is that of a useful but contingent means to a sought end—contingent both upon our seeking this particular end, which is a characteristic of the present evolutionary state, and upon our choosing the most efficient of the several available means. Thus, in the doubt–belief theory, logic loses that necessary relation to all possible knowledge which is asserted by the architectonic theory and required to prove the universality of the categories.

Classification of knowledge. Throughout the 1890s Peirce labored at the problem of reconstructing the architectonic theory. Since the architectonic theory presupposes a classification of knowledge into two classes—logic, and all other knowledge—Peirce's problem was to develop this classification so as to ensure the universality of the categories, while at the same time not contradicting his theory of inquiry. The final system of classification was not attained until 1902. In that system, Peirce divided knowledge into practical (or applied) and theoretical sciences, and then further subdivided the theoretical sciences into sciences of discovery and sciences of review (the latter merely summarizing the findings of the sciences of discovery). The major portion of the classification thus deals with the sciences of discovery. The classification is by presupposition.

The first science is mathematics, which Peirce regarded as presupposed by all others. Mathematics is divided into three branches: mathematics of logic, mathematics of discrete series, and mathematics of continua. It is to the

mathematics of logic that Peirce assigned the threefold classification of relations which constitutes the formal aspect of the categories. Next after (and presupposing) mathematics comes philosophy, which Peirce divided into phenomenology, normative science, and metaphysics. Phenomenology, which here appeared in Peirce's writing for the first time, is defined as the study of all that can be before the mind, but in practice, it is devoted to proving that all phenomenal experience is resolvable into three factors, which are the material aspects of the three categories. Thus Peirce sought to show that his categories, in both their formal and material aspects, are presupposed by all other knowledge.

Normative science has three divisions: aesthetics, ethics, and logic. In this classification logic appears explicitly as the science of how we ought to reason in order to obtain our objectives—whatever they may be. Thus the contingent and utilitarian aspect of logic, first brought out by the doubt–belief theory, is here made central. But reasoning as we ought is only one aspect of acting as we ought, which is the proper subject of ethics: hence, logic presupposes the science of ethics, or the science of how conduct should be regulated to attain our ends. But what our conduct ought to be depends on our aims, and these Peirce held to be the subject of aesthetics, which is the science of what is desirable in and of itself. Hence Peirce subscribed to an aesthetic theory of goodness and made the good and the beautiful coincide.

Following and presupposing philosophy is idioscopy, which Peirce subdivided into the physical and psychical sciences. Each division is further subdivided to yield what we would ordinarily regard as the physical, biological, and social sciences. All domains of science thus fall within the classification, and so depend upon the categories. The classification thus serves the purpose of preserving the architectonic while ensuring the normative role of logic.

Perception. Peirce's determination to preserve both the universality and phenomenal observability of the categories as well as the normative character of logic is evident in the theory of percepts and perceptual judgments which he propounded at this time. According to Peirce, physiology and psychology tell us that our percepts are synthesized from the myriad neural stimuli which assail us from without. Of these neural stimuli themselves and of the process of synthesis we are entirely unaware; the earliest step in cognition of which we are at all conscious is the percept. But we cannot really be said to know the percept; what we know is a perceptual judgment, which is a proposition telling us what the nonlinguistic percept was. The perceptual judgment, such as "red patch here now," is a hypothesis that explains the percept, but it is a peculiar hypothesis, since it is immediate and indubitable. Even if the perceptual judgment is immediately followed by a contradictory perceptual judgment, still that second perceptual judgment relates to a later percept, and it remains indubitable that my first and now forever vanished percept was truly red. Perceptual judgments, therefore, form the real starting point in knowledge and must be taken as the ultimate evidence statements.

Peirce described the processes of synthesis which precede and lead to the perceptual judgment as unconscious inference. Their inferential character is defended, here as in his earlier writings, by an argument that identifies the psychological processes of association with the forms of inferences. But since these processes are unconscious, they are beyond our control and thus are not subject to logical criticism—for logical criticism, being normative, is applicable only to voluntary and controllable behavior. On the other hand, conscious inferences, such as the processes whereby we derive knowledge from the perceptual judgments, are thoroughly subject to logical criticism. Accordingly, Peirce could hold both that there is no first impression of sense and that the object (percept) is given to us by a synthesis in intuition. He could further hold that our knowledge has a definite starting point in propositions which give direct reports of phenomenal observation and that whatever is asserted in those judgments of perception must be accepted as given. Thus, in the theory of percepts and perceptual judgments, Peirce tried to reconcile his denial of first impressions with his doctrine of direct phenomenal contact with the world.

On the basis of this theory, Peirce held that the material aspects of all three categories are empirically observable. Quality and *haecceity* are argued to be directly observable aspects of the percept. But so, too, according to Peirce, is Thirdness, for what is asserted in the perceptual judgment is necessarily true, and the perceptual judgment, being a proposition, has a predicate which is general. Since the generality is given in the perceptual judgment, and since criticism cannot go behind the perceptual judgment, this generality must be regarded as given in perception, and hence as being observable. Thus, by phenomenological analysis, all the categories can be shown to be present in experience.

Reality. In the course of his study of the logic of relations, Peirce noted that the analysis of certain relations leads to an infinite regress. Thus the relation "in the relation R to" must itself be related to its subjects by the same relation, for example, "in the relation 'in the relation R to' to," and so on. Such relations, which can be analyzed only into relations of the same sort, Peirce called continuous relations, since they fit the definition of the continuum as that of which every part is of the same nature as the whole. They are, according to Peirce's theory, pure triadic relations; therefore their irreducibility follows from the irreducibility of Thirdness. Moreover, since every relation must be related to its subjects by some such relation, Peirce drew the conclusion that all relations involve a continuous relation.

Continua. During the 1880s, Peirce had become acquainted with Georg Cantor's work on set theory, which bears directly on the problem of continuity. Recognizing at once the great importance of Cantor's work for both logic and mathematics, Peirce undertook the study of the foundations of mathematics and attempted to construct his own theory of cardinal and ordinal numbers. Peirce's papers on this subject are highly technical, and only the briefest summary of them can be given here. In developing his theory of cardinal numbers, Peirce discovered a form of the paradox of the greatest cardinal. His efforts to solve this paradox led him to the erroneous conclusion that the series of transfinite cardinals is only countably infinite and has an

upper limit which is the power of the linear continuum. It follows that if the continuum consisted of discrete elements, then there would exist a greatest cardinal, and to avoid this conclusion he held the continuum to be a "potential" set consisting of possible points. Accordingly, although subsets of any multitude may be actualized from the continuum, nevertheless, not all of the possible points are actualizable, since if they were, we should have a greatest cardinal and hence a contradiction. Peirce believed that by such arguments he had established that whatever is truly continuous involves unactualized possibility; hence the problem of the existence of real possibility, which he had found insoluble in the 1870s, was now reduced to that of the reality of continuity. Peirce used the arguments of Zeno in an attempt to prove that space and time must be truly continuous in his (Peirce's) sense, and he went on to argue that continuous relations are truly continuous both intensively and extensively. In defining the continuum as that of which every part is the same sort as the whole, Peirce was brought to the conclusion that real relations, and so real laws, are in some sense continua.

Synechism. The doctrine that the world contains real continua Peirce called synechism. He regarded this as his most important philosophical doctrine and preferred to have his whole philosophy called by this name. He also asserted that it was a modern form of scholastic realism. Scholastic or not, it is certainly realistic, for it holds that the external referents of true laws are real continua which, since they involve unactualized possibilities, contain real generality. To support this doctrine, Peirce had to define an ontology which would explain what those referents might be. Peirce was no stranger to such an enterprise. He began his work in philosophy in the 1850s, with the doctrine of the three ontological categories, and although he subsequently redefined the categories several times in less ontological fashion, he never forgot the question of what realities lay behind his categories. It is therefore not surprising that following the 1885 revision of the categories, Peirce returned to the problem of ontology, and this soon led him to propound an evolutionary cosmology.

Evolutionary cosmology. Peirce had several reasons for formulating an evolutionary cosmology in the 1890s. Not only did synechism require a clarification of his ontological commitments, but he was also impelled toward such a formulation by problems arising within the theory of cognition. First, the doubt–belief theory, by imbedding inquiry within an evolutionary context, made the utility of scientific method relative to a particular evolutionary adaptation, the permanence of which is by no means guaranteed and must therefore be investigated.

A second reason for Peirce's formulating an evolutionary cosmology in the 1890s springs from his doctrine of critical common sense. Like all students of scientific method, Peirce was perplexed by the problem of how we discover true hypotheses. Considering the infinity of possible false hypotheses, it is evident that not even Peirce's theory of synthetic inference could account for the remarkable frequency with which we do, in fact, find a true explanatory hypothesis. Utilizing the evolutionary doctrines current at the time (including the inheritance of acquired characteristics), Peirce argued that the human mind must possess some innate adaptation which enables us to guess the correct laws of nature more readily than pure chance would allow. Such an adaptation would mean that true hypotheses appear to us peculiarly simple and natural. According to Peirce, it follows, then, that judgments of common sense, conceived through the mechanism of the inheritance of acquired characteristics as quasi-instinctual beliefs that have been built up through centuries of experience, should have a greater probability of being true than have parvenu doctrines. But this probability is at best low, so that common-sense judgments cannot be accepted without critical analysis and careful test. Thus Peirce's doctrine of common sense is thoroughly critical: common sense is to be regarded as a likely source of true hypotheses, but no hypothesis is to be accepted without empirical validation. But in terms of the doubt–belief theory, this doctrine leads to a serious problem. Should the course of evolution alter significantly, our innate adaptation, which has proven so useful in the past, would become positively harmful, since it would direct us to seek explanations in terms of an adaptation that no longer obtains. Accordingly, it becomes a question of considerable moment to inquire what the future course of evolution will be.

The continuous external referent. In the doubt–belief theory, Peirce had formulated the principle that a law, which he conceived as governing the behavior of an organism, is a habit. Now a habit, considered as a psychological entity, is a connection among feeling states and actions, and this connection, Peirce held, must consist in an actual substantive continuity among them. Peirce based this assertion on a variety of arguments, including the felt continuity of mental phenomena (the impossibility of memory without continuous connection between past and present) and certain arguments drawn from the behavior of protoplasm under stimulation. It was therefore Peirce's doctrine that habit, considered as a psychological entity, is a continuum corresponding to a law that is conceived as governing behavior. To find continuous external referents for all laws, Peirce asserted that the universe is itself a living organism possessed of feelings and habits and that our laws of nature describe the habits of the universe. Thus, after 1885, the subjective idealism of Peirce's early writings became an extreme form of objective idealism.

Knowledge, feeling, volition. From the position that the universe is an organism, it follows that all our experience of the external world must be describable as experience of some state or behavior of this organism. But the possible forms of experience are defined by the material aspects of the categories, while Peirce took the possible components of mind to be defined by the traditional division into knowledge, volition, and feeling. He had already identified knowledge with belief-habit and made it the correspondent of law, or Thirdness. He now identified feeling as the correspondent of Firstness and volition as the correspondent of Secondness. But the doctrine asserts more than mere correspondence, for Peirce seeks to account for the fact that all our experience can be classified by the categories, and his explanation for this fact is that what is for the cosmic organism feeling, volition, and belief is experienced by the individual as Firstness, Secondness, and Thirdness.

Chaos and order. The habits created through inquiry are, objectively viewed, laws of behavior. What then, according to Peirce, is doubt, or the absence of belief? In the state of doubt, there will be feeling, but no habit and no order—hence, objectively viewed, the state of doubt will appear as purely random or chance behavior. Thus, objective orderliness or randomness corresponds to states of the universe in which habit is either strong or weak. The irritation of doubt is redefined as an intense consciousness associated with states of unordered feeling; as order or habit increases, the intensity of consciousness declines until, in the case in which virtually complete regularity has been established, it is so low as to be all but undetectable. Mind that is so hidebound with habit we regard as dead matter.

When the doubt–belief theory is applied to the organic universe itself, the result is an evolutionary cosmology. In the beginning, Peirce held, there is nothing but an undifferentiated continuum of pure feeling wholly without order—a primal chaos. From this starting point, the universe evolves by means of the development of habits. We have here the typical Spencerian passage from homogeneity to heterogeneity, but without benefit of Spencer's mechanical model. In the course of time, the universe becomes ever more orderly, but at any given time its habits remain less than perfectly regular and there are still areas requiring the further fixation of belief.

This cosmology is the basis for Peirce's doctrine of tychism—that there is absolute chance in the universe. For as law is the objective manifestation of habit, so chance is the objective manifestation of lack of habit; hence the primal undifferentiated continuum of feeling is literally a world of pure chance. Evolution constantly diminishes the amount of objective chance in the universe, but only in the limit does it wholly disappear. At any given time, some chance remains, and the laws of nature are not yet wholly exact.

Pragmatism and universal evolution. The doubt–belief theory describes inquiry as an attempt to escape the irritation of doubt. But it is hardly proper to say that the universe seeks to escape from doubt, and some better motive is required. The state toward which the universe is evolving is, according to Peirce's theory, one of complete order. Since such a state involves the complete subjection of feeling and action to belief, Peirce regarded it as the realization of rationality in the concrete, or, in his terms, of "concrete reasonableness." But it is also a state of maximum beauty, for Peirce's aesthetic is a coherence theory of beauty. Accordingly, the normative theory of inquiry may be brought to bear in explaining the evolutionary process. The end sought is concrete reasonableness; the means, supplied by ethics, is the regulation of conduct by this aim. In the area of inquiry, this implies the discovery of those laws necessary to regulate behavior. Thus pragmatism, or pragmaticism, as Peirce renamed his doctrine after 1905 in order to distinguish it from James's, also serves the cause of evolution, for in translating the concept into a set of habits we discover the practical effects of the object—that is, how our conduct is affected. It remains for scientific inquiry, then, to discover the truth or falsity of potential habits and hence to fix belief. Thus the course of universal evolution and our modes of inquiry must remain ever in harmony, for the objective logic of evolution is identical with the logic of discovery. All nature works by a common process to a common end, and the duty of the individual man is to aid that process by devoting himself to scientific inquiry.

Works by Peirce

The Collected Papers of Charles Sanders Peirce, Vols. I–VI, Charles Hartshorne and Paul Weiss, eds., Cambridge, Mass., 1931–1935; Vols. VII–VIII, Arthur Burks, ed., Cambridge, Mass., 1958. This is the basic published collection of Peirce's writings. (The usual method of citation to these volumes is by volume number, followed by a decimal point and the paragraph number—for example, 3.456.)

Charles S. Peirce's Letters to Lady Welby, Irwin Leib, ed. New Haven, 1953. These letters, written between 1903 and 1911, are largely devoted to the theory of signs and contain some of Peirce's best writings on that subject.

Works on Peirce

Buchler, Justus, *Charles Peirce's Empiricism.* New York, 1939. An incisive study of Peirce's more empirical doctrines, with particular emphasis on pragmatism and common-sensism.

Feibleman, James, *An Introduction to Peirce's Philosophy, Interpreted as a System.* New York, 1946. A broad but superficial survey.

Gallie, W. B., *Peirce and Pragmatism.* Harmondsworth, England, 1952. A thoughtful book devoted chiefly to Peirce's pragmatism.

Goudge, Thomas A., *The Thought of C. S. Peirce.* Toronto, 1950. Goudge holds that Peirce's work contains two contradictory positions, which he calls naturalism and transcendentalism. The book is an exposition of this thesis and of its implications.

Lewis, Clarence I., *A Survey of Symbolic Logic.* Berkeley, 1918. Ch. 1, Sec. 7. This is still the best essay on Peirce's work in logic.

Moore, Edward C., and Robin, Richard S., eds., *Studies in the Philosophy of Charles Sanders Peirce, Second Series.* Amherst, Mass., 1964.

Murphey, Murray G., *The Development of Peirce's Philosophy.* Cambridge, Mass., 1961. An attempt to interpret Peirce's work chronologically and systematically through the architectonic principle.

Thompson, Manley, *The Pragmatic Philosophy of C. S. Peirce.* Chicago, 1953. A thoughtful and systematic study of Peirce's pragmatism and related problems.

Wiener, Philip and Young, Harold, eds., *Studies in the Philosophy of Charles Sanders Peirce.* Cambridge, Mass., 1952. This collection of essays on Peirce's philosophy is extremely uneven: it contains some excellent articles and some very poor ones. The papers by Savan, Thompson, Fisch and Cope, and Weiss are particularly good.

Weiss, Paul, "Charles Sanders Peirce," in *Dictionary of American Biography.* New York, 1934. Vol. XIV. A very fine biographical article on Peirce.

MURRAY G. MURPHEY

PELAGIUS AND PELAGIANISM. Pelagius (c. 360–c. 431), said to be of British origin, was a highly educated man who was well versed in Latin and Greek and had an extensive knowledge of Scripture. Although he was a prolific writer, most of his works have perished. There is no certain evidence that he was ever ordained or a member of a religious order, but all authorities agree on his highly moral character. Augustine, to whom we owe much of our knowledge of Pelagius, calls him "a saintly man."

Pelagius went to Rome in 384 and remained there until 410. During this period he composed, among other works, his *Commentary on St. Paul.* It was also at this time that he met Celestius, a young Roman lawyer who became his first disciple and devoted his considerable dialectical skill to the propagation of Pelagius' ideas. In 410, with the invasion of the Vandals, the two men went to Carthage. Pelagius then moved on to Palestine, where he was favorably received. Celestius, however, was tried and excommunicated by the Council of Carthage in 411 for preaching the Pelagian doctrine. The ideas of Pelagius also became suspect in Palestine, but a synod in Jerusalem refused to act and later in 411 Pelagius was acquitted at Diospolis of the charge that he had denied the necessity of grace. Pelagius himself fervently denied any charge of heresy and always insisted on his Christian fidelity. He stayed in Palestine, but there is no account of his activities after 418.

Theological doctrine. The heretical error of Pelagius was his devaluation of the importance of grace. In his *Commentary on St. Paul,* his most significant work, he was more concerned with an exhortation to virtue and moral progress than with the development of Christian doctrine. An ascetic himself, he expressed in his actions and his preaching the conviction that man could achieve salvation and the good life without the special help or grace of God. This necessitated a radically different conception of the nature of man than was found in Christian doctrine. Pelagius completely rejected the doctrine of original sin, holding that man is inherently good and that the sin of Adam was not transmitted to posterity. That sin appears to be universal among men is due more to Adam's bad example than to the taint of original sin. The further implications are drawn that it is false that mankind suffered spiritual death through the sin of Adam and that the redemption of man is not due to the grace given by Christ but to the value of Christ's moral teachings. All this entailed that infants do not require baptism for the remission of original sin. These are the basic points of Pelagius' doctrine, contained in the first condemnation of Celestius at the Council of Carthage.

Augustine immediately took issue with the Pelagian doctrine, and one of the most significant contributions of the heresy was the stimulation it gave to Augustine's development of the Christian doctrine of grace. In the several years following the first condemnation of Pelagianism, Augustine was at the center of the controversy, and the subsequent condemnations of Pelagianism at the Councils of Carthage in 417 and 418 were largely due to his influence. Augustine asserted that through sanctifying grace man achieves a spiritual rebirth, not merely a remission of original sin and its effects. Man is created again in the divine likeness and finds his nature perfected so that he may share in the divine supernatural life.

However, the more significant problem for Pelagius was "actual" grace, which he rejected without qualification. Augustine held that actual grace gives man the power or freedom (*libertas*) to choose the good and to effect good works. Augustine never denied the freedom of the will—it is real and active under grace, and it is accommodated to the divine sovereignty. "Freedom is sufficient for evil; for good it is not enough unless it be empowered by the Omnipotent who is good." Actual grace is first active in faith and conversion and is necessary to "final perseverance," or the continuation of the virtuous life. The actions and decrees of the church councils followed this Augustinian doctrine in branding Pelagianism a heresy and in effectively suppressing it.

Philosophical implications. The philosophical significance of the Pelagian doctrine lies largely in the autonomy it conferred upon ethics. Pelagius did not deny the value and inspiration of religious truths, and he considered himself a true Christian; but he did reject the subordination of ethics to religious dogma. The autonomy of ethics followed from the autonomy of man. For Pelagius freedom was an inescapable fact of our experience, and freedom means that man has the power to choose either the good or the evil. It is true that God may help man by endowing his nature with the possibility of sinlessness and the ability to accomplish good works, but no special grace from God is needed to attain the virtuous life. The initiation of ethical activity lies within man.

By contrast, Augustine stressed the divine initiative, and his ethics was essentially a religious one. Pelagianism, in its emphasis on personal discipline, the attainment of the virtuous life, and the freedom of the will, had much in common with the Stoic ethics and the ideal of the wise man. Finally, it may be noted that, in denying the theological doctrine of original sin and in asserting the inherent goodness of man, there was a tendency in Pelagianism to subordinate the supernatural to the natural. Man is by nature good, and through the moral strength and freedom of his will he can attain the highest good, and even supernatural salvation, without the grace of God.

Works by Pelagius

"Libellus Fidei ad Innocentium Papam," in J. P. Migne, ed., *Patrologia Latina*. Paris, 1844–1864. Vol. XLVIII, pp. 488–491.
Pelagius' Expositions of the 13 Epistles of St. Paul, Alexander Souter, ed. *Texts and Studies*, Vol. IX. Cambridge, 1926.

Works on Pelagius

Ferguson, John, *Pelagius*. Cambridge, 1956.
Plinval, Georges de, *Pélage*. Lausanne, 1943. Both this and the Ferguson work contain excellent bibliographies.

JOHN A. MOURANT

PERAS. See APEIRON/PERAS.

PERCEPTION. The term "perception" may be used generally for mental apprehension, but in philosophy it is now normally restricted to sense perception—to the discovery, by means of the senses, of the existence and properties of the external world. Philosophers have been concerned with the analysis of perception—that is, the study of its nature and of the processes involved in it—and with its epistemological value—that is, how far, if at all, it can be regarded as a source of knowledge about the world. Their answers to these closely interrelated questions have been formulated in various theories: the common-sense theory and other kinds of direct realism, the representative or causal theory, critical realism, the sense-datum theory, and phenomenalism. This article will be devoted to the main features of perception that underlie the various theories and that have raised philosophical problems and controversy. It will discuss both the initial evidence that may be analyzed without recourse to scientific findings and the causal and psychological process revealed by scientific investigation.

INITIAL EVIDENCE AND ANALYSIS

Reflective examination. As percipients we are all familiar with perception, and so the first evidence should come from reflection on our own experience. The following points may thus be made about perception.

First, it is awareness of the external world—of material objects, to use a technical term for physical objects in general, animals, plants, and human beings insofar as they are perceptible (their bodies, in fact). The main characteristics of such objects are that they are external, independent of the percipient, and public, meaning that many people can perceive them at once. Perception, in being the awareness of such objects, may be contrasted with imagery, bodily sensations, or having dreams.

Second, perception is, or seems to be, intuitive—immediate and normally undoubting, a direct face-to-face confrontation with the object in sight or a direct contact in touch. Nor are we normally conscious of any processes of reasoning or interpretation in it. On the rare occasions when we reason or we have doubts about what an object is, the reasoning or doubts are about the identity or character of something already perceived—for instance, a rectangular red object or something white on the hillside.

Third, perception is variable in quality and accuracy; we may fail to notice something, to see clearly, to hear distinctly, and so forth. Three types of variation may be involved: variations in attention, in what we notice or discriminate; variations in quality or distinctness (for instance, where there is nearsightedness or fog); and variations in liability to err—we may misidentify what we perceive or mistake its qualities.

Fourth, perception nevertheless normally gives us knowledge of material objects and properties. With a few fairly obvious tests, like touching and looking closely, or using the evidence of other percipients, we can establish certainty or else correct the first sight or hearing.

Fifth, perception often issues in some judgment or assertion (to others or perhaps only to oneself)—for example, "There is a green fly on the roses" or "Here's the milkman"—but it may not.

Illusions. Illusions, comprising illusions proper, hallucinations, and cases of the relativity of perception, have traditionally been the most important origin of the major problems of perception. (See ILLUSIONS, which discusses their details and the argument from illusion; it is presupposed and only briefly summarized here.) The two main claims of the argument from illusion are (1) illusions show that perception is never absolutely certain, that tests are never final, and (2) the appearances we are aware of in illusions, especially hallucinations, cannot be identified with the real properties of objects and must therefore be private objects of awareness, or sensa (indeed, all perception involves awareness of sensa which in correct, or veridical, perception belong to the object or correspond to its properties).

The first claim was long thought to rule out perceiving as a source of knowledge; instead, one had to turn to pure reason, or rational intuition, which was held to provide mathematical knowledge. But, since the absolute certainty of mathematics came to be generally ascribed to its ultimately analytic, or even tautological, character, the tendency now would be to stress the negligibility of the possibility of error in tested perception and to use a different standard of certainty and knowledge concerning matters of fact, one which allows perceptual statements to qualify.

The second claim, concerning the existence of sensa, is vital in that almost all theories of perception either found their analyses on it (as does the sense-datum theory) or seek to controvert it or explain it away (as does common-sense realism). The seeds of this conflict already lie in the results of the reflective examination. Insofar as perceiving seems to vary in quality and accuracy, it is easy to say that in illusions we merely see the object looking different from what it is. But if perception is a direct intuitive confrontation, the illusory appearance must be a genuine existent, perceived as it really is, a sensum in fact; "looking different from what it is" must be interpreted as "presenting sensa different from the standard ones." In any case, some phenomena—for example, the integration of hallucinatory images with a perceived background—are difficult to explain without supposing awareness of private sensa in all perception, and almost all the phenomena require scientific and psychological findings for their full explanation, thus pointing beyond this initial evidence.

Perceptual consciousness and perceiving. The occurrence of illusions may lead to ambiguity in the use of "perceive" and allied terms. Thus, in double vision a man may be conscious of two bottles where there is only one. Do we say "He perceived two bottles" or "He perceived one bottle"? Each alternative has been adopted philosophically, and to avoid ambiguity, it is safer to distinguish (1) "X is perceptually conscious of Y" from (2) "Y is present to X's senses (or light from it is acting on his sense organs)" and use "X perceives Y" only when both are meant.

This recommendation is claimed to have the further advantage of enabling us to discuss as perceptual consciousness the state of mind (or mental act) occurring in both veridical perceiving and illusions. Perceptual consciousness of, for example, a dagger might occur when only a stick was present or even, as in Macbeth's case, when nothing was there. The notion of such consciousness as a common factor in perceiving a real dagger, in having hallucinations of one, and in mistaking something else for one fits in best with dualist theories, such as the sense-datum theory (especially H. H. Price's version) or critical realism, since it suggests that the contents of such consciousness differ from the external object perceived. Direct realists are suspicious of it; for them having hallucinations is something (imagery, perhaps) quite different from normal perception, even if confused with it, whereas in illusions they want to stress that one is perceiving the real object present—seeing a stick *as* a dagger or the round table *as* elliptical. But even if perceiving a round table as round or in perspective as elliptical is taken as immediate confron-

tation needing no further analysis, seeing a stick as a dagger (or a piece of wax as a tomato or a bush in a fog as a man) can hardly be equally simple and immediate. In such cases and in hallucinations one has to admit that one seems to see an object quite different from that present to the senses. This can fairly be described as perceptual consciousness of the (ostensible) object (dagger, wax, or man) and distinguished in analysis from actually perceiving an object (dagger, wax, or man). And in view of the subjective similarity it is but a short step to suppose that perceptual consciousness of X also occurs in perceiving X as X, the difference between illusory and veridical perception of an X lying not in this common consciousness but in whether X is present and acting on the sense organs. Any philosophy of perception should analyze this perceptual consciousness and explain how it may occur without the presence of the corresponding object.

Analyses of perceptual consciousness. Three major analyses are integral parts of the theories of perception mentioned above. First is the traditional notion that perceiving—that is, perceptual consciousness—is the interpretation of sensations as properties of external objects. Second, the sense-datum theory claims that perceptual consciousness is taking for granted that the sense datum one is sensing belongs to a material object (on both these, see SENSA). Third, the analysis of the critical realists, though stated as an analysis of perceiving, amounts to saying that perceptual consciousness is taking an intuited datum or character complex to characterize an external object (see REALISM).

The essential difficulty in these three analyses is that they contradict introspective evidence by splitting up perceptual consciousness into the awareness of some private data, recognizable by analysis as such, and the act of interpreting them as, or taking them to be, objects or object properties. In experience there is no such core of sensing or intuiting data distinguishable from the consciousness of a material object, even if only subsequently; still less is there any passage of the mind from awareness of sensation as such to object perception. And if some critical realists are less liable to this difficulty because they do not treat their data or character complexes as existents readily distinguishable from material objects, they do this only at the expense of obscurity or disagreement as to what the data are. Attempts at a remedy must be postponed until the psychological processes in perception are considered.

A fourth analysis is the idealist claim that all perceiving is judging, which is really an analysis of perceptual consciousness but is easier to follow if stated in terms of perceiving. It is that perceiving (perceptual consciousness) consists in making a judgment, which has an implicit sensory basis, about the real existence of an object or property. Thus, perceiving a tomato on a plate or perceiving that the dog has hurt its leg are the sensorily grounded judgments "There is a tomato on a plate" or "The dog has hurt its leg." The "perceiving that" description of a perception (for example, "He saw that the dog was hurt") certainly seems to suggest judgment, though the form may be misleading and may only be for emphasis of the feature noticed. But the main reasons for this analysis are (a) that perceiving is true (veridical) or false (erroneous) and only judgments or assertions can be true or false and (*b*) that perception is more than just sense experience, for we identify and interpret what is given (that is, it involves inference from implicit data, and the conclusion of such an inference must be a judgment). One may object that truth characterizes what is asserted, not the asserting—the judgments, in the sense of propositions, to which perceiving may lead, but not the act of perceiving itself. Perceiving may be proper, correct, clear, or accurate, but not true or false. Many other things we do may be done correctly and be liable to errors without being forms of judging, such as playing the piano, playing games, tying knots. False judgment is not the only form of error. Also, the idealist doctrine that all perceiving is judging is open to the general objection to the first three analyses above, particularly because the nature of the implicit data or sensory grounds is very obscure. Attempts to elucidate it—for example, Brand Blanshard's—turn them into sensa. Furthermore, the term "judgment" suggests something intellectual, explicit, and considered, with consciousness of the evidence for the assertion—conditions inappropriate to much perception. Also, we may correct a faulty judgment on learning the truth, but such knowledge does not enable us to correct illusory perceptions; we still see the mirage, and the railroad tracks still appear to meet in the distance.

Fifth, there is a causal analysis of perceptual consciousness—namely, that it is inferring that one's sensa are caused by an external object. This may be associated with representative realism but is not essential to it; representative realism's main thesis is that the sensa and the consciousness are externally caused by objects that the sensa "represent." One may accept this thesis along with any of the analyses of perceptual consciousness—the causal inference it involves is subsequent to the perceiving, and so is a claim about perception. The difficulties of supposing that perceptual consciousness *consists in* such an inference from effect to cause are that (*a*) we are not conscious of such an inference; (*b*) if we started only with private sensa, any inference to external causes would be too difficult and complex to be automatic and unconscious—it would *have* to be conscious; and (*c*) it leads to paradoxes, such as that children, being ignorant of the supposed causation of perception, cannot therefore perceive or be perceptually conscious of anything.

Conceptual analysis of perceiving. A rather different approach to perceiving is adopted by those who advocate conceptual analysis—that is, a close study of the ordinary meaning (or use) of expressions. This analysis is naturally associated with common-sense realism, for ordinary language tends to reflect ordinary views on perception or at least what once were such views. Such analysis, however, may well indicate features of perception which are not normally realized and so supplement or even correct reflective examination of an introspective kind.

Much attention along these lines has been directed to the categorization or classification of perceiving. Previous philosophers have referred to perception in various ways: as an act, even an operation, as a process, and as a mental state. None of these is satisfactory. "Act," at least as activity or operation, suggests listening or watching rather than just hearing or seeing; "state" and "process" suggest something long-term, and "process," like "activity," suggests something open to public observation—yet whereas one may observe *X* looking at *Y* one cannot observe *X* seeing *Y*. (One can perhaps claim that the best description of perception is "mental act," which would put perceiving in a special category with realizing, noticing, deciding and so on, but mental acts as such are suspect to these philosophers.) One suggestion is that perceiving is simply having an experience, but this neglects the active side of recognizing and identifying involved in it. A more popular suggestion is that perceiving is a skill or art, or, rather, since seeing *X* or hearing *Y* occur at a definite time, perceiving is the exercise of a skill. Oddly enough, the evidence for this is not linguistic. We may speak of a skilled observer, one who can direct and coordinate a series of perceptions, but not a skilled perceiver; we do not say that *X* is an expert at the art of seeing or hearing things. Rather, this suggestion is based on the fact that perceiving can be improved by learning and experience, so that one recognizes things easily, avoids mistakes, or can make allowances for such factors as distance. Although this may occur to one on reflection, however, its full and precise extent has been established only by psychological investigation. As soon as one seeks out this and other psychological evidence about perceiving or even asks how one learns by and exploits experience in perceiving, one is carried far beyond language and conceptual analysis to a scientific study of the subject. Also, to maintain that perceiving is the exercise of a skill brings one back to the suggestion that it is an operation or activity.

More striking perhaps was the earlier claim of Gilbert Ryle that "perceiving" is an achievement verb, like "finding" or "winning," and indicates the scoring of an investigational success. This means that perceiving is not an activity or process, though it may be the successful termination of the activity of looking for something; it is instantaneous, not something which takes time or can be observed. Ryle's aim was to attack representative realism and its associated dualisms of mind and body, sensa and object, by claiming that (*a*) perceiving, usually thought to be a private mental activity because it is not an overt one, is not an activity at all and thus provides no evidence of a mental world and that (*b*) since it is not a process, perceiving is not the final stage or effect of a process, particularly not of the causal process from object to person. Hence, there is no need to suppose that science proves that perceiving is awareness of private sensa. These are not very convincing arguments. As to the first, winning or scoring involves some activity such as kicking a ball. Likewise, perceiving involves experiences of colors or sounds and the psychological processes discussed below; these are normally claimed to be mental. The second is a *non sequitur*—instantaneous success may be the end and result of a causal process. Thus, scoring and finding may be observed and may be the result of a process or series of activities; other conditions may also be required but do not rule out their being effects. More generally, if perceiving is an achievement, what are misperception, illusion, failure to see properly, a casual glance? An analysis of perceiving must take these into account and not apply only to veridical perception. Ryle also failed to show how perceiving is related to the causal processes representative realism emphasizes. Thus, if instantaneous, perceiving can no longer be the relation across time and space which direct realism would need to claim in view of the factually verified time lag, the time taken by the causal transmission from a distant object. Indeed, contrary to Ryle's intention, a dualist interpretation of his claim is possible. Perceptual consciousness is instantaneous; when it is also successful, that is, when its content corresponds to the properties of the object causing it, it is perceiving; when unsuccessful, it is misperception or illusion.

THE CAUSAL PROCESSES IN PERCEPTION

The causal chains. The causal processes involved in perception form causal chains from the external object to the percipient's brain. In sight a complex system of light waves, sometimes emitted by the object but normally a differential reflection of light from the object's surface, travels from the object to the percipient's eyes. This system is diversified in intensity and wave length according to the shape, brightness, and color of the object surface and, on striking the eyes, is focused so that an image of the object is cast (upside down) on each retina. Each retina has a mosaic of over 120 million receptors, which are activated by the light cast on them in this image. The light causes chemical changes in the receptors; these changes, in turn, cause electrical impulses to pass along the nerve fibers which lead from the receptors to one of the two visual receiving areas of the brain. The impulses set up activity there and in certain other association areas; this done, the person then sees the object. Over one million such fibers form the optic nerve from each eye, and each fiber consists of a succession of cells that are made to conduct by a chain reaction; the resultant impulses can be picked up and reproduced on a cathode-ray tube.

In hearing, a pattern of sound waves is emitted or reflected from the object and strikes the eardrum; this causes vibrations to be transmitted through a series of bones to the liquid filling in the inner ear, thereby setting up vibrations in the basilar membrane of the cochlea according to the frequency (waves per second, corresponding to pitch) and intensity of the sound. The receptors in the cochlea then transmit electrical impulses along the nerve fibers to another receiving area in the brain. (These impulses are *not* at the frequency of the incoming sound.)

In smell and taste there is a chemical stimulation of receptors in the nose and tongue by particles of the substance perceived, and the receptors, in turn, send neural impulses to another area of the brain. For touch, the brain is linked to receptors all over the skin, some of which respond to the pressure of direct contact with the object, some to heat, and some to cold (or, rather, to rate of change in skin temperature). Other receptors in the skin and the body respond to a wide range of stimuli by transmitting to the brain impulses which ultimately cause a sensation of pain. There are also other senses—for example, a kinesthetic sense by which receptors in the muscles send impulses to the brain so that the position of the limbs is sensed or unconscious adjustments are made to guide and make efficient voluntary movement. There are also receptors

in the vestibule and semicircular canals behind the ear which assist balance and give us information about head position.

The chain process (object–[waves]–receptor–nerve impulses–brain activity) is a necessary condition of perception of an external object, for if it is interrupted by damage to the sense organ, no perception occurs. It is not a fully sufficient condition in that other areas of the brain must be suitably active so that the person is conscious and minimally attentive—that is, not wholly absorbed in thought. The interesting question is whether or how far the chain process is necessary and sufficient for perceptual consciousness of an object, granted conditions of consciousness and attention. At least the brain activity is clearly necessary, but theoretically one might insert stimulation at some point on the chain and thus cause experiences the same as those which would normally be attributed to the external object. This apparently happens naturally in illusions and hallucinations, including phantom limbs, and electrical stimulation of the appropriate areas of the brain may cause sensations of color, smell, or touch. (The sensations are not like the contents of perceptual consciousness of objects, but this difference may be due to the comparative crudity of the artificial stimulation by an electrode; also, activity in the association areas is necessary for normal perception.) Thus, it seems probable that suitable activity in the nervous system is a necessary and sufficient condition of perceptual consciousness, though it may be that some kind of external stimulation, even one quite unlike the object perceived, is required to trigger it.

Time lag. Causal processes take time. In the case of distant objects this is marked. Thus, because sound waves travel much more slowly than light waves, the flash of some distant gunfire or explosion may be seen appreciably before the sound is heard. Even at its great speed light takes eight minutes to reach us from the sun and four years and four months from the nearest star. Consequently, we may well be "seeing" a star long after it has disintegrated, for the perceptual consciousness occurs at approximately the time of the arrival of the star's light on earth. But as time is required for the sense organ to be activated and for the nerve impulses to travel to and spread in the brain, there is a slight but variable time lag in all perception; an accurate estimate is not possible but the delay is probably of the order of one-tenth of a second for nearby objects.

Uniformity of nerve impulses. One surprising fact is that the nerve impulses are of a similar type for all the senses. All that travels along any nerve from any receptor to the brain is a sequence of such impulses varying normally between 10 and 100 a second. The frequency variation is, in fact, a mark of intensity; the stronger the stimulus, the more impulses per second. Consequently, what distinguishes causation of an experience of sound from that of smell or an experience of a high pitched sound from that of a low one is not the impulse itself but the connections of the nerve fibers excited and conducting—where they start in the sense organ and where they end in the brain. (Though if one imagines a cross section across a bundle of nerve fibers, the pattern of some conducting and some not conducting can be regarded as a changing code.) Thus, excitation by nerve impulses of one tiny portion of the brain results in awareness of a loud shrill sound, excitation of another in awareness of a blue line. Various areas of the body are mapped in the brain, a group of receptors (or sometimes an individual receptor) in the skin and tissues corresponding to each point in the cerebral receiving area. Similarly, the retinal image is reproduced point by point in the brain, though with each half reproduced in a separate area, duplicated there, and distorted. Again, a strip of brain tissue is activated at different points according to the frequency of the sounds heard, as if it were a keyboard.

Complexities. There are nevertheless many complexities in the system, only a few of which we can mention here.

The nerve connections are intricate, with feedback fibers from the brain to the incoming sensory fibers and cross connections between the sensory fibers; in the grouping of receptors and in the brain there is summation—several nerves join one which conducts only when all or most of them do. (In fact, neurologists constantly use terms like "selecting," "integrating," "summating," and "coding.")

Binocular vision involves retinal disparity (a slight difference in the images cast on the two retinas) and the operation of two visual receiving areas reached by crossed-over nerve fibers so connected that the left-hand receiving area receives the signals coming from the right half of each retina and the right-hand area receives those of the left half. As a result we somehow normally see one object with depth and solidity rather than two two-dimensional ones.

Constant small eye movements are necessary for vision, with a shifting of the retinal image and of the resultant pattern of impulses in the fibers of the optic nerve, yet the object is seen as steady.

Most of the impulses reaching the brain from the eye come from a small portion of the retina (the fovea) which has relatively many receptors giving great distinctness; for exact vision the image is focused on the fovea by eye movement.

Color vision is particularly complex, and its mechanism is disputed. All the colors we know can be produced by suitable mixtures of red (long-wave), green (medium-wave), and blue (short-wave) light. White light can be formed by an appropriate combination of three colors or even of two widely separated ones. (Light, or "spectral" colors, mix differently from paint colors.) The simplest theory is that there are receptors in the eye reacting to each primary light color (red, green, and blue) and the brain, by summating the three color inputs, is enabled to cause the final color sensation. Thus, grass looks green because it absorbs red and blue light but reflects green, and a buttercup is yellow because it absorbs blue but reflects green and red, which combine to produce yellow. There are many difficulties in this theory. For instance, no receptors for blue can be positively located in the eye, only for red and green ones; the light from a green surface actually contains a mixture of wave lengths, with green predominating; the light wave lengths cover the spectrum of all the colors of the rainbow; the brightness and purity of the color also affect its hue. A final theory must therefore be very complicated.

The auditory receiving area gets impulses from both ears. This enables us to locate the source of a sound. If a sound is to the left, then sound waves reaching the left ear differ in phase (that is, timing of the wave crests) and in intensity from those reaching the right ear. The brain apparently combines the different inputs so that the location is done unconsciously and we just hear the sound as if it came from a certain direction.

Limitations of the senses. Radiant energy is known to range from short cosmic rays to long radio waves, but the eye responds only to visual light, which is a narrow band occupying about one-seventieth of the whole range. Even then we cannot distinguish light of different polarizations, as bees and birds apparently can, or see very small objects or fine structures. Similarly, in hearing we can distinguish only waves between 20 and 20,000 cycles per second; dogs, cats and rats can hear higher notes. Our sense of smell is obviously very inefficient compared with that of most other animals. Hence, though we can extend our range of observation by microscopes, infrared or X-ray photographs, radiotelescopes, and so on, it is clear that our senses themselves are very limited as a direct source of knowledge of the external world.

The causal argument. The causal argument maintains that the existence and character of these causal processes refute direct realism and force the adoption of a dualist position. Perception of an external object cannot be the direct contact or immediate confrontation it seems to be, since it requires this causal chain from object to the percipient's brain and is prevented if that is interrupted—for instance, if the optic nerve is cut or one of the small bones in the ear does not move properly. In this sense directness or immediacy must mean no intermediary and no possibility of interruption. The causal chain suggests that perceptual consciousness and its objects are generated, or brought into being, by the causal process, presumably by its last stage, the brain activity. In other words, insofar as perceptual consciousness is intuitive, it is awareness of some content or object quite distinct from the external object. This suggestion is supported by various points. First, the time lag—perceptual consciousness may occur after the external object has disappeared or moved, so its content cannot be identified with the object. Second, the possibility of perceptual consciousness without any external object at all or without one at all similar seems confirmed by the production of sensations by stimulation of the cerebral cortex and seems actualized in hallucinations. Third, the enormous complexity involved shows that the subjective simplicity of perception is illusory, at least insofar as a relation to an external object is concerned. Fourth, illusions and the relativity of perception are often explicable in terms of the causal processes. Unless the contents of perceptual consciousness are generated and conditioned by the causal process, one has to attribute bizarre and contradictory properties to the external object (see the discussion of the selective theory in REALISM). Fifth, the simplicity and uniformity of nervous impulses show that they cannot transmit all the various secondary qualities which make up objects as we know them (this point is elaborated in PRIMARY AND SECONDARY QUALITIES). These qualities must thus characterize contents of consciousness generated by the causal process. (This point is supported by such other limitations as the purely mechanical transmission through the bones of the ear.) Hence, it follows from the fourth and fifth points that one must abandon the other assumption of direct realism—that even when we are not perceiving them, objects continue to exist with the exact qualities we normally observe in them.

There is a good deal of resistance to these conclusions. One obstacle is that they seem to require a self-refuting type of representative realism. This fear is unjustified. It must also be noted that granted the dualist conclusion that the causal process generates the sensory experience whose content is (numerically) different from the external object, the nature of that experience and its content is still open. It may be that the awareness is of sensa, or it may be a full-fledged perceptual consciousness of percepts or ostensible objects. One is not even forced to adopt a mind–body dualism, though it is normally thought that sensa or percepts are mental. One might claim that though apparently distinct objects, they are in fact only the contents of sense experience, not existing apart from the sensing of them (adverbial analysis), and that they and the brain activity are two aspects of the reaction of the organism or person as a whole. This would mean that sensa are only a correlated aspect of brain activity, not effects of it, though still conditioned by the rest of the chain. In this way one might bypass one of the notorious difficulties of ordinary dualism—the unique and obscure causal relation supposed to exist between material brain and immaterial mind.

Sometimes, however, the opposition takes the form of denying the relevance of the scientific evidence to philosophy; it tells us only what the causes of perceiving are, not what perceiving itself is. Philosophers must investigate the latter and leave the causal processes to the scientist. But scientists normally hold that these processes require the adoption of representative realism, thus giving them philosophical relevance; also, those philosophers who wish to concentrate on the nature of perception alone usually come up with some answer (the sense-datum analysis or a view that perceiving is the exercise of a skill or an investigational success) which is compatible with or even supports a dualist interpretation of the causal processes. But, above all, to achieve full understanding of anything so vital as perception, one must consider its causes and conditions, particularly as their study has traditionally been claimed to transform our concepts of perceiving itself and of our knowledge of the external world.

THE PSYCHOLOGICAL PROCESSES

It is clear from experimental psychology that perceptual consciousness involves a whole range of adjustments and selective or quasi-interpretative processes. The main evidence for this lies in differences between what psychologists often call the phenomenal properties of an object (those we are perceptually conscious of) and its stimulus properties. In this context the stimulus is the pattern of light rays from the object striking the eye, of sound waves striking the ear, or of heat or pressure from touching the object. The stimulus properties are those which we should observe in the stimulus (such as shape, color, pitch) could we observe it directly and in itself. This is difficult to

achieve, and in fact the evidence of cameras, tape recorders, and other instruments is used, plus knowledge of the nature of the object and reasoning from the laws of perspective or of physics generally. The difference between the two kinds of property is presumed to be the result of modifications by the percipient.

Attention and selection. It is a simple fact of experience that the quality and accuracy of perception vary with our attention. We often look inattentively and fail to notice pronounced features of a scene, yet we may carefully observe and thus notice unexpected details—a mark on the wallpaper, a printer's error, a wrong note in a recorded symphony. From the evidence of other people, from photographs, and from other means there may be no doubt that these features appeared all the time in the stimulus properties even when we were unconscious of them. Besides confirming this, psychologists have shown how greatly what we do or do not notice depends on habits of attention or interests, on often unconscious "priming" or "set." A mother will hear her baby cry but not notice much louder noises; an architect may notice features of buildings, and a boy notices makes of cars, both being oblivious to much else. Thus, perceptual consciousness is very selective, and this selection is usually largely unconscious, though voluntary attention can greatly modify it. One special case of voluntary attention is of importance—"perceptual reduction" or "phenomenological observation," where we concentrate on the sensible qualities of what we perceive and not, as is usual, on the identification of the object concerned. An artist must do this when he has to paint a scene, and this kind of observation may reveal all sorts of previously unnoticed details of color, shape, and so on. It is open to question whether this kind of reduction reveals an element present in all perception—namely, sensing—or whether, and this is more plausible, it is simply a special kind of perception of external objects not found in normal perceiving.

Errors and enrichment. Some errors in perception can be attributed to psychological factors—misidentifications because of careless observation, seeing what one expects to see rather than what is actually present, thinking that one hears the expected visitor coming when no one is there, and the like. These point to a common characteristic of perception and one apparent only when it goes wrong—the enrichment of perception by imagery and thought. Many psychological experiments have been concerned with this. For example, vague or ambiguous stimuli (pictures or sounds) are presented to different groups of people who see or hear them as definite objects or words, and the direction in which they are thus unconsciously supplemented or altered can be shown to be caused by suggestion or by the interests, emotional state, or physical state of the person. Another kind of case is the divergence between several eyewitnesses' accounts of an incident, which may all differ from a filmed record. Again, blind spots or other visual defects are often not apparent to the subject, who unconsciously fills in the gap (this happens to us all if we look with one eye, for there is a blind spot where the optic nerve leaves the retina). Extreme cases are hallucinations where the apparition is integrated with the background or casts shadows. Unnoticed supplementation by imagery, which is admittedly private and mental, seems strong evidence for the dualist claim that the contents of perceptual consciousness are similarly private and must be distinguished from object properties.

Learning and cues. Our perception is clearly affected by learning and experience. Identification and discrimination afford obvious examples; one can learn to identify objects seen or photographed from unusual angles, to detect animals in natural camouflage, to distinguish different birds' songs. Driving a car involves perceptions of distance and relative speeds, perceptions that are acquired by experience. Psychological investigation has shown the role of learning to be far greater than this. Perception of spatial relations generally depends to a large extent on learning (normally unconscious and in childhood) to harmonize sight and touch and to use various cues. This is shown by various experiments, such as those with distorted rooms or inverted spectacles, and by the evidence of blind men who recover their sight. Among the various cues used for perception of distance and of solidity are shadows, aerial and linear perspective, parallax (or relative movement), and the interposition of objects. These assist binocular vision and enable us to see depth even with one eye.

Figure–ground and Gestalt. In perception our immediate consciousness is of an organized or structured whole. Some shape or feature stands out and is seen as the figure against a background, and if discrete units such as dots are presented, we see them as grouped or patterned in some way. This characteristic of experience has been particularly stressed by Gestalt psychologists, who produced much experimental evidence to show that we see wholes or structures (Gestalten, literally, "forms") and that perception develops by discriminating these in and from a background and not by synthesis of atomic elements or point sensations first perceived separately. Such organization of the visual field, though little affected by learning, is nevertheless largely the result of processes in the percipient himself. The clearest evidence of this comes from the reversals, or "alternating illusions," where the stimulus (picture or succession of sounds) is constant but is perceived differently at different times; thus, sometimes one pattern or shape stands out as the figure, sometimes another. Examples are the goblet that may appear as two faces in profile, Edwin Boring's wife–mother-in-law figure, Ludwig Wittgenstein's duck-rabbit, and the staircase which seems to be seen now from above, now from below.

Perception of motion. Perception of motion was closely investigated by the Gestalt psychologists, who drew attention to the Phi phenomenon, which is the impression of movement between adjacent stationary stimuli that are activated in succession. This underlies the consciousness of movement on a motion picture or television screen and is used in illuminated advertisements in which if groups of lights are successively switched on for a brief time, one is perceptually conscious of a moving figure or even of words moving along. Intermittent illumination may also make moving objects appear stationary. Thus, when illuminated by the flashing light of a stroboscope, a moving crank in a machine may, if the flashing is properly adjusted, be seen as stationary and examined for defects; if there is a slight maladjustment of the flashing, it may seem to rotate slowly backward like the wheels of coaches in Western films. There is a clear distinction in these cases between the properties of the stimulus and the contents of consciousness. Figure–ground effects also occur in movement perception, such as when the moon seems to sail through the clouds or when one's stationary train seems to move if an adjacent one starts.

Object constancy. The widespread phenomenon of object constancy in perception differs from the above in that the phenomenal properties of an object tend to remain constant or nearly so even though the stimulus properties vary considerably. Thus, when we look at a round object—for example, a dish—from an angle, it often still looks round and not elliptical, although by the laws of perspective the stimulus (light-ray pattern) or retinal image is elliptical, as would appear on a photograph taken from the percipient's viewpoint. (This causes complication in stating the argument from illusion and perspective realism.) Only if the angle is very marked does the dish look elliptical. ("Look" here refers to the sensible quality, not to what we judge to be the object's shape.) Similarly with size, brightness, and color—a man looks much the same size at ten yards' distance as at five even though the image cast on the retina is half as high in the former case; a white patch in the shade reflects less light than a dark one in bright sunlight, but it still looks white; a white patch in a yellowish light still looks white although it is reflecting yellowish light (one may be surprised by color photographs taken in the evening, for the camera cannot adapt itself to the yellower light). In general, over a range of varied stimuli we tend to see something corresponding to the property of the object or at least some compromise between this and the stimulus property. Experiments show that this constancy depends not on knowledge of the object but on the visibility of its background, for if the background is cut off by a screen so that only the object is visible, constancy does not hold and the stimulus property is seen. It is as though we made unconscious allowance for distance, angle of sight, and illumination as revealed by the whole scene. But this is not a learned or intelligent adjustment; children and even chickens or fish apparently see things with constancy, though to some extent it can be counteracted by adopting a stimulus attitude (trying to see the stimulus property).

Philosophical significance. The existence of these many complex processes which underlie perceptual consciousness and affect its content reinforces the causal argument by making even more incredible the direct-realist notion of perceiving as a straightforward direct confrontation with the actual properties of objects. If perception were a simple intuitive awareness of such properties, there would be no place in it for variations in quality; for the effects of interests, priming, and learning; and for the use of cues for enrichment by or integration with supplementary imagery, for constancy adjustments (especially where they produce a compromise between object and stimulus properties), for changing figure–ground effects, or for the Phi phenomenon.

The range of these processes is far greater than that which would be compatible with the usual analyses of perceptual consciousness—namely, that it is the interpretation of sensations (or inference from implicit grounds) or the taking for granted that a sensed datum belongs to an object. These views were mainly influenced by the possibility of error in perception, particularly in identification, although they took some account of the use of cues and of the role of learning. But they seem inadequate to cover the part played by attention and unconscious selection or by such organization adjustments as figure–ground, grouping, object constancy, or the Phi phenomenon, whereas some of the imaginative supplementation goes far beyond what can be called interpreting a datum. It is sometimes claimed that these adjustments are interpretations. But this is implausible, for they seem little affected by learning and are not intelligent since lower animals make them. Nor can many of the illusions or adjustments be overcome by knowledge of the facts or by conscious interpretation; where some counteraction is possible, as in object constancy, it is very difficult, and for most people the presence or absence of screens in experiments is compelling in its effect. The final objection to such analyses concerns the alleged pure sensory data; interpreting or taking for granted, insofar as we are aware of it, is of something we are conscious of as distinct and external and which is thus already the effect of many of these processes. Normally, however, perceptual consciousness seems intuitive—that is, without interpretation and quite unanalyzable; except in perceptual reduction its content almost always consists of ostensible objects. All the same, psychological evidence shows that there is a range of subjective processes. The only answer seems to be a genetic hypothesis, not an analysis into elements. Perceptual consciousness is introspectively a whole but must be supposed to be a product of a range of selective, supplementary, integrative or organizational, and quasi-interpretative processes acting on a supposed basic sentience. But—and this is the point—both processes and sentience are unconscious and so may plausibly be regarded as cerebral activities or adjustments of the nervous system. However, since we cannot as yet give any precise neurological statement of these processes, we have to describe them as if they were conscious, basing the description on the difference between the input to the senses and the finished product, but this product (perceptual consciousness) does not reveal within itself the processes that may be supposed to form it.

The suggestion that perceptual consciousness is the product of many unconscious processes is controversial, and any general conclusions about perception are bound to be personal. Hence, the main attention in this article has been on the facts which have to be taken into account in any fully adequate view of perception, and the reader is also referred to the statement of the various theories here and in other related articles. In this way he has the material for assessing the general view here adopted—namely, that the causal and psychological processes essential to perception, as well as its liability to illusion, require abandonment of direct realism for a dualist position. One must distinguish perceptual consciousness, whose content or objects are subjective and private to the percipient, from perception which occurs when this perceptual consciousness is caused by an external object with properties corresponding to its content. But one must not confuse this dualism with the traditional representative realism, which is only a variant of it, some form of critical realism being superior; the sense-datum theory's dualism of sense data and objects (perceptual consciousness is not thus analyzable, and its content consists of ostensible material objects); or the Cartesian mind–body dualism (it is possible also to adapt this view of perception to a double-aspect account of mind and body).

Bibliography

For discussions of other aspects of the philosophy of perception see ILLUSIONS; PHENOMENALISM; PRIMARY AND SECONDARY QUALITIES; REALISM; and SENSA and their bibliographies.

GENERAL INTRODUCTIONS

Perception is discussed, though usually less extensively than in the related articles in this encyclopedia, by most introductory books on philosophy. For example, see Bertrand Russell, *Problems of Philosophy* (London, 1912) and *Outline of Philosophy* (London, 1927); Charles Harold Whiteley, *Introduction to Metaphysics* (London, 1955); John Hospers, *Introduction to Philosophical Analysis* (New York, 1953; London, 1956); and Arthur Pap, *Elements of Analytic Philosophy* (New York, 1949). A clear and useful outline with emphasis on the associated epistemological problems is A. J. Ayer's *The Problems of Knowledge* (London, 1956). A more detailed introductory treatment is given by R. J. Hirst, *The Problems of Perception* (London, 1959), Chs. I–VI; the later chapters of this book develop a more advanced treatment of perceptual consciousness and the scientific evidence on the lines adumbrated here.

PERCEPTUAL CONSCIOUSNESS

For analyses of perception in the sense of perceptual consciousness, see H. H. Price, *Perception* (London, 1932) on the sense-datum theory; Durant Drake and others, *Essays in Critical Realism* (New York and London, 1920), and Roy Wood Sellars, *The Philosophy of Physical Realism* (New York, 1932), on critical realism; Brand Blanshard, *The Nature of Thought*, Vol. I (London, 1939), on idealism; and Roderick M. Chisholm, *Perceiving* (Ithaca, N.Y., 1957), which is a causal analysis with a general consideration of perceiving and epistemological questions. Roderick Firth, "Sense-data and the Percept Theory," in *Mind*, Vol. 58, No. 232 (1949), 434–465, and Vol. 59, No. 233 (1950), 35–36, is critical of any such analyses.

CONCEPTUAL ANALYSIS

For the approach by conceptual analysis see "On Seeing and Hearing" by Winston H. F. Barnes, "Identification and Existence" by Stuart Hampshire, and "Sensation" by Gilbert Ryle in H. D. Lewis, ed., *Contemporary British Philosophy*, Vol. III (London, 1956); Gilbert Ryle, *The Concept of Mind* (London, 1949), Ch. 7, and *Dilemmas* (Cambridge, 1954); Anthony M. Quinton, "The Problem of Perception," in *Mind*, Vol. 64, No. 253 (1955), 28–51; and D. W. Hamlyn's discussion of psychological theories, *The Psychology of Perception* (London, 1956). John Langshaw Austin's *Sense and Sensibilia* (London, 1962) is an outstanding defense of common sense against the argument from illusion, but unfortunately he does not discuss the scientific evidence. Another direct-realist study is David M. Armstrong's *Perception and the Physical World* (London and New York, 1961).

SCIENTIFIC BACKGROUND

Useful elementary accounts of the causal and psychological processes are given in such textbooks as Ernest Ropiequet Hilgard, *Introduction to Psychology* (New York, 1953); David Krech and Richard Stanley Crutchfield, *Elements of Psychology*, 3d ed.

(New York, 1962); and Robert Sessions Woodworth and D. G. Marquis, *Psychology* (New York, 1947; London, 1949). Rather more detail, with a philosophical discussion as well, is given in George McCreath Wyburn, Ralph William Pickford, and R. J. Hirst, *Human Senses and Perception* (Edinburgh, 1963). Two significant but unconventional psychological books which raise philosophical questions of interest to the advanced student are James Jerome Gibson, *The Perception of the Visual World* (Boston, 1950), and Friedrich August von Hayek, *The Sensory Order* (Chicago, 1952; London, 1953).

INTERPRETATIONS OF SCIENTIFIC EVIDENCE

See the works by Price, Chisholm, Hirst and the critical realists mentioned above and Arthur O. Lovejoy, *The Revolt Against Dualism* (New York, 1930), also a critical realist. C. D. Broad's *Perception, Physics and Reality* (Cambridge, 1914) and *Scientific Thought* (London, 1923), sense-datum analyses, are very technical at times. William Pepperell Montague, *The Ways of Knowing* (London and New York, 1925), gives a general comparison of the different realist (and other) views. See also the more sophisticated types of representative realism—namely, John Raymond Smythies, *Analysis of Perception* (London, 1956), or Bertrand Russell, *Analysis of Matter* (London, 1927) and *Human Knowledge* (London, 1948). Of Russell's two books, the first is often difficult, and the second is more for the general reader.

R. J. HIRST

PERCEPTUAL CERTAINTY. See ILLUSIONS.

PERCEPTUAL CONSCIOUSNESS. See PERCEPTION.

PERFECTION. The concept of perfection has two closely allied and often overlapping meanings. First, it means "completeness," "wholeness," or "integrity": *X* is perfect when he (or it) is free from all deficiencies. Second, it means the achievement of an end or a goal. This meaning emerges most clearly from the connection between the Greek words *teleios* ("perfect") and *telos* ("end" or "goal"). An entity is perfect (to use Aristotelian terms) when it has achieved its goal by actualizing its potentialities and realizing its specific form. Bringing these two meanings together, one would say that a thing is complete or entire when it has fulfilled its nature and thereby reached its "end." The concept is best examined first under its religious, and second under its moral, aspect.

Divine perfection. It has not always been believed that God (or, more generally, "the divine") is perfect. Thus, the deities of the Homeric pantheon were both ontologically and morally deficient. They differed from men only in being "deathless" (*athanatoi*). But in Christian theology the perfection of God has always been affirmed by orthodox writers. In St. Anselm's celebrated definition, God is *id quo nihil maius cogitari possit* ("that than which nothing greater can be conceived"). St. Thomas Aquinas later maintained that since God is self-existent, he must be infinite (or limitless) in intelligence, goodness, and power. He also claimed, in the fourth of his five Ways, to prove the existence of God as absolute perfection from the limited degrees of perfection in creatures. Thomists hold that by the "analogy of proportionality" we can attribute to God "in a more eminent way" (*eminentiori modo*) every "pure" perfection that exists in creatures (that is, every perfection

that is capable of pre-existing in an infinitely spiritual degree).

Those who hold this view of God's infinity must face two questions that have continually perplexed Christian philosophers. First, can we intelligibly assert that all perfections coexist infinitely in a single being? Thus, can God be both infinitely just and infinitely merciful? Second, if God is both infinitely powerful and infinitely good, how can we explain the presence of evil in the world?

Moral perfection. Ever since men began to reflect on the moral life, they have been aware of some perfect ideal of character and conduct toward which they must strive. Thus, in the Greco-Roman world the Stoics wrote copiously of the "perfect" (*teleios*) man. In their view perfection consisted in the subjugation of the passions to reason (*logos*) in a state of "self-sufficiency" (*autarkeia*). Sometimes they regarded moral virtue as the imitation of divine perfection, and sometimes they held out a human figure (especially Socrates) as the model of excellence; but more often they wrote abstractly of their ideal "wise man."

There can be no doubt that Jesus required moral perfection of those who would follow him. Thus, in the Sermon on the Mount, he told his disciples, "You, therefore, must be perfect, as your heavenly Father is perfect" (Matthew 5.48). In saying this Jesus reaffirmed the Old Testament, in which the Jews, as the people of the covenant, are required to be perfect (or "holy") by obedience to the law (*Torah*) which embodies God's will and reflects his character. The above-mentioned verses (Matthew 5.38–47) show that love, especially love of one's enemies, is the element in divine perfection that disciples are to imitate. Jesus' moral perfectionism was further expressed in his demands for complete inward purity (Matthew 5.21–22, 27–28) and self-renunciation (Mark 8.34–38).

Inevitably, theologians have affirmed that moral perfection is the goal of the Christian life. In the New Testament epistles perfection has three main characteristics. First, the norm of perfection is Christ himself, as the Incarnation of God. Second, the essence of perfection is love—the divine love revealed in Christ and made available to believers through the Spirit. Thus, St. Paul, having listed several virtues, wrote, "And above all these put on love, which is the bond of perfectness" (Colossians 3.14). Third, perfection is corporate. Thus, the author of Ephesians looks forward to the time when "we all attain to the unity of the faith and of the knowledge of the Son of God, to perfect manhood, to the measure of the stature of the fulness of Christ" (4.13). Post-Biblical theologians (for example, St. Augustine and Aquinas) continued to give primacy to love, by which all the natural virtues are supernaturally perfected.

Two comments on this Christian scheme are relevant. First, as early as St. Ambrose there emerged a distinction between the basic "precepts" according to which all Christians were expected to live and the "counsels of perfection" that only a few ("the religious") could follow. This distinction, which persisted throughout the Middle Ages, was based on such texts as Matthew 19.16–22 and could be plausibly represented as an attempt to combine adherence to Christ's absolute demands with a realistic attitude toward the spiritual capacities of the average

Christian in a secular occupation. But it was rejected by the Reformers, and with special vehemence by Luther.

Second, although some Christians have held that it is possible to achieve perfection (that is, sinlessness) in this life, the majority have held that the strength of original sin makes this impossible. Moreover, many Biblical texts (particularly I John 1.8–10) imply the Lutheran view that all Christians remain throughout their mortal lives *simul justi et peccatores* ("at the same time justified and sinners"). From a purely philosophical standpoint Kant held that since the moral law requires holiness, and since we cannot achieve it in this life, we must postulate another life in which an infinite progress toward it will be possible (*Critique of Practical Reason,* translated by T. K. Abbott, London, 1909, p. 218).

Finally, if we take human perfection in its widest sense to mean an ideal that satisfies man's deepest needs or fulfills his "true" being, we can see clear points of similarity between Christian and non-Christian systems. Thus, although humanists, Buddhists, and Christians have in common many virtues that they regard as normative, they put them in differing contexts. These virtues are practiced by the humanist as self-sufficient ends, by the Buddhist as means of entrance to nirvana, and by the Christian as both the outcome of present faith in God and a preparation for a future vision of him "face to face."

Bibliography

Flew, R. N., *The Idea of Perfection in Christian Theology.* Oxford, 1934.

Kirk, K. E., *The Vision of God.* London, 1931.

Niebuhr. Reinhold, *An Interpretation of Christian Ethics.* London, 1936. An important examination of Jesus' perfectionism and the problems that it raises.

Saunders, Kenneth, *The Ideals of East and West.* Cambridge, 1934.

H. P. OWEN

PERFECTION, DEGREES OF. See DEGREES OF PERFECTION, ARGUMENT FOR THE EXISTENCE OF GOD.

PERFORMATIVE THEORY OF TRUTH. Until relatively recently, it was taken for granted by all philosophers who wrote on the subject of truth, regardless of their differences on other matters, that words like "true" and "false" were descriptive expressions. This presupposition has been challenged by P. F. Strawson, who developed the theory that "true" is primarily used as a performative expression. A performative utterance may be understood by considering a paradigm case: "I promise." To say "I promise" is not to make a statement about my promising but simply to promise. To use a performative expression is not to make a statement but to perform an action. Strawson, in his essay "Truth," holds that to say that a statement is true is not to make a statement about a statement but to perform the act of agreeing with, accepting, or endorsing a statement. When one says "It's true that it's raining," one asserts no more than "It's raining." The function of "It's true that" is to agree with, accept, or endorse the statement that it's raining.

Strawson's performative analysis of "true" was conceived as a supplement to F. P. Ramsey's assertive redundancy, or "No Truth," theory of truth. Ramsey claimed that to say that a proposition is true means no more than to assert the proposition itself. "It is true that Caesar was murdered" means no more than "Caesar was murdered." "It is false that Caesar was murdered" means no more than "Caesar was not murdered." According to this view, "true" has no independent assertive meaning, and the traditional notion of truth as a property or relation is misguided. Ramsey suggested that "true" is used for purposes of emphasis or style, or to indicate the position of a statement in an argument.

Criticism of semantic theory. Strawson set himself the positive task of explaining the use of "true" in ordinary language and criticizing the metalinguistic or semantic theory of truth, which has an affinity with Ramsey's view. Philosophers like Rudolf Carnap, who hold the metalinguistic position, agree with Ramsey that to say that an assertion is true is not to make a further assertion. However, these philosophers claim that truth is a metalinguistic property of sentences, which means that to say that a statement is true is to make a statement about a sentence of a given language. According to this thesis, the statement that it's true that it's raining should, strictly speaking, be written: " 'It's raining' is true in English."

Strawson argues that translation practice shows the metalinguistic thesis to be false. He points out that a translator would not handle a truth declaration as if it were a sentence description. Consider the manner in which a translator would handle a case where it is perfectly clear that one really is speaking about an English sentence:

(1) "It's raining" is a grammatical English sentence.

Suppose a translator wanted to translate (1) into a different language. He would retain the constituent "It's raining" in its original English, in order to show that (1) is a description of an English sentence. But consider

(2) It's true that it's raining.

There would be no hesitation in translating the whole statement, including the constituent "It's raining." This shows that (2) is not, as the metalinguistic thesis claims, a description of an English sentence. Hence, "true" is not a metalinguistic predicate.

Philosophers who maintain that "true" is a descriptive expression have been misled by grammatical form. "True" is a grammatical predicate, but it is not used to talk about anything. Strawson compares "true" with "Ditto." *A* makes an assertion. *B* says "Ditto." Insofar as *B* talks about or asserts anything, he talks about or asserts what *A* talked about or asserted. *A*'s assertion is the occasion for the use of "Ditto," but because "Ditto" is not composed of a grammatical subject and predicate, one is not tempted to think that in uttering "Ditto" *B* is making an additional statement.

The parallel with "Ditto" illuminates the tie between statements and "true." The making of a statement is the occasion for, but not the subject of, a truth declaration. "True" has no statement-making role. To say that a statement is true is to perform the act of agreeing with, accepting, endorsing, admitting, confirming, or granting that statement. Expressions like "I grant . . . ," "I confirm . . . ," and "Yes" are perfectly capable of substituting for "The statement is true."

Expressive use of "true." While Strawson emphasizes the performative role of "true," he also calls attention to another kind of use, which he calls expressive. This use is often found in sentences beginning "So, it's true that . . . ," "Is it true that . . . ," and "If it's true that . . . ." In these utterances, "true" functions like the adverb "really," to express surprise, doubt, astonishment, or disbelief. However, "true" has only an expressive function in these utterances. It does not contribute, in either its expressive or its performative role, to the assertive meaning of what is said. Thus Strawson's thesis remains compatible with Ramsey's view. "True" does not change the assertive meaning of a statement. It has no statement-making role.

Resolution of "Liar" paradox. The performative analysis of a truth declaration enabled Strawson to offer an original resolution of a well-known paradox that arises when one says:

(3) What I am now saying is false.

If (3) is true, then it is false; and if it is false, then it is true. Hence, we arrive at a paradox whose resolution has been one of the achievements of the metalinguistic analysis of "true." According to this analysis, (3) is read in the following manner:

(3a) The object-language statement I am making now is false.

Since (3a) no longer refers to itself, the contradictory consequences disappear. Strawson dispenses with the metalinguistic solution and dissolves the paradox in a manner consistent with his own analysis of "true." To utter (3) is like saying "Ditto" when no one has spoken. It is not to make a statement but, rather, to produce a pointless utterance. Since (3) is not a statement, it is not a statement that implies its own denial. Hence, the paradox disappears without the necessity for metalinguistic machinery.

Objections to Strawson's analysis. Strawson does not distinguish a truth declaration from expressions like "I grant . . . ," "I accept . . . ," "I concede . . . ," "I admit . . . ," "I insist . . . ," "Yes . . . ," or "Ditto." It should be noted, however, that there are differences between using these expressions and saying that a statement is true. Expressions like "I grant . . . ," "I concede . . . ," "I accept . . . ," "I admit . . . ," and "I insist . . ." suggest a "me versus you" background. They underline the act performed as *mine*. This is not the role of "That's true." Moreover, one should distinguish between expressions like "Yes," which simply register bare assent, and "The statement is true." If asked whether I agree with Smith's statement, I may say, "Yes, but my opinion isn't worth very much; I haven't studied the evidence." However, to say "His statement is *true*, but my opinion isn't worth very much; I haven't studied the evidence" sounds unnatural. "True," unlike "Yes," has the force of adequate evidence.

Geach's criticism. P. T. Geach offered the following criticism of Strawson's analysis of "true" ("Ascriptivism," p. 233). Consider arguments of this pattern.

If *x* is true, then *p*;
x is true;
Ergo p.

Strawson claims that the second premise, "*x* is true,"

should be analyzed as an agreeing performance. However, it cannot be claimed that in the hypothetical premise "If *x* is true, then *p*," the constituent "*x* is true" is an agreeing performance. If I say, "If *x* is true, then *p*," I am not agreeing with or accepting *x*. Hence, the explanation of "true" in the hypothetical premise must differ from its explanation in the second categorical premise. However, if the explanation of "true" changes from one premise to another, the argument would be invalid, since the fallacy of equivocation has been committed. However, the argument is clearly valid. Hence, Strawson's analysis of "true," which implies that a different explanation is required for occurrences of "true" in hypothetical and categorical statements, must be wrong.

Geach's criticism, however, appears to rest on a misunderstanding of the behavior of performatives in logical arguments. Take a clear case of a performative, "I promise to help you." Now consider the following argument.

If I promise to help you, then I'm a fool;
I promise to help you;
Ergo I'm a fool.

There is a performative occurrence of "I promise" in the second premise, but not in the first. When I say, "If I promise to help you, then I'm a fool," I am not promising to help you. Hence, the use of "I promise" in the first hypothetical premise requires an explanation that differs from the explanation of "I promise" in the second hypothetical premise, yet the argument remains perfectly valid. A fallacy of equivocation is not committed simply because an expression has a performative use in one premise of a logical argument and a nonperformative use in another.

Occurrences of "true" in hypotheticals do not fit a performative analysis, but it must be remembered that while Strawson emphasizes the performative use, he does not claim that this is the whole story. The nonperformative use of "true" in hypothetical statements may be considered to fall under what Strawson calls the expressive use. What is the difference between the following statements?

(4) If Khrushchev's statement is *true*, there are no missile bases in Cuba.

(5) Khrushchev's statement implies there are no missile bases in Cuba.

While (4) and (5) have the same assertive meaning, (4) suggests that Khrushchev's statement is in doubt. Hence "true" in (4) contributes only to the expressive quality of the statement. Since "true" in (4) has only an expressive function, but not a statement-making role, (4) does not constitute an exception to Strawson's analysis.

"Blind" uses of "true." An interesting challenge to Strawson's position is found in "blind" uses of "true." This use of "true" is exemplified when a person applies "true" to a statement without knowing what the statement is. For example, suppose a man says, "Everything the pope says is true." Presumably he does not know every statement the pope has made. It cannot, therefore, be claimed that he is making the statements made by the pope. One cannot substitute the pope's statements for "Everything the pope says is true" without a change in meaning. Hence, "Everything the pope says is true" does not, as Strawson claims, have the same assertive meaning as the pope's statements. The notion, which Strawson takes over from

Ramsey, that a truth declaration has the same assertive meaning as the statement dubbed true, does not hold for blind uses of "true."

It may be argued that the speaker is blindly endorsing all the pope's statements. In that case, "Everything the pope says is true" would be analyzed as a performative use of "true" which falls outside the range of Ramsey's thesis. But this analysis could not be maintained for blind uses like "I hope that what Jones says will be true." The speaker is plainly not endorsing what Jones will say. Moreover, since "true" in this case does not function like the adverb "really," it cannot be maintained that "I hope that what Jones will say is true" exemplifies an expressive use of "true" either. Hence, neither Strawson's nor Ramsey's position seems to hold up for blind uses of "true."

Strawson, however, has analyzed blind uses of "true" in what he takes to be a Ramsey-like method. In his later paper, "A Problem About Truth—A Reply to Mr. Warnock," Strawson shifts from his original position and grants that "at least part of what anyone does who says that a statement is true is to make a statement about a statement" (p. 69). This is a departure from his earlier view that "true" has no statement-making role. For the blind truth declaration "Everything the pope says is true," Strawson would offer the following Ramsey-like paraphrase: "Things are as the pope says they are." According to Strawson, this paraphrase is a statement about the pope's statements, but it also conforms to the spirit of Ramsey's view. Presumably, Strawson considers this analysis to be a Ramsey-like analysis because "true" is eliminated from the paraphrase. It must be remembered, however, that Ramsey held "true" to be eliminable because "true" is a "superfluous addition" to a statement ("Facts and Propositions," p. 17). Hence, one can always substitute P for "P is true" without loss of assertive meaning. While Strawson has eliminated "true" from "Everything the pope says is true" in the paraphrase "Things are as the pope says they are," he has not fulfilled Ramsey's claim that "true" is superfluous. A philosopher who holds the correspondence theory of truth can also eliminate "true" by substituting "Everything the pope says corresponds to the facts" for "Everything the pope says is true." However, this surely would not be a Ramsey-type elimination. Since "true" is not a superfluous addition to a blind truth declaration, it does not seem that blind uses can be paraphrased in the spirit of Ramsey.

Bibliography

Ezorsky, Gertrude, "Truth in Context." *The Journal of Philosophy*, Vol. 60, No. 5 (Feb. 28, 1963).

Geach, P. T., "Ascriptivism." *The Philosophical Review*, Vol. 69 (April 1960).

Kincade, J., "On the Performatory Theory of Truth." *Mind*, Vol. 67 (1958).

Ramsey, F. P., "Facts and Propositions." *PAS*, Supp. Vol. 7 (1927). Reprinted in George Pitcher, ed., *Truth*. Contemporary Perspectives in Philosophy Series. Englewood Cliffs, N.J., 1964. P. 16.

Searle, J. R., "Meaning and Speech Acts." *The Philosophical Review*, Vol. 71 (1962).

Strawson, P. F., "Truth." *Analysis*, Vol. 9, No. 6 (1949). Reprinted in Margaret MacDonald, ed., *Philosophy and Analysis*. Oxford, 1955. Pp. 260.

Strawson, P. F., "A Problem About Truth—A Reply to Mr. Warnock," in George Pitcher, ed., *Truth* (see above). P. 68.

Strawson, P. F., and Austin, J. L., "Truth." *PAS*, Supp. Vol. 24 (1950).

Walsh, W. H., "A Note on Truth." *Mind*, Vol. 61 (1952).

Warnock, G. J., "A Problem About Truth," in George Pitcher, ed., *Truth* (see above). P. 54.

Ziff, Paul, *Semantic Analysis*. Ithaca, N.Y., 1960. P. 118.

GERTRUDE EZORSKY

PERFORMATIVE UTTERANCES. As a philosophical term "performative utterances" was introduced by the late Oxford philosopher John Langshaw Austin (see AUSTIN, JOHN LANGSHAW).

The characteristics of performative utterances can be explained as follows. Many verbs are used to describe or to report something. Verbs such as "to write," "to walk," "to eat," and "to look" can be, and almost always are, used to describe or to report that somebody is writing, walking, eating, or looking. These verbs can all be used in the first-person present progressive tense. To the question "What are you doing?" it is grammatically correct to answer "I am writing," "I am walking," "I am eating," or "I am looking." Such answers will be either true or false. If in fact I am writing, the answer "I am writing" is true; if not, it is false. Now compare these verbs with such verbs as "to apologize," "to name," "to swear," and "to guarantee." If a person hurts another person unintentionally, he may say "I apologize." In this situation the sentence "I apologize" is not used to describe or to report that he is apologizing; instead, it is used to apologize. The person apologizes by saying "I apologize." The sentence is used not to *describe* the performance of an act but to *perform* an act. The sentence has a performative use; it is a performative utterance. Likewise, if, in the appropriate situation, somebody says "I name this ship *Neptune*," he is not describing the act of naming a ship but is performing the act of naming it. By using the sentence "I name this ship *Neptune*" he is not reporting that he is naming; he *is* naming. Or, if in a courtroom the defendant says, "I swear that I did not do it," he is not describing what he is doing by the use of the sentence "I swear that I did not do it." He is not saying what he is doing; he is doing something by saying something. The use of the sentence is his swearing. The sentence is a performative utterance.

Very generally, performative utterances are in the first-person present tense. The sentences "I apologized" and "He is swearing" are not performative utterances. In most contexts the use of the sentence "I apologized" is to report that the person using the sentence apologized, and in most contexts the use of the sentence "He is swearing" is to report that the person talked about is swearing. As reports they are either true or false. But performative utterances are neither true nor false. The person who in the appropriate situation says "I apologize" is not asserting anything; he is not, therefore, saying anything that could be either true or false.

Although a performative utterance can be neither true nor false, it may be what Austin calls an infelicity or a misfire. It is surely not always the case that the use of performative sentences has the intended result, that is, results in the performance of an act. If Mrs. X telephones Mrs. Y and says that she invites her to dinner, Mrs. X has issued an invitation. But if Mrs. X's five-year-old son suddenly says to Mrs. Y, "I invite you to dinner," no dinner invitation has been issued, because the five-year-old son has no authority to issue such invitations. In order that a performative utterance should not be an infelicity or a misfire, the circumstances must be appropriate. But this does not mean that it is possible to specify a set of necessary and sufficient conditions that must be fulfilled in order that the circumstances can be counted appropriate.

Whether or not the use of sentences like "I apologize," "I name," "I invite you," and "I promise" results in a performance cannot be proved by pointing to certain facts which allegedly constitute the necessary and sufficient conditions. Rather, the claim that the use of a certain type of sentence results in a performance is a *defeasible* claim. The claim holds until it has been defeated. The claim of the five-year-old boy to have issued an invitation is defeated by the fact that he is not in a position to issue such an invitation. The claim that Mrs. X has invited Mrs. Y to dinner holds because there is nothing to defeat it.

Austin introduced the concept of performative utterances in his famous essay "Other Minds." In this essay Austin compares the use of the sentence "I know" with the performative utterance "I promise." There is a logical difference between saying "I shall do *X*" and saying "I promise to do *X*." In saying "I shall do *X*," I announce my intention. I announce that I intend to do *X*. But in saying "I promise to do *X*," I do something different. As Austin says, "A new plunge is taken." I have performed an act, I have made a promise. But I have performed no act by announcing my intention through the use of the sentence "I shall do *X*." There is a similar difference between saying "I feel absolutely sure" or "I am fully convinced" and saying "I know." To say that I feel absolutely sure or that I am fully convinced may be taken as a report of my psychological state. If my conviction proves to be wrong, I may be reproached for being naive but not for having said anything wrong; I was in fact convinced. But it is otherwise with the use of the sentence "I know." To say that I know is not to make a report of my psychological state. If that which I claim to know turns out not to be the case, I have said something wrong: I did *not* know. The use of the sentence "I know" is in many respects just like the use of a performative utterance. By saying that I know, I give others my word. I give others my authority for asserting the truth of the proposition I claim to know.

Applications and extensions. It has been argued by P. F. Strawson that the phrase "is true" has a performative use (see STRAWSON, PETER FREDERICK). To say "That is true" is not to make a statement or an assertion but to perform an act. According to the context, it may be to admit, to confess, to support, or to underline. By arguing that the phrase "is true" has a performative function, Strawson is opposing the view, held by Alfred Tarski, that a sentence containing that phrase is a metastatement, that is, a statement about a statement (see PERFORMATIVE THEORY OF TRUTH).

Also of philosophic interest is the performative use of a class of sentences that H. L. A. Hart has discussed. If a father hands over his watch to his son, saying "This is

yours," he does not describe or report anything. By uttering these words in such a situation, the father transfers a right to the son. According to Hart, sentences like "This is yours," "This is mine," and "This is his" are primarily (though not exclusively) used to claim proprietary rights, to confer or to transfer them, or to recognize or to ascribe them. In the appropriate situations the use of such sentences is not a report of an act of conferring or of transferring of some right; it is the very act itself.

In his William James lectures, delivered at Harvard University in 1955 and posthumously published in 1962, Austin elaborates and modifies the distinction between performative utterances and utterances that are either true or false (utterances Austin calls *constatives*). The distinction between a performative utterance and a constative one turns out not to be a clear-cut one. If in an appropriate situation I say "I promise," I have said something neither true nor false but have performed an act. If I say that the cat is on the mat, I am saying something either true or false; I have also performed an act insofar as I have succeeded in saying something—an act of saying something. So, in a way, whenever we say things, we perform acts— acts which Austin calls *locutionary* acts. But in saying something (that is, performing a locutionary act) we perform still another kind of act. If I say "What is your name?," I have performed a locutionary act and I have also asked a question. In performing locutionary acts we also succeed in performing such acts as asking questions, making promises, issuing warnings, making statements, and so forth. Such acts Austin calls *illocutionary* acts, and each locutionary utterance, as a meaningful utterance, has an illocutionary force.

Finally, any locutionary utterance, besides having an illocutionary force, may also have what Austin calls a *perlocutionary* force. An utterance may have a certain effect upon the feelings, thoughts, or actions of the audience or of the speaker. To affect such feelings, thoughts, or actions is to perform an act. Accordingly we may say that we have performed a perlocutionary act.

Although in saying something we always perform an illocutionary act (and so the dichotomy between performative and constative utterances loses much of its power), nevertheless we may still speak of constative and performative utterances. A constative utterance, then, is an utterance which we abstract from its illocutionary force; and a performative utterance is an utterance which we abstract from its correspondence with facts and attend as much as possible to its illocutionary force. A constative corresponds, or fails to correspond, to facts and is, accordingly, either true or false. A performative (or, rather, the performatory aspect of an utterance) cannot be said to correspond to facts but, if felicitous, to constitute facts and cannot be said to be either true or false in the same sense in which a constative is either one or the other.

Bibliography

Austin's essay "Other Minds," which originally appeared in *PAS*, Supp. Vol. 20 (1946), has been reprinted in A. G. N. Flew, ed., *Logic and Language*, 2d series (Oxford, 1953), and is also contained in Austin's *Philosophical Papers*, edited by J. O. Urmson and G. J. Warnock (Oxford, 1961), pp. 44–84. Austin's talk on performative utterances delivered on the BBC Third Programme in 1956 can also be found in *Philosophical Papers*, pp. 220–239. His William James lectures have been published under the title *How To Do Things With Words* (Cambridge, Mass., 1962).

The performative theory of truth is argued by P. F. Strawson in *Analysis*, Vol. 9 (1949), reprinted in Margaret MacDonald, ed., *Philosophy and Analysis* (Oxford, 1955). H. L. A. Hart's essay on the performative character of the ascription of rights originally appeared in *PAS*, Vol. 49 (1948/1949), 179–194, and is reprinted in *Logic and Language*. Mats Furberg's *Locutionary and Illocutionary Acts* (Goteborg, Sweden, 1963) is a penetrating analysis of certain aspects of Austin's philosophy. *Theoria* (1963) contains a symposium on performatives. The symposiasts are Ingemar Hedenius ("Performatives"), G. H. von Wright ("On Promises"), and Justus Hartnack ("The Performatory Use of Sentences"). Austin's *How To Do Things With Words* is reviewed by Alan White in *Analysis*, Supplement (January 1963).

JUSTUS HARTNACK

PERGAMUM, SCHOOL OF. See NEOPLATONISM.

PERIPATETICS. The original meaning of the word *peripatos* was "a covered walking place." The house which Theophrastus provided for the school of Aristotle contained such a *peripatos*. This yielded a proper name for the school itself—the Peripatos—and its members came to be known as "those from the Peripatos" or "Peripatetics." This derivation should be preferred to that previously current, according to which the term "Peripatetic" referred to a method of teaching while walking about, known to have been used by Protagoras, for example, and assumed to have been adopted by Aristotle. Although this view goes back to Hermippus at the end of the third century B.C., it is now generally regarded as a mistaken inference, based on nothing more than the name itself.

The history of the Peripatetics can be divided into two periods—that immediately following the death of Aristotle and that following the revival of interest in Aristotelian studies resulting from the edition of the treatises by Andronicus of Rhodes in the time of Cicero or a little later. When Theophrastus became president of the school in the year before Aristotle's death, he continued to show an interest in virtually the whole range of Aristotelian studies. But whereas it is now generally supposed that Aristotle retained a keen interest in metaphysical questions to the end of his life, it was the shift of emphasis away from Platonic otherworldliness to the phenomena of the world around us, a subject also found in Aristotle, which seems to have attracted Theophrastus most. Strato, Theophrastus' successor, made important developments in physical theory, transforming Aristotle's doctrine into a fairly full-blooded materialism. But after Strato's death about 269 B.C., his successors became almost exclusively concerned with questions about the content of the good life and the way to reach it, with questions of rhetoric, and with the distinctively Hellenistic interest in anecdote, gossip, and scandal. Many of the specifically Aristotelian doctrines were abandoned, and the school had become very much the same as a number of others in Athens by the end of the second century B.C.

The reasons for this disintegration are uncertain. It may be that the concentration of interest upon empirical questions discouraged speculation. Empiricism as such, however, has interested philosophers intensely at other periods of history. Some have supposed that the disintegration was part of a philosophic failure of nerve characteristic of the Hellenistic age as a whole. But this view of the Hellenistic age is probably incorrect, and in any case such a failure of nerve clearly applied less to Stoics, Epicureans and Skeptics of the period than it did to the Peripatetics. Thus, their fate would remain unexplained. It may be that the history of the Aristotelian writings had something to do with what happened to the Peripatetics. According to the well-known story, on Theophrastus' death his copies of Aristotle's writings went to Neleus of Scepsis in the Troad (Asia Minor). In one extreme view this meant that the Peripatetics in Athens thereafter had access only to the published works of Aristotle—namely, the dialogues. In fact, there seem to have been copies of at least some of the treatises available in Alexandria, in Rhodes, and probably in Athens throughout the Hellenistic period. They do not appear to have been much studied in the Peripatos, however, where knowledge of Aristotle came primarily from the writings of Theophrastus when not from the dialogues. Indeed, in a sense the school of Aristotle might more correctly be called the school of Theophrastus. The weakness of its links with Aristotle's own thought may explain its relative failure in philosophy.

Andronicus of Rhodes wrote a special study on the order of Aristotle's works and published an edition of the treatises in the order in which they have survived to us. His edition is the source of all subsequent ones. Andronicus is sometimes dated as early as 70 B.C., but as Cicero never refers to his edition, it may not have been published until after Cicero's death in 43 B.C. Andronicus initiated a revival in Aristotelian studies, and the Peripatos flourished at least down to the time of Alexander of Aphrodisias (about A.D. 200). Among those influenced by this revival were the geographer Ptolemy and the physician Galen. Alexander wrote important commentaries on the main Aristotelian treatises, and the tradition of writing such commentaries continued into the Byzantine period through such scholars as Themistius, Ammonius, and Simplicius, who must be classed as Platonists rather than as Aristotelians. All the commentators treated Aristotle's writings as a systematic corpus, and from the start all were influenced in varying degrees by both Stoic and Platonist doctrines.

The general approach, apart from certain unintended distortions, was intensely conservative. From time to time modifications of interest were proposed, however. The successor of Andronicus, Boëthus of Sidon (who is not to be confused with the earlier Stoic of the same name), rejected the doctrine that the universal is prior by nature to the particular and would not grant to form the title of primary substance. In so doing, he took a big step in the direction of medieval nominalism. The pseudo-Aristotelian treatise *De Mundo* is often regarded as a product of this period. It culminates in a theology in which a transcendent deity maintains order in the cosmos by the exercise of an undefined power, and in a general way the work has affinities with both Stoic writers like Posidonius and Neoplatonists. However, it seems to imitate the Aristotle of the dialogues rather than the treatises, and it may antedate the edition of Andronicus.

Bibliography

The earlier Peripatetics, fragments and testimonia, are in F. Wehrli, ed., *Die Schule des Aristoteles*, 10 parts (Basel, 1944–1959). See also P. Moraux, *Les Listes anciennes des ouvrages d'Aristote* (Louvain, Belgium, 1951); I. Düring, *Aristotle in the Ancient Biographical Tradition* (Goteborg, Sweden, 1957), Part III, Chs. XVII and XVIII, and Part IV; and C. O. Brink, "Peripatos," in A. Pauly and G. Wissowa, eds., *Realencyclopädie der classischen Altertumswissenschaft*, Supp. Vol. VII (Stuttgart, 1940). See also the Aristotelian commentators in *Commentaria in Aristotelem Graeca*, 23 vols. and 3 supp. vols. (Berlin, 1882–1909). *De Mundo* is translated by D. J. Furley with Aristotle's *On Sophistical Refutations;* translated by E. S. Forster (Cambridge, Mass., and London, 1955).

G. B. KERFERD

PERRY, RALPH BARTON (1876–1957), American realist philosopher. Perry was born in Poultney, Vermont, and attended Princeton University, where he received his B.A. in 1896; he received his M.A. from Harvard in 1897 and his Ph.D. in 1899. For a brief period he taught at Williams and Smith colleges. From 1902 to 1946 he taught at Harvard, where, after 1930, he was the Edgar Pierce professor of philosophy. He was Hyde lecturer at various French universities during the year 1921/1922. In 1920 he was elected president of the eastern division of the American Philosophical Association, and he served as Gifford lecturer from 1946 to 1948.

Perry was the author of some two hundred essays and two dozen books, in addition to countless lectures and letters to newspapers, and he was considered the chief living authority on William James. Perry believed that a comprehensiveness of view is philosophy's contribution to human wisdom; in his own work he willingly risked inaccuracy to range over every province of science, art, philosophy, and religion. He insisted on the merit of this venture, insofar as it was an attempt to achieve systematic unity in a field that would otherwise be divided between experts who were unaware of one another's achievements.

Reaction against idealism. As an early polemicist against idealism, Perry claimed that the relationship of the world to the mind is an accidental or subordinate aspect of the world. He argued that the relationship of knowing the world is not like the relationship of owning an object. An object owned becomes in a sense a part of the owner, whereas the world, although it lends itself to being known, does not thereby become entirely a part of the knower. It is not exhaustively defined by the relationship of being known. This claim became one of the basic tenets of what Perry and five other young American philosophers formulated as New Realism in their cooperative volume *New Realism* (1912). They argued that the world is real and independent of mind, and that it is directly present or "immanent" to the mind in knowledge and consciousness. Together these tenets formed their "cardinal principle"—the "independence of the immanent."

In his article "The Ego-centric Predicament" (1910), Perry had shown how this "predicament" had been used illicitly to argue for idealism. The idealist argument begins with the predicament that "it is impossible for me to discover anything which is, when I discover it, undiscovered by me," and concludes that "it is impossible to discover anything that is not thought." The idealist, Perry claimed, has confused the statement that "everything which is known, is *known*" with the claim that "everything which *is,* is known." Perry maintained that the predicament was simply methodological: the extent to which knowledge conditions any situation in which it is present cannot be discovered by the simple and conclusive method of direct elimination.

Perry did not deny that this predicament presents a real difficulty, but he did deny that it argues either for idealism or realism. He never suggested what could be done to overcome the difficulty, but he did not think there were other than methodological implications in it. Instead, Perry argued that the objects of knowledge and experience are independent of egocentricity. "Independence" here refers not to a particular kind of relation but rather to the absence of one. Perry defined it as nondependence. The independent object may be related or not, provided that it is not related in the way the dependent object is. The independent object can be related to consciousness, or mind, but not be dependent on that relationship for its existence.

However, as Perry developed his position (in *Present Philosophical Tendencies,* 1925), it turned out that independent objects of knowledge are not the real independent objects of the common-sense world but "neutral entities" indifferent to both the subjective and the physical (or objective) relations in experience. They do not exist in any place; they exist only in the logical sense, as either a class or members of a class. They are therefore pre-eminently independent of consciousness. The propositions of logic and mathematics are typical of such entities, and Perry contended that analysis of such propositions reveals neither a knowing relation nor reference to a knower.

In taking this position, Perry had adopted James's neutral monism, and although he eventually abandoned it, he continued to describe his own philosophy as, among other things, "neutralism." Perry's move away from neutral monism and New Realism is best seen in his two works on value theory, *General Theory of Value* (1926) and *Realms of Value* (1954). The first work sets forth Perry's theory of the generic nature of value, while the second details the varieties and types of this value as they appear in the major human institutions, or "realms of value."

THEORY OF VALUE

Believing that value was neither unanalyzable nor purely emotive, Perry formulated his well-known definition, "Any object, whatever it be, acquires value when any interest, whatever it be, is taken in it." Value is that which attaches to any object of any interest. Interest is defined as that which is characteristic of the motor-affective life, namely, instinct, desire, feeling, will, and all their states, acts, and attitudes. A thing is an object of interest when its being expected induces actions that anticipate its realization or nonrealization. Interested action is thus actively selective, tentative, instrumental, prospective, and fallible.

According to Perry, this theory did not conflict with the "independence of the immanent," because the latter, being restricted to knowledge, did not demand that values be conceived as independent. Yet Perry's theory included a cognitive element in all value or interest. Cognition gives the interest its object, Perry said, and the character of the object of interest is essentially the same as that of the object of cognition. The "mediating judgment" in interest and cognition is expectation and belief, and without belief there would be no basis for truth and error. All interest is characterized by expectancy, but it differs from cognition in that it also includes being for or against, favoring or disfavoring, the expected. Since both interest and cognition have this element of expecting something and being prepared to cope with it, expectancy is the key to understanding both.

Because expectancy looks forward and does not disclose itself except through a train of subsequent events, the object of interest and of cognition can be conceived of only as an ideal or "problematic" object, possessing the ambiguity or dual possibility of truth and error. This object is "internal" to the act or cognition and must be distinguished from its "external" referent, that which confirms or fails to confirm the expectation of the problematic object. Expectation is the meaning of an object.

Perry pointed out that during the process by which a sensory stimulus leads to an eventual sense perception, not only muscles and nerves, but attitudes, meanings, and interpretations are oriented toward the stimulus. Thus, when the ear is assailed by a stimulus, the organism listens toward the source and acts, or prepares to act, both upon that source and upon its context. At this point a conversion takes place: one hears the sound there and then perceives it as a bell having further characteristics. Thus, a stimulus touches off a reaction, and then the stimulus is superseded by thought, which now has an object, although the original stimulus has ceased to exist. The stimulus has been converted into an object; the sound has been converted into a bell, or in other words, into what it means, what is expected of it. This is the "perceptual object," that part of the total surrounding field to which the organism alerts itself, embracing what is expected of the sensory object.

This object is characterized both by meaning—that is, by what the organism expects of it—and by being part of the surroundings. When Perry went on to describe its status further, his monistic bias became apparent. He maintained that if the ideal object is not somehow present in nature, it would be impossible to affirm that nature is as it is "represented" in the finished product of scientific inquiry. If the logical and mathematical structures of knowledge are to be true of nature, they must be *in* nature; the laws of nature reign in the realm of nature and not in the realm of natural science, which discovers them.

Moral value. Having offered his theory of value, Perry went on to show in what sense we can say one value is "better" or "worse" than another. This too, he thought, called for a definition—that is, a descriptive account of the meaning of "better" and "worse." For Perry, that meant a description of those conditions that would enable us to say with justification that one object of an interest was better (or worse) than another.

The key to this problem of value was integration or harmony of interests. To integrate or harmonize interests is to remove from them such qualities as independence, irrelevance, dissimilarity, opposition, indifference, antagonism, or incompatibility. Harmony in place of conflict is Perry's *summum bonum*. Morality takes the conflict of interests as its point of departure. What Perry called the moralization of life—the harmonizing of interests for the sake of the interests harmonized—is effected through "reflective agreement" between the personal and the social will. "Harmonious happiness" is justified by its provision for the several interests that it harmonizes. Ought and obligation, then, are not moral ultimates but are justified by the good end.

That Perry's moral criterion was an absolute in an otherwise nonabsolutistic theory did not occur to him. However, he did assert that the criterion must agree with human nature and the circumstances of human life in such a way that men can adopt it and be governed by it. It must also possess qualifications for being accepted in lieu of other standards. Perry thought his concept of harmony, in its appeal to each knower's will, did possess universality because it embraced all interests—that is, that it was to some extent applicable to everybody's interest.

The adequacy of Perry's theory rests therefore on his assumption that for all men "better" signifies a greater inclusiveness and harmony of values. Perry was by no means unaware of the need for social arrangements that would render the interests of individuals mutually innocent and cooperative. Almost half of his books were devoted to some aspect of this problem, and they were often written in response to the problems facing his country at the time. He brought to all of them his standard of harmonious happiness, or reflective agreement, a "creed of inclusiveness" that excluded only hatred and personal aggrandizement.

Works by Perry

"The Ego-centric Predicament," in W. G. Muelder and L. Sears, eds., *The Development of American Philosophy.* Boston and New York, 1940. Reprinted from original article in *Journal of Philosophy,* Vol. 7, No. 1 (1910), 5–14.

"A Realistic Theory of Independence," in E. B. Holt et al., *The New Realism.* New York, 1912. Pp. 99–151.

The Present Conflict of Ideals; A Study of the Philosophical Background of The World War. New York, 1918.

Present Philosophical Tendencies; A Critical Survey of Naturalism, Idealism, Pragmatism and Realism Together With a Synopsis of the Philosophy of William James. New York, 1925.

General Theory of Value; Its Meaning and Basic Principles Construed in Terms of Interest. New York, 1926; reissued in 1950.

Philosophy of the Recent Past; An Outline of European and American Philosophy Since 1860. New York and Chicago, 1926.

"Realism in Retrospect," in G. P. Adams and W. P. Montague, eds., *Contemporary American Philosophy.* New York, 1930. Vol. II, pp. 187–209.

The Thought and Character of William James, as Revealed in Unpublished Correspondence and Notes, Together With His Published Writings, 2 vols. Boston, 1935. A Pulitzer Prize biography.

Our Side Is Right. Cambridge, Mass., 1942.

Puritanism and Democracy. New York, 1944. Best single statement of Perry's social and political philosophy.

The Citizen Decides, A Guide To Responsible Thinking in Time of Crisis. Bloomington, Ind., 1951.

Realms of Value; A Critique of Human Civilization. Cambridge, Mass., 1954.

Works on Perry

Boman, Lars, *Criticism and Construction in the Philosophy of the American New Realism.* Stockholm, 1955. Mainly an exposition of Perry and other New Realists that utilizes the tools of modern philosophical analysis.

Harlow, Victor, *A Bibliography and Genetic Study of American Realism*. Oklahoma City, 1931.

Hill, Thomas English, *Contemporary Theories of Knowledge*. New York, 1961. Critical discussion of Perry as a "polemical" New Realist.

THOMAS ROBISCHON

PERSONAL IDENTITY. One of the commonest of daily experiences is that of recognizing our friends. A less common, though still fairly familiar, experience is the decision that a certain person is or is not the person he claims to be. The problem of personal identity is that of clarifying the principles behind these indispensable processes of reidentification. To reidentify someone is to say or imply that in spite of a lapse of time and the changes it may have wrought, the person before us now is the same as the person we knew before. When are we justified in saying such a thing, and when are we not?

The basic problems. Some philosophers have said that we are never justified because sameness and change are, in themselves, incompatible. They have argued that it is almost paradoxical to say that something has changed and yet is still the same. There is nothing special about the case of persons in this connection, except, of course, that we might, as persons ourselves, be expected to be more concerned about this case or might be expected to have access to some of the facts needed to deal with it. One set of such facts is the private set of thoughts, feelings, and images that each of us has, and such philosophers as Hume have emphasized how constant and rapid are the changes in them with which our identity has to contend. The problem generated by this alleged paradox will be referred to as the problem of the unity of a person through change or, more briefly, as the problem of unity.

Most discussions of personal identity, however, have taken it for granted that sameness and change are, at least, often compatible and have concentrated on the conditions under which reidentification of persons can take place. What enables us to say, in spite of the changes wrought by time, that person *A*, before us now, *is* the person *B* whom we formerly knew and that person *C*, also before us now, is not?

The problem of the conditions for reidentifying persons should be distinguished from the problem of individuating persons. To individuate among a class of beings is to pick out one from another; to reidentify a member of a class of beings is to recognize him as the same as someone known at an earlier time. It is, of course, unlikely that these two notions can be kept separate, since, on the one hand, one has to be able to pick out a being from among his contemporaries before one is able to identify him with a past member of his class (which, in turn, had to be picked out) and since, on the other hand, it is hard to see how a being that exists in our world of time and change can be picked out, at least in the deeper sense of being recognized, without being picked out as a being with a certain history. It is not accidental that the world "identify" can sometimes mean the one procedure and sometimes the other. This article will be concerned directly only with the problem of the reidentification of persons, which will be called the problem of criteria.

It has had two main competing answers. One is that the criterion of the identity of a person is the identity of the body which he has—that it is either a necessary or a sufficient condition of saying correctly that this person before us is Smith that the body which this person before us has is the body that Smith had. The other answer is that the criterion of the identity of a person is the set of memories which he has—that it is either a necessary or a sufficient condition of saying correctly that this person before us is Smith that he should have memories of doing Smith's actions or of having Smith's experiences.

It is clear that in practice we settle problems of identification in both ways. But we can still ask of each one whether it is necessary or sufficient; we can ask whether each is independent of the other; and we can ask whether one is more fundamental than the other. It is in connection with these questions that we find what are usually called puzzle cases. These are stories, sometimes true but usually imaginary, which are thought to contain prima-facie conflicts between the two criteria. In deciding how the conflict is to be resolved, it is thought that we show the order of priority of the two criteria. For instance, there are the cases of ostensible "bodily transfer," like that of the cobbler and the prince mentioned by Locke. In this story what physically seems to be a cobbler wakes one morning with all the apparent memories of a prince, with no knowledge of shoe mending, and with disgust at his present sordid surroundings. We might make the story harder by imagining that at the same time what looks like the prince wakes up in the royal palace with cobbler memories. In a story like this, persons seem to recall actions and events associated with a body other than the one they now have. Should we say that they are the persons who their supposed memories suggest they are or the persons who they physically seem to be? To decide this entails deciding on the relative importance of the two criteria of identity.

Related issues. The two problems I have distinguished are bound to and do overlap in the literature. The difficulty and importance of the question of personal identity, however, are greatly increased by the fact that it lies at the point of intersection of several major lines of philosophical inquiry.

Influence of dualism. The problem of personal identity has traditionally been raised in a dualist context. Those who have discussed it have been greatly influenced by the picture of a person as composed of two entities—body and mind—which are only contingently related to each other. This has restricted the problem of unity so that it has become the problem of how one can be justified in attributing unity to the mind. This looks much harder than the problem in its more comprehensive form, since the thoughts, feelings, and images a person has are far less stable than is his body and since it is, to say the least, not easy to find what Hume calls "the bond that unites" them. Failing to find it, a philosopher may resort to a doctrine of spiritual substance and say that within each person there is some central component which preserves his identity because it never changes as his thoughts and feelings do; the philosopher must then decide whether this component can be detected by introspection or is unknowable. If he rejects this doctrine, as Hume did, he may give way to complete skepticism about identity.

Self-knowledge. The second issue with which the problem is involved is the relation between the knowledge a person has of himself and the knowledge that others have of him. There are a great many facts about a person which others can learn, it is often said, only by inference but to which he himself seems to have direct and privileged access. The usual examples are facts about his present thoughts, feelings, and intentions. But it looks as though something similar may be true about the past. Although others may have to ascertain whether I am a certain previously known person or did a certain past action by reference to external records or to my observable appearance, I seem to know this directly, in memory. This bears on the puzzle stories. It seems absurd, if we imagine ourselves as one of the participants in these tales, to suggest that someone else might know better than we who we are. If this is really absurd, the puzzles have to be settled in favor of memory; if it is not, we have to explain our natural tendency to want to settle them this way.

Immortality. A third connected issue is the possibility of survival. If the unity of a person is necessarily connected with the continuance of his body through time, then it is logically impossible for a person to survive the death of his body. If bodily identity is a necessary criterion of personal identity, then even if it could be shown that some nonphysical characteristics of a person continued after his bodily death, the person himself would not have been shown to have survived any more than (to use Antony Flew's example) he would have been if it had been possible to preserve his appendix in a bottle. On the other hand, if bodily identity is not a necessary criterion of personal identity, perhaps bodily death is merely one major event in a person's history and not the end of him. And if the fundamental criterion of identity is memory, it would seem to follow that a person might be known, at least to himself, to have survived death because he continued to have memories in his disembodied state.

Moral considerations. The concept of a person has moral connections. Problems of reidentification arise in practice largely when we have to decide questions of right or responsibility, such as right to inheritances or responsibility for crimes. Identity is a necessary though not a sufficient condition of someone's being accorded rights or being made to shoulder penalties. This applies in the afterlife, too. Only if beings who exist after our death can be identified with us can they rightly be held heirs to our merit or blame. A theory of personal identity must take this fact properly into account.

The "self." One result of these wider connections has been an unfortunate technical restriction on the language in which personal identity has come to be discussed. It has been referred to as the problem of the self. This word is sometimes used to mean the whole series of a person's inner mental states and sometimes, more restrictedly, the spiritual substance to which the philosopher says they belong. The use of the word "self," however, has the effect of confining the question to the unity of the mind and of preventing the answer from relying on the temporal persistence of the body. This has made the unity problem seem intractable, especially when the fleetingness of mental images, feelings, and the like is contrasted with the

temporal persistence their owner needs in order even to engage in the relatively lengthy processes of dreaming, reasoning, or scrutinizing the external world. This article therefore avoids a terminology that has ruled out one line of solution *ab initio* by making it impossible to endow the owner of mental processes with physical characteristics.

By far the most important classical discussions are those of Locke and Hume, and it is therefore useful to begin consideration of the problem of personal identity by reference to their attempts to solve it.

LOCKE

Incompleteness of the concept of identity. Locke began his discussion of identity in Chapter 27 of the *Essay Concerning Human Understanding* by pointing out a vital fact which others, including Hume, have since neglected. The concept of identity has to be joined to some substantive notion like that of a tree or a person in order to have any use at all. What makes us say that a given entity is the same depends on what sort of entity it is. This implies an answer to the unity problem—an entity of any sort can remain the same throughout its changes provided that the changes that take place in it are characteristic of entities of that sort and are allowed for in their concept. Over the years a tree can double its size and remain the same tree since this sort of change is characteristic of trees and is allowed for in the concept of a tree. It cannot, however, sprout wings and fly or burn to ashes and still remain a tree, for changes of these kinds are not allowed for. This being so, no hidden substance is necessary for the retention of its identity since there is no need of the unchanging character which this is said to provide. The same is true, presumably, of persons, and all that seems to remain is the much harder question of what changes are allowed for in this concept—the problem of the criteria of identity. Locke characteristically failed, however, to follow through the implications of his own insight. Although he saw the inutility of the concept of substance, he still retained it and led himself into some confusions.

These confusions are partly engendered by his apparent assumption that is it possible to find one single criterion of identity for each sort of being. Our concepts are not as tidy as this. When the assumption is brought to bear on the very untidy concept of a person, the result is a distortion of the concept's logical character. This takes the form of a supposed distinction between "person" and "man."

"Man" and "person." A man, according to Locke, is a certain sort of living organism whose identity depends on its biological organization. On the other hand, he defined a person as "a thinking intelligent being, that has reason and reflection, and can consider itself as itself, the same thinking thing, in different times and places; which it does only by that consciousness which is inseparable from thinking and essential to it." Further, "as far as this consciousness can be extended backwards to any past action or thought, so far reaches the identity of that person." To sever the two notions in this way is a radical departure from ordinary usage, in which the two words are often interchangeable. Locke admitted this, without, however, seeing that the admission conceded that his account must be inaccurate as a description of the two "ideas." Of course, there is a point in the division; behind it lies the recognition that there are two criteria of identity for persons. This Locke tried to accommodate to his belief that for each sort of entity there is one criterion only, by arguing that there are two distinct concepts, each of which has its own unique criterion, rather than one concept with two criteria. But Locke was not trying merely to be tidy; more important is the motive supplied in his claim that "person" is what he called a "forensic" term. A person is a morally responsible agent. It is clear that to establish by physical evidence that the man before us in the dock is the one who did the deed is not sufficient to show that he should suffer the penalty (though it is surely sufficient to show that no one else should, unless he instigated or compelled the deed). Locke wanted to mark this fact by a special restriction on the notion of a person, so that to state that someone is the same person who did the deed is to imply accountability without room for more (or much more) dispute. He thought it obvious that what makes people accountable for their actions is their ability to recognize them as their own. This seems to mean two things: first, an awareness of what one is doing when one is doing it and, second, an ability to remember having done it. Hence, he said that the criterion for the identity of persons, as distinct from men, is consciousness, a concept intended to embrace both awareness and memory. The fact that the same *man* is before us does not mean that the same person is, since the *man* may not be conscious of having done the deed in question and if the *man* is not conscious of having done it, then the *person* did *not* do it. Here Locke brought in the puzzle cases:

> Should the soul of a prince, carrying with it the consciousness of the prince's past life, enter and inform the body of a cobbler, as soon as deserted by his own soul, everyone sees he would be the same *person* with the prince, accountable only for the prince's actions . . . . Had I the same consciousness that I saw the ark and Noah's flood, as that I saw an overflowing of the Thames last winter, I could no more doubt that I who write this now, that saw the Thames overflowed last winter, and that viewed the flood at the general deluge, was the same *self* . . . than that I who write this am the same *myself* now whilst I write . . . that I was yesterday.

Locke was misconstruing the facts to which he draws our attention. Even granting that only persons are accountable, persons are still men (for men are accountable). We may be morally right in making the memory of crimes a condition for punishment, but memory does not thereby become the sole criterion of identity, for physical presence at the crime is also a condition of responsibility for it. Both the criteria are used together, and the most Locke has shown is that the satisfaction of only one is not, for moral purposes, enough; he has not shown that each serves a different concept. One is tempted to sever them only because of the puzzle stories. These, however, do not represent the conditions under which our concepts have been evolved but, rather, imaginary new conditions which might force us into the decision to change them. As things now stand, we have one complex concept, represented variously by words like

"person," "man," or "human being" and embedded in the specific notions of cobbler, prince, beggar, or thief. This concept has two complementary criteria of identity. If we allow ourselves to be forced to say that there are two concepts, each with one criterion, we are saying that our criteria here and now allow us to hold that the memory of a crime, even without physical presence, is enough to establish responsibility for it.

There is a possible Lockean reply to this. It is to say that when a person remembers his deeds but clearly does not have the body that performed those deeds, the deeds can nevertheless still be his because he may have done them in a previous body and have inherited another since. The same person will then no longer be the same man. This cannot be evaluated until we have considered the puzzle cases at some length. For the present let us turn to Locke's attempt to make memory the single necessary and sufficient criterion of personal identity. If this attempt is successful, his treatment of the puzzles is made highly plausible; if not, it becomes highly suspect.

Identity as memory. That there is a big difficulty in the problem of identity as memory was clear to Joseph Butler and has recently been very skillfully argued by Antony Flew. Locke wished to say that Smith is the same person who did or witnessed X if, and only if, Smith has the memory of doing or witnessing X. But this is unclear. The verb "remember" and its cognates have a strong and a weak sense. In the strong sense, to say that someone remembers something is to imply the correctness of his recollection (at least in all but minor details). To say in this idiom that someone's recollection is erroneous is to say that he does not really remember, but only seems to. In the weak sense, to say someone remembers something is merely to say that he sincerely claims to remember it (in the strong sense). In the weak sense, memories can be mistaken. Now, it is clear that even though we do pay special attention to what people claim to remember when settling questions of identity, the fact that someone claims to remember doing or witnessing something does not show that he did it or witnessed it. Even though sincere, he might be mistaken. Thus, to say that Smith is the same person if he has the memory of X must, it seems, mean that he has to remember X in the strong sense of "remember." But here a twofold difficulty arises.

How are we to decide between a genuine and an apparent memory in any given case? The candidate's inner conviction is unreliable. We seem to have to resort to more than the memory claims themselves. And the critical evidence would seem to have to be evidence of the person's physical presence at the scenes he describes. This suggests that the memory criterion is not self-sufficient, as Locke says it is, for in order to know that it is satisfied on a given occasion, we seem to have to use the bodily criterion first.

Apart from this it is much too stringent to restrict personal identity to cases where a person can actually recall his past actions or experiences. People forget. Therefore, we must alter our wording. Smith, we have to say, is the same person who did or witnessed X if, and only if, he could remember it. But what does "could" mean here? Taken in a practical sense, it seems too strong, for this would imply that if Smith did do or witness X, there is some actual set of procedures which, if we applied them, would enable him to recall it. But this may not be so; even psychoanalysts fail. If, on the other hand, "could" is not given this sort of sense, it is hard to see what its use here contributes, unless it is merely another way of saying that Smith is the one who did or witnessed X if, and only if, he is the person to whom the application of procedures designed to induce recollection is appropriate. Unfortunately, this is either straightforwardly untrue (since before we discovered who did or saw X, it would be appropriate to apply such procedures to all likely candidates, not just to Smith) or merely a concealed way of saying that Smith is actually the person who did it, so that *no one other than he could* remember it. Thus, the concept of memory seems, in this argument, to presuppose that of personal identity, rather than the reverse.

These arguments show that Locke was mistaken in trying to define personal identity in terms of memory because such a definition is necessarily circular. In at least this sense Butler was correct when he said that memory presupposes, and does not constitute, personal identity. Some philosophers have gone on to say that memory is not a criterion of identity for persons at all, since, they say, we cannot know whether someone's apparent memories are real without knowing by physical means that he is the person who was involved in the events he recalls. But this, it will be argued later, is also a self-defeating move. For the present it can be seen that Locke was undoubtedly wrong in holding that memory could be the *sole* criterion of identity for persons.

Spiritual substance. A great deal of the argument of Locke's chapter is designed to reconcile his preference for memory with his doctrine of spiritual substance. The doctrine of spiritual substance is inherited from his view that some doctrine of substance is necessary to account for the fact that the qualities of an object cohere. This is presumably intended to account for their exhibiting a permanent ownership through time, as well as their belonging together in one region of space. Yet, Locke denied that we have any knowledge of what substance is like, since our knowledge is restricted to the qualities of things. In the case of persons the doctrine is one of spiritual rather than material substance (whatever the difference between two unknowns may be). But it is clear that nothing whose character is totally unknown can be detectable by the senses or by introspection, so that the doctrine of substance, as Locke held it, cannot provide any answer to the problem of criteria. No one could be said to be applying a concept on the basis of facts to which he has no access. An intractable problem now arises. Granting for the moment that memory is the sole criterion of identity, what is the relation between this fact and that of the existence of the underlying substance? Is it not possible that the application of the memory criterion might lead us to ascribe identity when this was not metaphysically backed by the continuance of one substance? If this should happen, would we have made a mistake?

The most straightforward answer is the paradoxical one of saying that the memory criterion is merely a guide for making identity judgments and that their ultimate meta-

physical justification must forever elude us—which would mean that we could never be more than roughly sure we were punishing the right people for crimes. Locke sought to soften this by two devices. One was to sever "substance" and "person" in the same way that he severed "man" and "person" and to insist that only persons are bearers of responsibility, the concept of substance being obscure and irrelevant. The difficulty with this is that it leaves the doctrine of substance without any connection to those entities whose unity it was supposed to explain. The other device was to say that it is the "more probable opinion" that the consciousness which makes for personal identity is "annexed to" one immaterial substance rather than a plurality and to found the faith in its not being otherwise on the goodness of the Deity "who, as far as the happiness or misery of any of his sensible creatures is concerned in it, will not, by a fatal error of theirs, transfer from one to another that consciousness which draws reward or punishment with it."

But these are no more than devices and have to be used only if we represent the identity of persons as composed of one kind of fact yet recognized through another. For Locke himself, in his early comments on the varying criteria of identity for objects of different kinds, has provided us with a demonstration of the total inutility of the doctrines of substance. We do not need them to account for our ascriptions of identity through change; these rest upon our noticing characteristic patterns of sequence in things. But these patterns do not just supply the criteria for ascribing continuance. They are also the reasons for our doing so at all. In other words, the answer to the unity question lies in the same facts which yield the answer to the criteria question. The invention of substance was intended to explain a practice whose explanation Locke had himself provided in another way. That he did not draw the moral and altogether abandon this invention may in part be the result of his having inherited it from others and in part the result of the incompleteness of his account of the criteria of personal identity.

In Locke, then, we find: one answer to the unity problem in terms of substance and another in terms of the objects' characteristic patterns of change, which renders the first answer unnecessary; a clear recognition of the connection between problems of practical identification and moral responsibility, which is exaggerated to the point of caricature by the separation of the concepts of a person and a man; an unambiguous claim for the priority of the memory criterion of identity for persons, which seems on superficial examination to lead to circularities; and an introduction of the puzzle cases to force a decision in favor of the last claim. With the lessons of Locke's insights and errors behind us, we turn to Hume.

HUME

In Hume's famous section on personal identity (*Treatise of Human Nature*, Book I, Part IV, Sec. 6), we find a treatment of the topic which is, as would be expected, more polished and consistent than that of Locke. But since it is also radically defective, its very tidiness makes it less fertile. It has had a baffling effect on generations of readers because of Hume's ability to destroy metaphysical palliative solutions to problems without uncovering the confusions which give rise to them. This, in turn, issues in a paralyzing skepticism which rendered Hume even less capable than Locke of reaching a clear understanding of the conceptual structure he examines.

Hume began by attacking the spiritual-substance solution to the problem of unity, as it appears in the claim that there is a unique and simple "self" which each person is able to detect within himself. He argued with effective simplicity that he was unable to detect it in himself. He was accordingly forced to conclude that the belief in personal identity, since it lacks this justification, is erroneous. People are "nothing but a bundle or collection of different perceptions" in a constant state of change—for perceptions are all that Hume *could* detect in himself. In this situation all that a philosopher can do is examine how it is that men (himself included) "suppose ourselves possessed of an invariable and uninterrupted existence through the whole course of our lives." This psychological objective Hume tried to attain by uncovering a basic conceptual confusion which he claimed we all fall into. We fail, he said to distinguish properly between two things—the "idea of an object, that remains invariable and uninterrupted thro' a supposed variation of time" (which is the prototype of identity) and the "idea of several different objects existing in succession, and connected together by a close relation" (which is as good an example as any other of diversity). We confuse these two ideas because of the mental laziness which makes us content with their superficial similarity. Strictly ("to an accurate view"), change destroys identity, but we are easily beguiled into overlooking that change has occurred. Once launched upon this convenient path of error, the mind is led further and further along it by certain recurring facts—it is easier for us to overlook than notice gradual changes, changes that are characteristic of certain objects, and changes that occur according to certain smooth and regular patterns, and so we choose to overlook them. Everyone is prone to this error, which therefore acquires the dubious sanction of custom. Sooner or later, however, philosophers arrive on the scene and notice the recurrent paradox in which men have thus involved their thinking. They see both that we do ascribe identity to changing things and that we have no apparent ground for doing this. The result is that since they cannot *find* such a ground, they *invent* one. Hence, the metaphysical fancies of substance and the self. But these are hollow solutions; there is no discernible bond uniting a person, though there are sufficient interrelationships between his thoughts, feelings, and memories to explain why we erroneously ascribe unity to him. Hume had no consolation to offer us in this alleged predicament other than his usual one: Even though philosophical constructions cannot justify custom, philosophical criticism cannot dislodge it. For philosophical reasonings have power only in the study, not at the backgammon table.

Sameness and change. Given the premise that Hume shared with the philosophers of substance, his conclusions follow only too clearly. This premise is that there is indeed a paradox in ascribing both change and identity to the same subject, since to ascribe change is to deny that we *have* the same subject. To agree to this is to deny that there can be any genuine solution to the problem of unity and to show that even a substance solution is at best a palliative—and a misleading one. But this is a very odd premise to concede without a battle. It has the extreme, language-destroying consequence that no predicates which cannot be simultaneously ascribed to one subject can be ascribed to a subject at two different times. If it is a mere matter of custom that we violate this principle, at least the custom is indispensable. Surely, much argument is needed to show that the custom is paradoxical and the principle necessary. And there is very little argument in Hume to this effect. His account of the fundamental confusion he claimed to have detected is made plausible only by its vagueness. It looks reasonable to say there is a contrast between one continuing object and a succession of related objects, but this is so only if "object" is tacitly replaced by the same noun in each case. There is a contrast between one continuing note and a succession of related notes (and who would confuse one with the other?) but not between one continuing tune and a succession of related notes. It is by means of the second sort of arrangement, not the first, that we incorporate change into our language. In order to understand the unreality of the contrast which Hume was foisting upon himself, one has merely to recall Locke's principle that "same" is an incomplete term that functions only in conjunction with substantives. There are some conjunctions which would yield the contrast—"same note" and "succession of different notes" is obviously one. It is equally obvious that "same tune" and "succession of different notes" is not one. Thus, Hume was wrong to look for the source of the contrast, when it does exist, in the concepts of identity and diversity considered alone. The concepts do not operate alone and yield his conflict only in those cases where they are joined with the right substantives. In most cases it does not exist, because most substantive concepts (including that of a person) are designed to incorporate changes.

There is, of course, one sense of the words "same" and "identical" in which sameness and change are incompatible. This is the sense of "same" in which, if applied to two distinct things, it means "alike" and, if applied to one thing at different times, it means "unaltered." This we might call the comparative sense of the word. It is to be distinguished from the numerical sense, in which two things said to be the same are said not to be two, but one. Clearly, one thing cannot be said to be both changed and the same if the comparative sense is intended, but this is not the sense we intend when we wonder whether we are entitled to consider someone the same throughout changes. Once this is noted, we can easily see that there is no need to assume that "to an accurate view" an object has to be the same in the comparative sense to remain the same in the numerical sense. If this is missed, a sense of paradox will be only too easy to sustain.

On the other hand, our concepts do not allow all kinds of change indiscriminately. How much is allowed depends on the concept in question. A man can change in more ways before he is destroyed than a chair can. To know what alterations are and are not allowed is to know, among other things, what the criteria of identity are for the class of entities grouped under the concept in question. These matters may not always be easy to settle precisely. We may not be in a position to say whether we have the same things on certain occasions. When the roof is removed, does the house still exist, or are we left with something else? If the walls are torn down and rebuilt, do we have the same house or another? Sometimes the only answer at such a point is a decision on the scope of the concept. But for general purposes usage over the years has provided us with rough and ready conventions which (this is a truism) language-users know.

Hume was aware of this fact, but the logic of his position forced him to misrepresent it. Instead of presenting us with some general indications of the sorts of change which tend to be allowed under concepts (changes which are gradual, small, functionally absorbable into the whole, and so on), he claimed to present us with the factors which, in his view, beguile us most regularly into the habit of ignoring the changes which are taking place in objects right under our noses. But these factors (which do not at all conceal the changing character of our world from us) are the same ones which appear without this disguise in a correct account of the situation. It is from a detailed knowledge of the very facts he outlined that we derive the criteria for those very identity judgments which he declared to be always unjustified. This is not the first or last time a philosopher has drawn our attention to facts supposed to support one theory when they in fact support another.

Similar considerations apply to what Hume said about the creation of substance doctrines. It is probably true that philosophers have invented these in order to answer the unity problem, and it is, of course, a merit in Hume that he saw that there is no independent evidence for the truth of such doctrines. But he did not see that the primary objection to them is not that they cannot be shown to be true, but that they are unnecessary. They are invoked to soften a paradox that does not exist. There is no contradiction between saying a thing or person has changed and remains that same thing or person if the changes are characteristic of that sort of thing or of persons. If there is no paradox here, there is no need of any metaphysical postulate to conceal it. If Hume had seen this, he would not have tried to render more palatable the skepticism to which he was led by rejecting the doctrine of substance, for such skepticism could arise only if the doctrine were thought to be both false *and* necessary. But it is only false. The substantialists do not vindicate the ordinary language-user, and Hume does not convict him. Both have misdescribed what he is doing.

Persons. In the specific comments that Hume made about the identity of persons, he was clearly working, as was Locke, in the restricted framework in which "person" means "mind." Only thus can we read his statement that people are nothing but bundles of perceptions. The restriction makes him exaggerate for skeptical purposes the discontinuity he claimed to have discovered in the life histories of persons—a discontinuity which does not exist if we include the history of each person's body as well as that of his mind.

But this error hides a deeper one. There is a curious unreality about Hume's discussion of whether we can observe any real bond between the perceptions of a person. This question cannot, of course, be raised unless we can already distinguish between one person and another. Hume, that is to say, was asking whether there is any uniting bond among those perceptions that belong to one person. But why should this question puzzle him if he can already distinguish between those perceptions that belong to one person and those that belong to another? It is at least likely that those features of persons which enable us to distinguish one from another (to individuate) at any one time should also enable us to reidentify people after lapses of time. Yet these features are, and have to be, largely physical ones. For each of us can have (or perceive) only his own perceptions, and without the recognition of the bodies of others, there would be no question of the ownership of perceptions other than one's own ever arising (or, therefore, of the ownership of one's own). In asking his question, Hume was assuming that the perceptions which persons are alleged to consist of are somehow known to be in parallel strings, so that the only question remaining is what unites those perceptions that belong on any one string. But if, as he saw, there is no clear psychical factor uniting them, it might still be true that whatever determines their belonging to a particular string also serves to join them together along it. And this, after all, is part of what the body does. His puzzle arises in the form that baffled him only if we first differentiate persons from one another on the basis of their bodies and then, forgetting that we have done it this way, look for some substitute for this principle among the contents of the mind. The principle which the question throws into doubt has to be assumed for the question to be raised.

In Hume, therefore, we find a dismissal of metaphysical construction and an awareness of the general characteristics of the complex facts out of which we forge our criteria of identity. These, however, are rendered completely sterile by the skeptical use to which Hume had to put them. The skepticism is, in turn, the result of a rationalistic oversimplification of the notion of identity which prevented Hume from discovering the muddle at the heart of the unity puzzle and of the dualistic framework of thought within which he worked.

SOME INTERIM CONCLUSIONS

We can now draw some conclusions from this investigation of the two main classical discussions of self-identity. The first is that the problem of the unity of persons is a spurious problem which rests upon two errors concerning the idea of identity. One of the errors is the failure to take enough note of the distinction between comparative and numerical identity. The other is the failure to note that the concept of numerical identity works in harness with substantive class concepts that provide those who know how to employ them with rules for making correct identity judgments on entities within their classes.

The second conclusion is that the concept of spiritual substance is not only unverifiable (as Hume saw) but also unnecessary (as Locke saw and Hume did not).

The third conclusion is that the unity problem has acquired a specious appearance of difficulty because of a tacit restriction placed by philosophers on the concept of a person. Since only the psychical components of the person are considered, a picture of change and discontinuity is conjured up which makes the fictitious contrast between identity and change seem even more alarming.

This leads naturally into the fourth conclusion—that it is salutary to remind ourselves that our actual concept of a person is of a psychophysical being. Hence, talk of the criteria of identity for purely psychical beings is not talk of the concept of a person that we actually have. How far they would differ has yet to be decided, but we must at least begin by asking what the actual criteria for embodied human beings are. Here we must bear in mind the apparent circularity of the view that memory is the sole criterion for the identity of human beings. The examination of Locke suggested that in order to apply it some covert reference to the identity of the body has to be made. We must first examine this suggestion with some care.

We shall begin by trying to clarify further the notion of a criterion. It will then be argued that the bodily criterion of identity is in certain important ways more fundamental than the memory criterion in present discourse, although memory is still properly called a criterion in spite of Locke's failure. It could not, however, be the sole criterion. We shall finally consider the puzzles and argue that although they present us with some difficult conceptual decisions, they would not *necessitate* a change of convention in favor of memory, although this is a *possible* response to them. An attempt will be made to show that the response, if made, is innocuous, so that the puzzles are devoid of the wide implications philosophers have thought them to have.

CRITERIA

Thus far, two things have been meant in calling bodily identity and memory criteria of personal identity. One is that it is by reference to one or the other of these facts about people that questions of identity are usually settled. The other is that practical knowledge of how to settle these questions in these ways is a necessary part of having the concept of a person. More needs to be said than this.

There are two areas where the notion of a criterion has been of special concern in recent philosophy. One is the problem of the knowledge of the mental life of other persons. It has been said by some, following Wittgenstein, that we can have this knowledge because people's behavior is able to supply us with criteria for saying correctly that they have certain mental states. The other is the problem of the relationship between judgments of fact and evaluative judgments. It has been said by Urmson, Hare, and others that certain facts about things or people serve as criteria for evaluating them as good or bad. In both these cases the relationship the word "criterion" names is thought to be tighter than an inductive one and yet looser than a deductive one. In this discussion the word will not be used in this sense, since the relationship between bodily identity and memory, on the one hand, and personal identity, on the other, seems to be closer than this; it seems, in fact, to be straightforwardly deductive. In the

discussion of Locke we saw that saying someone remembers something in the strong sense entails that it forms a part of his life history. It is now claimed that if a person before us has the body that Smith used to have, it follows that he is Smith.

Two comments are necessary. First, this does not commit us to any view about how we know that the criteria are satisfied. To explain how we discover that this man really remembers or really has Smith's body, it might be necessary to use the notion of a criterion in some other, weaker sense—to say, for example, that a certain accumulation of evidence left no more room for reasonable doubt on the matter. But this is another issue. Second, an objection has to be countered. It might be objected that if the relationship between memory or bodily identity and personal identity is deductive, then the criteria are sterile and unusable. For, the argument might go, if either of these facts entailed that this was the same person, we would have to know independently who it was before we could be sure the criterion was satisfied. (This is the objection mentioned in the case of Locke.) This is not a genuine difficulty, but it is instructive. The reason for introducing it can only be the doctrine that if one proposition, *P,* entails another, *Q,* then it is impossible to know *P* without first knowing *Q.* But this is only a dogma that has to be tested against the facts, which do not bear it out.

The difficulty can teach us, however, that the standard objection to Locke is too simple. Even though the fact that memory entails personal identity prevents us from defining one in terms of the other without a circle, it is still possible that we may sometimes know that a person remembers without having previously checked on his identity. If this were not so, then memory could not serve as a criterion, for it is an additional part of the notion of a criterion, as all philosophers have used the term, that it can be applied. I shall shortly argue that this knowledge is possible.

Bodily identity. Some philosophers have said that the bodily criterion is not a criterion at all because there are some occasions in which we find human bodies that are not persons—that is, dead bodies or bodies that are biologically alive but incapable of exhibiting personality. But my thesis is that bodily identity is a sufficient criterion for reidentifying persons and by hypothesis these are not persons. If we are asking whether *X* before us, who is a person, is the same as Smith whom we once knew, who was a person, it is a sufficient condition of an affirmative answer to know that *X*'s body is Smith's body.

A more serious-looking argument against bodily identity comes from the puzzles. It might be said that when we use the bodily criterion, we are covertly assuming that there has not been any bodily transfer. This raises an important point of method: How are the puzzles to be treated? We shall treat them as cases of proposed conceptual innovation, as if those who invent them do so to make us imagine circumstances which would force us to change our conceptual habits and rely on one criterion alone, even though we now use two. I have argued that in using two criteria, we have not faced the sorts of problems the puzzles present. If this is right, then no proviso against them can be embodied in our present thinking, even covertly. (If anyone considers that such contingencies *are* already provided for, then what is said below about the puzzles can probably be transposed into the key needed to examine his view of what sort of provision we make.)

There are several ways in which the bodily criterion is more fundamental than the memory criterion. In the present thesis these statements should seem like truisms.

Although both criteria are sufficient, only bodily identity is necessary. "This is the person who fired the shot" is entailed equally by "This person has the body of the person who fired the shot" and "This person remembers firing the shot"; but although the third statement entails the first statement, it does not entail the second.

The bodily criterion is more extensive. It is a matter of chance that men remember the tracts of their lives that they do remember rather than those that they do not, and we can apply the memory criterion only when there are memories to use. But in a clear sense the bodily criterion can always be used, for the body is present whenever the person is.

The bodily criterion is more varied. There are more ways in which we can determine whether a person is physically the same as someone than there are ways of determining whether his recollections are genuine. There are blood tests, fingerprints, photographs, the testimony of witnesses, and much else. Of course, a candidate's memory claims can be used to support this evidence, just as physical evidence can be used to support memory claims. The resort to physical tests when the memory claims are in doubt, however, is much more nearly inevitable than the resort to memory claims when physical evidence is inconclusive, since there are so many ways of adding to the physical evidence and it is free from the nagging thought that there is more than one way of coming by information about the past.

These examples are enough to show that we should regard overconfident readings of the puzzle cases with some suspicion, since the normal order of priority between our criteria is not what these readings suggest that it is.

Memory. It has already been suggested that even though Locke was mistaken in thinking that he could define personal identity in terms of memory, it does not follow that he was wrong to think of memory as a genuine criterion of personal identity. It might be possible to know that someone remembered without first ascertaining in another way who he is. But if this is possible, it has to coexist with the fact that when men's memory claims are in doubt, decision hinges for the most part on physical tests.

One way of trying to relate these two is to say that when we accept a memory claim unchecked, as we often do, we are relying on an inductive connection between the memory claims of a person and the events he refers to. We have found, that is, that this man's memory claims are usually true or, perhaps, that most people's are usually true. We now accept his word on this basis. Sydney Shoemaker has argued persuasively that this is too simple. He has claimed that it is a logical truth that memory claims are usually true, not an inductive one. Following are his arguments. (1) If someone frequently said with sincerity that he remembered events which did not occur, we would be justified in concluding that he did not know how to use the

word "remember." (2) If a child learning the language were to behave in this way with the word "remember" or one of its cognates, we would tell him that he had not learned how to use it. (3) If we were translating an unknown language and were inclined to translate certain expressions in it as memory expressions, our decision whether to do so would have to hinge in part upon the truth or falsity of the statements beginning with those expressions; if they were generally false, we could not translate them in this way.

If these arguments are accepted, it should probably be added that in order to understand memory claims at all, we must be able to recognize cases of genuine memory, so that there must be *some* such cases and also that just as lies and false promises must be in the minority to succeed, so must insincere or mistaken memory claims. These arguments appear enough to refute any generalized skepticism about memory, unless the skeptic is prepared to deny that our language has those features on which these arguments depend—that its users are generally successful in communicating by means of it and that it is learned and not instinctive. We shall not investigate how far it is correct to regard something established by this sort of argument as a "necessary truth." Although the arguments do depend upon features of language which might be argued to be contingent ones, it is still clear that the conclusions are not straightforwardly inductive, and for this reason I shall allow the label to stick.

It is, then, a necessary truth that memory claims are usually true, from which it follows that they can usually be relied upon in practice. But this does not tell us whether any given memory claim is true. The situation here is, rather, that we are justified in accepting someone's memory claims unless there is some reason to doubt them. Only when there is such a reason do we need to check them. It is this which enables memory to serve as a criterion of identity.

But this is a far cry from Locke's theory that memory is the sole criterion. The very facts which show it to be a criterion at all show that it could not be the only one. We must be able to use the distinction between true and false memory claims (even to learn memory language), and this means we must have at our disposal a way or ways of checking the claims that are made. This implies, of course, that we must be able to discover whether the speaker was, indeed, present at that which he describes. Thus, the availability of the bodily criterion of identity is a necessary condition of our having made the distinction between genuine and false memories, even though it often must, from our previous arguments, be in order not to resort to it but to accept memory claims at their face value. Memory is thus a criterion of identity, but it is absurd to suggest it could be the only one, for without the ability to use another we would lack the ability to use it.

This bears out the view that the bodily criterion is more fundamental. There are arguments in Shoemaker, however, which suggest that just as the memory criterion depends on the bodily criterion in the way we have seen, a similar dependence exists the other way. There is a dependence the other way, but it is not a parallel one. The dependence is one found in all cognitive procedures.

Unless people had memories, they could not know past facts. If they did not know past facts, they could not know past facts about themselves or other persons, for we have to depend on either our own recollections or those of other witnesses to learn about the past of a human body. At some point memory testimony has to be accepted without further question, and to accept someone's testimony is to accept that he was indeed a witness to some past event. This is true and supplies us with one more argument to show that memory claims must usually be correct, but it does not establish parity between the two criteria because it does not show that in dealing with a problem of re-identification, it is impossible in theory to dispense with the memory claims of the candidate himself. This is possible, however, and is one of the reasons for the greater importance of the bodily criterion.

In spite of this many philosophers have accorded memory greater weight than the bodily criterion. This seems to be a result of what I shall call the "internality" of memory. In remembering, a person seems to have direct, rather than inferential, access to his own past, to know past facts about himself from the inside. This view of memory is reinforced by the fact that most people would admit to having quasi-perceptual experiences in the form of mental imagery when they remember. Most readers unhesitatingly follow the writers of bodily-transfer stories in assuming them to be intelligible—for how could someone who had systematic recollections of this kind be proved wrong about his own identity by outsiders?

This attitude is not shaken as much as it should be by the fact that in ordinary unsystematic cases we frequently find that even the most vivid recollections are illusory. This is presumably because of the traditional picture of memory as some sort of introspective contemplation of imagery. But what brings memory into the public arena and enables us to use it as a criterion of identity is not this or that sort of private experience but the claims made as a result of it. Indeed, the memory claims of those who deny having memory images are as negotiable in common speech as those of the rest of us. If someone were to claim that he remembered an event and if we were able to determine that he had indeed witnessed it, could give us correct information about it, and could not have come by this information through later research or hearsay, there could be no doubt that he did remember it. The presence or absence, vividness or faintness, of his private images would be of no interest.

It is nevertheless characteristic that when people remember, they have images. If it were not, it is hard to see how the traditional picture of memory could have gained currency. It is true that memory claims are corrigible public claims to knowledge about the past and true that those who make them usually seem to have memory images. It is the first claim that explains why memory has the status it has as a criterion of personal identity. It is the second claim that helps us to understand why some have thought it more fundamental a criterion than it is. For although the subject's unique possession of his images does not confer immunity on the claims he makes, it may have much to do with the fact that he makes them. And it is easy to imagine cases where someone has such experiences and makes the memory claims which they characteristically engender only to find out afterward that these claims are unfounded. This is common enough. It is an easy extension of this to imagine situations in which the events described by such a person did in fact take place, but in the presence of a human body other than the one he has. We then have a typical philospher's puzzle case. In such a situation characteristic image-laden experiences might take place, and the customary memory claims might be uttered, yet the contextual conditions surrounding correct memory claims would not exist. To allow in some such cases that the speaker really does remember is to change the meaning of this word, but the characteristic intimacy and feeling of conviction which such inner experiences engender might hide this fact from those imagining such examples.

BODILY TRANSFER

It is now time to look at the puzzles. There are, however, a great variety of these, and without deliberate restriction it is impossible to produce any example of the intricate conceptual decisions involved in them. We shall accordingly leave aside puzzle stories of persons who seem to vanish and reappear or who seem to be reincarnations of someone dead and keep to the case of apparent bodily transfer. What is said here is probably comparable to what could be said in these other cases.

Let us take a story in which the servants in a royal palace waken a person who looks as if he is the prince but who evinces complete bewilderment at his surroundings, utters memory claims befitting a cobbler, is astonished on looking into the mirror, and so on. At the same time a man who looks as if he is the cobbler produces princely reactions and memory claims and demands to be returned to the royal palace. What should we say?

B. A. O. Williams has pointed out that the puzzle cases are harder to state in detail than is usually thought. Are we really able to imagine a person with the cobbler's memories (which will include some acquired skills and personality traits) and the prince's body? I shall ignore this complication, though in fact it tends to support what I shall argue to be the best solution.

The first thing to notice about such a puzzle is that it is puzzling. We are torn two ways over it, as we would expect to be if we have two criteria in apparent conflict. On reflection, however, it is more puzzling because if what I have said above is correct, the bodily criterion is the more fundamental of the two, so that the priorities in present practice would lead one to expect that the puzzle should be settled in its favor. Yet those such as Locke, who invent these stories, take it for granted that our temptations are to settle it in favor of memory. And as far as their judgment of the temptations of most readers goes, they seem to be right. Any answer to the puzzle must take both sides of this paradox into account and try to reconcile them.

Priority of bodily criterion. Let us first consider the recommendation that our cobbler-prince episode should make us abandon the bodily criterion in favor of the memory criterion.

Put in this bald way, the proposal is absurd. We have already seen reason to say that memory could not be the sole criterion for the identity of persons because using it requires the availability of another. But this, although true, is far too brusque a reaction to the puzzle, which could be used to argue a more modest proposal—to *weaken* the bodily criterion in certain circumstances.

The advocate of bodily transfer could begin his case by making certain admissions and could then say that they do not destroy the case for it. The admissions would be these.

First, in order to set up any case at all, we have to have someone who now makes memory claims that fit a body other than the one he now has. This requires that he should be reidentifiable as the same throughout the period during which he utters the claims. The claims have to be systematic in the circumstances, so the period has to be considerable. For such reidentification the criterion of bodily identity would be necessary.

Second, in order to set up any case at all, we have to know that there was actually a person in the past about whose life these memory claims seem to be accurate reports and that all the claims fit the life history of the *same* person in the past, who *was* the person the claimant now says he *is*. This can be known only if in the past we were able to reidentify that person over the period of his life. This requires the past availability of the bodily criterion.

But when these admissions are made, the advocate of bodily transfer need go no further; he can hold his ground here and say that bodily transfer is still possible. If we had a case where the memory claims of the man who seemed to be the cobbler systematically fitted the past of the prince and vice versa, these claims could be checked up on in detail. And they would be found, *ex hypothesi*, to fit a past human body; the only difference from normal would be that the body which they fitted was not the body uttering them. Yet the past of the body uttering them would itself be taken care of by a systematic set of memory claims now uttered by that body which they did fit. In such circumstances it surely would be wholly natural to say that the two men had exchanged bodies.

In spite of much recent writing on the puzzles, there seems to be no satisfactory demonstration that the change in convention that would follow on our saying a transfer had occurred would lead to absurdities. It is therefore a possibility. If we make this decision, we would be forced to so weaken the bodily criterion that we were entitled to infer from its being the same body to its being the same person only if there were no (systematic) memory claims which pointed to its being another person. This would place the two criteria in a position of relative parity, for the memory criterion would hold in normal circumstances subject to bodily checks and the bodily criterion would hold except in those abnormal cases where there were detailed and systematic memory claims that conflicted with the normal reading of the bodily evidence.

Having allowed this, we must now emphasize two things. One is that other readings of these cases could be made, as will shortly be argued. The other is that even the adoption of the bodily-transfer reading of them does not have the exciting implications most have thought.

We have already seen that it lends no support to the view that memory either is or ever could be the sole criterion of identity for persons.

It also does nothing to support the suggestion that people could exist with no bodies at all or to give concrete meaning to the common picture of bodily transfer as someone's *going out of* one body *into* another.

Transfer cases, even if allowed, could only be exceptional. If they were not, we would have a world in which the procedures for applying memory concepts would be much more complex than they now are and virtually impossible to learn. I do not think we could come to learn memory language if the basic use of the word "remember" were one in which it could refer not only to the past of the body uttering it but also to the past of another body (which, in turn, it could be allowed to "fit" only if it were certain that there were no other systematic memory claims to fit the same period available from that body itself). A concept as epistemologically fundamental as that of memory has to be more easily come by than it would be in this sort of world. But granted that it is simpler and has been learned in more straightforward ways, as at present, then it could be stretched to subsequently cover the exceptional cases.

The conclusion is, therefore, that although the logical possibility of bodily transfer has to be admitted, the implications are small and the wisdom of this particular change in our conventions is not self-evident.

Abandoning the memory criterion. We shall now consider the reverse suggestion—that in the face of such a puzzle we abandon the memory criterion and keep the bodily criterion.

It is not immediately obvious what could be meant by this. If it means that we should ignore the memory claims of candidates for reidentification, this is something we could do in any case; the point at issue is the status of those claims when they are considered. If it means that we should reject memory claims that clash with the bodily facts, then this is something we do already and no change in conventions is implied in it. It must mean that we disallow the inference from "He remembers *X*" to "*X* formed part of his life history." But the difficulty here is that in order even to gather the bodily facts, we need to learn about the pasts of others, we have to use either our own memories or those of witnesses, and checks on one set of memories, as we saw earlier, require reliance on other sets. So a change of convention here must allow for the continuance of this reliance.

It seems possible to allow for it in only one way—to continue to say that memory claims are generally correct accounts of past actions or events but to add that these actions or events may have formed part of the life of a person other than the one now making memory claims about them. People, in other words, would be allowed to recall events in the lives of others. Two comments may be made here.

For reasons which would parallel those in the previous section, it seems that cases where people *did* recall events in the lives of others would have to be rare.

Suppose that in spite of his protestations *X* was just admitted to be the prince because he has the prince's body. He now says, "But I remember mending the shoes last night." Suppose *X* finally gives in and concedes that he must be the prince although it is still agreed on all sides that the cobbler did mend the shoes last night. *X* cannot just say, "Oh, I really remember the cobbler's mending the shoes, not myself." This will not do because it fails to distinguish between the new, special case in which one person remembers the deeds of another without having done them (or even having been present) and the familiar case in which one person remembers another's deeds through having witnessed those deeds. It is the second case that would be conveyed by a sentence like "I remember the cobbler's mending the shoes." I am not sure how far this difficulty could be removed by verbal adjustment, but it is at the minimum an inconvenience under the new convention.

The conclusion is as before.

Denial that one criterion is satisfied. There would thus seem to be two possible alternative conceptual changes that we could make, each of which would weaken a familiar inference and each of which would be awkward, though not demonstrably impossible. As a matter of fact, however, we already have at our disposal a much simpler device for dealing with such puzzles. Instead of pretending to abandon or to alter one criterion, we can refuse to allow that one of them is satisfied. This need not be thought of as merely a temporary device. If we were to come across odd examples of pieces of iron that did not obey the lodestone but seemed otherwise to satisfy tests for being iron, we could postpone conceptual change for some time by insisting either that the tests had not been properly administered or that it was not really a lodestone. Such moves would become irrational only if maintained in the face of repeated examples. It is hard to admit that the point of irrationality could ever be reached in the present case.

There are clearly only two moves of this sort here. We can deny that it is really the same body, on the grounds that the memory claims it utters fit another, or we can deny that it is really the case that the speaker remembers, because it was not the body before us that was present. Note that neither move involves denying a criterion as the term is being used here. It merely involves refusing to accept that one criterion is satisfied in those cases where accepting that both were satisfied would land us in direct contradiction. There seem to be insuperable obstacles in adopting the first move. For one thing, it would require us, in the case of human bodies, to adopt standards of re-identification that differ from those we accept in the case of all other physical objects. (And if we disregarded this and insisted on behavioral or memory criteria for the identity of human bodies, we would destroy the distinction between a human body and a person.) For another, we would find ourselves led straight into an absurdity. Note again that we are retaining the bodily criterion while making this move. If what is known to be spatiotemporally continuous with the prince's body utters cobblerlike memory claims and if for this reason we say that it is not really the prince's body, we are not able to go on to say that it is, instead, the cobbler's body; for, by hypothesis, it is not spatiotemporally continuous with the cobbler's body and is therefore *not* the same physical object as that body. Thus, it is nobody's body at all, which is absurd. Hence, we are not able to make the move of denying that it is the body it seems to

be. But there is nothing to prevent us from making the other move—of saying that unless the bodily facts at least coincide with the memory claims a person utters, then these claims are false, however closely they fit the past of someone else. This would merely be the determined application to special cases of a procedure we now follow.

We could not, of course, stop there, for we would have to explain how the person came to forget his own past and have so much accurate information about another's. Heroic hypotheses of retrocognitive clairvoyance would have to be brought forward to deal with such strange things. Such hypotheses would have to explain how it was that a person could have information about someone else's past in a manner so phenomenologically similar to the way in which he normally remembered his own. But no greater heroism would be called for here than would be called for by accepting that one person could exchange bodies or memories with another—for the second idea would require much the same sort of hypothesis as the one I have mentioned, and the first would make it puzzling that people should remember their own pasts. Of course, each would introduce a difficult conceptual change.

Puzzle cases becoming common. But would we not be forced into a conceptual change if such cases became common? For once, the complexities of our problem make it easier to deal with and enable us to give a negative answer. This can be understood from two sides. It has already been argued that either of the possible conceptual changes would require that the cases of bodily transfer or memory exchange be rare; otherwise, we would not have the memory concepts we do have. Yet in order even to state the problem, we must use memory concepts. From the other side, we have to remember that if we were to adopt the device recommended, then in cases like the one in our story we would say of the characters not that they remembered but that they "retrocognized." If such a convention were adopted, however, it would become the appropriate language for the persons to use in such situations. For what makes our problem is what makes the memory criterion possible—the occurrence of memory claims. These are made in public memory language. If the public language changed so that the inappropriateness of a standardly worded memory claim for such circumstances became generally recognized, then the persons themselves, on discovering that the bodily facts did not fit, would not say that they remembered but that they "retrocognized." Thus, by the time the cases became common, they would cease to exist in the logically puzzling form, because they would cease to be heralded by claims to remember. Pieces of iron do not talk; people are different, and the very data of the puzzles would change if the cases occurred frequently.

Primacy of memory. The solution has now to contend with the fact that we do feel a genuine compulsion to read these puzzle stories in some way that favors memory and to say that the claimant himself must know who he is better than others ever could. There are two reasons for this compulsion. One derives from the internality of memory, the other from psychophysical dualism.

On the internality of memory it is enough to repeat that although it is people's public memory claims which relate to decisions about their identity, such claims seem to be made for the most part when people have had characteristic image-laden experiences. Many philosophers consider these to be more closely related to the logic of remembering than they really are, and since the privacy of imagery places reports of it in an epistemologically privileged position, this privilege is erroneously thought to extend to memory claims—overlooking the fact that memory claims are not reports of imagery. When a person imagines himself being involved in a puzzle story, he supplies himself with vivid and systematic imagery to occasion memory claims that do not fit his present body, and he forgets that the persistence and vividness of the memory could not override the impact of the public physical checks that are a necessary part of the conventions governing memory claims.

As for the theoretical dualism which lies behind so many arguments about personal identity, it has here been argued that however we read them, the puzzles do nothing to support dualism. But the investigation of them has been conditioned in many cases by dualist preconceptions.

Shoemaker correctly remarked that the concept of bodily transfer is compatible with a behavioristic view of the mind, for one might mean when saying that the cobbler and prince had exchanged bodies, that in the case of each person his distinctive behavior patterns (including his memory claims and behavior) were to be found in a body other than the one in which they used to be found. This is true, but if this solution to the puzzles were urged upon us in conjunction with an overtly behaviorist view of personality, it seems plain that there would be no special obviousness in or compulsion toward this solution as opposed to the others, even though it would still be a possible one. The reason that we all feel some degree of compulsion toward accepting the bodily-transfer solution is that dualist preconceptions intrude themselves when we investigate the stories. It is taken for granted that we have an independently clear concept, with recognized criteria of identity, of a soul, spirit, or mind, which can be thought of as having a purely contingent relationship to the body, which it may abandon in favor of another body. (Locke's phraseology in introducing the puzzle is to the point: "Should the soul of a prince . . . enter and inform the body of a cobbler. . . .") The only available criterion for such a purely psychical being is presumably memory, but we have already seen that it cannot be self-sufficient in the way it would have to be for us to conceive such an entity independently. Yet this is necessary to justify otherwise vacuous talk about such an entity's entering one body, leaving another, and the rest. Anyone feeling impelled to read the puzzles in favor of memory is probably making covert use of this illegitimate picture.

An important objection could now be raised. It might be said that even though much reflection has been infused with a dualist theory, this is a linguistic fact of life that philosophers must accept without complaint, for all language-users, not just philosophers, tend to be dualists. Thus, all language-users, if faced with the puzzles, would tend to opt for the memory solution. If so, how can a philosopher cavil at this solution? For what we *should* say is usually to be determined by a decision as to what we *would* say.

This raises the difficult general question of how to react to a misleading theory that has filtered into ordinary discourse. In the present case we could argue as follows. Philosophers like Ryle have exposed many errors and confusions in traditional dualism. But they have spoiled their own case by representing themselves as champions of the common man against the professional philosopher. It is easy enough to show that nonphilosophers are dualists, too. However, the common man is a dualist in the same sense in which the philosopher is one—when he interprets his own thinking about mental qualities and conduct. What the antidualist arguments show is that laymen misconstrue in their interpretative moments the utterances and thoughts that they engage in in their day-to-day existence. (We could say that all of us are occasionally philosophers, when we think about our ordinary mental concepts, but most of us are bad philosophers because we misinterpret them.) These common theoretical misconstructions, though inconsistent with our daily use of such concepts, are usually harmless because of the merciful logical dispensation which allows us to make good sense with our concepts while talking nonsense about them. Occasionally, however, the prolonged continuance of the misguided theory can infect the practice. One such occasion is the present one, where the tacit appeal to the illegitimate concept of an independently identifiable psychical entity exerts a compulsion upon the reader of a puzzle story to interpret that story as a case of bodily transfer. Here it seems legitimate to replace bad theory by better and to argue against taking this solution for granted. The memory solution the dualist reading implies is at best one competitor among others, and one is led to think it is required only by our use of concepts on more normal occasions if one has misunderstood those occasions.

CONCLUSIONS

Of the two problems distinguished at the outset, this article has tried to show that the first, the unity problem, is spurious, since the paradox on which it rests is only apparent. The criteria problem admits of no such clear-cut solution, since it is clear on examination that both the bodily criterion and the memory criterion are ineluctable components of our concept of a person. The bodily criterion is more fundamental, but the memory criterion is, in its own way, indispensable because of the basic epistemological status of memory itself. This is one of the many facets of the irreducibly psychophysical nature of persons. One important result of this conclusion is that it is absurd to consider memory as the sole necessary or sufficient condition of identity. Thus, it would not even seem possible to construct a coherent concept of an independently identifiable bodiless person of whose identity memory would be the sole criterion. It would seem to follow that disembodied survival is logically absurd. It is impossible to decide here whether the doctrine of bodily resurrection fares better. Our examination shows that the puzzle stories can at most embody situations in which the relationships between the two criteria could be altered by conceptual decision. They could not embody situations in which either could be abandoned in favor of the other.

Bibliography

The literature devoted explicitly to the problem of personal identity is fairly small, but the amount that is devoted to related questions is immense. These works were made direct use of in the article: John Locke, *Essay Concerning Human Understanding*, edited by Campbell Fraser (Oxford, 1894), Book 2, Ch. 27; David Hume, *A Treatise of Human Nature*, edited by L. A. Selby-Bigge (Oxford, 1896), Book I, Part 4, Sec. 6; Joseph Butler, "Of Personal Identity," appendix to *The Analogy of Religion*, edited by W. E. Gladstone (Oxford, 1897), Vol. I, pp. 385 ff.; Antony Flew, "Locke and the Problem of Personal Identity," *Philosophy*, Vol. 26 (1951), 53–68; Terence Penelhum, "Hume on Personal Identity," *Philosophical Review*, Vol. 64 (1955), 571–589, and "Personal Identity, Memory, and Survival," *Journal of Philosophy*, Vol. 56 (1959), 882–903; B. A. O. Williams, "Personal Identity and Individuation," *PAS*, Vol. 57 (1956–1957), 229 ff.; Sydney Shoemaker, "Personal Identity and Memory," *Journal of Philosophy*, Vol. 56 (1959), 868–882.

The most important classical discussion that is not discussed in this article is Thomas Reid, *Essays on the Intellectual Powers of Man* (Edinburgh, 1785), Essay III, especially Chs. 4 and 6. Reid has some admirable criticisms of Locke, but he is too wedded to the concept of substance to see that Locke's departures from common conceptual practice are not remedied by the use of it.

Another classic discussion is Immanuel Kant, *Critique of Pure Reason*, translated by Norman Kemp Smith (London, 1929), pp. 341 ff.

There are some recent books whose discussions repay close study. See C. D. Broad, *The Mind and Its Place in Nature* (London, 1937), Sec. E, pp. 553 ff. For stimulating arguments in favor of the notion of a substantial self, see C. A. Campbell, *On Selfhood and Godhood* (London, 1957). Risierei Frondizi, *The Nature of the Self* (New Haven, 1953), contains interesting discussions of Locke and Hume, but its positive discussion seems to be vitiated by the restrictions of the terminology in its title. P. A. Minkus, *Philosophy of the Person* (Oxford, 1960), is obscure to a degree but has the only extended discussion of Reid. See also Sydney Shoemaker, *Self-Knowledge and Self-Identity* (Ithaca, N.Y., 1963), and his article MEMORY in this encyclopedia.

The following articles take positions that radically differ from the arguments of the present article. H. P. Grice, "Personal Identity," *Mind*, Vol. 50 (1941), 330–350, argues that the "self" is a logical construction consisting of experiences linked conceptually by memory. An authoritative presentation of the Kantian thesis that perceptual acts require a persisting subject or owner is found in H. J. Paton, "Self-Identity," in his *In Defence of Reason* (London, 1951). J. R. Jones, "The Self in Sensory Cognition," *Mind*, Vol. 58 (1949), 40–61, attempts to dispense with the notion of a subject of perceptual acts. This paper generated an exchange on the concept of the self between its author and Antony Flew; see Antony Flew, "Selves," *Mind*, Vol. 58 (1949), 355–358, and J. R. Jones, "Selves: A Reply to Mr. Flew," *Mind*, Vol. 59 (1950), 233–236. This article has not been able to deal with the detail of the arguments presented in these papers but would hold that each in its own way is handicapped by the restrictions placed on the discussion of personal identity by Hume and by the use of the terminology of the "self." On the perplexities surrounding the notion of a purely mental subject, rather than the psychophysical person, as the owner of mental acts and events, see Ch. 6 of Gilbert Ryle's *The Concept of the Mind* (London, 1949), and Ch. 3 of P. F. Strawson's *Individuals* (London, 1959). Both of these books have strongly influenced this article.

Other helpful recent treatments are C. B. Martin, *Religious Belief* (Ithaca, N.Y., 1959), Ch. 6, and A. M. Quinton, "The Soul," *Journal of Philosophy*, Vol. 59 (1962), 393–409.

TERENCE PENELHUM

PERSONALISM is a philosophical perspective or system for which person is the ontological ultimate and for which personality is thus the fundamental explanatory principle. Explicitly developed in the twentieth century, personalism in its historical antecdents and its dominant themes has close affiliations with and affinities to other (mainly idealist) systems that are not strictly personalist. This article will concentrate on American personalism, although the movement is not only American; there are and have been advocates of personalism or closely related positions in Europe, Great Britain, Latin America, and the Orient.

Background of the term. The term "person" comes from the Latin word *persona*, meaning mask and/or actor. It came to refer to a role and to a man's dignity in relation to other men. This usage is reinforced by theological language for which *persona* is the Latin equivalent of the Greek *hypostasis* (standing under) and for which both *persona* and *hypostasis* are closely related to *ousia* (substance). These associations foreshadow the ultimacy that personalism attaches to personality, both in value (a person is identified with his dignity) and in being (person is substance). On this basis we can understand the importance that personalists have attached to Boethius' definition of person as an individual substance of a rational nature (*Persona est naturae rationabilis individua substantia*). The effect of the modern critique of the concept of substance on the definition of person will be considered later.

In comparison with *persona*, the term "personalism" is relatively recent. Walt Whitman and Bronson Alcott both used the term in the 1860s; early in the twentieth century it was adopted and applied more systematically. In France, Charles Renouvier wrote *Le Personnalisme* in 1903; in Germany, William Stern developed critical personalism in *Person und Sache* (1906). In the United States, Mary Whiton Calkins began to use the term in 1907 and Borden Parker Bowne adopted it the following year. Bowne said of himself, "I am a Personalist, the first of the clan in any thorough-going sense." About this time, personal idealism established itself in England. Shortly thereafter, Neo-Scholastic (and hence, more realistic) versions of personalism emerged, especially in France.

Historical antecdents. The historical antecdents of these personalistic philosophies are so pervasive and for the most part so well-known that they need not be discussed in detail here. A. C. Knudson supplies abundant historical background in *The Philosophy of Personalism* (1927). In general, personalism has been decisively influenced by both the Greek metaphysical and Biblical religious motifs of the dominant Western theological tradition. With the notable exception of J. M. E. McTaggart's atheistic personalism, personalism in virtually all its forms has been integrally connected with theism. Nevertheless, it has usually considered itself a system defensible on philosophical grounds and not one based merely on theological presuppositions.

Recognition of the dominant historical influences on personalism would not, therefore, be complete without mention of several modern philosophers. Following Descartes, the primacy and indubitableness of personal experience and its identification as mental substance have exercised a decisive influence on nearly all forms of personalism. The Cartesian principle is apparent in Brightman's definition: "A person . . . is a complex unity of consciousness, which identifies itself with its past self in memory, determines itself by its freedom, is purposive and value-seeking, private yet communicating, and potentially rational" (in V. Ferm, ed., *A History of Philosophical Systems*, p. 341).

Leibniz is sometimes spoken of as the founder of personalism. His doctrine that all reality is composed of monads (psychic entities) without remainder and that monads are essentially centers of activity has been particularly influential on idealistic personalists of pluralistic and panpsychistic types.

The influence of George Berkeley converged with that of Leibniz in providing an impetus to idealistic personalism. Material substance is reinterpreted as the "language" of the Divine Person. Further reinforcement for this theme is found in Kant's doctrines of the phenomenality of the sense world and the primacy of the practical reason. It is only in the personal world of the practical (moral) reason that one has access to the noumenal. This Kantian direction has had enormous influence on what might be called ethical personalism.

Hegel was the single most important influence in the development of absolute idealism (absolutistic personalism). His emphasis on dialectical movement toward wholeness, on the concrete universal, and on the ultimacy of spirit has had a decided influence on other forms of idealistic personalism, notably that of E. S. Brightman.

One thinker who does not compare with the foregoing figures in eminence deserves to be mentioned because of his influence on such American personalists as B. P. Bowne and G. T. Ladd. He is Hermann Lotze, whose main work is *Mikrokosmus* (1856–1858).

Types of personalism. In characterizing more precisely the systematic position of personalism, it will be helpful to distinguish two major forms: realistic personalism and idealistic personalism. The former can best be understood in the context of supernaturalism or traditional metaphysical realism, and the latter in terms of metaphysical idealism.

Realistic personalism. For realistic personalists, personality is the fundamental being. That is, ultimate reality is a spiritual, supernatural being. There is also, however, a natural order of nonmental being, which although created by God, is not intrinsically spiritual or personal. Many Neo-Scholastics, for example J. Maritain, E. Gilson, and E. Mounier, identify themselves as personalists in the realistic sense. In fact, realistic personalism has been developing with remarkable vitality both in Europe and America in conjunction with the resurgence of Catholic theological thought. There are, however, some realistic personalists who do not stand in the scholastic tradition; among them may be mentioned N. Berdyaev, J. B. Pratt, D. C. Macintosh, Georgia Harkness, and A. C. Garnett.

Idealistic personalism. Excluding Platonism and Kantianism, there are three main types of idealism: absolute idealism, panpsychistic idealism, and personal (pluralistic) idealism. Although there are no neat lines of demarcation separating these types, oversimplification can in this case be illuminating.

(1) Absolute idealism (or absolutistic personalism) is the view that reality is one absolute mind, spirit, or person. All finite beings, however otherwise designated (for example, as physical things, logical entities, or human beings), literally participate in this absolute being; they *are* ontologically by virtue of their being manifestations or activities of the absolute mind. Since this is so distinctive a philosophical tradition, it receives full treatment elsewhere. Representative thinkers who have either had influence on or association with other personalistic positions are Edward Caird, T. H. Green, Josiah Royce, A. E. Taylor, Mary W. Calkins, and W. E. Hocking. With reservations, C. A. Campbell, Brand Blanshard, Paul Tillich, and Gabriel Marcel may also be included here.

Absolute idealism has not commended itself to personal idealism which, in opposing complete immanence or monism, is closer to realistic personalism and related theistic positions.

(2) For panpsychistic idealism, Leibniz' monadology is the paradigm. Reality is a hierarchy of psychic beings (monads) determined by the degree of consciousness possessed by any monad. The supreme monad (God) has created all other monads in pre-established harmony. Panpsychism has been developed in various ways by James Ward, F. R. Tennant, H. W. Carr, A. N. Whitehead, and Charles Hartshorne.

In many respects, panpsychistic idealism may be considered to be continuous with personal idealism. Although personal idealists do not deny the possibility that there are more grades of self or mind than the human and the divine, they tend to believe that panpsychists have not adequately resolved the tension between pluralistic and monistic strains in their position.

(3) Personal idealism is usually considered the most typical form of personalism. It is idealistic: all reality is personal. It is pluralistic: reality is a society of persons. It is theistic: God is the ultimate person and, as such, is the ground of all being and the creator of finite persons. Henceforth "personalism" will be used to mean personal idealism.

Systematic themes. Among the first generation of American exponents of personalism the most significant were George Holmes Howison (1834–1916) and Borden Parker Bowne (1847–1910).

In the 1860s Howison was a member of the St. Louis Philosophical Society. The discussion of Hegelian idealism, to which this group devoted so much of its time, led Howison to reject what he considered the submerging of the finite individual in the Absolute.

His basic metaphysical position is stated categorically: "All existence is either (1) the existence of *minds,* or (2) the existence of *the items and order of their experience;* all the existences known as 'material' consisting in certain of these experiences, with an order organized by the self-active forms of consciousness that in their unity constitute the substantial being of a mind, in distinction from its phenomenal life" (in J. W. Buckham and G. M. Stratton, eds., *George Holmes Howison*, p. 128). Howison's unswerving pluralism led him not only to reject pantheism but also to deny creation. "These many minds . . . have no origin at all—no source in *time* whatever. There is nothing at all, prior to them, out of which their being arises. . . . They simply *are*, and together constitute the eternal order" (*ibid.*, p. 129). Howison's "eternal republic" is reminiscent of Royce's community.

Bowne taught philosophy at Boston University from

1876 until his death. Berkeley, Kant, and Lotze were the major influences on his thought. Like Howison, Bowne was a pluralistic idealist, but unlike Howison, he was explicitly theistic. The Divine Person is not only the creator of finite selves or persons but is also the "world ground," whose "self-directing intelligent agency" shows itself in the order and continuity of the phenomenal world.

Bowne's famous chapter in *Personalism* on "The Failure of Impersonalism" expresses his basic polemic against Hegelian absolutism, Spencer's evolutionism, associationism, and materialism. At the same time, he fought just as hard against fundamentalism and dogmatic supernaturalism. Through his influence on many generations of students at the Boston University School of Theology, he contributed decisively to liberalizing the leadership of the Methodist church.

Three of Bowne's students were the leading exponents of personalism in the period following World War I. Albert C. Knudson (1873–1953) continued the personalist tradition in theological context at Boston University School of Theology. Ralph Tyler Flewelling (1871–1960) developed the School of Philosophy of the University of Southern California and also founded and edited the journal *The Personalist*.

Edgar Sheffield Brightman (1884–1953), the most important of Bowne's students, taught at Boston University from 1919 until his death. Brightman, a creative and original thinker, developed a comprehensive and coherent personalistic system.

Brightman espoused an epistemological dualism of "the shining present" (or "situation-experienced") and "the illuminating absent" (or "situation-believed-in"). Immediate experience is the inescapable starting point, but experience always refers beyond itself (self-transcendence). The possibility of reference is found in the activity of the mind in knowing; the adequacy of reference is determined by the criterion of coherence. Maximum coherence in interpreting experience is maximum truth. In his emphasis on the tentativeness and testing of hypotheses, Brightman is empirical; in his emphasis on system and inclusive order, he is rationalistic.

In metaphysics, Brightman maintained that "everything that exists [or subsists] is in, of, or for a mind on some level." He defined personalism as "the hypothesis that all being is either a personal experient (a complex unity of consciousness) or some phase or aspect of one or more such experients" (*Person and Reality*, p. 135). The natural world is understood as an order within or as a function of the mind of God. Finite persons are created by the uncreated Person. Human persons are, therefore, centers of intrinsic value.

Brightman might be called a value empiricist. His *Moral Laws* (1933), which has not received the attention it deserves, works out an impressive ethical theory. In his philosophy of religion values have a central place. The value dimension of human experience provides the evidence of a religious dimension of reality. Hence, generically, God is the source and conserver of values.

The most distinctive aspect of Brightman's thought is his revision of the traditional idea of God. He argued that if we are to take personality seriously as the basic explanatory model, then we must accept a temporalist view of God. If God is personal, he is omnitemporal, not timeless. Brightman also argued that the traditional conception of divine omnipotence could not be maintained without seriously qualifying the divine goodness. His penetrating consideration of evil, suffering, and death led him to conclude that the will of God is limited by nonrational conditions (the Given) within the divine nature that are neither created nor approved by that will. God maintains constant and growing—although never complete—control of the Given. Some personalists, including L. Harold DeWolf, prefer to follow Bowne's more traditional view of God's eternity and omnipotence. Others, like Peter A. Bertocci, find in Brightman's revisions the conditions of an intelligible and cogent theism.

Current developments. In recent years, personalism may seem to have been eclipsed by the rise of existential and analytic philosophies. However, many of the doctrines and motifs of personalism have been or are being appropriated and elaborated by other positions. Existentialism and the phenomenological movement have turned to the exploration of personal existence in ways that will be gratifying to most personalists. This movement should be particularly fruitful for personalists since it grapples in new ways with the relation of the body to the person, a problem that has caused a long-standing ambiguity in personalistic thought. Both realistic and idealistic personalists have stumbled over this problem. Phenomenological investigations may therefore provide an impetus for new conceptions of personality.

The analytic concentration on language also contributes to an improved understanding of personal symbolizing and communication, and the renewed interest in philosophy of mind, stimulated by recent psychological theories, again provides material that is important in the development of personalist thought. Personalists would seem to have an advantage in being willing to risk a systematic conception of the total person which would combine surface experience (sense) and depth dimension (value).

Among the large number of Brightman's students who have been developing various facets of personalistic thought, the best-known is Peter A. Bertocci, Brightman's successor as Borden Parker Bowne professor of philosophy at Boston University. Other contemporary personalists also continue to demonstrate that personalism can be a viable alternative among persistent philosophical perspectives.

Bibliography

GENERAL WORKS

Brightman, E. S., "Personalism (Including Personal Idealism)," in V. Ferm, ed., *A History of Philosophical Systems*. New York, 1950. Pp. 340–352.

Flewelling, R. T., "Personalism," in D. D. Runes, ed., *Twentieth Century Philosophy*. New York, 1947. Pp. 323–341.

Knudson, A. C., *The Philosophy of Personalism*. New York, 1927.

AMERICA

Beck, Robert N., *The Meaning of Americanism*. New York, 1956.

Bertocci, P. A., *Introduction to the Philosophy of Religion*. New York, 1951.

Bertocci, P. A., and Millard, R. M., *Personality and the Good*. New York, 1963.

Bowne, B. P., *Metaphysics*. New York, 1898.

Bowne, B. P., *Theism*. New York, 1902.

Bowne, B. P., *Personalism*. Boston, 1908.

Brightman, E. S., *A Philosophy of Religion*. New York, 1940.

Brightman, E. S., *Person and Reality*. New York, 1958. Edited after Brightman's death by P. A. Bertocci; contains a selected bibliography of Brightman's writings compiled by J. E. Newhall.

Buckham, J. W., *The Inner World*. New York, 1941.

Buckham, J. W., and Stratton, G. M., eds., *George Holmes Howison, Philosopher and Teacher*. Berkeley, 1934.

Čapek, Milič, *The Philosophical Impact of Contemporary Physics*. Princeton, N.J., 1961.

DeWolf, L. H., *The Religious Revolt Against Reason*. New York, 1949.

Flewelling, R. T., *Creative Personality*. New York, 1926.

Flewelling, R. T., *The Person or the Significance of Man*. Los Angeles, 1952.

Howison, G. H., *The Limits of Evolution*. New York, 1901.

Muelder, W. G., *Foundations of the Responsible Society*. New York, 1959.

Munk, Arthur W., *History and God*. New York, 1952.

White, H. V., *Truth and the Person in Christian Theology*. New York, 1963.

Closely related positions are developed in the works of J. E. Boodin, J. S. Moore, D. S. Robinson, J. S. Bixler, and C. Hartshorne.

ENGLAND

Carr, H. W., *The Unique Status of Man*. London, 1928.

Carr, H. W., *Cogitans Cogitata*. Los Angeles, 1930.

Oman, J., *Grace and Personality*. Cambridge, 1917.

Sturt, H., ed., *Personal Idealism*. London, 1902.

Webb, C. C. J., *God and Personality*. London, 1919.

Note also the writings of H. Rashdall, W. R. Sorley, and F. C. S. Schiller.

GERMANY

Eucken, Rudolf, *Die Einheit des Geisteslebens in Bewusstsein und Tat der Menschheit*. Leipzig, 1888.

Lotze, H., *Mikrokosmus*. Leipzig, 1856–1858.

Stern, William, *Person und Sache*. Leipzig, 1906.

Note also the writings of Max Scheler.

FRANCE

Brunner, A., *La Personne incarnée*. Paris, 1947.

Lahbari, M. A., *De l'Être à la personne: Essai de personnalisme réaliste*. Paris, 1954.

Maritain, J., *The Person and the Common Good*. London, 1948.

Mounier, E., *A Personalist Manifesto*. Paris, 1936.

Mounier, E., *Le Personnalisme*. Paris, 1950.

Nedoncelle, M., *Vers une Philosophie de l'amour et de la personne*. Paris, 1957.

Ravaisson, F., *De l'Habitude*. Paris, 1933.

Renouvier, C., *Le Personnalisme*. Paris, 1903.

Note also the writings of Henri Bergson.

ADDITIONAL WORKS

Berdyaev, N., *The Destiny of Man*, translated by N. Duddington. London, 1937.

Buber, Martin, *I and Thou*. Edinburgh, 1937.

Romero, Francisco, *La filosofia de la persona*. Buenos Aires, 1938.

Stefanini, L., *Personalismo filosofico*. Rome, 1954.

JOHN H. LAVELY

PERSONS. Neither in common usage nor in philosophy has there been a univocal concept of "person." Rather, the word "person" and its almost exact cognates in the modern Western languages, as well as in Sanskrit (*puruṣa*), have numerous uses which at best seem only to border on one another. In recent common usage, "person" refers to any human being in a general way, much as the word "thing" refers unspecifically to any object whatsoever. Usually, indeed, "person" contrasts with "thing" exclusively, and when it is not used referentially (as in "Jane is an interesting person"), it is most commonly used emphatically, to draw attention to the fact that whoever is so designated is, after all, a human being and ought to be treated accordingly.

Persons and things. That a person is distinct from a (mere) thing, and that any human being, insofar as he is a person, is in consequence of this status to be treated in a special manner, are two of the main logical features of this concept, and they carry over from ordinary to philosophical usage. Thus, Kant, for example, only reflected and rendered explicit distinctions and attitudes that were already current when he stipulated that persons, as contrasted with things, are of an unconditional worth and that respect is an attitude which has application to persons only and never to things.

Persons as ends-in-themselves. In view of the above, things may be pre-empted for our own purposes; their value depends upon the degree and kind of service they may be to us in the execution of our aims. *Persons*, however, must not be used (merely) as means to someone's end; they are, in Kant's famous phrase, "ends-in-themselves and sources of value in their own right."

Legal persons. A slave, to be sure, is by definition used as a means to another's ends, but in ancient legal tradition slaves had no rights in the eyes of the law and were therefore not regarded as persons. Aristotle, who supposed that there were natural slaves, would have regarded them as not human beings anyway, but as "[living] instruments for the conduct of life," and hence not persons in even the most generic sense. This brings us to a third feature of the concept of person, in accordance with which a person simply is any being having legal rights and duties. But in this respect, not every human being is legally a person (children and idiots are not persons), and not every legal person is a human being (a corporation is considered to be a juridical person).

Persons and roles. In a fourth use, now somewhat archaic, "person" is synonymous with "role" or "part" (cf. *dramatis personae*); it was originally used this way in connection with the theater and later in a more general sense. The English word "person," in fact, is alleged to have derived from the Latin *persona*, which was the mask worn by actors in dramatic performances. It has been suggested, in turn, that *persona* is a substantive derived from the participial *per-sonando* ("sounding through"), although this etymology has been challenged as being quantitatively impossible in Latin. Nevertheless, it is plausible enough to have gained even modern philological supporters. Added to this is the fact that *persona* sometimes seems to have stood for the person speaking through the mask and sometimes for the mask through which the voice came, an ambiguity similar to that generated by our word "speaker" and one which perhaps accounts for a great deal of the interesting ambiguity that the concept retains to this day. Thus, from *persona* we may derive, by nuanced steps, a variety of further uses, each perhaps best marked by synonyms, the differences between these synonyms serving to bring out a different sector in this word's range of meaning. Thus, from "role" we may proceed in one direction to "function," "office," and "capacity" (since certain rights go with certain offices, this is the legalistic direction), while in another direction we proceed to "guise," "semblance," "appearance," and "personification." Thus, an individual may speak as an actor, as a *dramatis persona,* or as himself ("in person"); the term is sufficiently accommodating to cover all of these uses. Accordingly, we can use it to mean "self," the individual as such (to treat someone as a person is to treat him as an individual), or, as distinct from the self, simply a role played or an office discharged—the uniform, so to speak, in contrast with the man who wears it. According to an influential theological interpretation, Christ, in this sense, was one of the three *persons* of the Trinity, which remained nevertheless one *substance* only. Indeed, Christ was the divine substance which, according to Clement of Alexandria, "assumed the human mask" (τὸ ἀνθρωπου προσωπεῖον), *prosopon* being the mask worn by Greek actors.

Self-consciousness. Doubtless there is a connection among the myriad usages mentioned above. We speak of a citizen as one who, ideally, plays a role or takes part in the life of the community of which he is a member, and to this extent the dramatic and legalistic senses of the word are connected. Ideally, again, the citizen's private life is his own; his citizenship is only the face he presents to the public (only the Roman citizen was entitled to wear the toga, but the toga was not worn in private life). However, not everyone who might be *de facto* a member of the community is recognized as being fit to play a role in its public life: there are criteria of enfranchisement, and satisfaction of these criteria constitutes someone a citizen or a person in the legal sense. Commonly, a necessary condition for having rights is being responsible for one's acts: rights are ascribable only to persons, and, accordingly, persons alone are responsible (hence, children and idiots are not persons).

At this juncture we may begin to sense something of what motivated certain philosophical characterizations of persons—for example, that a person is a being conscious of its identity through time. Kant mentioned a theory in which "that which is conscious of the numerical identity of itself at different times is insofar a *person,*" but he did not make clear why it should have been important for persons to be so. For clarification of this issue we must look to Leibniz, who characterized a person as that which conserves "the *consciousness,* or the reflective inward feeling of what it is: thus it is rendered liable to reward and punishment." His follower Christian Wolff explained the fact that animals are not persons and that human beings are simply on the grounds that the latter have, as the former do not, "a consciousness of having been the same thing previously in this or that state." Plainly, if I am to be responsible for my actions, I must continue to exist and to be capable of acknowledging that I am the same individual who performed them: otherwise I would be punished for acts that are not mine. But it is common legal (and philosophical) usage to insist that rationality is a precondition for responsible action. Responsible agents must know what

they are doing and must be able to give reasons for their having chosen to act so. It is responsible agents, executing their own purposes, who are regarded as persons—which brings us back to the Kantian notion of persons as ends-in-themselves. Thus, by easy associations one may pass from sector to sector of this concept.

PHILOSOPHICAL EXPLICATIONS

Self-awareness and especially rationality have figured in most philosophical characterizations of personhood from Boethius (*Persona est naturae rationalis individua substantia*) through Locke to nearly contemporary times. Locke defined "person" as "a thinking, intelligent being, that has reason and reflection, and can consider itself as itself, the same thinking thing, in different times and places; which it does only by that consciousness which is inseparable from thinking, and seems to me essential to it." For Locke, accordingly, "person" and "self" became near synonyms. It must be emphasized that Locke's characterization of "person" was dictated by systematic considerations and is to be taken as an explication of the concept as it functions in ordinary usage, in that sense of "explication" in which a more or less vague term in a natural language is reconstructed and given a measure of precision by being located within a set of terms that will constitute the vocabulary of a scientific or philosophical theory. It is no objection against Locke that his explication should contain both more and less than is to be found in the complex pattern of usage which the natural languages exhibit. However, it is again somewhat misleading to speak of Locke's, or any philosopher's, theory of persons, for there is no antecedently agreed upon definition of what these should be theories of. Rather, we must at best speak of this or that philosopher's *use* of "person" as a semitechnical term in his system. There must, of course, be some connection between this philosophical term and the ordinary concept or there would be little justification for using this word rather than another; but we cannot criticize a philosophical use of the term by citing, say, certain facts about persons that the theory in which it is used fails to account for or accounts for incorrectly. We may criticize it only by showing that its rules of usage are incoherent in one or another way or that there is nothing in the world which satisfies the characterization of "person" given by the theory. This must be the structure of philosophical discussion of this topic until "is a person," like "is a mammal," has a generally accepted meaning and denotation: *after* this, perhaps, there may be *discoveries* with regard to persons. On the other hand, we must not overlook the possibility that the seemingly complex and even ambiguous structure of the ordinary concept of "person" might really characterize the sorts of entities we shall decide that persons are, since it might be a failure on our part to suppose that the concept requires explication. Let us consider some cases.

Immaterial entities. "I know," Locke wrote, "that in the ordinary way of speaking, the same person and the same man stand for one and the same thing." Yet he believed that these two expressions stand for quite distinct ideas, "person" having to do with a rational self and "man" having to do simply with a certain physical shape. A rational parrot, he argued, would not be called a man, nor would a nonrational human be called anything but a man: the former, however, might be a person, while the latter, failing in rationality, might not be. A person, then, is *not* a rational man, since "man" has reference to corporeal form, and this is not, as he saw it, part of the meaning of "person" at all. But he then inferred that "person" must denote something *incorporeal* and indeed invisible. This deviates from common usage to the extent that according to one entry in a standard dictionary, "person" means "the bodily form of a human being": we speak of someone as being "comely of person" and of physical assaults as "crimes against the person," but neither usage is conveyed in Locke's explication. For him, identity of person was simply identity of consciousness, so that I remain the same person if I am conscious of being so, even though my body should change drastically and be diminished through age, disease, or amputation.

Logically, indeed, I should remain the same person even though I am altogether disembodied. Thomas Reid even regarded the idea of a person losing a part of himself as impossible: persons, he contended, are indivisible, the expression "part of a person" being "a manifest absurdity." One of his arguments was that if an amputated member were part of a person, "it would have a right to part of his estate and be liable for part of his engagements." We cannot but hear in this an echo of the legal usage of "persons" as those with rights and responsibilities, which in this instance is being weirdly called upon to support a metaphysical conclusion that it is pathetically inadequate to sustain.

For Reid and Locke, as for Leibniz and Wolff, persons were essentially covert, noncorporeal (though temporal), simple entities. It is precisely this notion of person which Kant attacked in the "Paralogisms of Pure Reason," but it becomes exceedingly difficult here to distinguish persons, so construed, from metaphysical selves, transcendental egos, *res cogitantia,* pure acts, spirits, mental substances, souls, and other similar philosophical fauna of the immaterial world. Brought in to account for certain features of persons as they are spoken of in theater, law court, *salon,* and market place, these concepts acquire a theoretical life of their own, and only the word remains as a vestigial remnant of their conceptual provenance.

P. F. Strawson's theory. The unappealing idea that in ascribing rights and responsibilities to human beings, we are implicitly referring to some bodiless entity perhaps marks the starting point for contemporary discussion. P. F. Strawson has adopted the term "person" for a philosophical use which comes rather closer to common usage than did Locke's interpretation; while it raises philosophical problems of its own, it is perhaps less disreputable than the metaphysical entities heretofore technically designated as persons. A Strawsonian person, to begin with, is to be understood as distinct from a (mere) material body, which retains the contrast customarily observed between persons and things. For Strawson, a thing, or material body, is a basic particular, specifically in the sense that we can identify and reidentify material bodies without having to

make reference to any kind of particular other than just material bodies. If we could not identify or reidentify anything, we could scarcely get about in the world; and *these* particulars are basic to *our* schemes of identification. But if our ideas were only of what we experienced, and if we experienced only material bodies, the question arises of whence derives the idea of that which *has* these ideas. How do we identify ourselves as distinct from the particulars which we identify and reidentify?

It would seem to follow from certain obvious answers to these questions that *we* are not material bodies and that our idea of ourselves is not the idea of a material body. This, in fact, is Strawson's view, but he desists from following the tempting path, followed by Locke, which leads to the conclusion that we are immaterial entities; instead, he emphasizes that many of the terms which are correctly applicable to material bodies are also, and according to exactly the same criteria, correctly applicable to ourselves as *persons*. Thre are two classes of terms, M-predicates and P-predicates, applicable respectively to material bodies and to persons; but there is an overlap, in that some M-predicates (perhaps all M-predicates) are applicable to persons, although there are some P-predicates that we "would not dream of applying" to material bodies (among the latter would be ascriptions of states of consciousness). If it is sensible to say of a person that he is sad, it is no less sensible to say of that very same person that he weighs three hundred pounds and even that he is the first because he is the second. Persons, then, are distinct from material bodies, but they are not therefore immaterial bodies or incorporeal nonbodies. A person has states of consciousness as well as physical attributes and is not merely to be identified with one or the other.

Persons are irreducible to parts of themselves and are thus "primitive" in just the same ways in which material bodies have been said to be. This means that our ability to identify and reidentify material bodies is insufficient for identification and reidentification of persons, for we might exhaustively identify an individual x under all the M-predicates true of x without thereby identifying x as a person. P-predicates are accordingly indefinable in terms of, and are not to be reduced to, M-predicates. We have not identified x as a person until we have correctly ascribed to him at least one P-predicate.

Ourselves and others. It is crucial in Strawson's account that P-predicates should be of the same logical kind independently of whether we ascribe them to ourselves or to others, so that "angry" means the same thing no matter which personal pronoun and which person (in the grammatical sense) of the copulative verb it is preceded by. Thus, a difference in the reference of a sentence using a P-predicate entails no difference in the predicate itself. Nevertheless, criteria for the applicability of the P-predicate will ordinarily vary with difference in pronominal reference. My criterion for self-ascription will consist simply in being aware of the state I ascribe to myself. But this cannot be my criterion for ascription of the same P-predicate to another person, for I (logically) cannot in this sense of "aware" be aware of his state: I do not feel his anger or his pain. I must accordingly have some "logically adequate" criterion, usually expressed in behavioral terms, for ascribing to another the same predicate I ascribe to myself on the basis of sheer awareness; and I do not ascribe (these) *P*-predicates to myself on the basis of observing my own behavior.

Philosophers have often supposed that while I am certain that I am in pain when I am in pain, I hardly have comparable certainty of the feelings (or mental states in general) of others. At best their states are known to me through evidence which, for technical reasons, is always less than adequate and, on some accounts, never more than perfectly inadequate. Or, according to a more sophisticated analysis, if the meaning of an expression is its mode of verification, "I am in pain" and "He is in pain" differ in meaning; and if we restrict verification to the having of certain experiences, "He is in pain" is meaningless if I cannot experience *his* pain. Hence, ascriptions of inner states to others are meaningless or else neither knowable nor rationally believable. Strawson's introduction of "logically adequate criteria" is meant to circumvent this skepticism, and his insistence that a *P*-predicate is univocal even if it has differing criteria of applicability is meant to counteract verificationism. Indeed, he insists that to know the use of a *P*-predicate is to recognize that it has two sorts of criteria: I cannot ascribe *F* to myself unless I am able or know how to ascribe it to others (he is not explicit regarding the converse of this); thus, skeptic and solipsist alike in fact require the precise concepts they would impugn.

This account has been challenged on a variety of points. It has been held that a pair of criteria for a predicate which are not equivalent to each other is an inconsistent notion. But this may be countered simply by showing that even if *p* implies *r* and *q* implies *r*, it does not follow that *p* implies *q*. Again, it has been contended that *P*-predicates are essentially ambiguous, since they satisfy disjoint classes of conditions. But this presupposes that a criterion for a predicate exhausts the meaning of that predicate, which is wrong: a predicate may have any number of criteria, as an event may have any number of sufficient conditions—although not every criterion or every sufficient condition need hold at once. And Strawson might at any rate point out that self-ascription of *P*-predicates is not done on the basis of criteria: one is in direct contact with what one ascribes to oneself, not merely with an external criterion, however logically adequate. However, the notion of logical adequacy has been attacked in the case of ascriptions to others. Surely a man may feign that behavior which is held to be logically adequate grounds for saying that he is in just the condition he pretends to be in: therefore, skepticism remains open. To this Strawson could reply that it remains open but uninteresting, since feigning itself is successful only insofar as the criteria that are acknowledged are those which, if feigned, might mislead someone. Even if these contested points in the theories of meaning and of knowledge be decisive, however, the metaphysical notion of persons as logically primitive would remain unaffected.

Here, of course, problems enough persist. Must at least one *M*-predicate be true of *x* if *x* is to be a person? If not, then "is a person" would be independent of any bodily criterion, and there could be disembodied persons, in which case one might well ask, as Locke might have, to what extent *M*-predicates after all enter into our concept of a person. Someone (a Heideggerian, for example) might say that, strictly speaking, *M*-predicates have no application to persons as such, that a person is never in a drawing room in the way in which, say, a moth is in one, so that the two classes of predicates are completely disjoint.

Even so, it is instructive to note how close Strawson's concept is to the *whole* concept of a person in ordinary usage. And some contemporary writers (the scientist Michael Polanyi, for instance) would emphasize that this ordinary concept cannot, at present, be rendered comprehensible in scientific terms, and that relative to the known laws of physics and chemistry, persons are indeed primitive and irreducible entities. And it is precisely the ambiguity we have noted in the ordinary concept which serves to define persons in the metaphysical sense. A person *is* the body (the victim of a crime against the person); *is* the appearance (the comely person); *is* the self-conscious and rational individual; *is* the source and object of rights and obligations; *is* that which takes roles and discharges functions. It is only a weak sense of complexity, perhaps, or a commitment to one or another reductionist program, which leads us to regard the concept as incoherent. Persons may indeed, then, be ontologically primitive as "wavicles" (not waves and not particles, but both together) are perhaps physically primitive. They may or may not be, but should we accept this possibility, we might also find in it some confirmation of the view that understanding our language is not an inauspicious beginning for attaining philosophical truth.

Bibliography

See the entry "Person" in the *Oxford English Dictionary* for the chief meanings of the term. See also Adolf Trendelenberg, "A Contribution to the History of the Word Person," in *Monist*, Vol. 20 (1910), 336–363; and F. Max Müller, "Persona," in *Collected Works of F. Max Müller* (London, 1912), Vol. X, pp. 32 and 47.

Traditional discussions are Boethius, *Contra Eutychen et Nestorium*, Sec. III; John Locke, *Essay Concerning Human Understanding*, Book II, Ch. 27, Para. 9; G. W. Leibniz, *Theodicy*, Sec. 2, 89; Christian Wolff, *Vernünftige Gedanken*, Sec. 924; Thomas Reid, *Intellectual Powers of Man*, Essay III, Ch. 4; Immanuel Kant, "The Paralogisms of Pure Reason," in *Critique of Pure Reason*, especially Paralogism III, *Fundamental Principles of a Metaphysic of Morals*, Sec. II, and *Critique of Practical Reason*, Ch. III. A critique of Locke and Reid is in Peter Minkus, *Philosophy of the Person* (Oxford, 1960), Ch. 1, Parts 2 and 4. Strawson's views are in his *Individuals: An Essay in Descriptive Metaphysics* (London, 1959), pp. 87–116 and *passim*. See the reviews of this by J. O. Urmson, in *Mind*, Vol. 70 (1961), 258–264; D. F. Pears, in *Philosophical Quarterly*, Vol. 11 (1961), 172 ff.; and B. A. O. Williams, in *Philosophy*, Vol. 36 (1961), 20–39.

For further criticisms, see C. D. Rollins, "Personal Predicates," in *Philosophical Quarterly*, Vol. 10 (1960), 1–10; Robert Rosthal, "Ascription of Mental Predicates," in *Philosophical Studies*, Vol. 12 (1961); R. Freed and Jerry Fodor, "Pains, Puns, Persons, and Pronouns," in *Analysis*, Vol. 20 (1961), 6–9, and "Some Types of Ambiguous Tokens," in *Analysis*, Vol. 14 (1963), 19–23; D. Mannison, "On the Alleged Ambiguity of Strawson's P-Predicates," in *Analysis*, Vol. 23 (1962); G. Iseminger, "Meaning, Criteria, and P-Predicates," in *Analysis*, Vol. 24 (1963), 11–18; S. C. Coval, "Persons and Criteria in Strawson," in *Philosophy and Phenomenological Research*, Vol. 24 (1964), 406–409.

For more specific reference to the antiskeptical maneuver, see M. C. Bradley, "Mr. Strawson and Skepticism," in *Analysis*, Vol. 20 (1959), 14–19; and A. J. Ayer, *The Concept of Person* (London, 1963), Ch. 4. Polanyi's views are in his *Personal Knowledge* (Chicago, 1958), *passim*.

Arthur C. Danto

PERSPECTIVE REALISM. See Realism.

PESSIMISM AND OPTIMISM. Pessimism and its opposite, optimism, are only secondarily philosophical theories or convictions; primarily they are personal opinions or attitudes, often widely prevalent, about the relative evil or goodness of the world or of men's experience of the world. As such they vary with the temperaments and value experiences of individuals, and with cultural situations far more than with philosophical traditions.

Both pessimism and optimism in the above sense may be reactions to experiences that vary in scope and content. Four types of reactions or judgments may be distinguished: (1) psychological or anthropological (involving judgments about the dominance of evil or good in one's own experience or in human experience generally); (2) physicalistic (judging the physical world to be dominantly evil or good); (3) historicistic (based on appraisals of the evil or goodness of a historical or cultural period or of the forces and institutions which determine history); and (4) universal, or cosmic (involving judgments about the dominance of evil or good in the universe as a whole).

Since the issue of the goodness or evil of human life involves belief in beneficent or malevolent forces upon which man's well-being is dependent, optimism and pessimism are prominent aspects of religious beliefs, and these beliefs may involve many or all of the above types of judgments.

Philosophical pessimism and optimism result from the critical analysis and clarification of judgments of the dominance of good or evil, an evaluation of the experiences upon which these judgments are based, and the presentation of reasons to justify or refute such statements. There is widespread doubt whether the terms "optimism" and "pessimism" are sufficiently precise for philosophical purposes and also whether optimistic and pessimistic beliefs are philosophically justifiable. This article will be concerned chiefly with philosophical formulations and arguments for optimism and pessimism with some reference to their manifestations in religion.

Optimistic and pessimistic attitudes and theories are much older than the terms used to describe them. The term *optimisme* was first used in the Jesuit journal *Mémoires de Trévoux* in 1737 to designate Leibniz' doctrine (which appears in his *Théodicée* and in other of his philosophical writings) that this is the best of all possible worlds. Leibniz himself used the term "optimum" in a technical sense that applied to the unique maximal or minimal instance of an infinite class of possibilities, and he held that this principle of the optimum was applied by God in the creation of the world. *Optimisme* was admitted by the French Academy to its dictionary in 1762. The first known appearance of the term "optimism" in English was in 1759, also in reference to the system of Leibniz.

"Pessimism" came into general use only in the nineteenth century, although its first known appearance in English was in 1795 in one of Coleridge's letters.

The superlative form of the Latin adjectives *optimus* and *pessimus* is not generally justified by any form of philosophical optimism or pessimism. It is true that Leibniz defended an optimal position in the formula "the best of all possible worlds," but this use of the superlative did not prevent his acknowledging the existence of much evil—indeed, the necessity of evil in all finite existence. Similarly, Schopenhauer affirmed that this is the worst of all possible worlds, but his chief philosophic concern was with finding a way of salvation from the evil of the world through art, a morality of sympathy, and philosophic and religious contemplation. The most thoroughgoing philosophical pessimist of the nineteenth century, Eduard von Hartmann, held that this is the best of all possible worlds; yet evil necessarily outweighs good in it, and it would be better if there were no world at all.

The philosophical issues might better have been served by the comparative forms "meliorism" and "pejorism" ("betterism" and "worsism"). Although the verb forms "meliorate" and "pejorate" did appear in the sixteenth and seventeenth centuries respectively, "pejorism" has found no acceptance, while "meliorism" has been used, following William James, to express the view that although the world is a mixture of good and evil, it can be bettered by man's moral efforts to improve it.

RELIGIOUS AND PHILOSOPHICAL ISSUES

Optimism and pessimism are thus relative terms; the former theory undertakes to give philosophical reasons for assuming that in whatever horizon or context is involved, good preponderates over evil, while the latter theory attempts to show that evil preponderates over good. The arguments in each case may be efforts to generalize from experiences of good and evil, or they may, and usually do, also involve a priori factors, basic definitions, and theological or metaphysical doctrines.

Empiricism and rationalism. A primary consideration in discussing optimism and pessimism is the definition and criteria of good and evil. Empiricists have generally adopted a hedonistic definition of good, and hedonism has frequently ended in pessimism: the universe seems not to be constituted to provide man with more pleasure than pain. But it has proved difficult to reduce normative judgments of value to the psychological measures of pleasure and pain, joy and sorrow, or satisfaction and dissatisfaction. Other criteria are also involved—for example, the conservation or destruction of life, the progress or decay of cultural institutions and values, human freedom and bondage (in various senses), and the just control of power.

While empiricism shows an inclination toward pessimism (and skepticism), rationalism operates with normative principles that have an affinity with affirmations of the identity of reality and goodness. Nevertheless, exponents of hedonism are driven to recognize qualitative distinctions between pleasures and pains and the complex interplay of pleasures and pains that makes possible greater goods, while beneath the most rational and optimistic systems of modern thought lurks the shadow of fear, if not of despair. Leibniz wrote during a period of devastating European wars and intended his thought to serve as the foundation for a European culture that would protect Europe against the threat of a new barbarism. Voltaire, Gibbon, and Pierre Maupertuis expressed the same fears, and in America, Franklin, Jefferson, Hamilton, and Adams had forebodings of the dangers of revolution and the collapse into barbarism that might follow a failure to establish a sound political order.

Religion. Religion involves both optimistic and pessimistic aspects. Since the essence of religion is salvation from evil, an optimistic element is essential to it; yet not all individuals or groups are saved. The magical component in religion is optimistic, since it promises success in the achievement of desired values; yet the failure of religious rites or prayers is common enough to support pessimism. Salvation is postponed to a future life, and the present world is viewed as a vale of tears, or as the historical conflict between good and evil, or as a source of desires to be resisted, or as an illusory order that possesses no substance. Yet in all religion there is also a joyous world-affirming element that expresses itself in community life and mystical or prophetic exaltation. Eschatological religions combine pessimism about a temporal world that is destined to end with joyous optimism about the new life that will follow.

Metaphysics. If hedonistic criteria of good and evil are a common source of pessimism, those systems of thought that hold to an ultimate identity of existence and value are the mainstay of optimism. Two philosophical convictions in particular have supported optimistic convictions in Western thought. One rests upon the Platonic and Aristotelian ideal of the perfectibility of man. It regards all the powers of man as capable of control and harmonization (without great resistance from senses and impulses). The other is metaphysical but has the same sources. Regarding the universe as a hierarchy of being and goodness, ordered from infinite perfection though all levels of particularization to the total formlessness of matter, or mere potentiality, it finds all evil and error to consist in a negation or privation of being.

Other traditions also have a bearing upon optimism and pessimism. Efforts to interpret the universe as normatively indifferent (traditional materialism, for example) usually end in pessimism. Dualisms of various kinds, on the other hand, whether they distinguish between cosmic powers of good and evil or between a real order of value and a phenomenal order of fact, tend to end in optimism.

Science. Finally, natural science has presented considerations which affect the problem of optimism and pessimism. Fires, earthquakes, floods, storms, diseases, and, ultimately, death have always been regarded as evil because they interfere with human purposes and hopes. But the theory of natural selection and the second law of thermodynamics, which has been held to imply an end to the universe at a finite time in the future, have put the issue of the destructiveness of natural powers, animate and inanimate, on a more objective basis by casting serious doubts upon the possibility and the goodness of evolution and progress.

HISTORY OF PESSIMISM AND OPTIMISM

Religious pessimism. Religion is relevant to the problem of optimism and pessimism insofar as it offers salvation to men, evokes attitudes of world-affirmation and world-renunciation, and involves beliefs about the place of man and his hopes in the world. In this sense Schopenhauer was justified in calling religion the metaphysics of the people. Most religions combine a certain joyous response to divine grace with a sense of anguish and guilt at man's failures. Most advanced religions reflect a deeply rooted intuition of natural and historical evils and of the human limitations to which man is subject.

Indian thought. When the Brahmanic tradition in India emerged from the earlier Vedic religious forms, it partly concealed an underlying pessimism with the doctrine of maya—namely, that the world in which man suffers is a world of illusion, and release follows from recognizing this and the supplementary truth that man's true nature is one with the Brahman. This Brahmanic tradition was supplemented by a popular polytheistic religion that combined an easy tolerance of the diversity of natural delights and griefs with a singleness of purpose in carrying out those disciplines (whether physical, moral, intellectual, or mystical) that assure the self of its ultimate release and redemption. The fatalistic doctrine of the eternal cycle of rebirth, together with the doctrine of karma, intensifies a mood of pessimism, since this cosmic law of justice sentences most men to relive the deceptions of life again and again.

This element of pessimism implicit in Hinduism became the driving force of Buddhism in its various forms. The fourfold truth revealed to Gautama under the Bo tree begins with the misery of human existence, caused by desire, and offers as salvation only the renunciation of desire and the attainment of that state of negation which is the highest bliss.

Western religions. As the Eastern religions show, the religious source of pessimism is to be found in the emergence of man's self-consciousness at a level at which he feels his isolation and estrangement in a world in which sickness, suffering, and death interfere with, and ultimately nullify, his hopes for a desired future. This mood showed itself in early Babylonian and Egyptian literature, as well as in the Hebrew Scriptures and in the Greek conception of life as being lived in the shadow of a fate (*moira*) from which death itself fails to offer a complete escape. Homer, although generally healthy-minded, judged that "there is nothing more wretched than man, of all things that breathe and are" (*Iliad* XXIV, 446 ff.), and Sophocles wrote, in *Oedipus at Colonus,* "Not to be born is the most to be desired; but having seen the light, the next best is to go whence one came as soon as may be." In the Old Testament, the books of Job and Ecclesiastes reflect the same struggle with the meaninglessness of life.

However, the Judaeo-Christian tradition is generally regarded as being optimistic. It applied a theistic view of Providence first to the history of a "chosen people" and then more universally to the moral interpretation of human history and of divine justice. The meaning of history is the redemption of God's people and, more generally, the

Kingdom of God or the Reign of Grace. Moreover, although the Hebrews had only a vague conception of life after death, Christianity offered the assurance of a blessed life—an assurance based neither upon a concept of strict justice, as in karma, nor upon works, but on divine Grace.

However, much Christian eschatology has condemned the present world to destruction and the people in it to judgment and condemnation. The division of people into saints and sinners has often comforted those conscious of their sainthood but has not generally strengthened the ideal of a great community of love. Doctrines of original sin and predestination of the damned, of apocalyptic horrors terminating history, and of the complete alienation of man from the world (the despair of life) have been a part of the Christian tradition and have been revived in our own time, when the consciousness of guilt and of alienation has been reinforced by the secular study of modern man.

Thus, most religion, in different contexts, emphasizes both good and evil in man, the universe, and history.

Ancient philosophical views. The Greeks, whose thought turned about the polarities of matter and form, impulse and reason, power and justice, freedom and order, and the transient and the permanent in experience, came to conclusions that have influenced all later discussions of the problem of good and evil in Western culture. When Nietzsche condemned Socrates for making the Apollonian mood supreme in Greek art and thought, he attributed to him a type of serene intellectualistic optimism that has formed much of Western culture, particularly through its elaboration and systematization by Plato and Aristotle, who by ultimately identifying existence and value and supporting the ideal of rational perfectibility, provided the philosophical grounds for Western optimism. But Plato was not so one-sidedly optimistic as Neoplatonism later became. The *Republic*, for instance, recognizes the possibility for man and society to attain justice and happiness, but it imposes harsh conditions for their attainment and is pessimistic about their ever being achieved by more than a select few.

In Hellenistic and Roman thought the nature of evil was a persistent problem that was shared by Epicureans, Stoics, Skeptics, and eclectics. Skepticism is often regarded as the intellectualistic counterpart of pessimism, but it has also often been the basis for an optimistic fideism. Although Epicureans and Stoics answered the question of the nature of evil differently, both the qualified hedonism of the one and the rejection of all external goods and emphasis upon self-sufficiency of the other tended to support a cultured tranquillity of contented, sometimes even grateful, acceptance. Both denied the evil of death, and the Stoics denied the evil of pain as well. While the Stoics relied upon determinism, and the Epicureans upon indeterminism, both denied that the gods were in any way connected with, or cognizant of, man's good. From Plutarch's *De Stoicorum Repugnantiis* (first century A.D.) to Vanini's *Amphitheatrum Aeternae Providentiae* (1615), the Stoics were charged with attributing evil to divine Providence, while the Epicureans grounded their conception of the contentment of the wise man upon his freedom from interference by the gods.

The decline and fall of Rome brought to consciousness a new dimension of pessimism—the despair evoked by the collapse of a historical order that had claimed eternity and universality. The relativity of good and evil to historical change provided the individual with a mode of adjustment to the evils of social and institutional decline. St. Augustine's great adaptation of Platonism to a Christian solution to this problem has been the source not only of most later religious optimism, but also of the great theodicies of the West, from the medieval and Renaissance Platonists to Leibniz and Hegel.

Early modern views. The Middle Ages have often been regarded as having been clouded with pessimism (they provided Hegel with the cultural type that he described as "the unhappy consciousness"), while the Renaissance and seventeenth century have been regarded as comparatively optimistic, culminating in baroque exuberance. But recent scholarship views the medieval and Renaissance periods as a cultural continuity moving toward "modernity." In the face of a deep concern for the physical, social, and moral evils of Europe, intellects in both periods were engaged in a concerted effort to lay a rational Christian foundation for human happiness and harmony. While the political and social conditions varied, and the ideal of transformation changed from an eschatological revolution to continuous progress, Greek and Roman intellectual traditions continued to limit the philosophical effort to synthesize science, moral rationalism, and religious faith. Science and technology, nationalism, new ideals of individual freedom and toleration, and contact with new lands and cultures shifted and enlarged the scope of inquiry and intensified the problems, but the differences between Abelard, Thomas Aquinas, Scotus, and Ockham on the one hand, and Descartes, Spinoza, Bacon, and Locke on the other are far more superficial than the continuity of their problems and their tradition.

Seventeenth-century discussions of the dominance of good or evil were affected by the new perspectives on human life that evolved in the Renaissance—notably, the emphasis upon individualism; the conflict about the nature of human freedom; the problem of the control of political power, which resulted from the collapse of the medieval synthesis and the multiplication of small states; and the ideal of a rule of reason, strengthened by the successful combination of mathematics and experimentation in the scientific mastery of nature.

Developments in psychology. The discussion of optimism and pessimism was affected by two developments in psychological thought: Galen's doctrine of the four humors was applied to man's reactions to good and evil, and there was a wide recognition of the role of the affections and appetites in human life. A comparison of Albrecht Dürer's famous engraving of Melancholia (1514) with Robert Burton's *Anatomy of Melancholy* (1621) is revealing. In Dürer's time the dominance of the melancholy humor was held to be the source of contemplation and therefore of mathematical and other forms of learning; Burton treated melancholia as pathological and analyzed its types, causes, and cures. Unfortunately, there is no work analogous to Burton's erudite essay that deals with the dominance of the opposing humor, the sanguinary. But the use of the humors to explain pessimism and optimism initiated a long tradition of distinctions that includes Shaftesbury's and Rousseau's theories of the natural affections, the *Weltschmerz* and *Weltfreude* of the German romantics, and after Schopenhauer, the psychoanalytic classifications of Freud and Adler and the psychological typologies of world views by William James, Wilhelm Dilthey, Max Scheler, and others.

A closely related trend was the growing recognition of the role of the affections in determining human attitudes and conduct. The third book of Luis Vives' work on the mind (*De Anima et Vita Libri Tres*, 1538) was an important source for later attempts by such thinkers as Descartes, Spinoza, and Hobbes to explain human actions in terms of feeling and desires. In Hobbes the result was a pessimistic theory of human nature; in Montaigne, Pascal, and thinkers of the libertine tradition, it was a relativization of human ends that undermined the absoluteness of goods and evils; but in the thinking of Vives himself and in the rationalistic tradition of the seventeenth century (for example, Descartes, Spinoza, and Leibniz), an idealistic optimism resulted from the doctrine that the affections are docile and readily moldable into socially constructive attitudes.

Politics and history. The problem of power (particularly political power) and its responsiveness to reason was a second noteworthy development affecting the estimation of good and evil. Machiavelli had formulated the fundamental theory of a *raison d'état* in a way that provided pragmatic support for the principle of the divine right of rulers. The series of disastrous wars that swept over Europe, however, intensified a mood of eschatological expectation and heightened the fear or hope of revolution and an overthrow of the existing order. The transfer of the eschatological hope from an afterlife to the temporal world, and the resulting faith in human progress, were the result primarily of the increase of scientific and technological knowledge and the wider expansion of faith in reason. Hobbes entirely restricted his realistic definition of justice as the power of the strongest to the limits of the present historical order, thus secularizing St. Augustine's pessimistic appraisal of the City of Man and providing a modern ancestry for pessimistic interpretations of history.

Rationalism. From the metaphysical point of view, however, the rationalistic tradition of the seventeenth century may be regarded as optimistic; it constituted an effort to bring the real into harmony with the ideal or the normative. This effort concentrated on the law of nature and on the individual's relation to the absolute source of power and wisdom. In Descartes, human passions are regarded as supporting the ideal of *generosité* and *honnêteté*; in Spinoza, actuality is generalized into possibility, and passive affections are shown to be imperfect but corrigible through active affections; in Leibniz, truths of fact are held to be grounded in truths of reason, if we could only completely analyze the former. This optimistic doctrine of reality is supported in these thinkers by the conviction that evil is finitude or limitation and that as our ideas move from confusedness, indistinctness, and inadequacy toward clarity, distinctness, and adequacy, the goodness of the world and of our life is brought to light in an absolutely convincing way. Not all thinkers, of course, accepted this optimistic metaphysical resolution of the

problem. Pascal was driven by his perception of the finiteness of man and the terror in which this finiteness involves him to a philosophy in which the heart, not the intellect, provides knowledge about ultimate reality. Pierre Bayle had recourse to a combination of skepticism and Manichaean dualism, while Locke was attracted on the one hand to libertinism, pluralism, and toleration, and on the other hand to arguments for faith in a determining divine Providence.

Leibniz and the Enlightenment. Gottfried Wilhelm Leibniz (1646–1716) is generally regarded as the outstanding modern philosophical optimist. His *Théodicée* (1710) is a prolonged argument for the rationality of Christian faith, the reasonableness of creation, and the view that this is the best of all possible worlds. The argument of this work is supported by a large body of writings which aimed at a *philosophia perennis* (a synthesis of the truth in all of the classical systems of thought) as well as a harmonious ordering of scientific, philosophical, and theological truth. This philosophical system, in turn, was intended to serve as the ethical basis for the great Leibnizian projects for engaging the leaders of Europe in the restoration of peace through the advancement of science and technology, the reform of the law, the perfection of logical and mathematical tools of learning and a universal encyclopedia, the reuniting of the churches, and the Christian conquest of the pagan parts of the world. Thus, Leibniz' optimism, although grounded on one of the most remarkable philosophical systems of Western thought, was also ideological; it aimed at concerted action in a variety of related fields, and in this sense it presupposed a deep sensitivity to the existing evils that were to be overcome.

In general, Leibniz' argument is that the man of good will (*homo honestatis*) should find his greatest happiness ("toute la joie dont un mortel est capable") in the recognition that in spite of its glaring evils this is the best of all possible worlds, because its creation involved the fullest possible realization of the divine attributes. He should also recognize that there prevails in the world a divine harmony that requires evil not only for the full manifestation of the infinite greatness of the world's Creator but also in order that this evil may contribute to a greater good than would otherwise be possible. The conception of evil involved in this argument combines three theories: the privative theory (supported by Leibniz' essentialist metaphysics) that the complete notion or law of every individual monadic series is a finite combination (erected by God) of its own simple perfections; a legalistic moral theory somewhat inconsistent with this, according to which justice requires retribution for man's sins and compensation for man's suffering; and an aesthetic theory that finds limited evil necessary (like the dark parts of a painting) for the perception of a more complete and inclusive good. Leibniz' defense of God is brilliant, and the many editions through which his *Théodicée* passed in the original French and in Latin and German translations produced an extensive following on the Continent and even in England, where it may have influenced the optimistic thought of Lord Bolingbroke, Alexander Pope, and others. Yet his argument is defective, most notably in his failure successfully to reconcile human freedom and responsibility with the determinism of the divine creation, and in his general inclination to explain what is in terms of what ought to be. Many readers have agreed with Jean Guitton (*Pascal et Leibniz,* Paris, 1951, p. 121) that "one would have to change very little to transform this supreme joy (in the supreme goodness of things) into a radical despair."

Deism. The optimism of the eighteenth century, influenced by Leibniz' defense of God rather than by his more subtle metaphysics, was deistic, and much of its thought followed the five creedal points of Lord Herbert of Cherbury, who asserted an instinctive faith in the law of nature that dictates belief in one God, a divine order of justice, a moral imperative, individual immortality subject to a system of rewards and punishments, and a condemnation of "enthusiasm" as divisive and disruptive of true religion. The spirit of deism was activistic, sometimes revolutionary, and intent upon scientific progress and the dissipation of superstition. In this sense it was optimistic.

Maupertuis. The eighteenth century was also the breeding ground of modern pessimism. Voltaire's shocked reaction to the Lisbon earthquake and his satirical attack on the Leibnizian formula in *Candide* stimulated the change in mood, but even more significant was the influence of Pierre Louis Moreau de Maupertuis (1698–1759), to whom both the utilitarian Jeremy Bentham and the philosophical pessimist Eduard von Hartmann were indebted for their conception of a "balance of pain and pleasure." In his *Essai de philosophie morale* (1749), Maupertuis proposed a measure of good and evil in terms of *plaisir* and *peine.* (The French terms, their English equivalents "pleasure" and "pain," and the German words *Lust* and *Unlust* have somewhat different psychological connotations that must here be ignored.) Maupertuis defined these terms functionally: *plaisir* is any "perception" that the soul prefers to experience rather than not to experience; *peine* is the opposite. An examination of life in terms of moments of pleasure and pain, Maupertuis concluded, shows in a frightening way how preponderant pain is. Life is a constant wish to change one's perceptions in order to achieve fulfillment and to see the intervening times destroyed (*anéantir*). But if God were to abolish these intervening periods from even the longest life, only a few hours would remain. "In the usual life the sum of evil is greater than the sum of well-being."

Kant. If the optimism of the Enlightenment found the goodness of creation revealed both in nature and in historical progress, the decline of this tradition and the growth of a new pessimism grounded in the romantic movement may be traced in the thought of Immanuel Kant. The *Versuch einiger Betrachungen über den Optimismus,* written in 1759, argued for the Leibnizian "best of all possible worlds" in two steps: first, there must be one possible world which is the best, and second, it is necessary that this existing world is that best of all possible worlds. Kant urged the faith that each human being, recognizing "that the whole is the best and everything is good for the sake of the whole," should find his small place in this world. But in his critical period, after 1781, he found the fact of evil decisive in invalidating the Teleological Argument and recognized a "radical evil" in man that prevents him from exercising the good will and doing his duty. In the short

paper of 1785, *Muthmasslicher Anfang der Menschengeschichte,* Kant could only advise maintaining one's courage in the face of life's tribulations.

Romanticism and idealism. The shift in attitude noted above deepened into the pronounced pessimism of the romantics, many of whose writings reflect a feeling of overwhelming anguish at man's situation in the world. Goethe's early works (especially the *Sorrows of Young Werther*) reveal this *Weltschmerz,* as do the works of Heine, Byron, and Leopardi. However, the German idealist philosophers struggled against it through various forms of voluntarism—a voluntarism that encompassed the cosmos in Fichte, was involved in history through great individuals in Hegel, and developed into a theory of emerging personal creativity in the context of chaos in Schelling's philosophy of freedom. Thus, Eduard von Hartmann and Olga Plümacher were unjust to the influence of this *Weltschmerz* when they excluded it from consideration as a form of philosophical pessimism. In a real sense it anticipated, and was the historical forerunner of, the twentieth-century irrationalist philosophies and philosophies of despair.

Schopenhauer and von Hartmann. The greatest philosophical protagonist of the pessimistic tradition is, of course, Arthur Schopenhauer (1788–1860), who gave expression to it in the context of the Kantian distinction between a phenomenal nature and a real intelligible world in which the moral will and an interpersonal society of willing beings are primary. Schopenhauer interpreted the realm of phenomena as "illusory" and as the result of human conceptualization; the real world is irrational will-to-live, known intuitively through man's perception of his own nature. To discover this world is to recognize the ultimate and inescapable evil of existence.

Man's life, Schopenhauer held, is permanently condemned to be in bondage to the will-to-live. As the Indian thinkers discovered, the essential nature of every human life is desire, and this desire is never stilled, since even its satisfaction results in increased desire or ennui. The world as will, therefore, is unmitigated evil; good is illusory, but man, by his very nature as an intelligent, feeling animal, and facing inevitable death, is driven beyond this illusion to discover his own plight. This is therefore the worst of all possible worlds, since there is no good in it. The only escape is through renouncing will, but only the great artists, thinkers, and prophets are capable of doing this—and only in a finite and impermanent degree. There is, however, an ethics involved in this pessimism; it is the ethics of sympathy and amelioration of the suffering of one's fellows.

Von Hartmann. Eduard von Hartmann found Schopenhauer's pessimism to be the ultimate expression of a romantic *Weltschmerz* in which a sense of guilt over the quest for pleasure was implicit. Although he adhered generally to Schopenhauer's metaphysics (supplementing the will, however, with a parallel order of ideas, both will and ideas having their seat in the unconscious), he modified his own theory of conflict in nature by stressing the purposiveness of every individualized act of will. He also rejected the Darwinian theory of change through struggle and survival in favor of a theory of evolutionary creativity in which new forms arise in the germ plasm of the old. In contrast to Schopenhauer's pessimism, von Hartmann claimed that his was a "powerful, energetic pessimism, filled with the joy of action," whose historical antecedent is to be found in Kant, not Maupertuis. This is not the worst of all possible worlds; the logical element (i.e., the ideas) ensures that the world is a best possible world. Yet it would be better if there were no world at all, and this is in truth the end to which the universal will, spatialized, and individualized through the particularizations of intellect, is driving—the total negation of all will through the fulfillment of its purposes.

Although von Hartmann argued that his metaphysical system of the unconscious would be valid without his pessimism, it is apparent that the converse is not the case: his pessimism rests directly upon his metaphysics of the unconscious. Yet he supported his pessimism by a comprehensive examination of empirical arguments from neurology, psychology, and the history of culture. The optimistic illusion takes form in three stages: first, the belief that happiness is attainable in the present world; second, that there will be a future otherworldly life in which the good will be attained; and third, that the surplus of happiness will be achieved sometime in this world's future history. The transition from each stage of optimism to the next already involves a surrender of hope. Von Hartmann's refutation of optimism is not merely negative but consists of a constructive argument for three corresponding levels of pessimism, which he labeled empirical, transcendental, and metaphysical respectively. Transcendental pessimism involves the denial of life after death, a conclusion von Hartmann undertook to prove through a metaphysical argument for the inseparability of body and mind. Metaphysical pessimism is supported a priori by the inevitability of misery in a world of will individuated by ideas and by the total lack of feeling of the will after all existents have ceased to be. It is also shown, however, by the finiteness and ultimate failure of all the values of human life—particularly the ethical, religious, and aesthetic values.

It is in his argument for empirical or eudaemonistic pessimism that von Hartmann showed his greatest skill in penetrating human motives and the interaction between pleasure and displeasure in human action. Twelve arguments, cumulative in force, were offered for the preponderance of pain over pleasure. On the simplest level, the growing fatigue induced by nervous processes diminishes the effort to retain pleasures, and as the fatigue grows, it increases the resistance to pleasure. Moreover, most pleasure is merely the negative kind that results from the cessation of positive unpleasantness or pain; thus, it can in no way equal the unpleasantness that it terminates. Displeasure coerces consciousness in a way that pleasure cannot, since pleasure must consciously be sought and discovered and occurs only when there is conscious motivation or desire for it. In shared experiences of pleasure the sense of solidarity and sympathy may momentarily intensify that pleasure, but this intense pleasure is correspondingly sooner exhausted than unintensified pleasure. In shared suffering or displeasure this sympathetic response may also occur, but it is overbalanced by callous and egoistic reactions. Moreover, history shows that as

cultures advance in sensitivity and refinement, this overbalance of suffering increases proportionally. Such arguments, von Hartmann held, conclusively establish an excess of *Unlust* that confirms eudaemonistic pessimism.

In his late work on the history and foundation of pessimism (2d ed., 1892), von Hartmann modified his theory through an analysis of the different measures of value (*Wertmassstäbe*), of which pleasure is only one, the others being purposiveness, beauty, morality, and religiosity. These independent measures of value in themselves point to an optimistic view of life. Thus, he now called his thought a "eudaemonological pessimism" but a "teleologico–evolutionary optimism"; yet the new measures are themselves not unmixed with the subjective feeling dimension, so that we must conclude that the over-all balance of pleasure in the world is negative.

Von Hartmann's influence. Unlike Schopenhauer's pessimism, which was slow in gaining acceptance, von Hartmann's *Die Philosophie des Unbewussten* (Berlin, 1869; 9th ed. translated by W. C. Coupland as *The Philosophy of the Unconscious*, 3 vols., London, 1884) met with an immediate favorable response because of the changing intellectual and cultural mood of the last half of the century. The worst effects of the industrial revolution had become too conspicuous to be overlooked; colonialism involved nations in guilt; utopian reforms frequently ended in disillusionment; socialism shifted from its philanthropic to its "scientific" stage (von Hartmann himself was one of the early critics of social democracy); Darwinism intensified the perception of suffering and struggle in animate nature; and the romantic mood collapsed into a new naturalism according to which man was held in bondage to social forces and unconscious powers beyond his control. Novelists like Dickens, whose early works radiated Mr. Pickwick's cheerful vision of life, turned to the wretchedness of life and the irreducible evil of actual educational, penal, and political systems. Hawthorne and Melville in America and Thomas Hardy in England reflected different aspects of this pessimistic movement, which mounted in strength until it developed into the *fin de siècle* mood of disillusionment, mortification, and decadence described and criticized by Cesare Lombroso, Max Nordau, and others.

Several of von Hartmann's followers carried his pessimism to the limit of nihilism. Julius Bahnsen (1830–1881) analyzed the "dominance of the offended spirit" (*das angekränkelte Gemüth*) that is split by hate, malcontent, and horror, and Philipp Mainländer (pseudonym of Philipp Batz, 1841–1876) pushed pessimism to its ultimate conclusion in total annihilation. In his *Philosophie der Erlösung* (2 vols., Berlin, 1876–1886) Mainländer held that the will to annihilation (*Vernichtungswille*) is included in the nature of every individual being, inorganic as well as organic, and that the ethics of the individual is egoistic and implies virginity and suicide as means of world salvation (i.e., annihilation).

Von Hartmann's pessimism, although more critical and balanced than Schopenhauer's, also received extensive philosophical criticism. James Sully in England, Johannes Volkelt, Johannes Rehmke, Hermann Lotze, and Gustav Fechner in Germany, the spiritualists in France, and William James and others in America replied in terms of a more positive voluntarism or a more positive theory of value, thus laying the basis for a restoration of constructive liberalism in the twentieth century.

Nietzsche. The influence of Schopenhauer upon Friedrich Nietzsche was described by the latter in detail and is well known. He agreed with Schopenhauer's view that life is filled with suffering and a preponderance of evil, but rejected his ethics of resignation and of sympathy that was based upon it, as he also came to reject the metaphysical doctrine of will upon which it rested. Instead, Nietzsche's doctrine of the Dionysian man, or the superman, demanded a vigorous affirmation of life and power that would transcend both the "weakness doctrines of optimism" and tragedy as "the art of metaphysical comfort." In his "Versuch einer Selbstkritik" (1886; English translation in *The Philosophy of Nietzsche*, Modern Library edition, New York, pp. 934–946) Nietzsche corrected his earlier romantic reliance upon the ideal of "a pessimism of strength" that he found in Greek tragedy (*The Birth of Tragedy*), replacing it with an affirmation of man's powers of joyous creativity—the "laughter of Zarathustra." Although Nietzsche's ideal of a life "beyond good and evil" is ambiguous and easy to misread, he clearly transcended traditional conceptions of pessimism and optimism, pressing from the conceptual to the realm of personal living and valuing. His superman is a mixture of the rejection of accepted contemporary values, a rigorous discipline of the self in loneliness, and the joy of creativity and the hope of a new aristocracy of creative individuals.

Nietzsche's criticism of modern culture as nihilistic is beyond pessimism in the same sense that his ethics is beyond good and evil. Abstract theories of the balance of good and evil fall far short of reflecting the plight and the opportunity of modern man, upon whose will to power the civilization of the future must rest.

Santayana and Freud. Two thinkers who differed greatly in their theoretical and practical approaches to human problems, Santayana and Freud, developed pessimistic theories which were similar in important respects to the pessimism of Schopenhauer. (Freud arrived at his pessimism independently and did not read Schopenhauer until late in life.)

Santayana found in metaphysical matter what Schopenhauer found in will—the ultimate ground of all permanence, power, and life and therefore the ultimate ground of the tragedy which is involved in man's efforts to live the life of reason and spirit. Through concrete personal vision Santayana transcended the old debate between optimism and pessimism. Unlike Nietzsche, he found his personal resolution of the problem of evil not in the egocentric ideal of the superman but in an ideal of stoic acceptance and self-sufficiency.

In Freud's work the libido and, later, the id play a role similar to that of the will in Schopenhauer's system. The failure to gratify the impulses emanating from the id produces basic dislocations in the "libido economy" and thus leads to suffering and illness. In *Das Unbehagen in der Kultur* (Vienna, 1930 [1929]; translated by Joan Riviere as *Civilization and Its Discontents*, London, 1930) Freud traces human suffering to three sources—the superior power of nature, the decay and death of our own bodies, and the shortcomings of social relations and institutions.

Of these, the first two are insurmountable, and the third inevitably results in unhappiness and alienation from man's culture. Moral judgments are merely "the effort to support illusions with argument." The illusory world of subjective imagination and thought sometimes offers successful sublimations and corrections, but the ultimate way to soundness can be found only (if at all) by a return to the natural and cultural roots of our being through psychoanalytical techniques. In an earlier work, *Die Zukunft einer Illusion* (Vienna, 1927; translated by W. D. Robson-Scott as *The Future of an Illusion*, London and New York, 1928), Freud held out much hope for this ideal through the elimination of religion, which he saw as likely to accompany the progress of science.

The twentieth century. In the twentieth century, with its dislocation and destruction of human life and values, the tremendous potentialities of its technological advances, its moral and cultural uncertainties, and its rifts in the texture of human society, the problem of optimism and pessimism has shifted from an attempt to determine the relative goodness and badness of the world to an attempt to face the plight of modern man—his situation and his powers and resources for achieving good. This is a shift from conceptual modes of assessing the goodness of man, nature, and the universe to cautious nominalistic and phenomenological analysis of the individual.

It is true that a moralistic optimism has found strong defense and influence through the work of William James and John Dewey, while Alfred North Whitehead and others have offered metaphysical support of rationality, creativity, and the discovery of values in general. On the other hand, Bertrand Russell, in "A Free Man's Worship" (1903), gave moving expression to a naturalistic pessimism that regards man's existence in an indifferent universe as brief and without meaning, yet exhorts him to resist these natural powers with all the force of a living and vigorous faith in himself and in the powers of man. More commonly, the prevailing temper is to ignore the natural order as being neutral toward good and evil, and to show concern rather for the human person as a self-conscious being cast in a given historical situation. Man's natural environment, which John Dewey (in agreement with Hegel) found to be an aspect of the situation in which man is to achieve his freedom, is now taken by many as an aspect of the situation into which man is "thrown," but which he transcends in his capacity as insular self-consciousness, will, decision maker, or confronter of the divine.

Existentialism is the final expression of the inverted romantic spirit that began with Schopenhauer. Rousseau's attack on civilization is broadened and shifted: it is not just civilization that debases man; the entire situation in which *Dasein* finds itself forces upon it a sense of aloneness, alienation, and despair. But this is not pessimism; conceptual theory is irrelevant. The person's response must be "existential," taking the form of a blind affirmation of will or a surrender to a confrontation (whether with Christ or communism). Such a response is beyond optimism as well. According to the existentialist, no theory of the goodness of the world is relevant, but only unreasoning hope. Although the works of Heidegger and Sartre are replete with themes that evoke reactions of pessimism and optimism, they significantly avoid raising the old issues concerning the relative predominance of good and evil in the world. Gabriel Marcel has eloquently made the distinction between optimism and hope in *Homo Viator* (Paris, 1944, Ch. 2). The more completely irrationalistic followers of the existentialist movement (Jean Genêt, for example) push this rejection of the traditional philosophical issue further into an ultimate reversal of good and evil and a doctrine of redemption through evil.

Although optimism and pessimism are terms that are useful in expressing fundamental human attitudes toward the universe or toward certain aspects of it, they have an ambiguity and relativity that makes them useless for a valid philosophical analysis. The question of the relative amounts of good or evil in human life and its environment is too involved to be resolved with existing philosophical tools. The dominant movements in contemporary philosophy prefer to describe and analyze the human situation more carefully in order to achieve greater understanding of the elements involved in it. That this must be done in cooperation with psychology and the natural and social sciences seems obvious; yet there are distinctively philosophical issues involved (some of which are very old) that are receiving more fruitful analysis with recent philosophical techniques. Until the basic concepts involved in a philosophical anthropology have received such analysis, the terms "optimism" and "pessimism" might wisely be avoided.

Among analytic philosophies, the empirical and positivistic trend that brushes aside all metaphysical and ethical issues as unphilosophical offers little help in this undertaking, although the old issue of a pleasure–pain balance may be regarded as an important attempt to meet analytical and empirical requirements of method. On the other hand, contemporary linguistic analysis is seeking firm ground for some of the ethical and axiological terms upon which discussions of good and evil must be based. But the analytic movement has been cautious in moving toward the metaphysical decisions upon which the resolution of these complex problems depend. It may be conjectured that when the present interest in analytic and phenomenological exploration develops into a bolder metaphysical phase, the terms "optimism" and "pessimism" may survive as descriptions of dominant human attitudes, but they may be superseded as philosophical theories by more adequate and more complex conceptual formulations of the meaning of human life and history.

(See also LIFE, MEANING AND VALUE OF and NIHILISM.)

Bibliography

HISTORY OF PESSIMISM AND OPTIMISM

Billisch, Friedrich, *Das Problem des Übels in der Philosophie des Abendlandes,* 3 vols. Vienna, 1959.

Diels, Hermann, *Der antike Pessimismus.* Berlin, 1921.

Hartmann, Eduard von, *Zur Geschichte und Begründung des Pessimismus,* 2d ed. Leipzig, 1892.

Plümacher, Olga, *Der Pessimismus in Vergangenheit und Gegenwart. Geschichtliches und Kritisches.* Heidelberg, 1884.

Siwek, Paul, "Optimism in Philosophy" and "Pessimism in Philosophy," in *New Scholasticism,* Vol. 23 (1948), 239–297, 417–439.

Sully, James, *Pessimism: a History and a Criticism.* London, 1877.

Tsanoff, Radoslav A., *The Nature of Evil.* New York, 1931.

Vyverberg, Henry, *Historical Pessimism in the French Enlightenment.* Cambridge, Mass., 1958.

NINETEENTH-CENTURY VIEWS

Bailey, Robert B., *Sociology Faces Pessimism: A Study of European Sociological Thought amidst a Fading Optimism.* The Hague, 1958.

Caro, Elme Marie, *Le Pessimisme au XIXᵉ siècle: Leopardi—Schopenhauer—Hartmann.* Paris, 1878.

Copleston, Frederick, *Arthur Schopenhauer: Philosopher of Pessimism.* London, 1946.

Dorner, August, *Pessimismus: Nietzsche und Naturalismus, mit besonderer Beziehung auf die Religion.* Leipzig, 1911.

Gass, W., *Optimismus und Pessimismus.* Berlin, 1876.

Nordau, Max, *Entartung.* Berlin, 1892. Translated from the second German edition as *Degeneration.* New York, 1895.

Petraschek, Karl, *Die Logik des Unbewussten.* Munich, 1920. Vol. II especially.

Petraschek, Karl, *Die Rechtsphilosophie des Pessimismus.* Munich, 1929.

CONTEMPORARY ISSUES

Marcel, Gabriel, *Homo Viator.* Paris, 1944. Translated by Emma Craufurd as *Homo Viator.* Chicago, 1951.

Marcuse, Ludwig, *Pessimismus: ein Stadium der Reife.* Hamburg, 1953.

Unamuno, Miguel de, *Des sentimiento trágico de la vida en los hombres y en los pueblos.* Madrid, 1913. Translated by J. E. Crawford Flitch as *The Tragic Sense of Life in Men and in Peoples.* London, 1921.

L. E. LOEMKER

PESTALOZZI, JOHANN HEINRICH (1746–1827), Swiss educator whose views have profoundly affected the history and philosophy of education. Pestalozzi's father, a clergyman in Zurich, then the most lively center of awakening German culture and literature, died when his son was six years old. Pestalozzi's profound piety, the desire to love and to be loved, his compassion for suffering—and his extreme sensitivity and awkwardness in dealing with the practical affairs of life—were due largely to the exclusive upbringing of his pious mother.

After graduating from the Collegium Humanitatis (a secondary school), he turned to agriculture and experimented at his newly acquired farm, the Neuhof, with a school for the children of the neighboring farmers which was to combine elementary education with practical work. The Neuhof enterprise was a failure, financially as well as educationally, but it brought him the insights that determined his later educational, social, and religious theory and practice. These insights are jotted down in aphoristic style in *Die Abendstunde eines Einsiedlers* ("Evening Hour of a Hermit," 1780), one of those astounding works of sudden illumination which we sometimes find in the lives of men of rare genius.

As a young man, Pestalozzi sympathized with a liberal student movement which was considered subversive by the patrician government of Zurich. He also sympathized actively with the Swiss and French revolutions at the end of the eighteenth century but was soon disappointed in the development of both.

In 1789 he took over the education of the desolate children of the town of Stans, which had been the scene of a battle between the French and the Swiss and had been badly ransacked by the French victors. Later he founded schools at Burgdorf and Münchenbuchsee, and finally at Iverdon on the shore of the Lake of Neuchâtel, attracting increasingly the attention of reform-minded men and women all over Europe. "Pestalozzianism," as a method of education that emphasized the importance of individual differences and the stimulation of the child's self-activity as against mere rote learning, was transferred also to the United States and resulted, about 1860, in a thorough reorganization of its elementary schools.

Like Comenius (whom he mentions, without being influenced by him), Pestalozzi was able to fuse his Christ-centered piety with a romantic concept of nature. First impressed by Rousseau, whose ideas he later rejected, he used the term "nature" as synonymous with all that is genuine, authentic, and free from artificiality. He regarded it as the function of education, as of all other social activities, to find the "organic" or "elemental" principles by which the inherent talent of every person could be developed to his fullest individuality, or to his "truth." His concept of truth, therefore, does not aim at logical universality; rather, it is, to use a modern term, "existential." A person can be educated toward maturity only if he has been allowed to sense in his earliest infancy and under the care of his mother and his family the vital element in all human relations, altruistic love. And he can safely pass over to his next developmental stage only if he has fully mastered the experiences and tasks of the preceding stage, if the whole of his personality has been formed by the "education of the heart, the hand and the mind," if the things he has learned have become really his own and have aroused a sense of commitment, and if, finally, he discovers the vertical line, his personal relation to God, without which all relations between man and man, man and nature, and man and knowledge remain empty and meaningless. According to Pestalozzi, it is the curse of modern civilization that its hasty and primarily verbal education does not give man enough time for the process of *Anschauung,* a term perhaps best translated as "internalized apperception," or as dwelling on the meaning and challenge of an impression. Thus modern civilization leads a person more and more away from his deeper self into a tangle of self-perceptions, of useless, if not dangerous, knowledge, and of false ambitions, which will make him unhappy.

As in many similar cases, Pestalozzi's fame as an educator has prevented the scholarly world from recognizing the full scope and depth of his interests. Besides a few and often inadequate accounts, little attention has been paid to Pestalozzi as a man of passionate concern for social justice and for new forms of religious education which were intentionally prevented by corrupt ecclesiastical institutions.

Nor has his essay "Meine Nachforschungen über den Gang der Natur in der Entwicklung des Menschengeschlechtes" ("On the Path of Nature in the History of Mankind") received sufficient attention, although it is profounder and more realistic than the contemplations on human progress by Condorcet, Turgot, and other philosophers of the Enlightenment. According to Pestalozzi, the develop-

ment of the human race is reflected in the life of every person. Each of us has in himself the primitive, the social, and the ethical man. Injustice, therefore, will remain, although we may profit from the experiences of earlier generations. But the state of moral freedom will be achieved by only a few chosen individuals, and they (in this sentence he refers to his own life) will hardly find a niche in the house of mankind.

Works by Pestalozzi

GERMAN EDITIONS

Sämtliche Werke, A. Buchenau and others, eds. Berlin, 1927—. Critical edition, not yet completed.
Gesammelte Werke in zehn Bänden, Emilie Bosshart and others, eds. Zurich, 1944–1947.
Werke, Paul Baumgartner, ed. Zurich, 1944–1949.

TRANSLATIONS

Leonard and Gertrude, translated by Eva Channing. Boston, 1885.
How Gertrude Teaches Her Children, Ebenezer Cooke, ed., translated by L. E. Holland and Francis Turner. London, 1894.
Pestalozzi's Main Writings, J. A. Green, ed. New York, 1912.

Works on Pestalozzi and Selections

Anderson, L. F., ed. *Pestalozzi.* New York, 1931.
Silber, Käte, *Pestalozzi: The Man and His Work.* London, 1960.
Ulich, Robert, *History of Educational Thought.* New York, 1950. Pp. 258–270.
Ulich, Robert, *Three Thousand Years of Educational Wisdom.* Cambridge, Mass., 1959. Pp. 480–507.

ROBERT ULICH

PETER AUREOL (or Petrus Aureolus, Petrus Aureoli, Peter Oriole, etc.), French Franciscan philosopher and theologian called "Doctor Facundus," was born near Gourdon, Lot, between 1275 and 1280 and died in 1322. He entered the Franciscan order before 1300, probably at Gourdon, and was assigned to the province of Aquitaine. In 1304, Peter was at Paris, but whether he studied under Duns Scotus is uncertain. His first work was *Tractatus de Paupertate* (1311). In 1312 he was lector at the *studium generale* at Bologna, where he composed his only purely philosophical work, the unfinished *Tractatus de Principiis Naturae* in four books. From 1314 to 1315, as lector at Toulouse, he wrote the original and influential tract *De Conceptione B. M. V.* and the *Repercussorium* against certain opponents of the tract. From 1313 to 1316, probably also at Toulouse, he composed his extensive *Scriptum Super I Sententiarum,* dedicated to John XXII. At the Chapter General of Naples in 1316, Peter was nominated to lecture on the *Sentences* at Paris. The newly elected general of the order, Michael of Cesena, who had just finished his own *Sentences* at Paris, gave his consent as required although Peter openly opposed him. Peter lectured at Paris from 1316 to 1318; his *Reportata,* formerly called "the first redaction," is now believed to belong to this period. In a letter dated July 14, 1318, John XXII asked the chancellor of Paris to grant Aureol the licentiate. Peter is later mentioned (November 13, 1318) as among the master regents. For the next two years he taught Scripture at Paris while composing his often-published

Compendium Sensus Litteralis Totius Scripturae (1319). At the end of 1320, Peter became provincial of Aquitaine but was nominated archbishop of Aix and consecrated by the pope himself in 1321. He died either at Avignon or at Aix.

Although Peter's doctrines have never been thoroughly studied, he has long been regarded as a highly critical thinker who often discarded as useless philosophical theories of his time—for example, he rejected contemporary opinions on the cosmic influence of the intelligences. In particular, he criticized many theories of Thomas Wylton and Hervaeus Natalis. He often attacked Scotus, yet he also frequently followed and defended him.

Peter's own philosophical system is characterized by skeptical and empirical traits. In epistemology he supported a form of conceptualism—a doctrine midway between the realism of the great Scholastics and the nominalism of William of Ockham—in which the intelligible species is not merely the *medium quo* but itself the immediate object of our knowledge. Universal concepts have some psychic reality but no objective foundation; any principle of individuation is thus rendered superfluous. Knowledge of the individual, because of its high degree of clarity and truth, is to be preferred to knowledge of the universal. In keeping with the principle of economy often called Ockham's razor, the constitutive elements of beings are to be limited, so that without extremely cogent reasons we should not accept a plurality of "realities" in a thing. In other philosophical fields Peter had many theories of his own. He defended the existence of neutral propositions, neither true nor false, and this led him to think that God cannot know with certainty future contingent events. Peter emphasized that man's knowledge of God is largely dependent upon the psychological dispositions of the individual; moreover, ontologically there is no common ground of being between men and God. In cosmology Peter had his own opinions on the plurality of forms, the notion of an infinite, the subjectivity of time, and the meaning of movement. He thus bears witness to the fact that there was no dogmatic uniformity in medieval Scholasticism.

Bibliography

Peter's *Tractatus de Paupertate* was edited in *Firmamenta Trium Ordinum B. P. N. Francisci* (Paris, 1511), Part IV, folio 116r–129r. The *Tractatus de Principiis Naturae* is preserved only in manuscript. *De Conceptione B. M. V.* and the *Repercussorium* were edited at Quaracchi, Italy, in 1904. The *Sententiarum* was edited in Rome in 1516; the critical edition by E. M. Buytaert, in 2 vols. (to date), (St. Bonaventure, N.Y., 1953–1956), includes the Prologue and Book 1 (Distinctions 1–8), and the difficult question of the double redaction of the *Sentences* is discussed in the Introduction. The *Reportata* was edited in 2 vols. (Rome, 1596–1605). The *Compendium* was edited by P. Seeboeck (Quaracchi, 1896). Peter's other works include *Compendiosa Expositio Evangelis Joannis*, Friedrich Stegmüller, ed., in *Franziskanische Studien*, Vol. 33 (1951), 207–219; *Recommendatio et Divisio S. Scripturae*; *Commentariorum in Isiam*; one *Quodlibet* (1320) of 16 questions (edited Rome, 1605); and unedited questions and sermons.

SECONDARY SOURCES

Barth, T., article on Peter in *Lexikon für Theologie und Kirche*, 2d ed., Vol. VII (1963), p. 350.

Beumer, J., "Der Augustinismus in der theologische Erkennt-

nislehre des P. A." *Franziskanische Studien*, Vol. 36 (1954), 137–171.

Gilson, Étienne, *History of Christian Philosophy in the Middle Ages.* New York, 1955. Pp. 476–480, 777–779.

Maier, Anneliese, article on Peter in *Enciclopedia cattolica*, Vol. II (1949), pp. 409–411.

Maier, Anneliese, "Literarhistorische Notizen über P. A." *Gregorianum*, Vol. 29 (1948), 213–229.

Pelster, Franz, "Estudios sobre la transmisión manuscrita de algunas obras de P. A." *Estudios eclesiasticos*, Vol. 9 (1930), 462–479, and Vol. 10 (1931), 449–474.

Pelster, Franz, "Zur Überlieferung des Quodlibet und anderer Schriften des P. A." *Franciscan Studies*, Vol. 14 (1954), 392–411.

Pelster, Franz, "Zur ersten Polemik gegen Aureoli." *Franciscan Studies*, Vol. 15 (1955), 30–47.

Stegmüller, Friedrich, *Repertorium Biblicum*, Vol. IV, notes 6415–6422.

Stegmüller, Friedrich, *Repertorium Comment. in Sententiae Petri Lombardi*, 2 vols. Würzburg, 1947. Vol. I, notes 314–318, 657–663.

Teetaert, A., "Pierre Auriol," in *Dictionnaire de théologie catholique*, Vol. XII. Paris, 1935. Cols. 1810–1881.

A. EMMEN, O.F.M.

PETER DAMIAN (1007–1072), one of the greatest churchmen of the eleventh century, was born in Ravenna. After studying and teaching the liberal arts in several Italian cities, he joined a community of hermits at Fonte Avellana, near Gubbio, in Umbria (c. 1035), and became prior about 1040. He was soon called from the monastic life, however, to become an active leader in the growing movement of ecclesiastical reform. He became cardinal bishop of Ostia in 1057 and was sent on papal missions to Milan (1059), France and Florence (1063), Germany (1069), and Ravenna (1072). He died at Faenza.

Damian's attitude toward the humanistic culture of his time was ambiguous. Although he was a fine Latin stylist in both prose and verse, and a master of argument, he nevertheless belittled both grammar and dialectic. He argued, for example, that the study of grammar had begun badly when the devil taught Adam and Eve to decline *deus* in the plural (Genesis 3.5, "Ye shall be as gods"). As for dialectic, it could be nothing more than the "handmaid" (*ancilla*) of theology, and its usefulness even in that office was strictly limited.

The ascetic tradition of disdain for the world (*contemptus saeculi*), stemming from early Christian opposition to the naturalism and hedonism of pagan culture, dominated Damian's life and his pastoral care of others. His hostility to literary and logical studies was rooted in the conviction that the true purpose of human existence is to be found in the contemplation of God. Because he believed that religious communities should be nurseries of contemplatives, he was especially critical of the pursuit of secular studies by monks.

The intellectual conflicts of the age confirmed Damian in his opposition to dialectic. Theologians skilled in elementary Aristotelian logic were applying their analytical methods to major Christian doctrines, with more or less destructive results. While some defenders of orthodoxy responded to this challenge by attempting to formulate a rational apologetic for Catholic dogma, others (including Damian) were convinced that the pretensions of the dialecticians must be countered by unequivocal condemnation.

Peter Damian's most radical critique of human reason appeared in his major theological work, *De Divina Omnipotentia*. Here he argues not only that Christian dogma, being based on divine revelation, is beyond the range of rational demonstration but also that the norms of human rationality need not apply to the content of dogma. Indeed, his fundamental theological principle excluded any reasonable assurance that human experience as a whole could be orderly and intelligible. For Damian, the entire created order depends simply on the omnipotent will of God, which can even alter the course of past history.

Bibliography

For works by Peter Damian, see S. *Pier Damiani, De Divina Omnipotentia ed altri opuscoli*, edited by P. Brezzi (Florence, 1943), and *St. Peter Damian: Selected Writings on the Spiritual Life*, translated and edited by Patricia McNulty (London, 1959).
Works on Peter Damian include J. A. Endres, *Petrus Damiani und die weltliche Wissenschaft* (Münster, 1910).

EUGENE R. FAIRWEATHER

PETER LOMBARD (c. 1095–1160), theologian and bishop of Paris, was born at Lumellogno, Lombardy. He was elected bishop in 1159 and died the next year in Paris.

Born of a Longobard family (hence his "surname"), Peter probably studied at Bologna. He went to France about 1134, first to Rheims and then to Paris, where he soon became a teacher at the school of Notre Dame. By 1142 he was known as a "celebrated theologian," and in the same year Gerhoh of Reichersberg mentions his gloss on St. Paul, which had been preceded by a commentary on the Psalms (both works were soon adopted as the standard Scripture gloss). His fame rests chiefly on his *Book of Sentences* (*Libri Quatuor Sententiarum*), finished in 1157 or 1158.

The "Sentences." The fruit of Lombard's patristic studies, scholastic lectures, and long familiarity with theological literature and problems was the *Book of Sentences*. After a classical prologue, it treats of the Trinity and the divine attributes, of creation and sin, of the Incarnation and the life of grace and virtues, of the sacraments and Last Things. It seems to have received certain retouching and additions at the hands of the author before it was published in final form. Since it surpassed all other *summae* of the twelfth century in clarity of thought and didactic practicality, as well as in the range of its subject matter, it soon acquired great popularity. After 1222, when Alexander of Hales used it as the basis of his own theological course, it obtained official standing at Paris and other medieval universities; all candidates in theology were required to comment on it as preparation for the doctorate.

The work is basically a compilation, with numerous citations of the "sentences" of the Fathers and generous and often literal borrowings from near contemporaries: Anselm of Laon, Abelard's *Theology*, the anonymous *Summa Sententiarum*, Hugh of St. Victor's *De Sacramentis Fidei Christianae*, the *Decretum* of Gratian, and the *Glossa Ordinaria*. Not all Lombard's opinions found acceptance: lists of his positions not commonly accepted abound in medieval manuscripts. However, this did not lessen the work's influence in shaping scholastic method and thought for four or more centuries. Scholastic theology flourished within the framework of the *Sentences* but also suffered from the defects and limitations of this work. Because Lombard failed to treat certain questions, such as the nature and constitution of the church, the role of Christ's resurrection in the economy of salvation, and certain other aspects of Christology, these subjects were not developed in the scholastic period.

The scholastic method. Despite his overt criticism of dialectics, Lombard was largely responsible for introducing the scholastic method into the schools. Anselm of Laon (d. 1117) and his school had begun a more systematic approach to the questions of theology as a result of the growth of dialectics in the eleventh century. This approach was perfected by Peter Abelard, whose *Theologia Scholarium* is a reasoned study of theological doctrine, and whose *Sic et Non* is a vast assemblage of scriptural, patristic, and canonical material used in arguing for and against specific questions. In the prologue of the latter work, Abelard proposed principles for the reconciliation of opposing texts by semantic analysis, the authentication of texts, possible changes of opinion on the part of an author, and so on. Although critical of Abelard on many doctrinal positions, Lombard was thoroughly influenced by his method of contrasting authorities and arguments, interpreting their meaning, analyzing words, and drawing conclusions. As this method passed to the great Scholastics of the thirteenth through fifteenth centuries, it eventually led to the neglect of Scripture as the core of theological studies. Roger Bacon was to complain in 1267 that a "fourth sin" of contemporary theologians was their use of a *Summa magistralis*, the *Sentences*, in place of the Bible as the text of the faculty of theology.

Doctrines. To dismiss Lombard, as some authors have done, as primarily an unoriginal compiler almost completely lacking any philosophical foundations, and of historical importance only through the popularity his work attained, is not exactly a just judgment. Certainly Peter did not possess the deep speculative mind of, for example, his contemporary Gilbert of Poitiers or the dialectical keenness of Abelard. He made no pretense of being a philosopher, whatever he may have known of philosophical tradition. Rather, his work seems consciously to exclude the speculations of philosophy and to be primarily, if not exclusively, a work of theology based on Scripture and the doctrines of the Church Fathers. Lombard was undoubtedly a compiler, yet a compiler who was master of his sources and of his own thought. Often enough, his doctrinal importance emerges only when his teachings are examined against the background of his times.

On the nature of God, for example, Lombard is much more precise than the anonymous *Summa Sententiarum*. While the latter is inclined to speak of the divine essence or substance, the *Sentences*, following Augustine, makes it clear that, properly speaking, "substance" should not be predicated of the divine nature because it carries the connotation of accidents; rather, "essence," in the sense of absolute and total "beingness," or subsistent "being" (*esse*), is the proper name of God. From this Lombard deduces the corollary that immutability is primary among the divine attributes. From God's immutability follows his simplicity, in marked contrast to the multiplicity which in one form or another characterizes all created beings. If other attributes are predicated of God—that he is strong or wise or just—these imply no division, composition, or distinction which would militate against his absolute self-identity. Hence, while God knows all things in one perfect, unchanging act of knowledge, things do not thereby exist in God in such a way that they share his essence. Here, however, Lombard provides but the barest minimum on a question that was to receive much attention in the late thirteenth and early fourteenth centuries, the being of intelligibles.

When the creation of the world is considered in the first pages of Book II, Peter seems to react against the loquacity and daring speculation of some contemporary theologians in explaining Genesis; to all appearances, he deliberately avoids the teachings of the School of Chartres and follows Augustine's exegesis of the hexaemeron (through the *Glossa Ordinaria*), the *Summa Sententiarum*, and Hugh of St. Victor. His thought hesitates between the literal interpretation of the six days and the possibility of a simultaneous creation; although inclined to hold to the letter of the Scripture, Lombard leaves the way open to the position that creation was a single act and that matter later developed according to the capacities implanted in it. Far less attention is given to the nature of man and the soul than to the purpose of man's creation and his dignity as the image of God. With a certain vehemence Peter insists on creation rather than emanation or traducianism to explain the origin of the soul. The powers of soul on the levels of sense, reason, and free will are considered almost exclusively in their relation to divine grace.

The same disregard for philosophical questions characterizes Peter's moral doctrine, which is based far less on simply rational standards of human nature or of law than on man's natural dignity as the image of God, the supernatural gift of grace, and the indwelling of the Spirit. Unlike Abelard, whose moral doctrine is man-centered in the Aristotelian tradition, Lombard proposes an ethic based on God, with likeness to God as the goal of ethics and human life. If, as a theologian, he emphasizes man's absolute need of grace for virtuous acts, he lays equal stress on man's ability, under grace, to do good despite the weaknesses of human nature. The result is a moral doctrine that is far more positive than negative in character, an ethic of dignity.

Works by Lombard

"Gloss on the Psalms" (c. 1135–1137) may be found in J. P. Migne, ed., *Patrologia Latina* (Paris, 1844–1864), Vol. 191, pp. 55–1296; "Gloss on the Epistles of St. Paul" (1139–1141), *ibid.*, pp. 1297–1696 and Vol. 192, pp. 9–520. Some 29 sermons published under the name of Hildebert of Lavardin are contained in *Patrologia Latina*, Vol. 171, pp. 339–964. The *Libri Sententiarum* is available in many old editions; a critical edition was published at Quaracchi (Florence) in 1916, and a new edition is in preparation there for publication in 1966–1967.

Works on Lombard

Among the important articles in *Miscellanea Lombardiana* (Novara, 1957) are L. Ott, "Pietro Lombardo: Personalità e opera," pp. 11–23; S. Vanni Rovighi, "Pier Lombardo e la filosofia medioevale," pp. 25–32; R. Busa, "La filosofia di Pier Lombardo," pp. 33–44; Stanley J. Curtis, "Peter Lombard, a Pioneer in Edu-

cational Method," pp. 265–273; and A. Gambaro, "Piero Lombardo e la civiltà del suo secolo," pp. 391–402.

Many articles of interest also appeared in the now defunct review *Pier Lombardo* between 1957 and 1962. Among them are E. Bertola, "La dottrina della creazione nel *Liber Sententiarum* di Piero Lombardo," Vol. 1, No. 1 (1957), 27–44; E. Bertola, "La dottrina lombardiana dell'anima nella storia delle dottrine psicologiche del XII secolo," Vol. 3, No. 1 (1959), 3–18. G. De Lorenzi, "La filosofia di Pier Lombardo nei Quattro Libri delle Sentenze," Vol. 4 (1960), 19–34; C. Fabro, "Attualità di Pietro Lombardo," *ibid.*, 61–73; and I. Brady, "A New Edition of the Book of Sentences," Vol. 5, Nos. 3 and 4 (1961), 1–8. The Brady article is a sort of prospectus of the forthcoming Quaracchi edition of the *Sentences*. All of *Miscellanea* and *Pier Lombardo* are of interest.

See also P. Delhaye, *Pierre Lombard, sa vie, ses oeuvres, sa morale* (Montreal and Paris, 1961).

IGNATIUS BRADY, O.F.M.

PETER OF SPAIN, or Petrus Hispanus, Petrus Juliani (1210/1220–1277), logician, physician, philosopher, and pope. Born in Lisbon, he became a student and, briefly, a master at the University of Paris. There he evidently studied Aristotle's physics and metaphysics under Albert the Great, medicine and theology under John of Parma, and logic under William of Sherwood. His works on logic (the famous *Summulae Logicales*, a *Syncategoremata*, and a *Tractatus Maiorum Fallaciarum*) were probably written before he left Paris in 1245/1246 for Siena, where he practiced and taught medicine until sometime after 1250. His most important philosophical work, the *Scientia Libri de Anima*, was very likely written before 1261, when he became dean of the cathedral church of Lisbon. In 1272 he was appointed physician to Pope Gregory X, in 1273 he became a cardinal, and in September 1276 he was elected pope (John XXI). In order to continue his studies, he had a private chamber added to the papal palace at Viterbo, but while he was using his new room, its ceiling collapsed, and he died of his injuries on May 20, 1277.

His brief papacy has considerable importance for the history of philosophy, for during it occurred "the doctrinal storm of 1277 which brought the summer of scholasticism to an end." In January 1277 the philosopher-pope commissioned the bishop of Paris, Étienne Tempier, to investigate the teachings of the radical Aristotelians at the University of Paris, where men such as Siger of Brabant were pursuing philosophy as an end in itself and setting philosophical truths against revealed truth. Tempier was to report to the pope, but he exceeded his commission and issued the famous condemnation of March 7, 1277, in which 219 propositions of "Latin Averroism" and other forms of Aristotelianism taught at Paris were declared inimical to the faith. It is not clear whether the pope ever approved of or even knew of the condemnation. However, its short-term effect was the victory of Augustinianism over the Aristotelianism of Siger and Thomas Aquinas, and Peter of Spain was certainly an Augustinian philosopher himself. He could not have foreseen or approved of the long-term effect of the condemnation, for after 1277 theologians and philosophers grew increasingly distrustful and independent of one another, and Peter of Spain may fairly be said to have presided over the beginning of the divorce of reason from faith.

As a treatise on logic Peter's *Summulae Logicales* is in

some ways decidedly inferior to the productions of other terminist logicians. For example, although Peter covers much the same ground as does his teacher William of Sherwood, he avoids the philosophical problems discussed at length by William. For that reason and because it was simply written and contained a number of ingenious mnemonic devices, the *Summulae Logicales* was a better textbook than it was a treatise. Moreover, it appeared early enough in the development of the *logica moderna* to become *the* introductory logic text for the next three hundred years, surviving in no fewer than 166 editions, exclusive of manuscripts.

Several passages in his logic show that Peter is a realist in theory of universals, and his treatise *Scientia Libri de Anima* also places him squarely in the Platonist-Augustinian-Avicennian tradition. The soul is a substance, complete in some sense (*quodam modo completa*) but not separate. Nevertheless, it is capable of existing without the body simply by virtue of being a substance. Soul and body are united in life by the interaction of spiritual and corporeal light and heat, an Avicennian doctrine attacked by Peter's contemporary, Aquinas, as "fictitious and ridiculous" (*Summa Theologica* I, 76, 7).

Works by Peter of Spain

Comentario al "De Anima" de Aristoteles, Manuel Alonso, ed. Madrid, 1944.

Expositio Libri de Anima, De Morte et Vita, De Causis Longitudinis et Brevitatis Vitae, Liber Naturalis de Rebus Principalibus, Manuel Alonso, ed. Madrid, 1952.

Scientia Libri de Anima, Manuel Alonso, ed. Madrid, 1941.

Summulae Logicales, translated by Joseph P. Mullally, ed. Notre Dame, Ind., 1945. Edition and translation of the distinctively terminist portions of the book, including the *Tractatus Exponibilium,* which are omitted from the Bocheński edition, below.

Summulae Logicales, I. M. Bocheński, ed. Rome, 1947.

Tractatus Syncategorematum and Selected Anonymous Treatises, translated by Joseph P. Mullally, ed. Milwaukee, Wis., 1964. Introduction by Mullally and Roland Houde.

Works on Peter of Spain

Grabmann, Martin, "Handschriftliche Forschungen und Funde zu den philosophischen Schriften des Petrus Hispanus, des späteren Papstes Johannes XXI (+ 1277)," in *Sitzungsberichte der Bayerischen Akademie der Wissenschaften, philosophische-historische Abteilung, Jahrgang 1936,* Vol. IX. Munich, 1937.

All editions cited above also have extensive bibliographies.

NORMAN KRETZMANN

PETRARCH, or Francesco Petrarca (1304–1374), the Italian humanist, poet, and scholar, was born in Arezzo into an exiled Florentine family. He was taken to Avignon in 1312, and there he spent most of his life until 1353, except for a period as a student of law at Montpellier and Bologna and several long journeys to Italy. After 1353 he lived in Italy, mainly in Milan, Venice, and Padua; he died in Arquà near Padua. Petrarch held several ecclesiastical benefices and also enjoyed the patronage of the Colonna and the Visconti.

Petrarch's fame rests first on his Italian poems and second on his work as a scholar and Latin writer. His Latin writings include poems, orations, invectives, historical works, a large body of letters, and a few moral treatises.

Among the treatises we may mention especially *De Remediis Utriusque Fortunae* ("On the Remedies of Good and Bad Fortune," 1366), *De Secreto Conflictu Curarum Mearum,* better known as *Secretum* ("On the Secret Conflict of My Worries," completed before 1358), *De Vita Solitaria* ("On the Solitary Life," 1356), and *De Sui Ipsius et Multorum Ignorantia* ("On His Own and Many Other People's Ignorance," 1367).

Petrarch was no philosopher in the technical sense, and even his treatises on moral subjects are loosely written and lack a firm structure or method. Much of his thought consists of tendencies and aspirations rather than of developed ideas or doctrines, and it is inextricably linked with his learning, reading, tastes, and feelings. Nevertheless, it would be wrong to underestimate Petrarch's impact on the history of Western thought. He was the first great representative of Renaissance humanism, if not its founder; as a poet, scholar, and personality, he had a vast reputation during his lifetime and for several subsequent centuries. In many ways he set the pattern for the taste, outlook, and range of interests that determined the thought of Renaissance humanism down to the sixteenth century. Petrarch was regarded, by himself and by his contemporaries, not only as a poet, orator, and historian but also as a moral philosopher, and many of his attitudes were to receive from some of his successors the intellectual and philosophical substance which they seem to lack in Petrarch's own work.

One important aspect of Petrarch's thought which was to be developed by many later humanists was his hostility toward Scholasticism—that is, the university learning of the later Middle Ages. He attacked astrology as well as logic and jurisprudence and dedicated entire works to criticizing the physicians and the Aristotelian philosophers. These attacks, though sweeping and suggestive, are highly personal and subjective and rarely enter into specific issues or arguments. When Petrarch rejects the authority of Aristotle or of his Arabic commentator Averroës, he does so from personal dislike, not from objective grounds; when he criticizes such theories as the eternity of the world, the attainment of perfect happiness during the present life, or the so-called theory of the double truth (that is, of the separate validity of Aristotelian philosophy and of Christian theology), his main argument is that these doctrines are contrary to the Christian religion.

Yet the positive value that Petrarch opposed to medieval science was neither a new science nor mere religious faith but the study of classical antiquity. All his life Petrarch was an avid reader of the ancient Latin writers; he copied, collected, and annotated their works and tried to correct their texts and appropriate their style and ideas. He felt a strong nostalgia for the political greatness of the Roman Republic and Empire, and the hope to restore this greatness was the central political idea that guided him in his dealings with the pope and the emperor, with the Roman revolutionary Cola di Rienzo, and with the various Italian governments of his time.

Of the ancient Latin writers, Cicero and Seneca were among Petrarch's favorites. His polemic against dialectic and other branches of scholastic learning and his emphasis on moral problems seem to be modeled after the more moderate skepticism which Seneca expresses in his *Moral Epistles* with reference to the subtle dialectic of the older Stoics. To Seneca, Petrarch owes his taste for moral declamation and the Stoic notions that appear in his writings—the conflict between virtue and fortune, the contrast between reason and the four basic passions, and the close link between virtue and happiness. Even greater is Petrarch's enthusiasm for Cicero, to whom he owes the form of the dialogue and much of his information on Greek philosophy. We might even say that Petrarch and other humanists owe to their imitation of Cicero and Seneca not only the elegance of their style, but also the elusive and at times superficial manner of their reasoning.

Petrarch could not fail to notice the numerous references to Greek sources in the writings of his favorite Roman authors. He made an attempt to learn Greek, and although he did not progress far enough to read the ancient Greek writers in the original, his awareness of Greek philosophy and literature did affect his outlook and orientation. He owned a Greek manuscript of Plato and read the *Timaeus* and *Phaedo*, which were available to him in Latin translations. He also gathered information on Plato in Cicero and other Roman authors and cited some Platonic doctrines. However, more important than these occasional references to specific theories is Petrarch's general conviction that Plato was the greatest of all philosophers, greater than Aristotle, who had been the chief authority of the later medieval thinkers. "Plato is praised by the greater men, whereas Aristotle is praised by the greater number." In his *Triumph of Fame,* Petrarch places Plato before Aristotle, and his lines appear to be a conscious correction of the praise Dante had given to the "master of those who know." Petrarch's Platonism was a program rather than a doctrine, but it pointed the way to later humanist translations of Plato and to the Platonist thought of the Florentine Academy.

Petrarch assigned second place to Aristotle, but he was far from holding him in contempt. He knew especially Aristotle's *Ethics,* and he repeatedly suggested that the original Aristotle may be superior to his medieval translators and commentators. Petrarch thus pointed the way to a new attitude toward Aristotle that was to take shape in the fifteenth and sixteenth centuries. Aristotle was to be studied in the original Greek text and in the company of other Greek philosophers and writers; his medieval Latin translations were to be replaced by new humanist translations, and his medieval Arabic and Latin commentators were to give way to the ancient Greek commentators and to those modern Renaissance interpreters who were able to read and understand Aristotle in his original text. Thus, Petrarch was the prophet of Renaissance Aristotelianism, as he had been of Renaissance Platonism.

Although Petrarch opposed the classical authors to the medieval tradition, he was by no means completely detached from his immediate past. Christian faith and piety occupy a central position in his thought and writings, and there is no reason to doubt his sincerity. Whenever a conflict between religion and ancient philosophy might arise, he is ready to stand by the teachings of the former. The *Secretum,* in which Petrarch subjects his most intimate feelings and actions to religious scrutiny, is a thoroughly Christian work, and his treatise *De Remediis Utri-* *usque Fortunae* is equally Christian, even specifically medieval. His treatise *De Otio Religioso* ("On the Leisure of the Monks") belongs to the ascetic tradition, and even Petrarch's polemic against Scholasticism in the name of a genuine and simple religion continues or resumes that strand of medieval religious thought which found expression in Peter Damian and St. Bernard. In his treatise on his ignorance, Petrarch goes so far as to oppose his own piety to the supposedly irreligious views of his scholastic opponents. This shows that it was at least possible to reject Scholasticism and remain a convinced Christian, and to reconcile classical learning with religious faith. In accordance with this attitude, Petrarch liked to read the early Christian writers, especially the Church Fathers, along with the pagan classics but without the company of the scholastic theologians. His favorite Christian author was St. Augustine, who occupies a position of unique importance in his thought and work. Aside from numerous quotations scattered in Petrarch's writings, it is sufficient to mention two notable instances. Petrarch's *Secretum* takes the form of a dialogue between the author and St. Augustine, who thus assumes the role of a spiritual guide or of the author's conscience. And in the famous letter in which Petrarch describes climbing Mont Ventoux, he expresses his feelings by a quotation on which his eyes chanced to fall in his copy of Augustine's *Confessions:* "And men go to admire the high mountains, the vast floods of the sea, the huge streams of the rivers, the circumference of the ocean, and the revolutions of the stars—and desert themselves" (*Confessions* x, 8, 15).

Besides these and a few other general attitudes, there is at least one theoretical problem on which Petrarch formulates views akin to those of many later humanists. He keeps asserting that man and his problems should be the main object and concern of thought and philosophy. This is also the justification he gives for his emphasis on moral philosophy, and when he criticizes the scholastic science of his Aristotelian opponents, it is chiefly on the grounds that they raise useless questions and forget the most important problem, the human soul. This is also the gist of the words with which Petrarch describes his feelings when he had reached the top of Mont Ventoux. The words are Petrarch's, and they express his own ideas, but they are characteristically interwoven with quotations from Augustine and Seneca.

Petrarch expresses for the first time that emphasis on man which was to receive eloquent developments in the treatises of later humanists and to be given a metaphysical and cosmological foundation in the works of Ficino and Pico. This is the reason that the humanists were to adopt the name "humanities" (*studia humanitatis*) for their studies—to indicate their significance for man and his problems. Yet behind Petrarch's tendency to set moral doctrine against natural science, there are also echoes of Seneca and St. Augustine and of Cicero's statement that Socrates had brought philosophy down from heaven to earth. When Petrarch speaks of man and his soul, he refers at the same time to the blessed life and eternal salvation, adding a distinctly Christian overtone to his moral and human preoccupation. He thus comes to link the knowledge of man and the knowledge of God in a distinctly

Augustinian fashion and also to discuss an important problem of scholastic philosophy that had its root in Augustine: the question of whether the will or the intellect is superior. In discussing this scholastic problem, Petrarch follows the Augustinian tradition, as other humanists and Platonists were to do after him, in deciding the question in favor of the will.

Petrarch, the great poet, writer, and scholar, is clearly an ambiguous and transitional figure when judged by his role in the history of philosophical thought. His thought consists in aspirations rather than developed ideas, but these aspirations were developed by later thinkers and were eventually transformed into more elaborate ideas. His intellectual program may be summed up in the formula which he uses once in the treatise on his ignorance: Platonic wisdom, Christian dogma, Ciceronian eloquence. His classical culture, his Christian faith, and his attack against Scholasticism all have a personal, and in a way modern, quality. At the same time everything he says is pervaded by his classical sources and often by residual traces of medieval thought. In this respect, as in many others, Petrarch is a typical representative of his age and of the humanist movement. He did not merely anticipate later Renaissance developments because he was unusually talented or perceptive; he also had an active share in bringing them about, because of the enormous prestige he enjoyed among his contemporaries and immediate successors.

Works by Petrarch

Petrarch's Italian poems have been printed in numerous editions and translations; see also Roberto Weiss, *Un inedito Petrarchesco* (Rome, 1950). Of the *Edizione nazionale* of his collected works only six volumes have appeared, containing his poem *Africa*, a part of his letters—*Le familiari*, V. Rossi and U. Bosco, eds., 4 vols. (Florence, 1933–1942)—and the *Rerum Memorandarum Libri*, Giuseppe Billanovich, ed. (Florence, 1943). See also K. Burdach, *Aus Petrarcas aeltestem deutschen Schuelerkreise* (Berlin, 1929); *Petrarcas "Buch ohne Namen" und die päpstliche Kurie*, P. Piur, ed. (Halle, Germany, 1925); and *Petrarcas Briefwechsel mit deutschen Zeitgenossen*, P. Piur, ed. (Berlin, 1933).

The recent collection of *Prose*, G. Martellotti et al., eds. (Milan and Naples, 1955), contains the *Secretum*, *De Vita Solitaria*, and selections from the invectives and other treatises. *Le Traité De Sui Ipsius et Multorum Ignorantia*, L. M. Capelli, ed. (Paris, 1906), is the only complete modern edition of this important treatise. For many other Latin works of Petrarch the old edition of his works, *Opera* (Basel, 1581), must still be used. See also *Scritti inediti*, A. Hortis, ed. (Trieste, 1874).

English translations are available for the *Secret*, translated by William H. Draper (London, 1911); *The Life of Solitude*, translated by Jacob Zeitlin (Urbana, Ill., 1924); *On His Own Ignorance*, translated by H. Nachod, who added the letter on the ascent of Mont Ventoux and excellent notes, in Ernst Cassirer, Paul Oskar Kristeller, and John H. Randall, Jr., eds., *The Renaissance Philosophy of Man* (Chicago, 1948), pp. 36–133; the *Testament*, translated by Theodor E. Mommsen (Ithaca, N.Y., 1957); and for many letters—*Petrarch, the First Modern Scholar and Man of Letters*, 2d ed., translated by James Harvey Robinson (New York, 1914), *Petrarch's Letters to Classical Authors*, translated by Mario E. Cosenza (Chicago, 1910), and *Petrarch at Vaucluse*, translated by Ernest H. Wilkins (Chicago, 1958).

Works on Petrarch

From the vast literature on Petrarch only a few works can be mentioned; for a bibliography, see N. Sapegno, *Il trecento* (Milan, 1948). For Petrarch's life and works see Edward H. R. Tatham, *Francesco Petrarca*, 2 vols. (London, 1925–1926); U. Bosco, *Pe-*

trarca (Turin, 1946); Morris Bishop, *Petrarch and His World* (Bloomington, Ill., 1963); and, above all, numerous books and articles by Ernest H. Wilkins: *Studies in the Life and Works of Petrarch* (Cambridge, Mass., 1955), *Petrarch's Eight Years in Milan* (Cambridge, Mass., 1958), *Petrarch's Later Years* (Cambridge, Mass., 1959), *Petrarch's Correspondence* (Padua, 1960), and *Life of Petrarch* (Chicago, 1961).

For Petrarch as a scholar see Pierre de Nolhac, *Pétrarque et l'humanisme*, 2 vols., 2d ed. (Paris, 1907), and "de Patrum et Medii Aevi Scriptorum Codicibus in Bibliotheca Petrarcae Olim Collectis," in *Revue des bibliothèques*, Vol. 2 (1892), 241–279; numerous studies by Giuseppe Billanovich, especially *Petrarca letterato*, Vol. I, *Lo scrittoio del Petrarca* (Rome, 1947), and "Petrarch and the Textual Tradition of Livy," in *Journal of the Warburg and Courtauld Institutes*, Vol. 14 (1951), 137–208. See also J. H. Whitfield, *Petrarch and the Renascence* (Oxford, 1943).

For Petrarch's political thought see Theodor E. Mommsen, *Medieval and Renaissance Studies*, Eugene F. Rice, ed. (Ithaca, N.Y., 1959); Aldo S. Bernardo, *Petrarch, Scipio and the Africa* (Baltimore, Md., 1962); Jules Alan Wein, *Petrarch's Politics* (unpublished thesis, Columbia University, 1960); and Mario E. Cosenza, *Petrarch and the Revolution of Cola di Rienzo* (Chicago, 1913).

For Petrarch's religious and philosophical ideas see Armando Carlini, *Il pensiero filosofico religioso di Francesco Petrarca* (Iesi, Italy, 1904); Elena Razzoli, *Agostinismo e religiosità del Petrarca* (Milan, 1937); P. P. Gerosa, *L'umanesimo agostiniano del Petrarca* (Turin, 1927); K. Heitmann, *Fortuna und Virtus* (Cologne, 1958); William Granger Ryan, *Humanism and Religion in Petrarch* (unpublished thesis, Columbia University, 1950); and N. Iliescu, *Il canzoniere petrarchesco e Sant'Agostino* (Rome, 1962).

PAUL OSKAR KRISTELLER

PETRONIEVIĆ, BRANISLAV (1875–1954), Yugoslav philosopher and paleontologist, was born in Sovljak, Serbia. He taught as a professor of philosophy at the University of Belgrade and was a member of the Serbian Academy of Science and Arts. In paleontology, Petronievi´ was the first to distinguish between the genera Archaeopteryx and Archaeornis; he also discovered new characteristics of the genera Tritylodon and Moeritherium.

Petronievi´ systematically treated many problems, both in pure philosophy and in scientific methodology. He considered himself a "born metaphysician" and devoted himself to constructing his own metaphysical system. But, although original, it grew out of the nineteenth-century empirical metaphysics of Hermann Lotze, Eduard von Hartmann, and Petronievi´'s teacher, Johannes Volkelt.

Petronievi´'s epistemological theory of empiriorationalism claimed that all contents of consciousness are absolutely real in the same sense as things per se. Thus there can be no absolute or immanent or transcendental illusion. Petronievi´ rejected phenomenalism also, specifically Kant's. He claimed that an analysis of directly given empirical contents of consciousness shows that there are qualitatively simple evidences of experience, the "givenness of something"—the givenness of simple sensuous qualities as basic correlates of the laws of thought. Thought and being are identical, and apodictic knowledge of being itself is possible.

In his main philosophical work, *Principien der Metaphysik*, Petronievi´ claimed that the basic task of metaphysics is to explain the structure of the "world of multitude, diversity, and change" as the "pre-evidence" of the directly given empirical and transcendental reality. According to Petronievi´, the world is a manifold of "discrete points of being" and of quality, of will, etc. The world as a manifold is possible only because the real points of being are separated by real "acts of negation," which determine the qualities of being and without which being would be absolutely homogeneous. Petronievič regarded the principle of negation as "the absolute principle of the world," of both being and thought; only on the basis of this principle can the diversity and multiplicity of the world be deduced and explained. On similar grounds Petronievič considered the principle of sufficient reason the fundamental law of true knowledge.

Petronievič synthesized Spinoza's monism and Leibniz' monadological pluralism in his monopluralism. His original and profound "hypermetaphysical" teachings on the origin and development of the qualitative and quantitative manifoldness of the world have yet to be studied and evaluated. His views on real space and real time, which he regarded as discreta rather than abstract continua, deserve special attention. He constructed a new geometry of real discrete space.

Petronievič's view was essentially idealistic, since he held that absolutely unconscious atoms are impossible and that the soul, which is immortal, is a conscious monad.

Petronievič upheld an ethical theory of transcendental optimism and free will. He devoted a number of studies to aesthetics, particularly in the work of the Yugoslav poet Petar II Petrović-Njegoš and of Leo Tolstoy.

Among his most notable contributions to the logical foundations of mathematics are his work on typical geometries, on the problem of the finitude or infinitude of space, the three-bodies problem, on differential quotients, and on mathematical induction. In psychology he developed theories about the observation of the transparent and on the depth and observation of compound colors. In the history of science his most notable works were on the methodology of Newton's discovery of the law of gravitation, on Galle's and Leverrier's discovery of Neptune, and on Mendeleev's discovery of the periodic system of elements.

Works by Petronievič

Der ontologische Beweis für das Dasein des Absoluten. Leipzig, 1897.
Der Satz vom Grunde. Belgrade, 1898.
Prinzipien der Erkenntnislehre. Berlin, 1900.
Prinzipien der Metaphysik, 2 vols. Heidelberg, 1904–1911.
Die typischen Geometrien und das Unendliche. Heidelberg, 1907.
L'Évolution universelle. Paris, 1921.
Résumé des travaux philosophiques et scientifiques de Branislav Petronievič. Academie Royal Serbe, Bulletin de l'Academie des Lettres, No. 2. Belgrade, 1937.

Works on Petronievič

Spomenica Branislav Petronijević. SAN No. 13. Belgrade, 1957.
Articles on Petronievič by various authors.

BOGDAN ŠEŠIĆ

PETROVIĆ-NJEGOŠ, PETAR (1813–1851), Prince Petar II of Montenegro, was born in the village of Njegusi near Cetinje. As the government of Montenegro was then a theocracy, Njegoš, who ruled from 1830 to 1851, had to act as high priest, much against his own views and wishes. He was religious by conviction, but opposed to any religious fanaticism or formalities. By setting up a number of civil and cultural institutions, he transformed Montenegro from a tribal to a modern state.

Njegoš was one of the greatest Yugoslav poets. His principal works are *Slobodijada* ("Ode to Liberty"), *Gorski Vijenac* ("The Mountain Wreath"), *Luča Mikrokozma* ("The Ray of the Microcosm"), *Šćepan Mali* ("Schepan the Small"), and a number of minor poems, the best of which is the reflective poem *Misao* ("The Thought"). His main themes were man's destiny, marked by struggle and suffering, and freedom, which he understood as partly the struggle for national liberty. The elaboration of these themes led Njegoš to many philosophical thoughts and meditations. Being predominantly a poet, he presented these thoughts in poetic images and visions. The philosophical conception implicit in these images is a Platonic dualism. God and matter are coeternal. Mind and body are opposed principles both ontologically and axiologically. Mind originates in heaven, whereas body belongs to the "realm of decay." The body is "the physical shackles of the soul"; passions "lay man below the beast," whereas mind makes him "equal to immortals." In *Luča Mikrokozma* Njegoš interpreted the union of mind and body as a consequence of sin and the Fall. The first man, Adam, was once pure spirit, but he joined Satan in his rebellion against God, although he soon repented. He was then "clad in a body" and cast upon the earth, which was created by God as a place of expiation after man's sin. Thus, Njegoš's Adam, unlike Milton's or the Adam of official church doctrine, sinned prior to his bodily creation.

Luča Mikrokozma can be seen as providing metaphysical and religious reasons for the inevitability of suffering. *Gorski Vijenac* is a mighty hymn to the national struggle for liberation and to the struggle against evil in general. To justify this struggle Njegoš elaborated a dynamic and basically dialectical conception of the world. The world is made up of opposed and dangerous forces at permanent war. Through this struggle, order emerges out of chaotic disorder, and spiritual power triumphs over great confusion. Struggle and suffering are not mere evils but have a positive, creative aspect as well. The spark appears only after the flint is struck hard, and the soul that has endured temptations "nourishes the body with internal fire." Heroism is the master of evil, and human life has an aim only if it contributes to the realization of liberty, honor, and dignity. Njegoš's ethics were essentially derived from his people and, in turn, had a powerful influence on them in all the trying moments of their history.

Works by Petrović-Njegoš

Cjelokupna Djela, 9 vols. Belgrade, 1951–1955.

Works on Petrović-Njegoš

Djilas, Milovan, *Legenda o Njegošu.* Belgrade, 1952.
Latković, Vido, *Petar II Petrović Njegoš.* Belgrade, 1963.
Petronijević, Branislav, *Filozofija u "Gorskom Vijencu" i "Luči Mikrokozma."* Belgrade, 1924.
Šmaus, A., *Njegoševa "Luča Mikrokozma."* Belgrade, 1927.
Velimirović, Nikolaj, *Religija Njegoševa.* Belgrade, 1921.

VUKO PAVIĆEVIĆ

PETZOLDT, JOSEPH (1862–1929), German empirio-critical philosopher, was born at Altenburg and taught mathematics and natural science at a Gymnasium in Spandau. In 1904 he became *Privatdozent* at the Technische Hochschule in Berlin-Charlottenburg, and in 1922 he was named associate professor. For a number of years he was chairman of the Gesellschaft für positivistische Philosophie.

Petzoldt was indebted to Ernst Mach's positivism, to the immanence philosophy of Wilhelm Schuppe, and above all to the empiriocriticism of Richard Avenarius. Petzoldt presented Avenarius' difficult philosophy in a popular form and developed it independently. For example, he offered a psychological explanation of the "narrowness," and therewith the unity, of consciousness; he tried to demonstrate the unlimited validity of psychophysical parallelism; and he analyzed ethical and aesthetic values and proposed a theory of the ethical and aesthetic permanence, or maximum stability, of mankind. According to this theory, all evolutionary processes end in states of permanence. Hence, human evolution is also heading toward a state of complete stability and toward the marking out of defining forms of permanence, that is, of invariably repeatable, fixed components of mental acts. The most basic feature of all the goals of our thought and creative work is permanence or durability—the realization of ever recurrent, repeatedly used ways of acting and the establishment of enduring forms amidst the profusion of particular configurations. An example of this is the tendency of thought toward stability, the striving for a stable conceptual system.

Petzoldt called his philosophy a "relativistic positivism." According to this view, both causality and substantiality are untenable and unnecessary categories, and the difference between the mental and the physical reduces to a difference in the "mode of interpretation." Petzoldt, like Avenarius, held that the concept of cause should be replaced by the mathematical concept to functional dependence, or uniqueness of coordination. According to Petzoldt, the causal relation is fully exhausted in a "law of uniqueness," which holds that for every process, the elements that exclusively determine it should be specified. Because there is thus nothing in the real world corresponding to the "animistic" concept of cause, this concept should be eliminated. The demand for a causal explanation that goes beyond the complete and simplest description of processes rests on misunderstandings; such an explanation is in principle unrealizable and is therefore meaningless.

The concept of substance, according to Petzoldt, originates from a need for stability in thinking. There are no absolute substances but only relatively constant complexes of sensory qualities. Since all properties hold good only relative to a subject, the idea of an absolute, nonrelative being should be discarded, and with it the category of substance. There is no "world-in-itself"; there is only a "world-for-us," whose elements are sensations, even though "things" are to be thought of as "continuing to exist" even when we do not perceive them. The world-for-us is apprehended as being mental insofar as it is perceived and as being physical insofar as it is known as a correlation of elements. That which is ultimately "given" is thus neither mental nor physical, neither immaterial nor material, neither "internal" nor "external," neither thing-in-itself nor phenomenon. These antitheses are merely relatively valid limiting concepts, intelligible only in their interrelation; they are formed only subsequent to, and on the basis of, the primordial unitary experience. Petzoldt's conception resembled Bertrand Russell's neutral monism.

Petzoldt's philosophy culminated in an evolutionary naturalism. "Man is not a permanence type, but an organism in a state of very active development; yet, like all other organisms and like self-developing systems generally, he is headed toward a form of permanence" (*Einführung in die Philosophie der reinen Erfahrung* ["Introduction to the Philosophy of Pure Experience"], Vol. 2, p. 3). Just as organic evolution tends toward the production of permanence states and "man's brain approaches more and more a form of permanence," the spiritual and intellectual evolution of man likewise tends to permanence states. We strive for the completion of science, for the perfection of social institutions and customs by a progressive adjustment of national and social differences, and for the fulfillment of art through "emphasis on the typical and essential in the phenomena."

The goal of ethics is that in all that we do and think we help to realize the future permanence state that flows from the nature of man and his environment (*ibid.*, p. 206). This is the state of maximum utilization of powers, and hence of maximum stability, toward which all evolution strives. Each of us must risk everything "in order to perfect his personality in accordance with the nature and extent of his abilities and to place himself entirely at the service of human society" (*ibid.*, p. 212).

Bibliography

Works by Petzoldt include *Maxima, Minima und Oekonomie* (Altenburg, 1891); *Einführung in die Philosophie der reinen Erfahrung*, 2 vols. (Leipzig, 1900–1904); *Das Weltproblem vom Standpunkte des relativistischen Positivismus aus historisch-kritisch dargestellt* (Leipzig, 1906); *Die Stellung der Relativitätstheorie in der geistigen Entwicklung der Menschheit* (Dresden, 1921); and *Das natürliche Höhenziel der menschheitlichen Entwicklung* (Leipzig, 1927).

An article on Petzoldt is Christian Herrmann, "Nachruf: Joseph Petzoldt," in *Kant-Studien*, Vol. 34 (1929), 508–510.

FRANZ AUSTEDA
Translated by *Albert E. Blumberg*

PHENOMENALISM. Most philosophers have been led by the argument from illusion, by the causal argument, or by the introspective analysis advocated in the sense-datum theory to conclude that our immediate awareness in perception is not, as direct, or common-sense, realism claims, of material objects (of distinct, external physical entities perceptible by different persons at once) but of sensa (private, transitory, probably mental existents that may also be called sensations, sense data, ideas, representations, or impressions). Once this position is adopted, a serious difficulty arises concerning the nature and status of material objects. Representative realism claims that they exist external to us and cause the sensa or representations which correspond to them. The notorious difficulty of this view is that if all our direct awareness is concerned with the alleged effects, or sensa, how do we ever find out that material objects exist as their causes or what characteristics they possess? The theory seems to make material objects unobserved, and indeed unintelligible, causes of our perception. Although representative realism, especially in modern versions, tries to deal with this difficulty, it is still widely felt to be unsatisfactory. Therefore, alternative attempts have been made to deal with the problem of the nature of material objects. One such approach, which may loosely be called phenomenalist, is to reduce material objects to sensa, that is, to explain them as consisting solely of sensa or as being primarily groups or patterns of them. This approach results in slightly varying views, and when the term "phenomenalism" is used, reference is very often intended only to what we here call linguistic phenomenalism.

To introduce these variants of phenomenalism, we may consider one central problem that faces any attempt to reduce material objects to sensa, namely, the fragmentariness of perception. Any material object is believed to exist for long periods when it is not observed—for example, the furniture in an empty room, the beams in the roof, and so on—and some objects, such as rocks in Antarctica or under the ocean, may never have been observed. Yet when they are not observed, material objects cause no sensa, have no sensa belonging to them or constituting them. Hence, if material objects are reduced to actual sensa and consist only of them, they must cease to exist when unobserved, and those never observed must never have existed. Worse still, the material objects in a room must apparently come into and go out of existence as one looks at or away from them—the blinking of a human eye can destroy or create them. This seems such an intolerable paradox that Berkeley, though tempted to say that material objects are simply collections of ideas, had to introduce God as their continuing basis or cause. True phenomenalism, however, can no more allow unobserved divine causes than unobserved material ones.

PROBLEM OF FRAGMENTARINESS

Several approaches to the problem of fragmentariness may be taken.

Hume. One might accept fragmentary existence, though saying it is no insuperable paradox: objects are no more than groups or patterns of sensa, but owing to the regularity with which the same or similar series of sensa occur, we imaginatively fill in the gaps and falsely suppose that continuously enduring objects exist. This was Hume's official view. One may say that just as a tune may bridge various pauses when no sound occurs and thus be a pattern of sounds with intervening gaps, so an object may be a group or pattern of sensa and gaps. Nevertheless, the theory is incredible and is only on the fringe of the phenomenalist group of theories. For one thing, it is difficult to see why sensa recur in groups or patterns if nothing exists in between; the existence of some continuant basis or focus of them seems a far simpler and more plausible hypothesis than what would be a series of unexplained coincidences.

Sensibilia. Hume himself toyed with the supposition that impressions might exist unobserved—that the gaps might be filled with unsensed sensa—and if H. H. Price is right, Hume should have developed this as his official theory. Such a development was explicitly formulated by

Bertrand Russell in his *Mysticism and Logic,* where he gave the name "sensibilia" (singular, sensibile) to these "objects which have the same metaphysical and physical status as sense-data without necessarily being data to any mind." Russell regarded sensibilia as the ultimate constituents of matter; thus, objects consist of systems of sensed sensibilia (that is, sensa) and unsensed ones.

However, he soon abandoned this position, which seems untenable on two main grounds. First, it cannot explain the causal processes in perceiving. How does the sensing of sensibilia bring sensa into being? The evidence of the causal processes and of the conditioning of perception by the state of the nervous system and sense organs suggests that sensa are "generated," that is, brought into being, by events in the brain; this seems incompatible with the view that they existed as sensibilia before they were sensed. Second, what evidence is there of the existence or the nature of sensibilia? One cannot observe that such entities fill gaps between actual sensa; they are just as obscure and hypothetical as the unobserved material objects of representative realism and, in fact, introduce the very difficulty that they were intended to avoid.

Factual phenomenalism. Factual phenomenalism attempts to fill the gap between actual sensa with possible ones by defining material objects as groups of actual and possible sensa. This view was originated by J. S. Mill, who held that matter consists of "groups of permanent possibilities of sensation." Unfortunately, this theory also leaves quite obscure what possible sensa could be and adds the further implausibility that the gap-filling entities are purely possibilities and not actualities at all. If taken strictly, this should mean that nothing actually fills the gaps. To say that something, for instance, an accident, is possible implies that it is not actual, though it might be claimed that a possible X is an actual Y; for instance, the possible winner of a race is an actual horse, in which case once again matter will consist largely of unknown and unobservable entities. The view is also open to many of the objections to phenomenalism stated below.

Linguistic phenomenalism. Linguistic phenomenalism sees the basic problem before it in a different light, as one not of stating the constituents of matter but of elucidating the concept of a material object, of defining it in terms of sensa; and it seeks to achieve this not by formal definition but by a "definition in use," that is, by providing translations of statements about material objects into equivalent sets of statements about sensa. Thus, it is intended to show that what is meant by talking about tables, chairs, or similar objects can be expressed solely by talking about sensa; sometimes this is expressed by saying that material objects are logical constructions out of sensa. The underlying position is, in essence, that of Hume—that all we know to exist are sensa occurring in various patterns or sequences—but one main difference lies in the claim that these regular relationships between sensa are not something to be supplemented by imagination but are actually what we indirectly refer to by talking of material objects. Such objects are in fact coordinating concepts, devices that enable us to group and correlate our sense experiences, to identify and to refer to patterns in them.

The other main difference from Hume's position is in the linguistic presentation, the attempt to elucidate the concept by translation into a set of equivalent statements. This is in accordance with the linguistic approach contemporary with the heyday of phenomenalism, and it was held that statements about material objects and statements about sensa are simply two different ways of describing the same set of facts (facts that really concern sense experiences, their patterns and sequences). However, the sets of sensum statements not only are translations but also have a special form. Insofar as the object is observed, they are all categorical, but when it is unobserved, they are hypothetical. Thus, "I see a book on the table" is equivalent to "I have sensa *XYZ*," where *XYZ* might stand for "of a rectangular, red, solid-seeming shape on a flat brown expanse." However, "There is a book on the table in the next room" is equivalent to "If you were in the next room, you would have sensa *XYZ*." This introduces the notion of possibility that was not in Hume and that factual phenomenalism expresses so implausibly. It has the great advantage of expressing the possibility of sensa in the hypothetical form of the statement without suggesting that possible sensa are somehow constituents, perhaps the sole ones, of actual objects. Also of interest is that this approach was anticipated but not developed by Berkeley (*Principles*, Secs. 3 and 58), and occurs in places in J. S. Mill.

The result is an ingenious theory that transforms the problem of producing a viable alternative to representative realism. If successful, it would be an enormous theoretical economy; it would enable the facts of experience to be accounted for solely in terms of one type of existent, sensa, without any need to go beyond them and postulate other orders of material existence behind them. Indeed, it could further claim to be neutral between the sense-datum and adverbial analyses of sensing, for one could, as Ayer did, translate material-object statements into statements about "sense contents," a term used to describe *how* we sense but not to refer to separate entities.

This version of phenomenalism achieved great popularity from about 1930 to 1950, particularly because it was associated with (1) logical positivism and operationalism, the meaning of material-object statements being held to lie in their mode of verification, that is, in the sensum statements which verify them; (2) Russell's analysis of abstract terms, for instance, that space is not an entity but a logical construction out of observations and measurements; (3) a way of dealing with unobserved entities in physics, namely, that electron statements are equivalent to, are logical constructions out of, sets of statements about physicists' observations. However, in the last two cases the data for the construction are prima-facie observations of material objects, and the construction is thus at a different level. Furthermore, the third case gains plausibility from the fact that electrons are agreed to be unobservable; but no such unobservability belongs to tables and chairs.

DIFFICULTIES IN PHENOMENALISM

Because of its merits, linguistic phenomenalism became the dominant version of phenomenalism (so much so that the qualification "linguistic" may seem pedantic). All the same, many difficulties soon appeared in it and defied ingenious, almost desperately ingenious, attempts to deal with them. Further, the theory presupposed that our direct

awareness is entirely of private sensa; consequently, it has suffered from the recent revival in direct realism. Without questioning that presupposition (discussed at length in SENSA), we shall now consider the general difficulties in the theory.

Lack of equivalence. The original aim of linguistic phenomenalism was to give a fully equivalent translation of a material-object statement into sets of sensum statements, thus proving that it meant no more than is meant by a series of such statements. For various reasons this seems impossible. In the first place, according to the basic supposition of the sense-datum theory that is shared by phenomenalism, there is a different sensum for every different look, sound, feel, or other appearance of a material object. When a dish looks elliptical, one sensum belonging to it is obtained; when it looks round, another one is obtained; when it is felt, yet another; and so on. When one considers all the different points of view from which the dish can be seen and can look different, and then adds all the variations possible for the other senses and for other conditions of lighting and such, it would seem that the number of sensa belonging to the dish, and therefore the number of sensum statements necessary to produce a full analysis or translation of "There is a dish on the table," would be very great. Sometimes it is said that the number would be infinite because the different points of view are infinite in number; but this is dubious, for owing to object constancy (see the discussion of psychological processes in PERCEPTION), a slight change in point of view would not necessarily mean a different sensum. At any rate, the list of sensum statements would have to be far longer than can be achieved in practice. Furthermore, if the analysis is really to be adequate, it must be systematic: the sets of sensum statements must be so ordered as to show something of the patterns or correlations that justify the material-object concept; but far from doing this, phenomenalists usually give up after one or two of the sensum statements have been formulated.

Equivalence has also been denied on the ground of difference in form. The original material-object statement is a categorical one, clearly stating that something actually exists. However, the translation is a series of hypothetical statements, and even when the apodoses of these describe experiences, their normal function seems to be either to avoid asserting actual existence (or occurrence) or to convey something quite different, such as a promise or a warning—"If you touch that, you will get burned." Indeed, "If you go to the next room, you will see a book on the table" may function as a request or a suggestion that the person go there. Worse still, in the counterfactual statements that form the translation offered about past events, actual existence is denied by implication. Thus, "Pterodactyls lived in the Mesozoic era" would probably be translated "If an observer had been present in the Mesozoic era, he would have had pterodactyl-like sensa." However, there was no observer at that time—in fact, no human beings at all—and no sensa as we know them. Thus, the assertion of actual existence is replaced in the alleged translation by assertions about what might have happened but did not.

Another bar to the claim of equivalence is that there is not full mutual entailment of original and translation. On the one hand, there might be some illusion or hallucination in which the sensum statements would be true and the material-object statement false: all the red booklike sensa might be present, and yet the object might be a box covered and shaped to look and feel like a book. This can, no doubt, be ruled out in practice by getting enough sensa, especially those resulting from such tests as opening the book, but it is doubtful how far results of such tests are really part of the *meaning* of the material-object statement and are therefore true features of the translation. On the other hand, the material-object statement might be true and the sensory ones false. There might be a book on the table, and yet you might not get sensa of it—the light might fail, you might be taken ill suddenly or be careless and inattentive, the book might be covered by other objects, and so on. There is a large range of conditions that would have to be stated to ensure the truth of the sensum statement. This is particularly true if the object is a small one: "There is a needle in this haystack." If you looked, would you get the needle-like sensa?

Impurity of analysis. A troublesome practical difficulty facing phenomenalists is that it is impossible to specify more than a few sensa without recourse to material-object language (and not always then). Since in considering a book, the formula "sensa of a rectangular, red, solid-seeming shape on a flat brown expanse" would not differentiate the book from, say, a chocolate box, the temptation is to say "a red, rectangular, booklike sensum." But then one no longer has a translation, and the analysis is impure; it is like saying that in French *cheval* means an animal of a *cheval*-like nature. Most phenomenalists succumb to this temptation and blame it on the poverty of language, which was designed for speaking about material objects; they say, not very convincingly, that they could invent a proper terminology for describing sensa accurately but that it would take too long.

Another type of impurity in phenomenalistic analyses lies in the protases of the hypotheticals, where reference is normally made to observers and landmarks, for example, "If you go to the next room, you will get sensa *XYZ*." Even if only your body is a material object, you are at least not a sensum; and similarly, the room is physical and material. Thus, such a hypothetical statement is not a pure sensum statement. Even giving directions by compass points, for example, "If you look north . . . ," would seem to involve some dependence on material objects, such as the sun or a compass. Ayer suggested an ingenious way out of this difficulty: Instead of mentioning the observer and others, you describe the available sensa of the room or location, thus getting "Given sensa *ABC*, then sensa *XYZ* are obtainable," where *ABC* are "interior-of-roomlike sensa" and *XYZ* are "booklike sensa." (This also slightly mitigates the difficulty about standing conditions mentioned with respect to mutual entailment: if roomlike visual data are given, at least there is light enough to see large objects.) But once again, specifying the roomlike data without mentioning the room, though perhaps theoretically possible, presents great practical difficulties that no one has tried to surmount. Nevertheless, this second impurity problem has at least been reduced to the first one.

Publicity and persistence of objects. In view of the great difficulties facing any attempt at a fully equivalent and pure translation, the phenomenalist may modify his aims. He may say that by producing a few sentences of the translation and by using such short cuts as "booklike sensa" he can show the form a full analysis would take; he can give a schema or blueprint of it sufficient to show that a material-object statement really means no more than a set of sensum statements and to reveal the kind of relation between sensa which justifies the material-object concept. Others would argue that this is to abandon the real aim of phenomenalism: unless one produces a fully equivalent translation, one cannot be sure that there is not some characteristic of material objects which cannot be rendered in terms of sensa. This objection is supported by drawing attention to several features of the ordinary concept of a material object that seem particularly resistant to phenomenalist analysis.

The first of these are the publicity of material objects (the fact that many people can perceive them at once) and their persistence or relative durability. Sensa are private and transitory, so how can statements about them convey the meaning of statements about objects? A phenomenalist answer would be that all we mean or are entitled to mean by saying that an object is perceived by two people at the same time is that they simultaneously sense similar sensa. This can be formulated as: observer *A* has sensa *XYZ* at time *t*; observer *B* has sensa *X'Y'Z'* also at time *t*; and both sets of sensa are located similarly with respect to other background sensa. The analysis can be supported by saying that when *B* senses visual and tactile data describable as data of his touching the object, then *A* gets visual data describable as data of *B* touching it. As to the persistence of objects, all this amounts to is that sequences of similar data recur. In development of this point, Hume claimed that it involves constancy (recurrence of the same data each time you look) and coherence (sequences of data changing in an orderly manner); Ayer, however, put most emphasis on the recurrence of reversible series of data, as when you look round the room and then back again.

But these answers are inadequate for the following reasons.

(1) They make the analysis impure by reference to observers: the whole point in the publicity of material objects is that two observers have similar sensa, as opposed to a case of double vision, where one person has two sets of sensa; in the persistence of material objects it is that one observer has the recurrent or reversible series of sensa. (Actually, the best evidence of persistence would be that *A* sees the object during the gaps in *B*'s observation of it, for which mention of observers is clearly essential.)

(2) A more fundamental objection is that the assertion of the publicity and persistence of material objects is meant to convey more than the assertion of sets of sensa: one is maintaining, first, that a public object exists as the focus of two persons' perceptions and, second, that such an object continues to exist during the gaps between series of perceptions. ("Focus" here means either a common object of both perceptions, as in direct realism, or the common cause of the different sensa, as in representative realism.) It might be objected that this is simply putting forward an alternative to phenomenalism, but it seems fair to say that something like this realist claim is what we mean by a material object. Without the notion of focus or continuant, the agree-

ment of different people's sensa or the recurrent sequences of one person's sensa are incredible series of coincidences. Why, for example, are such agreements so common in perception of objects but so rare in pains or dreams or imagery? Surely because there is something *besides* the sense experiences responsible for the agreement, namely, a common object or cause.

(3) Furthermore, the fragmentariness of our perception of an object is closely correlated with our own actions, as are Ayer's reversible series. If sensa of a table are replaced by sensa of the view outside the window, we must have moved our head and have looked out of the window; if we get sensa of the interior of the room after an hour's gap, we must have dozed off or have gone out and returned. This seems to show that the sensa are caused by continuing objects, the room and furniture; since the fragmentariness of our observation of these objects is explained by our actions, we do not have to assume that the objects are fragmentary as well—indeed, if they were, we should find them and their sensa appearing and disappearing without any action on our part, like the Cheshire Cat in *Alice in Wonderland.*

Causal properties and processes. Any material object is thought to possess and to exercise many causal properties (its various powers to affect other objects by heat, propulsion, impact, pressure, chemical or electrical properties), and the concept of such an object may be claimed to involve them. They are so important that for many philosophers (for example, Price) they form the main stumbling block to the acceptance of phenomenalism, at least of the factual kind. Not only are these causal properties regularly exercised when the object is unobserved (fire still boils the water when the cook is not looking, beams still support the floor and roof even when quite hidden, and so on) but the properties and processes involved in the causation of perception—the events in the eyes and nerves of percipients—are also rarely if ever observed, and then only by scientists with special equipment. Thus, one may often perceive or experience the effects of unobserved causal properties; hence, actual sensa may be causally dependent on what are only possible ones—which is absurd.

Followers of linguistic phenomenalism may claim to avoid this. The observed movement of the hands of a clock caused by unseen works inside it, for example, is not a case of actual sensa due to possible ones. What one should say, rather, is that sensa of hands moving are sensed, and if one were to get sensa of the back of a clock with the cover removed, one would get sensa of cog wheels and shafts moving; or, more generally, given sensa of the effect, then if certain other sensa occur, sensa of the cause would also occur—S_e, and if S_x, then S_c. It must be noted that such an analysis presupposes the Humean, or regularity, view of causation, in which all that a causal relation amounts to is that the "effect" has been observed regularly to follow the "cause" (C causes E means whenever C, then E)—any conviction that the effect is brought about by some force in the cause which compels it to happen is mere superstition or is to be explained psychologically as the projection of our feeling of expectancy. However, this analysis will not satisfy those who maintain other theories of causation.

But even granting the regularity view, there is a special difficulty for phenomenalism. Presumably the "ifs" in the phenomenalist analyses are equivalent to "whenever" and themselves state regularities; whenever the floor board is taken up, one sees the beams supporting the floor. Hence, if causal relationship means no more than regularity or constant conjunction, the formula "S_e, and if S_x, then S_c" amounts to "S_e, and whenever S_x, then S_c" or "S_e, and S_x causes S_c." However, this expresses a causal relationship different from the original one; it concerns X and C rather than C and E, and, more important, expresses a relation between sensa, suggesting that one lot of sensa causes another. Indeed, this last conclusion must follow if nothing but sensory experiences exist. Thus, "The beam supports the floor" becomes "If (whenever) you have under-floor sensa, you have beam sensa," and hence, "Under-floor sensa cause beam sensa"—which is far from the original. (This point applies with greater force to the causation of perceptions; the causal properties of the percipient's nervous system must be expressed in terms of the sensa of some other person entirely—namely, the physiologist, who can observe them.)

It has been objected that all this is unfair; the causal language belongs only to material-object language, and causal relations are between material objects and events, while in the sensum language and analysis they are expressed as equivalent correlations. However, according to the regularity view of causation there is no reason why the relevant sensa, which are events and are regularly correlated, should not be causally connected. Hence, the difficulty illustrated by "under-floor sensa cause beam sensa" still stands; it suggests that causal connections are more than relations of sensa, and thus that phenomenalism is false.

Quite apart from this special difficulty, the proposed analyses of causal properties are open to the general difficulties of the phenomenalist account of the existence of objects. There is a similar impurity, particularly with respect to the causation of sense experiences, analysis of which involves reference to different observers. Equivalent translation is even more clearly ruled out: since causal properties involve other objects as well as the object analyzed, they are more complex than such simple, sensible ones as color or shape and thus require a longer and more intricate set of sensum statements for their analysis. They also produce their effect only when a whole range of standing conditions holds, for instance, the spring will not drive the clock if the bearings are clogged with dirt. All these conditions would have to be specified for the mutual entailment of a causal material-object statement and a set of sensum statements.

Bibliography

STATEMENTS AND DEFENSES

In addition to Hume's own writings, of special interest are attempts to modernize and improve on Hume: Henry Habberley Price, *Hume's Theory of the External World* (London, 1940), and Alfred Jules Ayer, *The Foundations of Empirical Knowledge* (London, 1940).

On sensibilism, see Bertrand Russell, *Mysticism and Logic* (London, 1918), and Price's *Hume's Theory of the External World.* Russell's theory developed from the phenomenalistic views he put forward in *Our Knowledge of the External World* (London, 1914), which were criticized by C. D. Broad in "Phenomenalism," in *PAS*, Vol. 15 (1914/1915), 227–251.

Factual phenomenalism is expounded by John Stuart Mill in *An Examination of Sir William Hamilton's Philosophy* (London, 1872), Ch. 11 and Appendix to Ch. 12. H. H. Price, *Perception* (London, 1932), is sympathetic, though Price finally abandons factual phenomenalism. For allied views, see Karl Pearson, *The Grammar of Science*, 3d ed. (London, 1911), or Ernst Mach, *Contributions to the Analysis of Sensations* (Chicago, 1897; London, 1900).

Linguistic phenomenalism, including criticisms of earlier variations, may be found in A. J. Ayer, *The Foundations of Empirical Knowledge* (see above), and "Phenomenalism," in *PAS*, Vol. 47 (1946/1947), 163–196, reprinted in his *Philosophical Essays* (London, 1952); however, his latest views in *The Problem of Knowledge* (London, 1956) involve some recantation. Also useful is D. G. C. MacNabb, "Phenomenalism," in *PAS*, Vol. 41 (1940/1941), 67–90. Compare the sophisticated version by Clarence Irving Lewis in his *Analysis of Knowledge and Valuation* (La Salle, Ill., 1947)—comments on this in Roderick M. Chisholm, "The Problem of Empiricism," in *Journal of Philosophy*, Vol. 45, No. 19 (1948), 512–517; a reply by Lewis, *ibid.*, 517–524—and Roderick Firth, "Radical Empiricism and Perceptual Relativity," in *Philosophical Review*, Vol. 59 (1950), 164–183 and 319–331.

GENERAL CRITICISMS AND DISCUSSIONS

Introductory surveys are given by John Hospers, *Introduction to Philosophical Analysis* (New York, 1953; London, 1956), and Charles Harold Whiteley, *Introduction to Metaphysics* (London, 1955). There is a general discussion by A. C. Ewing, R. I. Aaron, and D. G. C. MacNabb in the symposium "The Causal Argument for Physical Objects," in *PAS*, Supp. Vol. 19 (1945), 32–100.

More advanced and definitely critical are Rodney Julian Hirst, *The Problems of Perception* (London, 1959); Alfred Cyril Ewing, *Idealism, A Critical Survey* (London, 1934); David Malet Armstrong, *Perception and the Physical World* (London, 1961); J. J. C. Smart, *Philosophy and Scientific Realism* (London, 1963); Wilfrid Sellars, *Science, Perception and Reality* (London, 1963), Ch. 3; Richard Bevan Braithwaite, "Propositions About Material Objects," in *PAS*, Vol. 38 (1937/1938), 269–290; R. I. Aaron, "How May Phenomenalism Be Refuted?" in *PAS*, Vol. 39 (1938/1939), 167–184; George Frederick Stout, "Phenomenalism," *ibid.*, 1–18; Isaiah Berlin, "Empirical Propositions and Hypothetical Statements," in *Mind*, Vol. 59, No. 235 (1950), 289–312; W. F. R. Hardie, "The Paradox of Phenomenalism," in *PAS*, Vol. 46 (1945/1946), 127–154; and Paul Marhenke, "Phenomenalism," in Max Black, ed., *Philosophical Analysis* (Ithaca, N.Y., 1950).

R. J. HIRST

PHENOMENOLOGY is a term that has been used in as many widely varying senses in modern philosophy as has the term which names the subject matter of this science, "phenomena."

Johann Heinrich Lambert, a German philosopher contemporary with Kant, first spoke of a discipline that he called "phenomenology" in his *Neues Organon* (Leipzig, 1764). He took "phenomenon" to refer to the illusory features of human experience and hence defined phenomenology as the "theory of illusion." Kant himself used "phenomenology" only twice, but he gave a new and broader sense to "phenomenon" that, in turn, resulted in a redefinition of "phenomenology." Kant distinguished objects and events as they appear in our experience from objects and events as they are in themselves, independently of the forms imposed on them by our cognitive faculties. The former he called "phenomena"; the latter, "noumena," or "things-in-themselves." All we can ever know, Kant thought, are phenomena.

The next generation of philosophers, notably Hegel, was at great pains to show that this was a mistake. Hegel's first major work, *Phenomenology of the Spirit* (1807), traced the development of Spirit (or Mind) through various stages, in which it apprehends itself as phenomenon, to the point of full development, where it is aware of itself as it is in itself—as noumenon. Phenomenology is the science in which we come to know mind as it is in itself through the study of the ways in which it appears to us.

In the middle of the nineteenth century, the definition of "phenomenon" was further extended until it became synonymous with "fact" or "whatever is observed to be the case." As a consequence, "phenomenology" acquired the meaning that it possesses most frequently in contemporary uses—a purely descriptive study of any given subject matter. In this sense, Sir William Hamilton, in his *Lectures on Metaphysics* (1858), spoke of phenomenology as a purely descriptive study of mind. Similar was Eduard von Hartmann's use of the word in the title of his book *Phenomenology of Moral Consciousness* (1878), which had as its task a complete description of moral consciousness. When the American philosopher C. S. Peirce used the term "phenomenology," he had in mind not only a descriptive study of all that is observed to be real but also of whatever is before the mind—perceptions of the real, illusory perceptions, imaginations, or dreams. It was the task of phenomenology to develop a list of categories embracing whatever can be included in the widest possible meaning of "to be." Peirce introduced this sense of the term in 1902.

The changes described so far are all due to extensions of the meaning of "phenomenon," but phenomenology, the science of phenomena in these different senses, remained one field of study among others, having a relation to philosophy as a whole comparable to those of logic, ethics, and aesthetics. Frequently it was recommended as a descriptive study that was to precede any attempt to provide explanations of the phenomena. But since Husserl employed the term in the early 1900s, it has become the name of a way of doing philosophy—by using the phenomenological method. For the phenomenologists, who regard their method as the only correct way of proceeding in philosophy, phenomenology is therefore the best and perhaps the only legitimate way of philosophizing today. For other philosophers, phenomenology is one school or movement in philosophy today. At the same time, however, the older sense of the term persists. "Phenomenology" is therefore used in two distinct senses. In its wider sense it refers to any descriptive study of a given subject. In the narrower sense it is the name of a philosophical movement. This article will deal with phenomenology in the second sense.

The movement and its origins. "Phenomenology" became the name of a school of philosophy whose first members were found in several German universities in the years before World War I, notably at Göttingen and Munich. Between 1913 and 1930 this group published a series of volumes of phenomenological studies entitled *Jahrbuch für Philosophie und phänomenologische Forschung*, whose editor in chief was Edmund Husserl, the most original and most influential thinker of the group. Most of the better-known members of the phenomenological movement—Moritz Geiger, Alexander Pfänder, Max Scheler, and

Oscar Becker—were coeditors, at least for a time. Martin Heidegger was another coeditor, but he cannot be counted among the phenomenologists without serious qualifications. Other major figures in the movement were Adolf Reinach and Hedwig Conrad-Martius.

The contributions to the *Jahrbuch* ranged from Husserl's writings about the foundations of phenomenology, to essays in the philosophy of mind and Scheler's major work on ethics, to pieces on the nature of analytic judgments and the paradoxes in set theory. As the interests of the various phenomenologists differed, so did their conceptions of phenomenology. These disagreements emerged only gradually, as Husserl developed the theory of the phenomenological method further and encountered a progressively more critical reception among his fellow phenomenologists. At the outset, there was general agreement that phenomenology was to be descriptive and that it was to describe phenomena by means of direct awareness (*Anschauung*). It is best to begin to clarify these terms by showing what they could, but do not, mean.

DESCRIPTION

The terms "descriptive," "phenomenon," and "direct awareness" all suggest that phenomenology is here used in its wider sense as a purely descriptive science of observable phenomena. But this wider sense of the term does not include what for the phenomenologists is the most important feature of phenomenology—that it is a nonempirical science. From the very beginnings of the phenomenological movement, when the conception of phenomenology was otherwise still quite vague, there was general agreement that phenomenology does not describe empirically observable matters of fact. Insisting on this, the early phenomenologists took a stand in opposition to philosophical views then in vogue.

Kant had distinguished three kinds of statements: empirical statements, statements true by definition (which he called "analytic"), and a third kind which he called "synthetic a priori." After being temporarily eclipsed by the German idealism of the early nineteenth century, Kant found many vigorous adherents in the later decades of that century. But there were also many philosophers who found Kant's account of the third type of statement—the statements that are neither empirical nor analytic—profoundly unsatisfactory and who, instead of attempting to supply an alternative account, rejected the tripartite classification altogether. This was done, for instance, by the German positivists Ernst Mach and Richard Avenarius, who insisted that there are no nonempirical statements which are not analytic. Of equal, if not greater, importance were those philosophers who regarded *all* statements as empirical. Analytic statements seemed to them clearly to rest on "the artful manipulation of language" (Mill's phrase), and they thought it therefore implausible that the statements of logic and/or mathematics should be analytic, that they should be true, and, more important, that they should be applicable to objects of everyday experience and science merely by virtue of an arbitrary choice of definitions. Accordingly, John Stuart Mill in England and Christoph Sigwart in Germany, among others, sought to show that statements in logic and mathematics are no less empirical than statements in the sciences.

In the case of logic, the most plausible argument for such a view begins with the observation that logic deals with correct and incorrect thinking. Thinking is a mental or psychological activity and must, therefore, be studied in psychology just as any other mental or psychological activity. It seems to follow, then, that logic is either a special field within empirical psychology or a practical discipline whose theoretical foundations are supplied by empirical psychology. In the former case, the relation of logic to psychology is comparable to that of learning theory or abnormal psychology to psychology as a whole. In the latter view, logic is related to psychology as surveying is to geometry or accounting to arithmetic.

Opposition to psychologism. The phenomenologists were not the first to question the identification of logical with psychological statements—a view they called "psychologism." But while some other philosophers had approached the issue by distinguishing logic from psychology in terms of the distinction between theoretical and practical disciplines, the phenomenologists attacked the identification of logical with psychological statements on the grounds that the latter are empirical statements and the former are not. The most sustained and painstaking critique of psychologism is contained in the first volume of Husserl's *Logische Untersuchungen* ("Logical Investigations," Halle, 1900–1901), and the arguments in that book served as a first rallying point for phenomenologists.

Husserl's attack on psychologism had a special edge to it because his *Philosophie der Arithmetik* ("Philosophy of Arithmetic," Vol. I, Halle, 1891; the projected second volume was never published) had been a frankly psychologistic account of arithmetic. His change of heart was in part occasioned by a controversy with the German mathematician and philosopher of mathematics Gottlob Frege, in which Frege had insisted that a sharp line be drawn between psychological statements, on the one hand, and logical and/or mathematical ones, on the other.

Husserl devoted an entire book to the detailed examination and refutation of every variety of psychologistic doctrine, taking careful account of each view and trying to show its inadequacy. Underlying all his arguments, however, were a few general principles to which he appealed again and again in the course of his discussion:

(1) Psychology deals with facts; therefore its statements are empirical. It has not, until now, produced any precise scientific laws, and its generalizations are vague. The rules of logic, on the other hand, are precise. Hence, psychological generalizations can neither be identical with logical laws nor be premises from which they may be derived.

(2) Empirical statements are probable, at best, for there is always a real possibility that further evidence will show them to be false. Logical truths are necessary truths. A logical principle like *modus ponens* ("Given that 'If *p*, then *q*' is true and that '*p*' is true, '*q*' is true") is not probable; it is necessarily valid.

(3) Closely connected with (1) and (2) is the argument that empirical generalizations rest on induction; they are derived from a number of individual cases. This is not true of logical rules.

Both (2) and (3) are supported by pointing out that where there is a conflict between a logical principle and an empirical generalization, the logical principle will always emerge victorious because necessary truth is not to be refuted by a probable statement and logical truth cannot be shown to be false by an inductive generalization.

(4) The empirical generalizations of psychology produce, at best, causal laws, and logical principles are not causal laws. Premises and conclusions of an argument are not related as cause and effect; the truth of a conclusion is not the effect of the truth of the premises. Causal relations hold between events, and events happen at definite times in definite places. But the premises of an argument do not "happen," nor does the conclusion; they are either true or false. In a valid argument the truth of the conclusion "follows" from the premises; it is not the effect of events called premises.

(5) Empirical laws imply matters of fact; logical rules do not. Since empirical laws are, presumably, derived from the observation of particulars, the existence of such particulars in some place and at some time can be inferred from the truth of the empirical law. *Modus ponens*, on the other hand, does not imply that there exists, in a particular place and at a particular time, a pair of statements of the form "If *p*, then *q*" and "*p*." Nor are any corresponding facts implied by any other logical law. This point is sometimes stated in a phrase, borrowed from Leibniz, that empirical laws are true only for this actual world; logical laws are true "for all possible worlds."

The upshot of these arguments is that logical and empirical statements differ in kind. Logical statements are precise, necessarily true, and not derived inductively from particulars. They are, or give rise to, logical rules, not causal laws, and they do not imply matters of fact. Empirical statements, on the other hand, are vague, probably (but not necessarily) true, and based on inductive generalizations. They are, or give rise to, causal laws and imply the existence of matters of fact. Quite clearly, in the refutation of psychologism, the decisive argument, for Husserl, consisted in showing that there are two kinds of statements: empirical and nonempirical. Phenomenological statements are to be nonempirical.

To deny that phenomenological statements are empirical is to deny that their truth or falsity depends on sensory observation. But if not on sensory observation, on what does their truth depend? Some philosophers might be inclined to say that phenomenological statements are analytic. Insofar as only those statements are analytic which are true by virtue of explicit definition of terms, phenomenologists deny that their statements are analytic. We shall have abundant evidence that they are right in this, for phenomenological statements are not true by virtue of stipulation of meaning. But insofar as "analytic" is used in some other sense, it is not helpful either to assert or to deny that phenomenological statements are analytic; the meaning of the term "analytic" is much debated in contemporary philosophy and has therefore become extremely obscure. It is more profitable to ask the phenomenologists about the truth conditions of their statements. Their preliminary answer to this question consists in introducing the term "phenomenon" by saying that phenomenological statements are true if they accurately describe phenomena. This answer, however, remains merely a verbal maneuver unless "phenomenon" can be shown to have a clear and definite meaning.

PHENOMENA

We have seen that "phenomenon" is a technical philosophical term which different philosophers have used in very different senses. The phenomenologists sometimes say that "phenomenon" is their name for whatever appears to us in "immediate experience." By "immediate experience" they do not mean sensory observations that have not been interpreted or classified under general concepts ("raw sense data"). Like many other contemporary philosophers, the phenomenologists are not at all sure that there are for us any sensory observations which are not interpreted or classified under general concepts. The appeal to phenomena or to immediate experience is therefore not an appeal to simple, uninterpreted data of sensory experience. Furthermore, the appeal to phenomena does not presuppose the existence of a special class of objects called "phenomena." The phenomenologists do not claim to have discovered that besides all the kinds of entities found in this world (physical objects, thoughts, numbers, feelings, poems, etc.) there is one other class, phenomena. Any object is a phenomenon if looked at or considered in a particular way. This particular way of looking at all kinds of objects is recommended in the slogan "Zu den Sachen!"

Literally translated, this slogan means "To the things!" where "things" must be taken in the widest possible sense to embrace all possible kinds of objects. Like other slogans, moreover, this one gains its force from having more than one meaning. If a German says to someone, "Zur Sache!" he is exhorting him, as we would say, "to get down to business." "Zu den Sachen!" admonishes one to get down to the proper business of the philosopher by examining and describing all kinds of objects in the particular way that reveals them as phenomena.

This explication of "phenomenon" is, so far, circular. To clarify what is meant by that term, we must therefore explain what alternative ways of doing philosophy are excluded by telling us to examine and describe phenomena. We must explain the polemical import of the slogan "Zu den Sachen!" Once this is done, we must pursue the concept of phenomenon further by attempting to clarify the nature of the examination and description that shows all kinds of objects as phenomena.

Opposition to reductionism. The polemical import of "Zu den Sachen!" is readily made clear. In it the phenomenologists expressed their opposition to all reductionism, or, as Adolph Reinach called them, "nothing-but philosophies." Such philosophies are couched in sentences like "Logical laws are nothing but psychological laws," "Moral laws are nothing but the expressions of the mores of a given society," and "Aesthetic judgments are nothing but expressions of personal taste." To oppose all views of this sort would seem dogmatic. Some "nothing-but" statements may be false, but perhaps others are true; and one would think that each would have to be examined on its merits rather than be rejected summarily as an example of reductionism. However, the phenomenologists did not attack these "nothing-but" views on the grounds that they are false but on the grounds that the philosophers who held them, held them for the wrong kinds of reasons.

Psychologism, which is just one example of reductionism, did not assert that logical laws are nothing but psychological laws in the light of a thorough examination of the nature of logical laws which proved that they are identical with psychological ones. If someone challenged the psychologistic philosopher's views, he was not invited to examine for himself the nature of logical laws and to discover that they did not differ from those in psychology. Instead, he was given an argument from which it followed that logical laws "must" be psychological ones. Psychologistic assertions about logical and psychological laws do not result from an examination of laws in logic and psychology but are the logical consequences of certain more general assumptions. These assumptions themselves are not examined but are taken as self-evident.

Reductionism as attacked by the phenomenologist is the outcome of accepting certain statements that have not been examined carefully. If the implications of these assumptions are shown to conflict with facts about the world, the reductionist does not, the phenomenologists say, reexamine his original assumptions. Instead, he redefines the terms used to describe the facts about the world in such a way that the contradictions between these descriptions of facts and the implications of the original assumptions disappear. The redefinitions necessitated by the conflict between assumptions and facts are expressed in the "nothing-but" statements.

Opposition to phenomenalism. An example of a specific reductionist view attacked by the phenomenologists will clarify the process. Hume's empiricism was attacked for its phenomenalism, that is, for its view that physical objects, as well as human beings, are no more than collections of their observable properties. ("Phenomenology" must not be confused with "phenomenalism.") "Observable properties" in this context refers exclusively to sensory qualities like shape, color, sound, etc. This view of Hume's did not issue from a careful examination of the nature of physical objects. Instead, it was a product of his psychological theories about the origin and meaning of concepts and words. Hume held that all concepts are either derived directly from sensory experience or are complex collections of such concepts. He regarded it as a consequence of this view that all concepts refer either to sensory qualities like shape, color, and sound or to complex collections of these. He also thought that all nouns are the names of concepts. It follows from this that all nouns naming physical objects refer to concepts that can be completely analyzed into simple concepts referring to sensory qualities. Hence physical objects—what is named by physical object nouns—are no more than complex collections of sensory qualities. However, this view is not supported by a careful examination of physical objects themselves but follows from, and hence "must" be true in the light of, Hume's psychology and views on the meanings of words.

Opposition to psychological atomism. Another target of the antireductionist polemic was the then popular attempt by philosophical psychologists like Wilhelm Wundt to define consciousness as a set of contents—sensations, feelings, affects—on which operations—association and apperception—are performed. This view was not the product of careful examination and description of the series of phenomena that we call consciousness but was a logical consequence of more general assumptions about the world. It missed, the phenomenologists maintained, the essential characteristic of consciousness which they, following Franz Brentano, called "intentionality."

Opposition to scientism. Also objectionable was the so-called "scientism" of the positivists Mach and Avenarius. Scientism regarded scientific statements as premises in philosophical arguments such that the truth of statements in philosophy depends on the truth of scientific statements. This view was a direct consequence of two assumptions: that all statements are either empirical or analytic, and that all empirical statements are, at least ideally, statements in science. Given these assumptions, there is a choice between restricting philosophy to the practice of logic, in which statements are often thought to be analytic, or saying that philosophical truths are empirical. If we choose the latter alternative, philosophical statements "must" have scientific premises.

But this conclusion, phenomenologists held, was drawn without paying careful attention to actual and possible functions of philosophy, which, they held, is independent of science. In this they were not motivated by any hostility toward science; on the contrary, their aim was to establish philosophy as a "rigorous science" by means of the phenomenological method. Husserl had discussed this aim at some length in his article "Philosophie als strenge Wissenschaft" ("Philosophy as Rigorous Science," in *Logos*, Vol. I, 1910–1911, 289–341). This phenomenological and rigorously scientific philosophy was expected to provide the foundations for the existing sciences by providing clear explications of the concepts which the sciences use but do not themselves explicate. For instance, the definition of number, in which Reinach was interested, was considered a task for phenomenology. Husserl was concerned with clarifying epistemological terms like "meaning" and "truth." So conceived, phenomenology had to be independent of the existing sciences because it was to explicate the concepts and procedures presupposed by them. To consider philosophy a branch or subsidiary of existing science was one more example of "nothing-but" philosophy.

Presuppositionless inquiry. Here it must be asked whether philosophers must not make certain assumptions. We cannot, it would seem, show that all statements are true by reference to the truth of other statements; some we must merely assume to be true. But phenomenologists are unconvinced by this sort of argumentation. Statements in phenomenology are not true because certain other statements are true; they are true because they describe the phenomena correctly. In order to achieve true description, the phenomenologist must resist the temptation to make assumptions and, afterward, to define his terms in such a way as to make the descriptions of facts consistent with the assumptions and what must be inferred from them. The phenomenologist does not frame theories; he merely examines and then describes phenomena as they present themselves to his unprejudiced view. Having no theoretical commitment and only one practical one—to examine all phenomena carefully and to take none of them as familiar or understood until they have been carefully explicated and described—the phenomenologist says that his science is descriptive and that it is presuppositionless. This obviously does not mean that at any given time the phenomenologist may not be operating with certain unexamined assumptions—this can always happen. The claim of presuppositionlessness expresses the resolution to eschew all unexamined assumptions and the belief that such assumptions are unnecessary; No statement must be taken as true without examination. Phenomenology does not need any true but unexamined premises; the truth of all its premises can be tested by examining the phenomena.

This sheds some light on the second, affirmative sense of the slogan "Zu den Sachen!"—an exhortation to examine phenomena and to make them the sole touchstone of the truth of philosophical statements. But the precise import of this exhortation remains unclear until the meaning of "phenomenon" has been explicated, so this is a pressing question. It is also a question fraught with particular difficulties. Phenomena, as was stated, are those aspects of objects of every kind which are revealed by a particular way of looking at objects. The phenomenal aspects of objects are not revealed by ordinary empirical observation but only by looking at them *as* phenomena. The meaning of "phenomenon," on the other hand, cannot merely be stipulated in analytic statements. Hence, explications of "phenomenon" must result from using the phenomenological method and must be couched in phenomenological statements. But what these statements are cannot be made clear until it is clear what a phenomenon is, nor do we know what the phenomenological method is until we know what a phenomenon is.

"Methodological circle." The entire phenomenological enterprise is involved in a circle that can be called the "methodological circle." This methodological circle does not differ formally from the circle involved in any kind of logical investigation where the rules of inference, for instance, which the completed investigation hopes to formulate and justify must be employed during the course of the investigation itself so that its result, the logical rules, is the product of the application of the rules to themselves. The existence of this circle does not prove that logic is an impossible or unjustifiable discipline, nor does its presence in phenomenology support an analogous argument against it.

The occurrence of this circle should, however, put one on his guard against taking for completed analyses statements made by phenomenologists that are, in fact, merely gropings toward and anticipations of what phenomenology, its method, and the completed theory of method will be like in some indefinitely remote future. Phenomenology does not exist as a set of doctrines but at best as a method—and this method is to be developed by applying phenomenology to itself. Hence, even the phenomenological method is still in the process of being clarified, properly described, and elaborated; it is, at least to date, quite incomplete.

Husserl liked to refer to himself as a "perpetual beginner," an expression that meant several things to him. In one of its senses, it expressed what was just said about phenomenology: it is a method that can only be progressively developed by applying it to itself. Accordingly, most of Husserl's published works are discussions of the phenomenological method. This has sometimes been taken as a symptom of an excessive fondness for writing manifestoes, but discussions of phenomenological method are not of the nature of manifestoes prior to doing phenomenology, nor are they propaedeutics. Only while doing phenomenology can we clarify its method. To write about it was, in Husserl's case, to do phenomenology.

THE INTUITION OF ESSENCES

The preceding discussion has brought to light three properties of phenomenological statements:

(1) Phenomenological statements are nonempirical.

(2) Phenomenological statements are descriptive.

(3) Phenomenological statements describe phenomena.

These leave the task of making clear what phenomena are, a matter of disagreement among phenomenologists: most of the schisms within the phenomenological movement originate in disagreements about the set of conditions necessary for anything to be a phenomenon. We shall examine a variety of conditions proposed, beginning with the most simple and proceeding to more complex sets as the simpler ones turn out to be incomplete. The criterion of completeness for this set of necessary conditions is that any set of conditions required for anything to be a phenomenon must at least be consistent with the first requirement for phenomenological statements—that they be nonempirical. Hence, the set of conditions laid down for anything to be a phenomenon must clearly rule out any possibility that phenomena can be described in empirical statements.

The simplest specification of phenomenon, given by some early phenomenologists, contains only two conditions:

(1) Phenomena are essences.

(2) Phenomena are intuited.

The reason for identifying phenomena with essences is instructive. As we saw, it was claimed that there are some entities by virtue of which statements in phenomenology are said to be true or false. These entities (or phenomena) are not particular observable objects by reference to which empirical statements are confirmed or disconfirmed. Instead, the phenomenologists say, they are the necessary and invariant features of objects. Phenomenology explicates those features of any given object without which it could not truly be said to be the object that it is. These most general, necessary, and invariant features of objects have been called "essences" by other philosophers, and, following that terminological tradition, the phenomenologists also talk about essences.

Many philosophers in the past have held that statements about essences are empirical statements, arrived at by comparison of many examples of a type of object and extracting from the descriptions of all these examples the common features by means of some kind of generalization. Such a process has often been called abstraction. Abstract statements, since they are logically dependent on empirical descriptions of particular cases, are themselves empirical statements. Phenomenological statements, on the other hand, are, for the reasons given, not empirical statements. Hence, phenomenological statements are not reached by abstraction. They are, phenomenologists say, derived from a scrutiny of particular cases by seeing, intuition, or intuition of essences (*Wesensschau*).

The identification of phenomena as essences brings us one step closer to the goal of clarifying the particular way of looking at objects that reveals objects as phenomena. It turns out to be a species of intuition. Phenomenology is a form of intuitionism and has, accordingly, acquired the ill repute of all intuitionisms of being no more than a veiled refusal to provide evidence for one's philosophical statements. But sometimes such a refusal can be justified. Intuitionism is objectionable only if the philosopher is not willing to argue either about the nature of his intuition or about the justification for appealing to it in this case—if his appeal to intuition is merely intended to terminate philosophical debate. The phenomenologists' appeal to intuition is not of this kind. Hence more can, and must, be said about intuition.

Intuition seems to be a psychological term. Its German counterpart, *Anschauung,* often means no more than "seeing." The objects of seeing, in its ordinary sense, are empirical objects. Essences are not empirical objects, so they cannot be seen in any ordinary sense of that term. Hence, intuition must be seeing of some extraordinary kind. One might suggest that the phenomenologists claim to have discovered one more human cognitive faculty than had been known before, but such a discovery of an actual human faculty would have to be couched in empirical statements. Phenomenologists do not make empirical statements, so they cannot claim—nor do they—to discover previously unknown cognitive faculties.

The point of introducing intuition is not psychological but epistemological. To appeal to intuition is not to make a psychological statement about the causal origins of certain statements but an epistemological one about the sort of evidence that will be relevant to them. To say that we know essences by intuition is to say, negatively, that the truth or falsity of statements about essences is not dependent on the truth about empirical statements.

The appeal to intuition makes another positive, epistemological point: Our acquaintance with essences possesses an epistemological feature also possessed by our sensory acquaintance with empirical objects. This logical feature is sometimes described by saying that what we see is described in self-validating statements. A statement, "*P,*" about particular objects is self-validating if the strongest evidence that we can adduce for it is a statement like "I have seen that *P*" or "I have observed that *P.*" We cannot, therefore, claim that "*P*" is true because there is some other true statement, "*Q,*" from which "*P*" can be inferred and which is not equivalent to "*P.*" Statements about essences are self-validating in the same sense. Given any statement, "*E,*" of the form "_____ is the essence of _____," we cannot claim that "*E*" is true because there is some other true statement, "*F,*" which is not equivalent to "*E*" and from which we can infer "*E.*" Of course, some statements about the existence of particular objects may be deducible from other statements, and it is similarly true that some statements about essences may be deducible from other statements. But such a deduction does not provide stronger

evidence for statements about empirical existence or about essences than do self-validating statements.

Phenomenological statements are not derived by means of abstraction from particular statements, since, if they were so derived, they would not be self-validating. But they are not the only self-validating statements; empirical statements are also self-validating. An adequate account of phenomena must state more than that phenomena are revealed in the intuition of essences; it must specify this intuition to clarify in what respects it differs from the simple seeing of objects of sensory observation.

BRACKETING EXISTENCE: FREE IMAGINATIVE VARIATION OF EXAMPLES

In the light of the problem about the meaning of intuition, the reason for introducing a further condition defining "phenomenon" becomes clearer. This condition is not accepted by all phenomenologists but was regarded as necessary by Husserl, Pfänder, Reinach, and Scheler. We are in a position, they said, to describe objects *as* phenomena only after we have "bracketed existence" or "suspended our belief in the existence of objects." Husserl calls this the "phenomenological epoche" or the "phenomenological reduction." "Epoche" was borrowed from the Skeptics, but Husserl's use of it differed from theirs.

These references to "bracketing" or "suspending belief in existence," together with the talk about essences, led to the view that phenomenology is a kind of essentialism and, as such, is diametrically opposed to existentialism. There is no room here to bring out all the confusions that produced this fairly common interpretation; suffice it to say that the phenomenological epoche is *not* achieved by resolving to make no more statements about existence or what exists. To bracket existence is not to eliminate existence in general or existing entities in particular from the list of possible objects for phenomenological study.

In the light of Husserl's repeated insistence on the close similarities between his phenomenology and Descartes's methodical doubt, the phrase "suspending belief in the existence of objects" is often taken as a description of Cartesian doubt. But this is a misunderstanding, for Husserl insisted on distinguishing suspending belief in existence from doubting existence. This distinction cannot, therefore, be simply ignored.

Suppose a young woman states that she has direct evidence that she is terribly attractive to red-haired men. Her statement is not derived from a psychological law about the preferences of red-haired men or from a physiological one about their exceptional susceptibility to her figure and coloring. Her statement, a direct inductive generalization, is the result of her own experiences with red-haired men and tells us something about many or all of the members of the class of red-haired men. Besides all being red-haired and male, they have one further property: they cannot resist the charms of this young woman. In order to substantiate such a statement, she would have to cite cases of a number of red-haired men who at various times, under various circumstances, have given indubitable proof of their devotion. Two things are important here: that the red-haired men really exist and that their devotion to her is real. The truth of the inductive generalization depends at least on those two conditions. On the other hand, if the generalizations are correct, it follows that there exist (or existed) several red-haired men in this particular condition. If, however, the red-haired men do not exist or if their attachment is a figment of this young woman's imagination, then the general statement is false (unless evidence of a different kind can be found).

The story of this young woman was told in order to exemplify the relation of empirical generalizations to particular empirical statements—of "I am irresistible to red-haired men" to, for instance, "A red-haired matinee idol in New York committed suicide over me," and of both of these to the facts of the case. These relations were exemplified with an imaginary example, for it is quite unimportant that I do not know any young woman of this description. Where a description serves as an example in this sense ("example" is an ambiguous word), it is quite irrelevant whether the object described exists or not. If, on the contrary, I am interested in making a general statement about objects observed, it makes all the difference in the world whether the particular objects covered in my generalization exist and exist as described.

This is one sense of "bracketing existence." When existence has been bracketed in this sense, the descriptions of objects or situations do not serve as premises for an inductive generalization (or an abstraction), but as examples. But "example" is used in several senses. Sometimes it is used to designate one instance of an empirical generalization, but this is not the sense used here. At other times, examples serve a merely pedagogical function. I might have told my story about the young woman merely to provide a concrete illustration of abstract truth about empirical generalizations, in order to make the abstract statement easier to understand. In a third sense—"example" is used in phenomenology in this sense—the example both serves as an illustration and has evidential functions. In that case, the truth of the statement about empirical generalizations depends on the accuracy of the description of the example. I claim that my general statement is true because the description of the particular example is accurate, but how do I know whether a description is accurate so that it can have evidential force as an example? Since we have bracketed existence, I cannot say that the description is accurate because the case described has actually been observed to exist in a particular place and at a particular time, for examples need not be actual existents.

In order to understand this sense of bracketing existence, we must be able to answer two questions: (1) When can the description of an example rightly be said to be accurate? (2) How is a phenomenological statement to be derived from an example?

In this context Husserl talked about a procedure that he called "free imaginative variation," comparable to what Anglo-American philosophers call the method of "counterexamples." Here we describe an example and then transform the description by adding or deleting one of the predicates contained in the description. With each addition or deletion, we ask whether the amended description can still be said to describe an example of the same kind of object as that which the example originally described was said to exemplify. Sometimes we shall have to say that if we add this predicate to the description or take that one away, what is then described is an example of a different kind of object from that exemplified by the original example. At other times the additions or deletions will not affect the essential features of the kind of object exemplified by the different examples.

In this way we discover the necessary and invariant features of a given kind of thing that the example must possess in order to be an example of that kind of thing. We also discover which features are accidental and hence irrelevant to the question whether this object, as described, is or is not an example of a certain kind of thing. What we discover is what phenomenologists call the "essence" of objects.

For example, let us suppose that we meet someone who does not have the usual five senses but only three: sight, touch, and hearing. We might be perplexed, but we should still call him a person. The same would hold if he had three more senses than normal persons. But suppose we met someone who looked like a person but seemed to be deaf and blind, and without any tactile, olfactory, or gustatory sensations. He would still be regarded as a person, although as a seriously defective one. But suppose further that we find that this creature looks like a human being except that it has no sense organs at all. Would he nonetheless be called a person? No. An animal? No. A plant? Not really. We have no word in our language for such a being. We would not know what to say about it.

Here we have varied in imagination an example of a person with reference to one predicate, "possessing sense organs." We find that in order for anything to be a person, it must have sense organs of some kind; there is an essential (necessary and invariant) relation between "person" and "possessing sense organs." The results of free imaginative variation are statements of such essential connections. Since statements about phenomena are one kind of statement about essences (and vice versa), the statements resulting from this procedure are phenomenological statements.

"Epistemological circle." Phenomenological statements are made while existence is and remains bracketed. If true, they are so not because they describe something that we have directly observed. Nor are they true because they are warranted by a series of observations of particular objects or events. Hence, they do not imply the past or present existence of particular objects in just the way in which empirical generalizations imply it. All that is asserted in the phenomenological statement is that if any being is an example of a person, then it must have sense organs. We are, therefore, making an assertion about the necessary relations of properties: Whatever has the property of being a person must also possess the property of having sense organs.

This is the method of free imaginative variation. It would seem to provide an answer to the second question raised earlier—how a phenomenological statement is to be derived from an example. But the same procedure can also be said to provide an answer to the first question, how we decide whether an example is described accurately—whether the description contains all the essential predicates so that the thing described may rightly be said to be an example of a certain kind of object. For, once we have made clear the invariant features of the sort of thing exemplified, we are in a position to say whether the example contains all those necessary features. But to use free imaginative variation to answer both questions is, of course, circular; we derive the phenomenological statement from any given example by means of free imaginative variation and then confirm that the original example was accurately described because it possesses the invariant features expressed in the phenomenological statement. It would seem that we need an independent criterion for deciding the accuracy of the description of any given example, but there is no discussion of such an independent test in the writings of the phenomenologists. The phenomenological method appears, therefore, to be circular in a second sense that might be called the "epistemological circle."

Phenomenology, as we saw, is circular because it clarifies its own method while using it (the methodological circle); it is also circular, we see now, because it confirms its statements by reference to examples and then attests the accuracy of the descriptions of these examples by reference to the statements derived from them (the epistemological circle). We must now show that what we claimed earlier for the methodological circle—that its presence cannot be construed as an argument against phenomenology—is true for the epistemological circle as well. This will be argued for by an examination of a second sense of "bracketing existence." In this second sense, "bracketing existence" refers to the transition from nonreflective to reflective thinking.

BRACKETING EXISTENCE:
PHENOMENOLOGY AND REFLECTION

In free imaginative variation we ask ourselves about any given property of an example, "Is this a necessary feature for being a such and such? Is that?" For our answer we do not appeal to empirical observation. Neither do we give an answer simply by deciding to regard some particular feature as essential. We do not define our terms arbitrarily; instead, with each variation, we ask ourselves whether the example described could still be recognizable as an example of the same sort of thing as that exemplified before. We ask ourselves what features an object must have in order to be recognized as an example of a certain kind of object. What we discover are necessary conditions for recognizing a certain kind of thing.

But recognition presupposes previous acquaintance. I cannot recognize someone whom I meet for the first time, unless I have seen pictures of him or have been given his description or perhaps dreamed of him before. But if we can recognize only what we know already, then we must already know the necessary features of the objects which we are able to recognize. In that case, there would seem to be no need to bracket existence and to vary the examples freely in imagination in order to discover their essential features, since the entire procedure presupposes that we know these essential features all along.

The resolution of this difficulty comes when we consider that the word "know" has two radically different senses, which some English philosophers have called, respectively, "knowing how" and "knowing that." The latter refers to knowledge expressed in statements. To "know that" something is the case is to be able to put what is known into words. I can show that I know a person by describing his looks; however, it is of course also possible that I should know a person and yet be quite unable to give any sort of adequate description of his looks. It is often very difficult to give a good description of those persons whom we know very well. I know them, not in the sense that I can describe them but that I could recognize them anywhere. I can pick them out of a crowd without hesitation. I can identify them by their voice or their walk, although I might be hard put either to describe in words or to imitate them. This second kind of knowledge is "knowing how"; in the example, I know how to recognize a person.

These two kinds of knowledge are independent of each other. It is not a necessary condition for being able to do something, such as recognize someone, that I should be able to *say* that he is a person of a certain description. Conversely, it is not necessary that I should be able to do a certain kind of action, such as ride a bicycle, in order to be able to give a detailed and accurate description of riding a bicycle. It is, furthermore, possible that for certain kinds of knowing how there is no corresponding knowledge that.

Of some performances I can say: This time I did it right; last time I did it badly. Therefore, I possess criteria for proper performance. If asked what these criteria are, I may not be able to put them into words, but I know them in the sense that I use them and, in many cases, I can, upon reflection, state what they are. I have then, by means of reflection, produced knowledge that _____ corresponding to the knowledge how _____ which I possessed all along. This is what happens when I vary an example freely in imagination: I am always able to discriminate between the thing that I would recognize as a certain object and the thing that I would either take as a different kind of object or about which I would not know what to say. But only upon reflection can I verbalize the criteria implicit in such a recognition by stating the essential features of any given kind of object.

Reflective thinking. When I vary examples freely in imagination, I reflect about the criteria implicit in my ability to recognize examples of the given sort of object; I now put into words the criteria that previously were merely implicit in my performances. This description of the two sides of the process called "bracketing existence" accords perfectly with Husserl's explanations of it. Phenomenology, he stated, is a reflective enterprise. In its reflection it brings to light what was previously "anonymous" or "latent" in our "performances" (*Leistungen*). But phenomenological reflection is a very special kind of reflection. In phenomenology we do not reflect about facts ("Did I see right? Was that really Jones lying in the gutter?") or about specific actions ("Should I have lectured Jones on the evils of drink?"). Phenomenological reflection does not produce any factual statements, nor does it employ factual statements as premises or as the starting points of reflection. In phenomenology we reflect about examples, in the sense explained; the result of such a reflection is not a factual statement or an empirical generalization but a statement about the necessary conditions for any object's being an example of the sort of thing considered in our reflection.

"Bracketing existence" and the other phrases applied in this context are used ambiguously. Why did Husserl fail to distinguish these two senses? We have already uncovered one source of this ambiguity by showing that we can employ the method of free imaginative variation of an arbitrarily chosen example in order to clarify the essential feature of any object only if we reflect about the example. Hence, treating a given case merely as an example (bracketing in the first sense) presupposes that we have made the transition from nonreflective to reflective thinking (bracketing in the second sense). Although the two kinds of bracketing are distinct, they must occur together. But there is a second source of the ambiguous use of all these phrases. "Bracketing existence" and "suspending our belief in the existence" of an object seem to be particularly apt in describing important features of the transition from nonreflective to reflective thinking. Reflection involves questioning—more specifically, questioning something which I believed before or regarded as properly done. When I reflect, I ask, "Was that really Jones in the gutter?" or "Should I have helped him up?" Such questioning requires awareness that there are questions to be asked in this situation and that they are not pointless. Before I can reflectively question my earlier belief that it was Jones whom I saw lying in the gutter, I must be open to the possibility that it was not Jones. Hence, as I begin to reflect, I suspend my belief in the existence of Jones in that condition in that place, or I put his existence in brackets. "Bracketing" in this sense means that I become aware of the possibility that something which I believed to exist does not exist as I thought it did, that a statement which I considered true is not, or that some act which I considered right when I did it might have been wrong. Once I have become aware of that possibility, I am ready to reflect.

The insight that phenomenological statements are the product of reflection resolves the methodological and the epistemological circles. The methodological circle arises because the method must be used to clarify what the method itself consists of. It seems, therefore, that we can use the method only if we know what it consists of, but we can know what it consists of only if we have already used it. Therefore it would seem that we can never get started. But since phenomenology is reflective, it does not presuppose knowledge that the phenomenological method consists of certain procedures; it only presupposes that we know how to use it (to reflect about the essential features of arbitrarily chosen examples), even if we cannot describe it. Such a description is not a necessary condition for using the method, so there is no problem here.

The epistemological circle is resolved in a similar manner. In the method of free imaginative variation, it seemed that we could know that a given phenomenological statement, "*P*," is true only if we know that the description, "*E*" of the corresponding example is accurate. But we can know that "*E*" is accurate only if we know that "*P*" is true. Hence, it would seem that we cannot know either that "*P*" is true or that "*E*" is accurate. But phenomenological

reflection begins with my being able to recognize the example described in "*E*." I know that I describe the example accurately to the extent that I recognize the object in my description of it. Both the accuracy of "*E*" and the truth of "*P*" are tested by the criteria implicit in my ability to recognize the object. Hence, there is no difficulty in this case either.

Nonempirical status of phenomena. In the search for a complete definition of phenomenon we have now discovered three conditions defining phenomena: (1) phenomena are essences, (2) phenomena are intuited, (3) phenomena are revealed by bracketing existence. The third requirement is twofold: Phenomena are known only upon reflection of a specific sort, namely, reflection about the essential features of arbitrarily chosen examples. Once again the question must be raised whether this definition of phenomena is complete. The criterion of completeness used earlier was that a definition of "phenomenon" is complete only if it is consistent with the first of the three requirements for phenomenological statements— that they are nonempirical. We must ask, therefore, whether phenomena as defined can be described in empirical statements or whether our definition has ruled out that possibility.

It may seem obvious that the definition of phenomenon is complete by this criterion because it seems impossible that phenomena as defined—as being revealed only by bracketing existence—could be described in empirical statements, for statements about phenomena are not statements about single, observed particulars or about series of such single, observed particulars. They are, rather, statements about the necessary relations between the properties of some example of a certain kind of thing in which we do not consider whether the description of our example refers to an actually existing object. But can we really conclude from this fact, namely, that no observation of actually existent objects is consulted in phenomenological reflection, that the truth of phenomenological statements is independent of the truth of empirical observation statements? We must distinguish between the description of the process by which we arrive at phenomenological statements and the logical conditions that these statements must fulfill in order to be true. The former merely describes how I discover certain statements, but it reveals nothing about the truth conditions of my statements. It is said, for instance, that some Greek geometers discovered certain statements about plane figures by measuring and weighing actual plane figures of tin. They arrived at their statements by means of observations; they were able to make certain statements in geometry after observing actual physical objects, but their statements are no more empirically true (or false) than are the same statements when they appear as theorems in Euclid's *Elements*.

This example presents a case in which statements whose truth or falsity is independent of empirical observation are discovered through empirical observations. It is possible that statements about phenomena constitute a converse case where empirical statements are discovered without explicitly consulting observation of sensory particulars. For instance, it was stated in the preceding section that the phenomenologist does not necessarily consult actual observations when he describes phenomena; his example may be purely imaginary. But it is possible that the statements which he is thus able to make are nevertheless empirical statements. All that was said was that the making of a phenomenological statement is not immediately preceded by observations of existent objects. Perhaps, however, this is not necessary, since we know the necessary conditions for anything to be an example of a certain kind of thing because we have observed examples of this kind of thing many times and have, as it were, performed an unconscious induction all along. If this is true, then phenomenological statements may still be empirical statements. That they are not empirical statements has not been proved by stating that they are not discovered by means of explicit and deliberate observation of existing objects. The description of "bracketing existence" and of the subsequent reflection has revealed something about the method of discovering statements in phenomenology, but it has not shown that the statement so discovered may not nevertheless be empirical in the sense of being either verifiable by reference to observations of particulars or confirmable or at least refutable by reference to such observations.

There is reason to suspect that the phenomenologists who required that existence be bracketed in phenomenology thought that this requirement assured them that the statements so discovered would not be empirical in any of the senses mentioned. But, as has been shown, they have no such assurance. Hence, they can have no assurance that what is discovered once we have bracketed existence is a phenomenon, in the sense of being the referent of a nonempirical statement. We need further argument to show that bracketing existence does reveal phenomena in the required sense, in all or at least in some cases. Some of the phenomenologists, notably Husserl, have brought forward a number of considerations that provide the arguments needed here. These considerations can best be approached by considering intentionality.

INTENTIONALITY

It was said earlier that reflection undertaken after we have bracketed existence yields, if successful, descriptions of activities which we perform with ease in everyday life but are not able at the same time to describe. Concerning such activities we also know when they miscarry, when they are performed incorrectly or in an improper context, or when someone mistakes such an activity for a different one. We possess criteria for correct and appropriate performance and identification of such activities but are, ordinarily, unable to formulate them. Reflection subject to bracketing of existence yields formulations of these criteria. The phenomenologists regarded all statements resulting from such reflection as nonempirical, but there is no ground for thinking that this is true. These phenomenologists also believed that all the activities which are reflectively described and clarified after bracketing existence are intentional activities. This view can also be shown to be open to objections, but from these two doubtful assertions we can extract a more defensible characterization of phenomena than the one reached so far. So far three necessary conditions for phenomena have been

listed: (1) They must be essences which are (2) intuited (3) as the result of the exemplary reflection that requires bracketing existence. We now add a fourth condition, namely, that statements about phenomena must be limited to statements about intentional acts.

The noun "intentionality" does not refer to a thing (as does, for instance, "sodality") but to the state of an entity—the state of being intentional. Although Husserl used "intentional" in all kinds of contexts, in its primary sense it is an adjective modifying "act"; being intentional is a characteristic of acts. In this employment, "intentional" has an ordinary meaning as a synonym for "deliberate" or "done on purpose," and a philosophical meaning different from, although related to, its ordinary, nonphilosophical meaning. The philosophical use of the term dates back to scholastic philosophy. Later, it completely disappeared from the philosophical vocabulary until it was reintroduced in 1874 by the Austrian philosopher Franz Brentano. Husserl, a student of Brentano's, gives credit to Brentano for reintroducing intentionality into philosophical discussion but adds that intentionality became a fruitful philosophical concept only in phenomenology.

Intentional acts have four aspects, and there are four distinct questions we can ask about them. The sentence "Luther thought that the devil was in his cell" is the complete description of an intentional act. We can ask who is performing an intentional act, and the answer consists of a proper name ("Luther"). It could also be a personal pronoun ("I" or "we") or a definite description ("the father of the Reformation"). We can, in the second place, ask what this person is doing, and the answer will consist of the inflected form of a verb ("thinks," "thought"). The third question concerns the intentional object of the act, what the act is about. In the example, Luther is thinking about the devil. Finally, we can ask in what manner or under what description the intentional object is object of the act; in the example, what is Luther thinking about the devil? "The devil is in my cell."

The intentional act, having four elements, is a tetradic relation. So, for instance, is the relation described in the sentence "I place the book on the table." Here also there are four elements: the subject or agent (myself), my action (placing), what I place (the book), and the table on which I place it. There is, however, an important difference between the two cases. The second statement is false unless there is a table on which I place the book. If the statement as a whole is true, the final of the four terms in the tetradic relation must also exist. It would be self-contradictory to say "I place the book on the table . . . but there is no table."

We can therefore infer the existence of the table from the truth of the statement "I place the book on the table." This is not so in the case of intentional acts. If it is true that Luther thought that the devil was in his cell, it is not therefore true that the devil exists, let alone that he was in Luther's cell. Luther might have had hallucinations; he might have been the victim of religious madness; or he might have been drunk. All three of these are situations in which we are inclined to see things that are not there or to believe that things exist which in fact do not. Nor can we conclude from the truth of the original sentence that the devil does not exist or was not in Luther's cell. The same holds of whatever is thought or believed to be the case. A belief that my wallet was stolen or that there are leprechauns does not allow the inference that there was a thief who stole my wallet or that there are leprechauns. The same is true of perceiving, of hoping, expecting, doubting, fearing, and all similar activities. The truth of a statement describing someone's intentional act does not allow the inference of either the existence or the nonexistence of what the act is about. This distinguishes intentional acts and their four elements from genuine tetradic relations, where the existence of all four elements can be inferred from the truth of a description of the relation.

The noninference criterion. The usual discussion of Husserl's doctrine of intentionality presents intentionality as (1) the defining characteristic of consciousness in the ordinary sense of that term, which (2) consists in the fact that all consciousness is consciousness *of* something. The first point is false; the latter is true but trivial. It merely asserts that to be conscious is to be related to something. But I am also related to something if, for instance, I own property. In that case I am the owner *of* something. But being the owner of something is not an intentional act because the existence of the object owned can be inferred from the fact that I own it. The existence or nonexistence of the object of the intentional act, however, cannot be inferred from the true description of that act. (We shall call this the "noninference criterion"). This, rather than merely being related to an object, is the property of intentional acts that distinguishes them from all other kinds of tetradic relations. Hence, it is a defining characteristic.

Two examples will show that intentionality is not the exclusive property of consciousness. Consider the sentences "Luther threw an inkwell in order to injure the devil" and "The rat pushes the lever in order to obtain food." Both sentences express tetradic relations: the agent (Luther, the rat), what he does (throwing, pushing), what he does it with (the inkwell, the lever), and the object of the activity (injuring the devil, obtaining food). It may be said that these are not intentional acts because the object in each case is not what the act is about but is, rather, an aim or a purpose. The acts described in these two sentences are intentional in the ordinary sense of being purposive, but according to the noninference criterion, they are also intentional in the philosophical sense because we cannot infer from the first sentence that the devil was injured and hence we cannot infer that the devil exists or does not exist, nor can we infer from the second that food was obtained by pushing the lever.

The acts described in the two sentences are not acts of consciousness or mental acts in the traditional sense. Throwing and pushing have traditionally been regarded as physical acts, but they differ according to the purpose served. When throwing something at a person in order to injure, one throws differently (much harder, for instance) than when one throws someone a cigarette in order to be helpful. Although physical, both of these acts are intentional in the philosophical sense. Hence intentionality is not, as Brentano thought and Husserl thought at certain times, the defining characteristic of consciousness in the ordinary sense. Husserl became aware of this and

redefined "consciousness," in his later writings, by extending the term beyond its ordinary meaning to apply not only to mental acts but also to all kinds of activities, even to those usually regarded as physical, as long as they are intentional. Here intentionality became the defining characteristic of consciousness because this was how consciousness was defined. Husserl would perhaps not have wanted to apply "consciousness" to the behavior of animals, but his views on this point are not well known.

Inference. The verb "to infer" is used in a variety of senses in English, so it must be made clear in what sense it is used in the formulation of the noninference criterion. Suppose I see my foot as it sticks out unshod from my trouser leg and I say, "There's my foot." If someone asks me why I think that my foot is there (exists), I answer, "Because I see it" (or "Because I see something that looks like my foot"). In a loose sense of "infer," I may be said to infer the existence of my foot from the fact that I see it. In this sense of "infer," therefore, the correct description of an intentional act ("I see what looks like my foot") allows me to infer the existence of what I see (my foot). But this is inference in a loose sense. The conclusion does not follow necessarily from the premises. It is possible that the premise should be true and the conclusion false, as happens, for instance, when I am having hallucinations. There I see what looks like my foot, but the foot is not there. Common examples of this are the so-called phantom feelings—an amputee feels his foot long after it has been amputated. It is true that he feels his foot, but it is false that his foot is there. But if I say that I know my foot is under the table because I feel it, the inference (in the loose sense) is correct.

The sense of "to infer" used in the noninference criterion is stricter. In this sense we say that something is inferred from a premise or set of premises if the falsity of the conclusion is incompatible with the truth of the premise(s). In this sense it was said earlier that we can infer from the truth of "I place the book on the table" that there is a table. It would be self-contradictory to say "I place the book on the table . . . but there is no table" and to claim that both parts of this compound statement are true. It is in this stringent sense of "to infer" that the noninference criterion denies that we can infer the existence of the object of the intentional act from a true description of the act itself. The noninference criterion does not deny that feeling my foot, for instance, is often sufficient ground for saying that my foot is there. But it does deny that my foot must exist necessarily if I feel it. Intentional acts differ from other tetradic relations in that it is not inconsistent in the case of intentional acts to deny the existence of the final term of the four-term relation and to assert that the relation is described truly, but it is inconsistent to do this in the case of all nonintentional four-term relations.

Criterion is nonempirical. It is now easy to show that a statement of the noninference criterion is a nonempirical statement in the sense that no empirical statement can show it to be false. In this sense mathematical statements are nonempirical—no measurement of angles or lines in a triangle can show that geometrical statements about triangles are false. If there does appear to be a conflict between actual measurements and measurements predicted on the basis of certain geometrical propositions, we do not reject the geometrical proposition underlying our prediction; rather, we conclude that the measurements are false. The reason for this is, of course, that the procedures used in measuring presuppose the truth of the pertinent statements in geometry. In order to show that the statement of the noninference criterion is false, there must be at least one intentional act in which the existence of what the act is about or aims at follows with necessity from a true description of the act. But philosophers agree that no necessary relations are observed, or can be inferred from observations, so no statement about a necessary relation can be an empirical statement. Hence, the case needed to refute the noninference criterion cannot be described in empirical statements. It follows that the statement of the noninference criterion, not being refutable by means of an empirical statement, is not itself an empirical statement.

Intentionality as a phenomenon. The statement of the noninference criterion satisfies the fourth condition laid down for phenomena: it is a statement about intentional acts. It is easy to show that it also satisfies the other three conditions for phenomena: (1) The preceding analysis consisted of reflection subject to bracketing of existence. (2) It brought to light certain essential features of intentional acts. (3) The truth of the statements rests on intuition, in the sense discussed earlier. Intentionality is, therefore, not only one mark of phenomena but is also itself a phenomenon. It has also been shown that the description of this phenomenon contains at least one nonempirical statement, namely, the noninference criterion. There is, then, at least one statement about phenomena, as now defined, that is nonempirical. This suggests that the four conditions for phenomena constitute a complete definition. However, the four conditions for phenomena are not sufficient for a complete definition, so a fifth condition must be added—that, with respect to intentional acts, phenomena serve as criteria of coherence.

CRITERIA OF COHERENCE

Intentional acts are of two kinds; they are either purposive or about something. Purposive acts may be said to be adequate to their intentional object if the means chosen accomplish their purpose. Acts that are about some intentional object may be said to be adequate if what is believed or asserted about an object is really true, if what is questioned is questionable, if what is doubted is doubtful. Whether a given purpose is pursued correctly by using certain means depends on the nature of the purpose and of the means chosen, and on the way the means are used. Whether Luther throws the inkwell correctly at the devil depends on the weight of the inkwell, the distance between him and the devil, and how he throws. There are correct and incorrect ways of throwing inkwells or anything else. Which ways are correct and which are not is a matter of empirical fact, to be discovered by empirical study. Hence, rules about correct performance of this kind of intentional act are empirical rules. Similarly, it is in many cases an empirical question whether my beliefs are true, whether what I question is questionable, or whether

what I doubt is doubtful. It can be shown that at least some of these rules satisfy all four defining conditions for phenomena; hence, they can be regarded as statements about phenomena, as defined so far. This, in turn, shows that the four conditions laid down do not constitute a complete definition of "phenomenon," for phenomena, under this definition, are capable of being described in empirical statements. We need a fifth condition.

The following consideration will yield the required fifth condition for a complete definition of "phenomenon." Before we can ask whether any given intentional act is correctly performed—whether it is adequate to its intentional object—we must be certain that what we are asking about is a genuine intentional act. Since intentional acts have four elements—the subject (or agent), the action, the intentional object, and either the means used or what is asserted about the intentional object—we need certain rules to determine which subject can be combined with what actions, which intentional objects, and which means or assertions to form coherent intentional acts. Not just any member of each of these four classes of elements can be combined with any other to form a coherent and intelligible intentional act.

Coherence and intelligibility. The meanings of "coherent" and "intelligible" are best indicated by examples of their opposites, intentional acts that are incoherent or unintelligible. Purposive acts are not coherent and not intelligible (they "make no sense"), for instance, where the action and the means used are inappropriate to the intentional object. Someone might have said to Luther that it made no sense to throw anything at the devil because the devil is not a person but merely a symbol of evil. Not being a person, the devil has no body—and hence no location—and therefore cannot be made the target of any physical missile. A different case of an incoherent purposive act is that in which the means are inappropriate to the action. "Killing a person with kindness" is a metaphorical expression precisely because it literally makes no sense; the means chosen for killing a person are utterly inappropriate. They are not inappropriate merely in the sense that someone might try to use kindness as a murder weapon and discover that it does not do the job. It is not at all clear how one would proceed literally to try to kill someone with kindness. "Killing a person with kindness" is therefore not an intelligible or coherent intentional act. Similar incoherences can be found in the other relations among the four elements of intentional acts.

Corresponding incoherences appear in intentional acts that are about something. If what I believe about something is utterly inappropriate to its intentional object, such as "The Pythagorean theorem is mellifluous and sweet-smelling," there is no way of telling or even of finding out whether the statement is true. Asserting this sentence is not an intelligible intentional act, and hence the assertion is neither true nor false. Similar incoherences can occur between the action (for instance, "I predict") and its intentional object (for instance, some past event) or what is being predicted (that something happened yesterday).

So far the notions of coherence and incoherence, of intelligibility and unintelligibility, have been exhibited within single intentional acts. Husserl pointed out that there is also coherence and intelligibility of series of acts.

Suppose that Luther, rage suffusing his face, threw an inkwell at the devil with all his might and the very next moment rushed up to him, saying, "My dear fellow, I am so sorry. How very clumsy of me. Here, let me help you." This would be very surprising because the first action seemed clearly intended to injure, the second to placate. The change between the two is unmistakable and can be described by saying that the second act has a different intentional object from the first. As juxtaposed, the two acts make no sense because they seem to be members of two incompatible series of acts. The first act seems part of a series intended to enrage or injure the devil, and the second seems part of a different series aimed at mollifying the devil. The first action clearly leads to the expectation of another angry action. The second one disappoints that expectation, so the two actions make no sense, although each by itself makes sense. As single acts they are intelligible or coherent, but they do not make sense when they come in the above order. No one can understand what Luther is up to. We know what a man is up to if we understand a sequence of his actions and have correct expectations about what he is going to do next. If our expectations are disappointed, we may conclude that the agent has changed his mind or that we did not understand him to begin with. We understand or do not understand what someone is up to if his purposive actions form a coherent or incoherent series, respectively.

All this is true irrespective of whether the series of acts is performed well or badly. Hence, there are two sets of rules governing series of acts that correspond to the two sorts of rules governing individual acts: those which govern the coherence of act series and those which govern the adequacy of the act series to its collective purpose. What a man is up to in a series of acts can be inferred only from the sequence of acts performed. But not all sequences of acts are coherent. There are, therefore, rules about intentional acts determining the conditions for coherence of any series of intentional acts. Only if a series is coherent corresponding to the rules governing coherence can the question whether the actions and the means chosen are adequate to the aim pursued in the whole series be answered in the light of the relevant facts. Empirical statements about the adequacy of actions and means to their collective end are to be distinguished from statements about the coherence of such collections of acts.

It is not necessary to cite more examples to show that a series of acts which are about something are coherent or incoherent, intelligible or unintelligible, in analogous ways. A single act of belief, assertion, or questioning may be perfectly coherent and intelligible by itself but may be entirely out of context with what precedes or follows, and it is not understood what this person, in this act, is talking about, what he is trying to say.

"Horizon." Husserl used the term "horizon" to refer to the relations of coherence and incoherence of intentional acts. "Horizon" was not intended to refer to the place where sky and earth meet but to the edge of the perceptual field, which moves and changes with movements of the head or of the entire body. The horizon metaphor suggests that as the edge of the perceptual field (the horizon) leads us to expect a continuation of what lies before us, so any given intentional act suggests further acts that would be continuous or coherent with it. What is said in one act or done in one purposive action leads one to expect a second assertion or a second action continuous with the first. The second statement is continuous with the first if it is about the same object as the first; if in the second action one is up to the same thing as in the first, the two are continuous. I know what you are talking about or what you are up to when I know what sort of thing you will say or do next.

The horizon metaphor also implies that these relations between intentional acts are necessary conditions for any act being intentional, just as it is a necessary condition for the existence of a perceptual field that it have a horizon. Something is an act of asserting, for instance, if and only if I can repeat what I said in another way; if I can amplify, clarify, explain what I said; or if I can confuse, muddle up, and utterly obfuscate what my assertions are about. It is impossible that an intentional act should be without horizons, that is, unrelated to any other intentional act.

Criteria of coherence. As the horizons of the perceptual field are to some degree indefinite, so are the horizons of intentional acts. I cannot infer from any given assertion or activity of yours that you will next assert one particular statement or do some particular action and no other. When I see a church steeple on the horizon, I know that, when I come closer, I will not see a hippopotamus at its base. But there is definitely a point in coming closer to discover what the church or the building that resembled a church from a distance looks like. Similarly, there is a point in listening to you to find out what your next statement is going to be or in watching what you are going to do. If I understand what you are talking about or what you are up to, I have some idea of what you are going to say or do next. I know the minimum conditions for your next statement and action; I know the limits beyond which your next action will not be continuous with the last or your next statement will not be about the same object as the last. Horizons are the necessary conditions for any series of assertions or activities to be intelligible. Different kinds of intentional acts have different kinds of horizons. Linguistic acts are related in terms of their meaning; purposive activities, by reference to the purpose. It is the task of phenomenology to clarify the different sorts of horizons (conditions for intelligibility) and to put into words what the horizons of individual examples of each kind of act are. Husserl called the clarification and formulation of horizons "intentional analysis." The results of such intentional analyses are statements of the criteria for the coherence of intentional act series.

Having understood what Husserl meant by "horizon" and that there are criteria for the coherence of single acts corresponding to the horizons in act series, we have found the fifth condition defining "phenomenon." Statements about phenomena must, besides satisfying the first four conditions, be about the criteria of coherence of single intentional acts or of sequences of intentional acts. When we look at any object as a phenomenon, we are trying to discover the criteria for coherence of those intentional acts in which the object (or its name or description) can figure.

ARE PHENOMENOLOGICAL STATEMENTS A PRIORI?

Traditionally philosophers have called statements "a priori" if they are (1) nonempirical and (2) necessarily true. Phenomenologists have always held that their statements are a priori. The two parts of this claim must be examined separately.

It has been shown that phenomenologists agree that their statements are nonempirical, although they disagree about the description of phenomena. Some phenomenologists were content to describe them as essences intuited, but others regarded this as insufficient and added that phenomenological descriptions must be preceded by bracketing existence. But bracketing existence also turned out to be an inadequate guarantee that phenomenological statements are nonempirical. Therefore some members of the phenomenological movement, notably Husserl, added further requirements for statements about phenomena. The preceding discussion can be summarized by stating the five conditions that any statement must satisfy if it is to be a statement about phenomena:

(1) It must be about essences.
(2) It must be self-validating (intuitive).
(3) It must be the result of bracketing existence.
(4) It must be about intentional acts.
(5) It must lay down the criteria of coherence (or intelligibility) of intentional acts.

We must now, once again, ask: Are statements of this kind nonempirical?

The senses of "empirical." The above question is not easy to answer because the term "empirical" has several meanings. We must examine some of them.

Statements asserting particular matters of fact, such as "There is a fire burning in the fireplace," are true if observation shows them to be true and false if observation shows them to be false (for instance, that the fire has gone out). They are empirical because one observation will show them to be true or false.

General statements, such as "Continuous nervous tension produces high blood pressure," are neither confirmed nor refuted by one observation or even by a few observations but only by a series of carefully controlled observations. This case concerns generalizations about observable connections.

There is a further sense of "empirical" that applies to statements about objects which are in principle nonobservable, such as "ideal gases" or "perfectly elastic bodies." Such entities cannot be observed because they do not exist, and hence we cannot frame empirical statements about them in either the particular or the general sense of "empirical." These entities, which cannot be described in observation statements, are instead defined in a series of statements constituting a scientific theory. From such a theory statements can be deduced which can be tested by reference to direct experience. If observation shows the deduced statements to be false, we must reject the theory, and hence our theoretical statements about the unob-

servable entities are indirectly refuted by observation. These statements are therefore, in this indirect way, empirical because observations can serve to show them to be false.

Phenomenological statements. Phenomenological statements, as described in the preceding sections, are not empirical in the first two senses of the term. They are not empirical in the first sense because they are never statements about individual existing intentional acts but only about the criteria governing types of acts; only particular statements are empirical in the first sense. Empirical in the second sense are generalizations derived by induction from a series of observations of particulars. Such inductive generalizations presuppose that we know what particulars belong to the class of objects to be observed. If we want to make a generalization about the relation between nervous tension and high blood pressure, we must have a very precise idea of what must count as examples of nervous tension and what blood pressure counts as "high" blood pressure. Similarly, we cannot inductively arrive at statements about intentional acts unless we are already able to differentiate a coherent intentional act from an incoherent collection of each of the four kinds of elements of intentional acts. The same applies to generalizations about coherent series of intentional acts. Nothing said by the phenomenologists should exclude the possibility of framing empirical (in the general sense) statements about intentional acts. All that is argued is that the criteria of coherence of individual acts as well as of series of acts are presupposed and therefore are not established by such inductive generalizations. Therefore, statements formulating these criteria cannot themselves be empirical generalizations.

It is undoubtedly a task for phenomenology to differentiate the different senses of "empirical," that is, to describe the different kinds of intentional acts involved in what we call experience and the criteria of coherence belonging to each kind of act. Oddly enough, the phenomenologists so far have barely begun to undertake such an examination, and hence their conviction that statements about phenomena, as now defined, are nonempirical is not supported by adequate phenomenological analyses. This important shortcoming in the theory of the phenomenological method is all the more serious because there are good reasons for thinking that there is one perfectly good sense of the words "experience" and "empirical" in which statements about phenomena, as defined, *are* empirical.

Empirical phenomena statements. In a scientific theory, the terms are defined in relation to one another in such a way that if we alter the definition of one term, the definitions of some of the other terms are also changed. The effect of such a set of interrelated definitions is to limit the contexts in which these terms may be applied. A set of phenomenological statements has a similar function; it limits the contexts in which given intentional acts may be performed. The limits imposed on these intentional acts in the phenomenological statements are interrelated as the definitions in a theory are. If we alter the limits of one intentional act, those of other acts are also changed. History and ethnology provide many examples of such changes. Among the Trobriand Islanders, for instance, successful gardening requires the use of magic. Before seedlings are planted, a spell must be spoken over them. It is very important that the magician's mouth be as close as possible to the seedlings, for otherwise some of the power of the spell will be dissipated. The power of the spell resides not in the sound waves produced by the magician but in the meaning of the terms used, something which we would not regard as a physical phenomenon. Yet the power of the magical words is here treated as if it were a physical force that varies with the distance from the object it affects. It is clear that the Trobriander does not draw a distinction between the physical and the mental, so it makes perfect sense for him to say something that makes no sense to us—that the spell must be spoken as close as possible to the seedlings in order to be effective. He imposes different limits on his intentional acts—what makes literal sense to him is to us at best symptomatic of the confusions of the "primitive" mind—and these various limits are interrelated. We can formulate them in a set of phenomenological statements that we regard as false and he regards as true. This example shows the analogy between the limitations imposed on theoretical terms by their implicit definitions in a scientific theory and the mutual limitations imposed on intentional acts and expressed in phenomenological statements.

Statements in a scientific theory limit the application of the terms. If the limits imposed allow the use of the terms in false factual statements, these limits must be altered; the theory is invalid. In analogous ways phenomenological statements may be invalidated by experience. Phenomenological statements express the limits imposed on intentional acts, and if these limits are such that we cannot distinguish true factual statements from false ones, the limits must be altered; the phenomenological statements are invalid.

In order to make true generalizations about gardening and distinguish them from false ones, we need a clear notion of causation. Causal relations as discussed in science exist only between spatiotemporally contiguous events, and this implies that only spatiotemporally located events can be either causes or effects. A clear notion of causal relations, therefore, presupposes a clear distinction between events that are and those that are not spatiotemporally located, or between physical and mental events. Where such a distinction is not drawn, no clear understanding of causal relations is possible. The Trobriander does not differentiate physical events from mental events (and forces); hence he cannot clearly differentiate causal relations from noncausal relations. As a result, he cannot make general statements about gardening that are always true or always false as tested by the information available to us. They may, of course, be always true (or false) tested by what he knows. His generalizations are about classes containing very heterogeneous types of relations, both causal and noncausal. Statements about the causal are true under very different conditions from statements about the noncausal, so his generalizations are sometimes true and sometimes false, and he does not have the vocabulary necessary to reformulate them in such a way that they are always true or always false. This shows that the Trobriander's lack of scientific information about biology is not

accidental. It is impossible for him to do natural science because his language lacks the requisite distinctions. Scientific statements cannot be made in his language, which is clear proof that it is inadequate and that the phenomenological statements describing his linguistic acts as well as the nonlinguistic ones, such as those associated with garden magic, are therefore invalid.

This argument as stated is not conclusive, but it can be strengthened to make a rather formidable case for holding that the phenomenologists are mistaken in their claim that their statements about phenomena are nonempirical in *all* senses of that term. This conclusion shows that the question asked at the very outset—what are the truth conditions of phenomenological statements—remains unanswered. In the preceding a good deal has been said about these truth conditions, but it has been shown that that answer is incomplete. The phenomenologists' account of their method not only lacks a complete theory of experience in its different forms but also a complete theory of truth, at least as that term applies to the statements in phenomenology.

The senses of "necessary." The second aspect of a priori statements is their necessity.

A priori statements are necessary because they are nonempirical; if they are true at all, they are true independently of facts about the world. Even if all the statements about this world that are now true were false, and if, therefore, our world were very different from what it is now the a priori statements would still be true. They are true whatever happens to be the case in the world. Hence we may say that, if true at all, they *must* be true regardless of any facts. For this reason the term "necessary" has often been explicated as "true for all possible worlds." A different world from ours is one whose description requires factual statements to be true that are false of our world. Since necessary statements are true whatever factual statements may or may not be true, they are true for all possible worlds. A statement is necessary, therefore, to the extent that its truth is logically independent of the truth or falsity of empirical statements. It follows that there are different senses of "necessity" to correspond to the different senses of "empirical." There are, therefore, also different senses of "a priori." Hence, phenomenological statements are clearly a priori insofar as they are not empirical in the first two senses of that term. But phenomenological statements are empirical in a third sense and are therefore not a priori in that sense of "a priori" which contrasts with this third sense of "empirical."

Necessary phenomena statements. In the sense explained, statements are necessary if they are *true* necessarily. But if statements about phenomena are a priori— necessarily true *and* nonempirical—they are necessary in a second sense: their truth is a necessary condition for any empirical statement to be *capable* of being either true or false. An empirical statement can be either true or false only if it is meaningful, and that depends on the coherence of the intentional act and of the intentional act series in which it is asserted. But as was seen, the coherence of such acts and act series is presupposed by any question about the adequacy of intentional acts to their intentional objects. Hence the statements that lay down the criteria for coherence of all kinds of intentional acts, including acts of asserting, must be true if we are to be able to decide whether any given intentional act is adequate to its intentional object—for instance, whether an assertion is true or a purposive action is successful. Insofar as phenomenological statements are a priori, they are, therefore, necessary in this second sense; they are presuppositions for the adequacy or inadequacy of any intentional act to its intentional object. The truth of phenomenological statements is logically prior to the truth or falsity of all empirical statements and to the correctness of all purposive actions.

CONTEMPORARY PHENOMENOLOGY

Political events in Europe and the shifting winds of doctrine caused the phenomenological movement to lose much of its original momentum after Husserl's death in 1938. The best-known contemporary philosophers who have used the term "phenomenology" in descriptions of their own work are Martin Heidegger in Germany and Jean-Paul Sartre and Maurice Merleau-Ponty in France. All three use the term "phenomenology" in appreciably different senses from the phenomenologists previously discussed.

Heidegger. Heidegger was a student of Husserl's and at one time was a coeditor of the *Jahrbuch*. In that journal (Vol. 8, 1927) appeared his first major work, *Sein und Zeit* (translated by J. Macquarrie and E. Robinson as *Being and Time*, New York, 1962). The phenomenologists so far discussed all agreed that it is the task of phenomenology reflectively to bring to light the criteria implicit in the intentional acts we perform in everyday life, in which we act in, get to know about, and learn to master that everyday world which Husserl christened the *Lebenswelt* ("world in which we live"). The emphasis here is on putting into words what is commonly and familiarly done without one's knowing how to describe accurately what he is doing. Heidegger also regards phenomenology as a sort of reflection but not a reflection designed to put into words what is familiar in performance.

On the contrary, Heidegger's brand of phenomenology tries to open the way back to what has, he thinks, become completely unfamiliar, what he calls *Sein* (being). He recognizes that "being" has become a philosophically empty word. Hence we cannot gain a better understanding of being by reflecting only about the world insofar as it is familiar to us, for in that world "being" has become almost meaningless; there are very few contexts in which it makes sense to talk about "being." Thus, reflection about the criteria of intelligibility, which we use now, will not reveal much about being. Rather than reflect on these criteria, Heidegger proposes to ask why "being" has become almost meaningless to us. But since a question is intelligible only to the extent that we can specify the sort of answer we expect, and since an answer to Heidegger's question would require a language in which "being" is meaningful, even an intelligible formulation of his question involves him in the attempt to re-create a very different language, in which "being," far from being an empty word, is the richest and most important concept. This language, he believes, is the language used by the pre-Socratic philosophers. Heidegger's phenomenology thus leads him into an

enterprise utterly unfamiliar to the other phenomenologists, the attempt to develop a new philosophical language by re-creating that of the pre-Socratic philosophers.

Sartre. Sartre's major work, *L'Être et le néant* (Paris, 1943; translated by H. E. Barnes as *Being and Nothingness*, New York, 1957), bears the subtitle *An Essay in Phenomenological Ontology*. The work does not, however, contain any explicit discussion of phenomenology, nor has Sartre explained his conception of phenomenology at length in any other work. More than once he has differentiated phenomenology from science by saying that phenomenology makes statements about essences; science, about facts. In one long essay, "Là Transcendence de l'égo" (*Recherches Philosophiques*, Vol. 6, 1936–1937; translated by F. Williams and R. Kirkpatrick and published in book form as *The Transcendence of the Ego*, New York, 1958), he takes sharp issue with Husserl's transcendental phenomenology, particularly with the claim that in phenomenology we discover that there is a transcendental ego. It would seem, then, that Sartre is a phenomenologist who, like many others, adopts the descriptive approach to essences but refuses to follow Husserl in his later developments of the theory of the phenomenological method. But Sartre differs radically insofar as he is not averse to constructing philosophical theories. His major work is an example of constructive philosophy in precisely that sense in which phenomenologists attacked it in their polemic against reductionism. Sartre's conception of phenomenology is no clearer if we look at his actual practice of the method than if we consider his sparse statements about it. If Sartre practices phenomenology at all, the term as used by him and as applicable to his procedures has a different meaning from the one explicated in this discussion.

Merleau-Ponty. Merleau-Ponty's major work bears the title *Phénoménologie de la perception* (Paris, 1945; translated by Colin Smith as *Phenomenology of Perception*, London, 1962). Unlike Sartre, he includes an introduction devoted to a clarification of "phenomenology." The clear and explicit result of this discussion is that Merleau-Ponty has interpreted the notion of phenomenology in a sense rather different from that subscribed to wholly or partly by members of the phenomenological movement, as well as from that used by either Heidegger or Sartre.

These three philosophers use "phenomenology" in appreciably different ways from those in which it has been used by the phenomenologists discussed. To be sure, there were also radical and profound disagreements among the latter about the nature and presuppositions of the phenomenological method, but they regarded these differences as different results arrived at by applying the same method. In this sense these philosophers—Husserl, Pfänder, Geiger, Becker, and Reinach, among others—can be regarded as belonging to one school of philosophy. All of them shared certain common views at the outset, and they believed that they were using the same method. But Heidegger, Sartre, and Merleau-Ponty begin doing their respective brands of phenomenology by explaining what they consider phenomenology to be and how their conception differs from that of Husserl. They do not begin with the same common views, as did the earlier phenomenologists; and they do not regard their method as identical with that of Husserl and the other phenomenologists. For this reason they do not belong to the same school of philosophy.

(See also the articles BINSWANGER, LUDWIG; BRENTANO, FRANZ; EXISTENTIALISM; EXISTENTIAL PSYCHOANALYSIS; HEIDEGGER, MARTIN; INTENTIONALITY; LIFE, MEANING AND VALUE OF; PSYCHOLOGISM; SARTRE, JEAN-PAUL; SCHELER, MAX; TIME, CONSCIOUSNESS OF. See Phenomenology in Index for articles on philosophers who are commonly classed as phenomenologists.)

Bibliography

ORIGINAL WORKS IN GERMAN

Husserl, Edmund, *Husserliana*, Vol. I, *Cartesianische Meditationen.* The Hague, 1950. The shortest, though not always easy, introduction to Husserl's mature conception of phenomenology.

Husserl, Edmund, *Husserliana*, Vol. VI, *Die Krisis der europäischen Wissenschaften und die transcendentale Phänomenologie.* The Hague, 1954. A very late work of Husserl's; introduces the important notion of the *Lebenswelt*, the world of everyday life.

Husserl, Edmund, *Husserliana*, Vols. VII and VIII, *Erste Philosophie.* The Hague, 1956–1959. Husserl's lectures on the history of philosophy and phenomenology; more accessible than many of his other writings.

Husserl, Edmund, and others, eds., *Jahrbuch für Philosophie und phänomenologische Forschung*, 11 vols. Halle, 1913–1930. Contains representative writings of all the major phenomenologists.

Reinach, Adolf, "Über Phänomenologie," in his *Gesammelte Schriften*, Hedwig Conrad-Martius, ed. Munich, 1921. A brief and very lucid statement of an early conception of phenomenology.

ORIGINAL WORKS IN TRANSLATION

Husserl, Edmund, "Phenomenology," translated by C. V. Solomon, in *Encyclopaedia Britannica*, 14th ed. 1927. Vol. XVII, pp. 699–702.

Husserl, Edmund, *Cartesian Meditations*, translated by Dorion Cairns. The Hague, 1960.

Husserl, Edmund, *Ideas*, translated by W. R. Boyce Gibson. New York, 1931.

Husserl, Edmund, *The Idea of Phenomenology*, translated by William P. Alston and George Nakhnikian. The Hague, 1964. Translates a series of lectures given in 1907 in which the transcendental-phenomenological reduction is introduced.

Husserl, Edmund, *Phenomenology and the Crisis of Philosophy: Philosophy as Science and Philosophy and the Crisis of European Man*, translated with notes and introduction by Quentin Lauer. New York, 1965. Contains a long essay, published in 1910, in which Husserl provides an expanded version of his earlier polemics against psychologism. This book also translates portions of Husserl's late work, *Krisis*.

BOOKS ON PHENOMENOLOGY

Bachelard, Suzanne, *La logique de Husserl*. Paris, 1951. A lucid and detailed discussion of Husserl's *Formale und Transcendentale Logik* (1929).

Berger, Gaston, *Le Cogito dans la philosophie de Husserl*. Paris, 1941. One of the earliest and still one of the best monographs on one aspect of Husserl's thought.

Brand, Gerd, *Welt, Ich und Zeit*. The Hague, 1955. Attempts a summary of Husserlian phenomenology on the basis of unpublished manuscripts. Rather general but often illuminating.

Farber, Marvin, ed., *Philosophical Essays in Memory of Edmund Husserl*. Cambridge, Mass., 1940. A collection of stimulating and sometimes informative essays on different aspects of Husserl's work.

Mohanty, J. N., *Edmund Husserl's Theory of Meaning*. The Hague, 1964. An interesting discussion of Husserl's early work in the light of the treatment given the same questions by Russell, Moore, and others.

Spiegelberg, Herbert, *The Phenomenological Movement*, 2 vols. The Hague, 1960. Discusses phenomenology in general as well as individual contributors to the movement. Extremely informative.

ARTICLES ON PHENOMENOLOGY

Ayer, A. J., and Taylor, Charles, "Phenomenology and Linguistic Analysis." *PAS*, Supp. Vol. 33 (1959).

Boehm, Rudolf, "Basic Reflection on Husserl's Phenomenological Reduction." *International Philosophical Quarterly*, Vol. 5 (1965), 183–202.

Downes, Chauncey, "On Husserl's Approach to Necessary Truth." *The Monist*, Vol. 19 (1965), 87–106.

Findlay, J. N., "Phenomenology," in *Encyclopaedia Britannica*, 1965 ed.

Ryle, Gilbert, "Phenomenology." *PAS*, Supp. Vol. 11 (1932).

Spiegelberg, Herbert, "Toward a Phenomenology of Experience." *American Philosophical Quarterly*, Vol. 1 (1964), 1–8.

RICHARD SCHMITT

PHILO JUDAEUS (fl. 20 B.C.–A.D. 40), Jewish Hellenistic philosopher. The son of a wealthy and prominent Alexandrian family, Philo was well educated in both Judaism and Greek philosophy. Little is known about the actual events of his life except that in A.D. 40 the Jewish community of Alexandria sent him as the head of a delegation to Emperor Caligula to seek redress from the wrongs which the gentile population inflicted upon the Jews. His *Legacy to Gaius* tells the story of this mission. Although he also wrote moral and philosophic treatises on problems then current, the main bulk of his writings are philosophic discourses on certain topics of the Hebrew Scripture. In content they are, on the one hand, an attempt to interpret the scriptural teachings in terms of Greek philosophy and, on the other, an attempt to revise Greek philosophy in the light of those scriptural traditions.

The scriptural teachings with which Philo set out to revise Greek philosophy contained certain definite conceptions of the nature of God and his relation to the world but only vague allusions to the structure and composition of the world. In dealing with the latter, therefore, he felt free to select from the various views of Greek philosophers whichever seemed to him the most reasonable, although occasionally he supported the selection by a scriptural citation. In dealing with the conception of God, however, he approached Greek philosophic views critically, rejecting those which were diametrically opposed to his scriptural traditions and interpreting or modifying those which were plastic enough to lend themselves to remolding.

God, Platonic ideas, creation. Of the various conceptions of God in Greek philosophy, Philo found that the most compatible with scriptural teaching was Plato's conception, in the *Timaeus*, of a God who had existed from eternity without a world and then, after he had brought the world into existence, continued to exist as an incorporeal being over and above the corporeal world. But to Plato, in the *Timaeus*, besides the eternal God, there were also eternal ideas. Philo had no objection to the existence of ideas as such, for he held that there was a scriptural tradition for the existence of ideas. But he could not accept the eternity of the ideas, for, according to his scriptural belief, God alone is eternal. By a method of harmonization that had been used in Judaism in reconciling inconsistencies in Scripture, Philo reconciled the *Timaeus* with the scriptural tradition by endowing the ideas with a twofold stage of existence: first, from eternity they existed as thoughts of God; then, prior to the creation of the world they were created by God as real beings. He may have found support for the need of such a harmonization in the many conflicting statements about the ideas in Plato's dialogues.

The ideas, which in Plato are always spoken of as a mere aggregation, are integrated by Philo into what he terms "an intelligible world," an expression that does not occur in extant Greek philosophic writings before him. Then, following a statement by Aristotle that the "thinking soul" (that is, nous), "is the place of forms" (that is, ideas), Philo places the intelligible world of ideas in a nous, which, under the influence of scriptural vocabulary, he surnamed Logos. Accordingly, he speaks also of the Logos as having the aforementioned two stages of existence.

For the same reason that he could not accept the view that the ideas are eternal, Philo also could not accept the view commonly held by contemporary students of Plato that the pre-existent matter out of which, in the *Timaeus,* the world was created was eternal. But as a philosopher he did not like to reject altogether the reputable Platonic conception of a pre-existent matter. And so here, too, he solved the difficulty by the method of harmonization. There was indeed a pre-existent matter, but that pre-existent matter was created. There were thus to him two creations, the creation of the pre-existent matter out of nothing and the creation of the world out of that pre-existent matter. For this too, it can be shown, he may have found support in certain texts of Plato.

In the *Timaeus,* Plato describes the creation of the world as an act which God "willed" ($\dot{\epsilon}\beta o\nu\lambda\dot{\eta}\theta\eta$), and similarly the indestructibility of the world is described by him as being due to the "will" ($\beta o\dot{\nu}\lambda\sigma\iota\varsigma$) of God. Presumably, by will in its application to God, Plato here means the necessary expression of God's nature, so that the creation of the world, and of this particular world of ours, was an act that could not be otherwise; and similarly the indestructibility of the world is something that cannot be otherwise. Philo, however, following the scriptural conception of God as an all-powerful free agent, takes the will by which God created the world to mean that had God willed, he could have either not created the world or created another kind of world. And similarly, if it be his will, he can destroy the world, although, on the basis of a scriptural verse, Philo believed that God would not destroy it.

Laws of nature, miracles, providence. The scriptural conception of God as an all-powerful free agent is extended by Philo to the governance of the world.

Finding scriptural support for the belief in causality and in the existence of certain laws of nature current among Greek philosophers, except the Epicureans, Philo conceived of God's governance of the world as being effected by intermediary causes and by laws of nature which God had implanted in the world at the time of its creation. He even tried his hand at classifying the laws of nature which happen to be mentioned by various Greek philosophers. But in opposition to the Greek philosophers, to whom these laws of nature were inexorable, he maintained that God has the power to infringe upon the laws of his own making and create what are known as miracles. These miracles, however, are not created arbitrarily. They are always created with design and wisdom for the good of deserving individuals or deserving groups of individuals or mankind as a whole, for, to Philo, God governs by direct supervision not only the world as a whole but also the individual human beings within the world. To express this particular departure of his from the generality of Greek philosophers, Philo gave a new meaning to the Greek term $\pi\rho\acute{o}\nu o\iota\alpha$, "providence." To those Greek philosophers who made use of this term it meant universal providence, that is, the unalterable operation of the inexorable laws of nature whereby the continuity and uniformity of the various natural processes in the world are preserved. To Philo it means individual providence, that is, the suspension of the laws of nature by the will and wisdom and goodness of God for the sake of human beings whose life or welfare is threatened by the ordinary operation of those laws of nature. With this conception of individual providence, Philo takes up the discussion of the human soul.

Soul and will. On the whole, Philo's conception of the soul is made up of statements derived from various dialogues of Plato. He distinguishes between irrational souls, which are created together with the bodies of both men and animals, and rational souls, which were created at the creation of the world, prior to the creation of bodies. Of these pre-existent rational souls, some remain bodiless but others become invested with bodies. The former are identified by Philo with the angels of Scripture. Having in mind certain passages in Plato where such unbodied souls are identified with the popular Greek religious notions of demons and heroes, but knowing that Plato himself and also Aristotle and the Stoics dismissed these popular notions as mere myths, Philo says that the angels of Moses are what philosophers call demons and heroes, but he warns the reader not to take the existence of angels as mere myths. With regard to the pre-existent rational souls that become embodied, he says, following Plato, that they are equal in number to the stars and are to be placed in newly born human beings whose bodies are already endowed with irrational souls. Again following Plato, Philo says that the irrational souls die with the bodies, whereas the rational souls are immortal. But he differs from Plato in his conception of the immortality of the soul. To Plato, the soul is immortal by nature and is also indestructible by nature. To Philo, immortality is a grace with which the soul was endowed by the will and power of God, and consequently it can be destroyed by the will and power of God if it has proved itself unworthy of the grace bestowed upon it.

A similar revision was also introduced by Philo into the Greek philosophic conception of the human will. In Greek philosophy, a distinction is made between voluntary and involuntary acts. But since all the Greek philosophers, except the Epicureans, believed in causality and in the inexorability of the laws of nature, for them the human will, to which they ascribed the so-called voluntary acts, is itself determined by causes and is subject to those inexorable laws of nature which govern the universe, including man, who is part of it. To all of them, except the Epicureans, no human act was free in the sense that it could be otherwise. The term "voluntary" was used by them only as a description of an act which is performed with knowledge and without external compulsion. To all of them, therefore, there was no free will except in the sense of what may be called relative free will. To Philo, however, just as God in his exercise of individual providence may see fit to infringe upon the laws of nature and create miracles, so has he also seen fit to endow man with the miraculous power to infringe upon the laws of his own nature, so that by the mere exercise of his will man may choose to act contrary to all the forces in his nature. This conception of free will is what may be called absolute free will.

Knowledge. Philo also revised the philosophic conception of human knowledge, including the philosophic conceptions of man's knowledge of God. Human knowledge, like all other events in the world, including human actions, is, according to Philo, under the direct supervision of God. Like all other events in the world, which are to Philo either natural, in the sense that they are operated by God through the laws of nature which he has implanted in the world, or supernatural, in the sense that they are miraculously created by God in infringement upon those laws of nature, so also human knowledge is either natural or supernatural, called by Philo "prophetic," that is, divinely revealed.

Under natural knowledge, Philo deals with all those various types of knowledge from sensation to ratiocination that are dealt with by Greek philosophers, especially Plato and the Stoics. He presents prophetic knowledge as a substitute for that type of knowledge which in Greek philosophy is placed above the various senso-ratiocinative types of knowledge and is described as recollection by Plato, as the primary immediate principles by Aristotle, and as the primary conceptions by the Stoics. Like all miracles, prophetic knowledge is part of God's exercise of his providence over individuals, groups of individuals, or mankind in general. An example of prophetic knowledge due to God's exercise of his providence over individuals is Philo's account of his own experience: often, in the course of his investigation of certain philosophic problems, after all the ordinary processes of reasoning had failed him, he attained the desired knowledge miraculously by divine inspiration. An example of prophetic knowledge due to God's exercise of his providence over a group of individuals, as well as over mankind in general, is Philo's recounting of the revelation of the law of Moses.

Man's knowledge of God. Corresponding to the two kinds of human knowledge are two ways by which, according to Philo, man may arrive at a knowledge of God—an indirect ratiocinative way and a direct divinely revealed way. Philo describes the indirect way as the knowledge of the existence of God which the "world teaches" us, and he deals with the various proofs for the existence of God advanced by Greek philosophers. Most acceptable to him is the Platonic form of the cosmological proof in the *Timaeus,* inasmuch as it is based on the premise of a created world. He modifies the Aristotelian form of the cosmological proof so as to establish the existence of a prime mover, not of the motion of the world but of its existence. He similarly modifies the Stoic proof from the human mind to establish the existence not of a corporeal God immanent in the world but of an incorporeal God above the world.

In his discussion of the direct way of knowing God, however, Philo makes no mention of the Stoic proof of the innateness of the idea of God. His own direct way of knowing God he describes as a "clear vision of the Uncreated One." But as he goes on to explain it, this direct way of knowing God is only another version of the various indirect ways of knowing him and is similarly based upon the contemplation of the world. The difference between the indirect and direct ways is this: in the case of the various indirect ways, both the knowledge of the world and of the existence of God derived therefrom are attained laboriously by the slow process of observation and logical reasoning; in the case of the direct way, both the knowledge of the world and of the existence of God derived therefrom are flashed upon the mind suddenly and simultaneously by divine inspiration.

But the knowledge of God which man may gain by either of these two ways is, according to Philo, only a knowledge of his existence, not a knowledge of his essence; for as Philo maintains, "it is wholly impossible that God according to his essence should be known to any creature." God is thus said by him to be "unnamable" (ἀκατόνομαστος), "ineffable" (ἄρρητος), and "incomprehensible" (ἀκατάληπτος). This distinction between the knowability of God's existence and the unknowability of his essence does not occur in Greek philosophy prior to Philo. In fact, in none of the extant Greek philosophic literature prior to Philo do the terms "unnamable," "ineffable," and "incomprehensible," in the sense of incomprehensible by the mind, occur as predications of God. Moreover, it can be shown that both Plato and Aristotle held that God was knowable and describable according to his essence. Philo was thus the first to introduce this view into the history of philosophy, and he had arrived at it neither by Scripture alone nor by philosophy alone. He had arrived at it by a combination of the scriptural teaching of the unlikeness of God to anything else and the philosophic teaching that the essence of a thing is known through the definition of the thing in terms of genus and specific difference, which means that the essence of a thing is known only through its likeness to other things in genus and species. Since God is unlike anything else, he is, as Philo says, "the most generic being" (τὸ γενικώτατον), that is, the *summum genus,* and hence he cannot be defined and cannot be known.

As a corollary of this conception of the unknowability and ineffability of God, it would have to follow that one could not properly speak of God except in negative terms, that is, in terms which describe his unlikeness to other things. But still Scripture repeatedly uses positive terms as descriptions of God. All such terms, explains Philo, whatever their external grammatical form, whether adjectives or verbs, are to be taken as having the meaning of what Aristotle calls property, and the various terms by which God is described are to be taken as mere verbal variations of the property of God to act, in which he is unlike all other beings. For to act is the unique property of God; the property of all created beings is to suffer action.

Theocratic government. Philo widened the meaning of the conception of natural law in its application to laws governing human society. To Greek philosophers, with the exception of the Sophists, this application of the conception of natural law (or, as they would say, law in accordance with nature) meant that certain laws enacted by philosophers in accordance with what they described as reason or virtue were also in a limited sense in accordance with nature, that is to say, in the mere sense that they were in accordance with certain impulses, capacities, rational desires which exist in men by nature. The Greek philosophers assumed, however, that no law enacted for the government of men, even when enacted by philosophers in accordance with reason and virtue, can be regarded as natural law in the sense of its being fully in harmony with the eternal and all-embracing laws of nature by which the world is governed. Philo agrees with the philosophers as to the limited sense in which enacted human law may be regarded as natural law but argues that a law revealed by God, who is the creator of the world (as, to Philo, the law of Moses was), is fully in harmony with the laws of nature, which God himself has implanted in the world for its governance. To Philo, therefore, natural law came to mean a divinely revealed law.

This widened conception of natural law led Philo to answer the question raised by Greek philosophers as to what was the best form of government. To both Plato and Aristotle no form of government based upon fixed law can be the best form of government, and Plato explicitly maintains that the best form of government is that of wise rulers who are truly possessed of science, whether they rule according to law or without law and whether they rule with or without the consent of the governed.

Against this, Philo argues that the best form of government is that based upon fixed law, not indeed upon man-made fixed law, but upon a divinely revealed fixed law. In a state governed by such a divinely revealed law, every individual has his primary allegiance to God and to the law revealed by God. Whatever human authority exists, whether secular, governing the relation of man to man, or religious, governing the relation of man to God, that authority is derived from the law and functions only as an instrument of the application of the law and its interpretation. Such a state, whatever its external form of government, is really ruled by God, and Philo came near coining the term "theocracy" as a description of it; the term was actually so coined and used later, by Flavius Josephus. But Philo preferred to describe it by the term "democracy," which he uses not in its ordinary sense, as a description of a special form of government in contradistinction to that of monarchy and aristocracy, but rather as a description of a special principle of government, namely, the principle of equality before the law, which to him may be adopted and practiced by any form of government.

Virtue. In the course of his attempt to analyze the laws of Moses in terms of Greek philosophy, Philo injects himself into the controversy between the Peripatetics and the Stoics over the definition of virtue. Guided by scriptural tradition, he sides with Aristotle in defining virtue as a mean between two vices; hence, in opposition to the Stoics, he maintains that virtue is not the extirpation of all the emotions, that some emotions are good, that there is a difference of degree of importance between various virtues and various vices, and that the generality of human beings are neither completely virtuous nor completely wicked but are in a state which is intermediate between these two extremes and are always subject to improvement. He maintains, however, that by the grace of God some exceptional persons may be born with a thoroughly sinless nature.

Following Plato and Aristotle, both of whom include under the virtue of justice certain other virtues which they consider akin to justice, but guided also by scriptural tradition, Philo includes under justice two virtues that are entirely new and are never mentioned in any of the lists of virtues recorded under the names of Greek philosophers. Thus, on the basis of the scriptural verse (Genesis 15.6) that "Abraham had faith ($\epsilon\pi i\sigma\tau\epsilon\nu\sigma\epsilon\nu$) in God and it was counted to him for justice ($\delta\iota\kappa\alpha\iota\sigma\sigma\nu\nu\eta\nu$)," Philo includes "faith" ($\pi i\sigma\tau\iota s$), which he takes to mean faith in the revealed teachings of Scripture, as a virtue under what the philosophers call the virtue of justice. Similarly, because the Hebrew term ṣedakah in Scripture is translated in the Septuagint both by $\delta\iota\kappa\alpha\iota\sigma\sigma\nu\nu\eta$, "justice" (Genesis 18.19) and by $\epsilon\lambda\epsilon\eta\mu\sigma\sigma\nu\nu\eta$, "mercy," "alms" (Deuteronomy 6.25, 24.13), Philo includes "humanity" ($\phi\iota\lambda\alpha\nu\theta\rho\omega\pi i\alpha$), in the sense of giving help to those who are in need of it, as a virtue under the philosophic virtue of justice. But on the basis of Scripture only, without any support from philosophy, he describes also "repentance" ($\mu\epsilon\tau\alpha\nu\sigma\iota\alpha$) as a virtue. In Greek philosophy, repentance is regarded as a weakness rather than as a virtue.

His scripturally based conception of free will as absolute led Philo to give a new meaning to the voluntariness of virtue and the voluntariness of the emotion of desire as used in Greek philosophy. Both Aristotle and the Stoics, using the term "voluntary" in the relative sense of free will, agree that virtue is voluntary, but they disagree as to the voluntariness of the emotions. To Aristotle, all emotions are involuntary, except the emotions of desire and anger, the latter of which by the time of Philo was subsumed under desire; to the Stoics, all emotions are voluntary. Philo, however, using the term "voluntary" in its revised sense of absolute free will, maintains that in this revised sense the term "voluntary" is to be applied, as in Aristotle, to virtue and to the emotion of desire.

Philo similarly gave a new meaning to the philosophic advice that virtue is to be practiced for its own sake. To Plato, Aristotle, and the Stoics, this advice was meant to serve as a principle of guidance to those who, like themselves, did not believe in individual providence and were not impressed by the explanations offered in the popular Greek religious theodicies as to why virtue is not always rewarded and vice not always punished. The reason underlying this advice was that since there is no certainty as to what external goods or evils would follow the practice of either virtue or vice, it is preferable for man to take his chance on the practice of virtue. This reasoning was presumably based on the common human experience that it is easier for one to induce in himself a feeling of happiness in the misery that may follow a life of virtue than it is to induce in himself a feeling of happiness in the misery, and sometimes even in the joy, that may follow a life of vice. To Philo, however, the advice to practice virtue for its own sake is based upon his belief that providence is individual;

that, despite common observation to the contrary, no virtue goes unrewarded; that acts of virtue are of graded merits; and that the reward is always in accordance with the merit of the act. With all this in the back of his mind, Philo's advice to practice virtue for its own sake (which he expresses in a different context by the statement that man is to serve God out of love and not out of expectation of a reward) means that such a practice of virtue is of the highest degree of merit, and the reward for it, which ultimately is of a spiritual nature in the hereafter, will be in accordance with its merit.

Philosophy of history. Finally, Philo's belief in God as a free agent who acts by will and design in the world as a whole, as well as in the life of individual human beings, has led him to a theo-teleological philosophy of history. Alluding to passages in Polybius' *Histories,* in which the rise and fall of cities, nations, and countries are explained by analogy to the Stoic conception of cosmic history as a cyclical process which goes on infinitely, by necessity and for no purpose, Philo describes the cyclical changes in human history as being guided by "the divine Logos" according to a preconceived plan and toward a goal which is to be reached in the course of time. The preconceived plan and goal is that ultimately "the whole world may become, as it were, one city and enjoy the best of polities, a democracy." His description of the ultimate best of polities is an elaboration of the Messianic prophecies of Isaiah and Micah as to what will come to pass in the end of days.

This is a brief synopsis of Philo's revision of Greek philosophic conceptions of the nature of God and his relation to the world and man. The historical significance of Philo is that his revision became the foundation of the common philosophy of the three religions with cognate Scriptures—Judaism, Christianity, and Islam. This triple religious philosophy, which originated with Philo, reigned supreme as a homogeneous, if not a completely unified, system of thought until the seventeenth century, when it was overthrown by Spinoza, for the philosophy of Spinoza, properly understood, is primarily a criticism of the common elements in this triple religious philosophy.

Bibliography

The present article is based upon H. A. Wolfson, *Religious Philosophy: A Group of Essays* (Cambridge, Mass., 1961), and *Philo: Foundations of Religious Philosophy in Judaism, Christianity and Islam,* 3d ed., rev., 2 vols. (Cambridge, Mass., 1962).

Philo's writings have been translated in the Loeb Classical Library: *Philo,* translated by F. H. Colson and G. H. Whitaker, 10 vols., and 2 supp. vols. translated by Ralph Marcus (Cambridge, Mass., and London, 1929–1962). *Selections from Philo,* edited with an introduction by Hans Lewy, are available in paperback in *Three Jewish Philosophers,* edited by Hans Lewy, Alexander Altmann, and Isaak Heinemann (New York and Philadelphia, 1960).

Works on Philo written from various points of view and of interest to students of philosophy are N. Bentwich, *Philo-Judaeus of Alexandria* (Philadelphia, 1910); Émile Bréhier, *Les Idées philosophiques et religieuses de Philon d'Alexandrie,* 2d ed., rev. (Paris, 1925); J. Daniélou, *Philon d'Alexandrie* (Paris, 1958); J. Drummond, *Philo Judaeus,* 2 vols. (London, 1888); E. R. Goodenough, *By Light, Light; the Mystic Gospel of Hellenistic Judaism* (New Haven, 1935); Isaak Heinemann, *Philons griechische und jüdische Bildung* (Breslau, 1932); E. Herriot, *Philon le juif* (Paris, 1898);

C. Siegfried, *Philon von Alexandria* (Jena, 1875); M. Stein, *Pilon ha-Alexandroni* (Warsaw, 1937); and W. Völker, *Fortschritt und Vollendung bei Philon von Alexandrien* (Leipzig, 1938). See also H. L. Goodhart and E. R. Goodenough, "A General Bibliography of Philo," in E. R. Goodenough, *The Politics of Philo Judaeus* (New Haven, 1938), pp. 125–348.

HARRY A. WOLFSON

PHILOLAUS OF CROTON, influential Pythagorean of the fifth century B.C. There is evidence that he was one of the few survivors of the persecutions of Pythagorean societies in southern Italy during the middle of the century and that he was responsible for the transmission of Pythagoreanism to the mainland of Greece. Plato mentions his name once in a discussion about the nature of the soul and the justification of suicide, and Aristotle makes reference to him in passing. The remaining references, together with 23 fragments attributed to him, come from later doxographic and Neo-Pythagorean authors. The impression given by these reports is that Philolaus was a thinker trained in the religious-scientific fraternity of Pythagoras; he was evidently known and respected in exile as a spokesman of his school and was the originator, after his return to Italy, of scientific doctrines, especially in embryology and pathology.

Doubts about the authenticity of Philolaus' fragments forced several modern interpreters to argue for a conservative account. They pointed out that most citations associated with the name Philolaus are of late origin and, strangely, there is silence about him among his contemporaries. These critics contend that any attempt to prove the authenticity of the fragments must rely on Plato's and Aristotle's responses to Pythagoreanism; such efforts should also be consistent with the temper of philosophy in Magna Graecia at the end of the fifth century. With such provisions in mind, Philolaus' contributions can be summarized under four or five general topics: his belief in the immortality of the soul, his theory about numbers and the construction of geometrical figures, his astronomical innovations, and his physiological and medical observations. A reconstruction along these lines reveals a philosopher of boldness and subtlety.

In the spirit of Ionian cosmogonists, Philolaus tried to explain the genesis and nature of the world by means of the infinite and the finite. He held that the world and everything in it had been constructed through the interaction of these mutually opposed principles, which sustained cosmic balance through *harmonia.* Numbers were constitutive of things and expressive of the universal order that evidenced the kinship of everything to everything. In the light of this striking doctrine, Philolaus seems to have originated the theory that the human soul is an attunement, and the body is the tomb of the soul. Most likely, the complementary religious contention that true philosophy is the study of death was also a doctrine that he proposed.

He held that we know through numbers, that all numbers relate to oddness and evenness, that the decad has unique properties, and that arithmetic is especially suited to the search for truth. Within the same framework, he suggested that the point, the "first principle leading to magnitude," generates a line (associated with the number two), a line generates a surface (classed under the number three), and a surface generates a solid (the number four). Given these properties, the elements of the world—earth, water, air, and fire—could easily be correlated to the newly discovered regular solids: the cube, icosahedron, octahedron, and tetrahedron, respectively. From such illuminating associations of ideas, together with empirical observation, Philolaus inferred a planetary earth circling a central fire, the existence of a counterearth (*antichthon*), a mirror-like reflecting sun, the "sphere of the whole" (perhaps composed of a fifth element), and the harmony of celestial motions. Through a critical use of the macrocosm–microcosm analogy he made important observations on embryological and pathological matters.

Philolaus' philosophy was the last formulation of Pythagoreanism as a comprehensive cosmological doctrine. What survived its break-up soon found a better place in the natural sciences of the fourth and third centuries B.C. and in the Platonism of later thought.

Bibliography

Burnet, John, *Early Greek Philosophy*, 4th ed. London, 1930. Pp. 276–309.

Bywater, I., "On the Fragments Attributed to Philolaus the Pythagorean." *Journal of Philology*, Vol. 1 (1868), 20–53.

Cornford, F. M., *Plato and Parmenides*. London, 1939.

Diels, H., and Kranz, W., eds. *Fragmente der Vorsokratiker*, 10th ed. Berlin, 1961. Vol. I, pp. 398–419.

Guthrie, W. K. C., *A History of Greek Philosophy*, Vol. I. Cambridge, 1962.

Heidel, W. A., "Notes on Philolaus." *American Journal of Philology*, Vol. 29 (1908).

Heidel, W. A., "The Pythagoreans and Greek Mathematics." *American Journal of Philology*, Vol. 61 (1940), 1–33.

Kirk, G. S., and Raven, J. E., *The Presocratic Philosophers*. Cambridge, 1957. Pp. 307–313.

Mondolfo, R., "Sui frammenti di Filolao." *Rivista di filologia*, Vol. 65 (1937).

Raven, J. E., *Pythagoreans and Eleatics*. Cambridge, 1948.

P. DIAMANDOPOULOS

PHILOPONUS, JOHN, sixth-century philosopher, commentator on Aristotle, grammarian, and theologian. Almost nothing is known about him except a few remarks by him and some of his contemporaries and the dates of two of his works. He was born probably in the late fifth century in Caesarea and died early in the second half of the sixth century in Alexandria, where he was one of the last holders of the chair of philosophy as the successor of Ammonius the son of Hermias. Philoponus' philosophical background was Neoplatonic; he was, probably from birth, a Christian who adhered to the Monophysite sect, which was declared heretic in the seventh century.

Philoponus' significance lies in his being, at the close of antiquity, the first to undertake a comprehensive and massive attack on the main tenets of Aristotle's physics and cosmology, an attack which was not repeated in thoroughness until Galileo. The essential part of his criticism is to be found in his commentary on Aristotle's *Meteorology*, in his book *On the Eternity of the Cosmos Against Proclus*, and in fragments of his last book against Aristotle's cosmology. This last work was quoted by his pagan adversary Simplicius in his commentaries on Aristotle's *Physics* and *On the Heavens*.

The starting point of Philoponus' natural philosophy is his monotheistic belief in the universe as a creation of God; this implies a rejection of the Greek belief in the divine nature of the stars and his subsequent assumption that there is no essential difference between celestial and terrestrial objects. The object of his attack was the dominant Aristotelian view that postulated the eternity of the universe and the dichotomy of heaven and earth, and ascribed an invariable structure to the celestial region. Denying these a priori assumptions, Philoponus supported his views by physical arguments. Against the doctrine that the celestial bodies are made of the indestructible ether (the fifth element whose natural movement is circular), Philoponus pointed to the complexity of planetary motions, which does not conform to the conception of a simple movement that Aristotle attributed to each element. The sun and stars must be composed of fire, and their different colors indicate differences in material composition; this can be inferred from the dependence of the color of terrestrial fires on the nature of their fuel. Furthermore, the different individuality of each of the celestial bodies proves their perishable nature—regardless of what matter they may be made of—and if one abstracts from their various shapes, they all possess a tridimensional extension in common with terrestrial bodies.

Against the Aristotelian and Neoplatonic belief in the eternity of the world, supported by the apparent changelessness of the heaven, Philoponus again adduces physical arguments. The universe, like every organic entity, is composed of parts that change at different and sometimes very low rates; furthermore, the greater the quantity of matter, the slower its rate of change. This applies to the immense celestial bodies as well as to terrestrial objects; although the ocean does not seem to change when seen as a whole, if it were divided into a sum of small volumes of water, the water in each container would exhibit rapid change.

In order to conceive the universe as a creation of God, Philoponus applies to it the Aristotelian category of privation. Like every physical form, the universe presupposes its privation, a nonuniverse, out of which it was created and into which it must perish. Together with this assumption of a *creatio ex nihilo*, in which God is put above nature and transcends all creations, Philoponus conceived the universe as a vast mechanism functioning according to physical laws with which matter was imbued by God at the moment of creation.

Among the many physical doctrines of Aristotle challenged by Philoponus is the concept of natural movement. By pointing out the downward motion of air rushing to fill the place of a body that is being removed beneath it, Philoponus hints at the possibility that the natural movement of air upward may also be caused by an empty space created in a higher region. Of great importance is his theory of the impetus, in which he developed earlier ideas of Hipparchus and Ptolemy and rejected the Peripatetic conception that a body can perform a motion other than its natural one only as long as a force is acting on it. It was supposed, for example, that a projectile was kept moving by the constant push of the air behind it. Philoponus' theory, supported by impressive arguments, is that an "immaterial kinetic power" is imparted by the thrower to the object thrown. This impetus keeps the projectile moving until it is consumed, whereupon it resumes its natural movement downward. Philoponus' theory of the impetus, a kind of precursor of the modern concept of momentum or kinetic energy, was taken up by Islamic philosophers in the twelfth century and later by the Western Schoolmen (Ockham, Jean Buridan, and Nicholas Oresme). Philoponus' theory of light is also related to his concept of the impetus, in that he regards light as an impetus emitted from a luminous body and propagated to the eye according to the laws of geometrical optics. This conception is opposed to that of Aristotle, who regarded light as the actualization of the potential state of a transparent medium, thus in no way associating it with motion.

Bibliography

Philoponus' main doctrines are contained in his commentaries on Aristotle, published by the Berlin Academy (1887–1901), in particular the commentaries on the *Physics, Generation and Corruption, Meteorology,* and *On the Soul.* See in addition his works *On the Eternity of the Cosmos Against Proclus* (Leipzig, 1899) and *On the Creation of the World* (Leipzig, 1897), both in Teubner's edition.

For further details of his philosophy see Gudeman, "Ioannes Philoponus," in A. Pauly and G. Wissowa, eds., *Real-Encyclopädie der classischen Altertumswissenschaft,* Vol. 18 (Stuttgart, 1916), Cols. 1764–1793; H. D. Saffrey, "Le Chrétien J. Philopon et la survivance de l'école d'Alexandrie," in *Revue des études grecques,* Vol. 67 (1954), 396–410; and S. Sambursky, *The Physical World of Late Antiquity* (London and New York, 1962).

SAMUEL SAMBURSKY

PHILOSOPHER-KINGS. The term "philosopher-king" was a suggestion of Plato's, introduced apologetically as "a very paradoxical saying" in the *Republic* (Book V, 473), developed in some detail in *Politicus,* and abandoned as unfortunately impossible in the *Laws.* In what may have been an attempt to implement his idea, Plato went to Syracuse in 367 and 361 B.C. to help his friend Dion in the education of the young king Dionysius. Plato failed in his efforts to train Dionysius in his ideals, however, and left Sicily disappointed. One of his purposes in founding the Academy may have been to train philosopher-statesmen; in fact, four (perhaps six) of its graduates became rulers. A good statement of Plato's theory is in his *Seventh Letter* (325D–326B): "Hence I was forced to say in praise of the correct philosophy that it affords a vantage point from which we can discern in all cases what is just for communities and for individuals; and that accordingly the human race will not see better days until either the stock of those who rightly and genuinely follow philosophy acquire political authority, or else the class who have political control be led by some dispensation of providence to become real philosophers."

A few later writers have expressed similar ideas, but the consensus of philosophical (not to mention kingly) opinion has been overwhelmingly against Plato's proposal. The rationalistic Kant said: "That kings should philosophize or philosophers become kings is not to be expected. But neither is it to be desired; for the possession of power is inevitably fatal to the free exercise of reason" (*Perpetual Peace,* Second Supplement). Spinoza, like Machiavelli and Hobbes, held that men and states are governed by passion, not reasons. Therefore, he claimed: "Such as persuade themselves that . . . men distracted by politics can ever be induced to live according to the bare dictates of reason must be dreaming of the poetic golden age or of a stage play" (*Political Treatise* I, 5). Kant claimed that ruling is dangerous for philosophy; Spinoza held that philosophizing is dangerous for ruling. Later thought has, if anything, heightened this contrast, on the one hand by emphasizing the philosopher's need of complete independence from authority, and on the other hand by showing that a good ruler has regard for such nonrational factors as popular wishes and national traditions. Nevertheless, all of the foregoing is compatible with the view that kings and philosophers are accountable to each other, that is, that philosophers have political functions or responsibilities, and rulers have an obligation to rationality and to ethics. Thus, violent criticism of Plato's conjunction of philosophy and kingship is generally in error. For example, when Eduard Spranger (*Lebensformen,* Part II, Chs. 1 and 5) systematically contrasted the theoretical and political types of men, and when Oswald Spengler in *Man and Technics* described an age-old struggle between kingly warriors and plebeian philosophers, they were foreshadowing the Nazi doctrines that philosophers are futile and unnecessary and that political rule is a blind, irrational, vital force.

For various reasons, then, and with varying degrees of vigor, philosophers of succeeding ages have dismissed Plato's philosopher-king as an unpractical and possibly dangerous freak. To see fully why they did so, as well as to account for the few exceptions to that generalization, one must distinguish the philosopher-king idea from other, more successful beliefs. First, it has nothing to do with the highly successful doctrine of "reason of state," the personification of the state as a rational being whose acts have reasons that individual intelligences cannot always grasp. As Louis XIV of France stated this theory "Those acts of kings that are in seeming violation of the rights of their subjects are based upon reason of State—the most fundamental of all motives, as everyone will admit, but one often misunderstood by those who do not rule." Plato's philosopher-kings, as he showed in the *Republic,* would have made frequent and unscrupulous appeal to reason of state, but most rulers have done the same without pretending to be philosophical.

Second, although Plato's philosopher-rulers (he allowed they might be one or several, a monarch or a ruling class) would constitute an elite, modern elitists have not regarded the Platonic concept as a political possibility. Gaetano Mosca held that knowledge and power were seldom (in modern times, never) fused in a ruling class, and that the best hope was that a scholarly elite might retain its independence of the intellectually undistinguished ruling elite. Vilfredo Pareto's elites consisted of those persons who managed to get to the top by any means whatever (economic, military, or religious); and although such elites might contain scientific or artistic groups, those groups never actually ruled (*Sociologia generale,* Sec. 2032). C. Wright Mills (*The Power Elite*) feared that any measure of independence for intellectuals has now disappeared and that learning's only role in society today is that of the "hired man, the well-paid expert, the mere tool of power."

Last, the rule of philosophers would not be (indeed was conceived precisely in opposition to) rule by experts. In Plato's day the would-be technocrats, the candidates for jobs as scientist-kings, sociologist-kings, or economist-kings, were the Sophists and their pupils, and Plato (in the *Gorgias*) dismissed their claims as unphilosophical, in the sense of not being based on universal principles. Even more scornfully he rejected the mere politician, whose claim to office was the cunning and tact he had acquired by long experience in political manipulation. Thus, Plato denied in advance Machiavelli's *arte dello Stato*, the art of ruling that is learned empirically in political practice.

For Plato all such technical knowledge was not only subsidiary to but also an obstacle to, the philosophical wisdom the true king needs. He contrasted opinion and knowledge, the former relating to the changing appearances of the world, the latter to the eternal Forms, or Ideas. Some such doctrine is needed if the philosopher-king suggestion is to have any plausibility. Experience shows that philosophers are inept at politics and that rulers are indifferent to philosophy; but if we believe that man and the state have a perfect, ideal model known to the philosopher but obscured by empirical variety and confusion, then we must invite the philosopher to rule, or at least to advise rulers. The more a man knows about public life, the less he may know about the ideal natures of man and the state, for he will not have had the leisure and training to contemplate those suprahistorical realities, the Forms. He will possess opinions and rules of thumb, but he will not be familiar with the heavenly original, the ideal state, of which any stable polity must be a true copy. The true philosopher, according to Plato, does have that knowledge; therefore, no law should limit his power to mold men and the state in the image of the ideal.

The philosophy that most nearly approached the supposition in the theory of Forms of two levels of being was natural-law theory. This theory, too, led in the eighteenth century to the aspiration for philosophical rule. Natural-law theorists held that society had a natural constitution which was known to reason but which was not being applied because of ignorance, tradition (called "superstition"), and wickedness. "Natural" in this theory had much the same meaning as "ideal" in the Platonic philosophy, that is, it referred to a superior reality capable of being empirically imitated. It was alleged in the eighteenth century that the sort of law made manifest by Newton in physics also existed in politics, but that it was obscured there. A terrestrial divinity was needed to complete nature's work by setting in operation the laws laid down for the proper regulation of society. Rousseau and Mably called him the Legislator, and the physiocrats called him the enlightened despot; he was the reincarnation of the philosopher-king.

In the main, the Enlightenment opposed absolutism, inequality, hereditary privilege, or kingship of any sort. Most *philosophes* put their trust in education, liberalization, and reform from below, but some hoped for a despot who would translate the laws of nature ("dictates of reason") into political practice. Their chance of finding a reigning sovereign ready to act as the omnipotent embodiment of reason, as the executive agent of natural law, would have been slight were it not for the historical accident that the state, at just this time, was struggling to free itself of the restraints imposed on power by religion, custom, and tradition. Ambitious monarchs, such as Frederick the Great in Prussia and Catherine the Great in Russia, and their ministers, like the Marquis de Pombal in Portugal, saw in the *philosophes* useful allies in the fight against such "irrational" feudal vestiges as the church, the nobility, *parlements*, private corporations, and local liberties. There ensued one of history's curious misunderstandings, the alliance of Machiavellian monarchs with the disciples of Locke, the admirers of the English constitution. The philosophers thought they could use the kings, and the kings that they could use the philosophers. Both were wrong, as the French Revolution and its consequences showed: thrones toppled, undermined by rationalism, while *philosophes* (become *idéologues*) were jailed and exiled and rationalism was swamped in a romantic reaction.

That the philosopher-king alliance had been an illusion was proved when Napoleon Bonaparte carried much further all the progressive "rational" reforms that the enlightened despots had initiated in education, defense, finances, and administration without the aid of philosophers—indeed while ridiculing and persecuting philosophers. Hegel's explanation of this paradox marked the end of the philosopher-king illusion: Reason, he said, worked in history "immanently" and had no need of philosophizing kings. Indeed, reason could utilize antiphilosophical tyrants for its own purposes.

A similar demonstration of the vanity of intellectualism was made by Aristotle, only a few years after Plato first suggested the notion of philosopher-kings. Aristotle saw that one could not, like Plato, oppose nature and convention and thus separate the knowledge of the statesman from the reason incarnate in the law and custom of his society. He added that even the cleverest lawgiver could not surpass the anonymous wisdom of the laws and customs of a community with a long civilized tradition. In any case, it is a sufficient criticism of the proposal that philosophers rule to show that they do not have any sure knowledge of an ideal or natural society that existing societies must imitate. It is not philosophers but social movements that postulate and work for ideals of a "better" society, and there is no scientific way of choosing between their various proposals. One must avoid the Nazi error of saying that reason is irrelevant to politics or the claim of Sorel that social myths are beyond rational discussion, but philosophical discussion will never settle contests between rival social movements because there are no adequate neutral criteria for reaching a conclusion.

To say that philosophers would do better at deciding such contests than other people only transfers the problem to another level. From how to settle disputes, the problem becomes one of choosing the philosophers who will settle them. And this is as difficult as the first problem. As two millennia of critics have noted, Plato's suggestion is wrecked on the question of how to recruit the philosopher-rulers. Plato thought he had anticipated this objection because the first philosopher-ruler (he may have cast himself for the role) would have seen not only the model or form of the perfect state but also the model of perfect or ideal man, and he would instantly recognize this innate perfection in candidates. That is, Plato claimed that philosophy revealed ethical as well as political perfection. Thus, the assumptions required for the doctrine of philosophical rule are so extraordinary in extent and so adventurous that (quite apart from the almost unanimous dissent of philosophers) they would disqualify as unfit to rule any man presumptuous enough to make them.

Bibliography

Bambrough, Renford, "Plato's Political Analogies," in Peter Laslett, ed., *Philosophy, Politics and Society*. Oxford, 1956.

Bottomore, T. B., *Elites and Society*. New York, 1965.

Cobban, Alfred, *Dictatorship*. London, 1939. Eighteenth-century theories.

Crossman, R. H. S., *Plato Today*, 2d rev. ed. London, 1959. One of Plato's most hostile critics.

Hazard, Paul, *La Pensée européenne au XVIIIᵉ siècle*. Paris, 1946. Translated as *European Thought in the Eighteenth Century*. Cleveland, 1963. Eighteenth-century theories.

Mosca, Gaetano, *Elementi di scienza politica*. Rome, 1895. Translated from the 3d ed. by Hannah D. Kahn as *The Ruling Class*. New York and London, 1939.

Mills, C. Wright, *The Power Elite*. New York, 1956.

Pareto, Vilfredo, *Trattato di sociologia generale*, 2 vols. Florence, 1916. Translated by Andrew Bongiorno and Arthur Livingston as *The Mind and Society*, 4 vols. New York, 1935.

Plato, *Republic*.

Plato, *Politicus*.

Plato, *Laws*.

Popper, Karl, *The Open Society and Its Enemies*, 2d rev. ed., 2 vols. London, 1952. One of Plato's most hostile critics.

Spengler, Oswald, *Der Mensch und die Technik*. Munich, 1931. Translated by C. F. Atkinson as *Man and Technics*. London and New York, 1932.

Spranger, Eduard, *Lebensformen*. Halle, 1914.

NEIL McINNES

PHILOSOPHICAL ANTHROPOLOGY. Modern philosophical anthropology originated in the 1920s. During the 1940s it became the representative branch of German philosophy. It arose with, and has absorbed, *Lebensphilosophie*, existentialism, and phenomenology, although it is not identical with them. It has affinities with pragmatism and the sociology of knowledge. Although it is historically based on certain German traditions, it is also indebted to, and largely anticipated by, the eighteenth-century "science of human nature." It combines the critical traditions of the Enlightenment with an emphasis on dogmatic certitude.

HISTORICAL BACKGROUND

Following Bernhard Groethuysen, philosophical anthropology is often conceived as embracing all previous philosophy, insofar as previous philosophy dealt with man's place in the world. But this wide conception blurs the distinctive features of philosophical anthropology. Its history is best restricted to those authors and ideas whose impact is either admitted or can be traced in the literature of modern philosophical anthropology.

The impact of Kierkegaard, Marx, and Nietzsche is pervasive. Other generally acknowledged forerunners are Pascal, Herder, Goethe, Kant, Hegel, and Feuerbach. Pascal's influence is discernible in philosophical anthropology's conception of man as self-contradictory and mysterious, capable of surpassing his natural limits in quest of authenticity. Pascal's distinction between the organic *esprit de finesse* and the abstract and lifeless *esprit géométrique* was accentuated by Kant's distinction between the phenomenal world of the senses, with its quest for happiness (in the sense of egotistic pleasure), and the noumenal world of the thing-in-itself, between a world of determinate law and a world of transcendental choice. These concepts reveal themselves in the philosophical anthropologists' assumption of an unbridgeable gap between value and reason, between the ideal and the practical. Kant's basic questions—"What can I know? What ought I to do? What may I hope?"—are universally accepted in philosophical anthropology.

Herder was the first German author to correlate biology and the philosophy of man. From him stems the conception of man as a deficient being who must compensate for his lack of natural tools and weapons by the creative use of weapons and technology. Hegel's theory of alienation and its Marxist version have become a vital element in philosophical anthropology's comprehension and critique of society. Feuerbach formulated the claim that man can be used as the common denominator of philosophy, the true *ens realissimum*, embracing reason, will, and emotion. He held that philosophical anthropology was to take the place of theology; and indeed, contemporary philosophical anthropology may be regarded as secularized theology. Feuerbach conceived of God as a projection and objectification of the human spirit, reflecting the categorial structure of the human mind and its conceptual tools. This, as well as the corresponding Hegelian view of the divine spirit as being reflected in human history, is one of the recurring themes of cultural philosophical anthropology.

In a specifically German version and modified by the methodology of the practitioners of the *Geisteswissenschaften*, the "science of human nature," which stemmed from Hobbes, Locke, and Shaftesbury and reached its culmination in the eighteenth century, is the principal root of philosophical anthropology. Hume's *Treatise of Human Nature* provided a program for philosophical anthropology. "There is no question of importance whose decision is not comprised in the science of man. . . . In pretending to explain the principles of human nature we in effect propose a complete system of the sciences" (Everyman ed., Vol. I, p. 5). Philosophical anthropology took up Hume's empiricism with regard to the moral sciences, as well as his conception of religion.

Adam Smith's spectator theory of the moral sentiments was an early statement of the excentric position of man. The "Newtonian–Baconian" school of Scottish and French social thought of the eighteenth century (Francis Hutcheson, Adam Ferguson, John Millar, Dugald Stewart, Maupertuis, Diderot, and d'Alembert) which culminated in John Stuart Mill's sociology, was a direct precursor of philosophical anthropology in its aim of putting the study of man on an empirical biological basis. This school sought to elucidate and bridge the gap between man's distinctive nature and the sociocultural order in ". . . the belief that it was natural for man to make an order of life different from that in which the race was nurtured earlier, that it was in the nature of his equipment that he should react intelligently and creatively to the situations in which he found himself" (G. Bryson, *Man and Society,* Princeton, 1945, p. 173).

The more widely recognized forerunners of philosophical anthropology—Herder, Christian Garve, and Wilhelm von Humboldt—were directly influenced by the Scottish and French anthropologists and Encyclopedists, who had undermined Cartesian dualism. Thus, at the end of the eighteenth century, there was a wide acceptance of certain propositions concerning man's creative powers, his individuality, and his sociability. The Scottish and French precursors, however, had intended to develop more rigorous methods of investigation than those used by contemporary philosophical anthropologists.

SUBJECT MATTER, ATTITUDE, AND GOAL

Like existentialism and *Lebensphilosophie,* philosophical anthropology studies man's existence, his experiences, and his anxieties, combining the subjectivism of existentialism with the cultural objectivism of *Lebensphilosophie.* It uses the phenomenological methods of *Verstehen* and reduction. Philosophical anthropology shares with existentialism, phenomenology, and *Lebensphilosophie* a critique of society. Yet these currents are not identical; Heidegger and Jaspers, for example, refuse to be identified with philosophical anthropology, despite their great impact on it.

Philosophical anthropology seeks to interpret philosophically the facts that the sciences have discovered concerning the nature of man and of the human condition. It presupposes a developed body of scientific thought, and accordingly, in its program it aspires to a new, scientifically grounded metaphysics. It seeks to elucidate the basic qualities that make man what he is and distinguish him from other beings. It combines, and mediates between, what Kant designated as physiological and pragmatic anthropology.

Physiological anthropology studies man's natural limitations; pragmatic anthropology deals with man's potentialities, with what he, as a free agent, makes of himself, or is able and ought to make of himself. Thus, philosophical anthropology studies both man as a creature and man as the creator of cultural values—man as seen by a scientific observer and man as interpreted by himself (*Aussen-* and *Innenansicht*). Accordingly, most philosophical·anthropologists wish to combine scientific methods with an imaginative philosophical approach.

Philosophical anthropology seeks to correlate the various anthropologies that have developed with the specialization of the sciences. Max Scheler distinguished between scientific, philosophical, and theological anthropologies, or interpretations of the fundamental structure of human activities, which know nothing of one another. In order to stem what its followers describe as anarchy of thought and the "loss of the center," philosophical anthropology offers itself as a coordinating discipline. With the dissolution of traditional beliefs in guidance by gods, by kings and feudal leaders, by God, or by nature, there is today a general lack of direction. Man is now, as he was for Protagoras, the only possible measure. By coordinating and interpreting fragmented knowledge, philosophical anthropology aims at a new understanding of man's essential qualities and potentialities. It aims to accomplish this by the development of suitable methods, by a factual elucidation of the perplexities inherent in human institutions, and by borderline research (coordinating different branches of the sciences) used as a basis for a new "map of knowledge."

Since philosophical anthropology arose as an interpretation of various scientific disciplines, it has practitioners in many fields. Although there are only a few academic chairs of philosophical anthropology (Göttingen, Nijmegen), the number of professed philosophical anthropologists is large, chiefly in the German-speaking countries, but also in the Netherlands, Spanish-speaking countries, the United States, and France. Modern French humanism, whether existentialist, religious, or Marxist, is both historically and analytically allied with philosophical anthropology. Many philosophical anthropologists stress that they are theological, historical, political, juristic, biological, phenomenological, or cultural philosophical anthropologists. Much so-called philosophical anthropology is best treated under metaphysics, ontology, theory of value, epistemology, theology, philosophy of science or of history, or under the related contemporary philosophies. This article will discuss only the distinctive features.

Philosophical anthropology embraces most of the social sciences. Some leading practitioners, such as Arnold Gehlen, emphasize the concept of action, rather than man, as the distinguishing feature of philosophical anthropology, and define it as a new empirical discipline, *Handlungswissenschaft* (similar to "behavioral science" and the "theory of action"), as distinct from the natural sciences and the *Geisteswissenschaften.*

Philosophical anthropology is an attempt to construct a scientific discipline out of man's traditional effort to understand and liberate himself. At the same time, however, it is pervaded by the same antiscientific currents that mark existentialism, *Lebensphilosophie,* and phenomenology. But it is its dialogue with science that gives philosophical anthropology its peculiar character.

THE CRISIS OF SCIENCE

Philosophical anthropologists see a "crisis of science," a crisis first brought into view by three "humiliations of man." First, the humiliation of Copernican astronomy removed man's habitat, the earth, from the center of the universe; second, Darwin's biological evolutionism "shamed and degraded" man; and third, the historical schools revealed the relativity of religious and national cultural values. The crisis in science has been brought to a head by modern developments in depth psychology, post-Euclidean mathematics, and the indeterminacy principle in nuclear physics. From the scientific point of view, these developments represent advances rather than a crisis. However, German philosophers since Kant have conceived of science as being fixed in a rigid mathematico-mechanical determinism. According to philosophical anthropologists, this basic concept has broken down. There is a wide consensus among Continental thinkers that nineteenth-century materialism has been overcome and that the methods of the *Geisteswissenschaften* and phenomenology have been vindicated.

These methods seek the meaning immanent in events and in the works of man rather than the causal nexus between events. They aim to interpret other minds (both individual and collective), their peculiar intentions and tendencies, and the institutions through which their ideas have found expression. They investigate the conscious and unconscious actions of human beings and the structure of interpersonal (social and cultural) relationships. These methods are descriptive, interpretative, organic, and concrete, rather than explanatory, mechanical, and abstract, as in the natural sciences. This distinction of two methodologies—causal explanation on the one hand and *Verstehen* and phenomenological reduction on the other—takes up the emphasis of what is known in English as the Germano-Coleridgean school on, in the words of J. S. Mill, a philosophy of society in the form of a philosophy of history seeking a philosophy of human culture.

THEORY OF KNOWLEDGE

The crisis of science, according to philosophical anthropologists, evinces a deep crisis in the theory of knowledge—a crisis that makes imperative the adoption of pragmatic theories of truth. Traditional epistemology, they claim, was occupied with only one of the functions of consciousness. It failed to take into account what Pascal called the *logique du coeur* or *esprit de finesse*, which was akin to Coleridge's "imagination" and Newman's "illative reason." And consciousness itself is only a part of the forces that shape human reasons. For philosophical anthropologists, as for sociologists of knowledge, knowledge is determined by dispositions and by outside factors. Erich Rothacker claims that all knowledge is based on the particular ways of thought (*dogmatische Denkformen*) of national and sectional cultures, which determine both the questions asked and the answers given. Questions and answers have no validity apart from their appropriateness to the cultural environment (*Umwelt*). On the other hand, Scheler sought to establish an objective scale of values that would take into account nonrational elements. He distinguished in an ascending order the strata of vitality, intellectuality, and holiness (*Herrschaftswissen, Leistungswissen,* and *Heilswissen*). Despite his epistemological relativism, Rothacker has applied a similar scheme of "lower" and "higher" values in his psychological theory. Although most philosophical anthropologists profess value relativism, implicit value scales may be discerned underlying their methodological views and cultural criticism.

METHODOLOGY

Philosophical anthropology rejects the Cartesian dualism of body and soul: man is not part animal and part spirit but a being *sui generis*, distinct from animals in physical condition and in aspirations. This attitude, together with philosophical anthropology's theological roots, may account for a nearly universal (although currently weakening) rejection of Darwin and Freud for allegedly appealing to the forces of primitivism and animality in man. At the same time, many philosophical anthropologists reject modern intellectualism; their rejection of rationality, like that of many existentialists and *Lebensphilosophs,* has its roots in the romantic reaction to the Enlightenment and the French Revolution. In its suspicion of *Verwissenschaftlichung* ("scientism"), philosophical anthropology perpetuates the traditional German attacks on *Reflexionsphilosophie,* in which the nonrational aspects of reality are alleged to be ignored.

Philosophical anthropology's conception of method was formulated by Wilhelm Dilthey and Edmund Husserl. Husserl's nonempirical phenomenological approach to philosophical questions was claimed to be presuppositionless, wholly scientific, and logically prior to the natural sciences. It is concerned with meanings, an intuitive comprehension of directly experienced essences, and it involves a distinct method for "analyzing" (or rather, interpreting) facts, qualities, relationships, and the basic categories of human nature and culture—a method of analysis different from that which results in an explanatory theory. However, such thinkers as the biologist Adolf Portmann and the psychologist Karl Jaspers attempt to combine the scientific and interpretative approaches.

Ludwig Binswanger, for example, does not exclude the methods of natural science, but raises two objections to reveal their inherent limitations. One is that all abstractions are transpositions and simplifications of reality. The other is that the registration of stimuli in experimental psychology restricts the field of investigation so as to make the perception of meaningful wholes impossible; it precludes the essential selective and synthesizing activities.

Helmuth Plessner sees philosophical anthropology as the paradigm of borderline research. Although there is still a methodological gap between the physical and the social sciences, there has been spectacular progress toward methodological and substantive unification of physics, chemistry, and mineralogy, and of physiology and biochemistry. This progress supplies a model for philosophical anthropology. In its physical concerns, philosophical anthropology should correlate the work of medicine, zoology, chemistry, and physics, and in its nonphysical concerns, it should correlate the work of psychology, psychoanalysis, psychiatry, and the cultural sciences.

The physical and nonphysical concerns correspond to the traditional divisions of body and soul and of empiricism and subjective idealism. The division between body and soul emphasizes the ineluctable natural limitations of man and the determined aspects of his nature, and thus ignores his freedom and historicity, while the division between empiricism and subjective idealism has traditionally lost itself in metaphysical speculation. Philosophical anthropology tries to avoid both extremes; it sees man as essentially *homo absconditus*, inscrutable, an open question. Man must formulate his destiny so that he is not held rigidly in one role but safeguards his creative freedom. The direction in which this freedom permits man to fulfill himself is not amenable to scientific discovery, and thus science is devalued. Man's choices depend on his philosophical understanding of his own position in the world.

An infinite variety of choices is open to man. What distinguishes man's nature is not how he chooses, but that he does choose—that he is not determined by his biological and physiological constitution but is formed in the light of cultural values he himself has created and internalized. Philosophical anthropology's contribution to the study of cultures is its emphasis on the creative element in the unfolding of the various conceptions of man's position in the world. Therefore, man's self-understanding, or self-image, is a central theme of philosophical anthropology.

THE SELF-IMAGE OF MAN

Formerly, man was threatened not primarily by man, but by nature. Today, through science, nearly all natural phenomena have been or can be brought under man's control. Man is threatened neither by nature nor by the God who made nature, but by his own use of nature. Man's enemy is man, man-made structures, or the God who made man.

Again, even in coming to know nature, man (or his scientific representatives) meets himself rather than nature. Man no longer seeks nature as such, but nature as we question it for specific scientific purposes and in the specific contexts of axiomatic frameworks that we ourselves have determined.

Thus, man is inescapably confronted by man. We have reason to ask, What is this man? But what causes us to ask questions about the form in which man's subjective image of himself appears in his consciousness?

Man's subjective image determines what he makes of himself. Animals are as nature has created them, but man must complete his character; nature has supplied only the rudiments of it. Man must form his own personality, and he does so according to his image of what he can and should be. Scheler has delineated a historical typology of Western man's self-images, or "reality-worlds."

Man first saw himself as *homo religiosus,* a view based on the Judaeo-Christian legacy of supernaturalism and its ensuing feelings of awe and of inherited guilt. The next stage was *homo sapiens,* rational man in harmony with the divine plan. Since the Enlightenment, this image has been largely superseded by the naturalistic, pragmatic image of *homo faber*—man as the most highly developed animal, the maker of tools (including language), who uses a particularly high proportion of his animal energy in cerebral activities. Body and soul are regarded as a functional unity. Human being and development are explained by the primary urges of animal nature—the desire for progeny and the desire for food, possessions, and wealth. Machiavellianism, Marxism, racism, Darwinism, and Freudianism, it is claimed, are based on this interpretation of man.

These three self-images of man have in common a belief in the unity of human history and in a meaningful evolution toward higher organization. The images of *homo dionysiacus* and *homo creator* break with this tradition and herald a new orientation of anthropological thought. In the image of man as *homo dionysiacus,* man sees decadence as immanent in human nature and history. Typical exponents of this view are Schopenhauer, Nietzsche, and neoroman-

tics like Ludwig Klages, Spengler, and Leo Frobenius. Man is seen as the "deserter" or the *faux pas* of life; as a megalomaniac species of rapacious ape; as an infantile ape with a disorganized system of inner secretions; or as essentially deficient in vital powers and dependent for survival on technical means. Man's power of thought is an artifical surrogate for missing or weak instincts, and his "freedom to choose" is a euphemism for his lack of direction. Human social institutions are pitiful crutches for assuring the survival of a biologically doomed race. Reason is regarded as separate from the soul, which belongs to the vital sphere of the body. Reason is the destructive, "demoniac" struggle with, and submergence of, the healthy activity of the soul.

The image of man as *homo creator* is likewise derived from Nietzsche, and also from Feuerbach. But the Nietzschean superman has been transformed into a stricter philosophical conception by Nicolai Hartmann, Max Scheler, and the Sartrean existentialists. Scheler called this view a "postulatory atheism of high responsibility." Man has no ontological knowledge of an ultimate being. Contrary to Kant's postulate of the ethical need for a God, in the new view there must be no God—for the sake of human responsibility and liberty. Only in a mechanical, nonteleological world is there the possibility of a free moral being. Where there is a planning, all-powerful God, there is no freedom for man responsibly to work out his destiny. Nietzsche's phrase "God is dead" expresses the ultimate moral responsibility of man; the predicates of God (predestination and Providence) are to be related to individual man.

Man's awareness of his own self-images illuminates the whole range of his genuine potentialities so that his choice of an authentic form of life is not restricted by narrowness of view.

THE MAJOR BRANCHES

Philosophical anthropology shares with French humanism a particular critical analysis of society, but before this analysis can be presented, it is necessary to make a survey of the important branches of philosophical anthropology and of their results.

Biological philosophical anthropology. The reaction to determinism in the physical sciences has given rise to biological philosophical anthropology, or bio-anthropology. Bio-anthropology scrutinizes biological theories philosophically, primarily to correlate man's creative achievements and attitudes with his physiological organization. Man's cultural role—his character as a symbol-making being capable of abstraction, forethought, language, and intersubjective communication—is depicted as an irreducible function of his physiological constitution.

Among many important practitioners of bio-anthropology are the biologists F. J. J. Buytendijk and Adolf Portmann and the philosopher Arnold Gehlen. Important starting points of bio-anthropological thought have been Walter Garstang's concept of paidomorphosis and Jakob von Uexküll's concept of milieu (*Umwelt*), which was developed earlier, in philosophical terms, by Edmund Husserl. Paidomorphosis emphasizes the embryonic qualities that are preserved in man but lost in adult animals, as well as man's retarded extrauterine development. Gehlen has used the concept of man as a fetal ape to account for man's cultural achievements which, he claims, are conditioned by man's helpless status in the world. Devoid of instincts and of natural weapons and tools, man has been compelled to compensate for his shortcomings by active responses to the challenges of his environment and of his physiological urges. Man defends himself by his actions, whose scope, direction, and intensity, in contrast to instinctive reactions, are within his discretion. He transforms the natural environment into a system of action (*Handlungskreis*), the responses to which are perpetuated in institutions and language. Man's cultural environment is thus both a physiological condition of his survival and a distinctive criterion of his nature.

Uexküll. From his investigations into animal physiology, Uexküll derived a theory of the specific environmental determination of human life. Each species of animal lives in its own *Umwelt;* its consciousness of sense data is strictly limited by its innate capacities of perception. The range of these capacities corresponds to the teleology immanent in the "life plan" of different animals and is strictly limited to the life plan's specific tasks. Uexküll started from Kant's theory that the categories of the understanding determine the perception and conception of the data of the senses. It was Uexküll's teleological interpretation that distinguished his work from that of Western contemporaries who independently developed the sociology of animals. In the German romantic tradition, Uexküll was concerned with fighting the "mechanistic," positivistic conception of science that he saw represented in biochemistry and behaviorism.

Buytendijk. Buytendijk's physiological and psychological investigations have been undertaken in close contact with such phenomenologically oriented thinkers as Scheler, Helmuth Plessner, Viktor von Weizsäcker, and V. E. von Gebsattel. Like Uexküll, Buytendijk rejects Cartesian dualism and its mechanical interpretation of bodily processes; unlike Uexküll, he rejects the hypothesis that man is determined by his *Umwelt.* Through his detailed comparisons of animal and human physiology and psychology, Buytendijk has sought to work out man's unique condition as expressed in his capacity for abstraction and symbolization (the ability to create signs representing what is bodily absent), and in his capacity for the logical correlation of signs. For Buytendijk, biology is a historical science that must be understood in motivational, teleological terms. He conceives of motives and processes as value-related and spontaneous, derived from the built-in planning capacity of a self-structuring organism. Parallels with *verstehende* sociology are obvious, but Buytendijk's impressive ability to rest his philosophical views on a biological basis cannot conceal the fact that he held his views prior to his scientific illustration and testing of them.

Portmann. Adolf Portmann's work represents the culmination of bioanthropology. It aims at an integration of biological with psychological, sociological, and anthropological thought. According to Portmann, human biology has turned into anthropology, because the life of man, despite superficial similarities to animal life, is something *sui generis.* Portmann emphasizes the uniqueness of human action, language, foresight, and upright carriage, and of the human growth rhythm—duration of pregnancy, bodily proportions, extrauterine babyhood, and late formation of the female pelvis. These qualities, he claims, arise from a characteristic interpenetration of the hereditary process and teleological, sociocultural processes. Man's individuality (which continues to grow while the body decays) and man's sociability combine to establish his undetermined "openness," in contrast to determination of the animal by his *Umwelt.*

Portmann's central concept is "internality," the fact that individuals are centers of purposeful activity who use the external shell of the body as a means of self-expression and of communication with other individuals. Portmann does not claim that the affirmation of man's individuality and sociability provides the "meaning of life." Although specific mysteries of man's biological structure have been solved, he claims, the "basic fact" for philosophical anthropology continues to be man's "mysteriousness." Man has no built-in evolutionary mechanism leading to an equilibrium; there is only a creative variability (*Disponibilität*) of the human situation. Man's spontaneous individuality creates new self-images; his sociability spreads and maintains them.

Portmann has sought, however, to advance beyond the limits of functional morphology to a vantage point that will illuminate the hierarchy of values—a vantage point whose need has increased in view of the tremendous potential power of biotechnical advances to influence and change the human condition, and perhaps human nature. However, as in the biophilosophies of Henri Bergson, Pierre Teilhard de Chardin, and Julian Huxley, it is easier to discern the philosophical basis of Portmann's biological hypotheses than it is to discover any positive contribution that biology has made to his philosophical thought. He first developed his conception of man as functional unit as a philosophical hypothesis. "Openness" has been a theme of philosophical anthropology since the time of Herder and Kant.

In general, it must be said that no substantive lesson is to be drawn from either functional or analytical biology, except that it is of man's essence to create structured and meaningful systems of action. The biological foundation of man's creativity entails no concrete guide to what man ought to do. Nothing would appear to follow from the fact that creativity has biological roots except that man cannot permit himself to be altogether determined by any given environment. He must transcend it creatively, and he must be guided by ideas and leitmotifs rather than by instincts, by decisions rather than by reactions to stimuli. But the questions of what decisions man will take and what ideas he will adopt are not answered by bio-anthropology, which emphasizes the malleability of human nature as a basic fact. Any insight into the potential content of human achievement must therefore be based on the plurality of the cultures that have unfolded in history. Bio-anthropology thus leads into cultural philosophical anthropology.

Cultural philosophical anthropology. Like American cultural anthropology, cultural philosophical anthropology is concerned with man and his works, with culture history and culture sociology, and with historical morphology and the philosophy of history. It is interested primarily in developed societies—"high cultures" that have created a style of their own beyond the biological and trivial uniformities of the tribal state. Like German sociology, it emphasizes the multiformity rather than the uniformity of human nature, and the history rather than the theory of cultures. Like Portmann's bio-anthropology, it finds an ultimate mystery in man—the mystery of archetypes and racial dispositions.

Cultural anthropology combines Dilthey's historicism with the phenomenological method. Man comes to know and liberate himself through history. A comparative study of societies elucidates the human situation and the human predicament. But this study results in the same merely formal characteristics elaborated by bio-anthropology—the adaptability of the human mind, the need for a "sane" world view, sociability with its ensuing problems, a common growth rhythm, and common basic physiological urges.

Arnold Gehlen and Erich Rothacker are the most representative cultural philosophical anthropologists, while Werner Sombart is the most opinionated. Gehlen and Rothacker present integrated theoretical systems that have an ultimately psychological basis. Their psychologies, like that of Dilthey, are essentially descriptive and interpretative, and their psychological interpretations mirror their cultural philosophies.

Rothacker has classified cultural factors in a scale by "laws of polarity." He seeks to understand individual cultures by a process of "reduction" to "national souls" (attitudes and dispositions that generate *Weltanschauungen*) and to myths. These ur-experiences are not further reducible; they are embodied in the racial inheritance. Therefore, although people do create and develop the *Umwelt* of their national cultures, the possibilities that are thereby realized are ultimately determined. Rothacker's historicist relativism is less free from ethnocentrism than one might be led to expect by the emphasis of philosophical anthropology on the openness of man.

Gehlen's psychology is rooted in the archaic stage of cultural development. The values of this stage serve as criteria for the evaluation of late cultures, which accordingly appear as falls from grace.

In Sombart's anthropology ethnocentric traits are also emphasized. Thus, man's irreconcilable diversity rather than his potential openness is seen as distinguishing the human situation.

Ernst Cassirer, on the other hand, sought to discover the basic function of human cultural achievements (language, myth, religion, art, science, history) behind their innumerable forms and to trace them to a common origin in man's symbol-making power—the power to build up an "ideal world" of his own.

Psychological philosophical anthropology. Bio-anthropology and cultural philosophical anthropology are the most important branches of philosophical anthropology. Among other branches, only psychological philosophical anthropology and theological philosophical anthropology require separate mention.

Psychological philosophical anthropology is the most successful post-Freudian development in psychiatry on the Continent and, through existential psychoanalysis, is exerting considerable influence in the English-speaking world. The outstanding figures in this movement are Ludwig Binswanger, Erwin Straus, and Medard Boss. Erich Fromm seeks to incorporate his psychology within philosophical anthropology, and Rollo May in the United States and R. D. Laing in Britain follow similar lines. Their common belief is that traditional experimental psychology requires the assistance of philosophical thought to arrive at satisfactory results. Some psychological philosophical anthropologists oppose the empirical hypotheses and inductive statistical methods of experimental psychology; most of them combine experimental methods with a specific philosophical or phenomenological approach.

Since psychological philosophical anthropology deals with individual cases, it lends itself to concrete and descriptive investigations. Analyses have been made of laughter and weeping, fantasy, shame, resentment, pleasure, love, and fear. These analyses do not consist in mere registration of stimuli but in selective and synthesizing acts of interpretation by phenomenological "reduction" to an intuition of essential qualities. Plessner has traced the capacity for laughter and weeping to man's "excentricity," his ability to transcend his innate nature and to observe, judge, and respond to situations. Human moods (*Stimmungen*) are typically described as obstacles to the achievement of authenticity. The irrational elements in moods undermine the continuity of character, which is man's potential ability to give meaning and direction to his life. Accidental attitudes that arise from the challenge of situations thus deprive man of his right to make responsible choices; they tie him to an impoverished, one-sided anthropology.

Binswanger developed existential analysis from Freud's psychoanalysis. He describes Freud's positivist, "utilitarian" anthropology as one-sided and negative. Its culture concept, he claims, concentrates negatively on the taming of natural urges rather than positively on a teleological image of man's potentiality. Freud's "somatographic" or "somatomorphic" conception of existence stresses the scientific analysis of sleep, dream, passion, and sensuality while, according to Binswanger, it neglects the historical and cultural aspects of existence, such as religion, art, ethics, and myth, all of which are as important as science. In Binswanger's view psychological investigation should be directed toward the self-transcending exercise of man's liberty to make authentic choices. The psychologist's task is to illuminate the "inner life history" of the patient, his self-structuring in the light of his inner motivation. Self-structuring is equivalent to character or to the response that the individual makes to the challenge of the world around him. St. Augustine, to whom we owe the beginnings of autobiography, is a case in point. Illness prevented him from carrying out his ambition to become an orator. He transcended his natural disability by turning toward the spiritual world and thus arrived at his essential "real being." He could have reacted otherwise—by resentment or frustration, by neurosis or suicide. These and other potentialities held out to Augustine the temptation to restrict his character by the impoverishment inherent in giving in to an irresponsible choice—a choice suggested by the logic of the situation. Augustine chose an autonomous life that preserved his access to a full range of human values. Psychosis is explained as an "abortive encounter" with existence, or a form of existential misdirection. Diagnosis of a psychosis therefore depends on a valid interpretation of what constitutes an authentic existence. An authentic existence, according to Binswanger, consists in a life in keeping with a legitimate cultural (religious or national) tradition; in a dialogue with other beings (the "Thou"); or in the ability to act in character in the face of situational challenges.

However, the first of these criteria depends on values that are subject to unresolved doubt; the other two are so devoid of specific content that they hardly invite contradiction. Existential analysis, even more than psychoanalysis, obliterates the line between the normal and the abnormal and reduces psychological problems to questions of *Weltanschauung.*

Viktor von Weizsäcker, V. E. von Gebsattel, Erwin Straus, and Harald Schultz-Hencke have carried out structural analyses of inhibited character types and, in particular, of sexual perversions. Health is defined as openness to all potentialities of life, and obsessional urges are therefore interpreted as disturbed world views that enslave the individual in rigid, one-sided, compulsive attitudes and interfere with his social "I–Thou" relationships. Sexual perversions, in particular, have been construed by Gebsattel as obsessional urges that preclude a lasting I–Thou relationship based on mutual freedom, and as thus being incapable of providing ultimate satisfaction. Medard Boss, however, arguing from an equally existential basis, stoutly rejects this view. Gebsattel's apotheosis of the procreative element in love, however, points to the close affinity of philosophical anthropology with "secularized theology."

Theological philosophical anthropology. Theological anthropology emphasizes the Biblical conception of man in a dialogue with God. Martin Buber, Emil Brunner, and Dietrich Bonhoeffer are remarkable representatives of this movement, although their work is best studied in its theological context. However, the openness of man and his individuality and sociability are dominant themes of their work. The human difficulty of making the right choices is paralleled by the theological conception of man as simultaneously just and sinning.

A merely intellectual and logical exposition of God's message, in their view, is not enough for an understanding of God's revelation. An emphatic existential I–Thou relationship between man and God, based on the *logique du coeur,* is required. What matters is not that something is true, but how it can be made to come true. Belief in God has been explained by theological philosophical anthropologists, following Feuerbach, in terms of the self-understanding and the creative self-image of man.

The need for a postscientific interpretation of the Creed that is appropriate to a "mature" humanity and avoids theological sophistry has become a leading motif of theological anthropology, and this makes it difficult to distinguish between its tenets and those of secular philosophical anthropologies.

CRITIQUE OF SOCIETY

Philosophical anthropology shares with contemporary French humanism the conception that there is a crisis of the sciences that reflects a radical crisis of European society. It rejects contemporary bourgeois society, from either a romantic or a Marxist viewpoint, for the alleged dehumanizing tendencies it has developed in the process of rationalization following the breakup of feudal and religious institutions.

The rise of scientific rationalism is not regarded as a process of liberation from the shackles of superstition, conventions, and fallacies, but as a process that has deprived Western man of his "center of gravity" and has alienated him from his authentic nature through the replacement of value by "means–end" relationships, by neutral experiment, and by mechanico-mathematical abstraction. In the view of philosophical anthropologists, the "age of transition," or "age of crisis," which heralded the acceptance of utilitarianism in the English-speaking world, is still unresolved. Man's salvation from alienation is not seen as a continuous process of improvement or of piecemeal social engineering but as a radical challenge that is less concerned with practical reform than with a utopian rejection of the modern world.

The central theoretical insights of philosophical anthropology consist in an affirmation of the individuality and sociability of man as ultimate values. This theory would seem to suggest a social organization that combines an optimum of free choice with the minimum encroachment on individual liberty that is compatible with a viable social coexistence. This is in fact the utilitarian image of man that has prevailed since the early nineteenth century in the English-speaking world, where this image of man has been internalized to such an extent that the discussion of ultimate metaphysical questions has predominantly given way to the discussion of means to assure the accepted end of mutual accommodation and individual discretion. By contrast, on the Continent, and especially in Germany, the romantic reaction to the French Revolution precluded the acceptance of the philosophy of the Enlightenment. No commonly accepted concept of society was developed to counterbalance an unbridled individualism except the radical panaceas of nationalism and totalitarianism. By emphasizing the importance of both individuality and sociability, philosophical anthropology is returning to the type of position that gave birth to utilitarianism, and it may therefore be a step toward a utilitarian view of the world. Although most of its representatives present ethnocentric or nihilistic conclusions, these are not inevitable consequences of philosophical anthropology's affirmation of the creativity and sociability of man.

(See Philosophical Anthropology in Index for articles on philosophers who have especially concerned themselves with the topic.)

Bibliography

GENERAL AND HISTORICAL

Bryson, Gladys, *Man and Society.* Princeton, 1945.
Groethuysen, Bernhard, *Philosophische Anthropologie: Handbuch der Philosophie.* Munich and Berlin, 1928. Part III, pp. 1–207.
Häberlin, Paul, *Der Mensch: Eine philosophische Anthropologie.* Zurich, 1941.
Landmann, Michael, *De Homine.* Freiburg and Munich, 1962. Pp. 543–614. A comprehensive bibliography.

Landmann, Michael, *Philosophische Anthropologie*. Berlin, 1955.

Landsberg, P. L., *Einleitung in die philosophische Anthropologie*. Frankfurt, 1949.

Lipps, Hans, *Die Wirklichkeit des Menschen*. Frankfurt, 1954.

Litt, Theodor, *Die Selbsterkenntnis des Menschen*. Leipzig, 1938.

Löwith, Karl, *Das Individuum in der Rolle des Mitmenschen*. Munich, 1928.

Pappé, H. O., "On Philosophical Anthropology." *Australasian Journal of Philosophy*, Vol. 39 (1961), 47–64.

Pfänder, Alexander, *Die Seele des Menschen*. Halle, 1933.

BIOLOGICAL PHILOSOPHICAL ANTHROPOLOGY

Buytendijk, F. J. J., *Allgemeine Theorie der menschlichen Haltung und Bewegung*. Berlin, 1956.

Buytendijk, F. J. J., *Mensch und Tier*. Hamburg, 1958.

Portmann, Adolf, *Die Biologie und das neue Menschenbild*. Bern, 1942.

Portmann, Adolf, *Zoologie und das neue Bild des Menschen*. Hamburg, 1956.

Pringle, J. W. S., *The Two Biologies*. Oxford, 1963.

PSYCHOLOGICAL PHILOSOPHICAL ANTHROPOLOGY

Bally, Gustav, *Der normale Mensch*. Zurich, 1952.

Boss, Medard, *Psychoanalyse und Daseinsanalyse*. Bern, 1957. Translated by Ludwig B. Lefebre as *Psychoanalysis and Daseinsanalysis*. New York and London, 1963.

Gebsattel, V. E. von, *Prolegomena einer medizinischen Anthropologie*. Berlin, 1954.

Laing, R. D., *The Divided Self: A Study of Sanity and Madness*. London, 1960.

May, Rollo, ed., *Existence*. New York, 1958.

Schultz-Hencke, Harald, *Der gehemmte Mensch*. Leipzig, 1940.

Strasser, Stefan, "Phenomenological Trends in European Psychology." *Philosophy and Phenomenological Research*, Vol. 18 (1957), 18–34.

Weizsäcker, Viktor von, *Der kranke Mensch: Eine Einführung in die medizinische Anthropologie*. Stuttgart, 1951.

THEOLOGICAL PHILOSOPHICAL ANTHROPOLOGY

Kuhlmann, Gerhardt, *Theologische Anthropologie im Abriss*. Tübingen, 1935.

Loewenich, Walther von, *Menschsein und Christsein bei Augustin, Luther und J. Burckhardt*. Gütersloh, 1948.

Michel, Ernst, *Ehe: Eine Anthropologie der Geschlechtsgemeinschaft*. Stuttgart, 1948.

Rosenstock-Huessy, Eugen, *The Christian Future*. New York, 1946.

H. O. PAPPÉ

PHILOSOPHICAL BIBLIOGRAPHIES. Lists of philosophers and the titles of their works were for the most part provided only *en passant* by ancient and medieval writers and scholars, as in the brief citations scattered through the first book of Aristotle's *Metaphysics* and throughout Aquinas' *Summa Theologica*. It is true that Diogenes Laërtius' listing was somewhat more systematic, but philosophical bibliographies fully worthy of the name date from more recent times.

Modern philosophy has been well supplied with bibliographies in the general sense of the term, as will be noted in the present survey, but it has been weak in a special variety of bibliographical literature, namely, journals of abstracts. The two main journals containing abstracts of current work in philosophy—the *Bibliographie de la philosophie* and the *Bulletin signalétique: Philosophie, sciences humaines*—have done and are doing a good job as far as they go, but the scope of each is limited: the first covers books only, and the two-line précis in the second are enough only to whet a desire for more.

Modern bibliographies of philosophy are of four kinds: general bibliographies; those covering a specific region or country; those covering a particular period, movement, or philosopher; and those covering a specific philosophical discipline.

GENERAL BIBLIOGRAPHIES

Bibliographical books and pamphlets. One of the earliest of the general bibliographies of philosophy is the *Bibliotheca Philosophorum Classicorum Authorum Chronologica; in qua Veterum Philosophorum Origo, Successio, Aetas, & Doctrina Compendiosa, ab Origine Mundi, Usq. ad Nostram Aetatem, Proponitur; Quibus Accessit Patrum, Ecclesiae Christi Doctorum a Temporibus Apostolorum, Usque ad Tempora Scholasticorum ad An. Usq. Do. 1140, Secundum Eandem Temporis Seriem, Enumeratio*, by Johann Jacob Fries (Zürich, 1592, 110 pages), with about 2,500 entries. Three of its significant successors in the next three hundred years are the *Bibliotheca Realis Philosophica*, by Martin Lipen (2 vols., Frankfurt, 1679), with about 40,000 entries, some on subjects no longer regarded as philosophical in a strict sense; the *Bibliotheca Philosophica*, by B. G. Struve (Jena, 1704; 5th ed., 2 vols., 1740), containing about 4,000 entries; and the *Systematisch-alphabetischer Hauptkatalog der Königlichen Universitätsbibliothek zu Tübingen; Erstes Heft; A. Philosophie* (Tübingen, 1854, 63 pages), with about 3,000 entries and with annual supplements to 1880.

Of the four pre-twentieth-century bibliographies mentioned, all are available at the Library of Congress in Washington and at the British Museum in London. The last-named item is also available at the New York Public Library and at the Library of the University of Illinois.

In the twentieth century four main general philosophical bibliographies have been compiled. The first is the *Bibliography of Philosophy, Psychology, and Cognate Subjects*, by Benjamin Rand (2 vols., New York, 1905), which has about 70,000 entries and is a major work of scholarship. It was published as the two-part Volume III of the *Dictionary of Philosophy and Psychology*, edited by James M. Baldwin (3 vols., New York, 1901–1905). Part I of the two-part *Bibliography* covers histories of philosophy and works by and about philosophers from Abel to Zwingli, and Part II is systematic.

Second among the main general bibliographies of the present century is the *Bibliographische Einführung in das Studium der Philosophie*, edited by I. M. Bocheński, which consists of 20 fascicles (24 to 85 pages each) published at Bern from 1948 to 1950 and which covers philosophy in certain periods (ancient and medieval philosophy), countries (modern Italian, French existentialist, and American philosophy), religious and ethnic groups (Buddhist, patristic, Jewish, and Arabic philosophy), systems and disciplines (philosophy as a whole, symbolic logic, and logical positivism), and individuals (Plato, Aristotle, Augustine, Aquinas, and Kierkegaard).

The third principal source of this kind is Gilbert Varet's

Manuel de bibliographie philosophique (2 vols., Paris, 1956), which contains about 25,000 entries, Volume I being historical and Volume II systematic.

Finally, there is Wilhelm Totok's *Handbuch der Geschichte der Philosophie* (Frankfurt, 1964——), of which the first volume, *Altertum* (400 pages), covers works on Indian, Chinese, Greek, and Roman philosophy, with an introduction listing works on the methodology of research in philosophy and on the general history of philosophy, dictionaries of philosophy, introductions to philosophy, and works on the philosophical disciplines. Articles from over 400 periodicals are cited.

Bibliographical serials. Apparently the earliest general serial covering works in philosophy was the *Allgemeines Repertorium der Literatur; . . . philosophische Literatur,* by J. S. Ersch (Jena and Weimar, one volume each for 1785–1790, 1791–1795, and 1796–1800). Partly overlapping it in time was the *Lehrbuch der Geschichte der Philosophie und einer kritischen Literatur derselben,* by J. G. Buhle (Göttingen, one volume for each year from 1796 to 1804). After a gap of 87 years, the *Critical Review of Theological and Philosophical Literature,* edited by S. D. F. Salmond, was published at Edinburgh, covering the years 1891 to 1904. It was succeeded by the *Review of Theology and Philosophy,* edited by Allan Menzies, also at Edinburgh, which covered 1905/1906 to 1914/1915.

Meanwhile, in 1895 at Louvain a periodical was begun which was entitled the *Sommaire idéologique des ouvrages et des revues de philosophie.* After a number of changes (and with no volumes published from 1915 to 1933 and from 1941 to 1945), this periodical is now entitled the *Répertoire bibliographique de la philosophie.* It is issued four times a year and is one of the three general bibliographical serials now being published in the field of philosophy; it covers both books and periodical articles. (It is reproduced *in toto,* with Dutch headings replacing the French headings, in the *Tijdschrift voor Filosofie,* published quarterly at Louvain.) A second of the three leaders in this category is the *Bibliographie de la philosophie,* begun in 1937 as a semiannual by the International Institute of Philosophy, continued (with the omission of the years 1939 to 1945) until 1953, and issued since 1954 four times a year by the International Federation of Philosophical Societies; it covers books only, with a summary of each.

The third is the *Bulletin signalétique: Philosophie, sciences humaines* (entitled the *Bulletin analytique: Philosophie* from 1947 to 1955), published quarterly at Paris by the Centre de Documentation du Centre Nationale de la Recherche Scientifique; it is the only world-wide source of its kind which not only covers both books and periodicals but also contains a succinct abstract of each entry.

Remaining to be mentioned, as regards serial bibliographies of philosophy, are a number of sources which are either limited in scope in one way or another or are no longer issued.

A general world-wide serial no longer issued but useful for works published in the period in which it appeared is *Philosophic Abstracts,* published for the most part quarterly at New York from 1939 to 1954, with an index covering 1939 to 1950. It contains abstracts of books and lists of periodical articles.

There are two important serials, of a quasi-bibliographical character, devoted exclusively to critical reviews of philosophical books: The *Philosophischer Literaturanzeiger,* published eight times a year at Meisenheim am Glan (begun in 1949 at Schlesdorf am Kochelsee), which contains about 15 reviews in each issue; and *Philosophical Books,* issued quarterly since 1960 at Leicester, England, which contains about a dozen reviews in each issue, written largely from the viewpoint of analytical philosophy. Also deserving of mention, as regards coverage of books only, is *Scripta Recenter Edita,* issued ten times a year since 1959 at Nijmegen, the Netherlands, which is a list of books on philosophy and theology (each issue containing about 400 entries with emphasis on theology), designed especially for use by acquisitions officers of libraries.

Periodicals. It may be added, as regards serial bibliographies, that selective lists or reviews (and, in a few cases, abstracts) of current philosophical books, plus lists of periodical articles in some cases, are published either in each issue or annually or from time to time in many philosophical periodicals, and the coverage is in some cases fairly comprehensive. (For the names of periodicals in this field, see *Philosophical Periodicals, An Annotated World List,* by David Baumgardt, Washington, 1952, 89 pages, 489 entries; the list, with 157 entries, which appears under the heading "Philosophy" in *Ulrich's Periodicals Directory,* 10th ed., New York, 1963, 667 pages; and the article PHILOSOPHICAL JOURNALS in this Encyclopedia.) Especially strong in book reviews and abstracts are the German philosophical periodicals.

Of the currently published annual bibliographies in philosophical periodicals, mention may be made of the one which appears in the *Deutsche Zeitschrift für Philosophie,* published in East Berlin. Although generally global in coverage, it emphasizes works on dialectical materialism written in Eastern Europe.

Finally, topical, regional, or other summaries and evaluations of current philosophical literature (as distinguished from lists, reviews, or abstracts) appear regularly or occasionally in *The Hibbert Journal* (world-wide), *Cross Currents* (world-wide), *Philosophy* (selected countries), the *Revue philosophique de la France et de l'étranger* (selected countries), and the *Revue des sciences philosophiques et théologiques* (world-wide).

Bibliographical sections of books. Many of the standard histories of philosophy contain bibliographical sections. The most important source of this kind is the voluminous bibliographical material in the *Grundriss der Geschichte der Philosophie,* by Friedrich Ueberweg and others (12th ed., 5 vols., Berlin, 1923–1938). The handiest is the series of lists of philosophers preceding each main part of the *History of Philosophy,* by Wilhelm Windelband, translated by James H. Tufts (2 vols., New York, 1958, paperback reprint of the rev. ed. of 1901). Also useful for the history of philosophy are the bibliographical lists (usually divided into "Fonti" and "Studi") at the ends of the chapters of the *Guida storico-bibliografica allo studio della filosofia,* by Carmelo Ferro (Milan, 1949?).

In addition, many introductory works on philosophy contain bibliographical guides. An outstanding example is the discussion of philosophical books, periodicals and dictionaries in Louis de Raeymaeker's *Introduction to Philosophy*, translated by Harry McNeill (New York, 1948, 297 pages), on pp. 196–258.

NATIONAL OR REGIONAL BIBLIOGRAPHIES

Bibliographical books and pamphlets. A convenient list of the bibliographies of philosophy which are national in scope, covering some twenty countries or groups of countries, will be found in *A World Bibliography of Bibliographies*, by Theodore Besterman (4th ed., 4 vols., Lausanne, 1965–1966), Volume III, Columns 4809–4827. Outstanding among these country guides are the *Manuel de la recherche documentaire en France; . . . Philosophie,* by Raymond Bayer (Paris, 1950, 410 pages), with about 6,000 entries; the *Repertorium der Nederlandse Wijsbegeerte,* by J. J. Poortman (Amsterdam, 1948, 404 pages), with about 20,000 entries and a 168-page supplement published in 1958; the *Bibliografia filosofica italiana del 1900 al 1950* (4 vols., Rome, 1950–1957), with about 50,000 entries; the *Bibliografia filosófica española e hispanoamericana (1940–1958),* by Luis Martínez Gómez (Barcelona, 1961, 524 pages), 10,166 entries; and the anonymous *Philosophie und Grenzgebiete, 1945–1964* (Stuttgart, 1964, 434 pages), covering philosophical works in the German language, with a list of periodicals. Also deserving of mention, as regards French philosophy, are the fascicles entitled "Logique et philosophie des sciences," by Robert Blanché (1959, 54 pages), and "Morale et philosophie politique," by Georges Bastide (1961, 92 pages), in the *Bibliographie française établie à l'intention des lecteurs étrangers* (Paris).

Two volumes of a *Bibliografia Filozofii Polskiej,* covering 1750–1830 and 1831–1864, were published at Warsaw by the Polska Akademia Nauk in 1955 and 1960 (1,241 and 3,771 entries, respectively). The first volume of a *Bibliographie der sowjetischen Philosophie* (listing the articles which appeared in the Soviet periodical *Voprosy Filosofii* from 1947 to 1956; 906 entries) was compiled under the direction of I. M. Bocheński and published in 1959 by the Ost-Europa Institut at the University of Fribourg, Switzerland; four subsequent volumes, published from 1959 to 1964, covered books of 1947 to 1960 and articles of 1957 to 1960.

Bibliographical serials. Serials (mostly annuals) devoted to philosophical works issued in particular countries include the following:

Abstracts of Bulgarian Scientific Literature; Philosophy and Pedagogics (Sofia; one volume for each year since 1958).

Bibliografia filosofica italiana (Milan; one volume for each year since 1949).

Bibliography of Current Philosophical Works Published in North America, issued as a supplement to certain issues of *The Modern Schoolman* (St. Louis, Mo.) and covering mainly the United States.

Die deutschen Universitätsschriften zur Philosophie und ihre Grenzgebieten, edited by Kurt Gassen (published annually at Erfurt from 1924 to 1930).

Literarische Berichte aus dem Gebiete der Philosophie, edited by Arthur Hoffman (published semi-annually at Erfurt from 1923 to 1932), which covered current German periodical publications, with special retrospective bibliographies on Hegel, Nietzsche, and others.

"Thèses de doctorat concernant les sciences philosophiques et théologiques soutenues en France," published each year since 1954 in a spring or summer issue of the *Revue des sciences philosophiques et théologiques* and covering the preceding year.

The annual *Handbook of Latin American Studies* (published since 1935, originally and now again at Gainesville, Fla.) regularly contains a chapter on philosophical studies. A "Scandinavian Bibliography," covering philosophical works published in Denmark, Finland, Norway, and Sweden, appears once a year in *Theoria* (Lund, Sweden). The *Heythrop Journal* (Oxford, quarterly) regularly contains a "select list of British books on philosophy and theology."

Bibliographical sections of books. Many of the standard historical, critical, or documentary treatments of philosophy in particular countries or regions (American, British, French, German, Indian, etc.; and Latin American, Anglo-American, European, Scandinavian, Western, Oriental, etc.) include extensive bibliographical sections, either at the end of the book or at the end of each chapter. Examples are the bibliographies in the introductions to the several parts of the anthology *The Development of American Philosophy,* edited by W. G. Muelder and others (2d ed., Cambridge, Mass., 1960), with about 500 entries, and the bibliography at the end of Chandradhar Sharma's *Indian Philosophy* (New York, 1962, paperback reprint of the Benares edition of 1952), with about 300 entries.

PERIOD OR MOVEMENT BIBLIOGRAPHIES

Bibliographical books and pamphlets. Noteworthy among the philosophical bibliographies which cover a particular period are one on antiquity, one on the Renaissance, one on an 11-year period of the twentieth century, and one on the twentieth century as a whole:

Guía Bibliografia de la Filosofia Antigua, by Rodolfo Mondolfo (Buenos Aires, 1959, 102 pages), which is a worthy extension of the author's many substantive contributions to philosophical scholarship.

A Catalogue of Renaissance Philosophers (1350–1650), by John O. Riedl and others (Milwaukee, 1940, 179 pages), dealing with about 2,000 philosophers, with lists of writings in some cases.

Bibliographia Philosophica, 1934–1945, by G. A. de Brie (2 vols., Brussels and Antwerp, 1950–1954), Volume I historical and Volume II systematic; 48,178 entries.

Bibliografia filosofica del siglo XX.; Catalogo de la Exposición Bibliografica Internacional de la Filosofia del Siglo XX. (Buenos Aires, 1952, 465 pages), with 4,011 entries.

A period bibliography which is specialized in two senses (limited with respect to the period when the items were published and to the period with which the items deal) is the *Thomistic Bibliography, 1920–1940,* by Vernon J. Bourke (St. Louis, Mo., 1945; supplement to Vol. 21 of *The Modern Schoolman*), with about 5,700 entries. It lists a number of earlier bibliographies of scholastic philosophy.

Illustrative of bibliographies covering philosophical movements is the "Bibliographie der Geschichte der idealistischen Philosophie," in *Idealismus; Jahrbuch für die idealistische Philosophie* (Zurich), Vol. I (1934), pp. 217–256 (about 350 entries). Bibliographies covering philosophical movements in particular countries include V. E. Harlow's *Bibliographical and Genetic Study of American Realism* (Oklahoma City, Okla., 1931, 132 pages), with some 700 entries, and Vito A. Belleza's "Bibliografia italiana sull'esistenzialismo," in *Archivio di filosofia*, Vol. 15 (1946), 171–217, with over 700 entries. Works dealing with problems of philosophy and the history of philosophy from the standpoint of Marxism are listed in *O Marxistickej Filozofii a Vedeckom Komunizme*, compiled at the University of Bratislava (Bratislava, 1962, 146 pages), with over 400 entries.

Bibliographies covering individual philosophers are very numerous. They are listed in the appropriate sections of the general bibliographies mentioned earlier. For contemporary philosophers, the comprehensive bibliographies in the volumes of the Library of Living Philosophers, edited by Paul A. Schilpp (now published in La Salle, Ill.), are especially worthy of mention; the series covers C. D. Broad, Rudolf Carnap, Ernst Cassirer, John Dewey, Albert Einstein, Karl Jaspers, G. E. Moore, Sarvepalli Radhakrishnan, Bertrand Russell, George Santayana, and A. N. Whitehead, and volumes on others are in preparation.

Bibliographical serials. The main bibliographical serial covering a specific period or movement in philosophy is the annual *Bibliographia Patristica; Internationale patristische Bibliographie,* by Wilhelm Schneemelcher (Berlin, begun with a volume for 1956 published in 1959), with about 1,000 entries in each volume.

Bibliographical sections of books. Many of the standard works on the philosophy of a particular period or movement include extensive bibliographical sections either at the end of the volume or at the end of each chapter. As regards books on particular periods, mention may be made, for example, of Maurice de Wulf's *History of Mediaeval Philosophy*, 3d English ed., based on the 6th French ed., translated by E. C. Messenger (2 vols., London, 1935–1938; reprinted 1952); it contains (1) in Volume I an introductory chapter entitled "General Bibliography," with sections on research methods, auxiliary sciences, dictionaries and encyclopedias, collections, monographs on problems, etc. (totaling over 500 entries), and (2) at the end of each major section in each chapter a bibliographical discussion (for example, about 25 entries on John Scotus Erigena).

As regards books on particular movements, mention may similarly be made, for purposes of illustration, of *Logical Positivism* (Glencoe, Ill., 1959), edited by A. J. Ayer, which contains on pp. 381–446 a section entitled "Bibliography of Logical Positivism" (over 2,000 entries), covering not only logical positivism strictly interpreted but also "all types of analytical philosophy." Ayer's book is part of the series entitled Library of Philosophical Movements; the other books in the series (on existentialism,

Scholasticism, "realism and the background of phenomenology," etc.) also contain extensive bibliographies.

BIBLIOGRAPHIES OF SPECIFIC DISCIPLINES

Among the bibliographies covering specific philosophic disciplines are the following:

I. M. Bocheński's bibliography of the history of formal logic in his *Formale Logik* (Fribourg, 1956), pp. 531–605 (over 2,000 entries), which was reproduced photographically in the English translation by Ivo Thomas, *A History of Formal Logic* (Notre Dame, Ind., 1961), on pp. 460–534, with English section headings substituted for the German headings and 34 additions to the bibliography given on p. 567.

Alonzo Church's "A Bibliography of Symbolic Logic," in *Journal of Symbolic Logic*, Vol. 1 (1936), 121–218 (about 1,800 entries), which is supplemented by abstracts of books and periodical articles on symbolic logic in each issue of the *Journal of Symbolic Logic*. Vol. 3 (1938), 178–212, contained the section "Additions and Corrections," applicable to the basic bibliography.

William A. Hammond's *A Bibliography of Aesthetics and of the Philosophy of the Fine Arts From 1900 to 1932* (rev. ed., New York, 1934, 205 pages, 2,191 entries), which also has a continuing supplement in the "Selective Current Bibliography for Aesthetics and Related Fields," now published annually in June in the *Journal of Aesthetics and Art Criticism* and originally published quarterly, under the title "Quarterly Bibliography of Aesthetic Theory, Criticism, and Psychology of Art," from the beginning of the issuance of the periodical in 1941.

Ethel M. Albert and Clyde Kluckhohn's *A Selected Bibliography on Values, Ethics, and Esthetics in the Behavioral Sciences and Philosophy, 1920–1958* (Glencoe, Ill., 1959, 342 pages), which contains 600 items in Chapter 6, "Philosophy."

John C. Rule's *Bibliography of Works in the Philosophy of History, 1945–1957* (The Hague, 1961, 87 pages, 1,307 entries), which excludes Marxist interpretations of history in the expectation of covering them separately later.

Amedeo G. Conte's "Bibliografia di logica giuridica (1936–1960)," in *Rivista internazionale di filosofia del diritto*, Vol. 38 (1961), 120–144 (about 250 entries). Addenda appeared in Vol. 39 (1962), 45–46.

For a discussion of some of the bibliographies mentioned in this article, from a librarian's standpoint, see Wilhelm Totok, "Die bibliographische Situation auf dem Gebiet der Philosophie," in *Zeitschrift für Bibliothekswesen und Bibliographie,* Vol. 5 (Frankfurt, 1958), 29–43; and his *Bibliographischer Wegweiser der philosophischen Literatur* (Frankfurt, 1959, 36 pages). See also the section on bibliographies of philosophy in Jean Hoffmans, *La Philosophie et les philosophes; ouvrages généraux* (Brussels, 1920, 395 pages).

WILLIAM GERBER

PHILOSOPHICAL DICTIONARIES AND ENCY-CLOPEDIAS. Aristotle compiled the first dictionary of philosophy. Other outstanding philosophers who either wrote such works or made slight beginnings in that direction include Avicenna, Leibniz, Voltaire, and Dewey. Kant lectured on *philosophische Enzyklopädie,* but his topic was really the encyclopedic scope of philosophy; Hegel wrote an "encyclopedia" of philosophy which was not an encyclopedia in the ordinary sense. Indeed, what constitutes a dictionary or encyclopedia of philosophy deserves discussion. First, it will be helpful to inspect early examples of such works as well as what might be called embedded dictionaries—the philosophical articles, alphabetically arranged but separated by nonphilosophical material, in general encyclopedias.

In Book V of Aristotle's *Metaphysics* each section consists of a definition and discussion of a philosophical concept. The various sections begin, for example, "Beginning means . . . ," "Cause means . . . ," "Element means . . . ." He thus covered 29 topics in this first dictionary or quasi dictionary of philosophy: beginning, cause, element, nature, necessity, one, being, substance, sameness and difference, limit, that in virtue of which (or reason why), disposition, priority and posteriority, potency, quantum, quality, relation, completeness (or perfection), state, being affected, privation, possession, derivation, part, whole, mutilation, genus, falsity, and accident. The rationale for the order of topics can only be conjectured.

After Aristotle dictionary-type or encyclopedic compendiums were produced by Alexandrian, Roman, and Byzantine lexicographers and doxographers, covering, for the most part, philosophy among other domains of knowledge, not philosophy exclusively. Many of these compendiums were arranged in an order other than alphabetical. Thus, in his *Bibliotheca,* or *Myriobiblion,* Photius (c. 850) summarized, in no special order, some 280 philosophical and nonphilosophical books, including works by Philo Judaeus, Justin Martyr, Origen, and Gregory of Nyssa but none by Plato or Aristotle, although he mentions having read books by Timaeus, Boëthus, and Dorotheus on Plato's use of words.

By contrast Suidas' *Lexicon* (c. 950) is arranged alphabetically. It contains articles on Aristotle (about 150 words), Zeno of Elea (about 75 words), and numerous other philosophers, as well as many topical entries, such as those on *physis, physikos,* and related terms (about nine hundred words in this group). After Suidas, however, through the rest of the medieval period and the Renaissance, most of the summaries of knowledge reverted to the nonalphabetical arrangement.

In modern times the alphabetical arrangement has been dominant in general compendiums of knowledge, and useful philosophical articles have frequently been included in them. It will be instructive, before examining the separately published dictionaries of philosophy, to survey the embedded dictionaries of philosophy.

PHILOSOPHICAL ARTICLES IN GENERAL ENCYCLOPEDIAS

From the standpoint of embedded philosophical material four French, six English, and seven other encyclo-pedias are especially worthy of comment. In addition, readers may note (*a*) the interest of various prominent philosophers in general encyclopedias, as illustrated by Leibniz' proposal to Louis XIV around 1675 that a group of learned persons "extract the quintessence of the best books, add the unwritten observations of experts, and thus build systems of knowledge based upon experience and demonstrations"; (*b*) the role of the *philosophes* in the work on the *Encyclopédie;* and (*c*) Giovanni Gentile's role in the Italian encyclopedia of 1929–1939.

French general encyclopedias. Moreri, Bayle, Diderot, and Larousse are the key figures in the history of French encyclopedias. Of these four Louis Moreri and Pierre Bayle each produced an entire encyclopedia single-handedly.

Moreri. Moreri's *Le Grand Dictionnaire historique* (1st ed., Lyon, 1674, 1,346 pages; 20th ed., 10 vols., 1759) was translated twice into English and at least once into German, Italian, and Spanish. Reprintings and supplements continued to be published until 1845. By contrast with many dictionaries of philosophy which cover only topics, not individual philosophers, Moreri, in his articles on philosophy, covered many of its practitioners but offered no separate treatments of philosophical domains, problems, schools, or technical terms. Moreover, his articles on the philosophers are so thoroughly oriented toward biography that little attention is paid to doctrines.

Bayle. Bayle's *Dictionnaire historique et critique* (1st ed., 2 vols., Rotterdam, 1697; 5th ed., 5 vols., 1734; annotated ed., 16 vols., Paris, 1820–1824), two editions of which were translated or paraphrased into English, contains some basic facts plus philosophical or critical (usually impish and skeptical) comments for each entry. The comments on both the philosophical and the nonphilosophical topics support atheism, hedonism, and skepticism. As professor of philosophy at Sedan, France, and at Rotterdam, Bayle possessed the necessary technical equipment with which to support his trenchant skepticism. Acknowledging the roar of disapproval which greeted the first edition, Bayle made some revisions in the articles, but the second edition was no less outspoken than the first.

New English translations of selected articles from the *Dictionnaire* were published at Princeton in 1952, edited by E. A. Beller and M. du P. Lee, Jr., and at Indianapolis in 1965, edited by Richard H. Popkin.

"Encyclopédie." The third French general encyclopedia with significant philosophical articles was the one called simply, by common consent, the *Encyclopédie.* Its full title was *Encyclopédie, ou Dictionnaire raisonné des sciences, des arts et des métiers, par une société de gens de lettres,* edited by Denis Diderot and Jean d'Alembert.

The *Encyclopédie* had a stormy history. It was originally conceived by André F. Le Breton as merely a translation of Ephraim Chambers' *Cyclopaedia* of 1728 (described below), but the character of the project changed, especially after Diderot was put in charge. A corps of contributors was rapidly enlisted which included men of the caliber of Rousseau and Voltaire.

Among the vicissitudes which followed were the periodic banning of the work as irreligious or politically dangerous after the publication of the early volumes and the discouraged resignation of d'Alembert from the project. In 1764, while the manuscript for the final volumes was being edited, Diderot learned to his consternation that Le Breton was toning down the language in order to obviate further prosecution; some of Le Breton's most extensive changes were made in Diderot's own article "Pyrrhonienne ou sceptique philosophie," containing Diderot's most cherished ideas. The original proofs, showing Le Breton's changes and deletions, were discovered in 1933.

The *Encyclopédie* contains no articles on philosophers as such. Among its main articles dealing with philosophical schools or otherwise of philosophical interest are those on Socratic philosophy, Aristotelianism, Epicureanism, and skepticism. The spirit of the philosophical and ethical articles in the *Encyclopédie,* many of which were written by Diderot himself, was antidogmatic, but it was not atheistic or consistently skeptical. Voltaire's 40-odd articles, written in this vein, included 3 in the *E*'s ("Élégance," "Éloquence," and "Esprit"), 21 in the *F*'s ("Félicité," "Finesse," "Fornication," and so on), 11 in the *G*'s ("Goût," "Grandeur," and so on), 5 in the *H*'s ("Heureusement," "Histoire," and so on), "Idolatrie" in the *I*'s, and "Messie" (Messiah) in the *M*'s.

Rousseau wrote the articles on economics (in which he laid the groundwork for his *Contrat social*) and music. Baron de Montesquieu declined the invitation to write on democracy and despotism but promised an article on taste; the portion of it which he had finished before his death in 1755 at the age of 66 was published in Volume VII immediately after Voltaire's article on the same subject.

Eight articles from the *Encyclopédie* on ethical subjects (calumny, unhappiness, and the like) were translated by Ivan Vanslov into Russian and published in 1771 at St. Petersburg by the Imperial Academy of Science as a 21-page dictionary of ethics.

(For a full discussion of the purpose, influence, and philosophic content of the *Encyclopédie,* see ENCYCLOPÉDIE.)

Larousse. .The excitement aroused by Diderot's original *Encyclopédie* and by the revised editions which followed it eventually subsided, and a calm period in this field ensued. The fourth main French encyclopedia, Larousse's, had its birth in the second half of the nineteenth century. Several encyclopedias bear the name Larousse, beginning with the 15-volume *Grand Dictionnaire universel du XIXᵉ siècle* sponsored by Pierre Larousse (Paris, 1865–1876; 2-vol. supp., 1878–1890) and extending through *Larousse de XXᵉ siècle,* compiled by Paul Augé and published in Paris by the Librairie Larousse (6 vols., 1928–1933; supp., 1953), and the *Grand Larousse encyclopédique,* also published by the Librairie Larousse (10 vols., 1960–1964).

In the *Grand Dictionnaire* the article on philosophy, which covers only the history of philosophy, is curiously followed (perhaps to compensate for the lack of topical discussion) by 51 extensive articles on books with *philosophie* as the first or principal word of the title, such as "Philosophie (Principes de)," by Descartes; "Philosophie morale (Principes de)," by Shaftesbury; "Philosophie première, ou Ontologie," by Wolff; "Philosophie de la vie," by Schlegel; and "Philosophie de l'art," by Taine. This is hardly the best way to cover philosophy in an encyclopedia.

The current *Grand Larousse encyclopédique* contains numerous philosophical articles, both topical and biographical, which, although pithy, are excessively brief; for example, Bergson is covered in eight hundred words and logic in nine hundred. The space devoted to the separate articles "Logique (Grande), ouvrage de Friedrich Hegel," "Logique déductive et inductive (Système de), par John Stuart Mill," and "Logique de Port-Royal ou Art de penser" (after the fashion of the nineteenth-century edition) could have been far better used in the article on logic.

English general encyclopedias. Of the numerous English-language encyclopedias mention may be made of Harris' and the two Chambers', which are mainly of historical interest, and the *Britannica,* the *Americana,* and *Collier's,* which are influential today.

Harris. The *Lexicon Technicum, or an Universal English Dictionary of Arts and Sciences,* by the clergyman John Harris (1st ed., London, 1704; 5th ed., 2 vols., 1736; supp. vol., 1744), is called by the *Encyclopedia Britannica* the first alphabetical encyclopedia in English, although there seem to be other claimants to this honor. Harris wrote in the Preface, "In Logick, Metaphysicks, Ethicks, Grammar, Rhetorick, &c. I have been designedly short; giving usually the bare meaning only of the Words and Terms of Art, with one or two instances to explain them, and illustrate them."

The book contains no articles on individual philosophers, and the articles on philosophical topics show a popular rather than a technical understanding (or misunderstanding) of the subject. For example, the article "Logick" (32 lines, mainly laudatory and, curiously, ascribing to logic our ability to explain why we dislike a painting) refers the reader, for details, to the articles "Apprehension" (7 lines), "Discourse" (5 lines defining the term as if it were a synonym of "inference"), "Judgment" (12 lines), and "Method, or Disposition" (40 lines, outlining Descartes's four methodological precepts, with condescending comment) but does not refer the reader to the articles "Conditional Propositions" (8 lines) or "Definition" (19 lines). There is no article on fallacy or syllogism.

Chambers' "Cyclopaedia." A quarter of a century after the appearance of the Harris volume Ephraim Chambers published the *Cyclopaedia, or an Universal Dictionary of Arts and Sciences* (1st ed., 2 vols., London, 1728; 5 other eds., 2 vols., London, 1739–1751/1752, and another 2-vol. ed., Dublin, 1742); supplements were published at various times from 1738 to 1753. Later editions were reportedly used in an unpublished French translation by the writers of the French *Encyclopédie.* Chambers was a freethinker, but many of his articles repeat superstitions and preposterous medical marvels as fact. The *Cyclopaedia* contains succinct articles on essence, ethics, God, knowledge, logic, metaphysics, philosophy, Sophists, truth, and will, as well as on Academic, Cartesian, Epicurean, Platonic, Pyrrhonian, Socratic, and Stoic philosophy, among others. It does not cover individual philosophers.

"Chambers's Encyclopaedia." The so-called *Chambers's Encyclopaedia, a Dictionary of Universal Knowledge for the People* (10 vols., London and Edinburgh, W. & R. Chambers, 1860–1868; rev. eds. issued periodically to 1935) was not a new edition of Ephraim Chambers' *Cyclopaedia* but a new work, written by over one hundred contributors and influenced greatly by the 15-volume tenth edition of the *Conversations-Lexikon* published from 1851

to 1855 by F. A. Brockhaus at Leipzig. The philosophical articles in *Chambers's Encyclopaedia* are uneven. Anaximander is allotted ten times as much space as Anaximenes. The article on the Gnostics is scholarly (although the author wrongly says that they "feigned a naive surprise" at not being accepted as Christians), whereas other articles are more popular in style. The article on Pascal is wholly biographical, but the one on Plotinus covers both his life and his teaching.

The current *Chambers's Encyclopaedia* (15 vols., London, George Newnes, 1950; rev. ed., 1959) is a successor of the 1860–1868 work, not of Ephraim Chambers'. Its advisers on philosophy were John Laird and A. C. Ewing. The articles on Greek philosophy incorporate recent scholarship; the one on Antisthenes, for example, avoids the error, embodied in many earlier treatments, of calling him the first Cynic. It seems odd, however, to find the intellectual work of Mohandas Gandhi and Sarvepalli Radhakrishnan discussed in A. B. Keith's article on Hinduism, which is concerned mainly with the Hindu religion, rather than in S. N. Dasgupta's article on Indian philosophy. The index volume contains a useful classified list of the philosophical articles: 29 on philosophy, metaphysics, and epistemology; 32 on logic; 8 on ethics; 41 on systems and schools; and over 200 on individual thinkers.

"Encyclopaedia Britannica." The last edition of Ephraim Chambers' *Cyclopaedia* was published in the 1750s, and the French *Encyclopédie* had appeared in the 1750s and 1760s. In the middle or late 1760s William Smellie, a printer, historian, and naturalist, wrote most of the articles for a new compendium, the *Encyclopaedia Britannica, or Dictionary of Arts and Sciences* (1st ed., 3 vols., Edinburgh, A. Bell and C. Macfarquhar, 1768–1771). It was issued in installments beginning in December 1768, and subsequent editions, some with supplements, were issued by various publishers. The numbering of the editions was discontinued after the fourteenth edition, which appeared in 1929. The *Britannica* is now published, with continuous revisions, in Chicago by William Benton.

The most famous (and on some topics the most scholarly and comprehensive) edition of the *Britannica* is the eleventh (29 vols., London and New York, 1910–1911). It was sharply attacked by Willard H. Wright (better known by his pseudonym S. S. Van Dine, under which he wrote best-selling murder mysteries) in *Misinforming a Nation* (New York, B. W. Huebsch, 1917), which made several points in Chapter XI, "Philosophy." The *Britannica* is provincial, he claimed, as in its description of Locke as "typically English in his reverence for facts"; dogmatic, as in the statements that Berkeley "once for all lifted the problem of metaphysics to a higher level" and that Hume "determined the form into which later metaphysical questions have been thrown"; and patronizing, as in the statement that Condillac's thought "was by no means suited to English ways of thinking." Wright also pointed out that the eleventh edition contained no articles on Bergson, Bradley, Dewey, Royce, or Santayana, and only 1 column on Nietzsche, as compared to 3 on Samuel Clarke, 5 on Spencer, 7 on Fichte, 11 on Cousin, 14 on Hume, 15 on Hegel, 15 on Locke, and 19 on Newton.

Edmund Husserl's article on phenomenology, first published in the 14th edition (1929), was included in the various printings through 1955. It was also reproduced in *Realism and the Background of Phenomenology* (Roderick M. Chisholm, ed., Glencoe, Ill., Free Press, 1961). In subsequent printings of the *Britannica* the article on phenomenology was written, at first, by J. N. Findlay and, currently, by Herbert Spiegelberg.

Many of the philosophical articles in the *Britannica* were rewritten around 1957. Some of the topical articles reflect the current Oxford philosophy. Of the current revision (1966), which for the most part reproduces the recently rewritten articles, the editors and advisers for articles on philosophy are Alonzo Church of Princeton, W. C. Kneale and W. H. Walsh of Oxford, and Sarvepalli Radhakrishnan, president of India. Contributors near the beginning of the alphabet include A. J. Ayer, Max Black, and Brand Blanshard and near the end I. A. Richards, Gilbert Ryle, A. E. Taylor, Wilbur M. Urban, and Abraham Wolf.

In the current revision Thomas E. Jessop is lively as well as scholarly on Hume. The article on Plato, by A. E. Taylor and Philip Merlan, is a comprehensive monograph of the highest value; the bibliography of over 125 items covers manuscripts, editions, commentaries, translations, and analyses. The article on aesthetics, by Thomas Munro, and "Aesthetics, History of," by Helmut Kuhn, which refer to each other, overlap somewhat; for historical data one should consult both. In his article on metaphysics Gilbert Ryle presents a penetrating survey of the status of metaphysics from the origin of the term through the twentieth-century attacks on the discipline; he predicts that the term may "come back into ordinary or pedagogic use" when the motives which generate synoptic world views swing once more into prominence.

"Encyclopedia Americana." Another major English-language encyclopedia, the *Encyclopedia Americana,* edited by Francis Lieber and Edward Wigglesworth (13 vols., Philadelphia, Carey, Lea and Carey, 1829–1833), was originally in large part a translation of the seventh edition (1827–1829) of the *Conversations-Lexicon* published by Brockhaus. Subsequent unnumbered editions, some with supplements, have been issued by various publishers. Now published in New York by the Americana Corporation, the encyclopedia is continuously revised, and each revision is referred to as an edition.

The current edition of the *Americana* (1966) has Morton G. White of Harvard University as the philosophy member of its editorial advisory board. Among the principal contributors are Brand Blanshard on idea and idealism, Richard B. Brandt on duty and ethics, Herbert Feigl on the Vienna circle, Carl G. Hempel on meaning, Walter Kaufmann on Nietzsche, C. I. Lewis on philosophy, Kingsley Price on fine arts, and Donald C. Williams on conceptualism, free will, innate ideas, mechanism, and pluralism. The article on logic, by Ernest Nagel; "Logic, Symbolic," by W. V. Quine; and the "Logic Glossary," by Arthur Danto, excel in covering a broad range of technical data briefly but comprehensibly. Some of the articles need updating; for example, the death of G. E. Moore, which is mentioned in Volume XIX, has not yet occurred in the article on common sense in Volume VII. The unsigned article on Santayana is philosophically weak.

"Collier's Encyclopedia." Collier's Encyclopedia (20 vols., New York, P. F. Collier & Son, 1950–1951; rev. ed., 24 vols., 1962), now published by Crowell Collier and Macmillan, is revised annually. It has T. V. Smith as its adviser on philosophy. Among its American contributors in the field of philosophy are Max Black, Brand Blanshard, George Boas, Roderick M. Chisholm, Raphael Demos, C. J. Ducasse, Marvin Farber, Carl Hempel, Sidney Hook, C. I. Lewis, Ernest Nagel, and Herbert W. Schneider. There are also philosophical articles by such eminent foreigners as T. M. P. Mahadevan and John Passmore. *Collier's* is stronger on the philosophical disciplines than on the schools. It contains first-class articles on aesthetics, by Van Meter Ames; epistemology, by Roderick M. Chisholm; history of ethics, by R. A. Tsanoff; logic, by I. M. Copi; metaphysics, by Blanshard; and philosophy, by a group including Blanshard, Demos, and C. W. Hendel. However, there is no article on realism, the one on naturalism has 1 paragraph, the one on monism 2 paragraphs, and the one on pragmatism 3 paragraphs. Existentialism, however, has 12 paragraphs. The bibliography of philosophy in the final volume lists over four hundred books.

Other general encyclopedias. Of the numerous other modern encyclopedias, mention may be made of seven—three in German, one each in Italian and Spanish, and two in Russian—which are perhaps the most prominent.

German. The *Grosses vollständiges universal Lexicon,* edited by Johann Heinrich Zedler and Carl G. Ludovici (64 vols., Halle and Leipzig, 1732–1750; reprinted, 1959), was the first encyclopedia compiled on a cooperative basis. The number of its collaborators, nine, was meant to correspond to the number of the Muses. The articles display an orthodox and partly medieval point of view, acknowledging the existence of the devil and of miracles, accepting astrology ("the influence of the planets must be conceded"), and stressing the scientific contributions of Roger Bacon and Albert the Great.

Der grosse Brockhaus (16th ed., 12 vols., Wiesbaden, F. A. Brockhaus, 1952–1957; supp. vol., 1958) is the current progeny of the Brockhaus-sponsored *Conversations-Lexikon.* It is especially strong on bibliography. The bibliographical sections of some of the philosophical articles, especially those on individual philosophers, constitute one-third or more of the entire text. The bibliographical section of the article on philosophy contains seven subsections, including one on dictionaries, which lists 12 items (9 German, 2 English, and 1 French).

Of the series of encyclopedias begun by Joseph Meyer as *Das grosse Conversations-Lexicon für die gebildeten Stände* ("The Great Encyclopedia for the Educated Classes," 38 vols. in 46, Philadelphia and Hildburghausen, Germany, Bibliographisches Institut, 1840–1853; 6-vol. supp., 1853–1855) the various editions, most of which were published at Leipzig and Vienna, included, for the most part, very creditable articles on philosophers and philosophical topics. The eighth edition, called *Meyers Lexikon* (Leipzig, Bibliographisches Institut, begun 1936; Vol. XII, an atlas, published 1936), was abandoned in 1942 with the ninth volume, covering *R* and *S.* This edition showed decided Nazi influence, using, for example, the exclamation point of sarcasm in noting, in a discussion of

Jewish thought, Spinoza's doctrine that God and nature (and substance also, according to the author of the article) are "identisch(!)" and in referring, in the article on Salomon Maimon, "Philosoph, Ostjude," to the baleful influence of his "Ghetto-Intellekt" on Neo-Kantianism.

Italian. Giovanni Gentile was a director and later a vice-president of the organization which produced the *Enciclopedia italiana di scienze, lettere ed arti* (36 vols., Milan and Rome, Istituto Giovanni Trecanni, later the Istituto della Enciclopedia Italiana, 1929–1939; supp. vol., 1938; 2-vol. supp., 1938–1948). The philosophical articles often include special features. For example, the one on Socrates offers a detailed analysis and appraisal of the sources, the one on Aristotle contains a section on medieval legends about Aristotle and Alexander, the one on Bruno discusses *la libertà filosofica,* and the one on *filosofia* (almost 100,000 words) quotes from a large number of writers on the nature of philosophy. Mussolini was the author of the article on fascism.

Spanish. In the Spanish *Enciclopedia universal illustrada europeo-americana* (70 vols., in 72, Bilbao, Spain, Espasa–Calpe, 1905–1930; 10-vol. appendix, 1930–1933; supp., usually biennially) many of the articles on philosophical schools or positions—materialism, utilitarianism, and so on—are usefully divided into two sections, exposition and criticism. In the article on pragmatism, for example, the sections on Anglo-American pragmatism and French pragmatism are each so divided.

Russian. The outstanding encyclopedia of prerevolutionary Russia was the *Entsiklopedichesky Slovar'* ("Encyclopedic Dictionary"), edited by Ivan E. Andreyevsky and others (43 vols. in 86, St. Petersburg and Leipzig, F. A. Brockhaus–I. A. Ephron, 1890–1907). Its philosophy articles were edited by Vladimir S. Solovyov, one of Russia's greatest philosophers, until his death in 1900 and then by Ernest L. Radlov, author of a philosophical dictionary published in 1911 (mentioned below). Solovyov himself wrote the articles on actuality, Campanella, cause, Comte, Duns Scotus, eternity, freedom of the will, Gorgias, Hartmann, Hegel (22 columns), Indian philosophy, Kant, Lully, Maine de Biran, Malebranche, metaphysics, nature, optimism, pessimism, Plato (28 columns), Plotinus, space, time, Vedānta, world process, and others.

The first edition of the *Bol'shaya Sovetskaya Entsiklopediya* ("Great Soviet Encyclopedia") was published in Moscow from 1926 to 1947 in 66 volumes. The second edition, whose chief editor was S. I. Vavilov, was published in Moscow by the Soviet Encyclopedia Publishing House from 1950 to 1958 in 53 volumes. Stalin's death during the course of publication of the second edition led to a change in the tone in the later volumes, where, for example, the cult of personality is rejected. In 1964 *Pravda* announced plans for a third edition.

The philosophical articles in both editions of the "Great Soviet Encyclopedia" are characteristically Marxist in viewpoint. Thus, Rudolf Carnap's philosophy is branded as "a typical example . . . of subjective idealism under the new labels adopted by the ideologists of the imperialist bourgeoisie in the struggle against the scientific materialist world view." In the allocation of space Hegel gets 5 pages, Kant 4, Spinoza 2, Plato 1, and G. E. Moore none;

dialectical materialism gets 19 pages, philosophy 17 pages, and pragmatism half a page.

Some of the philosophical articles of the "Great Soviet Encyclopedia" were translated into German and issued in separate brochures (one each on Aristotle, Hegel, Voltaire, and idealism; one covering Bacon, Berkeley, and Bruno; and one covering Helvétius, Heraclitus, Hobbes, and Holbach) in a series entitled *Grosse Sowjet-Enzyklopädie: Reihe Geschichte und Philosophie* (Berlin, Aufbau-Verlag, 1953–1955).

Encyclopedic dictionary. Well deserving of mention is the fact that Charles S. Peirce wrote the definitions of terms in metaphysics, logic, mathematics, and other subjects and Lyman Abbott was responsible for those in theology in *The Century Dictionary; An Encyclopedic Lexicon of the English Language,* edited by William D. Whitney (8 vols., New York, Century, 1891; issued, together with *The Century Encyclopedia of Names* and an atlas, as a 10-vol. work entitled *The Century Dictionary and Encyclopedia* in various years, with revisions, to 1911; issued in condensed form as *The New Century Dictionary,* 2 vols., D. Appleton–Century, 1943 and later years). According to the Preface, "Though it has not been possible to state all the conflicting definitions of different philosophers and schools," nevertheless, ". . . the philosophical wealth of the English language has, it is believed, never been so fully presented in any dictionary." Peirce's fine hand is evident not only in the choice of illustrative quotations but also in the breakdown of terms into subcategories; for example, the article on being includes definitions of actual being, accidental being, being in itself, connotative being, and so on.

Semigeneral encyclopedias. The following constitute bridges between the dictionaries of philosophy embedded in general encyclopedias and the separate dictionaries of philosophy.

"Cyclopedia of Education." Articles on 114 philosophers or groups of philosophers "whose systems have educational significance" and on 29 "philosophic views bearing on the nature of education" (atomism, determinism, dualism, empiricism, and so forth) appear in *A Cyclopedia of Education,* edited by Paul Monroe (5 vols., New York, Macmillan, 1919). John Dewey was the departmental editor for philosophy of education, and he wrote the articles on determinism, positivism, and many others. Other contributors include John Burnet, Paul Carus, Morris R. Cohen, Arthur O. Lovejoy, I. Woodbridge Riley, Frank Thilly, and Frederick J. E. Woodbridge. Cohen's article on philosophy is one of the best sources for the history of the teaching of philosophy; its bibliography contains 45 painstakingly assembled entries on philosophy in American, British, and Continental colleges, on philosophy in the secondary school, and so on.

"Encyclopaedia of the Social Sciences." The *Encyclopaedia of the Social Sciences,* edited by Edwin R. A. Seligman and Alvin Johnson (15 vols., New York, Macmillan, 1930–1935; reissued in part or in whole in various years), of which John Dewey was the advisory editor for philosophy, had over a dozen philosophers among its editorial consultants, including Morris R. Cohen, Benedetto Croce, Arthur O. Lovejoy, Ralph Barton Perry, Herbert W. Schneider, and T. V. Smith. This encyclopedia contains some extraordinarily illuminating articles on philosophical subjects.

Among the contributors of philosophical articles were George Boas on Berkeley; Léon Brunschvicg on Pascal and on Plato and Platonism; Ernst Cassirer on Kant; Cohen on atheism, belief, Bradley, Descartes, fictions, Hegel, and scientific method; Dewey on human nature, logic, and philosophy; Sidney Hook on Engels, Feuerbach, materialism, and violence; Hu Shih on Confucianism; Horace M. Kallen on behaviorism, James, modernism, morals, pragmatism, and radicalism; Lovejoy on academic freedom; Richard McKeon on Albert the Great, Anselm, Averroës, and Peter Lombard; C. R. Morris on Locke; M. C. Otto on hedonism; J. H. Randall, Jr., on Copernicus and on deism; F. C. S. Schiller on humanism; Herbert Schneider on Christian socialism, ethical culture, and transcendentalism; T. V. Smith on common sense, duty, ethics, and honor.

Dewey's article on human nature (ten columns) sets forth with clarity and force the principal meanings of the term *human nature,* the basic questions which may be asked about human nature, and the history of the understanding of human nature; his 21-item bibliography begins appropriately with his own *Human Nature and Conduct* (1922). Cassirer's article on Kant (eight columns) highlights Kant's significance for social thought and succinctly traces his impact through Fichte, the Hegelians, and the socialists; the 39-item bibliography begins with Cassirer's ten-volume edition of Kant's *Werke.* McKeon's article on Anselm brings out Anselm's little-known contribution to the problem of church–state relations.

"International Encyclopedia of the Social Sciences." The *International Encyclopedia of the Social Sciences,* a completely new encyclopedia, edited by David L. Sills, is a lineal descendant of the *Encyclopaedia of the Social Sciences.* It is scheduled for publication in 1968 by the Macmillan Company and the Free Press. This encyclopedia is devoted primarily to the fields of anthropology, economics, political science, psychology, sociology, and statistics. However, many of its articles are of direct relevance to philosophy; others describe the relevance of philosophical concepts to the social sciences. There are also many biographical articles on philosophers who have made significant contributions to the social sciences.

EARLY DICTIONARIES OF PHILOSOPHY

What is to count as a dictionary of philosophy and the difference between a dictionary of philosophy and an encyclopedia of philosophy are largely matters of definition. Two definitions seem most useful for the present purpose. First, a dictionary of philosophy is an expository work setting forth information about philosophical ideas in an arrangement which either is alphabetical (as in the embedded dictionaries of philosophy already mentioned and in most of those described below) or is based on key words or concepts (as in Aristotle's "dictionary" mentioned above and the first few of those mentioned below) rather than on a systematic division of philosophy into its disciplines or parts. Second, an encyclopedia of philosophy is a comprehensive dictionary of philosophy in which various articles are monographic in scope.

Dictionaries of philosophy range from those which are purely factual through those which are partly interpretive or evaluative to those, such as Voltaire's, which present rhapsodic or satirical reflections on key general topics. Divergences from this broad range of varieties also occur—for example, a "dictionary" which merely lists philosophical terms in one language with equivalents in other languages, a "dictionary" which presents for each important philosophical term a suggested usage rather than a statement of actual usage, and an anthology of philosophical quotations arranged alphabetically by topic. Over one hundred dictionaries of philosophy of one sort or another have been published. Most have been soon forgotten, but some have gone through multiple editions over many decades.

Middle Ages. Of the medieval works which may be counted as dictionaries of philosophy perhaps those of Isaac Israeli and Avicenna are most worthy of note. Israeli (c. 855–c. 955), the first Jewish Neoplatonist, wrote, in Arabic, *Kitāb al-Hudūd wal Rusum* ("Book on Definitions and Descriptions"), later translated into Latin and Hebrew. This work contains definitions, with comments thereon, of topics grouped roughly as intellect, soul, vital spirit, and so on; reason, knowledge, opinion, memory, deliberation, and so on; division, syllogism, demonstration, truth, falsehood, necessary, impossible, and so on; imagination, estimation, and sense perception; love, passion, and desire; innovation, creation, coming to be, passing away, and so on; time, eternity, and perpetuity; and other topics. The influence of al-Kindī in some 20 of the 56 sections has been noted by the latest editors of Israeli's work, A. Altmann and S. M. Stern.

Avicenna's *Kitāb al-Hudūd* ("Epistle on Definitions") contains, after an introduction on the pitfalls of the process of defining, definitions—extracted in part from Avicenna's other works—of accident, body, cause, continuous, creation, definition, form, individuality, intelligence, limit, motion, nonbeing, place, prime matter, priority, rest, soul, substance, time, universe, and other subjects. Terms having obvious mutual relations are grouped. The definitions are close to Aristotelianism in tenor.

An anonymous *Compendium Philosophiae*, based mainly on Aristotle and Albert the Great, written (probably in France) about 1327 and as yet only partly edited and published (Paris, 1936), was one of the last medieval dictionaries of philosophy. In topical groups it contains, in Books I to V, brief discussions of God, the physical features of the world, plants, animals, and man and, in Books VI to VIII, scholastic-type discussions of accident, actuality, art, becoming, being and nonbeing, cause, fate, free will, identity, language, law, motion, names, necessity, perfection, philosophy, place, potentiality, quality, quantity, relation, science, substance, time, truth and falsity, virtue and vice, and wisdom, as well as other subjects.

Sixteenth century. After the revival of learning and the invention of printing there appeared a number of compendiums of philosophical information. Apparently, the first formal dictionary of modern times devoted exclusively to philosophy was Giovanni Baptista Bernardo's *Seminarium*

Totius Philosophiae (3 vols., Venice, Damian Zenarius, 1582–1585; 2d ed., 3 vols. in 2, Geneva, Jacob Stoer and Franc. Faber, 1599–1605), later referred to as the *Lexicon Triplex*. In separate alphabetical dictionaries the three volumes cover, respectively, Aristotelian, Platonic, and Stoic philosophy in the writings not only of Aristotle, Plato, and the early Stoics but also of other philosophers, Greek, Roman, Christian, and Arabic. Thus, the first volume contains articles on Aristotelian philosophy from "Abstractio," "Accidens," "Actus," and other topics in the A's to "Zeleucus," "Zephirus," "Zodiacus," and other topics in the Z's.

The article "Definitio" in Volume I contains 333 paragraphs summarizing or quoting specific passages on the subject in Aristotle, Ammonius, Alexander of Aphrodisias, Themistius, Simplicius, Boethius, Averroës, Alexander of Hales, Albert the Great, Thomas Aquinas, and others. A similar approach—abstracting specific passages—is used throughout the three volumes. Accordingly, the work is essentially useful as a thorough guide to the sources but not as a synthesis.

Seventeenth century. The seventeenth century provided nine principal dictionaries of philosophy, all in Latin.

1610—Nicolaus Burchardi. Buchardi's *Repertorium Philosophicum, Quo Omnes in Universa Philosophia Subinde Occurrunt Termini Perspicue Traduntur* (Leipzig, 573 pages) appeared in 1610. It was also issued at Grimma in 1613 and at Gera in 1614, 1615, and 1616. Only two copies of this work are known to exist, having been located, after many fruitless searches elsewhere, in the Universitätsbibliothek in Marburg, West Germany (the 1614 printing), and in the Sächsische Landesbibliothek in Dresden, East Germany (the 1616 printing). A microfilm copy of the 1616 printing was procured and is filed in the Public Library of the District of Columbia.

The main part of the book is not arranged alphabetically. It treats exactly one hundred topics, from philosophy, logic, metaphysics, art, nature, and word, near the beginning, to infinite soul, theology, and God, at the end. The articles are superficial in their analysis but reflect wide reading in the classic sources. An alphabetical index of topics (*abstractum, ars,* and so on) appears at the beginning, and the book ends with an alphabetically arranged index of themes discussed in the articles—for example, *abstracta saepe ponuntur pro concretis* ("the abstract is often substituted for the concrete") and *amicitia honesta cur rara* ("why true friendship is rare").

1612—Henri Louis Chasteigner. Chasteigner's *Celebriorum Distinctionum tum Philosophicarum tum Theologicarum Synopsis* (Poitiers, A. Mesner, 1612, 71 pages; subsequent eds. or reprints, various places, 1616, 1617, 1619, 1623, 1635, 1645, 1651, 1653, 1657, 1658, 1659, and 1667) made a beginning in the provision of syntheses that Bernardo's work lacked. Thus, absolute is explained as in one sense opposite to relative; in another, to dependent; and in still another, to restricted. Abstraction is broken down into real (when the thing abstracted can exist separately) and rational; rational abstraction, into negative (or divisive) and precise (or simple); and precise abstraction, finally, into physical, mathematical, and so on. A prefatory alphabetical list names 48 authors—Alexander of Hales, Aristotle, Bonaventure, Buridan, Duns Scotus, Suárez, Thomas Aquinas, William of Ockham, and so on—whose writings were chiefly used in compiling the work.

1613—Rudolf Goclenius the elder. The *Lexicon Philosophicum* (Frankfurt, Matthias Becker, 1613, 1,143 pages; additional printings or eds., Marburg, 1613, 1615 and Frankfurt, 1633, 1634; Frankfurt 1613 ed. reissued in facsimile, Hildesheim, 1964) opens with four tributes to Goclenius (Rudolf Goeckel) in Latin verse. There follow articles on terms beginning with the vowels—*absolutum, existentia, idea, obligatio, unitas,* and the like—and then articles on terms beginning with the consonants—*beatitudo, causa,* and so on. The articles are informative, presenting standard scholastic breakdowns and definitions. As has been noted by José Ferrater Mora, Goclenius, although he was the first to use the term *ontologia* (in Greek letters), did not make significant use of the term. Goclenius is cited for support on a particular point in a work as late as Eisler's *Wörterbuch der Philosophie* (1899).

1626—Johann H. Alsted. Alsted's *Compendium Lexici Philosophici* (Herborn, Germany, Georg Corvin and J. G. Muderspach, 1626, 720 pages) is a group of dictionaries on about thirty separate disciplines—anatomy, arithmetic, astronomy, and so on in nonalphabetical order—including ten on philosophy covering ethics, logic, metaphysics, philosophical "archelogy" (basic terms), philosophical didactics (teaching of philosophy), philosophical "hexilogy" (mental faculties involved in philosophy), philosophical method, pneumatics (study of spiritual beings), poetics, and politics. Some parts of the dictionaries are alphabetical; others are not. Of the ten philosophical dictionaries, the one on logic, which is 26 pages long, is perhaps the best, but most of the material in it is not arranged alphabetically and is therefore difficult to follow.

1629—George Reeb, S.J. Reeb's *Distinctiones Philosophicae* (Ingolstadt, Germany, Gregory Haenlin, 1629, 167 pages; 2d ed., Cologne, 1630) was reprinted in 1653, 1657, and 1658 in the same volume as Chasteigner's *Synopsis.* With Reeb's *Axiomata Philosophica* it was reissued under the editorship of J. M. Cornoldi, S.J. (Bressanone, Italy, 1871 and Paris, 1873, 1875, 1891), under the title *Thesaurus Philosophorum, seu Distinctiones et Axiomata Philosophica.* Reeb's work, written from a scholastic viewpoint, discusses, as philosophical topics, such adverbial opposites as absolutely and dependently, in act and in potency, artificially and naturally, collectively and distributively, concretely and abstractly, and so on.

1653—Johann Micraelius. The *Lexicon Philosophicum Terminorum Philosophis Usitatorum* of Johann Micraelius (Jena, Jeremiah Mamphras, 1653, 667 pages; 2d printing, 1662) contains explanations of the terms used in philosophy, broadly understood; a 51-page appended outline, by discipline, of the topics covered; a 30-page index of Greek terms; and 17 pages of illustrations, mostly geometric figures. Many articles begin with what Aristotle said on the subject and continue with the scholastic elaborations of what Aristotle said. The article "Deus," however, begins by saying flatly that Aristotle was right in calling God the prime mover but was wrong in denying God's creation of the world, God's omniscience, and so on.

1658—Johann Adam Scherzer (Schertzer) and others. Scherzer and others' *Vade Mecum, Sive Manuale Philosophicum Quadripartitum* (Leipzig, Christian Kirchner, 1658) has four parts separately paged but bound as one volume. Part I, by Scherzer, entitled *Definitiones Philosophicae,* is a scholastic-type alphabetical dictionary, with definitions, for example, under *necessarium,* of absolute, hypothetical, physical, moral, and logical kinds of necessary thing. Part II consists of Chasteigner's *Synopsis* and Reeb's *Distinctiones Philosophicae.* Part III, by Scherzer, entitled *Axiomata Resoluta,* presents a system of rules of thought (a thing cannot be and not be, a proposition must be true or false, and so on). Part IV, by Scherzer, entitled *Aurifodina Distinctionum* ("Gold Mine of Distinctions"), discusses selected distinctions in an alphabetical arrangement (for example, intrinsic and extrinsic accidents among the *A*'s and remote and proximate cause among the *C*'s). Scherzer's project was ambitious, but the resulting complex was too cumbersome for convenience.

1675—Heinrich Volckmar. The *Dictionarium Philosophicum, Hoc Est Enodatio Terminorum ac Distinctionum* of Heinrich Volckmar (Frankfurt, Jacob Gottfried Seyler, 1675, 798 pages; 2d printing, 1676) is in Latin, but the author sprinkles a little German here and there. Thus, in citing the tenet "Credo quod Deus creavit me" under "Creatio," he translated it (as if it were difficult Latin) "Ich gläube dass mich Gott geschaffen hat." In an epilogue he asked the reader to ascribe any omissions not to negligence but to the enormity of the field to be covered, and he named as predecessors Chasteigner, Goclenius, Reeb, Micraelius, and Scherzer but not Alsted.

1692—Étienne Chauvin. In Chauvin's *Lexicon Rationale, Sive Thesaurus Philosophicus Ordine Alphabetico Digestus* (Rotterdam, P. van der Slaast, 1692, 756 pages; 2d ed., entitled *Lexicon Philosophicum,* Leeuwarden, Netherlands, Franciscus Halma, 1713, 719 pages) philosophy includes natural science. Thus, there are articles, in their Latin equivalents, on acceleration, fire, meteors, and the stomach, as well as on Aristotle, Descartes (a particularly laudatory article), other philosophers, and *cognitio, simplicitas, subsistentia,* and other philosophical concepts. Cartesian influence is apparent in many of the articles.

"Nondictionaries." Mention may also be made of an unalphabetical "lexicon" of this period by Pierre Godart. The second edition of his *Totius Philosophiae Summa* (Paris, L. Billaine, 1666, 245 pages) was entitled *Lexicon Philosophicum* (2 vols. in 1, Paris, J. and R. I. B. de La Caille, 1675) although it was not really a dictionary. After an introduction on philosophy and its divisions, the philosophical schools, and some principles of philosophy the book discusses being, causes, properties, and species; physics, including matter, motion, soul, sensation, and so on, with an attack on Cartesian philosophy; economics and politics; and logic. The alphabetical index in the second edition is 47 pages long.

Wolter Schopen's *Alphabetum Philosophicum* (Nissa, John Joseph Krembsl', 1696, 105 pages), although sometimes referred to as a dictionary of philosophy, is, like Godart's *Lexicon,* not a dictionary. It is a straight exposition of twenty-odd philosophical topics, such as what a definition is, what conversion and opposition of propositions are, and how many kinds of syllogism there are, each topic being designated by a letter of the alphabet (*A, B, C,* and so on).

Leibniz and after. Among the fragments of Leibniz edited in 1903 by Louis Couturat and assigned to the period 1670–1704 are two which show an interest in the Alsted work mentioned above and several which consist of lists of definitions of terms, as if Leibniz were thinking of compiling a dictionary of philosophy apart from the general encyclopedia which he had discussed with Louis XIV. One of these lists of definitions, for example, is headed "Introductio ad Encyclopaediam Arcanam." It contains definitions of *conceptus clarus, conceptus distinctus, conceptus adaequatus, conceptus primitivus,* and the like. Another, untitled, contains definitions of *amor* (love), *sapientia* (wisdom), *laetitia* (joy), *perfectio* (perfection), and so on. Illustrative are his definitions of love, the emotion by which it happens that the good or evil of another is considered part of our own, and of wisdom, the science of happiness. If Leibniz had completed a dictionary of philosophy along these lines, it would probably have constituted a vade mecum to his own philosophy rather than an exposition of historical viewpoints in philosophy.

In 1716, the year of Leibniz' death, there appeared the last Latin dictionary of philosophy before the first modern-language dictionaries. It was the *Lexicon Philosophicum; Sive Index Latinorum Verborum Descriptionumque ad Philosophos & Dialecticos Maxime Pertinentium* (The Hague, Henri du Sauzet, 322 pages), of which the author is listed on the title page as Plexiacus ("Auctore Plexiaco"). Plexiacus has been identified as Charles Du-Plessis d'Argentre or Michèle Toussaint Chrétien Duplessis (or du Plessis), but the best scholars attribute the work to one Michel Brochard. Following an extended systematic treatment of argumentation, definition, words and things, distinctions, and so on, the author presents, in an alphabetical arrangement, numerous philosophical terms and their definitions. The systematic treatment in the first part of the book, which leans heavily on the writings of Cicero, is more interesting than the somewhat routine definitions in the lexicon proper.

A Latin quasi dictionary of philosophy that may deserve mention here is the book *Philosophia Definitiva, Hoc Est Definitiones Philosophicae,* by Frederick Christian Baumeister (Wittenberg, Germany, J. J. Ahlfeld, 1738, 252 pages; 7th ed., 1746; enlarged ed., 1767), which contains definitions, grouped according to subject, of 329 logical terms, 233 terms in ontology, 95 terms in cosmology, 264 in psychology, 53 in natural theology, 182 in ethics, 69 in political philosophy, and 35 in physics, with a consolidated alphabetical index. The definitions, based in large part on the philosophy of Christian Wolff, are useful but not profound.

FIRST MODERN-LANGUAGE DICTIONARIES

In 1715 there appeared a work by J. H. (Johann Hübner) entitled *Compendieuses Lexicon Philosophicum* (Frankfurt and Leipzig, B. P. C. Monath, 208 pages; 2d ed., 1717).

The title of the second edition, varying slightly from that of the first, was *Compendieuses Lexicon Metaphysicum, zum besondern Nutzen aller Studierenden, vornemlich aber der politischen Wissenschaften befliessenen zusammen getragen* ("Compendious Metaphysical Lexicon, for Special Uses by All Students, but Chiefly Those Specializing in Political Sciences Taken as a Whole"). Although the work is in German, it discusses only Latin philosophical terms in nonalphabetical order. It begins with *ens* (a being) and among other things points out, with German examples, the distinctions among *ens, res* (a thing), and *reale* (a real thing). Other terms discussed include *verum* and *bonum* (true and real), *ubi* and *quando* (where and when), and the four causes. An alphabetical index at the end contains over four hundred entries, including about fifty under *causa—efficiens, in sensu juridico, necessaria, proxima,* and so on. The treatment is elementary, the analyses are not sharp, and the work has only historical interest today.

The first alphabetically arranged dictionary of philosophy in a modern European language appears to be Hubert Gautier's *La Bibliothèque des philosophes, et des sçavans, tant anciens que modernes* (2 vols., Paris, André Cailleau, 1723). Chauvin had treated philosophy as including the natural sciences; Gautier treated it as including the natural sciences and the humanities. Thus, his book contains articles on Alexander the Great, Copernicus, and La Fontaine, as well as on Avicenna, Descartes, Porphyry, and many others, plus a smaller number of topical articles, such as those on the Académie Royale des Sciences, *homme* (man), and *terre* (earth). Each volume has a topical index. Today, the work has interest mainly as a curiosity rather than for the information it provides.

Strictly speaking, the first dictionary of philosophy in a modern language appears to be the *Philosophisches Lexikon,* by Johann Georg Walch (Leipzig, 1726, 3,048 cols.; 2d ed., 1733; 3d ed., 1740; 4th ed., 2 vols., 1775), which set a new standard of comprehensiveness and scholarship for works of this kind. It reflects in part the ideas of Leibniz and Wolff, quoting or citing them in various articles as authorities. Among the more intriguing articles in this *Lexikon* are those on atheism (16 cols.), discussing arguments derived from the existence of evil, the eternity of the world, the sufficiency of nature as an explanation of events, the anthropomorphic character of our idea of God, and so on; self-knowledge, knowledge of others, knowledge of nature, and knowledge of God; fate, with summaries of the views of Parmenides, Democritus, Plato, Aristotle, the Stoics, the Epicureans, the Chaldeans and other Oriental peoples, Sextus Empiricus, Leibniz, and others; and freedom of thought (25 cols.), discussing the ipse dixit principle, freedom of interpretation, freedom of belief, the role of reason, the fate of Spinoza, the right to know the truth, and other aspects of the topic.

An appendix covers philosophers from Abelard, Albinus, and others at the beginning to the two Zenos and Zoroaster at the end. These biographical sketches are of decidedly less interest than the vivid expositions in the topical articles. Many of the biographical sketches begin, repetitiously, ". . . one of the most famous philosophers of" such-and-such a country.

In 1963 the Stuttgart firm of Friedrich Frommann Verlag was planning to issue a facsimile reprint of the fourth edition of Walch's *Philosophisches Lexikon.*

Walch's work was followed by one which originated the exact title used shortly thereafter by Voltaire. This was the *Dictionnaire philosophique portatif, ou Introduction à la connoissance de l'homme,* by Didier Pierre Chicaneau de Neuville (London, J. M. Bruyset, 1751, 381 pages; 2d ed., Lyon, J. M. Bruyset, 1756; Italian translation of 2d ed., Venice, 1756; 3d ed., Paris, 1764). In de Neuville's pioneering French philosophical lexicon many of the articles are, or begin with, dictionary-type definitions, but the further explanatory material (including quotations from Boileau, Pope, Rousseau, and the early writings of Voltaire) is sometimes piquant.

VOLTAIRE AND AFTER

On September 28, 1752, Voltaire and other intellectual companions of Frederick the Great were dining with the king at Potsdam. Someone, perhaps Frederick himself, mentioned the idea of producing a philosophical dictionary on which men of letters, including Frederick, would collaborate. Voltaire began work on the project the next day and soon showed the article "Abraham" to Frederick, who considered it good and asked Voltaire to set up a list of proposed articles for the work. Voltaire instead quickly produced articles on *âme* (soul), *athéisme, baptême,* and so on, and Frederick commented that the whole book would soon be finished. Voltaire, however, interrupted the project some months later, when he left Potsdam following his break with Frederick, and he presently became involved in preparing articles for Diderot's *Encyclopédie.*

Early in 1760 Voltaire resumed work on his own dictionary. He wrote to the marquise du Deffant on February 18, "I am absorbed in rendering an alphabetical account to myself of everything that I think about this world and the other, entirely for my own use, but (perhaps after my death) for that of honest people."

In the summer of 1764 the *Dictionnaire philosophique portatif,* which was 344 pages long and contained 73 articles, was printed anonymously at Geneva with London given as the place of publication. There was a second printing later in the year. The book was banned by the Parlement of Paris on March 19, 1765, and was placed on the Index of prohibited books by the pope on July 8, 1765. Voltaire denied authorship of the book in 68 letters between July 1764 and February 1768.

A second edition was published at London in 1765 in four printings (varying from 308 to 364 pages), with eight additional articles. Three of these four printings were subsequently counted as the second, third, and fourth editions. A printing which was counted as the fifth edition was issued at Amsterdam in 1765 in two volumes with 15 additional articles. An edition specifically labeled "Sixième Édition," with 34 additional articles, was published at London in 1767 in two fascicles bound as one volume. Another edition, also called the "Sixième Édition," was printed at Geneva in 1769 under the title *La Raison par alphabet,* with further additions, in two volumes.

Subsequent editions continued to appear both during and after Voltaire's lifetime under various titles, sometimes including the articles prepared by Voltaire for the *Encyclopédie;* Voltaire's *Questions sur l'Encyclopédie,* an alphabetically arranged set of comments; *L'Opinion par alphabet,* a manuscript found after Voltaire's death; or a combination of the foregoing. One of the most useful editions was edited by Julien Benda (2 vols., Paris, Garnier Frères, 1936). Of the English versions, complete or abridged, the first appeared in 1765; a noteworthy successor appeared in 1824 (6 vols., London, J. and H. L. Hunt), comprising about three-fourths of the original, the remainder being, according to the anonymous translator, repetitive. In 1901 an "unabridged and unexpurgated" edition was translated by William F. Fleming (10 vols., London, E. R. DuMont); the latest edition, translated by Peter Gay with a preface by André Maurois, was published in 1962 (2 vols., New York, Basic Books).

Voltaire's dictionary covers primarily topics, almost totally excluding individual philosophers; among the few philosophers accorded separate treatment are Arius and "Julien le Philosophe." The topical articles are largely in the nature of discursive essays, occasionally in dialogue form, rather than directly informative expositions, but they nevertheless reflect extensive research and critical analysis. In the article on miracles Voltaire made such points as the following: if a miracle is an event to be marveled at, then everything is a miracle; if a miracle is a violation of an eternal (inviolable) law, then it is a contradiction in terms; it is a strange God who is so incapable of achieving his purposes through his own laws of nature that he must resort to changing his own "eternal" ways.

The topics covered are, for the most part, in the field of popular philosophy or religious controversy, such as Adam, apocalypse, *tout est bien* (all is good), confession, *enfer* (hell), inquisition, and so on. A few touch on technical philosophy; examples are those on *âme* (soul), *beauté* (beauty), *chain des êtres créés* ("great chain of being"), *destin* (fate), and *nécessaire* (necessary). Of the articles in his own dictionary Voltaire submitted only the one on idolatry intact to Diderot for inclusion in the *Encyclopédie.* It was reprinted there without change.

Various literary scholars have studied the sources of Voltaire's dictionary. Although Voltaire acknowledged his indebtedness to Bayle's *Dictionnaire historique et critique* and the title of his dictionary is identical with that of the one de Neuville published in 1751, it appears that he owed more to the English deists and the early French deists. As André Maurois has observed, the ideas in Voltaire's dictionary "were clichés in its epoch. Gassendi, Fontenelle, Bayle, had said all that." But the form in which the ideas are clothed in Voltaire's dictionary is inimitably adroit, vivid, chatty, anecdotal, and essentially consistent in its rough humaneness and urbanity though inconsistent in details.

Reaction to Voltaire. Reacting with indignation to the religious skepticism of the *Dictionnaire philosophique portatif* and without knowing that Voltaire was the author of the work, Louis M. Chaudon published—also anonymously—the *Dictionnaire anti-philosophique, pour servir de commentaire & de correctif au Dictionnaire philoso-*

phique & aux autres livres qui ont paru de nos jours contre le christianisme (Avignon, 1767, 451 pages; 4th ed., 2 vols. in 1, Avignon, La Veuve Girard, 1775). Among the approximately 150 articles in the first edition are those on soul, atheism, Bayle, *Encyclopédie*, faith, hell, miracles, natural law, and reason; new articles in subsequent editions include those on deists, Spinoza, suicide, theater, and tyrannicide. Some of the articles are in two sections, presenting the orthodox view of the subject and replying to the skeptics' objections. After the alphabetical part of the work is a summary headed "Résultat des réflexions répandues dans ce *Dictionnaire*." Chaudon's defense of religion in general and of Christianity in particular was spirited and literate.

Other eighteenth-century dictionaries. Between Voltaire and Chaudon and the end of the eighteenth century six dictionaries of philosophy appeared—three in French, two in German, and one in English—plus a number of works which have promising titles but are not dictionaries of philosophy.

French. In 1772, eight years after the first appearance of Voltaire's dictionary, a work comparable in outline, *La Petite Encyclopédie, ou Dictionnaire des philosophes,* by Abraham J. de Chaumeix, a Frenchman, was published anonymously and posthumously (Antwerp, Jean Gasbeck, 136 pages). It contains only topical articles, none on philosophers, and the articles are popular rather than strictly philosophical in tenor. The motto at the end of the book is a misquotation from Virgil, "Heu! Ubi prisca fides?" ("Alas! Where now is your former faith?").

The other two of the three French dictionaries were parts of a 166-volume rearrangement, by disciplines, of the material in the Diderot *Encyclopédie*. The rearrangement, entitled *Encyclopédie méthodique* (Paris, C. J. Panckoucke and others, 1782–1832), consisted of about fifty separate dictionaries. One of these was *Logique, métaphysique et morale,* edited by Pierre L. Lacratelle (4 vols., 1786–1791). The Lacratelle work started out to cover only logic and metaphysics, and a complete alphabetical arrangement of topics in those two disciplines was presented, from absolute (in logic, 2 cols.) and abstraction (19 cols.) at the beginning of Volume I to sensation (230 cols.) and systems (41 cols.) near the end of Volume II; however, the scope was then changed to include ethics, and the remainder of Volume II and Volumes III and IV contain an alphabetical series of articles on ethics. Volume III was the first volume to include ethics on the title page.

Immediately adjacent to the Lacratelle work in the *Encyclopédie méthodique* is *Philosophie, ancienne et moderne,* edited by Jacques A. Naigeon, an atheist who considered himself Diderot's successor (3 vols., 1791–1793). The topics range from Academics (352 cols.) to Academy (2 cols.) in Volume I to Zend-Avesta (10 cols., Diderot's article on the subject transplanted intact from the *Encyclopédie*) in Volume III. The third volume also contains, on pages 767–945, articles omitted from the first two volumes.

German. Various giants in the history of philosophy—Aristotle, Leibniz, and Voltaire—have thus far entered this record as contributors to the development of dictionaries of philosophy. Another giant—Kant—enters the record by a quirk of terminology. Kant lectured on the subject *philoso-*

phische Enzyklopädie ten times from 1767/1768 to 1781/1782 and advertised lectures on this subject for 1785/1786 and 1787, although these did not materialize. A set of his lecture notes on *philosophische Enzyklopädie,* probably dating from the winter semester of 1781/1782, was edited by the Deutsche Akademie der Wissenschaften zu Berlin and published for the first time in 1961 in East Berlin. But the work actually deals with what might suitably be called philosophy as an encyclopedic discipline rather than philosophy expounded in encyclopedic form. It presents a structured (not alphabetical) outline of philosophy in its broadest ramifications, based on J. H. Feder's *Grundrisz der philosophischen Wissenschaften* ("Foundation of the Philosophical Sciences," Coburg, Germany, J. C. Findeisen, 1767; 2d ed., 1769).

Thus, Kant did not write a dictionary of philosophy. However, his admirer Salomon Maimon did. Maimon was the author of *Philosophisches Wörterbuch, oder Beleuchtung der wichtigsten Gegenstände der Philosophie, in alphabetischer Ordnung* ("Philosophical Dictionary, or Illumination of the Most Important Themes of Philosophy, in Alphabetical Order," Berlin, Johann F. Unger, 1791, 222 pages). This work is an impressionistic presentation of various philosophical topics, in substance less iconoclastic than Voltaire's dictionary but just as unconventional stylistically. One of the articles, for example, includes separate vehement apostrophes, each beginning "Meine Herren!," to "die Dogmatiker oder Antikantianer" ("dogmatic philosophers or anti-Kantians") and "die kritischen Skeptiker oder Kantianer" ("critical skeptics or Kantians").

Another German dictionary of philosophy in this period, also impressionistic, was Carl Ludwig Friedrich Rabe's *Gedanken und Urtheile über philosophische, moralische und politische Gegenstände, aus guten Schriften gezogen, alphabetisch geordnet* ("Thoughts and Judgments on Philosophical, Ethical and Political Themes, Deduced From Reliable Publications, Alphabetically Arranged," Stendal, Germany, D. C. Franzen and J. C. Grosse, 1789–1790, 2 vols.). This work is even rarer than the Burchardi book of 1610. The Royal Library at Copenhagen possesses what may be the sole extant copy of it, located after the trail had run dry in many other directions. A microfilm of the Copenhagen copy is now available at the Public Library of the District of Columbia.

Volume I of Rabe's *Gedanken* contains reflections on topics with initial letters from *A* to *Z,* and Volume II likewise begins at the beginning of the alphabet and goes through to *Z.* Among the topics discussed are antiquity, art, business, culture, death, despotism, freedom of the press, God, guilt, happiness, language, man, religion, republic, *Schmerz,* science, soul, and time. Articles range from one or two lines to three or four pages in length. The one on freedom of the press reads, in translation, "Without freedom of the press, the soul is crippled. Freedom to think, without freedom to say, is no better than being in a straitjacket." The article on *Held* (hero) reads, "Ein Held wird nicht geformt, er wird geboren" ("A hero is born, not made").

Toward the end of the eighteenth century, there appeared two other documents like Kant's with titles that sound relevant to the story of dictionaries of philosophy but which turn out to have no relevance to the subject. The first of these was Johann Georg Büsch's *Encyclopädie der historischen, philosophischen und mathematischen Wissenschaften* (2 vols. in 1, Hamburg, Heroldsche Buchhandlung, 1775), which presents its material not in an alphabetical but in a systematic arrangement, Volume I covering history and philosophy and Volume II mathematics. The section on philosophy stresses the contributions of Descartes and Wolff and discusses philosophy in general, logic, theology, philosophical psychology, ethics, politics, economics, and related topics.

The second was the *Encyclopädische Einleitung in das Studium der Philosophie*, by Karl Heinrich Heydenricks (Leipzig, Weygandsche Buchhandlung, 1793, 249 pages), which is a systematic, nonalphabetical exposition of the nature of philosophy, systems of philosophy, the bearing of philosophy on other disciplines and on life, and the way to study philosophy.

English. In 1786, *The Philosophical Dictionary, or The Opinions of Modern Philosophers on Metaphysical, Moral, and Political Subjects,* by François Xavier Swediaur, was published (4 vols., London, G. G. J. and J. Robinson, 1786) with "F. S******r, M.D." at the end of the Preface as the only indication of the author or compiler. Many of the articles bear at the end the name of an author (Gibbon, Helvétius, Hume, Locke, Rousseau, Voltaire, and others) from whose writings the article was adapted. Swediaur did not show much understanding of or sympathy for technical philosophy. His article "Ancient Greek Philosophy" mentions Hesiod and Theognis but not Socrates, Plato, or Aristotle.

NINETEENTH CENTURY

Dictionaries of philosophy, or works purporting to be such, appeared in German, English, French, Italian, Latin, and Russian in the nineteenth century.

German. Initiating the contributions of the century to the library of dictionaries of philosophy, J. C. Lossius published *Neues philosophisches allgemeines Real-Lexikon* (4 vols., Erfurt, Germany, J. E. G. Rudolph, 1803–1805). It contains no articles on individual philosophers. Many of the articles are written from a Kantian point of view. The topics treated include not only such philosophical concepts as *angebohrne Begriffe* (innate ideas) and *cogito ergo sum* but also concepts in anthropology, mathematics, and other disciplines.

Lossius' four-volume work was followed soon after by two other works, both of which were left incomplete.

The first of these, Georg S. A. Mellin's *Allgemeines Wörterbuch der Philosophie, zur Gebrauch für gebildete Leser* ("General Dictionary of Philosophy, for Use by Educated Readers," 2 vols., Magdeburg, Germany, Ferdinand Matthias, 1806–1807), covers the letters *A* and *B*; no more volumes were published. The work is thoroughly Kantian, as is evidenced particularly in such articles as those on apperception, on the various aspects of *Begriff* (concept), and on the various kinds of concepts.

The other, Gottfried Immanuel Wenzel's *Neues vollständiges philosophisches Real-Lexikon* ("New Complete Philosophical Encyclopedia," 2 vols., Linz, Austria, Akade-mische Buchhandlung, 1807–1808), was planned in four volumes, but the author died before the work was completed, and only two volumes (covering *A* to *H*) appeared. The quaint subtitle gives an adequate, if overstated, description of the work. Literally translated, the subtitle reads: "In Which the Materials and Technical Terms Appearing in All Parts of Recent and Most Recent Philosophy Are Explained, Being Developed From History Where Necessary; Disagreements of Philosophers Are Expounded and Analyzed, Many Propositions Thereof Being Corrected, Made Precise, or Expanded; Obscurities Are Lifted; New Contributions to the Stock of Philosophical Knowledge Are Presented; and Higher Pedagogy and the Science of Intellectual Excellence [*Klugheitslehre*] Are Similarly Treated."

Original works of encyclopedic scope. Each of three German works published in the subsequent years of the nineteenth century, although denominated an encyclopedia of philosophy, presented its material nonalphabetically. The works are Gottlob E. Schulze's *Enzyklopädie der philosophischen Wissenschaften, zum Gebrauche für seine Vorlesungen* ("Encyclopedia of the Philosophical Sciences, for Use With the Author's Lectures," Göttingen, Vandenhoeck and Ruprecht, 1814, 150 pages; 2d ed., 1818; 3d ed., 1823, 1824); Georg Friedrich Hegel's *Encyklopädie der philosophischen Wissenschaften im Grundrisse* ("Encyclopedia of the Philosophical Sciences in Outline," Heidelberg, A. Oswald, 1817, 288 pages; 2d and 3d eds., 1827, 1830; 4th ed., 3 vols., Berlin, issued by Hegel's students with their lecture notes and other materials, 1840–1845); and Johann F. Herbart's *Kurze Encyklopädie der Philosophie aus praktischen Gesichtspuncten entworfen* ("Short Encyclopedia of Philosophy Designed From the Practical Standpoint," Halle, Germany, C. A. Schwetschke und Sohn, 1831, 405 pages; 2d ed., 1841), which is reprinted in the various editions of Herbart's collected works.

Other dictionaries. German dictionaries of philosophy, more properly so designated, were written after the earliest years of the century by Krug, Furtmair, Hartsen, Noack, and Kirchner (as well as by Eisler, who wrote a landmark work described in a section below). Of the works referred to the first four are of mainly historical interest.

The first is Wilhelm T. Krug's *Allgemeines Handwörterbuch der philosophischen Wissenschaften, nebst ihrer Literatur und Geschichte, nach dem heutigen Standpuncte der Wissenschaft* ("General Concise Dictionary of the Philosophical Sciences, Including Their Literature and History, From the Present Standpoint of Science," 4 vols., Leipzig, F. A. Brockhaus, 1827–1829, plus supp., 1829; 2d ed., 4 vols., 1832–1833, plus supp., 1838). Krug succeeded Kant in the chair of philosophy at Königsberg. Among the more interesting and unusual articles of Krug's book, all competently written, are "Aegyptische Weisheit" (Egyptian wisdom), "Baccalaureus der Philosophie" (Ph.B. degree), "Freund und Freundschaft" (friend and friendship), "Immoralität" (immorality), "Ontologischer Beweis für's Dasein Gottes" (Ontological Proof of God's existence), "Schöne Kunst" (fine art), and "Supernaturalismus" (supernaturalism). The collaborators who produced the Adolphe Franck dictionary of 1844–1852 mentioned below and Pierre Larousse of the French encyclopedia firm criticized Krug more sharply than seems warranted for working, as far as they could see, without plan or method, for giving more emphasis to the history of philosophy than to philosophy itself, and for showing, in their opinion, insufficient gravity in his style.

Another dictionary was Max Furtmair's *Philosophisches Real-Lexikon* (4 fascicles in 1 vol., Augsburg, Karl Kollmanschen Buchhandlung, 1853–1855). The third and fourth fascicles were prepared with the collaboration of Johann N. Uschold. The author, inviting attention to his title, said that his aim was to clarify not words but things. What he presented, however, is indistinguishable from the contents of lexicons with more modest pretensions. His heavy indebtedness to Krug, which he acknowledged, is evidenced by, among other things, his inclusion of the articles "Aegyptische Weisheit," "Baccalaureus der Philosophie," "Freundschaft," and others on topics suggested by Krug's work.

In 1877 appeared Frederik A. Hartsen's *Ein philosophisches Wörterbuch* (Heidelberg, Carl Winter, 45 pages). The terms defined in this work are generally philosophical expressions rather than single terms. An example is *Betrachten etwas* (A) *als etwas* (B) ("considering something [A] as something [B]"). In some cases the definitions are of the dictionary type, with little philosophical depth.

There is also Ludwig Noack's *Philosophie-geschichtliches Lexikon* (Leipzig, Erich Koschny, 1879, 936 pages). This work emphasizes individual philosophers and is especially useful for little-known Renaissance and early modern thinkers. Although some topics—the Academy, eclectics, French philosophy, Cabala—are covered, there are no articles on the philosophical disciplines—ethics, logic, metaphysics, and so on. In 1963 the Stuttgart firm of Friedrich Frommann Verlag was planning to issue a facsimile reprint of this work.

Friedrich Kirchner, author of philosophical monographs and textbooks, including a history of philosophy which went into several editions and was translated into English, wrote a *Wörterbuch der philosophischen Grundbegriffe* (Heidelberg, G. Weiss, 1886, 459 pages), which also appeared in second and third editions (1890 and 1897), by Kirchner, and in fourth, fifth, and sixth editions (1903, 1907, 1911), revised by Carl Michaëlis. The first fascicle, 96 pages, of a projected Russian translation was published at St. Petersburg by Brockhaus–Ephron in 1913. Kirchner's work contains no articles on individual philosophers. The articles are scholarly but not penetrating; the one on logic, for example, is mainly historical and biographical.

English. The four English dictionaries of philosophy published in the nineteenth century are now outmoded.

The first one, Isaac Taylor's *Elements of Thought, or First Lessons in the Knowledge of the Mind* (London, B. J. Holdsworth, 208 pages), appeared in 1822. With some changes in the subtitle this work went through 11 British editions (11th ed., 1866) and two American editions (2d American ed., New York, 1851). Part II contains an exposition, in alphabetical order, of about ninety topics—analysis, argument, art, axiom, being, belief, cause, and so on—bearing upon "the nature and operation of the intellectual powers."

In 1857 William Fleming's *The Vocabulary of Philoso-*phy, *Mental, Moral, and Metaphysical, With Quotations and References, for the Use of Students* (London and Glasgow, Richard Griffin, 560 pages) was published. Subsequent editions included the second (1858), an American edition, edited by Charles P. Krauth (Philadelphia, 1860; reissued 6 times, 1866–1873); a third, edited by Henry Calderwood (1876); another American edition edited and entitled *A Vocabulary of the Philosophical Sciences* by Krauth (1878; reissued, 1879); another American edition edited by Calderwood (New York, 1887, 1890); and a work by Calderwood entitled *Vocabulary of Philosophy and Student's Book of Reference, on the Basis of Fleming's Vocabulary* (1894). The illustrative quotations in the various articles are taken mainly from English writers such as Berkeley, Hume, Jeremy Taylor, Sir William Hamilton, and J. S. Mill, but there are quotations from Kant (in English) in the article "A Priori," from Cicero (in Latin) in "Faculty," and from other foreign thinkers in other articles.

In *A Dictionary of English Philosophical Terms* (London, Rivington, 1878, 161 pages) Francis Garden undertook to present a more general and less technical account of philosophical topics than had appeared in Fleming's work. Like Fleming, however, he leaned heavily on Hamilton for arguments, illustrations, and even topics, including, for example, the article "Worse Relations" (that is, more distant relations) in logic, which is written chiefly according to Hamilton's views.

Edwin S. Metcalf's *Olio of Isms, Ologies and Kindred Matter, Defined and Classified* (Chicago, L'Ora Queta P. and J. Co., 1899, 158 pages) is an elementary and popular manual. In the section "Doctrinal and Sectarian Isms" it has articles on agnosticism, antinomianism, Arminianism, and the like; the section "Civic Isms" has articles on topics like anarchism and collectivism; "Ologies" deals with such topics as aetiology and cosmology. A section headed "Miscellany" treats altruism, analogy, art, and so forth, and "Divination" has articles on aruspicy (art or practice of divination), bibliomancy, and similar topics.

The work entitled *A Dictionary of Philosophy in the Words of Philosophers*, compiled by John R. Thomson (London, R. D. Dickinson, 1887, 479 pages; 2d ed., 1892), is not a dictionary. Its material is arranged according to a strange outline the logic of which leaves much to be desired. In some cases it is not clear whether the material presented is in Thomson's words or in those of the philosopher who is under discussion.

French, Italian, and Latin dictionaries. Adolphe Franck, a disciple of Victor Cousin, and more than fifty collaborators, including A. A. Cournot, Paul Janet, and Ernest Renan, produced the *Dictionnaire des sciences philosophiques* (6 vols., Paris, Librairie Hachette, 1844–1852; 2d ed., 1 vol., 1875; 3d ed., 1 vol., 1885); the second and third editions had an analytical guide to the alphabetical articles. In matters touching on religion the authors of the articles, as pointed out by Pierre Larousse in 1865, showed restraint and circumspection; indeed, in the Preface they acknowledged reverence as one of their key principles. The work is still useful today for its extensive articles on less well-known philosophers. It contains, for example, individual articles on 12 Sophists, 11 Cyrenaics,

6 Pyrrhonists, 13 Greek Stoics, 15 Roman Stoics, and 21 members of the school of Leibniz and Wolff.

Of the other French-language dictionaries of philosophy published in the nineteenth century, one was a Belgian product, and three were Parisian.

The Belgian work, (Louis J. A.) de Potter's *Dictionnaire rationnel des mots les plus usités en sciences, en philosophie, en politique, en morale et en religion* (Brussels and Leipzig, August Schnée, 1859, 348 pages), began as a glossary at the end of the author's *La Réalité déterminée par le raisonnement* (Brussels, 1848). The glossary was reprinted under the title *A, B, C de la science sociale* (Brussels, 1848) and was then extensively elaborated into the *Dictionnaire rationnel*. The author defended middle-class conservatism in religion, politics, morals, and economics. He decried the intellectual elite and the democratic masses, the philosophical skeptics and the radical innovators.

In 1877 Bernard Pérez wrote the 16-page *Petit dictionnaire philosophique* (Paris, A. Morant). This work, intended for baccalaureate candidates, contains mostly two-line to four-line definitions or explanations of technical terms (plus identifications of a few philosophers), from *acatalepsie, actuel,* and *animisme* to *vitalisme,* Xenocrate, and *zététique* (persistent skepticism). Pérez also produced a similar work, *Dictionnaire abrégé de philosophie* (Paris, Félix Alcan, 1893, 90 pages).

Pages 483–521 of Henri Marion's *Leçons de psychologie appliquées à l'éducation* (Paris, Armand Colin, 1882, 538 pages; 13th ed., 1908) contained a "Vocabulaire des noms propres et des expressions philosophiques." This vocabulary covers topics in philosophy and other fields, including art, religion, and science.

Alexis Bertrand's *Lexique de philosophie* (Paris, P. Delaplane, 1892, 220 pages) has had at least four printings. This work covers topics only, on an elementary level, but the explanations are not always clear.

There were one Italian and two Latin works of this kind published in the nineteenth century.

The first Latin work was J. A. Albrand's *Lexicon Philosophicum, Quo Verba Scholastica Explicantur,* a work 68 pages long printed on pages 557–624 of Volume IV of Albrand's edition of the *Theologia Dogmatica,* by Thomas ex Charmes (4 vols., Paris, Louis Vivès, 1856–1857). The articles, explicating *absolutum, beatitudo, esse,* and so on, provide, in prosy Latin, the standard scholastic definitions of the regular scholastic philosophical terms. The *Lexicon* was intended for the use of theological students, especially those trying to understand the system of the eighteenth-century theologian Thomas ex Charmes (also called Thomas a Charmes). Of the several reprints of Albrand's edition of Thomas' *Theologia* (6, 7, or 8 vols.) some do and some do not include Albrand's *Lexicon Philosophicum.*

The Italian work was Luigi Stefanoni's *Dizionario filosofico* (2 vols, in 1, Milan, Natale Battezzati, 1873–1875). Some of the articles—for example, those on immaculate conception, matrimony, molecule, pope, and Shakers—are a bit unusual in dictionaries of philosophy, but the articles on technical philosophical subjects are useful and contain a significant amount of detail. A pro-Catholic bias is evident in the articles on theological subjects.

The second Latin work, Niceto A. Perujo's *Lexicon Philosophico-theologicum* (Valencia, Spain, Friedrich Domenech, 1883, 352 pages), had a scholastic orientation. It contains 1,364 articles, including explanations not only of terms but also of such common philosophical propositions as "Dato uno absurdo, sequitur aliud" ("If one absurdity is granted, another follows"). Some of the explanations are supported by extensive quotations from Aquinas, Bonaventure, and others.

Russian. A number of notable dictionaries of philosophy were written in Russia in the nineteenth century.

In 1819 appeared Alexander I. Galich's *Opyt Filosofskogo Slovaria* ("Toward a Philosophical Dictionary," St. Petersburg), the second fascicle of a larger work on the history of philosophical systems. This dictionary contains 217 articles, from "Absolute" to "Theurgy." The topic headings are given in the Latin alphabet—for instance, "Absolutum"—and the explanations in Russian. Special attention is paid to new philosophical terms.

Alexander I. Galich's *Leksikon Filosofskikh Predmetov* (Vol. I, No. 1, St. Petersburg, Tip. Imp. Akad. Nauk, 1845, 298 pages) is the first fascicle of a proposed set of nine (three volumes with three numbers in each). It covers about 170 terms beginning with *A* or *B* in aesthetics, ethics, logic, and metaphysics. The project was discontinued when the author's notes were destroyed in a fire.

S. S. Gogotsky's monumental work *Filosofsky Leksikon* (4 vols., Kiev, University of Kiev and other publishers, 1857–1873; 2d ed., 1 vol., St. Petersburg, I. I. Glazunov, 1859) contains about twelve hundred articles. The articles on philosophical method, such as those on analogy, classification, dialectic, dogmatism, and method in general, are especially noteworthy. In 1876 Gogotsky produced *Filosofsky Slovar'* (Kiev, Tip. Red. "Kievsk Telegrafa," 146 pages), a one-volume condensation of his lexicon, containing approximately the same number of articles.

Eisler. Rudolf Eisler produced his *Wörterbuch der philosophischen Begriffe und Ausdrücke* ("Dictionary of Philosophical Concepts and Expressions," Berlin, E. S. Mittler und Sohn, 1899, 956 pages), which, following the setup of the *Wörterbuch* by Friedrich Kirchner, has no articles on individual philosophers. Of the three volumes of the fourth edition, whose title was shortened to *Wörterbuch der philosophischen Begriffe* (Berlin, E. S. Mittler und Sohn, published with the cooperation of the Kantgesellschaft, 1927), the second and third were edited with the assistance of Karl Roretz, Eisler having died after the work on the first volume was completed.

This is perhaps the best technical dictionary of philosophy produced up to its time. Even now, it is probably one of the ten best available dictionaries of philosophy, ranking along with the better works of the twentieth century. Its articles contain terse definitions and are rich not only in relevant quotations in the original languages, including English, but also in bibliographical citations. On Oriental subjects the articles were weak in the first edition (Sāmkhya being dismissed with the statement that it is the system of the Indian thinker Kapila) but were strengthened somewhat in subsequent editions. The later editions, although expanded in coverage, contain fewer quotations in languages other than German.

In 1964 the Basel firm of Benno Schwabe had in preparation a new edition of the *Wörterbuch* under the editorship of Joachim Ritter.

For use by students Eisler summarized the main articles of his large dictionary in the *Handwörterbuch der Philosophie* (Berlin, E. S. Mittler und Sohn, 1913, 801 pages), of which a second edition, supervised by Richard Müller-Freienfels, was issued not only as a regular book in 1922 but also as a "microbook" (Düsseldorf, Microbuch- und Film Gesellschaft, 1922, 785 pages on 88 sides).

Eisler also produced the *Philosophen-Lexikon: Leben, Werke und Lehren der Denker* ("Dictionary of Philosophers: Lives, Works and Doctrines of the Thinkers," Berlin, E. S. Mittler und Sohn, 1912, 889 pages) to make up for the lack of treatment of individuals as such in his *Wörterbuch*. The *Philosophen-Lexikon* was the first modern biographical dictionary of philosophers. Although its articles are shorter, more numerous, and alphabetically arranged, it recalls the useful work of Diogenes Laërtius. From Anathon Aall of Norway to Ulrich Zwingli, the Reformation figure, some four thousand philosophers are identified and, when appropriate, discussed, with their main writings and writings about them listed. Eisler could perhaps be excused for according some emphasis to German philosophers, and it is not strictly fair to criticize comparative comprehensiveness on the basis of lines of print, especially since most of Eisler's allocations of space seem right; nevertheless, one may perhaps with some warrant complain that Kant gets 33 pages, Wundt 16, Spinoza 11, Plato (as well as Hegel and Leibniz) 10, and Aristotle 9 and that Hermann Cohen gets more space than Augustine, Fichte more than Descartes, Herbart more than Hume, Lotze more than Locke, Maimon more than Maimonides, and Meinong more than Bentham.

EARLY TWENTIETH CENTURY

In 1901 an important dictionary was published, and an important dictionary was begun. The early twentieth century also saw the publication of dictionary-type or supposedly encyclopedic treatments of philosophical topics by Lalande, Windelband, and less well-known writers.

Goblot. Edmond Goblot issued *Le Vocabulaire philosophique* (Paris, Librairie Armand Colin, 1901, 513 pages; 6th ed., 1924), in which he tried not only to record the actual meanings of terms but in part to correct confused usages by suggesting, for example, separate meanings for *général* and *universel;* for *particulier, individuel,* and *singulier;* and for *mémoire* and *souvenir.* But philosophers being the individualists that they are in the use of words, their degree of acceptance (if any) of his commendable suggestions is not perceptible. Spanish translations of this work were published at Barcelona in 1933 and at Buenos Aires in 1942 and 1945.

Baldwin. The other important work of 1901 was Baldwin's. James M. Baldwin, a psychologist, edited, with the collaboration of an international board of advisers and contributors that included Bosanquet, Dewey, William James, Janet, Lloyd Morgan, Moore, Münsterberg, Peirce, Pringle-Pattison, Royce, Sidgwick, Stout, and Urban, the *Dictionary of Philosophy and Psychology* (3 vols. in 4, New York, Macmillan, 1901–1905; reprinted with correc-

tions several times, in part or in entirety, by the same firm, in some cases with the designation "New Edition"; also reprinted by Peter Smith twice, partly at New York and partly at Gloucester, Mass., 1940s, 1950s). Volume III, in two parts, is a bibliography of philosophy and psychology, by Benjamin Rand, to which there were annual supplements in the *Psychological Index* from 1901 to 1908.

In the Preface the editor stated that a dictionary of terms used in Greek and scholastic philosophy "is much needed: but we have not attempted it." The dictionary does, however, include articles on Greek terminology (8 pages, by Royce) and Latin and scholastic terminology (11 pages, by Royce), as well as on analogy, nous (mind), and other special terms. Moreover, the editor aimed "to present science—physical, natural, moral—with a fullness and authority not before undertaken in a work of this character." Thus, there are articles on anthropology, brain, case law, hybrid, money, peace, pupa, and others. Like Goblot, Baldwin futilely suggested that his readers follow the recommendations made in some of the articles for preferred philosophical usage. For many entries German, French, and Italian equivalents are recommended. In addition, at the end of Volume II there is an index of Greek, Latin, German, French, and Italian terms, including those covered by separate articles on the terms as such and those merely mentioned as recommended equivalents.

Philosophically, the articles in the Baldwin dictionary are of uneven value. Some, especially the biographical articles, are too short, and there are no articles at all on Maine de Biran, Renan, and Saint-Simon. Others are broken down too minutely into terms rarely encountered, including Peirce's articles on particulate, *parva logicalia,* philosopheme, predesignate, and prosyllogism. In others there is cavalier treatment of the philosophical aspects of a subject, as in the psychologically oriented article on the self. Some articles, however, are excellent, especially the longer ones by Dewey—for example, those on nature, pluralism, and skepticism; those by Moore on cause and effect, change, nativism, quality, real, reason, relation, relativity of knowledge, spirit, substance, teleology, and truth; and the longer ones of the approximately 180 written by Peirce, including his 23 columns on syllogism, 10 columns on uniformity, and 10 on matter and form. Peirce's articles (the preparation of which, from 1901 to 1905, constituted his last steady employment) were mainly fragments of a book on logic which he never finished; only about half of these articles were reprinted in the Harvard *Collected Papers* of Peirce. Moore's 12 articles, which he later, with undue modesty, called crude, have not been reprinted.

Lalande. With the collaboration of others André Lalande, a professor at the Sorbonne, issued the *Vocabulaire technique et critique de la philosophie* (21 fascicles, Paris, Félix Alcan, 1909–1922; revision of fascicle covering A in *Bulletin* of Société Française de Philosophie, 1923; 2d ed., 2 vols., 1926; 3d ed., 2 vols., 1928; 4th ed., 3 vols., 1931, reissued in 1932, Vols. I and II reissued, 1938; 5th–9th eds., 1 vol., 1947, 1950, 1956, 1960, 1962; 5th ed. translated into Spanish, Buenos Aires, 1953, with 2d ed., Buenos Aires, 1964, 1,502 pages). Lalande was 95 years old when the ninth edition of the *Vocabulaire* was published. At the bottom of most of the pages appear the comments of members of the Société Française de Philosophie, including Peano and Russell among the foreign members, on the articles. The emphasis of the articles is on clarifying the meanings of terms and the usage of expressions rather than on the imparting of historical or technical information.

Original works of encyclopedic scope. Just as, early in the nineteenth century, the works of Schulze, Hegel, and Herbart were published as encyclopedias of the philosophical sciences, so early in the twentieth century three works of this kind were published or begun. The first "nonencyclopedia" was a series of works, edited by H. Renner and published at Charlottenburg, Germany, by O. Günther beginning in 1907, under the general title *Encyklopädie der Philosophie*. It included, for example, an introduction to philosophy and volumes on the philosophy of Rudolf Stammler and Rudolf Eucken.

Second of the three nonencyclopedias was August J. Dorner's *Encyklopädie der Philosophie* (Leipzig, Verlag der Durr'schen Buchhandlung, 1910, 334 pages); in Kantian fashion it dealt with phenomenological investigations, the construction of empirical science, and similar topics.

The third was a proposed *Encyklopädie der philosophischen Wissenschaften,* of which the first volume, *Logik,* was published in 1912, edited by Wilhelm Windelband and Arnold Ruge (Tübingen, Germany, J. C. B. Mohr, 275 pages), containing expositions of the principles of logic by Windelband, Josiah Royce (translated from English), and Louis Couturat (translated from French); of the task of logic by Benedetto Croce (translated from Italian); of the problems of logic by Federigo Enriques (translated from Italian); and of the bearing of the concepts of consciousness on logic by Nicholas Lossky (translated by Lossky himself from the original Russian).

An English edition of the Windelband–Ruge encyclopedia was projected under the editorship of Sir Henry Jones, and the first volume, *Logic,* was published in 1913 (London, Macmillan, 269 pages). For the English edition Royce's English version was available, Couturat's article was done into English from the original French rather than from the published German version, and the German of Lossky's article was his own; therefore, as the translator, B. Ethel Meyer, pointed out, only Croce's and Enriques' articles "suffered a double process of translation."

The onset of war in 1914 and the death of Windelband in 1915 resulted in the abandonment of the project. Windelband's contribution to the first volume, issued separately in German in 1913, was republished in English years later as *Theories in Logic* (New York, Philosophical Library, 1961, 81 pages). Royce's contribution was also published separately, as *The Principles of Logic* (New York, Philosophical Library, 1961, 77 pages).

Other works. The works of the early twentieth century by less well-known writers in Italian, French, German, English, Russian, and Japanese were numerous.

In Italian there was Cesare Ranzoli's *Dizionario di scienze filosofiche* (Milan, Ulrico Hoepli, 1905, 683 pages; 2d ed., 1916, 1,252 pages; 3d ed., 1926, 1,207 pages; 4th ed., Maria P. Ranzoli, ed., 1943, 1,360 pages; 5th ed., Maria Ranzoli, ed., 1952, 1,313 pages). Covering only topics, not

individual philosophers, the book contains articles on Pyrrhonism and Pythagoreanism (and later editions cover existentialism), but there is none on Platonism. The articles are of high quality.

In 1906 appeared Élie Blanc's *Dictionnaire de philosophie ancienne, moderne et contemporaine* (Paris, P. Lethielleux, 1,248 cols.; supp., for 1906–1907 and 1906–1908; consolidated ed., 1909). Blanc also published a vocabulary of scholastic and contemporary philosophy, presented at the beginning of his *Traité de philosophie scolastique* (3 vols., Lyon, Emmanuel Vitte, 1889; 3d ed., Paris, 1909), and the *Dictionnaire universel de la pensée, alphabetique, logique et encyclopédique* (2 vols., Lyon, Emmanuel Vitte, 1899), which was a thesaurus-type classification of words, ideas, and things. In the *Dictionnaire de philosophie* his Catholic viewpoint is evident in many places; indeed, his starting point, he said, is moderate dogmatism.

In Germany Rudolf Odebrecht produced the *Kleines philosophisches Wörterbuch; Erklärung der Grundbegriffe der Philosophie* (Berlin, Buchverlag der "Hilfe," 1908, 83 pages; 6th ed., Leipzig, Felix Meiner, 1929). The choice of topics in this highly condensed wordbook was in some cases injudicious. There are entries on *heliozentrisch* (heliocentric) and *Hypnose* (hypnosis) but none on the Academy, Epicureanism, or Taoism.

A pocket volume, about $2\frac{1}{2}$ inches by 4 inches, one of a series of about fifty covering literary terms, commercial terms, art terms, and so on was edited by Arthur Butler, *A Dictionary of Philosophical Terms* (London, G. Routledge and Sons, and New York, E. P. Dutton, 1909, 114 pages). The *Dictionary of Philosophical Terms* depends heavily on Kant, who is cited in ten of the first fifty articles. Among the topics treated are a number of German terms, such as *Anschauung* (outlook), *Begriff* (concept), and *Ding an sich* (thing-in-itself).

In 1909 also appeared Arturo Mateucci's *Vocabolarietto di termini filosofici* (Milan, Casa Editrice Sonzogno, 63 pages; 2d ed., 1925). Intentionally elementary in its treatment, in many cases this work contains little more than dictionary definitions of the concepts covered. Some 75 per cent of the articles consist of only one, two, or three lines.

Fritz Mauthner edited the *Wörterbuch der Philosophie* (2 vols., Munich, G. Muller, 1910–1911; 2d ed., 3 vols., Leipzig, Felix Meiner, 1923). Mauthner was a literary critic and nonacademic philosopher who contributed pioneering insights on the question of what, if anything, ordinary language reveals about the world, whether the distinction between analytic and synthetic propositions is tenable, and so on. His *Wörterbuch,* after a rambling introduction of 96 pages, presents a mixture of very odd items and very useful, though informal, ones. The odd items include the articles "Babel," "Bacon's Gespensterlehre" (Bacon's study of ghosts), "Form" (40 cols., with only a passing reference to Aristotle), and "Graphologie." The more useful ones include "Geschichte" (history, 68 cols.), "Natur" (nature, 29 cols.), "Nichts" (nothing, 14 cols.), and "Spinoza's 'Deus'" (Spinoza's "God," 19 cols.); even these, however, should be used with caution, for they contain some questionable material.

Ernest L'vovich Radlov's *Filosofsky Slovar'* (St. Petersburg, Brockhaus–Ephron, 1911, 284 pages; 2d ed., Moscow, G. A. Leman, 1913) covers aesthetics, ethics, logic, psychology, and the history of philosophy. It is of only limited usefulness.

Tetsujiro Inouye, Yujiro Motora, and Rikizo Nakashima edited the *Dictionary of English, German, and French Philosophical Terms, With Japanese Equivalents* (Tokyo, Maruzen Kabushiki–Kaisha, 1912, 205 pages), written in English. This is the definitive edition of the *Dictionary of Philosophical Terms* first brought out by Inouye and others in 1881 and issued in a second edition in 1884. For topical entries, including some in Arabic, Greek, and Latin besides the languages listed in the title, only the Japanese equivalents are given; the personal entries also provide identifying information.

Julius Reiner's *Philosophisches Wörterbuch* (Leipzig, Otto Tobies, 1912, 295 pages) is an elementary work in which, for example, the article on *Ambiguität* (ambiguity) consists of one word, *Zweideutigkeit* (having two meanings), and the article on *Intellekt* (intellect) consists of two words, *Geist, Verstand* (spirit or mind, understanding). Other articles, however, such as those on *Darwinismus* and *Ethik* (Darwinism and ethics), go more deeply into the subject.

Another German work was Heinrich Schmidt's *Philosophisches Wörterbuch* (Leipzig, Alfred Kröner, 1912, 106 pages; 8th ed., 1930). This was republished in the United States in 1945 by authority of the alien property custodian and went through several editions; the tenth edition (1943) was reprinted in the United States without the authority of the alien property custodian; the sixteenth edition appeared in 1961. The editions which appeared after the death of the author in 1935 were supervised by various editors. The numerous editions of this work had a vast circulation in all German-language areas. Indeed, it is perhaps the most widely used philosophical dictionary in any language at any time, the Eisler work being its main rival for this distinction. In the ninth edition (1934), while Schmidt was still alive, some pro-Nazi and anti-Jewish comments were included, and in the tenth edition (1943) the desecration of scholarship was compounded with obsequious compliments to insignificant Nazis and truly monstrous articles on Bergson, Freud, Husserl, and others. Recent editions bend over backward to rectify these aberrations.

Paul Thormeyer's *Philosophisches Wörterbuch* (Leipzig, B. G. Teubner, 1916, 96 pages; 4th ed., 1930) is an uncommonly useful short reference work. It is well organized and was up-to-date at the time it was issued.

THE NINETEEN-TWENTIES

Anglo-Saxon silence. In the 1920s 12 dictionaries of philosophy appeared or were begun—4 in German and 1 each in Hungarian, Swedish, Dutch, French, Spanish, Hebrew, Japanese, and Chinese. Not one was published in the United States or Great Britain. Indeed, the only English-language work deserving of mention here published between Butler's *Dictionary* of 1909 and Runes's

Dictionary of 1942 was a quasi encyclopedia, the *International Encyclopedia of Unified Science,* begun in 1939. The Anglo-Saxon silence can only be recorded here. The explanation of it requires more data than are readily at hand.

German. Of the German works published in the 1920s three were published in 1923. The *Systematisches Wörterbuch der Philosophie,* by Karl W. Clauberg and Walter Dubislav (Leipzig, Felix Meiner, 1923, 565 pages), is systematic to a fault, many of the articles being broken down into standard subdivisions—for example, definition, statement, addition, and example—in a somewhat rigid fashion. Dubislav, who was a professor of philosophy at the University of Berlin, had a continuing interest in the clarification of concepts. He was close to logical empiricism and wrote the comprehensive *Die Definition* (Leipzig, Felix Meiner, 1931, 160 pages); he also made notable contributions to the philosophy of method, mathematics, and science.

In Rudolf Wagner's *Philosophisches Wörterbuch* (Munich, Rösl, 1923, 148 pages) articles range in length from one-word or two-word definitions or identifications to the six-page article on the history of philosophy, which consists mainly of a five-page outline taken from Wilhelm Wundt's *Einleitung in die Philosophie* (1914); individual philosophers are not accorded separate treatment.

In most dictionaries of philosophy that cover both topics and persons, the articles on topics are far more numerous than those on people; in Alfred Sternbeck's *Führer durch die Philosophie; Philosophenlexikon und philosophisches Sachwörterbuch* (Berlin, Globus Verlag, 1923, 306 pages), however, those on people almost equal the topical articles in number. Moreover, whereas some of the topical articles are elementary, containing little more than dictionary definitions, the biographical articles are more substantial.

Two years later, there was published the last of the German works of the 1920s, *Klare Begriffe! Lexikon der gebräuchlicheren Fachausdrücke aus Philosophie und Theologie,* by Theodor Mönnichs, S.J. ("Clear Concepts! Dictionary of the Most Common Technical Terms of Philosophy and Theology," Berlin, Ferdinand Dümmlers Verlag, 1925, 170 pages; 2d ed., 1929). This work was written, according to the author, from the standpoint of *philosophia perennis* and Catholic theology. The longest article is the sixty-line one on religion. The pervasive scholastic emphasis in the book is indicated by the fact that many articles begin with the Latin equivalent of the term being covered, and the second edition contains, as an appendix, a 20-page alphabetical list of Latin philosophical terms with their German equivalents.

Hungarian. The Hungarian work of the 1920s was *Philosophiai Szótár,* by Enyvvári Jenő (family name Enyvvári), published at Budapest by Franklin-Társulat (1923, 187 pages). The articles in this work show a creditable familiarity with West European scholarship. The titles of many of the articles are in languages other than Hungarian—for example, "Élan vital," and "Moral Insanity." Appended are a list of philosophers and a competent discussion of philosophical bibliographies.

Swedish. Sweden contributed the *Filosofiskt Lexikon,* edited by Alf Ahlberg (Stockholm, Bokförlaget Natur och

Kultur, 1925, 207 pages; 3d ed., 1951). In this work Swedish philosophers were given fuller treatment than others—C. J. Boström, 15 cols.; E. G. Geijer, 10 cols.; Aristotle and Plato, 6 cols. each.

Dutch. The Dutch work of the period was C. J. Wijnaendts Francken's *Koort Woordenboek van Wijsgeerige Kunsttermen* ("Short Dictionary of Philosophical Terms," Haarlem, D. H. Tjeenk Willink & Zonen, 1925, 157 pages). It covers topics only, in a fairly popular style, and the choice of topics is liberal, making room for such terms as *kosmopolitisme, opportunisme,* and *sarcasme,* along with more technical philosophical terms.

French. In France appeared Armand Cuvillier's *Petit Vocabulaire de la langue philosophique* (Paris, Librairie Armand Colin, 1925, 109 pages; 13th ed., 1953). It was subsequently translated into Turkish (Ankara, 1944) and Portuguese (São Paulo, Brazil, 1961). This work was intended by its author to be at once *élémentaire* and *précis.* In large measure it succeeded in achieving both objectives.

Spanish. Begun in Spain was the *Diccionario manual de filosofía* by Marcelino Arnáiz and B. Alcalde (Madrid, Talleres Voluntad, 1927——). Volume I, "Vocabulario Ideario" (659 pages), is rich in bibliography, and many of the articles contain sound historical data in addition to the conceptual explanations which the volume was essentially intended to provide. A projected second volume, covering the history of doctrines, biographies, and bibliography, was not published.

Eastern languages. In the 1920s dictionaries of philosophy appeared in three Eastern languages, apparently for the first time (aside from translations).

Hebrew. The Hebrew dictionary of philosophy begun in the 1920s was the *Otsar ha-Munahim ha-Filosofiyim ve-Antologiyah Filosofit* ("Thesaurus of Philosophical Terms and Philosophical Anthology"), by Jacob Klatzkin (4 vols., Leipzig, August Pries, 1928–1933); an introductory volume, published in Berlin by "Eschkol" Verlag in 1926, contains an anthology of Hebrew philosophy. Each of the four regular volumes has, as an added Latin title, *Thesaurus Philosophicus Linguae Hebraicae et Veteris et. Recentioris;* Volumes III and IV had M. Zobel as coeditor. The dictionary articles are on topics only, not philosophers or schools of philosophy. Many of the articles contain the German or Latin equivalent of the title of the article; indeed, the purpose usually seems to be to explain the use of terms rather than to convey historical information on the topic as a topic, although the usage of historical writers on the subject is often indicated.

Japanese. A 1,026-page work entitled *Tetsugaku dai-Jisho* ("Dictionary of Philosophy") was published at Tokyo in 1924 by Dai Nippon Hyakka Jisho (Japanese Encyclopedia). The eighth edition (1928) consists of three volumes of text, an index volume, and a supplement. In the text volumes and in the supplement each article begins with the title in Japanese, followed usually by English, German, and French equivalents of the title. Thus, the first article in the first volume is headed, after the Japanese title, "Love. Liebe. Amour." The next several articles deal with patriotism, agape (listed alone after the Japanese title), affection, love and hate (with the Greek equivalents, φιλότης and νεῖκος), Aitareya Upanishad, idealism, vague

dualism, pity, and Augustine. Some of the articles, including the one on religion, are extensive, and many include references to European works.

The index volume of this Japanese dictionary has a title page in German ("Encyclopaedia Japonica, *Enzyklopädische Wörterbuch der Philosophie . . . Register . . .* Tokyo: Dobunkwan"). In addition to a Japanese index, it contains English, French, German, Latin, Pali, Sanskrit, and Chinese indexes and a *Namenregister* (index of names). In the English index approximately 35 of the first 100 entries are strictly philosophical—absolute, abstract, Academy, accident, actual, and so on; most of the others pertain to psychology. In the *Namenregister,* too, about 35 of the first 100 entries are standard names in philosophy—Abelard, Aenesidemus, Albert the Great, al-Fārābī, and so on.

Chinese. In *Chê Hsüeh Tz'ŭ Tien* ("Dictionary of Philosophy"), by Fan Ping-ch'ing (Shanghai, Commercial Press, 1926, 1,110 pages; 2d ed., 1935; 3d ed., 1961), the title of each article is given in Chinese, English, French, and German. The dictionary begins with an article on monism and continues with articles on monotheism, Monophysites, the seven liberal arts, the seven wise men, dualism, dilemma, antinomy, ethnology, subconscious, Albert the Great, major term, minor term, asymmetry, *credo quia absurdum,* medieval philosophy, Pascal, Parmenides, and so forth. The content is scholarly, but there are numerous errors in the Western languages. The work closes with an alphabetical index of names (in which Abelard has 8 references, Aristotle 45, Kant 28, and Marx 5) and an alphabetical index of topics from abiogenesis (1 reference) to *Zwecksystem* (1 reference).

THE NINETEEN-THIRTIES

In the 1930s there appeared four Italian and two Russian works. During this period a number of works in other languages were also published.

German. Germany began the decade with Max Apel's *Philosophisches Wörterbuch* (Berlin and Leipzig, W. de Gruyter, 1930, 155 pages). The fifth edition, which was revised by Peter Ludz, appeared in 1958, and a Spanish translation was published at Mexico City in 1961. Editions of Apel's work published since World War II are pro-Soviet.

Dutch. In the Netherlands appeared the *Encyclopaedisch Handboek van het Moderne Denken,* edited by Willem Banning and 41 collaborators (2 vols., Arnhem, Van Loghum Slaterus, 1930–1931; 2d ed., 1 vol., 1942; 3d ed., 1 vol., 1950). Although the third edition emphasizes such modern ideas as anarchism, Gestalt theory, phenomenology of worship, quantification of the predicate, and the United Nations, the work does not neglect such standard philosophical ideas as category, natural law, and thing.

English. A United States contribution, a quasi encyclopedia, in the 1930s was the inauguration of the *International Encyclopedia of Unified Science,* by Otto Neurath, Rudolf Carnap, and Charles Morris in 1936/1937 at the University of Chicago. This work, carried on after Neurath's death in 1945 by the Institute for the Unity of Science in Boston under the joint editorship of Carnap and

Morris, consists thus far of 15 fascicles, of which Volume I, Number 1 (1938), contained articles by Niels Bohr on analysis and synthesis in science, by Carnap on logical foundations of the unity of science, by John Dewey on unity of science as a social problem, by Morris on scientific empiricism, by Neurath on unified science as encyclopedic integration, and by Bertrand Russell on the importance of logical form. The other 14 are monographs by individual authors. To each of these a volume and a number are assigned. The latest numerically is Volume II, Number 9 (1951), a study by Jørgen Jørgensen on the development of logical empiricism. The latest chronologically, Volume II, Number 2 (1962), is a monograph by Thomas S. Kuhn on the structure of scientific revolutions.

Thus, this "encyclopedia," like Hegel's, Herbart's, Contri's (see below), Windelband–Ruge's and the *Nouvelle Encyclopédie philosophique,* is a compendium but it is not alphabetical. The announced topics of the volumes are foundations of the unity of science, Volumes I and II; theories, induction, probability, and so on, Volume III; logic and mathematics, Volume IV; physics, Volume V; biology and psychology, Volume VI; social and humanistic science, Volume VII; and history of the scientific attitude, Volume VIII. This project, inspired by logical positivism and designed by Neurath to show that all the sciences speak the same language—essentially, physicalism—was overambitious.

French. France's contribution in the 1930s was Jean B. Domecq's *Vocabulaire de philosophie* (Tours, Alfred Cattier, 1931, 208 pages), which has separate alphabetical arrangements of topics for logic, ethics, and metaphysics and a consolidated index at the end. The author was an abbot, and the work has a Catholic orientation.

Mention may also be made of a series of monographs inaugurated in Paris in 1934 by the Presses Universitaires de France, *Nouvelle Encyclopédie philosophique,* which do not constitute an encyclopedia in the strict sense. Among the monographs published thus far are, for example, Louis Lavelle's *Introduction à l'ontologie* (No. 41, 1947) and Robert Blanché's *Les Attitudes idéalistes* (No. 45, 1949).

Italian. Four Italian dictionaries of philosophy appeared or were begun in this period. The first was Giovanni Semprini's *Piccolo dizionario di coltura filosofica e scientifica* (Milan, Edizioni Athena, 1931, 502 pages). This was revised as *Nuovo dizionario di coltura filosofica e scientifica* (Turin, Società Editrice Internazionale, 1952, 470 pages). The work covers topics and individuals in philosophy, science, and education.

In 1933, Antonio Bettioli's *Il pensiero filosofico attraverso i secoli* (Urbino, Editoriale Urbinate, 234 pages) was published. The articles are grouped into schools and systems of philosophy—for example, the Academy, eclectics, idealism—and individual philosophers—113 names, including Dante, Feuerbach, Goethe, Leonardo, Swedenborg, and Tolstoy but not Bergson, Dewey, Husserl, Origen, Philo, or Proclus. The book is of limited value.

An elementary work with little penetration, Francesco Varvello's *Dizionario etimologico filosofico e teologico* (Turin, Società Editrice Internazionale, 406 pages), appeared in 1937, with a second edition in 1938. Fascism is lauded as the opposite of various false forms of government. According to the author, Marx (described as a Jew) rejected the idea that man does not live by bread alone. The articles on religion are pro-Catholic.

There was also Emilio Morselli's *Piccolo dizionario filosofico* (Milan, Carlo Signorelli, 1938, 104 pages). In this book the author aimed to help young readers who encounter in the classics of thought special philosophical expressions, expressions whose meanings differ not only from what they are in ordinary discourse but also from period to period.

An Italian work of the 1930s which called itself an encyclopedia of philosophy but which was not arranged alphabetically was Siro Contri's *Piccola enciclopedia filosofica* (Bologna, Costantino Galleri, 1931), of which only the first volume, on logic and the philosophy of science, was published.

Portuguese. In Brazil appeared Renato Kehl's *Bioperspectivas; dicionário filosófico* (Rio de Janeiro, Livraria Francisco Alves, 1938, 187 pages), which is a series of Voltairian musings on art, the categorical imperative, civilization, death, education, free will, God, history, intelligence, original sin, personality, philosophy, politics, progress, work, and other subjects.

Russian. The first of the two Soviet contributions of the 1930s was Timofei S. Ishchenko's *Kratky Filosofsky Slovar'* (Moscow, Moskofsky Rabochy, 1931, 200 pages), which gave more space to Stalin (four cols.) than to Plato, Aristotle, Kant, Hegel, or Marx. Other Marxist topics, such as dictatorship of the proletariat, were accorded correspondingly disproportionate treatment with the usual positive bias. The three items in the bibliography on Aristotle are by Marx, Engels, and Stalin, respectively.

The second was a work by Mark M. Rozental' and Pavel F. Yudin, likewise entitled *Kratky Filosofsky Slovar'* (Moscow, 1939; 2d–4th eds., 1940, 1951, 1954, each of which was reprinted the following year). A new edition appeared in 1963 with the title modified by the omission of the first word, which means "short," although the 1963 edition of 544 pages is actually shorter than the previous edition, which had 567 pages. The encyclopedia was translated into Spanish in 1945, Bulgarian in 1947, English in 1949, Ukrainian in 1952, Hebrew in 1954, and Chinese, French, Polish, and Rumanian in 1955. Reportedly, 2 million copies of the Russian original were sold in the first ten years after publication, and the press run of one of the printings in the 1950s was 500,000. The English version, adapted and translated by Howard Selsam (New York, International Publishers, 1949, 128 pages), stated in the Preface that the volume reflects Marxist partisanship (for materialism and for socialism) as contrasted with the lack of a "common approach" and the "alphabetic disorder" of other dictionaries of philosophy.

Illustrative of the topical entries in the English version are those in the E's: "Eclecticism," "Economic Bases of Society," "Economic Determinism," "Economics and Politics," "Empiricism," "Empirio-criticism," "Energism (metaphysical)," "Epistemology," "Equality," and "Equilibrium, Theory of." The men treated in the S's are Saint-Simon, Schelling, Spencer, Spinoza, and Stalin, and the article on Stalin is the longest of these.

The article on Kant in the English version dutifully

quotes from Lenin, and those on Campanella and dualism, among others, drag in quotations from Stalin. Many of the articles on individual philosophers vapidly make a point of recounting what Marx, Engels, Lenin, or Stalin thought of the philosopher or even reverently disinter a colorless quotation from Stalin summarizing what Marx or Lenin thought of the philosopher. The article "Partisanship of Philosophy" states that the class struggle is always behind the scenes in the open struggle of philosophical opinions.

According to Alexander Philipov, a former professor of philosophy at the University of Kharkov who now lives in the United States, for the English version Selsam watered down two features of the original—its invective and its extravagant praise of Lenin and Stalin—in order to make the edition less offensive to Western readers.

A significant feature of the original is the fact that the article on Stalin in the fourth edition (1954) ended with a sentence which may be translated "The immortal name of Joseph Stalin will live forever in the minds and hearts of the Russian people"; that sentence vanished without a trace in the 1955 printing of the same edition. In the 1963 edition, of which 400,000 copies were printed and which had about 160 collaborators (including most of the important figures in current Soviet philosophy), there is no article on Stalin, and the Preface acknowledges the "enormous harm" resulting from the cult of Stalin. The 1963 edition is stronger than its predecessors in coverage of linguistic philosophy, logical positivism, and logic.

Lithuanian. Lithuania's contribution to the history of philosophical dictionaries is a 97-page article entitled "Bendroji Filosofijos Terminija" ("General Terminology of Philosophy"), by Stasys Šalkauskis; it constituted an entire issue of the periodical *Logos; Filosofijos Žurnalas* (Kaunas), 1937. The article listed some fifteen hundred Lithuanian terms useful in philosophical discussions, with their equivalents in French, German, and Russian. The list was supplemented by a discussion of synonyms of various philosophical terms in Lithuanian. In a 1938 issue of the same periodical Šalkauskis presented a list of over fifteen hundred German philosophical terms with their Lithuanian equivalents.

Hebrew. In Palestine, Zvi Hirsch Rudy produced the *Leksikon le-Filosofiyah* (Tel Aviv, Dvir, 1939, 816 cols.), with an added title page in Latin, *Philosophiae et Scientiarum Propinquarum Lexicon Hebraicum*. This work is generous with Latin terms, as the titles of articles—for example, "Actus purus," in Hebrew transliteration; as the Latin equivalents of the Hebrew titles of topical articles—for example, "Natura Naturans" as the equivalent of "Teva Tovei"; and as the titles of works cited—for example, works by Abelard and Augustine cited in the articles on those thinkers. Contemporary writers, such as Dewey and Meyerson, and topics of current interest, such as absurd and *élan vital*, are also included. The articles lack penetration. The Bibliography at the end is erratic in including, along with students' handbooks, a poorly balanced small selection of specialized monographs.

Chinese. In 1934 appeared a new Chinese dictionary, not so strictly confined to philosophy as was the 1926 Chinese work. This was the *Ssu Hsiang Chia Ta Tz'ŭ Tien* ("Dictionary of Great Thinkers"), by P'an Nien-chih

(Shanghai, Shih Chieh, 1,062 pages), which contains over five hundred articles on philosophers, writers, artists, musicians, and others. Mo Tzu quite properly is accorded 12 columns, but in the modern period Kant and Mill get only 5 columns each while Mussolini rates 6. Many names are misspelled.

THE NINETEEN-FORTIES

The 1940s saw six philosophical dictionaries in Spanish, five in English, five in German, two in Italian, two in French, and one each in Hungarian and Turkish.

Ferrater Mora. José Ferrater Mora began the decade by producing the *Diccionario de filosofía* (Mexico City, Editorial Atlante, 1941, 598 pages; 2d ed., 1944; 3d–4th eds., Buenos Aires, Editorial Sudamericana, 1951, 1958; 5th ed. in preparation). It is one of the most useful dictionaries published in the twentieth century. From the technical standpoint it may be mentioned that the author used a sensible system of cross references which eliminates the need for an index; he chose as topics for articles units which are neither too large nor too small. The bibliographical citations provided at the ends of some articles are judiciously selected.

The writing shows a philosophical understanding decidedly above the average for writers of philosophical dictionaries. Ferrater Mora was equally strong in his knowledge of modern logic and positivism and in the more traditional philosophical trends and developments associated with Continental metaphysics. The comprehensiveness of his scholarship and the soundness of his judgment have combined to create a monumental one-man contribution to the library of dictionaries of philosophy.

Other Latin American works. In the same year, 1941, two other dictionaries were published in Latin America. One was Martín T. Ruiz Moreno's *Vocabulario filosófico* (Buenos Aires, Editorial Guillermo Kraft, 1941, 156 pages; 2d ed., 1946, 302 pages). Among the articles of special interest in it are "Angustia" (anguish), which sets forth the viewpoints of Kierkegaard and Heidegger, and "Cosa" (thing), which distinguishes the philosophical, the (Argentine) juridical, and the economic uses of the term.

The other dictionary was César A. Guardia Mayorga's *Léxico filosófico* (Arequipa, Peru, 1941, 138 pages). A second edition was published in Arequipa in 1949 under the title *Terminología filosófica*. This work allots more space to Oriental subjects than does Ruiz Moreno's.

A work of the 1940s described as a dictionary of Argentine thought—Florencio J. Amaya's *Diccionario político, sociológico y filosófico argentino* (Mendoza, Argentina, Editorial Cuyo, 1946, 520 pages)— is more general than its title indicates. The philosophical articles are mainly subjective reflections (in the manner of Voltaire but more conservative) with occasional references to historic positions. The author's declared intention to produce sequels 6 and 12 years later (described on the title page of this book as Volumes II and III) was not carried out.

In 1947 appeared the anonymous *Pequeño diccionario de filosofía* (Buenos Aires, 156 pages), issued by Ediciones Centurión for use in conjunction with Emilio Gouiran's *Historia de la filosofía* (Buenos Aires, 1947), published by the same house. The *Pequeño diccionario* consists of two parts, one on philosophers from Peter Abelard to Xavier Zubiri, with indications of their dates and their principal works, and the other on philosophical terms, from Academia (the Academy) to *univoco* (univocal), with explanations ranging from 1 to 29 lines.

Spanish – Spain. In José M. Rubert Candau's *Diccionario manual de filosofía* (Madrid, Editorial Bibliográfica Española, 1946, 658 pages) the main topics of philosophy are dealt with in extensive articles or groups of articles, and the less important topics are given merely as entries with references to the main articles where they are treated. Thus, there are articles on being (5 cols.), supreme modes of being (21 cols.), and transcendental properties of being (27 cols.); the entry "Categorías supremas" refers the reader to the articles on supreme modes of being and on predicables and predicaments. This work deserves to be better known for its clear and systematic exposition of complex subject matter, especially on topics where its Catholic orientation is not a factor.

Italian. Alfredo Galluccio's *Dizionarietto dei principali vocaboli filosofici* (Cava de' Tirreni, Italy, Editore Coda, 1942, 23 pages; 3d ed., Naples, 1952) covers only topics. Most of the eight hundred articles in the third edition are only a few lines long and are intended to identify unfamiliar terms which students may encounter in their philosophical reading.

Another miniature dictionary is Paolo Rotta's *Dizionarietto filosofico* (Milan, Carlo Marzorati, 1944, 125 pages; 5th ed., 1953), which likewise covers only topics, including concepts, problems, and movements. Many of the almost five hundred articles in the fifth edition present Kant's ideas on the subject at hand.

French. Régis Jolivet, dean of the faculty of philosophy of the Catholic University of Lyon, produced the French contribution of the 1940s, *Vocabulaire de la philosophie* (Lyon, Emmanuel Vitte, 1942, 207 pages; 2d–4th eds., 1946, 1951, 1957; Spanish translation, Buenos Aires, 1953). The articles are brief (4 lines for "Thomisme" but 53 for "Liberté" and 52 for "Nature"). A 17-page appendix presents a "tableau historique des écoles de philosophie," showing, in conventional groupings, the dates and (in 1–11 lines) the "écoles et doctrines" of about 250 philosophers from Zoroaster to Wittgenstein.

A book described in its foreword as a "dictionnaire abrégé" is Georges Barbarin's *L'Ami des heures difficiles; un consolateur et un guide* (Paris, Éditions Niclaus, 1946, 173 pages). The author presents conventional advice, constituting a popular philosophy or a popular psychology, on more than 130 problems of life—adversity, anxiety, despair, humiliation, injustice, pain, remorse, scandal, and seduction, among others. A seduced and betrayed woman is advised to look inward and find the Divine Friend in her own soul. The friend (*Ami*) mentioned in the title is not the book but God.

English. The *Dictionary of Philosophy* (343 pages), edited by Dagobert Runes, was published at New York by the Philosophical Library in 1942. The list of 72 contributors included some outstanding American philosophers plus a few noted Europeans. When the work was published, 13 of the contributors—C. A. Baylis, A. C. Benja-

min, E. S. Brightman, Rudolf Carnap, Alonzo Church, G. W. Cunningham, C. J. Ducasse, Irwin Edman, Hunter Guthrie, Julius Kraft, Glenn R. Morrow, Joseph Ratner, and J. R. Weinberg—declared their disapproval of it. Their statement, published in various periodicals including the *Philosophical Review* and *Mind,* read in part: "We objected to the publication of the work in its present form, and some of us made vigorous efforts to persuade Mr. Runes to delay publication until it had been very materially revised. These efforts were to no avail." They added that their own articles had been altered without their consent and that although they were listed as associate or contributing editors, they "feel obliged to make a public disavowal of any editorial responsibility for it."

Despite the important defects of this work, chiefly imbalance, there are many pithy, useful identifications, descriptions, and discussions in it, especially those by Church on topics in logic. Indeed, the collection of Church's contributions to the dictionary and their issuance in a separate volume on issues and methods in logic would be a worthwhile project.

A new edition of the Runes dictionary has been issued every few years (16th ed., 1960); these are, however, essentially reprints, containing only minor variations from the first edition. At least one edition, or reprint, was issued overseas (Bombay, Jaico Publishing House, 1957).

Runes also edited *Who's Who in Philosophy,* Vol. I, *Anglo-American Philosophers* (New York, Philosophical Library, 1942, 193 pages), a biographical dictionary of over five hundred living thinkers, covering not only Americans and Britons but also Indians, Europeans who came to the United States or England during Hitler's regime, and others. A contemplated second volume, for other parts of the world, was not issued. An unusual feature of the work is the listing of numerous periodical articles, as well as the major books, written by the philosophers included. Thus, the entry on Dewey runs to over 650 lines, listing over 50 books and over 250 articles.

In 1946, Father William D. Bruckmann published the third of the four American dictionaries of philosophy of this period, a volume entitled *Keystones & Theories of Philosophy* (New York, Benziger Brothers, 230 pages). This work includes comprehensive explanations—from the standpoint of Catholic philosophy—of concepts from *abstractio* (abstraction), to *voluntas* (will), of theories from absolutism to voluntarism, and of technical terms from *ab intrinseco–ab extrinseco* (from the intrinsic–from the extrinsic) to *ut sic* (as such). It also lists chronologically 121 philosophers with very brief indications of their viewpoints. The bulk of the work is devoted to concepts, only 19 pages being given to the individual philosophers.

Finally, John Dewey and Arthur F. Bentley, in an article in the *Journal of Philosophy* (Vol. 44, 1947, 421–434), "Concerning a Vocabulary for Inquiry Into Knowledge," presented what may, by a broad interpretation, be counted as a dictionary of philosophy. It is an array of ninety terms in alphabetical order, from *accurate, action, activity, actor, application,* and *aspect* near the beginning to *thing, trans* (as a prefix), *transaction, true, truth,* and *word* near the end. Although the entry for *mental* begins "This word is not used by us" and continues that the word usually "indicates a hypostatization arising from a primitively imperfect view of behavior," the remainder of the entry sanctions the use of the word for "emphasizing an aspect of existence." The entry for *real* reads: "Its use is to be completely avoided when not a recognized synonym for genuine as opposed to sham or counterfeit." The other entries show a similar striving for clarity and rigor.

A British dictionary of philosophy published in the 1940s is *A Rationalist Encyclopaedia: A Book of Reference on Religion, Philosophy, Ethics, and Science* (London, Watts, 1948, 633 pages; 2d ed., 1950), by Joseph McCabe, a former priest. McCabe debunks Aquinas as bracketing "serfs and animals," Aristotle as having had almost no influence for several centuries and then a deleterious influence on science, Augustine as writing poor Latin, Avicenna as sensual and dissipated, Bacon as hypocritical, Bergson as using largely inaccurate scientific material, Buddha as unoriginal, and so on. He generally lauds philosophers who were agnostics or deists. Some of the topical articles, while equally tendentious, contain useful criticism.

German. The Kirchner work of 1886 as revised by Michaëlis in 1903 was the basis of the *Wörterbuch der philosophischen Begriffe,* by Johannes Hoffmeister (Leipzig, Felix Meiner, 1944, 776 pages; 2d ed., 1955, 687 pages). The 1944 edition shows the influence of Adolf Hitler's regime. For example, the article "Volk" (folk) in the 1944 edition includes a lyrical exposition of the meaning of membership in a tight ethnic group and cites Hitler's *Mein Kampf* and Alfred Rosenberg's *Der Mythus des 20. Jahrhunderts,* but in the 1955 edition that exposition and those citations have vanished. The 1944 article "Rassenbiologie" (racial biology) does not appear in the later edition. The 1944 article "Demokratie" (democracy) says that pure democracy is impossible to achieve because it falsely assumes the equality of individuals; that statement is omitted in the 1955 edition. The article "Relativitätstheorie" in the 1944 edition refers to "der jüd. Gelehrte Einstein," but in the 1955 edition it says simply "Einstein"; the articles "Marxismus," "Spinozismus," and others show the same difference in the two editions.

In 1945 the Zurich firm of Rudolf Schaltegger published the first of the new German-language dictionaries of the decade, the *Ruscha Fachwörterbuch der Philosophie* ("Ruscha Dictionary of Technical Terms in Philosophy," 147 pages), in which the entries are, for the most part, a few lines long. The book would be of use to only the most elementary students.

Three years later Erwin Metzke published *Handlexikon der Philosophie* (Heidelberg, F. H. Kerle Verlag, 1948, 457 pages; 2d ed., 1949). The wealth of topics it covers may be noted, for example, in the *L*'s, where one finds the articles "Leben" (life), with four meanings distinguished, three of them broken down into submeanings; "Lebensanschauung" (outlook on life), two meanings; "Lebensform" (form of life), two meanings; "Lebensgefühl" (feeling toward life), three meanings; "Lebenskraft" (vigor), two meanings, with cross references to "Vitalismus" (vitalism) and "Vitalität" (vitality); and "Lebensphilosophie" (philosophy of life), six meanings. A 138-page appendix consists of 1-line to 34-line identifications or brief accounts of almost two thousand philosophers, many of them living, with Americans well represented.

Walter Brugger, S.J., is the principal author of the *Philosophisches Wörterbuch,* prepared with the collaboration mainly of his colleagues at the Berchmans-Kolleg near Munich (Vienna, Herder Verlag, 1948, 532 pages). This work went into 11 editions published in various years to 1964; it was also translated into Italian (Turin, 1959) and Spanish (4th ed., Barcelona, 1964). Many of the more than two thousand articles contain bibliographical references, mostly to German works. The Catholic viewpoint from which the book was prepared is not conspicuous, and the topics are treated factually, with a minimum of controversial interpretation. An appendix of over one hundred pages (including an index of about two thousand names) presents an outline history of philosophy.

Six fascicles, covering *A* to *J*, of the *Philosophen-Lexikon* were issued in 1936–1937 by various publishers in Berlin, having been prepared under the editorship of Eugen Hauer, Werner Ziegenfuss, and Gertrud Jung. The completed work was issued in 1949–1950 by Ziegenfuss, with the collaboration of Gertrud Jung, under the title *Philosophen-Lexikon: Handwörterbuch der Philosophie nach Personen* (2 vols., Berlin, Walter de Gruyter). Most of the articles contain biographical data about the individual covered, an indication of his contribution to philosophical thought, the titles (and years of publication) of his principal works or the principal collections of his works, and the titles of selected writings about him. Some articles, such as those on von Hartmann, Friedrich Schiller, and Unamuno, present significant quotations from their writings. For Karl Barth there are, atypically, only 3 lines of text, followed by a 24-line bibliography of his writings and a 12-line list of writings about him.

The two volumes of the Ziegenfuss work are remarkably comprehensive. They are also accurate and relatively cosmopolitan. Germans, it is true, get more space than others—for example, 5 pages for Benno Erdmann, who was Gertrud Jung's teacher, and 6 pages for Fechner, compared with 1 for Democritus and 3 for Socrates. A few Marxists also get disproportionate coverage—4 pages for Lenin and 5 for Marx—and contemporaries likewise are given some preference—for example, 6 pages for Berdyaev, compared with 1 for Bentham. One is surprised to see 5 pages devoted to the racist Houston Stewart Chamberlain. But Americans are given fairly good coverage—1 page for Peirce, 3 for Emerson, 3 for James, 2 for Dewey, and 1 for Royce.

A few of the articles in the Ziegenfuss work (for example, those on Nicolai Hartmann, 17 pages; P. A. Sorokin, 3 pages; and Erich Rothacker, 7 pages) were written by the subjects themselves.

Hungarian. Volume I ("Aall" to "Avicebrón") of Pal Sandor's *Filozofiai Lexikon* (Budapest, Faust Kiadás, 64 pages) appeared in 1941. No further volumes seem to have been published. This is a biographical dictionary of philosophers with some emphasis on nineteenth-century and twentieth-century thinkers—Erich Adickes, four men named Adler, Samuel Alexander, and so on—and with considerable space devoted to selected great figures of the past—Anselm, Antisthenes, Aquinas, Aristotle (32 cols.), and others.

Turkish. The *Felsefe ve Gramer Terimleri* ("Dictionary of Philosophy and Grammar," Istanbul, Cumhuriyet Basimevi, 1942, 318 pages), prepared by the Türk Dil Kurumu (Turkish Language Society), contains a series of alphabetical three-language lists of equivalent terms (Turkish, Osmanli, French; Osmanli, French, Turkish; and French, Osmanli, Turkish) and three corresponding lists of grammatical terms. (Osmanli is a Turkish dialect.) The philosophical lists usefully include over one thousand terms in cosmology and metaphysics—*causality, demiurge,* and so on; ethics—*altruism, deontology,* and so on; logic—*amphibology, contraposition,* and so on; and other domains of philosophy, plus terms in psychology—*abulia, claustrophobia,* and so on.

THE NINETEEN-FIFTIES

The flowering begun in the 1940s continued in the 1950s. Where the previous decade saw 22 new dictionaries of philosophy that have come to the writer's attention, 24 were published in the 1950s. Nine languages were represented: English, Gaelic, German, Dutch, French, Italian, Spanish, Portuguese, and Turkish. The great landmark of the 1950s is the monumental four-volume Italian encyclopedia of philosophy written by scholars at Gallarate.

English. A philosophical dictionary vastly different from most is *The Great Ideas: A Syntopicon of Great Books of the Western World,* compiled under the direction of Mortimer J. Adler (Chicago, Encyclopaedia Britannica, 1952), comprising Volumes II and III of the publisher's 54-volume "Great Books of the Western World." It covers 102 "great ideas," including art, being, cause, chance, change, democracy, eternity, form, God, good and evil, idea, knowledge, logic, love, matter, metaphysics, mind, nature, necessity and contingency, one and many, reasoning, sense, sign and symbol, soul, space, time, truth, will, wisdom, and world.

For each idea the work presents an analytical and expository introduction, followed by a list of elements of the idea with a series of references to pertinent passages in the great books for each element. There is also a list of related great ideas and finally a list of additional readings on the subject in classics which are not included in the "Great Books" collection. At the end of the second volume of the *Syntopicon* there are a bibliography consolidating the lists of additional readings, a discussion of "syntopical construction" (which lists, among the ideas originally considered for inclusion but rejected, becoming, belief, deduction, doubt, essence, probability, purpose, reality, self, spirit, substance, value, and many others), and an "inventory" (index) of eighteen hundred terms.

A more self-conscious book could scarcely be imagined. Virtually every portion of the book is preceded by an explanation of why that portion was formed in the way in which it was formed and not otherwise. Critics are answered before they have a chance to formulate criticisms. The reader is everywhere shown the scaffolding, and his attention is invited to a close inspection of its features.

Nevertheless, the book is highly useful. For the elements of the idea of form, for example, the reader is referred to specific passages in Plato, Aristotle, Lucretius, Augustine, Aquinas, Bacon, Descartes, Locke, Berkeley, Kant, Hegel, William James, and others. The analytical and expository introductions are for the most part general

rather than technical, but they go as deeply into a subject as a thoughtful, educated reader may desire. All in all, this unique work was decidedly worth undertaking and was competently executed.

The only other English dictionary of philosophy published in the 1950s was Michael H. Briggs's *Handbook of Philosophy* (New York, Philosophical Library, 1959, 214 pages). It is difficult to see the usefulness of the article "Future," which reads, in its entirety, "Those events that will happen in time to come," or of the opening definition of the article "Change"—namely, "A constant alteration of states of the universe so that specific combinations of events do not persist." Several other articles in this handbook are equally unenlightening.

Gaelic. The *Focloir Fealsaimh* ("Vocabulary of Philosophy"), by Colmán O Huallacháin, O.F.M. (Dublin, An Clóchomhar, 1958, 169 pages), begins with a preface in French by Monsignor Louis de Raeymaeker of the University of Louvain. The book presents brief Gaelic descriptions or explanations of about two thousand Gaelic terms in philosophy and related humanistic disciplines, with the equivalent terms in German, English, French, and Latin. At the end of the book are four reciprocal word lists—German, English, French, and Latin—with the Gaelic equivalent of each word. The English word list includes not only such specifically philosophical terms as *Absolute, actual, aesthetics, agnostic,* and *aseity* but also such terms as *abnormal, acoustics, agoraphobia, anthropology,* and *atavism.*

German. In Germany and Switzerland five works were produced or begun, not counting a nonalphabetical so-called encyclopedia published in 1959. First, Carl Decurtins produced the *Kleines Philosophen-Lexikon* (Affoltern am Albis, Switzerland, Aehren Verlag, 1952, 312 pages), containing biographical sketches of three hundred individuals, among whom are not only the main figures in the history of philosophy strictly conceived but also Helena P. Blavatsky, Karl von Clausewitz, Lenin, Mussolini, the racists Chamberlain, Gobineau, and Alfred Rosenberg, as well as Jesus Christ, Dostoyevsky, Emerson, and Omar Khayyám. Chamberlain gets more space than Jesus Christ.

In 1954, Franz Austeda wrote the *Kleines Wörterbuch der Philosophie* (Frankfurt, Humboldt-Verlag, 188 pages; 2d ed., entitled *Wörterbuch der Philosophie,* Berlin and Munich, Verlag Lebendiges Wissen, 1962, 270 pages). This work contains over eighteen hundred articles, including eight hundred which are biographical. It is a highly sensible and sound short reference work, with a reasonable proportion of space allotted to each of the standard topics in philosophy and the principal philosophers of the past and the present, as well as topics in less standard fields, such as Oriental philosophy, disciplines close to philosophy, and even old saws like Terence's "Homo sum; humani nihil a me alienum puto" ("A man am I; nothing human do I consider alien to me").

On behalf of the Kommission für Philosophie der Akademie der Wissenschaften und der Literatur zu Mainz, Erich Rothacker undertook a series of volumes under the general title *Archiv für Begriffsgeschichte; Bausteine zu einem historischen Wörterbuch der Philosophie* ("Archive for History of Concepts; Building Stones for a Historical Dictionary of Philosophy," Bonn, H. Bouvier, 1955——).

Among the volumes which have appeared are Volume II (Part 2), *Kosmos* (1958, 168 pages), by Walther Kranz; Volume III, *Gewohnheit* ("Custom," 1958, 606 pages), by Gerhard Funke; Volume IV (1959, 239 pages), containing discussions by eight writers regarding various concepts or suggested texts of articles for the *Wörterbuch;* Volume V (1960, 718 pages), containing, under the headings "Absolut," "Abstrakt, Abstraktion," and "Aktivität, aktiv – passiv," the *Bibliographie deutscher Hochschulschriften von 1900 – 1955*, by Hans Flasche and Utta Wawrzinek; Volume VII (1962, 325 pages), containing discussions by a number of writers on such concepts as the Kantian *Analytik* and *Dialektik;* and Volume VIII (1963, 398 pages), by Karl Otto Apel, on the idea of language in the humanistic tradition from Dante to Vico. This is an ambitious and useful undertaking. Although it may not eventuate in an actual dictionary of philosophy, future writers of such dictionaries should feel obliged to utilize its findings.

In 1958, Max Müller and Alois Halder produced the paperback *Herders kleines philosophisches Wörterbuch* (Freiburg, Verlag Herder, 204 pages; 7th ed., 1965), with a bibliographical appendix citing various histories of philosophy and journals of philosophy and nine earlier dictionaries of philosophy. Portraits of Aristotle, Plato, Augustine, Aquinas, Descartes, Leibniz, Kant, Hegel, Husserl, Bergson, Heidegger, and Jaspers appear on the back cover. The articles on medieval, modern, and contemporary thinkers are especially useful; Nicholas of Cusa is given 76 lines, Unamuno 34 lines, and Buber 28 lines.

The last of the German-language contributions of the decade is Volume II of *Das Fischer Lexikon, Enzyklopädie des Wissens*, a compilation entitled *Philosophie*, edited by Alwin Diemar and Ivo Frenzel (Frankfurt, Fischer Bucherei, 1958, 376 pages). This paperback book was reprinted in 1959 and 1960, and an English version translated by Salvatore Attanasio and prepared under the direction of James Gutmann was published as *Philosophy—A to Z* (New York, Grosset and Dunlap, 1963) in hardback and paperback editions. The collaborators consisted of 15 German authorities plus Paul K. Feyerabend of the United States. The work presents a small number of comprehensive articles—26—on such broad topics as anthropology, aesthetics, and Chinese and Japanese philosophy rather than a multitude of short ones. Historical information is given where necessary, but the emphasis is on concepts and problems. The articles show originality and penetration.

A nonalphabetical so-called encyclopedia was *Die Philosophie im XX. Jahrhundert: Eine Enzyklopädische Darstellung ihrer Geschichte, Disziplinen und Aufgaben*, edited by Frederick H. Heinemann ("Philosophy in the Twentieth Century; An Encyclopedic Presentation of Its History, Disciplines and Formulations," Stuttgart, Ernst Klett Verlag, 1959, 600 pages; 2d edition, 1963). Heinemann begins with a discussion of the term *encyclopedia* which de-emphasizes the alphabetical order of topics, and he continues with chapters, written by himself or others, on Oriental, ancient, medieval, and modern philosophy; on movements in twentieth-century philosophy; and on epistemology, logic, philosophy of mathematics, metaphysics, philosophy of nature, and other philosophical disciplines.

The treatment of the topics is mainly interpretive and constructive, rather than purely expository, especially in the chapters on the philosophical disciplines.

Dutch. The Dutch work of this decade was edited by Johan Grooten and G. Jo Steenbergen. It is *Filosofisch Lexicon* (Antwerp, Standaard-Boekhandel, 1958, 331 pages), written by 32 collaborators, of whom the best known are perhaps E. W. Beth and Louis de Raeymaeker. The book begins with an explanation of how the topics are broken down, what type of spelling is used, how to find medieval names, and how the cross references are shown. The articles themselves are scholarly and well balanced.

French. Armand Cuvillier's *Nouveau Vocabulaire philosophique* (Paris, Librairie Armand Colin, 1956, 203 pages; 3d ed., 1958) is a worthy successor to his *Petit Vocabulaire*, which went through 13 editions from 1925 to 1953. The new work includes a number of terms borrowed from other languages, such as *Erlebnis* (experience), *Dasein* (existence), and *pattern*. A number of articles, à la Goblot and Baldwin, set forth more than one meaning and then discourage the use of the term in one of the senses. For example, under "Empirique" (Empirical), the third meaning is "fondé sur l'expérience en général . . ." ("founded on experience in general"), but the author comments, "impropre au sens 3; dire expérienciel" ("improper in sense 3; say experiential"). A Spanish translation, entitled *Diccionario de filosofía*, was published at Buenos Aires in 1961.

J. Claude Piguet's *Le Vocabulaire intellectuel* (Paris, Centre de Documentation Universitaire et S.E.D.E.S. Réunis, 1957, 112 pages; reprinted, 1960, backstrip title, *Vocabulaire de philosophie*) disclaims being a dictionary in the sense of a list of pat definitions. It aims, instead, to stimulate students' thinking, partly by provocative opposition. For many terms an antonym is given, or two or more "opposites" are cited; for example, the article on absolute contrasts absolute with relative, and the article on duty contrasts duty not only with moral indifference but also with right. The book is probably of use mainly to students specializing in subjects other than philosophy.

Italian. Of the seven Italian works of the period, three were published in 1951. Eustachio P. Lamanna and Francesco Adorno produced the *Dizionario di termini filosofici* (Florence, Felice le Monnier, 1951, 104 pages; 9th ed., 1960), in which the articles are brief, ranging from 1 line for "Verbo, (il)," ending with a cross reference to "Logos," to 47 lines for "Intelleto."

Giovanni Semprini compiled the *Nuovo dizionario di coltura filosofica e scientifica* (Turin, Società Editrice Internazionale, 1951, 470 pages), which chiefly has articles on philosophical subjects, with errors in various articles on British and American philosophy, but also covers topics in the empirical sciences; for example, there are articles on anesthesia, clan, geology, and Mesmer.

Mario A. Boccalaro's *Dizionario filosofico* (Bologna, Licinio Cappelli, 1951, 91 pages) covers topics only. Its articles, generally a few lines long, are carefully and accurately phrased.

In 1952, Vincenzo Miano and 12 Italian collaborators produced the *Dizionario filosofico* (Turin, Società Editrice Internazionale, 1952, 693 pages), written with a Thomistic approach. Only topics are treated, but the appended

"Schema della storia della filosofia" shows the name of the article in which each important philosopher is discussed; over 150 thinkers are included in the list.

Umberto Cantoro's *Vocabulario filosofico* (Bologna, Casa Editrice N. U. Gallo, 1955, 283 pages) began with an introduction on the philosophical disciplines and continued with an alphabetically arranged vocabulary which purportedly emphasized terms in common usage that have a special meaning in philosophy—for example, *absolute, concrete,* and *criticism*—but actually devoted most of its pages to the usual philosophical terms—*agnosticism, ambiguity, anguish, free will,* and the like. Psychology was taken by the author to be a philosophical discipline.

The *Dizionario di filosofia,* edited by Andrea Biraghi with contributions by 29 Italian collaborators (Milan, Edizioni di Comunità, 1957, 787 pages), is not strictly a dictionary since the materials in its two parts (on the history and problems of philosophy, respectively) are arranged in a nonalphabetical order, but it contains, as appendixes, three features which put it in the broad stream of dictionaries of philosophy: a dictionary of Greek terms, a dictionary of German terms, and a comprehensive alphabetical index.

The Gallarate landmark. In 1957 a group of Italian scholars in the Centro di Studi Filosofici di Gallarate, together with a few foreign collaborators, produced the *Enciclopedia filosofica* (4 vols., Venice and Rome, Istituto per la Collaborazione Culturale for the Ministry of Public Education and the Giorgio Cini and the Enrico Lossa foundations), which for the first time in half a century outshone the Baldwin work in comprehensiveness and up-to-date scholarship. The directing committee aimed to produce not "un mero *dizionario* filosofico" but a true encyclopedia of philosophy which would go beyond the dry explanation of the usages of terms and would present deeper analyses of the elements and implications both of individual problems and ideas and of more general points of view.

Each volume contains a number of full-page illustrations (mostly portraits of philosophers), and many of the articles contain bibliographical references at the end. This colossal work, totaling some 6 million words, is a basic landmark in the field of philosophical reference works, far outstripping its nearest competitors in magnitude. Physically, also, it is outstanding; the print and the 233 illustrations are not only tasteful but in some ways sumptuous. The work contains about twelve thousand articles, of which seven thousand are historical (on individual philosophers, movements, and the like) and five thousand are analytical (on concepts, problems, and the like). There are, for example, over 130 articles on past and present Russian philosophy, 82 on individual philosophical journals, over 80 on twentieth-century American philosophy, 74 on Indian philosophy, and 55 on subtopics of deduction and induction.

The contributors are mainly professors in Italian universities. Their contributions are factual, reliable, and broad in scope. The article on Aristotle (27 cols., with a full-page glossy reproduction of Raphael's head of Aristotle in the "School of Athens") is followed by articles on Pseudo-Aristotle (1 col.), Aristotle in Latin (2 cols.), and Aristotelianism (6 cols.), all of them rich in content and based on vast learning. There are worthwhile articles on neo-

classicism, neocriticism, neo-empiricism, Neo-Guelphism, Neo-Hegelianism, Neo-Lutheranism, Neo-Malthusianism, Neo-Pythagoreanism, Neoplatonism, neopositivism (16 cols.), neorealism, Neo-Scholasticism, and neo-humanism.

There is some bias toward religious and idealistic positions in philosophy. Moreover, more Italian twentieth-century philosophers are treated in separate articles than either French or British. G. E. Moore gets only a column, which is less than the space assigned to Bernardo Varisco or Michele F. Sciacca, and a number of eminent American philosophers—Brand Blanshard, C. I. Lewis, Arthur O. Lovejoy, and R. W. Sellars—get less than a column.

The encyclopedia also goes far afield in including material on economics, pedagogy (with articles on *scoutismo*—the boy scouts—and on coeducation), and literary art (with articles on Joseph Addison, Sir Philip Sidney, and Jonathan Swift). Moreover, there are many minute articles which could profitably have been combined into more meaningful longer articles. However, weighing the encyclopedia's many merits against its few shortcomings, one must conclude that the work represents a highly laudable achievement, destined to be useful over a prolonged period.

Spanish. Of the two Spanish-language dictionaries of philosophy produced in the 1950s, the first was published in Argentina and the second in Spain. Julio Rey Pastor and Ismael Quiles directed five editors and ten collaborators in the production of the *Diccionario filosófico* (Buenos Aires, Espasa–Calpe Argentina, 1952, 1,114 pages), in which the material is arranged according to a systematic outline of topics in 18 chapters instead of in alphabetical order. The 18 chapters are headed "Introducción á la historia de la filosofía"; "Lógica"; "Teoría del conocimiento"; "Epistemología y teoría de la ciencia"; "Logística, Lógica Simbólica o Lógica Matemática"; "Ontología," with 19 subheads, including "Ser," "Ente," "Existencia," and "Esencia"; "Metafísica general" (nature and structure of being and individuality); "Metafísica especial" (matter, life, mind, and spirit); "Filosofía de los valores"; "Filosofía de la religión"; "Ética"; "Estética"; "Filosofía del arte y poética"; "Psicología"; "Antropología filosófica"; "Concepción del mundo"; "Sociología"; and "Filosofía del derecho." At the end are the 45-page "Vocabulario filosófico," alphabetically arranged, and the 17-page "Equivalencias idiomáticas" (German–Spanish, English–Spanish, French–Spanish, and Italian–Spanish).

Juan Zaragüeta Bengoechea, director of the Luis Vives Institute of Philosophy in Madrid, is the author of the *Vocabulario filosófico* (Madrid, Espasa–Calpe, 1955, 571 pages), in which almost every article begins with the German, French, English, and Italian equivalents of the term being discussed. The terms are defined and explained from a scholastic point of view, generally without historical references. The articles are weak on contemporary philosophy, the one on *logística,* for example, merely setting forth in 20 lines what symbolic logic is about.

Portuguese. Three Portuguese-language dictionaries of philosophy were published or were begun and dropped in the decade of the 1950s. Volume I (*A–D*) of the *Dicionário de filosofia,* by Orris Soares, was published at Rio de Janeiro in 1952 by the Instituto Nacional do Livro of the Ministério da Educação e Saúde. No other volumes have appeared. At the beginning of many of the articles are the equivalents of the term being covered in one or more of the following languages—Greek, Latin, French, Italian, English, and German. The article on Aristotle runs to more than 25 columns, with subtopics arranged alphabetically (for instance, "Aristóteles e a alma" and "Aristóteles e a astronomia"). To take the *D*'s for an example, there are useful articles on Dalton, Dante, Darwin, Descartes (15 cols.), Diogenes (four persons so named), Driesch, Duhem, Dühring, Duns Scotus, Durkheim, and others but none on Dewey.

Published at São Paulo were the first fascicle, covering the letter *A*, of the *Dicionario de filosofia,* by Luís Washington Vita, reprinted from the *Revista do Arquivo Municipal* (1950, 48 pages), and the *Vocabulário filosófico,* by Carlos Lopes de Mattos (Edições Leia, 1957, 387 pages). Both cover only topics but include among the topics the philosophy of some individuals, in the articles on Aristotelianism, Averroism, and so forth. Vita modestly ascribes any errors which may appear in his work (of which no more has been published) to the fact that his is the first dictionary of philosophy in the Portuguese language; thus, he does not count the Voltairian 1938 work of Renato Kehl as a true dictionary of philosophy. Vita includes and Mattos excludes fields akin to philosophy. For many of his terms Mattos gives the equivalents in Esperanto, French, German, Greek, Italian, Latin, and Spanish and enumerates in the Bibliography 17 earlier dictionaries of philosophy.

Turkish. Of Cemil Sena's *Büyük Filozoflar Ansiklopedisi* (Istanbul, Negioğlu Yayinevi, 1957——), only one volume, covering *A* to *D*, appeared. This work is a dictionary of philosophers which ranges from technical philosophers like Anaxagoras (12 cols.) to popular philosophers like Angelus Silesius and Will Durant, natural scientists like Ampère, and sociologists like Durkheim. The articles—some of them illustrated—are well balanced between biography and doctrine. Appended to Volume I are a glossary of Turkish philosophical terms with their French equivalents and an index of persons mentioned, showing, for example, 130 pages of the 642 pages in Volume I as containing references to Plato.

URMSON, ABBAGNANO, AND AFTER

English. *The Concise Encyclopedia of Western Philosophy and Philosophers* (New York, Hawthorn Books, 1960, 431 pages), edited by James O. Urmson, contains over 150 articles on individual philosophers and about 65 articles on philosophical topics and schools. It also includes over one hundred full-page illustrations, mostly portraits of philosophers, of which eight are in color. It closes with an 11-page bibliography. Many outstanding contemporary British and American philosophers are among the 48 contributors. In the Preface the editor set forth his principles. Where it was difficult to summarize the views of a philosopher briefly, he was to be given enough space to make his position intelligible (six thousand words for Kant). More generally, it was deemed better to have fewer and longer articles than many short ones of doubtful utility. Philosophy was interpreted narrowly, excluding such popular topics as the philosophy of life. Eastern thinkers were excluded be-

cause, according to Urmson, they are philosophers in the popular, and not in the technical, sense. In recapitulation, however, he gives as the reason for their omission the fact that "their achievement is not closely related to that of western philosophers." Exception could be taken to the former of these justifications for the omission of Oriental philosophy, but the addition of the latter makes it hard to object.

Although the articles in the Urmson work are not signed, the authorship of some has become known—for instance, the article on epistemology is by Gilbert Ryle, on ethics by R. M. Hare, on Heidegger by Walter Kaufmann, and on logic by D. J. O'Connor. The articles on epistemology and ethics display a freshness seldom found in encyclopedias; they are readable, free of academicism, informative, and challenging. Many other articles are also both brilliant and original. However, the article on Heidegger not only, with some justification, makes much of his welcome of Hitlerism but also, with less warrant, dismisses the fabric of his thought as comparable to the nonexistent clothes of Hans Christian Andersen's fairy-tale emperor.

Urmson's choice of topics is questionable. Although topics outside technical philosophy were to be excluded, Karl Marx is covered in an article of fifty-three hundred words, of which the first sentence is "Marx was not primarily a philosopher." Many of the contributors are themselves the subjects of articles, but one does not find any article on Gödel, Tarski, or, among thinkers of the past, Bayle or Voltaire. Among the topical articles one does not find any on belief, causation, error, existence, identity, necessity, philosophy of history, negation, self, or vitalism.

Another English work of the 1960s was Henry Thomas' *Biographical Encyclopedia* (New York, Doubleday, 1965, 286 pages). This is a work for the general reader, not for the specialist in philosophy. For example, the more than four hundred thinkers covered include a generous selection of poets (Horace, Omar, Byron, Shakespeare), social commentators (Benjamin Franklin, Oliver Wendell Holmes, Jr.), and theosophists (Annie Besant, Helena P. Blavatsky) but not Ayer, Carnap, Jaspers, Lovejoy, Meinong, Moore, Reichenbach, Ryle, or Schlick. The expositions and evaluations are likewise on a popular level.

Another popular biographical work is Thomas Kiernan's *Who's Who in the History of Philosophy* (New York, Philosophical Library, 1965, 185 pages). The expositions of the doctrines of some of the philosophers covered are naive. For example, Aquinas is said to have redirected Aristotelianism "towards truth and away from doubt," and Mill's inductive methods are said to be based on his "advocacy of the law of the uniformity of nature."

Russian. The year 1960 saw the first volume (*A* to "Diderot") of a new Russian dictionary of philosophy, the *Filosofskaya Entsiklopediya,* edited by F. V. Konstantinov and others (Moscow, "Soviet Encyclopedia" Publishing House). The second volume (covering "Disjunction" to "The Comic") of the four projected volumes was published in 1962. Volume I includes four articles—"Democracy," by L. Denisova; "Dialectics," by P. Kopnin; "Humanism," by L. Denisova; and "Dialectical Materialism," by A. G. Spirkin—which are available in English, the first three having been translated by William Mandel in the quarterly *Soviet Studies in Philosophy* (Vol. I, Spring 1963) and the fourth having been translated for *Russian Philosophy: A Book of Readings,* edited by James M. Edie and others (3 vols., Chicago, Quadrangle Books, 1965).

The article on democracy attempts to show that bourgeois democracy is dictatorship of the capitalist class, with illusory freedoms, whereas socialist democracy is dictatorship of the proletarian class, with genuine freedom of speech, the press, assembly, and demonstration. The truth is also labeled elsewhere in the encyclopedia, as in the article on absolute idealism, which is described as based on "the false assumption of the existence of an absolute idea." On the positive side may be mentioned the numerous good articles on logic, the broad coverage of both topics and persons (except that Bukharin and some other heretic Marxists are omitted), and the many halftone cuts. Such sociological topics as marriage are included.

Karl G. Ballestrem's *Russian Philosophical Terminology* (Dordrecht, D. Reidel, 1964, 116 pages) contains a glossary of about one thousand philosophical terms in Russian, with English, French, and German equivalents. Emphasis is placed on terms having a special use in Soviet philosophy.

Italian. Nicola Abbagnano published the *Dizionario di Filosofia* (Turin, Unione Tipografico, 1961, 905 pages; Spanish translation, Mexico City and Buenos Aires, 1963) with the collaboration of Giulio Preti on topics in the field of logic. Abbagnano is a distinguished figure in contemporary philosophy and philosophical scholarship. His dictionary, covering only topics, shows vast erudition and commendable acumen in appraising tendencies and movements in philosophy. It gives, for example, a fair and thoroughly knowledgeable treatment to contemporary Anglo-American and positivistic philosophy. In the admiring words of Urmson, who noted a few inaccuracies in the Abbagnano work in a review in *Mind* (Vol. 71, 1962, 425), Abbagnano "refers as readily to the latest numbers of American journals as to the works of Plato."

Topics for which the standard name is in a language other than Italian—for example, *Erlebnis* (living experience), *Gegenstandtheorie* (object theory), and *Weltanschauung* (world outlook)—are treated by Abbagnano or cross-referenced in their regular alphabetical order. For many of the Italian words he also gives equivalents in Greek, Latin, English, French, and German. This work is one of the outstanding dictionaries of philosophy of our time. An English translation is scheduled to be published by the University of Chicago Press.

Dutch. K. Kuypers is the editor of a Dutch work, *Elseviers Kleine Filosofische en Psychologische Encyclopedie* (Amsterdam, Elsevier, 272 pages), that appeared in 1960. Short but useful articles are presented on obscure as well as prominent thinkers and topics. Some topics—for instance, the Gifford lectures—are not often found in dictionaries of philosophy. Appended are a 15-page historical outline showing the schools or other groupings of over five hundred philosophers; a bibliography; and a selected list of philosophical journals and organizations.

Danish. A work of this period is Henrik Thomsen's *Hvem Taenkte Hvad; Filosofiens Hvem-Hvad-Hvor* (Copenhagen, Politikens Forlag, 1961, 390 pages), with an introductory note by Justus Hartnack. The book contains a thumbnail history of philosophy from the pre-Socratics to Husserl, Wittgenstein, and Russell; numerous illustrations and two maps; a who's who of philosophy with illustrations of Augustine reading and Heidegger hiking; a dictionary of technical terms; and a bibliography.

German. Joseph Münzhuber wrote the *Kleines Wörterbuch der Philosophie, zum Gebrauch an Schulen* (Düsseldorf, Pädagogischer Verlag Schwann, 1962, 45 pages). This work contains about 135 articles ranging from the 2-line "Transintelligibel" to the 48-line "Existenzphilosophie." Among the more unusual articles are "In-der-Welt-Sein" (being-in-the-world) and "Unschärferelation" (Heisenberg's uncertainty relation).

Anton Neuhäusler wrote *Grundbegriffe der philosophischen Sprache: Begriffe viersprachig* (Munich, Ehrenwirth Verlag, 1963, 276 pages). The length of the article on any topic covered by Neuhäusler is based not on the topic's importance but on its "Klärungs-bedurfigkeit und -schwierigkeit" ("need and difficulty of explanation"). Each entry includes the English, French, and Italian equivalent of the term; an indication of the origin of the term (if this is relevant); a sophisticated but clear discussion of the use of the term; and a brief bibliography. An appendix presents a decimal classification of philosophical concepts—for example, 1 for philosophy itself; 11 for metaphysics; 11.1 for ontology; 111.11 for existence, *Dasein,* and reality; 19 for history of philosophy; 2 for theology.

In 1964 there appeared another *Philosophisches Wörterbuch* (Leipzig, VEB Bibliographisches Institut, 650 pages; reprinted 1965), edited by Georg Klaus and Manfred Buhr. It was a joint project of the Institute for Philosophy of the German Academy of Sciences in Berlin and the professorial chair for philosophy of the Institute for Economics of the Central Committee of the German Socialist Unity party. The Marxist–Leninist slant is sometimes blatant, as in the article "Demokratie," where bourgeois democracy is characterized as a form of government in which everything is subordinated to profit. Among the examples presented to illustrate the use of "is" in the article "Kopula" are (in translation): "Marx is the author of *Capital*" and "Marx is one of the greatest thinkers of mankind."

French. In 1962, Paul Foulquié, with the collaboration of Raymond Saint-Jean, produced the *Dictionnaire de la langue philosophique* (Paris, Presses Universitaires de France, 1962, 776 pages), which, as the Preface states, is heavily indebted to Lalande's work. Since Foulquié's is a dictionary of concepts, there are no articles on schools or viewpoints, such as Aristotelianism and Eleaticism. Although the basic arrangement is alphabetical, related concepts are in some cases grouped around a generic term—for example, *étant, entité, essence, exister,* and *existentialisme* around *être.* Many of the articles quote texts to support the definitions presented.

The anonymous *Dictionnaire des philosophes* (Paris, Collection Seghers, 1962, 383 pages; binder's title, *Dictionnaire illustré des philosophes*) contains biographical statements regarding approximately six hundred standard Western philosophers and philosophic thinkers, such as Ruth Benedict, Karen Horney, and Kurt Lewin, in allied fields. There follow references to about thirty Oriental thinkers and a vocabulary of some five hundred terms, most of them defined in a few lines. Scattered in the book are 64 portraits.

According to Didier Julia, the purpose of his *Dictionnaire de la philosophie* (Paris, Librairie Larousse, 1964, 320 pages) is the disclosure of eternal truths as being applicable to daily life. In keeping with that purpose, the illustrations are popular: an abstract painting, a scene in Paris after the explosion of a plastic bomb, a child peering through curtains (illustrating "Attention"), a Buddhist immolating himself at Saigon, and others. Marx gets more space than anyone else, and Trotsky gets more than Aristotle. Maimonides and Peirce are among the omissions. It is doubtful that the announced purpose of the work was achieved.

Spanish. Paul Henri Boyer's *Diccionario breve de filosofía* (Buenos Aires, Club de Lectores, 1962, 187 pages) has some material of questionable validity. There is only one article on Oriental philosophy, on nirvana, which is wrongly defined as negation of the will to live. The spelling of non-Spanish names in the work is not reliable.

Oriental languages. Three Asian countries—nationalist China, Japan, and, most notably, Korea—have made significant contributions in the 1960s.

Chinese. The Chinese dictionary is *Chê Hsüeh Ta Tz'ŭ Tien* ("Comprehensive Dictionary of Philosophy," Taipei, Ch'i Ming Shu Chü, 1960, 464 pages), containing about one thousand five hundred articles, each printed with the equivalent of the term in at least one Western language. The first entry is on monism, and the last is on "idealrealism." The rest cover the standard philosophical and psychological topics and personalities plus such unusual topics as dilemmatic proposition and "summists" (authors of works entitled *Summa*). Two indexes in Western languages (and roman type) list topics and personal names.

Japanese. Naomichi Takama's *Tetsugaku Yogo No Kiso Chishiki* ("Philosophical Terminology," Tokyo, Seisun Shuppan Sha, 242 pages), a Japanese work, was published in 1961. The title of each article is given with English and German equivalents. There are articles on patriotism, happiness, justice, human nature, freedom of the will, suicide, space, time, dialectical materialism, scholastic philosophy, and many other popular and technical topics. Some of the articles show an undue influence of Marxism.

Another Japanese work was edited by Yasumasa Oshima—*Shin Rinri Jiten* ("Dictionary of Ethics," Tokyo, Sobun Sha, 1961, 472 pages). The scope of this work is broader than its title indicates. Some of the articles are on ethical subjects, including agape, evil, ataraxia, will, Epicureanism, and human rights, but others transcend the domain of ethics, including those on atman, Aristotle, either–or, a priori, causality, Eleatics, entelechy, and *Dasein*. In general, this is the more scholarly of the Japanese works.

Korean. One hundred and four Korean scholars worked on the *Dictionary of Philosophy: Ch'ŏrhak Taesajŏn* (Seoul, Hagwŏnsa, 1963, 1,376 pages). A monumental job of scholarship and printing, this work contains, for many entries, the Korean expression followed by equivalents in other pertinent languages, the article in Korean with romanized transliterations where needed, and a bibliography. The field covered includes philosophy, psychology, and sociology, and the articles are of exceptionally high

quality. Among the added features are about four hundred pictures of philosophers; other illustrations, including Wittgenstein's duck-rabbit and four full-page maps; a uniquely rich year-by-year chronology of philosophy, showing, for example, 1905 as the year of the inauguration or publication of specific works by 22 philosophers; and an index of about five thousand terms in Western languages.

A "nonencyclopedia." From time to time we have paused to poke a curious finger into works which are called dictionaries or encyclopedias of philosophy but which are not arranged alphabetically. The latest of these is Ramón Conde Obregón's *Enciclopedia de la filosofía* (Barcelona, De Gassó Hernanos, 1961, 363 pages). The first four parts of the book are on philosophy in general, prephilosophy, Western philosophy, and Oriental philosophy; the fifth is headed "Conclusion." Conde's work will probably not be the last, in the march of philosophical exposition, to exploit the perennial intellectual magnetism of the term *dictionary* or *encyclopedia*.

DICTIONARIES OF SPECIAL PHILOSOPHICAL TOPICS

There are dictionaries which cover one or more philosophical disciplines, periods, and schools, as well as individual philosophers. The listings presented here are merely illustrative; complete coverage is not attempted.

Disciplines. Some dictionaries cover a single discipline, such as aesthetics, ethics, logic, or theology; others cover a combination, such as ethics and theology or logic and philosophy of science.

Aesthetics. Among the dictionaries of aesthetics is Ignaz Jeitteles' *Aesthetisches Lexikon: Ein alphabetisches Handbuch zur Theorie der Philosophie des Schönen und der Schönen Künste* ("Dictionary of Aesthetics: An Alphabetical Handbook of the Theory of the Philosophy of Beauty and the Fine Arts," 2 vols., Vienna, Carl Gerold, 1835–1837). This is a capably written reference work, covering numerous topics in architecture, the dance, drama, drawing, music, painting, poetry, rhetoric, sculpture, and other arts, as well as topics applicable to natural beauty or to more than one of the arts. An 84-page appendix reviews the classic literature on aesthetics.

In 1946 Roger Caillois produced the *Vocabulaire esthétique* (Paris, Éditions de la Revue Fontaine, 141 pages). In addition to whole chapters on nature and art, this work contains articles on art for art's sake, authority, image, order, originality, sincerity, and other topics in nonalphabetical order. Each article is a discursive essay rather than a systematic treatment.

A curiosity among dictionaries of aesthetics is Paolo Mantegazza's *Dizionario delle cose belle* (Milan, Fratelli Treves, 1891, 346 pages; German translation, 2 vols., Jena, 1891–1892). After an introduction on elements of beauty (color, symmetry, and so on) constituting about a third of the book, the author presents over one hundred articles in alphabetical order on "beautiful things"—alabaster, eagle, gazelle, jasmine, lark, lion, moon, snow, stars—with rhapsodic comments on each.

Ethics. Among the dictionaries of ethics, mention may be made of two in particular. The first is *Dictionnaire des passions, des vertus, et des vices* (2 vols., Paris, Chez Vincent, 1769), published anonymously by Antonio F. Sticotti and Antoine Sabbatier. Discussing such topics as abasement, abominable, admiration, and adultery near the beginning of the alphabet and urbanity, utility, vivacity, and volition near the end of the alphabet, the authors epitomized the comments of famous writers—Aristotle, Bacon, Confucius, Diderot, Locke, Pascal, Voltaire, and others—on these topics.

In 1956 Vergilius Ferm's *Encyclopedia of Morals* (New York, Philosophical Library, 682 pages) appeared. The contributors to this scholarly and well-balanced volume include Lewis White Beck on Nicolai Hartmann; William K. Frankena on Ross, Sidgwick, and moral philosophy in America; Lucius Garvin on major ethical viewpoints; Walter Kaufmann on Freud, Goethe, Hammurabi, and Nietzsche; George L. Kline on current Soviet morality; Clyde Kluckhohn on Navaho morals; Swami Nikhilananda on Hindu ethics, and Frederick Sontag on Socrates, Plato, and Aristotle. Most of the articles are of substantial length and rich in content; some are a bit pedestrian.

Logic. In logic there is a Spanish *Vocabulario de Lógica*, by Baldomero Diez y Lozano (Murcia, Spain, Imp. Lourdes, 1925, 198 pages; 2d ed., 1928), which contains about five hundred articles covering not only topics in traditional logic, such as absurd, affirmation, a fortiori, but also topics in related philosophical fields, such as change, causality, phenomena, tree of Porphyry. Given the brevity of the articles, the treatment is necessarily superficial, but the identifications of the more obscure terms are useful.

Theology. Dictionaries of theology are fairly numerous. Among them, some warrant special mention.

From 1908 to 1914 was published a work edited by Samuel M. Jackson and others, *The New Schaff–Herzog Encyclopedia of Religious Knowledge* (13 vols., New York and London, Funk and Wagnalls; reprinted, Grand Rapids, Mich., Baker Book House, 1949–1950). This work was based on the nineteenth-century works in this field edited by Philip Schaff and Johann J. Herzog. The Preface lists numerous preceding Catholic, Protestant, Anglican, Jewish, Muslim, and other theological dictionaries. More of the articles are on individuals—prophets, religious leaders, and theologians—than on topics. Most articles of philosophical interest, such as those on dualism, duty, ethics, freedom of the will, gnosticism, philosophy of religion, positivism, probabilism, Stoicism, utilitarianism, and others, as well as on individual philosophers, were written by specialists in religion; a few, however, such as those by Troeltsch on British moralists, deism, the Enlightenment, idealism, and so on, are philosophically penetrating. The 13-volume work was condensed and brought up to date in the *Twentieth Century Encyclopedia of Religious Knowledge,* edited by Lefferts A. Loetscher (2 vols., Grand Rapids, Mich., Baker Book House, 1955).

Joseph Bricout edited the *Dictionnaire pratique des connaissances réligieuses* (7 vols., Paris, Letouzey et Ané, 1925–1933). In this Catholic-sponsored work the articles of philosophic interest—prepared mostly by professors at the Séminaire des Missions located at Vals in southern France—include those on aesthetic sense, agnosticism, atheism, belief, categories, criteria of truth, deism, doubt, efficient cause, empiricism, and others, plus about 230 articles on philosophers, theologians, and schools of thought. The articles on non-Catholic viewpoints are factual and fair.

Joseph Höfer and Karl Rahner edited the *Lexikon für Theologie und Kirche* (10 vols., Freiburg, Verlag Herder, 1957–1965), a revision of the work of the same title, edited by Michael Buchberger (10 vols., 1930–1938), which was itself referred to as the second edition of Buchberger's two-volume *Kirchliches Handlexikon* (Munich, Allgemeines Verlags-Gesellschaft, 1907–1912).

The work on the philosophical articles was coordinated by Bernhard Welte of Freiburg. The Catholic viewpoint is supported throughout, but the presentation of other viewpoints is informative.

The dictionary edited by Everett F. Harrison, *Baker's Dictionary of Theology* (Grand Rapids, Mich., Baker Book House, 1960, 566 pages), includes articles on movements of theological thought—for example, Calvinism, Lutheranism, and Thomism—but none on individual thinkers as such. Only those philosophical topics which are theological in a strict sense are dealt with. The orientation is that of sophisticated fundamentalism.

In 1962 was begun *A Catholic Dictionary of Theology* (Edinburgh, Thomas Nelson and Sons), edited by Monsignor H. Francis Davis and others. One volume of the four projected volumes has been issued thus far. Very Reverend Ivo Thomas is among the editors, and Father F. C. Copleston is among the better-known contributors. Instead of the usual prosaic and often uninspired articles on individual thinkers, Volume I contains articles on special features, such as Augustine and his influence, Berkeley and Catholicism, and the system of Boscovich. The writing is lively, and the authors do not hesitate to propound new theories.

Dictionaries or encyclopedias of specific religions and denominations are also available and contain articles on theological and even general philosophical topics. Several of these sectarian dictionaries of philosophy are outstanding.

The Jewish Encyclopedia, edited by Cyrus Adler and others (12 vols., New York and London, Funk and Wagnalls, 1901–1906; reprinted in various years), contains rewarding articles on Aristotle in Jewish literature, the influence of Arabic philosophy on Judaism, Maimonides (21 cols.), Spinoza (17 cols.), ethics, theology, and numerous other topics of philosophical relevance.

The Universal Jewish Encyclopedia, edited by Isaac Landman (10 vols., New York, Universal Jewish Encyclopedia, 1939–1943), had significant contributions by Isaac Husik, perhaps the greatest historian of medieval Jewish philosophy. This encyclopedia is a worthy successor to *The Jewish Encyclopedia.*

The Catholic Encyclopedia, edited by Charles G. Herbermann and others (16 vols., New York, Robert Appleton, 1907–1912; reprinted, 1913; supp., 1917, 1922, 1954), contains over five hundred articles on cosmology, theology, metaphysics, epistemology, logic, ethics, and individual philosophers. The articles expound these topics with clarity and vigor. Noteworthy contributors include Émile Bréhier, Pierre Duhem, and Maurice de Wulf. Comparable works exist in French, German, and Italian.

Of projected works the *New Catholic Encyclopedia* being edited at the Catholic University of America, Washington, D.C., will devote about 1 million of the total of

14 million words to subjects pertinent to philosophy. *Je sais, je crois: Encyclopédie du catholique au XXᵉᵐᵉ siècle,* edited by Henri Daniel-Rops (Paris, Librairie A. Fayard, 1956—), is scheduled to comprise 150 volumes (more than 130 have been published as of 1965); it is being translated into English as *The Twentieth Century Encyclopedia of Catholicism* (New York, Hawthorn Books). It is arranged by topic rather than alphabetically. Among the volumes of philosophical interest are Claude Tresmontant's *Les Origines de la philosophie chrétienne,* Vol. XI (1962), Philippe Delhaye's *La Philosophie chrétienne au moyen âge,* Vol. XII (1959), and Régis Jolivet's *L'Homme métaphysique,* Vol. XXXV (1958).

Theology and ethics. Of the dictionaries that cover two philosophical disciplines, chief among those covering theology and ethics is the *Encyclopedia of Religion and Ethics,* edited by James Hastings and others (13 vols., Edinburgh and New York, T. and T. Clark and Charles Scribner's Sons, 1908–1926; reprinted in whole or in part in various years). This is one of the great encyclopedias of all time. In conception it is original and imaginative; in execution, apt. The choice of topics is sagacious; the research has weathered the test of time; the analyses are thorough and penetrating. Among the philosophical contributors are John Burnet on the Academy, skeptics, and Socrates; C. D. Broad on reality and time; A. F. R. Hoernlé on solipsism; the Reverend William R. Inge on logos and Neoplatonism; Rufus M. Jones on mysticism; John Laird on will; J. M. E. McTaggart on personality; John H. Muirhead on ethics and rights; Josiah Royce on axiom, error and truth, mind, monotheism, negation, and order; F. C. S. Schiller on humanism, pragmatism, spiritualism, and values; A. E. Taylor on identity and theism; Ernst Troeltsch on idealism and Kant; Frederick J. E. Woodbridge on Hobbes, Hume, and pluralism; and Maurice de Wulf on aesthetics and beauty. The orientation in the articles on religion is generally that of liberal Protestantism, but opposing points of view are presented fairly. The bibliographies are compact and useful.

Also deserving of mention as covering both theology and ethics is *A Dictionary of Religion and Ethics,* edited by Shailer Mathews and Gerald B. Smith (New York, Macmillan, 1921, 513 pages), which had as contributors Franz Boas, Edgar J. Goodspeed, Rufus Jones, Eugene Lyman, George Herbert Mead, Roscoe Pound, James B. Pratt, James H. Tufts, and others. For less important topics the articles present dictionary-type definitions or identifications and little more. Imbalance in some of the articles may be illustrated by the fact that the 800-word article on Aristotle presents only one sentence on his ethics. There is a bibliography at the end, containing almost two thousand items.

Logic and philosophy of science. Major topics of another pair of philosophical disciplines—logic and the philosophy of science—are covered, though inadequately, in the *Harper Encyclopedia of Science,* edited by James R. Newman (4 vols., New York, Harper and Row, 1963), which had Ernest Nagel as its consultant on the philosophy and history of science. Among the contributors to the Newman work besides Nagel were Max Black, Irving M. Copi, Arthur C. Danto, and Milton K. Munitz. However, the philosophical articles are for the most part excessively brief.

Exceptions include those on logic (four thousand words) and logical empiricism (almost five hundred words).

Periods. There are dictionaries covering the philosophy of specific periods, including, for example, the *Lexicon Philosophicum Graecum,* by Rudolf Goclenius the elder (Marburg, Rudolf Hutwelcker, 1615, 390 pages; 2d ed., Frankfurt and Paris, S. Celerius, 1634), in which the terms defined are in Greek and the definitions and explanations are in Latin. Sources used by the author include the Greek philosophical classics, the New Testament, and the writings of the Greek Fathers of the Church.

The *Index zu philosophischen Problemen in der klassischen griechischen Literatur,* by Georg T. Schwarz (Bern, Francke Verlag, 1956, 109 pages), is a list of about 280 topics, such as being, definition, democracy, good, idea, life, love, philosophy, and reason, with an indication of where and how each one is discussed in pre-Aristotelian Greek literature and philosophy. Its limited objective is well carried out.

The *Dictionnaire de philosophie et de théologie scolastique, ou Études sur l'enseignement philosophique et théologique au moyen âge,* by Frédéric Morin, is included in the *Encyclopédie théologique,* edited by J. P. Migne (168 vols. in 170 in 3 series, Paris, 1844–1866), as Volumes XXI and XXII (1856–1857) of the third series. This dictionary covers adequately the medieval Scholastics, the main Arabic thinkers (but no Jewish philosophers), and the more important topics, problems, and movements of medieval philosophy. (The Migne encyclopedia is an unsystematic collection of dictionaries of aspects of religion—the Bible, church history, liturgy, saints, and so on.)

Schools. Movements or schools in philosophy are covered by various works. Among these is *A Biographical Dictionary of Modern Rationalists,* by Joseph McCabe (London, Watts, 1920, 934 pages). Rationalists are defined here as those who "uphold the right of reason against the authority of Church or tradition." Included are biographies of philosophers—for example, Bergson, Bradley, Lovejoy, and Moore; statesmen—for example, John Adams and Clemenceau; writers—for example, Balzac and Keats; musicians, artists, scientists, inventors, historians, sociologists, and so on.

Another school is covered in the *Dictionary of Scholastic Philosophy,* by Bernard Wuellner (Milwaukee, Wis., Bruce Publishing Co., 1956, 138 pages). Many of the articles are merely definitions. For example, the article on belief consists simply of the synonym *faith* and the article on faith gives only dictionary-type definitions of *faith* and *divine faith,* with references to two works of Aquinas. However, the book contains 33 interesting diagrams and charts, which show the subdivisions of act and potency, the categories of being, the kinds of evil, and the like.

A Concise Dictionary of Existentialism, edited by Ralph B. Winn (New York, Philosophical Library, 1960, 122 pages), contains quotations from six thinkers—Kierkegaard, Heidegger, Jaspers, Marcel, Sartre, and de Beauvoir—on anguish, being, boredom, choice, encounter, and other topics. Some of the quotations are epigrammatic; others are more extensive.

Philosophers. Dictionaries devoted to the thought of individual philosophers are numerous. Aquinas, Aristotle,

Bonaventure, Kant, Hegel, Maimonides, Plato, Russell, Schopenhauer, Spinoza, Teilhard de Chardin, and Wolff are among the main figures having special dictionaries devoted to their work. Aristotle, for example, is covered by four works.

First was Hermann Bonitz' *Index Aristotelicus* (Berlin, G. Reimer, 1870, 878 pages), which was reprinted from Volume V of the Academia Regia Borussica edition of Aristotle (5 vols., Berlin, G. Reimer, 1831–1870), with Greek texts edited by Immanuel Bekker. The index was reprinted in 1955 by the Akademie-Verlag in East Berlin. It is a complete concordance, indispensable to Aristotle scholars working with the original Greek.

Matthias Kappes' *Aristoteles-Lexikon* (Paderborn, Germany, Ferdinand Schöningh, 1894, 70 pages) contains a discussion in German of about four hundred Greek words used by Aristotle, with references to the main passages where those words play a part in his philosophy. On the basis of the 11-volume Oxford translation of Aristotle, Troy W. Organ's *An Index to Aristotle in English Translation* (Princeton, N.J., Princeton University Press, 1949, 181 pages) covers about four thousand English words, from Abdera, abdomen, and abortions to Zeno, Zeus, and zodiac, with references to the passages where they significantly occur.

In 1962 there appeared the *Aristotle Dictionary*, edited by Thomas P. Kiernan (New York, Philosophical Library, 524 pages), which has passages from Aristotle's writings, translated by H. E. Wedeck and others. It begins with a 161-page summary of the individual writings of Aristotle and continues with quotations under alphabetically arranged topic headings. The quotations chosen are not always apt; for example, the five sentences quoted under "Form" do not represent Aristotle's philosophy of form.

Plato, Aquinas, and Kant are similarly covered by three or more dictionaries each; one of the Kant dictionaries is in Russian.

CONCLUSION

In the past it was possible for a scholar to encompass in a lifetime of learning the whole of a broad domain of human interest, such as philosophy. It was possible for one man to read all the important sources, major interpretations, and critiques of the sources. A man could then write a thorough, well-balanced, and accurate dictionary of philosophy for his less knowledgeable colleagues.

However, with the democratization of education and the spread of intellectual activity the philosophical sources and the critical works have become too voluminous for one man to master. The truly comprehensive study of what philosophers have thought and said has therefore necessarily become a cooperative venture. Although some commendable dictionaries of philosophy have been produced by great scholars singlehandedly in the twentieth century, the scholarship of a single individual is, after all, limited.

Periodically, therefore, the need arises for expert summaries and appraisals of the philosophical books and articles that rush from the presses. Thus, cooperative summings up have appeared with some regularity. This *Encyclopedia of Philosophy* is intended to provide a new, more inclusive treatment of a wide variety of philosophical topics and to be a repository of up-to-date, detailed scholarship for the use of researchers and creative philosophers alike.

Bibliography

ON GENERAL ENCYCLOPEDIAS

Especially useful are the articles on encyclopedias which appear in the *Encyclopaedia Britannica*, 11th ed., 29 vols. (Cambridge and New York, 1910–1911); in the *Encyclopedia Americana*, 30 vols. (New York, 1966); and in *Chambers's Encyclopaedia*, 15 vols. (London, 1959).

OLDER LISTS

Some 20 dictionaries of philosophy, of ethics, or of individual philosophers are listed in Johann A. Fabricius, *Abriss einer allgemeinen Historie der Gelehrsamkeit*, 3 vols. (Leipzig, 1752–1754), Vol. I, p. 422. Shorter, evaluative lists of dictionaries of philosophy appear in the Preface to the first edition of Franck's *Dictionnaire des sciences philosophiques*, 6 vols. (Paris, 1844–1852), and in the Preface to Larousse's *Grand Dictionnaire universel du XIXᵉ siècle*, 15 vols. (Paris, 1865–1876), Vol. I, pp. xli–xlii.

TWENTIETH-CENTURY LISTS

The section "Dictionnaires de philosophie" in Jean Hoffmans, *La Philosophie et les philosophes: Ouvrages généraux* (Brussels, 1920), pp. 1–4, lists, along with 11 general dictionaries of philosophy, about 80 specialized dictionaries, on topics like ethics and aesthetics. See also the lists of philosophical dictionaries in the Alcalde *Diccionario* (Madrid, 1927), Vol. I, pp. 12–15; the section on dictionaries in the *Allgemeine philosophische Bibliographie*, by I. M. Bocheński and Florenzo Monteleone (Bern, 1948), pp. 32–33; the section on dictionaries in Carmelo Ferro's *Guida storico-bibliografica allo studio della filosofia* (Milan, 1949), pp. 187 ff.; and the section "Philosophie" in the *Index Lexicorum*, by Gert A. Zischka (Vienna, 1959), pp. 40–43.

DISCUSSIONS

André Lalande, in "Les Récents Dictionnaires de philosophie," *Revue philosophique de la France et de l'étranger*, Vol. 56 (1903), 628–648, and Frederick H. Heinemann, in "Die Aufgabe einer Enzyklopädie des XX. Jahrhunderts," pp. 1–22 of his compilation *Die Philosophie im XX. Jahrhundert*, 2d ed. (Stuttgart, 1963), provide thoughtful comments. Also provocative is Benedetto Croce's "Un Vocabolario della lingua filosofica italiana," *La Voce*, Vol. 1 (1909), 42; in it he urged the need for historical and analytical work on philosophical terminology which would not be a mere "dizionario filosofico," with its dismembered alphabetical order; he suggested, rather, a work like "una enciclopedia filosofica," having some of the attributes of Hegel's *Encyklopädie*. The editors of the Gallarate encyclopedia, in offering more than "un mero *dizionario* filosofico" may have had Croce specifically in mind.

WILLIAM GERBER

PHILOSOPHICAL JOURNALS. The learned journal was one of the major cultural innovations of the seventeenth century. Of the pioneering scholarly journals inaugurated during that century, the earliest one that regularly presented philosophical material is, remarkably, still being published, but, unhappily for our story, it now deals mainly with philology and related fields. This patriarch of professional periodicals, 300 years old and still lively, is the *Journal des savants* (Paris, 1665——), issued quarterly, with variations. The title was *Journal des sçavans* from 1665 to 1792. Publication was suspended from 1797 to 1816. The journal was devoted originally to book reviews, bibliographies, and news notes on philosophy, science, and literature.

In the same century similar learned journals, commenting on new books in philosophy and other fields, were issued for various periods in a number of cultural centers besides Paris. Indeed, on October 22, 1668, Leibniz wrote to Emperor Leopold I, taking note of the fact that the rival French nation had inaugurated the *Journal des sçavans* and declaring that Germany needed a similar medium of intellectual communication; Leibniz asked for a license to issue such a periodical, and the issuance of *Acta Eruditorum* beginning some 14 years later (see below) may have been the result. Prominent among the early learned journals issued outside of France which covered philosophy among other subjects were:

> 1668–1690. *Giornale de'letterati* (Parma), monthly. Suspended 1679–1686. Periodicals with the same title were also published in other Italian cities, including Rome, for various periods.
>
> 1681–1683. *Weekly Memorials for the Ingenious* (London), weekly.
>
> 1684–1718. *Nouvelles de la république des lettres* (Amsterdam), originally issued monthly, later issued six times a year. Founded by Pierre Bayle during his exile from France and edited by him from 1684 to 1687. Suspended 1689–1698 and 1711–1715.
>
> 1688–1690. *Freymüthige lustige und ernsthaffte Monats-Gespräche* (Halle), monthly.

In Latin, philosophical and other material appeared in *Acta Eruditorum* (Leipzig, 1682–1776), issued monthly. The title was *Nova Acta Eruditorum* from 1732 to 1776. This periodical, founded by Otto Mencke, Leibniz' friend, contained many contributions by and about Leibniz, and some authorities even say it was founded by Leibniz; he probably at least had a hand in Mencke's establishment of it. In this vehicle Leibniz first gave the world his notions respecting the differential calculus, and in it raged the controversy, beginning in 1699, over whether Leibniz or Newton first discovered the principles of the calculus.

Beginning in the eighteenth century a number of learned journals were devoted exclusively or largely to philosophy. These were the earliest instances of philosophical journals in a strict sense.

Definition of a philosophical journal. A philosophical journal, for the purposes of this article, is a publication that fulfills the following criteria:

(1) It is devoted to the whole field of philosophy (and nothing else) or, more narrowly, to a part of the field of philosophy (for example, symbolic logic or Thomism) or, more broadly, to the whole field of philosophy plus one or two other fields of interest (philosophy and psychology, philosophy and theology, and so forth). The specification "part of the field of philosophy" is taken strictly, thereby excluding philosophy of education and pure theosophy, but it includes political and social philosophy. Magazines of popular philosophy or popular morals—such as Addison and Steele's *Spectator* (founded 1710), *Der Leipziger Diogenes* (founded 1723), and *Der Dresdnische Philosoph* (founded 1737)—are excluded. Student journals, such as the *Graduate Review of Philosophy* (Minneapolis), are

also excluded. One theosophical journal, however, *The Aryan Path,* which contains many strictly philosophical articles, is included here.

(2) It is issued at stipulated intervals of less than a year. Thus, the intent reader will notice that this account does not mention bibliographical yearbooks, annual collections of studies, annual proceedings of philosophical societies, or irregular collections of articles (such as the quasi journal *Polemic,* of which eight issues were published at London at irregular intervals, from 1945 to 1947). In a few cases, however, a publication which, although it had no stipulated frequency, was actually issued (say) four times a year for a period of years, is counted as a regular journal.

(3) It has survived longer than a year. This requirement leads to the exclusion of, for example, *Symposion; Philosophische Zeitschrift für Forschung und Aussprache* (Erlangen), edited by Ernst Cassirer, Hans Driesch, and others, since only four issues were published, in 1926. In the case of periodicals inaugurated just prior to the completion of this article, however, the requirement of more than a year's duration is relaxed.

Strict adherence to the second criterion listed above has led to the exclusion of at least one vitally important medium of philosophical discussion—*Proceedings of the Aristotelian Society* (London), issued annually (referred to in this Encyclopedia as *PAS*). Since its founding in 1891 this periodical has presented numerous important articles, including papers by Bertrand Russell, Gilbert Ryle, J. L. Austin, Ludwig Wittgenstein, G. E. Moore, and many others.

In our account of significant journals devoted to the whole of philosophy, we have attempted to be comprehensive. It is probable, however, that a considerable number of obscure, though worthy, journals have slipped through our net and that on our strict criteria a few borderline semiprofessional journals are omitted which may have merited inclusion. Therefore, the statistics offered from time to time in this article (for example, that so many journals originated in a certain period) are based on our particular standards and should be taken as approximate. For fairly complete details about philosophical journals devoted to the whole of philosophy which are still being issued, the reader is referred to the *International Directory of Philosophy and Philosophers,* edited by Gilbert Varet and Paul Kurtz (New York, 1966).

For journals devoted to a part of philosophy or to philosophy and other disciplines, the present list is definitely incomplete. For example, there have been over a hundred theological journals, past and present, but only some fifty are mentioned as outstanding examples.

Regarding each journal mentioned in this article, four facts are ordinarily presented: the year it began publication (and, if it is no longer issued, its last year of publication), its title, its place of publication, and the frequency of its issuance. Other facts, such as historic figures who were editors, periods of suspension, and changes of title, are sometimes noted, but these additions are illustrative rather than complete.

In the case of journals that have changed their titles, the latest title is usually given as the main entry, and earlier titles are noted. Where one journal has succeeded another with some definite contact or relationship between them, they are considered as a single journal with a changed title. Thus, *Ratio* is considered as continuous with its earlier incarnation and appears below as one of the two oldest living philosophical journals.

In several instances some outstanding articles that the periodicals have published or striking facts about their influence in the philosophical world are set forth. Other periodicals, such as *Philosophy* (1926——), *Voprosy Filosofii* (1947——), and some German and Italian periodicals, could also have been appropriately singled out for such an exposition, had space permitted.

Statistical conspectus. From the eighteenth century to the present, approximately 70 philosophical journals have been born with more or less fanfare, have survived for a period, and have given up the ghost. About 180 others, however, are still alive, some flourishing, some manfully keeping their heads above water, some pitifully gasping for breath.

Of the philosophical journals published today, two are more than a century old, and four others are over 90 years old; their average life span, however, is about 28 years. Of those which no longer exist, the longest-lived at the time of its death was 81 years old: the *Zeitschrift für Philosophie und philosophische Kritik*, founded by the younger Fichte in 1837 and discontinued in 1918.

More births of philosophical journals occurred in the 1950s (55) and the 1940s (49) than in any other decades, but likewise more deaths of philosophical journals occurred in the 1950s (19) and the 1940s (17) than in any other decades. During World War I about 12 per cent of the philosophical journals in existence in 1914 ended their lives; during World War II about 15 per cent of those in existence in 1939 were terminated.

EARLY JOURNALS

Early quasi journals. Publications devoted to philosophy that were intended to be issued from time to time (more than once a year) but not at uniform intervals may be denominated "quasi journals of philosophy" since they do not conform to the requirement of a set frequency of issuance. A number of these quasi journals came into being from about 1715 on, especially in Germany, and lasted for varying periods. The following may serve as examples:

1715–1726. *Acta Philosophorum* (Halle). In German. Covered books on the history of philosophy. Probably the earliest quasi journal of philosophy.

1741–1744. *Philosophische Büchersaal* (Leipzig). Eight issues were published.

1789–1790. *Neues philosophisches Magazin; Erläuterungen und Anwendungen des Kantischen Systems bestimmt* (Leipzig). Two volumes, each with four issues, appeared.

1790–1850. Of seven genuine philosophical journals that saw the light before 1850, two—the *Theologische Quartalschrift* and *Ratio*—still survive, but the continuity of *Ratio* with its origin is tenuous. Chronologically, the seven pre-1850 journals fall into two groups. Those in the first group are:

1794–1807. *Revue philosophique, littéraire et poli-*

tique (Paris), issued three times a month, with variations. Title was *Décade philosophique, littéraire et politique* from 1794 to 1804 and became *Revue, ou Décade philosophique* late in 1804. Merged in 1808 with the *Mercure de France* (Paris, 1672–1820) and at that point may be considered to have lost its standing as a philosophical journal.

1795–1800. *Philosophisches Journal einer Gesellschaft teutscher Gelehrten* (Neustrelitz, 1795–1796; Jena and Leipzig, 1797–1800), monthly. J. G. Fichte was coeditor from 1797 to 1800. An article that Fichte published in the *Journal* in 1798 regarding the grounds of our belief in a divine government of the universe (defining God as the moral order of the universe) caused a cry of atheism to be raised and led to the suppression of the *Journal* in all the German states except Prussia, as well as to Fichte's resignation in 1799 from his teaching position at the University of Jena (see ATHEISMUSSTREIT).

1802–1803. *Kritisches Journal der Philosophie* (Tübingen), issued five times in 1802 and once in 1803. Editors, F. W. J. von Schelling and G. W. F. Hegel. Included a number of articles by Hegel.

1819——. *Theologische Quartalschrift* (Tübingen; later Ravensburg; now Stuttgart), quarterly. Suspended 1945.

The following journals belong to the second pre-1850 group:

1832–1852. *Zeitschrift für Philosophie und katholische Theologie* (Cologne, 1832–1836; Coblenz, 1836–1839; Cologne, 1840–1841; Bonn, 1842–1852), quarterly, with variations.

1837–1918. *Zeitschrift für Philosophie und philosophische Kritik; Vormals Fichte-Ulricische Zeitschrift* (Bonn, 1837–1842; Tübingen, 1843–1846; Halle, 1847–1890; Leipzig, 1891–1918), quarterly, with variations. Title was *Zeitschrift für Philosophie und spekulative Theologie*, from 1837 to 1846; subtitle varied. Founded by I. H. von Fichte (son of J. G. Fichte); later edited by him and Hermann Ulrici. Supported Christian and Hegelian views.

1847——. *Ratio* (Oxford and Frankfurt; formerly Göttingen), semiannual, with variations. Title was *Abhandlungen der Fries'schen Schule* from 1847 to 1936. Suspended 1850–1903, 1915–1917, 1919–1928, and 1937–1956. Now issued in English and German editions.

1850–1900

Of the decades from 1850 to 1899, the first produced 1 new journal of philosophy, the second and third a total of 11, and the fourth and fifth a total of 19. The lone philosophical journal born in the 1850s was *La Revue philosophique et religieuse* (Paris, 1850–1858), issued monthly.

The 1860s. In the 1860s seven philosophical journals were begun—three in Germany and one each in Belgium, France, Switzerland, and the United States. The first four journals to appear in this decade, including the first English-language journal of philosophy, are now defunct.

1861–1914. *Zeitschrift für Philosophie und Päda-*

gogik (Leipzig; later Langensalza), monthly, with variations. Title was *Zeitschrift für exakte Philosophie im Sinne des neuern philosophischen Realismus* (and the journal was, for the most part, a quarterly) from 1861 to 1896; suspended 1876–1882. Merged in 1896 with the *Zeitschrift für Philosophie und Pädagogik,* which had been issued since 1894; the combined publication took the title of the latter *Zeitschrift.*

1862–1864. *Athenäum; Philosophische Zeitschrift* (Munich), quarterly.

1867–1913. *L'Année philosophique* (Paris), issued annually and therefore not a "periodical" in the required sense, from 1867 to 1869 and again from 1890 to 1913, but it was a weekly (with variations) from 1872 to 1885 and a monthly from 1885 to 1889. Title was *La Critique philosophique* when the publication was issued weekly or monthly, from 1872 to 1889. C. B. Renouvier was a coeditor from 1890 to 1900.

1867–1893. *Journal of Speculative Philosophy* (St. Louis, Mo., 1867–1880; New York, 1880–1893), quarterly, with variations. Apparently the first philosophical journal in the English language. Founded by William T. Harris. Organ of the St. Louis Philosophical Society. Served as the vehicle for the first published writings of James, Royce, and Dewey. Its motto was "Philosophy can bake no bread, but she can procure for us God, freedom, and immortality."

The three philosophical journals of this period which have survived are German, Swiss, and Belgian, respectively:

1868——. *Archiv für Geschichte der Philosophie* (Berlin; previously Leipzig and Heidelberg), quarterly, with variations. Title was *Philosophische Monatshefte* from 1868 to 1887, *Archiv für Geschichte der Philosophie* from 1888 to 1894, *Archiv für Philosophie* from 1895 to 1926 (in this period the periodical was issued in two parts, *Archiv für Geschichte der Philosophie* and *Archiv für systematische Philosophie*), title was *Archiv für Philosophie und Soziologie* from 1927 to 1930 (again issued in two parts, *Archiv für Geschichte der Philosophie und Soziologie* and *Archiv für systematische Philosophie und Soziologie*), title reverted to *Archiv für Geschichte der Philosophie* in 1931; suspended 1933–1959. Original editor was Ludwig Stein, with the collaboration of Hermann Diels, Wilhelm Dilthey, Benno Erdmann, and Eduard Zeller. Paul Natorp became coeditor of the combined publication in 1895 and editor of the systematic part. Has contained articles in English, French, German, and Italian since 1895.

1868——. *Revue de théologie et de philosophie* (Lausanne), issued six times a year from 1868 to 1920, quarterly since 1921. Title has varied.

1869——. *Nouvelle Revue théologique* (Louvain, Belgium), monthly. A Jesuit organ.

The 1870s. The 1870s are remembered as the decade which produced the *Revue philosophique de la France et de l'étranger* and *Mind.* However, two other journals were inaugurated during the decade:

1870——. *Rivista di filosofia* (Turin; previously Bologna–Modena, Florence, Forli, Genoa, Pavia, Rome, and Milan), quarterly, with variations. Title was *La filosofia delle scuole italiane* (Florence; then Rome), 1870–1885; title was *Rivista italiana di filosofia* (Rome) from 1886 to 1898; became two separate periodicals, *Rivista di filosofia e scienze affini* (Bologna), 1899–1908, and *Rivista filosofica* (Pavia), 1899–1908; combined under the title *Rivista di filosofia* in 1909. Suspended 1922. In 1963 it absorbed *Il pensiero critico,* a quarterly published at Milan since 1950.

1877–1916. *Vierteljahrsschrift für wissenschaftliche Philosophie und Soziologie* (Leipzig), quarterly. Title was *Vierteljahrsschrift für wissenschaftliche Philosophie* from 1877 to 1901. Coeditors at various times included Richard Avenarius, Ernst Mach, and Wilhelm Wundt.

"Revue philosophique." The *Revue philosophique de la France et de l'étranger* (Paris, 1876——) was originally issued monthly and later issued six times a year; it is now issued quarterly. The *Revue's* first editor, Théodule Ribot, served for 40 years, until his death in 1916. Under his direction the *Revue* gave primary emphasis to articles on psychology. Philosophy began to gain predominance under Ribot's successor, Lucien Lévy-Bruhl, who was also a long-lived editor, conducting the periodical for 23 years until his death in 1939. The editors in succeeding years, when philosophy was fully established as the main arena of discussion in the *Revue,* were Émile Bréhier and Paul Masson-Oursel (1940–1952), Masson-Oursel and Pierre-Maxime Schuhl (1952–1956), and Schuhl alone (since 1956).

Even now the *Revue's* strongest contribution is represented not so much by publication of original hypotheses as by careful analysis and criticism of old and new viewpoints. Useful articles, for example, have been published on Leibniz, Hume, and English linguistic philosophy. An entire issue was devoted to Lévy-Bruhl in 1957 on the one hundredth anniversary of his birth. The coverage of philosophy "de l'étranger" has consisted in large part of some translations from English and German, extensive critical reviews of books, and summaries of periodical articles.

Among the more original contributions in the *Revue* have been C. S. Peirce's "La Logique de la science" (1878–1879), Étienne Gilson's "Essai sur la vie intérieure" (1920), Raymond Ruyer's "Ce qui est vivant et ce qui est mort dans la matérialisme" (1933), and Georges Gurvich's "Le Problème de la sociologie de la connaissance" (1957–1958). Famous contributors have included Rudolf Hermann Lotze, Herbert Spencer, J. S. Mill, Wilhelm Wundt, Henri Bergson, and Georges Sorel.

"Mind." *Mind; A Quarterly Review of Psychology and Philosophy* (originally London, later Edinburgh, now Oxford, 1876——), is issued quarterly.

In 1874 Alexander Bain broached the idea of establishing the first British philosophical journal to his pupil George C. Robertson, who suggested the title *Mind.* Bain appointed Robertson editor and supported the journal financially, sinking almost £3,000 into it in 15 years, until Robertson resigned in 1891.

Robertson, on laying down his mantle as editor, lamented that the journal had attracted more attention from "the lay student" than from those "whose regular business is with Philosophy." G. F. Stout, when he succeeded Robertson in 1892, wrote that "what is of prime importance is that our pages shall be filled with genuine work to the exclusion of merely dilettante productions." The implication here is curious when one considers that among the contributors to *Mind* during Robertson's stewardship were philosophers of the caliber of Samuel Alexander, A. W. Benn, Bernard Bosanquet, F. H. Bradley, T. H. Green, William James, C. Lloyd Morgan, Hastings Rashdall, Josiah Royce, Henry Sidgwick, and John Venn.

Sidgwick, who succeeded Bain as the financial "angel" of *Mind*, died in 1900. It was then that, pursuant to a suggestion made by Sidgwick in 1899, the Mind Association was formed (with Edward Caird as the first president) to support the journal. Meanwhile, G. E. Moore and Bertrand Russell had published their earliest contributions in *Mind* in the 1890s, and the periodical was well on its way to becoming what it is now, one of the dozen most influential journals of philosophy in the world. Stout relinquished the editorship in 1920; his successors were Moore, 1921 – 1947, and Gilbert Ryle since 1948.

Over the decades *Mind* has published many highly influential articles, such as Moore's "The Refutation of Idealism" (1903), Russell's "On Denoting" (1905), and H. A. Prichard's "Does Moral Philosophy Rest on a Mistake?" (1912). During Moore's editorship the journal set a particularly high standard, publishing such papers as W. T. Stace's "The Refutation of Realism" (1934), A. J. Ayer's "Demonstration of the Impossibility of Metaphysics" (1934), C. L. Stevenson's "Persuasive Definitions" (1938), Norman Malcolm's "Are Necessary Propositions Really Verbal?" (1940), John Wisdom's eight articles entitled "Other Minds" (1940–1943), and Frederick Will's "Will the Future Be Like the Past?" (1947). More recently (under Ryle's editorship), *Mind* has presented such important articles as J. N. Findlay's "Can God's Existence Be Disproved?" (1948), R. M. Hare's "Imperative Sentences" (1949), Paul Edwards' "Bertrand Russell's Doubts About Induction" (1949), P. F. Strawson's "On Referring" (1950), A. J. Ayer's "Individuals" (1952), G. E. M. Anscombe's "Aristotle and the Sea Battle" (1956), Nelson Goodman's "About" (1961), and many papers—written by Wittgenstein's disciples—that helped·to establish Wittgenstein's reputation before the posthumous publication of his books.

A public controversy occurred when *Mind* declined to publish a review of Ernest Gellner's *Words and Things* (London, 1959), which was critical of the ordinary-language school. Bertrand Russell, in a letter to the London *Times,* on November 5, 1959, protested against *Mind*'s decision.

Ryle's policy as editor has been to give some preference to philosophers who have not previously appeared in print. This policy, while testifying to the kindness of the editor and his concern for providing needed encouragement to tomorrow's leading spirits, has made it difficult to maintain the Olympian level of quality to which readers became accustomed during Moore's period as editor.

The 1880s. Of the nine journals of philosophy generated in the 1880s, five are still functioning, *The Monist* being perhaps the best known. One of the nine, among the oldest Italian philosophical journals, is *Divus Thomas;* another, a Swiss product, has had *Divus Thomas* as its subtitle or (for a time) as its main title. Japan and Russia gave birth to journals of philosophy in this decade, and the Japanese entry is still in the field.

American and British. Paul Carus was associated with two of the three English-language journals begun in this decade.

> 1886 – 1915. *Review of Theology and Philosophy* (Edinburgh), quarterly. Title was *Theological Review and Free Church College Quarterly* from 1886 to 1890 and *Critical Review of Theological and Philosophical Literature* from 1890 to 1904.

> 1887 – 1936. *The Open Court* (Chicago), issued every other week from 1887 to 1888; weekly from 1888 to 1896; monthly from 1897 to 1933; quarterly from 1934 to 1936. Successor to *The Index* (published weekly at Toledo, Ohio, and later at Boston, 1870 – 1886), organ of the Free Religious Association. *The Open Court* was founded by Paul Carus. Devoted to the establishment of ethics and religion on a scientific basis, it was more clearly a philosophical journal than was *The Index.*

> 1888——. *The Monist; An International Journal of General Philosophical Inquiry* (La Salle, Ill.; previously Chicago), quarterly. Suspended 1937 – 1963. International editorial board. Each issue now devoted to a specific topic. Edited by Paul Carus from 1888 to his death in 1919. Contributors have included Peirce, Dewey, Bosanquet, and Russell.

European. Two of the journals first issued in the 1880s are products of Italy and two are German-language publications.

> 1880——. *Divus Thomas; Commentarium de Philosophia et Theologia* (Piacenza), issued six times a year. Articles in English, French, Italian, and Latin. Suspended 1906 – 1923.

> 1881 – 1900. *Rivista speciale di opere di filosofia scientifica* (Milan), monthly. Title was *Rivista di filosofia scientifica* from 1881 to 1891.

> 1886——. *Freiburger Zeitschrift für Philosophie und Theologie* (Fribourg, Switzerland), quarterly, with variations. Title was *Jahrbuch für Philosophie und spekulative Theologie* (Paderborn; later Vienna) from 1886 to 1922, with the subtitle *Divus Thomas* from 1914 to 1922; title was *Divus Thomas* from 1923 to 1953.

> 1888——. *Philosophisches Jahrbuch* (Munich; previously Fulda), semiannual, with variations. Title has varied. Catholic-oriented.

Japanese and Russian. The Japanese journal begun in the 1880s is still being issued. The Russian journal, *Voprosy Filosofii i Psikhologii,* died in 1917, but a new *Voprosy Filosofii,* as will be noted later, arose from its ashes 30 years later, in 1947.

> 1887——. *Tetsugaku Zasshi; Journal of Philosophy* (Tokyo), quarterly, with variations. Journal of the Philosophical Society of Tokyo University. Titles of articles in English.

> 1889 – 1917. *Voprosy Filosofii i Psikhologii* (Moscow),

issued six times a year by the Moskovskoe Psikhologicheskoe Obshchestvo.

The 1890s. The 1890s constituted the fertile decade of *Ethics* and *The Philosophical Review*, of the *Revue de métaphysique et de morale*, of the *Revue philosophique de Louvain*, and of *Kant-Studien*, all of which are on the scene today, plus the oldest Indian and Polish philosophical journals, which also continue to appear.

Louvain was the parent of a pair of French-language journals, both flourishing today:

1894——. *Revue philosophique de Louvain* (Louvain), quarterly. Founded by Cardinal Mercier. Published by the Société Philosophique de Louvain. Neo-Scholastic. Suspended 1915–1918 and 1941–1944. Title was *Revue néo-scolastique* from 1894 to 1910, *Revue néo-scolastique de philosophie* from 1910 to 1933, and *Revue néoscolastique de philosophie* from 1934 to 1945. A *Répertoire bibliographique* has been published as an adjunct of the *Revue* since 1895; since 1938 it has been published separately, and since 1949 it has been administratively separate. Some articles in English; others in French with English summaries.

1895——. *Répertoire bibliographique de la philosophie* (Louvain), quarterly. Title was *Sommaire idéologique des ouvrages et des revues de philosophie* (with variations) from 1895 to 1914. Suspended 1915–1933 and 1941–1945. Reproduced *in toto*, with Dutch headings, in the *Tijdschrift voor Filosofie* (Louvain, 1939——).

Two of the journals that started publication in the 1890s have ethics as their subject matter, ethics alone in one case and ethics plus metaphysics in the other:

1890——. *Ethics; An International Journal of Social, Political and Legal Philosophy* (Chicago), quarterly. Established, under the title *The International Journal of Ethics*, as an outgrowth of *The Ethical Record*, organ of the Ethical Societies; responsibility assumed by the University of Chicago in 1923; name changed to *Ethics* in 1938.

"Revue de métaphysique et de morale." The *Revue de métaphysique et de morale* (Paris, 1893——) has been issued quarterly since 1920 (previously issued six times a year). This *Revue*, now the principal French philosophical journal, was established by Xavier Léon, with the collaboration of Élie Halévy. The title of the publication reflected not only a reaction against positivism but also, affirmatively, a belief that the conclusions of speculative philosophy could have a practical value. Léon (who also founded the Société Française de Philosophie in 1901 and organized various international congresses of philosophy) served as editor of the *Revue* until his death in 1935, when he was succeeded by Dominique Parodi. Parodi died in 1955, and Jean Wahl (who had assisted Parodi on the *Revue*) took over.

Until World War II special numbers of the *Revue* were occasionally devoted to a single topic. For example, issues were devoted to Kant (1904, the centennial of his death), Rousseau (1912, the bicentennial of his birth), American philosophy (1922, with articles by John Dewey, W. E. Hocking, C. I. Lewis, R. B. Perry, and others), Pascal (1923, the tercentenary of his birth), Hegel (1931, the cen-

tennial of his death), and Descartes (1937, the tercentenary of the *Discourse on Method*).

The journal's contributors have included all French philosophers of note as well as many eminent foreigners, such as Bertrand Russell, A. N. Whitehead, and Bernard Bosanquet; Benedetto Croce and Giovanni Gentile; Miguel de Unamuno; and Edmund Husserl. Among the articles of more than ordinary interest which have appeared in the journal are Henri Poincaré's "La Logique de l'infini" (1909), Henri Bergson's "L'Intuition philosophique" (1911), Étienne Gilson's "Art et métaphysique" (1916), Gabriel Marcel's "Existence et objectivité" (1925), Léon Brunschvicg's "Religion et philosophie" (1935), José Ferrater Mora's "Philosophie et architecture" (1955), and Wahl's "Physique atomique et connaissance humaine" (1962).

"The Philosophical Review." Two of the major philosophical journals now on the scene had their origin in the *fin de siècle* decade. One of these was American, *The Philosophical Review* (Ithaca, N.Y., 1892——), which is now issued quarterly. It was previously issued six times a year. It is published by the Sage School of Philosophy at Cornell University.

The Philosophical Review was relatively undistinguished until the late 1940s. Among the few important articles that preceded the late flowering of the journal were C. I. Lewis' "Experience and Meaning" (1934) and Moritz Schlick's reply, "Meaning and Verification" (1936), which is commonly regarded as Schlick's most telling contribution to contemporary philosophy.

The *Review's* recent burgeoning took place under the guidance of Max Black and his colleagues on the philosophy staff at Cornell. Significant contributions in this period include W. V. Quine's "Two Dogmas of Empiricism" (1951), Black's "Definition, Presupposition, and Assertion" (1952), Gilbert Ryle's "Ordinary Language" (1953), H. P. Grice and P. F. Strawson's "In Defense of a Dogma" (1956), Stuart Hampshire's "On Referring and Intending" (1956), various articles by John Rawls on justice (1958–1963), J. J. C. Smart's "Sensations and Brain Processes" (1959), Norman Malcolm's "Anselm's Ontological Arguments" (1960), and Richard Taylor's "Fatalism" (1962).

Other prominent philosophers whose work has appeared in *The Philosophical Review* include George Boas, R. M. Chisholm, P. T. Geach, Nelson Goodman, Arthur E. Murphy, Ernest Nagel, and J. A. Passmore.

"Kant-Studien." The other famous journal founded in the last decade of the nineteenth century was German: *Kant-Studien; philosophische Zeitschrift* (Hamburg and Leipzig; later Berlin; now Cologne, 1896——), issued quarterly, with variations. The title was originally spelled *Kantstudien*. This journal has been the organ of the Kant-Gesellschaft since 1904. It was suspended twice, from 1937 to 1942 and from 1945 through 1953.

Hans Vaihinger founded *Kant-Studien* and was its editor, alone or with one or two coeditors, until 1922; Max Scheler was coeditor in 1902/1903. The periodical has published articles in English, French, German, and Italian by outstanding scholars and philosophers, including Erich Adickes, Émile Boutroux, Edward Caird, Ernst Cassirer, Rudolf Eucken, and Norman Kemp Smith. Although the periodical is specifically oriented toward Kant, it includes in its purview current thought on questions raised by Kant, pre-Kantian philosophy as part of the background of Kantianism, and other liberal extensions of the frame of reference.

For many years *Kant-Studien* published abstracts of new books in philosophy on a unique basis: the abstracts were written by the authors themselves. As another special feature, 86 separate monographs have been issued under the auspices of the journal.

During the short-lived revival of *Kant-Studien* in 1942–1944, the journal was not uninfluenced by Nazism. In 1954, however, on the 150th anniversary of Kant's death, the periodical was reborn in a new setting (Cologne), and since then it has regained its international reputation.

Other journals. Additional journals which arose in the 1890s were the following:

1893——. *Revue thomiste; Revue doctrinale de théologie et de philosophie* (originally Brussels; now Toulouse), quarterly. Founded by the Dominican order.

1895——. *The Vedanta Kesari* (Madras), monthly, with variations. Title was *The Brahmavadin; A Fortnightly Religious and Philosophical Journal* from 1895 to 1914. Organ of the world-wide Ramakrishna order.

1896–1915. *Neue metaphysische Rundschau* (Berlin), monthly. Title was *Metaphysische Rundschau* from 1896 to 1897.

1897–1949. *Przegląd Filozoficzny* (Warsaw), quarterly. English summaries of articles in some issues; table of contents also printed in French. Suspended 1940–1946. Issuance stopped by the government at the beginning of the period of militant Marxist domination of Polish philosophy (first half of the 1950s). Replaced (not succeeded) by the periodical now called *Studia Filozoficzne; Kwartalnik* (1951——).

PREWAR PERIOD

The vital statistics for the period from 1900 to 1914 show 19 journals born, 12 of which have survived. This is the period of *The Hibbert Journal, The Journal of Philosophy, The Harvard Theological Review,* and the first of various journals called *Logos.* Czechoslovakia, Ireland, the Netherlands, and Spain are represented for the first time in this period.

Theology. The prewar period was exceptionally rich in journals which emphasized theology or the philosophy of religion:

1900–1939. *Revue de philosophie* (Paris), issued six times a year. Thomist-oriented.

1902——. *The Hibbert Journal; A Quarterly Review of Religion, Theology and Philosophy* (London), quarterly; originally issued monthly. Treats religious and humanistic questions from a philosophical or cultural point of view. Contributors have included Henri Bergson, Sarvepalli Radhakrishnan, Bertrand Russell, Rabindranath Tagore, and Leo Tolstoy.

1905–1910. *Rivista storico critica delle scienze teologiche* (Rome), monthly.

1907——. *Revue des sciences philosophiques et théologiques* (Étiolles, Soisy-sur-Seine), quarterly, with variations. Founded by the French Dominicans of the Facultés de Philosophie et de Théologie du Saulchoir. Suspended 1915–1919 and 1943–1946.

1908——. *The Harvard Theological Review* (Cambridge, Mass.), quarterly.

1909——. *Rivista di filosofia neo-scolastica* (Milan), issued six times a year, with variations. Organ of the Istituto di Filosofia, Università Cattolica del Sacro Cuore.

1910——. *La ciencia tomista* (originally Madrid; now Salamanca), issued six times a year from 1910 to 1949, quarterly since 1950. Edited by the Spanish Dominicans.

Social philosophy and aesthetics. Journals of ethics, social philosophy, philosophy of culture, and aesthetics were fostered in the prewar period in Germany and Italy:

1906–1926. *Zeitschrift für Ästhetik und allgemeine Kunstwissenschaft* (Stuttgart), quarterly. Max Dessoir, editor.

1907——. *Archiv für Rechts- und Sozialphilosophie* (Neuwied; previously Munich), quarterly. Title has varied. Contains articles mainly in German and English.

1906——. *Rivista rosminiana di filosofia e di cultura* (Milan; formerly published at Pallanza and other Italian cities), quarterly, with variations. Edited by Giuseppe Morando from 1906 to his death in 1914; edited by his son Dante since 1937. Combats positivism and subjectivism.

1910–1941. *Zeitschrift für deutsche Kulturphilosophie; Neue Folge des Logos* (Tübingen), issued three times a year. Title was *Logos; Internationale Zeitschrift für Philosophie der Kultur* from 1910 to 1933. In 1934, when the journal was completely Nazified, Richard Kroner was replaced as editor in chief (a post which he had held since 1910) and Ernst Cassirer, Edmund Husserl, Friedrich Meinecke, and Rudolf Otto were summarily removed from the roll of collaborating editors.

General philosophy. Several of the prewar journals were general in their philosophical coverage. Two were Italian:

1903–1951. *Quaderni della critica* (Naples), issued six times a year, with variations. Founded by Benedetto Croce. Title was *La critica; Rivista di letteratura, storia e filosofia* from 1903 to 1944. Contained many articles by Croce and by Gentile.

1908–1925. *Bollettino filosofico; Organo della Biblioteca Filosofica di Firenze* (Florence), monthly, with variations. Suspended 1910, 1913–1915, and 1917–1923.

France and the Netherlands gave rise to two others:

1900——. *Bulletin de la Société Française de Philosophie* (Paris), quarterly. Contributors have included Bergson, Louis de Broglie, Brunschvicg, Croce, Einstein, and Russell.

1907——. *Algemeen Nederlands Tijdschrift voor Wijsbegeerte en Psychologie* (Assen; formerly Amsterdam), issued five times a year. Organ of the Algemene Nederlandse Vereniging voor Wijsbegeerte. Title was *Tijdschrift voor Wijsbegeerte* from

1907 to 1934. From 1934 to 1938 this periodical included, as a separate section, *Annalen der Critische Philosophie* (Assen, 1931–1938), which was also published separately and was succeeded by *Annalen van het Genootschap voor Wetenschappelijke Philosophie* (Assen, 1939–1959), which was likewise published separately in addition to being included in this periodical. Suspended 1944–1946.

One periodical begun in this period originated in what is now Czechoslovakia, and one in what is now Poland:

1902–1937. *Česká Mysl; Casopis Filosofický* (Prague), quarterly, with variations.

1911——. *Ruch Filozoficzny* (Torun; previously Lvov), originally monthly; now quarterly. Was a supplement to *Przegląd Filozoficzny* (Warsaw, 1897–1949) from 1911 to 1914. Suspended 1915–1919, 1939–1947, and 1951–1957 (the third period being one of militant Marxist domination of Polish philosophy). Organ of the Polskie Towarzystwo Filozoficzne.

Two of the general prewar products were English-language journals. One was an Irish intellectual quarterly:

1912——. *Studies; An Irish Quarterly Review of Letters, Philosophy & Science* (Dublin), quarterly. Title on individual issues is now *Studies; An Irish Quarterly Review*, but the annual title page for bound volumes continues to use the full title.

The other English-language philosophical periodical of a general character has been associated from the start with Columbia University.

"The Journal of Philosophy." The *Journal of Philosophy* (New York, 1904——), issued fortnightly, was founded by Frederick J. E. Woodbridge and Wendell T. Bush. The title was *Journal of Philosophy, Psychology, and Scientific Methods* from 1904 to 1920. Provocative articles by William James, Arthur O. Lovejoy's "The Thirteen Pragmatisms" (1908), the "First Platform and Program of the New Realists" (1910), and numerous other notable articles have appeared in its pages. Dewey was a frequent contributor, and his philosophy has been analyzed and appraised in the *Journal* from many angles.

A few of the other important articles, on a variety of subjects, that have appeared in the *Journal* are C. I. Lewis' "A Pragmatic Conception of the A Priori" (1923), Herbert Feigl and Albert Blumberg's "Logical Positivism, A New Movement in European Philosophy" (1931), which introduced the term "logical positivism," Ernest Nagel's "Impressions and Appraisals of Analytic Philosophy in Europe" (1936), W. V. Quine's "Designation and Existence" (1939), C. G. Hempel's "The Function of General Laws in History" (1942), Nelson Goodman's "The Problem of Counterfactual Conditionals" (1947), and Norman Malcolm's "Knowledge of Other Minds" (1958). Also noteworthy are Nagel's penetrating reviews, which were frequently featured in the *Journal* in the 1930s and 1940s.

From 1933 to 1936 the *Journal* published annual world-wide bibliographies of philosophy. In more recent years it has carried texts of papers presented at the annual meetings of the Eastern Division of the American Philosophical Association. In 1963/1964 the *Journal* was involved in a minor *cause célèbre* when, after publishing an article by one of its editors on the discussion between non-Soviet and Soviet philosophers at the Thirteenth International Congress of Philosophy (Mexico City, 1963), it declined to provide equal space, although it offered some space, for an article giving a contrary view of the same discussion.

WORLD WAR I TO 1928

During World War I two new philosophical journals were begun in Europe and one each in Argentina and Japan. Only the Japanese journal is still being published. One of the European journals was a new *Logos*.

1914–1943. *Logos; Rivista trimestrale di filosofia e di storia della filosofia* (Perugia; later Naples and Florence; then Rome), quarterly. International board of editors. Suspended 1916–1919. Title was *Logos*, without the subtitle, from 1914 to 1938.

1915–1929. *Revista de filosofía, cultura, ciencias, educación* (Buenos Aires), issued six times a year, with variations.

1916——. *Tetsugaku Kenkyu; Journal of Philosophical Studies* (Kyoto), monthly. Organ of the Philosophical Society of Kyoto University. Contributors have included Heidegger and Jaspers.

1918–1943. *Blätter für deutschen Philosophie; Zeitschrift der Deutschen Philosophischen Gesellschaft* (Erfurt; later Berlin), quarterly. Title was *Beiträge zur Philosophie des deutschen Idealismus* from 1918 to 1927.

The years from 1919 to 1928 saw 32 new journals of philosophy roll off the presses, the largest quota in any ten-year period up to that time. Included were *The Personalist*, the first Chinese philosophical journals, another *Logos, The Australasian Journal of Philosophy, Philosophy,* and *The New Scholasticism*. Of the total of 32, 7 were Italian (5 survive), 5 German (2 survive), 5 French (all survive), and 4 American (all survive); the rest were scattered among China (3, none surviving), Czechoslovakia (2, none surviving), and Australia, Great Britain, India, Lithuania, the Netherlands, and Poland.

Italian. Three of the Italian journals of the postwar decade have Latin names and concern theological matters chiefly:

1920——. *Gregorianum* (Rome), quarterly. Published by the Università Gregoriana di Roma. Articles in English, French, German, Italian, Latin, and Spanish.

1924——. *Angelicum* (Rome), quarterly. Journal of the Faculty of Theology, Canon Law, and Philosophy, Pontificium Athenaeum Angelicum. Articles in French, German, Italian, and Latin.

1926——. *Antonianum; Periodicum Philosophico-theologicum Trimestre* (Rome), quarterly. Published by the Athenaeum Antonianum de Urbe. Articles mainly in Latin; those in other languages are summarized in Latin.

The other Italian philosophical journals of the period cover various fields:

1920–1923. *Rivista trimestrale di studi filosofici e religiosi* (Perugia), quarterly.

1920——. *Giornale critico della filosofia italiana* (Florence; previously Messina, Milan, Rome, and elsewhere), quarterly, with variations. Founded by Giovanni Gentile and edited by him until his assassination in 1944.

1921——. *Rivista internazionale di filosofia del diritto* (Milan), issued six times a year, with variations.

1924–1945. *L'idealismo realistico; Rivista di filosofia mazziniana* (Rome), monthly.

German. *Erkenntnis* (see below) was the most important journal of the postwar decade, but four other German journals also merit attention.

1919–1924. *Grundwissenschaft; Philosophische Zeitschrift der Johannes-Rehmke-Gesellschaft* (Leipzig), quarterly. Subtitle varied.

1923–1932. *Literarische Berichte aus dem Gebiete der Philosophie* (Erfurt), semiannual, with variations. Title was *Literarische Berichte der Deutschen Philosophischen Gesellschaft* from 1923 to 1924.

The two German journals begun in this period that are still on earth are concerned with heavenly matters:

1923——. *Neue Zeitschrift für systematische Theologie und Religionsphilosophie* (Berlin; originally Gütersloh), issued three times a year; formerly quarterly (irregular 1956–1959). Title was *Zeitschrift für systematische Theologie* from 1923 to 1958, and *Neue Zeitschrift für systematische Theologie* from 1959 to 1962. Suspended 1944–1949.

1926——. *Scholastik; Vierteljahresschrift für Theologie und Philosophie* (Frankfurt; previously Freiburg im Breisgau), quarterly. Published by the Jesuits of the faculties of philosophy and theology, Hochschule St. Georg, Frankfurt, and Berchmanskolleg, Pullach-am-Main. Suspended 1941–1943; combined with the *Theologische Quartalschrift* (1819——) for one year, 1944; suspended 1945–1948.

"Erkenntnis." The *Journal of Unified Science* (*Erkenntnis*) (Leipzig; later The Hague and Chicago, 1919–1940) was issued six times a year, with variations. Its title was *Annalen der Philosophie, mit besonderer Rücksicht auf die Probleme der als ob Betrachtung* from 1919 to 1923, *Annalen der Philosophie und philosophischen Kritik* from 1924 to 1930, and *Erkenntnis, zugleich Annalen der Philosophie* from 1930 to 1939. Hans Vaihinger was coeditor from 1919 to 1930. From 1930 to 1940 the editors were Rudolf Carnap and Hans Reichenbach (but Carnap alone in 1937/1938).

In the 1930s *Erkenntnis* was perhaps the most influential philosophical periodical ever published. The Vienna circle of logical positivists took over the journal, then entitled *Annalen,* in 1930 (Vaihinger, its coeditor, was then 78 years old), renamed it *Erkenntnis,* and transformed it into a medium—which struck sparks of fire in the philosophical world—for the discussion and propagation of the circle's theses. The first issue of *Erkenntnis* contained Moritz Schlick's "Die Wende der Philosophie" ("The Turning Point in Philosophy") as the opening article and also Carnap's "Die alte und die neue Logik" ("The Old and the New Logic"). In quick succession, in the early 1930s, the periodical published Carnap's "Überwindung der Metaphysik durch logische Analyse der Sprache" ("Elimination of Metaphysics Through Logical Analysis of Language"),

probably his most famous paper; Schlick's "Positivismus und Realismus" ("Positivism and Realism") and "Über das Fundament der Erkenntnis" ("On the Foundation of Knowledge"); Otto Neurath's "Protokollsätze" ("Protocol Sentences"); and Ernest Nagel's "Measurement."

Other notable articles which appeared in *Erkenntnis* are Hans Reichenbach's "Wahrscheinlichkeitslogik" ("Logic of Probability," 1935) and others by him on probability theory, Max Black's "Relations Between Logical Positivism and the Cambridge School of Analysis" (1939), and articles by Niels Bohr and other famous scientists and mathematicians, not all of whom were logical positivists. Various issues of *Erkenntnis* contained the proceedings of the Tagung für Erkenntnislehre der Exakten Wissenschaften (1929–1930), and of the International Congress for the Unity of Science (1934–1938).

Many of the articles published in *Erkenntnis* were translated into English and other languages and published in collections of the foundation papers of the logical positivist movement. Indeed, the journal had its greatest impact on philosophers in England and the United States rather than on those in continental Europe, many of whom had fallen under the spell of Martin Heidegger's *Dasein.*

French. Two of the French periodicals of the first postwar decade are religiously oriented.

1921——. *Revue d'histoire et de philosophie religieuse* (Strasbourg), quarterly. Published by the Faculté de Théologie Protestante de l'Université de Strasbourg.

1924——. *Bulletin thomiste* (Étiolles, Soisy-sur-Seine), quarterly, with variations. Organ of the Société Thomiste.

The other three are secular and humanistic.

1923——. *Archives de philosophie* (Paris), quarterly, with variations. Suspended 1953–1954.

1926——. *Les Études philosophiques* (Paris), quarterly, with variations. Founded by Gaston Berger.

1927——. *Revue des sciences humaines* (Lille and elsewhere), quarterly, with variations. Title was *Revue d'histoire de la philosophie* from 1927 to 1931 and *Revue d'histoire de la philosophie et d'histoire générale de la civilisation* from 1933 to 1946. Suspended 1932, 1940–1941, and 1945.

Eastern European. During the 1920s Prague was the birthplace of two philosophical journals and Kaunas and Cracow of one each (including another *Logos*):

1920–1939. *Ruch Filosofický* (Prague), issued six times a year, with variations.

1921–1938. *Logos; Filosofijos Laikraštis* (Kaunas), semiannual.

1922–1950. *Kwartalnik Filozoficzny* (Cracow), quarterly. Published by the Polskiej Nakładem Akademii Umiejętności. Suspended 1934 and 1940–1945. Editor in the last years of the periodical was Roman Ingarden. Emphasis on phenomenology and conceptual analysis.

1927–1929. *Filosofie* (Prague), issued ten times a year. Published under the auspices of the Ministerstvo Školstvi a Národní Osvěty of Czechoslovakia.

American. In the United States a personalistic magazine and three religious journals were founded and are still being issued:

1920——. *The Personalist* (Los Angeles), quarterly. Issued by the University of Southern California.

1923——. *The Modern Schoolman* (St. Louis, Mo.), quarterly.

1926——. *Thought; A Review of Culture and Idea* (New York), quarterly. Founded by the Jesuit periodical *America;* directed since 1940 by Fordham University. Subtitle was *A Quarterly of the Sciences and Letters* from 1926 to 1939.

1927——. *The New Scholasticism* (Washington), quarterly. Organ of the American Catholic Philosophical Association. This periodical is one of the two best sources of philosophical news (teaching appointments, publication projects, congresses, etc.), the other being the *Revue philosophique de Louvain* (1894——).

Asian and Australasian. The three Chinese journals of philosophy that were introduced in the 1920s are:

1921–1927. *Chê Hsüeh* ["Philosophy"] (Peking), issued six times a year, with variations. Generally referred to as *Chê Hsüeh Tsa Chih* ("Philosophical Journal").

1926–1930. *Chê Hsüeh Yüeh K'an* ["Philosophical Monthly"] (Peking), monthly, with variations.

1927–1944. *Chê Hsüeh P'ing Lun* ["Philosophical Review"] (Peking), issued six times a year, with variations.

A journal published in India continues to be active:

1925——. *Philosophical Quarterly* (Calcutta; later Amalner), quarterly. Organ of the Indian Institute of Philosophy and the Indian Philosophical Congress.

"The Australasian Journal." One journal published in Australia merits a pause for special comment: *The Australasian Journal of Philosophy* (Glebe, New South Wales, Australia, 1923——), issued quarterly from 1923 to 1937 and three times a year since 1938. It is the organ of the Australasian Association of Psychology and Philosophy. The title was *The Australasian Journal of Psychology and Philosophy* from 1923 to 1946.

The *Journal* announced in its first issue that some of its articles would be technical and addressed to a few experts, whereas others would treat of "topics of universal interest, ranging from the high metaphysical quest of the secret of the Absolute, to concrete problems of social and political ethics." It undertook not to "scorn the old fogey in Philosophy, or disdain the new faddist." Bertrand Russell helped the *Journal* get off to a flourishing start by publishing in its first volume (second issue) a little-known but important article of his, "Vagueness."

In 1935 John Anderson, a controversial philosopher of Scottish origin, became the editor of the *Journal.* He thereafter exerted a strong influence not only on the *Journal* but also on the thinking of philosophers in his part of the world. The legislators of New South Wales, shocked by Anderson's militant atheism, unsuccessfully demanded his removal from his teaching post at the University of Sydney.

The current editor of *The Australasian Journal of Philosophy* is A. K. Stout, son of G. F. Stout, former editor of *Mind.* This is the third notable case in which a son followed his father's trade as editor of a philosophical journal, the other such families being the Fichtes, who respectively edited the *Philosophisches Journal,* 1795 ff., and the *Zeitschrift für Philosophie,* 1837 ff.; and the Morandos, who were editors at different times of the *Rivista rosminiana,* 1906 ff.

Among the challenging and widely discussed papers that Anderson on his pluralistic, positivistic realism; the last pieces by the elder Stout; some of the most celebrated articles by J. N. Findlay and others in the early 1940s on the philosophy of Wittgenstein; J. A. Passmore's three articles entitled "Logical Positivism" (1943, 1944, and 1948) and his "Christianity and Positivism" (1957); J. J. C. Smart's "The Reality of Theoretical Entities" (1956); A. N. Prior's "The Autonomy of Ethics" (1960); and Keith Lehrer's "Doing the Impossible" (1964). The *Journal's* influence reached a particularly high level in the period beginning about 1955.

British and Dutch. The remaining examples of journals begun in the first postwar decade have had London and Hilversum as their headquarters:

1926——. *Philosophy* (London), quarterly. Organ of the British Institute of Philosophy. Title was *Journal of Philosophical Studies* from 1926 to 1931. Contributors have included Samuel Alexander, George Dawes Hicks, and Bertrand Russell.

1926–1944. *Denken en Leven; Wijsgeerig Tijdschrift* (Hilversum), issued six times a year.

1929–1938

From 1929 to 1938, 25 new journals of philosophy sought subscribers. Of these, 8 have fallen by the wayside, 6 being casualties of World War II. Among the new journals of this period were a Yugoslav quarterly, the first journals covering the philosophy of science and symbolic logic, and *Analysis.* Italy produced the most new philosophical journals (10); Germany produced none.

Idealistic, religious, and mystic. Two publications on nonworldly philosophy were established in India:

1930–1935. *Review of Philosophy and Religion* (Poona), semiannual. Organ of the Academy of Philosophy and Religion.

1930——. *The Aryan Path* (Bombay), monthly. Popular ethics and mysticism, with emphasis on Indian philosophy.

The remaining examples of this kind of journal had their homes in Belgium, Italy, the Netherlands, and the United States, respectively:

1929——. *Recherches de théologie ancienne et médiévale* (Louvain), quarterly.

1934——. *Doctor Communis; Acta et Commentationes Pontificiae Accademiae Sanctae Thomae Aquinatis* (Rome; previously Turin), issued three times a year. Title was *Acta Pontificiae Accademiae Sanctae Thomae Aquinatis* from 1934 to 1947. Articles mainly in Latin; those in other languages are summarized in Latin.

1938——. *Bijdragen van de Philosophische en Theologische Faculteiten der Nederlandsche Jezuieten* (Maastricht), issued three times a year, with variations. Title has varied.

1938——. *Vedanta and the West* (Hollywood, Calif.), issued six times a year. Emphasis on mysticism. Sponsored by the Vedanta Society of Southern California.

Logic and related disciplines. Balancing the inaugurations of religious periodicals were those of periodicals on logic, philosophy of science, and language analysis. The two most influential were *Analysis* and the *Journal of Symbolic Logic*.

"Analysis." *Analysis* (Oxford, 1933——) is issued six times a year, with variations. The journal was suspended from 1940 to 1947. This periodical was founded by a number of younger philosophers under the influence of G. E. Moore, Bertrand Russell, and Ludwig Wittgenstein. It was intended mainly as a medium for short analyses and discussions. A group of supporters pledged to pay £5 each if the venture should so require, but the journal paid its way. In 1936 an Analysis Society was formed, also aimed at guaranteeing the financial stability of the journal, but it went out of existence a few years later; some of the papers read at its meetings were published in *Analysis*.

Max Black, in America, was closely associated with the journal from its foundation, and Rudolf Carnap, Carl Hempel, and Moritz Schlick, of the Vienna circle, contributed articles to early issues. Among the memorable articles that *Analysis* has published are A. J. Ayer's "The Genesis of Metaphysics" (1934), Schlick's "Facts and Propositions" (1935), Margaret Macdonald's "Necessary Propositions" (1940), Black's "The Semantic Definition of Truth" (1948), Friedrich Waismann's six articles entitled "Analytic–Synthetic" (1949–1953), P. T. Geach's "Russell's Theory of Descriptions" (1950), Alonzo Church's "On Carnap's Analysis of Statements of Assertion and Belief" (1950), Gilbert Ryle's "Heterologicality" (1951), Karl R. Popper's "A Note on the Body–Mind Problem" (1955), Yehoshuah Bar-Hillel's "New Light on the Liar" (1957), Peter Achinstein's "The Circularity of a Self-supporting Inductive Argument" (1962), and Keith Gunderson's "Interview With a Robot" (1963).

Many highlights from the journal were reprinted in *Philosophy and Analysis* (New York, 1954), edited by Margaret Macdonald, who was editor of *Analysis* from 1948 to her death in January 1956. For a time in the 1950s, *Analysis* conducted "competitions" and published the best short answers to such questions as "Does it make sense to say that death is survived?"

Especially in the early years of *Analysis*, its pages crackled with iconoclasm, terseness, and wit. Currently, some of the articles are longer than the average of the early years, and a supplement containing extended articles is now issued annually.

"Journal of Symbolic Logic." The *Journal of Symbolic Logic* (Providence, R.I.; previously Menasha, Wis., and Baltimore, Md., 1936——), issued quarterly, publishes articles in English, French, and German. It is the organ of the Association for Symbolic Logic.

This journal was the first one to be devoted exclusively to its field. In April 1934, Paul Weiss called attention to the fact that papers on logic were scattered in heterogeneous periodicals, and (without specifically proposing a new periodical) he suggested the formation of a logic association. Later in the year, C. J. Ducasse and C. A. Baylis explicitly urged the establishment of a journal of symbolic logic, to be supported by an association for symbolic logic. The response was encouraging, and the venture was undertaken.

Financing the *Journal* was a problem in the early years, and it was uncertain, after the publication of the third issue, whether the publication could continue. Happily, subventions were obtained from a number of universities, and dues payments accumulated sufficiently to enable the *Journal* to meet its bills.

Aside from the high quality of many of the articles, the *Journal* is noted for an exceptionally useful section devoted to reviews and abstracts of current literature. These reviews and abstracts purport to cover all pertinent books and articles which have come to the attention of the editors; the frame of reference of publications pertinent to symbolic logic is interpreted broadly. The reviews and abstracts constitute a continuation of Alonzo Church's nonpareil bibliography of symbolic logic from 1666 to 1935 which appeared in the issue of December 1936, with a supplement in the issue of December 1938.

The well-deserved international reputation of the *Journal* derives in large part from the vast knowledge and logical acumen of Church, who is the principal editor. Among the many articles of enduring worth which have appeared in the *Journal* are Church's "A Note on the *Entscheidungsproblem*" (1936), Barkley Rosser's "Extensions of Some Theorems of Gödel" (1936), W. V. Quine's "On the Theory of Types" (1938) and his "On Universals" (1947), Carl G. Hempel's "A Purely Syntactical Definition of Confirmation" (1943), Rudolf Carnap's "Modalities and Quantification" (1946), Wilhelm Ackermann's "Begründung einer strengen Implikation" (1956), Gordon Matheson's "The Semantics of Singular Terms" (1962), and Frederic B. Fitch's "A Logical Analysis of Some Value Concepts" (1964).

Other journals. Other journals on logic, analysis, and so forth, were published in Poland, the United States, and the Netherlands:

1934——. *Studia Logica* (Warsaw), semiannual, with variations; formerly an annual. Suspended 1937–1952. Sponsored since 1953 by the Komitet Filozoficzny, Polska Akademia Nauk. Articles in English, French, German, Polish, and Russian, each with summaries in two other languages. In 1953 it absorbed the irregularly published *Studia Philosophica* (Warsaw, 1935–1951, four volumes).

1934——. *Philosophy of Science* (East Lansing, Mich.), quarterly. Organ of the Philosophy of Science Association.

1936——. *Synthese; An International Quarterly for the Logical and the Psychological Study of the Foundations of Science* (Dordrecht; previously Utrecht), quarterly, with variations. Subtitle has varied. Suspended 1940–1945 and 1964–1965. Articles in English, French, and German (originally, mainly in Dutch). Various issues have included a section (sometimes separately paged) entitled "Communications of the Institute for the Unity of Science" or "Unity of Science Forum."

Social and moral philosophy. Italy produced three, and the United States one, of the social and moral periodicals that started in this prewar period:

1932–1943. *Archivio della cultura italiana* (Rome), quarterly. Title was *Archivio di storia della filosofia italiana* from 1932 to 1938.

1935–1941. *Rassegna di morale e di diritto* (Rome), quarterly.

1935–1942. *Journal of Social Philosophy & Jurisprudence; A Quarterly Devoted to a Philosophic Synthesis of the Social Sciences* (New York), quarterly. Title was *Journal of Social Philosophy* (with the same subtitle as later) from 1935 to 1941.

1935––. *Rivista internazionale di filosofia politica e sociale* (Genoa; formerly Padua), quarterly. Suspended 1944–1963.

Philosophy, history, and letters. Italy fathered three journals linking history and literature with philosophy:

1929–1943. *Civiltà moderna; Rassegna bimestrale di critica storica, letteraria, filosofica* (Florence), issued six times a year.

1929––. *Convivium; Rivista di lettere, filosofia e storia* (Turin), issued six times a year. Suspended 1944–1946. Subtitle has varied.

1931––. *Ricerche filosofiche; Rivista di filosofia, storia e letteratura* (Messina), semiannual, with variations. Since 1948 it has been the organ of the Società Filosofica Calabrese, founded in that year.

General. Seven regular academic or professional periodicals devoted to philosophy in general were begun in this period:

1931–1959. *Annalen van het Genootschap voor Wettenschappelijke Philosophie* (Assen), issued five times a year. Title was *Annalen der critische Philosophie* from 1931 to 1938. In 1959 absorbed into *Algemeen Nederlands Tijdschrift voor Wijsbegeerte en Psychologie* (Amsterdam and later Assen, 1907––), after having been published both separately and as a section of that periodical from 1934 to 1959.

1931––. *Archivio di filosofia* (Rome), issued three times a year, with variations. Originally the organ of the Società Filosofica Italiana; more recently the organ of the Istituto di Studi Filosofici and the Associazione Filosofica Italiana. Suspended 1943–1945.

1933––. *Sophia; Rassegna critica di filosofia e storia della filosofia* (Rome; formerly Palermo, Naples, and Padua), quarterly. Became international in 1935. Subtitle has varied. Contains articles in English, French, German, Italian, and Spanish, with subtitles in these languages.

1935–1940. *Bollettino filosofico* (Rome), quarterly.

1935––. *Theoria* (Lund, Goteborg, and Copenhagen; previously Goteborg), issued three times a year. Contains articles in English, French, and German (before 1937, in Danish, Norwegian, and Swedish).

1936–1940. *Philosophia; Philosophorum Nostri Temporis Vox Universa* (Belgrade), quarterly, with variations. Contained articles in English, French, and German.

1938––. *Revue internationale de philosophie* (Brussels), quarterly, with variations. Suspended 1939–1948. Each issue is devoted to a movement, problem, or philosopher, with a comprehensive bibliography.

WORLD WAR II

In the seven years from 1939 to 1945, 21 journals of philosophy came into being. Fully 16 of these have survived, and they include a number of today's outstanding philosophical journals.

North American. Canada, the United States, and Mexico produced a total of eight philosophical journals during World War II. Canada gave us a new medium for discussions of theology and philosophy, *Laval théologique et philosophique* (Quebec, 1945––), issued semiannually. This journal is published by the Facultés de Théologie et Philosophie de l'Université Laval de Québec.

In Mexico, for 17 years, a university review of philosophy and letters was published: *Filosofia y letras* (Mexico City, 1941–1957), issued quarterly, with variations. It was the organ of the Facultad de Filosofía y Letras, Universidad Nacional Autónoma.

In the United States six periodicals, varying widely in their character and in their topical focus, began in the period from 1939 to 1945. Five of these were:

1939–1954. *Philosophic Abstracts* (New York), quarterly, with variations.

1939––. *The Thomist; A Speculative Quarterly Review* (Washington; formerly New York), quarterly. Edited by the Dominican Fathers of the Province of St. Joseph.

1940––. *Journal of the History of Ideas* (New York), quarterly.

1941––. *Journal of Aesthetics and Art Criticism* (Baltimore Md.), quarterly. Organ, since 1945, of the American Society for Aesthetics. Contributors have included Croce, Dewey, and Santayana.

1943––. *Etc.: A Review of General Semantics* (San Francisco; formerly Bloomington, Ill.), quarterly. Organ of the International Society for General Semantics. Anthology volumes, consisting of selections from *Etc.*, were published in 1954 and 1959.

"Philosophy and Phenomenological Research." The most influential journal begun during World War II was *Philosophy and Phenomenological Research* (Buffalo; then Philadelphia; now Buffalo again, 1940––), which is issued quarterly. This journal is an outgrowth of the *Jahrbuch für Philosophie und phänomenologische Forschung* (Halle, 1913–1930), which was founded by Edmund Husserl.

Husserl died in 1938. In the following year the International Phenomenological Society was formed in New York City to further the understanding, development, and application of phenomenological inquiry as inaugurated by Husserl. The Society's journal, *Philosophy and Phenomenological Research,* although taking Husserl's philosophy as "the point of departure," announced at the outset that it would represent "no special school or sect." Its editor for a quarter of a century, Marvin Farber, has kept the journal's pages open to diverse points of view.

Philosophy and Phenomenological Research published the proceedings of the First Inter-American Conference of Philosophy (held at Yale University in 1943) and several stimulating symposia. The symposia dealt with meaning and truth, with articles by C. A. Baylis, C. J. Ducasse, Felix Kaufmann, C. I. Lewis, Ernest Nagel, R. W. Sellars, Alfred Tarski, W. M. Urban, A. Ushenko, and John Wild (1943–1945); probability, with articles by Gustav Bergmann, Rudolf Carnap, Kaufmann, Richard von Mises, Nagel, Hans Reichenbach, and Donald Williams (1945–1946); Russian philosophy and psychology, educational philosophy, "philosophy of freedom," and the philosophy of Arthur O. Lovejoy (various years in the 1940s and 1963); and "logical subjects and physical objects," with articles by Wilfrid Sellars and P. F. Strawson (1957).

Among the memorable individual articles in the journal were three little-known papers by Husserl entitled "Notizien zur Raumkonstitution" (Nos. 1 and 2, 1940), "Phänomenologie und Anthropologie" (1941), and "Persönliche Aufzeichnungen" (1956). Others include Paul Weiss's "The Meaning of Existence" (1940), Ernst Cassirer's "The Concept of Group and the Theory of Perception" (1944), Arthur Pap's "Logical Nonsense" (1948), Richard McKeon's "Dialogue and Controversy in Philosophy" (1956), Lewis S. Feuer's "The Bearing of Psychoanalysis Upon Philosophy" (1959), Nagel's "Determinism in History" (1960), and Nicholas Rescher's "On the Logic of Presupposition" (1961). The journal publishes Spanish abstracts of its articles.

South American. In 1944 two philosophical periodicals were established in Argentina:

1944——. *Stromata: Ciencia y fé* (Buenos Aires), issued quarterly by the Facultades de Filosofía y Teología, Colegio Máximo de San José, San Miguel. Title was *Ciencia y fé* from 1944 to 1964. Now considered to be the successor to *Fascículos de biblioteca* (1937–1943) and *Stromata* (1938–1943).

1944——. *Philosophia* (Mendoza, Argentina), semiannual. Issued by the Instituto de Filosofía y Disciplinas Auxiliares, Universidad Nacional de Cuyo.

Western European. Despite the atmosphere of war or preparations for war, new journals for philosophical discussion were begun in Belgium and France and in Spain and Portugal:

1939——. *Tijdschrift voor Filosofie* (Louvain), quarterly. Articles in English, Dutch, French, and German, with English, French, or German summaries of the articles in Dutch. Editors are chosen from Netherlands universities and Dutch-language universities of Belgium.

1942——. *Revista de filosofía* (Madrid), issued three times in 1942, quarterly since 1943. Organ of the Instituto de Filosofía Luis Vives. Scholastic. Some foreign contributors.

1945——. *Pensamiento; Revista de investigación e información filosófica* (Madrid), quarterly. Organ of the Facultades de Filosofía, Compañía de Jesús en España. Strong on the bibliography of Spanish and Latin American philosophy.

1945——. *Revista portuguesa de filosofia* (Braga; formerly Lisbon), quarterly. Organ of the Faculdade Pontifícia de Filosofia of Braga, a branch of the Society of Jesus.

1945–1955. *Dieu vivant; Perspectives religieuses et philosophiques* (Paris), quarterly, with variations.

Central and southern European. Contributions of Italy and neutral Switzerland were:

1940–1943. *Bollettino dell'Istituto di Filosofia del Diritto dell'Università di Roma* (Rome), issued six times a year.

1940–1949. *Studi filosofici; Problemi di vita contemporanea* (Milan), quarterly. Pro-Marxist from 1946 to 1949. Subtitle varied.

1945——. *Methodos; Linguaggio e cibernetica* (Milan; previously Rome), quarterly, with variations. Title was *Analisi; Rassegna di critica della scienza* from 1945 to 1947 and *Sigma; Conoscenza unitaria* from 1947 to 1948. Subtitle has varied. Contains articles in various languages. International editorial board. Organ, since 1959, of the Centro di Cibernetica e di Attività Linguistiche, Università di Milano, and of the Consiglio Nazionale delle Ricerche.

1945——. *Theologische Zeitschrift* (Basel), issued six times a year.

Bulgarian and Israeli. In Bulgaria and Israel the following journals came into being:

1945——. *Filosofska Mis'l* (Sofia), issued six times a year. Table of contents also in English, French, German, and Russian; summaries in English and Russian. Issued since 1952 by the Institut po Filosofia, Bulgarska Akademiia na Naukite.

1945——. *Iyyun* (Jerusalem), quarterly. Irregular 1945–1948; suspended 1949–1950. Contains English summaries.

POSTWAR PERIOD

In the early postwar years philosophical journals were founded at an unprecedented pace. They numbered 11 in 1946 (of which 9 have survived); 8 in 1947 (6 still alive); 5 in 1948 (4 still alive); and 7 in 1949 (3 still alive). Among them was another *Logos*.

1946. Three products of the first postwar year had humanistic titles:

1946——. *Teoresi; Rivista di cultura filosofica* (Catania; formerly Messina), quarterly, with variations. Emphasizes the synthesis of idealism and realism.

1946——. *Sapientia* (Buenos Aires), quarterly. Organ of the Facultad de Filosofía, Universidad Católica Argentina. Thomist. International contributors.

1946——. *Humanitas* (Brescia, Italy), monthly. In four parts, of which the part on philosophy is edited by Michele Federico Sciacca.

Four journals, including two from Japan, had standard, traditional titles:

1946–1949. *Tetsugaku Hyôron; Philosophical Review* (Tokyo), monthly.

1946–1949. *Tetsugaku Kikan* ["Quarterly Review of Philosophy"] (Kyoto), quarterly.

1946——. *Giornale di metafisica* (Turin), issued six

times a year. Founded and edited by M. F. Sciacca. From 1946 to 1948 published by the University of Pavia; since then, by the University of Genoa. Has been described as following the Plato–Augustine–Rosmini tradition. Contributors include Maurice Blondel, Gabriel Marcel, and Jacques Maritain.

1946——. *Zeitschrift für philosophische Forschung* (Meisenheim am Glan, Germany; formerly Wurzach), quarterly.

The others cover a variety of fields:

1946——. *Otázky Marxistickej Filozofie* (Bratislava, Czechoslovakia; formerly Prague), issued six times a year, with variations. Title was *Philosophica Slovaca* from 1946 to 1949 (issued annually); *Filozofický Sborník* from 1950 to 1952 (issued annually); *Filozofický Časopis* from 1953 to 1955 (quarterly); and *Slovenský Filozofický Časopis* from 1956 to 1960 (quarterly). Issued by the Slovenská Akadémie Vied. Table of contents also in English, German, and Russian. Emphasis on historical materialism.

1946——. *Rassegna di scienze filosofiche* (Naples; previously Bari and Rome), quarterly. Title was *Noesis; Rassegna internazionale di scienze filosofiche e morali* in 1946. Suspended 1947. Neo-Scholastic.

1946——. *Rivista critica di storia della filosofia* (Milan), quarterly. Title was *Rivista di storia della filosofia* from 1946 to 1949.

1946——. *Nederlands Theologisch Tijdschrift* (Wageningen), issued six times a year.

1947. Two of the 1947 products expired within 3 to 11 years:

1947–1949. *Tetsugaku* ["Philosophy"] (Tokyo), quarterly.

1947–1958. *Wiener Zeitschrift für Philosophie, Psychologie, Pädagogik* (Vienna), semiannual.

The ones that are still alive include two that are general in their scope:

1947——. *Archiv für Philosophie* (Stuttgart), quarterly. Not to be confused with the *Archiv für Geschichte der Philosophie* (Berlin, 1868——), which was entitled *Archiv für Philosophie* from 1895 to 1926. Some issues of the Stuttgart periodical, beginning in the late 1940s, incorporated issues of the irregularly published *Archiv für mathematische Logik und Grundlagenforschung*.

1947——. *Voprosy Filosofii* (Moscow), monthly, with variations. Issued by the Institut Filosofii, Akademiia Nauk SSR. Contains summaries in English and titles in English, French, German, and Spanish.

"Review of Metaphysics." The *Review of Metaphysics* (New Haven, 1947——), published quarterly, is one of the major media of discussion of the perennial problems of metaphysics. In addition, it publishes annual lists of doctoral dissertations accepted by philosophy departments in the United States and Canada, of professors who have become emeritus in philosophy, and of visiting philosophy professors from abroad. Beginning with December 1964, each issue contains abstracts of articles in certain philosophical periodicals, written (as in the case of the book abstracts formerly published in *Kant-Studien*) by the authors of the articles themselves. In earlier years the *Review* conducted competitions, comparable to those in *Analysis* (1933——), for the best short answers to piquant questions, such as why there has never been a great woman philosopher.

Outstanding among the many important articles that have appeared in the *Review* are Paul Weiss's "Being, Essence and Existence" (1947), W. V. Quine's "On What There Is" (1948), Charles Hartshorne's "The Immortality of the Past" (1953), Nathan Rotenstreich's "The Genesis of Mind" (1962), and Wilfrid Sellars' "Abstract Entities" (1963). The discussion section of the *Review* has also provided a large number of valuable contributions to current thought.

Two of the 1947 periodicals concern the philosophy of science or the unity of the sciences, and one is bibliographical:

1947——. *Dialectica; International Review of Philosophy of Knowledge* (Neuchâtel, Switzerland; and Paris), quarterly. Emphasis on philosophy of science.

1947——. *Studium Generale; Zeitschrift für die Einheit der Wissenschaften im Zusammenhang ihrer Begriffsbildungen und Forschungsmethoden* (Berlin), monthly. Articles in English, French, and German.

1947——. *Bulletin signalétique: Philosophie, sciences humaines* (Paris), quarterly. Title was *Bulletin analytique: Philosophie* from 1947 to 1955. Contains abstracts of books and articles on philosophical subjects. Published by the Centre de Documentation du Centre Nationale de la Recherche Scientifique.

1948. Three journals begun in 1948 were founded on the European continent:

1948——. *Revue d'esthétique* (Paris), quarterly.

1948——. *Sapienza; Rivista di filosofia e di teologia dei Domenicani d'Italia* (Naples), issued six times a year. Since 1956 the organ of the Centro Italiano di Studi Scientifici, Filosofici e Teologici. Subtitle has varied.

1948——. *Roczniki Filozoficzne* (Lublin), quarterly.

The others were issued in South America:

1948–1950. *Revista colombiana de filosofia* (Bogotá), issued six times a year. Emphasis on Thomism and phenomenology.

1948——. *Filosofía, letras y ciencias de la educación* (Quito), semiannual. Published by the Facultad de Filosofía, Letras y Ciencias de la Educación, Universidad Central, Quito. Title has varied.

1949. Another *Logos* appeared in 1949, along with two periodicals called "philosophical studies" (in German and in English), and four other journals:

1949–1951. *Logos* (Mexico City), quarterly. Published by the Mesa Redonda de Filosofía, Facultad de Filosofía y Letras, Universidad Nacional Autónoma de Mexico.

1949–1952. *Philosophische Studien* (Berlin), quarterly, with variations.

1949——. *Philosophical Studies* (Minneapolis), issued six times a year. Brief articles. Many distinguished contributors.

1949–1953. *Revista de filosofía* (Santiago, Chile), quarterly. Organ of the Sociedad Chilena de Filosofía and the Universidad de Chile.

1949–1954. *Notas y estudios de filosofía* (Tucumán, Argentina), quarterly.

1949——. *Philosophischer Literaturanzeiger* (Stuttgart; formerly Schlesdorf am Kochelsee, then Stuttgart, then Meisenheim am Glan), issued eight times a year.

1949——. *Analele româno-sovietice; Filozofie* (Bucharest), quarterly, with variations. Table of contents also in Russian. From 1949 to 1951 it was a part of *Analele româno-sovietice; Seria istorie-filozofie* (quarterly; issued six times in 1951; title also in Russian), which itself had been a part, from 1946 to 1949, of *Analele româno-sovietice* (issued irregularly; title also in Russian).

THE NINETEEN-FIFTIES

The decade of the 1950s saw 11 new English-language journals, 13 Spanish-language journals, 11 Italian, 4 Portuguese, 4 French, 3 German, 2 Dutch, and 1 each in Hungarian, Rumanian, Polish, Serbo-Croat, Russian, Chinese, and Japanese. As in two earlier periods, Italy was the leading or a leading producer of new philosophical journals.

English. In continental United States and Hawaii the following journals were introduced:

1951——. *Philosophy East and West* (Honolulu), quarterly. Emphasizes Oriental and comparative thought. Suspended from 1964 to 1966.

1957——. *Philosophy Today* (Celina, Ohio), quarterly. Mainly contains reprints or translations of articles appearing elsewhere. Religious emphasis.

In Scotland are published a journal for the philosophy of science and a quarterly which has the same title as a living Indian journal begun in 1925:

1950——. *British Journal for the Philosophy of Science* (Edinburgh), quarterly.

1950——. *The Philosophical Quarterly* (St. Andrews, Scotland), quarterly. Published for the Scots Philosophical Club.

The Commonwealth countries of Canada, India, and Pakistan produced the following periodicals:

1953——. *Diogenes; An International Journal for Philosophy and Humanistic Studies* (Montreal; formerly New York), quarterly. Published under the auspices of the International Council for Philosophy and Humanistic Studies with the assistance of UNESCO.

1953——. *Journal of the Philosophical Association* (Amraoti, India; later Nagpur), quarterly. Organ of the Indian Philosophical Association. Contributors outside India have included P. T. Geach, Elizabeth Anscombe, and A. N. Prior.

1956——. *Indian Philosophy and Culture* (Vrindaban, India), quarterly. Issued by the Vaishnava Research Institute.

1957——. *Pakistan Philosophical Journal* (Lahore), quarterly.

1959——. *The Indian Journal of Philosophy* (Bombay),

quarterly; formerly issued three times a year. Published for the Association for Philosophical Research.

From the Netherlands and Norway we have the following:

1956——. *Phronesis; A Journal for Ancient Philosophy* (Assen), semiannual.

1958——. *Inquiry; An Interdisciplinary Journal of Philosophy and the Social Sciences* (Oslo), quarterly. Emphasis on analytic philosophy.

Spanish. In South America five periodicals sprang to life, including one which repeated the title (*Humanitas*) of an Italian journal begun in 1946:

1950–1954. *Revista de filosofía* (La Plata, Argentina), quarterly. Issued by the Instituto de Filosofía, Universidad Nacional de La Plata.

1951–1954. *Ideas y valores* (Bogotá), quarterly. Issued by the Facultad de Filosofía y Letras de la Universidad Nacional. Title varied slightly.

1952——. *Arkhé; Revista americana de filosofía sistemática y de historia de la filosofía* (Córdoba, Argentina), semiannual (formerly issued three times a year). Suspended 1955 to mid-1964. Title was originally *Arqué;* subtitle varied.

1953——. *Filosofía; Revista semestral* (Quito), semiannual. Organ of the Sección de Ciencias Filosóficas y de la Educación de la Casa de la Cultura Ecuatoriana.

1953——. *Humanitas; Revista de la Facultad de Filosofía y Letras, Universidad Nacional de Tucumán* (San Miguel de Tucumán), issued three times a year, with variations.

In Central America and the Caribbean, two university *Revistas* appeared:

1956–1958. *Revista dominicana de filosofía* (Ciudad Trujillo, now called Santo Domingo), semiannual, with variations. Organ of the Facultad de Filosofía of the Universidad de Santo Domingo.

1957——. *Revista de filosofía de la Universidad de Costa Rica* (San José), semiannual.

In Spain itself six periodicals arose, including one which repeated the title (*Convivium*) of a journal begun at Turin in 1929:

1951——. *Estudios filosóficos; Revista de investigación y crítica* (Las Caldas de Besaya, Spain), issued three times a year. Organ of the Spanish Dominicans.

1951——. *Archivum; Revista de la Facultad de Filosofía y Letras, Universidad de Oviedo* (Oviedo), semiannual, with variations.

1952——. *Espíritu; Cuadernos del Instituto Filosófico de "Balmesiana"* (Barcelona), semiannual, with variations.

1954——. *Crisis; Revista española de filosofía* (Madrid), quarterly. Emphasizes Christian existentialism.

1956–1957. *Convivium; Estudios filosóficos* (Barcelona), semiannual. Issued by the Facultad de Filosofía y Letras, Universidad de Barcelona.

1956——. *Augustinus* (Madrid), quarterly. Many foreign contributors.

Italian. Three of the births of Italian philosophical journals took place at Milan: one each in 1950, 1951, and 1952.

1950–1962. *Il pensiero critico* (Milan), quarterly. In 1963 absorbed into the *Rivista di filosofia* (Milan, 1870——).

1951——. *Aut Aut; Rivista di filosofia e di cultura* (Milan), issued six times a year. Title is based on the Kierkegaardian *Either/Or.*

1952——. *Bollettino della Società Filosofica Italiana* (Milan), quarterly.

Three births also occurred at Rome, including that of a journal with a Latin title which contains articles in Italian and other languages:

1952——. *Rassegna di filosofia* (Rome), quarterly. Organ of the Istituto di Filosofia, Università di Roma.

1955——. *La nuova critica; Studi e rivista di filosofia delle scienze* (Rome; formerly Florence), semiannual. Articles mostly in Italian, but with some in English and French. International board of editors. The title may reflect a desire for association with Croce's Naples journal *La critica* (1903 ff.), which, under a slightly different title, had died in 1951.

1958——. *Aquinas; Ephemerides Thomisticae* (Rome), issued three times a year, with variations. Subtitle has varied. Now issued by the Faculty of Philosophy, and the Patristic–Medieval Institute "Joannes XXIII," of the Pontificia Universitas Lateranensis. Articles in English, French, Italian, Latin, and Spanish.

The locale of two births was Turin; of two others, Padua; and of one, Bologna:

1950——. *Filosofia* (Turin), quarterly.

1951——. *Il saggiatore; Rivista di cultura filosofica e pedagogica* (Turin), quarterly.

1954——. *Studia patavina; Rivista di filosofia e teologia* (Padua), issued three times a year; formerly a quarterly.

1956——. *Rivista di estetica* (Turin; formerly Padua), issued three times a year.

1957——. *Il dialogo* (Bologna), quarterly, with variations.

Portuguese. The Portuguese-language journals which were brought into being in the 1950s were:

1951–1959. *Revista filosófica* (Coimbra, Portugal), issued three times a year, with variations.

1951——. *Revista brasileira de filosofia* (São Paulo), quarterly. Organ of the Instituto Brasileiro de Filosofia. Chiefly in Portuguese, with some articles in English, French, Italian, Spanish, and other languages.

1954——. *Filosofia; Revista do Gabinete de Estudos Filosóficos* (Lisbon), quarterly. Subtitle has varied.

1959——. *Organon; Revista da Faculdade de Filosofia da Universidade do Rio Grande do Sul* (Pôrto Alegre), quarterly, with variations.

French. Four new journals of philosophy in the French language appeared in the 1950s, including two published in Belgium (one with articles in English, French, and German) and one published in the Saar (with articles in French and German), which are included here among the French journals, since the titles of two are in French, and the title of the third is in Latin and French:

1951——. *Morale et enseignement* (Brussels), quar-

terly, with variations. Published by the Institut de Philosophie, Université de Bruxelles.

1951——. *Revue de l'enseignement philosophique* (Paris), issued six times a year, with variations. Organ of the Association des Professeurs de Philosophie de l'Enseignement Public.

1952——. *Annales Universitatis Saraviensis; Philosophie–lettres* (Saarbrücken), quarterly, with variations. Published since 1957 by the Philosophische Fakultät, Universität des Saarlandes. Articles in English, French, and German.

1954——. *Logique et analyse* (Louvain), quarterly, with variations. Articles in English, French, and German. Organ of the Centre National (Belge) de Recherches de Logique; issued only to members from 1954 to 1957 under the title *Bulletin intérieure.*

German and Dutch. Three new journals of philosophy in the German language appeared during the 1950s:

1950——. *Philosophia Naturalis; Archiv für Naturphilosophie und die philosophischen Grenzgebiete der exakten Wissenschaften und Wissenschaftsgeschichte* (Meisenheim am Glan), quarterly, with variations.

1953——. *Philosophische Rundschau* (Heidelberg), quarterly, with variations. Reviews of current books. Concerned largely, in its early years, with surveys of new philosophical literature, this is now a general philosophical journal. Contains occasional articles in English.

1953——. *Deutsche Zeitschrift für Philosophie* (East Berlin), monthly, with variations (quarterly, 1953–1954; issued six times a year, 1955–1959). Table of contents also in English, French, Russian, and Spanish.

The Dutch-language journals of the 1950s include one with a Dutch title and one with a Latin title:

1959———. *Dialoog; Tijdschrift voor Wijsbegeerte* (Antwerp), quarterly.

1959——. *Scripta Recenter Edita* (Nijmegen), issued ten times a year. Contains a list of books on philosophy and theology, with emphasis on theology.

Rumanian, Hungarian, and Slavic. The period produced one Rumanian and one Hungarian organ, each issued for the most part four times a year:

1954——. *Cercetări filozofice* (Bucharest), quarterly, with variations. Table of contents also in French and Russian; summaries in French or German and in Russian.

1957——. *Magyar Filozófiai Szemle* (Budapest), quarterly, with variations. Table of contents, and summaries, in English, German, and Russian. Organ of the Magyar Tudományos Akadémia Filozófiai Intézetének Folyóirata.

Of the Slavic languages, Polish, Serbo-Croatian, and Russian are represented once each in the new philosophical journals of the 1950s.

1951——. *Studia Filozoficzne; Kwartalnik* (Warsaw), quarterly, with variations. Title was *Myśl Filozoficzna* from 1951 to 1955 (issued six times a year). Sponsored from 1952 to 1955 by the Komitet Filozoficzny, Polska Akademia Nauk. Suspended

1956. Published by the Instytut Filozofii i Socjologii, Polska Akademia Nauk. Table of contents and summaries of articles in English and Russian. This periodical replaced *Przegląd Filozoficzny* (1897–1949) at the beginning of the period of militant Marxist domination. According to an article in a 1963 issue of *Studia Filozoficzne*, it was Lenin who first solved Zeno's antinomy of the arrow in flight.

1953–1958. *Filozofski Pregled* (Belgrade), issued three times a year, with variations.

1958——. *Nauchnye Doklady Vysshei Shkoly; Filosofskie Nauki* (Moscow), issued six times a year; originally issued quarterly. Often cited as *Filosofskie Nauki,* without the series title ("Scientific Reports of the Higher School") represented by the first four words.

Japanese and Chinese. Also begun in the 1950s were *Bigaku; Aesthetics* (Tokyo, 1950——), issued quarterly, and *Chê Hsüeh Yen Chiu* ["Philosophical Research"] (Peking, 1955——), issued six times a year; formerly quarterly.

THE NINETEEN-SIXTIES

The early years of the 1960s were fruitful in the production of new journals of philosophy, but not as fruitful as the record year of 1946 (11 journals). The year 1960 brought forward 9; 1961, 4; 1962, 6; 1963, 5; 1964, 3; 1965, 6; and 1966, 1 (as of the time of the completion of this article).

1960. Three philosophical journals which were started in 1960 had their origin in England:

1960——. *The Heythrop Journal; A Quarterly Review of Philosophy and Theology* (Oxford), quarterly. Issued by the Jesuit Faculties of Philosophy and Theology, Heythrop College, Oxford.

1960——. *The British Journal of Aesthetics* (London), quarterly. Published for the British Society of Aesthetics.

1960——. *Philosophical Books* (Leicester, England), originally a quarterly; now issued three times a year.

Three had their origin in the United States:

1960——. *Notre Dame Journal of Formal Logic* (Notre Dame, Ind.), quarterly.

1960——. *Studies in Philosophy and Education* (Toledo, Ohio; previously New Brunswick, N.J.), quarterly, with variations.

1960——. *Journal of Existentialism* (New York), quarterly. Title was *Journal of Existential Psychiatry* from 1960 to 1964.

Amsterdam, Madrid, and Rome fathered one philosophical journal each in 1960:

1960——. *Wijsgerig Perspectief op Maatschappij en Wetenschap* (Amsterdam), issued six times a year. Each issue devoted to a specific topic.

1960——. *Noesis; Revista de filosofía y arte* (Madrid), quarterly. Suspended 1962–1963. *Noesis* had previously been the title of a philosophical journal in Italy in 1946.

1960——. *Filosofia e vita; Quaderni trimestrali di orientamento formativo* (Turin; previously Rome), quarterly.

1961. Two journals of philosophy were inaugurated in the United States, and one each in India and the Netherlands, in 1961:

1961——. *Journal for the Scientific Study of Religion* (New Haven), semiannual.

1961——. *International Philosophical Quarterly* (New York and Heverlee–Louvain), quarterly. Edited by the department of philosophy of Fordham University and the professors of philosophy, Berchmans Philosophicum, Heverlee, Belgium.

1961——. *Darshana* (Moradabad, India), quarterly. International board of consultants.

1961——. *Studies in Soviet Thought* (Dordrecht), quarterly. Published by the Institute of East-European Studies, University of Fribourg, Switzerland. Articles in English, French, and German.

1962. Two more journals were inaugurated in the United States, and one each in Argentina, Canada, Italy, and Australia, in 1962:

1962——. *Pacific Philosophical Forum* (Stockton, Calif.), quarterly. Each issue devoted to a specific subject, with a set format (thesis and countertheses).

1962——. *Soviet Studies in Philosophy* (New York), quarterly. Contains translations from Soviet publications, mainly Soviet periodicals.

1962——. *Cuestiones de filosofía* (Buenos Aires), quarterly.

1962——. *Dialogue; Canadian Philosophical Review; Revue canadienne de philosophie* (Montreal), quarterly. Articles in English and French. Sponsored by the Canadian Philosophical Association.

1962——. *De Homine* (Rome), quarterly. Issued by the Centro di Ricerca per le Scienze Morali e Sociali, Istituto di Filosofia, Università di Roma.

1962——. *Sophia; A Journal for Discussion in Philosophical Theology* (Melbourne), issued three times a year. An Italian *Sophia* began publication in 1933.

1963. As in 1961 and 1962, two journals of philosophy were inaugurated in the United States in 1963; in addition, two were inaugurated in India and one in the Netherlands:

1963——. *Southern Journal of Philosophy* (Memphis, Tenn.), quarterly.

1963——. *Journal of the History of Philosophy* (Berkeley), semiannual.

1963——. *Indian Journal of Philosophic Studies* (Hyderabad), semiannual. Published for the Andhra Pradesh Philosophical Society by the department of philosophy of Osmanian University, Hyderabad.

1963——. *Research Journal of Philosophy and Social Sciences* (Meerut, Uttar Pradesh, India), semiannual, with variations. International editorial board. Each issue contains about 200 pages on a particular subject.

1963——. *Vivarium; A Journal for Mediaeval Philosophy and the Intellectual Life of the Middle Ages* (Assen), semiannual.

1964. Three new contributions appeared in the year 1964:

1964——. *American Philosophical Quarterly* (Pittsburgh, Pa.), quarterly. International board of consultants. Articles only; no book reviews.

1964——. *The Philosophical Journal* (Edinburgh), semiannual. Issued by the Royal Philosophical Society of Glasgow. Although mainly concerned with scientific matters, the *Journal* also contains some valuable philosophical articles.

1964——. *Documentación crítica iberoamericana de filosofía y ciencias afines* (Seville), quarterly.

1965. The following journals began publication in 1965:

1965——. *Concilium; An International Review of Theology* (London), issued ten times a year.

1965——. *Foundations of Language; International Journal of Language and Philosophy* (Dordrecht, Netherlands), issued quarterly.

1965——. *Information aus dem philosophischen Leben der Deutschen Demokratischen Republik* (East Berlin), issued quarterly.

1965——. *Religious Studies* (London), semiannual. Articles on philosophy of religion and history of religion.

1965——. *Transactions of the Charles S. Peirce Society* (Amherst, Mass.), semiannual.

1965——. *Revue universitaire de science morale* (Geneva), issued three times a year.

1966. One philosophical journal began publication in 1966 before the present article was completed:

1966——. *The Bulletin of Philosophy* (Washington), issued eight times a year. Contains news of interest to philosophers.

The expansion in the twentieth century of the number of currently published journals of philosophy has roughly paralleled the growing interest in philosophy as an academic discipline.

Bibliography

Four authors have studied philosophical journals in general. In chronological order, their reports on this field are Friedrich Medebach, "Die philosophische Fachzeitschrift," in *Zeitungswissenschaft*, Vol. II (Berlin, 1936), 210–214; David Baumgart, *Philosophical Periodicals; An Annotated World List* (Washington, 1952); Augusto da Silva, *Revistas de filosofía* (Braga, Portugal, 1955); and Tóth Ilona Kovácsné, "A Magyar Közkönyvtarakban Megtalálható Kurrens Filozófia Periodikák" ("Current Philosophical Periodicals Available in Public Libraries in Hungary"), in *Magyar Filózofiai Szemle*, Vol. 8 (Budapest, 1964), 574–601.

Three sources cover philosophical journals in particular countries: Paul Feldskeller, "Das philosophische Journal in Deutschland," in *Reichls philosophischer Almanach* (Darmstadt, 1924), pp. 302–458; Enrico Zampetti, *Bibliografia ragionata delle riviste filosofiche italiana del 1900* (Rome, 1956), and the highly knowledgeable passages on periodicals in Max Rieser, "Polish Philosophy Today," in *Journal of the History of Ideas*, Vol. 24 (1963), 423–432.

Short articles on 83 periodicals appear in the *Enciclopedia filosofica*, 4 vols. (Venice and Rome, 1957). Other pertinent sources are the list, published annually in the *Répertoire bibliographique de la philosophie*, of periodicals covered by the *Répertoire*, and the list headed "Philosophy" in *Ulrich's Periodicals Directory* (New York, 1932; 10th ed., 1963).

The titles appearing in the philosophy category in the monthly *New Serial Titles; Classed Subject Arrangement* (Washington, 1955——) are useful, as is also the record of births and deaths of periodicals (as well as of libraries which possess complete or partial sets of the periodicals) in the *Union List of Serials in Libraries of the United States and Canada*, edited by Edna Brown Titus, 3d ed., 5 vols. (New York, 1965), continued as *New Serial Titles*, which was begun by the Library of Congress in 1953 and is published monthly.

WILLIAM GERBER

PHILOSOPHY. The Greek word *sophia* is ordinarily translated into English as "wisdom," and the compound *philosophia*, from which "philosophy" derives, is translated as "the love of wisdom." But *sophia* had a much wider range of application than the modern English "wisdom." Wherever intelligence can be exercised—in practical affairs, in the mechanical arts, in business—there is room for *sophia;* Homer used it to refer to the skill of a carpenter (*Iliad* XV, 412). Furthermore, whereas modern English draws a fairly sharp distinction between the search for wisdom and the attempt to satisfy intellectual curiosity, Herodotus used the verb *philosophein* in a context in which it means nothing more than the desire to find out (*History* I, 30). Briefly, then, *philosophia* etymologically connotes the love of exercising one's curiosity and intelligence rather than the love of wisdom. Although philosophers have often sought to confine the word "philosophy" within narrower boundaries, in popular usage it has never entirely lost its original breadth of meaning.

According to a tradition deriving from Heraclides Ponticus (a disciple of Plato), Pythagoras was the first to describe himself as a philosopher. Three classes of people, he is alleged to have said, attend the festal games: those who seek fame by taking part in them; those who seek gain by plying their trade; and those ("the best people") who are content to be spectators (Diogenes Laërtius, *De Vita et Moribus Philosophorum* I, 12). Philosophers resemble the third class: spurning both fame and profit, they seek to arrive at the truth by contemplation. Pythagoras distinguished the *sophia* sought by the philosopher (knowledge based on contemplation) from the practical shrewdness of the businessman and the trained skills of the athlete. Whether or not these distinctions date back to the historic Pythagoras, they can certainly be found in Plato, who was much preoccupied with the question of what philosophy is and how it differs from other forms of inquiry. Some of Plato's contemporaries had thought of his master, Socrates, as a sage, some thought of him as a Sophist, and some thought of him as a cosmologist. In Plato's eyes, Socrates was none of these; he was a philosopher. But what made him different?

The Platonic conception of philosophy. For Plato, the first characteristic of philosophical wisdom is that it can face the test of critical discussion. As is suggested in the *Apology* (22), this criterion at once rules out almost every type of what is ordinarily called wisdom. Neither the statesman nor the artisan nor the poet can explain why he is doing what he is doing; none of them has formulated a clear, articulate, discussible system of ideas and principles. That a man sometimes does the wise or right or beautiful thing is no evidence that he possesses philosophical wisdom; he must be able to give grounds for his action that will stand up to cross-examination.

Second, philosophy, according to Plato, makes use of a method peculiar to it, which he calls "dialectic." The exact nature of the Platonic dialectic is obscure, but this much is clear: philosophy proceeds by criticizing received opinions. Even mathematics, the most developed of the sciences, is subject to philosophical criticism. According to Plato, mathematics rests on inarticulate assumptions, and it is the philosopher's task to bring these into the open and examine them critically. Philosophy is the highest form of inquiry, just because it alone involves no presuppositions.

Third, Plato suggests, the philosopher has direct access to "true Reality," as distinct from the ordinary world of ever-changing things. That is precisely why he can offer the final criticism of received opinions. Having direct access to reality, he has no need of assumptions or guesswork. Philosophy concerns itself with the relationship between eternal and unchanging entities—the only entities about which it is possible to have "knowledge," as distinct from mere belief or "opinion." Hence, the philosopher seeks wisdom of a very special kind—certainty about the true nature of reality.

Fourth, to apprehend the true nature of reality is to know what everything is for. To understand the real nature of man, for example, is to know toward what ideal it is man's nature to strive. In the *Phaedo* (98–99), Plato suggests that the Ionian cosmologists did not possess philosophical wisdom, precisely because they had no understanding of purposes. They could not explain why, for example, Socrates did not run away from prison; to understand Socrates' behavior they would have had to take account of Socrates' ideals, as distinct from the structure of Socrates' body.

Fifth, it is on account of his knowledge of ideals that the philosopher knows how men ought to live. The Sophists professed to teach their pupils how to make immediate gains, how to win friends and influence people. This, Plato says, cannot be done. The art of making immediate gains is not a form of knowledge; it involves quick wits and rapid judgment. In such contexts the philosopher may well look like a fool. But when it is a question of understanding the general nature of man—and, in consequence, of human society—men must turn to philosophy. That is why the ideal ruler would be a philosopher.

Philosophy as the knowledge of ultimates. When the Shorter Oxford Dictionary defines philosophy as "that department of knowledge which deals with ultimate reality, or with the most general causes and principles of things," it is substantially following Plato. The presumption is that science, inheriting the cosmological tradition, does not offer us a knowledge of ultimate reality: only philosophy can do this.

On the face of it, this is a very peculiar doctrine. It is scientists who tell us, insofar as the locution is a proper one at all, what "the ultimate reality" of the things around us consists in. The assertion that science can only tell us *how*, whereas philosophy can tell us *why*, things happen as they do, is in conflict with our everyday habit of turning to science precisely in order to find out why things happen. However, Plato and philosophers in his tradition (such as Louis de Raeymaker) would reply that the "general causes and principles" of the philosopher are "higher" and "more ultimate" than the causes and principles that science reveals to us.

Whether there are such higher principles, however, is itself a philosophical issue. It is obviously as improper to define philosophy in this way as it is to presume that a particular philosophical doctrine is true. Doubtless, philosophers have very often set out in search of ultimates— sometimes ultimate explanations, sometimes ultimate foundations for knowledge, sometimes ultimate reference points for meaning. But philosophers also have sought to show that this whole project is a mistaken one. For instance, Wittgenstein is no less a philosopher in the *Philosophical Investigations,* where he argues that the philosopher's belief that there must be ultimate simples rests on a confusion, than he is in the *Tractatus Logico-philosophicus,* where he tries to show that ultimate simples must exist. The Platonic-type definition of philosophy as an attempt to discover ultimates is, in other words, at best too narrow. Philosophy can survive the abandonment of the doctrine that there are any "ultimates" in the metaphysical sense.

The philosopher and the sage. Plato's distinction between philosophy and the pursuit of worldly success is now generally accepted. His distinction between philosophy and poetry—or, more generally, between the philosopher and the sage—has not won the same degree of acceptance.

The latter distinction is weakened by Plato's own concessions. In his earlier dialogues (*Ion, Apology*) he regularly suggests that true wisdom, as distinct from the inspired guesses of the poet-sage, must be clear and communicable. But when he professes to be describing the supreme end of philosophical inquiry ("the form of the good"), in the *Republic* (509), he speaks of it in the manner of a sage rather than of a philosopher. The form of the good lies "beyond all knowledge and being." It would seem that at the culminating point of philosophical inquiry, the philosopher has to abandon critical discussion and, like a sage, fall back on direct intuition.

Indeed, any Platonic-type metaphysics is forced to this conclusion. About the "ultimate" no further questions can be raised; if we can ask questions about it, as we can about everything else, it would cease to be ultimate. Yet it must be possible to ask questions about it, if anything definite can be said about it at all; any nontautological statement can be met with the question "Why shouldn't it be otherwise?" So the metaphysician is forced to conclude that nothing, or nothing clear, can be said about his ultimates. F. H. Bradley's "Absolute" and Wittgenstein's "totality of facts" (as Wittgenstein was well aware) share with Plato's "Form of the Good" the characteristic that they can be apprehended only "mystically." The paradox of Platonic-type metaphysics, indeed, is that what is supposed to make everything clear must itself be unintelligible, or, to give it its technical name, "transcendental."

When the critics of traditional philosophy, such as Friedrich Lange and A. J. Ayer, lay stress on its resemblance to poetry, they are identifying philosophy with transcendental metaphysics. Even so, they are mistaken: transcendental metaphysics incorporates a great deal of serious argument that must be seriously considered. But they have noticed that at its culminating point it abandons the method of critical discussion. What is true of transcendental metaphysics, however, is not true of philosophy as a whole.

In countries where the critical tradition is strong, the contrast between the sage and the philosopher is now fairly well established. However, the critical tradition is powerful in only a few parts of the world: what is commonly called "Chinese philosophy," for example, consists almost entirely of the pronouncements of sages. Neither in Russia nor in China has the tradition of critical discussion ever established itself. In France it has been greatly weakened as a result of the influence of Henri Bergson, followed by that of Martin Heidegger.

In fact, two very different forms of activity now go under the name of "philosophy": one is essentially rational and critical, with logical analysis (in a broad sense) at its heart; the other (represented by Heidegger, for example) is openly hostile to critical analysis and professes to arrive at general conclusions by a direct, essentially personal intuition. It is important to distinguish these two forms of activity from each other, even though they have sometimes been conjoined in the work of a single person. There is no value judgment involved in describing practitioners of the first kind of activity as "philosophers" and practitioners of the second as "sages." There are bad philosophers—unimaginative, pedantic men whose criticisms are captious and devoid of understanding. There are also good sages—men who bring us to a greater understanding of human life, even though they are neither systematic theorists nor careful analysts.

C. D. Broad draws a sharp distinction between "critical" and "speculative" philosophy. This might appear to coincide with our distinction between philosopher and sage; indeed, some of Broad's successors have suggested that, or have at least proceeded as if, critical analysis is the only sort of philosophy there is. But it is certainly not the case that philosophers in general, in our own time or in any other, have been unimaginative or unwilling to speculate. Philosophy, like science, is neither pure speculation nor pure criticism; it is speculation controlled by criticism. Recent philosophy—as exemplified in, for example, Gilbert Ryle's *Concept of Mind* or Wittgenstein's *Philosophical Investigations*—is quite as speculative as it ever was, although not about the "transcendental." The difference between sage and philosopher is not that the sage is imaginative and the philosopher unimaginative; it is that the philosopher submits his speculations to the discipline of close criticism.

The idea of a philosophical method. To say that in philosophy speculation is controlled by critical discussion is not to define philosophy; the same can be said of any rational inquiry. Critical discussion takes many different forms. In science it often consists in the testing of hypotheses by experiment, while in mathematics it consists in the probing of propositions to see whether they lead to contradictions. Has philosophy a method of its own? Plato and Hegel thought so; they disagreed about its nature but agreed in calling it "dialectic." For Bergson it was intuition, for Wittgenstein the uncovering of nonsense, for Moritz Schlick clarification, and for Husserl phenomenological description. Hume, on the other hand, thought that the philosopher should imitate the methods of experimental inquiry, while Spinoza believed that the philosopher should imitate the geometrician.

The diversity of these opinions would strongly suggest that to define philosophy in terms of any particular method is to take sides in a philosophical dispute. Historically speaking, philosophers have made use of a great variety of procedures. Some of their arguments have been formal in character, reminiscent of mathematics; some of them have been attempts to overthrow hypotheses by appealing to everyday observations; sometimes they have pointed to ambiguities, obscurities, and confusions. When we look in detail at claims for the discovery of the correct method of proceeding in philosophy, we always find that they are not borne out by the writings of the philosopher who makes them. Thus, for example, Descartes's doubts are anything but universal, Hume's own arguments are not experimental in character, and Wittgenstein's *Tractatus* does not consist, for the most part, in the uncovering of nonsense. In other instances the method itself is suspect; this is certainly true of Hegel's dialectic or Husserl's "method of bracketing." Furthermore, the view that there is only one correct method of philosophizing always rests on philosophical doctrines that are not themselves derived by that method, such as the distinction between the given and its interpretation (phenomenology) and the distinction between ultimate simples and the complex (analysis).

In general, the methods actually used by philosophy overlap with those used outside philosophy. Some types of argument (for example, the appeal to vicious infinite regresses) may be peculiar to philosophy, but the philosopher is free to use, and does use, any type of critical discussion that promises to throw light on the problems confronting him. It would now be generally agreed that certain methods that have been advocated in the past are in fact useless: philosophers cannot arrive at the sort of conclusions which interest them by deductions from self-evident principles; philosophy cannot have the same sort of general structure as a natural science. But these negative points do not amount to a demonstration that there is a single philosophical method.

Philosophy and value. The Platonic view that philosophy is concerned with purposes or values was revived in the nineteenth century (e.g., by Rudolf Hermann Lotze and James Ward) in response to the rise of the natural sciences. Science, it was argued, can tell us only what the world is like and how it operates, whereas philosophy can tell us what life and nature "mean," what value or purpose they have. The various branches of philosophy, according to this view, are each concerned with the "meaning" of a particular form of activity or class of thing: the philosophy of history is concerned with the meaning of history, and the philosophy of law with the meaning of law. In its most general form, philosophy elucidates the meaning of the "universe as a whole."

Once again, however, this definition of philosophy rests upon special philosophical assumptions. Some philosophers (for example, Dewey) completely reject the antithesis between facts and their value or meaning; others, even if they allow such a contrast within the limited sphere of human affairs, will certainly not grant that there is anything that can be described as the meaning of life, of history, or of the "universe as a whole," or indeed, anything answering to such descriptions as "the universe as a whole" or "the total movement of history." If it is possible to be a philosopher and at the same time to deny that the universe has a meaning, or to be a philosopher of history without admitting that history has a meaning, then philosophy certainly ought not to be defined in terms of the search for meanings.

The philosopher as adviser. The final question that arises from the Platonic description of philosophy is whether it is the philosopher's responsibility to give advice. In the Alexandrian period, Stoic, Epicurean, and Skeptic all agreed that philosophy's main objective is to show men how to achieve peace of mind. Their practical approach appealed to the Romans: Cicero defined philosophy as "the art of life." During the Renaissance the Ciceronian conception of philosophy came to be predominant, at least among ordinary cultivated men; as late as the seventeenth century John Selden wrote that "philosophy is nothing else but prudence," by which he meant that prudence is the art of life. The popular conception of the philosopher, as embodied in the phrase "taking things philosophically," indicates a similar attitude. Many of the best-known philosophers have offered practical advice that is very closely related to their general philosophical views (for example, John Locke in *Some Thoughts concerning Education*).

When Russell argued that philosophy should be neutral, he was not suggesting that the philosopher should be less ready to offer advice than are other people. Indeed, few philosophers have been as ready as Russell to give advice on the conduct of life. As a person unusually practiced in critical discussion, the philosopher may well have a special responsibility to do so. Furthermore, it would be very strange if, merely in virtue of his investigations, he were not sometimes in an unusually good position to offer advice. Even if the philosopher can do no more than show people that they are talking nonsense, as Wittgenstein once thought, this can be made the basis for advice on how to avoid talking nonsense. In all such cases, however, the advice rests upon, but does not constitute, the successful completion of a philosophical task. In this respect, too, the philosopher differs from the sage: not uncommonly the whole content of the sage's "wisdom" consists in advice.

Philosophy and the special sciences. In Plato's dialogues (except in the special case of the *Timaeus*), the range of subjects considered is relatively small, and most of these subjects still fall within the province of philosophy. Aristotle, on the other hand, discussed almost everything. In the Middle Ages his work was read as an encyclopedia of philosophy, when he wrote about anatomy as well as when he wrote about logic or metaphysics. Aquinas was scarcely less encyclopedic than his master; Bacon, Hobbes, and Descartes all defined philosophy in encyclopedic terms, as did Leibniz and Wolff. To be sure, they did distinguish between "moral" philosophy, "natural" philosophy, "civil" or "political" philosophy, and "first" philosophy, or metaphysics. But in general they used "philosophy" as often to refer to what we now call "science" as to refer to what we now call "philosophy."

Only gradually did the "sciences" (a word that did not come into general use until the early nineteenth century) become separate from philosophy. Even now the boundaries of philosophy are by no means clear. If J. L. Austin is right in suggesting that philosophy is in process of giving birth to a new type of linguistic theory, no doubt many works which we still think of as forming part of philosophy (Plato's *Cratylus* or the third part of Locke's *Essay*, for example) will come to be thought of as stages in the history of the development of that linguistic theory. We can at least be reasonably confident that there are a good many questions which we now consider to belong to philosophy but which will some day not be so regarded—although we are, of course, in no position to say what those questions are.

Philosophy as the science of man. When it came to be realized that physics was an independent inquiry, philosophers, especially in Great Britain and France, turned their attention away from nature to man. Descartes's sharp distinction between mind and matter made it appear that there could be an inquiry into "the inner world" which would be wholly distinct from inquiries into "the outer world." Philosophy came to be thought of as running parallel to physics—the science of man as contrasted with the science of nature.

This supposed parallelism reaches its extreme in Hume. Hume quite explicitly asserts that once the nonsensical ingredients are removed from philosophy, it can wholly be identified with what he calls the moral sciences, or the science of human nature. Yet in some measure he retained the view that philosophy is the "first science" by arguing that every other branch of inquiry, precisely because it is a creation of the human mind, is dependent upon the science of human nature for its foundations. In Great Britain in the nineteenth century it became the standard doctrine that philosophy consists, as Dugald Stewart put it (*Encyclopaedia Britannica*, 8th ed., Vol. I, p. 227), in "all those enquiries which have for their object to trace the various branches of human knowledge to their first principles in the constitution of our nature." Both J. S. Mill and Sir William Hamilton, however opposed they may have been in other respects, agreed in defining philosophy as, in Mill's words, "the scientific knowledge of man." But this is certainly an unsatisfactory definition. Hume and his successors were not able to show that notions as causality and identity can be clarified by tracing the workings of the human mind. This mistake, like that of confusing cosmology with metaphysics, was an important one in the sense that it led to the development of psychology as a form of inquiry. However, it also had the effect of completely obscuring what we are now able to see as a distinction between philosophical and psychological inquiries. Contemporary philosophers, such as Edmund Husserl and Alexius Meinong, began by insisting that philosophy had to be sharply distinguished from psychology—a declaration of independence facilitated by the emergence of a truly experimental psychology as distinct from what Hume had called "psychology."

Philosophy as the science of sciences. Could philosophy entirely disintegrate into special sciences? William James thought so. He defined philosophy as "a collective name for questions which have not been answered to the satisfaction of all that have asked them," with the suggestion that once satisfactory answers were found, they would form part of a special science. In this way philosophy slowly digs its own grave.

Yet there are philosophical questions that we could scarcely contemplate as forming part of any specialized inquiry, just because they have application to any form of inquiry whatever. Aristotle thought that questions of this sort constituted what he called "the first and last science"—the first science because it is logically presupposed by every other science, the last because in order to understand it we must in some measure have mastered other sciences. He defined it as follows: "There is a science which investigates being as being, and the attributes which belong to this in virtue of its own nature. Now this is not the same as any of the so-called special sciences, for none of these treats universally of being as being. They cut off a part of being and investigate the attribute of this part" (*Metaphysics* 1003a18–25).

This definition would still be accepted in some quarters (although with reservations) as a satisfactory definition of philosophy, or at least of metaphysics. However, it has its difficulties. It rests on the assumption that "being" is the highest predicate in a series of predicates such as "mammalian vertebrate living being," "vertebrate living being," "living being," "being." However, as Hume and Kant pointed out, "being" is not an attribute in the sense in which "living being" is an attribute. Nor has it attributes; pure being is indistinguishable from nothing. Only if "theory of being as being" is given a somewhat special interpretation (as often happens) can it be saved from emptiness. Thus, Samuel Alexander identifies the definition of philosophy as the theory of being with the very different definition suggested by Francis Bacon, for whom the task of "first philosophy" is to coordinate the axioms of the various specialized segments of philosophy. Herbert Spencer, in the same tradition, defines philosophy as "completely unified science." Henry Sidgwick took over and modified Spencer's definition, suggesting that the philosopher's task is to "coordinate the most important general notions and fundamental principles of the various sciences."

This way of putting the matter, however, claims at once too little and too much for philosophy. It claims too little because the philosopher does not restrict his attention to the sciences; he asks questions about the relations between science and everyday belief, between science and religion, or, as we are now doing, between science and philosophy. It claims too much, because, although our own century has witnessed enormous advances in the coordination of the "special notions" and the "fundamental principles" of the sciences, this has resulted from, and could only result from, the work of biochemists, biophysicists, and physical chemists. Philosophers are in no position to coordinate, say, molecular structure and biological activity.

What sort of coordination, then, is left for the philosopher? One possible answer (suggested by Hegel and Croce) is that the philosopher is interested in coordinating art, economics, religion, and philosophy as forms of human activity, or modes in which the human spirit comes to an awareness of its own potentialities. This account of the philosopher's task, which equates philosophy with the theory of culture, is widely influential on the Continent. Contemporary British philosophers either frown upon such

inquiries or do not consider them to lie within their competence. According to them, if these inquiries are anyone's responsibility, they fall within the province of the sociologist. But in practice, of course, the sociologist does not discuss the sort of issue raised in R. G. Collingwood's *Speculum Mentis* or Croce's *Philosophy of the Spirit*. He does not ask himself, as they did, how the theoretical and practical activities of mankind are interrelated, how religion differs from science or how both differ from philosophy. Indeed, even if these problems are not the very center of philosophy or its sole content, they may still be in some measure the philosopher's responsibility. This is a matter to which we shall return.

Philosophy as speculative cosmology. One objection to the identification of philosophy with the study of culture is that it is unduly anthropomorphic. Philosophy's real concern, it might be said, is not particularly with the human spirit, except on the very special assumption that "nature" itself is in some sense a reification of that spirit, as the Italian idealists in fact argued. Once this assumption is rejected, it is no longer at all plausible to restrict philosophy to the realm of culture. As A. N. Whitehead and Karl Popper have maintained, everything, not only the human spirit, falls within philosophy's sphere; indeed, like science, it is a contribution to cosmology. According to a common view of the matter, this is certainly the form in which philosophy first arose: Anaximander, for example, might accurately be described as a "speculative cosmologist." But it has often been questioned whether Anaximander was a philosopher; there are good grounds for thinking of him as a scientist, or perhaps as neither philosopher nor scientist but a precursor of both philosophy and science. On the other hand, Parmenides' *The Way of Truth* is unmistakably philosophy.

What makes the difference? Suppose we interpret Thales as asserting that everything is made of water and Anaximenes as denying this and saying that things are made of air. These hypotheses are in important respects of the same type as the hypothesis that everything is made of electrons; the theories of Thales and Anaximenes are speculative cosmology in the same sense that Descartes's theory of vortices or Newton's theory of gravitation are speculative cosmology. If, when Parmenides denied the existence of "not-being," he simply meant to deny that there is empty space, then he was working in the same tradition.

But in fact he was doing something very different. In support of his cosmological theory, Thales might have adduced such "facts" as that when men get hot their flesh turns to water. Parmenides could produce no comparable evidence to prove that there is no such thing as not-being. His argument is of a quite different kind: "Thou canst not know that which is not (that is impossible), or utter it; for the same thing can be thought as can be." The speculative cosmology of the physicist describes the world in terms of special types of physical objects and physical processes; the speculative cosmology of the philosopher (let us rather say, following P. F. Strawson, the philosopher's "descriptive metaphysics") is expressed in terms of such logical concepts as thing, property, substance, individual, and process. These are concepts which can easily be applied to the nonphysical, should it turn out that anything is nonphysical.

If Heraclitus took the view that everything is made of fire, he was a speculative cosmologist; if he took the view that everything is in process, he was a descriptive metaphysician. (Of course, he might have been both or he might not have been sure of what he was doing.) The difference between Russell's "logical atomism," which is descriptive metaphysics, and the atomism of the physicists, which is speculative cosmology, is quite apparent. Descriptive metaphysics, we might also say, is what Aristotle's definition of "first" philosophy as an inquiry into *being as being* reduces to, once we get rid of the notion that being is either a predicate or an attribute; it is what G. E. Moore had in mind when he said that philosophy is an attempt to arrive at "a general description of the whole universe."

If we can now distinguish with sufficient clarity between cosmological speculation and descriptive metaphysics, the fact remains that, as we can see from Aristotle's *Physics,* the distinction was not an easy one for men to make. Indeed, the philosophers' failure to distinguish clearly between speculative cosmology and descriptive metaphysics was one of those fruitful mistakes which, as Leonard Goddard has suggested, are largely responsible for the emergence of sciences within philosophy. It is because philosophers did not know quite what they were doing—in what sense, for example, the concept of motion was important to them—that they continued to work at what we now describe as problems in physics.

Philosophy as a theory of language. What sort of inquiry, then, is descriptive metaphysics? It is easy enough to see how we can discuss the question whether everything is made of water, but how are we to discuss whether, for example, things are reducible to complexes of qualities? In his *Logical Syntax of Language,* Rudolf Carnap suggested that descriptive metaphysics is about the language in which we describe the world, whereas cosmology is about the world itself. Carnap admits that "thing," "property," and "relation," are not on the face of it names for elements in a language. But this, he argued, is precisely why philosophers in the past have gone astray. Although they have written as if they were talking about the world, what they have said makes sense, insofar as it does make sense, only if it is reformulated as a statement about language. For example, to ask whether things are reducible to complexes of qualities is simply to ask whether language—or, more precisely, some particular language—contains distinct thing-words or only conjunctions of quality-words. Quite generally, the task of philosophy is to describe the (actual or possible) language of science.

In a less formal way, the doctrine that the distinctive feature of philosophy is its concern with language has also been characteristic of twentieth-century philosophy in Great Britain. In both cases the influence of Wittgenstein has been predominant. But whereas for Carnap the philosopher is interested only in the language of science (and this is obviously too narrow a definition of the philosopher's task), in Great Britain the stress has been on "ordinary language." British philosophers have continued to work on the assumption that philosophy is as much about religion, morality, or indeed about common-sense beliefs as it is about science. But the attempt to show that philosophy is only about "the language" of these forms of inquiry gives rise to an intolerable stretching of the word "language."

The general thesis that philosophy is "really about language" may well turn out to have the same fate as the thesis that philosophy is "really about human nature." It arose in much the same way. When, in the nineteenth century, the "moral sciences" were gradually transformed into psychology and the social sciences, and even logic, in its more technical sense, was converted into a branch of mathematics, the philosopher seemed to be left with nothing to do. The distinction between "language" and "the world" has, in an important sense, replaced the older distinction between the inner world and the outer world. It provided the philosopher with an area in which to work— one that satisfied the traditional requirement of width of scope and at the same time left "the world" to science. There was, it is true, some difficulty in explaining just how the philosopher's concern with language differed from the philologist's. But as long as philology was largely etymology, the distinction, although hard to pin down, at least had some justification. Now that philosophy has helped to create new forms of linguistics, however, the exact manner in which philosophy can be "about language" without being a scientific discipline has become more and more obscure. Once again, the attempt of the philosopher to carve out a special field for himself has been frustrated by the growth of science, and once again, that attempt assisted the development of the science which superseded it.

Philosophy as the theory of critical discussion. "Every philosophical problem," Russell wrote in *Our Knowledge of the External World,* "when it is subjected to the necessary analysis and purification is found to be not really philosophical at all, or else to be, in the sense in which we are now using the word, logical." (By calling it "logical" he meant that it "arises out of the analysis of propositions.") Post-Russellian philosophers have substituted "analytic," "conceptual," or "linguistic" for Russell's "logical." The resulting definition, we have been suggesting, is at once too broad and too narrow: not all conceptual, analytic, or linguistic problems are philosophical and not all philosophical problems are conceptual, analytic, or linguistic—that is, they cannot be solved merely by getting clearer about the way in which an expression is used, by removing an ambiguity, or by drawing attention to a temptation implicit in our ordinary ways of talking.

Russell's original definition, on the face of it, suffers from the same defect: controversies about explanation, for example, do not "arise out of the analysis of propositions." Perhaps we can modify Russell's definition by suggesting that the central problems of philosophy—although not all problems of philosophy—turn around the analysis of critical discussion. This is the view, which this article will now develop and defend, that the peculiarity of philosophy as a form of critical discussion lies in its being a critical discussion *of* critical discussion.

This, at least, is the philosopher's home ground, the area in which he must be expert. From it he can move out into a wider variety of problems, although always with reference to the way in which discussion operates. Thus, for example, most books about art are not philosophical, but a philosopher may choose to write about art. If he does so, however, he will take as his central point of reference such problems as these: how it is possible to discuss fruitfully the character and the qualities of a work; whether a work of art can itself be true or false; and whether appreciating a work of art involves a peculiar (or any) sort of knowledge. That is why a philosopher can make important contributions to the philosophy of art without being in any sense an expert on art. These are questions which arise as much in relation to a comic strip or a chocolate-box landscape as in relation to *Hamlet* or *Guernica*.

The view that we are suggesting accords with recent discussions about the nature of philosophy insofar as it regards philosophy as being a "meta-inquiry" (an inquiry about inquiry) rather than as running parallel to science and to history, differing from them only in subject matter and method. It allows that the philosopher needs to engage in investigations which are in a broad sense "linguistic," but only insofar as an understanding of how language works is essential to an understanding of discussion. It also allows that the philosopher makes use of, and is interested in, methods of analysis; but it does not see in the practice of analysis the distinguishing mark of philosophical inquiry. Since historical, legal, scientific, and moral discussions certainly have peculiarities that require independent investigation, this view leaves room for a philosophy of history, of law, of science, and of morals. However, it does not allow that the philosopher's concern is with the "meaning" of these activities.

On the face of it, no doubt, this definition also is unduly narrow. Although philosophers have devoted a good deal of attention to truth and falsity, and to meaning, evidence, and proof (all of which are involved in an analysis of discussion), they have also, for example, written at length about the theory of perception. To discuss perception is not, at first glance, to advance the understanding of discussion. But if we look at the way in which problems of perception arise for the philosopher, we see that they are intimately linked to the analysis of discussion.

In discussion we commonly regard certain types of remarks as clinching statements. At a popular level, such remarks would include "I saw it with my own eyes." Very early, however, the development of Milesian cosmology cast doubt on the reliability of sensory perception; it was generally agreed by the cosmologist that whatever the world is like, it is certainly very different from what we ordinarily take it to be. In Plato's *Theaetetus,* the point at issue between Protagoras and Plato was whether "perception is knowledge" or, as we might put it, whether problems can be decisively settled by an appeal to what we perceive. Plato argued that the appeal to perception is useless for this purpose, and that indeed the whole conception of a rational discussion collapses if perceptual judgments are taken as final.

In order to make his point, he was obliged to work out a relatively detailed theory of perception; in this he was imitated by his successors. As a result, many issues which were later to form part of psychology were first discussed by philosophers. But what, in general, philosophers were looking for in their epistemological writings were substitute clinching statements. Recognizing that "I saw it with my own eyes" is not decisive, they went in search of propositions (for example, "There is now a red sense datum") that would be decisive. The central points at issue in epistemology are whether "I see a table in the room" is or is not an inference; whether "I remember that happening" has a different evidential value from "I can see that happening"; and whether there are clinching statements which are not statements of perception. If we ask at what point the details of perception cease to be of importance to the philosopher, the answer is that they cease to be of importance to him when they no longer affect such questions as whether "I saw a table" is an inference. But there is no way of telling in advance what that point will be: a particular philosopher may penetrate deeply into physiology and psychology in pursuit of the answer to the problems which trouble him.

For this reason, the contrast between philosophy as "about inquiry" and science as "about the world" must not be made too sharply. Critical discussion is one way in which human beings try to come to terms with the things around them; it is only to be expected that the analysis of discussion will lead, at many points, into statements about "the world." Even if the philosopher of art can make important contributions to the philosophy of art without being an expert on art, as was suggested above, it by no means follows that he will never be led into a discussion of the qualities of a particular work of art. The peculiarity of philosophy consists only in the fact that the questions it asks about the world refer back to, and are considered with reference to, the general character of discussion.

Fields of philosophy. There are important parallelisms between the main concepts philosophers use in analyzing a discussion and the concepts they use in descriptive metaphysics. If, for example, the philosopher embarks upon a discussion of explanation, he soon finds himself confronted by the question whether there is a peculiar kind of explanation describable as "causal" explanation, and if so, what its peculiarities are. Again, in analyzing discussion it is natural to draw a distinction between what a person is talking about and what he says about it; such descriptive-metaphysics distinctions as those between substance and attribute and between objects of acquaintance and objects of description arise naturally out of, and are only discussible in relation to, the analysis of discussion. In *Theaetetus,* Plato argued, against Heraclitus, that unless there are unchanging entities, there can be no such thing as discussion. Wittgenstein maintained in the *Tractatus* that the world must consist of simples, because otherwise none of our statements could be intelligible. Without begging the question whether descriptive metaphysics is simply reducible to a set of assertions about the elements in a fruitful discussion, we can say at least that the two are related to each other in a very intimate way, so much so that to regard the central problems of philosophy as turning on the analysis of discussion does not exclude descriptive metaphysics from philosophy.

Nor does it even exclude, at the outset, transcendental metaphysics. For the transcendental metaphysician commonly sets out to show that the existence of transcendental entities is implicit in the practice of critical discussion. He tries to show, for example, that there must be a single subject which all our statements are about, or else they will turn out not to be about anything; that in our practice of seeking explanations, there is implicit the assumption that there is an ultimate explanation, something whose nature is such that it must exist; that it is nonsense to say that ethical controversies about what is right can be settled by an appeal to ends, unless there is an ultimate end, and so on. We might go on to reject transcendental metaphysics on the ground that in fact it professes to, but cannot possibly, solve problems about discussion by appealing to the undiscussible. But our definition does not rule out transcendental metaphysics a priori.

Of all forms of critical discussion, the most developed is certainly science. It is not surprising, therefore, that philosophers have taken a quite special interest in the structure of scientific discussion. At the other extreme, ethical, aesthetic, and political discussions are notoriously unsatisfactory. The philosopher interests himself in such topics as the good, the beautiful, and the public interest, just because the mechanism for discussing differences of opinion about them strikes him as being inadequate. Such discussions, however, are so confused that the philosopher may find himself obliged to look in more detail at the whole character of ethics, of aesthetics, and of political theory. He can discuss science on the presupposition that everybody knows what a scientific problem is and would agree that such and such scientific statements are accepted as being true. He cannot with the same confidence set about discovering the characteristics of a successful ethical, aesthetic, or political discussion; he has to consider which, if any, statements in these fields are true and what the subject, as a whole, is attempting to do. In fact, insofar as ethics is concerned, the subject still lies almost entirely in the hands of philosophers. But except for the fact that the nature of moral discussion is particularly difficult to analyze, on the face of it there is no reason why philosophers should take any special interest in rectitude or goodness, and many philosophers have not done so.

Legal discussion falls, in some respects, between aesthetic discussion and scientific discussion. Within a legal system, there is fairly general agreement about what is and what is not "a good discussion"; what counts as evidence; and under what circumstances somebody's conduct can be held to explain why a subsequent course of action occurred. At the same time, however, legal criteria may be difficult to reconcile with our more general views about, for example, causal explanations of conduct. The philosopher will need to look very carefully at the workings of a legal system before he can pronounce on such points. Insofar as legal systems form part of "the world," he has to examine "the world" in order to understand their peculiarities. Indeed, it is impossible to talk fruitfully about any form of discussion without considering to some degree its nature as a mode of life and its general aims and character. This is one reason that investigations along the general lines of "philosophies of the spirit"—although without their idealistic presuppositions—are of more than marginal interest to the philosopher.

Many philosophers have taken a special interest in such social institutions as education and censorship. This is not surprising. Education itself is, or can be, a training in critical discussion. Furthermore, the discussion of education and the attempt to settle controversies about the organization of educational institutions not uncommonly involve a confusion of theoretical, practical, and moral issues, which a philosopher may properly attempt to disentangle. Similarly, defenses of censorship often rest on a doctrine of "sacred truths" or of undiscussible issues, which are naturally of importance to the analyst of discussion.

The philosophical problems which seem most remote from the analysis of discussion are those which turn around what are often called the great issues—God, freedom, and immortality; mind and nature. But consider, for example, the difference between a neurophysiologist talking about mind and body and a philosopher talking about the same topic. The neurophysiologist tries to find out which cells in the brain are involved in particular forms of mental activity. The philosopher is concerned with quite different questions, such as whether everyday explanations of human behavior in terms of reasons, motives, and intentions are or are not compatible with explanations of human behavior in physiological terms. It is the meshing of two different types of explanations that presents him with his problem.

Similarly, God is important to the philosopher in three ways—first, insofar as it has been argued that the proposition "God exists" is both existential and indubitable; second, insofar as "God" is an explanatory concept and the use of God as an explanation involves peculiar difficulties; third, insofar as the question can be raised whether God's existence and nature are discussible at all. "God" is a metaphysical concept of such historical importance in Western culture that the philosopher may well pay more than ordinary attention to it. But God is not *intrinsically* of greater philosophical interest than, let us say, Bradley's Absolute or the Cartesian *cogito*.

Similarly, in the case of freedom, the question is whether our habit of discussing human behavior in a special kind of way (regarding as a real issue whether somebody is deserving of praise or blame) is compatible with the supposition that there are sufficient and necessary conditions for a person to act as he does—that is, with the possibility of explaining his behavior in the ordinary scientific fashion. As for immortality, there have often been doubts about whether this is really a question for philosophy. But insofar as it is, the question is whether it is possible to identify the being who is said to live after death with the living being by any of the ordinary means used in identification—that is, the means by which we determine whether we are both talking about the same person. Philosophy has only slowly discovered how such issues can be discussed, as distinct from merely being pronounced upon. This process of discovery has gone hand in hand with philosophy's creation of new fields of inquiry, which have brought philosophers face to face with the problem of how their investigations differ from the investigations of the scientist on the one side and the pronouncements of the sage on the other.

Philosophical problems are so interconnected that one could perhaps take some group of topics other than those relating to discussion and show how they can be expanded to fall within the province of traditional philosophy. But there are certain advantages in treating the analysis of discussion as central. For one thing, there can be no doubt that explaining, criticizing, and claiming to know are activities that actually go on, in a sense in which, for example, there can be doubt whether there are ultimate principles. Yet to define philosophy in terms of discussion does not rule out *ab initio* the search for ultimate principles.

Again, while the definition of philosophy as descriptive metaphysics has its attractions, it is certainly a matter of controversy—philosophical controversy—whether there can be such a subject, and how it can be developed. Nor, beginning at this point, is it at all easy to understand how there can be such subjects as "the philosophy of law" or "the philosophy of history," except insofar as a particular theory of law or history raises metaphysical issues. One can see why, for example, philosophers should be interested in what is meant by saying that "good is a nonnatural property," but not in why they should carry their interest in ethics beyond this point. In contrast, as Hare has pointed out, to begin from the nature of ethical discussion is to be led into the very heart of ethics.

Description, prescription, and rational reconstruction. If we say that philosophy is concerned with types of inquiry, we still have a problem to face: Does it merely describe what goes on in these forms of inquiry? It was stated above that aesthetic discussions were unsatisfactory, and it was presumed that scientific discussions were satisfactory. On the other hand, a good many philosophers (for example, James Ward) would not accept this account of the matter. Scientific discussions, they would argue, are profoundly unsatisfactory unless the question at issue is a purely technological one. The scientist never actually describes the concrete things he purports to be describing: his descriptions are wholly abstract, whereas the things he is describing are concrete. Many of these philosophers would add that aesthetic discussions do not suffer from this defect. Indeed, at any but the abstract technological level, scientific discussion itself is about whether to choose one theory or another; and in the end, this comes down to an aesthetic choice, since it is a mere pretense that argument, whether in the form of calculation or in the form of observation and experiment, can decide the issue.

When faced with such an opposition, how is the philosopher to proceed? One suggestion is that he should not allow himself to call one kind of discussion satisfactory and another unsatisfactory; it is his job, simply, to describe how aestheticians argue, how theologians argue, what considerations they accept, and what forms of reasoning they regard as decisive. This way of looking at the matter, which may be christened "descriptionist," is a natural reaction against the "prescriptionism" of classical rationalism. Classical rationalism begins from the notion of *real*

proof or *real* explanation or *real* knowledge. Sometimes it derives this ideal concept from some existing form of inquiry (for example, proof from axiomatic geometry or explanation from physics), and then proceeds to complain that there are no proofs (that is, axiomatic deductions) in philosophy and no explanations (that is, statements of necessary and sufficient conditions) in history. In even more extreme instances (in the case of F. H. Bradley, for example), classical rationalism begins from some supposed "requirement of the intellect" and then asserts that not even mathematics really proves and not even physics really explains—much as for Russell not even our best friends are "objects of acquaintance" and not even "Socrates" is really a proper name.

It is easy to understand why, in reaction to this attitude, philosophers should begin to argue that the philosophers' concern is to describe how, let us say, historians *actually* reason, without attempting to impose on historians a concept of good reasoning derived from "ideal considerations." Yet even if he wishes to, the philosopher cannot restrict himself to mere description. Suppose, for example, the philosopher of science attempts to "describe what the scientist does." Then he has first to determine what he is going to count as science. Is he going to include Marxism and Freudian psychology or will he, with Karl Popper, exclude them from science? To say that he will let the scientists "determine what is to count as science" is to be involved in a vicious circle, for how is he to decide who are the scientists? Hence, a "pure descriptionism" could never even get started.

But this does not mean that we are forced back to prescriptionism. There is a third possible approach, "rational reconstruction." To employ the method of "rational reconstruction" is neither simply to prescribe nor simply to describe. A satisfactory reconstruction of explanation, for example, will almost certainly not apply to everything which has previously gone under that name. It may well reject, for example, explanations in terms of the guiding hand of Providence, not on the ground that they are false but because they are not the sort of thing which ought to be reckoned as an explanation; they do not enable us to account for the fact that things happen in one way rather than in another.

So far, rational reconstruction is prescriptionistic, but not arbitrarily so. The rational reconstructor will try to show that there is no way of distinguishing between explaining and other forms of human activity (for example, reasserting), unless some of what have ordinarily been called explanations are excluded as pseudo explanations. Quite similarly, the test of whether a "rational reconstruction" of philosophy is a reasonable one is whether it provides us with a method of demarcating philosophy from other forms of inquiry, even if in order to do so it is obliged to exclude much that ordinarily passes as philosophy. The rational reconstructor is not so much prescribing as drawing attention to a difference.

Furthermore, he is a descriptionist to the extent that he will expect his theory of explanation, for example, to apply to a wide range of what have ordinarily been called explanations. He bases his reconstruction, not on a priori views about what kind of explanation would be fully satisfactory to the intellect, but rather on what counts as an explanation in developed forms of inquiry. His rational reconstruction of philosophy may exclude Kierkegaard but must apply, at least in large measure, to the work of Plato, Aristotle, Descartes, Hume, and Kant.

Obviously, there can be disagreement about whether a reconstruction is rational. Some people will think it so intuitively obvious that Kierkegaard and Kant are both engaged in the same sort of activity that they will reject as prescriptionist any rational reconstruction which has the effect that Kierkegaard is not a philosopher; or they will think it so obvious that Marxism explains what happens in history that they will reject out of hand any theory of explanation which denies that the materialist interpretation of history can serve as an explanation. Controversy on this point is all the more difficult because words like explanation, philosophy, science, and knowledge are used eulogistically. But this is only to say that agreement in philosophy is difficult to secure—which is scarcely news.

The variety of philosophical tasks. The analysis of discussion raises problems of such proportions that difficulties arising out of an attempt to solve them, rather than the original problems themselves, can come to be the sole preoccupation of philosophers. To take an instance, many philosophers have greatly interested themselves in the peculiarities of mathematical discussion. A philosopher may well restrict his attention almost entirely to the analysis of that particular variety of discussion, asking what conditions have to be fulfilled by an adequate proof, what role is played by axioms and by definitions, what exactly mathematical propositions tell us, and so forth. In the course of such a critical discussion of mathematics particular suggestions are made—for example, that mathematical propositions have the peculiarity of being synthetic a priori or of being tautologies. A philosopher may choose to concentrate almost entirely upon the question whether, and how, it is possible to distinguish between synthetic a priori propositions and analytic propositions.

What he says in the course of his attempt to settle this question may provoke further controversy about whether, for example, analytic propositions are "really about language." In the end the philosopher may be engaged in highly technical controversies which seem to have very little to do with the theory of discussion. But the point of such controversies, the reason that they are something more than technical exercises, is the light they throw on the connection and distinction between mathematical and scientific reasoning.

Similarly, a philosopher may concentrate his attention upon the problem of "counterfactual conditionals." But in this case, too, the point at issue is how a person who utters such a counterfactual conditional as "If Caesar had not crossed the Rubicon, the Republic would still have fallen" can, by that means, make a contribution to discussion. If this question is forgotten, controversy about counterfactual conditionals can easily collapse into scholastic pedantry.

With this reservation, however, it is quite natural that there should be a great many philosophers with interests of a highly technical nature that find expression in short studies on technical points rather than in large-scale constructions. At the other end of the spectrum, there are philosophers whose main interest is in the interrelation of such forms of human activity as religion, science, and art. These philosophers run the serious risk of woolliness, emptiness, or arbitrariness, unless they take as their central point of reference the structure of religious, scientific, and aesthetic discussion. There is room within philosophy for an immense variety of types of investigation, some very minute and some highly generalized. Nor is it a matter of any importance if a philosopher, in trying to solve a particular problem, passes outside the boundaries of philosophy altogether. In the end, it is problems, not the divisions between subjects, that are crucial.

Bibliography

Alexander, Samuel, *Space, Time and Deity*. London, 1920.

Austin, J. L., "Ifs and Cans," in *Philosophical Papers*. Oxford, 1961. Pp. 179–180.

Ayer, A. J., *Language, Truth and Logic*. London, 1936.

Bacon, Francis, *De Dignitate et Augmentis Scientiarum*. London, 1623. Especially Book III, Ch. 1.

Bergson, Henri, "L'Intuition philosophique," in *La Pensée et le mouvant*. Geneva, 1934. Translated by Mabelle L. Andison as *The Creative Mind*. New York, 1946.

Bradley, F. H., *Appearance and Reality*. London, 1893.

Broad, C. D., "Speculative and Critical Philosophy," in J. H. Muirhead, ed., *Contemporary British Philosophy*, First Series. London, 1924.

Carnap, Rudolf, *Logische Syntax der Sprache*. Vienna, 1934. Translated by Amethe Smeaton as *Logical Syntax of Language*. London, 1937.

Cicero, Marcus Tullius, *De Finibus* ("Concerning Ends"), translated by H. Rackham. Loeb Classical Library, No. 40. Cambridge, Mass., 1914. III, 2, 4.

Collingwood, R. G., *Speculum Mentis*. Oxford, 1924.

Croce, Benedetto, *Filosofia come scienza dello spirito*, 5 vols. Bari, Italy, 1909–1917. Translated by D. Ainslie as *Philosophy of the Spirit*. London, 1909–1921.

Descartes, René, *Philosophical Works*, 2 vols., translated by E. S. Haldane and G. R. T. Ross, Cambridge, 1911. Vol. I includes *Meditationes de Prima Philosophiae* (1641) and the Preface to the French translation of *Principia Philosophiae* (1650).

Dewey, John, *Reconstruction in Philosophy*. New York, 1920.

Ducasse, C. J., *Philosophy as a Science*. New York, 1941. Contains the best general discussion of the word "philosophy."

Goddard, Leonard, *Philosophical Thinking*. Armidale, New South Wales, 1962. Inaugural lecture.

Hamilton, William, *Lectures on Metaphysics and Logic*, 4 vols. Edinburgh, 1859–1860.

Hare, R. M., *Freedom and Reason*. Oxford, 1963.

Hegel, G. W. F., *Encyclopädie der philosophischen Wissenschaft*. Heidelberg, 1817. Part III. Translated by William Wallace as *Hegel's Philosophy of Mind*. Oxford, 1894.

Heidegger, Martin, *Was ist das—die Philosophie?* Pfullingen, 1956. Translated by W. Kluback and J. T. Wilde as *What Is Philosophy?* London, 1958.

Hobbes, Thomas, *De Corpore*. London, 1655. Translated as *Concerning Body*. London, 1656.

Hume, David, *A Treatise of Human Nature*. London, 1739.

Husserl, Edmund, *Logische Untersuchungen*, 2 vols. Halle, 1900–1901.

Husserl, Edmund, *Ideen zu einer reinen Phänomenologie und phänomenologischen Philosophie*, Vol. I. Halle, 1913. Translated by W. R. Boyce Gibson as *Ideas*. London, 1931.

James, William, *Some Problems in Philosophy*. New York, 1911.

Lange, F. A., *Die Geschichte der Materialismus*, 2d ed. Leipzig, 1873–1875. Translated by E. C. Thomas as *History of Materialism*. London, 1877.

Leibniz, G. W., *De Vita Beata* ("Concerning the Blessed Life"), first published in *Opera Philosophica*, J. E. Erdmann, ed. Berlin, 1840.

Lotze, (Rudolf) Hermann, *Metaphysik*. Leipzig, 1841. Translated and edited by Bernard Bosanquet as *Metaphysic*, 2 vols. Oxford, 1884.

Meinong, Alexius, *Untersuchungen zur Gegenstandstheorie und Psychologie*. Leipzig, 1904.

Mill, J. S., *Auguste Comte and Positivism*. London, 1865.

Moore, G. E., *Some Main Problems of Philosophy*. London, 1953.

Passmore, J. A., *Philosophical Reasoning*. London and New York, 1961.

Passmore, J. A., "The Place of Argument in Metaphysics," in W. E. Kennick and Morris Lazerowitz, eds., *Metaphysics*. Englewood Cliffs, N.J., 1966.

Popper, K. R., *Logik der Forschung*. Vienna, 1935. Revised English version, *The Logic of Scientific Discovery*. London, 1959.

Popper, K. R., *Conjectures and Refutations*. New York, 1962.

Raeymaker, Louis de, *Introduction à la philosophie*. Louvain, 1938.

Russell, Bertrand, *Our Knowledge of the External World*. London, 1914.

Schlick, Moritz, *Gesammelte Aufsätze*. Vienna, 1938.

Sidgwick, Henry, *Philosophy, Its Scope and Relations*. London, 1902.

Spencer, Herbert, *First Principles*. London, 1862.

Spinoza, Benedict, *Ethica*, in *Opera Posthuma*. Amsterdam, 1677. Translated by W. H. White and A. H. Stirling as *Ethics*. Oxford, 1927.

Strawson, P. F., *Individuals*. London, 1959.

Ueberweg, Friedrich, *Grundriss der Geschichte der Philosophie*, 3 vols. Berlin, 1862–1866. Translated by G. S. Morris as *The History of Philosophy*. London, 1871. Contains a discussion of the word "philosophy."

Walsh, W. H., *Metaphysics*. London, 1963. Contains one of the best general discussions of the word "philosophy."

Ward, James, *Naturalism and Agnosticism*. London, 1899.

Whitehead, A. N., *Process and Reality*. Cambridge, 1929.

Wittgenstein, Ludwig, *Tractatus Logico-philosophicus*, translated by C. K. Ogden. London, 1922. Corrected translation by D. F. Pears and B. F. McGuinness. London, 1961.

Wittgenstein, Ludwig, *Philosophical Investigations*, translated by G. E. M. Anscombe. Oxford, 1953.

Wolff, Christian, *Philosophia Rationalis*. Frankfurt, 1728.

JOHN PASSMORE

PHILOSOPHY, HISTORIOGRAPHY OF. Books and articles about past philosophical theories may take any of a number of different forms. Sometimes their object is to defend or attack a particular philosophical theory, that is, they are polemical rather than historical in intent. Or they may be purely doxographical, content to describe or summarize what philosophers have said. On occasion they set out to show by what steps philosophy has now arrived at the truth ("retrospective" histories). They may classify past theories into different types, or they may consider theories as a reflection of the time at which they were written ("cultural" histories). Finally, they may try to show how theories arose out of an attempt to solve specific philosophical problems. We shall consider each of these types of historical work in turn.

HISTORY AND POLEMICS

An exclusively polemical treatment of past events may have its philosophical advantages, but it is liable to result in either inaccurate or unduly prejudiced history. The polemicist is primarily concerned with advancing his own ideas and tends to regard himself as not bound by the ordinary canons of historical interpretation. Plato, for exam-

ple, had much to say about his predecessors, but his attitude toward them was polemical rather than historical. He tells us very little about their intellectual background or their relationships to one another. He does not hesitate, even, to ascribe to them views they certainly did not hold, if by so doing he can represent them as more completely exemplifying a philosophical position he wishes to defend or to controvert.

Many modern commentaries, nominally devoted to the elucidation of a particular philosopher or series of philosophers, exhibit the same polemical attitude. For a number of commentators "Plato" is simply a name for a set of doctrines only loosely linked with Plato's dialogues. The real object of the commentator is to expound his own philosophical ideas or to attack his contemporaries.

The polemical approach has been explicitly defended by C. D. Broad, in his *Five Types of Ethical Theory* (London, 1930). Here Broad sharply distinguishes the "philosophical" from the "philological" approach to philosophical texts. Scholarship, Broad suggests, is of no concern to the philosophical critic, who is interested in his predecessors only because "the clash of their opinions may strike a light which will help us to avoid the mistakes into which they have fallen." Against Broad, however, it must be pointed out that if the polemicist is wholly innocent of scholarship he is very likely to direct his criticisms against positions which nobody has ever been tempted to hold. Such straw-man polemics will almost certainly be philosophically less interesting than criticism based on a scholarly interpretation of what some important philosopher has actually said. In fact, though, scholarship and polemics need not be divorced; in, for example, N. Kemp Smith's *Studies in the Cartesian Philosophy* (London, 1902), they are intimately and fruitfully wedded. We can come to understand a philosopher by trying to see what went wrong with his arguments, but we can do this only if we take seriously the attempt to discover what those arguments actually were.

DOXOGRAPHICAL HISTORIES

The doxographical approach dominated early histories of philosophy. Theophrastus (c. 350 B.C.), the first to undertake systematic historical work in philosophy, wrote 16 books under the general heading "Opinions of the Physicists." In his first book he outlined the teachings of his philosophical predecessors, adding brief biographical annotations. Each of his later books was devoted to a particular topic, expounding and criticizing the views of his predecessors on that topic. (Only *Of Sensation* survives, and that not in its entirety.) This "topic" method of organizing the history of philosophy has rarely been adopted in modern times, but the method of summarizing "teachings" adopted in Theophrastus' first book set the pattern for all doxographical histories.

Influence of Diogenes Laërtius. Of the ancient doxographical histories Diogenes Laërtius' *Lives and Opinions of the Famous Philosophers* (third century?) exerted the greatest influence in the modern world. Diogenes, imitating Sotion of Alexandria (c. 200 B.C.), modified Theophrastus' purely chronological ordering. He divided philosophers into "schools" and disregarded all chronological relationships except those involved in successive membership in the same school. Thus, although the teachings of Plato are described in Book III, Pythagoras appears for the first time in Book VIII and only in Book IX do the names of Parmenides and Heraclitus finally appear. The sequence of argument is irretrievably obscured; Diogenes makes no attempt to explain why a philosopher argued as he did, what his problems were, why he was dissatisfied with the current solutions. For the doxographer a philosopher is an "interesting person"—Diogenes delights in biographical, especially scandalous, details.

Walter Burleigh, responding to the fourteenth-century revival of interest in philosophers of antiquity, compiled a free and highly unreliable version of Diogenes on *De Vita ac Moribus Philosophorum*. First printed at Cologne in 1470, this proved highly popular. For about two centuries it served as the only general history of philosophy. Francis Bacon in his *De Dignitate et Augmentis Scientiarum* (1623) called for a new history of philosophy which would be something more than a mere list of names and opinions, but he still thought of such a history as being concerned with "sects, schools, books, authors and successions" rather than with problems and the attempt to solve them.

A similar attitude is revealed in the title of the first general history of philosophy in the modern period, Georg Horn's *Historiae Philosophicae de Origine, Successionis, Sectis et Vita Philosophorum ab Orbe Condito ad Nostram Aetatem Agitur* (Leiden, 1655). But Horn's book is distinctly idiosyncratic in its organization. He makes use of the doctrine, popular with seventeenth-century scholars, that all philosophy was known to Adam, that the division of philosophers into sects is a sign of the Fall, and that the main clues to the true, primitive philosophy are to be found in the Old Testament. The history of philosophy— Horn was himself no philosopher—is presented as an attempt, aided by Christian revelation, to rediscover the original unity of thought. The major part of Horn's book is devoted to Old Testament and to Christian "philosophy"; the Greeks have a place in it only as illustrations of the pagan multiplication of sects.

Thomas Stanley's *History of Philosophy* (London, 1655), which largely restricts itself to the Greeks, was less unconventional and more widely read. Stanley did not, as is often said, simply reproduce Diogenes; he added material from other sources, taking as his acknowledged exemplar Pierre Gassendi's *De Vita, Moribus et Doctrina Epicuri* (Leiden, 1647). Nevertheless, he adopted the general structure, the biographical emphasis, the doxographical method characteristic of Diogenes. Stanley's history ran into four editions in England between 1655 and 1743 and was translated into Latin and published in that language at Amsterdam in 1690, Leipzig in 1711, and Venice as late as 1733. In short, until the mid-eighteenth century, the history of ancient philosophy was substantially that of Diogenes Laërtius.

Brucker. In 1742–1767 Jakob Brucker published at Leipzig the massive five volumes of his *Historia Critica Philosophiae, a Mundi Incunabulis ad Nostram usque Aetatem Deducta*. For Kant and for the French Encyclopedists Brucker's immensely learned and detailed history

was the principal authority. Freely adapted into an English form by William Enfield as *The History of Philosophy* (London, 1791), it was a standard text in England for another thirty years.

In the true doxographical manner, Brucker sets out a philosophical theory as though it were a collection of apothegms. But he is much more responsible philosophically than Diogenes or Stanley and is skeptical about the traditional sources. However, although his title promises a critical history, Brucker's "criticism" consists of praise or blame; he does not try to examine in detail the arguments philosophers have put forward. For him, as for Bacon, error is simply to be castigated as a sign of prejudice or bad faith. The Neoplatonists, for example, were wicked men who sought to subvert Christianity in the interests of paganism. There is never any question, in this view, of understanding why, in an intellectual sense, people developed their doctrines in the way in which they did. Still, Brucker's solid scholarship, for all the defects inherent in his doxographical method, was an important step on the path to more satisfactory histories of philosophy.

HISTORY AS THE PASSAGE TO TRUTH

Stimulated by Brucker's successes and failures, Germany in the last half of the eighteenth century witnessed a vigorous controversy about the nature of the history of philosophy. This gave birth to a number of large-scale histories designed on a new plan. Dietrich Tiedemann's *Geist der spekulativen Philosophie* (6 vols., Marburg, 1791–1797) is, in conception and design, the first history of philosophy in the modern manner. Only the last volume, however, is devoted to modern philosophy. Tiedemann begins with the Greeks, rather than, in Brucker's fashion, with "philosophy before the flood"; he abandons, as Brucker had not, Diogenes' method of dividing philosophers into "schools," so that for the first time the development of philosophy from Pythagoras, Heraclitus, and Parmenides to Plato can be made apparent. Tiedemann tries to discover the "leading principle" in each philosophy, rather than simply to summarize its principal doctrines; he relates philosophical ideas, however loosely, to the forms of social and religious life within which they emerged. In short, Tiedemann made the step forward beyond doxography, however unsatisfactory his history may be in detail. His weakness lies in a tendency (often to be found in later historians) to impose regular "systems" on philosophers who were certainly innocent of any such systematic ambitions.

Gottlieb Tennemann carries further Tiedemann's achievement. His *Geschichte der Philosophie* (11 vols., Leipzig, 1789–1819) begins with lengthy essays on the aims and methods of a history of philosophy. Tennemann says his object is not solely to collect sources or to summarize philosophical systems; he hopes to show how the philosophical spirit, although not without periods of decline, has gradually worked toward a scientific form by way of a logical development from one system to another.

Hegel. Both Tiedemann and Tennemann influenced Hegel; indeed, they anticipated many of the most characteristic teachings of Hegel's *Vorlesungen über die Ge-*

schichte der Philosophie (Berlin, 1833–1836). Hegel is less than generous in his references to them, but he is correct in suggesting that they did not succeed in showing how one philosophical theory arose historically out of another. They are content to point to "anticipations" of the truth when, Hegel says, the historian ought to show how the truth was actually arrived at.

The doxographical historian, Hegel argues (and he is particularly severe on Brucker, although in fact he borrows a great deal from him) offers us only bare unrelated facts; nothing could be more useless than knowing only when and how a philosopher lived and that he said such-and-such. A true history of philosophy, in contrast, will show us how each significant philosophy grew out of the spirit of the age, as part of the movement of the human mind toward truth. Hegel presents his own philosophy—in the modest guise of "the philosophy of the present"—as the culmination of the past, absorbing into a higher and final form whatever was of value in the work of his predecessors. Unlike Brucker, he does not condemn the doctrines of his predecessors as false. Their defect, in his view, is that they are "one-sided," as at their stage in the historical process they could not help but be.

Hegel's work is important insofar as he saw his predecessors as men struggling with problems, not simply as holding views. But his attempt to show that they were unconsciously moving toward Hegelianism leads to a falsification of the processes of history. Philosophies which will not fit into that pattern are dismissed as "perversities" or, as in the case of Berkeley and Hume, are very lightly touched upon; "philosophers" like Jakob Boehme, who suit Hegel's scheme, are discussed at disproportionate length.

Hegel's method, like Aristotle's before him, is retrospective; he looks upon the past from the standpoint of the present and as leading up to it. This, it might be argued, is inevitable; when we look at the past, we naturally emphasize in it what now interests us. For example, recent developments in logic have led the historian to reconsider medieval logic completely and to see in it anticipations of contemporary mathematical logic. But this is not to say that the historian should think of past philosophers as Hegel did—as striving to be where we now are—or of their doctrines as being wholly absorbed into our own point of view. The historian will be interested in philosophical movements which have certainly not been absorbed by any contemporary position, except in that peculiar Hegelian sense in which philosophy "absorbs" everything that it reacts against. Nor is there any single "philosophy of the present" from which the past can be regarded. When a historian chooses to write an account of the way in which a particular philosophical movement reached its present condition, he is not writing the history of *philosophy;* he will in fact be ignoring, deliberately, much of what was philosophically interesting in the past.

CLASSIFICATORY HISTORY

It is essential to Hegel's view that no philosophical ideas are in a strict sense contradictory, that they can always be reconciled into a higher unity. Charles Renouvier, in his *Esquisse d'une classification systématique des doctrines philosophiques* (2 vols., Paris, 1885). rejected this assumption, arguing that the history of philosophy describes the conflict between quite irreconcilable tendencies in human thinking—what William James was to call "tough-minded" and "tender-minded" philosophies. In this view philosophy has, in a way, no history. The historian classifies rather than relates historically. Renouvier's approach cannot be lightly dismissed; one cannot but be struck by the recurrence in the history of philosophy of certain fundamental disputes. But if, for example, the historian descries a conflict between "nominalists" and "realists" in contemporary as in medieval logic, it would still be quite wrong to say that all that has happened is that the disputants once wore cassocks and now wear suits. The modern realist does not merely use a different philosophical terminology from Plato's; he uses different arguments, designed to meet the classical objections to Platonism. The historian has to concern himself at least with the ways in which classical debates are reshaped under the pressure of argument. So the historical sequence of ideas is of the first importance to him.

CULTURAL HISTORY

That the historical sequence is of any real importance is substantially denied not only by Renouvier but by the "cultural historians." Although Hegel had officially taken the view that the philosophy of a period reflects the spirit of the age in which it was put forward, in practice he paid very little attention to anything except the internal logical relations between theories. Much the same is true of Bertrand Russell's *History of Western Philosophy* (New York, 1945), even though Russell tells us that he has tried to "exhibit" each philosopher as the product of and spokesman for his social environment.

The cultural historian proper takes much more seriously the sociohistorical affiliations of the philosophers he is discussing. The polemicist writes about Plato as if he were a colleague who might throw light on the philosophical problems which now confront us; for the cultural historian, Plato's whole concern is with problems set for him by the changing conditions of Greek society. "The philosophical problems of one age," writes John Herman Randall in his *The Career of Philosophy* (New York, 1962), "like the cultural conflicts out of which they take their rise, are irrelevant to those of another."

R. G. Collingwood, adopting in his *Autobiography* (London, 1939) a similar view, concludes that the polemical approach to past philosophers is wholly valueless. This seems, however, to exaggerate the actual position. No doubt, for example, Greek mathematics was very different from modern mathematics; the problems which confront the modern philosopher of mathematics are therefore in many respects different from the problems which confronted Plato; and it would be absurd to criticize Plato for not solving problems which did not confront him. But his problems and ours are not entirely different. Philosophers of mathematics can still ask themselves how Euclidean geometry is related to the world and can learn something by examining Plato's discussion of that same problem.

If the cultural historian is correct, the history of philosophy has to be written "horizontally," with reference to its setting, and not "vertically," with reference to the philosopher's predecessors. The practical effect of the cultural approach is that what, from the traditional standpoint, have always been regarded as minor philosophers move into the historical forefront, just because they faithfully represent the tendencies of their age. The more major figures, displaying more intellectual independence, are lightly discussed. Thus, for example, in his *The Seventeenth Century Background* (London, 1934) Basil Willey devotes 32 pages to Joseph Glanvill and only 16 to Descartes. Furthermore, the distinction between philosopher and sage tends to disappear. The philosopher's arguments are of no interest to the cultural historian; like the doxographer he is interested only in opinions.

The cultural historian tends, too, to lay stress on such periods as the early Renaissance and the French Enlightenment, during which philosophy, literature, theology, and social change were very closely related one to another but which, from the point of view of the professional philosopher, are of very slight interest. When the cultural historian is a trained philosopher, his history of philosophy tends to be more orthodox in practice than one would expect from his initial pronouncements. But a good deal of recent historical work on philosophy has been written by men whose training was in literature; in such cases the "horizontalizing" tendencies reach their most extreme expression.

The cultural historian is certainly correct in rejecting the view that philosophy is wholly autonomous. Nowadays few historians of philosophy, as distinct from mere polemicists, would discuss Hume without referring to Newton, Pierre Bayle, or the Scottish Enlightenment—in opposition to the older tendency to think of Hume's intellectual environment as consisting solely of Locke and Berkeley. But it is another matter to suggest that Hume's problems are not at all continuous with those of Plato, or Russell's with Hume's; that there is in no sense an independent philosophical tradition.

PROBLEMATIC HISTORIES

The importance of the Hegelian approach is that it emphasizes the fact that the philosopher begins from a problem. The "problematic" approach to philosophy is advocated by Wilhelm Windelband in *Geschichte der Philosophie* (Freiburg, 1892) and, freed from Windelband's Hegelian framework, is characteristic of much of the best historical writing of our time.

It is true that historical work in philosophy is still often doxographical. General histories of philosophy, in particular, may be little more than chronologically arranged reference books. This is in some degree inevitable; indeed, our historical knowledge is always doxographical at its margins. We always know of some philosophers nothing more than when they lived, what they wrote and, in very general terms, what they said.

Histories of philosophy which are genuinely illuminating, historically and philosophically, try to move beyond that point. Such works try to help us understand why men came to think as they did; why they did not even consider alternative possibilities which seem obvious to us; why certain types of problems and certain patterns of solutions obsessed them; out of what intellectual and social situations their problems arose; in what respects their discussion of these problems advanced inquiry.

The possibility of such a history depends upon there being, in some degree, progress in philosophy. Kuno Fischer in his *Geschichte der neueren Philosophie* (Mannheim, 1854–1877) raised the question how philosophy can have a history, since it claims to arrive at the truth and truth can have no history; on the other hand cultural historians not uncommonly deny that there can be any objective advances in philosophy, just because there are no philosophical truths.

We need not now face that question in its full complexity. We need only grant that there can be advances in philosophical understanding, in the sense of philosophers coming to see more clearly what their problems are, why certain seemingly plausible solutions will not suffice, and how such problems are affected by new developments in science, in religion, in society. (Of course there can also be declines in philosophical understanding; but the historian of philosophy, unlike the cultural historian, is particularly interested in periods of advance.)

To write a problematic history is to write about philosophy in a philosophic manner. Unless the historian has a genuine interest in philosophy, he is unlikely to have a full understanding of what it is to be troubled by a philosophical problem and to try to find a solution to it. The philosopher writing the history of philosophy is, no doubt, likely to distort it, just because he has strong views of his own. But the pure historian with no philosophical enthusiasm is almost certain to compose a doxography; or else, in the manner of the cultural historian, to see philosophy as a social symptom rather than as an activity with its own traditions and its own standards of success and failure.

Bibliography

The following are English translations of histories mentioned in the text: *Of Sensation*, in George Malcolm Stratton, *Theophrastus and the Greek Physiological Psychology Before Aristotle* (London, 1917); Georg Wilhelm Friedrich Hegel, *Lectures on the History of Philosophy*, translated by E. S. Haldane and F. H. Simson (London, 1892–1896); Wilhelm Windelband, *A History of Philosophy*, translated by James H. Tufts (New York, 1893); Kuno Fischer, *History of Modern Philosophy: Descartes and His School*, translated by J. P. Gordy (London, 1887); Gottlieb Tennemann, *A Manual of the History of Philosophy*, translated by A. Johnson, revised by J. R. Morell (London, 1852), the best English source for Tennemann's *Grundriss der Geschichte der Philosophie* (3rd ed., Leipzig, 1820), a manual based on the *Geschichte*.

For an extensive bibliography, see Friedrich Ueberweg, *Grundriss der Geschichte der Philosophie*, 12th ed. (Berlin, 1926), Vol. I, pp. 1*–8*. Other histories include Geoffrey Stephen Kirk and John Earle Raven, *The Presocratic Philosophers* (Cambridge, 1957); Émile Bréhier, *Histoire de la philosophie*, Vol. I (Paris, 1926), introduction and Sec. 3, pp. 523–787, and the same author's "The Formation of Our History of Philosophy" in *Philosophy and History*, Raymond Klibansky and Herbert James Paton, eds. (Oxford, 1936), pp. 159–172.

For general discussions of the historiography of philosophy, see these works (listed in order of publication):
Robin George Collingwood, *An Autobiography* (Oxford, 1939); Étienne Gilson, *History of Philosophy and Philosophical Educa-*

tion (Milwaukee, 1948); W. von Leyden, "Philosophy and Its History," *PAS*, Vol. 54 (1954), 202–208; Émile Bréhier, "Comment Je comprends l'histoire de la philosophie," in *Etudes de philosophie antique* (Paris, 1955), pp. 1–9; Enrico Castelli and others, *De la Philosophie et l'histoire de la philosophie* (Paris, 1956); Paul Kristeller, "The Philosophical Significance of the History of Thought," in *Studies in Renaissance Thought and Letters* (Rome, 1956); Ladislas Tatarkiewicz, "The History of Philosophy and the Art of Writing It," *Diogenes*, No. 20 (Winter 1957), 52–67; Harold Robert Smart, *Philosophy and Its History* (La Salle, Ill., 1962); Leonard Nelson, "What Is the History of Philosophy?," *Ratio*, Vol. 4 (June 1962); John Arthur Passmore, "American Philosophical Scholarship," in the philosophy volume of the *Princeton Studies* (Princeton, N.J., 1964); articles by Eugene Kamenka, Maurice Mandelbaum, John Arthur Passmore, William Henry Walsh in *Philosophy and the History of Philosophy*, J. A. Passmore, ed., Supplement No. 5 to *History and Theory* (The Hague, 1964).

JOHN PASSMORE

PHILOSOPHY OF EDUCATION, HISTORY OF.

There was probably a time when human culture was transmitted spontaneously from one generation to another. The young of the species cannot survive to maturity unless they assimilate some beliefs about the world, some attitudes toward it, and some skill in solving the practical problems it presents; and the only source from which they can derive this minimal wisdom is the culture of their elders. The tendency to imitate offers a ready-made mechanism for inheritance, and in primitive communities, where benign surroundings allowed a leisurely and spontaneous association with children or where a harsh environment spared no time from the effort to keep soul and body together, the education of the young must have proceeded without much thought or care. In societies that were a little more advanced, the need for instruction in tribal ceremonies and the apprenticeship of sons to fathers and of daughters to mothers may have covered spontaneous education with a thin veil of deliberateness. Still, in uncivilized communities generally, culture must have been passed on without the agency of persons especially devoted to that purpose.

Through time, beliefs accumulate, attitudes grow more diversified, skills become more numerous and more complex. This increase in the volume of culture must have rendered obsolete the deliberate spontaneity of its transmission. Mastering what there was to know required special and enduring effort; teaching others to master it demanded more than a casual supervision of their lives. A culture thus enhanced could find lodgment only in a special class of persons—those who were able to encompass it. And this class—seers, priests, and scholars—must have become its chief dispenser to succeeding generations.

BEGINNINGS IN GREECE

There are two important consequences of the concentration of culture in the hands of a specialized class. Conscious of their possession, scholars naturally came to ask how it might be improved and purified; and this question led to the beginning of research. Second, because they were held responsible for instruction, both scholars and laymen came to expect that some good purpose should be served by their teaching—that it not only should preserve and extend culture but that teaching should serve some other purpose as well.

The earliest records show that the first of these effects, the beginning of research, began to appear in Europe near the beginning of the sixth century B.C. For a long time, no doubt, the learned had looked upon the things of sensory experience as irreducible constituents of the world and, relying upon ancient religious belief, had explained the origin and changes of those things by reference to the gods who presided over them. Now, however, a torrent of speculation deprived sensory things of their irreducible reality and the gods of their explanatory force. Water, pure matter, air, fire—each was advanced as the ultimate stuff of things by some. Other thinkers preferred a substance which possessed all the qualities of sensory things and that was broken into many small bits. Some regarded sensory things as nothing but atoms moving in the void; others resolved their hitherto independent reality into numbers or mathematical structures. And others, still, saw their independence disappear into the absolute unity which was the only reality. Almost all saw the things of ordinary sensory experience as resulting from natural forces working upon the elements or somehow breaking up the unity. The more ancient wisdom was improved by pointing out that the world was really something different from what it seemed to the senses and by disallowing any explanatory value to myth.

Sophists. The second effect of the concentration of culture, the desire to serve a higher purpose, began to appear about the middle of the fifth century B.C. The diversity of opinions concerning the nature of things, their origin and change, and related topics, led in some minds to a profound skepticism. Gorgias (c. 480–380 B.C.) argued that nothing exists; that if something did, no one could know it; and that if one could know it, he could communicate his knowledge to no one else. Protagoras (c. 490–c. 421 B.C.) held that man is the measure of all things. Each concluded that belief is properly an individual concern and that what is good and right is similarly dependent upon individual interests. They did not draw the conclusion that one might do as he pleased, however; they urged, rather, that conformity to custom and convention furthers the interest of the individual person more than flouting does. They and their fellow Sophists moved through the cities of Hellas, giving instruction in the practical arts, in the humane and literary subjects, in rhetoric, in law and politics, and in the more theoretical considerations out of which their natural and egoistic principles grew. They asked a fee for their instruction, and that procedure was an innovation. But an even greater novelty was their view of their own function as teachers—a view of the transmission of culture not for its own sake merely, or for *ad hoc* purposes, but in order to help their pupils achieve the comprehensive goal of a practically successful life at home, in the court, or in the legislative assembly.

Socrates. Socrates (c. 470–399 B.C.), to judge from Plato's presentation of him, was even more conscious of his mission as a teacher than were the Sophists. He shared their skepticism toward physical and cosmological theories, but unlike them he refused to leave unchallenged any dogmatic trust in conventional morality. In his hands rhetoric became dialectic; and in his teaching the purpose to which the pupils of the Sophists put the former—the persuasion of others to whatever view the speaker finds most useful—became the discovery of truth, in the dialectical search for which all barriers of personal prejudice and social dogma must give way. He was convinced that the human mind could discover the truth about the physical world and about the life of man in it, although he was equally certain that no one had yet achieved this knowledge. His mission as a teacher, he thought, was to free his pupil's mind from confusion and dogma in order that it should be able to find and recognize the truth—especially the truth about the good or virtue. Confusion and dogma would disappear upon examination of the unclear and unfounded ideas that constituted them. Thus, although Socrates' purpose was positive, his teaching often shows a primarily negative aspect. The skepticism and conventionality of the Sophists brought an objective of prudence to their education; but the skepticism and rationality of Socrates gave to his instruction the purpose of a life of virtue whose discovery required a clarification of the ideas involved in ordinary discourse.

Plato. Plato (427–347 B.C.), influenced by the Sophists as well as by the speculative scientists and metaphysicians and inspired by the instruction of Socrates, gave us the first fully developed philosophy of education—that is, the first explicit, philosophical justification of a theory of education. In his *Republic,* on the basis of observation, he ascribed to all human beings, but in varying degrees, three distinct abilities: the ability to reason, which seeks the good life, the ability for appetition, which is connected with the body and is somewhat wayward, and the ability to enforce the decisions of reason about what is good against the inclination of appetites. He ascribed to all states, on a similar basis, three functions: that of legislation, that of economic production and distribution, and that of armed enforcement of law and foreign policy.

Plato recommended that education be employed as the chief method of reforming both the individual's character and the state. In a just character each of the three abilities is exercised to the height of its power: reason recognizes what is good, the appetites freely conform, and the ability to enforce the decisions of reason assures that conformity. In a just state each adult citizen performs that function for which he is best fitted: the highly rational engage in legislation, the predominantly spirited (Plato's name for the ability to enforce reason's decisions about the good) enforce it, and the chiefly appetitive operate the economy. Justice consists in a harmony which results when each part of a thing performs the function proper to it and refrains from interfering with the function of any other part. Reform in individual character and in the state is movement toward personal and social justice.

A system of universal, compulsory, public education from birth to maturity ought to be instituted to bring about this individual and social improvement. All should be taught to read, to write, to count, to appreciate the traditional poetry and drama (highly censored for the young), and to engage in gymnastic exercise. Some should learn the military art, and others should study the sciences and dialectic—the search for the fundamental principle that explains all reality and value. Each student should be tested to discover which ability dominates his soul and should be sent into the state to perform the function appropriate to it when he reaches the limit of his develop-

ment, which the testing reveals. Thus, each class in the state would be recruited from those best fitted to perform its function. Such a system of education would produce individuals whose souls are as just as their abilities allow and a state whose parts or classes are similarly harmonious.

Plato's philosophical justification of his theory of education consists of three parts. First, he shows that the just state or republic and the just individual are good. For every class of things, there is a Form, or Idea, existing in a supernatural realm, resemblance to which determines the class. The resemblance between a member of the class and its Form is its goodness. The Form for the class of states is that pattern into which the three constituent classes fall when each performs its proper function. The Form for the class of human beings is that pattern into which the parts of the soul fall when each is properly developed. Thus, insofar as a person is just, he is also good, for he resembles the Form of humanity. And insofar as the state is just, it is also good, for it resembles the Form of states. The goodness of a just character and of a just state warrants Plato's recommending them to our efforts.

Besides this ethical support for his recommendations Plato provides a metaphysical explanation for the facts upon which he rests them—the facts of human nature and of society. Every particular falls into some class, and the class is made what it is by virtue of the Form copied by all the members of that class. If we ask, then, why every human being should possess the three abilities (reason, appetite, and spirit) and why every state should perform the three functions (legislation, economic production and distribution, and law enforcement), the answer is that they cannot fail to possess and perform them since exactly that is required by their Forms.

Plato's epistemology gives a third support to his theory of education. First, his contention that we can know only the Forms in their logical connections, coupled with the view that the entire realm of becoming is a copy of that of the Forms, leads to the conclusion that even though knowledge is not an infallible guide to the course of nature it is more useful than mere opinion. In this way he argues that knowledge is useful in the pursuit of justice. He holds, second, that the only method appropriate to acquiring knowledge is that of purely rational inference. Assuming that the method of learning is identical with that of discovering truth, he argues that instruction should follow the path of deduction wherever that is possible.

Plato's philosophy of education resembles in some respects the thought of the metaphysicians and physicists of the fifth and sixth centuries; with them it shares the faith that the human mind can achieve knowledge of what exists. It resembles the thought of the Sophists in its insistence that the world of ordinary sensory experience cannot be known. But of their reliance on conventional morality, it shows no trace at all. Rather, Plato shares with Socrates the conviction that virtue can be known and that it is the business of education to reform conventional morality in its direction.

Definition of "philosophy of education." Plato's work, especially in the *Republic,* serves as a paradigm of a definition of the phrase "philosophy of education." He sets forth an educational theory—that is, a view about the facts of human nature and society on which are based recommendations about the curriculum, the methods, and the administration of education, regarded as means to the ultimate goal of just and good citizens living in a just and good society. His ethical theory justifies this goal; his metaphysical theory supports the recommendations ancillary to the goal; and his epistemology explains the effectiveness of some of the teaching methods he advocates as well as our capacity to perceive truth generally. "Philosophy of education" means any body of thought like this one—any body of thought that includes a theory of education, an ethics that justifies the goal that the theory adopts, a metaphysics that explains the psychological and sociological parts of the theory of education, and an epistemology that explains why certain methods of teaching and learning are effective and demonstrates our ability to know the truth of any thought whatsoever.

Many philosophies of education do not contain reference to all the subjects with which Plato was concerned. Nonetheless, his reflections on education fix the meaning of the phrase by constituting a model, resemblance to which (at least to some degree and in some respect) allows any body of thought to be called philosophy of education.

Hellenistic thought. After Plato's work, nothing very novel was added to philosophy of education for some seven centuries. There is extant some work of Aristotle's (384–322 B.C.), but it is fragmentary and a part of a theory of education rather than a philosophical treatment of such a theory. Epicurus (341–270 B.C.) and his followers Zeno of Citium (336?–265? B.C.) and the Stoics advocated a tranquillity in life—the Epicureans through cultivation of quiet pleasures easily obtained, the Stoics through willing acceptance of the lot for which one is necessarily determined and (among the later members of the school) through a love for all mankind viewed as a brotherhood. But Epicureans and Stoics, as far as we know, themselves developed neither a theory nor a philosophy of education. In the first century A.D., Quintilian (c. 35–c. 95) published his *Institutio Oratoria* (*The Training of an Orator*). Quintilian recommends that in his training an orator be given appropriate objectives toward which he can direct his native but unformed impulses. The life of the orator, he dimly suggests, is good because it meets the Stoic requirements of indifference to external circumstance and utility to fellow citizens. His book harks back to the humanistic curriculum of the educator and orator Isocrates (436–338 B.C.) and to the Sophists. It was of much influence in later antiquity and again, after its rediscovery, on humanistic education in the Renaissance, but it embodies a theory of education rather than philosophical reflection upon education. Other authors, for example, Plutarch (c. A.D. 46–120) and Tertullian (c. 160–c. 220), comment on education, but not in a philosophical way.

Although the literature of the Hellenistic age shows little that is new in philosophy of education, two ideas of great importance for change in that philosophy were, nonetheless, gradually coming to dominate men's minds. One is the idea that a chief factor in the good life is obedience to law; the other, that a necessary ingredient in that same life is the happiness of a love that unites all those who obey the law as well as each of them to the lawgiver himself. The Christian ideal of the brotherhood of men

under God, their creator, is the expression these ideas assumed, and the movement of Christianity, although influenced by Plato, not to mention Plotinus (205–270), produced a new philosophy of education.

MIDDLE AGES

Augustine. The new philosophy is the work of St. Augustine (354–430). Human nature, according to his view, must be described in terms of substance and faculties influenced by historical forces. Every human being is a combination of body and soul; the soul possesses the faculties of knowing, feeling, and willing. The first enables us to know whatever we sense and remember to have sensed, certain abstract principles which the mind carries within itself, and the world of sensible things as they are ordered by those principles. The faculty of feeling enables us to desire and to feel emotions which center on desires. The faculty of willing enables us to choose from among differing desires those we want to realize—an ability which exercises itself freely and which, when exercised correctly, employs rules of choice that flow from divine commands.

Human nature cannot be accounted for in terms of substance and faculties alone, however. A historical force always determines how these faculties operate. Before the Fall, Adam and Eve used their faculties in the right way—especially their faculty of desire, directing its operation upon what they ought to desire, centering their love on God and on one another in communion with him, and choosing freely to obey his commands whenever the clamor of bodily appetite opposed itself to the right. But from their original sin, of which the Fall was a natural consequence, flows the force which determines their descendants to act as sinfully as they—to choose freely to disobey God's command by selecting egoistic and carnal desires for realization. Human nature must be painted in terms of substance and faculties corrupted by early events in human history.

Human society is constituted by the direction of the activities of its members toward a single goal, but, like the human soul, it cannot be understood merely in terms of this abstract function. The unity of purpose which in principle constitutes the family, the city, the empire, and the community of men and angels is disrupted by inherited self-seeking. Another historical force determines two other communities—the city of earth and the city of God—each of which is reflected in the four just mentioned. The advent of Christ signifies God's wish to enable men, despite their sinfulness, to merit salvation. The city of earth is made up of those who refuse to believe in Christ's mission and to repent; its members will not be saved. The city of God is composed of those who believe in that mission and feel genuine repentance; its members will enter upon eternal communion with God after the day of judgment.

The ultimate objective of education grows out of the corruption of human nature and God's concern over it. Like the ultimate objective of the church, that of education is conversion and repentance. On the elementary level the curriculum should be the seven liberal arts—a program of studies prefigured by Plato's curriculum; on the advanced level it should consist in philosophy and theology. The method appropriate to the lower level involves censorship and the prevention of idleness in order to stifle sinful desires. The liberal arts should be taught in an authoritative manner because not all who seek elementary instruction are sufficiently rational to know the truth and since no more than belief is required for salvation. On the higher level, authority gives way to proof since those who advance thus far are able to achieve knowledge. The liberal arts, coupled with religious worship and instruction, ensure correct belief about the nature and order of the universe and about God's relation to man; philosophy and theology show the more able—those destined for the hierarchy of the church—why those beliefs are true.

Augustine's philosophical reflections upon his theory of education stem from his conception of God. He advances, first, a theory of language according to which every word means what it names, and every sentence, the combination of things named by its component words. He concludes that since on this theory no one can tell someone else what he does not already know, each man must learn for himself by consulting things as they are illuminated in a light of divine origin. Teaching is not informing; it is reminding others or ourselves of the knowledge supplied by God.

Second, from the concept of God flows the justification of the objective of education. The goodness of each created thing consists in its resemblance to the idea held before God's mind as the pattern for its creation; this idea is its exemplar. The exemplar for men is the obedience to God's commands and love for him and for one another in him that gave perfection to life before the Fall. To be happy is to possess what one wants at the time of wanting it; since God is the only eternal thing, he is the only dependable object of desire. To be happy is to illustrate the exemplar for man, and conversion, the objective for education, consists in achieving that condition.

Augustine finds in God, also, a metaphysical explanation of human nature and society. In the first moment God created everything either in actuality or in potentiality. All history—each man's repentance or failure to repent, each society's deeds, both good and bad—is the unfolding of what was first merely potential; what happens is what must happen because of the initial creation and God's all-comprehending providence. Human nature and society must be corrupt; hence, conversion must be the ultimate purpose of education.

Later medieval thought. During the centuries that followed the death of Augustine the interest in another world came so to dominate men's minds that education diminished in importance, and reflection upon it very nearly ceased. Attention was centered on the otherworldly results of repentance or its failure at the expense of training for terrestrial existence; and so dogmatic was the assurance of the need for conversion that any effort to justify this objective appeared useless if not impious. The clergy, then Europe's teacher, offered a meager training to those working toward holy orders and some understanding of religious ritual to the laity. But the transmission of culture diminished greatly. The widespread acceptance of the otherworldly objective of education stifled philosophical reflection upon it. Comment on education is found in the writings of the Venerable Bede (673?–735), of Alcuin (735–804), and of Hrabanus Maurus in the early ninth century; but they are at most casual and at least unphilosophical. Thomas Aquinas (1224?–1274) devoted some systematic attention to the philosophy of education, but his chief contribution to it concerns not the objective of training but the nature of teaching—a discussion which continues the thought of Augustine on that subject.

Renaissance. With the Renaissance came a revival of interest in ancient learning and a recognition of value in terrestrial life. In accord with this change of outlook some writers assigned to education an egoistic and prudential purpose like that of the Sophists. Reformationist thought—at least in Luther's case—demanded universal, compulsory, state-controlled education in order that religion should be national and God's word available directly to all. Ignatius Loyola (1491–1556), through the Society of Jesus, established a widespread system of schools and universities; and in 1599 the society established a plan of education for them (*ratio studiorum*) that exercised much influence on Catholic education. But Reformationist and Counter-Reformationist literature reveals much more polemic and dogma than philosophical reflection upon education.

MODERN PERIOD

Comenius. In the seventeenth century, philosophical reflection upon education began anew, and its history from that time to the present is that of the gradual secularization and naturalization of the Christian objective assigned to education by Augustine. The work of John Amos Comenius (1592–1670) begins this process. (In particular, see his *The Great Didactic* and *The Way of Light*.)

Like Augustine, Comenius holds that human nature is corrupted by inherited sin, but he also asserts that it is capable of absolute perfection. The soul contains the possibilities of erudition (perfect knowledge), of virtue (adherence to the rules of right conduct), and of piety (love of God, the author of mankind). Like Augustine, Comenius viewed history as a decline from innocence, but he held, nonetheless, that there is a zigzag pattern in history, leading to an age of perfect terrestrial existence before the last judgment devoid of international strife and ruled over by Christ. In this last age the possibilities in the human soul realize themselves in perfect knowledge, virtue, and piety, and all societies unite in a single international brotherhood. The reward for striving after this perfection is immortal blessedness. Comenius held that a system of public, universal, state-supported schools, from childhood to maturity, should further the full actualization of the soul's possibilities and assist history toward its goal. The curriculum should constitute a cyclical development from the simple and abstract elements of science, art, language, literature, and religion to their complex and concrete forms. The methods of instruction should consist in the uniform application to the young of the human species of principles observed in the development of the young of other species, both plant and animal.

Comenius' philosophical reflection on his theory of education centers, like Augustine's, around the notion of God. God made man in his own image, and, because God is perfect, man may become so as well. To achieve perfect knowledge is to make perfectly clear to ourselves the things our sensations reveal and to order them according to innate principles which reason brings to light. To perfect conduct is to identify the rule of one's will with a command of God, and to perfect piety is to love God in one's obedience to him. Human nature and human history find a metaphysical explanation in divine providence, which manifests itself through the opposed forces of light and darkness. The business of education is to perfect men in the three ways mentioned. It also makes the personal life of each human being perfectly Christian and aids history in its progress toward final social perfection.

Locke. Late in the seventeenth century, not long after Comenius, John Locke (1632–1704) published *Some Thoughts Concerning Education.* In this book, in *An Essay Concerning Human Understanding*, and in *Second Treatise of Civil Government*, he carried further the secularization of the objective of education started by Comenius. With Augustine and Comenius, Locke held that man is free, but in opposition to them he denied that man is inherently sinful by virtue of his racial history. Each man is a mental substance joined to a bodily substance, as Augustine asserted; mental activity, however, can be described wholly without reference to substance, in terms of two faculties, understanding and will. The faculty of understanding enables man both to know and to desire, but what man knows is determined by the ideas his environment allows to enter his mind, and what he desires is determined by the objectives his environment supplies to a few native instincts. The second faculty is the will, and its exercise consists in choosing desires for realization where they conflict.

Society in the state of nature is based on a natural division of labor and on the need to care for offspring. In that state the original "common" of the world was largely transformed into private property, and the function of primitive society was to enforce natural law, or the law of God according to which private property ought to be respected. Disputes inevitably arose, and, since all men possessed the power to enforce the law of nature, they often could not be settled amicably. Political society came into existence as a guarantee against such disputes. It is based upon a contract or agreement between the community and others according to which each member of the community agrees not to exercise his power to enforce natural law provided that the others who constitute the government will exercise it for him. It follows that the exercise of governmental power is legitimate only where it protects private-property rights. A government of the kind instituted after the Glorious Revolution, having popular representation, Parliamentary determination of the sovereign, majority rule, and separation of legislative from executive power, Locke held, is best suited for achieving this objective because it can most efficiently check unnecessary governmental activity.

The purpose of education is to produce men who will advance the happiness of the community. They must be of good character and properly disposed toward learning. Good character consists in the habits of acting virtuously, prudently, and with good breeding. The proper disposition toward learning is not possession of it but an esteem for it and the habit of acquiring it when the need arises. These habits and dispositions can best be acquired by a tutorial education at home, by a method of pitting one instinctual desire against another in order to establish them, and by presentation of clear and distinct ideas to the pupil in the order and connection possessed by their objects. In both moral and intellectual training one should appeal to the interests of the child, bring him to learn for himself, and give public approbation to his success. The child who will benefit from such instruction and who will contribute to the happiness of the community is the son of landed gentry, who can look forward to a place in government. The poor should be given sufficient education to make them religious and self-supporting.

The production and maintenance of a good society is the chief objective of Locke's theory of education. Such a society is one in which men find pleasure or happiness in the performance of duty, and Locke's ethical reflection endeavors to justify this conception of the good life. Duty is obedience to natural law as embodied in civil law concerning the protection of private property. Like all moral principles, it can be known with certainty to be valid; it can be demonstrated from the ideas of God, of his creature man, and of the relation between them. The moral and intellectual training of the gentleman will cause him to find his pleasure in doing his duty; the exercise of this duty through government as well as through more informal social controls will spread a similar happiness throughout all levels of society.

Locke's theory of knowledge led him to conclude that we can be perfectly certain of any proposition whose truth we can intuit, demonstrate, or perceive through our senses or through our memory of such perception. Since the validity of duty can be demonstrated, we can know that it is right to perform it; and in this way, his emphasis on moral education is justified. Since the theory holds that we can know very little of the sensible world—only what we remember having perceived through our senses or are now perceiving through them—the de-emphasis of intellectual pursuits is also justified. We must accept many propositions about nature on faith or as merely probable; hence, we do not need to busy the heads of the young with any detailed consideration of them.

Rousseau. Jean-Jacques Rousseau (1712–1778) advanced three distinct philosophies of education; in the most influential of the three he varied the social theme found in Locke's thought. In his discussion of a new constitution for Poland he advocated a highly nationalistic program on the ground that where a nation's institutions are in good health, education should support and renew them. In *Émile*, he set forth a program appropriate to women, holding that their education should give them charm, ability for household management, and thoroughgoing dependence on their husbands in matters not pertaining to the home. But the major part of *Émile* deals with the education of gentlemen, embodies a theory of education that has exerted much influence upon educational practice, and assigns to education a social ideal quite as secular and political as Locke's but applied in an altogether different way.

Rousseau described human nature, as did Locke, as independent of historical influences and as initially perfectly innocent. A human being is a substance with faculties—those of pleasure and pain, of sense, of reason, of desire and emotion, and of will. These faculties emerge clearly at different stages in the life of the individual according to a general pattern, and the personality is more or less stable according as the newly emerged faculty is made to harmonize with the exercise of others already established. Despite the general pattern, each individual differs from others and must achieve stability through a procedure adapted to his own case.

In the early history of mankind there was no society. Men were independent and therefore equal. With improvement in techniques of hunting, fishing, and farming, they acquired property; with property, they acquired families, differentiation of economic function, interdependence, and inequality. As society became more complex, greed, ambition, and deliberate selfishness entered the soul; in time, men developed government and law in order to protect the property of the wealthy against one another's greed and against the greed of the poor. Inequality is fixed in the structure of eighteenth-century society and is due for removal by revolutionary action.

Rousseau presented detailed recommendations for educating gentlemen to live happily in these circumstances. They differ for each stage of development, but he urged that in all the child must learn for himself through personal observation of and active participation in the world of nature and society. A tutor who devotes his entire career to one pupil should attend to the pupil's individual interests and instruct him by rousing those interests into activity. The young man who completed this education would have enjoyed to the full each of the stages in his development and would be possessed of a strong body and stable mind. This stability would consist in his possessing no desire for whose realization he did not also possess the requisite power. It would make him neither learned nor urbane, but it would lead him to adopt a rural life in which he could survive the social storm Rousseau anticipated.

Rousseau advanced three criteria for knowledge: sensory experience of the consequences of action, the dictates of the heart, and practical utility. The first he transformed into a method of instruction—the method of letting the child experience for himself the consequences of acting upon his ideas in order to learn what is true about nature and society. The second he employed to warrant his inclusion in education of a considerable amount of simple religious doctrine. The third he relied upon to exclude from education a great deal of philosophy and other literature that he found devoid of practical consequence.

Rousseau's metaphysical reflection led him to hold that all of nature, including men's bodies and their actions, is governed by law but that since duty often requires one to act in ways other than those determined by this law, there is a supernatural realm in which duty presides. To act according to duty is to use the right rule for selecting one desire from among many as a basis for action, and since this selection and realization runs counter to nature, we must be exercising free will when we act rightly.

Rousseau's thought about morality concluded with the view that the good life is one in which there is neither the shallowness of desires that have been multiplied to match excess in power nor the discontent of an excess of power over desires but the happiness which occurs when power to fulfill desires equals the desires one harbors and is exercised to realize only those which are in accord with duty—a view not unlike Locke's. Duty Rousseau understood in terms of the general will. This is the welfare of the nation as opposed to the corporate will, or the welfare of a smaller group, and to the particular will, or the welfare of the individual.

It is our duty to act for the general will where that is possible. But in the major nations of Europe all institutions have been subverted to the service of corporate and particular wills. The social contract (which is, whatever the historical account of it may be, the agreement to act in accord with duty rather than for some lesser goal) has been betrayed by those in authority. Consequently, the ideal of duty cannot serve as the purpose of education generally. The realization or preservation of one's own will must be put in its place. In this way Rousseau justified the individualistic effort at internal peace that informs the theory of education with which he was most concerned.

Pestalozzi. The educational proposals of Heinrich Pestalozzi (1746–1827), unlike those of Rousseau, whom he greatly admired, bear no trace of direct revolutionary inclinations. But he had a warm sympathy for the downtrodden, and he advocated education for all as a condition of social reform. By his example and his books he contributed greatly to the common-school movement in Europe and America. The influence of Rousseau on his thought is evident chiefly in Pestalozzi's insistence on treating children in ways appropriate to the process of development through which they all must pass.

This process exhibits three stages. The contents of the child's mind are at first blurred and indistinct. Next, objects stand out in consciousness characterized by explicit forms and qualities. Last, these objects are understood as examples of general concepts; they are, to use Pestalozzi's word, defined. Throughout the process the person is himself active in securing and clarifying images and in transforming them into ideas that contain knowledge. Each child should be dealt with in accord with the place he occupies in this threefold process, and a major part of teaching consists in enabling him to work out for himself his own knowledge or definition of things.

Knowledge always contains three elements: the number of things known, the form they exhibit, and the language that embodies them. Pestalozzi concluded that learning must start with the elements into which each of these may be analyzed. The elements of number are units, and arithmetic (operations with units) must be mastered in order to understand number. Form Pestalozzi seems to have thought of as visual and tactual; its elements, consequently, are lines, angles, curves, etc. The student must understand these elements before he can understand form. The elements of language are ultimately letters, and the mastery of language depends on mastering their spoken and written forms.

Pestalozzi set forth detailed methods for teaching the elements of number, form, and language. They grew out of those he thought natural to a mother's dealings with her children. In the family situation a mother can know in what stage of development each of her children finds himself; she can teach him to count, to draw, etc., through use and observation of ordinary materials in the context of the economic employment, such as spinning and weaving, in which the family engages; and she can assure herself that he comes to perceive objects clearly and to define them for himself according as his stage of growth permits. These methods, directed toward enabling each child to acquire knowledge based on his own perception (*Anschauung*) of things, Pestalozzi thought could be employed in a school situation. The schools he operated in Switzerland, taking the Swiss village family as their model, attracted imitators from many parts of Europe and America.

Besides knowledge of things, teaching should bring children to a knowledge of skills which exhibit their physical or motor capacities as knowing does their intellectual abilities; and Pestalozzi thought that the performance of deeds could be analyzed into elements just as knowledge could. He was convinced that learning how to do things required the mastery of elementary motions, just as coming to know required the mastery of the elements of number, form, and language. The teaching of morality and religion—more important than that of knowledge and skill—involved transferring the child's feelings of dependence on the mother to other persons in society and to God. But Pestalozzi's treatment of the development of the motor and moral capacities is not so detailed and clear as his discussion of the education of the intellect although he insisted upon the inseparable unity of the three capacities.

The direct influence of Pestalozzi on philosophy of education is negligible. He was not interested in it. Still, his schools and his writings on the theory of education strongly influenced some who were.

Froebel. Pestalozzi's younger contemporary Friedrich Froebel (1782–1852) spent several years working in one of Pestalozzi's schools. Froebel was also much given to philosophical reflection, upon which, he thought, the theory and practice of schools depended—especially that of the kindergarten, which he invented almost singlehanded.

Froebel's speculations found the goal of education in the full and integrated development of all the powers of the individual and in the internal harmony, as well as the harmonious relations with society, nature, and God, that this development assures. This goal cannot be imposed upon the student; he must achieve it for himself through activities expressive of the powers he harbors. One who has accomplished the goal exhibits a steadiness and solidity of character that gives him integrity in all situations and the intellectual habits (not a store of remembered facts) that enable him to acquire knowledge when necessary.

The process by which this goal may be reached, the process of education, consists in the unfolding of what is present in infancy. Each person is like a plant, and as a plant develops toward a given stage of maturity, so the life of each human being consists in the filling out, through increase of varied detail, of a pattern present from the start. This process is also one of increasing clarity of self-expression and culminates in a clear consciousness of the self. The development of the individual is altogether con-

tinuous, and the stages of infancy, childhood, boyhood, youth, and maturity into which it is divided are characterized not by the emergence of novelties, as Rousseau had suggested, but by an increase of clarity in consciousness of the tendencies present in all.

Froebel worked out methods of education in accord with this view of individual development. The methods applicable in the earlier stages should merely enable spontaneous expression of the pupil's self; methods applicable to the later stages should supervise and direct that development. His treatment of the stage of childhood amounts to the nearly singlehanded invention of the kindergarten—an institution which spread quickly, especially throughout the United States. His treatment of boyhood involved considerable innovation in the methods, materials, and curriculum of elementary schools.

In the first stage, the infant should be nurtured and cared for. In the second, the senses and language develop, and the child's tendencies toward this development should be permitted free expression. Play is the most important method for this expression. Froebel invented various apparatus (called "gifts") to serve as educative toys; introduced activities (called "occupations"), such as drawing and clay modeling, which, along with the gifts, develop sense perception; emphasized song and spontaneous conversation to develop language and prescribed games, often played in a circle (to which figure he attached cosmic if obscure significance), to develop the sociality inherent in the child.

The stage of boyhood should be developed by instruction. The boy is becoming self-conscious; in order to develop steadiness of character, he should participate in the administration of the school through school government. The study of nature, stories, learning in groups, family work, making things—all these further steadiness of character and habits of intellectual readiness. Froebel insisted that instruction, the direction of development, should not aim at the practically useful but at that self-consciousness of integrated and developed powers which is the proper objective of individual and social evolution. About the stages of youth and maturity Froebel had little comment.

Froebel saw education—the early, spontaneous, and the later, but directed, unfolding of the essential powers of each individual—in a metaphysical setting, tinged with mysticism, obscurantism, and incoherence and indebted heavily to the absolute idealism of his day. The Absolute embraces everything and is continually evolving as force in nature and as mind in man. This cosmic evolution proceeds from action to reaction to equilibrium, from simple to complex, from unconsciousness to self-consciousness. Froebel identifies the Absolute with God and its evolution with his creation. Everything has a purpose that unifies it and that binds it into larger organic wholes, by virtue of evolution or creation. The evolution of the Absolute is reflected in miniature in that of humanity. The human race has developed through five stages, and the life of each individual reflects this racial and cosmic evolution. Education, Froebel thought, ought to enable this process to fulfill itself in each person without hindrance. It ought to be the minister to individuals of a cosmic and racial evolution.

The best life for man is the fullest realization of a consistent will—the consciousness of the best self that he can develop. This self-consciousness is awareness of purposes inherent in him; in becoming aware of them, man becomes free. Evil is the distortion by some external factor of a tendency native to the self; all tendencies are naturally good if allowed to develop into self-conscious, harmonious freedom. Although some education should direct, the fundamental early education is chiefly negative; that is, preventive of external obstruction to the development of natural tendencies.

Froebel's metaphysical and ethical doctrines inspired him to activity that had enormous practical effect upon the schools directly, and while the chief influence on his thought lies in the practical work of Pestalozzi, Kant influenced it indirectly, at least through the pervasive effect of his theories on German thought in general.

Kant. The impact on educational theory of the work of Pestalozzi and Froebel was an emphasis on developing individuality in the student, and this impact may be traced to the thought of Rousseau. In the work of Immanuel Kant (1724–1804) a greater optimism than Rousseau's gave a less individualistic objective to education.

Kant conceived of human nature in terms of three faculties: cognition, which organizes sensory elements into the orderly world of experience; desire, which exercises itself in an instinctive effort at lawless, egoistic domination over others; and will, which selects desires for realization according to a rule. Human society grows out of the exercise of these faculties. The instinctual desire for domination leads to conflict between individuals; the faculty of cognition yields knowledge about how this conflict can be avoided—by association in republics; and the will leads to actual societies of this kind for mutual protection. But between republics conflict breaks out anew; and in order to avoid it, these states tend to unite in a peaceful international community. This community is the natural result of the unimpeded development of human faculties; and since we must believe that all things develop their capacities fully, we must believe that it stands at the end of historical progress.

It is the ultimate objective of education not to advance the welfare of individual students, but to promote the realization of the peaceful international state as the embodiment of human perfection. Accordingly, teachers should not regard the economic or other success of their charges but should center attention upon the fullest possible development of their faculties. This development can be assured by supplying to the cognitive faculty the general truths it should use to organize sensory elements into nature as we experience it, by rigorously disciplining the faculty of desire in order to eliminate the instinct for lawless behavior, and by enabling the will freely to use the right rules in organizing the remaining desires. The result of such instruction will be a perfected character and intellect, which, through the progress of generations, will assist history to realize the educational ideal.

Kant's ethical theory supplies a criterion for the kind of conduct which makes the international state possible. It is conduct which embodies rules that can be generalized without absurdity—rules which fit into the famous "categorical imperative." "Break your promise when you wish to" is not such a rule; for if instead of applying it to your own desires alone, you try to imagine all persons using it in selecting some for realization, the notion of a promise completely disappears. The rule degenerates into the nonsensical "Break a promise which no one ever takes to be a promise when you wish to." "Always keep your promise" is a necessary moral rule, and like all rules which fit the categorical imperative it is so because we cannot imagine the generalization of its opposite without imagining something rationally absurd. In the international state the character of each person will be so perfected that each will act upon such a rule when it is necessary to make a moral choice. Thus, the state will be both realized and preserved. Kant's philosophy of morals, in this way, clarifies part of the notion of an ideal social order which education should subserve.

Kant's metaphysics makes a great deal of the distinction between two realms—the realm of things we can experience, or phenomena, and the realm of things which transcend experience, or noumena. Following Rousseau, Kant held that men dwell in both realms and that in the former their desires and actions are determined by natural laws, whereas in the latter they are governed by right rules or duties. To act rightly requires that a person freely employ a right rule and that he not act in a way determined by a law of nature. Hence, whenever one acts rightly he acts as a free citizen of the noumenal world—he freely applies a rule to his desires to decide which one to act upon. This proposition of Kant's ethical theory illumines his method of training the will; that is, his method of preventing the growth of habit and of requiring that children freely adopt a rule in some hypothetical situation of choice.

Kant's views about history provide a goal for his theory of education, and his ethical and metaphysical theories explain part of that ideal and the method proposed for arriving at it.

Fichte. Rousseau's despair of achieving the national welfare led him to advocate the cultivation of individual self-sufficiency; and while it was no part of their theories, the effect of the work of Pestalozzi and of Froebel was to further attention to the individual student in the practice of education. Kant's enthusiasm for international well-being led him to advocate a future achievement for the entire race through the fostering of universal faculties rather than through the development of individuality. Enthusiasm for national existence as opposed both to individuality and to internationalism brought Johann Gottlieb Fichte (1762–1814) to advocate an objective more like the one Rousseau would have recommended if he had been more hopeful about the national institutions of his day.

Addressing the German people during the subjection of Prussia to Napoleon, Fichte urged that education be used to unite all Germans in a state that, through purity of race and character, would lead the world. Education was the only independent action allowed by the French; if all German children were separated from their parents, reared in a partially self-governing community in which each individual might learn directly the responsibilities of citizenship, taught through the energizing force of interest rather than by reward and punishment, and thus prepared for an adult life of wholehearted and unswerving duty, this possibility of independent action could be turned to the advantage of all Germany. It would lead to the creation of a reformed and unified German state, devoted to the right, and worthy (unlike others) of world dominance. This nationalistic objective of his somewhat fanciful proposals Fichte might have supported by his view that the best state is highly authoritarian—one in which the fulfillment of each man's duty to work is made possible by the state's provision of the opportunity and compensation for work and the complete control of the economy required by that guarantee. This socialistic ideal, in turn, he might have supported by his view that the physical world must be understood as the means and medium by use of which and in which duty becomes embodied in fact. This view is consonant with his metaphysical idealism, according to which the ego posits itself and its objects for the purpose of doing what it ought—a position Fichte developed out of his criticism of Kant's doctrine concerning noumena.

Herbart. Like Fichte, Johann Friedrich Herbart (1776–1841) gave much thought to the doctrine of noumena; but unlike him, he arrived at a kind of realism, to be described later, opposed to the metaphysical idealism Fichte, Hegel, and others made current in the Germany of his day. He relied upon it to advance an objective of education which assigns importance both to individuality and to sociality—both to being a person of the best possible sort and to being a citizen of the best possible society.

There are five criteria, the "moral ideas," all of which must be exhibited by a person with the best possible character and a society of the best possible sort. Applied to a person, the first two of these ideas are relations between his will and other aspects of his character, while the last three are relations between his will and other persons. When one knows what he wills and approves of it, he is "inwardly free," and inward freedom is the only freedom men enjoy. When one's will is strong, directed toward many things, or "many-sided," and constituted by inclinations toward objectives systematically ordered by the teleological relations they bear to one another, he possesses "perfection." When one directs his will toward enabling the wills of others to be realized, for the sake of that realization rather than for his own benefit, he is "benevolent." The remaining two ideas apply not to wills alone but to the embodiment in action of one person's will with respect to others. When several persons deliberately live according to a principle or law, thus preventing conflict, each individual acts "rightly"; and when a person willfully benefits or harms another, the idea of "equity" or "requital" requires that a corresponding benefit or injury be visited upon the doer of the deed.

A society—a political state or group of any kind—to which the five moral ideas apply is one in which law prevails because of the general relinquishment of rights whose exercise leads to conflict; one in which there is a system of rewards which makes requital to each citizen for that relinquishment; one in which an administrative system exhibits benevolence by assuring to all the greatest satisfaction of will; one in which many interests or wills, both individual and collective, find coherent realization or perfection in a cultural system; and one in which the soci-ety, being "inwardly free," knows its own will and approves of it—a trait that requires a soul for society not unlike that of the individual person.

Assuming that if the individuals in a group acquire the moral ideas the group will also, Herbart holds that the immediate objective of education is to produce individuals who exhibit them; and the production of such persons consists in the appropriate use of truths of psychology. These truths describe the relations of ideas or representations, and Herbart is distinguished in the history of psychology as having been among the first to have endeavored to state those relations in a rigorous, mathematical way. He regarded the propositions of his psychology as based on introspection and as justified by metaphysical reflection. Released from its technical form, his psychology may be stated, in part, as follows.

Each idea, Herbart held, endeavors to preserve itself and succeeds in that endeavor to some degree, i.e., *is* itself, more or less. The degree of its success depends upon its relations to other ideas, and these are of three kinds: of opposition, of mere dissimilarity, and of similarity. Red and blue (not-red) are opposed to each other, and short of some third idea that combines them, such as the idea of a substance red on one surface and blue on another, they cannot both be present in the same consciousness. Red and circular are merely dissimilar; consequently, they may both present themselves either in combination in a red circle or in simple juxtaposition or may be present separately. A red rose and a red apple are similar ideas; consequently, one may come to be attached to the other. The effort of each idea to preserve itself—an effort which cannot be completely canceled—succeeds insofar as we are conscious of the idea. The greater the success, the greater is the clarity of our awareness of it; the less the success, the dimmer our consciousness of it. But the degree of the success of any idea depends upon the aid and attack it sustains from others; so that the clarity or obscurity of any idea—its place with respect to the threshold that separates conscious from unconscious ideas (a piece of psychological apparatus made current by Herbart)—depends upon the context of other ideas in which it occurs. Where they oppose it.and are stronger than it is, it disappears into unconsciousness and becomes an unconscious impulse, striving to emerge into consciousness the moment it is not prevented by the occurrence there of its stronger opposites. Where the context includes merely dissimilar ideas, it may remain in consciousness, but not for long. The flux of experience will soon bring ideas into consciousness that will drive it down into the dark through opposition or keep it in the light by uniting with it through similarity. Where other ideas are similar, they come to its aid, forming a strong union which, so long as it remains, draws to itself its similars, inward from new sensory perceptions and upward from the storehouse of unconscious old sensations. Such a union of ideas is an "apperceptive mass" or "circle of thought"—another piece of psychological apparatus Herbart helped to make current. The psychology upon which Herbart based his educational procedures informs us that new pieces of information can be mastered only insofar as they become united with some apperceptive mass of ideas and that insofar as they are not so united, they are transformed into unconscious strivings, able to present themselves to consciousness only when a lack of their opposites there allows it or the presence of their similars there draws them up into it.

A person consists of ideas that dwell on two levels. On the level of consciousness he is a succession of ideas, each of which originates either in physiological activity or in sensation and quickly unites with some apperceptive mass or is pressed down into unconsciousness by the success of others striving to occupy consciousness. On the level of unconsciousness are all the ideas whose weakness or whose lack of similarity to those in consciousness chains them in that dark domain. On the level of consciousness the succession of ideas is punctuated by acts of attention. These are simply ideas in which we are, more or less, completely "absorbed." Some, like loud sounds, are involuntary; others, like highly discriminated shades of color or purposefully held thoughts, are voluntary. As objects of attention these ideas are isolated, but they either quickly become unconscious or acquire "meaning" and connection by drawing up into consciousness those "circles of thought," or apperceptive masses of similar ideas, in whose context they acquire significance. An idea attended to much or clearly, together with its circle of thought, is an interest—a desire to bring into existence that which it represents in some future time. The apperceptive mass to which the idea belongs, together with the relations of that mass to others, presents a framework for its suppression, its mere entertainment, or its realization and makes it a desire rather than a free-floating fancy—a part of the person rather than a casual caprice. An act of will is a desire together with the intention that what it refers to should occur. The ego is the central point of the person—the present idea from which memories radiate into the past, interests (desires, acts of will, etc.) into the future, and to which entire apperceptive masses are drawn from the domain of the unconscious or forced down into it.

Ideas, thus arranged and centered, exhaust the person as an introspectible entity. They result from the exercise of no faculties (Herbart seems both to have used this concept and to have declared it nonsignificant), for the soul possesses none. To think of something, to desire it, to will it, to have a feeling toward it—all this is nothing but, in different ways, to be conscious of an idea as connected with others.

Herbart's view of the nature of a person provided him with a method of education which became widespread both in theory and in practice. Education, he held, is instruction, and instruction should consist in four steps. (His followers made them five, prefixing "preparation" for it to "presentation" of an idea.) First, the idea or information to be learned must be "presented" to the student's clear attention; second, the idea thus presented must be allowed to draw up from the student's unconsciousness all ideas whatsoever whose similarity attracts them to it; third, through comparison most of these associations should be eliminated in favor of those which give the idea its proper meaningfulness in a circle of thought; last, to strengthen the idea's bonds in that circle, the student should be brought to "apply" the idea to new situations. This procedure, based upon the flux of ideas from the center of atten-

tion into the apperceptive mass to which they belong, gives the student mastery over new information; and mastery, or the ability to reproduce ideas, is the purpose of instruction.

To instruct a person is to construct him; since feelings, desires, etc., are all ideas, providing the student with ideas is providing him with all the materials of personality. But the instructor, by arranging the conditions in which the student acquires new ideas, determines not merely the materials out of which he is formed but also the organization or form those materials assume. And a person, as we have seen, is simply ideas organized in a certain way.

But education is not merely the construction of a person; it is also the effort to construct one who exhibits the five moral ideas. Herbart refers to this aim as the production of "character," and he deals chiefly with the production of "perfection," or "many-sidedness." If the child's attention is called to many things in his own experience, and if the store of this experience is supplemented vicariously through communication with other persons—a communication based on sympathy with them—his interests will naturally become numerous, and by control of the natural mechanism of apperception, well organized and strong. Perfection of will or character, tinged with an inevitable individuality, is a necessary ingredient in the objective of education, but it is also essential to sensible choices in adult life.

Herbart advanced a metaphysical view as a ground for his psychology. Reality is neither mental, as the prevalent idealism held, nor physical in the sense of being extended in space and time. Its characteristics are quite unknowable except for those of being independent of our minds and composed of perfectly simple entities (*Realen*), not unlike the monads of Leibniz. These simple reals conflict with one another from time to time, and on such occasions, there occurs an effort on the part of each to preserve itself from destruction. In a body, this act of self-preservation is its state; in a soul, such an act of self-preservation is an idea that represents, so far as that is possible, the attacking entity. Being simple, the soul cannot engage in more than one act at once; hence the struggle of ideas against one another and the inevitable fall into unconsciousness or into the unity of some apperceptive mass.

The ethical theory by which Herbart justified the five moral ideas as the standard for personal and social existence is one which holds that moral judgments are a species of aesthetic judgments. As such, they neither need nor can be given justification. The human taste prefers persons and societies that live up well to the five ideas, but the validity of the standard by which they are measured is still nothing different in kind from the taste we enjoy for music, painting, and the natural landscape.

J. S. Mill. In determining the objective for education, John Stuart Mill (1806–1873) disregarded several distinctions emphasized by his predecessors. He ignored the distinction between national and international well-being, speaking of society without qualification, and he argued that individual and social interests might be identified. But his work resembles that of Herbart in some ways: He endeavored to make use of psychology to achieve his educational objective, and the psychology he employed, although it regarded the elements of the mind in a different way, attributed relations to them—those of association—not altogether unlike those Herbart thought he had found.

Mill conceived of a human being in terms of a body and mind, but although they occur in his thought he scarcely makes use of the ideas of substance and of faculty in understanding human nature. The body, with the help of external things, determines what our sensations are like, and it harbors physiological structures which cause us to find activities and things of certain kinds instinctually pleasant or painful. The mind is a series of sensations and ideas with attendant feelings and emotions, held together by connections of an associative kind. Conscious elements are connected in these ways when they have been associated in past experience in certain circumstances. Under these conditions, when one element recurs in consciousness it brings its associates with it. The conditions of association are never repeated from one person to another; hence, every human being is unique.

In his *Utilitarianism* Mill holds that the best society is one in which there is the greatest amount of happiness for the greatest number of people. He understands happiness as constituted by pleasure properly proportioned between higher and lower activities, individual self-realization, and fulfillment of duty.

The chief purpose of education is to bring men closer to this social ideal. Careful attention to the content of the curriculum can develop the proper proportion between higher and lower desires and consequently between higher and lower pleasures. The method of instruction can ensure individual self-realization by making room for free discussion and personal discovery of truth. The most difficult task is so to associate egoistic pleasures with fulfillment of duties as to connect them in all subsequent experience. The success of this effort will be a person who finds pleasure in doing what he ought even though doing so involves personal sacrifice. Compulsory elementary education for all and higher education for those who can benefit from it will go a long way toward a society in which happiness is at its maximum.

Mill supported his theory of education by providing a justification of the utilitarian ideal by a theory of meaning according to which free discussion of the consequences of our ideas is the best way to make their meaning clear and by a theory of knowledge according to which we can, by using his famous canons of empirical inquiry, come to be perfectly certain about the sequences of things in nature whose use enables the development of that type of character which will advance the good society.

Spencer. Herbert Spencer (1820–1903) advanced as the objective for education a life for the individual suffused with pleasure and as full as possible. Its fullness consists in the satisfaction of five kinds of interests, listed here in order of decreasing importance: those pertaining to one's own preservation directly, to it indirectly as does making one's living to begetting and rearing a family, to political and social affairs, and to aesthetic enjoyments. The only knowledge which enables the adequate satisfaction of these interests is scientific, and education of the intellect should be concerned to propagate it rather than knowledge

of the classics. Moral education should consist in allowing the natural consequences of mistakes to strengthen knowledge of how to satisfy these interests, and physical education should provide a body that would further their satisfaction. Each individual is charged with finding his own happiness, and the function of government should be merely that of preventing others from infringing upon his pursuit of it. Consequently, education itself should be privately sought and conducted rather than socially compelled and supported.

Spencer held the metaphysical view that reality is unknowable, that it manifests itself in the individual life as phenomena—some vivid and some faint—and that it is expressed in the cosmic dimension as evolution—as change from homogeneous to heterogeneous conditions through differentiation and integration. In evolution survival goes to the fittest; and the fittest are those who find the phenomenon of vivid pleasure associated with the useful and utility in those actions that bring about or constitute "complete living." Education should assist in realizing this end that, in any case, evolution marks out for man.

Dewey. In the work of John Dewey (1859–1952), the most influential of the twentieth-century philosophers of education, Mill's ideal for education is somewhat simplified and his doctrine of the meaning of ideas, together with Spencer's emphasis on the utility of knowledge, transformed into a criterion for distinguishing knowledge from belief. As we have seen, Mill thought that happiness consists of three distinct factors—pleasure, duty, and self-realization—and he held that education should promote the greatest amount of happiness for the largest number of people. In the place of pleasure Dewey put activity that is satisfactory to the person acting; in the place of duty, the most satisfactory activity; and in the place of self-realization, the fact that the most satisfactory activity is that which the individual most genuinely prefers. The best life, Dewey held, is one in which the most genuinely satisfactory activity is most widespread throughout society. This view depends on his view of human nature.

Human nature cannot be understood in terms of substance and faculty, for there are no such things. Consequently, there can be no single set of activities that characterize all human life, as traditional philosophers and psychologists have supposed. All human beings begin life as biological organisms, filled with unformed energy or impulse, ready to assume whatever direction experience assigns; and since each environment generates a different experience of the world—a different set of patterns of response to it—human beings vary as much as do their environments. The habits which impulse takes on sometimes cease to provide a satisfactory release for it, and in these situations intelligence enters into life to solve the problems thus created. We form hypotheses as to how impulses can be reorganized, look forward to the consequences in action, select those whose anticipation makes us prefer them, act to secure them, and thus test the hypothesis from which they were inferred. Intelligence is the master habit of readjusting others when they break down, and while it characterizes human beings, it does so in no specific way since its possession brings with it no special knowledge but only the ability to acquire any knowledge whatever by finding it in the consequences of action.

Dewey thought of society in terms of group habits. A nation is composed of political parties, religious institutions, courts, etc., and each of these is a complex habit of acting in which many people take part. A society is a set of group habits or institutions which fit together. A good society is one which, by virtue of the ways in which its subordinate institutions fit together, enables growth in satisfaction for its citizens.

Education, according to Dewey, is the process of imposing on the impulse of infants the society or the set of group habits into which the infants are born; it is the perpetuation of society. But it is also a good deal more. For since one of the habits to be imposed upon impulse is that of acting intelligently, education must also foster the reform of society toward an ever better condition. To perpetuate intelligence is to begin its use, and the schools are thus the basis for social progress.

Since there is no single set of abilities running throughout human nature, there is no single curriculum which all should undergo. Rather, the schools should teach everything that anyone is interested in learning. Since a child can learn nothing without using his intelligence, and since this comes into play only when some habit breaks down, he should be inspired with interest in the subject matter he should learn and then made to feel some problem in not actuating that interest or habit. This method requires individual attention to discover particular interests and capabilities. Since the child learns best when he is working with others, he should be given a certain measure of participation in school affairs. In the light of these strictures on curriculum, method, and administration Dewey hoped to produce a child highly endowed with intelligence and disposed to reform society in the direction of the ideal of continually growing satisfactions.

Dewey's ethical ideal was advanced as a justification for this pedagogical objective. To be morally good is to be a set of consequences, deliberately intended and capable of satisfying impulse better than would any other set to which it is preferred; it is a preferred activity. To say that such activity satisfies impulse better than does some other which is rejected is to say that it makes possible more satisfactions in oneself and others than does the other—that it contains the possibility of greater growth. Democracy is a better society than any other because it permits more satisfaction of impulse on the part of more people than does any other. And the intelligent person leads a better individual life than does one who acts from some other habit, such as superstition, because his life contains the opportunity for more satisfactions than does that of one who is hemmed in by dogma. The criterion of growth shows that the objective of education ought to be the democratic society and the intelligent man.

Dewey's theory of knowledge lends support to the reformist tendency in education. The truth of a proposition is its utility, and to know something is to be aware of how to use the known proposition to secure some desirable consequence. Consequently, any genuine teaching will result, if successful, in someone's knowing how to bring about a better condition of things than existed earlier. Knowledge is knowing how to do what is useful—a view that may have resulted from Dewey's consideration of Spencer and Mill. This theory of knowledge helps to give the pragmatic flavor to Dewey's philosophy of education.

Dewey's metaphysical reflection helps in the same direction. Traditional metaphysics, such as Plato's, has erred in supposing that truth is a passive apprehension of the real and that its object is eternally separated from the vicissitudes of experience. Traditional metaphysical reflection has forgotten that to mean something is to act to secure certain consequences, and it has therefore overlooked the truth that knowing what is real consists in meaning it or in acting in a certain way to bring about certain consequences. What is real is a set of experiences, each of which is meant by some agent and all of which are connected together in one thing or event by his activity. Dewey used this notion of what is real to justify his method of learning by doing, his view of the curriculum as whatever interests of each student enable him to organize into a unity on his own, and of method as the procedure for arousing interest in organizing or reorganizing the elements of a subject matter.

In Plato's philosophy of education the supernatural realm of the Forms, by lending validity to the just person and the just state, supported the program of education. In St. Augustine's work the educational ideal was organized wholly around God and the theological view of his relation to things; a similar description applies to Thomas Aquinas' thought about education. Comenius also centered his philosophy of education around religious and theological doctrines, but his insistence on the future perfection of human life on earth and on the observation of nature in the search for effective teaching methods marks a beginning in the process of naturalizing the wholehearted supernatural Christian ideal of his predecessors. Locke found a basis for the goal of education in God's will, but the national welfare, which God's law or the law of nature promotes, and the analysis of it partly in terms of pleasure are additional worldly conditions whose emphasis constitutes a different facet of the disintegration of the supernatural ideal. Rousseau held that God exists, but the chief justification of his objective for education—an internally peaceful life apart from society—lies not in God's having ordained it but in the notion of the general will and its absence from national institutions. Froebel, a follower of Pestalozzi and of Rousseau, made much use of religious language, but by identifying God and the Absolute he removed philosophy of education still further than did Rousseau from a religious center. Kant held that we cannot avoid belief in God, although he also held that the belief can have no experiential content; but this position effects his educational goal in no way. The chief moral component of that goal is the categorical imperative—a notion Kant wished to conceive wholly in logical terms. The peaceful international state is not justified by being God's will but by being the result of a social life which embodies duty and which constitutes the perfect realization of our intellectual and moral powers. Fichte found the ideal for education in a national existence that would assure Germany of a position of world importance, and Herbart held that individuals and societies that are morally worthwhile are those that satisfy the aesthetic demands of human beings. Spencer made no use of religious propositions in his philosophy of education; nor did Mill, although he regarded great religions as great works of the imagination. Dewey's ideal of a society, containing the possibility of most growth in satisfaction, is completely devoid of religious affiliation. He would probably have said that interest in achieving it can become religious—that, indeed, it should—but by "religious" he would have meant little more than enthusiastic.

The history of philosophy of education reflects a movement evident in other phases of thought—a successive contribution on the part of antiquity to the Christian ideal for transmitting culture from one generation to another and then a gradual elimination from that ideal of supernatural and Christian elements. Of course, at no time has there been a wholehearted and single-minded devotion to any ideal, and there are many who do not accept naturalism today. Nonetheless, one way of understanding the history of philosophy of education is to regard the attitude of philosophers toward the justification and explanation of educational theory as having been expressed first in Plato's classic supernaturalism, next in Augustine's Christian supernaturalism, and then as undergoing a gradual alteration into the wholly non-Christian and naturalistic view represented by John Dewey.

(See Education, Philosophy of, in Index for articles on figures who have made notable contributions to the philosophy of education.)

Bibliography

INDIVIDUAL WORKS

Augustine, "The Teacher," in Johannes Quasten and Joseph C. Plumpe, eds., *Ancient Christian Writers; The Works of the Fathers in Translation,* Vol. XI. *Greatness of the Soul [and] The Teacher.* Westminster, Md., 1950.

Augustine, "De Ordine," *ibid.,* Vol. V, *Lord's Sermon on the Mount.* Westminster, Md., 1950.

Comenius, John Amos, *The Great Didactic,* translated by M. W. Keatinge. London, 1896.

Comenius, John Amos, *The Way of Light,* translated by E. T. Campagnac. London, 1938.

Dewey, John, *Democracy and Education.* New York, 1916.

Fichte, Johann Gottlieb, *Addresses to the German Nation,* translated by R. H. Jones and G. H. Turnbull. Liverpool, 1922.

Froebel, Friedrich, *The Education of Man,* translated by W. N. Hailmann. New York, 1887.

Herbart, Johann Friedrich, *Science of Education, Its General Principles Deduced From Its Aim,* translated by Henry M. Felkin and Emmie Felkin. Boston, 1893.

Herbart, Johann Friedrich, *A Text-book in Psychology,* translated by Margaret K. Smith. New York, 1894.

Herbart, Johann Friedrich, *Outlines of Educational Doctrine,* translated by Alexis F. Lange. London, 1901.

Kant, Immanuel, "The Natural Principle of the Political Order Considered in Connection with the Idea of a Universal Cosmopolitan History," in *Kant's Principles of Politics,* edited and translated by W. Hastie. Edinburgh, 1891.

Kant, Immanuel, "Perpetual Peace," in *Kant's Principles of Politics,* edited by W. Hastie. Edinburgh, 1891.

Kant, Immanuel, "Lecture Notes on Pedagogy," in *The Educational Theory of Immanuel Kant,* edited and translated by Edward Franklin Buchner. Philadelphia, 1908. Also translated by Annette Churton as *Education.* Ann Arbor, Mich., 1960.

Locke, John, "Some Thoughts Concerning Education," in R. H. Quick, ed., *Locke on Education.* London, 1913.

Locke, John, *Second Treatise of Civil Government.*

Mill, John Stuart, "On Genius." *Monthly Repository,* Vol. 6 (1832), 649–659. Partly reprinted in Kingsley Price, *Education and Philosophical Thought.* Boston, 1962. Pp. 449–459.

Mill, John Stuart, *On Liberty.*

Mill, John Stuart, *Utilitarianism.*

Pestalozzi, Heinrich, *How Gertrude Teaches Her Children,* translated by L. E. Holland and F. C. Turner. London, 1894.

Plato, *Republic,* in *Dialogues of Plato,* translated by Benjamin Jowett, 4th ed. Oxford, 1953.

Quintilian, *Institutio Oratoria,* translated by H. E. Butler as *The Training of an Orator,* 4 vols. New York, 1920–1922. Loeb Classical Library.

Rousseau, Jean-Jacques, *A Discourse upon the Origin and Foundation of the Inequality Among Mankind.* London, 1761.

Rousseau, Jean-Jacques, "Considerations Concerning the Government of Poland and Its Projected Reform," edited and translated by Kingsley Price in Ch. IV of *Education and Philosophical Thought.* Boston, 1962.

Spencer, Herbert, *Education, Intellectual, Moral and Physical.* London, 1861; rev. ed., 1883.

HISTORICAL SURVEYS

Boyd, William, *The History of Western Education.* London, 1952.

Eby, Frederick, *The Development of Modern Education.* New York, 1952.

Laurie, S. S., *Studies in the History of Educational Opinion From the Renaissance.* London, 1905.

Windelband, Wilhelm, *A History of Philosophy,* translated by James H. Tufts. New York, 1950.

CONTEMPORARY LITERATURE

Adler, Mortimer J., and Mayer, Milton, *The Revolution in Education.* Chicago, 1958.

Bode, Boyd Henry, *Progressive Education at the Crossroads.* New York and Chicago, 1938.

Brameld, Theodore Burghard Hurt, *Patterns of Educational Philosophy; A Democratic Interpretation.* New York, 1950.

Broudy, Harry S., *Building a Philosophy of Education,* 2d ed. Englewood Cliffs, N.J., 1961.

Brubacher, John S., *Modern Philosophies of Education.* New York, 1939; 3d ed., 1963.

Dewey, John, *Experience and Education.* New York, 1938.

Henry, Nelson B., ed., *National Society for the Study of Education Forty-first Yearbook.* Chicago, 1941. Pt. I, *Philosophies of Education.*

Henry, Nelson B., ed., *National Society for the Study of Education Fifty-fourth Yearbook.* Chicago, 1955. Pt. I, *Modern Philosophies and Education.*

Hutchins, Robert M., *Education for Freedom.* Baton Rouge, La., 1943.

Kilpatrick, W. H., *The Philosophy of Education.* New York, 1951.

Maritain, Jacques, *Education at the Crossroads.* New Haven, 1943.

Morris, Van Cleve, *Existentialism in Education; What It Means.* New York, 1966.

Nunn, Thomas Percy, *Education: Its Data and First Principles,* 3d ed., rev. New York and London, 1962.

O'Connor, D. J., *Introduction to the Philosophy of Education.* New York, 1957.

Peters, R. S., *Authority, Responsibility and Education.* London, 1959.

Phenix, Philip H., *Philosophy of Education.* New York, 1958.

Price, Kingsley, *Education and Philosophical Thought.* Boston, 1962.

Reid, L. A., *Philosophy and Education.* London, 1962.

Scheffler, Israel, *The Language of Education*. Springfield, Ill., 1960.

Smith, B. Othanel, and Ennis, Robert H., eds., *Language and Concepts in Education*. Chicago, 1961.

Ulich, Robert, *Philosophy of Education*. New York, 1961.

Walton, John, and Kuethe, James L., eds., *The Discipline of Education*. Madison, 1963.

KINGSLEY PRICE

PHILOSOPHY OF EDUCATION, INFLUENCE OF MODERN PSYCHOLOGY ON.

"All things are good as they come from the hands of their Creator, but everything degenerates in the hands of man." From this premise, which introduces *Émile*, Rousseau argues that two great advantages will accrue to teachers who engage in careful observation of rustic, unspoiled children: first, teachers will be able to devise effective means to ensure that children do what they ought to do, and, second, teachers will have a basis sounder than mere social convention for determining what children ought to do.

The title of this article could well fit a general treatise of what has occurred in educational thought and practice during the past two centuries, a period in which Rousseau's advice has been universally acknowledged as sound—and occasionally even followed. But the treatment here is narrowly restricted to two major developments in twentieth-century psychology—psychoanalysis and behaviorism—and to some practical and theoretical consequences of each.

PSYCHOANALYSIS

One learns to see in children what one has first seen in adults. In *The Sexual Enlightenment of Children* Freud wrote that "there must be a possibility of observing in the child at first hand and in all the freshness of life the sexual impulses and conative tendencies which we dig out so laboriously from amongst their own débris in the adult—especially as it is also our belief that they are the common property of all men." Despite certain technical difficulties in the analysis of children, Freud's "possibility" became an oft-repeated actuality in the work of Anna Freud, Melanie Klein, Susan Isaacs, and many others. Careful observation of children in the clinic and in the experimental school provided both confirmation and correction of Freud's theories of infantile sexuality.

It was recognized from the very beginning that education and psychoanalysis were in practice inseparable. On one hand, psychoanalysis is itself an educational endeavor. Freud's often-quoted formula *analysis replaces repression by condemnation* states the matter succinctly. For condemnation is a rational activity; learning to condemn what we ought to condemn and to praise what we ought to praise is, as Aristotle recognized, the very heart of moral education. There may be useful divisions of labor among analyst, parent, and teacher, but each assists the same process.

On the other hand, psychoanalysis forces educators to recognize that there are dynamic (that is, libido-driven) psychological processes in even the most austere intellectual training. In schools, efforts to take these dynamic processes into account were of two sorts: between the two world wars the major tendency was toward the establishment of quite radical new schools, since then the major effect has been the penetration of psychoanalytic ideas and techniques into the "regular" schools.

According to Bertrand Russell (1916), the school is an agency for the inculcation of "creeds that hold men together in fighting organizations: Churches, States, political parties." On that view one could not expect religiously or politically regulated schools to direct their teaching at intellectual and emotional freedom. If one regards the sexual and political enlightenment of children as the prime duty of education, then one must get outside the ordinary school system to engage in education. Russell's own Beacon Hill School (1927–1934, continued by Dora Russell until 1943) was one such effort. Although Russell accepted the basic premises of psychoanalysis, Beacon Hill was not a therapeutic center for disturbed children. Rather, its purpose was to establish for children conditions of absolute intellectual honesty and the maximum possible degree of personal freedom, so that the dynamic processes of development could occur with a minimum of crippling aftereffects.

A. S. Neill's educational thought was deeply influenced by psychoanalysis, but, like Russell, he resisted making clinical, analytical techniques the central teaching procedures of his school, concentrating instead on making freedom the normal condition of life. Neill's unique contribution during the more than forty years of the Summerhill school's existence since its founding in 1921 has been just that: he has proved that it is possible for normal children and even for rather seriously disturbed children to live in freedom, particularly in matters concerned with psychosexual development. Children who are self-regulated can engage in masturbation and other forms of sexual behavior without guilt and repression; hence, they are unlikely to require the clinical services of psychoanalysts when they reach adulthood.

Neill proved himself not only a practical genius who succeeded (where Russell had failed) in keeping his school alive in a hostile environment but also a clear and forceful writer. In the sizable corpus of works by Neill we recognize how deeply he was influenced by the literature of psychoanalysis (for example, by Wilhelm Reich, from whom he borrowed the concept of self-regulation); we can also see how Neill's own beliefs changed—grew and atrophied, some ideas becoming stronger and more ramified while others dropped away—as he reflected at different times on his unique experiences as teacher and therapist. Homer Lane, Neill's mentor and analyst, lacked his pupil's capacity for clear and forceful writing. Lane's own extraordinary genius in teaching intractable youth and "re-educating" neurotic adults is scarcely explained by his ideas, which seem an astonishing mélange of Freud, the New Testament, and Rousseau. Perhaps his success followed more from faith than from reason: Lane could write, "Human nature is inherently good," despite the cruel and inhumane treatment he received from British authority.

Between the two world wars many schools were founded on more or less psychoanalytic principles and with varying degrees of success. The Children's School, now the Walden School, established in 1915 by Margaret Naumburg in New York was an early and for a time justly famed center for psychoanalytically based educational methods in the United States, although its being a day school lessened its ability to provide a total environment of honesty and freedom for its pupils. Schools devoted to psychoanalytic principles were to be found throughout Europe (for example, the Malting House School in England, the Kinderheim Baumgarten in Berlin). But appropriately enough it was in pre-Nazi Vienna that a deliberate attempt was first made to disseminate the effects of psychoanalytic pedagogy from the radically experimental situation to the "regular" schools. Later, Anna Freud brought her methods and message to London, where they have had a beneficent albeit limited effect on English education.

Since the end of World War II, psychoanalytic modes of speech and thought have lost their power to shock and (perhaps therefore) their power to stimulate radically new educational activities. Psychoanalysis has merged with a general latitudinarianism in sexual affairs. A general extension of sensibility has made children, with their sexual needs and desires, visible as human beings; psychoanalysis has been caught up, perhaps submerged, in that general movement. The "regular" schools of most nations are as devoted to economic and military purposes today as they were in 1916. Such schools are generally conducted on the assumption that children and adolescents are sexless creatures, but other "secular" agencies of education—particularly the mass arts and advertising—have learned certain practical lessons of psychoanalysis only too well.

Foundations of moral education. Freud's basic conservatism in morals and politics was continued by most of his pedagogical followers. But in theory psychoanalysis put in jeopardy the basic moral and political principles that schools were designed to transmit to children. The radically experimental schools could simply ignore those principles: for example, at Summerhill, if children learn to be loving toward other people, Neill is quite happy to leave their moral and political beliefs alone. But as Otto Rank pointed out, the psychoanalytic pedagogue, with his devotion to science, must have rationally defensible principles for authority, responsibility, obligation, and other restraints on behavior. Yet comparative psychoanalytic studies show that all societies use irrational repressions as the basis for social control, and if the psychoanalytic teacher rejects the use of repression, guilt, and shame (that is, rejects the use of destructively channeled libidinal energy) to control human action, then the teacher must offer some effective and rationally defensible substitute. Exaltation of love, self-regulation, and freedom will not suffice.

As R. S. Peters remarked in *Authority, Responsibility and Education*, ". . . in Freud there is no positive theory of the development of the ego," and despite the great growth of "ego psychology" and "cognitive studies," very little theoretical work since Freud really bears on the problem of establishing a psychoanalytic basis for moral education. An important reason for this neglect is that an adequate theory of moral education must have its foundations in politics as well as in psychology, but most psychoanalyti-

cally inclined educators are distrustful of and disgusted by politics. Thus, Erich Fromm and Paul Goodman, the latter clearly the major voice of educational protest today, can offer only an uncritical communitarianism as the political foundation for their moral education.

A practical consequence of such philosophical neglect is the current crisis in school counseling and guidance. This rapidly expanding field is manned by persons who have engaged in at least the academic study of psychoanalytic thought; it is their professional duty to be aware that there are dynamic, psychosexual forces in the lives of children and adolescents, even though they have neither the time nor the training to discover the precise nature of these forces in each of the youngsters who pass hurriedly through their offices. It is the guidance counselor, with his allegiance to the traditions of psychoanalysis, who has increasingly become responsible for upholding the school's conceptions of authority, responsibility, merit, and worth—conceptions he can neither reconcile with the more enlightened views derived from psychoanalysis nor replace with others he knows to be rationally defensible. He becomes the unwilling, unhappy agent of a system designed, as Freud said, to make life easy for adults, not healthy for children. His problem is essentially one of theory.

The dynamics of learning. As Socrates made clear in the *Symposium*, all learning that is really worthwhile begins with Eros. But that little god is notoriously irresponsible; he may lead one up the ladder to knowledge of the Good or he may leave one fixated with some quite primitive obsession. Again, Rank pointed out the unresolved theoretical question for psychoanalysis: Education *of* the sexual drives or education *by means of* sexual drives?

Is sexual enlightenment merely one particularly interesting instance of a general intellectual honesty in dealing with children? Or is sexual preoccupation the primordial matrix from which all curiosity and all energy for intellectual pursuits must be derived?

Psychoanalytic theory relies on the relatively undeveloped concept of "sublimation" to account for the general displacement of energy into intellectual as well as into other socially approved, productive endeavors. Interest in or curiosity about specific intellectual affairs is accounted for by appeal to particular facts in the psychosexual development of the individual. But the theory is deficient in filling in the rungs of Plato's ladder; thus, we do not know how to use Eros' energy to lead youngsters from the desire for objects to the desire for knowledge. Psychoanalytic theory has explained how sex should be studied, but it has not made clear how, or even whether, all intellectual study can be infused with sexual energy.

One consequence of this hiatus in theory has been to render the concept of "motivation" almost meaningless. The basic idea is simple common sense: it is preferable that learners not be forced to engage in study but rather that they do so because the activities of learning accord with their interests and needs. However, since regular schools cannot acknowledge that sexual interests and needs exist, it is rather futile to exhort teachers to motivate their students' learning.

Little of practical value on this question has come from

experimental schools; Neill was frankly uninterested in pedagogy, holding that a self-regulated child could and would learn, academically speaking, when and as he needed to learn. Susan Isaacs made very careful observations of the intellectual processes in children's learning, but she never tied together her study of sociosexual development and her study of intellectual growth. Presently fashionable pedagogical theory by and large answers the question of motivation by ignoring it.

Also requiring the insights of psychoanalysis is the question of transference and its role in intellectual growth. It appears that certain of the mechanical aspects of teaching can now be done, appropriately, by machines. This opens the possibility that the teacher–student relationship may become more personal and more humane than it ordinarily is when teachers are preoccupied with routine tasks. But just how are we to understand this relationship? What are its dynamics? How can it be used to accomplish intellectual or academic purposes? Can it be "used" at all without destroying the possibility of a genuinely personal and humane encounter between a more mature and a less mature human being?

Analogues to these fundamental questions for a philosophy of education have received detailed and continuing attention in the literature of psychoanalysis, where the relation of therapist and client is of central concern. The concept of transference as refined by study and debate seems to have great importance for understanding the teacher–student relationship, but to date little has been done to bring psychoanalytic insights to bear on the educational situation.

The future of psychoanalytic thought in educational philosophy is hard to foresee. Despite the inherent drift toward syncretism in all educational thought, psychoanalytic doctrines have never been domesticated as merely another element in "progressivism." Insofar as philosophy of education is concerned with the standard questions of pedagogy, even when these are given quite radical answers as in the works of John Dewey, it cannot adequately reconcile itself to those psychoanalytic thinkers who question the seriousness—that is, the reality—of the entire enterprise of pedagogy. A climate of concern for clear ideas and radical experimentation is requisite for a genuine synthesis of psychoanalytic thought and other streams in philosophy of education. But such a climate is not apparent in reliable forecasts for American education.

BEHAVIORISM

Until quite recently, the influence of behavioristic psychology on education was to foster conservatism in politics, callousness in pedagogy, and absurdity in philosophy. A particularly blatant case of the last was the doctrine of connectionism: an attempt to account for all human learning as a variant of reflex conditioning as in Pavlov's dogs, accompanied by a neurophysiological explanation that was pure myth. So long as such scientism dominated the language and literature of education, serious philosophical treatment of such educational concepts as "learning," "teaching," "thinking," and "practicing" was clearly impossible.

Today, however, philosophy of education is forced to take account of a rather more sophisticated behaviorism. In the realm of practice the new behaviorism has produced effective devices for teaching; decisions about how and whether to use these devices raise moral and philosophical questions of considerable depth and delicacy. In the realm of theory this behaviorism forces a particularly contemporary formulation of many of the traditional questions of philosophy of education—for example, Can virtue be taught?—formulations which philosophers cannot afford to ignore. In both realms B. F. Skinner's name must appear at the head of any list of contributors to the new behaviorism.

Programmed instruction and moral issues. In one of Skinner's first papers on education ("The Science of Learning and the Art of Teaching," 1954), he made the point that so long as no clear connection between ends and means had been demonstrated in education, one could talk about ends in quite lofty terms although the actual work of the teacher remained menial and ineffective. The practical behavioristic psychologist asks that the ends or goals of education be formulated as specific acts that one wishes the learner to be able to perform at the conclusion of the teaching sequence. The psychologist will then survey the present repertoire of knowledge and skills possessed by the learner and design a sequence of learning acts ("frames") that will move the learner from his present state to the desired state. In principle these "frames" can be automated; in practice a teacher is often necessary, but even so the teacher is performing a purely mechanical task.

In much of the outcry against the use of "teaching machines" one can hear the squeal of threatened vested interest. Nevertheless, genuine moral issues are raised by this way of looking at education, issues that were concealed so long as high "moral" aims could be propounded in a context quite apart from detailed, step-by-step planning of means to achieve them. For as the psychologist forces us to ask precisely what behavioral goals we seek to achieve, he also makes us ask whether an educational (as opposed to a training) endeavor can have precise, behavioral goals. Can a statement of aims be precise but not behavioral? Or vice versa? Apart from precise or behavioral goals, is it possible to talk rationally and responsibly about what we intend to do and what we ought to do in educational practice?

The new behaviorism has forced philosophers of education to try to find some solution to the paradox of educational freedom: All would agree that education ought to contribute to the freedom of those being educated; however, unless this "ought" can be translated into clear terms of educational goals and procedures, it remains merely empty talk. But if the idea of freedom is translated into precise descriptions of how the learner is to behave and how teaching will ensure that he does so, then how can education be said to contribute to his freedom? As someone once put it, education is that human enterprise which is necessarily either useless or immoral.

The above questions are of immediate practical import, for as second-generation, computer-based teaching machines become available—a development now accelerated by federal subsidy and heavy corporate investment—

responsible policy decisions must be made about their use. Philosophers of education who could contribute a certain subtlety and sensitivity to these decisions will find that they need to know a great deal about programming, both computer and curriculum. Since an integration of the science and philosophy of education is desirable on many grounds, this demand on philosophers of education may be counted among the beneficent consequences of the new behaviorism.

The education of personal feelings. The dynamics of love and hate among human beings and the quality of the inner life would surely be regarded by philosophers as being among the most significant topics to be considered in any discussion of education. The new behaviorism seems to question this consensus in the most radical way possible: by denying that love and hate are really basic human feelings and by denying that the inner, mental life exists. These denials may be more apparent than real—or they may be just as real as they seem.

Is Skinner's translation of "I love you" into "I find you positively reinforcing" merely the introduction of a new linguistic convention? Or is this a clear case of reductionism in the pejorative sense? Note that the new behaviorism does not simply deny that men and women love and hate; such a denial could be ignored as absurd. But to translate love and hate into the language of behaviorism means that these feelings are not basic, not given in human nature, as it were, but acquired, like any other behavioral tendency, by operant conditioning. Serious, patient work by philosophers of education is necessary in order to separate the questions of what in fact can or cannot be taught by operant conditioning from the linguistic questions of what we mean when we say that we love and hate, and more important, that we ought to love and ought not to hate.

The same line of argument applies to the behaviorists' denial of a private mental life. There is the patently absurd denial that human beings think, imagine, envision, and so forth. There is the sophisticated doctrine that everything one legitimately wants to say about such mental events can be said in (purely) behavioral terms. At a superficial level, educators are quick to adopt the attitude of behaviorism: it lends an air of science to their work, and it emphasizes the public character of their goals and procedures. But few have thought how limiting the language of behaviorism is. Is there anything meaningful that a teacher might want to say about his effect on the mind of a child that he could not say in the language of behaviorism? Assuming a negative answer can be sustained, the next question becomes What morally significant purpose can the teacher have to affect the mental life of his student, unless that mental life manifests itself in behavior? The argument concludes that what cannot be said in the language of behaviorism is of no concern in education. Thus, however paradoxical this may at first appear, behaviorism clearly becomes a safeguard for privacy: the private thoughts and feelings of students are protected from the teachers' purview. In an age which has seen the school take on a frighteningly totalitarian character in its dealings with children, the limitations which behaviorism places on educational ends are to be counted in its favor, as is the effectiveness of behavioristic tech-

niques in achieving those ends. Skinner's arguments need to be removed from the context of his polemical novel, *Walden Two*, and treated with serious philosophical criticism.

Psychoanalysis has made an impact on philosophy of education in practice as well as in theory. The most radical and experimental schools of the century have been guided by psychoanalytic concepts, aiming in the main to provide an environment of freedom and honesty in which children may escape the psychic distortions that produce neuroses in adults. There have been many efforts to apply similar ideas in the regular schools of many Western nations, but because these schools were founded to serve quite different political and religious purposes, their rules do not easily admit the introduction of psychoanalytic ideas and practices.

On the other hand, the new behaviorism has provided findings which are of immediate practical value for schooling, but it has also raised some basic philosophical questions in new and interesting ways. Skinner is as much involved in ethics as in psychology; the serious question is whether anyone speaking the language of behaviorism exclusively can be as competent in ethics as in psychology.

In any event, philosophy must continue to serve as a conscience to education in the tradition of Rousseau: not only must a child be educated, he must also be protected from "education." The impact of behaviorism and the impact of psychoanalysis are sometimes antithetical, but philosophy of education must be sensitive to both.

Bibliography

Ekstein, Rudolf, and Motto, Rocco L., "Psychoanalysis and Education: A Reappraisal." *Psychoanalytic Review*, Vol. 51, No. 4 (1964–1965), 569–582. Extensive textual references.

Freud, Anna, *Psychoanalysis for Teachers and Parents*. New York, 1935.

Freud, Anna, *The Psycho-analytical Treatment of Children*. London, 1946. The major lectures delivered first in German in 1926.

Freud, Sigmund, *The Sexual Enlightenment of Children*. New York, 1963. Contains several papers written between 1907 and 1913, including the classic "Phobia in a Five-year-old Boy."

Fromm, Erich, *The Sane Society*. New York, 1955.

Goodman, Paul, *Growing Up Absurd*. New York, 1960.

Hook, Sidney, ed., *Dimensions of Mind: A Symposium*. New York, 1960.

Isaacs, Susan, *Intellectual Growth in Young Children*. New York, 1930.

Isaacs, Susan, *Social Development in Young Children*. New York, 1933.

Komisar, B. Paul, and Macmillan, C. J. B., eds., *Psychological Concepts in Education*. Chicago, 1966. Extensive textual references.

Lane, Homer, *Talks to Parents and Teachers*. New York, 1949. Contains practically all Lane's writings: several chapters from an unfinished manuscript left by Lane when he died in 1925 and some transcribed notes from lectures given in London between 1917 and 1921. The preface is by Neill; a brief account of Lane's tragic life is provided by Dr. A. A. David, bishop of Liverpool.

Neill, A. S., *That Dreadful School*. London, 1937.

Neill, A. S., *The Problem Teacher*. London, 1939.

Neill, A. S., *Hearts Not Heads in the School*. London, 1945.

Park, Joe, *Bertrand Russell on Education*. Columbus, 1963. Excellent bibliography of Russell's educational writings. Also contains an objective account of the Beacon Hill School.

Peters, R. S., *Authority, Responsibility and Education*. London, 1959.

Prescott, Daniel A., *The Child in the Educative Process*. New York, 1957. Excellent bibliography of the child-study movement.

Rank, Otto, *Modern Education*. New York, 1932.

Reich, Wilhelm, *The Sexual Revolution*, translated by T. P. Wolfe. New York, 1945.

Reich, Wilhelm, *Der sexuelle Kampf der Jugend*. Berlin, 1932.

Rogers, Carl R., "Significant Learning: In Therapy and in Education." *Educational Leadership*, Vol. 16, No. 4 (January 1959), 232–249.

Russell, Bertrand, *Education and the Good Life*. New York, 1926.

Russell, Bertrand, *Why Men Fight*. New York, 1916.

Schofield, William, *Psychotherapy: The Purchase of Friendship*. Englewood Cliffs, N.J., 1964.

Skinner, B. F., *Cumulative Record*. New York, 1961. Contains a wide assortment of papers in both technical psychology and in educational theory, including the influential 1954 essay "The Science of Learning and the Art of Teaching."

Skinner, B. F., *Walden Two*. New York, 1948.

JAMES E. MCCLELLAN, JR.

PHILOSOPHY OF HISTORY. Two different but related branches of philosophical inquiry are commonly referred to as philosophy of history. One is the philosophical analysis of historiography: the logical, conceptual, and epistemological characterization of what historians do. The other is the attempt to discover, either in the over-all course of events or in the general nature of the historical process, some meaning or significance which transcends the intelligibility achieved by ordinary historical work. In contemporary literature the two branches are usually referred to as critical and speculative philosophy of history respectively, although the contrasts "analytical and synoptic" or "formal and material" are also found. The distinction is analogous to one generally drawn between philosophy of science and philosophy of nature.

CRITICAL PHILOSOPHY OF HISTORY

Development. Critical philosophy of history has developed chiefly over the last hundred years. Before the nineteenth century, few philosophers offered more than passing remarks about historical inquiry. These were generally derogatory, like Aristotle's comment that history provides knowledge inferior to that of poetry, or like Descartes's that it cannot picture the past as it really was, or Voltaire's that it is a pack of tricks we play upon the dead.

Two eighteenth-century philosophers probed more deeply. David Hume's celebrated argument against the credibility of miracle stories, in his *Enquiry Concerning Human Understanding* (1748), rests largely on the claim that such stories are ruled out by the presuppositions of science, this claim suggesting a general criterion of historical credibility. Giambattista Vico's recognition of a specifically historical type of understanding, in his *New Science* (1725), is based on the doctrine that man can fully understand only what he himself has created and that therefore the study of civil society promises us more than the study of nature ever could. But thorough and systematic analyses of historical thinking were scarcely to be expected before the full development of history itself as a discipline with accepted procedures and standards. Even G. W. F. Hegel's *Lectures on the Philosophy of History*

(1837) offered only a series of shrewd comments on various types of history writing.

The work of the "critical" historians—Barthold Georg Niebuhr, Leopold von Ranke, and their successors—afforded fresh materials for philosophical reflection about history in the nineteenth century. An independent stimulus to such reflection was also provided by the methodological writings of positivist philosophers seeking to establish the theoretical foundations of a new "social physics." Both Auguste Comte's *Course of Positive Philosophy* (1830–1842) and John Stuart Mill's *System of Logic* (1843) assumed the fundamental unity of inquiry and argued for the extension of the procedures of the established natural sciences into the developing field of social sciences. Both represented historical work as, ideally, the application of generalizations derived from the social sciences to particular circumstances in the past, although they differed about the role individual psychology ought to play in it.

Articulate protest against such a denial of the autonomy of historical studies arose first in Germany, where critical history had originated and where the idealist distinction between nature and spirit—with history falling into the latter realm—was widely accepted. From the 1880s on, a succession of theorists contrasted history with natural science on a number of grounds. Wilhelm Windelband argued that history was concerned only with delineating particular fact—it was "idiographic" rather than "nomothetic." Heinrich Rickert held in addition that, unlike the natural sciences, history was a value-judging rather than merely a fact-stating discipline. Wilhelm Dilthey insisted that history's proper mode of understanding, since it involved the interpretation of physical expressions of mentality, was "empathetic" rather than dispassionate and uninvolved. Dilthey, perhaps the most important critical philosopher of history in the nineteenth century, planned to make the latter doctrine the foundation of a great "Critique of Historical Reason" in the manner of Kant. Unfortunately, this work was left unfinished at his death.

Since the turn of the century, the philosophical description of history has been carried further by a number of idealist philosophers. After having, in earlier works, assimilated history first to art and then to philosophy, Benedetto Croce characterized historical reconstruction, in *The Theory and History of Historiography* (1916), as the re-creation of past experience in the mind of the historian—a doctrine popularly, although perhaps misleadingly, expressed in such slogans as "All history is history of thought" and "All history is contemporary history." In *The Idea of History* (1946), R. G. Collingwood elaborated a similar position. Historical inquiry, according to Collingwood, makes the following basic presuppositions: that there is a historical past localized in space and time; that its details can be inferred from present evidence; that these details consist of actions rather than mere events; and that actions have a "thought-side" which can be rethought by the historian. Collingwood took far more seriously than Croce the problem of *establishing* historical claims to have re-enacted the past. His solution was a hypothetico-deductive account of arguments from historical evidence in which general laws are alleged to have no necessary place.

Analytic philosophers in Great Britain and America have recently shown increasing interest in critical philosophy of history. Discounting much of the work of their predecessors either as mere psychological descriptions of the activities of historians or as premature statements of convenient metaphysical presuppositions, these philosophers conceive their primary task as the detailed analysis and clarification of the conceptual structure of historical thinking. Important in arousing this current of interest was Maurice Mandelbaum's discussion of historical relativism in *The Problem of Historical Knowledge* (1938), the first full-scale work on history by an American philosopher. Influential in giving it a fruitful direction was Carl Hempel's restatement of the positivist position as a logical theory of historical explanation, in "The Function of General Laws in History" (1942). In spite of its supposedly new "conceptual" emphasis, however, contemporary analytic literature continues to reflect the nineteenth-century dispute between positivists and idealists about the alleged "autonomy" of history. Perhaps this is only to be expected. For unless historical inquiry is, or ought to be, distinctive in important logical, conceptual, or methodological ways, there is little need for critical philosophy of history. A general theory of inquiry would suffice.

Problems. A survey of the specific problems which have generally been treated by critical philosophers in their attempts to clarify the idea of history is scarcely feasible in the present limited scope. Certain problems may, however, be selected for brief consideration as especially important or typical. The three discussed below have all been objects of considerable attention in recent analytic literature. Two of them bear directly on the question of logical differences between history and the natural sciences.

Historical explanation. Few problems have exercised critical philosophers of history more than the kind of understanding to be sought in historical studies. In particular, it has been asked whether the logical structure of acceptable explanations in history necessarily involves subsumption of what is to be explained under general laws, as is generally assumed to be the case in scientific inquiry. It has been argued that all explanation of events aims to show that what happened was to be expected, in view of the conditions which preceded it, and that rational expectation is possible only through the assumption of appropriate general laws, which themselves require empirical verification. In the ideal case the laws would render a historian's explanandum logically deducible from his explanans. Those who support such a claim—sometimes called the covering law theory—generally concede that historians seldom actually cite laws when offering explanations. But this, they argue, simply shows that most historical explanations are incomplete—the degree of understanding achieved nevertheless depending on the degree to which the conceptual ideal is realized.

Opponents of the covering law theory have sometimes denied its appropriateness in history, on the ground that historical events are unique and unrepeatable, laws being applicable to events only as members of classes. In explaining the outbreak of a revolution, for example, a historian will not explain it simply as a revolution; he will want to take account of its being different in historically interesting ways from all other revolutions. But covering law theorists do not regard this as a difficulty. All that historians can explain, they maintain, are events as they conceive and describe them; and the language of historical description, like all language, represents its referent as something of a certain kind. The descriptions of most historical events, it is true, are complex enough to justify our regarding the events as "unique" in the sense of there being no others falling under identical total descriptions. Such uniqueness, however, raises no theoretical barrier to subsumption under laws; and in practice, it is assumed, a thorough analysis of what is to be explained would in fact make possible its explanation by reference to a complex conjunction of laws.

Other opponents of the theory have based their objections less on the alleged uniqueness of the historian's subject matter than on its consisting of the actions of rational beings who are capable of deliberation and decision. Even without knowledge of general laws, they have maintained, it is possible to explain a human action in the sense of discovering the agent's reasons for doing what he did, thus making clear not the likelihood but the point or rationale of that action. Covering law theorists have argued that knowledge of an agent's reasons would be explanatory only on the assumption of general laws linking the recognition of such reasons with the performance of relevant actions, or on the assumption that the agent was rational in the sense of being disposed to act in accordance with good reasons. Their opponents have contended that good reasons make intelligible an agent's choosing to perform an action, even if all that can be assumed is the agent's capacity to act rationally. The latter claim, it might be observed, represents understanding of human actions as possible even on libertarian assumptions about human action. Just as the covering law theory does not argue from the assumption of determinism, however, so the contrary claim has generally been advanced without reference to metaphysical considerations.

Many contemporary philosophers, who would accept as basically correct the contention that explanation must always involve reference to empirically testable generalizations of some kind, have nevertheless objected that the covering law theory, as usually formulated, is not flexible enough to throw much light on actual historical cases. Some philosophers have therefore argued that satisfactory historical explanations can be probabilistic rather than deductive, employing statistical generalizations rather than universal laws. Others have contended that they may often be adequately supported by reference to "laws" which are, strictly speaking, neither universal nor statistical but represent what happened as what "normally" happens in such circumstances. Still others have insisted that the generalizations required for explaining the actions of individual historical agents or institutions may be singular and intended to show only that what was done was characteristic of a particular individual. It has been claimed, too, that typical explanations in history aim to discover not sufficient but only certain necessary conditions of what occurred, the probability of the occurrence being irrelevant to the kind of understanding sought in such cases.

Further difficulties for the application of the covering law theory to history have been cited by philosophers who point out that historians commonly give explanations in answer to questions other than why something in fact occurred. For example, historians often explain in the sense of making clear what something really was—a kind of explanation usually involving redescription of what happened rather than its subsumption under general laws. Explanations are also given, especially in the course of narratives, in response to the question how something could be so, the task being to resolve puzzlement generated by a contrary expectation. In such cases what is required to make what happened intelligible, it has been argued, is simply the rebuttal of the contrary expectation, not reference to general laws which would show the inevitability of what did occur. Covering law theorists tend to regard such suggestions as the conceptual exploitation of defective cases of explanation. To their opponents this looks like a doctrinaire failure to take seriously the logical variety of inquiry.

The historical individual. One of the objections often brought against the claim that historical explanations may be given by reference to the reasons of the agents rather than to empirical laws is that even if individual human actions can be explained in such a way, what historians are most often concerned about cannot. For history is not primarily about the actions of individual human agents. What historians study are large-scale social events and conditions like conquests and depressions, or the careers of empires, parliaments, and classes; and since such "social" individuals clearly do not reason or choose as human individuals do, it may be assumed that their "activities" can be explained only by reference to large-scale societal laws. Philosophers who support the latter assumption have been called methodological holists. Those who hold that the explanation of social phenomena can be found piecemeal in the actions of relevant human agents have been called methodological individualists. The issue between holists and individualists constitutes a second problem that has been much discussed in contemporary philosophy of history.

One argument of the individualists is that since social groups exist only as constructions out of the activities of human individuals, ultimately satisfactory explanation must be in terms of these activities. Conceding some kind of independent existence to social groups is ontologically unacceptable, even if it does not assume the form of a group mind theory. Individualists have sometimes added the claim that even if social events and conditions may properly be said to exist, they cannot provide satisfactory explanations because only the actions of individual men can be genuine causes. Holists have generally found neither argument convincing. Their own position, they contend, attributes no independent existence to social phenomena: the latter may be existentially dependent on human individuals acting in appropriate ways without being reducible to a mere collection of such actions. And to say that only individual human actions can be causes not only rebuts what historians commonly claim but also invites the suspicion of all those who would explicate the notion of cause in terms of the exemplification of law. For

it is an empirical question whether societal laws can be found. If they can be, holists insist, it is proper to speak of societal as well as individual causes.

Individualists have offered epistemological as well as metaphysical arguments in support of their position. They have argued, for example, that only by reducing social phenomena to their component human actions can they really be made intelligible. Holists who are also covering law theorists have objected that the issue here is really whether subsumption under laws achieves intelligibility at any level. If it does, and societal laws are available, then holistic understanding can be claimed. Individualists have contended, too, that human actions have explanatory primacy because assertions about social phenomena can be verified only by reference to the actions of relevant human beings, these actions alone being observable. Against this, some holists have argued that some social phenomena at least—parades, revolts, coronations, for example—*can* be observed. Others have denied that the need to verify social conditions individualistically commits us to individualistic explanation any more than the need to verify physical object claims through sense perception entails their reducibility to sensation claims or the impossibility of explanations given entirely at the physical object level.

Individualists have sometimes put their position in logical or semantic terms. They have claimed that, although this might often be inconvenient in practice, all societal concepts could in principle be eliminated ("by translation") from the statements of historians. The response of holists has generally been that actual attempts to perform this elimination encounter insuperable obstacles. It might be thought, for example, that the acceptance of a deposit by a bank teller could be explained by reference to what a human individual, the depositor, does in filling out his slip and presenting his cash or check. But it does not follow from this that societal terms could be eliminated from the explanans. "Deposit," "check," and the like all refer implicitly to the banking system; and without the assumption that what the individual did was done in a social context of banking, the citation of his actions would render the result neither intelligible nor a matter of rational anticipation. The problem recurs if an individualist reduction of the notion "banking system" is attempted.

In the face of such difficulties, methodological individualists have often reduced their conceptual claim: they have asserted only that what happened in history can be described exhaustively in terms of what human individuals did, even if this description requires the use of societal terms. For their main concern is to assert that social phenomena are explicable in terms of the motivations of individual men and women. They have also conceded that although identifiable individuals would sometimes have to be mentioned, the most that is normally possible in history is reduction to the actions of anonymous individuals. Holists have still objected that, even with such qualifications, few societal assertions could actually be translated into statements about what individuals did: the claim is most plausible when the assertion is largely statistical (as in "The Conservatives won the election"), least plausible when it is not (as in "The union was in a militant mood"). What methodological holists fear is that overemphasis on deflationary individualist ontology, with which they often agree, may obscure the important organizing function of holistic historical concepts.

Historical objectivity. A third fundamental question of critical philosophy of history is whether typical historical conclusions, holistic or not, can be represented as "objective" in the sense that the natural sciences are generally supposed to be. The most common reason given for doubting that historical conclusions can be objective is that the historian necessarily makes value judgments in arriving at them, it being generally agreed that scientific inquiry should not incorporate the moral or aesthetic appraisals of the inquirer. Those who deny the objectivity of history on this ground have often been called relativists, since it appears to be a consequence of their position that historical claims should be interpreted relative to some value scheme or cultural context.

There are at least three ways in which value judgment has been alleged to enter historical work. One is in the selection of items for inclusion in a historical account. Such selection is unavoidable, for a history is not composed of a haphazard conjunction of true statements about some period, people, or event. Every history implicitly claims to distinguish the important elements in what is known about its subject matter. All such judgments, relativists have argued, will be guided by a value scheme that historians bring with them to their inquiry.

Against this it has been objected that the implied contrast between objective and nonobjective inquiries is really a vacuous one. For *all* inquiries must surely be selective; none can proceed very far, for example, without selecting a specific problem to solve. Relativists claim, however, that selection enters history in the determining of solutions, not just in the choice of problems. If the historical problem is to trace the history of the labor movement in England, the selection of a topic, although it eliminates much, does not determine what deserves mention in the historian's narrative. This is even more obvious in history of the "period" type. Objectivists have sometimes replied that historical importance is properly interpreted as a causal notion and that there are objective criteria of causal connection. Even if this is true for history which aims primarily to explain, however, relativists deny it of history which aims primarily to report and describe. In such inquiry, they argue, it is an essential part of the task to discover what was intrinsically important in the development or period studied.

A second way in which value judgments have been said necessarily to enter historical work is in causal explanation itself. The discovery of causes, relativists have emphasized, is not simply a matter of discovering either sufficient or necessary conditions of what occurred, the procedure for which may be value-neutral. Historians normally want to distinguish not only between relevant and irrelevant conditions but also between relevant conditions which are properly regarded as causes and those which are not. The selection of one or a few relevant conditions as causes, it has been argued, involves considerations of value in many historical contexts. In selecting certain actions as the cause of a war's outbreak, for example, a historian will normally disqualify those which he regards as "forced" by the ac-

tions of others. This applies the common-sense notion of a cause as something which "makes" things happen, but in historical contexts who forced whom to act is often a quasi-moral question. Some objectivists have replied that causal explanation, so conceived, although it may be found in history, is really an illegitimate type of inquiry. Others have contended that in the notion of a cause as what "makes the difference"—the condition which is "abnormal"—historians have at their disposal a criterion of causal selection which does not raise moral issues.

A third way in which value judgments have been thought to enter historical work is in the very characterization of individual actions by historians. Human action, it has been claimed, is a value-impregnated subject matter. The very "facts" of history are murders, triumphs, oppressions, reforms, and the like, and these cannot adequately be described in morally neutral language. Objectivists have generally conceded that the language of historical description is, in fact, highly evaluative. They have sometimes conceded, too, that there is a sense in which the actions of historical agents positively invite the value judgment of the historian. But they have denied that such judgments necessarily enter into historical descriptions. They have argued that evaluative descriptions are always replaceable by nonevaluative ones.

Some critical philosophers have objected to the whole discussion of historical objectivity in terms of value-freedom or value-involvement. They have pointed out that when historians themselves ask whether a history is objective, what they have in mind is seldom whether it makes value judgments. What they want to know is whether it is biased, tendentious, or censorious. Thus, a Roman Catholic historian might well regard a Protestant account of the Reformation as "objective" even though he recognized—and disagreed with—certain value judgments he found implicit in it. If there is such an ordinary sense of "objective" current among historians, it is clearly a proper task of critical philosophy of history to examine it. Relativists, however, might still point out that if it is asked whether history *as a form of inquiry* is objective, it would be strange to interpret the question in this ordinary sense. For in this sense the answer to "Is history objective?" could only be "Some is, some isn't."

SPECULATIVE PHILOSOPHY OF HISTORY

Development. Discussion of the nature of historiography has not, for most of its history, formed the main stuff of what has been called philosophy of history. This has generally been inquiry of the material, speculative kind. Some speculative interest in history can, in fact, be traced back to the beginning of Western philosophy. It is present, for example, in Platonic and Aristotelian theories of the way forms of government characteristically succeed each other in the state. But it is less from Greek philosophy than from Judaic and Christian religion that most Western discussion of the meaning or significance of history derives. Where reason and observation could find, at most, the orderliness of historical cycles, the eye of faith discerned in a unique historical process the redemptive activity of God.

St. Augustine's *City of God* (412–426) is the classical

philosophical statement of such a view. The course of history is envisaged as a struggle between two communities, the Heavenly City and the Earthly City, roughly represented by, although not identifiable with, the visible church and state. What gives meaning to the struggle is the assurance, through revelation, of the final triumph of the Heavenly City—although Augustine's account is not, strictly speaking, a progress theory: the goal of history is beyond history, and the concern of divine providence is with salvation, not the course of secular events. The Augustinian scheme was dominant for over a thousand years. Bishop Bossuet's *Discourse on Universal History* (1681) still moves within it in representing the Pax Romana as a supreme instance of providence in history, on the ground that it made possible the rapid spread of the Christian message throughout the Mediterranean world. It is Augustinian also in being content to leave the *modus operandi* of divine providence shrouded in mystery.

The rise of secular philosophy of history has generally been regarded as a phenomenon of the Enlightenment. It was Voltaire, in fact, who first used the expression "philosophy of history," yet the contributions of the *philosophes* themselves were sketchy and intrinsically of minor importance. Voltaire's *Essay on the Manners and Morals of Nations* (1756) is notable mainly for shifting the focus of universal history toward the mundane details of human society, which Voltaire pictured, but scarcely explained, as moving from the darkness of superstition toward the ever-increasing light of reason. Marie-Jean-Antoine de Condorcet's *Sketch for a Historical Picture of the Progress of the Human Mind* (1795) is similarly of interest chiefly as an eloquent expression of faith in continuous human progress. Vico's *New Science* was more ambitious, seeking an explanation of the over-all course of history in a pattern of recurring yet cumulative cultural growth and decay, in which "providence," although acknowledged, was virtually identified with the laws of the process itself. Vico's work, however, was ignored by his contemporaries. It was left to the idealist philosophers of the late eighteenth and early nineteenth centuries, heirs of the Romantic movement as well as of the Enlightenment, to transmute divine providence into an immanent historical force. Of these the most influential were Herder, Kant, and Hegel.

Johann Gottfried Herder's *Ideas for a Philosophical History of Mankind* (1784–1791) emphasized the organic unity of human cultures and the unique contributions made by the "spirit" of each—even the Middle Ages—to the general development of mankind. Kant's *Idea of a Universal History from a Cosmopolitan Point of View* (1784) explained progress in history by reference to a "secret plan" of nature, man's "unsociable sociability" driving him, almost against his will, into building a rational civil order, both national and international. On such foundations Hegel developed the boldest metaphysical account of the historical process ever written. In his *Philosophy of Right* (1821), and in more detail in his posthumously published *Lectures on the Philosophy of History*, he declared the theme of history to be the actualization of the Absolute in time, the self-development of Spirit itself, through the careers of a number of world-historical peoples. Since the essence of spirit is freedom, the theme of world history is at the same time the development of human freedom, both quantitatively and qualitatively, in successive types of social organization.

The nineteenth century saw a number of avowedly "scientific" attempts to comprehend history as a whole—those of Comte and Herbert Spencer, for example—and it continued to feel the impact of Hegel through the writings of Marx. Comte's *Course of Positive Philosophy* set forth a fundamental law of human mentality, according to which human societies in all their aspects passed through theologically, metaphysically, and scientifically oriented phases—a law which the development of speculation about history might itself be said to exemplify. Spencer applied to history, in his *Principles of Sociology* (1877–1896) and other works, an allegedly cosmic law of evolution, according to which social development, like any other sort, moved "from an indefinite, incoherent homogeneity to a definite, coherent heterogeneity." In a number of his writings, Marx elaborated a materialist conception of history which he summarized in the Preface to his *Critique of Political Economy* (1859). Although centered on economic rather than "ideological" factors, this theory retained both Hegel's concern for human freedom, which was now conceived chiefly as freedom from exploitation, and his dialectical theory of historical change.

Twentieth-century system builders like Oswald Spengler and Arnold Toynbee have offered accounts of history with more obvious claims to "scientific" status. Both Spengler and Toynbee argue inductively to laws governing the standard development of cultures or civilizations and use them to predict the fate of their own. Both take seriously the task of exemplifying, if not rigorously testing, their large hypotheses in a wide range of historical materials: Toynbee especially has at his disposal a wealth of historical data never approached in the history of speculation. Spengler's *Decline of the West* (1918–1922) claims to discern, by aesthetic insight, a number of cultural organisms which are born, mature, grow old, and die after exhausting the possibilities of a characteristic style of life. Toynbee's *A Study of History* (1934–1954) finds in history a spiritual progress arising out of men's response to the challenge of the breakdown and disintegration of successive generations of civilizations. The twentieth century has also seen a revival of straightforwardly theological attempts to declare the meaning of history. The works of Reinhold Niebuhr, Paul Tillich, Christopher Dawson, and Herbert Butterfield are examples.

Problems. Professional philosophers have tended to regard speculative philosophy of history with misgivings—this being both cause and effect of its having been practiced, since the mid-nineteenth century at any rate, chiefly by social theorists, historians, and theologians. Critics, however, have not always made clear whether they question the acceptability of particular systems or the legitimacy of the enterprise itself. Nor have they always distinguished between several quite different tasks which speculative philosophers of history generally undertake, some of which they may perform more satisfactorily than others.

The pattern of the past. One task of speculative theorists is to discover some over-all pattern in the history of mankind. There are three possible basic patterns. Either history has proceeded in a certain direction, or it has repeated itself in succeeding peoples and periods, or it has been formless and chaotic. A linear theory may be progressive or regressive, but most such theories have in fact asserted human progress. The basic possibilities can also be asserted in various combinations. Thus, a theory which at one level regards history as chaotic may admit fragmentary developments of either cyclical or linear types at another level—like Spengler's account of cultures which spring up willy-nilly, without relation to each other, but once started on their careers, tend to exemplify a common pattern. A cyclical development may also be combined with a linear one to form a spiraling advance, like that asserted by Vico.

In fact, few philosophers of history can be classified without qualification as linear, cyclical, or chaos theorists. Hegel, for example, emphasized the linear development of freedom, but he also noted a recurring three-stage pattern in the stories of the various peoples who contributed to it. Toynbee at first saw history in terms of the rise and fall of civilizations, but he came to represent this rhythm as contributing cumulatively to the religious insight of the human race. Even Niebuhr, who denies that history has any significant over-all pattern at all from the standpoint of Christian faith, admits that certain lines of progress can be drawn through it: the line of technological development, for example.

Now, at any level of inquiry the question whether past events displayed a certain pattern, although it may be of intense philosophical concern, is essentially a historical question: this is as true for cyclical patterns as for linear ones. The speculative philosopher engages in *universal* history. This is a branch of historiography in which historians themselves are showing increasing interest. Indeed, one distinguished modern historian, Henri Pirenne, has declared that the idea of universal history, at least, is essential to historical work, in the sense that all histories must be judged at some point as contributions to it. For the most part, however, speculative philosophers have had to be their own universal historians, just as early philosophers of physical science had to be their own physicists. The criticisms they have received—Toynbee not excepted—from specialists in various fields of historical research suggest that as history their work has in fact been seriously defective.

More theoretical reasons, however, have often been given for distrusting speculative philosophy of history in its historical aspect. Some critics have claimed that universal history is impossible in principle, on the ground that history as a whole is not a whole, so that the universal historian—by contrast, say, with a historian of the French Revolution or of the colonization of America—lacks a proper object of study. Against this it may be argued that the problems of finding unity and continuity when writing the history of the world are logically and conceptually exactly the same as those of any period history—say, a history of Europe in the nineteenth century. The only sense in which history as a whole must be a whole to be historically investigated does not include its having a single unitary theme. Whether it has one is a fundamental question of universal history.

Equally inadmissable, many would claim, is the common objection that universal history "oversimplifies" what happened, or tears out of context what the investigator regards as important. For all historical synthesis, at any level of generality, is open to appraisal in such terms. When Marx declared that all history is the history of class struggle, he was not pointing out a common characteristic of all historical events; he was selecting what he conceived to have been especially important and thus was applying a scale of values to history as a whole. The same could be said of Augustine's account of the "central events" of history in terms of the religious value of "salvation" or of Spengler's claim that history is "about" cultures. To accept universal history as a legitimate type of inquiry of course does not commit one to accepting any particular account of it, nor to any particular metaphysical interpretation which philosophers may place upon a given pattern. A *philosophe*, for example, might agree with Hegel that, from the most general point of view, what matters in the past is the gradual achievement of human freedom, without accepting the further claim that this pattern represents the self-development of the Absolute.

The nature of historical change. Speculative philosophers do not seek simply to display the pattern of the past, whether characterized in metaphysical or more ordinary historical terms. They seek also to understand why and how that particular pattern prevailed. In this connection many have claimed to discover laws peculiar to the historical process. Some of these laws set forth the chief stages through which large-scale historical units are thought typically or invariably to pass, like Vico's cycle of national development from an early "heroic" barbarism, through several degrees of civilization, and back to a decadent neobarbarism of "reflection." Others are less general, like Toynbee's claim that the stimulus of new ground to a developing civilization is greater if it can be reached only by crossing the sea.

Again it may be observed that, in searching for historical laws, the task which the speculative theorist sets himself is not one that would ordinarily be regarded as especially philosophical. For insofar as his law assumes the form of an empirically verifiable hypothesis, he may be said, rather, to be engaged in a quasi-scientific inquiry. Some speculative philosophers, it is true, have claimed nonempirical support for their theories of historical development, just as others have tried at times to solve the problems of natural science by pure reason. Yet few have been prepared to rest their case entirely on such considerations. Kant, for example, found a "clue" to universal history entirely a priori, but he specifically charged his successors with the task of verifying his account empirically. Spengler and Toynbee made "comparative morphology" and "empirical survey" the chief bases of their claims to have discovered historical laws. Just as speculative philosophers of history have had to be their own universal historians, it might be claimed, so they have had to be their own social scientists. It is plausible to go on to argue—as even friendly critics have often done—that any value which speculative hypotheses about historical laws now have is to be determined by absorbing them into social science proper.

Attacks on speculative philosophies of history have not always clearly distinguished between claims to have discovered historical patterns and claims to have discovered historical laws. This is especially true of attacks by historians, who tend to use the term "metahistorian" to mark deviations from normal professional activity in either the law-seeking or the pattern-seeking direction. Yet if there is confusion on this point, speculative philosophers of history may themselves be at least partly to blame. For they have often seemed to pass from the claim to have found a pattern in the past to the claim to have found a directional law of history, whether linear or cyclical. Indeed, one of the most common complaints against speculative theories generally has been that they characteristically try in some such way to transmute mere "facts" into "necessities."

The problem is most obvious when a linear law is derived from the alleged trend of the historical process as a whole. Since the process is unique, this looks, at best, like generalizing from a single case—perhaps with the spurious support of the concepts of historical "forces" or "tendencies." Comte and Marx, for example, seem to have regarded history as moving inexorably toward the goals of positivity and the classless society, respectively; and Toynbee claimed to detect a "nisus" toward political unity in North America. Yet there are two considerations, some would insist, which have not always been kept sufficiently in mind in applying such criticism to specific systems. First, the extent to which the systems have actually asserted "necessity" has often been exaggerated: neither Hegel nor Toynbee, for example, appears to be a determinist. Second, few speculative theorists have simply extrapolated discovered trends: Kant, Marx, and Toynbee, in particular, have offered quite extensive accounts of the factors which led them to expect the trends to continue. Such accounts may not in fact have been satisfactory. They would appear, however, to render questionable any attack on the speculative enterprise as committed to a confusion of laws with trends.

Besides setting forth historical laws, in either of the senses indicated, speculative philosophers have generally offered theories of change of a higher order. Some of these theories endeavor to set forth the "most important causal factors" in the process. Marx's law of the explanatory primacy of economic factors over political ones is an example. Carlyle's "great man" theory of history is another. It is tempting to interpret such theories as simply setting forth, whether knowingly or not, causal apothegms on the model of everyday claims like "The most important factor in road accidents is excessive speed." If these theories could be so interpreted, they would be empirical generalizations from a large number of particular causal diagnoses independently arrived at, each involving a selection of important necessary conditions, whether on evaluative or statistical criteria. It is doubtful, however, that they can be so interpreted. Their aim seems to be not to describe the way explanations in history generally go but rather to prescribe the way they should go. Unlike historical laws in the protoscientific sense, their claims seem to go beyond anything

that could be established by empirical survey, and their authority seems to derive from some more general philosophical position.

This is even more obviously true of what might be called speculative models of historical change, like Hegel's notion of a progress in history through the tension and resolution of opposites in a "dialectic of national principles"; or Spengler's of a quasi-biological "destiny" determining the general shape of cultural developments and limiting the choices of individual members to cultural expressions of an appropriate phase and type; or Toynbee's theory of creative human action as a free response to a challenge which achieves a golden mean of severity; or Niebuhr's of a tension in history between divine sovereignty and original sin which shows itself in an irony of human pride frustrating its own designs. The way speculative philosophers have actually propounded such higher-level "laws" has in fact often raised elementary logical difficulties. Toynbee's principle of the golden mean, for example, easily degenerates into a mere tautology; yet one could hardly expect it to be open to verification in the same way as his law of the challenge of the sea. Nor should one expect to reach conclusions about the acceptability of determinism or of supernatural activity in history by reference to historical or scientific considerations alone.

Value, purpose, and meaning. Discovering the pattern of the past and explaining it by reference to its mechanism of change might be said to render the whole historical process meaningful in the sense of "intelligible." Speculative philosophers, however, have generally sought meaning in the further sense of assurance that the whole process has purpose or value. As Hegel put it, the ultimate aim of philosophical speculation about history is theodicy, the "justification of the ways of God" so that we may be "reconciled with the fact of the existence of evil in the world." Thus, Toynbee asks how any spiritually significant purpose can be served by the "vain repetitions" of the cyclic life of civilizations and concludes that they serve the purposes of emerging higher religions. And Marx, although he hated the exploitation in bourgeois society, justified that society in its own proper time as a necessary step toward the eventual ending of the alienation of man.

In asserting that history is meaningful because it has a purpose which can be approved, speculative philosophy of history clearly transcends historical or scientific concerns and becomes part of metaphysics, ethics, and religion. The systems of the various philosophers consequently cannot be finally assessed without considering the total world views on which they rest. Some of the best-known systems are, in fact, disappointing in this connection. By contrast with those of Augustine and Hegel, for example, the metaphysical bases of Toynbee's and Spengler's accounts are sketchy. Spengler talked vaguely of a "proto-spirituality" which from time to time "takes root on a natural landscape." Toynbee offers little more than mystical musing of a highly personal nature. Even where a philosopher's general position is well worked out, the relation of history to that position is sometimes far from clear. Kant, for example, leaves history a puzzling *tertium quid* between the worlds of nature and of morality.

Not all speculative theories, it should be noted, find meaning in the direction history is discovered to take; some call attention, rather, to its general nature as a process. Thus Niebuhr, for example, although he finds the meaning of history in its "telos," places the goal, as did Augustine, beyond achievement in time: he does not even expect significant approximations to it within history. Insofar as meaning is to be found in events themselves, it is to be found not in their course but in their reflecting or revealing the purpose of human life: the struggle against original sin under the conditions of grace. Secular analogues of the latter idea might regard history as meaningful, at least in the sense of valuable, in providing opportunities for human endeavor of certain approved kinds. Collingwood, for example, seems to have found history valuable because he found it precisely the type of process a rational being needs to live in, if he is to develop his potentialities. Existentialist views of history often display a similar emphasis.

Critiques of speculative philosophies of history should also recognize the difference between asking whether any value is achieved by history and asking whether history has the purpose of achieving this value. Many philosophers—methodological individualists, for example—would regard the latter question as illegitimate on grounds which would not excuse us from raising the former. They would argue that the purposes allegedly discovered by most speculative theorists are clearly not intended to be attributed to the human agents involved, and they would suspect that society or history has been hypostatized in order to furnish an appropriate agent. Thus Hegel, although he claimed that all that happens in history happens through the wills of individual human beings, nevertheless spoke of Spirit as achieving purposes which even world-historical individuals like Caesar and Napoleon did not grasp. It is quite possible, however, for a theory of history to point out that the historical process is such that it has value, without engaging in any such attribution of purposes. History can achieve value simply through having a certain nature or arriving at a certain state of affairs.

Bibliography

INTRODUCTIONS

Aron, Raymond, *Introduction à la philosophie de l'histoire.* Paris, 1938. Translated by G. J. Irwin as *Introduction to the Philosophy of History.* Boston, 1961.
Dray, W. H., *Philosophy of History.* Englewood Cliffs, N.J., 1964.
Teggart, F. J., *Theory and Processes of History.* Berkeley and Los Angeles, 1941.
Walsh, W. H., *Philosophy of History: An Introduction.* London, 1951; 2d ed., New York, 1960.

GENERAL WORKS: CRITICAL

Cassirer, Ernst, *The Problem of Knowledge: Philosophy, Science, and History Since Hegel,* translated by William H. Wogrom and Charles W. Hendel. New Haven, 1950.
Croce, Benedetto, *History as the Story of Liberty.* New York, 1955.
Danto, A. C., *Analytical Philosophy of History.* Cambridge, 1965.
Gallie, W. B., *Philosophy and the Historical Understanding.* New York, 1964.

Nagel, Ernest, *The Structure of Science.* New York, 1961. Chs. 13–15.
Popper, Karl, *The Poverty of Historicism.* London, 1957.
Randall, J. H., Jr., *Nature and Historical Experience.* New York, 1958.
White, M. G., *Foundations of Historical Knowledge.* New York, 1965.
Winch, Peter, *The Idea of a Social Science.* London, 1958.

GENERAL WORKS: SPECULATIVE

Flint, Robert, *History of the Philosophy of History.* Edinburgh, 1893.
Löwith, Karl, *The Meaning of History.* Chicago, 1949.

WORKS BY HISTORIANS

Bloch, Marc, *The Historian's Craft,* translated by Peter Putnam. New York, 1964.
Butterfield, Herbert, *History and Human Relations.* London, 1951.
Carr, E. H., *What Is History?* London, 1961.
Geyl, Pieter, *Debates With Historians.* London, 1955.
Trevelyan, G. M., *Clio, A Muse.* London, 1930.

ANTHOLOGIES

Dray, W. H., *Philosophical Analysis and History.* New York, 1966.
Gardiner, Patrick, *Theories of History.* Glencoe, Ill., 1959.
Hook, Sidney, *Philosophy and History: A Symposium.* New York, 1963.
Klibansky, Raymond, and Paton, H. J., *Philosophy and History.* Oxford, 1936; 2d ed., New York, 1963.
Meyerhoff, Hans, *The Philosophy of History in Our Time.* New York, 1959.

BIBLIOGRAPHIES

The anthologies by Gardiner and Meyerhoff contain good bibliographies on both the speculative and the critical aspects. The journal *History and Theory* has published detailed bibliographies of works published in the years 1945–1957 (Beiheft 1, 1961) and 1958–1961 (Beiheft 3, 1964).

W. H. DRAY

PHILOSOPHY OF LANGUAGE. See LANGUAGE, PHILOSOPHY OF.

PHILOSOPHY OF LAW, HISTORY OF. The problems of authority, law and order, obligation, and self-interest first became central topics of speculation in the thought of the Sophists (late fifth and early fourth centuries B.C.). The most famous Sophists all stressed the distinction between nature (*physis*) and convention (*nomos*), and they put laws in the latter category. They generally attributed law to human invention and justified obedience to law only to the extent that it promoted one's own advantage. Laws were artificial, arrived at by consent; the majority of acts that were just according to the law were contrary to nature; the advantages laid down by the law were chains upon nature, but those laid down by nature were free. In the time of the Sophists notions of law, justice, religion, custom, and morality were largely undifferentiated; yet in this same period some of the crucial problems of legal philosophy were first formulated, and attempts were made at a formal definition of law. Thus, Xenophon (*Memorabilia* I, 2) reported that Alcibiades, who associated with both

Critias and Socrates, remarked to Pericles that no one can really deserve praise unless he knows what a law is. Pericles replied that laws are what is approved and enacted by the majority in assembly, whereby they declare what ought and what ought not to be done. He admitted that if obedience is obtained by mere compulsion, it is force and not law, even though the law was enacted by the sovereign power in the state. Xenophon also reported an alleged conversation between Socrates and the Sophist Hippias in which both maintained an identity between law, or what is lawful, and justice, or what is right, while admitting that laws may be changed or annulled (*ibid.* IV, 4). Socrates claimed that there are "unwritten laws," uniformly observed in every country, which cannot conceivably be products of human invention. They are made by the gods for all men, and when men transgress them, nature penalizes the breach.

Socrates and the Sophists, as presented in Plato's dialogues, disagreed concerning human nature. The Sophists conceived of man as egoistically motivated and antisocial, whereas for Socrates, as for Plato and Aristotle, man was a social being with other-regarding as well as self-regarding motives, who finds fulfillment in social life. By contrast, the Sophist Callicles, in Plato's *Gorgias,* holds that man is no exception to the law of nature, according to which the stronger rules; man-made laws and social institutions violate human nature. The less radical Sophists, although they could not identify law with some feature of reality, still accepted its practical usefulness.

PLATO AND ARISTOTLE

Plato. There is hardly any problem of legal philosophy not touched upon by Plato. He wrote during the decline of the Greek polis, when law and morality could appear as mere conventions imposed by shifting majorities in their own interest and the harmony between the legal order and the order of the universe could not easily be maintained. Plato sought to restore, as far as possible, the traditional analogy between justice and the ordered cosmos. Justice, or right action, cannot be identified with mere obedience to laws, nor can a truly moral life be reduced to conformity with a conventional catalogue of duties. Duties involve a knowledge of what is good for man, and this bears an intimate relation to human nature. The question "What is justice?" dominates Plato's *Republic.* Plato conceived of justice as that trait of human character which coordinates and limits to their proper spheres the various elements of the human psyche, in order to permit the whole man to function well. In order to understand the operation of justice in the human soul, Plato examined human nature writ large, the city-state. The state functions well when it is governed by those who know the art of government, and the practice of this art requires a positive insight into the Good. In a just society every citizen performs the role of which he is best capable for the good of the whole. Similarly, in the moral economy of the individual's life, justice prevails when reason rules and the appetites and lower passions are relegated to their proper spheres. A just social order is achieved to the extent to which reason and rational principles govern the lives of its members.

Plato's emphasis on reason found its way into his definition of law. Law is reasoned thought (*logismos*) embodied in the decrees of the state (*Laws* 644D). Plato rejected the view that the authority of law rests on the mere will of the governing power. The *Laws* contains a detailed discussion of many branches of law and is an attempt at a formulation of a systematic code to govern the whole of social life. In contrast with the ideal polis of the *Republic*, in which there would be little need for legislation, in the *Laws* Plato accepted "law and order, which are second best" (*Laws* 875D).

Aristotle. Aristotle, who discussed law in numerous contexts, nowhere gave a formal definition of it. He wrote variously that law is "a sort of order, and good law is good order" (*Politics* 1326a), "reason unaffected by desire" (*ibid.* 1287a), and "the mean" (*ibid.* 1287b). However, these must be taken not as definitions but as characterizations of law motivated by the point Aristotle was making in the given context.

Following Plato, Aristotle rejected the Sophistic view that law is mere convention. In a genuine community—as distinguished from an alliance, in which law is only a covenant—the law concerns itself with the moral virtue of the citizenry (*Politics* 1280b). Aristotle sharply distinguished between the constitution (*politeia*) and laws (*nomoi*); the constitution concerns the organization of offices within the state, whereas the laws are "those according to which the officers should administer the state, and proceed against offenders" (*ibid.* 1289a). The constitution of a state may tend to democracy, although the laws are administered in an oligarchical spirit and vice versa (*ibid.* 1292b). Legislation should aim at the common good of the citizens, and justice—what is equal—should be determined by the standard of the common good (*ibid.* 1283a). Yet Aristotle recognized that the law is often the expression of the will of a particular class, and he stressed the role of the middle class as a stabilizing factor.

In his discussion of the forms of government in Book III of the *Politics,* Aristotle took up the Platonic problem of rule by the best man versus rule according to laws. A society of equals by its very nature excludes the arbitrary rule of one man. In any case, even the best man cannot dispense with the general principles contained in laws; and legal training helps to make better officers of government. Furthermore, administrators, like all men, are subject to passion, and it is thus preferable to be judged by the impersonal yardstick of the laws. This in no way conflicts with the need to change the law through legislation when it has been found by experience to be socially inadequate. But not all law is the product of legislation; customary law is in fact more important than the written law.

Aristotle's discussion of the judicial process foreshadows many modern notions. Although it is better to have written laws than to rely completely on discretion, "some matters can be covered by the laws and others cannot" (*ibid.* 1287b20). General rules are insufficient to decide particular cases (*ibid.* 1286a26), although "well-drawn laws should themselves define all the points they possibly can and leave as few as may be to the decision of the judges" (*Rhetoric* 1354a32). Aristotle seems to have had two considerations in mind. First, judicial decision-making is practical—it involves deliberation—and as such cannot be completely determined in advance. Second, the resolution of disputed issues of fact in a particular case, on which the decision depends, cannot be settled in advance by legislation. This stress on the insufficiency of general rules connects with Aristotle's influential discussion of equity (*epieikeia*). Equity is just, "but not legally just but a correction of legal justice" (*Nicomachean Ethics* 1137b10). Aristotle sometimes seems to suggest that equity comes into play when there are gaps in the law, so that it consists in the judge's acting as the lawgiver would act if he were present. Yet he also seems to suggest that equity corrects the harshness of the law when adherence to the written law would work an injustice. Principles of equity are thus closely related to the unwritten universal laws "based on nature," a "natural justice" binding on all men, even those who have no association or covenant with each other. Nevertheless, what is naturally just may vary from society to society.

The *locus classicus* of Aristotle's discussion of justice is Book V of the *Nicomachean Ethics*. Generically, justice has to do with one's relations to others, and there is a sense of "justice" that refers to the complete moral virtue of the member of the community in such dealings. There is also a sense in which "justice" refers to a particular virtue involving the fair dealings of individuals in matters handled by private law. Two kinds of rights fall under this special virtue: rights in division (where each individual claims his fair share of goods, honors, and so on) and rights in redress (for wrongs done by one individual to another, such as failure to fulfill a contract).

ROME

Stoics. The Stoics, who conceived of the universe as a single, organic substance, exercised a lasting influence on legal thought. Nature, which exhibits structure and order, and man both partake of intelligence, or reason (*logos*). An animal is directed by a primary impulse toward self-preservation which adapts it to its environment. In man, reason is the "engineer of impulse," and man's actions may be evaluated only within the framework of the whole of nature. The criterion of moral action is consistency with the all-determining law of nature (*koinos logos*). This conception of a law of nature that is the ultimate standard of human laws and institutions was combined with Aristotelian and Christian notions to form the long-standing natural-law tradition of medieval legal philosophy. Another important Stoic contribution was the belief in the equality of all men in a universal commonwealth and a rejection of Aristotle's doctrine of slavery.

Cicero and Seneca. The writings of Cicero (106–43 B.C.) were important in transmitting classical legal thought to the medieval world. Although he was a professional arguer of legal cases, Cicero's philosophical treatment of law in his *De Legibus* disclaims any interest in "clients' questions" or the "law of eaves and house-walls." His legal philosophy was essentially Stoic; he denied that the positive law of a community (written or customary), even when universally accepted, is the standard of what is just.

Nor is mere utility the standard: "Justice is one; it binds all human society, and is based on one law, which is right reason applied to command and prohibition" (*De Legibus* I, 15). An unjust statute is not a true law. Law and morality are logically connected, and only that which conforms to the law of nature is genuine law. This view exercised a lasting influence on natural-law thinking and reappeared in the thought of Thomas Aquinas.

Like Cicero, Seneca (c. 4 B.C.–A.D. 65) aided in transmitting Stoic notions to later thinkers. He reiterated the conception of the equality of all men under natural law, but perhaps more important was his conception of a golden age of human innocence, a prepolitical state of nature. Legal institutions became necessary as human nature became corrupted.

Roman law. The influence of Stoicism may be traced in pronouncements of the Roman jurists. It is disputed whether these were any more than remarks designed to ornament legal texts, but they nevertheless influenced the thought of later ages. The jurists distinguished three kinds of law: *jus naturale*, *jus gentium*, and *jus civile*. In practice, the last originally referred to the law of the city of Rome, but ultimately it was applied to any body of laws of a given community. The *jus gentium* first meant the law applied to strangers, to whom the *jus civile* was not applicable, and was later extended to those legal practices common to all societies. Gaius (mid-second century), who systematized the Roman law in his *Institutes*, identified the *jus naturale* and *jus gentium* as universal principles of law agreeable to natural reason and equity. Thus, law was not a mere expression of human will or institution but that which is rationally apprehended and obeyed. The *jus gentium* was not an ideal law by which the positive law was judged but the rational core of existing legal institutions.

Ulpian (c. 170–228) distinguished *jus naturale* from *jus gentium* by stating that *jus naturale* is not peculiar to human beings but is taught by nature to all animals. Thus, among animals there is an institution similar to human marriage. Slavery and its attendant rules are products of the *jus gentium*, for by the *jus naturale* all men were born free. It is not clear, however, that Ulpian regarded slavery as bad. To him we owe the oft-repeated definition of justice: "the constant wish to give each his due" (*Digest* I, 1, 10). Following Celsus (c. 67–c. 130), he defined law (*jus*) as "the art of the good and the equitable" (*ibid.* I, 1, 1). Again, it does not seem that Ulpian thought of the *jus naturale* as an ideal law opposed to the *jus civile* or to the *jus gentium*. It has been suggested that behind Ulpian's thought was a conception of a natural state antecedent to the conditions of organized society.

The doctrines of the Roman jurists owe their lasting influence to their incorporation into the *Corpus Juris Civilis* of Justinian (sixth century), principally in the section called the *Digest*. The compilers of Justinian's *Institutes* (a section of the *Corpus Juris*) seem to have distinguished the *jus naturale* from the *jus gentium* and seem to have regarded the former as a set of immutable divine laws by which the positive law may be morally evaluated (*Institutes* I, 2, 11; III, 1, 11). The *Corpus Juris* also preserved statements of the Roman jurists concerning the source of the authority to make and unmake the laws constituting the civil law. According to a number of these statements, this authority resides in the consent of the people; however, the statement that "what pleases the prince has the force of law" (*Digest* I, 4, 1) was probably a more accurate view of the facts. Justinian seems to have combined these views theoretically in his reference to a (nonexistent) "ancient law" by which the Roman people transferred all their powers to the emperor (*Codex* I, 17, 1, 7).

EARLY MIDDLE AGES

To the legal thought of the Stoics and the Roman philosophers and jurists the Church Fathers added a distinctively Christian element. The law of nature was no longer the impersonal rationality of the universe but was integrated into a theology of a personal, creative deity. The relationship among the Mosaic law, the Gospels, and natural law emerged as a specific problem; the notion of *jus divinum* (divine law) as a distinct type of law, along with the three recognized by the jurists, was crystallized. The notion of the fall of man from a state of perfection (which may be compared with the view of Seneca) played an important role. Thus, according to St. Ambrose (340–397) the Mosaic law—a law of sin and death (see Romans 8.2)—was given because man failed to obey the law of nature. The fact that many legal institutions, such as slavery and private property, deviate from this ideal law does not necessarily imply that they are unjust or illegitimate; for the natural law is adapted to man only in a condition of innocence.

Of the Church Fathers, St. Augustine (354–430) was perhaps the most original and complex: only one point in his thought will be noted here. Cicero maintained that nothing can be nobler than the law of a state (*De Legibus* I, 14) and that if a state has no law, it cannot truly be considered a state (*ibid.* II, 12). The law of the state must therefore embody justice, for without *justitia* there is no *jus*. Augustine considered this position in *The City of God*, Book XIX. According to Augustine, since Rome had no justice, Cicero's position has the inconvenient consequence that Rome was no state at all. We must therefore seek another definition of "state" (*populus*) in which justice is not an essential element. Augustine stressed the notion of order—"a harmonious multitude"—with the suggestion that legal order need not be moral or just. There are passages in Augustine, however, which seem to uphold a more orthodox natural-law position. In any event the terms of his discussions are somewhat different; his main points of contrast are divine and human law, rather than *jus naturale* and *jus civile*.

The sources of the natural-law theories which were to dominate Western legal philosophy for many centuries were the writings of the Greek and Roman philosophers and poets, Justinian's *Corpus Juris Civilis*, and the Church Fathers. Isidore of Seville (c. 560–636), an encyclopedist and an important transmitter of Roman thought to later writers, concisely expressed the natural-lawyer's ideal regarding positive law: "Law shall be virtuous, just, possible to nature, according to the custom of the country, suitable to place and time, necessary, useful; clearly expressed, lest by its obscurity it lead to misunderstanding; framed for no private benefit, but for the common good" (*Etymologies* V, 21).

MIDDLE AGES AND RENAISSANCE

Civilians and canonists. In the revived study of Roman law in the twelfth century, associated with the glossators, legal philosophy received a fresh stimulus. Of special interest are the attempts at reconciling differences among the Roman jurists on the definition of law and the classification of its branches. In the main, the civilians were in the broad tradition of natural-law thinking; *jus* flows from *justitia*, although it must always fall short of perfect justice, which is God's alone. Irnerius (c. 1050–c. 1130) thus claimed that statutes ought to be interpreted in the light of equity. Strict law requires that all agreements be kept, but equity allows exceptions to the rule. This equity, according to Azo (c. 1150–c. 1230), must be written, rather than a principle found in the judge's heart.

The middle of the twelfth century also saw the systematization of the canon law. In the *Decretum* of Gratian a high degree of jurisprudential competence was brought to this task. The tripartite division of law of the Roman lawyers was verbally accepted, but the leading conceptions were Augustine's *jus divinum* and *jus humana*. Natural law was identified with the former, while the distinctive feature of the latter (covering both *jus gentium* and *jus civile*) was custom. Natural law is contained in the Mosaic law and the Gospels; the command to do unto others what we would have them do unto us is its fundamental principle. Natural law relates to man's rational nature and is immutable; the *mistica*, the cultic regulations found in Scripture, are part of the natural law only in their moral aspect. The commentators on Gratian further divided natural law so as to include not only commands and prohibitions but also *demonstrationes*, which point to what is good for mankind, such as possession of all things in common. In man's fallen condition custom has legitimately modified the *demonstrationes* in permitting private property and slavery. The other branches of natural law may not be abrogated and are the standards by which even the ecclesiastical law must be judged. Gratian (if not all his commentators) seems to have generally maintained a clear distinction between natural (divine) law and canon law.

Aquinas. The rediscovery of Aristotle in the thirteenth century greatly influenced the further development of legal philosophy. The culmination of the natural-law tradition is the theory of Thomas Aquinas (1224–1274), who integrated Stoic, Christian, and Aristotelian elements within a comprehensive philosophic system. Laws are standards of conduct which have a binding, or obligatory, character. This can be understood only if laws have some kind of rational origin. Combining this view with a teleological conception of nature and social order, Aquinas regarded legal control as purposive. Laws, he concluded, are ordinances of reason promulgated for the common good by the legitimate sovereign. Four types of law may be distinguished: eternal law, an expression of God's rational ordering of the universe; divine law, which guides man toward his supernatural end; natural law, which guides man toward his natural end; and human law, which regulates through the prospect of punishment the affairs of men in a given community in the light of that community's special requirements. Crucial to the concept of natural law are the notions of natural inclinations and right reason. "All those things to which man has a natural inclination are naturally apprehended by reason as being good and consequently as objects of pursuit, and their contraries as evil, and objects of avoidance" (*Summa Theologiae* I–II, 94). The relationship between inclination and reason, accounting for the apprehension of the natural law, has been variously interpreted. The precepts of natural law have as their common foundation the principle "Do good and avoid evil." Natural law is a standard to which human law must conform, and Aquinas employed Aristotle's conception of practical reasoning in explaining the derivation of human law from natural law by the legislator, thus accounting for differences between legal systems and for the possibility that rational men should disagree as to what human laws ought to be. He affirmed the long-standing view that an unjust law is no law; but although an unjust law is not binding in conscience, considerations of utility may require one to obey it. Aquinas allowed that such "laws" may be said to possess a "legal" character insofar as they are promulgated under the color of law by the legitimate prince.

Aquinas discussed in detail and with great acuity all of the problems treated by his predecessors. His influence may be traced in the English writers John Fortescue (c. 1394–c. 1476), Thomas Hooker (c. 1586–1647), and Christopher St. Germain (1460–1540). According to St. Germain, natural law is nothing other than the common-lawyer's notion of "reasonableness." Recent Thomist thinkers, such as François Gény and Jean Dabin, have advanced novel ideals within the Thomistic tradition.

Ockham. Some medieval writers seem to have espoused a protopositivism in their emphasis on the primacy of the will; this is characteristic of the Augustinian–Franciscan tradition. Thus, William of Ockham (c. 1285–1349) regarded the divine will as the norm of morality. "By the very fact that God wills something it is right for it to be done." Nevertheless, it is doubtful that Ockham would have affirmed that what the sovereign commands is just. His position is somewhat unclear, however, for he—like all medieval writers—continued to use the rhetoric of natural law in his *Dialogus:* in one of its senses *jus naturale* is composed of universal rules of conduct dictated by natural reason. A right, such as the immutable right of private property, is a dictate of right reason.

Rise of absolutism. A tendency to combine natural-law doctrines with a theory of royal absolutism began in the fourteenth century. A group of civilians, known as the post-glossators, undertook to forge a workable system of law out of the older Roman law, which they regarded as the *jus commune* of Europe. The technically trained administrators in the rising nation-states, they were naturally concerned with fundamental problems of legal theory. Bartolus of Sassoferrato (1314–1357) maintained that the ruler is not bound by the laws, although it is "equitable"

that he should voluntarily submit to them. The *jus gentium,* however, is immutable. Lucas de Penna (1320–1390) discussed jurisprudential questions in detail. Law is the articulation of the ethical virtue of justice, and reason is the foundation of law. At the same time he maintained, as did many civilians, that the prince's lordship rests on divine authority. The ruler is responsible to God alone and not to the people; law is not the expression of the will of the community. Nonetheless, although the prince is unfettered by the laws, bad laws (those that contradict divine law) have no binding force. It is not clear, in Lucas' view, whether the obligation to obey law derives primarily from the rationality of law or from the divine grant of authority to the ruler.

LATER RENAISSANCE

Bodin. Jean Bodin (1530–1596), the great exponent of unlimited sovereignty under natural law whose views were apparently influenced by the fourteenth-century civilians, like them appears to have had difficulty in adapting Christian legal thought to the conditions of the secular nation-state. In his *Six Books of the Commonwealth* Bodin was emphatic that "law is nothing else than the command of the sovereign in his exercise of sovereign power." But although the prince "has no power to exceed the law of nature," which is decreed by God, it seems plain that Bodin no longer thought of right reason as linking natural and positive law. Bodin's endorsement of the command theory also appears in his treatment of custom. The relative weights of positive law and custom had long been debated by the medieval lawyers, but Bodin was one of the first to hold that custom owes its legal authority to the sufferance of the ruler. In this he anticipated the idea of tacit command expressed by Thomas Hobbes and John Austin.

International law. The emergence of nation-states also brought the problem of the rational foundation of international law to the forefront of legal thinking. This development may be seen in the writings of the Spanish Thomists Francisco de Vitoria (c. 1492–1546) and Francisco Suárez (1548–1617) and of Hugo Grotius (1583–1645), a Dutch Protestant jurist with broad humanistic leanings. According to Vitoria, the *jus gentium* either belongs to or is derivable from the natural law and consists in prescriptions for the common good in the widest sense, namely, for the international community. Rights and obligations are thus conferred upon nations acting through their rulers.

The conception of a law of nations was developed in great detail by Suárez. Although his *De Legibus* is Thomistic in many respects, Suárez explicitly stated that Aquinas' account of law is inadequate. Suárez began by distinguishing laws in the prescriptive sense from laws of nature in the descriptive sense, which are laws only metaphorically. (Many positivists trace the origin of natural-law thinking to the tendency to confuse these two types of law.) With regard to prescriptive laws, Suárez defined a law (*lex*) as "the act of a just and right will by which the superior wills to oblige the inferior to this or that" or as "a common, just and stable precept, which has been sufficiently promulgated" (*De Legibus* I, 12). The reference to stability is notable: laws generally survive both the lawgiver and the populace living when they are enacted, and they are valid until abrogated. Such considerations have led recent writers to reject the identification of laws with mere acts of will; but although Suárez rejected the voluntaristic notion of natural law associated with the Ockhamists, he held that the civil law is enacted "more by the will than by reason." It is not derived from natural law by logical inference but by "determination," and hence is, in a sense, arbitrary (*ibid.* II, 20). Most medieval writers tended to use *lex* and *jus* interchangeably; Suárez, however, defined the latter as "a certain moral power which every man has, either over his own property or with respect to what is due to him" (*ibid.* I, 2). Although Aquinas briefly discussed *jus naturale* as contrasted with *jus positivum* (*Summa Theologiae* II–II, 57), the concept of a "natural right" was almost entirely absent from his thought. It is clearly present in Suárez, who, in the style of Locke and the Enlightenment philosophers, formulated a list of natural rights. Nevertheless, the individualism of these writers is not present in Suárez. His attitude was quite remote from eighteenth-century natural-law and natural-right theorists, who thought that a perfect system of law could be deduced from the natural law.

Despite Grotius' tendency to underestimate his predecessors, his *De Jure Belli ac Pacis* (1625) clearly showed the influence of such writers as Vitoria and Suárez. He developed their notion of a "just war," a topic still discussed by Hans Kelsen and other twentieth-century theorists concerned with the problem of sanctions in international law. Just wars presuppose the existence of laws governing relations between sovereign states; such laws have their origin in natural law and in treaties, which in turn presuppose precepts of the law of nature. The denial of the existence of natural law supposes that men are egoistically motivated, accepting law as a "second best." However, following Aristotle and the Scholastics, Grotius held that man is social, altruistic, and rational. Therein lies the origin of law, which would be binding whether or not God exists. This statement has been regarded by historians as epoch-making; they claim that Grotius separated jurisprudence from theology. More important, perhaps, is the tendency in Grotius and others who followed him to identify natural law with certain rational principles of social organization, and thus to loosen its tie with the Stoic metaphysical conception of the law of nature.

SEVENTEENTH–LATE NINETEENTH CENTURIES

Hobbes and Montesquieu. Thomas Hobbes (1588–1679) was perhaps the most important of the seventeenth-century legal philosophers. His break with the tradition of natural law provoked much controversy. Hobbes employed the terminology of "natural right," "laws of nature," and "right reason." But the first was for him simply "the liberty each man hath to use his own power as he will himself, for the preservation of his own nature; that is to say, of his own life" (*Leviathan* 14); the second are principles of self-interest, which are often identified with the third. There is no right reason in nature (*Elements of Law* II, 10, 8). The natural condition of mankind is one of perpetual war, in which common standards of conduct are absent. There is no right or wrong, justice or injustice, mine or thine in this situation. The crucial steps in Hobbes's theory are the identifications of society with politically organized society and of justice with positive law. Laws are the commands of the sovereign; it is in reference to such commands that the members of a society evaluate the rightness or justness of their behavior. An "unjust law" is an absurdity; nor can there be legal limitations on the exercise of sovereign power. No writer has put forward a positivistic conception of law with greater style and forcefulness than Hobbes. Difficulties in his position emerge from his concession that although the sovereign cannot commit an injustice, he may commit iniquity; the idea of injury to God in the state of nature; and the treatment of conscience in *De Cive*. Hobbes solved the problem of the source of the obligation to obey the sovereign's command by his "social contract" doctrine, the interpretation of which is still discussed by scholars. His unfinished *Dialogue Between a Philosopher and a Student of the Common Laws of England* examines various doctrines of the English law as put forward by Sir Edward Coke, and it is notable for its critical examination of Coke's statement that reason is the life of the law.

The *Second Treatise of Civil Government* by John Locke (1632–1704), primarily an attack on Robert Filmer's "divine right" theory, contains certain implied criticisms of Hobbes. Its interest for legal philosophy lies in its use of a version of the social contract to treat the question of the obligation to obey the law, its conception of limitations on sovereign power, and its individualistic view of natural inalienable rights, particularly rights in property. Locke's influence was enormous, and his view of natural rights had a profound effect on the development of law in the United States.

A new approach to the understanding of law and its institutions was put forward by Montesquieu (1689–1755). He, too, spoke the language of natural law and defined laws as "necessary relations arising from the nature of things" (*The Spirit of the Laws* I, 1). But his special importance lies in his attempt to study legal institutions by a comparative historical method, stressing the environmental factors that affect the development of law. This suggestion had been anticipated by Bodin, and Giambattista Vico (1668–1744) had also applied a historical method to the study of Roman law, but Vico's work had little immediate influence. Montesquieu's doctrine of the separation of powers had an extraordinary influence. His sharp separation of judicial from legislative and executive power reinforced the conception that the judge is a mere mouthpiece of the law and that judges merely declare the existing law but never make it. In 1790, in his *Reflections on the Revolution in France*, Edmund Burke turned the historical approach to a practical political use when he protested against proceeding a priori in the "science of constructing a commonwealth."

Kantianism. Immanuel Kant (1724–1804) contributed to legal philosophy as he did to other branches of philosophy. The keynote of his legal philosophy was inspired by Jean-Jacques Rousseau (1712–1778), who set as the problem of his *Social Contract* the reconciliation of social coercion and individual freedom. Kant's legal philosophy may be called a philosophy of justice in which the concept of freedom plays a central role. Kant sought a systematic understanding of the principles underlying all positive laws which would enable us to decide whether these laws are in accordance with moral principles. Positive law "proceeds from the will of a legislator," and any viable legal system will take into account the particular conditions of the given society: with these conditions the theory of law has no concern. The theory is an application of the results of moral philosophy to the conditions of "men considered merely as men." This endeavor covers both the domain of law (*Recht*) and the domain of ethics; the principle that right action is action in conformity with universalizable maxims holds for both juridical and moral laws. A law (*Gesetz*) is a formula expressing "the necessity" of an action. Juridical and moral laws are distinguished in that the former regulate external conduct irrespective of its motives. (But this does not mean that a judge should necessarily ignore the lawbreaker's motives when passing sentence upon him.) Any man, as a morally free agent, is entitled to express his freedom in activity so long as it does not interfere with the similar freedom that others possess. This is the principle underlying all legislation and "right." Juridical law also involves the authority to compel conformity and to punish violations. The necessary and sufficient condition for legal punishment is that the juridical law has been broken. It must be recognized, however, that the domain of such law is restricted by the limits of compulsion. While it is morally wrong to save one's own life by killing another, even where this is the only expedient, it can never be made legally wrong to kill in such a case. The principle of law receives content in Kant's application of it to particular private rights in external things and in his analysis of the methods for acquiring such rights.

Kant's influence on jurisprudence, after being somewhat eclipsed by Hegelianism, re-emerged at the end of the nineteenth century. One of the most important Neo-Kantians was Rudolf Stammler (1856–1938), who invented, but eventually discarded, the phrase "natural law with variable content." Accepting the Kantian distinction between "form" and "matter," he attempted to discern the form of all laws. He defined law as "exceptionless binding volition." Just law is an ideal involving principles of respect and cooperation.

Utilitarianism and positivism. While Kant and his followers may be said to have fostered a variety of natural-law thinking (although different from the Stoic and Thomistic types), Jeremy Bentham (1748–1832) and his followers (notably John Stuart Mill) claim to have rejected such thinking entirely. Of the influences on Bentham, two may be briefly noted. David Hume (1711–1776) argued that moral distinctions are not derived from reason; passion, or sentiment, is the ultimate foundation of moral judgment. Justice is grounded in utility. Second, the Italian criminologist Cesare Beccaria (1738–1794), in his *Of Crimes and Punishments* (1764), subjected the existing institutions of criminal law and methods of punishment to relentless criticism. His standard of judgment was whether "the

greatest happiness of the greatest number" was maximized. Bentham acknowledged his debt to Beccaria, and this "principle of utility" was the base of Bentham's voluminous projected "codes." He did not, however, define the nature of law by reference to utility. In his *The Limits of Jurisprudence Defined* (published in 1945) he defined a law as the expression of "the will of a sovereign in a state." Bentham's views, which were well suited to deal with the problems engendered by the industrial revolution in England, were of immense importance in effecting legal reform. In 1832, the year of his death, the Reform Act was passed, largely as a result of the work of his followers. Mill's *On Liberty* (1859) is an attempt to treat the limits of legal coercion by the state along modified utilitarian lines.

In legal philosophy Bentham's influence affected the English-speaking world especially through the thought of John Austin (1790–1859), the seminal figure in English and American legal positivism and analytic jurisprudence. Austin tried to find a clear demarcation of the boundaries of positive law, which would be antecedent to a "general jurisprudence" comprising the analyses of such "principles, notions, and distinctions" as duty, right, and punishment, which are found in every legal system; these analyses in turn were to be employed in "particular jurisprudence," the systematic exposition of some given body of law. Austin began by distinguishing "law properly so called" and "law improperly so called." The former is always "a species of command," an expression of a wish or desire, analytically connected with the ideas of duty, liability to punishment (or sanction), and superiority. The last notion led Austin to his famous and influential analysis of "sovereignty"; "laws strictly so called" (positive laws) are the commands of political superiors to political inferiors. From this it follows that international law is merely "positive international morality" rather than law in a strict sense. (Some writers, viewing this as an unfortunate and perhaps dangerous consequence, were led to various revisions of Austinianism.) Austin's "separation" of law and morality is often taken as the hallmark of legal positivism. "The existence of law is one thing; its merit or demerit is another," he wrote in *The Province of Jurisprudence Determined* (V, note). Yet Austin was a utilitarian; in distinguishing between the law that is and the law that ought to be, he did not mean that law is not subject to rational moral criticism grounded in utility, which he took to be the index to the law of God. At this point Austin was influenced by such "theological utilitarians" as William Paley.

Austin's views were subjected to vigorous discussion both without and within the traditions of positivism and analytical jurisprudence. And as the disciplines of history, anthropology, and ethnology assumed an increasing importance during the nineteenth century, rival approaches to the understanding of law developed. Thus, Sir Henry Maine (1822–1888), who formulated the historical law that legal development is a movement from status to contract, argued in his *Early History of Institutions* (London, 1875) that the command–sovereignty theory of law has no application in a primitive community, where law is largely customary and the political "sovereign," who has the power of life or death over his subjects, never makes law. The Austinian view can be saved only by maintaining the fiction that what the "sovereign" permits, he commands. Nonetheless, Austin had many followers at the turn of the twentieth century, such as T. E. Holland (1835–1926) and J. W. Salmond (1862–1924), who attempted to preserve the imperative and coercion aspects of his theory while introducing revisions.

The role of the courts was increasingly emphasized. In the United States, John Chipman Gray (1839–1915) wrote *The Nature and Sources of the Law* (New York, 1909; 2d ed., New York, 1921), one of the most important American contributions to the subject. Acknowledging his debt to Austin, Gray defined law as "the rules which the courts [of the State] lay down for the determination of legal rights and duties." This required him to construe statutes, judicial precedents, custom, expert opinion, and morality as sources of law rather than as law. All law is judge-made. The machinery of the state stands in the background and provides the coercive element, which does not enter into the definition of "law." Gray's influence may be traced in the realist movement in the United States.

Hegelianism and the historical school. While England was largely under the sway of the utilitarians, Kantianism, Hegelianism, the historical school, and legal positivism flourished in Germany, both singly and in various combinations. In his *Philosophy of Right*, G. W. F. Hegel (1770–1831) developed some Kantian themes in his own characteristic way. Law and social–political institutions belong to the realm of "objective spirit," in which interpersonal relationships, reflecting an underlying freedom, receive their concrete manifestations. In attempting to show the rightness and the rationality of various legal relationships and institutions in given moments of the development of "spirit," and in seeing them as natural growths, Hegel formulated a theory of law and the state that was easily combined with various historical, functional, and institutional approaches to legal phenomena.

Friedrich Karl von Savigny (1779–1861) is often regarded as the founder of the historical school. His *Of the Vocation of Our Age for Legislation and Jurisprudence* (1814) was published before Hegel's work and was probably influenced by Fichte (but not by Fichte's *Grundlage des Naturrechts*, 1796), whose notion of the "folk-spirit" was widely known. Law, like language, originates spontaneously in the common consciousness of a people, who constitute an organic being. Both the legislator and the jurist may articulate this law, but they no more invent or make it than does the grammarian who codifies a natural language. Savigny believed that to accept his conception of law was to reject the older notions of natural law; nevertheless, it is often claimed that Savigny's conception was merely a new kind of natural law standing above, and judging, the positive law.

Otto von Gierke (1844–1921), the author of *Das deutsche Genossenschaftsrecht*, clearly fits into the tradition of the historical school. Gray, in *The Nature and Sources of the Law*, subjected the theories of Savigny and his American follower, James C. Carter (1827–1905), to severe criticism. It should be noted that Maine's views have nothing in common with those of Savigny; in Maine's work the metaphysics of the *Volksgeist* is entirely absent.

LATE NINETEENTH CENTURY–PRESENT

Jhering and German positivism. Rudolf von Jhering (1818–1892), eminent both as a historian of law and as a legal theorist, rejected both Hegel and Savigny: Hegel, for holding the law to be an expression of the general will and for failing to see how utilitarian factors and interests determine the existence of law; Savigny, for regarding law as a spontaneous expression of subconscious forces and for failing to see the role of the conscious struggle for protection of interests. However, Jhering shared the broad cultural orientation of many of the Hegelians, and he was grateful to Savigny for having overthrown the doctrine of "immutable" natural law. Jhering's contribution was to insist that legal phenomena cannot be comprehended without a systematic understanding of the purposes that give rise to them, the study of the ends grounded in social life without which there would be no legal rules. Without purpose there is no will.

At the same time there are strong strains of positivism in Jhering: law is defined as "the sum of the rules of constraint which obtain in a state" (*Der Zweck im Recht*, p. 320). In this respect he was close to the German positivists, who emphasized the imperative character of law. Karl Binding (1841–1920), an influential positivist, defined law as "only the clarified legal volition [*Rechtswille*] of a source of law [*Rechtsquelle*]" (*Die Normen und ihre Uebertretung*, p. 68). In this period the slogan of German positivism, "All law is positive law," emerged. Yet Jhering opposed many of the claims of the analytical positivists; his essay "Scherz und Ernst in der Jurisprudenz" (Leipzig, 1885) ridiculed their "heaven of jurisprudential concepts."

Sociological and allied theories. Jhering's work foreshadowed many of the dominant tendencies of twentieth-century legal philosophy. Hermann Kantorowicz regarded Jhering as the fountainhead of both the "sociological" and "free-law" schools. The former term covers too wide a group of writers to be surveyed here, some of whom were concerned solely with empirical work, while others combined empirical work with a philosophical outlook. Proponents of the jurisprudence of interests (*Interessenjurisprudenz*) eschewed Jhering's inquiries into the metaphysical and moral bases of purposes, claiming that he did not sufficiently attend to the conflict of interest behind laws; law reflects dominant interest. (Similar analyses were made in the United States; for example, the "pressure-group" theory of politics advanced by A. F. Bentley [1870–1957] in *The Process of Government*, Chicago, 1908.) Much attention was devoted to the analysis of the judicial process and the role that the "balancing" of interests plays in it. As Philipp Heck, one of its leading exponents, remarked: "The new movement of 'Interessenjurisprudenz' is based on the realization that the judge cannot satisfactorily deal with the needs of life by mere logical construction" (*Begriffsbildung und Interessenjurisprudenz*, p. 4).

This sentiment was endorsed by the closely allied

"free-law" movement. According to this group, "legal logic" and the "jurisprudence of conceptions" are inadequate for achieving practicable and just decisions. The judge not only perforce frequently goes beyond the statute law, but he also often ought to go beyond it. The "free-law" writers undertook the normative task of supplying guidelines for the exercise of judicial discretion, and the judicial function was assimilated to the legislative function. The focus on such problems reflected the enormous change, occasioned by the industrialization of Western society, in the functions of the state. No longer did the nation-state exist merely to keep the peace or protect pre-existing rights; rather, it played a positive role in promoting social and individual welfare. The philosophy of law thus became increasingly concerned with the detailed working out of the foundations of legal policy. The "free-law" theorist Eugen Ehrlich (1862–1922), who influenced such American theorists as Karl N. Llewellyn (1893–1962) and other representatives of legal realist tendencies, summarized his *Grundlegung der Soziologie des Rechts* as follows: "At the present as well as at any other time, the center of gravity of legal development lies not in legislation, not in juristic science, nor in judicial decision, but in society itself." He rejected the positivistic tenet that only norms posited by the state are legal norms, for in any society there is always more law than is expressed in legal propositions. The "inner order" of an association is the basic form of law. Ehrlich also engaged in empirical study of the "legal facts" (*Rechtstatsachen*) and "living law" of various communities in the Austro-Hungarian empire. Ehrlich may thus be said to have considered custom as law in its own right. However, many positivists would argue that he was not able to account for the normative character of custom.

Marxism. The Marxist stress on economic interests was often combined with the sociological and free-law views. Central to the Marxist position are the notions of "class" (usually defined in terms of legal relationship to property and the means of production) and "class interest," which leads to the analysis of the role of law in different societies with differing class structures. Addressing their critics, Marx and Engels wrote: "Your law [*Recht*] is but the will of your class exalted into statutes [*Gesetz*], a will which acquires its content from the material conditions of existence of your class" (*Communist Manifesto*, 1848). This suggests that law is merely part of the ideological superstructure and has no effect on the material organization of society. It raises the question of whether law exists in all societies—for instance, in primitive society or in the "classless" society arising after the triumph of socialism—and the further question of the nature and function of law in the transitional period from capitalism to socialism. The issue of "revolutionary legality" or "socialist legality" was treated by Lenin, E. Pashukanis, and Andrei Vishinsky. An important Marxist study of the relationship between law and the economy is that of the Austrian socialist Karl Renner (*Die Rechtsinstitute des Privatrechts und ihre soziale Funktion*, 1929).

Pure theory and relativism. Although the sociological approaches to law have many practitioners, the most controversial and perhaps the most influential twentieth-century view is that of Hans Kelsen, a leading exponent of legal positivism. Influenced by the epistemology of the Neo-Kantians, Kelsen distinguishes sharply between the "is" and the "ought," and consequently between the natural sciences and disciplines, such as legal science, which study "normative" phenomena. Legal science is a descriptive science—prescriptive and valuational questions cannot be scientific—and Kelsen's "pure theory" aims at providing the conceptual tools for studying any given legal system irrespective of its content. The theory is "pure" in that it is divorced from any ideological or sociological elements; it attempts to treat a legal system simply as a system of norms. Kelsen's view is thus similar to the analytical jurisprudence of Austin, but Kelsen regards legal norms as "de-psychologized commands." In order to understand an act of will as a norm-creating act, we must already employ a norm which serves as a "schema of interpretation." The jurist who seeks to understand legal phenomena must ultimately presuppose a basic norm (*Grundnorm*), which is not itself a positive legal norm. Legal systems are sets of coercive norms arranged in hierarchical fashion; lower norms are the "concretizations" of higher norms. In Kelsen's analysis the "dualisms" of state and law and public and private law disappear, and the relationship between international law and national legal systems is seen in a fresh light.

Unlike Kelsen, Gustav Radbruch (1878–1949) did not found a school. His position, which he called relativism, has many affinities with that of Kelsen; but Radbruch maintained that law, which is a cultural phenomenon, can be understood only in relation to the values that men strive to realize through it. He attempted to analyze these values in relation to legal institutions, showing the "antinomies" among these values that led to his relativism. World War II raised the question in the minds of many legal philosophers whether the separation of law and morals of legal positivism, which was popular in Germany, contributed to the rise of Nazism. Concern over this problem seems to have caused Radbruch to move away from his earlier relativism toward a kind of natural-law position.

Realism and other recent trends. In the United States, until very recently, legal philosophy has largely been the province of lawyers rather than of professional philosophers. This may account for its sociological and realistic tone. The erudite Roscoe Pound (1870–1964) was its most prolific writer. Pound recognized the influence of Josef Kohler (1849–1919) and his notion of jural postulates and, especially, of Jhering. The pragmatism of William James also contributed to the development of his views. In an early article, "Mechanical Jurisprudence" (*Columbia Law Review*, Vol. 8, 1908, 605–610), Pound argued for an understanding of the interests that the law seeks to protect. Introducing a distinction between "law in books" and "law in action," he maintained the need for a close study of the actual operation of legal institutions. On both scores his influence in the United States has been momentous, but it is difficult to summarize his position; he is often associated with a "social engineering" approach to law. Law contains both precepts and ideal elements. Among precepts Pound distinguished rules, principles, conceptions, doctrines, and standards. It is pointless to isolate some canonical form to which all laws are reducible. The ideal element consists of received ideals "of the end of law, and hence of what legal precepts should be and how they should be applied." Pound offered an elaborate, although tentative, survey of the individual, public, and social interests secured by law. This list was criticized and amended by Pound's Australian disciple Julius Stone (*The Province and Function of Law*, 1946). In his later years Pound moved toward a kind of natural-law thinking, arguing for a more intimate connection between law and morality; he abjured the realist tendencies, which had been influenced by his earlier thought, as "give it up" philosophies.

It is exceedingly difficult to characterize the legal realists; they disclaim a common doctrine but recognize an interest in a common set of problems. With J. C. Gray, the spiritual godfather of American legal realism was Justice Oliver Wendell Holmes, Jr. (1841–1935). In his seminal essay "The Path of the Law" (*Harvard Law Review*, Vol. 10, 1896, 457–478), he advocated viewing law as the "bad man" would, in terms of the practicable remedies afforded individuals through the medium of the courts. Holmes presented in that article his famous definition of law as "the prophecies of what the courts will do in fact." It may be argued, however, that this definition, while perhaps adequate from the advocate's viewpoint, can hardly apply to the judge. When the judge asks what the law is on some matter, he is not trying to predict what he will decide.

Joseph W. Bingham was one of the first realists. In "What Is the Law?" (*Michigan Law Review*, Vol. 11, 1912, 1–25 and 109–121), Bingham argued that legal rules, like scientific laws, have no independent existence, being simply mental constructs that conveniently summarize particular facts. Laws are really judicial decisions, and the so-called rules or principles are among the (mentally) causative factors behind the decision. This nominalism and behaviorism, which characterized much of early realist writing, was criticized by Morris R. Cohen (1880–1947), until recently one of the few academic philosophers in the United States concerned with legal philosophy. "Behavior analysis" was advocated by Karl N. Llewellyn, who extended it beyond judicial behavior to "official" behavior (*Jurisprudence*, Chicago, 1962; collected papers).

The so-called myth of legal certainty was attacked by Jerome Frank (1889–1957) in his *Law and the Modern Mind* (New York, 1930), which explained the genesis of the myth in Freudian terms. In the sixth edition (New York, 1949) Frank was somewhat friendlier toward natural-law thinking, characterizing his change of attitude as going from an earlier "rule-skepticism" to "fact-skepticism" (*Courts on Trial*, Princeton, N.J., 1949). Other important realists include Thurman Arnold, Leon Green, Felix Cohen, Walter Nelles, Herman Oliphant, and Fred Rodell. Both positivism and realism were attacked by Lon L. Fuller (*Law in Quest of Itself*, Chicago, 1940), a leading American exponent of non-Thomistic natural-law thinking (*The Morality of Law*, New Haven, 1964). The revival of natural-law doctrines is one of the most interesting features of current legal thought. Recent contributions and criticisms may be found in the journal *The Natural Law Forum*.

The Scandinavian countries are a center of legal philosophy, and many of their leading writers are realists. They are more consciously philosophical than their American counterparts. The leading spirit was Axel Hägerström (1868–1939), who rejected metaphysical presuppositions in legal philosophy and insisted on an understanding of legal phenomena in empirical terms. Many legal concepts can be understood only as survivals of "mythical" or "magical" thought patterns, which should ideally be eliminated. Vilhelm Lunstedt (*Legal Thinking Revised*, Stockholm, 1956) is most radical in his rejection of metaphysics. Values are expressions of emotion and should be excluded from legal science. The "method of social welfare" should be substituted for the "method of justice." Alf Ross (*On Law and Justice*, London, 1958) argues that the first method is as "chimerical" as the second and presents an analysis of legal policy-making as a kind of rational technology. Laws, Ross argues, are directives to courts. The concept "valid law" as used by jurists and legal philosophers cannot be explicated in purely behavioristic terms; inner psychological attitudes must also be included. A similar view is presented by Karl Olivecrona (*Law as Fact*, London, 1939), who has written important realist analyses of legal language and severely criticized command theories of law, such as Austin's. In *Inquiries Into the Nature of Law and Morals* (translated by C. D. Broad, Cambridge, 1953), Hägerström argued that Kelsen's "pure theory" never escapes the "will" element either, and hence it falls subject to all the criticisms that may be leveled against the command theories.

The most influential legal philosopher in the English-speaking world today is H. L. A. Hart. In his *Concept of Law* (Oxford, 1961) he develops a view of law as consisting of a "union of primary and secondary rules." The former are rules imposing duties; the latter are rules of recognition, change, and adjudication. The first of the secondary rules (those for recognizing the rules of a system) seems to be crucial to his account of all three. His position is in many respects similar to that of Kelsen. He gives an interesting analysis, allied to Ross's account, of what it means to say that a rule exists. Hart sees the relationship between law and morals as contingent, in contrast with the Thomistic view of a logical connection between the two; this leads him to an interpretation of natural law not unlike that presented by some Renaissance writers. In a number of important articles Hart has focused on the nature of definition in jurisprudence, the analysis of psychological concepts in the law, legal responsibility, and the principles of punishment.

Bibliography

Ago, Roberto, "Positive Law and International Law." *American Journal of International Law*, Vol. 51 (1957), 691–733.

Allen, C. K., *Law in the Making*, 7th ed. Oxford, 1964.

Berolzheimer, Fritz, *System der Rechts- und Wirtschaftsphilosophie*, 5 vols. Munich, 1904–1907. Vol. II translated by R. S. Jastrow as *The World's Legal Philosophies*. Boston, 1912.

Bodenheimer, Edgar, *Jurisprudence*. Cambridge, Mass., 1962.

Cairns, Huntington, *Legal Philosophy From Plato to Hegel*. Baltimore, 1949.

Carlyle, R. W., and Carlyle, A. J., *A History of Mediaeval Political Theory in the West*, 6 vols. Edinburgh and London, 1903–1936.

Cohen, M. R., *Law and the Social Order*. New York, 1933.

Cohen, M. R., *Reason and Law*. Glencoe, Ill., 1950.

Davitt, T. E., *The Nature of Law*. St. Louis, 1951.

Del Vecchio, Giorgio, *Justice*, translated by Lady Guthrie. Edinburgh, 1952.

Dias, R. W. M., *Bibliography of Jurisprudence*. London, 1964.

Ebenstein, William, *The Pure Theory of Law*. Madison, Wis., 1945.

Ehrlich, Eugen, *Grundlegung der Soziologie des Rechts*. Munich, 1913. Translated by Walter L. Moll as *Fundamental Principles of the Sociology of Law*. Cambridge, Mass., 1936.

Entrèves, A. P. d', *Natural Law*. London, 1951.

Friedman, Wolfgang, *Legal Theory*, 4th ed. London, 1960.

Friedrich, C. J., *The Philosophy of Law in Historical Perspective*, 2d ed. Chicago, 1963.

Gierke, Otto von, *Das deutsche Genossenschaftsrecht*, 4 vols. Berlin, 1868–1913. Partially translated by F. M. Maitland as *Political Theories of the Middle Ages*. Cambridge, 1900. Also partially translated by Ernest Barker as *Natural Law and the Theory of Society*. Cambridge, 1934.

Gurvitch, Georges, *Sociology of Law*. New York, 1942.

Hall, Jerome, *Studies in Jurisprudence and Criminal Theory*. New York, 1958.

Hamburger, Max, *The Awakening of Western Legal Thought*, translated by B. Miall. London, 1942.

Hart, H. L. A., "Philosophy of Law and Jurisprudence in Britain (1945–1952)." *American Journal of Comparative Law*, Vol. 2 (1953), 355–364.

Heck, Philipp, *Begriffsbildung und Interessenjurisprudenz*. Tübingen, 1952.

Jaeger, Werner, "In Praise of Law," in P. L. Sayre, ed., *Interpretations of Modern Legal Philosophies*. New York, 1947.

Jennings, W. I., ed., *Modern Theories of Law*. London, 1933.

Jhering, Rudolf von, *Die Normen und ihre Uebertretung*. Leipzig, 1872.

Jhering, Rudolf von, *Der Zweck im Recht*, Vol. I. Leipzig, 1877. Translated by I. Husik as *Law as a Means to an End*. Boston, 1913.

Jolowicz, H. F., *Lectures on Jurisprudence*. London, 1963.

Jones, J. W., *Historical Introduction to the Theory of Law*. Oxford, 1940.

Kantorowicz, Hermann, *The Definition of Law*. Cambridge, 1958.

Kelsen, Hans, *What Is Justice?* Berkeley, 1957.

Kocourek, Albert, "The Century of Analytical Jurisprudence Since John Austin," in A. Reppy, ed., *Law: A Century of Progress*. New York, 1937.

Lloyd, Dennis, *Introduction to Jurisprudence*. London, 1959.

Lottin, O., *Le Droit naturel chez saint Thomas d'Aquin et ses prédécesseurs*. Bruges, 1931.

Macdonnell, J., and Manson, E. W. D., eds., *Great Jurists of the World*. London, 1913. Biographical.

Morris, C., "Four Eighteenth Century Theories of Jurisprudence." *Vanderbilt Law Review*, Vol. 14 (1960), 101–116.

Paton, G. W., *A Text-Book of Jurisprudence*, 2d ed. Oxford, 1951.

Patterson, E. W., *Jurisprudence*. New York, 1953.

Pollock, Frederick, *Jurisprudence and Legal Essays*. London, 1961.

Pound, Roscoe, *Jurisprudence*, 5 vols. St. Paul, Minn., 1959. A collection of much of his work.

Renner, Karl, *Die Rechtsinstitute des Privatrechts und ihre soziale Funktion*. Tübingen, 1929. Translated by A. Schwarzschild as *The Institutions of Private Law and Their Social Function*. London, 1949.

Rommen, Heinrich, *Die ewige Wiederkehr des Naturrechts*. Leipzig, 1936. Translated by T. R. Hanley as *The Natural Law*. St. Louis, 1947.

Spencer, A. W., ed., *Modern French Legal Philosophy*. New York, 1921.

Stone, Julius, *The Province and Function of Law*. Sydney, 1946.

Ullmann, Walter, *The Mediaeval Idea of Law*. London, 1946.

Verdross, A., *Abendländische Rechtsphilosophie*. Vienna, 1958.

Villey, M., *Leçons d'histoire de la philosophie du droit*. Paris, 1957.

Vinogradoff, Paul, *Outlines of Historical Jurisprudence*, 2 vols. London, 1910–1922.

Wolf, Erik, *Griechisches Rechtsdenken*, 3 vols. Frankfurt, 1950–1956.

M. P. GOLDING

PHILOSOPHY OF LAW, PROBLEMS OF.

The existence of legal systems, even the most rudimentary, has afforded the opportunity for a variety of academic disciplines. Of these some are, or purport to be, empirical: they include the historical study of particular legal systems or specific legal doctrines and rules, and sociological studies of the ways in which the content and the efficacy of law and the forms and procedures of law-making and law-applying both influence and are influenced by their economic and social setting, and serve social needs or specific social functions. But since law in most societies soon reaches a very high degree of complexity, its administration requires the special training of judges and professional lawyers. This in turn has created the need for a specific form of legal science concerned with the systematic or dogmatic exposition of the law and its specific methods and procedures. For this purpose the law is divided into distinct branches (such as crime, tort, and contract), and general classifications and organizing concepts are introduced to collect common elements in the situations and relationships created by the law (such as rights, duties, obligations, legal personality, ownership, and possession) or elements common to many separate legal rules (such as act and intention).

No very firm boundaries divide the problems confronting these various disciplines from the problems of the philosophy of law. This is especially true of the conceptual schemes of classification, definition, and division introduced by the academic study of the law for the purpose of exposition and teaching; but even some historical and sociological statements about law are sufficiently general and abstract to need the attention of the philosophical critic. Little, however, is to be gained from elaborating the traditional distinctions between the philosophy of law, jurisprudence (general and particular), and legal theory, although importance has often been attributed to them. Instead, as with other branches of philosophy, it is more important to distinguish as belonging to the philosophy of law certain groups of questions which remain to be answered even when a high degree of competence or mastery of particular legal systems and of the empirical and dogmatic studies mentioned above has been gained. Three such groups may be distinguished: problems of definition and analysis, problems of legal reasoning, and problems of the criticism of law. This division is, however, not uncontroversial; and objections to it are considered in the last section of the article.

PROBLEMS OF DEFINITION AND ANALYSIS

The definition of law. All the obscurities and prejudices which in other areas of philosophy surround the notions of definition and of meaning have contributed to the endlessly debated problems of the definition of law. In early arguments the search for the definition of law was assumed to be the task of identifying and describing the "essence" or "nature" of law, and thus the uniquely correct definition of law by reference to which the propriety of the use, however well established, of the expressions "law" and "legal system" could be tested. It is frequently difficult to distinguish from this search for the essence of law a more modest conception of definition which, while treating the task as one of identifying and describing the standards actually accepted for the use of these expressions, assumes that there is only one "true," "strict," or "proper" use of them and that this use can be described in terms of a single set of necessary and sufficient conditions. A wide range of different considerations has shown how unrealistic or how sterile this assumption is in the case of law and has compelled its surrender. Among these considerations is the realization that although there are central clear instances to which the expressions "law" and "legal system" have undisputed application, there are also cases, such as international law and primitive law, which have certain features of the central case but lack others. Also, there is the realization that the justification for applying general expressions to a range of different cases often lies not in their conformity to a set of necessary and sufficient conditions but in the analogies that link them or their varying relationships to some single element.

Lexical definitions and deviant cases. The foregoing are difficulties of definition commonly met in many areas of philosophy, but the definition of law has peculiar difficulties of its own. Thus, the assumption that the definition of law either has been or should be lexical, that is, concerned with the characterization or elucidation of *any* actual usage, has been challenged on several grounds. Thus it is often asserted that in the case of law, the area of indeterminacy of actual usage is too great and relates to too many important and disputed issues, and that what is needed is not a characterization or elucidation of usage but a reasoned case for the inclusion in or exclusion from the scope of the expressions "law" and "legal system" of various deviations from routine and undisputed examples. These deviant cases include not only international law and primitive law but also certain elements found in developed municipal legal systems, such as rules to which the usual sanctions are not attached and rules which run counter to fundamental principles of morality and justice.

Pragmatic definitions. In the above circumstances some theorists disclaim as necessarily deceptive any aim to provide an analysis or definition of law which is a neutral description or elucidation of usage; instead, they speak of the task of definition as "stipulative," "pragmatic," or "constructive," that is, as designed to provide a scheme or model for the demarcation and classification of an area of study. The criterion of adequacy of such pragmatic definitions is not conformity to or the capacity to explain any actual usage but the capacity to advance the theorists' specific aims, which may differ widely. Thus, a definition of law to be used for the instruction or assistance of lawyers concerned primarily with the outcome of litigation or court proceedings will differ from the definition used to demarcate and unify the fruitful area of historical study and will also differ from the definition to be used by the social critic concerned with identifying the extent to which human interests are advanced or frustrated by modes of social organization and control.

Structural problems. Neither the legitimacy of pragmatic definitions nor their utility for deliberately chosen objectives need be disputed. But it is clear that they avoid rather than resolve many of the long-standing perplexities which have motivated requests for the definition of law and have made it a philosophical problem. The factors which have generated these perplexities may be summarized as follows: Notwithstanding the considerable area of indeterminacy in their use, the expressions "law," "a law," "legal system," and a wide range of derivative and interrelated expressions ("legislation," "courts of law," "the application of law," "legal adjudication") are sufficiently determinate to make possible general agreement in judgments about their application to particular instances. But reflection on what is thus identified by the common usage of such terms shows that the area they cover is one of great internal complexity; laws differ radically both in content and in the ways in which they are created, yet despite this heterogeneity they are interrelated in various complex ways so as to constitute a characteristic structure or system. Many requests for the definition of law have been stimulated by the desire to obtain a coherent view of this structure and an understanding of the ways in which elements apparently so diverse and unified. These are problems, therefore, of the structure of law.

Coercion and morality. Reflection on the operations of a legal system discloses problems of another sort, for it is clear that law as a mode of influence on human behavior is intimately related to and in many ways dependent upon the use or threat of force on the one hand and on morality and justice on the other. Yet law is also, at points, distinct from both, so no obvious account of these connections appears acceptable: they appear to be not merely contingent, and since they sometimes fail, the statement of these connections does not appear to be any easily comprehensible species of necessary truth. Such tensions create demands for some stable and coherent definition of the relationships between law, coercion, and morality; but definitions of law have only in part been designed to make these important areas of human experience more intelligible. Practical and indeed political issues have long been intertwined with theoretical ones; and as is evident from the long history of the doctrines of natural law and legal positivism, the advocacy of a submissive or a critical attitude to law, or even of obedience or disobedience, has often been presented in the form of a persuasive definition of the relationship between law and morality on the one hand and between law and mere force on the other.

The analysis of legal concepts. Although legal rules are of many different types and may be classified from many different points of view, they have many common constituents; and although the law creates for both individuals and groups a great variety of different situations and relationships, some of these are constantly recurrent and of obvious importance for the conduct of social life. Both lawyers and laymen have frequent occasion to refer to these common elements and situations, and for this purpose they use classifications and organizing concepts expressed in a vocabulary which has bred many problems of analysis.

These problems arise in part because this vocabulary has a more or less established use apart from law, and the points of convergence and divergence between legal and non-legal usage is not always immediately obvious or easily explicable. It is also the case that the ways in which common elements in law or legal situations are classified by different theorists in part reflect and derive from divergent conceptions of law in general. Therefore, although different writers use such expressions as "rights" and "duty" in referring to the same legal situations, they select different elements or aspects from these situations. A third factor calling for clarification is the fact that many of the commonest notions used in referring to legal phenomena can be explicated only when certain distinctive ways in which language functions in conjunction with practical rules have been understood. These problems of analysis are illustrated in the case of the concepts of (1) legal obligation or duty, (2) a legal transaction, and (3) intention. (Certain distinctions once made between the notions of a legal obligation and a legal duty are no longer of importance and will be disregarded.)

Legal obligations or duties. The situation in which an individual has a legal duty to do or to abstain from some action is the commonest and most fundamental of all legal phenomena; the reference to duty or its absence is involved in the definition of such other legal concepts as those of a right, a power, a legal transaction, or a legal personality. Whenever the law of an effective legal system provides for the punishment of those who act or fail to act in certain ways, the word "duty" applies. Thus, to take a simple example, if the law requires under penalty that persons of a certain age shall report for military service, then such persons have, or are "under," a legal duty to do so. This much is undisputed, however much theorists may dispute over the analysis of "duty" or its application to situations created not by the criminal law but by the law relating to torts or to contract.

However, even the above simple situation can be viewed from two very different standpoints that give rise to apparently conflicting analyses of duty. From one of these (the predictive standpoint), reporting for military service is classified as a duty simply because failure to report renders likely certain forms of suffering at the hands of officials. From the other standpoint (the normative standpoint), reporting for military service is classified as a duty because, owing to the existence of the law, it is an action which may be rightly or justifiably demanded of those concerned; and failure to report is significant not merely because it renders future suffering likely but also because punishment is legally justified even if it does not always follow disobedience.

From Jeremy Bentham onward the predictive analysis of duty as a chance or likelihood of suffering in the event of disobedience to the law has been advocated by important writers for a variety of theoretical and practical reasons. On the one hand it has seemed to free the idea of legal duty from metaphysical obscurities and irrelevant associations with morals, and on the other to provide a realistic guide to life under law. It isolates what for some men is the only important fact about the operation of a legal system and what for all men is at least one important fact: the occa-sions and ways in which the law works adversely to their interests. This is of paramount importance not only to the malefactor but also to the critic and reformer of the law concerned to balance against the benefits which law brings its costs in terms of human suffering.

By contrast, the normative point of view, without identifying moral and legal duty or insisting on any common content, stresses certain common formal features that both moral and legal duty possess in virtue of their both being aspects of rule-guided conduct. This is the point of view of those who, although they may not regard the law as the final arbiter of conduct, nevertheless generally accept the existence of legal rule as a guide to conduct and as legally justifying demands for conformity, punishment, enforced compensation, or other forms of coercion. Attention to these features of the idea of duty is essential for understanding the ways in which law is conceived of and operative in social life.

Although theorists have often attributed exclusive correctness to these different standpoints, there are various ways in which they may be illuminatingly combined. Thus, the normative account might be said to give correctly the meaning of such statements as that a person has a legal duty to do a certain action, while the predictive account emphasizes that very frequently the point or purpose of making such statements is to warn that suffering is likely to follow disobedience. Such a distinction between the meaning of a statement and what is implied or intended by its assertion in different contexts is of considerable importance in many areas of legal philosophy.

Legal transactions. The enactment of a law, the making of a contract, and the transfer by words, written or spoken, of ownership or other rights are examples of legal transactions which are made possible by the existence of certain types of legal rules and are definable in terms of such rules. To some thinkers, such transactions (acts in the law, or juristic acts) have appeared mysterious—some have even called them magical—because their effect is to change the legal position of individuals or to make or eliminate laws. Since, in most modern systems of law, such changes are usually effected by the use of words, written or spoken, there seems to be a species of legal alchemy. It is not obvious how the mere use of expressions like "it is hereby enacted . . . ," "I hereby bequeath . . . ," or "the parties hereby agree . . ." can produce changes. In fact, the general form of this phenomenon is not exclusively legal, although it has only comparatively recently been clearly isolated and analyzed. The words of an ordinary promise or those used in a christening ceremony in giving a name to a child are obvious analogues to the legal cases. Lawyers have sometimes marked off this distinctive function of language as the use of "operative words," and under this category have distinguished, for example, the words used in a lease to create a tenancy from the merely descriptive language of the preliminary recital of the facts concerning the parties and their agreement.

For words (or in certain cases gestures, as in voting or other forms of behavior) to have such operative effect, there must exist legal rules providing that if the words (or gestures) are used in appropriate circumstances by appropriately qualified persons, the general law or the legal position of individuals is to be taken as changed. Such rules may be conceived from one point of view as giving to the language used a certain kind of force or effect which is in a broad sense their meaning; from another point of view they may be conceived as conferring on individuals the legal power to make such legal changes. In Continental jurisprudence such rules are usually referred to as "norms of competence" to distinguish them from simpler legal rules that merely impose duties with or without correlative rights.

As the expressions "acts-in-the-law" and "operative words" suggest, there are important resemblances between the execution of legal transactions and more obvious cases of human actions. These points of resemblance are of especial importance in understanding what has often seemed problematic—the relevance of the mental or psychological states of the parties concerned to the constitution or validity of such transactions. In many cases the relevant rules provide that a transaction shall be invalid or at least liable to be set aside at the option of various persons if the person purporting to effect it was insane, mistaken in regard to certain matters, or subjected to duress or undue influence. There is here an important analogy with the ways in which similar psychological facts (*mens rea*) may, in accordance with the principles of the criminal law, excuse a person from criminal responsibility for his action. In both spheres there are exceptions: in the criminal law there are certain cases of "strict" liability where no element of knowledge or intention need be proved; and in certain types of legal transaction, proof that a person attached a special meaning to the words he used or was mistaken in some respect in using them would not invalidate the transaction, at least as against those who have relied upon it in good faith.

Attention to these analogies between valid legal transactions and responsible action and the mental conditions that in the one case invalidate and in the other excuse from responsibility illuminates many obscure theoretical disputes concerning the nature of legal transactions such as contract. Thus, according to one principal theory (the "will" theory) a contract is essentially a complex psychological fact—something which comes into being when there is a meeting of minds (*consensus ad idem*) that jointly "will" or "intend" a certain set of mutual rights and duties to come into existence. The words used are, according to this theory, merely evidence of this consensus. The rival theory (the "objective" theory) insists that what makes a contract is not a psychological phenomenon but the actual use of words of offer and acceptance, and that except in special cases the law simply gives effect to the ordinary meaning of the language used by the parties and is not concerned with their actual states of mind. Plainly, each side to this dispute fastens on something important but exaggerates it. It is indeed true that, like an ordinary promise, a legal contract is not made by psychological facts. A contract, like a promise, is "made" not by the existence of mental states but by words (or in some cases deeds). If it is verbally made, it is made by the operative use of language, and there are many legal rules inconsistent with the idea that a *consensus ad idem* is required. On the other hand, just because the operative use of language

is a kind of action, the law may—and in most civilized legal systems does—extend to it a doctrine of responsibility or validity under which certain mental elements are made relevant. Thus a contract, although made by words, may be vitiated or made void or "voidable" if a party is insane, mistaken in certain ways, or under duress. The truths latent among the errors of the "will" theory and the "objective" theory can therefore be brought together in an analysis which makes explicit the analogy between valid transactions made by the operative use of language and responsible actions.

Intention. The fact that the law often treats certain mental states or psychological conditions as essential elements both in the validity of legal transactions and in criminal responsibility has thrust upon lawyers the task of distinguishing between and analyzing such notions as "will," "intention," and "motive." These are concepts which have long puzzled philosophers not primarily concerned with the law, and their application in the law creates further specific problems. These arise in various ways: there are divergencies between the legal and nonlegal use of these notions which are not always obvious or easily understood; the law, because of difficulties of proof or as a matter of social policy, may often adopt what are called external or objective standards, which treat certain forms of outward behavior as conclusive evidence of the existence of mental states or impute to an individual the mental state that the average man behaving in a given way would have had. Although statutes occasionally use expressions like "maliciously," "knowingly," or "with intent," for the most part the expressions "intentionally" and "voluntarily" are not the language of legal rules but are used in the exposition of such rules in summarizing the various ways in which either criminal charges or civil claims may fail if something is done—for instance, accidentally, by mistake, or under duress.

The problems that arise in these ways may be illustrated in the case of intention. Legal theorists have recognized intention as the mental element of central importance to the law. Thus, an intention to do the act forbidden by law is in Anglo-American law normally the sufficient mental element for criminal responsibility and also is normally, although not always, necessary for responsibility. So if a man intends to do the act forbidden by law, other factors having to do with his powers of self-control are usually irrelevant, although sometimes duress and sometimes provocation or deficient ability to control conduct, caused by mental disorder, may become relevant. In fact, three distinct applications of the notion of intention are important in the law, and it is necessary to distinguish in any analysis of this concept (1) the idea of intentionally doing something forbidden by law; (2) doing something with a further intention; and (3) the intention to do a future act. The first of these is in issue when, if a man is found to have wounded or killed another, the question is asked whether he did it intentionally or unintentionally. The second is raised when the law, as in the case of burglary defined as "breaking into premises at night with the intention of committing a felony," attaches special importance or more severe penalties to an action if it is done for some further purpose, even though the latter is not executed.

The third application of intention can be seen in those cases where an act is criminal if it is accompanied by a certain intention—for instance, incurring a debt with the intention never to pay.

Of these three applications the first is of chief importance in the law, but even here the law only approximates to the nonlegal concept and disregards certain elements in its ordinary usage. For in the law the question whether a man did something intentionally or not is almost wholly a question concerning his knowledge or belief at the time of his action. Hence, in most cases when an action falling under a certain description (such as wounding a policeman) is made a crime, the law is satisfied, insofar as any matter of intention is concerned, if the accused knew or believed that his action would cause injury to his victim and that his victim was in fact a policeman. This almost exclusively cognitive approach is one distinctive way in which the law diverges from the ordinary idea of intentionally doing something, for in ordinary thought not all the foreseen consequences of conduct are regarded as intended.

A rationale of this divergence can be provided, however. Although apart from the law a man will be held to have done something intentionally only if the outcome is something aimed at or for the sake of which he acted, this element which the law generally disregards is not relevant to the main question with which the law is concerned in determining a man's legal responsibility for bringing about a certain state of affairs. The crucial question at this stage in a criminal proceeding is whether a man whose outward conduct and its consequences fall within the definition of a crime had at the time he acted a choice whether these consequences were or were not to occur. If he did, and if he chose that insofar as he had influence over events they would occur, then for the law it is irrelevant that he merely foresaw that they would occur and that it was not his purpose to bring them about. The law at the stage of assessing a man's responsibility is interested only in his conscious control over the outcome, and discards those elements in the ordinary concept of intention which are irrelevant to the conception of control. But when the stage of conviction in a criminal proceeding is past, and the question becomes how severely the criminal is to be punished, the matter previously neglected often becomes relevant. Distinctions may be drawn at this stage between the man who acted for a certain purpose and one who acted merely foreseeing that certain consequences would come about.

The second and third applications of the notion of intention (doing something with a further intent and the intention to do a future action) are closer to nonlegal usage, and in the law, as elsewhere, certain problems of distinguishing motive and intention arise in such cases.

PROBLEMS OF LEGAL REASONING

Since the early twentieth century, the critical study of the forms of reasoning by which courts decide cases has been a principal concern of writers on jurisprudence, especially in America. From this study there has emerged a great variety of theories regarding the actual or proper place in the process of adjudication of what has been termed, often ambiguously, "logic." Most of these theories are skeptical and are designed to show that despite appearances, deductive and inductive reasoning play only a subordinate role. Contrasts are drawn between "logic" and "experience" (as in Holmes's famous dictum that "the life of the law has not been logic; it has been experience") or between "deductivism" or "formalism" on the one hand and "creative choice" or "intuitions of fitness" on the other. In general, such theories tend to insist that the latter members of these contrasted sets of expressions more adequately characterize the process of legal adjudication, despite its appearance of logical method and form. According to some variants of these theories, although logic in the sense of deductive and inductive reasoning plays little part, there are other processes of legal reasoning or rational criteria which courts do and should follow in deciding cases. According to more extreme variants, the decisions of courts are essentially arbitrary.

Legislation and precedent. In Anglo-American jurisprudence the character of legal reasoning has been discussed chiefly with reference to the use by the courts of two "sources" of law: (1) the general rules made by legislative bodies (or by other rule-making agencies to which legislative powers have been delegated) and (2) particular precedents or past decisions of courts which are treated as material from which legal rules may be extracted although, unlike legislative rules, there is no authoritative or uniquely correct formulation of the rules so extracted. Conventional accounts of the reasoning involved in the application of legislative rules to particular cases have often pictured it as exclusively a matter of deductive inference. The court's decision is represented as the conclusion of a syllogism in which the major premise consists of the rule and the minor premise consists of the statement of the facts which are agreed or established in the case. Similarly, conventional accounts of the use of precedents by courts speak of the courts' extraction of a rule from past cases as inductive reasoning and the application of that rule to the case in hand as deductive reasoning.

In their attack on these conventional accounts of judicial reasoning, skeptical writers have revealed much that is of great importance both to the understanding and to the criticism of methods of legal adjudication. There are undoubtedly crucially important phases in the use of legal rules and precedents to decide cases which do not consist merely of logical operations and which have long been obscured by the traditional terminology adopted both by the courts themselves in deciding cases and by jurists in describing the activities of courts. Unfortunately, the general claim that logic has little or no part to play in the judicial process is, in spite of its simple and monolithic appearance, both obscure and ambiguous; it embraces a number of different and sometimes conflicting contentions which must be separately investigated. The most important of these issues are identified and discussed below. There are, however, two preliminary issues of peculiar concern to philosophers and logicians which demand attention in any serious attempt to characterize the forms of legal reasonings.

Deductive reasoning. It has been contended that the application of legal rules to particular cases cannot be regarded as a syllogism or any other kind of deductive inference, on the grounds that neither general legal rules nor particular statements of law (such as those ascribing rights or duties to individuals) can be characterized as either true or false and thus cannot be logically related either among themselves or to statements of fact; hence, they cannot figure as premises or conclusions of a deductive argument. This view depends on a restrictive definition, in terms of truth and falsehood, of the notion of a valid deductive inference and of logical relations such as consistency and contradiction. This would exclude from the scope of deductive inference not only legal rules or statements of law but also commands and many other sentential forms which are commonly regarded as susceptible of logical relations and as constituents of valid deductive arguments. Although considerable technical complexities are involved, several more general definitions of the idea of valid deductive inference that render the notion applicable to inferences the constituents of which are not characterized as either true or false have now been worked out by logicians. In what follows, as in most of contemporary jurisprudential literature, the general acceptability of this more generalized definition of valid inference is assumed.

Inductive reasoning. Considerable obscurity surrounds the claim made by more conventional jurisprudential writers that inductive reasoning is involved in the judicial use of precedents. Reference to induction is usually made in this connection to point a contrast with the allegedly deductive reasoning involved in the application of legislative rules to particular cases. "Instead of starting with a general rule the judge must turn to the relevant cases, discover the general rule implicit in them . . . . The outstanding difference between the two methods is the source of the major premise—the deductive method assumes it whereas the inductive sets out to discover it from particular instances" (G. W. Paton, *A Textbook of Jurisprudence*, 2d ed., Oxford, 1951, pp. 171–172).

It is of course true that courts constantly refer to past cases both to discover rules and to justify their acceptance of them as valid. The past cases are said to be "authority" for the rules "extracted" from them. Plainly, one necessary condition must be satisfied if past cases are in this way to justify logically the acceptance of a rule: the past case must be an instance of the rule in the sense that the decision in the case could be deduced from a statement of the rule together with a statement of the facts of the case. The reasoning insofar as the satisfaction of this necessary condition is concerned is in fact an inverse application of deductive reasoning. But this condition is, of course, only one necessary condition and not a sufficient condition of the court's acceptance of a rule on the basis of past cases, since for any given precedent there are logically an indefinite number of alternative general rules which can satisfy the condition. The selection, therefore, of one rule from among these alternatives as the rule for which the precedent is taken to be authority must depend on the use of other criteria limiting the choice, and these other criteria are not matters of logic but substantive matters which may vary from system to system or from time to time in the same system. Thus, some theories of the judicial use of precedent insist that the rule for which a precedent is authority must be indicated either explicitly or implicitly by the court through its choice of facts to be treated as "material" to a case. Other theories insist that the rule for which a precedent is authority is the rule which a later court considering the precedent would select from the logically possible alternatives after weighing the usual moral and social factors.

Although many legal writers still speak of the extraction of general rules from precedents, some would claim that the reasoning involved in their use of precedents is essentially reasoning from case to case "by example": A court decides the present case in the same way as a past case if the latter "sufficiently" resembles the former in "relevant" respects, and thus makes use of the past case as a precedent without first extracting from it and formulating any general rule. Nevertheless, the more conventional accounts, according to which courts use past cases to discover and justify their acceptance of general rules, are sufficiently widespread and plausible to make the use of the term "induction" in this connection worth discussing.

The use of "induction" to refer to the inverse application of deduction involved in finding that a past case is the instance of a general rule may be misleading: it suggests stronger analogies than exist with the modes of probabilistic inference used in the sciences when general propositions of fact or statements about unobserved particulars are inferred from or regarded as confirmed by observed particulars. "Induction" may also invite confusion with the form of deductive inference known as perfect induction, or with real or alleged methods of discovering generalizations sometimes referred to as intuitive induction.

It is, however, true that the inverse application of deduction involved in the use of precedents is also an important part of scientific procedure, where it is known as hypothetic inference or hypotheticodeductive reasoning. Hence, there are certain interesting analogies between the interplay of observation and theory involved in the progressive refining of a scientific hypothesis to avoid its falsification by contrary instances and the way in which a court may refine a general rule both to make it consistent with a wide range of different cases and to avoid a formulation which would have unjust or undesirable consequences.

Notwithstanding these analogies, the crucial difference remains between the search for general propositions of fact rendered probable by confirming instances but still falsifiable by future experience, and rules to be used in the decision of cases. An empirical science of the judicial process is of course possible: it would consist of factual generalization about the decisions of courts and might be an important predictive tool. However, it is important to distinguish the general propositions of such an empirical science from the rules formulated and used by courts.

Descriptive and prescriptive theories. The claim that logic plays only a subordinate part in the decision of cases is sometimes intended as a corrective to misleading descriptions of the judicial process, but sometimes it is intended as a criticism of the methods used by courts, which are stigmatized as "excessively logical," "formal," "mechanical," or "automatic." Descriptions of the methods actually used by courts must be distinguished from prescriptions of alternative methods and must be separately assessed. It is, however, notable that in many discussions of legal reasoning these two are often confused, perhaps because the effort to correct conventional misdescriptions of the judicial process and the effort to correct the process itself have been inspired by the realization of the same important but often neglected fact: the relative indeterminacy of legal rules and precedents. This indeterminacy springs from the fact that it is impossible in framing general rules to anticipate and provide for every possible combination of circumstances which the future may bring. For any rule, however precisely formulated, there will always be some factual situations in which the question whether the situations fall within the scope of the general classificatory terms of the rule cannot be settled by appeal to linguistic rules or conventions or to canons of statutory interpretation, or even by reference to the manifest or assumed purposes of the legislature. In such cases the rules may be found either vague or ambiguous. A similar indeterminacy may arise when two rules apply to a given factual situation and also where rules are expressly framed in such unspecific terms as "reasonable" or "material." Such cases can be resolved only by methods whose rationality cannot lie in the logical relations of conclusions to premises. Similarly, because precedents can logically be subsumed under an indefinite number of general rules, the identification of *the* rule for which a precedent is an authority cannot be settled by an appeal to logic.

These criticisms of traditional descriptions of the judicial process are in general well taken. It is true that both jurists and judges, particularly in jurisdictions in which the separation of powers is respected, have frequently suppressed or minimized the indeterminacy of legal rules or precedents when giving an account of the use of them in the process of decision. On the other hand, another complaint often made by the same writers, that there is an excess of logic or formalism in the judicial process, is less easy to understand and to substantiate. What the critics intend to stigmatize by these terms is the failure of courts, when applying legal rules or precedents, to take advantage of the relative indeterminacy of the rules or precedents to give effect to social aims, policies, and values. Courts, according to these critics, instead of exploiting the fact that the meaning of a statutory rule is indeterminate at certain points, have taken the meaning to be determinate simply because in some different legal context similar wording has been interpreted in a certain way or because a given interpretation is the "ordinary" meaning of the words used.

This failure to recognize the indeterminacy of legal rule (often wrongly ascribed to analytical jurisprudence and stigmatized as conceptualism) has sometimes been defended on the ground that it maximizes certainty and the predictability of decisions. It has also sometimes been welcomed as furthering an ideal of a legal system in which there are a minimum number of independent rules and categories of classification.

The vice of such methods of applying rules is that their adoption prejudges what is to be done in ranges of different cases whose composition cannot be exhaustively known beforehand: rigid classification and divisions are set up which ignore differences and similarities of social and moral importance. This is the burden of the complaint that there is an excessive use of logic in the judicial process. But the expression "an excessive use of logic" is unhappy, for when social values and distinctions of importance are ignored in the interpretation of legal rules and the classification of particulars, the decision reached is not more logical than decisions which give due recognition to these factors: logic does not determine the interpretation of words or the scope of classifications. What is true is that in a system in which such rigid modes of interpretation are common, there will be more occasions when a judge can treat himself as confronted with a rule whose meaning has been predetermined.

Methods of discovery and standards of appraisal. In considering both descriptive and prescriptive theories of judicial reasoning, it is important to distinguish (1) assertions made concerning the usual processes or habits of thought by which judges actually reach their decisions, (2) recommendations concerning the processes to be followed, and (3) the standards by which judicial decisions are to be appraised. The first of these concerns matters of descriptive psychology, and to the extent that assertions in this field go beyond the descriptions of examined instances, they are empirical generalizations or laws of psychology; the second concerns the art or craft of legal judgment, and generalizations in this field are principles of judicial technology; the third relates to the assessment or justification of decisions.

These distinctions are important because it has sometimes been argued that since judges frequently arrive at decisions without going through any process of calculation or inference in which legal rules or precedents figure, the claim that deduction from legal rules plays any part in decision is mistaken. This argument is confused, for in general the issue is not one regarding the manner in which judges do, or should, come to their decisions; rather, it concerns the standards they respect in justifying decisions, however reached. The presence or absence of logic in the appraisal of decisions may be a reality whether the decisions are reached by calculation or by an intuitive leap.

Clear cases and indeterminate rules. When the various issues identified above are distinguished, two sets of questions emerge. The first of these concerns the decisions of courts in "clear" cases where no doubts are felt about the meaning and applicability of a single legal rule, and the second concerns decisions where the indeterminacy of the relevant legal rules and precedents is acknowledged.

Clear cases. Even where courts acknowledge that an antecedent legal rule uniquely determines a particular result, some theorists have claimed that this cannot be the case, that courts always "have a choice," and that assertions to the contrary can only be ex post facto rationalizations. Often this skepticism springs from the confusion of the questions of methods of discovery with standards of appraisal noted above. Sometimes, however, it is supported by references to the facts that even if courts fail to apply a clearly applicable rule using a determinate result, this is not a punishable offense, and that the decision given is still authoritative and, if made by a supreme tribunal, final. Hence, it is argued that although courts may show a certain degree of regularity in decision, they are never bound to do so: they always are free to decide otherwise than they do. These last arguments rest on a confusion of finality with infallibility in decisions and on a disputable interpretation of the notion of "being bound" to respect legal rules.

Yet skepticism of this character, however unacceptable, does serve to emphasize that it is a matter of some difficulty to give any exhaustive account of what makes a "clear case" clear or makes a general rule obviously and uniquely applicable to a particular case. Rules cannot claim their own instances, and fact situations do not await the judge neatly labeled with the rule applicable to them. Rules cannot provide for their own application, and even in the clearest case a human being must apply them. The clear cases are those in which there is general agreement that they fall within the scope of a rule, and it is tempting to ascribe such agreements simply to the fact that there are necessarily such agreements in the use of the shared conventions of language. But this would be an oversimplification because it does not allow for the special conventions of the legal use of words, which may diverge from their common use, or for the way in which the meanings of words may be clearly controlled by reference to the purpose of a statutory enactment which itself may be either explicitly stated or generally agreed. A full exploration of these questions is the subject matter of the study of the interpretation of statute.

Indeterminate rules. The decisions of cases which cannot be exhibited as deductions from determinate legal rules have often been described as arbitrary. Although much empirical study of the judicial process remains to be done, it is obvious that this description and the dichotomy of logical deduction and arbitrary decision, if taken as exhaustive, is misleading. Judges do not generally, when legal rules fail to determine a unique result, intrude their personal preferences or blindly choose among alternatives; and when words like "choice" and "discretion," or phrases such as "creative activity" and "interstitial legislation" are used to describe decisions, these do not mean that courts do decide arbitrarily without elaborating reasons for their decisions—and still less that any legal system authorizes decisions of this kind.

It is of crucial importance that cases for decision do not arise in a vacuum but in the course of the operation of a working body of rules, an operation in which a multiplicity of diverse considerations are continuously recognized as good reasons for a decision. These include a wide variety of individual and social interests, social and political aims, and standards of morality and justice; and they may be formulated in general terms as principles, policies, and standards. In some cases only one such consideration may be relevant, and it may determine decision as unambiguously as a determinate legal rule. But in many cases this is not so, and judges marshal in support of their decisions a plurality of such considerations which they regard as jointly sufficient to support their decision, although each separately would not be. Frequently these considerations conflict, and courts are forced to balance or weigh them and to determine priorities among them. The same considerations (and the same need for weighing them when they conflict) enter into the use of precedents when courts must choose between alternative rules which can be extracted from them, or when courts consider whether a present case sufficiently resembles a past case in relevant respects.

Perhaps most modern writers would agree up to this point with this account of judicial decision where legal rules are indeterminate, but beyond this point there is a divergence. Some theorists claim that notwithstanding the heterogeneous and often conflicting character of the factors which are relevant to decision, it is still meaningful to speak of a decision as *the* uniquely correct decision in any case and of the duty of the judge to discover it. They would claim that a judicial choice or preference does not become rational because it is deferred until after the judge has considered the factors that weigh for and against it.

Other theorists would repudiate the idea that in such cases there is always a decision which is uniquely correct, although they of course agree that many decisions can be clearly ruled out as incorrect. They would claim that all that courts do and can do at the end of the process of coolly and impartially considering the relevant considerations is to choose one alternative which they find the most strongly supported, and that it is perfectly proper for them to concede that another equally skilled and impartial judge might choose the other alternative. The theoretical issues are not different from those which arise at many points in the philosophical discussions of moral argument. It may well be that terms like "choice," "discretion," and "judicial legislation" fail to do justice to the phenomenology of considered decision: its felt involuntary or even inevitable character which often marks the termination of deliberation on conflicting considerations. Very often the decision to include a new case in the scope of a rule or to exclude it is guided by the sense that this is the "natural" continuation of a line of decisions or carries out the "spirit" of a rule. It is also true that if there were not also considerable agreement in judgment among lawyers who approach decisions in these ways, we should not attach significance and value to them or think of such decisions as reached through a rational process. Yet however it may be in moral argument, in the law it seems difficult to substantiate the claim that a judge confronted with a set of conflicting considerations must always assume that there is a single uniquely correct resolution of the conflict and attempt to demonstrate that he has discovered it.

Rules of evidence. Courts receive and evaluate testimony of witnesses, infer statements of fact from other statements, and accept some statements as probable or more probable than others or as "beyond reasonable doubt." When it is said that in these activities special modes of legal reasoning are exhibited and that legal proof is different from ordinary proof, reference is usually intended to the exclusionary rules of the law of evidence (which frequently require courts, in determining questions of fact, to disregard matters which are logically relevant), or to various presumptions which assign greater or lesser weight to logically relevant considerations than ordinary standards of reasoning do.

The most famous examples of exclusionary rules are those against "hearsay," which (subject to certain exceptions) make inadmissible, as evidence of the facts stated, reports tendered by a witness, however credible, of statements made by another person. Another example is the rule that when a person is charged with a crime, evidence of his past convictions and disposition to commit similar crimes is not admissible as evidence to show that he committed the crime charged. An example of a rule which may give certain facts greater or less probative weight than ordinary standards do is the presumption that unless the contrary is proved beyond reasonable doubt, a child born to a woman during wedlock is the child of both parties to the marriage.

The application of such rules and their exceptions gives rise to results which may seem paradoxical, even though they are justifiable in terms of the many different social needs which the courts must satisfy in adjudicating cases. Thus, one consequence of the well-known exception to the hearsay rule that a report of a statement is admissible as evidence of a fact stated if it is made against the interest of the person who stated it, is that a court may find that a man committed adultery with a particular woman but be unable to draw the conclusion that she committed adultery with him. A logician might express the resolution of the paradox by saying that from the fact that p entails q it does not follow that "it is legally proved that p" entails "it is legally proved that q."

Apart from such paradoxes, the application of the rules of evidence involves the drawing of distinctions of considerable philosophical importance. Thus, although in general the law excludes reports of statements as evidence of the facts stated, it may admit such reports for other purposes, and in fact draws a distinction between statements of fact and what J. L. Austin called performative utterances. Hence, if the issue is whether a given person made a promise or placed a bet, reports that he uttered words which in the context amounted to a promise or a bet are admissible. So, too, reports of a person's statement of his contemporary mental states or sensations are admissible, and some theorists justify this on the ground that such first-person statements are to be assimilated to behavior manifesting the mental state or sensation in question.

PROBLEMS OF THE CRITICISM OF LAW

Analysis and evaluation. A division between inquiries concerned with the analysis of law and legal concepts and those concerned with the criticism or evaluation of law prima facie seems not only possible but necessary, yet the conception of an evaluatively neutral or autonomous analytical study of the law has not only been contested but also has been taken by some modern critics to be the hallmark of a shallow and useless legal positivism allegedly unconcerned with the values or ends which men pursue through law.

Objections to pure analysis. Many different objections to a purely analytical jurisprudence have been made. By some it has been identified with, or thought to entail commitment to, the view that a legal system is a closed logical structure in which decisions in particular cases are "mechanically" deduced from clear antecedent rules whose identification or interpretation presents no problem of choice and involves no judgment of value. Other critics have contended that any serious demand for the definition of a legal concept must at least include a request for guidance as to the manner in which, when the relevant legal rules are unclear or indeterminate, particular cases involving the concept in question should best be determined. It is assumed by these critics that any question concerning the meaning of expressions such as "a right" or "a duty," as distinct from the question of what rights or duties should be legally recognized, are trivial questions to be settled by reference to a dictionary. Still others have urged that since the maintenance of a legal system and the typical operations of the law (legislation, adjudication, and the making of legal transactions) are purposive activities, any study which isolates law or legal phenomena for study without considering their adequacy or inadequacy for human purposes makes a vicious abstraction which is bound to lead to misunderstanding.

Replies to objections. None of the above seem to constitute serious objections. The difficulties of decision in particular cases arising from the relative indeterminacy of legal rules are of great importance, but they are distinct from analytical questions such as those illustrated earlier, which remain to be answered even when legal rules are clear. Thus the isolation and characterization of the normative and predictive standpoints from which law may be viewed and the precise manner of interplay between subjective and objective factors in legal transactions are not things that can be discovered from dictionaries. But attention to them is indispensable in the analysis of the notion of a legal obligation, a legal right, or a contract. There is of course much justice in the claim that in order to understand certain features of legal institutions or legal rules, the aims and purposes they are designed to fulfill must be understood. Thus, a tax cannot be distinguished from a fine except by reference to the purpose for which it is imposed; but to recognize this is not to abandon an analytical study of the law for an evaluative one. The identification of something as an instrument for certain purposes leaves open the question whether it is good or bad, although such identification may indicate the standards by reference to which this question is to be answered. In any case, there are many features of legal rules which may profitably be studied in abstraction from the purposes which such rules may be designed to achieve.

Criteria of evaluation. Nonetheless, protests against the severance of analytical from critical or evaluative inquiries, even if misdirected in their ostensible aim, often serve to emphasize something important. These protests are usually accompanied by and sometimes confused with a general thesis concerning the standards and principles of criticism specifically appropriate to law. This is the thesis (which has appeared in many different forms in the history of the philosophy of law) that, whatever may be the case with value judgments in other fields or with moral judgments concerning the activities of individuals, the criteria which distinguish good law from bad do not merely reflect human preferences, tastes, or conventions, which may vary from society to society or from time to time; rather, they are determined by certain constant features of human nature and the natural environment with which men must contend.

The doctrine of natural law in its various traditional forms embodies this thesis. There are, however, obscurities and metaphysical assumptions involved in the use by natural-law theorists of the notions of nature and reason which make their formulations unacceptable to most modern secular thought; and they often confuse their important arguments concerning the principles by which law and social institutions should be judged with arguments designed to show that a reference to morality or justice must be introduced into the definition of law or legal validity. Nonetheless, it is possible to segregate these tangled issues, and some important modern philosophical arguments concern the possibility of restating in an acceptable form the claim that there are certain objective and rationally determined criteria for the evaluation and criticism of law. These arguments will be sketched here in relation to substantive law, procedural law, and the ideas of justice and utility.

Substantive law. The purposes which human beings pursue in society and for the realization of which they employ law as an instrument are infinitely various, and men may differ in the importance they attach to them and in their moral judgments about them. But the simplest form of the argument that there are certain constant criteria for the evaluation of a legal system consists in the elaboration of the truth that if law is to be of any value as an instrument for the realization of human purposes, it must contain certain rules concerning the basic conditions of social life. Thus it is not only true that the legal system of any modern state and any legal system which has succeeded in enduring have contained rules restricting the use of violence, protecting certain forms of property, and enforcing certain forms of contract; it is also clear that without the protections and advantages that such rules supply, men would be grossly hampered in the pursuit of any aims. Legal rules providing for these things are therefore basic in the sense that without them other legal rules would be pointless or at least would operate only fitfully or inefficiently. Criticism of a legal system on the grounds that it omitted such rules could be rebutted only by the demonstration that in the particular case they were unnecessary because the human beings to which the system applied or their natural surroundings were in some way quite extraordinary, that is, that they lacked certain of the salient characteristics which men and things normally have. This is so because the need for such rules derives from such familiar natural facts as that men are both vulnerable to violence and tempted to use it against each other; that the food, clothes, and shelter necessary to existence do not exist naturally in limitless abundance but must be grown or manufactured by human effort and need legal protection from interference during growth and manufacture and safe custody pending consumption; and that to secure the mutual cooperation required for the profitable development of natural resources, men need legal rules enabling them to bind themselves to future courses of conduct.

Argument along these lines may be viewed as a modest empirical counterpart to the more ambitious teleological doctrine of natural law, according to which there are certain rules for the government of human conduct that can be seen by men endowed with reason as necessary to enable men to attain the specifically human optimum state or end

(*finis, telos*) appointed for men by Nature or (in Christian doctrine) by God. The empirical version of this theory assumes only that, whatever other purposes laws may serve, they must, to be acceptable to any rational person, enable men to live and organize their lives for the more efficient pursuit of their aims. It is, of course, possible to challenge this assumption and to deny that the fact that there are certain rules necessary if fundamental human needs are to be satisfied has any relevance to the criticism of law. But this denial seems intelligible only as a specifically religious doctrine which regards law as the expression of a divine will. It may then be argued that men's lives should be regulated by the law not in order to further any secular human purposes but because conformity to God's will is in itself meritorious or obligatory.

A more serious objection to the empirical argument conducted in terms of human needs for protection from violence to the person and property and for cooperation is the contention that although these are fundamental human needs, the coercive rules of a legal system need not provide for them. It may be said that the accepted morality of all societies provides a system of restraint which provides adequately for these needs, and that the vast majority of men abstain from murder, theft, and dishonesty not from fear of legal sanctions but for other, usually moral, reasons. In these circumstances it may be no defect in a legal system that it confines itself to other matters in relation to which the accepted morality is silent.

It seems clear, however, that social morality left to itself could not provide adequately for the fundamental needs of social life, save in the simplest forms of society. It may well be that most men, when they believe themselves to be protected from malefactors by the punishments, threats of punishment, and physical restraints of the law, will themselves voluntarily submit to the restraints necessary for peaceful and profitable coexistence. But it does not follow that without the law's protections, voluntary submission to these restraints would be either reasonable or likely. In any case, the rules and principles of social morality leave open to dispute too many questions concerning the precise scope and form of its restraints. Legal rules are needed to supply the detail required to distinguish murder and assault from excusable homicide and injury, to define the forms of property to be protected, and to specify the forms of contract to be enforced. Hence, the omission of such things from the legal system could not be excused on the ground that the existence of a social morality made them unnecessary.

Procedural law. Laws, however impeccable their content, may be of little service to human beings and may cause both injustice and misery unless they generally conform to certain requirements which may be broadly termed procedural (in contrast with the substantive requirements discussed above). These procedural requirements relate to such matters as the generality of rules of law, the clarity with which they are phrased, the publicity given to them, the time of their enactment, and the manner in which they are judicially applied to particular cases. The requirements that the law, except in special circumstances, should be general (should refer to classes of persons, things, and circumstances, not to individuals or to particular actions); should be free from contradictions, ambiguities, and obscurities; should be publicly promulgated and easily accessible; and should not be retrospective in operation are usually referred to as the principles of legality. The principles which require courts, in applying general rules to particular cases, to be without personal interest in the outcome or other bias and to hear arguments on matters of law and proofs of matters of fact from both sides of a dispute are often referred to as rules of natural justice. These two sets of principles together define the concept of the rule of law to which most modern states pay at least lip service.

These requirements and the specific value which conformity with them imparts to laws may be regarded from two different points of view. On the one hand, they maximize the probability that the conduct required by the law will be forthcoming, and on the other hand, they provide individuals whose freedom is limited by the law with certain information and assurances which assist them in planning their lives within the coercive framework of the law. This combination of values may be easily seen in the case of the requirements of generality, clarity, publicity, and prospective operation. For the alternative to control by general rules of law is orders addressed by officials to particular individuals to do or to abstain from particular actions; and although in all legal systems there are occasions for such particular official orders, no society could efficiently provide the number of officials required to make them a main form of social control.

Thus, general rules clearly framed and publicly promulgated are the most efficient form of social control. But from the point of view of the individual citizen, they are more than that: they are required if he is to have the advantage of knowing in advance the ways in which his liberty will be restricted in the various situations in which he may find himself, and he needs this knowledge if he is to plan his life. This is an argument for laws which are general in the sense of requiring courses of action and not particular actions. The argument for generality in the sense of applicability to classes of persons is different: it is that such rule confer upon the individual the advantage of knowing the restrictions to which the conduct of others besides himself will be subject. Such knowledge in the case of legal restrictions which protect or benefit the individual increases the confidence with which he can predict and plan his future.

The value of the principles of natural justice which concern the process of adjudication are closely linked to the principles of legality. The requirement that a court should be impartial and hear arguments and proofs from both sides of a dispute are guarantees of objectivity which increase the probability that the enacted law will be applied according to its tenor. It is necessary to insure by such means that there will be this congruence between judicial decisions and the enacted law if the commitment to general rules as a method of government is taken seriously.

Care must be taken not to ascribe to these arguments more than they actually prove. Together they amount to the demonstration that all men who have aims to pursue need the various protections and benefits which only laws conforming to the above requirements of substance and procedure can effectively confer. For any rational man, laws conferring these protections and benefits must be valuable, and the price to be paid for them in the form of limitations imposed by the law on his own freedom will usually be worth paying. But these arguments do not show, and are not intended to show, that it will always be reasonable or morally obligatory for a man to obey the law when the legal system provides him with these benefits, for in other ways the system may be iniquitous: it may deny even the essential protections of the law to a minority or slave class or in other ways cause misery or injustice.

Justice and utility. The equal extension to all of the fundamental legal protections of person and property is now generally regarded as an elementary requirement of the morality of political institutions, and the denial of these protections to innocent persons, as a flagrant injustice. Even when these protections are denied, lip service is often paid to the principle of equal distribution by the pretense that the persons discriminated against are either criminal in intention, if not in deed, or are like children who are incapable of benefiting from the freedom which laws confer and are in need of some more paternalistic regime.

Inadequacy of utilitarianism. Different moral philosophies offer different vindications of the principle of equality. The matter is considered here in order to illustrate the philosophical problems which arose in the criticism of law concerning the relative place of the notions of utility and justice. The central principle of utilitarianism, insofar as it supplies a moral critique of law, may be stated as the doctrine that there is only one vice in legal arrangements, namely, that they fail to produce the greatest possible total of happiness in the population within their scope. The concept of a total of happiness or pleasure or satisfaction is of course open to well-known objections. But on any interpretation, utilitarian principles, if unrestricted, must endorse legal or social arrangements if the advantages they give to some persons outweigh the disadvantages imposed on others. For a consistent utilitarian there can be no necessary commitment to any principles requiring an equal distribution.

However, in some cases, if allowance is made for principles of diminishing marginal utility, it may be shown that an equal distribution is the most efficient, in the sense of producing the greatest total of happiness. But for the utilitarian this is a contingent matter to be established in each case, not a matter of moral principle or justice; and where the question concerns the distribution of the fundamental legal protections of person and property, there seems no compelling utilitarian argument in favor of an equal distribution. Thus, a slave-owning class might derive from the system of slavery benefits outweighing the misery of the slaves. Bentham urged that this was not the case, owing to the inefficiency of slave labor, and therefore he rejected slavery; but he rejected it as inefficient rather than as unjust. Plainly, this form of argument is a very insecure foundation for the principle that all men are morally entitled to the equal protection of the laws, and it seems clear that utilitarian principles alone cannot give any account of the moral importance attached to equality and in general to the notion of the just, as distinguished from an efficient, distribution as a means of happiness.

Moral argument for equality. The simplest moral argument in support of the equal distribution of the law's fundamental protections is one that combines the idea that no rational person could wish himself to be denied these fundamental legal protections with the principle of the universalizability of moral judgment: moral judgments concerning social and legal arrangements must conform to the requirement that no man could regard as morally acceptable the withholding from others with needs and in circumstances similar to his own of those benefits which he would not wish to be withheld from himself. If this principle is admitted, it follows that it cannot be a sufficient moral ground for accepting legal arrangements that the advantages they give to some outweigh the disadvantages for others. The equal extension to all of the law's protections satisfies both the principle of utility, which requires that the law should advance human happiness, and the independent principle of justice, that the gain in happiness should be distributed fairly. According to this qualified form of utilitarianism, the best legal and social arrangements realize the most efficient of just distributions.

More ambitious arguments have been advanced to show that in spheres other than the distribution of the fundamental protections of the law, utilitarianism is acceptable only if qualified by independent principles of just distribution, and also to demonstrate that the distribution required by justice is in all spheres prima facie that of equality, unless inequalities can be shown to work ultimately for the equal benefit of all. Whatever the strength of these more general arguments may be, it is true that in relation to many legal institutions, utilitarianism unrestricted by other principles of justice yields results which would not be regarded as morally tolerable. This is particularly true of punishment. In all civilized legal systems it is recognized that no man should be punished except for his own conduct, and (with certain exceptions in the case of minor offenses) only then for such of his actions as were voluntary or within his power to control. Such limitations on the scope of punishment seem obvious requirements of justice to the individuals punished, but it is at least doubtful whether they can be adequately supported on purely utilitarian grounds.

The obligation to obey the law. The philosophical investigation of the obligation to obey the law requires a distinction between the utilitarian and other moral aspects of this subject similar to that outlined in the case of justice. It seems clear that the mere existence of a legal system, irrespective of the character of its laws, is not sufficient in any intelligible theory of morality to establish that a person ought morally to do what its laws require him to do. Yet there are also powerful arguments against a purely utilitarian theory of the obligation to obey law which would regard this obligation as simply a special case of the obligation to promote happiness, with the corollary that disobedience to bad laws is justified if the consequences of disobedience (including any harm done to others through the weakening of the authority of the legal system) are better in utilitarian terms than the consequences of obedience. Among features of the moral situation for which this utilitarian theory fails to account there are two of peculiar importance. The first is that the obligation to obey law is one which is considered as owed by the citizen specifically to the members of his own society in virtue of their relationship as fellow members, and is not conceived merely as an instance of an obligation to men in general not to cause harm, injury, or suffering. Second, men are often held to be subject to an obligation to obey the law even though it is clear that little or no harm will be done to the authority of the legal system by their disobedience, as in cases (like that of the conscientious objector) where those who disobey the law willingly submit to punishment.

The theory of a social contract focused on these two aspects of the obligation of obedience to law, and it is possible to detach from what is mythical or otherwise objectionable in contract theory certain considerations which show that the obligation to obey the law may be regarded as the obligation of fairness to others, which is independent of and may conflict with utility. The principle involved, stated in its simplest form, is that when a number of persons restrict their liberty by certain rules in order to obtain benefits which could not otherwise be obtained, those who have gained by the submission of others to the rules are under an obligation to submit in their turn. Conflicts between this principle and the principle of utility are possible because often the benefits secured by such restrictions would arise even if considerable numbers failed to cooperate and submit to the rules in their turn. For the utilitarian, there could be no reason for anyone to submit to rules if his cooperation was not necessary to secure the benefits of the system. Indeed, if a person did cooperate, he would be guilty of failing to maximize the total happiness, for this would be greatest if he took the benefits of the system without submitting to its restraints. The consideration that the system would fail to produce the desired benefits or would collapse if all were to refuse their cooperation is irrelevant in a utilitarian calculation if, as is often the case, it is known that there will be no such general refusal.

Bibliography

DEFINITION OF LAW

The major classics of jurisprudence in which definitions of law are elaborated include Thomas Aquinas, *Summa Theologica* I, 2, 90–97; Jeremy Bentham, *The Limits of Jurisprudence Defined* (New York, 1945) and *The Comment on the Commentaries* (Oxford, 1928); John Austin, *The Province of Jurisprudence Determined* (London, 1832); J. C. Gray, *The Nature and Sources of the Law* (New York, 1909); and Hans Kelsen, *General Theory of Law and State,* translated by Anders Wedberg (Cambridge, Mass., 1945).

Recent contributions include Hermann Kantorowicz, *The Definition of Law* (Cambridge, 1958); H. L. A. Hart, *The Concept of Law* (Oxford, 1961); and Richard Wollheim, "The Nature of Law," in *Political Studies*, Vol. 2 (1954), 128–142.

ANALYSIS OF LEGAL CONCEPTS

On legal obligations and duties, see Jeremy Bentham, "Essay on Logic," in J. Bowring, ed., *The Works of Jeremy Bentham*, 11 vols. (Edinburgh, 1838–1843), Vol. VIII, pp. 213–293 and *Fragment on Government* (London, 1776), Ch. 6; and O. W. Holmes, Jr., "The Path of the Law," in *Collected Legal Papers* (New York, 1920), pp. 167–202.

On legal transactions, see Axel Hägerström, *Inquiries Into Law and Morals,* translated by C. D. Broad (Uppsala, 1953), Ch. 5; Morris R. Cohen, *Law and the Social Order* (New York, 1933), Ch. 2; and John L. Austin, *How To Do Things With Words* (Oxford, 1962).

On intention, see Jeremy Bentham, *An Introduction to the Principles of Morals and Legislation* (London, 1789), Ch. 8; John Austin, *Lectures on Jurisprudence* (London, 1869), Chs. 18–19; G. L. Williams, *The Criminal Law: The General Part,* 2d ed. (London, 1961), Ch. 2; and G. E. M. Anscombe, *Intention* (Oxford, 1957).

PROBLEMS OF LEGAL REASONING

On logic and law, see Julius Stone, *The Province and Function of Law* (London, 1947), Chs. 6–7; J. C. Jensen, *The Nature of Legal Argument* (Oxford, 1957); Norberto Bobbio, "Diritto e logica," in *Il problema della giustizia* (Milan, 1962), pp. 11–44; and Lars Bergstrom, "Imperatives and Ethics," in *Filosofiska Studier,* Vol. 7 (1962), 94 ff.

On rule and discretion in judicial decision, see John Dickinson, "Legal Rules: Their Function in the Process of Decision," in *University of Pennsylvania Law Review,* Vol. 79 (1931), 833 ff., and "The Problem of the Unprovided Case," in *Recueil d'études sur les sources de droit en honneur de F. Gény* (Paris, 1934), Vol. II; Jerome Frank, *Law and the Modern Mind,* 6th printing (New York, 1949); Edward Levi, *Introduction to Legal Reasoning* (Chicago, 1949); John Wisdom, "Philosophy, Metaphysics, and Psycho-analysis," in his *Philosophy and Psycho-analysis* (Oxford, 1952); and Richard Wasserstrom, *The Judicial Decision* (Stanford, 1961) and "The Obligation to Obey the Law," in *University of California Law Review,* Vol. 10 (1963), 780–807. Also see *Jurimetrics: Law and Contemporary Problems,* Vol. 28 (1963).

PROBLEMS OF THE CRITICISM OF LAW

On problems of the criticism of law, see Alf Ross, *On Law and Justice,* translated by Margaret Dutton (London, 1958); John Rawls, "Justice as Fairness," in *Philosophical Review,* Vol. 67 (1958), 164–194; H. L. A. Hart, *The Concept of Law* (Oxford, 1961), Chs. 8–9; Torstein Eckhoff, "Justice and Social Utility," in *Legal Essays: A Tribute to Frede Castberg* (Oslo, 1963), pp. 74–93; and Lon Fuller, *The Morality of Law* (New Haven, 1964).

H. L. A. HART

PHILOSOPHY OF RELIGION, HISTORY OF.

It is not easy to say when strictly philosophical thought about religion began, for religion has always involved thought or belief of some kind. Even in other fields much of our thought is incipiently philosophical, but this is much more so in an interest that tends to be all-embracing. Religion has always had a cognitive factor, observances of various kinds had a meaning and these would often be of a far-reaching kind, involving beliefs about an afterlife or the influence upon us of beings other than those who inhabit this world. At what stage such beliefs come to be questioned, and not just accepted as a matter of course or tradition, is difficult to determine. But there is evidence of early questioning of this kind, and of the consequent defense and speculation, in some cultures, for example in India. It is a moot point how much of this we would consider strictly philosophical. But it is certain that the period, from the eighth to the fourth century B.C., which saw such an upsurge of intellectual interest and culture simultaneously (and seemingly without much mingling of cultures) in different parts of the world, produced philosophical thought of a very explicit kind, including philosophical reflection about religion.

EASTERN TRADITIONS

Hinduism. Perhaps the earliest example of philosophical reflection about religion is found in the *Upaniṣads.* These were committed to writing about the eighth century B.C. but they reflect much that had been going on before. They are part of the corpus of Indian sacred writings known as the *Vedānta.* Even the earliest and simplest of these contain distinctive and shrewd anticipations of the views about life and the universe which came to be explicitly formulated in the *Upaniṣads,* and it would thus be misleading to say that religious thought began in India with the composition of the *Upaniṣads.* But it is in the body of writings known by that name that we have the first sustained and deliberate thought about religion in a form which has affinity with what we know as philosophy.

The *Upaniṣads* vary much in quality and purpose. There is also much variety within their more strictly philosophical content, but the dominant theme is that of the unity of the universe. This is sometimes thought of in a sense that eliminates all plurality, anticipating much that some mystics have held at later times. For others "the One" is involved in all things in a way which is transcendent and absolute but which leaves it vague what status is to be accorded to finite things. This comes closer to the way God's transcendence has been understood generally in Western thought. But on occasion the *Upaniṣads* venture to be more explicit; some of their themes come close to those of Hegel and of post-Hegelian idealists in the nineteenth century; there is a clear insistence on the interdependence of whole and part in an all-inclusive system of reality, and this led also to speculations about the nature of the system and the function of the parts within it which suggest much that we read in idealist writings in our own times. There are also parts of the *Upaniṣads* which come closer to the Western notion of God as creator of a world of beings distinct from Himself and from one another. This is not unlike Christian theism and, in this respect, some passages of the *Upaniṣads* anticipate much which has since been central in Christian thought.

"The One breathed breathless" is a typically cryptic summing up of much of the teaching of the *Upaniṣads.* What it expresses is the profound and persistent sense of some ultimate nature of reality which escapes our understanding. The world does not wholly explain itself, it is rooted in mystery, and this means more than that there are things which are beyond our particular understanding at a certain time. All things point beyond themselves to a mystery which is in principle beyond our grasp or to some unity of things in the universe which is in some way more complete and final than the interrelations of things as we trace them in our normal understanding of the world. This is the significance of the terms which occur so often in Indian thought—"not this, not that" and "I am that." In this context these reflect a sense of some ultimate transcendent reality which is very vigorously presented in the *Upaniṣads* and whose implications are sometimes very explicitly set forth. It is indeed a very significant fact that there should be so shrewd a philosophical grasp of this notion at such an early date, and this makes the *Upaniṣads* a work of considerable significance for our understanding of religion in general. They contain also much explicit philosophical argument which is highly relevant to philosophical controversies about religion today. This covers many aspects of religion besides those which directly concern the dominant theme of the unity of all reality.

The *Upaniṣads* contain also much reflection upon our practical attitudes. This tends to be of the "world-denying" type and severely ascetic; that is not surprising where the dominant theme is the ultimate oneness of all things. But we find also in the *Upaniṣads* much emphasis on social service, on compassion, virtue, and welfare. Even if the views adopted on such matters seem to Western eyes too strictly determined by the sense of ultimate union with the whole, and even if it is true, as even some leading Hindus have stressed, that the otherworldly feature of Indian religion has led to apathy and indifference to present concern, there is also much to be learned from the insights we find in the *Upaniṣads,* as in later Indian thought, about the true nature of compassion and selflessness.

Taoism and Confucianism. Not much later than the time the *Upaniṣads* were committed to writing, there appeared in China philosophical teaching and writing about religion which had also at the center of it a sense of some ultimate unity of all reality. This is the essential significance of the doctrines of Tao (expounded in the *Tao-te Ching* traditionally ascribed to Lao-Tzu—born 604 B.C.—and in later writings like those ascribed to Lieh-Tzu and Chuang Tzu); and this in turn reflects a generally more basic notion which lies behind most early Chinese thought about religion, the idea of a "heaven and earth relationship." What this implies is that there is some character of reality beyond what we find in the world around us but which cannot be explicitly defined or grasped. We can only know it in its requirements and in the sense of some kind of justice operative in the universe at large. The "beyondness" of the power which works for righteousness in this way is deliberately softened; it is almost as if it could only be known from within. But this is itself a very significant fact, and the elusiveness of the influence to which our lives are subject in this way in Chinese thought is no mean indication of the subtleness of their philosophical and religious insights. It has in fact led sometimes to the view that Chinese religion, and especially Confucianism, is entirely a moral or religious system. That impression could easily be derived from *The Analects* of Confucius (551–478 B.C.), since they are concerned mainly with ethical and social matters, especially those which concern the appropriate "orders" in society. But Confucianism is in fact extensively determined and overlaid by notions like that of a heaven and earth relationship mentioned above. The distinctive thing, for philosophy, about Chinese religion and thought about religion is the shrewd sense that the nature of what lies beyond present existence and gives it meaning is best discerned by following a Way or path. The goal is, as it were, best reflected for us in the way it is to be attained. If this is not the whole truth, it is a significant pointer to it.

Buddhism. At a slightly later date we have the founding of the Buddhist religion in India. This led to the composition of the Pali Canon, containing, it is alleged, the substance of the teaching of Buddha. The Canon was closed in the reign of King Aśoka (273–231 B.C.) but not commited to writing until the first century B.C. It is not implausible to conclude that it does reflect fairly closely the actual teaching of the historical Buddha. The Pali Canon is of exceptional interest to philosophers today. It contains acute philosophical thinking, and some incline even to think of Buddhism as being more a philosophical system than a religion. That is certainly a mistaken impression, but we have in Buddhism a very shrewd grasp of the nature of religion as philosophy illuminates it. The purport of this has often been grievously misunderstood, not least in the assumption that Buddhism is a religion without God. The mystery of transcendent being is at the center of Buddhism and has remained so through most of its history and in its many varieties. This may not take quite the same form as in the West or find closely parallel expressions elsewhere, but it is unmistakable to anyone who knows his way about the subject.

A peculiarly distinctive feature of the doctrines of the Pali Canon is the subtle understanding of the difficulty of characterizing a reality that is "beyond" in the sense in which the infinite must be. It is in this context that we are told that we must not say that God exists or that He does not exist. At one point we have a list of 62 typical metaphysical questions which must not be asked. This is closely in line with much that has been maintained today in various forms of antimetaphysical philosophy, and it is strange how little appreciation there has been, on the part of recent positivists and agnostics, of how much grist of a sort there is to their mill in the doctrines of the Pali Canon. But it might all the same not be grist they could altogether accept, least of all if they fully grasped its implications in its contexts. For here we have skepticism and positivism with a difference. It springs less from a radically empiricist outlook than from a profound sense of the elusiveness of transcendent reality, and this makes much of the teaching of the Pali Canon uniquely relevant to philosophical controversies about religion today. The account of such matters as Buddha's enlightenment reinforces this, for while this can plausibly in fact be given an atheistic interpretation, it does point suggestively to a subtle grasp of the transformation of present reality through the invasion of it by a reality of an entirely different order which beggars all description. In these and kindred ways the Pali Canon, like related further aspects of Buddhist and of Hindu thought, has close and instructive points of affinity with the cruxes of religious thought today; and this is being increasingly understood by some experts in this field.

Philosophers. There has been a long line of impressive Oriental thinkers who have attempted variations and refinements on the themes just outlined. Among the most important are Śankara (c. 788) and Rāmānuja (c. 1017). In recent times the more traditionalist type of Hindu thought is well represented in the works of Radhakrishnan, while we have in the very liberal writings of Śri Aurobindo an attempt at reform which is sharply opposed to the objectionably other-worldly aspect of Hinduism and which tries to come to grips with the notion of some divine disclosure which leaves the individual a free and responsible creature.

GREECE

In the Western tradition philosophy begins with the Greeks, and to give a full indication of the course of religious philosophy in the West would be to outline the main continuous progress of philosophy from the Greeks to the present day. For almost all the main philosophical notions and the main divisions of opinion in philosophy (realist, nominalist, idealist, and so forth) have entered into religious controversy in one way or another. The matters which can be noted in the remainder of this article must thus be highly selective.

Parmenides and Heraclitus. In Greek thought, as in that of the Orient, there has been a central preoccupation with the problem of the one and the many. In the work of Parmenides this took a very distinctive and influential form. He proceeded by way of analysis of the nature of thought. This he found to involve predication, the affirmation of one thing about something else. To think is to say of an identifiable A that it is B; it is some relating of terms in a system which makes the relations possible. But there is an element of exclusion in such predication. If I say that this book is blue, that precludes its being black, although of course it says nothing about its being round or square, etc. All determination, as it is put, is negation. But does not this raise peculiar problems? For negation seems to be some odd sort of affirmation of what is not the case. It appears thus to deal with what is not. But what is not, Parmenides thought, is just altogether unreal—and no one can think or affirm this. But if negation becomes impossible in these ways, affirmation appears also to stand condemned, and there seems thus to be something radically unsatisfactory about thought itself and about the world as thinking apprehends it. Parmenides concluded that it was a mistake to suppose that the universe was a system of terms in relation, of the many which change and come into being and go, and that we must therefore think of all reality as one undifferentiated whole—conceived by him also as a sphere extending in the same way in all directions. There was given in this way a logical form to a profound religious sense of some ultimate all-embracing unity.

By contrast we find, in the work of other Greek philosophers, an emphatic insistence on the reality of the here and now and the world of variety and change. Protagoras took this to the length of insisting, in anticipation of much later empiricism and relativism, that nothing is real except as it appears. Neither the external world nor our moral ideas have any independent or objective reality; and this view of things received distinctive expression also in the thought of Heraclitus, who insisted that all things were in flux and that "we cannot step twice into the same river." But this was supplemented by Heraclitus by the notion of a pattern of change in which some principle or "logos" was expressed. For him, as for Parmenides, this carried with it a poetically mystical religious undertone. The idea of fire, as a central element, functioned as a symbol of that.

Plato. In due course Plato was to take up the problems presented in the way described above. He carefully restated and developed the difficulties which troubled Parmenides and Heraclitus and started a program of reconstruction by dealing firmly with the problem of negation.

He observed that this does not involve reference to a wholly unreal, to mere nothing. It could be amply provided for within the notion of terms in relation, for to say that something is not is just to say that it is other than something else, to indicate precise location within a system of interrelations. But if thought, as involving determination of this kind, is to function accurately, the system within which it operates must be a strict and tight one. Where is this to be found? Plato thought he found it pre-eminently in mathematics, and he thus came to regard mathematics as the true propaedeutic to philosophy and a paradigm of its method. The realities which could be properly thought and known had thus to be quasi-mathematical ones, and they consisted of general forms or principles which were real in their own right and bestowed on all other things whatever reality those could properly claim. This left Plato with the hard problem of accounting for the particulars and the changing course of things in the world, and it is not certain that he arrived at a view of this question which contented him. He sometimes spoke of particulars imitating the forms and sometimes of their participating in the reality of the forms, but the individual and unique existent had never more than a problematic place in Plato's philosophy. Difficulties also arose in yet another way, for even in its more rarefied instances, as in mathematics, there appears to be something essentially inadequate about the process of relating terms in a system. Every relation, including the relation of whole to part, seems to require yet another, or another system, to make it possible. All explanations of one thing in terms of others leave us with further questions and matters unexplained—there is no natural limit to the process of thought—and for the Greeks in particular that which is without proper limit is unsatisfactory—evil, they said, is of the infinite. Plato was led in this way to the notion of some yet more perfect reality, some quite different mode of unified existence in which present imperfect relatedness disappeared, and he held that everything had its reality exhaustively determined by this ultimate nature of the universe. To this he gave the name "the Good," and he declared that, in the sense indicated, this Good was "beyond being and knowledge." He did not mean that it was not real, or a mere notion—far from it. But it could not be given the sort of determinate existence and intelligibility which we ascribe to the sort of entities our minds can understand and encompass.

This is the first explicit formulation in Western thought of the idea of transcendence as it came to dominate much subsequent thinking. It is evident that it owes much, not only to Parmenides' puzzles about predication and nonbeing, but also more directly to Parmenides' insistence on some ultimate all-encompassing unity of being. But it does not involve the elimination of all plurality. When his system seems to involve that, Plato turns back on himself in vigorous protest—as in the famous passage in the *Sophist* where he insists that there must be "place in that which is perfectly real" for "change, life, soul, understanding." The specific forms, metaphysical as well as mathematical, had their place in the one universe in which everything derived its significance from the central all-encompassing reality of the good, and these forms lent some sort of reality to the particulars and to individual lives in the normal sense. The relation of particular to universal and of this to the Good, the ultimate supreme reality, may not have been worked out in a satisfactory way. But at least we have the notion that all we find in the world derives eventually from some one transcendent source in which all imperfection is resolved.

The formulation of these ideas owed much to the influence upon Plato of the Eleusinian mysteries and Orphic cults with which he came into contact—and also to the religiously orientated teaching of Pythagoras. In turn, it affected his teaching on what may appear to be more specifically and recognizably religious conceptions, like his doctrine (in the *Timaeus* and the *Laws*) about the Demiurge who fashions the world according to the eternal patterns and his belief in pre-existence and immortality. But it is not primarily in what he says about these more conventionally religious notions that Plato shows his main penetration or had his more abiding influence on religious thought. His notion of a system of forms held together in the transcendent unity of the Good was a more radically instructive and formative notion—although the teaching of the *Laws* and the *Timaeus* prescribed much of the form of later natural theology. It accorded best also with the element of mysticism which tempered the rationalism of his precursor to whom he was deeply indebted, namely Socrates. It is thus in the notion of the Form of the Good that Plato comes nearest to the idea of God in subsequent theism, but his approach to the subject left him no way in which his supreme and central principle of the Good could acquire the character of a person. That was precluded by the severely rationalist nature of Plato's main approach to his task and the consequent exclusion of any kind of revelation of an active concern, which could only be mediated through the actual particulars of life and history which figured in such an ambiguous and unimpressive way in Plato's philosophic outlook.

Aristotle. Our next main landmark is the philosophy of Aristotle. He did not separate the universal as completely as Plato did from the particular, although it is a moot point, still much debated, how ultimate is the difference between Plato and Aristotle here. But the difference did lead in due course to notions of the union of form and matter and of mind as the informing principle of the body by which much subsequent thinking on questions of this kind was directed. For Plato the properly mental side of human life was sharply separated from the body, and along with this went a low estimate of the body—although the body was not thought to be evil, as in much subsequent teaching. The mind is apt to be thought of by Plato as imprisoned in the body and awaiting its release. On the slant given to the subject by Aristotle there is a much closer integration of mind and body and this has been the model for a great deal of later thinking about human personality and the belief in resurrection. The mind is thought to require at least some kind of body, and there are philosophers who regard mind and matter as coextensive in the universe in general. Others have taken the Platonic lead in propounding a very sharp dualism of mind and body.

In strictly religious matters the difference between Plato and Aristotle here seems to become narrow; for although we have no strict equivalent to the Form of the Good in Aristotle or the same insight into the transcendent character of the ultimate religious reality, we do have an "Unmoved Mover" whose relation to the course of events He affects is a somewhat remote and detached one. The God of Aristotle is little involved in the world; it would have been a sign of inferiority and imperfection for Him to be so. This reflected a typically Greek attitude. To be affected by something external to your self is an indication of weakness, and in Aristotle's ideal of the "Great-Minded Man" this is very marked—he will not be cruel to his inferiors just because they are beneath such notice. The Stoics came later to pride themselves on their independence and self-sufficiency. Likewise the God of Aristotle is absorbed in contemplation of His own perfection; He takes no overt interest in other things, but He moves all other things by attraction. This is in sharp contrast with subsequent Christian teaching and represents the main way in which Christianity is "foolishness to the Greek." But the idea of an Unmoved Mover did nonetheless have a very extensive influence on later religious thought. It provided the model for the famous causal arguments for the existence of God. We have somehow to account for the world, and since we cannot account for it in terms of the way events determine one another within the world, we must have recourse to some altogether different mode of determination and explanation; and in due course this consideration became one of the main ways in which religious thinkers presented the idea that the world as we find it is dependent on some reality which is altogether "beyond" or transcendent. Here, as elsewhere, Aristotle determined very closely the style, if not always the substance, of later religious arguments.

This is evidenced specially in the way some of the further leading notions of Aristotle's philosophy, such as his distinction of potential and actual and his analysis of four types of cause and his notion of substance, became formative ideas in the religious thinking of later Christian times. It is in these ways, more than by very distinctively religious insight, that Aristotle made his main contribution to the philosophy of religion.

There is one further notion of great importance which had its place in Aristotle's system and became subsequently very influential. It is the idea of a law of nature. At times this was understood in a very relativistic way. To "follow nature" was taken to mean abiding by your own whims or impulses. It was sharply contrasted with convention, and the latter came to be much derided in some quarters in the period after Aristotle and Plato in Greece—indeed earlier to some extent among the Sophists. Here we see again, in an extreme form, the ideal of being self-sufficient. This was carried by some of the Cynics and Epicureans and the early Stoics to the extent of trying to "return to nature" and doing without society and its irksome restrictions altogether—a cry which was also sounded vigorously again in the seventeenth century. But it came to be realized that this policy led to absurdity and chaos, in personal life and in society; and thus the idea of "Nature" underwent complete transformation—it came to be taught that there was a nature to the universe at large ("Nature" with a capital N, as it were) and that this disclosed itself to men's reason. This led, in the fusion of the idea of law of nature with the Roman idea of a "law of nations," to the conception of a number of basic moral principles which were bound up with our rational nature and which, for many, further owed their firmness and objectivity to their foundation in the ultimate nature of the universe. This notion had a long and varied history and played a very important part in Christian accounts of morality and its relation to religion. It has a close affinity with the teaching of early Chinese religions and the notion of some power from beyond the world working for righteousness within it and prescribing our basic moral principles. Reflection upon this affinity can be very fruitful in seeking the way forward with such problems in the way they present themselves today.

EARLY AND MEDIEVAL CHRISTIANITY

The thought of early Christian times was extensively affected by Greek philosophy. This is evident even in the New Testament itself, not only in the way its authors write about matters like soul and body, but also in the central theme of "the Word" or Logos which became flesh. The Greek notion of Logos provided the basic concept in terms of which the doctrine of the Incarnation was to be understood. Directly, the concept of Logos came into philosophical thought in Christian times from the Stoics, for whom it meant originally an immanent World-Soul. But it was later combined with the Platonic idea of *nous* and so was conceived as acting in accordance with archetypal patterns. The basic problem was how is it possible to have knowledge of a strictly transcendent being, and for this a solution was sought in terms of an intermediary, in this case a logos, which was also induced in due course to fill other roles and help in the solution of further problems. These procedures came into Christian thought in the first place through the work of a gifted Jewish philosopher of the first century, namely Philo, and it had a prominent place in the subsequent Christology of formative thinkers like the Alexandrians, of whom Origen has most interest for philosophers. But what we have in the main during early Christian centuries is not so much philosophy of religion in the strict sense as theological writings which make extensive use of philosophical concepts. There were also some theologians of this period, as there have been of later times, who resented the intrusion of philosophy into the domain of faith. Of these the most outstanding was Tertullian.

The main exception to the normal course of thought in the early Christian period was Neoplatonism. Here we revert again to a profound sense of the Oneness of the Universe in a way which puts particulars and plurality in jeopardy, as they had been to some extent in the philosophy of Plato. But some account must be given of particulars, and there was developed in this way the difficult notion of emanation. God is the ultimate unity and He transcends all the categories of thought, but finite beings exist in the form of some falling away from the original perfection. This comes to terms in some fashion with the facts of finite existence and the reality of evil which occupied the minds of thinkers of this period a great deal. But it is very hard to make sense of the notion of emanation without calling in question the all-embracing nature of the one ultimate reality. The insistence on the latter notion did, however, influence the course of mystical thought and practice extensively. It also led, as in the case of Oriental mysticism, to attempts to draw away altogether from our present existence, with its limitations and evil, and to pass beyond the world of intellect as well as sense into total union with ineffable Being.

In sharp contrast to this teaching we have the position of thinkers who reflected anew on the significance of the Hebrew–Christian doctrine of creation. The Hebrews had come early to understand the elusive and transcendent character of God, and this had found very remarkable expression in parts of the Old Testament, the most famous passage here being the story of Moses at the burning bush. But this carried with it in Hebrew thought a subtle appreciation of the way a true discernment of God's transcendence required the recognition of our own distinctness as beings dependent on God. This sharpened, however, the question how such beings could in any way come to know God. The Hebrew answer was in terms of God's disclosure of Himself in history and experience, and this was deepened and extended in specifically Christian claims about the work and person of Christ. In this context the problem of revelation becomes a crucial one, and it has remained at the center of Christian philosophy at all times except when insistence on the distinctness of faith precluded all rational consideration of it.

Augustine. Preoccupation with the way man, being finite, can come to know an Infinite Being lies at the center of the more specifically philosophical parts of the writings of Augustine. In his attack on the problem Augustine gives prominence to our reflection on what we find our own souls to be like as a clue to our understanding of the relation of God to the world. He set the pattern for much subsequent reflection on our own nature and started a concern for the inward aspect of personality which persisted through formative later thinkers, like Descartes and Berkeley, to nineteenth century theologians like F. R. Tennant and the phenomenologists and existentialists of the present day. This side of Augustine's achievement is, however, often obscured by another. For although he emphasized the distinctness and freedom of finite beings, he came in another way to put these ideas in considerable jeopardy. In seeking to account for the redemptive work of Christ he posited the notion of an initial abuse of man's freedom leading to subsequent enslavement to sin. This gave considerable impetus to a doctrine of the Fall which, although not prominent in this form in earlier Christian times, became a central theme of much later theology and Christian profession of faith. The personal experiences of Augustine and his African background are thought to have greatly influenced his view in these respects, and there have certainly been voices, like those of Pelagius in his own time and Abelard later, raised in sharp protest against the rigors of the Augustinian doctrine of man's sin. The doctrine of the Fall has also been invoked to simplify the problem of our knowledge of God by blunting the strictly epistemological character of the problem; this came about through emphasis on the way our own allegedly corrupted nature made us spiritually blind and stood in the way of a vision of God. In the same context the idea of a law of nature became the idea of what is practicable in the present sinful state of man and society by contrast with the ideal law of God. This distinction was given much prominence by St. Augustine and has been reaffirmed, in the sense in which he understood it, by his most notable followers to the present day.

Anselm. The question of particulars and universals became prominent again in the controversy of realism and nominalism in the early Middle Ages. It had many implications for religious thought. For example, the view that individuals do not exist in themselves was thought to culminate in pantheism in the sense that "all visible things pass into intellectual, and intellectual into God." This period also saw further attempts to provide a rational defense of the faith, although without denying that faith had a firm foundation of its own. An outstanding feature of this activity in philosophical thinking is the formulation of the Ontological Argument by St. Anselm. This was intended to show that sound understanding of the idea of God yields us the necessity of His existence. The idea of God, it was urged, is the idea of a being than whom nothing greater can be conceived. But a being which does not exist is inferior to one who has the additional attribute of existence. Many changes have since been rung on this argument and it is being much canvassed at the present day.

Aquinas. The most impressive achievements of the Middle Ages in religious thought came about initially through the work of Muslim scholars (al-Ghazālī and Averroës in particular) who were much concerned about the question of reason and revelation in their own faith. Among these there had also been preserved important works of Greek philosophy, especially those of Aristotle, which were not properly known by Christian scholars. There came about in this way a revival of the study of Aristotle and a new concern about the way a transcendent being could be known by limited finite ones. This culminated in the very comprehensive work of St. Thomas Aquinas, which ranged over most religious questions, seeking a synthesis of religious claims and established philosophical principles. It set up firmly one of the main forms of natural theology. For Aquinas this covered two things. First we have the attempt to establish the existence of God by argument. This took the form of the famous "Five Ways." The first three of these are variations on the Cosmological Argument, as the term came to be used in due course. They seek to pass from the limited or contingent nature of finite things to an ultimate First Cause or Ground. The least elaborate, and also the most plausible, is the third way, which proceeds directly from the contingency of the world to its absolute Source without presupposing any particular view of cause and effect as we understand it. This argument, in one form or another, has been central to a great deal of subsequent philosophy of religion. Many hold today that it gets us at least very near the truth about the initial relation of God to the world and the way we know this. The other two "Ways" depend on notions of a scale of being and value and on the adaptation of things to their purposes, which are at least alien to the way we normally think about the world today—though they have their defenders.

The second prong of natural theology was that which sought, through an extremely subtle and cautious doctrine of analogy, to determine the attributes of God more precisely. It was urged that we cannot know God as He is in Himself, we can only know that He must be; and because God is a transcendent Ground of all things, He cannot be mirrored in the world He has made in the way an effect normally tells us something about its cause. Aquinas and his followers were therefore well aware of the need to move very circumspectly here, and what they maintained was that God must be thought to have certain attributes, like goodness or power, in whatever way is necessary for Him to be the Author of those in the form in which they appear in the created world. In presenting this doctrine some very careful distinctions were drawn between various types of analogies. The main difficulty which this approach involves is that of determining whether anything of substance is added in this way to what is originally claimed in regarding God as a transcendent Being. There is in any case needed in addition extensive recourse to revealed truth to supply the particular affirmations of a faith like the Christian one. These truths of faith could not, according to Aquinas, conflict with the truths of reason, but they go beyond them.

Ockham. The most formidable opponent of natural theology was William of Ockham, who questioned the ability of natural reason to discover in any measure the inscrutable will of God or reduce the mystery of transcendent being. His methods of procedure, involving the reduction of our postulates to the minimum which the facts require, anticipates many features of modern thought where skepticism about affirmations and alleged entities which pass beyond the facts of sensible experience and science is sometimes combined with a dogmatic affirmation of faith in which reason plays no part.

MODERN PHILOSOPHY

Outstanding formative philosophers of the modern period, roughly the last five hundred years, were of two main sorts, rationalists and empiricists. The former, including Descartes, Spinoza, and Leibniz, had great confidence in the power of reason alone to establish ultimate metaphysical truths.

Rationalism. Descartes claimed to prove his own existence by the power of reason alone and drew a sharp distinction between mind and body. He then sought, by severely rational arguments, to prove the existence of God. Two of these arguments invoke the causal principle, although they require also our having the idea of God; the third is a special form of the Ontological Argument; it contends that if we think of a being who does not exist we are withholding from our conception of it a "perfection," namely existence, which is essential to our conception of a perfect being. These arguments are not usually thought to succeed as they stand, but they can nonetheless be thought to be significant as indications of the insight into there having to be an ultimate reality in which essence and existence are one. They also illustrate the futility of seeking to establish the existence of such a being by arguments involving consideration of what limited finite things are like. Descartes's causal arguments are particularly illuminating in this way, as he imports into his premises, at every step in an elaborate argument, certain considerations derived from the notion of an infinite being which it is the aim of the argument to defend.

A further feature of Descartes's work is the insistence on the freedom of the individual—"liberty of indifference." This is bound up with the insistence on the distinctness of persons as nonmaterial entities. The same theme is taken up in Leibniz' monadology, in which every being is a distinct mental monad. But the genuineness of our freedom is jeopardized by Leibniz in his doctrine of pre-established harmony and the way each monad consistently unfolds in its history some destiny which its own nature prescribes for it from the start. In the ingenious monistic system of Spinoza freedom comes to be thought of in terms of accepting our place and destiny in the universe with adequate understanding and forbearance rather than in the form of genuine "liberty of indifference." Descartes's doctrine of the self as a distinct mental substance has been subjected to considerable criticism from time to time, not least at the present day. But there are many also who consider it an essential ingredient in a sound understanding of the relations of God to man and who stress, as did Descartes, the "interiority" and unextended character of the mind.

Empiricism. Empiricism inclines to skepticism and is severely skeptical in its stricter forms. The great British empiricists did not all hold to their principle with the same consistency. We find Locke departing from his avowed aim of showing that knowledge derives from sense impressions, not only in his theory of knowledge and his account of material and mental substances, but also in his expressly religious thought where he claimed, for example, that the existence of One Infinite Mind can be proved with the same certainty as we find in mathematics. There is much in fact in Locke's presentation of the causal argument in Chapter X, Book IV, of his *Essay Concerning Human Understanding* that has close relevance to controversies about the subject today. Likewise Berkeley, while dispensing with the notion of independent material substances, found in his account of the world of nature as dependent on its being perceived a firm foundation for the belief in a Divine Being on whose Mind the whole world of nature depends. To Berkeley we owe also a subtle appreciation of the distinctiveness of the way minds are known and the essential inwardness of personality which is so central a feature of religious philosophy today.

Hume, however, was little attracted to these compromises and, although he confessed to some admiration for the argument which seeks to prove God's existence from the evidence of design in the universe, he adhered generally to a ruthlessly empiricist position. This involved total skepticism about God, immortality, and all properly religious notions. Hume contended that religion had started in a thoroughly naturalistic way with the personification of natural objects and so forth and that only at a late and sophisticated stage of culture did men arrive at some unification of religious notions and the belief in one God. His presentation of this view is delightfully lucid and it set the pattern for much of the anthropological treatment of religion later in the nineteenth century. In Hume's *Dia-logues* there are also canvassed some of the main arguments which are used to support or reject religious beliefs, ranging from the general belief in God to belief in miracle.

Kant's criticisms. The "critical" philosophy of Kant sought to arrest the skepticism of Hume without retreating to the strict rationalism of Descartes and his followers. Kant's main contention was that the sort of experience of the world which we undoubtedly have presupposes a unified world of objects presented to an abiding subject. The modes of unification thereby involved, the necessary conditions of experience, provided a new basis for confident belief in causality and substance, though not in the same sense as that of Descartes; but it was also implied that knowledge is confined to the world of our experience and the principles involved in this, sometimes thought to be imposed by the mind itself. This did certainly yield us the belief in an unobservable subject of experience, but nothing could be known of this beyond its being required to account for the sort of knowledge we have of the external world. There was also a tendency to isolate this inner self so completely from the external world of known reality that the functioning of the "pure self," especially as will or active agent, became very hard to conceive and set for Kant some of his main difficulties, especially in his ethics.

The limitations involved in the alleged "critical" account of knowledge were, however, extensively corrected by Kant in his insistence that we have certain grounds for "faith," which supplements what we can strictly know. These grounds of faith are found in the operation of our practical reason or moral awareness which sets before us certain moral obligations, largely in the form of strictly universal rules, which have in turn far-reaching implications. It was urged, for example, that there is a moral requirement that justice be rewarded, but that, since the ethical motive would be impaired if we set our own happiness as the aim of moral actions, God must be postulated to guarantee the eventual relation between happiness and virtue in the universe. Freedom and immortality were similar postulates of practical reason. These contentions have been subjected to much criticism, and doubt has been cast on the success of even the limited undertaking of postulating certain principles of a unified world of experience. Religious thinkers have urged that "faith" in its Kantian form has little in common with properly religious faith and that the severely rationalist character of the appeal to postulates of practical reason neglects the distinctively religious element in religious belief. On the other hand the prominence given to moral considerations in religious thought has been widely welcomed, and many writers have sought to provide versions of the moral and teleological arguments which are not open to the difficulties of those provided by Kant.

Idealist responses to Kant. A great deal of post-Kantian philosophy was concerned with the gap in the Kantian system between the world as we apprehend it and the ultimate or "noumenal" reality of the world as it really is. For Kant these tended to be two separate worlds, but many thought this unsatisfactory and sought in various ways to understand the ultimate reality or "thing-in-itself" as some completion of the world as we find it—a notion which is in many ways anticipated in some of Kant's own reflections.

There were thus initiated various metaphysical enterprises concerned especially with finding within the world of our own experience some reliable clue to the nature of the universe as a whole. The most influential of these was that of Hegel, who found the ultimate principle of reality in reason. We cannot exhaustively understand the universe but the universe is in principle capable of being understood through and through as a system where everything has its place and nature determined by rational necessity. Others (like Schopenhauer) gave to will the pre-eminent place as a metaphysical clue.

There were many variations on these themes in the nineteenth century, including the work of British idealists like Green, Bradley, and Bosanquet and of American thinkers like Josiah Royce. Idealism became the dominant philosophical view, and within the perspective of it many views were advanced about the relation of God to the world, taking distinctive features of our own experience as the clues to what lies beyond it. This tended to leave nothing essentially or irreducibly mysterious about religion. But the leading post-Hegelian idealist, namely F. H. Bradley, argued that there were radically contradictory features of present experience which implied that the ultimate nature of the universe was suprarational. And with this emphasis we come back again to the idea of some transcendent reality on which everything depends in some way which in principle we cannot understand. It was argued also, in criticism of the more rationalist type of idealism, that it left little room for the distinctness and freedom of the individual, since all beings came to be regarded as elements or "phases" or "appearances" of an ultimate all-inclusive system—and in the same way the problem of evil became a very acute one for idealist defenders of religion.

Natural theology. In correction of the rationalist temper of idealist philosophy many voices were raised from time to time during the nineteenth century, stressing the mystery and elusiveness of religion. The most impressive and influential of these were those of Friedrich Schleiermacher and Rudolf Otto, the former giving prominence to the "feeling of absolute dependence" in religion and the latter stressing our sense of the holy or the numinous, the *mysterium tremendum et fascinans.* Otto claimed, in sharp contrast to the earlier naturalistic theories of Hume and his nineteenth-century followers, that there was ample evidence of this sense of the holy in the rawest beginnings of religion and he sought to describe the way it became schematized and moralized to give riper and more distinctive forms of religion. Other writers sought to correct the somewhat a priori approach of idealist philosophers by resorting to what they described rather incorrectly as an empiricist defense of religion which consisted in drawing out the implications of various features of our experience. This was the form which much natural theology took in the late nineteenth century, exemplified especially in the work of F. R. Tennant. Even if this approach fails to do justice to the factor of transcendence in religion, it could nonetheless be thought to have provided many of the ingredients of a sound understanding of religious experience.

Toward the close of the nineteenth century and early in this one there appeared, however, a strong reaction against what was thought to be the facile and too liberal rationalization of religious philosophy at that time. This found expression most of all in the insistence, by Karl Barth and other eminent theologians like Reinhold Niebuhr and Emil Brunner, on the "wholly other" character of God and the need, as they understood it, to fall back on a dogmatically orthodox theological position in which the central place was accorded to the idea of an exclusive revelation. This presented considerable difficulties, not least on the ethical side where elementary ethical principles seemed to be put in serious jeopardy. But it did give prominence again to the idea of God's transcendence, which is a focus for controversies about religion among philosophers of the present day.

Philosophy of religion. The philosophy of our time has become extensively empiricist again. This trend had been preparing for some time in America in aspects of the work of William James and Peirce. But it gathered its momentum in the work of the Vienna circle and those, like Wittgenstein, who extended its influence in England, notably at Cambridge and Oxford. Recent empiricism represents a sharp reaction against the ambitious and occasionally turgid speculations of nineteenth-century metaphysical philosophers. It set a premium on clarity and claimed to be tough-minded and down to earth. Its policy was extensively that of Hume, and it reflected much of the skepticism of the period subsequent to World War I. To Hume's empiricism was added, however, an alleged linguistic technique which was intended, in its main early forms at least, to account for the persistence of seemingly bold nonempirical notions, like the idea of the soul or of God, by ascribing them to confusions engendered by misleading forms of speech. This set off a spate of philosophical criticism of religion aimed at showing that its basic conceptions were logically improper. This is sometimes known as the linguistic veto. A desperate attempt to save religion was undertaken by several other empiricist philosophers who seemed willing to sacrifice the strictly nonempirical elements in religion and reinterpret the main features of religious belief in terms of present experience—for example, by regarding religion as a matter of satisfying certain distinctive emotions or by identifying it, in essentials, with ethics.

There have been considerable recent variations on this theme of the attenuation of religious faith. The same method of apologetics has appealed also to many theological writers, some equating religion with morality and others finding the essence of religion in a certain depth and earnestness of our own activities. The most outstanding of these theologians have relied heavily on the work of existentialist philosophers who have brought into prominence the importance of certain searching present experiences and of deep inner aspects of them. Neither they nor their existentialist mentors are very systematic or lucid thinkers, and it is thus not very clear how far they mean to go in interpreting religion in terms of our human experience in the here and now.

Religious existentialism. A typically elusive representative of this kind of philosophical theology was Paul Tillich. It is never quite clear whether he meant by his central conceptions of "the Ground of Being" and the "New

Being" a transcendent reality (or some impact of this upon us) or some profound depth of our own experience and natures. Nor is it clear how far this skepticism about traditional beliefs, reinforced by much skepticism in the field of Biblical scholarship, is meant to go; for the writers in question often give expression to seemingly skeptical views in the language of orthodoxy. The position is not made easier by considerable borrowings from phenomenological thinkers like Heidegger who combine unusual perceptiveness with a veritable genius for elaborate and obscure modes of utterance.

Linguistic apologetic. Equally uncertain and difficult is the work of certain more strictly philosophical thinkers who take their start from a new emphasis in linguistic philosophy derived largely from the later and much modified form of Wittgenstein's work. They stress the open texture and varieties of language and, on this basis, press the claims of religious language to a status not impaired by its not complying with the conditions of ordinary language or scientific language. This leaves the door open for a cautious but less skeptical approach to religion. But the question remains how much is accomplished unless we indicate how the distinctive language of religion is to be understood and what criteria may be applied to it. There is a tendency for some linguistic apologists of religion to be content with stressing the alleged oddity of religious language and thereby also to conflate major notions, like freedom and immortality, and to leave it very unclear in what sense the various affirmations made in religion are to be understood. These writers also tend to draw much support from existentialist insistence on the importance of formative and challenging present experiences. The details of their work, as in the case of I. T. Ramsey, is illuminating and imaginative, but it is not clear how much it can accomplish until their kind of sensitivity to religious language is accompanied by rigorous heed to the centrality and discipline of the more strictly epistemological considerations.

Response to empiricist criticisms. Epistemological considerations have again been uppermost in the work of a further body of recent philosophers who have taken up the challenge of empiricist and linguistic critics more boldly. They have welcomed the challenge in particular as a way of sharpening the question of the place of evidence in religious belief. They maintain that evidence is not strictly relevant to the question of the existence of God; we apprehend the necessity of God's existence in the contingent character of everything else. This, they maintain, is the element of truth misleadingly presented in the traditional arguments. Pioneers of this position in recent philosophy are Austin Farrer and E. L. Mascall, while another severe critic of linguistic empiricism, C. A. Campbell, has arrived, by way of some modifications of Bradley's thought, at a not dissimilar renewal of the emphasis on the suprarational character of the object of religious worship.

This takes the sting out of the challenge, given sharpness by John Wisdom and later by Antony Flew, to indicate what would count for or against the existence of God. The answer, it is said, is "nothing," for we are not here accounting for the way the world goes or some particular feature of it, but for there being anything at all. The question "Why is there something rather than nothing?" is regarded even by some skeptical philosophers as a significant one. This new appreciation of the uniqueness of the idea of God and of God's relation to the world has opened the way also for subtler understanding of religions other than Christianity, especially Buddhism, and with this has come a renewed philosophical interest in world religions. This is a more discerning interest than the one motivated by superficial notions of syncretism at the turn of the century.

But there has been accentuated in turn the problem of particular religious affirmations. Some have attacked this afresh through new presentations of the traditional doctrine of analogy; some, like A. C. Ewing, persist in a cautious restatement of idealism; others turn to fresh examination of the nature and sanction of religious imagery. There has also been much recourse to the analogy with our knowledge of one another, and in this context it has been thought, by the present writer among others, that a fresh examination of the nature of religious experience and of features of it which could afford justification of the claim to revelation in Scriptures and history, holds the best promise of a solution of the epistemological problems of religious faith. Some who follow this course are apt to lapse from a steady epistemological study, which their initial problem requires, into a psychological or phenomenological one; but when they do so, in the case of Gabriel Marcel for example, they may nonetheless provide highly relevant material for those who manage to keep the epistemological task steadily in mind. That may also be supplemented by the perceptive analysis of those whose concern is not mainly religious or who may be strictly atheistic like Sartre. The work of Merleau-Ponty is thought by many to be especially suggestive and illuminating in this way.

Consideration of religious experience may thus prove the point of convergence of many of the approaches to religion which hold most promise today of deepening our understanding of its perennial problems. Advances in fields other than strictly religious studies, most of all perhaps the study of paranormal phenomena, will have much relevance to the present tasks of the philosophy of religion; and some writers, like H. H. Price, C. D. Broad and C. J. Ducasse, have considered closely the implications of matters like paranormal phenomena for our general view of the world and for relevance to specific questions like immortality. Psychological studies, notably those which investigate the unconscious and the unconscious matrix of conscious imagery, have considerable relevance to the philosophers' problems. A further major preoccupation of those who study the philosophy of religion today is the relation of ethics to religion, not only in the form of fresh examination of the problems of freedom and grace or of variations on the traditional "moral argument," but also in reflections on the role of moral experience within the totality of religious experience. There have likewise been fresh examinations of the claims made for mystical experience, and one writer at least, namely W. T. Stace, is prepared to defend a very extreme form of monism as the ultimate truth about the universe to which mystical experience points. Other philosophers, including some like J. N. Findlay who took their orientation at one time from Wittgensteinian philosophy, are beginning to embark on bold—too bold?—speculative ventures in the field of religious thought.

In these ways the philosophy of religion, of which fashionable philosophers fought very shy about twenty years ago, has become again one of the liveliest interests of philosophers. It is of considerable significance also that some of the major themes of contemporary fiction, including those which seem to have little overtly to do with religion, are found to bear closely on aspects of religion which have most importance for the philosophy of religion. In the blend of new philosophical investigations of religion, sharpened in the challenge and discipline of tough-minded philosophy, and a perceptive understanding of contemporary cultures (in their limitations as well as in their achievements) in other regards may be found a means of genuine advance in the life of religion itself which will enable it to have its place effectively in the sophistications of a developing culture and rapidly changing state of society.

(See also JEWISH PHILOSOPHY and ISLAMIC PHILOSOPHY.)

Bibliography

Allen, E. L., *Existentialism from Within*. London, 1953.

Blackham, H. J., *Six Existentialist Thinkers*. New York, 1952.

Campbell, C. A., *Selfhood and Godhood*. London and New York, 1957.

Ewing, A. C., *Idealism*. London, 1934.

Farrer, Austin, *Finite and Infinite*, 2d ed. Naperville, Ill., 1959.

Ferré, Frederick, *Language, Logic, and God*. New York, 1961.

Flew, A. G. N., and MacIntyre, Alasdair, eds., *New Essays in Philosophical Theology*. London, 1955.

Hartshorne, Charles, *The Logic of Perfection*. La Salle, Ill., 1962.

Henson, H. H., *Christian Morality*. Oxford, 1936.

Hepburn, Ronald, *Christianity and Paradox*. London, 1958.

Hick, John, *Philosophy of Religion*. Englewood Cliffs, N.J., 1963.

Hughes, E. R., and Hughes, K., *Religions in China*. London, 1950.

James, E. O., *The Worship of the Sky God*. London, 1963.

Jayatilleke, K. N., *Early Buddhist Theory of Knowledge*. London, 1963.

Knowles, David, *Evolution of Mediaeval Thought*. London, 1962.

Lewis, H. D., "Survey of the History of Religion." *Philosophical Quarterly*, No. 15 (April 1954) and No. 16 (July 1954).

Lewis, H. D., *Our Experience of God*. London, 1959.

Lewis, H. D., *Teach Yourself the Philosophy of Religion*. London, 1965.

MacGregor, Geddes, and Robb, J. W., *Readings in Religious Philosophy*. Boston, 1962.

Mascall, E. L., *He Who Is*. London, 1943.

Mascall, E. L., *Existence and Analogy*. London, 1949.

Mascall, E. L., *Words and Images*. London, 1957.

Mascall, E. L., *The Secularization of Christianity*. London, 1965.

Mitchell, Basil, ed., *Faith and Logic*. London, 1957.

Moore, Edward C., *American Pragmatism*. New York, 1961.

Murti, T. R. V., *The Central Philosophy of Buddhism*. London, 1955.

Paton, H. J., *The Modern Predicament*. London, 1955.

Perry, R. B., *Present Philosophical Tendencies*. London, 1929.

Philosophy, No. 122 (July 1957). On empiricism and religion.

Pringle-Pattison, Andrew Seth, *The Idea of God*. Oxford, 1917.

Ramsey, Ian, *Religious Language*. London, 1957.

Ramsey, Ian, *Prospect for Metaphysics*. London, 1961.

Rogers, A. K., *A Student's History of Philosophy*. New York, 1940.

Rose, H. J., *Ancient Greek Religion*. London, 1946.

Slater, R. H. L., and Lewis, H. D., *World Religions and World Community*. New York, 1963.

Smart, Ninian, *Reasons and Faiths*. London, 1958.

Smart, Ninian, *Historical Selections in the Philosophy of Religion*. New York, 1962.

Smith, John E., *Philosophy of Religion*. New York, 1965.

Taylor, A. E., "Theism," in James Hastings, ed., *Encyclopedia of Religion and Ethics*. New York, 1959.

Wolfson, H. A., *Religious Philosophy*. Cambridge, Mass., 1961.

H. D. LEWIS

PHILOSOPHY OF RELIGION, PROBLEMS OF.

The term "philosophy of religion" is a relative newcomer to the philosophical lexicon, but what is now so designated is as old as philosophy itself. One of the earliest spurs to philosophical reflection, in ancient Greece and elsewhere, was the emergence of doubts concerning the religious tradition; and religious beliefs and conceptions have always formed much of the staple of philosophical discussion.

If one surveys the various things philosophers have done in thinking about religion, it is difficult to find any unifying thread other than the fact that they all spring from reflection on religion. Philosophy of religion is occupied to a large extent with the consideration of reasons for and against various fundamental religious beliefs, particularly the various arguments for the existence of God. But we find many other matters treated in books that are regarded as being within the philosophy of religion. These include the nature and significance of religious experience, the nature of religion, the relation between religion and science, the nature of religious faith as a mode of belief and/or awareness, the nature of revelation and its relation to the results of human experience and reflection, the place of religion in human culture as a whole, the logical analysis of religious language, the nature and significance of religious symbolism, and possibilities for reconstructing religion along relatively nontraditional lines.

Central aim. Some justification can be found for grouping all these topics under the heading "philosophy of religion" if we view them all as growing out of a single enterprise, the rational scrutiny of the claims of religion—the critical examination of these claims in the light of whatever considerations are relevant—with a view to making a reasonable response to them. A highly developed religion presents us with a number of important claims on our belief, our conduct, our attitudes and feelings. It gives answers to questions concerning the ultimate source of things, the governing forces in the cosmos, the ultimate purpose(s) of the universe, and the place of man in this scheme. It tells us what a supreme being is like, what demands he makes on men, and how one can get in touch with him. It offers a diagnosis of human ills, and it lays down a "way of salvation" that, if followed, will provide a way to remedy these ills and satisfy man's deepest needs. All this is very important. If the claims of a given religion on these points are justified, discovering this is a matter of the greatest moment. At bottom the philosophy of religion is the enterprise of subjecting such claims to rational criticism.

It is worth noting that such claims are not made by religion in general but by particular religions exclusively and that although generally we can find claims of all these sorts in any given religion, the specific content will differ widely from one religion to another. This will have important consequences for the direction taken by the philosophizing that arises in response to each religion. This article is largely concerned with the Western tradition, and thus the philosophy of religion represented has grown out of concern with some aspect of the Judaeo-Christian tradition, either through support or opposition. Philosophical reflection on a very different religious tradition will give rise to different preoccupations. Thus, Western philosophers, unlike their Indian counterparts, are much concerned with arguments for and against the existence of a supreme personal deity and with whether or not the occurrence of miracles is compatible with the reign of natural law. However, in a religious tradition like the Hindu or the Buddhist, which does not feature the notion of a supreme personal deity who has active personal dealings with his creatures, these problems do not arise. Philosophers in such a tradition, by contrast, will be concerned with trying to clarify the relation of a supreme ineffable One to the various things in the world that constitute its manifestations and with considering arguments for the ultimate unreality of the empirical world. There is, however, enough in common among different religions to insure that all philosophy of religion will be directed to recognizably identical problems, though in very different forms. (See RELIGION for a discussion of common characteristics.)

Philosophers have raised critical questions about the justifiability and value of religious beliefs, rites, moral attitudes, and modes of experience. However, philosophers have largely focused their critical powers on the doctrinal (belief) side of religion. This selectivity might be attributed to an occupational bias for the intellectual, but there is a real justification for it. If our basic interest is in questions of justifiability, then it is natural that we should concentrate on the belief side of religion, for the justification of any other element ultimately rests on the justification of some belief or beliefs. If one asks a Roman Catholic why he goes to Mass, or what the value is of so doing, he would, if he knew what he was about, appeal to certain basic beliefs of his religion: that the universe, and all its constituents, owes its existence to and depends for its ultimate fate on a supreme personal being, God; that man inevitably fails to live up to the moral requirements God lays down for him; that God became a man in the person of Jesus of Nazareth and suffered death in order to save man from the fatal consequences of his sinfulness; that as a part of a program designed to enable men to benefit from this, God has ordained that they should participate in the rite of the Mass, in which, in some mysterious way, they actually incorporate the body and blood of Jesus and so partake of the salvation effected through him. The ritual, as conceived by the participants, is a reasonable thing to do if and only if these beliefs are justified.

However, the attention of philosophers is generally more narrowly concentrated than this. Not all the beliefs of a given religion, not even all the beliefs considered crucial by that religion, receive equal attention. In works on the philosophy of religion, one finds little discussion of relatively special doctrines that are peculiar to a given religion, such as the virgin birth of Jesus, the divine mission of the church, or the special status of the priesthood, how-

ever important these doctrines may be for the religion in question. Instead, attention is focused primarily on what might be called the metaphysical background of the doctrinal system, the world view of the religion—the view of the ultimate source and nature of the universe; the nature of man; man's place in the universe; the end to which man is, or should be, tending; and so on. This preferential treatment is partly due to a desire to make philosophical discussions relevant to more than one religion; for example, roughly the same world view underlies Judaism, Christianity, and Islam. It is also partly due to a conviction that philosophical reflection will yield definite results only with respect to the more general aspects of a religious outlook. Very few philosophers have supposed that one can establish the virgin birth by philosophical argument.

It might also be argued that if we abstract from commitment to any particular religion, the world-view aspect of religion is the most undeniably significant one. Without presupposing some particular religious beliefs, it would be difficult to show that the acceptance of elaborate theological dogmas like that of the Trinity, or participation in rites, or singling out certain objects as sacred is an essential part of a fully human life. However, it can be argued on the basis of facts concerning the nature of man and the conditions of human life that human beings have a deep-seated need to form some general picture of the total universe in which they live, in order to be able to relate their own fragmentary activities to the universe as a whole in a way meaningful to them; and that a life in which this is not carried through is a life impoverished in a most significant respect. This would seem to be an aspect of religion that is important on any religious position; and so it seems fitting that it should be at the center of the picture in a general philosophical treatment of religion.

Other investigations and the central aim. In presenting, defending, and criticizing arguments for and against such fundamental beliefs as the existence of a supreme personal deity, the immortality of the human personality, and the direction of the universe toward the realization of a certain purpose, philosophers are directly engaged in critical evaluation. The other major topics listed at the beginning of this article do not have exactly this status, but they are all directly relevant to rational criticism of fundamental religious beliefs. In order to conduct a systematic scrutiny of such beliefs, one must start with an adequate conception of the nature and range of religion, so that he can be sure that he is dealing with genuine religious beliefs and with those which are most fundamental for religion, and so that he will not be unduly limited by the particular interests with which he starts.

Moreover, one needs an adequate understanding of the nature of religious belief in order to filter out irrelevant considerations and arguments. The charge of irrelevancy has been most trenchantly leveled against the traditional enterprise of presenting metaphysical arguments for the existence of God by Søren Kierkegaard, who maintained that anyone who tries to give an argument for the existence of God thereby shows that he has misunderstood the special character of religious belief. Whether or not such charges are justified, the mere fact that they can be made with any plausibility shows that it is incumbent on the philosopher of religion to look into the character of religious faith and to try to determine its similarities to and differences from other modes of belief; for example, those in everyday life and in science. With an increasing realization of the way in which thought and belief are shaped by language, this kind of investigation has increasingly taken the form of an inquiry into the type of utterances that express religious belief, an attempt to make explicit the logic of religious discourse—the special ways in which terms are used in religious utterances, the logical relations between religious statements themselves and between religious statements and statements in other areas of discourse, the extent to which religious statements are to be construed as expressive of feelings or attitudes or as directions to action, rather than as factual claims. Also, an appreciation of the extent to which language is used symbolically in religion can easily lead to a general concern with the nature and function of religious symbolism.

All the concerns listed thus far involve investigation of the relation of religion to other segments of human culture, such as science, art, and literature. The question of the relation of science and religion has a special importance for one who is critically examining religious beliefs in our society. For the last few hundred years the main challenges to religious doctrine in Western society have been made in the name of science. With respect to many segments of science, from Copernican astronomy through Darwinian biology to Freudian psychology, it has been claimed that certain scientific discoveries disprove, or at least seriously weaken, certain basic religious doctrines. Discussions of whether this ever does, or can, happen—and if so, what is to be done about it—have bulked large in works on philosophy of religion.

Philosophers of religion also investigate the nature of religious experiences because it is often claimed that such experiences provide direct warrant for the existence of God, or of other objects of religious worship. One is naturally led into a survey of the types of religious experience and into questions of their psychological bases. Finally, if a philosopher has decided that the basic beliefs of the traditional religion(s) of his society are unacceptable, he is naturally faced with the question of what to do about it. If he feels that religion is a crucially important aspect of human life, he will want to find some way of preserving religious functions in a new form. Hence, naturalistic philosophers, who reject the supernaturalistic beliefs of our religious tradition, sometimes attempt to sketch the outlines of a religion constructed on naturalistic lines. This will usually involve the substitution of some component(s) or aspect(s) of the natural world for the supernatural deity of the Judaeo-Christian tradition. This may be Humanity (Comte), human ideals (Dewey), those natural processes which make a contribution to the realization of the greatest good (H. N. Wieman), or some combination of these.

Relations to other disciplines. The philosophy of religion is distinguished from theology and from sciences dealing with religion (such as psychology of religion and sociology of religion) in opposite ways. It is distinguished from theology by the fact that it takes nothing for granted, at least nothing religious; in the course of its examination it takes the liberty of calling anything into question. The-

ology, in a narrow sense of that term, sets out to articulate the beliefs of a given religion and to put them into systematic order, without ever raising the ultimate question of their truth. The philosophy of religion is distinguished from sciences of religion by the fact that it is addressed to questions of value and justification and tries to arrive at some sort of judgment on religious claims. The psychology of religion—for instance, when pursuing strictly psychological questions—studies religious beliefs, attitudes, and experiences as so many facts, which it tries to describe and explain, without attempting to pass judgment on their objective truth, rationality, or importance.

The philosophy of religion, conceived of as an attempt to carry out a rational scrutiny of the claims made by a given religion, will always start from concern with some particular religion or type of religion and will basically aim at a judgment of that religion. It certainly is historically accurate to think of philosophy of religion as arising in this way and, furthermore, it may be taken as its common and most basic form. However, it is also possible for a philosopher to concern himself directly with the fundamental issues involved in the religious claims in question—the ultimate source of things, the destiny of man, and cosmic purpose, for example—without approaching them through the consideration of answers given to these questions by some organized religion. Spinoza's *Ethics* is an outstanding example of this kind of investigation. Other examples are Samuel Alexander's *Space, Time and Deity* (2 vols., London, 1920) and Henri Bergson's *L'Évolution créatrice* (*Creative Evolution*, New York, 1911). Whether we call philosophizing of this kind philosophy of religion is not important, but it is important to realize that these questions can be considered outside the context in which we are explicitly concerned with religion as such.

Various approaches. One should not suppose that every philosopher of religion concerns himself with the whole range of problems. On the contrary, a given philosopher will usually restrict his attention because of his special interests, his conception of religion, and/or his general philosophical position. The second and third of these factors deserve further notice. Concerning the second, the types of problems that a given philosopher emphasizes will sometimes be influenced by the particular aspect of religion he regards as essential. Thus, the concentration on problems connected with religious belief in traditional philosophy of religion is partly due to the fact that most philosophers of religion have thought of religion primarily as a kind of belief (although this may, in fact, be less important than other factors). W. T. Stace in *Time and Eternity*, for example, considers mystical experience to be the essence of religion. Stace concentrated his main efforts on interpreting and justifying religious doctrine conceived as basically an expression of mystical experience. On the other hand, Kierkegaard thought of religion as basically a matter of an individual maintaining a certain general stance in life, and he devoted himself to an elaborate description of a variety of such stances, combined with indirect recommendations of one of these; he rarely mentioned any of the problems customarily discussed by philosophers of religion.

The operation of the third factor, the individual's philosophical position, is more apparent and, perhaps, more powerful. A few examples, selected more or less at random, will be helpful. Philosophers who are primarily speculative metaphysicians—Plato, Aquinas, Leibniz, Hegel, and Whitehead—naturally take very seriously the enterprise of constructing metaphysical arguments for or against the existence of God, whereas predominantly antimetaphysical philosophers—Hume, Kant, and Dewey—will either criticize such arguments or, as is more common in recent times, ignore them altogether. Those who subscribe to the thesis that the only proper job of philosophy is the analysis (clarification) of concepts will observe the appropriate restrictions when and if they turn their attention to religion. There is a great deal of work of this kind to be done with the concepts of God, creation, revelation, faith, and miracle, to name a few. Traditionally this has been done in connection with attempts to reach substantive conclusions on the existence of God, immortality, and other major issues, but if one thinks that conclusions on such matters cannot be attained by philosophical reflection, as analytic philosophers do, he may still seek to make explicit the concepts involved in religious belief. Such philosophizing will regard itself as a humble servant of theology or of more ordinary religious belief and will pretend to no judicial functions, except where it locates internal confusions or inconsistencies.

The influence of philosophical orientation is clearly exemplified in naturalistic philosophers, who generally rule out all supernaturalism on the basis of their general philosophical position, without giving particular supernaturalistic beliefs any detailed examination. Naturalists devote their energies to revising religious belief and practice so that they will be acceptable within a naturalistic framework.

Finally, one may consider Hegel, who devoted his lectures on the philosophy of religion to demonstrating a dialectical progression in the history of religion. This reflected Hegel's basic philosophical conviction that reality consists of the process of the Absolute coming to full self-consciousness, that this process exhibits a dialectical pattern, and that it is manifested in the history of every cultural form.

In the task of classifying the positions that have been taken in the philosophy of religion, one confronts the difficulty that not all philosophers of religion, even in a single religious tradition, are dealing with the same problems. However, there is a common task underlying all the different approaches. All philosophy of religion is ultimately concerned with arriving at a rational judgment of the religion under discussion and, if the judgment is negative, to present some sort of alternative. The initial principle of division can then be taken as the affirmative or negative character of this judgment. (This cannot be absolutely clear-cut, partly because often some part of the religion is affirmed and some is rejected, partly because it is not absolutely clear what is to be included in the religion in question.) It can then be asked of those whose judgment is affirmative what the basis of their judgment is.

One major group, which includes the great majority of philosophers of religion, presents various arguments in support of such beliefs as the existence of God and the immortality of the soul, arguments that take their start from premises that are not themselves religious doctrines and that, it is assumed, any reasonable man would accept. In other words, they attempt to support religious belief by resting it on nonreligious premises. A smaller but still considerable group regards religious belief as not needing any such support from the outside; they regard it as somehow self-justifying or at least as justified by something from within religion. Some of them (Bergson and James) suppose that the belief in the existence of God, for example, is justified by religious experience. One can directly experience the presence of God, and therefore one does not need to prove his existence by showing that he must be postulated to explain certain facts. Others regard religious faith as different from other modes of belief in such a way that it does not need support of any kind, either from argument from effect to cause or from direct experience. Kierkegaard, Emil Brunner, and Paul Tillich, for example, all take this position, though there are great differences between them. (The case of Tillich illustrates the point that in some cases it is difficult to distinguish between those who accept the religious tradition and those who reject it. Tillich considers himself a Christian theologian, but his interpretation of Christian doctrine is so unorthodox that many feel he has reconstrued it out of recognition and therefore should be classed with those who substitute a symbolic reinterpretation for traditional beliefs.)

In the other major group we can distinguish between those who simply reject traditional religion (Holbach and Russell) and those who in addition try to put something in its place. In the latter group we can distinguish between those who try to retain the trappings, perhaps even the doctrinal trappings, of traditional religion but give it a nonsupernaturalistic reinterpretation, usually as symbolic of something or other in the natural world (Santayana), and those who attempt to depict a quite different sort of religion constructed along nonsupernaturalistic lines (Comte, Dewey, and Wieman).

Outside this classification are those analytical philosophers who restrict themselves to the analysis of concepts and types of utterances. We may regard them as not having a major position in the philosophy of religion, but rather as making contributions that may be useful in the construction of such a position.

Bibliography

Edwin A. Burtt, *Types of Religious Philosophy*, rev. ed. (New York, 1951), and Robert Leet Patterson, *An Introduction to the Philosophy of Religion* (New York, 1958), are useful introductory textbooks. A wide variety of readings in the field can be found in George L. Abernethy and Thomas A. Langford, eds., *Philosophy of Religion* (New York, 1962), and in William P. Alston, ed., *Religious Belief and Philosophical Reflection* (New York, 1963).

The following works are important treatments of a wide variety of topics in this area: John Baillie, *The Interpretation of Religion* (New York, 1928); H. J. Paton, *The Modern Predicament* (New York, 1955); A. E. Taylor, *The Faith of a Moralist* (New York, 1930); and F. R. Tennant, *Philosophical Theology* (Cambridge, 1928). These works are written from a standpoint more or less sympathetic to traditional theism. For fairly comprehensive discussions from a more critical standpoint, see J. M. E. McTaggart, *Some Dogmas of Religion* (London, 1906), and Bertrand Russell, *Religion and Science* (London, 1935).

Works dealing with the nature and significance of religious experience include William James, *The Varieties of Religious*

Experience (New York, 1902), and Rudolf Otto, *The Idea of the Holy,* translated by J. W. Harvey (New York, 1958). The nature of religion is discussed in Josiah Royce, *The Sources of Religious Insight* (New York, 1912), and in Julian Huxley, *Religion Without Revelation* (New York, 1958). For the relation of religion and science, see Bertrand Russell, *op. cit.,* and Michael Pupin, ed., *Science and Religion; a Symposium* (New York, 1931). J. H. Newman, *A Grammar of Assent* (London, 1870), and Paul Tillich, *Dynamics of Faith* (New York, 1957), cover the nature of religious faith as a mode of belief and/or awareness.

In Emil Brunner, *The Philosophy of Religion From the Standpoint of Protestant Theology,* translated by A. J. D. Farrer and B. L. Woolf (Edinburgh, 1937), the nature of revelation and its relation to the results of human experience and reflection are considered. The place of religion in human culture as a whole is dealt with in G. W. F. Hegel, *Lectures on the Philosophy of Religion,* translated by E. B. Speirs and J. B. Sanderson, 3 vols. (London, 1895), and in George Santayana, *Reason in Religion* (New York, 1905). For the logical analysis of religious language, see A. G. N. Flew and Alasdair MacIntyre, eds., *New Essays in Philosophical Theology* (London, 1955), and C. B. Martin, *Religious Belief* (Ithaca, N.Y., 1959). Edwyn Bevan, *Symbolism and Belief* (Boston, 1957), and W. T. Stace, *Time and Eternity* (Princeton, N.J., 1952), discuss the nature and significance of religious symbolism. Possibilities for reconstructing religion along relatively nontraditional lines appear in Immanuel Kant, *Religion Within the Limits of Reason Alone,* translated by T. M. Greene and H. H. Hudson (La Salle, Ill., 1934); John Dewey, *A Common Faith* (New Haven, 1934); and Julian Huxley, *op. cit.*

William P. Alston

PHILOSOPHY OF SCIENCE, HISTORY OF. The philosophy of science, as a distinct branch of philosophical inquiry, is of fairly recent origin. Formerly, with the exception of the work of Francis Bacon, the philosophy of science formed part of the general theory of knowledge. In reading Locke, for example, one has to infer from his general epistemology what his views on the specifically systematic, experimentally controlled, critical exploration of nature are. The idea that there are logical, epistemological, and metaphysical problems that are peculiar to or particularly pressing in the systematic sciences and that differ from the corresponding problems in the more ordinary commerce of mind did not really take root until the early nineteenth century. To keep this survey both reasonably detailed and of manageable proportions, we shall begin with the first great controversy of the modern era, that between Whewell and Mill in the second quarter of the nineteenth century.

In the account which follows, a grand opposition is brought out by dividing most of the leading characters into two camps. On the one hand, there are those philosophers who see the generation and justification of hypotheses as inductive processes from particular items of evidence; who hold causation to be nothing but regularity of succession; and who aim at the reduction of all theoretical concepts to functions of those observables from which, by induction, theory is supposed to spring. In this camp since 1850 there have been J. S. Mill, Benjamin Brodie, Ernst Mach, Karl Pearson, Pierre Duhem, Philipp Frank, Carl Hempel, Rudolf Carnap, and R. B. Braithwaite. In opposition there have been William Whewell, Ludwig Boltzmann, N. R. Campbell, and lately a group of philosophers and scientists who hold that the processes of theory construction are more complex than inductivism will

allow; that the meaning of theoretical concepts is not exhausted by logical function and observational basis; and that actual procedures of science have more authority than formal logic has. It would seem that Rudolf Carnap, although originally belonging to the former, reductionist, camp, must now be said to belong to the latter, realist, group.

The operationist theory of Mach, lately expounded with vigor by P. W. Bridgman, lies at the far extreme of reductionism. This theory of science claims to reduce the meaning of all empirical statements to descriptions of experimental operations. At the other extreme lies the weak romanticism of Henri Bergson, a perennial temptation for those who leave the canons of formal logic too far behind. Finally, there should be mentioned the sophisticated *commodisme* of Henri Poincaré, a view not easy to classify, which has been understood as asserting that in formulating theory we are, under the guidance of convenience, choosing conventions rather than developing a picture of reality, or merely generalizing the results of observation into forms convenient for logical manipulation.

MILL AND WHEWELL

For Mill the central problem in philosophy of science was to give a correct account of the function of the particular facts of observation and experiment; for Whewell it was to give a correct account of the function of theory. For Mill all knowledge was sensory in origin; for Whewell some part of the items of knowledge was contributed by the knower. Unfortunately, the extremely suggestive and potentially fruitful works of Whewell were overshadowed by Mill's elegantly expounded but crude empiricism.

Whewell and Mill each brought into the philosophy of the nineteenth century a leading strand of eighteenth-century thought. Whewell was oriented toward Kant and Mill toward Hume, but both developed less rationalist versions of the doctrines of their philosophical progenitors. Whewell played down the a priori and deductive element that Kant had emphasized in the establishment of the categories in which knowledge is to be framed; Mill would not allow any necessary truths, not even the axioms of mathematics, which Hume had distinguished from "matters of fact and existence."

Knowledge, Whewell thought, was not derived entirely from the senses but was a product of sensations and ideas. A scientist makes a discovery when he finds that he can, without strain, add an organizing idea to a multitude of sensations. When Kepler, for instance, added the organizing concept of the ellipse, a particularization of the idea of shape, to the known astronomical data, he found that it organized them without strain. This is how we should understand his discovery of the elliptical orbit of Mars. Whewell called this organizing of data by ideas particularized into concepts the colligation of facts. The addition of new data to the scientist's stock of unexplained facts makes demands upon his stock of conceptions, which sometimes can be met from the stock on hand, but sometimes not. New data require that concepts be refined, analyzed, made more precise, in what Whewell called the explication of the conceptions.

Whewell thought that the relations found to hold among facts, and the ways in which facts can be colligated, are contingent. At any time facts may turn up that lead to the abandonment of previous colligations of the other facts in the field. But Whewell firmly insisted that the relations which hold among conceptions and ideas are necessary. That light travels in straight lines, that heat is a form of energy, that action is equal and opposite to reaction were all necessary truths for Whewell, since they express the relations between concepts and between ideas; but it would be contingent for Whewell whether these relations would serve for the colligation of facts. He seems to have thought that each branch of science has, like geometry, its axioms and definitions, which are, in themselves, necessary truths; but whether they are the appropriate axioms and definitions to bring order to a field of phenomena is contingent. This opinion seems to have been derived as much from Leibniz as from Kant. Leibniz chose to consider all relations among predicates as necessary, leaving only existential questions contingent, so that a Leibnizian scientist might be thought of as approaching the world with a pattern book already drawn; the only question he must answer is which pattern exists, is exemplified in nature. Whewell was both more of an empiricist and more of a historian than this, since he did allow, in the explication of conceptions, for an adjustment in patterns under the influence of facts.

It was in the matter of the necessity of the relations among ideas and conceptions, and in the nature of the relation between theories and facts, that Mill and Whewell began to disagree. Mill was not prepared to concede even the axioms of mathematics to Whewell as necessary truths, for he took them to be extremely well grounded generalizations of experience. As for Whewell's belief that there were necessary propositions involved in the foundations of all the sciences, Mill briskly dismissed this. He coined the slogan that conceptions are not added to the facts but seen in them. Mill argued that Kepler did not approach the jumble of Martian observations with the ellipse (all of whose properties follow of necessity from its definition) and then find that this concept unified the data. On the contrary, Kepler eventually saw an ellipse in the data. According to Mill, there are no necessary truths of the kind Whewell believed in, and a fortiori science cannot be said to be the putting of a mass of data into order by introducing into it relatively a priori conceptions.

Mill became popular; Whewell sank into relative obscurity. The realistic picture of scientific method as the testing of hypotheses became obscured by an exaggerated all-pervasive inductivism. Although Mill understood that scientists were seeking to explain as well as to predict and describe the course of nature, and that explanation involved the postulation of causes, so narrowly did he understand causation (as only a regularity of contiguous succession among events) that he thought the route to both explanation and prediction was the "rendering particulars general, by induction" that had been advocated by Newton; and he believed that the logician's task, in studying the intellectual processes of science, was to identify the schemata by which generalizations are properly drawn from particulars. Mill never explicitly claimed that explanation and predic-

tion are logically identical, but every opinion that he advocated leads to that most unfortunate conclusion.

In his pursuit of a total empiricism Mill made another unfortunate identification. Working from Richard Whateley's opinion that every induction is a syllogism with some version of the principle of the uniformity of nature as major premise, Mill took the principle of induction itself to be an inductive generalization from an original experience of observed regularities. It took philosophy of science a hundred years to break free of the futile discussions that this claim occasioned, for on Mill's point of view it is obviously impossible to assemble enough data to prove the very principle (the uniformity of nature) upon which proof depends.

REDUCTIONISM

Mill's antitheoretical and inductivist views were immensely influential. This can be illustrated by one of the most remarkable episodes in nineteenth-century science, the chemists' abandonment of the atom. Chemistry in the nineteenth century was strongly antitheoretical. There was an official prohibition on theoretical papers in the *Journal of the Chemical Society,* and there was also a strong tendency to dismiss the atomic hypothesis as potentially misleading and metaphysical.

Brodie. The culmination of these tendencies came in the 1870s in the magnificent, but now almost forgotten, chemistry of Benjamin Brodie. Using the logical calculus of George Boole, and basing himself upon Mill's view that the laws of nature are but the description of observational regularities "reduced to their simplest expression," Brodie built a chemical system without atoms. He argued that the real subject of chemistry was qualitative changes, as when a liquid and a solid yield a solid and a gas, and gravimetric changes, as when 12 grams of liquid and 18 grams of solid yield 24 grams of solid and 6 grams of gas. Therefore, every chemical fact should be expressible in two equations, one expressing the qualitative change and the other the gravimetric.

The basic principle of Brodie's calculus, the pairing of qualitative operation equations and gravimetric equations, was based upon the generalization (untrue in fact) that every qualitative complex has its characteristic weight per unit volume, supposing it to be in gaseous form. With immense industry and ingenuity, Brodie proceeded to express in his calculus nearly all the chemical facts known to him and to develop an axiomatic treatment of the formulas so obtained, using a development of Boole's logical calculus.

Although Brodie's system was something of a sensation in its time, its limitations in the form in which it was presented and the unfamiliarity (in 1875) of the Boolean approach to the axiomatization of theories prevented its widespread adoption. But in his primary aim, the disavowal of atoms, Brodie had many seconders. At one meeting of the Chemical Society in London in the mid-1870s, during a debate on Brodie's chemical system only one of sixty members present declared himself a believer in the reality of chemical atoms.

In Brodie's work the corpuscularian philosophy, and

particularly the material atom, came under severe attack. Scientists generally denied the reality of atoms, and Brodie denied even their utility. Brodie's chemical calculus expressed only the relations between the observed qualities and weights before and after a reaction, and it was assumed that nothing could be ascertained concerning the mechanism of the reaction. It remained for Mach to formulate the underlying philosophy, assumed by Brodie, with elegance and to express it in popular form.

Mach. According to Mach, science is the generalization of experience; and, although tempting, it is wrong to impute to science "the power of opening up unfathomable abysses of nature, to which the senses cannot penetrate." Natural laws are, he wrote (*Popular Scientific Lectures,* Ch. 8), nothing but "the mimetic reproduction of facts in thought." Explanation consists in the analysis of a field of phenomena in such a way that we see "everywhere the same facts." Scientific investigations do not penetrate nature; they organize in economical fashion that which experience presents to us. Causality is nothing but the habit of mind, described by Hume, that leads us to expect an "effect" following the occurrence of a "cause." In this, Mach's views are not different from Brodie's, except that Brodie spoke of qualities and weights of substances, which are independent of us and exist in their own right. Mach's epistemology, however, is directly derived from Hume. Experience is the stream of all our sensations, and bodies, mentally experienced as separate individuals, are just relatively stable groups of those sensations. It is not the qualities of bodies that are related in our laws; it is our sensations. This defines the goal of scientific investigations, which can only be to discover the relations between sensations, since sensations alone constitute the field of phenomena.

This view of Mach's was endorsed by Karl Pearson, whose widely read *Grammar of Science* was strongly attacked by Ludwig Boltzmann, who argued that not only are our nonphenomenological thing-concepts justified by their enduring practical value in scientific investigations but also that deeper hypotheses concerning the mechanisms of nature play an essential part in the growth of science. According to Boltzmann, the entities developed to explain phenomena are characteristic and essential objects of theoretical thinking. Mach, like Pierre Duhem, believed they were nothing but devices, heuristic models.

Mach's attitude toward entities referred to in theory but not obviously revealed in observation is summed up in a revealing remark in his *Popular Scientific Lectures:* "It would not become physical science," he said, "to see in its self-created, changeable, economical tools, molecules and atoms, realities behind phenomena . . . the atom must remain a tool for representing phenomena, like the functions of mathematics." Thus, theory is not a guide to further realities but an instrument for organizing our sensations. It leads from sensation back to sensation, and the ground it traverses in this journey is entirely imaginary. This famous doctrine was hinted at by Proclus in antiquity; it was embraced fervently by many of the astronomers of the sixteenth century; it was advocated by Duhem and again by the logical empiricists. It is not only famous; it has proved immensely attractive. Despite the fact that

Kepler exposed its inadequacies, Whewell displayed its irrationality, and, as we shall see below, Campbell demonstrated its poverty, it continues to exert a powerful influence.

Duhem. Pierre Duhem expressed the reductionist attitude in a form which has come to be particularly important in modern times. An important feature of actual scientific work is the use of models, either actual constructions like rafts of soap bubbles to represent the crystal structure of metals, or conceptual models like atoms and molecules to represent the causal structure underlying observable chemical phenomena. Expressing exactly the prevailing atmosphere of skepticism at the turn of the nineteenth century, Duhem declared that all models are simply heuristic devices, psychological aids, and not logically necessary; in making inferences from theory, models are dispensable. All that is really required in science, Duhem thought, is a formal system expressing the relations observed between phenomena, and whatever can be done by a model and analogical reasoning can be done more surely by a formal system and deductive reasoning.

Influence. By the beginning of the twentieth century the reductionist views of Mach, Pearson, and Duhem had been clearly and strongly formulated, and during the following thirty years they profoundly influenced the development of European philosophy. The logical positivism of the Vienna circle was entirely in the spirit of Mach, whose sensationalism gave authority both to the famous dictum that the meaning of a statement is its method of verification and to the metaphysics of phenomenalism, with which logical positivism quickly became linked. The net effect of this movement was a steady denigration of the power of theory in favor of logically ordered structures of empirical concepts. The marriage of Mach's views on science with Russellian logic initiated the era of hypothetico-deductivism, when a theory was thought to be an axiomatic structure, like formal logic or geometry. The fact that axiomatic structures can never lead into the new and hitherto unknown, that they are, precisely because of their logical coherence, quite unfruitful, does not seem to have bothered the advocates of the hypothetico-deductive view. The logicians of this era were apparently not interested in the question of theory origin or theory growth, but only in the question of the best mode of formalizing theories that were already known. The power and beauty of the Russellian logic in mathematics seems to have exerted a restricting effect upon the analytical methods of logicians interested in science.

REALISM

It is ironical that logicians of the present age should now look back to a moment just prior to the growth of logical positivism for the starting point of a view about the structure of theories that is in almost total opposition to the reductionist view.

Campbell. In 1920 N. R. Campbell's great book, *Physics: The Elements,* was published. It presents an elegant demonstration of the uselessness of theories constructed according to the hypothetico-deductivist principles and the outline of a more profound view.

What Campbell grasped was that a theory which is to be of any use is a multiple structure with four distinct parts. First, there are the empirical generalizations which express the results of experiment and observation in a suitably processed form. Then there are two other groups of statements, the "dictionary" and the "hypothesis." The hypothesis contains statements using theoretical concepts that are introduced for the purpose of the theory and are not derived by abstraction or schematization from the field of phenomena to which the theory applies. Junction with the field of phenomena is achieved by the use of the "dictionary," which correlates certain functions of the theoretical concepts with empirical concepts. The fourth element is the "analogy," by which we see that the relations between the theoretical concepts are like the relations between the empirical concepts of some already explored field of phenomena. We can then draw upon that field to expand the hypothesis in a plausible and consistent way.

Through the interplay between the analogy, the hypothesis, and the "dictionary" Campbell was able to explain the power of theories to cope with new information, to accommodate contrary instances in a new and more powerful synthesis, and to predict novel kinds of phenomena. Darwin's evolutionary theory can be nicely structured on Campbellian lines. The empirical generalizations describe the geological and geographical distribution of animals and plants. The hypothesis is "natural selection," the idea that the interplay between an environment and a population leads to progressive change in the population because the "struggle for existence" tends to favor the inheritance of those random mutations which are of advantage to an individual in the given environment. The "dictionary" contains such entries as "Two different but similar populations in the same environment at different times are related by evolutionary descent." By means of such "dictionary" entries the observed geological traces and other empirical data are related to the hypothesis of natural selection. The analogy in this case is well known, since Darwin himself described it beautifully in the *Origin of Species*. It is between natural selection and variation and domestic selection and variation, the causal relation between the latter pair being the basis, by analogy, for the alleged causal relation between the former pair.

Campbell himself used the kinetic theory of gases as his illustrative example, and hundreds of other examples are not hard to find.

But there are problems. First, how do we proceed when we seem to need a hypothesis that demands as analogies two incompatible parts of traditional physics—for instance, in the case of the conflict between wave and particle models for subatomic entities? This was the basis of the dilemma that concerned Niels Bohr and Werner Heisenberg and led to the complementarity principle, which in effect counseled the adoption of both analogies with a rule to prevent their being applied together. Second, the analogy, according to Campbell, gives a tincture of reality to the concepts of the hypothesis. But should we not ask whether the process of natural selection, for example, exists in nature? Or whether gases really are made up of molecules? In the case of quantum theory the incompatibility of the two analogies that seemed to be needed makes one hesitate to reify any entities to which the theoretical concepts seem to refer, but there is no such difficulty in the case of natural selection, or gas molecules, or radio stars. Nevertheless, Campbell was not prepared to allow the passage of favorable existential judgments on the alleged referents of theoretical concepts except in a very special sense.

One might think that existential judgments, favorable and unfavorable, add and substract identifiable individuals from the world as we believe in it. Campbell, however, took the assertion "There are molecules" to be saying something different. In his own words, "It is a very useful and compact way of calling to our minds all the assertions and implications of the dynamical theory of gases." Similarly, of "real" he says, "The something that is real is an idea of the hypothesis of the true theory." Existence and reality judgments are, then, for Campbell no more than picturesque ways of introducing theories and declaring their truth. He did not think that they express additions to our stock of things, properties, or processes.

Expressing Campbell's views in the terminology used by Duhem would yield the principle that models are logically necessary for prediction and explanation—that is, the growth of the hypothesis is an essential element in inferring from theory to particular fact—and that this growth occurs by the exploitation of analogy. But the models so constructed and so used are not candidates for reality. In this, Campbell drew back from the full development of a realist view.

COMMODISME

Closely related to the last-discussed aspect of Campbell's thought is Henri Poincaré's view that, in a certain sense, theories are linguistic conventions. Poincaré arrived at this view from the problem of the proper status of mathematical axioms, which Mill had rather implausibly declared to be empirical generalizations. The problem of the proper status of the axioms of geometry has concerned philosophers from time to time. Should one treat the criteria of congruence, for example, as definitions and thus necessary truths, or as statements of fact and thus contingent? Both alternatives raise difficulties. If the basis of geometry is definition, why are some definitions more satisfactory than others? And if geometry has a factual basis, how does one account for its apparent uniqueness? Poincaré introduced his theory of *commodisme* to resolve these apparent difficulties. One can choose one's geometry from the available alternatives, since geometry is a method of representation of spatial facts rather than a set of spatial facts. Choosing between Riemann and Euclid is like choosing between different projections for making a map of the world. According to the choice, the map will be different, but the continents are the same and bear the same relations to one another.

Poincaré's *commodisme* was quickly translated into a popular doctrine which for convenience of distinction can be called conventionalism. Conventionalism, as preached by Edouard Le Roy, maintained that not only is the language of science arrived at by convention but so are the facts which that language is used to express. The laws of nature are not truths but mere conventions.

In repudiating this development of his opinions,

Poincaré worked out his own position in more detail. The extreme conventionalist view implied that it did not matter which conventions were adopted; any one would be as good as any other. Of course, Poincaré was quick to point out, in science some conventions are better than others because some recipes are successful and others are not. There must be an empirical criterion which distinguishes good science from bad. The nature of this empirical criterion can be approached by noticing that although the facts which are ultimate criteria of truth may be the same, there are a great many ways of expressing them. A scientific fact differs from a "crude" fact, according to Poincaré, in the same way that a statement in German differs from a statement in French. The laws of nature are, as it were, the rules of synonymy of the scientific language; but they can nevertheless be revised, for they depend upon concordances of fact. Should the concordance fail, scientific language would contain an ambiguity and would have to be revised. "In sum, all the scientist creates in a fact is the language in which he enunciates it."

But of what sort are the "facts"? Anticipating Wittgenstein in this matter, Poincaré argued that facts cannot be the qualitative characteristics of sense impressions. Languages must be public, intersubjective systems, while the qualities of our sense impressions are necessarily intrasubjective and incommunicable. Something sensory can be communicated, however: the relations between the qualities of sense impressions. Color words, for example, in the public language must be understood as expressing the fact that such and such group of things produces the same sensations, not as names for the sensations which they produce, since, for all we know, they may be different in each of us.

Unfortunately, Poincaré's influence has been less than it might have been because philosophers have preferred to knock down conventionalism rather than to refine *commodisme*. Nevertheless, the marked linguistic bias of his philosophizing has been influential in directing philosophers' attention to the language in which scientific discoveries are expressed and theories formulated.

PROBABILITY AND INDUCTION

Twentieth-century methods in philosophy have been characteristically formal as well as linguistic. They have involved the construction of mathematical model languages and, when these have proved inadequate, the more ample linguistic analysis of the language of intellectual operations in a new domain of discourse has often led to formal innovations, as well as to the posing of problems of formalization which are, as yet, unsolved. To some extent the attraction of the powerful mathematical tools developed from the nineteenth-century inventions of Boole, Venn, De Morgan, Peano, and Frege has lately exerted a drag on the progress of logic. Those tools, although sophisticated, have proved inadequate to the complexity of the structures to be analyzed. Confirmation theory is not just the logic of probability statements, and the models and analogies used in theory construction are not of the same kind as mathematical models. The logic of confirmation of hypotheses by evidence and the logic of analogy cannot be expressed in those logical structures whose origins are in nineteenth-century mathematics. Nevertheless, modern logic has been of immense service to the philosophy of science, particularly in two aspects. The first is in the growth of probability theory brought about by the effort to create a logic of induction; the second is in the growth of formal logic into a system capable of creating model languages.

As mentioned earlier, Mill had generated a characteristically philosophical problem by claiming that the principle which would have validated inductive generalization was itself in need of proof by inductive generalization. It seemed that the inescapable conclusion must be that it is impossible to justify inductive inference. However, despite this pessimistic conclusion, the use of the calculus of chances, or "probability" theory, to provide an inductive logic began in the nineteenth century, particularly in the work of W. Stanley Jevons.

Jevons. W. S. Jevons denied in effect that there was any such process as inductive inference, the alleged passage from particular statements of fact to their generalizatons. In its place he reintroduced the hypothetico-deductive method of Descartes, which Mill had toyed with. Jevons called it inverse deduction. According to this doctrine, scientific reasoning does not consist in inferences from particular *to* general but, rather, in the deduction of the known particulars *from* a general hypothesis. Jevons saw that a great many general statements would suffice as hypotheses for deducing any particular statements expressing the results of observation and experiment.

How is one to decide among all those hypotheses which have adequate logical power with respect to any given set of particulars? Jevons' answer was, in effect, to say that in natural science it is not appropriate to choose one hypothesis and reject all others. Rather, all the logically possible hypotheses from which a certain set of particulars can be deduced should be ranked according to their probability. The probability of a hypothesis (within what must be assumed to be a finite set of hypotheses, if the device is to work) was to be determined according to the probabilities of the events mentioned in the particular statements entailed by the hypothesis. For instance, if I know the kettle has boiled, I might consider the following hypotheses: (1) the kettle has been on the stove; (2) the kettle has been in the refrigerator. Since it is extremely probable that the kettle would boil if it were on the stove, and extremely improbable that it would boil if it were in the refrigerator, the first hypothesis is highly probable. Much of the subsequent work on inductive reasoning has followed the lines Jevons initiated. In the works of J. M. Keynes, Richard von Mises, Hans Reichenbach, and Rudolf Carnap the probabilistic exegesis of the measure of inductive support has been developed.

Logical positivism. The advances in formal logic made during the nineteenth and early twentieth centuries made possible the development of probability theories more elaborate and sophisticated than Jevons' and also encouraged the quest for a "universal character," or perfect language for science. Despite Campbell's virtual demonstration of the uselessness of mere formalism and theory, the logical calculi and the intellectual restrictions which were conditions of their use became enshrined in the dogmas of an immensely powerful philosophical movement. They became the basis of logical positivism, which was developed from a marriage of Mach's views on science and Wittgenstein's and Russell's theories of logical atomism. The logical calculus of propositions, with its mechanical method of determining the truth or falsity of compound propositions on the basis of the truth and falsity of the components, strongly suggested that there were atomic propositions, that is, ultimate components of statements, the smallest units capable of truth and falsity. To each true atomic proposition there should correspond an atomic fact.

What were the atomic facts to be? Here Mach's sensationalism suggested an answer to the originators of logical positivism, the philosophers and scientists of the Vienna circle. The atomic facts were to be the momentary sensations in the sensory fields of individual persons. Science then would consist in the discovery of regularities among sensations, in the style of Mach, which would be described in an entirely clear and unambiguous formal language, in the style of Russell. Science, according to Wittgenstein's *Tractatus Logico-philosophicus,* was a net of propositions thrown over reality, and the simpler its constituents (the smaller the mesh), the better reality is portrayed. All this is in marked contrast with the ideas of Whewell, Campbell, and Poincaré. In the early days of the Vienna circle it seemed that the only function of science was to transfer the facts from the world to language, as one might use a method of projection in making a map of the world. Apparently the only criterion required was a safeguard against nonsense, a demarcation principle that would distinguish empirical propositions from metaphysical ones.

To the problem of demarcation the philosophers of the Vienna circle gave their famous answer that a proposition was empirically meaningful (worthy of consideration by scientists) if and only if a method for verifying (confirming, testing) it could be described (see VERIFIABILITY PRINCIPLE). In whichever form the criterion was formulated, it was a questionable principle because general propositions cannot be verified (proved true) by instances. It is to the great credit of Karl Popper that he was the first to see the weakness of the criterion and to propose his own, that empirical propositions should be known by their potential falsifiability. Unfortunately, while this criterion is entirely sound for single general propositions, it breaks down for theories which have too complex a logical structure. Nevertheless, it did mark a great step forward. Popper himself has developed the notion of falsifiability into a whole philosophy of science, notably advocating the view that the logic of science is essentially the falsification of conjectures.

Carnap and Popper, among others, also saw that while verification of general propositions (proving them true) was out of the question as a goal of empirical investigations, there remained the problem of how to assess the degree of confirmation or corroboration which favorable instances do lend to a hypothesis. Carnap and Popper both followed Jevons in trying to make use of some function of probability as a measure of confirmation or corroboration, but they disagreed as to the way a corroborative coefficient should be built out of a probability assessment. For example, Popper maintained that the more improbable a statement was, the more highly it would be corroborated by a favorable instance. It seems today that this is an unsolved

problem. Apparently it will have to be tackled afresh, free of the entanglements of the past.

It soon became clear to some members of the Vienna circle, notably to Carnap, that a crude sensationalism would not do for the basis of the analysis of scientific knowledge. For one thing, the most elementary science requires a certain regularity of behavior in the objects of perception, which, according to sensationalism, could be achieved only by the assertion of a potentially infinite set of propositions stating or predicting the momentary existence of sensations in anyone's sensory field. Physical objects as the objects of perception already have the required continuity. Physicalism was substituted for sensationalism. This theory envisaged the construction of an ideal form of the language of physics that would be translatable into the everyday language of statements concerning our experience of things, properties, and relations. The substitution so effected re-emphasized some important philosophical problems. Notably, it was very pertinent to ask whether the physicalist language would suffice for the whole of science. There has always been a body of opinion, sometimes small, sometimes large, which would credit biology with the need for concepts peculiarly its own, irreducible to the concepts of physics and chemistry. Even if it is conceded that the biological language is but a dialect of the physicalist language, many people would still reserve the independence of societal facts—for example, those concerning moral systems and behavior choices—from physical reduction. This also remains an unsettled issue in philosophy of science.

Recent developments. While the logicians of the Vienna circle were forging their physicalist language, the same problem concerning the relation between physical theory and observable reality was raised in another form by physicists. It had been found that in trying to predict the future behavior of the smallest known "objects" (the products of atomic disintegration) and even of the occurrence of atomic disintegrations themselves, unique prediction had to be given up in favor of a system that would give the relative probabilities of a certain class of outcomes (see QUANTUM MECHANICS, PHILOSOPHICAL IMPLICATIONS OF). It seemed to some scientists, notably A. S. Eddington and J. H. Jeans, that this could be interpreted as the appearance of indeterminism in nature. The appearance of indeterminism seemed to be the basis for advocating a Machian view of science as expressing nothing but the regular relations among phenomena. It seemed too that no single model or picture of reality would do for the whole of physics.

Theory did not, after all, lead to a plausible reality, although its power of unification of the known laws into a system was high. Indeed, theory seemed reduced to an elaborate logical bridge by which the existence of some phenomena could, with a certain probability, be inferred from the existence of certain others. It was perhaps the consciousness of these difficulties that led to the revival of an old theory, that explanation and prediction are logically identical, the former being the subsumption of a particular under a generalization, a mock prediction of that particular. The new form of this view was formulated in modern times by Carl Hempel and Paul Oppenheim in their famous paper, "Studies in the Logic of Explanation." These logicians advocated the view that an explanation of a fact should consist of an antecedent fact of a similar kind, together with a generalization by means of which one could predict the fact to be explained from the antecedent fact. Theory, on this view, consists of a logically constructed system of general statements structured according to generality so that from axioms of the highest generality the lower-order generalizations could be deduced. The meaning of theory would then be exhausted by the observational basis of the facts upon which it was based. It will be remembered that a severe criticism of this view had already been published by Campbell in 1920. One of the contemporary schools of philosophy of science, represented particularly by Mary Hesse and Rom Harré, starting from a critical attack upon Hempel's ideas initiated by Michael Scriven, Norwood R. Hanson, and others, has revised Campbell's theory and has seen in the analogy attached to the logical structure of theory a source of meaning by which theory can grow.

PHILOSOPHERS INSPIRED BY BIOLOGY

We have sketched above the main lines of development of the philosophy of science. Despite great differences of opinion, a recognizable unity appears in the central position given to physics (it is generally regarded as central either in content or in method) and in a preference for argument in a mathematical style. But there are biological and social sciences, and there are methods of advocating opinions that are literary rather than mathematical. Along with the triumphant progress of the physical sciences and the style of philosophy of science that is concordant with their aspirations and methods there has been an equally continuous, although less respectable, reaction on the part of those who believe that the physical sciences, in their analysis of nature, omit crucial features of reality and that the mathematical analyses distort the intellectual processes by which reasoning is carried on. This reaction has taken two forms: an antiscientific idealism which has contributed nothing to the philosophy of science and a genuine philosophy of science that takes biology as the archetypal science and aims at reconstructing physical concepts in terms of the categories that are thought to be characteristic of the biological and even of the psychological sciences. Despite the unpopularity of the latter position among professional philosophers, the influence which both its chief advocates, Bergson and Whitehead, have had on lay opinion makes it an important part of the history of the philosophy of science.

Physical science has imagined the world to be essentially particulate, analyzable into separate things, each having its own properties independent of other things. When mechanics has been the dominant form of physics, these individual things have been thought of as capable of inaction, of unchanging and independent existence unless subject to exterior influence. But it can be argued that this image of the world comes from the science of physics, not from nature. Biologists, in studying the anatomy and physiology of animals and plants, must consider each part of an organism in relation to the whole of which it is a part,

so that the relation becomes an essential element in understanding that part and responsible for the form it takes. There could not be an isolated organ, as there can be an isolated thing. It is only in relation to their organisms that organs have significance.

Similarly, ecology could be construed as a science which treats environments and populations in such a way that interrelations are of as much or more importance than the physical properties of individuals, since the interrelations are responsible for individual characteristics. The vitalist philosophy of Bergson uses the biological model of the organism as a model for all nature. Following this approach, we are asked to treat the universe more as an organism than as an electromechanical gadget. In giving explanations, we are asked in principle to take into consideration the whole state of the world, future and past, and to consider as far as possible the function or purpose of each part in that whole. Entities, including people, are not, on this view, isolated individuals but integral parts of a quasi-organic whole; and it is as parts relative to the whole that they have significance. Organic evolution is not to be understood as a physical process leading by the operation of physical laws to the differentiation of immensely complex, self-replicating protein molecules but as the striving of an *élan vital,* a mysterious life force, to realize itself.

This doctrine has never recommended itself to professional philosophers. It is essentially literary and romantic. In asserting that parts can be understood only in relation to wholes, it was necessary to grant priority to the intuitive apprehension of wholes, and "intuition" thereby became the fundamental source of knowledge. Connected with this was Bergson's other characteristic idea, that "change" should be a more fundamental category than "thing."

Whitehead. Whitehead has been less justly neglected, since his philosophy of science is neither literary nor romantic. Curiously enough, one of Whitehead's starting points was an issue that also seriously concerned the great mechanist, Hobbes. Hobbes saw that nature contains no ideal mathematical entities, such as points and lines, and he endeavored to construct a "real" mathematics in which lines were thick and points had extension. In a similar way Whitehead, starting from the fact that there are no mathematical instants in our experience, substituted a conceptual scheme based upon nonpunctiform events rather than instants. In his *The Principles of Natural Knowledge* he showed how such a conceptual scheme might work, and using the method of "extensive abstraction," he sketched a mathematical physics based upon the idea of overlapping events. In this, Whitehead presented a strong form of one of Bergson's characteristic theses: that nature is not constituted by the enduring things of traditional physics but rather by a continuous flux.

By starting with events, Whitehead freed himself altogether from the presuppositions of the older philosophy of matter but managed to retain a world independent of the perceiver. He was able to show how one might substitute relations for qualities as the constitutive characteristics of nature; time became more fundamental than space. In recent years some of the theorizing in fundamental physics has had a markedly Whiteheadian flavor; in particular there seems to have been a growing tendency to substitute relations for qualities and to play down atomistic conceptions of individuals. Whitehead, however, did not stop at this point. In *Process and Reality* he went further and chose to interpret his conceptual scheme in a more and more psychologistic way. In the process he lost the confidence of professional philosophers. This seems a pity, since there are surely ideas in his earlier books that are as suggestive for the future of the metaphysics of science as Campbell's have proved for the logic of science.

Bibliography

Alexander, Peter, "The Philosophy of Science, 1850–1910," in D. J. O'Connor, ed., *A Critical History of Western Philosophy*. New York, 1964. Pp. 402–425.

Ayer, A. J., *Logical Positivism*. New York, 1959. A collection of the classical texts which formed the basis of the movement.

Bergson, Henri, *Time and Free Will*, translated by F. L. Pogson. London, 1910; New York, 1959. An example of the literary tradition in philosophy.

Bohr, Niels, "Discussions With Einstein on Epistemological Problems in Modern Physics," in P. A. Schilpp, ed., *Albert Einstein: Philosopher-Scientist*, Vol. II. New York, 1959. Ch. 7. Bohr's paper expresses his own position very clearly, and the book as a whole is worth serious study.

Boole, George, *The Mathematical Analysis of Logic*. Oxford, 1948. Contains the original logical algebra from which most modern logic ultimately stems.

Braithwaite, R. B., *Scientific Explanation*. Cambridge, 1953. An elegant account of the hypothetico-deductive analysis of scientific theory.

Bridgman, P. W., *The Logic of Modern Physics*, 2d ed. New York, 1948. A comprehensive statement of operationism as a philosophy of science.

Brodie, Benjamin, *The Calculus of Chemical Operations*. London, 1876. An astonishing and detailed anticipation of aspects of the work of both Bridgman and Carnap.

Campbell, N. R., *Physics: The Elements*. Cambridge, 1920. Reissued as *The Foundations of Science*. New York, 1957. Remains the most intelligent and one of the most detailed expositions of the method of the physical sciences.

Carnap, Rudolf, "Testability and Meaning." *Philosophy of Science*, Vol. 3 (1936), 419–471, and Vol. 4 (1937), 1–40. An exposition of the central tenet of logical positivism as applied to the philosophy of science.

Duhem, Pierre, *The Aim and Structure of Physical Theory*, translated by P. P. Wiener. Princeton, N.J., 1954. Expounds the hypothetico-deductive method and denigrates the logical role of models.

Eddington, Arthur, *The Nature of the Physical World*. Cambridge, 1929. Contrasts the world of physics with that of sensation.

Frank, Philipp, *Foundations of Physics*. Chicago, 1946. An example of a positivistic exegesis of a science.

Harré, Rom, *Theories and Things*. London, 1961. A critique of positivist philosophy of science and a sketch of a more realistic system.

Heisenberg, Werner, *Physics and Philosophy*. London and New York, 1959. Describes the history of the Copenhagen interpretation of quantum theory.

Hempel, Carl G., and Oppenheim, Paul, "Studies in the Logic of Explanation." *Philosophy of Science*, Vol. 15 (1948), 135–175. Very clear statement of the hypothetico-deductive theory of explanation. Reprinted in *Aspects of Scientific Explanation*. Pp. 243–295.

Hempel, Carl G., *Aspects of Scientific Explanation*. New York, 1965. Contains an elegant exposition of the logical positivist principles of science and a candid appraisal of the difficulties into which it runs.

Hesse, Mary, *Models and Analogies in Science*. London, 1962. An argument for the logical indispensability of models in theories and a sketch of a logic of analogy.

Jeans, James, *Physics and Philosophy*. Cambridge, 1942. Illuminating as to what laymen were told about the relations between physics and philosophy.

Jevons, W. S., *The Principles of Science*, with Introduction by Ernest Nagel. New York, 1958. An early attempt to treat the logic of science in terms of probability theory.

Mach, Ernst, *The Science of Mechanics*, translated by T. J. McCormack, 6th ed. La Salle, Ill., 1960. Attacks and reduces unnecessary theoretical concepts to observables.

Mill, J. S., *A System of Logic*, 8th ed. London, 1872. In Book III science is seen as the result of organizing particular facts by means of inductive methods.

Mises, Richard von, *Probability, Statistics and Truth*, Hilda Geiringer, ed. London, 1957. Expounds the relative frequency model of probability.

Nagel, Ernest, *The Structure of Science*. London and New York, 1961. Quite the best single book on the philosophy of science. In it will be found expounded most of the views which have been held on the main topics of the philosophy of science in the past half century. The author's own view is a judicious balance with which it is very difficult to disagree.

Neurath, Otto, "Physicalism." *Monist*, Vol. 41 (1931), 618–623. Expounds the view that all science, including psychology, can and should be reduced to physics.

Pearson, Karl, *The Grammar of Science*, Everyman ed. London, 1937. An influential early account of positivist ideas in science.

Poincaré, Henri, *The Value of Science*, translated by G. B. Halsted. New York, 1958. Theories are different languages for describing the facts, and they differ only in their convenience.

Popper, Karl, *The Logic of Scientific Discovery*. London, 1959. Attempt to falsify rather than to confirm is the hallmark and the method of science.

Reichenbach, Hans, *The Theory of Probability*. Berkeley, 1949. Sophisticated use of the frequency theory.

Scriven, Michael, "Definitions, Explanations and Theories," in *Minnesota Studies in the Philosophy of Science*, Vol. II, *Concepts, Theories and the Mind–Body Problem*, Herbert Feigl, Michael Scriven, and Grover Maxwell, eds., Minneapolis, 1958. Pp. 99–195. Attacks the "covering law" model of theories and the explanation-prediction symmetry central to Hempel's theory of explanation.

Whewell, William, *The Philosophy of the Inductive Sciences*. London, 1840. Monumental exposition of the view that science consists in the interplay between ideas and facts.

Whitehead, A. N., *The Principles of Natural Knowledge*. Cambridge, 1919. A "hard" account, as opposed to his later "soft" accounts, of the reduction of things to events.

Whitehead, A. N., *Process and Reality*. Cambridge, 1929. A vast metaphysical work drawing upon his earlier logical investigations but going far beyond them in cosmological aspiration.

R. Harré

PHILOSOPHY OF SCIENCE, PROBLEMS OF.

The scope of the philosophy of science is sufficiently broad to encompass, at one extreme, conceptual problems so intimately connected with science itself that their solution may as readily be regarded a contribution to science as to philosophy and, at the other extreme, problems of so general a philosophical bearing that their solution would as much be a contribution to metaphysics or epistemology as to philosophy of science proper. Similarly, the range of issues investigated by philosophers of science may be so narrow as to concern the explication of a single concept, considered of importance in a single branch of science, and so general as to be concerned with structural features invariant to all the branches of science, taken as a class. Accordingly, it is difficult to draw boundaries that neatly separate philosophy of science from philosophy, from science, or even from the history of science, broadly interpreted. But we can give some characterization of the main groups of problems if we think of science as concerned with providing descriptions of phenomena under which significant regularities emerge and with explaining these regularities. Problems thus arise in connection with terms, with laws, and with theories where a theory is understood as explaining a law and a law is understood as stating the regularities which appear in connection with descriptions of phenomena.

Terms. Ordinary language provides us the wherewithal to offer indefinitely rich descriptions of individual objects, and, as a matter of logical fact, no description, however rich, will exhaustively describe a given object, however simple. Science chooses a deliberately circumscribed vocabulary for describing objects, and scientists may be said to be concerned only with those objects described with the vocabulary of their science and with these only insofar as they are so describable. Historically, the terms first applied by scientists were continuous with their cognates in ordinary speech, just as science itself was continuous with common experience. But special usages quickly developed, and an important class of philosophical problems concerns the relation between scientific and ordinary language, as well as that between those terms selected for purposes of scientific description and other terms which, though applicable to all the same objects as the former, have no obvious scientific use. Scientists from Galileo to Arthur Eddington have sometimes tended to impugn as unreal those properties of things not covered by scientific description or at least have thought that the question of which are the real properties is an important one. Certainly, it would destroy the very concept of science to suppose it possible to account for all the distinctions between things under all the descriptions of them which are feasible, but there is no recipe for selecting the scientifically relevant predicates.

In practice, terms have been chosen when there seem to be interesting and systematic patterns of change in the properties picked out by these terms—for instance, between the distance a body travels and the time it takes to do so, between the temperature and the pressure of a gas, between the density of a fluid and the deviation from a norm of a light ray passing into it, and so forth. It has often been immensely difficult to set aside manifest and cherished differences among objects and the subtle language for expressing these in favor of the spare vocabulary of science under which such seemingly crucial distinctions are obliterated, as, for example, between celestial and terrestrial objects or between "noble" and base metals. Not only do scientific terms cut across the distinctions of common sense, but they also permit distinctions not ordinarily made and allow comparisons more precise than ordinarily demanded—for example, between differential amounts and precisely determinable degrees. For the class of terms discussed here are those which may be said to apply or not to apply to a given object by means of an act of observation rendered precise through some device of mensuration—for example, that the distance traveled is n units along a scale, that the temperature of a gas is n degrees along another scale, that the density of a fluid is m grams per cubic centimeter. The last measurement, which involves reference to different scales—namely, measures

of mass and volume—is sometimes called a "derived" in contrast with a "fundamental" measurement, where only single scales are involved. But even when we speak of derived measurements, as with pressure (in terms of foot-pounds), velocity (in terms of feet per second), or stress (in terms of force per unit area), we remain within the domain of observation; the coincidence of a needle with a mark on a gauge, the angle of a balance, the appearance of a color, a bubble between lines, or a certain buzz, inform us that a given term is true or false with respect to whatever we are studying.

Philosophers may press for a further reduction of the observational language of a science to a favored idiom—for example, to a sense-datum language—but within science observational vocabulary enjoys a certain ultimacy. There are many questions as to whether observational language, thus construed, is sufficient for the entire conduct of science, whether the whole language of science can be expressed in purely observational terms so that recourse need never be made to covert entities, hidden processes, or occult structures unamenable to direct observation and measurement. This issue cannot be fruitfully discussed until we come to the topic of theories, but it has been recognized that while observation has an essential role to play as the occasion for framing and the basis for testing scientific hypotheses, the no less important feature of measurement sets a limit on the program of thoroughgoing observationalism. For the algorithms, in connection with which it first makes scientific sense to assign numerical values and to apply scales, require use of the real number system, the class of whose values has the power of the continuum. Hence, as Carl G. Hempel has remarked, "A full definition of metrical terms by means of observables is not possible." Nevertheless, it has been through the efforts of reductionists to assimilate the entirety of scientific language to observation terms that other sorts of terms, having logically distinct roles within science, have been discovered, and a main task in philosophy of science has been to identify and determine the relation between terms occurring at different levels, and variously related to observation, within the idiom of developed scientific theories.

Laws. One cannot very readily treat the syntactical features of laws in isolation from their semantic properties or, for that matter, from pragmatic considerations. Syntax here concerns the formal conditions of "lawlikeness" for sentences, and semantics concerns the truth conditions for lawlike sentences, it being customary to define a law as a true lawlike sentence. But some philosophers will reject this definition since it might rule out any sentence as having the status of a law, inasmuch as laws are not, they feel, the sorts of sentences which it makes sense to regard as admitting truth-values in the normal way or even at all; for these a law would be a lawlike sentence which has a certain use.

It is commonly supposed that a universally quantified conditional sentence—$(x)(Fx \supset Gx)$—is the simplest form with which a lawlike sentence may be expressed. The chief syntactical problems arise, however in connection with the nonlogical terms F and G. For an important class of cases these will be observational, so that it is in principle possible to determine whether a given instance is both

F and *G,* and the law is generally based upon some known favorable instances. Yet there are cases in which the terms satisfy observational criteria, in which there are a large class of favorable instances and no known counterinstances, and still the appearance of these terms in a lawlike sentence *L* disqualifies *L* as a law even if it is true. Such terms are unduly restricted in scope, whereas it is thought that the terms suitable for laws should be unrestricted in scope. "All the hairs on my head are black" employs the restrictive term "the hairs on my head" and thus is disqualified as a law. A criterion sometimes advanced for identifying restrictive terms as antecedents in possible laws is that if the requisite universal conditional supports a true counterfactual, it is a law, but if the counterfactual is false, as (with reference to a certain white hair) "If that hair were on my head, it would be black" is false, then the corresponding sentence is not a law, and the term is restricted. However, this criterion begs the question insofar as it seems that counterfactuals must be analyzed in terms of general laws; at any rate, the analysis of counterfactuals, as well as the basis for distinguishing true from false counterfactuals, remains to be given by philosophers. In what sense "the hairs on my head" is restrictive, whereas "ravens" in "All ravens are black" is not, is difficult to specify, though the former does refer to a specific object (my head) and it is believed that the terms in a law must not make such references. This restriction, on the other hand, makes Kepler's laws laws in name only and forestalls the possibility of any laws for the universe as a whole. And though Kepler's laws may be retained since they are derivable from laws which employ unrestricted and generally referential terms, the laws of the universe hardly could be thus derived; moreover, it could be argued that "All the hairs on my head are black" might be derivable from some general laws of hirsuteness, making use only of purely qualitative predicates. Thus, precise and rigorous criteria for lawlikeness are difficult to specify.

If the terms of a lawlike sentence *L* must be unrestricted, *L* cannot be known as true through induction by finite enumeration; since there must in principle always be uninspected instances under *F*, the law $(x)(Fx \supset Gx)$ cannot be known true no matter how many known favorable instances there are. Of course, laws are not always (and perhaps not even often) inductive generalizations from large samples—Galileo's laws, for instance, were based upon few observations indeed—and it has been maintained by anti-inductivists (chiefly Karl Popper and his followers) that observations function as tests rather than inductive bases for laws; in this view laws need not be generalizations from observation but only be in principle falsifiable on the basis of observation. Some lawlike sentences may be known false, at least to the extent that they admit of observational consequences, but often the antecedent of a lawlike sentence is sufficiently hedged with *ceteris paribus* riders, to which we may add indefinitely, that one need not surrender a law save as an act of will. This suggests that the criteria for accepting a lawlike sentence as a law are more complex than either inductivists or their opponents have recognized, and an instrumentalist position may be taken, in accord with which laws are nei-

ther true nor false but serve as instruments in the facilitation of inference—"inference-tickets," as Gilbert Ryle has put it. In this view, as Stephen Toulmin has pointed out, the question is not "'Is it true?' but 'When does it hold?'" Here laws are regarded not as sentences about the world but as rules for conducting ourselves in it, and semantic considerations thus yield to pragmatic ones in that there is surely some agreement that a criterion for accepting *L* as a law is that it should, in conjunction with information, furnish successful predictions. Whether, in addition, a successful law is true and, if so, in what sense it is true other than that it successfully enables predictions cannot be discussed independently of larger philosophical considerations.

Many laws in science are statistical in form, but the suggestion that a law may be truly scientific and yet affirm a merely probable connection among phenomena has been offensive to scientists and philosophers with antecedent commitments to determinism as a metaphysical fact or a scientific ideal. For these nothing less than deterministic (nonstatistical) laws are ultimately tolerable, so that statistical laws, while countenanced as interim makeshifts, are, ideally, to be replaced in every instance with deterministic ones. As a program, however, the projected reconstruction of statistical laws and the theories which contain them has encountered an impressive obstacle in the quantum theory of matter, upon which the whole of atomic physics is based, for the laws here are demonstrably irreducible to deterministic form. To be sure, there is a logical possibility that quantum theory could be replaced *in toto.* But there is no way—for instance through the discovery of hidden variables—in which its laws may be rendered deterministic, and since there is scant evidence for any alternative and the evidence for quantum theory is overwhelming, most members of the scientific community are reconciled to an obdurate indeterminism at the core of one of its most fundamental theories. If the quantum theory should be true, certain events are objectively probable, or indeterministic; that is, they are probable independently of the state of our knowledge or ignorance. An epistemological sense of probability, connected with our concepts of induction and confirmation, is not incompatible with determinism; we may even speak of the probability of a deterministic law, meaning that relative to our evidence its degree of confirmation is equal to a number between 0 and 1. It is nonepistemological probability, according to which we could conceivably be certain that a given event were objectively probable, which is allegedly repugnant to determinism. It should be pointed out, however, that indeterministic laws may be deterministic in at least the sense that the values of certain probability variables are precisely determined by the values of other variables. At any rate, the extent of incompatibility between determinism and indeterministic laws and the precise explication of the two kinds of probability are topics of continuing philosophical investigation and controversy.

Laws are believed to play an important role in explanation as well as in prediction. It has been maintained that a necessary condition for explaining an event *E* consists in bringing *E* under the same general law with which it could have been predicted. Hempel regards the temporal position of the scientist vis-à-vis the event as the sole difference between explaining and predicting that event. This symmetry has been challenged (notably by Israel Scheffler), but we might still maintain Hempel's thesis by distinguishing among laws. Not every law used in prediction has explanatory force if we think of explanations as causal explanations, for causal laws do not exhaust the class of scientific laws, which also includes functional expressions of covariation among magnitudes, statistical laws, and so on, all of which are used in predicting. Even so, it has been questioned whether even causal explanation requires the use of causal laws, either in science or in history or the social sciences, where this controversy has been chiefly focused. Be this as it may, the explanation of particular events has less importance in science proper than the explantion of regularities, and it is therefore the explanation of laws that characterizes scientific achievement in its most creative aspect. This brings us to theories, for it is commonly held that to explain a law *L* is to derive *L* from a theory *T* when *T* satisfies certain conditions.

Theories. Let us characterize a law all of whose nonlogical terms are observational as an empirical law. A theory may be regarded as a system of laws, some of which are empirical. Not every empirical law is part of a theory, nor are all the laws of a theory empirical, for some of a theory's laws employ theoretical terms, which are nonobservational. Theoretical terms, if they denote at all, refer to unobservable entities or processes, and it is with respect to changes at this covert level that one explains the observed regularities as covered by empirical laws. Thus one explains the regularities covered by the Boyle–Charles law (all the terms of which are observational) in terms of the (unobservable) behavior of the gas molecules of which the gas is theoretically composed. The status of theoretical terms (and the theoretical entities they would designate if they designated anything) has been the subject of intense philosophical investigation. It is not mere unobservability—Julius Caesar is at this point in time unobservable though his name is not a theoretical term—but unobservability in principle which characterizes these entities; it is unclear whether there would be any sense in speaking of observing, say, Psi-functions, electrons, fields, superegos, and the like. Moreover, the behavior of theoretical entities, supposing the theory to be true, is (as with certain fundamental particles) often so grossly disanalogous to the behavior of the entities they are invoked to explain that our ordinary framework of concepts fails to apply to them.

Yet theoretical terms seem deeply embedded in scientific language. Empiricist strategies of eliminating them by explicit definition in observational language or of tying them to observation by reduction sentences have failed, although there exist techniques by which they may be formally replaced with striking ease. William Craig has demonstrated that any theory containing both theoretical and observational predicates may be replaced with another employing only observational ones but yielding, nevertheless, all the observational theorems (or empirical laws) of the original. Craig's result, however, has not been a victory for empiricism; the reasons for this are somewhat obscure, but it is due in part at least to the realization that theoretical terms play a role and have a meaning in terms of the total structure of the theory and therefore cannot be neatly extricated to leave anything to be called a "theory." Indeed, it often happens that rather than theoretical terms being defined in observational terms, observational terms are defined with reference to the theoretical vocabulary, so that one must, in effect, master the theory in order to make the relevant observations. With the elaboration of a theory, however, the inferential route from observation to (predicted) observation becomes complex (there may be many intervening steps and intermediate computations) and far removed from the simple universal conditional used to represent a law. A theory, in Hempel's words, "may be likened to a complex spatial network [which] floats, as it were, above the plane of observation and is anchored to it by rules of interpretation." Theories, that is, impinge upon experience as wholes but not in all their parts, and the rules of interpretation, or correspondence, which permit them to be applied, are not part of the theory; indeed, the same formal theoretical network might, through different interpretations, have application to different domains of experience.

We may think of a theory as a formal system distinguishable, in principle, from its interpretation, regarding the former (in R. B. Braithwaite's terms) as a calculus and the latter as its model. In point of scientific history and practice, however, model and calculus emerge together. The distinction first began to be clear through the advent of non-Euclidean geometries and the consequent agitated question of which was physically descriptive, and geometry, perhaps because it has been almost paradigmatic of axiomatic systems, has served as a pattern, at least for analytical purposes, for the calculi of theories generally. Thus, philosophers think of theories as employing primitive and derived terms, primitive and derived sentences, satisfying explicit formation and transformation rules, and the like. But whether, apart from the purposes of philosophical representation, actual scientific theories exhibit axiomatized form and whether axiomatization is even a desideratum for scientific theory-formation are moot points.

At any rate, the framing of theories in the course of history has almost always involved some intuitive model on the scientist's part, the pattern of thought being (whether this is or is not the "logic of discovery" which N. R. Hanson has suggested) this, that the regularities for which explanation is sought would hold as a matter of course if certain states of affairs (those postulated by the theory) held in fact. Whether the theoretical states do hold in fact is, of course, the immediate question, and it is through the obligation to provide an answer that the scientific imagination is disciplined. Without the formal means of deriving testable consequences from a theory, the theory would merely be *ad hoc,* and one wants more than the mere deduction of the laws which the theory was intended to explain. Indeed, it is by and large the ability of a theory to permit derivations far afield from its original domain which serves as a criterion for accepting a theory, for in addition to the obvious fruitfulness such a criterion emphasizes, such derivations permit an increasingly broad and diversified basis for testing the theory. The great theories in the development of science—Newton's, Einstein's, Dirac's—have brought into a single comprehensive system great numbers of phenomena not previously known to have been connected.

It is impossible to say, of course, whether the whole of scientific knowledge might someday be embraced in a single unified theory, but piecemeal assimilation of one theory to another is constantly taking place, and the conceptual issues which arise through such reductions are of immense philosophical interest. The careful elucidation of the logic of scientific reduction—of thermodynamics to mechanics, of wave and matrix mechanics—draws attention to features which lie, far more obscurely, within the oldest philosophical problems and controversies: problems of emergence, of natural kinds, of free will and determinism, of body and mind, and so on. The treatment of these questions is often not so much philosophy of science proper as the philosophical interpretation of science, in which the philosophy of science serves as a technique of philosophical clarification, illuminating topics remote from the conceptual issues of science as such.

Bibliography

The literature on the philosophy of science is immense and often technical. Many influential papers are anthologized in Arthur C. Danto and Sidney Morgenbesser, eds., *Philosophy of Science* (New York, 1950), and in Herbert Feigl and May Brodbeck, eds., *Readings in Philosophy of Science* (New York, 1953).
    The following may be consulted as representative and excellent discussions. On preliminary definition of the field see R. B. Braithwaite, *Scientific Explanation* (Cambridge, 1953), pp. 1–9, and Israel Scheffler, *The Anatomy of Inquiry* (New York, 1963), pp. 3–15. On the observational bases of science see Carl G. Hempel, *Fundamentals of Concept Formation in Empirical Science* (Chicago, 1952), especially pp. 20–50, and Scheffler, *op. cit.*, pp. 127–222. On measurement see Ernest Nagel "Measurement," in Danto and Morgenbesser, *op. cit.*, pp. 121–140. On laws see C. F. Presley, "Laws and Theories in the Physical Sciences," in Danto and Morgenbesser, *op. cit.*, pp. 205–215; Ernest Nagel, *The Structure of Science* (New York, 1960), especially pp. 29–78; and Stephen Toulmin, *Philosophy of Science* (London, 1953), pp. 57–104. On the nonlogical terms of laws see Carl G. Hempel and Paul Oppenheim, "The Logic of Explanation," in Feigl and Brodbeck, *op. cit.*, pp. 319–352. On laws and falsifiability see Karl Popper, *The Logic of Scientific Discovery* (New York, 1959), pp. 27–48. On explanation see Hempel and Oppenheim, *op. cit.* On the parity between explanation and prediction see Scheffler, *op. cit.*, pp. 43–88. On theories see Braithwaite, *op. cit.*, pp. 50–114; Nagel, *The Structure of Science, op. cit.*, pp. 79–152; Presley, *op. cit.*, pp. 215–225; Toulmin, *op. cit.*, pp. 105–139. On Craig's theorem see Carl G. Hempel, "The Theoretician's Dilemma," in Herbert Feigl et al., eds., *Minnesota Studies in the Philosophy of Science*, Vol. II (Minneapolis, 1958), and Scheffler, *op. cit.*, pp. 193–203. On the logic of discovery see N. R. Hanson, *Patterns of Discovery* (Cambridge, 1958), *passim*. On reduction of theories and related issues, see Nagel, *The Structure of Science*, pp. 336–397.

ARTHUR C. DANTO

PHYSICAL REALITY. See LAWS AND THEORIES; PHILOSOPHY OF SCIENCE, HISTORY OF; PHILOSOPHY OF SCIENCE, PROBLEMS OF.

PHYSICAL SCIENCES. The Encyclopedia includes the following articles on concepts and theories that have played a prominent part in the physical sciences: ACTION AT A DISTANCE AND FIELD THEORY; ATOMISM; COSMOLOGY; DYNAMISM; ENERGY; ENTROPY; ETHER; EXTREMAL PRINCIPLES; FORCE; MASS; MATTER; MOTION; NEWTONIAN MECHANICS AND MECHANICAL EXPLANATION; QUANTUM MECHANICS, PHILOSOPHICAL IMPLICATIONS OF; RELATIVITY THEORY, PHILOSOPHICAL SIGNIFICANCE OF; SPACE; TIME; and VACUUM AND VOID. See Physical Sciences in Index for articles on figures who have made notable contributions to the development of the physical sciences.

PHYSICOTHEOLOGY is the aspect of natural theology that seeks to prove the existence and attributes of God from the evidence of purpose and design in the physical universe. The argument is very ancient, but it is from the Greeks that its medieval and modern forms principally spring. Socrates revolted against the materialist tendencies of earlier philosophers, and his pupil Plato sought to show that the order and harmony exhibited in the world sprang from the action of mind. Plato argued that since matter cannot move itself, motion is evidence of the presence of mind in nature. All the activity and change in the world have their origin in a supreme mind which moves itself and creates subordinate souls or gods, the heavenly bodies. The outer sphere of the universe is set in motion by the direct action of the changeless, transcendent God. Aristotle expounded more emphatically a teleological or purposive view of nature in which the members of the hierarchy of natural classes in the universe seek to realize their beings according to their stations. This perspective presupposes a rational design, a universal aspiration to fulfillment, and in one passage Aristotle describes God as the perfect being whom all things desire. The theological aspects of Greek views of nature passed into later science and were readily translated into Christian thought. The animistic view of natural knowledge may be seen in the work of Galen (second century), for whom the processes of the human body are divinely planned. During the earlier medieval period the natural world appeared to the eye of faith to be a scene of symbols and ciphers veiling moral and spiritual doctrines. Later medieval philosophers were fond of discerning marks of providential direction in the operations of nature, and Aquinas rests one of his proofs of the existence of God upon the cooperation of all types of natural objects to make the order of the world and the pointing of that order to an intelligent author who devised it. There was abundant recourse to this argument during the later Middle Ages.

Seventeenth century. The golden age of the Argument from Design was the two centuries following the rise of science in the seventeenth century, and it took place principally in England. The new philosophy of nature abandoned belief in the intrinsic teleology of physical objects. In place of the analogy with a creator of living organisms or an artist creating works of beauty it substituted the analogy of an inventor and manufacturer of elaborate machines. The new scientists combined faith in the sovereignty of God in nature and belief in the mechanistic bases of phenomena by conceiving the deity as the skillful contriver of instruments, a consummate engineer. In England the doctrine was promoted by two trends of thought, the Baconian gospel of controlled observation and the revival of Greek atomism. The Baconian method inspired groups of inquirers in London and Oxford to collect a mass of detailed information in which they saw the confirmation of their religious faith; and it was the descriptions of the zoologists and botanists, such as Nehemiah Grew and Francis Willoughby, that strikingly illustrated the marvelous skill of the Creator. The second doctrine, the atomic, or corpuscular, theory of matter, incurred charges of materialism and atheism from moralists because of its association with Epicurean atomism, and in order to divide themselves from these imputations the virtuosi were intent on attaching theological conceptions to the elements of the material world. They were also acutely sensitive to the materialist dangers in the dualist philosophy of Descartes. Neither their religion, which formed the frame of all their thought, nor their reason, which saw the marks of purpose and planning in nature, allowed them to accept the idea that the world originated in the chance combination of material atoms. Ralph Cudworth, in his *True Intellectual System of the Universe* (1678), spoke for all the experimental philosophers when he argued at length that greater perfections and higher degrees of being cannot possibly arise out of senseless matter. The ancient metaphysics of cause, securely rooted in Christian theology, precluded any doctrine of natural evolution, and it is interesting to observe that when writers on biology mentioned the hypothesis that creatures have been produced by "millions of trials," as did John Ray, the hypothesis was dismissed with scorn. Species had been finally and completely created. There was no conceivable alternative to the Argument from Design.

Robert Boyle. The Argument from Design was expounded with eloquence by Robert Boyle (1627–1691). In his multifarious researches he was concerned with the evidence of benevolent and ingenious contrivance in nature and found on all sides "curious and excellent tokens and effects of divine artifice." But first we may notice the way in which he associated the atomic view of matter with supernatural power. In embracing the corpuscular or mechanical philosophy, he writes, he is far from supposing with the Epicureans that atoms accidentally meeting in an infinite vacuum were able by themselves to produce a world and all its phenomena. The philosophy he pleads for teaches that in the beginning God gave motion to matter and so guided the motions of its parts as to "contrive them into the world he designed they should compose," establishing those rules of motion that we call the laws of nature (*The Excellence and Grounds of the Mechanical Philosophy*, 1674). In *The Origin of Forms and Qualities* (1666) he explains that the diversity of bodies must arise from motion and that motion in the beginning was from God, for it is not inherent in matter. In the realm of animate nature Boyle points to numerous instances of ingenious design, such as the human eye, and he constantly speaks of organisms as engines or machines. For him an animal as a whole is an engine, and each part of it is a subordinate engine excellently fitted for some subordinate use. Here he reverts to a famous analogy that in a simpler context goes back to Cicero and even to Xenophon, the analogy of organisms and the world with clocks and watches. In Boyle's day, clocks were the most complex examples of machines available for comparison, and he takes a celebrated clock as a model of the machine of the world, the cathedral clock at Strasbourg, in which "the several pieces making up that curious Engine are so fram'd and adapted, and are put into such motion, as though the numerous wheels and other parts of it knew and were concerned to do its Duty" (*The Usefulness of Experimental Natural Philosophy*, 1663). The popularity of the analogy between a watchmaker and the author of nature in the following age issued largely from the writings of Boyle.

Robert Hooke. During the early years of the Royal Society proofs of design multiplied. Robert Hooke's *Micrographia* (London, 1665) disclosed the astonishing beauty and ingenuity of the minute creatures revealed by the microscope, and in his Cutlerian lectures he spoke of the divine providence which in the eye "has so disposed, ordered, adapted, and empowered each part so to operate as to produce the wonderful effects which we see."

John Ray. Before the end of the century there appeared treatises by the greatest zoologist of the age that were wholly devoted to the evidences in nature of the existence of God. John Ray's *The Wisdom of God Manifested in the Works of Creation* was first published in London in 1691, enlarged in three later editions before Ray's death in 1705, and reprinted more than twenty times by the year 1846. In the preface he declares that his discourse will serve to demonstrate the existence of the Deity and illustrate his principal attributes, his infinite power and wisdom. He proceeds to show the futility of attributing the world to the operation of chance events; it manifests all the marks of deliberate creation. Inanimate bodies are reviewed in order, the system of the stars and their planets, and the services performed for animals and man by water, air, fire, meteors, rain, and winds. Passing to regions of life, he ascends through the vegetable and animal kingdoms, discovering everywhere a complex arrangement of parts that contribute to the welfare of the plant or animal and to the uses of man.

Ray was too close an observer of nature to accept the crude doctrine that organisms are complex machines constructed by a divine watchmaker. His physicotheology borrowed from Cudworth the theory of plastic nature or vital force by which the growth, adaptation, and instinctive activities of living creatures are directed. This plastic virtue acts sympathetically, without reason, informing the movements of material bodies. Ray therefore diluted his physicotheology with an immaterial energy, a form of animism. But the plastic nature is nonetheless a subordinate instrument of divine providence, although it transcends the operations of local motion. Its relative independence of the immediate direction of God allowed Ray to meet a cardinal difficulty in the Argument from Design; he could accept the aberrations of nature without making the Deity responsible for them. Faced with this problem, Boyle has preserved his mechanistic view of creation by asserting that the irregularities we find in nature may serve ends that lie concealed in God's unsearchable wisdom.

Ray presided over the subsequent course of the Argument from Design, and theologians drew freely on his

Wisdom of God in Creation. They studied also his *Three Physico-theological Discourses* (London, 1692), which supports the Biblical narratives of the creation, the deluge, and the final dissolution of the world by arguments from natural philosophy.

Newton. The appearance of Isaac Newton's *Principia* in 1687 had provided the argument with a great deal of new material. Natural theology became absorbed by the cosmology of the *Principia*, and preachers and poets acclaimed the almighty hand that "poised, impels and rules the steady whole." Newton's great treatises offered at many points notable arguments for the belief that the universe is the work of an intelligent being; indeed, Newton told Bentley that in writing the *Principia* he had had an eye upon arguments for a belief in a deity, and in the *Opticks* he declared that the main business of natural philosophy was to deduce causes from effects until we arrive at the First Cause, which cannot be mechanical. In the *General Scholium* added to the second edition of the *Principia* and in the *Queries* of the Latin translation of the *Opticks* (1706), he set forth the religious conceptions that underlay his mathematical physics of the universe. Why is it, he asks, that all planets move the same way in concentric orbits? What prevents the stars from falling on one another? And, with a glance at the evidence of Boyle and Ray, how, he asks, did the bodies of animals come to be contrived with so much art? Whence, in short, arose all that order and beauty that we see in the world? Does it not appear that there is a Being incorporeal, living, intelligent, and omnipresent, who created the world?

For Newton, however, the admirable system of nature was not imposed by the deity upon an infinitely complex material mechanism; immaterial forces were introduced into the heart of the mechanism of nature. Newton asserted the atomic theory of matter in the manner of Boyle: It seemed probable that God in the beginning formed matter in solid, massy, hard, impenetrable, movable particles, but the forces that cause the particles to cohere and to form larger bodies are immaterial. It is not the business of experimental philosophy to discuss the nature of these forces, but it is clear that they provide the world with its structure and order. They could not have arisen from chaos by the mere laws of nature; the wonderful uniformity of the planetary system, for example, must be the effect of choice and must proceed from the counsel and dominion of an intelligent and powerful Being.

Other fundamental principles of Newton's system of physics are associated with theology. Absolute space is immovable, homogeneous, indivisible, and distinct from matter; like other thinkers of the time, Newton accorded space some of the attributes of God. He described infinite space as the boundless sensorium of the omnipresent God, whereby he perceives all things. Motion also presupposes a metaphysical agent, for if the motion of moving bodies is derived from the impact of bodies already in motion, some other principle was necessary for putting bodies in motion in the first instance and for conserving the motion of those in movement. The agent must be an all-powerful immaterial being, for pressure is constantly brought to move bodies throughout the universe. Furthermore, the variety of motion is always decreasing because at every impact

between bodies, some motion is lost. It must be renewed by an immaterial power.

Eighteenth century. The natural theology of Newton crowned the Argument from Design, and by the beginning of the eighteenth century the main stock of theory and of evidence on which the argument relied had been provided. Numerous writers repeated and enforced the case pronounced by Locke that the works of nature everywhere sufficiently evidence a Deity. Prominent among those who vindicated the conclusions of the great men of the seventeenth century were the Boyle lecturers in the series instituted in Boyle's will with the purpose of confuting atheism. The lectures were inaugurated in 1692 by Richard Bentley, a renowned scholar who corresponded with Newton while preparing the lectures. In his letters to Bentley, Newton maintained that there are many features of the universe that cannot be explained in terms of mechanical principles, and he went on to assert that the cause that constructed the planetary system cannot be blind and fortuitous but must be one very skilled in mechanics and geometry. Bentley faithfully reported these opinions in the lectures.

Clarke and Leibniz. The second Boyle lecturer was the celebrated Samuel Clarke, who delivered the course called "A Demonstration of the Being and Attributes of God" in 1704, an excellent survey of the accepted picture, with some fresh touches. His famous correspondence with Leibniz on natural theology was published in 1717; he probably received advice from Newton in composing his replies, and the letters further reveal Newton's position on such important topics as the divinity of space. But the vital interest of this correspondence is the conflict between Leibniz' conception of nature as mechanical, determined, self-sufficient, and self-perpetuating and the doctrine, defended by Clarke, of God's providential guidance of the world. Leibniz rejected the Newtonian contention that God corrects aberrations of the cosmic order, such as certain inequalities of planetary motions, as a watchmaker cleans and mends a watch—a view that implies that the creation of the system was imperfect and that God is lacking in foresight. Clarke, on his part, accused Leibniz of restricting the liberty of God to act as he will, independently of the laws of nature; indeed, but for his constant intervention, the world would lapse into chaos. The doctrine of supernatural intervention began to recede from the physics of astronomy and found its home before the end of the century in the realms of geology and biology.

Joseph Butler. The deists, in their war against revelation, caught at the notion that God, having created the world in the distant past, had left it to the action of the laws of nature. Deism provoked a stream of hostile pamphlets and treatises, but orthodox churchmen who opposed deism continued to harp on law, order, and design and the divine artificer. The greatest of these apologists was Bishop Butler. *The Analogy of Religion* (1736) shows that he had closely studied Newton, but his natural theology rises above that of other writers of the age in its candid recognition of the defects of nature, which he ascribes to our ignorance of God's purposes.

Another Boyle lecturer was William Derham, whose *Physico-theology* (London, 1713) and *Astro-theology* (London, 1715) rehearsed the testimony of Ray and of Newton at prodigious length, with some superficial reflections of his own. Many other utterances must be passed over. It is interesting to observe the large number of writers who discussed Clarke's (and Newton's) theology of space.

Hume. In the later years of the eighteenth century, natural theology encountered the penetrating criticism of Hume, although few scientific theologians were shaken by it. In the *Dialogues Concerning Natural Religion,* published posthumously in 1779, Hume exploded the logic of the Argument from Design, especially in the form in which it was presented by the disciples of Newton, such as the Scottish mathematician Colin Maclaurin. Hume confronted the analogy between the maker of a machine and the maker of the world with the point that while scientists like Copernicus and Galileo made fruitful use of reasoning by analogy, the associations between cause and effect that provided the material of their arguments were derived from observation. The inference from machines and their makers to a world and its maker is not parallel. Order, arrangement, or the adjustment of final causes is not by itself any proof of design, but only insofar as it has been seen to be produced by design; since we have no experience of the invention and production of a world or of nature, we cannot maintain that an orderly universe must arise from thought or art. For all that we can know a priori, matter may contain the source of order within itself. Hume attacked this argument by a *reductio ad absurdum.* If we are confined to speculative, a priori explanations of the origins of the world, they can lead to disturbing conclusions. Some natural philosophers have found nature to resemble an organism, a vegetable or an animal, and its origin ought to be ascribed to generation and vegetation rather than to reason or design. When the analogy with the manufacturers of machines is pressed, we might infer that several deities combine in contriving and framing the world. Hume now introduced fatal evidence against the belief in a benevolent Creator. The curious artifices of nature embitter the life of every living being. "The whole presents nothing but the idea of a blind nature, impregnated by a great vivifying principle, and pouring forth from her lap, without discernment or parental care, her maimed and abortive children." Faced with these difficulties the defender of traditional doctrine in the *Dialogues* is compelled to admit that belief in a beneficent Creator of the world cannot be rationally sustained. The sources of such a belief are "temper and education," and the defender of the Argument from Design falls back on utilitarian supports; belief in divine design promotes morality.

Nineteenth century. Hume's *Dialogues Concerning Natural Religion* failed to confound the deep-seated prepossessions of the natural theologians, nor were they discomposed by the refutation of the Argument from Design by Kant in the *Critique of Pure Reason* (1781).

Paley. At the turn of the century the argument was revived in William Paley's *Natural Theology* (1802). It marks the apotheosis of the analogy between a watch and a natural object, opening, in fact, with the discovery of a watch lying on a heath. The instrument must have been made by a being who comprehended its construction and designed its use. If we suppose that the watch contains a mechanism by which it can produce another watch (a supposition that exhibits the deficiency of the mechanical analogy), our admiration of the maker's skill will increase. Paley proceeds to describe numerous examples of natural contrivances, drawn from anatomy, physiology, botany, and entomology: the eyes of fish, animals, and men, the construction of the ear, the webbed feet of water birds, the elongated tongue of the woodpecker, and a catalogue of other instances. These marvels of adaptation prove the existence of a superhuman designer, God. As for the suffering that nature displays, Paley attempts to minimize the spectacle; the pain of animals, he thinks, is exaggerated, and their happiness outweighs their pain. Even venomous bites and the preying of one species on another are shown to be necessary features of benevolent design.

Bridgewater Treatises. Leading men of science in this period duly acknowledged the action of divine providence in natural phenomena. In geology John Playfair and Sir Charles Lyell discovered in the adjustment of the strata of the earth to the accommodation of living creatures clear proofs of divine foresight, and James Prescott Joule saw in the interconvertibility of natural forces evidence of the sovereign will of God. The most sustained defense of the Argument from Design was advanced in the Bridgewater Treatises of the 1830s. Eight men of science, four of whom were clergymen, were chosen to discharge the intentions of the Earl of Bridgewater to explore "the Power, Wisdom and Goodness of God, as manifested in the Creation." These writers added a wealth of new information from astronomy, physics, chemistry, and anatomy to the old theses of Ray and Derham, and they outstripped Paley in showing how all aspects of nature have been thoughtfully arranged for the comfort of the world's inhabitants and especially for man. John Kidd, Regius professor of medicine in the University of Oxford, in *On the Adaptation of External Nature to the Physical Condition of Man* (London, 1833); Peter Roget, secretary to the Royal Society, in *On Animal and Vegetable Physiology Considered in Relation to Natural Theology* (London, 1834); and William Buckland, professor of geology at Oxford, in *On Geology and Mineralogy* (London, 1836), showed how climates have been fitted to the character of the various races of mankind, horses invented for man's transport, minerals for his adornment, and water for his ablutions. In short, much of the reasoning of these writers recalls that of the lady who praised the goodness of the Creator in causing a great river to flow through the main cities of Europe.

Sir Charles Bell, the most distinguished physiologist of the time, in his *The Hand, Its Mechanism and Vital Endowments as Evincing Design* (London, 1833), argues that species were successively created to fit the conditions of geological epochs, changes in their anatomy being deliberately shaped to meet the circumstances of the creatures' life. Man is the center of a magnificent system, which has been prepared for his reception by a succession of revolutions affecting the whole globe, and the strictest relation is established between his intellectual capacities and the material world. The celebrated William Whewell, in his *Astronomy and General Physics considered with Reference to Natural Theology* (London, 1833), makes play with the ambiguous sense of the word "law," a common procedure among scientific theologians of the period, confusing the idea of uniform sequence with the idea of legal and moral law; the confusion arose from Whewell's demonstration that the laws of nature, terrestrial and celestial, provide evidence of selection, design, and goodness. The tenacity and ingenuity with which the scientists vindicated the sovereignty of God over nature are illustrated in Charles Babbage's *Ninth Bridgewater Treatise* (London, 1837), where by means of his calculating machine he proves mathematically that miraculous interruptions of scientific laws can be predicted, and that the Being who called the laws into existence must have chosen them with the breaches of continuity in view.

The Bridgewater Treatises marked the final stage of the general confidence of men of science in the old natural theology, although religious thinkers long continued, and still continue, to appeal to it. However, when the treatises appeared the classical form of the Argument from Design was weakening. Whewell had difficulty in understanding the bearing of cosmology upon the support and comfort of sentient creatures, and geologists, led by James Hutton and Lyell, were abandoning the view that there had been sudden changes in the crust of the earth, occasioned by the mediation of God. The catastrophic picture of geological change was yielding to the uniformitarian view in which the laws operating at present could in the slow process of ages have caused all the changes of the past. The range of natural law in time and space was being extended, but the scientists failed to account for the processes by which fresh species had originated, and faith in the periodic agency of the Creator was encouraged.

Darwin. Charles Darwin opened a notebook on the transmutation of species in 1837, and in the unpublished "Essay on Species" of 1844 he proposed the machinery by which new species might result from the natural selection of fortuitous variations. The notion of special creations, he recorded in his private notebook, explains nothing, and the Essay concluded with a forceful *reductio ad absurdum* of the Argument from Design. *The Origin of Species* (1859) brought a wealth of material to substantiate the theory of natural selection in the evolution of species and in adaptations of the organs of living creatures to their circumstances, and it is interesting to see Darwin using the same examples that Paley did to show evidence of contrivances resulting not from purpose but from chance. By abolishing both transcendent and immanent teleology, Darwin undermined the ground on which physicotheology had stood since the seventeenth century. Yet in the last chapter of the *Origin* Darwin himself assumed a First Cause, though not a beneficent one, and he declared in 1873 that the impossibility of conceiving that this great and wondrous universe arose through chance seemed to him the chief argument for the existence of God. In the end, however, Darwin became a complete agnostic, as is shown most clearly in the unexpurgated edition of his *Autobiography* (first published in 1958).

J. S. Mill. In his *Three Essays on Religion,* published posthumously in 1874, J. S. Mill allowed some value to the Argument from Design, for the world contains marks of deliberate contrivance, and our experience of such devices is associated with an intelligent mind. Mill here seems to have exposed himself to Hume's objections against arguing from cases within the world to the world as a whole. But Mill recognized many features of the world that are incompatible with beneficent design, and he thought that God may be a limited Being circumscribed by matter and force. Mill maintained that if Darwin's doctrine of evolution were shown to be valid it would greatly weaken the evidence for the work of a divine intelligence in nature.

Support from scientists. Other scientists contrived to fit the theory of natural selection into the frame of divine purpose. Samuel Houghton, a fellow of the Royal Society, described expressions of supernatural intentions in his book *Principles of Animal Mechanics* (London, 1873). Another book that exercised great influence was Professors P. G. Tait and Balfour Stewart's *The Unseen Universe* (1875), in which it was contended that science upheld the ideas of religion on the transcendental world and its connection with the physical world. A succession of eminent scientists proclaimed that nature is the sacred book of God. The most popular and, it must be added, most muddleheaded work that applied evolution to theistic principles was Henry Drummond's *Natural Law in the Spiritual World* (1883). The tendency of these scientific writers was to assert the view that Darwin's theory had deepened and widened the belief in the operation of purpose in nature, a view that was characterized as misplaced zeal by those who stood more closely to Darwin's findings.

A number of physicists of the period also employed classical versions of the design argument. The Celestial Engineer was reinstated by O. M. Mitchell in his widely read *The Orbs of Heaven* (4th ed., London, 1853) at the middle of the century, in which, after the manner of Newton, the deity is invoked to secure the stability of the solar system. It was a notion of the earlier apologists that the identical character of the fundamental materials of the physical world in all parts of the natural order indicated the action of an intelligent maker. The idea had been adopted by Sir John Herschel in his *Study of Natural Philosophy* (1830), and it was now revived by the greatest mathematical physicist of the age, James Clerk Maxwell. At the meeting of the British Association in 1873, he pointed out that every type of molecule in the universe is identical with every other type; a molecule of hydrogen, whether it occurs in Sirius or in Arcturus, executes its vibrations in precisely the same time. No theory of evolution accounts for this identity, for the molecule is not subject to change. Its similarity to other molecules proves that it is the product not of chance but of design. It is a manufactured article, and because they are the work of a Creator, the foundation stones of the material universe remain, whatever catastrophes may occur in the heavens. Even the argument from miracles reappeared in the *Natural Theology* (London, 1891) of a later mathematical physicist, Sir George Stokes: "If the laws of nature are in accordance with God's will, he who willed them may will their suspension." Stokes assumed that God's action in nature cannot be detected within the laws of physics but by interventions from beyond. *Natural Theology* embraces the arguments of physicotheology in the period.

A monumental exposition in a modern setting of the Argument from Design appeared in *Philosophical Theol-*

ogy (London, 1928–1930) by F. R. Tennant. Recent discussions of the argument have abandoned the old mechanical analogies and have dwelled on the evidence for various types of vitalism in biology. On these views evolution is guided no longer from outside but by directive activities within organisms. In the human psychosocial phase of evolution these self-directed activities point toward moral ends; history becomes the education of mankind in the fulfillment of God's design. Teleological doctrines of this kind have drawn support from philosophers such as Samuel Alexander and A. N. Whitehead, who contend that the universe is informed by an immanent nisus to divinity. Present theological discussions, however, ignore natural theology, and for contemporary linguistic philosophers the Argument from Design possesses no validity whatsoever and is logically and morally indefensible, although it may serve to heighten religious emotions.

(For philosophical criticisms, see TELEOLOGICAL ARGUMENT FOR THE EXISTENCE OF GOD.)

Bibliography

In addition to original works mentioned in the text, the reader may consult the following works as guides to the immense literature on the subject.

The Bridgewater Treatises on the Power, Wisdom and Goodness of God as Manifested in the Creation, 12 vols. London, 1833–1836.

Burtt, E. A., *The Metaphysical Foundations of Modern Physical Science.* London, 1925.

Carré, M. H., "The Divine Watchmaker." *The Rationalist Annual* (1965), 83–91.

Cohen, I. B., and Jones, H. M., eds., *Science Before Darwin.* London, 1963.

De Beer, Gavin, *Charles Darwin.* London, 1963. Bibliography.

Flew, Antony, and MacIntyre, Alasdair, eds., *New Essays in Philosophical Theology.* New York, 1955.

Gillispie, Charles C., *Genesis and Geology.* Cambridge, Mass., 1951.

Hooykaas, R., *Natural Law and the Divine Miracle.* Leiden, 1959.

Hurlbutt, R. M., III, *Hume, Newton and the Design Argument.* Lincoln, Neb., 1965.

Koyré, Alexandre, *From the Closed World to the Infinite Universe.* Baltimore, 1957.

Metzger, Henri, *Attraction universelle et religion naturelle chez quelques commentateurs anglais de Newton.* Paris, 1938.

Mossner, E. C., *Bishop Butler and the Age of Reason.* New York, 1936.

Pilkington, Roger, *Robert Boyle; Father of Chemistry.* London, 1959.

Raven, C. E., *John Ray.* Cambridge, 1950.

Raven, C. E., *Natural Religion and Christian Theology.* Cambridge, 1953.

Strong, E. W., "Newton and God." *Journal of the History of Ideas,* Vol. 13, No. 2 (April 1951), 147–167.

Westfall, R. S., *Science and Religion in Seventeenth Century England.* New Haven, Conn., 1958.

MEYRICK H. CARRÉ

PHYSIS AND NOMOS.

Physis is related in Greek to the root of a verb that means "to grow" but of which some parts carry the meaning "to be." Since according to later writers the pre-Socratics were primarily concerned with investigating *physis,* its precise meaning is important. The general equation with nature is not in doubt. In one view it meant "what things really are," and this interpretation was associated with positivistic views of the pre-Socratics as the first scientists. In a famous controversy, initiated by W. A. Heidel's criticism of the interpretation given by John Burnet, it was argued against this view that the term meant originally "growth" and that in investigating *physis* the pre-Socratics were concerned with what they regarded as a growing quasi-living organism. A possible view might be that the term most usually meant simply "that which is" but that the pre-Socratics did commonly suppose that "that which is" in fact behaves hylozoistically (as though with a life of its own). The term is used both of the whole of nature collectively and also of separate objects, such as the nature of man.

For Plato *physis* as ultimate reality means the Forms. Aristotle (*Metaphysics* Δ.4) distinguishes several senses and defines his own use as "the essence of things which have in themselves as such a source of movement." For him physics is a branch of knowledge pursued for its own sake and is concerned with separate and changing entities, whether living or inanimate. For the Stoics *physis* is identified with god and the active principle, while for Epicureans it consists of atoms and void. From Aristotle onward physics was regarded as a major branch of philosophy, and its students were called physicists.

Nomos. Since according to the usual Greek view being is good, *physis* as ultimate reality is good and provides a standard of goodness in behavior. Life in accordance with nature is the principle of Stoic ethics, but the nature of man as a standard was recognized long before. *Physis* could thus be opposed to *nomos* (convention or law) when the latter diverged from nature. Most commonly the appeal was from *nomos* to *physis* as a standard, but in the Sophistic period the antithesis was greatly elaborated and *nomos* was sometimes raised above nature.

Bibliography

Burnet, John, *Early Greek Philosophy,* 4th ed. London, 1930. Appendix. Consult for the physis controversy.

Heidel, W. A., "A Study of the Conception of Nature Among the Presocratics." *Proceedings of the American Academy of Arts and Sciences,* Vol. 44, No. 4 (1910). Consult for the physis controversy.

Heinemann, F., *Nomos und Physis.* Basel, 1945.

Leisegang, H., "Physis" (2d article), in Pauly-Wissowa, *Realencyclopädie.* Stuttgart, 1941. Vol. XX, pp. 1130–1164.

Lovejoy, A. O., and Boas, G., *Primitivism and Related Ideas in Antiquity.* Baltimore, 1935. Appendix. Some meanings of nature.

G. B. KERFERD

PIAGET, JEAN, Psychologist and philosopher, was born in Neuchâtel, Switzerland, in 1896. He studied zoology at the university there and in 1918 received his doctorate for a thesis on the subject of land mollusks in the Valais Alps. He then studied psychology for a year at Zurich and, from 1919 to 1921, abnormal psychology, logic, and the philosophy of science at the Sorbonne. From 1921 to 1925, he was director of studies at the Institut J.-J. Rousseau (now the Institut des Sciences de l'Éducation) in Geneva; he was its assistant director from 1929 to 1932 and became codirector in 1932. In 1925 he was appointed professor of philosophy at the University of Neuchâtel; in 1929, professor of the history of scientific thought at the University of Geneva; and in 1940, professor of experimental psychology and director of the psychological laboratory at Geneva. Since 1955 he has been professor of child psychology at the Sorbonne and director of the Centre International de l'Épistémologie Génétique at Geneva. Piaget has also taken an active interest in international educational projects. He has been director of the Bureau International de l'Éducation since 1929 and was associated with UNESCO as its assistant director general.

Thought. Although Piaget is usually considered a psychologist working in the field of child thought, his interests have always been, broadly speaking, philosophical. As a young man he read widely in philosophy, and while in Paris he studied with André Lalande and Léon Brunschvicg. Even his earliest work, which appeared between 1925 and 1932, dealt with such topics as thought, causality, moral judgment, and the development of language. His logical and epistemological interests show themselves particularly in his later studies, starting about 1937. By means of simple, although highly ingenious experiments, Piaget set out to make a detailed investigation of the way in which logical, mathematical, and physical concepts develop in the individual. He thus studied experimentally many of the concepts and principles that philosophers had discussed in the past on a purely a priori level. Piaget would say that what he was really doing in this work was re-examining the whole question of the Kantian categories. This re-examination formed for him the basis of a new discipline that he called genetic epistemology.

In a series of studies Piaget examined in some detail the development not only of abstract concepts such as classes, relations, and numbers but also of physical concepts like space, time, speed, atomism, conservation, and chance, all of which he has regarded as constructed from our behavioral activities. In starting from the facts of observable child behavior rather than from adult introspections (or sensations), Piaget has differed from thinkers like Ernst Mach, Karl Pearson, and Bertrand Russell by the importance he attaches to the part played by overt activities in building up the conceptual machinery of thought. Throughout his work Piaget has placed considerable emphasis on the pragmatic aspect of logical and mathematical operations, as, for example, the way we actually handle symbols and formulas. From this point of view Piaget's account bears a marked resemblance to the views of Jules Henri Poincaré and the intuitionists; the construction of number, for example, has for Piaget a definite psychological aspect.

Abstract concepts. Piaget believes that logical and mathematical notions first show themselves as overt activities on the part of the child and only at a later stage take on a conceptual character. They are to be conceived as internalized actions in which things are replaced by signs, and concrete actions by operations on these signs. Rational activity occurs in the child when his trial-and-error gropings attain a definite pattern of order that may be inverted in thought. At this rational stage, if the child makes a mistake in performing a task, he is able to return to his starting point. This characteristic of thought that enables us to reverse a train of ideas or actions Piaget calls "reversibility." It is the basis of our ability to perform mental experiments, as well as the psychological foundation of the deductive process.

Piaget contends that the more elementary forms of logical behavior in which the child compares, distinguishes, and orders the objects around him are largely concerned with the creation of concrete classificatory and relational systems. It is from these systems that we develop our later, more abstract, logical and mathematical modes of thinking. Piaget would rather not speak of the intuition of number before the child has developed logical concepts of invariance and has thereby grasped the operation of reversibility. The transition to number occurs in the child just when his activities of classifying and ordering objects take on the form of simple logical systems. What emerges from Piaget's experimental researches is that numerical concepts in their psychological development are ultimately based on simple logical notions. There is thus some resemblance between the way number comes to be constructed in a child's thought and the attempt on a purely normative plane by Russell and others to define number in logical terms.

Physical concepts. Among the other concepts studied by Piaget, those of time and space are of particular philosophical relevance. Kant, for example, believed that these concepts were objects of an a priori intuition. Piaget, however, has found that the abstract notion of time arises at a relatively late stage; at first time is connected with space. For example, the child first confuses the notion of age with that of height or other visible signs of age. As far as space is concerned, his ability to make spatial judgments is initially fairly rudimentary. He can differentiate between open and closed figures but has difficulty in distinguishing one shape from another. He is also incapable of imagining a perspective other than his own. Only at a later stage is he able to take account of several relations at once (before and behind, right and left) and to coordinate them into a general system of perspectives.

Perception. For Piaget learning plays an important part not only in the elaboration of intellectual structures but also in the field of perception. It is this that distinguishes his view from that of the Gestalt psychologists. For the latter, the perceptual constancies of shape and size belong directly to the perceived objects and are independent of age and ability. For Piaget, however, perception of figures is built up as a result of a series of random eye and other muscular movements, which are gradually corrected. The young child does not attribute a constant size or even identity to the objects around him. Piaget believes that the logical forms of activity that emerge in child behavior, namely classifying, relating, and so forth, arise as a result of his trial-and-error activities.

Piaget's views on perception have certain philosophical implications. In the past, he points out, philosophers have assumed a definite psychology of perception in their epistemologies. A good example of this is Locke's sensationalism, in which it is assumed (1) that empirical facts are passively given in perception and (2) that they correspond to a certain range of linguistic expressions that designate them. For Piaget, however, even the notion of an object, one of the simplest forms of perceptual invariants, requires a definite learning process. Before the child is able to use linguistic expressions to refer unequivocally to definite objects, he must first have developed concrete classificatory and relational activities. Even the simple statement, "This is green," implies the acquisition of such skills and hence cannot be regarded as a reference to a simple perceptual datum. When we talk intelligently of green, this presupposes that we have learned to classify objects according to their color and to differentiate one color from another.

Behavior and logic. Piaget's work might be dismissed as philosophically irrelevant by philosophers of a Platonic turn of mind. It might be said that philosophical discussions of conceptual thinking are largely concerned with questions of validity and not with questions of origin. Piaget does not deny that logical notions as they appear in purely formal discussions differ from those occurring in ordinary thought. However, he asserts (1) that even our simpler kinds of intellectual performance have a logical character about them, which we can study formally, and (2) that when the logician constructs logical systems, performs deductions, tests for validity, and so on, his logical behavior can be studied in the same direct way as that of the child or unsophisticated adult. Piaget also believes that it may be illuminating to compare the simpler logical structures inherent in our behavior with the purely formal systems constructed by the logician, as we may find some continuity between them.

Works by Piaget

Piaget is a prolific writer, and among the numerous volumes he has written the following have a specifically logical or philosophical character:

Le Jugement et le raisonnement chez l'enfant. Paris, 1924. Translated by M. Warden as *Judgment and Reasoning in the Child.* London, 1928.

Le Langage et la pensée chez l'enfant. Paris, 1924. Translated by M. Warden as *The Language and Thought of the Child.* London, 1926. 2d ed. translated by M. Gabain. London, 1932.

La Représentation du monde chez l'enfant. Paris, 1926. Translated by J. Tomlinson and A. Tomlinson as *The Child's Conception of the World.* London, 1929.

La Causalité physique chez l'enfant. Paris, 1927. Translated by M. Gabain as *The Child's Conception of Physical Causality.* London, 1930.

Le Jugement moral chez l'enfant. Paris, 1932. Translated by M. Gabain as *The Moral Judgment of the Child.* London, 1932.

La Genèse du nombre chez l'enfant. Paris, 1941. Written with A. Szeminska and translated by C. Gattegno and F. M. Hodgson as *The Child's Conception of Number.* London, 1952.

Le Développement des quantités chez l'enfant. Paris, 1941. Written with B. Inhelder.

Le Développement de la notion du temps chez l'enfant. Paris, 1946.

Les Notions de mouvement et de vitesse chez l'enfant. Paris, 1946.

La Représentation de l'espace chez l'enfant. Paris, 1948. Written with B. Inhelder and translated by F. J. Langdon and J. L. Lunzer as *The Child's Conception of Space.* London, 1956.

La Géometrie spontanée chez l'enfant. Paris, 1948. Written with B. Inhelder and A. Szeminska and translated by E. A. Lunzer as *The Child's Conception of Geometry.* London, 1960.

La Genèse de l'idée de hazard chez l'enfant. Paris, 1951.

De la Logique de l'enfant à la logique de l'adolescent. Paris, 1955. Translated by Anne Parsons and Stanley Milgram as *The Growth of Logical Thinking.* London, 1958.

La Genèse des structures logiques elementaires. Paris, 1959. Written with B. Inhelder.

Works on Piaget

There have been few philosophical discussions of Piaget's work, but W. Mays, "The Epistemology of Professor Piaget," in *PAS* (London, 1953–1954) compares his epistemology with the views of contemporary philosophers. C. Parsons in "Inhelder and Piaget's 'The Growth of Logical Thinking: II.' A Logician's Viewpoint," in the *British Journal of Psychology* (1960), criticizes Piaget's logic from a theoretical standpoint.

John H. Flavell in *The Developmental Psychology of Jean Piaget* (Princeton, N.J., 1963) gives a good summary of Piaget's work from a psychological point of view. The book contains an excellent bibliography of primary and secondary sources. W. Mays, "How We Form Concepts," in *Science News* (1954) gives a simple introduction from a more philosophical viewpoint.

K. Lovell in *The Growth of Basic Mathematical Concepts in Children* (London, 1961) provides an introduction to Piaget's ideas from an educational standpoint. Z. P. Dienes in *Building Up Mathematics* (London, 1960) shows how Piaget's work has influenced the introduction of new methods in the teaching of school mathematics.

WOLFE MAYS

PICO DELLA MIRANDOLA, COUNT GIOVANNI

(1463–1494), Renaissance philosopher, was born in Mirandola, near Modena. He was a younger son in a family of feudal lords who ruled the small territory of Mirandola and Concordia in northern Italy. He seems to have received at an early age his first humanistic training in Latin and, perhaps, in Greek. Being destined by his mother for a career in the church, he was named papal protonotary at the age of ten and began to study canon law at Bologna in 1477. Two years later he began the study of philosophy at the University of Ferrara, which he continued at the University of Padua from 1480 to 1482. After a number of journeys that took him to Paris and repeatedly to Florence, he studied Hebrew and Arabic under the guidance of several Jewish teachers and in 1486 composed 900 theses, offering to defend them in Rome the following year in a public disputation to which he invited scholars from all parts of Europe. When some of these theses met with objections from various theologians, Pope Innocent VIII appointed a committee to have them examined. As a result of the investigation 7 theses were condemned as unorthodox, and 6 more were declared to be dubious. When Pico published a defense of these 13 theses, the pope condemned all 900, although Pico had signed an act of submission. Pico fled to France, where he was arrested in 1488 on the request of papal envoys. Upon the intervention of several Italian princes he was released from prison by King Charles VIII. He returned to Italy and was allowed by the pope to settle in Florence, under parole, as it were, and under the personal protection of Lorenzo de' Medici. Except for a few short visits to Ferrara, Pico spent the remainder of his life in Florence and there wrote, or began to write, his most important works, remaining in close touch with the circle of the Medici, with the Platonic Academy of Ficino, and with Savonarola. In 1493 he was acquitted of all ecclesiastical censures and restrictions by Alexander VI. He died in 1494 on the very day (November 17) on which Charles VIII of France made his entry into Florence after the expulsion of Piero de' Medici.

Pico's numerous writings reflect the wide range of his interests. He composed Italian and Latin poems of which only some have survived. A number of his humanistic letters were published posthumously, as was his famous *Oration,* originally composed for the projected disputation. To the scholastic aspect of his work we may assign the 900 theses (1486) and especially the *Apologia* (1487), his defense of the condemned theses. Another early work is his lengthy commentary on the Platonic love poem of his friend Girolamo Benivieni (1486). His mature philosophical works include the *Heptaplus* (1489), a sevenfold interpretation of the first verses (1.1–27) of Genesis, and his *De Ente et Uno* ("On Being and Unity"), written in 1491 but published posthumously. His most extensive work is his *Disputationes Adversus Astrologiam Divinatricem* ("Disputations Against Astrology"), in 12 books, published posthumously. To this we may add a few short religious and theological writings and several fragments of a commentary on the Psalms that have been preserved in a number of scattered manuscripts and are still for the most part unpublished.

A characteristic document of Pico's attitude on history and philosophy from his earlier years is his correspondence with Ermolao Barbaro (1485). Barbaro, a distinguished Venetian humanist and student of the Greek texts of Aristotle, had stated in a letter to Pico that the medieval philosophers were uncultured and barbarous and did not deserve to be read or studied. Pico replied in a long letter in which he praises and defends the medieval philosophers and insists with great eloquence that what counts in the writings of philosophers is not their words but their thoughts. Unlike Barbaro and many other humanists who despised the scholastic philosophers for their lack of elegance and classical learning, Pico is willing to recognize the solidity of their thought and to learn from them whatever truth they may have to offer. The line between humanism and Scholasticism, rhetoric and philosophy, is thus clearly drawn, and Pico, although deeply imbued with humanist learning, throws his weight on the side of Scholasticism or, at least, of a synthesis of both sides. Many years after Barbaro and Pico died, Melanchthon wrote a reply to Pico's letter in defense of Barbaro's position.

Syncretism. Pico's defense of the scholastic philosophers was merely a special instance of a much broader historical and philosophical attitude which has been rightly emphasized as his syncretism. Pico was convinced that all known philosophical and theological schools and thinkers contained certain valid insights that were compatible and hence deserved to be restated and defended. This was the underlying idea of his projected disputation, for the 900 theses relied on the most diverse sources— Hermes Trismegistus, Zoroaster, Orpheus and Pythagoras, Plato and Aristotle and all their Greek followers and commentators, Avicenna and Averroës and other Arabic philosophers, Thomas Aquinas and Duns Scotus and several other medieval Latin thinkers, and the Jewish cabalists.

In using all these sources, Pico wished to emphasize his basic conviction that all of these thinkers had a genuine share in philosophical truth. His notion of a universal truth in which each of the schools and thinkers participates to some extent constitutes an attempt to deal with the apparent contrasts and contradictions in the history of philosophy. It may be compared with the positions of the ancient eclectics and of Hegel, yet it differs from both of them. For Pico truth consists in a large number of true statements, and the various philosophers participate in truth insofar as their writings contain, besides numerous errors, a number of specific statements that are true. That this was Pico's intent we may gather from the second part of his *Oration*

and from a passage in the *Apologia* that repeats it almost verbatim. He insists that he is not bound by the doctrines of any master or school but has investigated all of them. Instead of confining himself to one school, he has chosen from all of them what suits his thought, for each has something distinctive to contribute.

Pico's syncretism presupposes that of Ficino, who had proposed a theory of natural religion; had traced the Platonic tradition back to Hermes, Zoroaster, and other early theologians; and had insisted on the basic harmony between Platonism and Christianity. Yet Pico made these notions part of a much wider and more comprehensive synthesis. He explicitly includes Aristotle and all his Greek, Arabic, and Latin followers, and he adds to these previously known sources the Jewish cabalists, with whom he became acquainted through his Hebrew studies, thus being probably the first Christian scholar to use cabalistic literature. This attitude toward Aristotelianism and cabalism clearly distinguished Pico from Ficino and other predecessors; it was to find further development in Pico's own later thought and to exert a strong influence on the philosophy of the sixteenth century. Pico's broad syncretism has been rightly praised by several historians as a steppingstone to later theories of religious and philosophical tolerance.

Pico's use of cabalism consisted not so much in accepting specific cabalist theories as in gaining recognition for cabalism in general. Some of the theories that he seems to have borrowed from cabalist authors were not necessarily of cabalistic origin, such as the scheme of the three worlds—elementary, celestial, and angelic—which he uses for the first three sections of his *Heptaplus*. Pico accepted the claim made by the followers of cabalism that their writings were based on a secret tradition that went back, at least in oral form, to Biblical times. Cabalism thus acquires a kind of authority parallel to that of the Bible and similar to that held by Hermes and Zoroaster in the eyes of Ficino and Pico. Moreover, Pico applied to cabalism a principle that had been used for the Old Testament by all Christian writers since St. Paul: he tried to show that the cabalistic tradition, no less than the Hebrew Scripture, was in basic agreement with Christian theology and hence could be taken as a prophecy and confirmation of Christian doctrine. With this argument he laid the foundation for a whole tradition of Christian cabalism that found its defenders in Reuchlin, Giles of Viterbo, and many other thinkers in the sixteenth and later centuries.

In Pico's own work the cabalistic influence is most noticeable, after the time of the 900 theses, in his *Heptaplus* and in his fragmentary commentary on the Psalms. In a manner which goes far beyond the usual medieval scheme of the four levels of meaning Pico assigns to the text of Scripture a multiple meaning that corresponds to the various parts of the universe. He also uses the cabalistic method of scriptural interpretation, which assigns numerical values to the Hebrew letters and extracts secret meanings from the text by substituting for its words other words with comparable numerical values.

The other distinctive aspect of Pico's syncretism, his tendency to assume a basic agreement between Plato and Aristotle, also remained one of his major preoccupations during his later life. We know that he planned to write an extensive treatise on the agreement between Plato and

Aristotle. The idea that Plato and Aristotle were in basic agreement, although differing in their words and apparent meaning, was not new with Pico. We find it in Cicero, who probably took it from his teacher Antiochus of Ascalon. It is also attributed as a program to Ammonius Saccas, the teacher of Plotinus, and endorsed by Boethius. We may also compare certain trends in recent scholarship that have attempted to bridge the gap between Plato's dialogues and Aristotle's extant later writings by interpolating the oral teaching of Plato and the lost early writings of Aristotle. Pico's approach is known to us through his *De Ente et Uno,* a small treatise composed toward the end of his life and the only surviving fragment of his projected larger work on the harmony of Plato and Aristotle. The question he discusses is whether being and unity are coextensive, as Aristotle maintains in the tenth book of the *Metaphysics,* or whether unity has a broader diffusion and higher status than being, according to the view of Plotinus and other Neoplatonists. Following the scholastic doctrine of the transcendentals, Pico sets out to defend the position of Aristotle. He then tries to prove that Plato did not hold the opposite view, as claimed by the Neoplatonists. In support of his claim Pico cites a passage from Plato's *Sophist* and dismisses the testimony of the *Parmenides,* arguing that this dialogue is merely a dialectical exercise.

In the course of his discussion Pico sharply distinguishes between being itself and participated being, and it is thus possible for him to maintain that God is identical with being in the first sense but above being in the second. The harmony between Plato and Aristotle which Pico tries to establish turns out to be Aristotelian, at least in its wording, but in another sense it is neither Platonic nor Aristotelian, and the distinction between being itself and participated being is evidently indebted to the same Neoplatonists whom Pico tries to refute on the major issue of the treatise. As a result Pico's position was criticized, on the one side, by Ficino, who, in his commentary on the *Parmenides,* defended Plotinus and, on the other, by the Aristotelian Antonio Cittadini, who formulated a series of objections that were answered first by Pico himself and then by his nephew and editor Gianfrancesco Pico.

Another aspect of Pico's syncretism is his treatment of classical mythology. An allegorical interpretation of the myths of the Greek poets had been developed by the ancient Stoics and Neoplatonists, and for them it had been a device for reconciling pagan religion with philosophical truth. When the medieval grammarians continued to interpret the classical poets in this manner, they minimized the pagan religious element and emphasized the implied universal, or even Christian, truth that would justify the study of these authors. The method was taken over and further developed by the humanists and Ficino. Pico tends to be even more elaborate in his discussion and interpretation of ancient myths, especially in his commentary on Benivieni's love poem. Here he repeatedly mentions his plan to write a treatise on poetic theology, a work that probably remained unwritten. Pico apparently intended to construct a detailed system of the theology implicit in the myths of the ancient poets and thus to include them in his universal syncretism.

Dignity of man. Much more famous than the ideas thus far discussed is Pico's doctrine of the dignity of man and

his place in the universe. The *Oration,* in which this doctrine is developed, is probably the most widely known document of early Renaissance thought. In many editions the work is entitled "Oration on the Dignity of Man," but this title properly belongs only to the first part of the oration; the original title was simply *Oration.* Man and his dignity are often praised by the early humanists, and some of them dedicated entire treatises to the subject. The topic was taken up by Ficino, who assigned to the human soul a privileged place in the center of the universal hierarchy and made it, both through its intermediary attributes and through its universal thought and aspirations, the bond of the universe and the link between the intelligible and the corporeal world. In his *Oration* Pico went beyond Ficino in several ways. He did not discuss the question merely in passing or in the context of a large work dedicated to other subjects but displayed it prominently in the opening section of a short and elegant speech. Moreover, he lays the accent not so much on man's universality as on his freedom; instead of assigning to him a fixed though privileged place in the universal hierarchy, he puts him entirely apart from this hierarchy and claims that he is capable of occupying, according to his choice, any degree of life from the lowest to the highest. He has God tell Adam:

> Neither a fixed abode nor a form that is thine alone, nor any function peculiar to thyself have We given thee, Adam, to the end that according to thy judgment thou mayest have and possess what abode, what form, and what functions thou thyself shalt desire. Constrained by no limits, in accordance with thine own free will, in whose hand We have placed thee, thou shalt ordain for thyself the limits of thy nature. . . . Thou shalt have the power to degenerate into the lower forms of life, which are brutish. Thou shalt have the power, out of thy soul's judgment, to be reborn into the higher forms, which are divine.

These words have a modern ring, and they are among the few passages in the philosophical literature of the Renaissance that have pleased, almost without reservation, modern and even existentialist ears. It is not absolutely certain that they were meant to be as modern as they sound, and it is hard to believe what has often been said—that when Pico wrote them, he had denied or forgotten the doctrine of grace. After all, the words are attributed to God and are addressed by him to Adam before the Fall. Yet they do contain an eloquent praise of human excellence and of man's potentialities, and they receive added vigor when we think of what the reformers, and even great humanists like Montaigne, were to say about man's vanity and weakness.

Some scholars have tried to minimize Pico's praise of human dignity and regard it as a piece of mere oratory. This view is refuted by the testimony of the *Heptaplus,* a work written several years later and for an entirely different purpose. Here again, Pico places man outside the hierarchy of the three worlds—the angelic, celestial, and elementary—treats him as a fourth world by himself, and praises him and his faculties, although within a more obvious theological context.

Pico's insistence on man's dignity and liberty also accounts, at least in part, for his attack on astrology, to which he dedicates his longest extant work, probably composed during the last few years of his life. The *Disputationes Adversus Astrologiam Divinatricem* is full of detailed astronomical discussions and displays an amazing mastery of the astrological and antiastrological literature of previous centuries. It has often been hailed by historians as a landmark in the struggle of science against superstition. In fact, Pico does state that the stars act upon sublunar things only through their light and heat, not through any other occult qualities that may be attributed to them, and this statement sounds very sober, if not necessarily modern. Moreover, we learn that even a scientist like Kepler at least modified his initial belief in astrology under the influence of Pico's treatise. In Pico's time, however, the belief in astrology was more than a superstition, and the rejection of it was not necessarily scientific. As a general system astrology was closely linked with the scientific cosmology of the age and hence widely accepted not only by quacks but also by serious thinkers. There is no evidence that Pico was especially guided by scientific considerations in his polemics against astrology, and we must face the fact that he accepted natural magic while rejecting astrology. We happen to know that his work against astrology was composed as a part of a larger work he planned to write against the enemies of the church. The basic impulse of his attack was religious and not scientific, and he indicates more than once what his chief objection to astrology was—the stars are bodies, and our selves are spirits; it cannot be admitted that a corporeal and, hence, lower being should act upon a higher being and restrict its freedom.

Pico's conception of the relation between philosophy and religion is also significant. He became increasingly concerned with religious problems during his later years, a development in which his shock at the papal condemnation of his theses and the influence of Savonarola must have played a part. The fact appears in the religious and theological content of several of his later writings and in the religious motivation of his treatise against astrology. It also finds an unexpected expression in certain passages of the *De Ente et Uno,* a work that deals fundamentally with a very different problem. Here Pico tells us that God is darkness and that philosophical knowledge can lead us toward God only up to a certain point, beyond which religion must guide us. Unlike Ficino, Pico seems to regard religion as a fulfillment of philosophy; religion helps us to attain that ultimate end for which philosophy can merely prepare us.

Pico did not live long enough to develop his ideas into a coherent system. Fragmentary as his work was, it had wide repercussions for a long time. His universal syncretism came closer to subsequent efforts at formulating a universal religion than that of any of his predecessors, including Ficino. His study of Hebrew and Arabic, although not entirely without precedents, served as a widely known example and gave a powerful impulse to these studies in Christian Europe, leading to a study of the Hebrew Scripture and to many new translations of Jewish and Arabic texts. His study of the cabala started a broad and powerful current of Christian cabalism, which flourished throughout the sixteenth century and included many distinguished scholars and thinkers. In his attempt to harmonize the traditions of Platonic and Aristotelian philosophy, of Her-

metic and cabalistic theology, and of the various strands of Arabic and scholastic thought with one another and with Christian doctrine, Pico pointed the way toward intellectual freedom and a universal truth that stands above the narrow limits of particular schools and traditions.

Works by Pico

Three volumes of a critical edition of Pico's works by Eugenio Garin have appeared: *De Hominis Dignitate, Heptaplus, De Ente et Uno, e scritti vari* (Florence, 1942) and *Disputationes Adversus Astrologiam Divinatricem,* 2 vols. (Florence, 1946–1952). For the other works (especially the *Conclusiones, Apologia,* and *Letters*) one of the numerous editions of Pico's works must be used. The earliest and best was published in Bologna (1496); the most accessible is the Basel edition of 1572. For additional letters and texts see Léon Dorez, "Lettres inédites de Jean Pic de la Mirandole," *Giornale storico della letteratura italiana,* Vol. 25 (1895), 352–361, and Eugenio Garin, *La cultura filosofica del Rinascimento italiano* (Florence, 1961). A few of Pico's letters and short religious works, along with the biography of Pico by his nephew, were translated by Sir Thomas More as *Pico, His Life by His Nephew,* J. M. Rigg, ed. (London, 1890). The commentary on Benivieni was translated by Thomas Stanley in 1651 and later appeared as *A Platonick Discourse Upon Love,* Edmund G. Gardner, ed. (Boston, 1914).

There is a modern English version of the *De Ente et Uno,* translated by Victor M. Hamm as *Of Being and Unity* (Milwaukee, Wis., 1943), and no less than three versions of the *Oration—The Very Elegant Speech on the Dignity of Man,* translated by Charles G. Wallis (Annapolis, Md., 1940); *Oration on the Dignity of Man,* translated by Elizabeth L. Forbes in Ernst Cassirer, Paul Oskar Kristeller, and John H. Randall, Jr., eds., *The Renaissance Philosophy of Man* (Chicago, 1948), and published separately with the Latin text (Lexington, Ky., 1953); and *Oration on the Dignity of Man,* translated by A. Robert Caponigri (Chicago, 1956). The correspondence with Ermolao Barbaro was translated by Quirinus Breen as "Giovanni Pico della Mirandola on the Conflict of Philosophy and Rhetoric," *Journal of the History of Ideas,* Vol. 13 (1952), 384–426.

Works on Pico

For Pico's thought the chief monograph is Eugenio Garin, *Giovanni Pico della Mirandola* (Florence, 1937). Important is Ernst Cassirer's "Giovanni Pico della Mirandola," *Journal of the History of Ideas,* Vol. 3 (1942), 123–144, 319–346. See also Giovanni Semprini, *La filosofia di Pico della Mirandola* (Milan, 1936); Eugenio Anagnine, *G. Pico della Mirandola* (Bari, Italy, 1937); Pierre Marie Cordier, *Jean Pic de la Mirandole* (Paris, 1957); E. Monnerjahn, *Giovanni Pico della Mirandola* (Wiesbaden, Germany, 1960); and Eugenio Garin, *Giovanni Pico della Mirandola* (Mirandola, Italy, 1963).

For Pico's sources see Pearl Kibre, *The Library of Pico della Mirandola* (New York, 1936). For the condemnation of his theses see Léon Dorez and Louis Thuasne, *Pic de la Mirandole en France* (Paris, 1897). For his scholastic background see Avery Dulles, *Princeps Concordiae: Pico della Mirandola and the Scholastic Tradition* (Cambridge, Mass., 1941). for the *De Ente et Uno* and its background see Raymond Klibansky, "Plato's *Parmenides* in the Middle Ages and the Renaissance," *Mediaeval and Renaissance Studies,* Vol. 1 (1941–1943), 281–330. For his cabalism see Joseph L. Blau, *The Christian Interpretation of the Cabala in the Renaissance* (New York, 1944); F. Secret, *Le Zôhar chez les kabbalistes chrétiens de la Renaissance* (Paris, 1958) and "Pico della Mirandola e gli inizi della Cabala cristiana," *Convivium,* N.S. Vol. 25 (1957), 31–47.

For Pico's influence on the iconography of Renaissance art see Edgar Wind, *Pagan Mysteries in the Renaissance* (New Haven, 1958).

Several long papers by Eugenio Garin, Robert Weiss, Paul Oskar Kristeller, and Frances A. Yates are included in *L'opera e il pensiero di Giovanni Pico della Mirandola nella storia dell'umanesimo. Convegno internazionale, Mirandola, 15–18 settembre 1963,* 2 vols. (Florence, 1965).

PAUL OSKAR KRISTELLER

PIETISM. Since the seventeenth century Pietism has been an important movement within German Protestantism, and it is still influential in some parts of Germany. It began as a reaction against the formal and conventional character that appeared in Protestantism in the aftermath of the Reformation. Pietism opposed on the one hand the intellectualism implicit in the orthodox tendency to equate faith with the giving of assent to correct doctrine, and on the other, the tendency to identify Christianity with conformity to the ecclesiastical establishments that had been set up in various parts of Germany. By stressing experience, feeling, and personal participation as essential to a true Christian faith, Pietists hoped to bring new life into the Lutheran church. One can point to similar movements in other parts of Christendom, in the English-speaking world the movement most akin to Pietism was Methodism.

The founder of German Pietism was Philipp Jakob Spener (1635–1705). Influenced by the extreme Protestant sect of Jean de Labadie, he undertook the task of raising the devotional level of his congregation in Frankfurt am Main and eventually, he hoped, of German Protestantism as a whole. Devotional meetings in his home were the beginnings of the famous *collegia pietatis.* At its meetings his sermons were considered, the New Testament was expounded, and there was conversation on religious topics. Spener gave clear expression to the aims of his movement in *Pia Desideria* (Frankfurt am Main, 1675), in which he laid down six goals to be realized: (1) greater study of the Bible but with the aim of personal devotion rather than academic competence; (2) a serious commitment to Luther's belief in the priesthood of all Christian believers, so that the laity might really participate in the life of the church instead of merely conforming outwardly; (3) a realization that Christianity is a practical faith rather than an intellectual belief and that this faith expresses itself in love; (4) corresponding to this, a new style in apologetics and controversy that must aim not so much at intellectual conviction as at winning the allegiance of the whole man; (5) following from the last two points, the reorganization of theological education in order to lay stress on standards of life and conduct rather than on academic achievement; (6) the renewal and revitalizing of preaching as an instrument for building up a genuine piety among the people. Spener continued to advocate his views in many other writings, including *Das geistliche Priesterthum* (1677), *Des thätigen Christenthums Nothwendigkeit* (1679), *Die allgemeine Gottesgelehrtheit aller gläubigen Christen und Rechtschaffenen Theologen* (1680), *Klagen über das verdorbene Christenthum* (1684), *Natur und Gnade* (1687), and *Evangelische Glaubenslehre* (1688) which were all published at Frankfurt. He became engaged in stormy controversies, both attracting supporters and arousing opposition. Through the support of the elector of Brandenburg, the University of Halle became a center for Pietist views. Spener himself seems to have been a reasonable man who avoided the extravagances of some of his followers and performed a genuine service for the Lutheran church.

Also important in the history of Pietism is August Hermann Francke (1663–1727). He taught at the University of Halle and is noteworthy for his development of the practical emphasis of Pietism. He founded a school for the poor and an orphanage and also took an interest in the cause of foreign missions. Like Spener, he encountered opposition, especially among some of the theologians, because of his indiscriminate attacks on intellectualism and his depreciation of the academic disciplines in the interests of devotion and philanthropy. Francke, however, had his supporters and was favored by King Frederick William I of Prussia. Mention should also be made of Count Nikolaus Ludwig von Zinzendorf (1700–1760), a pupil of Francke, who spread the spirit of Pietism to Holland, England, and North America by founding communities there. He maintained close relations with John Wesley and the Methodists. Like the other Pietists, he stressed feeling and personal devotion in what seems to have been a mixture of mysticism and emotionalism.

The chief characteristics of Pietism can be seen from this sketch of its origins and early history. It made claims for the affective and sometimes also the conative aspects of religion, in devotion and in practical service, at the expense of the cognitive element. While this may have been a healthy corrective to a sterile dogmatic orthodoxy, it tended to lead to dangerous excesses. Its insistence on intense inward experience could easily lead to the emotionalism that is common in evangelical religion and to the contempt for intelligence and common sense that sometimes accompanies it. The moralistic tone encourages utopianism. Some of those who have been caught up in the enthusiasm of Pietism have underrated the complexities of the moral life and the limitations of what is possible for man; as a result they have shared with the Methodists a belief in perfectionism. Apart from these dangerous excesses, Pietism has contended for the breadth of the human spirit and guarded against too narrow a rationalism. That the tenets of Pietism can receive a sober formulation worthy of respectful consideration is shown above all by the work of F. D. E. Schleiermacher, whose analysis of religion in terms of the feeling of absolute dependence is a direct reflection of the Pietist tradition in Germany.

The influence of Pietism on philosophy is largely indirect. The Pietists themselves tended to be antiphilosophical, but their spirit and teaching became part of the German heritage and eventually influenced even philosophy. This influence showed itself above all in the rise of *Lebensphilosophie* of which the religious variety, as expressed in the work of Rudolf Christoph Eucken, comes nearest to being a philosophical version of Pietism. Yet even the nonreligious varieties of this philosophy probably owe something to the anti-intellectualism that Pietism has encouraged.

Bibliography

Grünberg, P., *P. J. Spener,* 3 vols. Göttingen, 1893–1896.

Mahrholz, A., *Der deutsche Pietismus.* Berlin, 1921.

Nagler, Arthur W., *Pietism and Methodism.* Nashville, Tenn., 1918.

Pinson, Koppel S., *Pietism as a Factor in the Rise of German Nationalism.* New York, 1934.

Ritschl, A., *Geschichte des Pietismus,* 3 vols. Bonn, 1880–1886.

Sachsse, E., *Ursprung und Wesen des Pietismus.* Wiesbaden, 1884.

Schmid, H., *Die Geschichte des Pietismus.* Nördlingen, 1863.

JOHN MACQUARRIE

PISAREV, DMITRI IVANOVICH

PISAREV, DMITRI IVANOVICH (1840–1868), Russian literary critic and social philosopher. Pisarev was educated at St. Petersburg University (1856–1861). His studies were interrupted by a nervous breakdown requiring four months of institutionalization. At this time he twice attempted suicide. Pisarev was imprisoned from 1862 to 1866 for his outspoken criticism of the tsarist regime. He drowned while swimming in the Baltic Sea, under circumstances that suggest suicide, at the age of 28.

Pisarev called himself a "realist" and praised "fresh and healthy materialism," but his own philosophical position was a sense-datum empiricism. In his early writings on ethics and social philosophy, in the years 1859 to 1861, he advocated the "emancipation of the individual person" from social, intellectual, and moral constraints but particularly stressed the preservation of the wholeness of human personality in the face of the fragmenting pressures of functional specialization and the division of labor.

Among the constraints which the free individual must discard are those resulting from "the timidity of his thought, caste prejudices, the authority of tradition, the aspiration toward a common ideal" (*Polnoye Sobraniye Sochineniy,* Vol. I, Col. 339). Pisarev declared that common ideals have "just as little *raison d'être* as common eyeglasses or common boots made on the same last and to the same measure" (*ibid.,* Col. 267). Eyes differ, feet differ, individuals differ; hence eyeglasses, boots, and ideals (for "every ideal has its author") should be individually fitted. Pisarev's moral relativism anticipated contemporary emotivist or noncognitivist doctrines in ethics—the claim that moral judgments are expressions of individual taste or preference. "When it is a matter of judging port or sherry," Pisarev wrote, "we remain calm and cool, we reason simply and soundly . . . , but when it is a question of lofty matters, we immediately . . . get up on our stilts. . . . We let our neighbor indulge his taste in hors d'oeuvres and desserts, but woe unto him if he expresses an independent opinion about morals" (*ibid.,* Col. 266).

In his later writings Pisarev adopted a utilitarian ethics modified by the principle of "economy of intellectual energies." In the situation of cultural and intellectual deprivation of Russia at mid-century, he argued, the greatest-happiness principle precludes such luxuries as esoteric art that can be enjoyed "only by a few specialists" and abstruse science that is "in its very essence inaccessible to the masses" (*ibid.,* Col. 366).

Works by Pisarev

Polnoye Sobraniye Sochinenii ("Complete Works"), St. Petersburg, 1894. Six volumes.

Selected Philosophical, Social and Political Essays. Moscow, 1958.

Works on Pisarev

Coquart, Armand, *Dmitri Pisarev (1840–1868) et l'idéologie du nihilisme russe.* Paris, 1946.

Masaryk, Tomáš G., *Die geistigen Strömungen in Russland,* 2 vols. Jena, 1913. Translated by E. and C. Paul as *The Spirit of Russia: Studies in History, Literature, and Philosophy,* 2 vols. London and New York, 1955. Vol. II, pp. 53–81.

GEORGE L. KLINE

PLANCK, MAX

PLANCK, MAX (1858–1947), German physicist, discoverer of the quantum of action, also called Planck's constant. Born in Kiel, Planck studied physics and mathematics at the University of Munich under Philipp von Jolly and at the University of Berlin under Hermann von Helmholtz and Gustav Kirchhoff. After receiving his Ph.D. at Munich (1879), he taught theoretical physics, first in Kiel, then (starting in 1889) in Berlin, as Kirchhoff's successor. "In those days," he wrote later, "I was the only theoretician, a physicist *sui generis,* as it were, and this circumstance did not make my *début* so easy." At this time Planck made important, and indeed quite fundamental, contributions to the understanding of the phenomena of heat, but he received hardly any attention from the scientific community: "Helmholtz probably did not read my paper at all. Kirchhoff expressly disapproved of its contents." The spotlight was then on the controversy between Ludwig Boltzmann and the Wilhelm Ostwald – Georg Helm – Ernst Mach camp, which supported a purely phenomenological theory of heat. It was via this controversy, and not because of the force of his arguments, that Planck's ideas were finally accepted. "This experience," he wrote, "gave me an opportunity to learn a remarkable fact: a new scientific truth does not triumph by convincing its opponents and making them see the light, but rather because its opponents eventually die." Nevertheless, the discovery of the quantum of action in 1900 (see QUANTUM MECHANICS, PHILOSOPHICAL IMPLICATIONS OF), for which Planck received the Nobel prize in physics (1918), was a direct result of these earlier studies. In 1912 Planck became permanent secretary of the (then) Prussian Academy of Sciences, a post which he retained with only minor interruptions for the rest of his life. He used this position with excellent judgment for furthering the international collaboration of all scientists. From 1930 to 1935 he was president of the Kaiser-Wilhelm-Institut, which later became the Max-Planck-Institut.

Politically Planck was conservative, loyal to the Prussian ideas of the state and of honor, and loyal to Wilhelm II. During World War I he more than once expressed his devotion to the cause of the German people united in battle, and he received the order of "pour le mérite," one of the highest orders of Wilhelm's Germany. However, he opposed the Nazi regime. He defended Einstein, first against his scientific opponents, then against his political enemies. Despite severe criticism by Johannes Stark, Phillip Lenard, and Ernst Müller, he continued to defend Einstein and other Jewish scientists (such as Walther Nernst) even after 1933. He later personally demanded of Hitler that those scientists who had been imprisoned be freed; as a consequence he was removed as president of the Physical Society, was refused the Goethe Prize of the city of Frankfurt (he was awarded it after the war, in 1946), and finally was forced to witness the execution of his only son, who had been connected with the German resistance. Antiquated as some of his political ideas may have been, he nevertheless put individual justice above all and defended it even at the risk of his own life. At the end of the war he was rescued by the Allied Forces. He spent the last years of his life in Göttingen.

Approach to science. Planck's research was guided by his belief "of the existence in nature of something real, and independent of human measurement." He considered "the search for the absolute" to be the highest goal of science. "Our everyday starting point," he explained, "must necessarily be something relative. The material that goes into our instruments varies according to our geographical source; their construction depends on the skill of the designers and toolmakers; their manipulation is contingent on the special purposes pursued by the experimenter. Our task is to find in all these factors and data, the absolute, the universally valid, the invariant that is hidden in them."

This point of view was not allowed to remain a philosophical luxury, without influence upon the procedures of physics. One of the main objections which Planck raised against the positivistic creed was its sterility in the promotion of theory. "Positivism lacks the driving force for serving as a leader on the road of research. True, it is able to eliminate obstacles, but it cannot turn them into productive factors. For . . . its glance is directed backwards. But progress, advancement requires new associations of ideas and new queries, not based on the results of measurement alone."

Scientific discoveries. Of new ideas Planck himself produced essentially two. He recognized and clearly formulated those properties of heat which separate it from purely mechanical processes, and he introduced and applied to concrete problems the idea of an atomistic structure not only of matter but of radiation also. In his doctoral dissertation he had already separated thermodynamic irreversibility from mechanical processes and had interpreted Rudolf Clausius' entropy as its measure. Later he showed (independently of Willard Gibbs) that "all the laws of physical and chemical equilibrium follow from a knowledge of entropy." His conviction that the principle of the increase of entropy was a genuine and independent physical law and his belief in the universal (or, to use his term, "absolute") validity of all physical laws led him to apply thermodynamic reasoning in domains which until then had been regarded as inaccessible to it. For example, he determined that the lowering of the freezing point of dilute solutions could be explained only by a dissociation of the substances dissolved, thus extending the science of thermodynamics to electrically charged particles. This tendency to strain laws to the limit rather than to restrict them to the domain of their strongest evidence caused a temporary clash with Boltzmann, who was quite unperturbed by the fact that in his approach the entropy of a system could both increase and decrease. But it also led to Planck's greatest triumph—his discovery of the quantum of action. He was the only one to correlate the relevant features of radiation with the entropy, rather than the temperature, of the radiant body. "While a host of outstanding physicists worked on the problem of spectral energy distribution, both from the experimental and theoretical aspect, every one of them directed his efforts solely towards exhibiting the dependence of the intensity of radiation on the temperature. On the other hand I suspected that the fundamental connexion lies in the dependence of entropy upon energy. As the significance of the concept of entropy had not yet come to be fully appreciated, nobody paid attention to the method adopted by me, and I could work out my calculations completely at my leisure." These calculations furnished a formula which agreed with experiment and contained the existing theoretical results (Wien's formula and the Rayleigh–Jeans law) as limiting cases. In the attempt to find a rationale for this result, Planck utilized Boltzmann's statistical interpretation of entropy and was thus led to the discovery of the "atomic," or discontinuous, structure of action (energy).

Realism, determinism, and religion. The discovery of the quantum of action was brought about not only by the specific physical arguments used but also by the philosophical belief in the existence of a real world behaving in accordance with immutable laws. The intellectual climate of the late nineteenth century was opposed to such a belief (Boltzmann was almost the only other figure to uphold it). This climate not only found expression in the philosophical superstructure but influenced physical practice itself. Laws were regarded as summaries of experimental results and were applied only where such results were available. However, it was the "metaphysics" of Planck, Boltzmann, and, later on, Einstein (whom Planck interpreted as a realist from the very beginning) which made possible many of the theories that are now frequently used to attack realism and other "metaphysical" principles.

Planck never accepted the positivistic interpretation of the quantum theory. He distinguished between what he called the "world picture" of physics and the "sensory world," identifying the former with the formalism of the Ψ waves, the latter with experimental results. The fact that the Ψ-function obeys the Schrödinger equation enabled him to say that while the sensory world might show indeterministic features, the world picture, even of the new physics, did not. His belief in the existence of objective laws also provided him with an important steppingstone to religious belief. Planck argued that the laws of nature are not invented in the minds of men; on the contrary, external factors force us to recognize them. Some of these laws, such as the principle of least action, "exhibit a rational world order" and thereby reveal "an omnipotent reason which rules over nature." He concluded that there is no contradiction between religion and natural science; rather, they supplement and condition each other.

Works by Planck

Theory of Heat Radiation, translated by Morton Masius. Philadelphia, 1914; 2d ed., New York, 1959.

Eight Lectures on Theoretical Physics, translated by A. P. Wills. New York, 1915. Lectures given at Columbia University in 1909.

The Origin and Development of the Quantum Theory, translated by H. T. Clarke and L. Silberstein. Oxford, 1922. Nobel Prize address.

A Survey of Physics; A Collection of Lectures and Essays, translated by R. Jones and D. H. Williams. London, 1925. Reissued as *A Survey of Physical Theory*. New York, 1960.

Treatise on Thermodynamics, translated by Alexander Ogg. London, 1927; 3d rev. ed., New York, 1945.

Introduction to Theoretical Physics, translated by Henry L. Brose, 5 vols. London, 1932–1933; New York, 1949. Includes *Gen-*

eral Mechanics, The Mechanics of Deformable Bodies, Theory of Electricity and Magnetism, Theory of Light, and *Theory of Heat.*

Scientific Autobiography and Other Papers, translated by Frank Gaynor. New York, 1949.

The New Science, translated by James Murphy and W. H. Johnston. New York, 1959. Includes *Where Is Science Going?* (a defense of determinism with a preface by Albert Einstein), *The Universe in the Light of Modern Physics,* and *The Philosophy of Physics.*

Works on Planck

Schlick, Moritz, "Positivism and Realism," in A. J. Ayer, ed., *Logical Positivism.* Glencoe, Ill., 1959. This essay was a direct reply to the criticisms of positivism that Planck expressed in *Positivismus und reale Aussenwelt.* Leipzig, 1931.

Vogel, H., *Zum philosophischen Wirken Max Plancks.* Berlin, 1961. Excellent biography with detailed bibliography.

PAUL K. FEYERABEND

PLATO. Plato's life began some thirty years before the end of the fifth century B.C. and ended soon after the middle of the fourth century. Yet this rich literary epoch yields little direct information about Plato's life or personality. Partly, this lack of information is due to the code of the prose writers of that period against making explicit mention of living contemporaries. The orator Isocrates, who was Plato's contemporary, does not mention Plato by name in any of his numerous orations that have come down to us or even in his letters. Aristotle, who was 37 when Plato died, alludes anonymously to Plato, Speusippus, Xenocrates, Isocrates and other contemporaries far more often than he names them, and many of the passages in which he does name them were most likely written after their deaths. In some places Aristotle oddly refers to Plato under the name "Socrates," as when he speaks of Socrates composing the *Republic.*

Plato's own dialogues nearly always have Socrates for hero or at least as a minor character. As Socrates was executed in 399, these dialogues could not, without anachronism, have mentioned any incident belonging to the last 52 years of Plato's own life. In fact, Plato is mentioned by name only in the *Apology,* where he is listed with other adherents of Socrates as attending his trial. However, Plato does not altogether avoid anachronism in his dialogues. There are some clear allusions to historical events which took place many years after Socrates' death. In the *Republic* Socrates is made to approve a major development in geometry which was the work of Theaetetus, though Theaetetus was only in his teens when Socrates died; and in several dialogues Socrates is made the spokesman of the Theory of Forms, which, as Aristotle explicitly says, was not a Socratic, but a Platonic theory. Where some anachronisms are certain, others are likely. So it is justifiable to expect to find in the dialogues clues to Platonic, as distinct from Socratic history. But the strengths and weaknesses of these clues must always be debatable.

Diogenes Laërtius, in his *Life of Plato,* cites Plato's will verbatim. The will is interesting for two things. It indicates that when Plato drew it up, he was not wealthy, though also not in great poverty. Its total silence about the buildings, grounds, and contents of his school, the Academy, pretty well proves that by this time Plato had ceased to be the owner of the Academy. It must already have acquired the semi-religious, "college" status that the will of Theophrastus shows to have been the status of Theophrastus' school. This status was that of a dedicated and endowed foundation, legally under the control of a board of trustees. Plato did not bequeath the Academy to Speusippus, nor did Speusippus bequeath it to Xenocrates. These two were elected to its headship, and Speusippus seems to have resigned from its headship.

There have come down to us thirteen letters reputedly written by Plato. Most of these letters are unanimously rejected by scholars as forgeries or imitations. There remain Letters III, VII, VIII, and XIII, some or all of which are accepted as authentic by most, though not by all scholars. Of these four, Letter VII is by far the most important. It is or purports to be a piece of Plato's autobiography, giving a fairly general account of his career as a young man and a very detailed account of his last two visits to Sicily in 367–366 and 361–360 and of his relations with the tyrant of Syracuse, Dionysius the Younger, and with the tyrant's opponent, Dion. As it also contains an excursus on the Theory of Forms, this letter, if authentic, shows that Plato adhered to this theory at least until his mid-seventies. There exists, however, the skeptical minority view that this letter is also a forgery. It is unmentioned by Aristotle, even in any of the many passages in which he criticizes the Theory of Forms. Nor do all latter-day philosophers find the letter's exposition of the Theory of Forms genuinely Platonic either in doctrine or in argumentation. According to one variant of the skeptical view, this letter is, with Letters III, VIII, and XIII, a contemporary political forgery intended to misrepresent, for Sicilian political purposes, Plato's relations with Dion and Dionysius. It needs to represent Plato as the confidant and supporter of Dion and the critic and opponent of Dionysius just in order to put Dion's political actions and policies in a good light and those of Dionysius in a bad light. The letter concludes by stating that conflicting stories are already rife, as if, half a dozen years before Plato died, many people did not yet think of Plato as the supporter of Dion or the opponent of Dionysius.

Even if the skeptical view of the Seventh Letter and the other three letters were accepted, they would, if contemporary forgeries, continue to be useful sources of information. A forger, to remain undetected, must not deny or garble things already well known to the readers of his forgeries. So there are some things, including some biographically important things, said in these four letters which must be true, in substance if not in coloration, even if these letters are forgeries; *a fortiori* they will be true if the letters are authentic.

Aristotle, who was 37 when Plato died, had belonged to the Academy for the last twenty years of Plato's life. Yet in his voluminous writings that have come down to us there is next to no personal information about Plato. Aristotle constantly draws examples from Plato's dialogues and frequently criticizes Plato's doctrines, especially his Theory of Forms. But about Plato's character or about the course of his life we learn next to nothing from Aristotle.

Even our natural supposition that the young Aristotle and his fellow students had been taught philosophy by Plato has been attacked. Nowhere does Aristotle indisputably mention anything taught by Plato that could not have been learned from Plato's writings or else from the lecture (or lectures) on the Good that Plato on one occasion gave but did not transmit in writing to posterity. In his *Politics* Aristotle more than once criticizes Plato's *Republic* for being inexplicit about fairly cardinal arrangements in the Ideal State. None of Plato's students or colleagues seems to have asked Plato in person to fill these gaps.

Certainly Aristotle's lectures would not have been thought the proper places for casual anecdote or personal gossip; but we search them equally vainly for reports of Plato's replies to objections or of his developments or revisions of his earlier ideas. Hardly one whisper of the tutorial voice of Plato is relayed to us by Aristotle, even on philosophical matters.

The orator Isocrates lived in Athens for nearly a hundred years. Though he was born before Plato and outlived him, in his orations he never mentions by name Plato or the Academy or Speusippus, Xenocrates, Eudoxus or Aristotle or, for that matter, any contemporary politician or rhetorician. His speeches and letters do contain, however, a number of indubitable anonymous references, as well as many other likely or merely possible references to Plato and the Academy and even one or two to Aristotle. These references tend to be acidulated. A careful sifting, especially of his *Helen, Busiris, Antidosis,* and *Panathenaicus,* might give us more information about Plato than all that we can cull from Plato's other contemporaries.

Xenophon, who wrote three pieces about Socrates, mentions Plato only once, though he was alive until Plato was in his seventies. Demosthenes mentions Plato twice, but quite uninformatively.

For the rest we have to draw almost entirely on philosophers, historians, scholars and anecdote collectors who wrote three, four or more centuries after Plato's death. These writers had access to earlier sources that are lost to us, and some of these sources were good authorities. But Diogenes Laërtius, say, and Plutarch were not very critical. They transmit some gold but much dross. In particular, they and others of these late writers assumed the authenticity of Letter VII.

Plato's life. Plato died in 347 B.C. at the age of about 81. He never married. He came from an aristocratic and wealthy family, several members of which had been politically prominent on the anti-democratic side. The victory of the democratic cause left Plato and his surviving relatives without political influence or prospects. Plato's attitude toward the leaders of the democracy—that is, the demagogues—is what could be expected. The account in Letter VII of the frustration of Plato's political ideals and ambitions is likely to be true in substance. Plato certainly saw military service in the war against Sparta. It is probable that he belonged to the cavalry. He was a close associate of Socrates, anyhow during the last few years of Socrates' life, which ended when Plato was about 31. The story is quite likely true that after the execution of Socrates Plato and others of Socrates' circle found it politically expedient to take refuge in Megara, where Euclides seems to have had some sort of school.

Later, probably in the earliest 380s, Plato traveled to Egypt, among other places. During these travels he paid the first of his three visits to Syracuse in Sicily, where Diony-

sius the Elder was military governor, or tyrant. The often repeated stories of a quarrel between Plato and this tyrant deserve no credence; they are standard anti-tyrant stories. They are not even faintly echoed in Letter VII, though this letter is unsparing of invective against Dionysius' son, Dionysius the Younger.

At some time after Plato's first visit to Syracuse and before his second visit in 367 he founded the Academy. The still prevalent idea that he founded the Academy in the early 380s rests entirely on one vague phrase in Diogenes Laërtius' *Life of Plato,* suggesting that after his travels Plato lived at the Academy. "Academy" was the name of Plato's house, and we have nothing to indicate that Plato started his school in this house at the moment he began to reside there or even that he began to reside there immediately or soon after his return from his travels. There is some evidence that Plato was teaching young men at the Academy before the inauguration of the school that we think of as "the Academy," with the curriculum described in Book VII of the *Republic.*

It is often assumed that Plato began to compose his Socratic dialogues when he was in his thirties or even in his late twenties, before the death of Socrates. There is no evidence to support this idea. On the other hand there is some fairly strong internal evidence that Plato's *Euthydemus* and *Crito* were written at least some way on in the 370s, that the *Symposium* was written after 371, and that the *Phaedo* was written just before Plato left for Sicily in 367; so it may be that Plato's career as a writer of dialogues began fifteen or twenty years after the execution of their hero, Socrates, that is, when Plato was well past middle age.

In 367 Plato sailed again to Syracuse, where he stayed as the guest of Dionysius the Younger for over a year. Letter XIII is or purports to be, *inter alia,* Plato's thank-you letter. Its tone of voice toward Dionysius is quite incongruous with the story in Letter VII of a wide and deep breach between Plato and Dionysius over the young tyrant's maltreatment of Dion, whom, a few months after Plato's arrival, Dionysius had banished for treasonable correspondence with Carthage.

The story given in Letters III, VII and XIII is that Plato came to Sicily on the joint invitation of Dion and Dionysius the Younger after the latter's accession to the tyranny. As the death of Dionysius the Elder cannot have occurred more than a couple of months before Plato left Athens and may have occurred only a few days before Plato reached Syracuse, this story cannot be true. Plato's invitation to Syracuse must have come, not from Dionysius the Younger, but from his father, during 368 or 369. If so, these three letters must be forgeries, since Plato himself could not have got wrong the identity of his inviter. It happens that we possess a letter from Isocrates to Dionysius the Elder, written in 368, regretting that he cannot risk the long journey to Sicily. As two other philosophers or sophists from Athens, Aristippus and Aeschines, were in Syracuse with Plato, it looks as if Dionysius the Elder had in 368 or 369 invited several Athenian luminaries, including Plato, to visit his court in 367. If so, then the so-called Platonic letters are in error not only about the source of Plato's invitation but also about the reasons for it, since these reasons would presumably be the reasons also for the invitations to Isocrates, Aristippus and Aeschines.

In 361 Plato visited Syracuse for the third and last time and was again, for part of his sojourn, the personal guest of Dionysius the Younger. This time he came with Aristippus, Aeschines, Speusippus, Xenocrates and probably Eudoxus, the last three being teachers in the Academy. No mention is made in the so-called Platonic Letters of their presence, the reasons for which could not have been the reasons alleged by these letters for Plato's visit. On these grounds too, the letters must be forgeries, and they are likely to be pro-Dion propaganda forgeries, since the motives that they allege for Plato's visit are pro-Dion motives. Plato returned from Syracuse via Olympia, where he attended the Games of July 360.

Some time not long after his return to Athens, when he was nearly seventy, Plato suffered, according to Seneca, a serious illness caused by the hardships of his long voyages. He survived this illness and was able to go on working for quite a long time. He died, aged about 81, in 347. He was succeeded as Head of the Academy by his nephew Speusippus. At about the same moment Aristotle left Athens and did not return for several years.

There must have been other biographically important events in Plato's life, but most of these must either remain hidden from us or be inferred or conjectured from clues provided by his dialogues, with, at best, snippets of corroboration from outside sources. One such event is this: Diogenes Laërtius says that Dionysius the Younger gave Plato the enormous sum of 80 talents. The amount is doubtless exaggerated, but the story that Dionysius treated Plato very handsomely is borne out by a number of mostly malicious yarns from other sources, according to which Plato was the beneficiary of Dionysius. The so-called Platonic Letters, in their hostility to Dionysius, have to deny that Plato benefited from the tyrant's monetary lavishness, as if there were stories already current to the opposite effect, which needed to be denied. This story of Diogenes Laërtius and the account in Letter VII of Plato's relations with Dionysius the Younger cannot easily be reconciled, and Diogenes Laërtius makes no attempt to reconcile them.

SOCRATES AND PLATO

It is certain that during some of Socrates' last years before his execution in 399 Plato was closely associated with him. There was some sort of circle of adherents who loved Socrates as a person and both admired and studied his practice of the Socratic Method. Whether they or some of them were in any formal sense his pupils is debatable. In the *Apology* Socrates is made to deny that he had ever been a teacher of students, as well as to deny, somewhat inconsistently, that he had ever charged fees for his teaching. On the other hand Aristophanes in his *Clouds* certainly represents Socrates as conducting a school for young men, some of whom lived in Socrates' house. A writer of comedies can, of course, play fast and loose with fact, and we know that Aristophanes credits Socrates with theories really held by Diogenes of Apollonia; he also attributes to Socrates things for which Protagoras seems to deserve the credit or discredit. Nonetheless, the Athenian public

would have found less fun in a comic account of Socrates' school if he had been known not to have had one than in a caricature of a school which he was known to have.

Isocrates in his *Busiris* denies that Alcibiades had ever been a pupil of Socrates, not apparently on the score that Socrates had no pupils but only on the score that Alcibiades was not one of them. In his *Life of Socrates* Diogenes Laërtius says that Socrates taught, not philosophy or disputation, but rhetoric, though we hear nothing of this from Plato or Xenophon. We should therefore treat with some skepticism the *Apology*'s denial that Socrates was a teacher of students. Even if he did teach students, it would not follow that Plato's association with Socrates had been that of a pupil with his teacher.

Although our picture of Socrates derives chiefly from Plato's dialogues, especially his early dialogues, with some reinforcement from Xenophon's *Symposium, Apology* and *Memorabilia,* these sources give us very little factual information about Socrates. Only in his *Apology, Crito* and *Phaedo* does Plato mention Socrates' sons; only in his *Phaedo* does Plato mention Socrates' wife. He tells us nothing about Socrates' house and nothing about the profession or craft from which he made his modest living. The story that Socrates was a sculptor does not come from either Plato or Xenophon.

We know that Socrates was tried in the King Archon's Court for "impiety" or "irreligion" and that he was executed for this. He could hardly have been so prosecuted and convicted just for privately harboring heretical opinions. He must have made his opinions known to Athens and even have been thought to have indoctrinated his pupils with them. The second charge against Socrates was that of corrupting the young men. Plato's *Apology* purports to be the speeches made by Socrates in his own defense. Yet of its two dozen pages only two or three are concerned with the charge of "impiety." The bulk of Plato's *Apology* is given up to Socrates' defense of his practice of the Socratic Method—that is, his practice of cross-examining politicians, orators, poets and artisans and driving them by his chains of questions into logical *impasses.* Near the end of the *Apology* Socrates is made to say, by implication, that he is being executed for his practice of the Socratic Method. The King Archon's Court was empowered to try only for the two capital crimes of murder and impiety. Socratic questioning was not even illegal, but if it had been illegal, it could not have been a capital offense or, therefore, one tried in this particular court. So Plato's *Apology* must, in bulk, be totally unhistorical. Plato must have had special reasons for publishing a defense of dialectic, and he did this by putting into his dramatic hero's mouth only a perfunctory answer to the charge of impiety but a protracted defense of the practice of elenctic questioning.

In the *Gorgias* and *Meno* there are apparent references, dramatically in the future tense, to the trial and condemnation of Socrates. Not a word is said here or in a partly analogous reference in the *Politicus* about the accusation of impiety. There is much more fiction than is sometimes supposed in the dialogues' pictures of Socrates.

We have no good reason to doubt that the real Socrates did in fact practice the Socratic Method, save that Diogenes Laërtius in his *Life of Socrates* says nothing about it and that Isocrates in his *Against the Sophists* and *Helen* reprobates Protagoras and other practitioners of what he calls "eristic" without any mention of Socrates by name or any clear allusion to him.

The Socratic Method. Many years before the death of Socrates there had been introduced into Athens and probably into other Greek cities a special debating exercise, sometimes called "eristic," though called "dialectic" by Plato and Aristotle. There are fairly good reasons for thinking that it was the sophist Protagoras who introduced it into Athens and taught its procedures and techniques to students. Possibly he was its inventor.

The exercise took the following form. Two debaters or disputants, a questioner and an answerer, are put up. The answerer undertakes to defend a thesis or proposition; the questioner has to try to demolish it. The questioner may, with certain reservations, only ask questions and questions so constructed that the answerer can answer Yes or No to them. The answerer in his turn is, with certain reservations, allowed to give only Yes or No answers. The questioner tries to pose such chains of questions that some of the answerer's Yes or No answers will turn out to conflict with the thesis that he had undertaken to defend. If the questioner is successful, he has confuted his opponent. If the answerer remains unconfuted until the time is up, he is the victor. The tournament, or logic duel, is fought out before an audience, which may act as a sort of jury to decide who has won or whether one of the duelists has been guilty of a foul. These set combats may sometimes have been controlled by an umpire. We may borrow the title "moot" for these organized disputations. In moots the same thesis is commonly debated time after time. Today's questioner may, but need not be tomorrow's answerer, or a new questioner and a new answerer may be brought in. The thesis need not be something of which the answerer is himself convinced. He is only its advocate for today, charged with the task of making the strongest possible case for it. Similarly, the questioner is charged with, so to speak, the prosecution of the thesis. He may have no doubts of its truth. His business is the barrister-like one of making the strongest possible case against it. Today's disputation will partly follow the course taken in yesterday's debate of the same thesis. If a line of argumentation has proved efficacious, it can be re-employed, perhaps with some condensations. But if it has proved inefficacious or frail, it is either dropped or strengthened. Sometimes, if not usually, some kind of written record is kept of the course of the argumentation, so that tomorrow's questioner and answerer can take over, with or without their own modifications, the arguments of yesterday and last week. There is no personal property in arguments, any more than there is in chess moves. When a thesis has thus been debated many times, the final *pro* and *contra* arguments are crystallizations of the accumulated contributions of many different debaters.

If the questioner succeeds in confuting the answerer's thesis, the result of the duel is necessarily negative, in the sense that what has been proved is either that the thesis is false or that the answerer's case for it contains one or more logical flaws. When, for example, Socrates defeats Protagoras in Plato's *Protagoras,* he has proved either that virtue is

not teachable or that there is a fallacy in Protagoras' arguments in support of the thesis that virtue is teachable. An *elenchus,* or confutation, has to be a demolition. No constructive doctrines can be established in discussions of this pattern. In such discussions the questioners are in search of illogicalities in the answerers' cases for their theses. The debate is concluded when such illogicalities are found.

Protagoras taught the art of elenctic disputation to young men and did so for a fee; the teaching of this art subsequently became widespread. Often, if not usually, it was taught to students who were also studying rhetoric. Eloquence and clarity of presentation were reinforced by cogency in destructive argumentation. Probably Protagoras thought of this new exercise only as a good training for future politicians and "lawyers"; and, to start with, young men paid to be coached in the exercise partly because it was an amusing and exciting contest but chiefly because of its career value. What is of importance to us is that it proved to be the beginning of methodical philosophical reasoning.

In the early dialogues of Plato we find, presented in the form of mimes or dramas, discussions between Socrates and interlocutors, conducted not under formal moot conditions but in unplanned and even casual conversations. Socrates is usually the questioner and is usually victorious, though in the *Euthydemus* he is, for part of the time, a hapless answerer. We need to see Plato's Socratic dialogue against this background of the rule-governed dialectical moot. If, as some clues suggest, Plato himself did for some time coach young men in elenctic disputation, his early dialogues are likely to reflect, in their argument sequences, the recorded proceedings of moots steered, arbitered and perhaps minuted by himself.

The idea, deriving entirely from the *Apology,* that the real Socrates had practiced his method by cross-examining in the market place people whom he happened to come across there is not credible. In no Platonic dialogue nor in the Socratic writings of Xenophon do Socrates' questioner–answerer tussles take place in such unsuitable surroundings. Instead, the other Platonic dialogues represent the discussions as taking place in a private house, a lecture hall or a gymnasium, and very often the disputants and their listeners are described as sitting down. Like the other teachers of dialectic, probably including Plato himself and certainly including Aristotle, the real Socrates would usually have conducted dialectical disputations under formal moot conditions. It is for dramatic ends that these discussions are, in the dialogues, informalized and enlivened with interactions between interesting persons.

PLATO'S ACADEMY

When Plato was young there existed in Athens no organized higher education for lads who were finished with school, save for the few who were individually apprenticed, for example, to doctors or architects. This gap was partly filled by the sophists. A sophist was usually an itinerant lecturer who charged fees for the classes that he conducted. The main subject taught by sophists was rhetoric, the art of making forensic, political and panegyric speeches. Since most of the young men for whom the sophists catered came from the upper class, what they required was training for public life. The rhetoric taught by the sophists might include more than eloquence and clarity of presentation. Some sophists also taught embryonic linguistic subjects; some of them certainly taught eristic disputation; some of them seem to have taught literary criticism; and some, maybe, political history of a superficial sort. A few sophists taught scientific subjects. Hippias of Elis certainly taught astronomy and mathematics; others seem to have taught elementary medicine.

It seems that as a rule a sophist would flit from one city to another, giving the same lectures in each. The young Athenian might sit at the feet of Hippias or Prodicus of Ceos for a few days or weeks and then never hear him again, unless he attached himself as a fellow migrant to the sophist's retinue. A few sophists, like Gorgias, ultimately settled down in Athens and thus inaugurated the stationary "school" or "college." Aristophanes' *Clouds* makes it appear that Socrates conducted a static school. Antisthenes certainly did so. These were single-teacher schools. As far as is known, Socrates and Antisthenes employed no assistants. The static school of which most is known is that of Plato's contemporary, Isocrates, who taught rhetoric in Athens. His pupils may have remained under his tutelage for three or four years. Though apparently no fees were charged to the sons of Athenians, they were charged to the sons of non-Athenians, and Isocrates prospered from these fees. As Isocrates was far on in his nineties when he died, it is a plausible guess that the teaching in his school was, in his later years, partly done by subordinates.

Plato's Academy certainly resembled the school of Isocrates, presumably that of Antisthenes, and quite likely that of Socrates in providing a continuous education. Aristotle came to the Academy at the age of 17 and remained there for some years as a student and then for many years as a teacher. Nearly all of the Academy's students of whom anything is known came, like Aristotle, from cities other than Athens.

In two extremely important respects the Academy was unlike the school of Isocrates. First, the Academy was from its start a school with a many-sided curriculum and, correspondingly, with more than one teacher. The mathematician Theaetetus taught in the Academy and is said to have been there from its start. Probably the astronomer and mathematician Eudoxus was in the same position. He had previously had a school of his own at Cyzicus and seems to have migrated to Athens with several of his students, who then became members of the Academy. In Book VII of the *Republic* the higher education prescribed for the young men is an education that Theaetetus and Eudoxus alone could at that time have provided.

Second, where Isocrates' school trained young men in things necessary or helpful for subsequent careers in public life, the subjects taught in the Academy were, for a long time, quite unvocational—that is, "academic." It could and did produce scientists and mathematicians, but it was not at the start a seminary for future politicians, orators or "lawyers." It was left to Aristotle, in his middle twenties, to add rhetoric to the Academy's curriculum and so to bring the Academy into competition with the school of Isocrates.

It is often taken for granted that the young students in the early Academy were taught not only mathematics and astronomy but also, and above all, philosophy; Aristotle is accordingly often described as having been taught philosophy by Plato. But in Book VII of the *Republic* Socrates quite violently forbids the teaching of dialectic to young men. We have some external evidence that this was the policy of the early Academy. For whatever reasons the young Aristotles were not trained to thrash out conceptual questions according to the Socratic Method. It was Aristotle who in the fairly early or middle 350s first gave this training to the Academy's students. Xenocrates may have cooperated. Though Plato was the Head of the Academy, he did not teach his own forte, dialectic, in it.

It is not clear that Plato taught there at all. Certainly Aristotle knew the scientific content of Plato's *Timaeus.* He draws on and criticizes this dialogue far more often than he does any other Platonic dialogue. But not one of his numerous comments indicates that the *Timaeus* had been more than a basic textbook. He nowhere unmistakably suggests that Plato ever developed or modified anything in the book; or that Plato conducted *Timaeus* classes in which he told the students anything in addition to, or in correction of what is in the text of the *Timaeus.* Aristotle also shows good or moderate knowledge of many, though not all of Plato's philosophical and political writings. But of things said in class by Plato, whether in response to questions or in reply to objections, whether in jest or in annoyance, not one certain echo is transmitted by Aristotle. Our very natural and congenial idea that the Academy was a seminary in which the main teacher was Plato and the main subject taught and discussed was philosophy seems to be a long way wide of the truth.

When was the Academy founded? That is, when did Plato, Theaetetus and probably Eudoxus start, at Plato's residence, which was named "Academy," the school the curriculum of which is described and justified in Book VII of the *Republic*? The traditional story that it was started in the early 380s cannot be true. Theaetetus had conducted a school of his own at Heraclea on the Black Sea before coming to the Academy, and we know from Plato's *Theaetetus* that Theaetetus was only a lad in 399. If Eudoxus was a fellow founder of the Academy, which is not certain, then the Academy could not have been started until late in the 370s. Isocrates' *Helen,* which should probably be dated late, perhaps very late, in the 370s, seems to castigate Plato, though without mentioning him by name, for teaching eristic to young men, and eristic, or dialectic, is precisely what the Academy debars young men from learning. So the founding of the Academy must have been later than the *Helen.* It is arguable that the Academy began not twenty years, but only three, four or five years before Aristotle joined it in 367.

We have no information about the number of students studying in the Academy at any one time. The temptation to liken the size of the Academy to that of a modern university or even of a college needs to be resisted. The Academy's students in a given year could probably have been counted in two figures, and very likely in the not very high two figures. Nor should it be supposed that the Academy resembled modern or even medieval universities in their most characteristic features. Nothing like their degrees, examinations, halls of residence or professorial and sub-professorial ranks can be supposed to have existed in Plato's or in Aristotle's days. Continuing lecture courses were certainly given; Aristotle's surviving books largely consist of such lecture courses. He made use of the Greek counterpart of our blackboard, and references are made here and there to anatomical diagrams, maps and the astronomers' orreries. It is not certain that the Academy even had a library in its early years.

The students took down notes of the lectures that they heard, and therefore they listened sitting down. The fact that we neither possess nor hear of any students' notes of lectures by Plato, other than his public lecture on the Good, suggests that Plato himself did not often, if ever, give lectures.

Whether, like Isocrates' school, the Academy charged fees to the sons of non-Athenians cannot be decided. We know that neither Theaetetus nor Eudoxus had inherited any private wealth, and they are likely to have had to make their livings from their own earlier schools at Heraclea and Cyzicus. There is evidence of debatable strength that Plato had become a relatively poor man shortly before the Academy was founded. If so, then it would seem inevitable that the Academy would have charged enough fees to support its Head and its two other teachers. On the other hand in a letter of questioned authenticity Dionysius the Younger reproaches Plato's successor, Speusippus, for charging fees where Plato had not done so. Plato's will seems to show that the Academy became, some time before Plato's death, an endowed foundation, controlled by trustees. So perhaps the Academy had charged fees to start with and ceased to charge them when it got the endowment that enabled it to acquire "college" status. It is tempting to identify this postulated endowment with the bounty of 80 talents that Dionysius the Younger is alleged to have given to Plato. No such wealth is bequeathed in Plato's will.

PLATO'S DIALOGUES

Plato wrote some two dozen compositions, which are known as his dialogues. A few of these are not really dialogues but addresses in monologue with a bit of conversational preamble. The *Laws*, on which Plato was still working when he died, seems originally to have been a sequence of addresses. This, after its original composition, was, during Plato's last years, in process of being reconstructed into conversational shape, but this reconstruction was never completed.

The *Menexenus* seems to be an orthodox funeral oration, to which an incongruous conversational preamble and close were subsequently added. The *Apology* is Plato's version of Socrates' speeches at his trial. The *Symposium* is, save for some brief stretches of conversation and debate, a sequence of short orations given by seven different speakers. The unfinished *Critias* and the *Timaeus* are both addresses in monologue prefaced by a little conversation. There is no philosophy in the *Menexenus*, the *Apology* or the *Critias;* almost no philosophy in the *Laws*, except for Book X, or in the first six speeches in the *Symposium;* and almost none in the *Phaedrus.* The *Republic* is a mixed bag,

of which some of the contents, like its educational requirements and its political diagnoses and prescriptions, exhibit Plato as the designer of utopian policies of political reform. The program of the *Laws* is relatively unutopian, and probably Plato hoped that this program would be realized.

No contemporary testimony tells us how Plato and the many other writers of dialogues published their compositions. Nor have scholars given much consideration to the matter. What follows is a hypothesis, based on a lot of little individually tenuous clues. There was, of course, no printing in ancient Greece. Compositions published in book form were individually handwritten by scribes. There is the evidence of silence from Plato, Isocrates and others that in Plato's day there were no libraries. Very likely there were no bookshops displaying stocks of ready-made handwritten books. We do not hear of anyone browsing in such a bookshop until half a century after Plato's death. The number of individual collectors of books must have been very small. Reading books was a fairly rare thing. Inside the Academy itself the young Aristotle seems to have acquired the nickname "Reader" because he was exceptional in being a voracious reader.

The normal mode of publishing a composition, whether in verse or prose, was oral delivery to an audience. Conjecturally, the compositions of dialogue writers, including Plato, Antisthenes, Xenophon and Aristotle, were no exception. The public got to know a new dialogue by hearing the author recite it. Normally, Plato orally delivered the words of his dramatic Socrates. The dialogues were dramatic in form because they were composed for semi-dramatic recitation to lay and drama-loving audiences, consisting largely of young men. A dialogue had therefore to be short enough not to tax the endurance of its audience. The only two mammoth dialogues, the *Republic* and the incompletely conversationalized *Laws,* must have been intended for special audiences that would reassemble time after time to hear the successive installments. There are special reasons for thinking that of Plato's dialogues only the *Timaeus* and the second part of the *Parmenides* were composed just for Academic listeners.

It is customary, and not seriously misleading, to divide Plato's writing career into three periods.

The first period. The dialogues of Plato's earliest period are the *Lysis, Laches, Euthyphro, Charmides, Hippias Major* and *Hippias Minor, Ion, Protagoras, Euthydemus, Gorgias* and *Meno.* The *Alcibiades,* I and II, if Plato wrote them, are in this group also, as is the bulk of the first book of the *Republic,* which would seem to have been originally intended for an independent dialogue, the name of which would have been *Thrasymachus.* All these are dialectical or elenctic dialogues, in the sense that in all of them the debating exemplifies the Socratic Method.

Often in these early dialogues the answerer's thesis is a suggested definition of some general notion, like Piety or Valor or Beauty, but often it is a general proposition, such as "Virtue can be taught" or "It is worse to suffer than to do wrong." In either case the disputants are in search of knockdown arguments against these positions or of rebuttals of such arguments.

To us, as to some contemporary critics of Socrates and Plato, such dialectical checkmates are disappointing. We think of philosophers as trying to resolve *impasses,* not create them. But when Plato was composing these early dialectical dialogues, the word "philosophy" had not yet acquired the constructive connotations that it has for us and that it had for Aristotle and the terminal Plato.

Socrates must have trained his associates, including Plato, Antisthenes and Aeschines, in disputing according to the Socratic Method. Plato almost certainly and Antisthenes certainly subsequently trained pupils of their own in this method, as, later on, Aristotle did too. It is likely, therefore, that these early dialogues of Plato reflect, in dramatized form, moots conducted by Plato himself before the foundation of his Academy, in which dialectical disputation was forbidden to its young students. Plato nearly always puts the questioner's words into the mouth of his dramatic Socrates, but no Athenian would have expected of these dialogues much biographical fidelity to the real Socrates. The art of biography did not yet exist. The young men for whom these dialogues were chiefly written had not known Socrates, nor could they read any Socratic writings, since Socrates had published nothing.

The middle period. In his *Gorgias* and what probably was to have been his *Thrasymachus,* now Book I of the *Republic,* Plato reaches the peak of his genius in the combination of lively dramatization with powerful elenctic argumentation. Then quite suddenly this genre of argumentation almost vanishes from Plato's dialogues, until the very undramatic second part of his late dialogue, the *Parmenides.* Only here and there and only for short stretches is the Socratic Method now practiced; and the conversations between the discussion leader and his interlocutors are no longer duels and often not even debates. In the last eight and a half books of the *Republic* Glaucon and Adeimantus merely acquiesce most of the time, without any theses of their own to champion or to surrender.

It seems plausible to connect Plato's near-abandonment of the Socratic Method with Socrates' startling veto on the participation in dialectic of the young guardians-to-be (*Republic* VI, 537–539). As the description of the higher education of these guardians is the description of the initial curriculum of the Academy, we have to conclude that in the early Academy itself young men in their teens or twenties were not allowed to take part in dialectical moots. The young Aristotle was not taught philosophy during his student years. Plato's teaching of dialectical disputation stopped with the foundation of his Academy. His composition of dialectical dialogues seems to have stopped at the same time, presumably for the same unrecorded reason.

It is in dialogues immediately succeeding the last of the dialectical dialogues that we first hear of the famous Theory of Forms. Here for the first time we find Plato putting forward a positive philosophical doctrine.

If Plato's middle period can be demarcated by the virtual disappearance of the *elenchus* and by the presence of the Theory of Forms, then the *Timaeus* has to be dated fairly close to the *Phaedo* and the *Republic.* Most commentators, however, hold that the *Timaeus,* and with it the *Philebus,* are among Plato's latest compositions and consequently that the Theory of Forms remained Plato's doctrine from the beginning of his middle period to the end of his third period. They have, in consequence, to construe

Plato's criticisms of the theory in his *Sophist* and *Parmenides* as either unserious or merely peripheral. According to the other view, the minority view that is adopted here, the *Timaeus* was composed in close proximity to the *Symposium, Phaedo* and *Republic,* with the *Philebus* succeeding the *Timaeus* fairly closely, so that the middle period dialogues are these five plus the unphilosophical *Critias* and the unphilosophical *Phaedrus.* The original unconversational version of Books III–VII of our *Laws* seems likely to belong to this period also. This is also unphilosophical.

The third period. The dialogues of the third period are the *Theaetetus, Sophist, Politicus* and *Parmenides.* The *Cratylus* should probably be included, but this is a matter of controversy. The later books of the *Laws* would seem to have been composed during this period.

It is a new feature of these dialogues that they deal with sophisticated and semi-professional issues. For whatever recipients Plato ostensibly wrote them, he clearly had in mind Academic colleagues and students who were already discussing methodological and embryonically logical or semantic matters. The atmosphere of these dialogues is the atmosphere in which Aristotle was preparing his *Rhetoric, Categories, De Interpretatione, Topics* and *Peri Ideon.* The Academy's initial veto on the teaching of dialectic to young men has clearly been rescinded. Aristotle's *Topics* is a course of instruction in the techniques and rationale of elenctic disputation; in his *Parmenides* Plato makes old Parmenides advise the youthful Socrates to practice argumentation of the Zenonian pattern if he is to develop into a philosopher. In the *Sophist* and *Politicus* Plato exhibits at tedious length the division of generic concepts into their species and sub-species, and whole books of divisions were correspondingly composed by Aristotle, Xenocrates, Speusippus and Theophrastus.

In the *Cratylus, Theaetetus* and *Sophist* Plato, like Aristotle in, for example, his *De Interpretatione* and *Categories,* is beginning to consider grammatical and semantic questions about the elements and the compositions of truths and falsehoods and of the sentences that convey them. We know from Isocrates' *Antidosis* that dialectic, or eristic, was a part of the Academy's curriculum for young men by or before the middle of the 350s. It is to the 350s that Plato's third period dialogues seem to belong.

THE THEORY OF FORMS

It has been shown that the series of Plato's elenctic dialogues is abruptly terminated with the *Gorgias* or the unfinished *Thrasymachus,* which is now the substance of Book I of the *Republic.* No matter what sort of crisis this drastic change of direction was due to, Plato's succeeding dialogues are markedly different from their predecessors. Negatively, they differ in being devoid or almost devoid of argumentative checkmating; positively, they differ in presenting constructive philosophical doctrines. Of these by far the most famous is Plato's Theory of Forms.

This theory is first adumbrated in the *Symposium.* It is fairly fully stated, argued and exploited in the *Phaedo.* It is expounded and made use of in the *Republic.* It is rather briefly defended in the *Timaeus,* as if it had been already subjected to criticism; here not much positive use is made of the theory. It is mentioned with respect in the *Philebus,* but as a theory which is up against radical objections; the main arguments of this dialogue do not depend on it.

In the *Sophist* the Theory of Forms is treated quite unparentally, and a modification is required of it which, if accepted, would make it a very different doctrine. In the first part of the *Parmenides* old Parmenides not only marshals a battery of powerful, almost Aristotelian, objections to the theory but also adjures its youthful inventor, Socrates, to take serious training in dialectic if he wishes to become a philosopher. In the *Cratylus* and *Theaetetus* the theory is unmentioned and unused, save that one important strand of it is reaffirmed, though without reference to the theory as a whole.

Historians of thought and commentators are apt to speak as if the Theory of Forms was the whole of Plato's thinking. It was indeed of great importance, but it has to be remembered not only that the theory is unthought of in the elenctic dialogues and is either ignored or criticized in the late dialogues; but also that during the very heyday of the theory, from the *Symposium* to the *Timaeus,* the page space given to the theory is only a small fraction of all that Plato uses. In the *Phaedo,* which seems to have been the source of most of Aristotle's ideas of the theory, the theory is employed as providing only one or two among several disparate reasons for believing in the immortality of the soul. In six of the ten books of the *Republic* nothing is said or needs to be said about the Forms. "Platonism" was never the whole of Plato's thought and for much of his life was not even a part of it.

What was this Theory of Forms?

It originated out of several different and partly independent features of the general ideas or notions that constituted the recurrent themes of dialectical disputations.

Definitions. Every discussion of a general issue turns ultimately upon one or more general notions or ideas. Even to debate whether, say, fearlessness is a good quality is to work with the two general notions of fear and goodness. Two disputants may disagree whether fearlessness is a good or a bad quality, but they are not even disagreeing unless they know what fear and goodness are. Their debate is likely, at some stage, to require the explicit definition of one or more of the general terms on which the discussion hinges. They may accept a proffered definition, but even if a proffered definition is justly riddled by criticism, this criticism teaches what the misdefined notion is not. If "fearlessness" were misdefined as "unawareness of danger," the exposure of the wrongnesses of this definition would by recoil bring out something definite in the notion of fearlessness. The Socratic demolition of a proffered definition may be disheartening, but it is also instructive.

Standards of measurement and appraisal. Some general notions, including many moral notions and geometrical notions, are ideal limits or standards. A penciled line is, perhaps, as straight as the draftsman can make it; it deviates relatively slightly, sometimes imperceptibly, from the Euclidean straight line. The notion of absolute straightness is the standard against which we assess penciled lines as crooked or even as nearly quite straight. Rather similarly, to describe a person as improving in honesty or loyalty is to describe him as getting nearer to perfect honesty or loyalty.

Immutable things. Ordinary things and creatures in the everyday world are mutable. A leaf which was green yesterday may be brown today, and a boy may be five feet tall now who was two inches shorter some months ago. But the color brown itself cannot become the color green, and the height of four feet, ten inches, cannot become the height of five feet. It is always five feet minus two inches. A change is always a change from something *A* to something else *B,* and *A* and *B* cannot themselves be things that change.

Timeless truths. What we know about particular things, creatures, persons and happenings in the everyday world are tensed truths, and what we believe or conjecture about them are tensed truths or tensed falsehoods. The shower is still continuing; it began some minutes ago; it will stop soon. Socrates was born in such-and-such a year; the pyramids still exist today; and so forth. But truths or falsehoods about general notions such as those embodied in correct or incorrect definitions are timelessly true or timelessly false. Just as we cannot say that 49 used to be a square number or that equilateral triangles will shortly be equiangular, so we cannot say, truly or falsely, that fearlessness is now on the point of becoming, or used to be, indifference to recognized dangers. If this statement is true, it is eternally or, better, timelessly true. We can ask questions about fearlessness or the number 49 but not questions beginning "When?" or "How long?"

One over many. It is often the case that we can find or think of many so-and-so's or the so-and-so's, for example, of the numerous chimney pots over there or of the prime numbers between 10 and 100. Things, happenings, qualities, numbers, figures, can be ranged in sorts or characterized as sharing properties. Hence, where we speak of the so-and-so's—say, the storms that raged last week—we are talking of storms in the plural, and we are thereby showing that there is something, some *one* thing, that each of them was—namely, a *storm.* Or if there are twenty idle pupils, there is *one* thing that all twenty of them are—namely, *idle.* Sometimes we do not and even cannot know how many leaves, say, there are in a forest, and we may ask in vain, How many leaves are there? But however many or few there are, there must still be *one* thing—namely, *leaf*—which each of them is. It is one or singular; they are many or plural. We have not seen and may never see all or most of them. But *it,* that which each of them is, is in some way known to us before we could even begin to wonder how many leaves there are.

Intellectual knowledge. For our knowledge of, and our beliefs and opinions about the things, creatures and happenings of the everyday world, we depend upon our eyes, ears, noses and so on, and what our senses tell us is sometimes wrong and is never perfectly precise. There is nobody whose vision or hearing might not be even slightly better than it is. On the other hand, our apprehension of general notions is intellectual and not sensitive.

Conceptual certainties. Last, but not least in importance, dialectical debates are concerned only with general ideas, like those of fearlessness, goodness, danger and awareness. The answerer's thesis is a general proposition, such as "Virtue is (or is not) teachable" or "Justice is (or is not) what is to the advantage of the powerful." When such a thesis has been conclusively demolished, something, if only something negative, has been conclusively established about virtue or justice. In the domain of general ideas or concepts certainties, if seemingly negative certainties, are attainable by argument. About things or happenings in the everyday world no such purely ratiocinative knowledge is possible.

Ontology of Forms. Most of the above ways of characterizing general ideas or concepts had been brought out severally or together in Plato's elenctic dialogues. Yet his Socrates did not in these dialogues put forward the Theory of Forms. The Theory of Forms, as first fully developed in the *Phaedo*, is a unified formulation of these several points, but it is also more than this. For Plato now proffers an ontology of concepts. A general idea or concept, according to this new doctrine, is immutable, timeless, one over many, intellectually apprehensible and capable of precise definition at the end of a piece of pure ratiocination *because it is an independently existing real thing or entity*. As our everyday world contains people, trees, stones, planets, storms and harvests, so a second and superior, or transcendent world contains concept-objects. As "Socrates" and "Peloponnesus" name perceptible objects here, so "justice," "equality," "unity," and "similarity" name intellectually apprehensible objects there. Furthermore, as the human mind or soul gets into contact, though only perfunctory and imperfect contact, with ordinary things and happenings in this world by sight, hearing, touch and so on, so the human mind or soul can get into non-sensible contact with the ideal and eternal objects of the transcendent world. We are ephemerally at home here, but we are also lastingly at home there. The immortality of the soul is proved by our ability to apprehend the everlasting concept-objects that Plato often calls the Forms. For what reasons and from what intellectual motives did Plato take this big stride beyond anything that his Socrates of the elenctic dialogues had established about general notions or concepts?

It is often suggested that Plato derived his ontology of Forms from the following seductive, though erroneous, semantic considerations. All statements of truths and falsehoods, or at least the basic ones, can be analyzed into a subject of which something else is truly or falsely predicated and a predicate, or that which is truly or falsely predicated of that subject. As both the subject word of such a sentence and the predicate word or predicate phrase must be significant for the whole subject–predicate sentence to be significant, both this subject word ("Socrates," say) and the predicate word ("wise," say) must name, stand for or denote something. Now the name "Socrates" names or stands for the particular snub-nosed philosopher who died in 399 B.C. But the word "wise" names or stands for a spiritual quality which can be possessed or lacked by anyone at all of any date whatsoever. Wisdom, or what the word "wise" names or stands for, is an eternal or timeless entity and one in which the fifth-century man Socrates was just one temporary participant. He exemplified it for a time, but it was and is there to be exemplified, whether by Socrates or by anyone else, at all possible times.

It may be that Plato did unwittingly take for granted such a view of the anatomy of truths and falsehoods into subjects and predicates. But there is certainly a big anach-

ronism in the idea that Plato came to his Theory of Forms as a result of considering this semantic analysis. It is only in his late dialogues, the *Cratylus, Theaetetus* and especially the *Sophist,* that we find Plato inaugurating the analytical study of the structures of truths and falsehoods and the study of the grammatical parsing of Greek sentences. Here even the, to us, elementary distinction between nouns and verbs is, for the first time, being established by fairly complex arguments. The technical terminology of "subject and predicate" was the creation not of Plato but of Aristotle.

Rather, far from the Theory of Forms issuing out of the recognition of the subject–predicate structure of truths and falsehoods, this recognition seems to have been achieved only after the Theory of Forms had already been subjected to radical criticism. The task of distinguishing the subjects from the predicates of truths and falsehoods and the nouns from the verbs in sentences was undertaken partly in order to diagnose the ills from which the Theory of Forms had proved to be suffering. The theory that Socrates is one entity in this world and wisdom a second and separate entity in another world and that the former for a time "participates" in or "takes after" the latter came to grief partly because of the ambivalent nature of this bridge notion of "participating" or "taking after." It was because Plato did not and could not yet distinguish predicate expressions, like "is wise," from subject expressions, like "Socrates," that wisdom, say, seemed to be required to be an entity counterpart to, and existing separately from Socrates or anyone else who can be asserted to be or not to be wise. Plato did not deduce the Theory of Forms from the false premise that verbs and verb phrases function like extra nouns. Rather, it was because he had not and could not have thought about such semantic and grammatical matters that he was for a time unsuspicious of his independently based treatment of wisdom, say, and equality as transcendent things.

One consideration which certainly did move Plato in developing his ontology of Forms was that geometry and arithmetic were certainly sciences and sciences the certainties of which were higher than, or rather of an order different from the limited convincingness of the speculations of the natural scientists, such as the astronomers and the doctors. The lines, angles and areas, the numbers, equalities and ratios that we discover in our geometrical and arithmetical thinking are not particular penciled lines, sketched areas or assembled couples. When we prove that the two base angles of an isosceles triangle are equal, we are not finding out by more or less rough measurements that these two penciled angles are so nearly the same as to make no difference. Nor in calculating $7 \times 7 = 49$ are we finding out by more or less careful counting that the number of nuts or drops of water in this container matches the total number of nuts or drops of water that had previously been in those seven containers.

Geometry and arithmetic are sciences of the line, the angle, the area, number, the ratio and so on in abstraction from their more or less rough and unstable approximations in our penciled diagrams and manipulatable objects. A geometrical truth is true of, say, the base angles of all possible isosceles triangles. The objects of which geometry is the science are, in an essential way, general objects, or to put it in a later idiom, geometrical truths are unrestrictedly general truths embodying ideal limit concepts. Geometry and arithmetic are sciences, and what they are sciences of are realities exempt from the imprecisions and the instabilities that belong to the things and happenings of the everyday world.

Another consideration that influenced Plato was that in a dialectical disputation the questioner and answerer are concerned with such general notions or concepts as justice, friendship, beauty, unity, plurality, identity, pleasure and so on. Their debating about these notions requires extracting the implications and incompatibilities of truths or falsehoods embodying these concepts; and often, also, the testing and re-testing of various suggested definitions of such concepts. When a conclusive argument has been found, then something, even if only a negative something, has been established about one or more of the concepts operated on. Here too, as in a different way in mathematics, abstract truths are established with certainty by pure ratiocination. The conclusions of a dialectical argument seem consequently to be scientific conclusions; like theorems of mathematics, the conceptual points established by Socratic demolitions are of an unrestricted generality and of a precision unattainable by the most plausible findings of the observational sciences.

But if dialectic is, in this way, also a science, then, it seems, what it is the science of must also be realities or real things. As the would-be science of astronomy has the visible stars and planets for its objects, so the objects dealt with by the dialectician—namely, abstract concepts—must also be things in the real world, though in this case their real world is a transcendent world of timeless and purely intelligible entities.

The credentials of dialectic. It may be that Plato was considerably influenced by a special need to establish dialectic as an autonomous and paramount science. For the Theory of Forms appears in his dialogues so swiftly after his sudden divorce from the practice of elenctic disputation and the composition of elenctic dialogues that we may conjecture that this divorce was forced upon Plato against his will, and that he needed to justify the now ostracized practice of dialectic. He had to satisfy some of his fellow Athenians, but also to satisfy himself, that the Socratic Method was something much better than the youth-demoralizing game that its enemies took it to be. It was, rather, a science, with such a supremacy over the other sciences or would-be sciences that without it as their foundation they were without foundation. This hypothesis is partly borne out by the fact that the examples of Forms given in the middle period dialogues are nearly always concepts constantly operated on in actual dialectical debates. At this stage we hear little of the concepts of natural kinds, of kinds of artifacts, or of sensible qualities; that is, we hear little or nothing of the Forms of Dog, Tree, Silver or Water or, with one or two exceptions, of the Forms of Spade, Knife or Table or of the Forms of Green, Sour, Shrill or Rough. Only later did Plato see that the arguments for taking Justice, say, and Unity as Forms would establish Tree, Silver, Knife and Sour as Forms too. To start with, he was thinking, above all, of those concepts that must and do

get dialectical examination, as these other concepts do not. Socratic probings into the nature of Copper, say, or Elephant could get nowhere. It is for the metalworker and the zoologist to find out by experiment and observation what can be found out about such subjects. But Socratic probings do fix the boundaries between such concepts as virtue and knowledge or justice and skill.

It may be, therefore, that Plato's Theory of Forms was, in part, a defense of dialectic, which woefully needed defense. The partial parallels of geometry and arithmetic, which needed no such defense, were cited as providing collateral reinforcements for the defense of dialectic. As they were recognized sciences, so it was an unrecognized science. When dialectic was described in the *Republic* as "the coping-stone of the sciences," Plato was not just gratuitously complimenting his darling ratiocinative exercise; he was contrasting the intellectual homage which it deserved with the contempt and hostility with which his Athens actually treated it—and him. When Plato made Socrates sternly refuse participation in dialectic to his young guardians-to-be on the ground that early participation demoralizes its participants, we must suppose that Plato was being politic. His Academy would indeed forbid dialectic to its young students, but because Athens demanded this, not because Plato's heart endorsed this demand.

In his *Parmenides,* of perhaps a decade or more later, he makes Parmenides urge the youthful Socrates to take training in the dialectical exercise if he wishes to become a philosopher. The supposed risk of the young man's being demoralized goes unmentioned, just as in the early dialogues Socrates encourages lads to join in elenctic debates without any warnings of dangers to their morals.

Applications of the Theory. The Theory of Forms is put to an ancillary use in the *Republic,* Book VI, where Socrates is challenged to explain why he requires philosophers to rule the Ideal State, when in real life philosophers are notoriously devoid of worldly sagacity. Socrates concedes the depressing fact but claims that the true philosopher's apprehension of the Forms and especially of the Form of the Good is analogous to our vision of sunlit objects and of the sun itself. Cave dwellers, when first let out into the sunlight, are dazzled by the bright light, though they soon see more than ever before. Conversely, on their first return to their cave they are worse at discerning its dimly illuminated objects than are those who have never looked at anything lit by the rays of the sun. The intellect is subject to its counterparts of dazzlement and night blindness.

In Book X of the *Republic* the Theory of Forms is employed for another subsidiary task. Painters, actors, sculptors and dramatists are all producers of representations or "imitations." The picture of a tree is not itself a tree; the stage hero does not perform real acts of heroism. To this distinction between realities and representations of them there corresponds the distinction between the man who apprehends the realities and the man who attends only to the imitations—that is, between the philosopher and, say, the theatergoer. Truths about realities are not to be looked for in Homer or Euripides. This contrast of representation with reality is then given a further application. A painter may produce a likeness of the real bed that the carpenter manufactures. But the carpenter, in manufacturing beds, is in a supposedly analogous way "imitating" the concept of Bed. What he produces in wood is a good or a bad specimen of Bed. Socrates pretends that it stands to what it is a specimen of somewhat as the picture of a wooden bed stands to the actual bed. As the painter has to know things about the real bed if he is ever to try to produce a good likeness of it, so the carpenter has to know what a bed is if he is ever to try to make a good specimen of a bed. In the *Timaeus* God, the cosmic artificer, is similarly described as modeling the things in his new world after eternal or timeless thing-patterns.

For us, as for Aristotle, the cardinal task of the Theory of Forms is to answer the question How are Forms related to the particular things in our everyday world which partially or completely exemplify these Forms? But this question had not been the cardinal question for Plato at the start. Then, apparently, he had needed his separate world of concept-objects to give objectivity and autonomy to conceptual inquiries—that is, to dialectic. Only later did he come under pressure to reunite the conceptual with the factual, the other world with this world. Later still, in his *Sophist* and in *Parmenides*, Part I, he argues as forcibly as Aristotle against that very separateness of his concept-objects, which had, at the start, seemed requisite for the scientific primacy of conceptual inquiries.

PLATO AND NATURAL SCIENCE

Plato's own schooling can have contained no natural science, though he later read for himself books of Ionian cosmologists and he knew something of the contents of past and contemporary medical handbooks. He also picked up a little astronomy. He was better grounded in geometry and arithmetic, although we have no reasons for thinking that he was ever an original mathematician. His Academy became the main seedbed of original mathematicians, and Plato gave his support and blessing to their researches. But Theaetetus and Eudoxus were the teachers who instructed the new generation of mathematicians.

In the *Phaedo* Socrates is made to declare his personal renunciation of natural science and his resultant recourse to conceptual inquiries. With surprising inconsistency he almost concludes his conversation with an exposition of "someone's" geophysical theories about the spherical shape and internal structure of the earth, about its hydraulics and about the causes of volcanoes and earthquakes. Parts of this geophysics belong to a period well after the death of the real Socrates, so the passage is likely to record things that Plato himself had newly learned at about the time he completed the *Phaedo*. Socrates is careful to avoid saying that these geophysical ideas are his own. In the *Republic* the astronomy and harmonics prescribed for the education of the young guardians are to have no touch with stellar observation or with acoustic experiments. In a different context, also in the *Republic,* medical science is likewise treated very scathingly.

It is therefore a remarkable fact that by the time, whenever it was, that Plato wrote his *Timaeus,* his attitude toward natural science had been completely revolutionized. For the *Timaeus* is in large part a synoptic digest of contemporary Italian and Sicilian natural science. After an introductory story of creation, the allocution given by Timaeus, whose description is the description of Archytas of Tarentum, is devoted almost entirely to astronomy, theoretical chemistry, anatomy, physiology, pathology and the mechanism of sense perception. It is true that Timaeus does not claim for his doctrines anything higher than probability and that he professes that the study of nature is only a pastime. But Plato certainly intended his *Timaeus* to be used in the Academy for the instruction of students, and we know that Aristotle was in fact steeped in its scientific content. Aristotle does not treat very seriously its theology or cosmogony, but he takes very seriously and treats very critically such things as its geometrical atomism, anatomy, physiology and theory of visual perception.

Scholars disagree whether it was in the middle or at the end of his writing life that Plato composed the *Timaeus*. The view adopted here is that Plato composed the *Timaeus* during his second visit to Syracuse, in 367–366, that this was very shortly after he had composed the *Phaedo* and the political core of his *Republic;* and that Plato's *Philebus* and *Theaetetus* were written later than the *Timaeus* and contain echoes from it. But this is a minority view. The matter is of great importance. If the view here adopted is correct, Plato's later thinking differs drastically from his earlier thinking. In the *Phaedo* and the *Republic* knowledge or science is possible only of what belongs to the transcendent world of Forms, including the objects of pure mathematics. Of the mutable things and the dated happenings that constitute nature nothing better than opinion and conjecture is possible. Our world is one of mere semblances. But after Plato had learned what Archytas and Philistion had to teach, he no longer thought that knowledge of nature was unattainable and no longer thought that the temporariness of things and processes in our world was incompatible with our discovering truths about them. An important part of what is commonly meant by "Platonism" was not what Plato thought after the *Timaeus*. In the *Sophist* he argues explicitly against the "friends of the Forms" that temporal things and events are genuine realities—that is, that nothing prevents tensed truths from being perfectly true or certainly true. Plato may well have continued for some time to think that Forms are eternally or timelessly existing objects, but he no longer thinks of them as the only objects of which scientific knowledge is possible.

In the *Timaeus* itself Plato had defended the Theory of Forms, apparently against some of its critics, by the antithesis between what is known and what merely appears to be so-and-so, taking it that Forms and only Forms are accessible to knowledge and only to knowledge, while whatever exists or happens in our everyday world is a matter of mere belief or opinion. In the *Theaetetus* Plato argues conclusively that we can make mistakes about timeless objects like numbers and that we can know for certain truths about things and events in our everyday world. For example, the eyewitness to a crime, unlike the jurors, is not persuaded of what took place; he knows what took place.

In the *Philebus* Socrates is made to allow that as long as

knowledge of conceptual matters retains its primacy, subordinate inquiries can be admitted as authentic sciences. The reputed otherworldliness or epistemological utopianism of Plato really did belong to him when he wrote the *Phaedo* and the *Republic*. He is somewhat on the defensive about it in the earlier part of the *Timaeus*. If the *Timaeus* belongs to Plato's middle period, then after the *Timaeus*, and possibly because of its detailed, elaborate and copious exposition of Italian and Sicilian natural science, Plato ceases to think of this world as a place of unreliable semblances, in which the intellect of man is an exile, forever sick for its other home.

In the *Parmenides*, Part I, Plato deploys the young Socrates' arguments for, and the old Parmenides' arguments against the Theory of Forms. No student of the quality of the argumentation can doubt that Parmenides' arguments are Plato's arguments or that what Parmenides rejects is what Plato now rejects. Since the second part of the *Parmenides* is a protracted and highly scholastic exercise in two-way question–answer dialectic, we can take it that the veto on dialectic for the young men in the Academy has by now been lifted or forgotten. Plato no longer needs the Theory of Forms to vindicate dialectic against contempt and suppression; he no longer needs the Theory of Forms to represent genuine science against the unstable pretensions of the natural scientists. His own Academy, without Athenian hostility, now teaches dialectic, mathematics, astronomy, zoology and, most likely, anatomy and physiology. Utopia evaporates into a dream. The Academy of the late Plato is the Academy of the young Aristotle. The same air is breathed by both.

THEORY OF KNOWLEDGE AND LOGIC

In the early dialogues prior to the *Meno* problems in the theory of knowledge are hardly touched on, save for the recurrent question *Is virtue teachable?* and the ancillary question about the relation between possessing knowledge and possessing virtue. Here the puzzles canvassed are puzzles about the nature of virtue rather than about the natures of knowledge, learning and teaching.

In the *Meno* the situation changes. At one point, when Socrates wishes to investigate the nature of virtue, Meno puts forward a debater's teaser about investigations of any sort. If a man does not know something, how can his inquiry succeed? For he will not recognize whether what he arrives at is what he had been looking for. Alternatively, if he had known what he was looking for, he would not have needed to look for it. For example, if I do not know what 7×8 makes, then whatever number I get, I shall not recognize it for the required number; I cannot recognize 56 as the object of my search, since I searched in ignorance of this product. The conclusion of this obviously sophistical argument, if accepted, would show that it is never any use trying to find out anything. Neither thinking nor any other kind of investigation could possibly achieve its aim.

Doctrine of recollection. Socrates rejects this conclusion and argues for a positive doctrine about inquiry, thought and knowledge, the doctrine known as his doctrine of reminiscence or recollection. A slave boy who had been taught no geometry is cross-examined about a geometrical problem. To start with, the boy jumps to tempting but false answers. He is quickly satisfied that the answers are false and in the end comes out with the correct answer. Yet Socrates has told him nothing, but only asked him questions. In short, the boy thinks out a geometric truth that is new to him from considerations stimulated in him by Socrates' interrogations.

Socrates now argues that in some way this truth must already have been in the boy, since it was elicited from him by questions and not introduced into him by telling it to him. But if this geometrical truth was already in the boy and had not got into him by any new instruction in geometry, then he must have acquired it in a previous existence. It must have been latently in him when he was born—that is, innate. Socrates' questions served as reminders of things that the boy had known before but had forgotten in the passage from an earlier life to this life. Thus, an immortality of the soul is apparently proved, though not yet an eternal life after death or an endless series of lives after death, for it is only an eternal life or an endless series of lives preceding this life. This argument reappears in the *Phaedo*, now in association with the Theory of Forms, which had had no place in the *Meno*. The doctrine of recollection seems also to be alluded to in the *Phaedrus*.

How much does Socrates' argument prove? It certainly proves that if a slave boy, say, thinks out for himself a truth that no one has taught him, then this discovery was in some sense already "in" him. But in this sense a poet's compositions, a humorist's new jokes or an inventor's inventions were antecedently "in" their producers, for they possessed the intelligence and the equipment to compose new poems, make new jokes or invent new inventions. Today's poem was not previously lodged away, ready-made, inside the poet, like the seed inside a berry. What the poet possessed was the talent or ability, plus the vocabulary and the prosody, to compose new poems. In this sense of "in," the exploit of climbing this tree was "in" the strong and adventurous boy—namely, that he had it in him to climb it, that is, he possessed the requisite strength, dexterity and courage. So the slave boy had it in him to think out the solution to his geometrical problem because he possessed the intelligence, application and interest. That the solution was "in" him in any other way is not proved by Socrates' argument, which, in effect, reduces thinking something out to having one's memory refreshed, without any answer to the resultant question, How did it ever get into him, even in some previous life? But it cost Plato and especially Aristotle much intellectual effort to separate out the notions of ability, capacity and skill from the notions of performance, application and exercise. Only then was it possible to distinguish the qualities that must have been possessed by the slave boy for him to think out the solution from his being already in actual, though latent, possession of that solution.

Knowledge and opinion. Toward the end of the *Meno* Socrates, despairing of proving that virtue is teachable and is, consequently, a piece of knowledge, reminds Meno that in many daily affairs correct opinion, *doxa*, serves us just as well as knowledge. The guide who only thinks that this is the road to Larissa but is quite right gets us to Larissa as effectively as if he actually does know it. The defect of opinion, even when correct, is that, unlike knowledge, it can be shaken by criticism, conflicting evidence, authority, etc. This opposition of knowledge to opinion, even to correct opinion, is of great importance. Much of Plato's *Theaetetus* is given up to the discussion of the antithesis. For the moment it is necessary to point out that *doxa* covers a good deal more than our "opinion." It includes any case of something seeming or appearing. The seeming convergence of the receding railway lines would be a case of *doxa*, as well as its seeming that the earth is flat, that $7 \times 8 = 54$, or that this is the road to Larissa.

It is in the *Phaedo* that we first find Plato systematically contrasting intellectual apprehension with sense perception, knowledge of what is exact and timeless with the temporary and imprecise deliverances of our senses, the true and permanent home of the philosopher with the temporary habitat of sense-tethered men. Here we get the opposition between the equalities established in, say, geometry and the more or less rough approximations toward equality that are exhibited by our wooden sticks or our tape measures. In assessing this quantity as approximately the same as that one we are applying the ideal limit of absolute sameness of quantity. This absolute standard is prior to its rough approximations. It is what these approximate toward or diverge from. Soul and body, reason and sense, ideal limit and approximation, eternal and ephemeral, sunshine and twilight, heaven and earth, knowledge and opinion, reality and semblance, invisible and visible, imperishable and perishable, divine and earthy—all these dualities are one duality. The philosopher who dies in an Athenian prison this morning lives in the other world not only forever after but already. The true objects of his pure thought had never been on this earth.

There is no great difference on these matters between the *Phaedo* and the *Republic*, especially Book VI. At this stage Plato's need is to distinguish or separate the ideal from the actual, the intelligible from the sensible, thought from sense perception, the measure from the things measured. He needs to establish that there is a separate world, of the realities of which philosophy and mathematics are the sciences. Only later does he feel the need to reunite the other world to this world by, among other things, considering how thought and sense perception can and sometimes must cooperate if our mundane inquiries are to result in new knowledge. The very crevasse between Forms and particulars, between the one and the many, between the objects of knowledge and those of *doxa*, which had been opened in order to ensure the autonomy of reason and the separateness of its proper objects, later had to be bridged in order to make communications possible; for example, to make nature amenable to science.

Teleology. At one stage in the *Phaedo* Socrates recounts how, after having for a time been fascinated by the speculations of the cosmologists, he had come to renounce, for his purposes, their causal or mechanical explanations. The explanations that he required were teleological explanations, answers to the question, What for? and not to the questions, Owing to what? and By means of what? It is not clear that he thinks that mechanical explanations fail to explain anything. In the *Timaeus* they are allowed to be genuine explanations, but only auxiliaries to the ultimate explanation. There is no sign that Plato rejects such auxiliary explanations merely on the grounds that they are still purely speculative and unproved. Least of all is Socrates in the *Phaedo* forswearing explanations of what is temporal or this-worldly on the grounds that such things are not worthy or susceptible of explanation; for he contrasts a mechanical with a teleological explanation of his own recent decision to stay in prison and die. Rather, it seems that Socrates is telling why he himself had preferred to concentrate on conceptual or perhaps dialectical problems, above all, those hinging on concepts of value. Ultimate explanations must be answers to the question, What is the good of it?

Theory of the sciences. The *Republic*, Book VII, moves beyond the *Phaedo* in developing not so much a theory of knowledge as a theory of the sciences. The education prescribed for the young guardians-to-be, which reflects the initial curriculum of Plato's own Academy, is a training in mathematics, harmonics and astronomy. Harmonics and astronomy, however, are to be studied as branches of pure theory, without recourse to acoustic experiments or to stellar observations. Although, before they reach the age of 30, the students are forbidden to take part in dialectic, still dialectic is the "coping-stone of the sciences." Even the purely theoretical sciences of arithmetic and geometry remain merely provisional or hypothetical until dialectic gives its guarantee to their postulates or so-called axioms. These sciences, at present, rest only on "hypotheses" or "sub-theses," and their conclusions are necessarily insecure as long as their starting points are insecure. Only dialectic can make these secure, by trying to test them to destruction.

In the *Timaeus* the Theory of Forms is briefly stated and championed, apparently against some skeptics. The case for the theory here rests wholly on the antithesis between knowledge or reason and true opinion. This distinction is made to derive from the differences between the timeless and immutable objects of knowledge and the short-lived objects of sense-given opinion.

The *Timaeus* seems to have been used in the Academy as a basic textbook of natural science and to have been written for this end. As one part of it gives the results of observational astronomy and other parts the results of anatomical dissections, both probably learned by Plato from the scientists of Italy and Sicily, his strictures on the senses as incapable of yielding teachable knowledge must by now have been attended by some mental qualifications. He could not consistently have believed both that no teachable truths about nature existed and that, among other subjects, human anatomy could and should be taught out of his own *Timaeus* to the young Aristotles in his Academy.

Knowledge in the "Theaetetus." Plato's *Theaetetus* is a head-on inquiry into the notion of knowledge. It begins with a destructive examination of the theory that knowledge is sense perception, that is, that to know something is to be in receipt of a deliverance from the eyes, the ears, the nose, etc. It is not being debated whether human knowledge requires or depends on the receipt of these deliverances but whether knowing just amounts to such receipt. Socrates is not out to establish that we could know some things, or all knowable things, even though deprived of sight, hearing, touch and the rest, but only that knowing things is more than getting sensations. Among several powerful arguments, Socrates produces a conclusive refutation of the theory that knowing something is simply equivalent to having a sensation. What I have found out, he argues, I continue to know until I forget. I can know that there was a noise when my hearing of the noise is over. So I now know this truth, though I can no longer hear the noise. Knowing the truth about the noise is therefore not equivalent to hearing it, since the former continues to exist when the latter has ceased to exist. To know something is to retain what has been got, and this retaining cannot be equated with this getting, though it presupposes it. Correspondingly, an expert may know how something is going to taste, feel or sound. He knows this future-tense truth before he sees or hears the thing foretold. If the knowing exists already when the seeing or hearing has not yet occurred, then the knowing cannot be identified with the seeing or hearing, or else the date of the one would be the date of the other.

Socrates now establishes a positive or constructive point. When I find out something by using my eyes, ears or tongue, and even when, on using my eyes, ears or tongue, it just seems to me that something is the case, what I have come to know, or even merely surmise, always embodies some element or feature other than the colors, noises and tastes that my senses present to me. For example, I know or surmise that one thing is similar in color to another; or that one noise is shriller than, and therefore not identical with another; or I know or surmise that there are two or several specks of red or only one speck; or I know or surmise that something exists now, has existed or will still exist; or that something else is not occurring, has not occurred yet, but will shortly occur. But these elements or features conveyed by "similar," "identical," "single," "several," "two," "exist," "not occur," "was," "will" and others are not, like colors, sight-given as opposed to taste-given or, like noises, heard as opposed to smelled. They are not proprietary to any one particular sense. They are neutral as between the different senses. There is not one of them of which a man blind or deaf from birth is therefore uncognizant. Though unable to see or hear, he is, unless also a moron, cognizant of these non-proprietary, or "common," elements because he can think. They are thought-given, not sense-given. Value notions, like good, beautiful, and just seem to be, in the same way, "common" or sense-neutral. It follows that our knowledge even about what is visible, tangible or audible demands intelligence as well as eyesight, hearing, etc. Thus knowledge or opinion is the product of thought in cooperation with sense perception. So on this score too, bare sensing does not amount to knowledge. Our knowings, supposings, surmisings, our recognizings and even our misrecognizings must contain the element of the thinking of thoughts.

Thought. What then is thinking? This question is now explicitly posed. The young Theaetetus, abandoning the equation of knowing with sensing, suggests instead that knowing should be equated with thinking—or rather, since thinking can be mistaken, that knowing should be equated with unmistaken thinking or correct thinking. Patently, a person who knows that something is the case is not mistaken, or else he could not be said to know.

Socrates postpones discussing this new equation in its own right. He first discusses very exhaustively the interim question. How is mistaken thinking possible? The difficulty is this. The things that we see, touch, hear, eat, hold, meet and carry are there to be seen, carried, etc. But if, perhaps in a fog, I misidentify Theaetetus as Theodorus, this identity of Theaetetus with Theodorus is *not* there, since they are really two different people. So what I mistakenly think is not there for me to think it. Yet I cannot be thinking nothing. Indeed, if you, in the same fog, misidentify Theaetetus as Socrates, your mistake is a different mistake from mine. You think something different from what I think, yet neither the something that you think nor the something different that I think is there to be thought, since the identity of Theaetetus with Socrates is no more really there than is his identity with Theodorus. Similarly, if my memory is at fault, the event I misremember did not happen. So, it seems, this event, which is what I misremember, did not occur—and how can an event be without occurrence?

A person who knows neither Theodorus nor Theaetetus, or who knows one but not the other, cannot misidentify either as the other. If he does know both, he knows that they are different people and so are not one and the same person. He cannot then think the thought "Theaetetus and Theodorus are one and the same person." Yet, in a fog, he may very well think "That man yonder [who is actually Theaetetus] is Theodorus." The relative clause in the square brackets is not his rider, but ours.

Similarly, the child may very well think that $7 \times 8 = 54$ [though it actually is 56]; so he thinks that the product of 7 and 8 [which in fact is 56] is 54, without thinking, what he could not think, that the number 54 is the number 56. Again, I may not know who it is that is yonder in the fog, although I do know the man Theodorus [who is actually over there]. Thus I can mistakenly think that the man over there is Theaetetus, whom I know, when it is really Theodorus, whom I also know. In making this mistake, I am not thinking that Theodorus is Theaetetus, but that the man yonder [who is really Theodorus] is Theaetetus. In retrospect I shall never say, "I thought that Theaetetus was Theodorus," but only, "I mistakenly thought that the man looming out of the fog was Theaetetus, but to my surprise it now turns out that he was Theodorus." This sort of misidentification is possible and common, but it is quite a different sort of misidentification from the impossible one, easily confused with the first, namely, thinking that Theaetetus, whom I know, and Theodorus, whom I know, are the same person or that the number 54 is the number 56.

Socrates sees that underlying his question What is it to think falsely? or How can a person mistake something for what it is not? there is this perfectly general feature of thinking, whether correct or mistaken thinking: to think is to have an answer, correct or incorrect, to a question; the verbal expression of a thought must be a complete sentence. What I think is that this is the road to Larissa or that the product of 7 and 8 is 54. This already weakens the early argument that as what I see, hear, eat or carry must be there for me to see it, etc., then what I think must be there for me to think it. For what I see or eat is a thing, and what I hear or remember may be a happening. But what I think is not a thing or a happening; it is a truth or a falsehood about one or more things or happenings. I can meet or hear Theodorus, but I cannot think *him*, but only *that* he is approaching through the fog or *that* he is not a mathematician, etc.

Suppose that you and I both see a man in a fog, and you say and think correctly that it is Theaetetus while I say and think incorrectly that it is Theodorus. Then, in some way, Theodorus seems to have got into my words and my thought instead of Theaetetus. I have made some sort of inadvertent swap or substitution of Theodorus, who ought not to be there, for Theaetetus, who ought, though necessarily I know that they are different persons. I have jumbled them in my thought but not, of course, thought them to be identical with one another. Socrates deploys in great detail impossibilities and difficulties in this initially tempting theory of mistakes, namely, that in saying or thinking something false we somehow substitute one person or one thing for another person or thing. Socrates seems here to be testing to destruction a view about what was later to be labeled the subject–predicate structure of true and false statements, and therewith of correct and incorrect thoughts, the view, namely, that just as the subject expression in an elementary statement stands for or names a person or an animal or a thing, etc., so its predicate expression stands for or names a second person or thing or animal, etc. He does not even mention here what he had mentioned in the *Cratylus* and analyzes in the *Sophist,* that is, statements of which the predicates are verbs, like "runs" and "flew," which no one could take to be the names of particular persons, animals or things. In the *Theaetetus* he operates almost wholly with false or true statements of the pattern "That man yonder is Theodorus," "The sum of 7 and 5 is the number 11." In his so-called "dream" he expounds the theory that a statement, true or false, is a combination of the names of the basic elements of which reality consists, though in the preceding and succeeding dialogues an elementary statement is a combination, not of two names, but of a name with a verb or a verb phrase. Such a verb or verb phrase is, in the *Sophist,* rightly denied to function as the name of anything.

In the *Theaetetus,* therefore, Plato rightly argues that knowledge requires thinking; that thoughts, with the statements of them, can be false as well as true; that false thoughts are *not* thoughts of two different things, or persons, etc., treated as the same thing or person, etc.; that in a false thought about a real thing or person what is wrong is not any sort of a substitution of one thing or person for another different thing or person, that is, by implication, predicate expressions, unlike subject expressions, are not also names of things or persons, etc.

True belief plus a "logos." When the discussion at last reverts to the original question What is knowledge? it is quickly shown that knowledge is not to be equated, as Theaetetus had suggested, with correct opinion. The jurors may be persuaded of truths about an event that they have not witnessed. The eyewitness knows what happened, but they do not know it, but only believe correctly that what he reports to them did happen. So knowing is not the same as correctly believing. It is now suggested that knowledge must be not just true belief, but true belief *plus* something

else, namely, a *logos.* It is soon shown that "*logos*" has many different senses and that in three of its senses, which are not its only senses, possession of a *logos* is not enough to entitle a person who believes something and is right, to claim that he knows it. The original question What is knowledge? does not get its final answer—and, incidentally, it has not got it yet.

Theory of meaning in the "Sophist." In the succeeding dialogue, the *Sophist,* the central question discussed belongs not to the theory of knowledge but to logic, or rather, to a part of the theory of meaning that is prefatory to logical inquiries proper. For Plato is now explicitly considering, side by side, questions about the grammatical structures of sentences conveying elementary truths or falsehoods, and the structures of those truths and falsehoods themselves. In an elementary statement, like "Theaetetus is flying," the nominative expression names or denotes a particular person or thing, but the predicate expression, in this case the verb, cannot possibly be doing this, since a sequence of two names, like "Theaetetus – Theodorus," says nothing, true or false. It merely lists two persons. For a sentence to say something true or false about Theaetetus, its predicate expression, say, the verb, must convey something that Theaetetus is or is doing or is undergoing. Moreover, the verb is tensed. It conveys what Theaetetus was doing or will be undergoing or is now looking like, etc. Finally, a sentence like "Theaetetus is (or was) flying" says something true or else, as in this instance, something false which can be negated. "Not" can be attached to the predicate expression, as it cannot be attached to the subject expression. If a falsehood is negated, as in "Theaetetus was not flying," a truth results and *vice versa.*

The central problem of the philosophical core of this dialogue is the problem, How can a statement to the effect that something is *not* the case be a true statement and, therefore, one which says what *is* the case? How can it really *be* the case that Theaetetus is not flying, when his *not flying* seems to be an example of something *not* being done by Theaetetus? Yet even to word the issue in this way is to take part of the heart out of the puzzle as it existed at Plato's time. Its natural formulation then was, How can we tell or think what *is not?* or How can we tell or think something that *is not?* For surely there cannot be, that is, exist, non-existent somethings. We cannot eat or see or carry an apple that is not there, so how can we tell or think what is not? This question can be taken as asking how we can significantly assert or believe something *false;* or it can be taken as asking how we can significantly assert or believe a *negative* proposition, true or false. Plato moves from a discussion of the former issue to a discussion of the latter one, which underlies the former. The Eleatic thinker, Parmenides, had set the problem to which Plato's *Sophist* gives at least a big part of the correct answer. For Parmenides the problem was this: Since what is not, is not anything, it is not to be thought about or mentioned; so there can be no thought or statement that not so-and-so. No truth or falsehood can be negative. What is not cannot be what I think or declare, since it cannot be anything at all. Obviously even these statements of Parmenides' doctrine, being themselves negative, come under their own proscription.

Plato shows that this proscription is self-destroying by

this shrewd argument. To say anything at all about that which *is* not, or about things that *are* not, is to speak either in the singular or in the plural. But then there must *be* one or more than one of what are spoken of in the singular or the plural. Yet we cannot *not* use the singular or the plural; so we cannot even say, with Parmenides, that that which is not is unthinkable or that things which are not cannot be spoken of. Parmenides' problem has therefore to be reformulated. How can we think or say about something or some things that it is or they are not so-and-so? The problem is not the unstatable problem, How can there be negative things? It is rather, How can things be truly or falsely denied to be so-and-so? In Aristotelian parlance, "not" cannot be attached to the subject of a truth or falsehood; but it can be attached to what is predicated of that subject. We can say truly of Theaetetus that he is not flying or falsely of him that he is not sitting. What we cannot do is say anything at all about not-Theaetetus or un-Theaetetus. Statements can be negative, though their subject names cannot. So the authentic problem is, What is it to deny or to affirm something, truly or falsely, of, say, Theaetetus? It is at once clear that the part of the sentence by which something is affirmed or denied or even asked of a named subject cannot itself be a second subject name. To affirm or deny something of Theaetetus is not to affirm or deny some *thing,* but that he is or is not so-and-so. A proposition is not a conjoining of two named subjects. This is made very clear by examples of elementary propositions of which the predicate is a tensed verb, as in "Theaetetus was (or is) sitting." It is just because the contribution of the verb to the proposition is entirely different from the contribution of its subject name that we can, for example, say that Theaetetus is *not* flying, without entrapping ourselves in the Parmenidean idea that we are thereby mentioning an un-thing or a not-person.

In his very abstract and intricate discussion of the "highest kinds" Plato seems to be developing a positive answer to the ensuing question, What is it to attach a negated verb or predicate to a subject? The somethings that verbs convey belong to one or other of a set of "families," so that to deny something of Theaetetus is thereby positively to ascribe to him some other member of the family to which the negated something belongs. If Theaetetus is *not* a fish, then there is something else in the family of fish-or-bird-or-man, etc., that he *is.* The denial of one predicate entails the affirmation of some other "brother" predicate and *vice versa.* Negative truths are the obverses of affirmative truths and *vice versa.* Negativeness, far from being the death of thought and statement, is an essential part of their daily lives.

Here then we find Plato investigating the bi-polar structures of integral truths and falsehoods. He is no longer spellbound by the idea of special entities, such as the concept-objects, or Forms, of his earlier days. Indeed in one passage in the dialogue he seems to hold himself aloof from the "friends of the Forms," whom he criticizes for their reluctance to concede the reality of any objects other than their timeless concept-objects. Doubtless one thing that moved Plato in this new direction was the impotence of the Theory of Forms to cope with Parmenides' difficulties with negation. For if there cannot be negative things, there cannot be negative concept-objects either. But then

there would be no place in the reality constituted by these concept-objects for not being so-and-so; and consequently no negative truths, and therewith no affirmative truths, could be known or thought or stated about even these concept-objects themselves. Only if verbs or predicates are *not* names, even of concept-objects, can truth and falsehood, affirmation and negation, knowledge and opinion be accounted for. The road is now opened for Aristotle's inquiries into the implications and non-implications of truths by other truths.

MORAL AND POLITICAL THEORY

The dialogues of Plato's first period often have ethical subjects for their disputation themes. Sometimes, as in the *Laches* and *Charmides,* Socrates demolishes a succession of attempted definitions of moral virtues, for example, of courage and self-control. Sometimes, as in the *Protagoras* and *Meno,* Socrates discusses the thesis that virtue can be taught. But the subject of the *Lysis* is friendship, that of the *Hippias Major* is beauty, while the *Gorgias* is concerned with the nature and worth of rhetoric. These themes are not ethical.

As the finale of an elenctic debate is a confutation, a dialogue exhibiting the Socratic Method in action cannot yield a positive theory. It is often said that in these dialogues Socrates is made to teach the doctrine that virtue is knowledge. But in the *Protagoras* and *Meno* Socrates argues against this equation. For knowledge is what can be taught; so if virtue cannot be taught, it is not knowledge. Elsewhere, as in the *Euthydemus,* Socrates does argue in the other direction.

In the *Gorgias* the young interlocutor, Polus, champions the sub-thesis that it is better to do wrong than to suffer it, and Socrates duly confutes this sub-thesis. In the *Protagoras* Socrates had, to our surprise, argued for a hedonistic calculus, like that of Bentham, but in the *Gorgias* and the much later *Philebus* his arguments are anti-hedonistic. It is in the *Republic* that Plato first puts forward a constructive ethical theory. A dominant theme of the *Republic* is the nature and worth of justice. In Book I, which is of the familiar elenctic pattern, some cynical views are defended by the sophist Thrasymachus and are duly confuted, though some of Socrates' argumentative tactics leave us uneasy. In the remainder of the *Republic* there is almost no questioner–answerer disputation; instead Plato makes Socrates give a positive definition of justice. He defines it, as self-control had been defined in the *Charmides,* as "the performance of one's proper function"—almost as "minding one's own business."

Structure of the soul. Socrates builds up a description of the constitution of the human soul paralleling his description of the constitution of the Ideal State. As the Ideal State is a coordination or integration of three different classes, each with its own economic and political role, so the soul is an integration of three different parts or elements, each with a role proper to it in the conduct of personal life. All people have in them the appetitive or impulsive element, the element of thought or reason, and, between these two, an element capable of curbing impulses and cravings and capable also of taking orders from thought or reason. The name of the in-between element, *thumos,* is sometimes unsatisfactorily rendered by "anger," sometimes by "spirit" (in the sense in which a horse may be spirited). This tripartite structure of the individual soul matches, and not by accident, the tripartite structure of the Ideal State in which the auxiliaries—the soldier-police—keep the lowest class in order and are themselves subject to the direction of the educated governors or kings.

Justice and happiness. This political model gives Plato a sort of psychological schema for the conflicts and the controls which form the content of the moral life. Just as in his political thinking Plato sometimes treats the working class as a deplorable necessity, so in his ethical thinking he is inclined to treat our impulses and desires in similar fashion. "Desire" and "pleasure," like our term "passions," are often used as terms of abuse, as if the ideal life, if we could only attain it, would be purged of these anti-rational forces. His theory, however, does not require this hyper-puritanism. That a man should not be a mere weathercock to his fears, likings and hankerings does not entail that ideally he should be screened from them. Though gales may sink the ill-rigged or ill-steered sailing ship, no ship can sail without winds. Winds can be too weak as well as too strong.

Still applying his model of the Ideal State, Plato is now able to reach the ethical conclusion that as political well-being requires the regulated cooperation of its three classes, so personal well-being requires the rationally coordinated functioning of the soul's three parts or elements. This coordination of different functions, that is, justice, is not merely a means to a good life, which might, with luck, be had without it. The functionings of these parts or elements, in their proper coordination, are what constitute well-being—somewhat as harmony is not something that just happens to be necessary for music; it is the relation between the notes without which there would be no music.

Pleasure. Of great psychological as well as ethical interest are Plato's frequent discussions of the worth and nature of pleasure. In the *Protagoras* Socrates champions, with apparent seriousness, a hedonistic calculus according to which the goodness of anything reduces to the long-term excess of the pleasures over the pains that it causes. In this view, no pleasure could itself be bad; it could only be inferior to a greater or a more enduring pleasure. Yet in the *Gorgias* Socrates argues that some pleasures are not merely relatively inferior but are absolutely bad. In the *Republic, Timaeus* and *Philebus* Plato gives an account of what pleasure is. With his eye on the pleasantness of various kinds of replenishment and recuperation, like eating when hungry and resting when tired, Plato argues that, with certain reservations, pleasure *is* the process of being restored to a "natural" condition. Aristotle frequently criticizes this definition.

Partly, though not entirely, on the basis of this definition Plato, in his *Philebus,* argues that the place of pleasure in the best life, far from being paramount, is inferior and subordinate to the place of thought and knowledge. Neither is all-sufficient, but the contribution of pleasure is a lot lower on the scale than that of thought and knowledge. One reason for its relatively lowly placing is derived from the doctrine of the limit and the unlimited, the *peras* and

the *apeiron.* Some things, like temperature and weight, admit of continuous quantitative variation, in the sense that for a thing of any particular weight there are or might be things of greater and lesser weights. On the other hand, there are no degrees of such notions as one ton or seven pounds. The precise "How heavy?" of a thing fixes it at a determinate point on the scale of heavier–lighter. There is no more-or-less of this determinate weight. Impulses, desires, feelings, pleasure and pain are like weight or temperature. Things can give us more or less pleasure or pain, and we can be very or slightly scared or angry. If for a person in a particular situation there is a proper determinate degree of an impulse or a feeling, this determinate degree has to be fixed by some standard outside that variably intense impulse or feeling itself. Nor can the scale of temperature by itself determine which point on that scale is the right temperature for this or that end, for example, for baking bread or for bodily health or comfort. It is from this application of the general theory of the limit and the unlimited that Aristotle's doctrine of the mean is developed. Of course, the general theory of the limit and the unlimited has applications in fields quite remote from the special field of ethics. It is, for example, largely in terms of the two polar notions of the limit and the unlimited that Aristotle tries to refute Zeno's seeming proofs of the impossibility of motion.

However, for what concerns us here, Plato tries to show that the place of pleasure is lower than that of thought and knowledge, since the right "How much?" is fixed by thought and knowledge for, *inter alia,* pleasure. At the end of the *Philebus* Plato attempts to describe the Good, or what constitutes the best life, in terms of such notions as truth, beauty, measure, harmony, proportion and order. The description remains somewhat nebulous, but it is interesting in suggesting that Plato, like ourselves, has found that his earlier parallel accounts of the Ideal State and of the individual soul in terms of a coordinated division of labor had been inadequate. Regulated departmentalization may be a necessary, but it is not a sufficient condition of the best life.

Politics. We can be reasonably sure that for some period during his younger days Plato had not only had political ambitions but had also tried to engage in active politics. The triumph of the popular party shut the door on Plato's hopes and plans, and henceforth his unabating and often vitriolic opposition to the democratic cause had to be literary and pedagogic. The dialogues of his first period are almost entirely unpolitical, save for the finale of his *Gorgias,* his *Crito,* and some incidental animadversions, for example in the *Meno,* on Pericles and Periclean democracy. It is in his two mammoth dialogues, the *Republic* and the *Laws,* together with his *Politicus,* that we find Plato's political diagnoses and prescriptions, ideals and antipathies.

The Ideal State: the "Republic." In the *Republic,* and especially in the political core of Books II–V, Plato delineates his famous Ideal State, or "Callipolis." Starting from the elementary but developing economy of a normal rustic community, Plato moves on to design a full-fledged city-state, the like of which has never yet existed and may never exist in the future, though some of its features are borrowed from the constitution of Sparta. Applying the economic principle of the division of labor, Plato sets up in his utopia three classes: the guardians, or ruling class; the auxiliary class; and the laborers. Most of Plato's recommendations concern only the ruling class, i.e., the governors and their auxiliaries, the police-soldiers. Its members, women as well as men, possess complete political authority, in return for which they live a garrison life, with no private property and not even private families. Their posterity is arranged for on stud lines. The other members of the state have no say in its government and are not entitled to its higher education. Their whole mission is to be farmers and artisans, but, significantly, not sailors. The guardians are trained and employed for external warfare and internal police work, but not only for these functions. Unlike the rulers in Sparta, its rulers have to go through a grueling intellectual training, resulting, at least for the select few, in their becoming philosophers. The Ideal State depends both for its creation and for its preservation upon its kings' being philosophers or philosophers' being its kings. For they know and only they know wherein the public weal consists.

The Ideal State is therefore, constitutionally, a rigid aristocracy of power, intellect and breeding but not of estates or families. No provisions are made for any reforms being made to this constitution after its creation. It is of its *raison d'être* to be static and immutable. It is therefore disheartening to hear, in Books VIII and IX, that even this supposedly self-perpetuating aristocracy is doomed by some numerological mystery eventually to degenerate through plutocracy into democracy and tyranny. Apparently in these books Plato was thinking not so much of his dream constitution as of actual contemporary Greek states, although, as Aristotle proves in his *Politics,* it was not true in fact that democracies always declined into tyrannies or that tyrannies never emerged out of plutocracies or aristocracies. Presumably Plato's account of the single-track course of this inevitable degeneration was minatory in intent rather than diagnostic or prophetic. It was certainly not utopian.

Since Plato himself tells us in *Republic* VI that philosophers are generally held to be politically useless or even politically harmful, and since the Athenian aristocratic families had long since lost their powers, privileges, and very often their wealth, it is hard to suppose that Plato even hoped that his plan for his Ideal State would make any difference to the actual course of politics in Athens. So little is said in the *Republic* of the lives to be led by *hoi polloi* in Callipolis that Plato could not have been trying to attract the Athenian demos to his elite-governed model state. It is a relevant fact that in the whole of the *Republic* nothing is said of fleets or sailors forming any part of the war strength of the Ideal State. The guardians have had soldiers' training. They include no admirals, and Callipolis has no Piraeus.

Was the *Republic* no more than the compensation dream of a politically thwarted aristocrat who happened to be in love with philosophy? Or did Plato write his *Republic* to interest and in some degree to influence some state in which the great families were still dominant? Certain clues suggest that the *Republic*, or rather the political gist of

Books II–V, had originally been composed for delivery in Syracuse. In the conversational opening of the *Timaeus* Socrates gives his companions, of whom one is a Sicilian and another an Italian, a précis of a discourse that he had given on the previous day. This is a précis of the section of the *Republic* that has just been mentioned. Socrates' précis is then followed by the preamble to the unfinished *Critias*, which was to give the history of a war, "9,000 years ago," between Hellas, headed by Athens, and Atlantis. The description of Atlantis is an only slightly romanticized description of Carthage, against whose eastward expansion Syracuse, under Dionysius the Elder and his son, was the sole bulwark for the western Greeks.

Both Socrates' précis, and the preamble to the *Critias* are tacked, quite incongruously, on to the *Timaeus*, a cosmological and physiological address which we have independent reasons for thinking was composed by Plato in Syracuse in 367–366 and delivered before Dionysius the Younger near the end of Plato's sojourn in Syracuse. According to this interpretation the *Republic* would contain a positive political message—namely, that the Sicilian elite should preserve its dominance by giving up its possessions and eliminating its inter-family feuds and becoming instead an order or brotherhood of soldier-philosophers.

Plato vaults rather cavalierly from the economic principle that productive efficiency is maximized by coordinated specialization to the quite different principles (a) that each individual person is constituted by nature to perform just one social and economic role and not another; and (b) that people's souls are, in an analogous way, microcosms composed of parts or elements, each having its own natural function or role. Both political and individual well-being depend on the proper coordination of these constitutionally different roles. A society is healthy when each of its classes performs its peculiar function; and a soul or person is, so to speak, properly self-governed when each of its parts makes its peculiar contribution to its microcosmic commonwealth, without trespassing on the domains of the other parts. What his reason is to a man at his best, the guardians are to the Ideal State. Both individuals and states are organic wholes, and their parts stand to these wholes somewhat as the several organs of a creature stand to that creature—or rather as they stand if and only if all is internally well with it. This semi-biological view of the body politic is apt to appeal less to those who are told that they are constituted by nature to be only the body's thews or feet than to those who are assured that their role is that of the body's eyes or brain.

The avowed object of the *Republic* as a whole is to exhibit the nature of justice, both within the state and within the individual soul. Socrates undertakes the task of proving that justice is no mere means to well-being, as regular exercise is to health. It is, rather, an essential part of well-being. The man who thinks that if there were no risks of punishment or other ill consequences, he would choose to be unjust, shows that he does not realize that the idea of well-being without justice is like the idea, not of health without exercise, but of health without vigor. The elucidation of the concept of justice in terms of the coordination of specialized functions is meant both to give support to and to get support from the partly independent idea that in the Ideal State there would be three sharply demarcated classes of citizens, which in their disciplined coordination would render that state economically efficient, strong in war and safe from revolutions.

The "Laws." Plato's Ideal State is a fairyland model rather than a plan. His *Laws*, on the contrary, is a would-be practicable plan. Under this "second-best" constitution the elite may possess modest estates, and private families are allowed. The lower ranks of society now have some political rights and powers, though careful regulations ensure that they will not attain political control. The rulers, though decently educated, are not required to be philosophers. The women are not warriors. Much of the *Laws* is a sort of Blue Book, in which detailed rules and regulations are laid down for the conduct of elections, legal proceedings, religious ceremonies, markets, schools and irrigation. Even the regimen of pregnant mothers and the games of infants are all but ordained. Comparatively few general issues of political theory are discussed. As a whole the *Laws* is a piece of detailed programmatic legislation. As its spokesman declares that the polity that he is to design is only second best to the Ideal State, scholars have naturally tended to concentrate their attention on the more utopian of the two schemes.

Early in the *Laws* the discussion leader had surprised his interlocutors and us by asserting, in the teeth of Books VIII and IX of the *Republic*, that for the realization of his planned polity there was required the conjunction of a great legislator and a good tyrant. This, with some corroborative clues, suggests that Plato wrote his *Laws* for practical adoption by Dionysius the Younger and that he may have been invited or encouraged by the young tyrant to do so. If so, the defeat of Dionysius by Dion in 356 made this legislative program a dead letter. Plato's uncompleted conversationalization of the *Laws* may have been intended to salvage as literature a work which had been composed as a realizable constitutional blueprint.

The *Laws*, outside Book X, is not even intended for philosophers. In its concrete legal, social and administrative prescriptions, however, students of Greek history and politics can find a good deal of interest. For inevitably Plato sometimes copies and often just improves on laws, regulations, codes, customs and expedients already obtaining in Athens or other Greek states. Political actualities can be read through Plato's political recommendations. Plato's limitations as a political theorist can be detected in his unquestioning retention, in principle if not in detail, of Greek ways which do not seem to us necessary conditions of social and political life. The state that Plato is designing is still a city-state. That the heyday of the city-state was already over was never dreamed by Plato, any more than it was by Aristotle. No modern statesman or political theorist would suggest remodeling Canada, say, or Russia or Ghana according to the prescriptions of the *Laws*—or even, retrospectively, Macedon or Rome.

PLATO AS A WRITER

Greek prose reached its peak in the writing of Plato. His flexibility, his rich vocabulary, his easy colloquialism and his high rhetoric, his humor, irony, pathos, gravity, bluntness, delicacy and occasional ferocity, his mastery of metaphor, simile and myth, his swift delineation of character —his combination of these and other qualities puts him beyond rivalry.

Some of Plato's compositions, such as the *Menexenus, Apology, Symposium* and the first part of the *Phaedrus*, belong to rhetoric. In the *Critias* and much of the *Timaeus* the writing is descriptive. But it is Plato's philosophical writing that is historically of first importance. It is almost true to say that in this field Plato did not develop, he created the art of incarnating abstract argumentative thought in prose.

We should distinguish two steps in this creation.

(1) In his early, elenctic dialogues Plato gives dramatic form to dialectical debates. He does not, save often in the *Lysis* and occasionally elsewhere, just sandwich dialectic with drama; he so blends them that the tussle between persons is itself the pitting of counter-arguments against arguments. The conversations are duels, and the duelists' weapons are arguments. We hear the *pros* and the *contras* of the debate in the challenges and the resistances, the sarcasms and the sulks of the debaters. Their very tones of voice, petulant, scornful, complacent, worried, eager and flabbergasted, ring to us of the reactions of human disputants to the twists and turns of the argumentation. When a cogent argument is produced, a man has scored against a man; and when a man has lost a point to an opponent, a weak argument has been rebutted. The wits and tempers of the debaters and the logical merits and demerits of their arguments are depicted on one canvas and by the same brush strokes. In that moment when our hearts are for or against Socrates or Thrasymachus, our heads are for or against the conceptual points that they make against one another. We are in one breath partisans for or against persons and judges of their premises and conclusions. Our hero is also a dialectical tactician, and he is our hero partly because his dialectical tactics are good. He gets a dual allegiance from us; hence the wrench that we feel when we find Socrates occasionally scoring an invalid point against Protagoras or Thrasymachus. Our twin allegiances are here at variance. The young Athenians, for whom especially Plato wrote these dialogues, must, like us, have taken sides and must thereby effortlessly have made their hero's arguments their own. A dialogue did not have to be committed to memory. It could not be forgotten.

(2) In Plato's late dialogues the tussle between persons has nearly disappeared. Socrates in most of the *Philebus* and in much of the *Theaetetus*, and the Eleatic stranger in the *Sophist* and *Politicus* are not dueling, and their interlocutors are not being maneuvered into surrender. So little dramatic life is in these dialogues that we can wonder whether their recitals interested any of the auditors other than the philosophically sophisticated young men from the Academy. The Eleatic stranger and even the Socrates of the *Philebus* have almost no character. Much the same is true of the *Parmenides*. In the discussion in Part I old Parmenides is a powerful destructive philosopher, but one who strikes us as almost the pure professional philosopher. We do not like him or dislike him. In Part II, though the discussion reverts to the old pattern of question–answer disputation, it is completely formalized and depersonalized. Contradictory conclusions are deduced from theses, but there is no battling for these theses or against these

conclusions. Here the questioner and answerer have no tones of voice. This part of the dialogue must be literally an Academic exercise.

The undramatic character of these late dialogues should not, however, be construed as evidence merely of the failing literary powers of the now aged Plato. He is no longer wholeheartedly composing dialogues for the benefit of lay audiences, but this is only partly because he is losing his exoteric touch. He is now composing for the colleagues and the partly trained students in the Academy. These dialogues are, consciously or unconsciously, adjusted to recipients like those to whom Aristotle's lecture courses are given. For such sophisticated recipients abstract issues generate their own intellectual excitements and their own impersonal partisanships. The impersonality of Plato's late dialogues, like that of Aristotle's lectures, reflects the emergence of philosophy as an inquiry with an impetus, with techniques and even with an academic curriculum of its own. Plato is now creating professional philosophical prose. As disputing for the sake of victory gives way to discussion for the sake of discovery, so the literature of the elenctic duel gives way to the literature of cooperative philosophical investigation. The university has come into being.

Bibliography

EDITIONS AND TRANSLATIONS

A critical edition of the Greek text of Plato's works may be found in *Platonis Opera*, John Burnet, ed., 5 vols (Oxford, 1899–1907). There are improved Greek texts by various editors with French translations in the Budé series, 13 vols. in 25 parts (Paris, 1920–1956), and with English translations in the Loeb series, in 12 vols. (London and New York, 1921–1953). The dialogues in English may be found in *The Dialogues of Plato*, translated with analyses and introductions by Benjamin Jowett, 4th ed., rev., 4 vols. (Oxford, 1953), D. J. Allan and H. E. Dale, gen. eds.

Modern editions and translations of, and commentaries on, individual dialogues include the following: *Gorgias*, revised text with introduction, commentary, and appendix on Socrates, Callicles, and Nietzsche by E. R. Dodds (Oxford, 1959); *Plato's Phaedo*, translated with introduction, notes, and appendices by R. S. Bluck (London, 1955); *Plato's Phaedo*, translated, with introduction and commentary by R. Hackforth (Cambridge, 1955); *Plato's Phaedrus*, translated, with commentary, by R. Hackforth (Cambridge, 1952); *Plato's Examination of Pleasure*, translation of the *Philebus*, with introduction and commentary, by R. Hackforth (Cambridge, 1945); *Philebus and Epinomis*, translated, with introduction, by A. E. Taylor, edited by Raymond Klibansky with Guido Calogero and A. C. Lloyd (London and Edinburgh, 1956); *The Republic of Plato*, translated, with introduction and notes, by F. M. Cornford (Oxford, 1941); *Plato's Statesman*, translated by J. B. Skemp (New Haven, 1952); *Plato's Cosmology*, the *Timaeus* translated with running commentary by F. M. Cornford (London, 1937); *Plato's Theory of Knowledge*, the *Theaetetus* and *Sophist* translated, with commentary, by F. M. Cornford (London, 1935); *Plato and Parmenides*, the *Parmenides* translated, with running commentary, by F. M. Cornford (New York and London, 1939); *Plato's Cretan City: A Historical Interpretation of the Laws*, by G. R. Morrow (Princeton, 1960).

For the *Platonic Letters* see Ludwig Edelstein, *Plato's Seventh Letter* (Leiden, 1966), and G. R. Morrow, *Studies in the Platonic Epistles*, translation with commentary (Urbana, Ill., 1935).

GENERAL ACCOUNTS

Bluck, R. S., *Plato's Life and Thought*. London, 1949.
Field, G. C., *Plato and His Contemporaries*. London, 1930.
Field, G. C., *The Philosophy of Plato*. Oxford, 1949.

Grube, G. M. A., *Plato's Thought*. London, 1935.
Koyré, Alexandre, *Introduction à la lecture de Platon*, translated by L. C. Rosenfield as *Discovering Plato*. New York, 1945.
Robin, Léon, *Platon*. Paris, 1935.
Shorey, Paul, *What Plato Said*. Chicago, 1933.
Taylor, A. E., *Plato: The Man and His Work*. London, 1926.
Wilamowitz-Moellendorf, Ulrich von, *Platon*, 2 vols. Berlin, 1919; 3d ed., Vol. I, Berlin, 1948.
Zeller, Eduard, *Die Philosophie der Griechen*, 6th ed. Hildesheim, 1963.

PARTICULAR ASPECTS OF PLATO'S WORK

Allen, R. E., ed., *Studies in Plato's Metaphysics*. London, 1965. Reprints articles by Cherniss, Ryle, Vlastos, Geach, Owen, et al.
Bambrough, Renford, ed., *New Essays on Plato and Aristotle*. London, 1965. Contains articles specially written for it by Vlastos, Hare, Ryle, Owen, MacKinnon, et al.
Cherniss, H. F., *Aristotle's Criticism of Plato and the Academy*. Baltimore, 1944.
Cherniss, H. F., *The Riddle of the Early Academy*. Berkeley, 1945.
Gould, John, *The Development of Plato's Ethics*. Cambridge, 1955.
Lasserre, François, *The Birth of Mathematics in the Age of Plato*. London, 1964.
Merlan, Philip, *From Platonism to Neoplatonism*. The Hague, 1953.
Murphy, N. R., *The Interpretation of Plato's Republic*. Oxford, 1951.
Robinson, Richard, *Plato's Earlier Dialectic*, 2d. ed. Oxford, 1953.
Ross, W. D., *Plato's Theory of Ideas*. Oxford, 1953.
Ryle, Gilbert, "Letters and Syllables in Plato." *Philosophical Review*, Vol. 59 (1960), 431–451.
Skemp, J. B., *The Theory of Motion in Plato's Later Dialogues*. Cambridge, 1942.
Solmsen, Friedrich, *Plato's Theology*. Ithaca, N.Y., 1942.
Stenzel, Julius, *Plato's Method of Dialectic*, translated from the 2d German ed. (1931) by D. J. Allan. Oxford, 1940.
Stenzel, Julius, *Zahl und Gestalt bei Platon und Aristoteles*, 2d ed. Leipzig, 1933. Translated by D. J. Allan as *Number and Form in Plato and Aristotle*. Oxford, 1940.
Tate, J., "Plato and 'Imitation.'" *Classical Quarterly*, Vol. 26 (1932), 161–169.
Vlastos, Gregory, Introduction to *Plato's Protagoras*, Benjamin Jowett's translation, extensively revised by Martin Ostwald, edited by Gregory Vlastos. New York, 1956. Pp. 7–58.
Vlastos, Gregory, "Anamnesis in the *Meno*." *Dialogue*, Vol. 4 (1965), 143–167.
Wedberg, A. E. C., *Plato's Philosophy of Mathematics*. Stockholm, 1955.

BIBLIOGRAPHIES

Cherniss, H. F., "Plato Studies, 1950–57." *Lustrum*, Vol. 4 (1959), 5–308; Vol. 5 (1960), 323–648.
Rosenmeyer, T. G., "Platonic Scholarship, 1945–1955." *Classical Weekly*, Vol. 50 (1957), 172–182, 185–196, 197–201, 209–211.

GILBERT RYLE

PLATONISM AND THE PLATONIC TRADITION. There are several ways in which our interpretation of Plato differs from that of Platonism or the Platonic tradition. Although inspired by Plato, the tradition has not been concerned with historical details, with the circumstances under which Plato wrote and the contemporary problems which faced him but rather with what it has seen as a body of timeless truth or as a mental outlook of permanent validity. There are thus certain aspects of Plato's thought which Platonism has tended to ignore. It has looked for a static body of dogma (where it has not been content with inspiration of a poetic character), and thus it has tended to minimize the tentative and less systematic aspects of Plato's philosophizing. It has ignored the setting of Plato's thought in his reaction against the Sophistic movement and (usually) his attempt to grapple with the basic problems of Greek mathematics as that had developed down to his day; the crisis of the older cosmological movement, which helped to stimulate the "anthropocentric" reaction both in the Sophists and in Socrates; the origins of Plato's thought in the Socratic technique of question and refutation (the *elenchus*); the dialogue form of composition which he employed as reflecting that technique and his distrust of set discourses and dogmatic statements; and the stages in his philosophical development. Further, Platonism has on the whole tended to neglect both the political interest which is predominant in Plato's two longest works (the *Republic* and *Laws*) and elsewhere (though exception must be made of al-Fārābī among Arabic Platonists and of the Platonic influence in nineteenth-century England, especially on Ruskin and the English idealists) and, concomitantly, Plato's critical and often hostile interest in rhetoric.

The divergent tendencies and emphases in the Platonic tradition reflect different sides of Plato's own nature, which was poetic as well as philosophical; of his two main philosophical stimuli, one came from the realm of ethics and the other from that of mathematics. We can distinguish in the Platonic tradition one tendency which is mathematical and another which is religious and poetic; of these the latter has on the whole been the more prominent in recent centuries, but the two are found united in much of the Platonic tradition of later antiquity.

The essence of Platonism. It is hazardous to attempt to extract an essence of Platonism, but perhaps certain features can be isolated which, if not present universally, tend to be characteristic. Platonism has come to be thought of as exhibiting the very type of a metaphysical philosophy, particularly of one directed toward a transcendent reality. With this goes the rationalistic side of the Platonic tradition, a belief in the power of thought directly to grasp transcendent realities, as shown in Platonic theories of universals and of mathematical objects (though the intuition of a supreme entity may be conceived as suprarational); thus logic and mathematics are seen as providing keys to the structure of the universe. A further correlate is the belief in degrees of reality, and another is the Platonic doctrine of the immortality of the soul (though the persistence beyond death of any individual characteristics may be discounted): Platonism is strongly opposed to anything that can be called materialism. Again, Platonism holds that a valid system of moral conceptions will reflect the nature of the universe, and morality is thus seen as more than merely human. Correlatively, Platonic ethics stresses the importance for conduct of knowledge and enlightenment and tends to place the highest good for man in the contemplation of truth (the theoretical life); moreover, Platonic ethics lays less stress on duty and responsibility than on virtue and the realization of good (interpreted in a nonhedonistic manner). There is also a disposition sometimes manifested to assimilate the moral and the aesthetic (as through the notions of the fitting or the appropriate).

In general, an extreme antithesis to Platonism—in, at any rate, many respects—is found in the skeptical philosophy of later antiquity, and in Hume and the positivistic movements of recent centuries.

Platonism and religion. The characteristics of the Platonic tradition in the field of religion deserve special treatment. Plato and ancient Platonism generally were much under the influence of Pythagoreanism, which had a strongly religious aspect. Plato's *Republic* has a markedly religious tone in its treatment of the Idea of the Good (a tone found also in the cosmology of the *Timaeus* and the Platonic *eros* of the *Symposium* and *Phaedrus*), and both it and (especially) the *Laws* have a place for religious observance. The Platonism of later antiquity, especially Neoplatonism, followed suit, in Plotinus (c. 205–270) and especially in Iamblichus (died c. 330) and his followers, with whom it developed in the direction of a cultus. The position of the Platonic Academy at Athens as a bastion of paganism led to its closure by Emperor Justinian in 529. So far as philosophical theology goes, A. E. Taylor wrote of *Laws* X that it "is the foundation of all subsequent 'natural' theology, the first attempt in the literature of the world to *demonstrate* God's existence and moral government of the world from the known facts of the visible order" (Introduction to his translation of the *Laws*). In one way its argument looks back to the *Phaedrus* and *Timaeus;* in another, forward to Aristotle's *Physics* VIII and *Metaphysics* Λ.

A further development appears in the influence of Greek philosophy, and especially of Platonism, on the Hellenized Judaism of Philo of Alexandria (early first century). This foreshadows the philosophical influences on the Christian Platonists of Alexandria (Clement of Alexandria and Origen, second and third centuries). From that time the influence of Platonism on Christian theology, though not continuous and not always of the same kind, has been considerable; in late antiquity one may particularly mention the acknowledged debt of St. Augustine to Neoplatonism. Islamic philosophy, in al-Kindī (died after 870) and Avicenna (Ibn-Sīnā, 980–1037), was much influenced by Neoplatonism; but Islam, unlike Christianity, proved in the end unable to assimilate the philosophical tradition of Greek antiquity, and with the death of Averroës (1126–1198) the Islamic philosophical tradition came to an end, crushed by theological opposition.

On the influence of Platonism on theology, and in particular on Christian theology, it is difficult to draw conclusions which combine generality with precision. Such a theology must face problems about the relation of reason to revelation, and in the early centuries of Christianity (as previously in Philo of Alexandria) there was a strong temptation to allegorical interpretations of the Bible. (Precedent for this may perhaps be seen in the pictorial representation of philosophical truths envisaged in *Republic* II–III, though there is a warning against allegorical interpretation of traditional Greek legends in *Phaedrus* 229–230.) In later centuries one may say that, while the Thomistic tradition has drawn a sharp line between reason and revelation, seeing the latter as supplementing the former, and antirationalist theologians have contrasted the two to the disadvantage of reason, the Platonic tradition has hesitated to draw a hard and fast line. Insight and intuition have been stressed as providing the first principles from which ratiocination is to proceed. The Platonist rejects a Calvinist insistence on the corruption of human nature and welcomes the metaphor of a spark of divinity in man which provides discernment of moral and religious truth. He sets a high value on contemplation as well as action and sees the latter as proceeding ideally from the former. In revealed theology, he lays more stress than the Calvinist on the doctrine of the Incarnation (though this brings, for the Platonist above all, problems of a tension between time and eternity), and less stress than a Calvinist on a somewhat legalistically conceived atonement (Origen believed in the ultimate salvation of all). Further, the element of otherworldliness in his outlook combines with a disinclination to formal rules of conduct and observance, as found, for instance, in a legalistic sabbatarianism; while against the Bibliolater he stresses the "spirit" rather than the "letter," and again he attaches less importance than some to forms of ecclesiastical organization (being Greek, we might say, rather than Roman in his outlook).

For examples of this type of theology one may refer to W. R. Inge, *The Platonic Tradition in English Religious Thought* (London and New York, 1926), which also illustrates the tendency in the Platonic tradition (sternly repressed by Plato himself) to see poetry as a vehicle of philosophical and religious truth. Despite St. Augustine's debt to Neoplatonism, his teaching on original sin clearly marks him off from religious Platonism as here delineated. In the eighteenth century Kant's rejection of metaphysical theology, his assertion of the primacy of practical reason, and his definition of religion as the recognition of the moral law as a divine command contrast sharply with Platonism; however, there is a Platonic element in his dictum that the sources of our awareness of the divine are to be found in "the starry heavens above and the moral law within." Kant was the father of the anthropocentric *Religionsphilosophie* of the nineteenth century. A still sharper contrast with Platonism is to be found in Karl Barth's neo-Calvinist theology, with its anti-intellectualism, its rejection of human reason as corrupt and of philosophy and human values, and its exclusive appeal to a divine revelation.

The antecedents of Platonism. If we seek the antecedents of Platonism, we must look first at Pythagoreanism and at the Neo-Pythagoreanism of the early centuries of the Christian era, which was influential in Neoplatonic circles, not least on Porphyry (232–c. 300) and Iamblichus. The individual views of Pythagoras and the detailed history of Pythagoreanism, both matters of much dispute, need not concern us. Aristotle (*Metaphysics* A, 6, 987a29–31, 987b10–14) derived the Platonic theory of Ideas from the Pythagorean distinction of Limit and the Unlimited and from the theory of numbers as entities apprehended by the intellect and providing the key to the universe. Plato also derived from the Pythagorean tradition his doctrines of the immortality of the soul and of transmigration, his ethical concepts of harmony and limit, and, in politics, the picture of the philosopher-ruler. The branches of mathematical study in the "second education" of *Republic* VII (arithmetic, geometry, astronomy, and music), which later formed the medieval *quadrivium*, are of Pythagorean origin. Also, we know that Plato was friendly with the Pythagorean Archytas of Tarentum, and the Pythagorean communities of southern Italy may have provided a model for the Academy.

As important as Pythagoreanism is the influence of the dissident Pythagorean Parmenides. His philosophy proclaimed a One Being, utterly undifferentiated and changeless, which was contrasted with a changing world of appearance that was relatively unreal, the former the object of a direct intellectual grasp and the latter the object of opinion. Plato's respect for Parmenides (though his world of Forms has a plurality that contrasts with Parmenides' One) is shown both in his *Parmenides* and in his *Theaetetus* (183E) and *Sophist* (241D), while his philosophical position was more sharply defined by the correlative influence of Heraclitus, who proclaimed the familiar world to be a world of flux (*Cratylus* 401D–402A; *Theaetetus* 160D; Aristotle, *Metaphysics* A, 6, 987a32–987b1; M, 4, 1078b12–17) and called upon man to rely only on his reason (the accuracy of Plato's interpretation of Heraclitus is less important here than how Plato saw him). Among other pre-Socratic thinkers, Plato borrowed from Empedocles the principle "Like is known by like," which he applied in a radically different way in his distinction of metaphysical levels; also, despite his criticisms of Anaxagoras (*Phaedo* 97B–99D), he is reminiscent of him in emphasizing the transcendence of intellect (though he thought Anaxagoras defective in this regard) and in his bias toward teleological explanation.

Plato's debt to Socrates, his teacher, is naturally the most important of all. Aristotle says (*Metaphysics* M, 4, 1078b27–29) that Socrates was responsible for "inductive" arguments (that is, from the particular to the universal) and the search for definitions, and he remarks that these were conducted in the moral sphere (1078b17–19). It was to Socrates that Plato owed, besides the sources of his conception of philosophical method, his ethical concern and his attempt to provide a stable basis for morality against the relativism of Protagoras and the dissolving tendencies of the Sophistic movement generally.

All these aspects of Plato's inheritance are relevant not merely to him personally but to the Platonic tradition generally.

In Plato himself there were combined both the earlier cosmological interests and a lively concern with mathematics, as well as the supervening emphases on human life and the place of man in the city-state. But he never lost his conviction that the highest function of man lay in the contemplation of eternal truth. Chronologically, the Socratic influence on him came first, and it was later and in part from this that the metaphysical and epistemological interests developed. Though Socrates' interests had been largely moral, Plato came (as the *Phaedo*, among the earlier dialogues, shows most definitely) to assign the highest place to pure thought—an issue on which he never wavered thereafter. Consonantly with this, the dialogues of the middle period give a large share of their attention to logical and epistemological issues: philosophy as dialectic becomes the actual subject of the dialogues and is not merely employed in them.

The range of Socrates' influence was in fact multifarious, and Plato was not the only one who felt it; his personality impressed itself, in a different way, on Antisthenes and through him on the Cynic and Stoic traditions.

Plato and the Early Academy. About 387 B.C. Plato set up the Academy at Athens as a center for philosophy and mathematics; it had an unbroken career until it was closed by Emperor Justinian in 529. As a center of thought its rigorously intellectualistic ideals contrasted with those of a more rhetorical and conventionally cultural kind associated with the influence of Plato's contemporary Isocrates, which derived from the Sophistic tradition (especially Gorgias). But in the field of ethics Plato modified the extreme intellectualism of the Socratic equation of virtue with knowledge by allowing a place for true opinion (as in the *Meno*) and also by his tripartition of the soul, assigning to man's emotions an essential place in his moral nature; this feature of the Academic ethics was later to distinguish it from the austere rationalism of the Stoics. Similarly, the ascetic rejection of pleasure in the *Gorgias* and *Phaedo* is drastically modified in the *Philebus* and *Republic.*

Plato's political ideals expressed themselves not merely in his writings but also in his attempts to translate them into practice on his second and third visits to Syracuse (367–366 and 362–360 B.C.), and there are other instances of constitutional advice emanating from the Academy, urging mathematical and philosophic study upon rulers (see Plato, *Epistle VI;* and Werner Jaeger, *Aristotle,* New York and London, 1934, pp. 111–114).

After the *Republic,* Plato came (as is shown in the *Timaeus* and *Laws* X, and to some extent foreshadowed in *Republic* VII) to have an increasing interest in, and respect for, physical science or, at any rate, for astronomy; the Academy was an important center of mathematical and astronomical study, at different times numbering among its members the mathematician Theaetetus and the mathematician and astronomer Eudoxus of Cnidus, together with Heraclides Ponticus.

The Early Academy after Plato. When Plato died (348/347), he was succeeded by his nephew Speusippus, and thereupon two of the leading members of the Academy, Xenocrates and Aristotle, retired from Athens, feeling themselves out of sympathy with the strongly mathematical turn that the philosophy of the Academy was now taking. Aristotle seems to have been thinking of Speusippus when he wrote that for his contemporaries philosophy had become identified with mathematics (*Metaphysics* A, 992a32–33). Under Pythagorean influence (*Metaphysics* M, 1080b11–18), it would seem, Speusippus rejected the theory of Forms, retaining only mathematical (not ideal) numbers (*ibid.* 1086a2–5); he rejected the Platonic Idea of the Good, placing the One beyond Being and denying the status of the Good as an initial principle (see P. Lang, *De Speusippi Academici Scriptis,* Bonn, 1911). Aristotle found Speusippus' system of the universe insufficiently unified (*Metaphysics* Λ, 1075b37–1076a4), but the location of the One beyond Being may be important as a source of the Neoplatonic system.

On the death of Speussipus in 339, Xenocrates returned to Athens as head of the Academy, a position he held until his death in or about 315. He was morally respected, but Aristotle seems to have had no high opinion of him as a philosopher (*De Anima* I, 408b32 ff.), alluding to his theory of the soul. His first principles were the monad and the dyad, and he identified the Ideas with numbers (mathematical numbers, not the "ideal" numbers over and above them postulated in the Platonic school). Soul (which was immortal) he defined as a self-moving number (see the

reference to Aristotle above). In the sphere of ethics, like Plato he associated happiness with virtue. The whole, so far as we are able to judge, seems an uninspired reformulation of speculations familiar in Academic circles. (See R. Heinze, *Xenocrates.*)

Aristotle. Aristotle is the greatest of all Platonists, though in many respects he reacted against his master, and his natural tendency to emphasize points of difference is liable to obscure their similarities. He was a member of the Academy for twenty years (368/367–348/347) and began from a Platonic position, though it is clear that he was already somewhat critical during Plato's lifetime. Unfortunately, our interpretation of his development depends partly on controversial dating of his surviving treatises and partly on fragments of his early dialogues and other lost writings which are difficult to assess. (On the issues involved, see especially Werner Jaeger, *op. cit.;* P. Wilpert, *Zwei Aristotelische Frühschriften über die Ideenlehre,* Regensburg, 1949; D. J. Allan, *The Philosophy of Aristotle,* London, 1952; *Aristotle and Plato in the Mid-fourth Century,* a collection of essays edited by Ingemar Düring and G. E. L. Owen; and Ingemar Düring, *Aristotle's Protrepticus: An Attempt at Reconstruction,* Goteborg, 1961.)

Aristotle's drastic modification of the general position of the Platonic school derived from his dissatisfaction with the theory of Forms—with their separation from particulars as substances existing in their own right and with the attempt to see them both as universals and, at the same time, as perfect instances of themselves. The problems had been surveyed by Plato himself in the first part of the *Parmenides* (to 135c). Aristotle's solution asserted the substantiality of the concrete particular, seen as a compound of form and matter, and, correlatively, it both assigned a higher place to sense perception and treated the soul as the form of an organic body (*De Anima* II, 1, 412a19–b6). With the rejection of the Form of the Good (*Nicomachean Ethics* I, 6, 1096a11–1097a14; *Eudemian Ethics* I, 8), the philosopher's grasp of truth has lost its former relevance to the life of action, and greater emphasis was laid on social habituation. But knowledge still depended on a grasp of forms, as reinterpreted (*Posterior Analytics* I, 1; *Nicomachean Ethics* VI, 1140b31–32); intellect remained at least in part a transcendent and eternal substance (*De Anima* III, 429a10 ff.); and the life of contemplation was still held to be the highest (*Nicomachean Ethics* X, 1177a12–1178b32), with the second place assigned to the life of moral virtue. The new trend in Aristotle's world outlook doubtless owed much to his vast interest in the facts of physical science and especially of biology; but he was in the Platonic tradition in distinguishing three forms of theoretical knowledge: mathematics, physical science, and metaphysics—still, in the eighteenth century, the three claimants to the title of knowledge in Kant's *Critique of Pure Reason.*

The Later Academy. When Aristotle returned to Athens in 335, he set up his own school, the Peripatos, in the Lyceum, and the Platonic and Aristotelian traditions henceforward ran in divergent lines for some centuries. The chief success of the Peripatos lay in the pursuit of physical science, and the Academy fell into the background, overshadowed by two new schools, the Stoic and the Epicurean. It came to align itself with the tradition of the Skeptics, falling back on elements which had been present in the Academy from the start, the critical questioning of Socrates and the skepticism about the world of sensible particulars. This was its reaction to the confident dogmatism of the Hellenistic system builders, and it came to the fore, in particular, in Arcesilaus (died 241 B.C.) and in the so-called founder of the New Academy, Carneades (died 128 B.C.); they, especially Carneades, laid stress on suspension of judgment (*epoche*) and on probability as a guide to thought and action. The Stoics were the main target of Carneades' critical assaults.

The first century B.C. saw the beginnings of an important new trend in ancient philosophy, a tendency toward a partial harmonization of the Platonic, Aristotelian, and Stoic schools. The skeptical movement in the Academy was abandoned, and the steps toward a closer approximation were aided by a recognition of the close affinities of Plato and Aristotle (especially the Aristotle of the dialogues, better-known then than now), not least in psychology and ethics, which had come more to the center of philosophical interest. At the same time, the Stoic Posidonius of Apamea (130–46 B.C.) borrowed from the moral psychology of Plato, with its tripartition of the soul, in order to modify the austere rationalism of Stoic ethics as expounded by Chrysippus. It was, indeed, coming to be an eclectic period, in which it was commonly held that elements of value might be drawn from more than one of the major constructive efforts of the past; Cicero, not an original philosopher but in his youth a pupil of Posidonius, is in this respect typical. Also, the reconciliation of the Platonic and Stoic traditions was the avowed aim of Antiochus of Ascalon, who died about 68 B.C.

Middle Platonism, extending to the second century A.D., is a group of tendencies by no means easy to trace; they continue the already existing synthetic trend (and include at times the influence of Neo-Pythagoreanism), marked by the otherworldly religiosity characteristic of the period. A notable feature, found in Albinus (second century), is the reinterpretation of the Forms as thoughts in a supreme Divine Mind (Albinus, *Epitome* 9). A further feature of Middle Platonism (recalling a fanciful suggestion made by Plato, *Symposium* 202D–203A) is the interposition, between the supreme Divine Mind and mortal men, of intermediaries in the form of inferior gods or *daimones*.

The temper of Middle Platonism, and not least its religiosity, is best preserved for us in the essays (the *Moralia*) of Plutarch (c. 45–125), who has, however, no claim to be regarded as an original philosopher.

Neoplatonism. The decline of Stoicism in the later second century (the last Stoic of importance was Marcus Aurelius, who died in 180) and the increasingly otherworldly religiosity of the period left the intellectual arena clear for Platonism, and in particular for the Neoplatonic school, the last of the great philosophical schools of antiquity, founded by Plotinus (born in Egypt c. 205, died in Campania 270). He studied philosophy in Alexandria and was apparently influenced above all by a certain Ammonius Saccas, of whom, unfortunately, we know little or nothing else; from 244/245 onward he conducted his own philosophical school at Rome. Besides Plato, the influence of Aristotle upon Plotinus' thought is to be noted, especially in his psychology; his treatment of cosmic "sympathy" was indebted to the Stoics; and among thinkers of the second century he may well have owed much to Numenius (Porphyry, *Vita Plotini* 14), in whom Platonic traits were combined with Neo-Pythagoreanism—in particular, Numenius' three gods: the first, a supreme One; the second, Nous (Intellect); and the third, Nous as directed toward matter.

The philosophy of Plotinus was, nevertheless, overwhelmingly Platonic in inspiration, though Platonic in a sense marked by the qualifications indicated at the beginning of this article—more dogmatic and less tentative than Plato, concerned with constructing a system for which Plato's dialogues could provide "proof-texts." Much that is central is not, in its Plotinian form, to be found in Plato at all. The main conception is that of the three divine hypostases, or natures, which are, in descending order, the One, Intellect, and Soul. The One is that from which all else derives by a process of emanation, on which all else depends, and toward which all aspires to return. It is above the realm of Being, lying beyond the possibilities of thought and discourse, and is to be attained only by a rare ascent of mystical exaltation. The realm of Intellect is the realm of Being, and Intellect contains the system of Intelligibles within itself—here Plotinus diverges from Plato, who had set thought and its objects in contrast, and follows the Middle Platonic tradition seen in Albinus. Intellect turns back to the One in contemplation and derives thence its own productive power, while the intelligible world itself is seen not as static but as instinct with life. Soul derives from Intellect and looks toward it, and itself in turn gives rise to the world of nature; it is (importantly for Plotinus' psychology) at the level of Soul that we encounter time, which is the "life of the soul in movement" (*Enneads* III, 7, 11). Matter, unknowable in itself, represents the farthest limit to which the process of descent points; utterly negative, it is for Plotinus the source of evil. (Matter as so conceived is akin to the primary matter of Aristotle.) The ethical side of Plotinus follows from the metaphysical; the ordinary moral virtues have a cathartic function, purging man of the passions and thus aiding his ascent to the world of Intellect; and beyond that is the mystical "return of the alone to the alone" (VI, 9, 11), which is the ultimate bliss. For Plotinus, as for Plato and Aristotle, the theoretical life has primacy over the practical, and, as for Plato, it is a theoretical life seen at its highest in mystical terms.

It is unnecessary for us to dwell at length on the later Neoplatonists. Porphyry, who wrote, among other works, Plotinus' biography and also an *Introduction to Aristotle's Categories* that had great influence in the Middle Ages, intensified the ascetic strain and was to some extent under Neo-Pythagorean influence. Two significant points are that he was given to the allegorical interpretation of Homer and that he originated the anti-Christian tradition of later Neoplatonism. Iamblichus, who wrote also on mathematics, developed Neoplatonism in a theurgical and magical direction. The last of the major Neoplatonists was the systematizer Proclus (410–485), who left not only philosophical treatises but also extensive commentaries on Plato; he was the head of the Platonic Academy at Athens. With Iamblichus and Proclus we find centers of Neoplatonism spreading over the eastern Mediterranean, as at Alexandria and Antioch. Damascius was the head of the Platonic Academy at Athens when it was closed by Justinian in 529 and its members departed for the Persian court of Chosroes, but this was far from meaning the end of Neoplatonic influence.

Philo and Christian Platonism. A very different Platonic tradition was initiated by the voluminous Jewish writer Philo (died c. A.D. 40), who rethought the Hebrew religious tradition in the light of Greek philosophy, with which the culture of Alexandria had brought him into contact. The basis of his thought was the acceptance of the Jewish religious revelation, and his works took the form of expositions of the Hebrew scriptures. The Greek influence was shown in his tendency to allegorical interpretations of the Biblical narrative, while the influence of the Platonic theory of Forms appeared in Philo's account of the divine Logos by means of which God formed the world: the intelligible world, subsisting in the Divine Mind, served as a pattern for the production of the material universe.

Like Philo, the Christian Fathers found it necessary to come to terms with the world of Greek thought. Tertullian (though under Stoic influence) was openly hostile, but in the philosophical milieu of Alexandria there grew up the Christian Platonist school whose most important representatives were Clement of Alexandria (c. 150–c. 211) and Origen (c. 185–c. 254), who was an older contemporary of Plotinus. Like Philo, they drew no sharp line between reason and revelation, and as in Philo there was a certain luxuriance of allegorical fancy. Greek philosophy was held to be, like the Jewish law and prophets, a preparation for the Gospel. Origen's was the more original mind of the two; he borrowed from the Platonic tradition the doctrines, sharply at variance with the general tradition of Christianity, of the soul's pre-existence, of a cosmic Fall, and of reincarnation, while his treatment of the three Persons of the Trinity, subordinating the Son to the Father and the Holy Ghost to the Son, has an affinity with the hypostases of Neoplatonism.

St. Augustine and later developments. Like the Alexandrian school, St. Augustine (354–430) recognized no line of demarcation between philosophy and theology. His philosophical inheritance, unlike theirs, derived from the Neoplatonic tradition, as found in Plotinus and Porphyry. Platonic influence on his thought emerges in his interpretation of the doctrine of the Trinity (which draws upon the Neoplatonic hypostases), his doctrine that the true ultimate goal of knowledge is a state of beatitude, his theory of Ideas and eternal truths as subsisting in the mind of God, and his accounting for human knowledge through reference to an illumination by the Divine Mind. On the other hand, the aspects of his theology for which he is most widely known, his treatments of predestination, of original sin, and of divine grace, have a very different origin.

An important source for Neoplatonic influence in the Middle Ages is to be found in the writings which went under the name of the Dionysius the Areopagite of the Acts of the Apostles (17.34) but which embody a Christian-

ized version of the philosophy of Proclus and seem to have been composed about 500, perhaps in Syria. They are best known for their influential treatment of man's knowledge of God, divided into a negative theology denying the applicability to God of predicates applicable to finite beings (compare, for instance, Plotinus, *Ennead* VI, 8, 13, on the inadequacy of language for speaking about the One), and an affirmative theology applying appropriate predicates but in a superlative degree. Evil he viewed as negative or privative. A remarkable thinker who owed much to the pseudo-Dionysius was John Scotus Erigena, who was born in Ireland about 810, lived at the court of Charles the Bald, and seems to have died about 877, and who attempted in his *De Divisione Naturae* to restate the Christian faith in Neoplatonic terms, in which divine Ideas served as the patterns for natural species.

Platonism in Islamic philosophy. Meanwhile, a different series of developments had been proceeding in the Near East following the rise and expansion of Islam from the middle of the seventh century. Here there had long been established centers of Neoplatonic thought, the most important at Alexandria. From about 800 we find vigorous activity in the translation of Greek philosophical works into Arabic, especially at Baghdad, in the school of Hunain ibn-Ishaq (middle of the ninth century). From this, and from the attempt to harmonize the Greek (and especially the Neoplatonic) tradition in philosophy with the theology of Islam, there sprang a new philosophical tradition, which owed much to the pseudo-Aristotelian *De Causis* (in fact a Christianized epitome of Proclus' *Elements of Theology*). Its first representative is al-Kindī (died after 870), whose inspiration combines Neoplatonic elements with Aristotelian ones and in whose synthesis the Muslim religious revelation takes the place of the Platonic myths. There was also Platonic influence on al-Razi (died 923 or 932), who knew Proclus' works. The philosophy of al-Fārābī (died 950) is basically Aristotelian, but for his political theory he turned to Plato, giving a fresh turn to the Platonic tradition in propounding his theory of a philosopher-caliph. Avicenna (ibn-Sīnā, 980–1037), who had greater originality, combined the Platonic and Aristotelian traditions and endeavored, following a long line of predecessors, to reconcile philosophy and religion by means of allegorical interpretation. Averroës (ibn-Rushd, 1126–1198), the last and greatest of the Islamic philosophers, was primarily an Aristotelian; with him the philosophical tradition came to an end, crushed by the hostility of religious orthodoxy.

The Middle Ages in Europe. During the Middle Ages, Plato was best known in western Europe through Chalcidius' translation of the *Timaeus* (c. 350), while in the second half of the twelfth century Henricus Aristippus translated the *Meno* and *Phaedo*. In the fifteenth century Nicholas of Cusa was familiar with a Latin version of part of the *Parmenides* together with Proclus' commentary, made by the thirteenth-century scholar William of Moerbecke. In general, it may be said that, down to the revival of Aristotle in the thirteenth century, the main influences on medieval philosophy were directly or indirectly Platonic, not least through St. Augustine; in the mid-thirteenth century St. Bonaventure followed this tradition with the stress on divine illumination in his epistemology. At a later date the pseudo-Dionysius, with his mystical theology, influenced Jean Gerson (c. 1400) and the more important thinker Nicholas of Cusa (1401–1464), with whom we reach the fringes of the Renaissance. His *De Docta Ignorantia* exemplifies the *via negativa* in theology.

Renaissance Platonism. The main center of Renaissance Platonism was the Florentine Academy, founded in the middle of the fifteenth century by Cosimo de' Medici and placed under the guidance of the Byzantine scholar Giorgius Gemistus Pletho (died 1452), who took part as an enthusiastic Platonist in a lively controversy on the relative merits of Plato and Aristotle. The Academy's most celebrated members were Marsilio Ficino (1433–1499), who translated both Plato and Plotinus into Latin and developed in his *Theologia Platonica* an elaborate form of Christian Platonism which drew on many sources, and Giovanni Pico della Mirandola (1463–1494), a pupil of Ficino who drew both on the pseudo-Dionysius and on the Jewish cabalistic tradition.

In its spiritualization of the Christian tradition the movement of the so-called Oxford Reformers, especially John Colet (1466–1519, dean of St. Paul's from 1504), owed much to Florentine Platonism. Colet corresponded with Ficino, much admired Origen, and wrote at length on the pseudo-Dionysius. In the field of political thought Colet's friend Sir Thomas More (1478–1535) was greatly influenced by the communism of Plato's *Republic* in the ideal he set forth in his *Utopia*—as was also, at a later date, the Italian Dominican Tommaso Campanella (1568–1639) in his *Civitas Solis;* the very different *New Atlantis* of Francis Bacon (1561–1626), redolent of the new age of discovery in science and technology, takes its title from Plato's *Critias.*

Later developments. Renaissance Platonism may well be considered the last full flowering of the Platonic tradition, and certainly the developments of modern philosophy and science have, in general, been in very different directions—though the mathematizing impulse in Kepler and Galileo had Pythagorean and Platonic roots. But in any case there is more to be said.

In the first place, the Platonic tradition in religious thought revived, surviving the eclipse suffered by Aristotelian scholasticism, in the Cambridge Platonists of the second half of the seventeenth century. Ralph Cudworth (1617–1688), one of their leading representatives, looked back to the Platonic tradition, seeking there a mode of defense against the encroachments of Democritean and Epicurean doctrines, and especially against Hobbes—against his materialism in metaphysics, his conventionalism in ethics, and his Erastianism in religion. In general the Cambridge Platonists (besides Cudworth, such figures as Benjamin Whichcote, Henry More, and John Smith) were attracted by a tradition which turned from the warring strife of ecclesiastical parties to the inner life of the spirit, and might be more inclined to toleration and sweet reasonableness. There are affinities also in the Quaker movement, with its emphasis on an "inner light" not necessarily confined to Christians; and William Penn (1644–1718) alluded appreciatively to Greek philosophy in his writings, not least to the Platonic tradition.

In the nineteenth century the so-called Broad Church school in the Church of England, as found in J. C. Hare (1795–1855) and F. D. Maurice (1805–1872), emphasizing the spirit rather than the letter in their interpretation of Christianity, owed a good deal to the Platonic tradition; and B. F. Westcott (1825–1901), bishop of Durham, was an admiring student of Origen. More recently, W. R. Inge (1860–1954), dean of St. Paul's, was a profound student of Plotinus, whose deep influence is to be seen in the mystical emphasis in his theology.

Second, Platonism has at various periods since the Renaissance exercised a profound influence in the field of poetry, both through its conception of a realm of eternal reality and through its doctrine of *eros,* or love directed toward the divine, which had an important influence on Ficino. In the sixteenth century one may particularly note Spenser's "Hymn of Heavenly Love" and "Hymn of Heavenly Beauty," while in the seventeenth century the poems of Henry Vaughan breathe a Platonic spirit. Early in the nineteenth century the romantic movement saw a revival of Platonic influence, as in Wordsworth's *Ode on Intimations of Immortality,* influenced by the Platonic theory of recollection, and in the poetry of Shelley (who also translated the *Symposium*), as for instance the "Hymn to Intellectual Beauty" (1816) and "Adonais" (1821; see especially the lines beginning "The One remains, the many change and pass"). Nor was such influence confined to England: in the United States the transcendentalism of the poet and thinker Ralph Waldo Emerson stands in the Platonic tradition.

Platonism was in general uncongenial to the dry rationalism of the eighteenth century, but we find Richard Price (1723–1791), in his *Review of the Principal Questions in Morals* (1758), making use of the *Theaetetus* in his attack on the empiricism of Locke. In Germany, Moses Mendelssohn (1729–1786) composed an adaptation of the *Phaedo* (1767), now best known as criticized by Kant in the *Critique of Pure Reason;* but Kant also shows Platonic influence, most notably in his *Dissertation on the Sensible and Intelligible Worlds* (1770), which, contrasting the functions of sense and of thought, allows thought to penetrate to a realm of things-in-themselves in a way the *Critique of Pure Reason* would not allow. In a very different field, the social and political philosophy of Rousseau, with its emphasis on the state as a moral educator, owed much to Plato (see C. E. Vaughan's edition of Rousseau's political writings, New York, 1915, and C. W. Hendel, *Jean-Jacques Rousseau, Moralist,* New York, 1934).

The revival of Platonic studies was initiated by Friedrich Schleiermacher's German translation at the beginning of the nineteenth century, and Plato's influence can be seen in the philosophy of Hegel, who held the *Parmenides* and *Sophist* in special regard and devoted considerable attention to Plato in his lectures on the history of philosophy. From then on, the center of interest in Greek philosophical studies was Plato and Aristotle, and not (as so often in the seventeenth and eighteenth centuries) the Hellenistic schools; further, the study of Plato began to show much more historical insight and to take account of his intellectual development.

In England, Benjamin Jowett's translation of Plato (1871) had widespread influence. Moreover, the English idealists were not indebted only to Kant and the post-Kantian ide- alists of Germany; their political theory, hostile to the individualism of the Lockean and Benthamite traditions, looked back to Plato when they thought of the state as organic. Their qualified admiration of Rousseau was, in part, indirectly an admiration of Plato (see especially Ber- nard Bosanquet, *The Philosophical Theory of the State*, New York, 1899, and Vaughan's edition of Rousseau). In other circles, the interest in eugenics looked back to Plato as well as to Darwin and Spencer; and somewhat earlier, the social teaching of Ruskin (1819–1900) was avowedly influenced by Plato's educational ideals.

In metaphysics, the most strikingly Platonic construction in this century has been the system of J. McT. E. McTag- gart (1866–1925), as set out in *The Nature of Existence* (2 vols., New York and Cambridge, 1921–1927), which sees ultimate reality as a system of timeless souls; A. N. White- head (1861–1947), on the strength of his *Process and Reality* (New York and Cambridge, 1929), has been called "the last and greatest of the Cambridge Platonists." It was Whitehead who spoke of all subsequent philosophy as "a series of footnotes to Plato," and his complex and difficult cosmology, with its theory of "eternal objects" and their ingression into particulars, avowedly owed much to the *Timaeus*. His conception of a nonomnipotent God harks back to the "Demiurge" or "Divine Craftsman" of that dialogue, and in *Adventures of Ideas* (New York and Cam- bridge, 1933) he recalls the way it speaks of the persuasive powers of reason over necessity.

In the field of ethics, Platonic influence is clearly strong in the intuitionism of G. E. Moore's *Principia Ethica* (Cam- bridge, 1903). Moore, like Plato, placed good at the center of his ethics and held it not to be definable in terms of any- thing prior. Rejecting the hedonistic utilitarianism of Mill and Sidgwick, he insisted on a plurality of goods, referring to the *Philebus* (21A–D) to make his point, while his cri- terion for the rightness of actions and of rules of conduct lay simply in their conduciveness to the production of good. On the other hand, Moore was un-Platonic in his denial that ethical conclusions could be drawn from metaphysical principles. The intuitionism of *Principia Ethica* led to the unmetaphysical ideal of the later Moore, who saw philoso- phy as concerned above all with the analysis of a common sense which was not open to refutation on metaphysical grounds. This analytic program has a spirit akin to the early Socratic dialogues of Plato, with their attempts to pass from the ordinary man's recognition of instances of a uni- versal to the isolation and grasp of the universal itself.

The same spirit may be found in Wittgenstein, through- out his philosophical career, as when he declared in his *Tractatus Logico-philosophicus* (New York and London, 1922) that the object of philosophy lies in the clarification of propositions (4.112).

A similar intention is found in a great body of the analyt- ic philosophy of recent years; for instance, there is an analogy between the dialectic of the Academy and the investigation of the mutual compatibilities and incompati- bilities of concepts as envisaged in Gilbert Ryle's *Philo- sophical Arguments*. One may add that recently I. M. Crom- bie, in *An Examination of Plato's Doctrines* (2 vols., New York and London, 1962–1963), has set out a view of Plato which emphasizes the tentative and undogmatic strain in his thought.

Politically, Plato has in this century come under severe attack as an authoritarian, as in Bertrand Russell's essay "Philosophy and Politics" and his *History of Western Phi- losophy* (New York, 1945). But the most sustained and im- portant attack in this field is that of Karl Popper in *The Open Society and Its Enemies* (4th rev. ed., 2 vols., Lon- don, 1962), of which Volume I is devoted mainly to Plato. Popper sees Plato as not simply authoritarian but racialist (his vision is doubtless colored by the recollection of Na- tional Socialism), as breathing a dogmatic spirit inimical to progressive empirical science, and as denying in his poli- tics any scope for individuality or for change: what Plato envisages, Popper argues, is a perfect over-all plan incapa- ble of any modification, and this is a betrayal both of Soc- rates and of the tradition of Athenian democracy. Popper's treatment of Plato is countered on many points of detail by R. B. Levinson in his lengthy work *In Defense of Plato* (Cambridge, Mass., 1953), but Popper nevertheless did good service in emphasizing the contrasts between the Platonic ideal and that of liberal democracy.

Outside such contexts, and in the field of philosophical logic, the term "Platonism" has been much used in recent years to denote theories postulating the self-subsistent re- ality of universals or of logical or mathematical objects (see on this topic the writings of W. V. Quine, as in his collected essays, *From a Logical Point of View*, Cambridge, Mass., 1953, and the earlier controversy, in which Russell took part, over Alexius Meinong's theory of meaning). But at this point, despite Platonic affiliations, the direct con- nection with Plato himself becomes tenuous.

Bibliography

TRANSLATIONS AND TEXTS

Plato, *Dialogues*, Benjamin Jowett, ed., 4th ed., 4 vols. Oxford, 1953. Revised by D. J. Allan.

Schleiermacher, F. D. E., *Platos Werke*, 5 vols. Berlin, 1804– 1810; 2d ed., 6 vols., 1817–1828. Schleiermacher's translation of Plato.

Vogel, C. J. de, *Greek Philosophy: A Collection of Texts*, 3 vols. Leiden, 1950–1959. Vol. III includes texts of Albinus, Numenius, and Philo, with useful comments.

SURVEYS

Cassirer, Ernst, *The Platonic Renaissance in England,* translated by James P. Pettegrove. Austin, Texas, 1953.

Inge, W. R., *The Platonic Tradition in English Religious Thought.* New York, 1926.

Klibansky, Raymond, *The Continuity of the Platonic Tradition During the Middle Ages.* London, 1939.

Merlan, Philip, *From Platonism to Neoplatonism.* The Hague, 1953.

Muirhead, J. H., *The Platonic Tradition in Anglo-Saxon Philos- ophy.* New York, 1931.

Theiler, W., *Die Vorbereitung des Neuplatonismus.* Berlin, 1930. On Middle Platonism.

SPECIAL STUDIES

Armstrong, A. H., *The Architecture of the Intelligible Universe in the Philosophy of Plotinus.* New York, 1940.

Dodds, E. R. and others, *Les Sources de Plotin.* Geneva, 1960.

Düring, Ingemar, and Owen, G. E. L., eds., *Aristotle and Plato in the Mid-fourth Century.* Goteborg, 1960.

Heinze, R., *Xenocrates.* Leipzig, 1892. Includes text.

Inge, W. R., *The Philosophy of Plotinus*, 2 vols. New York, 1918.

Kristeller, P. O., *The Philosophy of Marsilio Ficino*. New York, 1944.

Miles, Leland, *John Colet and the Platonic Tradition*. La Salle, Ill., 1961.

Notopoulos, J. A., *The Platonism of Shelley*. Durham, N.C., 1947.

Witt, R. E., *Albinus and the History of Middle Platonism*. Cambridge, 1937.

Wolfson, H. A. *Philo: Foundations of Religious Philosophy in Judaism, Christianity, and Islam*. Cambridge, Mass., 1947.

D. A. REES

PLEASURE. The concept of pleasure has always bulked large in thought about human motivation and human values and standards. It seems clear to most people that pleasure and enjoyment are pre-eminent among the things worth having and that when someone gets pleasure out of something, he develops a desire for it. Moreover, from the time of Plato much of the discussion of the topics of motivation and value has consisted in arguments for and against the doctrines of psychological hedonism (only pleasure is desired for its own sake) and ethical hedonism (only pleasure is desirable for its own sake). One can make an intelligent judgment on these doctrines only to the extent that he has a well-worked-out view as to the nature of pleasure. Otherwise he will be unable to settle such questions as whether a putative counterexample, for instance, a desire for the welfare of one's children, is or is not a genuine example of desiring something other than pleasure for its own sake.

Demarcation of the topic. Pleasure and pain have usually been regarded as opposite parts of a single continuum. As pain diminishes, it tends toward a neutral point; by continuing in the same "direction" we move toward increasing intensities of pleasure. Thus Jeremy Bentham regarded amounts of pain as negative quantities to be algebraically summated with amounts of pleasure in computing the total hedonic consequences of an action or a piece of legislation. This was in accordance with the utilitarian principle that an action is justified to the extent that it tends to produce pleasure and the diminution of pain. Since "pain" is most commonly used as a term for a kind of bodily sensation, it is natural to think of pleasure as having the same status. And indeed there are uses of the term "pleasure" in which it seems to stand for a kind of bodily sensation. Thus we speak of "pleasures of the stomach" and thrills of pleasure. But as hedonists have often insisted, in any sense of the term in which psychological or ethical hedonism is at all plausible, the term "pleasure" must be used so as to embrace more than certain kinds of localized bodily sensations. When someone maintains that pleasure is the only thing which is desirable for its own sake, he certainly means to include states of the following sort:

(1) Enjoying (taking pleasure in) doing something, such as playing tennis.

(2) Getting satisfaction out of something, such as seeing an enemy humiliated.

(3) Having a pleasant evening; hearing pleasant sounds.

(4) Feeling good, having a sense of well-being.

(5) Feeling contented.

It seems clear that phenomena of these sorts do not consist in localized bodily sensations of the same type as headaches, except for being of an opposite quality. When someone has enjoyed playing tennis, it makes no sense to ask where (in his body) he enjoyed it. Nor does it make sense to wonder whether the pleasure he got from the tennis came and went in brief flashes, or whether it was steady and continuous; but these would be sensible questions if getting pleasure from playing tennis were a localized bodily sensation like a headache. This is not to deny that various localized sensations might be involved in his enjoyment of the game, such as a swelling in his chest after making a good shot, or a sinking sensation in his stomach after muffing a shot. The point is that his enjoyment of the game cannot be identified with such sensations, for he could be enjoying the game *throughout* its duration, even though such sensations cropped up only from time to time.

In fact we are confronted with two distinguishable positive–negative dimensions. There is the pleasure–pain dimension, a dimension of bodily sensations ranging from intense pains to intense localizable pleasures of the sort experienced in sexual orgasm. To specify the other dimension we need a terminological convention. We shall use the term "getting pleasure" as a general designation for an experience like those specified in the above list. Thus, enjoying listening to music and feeling good on arising in the morning are special forms of "getting pleasure." Getting pleasure can, then, be thought of as the positive segment of a dimension, the negative segment of which will be termed "getting displeasure" and will include such things as feeling bad, feeling discontented, having a miserable time, being uncomfortable, being displeased by someone's action, being "pained" or distressed at the sight of something, and so on. We have variations of degree in this "pleasure–displeasure" dimension, as well as in the "pleasure–pain" dimension. One can enjoy oneself more or less and be displeased at something more or less. Moreover, it would seem that there is an intermediate neutral point at which one is neither pleased nor displeased at what is happening, neither enjoying oneself nor feeling miserable, and so on. It is the pleasure–displeasure dimension which philosophers are really trying to understand when they discuss "pleasure and pain." Hence we shall take the problem of the nature of pleasure to be the problem of understanding what it is to "get pleasure." For simplicity of exposition we shall largely confine the discussion to the positive segment of the pleasure–displeasure dimension; when dealing with the entire dimension we shall use the term "hedonic tone."

It is important to realize that in posing the problem in this way philosophers (and psychologists) have assumed that there is something fundamental which is common to enjoying something, getting satisfaction out of something, being pleased at something, feeling good, and so on. It is conceivable that this assumption is mistaken, in which case virtually all the discussions of the problem have been misguided. In this article we shall follow tradition in supposing that there is an important common element to be found.

Pleasure as a nonlocalized sensation. Admitting all the above, it still might be supposed that pleasure is a nonlocalized bodily sensation on the order of fatigue or "feeling energetic." (If pleasure is a sensation, it must be a bodily sensation rather than visual, auditory, tactile, olfactory, or gustatory; for it is evident that pleasure is not simply a function of the stimulation of external sense receptors.) If so, to get pleasure out of playing tennis would be to have the pleasure sensation while playing tennis. This view has recently been made the target of some acute critical attacks, most notably by the Oxford philosopher Gilbert Ryle. The main criticisms are as follows:

(1) Any sensation can be either pleasant or unpleasant, depending on further features of the context. A thrill can be either a thrill of pleasure or a thrill of horror. A masochist even gets pleasure out of painful sensations. Some sensations are generally pleasant (moderate warmth), others generally unpleasant (strong electric shock); but the fact that what one enjoys in a particular case depends on factors other than the kind of sensation involved, shows that we cannot identify taking pleasure in something with having a certain kind of sensation.

(2) It would seem that any sensation, if it becomes sufficiently acute, will tend to monopolize consciousness and interfere with concentration on anything else. On the view under consideration, the more pleasure we get out of, say, playing the piano, the more intense the sensation of pleasure would become, the more our attention would be taken up with the sensation of pleasure, and the harder it would become to concentrate on the playing. But the reverse is the case. The more pleasure we get out of doing something, the easier it is to concentrate on *it*.

(3) Any kind of sensation could conceivably occur without its usual conscious accompaniments and could, indeed, occupy the whole of consciousness. Even if sinking sensations in the stomach normally coincide with a perception or thought of something as dangerous, it is quite possible for one to have such sensations without being aware of anything else at the moment. Thus, on the sensation theory one could conceivably have the pleasure of playing tennis all by itself, without having it in conjunction with one's awareness that one is playing tennis. Pleasures do not seem to be detachable in the way this theory requires them to be. However, to this argument the sensation theorist could reply that we do have cases in which the pleasure sensation occurs all alone, such as feeling good or having a sense of well-being without consciously feeling good *about* anything in particular. Of course we cannot get the enjoyment of playing tennis without playing tennis, but that is just because of the way the complex phrase "enjoying playing tennis" is defined. We would not label the pleasure we get "the pleasure of playing tennis" unless the pleasure sensation occurred in conjunction with the awareness that one is playing tennis. But this verbal point does not disprove the contention that what makes enjoying playing tennis a case of getting pleasure is the presence of the same sensation which occurs alone in feeling good (about nothing in particular).

(4) A more serious difficulty is posed by another respect in which the sensation theory represents enjoyment as loosely connected with what is enjoyed. According to the theory, to enjoy something is to have the pleasure sensation in conjunction with that something. But if "in conjunction with" means merely "in consciousness at the same time as," we are faced with the following difficulty. Let us suppose that while enjoying playing tennis at a given moment I am aware not only of playing tennis but also of oppressive humidity in the atmosphere and of a plane flying overhead. The pleasure sensation occurs in consciousness at the same time as all these cognitions. Therefore the sensation theory implies that I must be enjoying the oppressive humidity and the plane just as much as I am enjoying playing tennis. But this is contrary to the facts. A person knows immediately which of the various things he is aware of at the moment he is taking pleasure in; and the sensation theory can give no account of this discrimination. We must posit some more intimate connection between the pleasure and its object than simply being together in consciousness at the same time. But it seems that so long as we interpret getting pleasure as having a certain kind of sensation, no more intimate bond can be specified.

Variants of the "conscious-quality" theory. The heavy emphasis on the bodily sensation theory in recent philosophical discussion has tended to obscure the fact that there are a number of other theories that belong to the same family, some of which have been much more important historically than the sensation theory. The general sort of view, of which the sensation theory is a variant, can be described as the view that pleasure is one of the ultimate immediate qualities (or data) of consciousness (experience). To say that it is a quality of consciousness is to say that it constitutes one of the ways in which one state of consciousness differs from another with respect to its own intrinsic nature rather than its relations to other things. (To say that a state of consciousness is a visual sensation of redness is to say something about its intrinsic nature, while to say that it belongs to Jones is not.) It is an *immediate* quality of consciousness because one is aware of it immediately, just by virtue of its presence; nothing further is required to get at it. Analogously, in a visual sensation one is aware of the color just by virtue of having the sensation; the color is not something which could be there without being the object of awareness. It is an *ultimate* quality of consciousness, because it cannot be analyzed in any way with respect to its intrinsic nature. Again we may use the less problematic sensory qualities to illustrate the point. A felt pressure differs from a felt warmth, or a seen color from a heard sound, in a way which cannot be further analyzed. To know what the difference is, one must have experienced both. Henceforth, we shall use the terms "pleasantness" and "unpleasantness" for the supposed ultimate qualities, the awareness of which is, on this kind of theory, essential for getting pleasure or displeasure.

The thesis that

(A) Pleasure is a kind of bodily sensation (more exactly stated, a quality which defines a kind of bodily sensation)

is one variant of this view; for qualities which do define kinds of bodily sensation are ultimate immediate qualities of experience—tingling, nausea, dizziness, and so on. However, there are other variants which are deserving of more respect.

(B) Pleasure is a kind of feeling, or a quality which defines a kind of feeling, where feelings are taken to be elements of consciousness distinguishable from sensations, including bodily sensations.

(*C*) Pleasure is a quality which can occur only as one aspect or attribute of some larger conscious complex, as a certain pitch or timbre occurs only as an aspect of a sound which has other aspects. Theories of this sort differ according to the sort of conscious element pleasure is thought to qualify: sensations, complexes of sensations, feelings, and so on. However, once we abandon the project of identifying pleasure with a certain kind of mental element, there is no reason not to take the most liberal alternative and consider the quality of pleasantness attachable to any sort of conscious state. This would have the advantage of not forcing us to explain away the fact that thoughts, realizations, memories, and mental images all seem to be accompanied by pleasure in the same way as sensations. For purposes of further discussion we shall take as our formulation of (*C*): *Pleasure is a quality that can attach to any state of consciousness.*

Let us consider whether the arguments against (*A*) cited above have any force against (*B*) and (*C*). Both the first argument (that any sensation can be pleasant or unpleasant) and the second (that any sensation is capable of monopolizing consciousness) depend on specific features of bodily sensations; one could hardly expect them to have any bearing on theories which do not identify getting pleasure with having a certain kind of bodily sensation. With respect to thesis (*C*), it is not clear that every quality of conscious states is inherently neutral between being pleasant and unpleasant, nor is it clear that every quality of conscious states will monopolize attention in proportion to its degree. With respect to thesis (*B*), there are, of course, feelings which are, or essentially involve, bodily sensations (feeling nauseated, feeling tired), and the arguments do apply to these. But thesis (*B*) identifies pleasure with feelings which are distinct from bodily sensations. Apart from this qualification there are feelings, ordinarily so called, which, no matter how "strongly" one has them, do not tend to monopolize attention (feeling calm), and there are feelings which are not, by their nature, neutral between pleasantness and unpleasantness (feeling contented, feeling distressed). Such examples show that the consideration adduced in the first two arguments cannot be used to rule out the possibility that pleasure is some kind of feeling.

The third argument (that any sensation should be capable of occurring without its usual conscious accompaniments), on the other hand, does rule out the possibility of pleasure being a feeling, if a feeling is conceived as a mental element which could occur alone. However, we must remember that thesis (*B*) is distinguishable from thesis (*A*) only to the extent that it is restricted to feelings which are not identifiable, in whole or in part, with bodily sensations. And insofar as such feelings exist, it is doubtful that they are capable of occupying the whole of consciousness. To make this point more concrete, let us look at the way position (*B*) developed. Its historical roots are to be found in the tripartite division of the mind into faculties of cognition, will, and feeling, a scheme developed in Germany in the eighteenth century by such men as Moses

Mendelssohn and Immanuel Kant. Roughly speaking, the faculty of feeling is the faculty of being consciously affected, positively or negatively, by things of which one becomes aware through the faculty of cognition. Already the suggestion appears that a feeling is something which arises only in reaction to one or more cognitions and hence does not have the essential autonomy of a sensation. The introspective psychologists of the nineteenth and early twentieth centuries who tried to work out a doctrine of feeling as a distinctive kind of element of consciousness, most notably Wilhelm Wundt and E. B. Titchener, wound up with a notion of feelings as, in effect, simply hypostatized bearers of the supposed ultimate qualities of pleasantness and unpleasantness. Wundt, indeed, tried to incorporate other qualities into feelings, namely, the dimensions of strain–relaxation, and excitement–quiescence; but other workers in the field tended to regard these as features of associated bodily sensations. More generally, it seems likely that insofar as two feelings, ordinarily so called, differ in their immediate "feel," other than with respect to pleasantness and unpleasantness, this difference can be attributed to the bodily sensations involved. Thus, if we contrast feeling homesick and feeling relieved, or feeling distressed and feeling contented, the difference in "feel," apart from different degrees of pleasantness and unpleasantness, will come down to differences in the kinds of bodily sensations involved. Hence, we are left with pleasantness and unpleasantness as the only qualitative dimension of feelings, construed as elements distinguishable from bodily sensations. Since it was generally held that such feelings could occur *only* in reaction to "cognitive" mental elements, including sensations, the third argument has no force against the thesis that getting pleasure out of something consists in having a pleasant feeling in conjunction with that something. But immunity from those criticisms is purchased at the price of any significant distinction between theses (*B*) and (*C*). Instead of saying that pleasantness and unpleasantness are qualities of special mental elements termed "feelings," which can only occur in conjunction with other mental elements, we might just as well say that pleasantness and unpleasantness are qualities which can attach to any mental element. For since on the feeling theory nothing can be said about the intrinsic nature of feelings, other than that they "bear" the qualities of pleasantness and unpleasantness, it would be in principle impossible to determine by introspection whether, when I am relieved at discovering that my child is out of danger, the pleasantness I experience attaches to my awareness of the situation or to a feeling which occurs in response to my awareness. There would be a point in adopting the more complex categorization of the experience in terms of special feeling-elements if the postulation of such elements were needed for the construction of a theory as to the causes and/or effects of getting pleasure and displeasure. But the notion of feeling-elements has not so far demonstrated any theoretical fertility. Thus, when probed, thesis (*B*) reduces to thesis (*C*).

Thesis (*C*)—that pleasure is a quality that can attach to any state of consciousness—escapes the third and fourth arguments, as well as the first two. The third argument obviously has no application since, according to this thesis, pleasure can exist only as a quality of some more concrete entity. It escapes the fourth argument (that according to the sensation theory, pleasure would attach to any awareness present in consciousness at the same time) because it is possible that the quality of pleasantness would attach to one apprehension and not another, even if both are in the same consciousness at the same time. Thus, in the example given, pleasantness could attach to my awareness of playing tennis but not to my awareness of the humid atmosphere, even though I am aware of both simultaneously.

Thus thesis (C) emerges as the only serious contender from the ranks of quality-of-consciousness theories, and historically most such theories can be regarded as approximations to it. John Locke treated pleasure and pain as "simple ideas obtained both from sensation and reflection," and for David Hume pleasure and pain were "impressions of sensation." Neither Locke nor Hume distinguished in any systematic way between kinds of sensations, qualities of sensations, feelings, and qualities of feelings. If we look at the way they actually used the notions of an "idea of pleasure" or "impression of pleasure," we can see that in effect they took pleasure to be a qualitative feature which can attach to any state of consciousness. The "sensationist" psychologists, such as David Hartley and James Mill (whose psychology, in the hands of Jeremy Bentham and John Stuart Mill, became the basis of the utilitarian ethics and social philosophy), took pleasure and pain to be ultimate, unanalyzable properties of sensations, copies of sensations (ideas), and combinations of sensations and ideas; pleasure and pain were thought to be transferred, via association, to any mental content. None of these thinkers distinguished between the pleasure–pain and the pleasant–unpleasant dimensions, but once we clear up that confusion their view, as applied to the latter, can be seen to be a form of thesis (C).

Consideration of conscious-quality theory. The main support for the conscious-quality theory comes from the fact, already noted, that a person knows immediately when he is getting pleasure from something. He knows it in a way no one else could conceivably know it—just by virtue of being the one who is getting the pleasure. He has an epistemologically "privileged access" to the fact. Since it is natural to take the awareness of sensory qualities, especially visual ones, as a paradigm of immediate knowledge of one's psychological states, it is natural to construe what one knows when he knows that he is enjoying something as some ultimate quality of consciousness.

Nevertheless, on further probing, the thesis that pleasure is a quality that can attach to any state of consciousness is not very plausible phenomenologically. When we reflect on a wide variety of cases of getting pleasure, as indicated by the list at the beginning of this article, we are unable to isolate a felt quality which they all share, in the way in which we can easily isolate a quality of redness which a number of different visual sensations share, or a quality of painfulness which a number of different bodily sensations share. On the contrary, enjoying playing tennis feels very different from getting satisfaction out of seeing an enemy in distress, and both feel very different from the sense of well-being one has when, in good health, one arises care-free from a good night's sleep. Nor does it seem possible to

find *in* these experiences some respect in which they are qualitatively the same, as two sounds, otherwise very different, can be the same in pitch. Even if we stick to one term in the "pleasure family," such as "getting satisfaction," it seems equally implausible to suppose that there is some felt quality common to getting satisfaction out of seeing an enemy in distress and getting satisfaction out of the realization of a job well done. The enjoyment or satisfaction seems to take whatever felt quality it has from what one is enjoying or getting satisfaction from. Thus John Stuart Mill was on sound ground in insisting, against Jeremy Bentham, that there are qualitative differences between "pleasures."

These doubts are reinforced by the fact that here we are without external support for the postulation of basic conscious qualities. In the case of sensory qualities, at least those of the external senses, we can tie down the quality to a certain kind of stimulation; people ordinarily get red visual sensations when and only when their optic nerves are stimulated by stimuli of a certain physical description. Moreover, certain kinds of variations in the physical properties of the stimulus can be correlated with judgments of degrees of properties of the sensation, such as hue, saturation, and shade. These correlations support our confidence in purely introspective discriminations between visual qualities. Nothing of the sort is possible with pleasantness. This quality, if such there be, does not vary with variations in physical stimuli in any discernible fashion. Nor can anything much better be found on the response side. It is true that there are gross typical differences in bearing and manner between a person enjoying himself and a person having a miserable time, between a person satisfied with the way things are going and a person who feels terribly frustrated. On the positive side of these contrasts we are more likely to get relaxation, expansiveness, and smooth coordination; on the negative side tenseness, constriction, and disruption of ongoing activities. But these manifestations differ so much from case to case because of other factors—general personality characteristics and state of health, for example—that they cannot be taken as reliable indications of how much pleasure or displeasure a given person is getting at the moment.

Motivational theories. No doubt there is something which all the experiences we have classified under "getting pleasure" have in common. If it is not an immediately felt quality, what is it? In searching for an alternative we might well take note of a different tradition in which the notion of pleasure was analyzed motivationally, in terms of the realization of the good, of the object of striving. In many systematic schemes of the "passions of the soul," the basic notion is appetite, inclination, striving, or tendency of the person toward some object he apprehends as good or desirable. Pleasure, delight, or joy is then defined as the state in which this object is actually present, in which the appetite has reached fruition. Versions of this view are to be found in Thomas Aquinas, Thomas Hobbes, Benedict Spinoza, and many other philosophers, as well as in some recent psychologists, notably William McDougall. The basic presuppositions of this approach to the subject are quite different from those of Locke and Hume. For Locke and Hume, and British empiricists generally, the way to understand any psychological concept is either to find it among the immediate data of introspection or to show how it is to be analyzed into such data. This approach ultimately stems from the Cartesian insistence that one knows one's own states of consciousness better than anything else, in particular, better than physical objects and events, since it is possible to doubt the existence of all the latter but not of all the former. Hence it is natural for one in this tradition freely to posit immediate qualities of consciousness whenever there is any plausibility to doing so. Thinkers in the other tradition have a more objectively oriented epistemology, according to which conscious experience has no priority over, for instance, overt behavior as an object of investigation and an object of knowledge. This leaves them free to explore the possibility of analyzing the notion of pleasure in terms of notions like appetite, or tendency, which could not be regarded as immediate objects of introspection.

Their view of the nature of pleasure might be formulated as follows:

(*D*) To get pleasure is to be in a state of consciousness which includes the awareness that one has obtained something one wants.

There are serious difficulties with this version of a motivational theory of pleasure. No doubt there are many pleasures which do presuppose a want in the absence of which no such pleasure would be forthcoming. I would not take pleasure in the discomfiture or prosperity of a certain person unless I wanted him to be discomfited or to prosper, as the case may be. But it seems that there are many pleasures which do not presuppose any such pre-existing want. Simple sensory pleasures, such as the pleasure of eating a good steak, are the most obvious cases. Having found steak pleasant, we may then develop a desire for a steak; but here the want presupposes the prior experience of pleasure, not vice versa. The view under consideration does not deny that wants can be reinforced or strengthened by the experience of pleasure in their satisfaction. But it does deny that one can get pleasure from anything except by way of that thing satisfying some previously existing want. And this seems contrary to experience. Surely infants take pleasure in many things, such as throwing a ball, when they encounter them for the first time. Prior to this encounter they could not have had a desire for it, for they did not yet know what throwing a ball is. It is noteworthy that proponents of this position maintain it in the face of these difficulties only by generously positing instincts and other nonconscious "tendencies" and "strivings."

However, there are other versions of a motivational theory which do not presuppose a pre-existing desire for each pleasure. The most promising is a view put forward by Henry Sidgwick, among others:

(*E*) To get pleasure is to have an experience which, as of the moment, one would rather have than not have, on the basis of its felt quality, apart from any further considerations regarding consequences.

This account makes pleasure a function not of a pre-existing desire but of a preference one has at the moment of the experience. To say that one has the preference at the moment is not to say that one expresses the preference even to oneself; it is not to say anything about what is before one's consciousness at the moment. It is, rather, to say something dispositional—for example, that one would choose to have an experience just like this rather than not if one were faced with such a choice at this moment and if no considerations other than the quality of the experience were relevant. This, unlike thesis (*D*), allows for the possibility of taking pleasure in something one did not previously have a tendency to seek. On the other hand, it is also clearly distinct from the conscious quality theory. According to thesis (*E*), when one says that he is enjoying something, he is saying something about the quality of his experience; he is saying that the quality of his experience is such that on that basis alone he would prefer to have it rather than not to have it. But he is not saying what the quality of his experience is; he is saying, rather, how it is related to his preferences, likes, or desires. More particularly, he is not saying that there is some particular quality, "pleasantness," present in the experience. On this view, the felt qualities on the basis of which the experience is valued can be as diverse as the range of human likes. They can involve calm, excitement, warmth, cold, thrills, and sinking feelings.

It might seem that the strongest reason for the conscious-quality view, the fact that pleasure is something to which the subject has privileged access, would pose a difficulty for thesis (*E*), but this is not necessarily so. It is natural to think that the only things an individual can know about immediately, in a way no one else can, are the qualities of his experience; and indeed sensory qualities have this status. But there are many things to which an individual has privileged access that cannot be regarded as immediately felt qualities, such as intentions, attitudes, and beliefs. If I intend to quit my job tomorrow, I know that I have this intention without having to do any investigation to find out; I know just by virtue of having the intention; I know this as immediately as I know that I am now aware of a reddish patch. And it is in principle impossible for anyone else to know in this way that I have that intention. Yet an intention is neither a felt quality nor a complex of felt qualities. Hence the epistemological status of pleasure is not a conclusive reason for construing it as a quality of experience. The epistemological status of pleasure does place a constraint on the range of possible theories; we cannot identify pleasure with something to which the subject does not have privileged access, such as a certain pattern of neuron firings in the brain. However, among the nonsensory quality items to which a person has privileged access are his likes, preferences, and wants. It seems reasonable to suppose that a person's knowledge that he would choose to have an experience just like his present one on the basis of its felt quality can be just as immediate as his knowledge that he is aware of a red patch.

Motivational theories have the following superiority over conscious-quality theories. It does not seem to be merely a contingent fact that pleasure is desirable, or that the fact that an activity is enjoyable is a reason for doing it. "I get a lot of satisfaction out of teaching, but I see absolutely no reason to do it" sounds like a self-contradiction. This is not to say that the fact that one will get pleasure out of something is a conclusive reason for doing it; there may well be other considerations which outweigh this. I would enjoy playing tennis now, but if an urgent job has to be completed, that is a good reason for not playing tennis. What we are suggesting to be necessarily true is (P) the fact that one gets pleasure out of x is a reason for doing or seeking x. This reason must be put into the balance along with other relevant reasons in making a decision in any particular case. The conscious-quality theory can throw no light on this necessity. If pleasure is an unanalyzable quality of experience, there is nothing about the meanings of the terms involved in (P) that would make it necessarily true. Why should it be necessarily true that a certain unanalyzable quality of experience is something to be sought? It would seem that any such quality is something that would or would not be taken as desirable by a given person, or people in general, depending on further factors. A motivational theory, on the other hand, analyzes the concept of pleasure in such a way as to make principles like (P) necessary. If to enjoy an experience *is* just to be disposed to choose an experience exactly like it if nothing other than the felt quality is relevant, then it follows trivially that the fact that something involves enjoyment is a reason for choosing it.

Superficially it might appear that opting for a motivational theory would involve a commitment to psychological hedonism, but this would be a mistake. The motivational theory commits us to holding that pleasure is (always) intrinsically desirable, but it carries no implication that pleasure is the only thing intrinsically desirable. One could adopt thesis (E) as his theory of the nature of pleasure and still regard other things as intrinsically desirable, such as fulfillment of one's potentialities and intellectual consistency, independent of any pleasure they might bring. It is an analysis of desire in terms of pleasure that would stack the cards in favor of psychological hedonism. If we hold that to desire something is to think of it as pleasant, it does follow that we do not desire anything except pleasure or what is believed to lead to pleasure.

The measurement of pleasure. The problem of measuring hedonic tone has occupied both psychologists and philosophers. Psychologists have addressed themselves to such problems as the physiological basis of pleasure, the dependence of pleasantness on various aspects of sensory stimulation (such as contrast), and the effect of pleasure and displeasure on the speed and efficiency of learning. To deal with these problems they have to study the effect of variation of sensory stimulus conditions, for instance, on degree of hedonic tone, or the effect of variations in hedonic tone on something else, such as ease of recall of learned material. To do this, one must be able to specify the degree or amount of hedonic tone present at a given moment. Philosophical concern with the measurement of pleasure has grown out of utilitarianism and other hedonistic ethical theories. According to utilitarianism, an action is justified if and only if it will probably lead to a greater balance of pleasure over displeasure for everyone affected than any possible alternative action. Applying this principle to a particular case would involve estimating the total quantity of pleasure and displeasure that would be produced by each of the possible choices. To do this we

would first have to list the ways in which one choice or another would make the situation, patterns of activities, and so on of a given person different from what they would be if that choice had not been made. Second, we would have to obtain information concerning how much pleasure or displeasure that person has derived from the situations and activities in question. Third, we would have to project how much pleasure and displeasure the person would derive from each of these in the future, taking into account any changes in circumstances, age, and so on that could be expected to make a difference. Fourth, we would have to sum up the hedonic consequences for that person. Fifth, having done this for each person likely to be affected, we would have to sum these results, arriving at a figure representing the probable total hedonic consequences of that choice.

Some of the problems relevant to these procedures fall outside the scope of this article. These include the problem of determining just what the objective consequences of a choice are likely to be, the problem of determining what features of a situation are responsible for the pleasure or displeasure felt, and the problem of projecting probable future pleasure from past pleasures. These are all essentially general problems of inductive reasoning. The problems having to do specifically with the measurement of pleasure are (1) How can one determine the degree of pleasure or displeasure experienced by a given person at a given moment? (2) How can one compare the amount of pleasure felt by one person at a given time with the amount of pleasure felt by another person at a given time?

In everyday discourse we compare pleasures and displeasures. We say things like "I didn't enjoy that party as much as the last one," "I get more pleasure out of gardening now than I used to," and "That interview was not as unpleasant as I had expected it to be." Even granting the reliability of such comparative judgments, the utilitarian needs something more. He needs to be able to specify the hedonic value of particular experiences in numbers which he can meaningfully subject to arithmetical operations, so that if a person gets four positive units (pleasure) from one minute of playing tennis and one negative unit (displeasure) from the next minute of playing tennis, the total hedonic value of the two minutes is greater than that of two minutes spent lying in the sun, from which he derived one positive unit per minute.

An obvious move is to try to refine everyday comparative judgments in such a way as to yield these kinds of results. (In fact, all the methods which have actually been used have been of this sort.) We might ask the subject to consider a large number of his past experiences and to make a comparative judgment on each pair. Possibly after ironing out a few inconsistencies, we would arrange a series such that each experience is more pleasant, or less unpleasant, than any experience lower in the series. We could then have the subject locate a point of hedonic indifference, after which we could assign positive and negative integers to the ranks diverging in either direction from the point of indifference. This would constitute a hedonic scale for that individual. Any other experience would be assigned a number by matching it with an experience on the scale from which it is hedonically indistinguishable. (If it fell between two experiences on the scale, the scale would have to be revised.)

Even assuming that subjects make responses that would enable us to set up an unambiguous scale, one might still doubt that it provides an adequate measuring procedure. First, it relies heavily on the subject's memory of how much pleasure or displeasure he got out of something in the past, and such memories are notoriously fallible. Second, even if we have constructed a scale such that, given two adjoining experiences, the subject is unable to think of an experience which would lie between them, it is still an open question whether the intervals between the items are equal. We have as successive items (a) taking a shower after a game of tennis, (b) being complimented on a performance, and (c) seeing one of one's children receive a prize. What reason is there to think that (c) is just exactly as much more pleasant than (b) as (b) is than (a)? And yet we have to make that assumption if we are going to use the numerical assignments to compare one "sum" of pleasures with another.

A different procedure would be to have the subject rate an experience, when it happens, by an absolute scale, for instance, a nine-point scale ranging from +4 to −4. This would avoid the problem about memory, but it brings fresh difficulties in its stead. Why suppose that the subject is in fact using the same standards every time we get him to make a rating? For that matter, why suppose that ratings which people are forced to make on an artificially constructed scale correspond to any real differences in experience at all? Moreover, there is still the question of whether the intervals on our "absolute scale," as used by the subject, reflect equal differences in actual degree of hedonic tone. If one of these procedures yielded measurements that entered into well-confirmed hypotheses relating hedonic tone to, for example, various properties of learning, this would bolster our confidence in the procedure. At least it would show that we were measuring something important. But such results have not been obtained to any considerable extent.

Even if all the above problems were surmounted, it would still be very difficult to compare the amount of pleasure or displeasure experienced by two different people. Suppose that I am trying to determine whether the total balance of pleasure over displeasure (or the reverse) is greater for my wife or for myself with respect to a given party. Even if the foregoing problems could be surmounted and we could find a valid way of assigning a hedonic number for each of us, relative to a scale for each, how are we to calibrate the two scales? How are we to determine whether a rating of +3 on my scale represents the same amount of pleasure as a rating of +3 on her scale?

So long as we restrict ourselves to refinements of the method of introspective judgment, the problem of intersubjective comparison seems insoluble. On the other hand, if there were some intersubjectively measurable variable, or complex of variables, which we had reason to think is intimately related to hedonic tone and which correlated well enough with rough introspective judgments to be taken as a measure of hedonic tone, all problems would be solved. Such a development is still in the future. Attempts to correlate introspective hedonic judgments with gross physiological variables on the order of pulse rate or patterns of respiration have not been fruitful. There has been no end of speculation concerning the neurological basis of hedonic tone. Pleasantness has been thought to depend on the degree to which assimilation counteracts dissimilation in the activity of any group of central neurones (A. Lehmann), the degree of the capacity of a neural element to react to stimulation (H. R. Marshall), the average rate of change of conductance in the synapses (L. T. Troland), and so on. Thus far, none of these theories has yielded effective physiological measures.

Bibliography

Plato discusses the nature of pleasure in his dialogues *Philebus* and *Timaeus*. Aristotle's main discussion is in Book X of the *Nicomachean Ethics*. A very illuminating history of the topic is H. M. Gardiner, R. C. Metcalf, and J. G. Beebe-Center, *Feeling and Emotion, A History of Theories* (New York, 1937).

Important discussions by contemporary analytical philosophers include Gilbert Ryle, *The Concept of Mind* (London, 1949), Ch. 4, and *Dilemmas* (Cambridge, 1954), Ch. 4; a symposium, "Pleasure," between Ryle and W. B. Gallie in *PAS*, Supp. Vol. 28 (1954), 135–164; Terence Penelhum, "The Logic of Pleasure," in *Philosophy and Phenomenological Research*, Vol. 17 (1957), 488–503; Anthony Kenny, *Action, Emotion, and Will* (London, 1963), Ch. 6; P. H. Nowell-Smith, *Ethics* (London, 1954), Chs. 8–10; and R. B. Brandt, *Ethical Theory* (Englewood Cliffs, N.J., 1959), Ch. 12.

Karl Duncker's article "Pleasure, Emotion and Striving," in *Philosophy and Phenomenological Research*, Vol. 1 (1940), 391–430, is a brilliant phenomenological analysis of the varieties of pleasure and their relation to desire. The psychological research on hedonic tone is well summarized in J. G. Beebe-Center, *The Psychology of Pleasantness and Unpleasantness* (New York, 1932). More recent developments are surveyed in Beebe-Center's article "Feeling and Emotion," in Harry Helson, ed., *Theoretical Foundations of Psychology* (New York, 1951).

The measurement of pleasure is discussed in Jeremy Bentham, *Introduction to the Principles of Morals and Legislation* (2d ed., Oxford, 1907), Ch. 4; Henry Sidgwick, *The Methods of Ethics* (London, 1874), Book II, Chs. 2 and 3 (also good on the nature of pleasure); R. B. Perry, *General Theory of Value* (New York, 1926), Ch. 21; and Robert McNaughton, "A Metrical Conception of Happiness," in *Philosophy and Phenomenological Research*, Vol. 14 (1954), 172–183.

WILLIAM P. ALSTON

PLEKHANOV, GEORGII VALENTINOVICH

(1856–1918), Russian Marxist, revolutionary, philosopher, sociologist, and historian of social thought. Plekhanov was the son of a poor nobleman. After graduating from a military academy in Voronezh, he studied at the Mining Institute in St. Petersburg. As a student he joined the revolutionary movement and became one of the leaders of the revolutionary organization of the Narodniki (Populists), called Zemlya i Volya (Soil and Freedom). After Zemlya i Volya split into the terroristic Narodnaya Volya (People's Freedom) and the Bakuninist–anarchist Chernyi Peredel (Redistribution of Soil) groups, Plekhanov became the leading theoretician of the Chernyi Peredel group.

In the beginning of 1880, Plekhanov emigrated to France and then settled in Switzerland. Between 1880 and 1882 he turned from Populism to Marxism, and in 1883 he founded in Geneva the first Russian Marxist group, Osvobozhdenie Truda (The Emancipation of Labor). In the summer of 1889 he took part in the founding congress of the Second International. In the late 1890s Plekhanov was one of the first to criticize both the international revisionism of Eduard Bernstein and its Russian variant, "economism."

In 1900, Plekhanov's group joined forces with a new group headed by Lenin. The two groups organized the second congress of the Russian Social-Democratic Labor party in London in 1902. The congress accepted a party program written mainly by Plekhanov. Disagreements over the nature of the party led to the split of the party into Bolsheviks and Mensheviks. Plekhanov supported Lenin at the congress, but he became neutral soon afterward and even leaned to the Menshevik side.

During the first Russian revolution (1905), Plekhanov severely criticized the tactics of the Bolsheviks, but after the defeat of the revolution he again came closer to Lenin. The onset of World War I led to the final parting of Plekhanov and Lenin. Plekhanov urged socialists to support the Allied governments, but Lenin declared war on the imperialist war.

After the February revolution of 1917 Plekhanov returned to Russia. Believing that Russia was not yet sufficiently mature for socialism, he regarded the October revolution as a fateful mistake. Nevertheless, he refused to engage in active struggle against Soviet authority.

As the founder of the first Russian Marxist group, Plekhanov is rightly called the father of Russian Marxism and of Russian social democracy. He was also an outstanding leader of the Second International. But the workers' movement is indebted to Plekhanov for his theoretical work, especially in philosophy, even more than for his practical organizational activity.

General philosophical views. Plekhanov regarded himself as an orthodox follower of Marx and Engels and severely criticized those who tried to "revise" the basic teachings of Marx or to "supplement" them with the ideas of Kant, Ernst Mach, or some other philosopher. But he insisted that the views of Marx and Engels should be developed further.

In his early writings Plekhanov exhibited the tendencies to reduce philosophy to the philosophy of history and to regard philosophy as a preliminary to science. He later stressed the independent tasks and problems of philosophy and defined philosophy in a broader way, as a study of the basic principles of being and knowledge and of their mutual relationships. Whereas Marx and Engels often insisted on the methodological character of their philosophy, Plekhanov stressed its systematic character. Marxist philosophy, according to Plekhanov, is a system, which Plekhanov named dialectical materialism.

Following Engels, Plekhanov maintained that the basic question of every philosophy was "the question about the relationship of subject to object, of consciousness to being," and he regarded materialism and idealism as two basic answers to the question. Dualism was a possible, but weaker, answer. A consistent thinker must choose between an idealistic and a materialistic monism, but vulgar materialism is not the only alternative to idealism. The real solution is dialectical materialism.

As the concept of matter was not clearly defined by Engels, Plekhanov made several attempts to do so. His formulations were more or less modifications of the traditional materialist view that matter is what exists independently of man's consciousness, affects his sense organs, and produces sensations. Plekhanov tried to show that opposing philosophies that maintain the world exists only in the consciousness of one man (solipsism), only in the consciousness of mankind (solohumanism), or only in that of some superindividual objective spirit (objective idealism) all lead to contradictions. The belief in the existence of the external world is, according to Plekhanov, an unavoidable leap of philosophy. Lenin reproached Plekhanov for such Humean terminology, and Soviet philosophers later exploited this criticism to accuse Plekhanov of Humeanism.

In criticizing idealistic views that "mind," "spirit," "consciousness," or "psyche" (he used these terms more or less interchangeably) is the only reality, Plekhanov at the same time rejected the view of those materialists who regard mind as a part of matter or (as Engels did) as a form of the movement of matter. Nevertheless, he held that mind is one of the properties of substance, or matter. In some earlier writings Plekhanov affirmed that mind is merely a mode of matter, a property characteristic of matter organized in a certain way. Later he modified his view, maintaining that mind is an attribute of matter, a property which, at least to a minimal, nonobservable degree, belongs to all matter. This theory led to his being accused of hylozoism. Plekhanov first thought that mind could be regarded as a consequence of another, more fundamental property of matter, movement. Later he changed this view and asserted that consciousness is an "inner state" of matter in motion, a subjective side of the same process whose objective side is motion.

Accepting the traditional correspondence theory of truth, Plekhanov tried to explain in a more specific way the character of correspondence or agreement holding between thought and reality. Against naive realism he stressed that "correspondence" does not mean "similarity." He maintained that sensations are "hieroglyphs" because although they can adequately represent things and their properties, they are not "similar" to them. To avoid misinterpretation of his views, Plekhanov later renounced this terminology; nevertheless, he was severely criticized for it by some Soviet philosophers, who held that it was a concession to Kantianism.

Plekhanov often stressed that Marxist philosophy is *dialectical* materialism and that dialectics is the soul of Marxist philosophy. But in explaining his conception of dialectics, he added little to what had already been said by Marx and Engels. He was more original in his view of the relationship between formal logic and dialectics. Starting from Engels, who likened the relationship between the two to that between lower and higher mathematics, Plekhanov maintained that thinking according to the laws of formal logic is a special case of dialectical thinking. By the help of a number of distinctions, like those between motions and things, between changing and relatively stable things, and between simple and compound things, he tried to determine more precisely the limits of fields in which the two logics could be applied. These explanations, although they gave no final clarification of the problem, nevertheless were the most explicit treatment of the problem in classical Marxist literature and served as the starting point for many later discussions.

Philosophy of history. Plekhanov's views on the philosophy of history have sometimes been misinterpreted. The fault is partly his own. Trying to present Marx and Engels' view on the relations between the economic foundation and the superstructure in a simple schematic way, he produced a formula involving:

1. The state of the forces of production; 2. Economic relations conditioned by these forces; 3. The sociopolitical regime erected upon a given economic foundation; 4. The psychology of man in society, determined in part directly by economic conditions and in part by the whole socio-political regime erected upon the economic foundation; 5. Various ideologies reflecting this psychology. (*Fundamental Problems of Marxism*, D. Ryazanov, ed., p. 72)

This formula may be regarded as an adequate schematization of economic materialism, the theory according to which the economic factor (the forces of production) is ultimately predominant in history. However, in other places Plekhanov maintained that neither man as man nor society as society can be characterized by a constant relationship between economic and other factors because such relationships are always changing. He even explicitly criticized the view that the economic factor must always be decisive and called it a "libel against mankind." Plekhanov admitted that so far men have been the "slaves of their own social economy," but he insisted that "the triumph of human reason over the blind forces of economic necessity is possible" (*Izbrannye Filosofskie Proizvedeniya*, Vol. II, p. 233).

In his best writings Plekhanov criticized not only the theory of the predominant role of the economic factor but also the theory of factors as such. In polemics against those who attributed the theory to Marx, he maintained that genuine materialists are averse to dragging in the economic factor everywhere and that "even to ask which factor predominates in social life seems to them pointless" (*The Materialist Conception of History*, p. 13). The question is unjustified because, "strictly speaking, there exists only one factor of historical development, namely—social man" (*Izbrannye Filosofskie Proizvedeniya*, Vol. V, p. 363); different branches of the social sciences—ethics, politics, jurisprudence, political economy—investigate one and the same thing, the activity of social man.

Aesthetics. Plekhanov was one of the few Marxist thinkers interested in aesthetics and the sociology of art. Criticizing the view that art expresses only feelings, he insisted that it expresses both feeling and thoughts, not abstractly, however, but in lively pictures. He added that the pictorial expression of feelings and thoughts about the world is not an end in itself but is done in order to communicate one's own thoughts and feelings to others. Art is a social phenomenon.

The first task of an art critic, according to Plekhanov, is to translate the idea of a work of art from the language of art into the language of sociology in order to find what could be called the sociological equivalent of a literary phenomenon. After the first act of materialistic criticism,

the second act—the appreciation of the aesthetic values of the work in question—must follow.

Investigating the social roots of the theory of art for art's sake and of the utilitarian view of art, Plekhanov came to the conclusion that the inclination toward art for its own sake emerges from a hopeless separation of the artist from the surrounding social milieu, whereas the utilitarian view of art emerges when a mutual understanding between the larger part of society and the artist exists. The utilitarian view of art can thus be combined with both conservative and revolutionary attitudes.

The value of a work of art is primarily dependent on the value of the ideas it conveys, but correct ideas are not enough for a valuable work. A work of art is great only when its form corresponds to its ideas.

Importance and influence. Although Plekhanov is not one of those greatest of philosophers who have opened up new vistas to mankind, he was not a mere popularizer of Marxist philosophy. Starting from Engels' interpretation of Marxist philosophy, he improved it and developed it in many directions. He greatly influenced Lenin's conception of Marxist philosophy, and through both his own works and Lenin's he decisively influenced Soviet philosophy between the two world wars. The leaders of the Soviet "philosophical front" in the 1920s, A. M. Deborin and Deborin's most outstanding opponent, L. I. Axelrod, were Plekhanov's immediate disciples.

In 1930 a new period in Soviet philosophy began, a period which included severe criticism of Plekhanov. All kinds of accusations were made against Plekhanov, but the Stalinist criticism abated in the 1940s and 1950s, and Plekhanov's philosophical views survived. Nevertheless, the publication of previously unpublished writings of Marx in the 1930s and 1940s and new discussions of Marx's philosophy in the 1950s and the 1960s seem to have produced an interpretation of Marxist philosophy which is more profound than that offered by Engels and developed by Plekhanov and Lenin.

Works by Plekhanov

COLLECTIONS

Sochineniya ("Works"), D. Ryazanov, ed., 24 vols. Moscow and Leningrad, 1922–1927.

Literaturnoe Nasledie G. V. Plekhanova ("The Literary Heritage of Plekhanov"), 8 vols. Moscow, 1934–1940.

Izbrannye Filosofskie Proizvedeniya, 5 vols. Moscow, 1956–1958. Translated by B. Trifonov as *Selected Philosophical Works*, Vol. I. Moscow, 1961. Five volumes are projected.

OTHER WORKS

Sotsializm i Politicheskaya Borba ("Socialism and the Political Stuggle"). Geneva, 1883.

Nashi Raznoglasiya ("Our Disagreements"). Geneva, 1885.

Anarchismus und Sozialismus. Berlin, 1894. Translated by E. M. Aveling as *Anarchism and Socialism*. London, 1895.

K Voprosu o Razvitii Monisticheskogo Vzglyada na Istoriyu. St. Petersburg, 1895. Translated by Andrew Rothstein as *In Defense of Materialism: The Development of the Monist View of History*. London, 1947; 2d ed., published as *The Development of the Monist View of History*, Moscow, 1956.

Beiträge zur Geschichte des Materialismus. Stuttgart, 1896; Russian ed., *Ocherki po Istorii Materializma*, Moscow, 1923. Translated by Ralph Fox as *Essays in the History of Materialism*. London, 1934.

"O Materialisticheskom Ponimanii Istorii." *Novoe Slovo,* No. 12 (1897), 70–98. Translated as *The Materialist Conception of History.* New York, 1940.

"K Voprosu o Roli Lichnosti v Istorii." *Nauchnoe Obozrenie,* Nos. 3–4 (1898). Translated as *The Role of the Individual in History.* New York, 1940.

Kritika Nashikh Kritikov ("Criticism of Our Critics"). St. Petersburg, 1906.

Osnovnye Voprosy Marksizma. St. Petersburg, 1908. Translated by E. Paul and C. Paul as *Fundamental Problems of Marxism.* New York and London, 1929. Also, ed. by D. Ryazanov, New York, 1936.

Ot Oborony k Napadeniyu ("From Defense to Attack"). Moscow, 1910.

N. G. Tschernischewsky. Stuttgart, 1894; Russian ed., *N. G. Chernyshevskii.* St. Petersburg, 1910.

Istoriya Russkoi Obshchestvennoi Mysli, 3 vols. St. Petersburg, 1914–1916.

Works on Plekhanov

Baron, S. H., *Plekhanov: The Father of Russian Marxism.* Stanford, Calif., 1963.

Fomina, V. A., *Filosofskie·Vzglyady Plekhanova* ("Philosophical Views of Plekhanov"). Moscow, 1955.

Hook, Sidney, *The Hero in History.* New York, 1943.

Petrović, Gajo, *Filozofski Pogledi G. V. Plehanova* ("Philosophical Views of G. V. Plekhanov"). Zagreb, Yugoslavia, 1957.

Vaganyan, V., *Opyt Bibliografii G. V. Plekhanova* ("Bibliographical Essay on G. V. Plekhanov"). Moscow and Leningrad, 1923.

Vaganyan, V., *G. V. Plekhanov: Opyt Kharakteristiki Sotsialno-politicheskikh Vozzrenii* ("G. V. Plekhanov: An Essay on the Characteristics of His Sociopolitical Views"). Moscow, 1924.

Volfson, S., *G. V. Plekhanov.* Minsk, U.S.S.R., 1924.

Yovchuk, M. T., *G. V. Plekhanov i Ego Trudy po Istorii Filosofii* ("G. V. Plekhanov and His Works in the History of Philosophy"). Moscow, 1960.

Zinoviev, Grigori, *G. V. Plekhanov.* Petrograd, 1918.

GAJO PETROVIĆ

PLESSNER, HELMUT, was, with Max Scheler, the founder of modern philosophical anthropology. Born in 1892 in Wiesbaden, Germany, he studied medicine, and then zoology and philosophy, at the universities of Freiburg, Heidelberg, and Berlin. He received a doctorate in philosophy from Erlangen in 1916 and his *Habilitation* in philosophy with Scheler and Hans Driesch at Cologne in 1920. His academic career in Germany was terminated by the National Socialist regime, and in 1934 he went to Groningen, the Netherlands, first as a guest of the Physiological Institute (where he was associated with F. J. J. Buytendijk), then as Rockefeller fellow, and from 1929 to 1942 as professor of sociology. Again dismissed by the Nazis, he was reinstated at Groningen by the Dutch in 1945 and occupied the chair of philosophy from 1946 to 1951. In 1951 he accepted the chair of sociology at the University of Göttingen in Germany. He became professor emeritus in 1962 and lectured as a visiting professor at the New School for Social Research in New York in 1962/1963. He received an honorary doctorate from Groningen in 1964.

Plessner's work—he has published 12 books and approximately 90 monographs, essays, and papers—ranges over an extraordinarily wide area, including animal physiology, aesthetics, phenomenology, the history of ideas, the history of philosophy, sociological theory, sociology of knowledge, sociology of education, and political sociology. Most of these studies are linked to the problems of philo-sophical anthropology, the discipline to which he has devoted his most important publications. His background in zoology and physiology, his phenomenological training under Edmund Husserl, and his sociological orientation have led him to redefine the problems and findings of the modern sciences of man.

Plessner agrees with the view that man artificially creates his nature, or more precisely, that what man makes of himself is contingent on history. However, man is bound by the structural principle of his position in the world; in contrast to the centricity of animals, who are, simply, what they are as organisms, in their *Umwelt,* man is "eccentric." Plessner rejects the dualism of spirit and matter present in Scheler's anthropology. He sees man as *being* a body (with such organically determined traits as upright posture, impoverishment of instincts, and drive surplus) and consequently exposed to his environment, and also as *having* a body and acting by means of it, as being open, within certain limits, to the world. Man is both "inside" and "outside" himself. Social and historical order is based on the precarious balance of these two dialectical moments. This order enables man to maintain a distance from things, from situations, and from himself, making it possible for him to use language and to plan actions. Man's eccentricity leads him to enter history, "to make himself" in history. However, when man faces ambivalent or insuperable situations, the balance on which order is founded is disrupted; planned action, speech, and all historically determined "orderly" ways of coming to terms with the world are blocked. His indirect, socially mediated relationship with the world momentarily breaks apart. In such marginal situations man responds in a prehistorical, presocial, and yet peculiarly human manner: by laughter or by tears.

Bibliography

Plessner's most important works are *Die Einheit der Sinne* (Bonn, 1923), *Die Stufen des Organischen und der Mensch* (Berlin and Leipzig, 1928; 2d ed., Stuttgart, 1964), *Das Schicksal deutschen Geistes im Ausgang seiner bürgerlichen Epoche* (Zurich and Leipzig, 1935; 2d ed. published as *Die verspätete Nation,* Stuttgart, 1959), *Lachen und Weinen* (Munich, 1941), and *Zwischen Philosophie und Gesellschaft* (Berlin and Munich, 1953).

For literature on Plessner see Jürgen Habermas, "Anthropologie," in *Fischer Lexikon,* Vol. II, *Philosophie,* Alwin Diemer and Ivo Frenzel, eds. (Frankfurt, 1958).

THOMAS LUCKMANN

PLETHO, GIORGIUS GEMISTUS (c. 1355–1452), the leading Byzantine scholar and philosopher of the fifteenth century. He was born in Constantinople, the son of a cleric. Pletho is noted primarily for advocating a restoration of ancient Greek polytheism and, above all, for inspiring the interest of the Italian humanists of the *quattrocento* in the study of Plato. His studies followed the usual pattern of Byzantine education, emphasizing the classical Greek heritage. Influenced by certain of his teachers, Pletho became interested primarily in the philosophy of Plato, whose writings had again been brought into vogue in Byzantium during the eleventh-century renaissance under the influence of the Neoplatonic philosopher-statesman Michael Psellus. In 1380, Pletho went to the

Turkish court at Brusa, or Adrianople, where he is reputed to have studied under the Jewish scholar Elisaeus. There Pletho presumably received training in the Muslim commentators on Aristotle, in Zoroastrianism, and in Chaldaic astronomy and astrology and was encouraged by Elisaeus to further his study of Greek philosophy. Indeed, Gennadius Scholarius, who later condemned Pletho for his belief in polytheism, credits Elisaeus with leading Pletho to apostasy. About 1390, Elisaeus was burned at the stake by the Turks, probably for heterodoxy, and Pletho returned to Constantinople, from which he moved in 1393 to Mistra in the Peloponnese, near the ancient site of Sparta. It was at this administrative and cultural center of Mistra, which ranked second only to Constantinople and Thessalonica, that he spent the most important years of his life.

In 1438 Pletho appeared as adviser to the Greek delegation at the Council of Ferrara-Florence, convoked in order to effect a union between the Eastern and Western churches. An antiunionist and in some respects even anti-Christian, he took little interest in the council's proceedings. He preferred to consort with the Italian humanists, themselves fascinated by his knowledge of the works of Plato, which had for centuries been virtually unknown to the West. He left the council before the final ceremony of union to return to Mistra, where he remained until his death.

Pletho's works reveal a deep insight into Platonic philosophy and, remarkably, a devotion to Greece rather than to the crumbling Byzantine Empire. Many of his treatises aim at the revivification and restoration of Greece's ancient glory. In his famous tract "On the Differences Between Plato and Aristotle," he asserts the superiority of Platonism to Aristotelianism, and his *Laws*, inspired by Plato's *Laws* and *Republic*, advocates a return to the polytheism of ancient Greece. Two memoirs based on a Platonic reconstruction of the state present a systematic plan of social and economic reform for Greece. Pletho felt that the collapse of the Byzantine Empire was due primarily to Christianity, the adoption of which had caused the alteration of the institutions of ancient Greece. In order to restore Greece to its former greatness it was necessary to foster a return to the ancient religion and to adopt a philosophy based on Platonic principles, which could serve as a guide in the process of governing. Pletho's numerous works include treatises on Zoroastrianism, Chaldaic astronomy, music, history, rhetoric, the "philosophic virtues," geography, and various theological subjects. Among his theological writings is a treatise on the procession of the Holy Spirit composed in response to the Latin view presented at the Council of Ferrara-Florence.

Despite some modern opinion to the contrary, Pletho's apostasy from Christianity seems certain. Scholarius, his Aristotelian opponent, condemns him for advocating paganism in his *Laws*, and George of Trebizond quotes Pletho as asserting that a new religion, neither Christian nor Islamic but similar to that of the ancient Greeks, would sweep the world. Why then did Pletho attend the Council of Ferrara-Florence and evidently acquiesce in the act of union? Pletho was taken to the council by the Byzantine emperor John VIII, probably as a learned layman philosopher who could buttress the arguments of the theologians.

Pletho's opposition to union was more on nationalistic grounds than dogmatic. As a patriot he feared that the consummation of union would precipitate a fresh Turkish attack on Constantinople. Moreover, he seemed to fear the Latinization of the Greeks, as for example in the possible suppression of Greek in favor of Latin in the ritual of the church. Finally, as a propagandist for the formation of a "Greek" nation and a restored Hellenism (in contrast to a "Byzantine" or, more correctly, "Roman" state), he was opposed to the international papal control implicit in the union of the two churches. His acceptance of the union can then be explained only as an act of political expediency with the aim of aiding Greece, not as the result of conviction that any particular doctrinal position was correct.

Almost every Greek humanist scholar of the fifteenth century was in some way influenced by Pletho, the most notable being his pupil, Cardinal Bessarion. A great many Italian humanists were also influenced by his writings and presence at the council. Through Pletho, ancient doctrines of the Chaldeans and Pythagoreans were transmitted to the West. More important, he set in motion at Florence the passionate interest in Platonism that was soon to permeate much of western Europe. Marsilio Ficino credits Pletho with inspiring Cosimo de' Medici to found the famous Platonic Academy. By introducing into Italy (especially through Paolo dal Pozzo Toscanelli) the geographical concepts of Strabo, Pletho may have prepared the ground for the correction of Ptolemy's geographical errors. Pletho consequently helped to alter the Renaissance conception of the configuration of the earth, thus indirectly influencing Columbus, for whom Strabo was an important authority. The high esteem in which Pletho was held by the Italian humanists is attested by the transfer of his remains from Mistra to Rimini, where they were interred in the Church of St. Francis.

Bibliography

The *Laws*, written about 1440 and printed at Paris in 1541, was printed in a Latin translation at Basel in 1574. "On the Differences Between Plato and Aristotle" was printed at Basel in the same year. J. P. Migne, *Patrologia Graeca* (Paris, 1866), Vol. CLX, pp. 773 ff., presents these and other Greek works of Pletho with Latin translations. On Pletho's life and thought the best and fullest work is F. Masai, *Pléthon et le platonisme de Mistra* (Paris, 1956). See also C. Alexandre, *Pléthon: Traité des lois* (Paris, 1858); M. Anastos, "Pletho's Calendar and Liturgy," in *Dumbarton Oaks Papers*, No. 4 (Cambridge, Mass., 1948), 183–305; M. Anastos, "Pletho, Strabo and Columbus," in *Annuaire de l'institut de philologie et d'histoire orientales et slaves*, Vol. XII, 1–8; J. Mamalakis, "Georgius Gemistus Pletho," in *Texte über Forschungen zur Byzantinisch-neugriechischen Philologie*, No. 32 (Athens, 1939); F. Schulze, *Giorgios Gemistos Pletho* (Jena, 1871); J. W. Taylor, "Pletho as a Moral Philosopher," in *Transactions of the American Philosophical Association* (1920), 84–100; and J. W. Taylor, *Pletho's Criticism of Plato and Aristotle* (Menasha, Wis., 1921). For the Byzantine influence on the Italian Renaissance in general see D. J. Geanakoplos, "Greek Scholars in Venice," in *Studies in the Dissemination of Greek Learning from Byzantium to the West* (Cambridge, Mass., 1962).

DENO J. GEANAKOPLOS

PLOTINUS (205–270), usually considered the founder of Neoplatonism. Plotinus was probably born in Lykopolis, Upper Egypt, and he may have been a Hellenized Egyptian rather than a Greek. He turned to the study of philosophy when he was 28. Disappointed by several teachers in Alexandria, he was directed by a friend to Ammonius Saccas, who made a profound impresson on him. Of Ammonius' teachings we know extremely little, but a promising line of investigation has been opened up in a comparison of Plotinus' doctrines with those of Origen the Christian, also a student of Ammonius. Of other students of Ammonius, Origen the Pagan and Longinus deserve special mention. Plotinus was Ammonius' pupil for 11 years. He left Ammonius to join the expeditionary army of Emperor Gordianus III that was to march against Persia, hoping to acquire firsthand knowledge of Persian and Indian wisdom, in which he had become interested through Ammonius. When Gordianus was slain in Persia in 244, probably at the instigation of his successor, Philip the Arabian, Plotinus had to flee from the army camp—which could mean that he was politically involved in some way. Plotinus reached Antioch in his flight and from there proceeded to Rome, where he arrived in the same year. In Rome he conducted a school of philosophy and after ten years started writing. At about this time he gained influence over, or the confidence of, the new emperor, Gallienus, and it is possible that his philosophy was meant to aid the emperor in some way in his attempted rejuvenation of paganism. In any case, Plotinus asked the emperor to grant him land in order to found some kind of community, the members of which would live according to the laws (or *Laws*) of Plato.

Despite the emperor's favorable attitude, a cabal of courtiers brought the plan to nothing, indicating that they may have seen in it some political implications. However, because the contents of Plotinus' writings and some facts of his life seem to point to a complete absence of political interests, the problem of Plotinus' involvement in affairs of state is controversial. Nevertheless it is strangely coincidental that his literary activity began in the first year of Gallienus' rule. Moreover, when Plotinus died (probably from leprosy, about two years after the assassination of Gallienus), he was not in Rome but on the estate of one of his friends (of Arabic origin), and only one of his pupils, a physician, was present. These circumstances make it difficult to rule out the possibility that Plotinus had left Rome and that his pupils had all dispersed at the death of Gallienus (between March and August of 268) because he and they were afraid they would be affected by the anti-Gallienus reaction; this would again contradict a completely apolitical interpretation of Plotinus.

Plotinus' works, which were all written in the 16 years after 253, have come down to us only in the edition by his pupil Porphyry. Porphyry arranged the works according to content into six sections called enneads because each contains nine treatises; he arbitrarily created some treatises by dissecting or combining the originals. Independent of this arrangement, he indicated when each treatise was written by assigning it to one of three periods in the life of Plotinus: before Porphyry became Plotinus' student, 253–263; while Porphyry was his student, 263–268; after Porphyry left him, 268–270. Whether Porphyry numbered the treatises within each period in strictly chronological order is open to some doubt. The presentation of Plotinus

given here follows the three periods of Porphyry with only a few forward or backward references. The standard citation to Plotinus' work designates the number of the ennead first, by Roman numeral; the treatise second, by arabic numeral; and the place of the treatise in Porphyry's chronological enumeration third, in brackets. The chapter number and, where relevant, the line number are also given in addition to the standard citation.

Contrary to the frequent attempts to present Plotinus' philosophy as a consistent whole, this presentation will stress all tensions by which the philosophy is permeated and leave it an open question whether Plotinus succeeded in reconciling them.

Influences. To understand the philosophy of Plotinus, a knowledge of some of the doctrines of Plato, Aristotle, the Neo-Pythagoreans, and the Stoics is very important.

In his dialogues Plato divided all reality into the realm of ideas (intelligibles) and the realm of sensibles, treating intelligibles alone as that which truly is (*ousia*), which implied that they are eternal and changeless (but see below). One of these ideas, the idea of the Good, he elevated above others, calling it beyond being (*epekeina ousias*). Comparable to the sun, it is the source of being and cognizability of all existents. In a lecture (or a lecture course) he seems to have identified the Good with the One.

Plato discussed the concept of the One in his dialogue *Parmenides,* ostensibly without any conclusion. In one passage he asserts hypothetically that if the One existed, it would be ineffable and unknowable. Whether this assertion was supposed to reveal the self-contradictory and, therefore, unacceptable character of the One, or on the contrary to express Plato's positive assertion as to the character of the One, is controversial.

In another dialogue, *The Sophist,* Plato seems to contradict his standard doctrine concerning the unchangeable character of the ideas by ascribing life, change, and knowledge to the realm of ideas.

As to the realm of the sensible, Plato in his *Timaeus* explains the origin of the cosmos in the form of a myth—as the work of a divine artisan (demiurge) who uses an ideal cosmos as model and fashions it out of something Plato calls "receptacle" and describes as void of any qualities, after ideas have in some way "entered" this void and by so doing created rudiments of the four elements. In addition to the physical universe the demiurge also fashions a cosmic soul and the immortal part of individual souls. The cosmic soul and the individual souls consist of a mixture of the same ingredients, on which mixture the demiurge imposes a numerical and a geometrical structure.

The immaterial and substantial character of the individual souls (or at least part of them) guarantees their pre-existence and post-existence (immortality). They are all subject to the law of reincarnation.

In the *Second Letter* (the authenticity of which was never doubted in antiquity, though today it finds virtually no defender), Plato, in a brief, and entirely obscure passage, seems to compress his whole philosophy into a formula reading: There are three realms, the first related to "the king," the second to the second, the third to the third. Plotinus was convinced that Plato is here describing the three realms of the One, Intelligence, and the Soul (whereas many Christian writers were convinced that Plato must have darkly anticipated the doctrine of the Trinity).

From Aristotle, Plotinus drew an important presentation of Plato's philosophy, ostensibly different from the one professed by Plato in his dialogues. According to Aristotle, Plato had assumed a realm of mathematicals mediating between ideas and sensibles (other sources identified this realm with that of the soul). Aristotle also attributed to Plato the view that two opposite principles, the One and the Indeterminate Dyad, are the supreme principles constitutive of everything, particularly of ideas and mathematicals—a doctrine Aristotle related to a similar, equally dualistic doctrine of the Pythagoreans. Aristotle represented Plato as having identified the Indeterminate Dyad with the receptacle and as having seen in it the principle of evil.

Plotinus also adopted Aristotle's doctrine of Intelligence (nous) as superior to the rest of the soul. Aristotle implied that it alone is immortal, the rest being merely the "form" of the body, hence incapable of separate existence. Aristotle designated the supreme deity as Intelligence contemplating (that is, intelligizing) itself; the cognitive activity of the Intelligence differed from sensation in that its objects (immaterial intelligibles) are identical with the acts by which Intelligence grasps them.

Plotinus was also aware of Academic and Neo-Pythagorean attempts to take over and modify the two-opposite-principles doctrine by elevating the One above the Indeterminate Dyad (sometimes above another One, coordinated with the Dyad), which thus changed Plato's dualism into monism culminating in a transcendent One. Plotinus also knew of the syntheses of Plato's and Aristotle's philosophy attempted by some Platonists, especially of the second century A.D., most prominently Albinus and Apuleius. Another influence was the strictly materialistic and immanentistic Stoic doctrine of the omnipresence of the divine in the cosmos. Finally, two Neo-Pythagorean teachers are particularly relevant as sources for Plotinus: Moderatus, who seems to have taken his cue from Plato's *Parmenides,* distinguishing a first One above being from a second and a third; and Numenius, who distinguished the supreme god from the divine artisan, creator of the cosmos.

PLOTINUS' PHILOSOPHY FIRST PERIOD, 253–263

Plotinus subdivided Plato's realm of intelligibles into three: the One, Intelligence, and the Soul (presupposed in IV 8 [6], Ch. 6; V 4 [7], Ch. 1; VI 9 [9], Chs. 1 f.; V 1 [10], Ch. 10; V 2 [11]).

The One. Following what are at best hints in Plato, Plotinus developed a full-fledged theory of the One as the highest principle, or cause. Precisely because it is the principle of everything that is—and is therefore omnipresent—it is itself above being (absolutely transcendental: VI 9 [9], Ch. 4, ll. 24 f., Ch. 7, ll. 28 f.; V 4 [7], Ch. 1, ll. 4–8; V 2 [11], Ch. 1). Since it is above being, it is fully indetermined (qualityless), although it may be called the Good as the object of universal desire. Because it is one, it

is entirely undifferentiated (without multiplicity: V 4 [7]; VI 9 [9], Ch. 3, ll. 39–45). As every act of cognition, even of self-cognition, presupposes the duality of object and subject, Plotinus repeatedly and strongly states that the One is void of any cognition and is ignorant even of itself (VI 9 [9], Ch. 6, l. 42; III 9 [13], Chs. 7, 9). He tries to mitigate this statement in some places, hesitatingly attributing to the One some kind of self-awareness (V 4 [7], Ch. 2, l. 16) or quasi awareness of its "power" to engender being (V 1 [10], Ch. 7, l. 13). In other places he distinguishes the ordinary kind of ignorance from the ignorance of the One and says that there is nothing of which the One is cognizant but that there is also nothing of which it is ignorant (VI 9 [9], Ch. 6, ll. 46–50).

Intelligence. The realm of the One is "followed" by that of Intelligence (intellect, spirit, mind—all somewhat inadequate translations of the Greek word *nous*). Here, for the first time, multiplicity appears. Roughly, this realm (hypostasis) corresponds to Plato's realm of ideas and, therefore, to that of true being. But whereas Plato's ideas are self-sufficient entities outside the Intelligence that contemplates them, Plotinus develops a doctrine of the later Platonists (perhaps originating with Antiochus of Ascalon) which interpreted ideas as thoughts of God and insists that intelligibles do not exist outside the Intelligence (V 9 [5], Chs. 7 f.; III 9 [13], Ch. 1). The structure of the second hypostasis also differs from that of Plato's ideal realm in that Plotinus assumes the existence of ideas of individuals; the resulting difficulty that the infinity of individuals would demand an infinity of ideas Plotinus meets by assuming that the sensible world is, as the Stoa had it, subject to cyclical destruction and regeneration and that in each of these worlds the same indistinguishable individuals, for which one idea would suffice, would exist (V 7 [18], Ch. 1).

Another difference between Plato's and Plotinus' realm of ideas is that Plotinus assumed the existence of souls in this realm (IV 8 [6], Ch. 3). This doctrine creates a special problem. The ideal Socrates, unlike the soul of Socrates, must be composed of soul and body. It should follow that the soul of the empirical Socrates should be only a copy of that of the ideal Socrates, a consequence which, however, Plotinus rejects in places (V 9 [5], Ch. 13; VI 4 [22] Ch. 14) and approaches in others (III 9 [13], Ch. 3; V 2 [11], Ch. 1, l.19).

Finally, Plotinus' realm of Intelligence contains even archetypal matter.

Despite all this multiplicity Intelligence remains one. In it everything is contained in everything without losing its identity, just as in mathematics every theorem contains all the others and, thus, the totality of mathematics (V 9 [5], Chs. 6, 9; IV 3 [27], Ch. 2).

Plotinus found it necessary to relate his doctrine of the One and Intelligence to the doctrine of the two opposite principles that figures in Aristotle's obscure presentation of Plato's philosophy in the *Metaphysics* (A6, 987a29 ff.). In that difficult passage (the text of which may be faulty), Plato is said to have identified ideas with numbers. Plotinus also found it necessary to relate his philosophy to the doctrine identifying the soul with number, the best-known example of which was Xenocrates' definition of the soul as self-changing number. Thus, Plotinus calls the realm of Intelligence the realm of number and calls the soul number (V 1 [10], Ch. 5). But as he conceives number to be derived from the interaction of One with plurality and yet elevates the One above the realm of Intelligence (being), he seems to assign to his One a double role, a doctrine very close to the Neo-Pythagorean assumption of a double One, one superior and transcendental and another inferior, present in the realm of Intelligence, or number (V 1 [10], Ch. 5).

Soul. Below the hypostasis of Intelligence Plotinus locates that of the Soul. Some souls remain unembodied; others "descend" into bodies. These bodies are either celestial or terrestrial. Celestial bodies offer no resistance to the soul's dwelling in them and thus these souls do not suffer from their incarnation (IV 8 [6], Ch. 2); terrestrial bodies, however, do offer resistance, and governing them may involve the soul to such an extent that it becomes alienated from Intelligence, its true home, and thus "sinks." In addition to these souls of individual bodies, Plotinus also assumes the existence of a cosmic soul (IV 8 [6], Ch. 7; III 9 [13], Ch. 3; II 2 [14], Ch. 2; I 2 [19], Ch. 1); thus, the world at large is one living organism. Probably the realm of the Soul does not consist of these individual souls alone; rather, they are all only individualizations of something we could call Soul in general (compare IV 3 [27], Ch. 4). In any case, all souls form only one Soul, and this unity implies that all souls intercommunicate by extrasensory means (IV 9 [8]).

Plotinus sometimes proves, sometimes merely assumes, not only the incorporeality, substantiality, and immortality of all the individual souls of men, animals, and even plants (IV 7 [2], Chs. 2–8[iii], 14), but also proves or assumes reincarnation, in the course of which the same soul may pass from the body of a man into that of a beast or a plant (III 4 [15], Ch. 2). Plato's best-known proof of immortality is based on the absolute simplicity and, therefore, indissolubility of the human soul. But Plato also taught that the soul is tripartite, and perhaps in an effort to reconcile these two doctrines, Plotinus assumes that the simple and, therefore, immortal soul on its "way" to the body receives additional, lower parts as accretions. This seems to be similar to a doctrine usually associated with Gnosticism—a downward journey of the soul, during which it passes the several planetary spheres, each of which adds something to it.

Emanation. The explanation of the relation of the three hypostases to one another leads to one of the most characteristic doctrines of Plotinus, but it is a strangely ambiguous one. This relation is described as "emanation," or "effulguration," of Intelligence from the One and of Soul from Intelligence—an emanation which, however, leaves the emanating entity undiminished (VI 9 [9], Ch. 9; V 1 [10], Chs. 3, 5–7; compare III 8 [30], Ch. 8, l. 11). The emanating entity thus remains outside of its product and yet is also present in it (VI 4 [7], Ch. 3; VI 9 [9], Ch. 7), a position sometimes described as dynamic pantheism to distinguish it from immanentist pantheism. This emanation Plotinus describes as entirely involuntary: what is full must overflow, what is mature must beget (V 4 [7], Ch. 1,

ll. 26–41; V 1 [10], Ch. 6, l. 37; V 2 [11], Ch. 1, l. 8; compare IV 3 [27], Ch. 13). Seen in this way, there is no fault, no guilt involved in emanation, nor is any justification of why the One had to become multiple necessary. On the contrary, the process deserves praise; without it the One would have remained mere potentiality, and its hidden riches would not have appeared (IV 8 [6], Ch. 5 f.). But sometimes, particularly when discussing the Soul's descent, Plotinus speaks of emanation in an entirely different manner. Even the emanation of Intelligence from the One, let alone that of Soul from Intelligence, he describes in such terms as "apostasy" and "falling away." It is recklessness and the desire to belong to nobody but oneself that cause the Soul to break away from the One (VI 9 [9], Ch. 5, l. 29). The Soul is motivated to break away from Intelligence by the desire to govern, which causes the Soul to become too immersed in bodies; by a craving for that which is worse; by a will to isolation (V 2 [11], Ch. 1; IV 8 [6], Ch. 4, l. 10; V 1 [10], Ch. 1). Matter emanates from Soul as the result of the Soul's wish to belong to itself (III 9 [13], Ch. 3). The "lowest" kind of Soul (the vegetative) is called the most foolhardy (V 2 [11], Ch. 2, l. 6). Thus, instead of an outflow, we should speak, rather, of a fall—with all its implications of will, guilt, necessity of punishment, and so on. These two interpretations—we shall call the former optimistic and the latter pessimistic—are difficult to reconcile.

Intelligence and Soul. Let us now consider the constitution of the second and third hypostases in additional detail. On the whole, Plotinus teaches that the One is in no way engaged in producing Intelligence. But sometimes he speaks as if Intelligence were the result of some kind of self-reflection of the One: The One turns to itself; this turning is vision; and this vision is Intelligence (V 1 [10], 7, l. 6—but the text is uncertain). Once more, we see that it is not easy for Plotinus to deprive the One of all self-awareness (consciousness). In any case, Intelligence is already multiple and, thus, less perfect than the One. However, the outflow from the One would not be sufficient to produce Intelligence. Rather, this flow must come to a stop—congeal, as it were. Incipient Intelligence must turn back to its source to contemplate it, and only by this act does Intelligence become fully constituted (V 2 [11], Ch. 1, l. 10). The emanation continues, and Soul emerges, again constituted by its turning toward the source, which is Intelligence (V 1 [10], Ch. 6, l. 47; V 2 [11], Ch. 1, l. 18; III 9 [13], Ch. 5). In Soul, multiplicity prevails over unity, and perfection has therefore decreased.

From Soul emanates matter, the totally indetermined (III 9 [13], Ch. 3; III 4 [15], Ch. 1). Because Plotinus tends to split the Soul into a higher, lower, and lowest kind, it is only the lowest which is the source of matter. Matter, when illuminated by the Soul, becomes the physical world, the model of which is in the realm of Intelligence (Soul thus corresponds to Plato's divine artisan, the demiurge). Thus, Plotinus' system would seem to be entirely monistic. But sometimes Plotinus speaks as if matter existed by and in itself, "waiting" to be ensouled (IV 8 [6], Ch. 6, ll. 18–20; V 2 [11], Ch. 1).

Emanation must be described in temporal terms. But, of course, it is in fact an entirely timeless event (VI [10], Ch. 6,

l. 19). Once the sensible world, particularly the human body, has been constituted, the Soul in the acts of incarnation becomes submerged in the realm of the temporal. The clash between a pessimistic and an optimistic evaluation of the emanative process can now be repeated in Plotinus' evaluation of incarnation.

Incarnation. The Platonist cannot easily ignore either the myth of the *Phaedrus,* implying that souls "fall" by some kind of failing, or the otherworldly mood of the *Phaedo,* implying that the soul should try to flee the body and be polluted as little as possible by it. But just as it is difficult for a Platonist to forget that according to the *Timaeus,* the first incarnation of the soul is the work of the divine artisan himself and, thus, a blameless event, so it is equally difficult for him to forget the myth of the *Republic,* according to which embodiment seems to be the result of some universal necessity. As a result, Plotinus had to resolve a contradiction. Sometimes he did so by trying to prove that there is no true contradiction (IV 8 [6], Ch. 5). But recognizing that such an assertion is in the last resort unsatisfactory, even when it is assumed that only part of the Soul descends (IV 7 [2], Ch. 13, l. 12; IV 8 [6], Ch. 7, l. 7), he adopted a theory which he explicitly claims as his innovation (he otherwise presents himself as an orthodox Platonist). According to this theory, a true fall has never taken place. Actually, even when in a body, the soul still lives its original "celestial" life and remains unseparated from Intelligence. Only we are not aware of this "hidden" life of the soul; in other words, we are partly unconscious of what happens in our minds (IV 8 [6], Ch. 8). What is true of the Soul in relation to Intelligence is even truer of the relation between our embodied selves and Intelligence. Not even when present in us does Intelligence discontinue its activity (V 1 [10], Ch. 12).

Plotinus also makes an optimistic and a pessimistic evaluation of the deterioration which has taken place in the soul as a result of its incarnation. On the whole, he tries to prove that no real deterioration has taken place, but he often feels that he must find reasons why the soul should try to escape the body and return home. One of these reasons is that the body prevents the soul from exercising the activity peculiar to it (IV 8 [6], Ch. 2, l. 43), which means, of course, that some deterioration does take place.

Dualism. There are some dualistic traits in the philosophy of Plotinus, particularly the recognition of the Indeterminate Dyad (as opposed to the One), to which he also refers simply as the Indeterminate (II 4 [12], Ch. 11, l. 37). Aristotle presented Plato's philosophy as a dualistic system, identifying the Indeterminate Dyad with Plato's receptacle and also with matter, in his own sense of the word; in other words according to him, Plato's ideas, being the product of the interaction of the two opposite principles, contain matter. Aristotle furthermore asserted that the Indeterminate Dyad is also the principle of evil. Plotinus is willing to recognize the Indeterminate as a second principle and to see in matter the principle of evil, but he refuses to recognize the existence of evil in the realm of Intelligence (ideas). He is thus forced to recognize the existence of two kinds of matter, one in the realm of the sensible and the result of the last emanative step, the other

in the realm of Intelligence ("intelligible matter"), which does not have some of the properties usually associated with matter—specifically, it is not evil. He justifies this by the assumption that everything, including matter in the physical world, must have its archetype in the realm of Intelligence (II 4 [12], Chs. 2 f., 11, 14). Whether the assumption of intelligible matter can be reconciled with monism appears dubious; its "origin" is never made clear by Plotinus.

As to matter in the realm of the sensible, it is sheer indeterminacy, incorporeal, and, thus, different from the Stoic conception of matter (II 4 [12], Chs. 1, 4, 9, 10). It remains as unaffected by the ideas (or "ratios," *logoi,* by which Stoic term Plotinus often designates ideas as present in the soul qua formative powers) as the mirror is unaffected by what it reflects. Precisely because this matter is indeterminate, it is evil (II 4 [12], Ch. 16, l. 19), which means that evil is not something positive, but sheer privation.

There is a strange parallelism between matter and the One, because both are entirely indeterminate. Therefore, they both elude ordinary concepts, and Plotinus faces the question of what it means to know them. As far as matter is concerned, Plotinus likens it sometimes to darkness, and the mental act by which we grasp it to "unthinking thinking," or the soul's reduction to indefiniteness (II 4 [12], Chs. 6, 11)—concepts reminding us of Plato's pseudo thinking (*nothos logismos*), declared by him to be the appropriate way to think the receptacle.

Knowledge of the One. But much more important for Plotinus is the problem how the One, in spite of its being ineffable, can be known. In the pseudo(?)-Platonic *Epinomis* (992B), the author insists that in order to know the One (whatever "knowledge" means here), the soul must itself become one; the Platonic *Letters* also seem to teach some kind of suprarational insight. Perhaps starting from passages such as these and also from passages in Aristotle and Theophrastus in which some kind of infallible knowledge of certain objects is described as a kind of touching (*thinganein*), Plotinus asserts that to "know" the One means to become one with it, which the soul can accomplish only by becoming as simple or as "alone" as the One. In the moment of such a union the soul has become God or, rather, is God; the soul has reascended to its original source (VI 9 [9], Ch. 9 f.). Among the terms Plotinus uses to describe this condition are "ecstasy," "simplicity," "self-surrender," "touching," and "flight of the alone to the alone" (VI 9 [9], Chs. 3, 11). This ecstasy—repeatedly experienced by Plotinus himself—is undoubtedly the climactic moment of man's life. It is not expressible in words (compare Plato, *Epistle VII,* 341D); only he who has experienced it knows what it means to be ravished away and full of God.

For this reascent man prepares himself by the acquisition of all the perfections (virtues, *aretai*). However, each of these perfections acquires different meanings according to the level on which man's spiritual life takes place—thus, there is a social fairness, above it another kind of fairness, and so on. Man also prepares himself by the exercise of dialectics (I 2 [19]; I 3 [20]). The preliminary stages of achievement Plotinus calls "becoming Godlike" (I 6 [1],

Ch. 8), a condition often described by Platonists preceding Plotinus as the ultimate goal of Plato's philosophy.

Free will and demonology. Among the other topics treated in this period, Plotinus' defense of the freedom of the will—only "reasonable" souls are free; others are subject to fate, εἱμαρμένη (III 1 [3])—and his demonology deserve special mention. In regard to demonology Plotinus tries to steer a middle course between two theories, one identifying demons with the supreme parts of our soul, and the other assuming the existence of demons as extrapsychical beings (III 4 [15]).

SECOND PERIOD, 263–268

Polemics. More than two-fifths of Plotinus' total literary output was produced during the brief period between 263 and 268, when Porphyry was studying with Plotinus. Perhaps Porphyry's presence worked as a powerful stimulus. A considerable part of the output of this period is devoted to polemics with other schools, notably on the doctrine of categories and against Gnosticism.

Categories. Plotinus rejects both the Aristotelian and the Stoic versions of this doctrine, adhering to the principle that there can be no categories common to the realms of the sensible and the intelligible. In application to the realm of the sensible he corrects and modifies Aristotle's categories; to the realm of Intelligence he tries to apply Plato's five genera—being, identity, diversity, rest, and change (VI 1–3 [42–44]).

Ideal numbers. Aristotle presented Plato as professing the existence of ideal numbers (twoness, threeness, and so on, as distinguished from ordinary numbers—two, three, and so on). And he devoted much effort to the criticism of the theory of ideal numbers. Plotinus defends the theory of ideal numbers—which differ from nonideal numbers in that they do not consist of addible unities and are therefore not addible themselves (V 5 [32], Ch. 4)—and, objecting to any nominalist or abstractionist theory of numbers, attributes to them subsistence. Specifically, after having divided the realm of Intelligence into three layers—Being, Intelligence (in a restricted sense of the word), and the original Living Being—he assigns ideal numbers to the uppermost layer and explains that only because of their existence can Being divide itself into beings (VI 6 [34]), Chs. 8, 16). In this context he also introduces a peculiar concept of infinity: The truly infinite is a thing which has no limits imposed on it from without but only from within (VI 6 [34], Chs. 17 f., but compare V 5 [32], Ch. 4).

Polemic against Gnosticism. Of all the polemics of Plotinus, the most significant is the one against Gnosticism. One could say that when facing Gnostic pessimism point-blank, Plotinus overcompensates for the pessimistic and Gnostic strand present in himself and responds with an almost unlimited optimism. The fundamental mood underlying Gnosticism is alienation from a hostile world, and Gnosticism undertakes to explain this mood and to open the road to escape from the world. The explanation is in the form of a history of the origin of the visible cosmos; according to Gnosticism, this cosmos is the result of the activity of an evil god sometimes identified with the Creator-God of the Old Testament or with Plato's divine artisan. This evil god is only the last in a succession of beings. The manner in which this succession takes place consists in a number of voluntary acts by which divinities of an ever lower order originate. The relation between these deities is often personal, based on such traits as curiosity, oblivion, daring, ambition. Man, as he exists in this evil world, contains in himself a spark of what was his original, divine substance, now imprisoned in his body owing to the scheming of the evil god. At a certain moment a messenger–savior in some way breaks the power of the evil god and makes it possible for those who hear the whole story (acquire gnosis) to regain their original standing and free themselves from the tyranny of the evil god.

Plotinus treats Gnosticism as a strictly philosophic system. He simply compares its doctrines with his own and with those of Plato; its salvationary aspects are of little interest to him (compare III 2 [47], Ch. 9). In the succession of divine beings he sees only a superfluous multiplication of the three hypostases of his own system (compare V 5 [32], Chs. 1 f.). To the cosmic drama which results in the creation of the visible cosmos he opposes his view of a totally undramatic, unconscious emanation, a product of necessity without arbitrariness and, contradicting even Plato's *Timaeus* (40B–45A), without planning (V 8 [31], Ch. 7) and, therefore, entirely blameless. The cosmos, product of the activities of the Soul (or Intelligence or both), he considers to be beautiful. Whereas Gnosticism sees the visible universe filled with spirits inimical to man, most outstanding among them being the rulers of the celestial bodies (planets), Plotinus sees in these spirits powers related to man in brotherly fashion. What is true in Gnosticism can, according to him, be found in Plato. The Gnostic objection that Plato did not penetrate the mysteries of the intelligible world Plotinus considers ridiculously presumptuous (II 9 [33]; compare V 8 [31], Ch. 8).

Problems. In the second period Plotinus was also concerned with the problems inherent in his own system, especially with the relation between the intelligible world and the sensible world and with the structure of the intelligible world.

The One. First, Plotinus tries to elucidate the nature of the One still further. He does this particularly in the context of a discussion concerning the nature of human freedom, in which he also asks whether the One should be considered as a necessary being or as a free one (*ens necessarium* or *ens liberum*)—in theistic terms, whether God must exist or has freely chosen to exist. In what is perhaps his most profound theological discussion, Plotinus tries to establish the concept of the One as Lord of itself and thus not having to serve even itself, so that in the One freedom and necessity coincide (VI 8 [39], Chs. 7–21). And without any vacillation he excludes any kind of consciousness from the One (V 6 [24], Chs. 2, 4 f.).

Intelligence and Soul. As far as Intelligence is concerned, Plotinus reiterates his doctrine that it contains ideas within itself (V 5 [32], Chs. 1 f.), and he again tries to explain how, in spite of being one, it still contains multiplicity (VI 4 [22], Ch. 4; VI 5 [23], Ch. 6). With regard to souls Plotinus tries to explain how they can remain distinct from one another although they all are only one soul (VI 4 [22], Ch. 6; IV 3 [27], Chs. 1–8; compare IV 9 [8], Ch. 5).

Both Intelligence and Soul are supposed to be present in the sensible world and, therefore, present in what is extended, although they themselves are not extended. Starting from the famous discussion in Plato's *Parmenides* (131B), in which the attempt is made to explain how one idea can be present in many particulars, Plotinus tries to show that just because Intelligence and Soul are not extended, they can be omnipresent and ubiquitous in what is extended (VI 4 [22], especially VI 5 [23], Ch. 11). And also in this context he tries to establish the concept of differentiated unity (VI 4 [22], Ch. 4), that is, the noncontradictory character of "one" and "many."

Intelligence, Soul, change. Probably the most formidable difficulty facing Plotinus is the result of his theory treating Intelligence and Soul as metaphysical principles on the one hand and as present in man on the other (that is, as both transcendent and immanent) and, therefore, in some way engaged in mental life, particularly in sensing and remembering. As metaphysical principles—that is, members of the realm of the intelligible—Intelligence and Soul should be unchangeable, whereas in man they seem to be involved in change. From this difficulty Plotinus tries to extricate himself in many ways, of which two will be presented.

On the one hand he keeps even the human soul away as much as possible from the processes of sensing, remembering, desiring, experiencing pleasure and pain, and so on (III 6 [26], Ch. 1–5). Sometimes he insists that the soul simply notices all these processes without being affected by what it perceives (IV 6 [41]; IV 4 [28], Ch. 19). Sometimes he insists that it is not the soul itself but only some trace of it which is engaged in these activities (IV 4 [28], Chs. 18 f.; compare VI 4 [22], Ch. 15, l. 15), and this ties in with the theory that the soul did not really—or not in its entirety—descend (VI 4 [22], Ch. 16). Sometimes he introduces the concept of a double soul, a higher and a lower, with only the lower being changeable. This doubling of the soul Plotinus carries to such extremes that he assumes two imaginative faculties and two faculties of memory, each belonging to its respective soul and each remembering in a different manner and different events. This is particularly the case after man's death; the higher soul no longer remembers anything it experienced while in the body, whereas the lower soul still remembers (IV 3 [27], Chs. 25–32; IV 4 [28], Ch. 1, l. 5). Sometimes he suggests that all the mental activities involving change happen not to the soul but to the composite of soul and body (IV 4 [28], Ch. 17), leaving undecided how anything can affect a whole without affecting the part which belongs to it.

On the other hand, when it comes to Intelligence and Soul as metaphysical principles (and even to the world soul and astral souls), Plotinus disallows them memory entirely (IV 4 [28], Chs. 6–17). As to sensing, he distinguishes two kinds, one serving such practical purposes as self-preservation, the other purely theoretical; it is only the theoretical kind which he ascribes to metaphysical entities, the implication obviously being that this kind of sensation does not cause any change in the perceiver (IV 4 [28], Ch. 24). Why they should still be called Intelligence and Soul remains somewhat unclear.

Perhaps the most striking example of the real effects of the Soul's falling away from Intelligence (despite everything said by Plotinus to minimize these effects) is that the cosmic soul, as it falls away, engenders time because of an inability to contemplate the totality of Intelligence simultaneously (III 7 [45], Ch. 11).

Ethics. The difficulties created for the explanation of the cognitive aspects of man's mental life without the assumption of a real change (passibility) of the soul return with even greater significance in the field of ethics. If there is no actual fall of the soul and if no deterioration of its nature has taken place as the result of incarnation (III 6 [26], Ch. 5), why is purifying the soul necessary? Yet the concept of purification plays a central role in the ethics of Plotinus (compare I 6 [1]; I 2 [19]); he even describes the perfections—wisdom, self-control, justice, courage—as purifications. Plotinus tries to help himself by a metaphor: The soul is merely covered with mud, which, however, has never penetrated it. According to another explanation, what the soul has acquired because of its fall is nothingness, and all it has to do, therefore, is to get rid of nothing (VI 5 [23], Ch. 12, ll. 16–23).

Cosmic sympathy. The insistence that memory and sensation, in their ordinary senses, are absent from the realm of Intelligence and even from that of the celestial sphere Plotinus explains with his theory that the universe is one animated organism. The sympathy existing among parts of one organism make memory and sensation superfluous, since the mutual affection need not be perceived. This leads to characteristic explanations of the efficacy of magic, prayers, and astrology. All these activities (and prophecies) are made possible by the fact that each part of the universe affects the others and is affected by them, not by mechanical causation nor by influencing the will of deities—particularly stars—but exclusively by mutual sympathy (IV 3 [27], Ch. 11; IV 4 [28], Chs. 40 f.). In this doctrine of sympathy many scholars see the influence of the Stoa, particularly Posidonius, on Plotinus.

Matter. As to matter, Plotinus in the writings of this period—with less ambiguity than in other periods—characterizes it as the result of the last step of the emanative process, thus fully preserving the monistic character of his system (II 5 [25], Ch. 5; compare I 8 [51], Ch. 7).

Some other problems discussed by Plotinus are distinctly occasional pieces and somewhat peripheral with regard to the system. Thus, we find a theory of vision, explained by sympathy (IV 5 [29]; II 8 [35]); a discussion of the Stoic concept of the complete interpenetration of bodies (II 7 [37]); a cosmology without the assumption of ether (II 1 [40]).

THIRD PERIOD, 268–270

As is to be expected, some earlier themes recur in the third period. In fact, one of the essays of the third period (V 3 [49]) contains what is perhaps the most comprehensive presentation of the basic tenets of Plotinus' philosophy. Plotinus proves that there must be a One preceding all multiplicity and that this One must be ineffable (V 3 [49], Chs. 12 f., 17). To explain its presence in us and the fact that we know about it although we do not know it, he says that those full of and possessed by the divine also feel that something greater than themselves is present in them, although they cannot say what it is (V 3 [49], Ch. 14). Once more facing the problem of how the One, which is absolutely simple, can be the source of multiplicity, Plotinus is on the verge of admitting that the One is at least potentially (though it is a potentiality *sui generis*) many (V 3 [49], Chs. 15 f.; compare VI 5 [23], Ch. 9). The same essay contains what is probably the most detailed and the most impressive description of the upward journey of the soul to reach the goal of ecstatic union, described by the formula "through light light" (V 3 [49], Ch. 17, ll. 28–37; compare V 5 [32], Chs. 4–9). As advice on how to achieve this union, Plotinus says "strip yourself of everything" (V 3 [49], 17, l. 38). Furthermore, Plotinus still feels he must prove that ideas are not external to Intelligence (V 3 [49], Chs. 5–13).

On the whole, the writings of Plotinus' last period are dominated by two themes. The first concerns theodicy, the origin and justification of evil, and the second asks what man's true self is.

Theodicy. To explain the origin of evil, Plotinus tries to reconcile the view that matter, though void of any quality and actually only deficiency, is still evil in some sense of the word and is the source of all evil (I 8 [51], Chs. 8, 10). In so doing, he sometimes comes dangerously close to the Gnostic theory that matter imprisons the soul (I 8 [51], Ch. 14, ll. 48–50) and to a completely dualistic system (I 8 [51], Ch. 6, l. 33). Nevertheless, his optimism is particularly strong in this period; he has high praise for the beauty of the visible cosmos (III 2 [47], Ch. 12, l. 4), and rejects the idea of an evil creator of the cosmos (III 2 [47], Ch. 1). His theodicy is a blend of Platonic arguments, drawn especially from Book X of the *Laws*, and Stoic arguments. Perfection of the whole demands imperfection of the parts (III 2 [47], Chs. 11, 17; III 3 [48]) and the existence of evil (I 8 [51], Chs. 8–15). At the same time he minimizes the importance of evil by insisting that it exists only for the wicked one (III 2 [47], Ch. 6). Furthermore, he points out that the cosmic order rewards and punishes everybody according to his merits and assigns each one an appropriate place, thus making for a completely harmonious whole (III 2 [47], Ch. 4). Ultimately, his theodicy is based on convictions characteristic of most theodicies—that to designate a particular as evil is to lose sight of the whole, that everything participates in the good as far as it can, and that evil is only absence of the good (III 2 [47], Chs. 3, 5; I 8 [51], Chs. 1–5).

Providence. Closely connected with the problem of theodicy is the problem of providence. Plotinus insists on the all-pervasive character of providence, thus rejecting Aristotle's dichotomy of the universe into a sublunar sphere dominated by necessity and a supralunar world to which providence is restricted. He replaces Aristotle's distinction by the dichotomy of good and wicked men; only the wicked are subject to necessity (III 2 [47], Ch. 9; compare III 1 [3], Chs. 8–10). But this providence is entirely impersonal (compare VI 7 [38], Ch. 1) and actually coincides with the order of the universe.

True self and happiness. The second major theme of Plotinus' last period is that of ascertaining what man's true self is—that is, of ultimately obeying the divine command "Know thyself." Attendant subproblems are the explana-

tions of wherein man's true happiness consists and of the concept of self-knowledge. It is extremely difficult for Plotinus to give a consistent account of what constitutes man's true self. He cannot simply identify it with Intelligence or Soul (as he did in IV 7 [1], Ch. 1, l. 24 or in I 4 [46], Chs. 8–16, where it is identified with the "higher" soul), precisely because both, in their character of metaphysical entities, remain transcendent; however, he rejects the idea that man is truly the composite of soul and body (I 4 [46], Ch. 14, l. 1) because this would grant the body too much importance. One of the solutions favored by Plotinus is that Intelligence is man's true self, but only if and when he succeeds in identifying himself with it. On the other hand, no such identification is actually necessary, because Intelligence is always in and with us even though we are not aware of it. (*Mutatis mutandis* this can also be applied to the relation of man and whatever is to be conceived the highest divinity: compare VI 5 [23], Ch. 12). Once more the concept of the unconscious plays a decisive role in the system of Plotinus (I 4 [46], Chs. 9 f.; V 3 [49], Chs. 3 f.). All this ties in with the idea that self-knowledge occurs only when the subject, the act, and the object of knowledge coincide—which takes place only on the level of Intelligence—whereas neither man as a whole nor Soul can possess full self-knowledge (V 3 [49], Chs. 3, 6). The One is, of course, above any kind of self-knowledge (V 3 [49], Chs. 10–13).

The thesis that only Intelligence is man's true self (if and when he makes full use of it) serves also as a basis for a discussion of the problem of man's happiness. If by "man" we mean the composite of body and soul, man cannot experience happiness, nor can he if he is body alone. However, if by "man" we mean the true self, it is obvious that happiness consists in the exercise of Intelligence—that is, in contemplation. But as the activity of Intelligence is uninterrupted (here in the argument Plotinus switches from Intelligence as immanent to transcendent Intelligence; see I 1 [53], Ch. 13, l. 7) man is actually always happy, although he may remain unconscious of it (I 4 [46], Chs. 4, 9, 13–16). Why this should apply only to the sage remains unclear.

The formidable problem of how the soul, the essence of which is unchangeability, can ever become evil also vexed Plotinus to the end (compare I 8 [51], Ch. 4, 12, 15). In the work of his last period he explains that as the soul at its descent acquires additional parts, evil resides only in them. Thus, the ethical task of man is not so much to separate the soul from the body as it is to separate it from these adventitious parts (I 1 [53], Ch. 12, l. 18). In this context the problem of who is the subject of punishments in afterlife also emerges; Plotinus answers that it is that "composite" soul (I 1 [53], Ch. 12). Why we should call soul an entity which is or can become evil, "suffer" punishment, and so on, after Soul has been presented as belonging to the realm of the unchangeable, remains unanswered; so do virtually all questions resulting from the dual character of Intelligence and Soul as metaphysical (transcendental) entities on the one hand and human (immanent) entities on the other.

There is almost something providential in the fact that the very last of Plotinus' essays, written at a time when death was approaching him, reasserts that all things participate in the One (the Good) and discusses the question of how to reconcile the two theses that life is good and yet death no evil, though it deprives us of something good (I 7 [54], Ch. 3). The battle between the pessimistic and the optimistic strands in Plotinus continued to the very end of his activity. Optimism ultimately won: Life is good—though not for the wicked one; death is good, because it will permit the soul to live an unhampered life.

Works by Plotinus

When completed, the edition of Plotinus' *Enneads* by P. Henry and H. R. Schwyzer will replace the others. Of the *editio maior* (with full critical apparatus), two volumes, containing Enneads I–III and IV–V, have appeared (Paris, 1951, 1959); of the *editio minor* (with abbreviated apparatus), one volume (Oxford, 1964). For Ennead VI, in addition to older editions, see the one by Bréhier cited below.

Translations accompanied by Greek texts, with notes, are available in French by Émile Bréhier, in 6 vols. (Paris, 1924–1938), and in German by R. Harder, W. Theiler, and R. Beutler (Hamburg, 1956—), in progress. For translations without Greek texts, see the English by Stephen MacKenna and B. S. Page, 3d ed. (London, 1962), and the Italian (with commentary) by Vincento Cilento, 3 vols. (Bari, Italy, 1947–1949).

Works on Plotinus

For an introduction to all problems of Plotinian scholarship, the best is H. R. Schwyzer's article "Plotinus" in A. Pauly and G. Wissowa, eds., *Realencyklopädie der classischen Altertumswissenschaft*, Vol. XXI (1951), pp. 471–592. See also appropriate sections in Eduard Zeller, *Die Philosophie der Griechen*, Vol. III, Pt. 2, 4th or 5th ed. (Leipzig, 1903; 1923), and Friedrich Ueberweg and Karl Praechter, *Die Philosophie des Altertums*, 12th ed. (Berlin, 1926). Two works on Plotinus are William Inge, *The Philosophy of Plotinus*, 2 vols. (London, 1929), and Émile Bréhier, *La Philosophie de Plotin* (Paris, 1952; new ed. in prep.), translated into English by J. Thomas as *Philosophy of Plotinus* (Chicago, 1958). There is a bibliography in B. Mariën in Vol. III of the Cilento translation cited above; see also Wilhelm Totok, *Handbuch der Geschichte der Philosophie*, Vol. I (Frankfurt, 1964—).

PHILIP MERLAN

PLOUCQUET, GOTTFRIED (1716–1790), German philosopher and logician, studied philosophy and theology at Tübingen, experiencing both Wolffian and Pietist influences. After serving as a pastor, he was professor of logic and metaphysics at Tübingen from 1750 to 1782. He was elected to the Berlin Academy in 1748. Ploucquet was one of the few logicians between Leibniz and Boole to study a symbolic calculus. In metaphysics, despite his Wolffian training, he developed a quite personal position inspired by Descartes and Malebranche and aimed at revising Leibnizianism on a theological basis.

Ploucquet regarded the problems of theology, cosmology, and psychology as inextricably intertwined, with theology as the predominant discipline. There were some variations in Ploucquet's doctrines, but typically he held that a monad is a spiritual substance, and that even being is spiritual. Spiritual substances and material things can interact because God represents both and connects them. Human perceptions are an effect of God's "real vision." Spiritual and material things are both real because God represents them; material things are real in a further sense,

as *phaenomena substantiata*, insofar as God represents them as real. This divine representation is the cause of the real existence of things; but we perceive only an appearance of this real existence. Ploucquet showed, by an examination of the logical difficulties of the concept of infinity, that space and time cannot exist outside of human representation.

Ploucquet's philosophy was basically a pronounced metaphysical subjectivism and phenomenalism. But in order to escape the consequent idealism of this position, Ploucquet reintroduced a variety of realism based on God. Ploucquet's was one of the most significant attempts before Kant to develop a phenomenalism that asserted the real existence of things but denied (contrary to Leibnizian and Wolffian phenomenalism) that we can know such things on the basis of their appearances.

Principal Works by Ploucquet

Primaria monadalogiae capita. Berlin, 1747.
Principia de substantiis et phaenomenis. Frankfurt and Leipzig, 1752.
Fundamenta philosophiae speculativae. Tübingen, 1759.
Institutiones philosophiae theoreticae. Stuttgart, 1772.
Elementa philosophiae contemplativae. Stuttgart, 1778.
Sammlung der schriften, welche den logischen Calkul des Herrn Prof. Ploucquets betreffen, mit neuen Zusätzen, F. A. Böck, ed. Tübingen, 1773.
Commentationes philosophicae selectiores. Utrecht, 1781.

Works on Ploucquet

Aner, Karl, *Gottfried Ploucquets Leben und Lehre.* Bonn, 1909.
Bornstein, Paul, *Gottfried Ploucquets Erkenntnistheorie und Metaphysik.* Potsdam, 1898.

GIORGIO TONELLI

PLURALISM. See MONISM AND PLURALISM.

PLUTARCH OF CHAERONEA (c. 46–120), Greek biographer and moralist. Plutarch was born in Chaeronea, a town of Boeotia. He studied in the Academy at Athens and later established a philosophical school in Chaeronea. His travels included at least two trips to Rome. For twenty years or more he was a priest at Delphi. His extant writings include 48 biographies and 65 other works (*Moralia*) varying greatly in subject and form. Titles of many additional works no longer extant are known from the "Catalogue of Lamprias," which lists more than two hundred in all.

Sixteen of the preserved writings are dialogues, the majority of which portray Plutarch's circle of friends and students. The two anti-Epicurean dialogues *Reply to Colotes* and *The Epicurean Life* describe sessions at his school: the reading of a philosophical work, Plutarch's comments on it, and then a more general discussion. Several dialogues have Delphi as their setting and are concerned with the oracle and other religious problems. *Table-Talk* is a long collection of conversations on a wide range of questions, with varying speakers and settings. In *The Face on the Moon* a group of mathematicians and philosophers discuss problems that presuppose a technical knowledge of mathematics, astronomy, and optics. Three dialogues—*The Face on the Moon, The Divine Vengeance,*

The Sign of Socrates—contain eschatological myths that link the immortality of the soul to a religious cosmology.

In his other works, as in the dialogues, Plutarch's philosophical position is a Platonism enlarged to include borrowings from Pythagoreans, Peripatetics, Stoics, and even Epicureans and Cynics.

Intellectual position. Plutarch relished intellectual problems of all kinds. Did the chicken come before the egg? Why is alpha the first letter of the alphabet? Why do the Romans suppose that Janus has two faces? What was Socrates' sign? His answers testify to his broad knowledge and acute observation. He was fully conversant with the sciences of his day and drew on them in the construction of a unified world view. Often he resorted to symbolism and allegory, as in *Isis and Osiris*, to make popular beliefs and practices compatible with Platonism. In good Academic tradition he claimed only probability for his answers to traditional philosophical problems, as in his *Generation of the Soul in the Timaeus*, 1014A, and *Divine Vengeance*, 550c. Yet his commitment to the belief that the soul, properly nurtured and purified, may escape (with the help of *daimones*) from the changing world of appearance to a higher world that is eternal and divine was sufficiently strong to lead him to violent denunciation of philosophers who challenged such a view. His bitterest attacks were against Epicureans and Stoics; for anti-Stoicism, see for example *Stoic Inconsistencies* and the dialogue *Common Notions*.

Moral teachings. Plutarch's interest in problems of behavior is everywhere apparent. His *Lives* are essentially character studies; and some two dozen of the *Moralia* are on moral themes. Titles include *Advice to Bride and Groom, How to Tell a Flatterer From a Friend, Inoffensive Self-Praise, Exile, Compliancy, Superstition, Control of Anger, Tranquillity of Mind, Brotherly Love, Can Virtue Be Taught?* Moral considerations dominate his approach to literature in *How to Study Poetry*. He even wrote on the behavior of animals: *The Cleverness of Animals* and *Beasts Are Rational*. In the moral essays one encounters many commonplaces, richly embellished with anecdote and often given an unusual twist. The underlying point of view is one that combines the goods of this world with those of the next. Plutarch is at times otherworldly, as in the *Consolation to His Wife* on the death of their two-year-old daughter: the soul that departs early from the earth does not become warped and cramped by the body but returns to the other world unimpaired. Yet even here he finds in life on earth more good than evil: The pleasure in remembering their daughter more than offsets grief at her death. So too the exile enjoys pleasures that outweigh his pains. The greatest pleasures come from intellectual pursuits and virtuous actions; a life so spent brings happiness in this world and leads to eternal felicity in the next.

Bibliography

Among the more important spurious works included in the Plutarchean corpus are *Philosophical Opinions* (a doxography); *Music* (drawn from Peripatetic sources); *Fate* (a product of syncretistic Platonism of the second century A.D.); and, on the level of "popular" philosophy, *The Education of Children* and *Consolation to Apollonius*.

Two English translations of the complete *Moralia* have been published, that of Philemon Holland (London, 1603), and that "by several hands" (5th ed., London, 1718; American ed., with introduction by Ralph Waldo Emerson, Boston, 1871). The Loeb Classical Library has announced a complete edition and translation in 15 volumes; 10 volumes have appeared, 2 more are in press. Other editions and translations will be found mentioned in the Loeb edition, especially Vols. I and VII.

Two German works are especially useful. K. Ziegler, "Plutarchos von Chaironeia," in *Real-encyclopädie der classischen Altertumswissenschaft*, Vol. XXI, Part 1 (1951), Cols. 636–962 (also published as a monograph, Stuttgart, 1949), is a detailed and authoritative account of Plutarch's life and work. R. Hirzel, *Plutarch* (Leipzig, 1912) contains several chapters on Plutarch's influence in ancient, medieval, and modern times.

Among American publications, R. M. Jones, *The Platonism of Plutarch* (Menasha, Wis., 1916) is of major importance. H. A. Moellering, *Plutarch on Superstition* (Boston, 1962), contains an extensive bibliography on pp. 158–164.

P. H. De Lacy

PNEUMA in Greek originally meant breath and was early identified with the life principle. For Anaximenes air both surrounds and controls the universe and is the source of individual life; Diogenes of Apollonia made pneuma the source of a whole series of biological functions. Pneumatology became increasingly important in medical theory, and in Galen's physiology blood and pneuma are basic substances. Breathed pneuma joins with blood in the left ventricle to form "zotic" pneuma (vital spirit). From the brain psychic pneuma (animal spirit) is distributed by the nerves. Others added physical pneuma (natural spirit), located in the liver.

Empedocles describes the embryo as alive but non-breathing. Some have derived Aristotle's famous connate pneuma from this prerespiratory life force. For Aristotle this is the material cause of soul in semen, and its association with heat makes it analogous to ether. In the living creature it is centered in the heart and is fundamental to the mechanism of sensation. For the Stoics pneuma is one manifestation of the divine active principle in the universe, but early Christians distinguished a transcendent divine pneuma in addition to this immanent, essentially material cosmic pneuma. For St. Augustine, God as spirit has become both nonmaterial and nonspatial. Pneuma in the individual was only later fully spiritualized.

Bibliography

Jaeger, W., "Das Pneuma in Lykeion." *Hermes*, Vol. 48 (1913), 29–74.

Peck, A. L., "Aristotle," in *Generation of Animals* (Loeb Series). London, 1943. Appendix B.

Verbeke, G., *L'Évolution de la doctrine du pneuma du stoicisme à S. Augustin.* Paris, 1945.

G. B. Kerferd

POINCARÉ, JULES HENRI (1854–1912), French mathematician and philosopher, was born into a distinguished family at Nancy. His cousin Raymond was both prime minister and president of the Third French Republic. At an early age Poincaré showed an interest in natural history and the classics, and at the age of 15 he developed an interest in mathematics. However, he trained first as a mining engineer, studying mathematics on his own during this training. In 1879 he was appointed to teach courses in mathematical analysis in the Faculty of Science at Caen. In 1881 he moved to the University of Paris, where he was soon given charge of the courses in mathematics and experimental physics. He lectured on mechanics, mathematical physics, and astronomy. Poincaré wrote an enormous number of papers on mathematics and physics and several important books on the philosophy of science and mathematics, as well as popular essays on science. His most important mathematical contributions were in differential equations, number theory, and algebra. In 1887 he was elected a member of the Académie des Sciences, and in 1899 he was made a knight of the Légion d'Honneur for his work on the three-body problem. In 1906 he became president of the Académie des Sciences, and in 1908 he was elected to the Académie Française.

Poincaré's work in the philosophy of science was in the tradition of Mach and Hertz, and he admitted a debt to Kant. His work was clearly influenced by his mathematical approach, and his interest was largely in the formal and systematic character of theories in the physical sciences. He showed less concern with epistemological problems connected with their support and establishment although he did write on the psychology of discovery. Einstein had a profound respect for his work in both mathematics and the philosophy of science. He is often claimed as an ancestor of logical positivism, although the justification is not always easy to see.

Aims and general character of science. Underlying scientific procedures, Poincaré held, is a belief in a general order in the universe which is independent of us and our knowledge. This is what mainly distinguishes the sciences from mathematics, which presupposes, if anything, merely the ability of the human mind to perform certain operations. The aim of the scientist is to discover as much as possible of the order of the universe, a point which must be borne in mind when Poincaré's view is called "conventionalism."

The method of discovery is basically inductive, proceeding by generalizing from observed facts; its lack of finality is due to its basis in a belief in a general order, since we can never be sure that the discovered order is absolutely general. Modifications in scientific conclusions spring from the constant pursuit of this generality. The discovery of facts depends upon observation and experiment, but these, in turn, depend upon selection because scientists cannot observe and absorb everything at once. There must be some principle of selection, but this principle must not be one of morality or practical utility. The search for an acceptable principle of selection led Poincaré to the idea of simplicity and a somewhat unusual defense of this idea. The best scientists are motivated by disinterested curiosity about how the world is, and their interest in general truths leads them to select those facts which "have the greatest chance of recurring." These are simple facts—that is, facts with few constituents. On grounds of probability there is more chance of the recurrence of a few constituents together than of the recurrence of many constituents together. However, familiar facts are more likely to appear simple to us than are unfamiliar facts. This seems to involve an unresolved conflict between two conceptions of simplicity.

What did Poincaré mean by "facts"? This is a question to which he gave less attention than it deserves. He held that science is to some extent objective. He toyed with sensationalism, but as a means of obtaining the necessary objectivity, he asserted that many sensations have external causes. Thus, he cannot strictly be regarded as a sensationalist. Objects are groups of sensation but not merely this; the sensations are "cemented by a constant bond," and science investigates this bond, or relation. Our sensations reflect whatever it is in the external world between which relations hold; science teaches us not the true nature of things but only the true relations between things. Scientific conclusions may thus be true of the world since they can give us a picture of its structure, though not of its content. We should expect theories of light, for example, to tell us not what light is but only what relations hold between the various occurrences of whatever light is.

The two main aims of scientific investigations are to relate what previously appeared unrelated and to enable us, by using these relations, to predict new phenomena.

Conventions. Poincaré constantly compared the physical sciences with pure mathematics and said that their methods of discovery are similar even though their methods of supporting conclusions are different. His view of science emerges most clearly from his comparison of it with geometry, in *Science and Hypothesis*. The space of geometry is not the space of sense experience; we can arrange conditions so that two things which look equal to a third thing do not look equal to each other. The mathematical continuum is invented to remove this disagreement with the law of contradiction; then, in mathematics things equal to the same thing are equal to one another *whatever* our senses tell us. This is one of those axioms of analysis, not geometry, which Poincaré called "analytical a priori intuitions."

Some geometrical axioms look superficially like this—for example, the Euclidean axiom that through one point only one line parallel to a given line can be drawn. The development of non-Euclidean geometries has shown that such axioms do not, as was formerly supposed, state fundamental properties of observable space. Coherent systems of geometry can be constructed based on the denial of Euclid's axioms, and these new geometries, when suitably interpreted, are translatable into Euclidean geometry. Moreover, they have physical applications. The applicability of the various systems is a function of context, or scale. The representation is purely structural.

Poincaré concluded that geometrical axioms are not synthetic a priori truths, for they are not of necessity true, and not experimental truths, for geometry is exact. They are conventions, or disguised definitions. It does not follow, as some critics have supposed, that they are arbitrary, for our choice is controlled by observation, experiment, and the need to avoid contradictions; nevertheless, such axioms cannot be either true or false. They are adopted because in certain contexts they are useful for saying how the world is. For most purposes Euclidean geometry is the most convenient. The application of geometry to the world involves an idealization. "Thus we do not *represent* to ourselves external bodies in geometrical space, but we *reason* about these bodies as if they were situated in geometrical space." No experimental support for Euclidean or any other geometry is possible, since experiments tell us only about the relations between bodies and nothing about the relations of bodies to space or of one part of space to another.

The physical sciences contain a conventional element as well as experimental, mathematical, and hypothetical elements, a fact which has been missed by most scientists. For example, the principle of inertia, according to which a body under the action of no force can move only at a constant speed in a straight line, is neither a priori nor experimental. It was originally conceived as experimental but has become a definition and so cannot now be falsified by experiment. Scientific conclusions are always conventional to some extent since alternatives to any hypothesis are always possible and, other things being equal, we choose those which are most economical. Because we have no means of knowing that the qualitative features of our hypothesis correspond to the reality, it does not make sense to regard the chosen hypothesis as the one true hypothesis.

In the physical sciences there are two kinds of statement—laws, which are summaries of experimental results and are approximately verified for relatively isolated systems, and principles, which are conventional postulates, completely general, rigorously true, and beyond the reach of experimental testing because for reasons of convenience we have made them so. Science is not entirely conventional because it does not consist wholly of principles. We begin with a primitive law, or experimental conclusion, but this is broken up into an absolute principle (definition) and a revisable law. Poincaré's example is the empirical statement "The stars obey Newton's law," which is broken up into the definition "Gravitation obeys Newton's law" and the provisional law "Gravitation is the only force acting upon the stars." Gravitation is an invented, ideal concept, but the provisional law is empirical and nonconventional because it predicts verifiable facts. The law of the conservation of energy is an outstanding example of a convention; it defines the concept of energy.

Prediction involves generalization, and generalization involves idealization. We connect a number of points on a graph by a smooth curve which does not pass through every one of them, and so we presuppose that the law we seek is best represented by a smooth curve even if this does not exactly fit the experimental results.

Points chosen midway between the existing points have a much better chance of showing which curve we should draw by eliminating one of them. A hypothesis is most strongly supported when it passes the tests which it was most likely to fail.

Unity and simplicity. We can obtain new knowledge only through experiment, and the role of mathematics in the physical sciences is to direct our generalizations from experiment. But experiment and generalization depend on presuppositions, most of which we make unconsciously. Among our presuppositions the most important are beliefs in the unity and simplicity of nature. Unity involves the possibility that various parts of the universe act upon one another as do the various parts of the human body, in the limited sense that to understand and describe one phenomenon, we may have to investigate other, superficially unre-

lated phenomena. The presupposition of simplicity is weaker: We can generalize any fact in an infinite number of ways, and we actually generalize in the simplest way until we have evidence against this way.

Two opposing trends can be discerned in the history of science. There is a movement toward simplicity and unity when we discover new relations between apparently unconnected objects and a movement toward complexity and diversity when, with the help of improved techniques, we discover new phenomena. The progress of science depends upon the first tendency, for "the true and only aim is unity." The second tendency is important, but it must ultimately give way to the first. Poincaré argued, referring to the growing unification of the studies of light, magnetism, and electricity, that there are signs of a continued victory for the tendency toward unity. But there are also signs that this does not always go along with simplicity : unity can sometimes be achieved only by revealing increased complexity in things when shown to be related. However, unity is essential and simplicity merely desirable.

Poincaré's account, like many others, suffers from a lack of clarity concerning precisely what is meant by "simplicity."

Hypotheses. Poincaré distinguished three kinds of hypotheses. The first kind he called "natural and necessary," and they are the very general hypotheses which we use in making judgments of relevance—for instance, when in physics we judge that the effect of very distant bodies is negligible. These form the common basis of theories in mathematical physics and should be the last to be abandoned.

The second kind he called "indifferent," and these are useful artifices for calculation or pictorial aids to understanding. Hypotheses are of this kind when they are alternatives which cannot be distinguished by experiment. Thus, he said, the two hypotheses that matter is continuous and that matter has an atomic structure are indifferent because experiment cannot establish the real existence of atoms. Such hypotheses may be useful, but they may also be seriously misleading if they are not seen for what they are.

The third kind of hypotheses he called "real generalizations." They are direct generalizations from observations and are indefinitely open to further testing. Whether or not they are finally accepted, they are always valuable, if only for their suggestiveness.

Theories and the role of mathematics. The aim of experiments in physical science is to break up complex phenomena into simple ones with respect to time and space, to connect each moment in the development of phenomena with immediately contiguous moments and each point in space with immediately contiguous points. We also aim to break up complex bodies and events into elementary bodies and events. Because observable phenomena may be analyzed in this way and be regarded as the result of large numbers of elementary phenomena similar to one another, they are conveniently described by differential equations. This accounts for the ease with which scientific generalization takes a mathematical form. Mathematical physics depends upon the approximate homogeneity of the matter studied, since this enables us to extrapolate.

A physical theory may be superseded by another which uses qualitatively different concepts but the same differential equations; the equations are merely given different interpretations in the two theories. The superseded theory will be just as valuable for prediction because it contains the same relations as the new one, and as long as these stand up to testing, we can say that these are the real relations between things in the world. Both theories are true in the only way in which it makes sense to talk of the truth of a theory. Any advantage that the new theory has over the old will be merely psychological and will lie in its suggestions rather than in its implications. It is relatively unimportant that one theory of light refers to the movement of an ether and another refers to electric currents; what is important is the extent to which their equations agree, and it is on this that their truth must be judged.

Theories do not set out to explain, although they may provide possible explanations. They are devices enabling us to connect and predict phenomena but not to describe reality in all its details. The assertion that, for example, atomic theories explain the behavior of matter implies that we are able to establish the actual existence of atoms as delineated by the theories. But this is a metaphysical and not a scientific assertion because such existence can never be established by scientific means.

Mathematics and logic. In mathematics Poincaré was, on the whole, an intuitionist, holding that the integers are indefinable and that underlying all mathematics is the principle of mathematical induction whose validity is intuitively recognized—that is, synthetic a priori.

In his last years Poincaré made a lively attack on the logic of Peano, Russell, and others, especially on the logistic attempt to reduce mathematics to logic (*Mathematics and Science: Last Essays*, Chs. 4–5). He thought it important to study not only the consequences of adopting given conventions but also the reasons for adopting these conventions rather than others. He argued that it is impossible to derive all mathematical truths from the accepted logical principles without further appeals to intuition. He pointed, for example, to the difficulty of defining numbers without begging the question, and he saw even in the foundations of Russell's logic a reliance, inescapable on any satisfactory account, on synthetic a priori principles. He objected to the idea of an actual infinity, which he claimed was essential to Russell's system, and held that the logical paradoxes could be avoided by excluding nonpredicative definitions—that is, definitions of particular members of a class which refer to all the members of that class (*Science and Method*, Book II, Chs. 4–5). He expressed a general dissatisfaction with the extensional interpretation of logical constants.

Works by Poincaré

Oeuvres de Jules Henri Poincaré, 11 vols. Paris, 1928–1956. Contains all Poincaré's important scientific papers together with part of his own account of his work, a biography by G. Darboux (Vol. II), and centenary lectures on his life and work (Vol. XI).

La Science et l'hypothèse. Paris, 1902. Translated by W. J. Greenstreet as *Science and Hypothesis*. London, 1905. Poincaré's most important book on the philosophy of science and mathematics.

La Valeur de science. Paris, 1905. Translated by G. B. Halsted as *The Value of Science*. London, 1907.

Science et méthode. Paris, 1908. Translated by Francis Maitland, with a preface by Bertrand Russell, as *Science and Method*. London, 1914.

Dernières Pensées. Paris, 1912. Translated by John W. Bolduc as *Mathematics and Science: Last Essays*. New York, 1963.

"Analyse des travaux scientifiques de Henri Poincaré, faite par lui-même." *Acta Mathematica*, Vol. 38, (1921), 1–385. Partly reprinted in *Oeuvres*. This is a Poincaré issue of the journal and contains an extensive bibliography and appreciations by J. Hadamard, H. A. Lorenz, P. Painlevé, M. Planck, L. Fuchs, and others.

Works on Poincaré

Carnap, Rudolf, *Logical Syntax of Language*. London, 1937.

Einstein, Albert, "Geometry and Experience," in *Sidelights on Relativity*, translated by G. B. Jeffery and W. Perrett. London, 1922.

Frank, Philipp, "Einstein, Mach and Positivism," in P. A. Schilpp, ed., *Albert Einstein, Philosopher-scientist*. Evanston, Ill., 1949. Other articles also mention Poincaré.

Frank, Philipp, *Modern Science and Its Philosophy*. Cambridge, Mass., 1949. Logical positivism's debt to Poincaré.

Grünbaum, Adolf, "Carnap's Views on the Foundations of Geometry," in P. A. Schilpp, ed., *Philosophy of Rudolf Carnap*. La Salle, Ill., 1964.

Hadamard, J. S., *The Early Scientific Work of Henri Poincaré*. Rice Institute Pamphlet, Vol. 9, No. 3, Houston, Tex., 1922.

Hadamard, J. S., *The Later Scientific Work of Henri Poincaré*. Rice Institute Pamphlet, Vol. 20, No. 1, Houston, Tex., 1933.

Le Roy, Édouard, "Science et philosophie." *Revue de métaphysique et de morale*, Vol. 7 (1899), 375, 503, 706; Vol. 8 (1900), 37.

Popper, K. R., *The Logic of Scientific Discovery*. London, 1959. For a somewhat misleading criticism of Poincaré's conventionalism.

Revue de métaphysique et de morale, Vol. 21 (1913), 585–718. Obituary number of journal.

Rey, A., *La Théorie de la physique chez les physiciens contemporains*. Paris, 1907.

Schlick, Moritz, *Raum und Zeit in der gegenwärtigen Physik*. Berlin, 1917. Translated by H. L. Brose as *Space and Time in Contemporary Physics*. Oxford, 1920.

Volterra, V., "H. Poincaré." *Book of the Opening of the Rice Institute*, Vol. 3 (Houston, Tex., 1912), 899–928.

PETER ALEXANDER

POLISH PHILOSOPHY. Philosophy in Poland developed in close contact with the entire philosophical tradition of Western civilization. As elsewhere, this development did not merely consist of a series of answers to the same set of well-defined questions: the very conception of the nature, task, and proper methods of philosophy underwent significant transformations over the centuries. The general pattern of these changes was, on the whole, analogous, although not identical, to that which existed in other countries. The differences, at times sufficiently significant to endow Polish philosophy with a high degree of originality, were closely bound to the distinctive features of Polish social and political history; these, however, cannot be considered in the highly selective and unavoidably oversimplified account that follows.

Scholastic philosophy. The active participation of Polish scholars in the intellectual life of the medieval West began in the thirteenth century. The earliest philosopher of international significance was Witelo, *filius Thuringorum et Polonorum*, a contemporary of Aquinas and a friend of William of Moerbeke who was notable for his contributions to optics, his analysis of visual perception, and his Neoplatonic metaphysics of light (*Perspectiva*, 1270). Philosophy started to develop more systematically after the founding (1364) and reorganization (1400) of the University of Cracow, which in the course of the fifteenth century became an international center of learning, maintaining close contact with centers of Scholasticism abroad and engaging in frequent interchange of students and teachers. All currents of late medieval thought, from Thomism, Scotism, and Averroism to nominalism and the empirical tendencies of the *via moderna,* were reflected in the activity of Polish thinkers in the fifteenth century. On the whole, in the first half of the century the *via moderna,* particularly through the influence of Jean Buridan, Albert of Saxony, and Marsilius of Inghen, predominated. Some of the philosophers who, in different ways, represented these tendencies were Matthew of Cracow, Andrew of Kokorzyn, and Benedykt Hesse. The second half of the fifteenth century was marked by variously transformed influences of Thomism, Albertinism, and Scotism, and often reflected the contemporary controversies between Albertists and Thomists of Cologne. John of Głogów (c. 1445–1507) and Michael of Wrocław (c. 1460–1534) are usually classified as Thomists, although their writings contain many other, mostly Albertinian, elements. One of the best representatives of the distinctive Cracow version of Albertinism, which blended well with some humanist and scientific interests, was James of Gostynin (c. 1454–1506). Scotism was advocated by Michael of Bystrzyków (c. 1450–1520), a student and follower of Peter Tartaretus and John Magistri, and it was advocated in a more moderate form by his pupil John of Stobnica (c. 1470–1530), who was open to various outside influences. Later the nominalistic tendencies regained influence through John Szyling (died 1518) and Gregory of Stawiszyn (1481–1540), who were followers of Lefèvre d'Étaples. These schematic indications do not do justice to the work of the Polish thinkers of the period, to their role in contemporary Polish culture, or to their specific contributions, which in many cases went well beyond the traditional classificatory labels. Current research is throwing much new light on the entire period. Most important new information can be found in the periodicals *Studia Mediewistyczne* ("Medievalist Studies"), *Studia i Materiały Zakładu Historii Starożytnej i Średniowiecznej* ("Studies and Materials of the Institute of the History of Ancient and Medieval Philosophy"), and *Mediaevalia Philosophica Polonorum* (in French and Latin).

Renaissance, Reformation, return of scholasticism. The ideas and attitudes of the Renaissance began to penetrate Poland in the middle of the fifteenth century. They coexisted for a time with late scholasticism and later, sustained by lively contacts with Italy, permeated the entire culture of the Polish golden age, which was characterized by the flowering of arts and humanities, religious tolerance, and establishment of civil liberties within the framework of the Polish constitutional system, which, with all its limitations, was highly advanced in comparison with other European countries.

Humanism. As early as the fifteenth century the University of Cracow, where the interest in Buridan's theory of "impetus" and in terminist physics had always been strong, achieved international prominence in philosophy of nature and in natural sciences. The work of Copernicus, the most famous student of the university, was in part the product of this environment.

A new interest in a nonscholastic Aristotelianism was represented by Szymon Maricius (1516–c. 1573). The most important Renaissance Aristotelian and one of the outstanding thinkers of the period was Sebastian Petrycy of Pilzno (1554–1626), popularizer, translator, and empirically minded commentator on Aristotle, who was interested chiefly in ethics, political philosophy, and education. Platonism was echoed in a dialogue on immortality written around 1505 by Adam of Łowicz, an admirer of *divina illa philosophia Platonica,* as he called it.

Two learned humanists represented Renaissance Stoicism. Jakub Górski (1525–1585) in his main work, *Commentatorium Artis Dialecticae Libri Decem* (1563), went beyond the traditional confines of narrowly construed formal logic and made contributions to the analysis of various modes of reasoning in the sciences, law, and ethics; he was, however, free from the exaggerated and often spurious anti-Aristotelianism common among humanists at the time. Adam Bursius (c. 1560–1611) was connected with a new Academy at Zamość. In his *Dialectica Ciceronis* (1604), which attracted the attention of Justus Lipsius, the famous renovator of Stoicism, Bursius developed an empiricist, sensualist theory of knowledge and advocated the use of inductive methods. He was also clearly aware of the distinctive character of Stoic logic—a rare virtue before Łukasiewicz in the twentieth century—and considered the logic of propositions to be fundamental part of deductive logic.

In political philosophy Polish humanists produced several interesting works, such as Jan Ostroróg's early (around 1455) theory of a modern nation-state, which anticipated some of the later themes of Renaissance political philosophy. The most important was Andrzej Frycz-Modrzewski's *De Republica Emendanda* (1551), well received by humanists outside Poland and notable for its dominant concern with social justice, its advanced program of social reform, and its critique of custom and tradition as criteria of the excellence of social institutions.

Reformation. In the second half of the sixteenth and the first half of the seventeenth centuries Poland became an international center of a radical Reformation movement of anti-Trinitarians, *Fratres Poloni* (Polish Brethren). Strengthened by exiles from other countries (such as Faustus Socinus), the Polish Brethren produced several thinkers notable for the breadth of their intellectual interests, their contacts with Western philosophers, and the humanitarianism of their original moral and social doctrines that emphasized the ideals of nonviolence, social justice, tolerance, and freedom of inquiry. Their views on philosophical and social issues, never quite unanimous, produced lively polemics both in Poland and abroad (Hugo Grotius, Leibniz). Despite sharp opposition and later persecution by other denominations in Poland and abroad, the Polish Brethren, known in the West as Socinians, earned the admiration of many outstanding minds of the period and exerted a lasting influence on the religious, moral, and political thought of Europe.

Two thinkers connected with another Reformation center in Poland also deserve mention: Jan Jonston (1603–1675), a precursor of Spinoza both in the form and in the content of his work (*Naturae Constantia*, 1632), and Jan Placentinus-Kołaczek (1630–1683), a Cartesian who taught abroad.

Seventeenth-century scholasticism. Aside from the exceptions indicated above and a few eminent mathematicians and scientists, Polish thought in the seventeenth century was isolated from the achievements of the "century of genius." In many ways it was a period of retrogression and political and social deterioration. Philosophy came under the almost exclusive domination of a resurgent scholasticism cultivated chiefly by the Jesuit schools, which established a near monopoly of education. These *scholastici iuniores*, whose main center was at the Academy of Wilno, produced numerous textbooks, most of them devoid of any originality and representing an anachronistic type of scholastic formalism; some, however, were of more than local significance, such as Marcin Śmiglecki's (Martinus Smiglecius) *Logica* (1618), which was used at Oxford and was reissued there twice in the seventeenth century. There were no significant changes in the first decades of the eighteenth century, except for an increased polemic against the infiltration of "novelties," particularly against Descartes. The most notable polemicist was Jerzy Gengell (1657–1727).

Enlightenment and beginning of nineteenth century. A radical shift in the philosophical climate occurred around the middle of the eighteenth century, within a wider context of social change and in close connection with a sustained large-scale effort to reconstruct and modernize the entire fabric of Polish society, especially the educational system.

The earlier phase of the Polish Enlightenment was one of eclectic assimilation of a variety of modern thinkers, accompanied by lively polemics on topical issues in political and social philosophy and a sustained defense of the value and autonomy of rational inquiry. The patron saint of the movement was often Christian Wolff, whose ideas were popularized by Wawrzyniec Mitzlof de Kolof (1705–1770), and two very active and influential students of Wolff: Antoni Wiśniewski (1718–1774) and Piotr Świtkowski (1744–1793). Marcin Świątkowski (died 1790) emphasized the significance of Baconian methodology; Kazimierz Narbutt (1738–1774) wrote the first textbook of logic in Polish.

The later, more radical stage was characterized by a turn toward empiricism and contact with and influence of the Encyclopedists. Condillac's *Logic* of 1780, written as a textbook for Polish schools, exerted considerable influence both in its original and in its Polish (1802) versions; Locke's ideas were popularized by Andrzej Cyankiewicz and later by Patrycy Przeczytański; the Enlightenment approach to natural law was represented by Hieronim Stroynowski and other writers whose beliefs were related to those of the physiocrats. These tendencies were, in the last phase of the Enlightenment, tempered by variously transformed influences of Kant and of the Scottish philosophy of common sense.

Jan Śniadecki (1757–1830), a mathematician and scientist of broad interests and an enemy of obscurity and ob-

scurantism, was the most eminent personality in the Polish Enlightenment world of learning. A radical critic of speculative metaphysics, Śniadecki conceived of philosophy in a manner related to the "new way of ideas" of British empiricists and partly related to Reid, and he anticipated many themes of later positivist literature.

A similar general outlook characterized Stanisław Staszic (1775–1826) and Hugo Kołłątaj (1750–1812), the two leaders of the social reform movement and the most outstanding exponents of its ideology. In their philosophical works, devoted mostly to moral philosophy and philosophy of history, they moved, however, more decisively toward a naturalistic theory of man and culture. Staszic's monumental panorama of human history emphasized the significance of education and of the struggles of the oppressed against the oppressors in mankind's progress. Kołłątaj's synthesis of the inspirations coming from Condillac, Helvétius, and the physiocrats presaged many later nineteenth-century ideas in the area of theory of history and of culture.

Jędrzej Śniadecki (1768–1838), brother of Jan and also a prominent scientist, is sometimes classified as a Kantian because his views on the relation between reason and experience seemed to anticipate the physiological type of Neo-Kantianism found in Helmholtz. His later work, however, displayed a Scottish common-sense realism with materialistic tendencies that is sometimes reminiscent of Feuerbach.

Kant's influence. The opposition to the Enlightenment philosophy, never wholly absent, drew on various inspirations. In the later Enlightenment one of these inspirations was Kant. The attempts to enlist Kant in the ideological battles of the times on the side of an offensive against the social program of the Polish Enlightenment, sometimes in the somewhat strange company of the Polish defenders of "throne and altar," complicated the reception of his thought, which was sharply criticized by the most prominent thinkers of the period. Jan Śniadecki, who saw in Kant's philosophy an attempt to resurrect pernicious and socially harmful metaphysics, was in turn criticized for an inadequate grasp of Kant's thought. The most serious and productive advocate of Kantianism was Józef K. Szaniawski (1764–1843), who later abandoned not just Kant but all philosophy. Without ever becoming predominant, Kant's thought affected Polish thinkers in a variety of ways; often characteristically Kantian emphases were blended with the increasingly predominant Scottish philosophy of common sense, although other representatives of the latter view criticized Kant.

Beginning of romanticism. Toward the end of the period, in an atmosphere of rising romanticism, the critical attitude toward the Enlightenment spread beyond the socially conservative circles, and the tradition of cautious empiricism and common-sense philosophy gradually gave way to new trends—to the Schellingian glorification of feeling and intuition exemplified by both the revolutionary romanticism of Maurycy Mochnacki (1804–1834) and the idealist metaphysics of a student of Schelling, Józef Gołuchowski (1787–1858). The latter, however, is usually classified as a Messianist and belongs to the next period.

Nineteenth century. The period between Poland's two unsuccessful uprisings (1830–1863) produced a series of daring metaphysical systems, developed partly in Poland and partly by Polish exiles abroad and usually described as Polish Messianism. Various points of contact existed between Messianism and contemporary philosophies such as those of Schelling, Hegel, Krause, and Lamennais, and in some versions of it there were strong echoes of mysticism following Jakob Boehme, Louis-Claude de Saint-Martin, and Andrzej Towiański. Nevertheless, for the most part Messianic philosophies were a distinctly original contribution to metaphysical speculations of the period, largely molded by intense preoccupation with Poland's fate. Some Messianists claimed their philosophy was a unique expression of the nation's spirit. Like their well-known Western analogues, Messianic philosophies do not lend themselves to brief summaries; their more specific and often penetrating insights were not very well served by the language of the period and the elaborate architecture of the systems. The most characteristic Messianist doctrine was a prophetic philosophy of history that proclaimed the coming of a new epoch of freedom and justice for all in a commonwealth of free people, and it emphasized, in the style of the century, the unique historical destinies and tasks of different nations, ascribing the special role of Messiah of the new world to a selected historical agent, usually the Polish nation but sometimes philosophy itself. The philosophy of history was developed within the context of a supernaturalistic, theistic, and personalistic metaphysics and was accompanied by a deep conviction that it is the business of philosophy to change the world, not just to interpret it. Behind this common façade there were many differences concerning specific conclusions and methods, which ranged from plain irrationalism and exaltation of mystical intuition, through various adaptations of Hegelian dialectic, to independently evolved methods of metaphysical construction.

The earliest and the most original representative of this tendency was Józef Maria Hoene-Wroński (1778–1853), who spent most of his life as an exile in France. Wroński made important contributions to mathematics and other sciences, and was driven by an iron resolve to effect a complete reform and unification of human knowledge, which was to provide a basis for the transformation of the world and to bring about a universal rule of reason. In a manner resembling Hegel, but independently of him, Wroński transformed the Kantian heritage into an all-embracing and strikingly original system of "absolute philosophy" which occupies a distinctive place in the history of metaphysical speculations in the nineteenth century. In spite of his prolific writings (he published about a hundred works in French and left many more in manuscript) and of his boundless self-assurance and proselytizing zeal, Wroński's influence was quite limited. An attempt to revive Wroński's philosophy was made, without great success, by a group of his admirers in the twentieth century.

August Cieszkowski (1814–1894) developed and modified Hegelianism in a highly original way (*Prolegomena zur Historiosophie*, Berlin, 1838; *Gott und Palingenesie*, Berlin, 1842) and later stated his philosophy in Polish in the form of a voluminous commentary on the Lord's Prayer. In terms of the issues then dividing German Hegelians, Cieszkowski's religiously inspired position was closer to the Right Hegelians, but his extension of philosophy of history to include the future and his emphasis on the *Philosophie der Tat*—on the concrete action leading to a "fulfillment of philosophy"—had important repercussions also among Left Hegelians.

Bronisław F. Trentowski (1800–1869) wrote first in German and later exclusively in Polish, creating for his purposes a large fund of strange neologisms. His system of rationalistic metaphysics, dominated by the desire to transcend, in a Polish national philosophy, the one-sidedness which he saw in main types of contemporary European thought, may be described as an adaptation of Hegelian procedures to a theistic metaphysics and a Messianic philosophy of history.

Two other Messianists, Karol Libelt (1807–1875) and Józef Kremer (1806–1875), combined their own modified versions of Hegelianism with Messianic metaphysics and were also noteworthy for their interest in and contributions to aesthetics. An important role in the history of Messianism was played by the great romantic poets Juliusz Słowacki (1809–1849); Zygmunt Krasiński (1812–1859), who was in many ways close to Cieszkowski; and above all Adam Mickiewicz (1798–1855), to whom Hegel was the epitome of abstruse obscurity and who tended, particularly in his lectures at the Collège de France, to transform Messianism into a mystically colored national gospel with an emphasis on the necessity of moral regeneration.

Messianism was not the only philosophy of the period. Two other important thinkers shared most of the philosophical concerns of the Messianists and some of their presuppositions but developed in a different direction. Henryk Kamieński (1812–1865), who wanted to replace the Cartesian *cogito* with "I create, therefore I am," was one of the most philosophically interesting democratic thinkers of the time. His social philosophy and theory of history were closely connected with a broader conception of human creativity and man's relation to the natural and cultural reality. Edward Dembowski (1822–1846), a young revolutionary killed during a demonstration, was a radical egalitarian and an enemy of eclecticism and compromises. Dembowski transformed Hegelian inspirations into a theory of national and social revolution which saw the motive force of history in the masses and their conflicts with the oppressors, and the universal rule of the people as an inevitable outcome of human history.

Social philosophies of the period ranged from downright reaction to utopian socialism. Of those which can be related to philosophical issues, it must be said that the metaphysical lines of division did not always correspond to the political ones. The conceptions directly associated with Messianism ranged from conservatism through paternalistic reformism, and from different forms of democratic liberalism to the self-styled socialism of Adam Mickiewicz. Other social philosophies owed their originality to the peculiarities of the Polish experience but also—particularly among exiles—reflected various contemporary influences (such as those of the Saint-Simonians, the Fourierists, Philippe Buchez, and Pierre Leroux). Most of the social philosophies grew against the background of and in close contact with revolutionary Europe, and they characteristically linked the liberation of Poland with various programs of social reform, such as the philosophies of the Polish Democratic Society and populist socialism.

Other philosophical tendencies of the period were represented by a few minor Hegelians and several conservative Catholic thinkers who had in common deep religious convictions rather than systematically articulated doctrines. The tradition of empiricism did not vanish altogether but was continued by Dominik Szulc (1797–1860) and above all by Michał Wiszniewski (1794–1865), an admirer of Bacon who was also influenced by Reid and Dugald Stewart.

"Polish positivism." After the second unsuccessful uprising (1863) the philosophical atmosphere in Poland changed again with the appearance of the so-called "Polish positivism." The term does not refer to a technical philosophical doctrine but, rather, to a wider intellectual movement that grew out of a specific political and social situation. It was opposed to romanticism and romantically inspired political action, advocating instead a sober, painstaking reconstruction of society through "organic work": economic improvement, popular education, and piecemeal elimination of prejudices and obsolete social institutions. Within this general context the dominant trend in philosophy was a reaction against all forms of romantic *Schwärmerei* and speculative metaphysics, influenced by a variety of contemporary positivist, and sometimes materialist, approaches to various areas of philosophy. The most systematic formulation of the new philosophical program was given ·by Julian Ochorowicz (1850–1917), who advocated a sober and cautious empiricism, distrusted all metaphysics, and was heavily influenced by Comte and Mill. Although the general position of Polish positivism, and in particular its social and political conceptions, was soon challenged, the movement played a significant role in the history of Polish philosophy by reviving the empiricist tradition that was originated by Jan Śniadecki and by preparing, in this way, the ground for later developments.

Turn of the century. In Poland at the end of the nineteenth century, despite an often difficult political situation, philosophical activity was intensified. As in other countries, it was the time of new beginnings that were to determine the character of philosophy in the twentieth century. *Przegląd Filozoficzny* ("Philosophical Review"), the first Polish periodical in the field, was founded in 1898 by Władysław Weryho (1868–1917).

A broadly positivist and antimetaphysical point of view with Kantian overtones was systematically developed by the influential thinker Adam Mahrburg (1855–1913), and in different forms by Marian Massonius (1862–1945) and Władysław M. Kozłowski (1858–1935). Władysław M. Heinrich (1869–1957), a student of Avenarius, was a proponent of empiriocriticism, which also had other advocates. Heinrich, later the founder (1922) and editor of *Kwartalnik Filozoficzny* ("Philosophical Quarterly"), was interested primarily in psychology and its methodological issues and in the theory of science. Władysław Biegański (1857–1917), sometimes called "the Polish Claude Bernard," was the author of works dealing with logic, theory of knowledge, and ethics and advocated a theory of science that showed affinities with pragmatism. Catholic philosophy came increasingly under the influence of Neo-

Scholasticism, as is shown in the works of Franciszek Gabryl (1866–1914) and Kazimierz Wais (1865–1934).

Marxism (or, more specifically, historical materialism), which had attracted the attention of some philosophers and of the rising socialist movement, found an independent and original interpreter in the social scientist Ludwik Krzywicki (1859–1941) and in Kazimierz Kelles-Krauz (1872–1904).

Edward Abramowski (1868–1918), a social philosopher (first a socialist, later a theoretician of the cooperative movement) and a noted psychologist, supplemented his various specific contributions to psychology, aesthetics, and methodology of the social sciences with radically anti-intellectualist "experimental metaphysics," according to which the nonverbalized, nonconceptualized mental states, accessible to experimental examination, open the way to objective reality undistorted by the intellect.

Stanisław Brzozowski (1872–1911), a critic of positivism and naturalism and an original theoretician of art, was a thinker of many often incompatible intellectual passions (for Sorel, Nietzsche, Marx, and Newman). His restless travels over the entire contemporary philosophical landscape never resulted in a systematically stated position, but his writings, embodying elements which would be called existentialist today, had a strong, stimulating impact, particularly in literary circles.

Wincenty Lutosławski (1863–1954), who fascinated and puzzled James and exasperated Peirce, acquired fame through his book on the chronology of Plato (*The Origin and Growth of Plato's Logic,* London, 1897; reprinted 1964). Later he developed an ambitious system of spiritualistic metaphysics inspired by nineteenth-century Messianism and enriched with his own conceptions. The system, proclaimed to be the embodiment of the "Polish national philosophy," was distinguished by its emphasis on palingenesis and the metaphysical significance of national consciousness (*Seelenmacht,* Leipzig, 1899; *The World of Souls,* London, 1924; *The Knowledge of Reality,* Cambridge, 1930).

One of the most original and brilliant thinkers of the period was Leon Petrażycki (1867–1931). First a professor in St. Petersburg, where he influenced a large group of Russian scholars, and later a professor in Warsaw, Petrażycki was primarily a philosopher of law. However, in the process of criticizing the then prevailing views and formulating his own theory, he developed a wealth of new and fruitful ideas in areas ranging from the problems of concept formation and theory construction in the social sciences to psychology and ethics.

Many of the above-mentioned scholars remained active after 1918, and some continued to exert much influence. However, the thinker most responsible for shaping the future character of Polish philosophy was Kazimierz Twardowski (1866–1938); (see TWARDOWSKI, KAZIMIERZ).

Twentieth century: 1918–1939. In the interwar period Polish philosophy, developing in an independent Polish state, reached one of the high points in its history. The dominant tendencies, although on the whole derived from different sources, approached those which came to prevail in the English-speaking world through the influence of G. E. Moore and Bertrand Russell. Although these tendencies were to a large extent due to Twardowski's influence, his numerous students did not share a common philosophical creed but, rather, a broad methodological commitment to rigorous standards of clarity of thought and precision of expression, accompanied by an opposition to irrationalism and dogmatism and an emphasis on the fundamental continuity of philosophical and scientific inquiry. This attitude favored specialized research, particularly the precise conceptual analysis of Brentanist inspiration, which often stopped at the propaedeutic level of sharpening the tools but also could, as it in fact did, lead to divergent philosophical positions.

The Lwów school, which grew around Twardowski even before World War I, included most thinkers who were to teach later at other Polish universities. Some of them kept fairly close to Twardowski's initial themes and procedures, particularly the psychologists with philosophical interests, such as Władysław Witwicki (1878–1948), who translated Plato and was a lucid and original thinker. Witwicki in some ways anticipated Alfred Adler and also contributed to aesthetics, moral philosophy, and history of philosophy. The tradition of conceptual analysis, especially of mental concepts, which had been enriched by the new influences of Husserl and Ingarden, was continued by some younger scholars, particularly Leopold Blaustein (1905–1944).

Most of Twardowski's students, however, developed a distinctive approach best exemplified by, although not limited to, the Warsaw school—a direct descendant of the Lwów school—whose leading thinkers were Stanisław Leśniewski; Jan Łukasiewicz; Tadeusz Kotarbiński, the most influential and admired thinker of the period; and, later, Alfred Tarski (see KOTARBIŃSKI, TADEUSZ; LEŚNIEWSKI, STANISŁAW; ŁUKASIEWICZ, JAN; TARSKI, ALFRED). Similar methodological tendencies and somewhat similar interests were represented by Tadeusz Czeżowski (born 1889), Zygmunt Zawirski (1882–1948), and above all by Kazimierz Ajdukiewicz (see AJDUKIEWICZ, KAZIMIERZ). A distinctive trait of the school, characteristically a methodological rather than a doctrinal one, was the emphasis on the philosophical relevance of symbolic logic, accompanied by an early interest in semantics and the application of the new analytic tools in various areas of philosophy. Some of the leading thinkers of the group were indeed creative logicians of great accomplishments, although their technical work in logic frequently grew out of distinctly philosophical concerns. Logic, which attracted a great number of younger scholars, was, however, developing as an increasingly autonomous discipline, often in close symbiosis with the Warsaw school of mathematics. Most of the philosophers of the group strongly criticized the traditional ways of doing philosophy, kept in touch with the activities of the Vienna circle but were not logical positivists, and explicitly rejected the most characteristic doctrines of logical positivism.

Among the younger generation of scholars brought up in this intellectual climate, the most important original contributions were made by Stanisław Ossowski (1897–1963) in aesthetics and methodology of the social sciences; by Maria Ossowska in metaethics, psychology, and sociology of moral behavior; by Janina Sztejnbarg-Kotarbińska in the methodology and philosophy of science; and by Janina Hossiasson-Lindenbaum (1899–1942) in the problems of probability and induction.

Catholic philosophy had numerous representatives of its various twentieth-century trends, the largest and most influential being the Neo-Thomist school (notably Jacek Woroniecki, 1879–1949). An important development within Neo-Thomism was the attempt to utilize the techniques of modern logic for the purpose of Thomistic metaphysics, as is shown in the work of Jan F. Drewnowski (born 1901), Jan Salamucha (1903–1944), and I. M. Bocheński (born 1902). The latter two scholars, following the trail-blazing work of Łukasiewicz, devoted special attention to the history of logic.

The University of Cracow, traditionally a stronghold of historical studies, was for a time also an independent center of studies in logic and in philosophy of science. One of the most important works in this field was an extended examination of the problem of determinism in natural science by Joachim Metallmann (1889–1942). The most original thinker connected with Cracow was Leon Chwistek (1884–1944), a philosopher, mathematician, painter, and theoretician of art and one of the most colorful figures in Polish intellectual life (see CHWISTEK, LEON).

Phenomenology was represented by one of the leading contemporary thinkers, Roman Ingarden (see INGARDEN, ROMAN). A lasting influence on generations of students was exerted by Władysław Tatarkiewicz (born 1886), for a quarter-century the editor of *Przegląd Filozoficzny*; he is a scholar of broad interests (ethics, aesthetics, methodology of the cultural sciences, history of art) and the most distinguished Polish historian of philosophy, and his works are notable for their striking combination of erudition, lucidity, and literary skill. Stanisław Ignacy Witkiewicz (1885–1939), a painter, playwright, and aesthetic reformer whose entire creative life was permeated by profound philosophical concerns, developed an ambitious and in many ways unique system of "biological materialism," a sort of naturalistic monadology.

In philosophy of law and related fields the tradition of Leon Petrażycki was continued, chiefly by Jerzy Lande (1886–1954). A different approach was represented by Czesław Znamierowski (born 1888), who was interested primarily in precise analysis of fundamental concepts relating to social action.

In the large volume of works devoted to history of philosophy, the most notable was the work of Konstanty Michalski (1879–1947), who gained international recognition for his part in establishing the new picture of fourteenth-century thought.

1945 to the present. During World War II Polish philosophy suffered great losses as a result of a systematic German attempt to destroy the "inferior" Polish culture. The number of philosophers who were murdered in occupied Poland and in concentration camps, or who died in action, is indeed staggering. However, the established scholarly traditions survived, partly because of underground teaching. After the war Polish philosophy developed in new conditions determined particularly by the fact that political authorities were explicitly committed to a definite philosophical system—dialectical materialism in the form which it acquired in the Soviet Union. The postwar history of philosophy in Poland may be divided—like Polish political history—into three periods.

Renewal. The first period, which lasted until about 1949, was a time of strenuous and manifold efforts to rebuild a normal scholarly life. This period was characterized by an intense preoccupation with philosophy on many different levels, by the presence of a variety of philosophical trends that included all prewar traditions as well as new concerns, and by a continuous debate between the officially promoted philosophy of dialectical materialism, represented primarily by Adam Schaff (born 1913), and its various friendly and unfriendly critics. The most significant works, some of them written during the war, included new publications by Ajdukiewicz, Kotarbiński, Ingarden, Tatarkiewicz, Czeżowski, Maria Ossowska, and Andrzej Mostowski. Most prewar philosophical journals were revived. Catholic philosophers resumed their activity, chiefly at the Roman Catholic University of Lublin.

Political regimentation. The second period was one of exclusive monopoly of "institutional Marxism–Leninism–Stalinism" established by administrative measures. Dissenting voices were silenced; the existing periodicals were replaced by *Myśl Filozoficzna* ("Philosophical Thought"), a militant organ of officially approved views; philosophy was enlisted in the service of political myth-making. With a few exceptions the bulk of the philosophical publications acquired the quasi-theological character of exegesis and popularization of a politically approved body of doctrine. This was accompanied by the "offensive on the ideological front," whose prime target was the tradition of the Lwów and Warsaw schools. Logic remained untouched by political intervention; the multilingual periodical *Studia Logica* was founded in 1953. Some interesting work was done in certain areas of history of philosophy, although it was often marred by twisted perspectives and a simple-minded Manichaean attitude. A monumental project of translating philosophical classics was initiated.

Relaxation of political control. The third period, which began around 1955 and more decisively after October 1956, extends to the present time and consequently may be described only very sketchily. Relaxation of political control was followed by a resurgence of philosophical life and in particular by two fundamental changes: (1) the re-emergence of various philosophical trends, including most older traditions, which not only managed to survive but, as it turned out, *sub silentio* strongly affected the official philosophy, and (2) a considerable transformation of the Marxist–Leninist philosophy itself.

The first change found its expression in (1) several important new works of the leading thinkers (Ajdukiewicz, Ingarden, Kotarbiński, Tatarkiewicz, Maria Ossowska) and renewed teaching and publishing activities of many others; (2) the re-edition of the works of the twentieth century's most significant Polish thinkers; (3) the appearance of a fairly large group of younger scholars of high professional competence; and (4) intensified activities of Catholic thinkers in various areas ranging from Thomistic metaphysics to history of logic and philosophy of law and sometimes reflecting new influences, such as existentialism.

The second change was spearheaded by a remarkable outburst of criticism directed against political manipulation of philosophy and by a re-examination of foundations which produced far-reaching departures from previously mandatory doctrines and stimulated the attempts to broaden and modernize the once petrified orthodoxy. Although the themes of the ensuing debate were not new in the history of Marxism, many significant contributions to Marxist literature were made. Consequently the Marxist–Leninist philosophy, while retaining its privileged position as an officially recognized foundation of state ideology, lost its artificially maintained monolithic character and abandoned its not-so-splendid isolation. Ultimately, some of the original revisionist thunder was absorbed by the Marxist–Leninist philosophy, which then acquired some distinctive characteristics. The once narrow path between "dogmatism" and "revisionism" was widened enough to accommodate specific changes of technical points of doctrine (such as the relation of dialectic to logic), to recognize the differing trends within the school (as usual the Hegelian and the more numerous scientist wings), and to incorporate new inspirations (semantics, philosophical anthropology, and early writings of Marx). The leading thinker of the school remained, as before, Adam Schaff, assisted by a new generation working in various areas from theory of knowledge to ethics and aesthetics. However, the tension between the officially sanctioned ideology and fully autonomous philosophy did not wholly disappear. The most original transformation of the Marxist heritage into an independent conception which goes beyond the confines of any orthodoxy is represented by the philosophy of Leszek Kołakowski (born 1927).

As a result of the changes, the volume of philosophical production, both in systematic philosophy and in history of philosophy, has become considerable. The philosophical scene is characterized by a variety of trends, with Marxism–Leninism in an officially favored position, and an interpenetration of various Marxist and non-Marxist traditions. (See also LOGIC, HISTORY OF, section on the Polish logicians.)

Bibliography

BIBLIOGRAPHIES

Two bibliographies covering specific periods are *Bibliografia filozofii polskiej 1750–1830* ("Bibliography of Polish Philosophy 1750–1830," Warsaw, 1955), and *Bibliografia filozofii polskiej 1831–1864* ("Bibliography of Polish Philosophy 1831–1864," Warsaw, 1960). Bibliographies may also be found in Władysław Tatarkiewicz, *Historia filozofii*, 3 vols. (Warsaw, 1958). Current bibliographies are in the quarterly *Ruch Filozoficzny*.

WORKS ON ALL OR SEVERAL PERIODS

A concise account covering the period until World War II is Władysław Tatarkiewicz, *Zarys dziejów filozofii w Polsce* ("An Outline of the History of Philosophy in Poland," Cracow, 1948). Although old, Henryk Struve, *Historia logiki jako teorii poznania w Polsce* ("History of Logic Considered as Theory of Knowledge in Poland"), 2d ed. (Warsaw, 1911), is still valuable as a source of information. Maurycy Straszewski, ed., *Polska filozofia narodowa* ("Polish National Philosophy," Cracow, 1921), contains essays on major thinkers of the eighteenth and nineteenth centuries; his *Dzieje filozoficznej myśli polskiej w okresie porozbiorowym* ("History of Polish Philosophical Thought after the Partitions"), Vol. I (Cracow, 1912), covers the period up to 1831. A short account of the history of logic and some related fields is Tadeusz Kotarbiński, *La Logique en Pologne* (Rome, 1959).

COLLECTIONS OF HISTORICAL STUDIES

Special collections of historical studies include *Archiwum Komisji do badania historii filozofii w Polsce* ("Archives of the Committee for Research on History of Philosophy in Poland") 6 vols. (1915–1937); *Wiek 19. Sto lat myśli polskiej* ("The Nineteenth Century. One Hundred Years of Polish Thought"), 9 vols. (1906–1918); and *Z dziejów polskiej myśli filozoficznej i społecznej* ("From the History of Polish Philosophical and Social Thought"), 3 vols. (Warsaw, 1956).

TWENTIETH CENTURY

Information on Polish philosophy in the twentieth century may be found in Kazimierz Ajdukiewicz, "Der logistische Anti-Irrationalismus in Polen," in *Erkenntnis*, Vol. 5 (1935), 151–161; I. M. Bocheński, "La Philosophie," in *Pologne 1919–1939*, Vol. III (Neuchâtel, 1942), pp. 229–260; Daniela Gromska, "Philosophes polonais morts entre 1938 et 1945," in *Studia Philosophica*, Vol. 3 (1948), 31–97; Tadeusz Kotarbiński, "Grundlinien und Tendenzen der Philosophie in Polen," in *Slavische Rundschau*, Vol. 5 (1933), 218–229, and "La Philosophie dans la Pologne contemporaine," in Raymond Klibansky, ed., *Philosophy in the Mid-Century* (Florence, 1959), Vol. IV, pp. 224–235; Władysław Tatarkiewicz, ed., *Pięćdziesiąt lat filozofii w Polsce* ("Fifty Years of Philosophy in Poland"), a special issue of *Przegląd Filozoficzny*, Vol. 44 (1948); Z. A. Jordan, *Philosophy and Ideology* (Dordrecht, Netherlands, 1963); and Henryk Skolimowski, "Analytical–Linguistic Marxism in Poland," in *Journal of the History of Ideas*, Vol. 26 (1965), 235–258. Wincenty Lutosławski and others, "Die polnische Philosophie," in *Ueberwegs Grundriss der Geschichte der Philosophie*, 12th ed. (Berlin, 1928), Vol. V, pp. 299–334, is valuable for bibliographical information but otherwise is misleading. *Journal of Philosophy*, Vol. 57, No. 7 (March 31, 1960), is an entire issue devoted to Polish philosophy. It includes a survey and articles by Polish philosophers.

GEORGE KRZYWICKI-HERBERT

POLITICAL AND SOCIAL THEORY. The Encyclopedia features two detailed survey articles, POLITICAL PHILOSOPHY, HISTORY OF and POLITICAL PHILOSOPHY, NATURE OF. It also includes the following articles on political or social concepts and doctrines and on methodological problems of the social sciences: ANARCHISM; AUTHORITY; COMMUNISM; CONSERVATISM; CULTURE AND CIVILIZATION; CUSTOM; DEMOCRACY; ECONOMICS AND ETHICAL NEUTRALITY; ECONOMICS AND RATIONAL CHOICE; EQUALITY, MORAL AND SOCIAL; FASCISM; FREEDOM; FUNCTIONALISM IN SOCIOLOGY; GEISTESWISSENSCHAFTEN; GENERAL WILL, THE; GERMAN PHILOSOPHY AND NATIONAL SOCIALISM; HISTORICAL MATERIALISM; HISTORICISM; HOLISM AND INDIVIDUALISM IN HISTORY AND SOCIAL SCIENCE; IDEOLOGY; JUSTICE; LIBERALISM; LOYALTY; MYTH; NATIONALISM; NATURAL LAW; PHILOSOPHER-KINGS; POWER; PROGRESS, THE IDEA OF; PROPERTY; PUNISHMENT; RACISM; RIGHTS; SOCIAL CONTRACT; SOCIALISM; SOCIETY; SOCIOLOGY OF KNOWLEDGE; SOCIOLOGY OF LAW; SOVEREIGNTY; STATE; TOLERATION; TRADITIONALISM; and UTOPIAS AND UTOPIANISM. See Political and Social Theory in Index for articles on thinkers who have given special attention to political or social topics or to problems arising from the social sciences.

POLITICAL PHILOSOPHY, HISTORY OF. The history of political philosophy is the succession of notions about the actual and proper organization of men into collectivities and the discussion of those notions. It is philosophical in character, because it is concerned with obedience and justice as well as with description; the persistent preoccupation of political philosophers has been the definition of justice and of the attitude and arrangements which should create and perpetuate justice.

A distinctive characteristic of political philosophizing is that it has usually been undertaken in response to some particular political event, or possibility, or threat, or challenge. This has led to a raggedness, even an incoherence, in works devoted to it and to an emphasis on intuitive argument which compares unfavorably with the content of other philosophical literature. Political philosophy has sometimes been supposed to confine itself to a particular entity called "the state," but in fact political philosophers have always concerned themselves with the collectivity as a whole, even when they have drawn a distinction between "state" and "society."

Problems of definition and description might appear to be prior to problems of analysis and prescription in political philosophy. In fact, however, ethical doctrine has always had a powerful effect on the view which a political thinker takes of the collectivity; he has tended to see it in terms of what he thinks it ought to be. Nevertheless, it has become usual to separate the empirical element from the normative. Empirical study has been further divided into sociology and political science. These definitions and divisions are no more satisfactory than others devised for similar purposes, and although we talk with some confidence of "sociologists," "political scientists" have only very recently emerged as an independent class of thinkers.

It is often useful to look upon political philosophy as in some sense systematic, proceeding from a view of reality and knowledge (ontology and epistemology) to a view of the individual (psychology) and a view of the social bond (sociology), and so to a general ethic, a political ethic, and finally to a set of recommendations about the form of the state and about political conduct. The expression "political philosophy" will be used in this sense here, and it will be considered solely in terms of the Mediterranean–European tradition.

CRITIQUE OF THE SUBJECT

There are several ways in which the history of political philosophy has been found important. Every thinker who engages in speculating about state and society and in formulating principles concerning them is anxious to know of the performance of his predecessors, to learn from them and to share their minds. Every thinking citizen is in this position too, to some extent, at least in the democracies: the questions raised in political life are frequently philosophical questions. Both thinkers and citizens, moreover, have good reason to believe that the intellectual and cultural life which they share with their contemporaries, together with the institutions which make political and social life possible for them, in some sense embody notions inherited from past political philosophy and philosophies. Certainly neither political attitudes nor political behavior nor political machinery can be understood without knowledge of this kind.

These various requirements have led to differing stand-ards for the study. Insofar as it is the record of thought about state and society, its level of accuracy has to be as high as possible. For academic historical purposes, every word of the text of Aristotle, or Marsilius of Padua, or Jefferson must be correctly registered, his intentions known, the circumstances of the writing and publication of his work discovered and recorded. But neither the con-scientious citizen nor the inquiring political theorist need be much affected by the particular version of a given work which he reads, even if it is an indifferent version, clumsi-ly translated and abbreviated perhaps, or a brief and ten-dentious summary in a general history. The complete book need not be known, nor the attitude of its author. It may even help if little fables are allowed to grow up around such works. The misunderstanding of one political philos-opher by another, or the misreading of authoritative books by citizens and constitution makers, has often been fruitful.

Moreover, historians of thought and of society have not been content with the role of annalists or of mere recorders of what was once written. They have sought to discover why the works were composed at all, to trace interconnec-tions and influences covering whole generations, whole centuries of intellectual development. More recently they have been concerned to study literature in the light of ideology and to see in the writings of political philoso-phers especially the "reflection" or "expression" of the social structure at the time of writing, with its discontinui-ties, inconsistencies, and ambivalencies. Classics have come to be regarded not only as determined in this way but also as instruments in the social process, intellectual weapons in the hands of interested men and groups of men.

Although these differing motives can be distinguished in the historiography of political philosophy, individual com-mentators are seldom moved by one alone and often fail to see them as distinct. To this confusion must be added the unfortunate consequence of confining attention to a partic-ular selection of authorities, a selection perhaps made originally for good philosophical reasons but which per-sists for reasons of convenience, curriculum, or plain con-servatism. This, which is itself an example of a confusion between the interests and outlook of the historian and of the philosopher, has led to the creation of a canon of "classics" which alone go to make up "the history of polit-ical philosophy." Taken together, these circumstances are responsible for a number of persistent weaknesses in the study of this subject, some of which are listed below:

(1) The scripturalist tendency to criticize works as if their authors should have written out the final truth with complete coherence and as if, therefore, their failure to do so, their incoherencies and inconsequences must conceal some inner truth to be unraveled.

(2) The philosophizing tendency to relate the select thinkers to each other and to no others, as if contrasts be-tween them and them alone are significant and as if they can be thought of as addressing each other. The reader's task becomes that of welding the various works into some philosophic whole.

(3) The tendency to mistake the theoretical interest of a work for its significance in other directions. This tendency is the general form of the failure to distinguish the separa-ble interests and objectives of historians (as annalists and explainers), of philosophers, and of citizens.

(4) The tendency toward what might be called "naive sociologism": the particular circumstances of a thinker are seen as expressed in his thinking in a literal and uncon-vincing way, and the dominant social conditions of the present are read almost unchanged into apparently analo-gous conditions of the past.

Each of these tendencies can be disabling enough in itself; when they are present in combination, the results can be strange indeed. The search for Hobbist elements in Locke, for example (tendency 2), can become an attempt to prove that he was really a Hobbist altogether and that his work on government must be examined for cryptic signs of those elements. More familiar are the exaggerations which come from stressing the relations of influence be-tween the canonical works (tendency 2) and seeing all other intellectual elements as "anticipations" and "deriva-tions" of these to such an extent that the relationships between bodies of thought and past societies are entirely distorted (tendency 3). Worst of all, perhaps, is a commen-tator who allows his thought to be so dominated by his experiences as a citizen in his own day that he betrays himself into an extreme form of the fourth tendency. When this happens, not only do Plato's or Rousseau's politics appear "totalitarian," but they are also made distantly re-sponsible for the totalitarian proclivities of the twentieth century.

Weaknesses of this kind, however, do not necessarily deprive the commentaries concerned of their interest. In the historiography of political philosophy, as in many other inquiries, the intrusion of obvious but stimulating fallacies helps to maintain the enterprise.

GREEK POLITICAL PHILOSOPHY

The Greek city-state, or polis, gave us the word "politi-cal" and is usually supposed to have been the social or-ganization which provided the necessary conditions for men to take for the first time a rational–critical view of the relation of the individual to the collectivity. The claim might be made that only in completely autonomous, small-scale, urban societies, like those of the Mediterra-nean area from the tenth century before Christ on, could an attitude of this kind develop. Because of the small size of these political entities, deliberations could take place, and decisions be made, in face-to-face discussion among all citizens, who could also see their collectivity as parallel with numerous other collectivities of the same character. It is certainly the case that the mold in which political phi-losophy has been set ever since is patently recognizable as Greek, and the assumption of face-to-face discussion and decision persists to this day, with not entirely fortunate results.

Socrates and Plato. The issues of freedom versus tyr-anny, of the various forms of the state (monarchy, aristoc-racy, or democracy), and of the nature and operation of law are not certainly known to have been debated until very close to the time of Socrates, who was born about 470 B.C., well into the famous fifth century. The Sophists, or teach-ers of the art of rhetoric and persuasion for use in the law courts and in Greek public life generally, are usually credited with initiating political discussion properly defined. Although he was unsparing in his criticism of these professionals in the techniques of influence, of *sophistry* in fact, it is hard not to classify Socrates himself as a Sophist.

A determined effort has been made in our day, by Karl Popper and others, to separate the political doctrine of Socrates, the champion of the critical discussion of dogmas and of institutions, from that of Plato, "the enemy of the open society," and their thinking has been related to the political events of late fifth-century Athens in a way which betrays many of the weaknesses described above. It seems best, however, to take Socrates and Plato as the dual spokesmen in the first known critical inquiry into the nature of the collectivity, with the peculiarity that one of them, Plato, did all the recording. The point at issue was the perennial point of how justice can be secured between men, organized as they have to be for the purposes of making a livelihood, propagating their kind, and cultivating the humane arts and accomplishments.

The answer given in Plato's *Republic,* probably composed about 365 B.C. and the most powerful of his dialogues, is straightforward enough in principle, perhaps even a little banal, but it is argued on the very loftiest plane. Justice is secured only when every member of the polis is doing what he is best suited to do, and those who are best suited to do the ruling are the philosophers themselves—lovers of wisdom, those who really know. "Unless," says Socrates at the end of Book V, "either philosophers become kings in our states or those whom we now call kings and rulers take to the pursuit of philosophy seriously and adequately, and there is a conjunction of these two things, political power and philosophic intelligence, . . . there can be no cessation of troubles for our states, dear Glaucon, nor I fancy for the human race either."

The steps of the argument before and after this passage are by no means a matter of formal political-theoretical demonstration, and the *Republic* is at one and the same time many different treatises, a characteristic which it shares with most of its successors as classics of political philosophy. What has probably sunk deepest into the European political imagination is its utopian element, the description of an ideal condition of the collectivity when it is ruled by a select society of guardians.

The famous Platonic guardians were to be brought into the world in accordance with premeditated principles of eugenics and were not to know who their parents were. They were to live in conditions of complete communism and poverty, without privacy and outside the family; both men and women were to spend their whole lives in the service of the polis and to undergo thirty years of education—gymnastics and military training to prepare the body, music and philosophical instruction to prepare the mind. Although it is implied that the guardians would be a small minority of the whole population, and that their undisturbed rulership would ensure justice, their actual relationship with the other two elements in the polis, the soldiery and the consumers (by which term Plato presumably meant the mass of handicraftsmen and peasants, producing and consuming), is never specified. These divisions

of the polis are presented as analogues of the divisions of the soul; indeed, the polis is the soul writ large. Insofar as there is a positive political doctrine in this most famous of all works of political philosophy, it seems to be hypothetical—if the polis-soul could be constructed in this way, then all problems would be solved.

Several other Platonic dialogues are concerned with political issues, and the last of them, the *Laws,* can be looked upon as the complete recasting of the Socratic–Platonic political philosophy in the light of a lifetime's reflection and experience, some of it Plato's own practical experience in advising a pupil of the Platonic Academy in the administration of the polis at Syracuse, in Sicily. But although Plato's *Politicus* (otherwise called the *Statesman*) presents an account of political life and political ideals rather different from that of the *Republic,* and although his *Laws* clashes at certain points with the *Politicus,* the ideal state of the *Republic* is that element of the political thought of Socrates and Plato which has interested posterity and influenced its thinking, almost to the exclusion of their other views.

Aristotle. Aristotle, Plato's pupil, was the first of many later philosophers and thinkers who addressed themselves to the Platonic utopia, and he rejected a great deal of it. Aristotle was even more of a synoptic thinker than Plato and was much more interested in the amassing and classification of knowledge. The gathering of information about politics and political organization was, therefore, only one of the many tasks on which Aristotle spent his extraordinarily industrious life (384–322 B.C.), along with his Herculean studies of logic, psychology, biology, literature, economics, physics and other subjects. But there is evidence to show that, like Plato and other Greek thinkers, Aristotle considered politics the most important subject of all.

The Aristotelian treatises on political philosophy, the *Eudemian Ethics* and *Nicomachean Ethics* and the *Politics* itself, appear to have been based on a monumental assemblage of material of a political-scientific character, including a record of no fewer than 158 constitutions of Greek poleis. These writings had even more impressive experience behind them, because Aristotle, a Macedonian by birth, had actually been tutor to Alexander the Great, who in Aristotle's lifetime subjugated Greece and Athens. Nevertheless, Aristotle's political theory was properly philosophical, that is, it proceeded from a general view of the world and of knowledge.

He was no more disposed than any other citizen of the polis to see the individual as a reality apart from the collectivity, but he did provide a critique of the reasons why human life implied compulsory association. Man, he claimed, is a species of animal that possesses intelligence and is found in intelligently collaborative groups; therefore "man is a political animal." The natural unit of the human family forms part of the natural unit of the village, which in turn forms part of the natural unit of the polis; but the polis is not merely the family enlarged, it is an association for leading the good life, which is otherwise incapable of realization—and this means a difference in classificatory, in logical, order. States (poleis—Aristotle significantly dismisses all larger organizations as capable of ordered living only by religious means) must be judged by the extent to which they enable citizens to become virtuous and to live the good life, a life of moderation, the mean. This line of argument led Aristotle to sketch his own ideal state, but it also led him, in the *Politics*, to raise a series of crucial issues which have endured almost unchanged as decisive questions for political science as well as for political philosophy.

Probably the most conspicuous are the claims of fundamental inequality between humans: slaves and barbarians are by nature inferior to Greeks and to citizens, although Aristotle conceded that inequality in some respects does not mean inequality in all respects. Within every collectivity, however, quite apart from the division between citizens and those incapable of citizenship, there are three classes: an upper class of aristocrats; a middle class of substantial men, mainly merchants, craftsmen, and farmers; and a lower class of laborers and peasants. The interests of these classes conflict: in sharp contrast with Plato and his anxiety for a harmony, a unity, in the polis-soul, Aristotle recognized politics as a conflict-defining, conflict-resolving activity. The actual distribution of political power among these classes—Aristotle himself insisted on the political virtue of the middle class—together with the web of man-made laws, goes to make up the particular constitution (*politeia*, the same word as the Greek title of Plato's *Republic*) of that polis. In spite of his fundamental inegalitarianism and his Greek inability to conceive of consent or representation as relevant to politics, Aristotle has often been hailed as the initiator of constitutionalism, as "the first Whig."

JUDAIC AND CHRISTIAN POLITICAL PHILOSOPHY

It is conventional to reckon the death of the polis at the death of Aristotle in 322 B.C. and to believe that nothing new of importance to political philosophy appeared until the Roman Stoics evolved the universalistic dogmas of natural law. It is undoubtedly true that no systematic philosophical discussion of political principles can be traced in Judaic thought or in early Christian thought. But it is important to recognize that the symbols and the symbol system of subsequent political thinking derives from Judaic as well as from Greek sources and that its psychological assumptions are deeply tinged with Christian revelationism.

The three social institutions of the ancient Hebrews, whose significance for the history of political thinking has only recently come to be recognized, are patriarchalism, the sense of the people, and kingship. The text of the Old Testament which proclaimed the duty of obedience as the basis not only of political discipline but of all social order, including economic order, was the commandment "Honour thy father and thy mother." Throughout the Christian centuries, therefore, all questions of obedience were seen in a patriarchal context, and the political power of the Hebraic patriarch (Judah, who condemned his daughter to death for playing the harlot, or Abraham, with his fighting army of servants) was the model for the power exercised by kings and ministers. Quite as significant was the Judaic

sense of the chosen people, the people led by the hand of God through the wilderness because they had an enduring purpose and being. Whenever Christian political theorists thought of the people as having a voice in the appointment of a king or a regime, or of the king as having a duty to his people, their model was the peculiar people of Israel. European kingship was also conceived in Biblical terms, and the tribal hero-king whose actions committed the people before God and whose power came from God can be seen behind the western European dynastic regimes.

Even more authoritative, of course, were the words of Jesus himself on political matters, and the few texts which could be made to bear at all upon them have been perpetually cited throughout the Christian era. Christ's submission to the Roman authority, his use of an inscription on a Roman penny ("Render unto Caesar the things that are Caesar's"), and his repeated insistence that his kingdom was not of this world made it difficult to find authority in the New Testament for any doctrine of resistance. Saint Paul's sayings pointed in the same quietist direction ("The powers that be are ordained of God"). But more interesting to the twentieth century are those fragments of evidence from the apostolic era which make it possible to believe that Christ's immediate followers lived a communistic existence.

ROMAN STOICISM AND NATURAL LAW

The belief that there is a universal and eternal moral ordering which is common to all men and which therefore carries weight on certain issues in every collectivity is a widespread ethical and religious notion, and it need have very little specific content (see NATURAL LAW). Its origins have been sought in Plato's immutable Ideas and, further back, in Greek poetry. The source most often favored, however, is the religious–philosophical sect of the Stoics, who took their name from the *stoa,* or porch, before which Zeno, their reputed founder, preached and taught in Athens soon after the time of Aristotle, about 390 B.C. Stoicism was brought to Rome during the classical generations of Roman republicanism, and it continued to be a system widely accepted, although changing in content, from the time of the Scipios (about 100 B.C.) until about A.D. 200, when even the great Roman political families began to feel the attraction of Christianity.

The orator-statesman Cicero, although eclectic in his intellectual outlook and not usually thought of as a philosopher, wrote probably the most widely read of all works in political philosophy until recent times, *On the Laws* (*De Legibus,* c. 46 B.C.) and *On the Duties of the Citizen* (*De Officiis,* a year or two later). The *Laws* was composed in deliberate imitation of Plato and was intended to complement Cicero's *De Re Publica* (his *Republic* of a year or two before), a work which was lost until 1820. *De Re Publica* contains, however, the classic text for the universalistic theory of natural law as it entered into political philosophy:

True law is right reason in agreement with Nature; it is of universal application, unchanging and everlasting . . . there will not be different laws at Rome and at

Athens, or different laws now and in the future, but one eternal and unchangeable law will be valid for all nations and all times, and there will be one master and one ruler, that is, God, over us all, for He is the author of this law, its promulgator and its enforcing judge. (Book III, Ch. 22, Sec. 33)

The cosmopolitan character of this doctrine—a society of all humanity ruled by one God—is in sharp contrast with the earlier Greek outlook, which assumed that only the small-scale polis could embody political good. The individual is recognizably the unit of this universal society and is the subject of the rights conferred on all citizens, all Roman citizens, by the Roman law. The identification of law with reason must be noticed in this process; reason carries its own claims to the individual's obedience. The final sanction of law and authority is placed here outside the collectivity altogether, in the Deity. Nevertheless, nothing in Stoicism could be taken as an argument against the deification of the later emperors, and one of them, Marcus Aurelius, was himself a Stoic thinker. So also was Epictetus, who began life as a slave. A rough doctrine of original freedom and equality, even the use of the contractarian model for the collectivity (see SOCIAL CONTRACT), has been read into Stoic texts—"All seats," so the Stoic proverb went, "are free in the theatre, but a man has a right to the one he sits down in"—but it was religious rather than specifically social equality. Much of the intellectual groundwork, in fact, of subsequent political philosophy can be sighted in the intellectual–religious tradition of Stoicism, and it is only the philosophizing tendency of historians which has prevented its attracting more attention than it has done.

ST. AUGUSTINE

The City of God (*De Civitate Dei*), written between 410 and 423 by St. Augustine, bishop of Hippo in north Africa (354–430), traditionally occupies an important place in the canon of great works on political philosophy. This extraordinary treatise raises in an acute form the problem of the historical reputation and effect of a body of thought in contrast with its actual content and the intention of its writer. *The City of God* was undoubtedly read in medieval times and afterward as the authoritative statement of the superiority of ecclesiastical power over the secular, because it was believed to identify the visible Christian church with the mystical city of God, thought of as the bride of Christ or, even more mystically, as the body itself of the Christian Saviour. But it is very doubtful whether this was St. Augustine's intention or is even implied by his text. What is more, the conscientious political scientist finds it very difficult to decide whether *The City of God* contains any positive political doctrine at all, theoretical or otherwise.

Very recent political philosophy might, therefore, justifiably claim this work as an antipolitical classic, stating in very different terms the position sketched out by Marx and Lenin as "the withering away of the state." There is the same tendency to identify all arrangements in the collectivity with evil, with the unjustifiable exercise of

naked power, and the same confidence that in the fullness of time this monstrous regimentation will disappear. Moreover, Augustine was a historicist: he sought to show how God's plan to fill up the places left in Heaven when Satan and his angels revolted was being fulfilled. The creation of man and the world was intended to reveal candidates for the heavenly choir, and some few men on earth at any one time, the pilgrims (*peregrinati*), were destined at the last trumpet to be among them. They and they only were the living members of the City of God, but no one would know who constituted this select few until the judgment. It seems to have been a matter of almost complete indifference to St. Augustine how those who were to be saved behaved toward society, secular or spiritual, or what was the nature of political arrangements.

The occasion of Augustine's beginning *The City of God* was the sack of Rome by Alaric the Goth in 410, and the fall of the Roman Empire, which this event presaged, could not possibly affect the Christian who held such views about history, state, and society. The complement of the City of God was the city of the devil (*civitas diaboli*), and although it seems unjustifiable to identify the one city with the church, it seems that Augustine did quite often refer to the Roman Empire as the other. Since the heathen Romans could not possibly do justice to God and since kingdoms without justice are but great robberies (*Remota itaque justitia quid sunt regna nisi magna latrocinia?*— Ch. 4, Bk. 4), what could the Roman Empire be but thievery on a colossal scale? If by the Roman Empire Augustine implied all possible forms of the collectivity—and there are passages to confirm this assumption—then he must indeed be supposed to have had a completely negative political philosophy. Justice could never be found in any of them. In this final work of ancient political theory, then, the overriding concern is with justice, just as it had been with Socrates at the very beginning, but in it justice is viewed from an anarchist, antipolitical outlook.

MEDIEVAL POLITICAL PHILOSOPHY: POPE AND EMPEROR

Apart from the development of natural law in Christian form, the Middle Ages did not give rise to much speculation about the nature of the collectivity which has affected subsequent attitudes, nor to any great body of specifically political philosophy. Before the time of St. Thomas Aquinas in the thirteenth century, what little critical analysis there was seems to have been dominated by the Church Fathers and especially by Augustine. Although these early medieval thinkers knew of the great Greek philosophers, the actual treatises of Plato, Aristotle, and others had been lost in the West. There seems to have been a certain amount of political awareness among the subjects of the Germanic kingdoms which had come to spread over Europe, and during the nineteenth century a great deal was made of the primitive Germanic sense of community (*Gemeinschaft*), people (*Volk*, folk), and corporation (*Gesellschaft*). But unless jurisprudence is counted a part of political philosophy, neither these arrangements nor the universal social institutions associated with feudalism seem to have been the subjects of much corresponding theorization. It is remarkable how little headway the analysis of political theories in ideological terms has made with the Middle Ages.

St. Thomas. John of Salisbury's *Policraticus* (1159) was still Ciceronian and Augustinian in content, in spite of the fact that by his time the text of Aristotle had already reached the Latin West from the Arabs. It was left to St. Thomas to arrange the enormous access of Aristotelian information and principle in a form acceptable to a Christian Europe, which he did in his great *Summa Theologica*. The frank acceptance of natural man—man as revealed by Aristotelian science; man not incurably maimed by sin and therefore indifferent to social–political arrangement; man whose nature is perfected, not taken away by the grace of God (*gratia non tollit naturam, sed perficit*) —distinguished the sociology of Aquinas from that of his predecessors. But although of enduring importance for politics, indeed still the final authority for the Thomist thinkers of our own day, the *Summa* and its Christian doctrine of natural law contains no developed political philosophy. For this we must turn to the *De Regimine Principum* (*Of the Rulership of Princes*) and other works, including Aquinas' commentaries on Aristotle's *Politics* and *Ethics*.

In these works St. Thomas presented his theory of the relationship between pope and emperor, which had already preoccupied Christian Europe for centuries and would continue to do so until the end of the medieval period. He developed the traditional distinction of *regnum* and *sacerdotum* (secular and spiritual jurisdiction) in Aristotelian terms, in terms of ends, the ends of humanity. "We are confronted," as A. P. d'Entrèves says, "with the doctrine of the distinction and interrelation of two great spheres of human life within one single society—the Christian society, *respublica christiana*." But although Thomas is moderate in his claims for the pope against the emperor, although he never talks of the direct sovereignty of the pope, he is firmly convinced that all kings in Christendom should be subject to the Vicar of Christ as to Christ himself. Yet willing as he was to temper Aristotelian inegalitarianism with Christian grace, anxious as he was to give every Christian his share in the affairs of the collectivity, Thomas was absolutely intolerant of the Jew and the infidel: they remain outcasts in the Christian community.

Authority in St. Thomas' system must be legitimate, otherwise it may be resisted. An evil ruler exceeding his powers and burdening his subjects must be resisted—resisted not by the individual citizen in virtue of his individual rights (Thomas had no room for such rights) but presumably by the church. This is the sense in which St. Thomas' thinking has been hailed, like that of Aristotle, as the forerunner of constitutionalism.

Dante and Marsilius. The other two medieval thinkers usually accorded a place in the history of political philosophy are Dante Alighieri, the supreme poet of the city of Florence, whose political essay *Monarchia* was composed between 1310 and 1313, and Marsilius of Padua, whose *Defensor Pacis* ("Defender of Peace") was completed in 1324. Both were imperialists, on the opposite side of the pope–emperor controversy from St. Thomas, but both

were Aristotelians. Dante's work was an idealization of the position of the medieval European emperor, who was in fact a ruler of Germany to whom the traditional trappings of the Western Roman emperor still attached as the secular ruler of all humanity, whose powers were derived directly from God and not indirectly through the pope. Marsilius approached somewhat closer to realism and had a recognizably empirical sociology: he insisted on the Aristotelian class analysis of political society and regarded the clergy as one among the classes, and therefore not in the privileged position which papal theory claimed.

The twentieth-century observer is far more at home in the Greek polis or in a Roman province than at the papal *curia* or the court of a feudal king. So much was the medieval collectivity a religious whole, embracing not only all the territory occupied by Christians but also the whole of intellectual and cultural life, that it may be doubted whether there existed anything which corresponds to the term "state" as political philosophers ordinarily use it. Apart from the metaphysics of the papal– imperial argument, most "political thought" of the European Middle Ages is recognizable as advice to a ruler, wise reflections on commonplace situations that are entirely traditional in context and object and show no trace of the analytic attitude. Nevertheless, the medieval collectivity and the reflections of medieval theologians upon it can be appreciated under more headings than that of record.

Apart from the paradigm for the metaphysical approach to the final problem of ethics and politics provided by Aquinas, the medieval situation provides the extreme example of territorial political relationships, in which the psychological mechanism usually called religious can be seen most clearly at work in providing the consensus on which such collective action as went forward had to rely. Any properly empirical account of how a collectivity in fact works, at any time, has to recognize that this mechanism is still very much in operation and that the mistake of supposing it to be replaced by rational–technical cooperation has still to be properly appreciated.

MACHIAVELLI AND REALPOLITIK

Although the polis began to lose its independence of policy as early as the lifetime of Aristotle, the towns of the Roman Empire continued to maintain a collective life which differed very little from the life of the classical polis. The decline of the cities was the outstanding feature of the fall of the empire, but they never entirely disappeared, at least in Italy. By the time of Dante and Marsilius such cities as Florence, Venice, and Milan were again in the formal position which Athens had occupied: they were independent urban communities having diplomatic relationships with each other and with the territorial monarchies. The cities possessed their own hinterlands, too, and colonies. It is not surprising, therefore, that the rational– critical attitude reappeared and that a consuming interest in ancient culture, in Plato and Aristotle, in Rome and Greece, led to an appreciation of classical political philosophy on something like its own terms.

Nevertheless, Machiavelli's *The Prince* (written 1513,

first printed 1532), in some ways the most effective and interesting of all works of political philosophy, was in form merely one more piece of advice to a ruler. It was not presented as a philosophical work, and it contained neither abstract argument about politics nor any systematic discussion of the nature of state and society. Its analysis is confined to situations between a prince and his people and between princes (or cities) themselves. Its method is historical, the citing of significant instances. The outcome of discussion is advice, with occasional reflective aphorisms. Some of these aphorisms have become famous, and all of them show an astonishing realism and insight: "Above all a prince should abstain from the property of others; because men sooner forget the death of their father than the loss of their patrimony." "Whoever is responsible for another becoming powerful ruins himself." "Fortune is a woman and if she is to be submissive it is necessary to beat and coerce her." The headings of the 26 brief chapters of *The Prince* are even more significant than the sayings; Chapter 17 is entitled "Cruelty and Compassion, Whether It Is Better to Be Loved Than to Be Feared."

Machiavelli's well-known answer is that it is far better to be feared than to be loved, if you cannot be both. His cool discussion of the effects of cruelty and unscrupulousness, his detached attitude toward Christianity and the traditional virtues, and his professed admiration for men of his time who are known to have been villainous and contemptible, especially the political gangster Cesare Borgia, have given Machiavelli the reputation of being the theorist of power politics, deliberate immoralism, and irresponsible, tyrannical government. But the contents of his major work on politics, the *Discourses on Livy,* have been cited to show that he was a believer in republican, not monarchical, government, and they have been used with the famous last chapter of *The Prince* itself to demonstrate that he was in fact a virtuous, patriotic Italian, worthy of the reputation he enjoyed among the English Whigs, for example, for political probity and insight. It has even been suggested, not for the first time in our generation, that *The Prince* was a satirical work. But there can be no doubt that from the time of its appearance this book was regarded as a textbook for tyrants and an exposition of the principles of power politics.

THE REFORMATION AND SECULAR NATURAL LAW

If Machiavelli's writing is looked upon as philosophical in intent, its most remarkable feature is its failure even to mention the doctrine of Christian natural law, which since the time of Aquinas had dominated discussion of the nature of the collectivity and of the duties of citizens. The arrival of Protestantism raised the question of political obligation in an acute form for the first time in the history of political philosophy. It challenged a believing Lutheran or Calvinist to decide whether he should go on obeying a Catholic prince, and a Catholic subject to make the same decision about a Protestant prince. This had the effect of emphasizing, crystallizing, and codifying natural-law doctrine, since it was only under a legal or quasi-legal system of natural law that most citizens felt that they could claim a right to disobey and ultimately to resist political authority which commanded actions against their faith. Once this

codification was made, systematic reflection on the philosophical problems raised by political allegiance began in earnest, and in the process natural law began to lose its exclusively religious sanction and become secularized.

It took a long time for the breakdown of universal religious consensus to have effects of this kind, even though many other influences going far back into the Middle Ages tended toward the secularization of political life. Luther himself offered no systematic political teaching, certainly no doctrine of the right to resist princes for conscience' sake. In fact, in his treatise *Of Good Works* (1520) Luther wrote out traditional patriarchal rules for submission in a particularly emphatic form. Calvin preached nonresistance too, but the religious wars in France in the later sixteenth century gave rise to a multitude of theories of the social contract which provided justification for disobedience and even for revolution on the basis of natural law. In England the Calvinists went even further, or so it seemed to the great doctor of the English Reformed church, Richard Hooker, when he sat down to write *The Laws of Ecclesiastical Polity* (written in the 1590s, first four books published in 1594 but not in print complete until 1662). Hooker believed that the claims to inspiration made by the extreme Puritans amounted to a denial of the efficacy of reason itself and to a complete rejection of natural-law principles. His response was a majestic reformulation of St. Thomas' natural-law philosophy that took account of the changes brought about by the Reformation, particularly of the doctrine of the final sovereignty of each individual state and its ruler, which had come to replace the ultimate authority of emperor or pope in Christendom. The absolute sovereignty of the secular ruler, from whose decree there was no appeal, a doctrine which might be called that of ethical self-sufficiency of every political system, was given its classical expression in the *Six Books of the Republic,* published by the eminent French lawyer Jean Bodin in 1576.

Along with these developments went another which can be seen very clearly as early as Machiavelli. This was the recognition that the body politic—the people and their political instruments, such as their parliament or their local institutions—might itself be an object of governmental action, worked on and molded by an enlightened ruler, just as the body politic might in its turn take action against government, rebel against it, replace and change its constitution. Meanwhile, secular natural law was providing a framework within which such processes could go forward and within which—as a code of international law—the various sovereign states could negotiate with one another. By the time that Hugo Grotius came to write that source book of all subsequent international law, *De Jure Belli ac Pacis* ("The Law of War and Peace," 1625), these relationships had come to include Islamic and Buddhist societies and societies entirely alien to the Christian point of view, even societies with no apparent belief in a deity. Natural law therefore had to become independent of Christian revelation, and Grotius stated that his principles would endure even if God did not exist. The stage was set for the first great classic of modern European, as opposed to classical ancient, political philosophy, the *Leviathan* of Thomas Hobbes (1651).

HOBBES

Although Hobbes is rightly regarded as above all a philosopher, with his own view of knowledge and of the nature of the physical world, his point of departure was political, as much as Plato's or Aristotle's was. Hobbes's declared object was "to set before men's eyes the mutual relation between protection and obedience, of which the condition of human nature, and the laws divine require an inviolable observation." This relation required the absolute submission of each individual to the dictates of an arbitrary sovereign, of "That great LEVIATHAN, or rather (to speak more reverently) of that *Mortal God,* to which we owe under the Immortal God, our peace and defence" (*Leviathan,* Ch. 17). Political science—though Hobbes did not use the phrase itself, he insisted that the proper name for the knowledge he was examining was in fact "science," on the geometrical model then beginning to take hold on men's minds—implied absolutism, despotism.

But Hobbesian political doctrine was no doctrine of the divine right of kings, nor even of one-man rule, for in this system democracies, aristocracies, and monarchies should all equally be absolute sovereigns, whose every dictate is law. Monarchy was to be preferred, as might be expected, and democracy, "the government of a few orators," was least desirable. The power of government is a part of the divine providence, but its sanctions are much more tangible. They rest on the unqualified alienation of all the rights of every individual into the hands of the sovereign at the time of the making of the social contract—of compact, as Hobbes called it—and thereafter every attribute of every citizen, even his property, depended on the sovereign's will. So anxious was Hobbes to remove any possible grounds which might be used to justify resistance to authority that he advanced two positions entirely unacceptable to most of his contemporaries. One was the reformulation of natural law in a form which gave no rights to the citizen and the other was to confer on the sovereign the function of pronouncing on the interpretation of Scripture itself.

Perhaps the most famous element in the Hobbesian system was the account of the state of nature, and the best-remembered passage reads:

> . . . during the time men live without a common power to keep them all in awe, they are in that condition which is called war; and such a war, as is of every man against every man. . . . In such condition, there is no place for industry, because the fruit thereof is uncertain: and consequently no culture of the earth; no navigation, nor use of the commodities that may be imported by sea; no commodious building; no instrument of moving, and removing such things as require much force; no knowledge of the face of the earth; no account of time; no arts; no letters; no society; and which is worst of all, continual fear, and danger of violent death; and the life of man, solitary, poor, nasty, brutish and short. (*Leviathan,* Ch. 13)

If this fighting anarchy is in fact the natural state of man, then it does seem to follow that the only possibility of cooperation in the collectivity is by absolute submission, and every human value must depend on the existence and efficacy of "the great Leviathan." The law, or rather the laws, of nature did exist at that repulsive stage of human development but only as rules of prudence, for "Reason suggesteth convenient articles of peace, which otherwise are called the laws of nature." Whatever the status of these principles, they could not possibly be used to justify resistance to the sovereign, although Hobbes did provide for the transfer of allegiance to another sovereign when the one established can no longer provide protection. He also allowed to the individual the right to refuse to confess to a crime or to take his own life. The appeal to revelation and to conscience, which Hobbes believed was responsible for the political instability of his own time, and especially for the Puritan rebellion in England, was completely precluded by his interpretation of the claims of his sovereign.

In spite of Hobbes's confident belief that his elucidation of the true principles of political science would resolve conflict, his work aroused immediate opposition and has given rise to unending controversy. There is first the question of whether his state of nature, succeeded by a covenant, or social contract, was intended to be taken literally as a historical and anthropological claim, or whether it was simply hypothetical. A recent ideological interpretation has claimed that the state of nature was hypothetical but that the aggressive, competitive emphasis arose from Hobbes's observing the possessive individualism informing the increasingly capitalist society in which he lived. The second question concerns the continuity between his state of nature and his state of society. How could men with the characteristics Hobbes gives them ever form themselves into a collectivity? A third question is whether he ever intended men to be morally obliged to obey the sovereign, or, if this was his intention, whether he succeeded in tying them down ethically. A further question is how far he was indeed abandoning the whole natural-law position and advancing an entirely utilitarian political ethic; men obey always and only because they see it is to their advantage.

WHIG CONSTITUTIONALISM AND LOCKE

Hobbes was not the first writer to invoke what came to be called the "pleasure–pain principle" in political discussion, and his radical contemporaries, the Levellers of the English Civil War, also made claims which seemed to rest on strictly utilitarian grounds, although in an unphilosophical and unsystematic form. The appearance of writings of this character, which have claims to be the first emanating from the common man, raises an important issue about the career of political philosophy from the seventeenth century on. The Levellers were democrats, and the political rights they claimed were meant to be exercised by a far greater proportion of the population than ever had been previously contemplated, even by the English Parliamentarians locked in their struggle with the house of Stuart. It has been recently and justifiably questioned whether all individuals were intended to be covered by Leveller declarations, or even all male householders, but from that time on, there is a recognizable class content in the doctrines of the political philosophers. Until the late eighteenth century most thinkers continued to share the universal assumption that "citizen" must be confined to the fully literate, propertied, elite minority, but they showed an increasing awareness that this was a tiny minority and that the right of this minority to stand for the whole might need justification.

Paradoxically enough, this crucial question was raised in an awkward form by one of Hobbes's exact contemporaries, Sir Robert Filmer, a traditionalist rather than a progressive. Sovereignty is a patriarchal matter, Filmer claimed, a matter of natural subordination, and unless this is recognized, the inequality of distribution of property and the subjection of poor men, men without the vote, servants, and women could never be justified. Much of Filmer's thinking, and that of the commonsensical Englishmen who came to accept his authority, is present in the writing of Hobbes. Nevertheless, for historical reasons it was against Filmer rather than against Thomas Hobbes that in the years 1679 and 1680 John Locke wrote out the classic statement of Whig constitutionalism and government by consent, *Two Treatises of Government* (revised and published in 1689).

This modification of the accepted account of the relation of Locke to Hobbes is due to very recent scholarship, and the same evidence goes to show that the work of Spinoza, the only immediate follower Hobbes had among philosophers, was more of an intellectual preoccupation for Locke than Hobbes ever was. Spinoza (*Tractatus Theologico-politicus*, 1670; *Tractatus Politicus*, 1677), if easily the least influential, was in some ways the most engaging of all the political thinkers of the early modern age in Europe. Unfortunately, we cannot dwell here on his modification of the Hobbesian system; his overt insistence that the contract was hypothetical; his specific insistence that all obligations had to be utilitarian, based on self-interest; or his attempt to ensure that the enlightened sovereign must seek the welfare of his people.

Locke's *Second Treatise*, with its subtitle *Of Civil Government*, seems to have been the first composed of the two, and it begins with the following assertion against Filmer's claim that all men are born unfree, unequal, and in patriarchal subjection:

> To understand political power right, and derive it from its original, we must consider what state all men are naturally in, and that is, a state of perfect freedom to order their actions and dispose of their possessions, and persons, as they think fit, within the bounds of the law of nature, without asking leave, or depending on the will of any other man. A state also of equality, wherein all the power and jurisdiction is reciprocal, no one having more than another.   (Sec. 4)

The law of nature, then, was real, and it governed all men in the peaceable condition which preceded the foundation of the collectivity, when order was maintained by what Locke called "the executive power of the law of nature" in the hands of every man. This law of nature gave men tangible rights, even before the contract. It ensured them the right to their religious opinions (not argued for, or even mentioned, in the work on government but in a succession of *Letters on Toleration,* the first published in 1689); it guaranteed them the right to property, whose

acquisition was brought about by men "mixing their labour" with the goods of nature; it made it legitimate for every person to take some political responsibility and in due course to act as sovereign himself or as part of the sovereign power, for the vital political right was that of insisting that government rested on the consent of the governed, the consent of the majority expressed constitutionally through representation. The stage of contract came about because the predominantly peaceful state of nature was liable to war and because property was insecure under it. When it arrived, political power was "a right of making laws for the regulating and preserving of property, and of employing the force of the community, in the execution of such laws, and in defence of the commonwealth from foreign injury, and this only for the common good" (*Second Treatise*, Sec. 3).

Contract, to Locke, was an agreement to pool the natural political virtue of individuals and to establish a sovereign power thereby which was in a perpetual trust relationship with the people. If the trust was broken, the people had a right to cashier their governors and put others in their place or, if necessary, to alter the constitution, and all this without the return of the state of nature. In this sense, and in allowing a final appeal to God if the compact itself was dissolved, Locke can be said to have held to a doctrine of the sovereignty of the people and to a perpetual reserved right of revolution. He believed in a form of the separation of powers and in the rule of majorities, but he shows little sympathy with representative democracy.

Recent studies have shown that Locke's political philosophy, as contrasted with his general philosophy, was much less influential in the eighteenth century than had been supposed. Nevertheless, the Lockian outlook, along with that of his friend and contemporary Sir Isaac Newton, must be counted as the point of departure of the intellectual movement known as the Enlightenment.

THE ENLIGHTENMENT AND MONTESQUIEU

Locke could not deal adequately with Newtonian mathematics, but in spite of the intellectual barrier between them, the two men shared one passionate curiosity: to know all that could be known about societies, customs, and religions outside Europe. Confidence in the efficacy of mathematico-physical methods to solve all problems, including those of social and political organization, and cultural relativism leading to doubt about religious revelation and the necessary value of any familiar institution underlie much Enlightenment thought. Meanwhile, the steady spread of literacy and the consequent growth of the size of the politically conscious, curious, and ambitious community, especially in France and England, was changing the conditions of political and social speculation.

The result was a proliferation of works of political philosophy which from now on defeats the summary historian. Sir Isaiah Berlin has said that "the conflict of the rival explanations (or models) of social and individual life had by the late eighteenth century become a scandal." Except as a critical movement, compelling all established dogma to give an account of itself, the Enlightenment cannot be called a uniform current of thought at all. Of the multiple works of Voltaire, Montesquieu, Hume, Helvétius, Ferguson, Rousseau, Mably, D'Argenson, Price, Paine, Jefferson, Burke, and their successors, we can comment here on only one or two that find a place in the traditional canon.

Montesquieu. Charles Louis de Secondat, baron de Montesquieu, may serve as the example of the early sociological attitude, presented with great literary skill and at considerable length in his *Esprit des lois* (in preparation from 1734, published 1748). To Montesquieu, who sought to examine and record social uniformities, natural laws describe necessary human behavior, and because they are necessary, they also oblige men ethically, or, rather, they are the basis of legal systems which men are morally obliged to obey. At this point it is usual to say that Montesquieu's attitude touches that of David Hume in his *Treatise of Human Nature* (1739), containing his famous aphorism about all systems of morality imperceptibly changing from propositions containing "is" and "is not" to propositions containing "ought" and "ought not." But the French author's interest was not in obligation as such; rather, it was in the structure of the collectivities which men find themselves obeying and in the ways in which these structures or their "spirits" (*esprits*) express environment.

Rousseau and the general will. Montesquieu is scarcely representative of the most characteristic feature of the political philosophy of his age, at least when viewed from the somber century we now inhabit, because he was neither an optimist nor a believer in the perfectibility of man. Jean-Jacques Rosseau was skeptical of progress too, for in some moods he seems to have believed that human nature had once been perfect but had been corrupted by society. This was the position which he defended in his first *Discourse* (1751). In his second *Discourse,* the *Discourse on Inequality* (1755), not society but property was the evil attacked.

Neither of these works contained Rousseau's specific contribution to political philosophy. In the *Social Contract* (*Du Contrat social,* 1762) Rousseau elaborated a doctrine which was both original and potentially revolutionary; the relation of the individual to the collectivity was seen as a matter of will, not of agreement, and the solution of the problem of obligation was the discovery of a general will directed to universal moral ends, which the individual had only to obey in order to secure justice (see GENERAL WILL). Rousseau presented the general-will model in individualistic, contractarian terms:

Man was born free, and everywhere he is in chains. What is it that can make this legitimate? . . . The moment men leave the state of nature and set up society, that act of association brings into being a moral, collective body in the place of the particular persons of each contracting party, composed of as many members as there are voices in the assembly, which from this same act receives its unity, its common personality (*moi commun*), its life and its will. This passage from the state of nature to the state of society produces a very remarkable change in man, in substituting justice for instinct in his conduct, and giving to his actions the morality which before they lacked. (*Du Contrat social,* Book I, Chs. 1 and 6)

In spite of the care which Rousseau took to effect a moral reconciliation of the will of the individual and that of society, the collectivist possibilities of his approach to political obligation are evident. Since he insisted that a collectivity which has no general will is unworthy of the obedience of its citizens, its revolutionary potentialities are also obvious. The most conspicuous element supporting the interpretation that the *Social Contract* is a statement of tyrannical revolutionary nationalism is its final chapter, "The Civil Religion," which can be interpreted as justifying the condemnation to death of anyone who flouts Rousseau's own dogmatic statement about the relation of the individual to the state.

"The Federalist," Burke, and Paine. The supposed direct relationship of Rousseau's thinking with the revolutionary movements of the late eighteenth century, particularly with the American and French revolutions—even with the Reign of Terror and the despotism of Napoleon—is a conspicuous example of that interplay between intellectual speculation and political movement in which both citizens and historians seem to want to believe. It is of course doubtful whether any element from the multifarious theorization about politics which went on during the Enlightenment could ever be shown to be causally related to what happened in France after 1789, and it is certain that the rebelling American colonists took little trouble to justify their actions in philosophical terms. Nevertheless, the foundation of the American political attitude is of importance to political philosophy, and *The Federalist* (written jointly by James Madison, Alexander Hamilton, and John Jay in the form of a collection of papers published in the New York press in 1787 and 1788) is an outstanding instance of a book's being taken as a compendium of the theoretical content of a nation's political outlook. Max Beloff has said that the sociology of this work was static; in their day there had been founded in America a society, a prefabricated, premeditated structure which would endure unchanged forever. It had the characteristic common to all ethically justified institutions: "Justice is the end of government. It is the end of civil society. It ever has been and ever will be pursued, until it be obtained, or until liberty be lost in the pursuit." But justice is not the imposition of equality—it is the protection of the weak against the stronger. Government will otherwise be content to hold the ring, and liberty will be ensured by the separation of the powers and by the balance between the state and federal governments.

Edmund Burke was a champion of the Americans against the arbitrary powers of the British crown, and he must have approved of much of the argument of the *Federalist,* especially that concerning the benefits of unequal distribution of property. The exercise of political power was the greatest challenge to the wisdom and responsibility of an individual and to his capacity to decide weighty issues on behalf of others. Where were such men to be found but among those experienced in the proper administration of great possessions and of the people who went with them?

Each of Burke's voluminous writings on politics, which occupied his whole life, contains a remark or two of importance to the philosophy of politics. But the work which has caught the eye of posterity is the one he wrote in horrified protest against the actions of the French revolutionaries, *Reflections on the Revolution in France* (published in 1790). The famous passage remembered from this book goes as follows:

Society is indeed a contract. Subordinate contracts for objects of mere occasional interest may be dissolved at pleasure—but the state ought not to be considered as nothing better than a partnership in a trade of pepper and coffee, calico or tobacco, or some other such low concern, to be taken up for a little temporary interest, and to be dissolved by the fancy of the parties. It is to be looked upon with other reverence; because it is not a partnership in things subservient only to the gross animal existence of a temporary and perishable nature. It is a partnership in all science; a partnership in all art; a partnership in every virtue, and in all perfection. As the ends of such a partnership cannot be obtained in many generations, it becomes a partnership not only between those who are living, but between those who are living, those who are dead, and those who are to be born. Each contract of each particular state is but a clause in the great primeval contract of eternal society, linking the lower with the higher natures, connecting the visible and invisible world, according to a fixed compact sanctioned by the inviolable oath which holds all physical and moral natures each in their appointed place. (Pp. 163–164)

The extravagance of the language and the lamentable vagueness of the statements are typical of Burke, and typical also of the uncritical acceptance of the contractarian model long after it had become unnecessary. Indeed, Burke's account of obligation, insofar as he presented one at all, was far closer to Rousseau's general-will argument than he would have admitted.

But the phrases which have interested posterity are those which limit the freedom of each generation to act against the expectations of the past and the interests of the future, and those in which he condemns as immoral the action of any society which allows fundamental revolution. It was an offense against all humanity to act as the French revolutionaries were doing. The very language of abstract natural right was excoriated by Burke, and he challenged all subsequent political thinkers with the problem of the status of political principles in relation to political action and practice.

Burke's effusive, skeptical conservatism was too much for Thomas Paine, his acute Anglo-American contemporary, whose *The Rights of Man* (Part I, 1791, a direct answer to Burke) is often acclaimed a minor classic of political philosophy. There has been no writer more optimistic about the effects of violent political action, or more indifferent to the existence of established government. "The instant formal government is abolished, society begins to act. A general association takes place and common interest produces common security." But in the second part of *The Rights of Man* (1792) Paine identified himself with the nascent working class, and added to the responsibilities of government policies that were hitherto scarcely contemplated and are hailed in our day as the first discernible sign of welfare legislation, even down to family allowances and maternity benefits. The talk of property, representation, and the will and wants of all, which had increased steadily since the time of Hobbes, had issued at last into something like universalistic claims for participation in political activity, into that "numerical democracy" which has characterized the industrialized world ever since.

THE UTILITARIAN TRADITION

Bentham. "It is the greatest happiness of the greatest number that is the measure of right and wrong." This famous tag appears in the second paragraph of Jeremy Bentham's *Fragment on Government* (1776) and may be looked upon as the original formulation of the utilitarian principle for specifically political purposes, although Bentham had the law in mind. (Utilitarian ethics of course goes back as far as Hobbes, and Bentham's use of it may be directly referred to Hume.) Bentham went on to offer a definition of the collectivity which was followed more or less faithfully by all his successors in the utilitarian tradition: "When a number of persons (whom we may style subjects) are supposed to be in the habit of paying obedience to a person, or an assemblage of persons, of a known and certain description (whom we may call governors) such persons altogether (subjects and governors) are said to be in a state of political society."

The unsatisfactory character of crude utilitarian ethics is plain in Bentham's best-known book, the *Introduction to the Principles of Morals and Legislation* (1789). "It seems to me," John Plamenatz has said of this work, "that Bentham, without quite knowing what he is doing, is trying to reconcile two couples of irreconcilable doctrines; egoistic hedonism with utilitarianism on the one hand, and a psychological with an objective theory of morals on the other." But in clarifying legal principles and in giving directions to lawyers and politicians, Bentham was much more effective, perhaps the most effective writer of principle for the purpose of advice. So anxious was he to make it crystal clear what men should do tomorrow that he went so far as to proclaim that the motives from which men act are morally irrelevant; only the consequences matter. Carrying out this advice made Bentham into an advocate of the doctrine that government is a necessary evil, since all that government can do is to coerce, and coercion must be kept to that minimum (Bentham's coinage) which will prevent even greater pain. In this way, with Paine as well as with Bentham, utilitarianism was used to justify equality between citizens and representative democracy.

J. S. Mill. The logical difficulties of utilitarian ethics and the possible dangers of numerical democracy—leaving every man to make up his mind about his own and the general happiness and giving him an equal right to a part in decisions about them—are also evident in the classic statement of liberalism, John Stuart Mill's *On Liberty* (written 1854, published 1859). It was followed in 1861 by *Utilitarianism* and *Representative Government*.

Mill's *On Liberty* shares some of the social unreality which is so evident in Bentham's definition of the collectivity, but to a very much smaller degree. "Wherever," says Mill, "there is an ascendant class, a large portion of the morality of the country emanates from its class interests, and its feelings of class superiority." In his later life Mill might well have described himself as socialist. But the doctrinal legacy of his text is very different:

> The object of this Essay is to assert one very simple principle, . . . that the sole end for which mankind are warranted, individually or collectively, in interfering with the liberty of action of any of their number, is self-protection, . . . to prevent harm to others. . . . The only part of the conduct of any one, for which he is amenable to society, is that which concerns others. . . . The only freedom which deserves the name, is that of pursuing our own good in our own way, so long as we do not attempt to deprive others of theirs. . . . (*On Liberty*, Ch. 1)

This principle of other-regarding actions' being distinguished from self-regarding actions, and being alone amenable to control from outside, is one of extreme difficulty in practice but of great convenience in argument. With it goes a deep suspicion of the "tyranny of the majority," not simply as expressed in governmental action but even more in the form of intolerant conformism of opinion. Mill is at his most persuasive when he argues that "all silencing of discussion is an assumption of infallibility" and when he insists that it is to the universal advantage that the truth should be known. His book may be regarded as the most forceful of all pleas for freedom of thought and expression. He ends it by insisting on three very general reasons against "government interference." States should not do things better done by individuals, things which it is better for the individuals to do themselves, and things which might unnecessarily add to governmental power.

Sidgwick. Mill was by no means the last of the utilitarian thinkers, although the positive grounds for freedom and justice put forward by the idealists were already beginning to replace the negative arguments summarized above. Henry Sidgwick's *Elements of Politics* (1891) may be taken as the final statement of political utilitarianism, although in its later editions it is marked by repeated concessions to socialism, always referred to in quotes. Sidgwick's definition of the collectivity is still Bentham's, although he admits that the principles of politics are not absolutely true but are based on psychological propositions approximately true of civilized man. He adopts from the great utilitarian jurist, John Austin, the claim that in every state the legislature must be legally unlimited, but he also qualifies this. He comes down emphatically on the side of individualism, "which takes freedom—the absence of physical and moral coercion—as the ultimate and sole end of governmental interference."

GERMAN IDEALISM

Kant. The general-will model associated with Rousseau underwent some development at the hands of the great German philosopher Immanuel Kant in various works written in the 1780s and 1790s. His idea of a "general and public will" is not a particularly lucid concept, but it does express for political purposes the supreme ethical principles of the Kantian philosophy that each man should treat each other man as if he were an end, never as a means, and that each act should be such that it might become a universal law. V. F. Carritt has also praised him highly for the recognition that obligation is a condition of political societies, not a product of them. More influential for subsequent political philosophy, however, was Kant's theory of history. In the course of this complex argument he proposes that the attainment of political society which shall enforce justice requires that man have a master to force him to be free and that this master be the will of the community.

Hegel. Most philosophers have tried to bring to bear on the problems of political philosophy an over-all view of the world and of knowledge. No philosopher has been so devoted to system and the whole as Georg Wilhelm Friedrich Hegel. Political philosophy has its appointed and necessary place within the dialectic exposition of reality. Reality is spiritual, the Absolute, and collectivities have their part to play in the teleological "unfolding" of the Absolute. Collectivities—the family, "civil society," and the state—are manifestations of objective spirit, and the state is the culmination of objective spirit. Collectivities arise when the manifestation of objective spirit in the individual reveals itself as inadequate. The individual can be truly himself only in some society. Formal ethics is bare and empty, and it must be made concrete. Concrete ethics can only be social. Thus the family is a dialectical necessity.

But the family is not a permanent institution; although the members of the family are united in the family and hence are one, the children grow up and leave the family. This "negation" of the family is negated in a new collectivity, civil society. Civil society embraces the economic order and the economic organizations and institutions through which it is expressed, as well as the legal system and the enforcement facilities necessary to it. But the legal system implies something over and above civil society, namely, the state, without which a legal system is impossible. Family and civil society are both embraced within the state; they are at the same time fulfilled by it and manifestations of it. The same is true of the individual. In the state the individual rises above his mere particularity to become a person and truly free.

What the concept of a state fully embraces can be known only through the historical development of actual states. Among the many possible forms of the actual state, the most rational is a monarchy. A corporative state, in which individuals participate in governmental affairs by virtue of their standing in the corporative bodies of civil society rather than as individuals, is more rational than representative democracy, in which individuals are represented merely as individuals. Nevertheless, the constitution which is best for any particular state is that one which has developed slowly in that state over the course of centuries. A constitution imposed artificially is bound to fail.

It might seem that Hegel's conceptual scheme would require that the state be embraced in some other form of collectivity, but this is not the case. The state is the highest form of objective spirit, and, at this point of the dialectic, objective spirit is negated by absolute spirit—the realm of art, religion, and philosophy. Thus Hegel rejected the Kantian notion of a federation of states and regarded war as not only natural but the motive force of history.

GREEN AND BOSANQUET

The meaning and implications of Hegel's political philosophy provoked immediate and lasting controversy. The central points of discussion have been the relation of the individual to the collectivity, whether state, society, race, or nation; the meaning of the notion of state; and the application of dialectic to the discovery of a necessary pattern in political history. The first point was the dominant problem of the social thought of the British idealist philosophers of the later nineteenth and early twentieth centuries. In political philosophy the two chief figures, with rather opposed views, were T. H. Green and Bernard Bosanquet. Green undertook the task of updating British liberalism to meet the changing circumstances of a rapidly industrialized society. To do so, he sought to divorce liberalism from the ethical egoism of utilitarianism and the laissez-faire economic doctrines of David Ricardo and to replace them with an idealist theory of society based broadly on Kant and Hegel.

For Green, as for earlier liberals, the effect upon freedom was the criterion by which a piece of legislation was to be judged. Did it tend to enlarge or to restrict freedom? Green held that Benthamite liberals had arbitrarily identified freedom with absence of legal restraint, implying that any piece of legislation must necessarily restrict freedom. Green pointed out that it had become evident that a person could be legally free and still not have the power to act for his own benefit. Where one party to a contract has all the powers of coercion on his side and the other party cannot help but agree to the terms proposed by the first party, then the state has the right and the obligation to interfere to restore the original freedom. There are other restraints on freedom than those imposed by the state.

Nevertheless, freedom was not, for Green, a natural right, for he held that there are no natural rights in the eighteenth-century sense. No one possesses abstract rights independent of his membership in a society in which the members recognize some common good as their own ideal good. Thus Green, more a Kantian than a Hegelian, held that the basis of all political obligation is the moral obligation to treat the other members of one's own society as ends in themselves, as having wills whose realization should not be interfered with. The state, on Green's view, has the duty to foster the conditions which permit each member so to act, and to lead him to regard and treat the other members as ends. The members in turn obey the state because they recognize it as the embodiment of their common right.

Green's liberalism stressed the positive function of the state in supporting the moral well-being of all its citizens, and it was not far from the Fabian conception of a national minimum of physical well-being below which the state should not allow any of its citizens to fall—for otherwise they could not participate fully as moral and political beings in society. The liberal side of Green's thought has greatly influenced British political philosophy, which has tended to remain idealist or partially idealist long after idealism passed out of fashion in other areas of British philosophy. But it has been certain antiliberal tendencies

which have come to be generally thought of as most typical of idealist political thought, especially since the publication of L. T. Hobhouse's *The Metaphysical Theory of the State* (London and New York, 1918). This work was a direct attack on Hegel and on Bosanquet's *Philosophical Theory of the State* (London, 1899).

Bosanquet developed the notion of the relation between individual and society beyond Green's claim that individuals are individuals only insofar as they are social. He claimed that society itself is more real and more of an individual than any of its members can ever be. And within each member of society it is the social self, rather than any purely individual desires or aims, that is most real. The social self is somehow identical with society, and thus social coercion is coercion by the higher, social self of the lower, individual self. In short, social coercion is self-mastery and true freedom.

Hobhouse charged that this revival of Rousseau's (and Locke's) notion that a man can be forced to be free is in itself dangerous and illiberal. He further charged that this notion, combined with Bosanquet's failure to distinguish properly between society and the state, or indeed to give any clear or unambiguous definition of the state, leads to the doctrine that the state can do no wrong, and hence to the justification of almost any action on the part of the government in power. There is no doubt that idealist claims have in fact so been used; however, Bosanquet held not that individual governments can do no wrong but that they can do wrongs of a kind totally different from those which individuals can commit—a government can confiscate property, but it cannot commit theft. And individual states can be judged by how well or poorly they fulfill the functions of a state.

MARX AND MARXISM

The Marxian development of Hegelianism is of an entirely different order from the academic philosophies of Green and Bosanquet. The difference is epitomized in Marx's famous eleventh thesis on Feuerbach: "The philosophers have only *interpreted* the world, in various ways; the point is to *change* it."

Karl Marx, the great theoretician of socialism, applied the Hegelian dialectic of history to the Hegelian analysis of collectivities. Hegel's family, civil society, and state are not three eternal ideas partially or imperfectly manifested at all periods of history. Rather, they are abstractions from the particular socioeconomic arrangements of the period in which Hegel and Marx lived. Hegel was right in stressing the central role of the economic function in civil society and in holding that, as now constituted, civil society requires a police power and hence a state. But he failed to see that civil society is not necessarily the same as capitalist, bourgeois society (civil society and bourgeois society are designated by the same phrase in German), and he did not see that those who determine the economic arrangements of society are not abstract individuals but are those who exercise control over the economic resources and forces available at the time. Since all others are excluded from having a voice in these economic arrangements, the result is class divisions and the need for the dominant class to defend its economic and political position against the other classes. Thus, as Hegel said, the state is necessary, but it is necessary as an instrument of the oppression of one class by another and not as something inherent in the very notion of social life. If class divisions were done away with, then there would be no one to oppress and the state would disappear. Civil society would be all that there was.

Marx, of course, believed that although in all previous periods (except for an initial period of primitive communism) the state had been necessary, the economic forces of capitalism had so developed that it was not only possible but also necessary for the state to disappear. The complexity of previous class divisions was becoming polarized into two antagonistic classes: the bourgeoisie, who controlled the instruments of production, and the proletariat, who had no choice but to work for the bourgeoisie at subsistence wages. Once the proletariat rises up and takes over the means of production from the bourgeoisie, there will be no more classes to oppress. In the classless society the state, the government of persons, will be "replaced by the administration of things and by the conduct of processes of production" (Friedrich Engels, *Anti-Dühring*, Moscow, 1962, p. 364).

Three intellectual tasks emerge from this view of the historical situation: a study of the laws according to which one era passes into another; a study of the present bourgeois era to discover in it those forces and movements tending toward its breakup and the emergence of the inevitable next era of the classless society; and some sort of preparation and anticipation, however blind, of the period of transition and its aftermath. Thus, economic history and political sociology become pressing practical subjects, and the central problem of politics becomes that of revolution.

The problem of justifying revolution had often been raised before. For Marxists, justification is no longer in question; revolution is inevitable, and only its date is unknown. Marxists must know how to bring about a revolution, whether it must be violent, and whether the revolution can be hastened if the productive forces are not yet ripe. Marx was sure that the bourgeoisie would not yield power without a struggle and that the revolution must be violent. He also held that it could not be hastened: "No social order ever disappears before all the productive forces for which there is room in it have been developed" (*A Contribution to the Critique of Political Economy,* translated by N. I. Stone, Chicago, 1904, Preface).

Those later developments of Marxist thought which have been serious and not merely propagandistic justification of a position have generally been attempts at adjusting or revising the theory of revolution to changing historical situations—the growth of mass socialist parties with the apparent possibility of their coming into power by peaceful means; abortive revolutionary governments like those of the Paris Commune of 1870 and the soviets of workers and peasants of the Russian revolution of 1905 (both as interpreted somewhat mythically by Marxist writers); the rapid succession in 1917 of a bourgeois revolution in Russia by a proletarian one before all the possibilities of the bourgeois era could come to flower; the conspiratorial character ascribed to that proletarian revolution; the imposition of socialist regimes in eastern Europe by Soviet intervention;

and the greater or lesser success of Marxist-inspired revolutions in countries, notably China, where modern bourgeois capitalism had only the most tenuous foothold. These revolutions in countries with precapitalist economies were totally inexplicable on classical Marxist grounds, and interpretations of them generally rely on some variant of Lenin's doctrine that in the latter part of the nineteenth century capitalism developed into a higher, final phase of international imperialism, with a corresponding internationalized proletariat and an interaction between the proletariat of the imperialist states and of the populations of the colonies.

ANARCHISM

Socialism, both Marxist and non-Marxist, has since the time of Marx generally favored some sort of centralized control at least of economic life, despite the Leninist prominence given to Engels' phrase "the withering away of the state." Although in general it has been held impossible to predict the exact character of a communist society, it has not been claimed that there would be no central authority. In opposition to this collectivist view were most of those early socialists whom Marx classified as utopian, as well as the anarchists and the later guild socialists, such as G. D. H. Cole.

The anarchists differed enormously in their attitudes toward social and economic arrangements, especially in their attitudes toward the institution of private property, but they were united in their opposition to the state, and hence to any centralized authority and to any participation in governmental functions. Engels expressed the Marxist's difference with the anarchist ideal succinctly:

> In this society there will, above all, be no *authority,* for authority = state = absolute evil. (How these people propose to run a factory, operate a railway, or steer a ship without a will that decides in the last resort, without single management, they of course do not tell us.) The authority of the majority over the minority also ceases. Every individual and every community is autonomous, but as to how a society of even only two people is possible unless each gives up some of his autonomy Bakunin again maintains silence. (Letter to Theodor Cuno, January 24, 1872)

The anarchists see the primary fault of the present economic order not in the economic arrangements, as do socialists, but in the existence of the state. The state is to be overthrown (although many anarchists, despite the popular identification of anarchism with terrorism, would stop short of violence), and then society will take care of itself. The actual order which will emerge is variously pictured as anything from an extreme individualism to voluntarily cooperating groups of various sizes. Marxists deny this primacy to the state, which, they hold, will collapse when the economic order of which it is the instrument collapses.

Ideas resembling the doctrines of the anarchist thinkers can be found in writings of various periods from Greek times onward, but the first fully articulated anarchist theory is to be found in William Godwin's *Enquiry concerning Political Justice* (1793). Like later anarchists, Godwin was as much an ethical writer as a political theorist. All social organization, and especially all governments, are necessarily corrupting. Society creates prejudices—preconceived ideas. We see people in terms of their social function and status rather than as individuals. and we judge in terms of false ideals—honor in a monarchy and public-spiritedness, a concern for the good of the state rather than of the individual, in a republic. Neither is a substitute for the ideal of benevolence. Godwin's solution is a small, classless community without rules in which individuals cooperate without compulsion, out of friendship, understanding, and benevolence.

Pierre-Joseph Proudhon, a self-educated Besançon printer, was the first theorist to describe himself as an anarchist. Despite his famous definition, "Property is theft," Proudhon was not against property as such but only against its unequal distribution. His ideals were equality and independence. As political science discovers the natural laws according to which society functions, then the arbitrary laws of governments become unnecessary. Proudhon favored individual ownership of the means of production by peasants and artisans. As political science revealed their mutual interests to them, they would freely join together in an ever-widening system of interlocking economic contracts which would make government unnecessary. Only in the case of some large-scale industries and public utilities would workers' syndicates be necessary.

With Michael Bakunin anarchism became associated with the nineteenth-century revolutionary tradition. The son of a Russian nobleman, Bakunin was involved in a number of revolutionary movements from the 1840s on, took part in abortive revolutions in France, Prague, Dresden, and Bologna, and was imprisoned in Saxony, Austria, and Russia. Bakunin was influenced by Proudhon but also by Hegel, Comte, Arnold Ruge, Darwin, and Marx. Like Proudhon, he held that what is produced should be distributed according to the amount of labor the recipient has provided, but he differed in advocating public ownership of the means of production. He differed from Marx in advocating the early destruction of the state rather than its seizure by the workers.

Another Russian writer, Prince Peter Kropotkin, was also influenced by Proudhon. His chief differences from Proudhon and Bakunin were that he favored the small local community as the unit of social organization and argued that goods should be distributed on the basis of need rather than on the basis of what the recipient had produced. Thus he envisaged warehouses where goods would be distributed freely rather than earlier schemes of distribution based on some measure of the recipient's production. Kropotkin also tended to stress the notion that man is naturally social, which was a factor in earlier anarchist theories, even going so far as to find that cooperation, and not merely competition, is a factor in animal evolution.

Far too complex in his views to be classed merely as an anarchist is the French philosopher Georges Sorel. Sorel is important less for his programmatic views than for his analysis of social systems into consumers' and producers' societies, each with its own system of morality, and of the roles of violence and of political myths in revolutionary movements. In a consumers' society the good is things to be obtained—welfare, prosperity, distributive justice, or the classless society. The consumers' society is based on envy. A producers' society sees the good in the cooperative creative endeavor of self-reliant individuals. But this creative endeavor tends in the end to decay into a consumers' society. Violence is a sign of moral health in a revolutionary movement. It ranges from a violence of principles to, occasionally, physical violence. It is intended as much to discourage the "reasonable" sympathizer who feels the time is not ripe for revolution and the man of good will seeking reconciliation as it is to intimidate the enemy. A myth is the revolutionary morality stated in terms of a hoped-for future. Thus, the notion of the general strike may be self-contradictory, but this is beside the point. It is not scientific prophesy but the expression of the aspirations of the revolutionary masses.

FASCISM AND NATIONAL SOCIALISM

Marxism and anarchism are representative of a modern tendency to see political arrangements in terms of a program and often of one dominant idea. There have been others, notably racism and the various forms of nationalism, but only two can be mentioned here. Like Marxism, fascism and national socialism were official philosophies, justifications of particular revolutions and of the regimes which ensued from them. Unlike Marxism, they were not coherent doctrines, and their proponents never made more than a pretense of reconciling theory and practice. New situations called out new theoretical pronouncements in diametrical opposition.to earlier ones—but the earlier pronouncements were deliberately allowed to remain as part of the doctrine, with no attempt at harmonizing them with the new claims. Complicating any systematic interpretation is their deliberate irrationalism. Mussolini tended to glorify action—any action; Hitler relied on his own intuition.

Of these two ideologies, fascism had the twin advantages for clarity and consistency, if not for ideological use, of being largely confined to a conception of the right arrangement of politico-economic life and of having an official formulation compiled by a philosopher, Giovanni Gentile (although Gentile's formulation was worked over by Benito Mussolini himself). Both fascism and national socialism pretended to be nationalist and socialist. In Italy this meant the corporative state and the denial of class antagonisms. Political power was supposed to pass upward through organizations embracing all those who worked in an industry, workers and owners alike, but these organizations would naturally merge their own interests in the national interest. In practice, although not as efficiently as in Germany, this meant totalitarian political control. The fascist glorification of the leader and the attempted revival of the glories of the Roman Empire seem peripheral to fascism when compared with the role played by similar claims in national socialist doctrine.

The tenets of national socialism, unlike those of fascism, were purposely left vague and were allowed to shift as circumstances warranted. The actual doctrines could only be what Adolf Hitler said they were, yet he deliberately tolerated or encouraged conflicting outlines of national socialism by Rosenberg and others. Even statements by Hitler himself were authoritative for the doctrine only at the time they were made. What can be said is that national socialism, like anarchism, was an antipolitical doctrine, but at the same time it was paradoxically a doctrine that aimed at total control. It was antipolitical in that this control was centered outside the state even though it might work through the state. The authority of the governmental workers and even of national socialist party leaders was diffused, indistinct, and broken on the lower levels so that it could be centered at the top. Hitler's own authority was held to derive not so much from his political position as chancellor of the Reich as from his being the *Führer,* or leader, of the people. He somehow embodied, and knew nonrationally, their strivings and desires; his will was theirs.

Of the various doctrines of national socialism, the central one was undoubtedly that of the racial war between Aryans and Jews. In this war the Jews were seen as the aggressors. They were guilty of constant and unceasing conspiratorial attacks on the superior Aryan race, which in self-defense was forced to undertake their extermination. All other violence instigated by Hitler, both against other nations and against the Germans themselves, was an incidental means to the strengthening of the Aryan race in its main battle. Nevertheless, even the race doctrine could have been dropped unceremoniously, or aimed at some other target, if circumstances had seemed to warrant, just as, for expediency, Hitler dropped first the anticapitalist claims of national socialism and then its anti-Bolshevist ones.

RECENT POLITICAL THOUGHT

With the growing professionalization of political thought into political science and its various branches, and the development of related sociological disciplines, there has been a decline in the Anglo-Saxon countries of political philosophy in the tradition with which Hobbes, Locke, Burke, Mill, and Green are identified. Books of traditional political philosophy have continued to be written, but not generally by those who are writing the most vital works in the more central areas of philosophy, and the new works have not generally been regarded as major contributions to philosophy by those working in the newer analytic modes of philosophy. Perhaps only the subtle and persuasive Burkean traditionalism of Michael Oakeshott has attracted the continuing interest, if not the agreement, of contemporary analytic philosophers.

The dearth of major systematic treatises of the nineteenth-century kind written by contemporary philosophers does not mean that they have completely neglected political philosophy. Despite the recent claim that political philosophy is dead, contemporary philosophers have applied new techniques developed in other fields to the study of the political realm. The apparent death of one tradition of political philosophizing has perhaps been confused with the death of political philosophy. Two main contemporary trends, which overlap to some extent, can be distinguished.

Methodology. The first trend consists in the application of the insights gained by the logical positivists and other philosophers of science into the logical status of laws,

theories, and concepts in the physical sciences to the problems of political philosophy and to the methodology of political science. The most eminent representative of this trend is Karl Popper. Popper's conception of politics depends on his conception of scientific research, and its exposition is closely intertwined with his critique of earlier political philosophies. It is thus difficult to do justice to his view on how politics should be practiced without explaining his scientific methodology and his reasons for holding that the notions of historical development held by Hegel, Marx, Comte, and Mill are mistaken, and that therefore their notions of what the aims and methodology of the social and political sciences should be are fallacious. But in general he takes a cautious attitude toward social change. He uses the analogy of scientific investigations to advocate what he terms "piecemeal engineering"; small-scale social changes are to be preferred, because our predictions are always fallible, and mistakes on a small scale are more easily rectifiable than large-scale ones. A total change of society, or the prophecy of the results of a total change, is logically impossible; but the broader the change, the more factors which we must predict and which may go wrong or be overlooked. Connected with this viewpoint is his limited utilitarianism: It is better to attempt to alleviate pain by rectifying an existing evil than to try to increase pleasure by initiating some apparently beneficial change.

The writings of Popper and others on the logic and methodology of the social and political sciences has pioneered in a field that was little more than discovered in the nineteenth century by Mill, Comte, and Spencer—a field in which there is much important work to be done. For example, philosophers have begun to study the logic of political decision making, a subject that has heretofore been left largely to the political scientists themselves.

Analytic political philosophy. The other main trend in contemporary political philosophy consists in the manipulation of the methods of philosophical analysis developed in the English-speaking countries in the last few decades. However, neither the variety of philosophical tasks undertaken nor the results achieved present a unified picture, since the approach analytic philosophers take to political philosophy is no more unified than their approach to other groups of philosophical problems.

The first full-scale analytic treatment of the problems of political philosophy, T. D. Weldon's *The Vocabulary of Politics* (Harmondsworth, England, 1953), is popularly supposed to have proclaimed the death knell of political philosophizing. Weldon claimed that the various philosophical theories put forth as foundations for liberal democracy, communism, and authoritarianism cannot do what they are held to do. Either they are logically empty and thus have no consequences, or they are mistaken and harmful empirical generalizations open to refutation. Thus Weldon made short work of the social contract theory. Assume, he said, that the Mayflower Compact was shown to be a forgery and that the laws of Massachusetts are held to be based on it. If the citizens of Massachusetts then claimed that because the compact was a forgery, they had lost faith in their democratic institutions, we would feel that this reason was a cover for some other reason.

But despite his denial of the usefulness or the possibility of providing foundations for a political viewpoint, Weldon's alternative description of the political process is a good example of philosophizing about politics, and he himself claimed that "a great deal needs to be done about the language in which discussions of political institutions are conducted" (p. 172).

Other contemporary philosophers have not taken as negative an attitude toward traditional philosophizing about politics as Weldon's. Rather than rejecting out of hand notions like the social contract or general will, they have sought to give new interpretations of such notions, regarding them, for example, as models of the political process. When so interpreted, new sorts of questions arise, questions appropriate to the relation between a model and reality rather than to the analysis of an empirical description. Many other new analyses of traditional political problems and of earlier answers to them are being given, particularly of such problems as sovereignty and natural law, on the borderline between philosophy of law and political philosophy. But the variety of work being done precludes any over-all description.

Bibliography

GENERAL HISTORIES

The standard work is still G. H. Sabine, *A History of Political Theory* (New York, 1938, and revisions). More recent inclusive works, such as John Plamenatz, *Man and Society*, 2 vols. (London, 1963), tend to be much more restricted in range.

CRITIQUE OF THE SUBJECT

No reasoned survey has yet appeared, but in such works as Karl Popper, *The Open Society and Its Enemies* (Vol. I, *The Spell of Plato*, Vol. II, *The High Tide of Prophecy, Hegel, Marx and the Aftermath*, London, 1945; Princeton, N.J., 1950), and C. B. Macpherson, *The Political Theory of Possessive Individualism* (Oxford, 1962), examples of contemporary critical attitudes will be found. They are themselves instances of an approach criticized in the first part of the article; for works sharing the view taken there, see the continuing collections entitled *Philosophy, Politics and Society*, edited by Peter Laslett, W. G. Runciman, and others (Oxford, 1957——).

ANCIENT POLITICAL PHILOSOPHY

Ernest Barker's books are the most useful for the ancient period: *Greek Political Theory, Plato and His Predecessors*, 3d ed. (London, 1947), *The Politics of Aristotle* (Oxford, 1946), and *From Alexander to Constantine* (Oxford, 1956). The editions of the ancient classics are innumerable, but the student is recommended to use the Loeb editions if he possibly can, with the original and its English translation on facing pages. All the relevant works (Plato, Aristotle, Cicero, Augustine, etc.) are now in print, although the edition of *The City of God* has yet to be completed.

MEDIEVAL POLITICAL PHILOSOPHY

The great works on medieval political philosophy are those of R. W. Carlyle and A. J. Carlyle (*A History of Political Theory in the West*, 6 vols., London, 1903–1936) and of Ernst Troeltsch (*The Social Teaching of the Christian Churches*, translated by Olive Wyon, 2 vols., London, 1931). The books of Walter Ullmann, beginning with *The Medieval Idea of Law*, (London, 1946), contain a stimulating if highly individual interpretation. The important texts are available in Aquinas, *Selected Political Writings*, A. P. d'Entrèves, ed. (Oxford, 1948); Marsilius of Padua, *Defensor Pacis*, translated with an introduction by Alan Gewirth as Vol. II of his *Marsilius of Padua, Defender of Peace* (New York, 1956); and

Dante, *De Monarchia*, translated and annotated by P. H. Wicksteed (1896).

MACHIAVELLI AND THE SIXTEENTH CENTURY

The Prince was edited in Italian by L. H. Burd (Oxford, 1891), but there is a much more recent critical edition in English of the *Discourses* (by L. J. Walker, London, 1950) which is valuable for Machiavelli generally. A useful if uninspired book is J. W. Allen, *A History of Political Thought in the 16th Century* (reprinted London, 1957). Jean Bodin's *Republic* has recently been edited in English by K. D. Macrae (Cambridge, Mass., 1962). Hooker is still best read in John Keble's Victorian edition of his *Works*, 3 vols. (London, 1836).

THE SEVENTEENTH AND EIGHTEENTH CENTURIES

The general authority on the seventeenth and eighteenth centuries is Otto von Gierke, *Natural Law and the Theory of Society*, translated by Ernest Barker (Cambridge, 1934). Hobbes's *Leviathan* has been edited by Michael Oakeshott (Oxford, 1947); Spinoza's *Political Works* by A. G. Wernham (Oxford, 1958); Locke's *Two Treatises* by Peter Laslett (Cambridge, 1960); and Robert Shackleton has written a standard work on Montesquieu: *Montesquieu, a Critical Biography* (Oxford, 1961); Montesquieu's *De l'Esprit des lois* is available in English, edited by F. Neumann (New York, 1949). Rousseau studies are still dominated by C. E. Vaughan, *The Political Writings* (1915, reprinted Oxford, 1962); there is also a translation of the *Social Contract* by F. M. Watkins (London, 1953). There are many reprints, but so far no critical editions, of the books of Burke, Paine, Bentham, Mill, and Green quoted in the text.

THE ENLIGHTENMENT AND UTILITARIANISM

Ernst Cassirer wrote a definitive work, *The Philosophy of the Enlightenment*, translated by F. C. A. Koelln and J. P. Pettegrove (1932, English ed., Princeton, N.J., 1951), and J. L. Talmon one with a more tendentious if stimulating thesis, *The Origins of Totalitarian Democracy* (London, 1952). John Plamenatz prefixed a brilliant essay, "The English Utilitarians," to his reprint of Mill's *Utilitarianism* (Oxford, 1949). Élie Halévy, *The Growth of Philosophic Radicalism*, translated by Mary Morris (London, 1938), is still important.

HEGEL AND GERMAN IDEALISM

Hegel's main work on political philosophy is *Naturrecht und Staatswissenschaft im Grundrisse* (Berlin, 1821), 2d ed. edited by E. Gans as *Grundlinien der Philosophie des Rechts* (Berlin, 1833), translated by T. M. Knox as *The Philosophy of Right* (Oxford, 1942). His *Phänomenologie des Geistes* (Würzburg and Bamberg, 1807), translated by J. B. Baillie as *Phenomenology of Mind* (London 1910), and *Vorlesungen über die Philosophie der Geschichte*, edited by E. Gans (Berlin, 1837) and translated by J. Sibree as *Lectures on the Philosophy of History* (London, 1857), should also be consulted. See also *Hegel's Political Writings*, translated by T. M. Knox with an introductory essay by Z. A. Pelczynski (Oxford, 1964). On Hegel's political thought, see M. B. Foster, *The Political Philosophies of Plato and Hegel* (Oxford, 1935); Franz Rosenzweig, *Hegel und der Staat*, 2 vols. (Oldenburg, 1920); Eric Weil, *Hegel et l'état* (Paris, 1950), and the works by Popper and Plamenatz cited above.

Hermann Lübbe, ed., *Die Hegelsche Rechte* (Stuttgart and Bad Canstatt, 1962), and Karl Löwith, ed., *Die Hegelsche Linke* (Stuttgart and Bad Canstatt, 1962), contain selections from right-wing and left-wing German successors of Hegel, respectively. The second is more directly relevant to political philosophy. From the voluminous writing on this period, see Sidney Hook, *From Hegel to Marx* (New York, 1950); Georg Lukács, *Die Zerstörung der Vernunft* (Berlin, 1954); and Herbert Marcuse, *Reason and Revolution: Hegel and the Rise of Social Theory*, 2d ed. (New York, 1954). Johann Gottlieb Fichte was an idealist contemporary of Hegel whose writings are of considerable political interest. See especially his *Der geschlossene Handelsstaat* ("The Closed Commercial State," Tübingen, 1800).

BRITISH IDEALISM

Green's *Lectures on the Principles of Political Obligation* were first published in *The Works of Thomas Hill Green*, R. L. Nettleship, ed., 3 vols. (London, 1885–1888). See Melvin Richter, *The Politics of Conscience: T. H. Green and His Times* (London, 1964). On Bosanquet, besides Hobhouse, see F. Houang, *Le Néo-Hegelianisme en Angleterre: La Philosophie de Bernard Bosanquet* (Paris, 1954). For a general account of British Neo-Hegelian political and social thought, see A. J. M. Milne, *The Social Philosophy of English Idealism* (London, 1962). *The Philosophy of Loyalty* (New York, 1908) by the American idealist Josiah Royce shows a related development. On Royce, see J. E. Smith, *Royce's Social Infinite* (New York, 1950). Other works by Hobhouse are *Liberalism* (London, 1911) and *The Elements of Social Justice* (London, 1922). See J. A. Hobson and Morris Ginsberg, *L. T. Hobhouse, His Life and Work* (London, 1931). Of the many British political writings broadly following in the tradition of Green, the following may be mentioned: Ernest Barker, *Reflections on Government* (London, 1942); A. D. Lindsay, *The Modern Democratic State* (London, 1943); and J. D. Mabbott, *The State and The Citizen* (London, 1948). A curious wartime idealist work with an intent similar to that of Hobhouse's *Metaphysical Theory of the State* is R. G. Collingwood's *The New Leviathan* (Oxford, 1942).

MARXISM

Almost any writing of Marx or Engels is relevant to their political philosophy. See especially Marx's *Das Kapital*, 3 vols. (Hamburg, 1867–1894), translated by Samuel Moore, Edward Aveling, and Ernest Untermann as *Capital*, 3 vols. (Chicago, 1915); Marx and Engels' *Die deutsche Ideologie*, V. Adoratsky, ed. (Vienna, 1932), translated as *The German Ideology*, S. Ryazanskaya, ed. (Moscow, 1964); Marx and Engels' *Manifest der kommunistischen Partei* (London, 1848), translated as *The Communist Manifesto*, edited with an introduction by Harold Laski (London, 1948); and Engels' *Der Ursprung der Familie, des Privateigentums und des Staat* (Zurich, 1884), translated by Ernest Untermann as *The Origin of the Family, Private Property, and the State* (Chicago, 1902). Two convenient anthologies are Lewis S. Feuer, ed., *Marx and Engels, Basic Writings on Politics and Philosophy* (Garden City, N.Y., 1949), and T. B. Bottomore and Maximilien Rubel, eds., *Karl Marx. Selected Writings in Sociology and Social Philosophy* (London, 1956). Of the writings of Lenin, see especially *Chto Delat? (What Is to Be Done?*, Stuttgart, 1902), *Shag Vperyod, Dva Shaga Nazad (One Step Forward, Two Steps Back*, Geneva, 1904), *Imperializm, kak Vysshara Stadiya Kapitalizma (Imperialism, the Highest Stage of Capitalism*, Petrograd, 1917), and *Gosudarstvo i Revolutsiya (State and Revolution*, Petrograd, 1918). There are various English editions of all of these. Of the many other Marxist writers on political philosophy, one of the most interesting is Antonio Gramsci. See his *Opere*, 6 vols. (Turin, 1947–1954), and *The Modern Prince and Other Writings*, translated by Louis Marks (London, 1957). For other Marxist writings and for writings on Marxism, consult the bibliographies to the articles DIALECTICAL MATERIALISM, HISTORICAL MATERIALISM, and MARXIST PHILOSOPHY.

ANARCHISM

Among the chief anarchist works are William Godwin, *An Enquiry concerning Political Justice and Its Influence on General Virtue and Happiness* (London, 1793); the writings of Michael Bakunin, translations of which appear in *The Political Philosophy of Bakunin: Scientific Anarchism* (Glencoe, Ill., 1953); Prince Peter Kropotkin's *The State, Its Part in History* (London, 1898), *Mutual Aid, a Factor of Evolution* (London, 1902), and *Modern Science and Anarchism* (Philadelphia, 1903); Pierre-Joseph Proudhon's *Qu'est-ce que la Propriété?* (Paris, 1840), translated by Benjamin R. Tucker as *What Is Property; An Inquiry Into the Principle of Right and of Government* (New York, 1890); Henry David Thoreau, "Civil Disobedience," in *The Writings of Henry David Thoreau*, Vol. X (Boston and New York, 1863); Benjamin R. Tucker, *Instead of a Book: A Fragmentary Exposition of Philosophical Anarchism* (New York, 1897); and Georges Sorel,

Réflexions sur la violence (Paris, 1908), translated by T. E. Hulme and J. Roth as *Reflections on Violence* (New York, 1914). On anarchism, see George Woodcock, *Anarchism: A History of Libertarian Ideas and Movements* (Cleveland, Ohio, 1962); James Joll, *The Anarchists* (London, 1964); and Alexander Gray, *The Socialist Tradition* (London, 1946).

NATIONAL SOCIALISM AND FASCISM

For further pronouncements by national socialists, see Josef Goebbels, *Goebbels Tagebücher*, Louis Lochner, ed. (Zurich, 1948); Adolf Hitler, *Mein Kampf*, 2 vols. (Munich, 1925–1927), and *Hitler's Secret Conversations 1941–1944* (New York, 1953). GERMAN PHILOSOPHY AND NATIONAL SOCIALISM contains an extensive bibliography of relevant works, which may be supplemented by bibliographies in many of the works cited there. On fascism, consult Benito Mussolini, *Scritti i discorsi*, 12 vols. (Milan, 1934–1939) and *The Doctrine of Fascism*, translated in Michael Oakeshott, ed., *Social and Economic Doctrines of Contemporary Europe*, 2d ed. (New York, 1942); and Giovanni Gentile, *Che cosa è il fascismo* (Florence, 1925) and *Origini e dottrine del fascismo* (Rome, 1929).

CONTEMPORARY POLITICAL THOUGHT

The best picture of contemporary analytic political philosophy can be gathered from the series of collections entitled *Philosophy, Politics and Society*, edited by Peter Laslett, W. G. Runciman, and others (Oxford, 1957——). Popper's main works on political philosophy are *The Open Society and Its Enemies* and *The Poverty of Historicism* (London, 1957). Weldon also published *States and Morals* (London, 1946). On Oakeshott, consult his inaugural address in the first volume of *Philosophy, Politics and Society* and his *Rationalism in Politics* (London, 1962). Other examples are H. L. A. Hart, "The Ascription of Responsibility and Rights," *PAS*, Vol. 49 (1948/1949), 179–194, reprinted in A. G. N. Flew, ed., *Essays on Logic and Language* (Oxford, 1951); Margaret Macdonald, "The Language of Political Theory," in *PAS*, Vol. 41 (1940/1941), reprinted in Flew, *op. cit.*; J. W. N. Watkins, "Epistemology and Politics," in *PAS*, Vol. 58 (1957/1958), 79–102; and S. I. Benn and R. S. Peters, *Social Principles and the Democratic State* (London, 1959).

(Introduction through Kant)
PETER LASLETT
(Hegel through recent political thought)
PHILIP W. CUMMINGS

POLITICAL PHILOSOPHY, NATURE OF. One may discuss the nature of political philosophy in two ways. One way is to try to identify in the acknowledged classics of the subject—Plato's *Republic*, Aristotle's *Politics*, Hobbes's *Leviathan*, Locke's *Two Treatises of Civil Government*, Rousseau's *Social Contract*, Hegel's *Philosophy of Right*, and so on—the principal recurrent problems and the methods used to deal with them. The other way is to begin with a preconceived idea of what constitutes a philosophical inquiry, as distinct from a scientific, theological, or aesthetic inquiry, and then consider how such an inquiry might be pursued in the field of politics.

The first way acknowledges that political philosophy is a tradition of inquiry, with its own characteristic forms of argument and conceptual models, a tradition in which every innovation emerges from a critical dialogue between the author and his predecessors. For instance, Rousseau's conception of sovereignty in *The Social Contract* proceeds from Aristotle's conception of the role of the polis in the development of man's moral nature, as well as from the theories of sovereignty of Bodin and Hobbes. Unhappily the tradition is not methodologically homogeneous. The authors of the classics, less self-conscious purists than some recent philosophers, were ready to use whatever arguments were at hand and to follow whatever lines of inquiry seemed fruitful without asking whether what they were doing was, in a strict sense, philosophy. Thus much of Aristotle's *Politics*, Montesquieu's *L'Esprit des lois*, and the *Communist Manifesto* is protopolitical science or protosociology—conjectures about how political organizations actually work or about the causal connections between forms of institutions and the types of policies likely to be pursued or between economic structure and political power. These are questions of fact calling for empirical rather than philosophical investigation. On the other hand, much of the classical writings could be interpreted as straightforward conceptual analysis, of the kind that modern analytical philosophy regards as completely respectable. In this class would fall Hobbes's discussion of the nature of authority and law, and Aristotle's analysis of justice and equality. Valuable recent work in this genre, on the frontier between political and legal philosophy, has been done by Hans Kelsen and Herbert L. A. Hart.

But some political philosophers have been more ambitious. They have tried to place politics, as an activity, and political institutions, as social entities, in a broad metaphysical setting. Hegel is an obvious example: He claimed to show that the state was the culmination of a historical process fully intelligible only in metaphysical terms, as the concrete realization of the human spirit and, through it, of the Absolute in its progress toward complete self-consciousness. Not all political philosophers have married politics and metaphysics so closely; but many have offered broad interpretations of politics designed to include all political phenomena—interpretations which no empirical evidence could prove false but which seem, nevertheless, to be mutually exclusive. Burke's account of political society as a contract between the living, the dead, and the yet unborn is one example; Marx's account of it in terms of class conflict is another. Generally, a political philosophy of this kind has been closely tied to some view of the nature of man, either in the sense of a psychological theory of motivation, as with Bentham and Hobbes, or in the Aristotelian sense of "nature," whereby the nature of a thing consists in the characteristic excellence of which it is capable. Examples of political philosophies related to views of the nature of man in the Aristotelian sense are Aristotle's own account of man as by nature political, the conception of man presupposed by J. S. Mill's views on the value of representative government, Rousseau's idea of moral freedom, and T. H. Green's and L. T. Hobhouse's ideas on self-realization.

Finally, none of the writers mentioned so far (with the possible exceptions of Hart and Kelsen) would have doubted that political philosophy is a normative or prescriptive activity. Plato's *Republic* diagnosed the ills of the polis in its decline by comparing it with an ideal, healthy form. Hobbes was concerned to preserve the state of England, torn by religious dissension and civil war; Locke, to safeguard the rights of property under the rule of law from the dangers of royal absolutism. Political philosophy generally flourishes when the state is sick—its practitioners believing themselves qualified to prescribe and claiming objective validity for the reasons with which they support their prescriptions.

Such claims have been seriously shaken by recent analytical philosophers. Their general approach to the nature of philosophical inquiry denies that philosophers as such possess any special method for supporting commendations or prescriptions or that there could be a body of characteristically philosophical knowledge that could yield them. A philosophical inquiry, they maintain, is concerned with the conceptual structure of our thinking about the world; it yields no new knowledge of facts other than facts about the structure of language. Prescriptions for action and commendations of policies or institutions depend on factual estimates of their consequences and on evaluations. No analysis of language alone can yield an evaluation. It can dispel confusions or obscurities in thought, so that issues may be more clearly seen, but what to do is ultimately a matter not of knowledge but of choice. Given full knowledge of the facts and clear understanding of the issues to be decided, no man, because of philosophical skill, is better qualified than another to decide them.

Political philosophy, according to this account, is necessarily a second-order activity. It is concerned either with the conceptual structure and methodology of political science, in which case it is a particular branch of the philosophy of science, or it is concerned with the conceptual structure of political discourse and with the kinds of arguments used to propose, defend, or criticize political institutions and policies. In either case, it must be politically neutral; that is, it will have nothing to say about the substantive merits of a policy or about the arguments used to support it. Indeed, though the supporting arguments may be shown to be logically invalid or to rest on conceptual confusions, this would not necessarily imply that the policy should be given up.

POLITICAL SCIENCE AND PHILOSOPHY

The analysis of concepts. The distinction between first-order and second-order activities may, however, be too sharply drawn. Politics is an activity governed by rules and standards of propriety and success; how one understands such rules and standards affects how one acts and how one evaluates and responds to the actions of others. The clarification and criticism of such criteria is a philosophical activity which can yet have substantive consequences. For philosophical criticism, in politics as in ethics, explores what a man is committed to by the principles he avows, and tests how far such avowals are coherent. Though conceptual analysis alone may yield no particular prescription, it can force a choice between principles with incompatible commitments or require that a principle be reformulated to free it from some prima facie but unacceptable commitment. Thus A might say to B: "If you support course X by advancing principle P, you would appear to be committed also to defending course Y (which you would probably agree was indefensible)." Then B would either have to endorse Y or restate P so as to exclude Y while saving X. Admittedly, to press upon a man the need to reformulate his principles may not affect his intentions in this particular application of them; nevertheless, it can have the practical effect of altering the terms in which choices will present themselves to him in the future.

Constitutional interpretation provides an illustration of this procedure of clarification and criticism, and of its implications for action, at a fairly low level of generality. When the principles governing political action are formally stated in constitutional declarations of rights and procedures, analyzing and interpreting them is commonly regarded as a task for lawyers. Yet the interpretation of a concept like "due process of law" demands not simply a knowledge of statutes and precedents but an understanding of the point of a tradition and of the role played by the concept in relation to others, like judicial independence, the rule of law, and the rights of the individual. Some of these indeed may never appear in any formal constitutional statement, yet they operate nonetheless as norms of healthy functioning for the system. Principles with no legal standing at all, like civilian control of the armed forces or, in British practice, collective cabinet responsibility, are very important criteria for the criticism and assessment of constitutional trends or proposals for reform. For instance, proposals for a system of functional committees of the British House of Commons have been repeatedly rejected, on the grounds that because such a committee would form close ties with its corresponding department, the minister's responsibility for the department would be impaired. This objection is taken as sufficient to show that such a system would be incompatible with the health of the constitutional organism. Yet precisely what such responsibility entails is not laid down in any legal instrument.

Authorities on the constitution formulate statements of principles, from time to time, to accord with the acknowledged precedents and, making articulate the accepted practices and expectations, provide guides for future developments. Such formulations tend to become orthodoxies. However, because constitutions have to adapt themselves to changing social conditions, the practices themselves change, that is, people not only come to expect a different response to a given situation but treat the expected as also legitimate. Discrepancies between expectations and doctrine invite criticism and reformulation. This task calls for knowledge of the practices, but also for an insight into the tradition and an understanding of the point that the old orthodoxy sought to sustain. This is an inquiry into the meaning of concepts and principles, essentially philosophical rather than empirical. For it describes not merely what people habitually do, nor yet why they do it; rather, it takes account of what they think of themselves as doing.

Principles and practice. But what may set out to be simply a reformulation to align principles with acknowledged practices will serve also as a license for new practices in the future. And because a given set of practices can be consistent with a number of possible formulations, which may be extended to license different sets of future practices, the interpretation of present institutions may not be neutral in its political implications, however dispassionate it may be in execution. Thus the criticism of orthodoxies and the recommending of revised formulations merely on the grounds that they accord more closely with

what is already going on may nevertheless have a substantial impact on the further evolution of institutions. And at any given time there may well be a number of competing accounts of a system current in a society, which differ not so much in what they say actually goes on as in their modes of describing it and consequently in their views of what, under possibly different circumstances, these present practices would license.

People who are politically active within a given system have an idea (or maybe a range of competing ideas) of what it is like and how it works, of the practices it sanctions and of those it could not tolerate, and of the demands it makes on participants if it is to remain healthy. And these ideas themselves regulate the behavior of individuals in their institutional roles. This, perhaps, is the truth that Bernard Bosanquet perceived, if somewhat obscurely, when he described institutions as "ethical ideas." This applies, however, at various levels of generality—not only to particular institutions or particular political and social systems but also to whole classes of systems.

The democracy concept: an example. An outstanding instance is the change over the last decade or two in the concept "democracy," a change attributable to research into voting habits, public opinion, pressure groups, and parties. The belief that an indispensable constituent of a healthy democracy is a lively and politically conscious electorate; that apathy is a pathological condition, a malfunctioning of the electoral organ; that voters must be eternally vigilant to safeguard their rights and their interests against the ever-present danger of tyranny and corruption—all this has suffered a rude shock. For, in the first place, the systems we have been accustomed to think of as the paradigms of democracy turn out not to satisfy these conditions. But even more, we are led to ask whether any system could satisfy them, given continued respect for other values, like the right to develop one's own interests free of propaganda pressure, the rights of privacy, and so on. To analyze the traditional presuppositions, or norms of democratic health, in the light of our new knowledge of actual social behavior swiftly raises the doubt whether the old model can have any relation at all to reality, whether it does not make demands which in practice are mutually incompatible. In that case, the traditional theory of democracy would be simply irrelevant to our social situation.

New models of democracy. The new insight into democratic realities has led to attempts, by Joseph Schumpeter, Robert A. Dahl, and others, to reconstruct the model. They have tried to look afresh at the old one to see in what respects it does seem to correspond more or less with what actually goes on, to salvage whatever in it still seems relevant and important (for instance, governmental sensitivity to the interests of the governed, open discussion, criticism, and public justification of policies), and then to reformulate the democratic norms of health to continue to provide for these things, while yet not asking for the impossible—or for the positively undesirable. Whether this operation is an exercise in political science or political philosophy is hard to say. The vague term "political theorists" traditionally applied to those who work in the area places it on the frontier between empirical and philosophical studies. For political theories are not theories in the scientists' sense of the term (though political scientists have begun in recent years to use the term in that sense too)—their role is not so much to explain as to systematize and make articulate how people operating political systems think they work and should work and to relate these systems to more general principles, like freedom and justice, which are said to sanction them, and which, conversely, the systems are held to instantiate. Moreover, though such theoretical exercises may begin by analyzing principles and matching them up with facts, they lead on to new syntheses, models, or paradigms, which will almost certainly license practices different from the old. For instance, it would be far more difficult to ground a case for compulsory voting on a modern pluralistic view of democracy than it was on the older populistic model. Or again, whereas the older model tended, with Rousseau, to be suspicious of organized interests in politics, the newer makes them a condition for the healthy functioning of democracy. Whether this sort of political theory be considered political science or political philosophy, it cannot be treated as a purely second-order activity; it has clear prescriptive implications for political practice.

POLITICS AND METAPHYSICS

Political discourse has its characteristic vocabulary. Or to put the matter differently, politics goes on in a world organized into communities, institutions, and states, in which men possess power and authority, maintain order, and so on. Political philosophy traces the relations between these concepts—or, one might say, it maps this world and investigates the ontological status of its component entities. What kind of a thing is a society or a state? What are the conditions for saying that one exists, or for recognizing its continuing identity through time? Does it have parts, and are they rules, offices, and institutions, or are they men and women?

Political analogies. When Hobbes described the state as an artificial man, created by covenant, and Hegel described it as an organism, they were suggesting analogies to elucidate and explain the relation between social entities and their individual components. To object, against Hobbes, that there never was a covenant and that men in a Hobbesian state of nature would not know how to make one is to miss the point. Political theories of this kind present a global picture of society, government, and politics. They are not models of some particular state, or even some class of states, for they aim to be true of all states. Though they might be criticized for incoherence, it is difficult to see what empirical objections would be relevant to their truth or validity. Do they provide, then, some special sort of knowledge? And if they are constructed so as to be consistent with all possible political worlds, and with care to commit no logical solecisms, how should one choose between them, and what difference can it make?

Theories as regulative principles. The social-contract model was a way of defining the relations between individuals in a society—of interpreting their cooperation and their submission to authority, as well as the fact that they have private aims. But the effect of the model is to give the private aims a kind of teleological priority; for, according

to the model, only when these are given do social actions and purposes have any point at all. The organicist, on the contrary, is impressed by the fact that so-called private aims are particular instances of interests and ideals socially established and sustained, so that the individual becomes a particularization of a greater whole—in Hegelian terms, of a concrete universal—whose conduct is intelligible only when he is regarded as a bearer of roles. Both accounts could be made consistent and intelligible, and there is little profit in asking which is true. The difference between them lies in the orientation each gives to the facts: as Eric Weil has said, "They distinguish . . . the essential from the nonessential, deep forces from superficial events, decisive factors from epiphenomena" ("Philosophie politique, théorie politique," p. 282). Only, of course, what is essential for one theorist may not be essential for another. Global theories of this kind are ways of stressing certain features of the political universe and lightly regarding others, of organizing experience according to standards of what is important. In this respect such theories function, like Kant's "ideas," as "regulative principles," in one sense subjective, in that they are not logically necessary or presupposed by experience, yet in another sense claiming to be true for the whole human race; for they appeal to our experience of the world of politics and ask, Looked at like this, does it not make more sense?

Precisely because models of this kind purport to account for all forms of political existence and action, they cannot entail in a strict logical sense any one form or system more than another. Yet in some sense they do imply that some are more reasonable than others. For instance, anyone accepting Burke's claim that a divine purpose is manifest in the history of political society is not logically committed to repudiating revolution, for that too might be a move in the divine game; but he must surely approach social change with a reverential regard for traditions, rather than eradicate as so much lumber everything in which he can find no rational point. Or again, anyone accepting Rousseau's view that a political society possesses a general will for the public good, latent if not manifest, would be inclined to approve a system from which popular decisions emerged unequivocally, by referenda, for instance, rather than one that institutionalized group conflicts and reached decisions by compromise and negotiation.

New ways of seeing politics. Global political theories serve to open our eyes to dimensions of the world of politics that may have been overlooked or underrated. And this is one reason why the classics of political philosophy retain their interest; the conceptual structure of their political world is often unfamiliar, and their models stress aspects of that world that our present social situation encourages us to overlook. Sir Isaiah Berlin says of theories of this kind that the test of their adequacy "is ultimately empirical: it is the degree of their success in forming a coherent and enduring conceptual system" ("Does Political Theory Still Exist?," p. 25). But it is empirical, if at all, in a somewhat special sense; for Berlin appears to mean that a model may take too little account of differences that strike us as undeniably important or reduce to the same terms factors which we insist on distinguishing. For instance, Rousseau criticized Hobbes, not because there are facts left out of his model, but for using a model that "was inadequate in principle . . . because it was based on a failure to understand what we mean by motive, purpose, value, personality, and the like" (*ibid.*, p. 24). It was inadequate not because it ignored these things but because, by reducing them all to expressions of the desire for "felicity," dominated by the overarching desire to avoid sudden death, it blurred distinctions, like that between morality and prudence or between egoism and altruism, which make a subtler understanding of our world possible.

How one sees the world is not just a matter of accurate observation, or recording impressions. What one sees, to be "seen" at all, must mean something, that is, must be fitted into a given conceptual structure. Perception and understanding and willing are not independent activities or faculties, for to perceive an object is to perceive it as something, and this is already to relate it to the rest of the world, albeit in a minimal way. Moreover, the terms in which we see the world will reflect our interests in it—we may divide the world of plants into Liliaceae, Orchidaceae, and so on, or into border plants, rockery plants, and weeds. Nor can we escape the necessity to see the world under some such guise, for there is no neutral, objective way, independent of interests. It is not that Rousseau and Hobbes are pressing upon us ideological spectacles, where we could see better with the naked eye. For when we think we see with the naked eye, we are only oblivious of the particular spectacles we wear. We become conscious of our own conceptual commitments by exploring alternative ways of structuring the world. These may treat lightly things we esteem; yet to see the world organized according to a different order of importance is to discover something new about men and the possible conceptual worlds they create to inhabit and the kinds of satisfaction and fulfillment they can achieve.

POLITICAL PHILOSOPHY AND THE CONCEPT OF MAN

Philosophical understanding proceeds by systematic criticism of differing visions of the world; the social philosopher strives to understand the patterns taken for granted in his society and the way they relate to human interests. Experiencing the world through other eyes, one becomes more clearly aware of the characteristics and limitations of one's own point of view; thus one begins to understand what other interests are possible to man. Thereby one's conception of man is itself widened. Such may be the experience, for instance, of someone coming to Aristotle, Aquinas, or St. Augustine for the first time who has been accustomed to seeing society only in terms of contracts and market models or in the terms used by the welfare economists. But beyond the critical assessment of the present in the light of the past, there are those who, like Rousseau, Marx, and Freud—more prophets perhaps than philosophers—teach their contemporaries, and even more their successors, to see with new eyes, by redesigning the conceptual structure in terms of which man is understood. For instance, the ideas of Newton, Hobbes, and Locke suggested to the social philosophers of the

Enlightenment, like Helvétius and Holbach, that individuals in societies were not only analogous to the atomic constituents of physical wholes but were themselves intelligible in terms of a system of quasimechanical, hedonic attractions and repulsions. Given knowledge of the natural laws of human psychological mechanics, individual dispositions could be molded to a socially consistent pattern by an appropriate set of ideal institutions, and all would be happy. Such utopian social engineering depended not only on a boundless confidence in the power of knowledge to control and create but also on a somewhat undemanding standard of human excellence—unlimited contentment from the satisfaction of finite desires through technological development. Contemporary social theorists, more sophisticated and less rationalistic in approach, discuss the relation of individuals to their society in terms of the "internalization of social norms," and they diagnose social ills in terms of alienation and social maladjustment, of inner-directedness and other-directedness, of authoritarian personalities and democratic personalities. These concepts rely heavily on Marxian and psychoanalytic concepts of man, which have in common at least a conception of human freedom through self-knowledge and the transcending of conflict within the personality and within the society.

The philosopher is led back, then, to an understanding of what man characteristically and distinctively is and, even more, of what he is at his best. For some notion of this kind, however inarticulate and unrecognized, lies behind every political program and every critique of political institutions. It would be difficult to sustain a case for democracy, for instance, if one held with Plato that though every man was capable of excellence of a sort, the highest excellence is open only to an intellectual elite and that the ultimate test of political organization must be its capacity to safeguard a Socrates. Nor could one believe in human rights if one held, with Aristotle, that the only excellence of which some men are capable is in the use that others can make of them. Conversely, behind most forms of democratic doctrine lies a conception of man as not merely capable of reasonable choice and independent judgment but as displaying a characteristic excellence in exercising this capacity. And this involves a consequent commitment to oppose techniques of human manipulation or practices tending to diminish such capacities and to support forms of education and political opportunities likely to enlarge them. Criticism of a political doctrine will elicit in the end a concept of man, which the political philosopher as such may take for granted but which is itself a perennial subject for philosophical inquiry.

Political philosophy, then, operates at different levels of generality and abstraction. At the lowest it merges into political science and practical politics. The frontiers are blurred, and even at the level of pure conceptual analysis the philosopher may have a positive effect on the way politics is done. At this rather low order of abstraction philosophical analysis can result in quite specific recommendations for policy and institutions. They are, it is true, mostly hypothetical; they come from an argument of the form: "If you agree that you are committed to this, then you must also agree that you cannot be committed to that."

But political philosophy operates also at a higher level of abstraction, less tied to the contingent incidence of institutions and policies and aiming rather at global interpretation of political reality. Here the relation between philosophy and practice is logically more remote but may be the more generally pervasive on that account. Finally, the political philosopher is confronted with a theory of human interests which furnishes criteria for the general appraisal of social institutions.

As one would expect, the lower-order activity brings the philosopher into the closest touch with current political controversy, the higher is what gives him lasting interest. If this is true, then T. D. Weldon was wrong when he wrote, of the classical authors on political philosophy, that "In so far as these works are concerned with verbal definitions and foundations they have indeed little of value to offer and, unfortunately, it is these sections of them which receive most attention in commentaries. On the other hand what their authors have to say in the way of description and of actual or implied recommendations is often important and illuminating" (*Vocabulary of Politics*, p. 15). What Plato, Rousseau, or Burke had to say in the way of description and actual recommendation is probably now of little more than historical interest; it is what Weldon misleadingly called "verbal definitions and foundations" that provide the vision which can supplement or in some measure correct the particular squints which we suffer from as observers from this particular viewpoint in time and space.

Bibliography

For more or less traditional treatments of political philosophy, see Sir Ernest Barker, *Principles of Social and Political Theory* (Oxford, 1951), and J. D. Mabbott, *The State and the Citizen* (London, 1948).

For critical discussions of the scope and limitations of political philosophy, see Alfred Cobban, "The Decline of Political Theory," in *Political Science Quarterly*, Vol. 68 (1953), 321–327; G. C. Field, "What Is Political Theory?" in *PAS*, Vol. 54 (1953/1954), 145–166; Dante Germino, "The Revival of Political Theory," in *Journal of Politics*, Vol. 25 (1963), 437–460; Peter Laslett, ed., *Philosophy, Politics and Society*, First Series (Oxford, 1956), especially the editor's Introduction, Michael Oakeshott's "Political Education," and T. D. Weldon's "Political Principles"; Peter Laslett and W. G. Runciman, eds., *Philosophy, Politics and Society*, Second Series (Oxford, 1962), especially Sir Isaiah Berlin's "Does Political Theory Still Exist?" and W. G. Runciman's "Sociological Evidence and Political Theory"; H. J. McCloskey, "The Nature of Political Philosophy," in *Ratio*, Vol. 6 (1964), 50–62; Margaret Macdonald, "The Language of Political Theory," in A. G. N. Flew, ed., *Essays on Logic and Language*, First Series (Oxford, 1951), pp. 167–186; Michael Oakeshott, *Rationalism in Politics* (London, 1962); P. H. Partridge, "Politics, Philosophy, Ideology," in *Political Studies*, Vol. 9 (1961), 217–235; P. H. Partridge, "Political Philosophy and Political Sociology," in *Australian and New Zealand Journal of Sociology*, Vol. 1 (1965), 3–20; John Plamenatz, "The Use of Political Theory," in *Political Studies*, Vol. 8 (1960), 37–47—Plamenatz also has a valuable discussion of the nature of political theory in the Introduction to his *Man and Society*, 2 vols. (London, 1963); J. C. Rees, "The Limitations of Political Theory," in *Political Studies*, Vol. 2 (1954), 242–257; *Revue française de science politique*, Vol. 11, No. 2 (1961), an entire issue devoted to "La Théorie politique," including, among other articles, Henri Lefebvre, "Marxisme et politique. Le Marxisme a-t-il un théorie politique?," Eric Weil, "Philosophie politique, théorie politique," and Richard Wollheim, "Philosophie analytique et pensée politique"; W. G. Runciman,

Social Science and Political Theory (Cambridge, 1963); Leo Strauss, *What Is Political Philosophy?* (Glencoe, Ill., 1959); T. D. Weldon, *The Vocabulary of Politics* (Harmondsworth, 1953); Sheldon S. Wolin, *Politics and Vision* (Boston, 1960).

For discussions of the relations between politics and metaphysics, see Stuart Hampshire, *Thought and Action* (London, 1959); G. W. F. Hegel, *Vorlesungen über die Philosophie der Geschichte* (1837), in his *Sämtliche Werke* ("Collected Works"), H. Glockner, ed., 26 vols. (Stuttgart, 1927–1940; facsimile ed., 24 vols., 1958–1965), Vol. XII, translated by J. Sibree as *The Philosophy of History* (New York, 1944)—see especially the Introduction; Karl Popper, *The Open Society and Its Enemies*, 2 vols. (London, 1945; 4th rev. ed., London, 1962); J. W. N. Watkins, "Epistemology and Politics," *PAS*, Vol. 58 (1957/1958), 79–102.

For treatments that try to take account of recent developments in philosophy, see S. I. Benn and R. S. Peters, *Social Principles and the Democratic State* (London, 1959), reissued as *Principles of Political Thought* (New York, 1964); and H. R. G. Greaves, *Foundations of Political Theory* (London, 1958).

For discussions from the standpoint of political science, see G. E. G. Catlin, *Political and Sociological Theory and Its Applications* (Ann Arbor, Mich., 1964); G. E. G. Catlin, *Systematic Politics* (Toronto, 1962); and C. J. Friedrich, *Man and His Government* (New York, 1963), which includes an extensive bibliography.

STANLEY I. BENN

POMPONAZZI, PIETRO (1462–1525), Italian Renaissance Aristotelian, was born in Mantua. He studied philosophy at the University of Padua, where, after obtaining his degree, he became extraordinary professor of philosophy in 1488 and ordinary professor in 1495. When war caused the university to close in 1509, he left Padua. After a short period at Ferrara he became a professor of philosophy at the University of Bologna, where he taught from 1512 until his death. He married three times and had two children.

Of Pomponazzi's writings only a few were published during his lifetime. Best known is the treatise *De Immortalitate Animae* ("On the Immortality of the Soul," 1516), which immediately provoked a large controversy. It was publicly attacked by several philosophers and theologians and was followed by the author's two treatises in defense—the *Apologia* (1518) and the *Defensorium* (1519)—which were longer than the original work. Probably as a result of this experience Pomponazzi did not publish anything else except for a few short philosophical questions that he added to the 1525 reprint (*Tractatus Acutissimi*) of his three writings on immortality. Equally important are his treatises *De Incantationibus* ("On Incantations") and *De Fato* ("On Fate"), both written about 1520, which were published posthumously in Basel by a Protestant exile in 1556 and 1567 respectively. A sizable body of other writings has been preserved in manuscript, and the study and publication of this material have barely begun. The most important among these unpublished writings are questions on Aristotelian and other problems, which Pomponazzi probably worded himself and which therefore directly reflect his thought. A much larger group consists of his class lectures on various works of Aristotle. Since they were taken down by students and show a certain amount of oscillation from year to year and from copy to copy, they must be used with caution in any attempt to reconstruct Pomponazzi's thought and philosophical development.

Pomponazzi was a product and in many ways a typical representative of the tradition of scholastic Aristotelianism that flourished at Bologna, Padua, and other Italian universities from the thirteenth to the seventeenth century. This school, often referred to as Paduan Averroism, had no institutional or doctrinal connections with theology, as did its northern counterparts, but rather with medicine, and this accounts for its secular orientation. In the study of Aristotle, whose writings served as the prescribed texts for the teaching of the philosophical disciplines, the emphasis was, as in Paris and elsewhere, on logic and natural philosophy rather than on ethics and metaphysics. Pomponazzi's main sources were the writings of Aristotle and of his commentators, and his style, far removed from classical or humanistic elegance, is a rather harsh example of scholastic terminology and argument, although he was at times capable of concise formulation and caustic wit. His reasoning shows great subtlety and acumen, but he is repetitious and sometimes inconsistent. He obviously enjoyed spinning out an argument and following reason wherever it led, and out of intellectual honesty he was prepared to admit his puzzlement before certain dilemmas and to modify his views whenever he felt compelled to do so by some strong argument. Thus, we may well understand the outburst in *De Fato* (III, 7) in which he compares the philosopher with Prometheus. In his efforts to understand the secrets of God the philosopher is eaten up by his continual worries and thoughts; stops eating, drinking, and sleeping; is held up to ridicule by all; is taken as a fool and a faithless person; is persecuted by the Inquisition; and is laughed at by the multitude.

In spite of his general scholastic orientation Pomponazzi was by no means unaffected by other currents. He knew and respected Plato and was clearly influenced by Ficino (and Pico) in his remarks about the place of man in the universe and perhaps in his preoccupation with the immortality of the soul. Like the humanists he cultivated the monographic treatise in addition to the question and the commentary, occasionally injected personal remarks about himself, and cited such sources as Cicero and Plutarch. His doctrine that virtue is its own reward has Stoic rather than Aristotelian antecedents, and his insistence that the end of man consists in practical virtue rather than in contemplation is at variance with Aristotle and may owe something to Cicero and to such humanists as Bruni and Alberti.

One may even link with humanism Pomponazzi's interest in Alexander of Aphrodisias. Alexander was not entirely unknown during the Middle Ages, but his writings acquired a much wider diffusion through new translations around the turn of the sixteenth century. The label of Alexandrism often attached to Pomponazzi is dubious and misleading. We know from a question composed by Pomponazzi in 1504 that his view on the problem of immortality, as adopted in his treatise of 1516, was derived from that of Alexander. We also learn that the writing of his treatise *De Fato* was occasioned by his reading a new Latin translation of Alexander's treatise on the subject (Pomponazzi knew no Greek). However, *De Fato* is actually a defense of the Stoic position against Alexander.

Pomponazzi's *De Incantationibus* is an attempt to offer natural explanations for a number of occurrences popularly ascribed to the agency of demons and spirits. The effects ascribed to the stars by the astrologers form for Pomponazzi a part of the system of natural causes. This work is the only one by Pomponazzi that was once on the Index of Prohibited Books (it no longer is) because of its implied criticism of miracles. It contains an interesting passage on prayer which shows a certain affinity to some ideas expressed in the treatise on immortality. The value of prayer, he said, consists not in the external effects it may have but in the pious attitude it produces in the person who prays.

The *De Fato*, which is divided into five books, is by far the longest of Pomponazzi's works. He discusses in great detail and with a great number of intricate arguments the problems of fate, free will, and predestination. His conclusions are by no means simple or clear-cut, but it appears from his final remarks that he regarded the Stoic doctrine of fate, on purely natural grounds, as relatively free from contradictions. Yet, because human wisdom is subject to error, Pomponazzi was willing to submit to the teaching of the church and to accept the doctrine that God's providence and predestination are compatible with man's free will. However, he was not satisfied with the way in which this compatibility is customarily explained and tried to propose an explanation which he considered more satisfactory.

De Fato has been unduly neglected by students of Pomponazzi, perhaps because of its length and difficulty. It is now available in a critical edition and may be studied within the twofold historical context in which it belongs: first, the philosophical controversy between determinism and indeterminism as it appeared in antiquity in the works of the Stoics and Alexander and again in more modern discussions and, second, the specifically theological problem of reconciling providence and predestination with free will. The second question has occupied Christian theologians of all centuries; it had been discussed before Pomponazzi by Lorenzo Valla in his treatise on free will, and it was to be debated by Luther, Erasmus, and many other theologians during and after the Reformation.

Pomponazzi's treatise *De Immortalitate Animae* is much better known, and it had far wider repercussions during the sixteenth century and even later. Pomponazzi explains the origin of the treatise as follows: he had stated in a class lecture that Thomas Aquinas' view on immortality, though perhaps true, did not agree with Aristotle's, and he was subsequently asked by a Dominican friar who was his student to express his own opinion on the question, staying strictly within the limits of natural reason. In complying with this request, Pomponazzi begins with the statement that man is of a manifold and ambiguous nature and occupies an intermediary position between mortal and immortal things (Ch. 1). The question is in what sense such opposite attributes as mortal and immortal may be attributed to the human soul (Ch. 2). Pomponazzi first lists six possible answers, and after having discarded two of them because they had never been defended by anybody, he promises to discuss the remaining four (Chs. 2–3).

The first of the four answers is the view attributed to Averroës and others, according to which there is only one immortal soul common to all human beings and also an individual soul for each person, which, however, is mortal. Pomponazzi rejects this opinion at great length (Ch. 4). The Averroist position maintains that the intellect is capable of acting without a body and can therefore be considered as separable and immortal. Yet in our experience, Pomponazzi argues, the intellect has no action that is entirely independent of the body, and therefore we have no evidence that the intellect is separable. If we wish to understand the relationship of the intellect and the body, we must distinguish between being in the body as having the body for its organ or subject or substratum and depending on the body as having the body, its perceptions, and imaginations for its object. Pomponazzi insists that the intellect does not have the body as its subject as do the souls of animals and the lower faculties of the human soul. Yet the human intellect cannot know anything without the perceptions or imaginations offered to it by the body, and this fact alone proves that the intellect is not separable from the body.

Second, Pomponazzi discusses an opinion he attributes to Plato, according to which each person has two souls, one immortal and the other mortal (Ch. 5). This position is rejected on the ground that the subject of perception and that of intellectual knowledge must be the same and that it is therefore impossible to distinguish two separate natures within the human soul (Ch. 6).

Third, he examines the view, attributed to Thomas Aquinas, which holds that the human soul has but a single nature and that it is absolutely (*simpliciter*) immortal and only in some respects (*secundum quid*) mortal (Ch. 7). Elaborating on some of the arguments he had already advanced against Averroës, Pomponazzi insists that he finds no evidence to prove the absolute immortality of the soul. He has no doubt, he adds, that the doctrine of the absolute immortality of the soul is true, since it is in accordance with Scripture, but he wonders whether it is in agreement with Aristotle and whether it can be established within the limits of natural reason without recourse to the evidence of faith and revelation (Ch. 8).

Fourth, Pomponazzi discusses a position according to which the human soul, having only one nature, is absolutely mortal and only in certain respects immortal (Ch. 9). He then proceeds to defend this position, which he had identified elsewhere as that of Alexander of Aphrodisias. Insisting once more on the middle position of man, he argues that the human intellect, unlike that of the pure intelligences, always needs the body for its object and has no way of acting without the help of the images of sense or imagination. It must therefore be considered absolutely mortal and only relatively, or improperly speaking, immortal. On the other hand, unlike the souls of the animals, the human intellect does not have the body as its subject because it does not use a bodily organ in knowing. If it resided in an organ, the intellect could not reflect on itself or understand universals. The fact that the human intellect is capable of some knowledge of itself and of universals shows that it participates somewhat in immortality and, hence, that it is in some respect immortal. This interpretation of immortality is claimed to be more probable than the others and to be more in accordance with the teachings of Aristotle (Chs. 9–10).

Having reached this conclusion, Pomponazzi continues in good scholastic fashion to formulate several sets of objections to his view (Chs. 11 and 13) and to answer these objections in great detail (Chs. 12 and 14). In addition to repeating and elaborating some of the same arguments presented in the preceding chapters, he introduces, especially in Chapter 14, several new arguments and conclusions which are of great intrinsic interest.

Along with other objections to his view Pomponazzi cites (Ch. 13) the argument that, according to Aristotle's *Ethics*, the ultimate end of man is contemplation and that the satisfactory fulfillment of this end requires immortality. In his reply he states that man has a threefold intellect—speculative, practical, and technical. Only a few persons have a share in the speculative intellect, whereas the technical intellect is shared by some animals. We may thus conclude that the practical intellect, in which all human beings and only all human beings share, is the faculty peculiar to human beings. Every normal person can attain the practical intellect in a perfect way, and a person is called absolutely good or bad with reference to this practical intellect but merely in some respect good or bad with reference to the other two intellects. For a man is called a good man or a bad man with reference to his virtues and vices, yet a good metaphysician with reference to his speculative intellect and a good architect with reference to his technical intellect. However, a good metaphysician or a good architect is not always a good man. Hence, a man does not mind so much if he is not called a good metaphysician or a good architect, but he minds very much if he is called unjust or intemperate, for it seems to be in our power to be good or wicked, but to be a philosopher or an architect does not depend on us and is not necessary for a man. The ultimate end must thus be defined in terms of the practical intellect, and every man is called upon to be as virtuous as possible. By contrast, it is neither necessary nor even desirable that all men should be philosophers or architects but only that some of them should be. Moreover, since the perfection of the practical intellect is accessible to almost everybody, a farmer or a craftsman, a poor man or a rich man, may be called happy and is actually called happy and is satisfied with his lot whenever he is virtuous. In other words, Pomponazzi departs in this important respect from Aristotle and identifies the end of human life with moral virtue rather than with contemplation, because this end is attainable by all human beings.

There had been another objection—that God would not be a good governor of all things unless all good deeds found their reward and all bad deeds their punishment in a future life. To this Pomponazzi replies that the essential reward of virtue is virtue itself, and the essential punishment of vice is vice itself. Hence, it makes no difference whether the external or accidental reward or punishment of an action is sometimes omitted, since its essential reward and punishment are always present. Moreover, if one man acts virtuously without the expectation of a reward and another with such an expectation, the act of the latter is not considered to be as virtuous as that of the former. Thus, he who receives no external reward is more fully rewarded in an essential way than he who receives one. In the same way the wicked person who receives no external punishment is punished more than he who does, for the punishment inherent in guilt itself is much worse than any punishment in the form of some harm inflicted upon the guilty person.

Pomponazzi further develops this idea in reply to another objection. It is true that religious teachers have supported the doctrine of immortality, but they have done so in order to induce ordinary people to lead virtuous lives. Yet persons of a higher moral disposition are attracted toward the virtues by the mere excellence of these virtues and are repelled from the vices by the mere ugliness of these vices; hence, they do not need the expectation of rewards or punishments as an incentive. Rejecting the view that without a belief in immortality no moral standards could be maintained, Pomponazzi repeats that a virtuous action without the expectation of a reward is superior to one that aims at a reward and concludes that those who assert that the soul is mortal seem to preserve the notion of virtue much better than those who assert that it is immortal. In thus stating that moral standards, as defined by the philosopher, do not depend on religious sanctions, he does not deny the validity of religious beliefs but asserts the autonomy of reason and philosophy, drawing upon certain passages in Plato and above all on Stoic doctrine and anticipating to some extent the views of Spinoza and Kant.

Having presented all arguments against the immortality of the soul, Pomponazzi states in the last chapter that the question is a neutral one, as is that of the eternity of the world. That is, he does not believe there are any natural reasons strong enough to demonstrate the immortality of the soul or to refute its mortality, although he knows that many theologians, notably Thomas Aquinas, have argued otherwise. Since the question is thus doubtful on purely human grounds, it must be resolved by God himself, who clearly proved the immortality of the soul in the Holy Scriptures. This means that the arguments to the contrary must be false and merely apparent. The immortality of the soul is an article of faith, for it is based on faith and revelation. It must thus be asserted on this ground alone and not on the basis of inconclusive or unconvincing rational arguments.

This conclusion and a similar one found in the *De Fato* have given rise to a variety of interpretations on the part of Pomponazzi's contemporaries and of modern historians. The statement made by some that Pomponazzi simply denied the immortality of the soul is patently false. He merely said that the immortality of the soul cannot be demonstrated on purely natural grounds or in accordance with Aristotle but must be accepted as an article of faith. This position is widely and somewhat crudely referred to as the theory of the double truth. The term is inadequate, for neither Pomponazzi nor anybody else ever said that something is true in theology and its opposite true in philosophy. What Pomponazzi did say, and what many respectable thinkers before and after him said, is that one theory—for example, that of the immortality of the soul—is true according to faith but that it cannot be demonstrated on the basis of mere reason and that its opposite would seem to be supported by equally strong or even stronger probable arguments.

This view has been called absurd by many modern historians and, ironically, by some who actually take a similar position themselves, though perhaps on other issues and with different words. Yet the persistent charge made against Pomponazzi and against many other medieval and Renaissance thinkers who took a similar position has been that the so-called theory of the double truth is merely a hypocritical device to disguise their secret disbelief and to avoid trouble with the church authorities. Thus, in saying that immortality cannot be demonstrated and that mortality may be defended by strong rational arguments whereas immortality is to be held as an article of faith, Pomponazzi, according to these historians, merely concealed his opinion that the soul was really mortal and substituted for it a formula that would protect him against ecclesiastic censure or punishment.

This is a serious and delicate problem. We cannot deny that a thinker of the past may have entertained opinions which we do not find expressed in his writings or that he may have put into writing views which he did not hold in his innermost heart. On the other hand, unless we have some text or document in support of this assertion, we are not entitled to claim that a thinker held some specific views which he failed to express in his writings or that are even in contrast with his expressed views. As a theologian of the eighteenth century said on this matter, we must leave it to God to look into Pomponazzi's heart and to see what his real opinion was. The human historian has no basis other than the written document, and the burden of proof, in history as in law, rests with those who want to prove something that is contrary to the overt evidence. Neither innuendo nor the assertions made by unfriendly critics or extremist followers can be accepted as valid evidence in lieu of some original statement or testimony concerning the author's view.

According to this standard, we have no real grounds for maintaining that Pomponazzi was hypocritical. The position he takes in the treatise on the immortality of the soul is fundamentally retained in two lengthy works composed afterward in defense of the first and, with a few dubious exceptions, also in his questions and class lectures. He was attacked by some theologians but defended by others, and his treatise was not condemned by the church authorities. The general position that immortality could not be rationally demonstrated, if not all the specific opinions that Pomponazzi associated with it, was held also by Duns Scotus and even by the leading Thomist of Pomponazzi's time, Cardinal Cajetan. After the first excitement had passed, Pomponazzi continued to teach at a university located in the papal states, had among his students many clergymen who apparently found nothing offensive in what he said, and died peacefully as a widely respected scholar. The pupil who took his remains to his home town and erected a monument for him was Ercole Gonzaga, later a cardinal and president of the Council of Trent. If there is any presumptive evidence, it hardly favors the opinion that Pomponazzi was a secret disbeliever or atheist.

Influence. Pomponazzi's influence, although not easily traceable, was considerable. The school of Italian Aristotelianism to which he belonged flourished for a hundred years or more after his death, and within this tradition his name remained famous and his views on such questions as the immortality of the soul and the unity of the intellect continued to be cited and discussed, if not adopted. The posthumous publication of several of his writings later in the century also gives testimony to his continued fame. His lectures and questions were copied in a large number of manuscripts, an indication of his popularity among his students; moreover, a considerable number of manuscripts containing the *De Incantationibus* and the *De Fato* prove that these works circulated widely, although, or perhaps because, they were not published during the author's lifetime. A few anecdotes associated with his name that we find in biographies, short stories, and dialogues of the period suggest that he made some personal impression even on the larger public outside university circles. He obviously was read by students and writers who did not belong to the Aristotelian tradition, and we may cite as an example Giulio Cesare Vanini, who seems to have used him as one of his favorite sources.

During the seventeenth century the Aristotelian school that had dominated the teaching of philosophy for such a long time finally lost its hold, especially in the field of natural philosophy, which was gradually replaced by the new mathematical physics of Galileo and his successors. Aristotelianism persisted much longer in the fields of logic, biology, and metaphysics. Yet because physics was the center and stronghold of medieval and Renaissance Aristotelianism, especially in Italy, most of Pomponazzi's specific teachings lost their immediate validity when the Aristotelian system within which he had developed his ideas came to be abandoned. Nevertheless, we may say that his view of the relation between natural reason and faith was capable of being reformulated in terms of the new physics and that in certain instances this did happen.

Even more important is another development. The seventeenth century, and still more the eighteenth, witnessed the rise and diffusion of free thought and overt atheism, especially in France. Some of the freethinkers who set out to discard faith and established religion came to consider the Aristotelian rationalists such as Pomponazzi as their forerunners and allies. Pomponazzi's treatise on the immortality of the soul was praised by the free thinkers and condemned by Catholic apologists, although moderate thinkers like Bayle tried to preserve a proper perspective. Pomponazzi's treatise was even reprinted in a clandestine edition with a false early date.

The use to which the French Enlightenment put Pomponazzi and the other Italian Aristotelians has had a strong influence on modern historians of the school, beginning with Renan. Again, a distinction is needed. It is one thing to say that Pomponazzi and the Aristotelians held the same views as later freethinkers, and it is another to state that they represent an earlier stage in a development that was to produce the views held by the freethinkers. In the first sense Pomponazzi was a forerunner of the freethinkers; in the second sense the evidence says he was not. Hence, we should not praise or blame him, depending on our own preferences and values, for being a freethinker, since we lack the factual basis for judgment. Yet in a different sense we may praise him. He belongs to the long line of thinkers who have attempted to draw a clear line of distinction between reason and faith, philosophy and theology, and to establish the autonomy of reason and philosophy within their own domains.

Works by Pomponazzi

Pomponazzi's *De Immortalitate Animae* is available in several modern editions—edited by G. Gentile (Messina, 1925), by G. Morra (Bologna, 1954), and by W. H. Hay II in a facsimile of the original edition of 1516 (Haverford, Pa., 1938). It is also included, along with the *Apologia*, the *Defensorium*, and several shorter treatises, in the collection entitled *Tractatus Acutissimi* (Venice, 1525).

The *De Naturalium Effectuum Causis Sive de Incantationibus* was printed separately in Basel (1556) and with the *De Fato* in the *Opera* (Basel, 1567); the volume contains only these two works. There is also a French translation—*Les Causes des merveilles de la nature,* translated by Henri Busson (Paris, 1930).

There is a modern critical edition of the *De Fato* edited by Richard Lemay (Lugano, 1957). Of the *De Immortalitate* there is an English translation by W. H. Hay II, first published with the facsimile edition of the text and then in a revised and annotated version in Ernst Cassirer, Paul Oskar Kristeller, and John H. Randall, Jr., eds., *The Renaissance Philosophy of Man* (Chicago, 1948).

For the unpublished works of Pomponazzi see L. Ferri, "Intorno alle dottrine psicologiche di Pietro Pomponazzi . . . ," in *Atti della Reale Accademia dei Lincei, Memorie della classe di scienze morali, storiche e filologiche,* Series 2, Vol. 3 (1875–1876), Part III, 333–548; C. Oliva, "Note sull'insegnamento di Pietro Pomponazzi," in *Giornale critico della filosofia italiana,* Vol. 7 (1926), 83–103, 179–190, 254–275; Bruno Nardi, "Le opere inedite del Pomponazzi," in *Giornale critico della filosofia italiana,* Vol. 29–35 (1950–1956); and Paul Oskar Kristeller, "A New Manuscript Source for Pomponazzi's Theory of the Soul . . . ," in *Revue internationale de philosophie,* Vol. 2 (1951), 144–157, and "Two Unpublished Questions on the Soul of Pietro Pomponazzi," in *Medievalia et Humanistica,* Vol. 9 (1955), 76–101, and Vol. 10 (1956), 151.

Works on Pomponazzi

For the general background see Ernest Renan, *Averroès et l'averroisme* (Paris, 1852); Bruno Nardi, *Saggi sull'Aristotelismo Padovano dal secolo XIV al XVI* (Florence, 1958); and John H. Randall, Jr., *The School of Padua and the Emergence of Modern Science* (Padua, 1961).

For Pomponazzi's doctrine see Francesco Fiorentino, *Pietro Pomponazzi* (Florence, 1868); Andrew H. Douglas, *The Philosophy and Psychology of Pietro Pomponazzi* (Cambridge, 1910); E. Weil, "Die Philosophie des Pietro Pomponazzi," in *Archiv für Geschichte der Philosophie,* Vol. 41 (1932), 127–176; Ernst Cassirer, *Das Erkenntnisproblem in der Philosophie und Wissenschaft der neueren Zeit,* Vol. I (Berlin, 1922), 105–117; and Bruno Nardi, *Studi su Pietro Pomponazzi* (Florence, 1965). For the immortality controversy see Giovanni Di Napoli, *L'immortalità dell'anima nel Rinascimento* (Turin, 1963).

PAUL OSKAR KRISTELLER

POPE, ALEXANDER

POPE, ALEXANDER (1688–1744), England's leading poet of the Age of Reason, was born in London, the son of a prosperous Roman Catholic linen draper. His Catholicism barred him from public school and university; and he was educated by private tutors and by extensive reading and study on his own, largely at Binfield in Windsor Forest, where his father had retired. About the age of 12, a severe illness stunted Pope's growth and deformed his spine, and for the rest of his life he was infirm. His devotion to poetry came early, and his genius was immediately recognized by William Wycherley and William Walsh. Early publications of note include the *Pastorals* (1709), *An Essay on Criticism* (1711), *The Rape of the Lock* (1712, enlarged 1714), and *Windsor Forest* (1714). During frequent visits to London, he became the friend of many prominent literary figures: Jonathan Swift, Joseph Addison, Richard Steele, John Arbuthnot, John Gay, and Lord Bolingbroke. Although not an ardent party man, Pope inclined more to the Tory than to the Whig. In 1718, after the death of his father, he removed to Twickenham, on the Thames near London. Pope's translation of the *Iliad* (1715–1720) and the *Odyssey* (1725–1726) were well received and financially successful. The edition of Shakespeare appeared in 1725.

Author of the *Essay on Man* (1733–1734), *Moral Essays* (1731–1735), and *Imitations of Horace* (1733–1737), and of the *Dunciad* (1728–1743) and various other satires, Pope was a philosopher-moralist-poet. He was generally so regarded throughout the eighteenth century, both at home and abroad. There is little of the original in Pope's thought, nor did he pretend to any, the very notion of originality being distasteful to the rationalistic mind. In the *Essay on Criticism,* he stated that his aim was to present "What oft was thought, but ne'er so well expressed." His writing in general admirably fulfills this precept, and his memorable formulations of traditional and familiar ideas bear the stamp of literary genius.

Despite frequent allegations to the contrary, Pope was not a deist. Indeed, in the *Dunciad* he specifically attacks Anthony Collins, Bernard Mandeville, Thomas Morgan, Matthew Tindal, John Toland, and Thomas Woolston, the leading deists of the day. He eschewed the role of Christian (Catholic) poet, however, preferring to represent what he considered the best in Western thought, both pagan and Christian. His universality is best seen in the *Essay on Man,* where in Epistle I a rationalistic metaphysics is presented, centering on the "Great Chain of Being," a concept as old as Plato's *Timaeus* which was a part of the heritage of Western man and was influential until well into the eighteenth century. The rationalistic myth of a "chain of being" extending from the Godhead at the one extreme to the lowliest atom at the other, with man as the middle link between the pure reason of angelic spirits and the pure instinct of lower animals, is presented by Pope as a means of chastising presumptuous man for attempting to be too rational, for attempting to deny the earthbound aspect of his nature. Such generic "pride" on the part of man would necessarily push him into a higher link and thus destroy the entire chain. The moral is clear: "The bliss of Man (could Pride that blessing find)/Is not to act or think beyond mankind." Man must submit to his ordained place in the universe because "Whatever is, is Right."

Pope has been frequently ridiculed for ending Epistle I on this seeming note of "easy optimism," as it has been erroneously labeled. A moment's recollection, however, of the fact that Pope devoted much of his career to satirizing contemporary mores and morality will make it evident that his "optimism" was not ordinary or glandular optimism but strictly metaphysical optimism, which is not necessarily of any comfort to mankind. Granted the "chain of being" as ordained by Deity, that plan and that chain must be right, even though, according to the "principle of plenitude," evil is just as necessary as good. Thus, apart from

the totality of cosmic rightness, many circumstances of life may not be good for man himself. Small comfort, therefore, to man to be assured that what seems evil to him personally is actually good from the cosmological point of view: God, but not man, can afford to be optimistic. In fact, the theme of the entire *Essay* is the problem of reconciling the contrary, apparently irreconcilable elements of man's nature with the infinite wisdom of a God of order and harmony. Thus it is that in the opening lines of Epistle II, Pope makes an effort to dismiss the prior metaphysical optimism with the homely precept: "Know then thyself, presume not God to scan;/The proper study of Mankind is Man." The remainder of the *Essay* is concerned with the world of real existence, insofar as this is possible given the background of rationalistic formalism. Epistle II treats of man as an individual; Epistle III treats of man and society; and Epistle IV treats of man and happiness. Here there is little "easy optimism."

Pope teaches that self-love is superior to reason and that the passions are requisite for action. The "dominant passion" (which varies from man to man) rules life in different ways, and virtue and vice are joined in man's mixed nature. In the second epistle reason is "The God within the mind" that distinguishes between virtue and vice, to which in the third epistle are added instinct and social love. The fourth epistle, after much deliberation, declares that only in virtue is happiness to be found. Pope then ends the *Essay* with the affirmation that he has

> Shew'd erring Pride, *Whatever is, is Right;*
> That *Reason, Passion,* answer one great aim;
> That true *Self-Love* and *Social* are the same;
> That *Virtue* only makes our Bliss below;
> And all our Knowledge is, *Ourselves to Know.*

The major sources of Pope's philosophy have been much disputed, with Leibniz, Shaftesbury, Bolingbroke, and King the most frequently mentioned modern authors. There is no direct evidence that Pope knew Leibniz, and he specifically denied any influence by him. Pope had certainly read parts of Shaftesbury's *Characteristics* and undoubtedly acquired something from the reading. The case for Bolingbroke's *Fragments or Minutes of Essays* was widely accepted until recent investigations adduced evidence that the *Fragments* were composed later than Pope's *Essay;* what Pope may have received from Bolingbroke in the course of conversation, however, remains unknown. Archbishop King's *De Origine Mali* (1702), probably in Edmund Law's translation of 1731, contains much of the metaphysical thinking of the first epistle of the *Essay on Man;* and there is little doubt that Pope found much useful information and many references in Law's elaborate notes. Gleanings from the ancient Platonists, Neoplatonists, and Stoics are to be assumed, as are, of course, some from the Christian tradition.

The *Essay on Man* first appeared anonymously, and Pope did not claim it until 1735. On the Continent it was translated (poorly) into French prose in 1736 and the following year into French verse (even more poorly). It ran through several editions with considerable praise until attacked in 1737 by J. P. de Crousaz in his *Examen de l'essai de M. Pope sur l'homme*. The Swiss theologian, ignorant of English, deliberately used the poem as a means of assailing the Spinozistic and the Leibnizian philosophies, of which Pope was innocent. The attack was taken up by several English pamphleteers until William Warburton (later bishop of Gloucester and editor of Pope's *Works*), that colossus of controversy, came to the defense with a series of articles in the *History of the Works of the Learned*, published as a book in 1739 and revised in 1742. Warburton vindicated Pope against allegations of unorthodoxy, including that of deism.

Another Continental attack came in 1742 from Louis Racine in a poem entitled *La Religion*. In 1755 Gotthold Lessing and Moses Mendelssohn, in *Pope ein Metaphysiker!*, ridiculed both the Prussian Royal Academy for using a poet as the subject of a prize essay in philosophy and Pope for attempting to be a metaphysician in poetry. To Kant, on the contrary, Pope was a favorite poet from whom he quoted frequently and whose thought he took seriously. Arthur O. Lovejoy has ventured the statement that "it would be hardly excessive to say that much of Kant's cosmology is a prose amplification and extension of the 'philosophy' of the First Epistle of the *Essay on Man*." Scorned or admired, at any rate, Pope's venture into verse philosophy was exceedingly popular, as is indicated by its translation into at least 15 European languages and by scores of editions in English during the eighteenth century. And his century was the last that would have approved of such a venture.

Pope's original plan as poetical philosopher and moralist was ambitious, although somewhat vague. His magnum opus, to be entitled "Ethic Epistles," was to consist of four books: the *Essay on Man*, as we now have it in four epistles; four more epistles dealing with "the extent and limits of human Reason," arts and sciences both "useful" and "unuseful," "the different Capacities of Men," and the "Use of Learning," science and wit; the "Science of Politics," to treat "of Civil and Religious Society in their full extent"; and "Private Ethics or Practical Morality." The plan—but not the philosophy—is curiously reminiscent of that of Hume as stated in the "Advertisement" to the *Treatise of Human Nature* (1739). (Incidentally, Hume probably took from Pope such terms as "the science of man," "the science of human nature," "the soul's calm sunshine," and "the Feast of Reason.") In 1741 Hume was to devote an entire essay, "That Politics may be reduced to a Science," to the refutation of Pope's lines (*Essay on Man*, III, 303–304): "For Forms of Government let fools contest;/Whate'er is best admister'd is best."

The *Essay on Man* was the only part of the *magnum opus* completed as planned. However, the *Epistles to Several Persons*, commonly known as the *Moral Essays*, constitute part of the original design and would have been portions of the fourth book, "Private Ethics or Practical Morality." These four epistles or essays are "To Cobham" ("Of the Knowledge and Character of Men"); "To a Lady" ("Of the Characters of Women"); "To Bathurst" ("Of the Use of Riches"); and "To Burlington" (also "Of the Use of Riches"). Pope was always the philosopher-moralist-poet

whose description of his own career (*Epistle to Dr. Arbuthnot*, ll. 340–341) is essentially accurate: ". . . not in Fancy's Maze he wander'd long,/But stoop'd to Truth, and moraliz'd his song."

Bibliography

Primary sources include *The Twickenham Edition of the Poems of Alexander Pope*, John Butt, gen. ed., 6 vols. in 7 (London, 1939–1961), and *Pope: The Correspondence*, George Sherburn, ed., 5 vols. (Oxford, 1956).

Secondary sources include Arthur Friedman, "Pope and Deism," in J. L. Clifford and Louis A. Landa, eds., *Pope and His Contemporaries: Essays Presented to George Sherburn* (Oxford, 1949); Arthur O. Lovejoy, *The Great Chain of Being* (Cambridge, Mass., 1936); and Geoffrey Tillotson, *The Moral Poetry of Pope* (Newcastle upon Tyne, 1946), *On the Poetry of Pope*, 2d ed. (Oxford, 1950), and *Pope and Human Nature* (Oxford, 1958).

ERNEST CAMPBELL MOSSNER

POPPER, KARL RAIMUND, Austrian philosopher of natural and social science. Popper was born in Vienna in 1902 and was a student of mathematics, physics, and philosophy at the university there. Although he was not a member of the Vienna circle of logical positivists and was in sharp disagreement with many of its doctrines, he shared most of the group's philosophical interests and was in close touch with several of its members, having a considerable influence on Rudolf Carnap. His first book, *Logik der Forschung*, was published in 1935 in the circle's series Schriften zur wissenschaftlichen Weltauffassung. In 1937 Popper went as senior lecturer to Canterbury University College in Christchurch, New Zealand, and remained there until his move in 1945 to a readership at the London School of Economics in the University of London. Since 1949 he has been professor of logic and scientific method at the London School of Economics. He was knighted in 1964.

Rejection of verifiability theory. The foundation of Popper's wide-ranging but closely integrated philosophical reflections is the bold and original form he first gave in 1933 to the problem of demarcating science from pseudo science in general and from metaphysics in particular. The logical positivists had taken this problem to be one of distinguishing meaningful from meaningless discourse and had proposed to solve it by making empirical verifiability the necessary condition of a sentence's meaningfulness or scientific status—in their eyes one and the same thing. Popper dissented both from their formulation of the problem and from their solution. His view has always been that the important task is to distinguish empirical science from other bodies of assertions that might be confused with it: metaphysics, such traditional pseudo sciences as astrology and phrenology, and the more imposing pseudo sciences of the present age, such as the Marxist theory of history and Freudian psychoanalysis. To identify this distinction with that between sense and nonsense is, he holds, to make an arbitrary verbal stipulation. It is also an unreasonable stipulation because the line between science and pseudo science is neither precise nor impermeable. Pseudo science, or "myth," as he sometimes calls it, can both inspire and develop into science proper:

indeed, the general progress of human knowledge can be considered as a conversion of myth into science by its subjection to critical examination.

Falsifiability criterion. A crucial difficulty for the verifiability theory of meaning was Hume's thesis that inductive generalization was logically invalid. Being unrestrictedly general, scientific theories cannot be verified by any possible accumulation of observational evidence. Moritz Schlick sought to interpret scientific theories as rules for the derivation of predictive statements from observational ones and not as statements themselves at all, but this attempt came to grief on the fact that theories can be empirically falsified by negative instances. This logical asymmetry in the relation of general statements to observations underlies Popper's view that falsifiability by observation is the criterion of the empirical and scientific character of a theory. He maintains, first, that scientific theories are not, in fact, arrived at by any sort of inductive process. The formation of a hypothesis is a creative exercise of the imagination; it is not a passive reaction to observed regularities. There is no such thing as pure observation, for observation is always selective and takes place under the guidance of some anticipatory theory. Second, even if induction were the way in which hypotheses were arrived at, it would still be wholly incapable of justifying them. As Hume showed, no collection of particular observations will verify a general statement; nor, Popper adds, is such a statement partially justified or rendered probable by particular confirming instances, since many theories that are known to be false have an indefinitely large number of confirming instances.

For Popper the growth of knowledge begins with the imaginative proposal of hypotheses, a matter of individual and unpredictable insight that cannot be reduced to rule. Such a hypothesis is science rather than myth if it excludes some observable possibilities. To test a hypothesis, we apply ordinary deductive logic in order to derive singular observation statements whose falsehood would refute it. A serious and scientific test consists in a persevering search for negative, falsifying instances. Some hypotheses are more falsifiable than others; they exclude more and thus have a greater chance of being refuted. "All heavenly bodies move in ellipses" is more falsifiable than "All planets move in ellipses," since everything that refutes the second statement refutes the first but much that refutes the first does not refute the second. The more falsifiable a hypothesis, therefore, the less probable it is, and by excluding more, it says more about the world, has more empirical content. Popper goes on to show that the obscure but important concept of simplicity comes to the same thing as falsifiability and empirical content. The proper method of science is to formulate the most falsifiable hypotheses and, consequently, those that are simplest, have the greatest empirical content, and are logically the least probable. The next step is to search energetically for negative instances, to see if any of the potential falsifiers are actually true.

Corroboration. If a hypothesis survives continuing and serious attempts to falsify it, then it has "proved its mettle" and can be provisionally accepted. But it can never be established conclusively. The survival of attempted refutations corroborates a theory; the corroboration being greater to the degree that the theory is falsifiable. Popper's critics have fastened on this theory of corroboration as the point at which the inductive procedure he ostensibly rejects makes an implicit reappearance. Is there any real difference, they ask, between the view that a theory depends for justification on the occurrence of confirming instances and the view that it depends on the failure of falsifying ones to occur? Furthermore, his critics claim, there is apparently an inductive inference embedded in Popper's doctrine—the inference from the fact that a theory has thus far escaped refutation to the conclusion that it will continue to do so. Popper could reasonably reply that the formal likeness between confirming and falsifying instances conceals an important difference in approach—that between those who glory in confirmations and those who ardently pursue falsifications. However, a certain disquiet about the inductivist flavor of the positive support that his theory allows a hypothesis to derive from the failure of attempted refutations is expresssed in Popper's leanings toward a rather skeptical view of the status of unrefuted hypotheses: "Science is not a system of certain, or well-established, statements. . . . Our science is not knowledge (epistēmē): it can never claim to have attained truth, or even a substitute for it, such as probability. . . . *We do not know: we can only guess.*" (*The Logic of Scientific Discovery*, Ch. 10, Sec. 85, p. 278).

Empirical basis. To complete his account of the growth of scientific knowledge, Popper had to explain the empirical basis of the falsificatory operation, that is, he had to make clear the formal character of the observation statements that are logically deduced from theories. It follows from the falsifiability criterion that unrestricted existential statements of the form "There is (somewhere at some time) an X" are unempirical because however many spatiotemporal positions have been examined for the presence of an X, an infinity of further positions remains to be examined. This is not true, however, of circumscribed existential statements reporting the existence of something at a specified place and time. Popper takes the basic observation statements to be of this form, to refer to publicly observable material objects, and to be capable of being straightforwardly affirmed or denied as true or false. Such basic statements are motivated by perceptual experiences, but they do not, as they are held to in the usual empiricist tradition, describe them. They can themselves be empirically tested in the light of the further basic statements which follow from them, together with accepted scientific theories. The infinite regress that this conception involves is not a vicious one: it can be halted by a conventional assignment of truth to basic statements at any point. But this convention is not dogmatic, since it is only provisional; if the basic statements in question are challenged, they can always be exposed to empirical tests.

Epistemology. In recent writings Popper has drawn many further inferences from his initial body of ideas. One is that knowledge has no foundations or infallible sources, either in reason or the senses. He sees the rationalist and empiricist epistemologies of the modern age as united in a determination to replace one sort of authority—a sacred text or an institution—with another—a human mental capacity. Both kinds of intellectual authoritarianism hold the mistaken opinion that truth is manifest and consequently that error is a sin and its propagation the outcome of some kind of conspiracy to deceive. There is no more comprehensive critique of the quest for certainty in the work of any other modern philosopher.

A second conclusion Popper draws is that the traditional empiricist account of concept formation—essentially Hume's idea that concepts are acquired by perceiving the similarity of sets of particular impressions—is mistaken because it embodies the same inductivist error as Bacon's and Mill's accounts of scientific knowledge. Resemblance is not passively stumbled upon; rather, we classify things together in the light of antecedent preconceptions and expectations. Popper rejects innate ideas strictly so called but believes that we approach the world of experience with innate propensities—in particular, with a general expectation of regularity that is biologically explicable even if not logically justifiable. The influence of Kant is especially evident in this side of Popper's thought. In a sense the proposition that nature contains regularities is for him synthetic a priori: it is neither a logical truth nor an empirical truth (since it is unfalsifiable), but it has a kind of psychological necessity as a general feature of the active human intellect.

Theoretical entities. Popper's dissent from the usual empiricist and positivist view that private, experiential propositions constitute the empirical foundation of knowledge and his insistence on the provisional and incompletable nature of scientific theorizing together determine his attitude to the subject matter or ontological significance of scientific theory. He rejects the essentialism of the rationalist philosophy of science, which conceives the goal of inquiry to be a complete and final knowledge of the essences of things, on the grounds that no scientific theory can be completely justified and that the acceptance of a new theory creates as many problems as it solves. He is equally opposed to the instrumentalist or conventionalist doctrine of those who, like Ernst Mach, Henri Poincaré, and Pierre Duhem, take the theoretical entities of science to be logical constructions, mere symbolic conveniences to assist us in the prediction of experience. The entities of scientific theory (such as molecules and genes) are not distinguishable in nature from the medium-sized public observables (such as chairs and trees) referred to in basic statements: both are possible objects of genuine knowledge.

Probability. A difficulty arises for Popper's falsifiability criterion from the presence in normal scientific discourse of statements about probability in the sense of frequency. No finite sequence of A's of which none are B decisively refutes the proposition that most A's are B. In his first book Popper put forward a modified version of Richard von Mises' view that the probability of the occurrence of a property in an unrestrictedly open class is the limit of the frequencies of its occurrence in finite segments of the open sequence, a version that made probability statements accessible to decisive empirical refutation. More recently he has argued that probability statements, although they may rest on statistical evidence, should not themselves be interpreted statistically but rather as ascribing objective propensities to natural objects.

Determinism and value. Popper's conviction that the mind is essentially active in the acquisition of knowledge and that its progress in discovery cannot be subsumed under a law and made the subject of prediction has led him far beyond the philosophy of natural science, with which his central doctrines are concerned. Scientific knowledge is a free creation; it follows that the mind is not a causal mechanism. He contends that no causal model of the most elementary acts of the mind in empirical recognition and description can be constructed, since such a model would leave out the intention to name that is essential to any real act of description. Although the pursuit of knowledge is guided by an innate propensity to expect deterministic regularity in the world, the existence of knowledge as developed by a series of unanticipatable novelties is the strongest reason for rejecting general, metaphysical determinism.

Popper's theory of mind and knowledge also has ethical implications. Judgments of value are not empirical statements but decisions or proposals. Our valuations are not determined by our natural preferences but are the outcome of autonomous acts of mind—a further link with Kant. Popper's own basic moral proposal is, however, not very Kantian. Popper is a negative utilitarian for whom the primary moral imperative is "diminish suffering."

History and society. In *The Open Society and Its Enemies* (1945) and in *The Poverty of Historicism* (1957), Popper applies his theory of knowledge to man and society in the form of an attack on historicism, the doctrine that there are general laws of historical development that render the course of history inevitable and predictable. In *The Open Society* historicism is examined in three influential versions, those of Plato, Hegel, and Marx. In *The Poverty of Historicism,* historicism is formally refuted and attributed to two oppositely mistaken views about the nature of social science. The formal objection is that since the growth of knowledge exercises a powerful influence on the course of history and itself depends on the anomalous initiatives of original scientific genius, neither the growth of knowledge nor its general historical effects can be predicted. Some historicists have been motivated by the mistaken idea that a science of society would have a general evolutionary law as its goal. This is a naturalistic error. The evolutionary process is not a lawlike regularity at all; rather, it is a loosely characterized trend whose phases exemplify the laws of genetics, for example. The historicists who have made this error are right in believing that scientific method applies to society, but they have a false idea of what scientific method is. On the other hand, among historicists there are antinaturalists who hold that ordinary scientific method does not apply to society, for which laws of a special historicist form must be found. Popper asserts that scientific method applies both to nature and to society, and in the same way—to particular isolable aspects of the whole. Social science can discover laws that make clear the unintended consequences of human action, but there can be no laws of the whole system. It follows that social reform must proceed by piecemeal social engineering, not by total revolutionary reconstructions of the social order. Popper presents the central problem of politics in a characteristically falsificationist way: The question "Who should rule?," he says, should be replaced by the question "How can institutions be devised that will minimize the risks of bad rulers?"

Philosophy and knowledge. Popper does not believe, as do most analytic philosophers, that philosophy is sharply distinguishable from science, either in its methods—which, like science's, must be those of trial and error, conjecture and attempted refutation—or in its subject matter—which is not only language but also the world to which language refers. Furthermore, there is no uniquely correct philosophical method. Both the examination of actual language and the construction of ideal languages can contribute to the philosophical understanding of particular problems, but they are not universal keys to truth. Popper believes that if philosophy is to be of any general importance, it must stand in a close relation to the work of other disciplines. When it is isolated, as a special autonomous craft, from the general pursuit of knowledge, it degenerates into scholasticism and triviality.

Works by Popper

BOOKS

Logik der Forschung. Vienna, 1935. Translated by Popper, with the assistance of Julius Freed and Lan Freed, as *The Logic of Scientific Discovery.* New York, Toronto, and London, 1959.
The Open Society and Its Enemies, 2 vols. London, 1945; 4th, rev. ed., with addenda, London, 1961.
The Poverty of Historicism. London, 1957; 2d ed., with some corrections, 1961.
Conjectures and Refutations; The Growth of Scientific Knowledge. London, 1963. Collected essays.

ESSAYS

"Logic Without Assumptions." *PAS,* N.S. Vol. 47 (1946–1947), 251–292.
"New Foundations for Logic." *Mind,* N.S. Vol. 56 (1947), 193–235; corrections and additions, N.S. Vol. 57 (1948), 69–70.
"Indeterminism in Quantum Physics and in Classical Physics," I and II. *British Journal for the Philosophy of Science,* Vol. 1 (1950–1951), 117–133; 173–195.
"On the Theory of Deduction." Proceedings of the *Koninklijke Nederlandse Akademie van Wetenschappen,* Vol. 51, Nos. 1 and 2 (1948).
"Probability, Magic or Knowledge out of Ignorance?" *Dialectica,* Vol. 11 (1957), 354–374.
"The Propensity Interpretation of Probability." *British Journal for the Philosophy of Science,* Vol. 10 (1959), 25–42.

Works on Popper

Bunge, Mario, ed., *The Critical Approach to Science and Philosophy.* Glencoe, Ill., 1964. Contains 29 articles largely concerned with the whole range of Popper's views. Includes a bibliography of Popper's publications, complete up to the beginning of 1964.
Kaufmann, Walter, *From Shakespeare to Existentialism.* New York, 1959. Chapter 7, "The Hegel Myth and Its Method," is a sympathetic but powerful criticism of Popper's account of Hegel in *The Open Society.*
Levinson, Ronald B., *In Defense of Plato.* Cambridge, Mass., 1953. This substantial critique of Plato's modern opponents gives Popper pride of place.
Neurath, Otto, "Pseudorationalismus der Falsifikation." *Erkenntnis,* Vol. 5 (1935), 290–294.

Reichenbach, Hans, "Über Induktion und Wahrscheinlichkeit. Bemerkungen zu Karl Poppers *Logik der Forschung.*" *Erkenntnis,* Vol. 5 (1935).
Schilpp, P. A., ed., *The Philosophy of Karl Popper.* La Salle, Ill., forthcoming. A volume in the Library of Living Philosophers.
Warnock, G. J., review of *The Logic of Scientific Discovery. Mind,* N.S. Vol. 69 (1960), 99–101.

ANTHONY QUINTON

POPPER-LYNKEUS, JOSEF (1838–1921), Austrian inventor, social reformer, and philosopher. Now almost completely forgotten, Popper enjoyed great fame in the early years of this century and on several topics his writings are far from dated.

LIFE AND WORKS

Popper grew up in the ghetto of the small Bohemian town of Kolin. At the age of 16 he began his studies in mathematics and physics at the German Polytechnikum in Prague. Four years later he moved to Vienna, where he attended lectures first at the Imperial Polytechnikum and later at the University of Vienna. In spite of his acknowledged brilliance, Popper was not able to secure a teaching position, partly because he was Jewish and partly because of his radical opinions on religious and social questions. For some time he had a minor clerical job with the National Railways in southern Hungary. Returning to Vienna, he earned his living as a private tutor and as the owner of a scientific–technical literary agency. He attended scientific conferences and lectures, taking notes in longhand. These he wrote up, making 10 to 12 carbon copies which he sold to the city's newspapers. In his autobiography, Popper recalls that during those years his income barely equaled that of the lowest-paid unskilled laborer. Popper's extreme poverty came to an end at the age of thirty with his invention of the so-called *Kesseleinlagen*—a device which significantly improved the working capacity of engine boilers. Although this, as well as several other of Popper's inventions, became generally used, he did not acquire wealth and it was not until he was almost sixty that he could retire from active participation in the production and selling of his various appliances in order to devote himself to literary pursuits.

During the last twenty years of his life, when Popper's books on social and philosophical questions had a very wide circulation, he became the center of what amounted almost to a cult. Popper's books give the impression of a man of transparent honesty and uncompromising hostility to every kind of humbug, especially of the kind that infested German public life in the late nineteenth and early twentieth centuries, but they do not, according to those who knew him, convey an adequate idea of his character and personal impact. His friends and admirers included Ernst Mach, Wilhelm Ostwald, Einstein, Freud, Arthur Schnitzler, Hermann Bahr, Stefan Zweig, Philipp Frank, and Richard von Mises. Mach referred to him as a "genius of freethinking"; Einstein, who visited Popper when a young man, spoke of him as a "saintly and prophetic person"; and all who met Popper were impressed by his deep serenity, warmth, and unusual and genuine kindness.

Popper was not a scientist of the first rank, but several of his publications dealing with problems in physics are favorably mentioned in standard histories of the subject. He was the first person to suggest the possibility of transmitting electric power, he was a pioneer in aerodynamics, and he was one of the first to see the full implications of the work of Robert Mayer. Popper's treatise "Über die Quelle und den Betrag der durch Luftballons geleisteten Arbeit" ("On the Sources and the Amount of the Work Done by Balloons," *Sitzungsberichte der Kaiserlichen Akademie der Wissenschaften*, 1875) led to correspondence with Robert Mayer, who requested Popper to review the second edition of his *Die Mechanik der Wärme* (*Mechanics of Heat*, 1874). Popper's article, published under the title "Über J. R. Mayer's Mechanik der Wärme" in the periodical *Das Ausland* (1876), did not confine itself to a discussion of Mayer's conservation principle but also contained a statement of a phenomenalistic philosophy of physics. In its "sharpness and fresh originality," according to Philipp Frank, "it equals the best that is found in Mach's works." In this essay there are also some remarkably perceptive criticisms of the common view that the law of entropy implies the "heat-death" of the universe. In his later work, *Physikalische Grundsätze der elektrischen Kraftübertragung* ("Physical Principles of the Transmission of Electricity," Vienna, 1884), Popper emphasized the analogies between different forms of energy and suggested that every type of energy be regarded as a product of two factors, one of which can be regarded as a kind of quantity and the other as a "difference of level." This idea was subsequently employed in the "energetics" of Helm and Ostwald, both of whom made due acknowledgment to Popper.

Popper's first work dealing with religious and social questions was published in Leipzig on May 30, 1878, the hundredth anniversary of Voltaire's death. It was entitled *Das Recht zu Leben und die Pflicht zu Sterben, sozialphilosophische Betrachtungen, anknüpfend an die Bedeutung Voltaires für die neuere Zeit* ("The Right to Live and the Duty to Die, Social-philosophical Reflections in Connection With Voltaire's Significance for Our Times"). This work contains most of the ideas which Popper was to develop in later writings—a defense of the value of the individual in opposition to the national policies of all existing states, proposals for various social welfare measures totally at variance with the prevailing laissez-faire philosophy, recommendations for drastic reforms of the criminal law and judicial procedures, and reflections about the baleful influence of religion and metaphysics, accompanied by suggested methods for their elimination from the human scene. Both here and in a later more detailed study, *Voltaire, eine Charakteranalyse* ("Voltaire—A Character Analysis," Vienna, 1905), Popper went out of his way to rebut the charges of German nationalists and romantics about Voltaire's disruptive (*zersetzende*) influence on morals and society, praising Voltaire for his great honesty, humanity, and courage, which, in Popper's opinion, were not matched by any of his German detractors.

In 1899 Popper published, under the pseudonym of Lynkeus (Lynkeus was the helmsman of the Argonauts, famous for his keen sight), a two-volume book entitled *Phantasien eines Realisten* ("Fantasies of a Realist"), which consisted of eighty sketches in the form of short stories or dialogues, most of them centering on some controversial philosophical or social topic. One story, "Gährende Kraft eines Geheimnisses" ("The Fermenting Power of a Secret"), is set in fifteenth-century Florence and deals with the incestuous relations between a mother and her adolescent son, both of whom were burned at the stake. The *Phantasien* was banned in Vienna, and clerical members of the Austrian parliament demanded a criminal prosecution of the author. Since the book was published in Dresden and the German authorities took no action, it remained in circulation and went into no fewer than 21 editions. Philosophically of more interest than "The Fermenting Power of a Secret" are various sketches illustrating the influence of religion on human life, including an imaginary conversation between Hume, Diderot, Holbach, and other outstanding figures of the French Enlightenment. One of the stories, "Träumen wie Wachen" ("Dreaming Like Waking"), independently arrived at several of the key doctrines of Freud's theory about dreams. Like Freud, Popper insisted that there is a continuity between waking thought and dream content and that dreams cannot be dismissed as "nonsense." Freud did not read Popper's story until after the first edition of *The Interpretation of Dreams* had been published, but later he repeatedly complimented Popper on his insights.

Of Popper's other books, three deserve special mention. *Über Religion* (Vienna, 1924), which was written in 1905 but could not be published before the overthrow of the monarchy with its clerical censorship, contains the fullest statement of Popper's criticism of religion and metaphysics. *Das Individuum und die Bewertung menschlicher Existenzen* ("The Individual and the Evaluation of Human Lives," Dresden, 1910) is the most complete statement of Popper's individualistic ethics and his objections to the many theorists from Hegel to Nietzsche whose writings bristle with contempt for the common man. Popper himself regarded *Die allgemeine Nährpflicht* (Vienna, 1912) as his most important work. It develops in detail the system which, in Popper's words, should replace "our dreadful economic conditions" by such as are "good and moral." Society, according to Popper, has the duty to secure every individual against want, irrespective of his talents and qualifications. He classifies goods and services into "necessities" and "luxuries," the former including food, clothing, shelter, medical attention, and basic education. To ensure for every human being a "guaranteed subsistence-minimum," Popper proposes a term of labor service in the *Nährarmee* ("Nourishment Army"). Utilizing an elaborate analysis of agricultural and industrial conditions in Germany at the beginning of the century, he calculates that 12 years of service by men and 7 by women, working a 35-hour week, would be sufficient for this purpose. There is to be a double economy: the provision of necessities is to be regulated by the state, while private enterprise is to handle the production and distribution of luxuries. After a person has completed his term of service, he is free to work in any occupation he chooses, or not to work at all. In the latter event, he is still fully entitled to receive all "necessities." As technology advances, the period of service in the Nourishment Army will become progressively shorter. Popper deliberately used the term *Nährpflicht* (literally "the duty to furnish nourishment") to express the key concept of his program, since it rhymes with *Wehrpflicht*, the German for compulsory military service, which Popper resolutely opposed. Popper's idea of a "compulsory civil service" is similar to one proposed by William James in his essay "The Moral Equivalent of War," but Popper anticipated James by several decades. If Popper's ideas about the duty of society to secure the individual against economic uncertainty do not sound exciting to the contemporary reader now that the concept of the welfare state is accepted by the majority of the populations of western Europe and the United States, and even the notion of a guaranteed income is advocated by leading economists, it should be remembered that at the time of their first publication, these ideas were extremely radical and were in fact received with violent hostility. In 1878 the great majority of political theorists, economists, and statesmen still adhered to the view that people are poor because of their laziness and ineptitude and that any state intervention in economic matters is a highly dangerous tampering with natural laws.

In spite of his courage and independent spirit, Popper failed to emancipate himself in some important areas of thought from the prejudices of his times. For example, he accepted without any question the view that masturbation "shatters" (*zerrüttet*) the nervous system. He also had no doubt about the soundness of the prevailing hereditarian theories, according to which mental disturbances are largely the result of an innately weakened nervous system, and Popper frequently indulged in generalizations about the basically weak or strong nervous system of this or that national group. Although he knew of Freud's high esteem of his own work, Popper had no appreciation whatsoever of any of the ideas of psychoanalysis. Fritz Wittels, a psychoanalyst who was one of Popper's most devoted and trusted followers, called his attention to Freud's books and there was some polite correspondence between Popper and Freud. However, according to Wittels, Popper scarcely did more than look at Freud's books. In one case, when the subject was society (Freud's *Group-Psychology and the Analysis of the Ego*), Popper went to the trouble of reading the book. "I enjoyed what he quoted from the Frenchman [Le Bon]," he later told Wittels, but as for Freud's own theories, Popper added, "I must tell you that I did not understand one word."

THE SANCTITY OF HUMAN LIFE

None of Popper's theories is philosophically more interesting than the ethical individualism on which he bases his program of social reform. On the opening page of *Das Individuum und die Bewertung menschlicher Existenzen* (from now on referred to as *Das Individuum*) Popper announces what he calls his "motto," and the rest of the book consists of its elaboration and defense as well as of detailed criticism of the anti-individualist positions of various influential writers, including Hegel, Nietzsche, Carlyle, Spencer, Treitschke, and Popper's own friend Wilhelm Ostwald. Popper formulates the motto as follows:

BASIC PRINCIPLE OF A MORAL SOCIAL ORDER

When any individual, of however little account, but one who does not deliberately imperil another's existence, disappears from the world without or even against his will, this is a far more important happening than any political or religious or national occurrence, or the sum total of the scientific and artistic and technical advances made throughout the ages by all the peoples of the world.

Should anybody be inclined to regard this statement as an exaggeration, let him imagine the individual concerned to be himself or his best beloved. Then he will understand and accept it.

To make clear what he means, Popper lists a number of propositions which he terms "the value-arithmetic" of human lives. The valuation of a person's life by the person himself, he writes, is something indefinite, varying, according to the mental state of the individual, from nothing to infinity. His life means nothing to him in moments of extreme unhappiness or when he is willing to sacrifice it for a cause in which he believes; but in other circumstances he regards it as possessing infinite value. "From an ethical point of view," Popper writes, "the existence of a stupid peasant-boy is just as infinitely valuable as the existence of a Shakespeare or a Newton" (*Das Individuum*, p. 193). "There is not the remotest equivalence," he remarks, "between the existence of a human being who wants to go on living and who is not trying to destroy another one, and any other value; the former exceeds the latter infinitely" (*ibid.*, p. 189). Let us suppose that the angel of death were to allow Shakespeare and Newton, in the most creative periods of their lives, to go on living only on condition that we surrender to him "two stupid day-laborers or even two incorrigible thieves." As moral beings we must not so much as consider an exchange of this kind. It would be far better if Shakespeare and Newton were to die. One may call attention, as much as one wishes, to the pleasure produced in countless future ages by Shakespeare's plays; one may point to the immense progress of science which would be the consequence of the prolongation of Newton's life—by comparison with the sacrifice of a human being, these are mere "luxury-values."

However, all of these considerations, Popper repeatedly insists, apply solely to "non-aggressive individuals." A person whose life is threatened by another may, in self-defense, kill the aggressor without having to feel the slightest remorse or misgivings. In such a case, the person's own life rightly counts as something infinite, while the life of the aggressor, be he one or many, counts as nothing. It is in fact a person's *duty*, and not merely his right, to defend himself in such a case with all means at his disposal. In addition to helping himself, he also "exerts a beneficial influence on millions of others if he demonstrates to them by his example what importance and value a non-aggressive human being attaches to his life" (*ibid.*, p. 218). In one place Popper goes so far as to assert that it would be better if all the aggressors in the world, even if they numbered millions, were to be destroyed than if a single human being succumbed to them without resistance.

On occasions Popper concedes that his own principles cannot be proved and that the principles of his assorted opponents cannot be disproved, but for the most part he maintains that they can be shown to be "true" by means of an "evident deduction" from premises granted by most civilized men (*ibid.,* p. 64). He employs two types of arguments, the first of which consists in calling attention to the way in which civilized persons actually judge and behave in a great many situations, when their vision is not clouded by special bias or prejudice. Suppose, for example, a fire were to break out in the Louvre; in such a situation, Popper maintains, it would not occur to any of the firemen or any of the voluntary helpers to save the paintings in preference to the human beings present. If somebody were to save a painting and let a human being die, his behavior would be generally condemned and he might in fact be subjected to punishment. It is true, Popper admits, that sometimes when people *hear* that in a fire in some distant location a number of human beings perished but that certain valuable manuscripts or collections were saved, they respond with greater satisfaction than if it had been the other way around; but this only proves that distance from the place of a disaster produces indifference and makes people forget the enormous value of somebody else's life. "It becomes altogether different," Popper observes, "if one stands in front of the burning house" (*ibid.*). To take another illustration, in all civilized nations a person may not be subjected to vivisection or become the involuntary subject of a medical experiment, regardless of the benefits that might accrue to medical science and, indirectly, to future generations.

Popper also considers at great length another type of case which, in his opinion, shows particularly clearly that civilized people do in fact adhere to his principles. In fortresses or on ships, where the shortage of food may become so acute as to necessitate the sacrifice of some individuals, civilized men would always decide the issue by the casting of lots: in such a situation it would not occur to anybody to refer to the special literary or scientific talents of some member of the group. Shakespeare and Newton would here count no more than anybody else, and nobody would dare to propose that a less talented person be killed so that the great dramatist or the great physicist be kept alive instead. This is very evident in a case of this kind because "once the terror of death is so close, everybody perceives that the naked existence of a human being is something so elevated and infinite that compared with it everything else—be it genius, scholarship, or physical beauty—becomes quite inferior in value and a mere luxury" (*ibid.,* p. 208).

The analysis of these and many other cases makes it clear, Popper contends, that his principles, which seem so strange and unrealistic when first stated in general terms, are quite commonly invoked. It is true that they are widely ignored when it comes to certain questions, such as compulsory military service, the death penalty, and the duty of society to guarantee the basic subsistence of every human being. However, in these cases it can be shown that people are simply inconsistent and have not perceived the implications of their own principles.

Popper's second type of argument, which is already indicated in his "motto," is much more interesting and original. It may not unfairly be labeled an *ad hominem* technique. Arguments of this type consist of two steps: (*a*) if a person, *X*, recommends a policy which involves the killing of one or more nonaggressive human beings, we extract from him the admission that the policy would not be justified if he, *X*, were the individual to be killed; (*b*) we then extract from him the admission that other human beings have the same right to live and not to be sacrificed to some biological, cultural, or aesthetic goal. Popper observes that, except in special "periods of hate," most human beings are ready to make the latter of these admissions, at the very least for other members of their own nation or class. It does not, of course, mean, Popper explains, that a human being should mourn the death of any given person the way he mourns the death of somebody close to him; but human beings should realize that the mourning of somebody else in a similar situation is as justified as one's own and that to this other person his life or the life of somebody dear to him is more important than anything else in the world.

Popper employed his *ad hominem* strategy with relish in dealing with assorted philosophers and aesthetes who flaunted their readiness to approve the killing or enslavement of millions of ordinary human beings if this were necessary to achieve a biologically superior race or to produce great works of art. Thus, Popper devoted a good deal of attention to Spencer's conclusions that in giving artificial aid to the weakest members of a society, its physical and moral qualities are undermined and that, furthermore, all acts by the state to protect the weak and the sick are a "sin against the natural laws of life." After pointing out the dubious analogies on which such conclusions are based and the arbitrary preference for the value of future lives to those now in existence, Popper turns to his "frequently employed method." Suppose, he writes, Spencer or those taking such a "biological viewpoint" were themselves to become sick or unable to look after themselves. Would they approve of a society that turned to them and said: "Perish miserably! To help you is to make future generations less perfect." Will Spencer and his followers then be prepared to be treated as damaged goods, as refuse in a human breeding institution? Will they then still hold to the theories which they so calmly advocated while they were in good health and *others* were sick and in need of assistance?

Apparently nobody, not even the "monstrous" Nietzsche, irritated Popper more than the anti-Semitic historian and aesthete Heinrich von Treitschke, who in his essay "Der Sozialismus und seine Gönner" ("Socialism and Its Patrons") had claimed that "the one statue of Phidias more than makes up for all the misery of the millions of slaves in Antiquity." One may well believe, Popper comments, that Treitschke can look at the statue of Phidias with great delight when *others* were compelled to labor as slaves. "A person holding such a view," Popper proceeds, "ought to have his own principles applied to himself to determine whether he will adhere to them after he has come to feel in his own person what they mean" (*ibid.,* p. 166). It would have been a good idea to condemn Treitschke to five years of service as a slave and then offer him an apartment in the Berlin Museum, where he could spend all his days admiring antique statues. That would be the time to ask Treitschke how he feels about Phidias and the slaves. Perhaps this is the only method, Popper concludes, to make people like Treitschke have some respect for human life.

It would lead too far afield to attempt a detailed assessment of Popper's principles here, particularly of his rather curious "value-arithmetic" of human lives. A few words, however, are perhaps in order about his *ad hominem* technique, both because arguments of this kind are in fact very common (although few employ them with Popper's deliberateness and persistence) and because there may be a tendency to dismiss them too readily. Anybody with a training in logic is apt to regard all such arguments as flagrant instances of the fallacy of *ignoratio elenchi*. If a person makes a moral judgment but violates it in his own behavior, this is surely no argument against the soundness of the moral judgment. We all tend to smile at the familiar stage figure of the preacher of temperance who takes out his whiskey flask as soon as the congregation has departed, but his failure to practice what he preaches does not by itself invalidate his preaching—it does not even prove that he is insincere. A doctor, unable to break his own smoking habit, is not necessarily giving bad advice and also may be perfectly sincere when he advises his patients to stop smoking. Turning to one of Popper's examples, if Spencer, after becoming ill and helpless, were to abandon his views concerning the social or biological undesirability of aiding the weak, this would not disprove his views; nor, conversely, would it be evidence for Spencer's position if, upon falling ill, he refused all aid and cheerfully disintegrated in the belief that he was thereby promoting biological progress.

Yet surely this is not the end of the matter. In reading Popper, one cannot help feeling that he is doing a great deal more than expressing his indignation at the defenses of callousness and inhumanity by writers like Spencer, Nietzsche, and Treitschke. Granting that Popper's *ad hominem* arguments do not disprove the positions he attacks and that they do not prove his own ethical individualism, it might nevertheless be held that his strategy helps to bring out at least two points of some interest. In the first place, Popper may be said to call attention to a double use of "understand" and related expressions which seems of special importance in ethical controversy. Bernard Shaw once remarked that nobody should be allowed to be a judge unless he had spent at least six months in prison. The average judge, he explained, does not really know what he is doing when he sends a man to prison. In a sense this is no doubt false, but in another and deeper sense it may well be true. A judge can of course understand the statement "You are hereby sentenced to imprisonment for a period of five years" without having been a prisoner and even without having visited a prison—he obviously knows the difference in meaning between "two years" and "five years," and he also knows when to apply and when not to apply the word "prison." At the same time, however, he might not know what he is doing in the sense that he has no clear conception of what it is like to languish for years in prison—what conditions really prevail in most prisons and what such a term of imprisonment frequently does to a man's character. It may very plausibly be held that when intellectuals like Nietzsche, Spencer, and Treitschke advocate or condone the destruction or

enslavement of millions of men, they do *not*, in this latter sense of the word, understand what they are recommending and that they could properly understand their own recommendations only if they became slaves or if they themselves experienced the prospect of being forcibly done away with. If we are satisfied that a person who recommends a certain policy does not himself understand, in this deeper sense, what he is recommending, this does not indeed show his policy to be mistaken, but it does undermine his standing in the discussion. For it means that he is ignorant of relevant, perhaps crucially relevant, facts, and hence, on almost any normative theory, his recommendation would not be adequately supported.

Second, Popper's strategy may help to determine the true *status* of the recommendations under discussion. Most people would want to make a distinction between a genuine moral or evaluative judgment and the mere expression of a desire or feeling; and it is the mark of the former but not of the latter—so, at least, a defender of Popper would argue—that it is universalizable: in passing a moral judgment on somebody, one is, in virtue of its being a moral judgment, committed to passing the same judgment about *anybody else* in similar circumstances, including oneself and those one cares for. Now, the writers whom Popper was opposing presumably wished their pronouncements to be treated as genuine evaluative judgments, as the advocacy of certain ideals and not merely as expressions of their desires. However, unless they were willing to maintain that they, too, ought to be enslaved or killed or left without assistance in order to further the goals in question, their original assertions will not qualify as genuine evaluations.

It will be instructive to see how Popper's challenge, thus interpreted, helps to determine the status of Treitschke's recommendation. Treitschke, we will assume, has just declared that certain "inferior" human beings ought to be enslaved for the purpose of producing a sublime work of art. Let us also assume that, in the sense under discussion, Treitschke admits that he, as well as his children (whom he loves), is "inferior." Now, if Treitschke, in this hypothetical situation in which he imagines himself and his children to be inferior, is ready to maintain that he and his children, no less than other inferior human beings, ought to be enslaved, his original declaration has the status of a genuine evaluative judgment. If, however, Treitschke wishes to exempt himself and his children, not merely in the sense that he would resist any attempt to be sold into slavery but in the sense of declaring that he and his children, although inferior beings, ought not to be enslaved, it would follow that his initial statement was not a genuine evaluation—that "ought" was not used there in its moral or evaluative sense. (More accurately: it would follow either that Treitschke was not offering a genuine evaluation or that he was inconsistent in denying a proposition entailed by one asserted previously.) Popper would probably add to this that in actual fact the great majority of those who talk like Treitschke, and very likely Treitschke himself, would insist that they and those they love ought not to be enslaved or otherwise mistreated. While it may be disappointing to realize that the callous positions against which Popper wrote have not been refuted, it is not a mean achievement to have shown that certain pronouncements masquerading as value judgments are in fact nothing more than the expressions of certain desires.

ELIMINATION OF RELIGION AND METAPHYSICS

Popper's positivism, like that of Mach, may be regarded as a midway stage between the philosophy of Comte and the logical positivism of the Vienna circle. Although he knew a great deal about mathematics, Popper did not advance beyond Mill's position that mathematical statements are extremely well supported empirical propositions. Metaphysics he dismissed as futile, but he wavered between dismissing metaphysical questions as meaningless and treating them as meaningful but unanswerable.

He never wavered, however, in regarding metaphysics, and more especially the theological varieties associated with Western religions, as exceedingly harmful. No change in economic arrangements, however rational and beneficial it may be, can bring about a happy world unless all forms of supernaturalism are banished. There can be no peace in the world, Popper insists, as long as there is the slightest vitality in organized religious superstition, which is something "necessarily aggressive." Some of Popper's more conservative followers have done their best to play down his antireligious sentiments. It is therefore necessary to insist that he himself regarded the *Ausrottung* (extermination) of religion and metaphysics—and of all "enthusiasm for transcendent ideals"—as an essential part of his philosophical and social program, one that was necessarily implied by his humanitarian individualism. Margit Ornstein, his literary executor, relates how Popper, very shortly before his death, when he was revising the manuscript of *Über Religion,* remarked to her with a smile, "This is my Parthian arrow," adding, "When the Parthians left the battle scene they turned around once more to aim a final arrow at the enemy" (*Über Religion,* p. 3).

Purely ceremonial or "civil" religions, such as those practiced by the ancient Greeks and Romans or most of the people of China and Japan, are relatively harmless: unlike the religions which we know in the West, they lack any kind of metaphysical foundation, anything that can be called a theological system, and above all, they do not possess a powerful priestly caste. Religion begins to have an evil influence only when it is given a systematic formulation and when it becomes "an affair of the heart." Popper's condemnation is sweeping and is meant to apply to the kind of belief fostered by rationalistic theologians no less than to the pietistic enthusiasm found in many religious groups all over the world. "At first it [religious zeal] is just nonsense, then it becomes obstinacy and spite, and in the end it is wildness and insanity beyond all limits" (*ibid.,* p. 2). The harmfulness of religion is exactly proportional to the degree of religious fervor. Popper approvingly quotes Bayle's saying that "the person who is convinced that he is promoting the Kingdom of God by the extermination of heretics will step on all moral laws," and he offers numerous examples from the history of the "genuine positive," as opposed to the merely ceremonial and civil religions, to support his indictment that the former increase bad feeling in the world, that they encourage malicious tendencies which are then covered up and justified in high-sounding language, that they place love of man below the love of religious conceptions, that they multiply situations of strife and conflict by promoting the intervention of priests in even the most intimate details of everyday living, that they weaken and indeed destroy respect for truth and justice, and, finally, that they use, wherever they can, the power of the state for their purposes, especially in matters of education.

Popper disliked Christianity most of all, and in a section of *Das Individuum* ("A Digression on the Valuation of Human Lives in the Christian Religion") he undertakes to correct the long-standing and, he claims, erroneous notion that Christianity encourages respect for the individual. Christianity does indeed speak of the value of the individual *soul,* but both in doctrine and in practice this notion has coexisted with contempt for the individual's body and life here on earth. Popper does not deny that now and then religious belief has given people hope and consolation and that some of the expressions of religious devotion have been touchingly beautiful. However, such considerations must not be allowed to affect our over-all judgment—"the burning of one heretic more than cancels ten thousand beautiful and deep feelings" (*ibid.,* p. 72).

Popper had no doubt that the ideal of a "superstition-free culture," which, for him, meant a world without religion, was entirely attainable. He repeatedly takes issue with the widespread view that religious belief or religious needs are innate. This, he argues, is clearly disproved by the existence of entire nations without religion and of numerous persons in our own culture who are entirely devoid of religious belief and whose lives are no less happy or responsibly conducted than those of most believers. Moreover, the existing statistics on the prevalence of religious faith are suspect in the sense that, as far as religious issues are concerned, most people are not allowed to develop freely but live under the constant pressure of proreligious propaganda and the threat of social disapproval and economic loss if they avow their disbelief. "The masses of Europe," he writes, live in effect "in a religious penitentiary" (*ibid.,* p. 59). Once the social and political power of the churches is shattered and education, uninfected by proreligious bias, becomes universal, religious belief is bound to vanish. "A person who has learned about the history and origin of religions, including Christianity, who has absorbed the main results of the sciences and the relations of these to the claims of religion, will not for a moment be afraid of or express gratitude to imaginary entities or persons" (*ibid.,* p. 223). Prior to the elimination of religious influences from the public schools, freethinkers must band together into a powerful "International League for the Liberation from Superstition." Such a league would publish and obtain the vast circulation of what Popper calls "counter-books"—works written in simple and clear prose, which would refute point by point the fallacies, the lies, and the distortions in the religious and proreligious textbooks used in the schools. This league would also open "counter-schools" and train "wandering counter-preachers," whose function it would be to bring enlightenment to the peasant population. The counter-preachers would conduct meetings in the villages immediately after the Sunday services. In the beginning the peasants, incited by the priests, would try to chase away the "godless intruders," but with some courage and persistence it would be possible to receive a hearing, to catch the interest of the peasants, and in the end to make them see the soundness and good sense of the unbeliever's position. In his first formulation of this program in 1878, Popper estimated that such a "gigantic cleansing operation" would take several hundred years, but writing thirty years later, apparently encouraged by the constant decline in religious belief, he thought that a "few generations" would be quite sufficient.

In some places Popper admits that the teaching of science and of the history of religions and the exhibition of the conflict between scientific conclusions and religious assertions is not enough to banish supernaturalism. We also have to take into account the "metaphysical need" which is commonly found in Europeans, though it is for the most part lacking in the peoples of east Asia. This metaphysical need can be eliminated by "improved epistemological instruction." The metaphysical need is "nothing other than the longing to find a resting place in the exploration of the universe, to reach a stage at which there will be no urge to ask new questions" (*ibid.*, p. 62). It is however, a senseless drive and must be recognized as such if we are to have a healthy mental constitution. Our knowledge of the world consists in the establishment of functional relations between experienced data (Mach's "elements"). Knowing the world means discovering correlations and subsuming these under ever wider correlations. "We cannot do anything further," writes Popper, "than to determine ever richer relations between elements already known or to insert new ones as connecting links between them" (*ibid.*). The world may be likened to a carpet spread out in front of us, between whose webs we go on weaving ever-new webs without limit. It is a vain effort "to try to see behind the carpet," as the metaphysicians and mystics do, in the hope of finding there all kinds of wonderful happenings. In discovering causal relations, "we do not descend step by step into the Ground of the World . . . rather we crawl like an insect on that colorful carpet which we call the world and which, as a consequence of our explorations, becomes ever more dense" (*ibid.*, p. 63). This carpet has no "other side" transcending the one we explore.

Bibliography

In addition to the works by Popper mentioned in the body of the article, the following deserve to be mentioned. *Fürst Bismarck und der Antisemitismus* (Vienna, 1886) is an examination of the violent anti-Semitic fulminations of Dühring and Richard Wagner, as well as of the milder anti-Semitic arguments of Eduard von Hartmann. Popper's *Selbstbiographie* (Leipzig, 1917) reprints the complete text of "Über J. R. Mayer's Mechanik der Wärme," as well as the correspondence between Mayer and Popper. *Die Philosophie des Strafrechts* (Vienna, 1924) presents the details of Popper's objections to existing penal systems and his own alternative, based on his ethical individualism. Parts of a major epistemological treatise which Popper had planned to write were posthumously published under the title "Über die Grundbegriffe der Philosophie und die Gewissheit unserer Erkenntnisse" in *Erkenntnis*, Vol. 3 (1932/1933), 301–324.

Very little by Popper is available in English. "Dreaming and Waking," translated by A. A. Brill, can be found in *The Psychoan-*

alytic Review, Vol. 34 (1947), 188–197. The story about incest is translated by S. Rosenzweig as Appendix I of his article "The Idiocultural Dimension of Psychotherapy—Pre- and Post-History of the Relations Between Sigmund Freud and Popper-Lynkeus," in *Psychoanalysis and the Social Sciences*, Vol. 5 (1958), 9–50. Extracts from various of Popper's writings are translated in H. I. Wachtel, *Security for All and Free Enterprise; A Summary of the Social Philosophy of Josef Popper-Lynkeus* (New York, 1955), which has an introduction by Einstein.

A. Gelber, *Josef Popper-Lynkeus, sein Leben und sein Wirken* (Vienna, 1922), and F. Wittels, *Die Vernichtung der Not* (Vienna, 1922), are full-length studies of Popper's life and work. The latter is available in English, translated by Eden and Cedar Paul as *An End to Poverty* (London, 1925). There is a shorter but very informative study by Richard von Mises in Vol. VII of the series Neue Österreichische Biographie (Vienna, 1931), pp. 206–217. Popper's scientific work is discussed in P. Frank, "Josef Popper-Lynkeus zu seinem achtzigsten Geburtstag," in *Physikalische Zeitschrift*, Vol. 19 (1918), 57–59; and in T. von Karman, "Lynkeus als Ingenieur und Naturwissenschaftler," in *Die Naturwissenschaften*, Vol. 6 (1918), 457–463. Popper's contributions to "energetics" are discussed in G. Helm, *Die Energetik nach ihrer geschichtlichen Entwickelung* (Leipzig, 1898), Part VII, Ch. 2. A most interesting excerpt from the correspondence between Mach and Popper, containing a remarkable anticipation of the quantum theory, is reprinted in H. Löwy, "Historisches zur Quantentheorie," in *Die Naturwissenschaften*, Vol. 21 (1933), 302–303.

Freud's estimate of Popper is found in his article "My Contact With Josef Popper-Lynkeus," which is reprinted in Vol. V of Freud's *Collected Papers* (New York, 1959) and also in his *Character and Culture* (New York, 1963). Popper's remark about Freud quoted in this article will be found in F. Wittels, "Freud's Correlation With Popper-Lynkeus," in *The Psychoanalytic Review*, Vol. 34 (1947), 492–497.

In recent years there has been a good deal of discussion of *ad hominem* arguments of the kind employed by Popper against writers like Spencer, Nietzsche, and Treitschke. This discussion is in large measure due to the work of the influential British philosopher R. M. Hare, who in his *Freedom and Reason* (Oxford and New York, 1963) employed a strategy strikingly similar to that used by Popper. Among discussions of how much (or how little) can be established by means of such arguments, the following are especially noteworthy: A. C. Ewing, "Hare and the Universalization Principle," in *Philosophy*, Vol. 39 (1964), 71–74; D. H. Munro, "R. M. Hare's *Freedom and Reason*," in *Australasian Journal of Philosophy*, Vol. 42 (1964), 119–134; G. Madell, "Hare's Prescriptivism," in *Analysis*, Vol. 26 (1965), 37–41; and G. Ezorsky, "Ad Hominem Morality," in *The Journal of Philosophy*, Vol. 63 (1966), 120–125.

There is a complete bibliography of writings by Popper on philosophical, political, and scientific topics in H. I. Wachtel, *Security for All and Free Enterprise* (see above).

PAUL EDWARDS

POPULAR ARGUMENTS FOR THE EXISTENCE OF GOD. Argument about the existence of God is rare, for religious beliefs are effectively supported in our society by means that are not principally rational. It is common to answer the question "Why are you a believer?" with "Because I was taught to be," uttered in the tone of voice, or in the context, of one presenting reasons, not mere causes, of belief. It is even more common to speak of faith in God as if this were a specially compelling reason for belief and, moreover, one beyond logical criticism. Faith, however, is merely determination to believe and no kind of reason. Literature giving such justifications is not considered in this article. Despite this omission of the greater part of the popular writing and what one might call the traditional verbal folklore of religion, a vast quantity of material remains that can be considered argumentative. After omitting further the grossest absurdities among these arguments, it has still been necessary to choose in a rather arbitrary way what should be dealt with, and no claim to completeness is made.

General remarks. Most of the arguments in popular literature may be seen as variants of the more strictly philosophical arguments, such as the Cosmological and Teleological arguments, or those from morals and common consent. The variants are popular largely because they are posed as probable rather than as valid arguments; that is, they are not offered as arguments whose premises entail their conclusions. Almost all of them fall into a common class of arguments of the form "The universe contains some puzzling feature, *F* (design, an objective morality). God's existence explains *F*, and no other known hypothesis does. Therefore, God exists." That they have this form is a matter of no small importance; it affects the whole question of what kind of objection is likely to succeed against a given popular argument. It is beside the point to demonstrate the formal invalidity of such arguments, although their invalidity is very easy to show in almost every case. However, it is entirely relevant to require of such an argument that it should make clear just how God's existence explains *F*. (Similarly, the real force of the well-known infinite regress counter to the Cosmological, or First Cause, Argument, is that it demonstrates the failure of this argument to provide the promised explanation. The argument merely postpones the explanation. That God's nature is mysterious does not, of course, fill any explanatory bill.) On this score, popular arguments are universally unsatisfactory, appealing tacitly (for the most part) to the claim on the one hand that all things are possible to God and on the other that, God being a transcendental mystery, it is presumptuous to expect any account of his efficacy to be actually intelligible. As the substance of an explanation, this is thin. Further, it is an entirely relevant question to ask whether any explanation is required of some singled-out feature, and whether alternative explanations are simply not known or whether there appears to be a reason to suppose there are none.

Argument from common consent. The argument from common consent is an old and constantly recurring popular argument (see J. A. O'Brien, *God: Can We Find Him?*). The argument has a large measure of plausibility, despite the fact that it is formally invalid; for it is very often overwhelming evidence for some view that the majority holds it. For example, if a huge majority of spectators at a football game believes that a certain team won the game, that is exceedingly good evidence that this team indeed won it; and any minority dissent can be written off in some way, such as irrational partisanship for the beaten team. However, the proportion of majority to minority views is not the only, or by any means the most important, factor in such situations. It is also crucial whether the majority has any competence to judge the issue. On the outcome of football games the majority of spectators is well placed to judge, but on the significance of some scientific experiment the majority is not at all well placed. Obviously, the general run of mankind has always been and still is poorly placed to pronounce on such a question as the existence of a Deity. This requires a competence in logical reasoning on

highly abstract matters and an ability to assess complex evidence that the majority does not possess. Their vote carries no weight on this issue.

Argument from morals. An argument widely used, especially by evangelists who aim at the most general audience, is the argument from the intelligibility of morals. (On a more sophisticated level it has been argued by A. E. Taylor in *The Faith of a Moralist*.) Many who urge it seem to have dimly in mind an essentially rather sophisticated argument, encapsulated in naive remarks like "But if God doesn't exist, why do you not murder or plunder?" and "If God doesn't exist, then a morality could amount only to doing what you please." The rather sophisticated argument thus hinted at is as follows: to call an action moral (immoral) is, first, to provide a motive for doing (avoiding) it. Second, the claim that an action is moral can be a subject of rational dispute, which requires that the claim be not simply a disguised subjective remark about the speaker's tastes. The existence of God explains these two features of normal discourse. Therefore, God exists.

As was pointed out earlier, the first question must be "Does the existence of God explain these features of moral discourse?" If the question whether an action is moral is equivalent to the question whether the action is consistent with God's commands, then moral questions are not purely subjective. On the other hand, it is doubtful whether the theory accounts for the sort of discussion that actually goes on when moral issues are argued. God's commands must, according to the hypothesis, be arbitrary. It cannot be that he consults something beyond his own will, since that external thing or principle would then be the source of morality and God its mere interpreter and announcer, not its creator. However, moral reasoning surely requires empirical knowledge of other persons and the world generally—and a very great deal of intelligence if the reasoning is to be satisfactory. It is far from clear that the hypothesis allows for the relevant play of intelligence and knowledge in arriving at moral conclusions.

Again, it is rarely stated just which motive for behaving morally is provided under the hypothesis of God's existence. It cannot be suggested that we have a moral duty to obey God's commands because the whole point of the proposed explanation is that his commands are the source of all moral duties. It could be claimed that terror of punishment and desire for reward are perfectly adequate motives for obeying the commands. However, despite the undoubted efficacy of these motives, they are seldom urged because they do not adequately account for what we feel our motives really are in moral behavior. The most satisfactory suggestion as to the motive provided under the hypothesis seems to be that one obeys the commands out of love of God.

In sum, it is uncertain how the hypothesis clearly explains the required features of moral discourse. Further, it seems quite possible to account for them at least as well without being committed to the theistic view. For if love of God is an adequate motive for moral behavior, why should not love of one's fellows also be adequate? And if it is, then it further seems an objective empirical question which courses of action promote those almost universally desired ends of continuance of life, adequate food and shelter, and freedom from violence, as well as less fundamental and more subtle ends that promote smooth social intercourse.

Teleological arguments. Versions of the classical Teleological Argument are by far the most popular of all popular arguments. The variety of changes rung upon this old theme in respect of its premises is astonishingly wide, as may be gathered from the following brief examples: the smallness of the human gene has been cited by A. C. Morrison, for no very clear reason, as an instance of God's designing hand, and so has the immensity of the orbital velocity of an electron. More markedly odd are such suggestions as "This old world has three times as much water as land but with all of its twisting and turning not a drop sloshes off into space" (*Ebony* symposium, November 1962, p. 96) and that the annual progress of the earth round the sun, although it is much more rapid, is also much smoother than the most sophisticated jet airliner yet designed. Although it is difficult to see what relevance these considerations may be thought to have, they perhaps involve a confusion between a good argument to the conditional conclusion that if these things are designed, then the technology of their production is well beyond our present reach, and a bad argument to the conclusion that these things have, in fact, been designed.

An ingenious variant, heard in conversation but apparently never published, neatly turns the tables on a standard polemic against belief in a God that stems from Freudian psychology—that such belief is caused by a psychological mechanism arising from various sexual stresses in an infant's relationship with its father. This mechanism, it is claimed, far from showing that belief in God is pathological and irrational, really demonstrates his loving care for his creatures in providing a psychological mechanism that promotes belief, thus preventing the damnation of his creatures as heretics and infidels. This does not at all answer the point that insofar as belief depends upon the psychological stresses, it is irrational and pathological. (Irrational and pathological beliefs may, of course, be true.)

Arguments from the sciences. Only recent arguments taken from the biological and the physical sciences will be discussed.

First, however, there is a general argument from the very existence of science, or as it is more likely to be put, from the intelligibility of nature (see D. Elton Trueblood, *Philosophy of Religion*, pp. 94–98). It is felt that the universe must be rational if science, using logic and mathematics, is able to comprehend it. But logic and mathematics are concerned with deriving some propositions or formulas from others. It is not the conclusions or the premises of arguments that may properly be called rational, but only the procedure of deriving conclusion from premises. This procedure reflects no rational process in nature. It would be more accurate (although still not very accurate) to call this a linguistic procedure. We can move from "If there is lightning, then there is thunder" and "There is lightning" to the conclusion "There is thunder" by the rational procedure known as *modus ponens*, but it is not even intelligible to suppose that *modus ponens* is a natural physical process by means of which lightning produces thunder. Scientists may discover the important equation that relates the speed of a falling body to the square of the time of its fall. They may differentiate this equation, $v = t^2$, to show that the body's acceleration is constant. Differentiation is a mathematical procedure of derivation, but it is not intelligible to say that the body or the gravitational field in which it falls undergoes any such process of differentiation, or that it undergoes some nonmathematical counterpart of it.

Arguments from biology. It has been argued—by Lecomte du Noüy and Teilhard de Chardin, for example— that the pattern of evolution as displayed by modern biology shows clear marks of a designing hand. The direction of evolution, it is claimed, is toward progressively more intelligent life forms, thus showing the desire of the Creator (Omega, as Teilhard de Chardin called him) to bring about beings like himself. The claim is highly dubious. It induces "a certain shuffling of the feet" (to quote Medawar's review) in Teilhard, when he discusses the fact that insects and plants do not seem to evolve in this way at all. Lecomte du Noüy solved the difficulty by defining the problematic cases not as evolutions but as adaptations. The direction of adaptation is toward usefulness; that of evolution, toward liberty. Thus he made the claim perfectly, if trivially, safe. Even so, there is a difficulty, for if it is all a plan, why does God not bring about immediately and at a stroke the desired state of affairs now being so laboriously approached with such a plethora of wasteful products? Lecomte du Noüy's apparent answer is merely that since God is an eternal Being, what seems to us simple mortals as a drear immensity of wasted time is to him but the twinkling of an eye. The irrelevance of this to the original objection is obvious enough. The waste is still waste, and the existence of so many pointless dinosaurs (whose lives played no part in future evolution) can scarcely have escaped the attention of him who takes note of the fall of a sparrow.

One prevalent argument, put forward by Morrison, among others, is based on the allegedly remarkable hospitality of our planet to complex forms of life. Temperatures are neither too high nor too low, and there is an abundance of water and oxygen and an atmospheric blanket against lethal doses of cosmic radiation. But the argument inverts the situation. We now have good reasons (of a Darwinian kind) to believe that the surviving life forms are those which adapt to the environment rather than those for whom the environment has been adapted by a beneficent Overseer. So far as is known, only one of the nine major planets of our particular star is hospitable to complex life forms. It might be surprising if every planet of every star fulfilled the quite detailed set of conditions that favor life as we know it and that prevail over most (not all) of our planet. But that there is one such planet is not so surprising that we need recourse to metaphysical entities to explain it.

Similar arguments from alleged improbabilities also spring from biology. Lecomte du Noüy and others have claimed that life is inconsistent with the Second Law of Thermodynamics. This law states that entropy increases, which means, roughly, that in any isolated system energy breaks down from various differentiated forms that are usable in doing work to an undifferentiated state of uniform heat. In statistical thermodynamics, increase of entropy is defined roughly as increase of the randomness of systems, that is, their movement toward more probable forms. But, it is said, living organisms decrease in entropy as they grow; they build up differentiated forms of energy and hence are improbable structures.

However, the phenomena of life are quite consistent with the law, for living organisms are not thermodynamically isolated systems. In whatever way life may be improbable, it is certainly not improbable in any sense that makes it inconsistent with statistical thermodynamics.

A second, more plausible, claim of this kind is that even a simple protein molecule is a highly improbable structure, so improbable that it is simply incredible that it should ever have come into existence by pure chance. A calculation cited by V. H. Mottram puts the odds against a chance "manufacture" of a simple protein molecule as 10^{160} to 1, a small chance by any standards. Mottram also claimed that 10^{243} years would be needed for such an event to occur on this planet (a much longer period than that accepted for the cool earth) and that it would require sextillion sextillion sextillion times more material than is believed to be in the entire universe. Another calculation shows that the probability of such a molecule's arising by chance manipulation of amino acids (already quite complex structures) is still as low as $1:10^{48}$ and hence very improbable indeed.

The ways of statistical arguments are notoriously complex. We must always ask "Relative to what assumptions are these probability figures reached?" This was not made clear by Mottram. Presumably we are to assume at least that the atoms are rearranged in various positions by a process of mechanical shuffling of some sort in which all the rearrangements so envisaged are equally probable.

The possibility of such a rearrangement is very dubious. Even elementary chemistry informs us that certain combinations are not possible—for example, five hydrogen atoms may not be linked to one carbon atom. There is no evidence that such groups were excluded from the class of equiprobable arrangements considered in constructing this figure. If one considers the various linkages of more complex groups in which, say, a group of fifty atoms hooks on to another group of fifty, the number of chemically possible combinations is, presumably, very small. But this cannot have been taken into consideration in constructing the figures, because we do not have sufficient knowledge of the chemical possibilities at this level. The theists appear to have committed at this point the fallacy of assuming equal probabilities in cases where we have no positive knowledge of what the probabilities are.

Consider a liter of hydrogen containing, say, 10^{22} atoms. If we attempt to assign a number to all the conceivable arrangements of those atoms, the number is enormous. Yet we invariably find them divided into hydrogen molecules, 0.5×10^{22} pairs of atoms extremely close together. The improbability of this always coming about as a random arrangement of atoms is immense, and certainly far greater than any of the figures quoted by Mottram, yet this is presumably not evidence of design. Without more information

about and justification of the assumption of equiprobability on which Mottram's calculation is based, plainly no reliance can be placed upon it.

Arguments from physics. Perhaps even than biology, modern physics has given rise to a group of widely circulated arguments purporting to show that, despite the fact that God nowhere appears in the calculations of physicists, modern physics demands, suggests, or allows for the existence of God.

Although most apologists agree that the views of a scientist have no special authority outside the field of his expertise, this does not prevent their citing a vast mass of material produced by those physicists who spend their less strenuous hours philosophizing on their findings. The view almost universally favored among such writers, and perhaps most forcefully expressed by Sir Arthur Eddington and Sir James Jeans, is that modern physics establishes the subjectivity of all knowledge and that reality is mental, not material. It is often further concluded that physics has shown the world to be a nonrational place about which clear logical argument is out of place.

Relativity theories are alleged to have shown the subjectivity of all knowledge and to have confirmed Protagoras' doctrine that man is the measure of all things. But the special theory of relativity is concerned with relations between inertial systems (a notion definable wholly within objective dynamics). It is not at all concerned with any observers who may be reading clocks or using measuring rods within these systems. The general theory only extends the results of the special theory to cover relations between systems of a wider class. Neither theory is subjectivist or mentalistic.

A similar example of needless obscurantism concerns the primary place given the concept of energy by the relativistic notion that mass (matter) may be converted into energy, and vice versa. Few of us are sure just what energy is; and, when a scientist like E. J. Bing informs us that everything is energy, that it may exist in the form of electromagnetic vibration, and that it is a vehicle of universal thought (a gratuitous addition), we are apt to think that, while we do not know what this really means, perhaps everything is, in some obscure way, thought and hence in the mind of God.

Trueblood (*op. cit.,* pp. 102–105) has invoked the science of thermodynamics to yield a theistic conclusion. The Second Law of Thermodynamics shows that the universe is steadily increasing its thermodynamic randomness—it is dissipating its stores of differentiated energy usable in doing work. It also shows that, as we trace the history of the universe in time according to the law, we come to a state of minimum energy, a sort of beginning in time of the universe. But this is far from lending support to the theistic hypothesis. It simply means that the law leads us to a point beyond which it will not take us. It gives no warrant for the conclusion that the minimum entropy state has a supernatural cause.

The greatest number of arguments are derived from the difficult and puzzling field of quantum mechanics. It is possible to give some indication of the relevant state of affairs in physics in terms of two features: (1) The Schrödinger wave equation, which is fundamental to quantum physics, contains the Ψ function. This gives as its square the probability that an electron, for example, is in a certain spatiotemporal region. This feature leads to the result that the exact later states of electrons are unpredictable even from the fullest statement of their earlier states. (2) Beams of radiation or of electrons show some features characteristic of beams of particles but others characteristic of beams of waves, although their being particles is inconsistent with their being waves.

Feature (2) leads directly to such distortions as "If an electron can be two wholly inconsistent things, it is a little narrow to expect so much less of God." The electron, of course, is not, nor can it be, two inconsistent things—and (2) does not entail this. But the claim, together with the breakdown of the Laplacean view that given the complete mechanical state of the universe at any one time, any future or past state could be rigorously deduced in every detail, is generally hailed by religious apologists. Very few apologists claim that quantum physics actually provides evidence for God's existence. It is simply that in quantum theory mechanical determinism breaks down and there is no mechanical picture of quantum processes that is an adequate interpretation of the mathematical formalism of the theory. To religious apologists it appears that these facts allow for occult nonphysical causes and forbid rational understanding. They appear to feel that in the overthrow of reason itself lies their best defense.

More specific in their trend toward the admission of occult or physically transcendent causes are the following characteristic arguments. Arguing from the bad habit some physicists have of speaking about unpredictable electron jumps as the electron "choosing" one rather than another energy state, E. J. Bing wrote, "Let's call a spade a spade. To say that an electron 'chooses' to do anything *is to attribute free will to the electron.*" The theory gives no warrant for taking this obvious metaphor literally. It is quite unclear what real meaning there could be for such terms as "choice" and "free will" if their use is extended from describing living things to describing those that are nonliving. Such extension can result only in confusion.

Some physicists (Jeans, for example) have an equally deplorable habit of speaking of the Schrödinger wave equation as "waves of knowledge" in discussing the behavior of subatomic particles. This is presumably because the Schrödinger equation, which describes the behavior, is a wave equation and contains a function whose square is a probability. Apparently they regard probability as purely a matter of knowledge and thus suppose that some occult mental principle is at work in the quantum world. These suggestions win no assent from such authoritative quantum physicists as Niels Bohr and Werner Heisenberg, who have most strongly insisted on the indeterminacy of quantum physics. Their notion is not that quantum phenomena have occult causes (acts of free will on the part of electrons) or unknown causes, but that they have no causes at all. Although there have been many distinguished scientists, including Einstein, who believe it is possible that in the future we shall have a fully deterministic theory of the subatomic world, they have all taken for granted that the theory would postulate only physical causes.

Bibliography

FAVORABLE VIEWS

Bing, E. J., "Modern Science Discovers God." *American Mercury* (June 1941).

Corbishley, Thomas, *Religion Is Reasonable*. London, 1962.

Ebony, symposium, "Why I Believe in God" (December 1961 ff.).

Eddington, A. S., *Nature of the Physical World*. London, 1928.

Gittelsohn, R. B., "Have We Outgrown God?" *Saturday Review* (September 16, 1961).

Griffith, A. L., *Barriers to Christian Belief*. London, 1962.

Jeans, Sir James, *The Mysterious Universe*. London, 1930.

Lecomte du Noüy, Pierre, *Human Destiny*. London, 1947.

Lewis, C. S., *Miracles*. London, 1948.

Morrison, A. C., "Seven Reasons Why a Scientist Believes in God." *Reader's Digest* (October 1960).

Mottram, V. H., "Scientific Basis for Belief in God." *The Listener* (April 22, 1948).

O'Brien, J. A., *God: Can We Find Him?* New York, 1942.

Robinson, J. A. T., *Honest to God*. London, 1963.

Rosten, Leo, ed., *Guide to the Religions of America*. New York, 1955.

Taylor, A. E., *The Faith of a Moralist*. London, 1930.

Taylor, F. Sherwood, *Man and Matter*. London, 1951.

Teilhard de Chardin, Pierre, *The Phenomenon of Man*, translated by Bernard Wall. London, 1959.

Trueblood, D. Elton, *Philosophy of Religion*. New York, 1957.

Weaver, Warren, "A Scientist Ponders Faith." *Saturday Review of Literature* (January 3, 1959).

Whittaker, Sir Edmund, "Religion and the Nature of the Universe." *The Listener* (June 1, 1950).

SKEPTICAL VIEWS

Cohen, Chapman, *God and Me*. London, 1946.

Cohen, Chapman, *God and the Universe*. London, 1946.

Feyerabend, Paul, "Niels Bohr's Interpretation of the Quantum Theory," in Herbert Feigl and Grover Maxwell, eds., *Current Issues in the Philosophy of Science*. New York, 1961. The relevant features of quantum physics are well discussed in this difficult but not highly mathematical paper.

Jack, H., "A Recent Attempt to Prove God's Existence." *Philosophy and Phenomenological Research*, Vol. 25 (1965), 575–579. Critically discusses one of the arguments by A. C. Morrison and a very similar argument by Lecomte du Noüy in *Human Destiny*.

Medawar, P. B., "Critical Notice of 'Phenomenology of Man.'" *Mind*, Vol. 70 (1961), 99–106.

Russell, Bertrand, *The Scientific Outlook*. London, 1931.

Russell, Bertrand, *Religion and Science*. London, 1936.

Russell, Bertrand, *Why I Am Not a Christian*. New York, 1957.

Stebbing, L. Susan, *Philosophy and the Physicists*. London, 1937.

G. C. NERLICH

PORPHYRY, one of the principal founders of Neoplatonism. Porphyry was born of Syrian parents at Tyre about A.D. 232. He studied philosophy at Athens. In 263 he went to Rome, joined the group that regarded Plotinus as its master, and, apparently some years after Plotinus' death, took over his school. He died some time in the first six years of the fourth century.

Porphyry can be called a founder of Neoplatonism because, while the philosophy he upheld was in the main that of Plotinus, he made it possible for this philosophy to become, as it did, an institution throughout the Roman Empire. He arranged Plotinus' lectures for publication in their present form; he defended and developed their content in independent works of his own; third, he enabled some of the much more systematic, not to say more teachable, philosophy of Aristotle to be included even by Platonic professors in a university curriculum.

In the so-called *Sententiae ad Intelligibilia Ducentes* ("Aids to the Study of the Intelligibles," a short, difficult summary, incomplete as we have it, of Neoplatonism) he presents methodical proofs of two Plotinian theses which were unacceptable to the more conservative Platonists and to Porphyry himself when he first came to Rome: the independence and priority of the One to Being or Intellect, and the identity of Intellect or Thought with its objects. Plotinus, however, had been ambiguous over the extent to which the lower hypostases, Intellect (embracing the Platonic forms) and Soul (embracing nature and the Aristotelian forms), each existed in its own right. It is the monistic strand which seems to dominate in Porphyry: everything that is not the One is an appearance of the One and is the result of the inadequacy of our thought about the One. The serious consequence of this doctrine is for the ordinary notion of personality. The individual, embodied soul and intellect, themselves appearances (he also calls them parts) of some universal soul and intellect, will be unreal; Porphyry calls the individual soul "the soul in a relation"—for it is related to a body—which implies its nonsubstantiality according to Aristotle's doctrine of categories. This consequence was vigorously challenged by Iamblichus. Union with the One can be achieved, according to Porphyry, by the unaided effort of intellect, but we do not have enough evidence to know how he met the philosophical problems of this thesis even if he had a consistent doctrine about it.

Porphyry's ethics followed Plotinus in stressing the universal equation between pursuit of the good, becoming what one "essentially" is, the self-awareness that accompanies thought, and "reversion" to the "cause" of one's being. Evil, together with matter, was the result of a "deviation from reality." In schematizing *Ennead* I 2 [19], Porphyry gave Plotinus' scale of virtues a nomenclature which became conventional for later Neoplatonists. *A*, the virtues of the soul, are (1) civic, (2) purificatory; *B*, the virtues of the intellect, are (3) contemplative, (4) paradigmatic. Less abstractly and on less philosophical grounds he was attracted like many Neoplatonists by the asceticism and taboos of Pythagoreanism.

Nothing has survived of a book which Porphyry wrote comparing Platonism and Aristotelianism. It undoubtedly maintained that there was no substantial conflict between the two, which was commonplace for Platonists of the empire. His commentaries on Plato have perished too; so have those on Aristotle, except for the introduction to the *Categories* known as the *Isagoge* and an elementary commentary on the same work. But his views were often quoted; and it is clear that what is distinctive about his treatment of Aristotle is twofold—a facility in expounding him without trying to Platonize him or to score against him, and a remarkable gift of clear exposition that does not depend (as it does in some later commentators) on ignoring the difficult issues. Most of the formulas which aimed at accommodating the metaphysical presuppositions of Aristotle's logic to Platonism had probably been worked out already. But since it was only the metaphysics that was objectionable, the way was open to the full acceptance of a purely formal logic. This meant not the Aristotelian logic of terms from which the nonexistent, the negative, and the particular were excluded, but something roughly equivalent to the Boolean algebra of classes. This logic without metaphysics is roughly, too, what we find in Porphyry; and it is what has sometimes been inaptly called Porphyry's nominalism. With some debt to the Stoics, it enabled logic to develop as an autonomous science. For his *Isagoge* was translated into Arabic and Syriac as well as Latin, and his more advanced work was incorporated in Boethius' logic. The *Isagoge* is traditionally said to have made species a fifth predicable in place of definition. If it had it would have misrepresented Aristotle by implying that the subject was not a universal term, like those of the other predicables, but a particular. The implication might not have disturbed Porphyry, but in fact the *Isagoge,* or *Quinque Voces,* is not about predicables but what it says it is about, the five words which are essential to the understanding of the *Categories.* It does, however, introduce "inseparable accidents" which are an uneasy intermediate between essential attributes and pure or separable accidents.

Porphyry was a man of wide learning and wide interests. He studied many of the religious beliefs and practices with which he came into contact, and though generally sympathetic to them as various if inferior ways to salvation, he was renowned for centuries as the author of a detailed work against the Christians. But this and ventures of a more or less occultist nature—allegorical interpretations of poetry, descriptions of the soul's "vehicles," and the like—have mostly survived only in statements from controversial sources; and while respectable as philosophy in their day they are of small philosophical interest in the modern sense.

Bibliography

Porphyry's "Life of Plotinus" is included in editions of Plotinus' works. *Sententiae ad Intelligibilia Ducentes* ("Aids to the Study of the Intelligibles") has been edited by B. Mommert (Leipzig, 1907). For the *Isagoge,* with Boethius' translation, see *Commentaria in Aristotelem Graeca,* A. Busse, ed. (Berlin, 1887), Vol. IV, Part I. Excerpts from other works are available in Stobaeus' *Florilegium,* C. Wachsmuth and O. Hense, eds. (Berlin, 1884–1912), and in J. Bidez' *Vie de Porphyre, Le Philosophe néo-platonicien* (Ghent and Leipzig, 1913).

On Porphyry's life and works see, in addition to Bidez, R. Beutler, "Porphyrios" No. 21 in Pauly and Wissowa, *Realencyklopädie der classischen Altertumswissenschaft,* Vol. XXII, Sec. 1 (Stuttgart, 1953); T. Whittaker, *The Neo-Platonists,* 2d ed. (Cambridge, 1918; reprinted Hildesheim, 1961).

A. C. LLOYD

PORTER, NOAH (1811–1892), American Congregationalist clergyman, philosopher, and psychologist, and president of Yale College from 1871 to 1886. As a student in the Yale Divinity School, Porter had become a disciple of Nathaniel W. Taylor's modified version of New England Calvinism. For ten years he preached Taylorism at churches in New Milford, Connecticut (1836–1843), and Springfield, Massachusetts (1843–1846). He was then appointed Clark professor of moral philosophy and metaphysics at Yale, holding this chair throughout his tenure of the presidency of the college. On retiring from the office of president, he resumed a small teaching load until his death.

Porter's thought until 1853 was dominated by the conventional Scottish common-sense realism that pervaded American colleges. Then two years spent in Europe, largely in study at the University of Berlin, increased his familiarity with more recent and more daring philosophical systems. He became particularly interested, through the German philosopher Friedrich Adolf Trendelenburg, in the central epistemological problems of modern philosophy. Porter was convinced that these problems had to be solved before any advance in ontology could be expected. Moreover, he believed that the epistemological questions themselves required a foundation in scientific psychology.

This conviction and a much keener appreciation of the value of the history of thought than was usual among American philosophers of his time, led Porter to the preparation and publication of his important treatise *The Human Intellect*, the best work on psychology in English before William James. Porter presented and critically examined the leading ideas of both English and European (chiefly German) schools of psychology, as well as summarizing earlier work in the field. Because he regarded psychology as a necessary prelude to epistemology which, in turn, he considered prior to metaphysics, he insisted that psychology had to be an inductive science and roundly criticized Hegel for attempting to ground psychology in his metaphysical system. Although inductive, however, psychology cannot be a material or experimental science. Its subjects are the data of consciousness, which must be discovered introspectively; physiological experiments and investigations must be kept in mind by the psychologist, but these studies are ancillary to the direct study of the data of consciousness.

The influence of this major work and of Porter's many lesser writings was one of the chief forces in liberating academic philosophy in America from domination by naive realism and in introducing the study of German philosophy and psychology.

Among the nonphilosophical activities of Porter, special note should be taken of his editorship, with Chauncey A. Goodrich, of a revised edition of Noah Webster's *An American Dictionary of the English Language* (Springfield, Mass., 1864). This work was revised under Porter's sole supervision as *Webster's International Dictionary of the English Language* (1890).

Works by Porter

The Human Intellect. New York, 1868.
The American Colleges and the American Public. New Haven, 1870.
Science and Sentiment. New York, 1882.
The Elements of Moral Science. New York, 1885.
Kant's Ethics. A Critical Exposition. Chicago, 1886.

Works on Porter

Blau, Joseph L., *Men and Movements in American Philosophy*. Englewood Cliffs, N.J., 1952.
James, Walter T., *The Philosophy of Noah Porter*. 1951. An unpublished doctoral dissertation, available in typescript in the Columbia University library.

Merriam, George S., ed., *Noah Porter: A Memorial by Friends*. New York, 1893. Biographical and expository discussion.
Schneider, H. W., *A History of American Philosophy*. New York, 1946. Contains additional comment.

J. L. BLAU

POLLA. See HEN/POLLA.

PORT-ROYALISTS. See ARNAULD, ANTOINE; LOGIC, HISTORY OF; NICOLE, PIERRE.

POSIDONIUS of Apameia (135–51? B.C.), the Stoic philosopher, was famous in his own time and continued to influence writers into the first and second centuries A.D. Soon after, his writings seem to have been lost, and even his name is rarely mentioned. Known to modern historiography mainly from the mention of his views in Cicero, Strabo, Seneca, and Galen, he was considered from the Renaissance to the beginning of the nineteenth century as a minor figure in the development of Stoicism. Then his thought began to be discovered in an ever increasing number of writers, who were believed to follow him although they do not quote him, and he was established as the mediator between the Orient and the Occident, the reconciler of philosophy with religion and mysticism, the foremost representative of dualism. In the early twentieth century the reconstruction of Posidonius' work through *Quellenforschung* ("source criticism") was replaced by a reconstruction based on the inner form of his thought, and Posidonius was represented as a visual thinker, the defender of monism, the proponent of the doctrines of cosmic sympathy and vitalism, and the last Hellenistic philosopher. Both interpretations pay little attention to the fragments preserved under the name of Posidonius and therefore remain largely conjectural. What will be said here is based exclusively on the attested material.

This material leaves no doubt about the fundamentally dualistic character of Posidonius' system. His ethics, which is the best-known part of his thought, teaches, contrary to the general Stoic dogma, that passions are not simply false judgments but an irreducible force in human nature. This distinction is also echoed in Posidonian physics in the again unorthodox definition of matter as endowed with its own form and quality, which is merely reshaped and remodeled by divine reason. His logic establishes reason as a criterion of truth independent of sense perception. On the other hand, the duality of matter and reason is bridged by the realm of mathematical forms; among the Stoics only Posidonius was a mathematical realist. The macrocosm and the microcosm are in the end viewed as gradated, as hierarchies as it were, in which reason governs the subordinate irrational forces. God pervades the world; the passions follow the leadership of rational insight; man is here to contemplate and to act.

The Platonic and Aristotelian elements in this Stoicism were noted even by ancient critics. In Posidonius' opinion the founders of the Stoa, Zeno and Cleanthes themselves, had been Platonizing and Aristotelianizing. The strict monism of the school was due to Chrysippus, whose work Posidonius thought had to be undone. Yet although Posidonius harked back to the older teaching and in this sense remained in the Greek tradition—he was innocent of the later Orientalizing—he undoubtedly made an original contribution to philosophy. His ethics is a greatly refined analysis of the emotions which refutes the rationalistic position by pointing to its inner inconsistency and its inconsistency with observed facts. He stressed the importance of the will. Although only a few details of his physics can be rediscovered, it is clear that he was intent on explaining things; he was famous for his etiologies, and he carefully distinguished the various causes, assigning first place to teleology. Cosmic sympathy is but one of the factors he invoked in his exegesis of nature. His logical investigations furthered the understanding of syllogistic thinking, which seemed to him validated not by linguistic connections but by implied axioms. In short, his system marks a step forward in the history of Greek rationalism, and this is in accord with Posidonius' belief in the gradual development of knowledge and in the idea of progress, which he, like so many earlier Greek rationalists, upheld.

Posidonius' contributions were, however, not restricted to the field of philosophy proper. He wrote a history of his own time and in it, if not separately, dealt copiously with the rise of civilization, which he claimed began with practical inventions made by philosophers. In the historical process itself he detected the dominance of freedom over circumstance. Several of his books were devoted to natural sciences, such as astronomy and meteorology; he also investigated problems of mathematics and of military tactics. Perhaps the greatest significance of these works lies in the fact that they do not isolate scholarly and scientific research but put it in a philosophical framework. Events are seen as part of the history of the cosmos. Scientific explanations are hypotheses, the correctness and adequacy of which must be judged through philosophical reflection. It was as a philosopher that Posidonius felt impelled to reject the heliocentric theory in favor of the geocentric theory. Although he erred in this respect, he did enforce the idea of the hypothetical character of all scientific knowledge and did restore the unity of the sciences which Hellenistic thought had destroyed.

The stoa of the empire, initially influenced by Posidonius, tended more and more to follow Chrysippus. Thus, the philosopher Posidonius soon lost importance. His scientific writings kept the Greek heritage alive much longer and carried it, through Seneca's *Naturales Quaestiones,* into the Middle Ages. If one judges his achievement and his influence, one cannot compare him with Plato, Aristotle, or Democritus or with Zeno, Epicurus, or Plotinus. It is fair to say, however, that his personality, which he allowed to intrude into his work, makes him one of the most attractive figures among ancient philosophers. He was a man of dignity and not without a sense of irony and humor. He lived the dogma he preached, studying and teaching as well as participating in the political affairs of Rhodes, his adopted city. The variety of his gifts is amazing—his dialectical skill, traced by Galen to his mathematical erudition; the keenness of his powers of observation of men and things, which is especially marked in his reports on the travels that took him throughout almost the whole of the then-known world; and the strength of his analytical ability, along with his love of literature and art.

It was perhaps the universalism of his nature that made it possible for him not only to attempt a new explanation of the universe in all its aspects, doing justice to both man's cognitive and his practical concerns, but also to root human existence—for the last time in antiquity, it seems—in the world of reality without depriving this world of the reign of human reason, which he considered of the same nature as the divine spirit ruling the cosmos.

Bibliography

The approach of *Quellenforschung* has been criticized, and criticized fairly, by J. F. Dobson, "The Posidonius Myth," in *Classical Quarterly,* Vol. 12 (1918), 179 ff. For Posidonius as a monist see K. Reinhardt, *Poseidonios* (Munich, 1921); see also his *Kosmos und Sympathie* (Munich, 1926) and A. Pauly and G. Wissowa, *Realencyclopädie der classischen Altertumswissenschaft,* Vol. XXII (Stuttgart, 1953), Part I, Cols. 558–826. I. Heinemann, *Poseidonios' metaphysiche Schriften,* 2 vols. (Breslau, 1921–1928), considers Posidonius especially in relation to his predecessor Panaerius.

For a reconstruction of Posidonius' philosophy according to the attested fragments see Ludwig Edelstein, "The Philosophical System of Posidonius," in *American Journal of Philology,* Vol. 57 (1936), 286 ff. For the historical fragments see F. Jacoby, *Die Fragmente der griechischen Historiker,* Vol. II, No. 87 (Berlin, 1926). The collection of fragments by I. Bake, *Rhodii Reliquiae Doctrinae* (Leiden, 1810), is antiquated.

LUDWIG EDELSTEIN

POSITIVISM.   The term "positivism" was used first by Henri, comte de Saint-Simon to designate scientific method and its extension to philosophy. Adopted by Auguste Comte, it came to designate a great philosophical movement which, in the second half of the nineteenth century and the first decades of the twentieth, was powerful in all the countries of the Western world.

The characteristic theses of positivism are that science is the only valid knowledge and facts the only possible objects of knowledge; that philosophy does not possess a method different from science; and that the task of philosophy is to find the general principles common to all the sciences and to use these principles as guides to human conduct and as the basis of social organization. Positivism, consequently, denies the existence or intelligibility of forces or substances that go beyond facts and the laws ascertained by science. It opposes any kind of metaphysics and, in general, any procedure of investigation that is not reducible to scientific method.

The principal philosophical sources of positivism are the works of Francis Bacon, the English empiricists, and the philosophers of the Enlightenment; but the cultural climate that made it possible was that of the eighteenth-century industrial revolution and the grand wave of optimism to which the first successes of industrial technology gave rise. Positivism made this climate into a philosophical program—that is, a universal project for human life. It exalted science without concerning itself (as does contemporary positivism) with the conditions and the limits of the validity of science, and it claimed that not only ethics and politics but also religion would become scientific disciplines. In one direction, this led to an attempt to establish a "positive" religion in place of traditional theological religions.

Through its acceptance of the concept of the infinity of nature and of history and, therefore, of necessary and universal progress, positivism had affinities with the other important nineteenth-century philosophical movement, absolute idealism, and belongs with it in the general range of romanticism.

There are two fundamental kinds of positivism: social positivism, with a professedly practicopolitical character, and evolutionary positivism, with a professedly theoretical character. Both share the general idea of progress, but whereas social positivism deduces progress from a consideration of society and history, evolutionary positivism deduces it from the fields of physics and biology. Comte and John Stuart Mill are the principal representatives of social positivism, and Herbert Spencer of evolutionary positivism. A materialistic or spiritualistic metaphysics is often associated with evolutionary positivism. A third, critical type of positivism, also known as empiriocriticism, should be distinguished from both social and evolutionary positivism. Contemporary forms of positivism—logical positivism and neopositivism—are directly connected with critical positivism.

SOCIAL POSITIVISM

Social positivism arose in France through the work of Saint-Simon and other socialistic writers (Charles Fourier, Pierre Joseph Proudhon) and in England through that of the utilitarians (Jeremy Bentham and James Mill), who, in turn, considered their work closely associated with that of the great economists Thomas Malthus and David Ricardo. Social positivism sought to promote, through the use of the methods and results of science, a more just social organization. According to Saint-Simon, men now lived in a critical epoch because scientific progress, by destroying theological and metaphysical doctrines, had eliminated the foundation of the social organization of the Middle Ages. A new organic epoch, in which positive philosophy would be the basis of a new system of religion, politics, ethics, and public education, was required. Through this system society would regain its unity and its organization by basing itself on a new spiritual power—that of the scientists—and a new temporal power—that of the industrialists. In his last writing, *The New Christianity* (1825), Saint-Simon considered the new organic epoch to be a return to primitive Christianity.

Comte. Saint-Simon's ideas inspired the work of Auguste Comte. The point of departure of Comte's philosophy is his law of the three stages. According to this law, both the general history of humanity and the development of the individual man, as well as that of every branch of human knowledge, passes through three stages: the *theological,* or fictitious, stage in which man represents natural phenomena as products of the direct action of supernatural agents; the *metaphysical* stage, in which the supernatural agents are replaced by abstract forces believed to be capable of generating the observable phenomena; and, finally, the *positive* stage, in which man, refusing to seek the ultimate causes of phenomena, turns exclusively toward discovering the laws of phenomena by observation and reasoning. The positive stage is that of science, whose fundamental task is to predict phenomena in order to utilize them.

"Science whence comes prediction; prediction whence comes action" is the formula in which Comte epitomized his theory of science. The formula, as Comte himself recognized, expresses exactly Francis Bacon's point of view. The law of the three stages permits the classification of the sciences according to the order in which they entered into the positive phases—an order determined by the degree of simplicity and generality of the phenomena which are the objects of each science as it reaches the positive phase. Thus, according to Comte the following hierarchy constitutes "a necessary and invariable subordination": astronomy, physics, chemistry, biology, and sociology. Mathematics remains outside this order because it is at the basis of all the sciences; psychology, because it is not a science, also remains outside. Psychology should be based on introspective observation. But introspective observation is impossible, because the observed and observing organ would have to be identical. The apex of the hierarchy of sciences is sociology, or social physics, which Comte divided into social statics, or theory of order, and social dynamics, or theory of progress.

Progress is a necessary law of human history: the realization of progress is entrusted not to individuals, who are only the instruments of progress, but to the true subject of history—humanity, conceived as the Great Being in which past, present, and future beings partake. "We always work for our descendants, but under the impulse of our ancestors, from whom derive the elements and procedures of all our operations" (*Politique positive,* Vol. IV, pp. 34–35). Humanity is the continuous and uninterrupted tradition of the human race, and it is the divinity that must replace the God of traditional religions. The wisdom and providence of humanity preside infallibly over the realization of progress. At the end of progress there is sociocracy, a new absolutist social regime based on science and the religion of humanity and directed by a corporation of positivist philosophers. Sociocracy, by limiting liberties, will make impossible any deviation from the fundamental beliefs of the positivistic cult.

In his last work, *Philosophy of Mathematics* (1856), Comte proposed a new kind of religious trinity, the Great Being (humanity), the Great Fetish (the earth), and the Great Way (space). The religious aspect of Comte's philosophy drew a great number of followers and generated the greatest wave of enthusiasm. Pierre Lafitte and Émile Littré in France, Richard Congreve and G. H. Lewes in England were the most philosophical of Comte's first disciples. The influence of Comte's religious thought, however, rapidly exhausted itself, except among small groups of devotees, while his philosophical ideas (the law of the three stages; the conception of science as description and prediction; the theory of progress; and sociology as a positive science) have exercised a lasting influence on science and philosophy.

Bentham and the Mills. Comte's English contemporaries, the utilitarians Jeremy Bentham and James Mill, presented with equal force, although more modestly, the fundamental requirement of positivism: that every kind of valid knowledge be included within science. They sought to establish a science of mind based on facts, as is the science of nature, and tried to make ethics itself, as Bentham used to say, an "exact science." They considered the mind to be an associative mechanism, ruled by precise laws whose constitutive elements are sensations, which were regarded as the ultimate facts of mind. Traditional ethics was substantially a theory of the end of human conduct: It established by a priori means what that end was and deduced from it the rules of conduct. Bentham and Mill intended to substitute for traditional ethics a theory of the motives of conduct—that is, of the specific causes of conduct. If it were ascertained what are the motives and the rules that human beings obey, Bentham and Mill believed, it would be possible to direct human conduct in the same way that nature can be controlled by knowing its causal laws.

These principles remained fundamental in later developments of positivism, first in the work of John Stuart Mill, who was influenced by both Saint-Simon and Comte. Mill, like Saint-Simon and Comte, spoke of reorganizing society on new foundations. He rejected, however, the doctrinaire political and religious absolutism of Comte and defended instead the freedom and development of the individual, to whom he considered the social organization subordinate. Mill's classic *Principles of Political Economy* (1848) concluded by determining the limits of governmental intervention in economic affairs—limits required so that there would be in human existence "a sacred fortress safe from the intrusion of any authority."

Mill's *System of Logic* (1843), which is perhaps the most important work of nineteenth-century positivism, contains a fundamental correction of Comte's view of science. Comte had stressed the rational aspect of science and considered its experimental basis, the verification of facts, as merely preparatory to the formulation of laws. He had excluded the notion that once they were formulated, laws could again be subjected to the test of facts and eventually placed in question by "a too detailed investigation," and he had prescribed for scientific investigation a series of limitations to keep it from being transformed into "a vain and at times a seriously disturbing curiosity." Mill's logic, instead, appealed to a radical empiricism and avoided any dogmatizing of scientific results. The very principles of logic, according to Mill, are generalizations of empirical data, and induction is the only method that science has at its disposal. The basis of induction itself, the principle of the uniformity of the laws of nature, is, in turn, an inductive truth, the fruit of many partial generalizations. Prediction is possible in science only on the basis of past experience, which alone furnishes the evidence both for the major premise and for the conclusion of the traditional syllogism. "'All men are mortal' is not the proof that Lord Palmerston is mortal; but our past experience of mortality authorizes us to infer *both* the general truth and particular fact with the same degree of certainty for one and the other" (*System of Logic,* Bk. II, Ch. 3).

Like the other utilitarians, John Stuart Mill held that the human mind has the same structure as natural phenomena and is knowable in the same ways. "If we knew the person thoroughly, and knew all the inducements which are acting upon him, we could foretell his conduct with as much

certainty as we can predict any physical event" (*System of Logic,* Bk. VI, Ch. 2, 2). To make such predictions possible, he held that a new science, ethology, was needed to study the laws of the formation of character. Mill placed this science alongside Comtian sociology, to which he attributed the task of discovering the laws of progress that make it possible to predict social events infallibly (*ibid.,* Ch. 10, 3).

Mill held that even religion should be based on experience. Experience, by suggesting that there is a limited and imperfect teleological order in nature, permits belief in a divinity of limited power, a kind of demiurge. Such belief encourages a religion of humanity based upon an altruistic ethics and the "supernatural hopes" of mankind.

Social positivism in Italy and Germany. In Italy social positivism had two defenders, Carlo Cattaneo and Giuseppe Ferrari. Both were influenced by the work of Saint-Simon, and both saw him as a continuer of the work of Giambattista Vico, whom they credited with having founded "a science of man in the very heart of humanity."

The German social positivists Ernst Laas, Friedrich Jodl, and Eugen Dühring appealed to Ludwig Feuerbach rather than to Saint-Simon and Comte. But faith in science, in progress based on science, and in a perfect social form to which this progress must lead was the inspiration of all social positivists.

EVOLUTIONARY POSITIVISM

Evolutionary positivism shared the faith in progress of social positivism but justified it in a different way. Evolutionary positivism is based not on society or history but on nature, the sphere of physics and biology. Its immediate forerunners were the work of the geologist Charles Lyell and the doctrine of biological evolution. Lyell, in *The Principles of Geology* (1833), demonstrated that the actual state of the earth is the result not of a series of cataclysms (as Cuvier had argued) but rather of the slow, gradual, and imperceptible action of the same causes that are acting before our eyes. The doctrine of evolution triumphed in 1859 with the publication of Charles Darwin's *Origin of Species,* which first presented adequate proofs of biological evolution and formulated the doctrine in a rigorous way. Lyell's and Darwin's doctrines made possible the formulation of the idea of a natural and necessary progress of the whole universe, beginning with a cosmic nebula and, through the uninterrupted development of the inorganic and organic world, continuing into the "superorganic" development of the human and historical world. It is superfluous to note that the scientific theories which furnish the occasion for the rise of the idea of evolutionary positivism do not constitute the elements of a sufficient proof of it, since it is so highly generalized a hypothesis that it seems to be of a metaphysical nature. Darwin himself remained "agnostic" (to use the term created by another biological evolutionist, T. H. Huxley) with respect to all problems that concern the universe in its totality.

Spencer. The importance of Herbert Spencer, however, and the lasting influence of his work, depends on his defense of universal progress as a continuous and unilinear evolution from a primitive nebula to the more refined products of human civilization. Spencer used the term "evolution" in preference to progress in an early programmatic article of 1857, and even then he saw universal progress as modeled on biological evolution. His definition of evolution as "the passage from the homogeneous to the heterogeneous" or from the simple to the complex was suggested by the development of vegetable and animal organisms, whose parts are chemically and biologically indistinct at first but which then differentiate to form diverse tissues and organs. Spencer held that this process can be discovered in all fields of reality and that each of these fields has a specific science whose task is to recognize and clarify its characteristics. Philosophy is (as Comte conceived of it) the most generalized knowledge of the process of evolution. The role of philosophy begins with the widest generalizations of the individual sciences; from these generalizations it seeks to realize a "completely unified" knowledge. However, neither philosophy nor science, according to Spencer, can take the place of religion.

The truth of religion is that "the existence of the world with all that it contains and all that it encompasses is a *mystery* that always needs to be interpreted" (*First Principles*, London, 1862, Par. 14). All religions, however, fail in giving this interpretation; therefore, the sole task of authentic religion is to remind men of the mystery of the ultimate cause. The task of science, on the other hand, is to extend indefinitely the knowledge of phenomena. Like William Hamilton and Henry Mansel, Spencer held that human knowledge is enclosed within the limits of the relative and the conditioned, that is, within the limits of phenomena. Beyond these limits there is the unlimited and unknown force on which all phenomena depend. The unknowability of this force is revealed in the insolubility of certain problems at the limits of philosophy and science, such problems as those concerning the essence of space, of time, of matter, and of energy, the duration of consciousness (whether finite or infinite), and the subject of thought (whether it is the soul or not).

If Comte's religion of humanity had little success among philosophers and scientists, Spencer's agnosticism found many adherents among them, and for a few decades it was a required attitude for intellectuals generally. However, other positivists, like Roberto Ardigò, rejected agnosticism and denied that one could speak of an "unknowable" in an absolute sense. Ardigò, moreover, wanted to redefine the process of evolution by considering it as "a passage from the indistinct to the distinct," referring to psychological experience rather than to biology.

Spencer wrote on many fields of knowledge—biology, sociology, ethics, politics, and education. When he turned his attention to sociology, he attempted to rescue it from the practical and political task that Comte had assigned to it and to consider it as a theoretical discipline whose task is to describe the development of human society to its present state. This change was accepted by such positivist sociologists as John Lubbock, Edward Tylor, Émile Durkheim, and William Graham Sumner, who were strongly influenced by Spencer.

Evolutionary positivism is, in its more rigorous form, as far from materialism as it is from spiritualism. Spencer affirmed (*ibid.*, Par. 194) that the process of evolution can be interpreted both in terms of matter and movement and in terms of spirituality and consciousness: the Absolute which it manifests can be defined neither as matter nor as mind. Positivism embraces both trends which interpret the concept of evolution materialistically and trends which interpret it spiritualistically. The laws of the conservation of matter discovered by Antoine Lavoisier (1789) and the laws of the conservation of energy implicit in Robert Mayer's discovery of the equivalence of heat and work (1842) were taken as proofs of the hypothesis that a single substance, of which matter and energy are inseparable attributes, is the eternal subject of cosmic evolution and necessarily determines all its characteristics.

Haeckel and monism. The German philosopher Ernst Haeckel termed the view that matter and energy are inseparable attributes of one basic substance "monism" and utilized it to combat the dualism that he held was proper to all religious conceptions based on the duality of spirit and matter, of God and the world. Haeckel also found a decisive confirmation of biological evolution and of its necessity in what he termed the "fundamental biogenetic law" of a parallelism between ontogeny, the development of an individual, and phylogeny, the development of the species to which that individual belongs. Monism was accepted by many chemists, biologists, and psychologists and became popular through the diffusion of Haeckel's writings and of such other works as Ludwig Büchner's *Force and Matter* (1855).

Monism also inspired literary and historical criticism. A passage from the introduction to Hippolyte Taine's *History of English Literature* (1863) has remained famous as an expression of this tendency: "Vice and virtue are products just as vitriol and sugar are, and every complex datum is born from the encounter of other simpler data on which it depends."

Lombroso. The positive school of penal law, founded by Cesare Lombroso, drew its inspiration from materialistic and especially from deterministic positivism. This school taught that criminal behavior depends on inevitable tendencies which are determined by the organic constitution of the delinquent. The structures of this constitution would be analyzed by a corresponding science—criminal anthropology.

Wundt. Evolutionary positivism was also interpreted spiritualistically, notably by Wilhelm Wundt, who sought to substitute "psychophysical parallelism" for materialistic monism. Wundt's doctrine was that mental events do not depend on organic events but constitute a causal series by themselves and correspond point for point to the series of organic events. He made this doctrine the basis of his psychological investigations (Wundt founded the first laboratory of experimental psychology), and for many decades it remained the working hypothesis of experimental psychology. Wundt cultivated, moreover, a "psychology of peoples" which is descriptive sociology, in Spencer's sense. Like Spencer, Wundt intended it to be the study of the evolutionary process that produces institutions, customs, languages, and all the expressions of human society.

Influence of evolutionary positivism. Evolutionary positivism has left as a legacy to contemporary philosophy the idea of a universal, unilinear, continuous, necessary, and necessarily progressive evolution—an idea which forms the background and the explicit or implicit presupposition even of many philosophies which do not recognize their debt to positivism and which, in fact, argue against it. The idea of evolution is fundamental to the philosophies of C. S. Peirce, William James, and John Dewey, as well as to those of George Santayana, Samuel Alexander, and A. N. Whitehead. Some of these philosophers have sought to remove the necessitarian character from the idea of evolution and to include within it an element of chance or freedom (Peirce, James, Dewey) or of novelty and creativity (Henri Bergson, C. Lloyd Morgan). Bergson, who interpreted evolution in terms of consciousness and insisted upon its creative character, explicitly acknowledged his debt to Spencer (*La Pensée et le mouvant*, 3d ed., Paris, 1934, p. 8). It is not without reason that his disciple Édouard Le Roy termed Bergson's doctine a "new positivism," which means a new spiritualistic interpretation of cosmic evolution.

The vitality and the broad diffusion of the legacy of positivism is no sign of its validity. No scientific discipline is as yet able to adduce any sufficient proof in favor of a unilinear, continuous, and progressive cosmic evolution. In fact, in the very field where the phenomena of evolution have been most closely considered—biology—evolution seems to lack precisely those characteristics that positivism attributes to it.

CRITICAL POSITIVISM

Empiriocriticism. In the last decade of the nineteenth century, positivism took on a more critical form through the work of Ernst Mach and Richard Avenarius. In Germany and Austria this critical positivism was known as empiriocriticism. Mach and Avenarius both held that facts (which for them, as for the other positivists, constituted the only reality) were relatively stable sets or groups of sensations connected to and dependent on each other. Sensations are the simple elements which figure in the constitution both of physical bodies and of perceptions or consciousness or the self. These elements are neutral, neither physical nor psychical, and every substantial difference between the physical and the psychical disappears. From this point of view, a "thing" is a set of sensations and the thought of the thing is the same set considered as "perceived" or "represented." For Avenarius, however, the process of interiorization, which he called introjection, and by which the thing is considered as a modification of the subject or as a part of consciousness, is a falsification of "pure" (that is, authentic or genuine) experience. For Avenarius and Mach, science, and knowledge in general, is only an instrument which the human organism uses to confront the infinite mass of sensations and to act in the light of those sensations in such a way as to conserve itself. The function of science is, therefore, economic, not contemplative or theoretical. It conforms to the principle of least action, and its end is the progressive adaptation of the organism to the environment.

Theories concerning concepts, scientific laws, and causality very different from those of classical positivism are the chief results of empiriocriticism. According to Mach a concept is the result of a selective abstraction that groups a large number of facts and considers those elements of these facts that are biologically important—that is, those adapted to excite the appropriate reaction in the organism. Since the variety of the biologically important reactions is much smaller than the variety of facts, the first task is to classify and simplify the facts by means of concepts, each of which constitutes the project of an appropriate reaction. And since the interests with which men confront facts are different, there are different concepts which refer to the same order of facts. The laborer, the doctor, the judge, the engineer, and the scientist all have their own concepts, and they define them in those restricted ways which are appropriate for stimulating the reaction or set of reactions in which each is interested.

The concept of law, which classical positivism conceived of as a constant relationship among facts (a relationship which in turn was considered as a fact) underwent a radical transformation in critical positivism. The Englishman Karl Pearson, in *The Grammar of Science* (1892), gave a kind of *summa* of the fundamental principles of the science of the time. Although Pearson's work utilized Machian concepts, it supplied Mach himself with many inspirations. Pearson affirmed that scientific law is a description, not a prescription: It "never explains the routine of our perception, the sense-impressions we project into an 'outside world.'" Instead of description, Mach preferred to speak of a restriction that the law prescribes on our expectation of phenomena. In any case, he added, "Whether we consider it a restriction of action, an invariable guide to what happens in nature, or an indication for our representations and our thought which bring events to completion in advance, a law is always a limitation of possibilities" (*Erkenntnis und Irrtum*, Leipzig, 1905, Ch. 23).

Mach and Pearson sought to free the notion of causality from the notion of force, which they regarded as an anthropomorphic interpolation. Mach held that the mathematical notion of function should be substituted for that of cause. When science succeeds in gathering various elements into one equation, each element becomes a function of the others. The dependence among the elements becomes reciprocal and simultaneous, and the relation between cause and effect becomes reversible (*Die Mechanik in ihrer Entwicklung*, 4th ed., Leipzig, 1901, p. 513). From this point of view, time, with its irreversible order, is real at the level of sensations and as a sensation. The time of science is, on the other hand, an economic notion which serves for the ordering and prediction of facts.

Along the same lines, a disciple of Mach, Joseph Petzoldt, proposed to substitute for the principle of causality the "law of univocal determination," which would also be applicable to cases of reciprocal action. According to this law, one can find for every phenomenon means which permit determination of the phenomenon in a way that excludes the concurrent possibility of different determinations. According to Petzoldt this law permits the choosing, from among the infinite conditions that either determine a phenomenon or are interposed between it and its cause, of those conditions which effectively contribute to the determination of the phenomenon itself.

Pearson drew from his descriptive concept of law the consequence that scientific laws have only logical, not physical, necessity: "The theory of planetary motion is in itself as logically necessary as the theory of the circle; but in both cases the logic and necessity arise from the definition and axioms with which we mentally start, and do not exist in the sequence of sense-impressions which we hope that they will, at any rate, approximately describe. The necessity lies in the world of conceptions, and is only unconsciously and illogically transferred to the world of perceptions" (*The Grammar of Science,* 2d ed., London, 1900, p. 134).

The empiriocritical branch of positivism is the immediate historical antecedent of the Vienna circle and of neopositivism in general (see LOGICAL POSITIVISM). The sense impressions spoken of by Pearson and the sensations spoken of by Mach, Avenarius, and Petzoldt as neutral elements that constitute all the facts of the world, both physical and psychical, correspond exactly to the objects (*Gegenstände*) spoken of by Ludwig Wittgenstein in his *Tractatus Logico-philosophicus* as the constituents of atomic facts and to the elementary experiences (*Elementarerlebnisse*) spoken of by Rudolf Carnap in *Der logische Aufbau der Welt.* The restriction of necessity to the domain of logic, and the consequent reduction of natural laws to empirical propositions, is also a characteristic of the neopositivism of Wittgenstein, Carnap, and Hans Reichenbach. The critique of the principle of causality frequently recurs in neoempiricism reinforced by consideration of quantum mechanics (Philipp Frank, Reichenbach). The emphasis on prediction, important at all levels of science, is also a result of both empiriocriticism and logical positivism, as is the principle of the empirical verifiability of scientific propositions and the need to test and correct them constantly. What empiriocriticism lacks is the stress on logic and language that is central to contemporary neopositivism. This stress developed out of work done in mathematical logic, especially by Bertrand Russell. Empiriocriticism lacks the concern with logic and the preoccupation with the nature of mathematics and of logical principles that is characteristic of contemporary neopositivism. The view that the proper business of philosophy is the clarification of concepts or the analysis of meanings derives largely from Russell, as does the preoccupation with problems about the status of logical and mathematical principles. The so-called linguistic theory about the nature of logical and mathematical principles, although subsequently endorsed by Russell, was developed by Wittgenstein. The use of the verifiability principle to demarcate meaningful from meaningless sentences and questions derives ultimately from Hume's theory of impressions and ideas, but it is not to be found in any systematic form prior to the publications of the Vienna circle.

(See Logical Positivism and Positivism in Index for articles on philosophers who are frequently classed as positivists.)

Bibliography

There are no complete studies on positivism. For the individual philosophers, see J. Watson, *Comte, Mill and Spencer: An Outline of Philosophy* (Glasgow and New York, 1895); Leslie Stephen, *The English Utilitarians,* 3 vols. (London, 1900); D. G. Charlton, *Positivist Thought in France During the Second Empire, 1852–1870* (Oxford, 1959); and W. M. Simon, *European Positivism in the Nineteenth Century* (Ithaca, N.Y., 1963), which is limited to Comte's positivism and reactions to it.

NICOLA ABBAGNANO
Translated by *Nino Langiulli*

POSITIVISM, LEGAL. See LEGAL POSITIVISM.

POSITIVISM, LOGICAL. See LOGICAL POSITIVISM.

POSSIBILITY. The first known comprehensive discussion of possibility occurs in Aristotle.

Aristotle. According to the doctrine of *On Interpretation* (xiii, 22b), necessity is our basic modal notion, and possibility is to be understood by reference to it, "It is possible that *p*" meaning "It is not necessary that not-*p*." Necessity of this basic kind is absolute necessity, and a necessary proposition is one that truly predicates something of a thing's essence, such as "Every man is rational." Accordingly, a possible proposition is one that attributes an accident to a thing, an accident being a character that, because it is not excluded by a thing's essence, may or may not belong to it, as being seated may or may not belong to a man. Since for Aristotle necessary propositions state "real connections" between essences, they are either real definitions themselves (that is, definitions of a thing's essence) or they are based on real definitions. Propositions stating possibilities are based on real definitions since if the statements are true, they attribute to things only those characteristics whose possession is consistent with the things' essences.

Formal possibility. Although Aristotle's explicit remarks on absolute necessity relate to his theory of essences, he also uses a formal notion of necessity and, thus, of possibility, as when he argues that "Necessarily, every *S* is *L*" follows from "Necessarily, every *M* is *L*" and "Necessarily, every *S* is *M*." That the necessity—and, correlatively, the possibility—involved here is different from the real necessity and possibility just discussed comes out from the fact that the necessity of "Every *S* is *L*" (and the impossibility of "Some *S* is not *L*") is justified wholly by the logical connection signified by "Every . . . is . . ." and by the suboccurrences of "necessarily" in the modal syllogism. Important as this type of necessity and possibility obviously is to his theory of modal syllogisms, he does not seem, however, to have reached the point of formulating its meaning explicitly. (See the discussion of Aristotle's modal syllogisms in the work by William and Martha Kneale cited in the Bibliography.) There can be little doubt, though, that this formal notion of necessity is rooted in the necessity of the first principles of all reasoning, such as the principle of contradiction. These principles cannot, however, be demonstrated, for all demonstration presupposes them (see *Posterior Analytics* I, 3, 72b). They are, rather, known immediately and intuitively, and they cannot be consistently questioned.

Relative possibility. In the *Prior Analytics* (I, 19, 23a) Aristotle distinguishes absolute from relative necessity, and a similar distinction for possibility is implicit in various passages of the *Organon* (For instance, *De Sophisticis Elenchis* iv, 166a22–30). Thus, just as a proposition that does not state an absolute necessity may be considered necessary relative to certain other propositions (as a contingent statement constituting the conclusion of a valid deductive argument may be considered necessary relative to the truth of the premises), so a proposition like "Jones is walking" may be considered impossible relative to the proposition "Jones is sitting" and so "Jones is sitting" may be considered possible relative to "Jones is not running." Although this distinction is intuitively clear, Aristotle does not explicitly say whether relative necessity and relative possibility are to be understood by reference to the sort of real absolute necessity and possibility discussed earlier or whether, as is likely, they are to be understood in relation to the formal notions which he sometimes uses but does not explicitly define.

Potentiality. Another sort of possibility discussed by Aristotle is potentiality, for certain possibilities are said to exist as potentialities of concrete things. Thus, the possibility of a man's reading this or that may be understood in relation to a potentiality (we would say an ability) that he has. For Aristotle a man who can read is a potential reader. Although the notion of potentiality is basic to Aristotle's metaphysics, he thought it could be understood only by analogy: "As a man who is building is to one who knows how to build, as waking is to sleeping, that which sees to that which has sight but has eyes shut, that which is shaped out of matter to its matter, the finished product to the raw material, so in general is actuality to potentiality" (*Metaphysics* 1048b).

Megarians and Stoics. A definition of possibility widely accepted in the Hellenistic period was that of Diodorus Cronus of Megara, who said, "The possible is that which either is or will be true." This identification of possibility with, in effect, present and future actuality was challenged by the Stoics (for example, by Chrysippus), who defined "real" possibility as "that which is not prevented by anything from happening even if it does not happen." Since the Stoics tended to be strict determinists, holding that whatever happens is necessitated by something else, they typically argued that our assessment of nonactuals as possibles could be based only on ignorance, for any conceivable occurrence that does not take place at some time or other is presumably prevented from taking place by the course of nature. Accordingly, their conception of real possibility developed into a conception of what is now known as epistemic possibility, or possibility as consistency with our knowledge. However, because the Stoics were especially interested in formal logic, they had another conception of possibility. According to this conception, necessary propositions (that is, necessary sentences) are those that are always true, such as the propositions of logic and mathematics. Possible propositions are those that are sometimes true. Since today's utterance "A sea battle will occur tomorrow" is sometimes true according to the Stoics, then even though the course of nature may determine its truth with respect to tomorrow, the fact it states still belongs to the category of the possible (in the sense of sometimes true). It is perhaps worth adding that some commentators—for instance, Jaakko Hintikka—find this conception of possibility in Aristotle as well.

Neoplatonists. The next distinctive conception of possibility, which turned out to be of great importance in medieval and modern philosophy, was worked out by the Neoplatonists, though it can be said to have its roots in Plato. According to this tradition, possibilities are not facts or states of affairs (that is, items properly expressed by propositions) but beings or essences which belong to nous or intelligence, the "first emanation of the One." Aristotle had, of course, spoken of potential beings inherent in various matters—for instance, a statue of Hermes existing potentially in a chunk of marble—but the idea of a possible being which cannot be understood in relation to what substances or matters will become under certain conditions or when operated on in a certain way is evidently new. Admittedly, the idea may in a sense be traced back to Plato, for a possible being thus conceived is essentially something thinkable or intelligible, and Plato identified the intelligible with the world of Ideas or Forms. Still, Plato's Ideas were always general rather than specific, of man rather than of Socrates, and this means that the only possibilities, in this sense, that Plato could accommodate were kinds or species. Such Neoplatonists as Plotinus, however, admitted Ideas of individual souls, and these, being nongeneral, may be regarded as the prototypes of the possible beings that occur in such later philosophies as that of Leibniz.

An extremely important aspect of the Neoplatonist treatment of possibles is that all possible beings were held to be actualized; possibility and actuality were regarded, that is, as precisely coextensive. The basic reason for this was that the infinite perfection or "goodness" of the One, which "overflows" into the emanation constituting the world of diverse actuality, requires that every possible being be brought into existence or actualized. This principle of plenitude among actualities is necessary according to the nature of things, for it is an essential feature of the One's perfection "to produce otherness" and "necessarily to do this in the maximum degree."

The Neoplatonic conception of possibles as Ideas in a divine mind which, owing to the perfection of that mind, are necessarily actualized was a recurrent and problematic theme in medieval philosophy. As A. O. Lovejoy has pointed out in *The Great Chain of Being*, medieval writers tended to conceive the "love" or "goodness" of the Christian God (in whose mind the Ideas were now said to exist) as an "immeasurable and inexhaustible energy," a love of which "the only beneficiaries . . . were not actual sentient creatures or already existing moral agents, but Platonic Ideas, conceived figuratively as aspirants for the grace of actual existence" (p. 68).

Abelard. Abelard, writing in the early twelfth century, was led to maintain that what can be is the same as what can be produced by God and that "it is intrinsically impossible for God to do (or make) or to leave undone (or unmade) anything other than the things that he actually does at some time do or omit to do; or to do anything in any other manner at any other time than that in which it actually is done" (Lovejoy, p. 71).

Aquinas. Since Abelard's view of possibility and actuality seemed not only to deny God's divine freedom but also, in implying that the created world was so good that it could not be better, to "make the creation equal to the

Creator," it was regarded as heretical. Accordingly, other Schoolmen, who like Aquinas agreed that "all things pre-exist in God by their types (*rationes*)," had to maintain that the creation involved a selection among the Ideas. In this view not all possibles are actual, and what is actual is not necessary; there are, that is, possible beings that God could have created but did not create, and he did not have to create the things that he did create. In order to square this claim with God's goodness, Aquinas found it necessary to invoke the Aristotelian distinction between absolute and hypothetical (or relative) necessity and possibility, for although it is absolutely possible for God, good as he is, to have created other than what he did create, it may nevertheless be admitted that, relative to his choice, which was "becoming to" rather than necessary to his goodness, the existence of what is actual is necessary and could not be otherwise. That is, relative to this premise, it is impossible for anything to exist that does not sooner or later actually exist.

But even granting the distinction between absolute and relative possibility, it might be objected that Aquinas is still imposing a limit on God's freedom, since if what actually exists is determined by God's selection from a class of possibilities, it would appear that God could not, in an absolute sense, have created anything not belonging to this class. In answer to this, however, Aquinas maintained that what is absolutely impossible is actually self-contradictory and that what is self-contradictory is contrary to God's nature, repugnant to being, and, thus, not an object at all. ("So it is better to say that what involves a contradiction cannot be done rather than God cannot do it," *Summa Theologica* I, 25, 3–4.) In making this reply, Aquinas may seem to be introducing a formal notion of absolute possibility of the sort defended in more recent times. Yet, as with Aristotle, the category of possibility in question is grounded not in linguistic or purely logical considerations but wholly in intelligible essences ("intelligible forms"); in other words, the definitions with respect to which one determines the consistency or intelligible character of a term or idea are real rather than nominal, which means that the possibility in question is a species of "real" possibility, not the kind of formal possibility discussed in modern times.

Hobbes. In the modern period we find in Hobbes a view that not only contrasts vividly with the typical medieval one but which, confused as it is, is also occasionally defended even today. Hobbes's view contrasts with the medieval one because conceivable beings are not necessarily possible beings; the only inference Hobbes drew from the fact that a being is conceivable is that words standing for it are not gibberish. To be possible, the necessary conditions for a thing's existence must be satisfied. This being so, every possible being, event, or state of affairs is at some time or another actual, "for if it shall never be produced, then those things will never concur which are requisite for the production of it" (*Elements of Philosophy* X, 4). Since for Hobbes whatever exists does so in virtue of necessary causes, we can call something possible (or contingent), as opposed to necessary, only when we do not know the cause that will produce it. This view plainly goes back to that of the Stoics, for it implies that the only legitimate possibilities that are not also necessi-

ties are epistemic possibilities—that is, things or states of affairs whose existence is consistent with our knowledge at a given time.

Descartes. Descartes's approach to possibility is important mainly because it is essentially psychologistic: What is possible is what is clearly and distinctly conceivable. Descartes admitted, of course, that if the idea of a thing involves a contradiction, it is impossible as well, but this is because contradictory ideas cannot be clearly and distinctively conceived. The latter criterion is basic for Descartes because in his view not all impossibilities involve contradictions. He held that there are a priori truths which, though necessary and guaranteed by the goodness of God, are not analytic in the modern sense and that their denials, which state impossibilities, are not therefore invariably contradictory. To know whether a given idea—for instance, the idea of a circular rectangle—does represent a possibility, one must be able to form a clear and distinct idea of it; if one is able to form such an idea, one has the assurance of God's goodness that it does represent a real possibility, the sort of thing that God could actualize if he chose to do so.

Spinoza. According to Spinoza, "a thing is said to be impossible either because the essence of the thing itself or its definition involves a contradiction, or because no external cause exists determinate to the production of such a thing." Since Spinoza in effect adopted the Neoplatonic principle of plenitude, he held that if the idea of a thing does not involve a contradiction, it must be actual, in fact, necessary, for all self-consistent beings are determined to exist, and necessarily exist, by the very nature of reality, which he calls "God."

> [Accordingly, a] thing cannot be called contingent unless with reference to a deficiency of our knowledge. For if [and here Spinoza introduces the notion of epistemic possibility] we do not know that the essence of a thing involves a contradiction, or if we actually know it involves *no* contradiction, and nevertheless can affirm nothing with certainty about its existence because the order of causes is concealed from us, that thing can never *appear to us* as necessary or impossible, and therefore we call it either contingent or possible. (*Ethics* I, Proposition 33, Note 1; italics added)

Leibniz. Leibniz' view of possibility at first seems both simple and remarkably contemporary: Possible beings or possible states of affairs are simply beings or states of affairs whose conception is free from contradiction. In point of fact, however, Leibniz' views are neither simple nor contemporary. For one thing, since God's concept of a thing includes all facts about it, including such apparently accidental facts as that it once crossed a certain river in Peru or that it was once knocked over by a man named Jones, it turns out that if a thing is possible, it is so only relative to its place in a possible world, one including, for instance, certain possible rivers and certain possible men. Thus, a possible being is strictly a being whose existence is compossible with the existence of a class of beings, with the individual members of some possible world. Moreover, a Leibnizian possible being is, like a possible being of Plotinus, an idea in the mind of God, an idea which seems to strive for the perfection of actual existence. As a recent commentator has put it, "Leibniz thinks of creation as the removing of a hindrance to the exercise of a power which is latent in possible beings. . . . He seems to have the queer picture in mind of all possible beings waiting to have the bar to the exercise of their powers removed" (R. L. Saw, *Leibniz*, p. 83). Finally, Leibniz also seemed to regard the difference between possibility and actuality as a matter of degree, for having admitted that possibility is really a matter of compossibility, he went on to say, "The existent may be defined as that which is compatible with more things than is anything incompatible with itself" and even "I say therefore that the existent is the being which is compatible with most things, or the most possible being, so that all coexistent things are equally possible" (*ibid.*, p. 83). Since the ground of all possibility is, ontologically conceived, the divine essence, it follows that there is nothing in any way conventional about a Leibnizian possibility. His possibilities are conceived as "real" possibilities, and he is operating squarely in the tradition of Christian Platonism.

Hume. The British empiricists, typically rejecting the claims of conceptualism as defended by most rationalists, seemed to embrace more fully the idea that possibility is a matter of logical consistency. In remarking that "the contrary of every matter of fact is still possible, because it can never imply a contradiction," Hume appears firmly committed to a fairly up-to-date view of (formal) possibility. As Arthur Pap, however, has pointed out, in adding to the quoted sentence "and is conceived by the mind with the same facility and distinctness," Hume discloses his tacit commitment to a psychologistic conception of possibility (what is possible is what is conceivable), which was held not only by Descartes but which also has been endemic in recent discussion (see Pap, *Semantics and Necessary Truth*, pp. 75 ff., and Hume's *Enquiry Concerning Human Understanding*, Section IV, Part 1).

Kant. With Kant we have not only a clear identification of a priori possibility in something like its contemporary form, but we also find a careful distinction between logical and physical (or nomological) possibility. For men like Spinoza, who identified the logical with the real order, there was plainly no sense in this distinction, and there was little place for it in the philosophies of the Greek and medieval thinkers. It is, however, essential to the contemporary outlook. Kant expresses the distinction thus:

A concept is always possible if it is not self-contradictory. This is the logical criterion of possibility, and through it objects are distinguished from the *nihil negativum*. But it may none the less be an empty concept, unless the objective reality of the synthesis through which the concept is generated has been specifically proved; and such proof . . . rests on principles of possible experience, and not on the principle of analysis (the law of contradiction). This is a warning against arguing directly from the logical possibility of concepts to the real possibility of things. (*Critique of Pure Reason*, A597 – B625, note)

[Thus, the possibility of such concepts as] a special ultimate mental power of intuitively anticipating the future . . . [are] altogether groundless, as they cannot

be based on experience and its known laws; and without such confirmation they are arbitrary combinations of thoughts, which, though free from contradiction, can make no claim to objective reality, and none, therefore, as to the [real] possibility of an object such as we here profess to think. (*Ibid.*, A223 – B270)

To ascertain that such things are empirically, as opposed to merely logically, possible, "we must ascertain whether the nature of things so described agree with the formal conditions of actual experience."

Critical remarks. Not all the conceptions of possibility discussed in the preceding section on the history of philosophy are equally tenable; however, most of the conceptions that are tenable, or at least tenable from a contemporary point of view, have been alluded to in some way. Of course, the variety of things that might be meant by the word "possibility" in everyday life is very great, as are the possible meanings of the word "can" (see CAN). There are, however, five basic categories of possibility that are generally recognized today as both distinct and equally legitimate, and four of these have at least been mentioned in the short historical survey given above. These four are absolute possibility, both conceptual (or a priori) and nomological (that is, physical or "real"); relative possibility, both conceptual and nomological; epistemic possibility; and possibility as ability or capacity (this sense corresponds to Aristotle's potentiality). The fifth category of possibility, which seems not to have attracted the attention of traditional philosophers, may be described as possibility as minimal probability.

Absolute possibility. The notion of conceptual, or a priori, possibility is at present an extremely controversial one. Some philosophers, such as Quine, seem anxious to disown this sort of possibility, finding it both useless and mysterious (see *Word and Object,* pp. 195 ff.) Others, such as most logical positivists, accept the notion as legitimate only if it is taken as equivalent to logical, or formal, possibility, a formal possibility being a state of affairs the description of which is formally consistent—that is, such that, by reference only to basic logical principles and the explicit definitions (if any) of the terms occurring in that description, no formal contradiction is deducible. Others, such as Wilfrid Sellars, accept the notion of a priori possibility in a still broader sense, according to which anything consistent with basic conceptual necessities is declared possible. By a basic conceptual necessity we mean, roughly, a statement which, though not necessarily a formal truth in the above sense, may yet be said to be true *ex vi terminorum* (according to usage). An example of such a statement would be "Anything that is red all over cannot simultaneously be green." Exactly why and in what sense these statements are true *ex vi terminorum* are questions of dispute even among their champions. Here it is perhaps sufficient to say that they have been termed "meaning postulates" (Carnap), "object-language surrogates for linguistic rules" (Max Black), "implicit definitions" (Sellars), and the like. There can be no doubt that the notion of a conceptual necessity is an extremely problematic one, but if it is accepted as tenable, a priori possibility can be defined according to the Aristotelian schema: "It is a priori possible that *P*" means "It is not a priori (conceptually) necessary that not-*P*." It is clear that formal possibilities constitute a subclass of a priori possibilities in the sense defined.

The notion of nomological, or physical, possibility is, in matters of detail, almost as controversial as that of conceptual possibility. Here the difficulty concerns the identity and character of a law of nature, for however laws of nature are to be understood or analyzed (on this see LAWS OF SCIENCE AND LAWLIKE STATEMENTS), we commonly take them to rule out certain states of affairs as physically, or nomologically, impossible. Thus, it is by virtue of a law of thermodynamics that a perpetual motion machine is declared impossible, and it is by virtue of the law of gravity that it is impossible for unsupported bodies to dangle motionless above the surface of the earth. As in the case of a priori possibility, physical possibility is interdefinable with the appropriate kind of necessity, for it is the consistency of describable situations (states of affairs) with principles of nomological necessity (laws of nature) that determines their possibility.

Relative possibility. Relative possibility, whether conceptual or nomological, is definable with reference to absolute possibility, conceptual and nomological. A state of affairs is relatively possible (in either of these ways) just in case the state of affairs is possible relative to some hypothesis. Thus, to take two cases of conceptual possibility, Jones's sitting is impossible relative to the fact that he is standing, and relative to our present state of technology, it is nomologically impossible for a man to make a safe journey to the planet Saturn. Both of these cases are only relative possibilities, since neither is inconsistent with the appropriate necessities. That Jones is sitting is perfectly consistent with basic conceptual necessities, and a man's journeying safely to Saturn does not violate a law of nature.

Epistemic possibility. The notion of epistemic possibility is apparently clearer than possibility as ability (Aristotle's potentiality) and as minimal probability, but it actually presupposes them. A state of affairs is deemed epistemically possible if it is not ruled out by the knowledge, both a priori and scientific, that we happen to have at a certain time. In other words, if, relative to the knowledge we happen to have at a certain time, it would be inconsistent for us to admit a certain thing, event, or state of affairs as actual, then the existence of that thing, event, or state of affairs is epistemically impossible for us at that time. It is clear that because the state of our knowledge is constantly changing, what is epistemically possible at one time may be declared epistemically impossible at another time. And if our world is a deterministic one in the strict Hobbesian sense, then if we were Laplacean ideal knowers aware of all the laws of nature and all initial conditions, all epistemic possibilities would at some time have to be actual. Thus, the collapse of modal distinctions that in the opinion of Hobbes, the Stoics, and even some contemporary writers is forced upon us by a deterministic view of nature really affects the domain of epistemic, not nomological, possibilities, and it does this only on the hypothesis that we are ideal knowers.

Possibility as ability. Possibility as ability, which corresponds to Aristotle's potentiality, is perplexing mainly to the extent that the notion of a subjunctive conditional is perplexing (see IF). We often have this sense of possibility in mind when we wonder what a man can do under certain conditions—can he do twenty push-ups after that big meal? is it possible for him to do so many? Here the notion of possibility is bound up with the notion of an ability, a capacity, or a capability of doing something under certain circumstances. And, roughly speaking, to have such an ability, capacity, or capability is to be such that if in certain circumstances one were to want, will, intend, or so on to perform the action in question, one would be successful in performing it. Similarly, for inanimate things to have a certain ability, capacity, or even disposition is to be such that if under certain circumstances some specific thing were to happen or be done to it, a particular result (termed the manifestation of the capacity or disposition in question) would occur. In general, then, abilities, capacities, and dispositions, though there are important differences among them, may be said to be definable by sentences having the form of subjunctive conditionals. Accordingly, to the extent that the logic of sentences of this kind is well understood, the notion of possibility as capacity, ability, or propensity (either generally or in certain circumstances) may be said to be one of the least problematic categories of possibility.

Minimal probability. The final sense of possibility, the one that may be termed "minimal probability," rarely occurs in technical contexts, but it is familiar in everyday talk and, as Norman Malcolm has argued, it tends to turn up in philosophical discussions about verification and certainty. The peculiarity of this sense of possibility is that it admits of degrees ("There is a slight, as opposed to a very real, possibility that *P*") and that when people are asked to justify their claim that such-and-such is possible, they respond by citing evidence that provides some support for the actuality of what they term "possible." Thus, to take Malcolm's examples, if a man's wife tells him that their neighbor Mr. Jones will possibly visit them one evening, she might answer, on being asked why she thinks so, that the neighbor told her that he would visit them if he did not have to work that evening. Again, if a Greek scholar were to say to a colleague, "It is possible that Plato did not write the *Republic*," he might naturally back this claim by showing that there is some evidence, though admittedly very weak evidence, that Plato did not write the *Republic*. This sense of possibility is plainly different from the four senses described above since none of them implies that "it is possible" may have the force of "there is a slight probability."

Bibliography

Aristotle, *Basic Works,* Richard P. McKeon, ed. New York, 1941.

Bergmann, Gustav, *Meaning and Existence.* Madison, Wis., 1960.

Black, Max, *Models and Metaphors.* Ithaca, N.Y., 1962.

Carnap, Rudolf, *Meaning and Necessity,* 2d ed. Chicago, 1956.

Copleston, Frederick, *A History of Philosophy,* 7 vols. London, 1959——.

Descartes, René, *Philosophical Works,* E. S. Haldane and G. R. T. Ross, eds., 2 vols. New York, 1931.

Hintikka, Jaakko, "Necessity, Universality, and Time in Aristotle." *Adjatus,* Vol. 22 (1959).

Hobbes, Thomas, *Hobbes: Selections*, J. E. Woodbridge, ed. New York, 1930.

Hume, David, *An Enquiry Concerning Human Understanding*, L. A. Selby-Bigge, ed. Oxford, 1902.

Kant, Immanuel, *Critique of Pure Reason*, translated by N. K. Smith. London, 1961.

Kneale, William, and Kneale, Martha, *The Development of Logic*. Oxford, 1963.

Leibniz, Gottfried von, *Leibniz: Selections*, Philip P. Wiener, ed. New York, 1951.

Lovejoy, A. O., *The Great Chain of Being*. Cambridge, Mass., 1936.

Malcolm, Norman, "The Verification Argument," in Max Black, ed.,*Philosophical Analysis*. Ithaca, N.Y., 1950.

Pap, Arthur, *Semantics and Necessary Truth*. New Haven, 1958.

Quine, W. V., *Word and Object*. Cambridge, Mass., 1961.

Saw, R. L., *Leibniz*. Harmondsworth, England, 1954.

Sambursky, S., "On the Possible and the Probable in Ancient Greece." *Osiris*, Vol. 12 (1956), 35–48.

Sellars, Wilfrid, "Is There a Synthetic A Priori?," in his *Science, Perception, and Reality*. London, 1963.

Sellars, Wilfrid, "Meditationes Leibnizienses." *American Philosophical Quarterly*, Vol. 2 (1965), 105–118.

Spinoza, Baruch, *Philosophy of B. de Spinoza*, translated by R. H. M. Elwes. New York, 1955.

Thomas Aquinas, *Basic Writings*, Anton C. Pegis, ed., 2 vols. New York. 1945.

BRUCE AUNE

POTENTIALITY. See POSSIBILITY.

POWER. The meanings of "power," "influence," "control," and "domination" are uncertain, shifting, and overlapping. Although two of these words may be interchangeable in one context, in another context one of the words may refer to a genus and another to a species, or one may refer to a cause and another to an effect. To substitute "power" for "influence" would not matter much in the sentence "The United States has very great influence in South American politics," but to interchange them would radically change the meaning of the sentence "Colonel House's power derived not from any constitutional authority but from his influence over President Wilson."

Shifts like this account for much of the intractability of problems associated with power. For instance, power is often said to be a relation (H. Lasswell, C. J. Friedrich, P. H. Partridge), yet we talk about the distribution of power, about the power of speech, about seeking power as a means to future enjoyment (Hobbes), or about power as "the production of intended effects" (Russell). If power is a relation, between what kind of terms or things does it hold? Does power over men require a minimum of acquiescence, consent, or cooperation (Hume, Friedrich), or can it be analogous to a physical force acting on an otherwise inert object? Is to exercise power always to succeed in what one intends (Russell, Lasswell), or can a man exercise power in ignorance of what he is doing (R. A. Dahl, P. H. Partridge, F. E. Oppenheim), like a ruling elite that neither knows nor cares about the effects of its actions on other classes?

Instead of seeking a single analysis of "power," it is more helpful to think of diverse uses of "power" and of associated words like "influence" as instances of different members of a family of concepts that do not all share any one particular characteristic but have various relations and resemblances by which they are recognizably kin. One might construct a power paradigm combining as many of these family features as possible. Thus, "A, by his power over B, successfully achieved an intended result r; he did so by making B do b, which B would not have done but for A's wishing him to do so; moreover, although B was reluctant, A had a way of overcoming this."

There are five main features of this paradigm: (1) an intention manifest in the exercise of power; (2) the successful achievement of this intention; (3) a relationship between at least two people; (4) the intentional initiation by one of actions by the other; and (5) a conflict of interest or wishes engendering a resistance that the initiator overcomes. Not every feature would be present, of course, in every instance in which we properly speak of power; but we can examine how different instances are related to the paradigm and to one another, and thus throw some light on a few of the questions listed above.

Power and conflict. Some instances of power do not involve overcoming resistance to an initiative. A charismatic leader's power over his followers consists in being able merely by suggestion to move them to do willingly what he wants, even though their interests might have led them to act differently. The family of power concepts might be arranged along a conflict scale (Partridge): at the end at which conflict is least would lie instances of influence, while at the other end would lie instances of domination, and in between, instances of authority. In the extreme case, exercising influence would not involve overcoming resistance, for to manipulate a man's actions by shaping what he considers to be his interests is not to impose action upon him *in the face of* his interests. Yet this would still be an instance of power satisfying the first four features of the paradigm.

The limiting case at the end of the scale at which conflict is least would be rational persuasion, for to offer a man good reasons for doing something is not to exercise power over him, although it may influence his decision. One possible difference between influence and power, then, seems to be that power generally implies a difference of standing between the two parties: the one stimulates, the other reacts. Rational persuasion, on the contrary, to the extent that it criticizes and invites criticism, presupposes at least the possibility of a dialogue between equals. To the extent that persuasion is really rational, the influence is not so much that of the persuader as of his arguments; the same arguments from anyone else would do as well. (By contrast, a threat of violence is more effective coming from a strong man than from a weak man.) Of course, if A rationally persuades B to help him, A may get power—not over B, however, but over C or D, or even simply the power to do something he could not otherwise do.

Power, injury, and interest. In the case of the man who punishes another for disobedience, conditions (1), (3), and (5) of the paradigm would be satisfied, but not (2) and (4), for the initiative has been refused. Instead, it suffices for an instance of power if the power-holder successfully and intentionally makes the subject suffer for refusing the initiative. And by yet a further extension of meaning, one can exercise power over someone by deliberately making him suffer, whether or not he has refused an initiative. Just as in the limiting case of rational persuasion one could speak of influence but hardly of power, so at the other end of the scale one can talk of power but not of influence, for influence is manifest in what a man is, does, or believes, not in what is simply made to happen to him by another man.

A stoic would probably resist the extension of the concept of power to cover the mere infliction of suffering. By not caring about physical pain or external conditions, he might say, one can remove oneself from the power of another man. So too Luther believed that a true Christian is free because no outer things can touch him at any significant point. It would seem that what characterizes a power situation of this kind is not just the ability to make someone suffer, which after all a dentist possesses, but rather to do him harm—that is, to attack his interests. Thus, by revising the notion of a man's interests, and therefore the notion of harm, the stoic or the Christian can deny the reality of one man's power over another, since nothing that another man can do to me can affect my real interests; I am always free, if once I see what those interests are. This argument is a little odd, because the concept of power generally implies a restriction on choice; but according to the stoic or Christian view, one can always choose to make the restriction insignificant, and therefore one can choose whether to be in the power of another. In that case, there could not be a real restriction, and all power would be illusory. But then, what would power be like if it were real?

The stoic argument demonstrates, however, that whether one man has power over another depends not merely on what he can do to the other but also on the importance to be attached to his action and on whether the subject can reasonably be expected to disregard it. One would not say that X was in Y's power if one thought that what Y could do to X was trivial—something that X could or should readily ignore.

Again, although threats of real harm are an exercise of power, bribes or promises of reward are not, unless some special feature of character or situation makes them irresistible—that is, unless no one so placed could reasonably be expected to resist them (although some in fact might). This is not to say, of course, that a man cannot exercise power by bribery. However, it need not be power *over* his hirelings but power over others *through* them; or it may be power only in the still more general sense of an ability to bring about an intended result. Thus, we speak of power in situations in which a man could either successfully determine another's actions or do him harm. An ability to do him some good is not in itself power over him, although the threat of withholding a good that he has come to count on may well be.

Problems of power as a relation. Power may not be a relation between people but between a person and a thing. There is a nonsocial kind of power that is simply an ability to produce an intended result, like a tenor's power to smash a tumbler with a high C. And even in a social context, the financier's power to destroy a government comes very close to this, for in this instance too power is manifest merely in the active achievement of an intended result. Although the financier no doubt works by initiating actions

on the part of others, the relation between him and his object (the government) is that which exists between agent and patient. This case can be distinguished both from that in which power is exercised by punishing a subject for noncompliance and from that in which power is used to inflict deliberate injury. For in the present case the object of the exercise may be only to remove an obstacle. The manifestation of power does not consist in the government's being made to suffer, for it would be just as much a manifestation of power if the financier had chosen instead to prop it up or if the government welcomed its downfall as a blessed release from responsibility. Power is manifest simply in that what happens is the result of the financier's intentional action, just as the tenor's power is manifest in his being able to break a glass whenever he likes.

Power is of course relational in a logical sense in that it requires more than one term for a complete statement; and if more than one of the terms is a person, and the relation presupposes institutions, rules, and so forth, power will certainly be a social relation. But writers who stress that power is a relation usually mean that it is an initiative–response relationship of the kind that C. J. Friedrich had in mind when he wrote, "The power seeker must find human beings who value the things [he controls] sufficiently to obey his orders in return" (*Constitutional Government and Democracy*, p. 12).

Now, Friedrich's point is substantially true in those instances in which power implies a successful initiative and even perhaps in those instances in which power tends to injure its subject. To set about hurting someone, one must know how to get the right kind of response: there is no point in depriving nonsmokers of tobacco. It is not so clear, however, that the financier's power is of this type, for he does not secure a response from the government; he merely makes something happen to it. Although his agents respond to his initiatives, one must distinguish the power he has over them from the power he has over the government. These powers would be of the same kind only if he were able not just to destroy the government, but to use it as he wished. But it is presumably because he cannot do this that he uses his power to destroy it.

This analysis further elucidates the relation between power and consent. We have seen that at one extreme a man may exercise power over another by influencing his desires, or a man may do whatever he is told by another because he believes that he ought to do so, which is an instance of authority. Both cases imply some measure of consent or acquiescence, if not to the particular initiative, then to the right of the initiator to issue it. But in cases in which power depends on threats or on physical coercion, the subject's acquiescence amounts to no more than that he continues to value whatever is being used as a lever against him—an acquiescence that only the stoic, perhaps, would seriously regard as a matter of choice. However, political power cannot be entirely coercive. The few can rule the many because the many believe either that the few are entitled to do so or that they could harm them if they disobeyed. But they would not think that coercion were possible if they did not also believe that most of the people were prepared to obey without coercion. A political power situation, therefore, must almost always contain some elements of acquiescence as well as coercion—*almost* always because it is at least theoretically possible that a reign of terror might enslave a whole people simply by sowing such mistrust that its opponents could never know their own potential strength.

Power and intention. Still further from the paradigm is the case in which one says quite generally that a person is powerful, or that he seeks power, without specifying the range of possible intended action or the persons subject to the power. Usually it would not be difficult to supply terms to complete either one or both of these blanks. Political theorists commonly insist that comparisons of power, without reference to its "domain" and "scope," are meaningless (H. Lasswell and A. Kaplan, F. E. Oppenheim). However, some have tried to generalize the concept by disregarding intentionality. R. A. Dahl defines power as "the difference in probability of an event, given certain actions by A, and the probability of the event given no such action by A" ("The Concept of Power," p. 214). At this level of abstraction, "power" is freed not only from intentionality but also from achievement and conflict; what remains is a relation between a stimulus and a reaction. Elsewhere (*Modern Political Analysis*, p. 40), Dahl defines "influence" as a relation among actors in which one induces others to act in some way in which they would not otherwise act. Dahl would want to purge, if he could, the hint of intentionality in the word "induce." Like a field of force in mechanics, power is a potential for creating disturbance, like the potential of a stone cast in a pond for creating ripples. But this has some odd results. Instead of suffering a *loss* of power, the crashing financier who brings down thousands with him in his fall would be exercising a power that is perhaps greater than ever before. Admittedly, it is a mark of power if a man's actions cause disturbances, even if he is careless or even ignorant of them. Nevertheless, if powerful men cause incidental and unintended disturbances, they do so in the course of *getting what they want*. (C. Wright Mills's conception of a "power elite" seems to be of this kind.) One would not call someone powerful who, like a careless smoker constantly causing fires, was forever causing disturbances but never achieving anything he intended; nor is it clear that any useful methodological purpose in political science would be served by a definition of power that permitted the production of unintended effects alone to serve as a criterion.

To possess power or to be powerful is, then, to have a generalized potentiality for getting one's own way or for bringing about changes (at least some of which are intended) in other people's actions or conditions. "Influence," it is true, is used in a more general sense. If a parent has the unintended influence of stiffening his child's determination to be as different from him as possible, this would not be described as an instance of power: it is more like "the influence of climate on national character." The use of the term "influence" suggests that there is a causal relationship between the behavior of the parent and that of the child (cf. P. H. Partridge, "Some Notes on the Concept of Power," p. 114). "A writer's influence on succeeding generations" stands somewhere between this case and that of influence by rational persuasion. For a writer may have influence only to the extent that other writers recognize his merits and choose to imitate him. Although such influence may not be intended, still it is not a cause, at least in the sense that climate is a possible cause of national character. In any case, none of these is an instance of an influence in the sense that House *had* influence with Wilson. "To *use* one's influence" usually implies actively and intentionally working through or on other people, and one who can do this recurrently "*has* influence." Of course, people who have power (that is, who can do many things they want and induce many other people to accept their initiative) are likely on that account to influence (that is, to have effects on) other aspects of society in ways that neither they nor their social inferiors necessarily understand. Other classes, envying and admiring them, may imitate their tastes and practices, and in this sense they may be influenced by them. But this influence is not a manifestation of power; it is only one of its effects.

Bibliography

CLASSIC THEORIES OF POLITICAL POWER

Aiken, H. D., ed., *Hume's Moral and Political Philosophy.* New York, 1948.

Hobbes, Thomas, *Leviathan,* M. Oakeshott, ed. Oxford, 1946.

Hume, David, "Of the First Principles of Government," in *Essays Literary, Moral and Political* (1741). London, 1963.

Hume, David, *Treatise of Human Nature* (1740), L. A. Selby-Bigge, ed. Oxford, 1951. Book III.

Spinoza, Benedict de, *Tractatus Theologico-politicus.* Hamburg, 1670.

Spinoza, Benedict de, *Tractatus Politicus* (1677).

Spinoza, Benedict de, *The Political Works,* translated and edited by A. G. Wernham. London, 1958.

Plamenatz, John, *Man and Society,* 2 vols. London, 1963. A critical discussion of classic theories.

GENERAL PHILOSOPHICAL DISCUSSIONS

Acton, H. B., "Logique et casuistique du pouvoir," in *Annales de philosophie politique: Tomes I et II: Le Pouvoir,* 1956–1957. Vol. II, pp. 69–86.

Emmet, Dorothy, "The Concept of Power." *PAS,* Vol. 54 (1953–1954), 1–26.

Friedrich, C. J., "Le probleme de pouvoir dans la theorie constitutionnaliste," in *Annales de Philosophie Politique: Tomes I et II: Le Pouvoir.* Paris, 1956–1957. Vol. I, pp. 33–51.

Jouvenel, Bertrand de, *Le Pouvoir.* Geneva, 1945. Translated by J. F. Huntington as *On Power; Its Nature and the History of Its Growth.* Boston, 1962.

Jouvenel, Bertrand de, *Pure Theory of Politics.* Cambridge, 1963.

Partridge, P. H., "Some Notes on the Concept of Power." *Political Studies,* Vol. 11 (1963), 107–125.

Partridge, P. H., "Politics and Power." *Philosophy,* Vol. 38 (1963), 117–136.

Polin, R., "Sens et fondement du pouvoir chez John Locke," in *Annales de Philosophie Politique: Tomes I et II: Le Pouvoir.* Paris, 1956–1957. Vol. I, pp. 53–90.

Russell, Bertrand, *Power.* London, 1938.

SOCIOLOGY AND METHODOLOGY OF POLITICAL SCIENCE

Bierstedt, Robert, "An Analysis of Social Power." *American Sociological Review,* Vol. 15 (1950), 730–738.

Dahl, Robert A., "The Concept of Power," in Sidney S. Ulmer, ed., *Introductory Readings in Political Behavior.* Chicago, 1961.

Friedrich, Carl J., *Constitutional Government and Democracy.* Boston, 1950.

Friedrich, Carl J., *Man and His Government.* New York, 1963.

Lasswell, Harold D., and Kaplan, Abraham, *Power and Society: A Framework for Political Inquiry.* New Haven, 1950.

Merriam, Charles E., "Political Power," in H. D. Laswell, C. E. Merriam, and T. V. Smith, *A Study of Power.* Glencoe, Ill., 1950.

Oppenheim, Felix E., *Dimensions of Freedom.* New York, 1961.

Weber, Max, *From Max Weber; Essays in Sociology,* translated and edited by H. H. Gerth and C. Wright Mills. London, 1948.

Walter, E. V., "Power and Violence." *American Political Science Review,* Vol. 58 (1964), 350–360.

STANLEY I. BENN

PRAGMATICISM. See PEIRCE, CHARLES SANDERS; PRAGMATISM.

PRAGMATICS. See SEMANTICS.

PRAGMATIC THEORY OF TRUTH. Pragmatic theories of truth are best understood in the light of Charles S. Peirce's declaration, ". . . there is no distinction of meaning so fine as to consist in anything but a possible difference of practice" ("How to Make Our Ideas Clear," 1878).

Peirce's view of truth. The above quote from Peirce represents the claim that when one knows how an object will react to experimental handling, one has achieved a clear idea of that object. To say that a substance is hard is to say that it will not be scratched by other substances. Peirce's criterion of meaning was pointed against traditional Cartesian subjectivism. Descartes, as Peirce saw it, took an idea to be clear if it seemed clear to him, never considering the possibility that an idea may seem clear without really being clear. It is not surprising, therefore, that Peirce, in considering the meaning of truth, insisted on its public character, deploring the Cartesian view, according to which the individual judgment is the test of truth.

Peirce called philosophical disputes about truth absurd when truth is conceived apart from its practical bearings on the actual doubts and beliefs which frame human inquiry. He argued that metaphysical visions of truth and falsity that envisage them as something existing apart from the conduct of inquiry violate the principle of Ockham's razor. Moreover, the doubt that impels scientific investigation is real, but its philosophical counterpart, Cartesian doubt, is feigned. Philosophers who imagine that a man can simply will to doubt apparently think that doubting is as easy as lying, that one can do it simply by saying "I doubt." Men, however, seek belief, and the search for truth in practice is the search for belief. The experimental method attains those beliefs that will ultimately be accepted by the scientific community. "The opinion which is fated to be ultimately agreed to by all who investigate, is what we mean by the truth . . ." ("How to Make Our Ideas Clear"). If belief "were to tend indefinitely toward absolute fixity," we would have the truth ("What Pragmatism Is," in *The Monist,* 1905).

Peirce's definition was an attempt to clarify truth as it shows up in the practice of inquiry. Yet did it really accomplish this? By defining truth as "absolute fixity" of belief, Peirce set it apart from the fixed opinion of the scientific community, which is all that inquiry really yields. What pragmatic meaning can be attributed to notions such as "absolute fixity" or "the opinion which is fated to be ulti-

mately agreed to"? One would imagine that these concepts, too, would be unacceptable on the principle of Ockham's razor.

James's interpretation of pragmatism. William James and John Dewey applied the pragmatic method of framing concepts to the notion of truth. There is a marked difference, however, in the results achieved by James and Dewey. Under James's handling, Peirce's method suffered a crucial transformation.

Peirce had insisted that a clear concept must have practical bearings on conduct. But Peirce, it must be remembered, was thinking of the practice of an experimenter, for, as he saw it, only the sort of experience that might result from an experiment can have a bearing upon our practice. Moreover, this experience must be seen not as particular but as inescapably general. For example, it is the case that if I observe the outcome of applying most substances to this hard object, I will see that the hard object will not be scratched. But the definition of hardness must state a general regularity which holds not just for an individual but also for the community of observers. Practice for Peirce meant the repeatable experimental practice of the community of scientists.

James reworked Peirce's view in two ways. First, James declared that by "the practical" he meant "the distinctively concrete, the individual, the particular and effective as opposed to the abstract, general and inert" ("The Pragmatist Account of Truth and Its Misunderstanders," in *The Meaning of Truth,* pp. 209–210). Thus, James, a nominalist, explicitly denied what Peirce, a realist, had emphasized: the *generality* of meaning. Moreover, James's interpretation of practical consequences went far beyond Peirce's experimentalism. James approached philosophical questions from a human rather than a specifically philosophical perspective. He was interested in the import of metaphysical and theological "world formulae" in the life of the individual. If these formulae are not merely verbal, they must have effects on the practice of those who uphold them, and James insisted that such effects could be traced. The belief that a seeing force and not a blind one governs the universe creates optimism, and thus confidence in the future is the effective pragmatic meaning of the terms "cosmic design" and "divine creator." Whereas Peirce had construed practical consequences to be those which are experimentally and publicly determinable for the community, James interpreted "practical" to mean the particular import that a belief has in the life of the individual.

Truth and utility. James's notion of "pragmatic" meaning served to reinforce the theory of truth that sprang from his interpretation of the role of thinking. According to James the function of thought is not to copy or image reality but to form ideas in order to satisfy the individual's needs and interests. What practical difference does it make if an idea is true? In science the truth of an idea is determined by experimental verification. Since verified ideas serve our need to predict experience and cope with our environment, scientific truth fulfills our practical interests. Hence, in the context of investigation, the true and the verified are one.

Science, however, gives us no criteria for decision in the case of metaphysical and theological beliefs. Since the meanings of world formulae are their effects on the attitudes of an individual, the individual is justified in regarding such formulae as true insofar as they provide him with "vital benefits." Thus, "On pragmatic principles, if the hypothesis of God works satisfactorily in the widest sense of the word, it is 'true'" (*Pragmatism,* p. 299). In this way James brought pragmatic meaning into harmony with his notion of the role of thinking and produced the famous statement that shocked the philosophical community: "The true is only the expedient in our way of thinking, just as the right is only the expedient in the way of our behaving" (*The Meaning of Truth,* p. vii). In "The Will to Believe" (1896) James extolled the "vital benefits" gained by faith. Is not faith often "father to fact"? For example, train passengers who have faith in each other will rise in unison against a band of robbers and win the day. We know that the skeptic in society who churlishly demands proof of every word he hears cuts himself off from the social rewards raked in by a trusting spirit. The religious skeptic who shuts himself up in "snarling logicality" may lose the opportunity of meeting up with God. The English pragmatist F. C. S. Schiller developed a view of truth allied to that of James. Schiller declared that the conceptions of science and religion are regarded as broadly true because the material results of science and the spiritual results of religion show that both science and religion work.

Objections to James's view. Bertrand Russell and Arthur O. Lovejoy (among others) criticized James's view of truth. They argued that the notion of truth as what works is not clear to begin with, since the concept of "working" is ambiguous. Lovejoy pointed out that a belief may work in two very different senses. It may work by having its predictions fulfilled or by contributing to the energy, efficiency, or survival of those who hold it. A belief may work in one sense and not work in the other. For example, the belief that the Messiah would come worked for the Jews in the sense that it contributed to the energy and self-confidence of individual Jews. But it failed to work in the sense that the event predicted did not occur. Russell claimed that James had confused two different conceptions of "working." When the scientist says that a hypothesis works, he means that we can deduce a number of verifiable propositions from the hypothesis and that none of the contradictories of these propositions can be deduced. He does not mean that the effects of believing the hypothesis are good. James failed to make the distinction between these two senses of "working."

Furthermore, Russell found James's view of truth to be hopelessly inadequate since it ignored the meaning commonly given to the word true. Consider the following sentences: (1) "It is true that other people exist," and (2) "It is useful to believe that other people exist." If James were right, (1) and (2) would have the same meaning and would express one and the same proposition. When I believe one, I believe the other. Hence, there should be no transition in the mind from one to the other. But it is obvious that there is a transition, thus these sentences do not have the same meaning. In addition, Russell argued, James's notion of truth is so difficult to apply that it is practically useless. James wrote, in *Pragmatism,* that our truths "have only this quality in common, that they *pay.*"

This must mean that the consequences of entertaining the belief are better than those of rejecting it. But Russell pointed out that it is enormously difficult to know the consequences of holding many beliefs. For example, many men of the French Revolution believed in Rousseau's doctrines, and no doubt this belief had enormous effects on the subsequent history of Europe. But it is almost impossible to disentangle just what these effects have been. How, then, can we determine whether the effects of this belief have been good or bad? It is surely easier to determine whether the *contrat social* is a myth. Religious beliefs present the same problem. How are we to determine whether the effects of believing in Roman Catholicism are on the whole good· or bad? "It is far easier, it seems to me," wrote Russell, "to settle the plain question of fact: Have Popes always been infallible? than to settle the question whether the effects of thinking them infallible are on the whole good" (*Philosophical Essays,* p. 135).

Peirce dubbed James's doctrine "suicidal" and rebaptized his own philosophy as "pragmaticism." James found "pragmatic" meaning in traditional metaphysics, but for Peirce pragmatism showed that "almost every proposition of ontological metaphysics is . . . meaningless gibberish" (*Collected Papers of Charles Sanders Peirce,* Vol. V, p. 423). Dewey also disassociated himself from James on this matter. He disclaimed the notion that truth is what gives satisfaction and argued that James had arrived at this view by confusing the pragmatic meaning of an idea with its value. The intellectual task of a pragmatist philosopher should be to determine whether or not metaphysical theological beliefs have experimental meaning. By focusing attention on the value of holding these beliefs, James had simply bypassed this responsibility. In "What Pragmatism Means by Practical" (1916), Dewey wrote, ". . . it seems unpragmatic for pragmatism to content itself with finding out the value of a conception whose own inherent significance pragmatism has not first determined" (p. 316). He denied that the pragmatic method could be used to find meaning in a notion that can never be empirically verified; for example, the notion of eternal perpetuation.

Dewey: truth as warranted assertibility. Dewey developed a theory of truth consistent with the pragmatic method. He began with the assumption that if we are to understand the practical bearings our ideas have on our experience, we must see them at work in the contexts of their use, those of reflective thinking and problem solving. It is easy to subscribe to the formula that truth is the correspondence between ideas and facts. But what does this correspondence mean in practice? How do ideas and facts function in the conduct of investigation?

Dewey maintained that the conduct of an investigation is always inspired by an initial state of doubt and uncertainty. We cannot understand the investigator's use of ideas and facts unless we understand his purpose in undertaking the inquiry. Like Peirce, Dewey insisted that one does not will to doubt. On the contrary, one is caught by doubt, and the resulting uncertainty characterizes a "situation" which is obscure, confused, or conflicting. Dewey's claim that doubt and uncertainty are primarily ascribed to a situation may be understood by thinking of his own example in *Essays in Experimental Logic* of a man lost in the woods. Can the man's uncertainty be imagined as something distinct from the unfamiliarity of his surroundings? Could he remember his experience apart from the environment which held him? If he tried to separate his doubt from this setting, he might remember uneasy tremors but nothing more. The quality of uncertainty which pervaded his whole situation made it into a distinctive experience.

Ordered inquiry begins when the investigator structures his uncertainty into the form of a problem. Within that framework an idea is a suggested solution to the problem at hand. Dewey's concept of ideas was set in opposition to the empiricist theory that an idea is simply a representation of an immediate experience. When a man who is lost in the woods "gets an idea," the idea (if it is any good at all) is not limited to elements in the immediate environment. It must extend beyond what is directly perceived to what is not perceived—to the man's home or his starting point. The idea is not an image of the environment; rather, it is a plan that will help the man to find his way. In the context of an investigation, therefore, ideas are plans of action or proposals formed in the context of a problem as a possible solution. It is to be noted that Dewey spoke of ideas in a way that is strikingly close to their use in ordinary language. When we say an idea is good, fruitful, workable, feasible, practical, or suggestive, we have in mind not a copy or image of experience but a solution to the problem before us. Ideas as we conceive them in inquiry have all the prospective, leading character that Dewey claimed for them.

Facts are used in inquiry to set the terms of the problem by marking off what is secure and unquestioned. The facts of the case "must be reckoned with or taken account of in any relevant solution that is proposed" (*Logic: The Theory of Inquiry,* p. 109). Facts guide inference by suggesting ideas, while ideas "promise" new facts which in turn serve to test the validity of the ideas. Philosophers have recently debated the question "Are facts *things* that belong to the world?" Dewey's view of the matter suggests that the issue has been posed incorrectly. In a particular context—that of an inquiry—one may call a thing a fact. A detective may point to a footprint in the grass, an open window, or an empty wallet, saying, "Here's an interesting fact." Outside of inquiry, however, the idiom of things does not parallel the idiom of facts. Things, not facts, may fall on the floor, get in our way, be bulky, small, or round. In inquiry, however, both facts and things are studied, examined, selected, discovered, or overlooked. In the language of inquiry, a thing functions as a sign, evidence, something to be reckoned with in drawing inferences; in this context, the idiom of things merges with the idiom of facts.

Dewey derived the correspondence of facts and ideas from their working relationship in inquiry. An idea in practical and scientific investigation corresponds to the facts when "it has, *through action,* worked out the state of things which it contemplated or intended. . . ." The man lost in the woods uses his idea as a working hypothesis to guide his action. When he finds his way home, then he is in a position to say that his idea is true. It "agrees with reality."

Ideas become true when their "draft upon existence" is honored by the verifying facts they promise. According to Dewey's analysis of the working correspondence of idea and fact, the notion that truth somehow exists antecedent to and separate from inquiry is meaningless. For him truth was a mutable concept. Truth "happens to an idea" when it becomes a verified or warranted assertion.

Russell's objection. There are serious difficulties in Dewey's theory of truth, but let us first examine a criticism which seriously misinterpreted his view. Bertrand Russell (in *The Philosophy of John Dewey*) presented Dewey's notion of truth in the following fashion: For the pragmatist an idea is true when "the consequences of entertaining a belief are such as to satisfy desire." But Dewey never identified truth with the satisfaction of desire. He expressly repudiated this view of truth in his criticism of William James a quarter of a century before Russell wrote his interpretation. Indeed, Dewey confronted James with the sort of example that Russell used against Dewey. In the case of the man, Dewey wrote, who "drinks a liquid to test the idea that it is poison, does the badness of the consequences in every other respect detract from the verifying force of the consequences? . . ." ("What Pragmatism Means by Practical," in *Essays in Experimental Logic,* p. 320). Russell simply refused to recognize the distinction between James and Dewey on this issue.

Carnap's and Moore's objections. In the dispute that followed Russell's remarks, the real problem in Dewey's theory of truth was obscured. That problem may be put in the following way: Dewey saw truth as a property which accrues to an idea when it is confirmed by an investigator. He rejected the concept of antecedent truth in favor of truth as a time-dependent or acquired property; we make a hypothesis true when we verify it. Yet such a notion is hardly acceptable. Suppose that a crime was committed on Monday. If a detective confirms his hypothesis of Smith's guilt on the following Friday, then we may say that the statement "Smith committed the crime" became confirmed on Friday. But it hardly follows that this statement became true on Friday. Indeed, since the crime was committed on Monday, we should, following Dewey, have no reason to convict Smith, since by Dewey's reasoning it was not true on Monday that Smith committed the crime.

Both Rudolf Carnap and G. E. Moore presented arguments against the notion that truth is a mutable concept. Carnap pointed out that "true," unlike "confirmed," is a time-independent expression. One can say that a statement was confirmed at a particular time, but "one cannot say 'such and such a statement is true today (was true yesterday; will be true tomorrow)' but only 'the statement is true'" ("Truth and Confirmation," p. 119). Moreover, Carnap added, the pragmatic theory of truth would lead to the abandonment of the law of excluded middle. This law prescribes that for every statement, either it or its negation is true. Since, according to the pragmatist, "true" means the same as "confirmed," the law would mean that every statement or its negation is confirmed. But this version of the law is unacceptable because it is plainly false. We know of many statements that neither they nor their negations have been confirmed. For example, neither the statement that it rained on Manhattan Island five thousand years ago nor its negation has been confirmed. Yet it is surely the case that either the statement or its negation is true.

Moore suggested that there is only one sense in which we might say that we make a belief true. "I may have the belief that it will rain tomorrow. . . . We should say that I had a hand in making it true, if and only if I had a hand in *making the rain fall*" ("William James' Pragmatism," p. 141). Moore's argument was in fact directed against William James, but it applies equally well to Dewey's view.

Dewey's lasting contribution. Where did Dewey go wrong? This question may be answered by turning to a view of truth which seems at first sight very far from Dewey's. F. P. Ramsey argued that " 'It is true that Caesar was murdered' means no more than that Caesar was murdered, and 'It is false that Caesar was murdered' means that Caesar was not murdered" ("Facts and Propositions," in *PAS*, Vol. 7, 1927). From Ramsey's point of view "true" is an assertively redundant expression. P. F. Strawson has expanded Ramsey's thesis by pointing to the nonassertive performative uses of "true" ("Truth," in *Analysis*, Vol. 9, No. 6, 1949). He compares "true" to "ditto." "Ditto" does not describe a statement but requires that a statement be made as the occasion for its use. "True" has a similar function. By saying that a statement is true, we do not describe the statement; rather, we agree with, admit, concede, or confirm it. From the performative perspective on "true," we may see where Dewey went wrong, as well as the contribution he made to the problem of truth.

Dewey claimed that assertions become true when they are verified. But to say that *S* is *P* became true does not mean that *S* is *P* became verified. It can mean only that *S* became *P*. Yet the same argument can be used to reject the notion that an assertion is always true. To say that *S* is *P* is always true is merely to say that *S* is always *P*. Dewey, in rejecting truth as an immutable property ("always true"), saw no alternative but to argue that it was a mutable property ("became true"). He did not consider the possibility that "true" is not used to describe the condition of an assertion, either as it is always or as it has become. For all its radical perspectives on language, pragmatism retained the notion that a grammatical predicate must stand for something.

However, if one extracts Dewey's view from its traditional framework, his contribution to the problem of truth may be preserved. With the aid of Dewey, an expanded and more tenable version of Strawson's performative analysis may be developed. Strawson, taking off from Ramsey, explored the nonassertive functions of "true." The context of the use of "true" which Strawson emphasized was the statement-making occasion. Person *A* makes a statement. Person *B*, in ditto fashion, says "That's true." Dewey, on the other hand, probes the use of true in a less narrowly framed context, that of an inquiry, where an investigator, prompted by doubt, confirms a hypothesis and thereby transforms it into a warranted assertion. Following Dewey, one keeps the link between a truth declaration and warranting evidence in mind. From the perspective that he emphasized, a distinction between "true" and other agreeing performatives like "yes" or "I accept his statement" emerges. When asked if I agree with Jones, I may say, "*Yes,* but I haven't studied the evidence, so my opinion isn't worth very much," or "*I accept his statement,* but I haven't studied the evidence, so my opinion isn't worth very much." On the other hand, it would be most peculiar to say, "His statement is *true,* but I haven't studied the evidence, so my opinion isn't worth very much." Agreeing expressions like "Yes" or "I accept his statement" lend themselves to openly violating the canons of respectable evidence, but a truth declaration does not. It is not natural to accompany a truth declaration with a confessed ignorance of relevant evidence. "That's true" has Dewey's stamp of warranted assertibility.

Bibliography

PEIRCE

The Collected Papers of Charles Sanders Peirce, Charles Harts-horne, Paul Weiss, and Arthur W. Burks, eds., 8 vols. Cambridge, Mass., 1931–1958.
Philosophical Writings of Peirce, Justus Buchler, ed. New York, 1955. Includes "How to Make Our Ideas Clear."
Gallie, W. B., *Peirce and Pragmatism.* New York, 1952.

JAMES

James, William, *Pragmatism. A New Name for Some Old Ways of Thinking.* New York, 1907.
James, William, "The Will to Believe," in *Selected Papers on Philosophy.* New York, 1917.
James, William, *The Meaning of Truth.* New York, 1909.
Lovejoy, Arthur O., "The Thirteen Pragmatisms II." *Journal of Philosophy,* Vol. 5 (1908), 29–39. Reprinted in W. G. Muelder and L. Sears, eds., *The Development of American Philosophy.* New York, 1940.
Moore, G. E., "William James' Pragmatism," in *Philosophical Studies.* London, 1922.
Perry, Ralph Barton, *The Thought and Character of William James,* 2 vols. Boston, 1935.
Pratt, J. B., "Truth and Its Verification." *Journal of Philosophy,* Vol. 4 (1907), 320–324.
Russell, Bertrand, "Pragmatism" and "William James' Conception of Truth," in *Philosophical Essays.* London, 1910.
Schiller, F. C. S., *Studies in Humanism.* London, 1912.

DEWEY

Carnap, Rudolf, "Truth and Confirmation," in H. Feigl and W. Sellars, eds., *Readings in Philosophical Analysis.* New York, 1949.
Dewey, John, *Essays in Experimental Logic.* Chicago, 1916.
Dewey, John, *Philosophy and Civilization.* New York, 1931. Includes "The Development of American Pragmatism."
Dewey, John, *Logic: The Theory of Inquiry.* New York, 1938.
Hook, Sidney, *John Dewey: An Intellectual Portrait.* New York, 1939.
Russell, Bertrand, "Dewey's Logic," in P. A. Schilpp, ed., *The Philosophy of John Dewey.* New York, 1939.

GERTRUDE EZORSKY

PRAGMATISM was the most influential philosophy in America in the first quarter of the twentieth century. Viewed against the widely diversified intellectual currents that have characterized American life, pragmatism stands out as an energetically evolved philosophical movement. As a movement it is best understood as, in part, a critical rejection of much of traditional academic philosophy and, in part, a concern to establish certain positive aims. It is in these respects, rather than because of any one idea or exclusive doctrine, that pragmatism has been the most distinctive and the major contribution of America to the world of philosophy. Among the Continental thinkers it has influenced and with whose philosophy it has been in harmony are Georg Simmel, Wilhelm Ostwald, Edmund Husserl, Hans Vaihinger, Richard Müller-Freienfels, Hans Hahn, Giovanni Papini (leader of the Pragmatist Club in Florence), Giovanni Vailati, Henri Bergson, and Édouard Le Roy.

BACKGROUND

The origins of pragmatism are clear in outline, if not in detail. The familiar capsule description is as follows: pragmatism is a method of philosophizing—often said to be a theory of meaning—first developed by Charles Peirce in the 1870s; revived and reformulated in 1898 by William James, primarily as a theory of truth; further developed, expanded, and disseminated by John Dewey and F. C. S. Schiller.

This glossing of the facts is useful as a summary or for directing us where to look if we want to find out more about pragmatism. But it can be misleading. A re-examination or rewriting of the history is not to be embarked upon here; but the following cautionary points deserve mention. The specific formative conditions of the early evolution of pragmatism are not entirely clear for several reasons. The historical occasion of the birth of pragmatism is complicated by the fact that it was to some extent the product of cooperative deliberation and mutual influences within the "Metaphysical Club," founded by Peirce, James, and others in the 1870s in Cambridge. This may be one of the very few cases in which a philosophy club produced something notable philosophically (compare Locke's account of the "club" in the 1670s that stimulated the writing of his great *Essay*). But the paper (now lost) that Peirce drew up as a memento lest the club dissolve without leaving behind anything substantial, the paper in which pragmatism was first expressed, was not the free creation of one mind, even though the major credit surely goes to Peirce. Years later, undertaking to write on pragmatism, Peirce queried James: "Who originated the term *pragmatism*, I or you? Where did it first appear in print? What do you understand by it?" And James replied with the reminder: "You invented 'pragmatism' for which I gave you full credit in a lecture entitled 'Philosophical Conceptions and Practical Results.'"

In addition to some uncertainty as to the facts in the evolution of pragmatism, there are—as we shall see—several problems of interpretation. Peirce and James often gave very different accounts of what they understood by "pragmatism." Usually this is explained by holding James responsible for distorting or even misunderstanding Peirce's ideas. That there were differences between Peirce and James on this score is clear. Peirce, despairing of what James (and his followers) were making of the idea, rebaptized his own view as "pragmaticism," a word ugly enough, he commented, to keep it safe from kidnapers. Historians usually side with Peirce, tending to discredit James's overzealous pronouncements upon pragmatism and applications of it to issues of the moral value and truth of religious belief. But with equal justice it can be maintained that James was developing a substantially different approach to a different type of philosophical problem, related in some ways to Peirce's thought, but mostly superficially; only his habitual overgenerosity led him to call what he was doing "pragmatism" and to cite Peirce as the "inventor."

There is, however, a more serious and persistent problem of interpretation entrenched in the history of pragmatism. This is the problem of determining with some precision what "pragmatism" means or stands for as a philosophical doctrine. As already suggested, pragmatism, by virtue of being an evolving philosophical movement, is to be viewed as a group of associated theoretical ideas and attitudes developed over a period of time and exhibiting—under the differing influences of Peirce, James, and Dewey—rather significant shifts in direction and in formulation. We have the advantage of historical perspective and can make use of it to survey and select distinctive themes and phases in the formation of pragmatism, but a single definitive statement of a single thesis is not to be hoped for.

In the heyday of pragmatism its rapidly changing character proved to be a source of embarrassment and confusion to pragmatists and critics alike. Arthur O. Lovejoy, in a welcome effort at clarification, in 1908 distinguished 13 possible forms of pragmatism. And Schiller, in an almost intoxicating pluralistic spirit, commented that there were as many pragmatisms as there were pragmatists (at the time a considerable company). Additional confusion over pragmatism was caused by the tendency of its spokesmen to find the philosophical past well populated with pragmatists. Thus Socrates, Protagoras, Aristotle, Francis Bacon, Spinoza, Locke, Berkeley, Hume, Kant, Mill, and an assorted variety of scientists were included in the fold.

These perplexities, once hotly debated in the journals, are now only of historical interest. They need not concern us in surveying and assessing what are undoubtedly the leading ideas of pragmatism. It suffices to note the irony in the fact that while pragmatism was supposed to have made its appearance in the paper by Peirce entitled "How to Make Our Ideas Clear" (1878), pragmatists continued to have so much trouble in doing so.

CHARLES PEIRCE

What has come to be known as Peirce's pragmatism grew out of his study of the phenomenology of human thought and the uses of language. For Peirce, the investigation of thought and language—and, therefore, the way into specific studies of all kinds of claims, assertions, beliefs, and ideas—depended upon the understanding of "signs." One of Peirce's lasting ideals, resolutely pursued but never completely achieved, was to work out a general theory of signs—that is, a classification and analysis of the types of signs and sign relations and significations that, in the broadest sense, make communication possible. A sign is anything that stands for something else. While this ancient way of putting it admits of a trivial construction (signs are signs), for Peirce, the main thing was that signs are socially standardized ways in which something (a thought, word, gesture, object) refers us (a community) to something else (the interpretant—the significant effect or translation of the sign, being itself another sign). Thus, signs presuppose minds in communication with other minds, which in turn presupposes a community (of interpreters) and a system of communication.

Pragmatic method. Put roughly, Peirce's pragmatism is a rule of procedure for promoting linguistic and conceptual clarity—successful communication—when men are faced with intellectual problems. Because the emphasis is upon method, Peirce often remarked that pragmatism is not a philosophy, a metaphysic, or a theory of truth; it is not a solution or answer to anything but a technique to help us find solutions to problems of a philosophical or scientific nature.

One of Peirce's best-known statements of the technique was in "How to Make Our Ideas Clear" (1878): "Consider what effects, that might conceivably have practical bearings, we conceive the object of our conception to have. Then our conception of these effects is the whole of our conception of the objects." In a somewhat clearer account he said that "in order to ascertain the meaning of an intellectual conception one should consider what practical consequences might conceivably result by necessity from the truth of that conception; and the sum of these consequences will constitute the entire meaning of the conception" (*Collected Papers*, Vol. V, paragraph 9).

While Peirce often spoke of pragmatism as a method of clarifying the meaning variously of words, ideas, concepts (sometimes of objects), we can take his intended purpose to be as follows:

(1) Pragmatism is a method of clarifying and determining the meaning of signs. We must note the comprehensive status Peirce gives to signs in this connection, for example: "All thought whatsoever is a sign, and is mostly of the nature of language." The pragmatic method, however, does not apply to all the various kinds of signs and modes and purposes of communication. Peirce considered pragmatism "a method of ascertaining the meaning of hard words and abstract concepts" or, again, "a method of ascertaining the meanings, not of all ideas, but . . . 'intellectual concepts,' that is to say, of those upon the structure of which, arguments concerning objective fact may hinge."

(2) The aim of the method is to facilitate communication, and in particular cases, the degree to which this is accomplished determines the relevance and justification of the method. This aim takes two main forms illustrated in Peirce's writings. The first is of a critical nature: where disputes or philosophical problems seem to have no discoverable or agreed-upon solution, pragmatism advises that words are being used in different ways or without definite meaning at all. For example, says Peirce, pragmatism will "show that almost every proposition of ontological metaphysics is either meaningless . . . or else . . . absurd." And it is in this critical capacity that Peirce remarked: "Pragmatism solves no real problem. It only shows that supposed problems are not real problems."

But the second role the method performs is much less negative: where signs (that is, ideas, concepts, language) are unclear, the method supplies a procedure for reconstructing or explicating meanings. Here the method is directed to translating (or systematically replacing) unclear concepts with clearer ones. It is in this spirit that Peirce offered his explications of the concepts of "hardness," "weight," "force," "reality." His procedure consisted in translating and explicating a sign (a term, like "hard," or sentences of signs, such as "x is hard") by providing a conditional statement of a given situation (or class of situations) in which a definite operation will produce a definite result. Thus, to say of some object O that it is "hard" is to mean that "if in certain situations the operation of scratch-testing is performed on O, then the general result is: O will not be scratched by most substances." The sign (or concept) "hard" in statements asserting that some object is hard is replaceable and clarified pragmatically with a conditional statement of the sort just given. Peirce refers to this method of conditional explication of signs as a "prescription" or "precept." The conditionals are recipes informing us what we must do if we wish to find out the kind of conditions determining the meaningful use of a sign.

Meaning. For Peirce, two points are of considerable importance in the pragmatic procedure for determining meaning: (*a*) Where one cannot provide any conditional translation for a sign, its (pragmatic) meaning is empty. This is what Peirce intended by such characteristic statements as that our conception of an object is our conception of its "practical effects" or "sensible effects." He did not mean (as James sometimes did) that the meaning of a concept is the practical effect it has in particular cases when you use it. All Peirce argued was that a concept must have some conceivable consequences, or "practical bearings," and that these must be specifiable in the manner just discussed if the concept is to play a significant role in communication. (*b*) Peirce's pragmatism thus is offered as a schema for getting at the meaning, or empirical significance, of language. As a schema it is not a theory of meaning in the sense of some general definition of meaning; it is a theoretical device for getting at the empirically significant content of concepts by determining the roles they play in classes of empirically verifiable statements. This procedure, or schema, clearly foreshadowed the later programs of operationalism and the verifiability theory of meaning.

Despite some serious difficulties that jeopardize portions of Peirce's method, the general aspects of his approach appear to be sound canons of scientific practice. Peirce's recondite statements of pragmatism have created considerable confusion. But Peirce seemed less concerned with the problem of providing an accurate and complete statement of the "maxim" of pragmatism than with its use and justification. This he attempted to show in much of his later philosophical inquiries of a scientific and metaphysical sort.

Peirce's schema, or prescriptive method, for "determining the meaning of intellectual concepts" has several sources in additon to his familiarity with scientific technique. Suggestions of it are to be found in Berkeley and in Kant. Peirce's view that meanings take a general form expressed in schema or formulas that prescribe kinds of operations and results and *conceivable* consequences and rules of action was directly linked to Kant. Peirce says he was led to the method of pragmatism by reflecting on Kant's *Critique of Pure Reason* and on the Kantian use of *pragmatisch* for empirical, or experimentally conditioned, laws, "based on and applying to experience."

Inquiry and truth. It should be noted, finally, that Peirce's pragmatism is part of a more general account of "inquiry," aspects of which he elaborated with some care and most of which was taken up into Dewey's extensive construction of a theory of inquiry. Peirce described the function of thought as a form of behavior initiated by the irritation of doubt and proceeding to some resolution in a state of belief. Belief is a condition of organic stability and intellectual satisfaction, but these latter do not determine the truth of beliefs. Peirce outlined a scientific and pragmatic method of clarifying and justifying belief. It was this aspect of Peirce's analysis of inquiry and belief that suggested a pragmatic theory of truth. On this matter he was unclear and wavering. Sometimes truth and pragmatic meaning overlapped or coalesced in his discussions of them. But Peirce also argued that truth theory and pragmatism are entirely separate considerations. Generally, the idea of truth, for Peirce, is drawn from Kant and is to be understood as a regulative idea, one that functions solely to order, integrate, and promote inquiry. Taken as a "correspondence" or "coherence" theory—or criticized from the point of view of such theories—Peirce's account of truth looks strange, cumbersome, and naive.

WILLIAM JAMES

It was James who launched pragmatism as a new philosophy in a lecture "Philosophical Conceptions" in 1898; it was under his leadership that pragmatism came to be famous; and it was primarily his exposition that was received and read by the world at large.

Although Peirce and James were lifelong friends and exerted much intellectual influence upon each other, they differed in ways that had important effects upon their respective versions of pragmatism. Peirce was a realist (calling himself a scholastic realist); James was far more of a nominalist. Where Peirce sought meaning in general concepts and formulas of action, James sought meaning in experienced facts and plans of action. James looked to the concrete, immediate, practical level of experience as the testing ground of our intellectual efforts; for Peirce, the immediate sensory experience is all but destitute of "intellectual purport." Furthermore, while Peirce's pragmatism took a logical and scientific character, James, despite being an eminent man of science, was first and foremost a moralist in his pragmatism.

Value. Moral interests and moral language appear in almost every important passage of James's writing on pragmatism. In *Pragmatism* James made his moral conception of philosophy unmistakably evident in saying that "the whole function of philosophy ought to be to find out what definite difference it will make to you and me, at definite instants of our life, if this world-formula or that world-formula be the true one." The phrase "what definite difference . . . at definite instants of our life" is by and large James's way of critically judging the meaning and truth of ideas. For James, meaning and truth are included in a more fundamental category of value; to determine the meaning or truth of ideas one must evaluate their "practi-

cal consequences," "usefulness," "workability." In several famous pronouncements, James spoke of truth as what is good or expedient in our beliefs. In a phrase that permanently shocked some of his readers, James described the meaning and truth of ideas as their "cash value."

Generally, for James, the function of thought is that of assisting us to achieve and sustain "satisfactory relations with our surroundings." The value of ideas, beliefs, and conceptual dealings is to be determined accordingly, on each of numerous occasions, by their effectiveness and efficiency as the means of carrying us propitiously "from any one part of our experience to any other part, linking things satisfactorily, working securely, simplifying, saving labor."

James was thus primarily concerned with issues of belief and conceptual renditions of experience in their role of enabling men to deal with environments and to enrich the fare of daily experience. It is the level of life experience that interested James. Hence, his own statements of pragmatism resemble those of Peirce but emphasize the importance of immediate experience and practical consequences and clues to action. For James, our thoughts of an object pragmatically considered lead us to "what conceivable effects of a practical kind the object may involve—what sensations we are to expect from it, and what reactions we must prepare. Our conception of these effects, whether immediate or remote, is then for us the whole of our conception of the object." If we compare this statement from *Pragmatism* with those cited earlier from Peirce, it is not difficult to see that in James's pragmatism the emphasis is upon the way individuals interpret environing conditions for purposes of successful action. The passage also reflects how James's view differed from Peirce's Kantian conception; James explained "pragmatism" as coming from the Greek πράγμα, meaning "practice," "action." Indeed, so fundamental are action, exploration, and life experience in James's philosophy that some of his critics have taken great pains to demonstrate the value of inaction and the general uselessness of philosophy. In this endeavor, it may be said, they have been on the whole successful.

Belief. It was James's conception of truth that became a *cause célèbre* for pragmatism and its critics, until eventually James, tiring of the matter, turned his attention to other philosophical pursuits, leaving to Dewey the defense and development of pragmatism. Aside from truth, the other major critical issue in pragmatism was James's argument for the justification of moral and religious belief. James's interest in the meaning and function of belief was that of a skilled and perceptive psychologist and moralist. His general view was this: When, for a given person P, a belief B answers or satisfies a compelling need (of P to see or interpret the world in a certain way), the "vital good" supplied by B in the life of P (the difference it makes as a beneficial causal condition in the psychological and physiological behavior of P) justifies B. It must be noted that James argued for this justification procedure only when (a) the choice of B or not-B is, for a given individual at a given time, "live," "forced," and "momentous"; (b) the evidence for or against B is equal, or admits of no rational adjudication of one over the other; (c) the effect or consequences of

B are a "vital benefit." These three qualifications work against ascribing to James some popular defense or universal apologia for religious belief. He thought he was correct in pointing to a psychological and moral right to belief analogous to the justification of postulates or posits (in Kantian and Fichtean transcendental philosophizing) or of certain theoretical hypotheses in science.

Peirce and Dewey, among others, were highly critical of this defense of the will to believe. James the psychologist and literary artist brilliantly described the working consequences of types of religious belief for characteristic types of persons. But James the philosopher tended to confuse a descriptive analysis of how belief functions and why men believe with questions of the evaluation or verification of specific cases of belief. (Thus, for example, the fact that *B* answers a need of *P* is not of itself evidence that the content of belief *B* is warranted or that *P* has correctly understood his "need.")

However, it was this side of James that was enthusiastically received as the moral core of his pragmatism by F. C. S. Schiller in England and Giovanni Papini in Italy. Here also James's views have affinities with those of Henri Bergson, Hans Vaihinger, and Georg Simmel. James seemed to be a democratic, energetic, and lovable Fichte, an artist and scientist exhorting men to trust their beliefs and, above all, to leave the classroom and cloister and start living and acting in the world.

JOHN DEWEY

In the article "The Development of American Pragmatism," John Dewey described Peirce's views as stemming from an "experimental, not a priori, explanation of Kant" and James's pragmatism as inspired by British empiricism. But he also noted this difference: "Peirce wrote as a logician and James as a humanist." There was, in fact, a cross-fertilization of these strains; but the characterization is apt and traceable enough in the history of pragmatism and in Dewey, too, to be of expository aid. Dewey began to appreciate James while still under the influence of Hegelian and Kantian idealism; later he recognized the importance of Peirce, whose insights and ideas were in many respects anticipations of those Dewey had started to work out on his own. The Hegelian synthesis of the logical and humanistic sides of pragmatism was achieved by the disenchanted Hegelian Dewey.

Instrumentalism. Through Dewey's patient, critical, and indefatigable efforts, pragmatism was carefully and thoroughly reformulated into what Dewey called Instrumentalism, "a theory of the general forms of conception and reasoning." Instrumentalism was a single philosophical theory within which the two evolving aspects of pragmatism found coherent expression. Instrumentalism was both theory of logic and a guiding principle of ethical analysis and criticism. For Dewey, this theory bridged the most persistent and noxious of "dualisms" in modern thought—the separation of science and values, knowledge and morals.

Instrumentalism was Dewey's theory of the conditions under which reasoning occurs and of the forms, or controlling operations, that are characteristic of thought in establishing future consequences. In the paper cited above, Dewey wrote:

> Instrumentalism is an attempt to constitute a precise logical theory of concepts, of judgments and inferences in their various forms, by considering primarily how thought functions in the experimental determinations of future consequences . . . it attempts to establish universally recognized distinctions and rules of logic by deriving them from the reconstructive or mediative function ascribed to reason. It aims to constitute a theory of the general forms of conception and reasoning.

A suggestive and vital feature of this theory for Dewey was that while the subject matters of scientific inquiry and moral and social experience differ, the method and forms of thought functioning "in the experimental determinations of future consequences" do not differ in kind. The method of thought and the forms of reflective behavior exhibit a common functional pattern whenever problematic situations become resolved through inquiry yielding "warranted assertion."

Inquiry and truth. "Warranted assertion" is the term for Dewey's version of truth. Inquiry is initiated in conditions of doubt; it terminates in the establishment of conditions in which doubt is no longer needed or felt. It is this settling of conditions of doubt, a settlement produced and warranted by inquiry, which distinguishes the warranted assertion. Whereas Dewey once defined "truth" as the "working" or "satisfactory" or "verified" idea or hypothesis, he was led, later—partly as a result of several critical controversies over truth with Bertrand Russell during the 1930s and 1940s—to restate his view of truth as warranted assertion.

In his *Logic* Dewey gave his general definition of inquiry as "the controlled or directed transformation of an indeterminate situation into one that is so determinate in its constituent distinctions and relations as to convert the elements of the original situation into a unified whole."

The theory of inquiry was developed over many years and in many writings; into it went the products of Dewey's reflections on the nature of thought, his contributions to psychology and education, the influence of the biological and functional aspects of James's *Principles of Psychology*, and the influence of Peirce on the nature of scientific inquiry. In his analysis of the biological and cultural conditions of inquiry and in his account of intelligence as a function of these interacting conditions in a particular situation with respect to a problem and its outcome, Dewey was also guided by some of the basic ideas in the philosophical social psychology of G. H. Mead, once Dewey's colleague at Michigan and Chicago and one of his closest friends. The definitive statement of the theory is in Dewey's *Logic: The Theory of Inquiry* (1938).

For Dewey, the theory of inquiry is a generalized description of the organic, cultural, and formal conditions of intelligent action. Such action is provoked by problems of diverse kinds—political, ethical, scientific, and aesthetic. But irrespective of the specific content of human problems or the nature of problem situations, inquiry is a reflective evaluation of existing conditions—of shortcomings and possibilities—with respect to operations intended to actualize certain potentialities of the situation so as to resolve what was doubtful. The purpose of inquiry is to create goods, satisfactions, solutions, and integration in what was initially a wanting, discordant, troubled, and problematic situation. In this respect all intelligence is evaluative, and no separation of moral, scientific, practical, or theoretical experience is to be made.

So commanding an achievement was Dewey's last-mentioned work that "pragmatism" is often identified with the position he expounded there as a naturalistic logic for evaluating and reconstructing human experience.

RECENT TENDENCIES

A somewhat different articulation of pragmatism, deriving less from James and Dewey than from Peirce, was set forth by C. I. Lewis in the 1920s as "conceptualistic pragmatism." Lewis emphasized the role of mind in supplying the a priori principles and categories by which we proceed to organize and interpret sense experience. But he also stressed the plurality of categories and conceptual schemes by which experience can be interpreted and the evolutionary character of our systems. Because a priori principles impose no necessary order on the world or upon sense experience (determining only our ways of organizing experience), Lewis argued for a "pragmatic a priori." Decisions to accept or reject conceptual principles, indeed the very function of those principles, rest upon socially shared needs and purposes and upon our interest in increased understanding and control over experience. According to Lewis (in *Mind and the World Order*), "The interpretation of experience must always be in terms of categories . . . and concepts which the mind itself determines. There may be alternative conceptual systems giving rise to alternative descriptions of experience, which are equally objective and equally valid. . . . When this is so, choice will be determined, consciously or unconsciously, on pragmatic grounds."

Lewis' pragmatism resulted in a theory of conceptual and empirical meaning and in an analysis of empirical judgments as probable and evaluative modes of acting upon passing and future experience.

In recent literature, under the influence of Dewey and Lewis as well as Rudolf Carnap, Charles Morris, Ernest Nagel, W. V. Quine, and others, "pragmatism" connotes one broad philosophical attitude toward our conceptualization of experience: theorizing over experience is, as a whole and in detail, fundamentally motivated and justified by conditions of efficacy and utility in serving our various aims and needs. The ways in which experience is apprehended, systematized, and anticipated may be many. Here pragmatism counsels tolerance and pluralism. But, aside from aesthetic and intrinsic interests, all theorizing is subject to the critical objective of maximum usefulness in serving our needs: our critical decisions, in general, will be pragmatic, granted that in particular cases decisions over what is most useful or needed in our rational endeavors are relative to some given point of view and purposes.

An expression of this attitude that is of current interest was advanced by Peirce, James, and Dewey, as well as by F. P. Ramsey, the brilliant English philosopher influenced by Peirce and James. This is an interpretation of the laws and theories of science as "leading principles," or instrumental procedures, for inferring stated conditions from others. Construed as leading principles, theories function as guides for logical inference, indicating *how* certain formulations are to be derived from other formulations of events, rather than as descriptively true statements of reality serving as premises *from* which conclusions are deduced. Pragmatically, theories are inference policies, neither true nor false (except pragmatically) but nonetheless critically assessable as to their utility and clarity and the fruitfulness of the consequences that result from adopting them.

While there continues to be an interest in the philosophies of Peirce, James, Dewey, and Schiller, pragmatism as a movement, in the form outlined in these pages, cannot be said to be alive today. But pragmatism has succeeded in its critical reaction to the nineteenth-century philosophical background from which it emerged; it has helped shape the modern conception of philosophy as a way of investigating problems and clarifying communication rather than as a fixed system of ultimate answers and great truths. And in this alteration of the philosophical scene, some of the positive suggestions of pragmatism have been disseminated into current intellectual life as practices freely adopted and taken for granted to an extent that no longer calls for special notice.

The measure of success pragmatism has achieved in encouraging more successful philosophizing in our time is, by its own standards, its chief justification. To have disappeared as a special thesis by becoming infused in the normal and habitual practices of intelligent inquiry and conduct is surely the pragmatic value of pragmatism.

(See also PRAGMATIC THEORY OF TRUTH. See Pragmatism in Index for articles on philosophers who are commonly classed as pragmatists.)

Bibliography

GENERAL WORKS ON PRAGMATISM

Dewey, John, "The Development of American Pragmatism," in his *Philosophy and Civilization*. New York, 1931. Ch. 2.

Schneider, H. W., *History of American Philosophy*. New York, 1946. Chs. 39–41.

Thayer, H. S., "Pragmatism," in D. J. O'Connor, ed., *A Critical History of Western Philosophy*. New York, 1964. Pp. 437–462.

Thayer, H. S., *Meaning and Action: A Critical History of Pragmatism*. Announced for publication New York, 1966.

Wiener, Philip P., *Evolution and the Founders of Pragmatism*. Cambridge, Mass., 1949.

WORKS BY PEIRCE

Collected Papers, C. Hartshorne, P. Weiss, and A. W. Burks, eds., 8 vols. Cambridge, Mass., 1931–1958. Vols. V and VIII especially.

WORKS ON PEIRCE

Buchler, Justus, *Charles Peirce's Empiricism*. New York, 1939.

Gallie, W. B., *Peirce and Pragmatism*. London, 1952.

Murphey, Murray G., *The Development of Peirce's Philosophy*. Cambridge, Mass., 1961.

WORKS BY JAMES

The Will to Believe. New York, 1897.
"Philosophical Conceptions and Practical Results." University of California *Chronicle* (1898). Reprinted in his *Collected Essays and Reviews.* New York, 1920. Pp. 406–437.
Pragmatism. New York, 1907.
The Meaning of Truth. New York, 1909.

WORKS ON JAMES

Perry, R. B., *The Thought and Character of William James,* 2 vols. Boston, 1935.

WORKS BY DEWEY

Democracy and Education. New York, 1916.
Essays in Experimental Logic. Chicago, 1916.
Reconstruction in Philosophy. New York, 1920. Reprinted in paperback edition with a new introduction. New York, 1950.
Human Nature and Conduct. New York, 1922.
Logic: The Theory of Inquiry. New York, 1938.

WORKS ON DEWEY

Geiger, G. R., *John Dewey in Perspective.* New York, 1958.
Hook, Sidney, *John Dewey.* New York, 1939.
Thayer, H. S., *The Logic of Pragmatism.* New York, 1952.
White, Morton, *The Origins of Dewey's Instrumentalism.* New York, 1943.

OTHER PRAGMATISTS

Abel, Reuben, *The Pragmatic Humanism of F. C. S. Schiller.* New York, 1955.
Lewis, C. I., *Mind and the World Order.* New York, 1929.
Lewis, C. I., *An Analysis of Knowledge and Valuation.* La Salle, Ill., 1946.
Mead, George H., *Mind, Self and Society.* Chicago, 1934.
Mead, George H., *The Philosophy of the Act.* Chicago, 1938.
Mead, George H., *Selected Writings,* Andrew J. Reck, ed. New York, 1964.
Schiller, F. C. S., "Axioms as Postulates," in Henry Sturt, ed., *Personal Idealism.* London and New York, 1902. Pp. 47–133.
Schiller, F. C. S., *Studies in Humanism.* New York, 1907.
Schiller, F. C. S., *Logic for Use.* London, 1929.

H. S. THAYER

PRECOGNITION. Etymologically, "precognition" is simply the Latin equivalent of "foreknowledge." But it has come to have a more specialized meaning as a semitechnical term for one of the phenomena or putative phenomena of parapsychology (psychical research). This article touches on the wider issues of foreknowledge only insofar as they appear in a rather special form in the narrower context of parapsychology. Again, since the philosophical problems centering on some of the other concepts of parapsychology are examined at length elsewhere (see ESP PHENOMENA, THEIR PHILOSOPHICAL IMPLICATIONS), telepathy, clairvoyance, and psychokinesis are mentioned here only when necessary to the main goal of becoming clearer about the logical geography of parapsychological precognition. Nor will there be any discussion of what the facts actually are. We shall be concerned only with theoretical questions of implication and explanation.

"Precognition" is one of a group of terms that also includes "telepathy," "clairvoyance," and—more peripherally— "psychokinesis" (PK). Telepathy is thought of, initially at any rate, as consisting in the acquisition of information by one person from another without the use of any of the senses normally indispensable to communication. Clairvoyance, at the same initial stage, is conceived of as being generically identical with telepathy; the specific difference is that in the case of clairvoyance the information is supposed to be obtained not from another person but from an object. Telepathy would be termed "precognitive" if the information so acquired was not going to become available to the other person until later. Clairvoyance would be termed precognitive if the information so acquired was not, until later, even going to become available in things, as opposed to minds. It is thus possible to consider precognitive telepathy and precognitive clairvoyance as being two species of the genus precognition. Straight telepathy, straight clairvoyance, and both sorts of precognition are all supposed to be both nonsensory and noninferential. It is partly for this reason that all these alleged phenomena are frequently classed together as varieties of ESP. It is important to recognize that both these negative characteristics are in all four cases defining. To show that the information was acquired by the use, whether conscious or unconscious, of sensory cues, clues, or signs is a sufficient reason for disqualifying as genuine telepathy, or what have you, any ostensible case of telepathy or other such phenomenon. Similarly, to show that this acquisition was the result of a feat of inference, however heroic and remarkable in itself, again constitutes a completely sufficient reason for insisting that we are not confronted with a genuine case of precognition. At most we must describe it as a pseudo precognition, "precognition" only in quotation marks.

Suppose someone has an intuition or a dream or a waking vision that is found to correspond to some actual later happening. Suppose that it seems out of the question either (1) to account for the correspondence as the result of successful inference, conscious or unconscious, from materials available to the subject at the time, or (2) to trace it back to some causal ancestor common to both the "anticipation" and the "fulfillment," or (3) to say that the "fulfillment" was somehow a result of the "anticipation," or (4) even to refuse to account for the correspondence in any way on the grounds that it was just a coincidence. (The counterargument in this last case would be that some intuitions, dreams, visions, and so forth, are bound to prove veridical and that presumably this was just one of those striking cases that is—as the catch phrase has it—"by the law of averages" bound to occur occasionally.) If such an intuition, or what have you, were to occur we would—provided that all four conditions seemed to be met—have at least a prima facie case of precognition. Three theoretical questions must then be considered.

OPERATIONAL DISTINCTIONS

The first question is whether there are real operational distinctions to be made between all the supposed varieties of ESP or whether any of them can be regarded as alternative descriptions of the same logically possible phenomena. For instance, some ingenuity is required to work out an experimental design which would enable us to distinguish decisively between straight clairvoyance and precognitive telepathy.

To make this clear, consider a stylized ESP experiment. The experimenter equips himself with a pack of cards, perhaps the special Zener type, which consists of five suits of five identical cards. He devises a procedure for randomizing the order in which the cards are to be offered as targets. He recruits a subject whose function is to guess the values of the cards chosen as targets. The experimenter takes drastic and thorough precautions to ensure that it is quite impossible for the subject to tell by any combinations of inference and sensory perception what is or is going to be the value of any target card. (This is, of course, very much more easily said than done. But here our concern is with theory only.) The subject in due course makes his guesses, and these guesses are recorded. If enough guesses are made—provided always that the experiment has been properly designed and properly executed—we should expect "by the law of averages" that when the guesses are scored against their targets about one-fifth of the total will turn out to have been right and the remaining four-fifths wrong. But if significantly more hits have been scored than this mean-chance expectation, then it seems that *some* ESP factor must have been involved.

Suppose now that the experimenter has taken care to ensure that no one at all, himself included, should know, at the time when the subject makes his guesses, what is the value of each target card. It might seem that his experimental results can be interpreted as evidence only for clairvoyance and not for telepathy. But once we have allowed the possibility of precognition, then these same results can be described equally well in terms of precognitive telepathy. The subject is perhaps precognitively "picking" the brains of whoever later does the scoring.

The problem is further complicated if one is also prepared to allow the possibility of PK. Literally, "psychokinesis" means movement by the mind. The idea is that perhaps some people sometimes may be able, whether consciously or unconsciously, to move or otherwise affect things without pushing or pulling them and, indeed, without in any way touching either the things in question or any other things involved in the process. Perhaps, it is suggested, these people or, indeed, all of us really can in some conditions bring about changes in things by simply "willing," as a gambler might wish that by simply "willing" and without any detectable cheating he could get dice to fall in the ways he desires. Once this suggestion is allowed there seems to be room for an alternative description of many experiments which might otherwise have appeared to be unambiguous evidence of the reality of precognition. Such a description will be in terms of psychokinesis, guided perhaps by a measure of straight telepathy or straight clairvoyance. The subject may not, after all, really be precognizing the target. Perhaps he or somebody else is consciously or unconsciously influencing psychokinetically the target-determining mechanism in order to increase the degree of correspondence between the guess series and the target series. With appropriate alterations the same suggestion can be applied to spontaneous, as opposed to experimental, cases of ostensible precognition. The "fulfillment" or "fulfillments" become partly or wholly the results of the "anticipations," and, by specification, any such cases are disqualified from being classed

as genuinely precognitive. Confronted by this kaleidoscopically changing confusion of alternative descriptions, we need not wonder that PK was once described as the parapsychological equivalent of a universal solvent.

IMPLICATIONS

The second sort of theoretical question concerns the implications of precognition. Suppose it were to be established that there really is such a phenomenon, which actually does satisfy all the conditions stipulated; what would follow?

The future as present. One consequence which has often been thought to follow from the existence of precognition is that, sensationally, the future must somehow be already here—or at any rate 'there. This is usually derived from a conception of precognition as a mode of perception, of extrasensory perception. Thus, J. W. Dunne, in *An Experiment with Time* (3d ed., London, 1939, p. 7), claims that in precognition "we habitually observe events before they occur." By valid inference from this misdescription he concludes that the future must therefore really be present. Upon this absurdity he proceeds to erect his logical extravaganza "the serial theory of time." Or again, in a useful survey of the field, D. J. West remarks: ". . . precognition—foreseeing arbitrary events in the future that could not by any stretch of the imagination be inferred from the present—that is something which is almost impossible for our minds to grasp. How can anyone see things which do not yet exist?" (*Psychical Research Today,* London, 1954, p. 104).

Now it is necessarily true that if anything is to be seen or otherwise perceived—and not just "seen" or "perceived" (in discrediting quotation marks)—that thing must be presently available. (We ignore for present purposes the peripheral problems presented by very distant stars.) West is therefore more right than perhaps he realizes in suggesting that it is inconceivable that anyone should be able to see things which do not yet exist. Nevertheless, the correct conclusion to draw is not, as some have been inclined to think, that precognition is logically impossible. The correct conclusion is, rather, that if the phenomenon specified was to occur, it could not be conceived of as any sort of perception. The argument reduces to absurdity not the notion of precognition as such but the assumption that such precognition can be assimilated to perception. (There are indeed further reasons, applying equally to all varieties of ESP, which tend to destroy this analogy and therefore make unfortunate the use of the expression "extrasensory perception." But the present reason, applying only to precognition, is in this case by itself entirely decisive.)

Precognition as foreknowing. Suppose one begins by thinking of precognition not as foreseeing but as foreknowing. Suppose then that one happens to be one of those who conceives of cognition on the model of perception. This is, of course, a misconception, but one with a most ancient and distinguished pedigree. One relevant reason for insisting that this model is inapplicable is that whereas it is logically possible for me to know now that certain things happened in the past and that other things will happen in the future, it is not logically possible for me now to perceive anything but what is now available to be perceived. Thus, anyone who thinks of precognition as a form of knowing and of knowing as a sort of perceiving will arrive by a rather longer route at exactly the same conclusions—that the future is present—as the person who begins by thinking of precognition as a type of perception. In either case the treatment indicated is essentially the same.

C. D. Broad comments:

> The fact is that most people who have tried to theorize about non-inferential precognition have made needless difficulties for themselves by making two mistakes. In the first place, they have tried to assimilate it to sense-perception, when they ought to have assimilated it to memory. And, secondly, they have tacitly assumed an extremely naive prehensive analysis . . . [which] is simply nonsensical when applied to ostensible remembering or ostensible foreseeing. ("The Philosophical Implications of Foreknowledge")

By "prehensive analysis" Broad means believing, mistakenly, that for an occurrence to be remembered it must somehow be present.

Fatalism. The model of memory is, as Broad urged, much less inapt than that of perception. But it, too, has its dangers. It has beguiled some into thinking that precognition must necessarily involve fatalism. The suggestion is that precognition would be an exact analogue and complement of memory, but where memory operates backward, precognition would be remembering forward. (See, for instance, Lewis Carroll, *Through the Looking Glass*, Ch. 5.) Now, if someone remembers that he himself killed Cock Robin, and provided that he really does remember and that he is not merely claiming, mistakenly or even dishonestly, to remember that he committed this crime, then it follows necessarily that he did kill Cock Robin. But if he has done it, then he has done it, and it must now be too late for anyone to intervene to save the victim. It is, notoriously, a tautology that what is done is done and cannot be undone. The past is unalterable. The temptation is to argue that the same must, in exactly the same sense, apply to the future. If I can truly precognize that I will kill Cock Robin—provided that it really is a precognition and that I am not merely claiming mistakenly, or even dishonestly, to be precognizing—then it follows necessarily that I will kill Cock Robin.

The false step is to go on to urge that by parity of reasoning, since he will do it, then he will do it, and therefore it must now be too late for anyone to save Cock Robin. For the conclusion does not follow. From the proposition that he will kill Cock Robin we are entitled to infer that he will kill Cock Robin and hence that no one will in fact save the bird. But what we are not entitled to infer is that it must now be too late to take any steps to save Cock Robin, that no one could possibly do anything to help. It is one thing to know that some catastrophe will in fact occur; it is quite another to know that there is now nothing that anyone could do to prevent it, even if he so wished. To know that he will in fact do it, it is sufficient to know that he in fact will: tautology. It is not necessary also to know, what may very well not be the case, either that he would not have been able to do otherwise had he been going to want to or

that no one else would have been able to stop him had they been going to be so inclined.

This point is, of course, involved in the much wider question of whether foreknowledge in the general sense must carry any such fatalist implications. The wider question is beyond the scope of this article, but the argument offered here is as applicable to the wider context as to this narrower one. The problem remains why it should be thought, as obviously it often is, that to establish the reality of noninferential precognition, even as an extremely weak and rare faculty, ought to raise fatalist anxieties in a much more acute form than does, for instance, the present possibility of inferring the outcome of some not too distantly future election—on the basis of a knowledge of the present preferences, psychological traits, beliefs, and expressed voting intentions of the electors concerned.

The threat to autonomy. One possible suggestion is that it may be thought that whereas predictions on the basis of knowledge of human beings do not constitute any threat to the autonomy and dignity of the persons concerned, a precognitive forecast about someone's future actions, made without reference to his peculiar characteristics, plans, and desires, would tend to show that his decisions to act in those ways will not be as causally necessary as he might like to believe. To show that human wishes, plans, and decisions do not affect what happens would indeed be to demonstrate a fatalist conclusion; for this is precisely what "fatalism" means. But to show that someone can know, without reference to that other person's wishes and plans, what another person is going to do is, surely, not sufficient to show that those wishes and plans will not determine his course of action.

It might be argued that knowledge presupposes grounds and that, insofar as the grounds contain no reference to the wishes and plans of the agent, this shows that he cannot properly be held responsible for what he is going to do. This argument would have more force if knowledge of what is going to occur always had to be grounded on knowledge of the presence of particular causes sufficient to bring about the occurrence. But quite apart from any question of whether it is true that all knowledge must be grounded on something else, the argument must be ineffective as long as we have to allow that some knowledge is quite sufficiently grounded simply on a recognition of reliable signs. Suppose precognition does actually occur, and suppose that it is properly to be classed as a form of knowledge; then it can be only either a variety which is not grounded at all or one which is based upon just such a recognition of signs—the recognition, namely, that some particular class of guesses, intuitions, visions, or whatnot are in fact reliable pointers to the future. For any inference, whether conscious or unconscious, from any knowledge, however acquired, of the causes of what is going to happen to the true conclusion that just that is indeed going to happen must by definition disqualify that conclusion as a genuine noninferential precognition.

Perceptual model and fatalism. A second suggestion is that the special anxiety felt in this case of precognition is just one more consequence of thinking in terms of a perceptual model. If in having a precognitive experience you were, as it were, seeing the future, then indeed it would be absurd to insist, once that experience has taken place, that there are any steps which anyone could take that could prevent the fulfillment of the precognition. It would be absurd so to insist because on this assumption of a literal foreseeing, the event precognized would by now have been seen happening. But once an event has happened there cannot be anything that anyone could possibly do to prevent it from happening.

Precognitive infallibility. A third suggestion is adapted to a rather different conception of the problem. It is common enough to find people who (at any rate, in their most self-consciously philosophical moments) would be reluctant to concede that there is any such thing as real knowledge of future events, or at least of future human actions. To such a person precognition might appear to present a special problem precisely because of the analogy to memory. This might, of course, be because he naively assimilated memory to perception. But he might in a rather more complicated way be arguing that since from the occurrence of a genuine memory one is entitled to deduce that the past was as that memory represents it to have been, therefore the occurrence of an authentic precognition would, insofar as precognition is to be conceived on the model of memory, provide a similarly inexpugnable guarantee that the future must necessarily be as it is precognized to be going to be. The idea would be, presumably, that whereas inferences can be invalid and their conclusions false, memory is necessarily infallible. Thus, if precognition is a reality, and if it is a faculty exactly analogous to memory, then it, too, must be similarly infallible. In that case there can be nothing which anyone could do to prevent the fulfillment of any such precognitive anticipations.

Insofar as this claim really represents a different contention from any so far considered, and it is not altogether clear that it does, the crucial error seems to lie in a confusion between remembering and mistakenly or dishonestly claiming to remember. True memory is, if you like, infallible, but only in the weak sense that "I remember doing it" entails "I did it," not in the strong sense that "I claim to remember doing it" entails "I did it." This is because it is always possible that in making such a memory claim I may either be mistaken or be acting dishonestly. Thus, to be exactly analogous to memory, precognition would have to be infallible in this and only this sense. But this sort of infallibility pertains equally to knowledge: for "He knows that the dogmas of his Roman Catholic faith are true" entails "The dogmas of his Roman Catholic faith are true"; whereas "He claims with absolute conviction that he knows that the dogmas of his faith are true" is by itself not even evidence for "The dogmas of his faith are true." And we have already devoted enough space to urging that from the possibility of knowledge as such of future human actions no fatalist conclusions follow necessarily.

"Forward memory" and fatalism. Another, and perhaps the most important, consideration encouraging the idea that parapsychological precognition must constitute a fatalist threat more serious than any arising from ordinary possibilities of foreknowledge is that what we remember is always and necessarily something in which somehow we ourselves were previously involved: we remember, that is, only what we have learned or what happened to us or what

we did. Therefore, insofar as precognition is to be thought of as "remembering forward," its contents must be similarly restricted to what we shall later come to know by other means, to what will happen to us, or to what we will do. But now, as long as I remain the sort of creature that I am, it will clearly not be possible for me to precognize something very unpleasant as going to happen to me without my casting about for ways in which the unpleasantness may be avoided. Hence, if there is to be precognition, at least one of three further conditions must be satisfied: either (1) the contents of my precognitions must be restricted to terms which even in an unchanged universe would not provoke me to effective avoiding action, or (2) I as the precognizer must be so changed that I no longer attempt any avoiding action, or (3) the universe around me must be so changed that my attempts are all in fact now ineffective. Obviously both the second and the third of these options would constitute major steps towards a fatalistic universe. Yet neither of these represents a necessary corollary of precognition as such. On the other hand, to take the first option is to accept a limitation which drastically reduces the analogy between precognition and memory. The conclusion is that any fatalist consequences belong to precognition as a faculty fully analogous to memory, not simply to precognition as such.

Cause and effect. It has sometimes been suggested that to establish the reality of precognition would be to show that in some cases effects can precede their causes. Surprising and disturbing though the effects reported certainly are, this at least is something that neither these nor any other phenomena could ever establish. The reason is, quite simply, that "a cause must either precede or be simultaneous with its effect" is a necessary truth. It is no more possible to discover an effect preceding its cause than to light upon a bachelor husband—and the impossibility is of the same sort in both cases.

Someone who had appreciated this point might well be inclined to dismiss it as merely verbal and trifling. He might claim that nevertheless we have here some radically new and theoretically highly recalcitrant facts and that to take account of them we must revise some of our old ideas.

Not every verbal point is trifling, however, and not all matters of definition are mere matters of definition. What looks like a piece of obstructive lexicography can be justified at a deeper level. The implicit definitions to which appeal was originally made are grounded on a more fundamental necessity. We cannot simply brush off the objection by prescribing a small revision in usage whereby causes may in future be spoken of as succeeding their effects, and then proceed exactly as before. The crux is that causes are—and in principle can always be used by us as—levers for bringing about their effects. But a cause which succeeded its effect could not be, or be used as, a lever for producing it. Once the "effect" has happened it must be too late for any "cause" to bring it about—and too late also for it to be prevented by preventing the occurrence of this "cause." To make this suggested change in the usage of the terms "cause" and "effect" would be not to modify but to disrupt the concept of cause. The refusal to accept the claim that in precognition we would be confronted with causes operating backward in time may therefore spring from something less discreditable than complacency. It might even be one manifestation of a conviction that to accommodate such a phenomenon we should need something much more radical and much more ratiocinative than a paradoxical but really not particularly significant set of adjustments in the usage of one or two common terms.

POSSIBLE EXPLANATIONS

The third kind of theoretical question about precognition is "What sort of explanation or account could we hope to find, supposing it were to be definitely established that precognition does indeed occur?" Presumably this would have to cover whatever other parapsychological phenomena were also found to be genuine. To provide such a theory would be enormously difficult, if not impossible. In any case, in the present confusing and apparently contradictory state of the evidence in this field, a state which should no doubt be attributed (at least in part) to the lack of any theory adequate to serve as even the most tentative of working hypotheses, it is impossible to say with confidence and precision just what are the phenomena of which we need to take account. Nevertheless there are three suggestions which it may perhaps be useful to consider.

Causal explanation. The first suggestion concerns the possibility of interpreting precognitive correlations in causal terms. To give a causal account of the subsistence of a statistically significant correlation between two series of events A and B involves showing either (1) that A results from B, or (2) that B results from A, or (3) that both A and B result from some third cause or set of causes, or (4) that both A and B are causally independent results of separate chains of causation. Suppose A is a series of precognitive guesses or anticipations and B a series of fulfillments or verifications. Series A cannot result from series B, for that would involve the logical impossibility of future occurrences bringing about events in the past. Series B cannot result from series A, for if it does, then the case is *ipso facto* disqualified by definition. And A and B cannot both result from some third cause or set of causes, for if they do, then again the case is by definition disqualified from rating as genuinely precognitive. The only remaining possibility is to say that A and B are both the causally independent results of separate chains of causation.

But to say this is precisely not to display a causal connection between A and B; it is, rather, to imply that the statistically significant correlation between the two series is a coincidence. This conclusion may be disturbing, but at least it has the merit of not involving any actual self-contradiction. For to establish a statistically significant correlation between two series of events is not thereby and necessarily to establish that these series are in any way connected causally. In the face of any correlation, however perfect and however extended, it is always significant, although often foolishly misguided, to insist that there is nevertheless no causal connection. Statements of constant conjunction do not entail statements of causal connection. Anyone who insists on a stronger sense of statistical significance, which would entail the subsistence of a causal connection, and who then proceeds to stipulate that

a precognitive correlation would have to be statistically significant in this stronger sense, will succeed only in making his concept of precognition self-contradictory from the start.

Coincidence. It seems that any explanation or, if that now becomes too strong a word, any account of precognition as such will have to center on the notion of coincidence or of something very like it. The laws, if there are any laws to be discovered, will describe the conditions under which we may expect to find precognitive correlations. One is reminded of C. G. Jung's talk about "synchronicity phenomena." For "synchronicity phenomenon" is in fact only a pretentious neologism for "coincidence," with perhaps a built-in suggestion that such phenomena are both more common and also somehow more significant than might be thought. It is a similarity which might easily be overlooked because of Jung's terminological peculiarities, because he associates the idea with many of his own more bizarre inventions, and because he exploits it for his own, it seems, often willfully antiscientific and antirational ends. A law of the kind suggested might paradoxically but pointedly be characterized as a law about the regularities in the conditions for the occurrence of a certain sort of coincidence.

Statistical explanation. Theorists seem to have taken far too little notice of the surely remarkable fact that it seems to be impossible either for the subjects or for anyone else to achieve any significant success in identifying, without reference to the targets, the particular guesses which are going to prove to be hits. Another similar and similarly neglected fact is that even after the guesses have been scored against the targets we have no criterion for distinguishing any particular hit as precognitive. In each case the reason for talking of precognition is not that any particular guess can, at some stage, be identified as precognitive but that, after the guesses have been checked against the targets, the proportion of hits in a series of guesses is found to be significantly above mean-chance expectation. With appropriate alterations the same thing seems to be true of all ostensible parapsychological phenomena. It is usually argued that whereas this perhaps has to be allowed in the case of quantitative experiments in card guessing, dice throwing, and so forth, it does not apply at all to what appear to be spontaneous cases of telepathy and clairvoyance, precognitive or straight. But this is surely wrong. For suppose we find that someone who had no means of inferring that the *Titanic* might meet disaster nevertheless had a dream which is later found to have corresponded in amazing detail with what actually happened on the night when that great ship went down. Still, our only warranty for describing his dream as precognitive lies precisely in that extraordinary degree of correspondence: any single item of correspondence might be dismissed as something which was bound to happen "by the law of averages," and so no single item can be picked out as unequivocally precognitive.

Of course this situation may conceivably at any time be transformed by the progress of the research. But at the time of writing it remains true that all the putative varieties of ESP, precognition in particular, are and must be defined in essentially statistical terms. This is no reason to ignore or to dismiss the evidence. But it may very well prove to be a significant theoretical pointer.

Bibliography

For general discussion consult C. J. Ducasse, "Broad on the Relevance of Psychical Research to Philosophy," pp. 375–410, A. G. N. Flew, "Broad on Supernormal Precognition," pp. 411–436, and C. D. Broad, "A Reply to My Critics," pp. 709–830, in P. A. Schilpp, ed., *The Philosophy of C. D. Broad* (New York, 1959); and W. G. Roll, "The Problem of Precognition," in the *Journal of the Society for Psychical Research,* Vol. 41 (1961), 2 ff. Roll's article is valuable especially for its bibliography.

There have been many ingenious discussions of ways of making operational distinctions between the various forms of ESP phenomena in the parapsychological journals since about 1930. For an excellent example, see C. W. K. Mundle, "The Experimental Evidence for PK and Precognition," in *Proceedings of the Society for Psychical Research,* Vol. 49 (1949–1952), 61–78.

For a criticism of Dunne's "Serial Theory of Time," see A. G. N. Flew, *A New Approach to Psychical Research* (London, 1953), Appendix II: "An Experiment with 'Time.'"

C. D. Broad's "The Philosophical Implications of Foreknowledge" was published in *PAS*, Supp. Vol. 16 (1937), 177–209. Broad referred the empirically curious to H. F. Saltmarsh's "Report on Cases of Apparent Precognition," in *Proceedings of the Society for Psychical Research,* Vol. 42 (1934), 49–103. With Saltmarsh's paper one may compare D. J. West's considerably more skeptical "The Investigation of Spontaneous Cases," in *Proceedings of the Society for Psychical Research,* Vol. 48 (1948), 264–300. The weight of both evidence and research has now shifted away from ostensible spontaneous cases of ESP toward quantitative experiments in card guessing. The classic series is that reported by S. G. Soal and K. M. Goldney in "Experiments on Precognitive Telepathy," in *Proceedings of the Society for Psychical Research,* Vol. 47 (1942–1945), 21–150. This work was hailed by Broad in 1944 in "The Experimental Establishment of Telepathic Communication." Soal and Frederick Bateman have since produced a general survey, *Modern Experiments in Telepathy* (London and New Haven, 1954).

On the infallibility of precognitive experiences and on cause and effect, see M. A. E. Dummet, "Can an Effect Precede Its Cause?" in *PAS*, Supp. Vol. 28 (1954), 27–44, and the reply with the same title by A. G. N. Flew in that volume, on pp. 45–62. See also Flew's *Hume's Philosophy of Belief* (London, 1961), Ch. 6.

For a fuller criticism of Jung's theory of synchronicity phenomena, see A. G. N. Flew's "Coincidence and Synchronicity," in *Journal of the Society for Psychical Research,* Vol. 37 (1953–1954), 198–201.

ANTONY FLEW

PREDESTINATION. See DETERMINISM.

PREDICATE. See SUBJECT AND PREDICATE.

PRE-SOCRATIC PHILOSOPHY. "Pre-Socratic" is the term commonly used (and the one that will be used here) to cover those Greek thinkers from approximately 600 to 400 B.C. who attempted to find universal principles which would explain the whole of nature, from the origin and ultimate constituents of the universe to the place of man within it. Yet 400 was the last year of Socrates' life, and among the Sophists, who are also excluded, Protagoras and Gorgias were older than he and others were his contemporaries. "Pre-Socratic" therefore indicates not so much a chronological limit as an outlook and a range of interests. This outlook Protagoras and Socrates deliberately attacked, condemning natural philosophy as worthless compared with the search for a good life, the discussion of

social and political questions, and individual morality. Socrates also dismissed its explanations as inadequate because expressed predominantly in terms of origins and internal mechanisms. In his view explanation should be functional, looking to the end rather than the beginning. Thus, for the last sixty or so years of the fifth century, both points of view existed, and a lively controversy went on between them. It was not that the natural philosophers excluded human nature from their investigations but that they saw man and society in a larger framework, as a particular late stage in cosmic development, whereas the others deliberately turned their backs on the external world. The universal and speculative character of pre-Socratic thought was also combated by some of the fifth-century medical writers, and it was in the fields of physiology and hygiene that observational science reached its highest point in this period.

Nature of the evidence. Before attempting to describe the pre-Socratic doctrines, it is necessary to emphasize the peculiar nature of our sources of knowledge. None of the pre-Socratics' works has survived independently. We have a few references in Plato, some more systematic discussion in Aristotle, and information from later compilers and commentators of which the greater part goes back to a history by Aristotle's pupil Theophrastus. Actual quotations occur and are in some cases extensive, as with the prose fragments of Heraclitus and the 450 surviving lines of Empedocles. Yet, from Aristotle onward, the men who passed on this information were not historians in the modern sense but wrote from a particular philosophical viewpoint (most often Peripatetic), searching the past for anticipations of their own ideas and selecting and arranging their material accordingly. The task of reconstruction and interpretation is thus very different from and more precarious than that of interpreting a philosopher whose original writings are still available for study.

The Milesian school. Pre-Socratic philosophy differs from all other philosophy in that it had no predecessors. Philosophy has been a continuous debate, and even highly original thinkers can be seen developing from or reacting against the thought of a predecessor. Aristotle is unimaginable without Plato; Newton, without Descartes, Kepler, Galileo, and many others. But with the Greeks of the sixth century the debate begins. Before them no European had set out to satisfy his curiosity about the world in the faith that its apparent chaos concealed a permanent and intelligible order, and that this natural order could be accounted for by universal causes operating within nature itself and discoverable by human reason. They had predecessors of a sort, of course. It was not accidental that the first pre-Socratics were citizens of Miletus, a prosperous trading center of Ionian Greeks on the Asiatic coast, where Greek and Oriental cultures met and mingled. The Milesian heritage included the myths and religious beliefs of their own peoples and their Eastern neighbors and also the store of Egyptian and Babylonian knowledge—astronomical, mathematical, technological. The influence of this heritage was considerable. Yet the Milesians consciously rejected the mythical and religious tradition of their ancestors, in particular its belief in the agency of anthropomorphic gods, and their debt to the knowledge of the East was not a philosophic one. That knowledge was limited because its aim was practical. Astronomy served religion; mathematics settled questions of land measurement and taxation. For these purposes the careful recording of data and the making of certain limited generalizations sufficed, and the realm of ultimate causes was left to dogmatism. For the Greeks knowledge became an end in itself, and in the uninhibited atmosphere of Miletus they gave free play to the typically Greek talent for generalization, abstraction, and the erection of bold and all-embracing explanatory hypotheses.

Consciously, the revolt of the Milesian philosophers against both the content and the method of mythology was complete. No longer were natural processes to be at the mercy of gods with human passions and unpredictable intentions. In their place was to come a reign of universal and discoverable law. Yet a whole conceptual framework is not so easily changed. Poetic and religious cosmogonies had preceded the schemes of the Milesians, and the basic assumptions of these can be detected beneath the hypotheses of their philosophic successors. Nevertheless, the achievement of abandoning divine agencies for physical causes working from within the world itself can hardly be overestimated.

It was common to the mythologies of Greece and neighboring civilizations (and, indeed, to others) that the world arose from a primitive state of unity and that the cosmogonic process was one of separation or division. This was the first act of the Hebrew Creator. In the Babylonian *Enuma Elish* the original state of the universe was an undefined mass of watery cloud. The Greek theogony of Hesiod speaks of Heaven and Earth, conceived as anthropomorphic figures, lying locked in an embrace until their son forced them apart as Marduk formed heaven and earth by splitting apart the body of the monster Tiamat. Euripides relates an old tale according to which earth and heaven were once "one form" and after their separation brought to birth the whole variety of living things. In Egypt (like Babylonia, a river culture) everything arose out of the primeval waters.

Thales. It is not surprising, therefore, that the first men to seek a universal explanation of the world along rational lines assumed that it was in substance a unity from which its variety had been produced by some process of segregation. The key, they thought, lay in identifying the single substance which must satisfy the condition of being able to produce variety out of itself. Thales (active in 585 B.C.), who chose water or moisture, may still have had the myths at the back of his mind. For him the earth floated on water as it did for the Egyptians. Little else certain is known of him, and we can only guess at his reasons. Water can be seen as solid, liquid, and vaporous. Aristotle thought it more probable that Thales was influenced by the essential connection of moisture with life, as seen in such substances as semen, blood, and sap. With the removal of external personal agents, the world must initiate its own changes, and at this early stage of speculation the only possibility seemed to be that life of some kind is everywhere and that the universe is a growing, organic structure. This may be the explanation of the saying attributed to Thales: "Everything is full of gods."

Anaximander. With Anaximander, Thales' younger con-

temporary, there emerges the notion of the four primary opposites which later, when the concepts of substance and attribute had been distinguished, gave rise to the four elements adopted by Aristotle and destined for a long and influential history. Anaximander spoke of only the hot and the dry, which were inevitably in conflict with the cold and the wet. This led him to a momentous idea. The original substance of the universe could not be anything definitely qualified like water, for how could the cold and wet produce their opposites, the hot and dry? Water quenches fire; it cannot engender it. Prior to all perceptible body there must be an indefinite something with none of the incompatible qualities implied by perceptibility. Although still regarding all that exists as corporeal, Anaximander is the first to find ultimate reality in the nonperceptible.

This primary substance he called the apeiron, a word of many meanings all related to the absence of limits—everlasting, infinite, indefinite. Because it was imperishable, the origin of all things, and the author of their changes, he called it (says Aristotle) divine. From it all things have been "separated out," though in what sense they were previously "in" it while the apeiron itself remained a unity is a question which probably did not present itself to him. Somewhere in the apeiron, Theophrastus asserts, a "germ" or "seed" of hot and cold was separated off, and from the interaction of these two flowed the whole cosmic process. A sphere of flame enclosed a moist mass, more solid at the center where the earth formed, vaporous between. The sphere burst into rings around which the dark vapor closed, leaving holes through which we see what appear as sun, moon, and stars. Wet and dry continue to separate, forming land and sea, and finally life itself is produced by the same action of heat (sun) on the cold and moist portions of the earth. The first animals were born in water and crawled onto dry land. Human infants were originally born and nurtured within the bodies of fishlike creatures, for under primitive conditions unprotected babies could not have survived.

The earth, a flat cylinder, hangs freely in space because of its equal distance from all parts of the spherical universe. The sun is the same size as the earth. Eclipses are caused by the closing of the holes in the vapor tubes of the sun and moon. In this first of all attempts at a rational cosmogony and zoogony, the sudden freedom from mythical modes of thought is almost incredible.

Anaximenes. Further reflection led Anaximenes, the youngest member of the Milesian school, to a different conclusion about the primary substance: it was air. In its elusiveness and invisibility as atmospheric air, it could almost match the apeiron, and, whereas apeiron, once differentiated into a universe, could no longer be so called, air could become hotter and colder, rarer and denser, and still remain the same substance. Moreover, this theory allowed Anaximenes to break with the notion of separation, which was, at bottom, mythical, and account for the universe by the extension of a known natural process. This was condensation and rarefaction, the former of which he associated with cold and the latter with heat. Air as it rarefies becomes fire; condensed, it turns first to wind, then to cloud, water, earth, and stones. In other words, it is all a question of how much of it there is in a given space, and for the first time the idea enters science that qualitative differences are reducible to differences of quantity. This is Anaximenes' main achievement, although there is no evidence that he applied the principle with any mathematical exactness.

With air as his basic, self-changing substance, Anaximenes could find room for the ancient belief that life was identical with breath. Macrocosm and microcosm were animated by the same principle: "Just as our soul, which is air, integrates us, so breath and air surround the whole cosmos."

The few details that we have of his cosmology suggest that compared with Anaximander's, it was reactionary and timid. His contribution lies elsewhere.

The Pythagoreans. Pythagoras (c. 570–490) was also an eastern Greek but migrated from his native Samos to Croton in southern Italy. As a result the western or Italian Greek philosophers, even when not actual members of his school, became known for a characteristic outlook very different from that of the materialistic and purely rational Milesians and stamped with the impress of his remarkable genius. He founded a brotherhood dedicated to *philosophia* (the word was believed to be his invention) as a way of life, with a strong religious, and also a political, element. Philosophically, his importance lies in the shift of interest from matter to form. Inspired, it is said, by the discovery that the musical intervals known to the Greeks as consonant (and marked by four fixed strings on the seven-stringed lyre) were explicable in terms of ratios of the numbers 1 through 4, Pythagoras saw the universe as one glorious *harmonia*, or mathematico-musical structure. Number was the key to nature. This idea had incalculable consequences for science even if it led at the time to some rather fanciful equations of natural objects and moral qualities with particular numbers. In spite of that, by the time of Socrates the school had made real progress in mathematics. Since the cosmic harmony included everything, all life was akin. The soul was immortal and underwent a series of incarnations, both human and animal. Philosophy was the effort to understand the structure of the cosmic harmony, with the ultimate aim of integrating the philosophic soul more closely into that harmony on the principle that knowledge assimilates the knower to its object. This aim also demanded the observance of certain religious precepts of which the most important was abstention from animal food.

Heraclitus. Heraclitus (active c. 500) objected to the Pythagorean emphasis on harmony, maintaining that, on the contrary, strife and opposition were the life of the world. Life was maintained by a tension of opposites fighting a continuous battle in which neither side could win final victory. Thus, movement and the flux of change were unceasing for individuals, but the structure of the cosmos remained constant. This law of individual flux within a permanent universal framework was guaranteed by the Logos, an intelligent governing principle materially embodied as fire, the most subtle element and identified with soul or life.

Philosophy had thus far meant the search for an essentially simpler reality underlying the bewildering confusion of appearances. The answers fell into two broad categories, matter and form: reality was a single material substance (the Milesians) or an integral principle of structure which could be expressed in terms of numbers (the Pythagoreans). Heraclitus, with a statement like "You cannot step twice into the same river," reaches the logical conclusion of the materialistic answer. The water will be different water the second time, and, if we call the river the same, it is because we see its reality in its form. The logical conclusion of form-philosophy is the opposite of flux—namely, a belief in an absolute, unchanging reality of which the world of change and movement is only a quasi-existing phantom, phenomenal, not real. (This conclusion was reached in the idealism of Plato, which was largely of Pythagorean inspiration.)

Eleatic school: unity of reality. At this time the direction of philosophy was changed by the precocious and uncompromising logic of Parmenides of Elea, who was perhaps 25 years younger than Heraclitus. For the first time abstract, deductive reasoning is deliberately preferred to the evidence of the senses: "Ply not eye and ear and tongue, but judge by thought." He concluded that if there is any reality at all (in the language of his time, if "it is"), it must be (1) one only (for if more than one, its units could be separated only by "what is not"); (2) eternal and unchanging (for to speak of change or perishing is to say that reality at some time "is not" what it was, but to say of "what is" "it is not" is contradictory and impossible); (3) immovable (this follows from his statement that "all is full of what is"; since it cannot admit discontinuity or lack of homogeneity and since "what is not is not," the spatial requirements of locomotion cannot be provided). In this way he "proved" that, on the premise of his predecessors that reality is one, differentiation of the real can never occur. It remains one—a timeless, changeless, motionless, homogeneous mass, which he compared to a sphere. The multiple, changing world of appearances is an illusion of our senses. Only as a concession to human weakness, and in recognition of our practical need to come to terms with the show of a natural world, did he append a cosmology of the conventional type, beginning with two principles, heat-light and cold-darkness. Cosmogony from a single origin was no longer possible, yet he explicitly warns his hearers that reality is in truth a unity and that the cosmos is only a deceitful appearance to mortals.

It is disputed whether the One Reality of Parmenides is material. The question can hardly be answered, since we are still in a period before the distinction between material and nonmaterial could be drawn. The important thing is that it was nonsensible and could be reached only by thought. Parmenides was the first philosopher to distinguish explicitly between the sensible and the intelligible and to condemn the former as unreal. Plato himself, though fully aware of the distinction between material and spiritual, usually preferred to call them sensible and intelligible, and it is very doubtful whether the philosophy of Platonic idealism would ever have been possible without Parmenides.

Zeno and Melissus. Parmenides had two followers, who, with him, are known as the Eleatic school. Zeno of Elea (born c. 490) concentrated on a defense of the proposition that reality is one and immovable by the dialectical method of showing up absurdities in the contrary view. His famous paradoxes are aimed at demonstrating the impossibility of plurality and movement. Melissus of Samos (active in 440) modified Parmenides' ideas to the extent of saying that reality is infinite. He explicitly denied the possibility of empty space (which Parmenides had only hinted at) and said that if there *were* many things, each would have to have the characteristics of the Parmenidean One. It is therefore probable that the atomists had him especially in mind when they boldly explained the world in terms of space plus tiny entities, each of which had many of the Eleatic qualities—indivisibility, homogeneity, unalterability.

The naïveté of Parmenides' logic and the purely linguistic nature of some of his difficulties seem obvious now, but at the time his questions appeared unanswerable. There were only two ways out: either to abandon monism and admit the ultimate plurality of the real or to admit the unreality of the natural world. The latter solution was Plato's, with his contrast between "what always is and never becomes" and "what is continually becoming (like the flux of Heraclitus) but never truly is." The remainder of pre-Socratic thought is occupied with attempts to save the phenomena by adopting some form of pluralism.

The pluralists: Empedocles. The first of the pluralistic systems was that of Empedocles (c. 490–430), a Sicilian poet-philosopher steeped in the Western tradition, with its combination of rationalism and mystical religion so different from the purely scientific outlook of the Ionians. His proposal was the first clear enunciation of the four-element theory. Fire, air, water, and earth are the ultimate roots of all things, themselves ungenerated and indestructible. Everything in nature comes into being and perishes by the mixture and separation of these substances. The first premise is no longer "It is" but "They are." Thus, trees and animals, clouds and rocks, are not mere illusion. However, since they are only temporary combinations of the four "realities" in varying proportions, we can admit that they themselves are not "real." Nor need the forbidden concepts of "becoming" and "perishing" be invoked; mixture and separation will account for all. Locomotion is, of course, necessary, and, although he accepts the Eleatic denial of empty space, Empedocles seems to have thought that this could occur by some reciprocal and simultaneous exchange of place, the whole remaining full.

The four elements are not self-moving (another concept which Parmenides had rendered difficult), and the blend of mystic and rationalist in Empedocles appears especially in his motive causes. These were two, Love and Strife, the former bringing disparate elements together and the latter drawing them apart. They are in endless opposition and prevail in turn, bringing about a double evolutionary cycle. Under Love all four elements are indistinguishably fused in a sphere; under Strife the same sphere contains them in separate layers. During the contest, when neither Love nor Strife is in complete control and when the elements are partly joined and partly separated, a world like our own is formed. Nothing existent is as yet incorporeal, though Love and Strife are of finer and more tenuous substance than the elements. Their names are no metaphors, nor is

their action purely mechanical. Under Love the elements are dear to and desired by one another; Strife makes them grim and hostile. Nothing is purely inanimate, and everything has its share of consciousness. Besides his poem on nature, Empedocles also wrote a religious one, in which the moral character of Love and Strife is emphasized—Love is good, Strife evil. In the present world Strife is gaining, and men have fallen from a previous blessed state by giving themselves to Strife and sin, above all the sin of killing and eating animals. All life is akin, as it was to the Pythagoreans, and our souls are fallen spirits which must undergo a series of incarnations before they can win back their former state by abjuring Strife and cultivating Love. What the substance of the spirits was is not clearly stated, but most probably in their pure state they were portions of Love which are now contaminated with Strife.

Anaxagoras. Anaxagoras of Clazomenae (c. 500–428) brings us back to Ionia both geographically and in spirit. His motive is rational curiosity entirely uncomplicated by religious preoccupations. Even Parmenides, a Westerner like Empedocles, had written in verse and represented his deductive arguments as a revelation from a goddess. In his return to prose, as in his purely scientific aims, Anaxagoras is the heir of the Milesians. At Athens, where he lived until exiled for atheism, he was a member of the brilliant and freethinking circle of Pericles. His prosecution seems to have had a political flavor, but the charge is nevertheless significant: he declared the sun to be not a living divinity but a lump of incandescent rock larger than the Peloponnese.

To save the phenomena without admitting the coming into being or destruction of what exists, he adopted an extreme form of pluralism plus a first cause of motion, which he called Mind. It is described as knowing all things and having the greatest power, and, in order to control the material world, it is entirely outside the mixture of which the material world is formed. It is not easy to be sure whether Anaxagoras is at last trying to express the notion of incorporeal being without an adequate vocabulary or whether he still thinks of Mind as an extremely subtle and tenuous form of matter. At any rate, its separateness from the constituents of the cosmos is emphasized at every turn. In spite of the references to its knowledge and power, it action seems to be confined to the earliest stages of cosmogony, except in the case of living creatures. They are an exception to the rule that Mind is in nothing else, and them it still controls.

In the beginning "all things were together," a stationary mass in which nothing could be distinguished. Mind is the agent which has produced from this an ordered cosmos. It did so by starting a rotatory movement or vortex, which by its own increasing speed brought about the gradual separation of different forms of matter. Anaxagoras' highly subtle and ingenious theory of matter seems to have been especially prompted by the need to explain nourishment and organic growth: how can flesh and hair come out of the not-flesh and not-hair of the food we eat? After Parmenides the coming into being of new substances is disallowed. Anaxagoras answered that there is a portion of everything in everything—that is, every distinguishable substance, in however small a quantity, contains minute particles of every other but is characterized by that which predominates. He boldly asserted the existence of the infinitesimal (which Zeno had denied) in the words: "Of the small there is no smallest."

The atomists. Perhaps around 430 Leucippus promulgated the much simpler theory of atomism, which was further developed by his famous pupil Democritus of Abdera (born c. 460). Like the other theories, this one arose in direct response to the Eleatic challenge. Its most striking innovation for its time was the assertion of the existence of genuine empty space. Thus far, everyone had believed that "what is" must be some form of body, and, when Parmenides brought into consciousness the implicit consequence that space, not being "what is," must be "what is not" (that is, nonexistent), his conclusion seemed logically inescapable. Hence, even the atomists had to use the paradoxical expression that it is no more correct to say of "what is" than of "what is not" that it *is*. At this particular point in the philosophic debate, this was the only way of expressing the conviction that, though not any kind of stuff, space must be assumed if the plain facts are to be explained. Democritus, said Aristotle, is to be commended for refusing to be dazzled by the abstract logic of Parmenides and for relying on the kind of argument more proper to a natural scientist. Reality consists of innumerable microscopic and indivisible (*a-tomos* = uncuttable) bodies in motion in infinite space. They are solid and homogeneous but infinitely variable in size and shape. At different places in the infinite, they have collided and become entangled. Projections hook together, convex fits into concave, and so on. Their continued motion sets up a vortex in which the larger and heavier fall into the center and the smaller and lighter are extruded to the circumference; in this way a cosmos is formed. There are many worlds, and not all are similar to our own. The first atomists appear to have provided no separate cause of motion, perhaps because they deemed it sufficient to free the atoms by setting them loose in infinite space. After all, the chief Eleatic arguments against motion had been the continuity of being and the nonexistence of a void.

Only atoms and the void exist. Sensible qualities other than size and shape are subjective, caused by interaction between the atoms of external objects and those in our own bodies. This was worked out in considerable detail. For instance, hard objects have their atoms more closely packed than do soft. Sweet flavors are caused by smooth atoms, bitter and astringent by sharp or hooked. Colors vary according to the positions of surface atoms, which cause them to reflect in different ways the light that falls upon them. Objects are continually throwing off films of atoms, and sight is the reception of these films by the eye. The soul, or life principle, is composed of smooth, round atoms that are even more mobile than the rest and impart to the body the power of motion and cognition, for "soul and mind are the same"—that is, composed of the same kind of atoms. Soul is dispersed throughout the body, alternating with body atoms, but the mind appears to have been a collection of these finest particles that is located probably in the breast. Although the direct objects of

sight and hearing, taste and smell, are unreal, they lead the mind to the truth about reality, and Democritus quoted with approval a saying of Anaxagoras: "Phenomena are a glimpse of the unseen."

Ancient atomism (including its revival by Epicurus a century or more after Democritus) has acquired a partly adventitious reputation through its resemblances to nineteenth-century physical theories, but its hard, solid, unbreakable particles have little in common with the ultimate entities of modern science. Its most striking features are the distinction between primary and secondary qualities (upheld by Descartes, Galileo, and Locke), the explanation of directly observable objects by hypothetical constituents below the level of perception, and the outspoken championship of discrete quanta as opposed to a continuum. Its inadequacy in allowing no mode of action other than direct contact, collision, and interlocking was evident in some physical problems—for example, in its attempted explanation of magnetism and, most of all, in the effort to include within its purview the phenomena of life and thought. The atomic structure of matter has indeed been a fruitful hypothesis, but the intention of its authors is best understood in the context of their time and as an attempt to escape the Eleatic dilemma, rather than as an anticipation of postmedieval science.

Diogenes of Apollonia. The teleological explanation, which one would naturally associate with Anaxagoras' adoption of Mind as first cause, appears more strongly in the second half of the fifth century in a less gifted thinker, Diogenes of Apollonia. He put Mind back into the mixture by returning to Anaximenes' idea that the primary substance is air or breath and by identifying this air in its purest (dry and warm) state with intelligence. The regularity of cosmic events he regarded as evidence of intelligent control, going so far as to say that anyone who reflects will agree that all is arranged in the best possible way. Breath is also the life of men and animals, so that all owe their soul and mind to the same material principle—"a small portion of the god"—which they share in varying degrees of purity. He probably thought he avoided the Eleatic arguments against a materialistic monism by the admission of void, which, by the time he wrote (after Melissus and Leucippus), would in any case be recognized as necessary for the process of condensation and rarefaction by which air produced the variety of nature.

When we consider the grotesqueness of some of the mythological background from which the pre-Socratic thinkers started, we must be amazed by the intellectual insight and firm grasp of universal principles which at their best they were capable of displaying. But a dispassionate assessment of their contribution to the history of philosophy would probably show that, to use a metaphor, although they manufactured many of the pieces and set them on the board, Plato and Aristotle were the first players who learned the rules and started the game. The pieces are those opposed concepts by means of which philosophical discussion is maintained: being and becoming, sensible and intelligible, analytic and synthetic, appearance and reality, time and eternity, materialism and idealism, mechanism and teleology, and so forth. Once these stand out clearly, a philosopher may champion one or the other, but the pre-Socratics could not yet do this. One cannot speak realistically of a controversy among them between, say, materialists and idealists. The achievement of their intellectual effort and controversy was that by the end of this period a clear notion of what was meant by matter and mind, sensible and intelligible, phenomenal and real, and the rest was at last emerging, so that succeeding generations had the set in their hands and could begin the game in earnest. For the first of all philosophers, this was no mean achievement.

Their interests were, of course, in modern terms, as much scientific as philosophical, and in this sphere also they could claim some remarkable results. For instance, before the end of the period the true cause of both lunar and solar eclipses had been discovered (probably by Anaxagoras), and certain Pythagoreans had abandoned the geocentric cosmology, asserting that the earth, sun, and planets all circled round a central fire. But it is probably fair to say that their scientific discoveries appeared only as by-products of the main controversies and of the few universal principles from which they confidently deduced even the details of the physical world. The true and lasting discoveries were not picked up and developed as they would have been by post-Renaissance scientists because, owing to the different preoccupations of philosophy at their time, they had no firm basis in established fact and did not in any way stand out from other and, to us, more fanciful assumptions.

Bibliography

GENERAL WORKS

Burnet, John, *Early Greek Philosophy*, 4th ed. London, 1930. For long the standard work, now out of date in some respects.

Cornford, F. M., *Principium Sapientiae: The Origins of Greek Philosophical Thought*. Cambridge, 1952. For the transition from myth to philosophy.

Diels, Hermann, and Kranz, Walther, *Die Fragmente der Vorsokratiker*, 10th ed. Berlin, 1960. Comprehensive critical edition of Greek texts for classical scholars; with German translation.

Frankfort, H., and others. *The Intellectual Adventure of Ancient Man*. Chicago, 1946. Reprinted as *Before Philosophy*. Baltimore, 1949. Excellent account of the climate of thought in Near Eastern countries when Greek philosophy began.

Guthrie, W. K. C., *A History of Greek Philosophy*, Vol. I, *The Earlier Presocratics and the Pythagoreans*. Cambridge, 1962. Vol. II, *The Presocratic Tradition From Parmenides to Democritus*. Cambridge, 1965. Comprehensive but intended for general reading.

Jaeger, Werner, *The Theology of the Early Greek Philosophers*. Oxford, 1947. A very readable account.

Kirk, G. S., and Raven, J. E., *The Presocratic Philosophers*. Cambridge, 1957. Selection of texts with English translation and commentary.

PARTICULAR THINKERS OR SCHOOLS

Bailey, C., ed., *The Greek Atomists and Epicurus*. Oxford, 1928. Criticism and text.

Bignone, Ettore, ed., *Empedocle*. Turin, 1916. Full and scholarly account with translation of fragments and discussion of alternative views; in Italian.

Kahn, C. H., *Anaximander and the Origins of Greek Cosmology*. New York, 1960.

Kirk, G. S., ed., *Heraclitus: The Cosmic Fragments*. Cambridge, 1954.

Lee, H. D. P., ed., *Zeno of Elea*. Cambridge, 1936. Full text and translation of passages, with commentary.

Raven, J. E., *Pythagoreans and Eleatics*. Cambridge, 1948. For classical specialists; the Greek quotations are not translated.

W. K. C. GUTHRIE

PRESUPPOSING. The notions of presupposing and of contextual implication, which we shall compare and contrast in what follows, have come to play increasingly prominent roles in the philosophical literature of the English-speaking world during the past 25 years. This development is not accidental but arises from the stress the twentieth century puts upon analysis as a fundamental mode of philosophical inquiry. The notions of presupposing and of contextual implication play both negative and positive roles within this general orientation. Negatively, they are devices that contemporary thinkers employ in order to minimize the tendency of philosophers and other reflective persons to view the world in terms of oversimplified conceptual models. Positively, they function as instruments in the dissection and ultimate understanding of certain human activities, especially those that involve the efforts of human beings to communicate with one another, as in promising, stating, saying, implying, a task which, some philosophers feel, is hindered or obstructed by the natural disposition of reflective individuals to subsume such activities under excessively simple descriptions. The appeal to the notions of presupposing and of contextual implication has thus served to widen—and at the same time to make more accurate—our conceptions of the circumstances in which human communication takes place. This essay will describe the history (all of it very recent, of course) of the major developments that have taken place with regard to these subjects, and will in this way attempt to bring out their essential features.

Similarities and differences. It is no simple matter to show why presupposing and contextual implication are two separate concepts, since the differences between them are subtle. Most writers have, in fact, not discriminated between them, in part because both notions are slippery but also because they have similar functions. Their similarities may be elucidated as follows. If we distinguish between what a person explicitly states, or asserts, when he utters certain words in certain circumstances and what he (or perhaps his statement) implies, then the concepts of presupposing and of contextual implication belong to the latter category rather than to the former. This crude distinction must be refined further, however, for the sense of "implies" that is being marked out here is not that of logical implication in any of the various senses of that term—for example, the sense involved in saying that "X is a husband" implies "X is married." Indeed, both presupposing and contextual implication are to be contrasted with logical implication. The kinds of implications that fall into this category may be indicated by simple examples. In saying "alas!" in certain circumstances, I am normally taken as implying that I am unhappy. But I am not taken to be asserting that I am unhappy, as I would be if I were to utter the words "I am unhappy." Or, to vary the example, when a person says, "All my children are now in college," he is normally taken to be implying that he has children (although not to be asserting that he has), and his auditors are justified in making this assumption. Or again, when one says in such sorts of contexts, "Smith has just gone out," he implies, or his words imply, that he believes or knows that Smith has gone out, and those to whom he is speaking are justified in assuming that he does. That the sense of "implication" expressed by these examples is not that of logical implication may be illustrated by the observation that there is no formal contradiction in asserting "All my children are in college, but I have no children" or in asserting "Smith has gone out, but I don't believe he has." Indeed, in standard systems of mathematical logic, the first statement is true whenever the speaker has no children, and the second is true whenever Smith has gone out but the speaker does not believe he has.

Sentences like "All my children are in college, but I have no children" and "Smith has gone out, but I don't believe he has" thus satisfy the rules of logical syntax and, indeed, the rules for correct English. Yet they fall upon the ear as decidedly odd. If employed at all in everyday speech, they would occur only in unusual circumstances— "I don't believe he has" might be whispered as an aside to a confederate, for example. But except for situations like this, they would be perplexing things to say. What, then, is the source of their oddity, given that they do not involve any formal mistake?

It is now generally agreed that the oddity we feel upon hearing such sentences stems from a disparity between the conditions we assume will have been satisfied whenever someone is trying to communicate with another and the utterances we expect will be employed in those circumstances. In effect, this is to say that certain assumptions, or presuppositions, that communicating human beings make in the everyday give-and-take of verbal intercourse, assumptions that thus form the ground of such intercourse, fail to hold or are violated in such circumstances.

Talk about presuppositions and talk about what is contextually implied by a speaker's words thus have in common a reference to the background conditions normally expected to obtain when an utterance is made. If stating and asserting are conceived of as elements constituting part of the foreground of the situation in which communication takes place (that is, as activities that bring an item of information into the immediate focus of attention), then presupposing and contextual implication may be thought of as elements constituting part of the background of the situation (that is, as factors that remain implicit unless they are otherwise articulated but that nonetheless are essential factors in communication). Part of the task that faces the student of informal logic is to specify what these conditions are, how they contribute to the background that makes communication possible, and what sorts of relations exist between them and the utterances that occupy the foreground during the transmission of information.

Let us then call the concepts referring to such conditions background concepts. Because such concepts play covert roles in daily discourse and because their functions are remarkably similar, it is not surprising that many writers have failed to discriminate between them. But not all writers have blurred the distinction. Isabel C. Hungerland is one notable exception. In her important paper "Contex-tual Implication" (*Inquiry*, Vol. 4, 1960, pp. 211–258), she writes, "The relation (presupposing) defined by Strawson is *not* that of contextual implication. . . . The relation between the two may be indicated as follows: When S presupposes S', a speaker in making the statement S, contextually implies that he believes that S'" (p. 239). Following Mrs. Hungerland's suggestion and overlooking the many subtleties a full treatment of the subject would demand, we may say that the key distinctions that mark off the one notion from the other are those of scope: Neither the conditions subsumed under the two notions nor the range of entities to which the notions apply are in all cases the same.

Presupposing is a concept referring to those conditions that must be satisfied before an utterance can count as a statement, or if "statement" is so defined that statements need be neither true nor false (see P. F. Strawson, "Iden-tifying Reference and Truth-values," in *Theoria*, Vol. 30, Part 2, 1964), then presupposing applies to those conditions that must be satisfied before statements can be either true or false. Contextual implication, on the other hand, is a concept that applies to those conditions that must be satisfied before an utterance can count as "normal" in the circumstances in which it is made—that is, it applies to those beliefs a speaker has when he makes the utterance he does in certain circumstances and which rule out that he is lying or deliberately deceiving someone. The range of entities thus referred to by the concept of presupposing is either the class of statements as such or the class of those statements that are either true or false, whereas the range of entities referred to by the notion of contextual implica-tion is the class of beliefs held by the speaker (and, deriv-atively, by his auditors).

Examples may be invoked at this point to illuminate the above remarks. Suppose during the course of a conversa-tion I say, "The store on the corner sells such goods," not realizing that there is no longer a store on the corner. My remark in this circumstance is neither true nor false; as R. G. Collingwood puts it, the question of its truth or falsity "does not arise." For it is a presupposition of my using that utterance to make a statement (that is, an utterance that can be either true or false) that there be such a store. We may say in such a case that it is a condition of the truth or falsity of the remark that the store exist. But I may well believe that there is such a store, and in making the remark, I imply that I have this belief at the time of my utterance. One of the conditions for the normality of the remark (that is, that I was not lying) is that I had this belief at the time of say-ing what I did. We may say therefore that the conditions determining the normality of the background from which my remark issued and the conditions determining the background from which a statement would have issued are different conditions. It is this sort of difference in the background conditions that determines the difference between the concepts of presupposing and of contextual implication.

History of contextual implication. The genesis of the notions of contextual implication and of presupposing differs considerably. As a philosophical subject, contextual implication, under another name, has a longer traceable history in the modern period than does presupposing. The history of contextual implication is mainly connected with developments in moral philosophy, especially with efforts to give a correct analysis of the use of moral language. In G. E. Moore's *Ethics* (London, 1912), for example, we find the following comments:

> There is an important distinction, which is not always observed, between what a man *means* by a given assertion and what he *expresses* by it. Whenever we make any assertion whatever (unless we do not mean what we say) we are always *expressing* one or other of two things—namely, either that we *think* the thing in question to be so, or that we *know* it to be so." (p. 125)

In the subsequent history of moral philosophy the distinction referred to by Moore became the key distinction invoked by those authors who espoused the emotive theory of ethics. According to advocates of this doctrine, the sorts of utterances used in moral contexts ("That's good," "Stealing is wrong") are not being used to make assertions and hence are neither true nor false, as both naturalists and nonnaturalists had assumed. The primary use of such utterances is to express the attitude or the feelings of the speaker toward whatever he is talking about and to arouse comparable attitudes in the auditor. The later history of contextual implication is deeply concerned with the import of this distinction, and the main works in which it is discussed, sometimes critically, are *Language, Truth and Logic* by A. J. Ayer (London, 1936); *The Philosophy of G. E. Moore*, edited by P. A. Schilpp (Evanston, Ill., 1942), pp. 540–554; *Ethics and Language* by C. L. Stevenson (New Haven, 1944); *Ethics* by P. H. Nowell-Smith (Harmondsworth, 1954); *The Emotive Theory of Ethics* by Avrum Stroll (Berkeley, 1954); *The Logic of Moral Discourse* by Paul Edwards (Glencoe, Ill., 1955); and "Contextual Implication" by Isabel Hungerland (see above). Various formulas are proposed by some of these writers.

Nowell-Smith says, for example, "A statement *p* contextually implies *q* if anyone who knew the normal conventions of the language would be entitled to infer *q* from *p in the context in which they occur*" (*Ethics*, p. 80). According to Isabel Hungerland all such early attempts to characterize the relation that obtains between what a speaker expressly asserts and what he implies suffer either from vagueness or from mistakenly thinking that the relation is a special case of inductive inference. Her own contention is that it is neither vague nor a case of inductive inference, but is, rather, the presumption that in a situation of communication, acts of stating are normal. She thus likens contextual implication to the juridical principle that a man is presumed to be innocent until proved guilty, a principle which is not arrived at inductively, by surveying the evidence, but which serves to place the onus of proof in a legal contest upon the prosecution. As she puts it, "Contextual inference (if we wish to use the word) is a matter, rather, of a communal assumption in the absence of evidence to the contrary, that, in a situation of communication, acts of stating are normal" (p. 233). Her view is that contextual implication depends upon three factors: (1) The presence of a stating context (since the question of a man's believing what he says does not arise in a nonstating context); (2) the presumptions of normality (that is, that within

a stating context the implication holds only if the presumptions are principles of communication); and (3) rules for the correct use of an expression (that is, whether belief is implied when a man says *p* will be in part determined by rules for the correct use of *p*).

History of presupposing. Unlike contextual implication, the notion of presupposing has its genesis in logical theory, especially in those developments involving alternative accounts of Bertrand Russell's theory of descriptions and of the so-called square of opposition. The writer most closely identified with both of these matters is P. F. Strawson of Oxford University. He has dealt with the theory of descriptions in his papers "On Referring" (*Mind*, 1950), "Presupposing" (*Philosophical Review*, 1954) and "Identifying Reference and Truth-values" (see above) and in his book *Individuals* (London, 1959; Ch. 8 especially). In *Introduction to Logical Theory* (London, 1952) Strawson considers both the theory of descriptions and the square of opposition.

In the works that deal only with the theory of descriptions, Strawson rejects Russell's analysis of sentences containing definite descriptive phrases (that is, phrases of the form "the so and so" used in the singular in English). According to Russell, the analysis of a sentence like "The queen of England is beautiful" contains in part an assertion to the effect that the queen of England exists. Strawson argues, cogently, that this statement is not an explicit part of what is asserted by "The queen of England is beautiful" but is presupposed by a speaker who would use such a sentence in normal circumstances to make a statement. In *Introduction to Logical Theory*, Strawson goes on to define the statement "*S* presupposes *S'*" as follows: "The truth of *S'* is a necessary condition of the truth or falsity of the statement that *S*" (p. 175).

This characterization has been objected to by various writers, including David Rynin, who points out that when "necessary condition" and "truth or falsity of the statement that" are interpreted in the ordinary, truth-functional way, the definition has the paradoxical consequence that all presupposed statements are true. Rynin's demonstration is that $(S \supset S')$ and $(-S \supset S')$, but $(S \lor -S)$; therefore *S'*. Avrum Stroll has also suggested that Strawson's account suffers from the difficulty that if "The king of France no longer exists" is used to make a true statement, then by Strawson's criterion one who employs it thereby presupposes the existence of the king of France. It is now generally agreed that neither Russell's nor Strawson's analysis does full justice to all uses of sentences in everyday English containing "the" phrases in the singular. But regarded as proposals for the development of explanatory models for subparts of everyday discourse, each has considerable merit. In this interpretation Strawson's doctrine belongs to the logical tradition of analyzing descriptive phrases initiated by Frege in "Über Sinn und Bedeutung" (1892) and supported by Hilbert and Bernays in their *Grundlagen der Arithmetik* (Berlin, 1934; Vol. I, p. 384) and by Carnap in *Meaning and Necessity* (Chicago, 1947; pp. 33–42).

Strawson has also argued that if universal statements ("All my children are in college") are interpreted as presupposing the existence of the items mentioned by the subject term, paradoxes stemming from modern symbolic interpretations of the square of opposition can be eliminated without affecting the logical relations which one intuitively feels ought to hold between the elements of the square. This matter is persuasively discussed by S. Peterson in "All John's Children" (in *Philosophical Quarterly*, 1960).

Presupposing in metaphysics. The notion of presupposition plays an important role in various metaphysical constructions, including R. G. Collingwood's *An Essay on Metaphysics* (Oxford, 1940) and Michael Polanyi's *Personal Knowledge* (Chicago, 1958). Collingwood distinguishes (Chs. 3–4) between absolute and relative presuppositions, arguing that the former are neither true nor false and that metaphysics is the science that ascertains what these absolute presuppositions are. His view is that absolute presuppositions form the basis of the civilizations developed at various times in history and the ground of the science developed in such civilizations. When a civilization changes, its presuppositions change and are succeeded by others. According to this view, metaphysics is therefore a branch of the historical sciences.

Bibliography

Anscombe, G. E. M., *An Introduction to Wittgenstein's Tractatus*. London, 1959. Ch. II.

Baker, A. J., "Presupposition and Types of Clause." *Mind*, Vol. 65 (1956), 368–378.

Bar-Hillel, Yehoshua, "Analysis of 'Correct' Language." *Mind*, Vol. 55 (1946), 328–340.

Black, Max, *Problems of Analysis*. Ithaca, N.Y., 1954. Chs. 2–3.

Black, Max, *Models and Metaphors*. Ithaca, N.Y., 1962. Ch. 4.

Cavell, Stanley, "Must We Mean What We Say?" *Inquiry*, Vol. 1 (1958).

Collingwood, R. G., *An Autobiography*. Oxford, 1939. See especially pp. 66–76.

Donagan, Alan, *The Later Philosophy of R. G. Collingwood*. Oxford, 1962.

Frege, Gottlob, "Über Sinn und Bedeutung." *Zeitschrift für Philosophie und philosophische Kritik*, Vol. 100 (1892), 25–50. Translated by Max Black as "On Sense and Reference," in P. T. Geach and Max Black, eds., *Translations From the Philosophical Writings of Gottlob Frege* (Oxford, 1952).

Geach, P. T., "Russell on Meaning and Denoting." *Analysis*, Vol. 19 (1959), 69–72.

Grant, C. K., "Pragmatic Implication." *Philosophy*, Vol. 33 (1958), 303–324.

Griffiths, A. P., "Presuppositions." *Analysis*, Vol. 15 (1955).

Hall, Roland, "Assuming: One Set of Positing Words." *Philosophical Review*, Vol. 67 (1958), 52–75.

Hall, Roland, "Presuming." *Philosophical Quarterly*, Vol. 11 (1961), 10–21.

Hampshire, Stuart, "On Referring and Intending." *Philosophical Review*, Vol. 65 (1956), 1–13.

Hancock, Roger, "Presuppositions." *Philosophical Quarterly*, Vol. 10 (1960), 73–78.

Hart, H. L. A., "A Logician's Fairy Tale." *Philosophical Review*, Vol. 60 (1951), 198–212.

Kemeny, John G., *A Philosopher Looks at Science*. Princeton, N.J., 1959. Ch. 3.

Langford, C. H., "The Notion of Analysis in Moore's Philosophy," in P. A. Schilpp, ed., *The Philosophy of G. E. Moore*. Evanston, Ill., 1942.

Llewelyn, John E., "Collingwood's Doctrine of Absolute Presuppositions." *Philosophical Quarterly*, Vol. 11, (1961), 49–60.

Llewelyn, John E., "Presuppositions, Assumptions, and Presumptions." *Theoria*, Vol. 28 (1962), 158–172.

MacIver, A. M., "Some Questions About 'Know' and 'Think.'" *Analysis*, Vol. 5 (1937/1938).

Nelson, Everett J., "Contradiction and the Presupposition of Existence." *Mind*, Vol. 55 (1946), 319–327.

Nowell-Smith, P. H., "Contextual Implication and Ethical Theory." *PAS*, Supp. Vol. 36 (1962).

O'Connor, D. J., "Pragmatic Paradoxes." *Mind*, Vol. 57 (1948), 358–359.

Quine, W. V., "Meaning and Inference," in *From A Logical Point of View*. Cambridge, Mass., 1953. See especially pp. 164–166.

Rynin, David, "Donagan on Collingwood on Metaphysics." *Review of Metaphysics*, Vol. 18 (1964).

Sellars, Wilfrid, "Presupposing." *Philosophical Review*, Vol. 63 (1954), 197–215.

Shwayder, D. S., "Self-defeating Pronouncements." *Analysis*, Vol. 16 (1956).

Shwayder, D. S., "Uses of Language and Uses of Words." *Theoria*, Vol. 26 (1960).

Stroll, Avrum, "The Paradox of the First Person Singular Pronoun." *Inquiry*, Vol. 6 (1963), 217–233.

Urmson, J. O., "Parenthetical Verbs," in A. Flew, ed., *Essays in Conceptual Analysis*. London, 1960.

Wolterstorff, Nicholas P., "Referring and Existing." *Philosophical Quarterly*, Vol. 11 (1961), 335–349.

AVRUM STROLL
Bibliographic assistance by *J. Ornstein*

PRICE, RICHARD (1723–1791), Welsh dissenting preacher, moral philosopher, and actuary, was born at Tynton, Llangeinor, Glamorganshire. His father, Rees, was a dissenting minister with extreme Calvinist opinions. Price was educated at a number of different academies, finally entering Coward's Academy in London, where he remained for the years 1740–1744. He was ordained at the age of 21 and began his ministerial career as a domestic chaplain. He later served a number of London congregations, notably those at Stoke Newington, where he lived, and at the Gravel-Pit Meeting House in Hackney. Price was buried in the cemetery at Bunhill Fields; his friend Joseph Priestley preached the funeral oration.

In addition to his writings on moral philosophy, Price wrote with considerable influence on financial and political questions. His papers on life expectancy and on calculating the values of reversionary payments were instrumental in reforming the actuarial basis of the insurance and benefit societies of the time. His paper on the public debt is said to have led William Pitt, the prime minister, to re-establish the sinking fund to extinguish England's national debt. In his pamphlet *Observations on the Nature of Civil Liberty, the Principles of Government, and the Justice and Policy of the War with America* (London, February 8, 1776), Price defended the American cause. The widespread circulation and generally favorable acceptance of this work is said to have encouraged the American decision for a declaration of independence. Price had become friendly with Benjamin Franklin during the latter's stay in London, and in 1778 the Continental Congress moved to grant Price American citizenship if he would come to America and serve as an adviser on the management of American finances. He was grateful for the invitation but did not accept it. Price also regarded the French Revolution with approval, which he expressed, along with an appeal for reform in England, in his *Discourse on the Love of Our Country* (1789). Edmund Burke's *Reflections on the Revolution in France* (1790) was written in reply.

Price is also the author of *Four Dissertations:* I. "On Providence"; II. "On Prayer"; III. "On the Reasons for expecting that virtuous Men shall meet after death in a State of Happiness"; IV. "On the Importance of Christianity, the Nature of Historical Evidence, and Miracles" (London, 1767). In the fourth of these dissertations Price criticized David Hume's "Of Miracles." Hume was grateful for the civility with which Price argued, and he wrote to Price that the light in which he put this controversy was "new and plausible and ingenious, and perhaps solid. But I must have some more time to weigh it, before I can pronounce this judgment with satisfaction to myself."

Moral philosophy. Price's contribution to moral philosophy is *A Review of the Principal Questions in Morals* (London, 1758; corrected editions in 1769 and 1787). Price criticized the moral-sense doctrines of Francis Hutcheson in order to clear them away and make room for an account of immutable right and wrong, derived from Samuel Clarke.

Price says that we may have three different perceptions concerning the actions of moral agents. We may notice whether they are right or wrong, whether they are beautiful or ugly, and whether they are of good or ill desert. By talking of perceptions here, he shows that he has accepted the premise, of Lockean origin, that all knowledge is to be accounted for as some kind of perception by one of our faculties. Thus, Price's first question, "How do we know right?," is treated as a search for the faculty by means of which we obtain our ideas of right and wrong. He considers Hutcheson's answer that our moral ideas come to us by the way of a moral sense, and he understands Hutcheson to be claiming that this sense is "a power within us, different from reason; which renders certain actions pleasing and others displeasing to us." Price objects to this doctrine because of certain consequences which he believes are implied by it. Our approval and disapproval of actions appear to depend on the way our minds work or, to carry the matter back a step, on the way God has made them to work. Thus, our judgments of right and wrong depend on the mere good pleasure of our Maker, who created us in a certain way. But if he had pleased, he might have made us to be pleased or displeased by quite different actions, even actions contrary to those which now please and displease us. Thus, right and wrong would be only matters of taste, only a certain effect in us, and nothing in actions themselves.

For his part, Price is convinced that morality is equally unchangeable with all truth and that right and wrong are real characteristics of actions and not mere sensations derived from the particular way in which our minds are framed. To show the immutability of right and wrong, Price argues that these ideas are derived not from a special sense but from the understanding. As Price sees it, the only debatable issue in morals is not what actions are right and wrong but what is the faculty by which we discern right and wrong.

Price prefaces his argument for regarding the understanding as our moral faculty with the preliminary claim that the understanding is a source of new ideas. He objects to interpreting Locke as saying that sensation and reflection are the sources of all our ideas. Price argues that Locke may have meant only that all our ideas are ultimately grounded on ideas derived from sensation and reflection. Thus, Price makes room for certain new ideas which may arise as the understanding compares the objects of thought and judges them. Some of these new ideas are solidity, inertia, substance, accident, duration, space, cause or power, entity, possibility, and actual existence. Price locates these new ideas in a revised classification of simple ideas. He divides simple ideas into those implying nothing real outside the mind and those which denote real and independent existence distinct from sensation. The first class of simple ideas consists, on the one hand, of tastes, smells, and colors and, on the other, of such notions as order, happiness, and beauty. The second class of simple ideas has three subclasses: the real properties of external objects, such as figure, extension, and motion; the actions and passions of the mind, such as volition, memory, and so on; and those new ideas noted above which arise as the understanding considers the ideas it has been supplied with. It is important to note that Price does not regard the second class of simple ideas as constructions of the mind. The real properties of external objects are in the objects, and such new ideas as cause, duration, and space are of properties in a real world.

Armed with his reclassification of simple ideas, Price is now prepared to locate our ideas of moral right and wrong in the scheme and thus establish that they are perceptions of the understanding. Price first considers the question of whether moral right and wrong are simple ideas. He declares that they must be, for we cannot give definitions of them that are more than synonymous expressions. It is Price's recognition of this point which has led contemporary students to declare him one of the first to recognize the naturalistic fallacy, although he does not use that term. Having established that our ideas of right and wrong are simple ideas, Price then locates them in his scheme as two of those new ideas which arise in the understanding.

Hutcheson had simply assumed that if right and wrong are immediately perceived, they must be perceptions of an implanted sense. But the question of how we perceive these ideas may be settled by simply considering the nature of our own perceptions.

> Let anyone compare the ideas arising from our *powers of sensation,* with those arising from our *intuition of the natures of things,* and enquire which of them his ideas of right and wrong most resemble. . . . It is scarcely conceivable that anyone can impartially attend to the nature of his perceptions, and determine that when he thinks gratitude or beneficence to be *right,* he perceives nothing *true* of them, and *understands* nothing, but only receives an impression from a sense.

Price notes that some impressions of pleasure or pain, satisfaction or disgust, generally attend our perceptions of moral right and wrong; the proponents of a moral sense may have confused these impressions with our actual perceptions of right and wrong.

But there is an assumption in Price's own system on which much depends and for which he offers insufficient argument. He tells us that ". . . all actions undoubtedly have a *nature*. That is, *some character* certainly belongs to them, and somewhat there is to be *truly* affirmed of them." It is the task of the understanding to perceive these truths. Price regards actions in this way because it enables him to say that their rightness or wrongness is in them, not in the mind of the person judging the actions, but apart from noting the advantage to his own moral philosophy, Price offers no justification for the claim that actions have natures. It is unfortunate that he does not, for he rests his contention that morality is eternal and immutable on this claim.

When Price turns to our ideas of the beauty and deformity of actions, the second kind of perception of actions which he promised to account for, he finds that these perceptions are feelings of delight or detestation which may accompany our perceptions of the rightness or wrongness of actions. These feelings of delight and detestation are the effects on us of the actions we consider, and it is very likely that they arise from an arbitrary structure of our minds, which may be called a sense. Price allows that there is a distinction between noting that an action is right and approving it. We are made, however, in such a way that we cannot perceive an action to be right without approving it, for in men it is necessary that the rational principle, or the intellectual discernment of right and wrong, should be aided by instinctive determinations. When these feelings of the heart support the perceptions of the understanding, we are provided with the motivation for moral behavior. Here Price agrees with Hutcheson, pointing out that he has never disputed that we owe much to an implanted sense and its determinations. He means to resist only the claim that we owe our knowledge of right and wrong to such a sense.

Our ideas of the good and ill desert, the third sort of perception concerning actions which Price notes, carry the mind to the agent. He finds that we cannot but love a virtuous agent and desire his happiness above that of others. Quite apart from any advantage which we may gain from someone else's virtuous behavior, we have an immediate approbation of making the virtuous happy and of discouraging the vicious.

Price distinguishes between abstract and practical virtue. Abstract virtue denotes "what an action is independently of the sense of an agent; or what, in itself and absolutely, it is right such an agent, in such circumstances, should do." But Price recognizes that the actual practice of virtue depends on the opinion of the agent concerning his actions. Thus, an agent may be mistaken about his circumstances but sincere about what he believes he ought to do. In this respect practical virtue may diverge from abstract virtue but be no less obligatory insofar as the agent acts from a consciousness of rectitude. The ideal state of affairs is a correspondence of practical virtue with abstract virtue. Its achievement depends on the liberty and intelligence of the agent. These constitute the agent's capacity for virtue, and intention gives virtue actual being in a character. Price takes a short way with the question, "Why be moral?" "The knowledge of what is right, without any approbation of it, or concern to practise it, is not conceivable or possible. And this knowledge will certainly be attended with *correspondent, actual practice*, whenever there is nothing

to oppose it." Why a person chooses to do what he knows he should do is a question "which need not and should not be answered."

Benevolence is not the sole virtue. We also have duties to God and to ourselves, and there is room for many other sorts of good behavior, such as veracity, sincerity, and gratitude. As a measure of virtue Price offers the rule that "the virtue of an agent is always less in proportion to the degree in which natural temper and propensities fall in with his actions, instinctive principles operate, and rational reflexion on what is right to be done, is wanting."

Price discusses at length the relation of morality to the divine nature. Just as moral right and wrong are independent of man's mind, they are also absolutes for God. Were this not so, there would be no sense in which God's will could be good.

Freedom of the will. Price and Joseph Priestley published a set of letters as *A Free Discussion of the Doctrines of Materialism and Philosophical Necessity* (London, 1778). The correspondence had its origin in Price's criticism of Priestley's *Disquisitions Relating to Matter and Spirit*. The letters cover the nature of matter, the human mind, the mortality of the soul, the essence of the deity, and the doctrine of necessity. The last topic is the one that is treated in the most interesting way. Priestley contended that there can be no human liberty because "liberty" must mean someone's willing without a motive, which he regards as impossible. Price enlarges on the account of liberty which he offered in *A Review of the Principal Questions in Morals*. He argues that human agents are not physical objects but unique entities capable of self-determination. Consider the difference between a man who is dragged by a superior force and a man who follows a guide for a reward. Both of these examples may be certainties, but having different foundations, they are of totally different natures. "In both cases the man might in common speech be said to *follow;* but his following in the one case, however certain in event, would be *his own* agency: In the other case, it would be the agency of another. . . . In the one case, superior power moves him: In the other he moves himself."

Bibliography

Price's *Works* were published in 10 volumes (London, 1816), with a memoir of his life by W. Morgan. *A Review of the Principal Questions in Morals* has been published with a critical introduction by D. D. Raphael (Oxford, 1948). This is a reprint of the third edition (1787) with an Appendix and "A Dissertation on the Being and Attributes of the Deity."

For biography, see Carl B. Cone, *Torchbearer of Freedom, the Influence of Richard Price on Eighteenth Century Thought* (Lexington, Ky., 1952). Other works on Price include Joseph Priestley, A *Discourse on the Occasion of the Death of Dr. Price* (London, 1791); Leslie Stephen, *History of English Thought in the Eighteenth Century* (London, 1876; 2d ed., London, 1902); and Roland Thomas, *Richard Price* (London, 1924).

ELMER SPRAGUE

PRIESTLEY, JOSEPH (1733–1804), English scientist, nonconformist minister, educator, and philosopher, was born at Birstall, Yorkshire, the son of a cloth dresser. His mother died in 1740, and in 1742 Priestley was adopted by a childless well-to-do aunt, Mrs. Keighley, a convinced but unbigoted Calvinist. A sensitive child, Priestley suffered greatly because he could not convince himself that he had experienced the "new birth" essential, on the Calvinist scheme, for his salvation. As a result of these childhood miseries Priestley was left, he tells us, with "a peculiar sense of the value of rational principles of religion" as opposed to the "ignorance and darkness" of Calvinism.

Until the age of 16 Priestley was educated at a conventional grammar school. For the next three years, his health being too poor for regular studies, he in large part educated himself, reading his way into mathematics, physics, and philosophy and undertaking the study of European and Middle Eastern languages. In 1752 his health improved and he entered Daventry Academy, a university-type institution set up by nonconformists because Oxford and Cambridge would not admit nonconformists to a degree.

At Daventry the emphasis was on free discussion, and the curriculum was considerably broader than at Oxford or Cambridge. Priestley was introduced to David Hartley's *Observations on Man* (1749) and was at once—and permanently—converted to Hartley's general outlook. The simplicity and generality of Hartley's associationist psychology appealed to Priestley's maturing scientific instincts; it provided a theoretical foundation for his belief in perfectibility through education; and it offered a psychological alternative to the doctrine of free will, which Priestley's reading of Anthony Collins' *Philosophical Inquiry concerning Human Liberty and Necessity* (1714) had already caused him to reject.

In 1755 Priestley entered the ministry, taking over a decaying congregation at Needham Market, Suffolk. Stammering and unorthodox, he was not a success as a minister. He moved in 1758 to a more sympathetic but equally impoverished congregation at Nantwich in Cheshire. In an attempt to increase his income he set up a school where, perhaps the first to do so, he taught experimental science with the help of an "electrical machine" and an air pump.

Appointed in 1761 as "tutor of the languages" at Warrington Academy in Lancashire, Priestley taught oratory, literary criticism, grammar, history, and law, as well as languages. Characteristically, on all these latter topics Priestley developed ideas that he sooner or later published. *The Rudiments of English Grammar* (1761), many times reprinted, is typical of his innovating boldness, insofar as he tried to simplify English syntax by removing from it the complications introduced by classically trained grammarians. His *A Chart of Biography* (1765) and *A New Chart of History* (1769) were even more enthusiastically received; they won for him not only his sole academic distinction, the doctorate of laws of the University of Edinburgh, but also his fellowship of the Royal Society.

Priestley's days of relative isolation were now over. In 1762 he married an ironmaster's daughter, Mary Wilkinson, an intelligent woman with a sense of humor and considerable force of character—qualities she was to need in the years to come. His duties at Warrington left him free to visit London for a month each year, where he came into contact with an active group of scientists, philosophers, and political thinkers, including Benjamin Franklin and Richard Price. Franklin encouraged Priestley's project of writing a history of electrical experiments. The work that resulted, *The History and Present State of Electricity, with original Experiments* (1767), is a notable contribution to the history of science. Describing a number of important original experiments, it is also in some respects the most theoretically adventurous of Priestley's scientific works. It contains as well Priestley's reflections on the use of hypotheses in scientific procedures as a guide to experimentation.

Education and government. Like many of his fellow dissenters, Priestley was greatly interested in educational reform. Education had, he thought, thus far concentrated unduly on the needs of the clergy. His *An Essay on a Course of Liberal Education for Civil and Active Life* (1765) is a plea for a curriculum that should be suitable for men of affairs, emphasizing history and public administration rather than the classical languages. Priestley did much to encourage the teaching of history in the nonconformist academies. A set of lectures that he delivered at Warrington (published in 1788 as *Lectures on History and General Policy*) provided not only the academies but also the new American colleges with a text suitable for their needs; it was, indeed, recommended even at Cambridge. It is a summary account of the main historical sources, with an emphasis on commerce, law, and administration, rather than a historical textbook of the ordinary kind.

Priestley's political theory was closely related to his interest in education and his experience as a member of a minority group. In an appendix to his *Essay on a Course of Liberal Education* he developed an argument against the introduction of a state system of education, which would inevitably, he thought, favor the *status quo* and produce a quite undesirable uniformity of conduct and opinion. Like John Stuart Mill after him, Priestley gloried in diversity; uniformity, he said, is "the characteristic of the brute creation."

These reflections were more fully worked out in *An Essay on the First Principles of Government* (1768), which bears the subtitle *On the Nature of Political, Civil and Religious Liberty*. For Priestley, the preservation of civil liberty was the crucial political issue. Deciding who should participate in government—who, that is, should possess political, as distinct from civil, liberty—was, he thought, a practical matter, to be settled by considering what groups in the community are most likely, if they possess political power, to act for the greatest happiness of the greatest number. Such groups remain entitled to power only as long as they continue so to act. Legislation, on Priestley's view, should be kept to the minimum. What that minimum is cannot be determined a priori but only as a result of political experiment. But we can see at once, Priestley thought, that legislation that restricts civil and religious liberty is bound to be against the interests of the community. Unlike most nonconformist upholders of toleration and unlike his master John Locke, Priestley was uncompromising on this point; he upheld unbounded liberty of expression even to atheists and Roman Catholics.

In Priestley's eyes, the noblest of occupations was that of the clergyman, not the lecturer, and in 1767 he accepted a call to Mill Hill, Leeds, a congregation to whom his religious views were exceptionally congenial. The years Priestley spent at Mill Hill were extremely important in his development; his salary, although small, sufficed for his needs, and his duties left him considerable leisure.

Unitarianism. Priestley had long before abandoned both the doctrine of the atonement, on which he wrote critically in *The Scripture Doctrine of Remission* (1761), and orthodox Trinitarianism. Now he took what was to be the final step in his transition from Calvinism to Unitarianism. Christ, he argued, although the Messiah, was a man, and not even a perfect man. Priestley's subsequent theological writings were in large part an attempt to prove—most maturely in his *History of Early Opinions Concerning Jesus Christ* (1786)—that Unitarianism was the doctrine of the early church. He defended his unorthodoxies both against clerical attack, as in his *Letters to Dr. Horsley* (1783–1786), and, as in his *Letters to a Philosophical Unbeliever* (Pt. I, 1780; Pt. II, 1787), against those who, like Gibbon, could not understand why Priestley did not make a complete break with Christianity. Priestley valued his theological writings above all his other work. A firm belief in Providence is everywhere evidenced in his writings. Few men have committed themselves so often and so absolutely to the doctrine that "all is for the best in the best of all possible worlds," although he also believed that the future world could—and therefore would—be better.

Scientific achievement. It was as a scientist that Priestley won his international reputation. He published in 1772 what was intended to be the second section of a general history of science, *The History of the Present State of the Discoveries relating to Vision, Light and Colours;* but this work, invaluable though it still is to historians of science, did not arouse a great deal of interest. Priestley therefore abandoned his large-scale historical project and concentrated instead on chemistry. His first chemical publication, in 1772, was of an unusually practical character: it described a method of producing "mephitic julep," or soda water. But it was the paper "On Different Kinds of Air," which he read in that same year to the Royal Society," that at once established his reputation as a chemist. In 1774 he prepared the first edition of *Experiments and Observations on Different Kinds of Air;* this he republished in a series of editions, with important changes in contents, in method of organization, and even in title, until 1790.

By the end of that period Priestley, following up the work of Joseph Black and Henry Cavendish, had considerably enlarged our knowledge of the chemical properties of gases. He differentiated between nine gases, of which only three had previously been known to science, and described a method of collecting them. Of particular importance was his preparation of "dephlogisticated air" (oxygen), which he produced on August 1, 1774, by heating red mercuric oxide. It then became clear that air was not an element. Priestley went on to examine the properties of oxygen; in a series of chemicobiological experiments he brought out its importance for animal life.

As a resourceful experimenter, using simple and economical methods, Priestley has had few equals. But it was left to others, to Cavendish and Lavoisier, to appreciate the theoretical significance of his work. Priestley had isolated oxygen and had observed its importance in combustion; he had passed a spark through a mixture of hydrogen and oxygen and had noticed that dew was formed. Yet his last scientific work (1800) bore the title *The Doctrine of Phlogiston established and that of the Composition of Water refuted.* Although he had himself carried out important quantitative experiments, he did not appreciate the significance of the quantitative considerations by which Lavoisier overthrew the phlogiston theory.

Philosophy. Much of Priestley's most important scientific work was carried out at Shelburne, where from 1772 until 1780 he acted as "librarian and literary companion" to the earl of Shelburne. During these same years Priestley embarked upon his most substantial metaphysical works. He began in 1774 with *An Examination of Dr. Reid's Inquiry into the Human Mind on the Principles of Commonsense, Dr. Beattie's Essay on the Nature and Immutability of Truth, and Dr. Oswald's Appeal to Commonsense on Behalf of Religion,* commonly referred to as *An Examination of the Scotch Philosophers.* This is a vigorous polemic, which sets out to demonstrate the superiority of Hartley's psychology to the philosophy of the Scottish common-sense school, a philosophy that Priestley thought obviously reactionary insofar as it substituted for the simple Locke–Hartley theory of mind "such a number of independent, arbitrary, instinctive principles that the very enumeration of them is really tiresome." All the so-called "instinctive beliefs of common-sense" can, Priestley set out to show, be derived from the operations of associative principles working on the materials provided by sensation. He came to regret in later life the tone of this publication but never its doctrines.

Materialism. Hoping to make Hartley's views better known, Priestley published an abridged version of Hartley's *Observations on Man* in 1775 as *Hartley's Theory of the Human Mind on the Principle of the Association of Ideas.* In his Preface, Priestley somewhat tentatively suggested that all the powers of the mind might derive from the structure of the brain. Even as a suggestion this created a considerable uproar, but Priestley was not to be intimidated by clerical clamor. Convinced that materialism was the natural metaphysical concomitant of Hartley's associative psychology, he set out, therefore, in his *Disquisitions Relating to Matter and Spirit* (1777) to demonstrate that materialism was theologically, scientifically, and metaphysically superior to orthodox dualism.

On the theological side, materialism had commonly been objected to on the ground that it is incompatible with immortality. Man, Priestley replied, is not "naturally" immortal; he is immortal only because, as we know from revelation, God chooses to resurrect him; this resurrection is of the body and therefore also of the body's mental powers. As for the commonplace metaphysical objections to materialism, these are based, according to Priestley, upon an untenable conception of matter as being by nature inert and therefore incapable of exerting mental activity. To such a concept of matter Priestley opposed the physical theories of his friend and fellow scientist John Michell and the Jesuit mathematician Roger Boscovich. Material objects, on their view, are centers of force; if this is the nature of matter, Priestley argued, there is no good reason for denying that mental operations are part of the activity of a material object. On the other hand, there are very good reasons for objecting to the traditional dualism, which is quite incapable of explaining how mind and body can enter into any sort of relationship.

Determinism. Priestley had been a determinist long before he became a materialist, but not until 1777, in *The Doctrine of Philosophical Necessity Illustrated,* did he fully present his case against free will; indeed, even then he thought of himself as supplementing Hobbes, Collins, Hume, and Hartley with illustrations rather than as working out an entirely independent position. The doctrine of free will, he argued, is theologically objectionable because it cannot be reconciled with the existence of an all-seeing Providence; from a metaphysical standpoint, it makes human actions quite unintelligible, and ethics has no need of it. As a basis for our everyday moral judgments, the distinction between acting voluntarily and acting under compulsion is certainly important, but this distinction does not, according to Priestley, rest upon a metaphysical conception of free will.

Priestley's metaphysical unorthodoxies considerably disturbed his old friends, provoking a candid but good-tempered correspondence with Richard Price, published in 1778 as *A Free Discussion of the Doctrines of Materialism and Philosophical Necessity Illustrated.* Developing his views on the relation between moral judgments and determinism, Priestley admitted that the determinist will prefer to avoid describing men as blameworthy or praiseworthy. He will say of them, rather, that they have acted, or have not acted, from good principles—from principles, that is, that are conducive to the general happiness. But the determinist's different method of describing moral conduct has, Priestley thought, no practical consequences, and if determinism is in some respects inconsistent with everyday usage, this is even more true of libertarianism.

Later years. There was a real risk, however, that Priestley's reputation for materialism might endanger the earl of Shelburne's political ambitions. Perhaps for this reason Priestley and Shelburne parted amicably in 1780, when Priestley, refusing Shelburne's offer of a post in Ireland, took up residence in Birmingham. There he had a circle of congenial friends who were prepared to offer him financial as well as intellectual support. He became a member of the Lunar Society, with which were associated men of the caliber of Erasmus Darwin and James Watt, and he enjoyed the friendship and help of the scientifically minded potter Josiah Wedgwood, who supplied him with apparatus specifically designed for his chemical experiments. Much of Priestley's scientific work in this period, under Volta's influence, conjoined his two main scientific interests: electricity and gases. He examined the effect of passing electrical sparks through a variety of gases and studied their thermal conductivity.

He was by no means unsympathetic to the laissez-faire sociopolitical attitude of Birmingham industrialists. In *Some Considerations on the State of the Poor in General* (1787) he strongly criticized the poor laws and elsewhere opposed apprenticeship laws and laws for regulating interest rates. On his view, any sort of social welfare legislation "debased the very nature of man" by treating him as someone who had to be provided for. Although Priestley warmly supported schemes for cooperative insurance against hardship, he was opposed to any legislation that might diminish independence or increase the power of the state over individuals.

Political radicalism. In general terms, Priestley's life at Birmingham was a continuation and development of his earlier activities; theological controversy continued to be his main interest. But one event transformed his life and modified his political attitudes: the French Revolution. Reacting to that revolution, the British government became steadily more intolerant and conservative, and Priestley came to think that extensive political innovations were a necessary condition for the preservation of civil liberty. He moved toward political radicalism of the nineteenth-century kind in his *Letters to Edmund Burke occasioned by his Reflections on the Revolution in France* (1791) and in the anonymously published *A Political Dialogue on the General Principles of Government* (1791). He had formerly been accustomed to describe himself as "a Unitarian in religion but a Trinitarian in politics" because he had accepted the view that liberty rested on the balance between king, Commons, and House of Lords. He now came to feel that there should be but one source of political power, the will of the people as it would be represented in a reformed House of Commons.

On July 14, 1791, the Friends of the Revolution organized a dinner at Birmingham (Priestley was not present) in order to commemorate the fall of the Bastille. This was the last straw. With the encouragement, it would seem, of the authorities, an angry mob attacked the nonconformist chapels, then turned their attention to Priestley's house, destroying his books and furniture. Priestley was persuaded by his friends to leave Birmingham for London where he was, however, shunned by his scientific colleagues.

Life in America. For some years, Priestley had been contemplating migration to the United States, where his three sons had already gone. In 1794 he left for New York and finally settled in Northumberland, Pennsylvania. There, still supported by his old friends, he continued to experiment and to write, mainly on theological questions.

He was disappointed, however, by the orthodoxy of the American clergy and alarmed by the growth of intolerance in the United States. Although he took no part in politics, he wrote an uncompromising exposition of his political and religious views in *Letters to the Inhabitants of Northumberland* (1799). There was talk of his being deported under the Aliens Act, but Adams would not permit the application of the act to "poor Priestley." With the election of Jefferson to the presidency, Priestley was not only secure but also at last on good terms with authority. Jefferson consulted him on educational questions, and Priestley's *Socrates and Jesus Compared* (1803) precipitated Jefferson's "Syllabus" of his religious beliefs. Another of Priestley's works, *The Doctrines of Heathen Religion Compared with those of Revelation* (1804), awoke in Adams an enthusiasm for comparative religion. Priestley's last years, from 1801 until his death, were marred by ill health and bereavements, but his diversified intellectual interests remained with him until the end.

Bibliography

Priestley's scientific writings have never been collected. The standard edition of his philosophical, theological, and miscellaneous writings is *The Theological and Miscellaneous Works of Joseph Priestley*, John Towill Rutt, ed., 25 vols. in 26 (London, 1817–1832). John Arthur Passmore, *Joseph Priestley* (New York, 1965) includes a short list of Priestley's writings, an introductory essay, and selections from his major works.

See also Thomas Henry Huxley, "Joseph Priestley," in *Science and Culture* (London, 1881); Thomas Edward Thorpe, *Joseph Priestley* (London and New York, 1906); Edgar Fahs Smith, *Priestley in America, 1794–1804* (Philadelphia, 1920); Wallace Ruddell Aykroyd, *Three Philosophers: Lavoisier, Priestley and Cavendish* (London, 1935); Arthur Handley Lincoln, *Some Political and Social Ideas of English Dissent, 1763–1800* (Cambridge, 1938); Francis Edward Mineka, *The Dissidence of Dissent* (Chapel Hill, N.C., 1944); Stephen Edelston Toulmin, "Crucial Experiments: Priestley and Lavoisier," in *Journal of the History of Ideas*, Vol. 18, No. 2 (1957), 205–220; and the detailed bibliographies in the *Dictionary of National Biography* and the *Dictionary of American Biography*.

JOHN PASSMORE

PRIMARY AND SECONDARY QUALITIES. The distinction between primary and secondary qualities, first stated and thus named by Robert Boyle, received its classical formulation in Locke's *Essay*. There Locke states that apart from ordinary causal properties or "powers," material objects possess five primary qualities—extension (size), figure (shape), motion or rest, number, and solidity (impenetrability)—and many secondary qualities, such as color, taste, smell, sound, and warmth or cold. This distinction was made in the context of representative realism; that is, it was presupposed that the qualities of objects are quite distinct from, and are in fact causes of, "ideas" (representations or sensa), which are the only immediate objects of sensory awareness. The basis of the distinction was twofold. First, perceived size, shape, motion, number, and solidity are ideas caused by and exactly resembling the corresponding primary qualities of objects; perceived color, taste, smell, sound, and so on are caused by, but do not resemble, the corresponding secondary qualities. Second, the primary qualities are inseparable from matter and are found in every part of it; the secondary qualities are not true qualities of matter but are merely powers in the objects to produce sensory effects in us by means of the primary qualities in their minute parts. Thus, red as experienced (idea or sensum) is the effect of the secondary quality red, which is merely the power possessed by a special texture or surface structure of the object to reflect certain light frequencies and to absorb others.

This formulation is rather clumsy, and since Berkeley the custom has been to apply the first part of the distinction to the qualities of the ideas or sensa. The primary or spatiotemporal qualities of these data may then be said to characterize the object as well, for instance, the sensum is square and so is the object; but the secondary qualities are said not to characterize the object at all except in a derivative way, for instance, the sensa may be red and fragrant, but the object itself is intrinsically neither colored nor scented; it is red and fragrant only in the secondary sense that it causes the appropriate data of color and smell in the percipient. The doctrine is thus essentially the same as

Locke's, but the language is slightly different. This second formulation will be used here.

Though Boyle and Locke invented and popularized the distinction and the terminology of primary and secondary qualities, the distinction dates back in principle to Democritus, who said that sweet and bitter, warm and cold, and color exist only by convention ($\nu\acute{o}\mu\omega$), and in truth there exist only the atoms and the void (Fr. 9, Diels and Kranz). The distinction was revived by Galileo and accepted by Descartes, Newton, and others.

ARGUMENTS FOR THE DISTINCTION

Relativity and measurement. The relativity argument is the most important one: secondary qualities are affected by the condition of our sense organs and nervous system, by our distance from the object or its motion relative to us, by the lighting or by such intervening media as fog. Since secondary qualities thus vary according to, and depend for their nature on, factors quite external to the physical object, they cannot be intrinsic properties of it. This point was elaborated by Locke in various examples, two of which follow: (*a*) If one takes three bowls of water, one judged hot, one judged cold, and one judged medium, and places one hand in the hot water and the other hand in the cold, and then transfers both hands to the middle bowl, the water in that bowl will feel hot to the hand that has been in the cold water and cold to the hand that has been in the hot water. But since it cannot be both hot and cold, hot and cold are therefore not intrinsic properties of the water. (*b*) Marble is not colored in the dark; its color appears only in the light. But presence or absence of light cannot alter its real properties, so that the perceived color cannot be included among them.

If we grant the position of representative realism that hot, cold, and color, as experienced, are qualities of ideas or representations, then it is plausible to suppose on these grounds that they do not also characterize objects or resemble properties of objects. (Locke does not always make it clear that representative realism is to be presupposed). But this claim is apparently open to the insuperable objection, stated by Berkeley, that the primary qualities also vary: the object's apparent shape or size varies just as much as its color or sound. This would mean that shape and size as perceived do not characterize objects or resemble the actual properties of the object, thus subverting the whole basis of the distinction. That Locke did not see this may have been partly because he felt that he had to argue against the common-sense assumption that all sensible qualities characterize objects, and partly because the belief that primary qualities characterize all matter was apparently guaranteed by the physics of his day.

Although this objection is valid against Locke's position, it does not destroy the distinction between the primary and secondary qualities, which it is natural to recast and support by a revised relativity argument. This new point is that, in contrast with the secondary qualities, the main primary qualities—shape, size, and motion—can all be measured (solidity cannot, but it is dubious anyhow, in that most physical objects, even atoms, are far from solid or impenetrable; number, whether there is one object or two, seems scarcely a quality at all; strictly also in the case of shape, what is measured are various dimensions—diameters, angles, and so on—of the object, and supporters of the distinction must maintain that these are the differentiae of the shape). A plate may look elliptical, but by measuring its diameters and seeing that they are equal, we can establish that it is round; one man may look taller than another, but their relative heights may be settled by measurement, as can the speed of objects relative to the earth. The measured size and shape of a plate may thus be held to characterize it, and the sensible size and shape may agree with and resemble them, so that one can say that size and shape (and motion) are primary. Nevertheless, only in favorable circumstances does a given primary sensible quality also characterize the object (for instance, both object and sensum are round); otherwise, there is only a projective relationship, as between elliptical sensum and round object.

Measurement is objective and does not vary significantly because it is an operation that depends on the coordination of a number of separate perceptions and that may be performed by a number of different persons. Consequently, variations due to the measurer on any particular occasion are compensated for and do not affect the final result, and the various actions confirm that one is not simply establishing the qualities of representations. Measurement also leads to conclusions regarding the dimensions and positions of objects in physical space that can be verified by further activities or operations, such as fitting the objects together, moving one's hand between them, rolling an object to confirm that it is round, and so on. By contrast, the variation found in the sensory qualities seems to be caused by their being simply the content of one single act of perception limited to one person at one time.

If all this is so, the list of primary qualities must be somewhat amended. Shape, size, and motion remain, but one should substitute mass for solidity. Temperature is more difficult: since it can be measured, it seems at first primary. But what is measured is the property of causing expansion in fluid or metal; this property in no way resembles felt warmth, and in physical theory it is a form of energy. Hence, temperature should not be regarded as a separate primary quality. Material objects do, of course, possess many other properties—causal and dispositional ones, for example—as Locke realized by his doctrine of "powers," but part of the distinction is that only the primary ones are intrinsic (that is, possessed without reference to other objects) and that all such powers are ultimately due to patterns of primary qualities. Even so, the distinction would have difficulty in coping with some intrinsic "scientific" properties, such as energy or electric charge.

Apart from this, various objections have been made to the distinction in terms of measurement. First, measured motion and size must be stated in terms of some standard, such as a yard or meter; hence, they are purely relational and are not intrinsic properties of the object. But one can reply that it is only the description or labeling of the measurement that is thus relational; the motion or exten-

sion labeled, which is actually measured, seems intrinsic to the object.

Second, since colors and sounds may be measured, are they not also primary? But this objection seems based on a misunderstanding of the processes of measurement, for one way of "measuring" color might be to compare a given shade with a standard on a shade card; but that would be like comparing the sensible size of two objects, not measuring them. Proper measurement goes beyond this kind of sensory experience, and even if one gives the shade a number, one cannot calculate with the results as one can with the dimensions of objects. Normally, however, measurement of colors or sounds is either the measurement of the amplitudes or lengths of light waves or sound waves, or a mixture of wave measurement and the comparison of experiences. If one brings up a decibel meter and says that the sound to be measured is 80 decibels, it is the amplitude of the sound waves that is ultimately responsible for the movement of the pointer to 80. It should be noted, however, that the logarithmic scale is used because of a characteristic of human ears—that experienced loudness is related logarithmically to wave amplitude.

Third, measurement is a perceptual process—at least it relies on and largely uses perception—so it may be only producing various correlations of sensa and never getting through to the supposed properties of material objects at all. This objection is made from the point of view of phenomenalism, however, while the whole primary-secondary quality distinction presupposes representative realism. Supporters of the latter would say that the best explanation of the correlation is that the sense experiences arise in the measurement of actual physical objects.

Arguments from science. Science can adequately explain and describe the nature of the physical world solely in terms of primary qualities; hence, while primary qualities must characterize objects, there is no need to suppose that secondary qualities must also. The latter would be otiose, and on the principle of economy, or Ockham's razor (that entities should not be multiplied more than is necessary), it would be unscientific to suppose that they exist as intrinsic properties of objects. The objection to this argument is partly that the science of one's day is not final (thus, Locke was persuaded by seventeenth-century science to include solidity in the list of primary qualities), and mainly that scientific theory and description are not the whole truth—they describe only one aspect of the world, being limited by their quantitative approach and their instruments. Secondary qualities may thus be real properties of matter with biological or aesthetic functions; Ockham's razor oversimplifies the facts pertaining to living things.

Investigation of the causal processes on which perception depends shows that the only variables capable of transmitting information about the properties of external objects are spatiotemporal ones, which are associated with primary qualities. Thus, light waves (energy distributed in space and time) pass from the object to the percipient, but nothing resembling experienced color and sound is transmitted. But the main force of this argument, since it applies to all the senses, is neurological. The nerves from the different sense organs to the brain are all similar, and therefore the only variables are the frequencies of the impulses (which convey the intensity of the stimulus), their different neural pathways, and their different destinations in the brain. Indeed, it seems to be the different destinations that primarily govern the type and quality of the sensation. And although one can conceive of primary qualities being transmitted by spatiotemporal variables, it is difficult to conceive of color, warmth, taste, or smell being so transmitted. (It may be objected that radio and television can transmit color and sound by converting them into electrical impulses for transmission and then reconverting them. But, strictly speaking, what is converted is not color or sound but light waves or sound waves; moreover, the radio or television station must use microphones and cameras to effect the conversion, and there is no evidence of such conversion devices at the objects we see or hear.)

BERKELEY'S CRITICISMS

Berkeley's formidable criticisms of the distinction between primary and secondary qualities have convinced many people. We have mentioned his objection concerning relativity, which, though valid against Locke, can be avoided by restating the distinction on the basis of measurement. He also has nothing to say on the scientific considerations, which were not explicit in Locke. But he did have some further well-known criticisms. First, he stated, "An idea can be like nothing but an idea." In other words, our sensa, being private, mental, and directly perceivable, cannot resemble properties of material objects which are public, physical, and not objects of direct awareness. But resemblance is claimed only for primary qualities; and though sensa cannot be extended in physical space, it seems reasonable to claim a structural resemblance, a similarity in form, between the spatial relations that they sensibly possess and those attributed to objects by measurement; thus, it can be confirmed by measurement that various relations between the sides of a square sensum hold in the object. A similar resemblance seems plausible in the case of motion. There are, however, some underlying difficulties here. In the older representative realism, sensa were mental; and since the mind was held to be unextended, they could hardly have spatial relations. But newer versions would allow some sensible or subjective space different from physical space; certainly sensa seem spatial, and there seems to be no reason why what is directly perceivable and what is not should be unable to have a similar form or character.

Second, matter consisting only of primary qualities—for instance, possessing extension but no color, taste, sound or smell—is inconceivable. This objection is beside the point: admittedly one cannot conceive, in the sense of "imagine" or "picture to oneself" (Berkeley's sense of the word), any such thing, for what we can imagine is limited by past experience and perception. But the range of possible existents need not be confined to this, and there is much in science, particularly in modern physics, that cannot be imagined or pictured.

Bibliography

CLASSICAL WORKS

Anticipations of the distinction are to be found in Democritus, Fragments 9 and 125, in H. Diels and W. Kranz, *Fragmente der Vorsokratiker*; Galileo, *Il saggiatore* ("The Assayer," 1623), in his *Opere*, F. Flora, ed. (Milan, 1952), pp. 311–314; René Descartes, *Principles of Philosophy*, Part IV, Nos. 188–203, and *The World or Essay on Light*, Chs. 1–2. Robert Boyle adumbrated the distinction in his *The Origin of Forms and Qualities* (London, 1666), especially the section entitled "An Excursion about the Relative Nature of Physical Qualities"; John Locke stated it in his *Essay Concerning Human Understanding* (London, 1690), Book II, Ch. 8; Newton's view is best stated in his *Opticks*, Book I, Part II (paperback, New York, 1952, p. 124), but that was not published until 1704. Berkeley's criticisms are in his *Principles of Human Knowledge*, Secs. 9–20. Edwin A. Burtt, *The Metaphysical Foundations of Modern Physical Science* (London, 1925), contains useful discussion of the early versions.

MODERN WORKS

No book is devoted to the distinction, and substantial treatments are rare, but helpful contributions may be found in the following: A recent scientific comment on the distinction is Russell Brain, *Mind, Perception and Science* (Oxford, 1951). L. Susan Stebbing, *Philosophy and the Physicists* (London, 1937), attacks scientific versions of it, especially those of Newton and of Arthur S. Eddington (see his *The Nature of the Physical World*, London, 1928). Among the general works available are Charlie Dunbar Broad, *Scientific Thought* (London, 1923) and *The Mind and Its Place in Nature* (London, 1925); William Pepperell Montague, *The Ways of Knowing* (London and New York, 1925); Roderick Chisholm, *Perceiving* (Ithaca, N.Y., 1957); and more fully, R. J. Hirst, *The Problems of Perception* (London, 1959). D. M. Armstrong, *Perception and the Physical World* (New York, 1961), Chs. 14 and 15, discusses the subject from a direct realist position, and Gilbert Ryle's criticisms of the distinction in his *Dilemmas* (Cambridge, 1954) are well known.

Among articles on the distinction are Reginald Jackson, "Locke's Distinction Between Primary and Secondary Qualities," in *Mind*, Vol. 38, No. 149 (1929), 56–76; J. J. C. Smart, "Colours," in *Philosophy*, Vol. 36, No. 137 (1961), 128–142 (reprinted with additions in his *Philosophy and Scientific Realism*, London, 1963); Colin Strang, "The Perception of Heat," in *PAS*, Vol. 61 (1960–1961), 239–252; and for a more general treatment, W. C. Kneale, "Sensation and the Physical World," in *Philosophical Quarterly*, Vol. 1, No. 2 (1951), 109–126.

R. J. HIRST

PRINCIPLE OF LEAST ACTION. See EXTREMAL PRINCIPLES.

PRINGLE-PATTISON, ANDREW SETH (1856–1931), Scottish personal idealist, was born Andrew Seth, in Edinburgh. (He adopted the surname Pringle-Pattison at the age of 42 as a condition of inheriting a family estate in Scotland.) He studied philosophy at Edinburgh University under Campbell Fraser. Two years of study in Germany convinced him that it was the worst place for the study of German idealism but resulted in his completing, at 24, his Hibbert essay, *The Development From Kant to Hegel*. From 1880 to 1883 he served as Campbell Fraser's assistant at Edinburgh and then took the foundation chair of philosophy in the University College of South Wales at Cardiff. He left Cardiff in 1889 for the chair of logic and metaphysics at the University of St. Andrews. This he relinquished in 1891, when he succeeded Campbell Fraser at Edinburgh. In 1919 he resigned, after 39 influential years as a university teacher.

Philosophy for Pringle-Pattison was a serious enterprise of the human spirit, which he did not distinguish strictly from a statement of his own findings in religion and morality. His writing is clear and eloquent but not very original. He sought to advance his subject through critical interpretation of the great philosophers, especially Kant and Hegel. He was skeptical about the value of philosophical systems, holding that we cannot know the universe as we can know its individual parts; only God can do this. Rather, "the ultimate harmony may justifiably be spoken of as an object of faith—something which I am constrained to believe, even though I do not fully see it."

Pringle-Pattison was a Scottish Hegelian with a difference. Rebelling against the absolutism of Hegel and of such Hegelians as Bradley and Bosanquet, for whom the individual is merged in the universal, he insisted on the uniqueness of the individual person. It is only as knower that the self is a unifying principle. As a real being it is separate and distinct, impervious to other selves, even to God. "I have a centre of my own—a will of my own—a centre which I maintain even in my dealings with God Himself." We feel this to be so; it neither needs to nor can be established by argument. But God too is a Person; we cannot deny him self-consciousness, because this is the highest source of worth in ourselves. Hegel and the Hegelians were at fault here also.

Philosophy, Pringle-Pattison held, cannot do justice to "the individual within the individual—those memories, thoughts, and feelings which make each of us a separate soul" (*Hegelianism and Personality*, p. 217). Religion and poetry go further and deeper than philosophy, and this, as he said, is why he drew so frequently on the poets.

Our knowledge of the Absolute starts from experience—our experience "of the concrete worlds of morality, of beauty, of love or of the passion of the intellectual life." It is, however, a postulate of reason that the world is a cosmos, not a chaos, which we can gradually explore but never grasp in its entirety. Pringle-Pattison described his philosophy as "a larger idealism" that reconciles the dictates of morality and religion with the findings of science, purpose being the supreme category.

He was cautious in his claims about immortality. The nature of the soul is such that it is reasonable to entertain the hypothesis of its survival, and since human spirits must be "values for God" they were surely not made to be constantly destroyed and replaced by others. Yet if there is personal immortality, it is not the inherent possession of every human soul but must be won by the continuous effort needed to develop a coherent self. Morality does not depend on personal immortality, nor need immortality be the central article of philosophy or religion. In the apprehension of Truth, Beauty, and Goodness—eternal realities—man has already tasted eternal life and so should not be much concerned about personal survival.

Works by Pringle-Pattison

Scottish Philosophy: A Comparison of the Scottish and German Answers to Hume. Edinburgh, 1885.

Hegelianism and Personality. Edinburgh, 1887.
Man's Place in the Cosmos. Edinburgh, 1892.
The Idea of God in the Light of Recent Philosophy. Oxford, 1917.
The Idea of Immortality. Oxford, 1922.
Studies in the Philosophy of Religion. Oxford, 1930.
The Balfour Lectures on Realism (delivered 1891), with a memoir by G. F. Barbour, ed. Edinburgh, 1933.

A. K. STOUT

PRIVATE LANGUAGE PROBLEM. The private language problem is essentially the question of whether or not a language as a system of symbols which are means of thinking is, of necessity, a language as a system of symbols which are means of communication. Defining "private language" as language (in the sense of means of thinking) which in principle the speaker alone can understand (so that it cannot serve as a means of communication), our question is roughly equivalent to: "Is a private language possible?" Many philosophers, following Wittgenstein, have recently made the claim (here called the private language thesis, abbreviated PLT) that private languages are impossible. Armed with it, they have argued against solipsism, phenomenalism, the analogical or empirical view of one's knowledge of other minds, and against mind–body dualism. Some of them have gone on to argue for certain versions of philosophical behaviorism as well as for the view that the meaning of a word consists of its use or employment in a social practice and not in its referring to something or its designating a kind of entity. Thus, the PLT has been a central principle in the cluster of Wittgensteinian doctrines. It is not clear, however, that exactly the same thesis figures in all the arguments in question, since the idea of a private language varies in different contexts. There is, therefore, a multiple problem: First, to differentiate the several propositions which pass as the PLT by clarifying the sense of "private language" being used; second, to determine which ones are true; and third, to explain why they are supposed to be intimately related. These problems differ from the question, debated around 1930, of whether or not it is possible to start with a private language about one's sensations or "raw" feelings and arrive at the intersubjective and communicable language of science. (On this question, see Rudolf Carnap, "Psychology in Physical Language," and J. R. Weinberg, *An Examination of Logical Positivism.*)

The sense of "impossible." In all the interpretations of the PLT, the word "impossible" is understood in a strong sense which is not easy to characterize precisely. Some philosophers speak of "logical impossibility," but they do not necessarily mean that private languages are impossible in the sense that unbounded triangular figures are impossible. The expression "unbounded triangular figure" reduces to the formal self-contradiction "*unbounded* figures *bounded* by three lines" by means of a substitution allowed by the definition of "triangle." But few philosophers would suggest that there is a similarly ready definition of "language" by means of which we can produce a formal self-contradiction "private so-and-so which is not private." The impossibility at issue is like (1) the impossibility of unextended red things (that is, the impossibility that something be red and yet lack width or length), or (2) the impossibility of a cube with fewer than eight edges. These do not lead straightforwardly to formal contradictions, since there are no definitions for all the terms involved; they depend on implication relations which constitute the concepts involved in their statement. In the last analysis, the persistent rejection of (1) and (2) evidences the failure to understand the meanings of all the words involved, that is, the lack of some of the relevant concepts. But (1) is unprovable and obvious, and (2) only needs a trivial argument, while the PLT (if true) requires careful reasoning.

We shall speak of *conceptual impossibility* to refer to any formal self-contradiction, to any impossibility which entails a formal self-contradiction, and to any a priori impossibility such as that found in the above examples (1) and (2).

THE PRIVATE LANGUAGE THESIS

The most important propositions often discussed as the PLT, each embodying a different idea of private language, are the following:

PLT*: It is impossible for a man to use a word with a meaning that nobody else could, even in principle, understand.

PLT-1: It is impossible for a man to use words which refer to private objects, that is, objects which nobody else could—even in principle—know. (For subtheses arising out of the ambiguities of "know," see H.-N. Castañeda, "The Private-Language Argument.")

PLT-2: It is impossible for a man who has always lived in isolation to possesss a language, even if his sounds are understandable by another person.

Here the expressions "could not in principle" and "impossible" are meant to express conceptual impossibility. PLT* allows that a man may use words with meanings that nobody else in fact understands, provided that they are understandable to other people in the appropriate circumstances. PLT-1 allows that a man may refer to objects which, in fact, he alone knows, but again others must be capable of knowing them in the appropriate circumstances. PLT-2 allows that a man, like Robinson Crusoe, keeps possession of a language he learned previously while living in a community of speakers.

Many philosophers assume that it is conceptually impossible for two persons to share one and the same immediate sensation. Many also hold that, in a strict sense of "know," others do not really know whether one has a certain immediate sensation or not, precisely because they cannot share it. On these assumptions, a language about one's own immediate sensations would be a language of the sort that PLT-1 claims to be impossible. Indeed, such a language is customarily regarded as the would-be prototype of private language.

In general, on the assumption that (direct) knowledge of the referent of a word is required for understanding the meaning of the word in question, PLT* entails PLT-1. On this assumption, a language about one's own immediate sensations is also private in the way that PLT* claims to be impossible.

PLT-1 does not entail PLT*. A word might have a meaning understandable to only one person because the word itself is a private object in the sense of PLT-1, even though everybody may be acquainted with the physical objects it refers to. For example, the words of a person's language might all be mental images of German written words, so that all his thinking would be a sort of mental reading of German. In this case, the referents of the words would be public, but the words themselves would be private and hence unintelligible to others.

PLT-2 neither entails nor is entailed by PLT-1. If PLT-2 is true, then if on the previous assumptions about sensations, one's language about one's own sensations is private in the sense of PLT-1, then one could still, in principle, invent such a language. Conversely, the truth of PLT-1 does not by itself make it impossible for an isolated person to invent a language about physical objects. Similarly, PLT-2 neither entails nor is entailed by PLT*.

Applications of private language theses. The important claims made with the help of the PLT do require other assumptions, which in their turn play roles, as we shall see, in the defense of the PLT itself. The most natural and pervasive of these assumptions is the following:

(A) In the sense of "thinking" in which one can both have a false (or true) thought and draw inferences from what one thinks, it is conceptually impossible to think without possessing a language which is a means of thinking.

From this assumption and PLT-2, one can conclude that the fact that one thinks, guarantees the existence of other persons, namely, one's fellow speakers of the same language. Thus, the solipsist who merely asserted that it is possible that he alone exists at the time he is thinking would be contradicting himself (an argument of this sort can be constructed with premises suggested by Rush Rhees in "Can There Be a Private Language?"). Of course, many philosophers have serious objections to (A).

The existence of hallucinations, illusions, and visual perspective leads many philosophers to characterize every case of perception in terms of our apprehension of sense data or immediate impressions. Some have proceeded to espouse a phenomenalistic program of "logical reconstruction" of physical objects and minds as systems of sense data; others, however, have subscribed to some form of realism, that is, the complete irreducibility of physical objects and minds to sense data. But all of them have recently been criticized on the ground that the language of sense data is private in either the sense of PLT* or the sense of PLT-1. Here, in addition to (A), the critics need the following assumption:

(B) If it is conceptually impossible that there be a language about entities of a sort T, then there are no entities of sort T.

Again, some philosophers would claim against (B) that if PLT* or PLT-1 is true, then sense data or the given in experience are simply ineffable.

Many philosophers have subscribed to some form or other of a principle of verification, for example:

(C) It is conceptually impossible to understand a sentence without knowing what state of affairs would verify the statement made with it.

Assumption (C) leads to the view that language about states of consciousness is private, if we add to it and (A) and (B) the following principle:

(*P*) Only the person himself can verify conclusively and directly that he has certain experiences.

On this view, for instance, when someone else speaking about me says, "He is in pain," he cannot understand or mean exactly the same thing that I understand and mean when, of myself, I say, "I am in pain." But if PLT* is accepted, one is involved in a contradiction. Here many philosophers have given up (*P*), and in order to guarantee that everybody else can know what somebody is feeling or thinking, some philosophers have espoused some form of behaviorism, that is, a view according to which every description of a person's experiences or mental states is really shorthand for (synonymous with) a description of his bodily movements, his relations to other bodies, and his abilities to perform further movement. This is often supplemented with the supposition that first-person utterances like "I have a headache" do not make statements of direct knowledge but are, rather, learned responses, analogous to the natural responses of moaning, crying, and so on, which are said to constitute the person's ache. As is to be expected, other philosophers have preferred to keep (*P*) and reject one or more of the other premises, in particular (*C*) or PLT*. (See H.-N. Castañeda, *op. cit.*, Part B, for a discussion of the privacy of experiences.)

The main arguments for the PLT. There are many arguments seeking to prove that being private makes it impossible for a language to have a property required for the existence of a language. Most of the arguments depend on the following assumption:

(*D*) A language is a system of rules, and to speak or write a language is to follow rules.

On this assumption, it suffices to establish the PLT to show that a man (say, Privatus) cannot be following rules when he is using a private language (to be called Privatish). This is, in fact, what a series of arguments suggested by Wittgenstein purports to do. The gist of the argument is as follows: A rule is, by its very nature, the sort of thing that can be misapplied (or disobeyed), but Privatus cannot misapply the rules of Privatish; hence, when speaking Privatish, Privatus is not following rules. The specific arguments are meant to support the crucial premise:

(1) Privatus cannot misapply the rules of Privatish.

A fair objection to (1) is that Privatus can certainly make slips; he may call something of kind *A* "*B*," whatever "*A*" and "*B*" may mean in Privatish. Slips of the tongue are precisely ways in which one violates the rules (if there are such) of natural languages. For instance, if there are rules of English governing the application of color words to physical objects; whenever one commits a slip of the tongue and calls a red object "blue," then one misapplies either a rule governing the use of "red" or one governing the use of "blue."

This reply to (1) is often met by several rejoinders. The first claims both that a slip counts as a misapplication of a linguistic rule only if there is a way in which the speaker can in principle detect and correct his slip and that Privatus cannot detect or correct his slips. This rejoinder, however, changes the issue, since premise (1) says nothing about verifying the existence of a misapplication of a rule. Nevertheless, the rejoinder has a point, for if to use words is to apply rules, then one must at least sometimes be able both to know of one's misapplications of the rules for the use of one's words and to know how to make the appropriate corrections. The question of whether or not Privatish allows this is discussed below under premise (2).

The second rejoinder is that to obey a rule is a *custom* (use, institution), but Privatus' actions cannot constitute a custom (see Ludwig Wittgenstein, *Philosophical Investigations,* Sec. 199). This rejoinder would establish PLT-2 but not PLT* or PLT-1. For it may be a custom in a tribe that people use words which they alone understand in the ways required by PLT* or PLT-1. But as an argument for PLT-2 the rejoinder is by itself question-begging. It must be supported by an argument which shows that obeying a rule is indeed a custom.

The third rejoinder is that Privatus' slips do not count as violations of the rules of Privatish because we cannot be corrected or taught by others what is the correct thing to say (see Wittgenstein, *op. cit.,* Sec. 378, and Norman Malcolm, "Discussion of Wittgenstein's *Philosophical Investigations,*" pp. 536 f.). If the "cannot" here is taken to mean conceptual impossibility, the rejoinder does not apply to PLT-2. If it is taken in a weaker sense, that is, a sense in which a person may be in the position of being in fact corrected by other persons, then the rejoinder supports PLT-2, but it would not allow that there be just one language-user in the universe. Besides, it is not clear that it would allow that Antonia Udina, for example, used language when, as we normally say, he spoke Dalmatian as the last speaker of Dalmatian. Although a person who uses words must be capable of self-correction, it is not immediately obvious that a person's sounds cannot count as utterances of words if nobody else can (in some sense) correct him. The need for others' possible corrections has to be established by an argument. Thus, we are again thrown back to the other lines of reasoning.

The fourth rejoinder is that Privatus' slips do not count because another person, by noting Privatus' behavior and circumstances, cannot discover that his use of the word is correct or incorrect (adopting Malcolm, *op. cit.,* p. 537). This rejoinder also leaves PLT-2 unsupported if "cannot" is understood as expressing conceptual impossibility. While it must be conceptually possible for Privatus to know whether his uses of language are correct or incorrect, it is not at all clear that it must be possible for others to know this fact. The principle that it must be possible for others to know whether his uses of language are correct or incorrect requires an independent argument to support it. However, the present rejoinder has a point. It reminds us that if there is no way at all of telling, for any word of Privatish, whether or not Privatus used it correctly (however coherent the concept of a private language is), it would be a completely gratuitous hypothesis that Privatus spoke a private language. Although our topic here is only the conceptual possibility of private language, we should note that the claim that somebody's entire language is of the type described in PLT* is certainly gratuitous. Yet the claim that someone has a mixed language, part of which is private in the sense of PLT*, does not seem gratuitous.

The fifth rejoinder dismisses mere slips on the ground that they show at most a breakdown of a linguistic habit. The rejoinder asks us to consider the case of Privatus trying deliberately to apply a rule of Privatish and failing to comply with it. The rejoinder claims that, for Privatish, "thinking one was obeying a rule would be the same thing as obeying it," but "to *think* one is obeying a rule is not to obey a rule. Hence it is not possible to obey a rule 'privately'" (Wittgenstein, *op. cit.*, Sec. 202). This rejoinder does not require that every utterance of a word be a case of deliberately attempting to obey the corresponding linguistic rule(s). Conjoined with assumption (A), this view would lead to a vicious infinite regress. For then, in order to say something, one would have to be aware of the rules governing the words one intends to utter, and these rules in their turn would be formulated in some words the rules governing which one would have to be aware of through some other words, and so on *ad infinitum*. Therefore, to use language is, of necessity, to use most of the words from habit, not in intended obedience of the linguistic rules. The rejoinder cannot even demand that Privatus sometimes be aware of the rules of Privatish: a being might speak a language without ever rising to the level of formulating any of his rules. But if, by assumption (D), languages are made up of rules, then if it were conceptually impossible for Privatus to be at least sometimes aware of the rules of Privatish, Privatish would be a very defective language indeed, incapable of discharging the philosophical duties that private languages are alleged to discharge. Thus, the rejoinder is right in urging that

(a) For every rule R of a language L and every speaker S of L, it is conceptually possible that sometimes R applies to S's situation while S thinks that he is obeying R without S's actually obeying R.

Presumably, a rule of language is here of the form "If x is φ, you may (must) call it '. . . ,'" but the meaning of "call" is difficult. In one normal sense of "call," slips of the tongue are, again, ways in which (a) is true. Clearly, a person may think that he is calling a thing "red" in deliberate compliance with the English rule for "red," without realizing that he actually called it "blue" because he is deaf or because he simply did not hear what he said. In the same sense of "call," (a) can be true because the speaker deliberately calls a red thing "blue," if he thinks that the rule in question allows (or prescribes) his calling it "blue." In particular, suppose that the rule R allowing (or prescribing) that one call a thing "red" is the rule Gaskon typed yesterday and that today, confusedly, Gaskon thinks that the rule he typed yesterday allows (or prescribes) that a certain thing be called "blue," and he calls the thing in question "blue," thinking that he is complying with the rule. Here, in spite of his deliberately calling a certain thing "blue," Gaskon's use of "blue" and the rule he thinks he is complying with both satisfy (a). Both ways of satisfying (a) are open to Privatus. It might be argued that Privatus' deliberately calling one of his private objects "A" instead of "B" has no point or "function" (see Wittgenstein, *op. cit.*, Sec. 260), since he is not talking to others. This is, however, false. Privatus may very well play word games involving miscallings of things. But more importantly, whether or not there is a point in Privatus' flouting of the rules of Privatish has nothing to do with the issue about the possibility of private language.

The rejoinder often uses a stronger sense of "call." In this sense, by a natural development of assumption (A), to *think* that something is, for example, red is to call it "red." This stronger sense appears in an argument given in support of PLT-1. As said above, language about one's own immediate sensations is often regarded as the paradigm of private language in the sense of PLT-1. Now, one knows incorrigibly that one's sensations have immediately sensible qualities. That is to say, if one believes that one has a pain (itch, tickling, feeling of discomfort), then one knows that one has a pain (itch, tickling, feeling of discomfort). So it is impossible to have no pain while one thinks that one has a pain. Thus, if one thinks that one is obeying the rule of the form "If x is a pain, you may (must) call it 'pain,'" one surely thinks that one is in pain and the rule cannot fail to apply. Similarly, since one also has incorrigible knowledge of the absence of one's immediate sensations, if the objects that Privatus can think about in Privatish are only his immediate sensations, then when he thinks that a rule of Privatish does not apply, the rule does not, in fact, apply. But if "call" is taken in its normal sense, neither of these two features of the rules of Privatish implies that Privatus cannot think that he is obeying a rule (which then applies) without actually obeying it, since slips and deliberate miscallings are still available as violations of the rule. On the other hand, if "call" is taken in the strong sense (in which thinking can be calling), then if Privatus thinks that he is obeying a rule of the form "If x is A, you may (must) call it 'A,'" he surely thinks that the rule applies, that is, he thinks that the object x is A; if A is a sensible property of Privatus' immediate sensation x, then x is A, and Privatus is both calling x "A" and unavoidably obeying the rule. Thus, if Privatish is a private language about Privatus' immediate sensations and their sensible properties, then (a) above and (b) below are both false:

(b) For every rule R of a language L and every speaker S of L, it is possible that sometimes S thinks that he is obeying R while he is not.

Since (a) is true, Privatish is not a private language.

This argument does not by itself support PLT-2; it may or may not support PLT*, depending on how one interprets the phrase "knowing the meaning of a word."

There is, however, a difficulty with the above argument. Consider the rule of English: "If x is a cat, you may (must) call x 'cat'; that is, you may (must) think that x is a cat." This rule differs from the above rule for the Privatish word "A" in that thinking that one is obeying the rule for "cat" does not imply that the rule for "cat" applies to the situation in question. For to think that one is obeying the latter rule implies that one thinks that it applies, and this implies that one thinks that some object x is a cat. But surely one can be mistaken about x's being a cat. Yet the rule for "cat" also fails to satisfy condition (a). Suppose that the rule applies; then the object x in question is a cat. And suppose that one thinks that one is obeying the rule; then it is true that one thinks that if x is a cat one may (must) think that x is a cat, and that one thinks that x is cat. Thus, one is in fact obeying the rule! Therefore, the strong sense of "call" included in the concept of language rule R makes (a) an impossible condition.

Now, in the case in which a rule R does not apply to a man's situation, we are often reluctant to say that when such a man thinks that he is obeying *R,* he is not obeying *R.* But we could say this with no great distortion, and if we did, we could say that the above rule for the English word "cat" satisfies condition (*b*). For in a situation in which an object *x* is not a cat and the rule does not apply, we may very well both misperceive or otherwise think that *x* is a cat and think that, in accordance with the rule, we may (must) think that *x* is a cat. Thus, if we raise (*b*) as the crucial condition that linguistic rules must satisfy, then we can claim that PLT-1 is established in the sense that a pure language of sensations is impossible. But this answer is inconclusive. Besides the small amount of distortion involved, there is the fact that (*b*) is not a general condition of rules. This is shown by the following rule which a man might give to his son: "If you think that you need to delay your action, think that $1+2+3+\cdots+24=300$." Since to think that one thinks that *p* entails that one thinks that *p,* if the boy thinks that the rule applies, he thinks he needs to delay his action, and the rule applies. If he thinks that he is obeying the rule, he thinks both that it applies and that $1+2+3+\cdots+24=300$; hence he thinks that $1+2+\cdots+24=300$; hence, the rule applies and he obeys it. Thus, to defend PLT-1 by means of (*b*) requires an independent argument showing that rules of language must, in any case, comply with (*b*), distorted as suggested.

Let us turn now to a subtler line of argument. Some defenders of the PLT do not argue for (1) but for

(2) Privatus cannot distinguish his correct uses of Privatish words from his incorrect uses.

Suppose, then, that Privatus is debating whether something is *A* or not. Suppose that Privatish is private in the sense of PLT-1. Here the defenders of the PLT adduce (*a*) that Privatus lacks a *criterion* of correctness, that is, "something *independent* of his impression" that he is correctly using the Privatish rule governing the use of "*A*" by means of which he can "prove his impression correct" (Malcolm, *op. cit.,* p. 532), and (*b*) that his impression that he remembers what objects of kind *A* appeared like before is of no help, since memory "is not the highest court of appeal" (Wittgenstein, *op. cit.,* Sec. 56) and the "process [of checking memories] has got to produce a memory which is actually *correct*" (*ibid.,* Sec. 265). Now, these points exaggerate Privatus' predicament. Privatus' private objects may be related among themselves by entailment, by coexistence, by similarities, by causal relationships, and so on. Privatus can resort to any of these to test whether he is, on the present occasion, using the term "*A*" correctly. For instance, in Privatish, "being *A*" may be logically equivalent to "being *B* and becoming *C* in the presence of another *C*." Indeed, Privatus may even employ paradigms. The very first object he calls "*A*" may very well be enduring, so that he can compare the next objects of kind *A* with it. The same applies to languages of the type mentioned in PLT-2. Furthermore, memory *is* the highest court of appeal when it comes to our knowledge of the past. True, we have records and other historical evidence, but all of this only provides inductive evidence, not a proof, and our inductions involve the acceptance of unchallenged memories.

Nevertheless, Privatus is not only in no position to question the correctness of all of his uses of words, but he also cannot *prove* that the uses he questions are correct unless he is allowed the ability to identify certain proper-

ties of objects without criteria and without challenging his memory. But exactly the same happens with the speakers of *any* language. In the case of terms like "red" and "straight," for instance, there is nothing at all to which an English speaker *E* can resort in order to "prove" that he has correctly called an object red or straight. His fellow speakers may all utter in unison, "Not red but blue." Yet this choral utterance is not a proof; the speakers may be lying, may all be victims of a hallucination, or may just be rehearsing a new song—or the whole proceedings may be just *E*'s hallucination. In any case, for *E* to accept the correction, he must correctly identify the words expressing it without the use of criteria and remember correctly the meanings of these words. A vicious infinite regress would ensue if *E* were required to have a proof that he both remembers this correctly and identifies the objects the words apply to. Moreover, there is nothing to prove each corrector's use of words correct. Suppose, for example, that one corrector learned the meaning of "blue" with the help of object *O* and that he continuously stares at *O* during the preceding two minutes before correcting Privatus. He still must *remember* correctly that *O* has the same color it had two minutes before, that the color of *O* is called "blue," that the name of the color sounds "b–l–u–e," that the noise "red" uttered by *E* has the same meaning that makes red and blue incompatible, and so on. Thus, either somebody *just* identifies some words or objects correctly and remembers some qualities of objects and the meanings of some words correctly, or else nobody can be corrected by another speaker. In sum, demands (*a*) and (*b*) cannot be adduced against the possibility of a private language.

Logical words. Often it is claimed that a private language cannot have logical words or syntactical rules, both of which are necessary for the existence of logical relationships. Clearly, if a private language is allowed no implications or entailments, it would certainly be no language. But if "private language" is meant in the sense of PLT* or PLT-1 or PLT-2, this contention appears to be false. Often this contention is defended on the ground that a really private language does not have words with meanings in common with the words of another language (Wittgenstein, *op. cit.,* Sec. 261; Malcolm, *op. cit.,* p. 537). Now, private language in this sense is impossible. A language is a system of words of which some refer to objects, some signify properties or relations, and some express logical connections; the words expressing logical connections must be capable of being understood by anybody else and must, therefore, be common to all languages. This is an important result. But it is not the same as PLT*, which requires that every single word of a language must be understood by persons other than the speaker. Likewise, the impossibility of languages without logical words does not imply that a language cannot have some nonlogical words which refer to private objects, that is, it does not imply that PLT-1 is true. Again, that a language must have logical words implies nothing about the possibility of a single man developing a language for and by himself, that is, does not imply that PLT-2 is true.

"The same." Apparently Wittgenstein knew that there are no criteria (in the sense of something independent) which prove that words have been used incorrectly. He also knew that the correctness of an application of a word is not determined by a rule whose formulation serves as a recipe or canon. His fundamental opposition to private language derives from his profound investigations into the nature of concepts and his strong inclination toward an extreme nominalism. This opposition is never crystallized in a definite argument, but its gist is, in crude form, as follows. Postulate:

(E) The similarities and samenesses we find in things do not exist *in rerum natura,* that is, do not exist in things as we find them, independently of our finding them or of our referring to them in the way we do; they "come from the language" (Rhees, *op. cit.,* p. 80) and at bottom consist of the fact that we "call" the things in question the same (Wittgenstein, *op. cit.,* Secs. 146, 149, 185–190, 208–223, 348–352).

On a rigorous interpretation of (E), we find a rationale for assumptions (A), (B), and (C), as well as for the fact that the PLT has a chameleonlike and pervasive character. If we take (E) literally, then to find a property in several things is to find that we "call" the things in question "the same" or refer to them with the same word. Thus, it is impossible to think that something is such-and-such without a language in which there is an expression (even if a very long phrase) which "constitutes" the such-and-such in question. This is assumption (A). Also, (B), without an expression "constituting" a type T, there is no type T for things to belong to. Similarly, to understand an expression is not to apprehend an independently existing (or subsisting) property but simply to know how and to what to apply it, and this includes knowing how to call certain utterances "true" in which the expression is correctly applied. This is, in fact, a generalization of assumption (C).

We cannot say that a man in doubt about whether or not he used a word correctly must simply identify certain features of things without criteria and, armed with these identifications, test his uses of words. For on the extreme interpretation of assumptions (A) through (E) to identify a feature is to "call" a thing something. So, when the use of a word is at issue, the identification and nature of the thing is precisely what is at issue. The referents of one's previous uses of the word, as well as the uses themselves, are irrelevant. If one "calls" something "A," then it is A and *a fortiori* similar to the previous A's; if one withholds the name "A" from it, then it is not an A, and *a fortiori* it is dissimilar to all A's with respect to being an A. Clearly, it does not matter whether one's language is about private or about public objects; one's uses of words simply fail to be capable of being incorrect. They would seize reality so well that each "would have to be at once a statement and a definition" (Rhees, *op. cit.,* p. 82).

Thus, the following question arises. If, on assumption (D), language is a matter of rules and rules are the sort of thing that can be misapplied or not, how, then, is language possible after all? At this stage, obviously, we are not interested in proving anything but are anxious to find an explanation. Wittgenstein seems to suggest one: A man's uses of words can be incorrect only if they are compared with those of his fellow speakers. His "calling" something "A" is correct if his cospeakers now also call it "A." Then it is A and *a fortiori* similar to the things he and his cospeakers previously called "A." That is why obeying a rule of language is a practice (Wittgenstein, *op. cit.,* Sec. 202).

It is not necessary that the speakers of the language should call the thing in question "A" or that they call it "A" afterwards. Nor is it necessary that they call it "A" or anything at all, or that they call it the same thing. It is just a contingent fact that they coincide in calling it "A." But this coincidence (or agreement) is an empirical fact which is necessary for the existence of language.

Such is the underlying argument of Wittgenstein's remarks (*op. cit.,* Secs. 146, 149, 185–190, 208–223; for a discussion of the role of Wittgenstein's extreme nominalism in his views about necessary truth, see Michael Dummett's "Wittgenstein's Philosophy of Mathematics"). He builds a Heraclitean picture of language as something living only in our actual use of it and changing according to our needs. But is this a true picture of the connection between language and reality?

Here we cannot discuss the whole issue of nominalism, but to this writer it seems indefensible. We could doubtless have classified objects in entirely different ways from the ways we in fact do. For instance, we might have had no color words, no terms for species of plants or animals, and instead have used, say, "sha" for some elephants and white roses and reddish sand, and "sho" for female elephants, eggs, and rivers. But even so, we should have had to *find* features of similarity in the things so classified, and these features would have provided tests for the correct application of our words. At any rate, the view that things are the same because we "call" them "the same" or because we refer to them with the same words can get off the ground only by postulating our recognition of the samenesses of words, that is, the similarities of noises whose application to things constitutes the similarities of the latter. A serious infinite regress would ensue if we also hold that our words are similar only because we "call" them so.

The several propositions that are often debated as the claim that private languages are impossible can be linked to each other only under the assumption of extreme nominalism. None of the arguments given for the claim appear to be successful. There may be no conclusive way of either proving or refuting this claim. Perhaps the only course is to build detailed and rigorous philosophical views on each alternative and assess the adequacy of such views by their consequences. This topic continues to be widely discussed in the literature, and many philosophers adopt a position different from that advocated in the present article.

Bibliography

THE PROBLEM BEFORE WITTGENSTEIN

Carnap, Rudolf, "Psychology in Physical Language," in A. J. Ayer, ed., *Logical Positivism.* Glencoe, Ill., 1959. Ch. 8. Translated by Frederic (there called George) Schick from the German version, which appeared in *Erkenntnis,* Vol. 3 (1932/1933).

Weinberg, J. R., *An Examination of Logical Positivism.* New York and London, 1936. Ch. 11.

WITTGENSTEIN'S VIEWS

Albritton, Rogers, "On Wittgenstein's Use of the Term 'Criterion.'" *The Journal of Philosophy,* Vol. 56 (1959), 845–857. An excellent collation and exegesis of the passages in which Wittgenstein discusses criteria; brings out certain internal tensions in Wittgenstein's conception.

Dummett, Michael, "Wittgenstein's Philosophy of Mathematics." *Philosophical Review*, Vol. 68 (1959), 324–348.

Malcolm, Norman, "Wittgenstein's *Philosophical Investigations*." *Philosophical Review*, Vol. 63 (1954), 530–559. An extended review and discussion which presents Wittgenstein's arguments against the PLT, with emphasis on the private language speaker's lack of a criterion of correctness.

Rhees, Rush, "Can There Be a Private Language?" *PAS*, Supp. Vol. 28 (1954), 77–94. A symposium with A. J. Ayer containing an exposition of Wittgenstein's views on private language understood mainly as PLT-2; conveys Wittgenstein's nominalistic rationale very well, without discussing it as such.

Wittgenstein, Ludwig, *Philosophical Investigations*. German with facing translation by G. E. M. Anscombe. Oxford, 1953.

THE PROBLEM AFTER WITTGENSTEIN

Ayer, A. J., "Can There Be a Private Language?" *PAS*, Supp. Vol. 28 (1954), 63–76. A symposium with Rush Rhees in which Ayer criticizes the PLT and emphasizes the need for criterionless identification at some point.

Carney, James, "Private Language." *Mind*, Vol. 64 (1960), 560–565. Favors the PLT.

Castañeda, Héctor-Neri, "Criteria, Analogy, and Knowledge of Other Minds." *The Journal of Philosophy*, Vol. 59 (1962), 533–546. Discusses some problems of Malcolm's views on criteria.

Castañeda, Héctor-Neri, "The Private-language Argument." in C. D. Rollins, ed., *Knowledge and Experience*, 1962 Oberlin Philosophy Colloquium. Pittsburgh, 1963. A symposium with V. C. Chappell and J. F. Thomson; surveys critically the arguments for the PLT and also replies to the other symposiasts.

Chappell, V. C., "Comments," in C. D. Rollins, ed., *Knowledge and Experience*. Vigorously defends the PLT from criticisms raised by Castañeda's discussion.

Garver, Newton, "Wittgenstein on Private Language." *Philosophy and Phenomenological Research*, Vol. 20 (1960), 389–396. Favors the PLT.

Hardin, Clyde L., "Wittgenstein on Private Language." *The Journal of Philosophy*, Vol. 56 (1959), 517–528. Attacks the PLT.

Hervey, Helen, "The Private Language Problem." *The Philosophical Quarterly*, Vol. 7 (1957), 63–79. Accepts PLT* but claims that the real problem is whether or not one can recognize and classify one's sensations apart from their outward expression.

Tanburn, N. P., "Private Languages Again." *Mind*, Vol. 72 (1963), 88–102. Attacks PLT-2 and the thesis that all entities referred to in conversation must be publicly available.

Thomson, J. F., "Comments," in C. D. Rollins, ed., *Knowledge and Experience*. In his part of the symposium with Castañeda and Chappell, Thomson contends that the PLT is too unclear for decision.

Todd, W., "Private Languages." *The Philosophical Quarterly*, Vol. 12 (1962), 206–217. Argues that "a private language, in the sense of a personal sensation language, is logically possible," refutes certain arguments of Malcolm, and attempts to show that a private language need not lack criteria of correctness.

Wellman, Carl, "Wittgenstein and the Egocentric Predicament." *Mind*, Vol. 68 (1959), 223–233. Discusses critically some of Wittgenstein's arguments for the PLT in connection with the view that all knowledge is based on private experiences.

Héctor-Neri Castañeda

PROBABILITY. Our discussion of probability consists of three main parts. It seems advisable to trace in outline in the first part the "common sense of probability," the complex pattern of ordinary uses of "probably" and its semantic cognates that is the starting point for all attempts at philosophical analysis or reconstruction. Equally important is the well-established mathematical theory of probability, whose main outlines have been known for over two centuries and which is discussed in the second part. The concluding part outlines the main alternative types of philosophical interpretations of probability available at the time of writing. These three parts are relatively independent and can be read in any order. (The subject of probability is too broad to permit brief discussion. Reference is desirable to other relevant articles in this encyclopedia, especially CONFIRMATION: QUALITATIVE ASPECTS; CONFIRMATION: QUANTITATIVE ASPECTS; DECISION THEORY; and INDUCTION.)

The reader should be warned that the philosophy of probability is highly controversial and that the views expressed in this article would be rejected by many competent theorists.

It is unusual enough to be disconcerting when a philosopher, in his professional capacity, makes an assertion of the form "Probably *P*" or of the form "The probability of P_2, given *D*, is such-and-such." The natural context for a reference to probability is an assertion about matters of fact, about which philosophers are, by general consent, professionally indifferent. When a philosopher says that he hopes to have rendered it probable that arithmetic can be reduced to logic (Gottlob Frege) or urges that common sense has on the whole a higher probability of being right than any conflicting metaphysical theory (Bertrand Russell), he is perhaps merely reminding the reader of human fallibility. Indispensable references to probability are, however, a distinguishing feature of nondemonstrative arguments concerning matters of fact, which require more or less precise indications of the imputed reliability of both premises and conclusion. The rationale of nondemonstrative argument is a topic of great philosophical interest.

Corresponding interest in the concept of probability is heightened by its intimate connection with the still more elusive and important concept of rationality. Indeed, Pierre Simon de Laplace's dictum that the most important questions in life are usually those of probability is hardly overstated. Anybody who aspires to rationality must be guided by probabilities in the face of uncertainty: how this is to be done and with what justification are the main themes of the philosophy of probability.

Here, as elsewhere, the most pressing philosophical tasks are those of clarifying, analyzing, and, if need be, "reconstructing" the concept and its cognates. The "begin-all" of such work, as those who undertake it recognize, is the "ordinary" or "preanalytical" concept, whose relevant features are manifested in the accepted usages of the corresponding probability expressions.

COMMON SENSE OF PROBABILITY

An adequate survey of laymen's talk about probability must take account of the uses of the words "probably," "probable," and "probability," together with their numerous synonyms, antonyms, and paronyms. However, it is plausible to assign logical primacy to the use of the adverb, in combination with singular sentences or "that"-clauses. It is at any rate convenient to start with the ordinary uses of such a sentence as "Probably a black ball will be drawn," where what may be called the *kernel sentence* ("A black ball will be drawn") refers to a particular event (the drawing of a ball from a bag) whose *outcome* (relevant feature—whether the ball is black or white) is unknown at the time of utterance.

The following comments are at least plausible:

(1) "Probably" is semantically akin to "possibly" and "certainly." More precisely, "probably" usually fits any sentence frame into which the other two adverbs fit, so that one may be substituted for either of the others without violating syntax or logic.

(2) "Probably" implies "possibly" and excludes "certainly": what is probable is neither certain nor impossible. Anyone who says that a black ball will probably be drawn from an urn implies that it is possible for such a ball to be drawn and also that it is not certain that it will be—and similarly in other cases.

(3) In such contexts, the relevant sense of possibility is that of empirical, not "logical," possibility. A speaker who claims that a black ball may "possibly" be drawn is, to be sure, implying the absence of logical inconsistency between a statement of the known initial conditions (the nature and composition of the balls in the urn and the manner of drawing) and a prediction to the effect that a black ball will in fact be drawn. But he implies more. He means that in view of the urn's contents and the mode of selection the drawing of a black ball is not ruled out *by the facts* in the way that the drawing of a black bird would be. (Behind this is the idea that the nature of things excludes the occurrence of much that is logically possible.)

(4) As suggested by the last remark, there is implicit reference, in a statement of the form under consideration, to "initial conditions" (or, more colloquially, to the "way things are now"—that is to say, in advance of the trial). "Probably a black ball will be drawn" may be taken as elliptical for "Given that we have such-and-such an urn, containing such-and-such balls of known colors, etc., a black ball will probably be drawn." The initial conditions are identified by means of some abstract description: different descriptions of a state of the world may generate different estimates of probability. (Information about the electrical charge of the balls, for instance, may affect the probability of drawing a black one.)

(5) Often, a speaker will assert "Probably *P*" in partial or total ignorance of the initial conditions (with correspondingly weak reasons for his judgment); then the force of the statement is, approximately, "In view of the unknown state of the universe prior to the trial, a black ball will probably be drawn."

(6) Grammatically speaking, the adverb "probably" modifies the entire "kernel sentence" (or, in other contexts, the entire "that"-clause) to which it is attached. This is suggested in English, as in other languages, by the "parenthetical" nature of this adverb—its capacity to appear, without grammatical impropriety, almost anywhere between the words of the kernel sentence.

(7) If a kernel sentence by itself ("A black ball will be drawn") is taken to express the occurrence of some yet-to-be-realized event, situation, or state of affairs, we shall have to say, in the material mode, that probability, like possibility and certainty, is ordinarily attributed to such a "situation"—to something expressed by the sentence. Thus, "probably" belongs, prima facie, to the object language, not to a metalanguage in which features of verbal expressions are mentioned rather than used. It is therefore misleading to say, as some writers do, that probability is an attribute of propositions. If this kind of idiom is to be employed, accuracy requires us to say that probability judgments concern the probability of a proposition's *being true* rather than the probability of the proposition *simpliciter*.

(8) In some uses, at least, "Probably a black ball will be drawn" implies that a black ball *will* be drawn. (This point, more controversial than its predecessors, would be denied by many theorists.) There is an absurdity in saying "Probably a black ball will be drawn, but all the same a black ball will not be drawn." Although the speaker's use of "probably" is intended to intimate that the initial conditions are insufficiently strong to render the designated outcome empirically certain, the whole assertion, however guarded by acknowledgment of fallibility, is intended to commit the speaker to the kernel's truth. A layman, uninfluenced by the supposed demands of a correct philosophical analysis, will say, after drawing a white ball, "I was wrong"—falsity of the kernel counts as a setback, a failure. Of course the speaker may add, "But I was justified in saying what I did—namely, that a black ball would probably be drawn."

(9) We can accordingly distinguish between the appropriateness of a probability statement and its correctness. According to the view here recommended, a singular probability assertion has the double aim of seeking to make an appropriate attribution of probability while also seeking to predict the "outcome." Thus, the point of making a probability assertion is to make a prediction that is both sound (justified by the evidence) and successful (true); if it is the first it may be called warranted, if the second, fulfilled. (It is interesting to note that "true" and "false" seem incongruous modifiers of entire probability sentences.) The assertive aspect of an adverbial probability assertion is often suppressed in adjectival uses of "probable" and is almost invariably absent from substantival uses of "probability."

(10) "Probably" admits of adverbs of comparison—probability is "gradable." The supplementary question, "How probable?" always in order after a "probably"-assertion has been made, may be answered by "Rather probable," "Highly probable," "Almost certain," and even, in special contexts to be discussed below, by an indication of numerical chances, or odds.

(11) Possibility is gradable in approximately the same way that probability is: the question "How possible?," odd as it might seem to some philosophers, occurs in ordinary talk and can be answered by "Very possible," "Almost certain," etc. "Certainly," on the other hand, functions as a boundary, which possibility and probability may approach without reaching. In ordinary uses, certainty is not a special case of probability. "Close to being certain" and "nearly certain" are natural locutions, whereas "highly certain" and "rather certain" sound decidedly absurd.

(12) Gradations in probability, indicated by such rough expressions as "more probable than not," "somewhat probable," "very probable," and "so probable as to be almost certain," seem to correspond precisely to the corresponding gradations in possibility. (The awkwardness in saying, in English, "more possible than not" and "so pos-

sible as to be almost certain" can be discounted as resulting from accidents of idiom.)

It is worth considering, indeed, whether the common notion of probability is not merely that of greater or less possibility relative to the "initial conditions," considered in the light of its "distance" from certainty. This is, of course, unacceptable as an analysis, but perhaps no formal definition should be demanded; a sufficiently detailed description of the ramifying uses of "probably" and its semantic cousins is perhaps all that can be expected.

(13) On this identification of probability with empirical possibility, a question of the form "What is the probability of *P*, given *D*?" (when appropriate) asks for an estimate of the extent of the possibility for the truth of "*P*" left open by the truth of "*D*." Similarly, "What is the length of *B*?" asks for a measure of the extension of *B* along a certain direction. However, length is not to be identified with the numerical result of the comparison of extension with a standard body; nor is probability to be identified, as is too often done, with its numerical measure.

(14) The "assertive aspect" of ordinary uses of "probably" (see 8, above) is bound up, in ways that are hard to make precise, with the practical function of probability estimates within a general practice of acting upon the conclusions of nondemonstrative arguments. It would count as an absurdity in common contexts to say, for instance, "*P* is so probable as to be as good as certain, but I don't think that *P* will be the case." It would be equally absurd to say "*P* is as good as certain, but I propose to take no measures appropriate to *P*'s being the case." Roughly speaking, it is required by the general practice of drawing "risky inferences" to prepare for what is almost certain and to neglect what is extremely improbable. (The estimation of how improbable a conclusion has to be in order to be properly ignored must, in the end, be left to the judgment of the reasoner.)

A sufficiently detailed account of the uses of "probably" (which cannot be undertaken here) would require collateral exploration of the relevant uses of "expectation," "reasonable," and "justification."

(15) A paradigm case for the use of "probably" is the following: Imagine a marble contained in a box that is closed except for a hole large enough to permit the marble to pass. Imagine the box to be shaken vigorously for, say, thirty seconds. Common sense urges that the ball then "has a chance" of being shaken out, because it is possible for this to occur. That this empirical possibility is present can be shown by repeatedly shaking the box for the prescribed time: if the marble sometimes falls out, it was possible for it to do so; if this *never* happens, common sense will conclude that it is "impossible for the marble to escape" in the specified conditions. If a fairly long series of trials under the prescribed conditions results in the ball's being shaken out in a substantial majority of cases, common sense will conclude that the ball will "probably" be shaken out on the next trial.

(16) Suppose now that an extra hole of the same size is punched in the box. Then it looks "obvious" or "self-evident" that the marble has acquired "an extra chance" or extra possibility of escape and that, correspondingly, the

probability of its emergence has been raised (or, more cautiously, not lowered). But since empirical possibility is in question, the assumption can be put to empirical trial. If under the new conditions the marble is found on the whole to emerge in a substantially larger proportion of cases than before, the assumption that "its chances" of being shaken out have increased will be sufficiently verified. (If the new hole left the frequency of success unchanged, the conclusion would be that one hole somehow "interfered" with the other.) Observation of repeated trials provides evidence for probability judgments. To identify probability with proportionate frequency is, however, as implausible as to identify possibility with eventual occurrence.

(17) It will have been noted that we have been using "possibility" and its rough synonym "chance" as general nouns. In paradigmatic situations, common sense conceives of "chances," in the plural, as so many openings for bringing about a designated outcome (compare the common expression "Give me a chance," where "chance" has roughly the meaning of "opportunity"). If, given *D*, *P* is empirically impossible, then the initial situation that makes *D* true blocks all pathways to "success" (the marble is wholly enclosed in its box); if, however, the initial conditions are sufficiently relaxed, there is leeway for the outcome—the ball may or may not emerge, because there is now an exit, a tangible "chance" to get out. When one can justifiably say "Given *D*, probably *P*" the picture is one of "exits" predominating over "barriers."

(18) If a layman is pressed to explain in nonfigurative language what it means to say that exits "predominate" over barriers, a somewhat different picture may be offered. The "initial conditions" may now be conceived of as embodying forces or influences, some tending to bring about *P* but the others resisting. (The underlying picture is of something like a tug of war between allies and adversaries.) From this perspective, to say "Probably *P*" is to claim that on balance the propitious influences will prevail over their opponents.

In a case of empirical certainty the initial conditions (the effective part of the state of the universe at a given time *t*) wholly constrain and determine the outcome. In a case of empirical possibility, however, the initial conditions determine the outcome only partially, so that at the time of utterance, *t*, some situations can be realized and others cannot. Finally, a case of probability is such that among the set of possible outcomes left open by the initial conditions, one (the situation expressed by the kernel of the "probably"-statement) is on the whole favored by the initial conditions and may therefore on balance be expected.

(19) The foregoing references to "pictures" are justified by the extent to which laymen's talk about probability is dominated by pictorial imagery and crude mythology, lurking just below the surface.

It is unclear how much influence such imagery exerts. The dramatic conceptions of "favorable" and "adverse" chances, of tangible pathways to realization, and the rest (all of which are necessarily attenuated in situations where they fit less plausibly than in the paradigmatic situation already considered), seem to leave the relevant verification conditions untouched: a man who dismisses them as fairy tales will adopt the same procedures for arriving at probabilities that anybody else will.

But reference to empirical possibility is not to be set aside so lightly. Too many philosophers display an unreasonable *horror possibilitatis:* a tough-minded positivist, for instance, is apt to regard all talk about empirical possibility as no better than picturesque nonsense and will seek to purge ordinary talk about probability of all implicit reference to the unobservable-in-principle. Yet talk about empirical possibility and empirical necessity seems no more objectionable in principle than talk about persons or tables; nor does there seem to be any harm in admitting a notion of partial empirical determination. The "pictures" that underly ordinary probability talk, crude as they are, can perhaps be made as philosophically respectable as more fashionable general views concerning the universe.

(20) Conceptions of "partial determination," "favoring conditions," and the like, lend powerful support to certain general principles of probability that are needed in the mathematical theory of probability. Thus, it follows from what has already been said that any reinforcement of the "favoring chances" that leaves the original chances unimpaired cannot reduce the probability of *P.* (Hence, the second hole in the box could be expected not to diminish the chance of shaking the marble out.) This may be put more precisely, as follows: Suppose that *P* entails *Q*; then the probability of *Q*, given *D*, is not less than the probability of *P*, given *D*. Similarly, increase in the relative superiority or "strength" of the favoring conditions for *P* cannot diminish the probability that *P* will be the case. (In a tug of war, adding another man to one team cannot lessen the team's prospect of success as long as the new man does not get in the way of those who were there already.) Most writers have agreed in treating these principles as axiomatic.

(21) Some philosophers will say that the cash value of ordinary probability talk, infected as it is with dubious metaphor, can reside only in the corresponding verification conditions.

There seem to be two main types of verification. The most basic has already been illustrated: it consists of appeal to relative frequency of occurrence in similar cases. If in initial conditions *D*, *D'*, *D''*, · · ·, respectively, the outcomes *P*, *P'*, *P''*, · · · are realized substantially more often than not (where the *D*'s are all alike in relevant respects and the *P*'s are all alike in relevant respects), then this is taken to establish that given *D*, *P* has a better chance of being realized than not-*P*. It will be noticed that this type of verification procedure uses inductive inference and hence presupposes the soundness of inductive methods.

(22) Less direct modes of verification, in common use, are based upon inspection of the given initial conditions rather than upon an inductive inference from the consequences of repeated trials. A man may (or may seem to) conclude from mere knowledge of the defining conditions that there is a better chance of drawing a black ball from an urn containing 99 per cent black ones than there is of drawing one from another urn containing 50 per cent black ones. Closer examination of the assumptions behind such reasoning will reveal the essential role played by previous experience—for example, about how shaking or shuffling will favor "random" distributions of outcomes.

(23) The last point suggests that certain commitments to uniformity play a large part in the common-sense view. Built into the common talk about "forces," "reasons," and "determination," noted above, is the conception that like consequences must ensue upon like conditions. Thus, if a ball drawn in a certain way from a bag *B* that contains a given number of balls has a certain probability *p* of being black, common sense requires that a ball drawn in the same way from another bag *B'*, similar in all relevant respects, notably in having the same number of balls, will have the same probability of being black. The associated proportionate frequencies of occurrence are also taken to be approximately equal. Probability talk is based upon a generalization of determinism: like conditions are expected to go with like distributions of probabilities and with like distributions of associated frequencies.

(24) The foregoing remarks have concerned what might be called an absolute sense of "probably," where the "initial conditions" to which explicit or implicit reference is made are identified with the relevant features of the "state of the world" at the moment of utterance. Attention should now be paid to an explicitly relative sense, exemplified in such uses as "On the evidence, he is probably guilty" or "Given that he is a wealthy American, there is a high probability that he is a Republican."

The "absolute" use of "probably" previously discussed can be assimilated to the explicitly relative use in the following way: in the formula "On evidence *D*, probably *P* (to such-and-such a degree)," take "*D*" to refer to what were previously called the initial conditions. In this way the "absolute" use can be regarded as a special case of the "relative" use, when the datum is the (known or assumed) condition of the universe at the instant of assertion. We can therefore acknowledge the large measure of truth in the commonly accepted dictum that probability is always relative to evidence. This is correct in its implication that any probability assertion, whether explicitly relational or not, harks back to assumed enabling conditions—or, from another perspective, to conducive forces or propitious "chances"—that could be expressed in a more explicit version of the original assertion; it is, however, misleading if intended to imply that in the absence of such explicit indications of a basis, ordinary probability judgments are defective or in need of supplementation.

(25) The above view of ordinary uses of "probably" can be extended with little strain to cases in which the adverb is attached to a general statement. After inspecting a large and varied sample of crickets, a biologist may say, "Probably all crickets have ears on their legs." Common sense is inclined to think of the facts revealed in the examined sample as constraining and favoring a general possibility (that all crickets have ears on the leg) at the expense of competing possibilities. The available *information* about the universe now replaces the assumed initial conditions. In this use there need be no implication of objective uncertainty about the state of affairs to which probability is ascribed: a man who says, "On the evidence to hand, probably all *A* are *B*," may without inconsistency hold that

there are conclusive reasons "in the world" for all *A*'s being *B*. Thus, attributions of relative probability can be consistently made by a whole-hearted determinist, such as Laplace. That some general feature of "the facts" favors certain other large-scale features without wholly necessitating them is compatible with complete determination of the outcome in its full specificity. (This thought may have been behind Ludwig Wittgenstein's remark that probability assertions belong to a "myopic" view of the world.)

(26) The expression "it is probable that" sometimes functions as a synonym of "probably"; more characteristic, however, is its use to register the strength of the determining conditions as conducive, on balance, to the designated outcome. In many such cases the nonassertion of the kernel is patent.

With the use of the substantive, "probability," there is still greater epistemological distance from any act of assertion: to say something of the form "Given *D*, the probability that *P* is such-and-such" is to formulate a theoretical judgment about the strength of the enabling conditions without facing the question whether *P* should be expected with sufficient confidence for its assertion to be warranted. Still, to probability thus theoretically conceived something of the more full-bodied adverbial use still clings, and there are logical transitions from the substantival assertions to the adverbial ones. For instance, no intervening link is required for the logical transition from "Given *D*, the probability that *P* is overwhelming" to "Given *D*, probably *P*" with assertive force.

(27) The extent to which precise measures can be assigned to degrees of probability (or—what comes to the same thing, according to the view here taken—to degrees of possibility) is moot. In some cases at least, comparative judgments of probability (see, for instance, 16, above), when coupled with the generalized principle of uniformity (21, above), readily persuade the layman to assign determinate measures of probability.

Suppose, for example, that ten similar cards, each white on one side and black on the other, are pasted on a vertical glass screen so that five white sides and five black are in view: let a man *A* on one side of the screen be asked to choose a card at random, and let another man *B* on the other side be given the same task. Then common sense is almost irresistibly inclined to say that the situations of *A* and *B* are alike in all relevant respects and consequently that the chance of *A*'s choosing a white card is precisely the same as the chance of *B*'s choosing a black one. With the conventional allocation of unity to certainty, it then follows that the chance of either *A*'s or *B*'s choosing a white card is precisely 1/2. (This is an example of the use of the "principle of indifference," discussed in the final part of this article.)

If one asks instead for the probability of, say, finding life on Mars, it would be hard to suppose any definite measure appropriate. But here again a layman would confidently set the probability at less than 99/100. Behind such a judgment there may well be an imagined comparison with one's relative state of confidence in the occurrence of some designated outcome in a game of chance. If a man is convinced that he would rather bet on two consecutive sixes being shown by a fair die than on there being life on Mars,

he can at least set an upper bound to his confidence in the truth of the latter proposition (see the discussion, in the last part of this article, of "subjective" interpretations of probability).

The correct view seems to be that ordinary uses of probability (influenced, no doubt, by exposure to discussion of odds in games of chance) employ rudimentary and limited measures of probability, but are willing to be led, by suitable devices, to extend such estimations to any desired degree of precision. Mathematical theories of probability superimpose a numerical grid upon the partially unstructured comparative probability judgments of naive common sense. The relations between such mathematical calculations and the common-sense matrix may be plausibly compared to those between thermometric readings of temperature and crude judgments of "warmth."

Multiple senses of probability? The propriety of what seem to be radically different ways of verifying ordinary probability judgments (say, counting the number of pips on a die—as opposed to consulting mortality tables) has led a number of writers to claim that "probability" is an equivocal term. The preferred number of senses is two, although some writers have argued for as many as five. The absence of any generally accepted criteria for identity of senses or identity of concepts makes such claims hard to assess. The most influential case for the recognition of radically distinct senses of probability has been made by Rudolf Carnap, who wishes to distinguish sharply between probability as "rational credibility" and probability as "limiting relative frequency of occurrence." But his argument proves, upon examination, to be based solely upon the different modes of verification of two probability assertions, one held to be a priori, the other empirical (although he later offers a "logical" interpretation even of the latter). Writers who wish to argue that the existence of a priori as well as empirical probability assertions justifies attribution of plurality of senses might be asked to consider whether "two" has different senses in "Jones has two hands" and "Two and two makes four." There seem to be no compelling reasons for recognizing radically distinct senses of probability.

Structure of the common-sense view. In ordinary life, an assertion of the form "Probably *P*" where "*P*" expresses the realization of some possible event or situation has the function of committing the speaker to *P*'s being true, on the basis of the existence of "enabling initial conditions" that favor *P*'s realization without ensuring it. Thus, the use of the adverb signifies the supposed existence of such conditions and ensures that the assertion in which it occurs shall be circumspect, or "guarded." In the absence of other indications, the enabling conditions are understood to be the "state of the universe" (or the relevant part of it) at the moment of utterance. In explicitly relative probability assertions, however, the basis is expressed by a clause formulating information concerning some general feature of the universe, conceived of as favoring some other general feature (a relation of partial determination between attributes). In substantival uses ("Given *D*, the probability that *P* is such-and-such"), the assertive force of the adverbial use is bracketed or suppressed, the point of such uses being solely to estimate the strength with which the relevant enabling conditions (expressed by the reference to "*D*") favor the realization of the outcome *P*.

The view of probability here outlined differs from other current analyses in some or all of the following respects; (*a*) probability is not treated as an equivocal concept; (*b*) probability is regarded as legitimately attached to singular situations no less than to general features of the world; (*c*) probability is not identified with relative frequency or with some definable logical relation between propositions or with some imputed state of mind of an ideally reasonable judge.

It will be noticed that the common-sense conception of probability has been taken to be thoroughly objective. It has been argued that the layman thinks of his probability assertions as referring to "something out there" rather than to logical relations between propositions, conceived of as conceptual or verbal entities. Still less plausible is it from the common-sense point of view to think of assertions of probability as intended to express merely the speaker's "confidence" in the designated outcome. There are, to be sure, pragmatic rules that require the speaker to be conventionally invested with a degree of confidence corresponding to the character of the probability assertion uttered, but the expression of such confidence is not the primary purpose of such utterances.

It may be generally acceptable as a conclusion from the foregoing survey that the patterns of ordinary use of "probably" and its cognates are dishearteningly complex. However, the various subtle differences between roughly synonymous modes of expression in terms of "probably," "the likelihood is," "the chances are," "it is to be expected that," and the like, are normally of no consequence in primary contexts of circumspect commitment to uncertain outcomes. Nor is it usually important to distinguish between, say, the content of the probability assertion itself, the grounds for its assertion (characteristically although not exclusively based upon relative frequencies of occurrences in similar cases), the degree of confidence conventionally attributed to the speaker, and his approvable epistemic attitudes and actions. Some theorists have therefore been able to exploit, quite plausibly, a single feature of this tangled web, whereas others have hoped to divide and conquer by imputing a variety of senses.

Monolithic theories tend to distort obtrusive features of ordinary probability talk in the service of some philosophical preconception, whereas fragmenting approaches are hard pressed to show any principle of connection between the divorced senses. It seems implausible, however, to saddle ordinary probability talk with an inexplicable propensity for punning. A fully satisfactory theory, which is yet to be found, would do justice to both the variability and the unity of ordinary probability talk.

MATHEMATICAL THEORY OF PROBABILITY

Probability as a measure of sets. Mathematicians have clarified the foundations of the mathematical theory of probability (or the "calculus of chances") to a point at which it can be rigorously presented as a branch of pure mathematics—more specifically, as part of the general theory of additive functions of sets.

The leading ideas in this approach can be illustrated as follows: Suppose we have a number of sets, composed of any objects whatsoever—for instance, the sets that can be formed by taking some or all of the inhabitants of a certain village. Let us call such a set s_i. The set of all the inhabitants of the village—*S*, say—is then a special case of an s_i, as is Λ, the "null set" containing no inhabitants. We wish to find a way of assigning a number *m* to each *s*, to indicate what may provisionally be conceived of as the "spread" or "extent" of that set. In order to do this we shall certainly want the measure of a set obtained by combining two sets with no common members to be the sum of the measures of the two original sets. Let us call this the additive condition. We shall now adopt the convention that the measure of *S* itself, $m(S)$, is 1.

With these understandings, the most natural way of defining *m* would be to take its value each time to be simply the number of members of the set in question. It is easy to see, however, that as far as satisfying the proposed additive condition is concerned, the assignment of values to *m* can be made in a large variety of ways. (There might be some practical point, for instance, in giving a set composed of adults a measure higher than that of a set composed of the same number of children.) Suppose we assign an arbitrary "weight" to each inhabitant (with the sum of all the weights being 1) and take the measure of a set to be the sum of the weights of all its members; it is easy to see that the additive condition is then satisfied.

More generally, consider some set *S* containing as members a finite set of individuals $a_1, a_2, \cdots, a_m$. (The interesting general case, where the members of *S* form an infinite set, not necessarily countable, will be ignored here for the sake of simplicity.) Consider next the set *U* of all the subsets of *S*, with members $s_1, s_2, \cdots, s_n$. (Since *U* is taken, by convention, to include both *S* itself and the null set, Λ, it follows that $n = 2^m$.) Suppose, now, that each member s_i of *U* is to be assigned a definite nonnegative number, represented as $m(s_i)$, to be regarded as the "measure" of the set in question. Let each individual a_j be assigned a nonnegative "weight," $w(a_j)$. Finally, let $m(s_i)$ be defined as the sum of the weights of all the members of s_i. We add the convention that the measure of the set *S* (having all the a_i's as its members) is unity.

The following are almost immediate consequences of these stipulations:

(*a*) The measure of the null set is zero: $m(\Lambda) = 0$. (For Λ has no members at all.)

(*b*) The measure of a set and the measure of its complementary set, relative to *U*, add up to unity: $m(s) + m(\bar{s}) = 1$. (Here "$\bar{s}$" stands for the subset of *S* composed of all members of *S* that are not included in *s*.)

(*c*) The measure of a set composed by combining the membership of two sets is equal to the sum of their measures less the measure of their common part: $m(s_1 \cup s_2) = m(s_1) + m(s_2) - m(s_1 \cap s_2)$. (Here "$s_1 \cup s_2$" is used for the "union" of the two sets and "$s_1 \cap s_2$" for their "intersection," the set composed of their common members. The stated result follows at once from the adopted definition of measure.)

(*d*) In the special case in which the two sets have no common members, the measure of their union is the sum of their measures: If $s_1 s_2 = \Lambda$, then $m(s_1 \cup s_2) = m(s_1) + m(s_2)$.

Let us now introduce the notion of the relative measure of s_1 with respect to another set s_2, written $m(s_1|s_2)$. The definition is, simply, $m(s_1|s_2) = m(s_1 \cap s_2)/m(s_2)$—that is, the ratio of the measure of the intersection of the two sets to the measure of the reference class s_2.

(e) The measure of the intersection of two sets s_1 and s_2 is the product of the measure of the first and the relative measure of the second with respect to the first: $m(s_1 \cap s_2) = m(s_1|s_2) \times m(s_2)$. (This follows immediately from the definition of relative measure already given.)

We can easily apply this simple mathematical apparatus to an illustrative case in which probability calculations are performed. Suppose we are interested in calculating various odds connected with outcomes, defined as the simultaneous throws of two coins. Then the most specific ways of describing the outcomes are "*HH*," "*HT*," "*TH*," and "*TT*." Let us refer to these "basic outcomes" as a_1, a_2, a_3, and a_4, respectively, and think of them as constituting a set S. Suppose them to have been given probabilities of occurrence (how these probabilities are known we do not here inquire) that are, respectively, p_1, p_2, p_3, and p_4.

A typical (but trivial) problem in mathematical probability is to determine the chance that at least one head will appear when both coins are tossed. The elementary reasoning runs as follows: "The event in question may arise from a_1 or a_2 or a_3; hence its probability is 3/4." The analogy with the foregoing calculation of measures leaps to the eye. Think of any complex outcome as the set of all the basic outcomes compatible with it; identify the probabilities of the basic outcomes with weights; finally, identify probability and measure. Thus, we shall have

$$P(HH) = p_1 = w(a_1)$$
$$P(HT) = p_2 = w(a_2)$$
$$P(TH) = p_3 = w(a_3)$$
$$P(TT) = p_4 = w(a_4).$$

Since the complex outcome "at least one head" is compatible with a_1, a_2, and a_3, we shall have $P(HH$ or HT or $TH) = m(\{a_1, a_2, a_3\}) = w(a_1) + w(a_2) + w(a_3) = p_1 + p_2 + p_3$.

In short, such a calculation as is illustrated here can be conceived of as the determination of a measure, in the sense already explained, in accordance with the following dictionary:

possible, fully analyzed, or "basic" outcome (such as "*HH*")	member of a given set S
a generalized nonbasic outcome (such as "at least one head"), conceived of as a disjunction of basic outcomes	nonunit subset of S
the initial probability (p_1, p_2, p_3, or p_4) of a given basic outcome	weight of the corresponding member of S
probability of occurrence of a generalized outcome	measure of the corresponding subset of S
the probability of no basic outcome resulting is zero	$m(\Lambda) = 0$

the probability of any outcome and the probability of the complementary outcome add up to unity

$$m(s) + m(\bar{s}) = 1$$

and so on. This scheme can be at once extended to include "conditional" probability, of the form $P(O_1|O_2)$, read as "the probability of occurrence of O_1 if O_2 occurs":

$P(O_1|O_2)$, where O_1 and O_2 are the outcomes corresponding respectively to s_1 and s_2.

$$m(s_1|s_2)$$

On this interpretation, propositions (c) and (e), above, correspond, respectively, to the "general addition theorem" and the "general multiplication theorem" that are the basic principles of the calculus of chances:

$$P(O_1 \text{ or } O_2) = P(O_1) + P(O_2) - P(O_1 \text{ and } O_2);$$
$$P(O_1 \text{ and } O_2) = P(O_1 \text{ given } O_2) \times P(O_2).$$

These fundamental propositions look almost self-evident on the suggested interpretation.

The suggested transition from preanalytical ideas about probability to the abstract theory of measure has here been made via the notion of given basic outcomes, conceived of as abstract realizable features of a given configuration (the tossing of two coins, say). It is, however, possible to connect probability ideas with the abstract calculus in a variety of other ways. Suppose, for instance, that the desired weights are derived from observations of relative frequencies, so that to say $P(HH) = p_1$ is to claim that in a certain series of trials with the two pennies, HH turns up in the ratio $p_1 : 1 - p_1$—and similarly for p_2, p_3, and p_4. Then the transition to the calculus will be as feasible as before, for all that is needed for such a transition is that the individuals answering to the basic outcomes shall have numbers assigned to them in advance (and such that all these weights total unity). This very modest requirement can also be satisfied by somebody who purports to have a priori access to the requisite "weights"—or, again, by somebody who claims to be able to measure degrees of "rational confidence," or the like. Provided these competing philosophical interpretations issue, as they commonly do, in determinate measures of probability (however construed) satisfying the basic "additive condition" mentioned above, it will be possible to view the matter through the lenses of the set-measure conception. (The difficulty of directly connecting philosophical theories of probability with the mathematical theory will be precisely proportional to the extent that they imply that such measures cannot be provided. This is partly true, for instance, of J. M. Keynes's system of probability and to some extent true of Harold Jeffreys' system.)

The mathematical theory, accordingly, may be properly regarded as almost wholly neutral with respect to the conflicting philosophical analyses of the probability concept. It simply provides an abstract (but astonishingly fruitful) framework for calculating the values of complex probabilities in terms of the values of related ones. It gives us the former as calculable functions of the latter, ignoring any determinate values that either may have.

The last point can hardly be overemphasized, for its neglect has often invited fallacy. The set-measure conception assumes that the weights are assigned (subject to stated restrictions) from "outside the theory": values of the probabilities of "basic" outcomes must be supplied *to* the theory and cannot be determined *inside* it. Nothing in the mathematical theory of probability is competent to settle the "proper" values of such probabilities. Now in all problems of application of the pure mathematics, determination of the values of these "basic" probabilities plays an essential part.

The mathematical theory of probability can be usefully compared to a (hypothetical) theory of length in which no determinate measures of lengths are available. Such a theory could show how the lengths of compound lines are related to the lengths of their components—$l(AB)+l(BC)=l(AC)$, when A, B, and C are collinear, to take a simple example—but would be incompetent to determine the length of even a single segment. Were such a theory supplemented by conventions of congruence, permitting tests for equality of lengths, measurements would rapidly become possible. Precisely the same thing can be said for the theory of chances: in order to determine the requisite "weights" of basic outcomes it is sufficient—at any rate, in a large class of cases—to be able to determine when given outcomes are to be regarded as *equally* probable. (If certainty can be partitioned into a finite set of n equiprobable alternatives, each of these will then have the determinate probability $1/n$ and the rest will follow without difficulty.) Equiprobability plays the same role in the pure theory of chances that congruence does in the mathematical theory of linear mensuration. In both cases the pure theory can receive specific application only by means of additional conventions not derivable from purely mathematical considerations. (This is a special case of the principle that pure mathematics cannot apply to the world without a nonmathematical link.)

Inverse probability and Bayes' formula. A problem of calculation that constantly arises in practice is that of "inverting" a probability—that is, of computing the value of $P(K|L)$ when the value of $P(L|K)$ is known. Such a calculation—or something equivalent—is needed to perform the important task of inferring from observed frequencies to associated probabilities.

The calculation can be illustrated by the following simple example. Suppose that of a certain set of men 90 per cent own an automobile and that among those automobile owners 10 per cent also own a bicycle, whereas among the non-automobile owners 20 per cent own a bicycle. We wish to know the probability that a man in the set considered, who owns a bicycle, also owns an automobile.

Writing "A" for "x owns an automobile" and "B" for "x owns a bicycle," we have:

$$p_1 = P(A) = .9 \qquad p_2 = P(\bar{A}) = .1 \text{ (given)}$$
$$q_1 = P(B|A) = .1 \qquad q_2 = P(B|\bar{A}) = .2 \text{ (given)}.$$

Here p_1 and p_2 may be called the "prior" probabilities (a label to be preferred to the classical "a priori probabili-

ties") and q_1 and q_2 the (conditional) "forward" or direct probabilities (sometimes called the likelihoods).

In this example, by the multiplication and addition rules we have:

$$P(AB) = p_1 q_1 = .9 \times .1 = .09$$
$$P(\bar{A}B) = p_2 q_2 = .1 \times .2 = .02$$
$$P(B) = P(AB) + P(\bar{A}B) = .09 + .02 = .11.$$

In order to find the "backward," or inverse, conditional probability, $P(A|B)$, we use the multiplication formula

$$P(A|B) \times P(B) = P(AB).$$

Writing "r_1" for "$P(A|B)$" and using the results already obtained, we rewrite the last equation as

(*) $$r_1 = (p_1 q_1)/(p_1 q_1 + p_2 q_2).$$

In the special case considered, we find that r_1, the inverse probability that a bicycle owner will also be an automobile owner, has the value $(.09)/(.11)$, or $9/11$. Similarly, the complementary probability that a bicycle owner will not also be an automobile owner is $2/11$.

The elementary formula (*) is a special case of the so-called Bayes' formula. Its essence is that the backward probability is proportional to the product of two numbers: the forward probability, q_1, and the corresponding prior probability, p_1. (This agrees with the "good sense" that Laplace wished to reduce to calculation. Common sense requires the chance that a bicycle owner shall also be an automobile owner to depend on two things—the prior probability that a man owns an automobile as well as the conditional probability that an automobile owner owns a bicycle. Formula (*) expresses this idea in a precise numerical form.)

The more general case, where we start with n prior probabilities, p_i, and n corresponding forward probabilities, q_i, follows by the same simple arithmetic. The corresponding value for the backward probability, r_1, is obviously

(**) $$r_1 = (p_1 q_1)/(p_1 q_1 + p_2 q_2 + \cdots + p_n q_n).$$

Given the values of the p's and q's, the value of each r_i is readily obtained by simple arithmetic.

Bayes' formula, (**), is obviously legitimately applicable in the example illustrated. This is more than can immediately be said in instances where the values of the prior probabilities are unknown.

Consider the following example. A bag is known to contain 100 balls, all of which are either black or white. Of 10 balls drawn at random with replacement, 6 are found to be black and 4 white; it is required to calculate the (inverse) probability that the bag contains black and white balls in equal numbers.

Here there are 99 alternatives to be considered, corresponding to the 99 different possible compositions of the bag's contents. For each such alternative, the "forward" probability, q_i, can be computed. However, in order to apply Bayes' formula, we also need to know the prior probabilities of each of these alternatives. Thus, in computing the backward probability that on the evidence (6 black, 4 white balls in the sample) the original population was evenly divided between black and white balls, we need to know the respective prior probabilities that the bag was composed of 99 white and 1 black, of 98 white and 2 black, and so on. Now, on the data given, no values can be assigned to these prior probabilities—not because we are ignorant but rather because the meaning of "prior probability" has not yet been established; hence, the problem is indeterminate and cannot be solved without further data.

In the earlier uses of Bayes' formula the assumption was made in such cases that in the absence of any specific knowledge of the prior probabilities, we are entitled to treat all of them as equal in value. It is easily seen that Bayes' formula then reduces to the special form

$$(\dagger) \qquad r_i = (q_i)/(q_1 + q_2 + \cdots + q_n).$$

Since the p_i's have now dropped out of the formula, the calculation is readily performed. It is, however, hard to see what sense, let alone what justification, can be given to the assumption of the equality of the prior probabilities. Such a sense could be supplied in this particular illustration if a large number of similar drawings were made on other occasions from bags of different compositions. The requisite prior probabilities would then correspond to the proportionate frequencies of occurrence of differently composed bags in the series of trials considered. This resource will not, however, be available in the general case now to be considered.

The general situation in which considerations of inverse probability arise is one in which a number of hypotheses H_i are compatible with given evidence E and in which the forward probabilities $P(E|H_i)$ are known or are computable. If one, or a certain subset of the H_i could be selected as relatively best-supported by E, it would then be possible to compute the forward probability that further data D would be found. In short, the situation is the basic one of inference from sample consequences to best-supported hypothesis and so, indirectly, to further consonant observations.

Here the analogy with the bags of balls, used above, breaks down. Variously composed bags may indeed be used on different occasions, but universes are not available for inspection in repeatable series of trials. Since precisely one of the competing hypotheses H_i is in fact true in this one and only universe, no good sense can be given, in general, to the ascription of an associated prior probability, and a fortiori no good sense can be given to the assumption of equality of such imputed probabilities.

This objection seems decisive against such uncritical use of Bayes' formula (or the interesting variants derivable from the assumption of infinitely many alternative hypotheses). Discussion of the subject has in the past sometimes paid undue attention to the supposedly absurd consequence known as Laplace's rule of succession—if a successes have been observed in $a + b$ independent trials, the probability of success in a new trial is $(a + 1)/(a + b + 2)$. It would indeed be disquieting if we had to suppose that

after rain on three successive days the chance of rain on the next day must be exactly 4/5—but it may be doubted that the conditions for use of the rule of succession have here been satisfied. The objection previously formulated seems in any case more fundamental.

One nontrivial consequence of Bayes' formula is important to such theorists as the defenders of the "subjective" interpretation of probability to be discussed below, who still rely upon circumspect uses of inverse probability. We have seen that in such an example as the drawing of samples with replacement from a bag of unknown composition, the calculation from the composition of the sample to the backward probability depends on the unknown prior probabilities as well as on the conditional forward probabilities. It can be shown, however, that (speaking roughly) the influence of the values of the prior probabilities on the magnitude of the backward probability diminishes progressively as the size of the sample increases. Thus, a case can be made for arguing that an arbitrary but fixed distribution of the prior probabilities of the hypotheses considered will suffice for application of Bayes' formula if we are content to get results acceptable in the long run.

The issues are too technical and controversial for discussion here. Many, if not most, statisticians regard as dubious arguments from inverse probabilities in something like the traditional style. In many situations, at least, they can be bypassed in favor of "tests of significance," whose rationale is substantially different.

Suppose we are considering, in our example of the bag of colored balls, whether the evidence to hand (composition of a sample) will justify acceptance or rejection of a given hypothesis (say, that 90 per cent of the balls in the bag are black). Suppose the forward probability $P(E|H)$ is very low—say, less than .01. Then we may feel justified in rejecting H on the ground that it is unreasonable to believe in H if it commits us to the occurrence of so unlikely a consequence. If we were to accept H we would have to believe that some very improbable consequence (one whose probability of occurrence given H was less than .01) would have occurred—which may be enough to warrant our looking elsewhere for some other hypothesis compatible with the evidence.

The leading idea in this highly simplified train of thought is characteristic of much refined contemporary statistical method based upon the use of "confidence intervals" and "tests of significance." Its philosophical interest lies in its apparent avoidance of any dubious appeals to inverse probability. There does remain, however, the question of what justification, if any, can be given for the neglect of small probabilities—or, what comes to much the same thing—what justification can be given for the conventional choice by statisticans of a determinate confidence level.

Law of large numbers. Let us suppose that a well-balanced, "fair," coin has been tossed a large number of times, n. Common sense would lead us to expect that the proportion of heads in the n trials—call it "p"—should be approximately 1/2 (that is, the same as the initial probability of a head). It is also reasonable to expect that the approximation gets "better" as n gets larger. Our common ideas about probability seem to commit us to this loose kind of connection between the initial probability, 1/2, and the approximate relative frequency of occurrence of heads in a long series of repeated trials. This important idea received exact mathematical expression in a striking result discovered by Jakob Bernoulli and often called Bernoulli's theorem.

The theorem applies to the present illustration in the following way: Suppose that after *n* tosses the proportionate frequency is found to lie between .5 + .1 and .5 − .1; let us then say that *p* has "*arrived* within .1 of the initial probability 1/2," and let us call .1 the corresponding "distance." For a given *n*, say 1,000, the chances that *p* will have arrived within the distance .1 of 1/2 can be calculated; similarly, the corresponding chances can be calculated for other values of *n* and other choices of the "distance." Let us call the chance in favor of *p*'s having arrived after *n* throws within a given distance of the initial probability (1/2) the corresponding "prospect." It is obvious that the prospect is a function, in general, of the number of throws and also of the chosen distance.

Bernoulli's theorem implies the following information about this interdependence: For any given and fixed distance, the corresponding prospect after *n* trials can be made indefinitely close to 1 as *n* increases. In other words, if we want *p* to be within a certain distance of 1/2, settled in advance, our chance of being satisfied converges to 1 as *n* increases.

An example may help to explain this. Let us take the distance to be 1 per cent. Then for *n* = 40,000, calculation shows that the odds in favor of the proportion of heads lying between .5 + .01 and .5 − .01 are better than 999 to 1 (that is, the prospect is then better than .999). Bernoulli's theorem assures us that had we held the 1 per cent distance fixed while considering a larger number of trials, the prospect would be even closer to 1 than .999. Indeed, for that choice of distance, the prospect could be made as close to 1 as we pleased by taking *n* to be sufficiently large. Had we chosen a smaller distance to start with, say .1 per cent, we would have needed a larger number than 40,000 trials to get equally favorable odds (999 to 1) in favor of the frequency's being within that distance of 1/2, but otherwise all that has been said would still apply. All of this follows by nontrivial mathematical calculation from the stated assumptions.

In this sketch the initial probability of 1/2 was chosen merely for the sake of simplicity in illustration. Had the initial probability been some other fraction, say 4/5, corresponding remarks would apply.

Complicated as the foregoing may seem, it has seemed worthwhile to state the general character of the "law of great numbers" correctly, in order to forestall the misunderstandings of it and the consequent abuses that are surprisingly common in the literature. It is, for instance, quite wrong to say categorically that in the long run the observed relative frequency of occurrence of a character *will* be approximately the same as its initial probability of occurrence in a single trial. The correct formulation, as we have seen, concerns the *chance* that this will be the case. There is no direct "bridge" between probability and relative frequency: the law provides a connection between initial probability and a related *probability* (that can be

made as close to unity as desired) of a certain specified kind of distribution of occurrences.

The validity of Bernoulli's theorem depends on two assumptions that restrict its usefulness in practice: (1) the initial probability of the single event (1/2 in our illustration) is assumed to be the same throughout; (2) the successive trials are assumed to be independent of one another. If a roulette wheel was to be continuously spun, without correction for wear and tear, the first condition would eventually be violated; if a dishonest croupier saw to it that no more than seven consecutive reds or blacks ever occurred, the second condition would be violated. (Modern refinements of Bernoulli's theorem, in which the two conditions can be somewhat relaxed, will not be considered here.)

It is possible to formulate a kind of inversion of the theorem, permitting a suitably circumspect inference from observed frequency to a prospect of the initial probability's being within a predetermined distance of the observed relative frequency *p*. This procedure has all the disadvantages of the "direct" use of Bernoulli's theorem.

The inference from "a posteriori probability" (that is, observation of relative frequency in a large number of trials) to approximate "a priori probability" (that is, "initial probability," in the terminology of the previous account) is, however, usually made in a somewhat different fashion. A certain hypothesis is considered concerning the approximate value of the unknown initial probability—call that hypothesis "*H*." Then the odds against the occurrence of the observed relative frequency are calculated on the assumption that not-*H* is the case—using Bernoulli's theorem or some consequence of it. If the odds against the observed distribution thus obtained are regarded as sufficiently high, not-*H* is rejected and *H* is accepted.

This may be regarded as the use of a "significance" test, for which the end of the section on inverse probability and Bayes' formula may be consulted. The basic methodological principle involved is—to speak roughly—that hypotheses that if true would make observed data sufficiently unlikely may be rejected. (To replace this crude formulation by precise procedures permitting reliable estimates of the risks involved is one of the main technical tasks of statistics.)

THE MEANINGS OF "PROBABILITY"

Whether or not probability is as much the "guide of life" as Bishop Butler thought, probability estimates are highly useful for making determinate judgments concerning unobserved events and unverified hypotheses. No uninterpreted or "pure" mathematical theory of chances can be useful in this way until its undefined terms are given definite "interpretations" (semantic definitions) that will convert the axioms of the calculus into fully meaningful assertions. The student can choose, at this point, from an embarrassing variety of plausible interpretations of the basic probability expressions.

In weighing the merits of the rival claimants it is appropriate to consider how well they answer the following basic questions: (1) How well does the theory succeed in certifying the axioms of the mathematical theory of chances as correct? (As already explained, this hinges essentially upon the definition of equality of chances that is offered.) (2) What connection, if any, does the theory establish between probabilities and observed frequencies? (It is quite certain that frequencies, empirically determined, in practice often do establish reasonable judgments of probability.) (3) Can the theory render intelligible and justify our trust in probabilities as a guide to the provisionally unknown? (This question is obviously connected with its predecessor.)

Mathematical dogmatism. Brief mention should be made of a view of a kind sometimes found in mathematical textbooks on probability and often recommended in the classroom. Roughly speaking, we are asked to conceive of probability as whatever can satisfy the axioms of the mathematical theory. The pure theory of chances is compared to a pure geometry, both viewed as "idealized models," having only a loose connection with reality, and the task of correlating the precise mathematical results with their imprecise counterparts in experience is held to be basically a practical one, needing no theoretical discussion.

As a solution to the problem of interpretation, this approach is merely an evasion. Formal obeisance to the "idealization" implicit in mathematical theory construction serves merely as an excuse for shirking the hard work of articulating the links between theory and practical applications.

Classical theory and the principle of indifference. The label "classical theory" usually alludes to the influential views expressed in Laplace's famous "Essai philosophique sur les probabilités" (1814) and adopted by a hundred writers since. The fundamental notion of deriving equalities of probability from parity of favoring reasons is, however, at least a century older, having been stated by Jakob Bernoulli in his posthumously published *Ars Conjectandi* (1713).

In the absence of explicit information in the writings of Bernoulli and Laplace, it is uncertain how these pioneers would have chosen to define probability. On the whole, however, their practice suggests that the basic conception was, in effect, one of *justified degree of belief*. Probability concerns the "degree of certainty" (Bernoulli) of an ideal rather than an actual belief; its value measures the strength of a belief that would be held by a thinker (a perfectly reasonable man) who correctly adjusted his expectation to the evidence at his disposal.

To determine how strongly such a thinker would believe in a given alternative (or how anybody *ought* to think), we turn to the celebrated "principle of indifference" (so called following Keynes; formerly known as the "principle of nonsufficient reason," with a possible allusion to Leibniz' "principle of sufficient reason").

Suppose the question is whether a certain man is in New York or Chicago, given that he must be in one place or the other, and suppose every reason in favor of his being in New York (for example, that he said he would be there) is matched by a reason of the same form in favor of his being in Chicago (for example, that he also said he would be in Chicago); we are then, it is said, entitled to regard the probabilities of the two mutually exclusive alternatives as equal.

More generally: if there are n mutually exclusive alternatives of the same form, backed by symmetrical reasons, then the n probabilities are to be taken as equal. From this there follows at once the definition of measure of probability, to be found in innumerable mathematical textbooks, ancient and modern, as "the ratio of the number of favorable cases to the total number of cases." (To compute the probability of a 6 turning up in three throws of a die, for instance, we assume that the principle guarantees equal probabilities of the die's showing a given number on any throw; the rest is then a simple exercise in permutations and combinations.)

The principle of indifference has been stated above in its most plausible form. When each reason we have for believing in A is matched by an exactly corresponding reason in favor of believing in B, common sense readily agrees that the probabilities properly assigned to the alternatives, on the evidence provided, should be equal. Less plausible is the application of the principle to cases where the required symmetry of supporting reasons derives from the total absence of reasons on either side. Arguments from what might be called "parity of ignorance" (which have seduced even so able a thinker as William Stanley Jevons) have tended to bring the principle into deserved disrepute. (It is hard, of course, to imagine a case in which the reasoner is *wholly* ignorant of evidence favoring either P or not-P and is therefore required to assign to each alternative the probability 1/2. Is the present reader of these lines of the male sex? The writer fancies that women read philosophical articles less often than men do; if so, the relevant reasons are asymmetrical and the principle fails to apply.)

Even in more plausible contexts use of the principle can rapidly generate absurdities. For instance, the "alternatives" to which the principle is supposed to apply can normally be classified in a number of different ways, resulting in incompatible probability values. Suppose we wish to compute the probability that two cards drawn at random from a set composed of two red and two black cards will have the same color; shall we consider as equally probable alternatives the six possible "constitutions" of the hands (counting hands as different if different cards are drawn) or shall we pay attention only to the "complexions" of such hands (the number of red and black cards)? If the first, the probability will be 2/6; if the second, 2/3. Appeal to "parity of reasons" offers no guide to the right answer.

Even stronger objections can be raised when the variable whose value is to be determined runs over a continuous domain. To determine the probable mass m of a body known to have a value between 0 and 1, shall we take it as equally likely that m lies in the intervals $(0,1/2)$ and $(1/2,1)$? But then we also have "parity of reasons" for a similar distribution of the reciprocal, $1/m$—which would produce a different answer. (This type of objection has been forcefully upheld by Keynes.)

It has also been objected that the principle is never strictly applicable since evidence is never perfectly symmetrical with respect to a number of alternatives and that it is in any case useless in the numerous cases in which the alternatives to be examined cannot be analyzed into a set of ostensibly parallel alternatives.

The somewhat naive attempts by earlier exponents of

the Bayesian approach to use the principle in the calculation of inverse probabilities (by assuming equiprobabilities of the hypotheses under test) have further contributed to the current ill repute of the principle.

It is clear that the principle is too weak to achieve unaided the desired results of assigning equiprobabilities. Some of the previously mentioned difficulties can perhaps be overcome by suitable supplementation of the principle. Variants of the principle of indifference will be found to figure prominently in the "logical" theories now to be discussed.

Logical theories. Any philosophical interpretation of probability deserves the title logical theory if its author claims that a basic probability statement, of the form "The probability of *P* on *S* is *p*," is true a priori. This distinctive feature, shared, for instance, by the well-known theories of Keynes, W. E. Johnson, Rudolf Carnap, and Harold Jeffreys, sets a "logical" interpretation apart from the "empiricist" and "subjective" views still to be considered. (Roughly speaking, an "empiricist" supposes a true basic probability statement to say something about the inanimate world, whereas a "subjectivist" takes it to say something about the belief or degree of confidence of an ideal reasoner.)

Logical theories are in direct descent from the "classical" standpoint of Bernoulli and Laplace, however superior they may be in sophisticated elaboration of explicitly invoked assumptions. Laplace and his followers, as we have seen, characteristically conceived of the degree of probability as being wholly determined by a calculable relation between *given* information (or the lack of it) and a given hypothesis, independently of appeal to associated frequencies or any other matters of fact. Like the Laplacians, latter-day advocates of "logical" theories typically construe probability as relative to evidence—indeed, the slogan "probability varies with the evidence" is commonly taken by them to be as good as self-evident.

Some confusion is often introduced by reference to "rational credibility," "warranted assertibility," or the like. This has the appearance of an implicit appeal to some ideal judge of strength of evidence, a perfectly reasonable man whose verdicts determine the "correct," "rational," or "justifiable" degree of probability. The fiction is, of course, transparent: the ideally rational man does not answer when summoned, and reference to him is merely a picturesque way of pointing to an imputed logical relationship supposedly holding between a pair of given propositions solely in virtue of their meanings. Indeed, the criteria of "rationality" include observance of proper rules for estimation of probabilities; there is no independent test for rationality. The "ideally rational man" is as irrelevant to "logical" theories as the "ideal calculator" would be to mathematics.

Keynes, whose eloquent defense of the logical approach against its rivals is largely responsible for its present vogue, wished to treat the ultimate relation between "proposal" and "supposal" as indefinable. This has the serious disadvantage of making the truth of the ultimate basic propositions available only to intuition, which is even more unreliable in matters of probability than it is elsewhere.

Later writers, such as Carnap, committed to constructing a definition of the ultimate logical relation, have typically invoked the notion of relative "range" (*Spielraum*) or something equivalent.

This can be briefly explained as follows. Suppose the indefinable, or "primitive," propositional functions of a given language *L* have the form $P_i(x_1, x_2, \cdots, x_n)$. For each P_i, form all possible values of these functions by inserting all possible choices of names of the individuals in the domain to which *L* refers. Call these the "atomic" sentences of *L*. Now form a conjunction in which every atomic sentence or its negation appears. This is a so-called state description. Each such state description may be regarded as expressing a "possible universe" relative to the choice of the language *L*, because it is the most specific description in *L* of what such a universe might be like. By suitably weighting such state descriptions, each proposition *P* can then be assigned a measure $m(P)$ and the degree of probability of *H* on *P* can be simply defined by the fraction $m(HP)/m(P)$. In this way it is theoretically possible to calculate the probability of *H* relative to *P* for every pair of propositions *H* and *P* expressible in *L*.

The arbitrariness in application of the "principle of indifference," previously noted, reappears here in the fact that the state descriptions can be weighted in infinitely many ways, each resulting in self-consistent attributions of probabilities to given pairs of propositions. (Carnap's detailed exploration of the consequences of such choices is a valuable contribution to this subject.)

Many critics regard the variability of the probability values relative to the choice of a language *L* as a further source of disquiet in Carnap's elaborate construction. (It should be noted, also, that Carnap has so far succeeded in developing his theory only in connection with certain very highly simplified "languages." Whether his methods can be extended to some language rich enough to approximate the contemporary "language of science" is still an unsettled question.)

The most difficult question that any "logical" theory has to answer is how a priori truths can be expected to have any bearing upon the practical problem of anticipating the unknown on the basis of nondemonstrative reasons.

Frequency theories. All probability theorists agree with the common-sense approach in recognizing that knowledge of relative frequencies of occurrence sometimes properly influences probability judgments. Were this not so, actuaries would deserve no more credit than soothsayers and their interest in statistical information would be an idle folly. The warmest advocate of a neoclassical analysis of probability in terms of the relative strength of reasons is bound to recognize that such strength is sometimes affected by relevant information concerning frequency. A well-balanced coin may, in the absence of further information, invite application of the principle of indifference, but when repeated trials with it show heads markedly predominating over tails, the evidence ceases to be symmetrical.

The root idea of a "frequency" theory is to deny the existence of any logical gap between frequency and reasons: probability is, in all cases, to be identified with some suitably defined relative frequency. (Sophisticated modern versions of this approach identify probability, instead, with the "limiting value" of such frequency.)

This idea has great intrinsic appeal to empiricists who,

hoping to interpret basic probability statements as contingent (and in this way guaranteeing their application to practice), have nowhere better to look than in the direction of observed frequencies.

An early and influential anticipation of "frequency" theories is Locke's characterization of probable argument as "proof . . . such as for the most part carries truth with it" (*Essay Concerning Human Understanding*, Bk. 4, Ch. 15, "Of Probability"). Locke, on the whole, with his definition of probability as "likeliness to be true . . . [of] a proposition, for which there be arguments or proofs, to make it pass or be received for true," is still close to the classical conception.

More than a century ago, Leslie Ellis proposed to make the theory of probabilities a "science relating to things as they really exist" by taking as axiomatic the principle that in a long series of trials "every possible event tends to recur in a definite ratio of frequency." John Venn used this suggestion in *The Logic of Chance* (1866), defined probability explicitly in terms of relative frequency of occurrence of events in "the long run" (Ch. 6, Sec. 35), and developed the consequences in much detail. C. S. Peirce, acknowledging indebtedness to both Locke and Venn, considered probability to belong to arguments rather than events. For him the relevant measure was the proportionate number of times that the argument leads from true premises to true conclusions and is to be established by empirical investigation of the "success" of the argument in the long run.

The most ingenious and persuasive advocate of a frequency view in modern times has been Richard von Mises. Central to his conception is the original but controversial idea of a *Kollektiv*, a series of events in which the characters of interest occur randomly. Von Mises' own definition of the desired type of randomness can, it seems, survive the accusations of inconsistency first leveled against it. Hans Reichenbach's very detailed investigations of probability purport to be able to dispense with von Mises' problematic conditions for randomness.

Although the frequency approach attracts working statisticians and other scientists concerned with large populations of events (for example, in "statistical mechanics"), it has the disadvantage, from the broader standpoint of an adequately comprehensive philosophy of probability, of denying any meaning to the probability of a unique event. Probability, according to frequentists, must always be construed as a global character of some indefinitely large class or indefinitely extended series of events. That such series are never to be found in experience makes probability statements, on this interpretation, neither strictly verifiable nor strictly falsifiable. This limitation and the necessary exclusion of probability statements concerning single events combine to restrict the scope of probability, so interpreted, too drastically for comfort.

A further difficulty is the implausibility of assigning probability, conceived in the frequentist fashion, to general assertions of law. For laws can hardly be conceived of as "occurring" as members of relevant classes. In spite of Reichenbach's valiant attempts to overcome this defect, the frequency interpretation must be held to reflect at best only part of the truth about probability.

Subjective theories. Let someone—S, say—be asked to consider how confident he would be of the truth of the proposition "A black ball will be drawn next" (H, say) if he knew the truth of the proposition "Ten balls drawn with replacement from a bag have all been black" (E, say). It seems certain that S's attitude of expectation toward H, in such cases, would vary with the evidence, E; for instance, if H' is the proposition obtained from H, above, by replacing "ten" by "a hundred," it seems certain that every S can be counted upon to say that his confidence in E, given H', is greater than his confidence in E, given H. On the assumption of such comparability of expectations, we may introduce the symbol "$c_S(H|E)$" to stand for the degree of S's confidence in H, given E. (Some authors prefer to say "degree of belief.") It may also be assumed, pending further discussion, that numerical values can sometimes be attached to degrees of confidence. (For different choices of S, the values of $c_S(H|E)$ must in general be expected to be different.)

An extreme form of a "subjective" interpretation would simply identify probability with c_S—that is, with a given person's intensity of confidence. No theorist has proposed this view, if only because it would make probabilities fluctuate too much to be worth considering.

The following modification has, however, been ably defended in recent times, notably by Leonard J. Savage and by Bruno de Finetti. Suppose our hypothetical subject, S, is called upon to make an indefinitely large number of judgments resulting in values of $c_S(H|E)$ for different choices of E and H. Some such assignments of values of c_S would prove to be inconsistent or "incoherent," in senses soon to be explained. Let him then adjust all his assignments of values of c_S in such a way as to remove such incoherence; his "confidence" in H, given E, may then be called "rectified" (most writers prefer some such term as "reasonable," which is here avoided because of its implications of some standard of objective rationality). The views to be discussed here identify probability with degree of rectified confidence. They are distinguished from all logical theories by the important assumption that rectified confidence (and hence probability) can vary from one person to another, without imputation of fault.

The requisite notion of "coherence" is broader than that of logical consistency, which is presupposed. (Thus, it is assumed that if E_1 is logically equivalent to E_2 and H_1 is logically equivalent to H_2, a given S will assign the same values to $c_S(H_1|E_1)$ and to $c_S(H_2|E_2)$.) Suppose a given S were willing to offer odds of two to one that H would be true, given E, and odds of three to one that not-H would be true, given E. Although this might be done without any formal contradiction resulting, a gambler, by accepting both bets at once, could be certain to defeat S. All he need do is to make E true and await the outcome: if H then proves to be true, he collects $3 - 1$ points, while if H proves false he collects $2 - 1$ points, ending as the winner in either case. In the jargon of the racetrack, this is called "making a Dutch book" against S.

Let us give the rectification of S's confidence values the following meaning: S will so choose these values that it will be impossible for anybody to "make book" against him, by accepting odds that will guarantee a net profit. It is surprising but demonstrably true that if *S*'s system of confidence values is coherent in this sense of rendering it impossible for anybody to make book against *S*, those values will obey the addition and multiplication rules of the mathematical theory of chances. This striking result gives the subjectivist access to the usual mathematical axioms and their consequences. By stipulating that the degrees of confidence in question shall be coherent in the sense now explained, the advocate of a subjective theory is able to find a firm foundation for the customary calculation of complex probabilities. All systems of rectified confidence-values will use the same calculations for deriving complex probabilities from simpler ones, however different their starting points.

Some reluctance may be felt in supposing that the "confidence-values" to which the theory refers can be accurately measured in all cases. The answer offered, based upon a suggestion of F. P. Ramsey, is, roughly speaking, to determine these values from a knowledge of the odds that the person in question would offer in betting for one outcome rather than another. Let *S* be asked to bet on the truth of *H*, given *E*: if he is willing to wager one dollar against fifty cents (or anything more, but nothing less), we may assume that his confidence in *H*, given *E*, is measured by the odds of 2 to 1 (or, in more conventional terminology, that he attributes to *H*, given *E*, the probability 2/3) and similarly in other cases. (The complications resulting from the "diminishing utility" of money wagers, and the like, will be passed over here, but the reader may consult the references in the Bibliography). Even propositions at first sight incomparable because of diversity of content may in this way, at least in principle, have their corresponding degrees of confidence brought into a single system. This behavioristic conception of degrees of confidence, when due allowance is made for the inevitable idealization required by any comprehensive theory, seems to provide an intelligible link with observable fact.

In their approaches to the crucial problems of inverse probabilities, subjectivists like Savage and de Finetti are Bayesians. Since the prior probabilities entering into the calculations are supposed to reflect only the varying *opinions* of different reasoners, it might be thought that no generally acceptable estimates of the strength of given evidence could result. De Finetti, however, relies upon the asymptotically diminishing effect of such varying assignments of initial probabilities as empirical evidence accumulates. He is able to show, in effect, that in a large number of interesting cases the choices made of the initial probabilities have, in the long run, negligible influence on the conclusions of statistical inference. (This part of his work, with its introduction of the interesting notion of "exchangeable events," has mathematical significance independently of any final appraisal of his philosophical position.)

In spite of the admirable ingenuity of its defenders, and their great resourcefulness in answering criticism, it is hard to believe that this type of theory is satisfactory from a philosophical standpoint.

For instance, it is not clear why the desire to prevent others from "making a Dutch book" against oneself should be regarded as a necessary criterion of rationality, to be accepted without further ado. It might be objected that to be willing to accept simultaneous bets for and against a certain outcome at the same stakes (and thus to be as coherent as subjectivists require) would be to destroy the point of betting by ensuring that no money would change hands. It is only bookmakers, who are bound to accept a variety of bets on both sides of a given outcome, who need fear a "Dutch book." And even they, like traders in foreign exchange, are not to be counted as irrational in buying at a lower price than that at which they would sell. In any case, behavior that is prudent for bookmakers seems an inadequate basis for an analysis of rationality in general. A man would not be irrational if he insisted on betting on only one side of a question; nor would he necessarily be irrational if he offered odds of 1:3 on *H* and odds of 1:2 on *H̄*, with the stipulation that wagers on *H* must be at least three times as large as those on *H̄*.

In general, it seems doubtful that the subjective view provides an even approximately correct analysis of what probability statements normally mean. When a man says, for instance, "The chance of my dying within the next ten years is even," does he *mean* something like "On the evidence to hand, suitably rectified to prevent anybody from winning money from me without risk, I find I would accept the same odds against my death that I would against a fair penny's showing heads on a single toss"? This seems very doubtful, if only because the implication in ordinary language of there being a *correct* answer to the question raised is absent. The departure from the preanalytical, common-sense concept seems too drastic to be ultimately acceptable.

Merits of the different theories. None of the chief types of interpretation of probability now in favor can be accepted as wholly satisfactory. One reason may be that an acceptable philosophy of probability is called upon to perform a number of tasks that are hard to reconcile: to show why some probability judgments are a priori whereas others are contingent; to provide a firm basis for a calculus of probability while recognizing probability judgments that are incorrigibly imprecise; to account for and to defend the connection between "rationality" and specifiable degrees of confidence in conclusions following with probability from given premises; and, above all, to show how and why it is justifiable to act on probabilities.

To the extent that the theories briefly examined in this article do not respond to such problems by denying their existence (on the old principle of going to bed until the desire for exercise vanishes), they may be said to have emphasized, in their different ways, plausible approaches to some of these tasks at the expense of the others. The fashionable response of some mathematicians, who are too "pure" to take problems of interpretation seriously, is simply to turn a blind eye to the tasks of the philosophy of probability. Empiricist views would succeed in providing an intelligible basis for contingent probability judgments were they not driven to postulate, in the form of limiting frequencies, series of observations that cannot be performed. Logical views readily certify the credentials of a priori probability judgments but are hard pressed to identify the rationale of appeals to frequencies. Subjective views pay more attention than their rivals do to the relevance of the reasoner's attitude but operate with so schematic a conception of rationality as to render their position suspect. That all the theories can, with greater or less display of ingenuity, provide a basis for the calculus of chances testifies only to the remarkable economy and simplicity of the needed axioms.

A remaining puzzle. What still remains to be done can perhaps be sufficiently illustrated by some concluding remarks concerning the problem of application.

Suppose that a philosopher has the choice of publishing his first book with one of two publishers, A and B. Suppose also that he knows that of first philosophical manuscripts published by A and B the chances of a second edition's being required are 9/10 in the case of publication by A but only 1/10 in the case of publication by B. On the assumption that the philosopher wishes to have a second edition of his work and knows nothing else that is relevant, everybody would agree that he ought to prefer publication by A to publication by B. But why? It is generally admitted that the truth of the judgment that the book has a 9/10 chance of having a second edition is logically compatible with its not in fact being reprinted. Thus, given that the author is interested in having his book continue in print and is not merely interested in the correctness of the probability estimate, why should he prefer A to B?

Peirce, Reichenbach, and many others, say that the answer is to be found by considering a class of similar cases and by being content to achieve one's practical aims "in the long run." But even in the long run there can be only high *probability* of success on the whole, so that the question of why one should be guided by considerations of probability is only postponed. In any case, the very definition of our situation excludes repetition.

Some defenders of a logical interpretation argue, in effect, that it is an analytic truth that one must be guided by probabilities in order to be considered rational. But then why should one be rational, if rationality has nothing to do with "success" and the attainment of practical aims?

A currently fashionable appeal to "maximizing expected utility" invites a would-be reasonable man to choose that course of action that will provide him with the highest calculable "expected" value—but this is, after all, merely to invite him to choose a way that will *probably* lead to more gain.

The subjectivist, if he says anything, tells our imagined author to follow whatever course he is inclined to follow—provided he allows nobody to "make book" against him—which is not much help.

It may be that the root of this intractable puzzle—in which action based on considerations of probability is justified only by further considerations which never satisfy, just because they still refer to probabilities—is to be located in a persuasive metaphysical conception that is unable to find any place in the universe for anything but categorical facts—or, what comes to the same thing, for propositions that are unqualifiedly true or false. If a philosopher has the unshakable notion that everything in the universe is what it is and no other thing, that events either occur or else they do not, and that it is absurd to think of some "middle ground," the basic notions of probability are bound to seem mysterious. Foiled in the attempt to explain

probability in terms of factual properties of aggregates or long-run sequences, he may revert, like many others, to thinking of probabilities as expressing degrees of ignorance or degrees of subjective belief or something of the sort. But then the problem of explaining why it should be rational to act on probability will seem even more intractable than ever.

Whatever may be the proper therapy for this philosophical "cramp," it still offers a formidable challenge to all students of the philosophy of probability and induction.

Bibliography

GENERAL WORKS

Anybody coming fresh to the subject might make a good beginning by consulting the books by Nagel, Kneale, Keynes, Carnap, Kyburg, and Smokler, listed below.

Ernest Nagel, *Principles of the Theory of Probability* (Chicago, 1939), written for the *Encyclopedia of Unified Science*, is still one of the best available short surveys of the entire field. Although Nagel writes as an empiricist, his account of the strengths and weaknesses of the alternative positions is very judicious.

Irving John Good, *Probability and the Weighing of Evidence* (New York, 1950), contains a good, concise analysis of the different interpretations of probability (pp. 6–12). Good defends a moderately "subjective" position.

G. H. von Wright, *The Logical Problem of Induction* (Helsinki, 1941; 2d, rev., ed., Oxford, 1957), is especially valuable for the history of the subject.

Rudolf Carnap, *Logical Foundations of Probabilitiy* (Chicago, 1950), is mainly a defense of the logical point of view. However, Carnap also provides thorough criticism of opposing viewpoints.

John Maynard Keynes, *A Treatise on Probability* (London, 1921), must be read by all serious students of the subject. Like von Wright's book, it is also valuable for its historical remarks.

William Kneale, *Probability and Induction* (Oxford, 1949), is perhaps the best available discussion of the entire range of the philosophy of probability.

Isaac Todhunter, *A History of the Mathematical Theory of Probability From the Time of Pascal to That of Laplace* (Cambridge and London, 1865), is a useful if somewhat pedestrian survey of mathematical theory, but neglects philosophical aspects.

THE COMMON SENSE OF PROBABILITY

Stephen E. Toulmin, *The Uses of Argument* (Cambridge, 1958), Ch. 2, "Probability," pp. 44–93, argues that to say "S is probably P" is to commit oneself guardedly, tentatively, or with reservations to the view that S is P and likewise guardedly to lend one's authority to that view. For criticism of Toulmin's view, see John King-Farlow, "Toulmin's Analysis of Probability," in *Theoria*, Vol. 29 (1963), 12–26. J. N. Findlay, "Probability Without Nonsense," in *Philosophical Quarterly*, Vol. 2 (1952), 218–239, is phenomenological in flavor: it shows good flair for some ordinary idioms. Kneale, *op. cit.* (especially p. 20), claims that in ordinary life "probable" means the same as "fit to be approved" or, more precisely, "such as a rational man would approve as a basis for practical decisions." He thinks, therefore, that a "suggestion of merit" attaches to the word. The notion of "probable" as implying a value judgment is pushed to extremes in John Patrick Day, *Inductive Probability* (London, 1961), especially pp. 29–39. For incisive criticism of Day's book, see, for instance, Wesley C. Salmon's review in *Philosophical Review*, Vol. 72 (1963), 392–396. For Carnap's discussion of the "Two Senses of Probability," see Carnap, *op. cit.*, Ch. II, Sec. 9, pp. 23–36, and Ch. IV, Sec. 42, pp. 182–192. See also John Wisdom, "A Note on Probability," in Max Black, ed., *Philosophical Analysis* (Ithaca, N.Y., 1950), pp. 414–420.

No systematic and comprehensive examination of the ordinary uses of "probably" and cognate terms has yet been published.

THE MATHEMATICS OF PROBABILITY

The classical work on the axiomatics of probability theory is A. N. Kolmogorov, *Foundations of the Theory of Probability* (New York, 1950). Among the standard works on mathematical aspects of the subject the following can be recommended: Harald Cramér, *The Elements of the Probability Theory* (New York, 1955); William Feller, *An Introduction to Probability Theory and Its Applications* (New York, 1950); and Thornton C. Fry, *Probability and Its Engineering Uses* (New York, 1937). The third of these is especially valuable to readers without much mathematical background. For philosophers interested in the foundations of statistics, Ronald A. Fisher, *Statistical Methods and Scientific Inference* (London, 1956), makes fascinating reading. It should be added that Fisher's views are not universally accepted by statisticians. A good elementary account of modern approaches to statistical theory is Herman Chernoff and Lincoln E. Moses, *Elementary Decision Theory* (New York, 1959).

CLASSICAL THEORIES

Jakob Bernoulli, *Ars Conjectandi* (Basel, 1713), has not been translated into English. However, there is a German translation by R. Haussner, under the title of *Wahrscheinlichkeitsrechnung*, 2 vols. (Leipzig, 1899).

Pierre Simon de Laplace, *A Philosophical Essay on Probabilities* (New York, 1952), is a readily available translation of the "Essai philosophique sur les probabilités" that appeared in the second edition (Paris, 1814) of Laplace's *Théorie analytique des probabilités* 1st ed., Paris, 1812).

LOGICAL THEORIES

Keynes, *op. cit.*, is still indispensable.

Carnap, *op. cit.*, is the most important book now available. Further references to discussions of Carnap's views can be found in the bibliography to the article INDUCTION.

Harold Jeffreys, *Scientific Inference* (2d ed., Cambridge, 1957) and *Theory of Probability* (2d ed., Oxford, 1948), are in the tradition of Keynes. The second is the more elaborate book; the former has more controversial philosophical comment.

It would be a pity to overlook W. E. Johnson's posthumously published articles "Probability: The Relations of Proposal to Supposal," in *Mind*, Vol. 61 (1932), 1–16; "Probability: Axioms," in *Mind*, Vol. 61 (1932), 281–296; and "Probability: The Deductive and Inductive Problems," in *Mind*, Vol. 61 (1932), 409–423.

Bertrand Russell, *Human Knowledge: Its Scope and Limits* (New York, 1948), contains seven chapters on probability (pp. 335–418).

C. I. Lewis, *An Analysis of Knowledge and Valuation* (La Salle, Ill., 1946), Ch. 10, "Probability," takes probability to be a "valid estimate of a frequency."

Henry E. Kyburg, Jr., *Probability and the Logic of Rational Belief* (Middletown, Conn., 1961), is one of the latest sophistications of the logical standpoint. The position, somewhat obscured by excessive symbolism, is more simply explained in the same author's "Probability and Randomness," in *Theoria*, Vol. 29 (1963), 27–55.

FREQUENCY THEORIES

John Venn, *The Logic of Chance* (London, 1866; 3d, rev., ed., 1888; reprinted, New York, 1962), one of the earliest presentations of a frequency theory, still makes good reading. For C. S. Peirce's view, see *Collected Papers of Charles Sanders Peirce*, Charles Hartshorne, Paul Weiss, and Arthur W. Burks, eds., 8 vols. (Cambridge, Mass., 1931–1958), especially Vol. II.

Richard von Mises, *Probability, Statistics and Truth* (2d, rev., English ed., New York, 1957), contains a relatively nontechnical account of von Mises' view and pungent criticism of alternatives. The somewhat similar views elaborately expounded in Hans Reichenbach, *The Theory of Probability* (Berkeley and Los Angeles, 1949), have received severe criticism. See, for instance, Arthur W. Burks, "Reichenbach's Theory of Probability and Induction," in *Review of Metaphysics*, Vol. 4 (1951), 377–393.

SUBJECTIVE THEORIES

The most valuable book on this topic is now Henry E. Kyburg, Jr., and Howard E. Smokler, eds., *Studies in Subjective Probability* (New York, 1964), which contains, among other useful materials, a translation by Henry E. Kyburg, Jr., of de Finetti's important memoir, "La prévision: Ses Lois logiques, ses sources subjectives" (in *Annales de l'Institut Henri Poincaré*, Vol. 7, 1937, 1–68), as "Foresight: Its Logical Laws, Its Subjective Sources," pp. 93–158. The editors' introduction is an able statement of the subjective standpoint.

For F. P. Ramsey's suggestion for measuring subjective probability, see *The Foundations of Mathematics and Other Logical Essays* (London, 1931). Ramsey's test for degree of belief is explained on pp. 174–182. The connection between "making a Dutch book" and satisfaction of the axioms of a calculus of probability is developed in John Kemeny, "Fair Bets and Inductive Probabilities," in *Journal of Symbolic Logic*, Vol. 20 (1955), 263–273; in R. Sherman Lehman, "On Confirmation and Rational Betting," in *Journal of Symbolic Logic*, Vol. 20 (1955), 251–262; and in Abner Shimony, "Coherence and the Axioms of Confirmation," in *Journal of Symbolic Logic*, Vol. 20 (1955), 1–28. The first may be especially recommended.

Leonard J. Savage, *The Foundations of Statistics* (New York, 1954), a pioneering defense of the subjective approach, continues to exercise a good deal of influence. It contains much material of philosophical interest. For valuable but difficult argument among statisticians about Savage's position see Savage and others, *The Foundations of Statistical Inference: A Discussion* (New York, 1962).

Some brief philosophical criticism may be found in G. H. von Wright, "Remarks on Epistemology of Subjective Probability," in Ernest Nagel, Patrick Suppes, and Alfred Tarski, eds., *Logic, Methodology and Philosophy of Science* (Stanford, Calif., 1962), pp. 330–339. For alternative approaches to subjective probability see, for instance, I. J. Good, *op. cit.*, and B. O. Koopman, "The Axioms and Algebra of Intuitive Probability," in *Annals of Mathematics*, Vol. 41 (1940), 269–292. Koopman differs from some other subjectivists in taking probability to be only partially measurable.

BIBLIOGRAPHIES

There are ample references in the books listed above by Keynes, Carnap, and von Wright. An excellent list, emphasizing subjective theories, is contained in Kyburg and Smokler, eds., *op. cit.*

Max Black, "Induction and Probability," in Raymond Klibansky, ed., *Philosophy in the Mid-century*, Vol. I (Florence, 1958), 154–163, is a critical survey of a decade's work, and, finally, Henry E. Kyburg, Jr., "Recent Work in Inductive Logic," in *American Philosophical Quarterly*, Vol. 1 (1964), 249–287, although largely concerned with problems of induction, is also useful as a survey of probability theory. It has a lengthy bibliography.

The bibliography to INDUCTION may be consulted with profit.

MAX BLACK

PROCESS. See CHANGE.

PROCLUS (c. 410–485), the last major Greek philosopher. He had been a well-to-do, handsome, healthy young man who intended to become a lawyer, when he experienced a conversion that turned him to philosophy, eventually to Neoplatonic idealism (this is reported by his pupil Marinus in his *Life of Proclus*). Instructed systematically by the elderly Plutarch of Athens and Plutarch's pupil Syrianus, Proclus was prepared to become, shortly after Syrianus' death, the "Platonic successor" (diadochos), or administrator of the Athenian School of Neoplatonism. Dedicating himself wholeheartedly, Proclus never married and lived as a vegetarian and semiascetic, constantly occupied with teaching, writing, and personal meditations and devotions. Though frequently high-strung, proud, and critical, he was loving to friends and pupils and generous to servants. By the time of his death he surely knew that he was an illustrious link in the "golden chain" of Platonism—but not that he was practically the final one.

Basic philosophy. The philosophy of Proclus, expressed most prominently in his *Stoicheiōsis Theologikē* (*Elements of Theology*), *Eis tēn Platōnos Theologian* (*Platonic Theology*), and numerous commentaries on the Platonic dialogues, offers a stimulating world vision to anyone in sympathy with idealism. Proclus assumes that reality is not fundamentally material but mental, or the substance of consciousness; thus every "thing" is ultimately a thought, and every thought is somehow real. And since even the distinction between anything and my thinking of it is also mental, not bodily, the process of knowing is practically identical with whatever is known.

But Proclus is an "objective" idealist because he regards *universal* consciousness as independent of any mind knowing it and human consciousness, therefore, as a separate reality moving from one thought to another within the existing totality. This doctrine of a universal consciousness–reality existing apart from any single mind was shared with other Platonists and many idealists. In Proclus' philosophy, however, it produces ambiguities, even inconsistencies, such as the detailed emphasis upon the "lesser realities."

There is only one true Reality for Proclus; it is the "One," beyond all possible description because it is the most fundamental thought conceivable (like "consciousness itself"). And Proclus asserts that the One already contains the whole universe, absolutely unified, within itself, leaving its oneness uninfected with plurality. Consequently, all other things, considered by themselves as if independent of the One, cannot be truly real but only more or less apparently real or "less real." Proclus' purpose is to explain how the eternal One seemingly declines into increasing plurality until it reaches our daily consciousness, the endless succession of only vaguely meaningful experiences, and, conversely, to explain how our ordinary consciousness can increasingly succeed in grasping the ultimate meaning of everything. The inconsistency is this: although the One is the only Reality, Proclus describes its apparent decline into plurality with highly detailed attention, thereby turning the focus away from the One to the neatly arranged successive states of "lesser realities" (increasing appearances), which are then carefully analyzed as if independent entities. This therefore is a doctrine of emanation according to which the single Reality radiates from itself innumerable lesser yet independent realities. (See EMANATIONISM; the doctrine stems from the objective–idealistic approach which, although it treats the substance of the universe as consciousness, regards the universe as existing apart from any knowing mind.)

Proclus' system is not, however, a typical doctrine of emanation because of an important principle which he was the first to apply throughout—namely, "all things are in all things, in proper manner" (see *Elements of Theology*, Proposition 103). According to this, every reality or consciousness is mirrored in and therefore appropriately colored by every other consciousness. For example, the One is known by the human mind but in a human manner, whereas the human appearance exists within the One Reality in its one real nature. By means of this principle the careful distinctions that Proclus otherwise constructs become blurred if not erased; the One becomes treated as disintegrating gradually, flowing into its many appearances, and the universe becomes a single organization of consciousness, an eternal "movement" of thought from higher to lower and back again. Both the objective, distinction-producing doctrine of emanation and the unifying "all-things-are-in-all-things" principle coexist in Proclus. But Proclus was the first to apply the latter doctrine fully, so we may speculate how he might have launched the philosophy of an organically interacting universe of consciousness had this possibility not been abruptly crushed by the Christian Emperor Justinian, who closed the Neoplatonic School not long after Proclus' death and caused its last adherents to flee to Persia.

Specific world picture. The very carefully arranged stages that Proclus inserted between the One Reality and the many appearances of daily consciousness were chosen by two standards: first, deduction from ontological principles and second, the voice of Platonic tradition. The principles called "ontological" (that is, those applying equally to all levels of reality) were largely original with Proclus and received his detailed and critical attention. Indeed, Proclus was an ontologist as much as a cosmologist; not only was he constructing a picture of the universe (cosmology, the main interest of Plato or Plotinus), but he was also expounding what he considered the all-pervading principles underlying this picture. Therefore, the following presentation of his three most important principles is necessary not only for understanding the stages of reality deduced from them but also for conveying the unique flavor of Proclus' whole philosophy.

Powers. Every reality has its own power, meaning primarily the power to imply or "cause" that which is derived from it (for example, the eternal concept of Identity, implying all particular cases of identity in the world, has the power to imply or "produce" them), and meaning also the power to be implied by, or the "Effect" of, that from which it is itself derived and, metaphorically, the power to "return" to this cause (for example, any two identical terms have the power to be identical, and by expressing identity, they point or "return" to the eternal Identity as their source). On the first principle see *Platonic Theology*, page 133; *Elements of Theology*, Proposition 31.

Activities. Between every reality and the one(s) derived from it there is a third, connecting reality called the activity of the first, or the process by which the first implies the second, and this activity has its own power. For example, the eternal Identity uses its power to make all particular cases of identity possible, and this possibility, in turn, has the power to make them actual. Although only a possibility, it is called the cause's "activity" since the effects already appear here in all their variety. The complete series becomes (1) the first reality, or cause; (2) its power to imply the second; (3) its activity, the process of implication, or the possibility of the second; (4) the power of this process actually to result in the second; (5) the second reality, or effect; and, less important, (6) the power of the second reality to be the effect of the first. (On the second principle see *Elements of Theology,* Proposition 77).

Characteristics. In answering the problem of how something can be something else—that is, how it can possess a characteristic or quality outside itself—Proclus asserts that every characteristic first exists in a perfect form, a reality prior to and the cause of all the many imperfect instances or examples of that characteristic, and that each of these individual, imperfect characteristics is in turn prior to and the cause of whatever "thing" happens to possess it. For example, the Perfect Unity produces the class of all the imperfect unities possessed by things, although the unity possessed by, say, a person is regarded as being his direct cause. Only imperfect characteristics are possessed by things; the original perfect form is not possessed by anything and is called the "unpossessed." (See *Elements of Theology,* Propositions 23–24 on the third principle.)

These three ontological principles explain most of the stages that Proclus inserts between the One Reality and the world of appearances. Since the One is (1) the cause of everything else, it should have (2) the power to imply all its effects; but if the One were a "reality having a power," it would acquire a particular description, whereas it must be absolutely universal and beyond all descriptions. For this reason Proclus places *two* concepts immediately after the One: first, the One's "reality" as distinct from the One itself and, second, its power. These concepts are respectively called "definiteness" and "infinity" (*Platonic Theology,* Book II, p. 132). After this necessary exception the deduction continues regularly. As the First Cause, the One has (3) its own activity, the process by which it implies everything else and within which the rest of the universe is already potentially contained, and (4) the power of this activity. The One's first effect (5) is the vast class of the "onenesses" or "unities" (a doctrine original with Proclus or his immediate teachers; see *Platonic Theology,* Book III, pp. 119–121). Here the One is considered the unpossessed, perfect form of unity, the most fundamental characteristic conceivable (like "the possibility of being conscious"), which must therefore be possessed by everything in the universe, so that all possessed, imperfect instances of unity are collectively the One's first effect. Each unity, in turn, is a cause having its own power, activity, and the power of this activity; the unity's own effect is that individual thing which possesses it. Hence, the universe, or the class of all things possessing the characteristic of unity, including the world's appearances, is the One's final effect.

Within this universe Proclus distinguishes five levels of reality, partly deduced from his ontological principles but partly reflecting Platonic tradition. Platonism asserted that there was a realm of Ideas; each Idea was the one eternal, perfect form of all examples of any one kind (like Proclus' "unpossessed"), but each Idea coexisted with all the many other Ideas in one realm, a logical bridge between the absolute One and the infinitely varied, fleeting appearances of daily consciousness. Between these Ideas and the appearances, Platonism placed another bridging concept—a World Soul, or energy moving through the world, copying the Ideas in the material of appearances, thus

transforming an unchanging, perfect Idea into its many changing, imperfect examples. Finally, there was this "material," not really matter, only the apparent potentiality to become any characteristic the World Soul assigned to it, the lowest level of reality. Proclus accepts these traditional concepts but incorporates them into a much larger system. His five levels of reality in the universe are highly integrated with one another because they are parts of a single cause-and-effect system; in the *Platonic Theology* (Books III–VI) they are called (1) Being, the cause; (2) Power, the power of this cause; (3) Mind, the activity of the cause, in which all the effects are potentially contained and part of which is identified with the realm of Ideas; (4) Soul and/or Nature, the power of this activity, one function of which is identified with the World Soul; and (5) Becoming, or the world of appearances, which are the effects. By an interesting and original insight, Proclus further analyzes the great variety of fleeting appearances into a descending series of increasingly weaker, more dependent but therefore simpler and eternal concepts (such as quantity, negation, and so on), which mirror in reverse the ascending series of stronger, clearer, and thus also simpler, eternal realities (see *Elements of Theology,* Propositions 56 ff., 70 ff.). The absolutely lowest concept is matter, which is merely (6) the power of everything to be caused by the One. Because of these two hierarchies, ascending and descending, Proclus' world picture becomes diamond-shaped: the highest eternal causes and the lowest yet also eternal effects are few in number, whereas the greatest variety occurs in the world of appearances. Thus, Proclus suggests a previously unsuspected close relationship between the so-called highest and lowest realities.

God and the gods. All readers of Proclus quickly discover that his metaphysical language constantly alternates with a religious, theological vocabulary. The basis of this correlation between philosophy and theology is that the One is God or the Godhead. Thus, all the eternal unities produced by the One become gods, and all other eternal realities, which must possess these characteristics of unity, become equated with particular divine beings of the Greek pantheon, their relationships being described in terms borrowed from Greek mythology, including the Orphic-Pythagorean tradition, or even the "myths" in Plato's dialogues.

In using religious language, Proclus' intentions were basically sincere. It has been the rule rather than the exception for idealists to identify the ultimate Reality with God, the object of worshipful and spirit-exalting attitudes. And, according to Marinus (*Life of Proclus,* Chs. 18–19, 28–33), Proclus was religious, performing daily devotions to the sun and moon and celebrating not only the Greek but also the Egyptian and other Near Eastern religious holidays. But Proclus was a philosopher, not a theologian; his "divine beings" are simply names associated with the existing concepts of his metaphysics and are described by means of these concepts. To some extent, therefore, Proclus may have been trying to furnish philosophical support for the Greek religion, which was then being increasingly persecuted by the Christians.

Ethics and mysticism. Proclus' ethics is founded upon the statement that the One is also the Good—that is, the final goal of all life's efforts. This means not only that we should consciously strive to reach the One but also that essentially we are always seeking it, even if subconsciously and, thus, randomly. For everything that is the effect of some cause is said automatically to "return" to that cause. Consequently, Proclus' ethics is almost nothing but his metaphysics in reverse—a retracing from the lowest human level to the highest Reality of the stages through which the highest originally declined into that lowest. Thus, we are urged to renounce the appearances of the body, meaning unnecessary physical desires, social relations, and political interests—indeed, all the misleading appearances of the senses, imaginations, and mere opinions (see *Commentary on the First Alcibiades*, Col. 518). Conversely, we are urged to concentrate on rational knowledge, which prepares the individual mind for intuitive knowing, or the ability to grasp such eternal ideal realities as Mind, Power, Being (*ibid.;* see also *Platonic Theology*, Book IV, pp. 186–194).

But how can human consciousness rise from particular realities, which are still objects of knowledge separate from the knower, to the One Reality itself, which is an all-inclusive unity? Between this unity and human consciousness the most direct links are the many unities, since each consciousness has its own unity; and that internal method by which each consciousness perceives its own unity or divinity Proclus calls "faith"—using the traditional term but defining it as a "higher kind of intuition" for which certain persons have an innate predisposition and which in others can be stimulated but not actually taught (*Chaldean Philosophy* II, IV). Perceiving its own unity, consciousness can mystically jump, in a fit of divine madness, into the unity of all things (the One), making contact with it, then approaching it, then uniting with it—the absolutely final goal of all life's previous efforts (*On Providence and Fate*, pp. 139–140; *Commentary on the Timaeus* I, p. 210).

Bibliography

Editions marked with an asterisk (∗) are those cited in the text.

ORIGINAL PHILOSOPHIC-RELIGIOUS WORKS

Elements of Theology, ∗Greek text with commentary and English translation by E. R. Dodds (Oxford, 1933), is of interest because of its construction as a system of propositions with deductive proofs but without definitions or axioms. It is the best source for Proclus' ontological principles. *The Platonic Theology*, ∗Greek text with Latin translation by A. Portus (Hamburg, 1618; Frankfurt, 1960), English translation by Thomas Taylor (London, 1816), is the basic source for Proclus' whole philosophy and was probably written in his most mature years. *De Providentia et Fato et Eo Quod in Nobis* ("On Providence and Fate"), *De Decem Dubitationibus Circa Providentiam* ("Ten Questions on Providence"), *De Malorum Subsistentia* ("The Existence of Evils")—the "three Latin works"—are thus called because until recently they were known only through the Latin translations of William of Moerbecke; there is a ∗Latin text with Greek fragments edited by Helmut Boese, *Tria Opuscula* (Berlin, 1955), and an English translation by Thomas Taylor (London, 1833). "Eighteen Arguments Supporting the Eternity of the World" is a polemic against the Christians known only from quotation in John Philoponus' *On the Eternity of the World, Against Proclus*, edited by H. Rabe (Leipzig, 1899), English translation by Thomas Taylor (London, 1825). *The Hieratic Art*, text with French translation by J. Bidez

(Brussels, 1928), and *The Chaldean Philosophy*, ∗text edited by A. Jahn (Halle, Germany, 1891), English translation by T. Johnson (Osceola, Mo., 1907), are two examples of Proclus' religious writings, the latter filled with intensity and enthusiasm.

COMMENTARIES ON PLATO

∗*Commentary on the Parmenides*, in Victor Cousin, ed., *Opera Inedita*, 2d ed. (Paris, 1864), has been translated into French by A. Chaignet (Paris, 1903) and photographically reproduced (Hildesheim, Germany, 1961); among the commentaries this is the most significant for metaphysics. *Commentary on the First Alcibiades*, ∗text edited by Victor Cousin, *op. cit.*, is the most significant for ethics. *Commentary on the Timaeus* has a ∗text edited by E. Diehl (Leipzig, 1906), English translation by Thomas Taylor (London, 1820). *Commentary on the Republic* has a text edited by W. Kroll (Leipzig, 1901), and *Commentary on the Cratylus* has a text edited by G. Pasquali (Leipzig, 1908).

MISCELLANEOUS WORKS

Proclus was also a polymath of his day and wrote treatises on mathematics and physical science (mostly astronomy), essays on the art of writing, and philosophic-religious hymns, the style of which has been praised by Charles des Guerrois in "Mémoires de la Société Académique de l'Aube," Vol. 72 (1908), as "deserving of any collection of Greek lyric poems." For a detailed discussion and annotated bibliography of all Proclus' writings see L. J. Rosán, *The Philosophy of Proclus* (New York, 1949).

CRITICISM

Among the more important writings about Proclus are A. Berger, *Proclus: Exposition de sa doctrine* (Paris, 1840), and H. Kirchner, *De Procli Neoplatonici Metaphysica* (Berlin, 1842), as well as articles by A. Taylor, "The Philosophy of Proclus," in his *Philosophical Studies* (London, 1934), and E. R. Dodds, Introduction and Commentary to his edition of Proclus' *Elements of Theology*. See also L. J. Rosán, *op. cit.* Since 1949 have appeared G. Martano, *Dio e uomo in Proclo* (Naples, 1952), a good analysis but sharply divided into psychology and metaphysics, with appended detailed discussion of Proclus' influence (Martano had not seen Rosán's book), and L. Grondijs, "L'Ame, le nous et les hénades dans la théologie de Proclus," in *Mededelingen der Koninklijke Nederlandse Akademie van Wetenschappen*, N.S. Vol. 23, No. 2 (1960), 27–42, which is based on the philosophy of Plotinus more than on that of Proclus but has a good section on Proclus' methods of mystical union.

LAURENCE J. ROSÁN

PRODICUS OF CEOS, Greek Sophist, was probably born before 460 B.C. and was still alive at the time of the death of Socrates in 399 B.C. He traveled widely as an ambassador for Ceos and also earned a great deal of money lecturing in various Greek cities, especially in Athens. His writings are known to have dealt with physical doctrines, with religious and moral themes, and above all with distinctions between the meanings of words usually treated as synonyms. Socrates attended a lecture by him on the last of these topics and regularly claimed to be a pupil of Prodicus in the art of synonymy (*Protagoras* 341A, *Meno* 96D).

In physics he appears to have treated the four elements of Empedocles as divine, and no doubt they formed the basis of the cosmology of Prodicus, to which Aristophanes refers in the *Birds* (1.692), although the fanciful cosmology which follows is probably not based on that of Prodicus. Prodicus further held that those natural objects and powers that are useful to human life were made the objects of cult and treated as gods by men. Inevitably, he was later classed as an atheist, but it is more likely that he offered an account of the origin of the gods which was not intended to deny their existence.

In a work entitled the *Horae* ("Hours") he included the since famous story "Heracles Where the Road Divides," of which we have a fairly full summary in Book II of Xenophon's *Memorabilia*. Vice and Virtue appear to Heracles personified as women and invite him to choose between them. Each describes what she has to offer, and Heracles chooses the arduous tasks of Virtue rather than the pleasures of Vice.

Of greater philosophic interest is the ethical relativism attributed to Prodicus in the pseudo-Platonic dialogue the *Eryxias*. There he is apparently quoted as arguing that what is good for one man is not good for another man, so that we cannot speak of anything as good *simpliciter*. On the other hand, the goodness of a thing does not depend on the goodness of the user (although some scholars have interpreted him this way). Rather, the value of a thing inheres in the thing itself in such a way that it will be good in relation to one person and not good in relation to another, according to the person and the way in which it is used.

The discussion of synonyms and the right use of words clearly involved fine distinctions of meaning between words. Many examples quoted are ethical, and a term of narrower application is commonly distinguished from one of wider application that includes in its range of meaning the meaning of the first term. The value of such distinctions is clear in rhetorical argument. But Prodicus was also eager to reject the kind of view found in Democritus, according to which there can be different names for the same thing since names are attached to things by convention only. Prodicus maintained, it would seem, that no two words have the same meaning, and in this he at least prepared the way for the search for precisely stated meanings which later fascinated Socrates and Plato.

Bibliography

Fragments and *Testimonia* are in H. Diels and W. Kranz, eds., *Fragmente der Vorsokratiker*, 10th ed. (Berlin, 1961), Vol. II.

See also M. Untersteiner, *I sofisti* (Turin, 1949), translated as *The Sophists* (Oxford, 1954); H. Mayer, *Prodikos von Keos* (Paderborn, Germany, 1913); and G. B. Kerferd, "The 'Relativism' of Prodicus," in *Bulletin of the John Rylands Library*, Vol. 37 (1954), 249–256.

G. B. Kerferd

PROGRESS, THE IDEA OF. In broad terms a popular belief in progress means the rejection of an attitude that has characterized most human communities throughout history. Normally, men have believed that the future would repeat the past. When they have expected that human life was going to change, they have usually supposed that this change was going to take place suddenly and radically, by supernatural intervention. And if they have permitted themselves to hope for the improvement of the human condition, the hope has commonly been directed toward salvation from the world rather than reform of the world. By and large, historical change, when men have been aware of it at all, has been viewed as a sign of mortality and the proof of a lapse from ideal standards.

Indeed, in many societies there has been a popular conviction that man's condition has changed in the course of history but for the worse. Characteristically, when men have believed in a golden age, they have put that age in the past rather than the future.

In contrast, in modern Western societies change and innovation have a different place in the popular imagination. Not everyone assumes that all change is necessarily for the better, but it is widely assumed, even by conservatives, that only a society which has a general capacity to change is capable of surviving. And despite wars and depressions a large proportion of the members of Western societies have tended to expect that, short of a cataclysm, their children would live happier and better lives than they. They have supposed that this improvement would be cumulative and continuing and that although temporary setbacks, accidents, and disasters might take place, human knowledge, power, and happiness would increase over the long run.

The emergence of this idea is the product of a variety of circumstances, such as the accumulation of an economic surplus, the increase of social mobility, and the occurrence of major inventions that have dramatically increased human power over nature. Over and above these, however, the idea of progress is peculiarly a response to the emergence of the unique social institution of organized scientific inquiry.

HISTORY OF THE IDEA

Seeds of the faith in progress can be found in the works of the two great spokesmen for the new science, Bacon and Descartes. The fundamental elements of the idea itself were developed in the course of the so-called quarrel of the ancients and the moderns, which occupied writers and critics in the last part of the seventeenth century. At the heart of this controversy was a dispute over the authority that should be attributed to the opinions and examples left by the ancient writers. Was it the task of learned men to stand as sentinels at the gate, guarding against innovation and protecting established styles and beliefs? The controversy implicitly raised not only literary questions but the larger question of what attitude toward the past should govern the intellectual life.

In developing their position, the moderns argued that the partisans of the ancients were misled by a false analogy. They looked upon the ancients as their forefathers and therefore thought of the ancients as older and, in consequence, wiser than themselves. But just as the individual grows older and presumably wiser as time goes by, so does humanity. The so-called ancients were really the young men of humanity, and those alive today were the true ancients. They stood on the shoulders of their predecessors and could see farther; their wisdom and authority was greater than the wisdom and authority of their predecessors. This argument was developed with particular force by Bernard de Fontenelle in his *Digression sur les anciens et les modernes* (published in 1683).

The analogy between the history of mankind and the life of an individual had already been developed, however, by a number of writers. Blaise Pascal, for example, used it in drawing a belief in intellectual progress from an examination of the nature of scientific inquiry. In 1647, Pascal had published a study, *Nouvelles expériences touchant le vide,* which encountered immediate objections from many scientists and philosophers, including Descartes, on the ground that it denied the time-honored truth that nature abhorred a vacuum. Pascal replied to one of his critics, Father Noel, that an appeal to inherited authority had no force where the study of physics was concerned. And in a longer essay, *Fragment d'un traité du vide,* he went on to give general reasons for moderating the respect for received authority. "The experiments which give us an understanding of nature multiply continually . . . ," he pointed out, "from whence it follows . . . that not only each man advances in the sciences day by day, but that all men together make continual progress in them as the universe grows older." Pascal believed, however, that such progress took place only where the experimental methods of the sciences were relevant. In theology received authority set the final limits to inquiry, for there the object was not to add to the knowledge provided by ancient authority but only to understand as fully as possible what that authority revealed.

During the eighteenth century, however, and particularly in France an increasing number of intellectuals came to believe that the methods and spirit of science should be applied to all fields. In consequence, the idea of progress came to include a concept of social and moral progress. The cumulative improvement in human knowledge and power which had been brought about in the physical sciences could also be brought about in the organization of human society and the character of human conduct, it was asserted, if only the barriers that existed against the employment of rational methods in morals, religion, and politics could be removed. The Encyclopedists, chief among whom were Denis Diderot and Jean d'Alembert, led in the dissemination of this point of view. The most complete and moving expression of this faith in progress was the marquis de Condorcet's *Esquisse d'un tableau historique des progrès de l'esprit humain,* written in 1793.

In the nineteenth century a new kind of historicist philosophy emerged which rejected the eighteenth-century conception of reason and the sharp dichotomy between the present and the past that had been made by believers in progress. This philosophy, best represented by Hegel, substituted the view that history followed its own inherent course of development and that this course of development embodied rational principles higher than those of merely human reason. Since this form of historicist philosophy identifies all conceivable changes as elements in an unfolding rational purpose, it deprives the idea of progress of definite meaning.

The more definite and combative eighteenth-century conception of progress, however, also continued to be a central theme in the thought of the nineteenth century. In one form or another, major figures of the century, like Karl Marx, Auguste Comte, and John Stuart Mill, all propounded the doctrine. Although Marx, Comte, and Mill were influenced, each in his own way, by historicist ideas, each retained the characteristic eighteenth-century emphasis on the struggle between reason and superstition, on the movement of mankind away from theological and metaphysical modes of thought to positive or empirical habits of mind, and on the importance of extending the standards and methods of the sciences to all domains.

In the twentieth century the idea of progress has continued to have adherents, particularly among American pragmatists, Marxists, and logical empiricists. For obvious historical reasons, however, advocates of the belief in progress have become steadily more modest in their claims since World War I, and during the past fifty years the idea of progress has been seized on by an increasing number of philosophers, theologians, and social critics as the prime fallacy of the tradition of liberalism and rationalism.

ANALYSIS OF THE IDEA

In tracing the history of the idea of progress, it is useful to distinguish between two motifs.

Generally speaking, the belief in progress has been supported by an appeal to the progress of the sciences. In many cases, however, this appeal has consisted in showing that the sciences—usually some particular science—had uncovered fundamental truths that had been previously unknown to man and that progress would now take place if only men accepted these truths as guides to practice. Thus, progress has been said to be guaranteed if men lived by the fundamental principles disclosed by the science of economics, if they accepted the laws of historical development revealed by a scientific approach to history, or if they extended to the government of human society the Darwinian doctrine of evolution by natural selection. Progress has also been thought to be guaranteed if men could only come to recognize certain rational moral principles, such as universal natural rights. Such universal principles, though antecedent to any particular science, were nevertheless closely identified with science, for it was assumed that their validity would be apparent to anyone who could disencumber himself from the superstitions and prejudices of the past and that this process of disengagement was immensely accelerated by the advent of science. This conception of the nature and conditions of progress lends itself to Utopian and Messianic interpretations of progress when understood as an ideal but to the reduction of the idea, in G. M. Young's phrase, "from an aspiration to a schedule" when associated with rigid, a priori approaches to the problem of improving the human condition.

A second motif in the theory of progress, however, has associated progress not with any particular discoveries of science or reason but with the unique, self-corrective methods of science. From this point of view the essential conditions for progress are the rejection of absolutes and fidelity to the principles of free, fallibilistic, experimental inquiry in all domains of thought and action. Even if we assume that it is valid to assert that the methods of science are universally applicable, this approach obviously imposes practical conditions for progress which are immensely difficult and perhaps impossible to realize. Accordingly, those who adopt this approach to the idea of progress can be taken to be saying only that there is a possibility of progress or, at best, a slow and uneven historical tendency which is characteristic only of societies possessing an appropriate ethic and social order and whose continuation is by no means ensured. In the past many proponents of the idea of progress undoubtedly underestimated the difficulties of domesticating within society at large the attitudes and habits of mind exemplified in scientific investigation. Nevertheless, insofar as their concept of progress depended simply on an appeal to the character of scientific procedure, they cannot be said merely to have offered a secularized version of older religious beliefs in a heavenly city, and criticisms of them for having done so, which are standard in much of the literature related to the history of the idea of progress, are a source of considerable confusion.

To be sure, the theories of progress that were developed in the eighteenth and nineteenth centuries are often based on a combination of these two motifs. In Condorcet's thought, for example, there can be found Utopian as well as realistic formulations of the idea of progress. Nevertheless, it is a mistake, on the whole, to associate the idea—particularly as it arose in eighteenth-century France—with the naive hope that human beings and human society could be made perfect. If we study the specific predictions that Condorcet made with regard to the future of humanity, for example, we find that he pointed ahead, with extraordinary prescience, to what are now such commonplace facts as the lengthening of life expectancy, social insurance, and the guarantee of equal legal rights to all citizens. Although none of these has brought the happiness and general reasonableness which Condorcet assumed they would, it was historical realism on his part, not juvenile innocence, to make such predictions. An inability to imagine the wretchedness of the past, not a cold, unillusioned understanding of the present, lies behind the failure to appreciate why reasonable men in the eighteenth and nineteenth centuries should have been rhapsodic about the possibility of changes in the human condition which, in the light of contemporary heightened expectations, may tend to appear fairly modest.

Scientific progress. What can be said with regard to the validity of the idea of progress? We must first ask what meaning can be assigned to the notion of scientific progress.

One frequent argument against the validity of the belief in scientific progress is that it contains a self-contradiction. The belief that there is scientific progress is usually attached to the argument that science is continually self-corrective. But if science never does anything but correct itself, is there any sense in speaking of scientific progress? Does not the concept of progress presuppose a fixed end or standard, and does not science, at any rate as interpreted by those who emphasize its fallibilism, deny that there can be fixed ends or standards? "Progress," in short, appears to be a term without meaning, according to this view, unless it can be attached to metaphysical standards, such as absolute truth, whose status is antecedent to science.

This view fails, however, once it is recognized that progress can also refer to the solution of particular problems, not only to the movement toward a general and abstract goal. For example, meaning can obviously be assigned to the statement that science has made progress in determining the causes of malaria or in describing the characteristics of the other side of the moon. Such statements mean that there are now answers to questions to which there were no answers before and that these answers are in accord with the procedures of inquiry in force among competent scientific investigators. Once scientific progress is defined in terms of the solutions to particular problems, sense can also be given to the notion of cumulative scientific progress, for the general scientific capacity to solve problems has also tended to grow.

Some doubt has been thrown on these conclusions, however, by recent philosophers of science. Karl Popper, for example, has argued that scientific theories and hypotheses are never genuinely confirmed but at best succeed only in resisting successive efforts to falsify them. Since the capacity of a scientific conclusion to survive a series of such efforts does not prove that it will always be able to do so, it would seem to make no sense to speak of successful or true solutions of scientific problems. Popper's view, however, seems to involve an unnecessarily paradoxical way of stating the truism that all scientific conclusions are subject to correction in the future. The survival of a scientific conclusion despite successive efforts to overthrow it adds to the degree of reliability that may reasonably be ascribed to it. It is just as possible to describe the critical position of scientists toward accepted conclusions as efforts to extend the range and reliability of these conclusions as it is to describe it as the expression of a compulsion to destroy what has been inherited. The accumulation of increasingly well-tested and continuously powerful ideas by the sciences is an obvious fact of their history, but as seen by Popper, it seems almost an accidental by-product.

Doubt has also been thrown on the belief in scientific progress by the view that the history of science is the record of revolutions in scientific theory so radical in character that it is impossible to establish the continuity between the ideas of one generation and the ideas of a later one. If this were true, it would be impossible a fortiori to establish a concept of progress, since such a concept presupposes a measure of continuity in the sequence of events under examination. Underlying this view is the thesis that the confirmation by experiment of particular hypotheses always entails the use of a specific theoretical framework. When this theoretical framework changes, observations are simply run through a different set of conceptual categories. Accordingly, it makes little sense, it is argued, to say that the sciences have improved or extended their knowledge, for all that has happened is that one body of beliefs has been substituted for another. This point of view raises epistemological and methodological questions of great complexity, and there is no room to discuss them sufficiently here. It appears to leave out of account, however, the consideration that, for example, fundamental principles of Newtonian physics can, with appropriate modifications, be absorbed into modern physical theories. It also appears to underestimate the implications of the fact that these principles, without substantial modification, continue to provide reliable instruments for the explanation and prediction of events in large sectors of macrophysics.

Social and moral progress. Assuming that both meaning and truth can be assigned to the idea of progress in science, what is the status of the belief in social and moral progress? Obviously, the answer to this question depends in part on the standards employed as the touchstones of progress. However, some of the difficulties involved in stating and defending such standards can be circumvented if in this sphere we also define progress in terms of the successful solution of specific problems. Thus, there has been striking progress in the control of disease, in methods of farming, in material productivity, in the reduction of backbreaking labor, in the techniques of rapid mass communication, in the spread of literacy, and probably in the reduction of the amount of violence in everyday life. Of course, it is theoretically possible to hold a moral code from whose standpoint one or more of these historical trends would be regarded as retrogressive rather than progressive. In fact, however, even though men in different contemporary cultures (and men in the same culture) hold widely disparate moral outlooks, there are few informed and disinterested observers, whatever their moral outlooks, who regard any of these trends, considered in themselves, as movements in the wrong direction. And most would also look upon many other historical trends that have characterized the modern world—for example, the development of more humane attitudes in penology, the abolition of slavery and serfdom, the spread of the doctrine of basic human rights—in a similarly favorable light. To this extent it is possible to speak with a measure of precision and truth of social and moral progress.

But this answer, of course, goes only part of the way. On at least two scores it is incomplete. First, it is reasonable to ask whether the gains that have been mentioned have not been bought at a cost which more than cancels them out; second, it is possible to ask how we are to vindicate the moral principles in terms of which we assess these gains as gains.

The cost of progress. It is not possible, of course, to give a wholly unequivocal answer to the question of the cost of progress. The notion that large-scale historical trends can be neatly categorized as good or bad belongs to eschatology, not to mature historical analysis. If the reduction of civil violence, considered in itself, is a progressive trend, contemporary mass warfare and genocide must be considered retrogressive; if rapid mass communication is a benefit to mankind, the use of the facilities of communication for totalitarian thought control is a calamity. Moreover, the successful solution of many problems often creates new and more difficult ones. The control of disease, for example, has created a serious threat of overpopulation. And by what calculus can one measure the gains brought about, for example, by industrial innovations against the losses brought about by mass warfare or cyclical unemployment? A moral accounting system for judging even much simpler matters than these does not exist.

Nevertheless, if the span of time we measure is sufficiently long, it remains true that on the whole the physical lot of most ordinary people has considerably improved in modern societies and that this has largely been due to the application of rational techniques to the economy. The cost has been grievous, and many of the sacrifices this progress has entailed could probably have been avoided if men had employed reasonable forethought

and had shown reasonable respect for the equities. Admittedly, too, it is difficult to say whether this physical progress has made men "happier"; indeed, it is doubly difficult to say this, for "happiness" is in part a function of what men expect, and physical progress has meant an enormous expansion of their expectations. Nevertheless, it is doubtful that most of those who put forward the view that the costs of material progress outweigh the benefits would willingly exchange places with any but the most privileged members of past societies if they actually had the chance.

Nor must we confine ourselves to a belief in purely physical or material progress. The role of fantasy, ignorance, superstition, and fanaticism in determining the world's affairs continues to be enormous. It is doubtful, however, whether so many members of human societies, from housewives to statesmen, have ever before thought it reasonable to make decisions on the basis of carefully acquired and sifted information, and never before have societies possessed as much knowledge about themselves and their workings as they do now, shaky and scattered though that knowledge is. Only if one thinks it morally dangerous to seek reliable information before making decisions or thinks it mistaken to try to employ rational methods in the study of human affairs can he declare such long-range social trends to be anything but progressive. Indeed, the very reason that the members of an educated modern society bear a particularly heavy burden of responsibility for the emergence of doctrines like Nazism is that they have opportunities to be informed and judicious which members of other societies did not have. In sum, although it is not possible to say in wholesale terms that there has been moral progress, it is possible to assert that the context of human behavior has changed and that the collective capacity to achieve human purposes, whether good or ill, has enormously increased. The expectations which it is reasonable to impose on modern social arrangements are therefore justifiably higher than those that may have been reasonable in the past. In this modified but important sense it is fair to speak of moral progress.

Justification of moral standards. All the preceding reflections, however, obviously presuppose the validity of a secular, liberal, and rationalistic moral code. In the end, as must be obvious, objections to the idea of progress usually turn on fundamental differences in values. Whether the validity of one fundamental moral outlook as against another can be demonstratively proved is an issue that falls beyond the scope of the present article. If we assume, however, that we cannot resolve these differences in a way that will satisfy traditional standards of demonstrative certainty, there is no so-called ultimate answer to the question of whether modern society has been the scene of genuine progress.

It is possible, however, to show that a relativistic moral philosophy is perfectly compatible with a belief in progress, for it is not true that a relativistic philosophy cannot make any meaningful statements about progress because it has to grant that there are different moral standards and that all are equally valid. First, even if there is no way of proving the absolute validity of a moral outlook, there is still a way of intelligently and objectively assessing its credentials. The moral ideals that underlie the indictment of modern civilization for its excessive individualism and egalitarianism made by T. S. Eliot, for example, would require, if they were to be seriously employed as positive programs for action, the dismantling of large segments of industrial society. Since we may assume that those who put forward such criticisms would wish medical science to continue its work, for example, and would accept a world population at something like its present size, we must conclude that their announced preferences are both unrealistic and incoherent because they are incompatible with other values which they also hold. An examination of available resources, of the costs of maintaining or instituting alternative systems of values, and of the utility of these systems as guides to the resolution of definite historical problems provides a way of choosing among competing moral outlooks and makes the choice something more than a matter of personal whim or social convention.

Second, although the philosophical relativist may believe that apart from the specification of definite problems in determinate historical contexts, there is no way of showing that a moral code is valid, this does not mean that he does not himself hold any moral standards or that he is any less attached to them than an absolutist would be. A twentieth-century American looking at slavery in ancient Rome, for example, will regard it as a change for the better that slavery is now illegal in Western society, and he will do so whether or not he is a relativist. And to say that he might feel different if he were a Roman is irrelevant, for he is a twentieth-century American, not a Roman, and it would be a different person with a different identity, not he, who felt different in the hypothetical circumstances. Similarly, if the standards of men in the future change, they may well disagree with us in regard to what has been progressive in history. But if these future judgments reverse present judgments, that does not bind a relativist living here and now to accept them. Nothing in his position requires him to say that progress is any historical trend that comes to be thought desirable.

Progress as a moral standard. As a final consideration, it is important to recognize that the idea of progress in its most important aspect is itself a regulative moral ideal, not simply a belief about history. It represents a directing principle of intellectual and social action, instructing men to regard all social arrangements with a critical eye and to reject any claim that any human problem has been finally solved or must be left finally unsolved. To the extent that this idea of progress is embodied in moral codes and social systems, these codes and systems will contain deliberate provision for self-reform. The idea of progress thus represents the social application of the principle that inquiry should be kept open and that no bounds can legitimately be set to the authority of such free inquiry. As such, it would appear to be an indispensable belief for a fully liberal civilization.

Bibliography

Alembert, Jean d', *Discours préliminaire de l'Encyclopédie*, edited by F. Picavet. Paris, 1894.
Becker, Carl, L., *The Heavenly City of the Eighteenth Century Philosophers*. New Haven, 1932.
Bury, J. B., *The Idea of Progress*. London, 1924.
Butterfield, Herbert, *The Whig Interpretation of History*. New York, 1951.
Comte, Auguste, *Cours de philosophie positive*. Paris, 1835–1852.
Condorcet, Marie Jean de, *Esquisse d'un tableau historique des progrès de l'esprit humain*, O. H. Prior, ed. Paris, 1933.
Fontenelle, Bernard de, *Digression sur les anciens et les modernes*, in *Oeuvres completes*, 5 vols. Paris, 1825. Vol. IV.
Frankel, Charles, *The Case for Modern Man*. New York, 1956.
Inge, W. R., *The Idea of Progress*. Oxford, 1920.
Maritain, Jacques, *True Humanism*, translated by M. R. Adamson. New York, 1954.
Mill, John Stuart, *A System of Logic*. London, 1961. Book VI, Chs. 10–11.
Niebuhr, Reinhold, *The Nature and Destiny of Man*. New York, 1951.
Pascal, Blaise, *Fragment d'un traité du vide*, in *Oeuvres*, Léon Brunschvicg and Émile Boutroux, eds. Paris, 1904–1914. Vol. II.
Rousseau, Jean-Jacques, "Discourse on the Arts and Sciences," in *The Social Contract and Discourses*, translated by G. D. H. Cole. London, 1913.
Spencer, Herbert, *Illustrations of Universal Progress*. New York, 1881.
Teggart, F. J., ed., *The Idea of Progress*, rev. ed. Berkeley, 1949. Introduction by George H. Hildebrand.
Todd, A. J., *Theories of Social Progress*. New York, 1919.
Turgot, A. R. J., *On the Progress of the Human Mind*, translated by McQ. de Grange. Hanover, N.H., 1929.

CHARLES FRANKEL

PROOF THEORY. See MATHEMATICS, FOUNDATIONS OF.

PROPER NAMES AND DESCRIPTIONS. The status of proper names has puzzled philosophers ever since the days of Plato. There seems to be no doubt that adjectives and common nouns like "red" and "table" have sense or meaning, and the same seems to hold fairly obviously for so-called definite descriptions like "the red flower" or "the man next to the table." But what about proper names like "Winston Churchill" and "San Francisco"? Do they have sense in the same way that adjectives, common nouns, and definite descriptions have sense? In the history of philosophy, answers to this question have been crucial to answering the general question of how words relate to the world.

Sense and no-sense theories of proper names. According to one widely held view, proper names simply stand for objects, without having any sense or meaning other than standing for objects. An early formulation of the germ of this theory is in Plato's *Theaetetus*, and the most sophisticated modern versions of the view are in Wittgenstein's *Tractatus Logico-philosophicus* and Russell's *Philosophy of Logical Atomism*. According to Wittgenstein, the meaning of a proper name is simply the object for which it stands. Perhaps the most famous formulation of this no-sense theory of proper names is Mill's statement that proper names have denotation but not connotation. For Mill a common noun like "horse" has both a connotation and a denotation; it connotes those properties which would be specified in a definition of the word "horse," and it denotes all horses. But a proper name only denotes its bearer.

The above is a famous and attractive theory of proper names, but there are certain notorious difficulties with it.

One is that sometimes one sees proper names in identity statements, statements of the form "*a* is identical with *b*." As Frege pointed out, if proper names simply stand for objects and nothing more, how could such statements ever convey any factual information? If we construe such statements as solely about the referent of the names, then it seems they must be trivial, since, if true, they say only that an object is identical with itself. If, on the other hand, we construe the statements as giving information about the names, then it seems they must be arbitrary, since we can assign any name we wish to an object. Frege's solution was to argue that besides the names and the objects they refer to, we must distinguish a third element, the sense (*Sinn*) of the name in virtue of which and only in virtue of which it refers to the object. In the statement "The evening star is identical with the morning star," the expressions "the evening star" and "the morning star" have the same referent but different senses. The sense provides the mode of presentation (*Art des Gegebenseins*) of the object; the object is, as it were, illuminated from one side (*einseitig beleuchtet*) by the sense of the expression; and it is because the two expressions have different senses that the statement can convey factual information to us. What the statement conveys is that one and the same object has the two different sets of properties specified by the two different senses of the two names, and thus such a statement can be a statement of fact and not a mere triviality or an arbitrary verbal decision. All proper names, for Frege, had senses in the way that the expressions "the evening star" and "the morning star" have senses.

This presents a completely different picture of proper names from the classical no-sense theory. According to the classical theory, names, if they are really names, necessarily have a reference and no sense at all. According to the Fregean theory, they essentially have a sense and only contingently have a reference. They refer if and only if there is an object which satisfies their sense. In the first theory proper names are *sui generis*, and indeed for Plato (in the *Theaetetus*) and Wittgenstein (in the *Tractatus*) they are the special connecting link between words and world; in the second theory proper names are only a species of disguised definite descriptions: every one is equivalent in meaning to a definite description, that definite description which gives an explicit formulation of its sense. According to the first theory, naming is prior to describing; according to the second, describing is prior to naming, for a name only names by describing the object it names.

Pros and cons of the theories. There is a straightforward clash between the classical no-sense theory and the Fregean sense and reference theory. Part of the charm of the problem presented by this clash is that each has interesting arguments in its favor.

Common sense seems to incline us toward the no-sense theory, at least as far as most ordinary proper names are concerned. Proper names are not equivalent to definite descriptions because, for example, calling an object by its name is not a way of describing it. Naming is a preparation for describing, not a kind of describing. Furthermore, we do not have definitions of most proper names; dictionary entries for proper names usually offer statements of contin-

gent fact describing the object referred to by the name. The descriptions are not definitional equivalents of the name, for they are only contingently true of the bearer. But the name is not "true of" the bearer at all; it is its name.

Not only do we not have definitional equivalents for proper names but also it is not at all clear how we could go about getting definitions of proper names if we wanted to. If, for example, we tried to present a complete description of the object as the sense of the name, odd consequences would ensue—for example, any true statement about the object that used the name as subject would be analytic, and any false one would be self-contradictory. The meaning of the name (and perhaps the identity of the object) would change every time there was a change in the object, and the same name would have different meanings for different users of the name.

Such common-sense considerations weigh heavily in favor of the no-sense theory, yet it too encounters serious difficulties. First, as has been shown, it cannot account for the occurrence of proper names in informative identity statements. Second, it is similarly unable to account for the occurrence of proper names in existential statements. In such statements as "There is such a place as Africa" and "Cerberus does not exist," the proper names cannot be said to refer, for no subject of an existential statement can refer. If it did, the precondition of its having a truth-value would guarantee its truth if it were in the affirmative and its falsity if it were in the negative. (This is just another way of saying that "exists" is not a predicate.) Every affirmative existential statement states in effect that a certain predicate or concept is instantiated. (As Frege put it, existence is a second-order concept.) An affirmative existential statement does not refer to an object and state that it exists; rather, it expresses a concept and states that that concept is instantiated.

Thus, if a proper name occurs in an existential statement, it seems that it must have some conceptual or descriptive content. But if it has a descriptive content, then it seems Frege's theory must be correct, for what could that descriptive content be except the sense of the proper name? Thus, the occurrence of proper names in existential statements poses another grave difficulty for the no-sense theorists. But worse is yet to come.

What account can the no-sense theorist give of the existence of the object referred to by a proper name? If one agrees with the Wittgenstein of the *Tractatus* that the meaning of a proper name is literally the object for which it stands, then it seems that the existence of those objects which are named by genuine proper names cannot be an ordinary contingent fact. The reason for this is that such changes in the world as the destruction of some object cannot destroy the meaning of words, because any change in the world must still be describable in words. But this seems to be forcing us into the view that there is a class of objects in the world whose existence is somehow necessary, those objects which are the meanings of the real proper names. Indeed, it seems, if we accept this view, that it could not make any sense to assert or deny the existence of the objects named by genuine proper names. As Plato remarked, we cannot say of an element that it exists or does not exist (*Theaetetus* 201D–202A).

There are at least two ways of dealing with this problem of the existence of the referent, a metaphysical way and a linguistic way. In the *Tractatus*, Wittgenstein adopts a metaphysical conclusion, saying that "objects form the substance of the world" (2.021). Their existence can neither be asserted nor be denied. In her book, *An Introduction to Wittgenstein's Tractatus*, G. E. M. Anscombe adopts a linguistic way out of the problem. She says simply that we must distinguish genuine proper names from apparent ones. Only expressions which have bearers are genuine proper names. It is indeed a necessary truth that a genuine proper name has a bearer, but this does not force us to accept the view that there is a class of objects which have a necessary existence; rather, it leads to the view that whether or not an expression is a proper name depends on whether or not its purported referent really exists (or at least has existed or will exist). Thus, if we discovered that Caesar never existed, we would in effect prove that "Caesar" was not a genuine proper name.

A consequence of the Wittgensteinian doctrine, accepted and elucidated by Russell in his logical atomism period, is that what in ordinary language we consider to be proper names are not proper names at all because the existence of their bearers is a contingent fact and in no way follows from the status of the expressions in the language. This is a somewhat ironical and unfortunate consequence, for the no-sense theory, which starts out as a common-sense account of ordinary proper names, when followed out on this track ends with the startling and implausible conclusion that ordinary proper names are not really proper names (not "logically proper names") at all but disguised definite descriptions.

Anscombe's view avoids the uncomfortable conclusion that no ordinary proper name is a genuine proper name, yet there are still compelling objections against it. She maintains that it is a criterion for an expression's being a proper name that it have a bearer. This has the odd consequence that membership in a syntactical category becomes contingent on the nonsyntactical relation of name-bearing. Furthermore, it has the odd consequence that many obvious proper names, such as "Cerberus" and "Zeus," are not really genuine proper names because Cerberus and Zeus do not exist. Her view is simply an arbitrary decision to use the expression "genuine proper name" in such a way that only expressions which have bearers are genuine proper names. But some such arbitrary and unsatisfactory decision seems to be forced upon us if we accept the no-sense theory and reject the Wittgensteinian doctrine of substance. In his later work Wittgenstein rejected his earlier view of proper names, saying that it confused the *bearer* of a name with the *meaning* of the name: "When Mr. N. N. dies one says that the bearer of the name dies, not that the meaning dies" (*Philosophical Investigations*, Para. 40).

Thus, at least initially, common sense seems to favor the no-sense theory, but it is unable to account for the occurrence of proper names in informative identity statements and in existential statements. Furthermore, for the no-sense theorist the nature of the existence of the referents of proper names raises serious problems. The sense theory seems implausible in claiming that proper names are simply shorthand definite descriptions, but it does at least have the merit of accounting for the problems about identity statements and existential statements.

A proposed solution. The antinomy posed by the two opposing views of proper names admits of a possible solution. We might rephrase the question "Do proper names have senses?" as "Do proper names entail any descriptive predicates?" or simply as "Are any propositions that contain a proper name as a subject and a descriptive expression as a predicate analytic?" But this question has a weaker and a stronger form: the weaker, "Are there any such analytic statements at all?" and the stronger, "Are there any analytic statements where the subject is a proper name and the predicate a description that is sufficiently specific to identify one and only one object (hereafter called an 'identifying description')?" It is characteristic of a proper name that it is used to refer to the same object on different occasions. The use of the same name at different times presupposes that the object is the same; a necessary condition of identity of reference is identity of the object referred to. But to presuppose that the object is the same in turn presupposes a criterion of identity, that is, it presupposes an ability on the part of the speaker to answer the question "In virtue of what is the object at time t_1, referred to by name N, identical with the object at time t_2, referred to by the same name?" To put it more simply, "The object at time t_1 is the same *what* as the object at time t_2?" The gap indicated by "what" is to be filled by a descriptive general term; it is the same mountain, the same person, the same river, and so on. The general term provides a criterion of identity in each case. This gives us an affirmative answer to the weaker question. Some general term is analytically tied to any proper name: Everest is a mountain, the Mississippi is a river, de Gaulle is a person. Anything which was not a mountain could not be Everest, and so on, for to secure continuity of reference we need a criterion of identity, and the general term associated with the name provides the criterion. Even if someone wanted to assert that de Gaulle could turn into a tree or horse and still be de Gaulle, there must be some identity criterion. De Gaulle could not turn into anything whatever and still remain de Gaulle, and to say this is to say that some term or range of terms is analytically tied to the name "de Gaulle."

One temptation is to say that if we continue to call an object "Everest," the property of being called Everest is sufficient to guarantee that it is the same. But the point of the above analysis is that we are justified in calling it "Everest" only if we can give a reason for supposing it to be identical with what we used to call "Everest," and to give as the reason that it is called "Everest" would be circular. In this sense, at least, proper names do have "connotations."

But the answer "Yes" to the weaker question does not entail the same answer to the stronger one, and it is the stronger form which is crucial for deciding whether or not a proper name has a sense, as Frege used the word. For according to Frege, the sense of a proper name contains the "mode of presentation" which identifies the referent, and of course a single descriptive predicate does not provide us with a mode of presentation (an identifying description). That Socrates was a man may be analytically true, but the predicate "man" is not a specific identifying description of Socrates.

Let us now consider the stronger formulation of the question. At least two considerations incline us to say that it might have something like an affirmative answer. First, we learn to use proper names and we teach others to use proper names only by ostension or description, and both methods connect the name to the object only in virtue of specifying enough characteristics of the object to distinguish it from other objects. Second, anyone who uses a proper name must be prepared to answer the question "Who or what are you talking about?," and answers to this question, where adequate, will take the form either of verbal identifying descriptions or of ostensive presentations of the object. Both considerations suggest a close connection between the ability to use the name and a knowledge of the characteristics of the object sufficient to distinguish it from other objects.

But how close is the connection? Suppose we ask the users of a proper name, say "Aristotle," to state what they regard as essential and established facts about him. Their answers would constitute a set of descriptions, many elements of which would be identifying descriptions and the totality of which would be an identifying description. For example, Aristotle was a Greek; a philosopher; the tutor of Alexander the Great; the author of the *Nicomachean Ethics,* the *Metaphysics,* and the *De Interpretatione;* and the founder of the school of the Lyceum at Athens. Although no particular single one of these descriptions is analytically tied to the name Aristotle, some indefinite subset of these descriptions is. A classical scholar might discover that Aristotle never tutored Alexander or that he did not write the *Metaphysics;* but if a classical scholar claimed to discover that Aristotle wrote none of the works attributed to him, never had anything to do with Plato or Alexander, never went near Athens, and was not even a philosopher but was in fact an obscure Venetian fishmonger of the late Renaissance, then the "discovery" would become a bad joke. The original set of statements about Aristotle constitute the descriptive backing of the name in virtue of which and only in virtue of which we can teach and use the name. It makes sense to deny some of the members of the set of descriptions of the bearer of the name, but to deny all of them is to strip away the preconditions for using the name at all.

To rephrase this point, suppose we have independent means of identifying an object. What, then, are the conditions under which I could say of the object, "This is Aristotle?" What is being claimed is that the conditions, the descriptive powers of the statement, are that a sufficient but so far unspecified number of these statements (or descriptions) are true of the object. In short, if *none* of the descriptions believed to be true of some object by the users of the name of that object proved to be true of any independently located object, then there is no object identical with the bearer of the name. It is a necessary condition for an object's being Aristotle that it satisfy at least some of these descriptions. This is another way of saying that the disjunction of these descriptions is analytically tied to the name "Aristotle"—which is a quasi-affirmative answer to the question "Do proper names have

a sense?" in its stronger formulation. It should be pointed out parenthetically that the description "called Aristotle," although it has a peculiar status, is no more crucial than any other description, for it is a contingent fact that Aristotle was and is called Aristotle.

The answer, then, to the question "Do proper names have a sense?"—if this asks whether or not proper names are used to describe or specify characteristics of objects—is "No." But if it asks whether or not proper names are logically connected with characteristics of the object to which they refer, the answer is "Yes, in a loose sort of way."

Some philosophers suppose that it is an objection to this sort of account that the same word is sometimes used as a name for more than one object, but this is a totally irrelevant fact and not an objection to this account at all. That different objects are named John Smith is no more relevant to the question "Do proper names have senses?" than the fact that both riversides and finance houses are called banks is relevant to the question "Do general terms have senses?" Both "bank" and "John Smith" suffer from homonymy, but one does not prove a word meaningless by pointing out that it has several meanings.

This solution is a compromise between Mill and Frege. Mill was right in thinking that proper names do not entail any particular description, that they do not have definitions, but Frege was correct in assuming that any singular term must have a mode of presentation and hence, in a way, a sense. His mistake was in taking the identifying description that can be substituted for the name as a definition.

This analysis of proper names enables us to account for all the difficulties raised earlier in this article. How can a proper name occur in an existential statement? A statement such as "Aristotle never existed" states that a sufficient, but so far unspecified, number of the descriptive backings of "Aristotle" are false. Which of these are asserted to be false is not yet clear, for the descriptive backing of Aristotle is not yet precise. Supposing that of the propositions believed to be true of Aristotle half were true of one man and half of another, would we say that Aristotle never existed? The question is not decided in advance. This means that insofar as "Aristotle" has a sense, it is much less precise than that of a definite description.

Similarly, it is easy to explain identity statements using proper names. "Everest is Chomolungma" states that the descriptive backing of both names is true of the same object. If the descriptive backing of the two names, for the person making the statement, is the same, or if one contains the other, the statement is analytic; if not, it is synthetic. Frege's instinct was sound in inferring from the fact that we do make factually informative identity statements using proper names that they must have a sense, but he was wrong in supposing that this sense is as straightforward as in a definite description. His famous "morning star –evening star" example led him astray here, for although the sense of these names is straightforward, these expressions are not paradigm proper names but are on the boundary line between definite descriptions and proper names.

The imprecision of proper names. We have seen that insofar as proper names can be said to have a sense, it is an imprecise one. We must now explore the reasons for this imprecision. Is the imprecision as to exactly what characteristics constitute the necessary and sufficient conditions for applying a proper name a mere accident, a product of linguistic slovenliness? Or does it derive from the functions which proper names perform? To ask for the criteria for applying the name "Aristotle" is to ask in the formal mode what Aristotle is; it is to ask for a set of identity criteria for the object Aristotle. "What is Aristotle?" and "What are the criteria for applying the name 'Aristotle'?" ask the same question, the former in the material mode, and the latter in the formal mode, of language. So if, prior to using the name, we came to an agreement on the precise characteristics which constituted the identity of Aristotle, our rules for using the name would be precise. But this precision would be achieved only at the cost of entailing some specific qualities by any use of the name. Indeed, the name itself would become logically equivalent to this set of descriptions, but if this were the case, we would be in the position of being able to refer to an object solely by describing it. In fact, this is just what the institution of proper names enables us to avoid and what distinguishes proper names from descriptions. If the criteria for proper names were in all cases quite rigid and specific, then a proper name would be nothing more than a shorthand for these criteria and would function exactly like an elaborate definite description. But the uniqueness and immense pragmatic convenience of proper names in our language lies precisely in the fact that they enable us to refer publicly to objects without being forced to raise issues and come to an agreement as to which descriptive characteristics exactly constitute the identity of the object. They function not as descriptions but as pegs on which to hang descriptions. Thus, the looseness of the criteria for proper names is a necessary condition for isolating the referring function from the describing function of language.

To put the same point differently, suppose we ask, "Why do we have proper names at all?" Obviously, to refer to individuals. "Yes, but descriptions could do that for us." But only at the cost of specifying identity conditions every time reference is made. Suppose we agree to drop "Aristotle" and use, say, "the teacher of Alexander." Then it is a logical truth that the man referred to is Alexander's teacher—but it is a contingent fact that Aristotle ever taught Alexander (although it is a necessary fact that Aristotle has the logical sum [inclusive disjunction] of the properties commonly attributed to him).

We might clarify some of the points made in this article by comparing paradigm proper names with degenerate proper names like "the Bank of England." For the latter limiting cases of proper names, it seems the sense is given as straightforwardly as in a definite description; the conditions of using the name are obvious. On the other hand, a proper name may acquire a rigid use without having the verbal form of a description: God is just, omnipotent, omniscient *by definition* for believers. To us, "Homer" simply means "the author of the *Iliad* and the *Odyssey*." The form may often mislead us; the Holy Roman Empire was neither holy nor Roman nor an empire, but it was, nonetheless, the Holy Roman Empire. Again, it may be conventional to name only girls "Martha"; but if I name my son "Martha," I may mislead but I do not lie. And, of course, not all paradigm proper names are alike with respect to the nature of their "descriptive content." There will, for example, be a difference between the names of living people, where the capacity of the user of the name to recognize the person may be an important "identifying description," and the names of historical figures. But the essential fact to keep in mind when dealing with these problems is that we have the institution of proper names to perform the speech act of reference. The existence of these expressions derives from our need to separate the referring from the describing functions of language. But reference never occurs in complete isolation from description, for without some description, reference would be altogether impossible.

Bibliography

Anscombe, G. E. M., *An Introduction to Wittgenstein's Tractatus.* London, 1959. Ch. 2.

Frege, Gottlob, "Sense and Reference," in P. T. Geach and Max Black, eds., *Translations From the Philosophical Writings of Gottlob Frege.* Oxford, 1952.

Mill, J. S., *A System of Logic.* Book I, Ch. 2, especially Sec. 5.

Plato, *Theaetetus.* 201D ff.

Russell, Bertrand, "The Philosophy of Logical Atomism," in his *Logic and Knowledge,* R. C. Marsh, ed. London, 1956. Pp. 200–201.

Searle, J. R., "Proper Names." *Mind,* Vol. 67 (April 1958), 166–173.

Wittgenstein, Ludwig, *Tractatus Logico-philosophicus,* translated by C. K. Ogden. London, 1922.

Wittgenstein, Ludwig, *Philosophical Investigations,* translated by G. E. M. Anscombe. Oxford, 1953. Paras. 40–79.

JOHN R. SEARLE

PROPERTY. The institution of property has interested social philosophers in part, at least, because it raises issues of justice. Like government, it is practically universal but varies enough in its particular arrangements to suggest the question What criteria are relevant in assessing the relative merits of various arrangements? Again, because it discriminates between rights and fortune, it invites moral criticism and the demand for justification.

Many of the classical accounts of the origin and function of private property have taken for granted that in nature all things were held "in common." This phrase, however, is ambiguous, for it often meant not a system regulating the use of goods by general agreement but a condition where, there being no rules, everything was *res nullius* (a thing belonging to no one) and the concept "property" was consequently irrelevant. How, then, it was asked, would men come to appropriate the land and its fruits? How could such appropriation be justified? What would be rational grounds for claiming exclusive possession? And could there be any limit on a man's right to do what he would with his own?

Theories of property. According to the Church Fathers, property was both the consequence and the social remedy for the sin of covetousness that came with the Fall. But since owners have appropriated what at one time belonged to all, they have a duty to administer it for the benefit of all. "Our property," said Gregory the Great, "is ours to distribute, but not ours to keep." The concept of the owner as steward is the core of the traditional Christian view of property.

Natural law and conventionalism. By the seventeenth century, property rights came to be grounded in the needs and accomplishments of the individual owner, and ownership implied a natural right to enjoy and dispose of its objects, limited only by the duty to respect the rather narrowly defined interests of others. In Locke's account, property as an institution is explained by human needs. Although God gave the earth and all its fruits to all men to preserve their lives, still this meant one's making the fruits of the earth exclusively his own, if only by eating them. However, what in nature entitled one to call something one's own was that one made the effort to make it so. To add one's labor to a *res nullius* was to create a title to the whole product. Locke limited this title to whatever one could use before it spoiled; appropriation for waste would be illegitimate.

To appropriate an object implied for Locke not merely a right to enjoy it but also to alienate it at will, so that although the appropriation of *res nullius* could legitimately be effected only by labor, the title, once established, could be freely transferred. It is questionable, however, whether Locke was justified in assuming that because we may appropriate what we need from the common stock, we may therefore transfer what we acquire, but do not need, to whomsoever we choose. Locke needed this right, however, if his theory was not to suggest, as did certain later writers on economic justice, that the laborer was entitled to the entire fruits of his master's fields, if not to the fields themselves. For where all land had long been appropriated, the titles of present owners would depend entirely on the legitimacy of such transfers in the past. So, since the land was no longer *res nullius*, all the laborer could claim was the value of his labor in wages. Moreover, in a market economy and with the introduction of money, wealth might be accumulated and stored indefinitely without spoiling; furthermore, since money had only a conventional value, hoarding it deprived no one of anything of natural value, and its distribution must be taken to be by common consent. Having accounted, then, for the existence of property, and for existing titles, with a theory of natural right, Locke overlaid the theory with a conventionalist theory which neutralized the limitations on appropriation that the original theory prescribed.

Nature and convention are to be found similarly blended, if in varying proportions, in Hugo Grotius, Samuel von Pufendorf, and William Blackstone. In Kant, too, there is a blend. Kant deduced the principle of first occupier from the autonomy of the will but conceded that only a universal legislative will—the civil state—could give binding force to the intention to appropriate.

Utilitarian positions. According to Hume, a man's creation ought to be secured to him in order to encourage "useful habits and accomplishments." Inheritance and the right to alienate were alike valuable as incentives to or conditions for useful industry and commerce. Property rested on convention in the sense of rules upheld by common interests commonly perceived. It was a law of nature, too, but in the sense that men were sufficiently alike the world over for the same general arrangements to be equally to the public advantage. Hume's argument, then, also blends natural law doctrine with conventionalism but reduces both to utilitarianism.

Bentham did little more than elaborate Hume's arguments. However, by introducing considerations of utility, Hume and Bentham pointed the way for criticism of the distribution of private property and, indeed, of the institution itself. Already in 1793 William Godwin was arguing that in a consistent application of the principle of utility "every man has a right to that, the exclusive possession of which being awarded to him, a greater sum of benefit or pleasure will result, than could have arisen from its being otherwise appropriated" (*Political Justice,* Book 8). J. S. Mill, though broadly committed to a belief in private property, held that, in the case of land at any rate, private ownership must be conditional on its expediency; the rights associated with it, especially the right to exclusive access and enjoyment, ought to be limited to whatever was required to exploit it efficiently. Mill recognized that the rights of property were not an inseparable bundle, to be justified en bloc; each constituent right had to be independently justified on grounds of utility.

However, Mill's belief that the institution of property would be justified provided that it guaranteed to individuals the fruits of their labor and abstinence is open to question. In a complex industrial society, "the fruits of one's labor" can mean only the value of a given worker's contribution to the finished product. But value derives from the relations of supply and demand, both for the commodity and for labor of the various kinds needed to produce it. "The fruits of one's labor," understood as one's share in a social dividend, will depend not only on one's efforts but also on the number of other people available to do the same job and on how badly consumers want it done. If for the time being a particular skill is in short supply, is it self-evident that this increases the value of its fruits or that those who have it should be the better off for it?

Marxist and Hegelian critiques. Again, the exclusive claims of labor take no account of what men owe to others and to the social interest. Durkheim, for instance, objected that "it is not enough to invoke the rights that man has over himself: these rights are not absolute but limited by the claims of the moral aims, in which a man has to cooperate." Marx was equally critical of the German Social Democrats' Gotha program of 1875, which claimed that labor should receive its produce "unabridged and in equal right." He charged that this formula ignored the need for capital replacement and development, social services, and the support of the incapable. In any case, he said, distribution proportional to contribution would still be only partial justice, bearing in mind differences in natural capacity on the one hand and need on the other. In the truly cooperative society, based on common ownership of the means of production, individual labor would be impossible to separate out, and distribution would be according to need alone. This would be possible, however, only because labor would have ceased to be a burden and would have become "life's principal end."

This last condition suggests why, in a period when hedonistic premises underlay a great deal of psychology, ethics, and economics, the necessary relation between labor and property should have been so generally accepted. On the assumption that work was painful, the only conceivable reason for working was a greater pleasure expected from its fruits. Marx argued that this account of labor was neither an explanation nor a justification, but a consequence, of the system of private property. The worker was alienated from his work, which appeared to him not as a fulfillment but as a burden; he was alienated, too, from the product of his work, which, passing to his employer in surplus value, confronted him as capital—that is, as an instrument of his own bondage.

Despite the stress on labor as the source of value that Marx shared with the English utilitarians and economists, his account of property derives at least as much from Hegel as from the English school. Like Kant, Hegel regarded property as necessary not because it helped to satisfy human needs but because "a person must translate his freedom into an external sphere in order that he may achieve his ideal existence" (*Philosophy of Right,* Sec. 41); because "property is the first embodiment of freedom and so is in itself a substantive end" (*ibid.,* Sec. 45). Plato erred, in Hegel's view, in denying private property to the guardians, for he was denying them the conditions necessary for giving concrete realization to their personalities and wills.

Marx and Hegel are alike in seeing the human will objectifying itself in its acquisitions and creations. If for Marx the process is not rationalizing and liberating but alienating and enslaving, it is because the property created is not and cannot be the worker's own. The laborer can transcend this alienation only in the communist society, in which, like Plato's guardians or the members of a monastic community, he gets caught up in a common enterprise where "mine" and "thine" are of no account because life is more than the satisfaction of material needs. In a world in which "sharing in" counted for more than "sharing out," property—like justice—would present no problems.

Economic and social significance. In the course of the past century, legal and social philosophers (Léon Duguit and Karl Renner, for example) have come to think of property increasingly as an institution with social functions and not, like Locke, as simply a guarantee of individual interest. Moreover, because property entails inequalities in power, in claims on the social product, in social status, and in prestige, it must be justified, and not merely in terms of the interests or natural rights of its immediate beneficiaries.

It is difficult, however, to see how any one theory could apply generally to all forms of private property and include all rights of ownership. Individual control of productive resources raises very different issues from the exclusive right to enjoy consumer goods like clothes and furniture. The right to control the use of mines and factories is not really an instance of the right of a Kantian rational and autonomous being to manipulate mere things for his own needs; it is also an exercise of power over other men. According to A. A. Berle, the United States is gradually extending to such property the limitations traditionally applied to state action in order to protect individual freedom.

Again, could one justify one's title to dividends on the ground that instead of enjoying the fruits of one's labor one had invested them? And would the same justification extend to a corporate title to the yield on investments financed out of undistributed profits? Such claims have certainly flourished under the umbrella of natural rights; but it is difficult to see how any but a utilitarian argument could seriously be proposed in defense of such arrangements.

Analysis of ownership. Talk of property often seems to be talk about things. Things constitute property, however, only inasmuch as they can be assigned to owners; to own something is to have, in respect to it, certain rights and liabilities vis-à-vis other persons or the public at large. Ownership, therefore, is a normative relation or a complex of such relations between owner, object, and third parties; and to refer to something as "property" is to locate it as a term in such a relationship. Some jurists, indeed, insist that "property" refers not to things at all but, rather, to a bundle of rights. And this is obviously true of income titles, such as securities and annuities, and of rights of control over "intellectual property," such as patent rights and copyrights; these are "things" only in a very abstract sense, as characteristic complexes of normative relations.

As the objects of property are diverse, so also are the rights constituting it. Landowners' rights are necessarily different from copyright owners', and the owner of a gun does not have the same unrestricted use and control of it as the owner of a table has of the table. Jurists have nevertheless tried to identify some right necessary to ownership. The rights of exclusive use, possession, or alienation seem to be likely candidates, but each can conceivably be detached (for example, by a lease or an easement, under the terms of a trust, or, in former times, by entail) without the owner's losing property in the object. Accordingly, Sir Frederick Pollock suggested that "we must look for the person having the residue of all such powers when we have accounted for every detached and limited portion of it." But this residue, as held, say, by a ground landlord with a thousand-year tenant, may be very slender indeed, and the owner to whom all the detached rights will revert when the encumbrances reach the end of their term will certainly not be the present owner.

A. M. Honoré suggests a way out of these difficulties by concentrating not on the difficult exceptions but on the standard instance. He defines ownership as "those legal rights, duties and other incidents which apply, in the ordinary case, to the person who has the greatest interest in a thing admitted by a mature legal system." Among the characteristic features are the right to possess and to be secure in possession, to use and to manage the property, to enjoy income arising from it and to alienate, consume, waste, or destroy the capital, and to transmit ownership to one's successors indefinitely; the absence of a fixed date on which the owners' interests terminate; the prohibition of harmful use; the liability of the property to execution for debt or insolvency; and the reversion to the owner on the termination of whatever lesser interests (leases, usufructs) encumber the property. Now, to say that *A* is the owner of *x* is not necessarily to say that he is the present subject of all these incidents; however, provided the kind of property in question can intelligibly be said to be the object of them and in the absence of special conditions or reservations, it is reasonable to infer that he is.

The Scandinavian legal realists—Karl Olivecrona and Alf Ross, for example—have been more radical in their analyses. According to Ross, ownership is "solely . . . a tool in presentation." Theoretically, one could enunciate a mass of directives to judges, each consisting of a conditioning fact or facts (*F*) and a legal consequence (*C*), such as (1) if a person has lawfully purchased a thing (F_1), judgment for recovery of possession should be given in his favor (C_1); (2) if a person by prescription has acquired a thing and raised a loan that is unpaid (F_2), the creditor should be given judgment for satisfaction out of the thing (C_2); and so on. Now, to introduce "ownership" is not, according to Ross, to add something that *accounts* for the connections between the F's and the C's but merely to indicate the systematic connection between them such that F_1, F_2, F_3, $\cdots$, F_p severally and collectively entail the totality of legal consequences C_1, C_2, C_3, $\cdots$, C_n. The word "ownership" in Ross's view is "without any semantic reference whatever"; it serves only to reduce the complexity of particular rules to a systematic order. There is nothing beyond or in addition to the rules.

Now, it is certainly true that only confusion can result from trying to identify some special kind of a thing, or some special quality of things, which is called "property." Nevertheless, "ownership" does not always imply the same bundle of rights. The possible conditioning facts and the legal consequences are not the same for every case in which one may say that X is the owner of P. And, therefore, since the relevant rules do not have the rigorous relation to one another that Ross suggests, one can identify them as the rules of property (as distinct from, say, personal rights) only by recognizing some sort of family resemblances between them. Indeed, the terms Ross uses in exemplifying his conditioning facts—"purchase," "occupation of *res nullius*," "acquisition by prescription"—are obviously already impregnated with ownership; to purchase something, for example, is to give money for it—that is, on the understanding that one acquires not merely possession, but also owners' rights, over it.

Deciding who is the owner of a piece of property is, of course, to decide on the basis of certain facts where certain powers and liabilities lie. But to reduce a legal concept like property to a finite set of directives to judges ignores the fact that judges are constantly having to reshape the rules in the very process of applying them. If the rules of ownership are treated as a more or less arbitrary agglomeration, it is difficult to see how judges could make rational decisions at all.

Ross's bundle of conditioning facts and legal consequences is significant, however, because it suggests how one goes about constructing a paradigm case of ownership, or, rather, a family of paradigms related by the fact that different conditioning facts entail broadly similar legal consequences. Deciding ownership in an atypical case would then involve deciding whether it can be assimilated to any of the available paradigms even though some characteristic ownership features are absent or other features that are out of character are present. A judge may have all kinds of reasons for making or refusing such an assimilation; but it is difficult to see how the problem could be presented to him at all without presupposing the standard cases of ownership as agreed starting points for discussion.

Bibliography

Dias, R. W. M., *A Bibliography of Jurisprudence*. London, 1964. Extensive annotated bibliography, mainly from the juristic standpoint.

GENERAL HISTORIES

Bartlett, J. V., and others, eds., *Property, Its Duties and Rights*. London, 1915.

Grace, Frank, *The Concept of Property in Modern Christian Thought*. Urbana, Ill., 1953.

Macpherson, C. B., *The Political Theory of Possessive Individualism: Hobbes to Locke*. Oxford, 1962.

Schlatter, Richard, *Private Property: The History of an Idea*. London, 1951.

CLASSICAL THEORIES

Hegel, G. W. F., *Grundlinien der Philosophie des Rechts*. Berlin, 1821. Translated, with notes, by T. M. Knox as *Hegel's Philosophy of Right*. Oxford, 1942.

Hume, David, *Treatise of Human Nature* (1640), L. A. Selby-Bigge, ed., 2d ed. Oxford, 1896.

Locke, John, *Two Treatises of Government* (1690), Peter Laslett, ed. Cambridge, 1960.

Marx, Karl, *Critique of the Gotha Programme*, in *Karl Marx and Friedrich Engels: Selected Works*, 2 vols. Moscow, 1949–1951. Vol. II.

Marx, Karl, "Oekonomisch-philosophische Manuskripte aus dem Jahre 1844," in D. Riazanovsky and A. Adoratski, eds., *Marx–Engels Gesamtausgabe*, Berlin, 1932. Part I, Vol. III. Edited and translated by T. B. Bottomore as "Economic and Philosophical Manuscripts" in *Karl Marx: Early Writings*. London, 1963.

Mill, J. S., *Principles of Political Economy*, 7th ed. London, 1871.

ECONOMIC AND SOCIAL SIGNIFICANCE

Berle, A. A., "Property, Production and Revolution." *Columbia Law Review*, Vol. 65, No. 1 (1965), 1–20.

Berle, A. A., and Means, G. C., *The Modern Corporation and Private Property*. New York, 1933.

Duguit, Léon, *Les Transformations générales du droit privé*. Paris, 1912.

Durkheim, Émile, *Leçons de sociologie physique des moeurs et du droit*. Paris, 1950. Translated by Cornelia Brookfield as *Professional Ethics and Civic Morals*. London, 1957.

Renner, Karl, *Die Rechtsinstitute des Privatrechts und ihre soziale Funktion*. Tübingen, 1929. Translated by Anges Schwarzschild as *The Institutions of Private Law*, Otto Kahn-Freund, ed. London, 1949.

ANALYSIS OF OWNERSHIP

Honoré, A. M., "Ownership," in A. G. Guest, ed., *Oxford Essays in Jurisprudence*. London, 1961.

Noyes, C. Reinold, *The Institution of Property*. New York, 1936.

Olivecrona, Karl, *Law as Fact*. London, 1939.

Pollock, Frederick, *Jurisprudence and Legal Essays*. London, 1961.

Ross, Alf, *On Law and Justice*. London, 1958.

Simpson, A. W. B., "The Analysis of Legal Concepts." *Law Quarterly Review*, Vol. 80 (October 1964), 535–558.

STANLEY I. BENN

PROPOSITIONS, JUDGMENTS, SENTENCES, AND STATEMENTS.

One of the most heatedly disputed questions in modern philosophy concerns whether there are propositions. Now, if we take the word "proposition" in its ordinary, nonphilosophical senses, there are obviously propositions, for it is a fact that there are propositions in mathematics textbooks which are to be demonstrated and propositions about which debaters argue. But, and this cannot be emphasized enough, the propositions for whose existence philosophers have argued are not of these common sorts. What, then, are these "propositions," and what function do they serve? These questions must be answered in reverse order since we cannot understand the nature and status of these propositions unless we first understand why certain philosophers have considered it necessary to introduce them.

As Gilbert Ryle has pointed out in his article "The Theory of Meaning," the necessity for introducing propositions is a result of two intimately related theoretical assumptions, one in philosophical psychology and the other in logic, which are shared by most philosophers of a realistic bent: (1) the theory of the intentionality of consciousness, requiring that every mental act be directed toward some object, and (2) the theory of meaning as naming, the meaning of an expression being the object named by it.

Theories (1) and (2) are intimately connected in that, as we shall see, it is one and the same *abstract* object, called a "proposition," that serves as both the intentional object of a mental act and the meaning of the sentence formulating this act. By upholding the objectivity and independence of the objects about which we think and speak, both theories are in opposition to the subjectivism of idealism and British empiricism. In spite of these convergent results they are distinct theories involving different theoretical assumptions, so that one could, without inconsistency, hold one of these theories and reject the other. For ease and clarity of exposition and critical evaluation of these theories they will be discussed separately. It will be seen that many philosophers of a nominalistic bent, who have assigned a more mundane status to the proposition, identifying it with a complex of empirical objects, mental images, or word complexes, and so on, have nevertheless accepted the basic assumptions of (1) and/or (2).

PROPOSITIONS AS INTENTIONAL OBJECTS OF MENTAL ACTS

Dyadic-relation theory of judgment. Franz Brentano claimed that all acts of consciousness are directed toward an object and called this directedness the intentional relation. To think, fear, or doubt is to think, fear, or doubt something. We shall call such verbs as "think," "believe," "judge," "guess," "hope," "wish," "fear," and the like propositional verbs, and the mental acts which they supposedly signify we shall call propositional acts or attitudes. It is a grammatical fact that such verbs can, and often do, take as their subject a pronoun or proper noun and as their accusative a noun "that" clause. The propositional acts or attitudes signified by these verbs are mental acts involving a dyadic relation between a subjective constituent consisting of the subject's mind and an objective constituent consisting of the complex entity named by the noun "that" clause. That this objective constituent, which we shall call a proposition, is other than the propositional act of which it is the accusative can be seen from the fact that we can say things about the one which cannot be said about the other—for example, my mental act of believing that Socrates wore a toga is an episode forming part of my mental history and occurs in 1964, whereas the fact that Socrates wore a toga is not part of my mental act of believing and does not occur in 1964. Judgment, like belief, has a double

sense in that it can mean either the act of judging or believing or that which is judged or believed.

Moreover, this objective constituent or proposition is not only other than, but also independent of, propositional acts. The following three arguments have been advanced to support this conclusion (see Ryle's "Are There Propositions?").

(1) There are three forms of the argument based upon the operation with identity.

(*a*) The publicity of our judgment requires that the content of different judgments be identical. Several persons can make the same judgment not in the logically impossible sense that their mental acts are numerically one but in the sense that what is judged in these different acts is identical. If there were no objective propositions common to different judgments, communication and science would be impossible.

(*b*) Because a person can think the same thing several times, there must be a temporally neutral proposition which is the common accusative of these acts. If there were no such temporally neutral propositions, a person could neither agree nor disagree with what he had previously believed.

(*c*) One person can have different propositional attitudes toward the same proposition at different times, and several persons can have different propositional attitudes toward the same proposition at the same and also at different times. Thus, propositions are neutral between different propositional attitudes.

(2) Independent propositions are required to account for the incompatibility between propositional acts. Propositional acts qua mental acts cannot be logically incompatible. As mental acts they are events, and events cannot be incompatible with one another. Therefore, the incompatibility between your belief that Socrates wore a toga and my belief that he did not must be between the propositions which serve as the objective constituents of our beliefs.

(3) The objective and timeless nature of truths and falsehoods requires that there be propositions which are timelessly true or false independent of their relation to propositional acts. There are objective truths in the formal and empirical sciences—for example, the Pythagorean theorem, that 2 plus 2 is 4, the law of gravity, that Columbus discovers America in 1492—which are discovered and not created by our minds. Moreover, these truths are timeless, not becoming true at the time we discover them or ceasing to be true when we no longer think about them. The propositional acts directed toward these propositions form part of the mental biographies of persons and so are necessarily dated. Therefore, these acts must be visitors to an independent realm of timeless truths and falsehoods. Propositions, then, as timeless truths and falsehoods are independent of acts and are in no sense a product of, or dependent upon, these acts, as a conceptualist might contend.

Thus far we have presented arguments to show the necessity for introducing objective propositions to serve as the intentional objects of propositional acts, but we have said nothing about their nature and ontological status. The defenders of the proposition theory are more clear as to what propositions are not than what they are. We are told that they are not sentences, images, or facts. Certainly, what I believe when I believe that Socrates was Greek is not a string of words or a psychical content of my mind. Nor can facts be the object of propositional acts, for it is all too sad a fact that such acts often have no factual accusatives, desires and wishes often go unfulfilled, and judgments often are false. But there must be some object for these unfortunate acts; otherwise, we would be desiring and judging nothing and therefore not desiring or judging at all. To account for erroneous judgments, we must find some nonfactual complex to serve as the object of judgment, just as, analogously, in order to account for erroneous sense perceptions, it was deemed necessary to introduce sense data. Since the object of a false judgment must be a proposition and since there is no intrinsic difference between a true and false judgment, it follows that the direct object of all judgments must be propositions. To answer the questions concerning the nature and status of these propositions, we shall now consider the views of the leading proponents of this theory, noting their similarities and differences.

Moore. G. E. Moore's theory of judgment developed in the course of his criticism of the idealist theory of judgment as an operation performed on ideas. In judgment, according to the idealists, we use some psychical content of our minds to signify or refer to reality. For Benno Erdmann and Christoph Sigwart it was the psychical content itself which is so used, whereas for F. H. Bradley and Bernard Bosanquet it was an abstracted part of it. For Bradley this abstracted content was predicated of reality as a whole, whereas for Bosanquet it was predicated of that fragment of reality with which we are in immediate contact. It was Bradley's definition of judgment as "the act which refers an ideal content (recognized as such) to a reality beyond the act" which served as Moore's immediate jumping-off-place. He claimed that Bradley had not successfully exorcised the ghost of Locke's ideas, for Bradley's definition is ambiguous, being either about what ideas mean or the idea as a psychic phenomenon. Is it the symbol or what is symbolized which is the content of judgment? For Moore it is an objective concept, having what Bradley called a "universal meaning," which is somehow attached to the psychic content or symbol. A concept is similar to a Platonic Idea, being eternal and immutable. In judgment two or more such concepts are joined to form a complex concept, this complex being the proposition. If I judge that there are unicorns, the concept of unicorn is joined to the concept of existence, and this complex subsists eternally, regardless of its truth-value and its being thought of by anyone.

A fact is nothing but a true proposition, truth being a simple, unanalyzable, intuitable property belonging to some propositions and not to others. All knowledge, even knowledge by sense perception, is nothing but cognition of a proposition. Propositions are timelessly true or false; judgments are true or false only in the derivative sense of having as their accusative a true or false proposition. These propositions or complex concepts serve as the objective accusatives of propositional acts, as required by the above three arguments. The relations which propositions have to

these acts are external and therefore do not alter their essential nature.

To establish the objectivity of propositions, Moore used an argument which parallels that used in his famed "Refutation of Idealism" (1903; in *Philosophical Studies,* London, 1922). There he argued that a preception of green qua conscious act of perceiving is not distinguishable from a perception of yellow but can be distinguished from it only in terms of a difference in the objective content of these perceptions. Similarly, he argued, a judgment (for example, that Socrates wore a toga) does not differ qua mental act of judging from another judgment (for example, that he wore a motorcycle jacket) but can be distinguished from it only in terms of a difference in their objective content—that is, what is judged or apprehended in these judgments.

Moore later attempted to get rid of such propositions but came to grief on the problem of false judgments.

> In order that a relation may hold between two things, both the two things must certainly be; and how then is it possible for any one to believe in a thing which simply has no being? This is the difficulty which seems to arise if you say that false belief does not consist merely in a relation between the believer . . . and something else which certainly *is*. . . . And I confess I do not see any clear solution of the difficulty. (*Some Main Problems of Philosophy,* p. 263)

Russell. Bertrand Russell followed Moore on all essential points. He used the word "term" in place of Moore's "concept" but meant the same thing by it. Propositions, then, are timeless complexes of terms, which possess a peculiar internal unity. False propositions, as well as true ones, have being, "since to be false a proposition must already be." Moreover, since false propositions, as well as true ones, logically imply one another, they must subsist eternally. Propositions serve the same function for Russell as they did for Moore, being the objective accusatives of propositional acts. "The object of a thought, even when this object does not exist, has a Being which is in no way dependent upon its being an object of thought." When we believe, we believe something: "The subsistence of the something . . . seems to follow from the fact that, if it did not subsist, I should be believing nothing, and therefore not believing" ("Meinong's Theory of Complexes and Assumptions," I, p. 510). It was this consideration which plagued Moore's attempt to dispense with propositions. Russell's four other theories of propositions and judgment will be discussed below.

Meinong. Alexius Meinong developed Brentano's doctrine of intentionality into a theory of objects. The objects of simple presentations, such as trees and horses, are said to exist or not to exist. But even nonexistent objects, such as unicorns and Santa Claus, seem to have some sort of being, for Meinong says that "there are objects of which it is true to say that there are no such objects." Judgment is the acceptance or rejection of a presentation. The objects of judgment are higher-order objects ("objectives"). Objectives are peculiar sorts of complex unities corresponding to the grammatical accusative of propositional verbs—that is, the noun "that" clause. Like numbers, they cannot be said to exist or not to exist but, rather, to be real (or subsist) or not to be real. Real objectives are those which are the case—in other words, which are facts. There can be real or subsistent objectives about nonexistent objects, even about objects whose existence is logically impossible. Objectives are said to be true when they have factuality and are the objects of a judgment.

Russell (in *Mind,* 1904) identified Meinong's objectives with his and Moore's propositions since both are abstract complex unities which have being whether true or false and are facts when true. This interpretation of Meinong has been challenged by Findlay in his book *Meinong's Theory of Objects* (pp. 83–86), but all he shows is that Meinong's objectives are not similar to propositions when these are defined as linguistic or psychological entities, not that they are not similar to the Platonic complexes of Moore and Russell. In his Introduction to *Realism and the Background of Phenomenology* Roderick M. Chisholm also questions Russell's interpretation because Meinong's objectives, unlike Russell's propositions, are not said to be real or have being when they are nonfactual. This difference, however, is only an apparent one and is due to a difference in terminology. If Meinong's nonfactual objectives do not possess some sort of being, how is it possible for them to play the role they do in his realistic philosophy as the objective accusatives of propositional acts? If Meinong did not intend to ascribe some sort of being to these objectives, he certainly used the most misleading language possible for stating his position. At any rate, it was the Meinong of Russell's interpretation who played such a prominent role in the history of philosophy and caused such furor. For these reasons we shall accept Russell's identification of objectives with propositions.

Husserl. In his *Logische Untersuchungen* (1900–1901) Edmund Husserl attacked psychologism, the doctrine that logic is based on empirical generalizations about how people think. Logic has for its subject matter a "third realm," composed of timeless meanings (nonphysical and nonmental essences) and propositions, which can serve as the independent objects of our intuitions. These intuitions are akin to knowledge by acquaintance and give us direct insight into these propositions and their relations. These semi-Platonic objects bear a strong family resemblance to Meinong's objectives. Husserl seemed to think of them as subsisting independently of our propositional acts, but in his later work he regarded them as intrinsic contents of such acts, thus departing radically from the extreme realism of Meinong, Moore, and Russell. Brentano also, in his later work, became a critic of extreme realism by rejecting his earlier doctrine that all mental acts have an object.

Stout. In accordance with the doctrine of intentionality, G. F. Stout claimed that what a person thinks of must have some reality of its own independent of its being thought of, for otherwise it could not be related to something else—namely, the person's thought. If we start with a disruption between our thoughts and reality, as representative theories do, there is no escaping from the prison of subjective ideas. In judgment the mind has before it a real object consisting of a complex which possesses a peculiar unity not found in a mere collection of objects. Stout, however, · assigned an ontological status to this complex different from that given it by the realistic philosophers previously mentioned. He claimed that it was a real possibility, relative to some actuality, inherent in the nature of things. In judgment the mind knows some determinate fact (for example, that there is a piece of paper in front of me) which is further determinable (the other side of this paper could have any one of the determinate shades of color), and it then selects one of these real possibilities as the actualized one. The alternative selected is a real possibility relative to the determinate fact and serves as the independent object of a judgment. A judgment is true if the alternative selected is identical with the realized possibility. It is hard to see how Stout's theory escapes the pitfalls of representative theories and also what the ontological status of an unrealized possibility is.

Multiple-relation theory of judgment. Although the dyadic-relation theory of judgment managed to find an intentional object for propositional acts and to answer the question "What is the object of a false judgment?," it left the status of propositions quite obscure. As it turns out, reality becomes an overcrowded slum, for it contains not only everything which is the case—facts—but also an infinite number of things which are not the case—nonfactual complexes. And this was more than the post-1904 Russell and others with a "robust sense of reality" were willing to stomach. Russell could no longer get himself to believe that in addition to facts, such as that Socrates was Greek, there are nonfactual entities, such as that Socrates was Chinese, that Socrates was an Eskimo, that Socrates was 10 feet tall, that Socrates was 11 feet tall, and so on. (It is interesting to note how an entire philosophical theory can be discarded merely because it is not in accord with our prephilosophical feelings of what is reasonable or plausible. This provoked Meinong to charge Russell with having a prejudice in favor of the actual.)

Russell's problem was this: Granted that propositional acts are intentional, can we find for these acts some object(s), other than propositions, that will not involve the absurdity of objective falsehoods? His answer was that a propositional act, such as judging, is a multiple relation which (1) has as its constituents a judging mind (the subject) and the elements of the proposition judged (the objects) and (2) which arranges them in a certain order. For example, Othello's belief that Desdemona loves Cassio has as its constituents *Othello* (the subject) and *Desdemona, loving,* and *Cassio* (the objects), which are cemented together in a particular order (in this case going from *Othello* to *Desdemona* to *loving* to *Cassio* rather than, say, from *Othello* to *Cassio* to *loving* to *Desdemona*) by the multiple relation of judging, so as to form a complex unity (the judgment complex). The judgment is true if there is a factual complex corresponding to the judgment complex in the sense that what are the objects in the judgment complex exist as a unity on their own and in the same order outside the judgment complex. If there is a factual complex consisting of Desdemona, loving, and Cassio and having the same order as these objects have in the judgment complex, then Othello's judgment is true; otherwise, it is false.

But how does this theory go beyond the dyadic theory in finding an intentional object for false judgments without positing the reality of false propositions? For Russell a judgment is meaningful only if the subject is acquainted with, has a direct cognitive relation to, the objects in the judgment complex. When Othello judged that Desdemona loved Cassio, he was acquainted with his Cartesian self, Desdemona, loves, and Cassio, each of which must therefore be an objective constituent of the judgment complex. Since Othello's judgment is meaningful, it must have as its intentional objects those real objects with which he is acquainted—*Desdemona, loves,* and *Cassio*—and this holds even if there is no factual complex consisting of Desdemona – loving – Cassio, in which case his judgment is false. The multiple-relation theory therefore differs from the dyadic-relation theory in giving us, instead of one internally complex object, several objects which may or may not exist as a unity outside of the judgment complex.

This theory, however, was not without its difficulties. First, Russell's analysis does not account for judgments with more than three objects in the proposition judged, nor does it account for cases in which this proposition is molecular. As Geach has pointed out in his book *Mental Acts* (p. 49), to overcome this difficulty, he would have to give some recursive procedure whereby the judging relations for more complex cases could be defined in terms of those for simpler cases.

Second, and more serious, his theory cannot account for the unity of the objects in the proposition judged. *Loves* is a constituent in the judgment complex consisting of Othello's belief that Desdemona loves Cassio, but in the factual complex it functions as a relation. How, then, can we say that the judgment complex corresponds to the factual complex? Moreover, since *loves* does not relate *Desdemona* to *Cassio* in the judgment complex, how can we explain the direction or sense which the objects have in the proposition judged—namely, that the direction is from Desdemona to loves to Cassio rather than vice versa? Russell's answer was that the mental act of judging places the objects in a certain order. But this is subject to all of the difficulties of the Kantian mental synthesis. Certainly, when I judge that John loves Mary, it is not my act of judging which places these objects in a certain order, whatever that could mean, for I believe that these particulars are related in a certain direction by the relation *loves* independently of my mental act. The elements constituting the proposition judged have a unity of their own. This can be seen by the fact that a judgment is formulated by a complete sentence having a peculiar internal unity and is not found in a mere collection of words. Russell is wrong, therefore, when he claims, "You cannot say when you believe, 'What is it that you believe?' There is no answer to that question, *i.e.*, there is not a single thing that you are believing." Furthermore, if the mind is successful in uniting the objects of the proposition judged into a unity having a certain direction, then what keeps this complex from being the factual complex, since all of its constituents have a reality of their own independent of the act of judging?

Psychological theory of propositions. Russell later acknowledged certain of these difficulties, but he was unable to resolve them. This, plus his growing doubts about the reality of the Cartesian subject, caused him to abandon the multiple-relation theory in favor of a psychological theory of propositions as complex images. When someone judges or believes something, there are (1) a complex image in his mind, (2) a sensation or feeling of belief, and (3) a relation subsisting between (1) and (2) consisting in the fact that the feeling of belief is connected with or directed toward the complex image.

Though Russell attempted to get rid of intentional mental acts by this theory, it is doubtful whether he succeeded. It seems that all he does is to give a different *object* for the mental event or act of judging or believing. Instead of saying that this object is a single abstract entity (the dyadic-relation theory) or a complex of empirical objects (the multiple-relation theory), he says that it is a psychical content (the complex image). This seems to be the meaning of condition (3) above, requiring that there be an actual relation between the feeling of belief and the psychical content. A further difficulty with this theory is its ultrasubjectivism. What does it mean to say that my belief has as its object a complex image in my mind? How can that be what I believe, except in cases where I am believing something about my own mind?

A proposition, in this theory, is true if it corresponds with or points toward a fact; it is false if it points away from this fact. Thus, contradictory propositions have the same fact as their objective—the fact by virtue of which one is true and the other false—but they have different relations to this objective. An image proposition (a complex image) can resemble or picture a factual complex, and in this respect it is superior to a word proposition (a sentence), for a word proposition contains one constituent too many—the word expressing the relation is an object in the word proposition but not in the factual complex.

Broad. C. D. Broad has attempted, within the framework of intentionality, a nominalistic solution to the problem of propositions. His theory, which is a synthesis of Stout's theory and the multiple-relation theory, claims that every belief is a complex state of affairs, in which we can distinguish the following factors: (1) acquaintance with some determinate fact whose subject or predicate is a determinable and lack of acquaintance with the more determinate fact in which this subject or predicate is specifically determined; (2) the same mind being acquainted with the fact that certain determinates of which it is thinking are specifications of this determinable; (3) the thought of one of these determinates' being marked out from the thoughts of the others by standing to the acts of acquaintance, already mentioned, in the special relation of being inserted in them. Broad holds that in a propositional act there must be some fact—a fact about a certain thought of the subject's being inserted in his acts of acquaintance— known by the mind. "In a judgment," Broad writes, "whether true or false, there really is a unique kind of complex object before the mind. But it is a fact, and not a proposition; it is known and not believed" (*Examination of McTaggart's Philosophy*, Vol. I, p. 76).

Behavioristic analysis. The evolution of Russell's theories of judgment from the dyadic through the multiple relation to the psychological represents a gradual shift toward behaviorism. He had always been fascinated by behaviorism but was unable to accept it, for he could not answer the objection to this theory that there could be conscious states of believing, desiring, and so on which resulted in no overt behavior. In his later work this objection did not appear insurmountable, and he attempted to work out a behavioristic analysis of judgment. A proposition is no longer said to be the object of a mental act, be it in the form of a single complex entity, a complex of empirical objects, or a complex of images or words; it is said to be nothing but the implicit behavior manifested by someone who believes it.

The main attraction of this analysis is that it answers the thorny question of how a sentence can be both meaningful and false. A sentence is meaningful if it is significant, and the significance of a sentence is nothing but the implicit behavior it causes in someone who accepts or believes it—that is, the physiological state of his organs, his readiness to perform certain actions, and so on. Different sentences can express or signify the same proposition in the sense that they produce similar physiological changes in persons who believe them. A sentence could be called true if the actions promoted by it in the believer are appropriate to the situation he is in. Russell saw difficulties with such an analysis and was still willing to allow for the existence of image propositions. The important point is that sentences signify something within the believer—either a physiological or psychological state—that accounts for meaningful false sentences.

The behavioristic analysis is very sketchy. We are to say that two persons believe the same proposition if their physiological (and/or psychological) states are similar in certain relevant respects. But what, exactly, are to count as relevant respects? A more basic objection is that the behavioristic reduction fails to get rid of mental acts, for in order to account for the different behavior manifested by two persons who believe the same proposition, considerations concerning differences in their desires or beliefs must be introduced.

Criticism. All of the theories of judgment and propositions considered thus far, with the exception of the behavioristic theory, have accepted the theory of intentionality, requiring that every propositional act be directed toward some object. They can be viewed as different answers to the same question, "What is the object of a judgment?," with the differences in these theories consisting in what sort of intentional object(s) they introduce. But if it can be shown, as we shall attempt to do now, that this question is meaningless, we shall have invalidated all of these theories, nominalistic as well as realistic.

It is important to distinguish between propositional verbs, such as "judge," "think," "believe," and so on, on the one hand, and what we shall call cognitive verbs, such as "know," "see," "hear," "feel," "taste," and "smell," on the other. The doctrine of intentionality, it will be argued, is based on the misleading surface grammatical analogy between these two types of verb—that both of them have grammatical accusatives. From this alone it would be wrong to assume that they must be alike in other relevant respects. Since there must be something in reality answering to or corresponding with the grammatical accusative of a cognitive verb, it seems to be assumed that the same must hold for a propositional verb, thus creating the pseudo question of what the object of a false judgment can be. One of the clearest examples of this confusion is found in Plato's *Theaetetus* (189A):

SOCRATES. And if he touches a thing, he touches something, and if something, then a thing that is.
THEAETETUS. That also is true.
SOCRATES. And if he thinks, he thinks something, doesn't he?
THEAETETUS. Necessarily.
SOCRATES. And when he thinks something, he thinks a thing that is?
THEAETETUS. Clearly.
SOCRATES. But surely to think nothing is the same as not to think at all.
THEAETETUS. That seems plain.
SOCRATES. If so, it is impossible to think what is not, either about anything that is, or absolutely.
THEAETETUS. Evidently.

Moore's analogy between judgment and sense perception rests on the same confusion. To dispel this misleading picture, which is rooted in an unfortunate grammatical analogy, we must investigate the "logical grammar," the rules or conventions controlling the use, of these two types of verb in order to see whether they behave the same way in all relevant respects.

One very significant difference between propositional and cognitive verbs is the fact that it is tautological to say, "If he *knows* (or *sees* and so on) that the cat is on the mat, then it is true that the cat is on the mat," whereas it is not tautological to say, "If he *judges* (or *believes* and so on) that the cat is on the mat, then it is true that the cat is on the mat." This is true because if one knows, sees, smells, hears, tastes, or feels something, it entails something which he knows, sees, and so on, whereas there need be no object of a propositional act. For this reason it is contradictory to say, "He *knows* that the cat is on the mat, and it is false that the cat is on the mat," whereas it is not contradictory to say, "He *judges* that the cat is on the mat, and it is false that the cat is on the mat."

Another important difference between propositional and cognitive verbs is that if we claim to know or see something and it turns out that we were mistaken, we withdraw our claim to know or see something, whereas there is no analogous way of our withdrawing our claim to have judged, believed, or thought something when it is discovered that such acts have no objects. For example, if I claim to see pink elephants on the wall and there are, in fact, no such beasts clinging to the wallpaper, I withdraw my cognitive claim to have seen something by saying, "Well, I only thought I saw (or it seemed to me then that I was seeing) pink elephants." To see something in a delusion is not to see something but merely to think that you are seeing something. But if a man erroneously judges or believes that there are pink elephants on the wall, we do not say that it only seemed or appeared to him then as if he were judging or believing something. To judge erroneously is nevertheless to judge, not just to think that you are judging.

But how can someone judge or believe without having a cognitive relation to something? As Russell pointed out in his multiple-relation theory, a judgment is meaningful only if the subject is acquainted with the objects of the proposition judged. This is ambiguous, meaning either (*a*) that in order to make a meaningful judgment, we had to have learned through sense experience the meaning of the words in which our judgment is formulated or (*b*) that at the time we make this judgment we must have a cognitive relation to these objects. The first alternative, which is a form of the empirical theory of meaning, may very likely be true, but it does nothing to establish the truth of the second alternative, that judgment involves a cognitive relation to objects at the time the judgment is made. Therefore, even if propositional acts presuppose prior cognitive experience, it does not follow that such acts are themselves cognitive, and evidence has been given to indicate that these acts are not cognitive in the sense of requiring objects.

The differences which we have pointed out in the logical grammar of propositional and cognitive verbs enable us to give a very simple answer to the question of how we can judge, believe, and the like something when there is nothing to serve as the object of these acts. We judge or believe because propositional verbs, unlike cognitive verbs, are used in such a way that there need not be anything *in rebus* answering to their grammatical accusatives. How is it possible for a horse not to win the Kentucky Derby? Very simply, because we use the word "horse" in such a way that what it designates need not be the winner of the Kentucky Derby. *That is the way we use these words.* There is no deeper mystery involved in the case of propositional verbs than in the case of horses if the above analysis is correct; for this reason there is no need to introduce Platonic complexes or anything else to serve as the object of propositional acts.

PROPOSITIONS AS MEANINGS OF SENTENCES

Even if the preceding argument is successful in disposing of propositions as intentional objects of mental acts, it in no way discredits the second theoretical assumption—the theory of meaning as naming—which has necessitated the introduction of abstract propositions. It is claimed that the meaning of a sentence is a semi-Platonic proposition which also doubles as the intentional object of a propositional act. Whereas the theory of intentionality claimed that a propositional act is a relation between a subject and a proposition, this theory claims that meaning is a relation between a sentence and such a proposition. Before considering this theory in detail, we shall consider the criticisms which its proponents have made of certain rival theories concerning the nature of sentences and propositions.

Nominalists identify a proposition with a declarative sentence in some language. By a sentence we mean a sentence-token, a concrete series of ink marks on a piece of paper or noises made on some occasion. The difficulty with this identification is that the things which we can say about a sentence cannot meaningfully be said about a proposition, indicating that they are two distinct things. A sentence is in a particular language, is so many inches long, in ink or chalk, but none of these things can be predicated of a proposition. Moreover, different sentences, whether in the same or in different languages, can have the same meaning and express the same proposition—for example, "Time flies" and "Tempus fugit." Thus, we must distinguish between the sentence, or sign vehicle, and its meaning. A more adequate definition of a proposition, originally offered by Boethius, is that a proposition is a declarative sentence taken with its meaning. It is possible for two instances (or tokens) of the same sentence type to have different meanings and thus express different propositions—for example, "I am hot" (uttered by two different persons). But this definition still has the undesirable consequence that a difference in sentences involves a difference in propositions even if the sentences mean the same thing—for example, "Jack is taller than John" and "John is shorter than Jack."

To overcome the inconvenience of having a proposition depend on the particular form of words used, the notion of a mental proposition and, later, of a judgment was developed. Ockham and later Scholastics distinguished, as did Aristotle, between spoken, written, and mental propositions. The written proposition means the spoken, and this in turn means the mental proposition. All written or spoken propositions thus presuppose mental propositions. Ockham did not raise the question of whether mental propositions do not equally involve spoken or written propositions. Post-Scholastic logicians defined a proposition as judgment, which is the mental act of assent or dissent. It was later defined as the verbal expression of a judgment. The trouble with mental propositions and judgments is that they make propositions subjective. To make propositions dependent on a psychic content is just as undesirable as making them dependent upon a particular language. As Alonzo Church has said:

> For some purposes at least there is needed a more abstract notion, independent alike of any particular expression in words and of any particular psychological act of judgment or conception—not the particular declarative sentence, but the content of meaning which is common to the sentence and its translation into another language—not the particular judgment, but the objective content of the judgment, which is capable of being the common property of many. ("Propositions," *Encyclopaedia Britannica*)

This common content of meaning is called an abstract proposition by Church.

This abstract sense of proposition goes back to the Stoic *lekta* ("meanings") and the *complexe significabilia* of the fourteenth- and fifteenth-century Scholastics. This notion fell into oblivion until 1837, when Bolzano reintroduced the distinction between the sentence (*Satz*) and the abstract proposition (*Satz an sich*) which it expresses. Bolzano claimed that this distinction was anticipated by Leibniz in his *Dialogus de Connexione Inter Res et Verba et Veritatis Realitate* and *Nouveaux Essais,* Book IV, Ch. 5, but this is doubtful, for whereas Leibniz held that there can be truths which no one knows, he nevertheless claimed that the property of being true belongs to possible thoughts or signs.

Frege. It was in the work of Gottlob Frege that the notion of the abstract proposition received its most articulate and searching analysis. Like Meinong, Husserl, and Russell, he was intent on establishing the objectivity of the empirical and formal sciences and, in particular, saving logic and mathematics from the combined empiricism and psychologism of J. S. Mill. Toward this end Frege made a careful distinction between (1) the sentence which is uttered or written, (2) the mental idea(s) accompanying it, and (3) the *Gedanke* (usually translated as "proposition" or "thought") which the sentence expresses. Ideas are subjective and private, but the proposition or thought is not, having no bearer or owner. It is an abstract entity similar to numbers and classes and enjoys the same sort of reality as a Platonic Idea. Frege spoke of it as belonging to a "third realm"—a timeless order of nonphysical and nonmental objects. When we understand a sentence, we apprehend the proposition it expresses; it is this which is the common content of meaning of synonymous sentences, whether in the same or in different languages. Propositions are true or false; sentences are true or false only in the derivative sense of expressing a true or false proposition. A true proposition is a fact.

A sentence, in addition to expressing a proposition, which Frege calls its sense (*Sinn*), also has a reference or denotation (*Bedeutung*), which is a truth-value or the circumstance that it is true or false. All true sentences have the same reference—the true—even though they may differ in sense, and, similarly, all false propositions have the same reference—the false. Frege's distinction between sense and reference is in some ways similar to Mill's distinction between connotation and denotation. What is unusual in Frege's treatment of sentences is his claim that they are names, which, like any name, have both a sense and a reference. His analogy between a sentence and a name becomes strained when one looks for the reference or denotation of a sentence. In making the reference of a sentence a truth-value, he did not make clear just what sort of an entity it is. If by the truth-value of a sentence he meant the circumstance that it is true or false, then he is inconsistent in saying that all true sentences have the same reference, for the circumstance "that Socrates was a Greek is true" differs from the circumstance "that Socrates was snub-nosed is true."

The motive behind Frege's rather strained analogy is his concern with developing an extensional logic. If two terms have the same reference, one can be substituted for the other in any sentence in which it appears without altering the truth-value of this sentence, and this holds even when these terms differ in sense. Sentences are analogous to terms in that if two sentences have the same reference (truth-value), one can be substituted for the other in any molecular sentence in which it appears without altering the truth-value of this molecular sentence, and this holds even when these sentences differ in sense. There are, however, certain nonextensional contexts—for example, sentences containing propositional verbs with a subordinate noun "that" clause—in which the truth-value of a sentence is not a function of or dependent upon the truth-value of the sentence appearing in the subordinate clause. For example, the truth-value of the belief sentence

"Copernicus believed that the planetary orbits are circles" is not a function of the truth of the sentence "The planetary orbits are circles"; if we substitute for it a sentence having the same truth-value but a different sense—for example, "The planets are made of pasta"—we cannot be sure that we shall not alter the truth-value of the whole belief sentence. Also, we could substitute for the sentence in the subordinate clause a different sentence having the same sense without altering the truth-value of the belief-sentence—"Copernicus believed that the orbits of the planets are circular." Frege handled such nonextensional contexts by making the reference of the sentence used in the subordinate clause the proposition it expresses—that is, what would be its sense in an extensional context. But a sentence, like any other name, cannot have a reference unless it has a sense. Frege claimed that the sense of a sentence when used nonextensionally is the sense of the words "The proposition that. . . ." What this could mean is far from clear.

Church. Frege's most faithful follower is Church. His main contribution has been his attack on the nominalistic treatment of sentences containing propositional verbs. He has attempted to show that these sentences must be analyzed in terms of Frege's abstract propositions. In order to prove that the object of a propositional act is a proposition, Church considers the way in which belief sentences are translated from one language into another. When we translate "I believe that he is here" into German, we translate the entire sentence into German—"Ich glaube er ist hier." But if the object of my belief were a sentence—for instance, "I believe the sentence 'He is here'"—then when we translate this, we would not translate the portion of the sentence within single quotation marks—"Ich glaube den Satz 'He is here.'" Since belief sentences are not translated in this manner, it follows that a proposition rather than a sentence is the object of a belief or other propositional act. These considerations show that we must distinguish a sentence from the abstract proposition it expresses. Thus, Church reaches the same conclusion as Frege, that the reference of a sentence in a nonextensional context is its meaning or sense. Attempts have been made by Israel Scheffler and W. V. Quine to meet Church's argument.

Carnap. In Carnap's *Introduction to Semantics* a sentence is said to designate a proposition, this term being identified by Carnap with Bolzano's "Satz an sich," Meinong's "objektiv," and Wittgenstein's "state of affairs" in the *Tractatus*. In a later work, *Meaning and Necessity*, Carnap developed a semantic method in which all terms, including sentences, are given both an intension and extension, which corresponds roughly to Frege's distinction between sense and reference. The extension of a sentence is a truth-value, and its intension is the proposition it expresses, which is something objective. But how can a false proposition be an objective entity when it is neither itself a fact nor exemplified by a fact? To answer this, Carnap draws an analogy between the property expressed by a complex predicator (name) and the proposition expressed by a sentence. A complex predicator, such as "golden mountain," has an objective property as its intension even though it is not exemplified by any individual; this is true because its components, "golden" and "mountain," do express properties which are so exemplified. "Analogously, the fact that some sentences are false does not exclude the explication of propositions as objective entities. Propositions, like complex properties, are complex entities; even if their ultimate components are exemplified, they themselves need not be" (p. 30). The difficulty with this solution, as Ryle pointed out in his review of *Meaning and Necessity,* is that it assimilates saying to referring (mentioning or denoting) and is therefore unable, in the same way as was the multiple-relation theory, to account for the peculiar internal unity of the sentence used to express a proposition. To say "Desdemona loves Cassio" is not just to mention three things—Desdemona, loves, and Cassio; that would be a mere laundry list.

Unlike Frege and Church, Carnap does not draw any Platonic metaphysical conclusions from his theory of meaning. In fact, he claims that the Platonist–nominalist controversy turns on the pseudo question "Do abstract entities exist?" In "Empiricism, Semantics, and Ontology" Carnap distinguishes between internal and external questions of existence. Internal questions of existence are answered by reference to some framework and, depending upon the nature of this framework, can be settled by either empirical or logical considerations. Questions concerning the existence of propositions can be answered by reference to some framework; if one adopts a language having a rule of meaning that gives an intension and extension to every term, then it is trivially true that they exist. External questions of existence are not theoretical; they are really practical questions concerning the pragmatic justification of adopting some particular framework.

Lewis. C. I. Lewis has also treated propositions as terms, which, like all terms, must have an intension and an extension. The intension of a proposition is an assertible content capable of signifying a state of affairs. The extension of a proposition is the actual world or it is empty. "All *true* propositions have the same extension, namely, this actual world; and all *false* propositions have the same extension, namely, zero-extension" ("The Modes of Meaning," in *Semantics and the Philosophy of Language,* p. 56). This is not too great a deviation from Frege in that the distinctive extensional property of a proposition is its truth-value. Lewis' rather paradoxical doctrine is similar to Bradley's because it means that the only particular having any properties is the whole universe. C. A. Baylis has revised Lewis' theory in order to bring it more into accord with common-sense beliefs. He draws a distinction between concrete and abstract states of affairs, assigning the former to the extension of (true) propositions and the latter to their intension. A proposition is true of those facts or concrete states of affairs which exemplify it; a false proposition, since it characterizes no fact, has a zero extension.

Criticisms. There are two main types of criticism that have been made to the theory of propositions as meanings of sentences: (1) propositions are redundant and therefore unnecessary and (2) meaning is not a relation between a sign and an object.

Propositions are redundant. Nominalists have tried to show the redundancy of propositions by analyzing them in terms of sentences, an example of which is Russell's anal-

ysis of a proposition as being a logical construction out of a class of synonymous sentences. This does not mean that a proposition is a collection of sentences but, rather, that to speak about a given proposition is a way of saying something, though not quite the same thing, about certain sentences. In *An Inquiry Into Meaning and Truth* Russell claimed that a proposition is what a sentence signifies. "We can make sure of *some* meaning for the word 'proposition' by saying that . . . it shall mean 'The class of all sentences having the same significance as a given sentence' " (pp. 208–209).

The difficulty with a nominalistic reduction of propositions to sentences, such as the above, is that in its analysis it must make use of the concept of two sentences either having the same significance (meaning the same thing) or being synonymous, two concepts which, a realist would contend, cannot be analyzed except in terms of abstract meanings—propositions. To date, no purely nominalistic analysis of these concepts has been successful.

Meaning is not a relation. Probably the most significant criticisms which have been made of the proposition theory concern the adequacy of the theory of meaning upon which it is based—that is, that meaning is a relation between a word or sentence, on the one hand, and its extension and intension, on the other. We have seen the difficulties and obscurities connected with the attempt to determine the extension or reference of a sentence and shall now concentrate on the question concerning the sense or intensional meaning of a sentence. Is it, as claimed by the proposition theory, a relation between a sentence and an abstract entity?

Several philosophers, among whom are Austin, Ayer, and Hampshire, have doubted the propriety of the question "What is the meaning of a sentence in general (no particular sentence)?," the question which the proposition theory answers. Their reason is that there is no one thing which all sentences mean, any more than there is any one thing that all words mean. Usually, when a speaker is asked what he means by some sentence, it is a request for him to make more explicit just what he is suggesting. If I say, "The building is inadequate," you might ask me, "How do you mean?" Am I talking about its size, its structure, or what? The question is sometimes prompted by the hearer's not knowing the meaning of a word in the sentence or understanding the grammatical construction of the sentence. Such a question, when raised in regard to a specific sentence, can be answered with another sentence which contains more familiar words or has a simpler grammatical construction. If such a procedure is not feasible, we could answer the question by pointing to something which the sentence in question would properly be used to describe. However, neither the method of giving a synonymous sentence nor pointing could be used to answer the question of what a sentence in general means. Since the question is in principle unanswerable, it is not a meaningful question. The question is the result of an illicit generalization—since we can ask for the meaning of any specific sentence, it is assumed that we can ask for the meaning of a sentence in general.

Those who ask for the meaning of a sentence in general assume that meaning is a relation between two things. It is assumed that a sentence is a name and that its meaning is the object named by it, just as, to use Ryle's example, Fido is the meaning of the name "Fido." But, as pointed out previously in our criticisms of the multiple-relation theory and Carnap, a sentence is used to say something, not just to mention or name some thing(s). A noun "that" clause or participial phrase can indeed be used as the subject or predicate term of a sentence, but when so used, it says nothing that is true or false; it merely does or does not refer successfully to some event or state of affairs. If "meaning something" is a "relation expression," how can a false sentence have a meaning? Someone who accepts this theory of meaning would have to say that a false sentence is only a quasi symbol, an unfortunate consequence which Ryle was led to accept in his very early paper "Are There Propositions?" (p. 121).

Meaning as use. To overcome the difficulties of the theory of meaning as naming, Wittgenstein, in his later writings, developed a theory of meaning based upon the use of an expression. His slogan "Don't ask for the meaning, ask for the use" cautioned philosophers not to look for the entity named by some expression but to see how it is used in various contexts, what its role or function is. Learning the meaning of an expression is learning how to operate with it, just as learning the meaning of the king in chess is learning what moves can be made with it. The meaning of an expression is contained in the rules or conventions controlling what can and cannot be said, asked, commanded, and so on with it. Ryle, in drawing out the implications of this theory, wrote: "If the meaning of an expression is not an entity denoted by it, but a style of operation performed with it, not a nominee but a role, then it is not only repellent but positively misleading to speak as if there existed a Third Realm whose denizens are Meanings" ("The Theory of Meaning," pp. 262–263).

It remains to be seen whether the Wittgensteinian use theory of meaning is successful in disposing of abstract propositions. A realist would argue that we must distinguish between the description of the use of a sentence and what is said by someone who uses this sentence on some occasion, this being the abstract proposition. For example, the description of the use of the sentence "It is now raining" states that this sentence is used to report an occurrence of rain in the vicinity of the speaker that is simultaneous with his utterance. But this is certainly not what someone says or states when he utters this sentence; he says that it is raining, not that the sentence "It is raining" is used to report. . . . To say the latter is to describe a move in the fact-stating language game, but it is not itself a move in the fact-stating game, for it asserts nothing about the weather. Not only must we distinguish the what-is-said or what-is-stated in a declarative speech act from the description of the use of the sentence employed in this speech act but also from the uttering of the sentence, the uttering of the sentence on that occasion, the sentence-token produced in this speech act, and so on. (For a far more detailed list see Richard Cartwright's "Propositions.") What is said—that it is raining—has no position in space or time and has no owner; however, these things can meaningfully be said about the linguistic event consisting in the uttering of the sentence on that occasion and the sentence-token produced. Moreover, there is a difference in arithmetic between the what-is-said and the particular sayings of it. There can be several different sayings (several different declarative speech acts) but only one what-is-said in these different sayings. Therefore, the what-is-said (or -stated) is an abstract entity that is quite distinct from and independent of declarative speech acts.

This new argument for abstract propositions based on the conceptual distinction between saying something and the what-is-said might be countered by calling into question its underlying assumption, that corresponding to every conceptual distinction there must be in reality two distinct and separate things. It is argued that because there is a conceptual distinction between saying something and what is said, which is borne out by the fact that we cannot meaningfully say and ask the same things about both of them, there must therefore be in reality two quite distinct and separate things—the declarative speech act and the what-is-said (the abstract meaning or proposition). That this assumption is false can be seen by the numerous exceptions to it; for instance, there are not in reality two separate and distinct things answering to the conceptual distinction between a body's shape and color or between dancing and the dance that is done. Just as there is a difference in arithmetic between speech acts and what is said in these acts, so, too, there is a difference in arithmetic between dancing and the dance that is done. Several people can be dancing the same dance—the waltz, for example.

To make the argument work, the realist must show that "say" and "state" are genuine dyadic relations between two distinct and separate things. The question of whether "say" or "state" is a dyadic relation between two things gets down to what sort of logical grammar the verb "say" or "state" has. Is it that of a propositional verb or that of a cognitive verb and other verbs, such as "meet" and "hit," that unquestionably do signify a relation between two distinct things? "Say" and "state" obviously do have the same logic as a propositional verb in that their correct use does not require that there be anything in reality answering to their grammatical accusative, as is the case for cognitive verbs and verbs like "meet." To misstate something is not a case of just thinking that you are making a statement or of its seeming to you then as if you were making a statement. The accusatives of such propositional verbs as "judge" and "say" are internal, just as "waltz" is an internal accusative to "dance" in "She is dancing the waltz." Cognitive verbs take external accusatives.

But, it might be asked, how can someone say or state what is not the case, since what we say or state is always a fact? This question is based on a confusion between (1) "He stated it as a fact" or "He made a factual assertion" and (2) "He stated a fact." Both (1) sentences indicate the particular use he made of language, the function which his utterance was intended to fulfill, whereas (2) says that his utterance was successful in fulfilling this function. If one overlooks the difference between (1) and (2), he could find a great paradox in a theater critic's review which began, "Last night a comedy, *Catch a Duck*, opened at the Baronet, and all I can say is that it wasn't the least bit comical," or with a sportscaster who said, "The blocking back for State has missed all of his blocks today." By saying that a play is a comedy or a football player is a blocking back, we are identifying their intended functions and are not thereby claiming that they are successful in achieving these functions. Similarly, when we say that a person stated something as a fact, we are identifying the particular function of his utterance and are not thereby saying that he was successful, that he actually stated a fact.

If it is true that "say" and "state" have the logic of a propositional verb, then it follows that saying or stating something is not a dyadic relation between two separate and distinct things. There is only one thing, the declarative speech act, and the what-is-said is a conceptually discernible aspect of this linguistic event. If this is so, we may conclude that the nominalists were right in denying the independent reality of abstract propositions but wrong in thinking that these propositions could be analyzed in terms of sentence-tokens or utterances of a sentence-token. The logic of cognitive verbs and verbs like "meet" licenses us to speak of their accusatives as existing outside of the relation; the existence of the accusative does not depend on its being a term in the relation. But the logic of a propositional verb is such that we cannot speak of its accusative, in the case of "say" it being the what-is-said, as existing or subsisting independently of its occurrence in the pseudodyadic relation of saying. Therefore, they cannot be propositions, in the sense of the what-is-said, which have reality even though no one ever says them.

Bibliography

IDEALIST THEORIES

For idealist theories see F. H. Bradley, *The Principles of Logic*, 2d ed. (London, 1922); Bernard Bosanquet, *Logic* (Oxford, 1888); H. H. Joachim, *The Nature of Truth* (London, 1906); J. M. E. McTaggart, *The Nature of Existence*, Vol. I (Cambridge, 1921).

Criticisms of Bradley's theory are found in G. F. Stout, "Mr. Bradley's Theory of Judgment," *PAS*, Vol. 3 (1902–1903); and J. C. Wilson, *Statement and Inference* (Oxford, 1926).

DYADIC-RELATION THEORY

For dyadic-relation theory see G. E. Moore, "The Nature of Judgment," in *Mind*, Vol. 8 (1899); "Truth," in James M. Baldwin, ed., *Dictionary of Philosophy and Psychology* (New York, 1901–1905); "Mr. Joachim's *Nature of Truth*," in *Mind*, Vol. 16 (1907); and *Some Main Problems of Philosophy* (London, 1952).

See also Bertrand Russell, *The Principles of Mathematics* (Cambridge, 1903), and "Meinong's Theory of Complexes and Assumptions," I, II, III, in *Mind*, Vol. 13 (1904); and Alexius Meinong, *Über Annahmen* (Leipzig, 1902), and his essay in Alexius Meinong, ed., *Untersuchungen zur Gegenstandstheorie und Psychologie* (Leipzig, 1904), reprinted in English in Roderick M. Chisholm, ed., *Realism and the Background of Phenomenology* (Glencoe, Ill., 1960). J. N. Findlay's *Meinong's Theory of Objects* (Oxford, 1933) clarifies and defends Meinong's position. See Edmund Husserl, *Logische Untersuchungen* (Halle, Germany, 1900–1901), parts of which are paraphrased in Marvin Farber's *The Foundation of Phenomenology*, 2d ed. (New York, 1962).

Brentano's theory of judgment is put forth in *Psychologie vom empirischen Standpunkt* (Leipzig, 1874), Book II, Ch. 7, reprinted in English in *Realism and the Background of Phenomenology*. Brentano's criticisms of Meinong's ultra realism are in the appendixes to *Von der Klassifikation der psychische Phänomene* (Leipzig, 1911) and the posthumous supplement "The Object of Thought," both in *Psychologie*. A linguistic restatement of his theory of intentionality is in Roderick M. Chisholm's "Sentences About Believing," *PAS*, Vol. 56 (1955–1956).

See also G. F. Stout, "The Object of Thought and Real Being,"

in *PAS*, Vol. 11 (1910–1911). A good critical analysis of the dyadic theory is in Gilbert Ryle's "Are There Propositions?," in *PAS*, Vol. 30 (1929–1930).

MULTIPLE-RELATION THEORY

See Bertrand Russell, *The Problems of Philosophy* (London, 1912); *Philosophical Essays* (New York, 1910); "Knowledge by Acquaintance and Knowledge by Description," in *PAS*, Vol. 11 (1910–1911); and "The Philosophy of Logical Atomism," Lecture III, in *Monist*, Vol. 29 (1919), reprinted in R. C. Marsh, ed., *Logic and Knowledge* (London, 1956). Similar views are expressed by F. P. Ramsey, "Facts and Propositions," in *PAS*, Supp. Vol. 7 (1927), reprinted in his *The Foundations of Mathematics*, R. B. Braithwaite, ed. (London, 1931); and John Wisdom, *Problems of Mind and Matter* (Cambridge, 1934).

Criticisms of the multiple-relation theory are in G. F. Stout, "Mr. Russell's Theory of Judgment," in *PAS*, Vol. 15 (1914–1915); Findlay, *op. cit.*; and William Kneale, "The Objects of Acquaintance, in *PAS*, Vol. 34 (1933–1934).

Attempts to extend and revise this theory are in D. Wrinch, "On the Nature of Judgment," in *Mind*, Vol. 28 (1919); A. D. Woozley, *Theory of Knowledge* (London, 1949); and Peter Geach, *Mental Acts* (London, 1957).

An interesting synthesis of Stout and the multiple-relation theory is in C. D. Broad's *Examination of McTaggart's Philosophy*, Vol. I (Cambridge, 1933).

PSYCHOLOGICAL THEORY

See Bertrand Russell, "On Propositions: What They Are and How They Mean," in *PAS*, Vol. 19 (1919), reprinted in *Logic and Knowledge* and *The Analysis of Mind* (London, 1921).

BEHAVIORISTIC THEORY

See A. Kaplan and I. Copilowish, "Must There Be Propositions?" in *Mind*, Vol. 48 (1939). This paper develops a behavioral analysis of propositions based on Charles Morris' theory of semiotics. It is critically discussed by Russell in *An Inquiry Into Meaning and Truth* (New York, 1948).

PROPOSITIONS AS MEANINGS OF SENTENCES

The writings of Moore, Russell, Meinong, and Husserl which are mentioned under dyadic theory are to be consulted in this connection. See also Bernard Bolzano, *Wissenschaftslehre* (Sulzbach, Germany, 1837). Gottlob Frege's 1892 article "Ueber Sinn und Bedeutung" is translated by Herbert Feigl in Herbert Feigl and Wilfrid Sellars, eds., *Readings in Philosophical Analysis* (New York, 1949). Frege's "The Thought" appears in English translation in *Mind*, Vol. 65 (1956). An excellent critical analysis of the views of Bolzano and Frege is in William Kneale and Martha Kneale's *The Development of Logic* (Oxford, 1962). See also Alonzo Church, "Propositions," in *Encyclopaedia Britannica*, 14th ed. (Chicago, 1958); "The Need for Abstract Entities in Semantic Analysis," in *Proceedings of the American Academy of Arts and Sciences*, Vol. 80 (1951); "On Carnap's Analysis of Statements of Assertion and Belief," in *Analysis*, Vol. 10 (1950); "Propositions and Sentences," in I. M. Bocheński et al., *The Problem of Universals* (Notre Dame, Ind., 1956); and *Introduction to Mathematical Logic*, Vol. I (Princeton, N.J., 1956). Critical discussions of Church's analysis of belief sentences are to be found in *Analysis* for 1954 and 1955. See also W. V. Quine, *Word and Object* (Cambridge, Mass., 1961); Rudolf Carnap, *Introduction to Semantics* (Cambridge, Mass., 1942), *Meaning and Necessity* (Chicago, 1947); "Empiricism, Semantics, and Ontology," in Leonard Linsky, ed., *Semantics and the Philosophy of Language* (Urbana, Ill., 1952); C. I. Lewis, "The Modes of Meaning," in *Philosophy and Phenomenological Research*, Vol. 4 (1944), and *An Analysis of Knowledge and Valuation* (La Salle, Ill., 1946); C. A. Baylis, "Facts, Propositions, Exemplification and Truth," in *Mind*, Vol. 57 (1948).

Others who have defended the proposition theory are Ralph M. Eaton, *General Logic* (New York, 1931), and Jenny Teichmann, "Propositions," in *Philosophical Review*, Vol. 70 (1961). Sellars'

"Quotation Marks, Sentences, and Propositions," in *Philosophy and Phenomenological Research*, Vol. 10 (1950), and "Truth and Correspondence," in *Journal of Philosophy*, Vol. 59 (1962), contain interesting approaches to the problem of propositions.

CRITICISMS OF PROPOSITIONS AS MEANINGS OF SENTENCES

Attempts to show that propositions are logical constructions out of synonymous sentences or judgments are in Wisdom, *op. cit.*; A. J. Ayer, *Language, Truth and Logic* (London, 1936); and Russell, *An Inquiry Into Meaning and Truth*. Attempts to show the pseudo nature of the question concerning the meaning of a sentence in general are in A. J. Ayer, *The Foundations of Empirical Knowledge* (London, 1940); Stuart Hampshire, "Ideas, Propositions and Signs," in *PAS*, Vol. 40 (1939–1940); and John L. Austin, "The Meaning of a Word," in J. O. Urmson and G. J. Warnock, eds., *Philosophical Papers* (Oxford, 1961). Criticisms of the theory of meaning as naming are in Ludwig Wittgenstein, *The Blue and Brown Books* (Oxford, 1958), especially pp. 31–43, and *Philosophical Investigations* (Oxford, 1953), especially paragraphs 91–96, 134–137, 428–465; Gilbert Ryle, "Meaning and Necessity," in *Philosophy*, Vol. 24 (1949), and "The Theory of Meaning," in C. A. Mace, ed., *British Philosophy in the Mid-century* (London, 1957).

SENTENCES AND STATEMENTS

An attempt to treat statements as declarative speech acts is in John Austin, "Truth," in *PAS*, Supp. Vol. 24 (1950), and is effectively criticized by P. F. Strawson in his contribution to this symposium. See also Richard Cartwright, "Propositions," in R. J. Butler, ed., *Analytical Philosophy* (Oxford, 1962).

RICHARD M. GALE

PROTAGORAS OF ABDERA in Thrace, most famous of the Sophists, was born not later than 490 B.C. and probably died soon after 421 B.C. According to Plato, he was the first to declare himself a professional Sophist. He went from city to city in the Greek world, offering instruction in return for money, and he undertook above all to train young men in the art of politics. He was well known in Athens, where he enjoyed the friendship of Pericles—he produced a theoretical basis for Periclean democracy and was asked by Pericles to draft the constitution for the new colony of Thurii in 443 B.C. He made contributions to grammatical and rhetorical theory, and his views on religion provoked charges of impiety against him in the courts, which led to his exile from Athens at the end of his life and to the public burning of at least one of his books.

His writings were numerous and included "On Truth," "On the Gods," and "Antilogic" (or "Antilogies"). Later writers probably took their information about him mainly from the accounts of Plato, Aristotle, and Sextus Empiricus, but one of his works was read by Porphyry in the third century A.D., and in the Hellenistic period he was regarded as sufficiently important for his statue to be set up, together with those of Plato, Aristotle, and other thinkers, in the Serapeum at Memphis in Egypt.

Since the time of Plato, Protagoras' main doctrines have been regarded as possessing considerable philosophical interest, even by those who deny philosophical importance to the Sophists in general; but very divergent interpretations have been propounded. With no surviving works and virtually no fragments, interpretation must depend upon the assessment of the evidence of Plato, Aristotle, and Sextus Empiricus. In what follows, the view is taken that Plato in the *Theaetetus* correctly states the basic position of Protagoras and then proceeds to distinguish certain possible developments of this position not held by Protagoras. The basic position was independently understood in the same way by both Aristotle and Sextus Empiricus, each of whose information was not simply derived from the *Theaetetus*. This would be denied by some scholars.

Epistemology. The starting point must be the famous contention that "man is the measure of all things, of things that are that [or "how"] they are and of things that are not that [or "how"] they are not." Theodor Gomperz maintained that "man" is to be understood collectively in the sense of "mankind as a whole" or "the human race." But against this, the evidence of the *Theaetetus* 152A–B seems to show conclusively that it is individual men that Protagoras had in mind in the first instance, although, as will be seen, his theory is capable of easy extension to groups of men, and he probably made this extension himself.

According to Plato's example in the *Theaetetus*, when the same wind appears cold to one person and warm to another person, then the wind is warm to the person to whom it appears warm and is cold to the person to whom it seems cold. It follows that all perceptions are true and the ordinary view is mistaken, according to which, in cases of conflict, one person is right and the other person is wrong about the quality of the wind or of anything else. This clearly was the position held by Protagoras, but it is not clear exactly how he came to this view. It is often held that his position is a kind of subjective idealism similar to that of Bishop Berkeley, according to which qualities in a thing *are* for the person to whom they seem, so long as they seem to him, but have no existence independent of their seeming. Against this view, Sextus Empiricus is explicit: all qualities perceived by different persons are actually present in matter. Sextus' introduction of matter may well be anachronistic, but his account suggests an alternative view, accepted by Cornford among others, according to which opposite qualities are copresent in objects, and in cases of conflict of perceptions between two persons, what happens is that we have a sort of selective perception—one person perceives one quality and the other its opposite, both qualities being present in the situation, waiting to be perceived, as it were, independently of any actual perceiving by a subject. This view seems to have the support of Aristotle, who always treats Protagoras' doctrine as involving the denial of the principle of contradiction, and the view coincides with incidental pointers in Plato's account ("the same wind"—152B; "perception, then, is always of something that is"—152C). It is true that in the "secret doctrine" attributed to Protagoras by Plato (152C ff.) the independent status of sense objects is undermined, but the fact that this is presented as a secret doctrine is surely conclusive evidence that it was a doctrine not publicly associated with Protagoras.

The "man-measure" doctrine is presented by Plato in the first instance as a doctrine about perception of sensible qualities. But it is clear that Plato supposed that for Protagoras it also applied to moral and aesthetic qualities such as "just" and "beautiful." It is especially in these cases that the extension of the doctrine to groups of men was made by Protagoras—"whatever seems just to a city is just for that city so long as it seems so." Probably Protagoras did not extend his doctrine to apply to all judgments; this was done immediately by his opponents in the famous *peritrope*, or "turning of the tables": let us suppose that whatever seems true to any person is true for the person to whom it seems so. If this is the doctrine of Protagoras, then Protagoras will hold that those who hold that Protagoras' theory is false are holding the truth (*Theaetetus* 171A). But Plato points out that if Protagoras could pop his head up through the ground, he would surely have an answer to this objection.

At the very least, Protagoras was clear about one point. In the case of conflict about perceived qualities all perceptions are true. But some perceptions are better than others, for example, the perceptions normally found in a healthy man as distinct from those found in a man who is ill. It is the function of a doctor, Protagoras held, to change a man who is ill so that his perceptions become those of a man who is well. Likewise, in moral, political, and aesthetic conflicts it is the function of the Sophist as a teacher to work a change so that better views about what is "just" and "beautiful" will seem true to the "patient"—better, that is, than those which previously seemed true to him. All the "patient's" views are equally true, but some are better than others. There is nothing to suggest that by "better" Protagoras meant what will seem better. Quite the contrary. Better views are views which have better consequences, and consequences which are better are so as a matter of fact, independently of whether a person thinks them better or not. In other words, Protagoras here made an exception to his "man-measure" doctrine. There is every reason to suppose that he would have excepted the class of judgments about the consequences of judgments from his principle. Indeed, there is no actual evidence in any ancient author that Protagoras himself ever applied his doctrine to statements other than those about perceived qualities and moral and aesthetic qualities treated on the same plane as visually perceived qualities. What probably happened was that he propounded his doctrine in certain general statements such as "whatever seems to anyone is so for that person," without adding the qualifications which he really intended; thus he gave a handle to his enemies, which enabled them to apply the *peritrope* and similar objections.

The above account rests primarily upon Plato's *Theaetetus*. To it may be added evidence from other sources. According to Diogenes Laërtius, Protagoras was the first to propound the theory that there are two *logoi*, or accounts, to be given about everything. This has sometimes been treated as simply the now familiar rhetorical doctrine that "there are two sides to every question." But this theory was used as a method of argument, and it should probably be related to the "man-measure" doctrine and to what Plato called "Antilogic," the probable title of one of Protagoras' treatises. In conflicts about perceived qualities, and also moral and aesthetic qualities, there might seem room for an infinite variety of "seemings," but if we take any one as a starting point, for instance, that the wind seems warm,

all other seemings may be expressed as the negative of this, namely "not-warm." This was clearly the way in which Plato tended to regard phenomena—as did the antilogicians, too—namely, as always being both "warm" and "not-warm." In this view, Plato was probably following Protagoras. It is possible that Protagoras associated with the two-*logoi* principle the prescription attributed to him by Aristotle "to make the lesser [or "the weaker"] argument the stronger." This may have been what the Sophist was expected to do when altering a man's opinions for the better.

Social theory. In Plato's dialogue *Protagoras* we are given a coordinated theory of the Sophist in relation to society and of a possible theoretical basis for a Periclean-style democracy. All is completely consistent with the positions attributed to Protagoras in the *Theaetetus*. When Protagoras professes to make men good citizens, Socrates objects that while the Athenians call in experts to advise on technical matters, they regard all citizens as capable of advising them on matters relating to the city. This seems to imply that Athenian democracy leaves no place for expert instruction in citizenship. Protagoras replies with a myth followed by a nonmythical exposition that while all men share in the qualities that make good citizens, they do not do so by nature but acquire these qualities by instruction and by practice. These qualities are beliefs and opinions about what is just and right. In a sense, the whole community teaches its members about these matters, and so all are rightly consulted about political matters. But the expert teacher, such as the Sophist Protagoras, can improve opinions on such matters, whether it be in the case of an individual or in the case of a whole community.

Other views. Protagoras' doctrines ranged beyond the topics discussed above to cover physical and mathematical problems as well, but it is no longer possible to state his actual teachings on these problems. He seems to have held that a tangent touches a circle not only at one point, but at more than one, clearly arguing from visual experience of drawn lines. Parmenides had rejected the world of seeming in favor of his world of being; Protagoras took the opposite path and attempted to expound a world in which all appearances were true and where there was nothing outside or beyond what appeared. This involved the copresence of opposed and contradictory qualities at many points. Protagoras was prepared to accept and explain this copresence through his "man-measure" principle, either on the basis of a theory of subjective idealism or, more probably, on the basis of a conception of a phenomenal world actually composed of opposites (a conception typical of the pre-Socratics). This conception seemed to Plato to be substantially correct for the phenomenal world, hence his great interest in Protagoras. But Plato felt that this view made it impossible to give any account or explanation of phenomena, and to be able to give an explanation seemed to him essential.

Diogenes Laërtius says that for Protagoras the soul is nothing apart from its perceptions. This suggests a phenomenalistic view of the soul as well as of everything else. Diogenes' account may be correct, although doubts have been cast upon it. If it is correct, however, it probably was not intended to imply any doctrine like the modern theory of neutral monism, but simply to deny the existence of any "submerged," or nonphenomenal, element in the soul.

Bibliography

Fragments and testimonia of Protagoras' work may be found in H. Diels and W. Kranz, eds., *Fragmente der Vorsokratiker*, 10th ed. (Berlin, 1961), Vol. II. A. Capizzi, *Protagora* (Florence, 1955), is probably the best full discussion, and it includes some material not in Diels and Kranz. See also F. M. Cornford, *Plato's Theory of Knowledge* (London, 1935); and G. B. Kerferd, "Plato's Account of the Relativism of Protagoras," *Durham University Journal*, Vol. 42 (1949), 20–26, and "Protagoras' Doctrine of Justice and Virtue in the 'Protagoras' of Plato," *Journal of Hellenic Studies*, Vol. 73 (1953), 42–45. The account in M. Untersteiner, *I Sofisti* (Turin, 1949), translated by Kathleen Freeman as *The Sophists* (Oxford, 1954), presents a number of special points of interpretation which have not won general acceptance. See also G. Vlastos' introduction to *Plato's Protagoras* (New York, 1956), translated by M. Ostwald.

G. B. KERFERD

PROTOCOL SENTENCES. See BASIC STATEMENTS.

PROUDHON, PIERRE-JOSEPH (1809–1865), has been called the father of anarchism, a title that is accurate insofar as organized anarchist movements throughout the world can be traced to his teachings and to the actions of his disciples. Proudhon was also the first writer deliberately to accept the title of anarchist, which he did in 1840. Before his time the term had been used to denote one who seeks to promote social disorder; Proudhon argued that it could be used with more justice to describe one who seeks social order without authoritarian government. "As man seeks justice in equality, so society seeks order in anarchy," he said. "Anarchy—the absence of a master, of a sovereign—such is the form of government to which we are every day approximating." Such doctrines were not entirely original; the English writer William Godwin had expounded them fifty years earlier without describing them as "anarchist," but Proudhon appears to have been uninfluenced by Godwin and to have reached his conclusions independently.

Proudhon prided himself on being a man of the people. He was born in Besançon, capital of Franche-Comté, of Jura peasant stock. His childhood was hard, and after a brief period at the college in Besançon, he received his education largely through his work as a printer; he taught himself Greek and Hebrew and developed a prose style that eventually won the admiration of Baudelaire, Flaubert, and Victor Hugo. The turning point in Proudhon's career came when he was awarded a scholarship by the Besançon Academy in 1838. This took him to Paris and gave him the leisure to formulate his ideas and to write his first important book, *Qu'est-ce que la propriété?* (*What is Property?*, Paris, 1840). This book, hailed by Marx as "the first decisive, vigorous and scientific examination" of the institution of property, gained notoriety because in one passage Proudhon defined property as "theft." The author's love of telling phrases distorted the nature of his argument, for *Qu'est-ce que la propriété?* was in fact an investigation of abuses that had entered into the institution of property rather than a condemnation of property itself. The arguments which Proudhon put forward in this early book, on the nature of property and the faults of government, are those which he elaborated and gave a deeper philosophical backing in his later works.

Proudhon attacked the existence of private property that allows the exploitation of the labor of others, such as the owning of land by those who do not work it; he had only approval for the "possession" that allows a worker to dispose of what his hands make. "The right to products is exclusive—*jus in re*; the right to means is common—*jus ad rem*." This is so because the means of production, the heritage of techniques and inventions, have been built up by human cooperation, and no man has a right to use them exclusively for his own benefit. However, for the sake of independence, Proudhon granted the need for each man to control the land or tools he can use. In this early book he still thought in terms of a peasant-and-handcraft society.

Proudhon attacked unreformed property because it negates equality, but he rejected the communist theories of his time (principally those of the French utopian socialists) because they denied independence. Here Proudhon came to the political aspect of his argument—both unreformed property and communism are dependent on forms of authority to maintain themselves. But how far is authority justified? Proudhon contended that it arises from the tendency of social animals and primitive man to seek leaders. As reason develops, criticism, protest, and rebellion arise. Emergent political science finds the laws by which society functions in the nature of things, not in the whims of rulers. At this point anarchy, administration without government, becomes possible. Proudhon, at this stage under the influence of Hegelian ideas imperfectly absorbed from French reviews, created a triad. The thesis is property, which destroys equality; the antithesis is communism, which denies independence; the synthesis is anarchy or liberty, which is embodied in a society of producers bound together by a network of free contracts. In the widening recognition of mutual interests, government becomes unnecessary.

During the 1840s Proudhon served for several years as office manager for a water transport firm in Lyons, work that allowed him to travel frequently to Paris. In these two settings his theory of mutualism—the form of anarchism particularly associated with him—developed. Political radicalism flourished in mid-nineteenth-century Lyons, and Proudhon encountered there the disciples of Étienne Cabet, Charles Fourier, Pierre Leroux, and other socialist prophets. He developed the idea of a world-wide working-class organization on an economic basis rather than a political one. This led him to place faith in various forms of mutual credit systems which might eventually make governmental administration unnecessary; he envisaged such associations as becoming world-wide. In Paris, Proudhon associated with some of the leading European revolutionary theorists, including Marx, Bakunin, and Herzen. However, his personal and theoretical incompatability with Marx soon became evident; the historic conflict between libertarian and authoritarian views of socialism began with the split between Marx and Proudhon, which dates from Marx's attack in *La Misère de la philosophie* (Paris, 1847) on Proudhon's *Système des contradictions économiques* (2 vols., Paris, 1846). Bakunin and Herzen, on the other hand, eventually became Proudhon's most important disciples.

During the 1840s Proudhon, an eclectic thinker, took what he found valid from the writings of Hegel, Feuerbach, Kant, and other German philosophers, as well as from Comte and the French utopians. He evolved a philosophy which left out the third term of the Hegelian triad, and accepted contradiction as an enduring force tending toward a dynamic equilibrium—the desirable condition of existence. He denied all absolutes, all utopian aspirations to permanent solutions, and, in his *Philosophie du progrès* (Paris, 1853) saw progress as "the affirmation of universal movement and in consequence the negation of all immutable forms and formulae, of all doctrines of eternity, permanence, or impeccability, and of every subject, or object, spiritual or transcendental, that does not change." He was, deliberately and avowedly, an antisystematic philosopher.

Proudhon assumed the standpoint of a critical independent, and as such he became the most outspoken journalist of the period, giving qualified support to the French revolution of 1848. His *Le Représentant du peuple* (1848) was the first anarchist newspaper published with any regularity; harried by suppressions and fines, it survived under various names for more than two years. Proudhon was elected in June 1848 to the Constituent Assembly, where he maintained an intransigent minority position. He also planned a people's bank, based on his mutualist ideas, which never materialized because he was imprisoned for attacks in his paper on Louis Napoleon, then president of the Republic.

Proudhon's three years of imprisonment were light: He was allowed occasional days out on parole, on one of which he married Euphrasie Piégard, and he wrote two of his most important books, *Les Confessions d'un révolutionnaire* (Paris, 1850), an analysis of the events of 1848 which states the aim of anarchist revolutionism as "no more government of man by man, by means of the accumulation of capital," and *Idée générale de la révolution au XIXe siécle* (*General Idea of the Revolution in the Nineteenth Century*, Paris, 1851). The latter book comes nearer than anything else Proudhon wrote to presenting his view of the ideal libertarian society, based on contract instead of laws, with authority decentralized in communes and industrial associations, with frontiers abolished and flexible federation replacing the centralized national state.

During the early years of the Second Empire, Proudhon was subjected to constant police persecution, and in 1858 he was again sentenced to three years' imprisonment for an offense against the press laws. He fled to Belgium, where, although pardoned in 1860, he lived until 1862. During his final years in Paris, he gained a considerable mutualist following among French workingmen, and before he died early in 1865, he learned that his followers had taken a leading part in the meetings that led to the founding of the International Workingmen's Association.

During his final years Proudhon wrote a number of books that elaborated important aspects of his doctrines. *Du Principe fédératif* (Paris, 1863) summarized his criticism of nationalism and developed his ideas of communal organization leading gradually to world federation. *De la Justice dans la révolution et dans l'église* (3 vols., Paris, 1858) opposed his own theory of an immanent justice to transcendentalist ideas of justice. *De la Capacité politique des classes ouvrières* (published posthumously in Paris, 1865) developed Proudhon's view of the power of the working class to achieve its own liberation by economic means.

Later anarchism and syndicalism were largely influenced by Proudhon's doctrines, as was the populist movement in Russia. As the Russian anarchist Mikhail Bakunin said, "Proudhon was the master of us all."

Works by Proudhon

Oeuvres complètes de P. J. Proudhon, 26 vols. Paris, 1867–1870.
Oeuvres complètes de P. J. Proudhon, C. C. A. Bouglé and Henri Moysset, eds., 11 vols. Paris, 1920–1939. Never completed.
Correspondance, 14 vols. Paris, 1874–1875.
What Is Property?, translated by Benjamin Tucker. Princeton, 1876.
System of Economic Contradictions, translated by Benjamin Tucker. Boston, 1888.
General Idea of the Revolution in the Nineteenth Century, translated by John Beverley Robinson. London, 1923.

Works on Proudhon

Brogan, D. W., *Proudhon*. London, 1936.
Dolléans, Édouard, *Proudhon*. Paris, 1948.
Lubac, Henri de, *Proudhon et le christianisme*. Paris, 1945. Translated by R. E. Scantlebury as *The Un-Marxian Socialist: A Study of Proudhon*. London, 1948.
Prion, Gaëtan, *Proudhon et syndicalisme révolutionnaire*. Paris, 1910.
Sainte-Beuve, Charles A., *P.-J. Proudhon*. Paris, 1872.
Woodcock, George, *Pierre-Joseph Proudhon*. London, 1956.

GEORGE WOODCOCK

PROUST, MARCEL (1871–1922), French author, was born and educated in Paris. He lived there all his life, leaving only for short holidays or artistic pilgrimages, most of which were to the great cathedral cities of France. His father, a professor of medicine, was Catholic; his mother, whom he adored, was Jewish. Both traditions, as well as his consuming interest in French history and culture, played important roles in his life and art, although he was neither religiously orthodox nor politically chauvinistic. He undertook a considerable and seemingly futile search for a vocation and did some writing, most of which was discarded drafts of his future novel. Suffering terribly from asthma and from certain guilts about his homosexuality, but with economic as well as spiritual means sufficient to indulge and transmute these ills, Proust ensconced himself in his famous cork-lined room to write his masterpiece, *A la Recherche du temps perdu*.

Philosophical themes. Although Proust compared a work of art in which there are theories to an object on which the price is marked, *A la Recherche* is, nonetheless, a philosophical novel. There are two major philosophical themes woven into the novel: that reality is composed of artistic essences and that the search for essences ends in their dissolution. Proust stated only the first theme; the second, however, is implied by much of the action of the novel.

In the last volume of the novel, *Le Temps retrouvé,* Proust, as narrator and participant, stated his theory of artistic essences as reality; this theory, because of its role in the context of the whole novel, must be understood as an integral part of it, along with the characterization, dialogue, and plot. According to Proust's theory, we live in a world of people, places, and things, all of which are organized spatially or temporally, in the ordinary sense of space and time, and which impinge on us. Most of us merely react to these phenomena. The true artist, however, like the scientists, attempts to find the laws that govern these phenomena. Whereas the scientist proceeds by his intellect, the artist cannot, for his laws are to be discovered only by intuition. The artist's intellect supplements, but it cannot supplant, intuition. Intuition is that state of mind in which the artist—rooted in past experiences, nourished by suffering, and graced by an involuntary memory of a past sensation joined with a similar present one—extracts the qualitative similarity or essence from these sensations in order to embody that essence in a metaphor which, like the essence, is not subject to the ravages of time. Thus, these essences are the only true reality, and their artistic expression the only true judgment on reality.

Proust, it is important to realize, did not deny the existence of temporal or spatial relations, but he rejected them as unreal. Hence, he must understand by "reality" something quite distinct from "existence": "reality" for him functioned as an honorific term denoting that which is salvageable from the past and which transcends the present—that, therefore, which is ultimate in the precise sense of being out of time. "Reality" in effect denotes the essences extracted by intuition from what exists in relation to what existed.

It has been claimed that Proust's conceptions of time and intuition are Bergsonian. It seems, however, that there are important differences. According to Bergson, time is essentially duration (*durée*). The concepts of the past, present, and future cannot apply to time because they spatialize it. Duration can only be experienced, not thought of or talked about; it is the indivisible, ultimate fact of process in the world, and intuition is the experience of duration, a direct acquaintance with it. For Proust, however, time is not duration; it consists of chronological relations among events. Nor is time ultimate; only the timeless essences are that. Finally, intuition for Proust is an extraction from, not an immersion in, time.

Nor is Proust's theory Platonic, as has sometimes been suggested. Plato's timeless essences are perfect and have their being absolutely independently of the spatial and temporal particulars of this world; the Proustian essences are at most more or less imperfect copies of the truly real forms.

Besides this aesthetic–ontological theme, which Proust integrated magnificently in the novel, there is the nether theme of the dissolution of essences in the very search for them. Although he never stated this theme, much of the novel embodies it. The treatment of love is probably the best single example. Through the narration of many different love relationships, commonly regarded as a major achievement of the novel, Proust dramatized that love has no essence, only an inexhaustible set of properties, none of which is necessary or sufficient. Here intellect supplants rather than supplements intuition. Proust's observations, analyses, and generalizations harvest a vast multiplicity of criteria that govern our understanding and concept of love. In effect, Proust showed through his characterization, monologue and dialogue, as well as through the plot, that the range of the experience of love renders impossible any traditional essentialist definition of it. To have discovered, explored, and artistically wrought this important truth about our conceptual life and to have shown it a full generation before philosophers stated it is not the least of Proust's accomplishments in his great novel.

Works by Proust

Portraits de peintres. Paris, 1896.
Les Plaisirs et les jours. Paris, 1896. Translated by Louise Varese and others as *Pleasures and Days,* with an introduction by F. W. Dupee. New York, 1957.
La Bible d'Amiens. Paris, 1904. A translation, with preface and notes, of John Ruskin's *Bible of Amiens.*
Sésame et lys. Paris, 1906. A translation, with preface ("Journées de lecture") and notes, of Ruskin's *Sesame and Lilies.*
A la Recherche du temps perdu (published by the *Nouvelle Revue Française*), 7 parts, 13 vols. Paris, 1919–1927. One volume had been published in 1913, at Proust's expense. Translated by C. K. Scott Moncrieff (the first 6 parts) and Stephen Hudson (last part only) as *Remembrance of Things Past.* New York, 1922–1931. Uniform edition, 12 vols. London and New York, 1941. Pléiade edition, 3 vols., Paris, 1954.
Chroniques. Paris, 1927.
Jean Santeuil, with introduction by André Maurois. Paris, 1954. Translated by Gerard Hopkins. London, 1955; New York, 1956.
Contre Sainte-Beuve. Paris, 1954. Translated by Sylvia Townsend Warner as *By Way of Sainte-Beuve.* London, 1958.

Works on Proust

Brée, Germaine, *Marcel Proust and Deliverance From Time.* New York, 1955.
Cocking, J. M., *Proust.* London, 1956.
Delattre, Floris, *Bergson et Proust.* Paris, 1948. Vol. I of *Les Études Bergsoniennes.*
Green, F. C., *The Mind of Proust.* Cambridge, 1950.
Maurois, André, *The Quest for Proust.* London, 1950.
Weitz, Morris, *Philosophy in Literature: Shakespeare, Voltaire, Tolstoy and Proust.* Detroit, 1963.

MORRIS WEITZ

PROVIDENCE. The idea of providence has three components—foresight, direction, and care. It is normally found in a theistic context. In its fullest sense it means that God foresees and governs (in a word, "provides for") the world which is the object of his care (or love). Divine providence was affirmed by Plato in his *Laws* (887–888), where he condemns the view, later held by the Epicureans, that the gods take no interest in human affairs. The most important later thought upon the subject arose in Stoicism and Christianity.

Stoics. The Stoics held a firm belief in the providence (*pronoia*) of God (or the gods). Thus, Epictetus uses an elementary form of the teleological argument to prove God's supervision of the universe (*Discourse* 1.16). But two factors prevented the Stoics from taking a fully personal view of providence. First, they often conceived God abstractly (as a cosmic logos) and even physically (when they identified him with nature's basic elements, air and fire). Second, and correlatively, they did not stress God's care for persons individually, nor, as a consequence, did they allow that God accomplishes his purpose in and through the free response of human wills to his initiative. On the contrary, they equated providence with destiny or fate (*heimarmene*). In the words of Cleanthes' Hymn to Zeus, translated by Seneca, *Ducunt volentem fata, nolentem trahunt* ("Fate leads the willing, drags the unwilling on," Epistles 107.11).

Christianity. Our primary evidence for Christianity is the teaching of Christ himself. Christ taught that God is a Father who cares for all his children individually. Therefore, they must not be anxious or distressed; rather, they must trust God absolutely (Matthew 6.25–33, 10.29–31). Furthermore, they must approach God freely in prayer in the confidence that he will answer their requests (Matthew 7.7–11). St. Paul made two basic assertions: first, that we know through Christ that God's sovereignty is one of love through which we are "more than conquerors" (Romans 8.35–39) and second, that God accomplishes his purpose by cooperating with our wills, not by demanding our submission to a *fait accompli* (Romans 8.14–16, Philippians 2.12–13). Hence, St. Paul, like Jesus, affirms the reality of, and the necessity for, petitionary prayer.

Attempts have been made to see providence in nature, history, and individual lives.

Nature. The theist maintains that God acts in nature both ordinarily, through those laws which science formulates, and extraordinarily, through miracles. Both modes of God's activity signify his wisdom and love to the believing mind. Furthermore, many theists, following Aquinas in his Fifth Way, believe that it is possible to base an argument for God's existence on the apparent traces of design in nature, but it must be admitted that the fact of evil constitutes prima-facie evidence against the existence of a Designer who is both omnipotent and good.

History. To what extent can we interpret God's purpose in terms of a "pattern," or "patterns," discernible in historical events? Here one can only summarize a general tendency among modern theologians. Most of them would say that our ability to perceive a pattern or plan is restricted to the main events of the Bible as interpreted by the prophetic and apostolic writers. Perhaps we also have a right to see a *preparatio evangelica* in the achievements of Greece and Rome, but we cannot perceive an analogous plan in either the secular or ecclesiastical history of the post-Biblical era. Thus, Josef Pieper writes, "Not that he who philosophizes could reach the point of being able to identify *in concreto* the character of an event in terms of salvation and disaster. We are moving here within the realm of the *mysterious*—in the strictest sense. And even for the believer, the history of salvation 'within' history is not to be apprehended concretely" (*The End of Time*, London, 1954, p. 23).

Individual lives. In regard to individual lives we must also distinguish between a general belief in providence and a detailed knowledge of its workings. St. Paul affirmed as a matter of faith that "we know that in everything God works for good with those who love him, who are called according to his purpose" (Romans 8.28). But in 1 Corinthians 13.12 he admits that all our knowledge of God is indirect, partial, and confused. Hence, any claim to see God's purpose in particular events is bound to be provisional and incomplete.

Bibliography

Caussade, J. P. de, *L'Abandon à la providence divine.* 1867. Translated by A. Thorold as *Self-Abandonment to Divine Providence*, 5th ed. London, 1955. A classic of spiritual theology.

Hazelton, Roger, *Providence.* London, 1958.

Laird, John, *Mind and Deity.* London, 1941. Pp. 173–201.

Pollard, William C., *Chance and Providence.* New York, 1958.

H. P. OWEN

PSEUDO-DIONYSIUS. The writings of Pseudo-Dionysius, first cited at the beginning of the sixth century, have attracted interest partly because the writer has been wrongly identified with Dionysius the Areopagite, who was converted by St. Paul at Athens, and also with St. Denis, the patron saint of France. However, neither of these identifications is possible.

While the thought of Pseudo-Dionysius was a continuation of the Christian Platonism of the early Church Fathers, it is directly influenced by the latest forms of Neoplatonism, as found in Proclus. No other early Christian writer was so clearly influenced by a particular philosopher. The influence of Pseudo-Dionysius on later theologians, philosophers, mystics, and poets was immense. John of Damascus and Thomas Aquinas were both strongly influenced by him. Peter Lombard, Robert Grosseteste, and Albert the Great also acknowledged their debt to him. The poetry of Dante and Milton reflects his heavenly hierarchy.

Four of his treatises—"The Celestial Hierarchy," "The Ecclesiastical Hierarchy," "The Divine Names," and "The Mystical Theology"—and ten of his letters are extant. The problem of the one and the many in the treatises is the problem of the relation of God to the universe, both visible and invisible. The basic propositions of Proclus were that every plurality participates in unity, is both one and not one, and is other than the one itself. The order of the universe is an order which depends on the ultimate unity. It is arranged in different orders of being which descend from and ascend to the first principle. This hierarchical view of the universe goes back to Plato and Aristotle and is found in Philo and the Gnostics, as well as in later Platonism. Proclus and Pseudo-Dionysius represent the final stage of the idea in the ancient world, and Pseudo-Dionysius is the chief transmitter of the idea to later times.

The four treatises exhibit the sequence of Dionysius' thought. Those on hierarchies show the descent and return of the divine goodness, "The Divine Names" shows the nature of God, and "The Mystical Theology" shows the way by which the knowledge of God may be found.

The hierarchies. "The hierarchy is a holy order, a knowledge and an activity which assimilates to the divine nature as far as possible and which through the light granted from God is raised in due proportion to the imitation of God" ("The Celestial Hierarchy" III, 1). The celestial hierarchy contemplates the divine perfection and shares in it, reflecting its light down through its several ranks: Seraphim, Cherubim, Thrones, Dominions, Powers, Authorities, Principalities, Archangels, and Angels. The members of the highest hierarchy are nearest to God and share most fully his vision and his likeness. The other members of the hierarchy become more symbolic and corporeal as they descend. Each member of the hierarchy comes directly from God, in contrast with the emanations of Proclus, which produce one another. The Christian doctrine of creation makes the unity of the hierarchy that of spiritual communion rather than that of progressive generation. On earth the ecclesiastical hierarchy continues the celestial hierarchy in visible form, with Jesus at the top of this hierarchy as God is at the summit of the celestial hierarchy. The members of the hierarchy in descending triads are chrism, communion, and baptism; bishops, priests, and deacons; monks, laity, and catechumens.

"**The Divine Names.**" The third treatise discusses the names given to God. These names cannot describe God but must be understood in a special sense, since God is above all reason, speech, being, and name. He is above being yet the cause of being, and may be said to be only in a higher sense. His names are not derived from himself but from the manifestation of his providence. He is both nameless and many-named. He is in the world, around the world, above the world, and above the heavens. He is sun, star, fire, water, wind, dew, cloud, stone, and rock—and none of them. Knowledge of God comes through prayer, which draws men to him so that they may know his goodness. How can such a God be the sovereign creator of a world in which evil exists? Only because evil is not real but simply the absence of good. "Evil is then a deprivation, defect, weakness, disproportion, error, and the absence of purpose, beauty, life, understanding, reason and perfection." When night falls, there is nothing positive in its darkness but simply the absence of light. Evil is simply the absence of goodness.

"**The Mystical Theology.**" "The Mystical Theology" describes the way to the knowledge of God by the Neoplatonic method of abstracting visible and invisible qualities until one comes to the knowledge of God by negation or removal. This knowledge of God is mystical and ineffable rather than philosophical and theological, and it involves complete cessation of thought and speech. One penetrates the darkness which is above intelligible things, and in absolute silence one is united to the ineffable. God is absolutely unknowable, and the ecstasy which unites with him is both total ignorance and a knowledge beyond reason.

The distinctive quality of Pseudo-Dionysius is found in the extreme statement of two things—the unity of the world and the unity of God. The unity and order which the divine goodness imposes on the universe is described most concretely and explicitly. The unity of God is described in negative terms which isolate it completely from all else. The extreme statement of these two opposite things enabled Pseudo-Dionysius to influence succeeding thinkers in their account of an ordered world and of a transcendent God. The opposition is inherent in all Pla-

tonism if not in all philosophy. Its explicit exposition is therefore of value.

Works by Pseudo-Dionysius

Works of Pseudo-Dionysius may be found in J. P. Migne, ed., *Patrologia Graeca*, Vol. III (Paris, 1857). Translations of his works include *The Celestial and Ecclesiastical Hierarchy of Dionysius the Areopagite*, translated by John Parker (London, 1894), and *Dionysius the Areopagite on the Divine Names and the Mystical Theology*, translated by C. E. Rolt, 2d ed. (London, 1940).

Works on Pseudo-Dionysius

Works on Pseudo-Dionysius are Hugo Koch, *Pseudo-Dionysius Areopagita in seinen Beziehungen zum Neuplatonismus und Mysterienwesen* (Mainz, 1900); René Roques, *L'Univers dionysien* (1954); and Walther Völker, *Kontemplation und Ekstase bei Pseudo-Dionysius Areopagita* (Wiesbaden, 1958).

E. F. OSBORN

PSEUDO-GROSSETESTE was the anonymous author of a *Summa Philosophiae*, written between 1265 and 1275. Because of the reference in the *Summa* to Simon de Montfort's death (1265), it could not have been written by Robert Grosseteste, who died in 1253. Bartholomew of Bologna, Robert Kilwardby, and a disciple of Roger Bacon have all been suggested as the author, but there is no consensus. It does seem probable, however, that he was English and was either a Franciscan or a secular.

The *Summa*, which begins with a history of philosophy similar to that found in Roger Bacon's *Opus Maius*, is a work of considerable subtlety and sophistication, an advanced product of the so-called Augustinian school. It holds that there is a universal wisdom in which both ancients and moderns share, perfected however by Christian revelation. Those concerned with wisdom are theosophists, to whom truth is directly revealed; theologians, who systematize and make more clear what has been revealed to the theosophists; and philosophers. The first two groups are concerned with the infallibly true, and their proper study is of matters relevant to human salvation. Philosophy, on the other hand, while it may often be in error, is completely unrestricted in its scope and may undertake to explain the natures and causes of all things whatsoever.

The *Summa* then treats the whole range of metaphysical questions in separate treatises, beginning with truth and the necessary existence of an uncreated being and ending with psychology, light, the four elements, meteors, and minerals. Its characteristic metaphysical positions are derived largely from the author's explicit hylomorphism. Every created thing is composed of matter and form. Prime matter, the mark of contingency, is not corporeal but is unextended and has three inseparable properties: it is in potency to every form; it has a desire for form; and it is privation of form. Insofar as it is privation of form it is the cause of instability; but its desire for form is a tendency toward stability. It first receives universal form, that is, substance. Substance, or substantial form, is either corporeal or incorporeal and individuates matter. It receives further perfections from other forms, so that there is a plurality of forms in any given body. This leads the author to reject the distinction (except as one of reason) between essence and existence. It also leads him to insist that the Intelligences are compounded of matter and form and differ both according to species and individuality. The human soul, like the Intelligences, is an incorporeal intelligent substance, but unlike them is capable of being joined to a body as well as of existing separately; it too is composed of matter and form. In these points, as in many others throughout the *Summa,* the author seems to be correcting what he considers the errors of Thomas Aquinas.

Bibliography

The text of the *Summa* is printed in L. Baur, *Die philosophischen Werke des Robert Grosseteste, Bischofs von Lincoln* (Münster in Westfalen, 1912), pp. 275–643. Parts are translated in R. McKeon, *Selections from Medieval Philosophers* (New York, 1929), Vol. I, pp. 290–314. An excellent analysis appears in C. K. McKeon, *The Summa Philosophiae of the Pseudo-Grosseteste* (New York, 1948). A good summary is in E. Gilson, *History of Christian Philosophy in the Middle Ages* (New York, 1955), pp. 265–274.

RICHARD C. DALES

PSYCHE in Homer first means life and later means a departed life or ghost. The first identification with soul in the sense of the conscious self is found perhaps in Ionia, and the earliest full identification with the rational as well as with the emotional side of personality has been attributed to Socrates. In all this there was no opposition between soul and body. The doctrine that the soul is a prisoner in the body that Plato took from Orphic doctrine had reached Greece, perhaps from Scythia, before the time of Pythagoras, probably in association with a doctrine of transmigration. Plato, in the *Phaedo,* while recognizing that most people do not believe in survival after death (80D), propounded a view that combines the Socratic and Orphic attitudes. In the tripartite soul of the *Republic,* however, it is the rational part alone that is immortal; this was also Aristotle's view.

The majority of the pre-Socratics regarded the universe as a quasi-living organism, and this view also found expression in Plato's doctrine in the *Timaeus* of a world soul as a source of orderly motion in the universe. Aristotle presented a developed human and animal psychology in his analysis of the soul in the *De Anima* and elsewhere. Whereas Plato regarded the soul as a substance separate from the body, Aristotle's final view treated it as the form of a living body. For the Stoics the soul is an aspect of the all pervading cosmic logos, while for the Epicureans it is a combination of especially smooth atoms. Within Christian theology Augustinians follow an essentially Platonist view, while Thomists prefer Aristotle's approach.

Bibliography

Burnet, J., "The Socratic Doctrine of the Soul." *Proceedings of the British Academy,* Vol. 7 (1915–1916), 235–259.
Rohde, E., *Psyche,* translated by W. B. Hillis. London, 1925.

G. B. KERFERD

PSYCHOANALYSIS, EXISTENTIAL. See EXISTENTIAL PSYCHOANALYSIS.

PSYCHOANALYTIC THEORIES, LOGICAL STATUS OF. Since psychoanalysis fails to conform to currently accepted methodological models, its prominence on the contemporary scene constitutes a challenge to the methodologist. He must either revise his canons or show the psychoanalyst the error of his ways. Both tacks have been tried, but thus far the second has predominated. This article will be confined to methodological problems raised by psychoanalytic theory, though as we shall see, such problems cannot be pursued very far without running into questions concerning the clinical interpretation of particular cases.

Content of psychoanalytic theory. Within psychoanalytic theory there are diverse strands, and the relations between them are by no means obvious. For one thing, there are theoretical ideas at different levels. Fairly close to actual clinical practice are found the concepts of repression, regression, projection, reaction formation, and transference. At a higher level there is a theoretical model of the mind in terms of psychic energy, which gets attached to various ideals, the transformations of which are governed by quasi-mechanical principles. This is, in fact, designed to be a perfectly general model of the mind, in terms of which, in the last analysis, all psychological processes and states may be conceived. At this level we have also the division of the psyche into the three systems—id, ego, and superego—together with an account of their properties and interrelations.

In addition to the distinction between levels, we have the distinction between developmental and dynamic theories. In the first group is the theory of psychosexual stages—oral, anal, genital—according to which there is a biologically determined order, beginning from infancy, in which first one, then another, area of the body is maximally sensitive to pleasurable stimulation and according to which certain personality traits predominate as one or another stage is prolonged or transcended only with difficulty. For example, passivity and lack of initiative are associated with the oral stage, during which sensuous pleasure comes mostly from taking things into the mouth.

By contrast, the dynamic theories have to do with processes that take place, or can take place, over a short span of time or at least within the same stage of a person's life. Under this heading we have, for example, the theory of defense mechanisms, according to which the person will defend himself against dangerous impulses by various devices—going to the other extreme (reaction formation), attributing the impulses to someone else (projection), and so on. One of the reasons that the distinction between developmental and dynamic theories is important is that many of the philosophical difficulties raised about psychoanalytic theory center on the notion of unconscious psychic processes, and such processes are more central in dynamic than in developmental theories.

In order to have something fairly definite to work with, let us take the following to be an oversimplified formulation of the psychoanalytic theory of psychic conflict, which is basic to all the dynamic theories.

(1) When it is very painful for a person to be aware of the fact that he has a certain desire, he represses it (prevents it from becoming conscious). The pain may stem

from a severe conflict between the desire and the person's standards for himself, from fear of the consequences of attempts to satisfy the desire, or from both.

(2) Repressed psychic material exhibits primitive, infantile features. These include the lack of sharp distinctions, which is in turn conducive to the formation of strong associations between a certain desire and many other, often irrelevant, things and a tolerance for lack of realism and for incompatibility of one's desires and thoughts.

(3) A repressed desire (which continues to exist as a desire) can be partially satisfied by happenings, in actual occurrence or in fantasy, which are associated with the object of the desire.

(4) When the substitute satisfactions themselves arouse too much anxiety, the person seeks to ward them off, often in equally derivative ways.

This basic theory is then applied to the explanation of dreams, slips of the tongue, and neurotic symptoms by studying the ways in which such phenomena constitute substitute satisfactions of repressed desires and/or defenses against such satisfactions.

An illustration of these ideas is presented by Freud in Lecture 17 of his *General Introduction to Psychoanalysis*. A girl has, for obvious reasons, repressed a strong desire for sexual intercourse with her father. In the unconscious, various things happen to this desire and the ideas involved in it. The dread of carrying out the act generalizes to a dread of sexual activity of any sort. An association is formed between sexual intercourse and breaking a vase. The bolster at the back of the bed is pictured as the girl's father and the back of the bed as her mother. The pressure of this repressed material becomes so great that the girl develops a compulsion to go through an elaborate ritual before going to sleep at night. She arranges the vases in her room so that breakage is impossible, thus symbolically guarding against sexual intercourse, and she takes care lest the bolster touch the back of her bed, thus achieving a substitute satisfaction for her desire to keep her father and mother apart.

Methodological problems. Some of the philosophical objections to psychoanalytic theory can easily be shown to have little or no force. For instance, some philosophers object that the theory postulates unobservable entities; others believe that it is self-contradictory to speak of unconscious mental processes, for what is mental is, by definition, conscious.

In answer to the first objection, it can be pointed out that this practice is common in the most respectable parts of science. Electromagnetic fields and energy quanta are as unobservable as unconscious fantasy. They are, nonetheless, scientifically legitimate because of the functions performed by the theories embodying them, a point to which we shall return. In answer to the second objection, it may be admitted that psychoanalytic theory involves some stretching of such terms as "desire" and "thought" (as in the unconscious thoughts believed to underlie the conscious content of a dream). But, again, this is standard practice in scientific theorizing. The submicroscopic particles postulated in the kinetic theory of gases are modeled on familiar physical objects, like baseballs, except that they lack some of the properties of baseballs, like color and

texture, and they possess perfect elasticity. One may as well say that it is a contradiction to speak of physical particles which have no color. Difference from familiar concepts is not in itself fatal. Again, the crucial question is what can be done with the concepts thus derived.

The serious difficulties emerge when we try to determine whether psychoanalytic concepts have the kind of status which is required for scientific validity and fruitfulness. This problem has two closely related parts. (1) Do psychoanalytic terms have any empirical significance, and if they do, how can it be exhibited? (2) How can theoretical principles couched in these terms be put to an empirical test? These questions become two sides of the same coin if we make certain assumptions which are widely shared by contemporary philosophers of science. First, a term has the kind of semantic status required for science if and only if statements in which it figures have implications for what would be experienced under certain circumstances. Second, one brings out a term's empirical or scientific significance, as contrasted with its pictorial associations, by tracing out such implications. Third, it is only if statements have such implications that they can be put to an empirical test. Given these assumptions, we can deal with the two questions simultaneously. By showing how statements involving the term "repress" give rise to implications of a sort that make an empirical test possible, we will at the same time be showing what scientific significance the term has over and above any of its pictorial associations—for example, a man firmly clamping a lid down on a pot of molten metal. With this equivalence in mind, the following discussion will be explicitly directed to the second question: How can the theoretical principles of psychoanalysis be empirically tested?

There is a commonly accepted doctrine, largely derived from a consideration of physics, according to which a theory involving unobservables gets empirical significance by virtue of the fact that it, together with subsidiary assumptions, implies various general lawlike hypotheses which can be directly tested empirically. In this way the theory can be assessed in terms of the extent to which it succeeds in explaining and unifying a variety of lower-level laws which have been empirically confirmed and, on the negative side, the extent to which it does not imply lower-level hypotheses which have been empirically disconfirmed. The Bohr theory of atomic structure, which represents an atom as a sort of miniature solar system with electrons revolving in orbits around the nucleus, cannot be tested directly, for an individual atom cannot be observed. However, from the theory we can derive a variety of testable hypotheses—for instance, those concerning the constitution of the spectrum of the light emitted from a given element.

Deriving testable hypotheses. One might well expect to have difficulty deriving testable hypotheses from psychoanalytic theory. The theory represents the postulated unconscious processes mediating between events which are accessible to either introspection or observation, just as do unobservable processes within the atom in the Bohr theory.

In a typical sequence we start with conscious Oedipal desires in a child. Tentative attempts at satisfaction of the desires are met with violent opposition, and as a result the child builds up strong fear and/or horror of the realization of the Oedipal desires. Thus far, everything is, in principle, directly accessible to one or more observers. Then, according to the theory, the complex of desires, fears, and guilt is repressed, whereupon it undergoes various transformations, the exact nature of which is influenced by things that happen to the person, these things again being directly observable. In particular, the associations formed in the unconscious are largely determined by conscious experiences of the person. Finally, the unconscious complex is manifested in various ways—dreams, memory failures, slips of the tongue, compulsions, obsessions, psychosomatic illnesses—all of which are again accessible to experience. This being the case, one would suppose that the theory would yield general hypotheses to the effect that whenever strong desires of a certain kind are met with strong internal and/or external opposition, then (perhaps with the further assumption of certain kinds of intervening experiences) abnormal symptoms of certain kinds will be forthcoming. In other words, since unconscious psychic processes are supposed to provide connecting links between observables, a theory about them should imply that certain antecedent observables would lead to certain consequent observables.

In fact, however, we find little of this. Some attempts have been made to derive hypotheses about statistical distributions from parts of the theory. For example, the theory of dreams holds that dreams partially satisfy repressed desires by representing them as satisfied. It would follow from this that if a group of people were prevented from dreaming for several nights, they would then show a higher average level of tension than a control group. This hypothesis has been tested, using eyeball movement as a criterion of the occurrence of dreams. Most efforts of this sort have stemmed from relatively peripheral components of the theory; in particular, virtually nothing has been done to derive testable hypotheses specifying sufficient conditions for the occurrence of abnormal symptoms. It is only if this were done that the theory could be used for the prediction of such phenomena. Perhaps this is because of the psychoanalyst's preoccupation with the treatment of particular cases rather than with controlled testing of general hypotheses.

There are other features of the situation which also make the formulation of testable hypotheses extraordinarily difficult. Psychoanalytic theory has not been developed to the point where one can give sufficient conditions for one outcome rather than another even on the theoretical level of unconscious processes. Repression is said to occur when a desire arouses great anxiety, but just how much anxiety is required? Obviously, the amount is crucial, but the measurement problem has yet to be solved. Again, given a certain level of anxiety aroused by Oedipal desires, repression is not the only possible outcome. There might, instead, be a regression to the oral or anal phase, or the libido might be redirected into homosexual channels. There are some suggestions about what makes the difference— for example, if one never fully outgrew an earlier stage, this makes regression more likely. But at present this is all rather loose. Moreover, once repression has occurred, the

repressed material may develop in a great many different ways. The fear of sexual contact with the mother may or may not generalize, and if it does, it may generalize along various dimensions. Thus, the person may develop a dread of sexual contact with anyone or only with anyone who is like his mother in some respect. A part of the complex may come to be associated with things which have little or no intrinsic connection with it, as the girl in the example cited above formed an association between sexual intercourse and the breaking of a vase. It may well seem impossible to develop principles which would take into account all the determinants of unconscious trains of thought in a way that makes possible, in principle, the prediction of such associations. This impression is reinforced by the fact that these associations are often powerfully influenced by the person's external experiences, which could not be predicted on the basis of psychological facts about him. Thus, in the above example the girl had once broken a vase and cut her finger, which had bled profusely, an incident which then was associated in her mind with the bleeding accompanying defloration.

But even if connections were strong on the level of unconscious processes, there would still remain the job of formulating sufficient conditions for the occurrence of the ultimate facts to be explained. One and the same unconscious complex, given our present powers of discrimination, may issue in a phobia, hysterical paralysis or anesthesia, obsessive concern over bodily symptoms, or a generalized feeling of unworthiness, to mention only a few possibilities. No doubt the choice of symptom is due to other factors, but the problem has not been investigated sufficiently to yield even promising general hypotheses.

Background for clinical interpretation. In view of the extreme difficulty of empirically verifying psychoanalytic theory, one might ask why it should be regarded as anything other than an imaginatively satisfying fantasy. Why does it seem to have an empirical foundation? The answer is that it has significant connections with empirical facts but not connections of the sort insisted on by philosophers of science who take their models from physical theory. Psychoanalytic theory has grown out of the clinical treatment of neurotics, and in that context it has the function of providing suggestions for the interpretation of particular cases. Thus, if we are dealing with a compulsion neurosis, the theory tells us that compulsive behavior simultaneously provides substitute satisfactions for repressed desires (through the realization of states of affairs unconsciously associated with the realization of the desires) and guards against the arousal and/or satisfaction of the desire. (See the clinical case described above.) Furthermore, the theory tells us what kinds of desires are most often repressed—incestuous, homosexual, aggressive. Also, psychoanalytic theory is associated with certain techniques—the analysis of dreams, of free associations, and of reactions to the analyst—for ferreting out repressed material in particular cases. Thus, the theory provides leads for the analyst. Insofar as it has this function rather than that of explaining and unifying testable hypotheses about the conditions under which, in general, we will get one outcome rather than another, it is no defect that it is largely made up of rather loose statements about what can happen, given certain conditions, and what can be responsible for a given symptom. In explaining an event, E, that has already occurred, our needs are simpler than when we are engaged in predicting or establishing general principles. In retrospective explanation we can take advantage of our knowledge that E has already occurred; we are reasoning backward to its sources. Therefore, provided we have a list of possible causes and some way of telling which of these are present, we have something to go on, even if each statement of possible cause is only to the effect that C can result in E. If we were setting out to predict, however, we would need a further specification of the conditions under which C will in fact lead to E. The knowledge that an unconscious desire for and fear of intercourse with the father, plus an association between intercourse and breaking a vase, can lead to a compulsive tendency to arrange vases so as to minimize chances of breakage is general knowledge of a sort, but not of the sort exemplified by the Newtonian theory of gravitation, in which the general principles enable one to predict one state of the system from any other state of the system.

Thus, one can say that psychoanalytic theory, given the way it has developed up to now, makes contact with empirical reality through being used as a basis for explanations of certain kinds of observable occurrences and that the theory receives empirical support to the extent that such explanations are adequate. To many methodologists this situation is profoundly unsatisfying. If a theory yields predictively confirmed hypotheses, we have a strong indication that contact with something real has been made, for by thinking in these terms, we have succeeded in anticipating the course of nature. But if the theory can provide only suggestions for retrospective explanations, it is not so clear what this shows. More specifically, many have suspected that the success of psychoanalysts in devising explanations of their patients' symptoms is more a function of the analysts' ingenuity than of the soundness of their theory. It is easy to get the impression that a plausible explanation in psychoanalytic terms could be framed for any behavior, no matter what the facts. If it is not a reaction formation from overattachment to mother, then it is a projection of a self-directed death wish, and so on.

Adequacy of clinical interpretations. Clearly, what is needed is a set of objective criteria for the adequacy of an explanation in terms of unconscious psychic factors, criteria which would permit us to assess a proposed explanation on some grounds other than the way it seems to make sense of the phenomena. If and only if such criteria can be formulated can explanations of particular cases provide any empirical basis for the theory.

Within the limits of this article, we can only touch briefly on the problems involved in formulating and defending such criteria. The problems fall into three groups.

Status of the data. Questions have often been raised about the status of the ultimate data to which the psychoanalyst appeals in justifying an interpretation. These consist of the behavior of the patient, verbal and otherwise, in therapeutic sessions. Criticisms have been of three sorts.

First, the data actually presented are a small sample of all the behavior engaged in by the patient in the presence of the analyst. We are almost never given any reason for supposing that this is a representative sample, that the analyst has not, perhaps unconsciously, selected those items which best support his hypothesis.

Second, a given patient is rarely, if ever, compared with controls who do not have his difficulties. Without this we cannot show that the data cited have bearing on the abnormalities to be explained. For example, if almost anyone would get annoyed when the analyst acts bored with the session, then the fact that patient A does so is not likely to reveal anything that is responsible for any idiosyncrasy of his.

Third, the analyst may often be guilty of contaminating the data through, perhaps unconsciously, tipping the patient off about his interpretation, thus implicitly inviting the patient to produce associations which will support that interpretation.

These are serious problems in data collection and assessment, and they will have to be solved if psychoanalysis is to become more respectable scientifically. But since it seems in principle possible to overcome them, they are less crucial for the logical status of the theory than problems in the other groups.

Unconscious causes. An explanation of E in terms of C is not warranted unless C actually exists. What objective tests are there for the actual existence of the unconscious psychic factors appealed to by the analyst? Analysts regularly use a number of detection procedures.

Among the things they consider significant are the following: (1) Patterns of behavior that are as they would be if A had a desire of which he is not conscious. For example, a 17-year-old girl devotes a great deal of time and energy to the small children of a youngish widower friend of the family, though she is not aware of being in love with him. (2) Patterns of feeling which have the same status. In the same example, the girl gets very depressed when the widower does not send her a birthday present. (3) Analysis of dreams and of free associations. Such analysis proceeds in a rather devious fashion and cannot be illustrated briefly. It is based on the principle that unconscious complexes influence conscious thought and fantasy, including dreaming, by producing relatively safe conscious derivatives of these complexes. (4) Final realization by the patient, after treatment, that he had the desire in question all along.

The inferences involved in the use of these procedures are extremely complex, and it is difficult to say just how conclusively anyone has ever demonstrated the existence of certain unconscious material in a given case. It is worth noting that the use of (3) and (4), unlike (1) and (2), requires the assumption of certain parts of the theory. Thus, for example, we cannot take dreams to reveal unconscious desires in the way analysts do unless we assume that dreams are formed in the manner postulated by the theory. This means that insofar as explanations which are supported in part by dream interpretation are adduced in support of the theory, we are going round in a circle.

Unconscious complexes and symptoms. The most difficult problem is that of showing that a given unconscious complex is responsible for certain symptoms. Granted that the girl does have a repressed desire for and dread of sexual intercourse with her father, why should we suppose that this is what led her to develop a compulsive tendency to arrange the vases in her room in a certain way before retiring? In order to answer this question, we shall have to decide what kind of explanation this is supposed to be. Freud often gives the impression that it has the ordinary pattern of an "in-order-to" explanation ("I went into the kitchen in order to get a bottle of beer" or "I went into the kitchen because I wanted a bottle of beer"), except that here the want is unconscious. But the ordinary "in-order-to" explanation carries the assumption that the agent believes that the action in question is, or may be, instrumental in the satisfaction of the want in question. Can we say that the girl unconsciously believed that preventing the vases from breaking would be instrumental in preventing intercourse with her father? A strange belief, but Freud did say that the unconscious is quite illogical. Or should we say, rather, that no belief is involved here but only an association between breaking a vase and intercourse? However this issue is resolved, this assimilation will not help us to justify the explanation, for the fundamental method of justifying an ordinary "in-order-to" explanation—getting a sincere report by the agent of why he did what he did—is not available here.

Freud might claim that an analogue is available—the realization by the patient, after treatment, that that was why she had to arrange the vases as she did. However, if one rests the adequacy of the explanation on the patient's posttherapeutic insight, he leaves himself open to the charge of undue influence on the source of data. Moreover, circularity comes up again, for if the patient came to have this conviction as a result of being presented with this explanation under hypnosis, this would not count in favor of the explanation. Only insight that comes after certain kinds of therapeutic interactions is relevant, and the claim that insight produced in that way is valid depends on the psychoanalytic theory about the effects which can be expected from psychoanalytic therapy. Thus, there are difficulties in construing the explanation on the model of "I went to the kitchen because I wanted a bottle of beer." On the other hand, if we take as our model an everyday explanation in terms of physical causation, like "The window broke because a baseball hit it," we will have to support it by reference to general principles to the effect that factors of the sort cited have results of the kind we are seeking to explain. And the absence of such tested generalizations in psychoanalysis has already been noted.

Thus, it would seem that before psychoanalytic theory can enjoy a firm empirical foundation, its practitioners must either develop explicit and workable objective criteria for the adequacy of interpretations of clinical phenomena in terms of unconscious factors, or do more to derive testable general hypotheses from the theory, or do both.

Bibliography

The basic expositions of psychoanalytic theory are to be found in the works of Sigmund Freud. See especially his *General Introduction to Psychoanalysis* (New York, 1949), *New Introductory Lectures on Psychoanalysis* (New York, 1933), *The Interpretation of Dreams* (New York, 1938), *The Ego and the Id* (London, 1927), *Inhibitions, Symptoms, and Anxiety* (London, 1961), and the theoretical essays in Vol. IV of the *Collected Papers* (London, 1948).

Important later additions include Anna Freud, *The Ego and the Mechanisms of Defence* (London, 1937), and the new developments in ego psychology to be found in two articles by Heinz Hartmann, "Comments on the Psychoanalytic Theory of the Ego," in *The Psychoanalytic Study of the Child*, Vol. V (New York, 1950), and "The Mutual Influences in the Development of the Ego and Id," *ibid.*, Vol. VII (New York, 1952).

Useful expositions are to be found in R. L. Munroe, *Schools of Psychoanalytic Thought* (New York, 1955); Otto Fenichel, *The Psychoanalytic Theory of Neurosis* (New York, 1945); C. S. Hall, *A Primer of Freudian Psychology* (New York, 1954); and David Rapaport, "The Structure of Psychoanalytic Theory," in Sigmund Koch, ed., *Psychology: A Study of a Science*, Vol. III (New York, 1959).

Methodological problems are explored in Sidney Hook, ed., *Psychoanalysis, Scientific Method, and Philosophy* (New York, 1959); B. F. Skinner, "Critique of Psychoanalytic Concepts and Theories," in *Minnesota Studies in the Philosophy of Science*, Vol. I (Minneapolis, 1956); Antony Flew, "Motives and the Unconscious," *ibid.*; Gustav Bergmann, "Psychoanalysis and Experimental Psychology," in M. H. Marx, ed., *Psychological Theory* (New York, 1951); Ch. 3 of R. S. Peters, *The Concept of Motivation* (London, 1958); a series of essays reprinted in Margaret Macdonald, ed., *Philosophy and Analysis* (Oxford, 1954)—Stephen Toulmin's "The Logical Status of Psycho-analysis," Antony Flew's "Psycho-analytic Explanations," and R. S. Peters' "Cause, Cure, and Motive"; and B. A. Farrell's articles "The Criteria for a Psychoanalytic Interpretation," in *PAS*, Supp. Vol. 36 (1962)—reprinted in D. F. Gustafson, ed., *Essays in Philosophical Psychology* (New York, 1964), pp. 299–323—and "Can Psychoanalysis Be Refuted?," in *Inquiry*, Vol. 4 (1961), 16–36.

Attempts to derive testable general hypotheses from psychoanalytic theory are canvassed in R. R. Sears, *Survey of Objective Studies of Psychoanalytic Concepts* (New York, 1943).

WILLIAM P. ALSTON

PSYCHOANALYTIC THEORIES OF THE UNCONSCIOUS. See UNCONSCIOUS, PSYCHOANALYTIC THEORIES OF THE.

PSYCHOKINESIS. See ESP PHENOMENA, PHILOSOPHICAL IMPLICATIONS OF.

PSYCHOLOGICAL BEHAVIORISM. The twentieth century has seen the development of a school of thought in psychology loosely known as behaviorism. Behaviorism has taken a number of forms and gone through a number of transformations, but certain basic ideas have remained throughout the changes.

Behaviorism has attempted to explain behavior of men and animals by theories and laws couched in concepts designating only physical things and events. The attempt is, therefore, to eschew concepts involving purpose, desire, intention, feeling, and so on. Such concepts are held to designate, if indeed they designate anything at all, unobservable things and events, whose locus is inside the organism. Put another way, the attempt is to avoid any reference to mental events or activity, such as thinking, expectation, understanding, and bafflement. In behaviorist circles "mentalistic" is a pejorative term. As Clark L. Hull put it, "Instead of furnishing a means for the solution of problems, consciousness appears itself to be a problem needing solution" ("Mind, Mechanism and Adaptive Behavior," in *Psychological Review*, 1937, Vol. 44, 1–32).

However, the intention has not been to produce a purely physiological theory of behavior and to absorb psychology into another science. Behaviorists have believed that a science of behavior could be built up on the level of the gross observable reactions of organisms dealt with by the everyday language of action concepts. That is, functional relations could be discovered in which these gross reactions would be the dependent variables. A science of this kind would be a "molar" science of behavior. Of course, it was generally believed that the functional relations discovered at this level could in all likelihood be accounted for in terms of physiological connections, by means of a "molecular" theory. But this was—at least during the heyday of behaviorism—generally held to be a separable operation.

A molar science was therefore justified in that it would allow us to advance our understanding of the determinants of behavior without having to wait for exhaustive research in physiology to produce detailed knowledge of the workings of the organism. Psychology thus defended itself as a separate science, but, most paradoxically, not on the grounds that it dealt with the psyche but rather as an objective science of behavior of a more coarse-grained, macroscopic kind.

The faith in an eventual physiological underpinning was expressed in the language of many psychologists of this school. Hull, for instance, spoke of "afferent impulses." But in fact these terms and all others used by thinkers of this school referred either to grossly observable behavior of organisms or features of the environment or to physiological happenings that were pure inferences from such behavior or overt features. The nature of the "afferent impulse," for instance, was inferred from that of the environment in which the organism was placed.

Behavioral science thus became an attempt to correlate the responses of an organism with features of the environment present and past, or, in the extended semiphysiological language used by thinkers of the school, to correlate "stimulus" and "response." Behaviorism is thus often referred to as S–R theory. Most theorists recognize, of course, that there are internal determinants of behavior as well as environmental ones. The most obvious of these is that which we call in unscientific language "desire." An animal, for instance, will not "respond" to the "stimulus" of food if he has just eaten and is not hungry. Variations in behavior of this kind have to be coped with by postulating other determinants (in this case, the usual term is "drive"). But in order to avoid reference to unobservable inner events (the avoidance of which was, after all, the aim in eliminating all reference to mind), the operation of these determinants is conceived of as being closely linked with certain external factors. Thus, for example, the hunger of the animal in the above example will be measured in terms of the hours since the last feeding, or something of the sort. Hence, behavior will be seen as a function either of features of the environment or of factors measured in terms of the organism's history, recent or remote.

Philosophical affinities. Behaviorism has deep roots in the Western philosophical tradition. One thinks of the developments that immediately preceded its rise in the early decades of the century, linked with the names of J. B. Watson and Edward L. Thorndike in the United States, Ivan Pavlov and V. M. Bekhterev in Russia, of the trend toward mechanism in biology during the latter part of the nineteenth century, of the growth of studies of animal behavior (which in the light of Darwinian evolutionary theory could be seen as the basis for the study of human behavior), and of the influence of pragmatism (in the United States). From a longer perspective, we cannot neglect the influence of physics, which, with its methods of exact measurement and intersubjective verification, set a model for science, one against which the uncertain and shifting results of the introspective psychology of Wilhelm Wundt and E. B. Titchener compared badly. Later we find physics providing a model in another way, too, for the "hypothetico-deductive" system of Hull.

The influence of physics on the science of human behavior goes back at least to Hobbes. In a more general sense, behaviorism has roots in the materialist tradition of Western philosophy which goes back to the Greeks. But, if a more particular philosophical affinity can be singled out, behaviorism's closest links are to the empiricist tradition.

Empiricism. The affinities between behaviorism and empiricism can be seen on two levels, both of which relate to the central idea of empiricism, its doctrine of experience. Empiricism, following Cartesianism, conceived of our experience of the world on the model of the interaction of bodies in space. If we are aware of our surroundings, it must be that they touch us in some way, that they make an impression on the mind. Hume used the word "impression," but Locke's "idea" served in part to convey the same notion. Experience is thus seen as caused by the surroundings; that is, the ideas or impressions in the mind are brought about by the features of the world around us that impinge on us. Perhaps not all those who have used the empiricist language of impression or idea or, more recently, "sense datum" would be willing to subscribe to a theory of experience as caused by the environment, but such a view is implicit in the thesis that experience can be understood as a series of events in the mind distinct from the events and things in the world "about" which experience claims to tell us something. The very thesis that experience has immediate objects that are not the objects of the public world, surely a central claim of empiricism, involving as it does a rigid separation between experience and world, poses the question of the relations between them in a way that predetermines the answer: if these relations exist at all (and the negative hypothesis always remains open to haunt empiricism), they must be such as to make experience the dependent term in a causal correlation.

From this central conception there are two lines of philosophical reflection, common in the tradition, which have both contributed to modern behaviorism. The first concerns the nature of the mind and its relation to the body. Empiricism has followed Cartesianism in that it has given rise to a dualism of mind and body. Experience is the dependent term in a causal relation of which the external world is the independent term. But in a sense the body, too, belongs to the "external world." Thus, there is inner experience or "reflection" as well as outer. To a large degree this results from bodily happenings just as my perception of the room around me results from the things in the room impinging on my receptors. Much of inner experience is affective, and thus feeling, too, insofar as we can account for it in terms of the body, is seen as a condition of the mind which has a cause outside it. The notion of mind and body thus becomes one of two entities related by causal links. Action, too, is construed on this model: an inner intention or desire is the cause of external movement.

The psychological theory that developed from traditional empiricism and that can be seen, for instance, in utilitarianism accounts for behavior by a chain of causal links crossing between external events and intramental happenings and back again. Mental contents that can act as motive forces for behavior are the ideas of pain and pleasure, Bentham's "two sovereign masters." Through experience certain other ideas become associated with these and thus acquire the power to initiate behavior. These ideas themselves are caused by the features of the surrounding world to which (we hope) they correspond. Thus, we react to an object in our surroundings, say a succulent morsel of food, because (*a*) the food gives rise to a sense datum of food in the mind, (*b*) this is linked by past experience to the idea of eating the food, which in turn is linked to the idea of pleasure, and (*c*) the idea of pleasure brings about the action of eating the food.

This conception was obviously bound to give rise to the problems concerning "other minds" that are characteristic of empiricism. For, on this view, where the mind is seen as the locus of events only causally linked with bodily happenings, it remains outside the field of observation. One can be said to observe movement, for instance, but not, strictly speaking, to observe action. Thus, the question always arises how we can manage to make and justify statements about the actions, feelings, thoughts, etc., of other people.

Behaviorist psychology draws on this conception. But in the name of science, and sometimes also of metaphysical simplicity, it suppresses the inner happenings of the mind and tries to relate directly the features of the environment and overt behavior. Thus, in the example above, we react to the morsel of food because (*a*) it impinges on the receptors, which (*b*) sets off the response of eating it. The traditional association of ideas has been replaced by an association between stimulus and response. What has become of the "idea of pleasure" which on the old view accounted for our acquiring the tendency to eat this food when we encounter it? It has become the "positive reinforcement" of modern theory. The conception involved here is that a response which occurs together with a stimulus and which is followed by satisfaction (say the reduction of a need) tends to be reinforced—that is, to occur in future when the stimulus is presented.

The link between the empiricist tradition and modern behaviorism can be seen in their historical development, where thinkers like Thorndike transformed the nineteenth-century explanation of learned adaptation in terms of pleasure into the law of effect, but it can also be seen in the assumption they share with their forebears that only external movement is observable, that the mental is the invisible. This thesis has acquired something of the status of a self-evident truth among thinkers of the behaviorist persuasion. It is largely taken for granted that, for example, " 'hear,' 'feel,' 'try,' 'need,' 'in order to,' and 'intention' cannot be included in the data language of a science of behavior . . ." (W. Verplanck, in Estes et al., *Modern Learning Theory*, p. 278).

This conception of the observable is supported by another line of reflection from the central doctrine of empiricism, an epistemological one. If experience consisted in the receiving of impressions, then any belief about the world must find evidence in impressions received on the mind. Every "idea" that was empirically founded must have a corresponding "impression." And if a distinction between two ideas was to be empirically founded, there must be a corresponding distinction between the impressions. On this view it is difficult to give sense to the notion of observing psychological events. We can see this with the concept of action. What is the impression from which the "idea" of action comes? It is clear that in the impression that it makes the execution of an action cannot differ in any way from the occurrence of the corresponding movements. If we interpret the notion of observation in terms of this concept of experience and think of observing as having certain impressions, then there is nothing that can count as observing an action which is not identical with observing the movements. On this view, then, we cannot, strictly speaking, be said to observe action: it becomes something inferred, and the same goes for other mental events that bear the same relation to their bodily expressions: we infer to them from the latter, more or less uncertainly.

Logical empiricism. It should not be surprising, then, that psychological behaviorism is very close to another offshoot of classical empiricism in the twentieth century, logical empiricism. Psychologists of this school have drawn heavily on the logical-empiricist theory of science in their theoretical reflections. Hull's conception of a hypothetico-deductive science, for instance, owes a great deal to the work of Moritz Schlick and other members of the Vienna circle. And the connection is clearly visible in the notion of the "data language," a basic stratum of concepts defined by the nature of observation to which all scientific terms must be reducible. This notion springs from and depends for its force on the traditional empiricist notion of experience as the reception of impressions, with its corollary that only certain ranges of concepts designate observables and that all others must be given an empirical meaning in terms of these concepts, by some such device as "operational definition" or "logical construction." In philosophy this has given rise to all the attempts by positivists to reduce concepts of one range to those of another and thus to achieve the unity of science. But whereas philosophers might have hesitated whether to adopt the sense-datum language as their privileged stratum, behavioral psychologists have latched firmly onto the "physical-thing language" as the basic currency of science. The influence of logical empiricism can be seen in the use of such concepts as the above and such others as "operational definition." Its influence can also be seen, along with the pull of modern physics, in the insistence that the crucial data of behavior theory be measurable.

The internal debate. The assumptions that come to behaviorism from traditional empiricism, and particularly its conception of the observable, have rendered behaviorist psychology largely impervious to criticism, even of the most probing and disturbing kind. Behaviorism exists in a field in which the major rivals are Gestalt theory and the different offshoots of psychoanalysis. Gestalt theorists are condemned for their use of such "cognitive" concepts as "insight," psychoanalysts for using a whole range of "mentalistic" concepts dealing with feeling, desire, unconscious and conscious purpose, and so on. Yet the successes achieved by these other schools and the criticisms they direct toward behaviorism—not to speak of the shafts aimed at it by mere philosophers who have criticized the empiricist notions of experience and action—have left its practitioners largely unconcerned. This is to a great extent because the firmly received conception of what a science of behavior must be, rooted in the concept of observability, rules out Gestalt psychology and psychoanalysis from the start as serious contenders, based as they are on "subjectivism," "anthropomorphism," or "introspection." Any objection they make must therefore be in principle surmountable, and their results may be admitted only if restated in behaviorist language (where this is possible).

Behaviorism is much more occupied with the discussion of inner differences. Quite apart from the methodological and metaphysical premises discussed above, there is a surprising degree of convergence in the views of thinkers of this school. Most of them attempt to tackle the problems of behavior by studying animal learning. Learning theory is essential to behaviorism since it is here if anywhere that it can account for adaptive behavior without using the concepts of purpose, intention, understanding, etc., or related ones, in the explanation. The aim is to account for learning and therefore for adaptation strictly in terms of "stimuli" and "responses."

Within this general framework, behaviorists differ on a number of questions, most notably the dispute centering on the law of effect. Some theorists explain the setting up of an S–R connection by the occurrence of the response in the presence of the stimulus in a context of reward (reinforcement theory, as found, for instance, in the work of Hull, B. F. Skinner, and Kenneth W. Spence); others account for it by the simple occurrence of R in the presence of S (contiguity theory, as found, for instance, in the work of E. R. Guthrie). The first view descends more or less from the work of Thorndike, the second from that of Watson and Pavlov. There are numerous variations within each school. Behaviorists also differ in the degree to which they make use of intervening variables or constructs in their theories. Hull's hypothetico-deductive system is at one extreme on this question; Skinner's parsimony at the other.

Another distinction which is perhaps of growing importance is that between "centralists" and "peripheralists." The former hold that behavior cannot be accounted for by correlations between stimuli and responses but that account has to be taken of central processes in the brain or nervous system that determine the course of both perception and response. To this extent they call in question the dominant view of behaviorism as a molar science of behavior correlating events at the "periphery" of the organism, that is, the stimuli impinging on it and the gross observable responses made. To what extent an approach of this kind would do away with psychology's independent identity as a discipline would depend on which directions of research prove most fruitful, if any. Thinkers of this orientation, of which D. O. Hebb is a prominent representative, are pursuing research on the borderline between neurophysiology and psychology, as well as examining cybernetics, information theory, probability mathematics, and the like in an attempt to discover a model for the central processes controlling behavior.

The present uncertainty. The centralist approach, or family of approaches, is taking on added importance, for the traditional molar behaviorism is having more and more difficulty maintaining itself. Many of the obstacles it is now trying to surmount were introduced by experiments made by Gestalt psychologists or by thinkers with a leaning in that direction (such as Edward C. Tolman), but for the reasons mentioned above these theories are not considered serious contenders and therefore do not reap what they have sown. Centralist theories benefit instead.

The difficulties for traditional behaviorism have been posed by examples of intelligent adaptive behavior which could not be put in the mold of S–R learning theory, in which the successful learned response is a repetition of one that has occurred in the learning history. The behaviors in question showed improvisation or insight, or understanding or orientation of some sort. Famous examples were the experiments of Wolfgang Köhler with chimpanzees and of Tolman with rats. S–R theory has tried to cope with findings of this kind, first by introducing more and more intervening factors (such as, for example, "fractional anticipatory goal responses" or other unobserved internal cues) whose empirical basis is dubious and whose mode of operation is unclear and often conceived in a contradictory way from one context to another; second, by extending the meaning of its basic concepts, such as "stimulus," "response," and "drive," in a way that renders the theory of questionable value by its own, and indeed by any, criteria.

Thus, the notion of a stimulus has to be extended to take in configurational properties, relational properties (such as "brighter than X"), and the like. And animals can be trained to respond to features of their environment that defy description in stimulus terms (for example, they can pick up the object resembling a standard one with respect to color as against one resembling it with respect to shape). The notion of response has been similarly extended so as implicitly to reintroduce the concept of action, or of behavior which is aimed at a certain result, whereas the notion of drive has come very close to reincorporating those features of the concept of desire that it was supposed to avoid. Instead of being characterized as a directionless "energizer" of behavior, it is often defined in terms of the goals to which it impels, just as desire is. Thus, we find new "drives" for money, achievement, friendship, and so on, being introduced by behavior theorists.

Difficulties of this kind have led to the invention of a host of secondary hypotheses, many of which have added as many difficulties as they solve and some of which seem incompatible with the goals of behaviorism once their meaning is clarified (for example, responses defined by their result, drives by their goal, stimuli by their relations with others). At the same time molar behaviorism has not lived up to its promise. Its results have been relatively meager and very disparate; they have not converged toward any systematic conception of human behavior, as earlier theorists had hoped. Indeed, the number of theories grows unceasingly. The behaviorist school of thought is thus for the first time entering a period of doubt and uncertainty which accounts for the increased emphasis on centralist theory mentioned above, but which may have more far-reaching effects.

Bibliography

Some general works by behaviorists are J. B. Watson, *Psychology From the Standpoint of a Behaviorist* (Philadelphia, 1919; 2d ed., 1924); C. L. Hull, *Principles of Behavior* (New York, 1943) and his *A Behavior System* (New Haven, 1952); B. F. Skinner, *The Behavior of Organisms* (New York, 1938) and his *Science and Human Behavior* (New York, 1953); and D. O. Hebb, *A Textbook of Psychology* (Philadelphia, 1960).

There is an interesting theoretical statement in C. L. Hull, "Mind, Mechanism and Adaptive Behavior," in *Psychological Review*, Vol. 34 (1937), 1–32. See also B. F. Skinner, "Critique of Psychoanalytic Concepts and Theories," in *Minnesota Studies in the Philosophy of Science,* Vol. I, Herbert Feigl and Michael Scriven, eds. (Minneapolis, 1956), pp. 77–87, and the critique by Michael Scriven, "A Study of Radical Behaviorism," in the same volume, on pp. 88–130.

A collection of articles and discussions of different views is S. S. Stevens, ed., *Handbook of Experimental Psychology* (New York, 1951); specifically in the field of learning theory, see E. R. Hilgard, *Theories of Learning*, 2d ed. (New York, 1956), and William K. Estes et al., *Modern Learning Theory* (New York, 1954); in the field of motivation, see Marshall R. Jones, ed., *Nebraska Symposia on Motivation* (Lincoln, Nebr., 1953+).

More recent collections that show a more critical bent are Sigmund Koch, ed., *Psychology: A Study of a Science*, 6 vols. published so far (New York, 1959————), and T. W. Wann, ed., *Behaviorism and Phenomenology* (Chicago, 1964).

Works by thinkers of a "centralist" orientation are D. O. Hebb, *The Organization of Behavior* (New York, 1949), and G. A. Miller, E. Galanter, and K. H. Pribram, *Plans and the Structure of Behavior* (New York, 1960).

A representative and influential article on the philosophy of science by a logical empiricist is Rudolf Carnap's "Methodological Character of Theoretical Concepts," in *Minnesota Studies in the Philosophy of Science*, Vol. I. (see above), pp. 38–76.

Discussions of the philosophy of science by behavior theorists can be found in the symposium on operationism in *Psychological Review*, Vol. 52 (1945), and in K. MacCorquodale and P. E. Meehl, "On a Distinction Between Hypothetical Constructs and Intervening Variables," in *Psychological Review*, Vol. 85 (1948), 95–107.

Works by contemporary philosophers which directly or implicitly call into question the main ideas of behaviorism are G. E. M. Anscombe, *Intention* (Oxford, 1957); R. S. Peters, *The Concept of Motivation* (London, 1958); A. Kenny, *Emotion and Will* (London, 1963); A. I. Melden, *Free Action* (London, 1961); and Charles Taylor, *The Explanation of Behaviour* (London, 1964).

Works by contemporary philosophers whose views are broadly sympathetic to behaviorism in the hostility to purposive or "mentalistic" explanations are W. V. Quine, *Word and Object* (Cambridge, Mass., 1960); J. J. C. Smart, *Philosophy and Scientific Realism* (London, 1963); and Herbert Feigl, "The 'Mental' and the 'Physical,'" in *Minnesota Studies in the Philosophy of Science*, Vol. II, Herbert Feigl, Michael Scriven, and Grover Maxwell, eds. (Minneapolis, 1958).

CHARLES TAYLOR

PSYCHOLOGISM is the term first used in Germany in the first half of the nineteenth century to designate the philosophical trend defended by Jakob Friedrich Fries (1783–1844) and by Friedrich Eduard Beneke (1798–1854) against the dominant Hegelianism. Fries and Beneke advocated a philosophical position based entirely on psychology. They held that the only instrument philosophical inquiry has at its disposal is self-observation (or introspection) and that there is no way to establish any truth other than by reducing it to the subjective elements of self-observation. Psychology becomes, from this point of view, the fundamental philosophical discipline. Logic, ethics, metaphysics, philosophy of law, philosophy of religion, and philosophy of education are all little more than psychology or applied psychology. Beneke wrote, "With all of the concepts of the philosophical disciplines, only what is formed in the human soul according to the laws of its development can be thought; if these laws are understood with certainty and clarity, then a certain and clear knowledge of those disciplines is likewise achieved" (*Die Philosophie in ihrem Verhältnis zur Erfahrung*, p. xv).

Fries and Beneke, who viewed Kant as their predecessor inasmuch as he defended the "rights" of experience, held, nevertheless, that he was mistaken in wanting to institute an inquiry independent of experience which would arrive at knowledge of the a priori forms of intuition and of the categories and in seeking the transcendental ground of truth—the objective validity of human knowledge. This inquiry, Fries claimed, is impossible. The critique of reason can only be a science of experience based on self-observation (*System der Metaphysik*, p. 110). In the same period Vincenzo Gioberti branded as psychologism all of modern philosophy from Descartes on. He meant by psychologism the philosophical procedure that claimed to go from man (that is, from experience) to God and contrasted it with ontologism, which is the movement from God to man.

The doctrine defended by Fries and Beneke has some connection with certain aspects of English empiricism from Locke to Hume in that in both theories experience is not only the instrument of control and the criterion of the truth of knowledge but also the psychological origin of knowledge itself.

Fries and Beneke were correct in accusing Kant of rejecting psychologism, since he had posited the premises for a critique of any psychologism by distinguishing (in a famous passage in the *Critique of Pure Reason*) the *quaestio facti* of the "physiological derivation" of a priori concepts—that is, of their occurrence in the mind or consciousness of man—from the *quaestio juris* of their validity, which demands as a response the transcendental deduction. This distinction, on the basis of which Kant criticized Locke, who would have answered only the first question, is one of the pivotal points of the whole Kantian doctrine—namely, that the truth of empirical knowledge does not depend on the psychological mechanism but on a priori conditions independent of this mechanism; that the validity of the moral norm does not depend on desires or appetites but is a priori as well; and that the validity of aesthetic judgments is in turn based on taste, an a priori faculty.

Toward the middle of the nineteenth century, psychologism was defended in the very field in which it would seem most foreign—logic and mathematics. In John Stuart Mill's *A System of Logic* it is explicitly stated that introspection is the only basis of the axioms of mathematics and the principles of logic; in Mill's *Examination of Sir William Hamilton's Philosophy* logic is classified under psychology and distinguished from it only as the part is distinguished from the whole or art from science. Many logicians in subsequent years accepted this point of view.

The Kantian point of view was developed systematically by Rudolf Hermann Lotze in his *Logik*. The psychological act of thinking is, according to Lotze, completely distinct from the content of thought. The psychological act exists only as a determinate temporal phenomenon, whereas the content has another mode of being—validity. A decade later Gottlob Frege defended the same point of view with regard to mathematics.

> Never take a description of the origin of an idea for a definition, or an account of the mental and physical conditions through which we become conscious of a proposition for a proof of it. A proposition may be thought, and again it may be true; never confuse these two things. We must remind ourselves, it seems, that a proposition no more ceases to be true when I cease to think of it than the sun ceases to exist when I shut my eyes. (*Die Grundlagen der Arithmetik*, Introduction)

In the last decades of the nineteenth century, the Neo-Kantians argued against the psychologistic presentation of philosophy. The Baden school (Windelband, Rickert) defended the independence of values from psychological experience, which could never establish their absoluteness and necessity, and the Marburg school (Cohen, Natorp) held, similarly, that the validity of science, like that of ethics and aesthetics, does not depend on psychological conditions but on the laws proper to these sciences—that is, on the methodological rules which govern their construction. Cohen and Natorp held, moreover, that "thought" or "consciousness" does not designate a psychic reality subject to introspection but the objectively valid content of knowledge—the totality of the possible objects of knowledge itself and the method used in the development of the sciences.

The systematic critique of psychologism in the fields of logic and mathematics is an important part of Husserl's *Logische Untersuchungen*. His main objections are that if logical laws were based on psychological laws, then (1) they ought to be, like the latter, vague and approximate, whereas, at least in part, they are so exact that they cannot be guaranteed by an empirical element; (2) they ought to be based, like all empirical laws, on induction, which yields only a probable validity and not the apodictic certainty they manifest; (3) they ought to imply the existence of such psychic events as representation and judgment, whereas they do not concern the reality of psychic life and of other facts (unlike the laws of nature, which are merely probable) but concern necessary relations independently of facts (*Logische Untersuchungen*, Vol. I, Secs. 21–24). Later in his career Husserl wrote, in terms very close to Frege's, "To refer to it [a number] as a mental construct is an absurdity, an offence against the perfectly clear meaning of arithmetic discourse, which can at any time be perceived as valid, and precedes all theories concerning it" (*Ideen*, Sec. 22). He warned against the tendency to "psychologize the eidetic"—that is, to identify essences, which are the authentic objects of knowledge, with the simultaneous consciousness of these essences (*ibid.*, Sec. 61).

The battle between psychologism and antipsychologism is sometimes fought among philosophers with the same point of view. Among the existentialists Heidegger, who adopted as his method Husserl's phenomenology, intended existential analysis as the uncovering of human situations in their essence, not in their psychic occurrence (*Sein und Zeit*, Halle, 1927, Sec. 7), whereas Sartre, speaking of existential psychoanalysis, seems inclined toward psychologism, although he tried to correct it by affirming that "consciousness is not a mode of particular knowledge but it is the dimension of transphenomenal being in the subject" (*L'Être et le néant*, Paris, 1943, p. 17).

Within logical empiricism the argument against psychologism is one of the fundamental points of Carnap's first work, *Der logische Aufbau der Welt*. The fundamental theses of *Logische Syntax der Sprache*, especially the principle of tolerance, are incompatible with psychologism, according to which, obviously, there could be only a single language—that determined by psychological laws. Carnap took the same line when he criticized Russell's thesis that propositions are mental events in "Empiricism, Semantics, and Ontology." Arguments against psychologism occur frequently in the writings of other logical empiricists, though traces of psychologism can be found in the thesis, deriving from Russell and held by many logical empiricists, of the immediate, private, and incommunicable character of the sense data that are at the basis of empirical propositions.

Works Favoring Psychologism

Beneke, Friedrich Eduard, *Die Philosophie in ihrem Verhältnis zur Erfahrung, zur Spekulation, und zum Leben.* Berlin, 1833.

Fries, Jakob Friedrich, *System der Metaphysik.* Heidelberg, 1824.

Gioberti, Vincenzo, *Introduzione allo studio della filosofia.* Brussels, 1840.

Lipps, Theodor, *Grundzüge der Logik.* Hamburg–Leipzig, 1893.

Lotze, Hermann, *Logik.* Leipzig, 1874. Translated by Helen Dendy as *Logic.* Oxford, 1884.

Mill, John Stuart, *A System of Logic,* 2 vols. London, 1843.

Mill, John Stuart, *Examination of Sir William Hamilton's Philosophy.* London, 1865.

Sigwart, Christoff, *Logik,* 2 vols. Tübingen, 1873–1878. Translated by Helen Dendy as *Logic,* 2 vols. London, 1890.

Works Critical of Psychologism

Carnap, Rudolf, *Der logische Aufbau der Welt.* Berlin, 1928.

Carnap, Rudolf, *Logische Syntax der Sprache.* Vienna, 1934. Translated by Amethe Smeaton as *The Logical Syntax of Language.* London, 1938.

Carnap, Rudolf, "Empiricism, Semantics, and Ontology." *Revue internationale de philosophie,* 4th year, No. 11 (1950), 20–40. Reprinted in Herbert Feigl and May Brodbeck, eds., *Readings in the Philosophy of Science.* New York, 1953.

Frege, Gottlob, *Die Grundlagen der Arithmetik.* Breslau, 1884. Translated by J. L. Austin as *The Foundations of Arithmetic.* Oxford, 1950.

Husserl, Edmund, *Logische Untersuchungen,* 2 vols. Halle, 1900–1901.

Husserl, Edmund, *Ideen zu einer reinen Phänomenologie und Phänomenologischen Philosophie,* Vol. I. Halle, 1913. Translated by W. R. Boyce Gibson as *Ideas—General Introduction to Pure Phenomenology.* London, 1931.

Pap, Arthur, *Elements of Analytic Philosophy.* New York, 1949.

NICOLA ABBAGNANO
Translated by *Nino Langiulli*